India

THE ROUGH GUIDE

There are more than sixty Rough Guide titles covering
destinations from Amsterdam to Zimbabwe & Botswana

Forthcoming titles include
Bali • Costa Rica • Goa • Hawaii • Majorca
Rhodes • Singapore • Vietnam

Rough Guide Reference Series
Classical Music • World Music

Rough Guide Phrasebooks
Czech • French • German • Greek • Italian • Spanish

India: Rough Guide Credits

Editor:	Greg Ward
Series Editor:	Mark Ellingham
Text Editors:	Greg Ward, Samantha Cook
Production:	Susanne Hillen, Andy Hilliard, Alan Spicer, Judy Pang, Link Hall, Nicola Williamson
Publicity:	Richard Trillo (UK), Jean-Marie Kelly (US)

Acknowledgments

The editor would like to thank Susanne Hillen for her organizational genius and patience, Sam Cook for skilful editing through a long summer, Paul Gray for diligent proofreading and editorial help, Alison Cowan for the horse sacrifice, Andy Hilliard and Link Hall for unflappable typesetting, and Micromap for creating great maps to a demanding schedule.

Thanks to the writers who contributed extra material, especially Daniel Jacobs for his superb work on *Basics*, and Dave Crawford the history man, Ravi S Vasudevan, Jameela Siddiqi, David Muddyman, Kim Burton and Tony Stones.

David: In the UK, thanks to Razz, for living with the book in Bath; to Sal for technical help; to Bru for the break at Easter; and most of all to Lis, for being cooped up with me during my long incarceration on Dartmoor. For help in India I am indebted to: Messrs Soni and Mishra, Bhubaneshwar; Yuvraj (Bubu) Padrole, Puri; Edith, Becka and Adrina, Leh; Alex Gedge, Anjuna; and Aadriaan Valkering, from Egmond, Holland.

Harriet: Bottomless thanks to Dee for his support, company and tolerance; to Claire for good times in London and Rajasthan; to Gabi for encouragement; Becca and Jeremy in London, and to Claus, Ollie and Ben for light relief in India.

Devdan: My part of the book is dedicated to Pauleen, whose encouragement, assistance, and criticism helped make it possible. Special thanks to Anupa Roy and Myra Belshaw for their vital help; Jai Chand Mahtab and family in Calcutta; Nisha and Rajiv Kehr in UP; Jume Lal; Amit Barua, Rajiv Barua and family; Peter Orchard and family; Puli and friends; Toshi Sabharwal; Bhairav Radia; Gunnar Bohnsack and his magic bus; Michael Garratt and Claire Plumley for good company; Heidi Fuchs, Chris Burgess and Alison Williams; and Jitendra Sharma in Patna, who became a friend.

Gareth: Gratitude to family and friends for their patient and practical support, especially Margaret Mattingly; Ronald and Muriel Williams; Nicholas Goodall and Neil Lawson. Respectful thanks to my teachers Naripatta Narayanan Namboodiri, John Marr and Rupert Snell. For help and advice in the UK: Jeya Arunagirinatham; Sue Rollin; Tim Ridley and Katrina Payne; Rick Wilson and Helen East. For hospitality, illumination and guidance in India I am very grateful to Dr BM Alur; Jaya and Kalpana Ashar; Jose Dominic; Diane Daugherty and K K Gopalakrishnan; PV Jayashankar; Shivanna Prabhappa Mulgund; Prof Vishnu Namboodiri; the Naripatta family; MG Shashi Bhooshan; LS Rajagopalan; Babu Verghese and everyone else who showed kindness.

All the authors would like to thank the entire *Rough Guides* team for making it all happen, especially Greg Ward, without whose inspired editing and unflagging commitment this book would not be in the fine shape it is. We all also received invaluable help from Dr Dandapani, of *SD Enterprises* in London, and Athul Seth of ITDC in New Delhi (with his family). A further list of those who helped us during our travels appears on p.iv.

The publishers and authors have done their best to ensure the accuracy and currency of all the information in *The Rough Guide to India*, however, they can accept no responsibility for any loss, injury or inconvenience sustained by any traveller as a result of information or advice contained in the guide.

This first edition published 1994 and reprinted in March 1995 by Rough Guides Ltd, 1 Mercer Street, London WC2H 9QJ.

Distributed by the Penguin Group:
Penguin Books Ltd, 27 Wrights Lane, London W8 5TZ
Penguin Books USA Inc., 375 Hudson Street, New York 10014, USA
Penguin Books Australia Ltd, 487 Maroondah Highway, PO Box 257, Ringwood, Victoria 3134, Australia
Penguin Books Canada Ltd, 10 Alcorn Avenue, Toronto, Ontario, Canada M4V 1E4
Penguin Books (NZ) Ltd, 182–190 Wairau Road, Auckland 10, New Zealand

Typeset in Linotron Univers and Century Old Style to an original design by Andrew Oliver.

Printed by Cox & Wyman, Reading, Berks. Illustrations in Part One & Part Three by Edward Briant.

1184pp, includes index

A catalogue record for this book is available from the British Library.

ISBN 1-85828-104-0

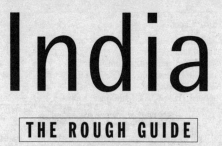

India

THE ROUGH GUIDE

Written and researched by
**David Abram, Harriet Podger,
Devdan Sen and Gareth John Williams**

THE ROUGH GUIDES

THANKS

As well as those listed on p.ii, the authors thank the staff of the national and state tourist offices throughout India; Anil of *Global Travel*); Shiv Khan; Snaylata Gohil; Dr Tariq Ali; Cecil Samuels; OP Garg and K Rajpoot and *Indian Airlines*; the Maharana of Udaipur, Maharaja Swaroop Singh and family, the *Bharatpur Forest Lodge* and *Andaman Beach Resort*; Srikanta Saha, Suranjan Saha and the lads of the *Mother India Biri Company*; Mr Lama and Mr Rama of *Gyabaree Tea Estate*; SS Pangtey, UP Hills; GMVN, and their driver, Sunderlal; AS Negi, Corbett National Park; B Sanghluna, Mizoram; Gautam Bannerjee, *Eastern Railways*; Lal Tharkimi and Lal Rampari Sailo; the Mohiuddin brothers of the *Dragon Hotel* in Leh; Indra Gomba in west Sikkim; Mur Guru S Chahal in Bhopal; Mr Dev Mehta; Mr Shriniwas and staff at the ITDC office in Churchgate, Bombay – particularly Rajan; Mr Geeta Ram in Shimla; and Mr Rupu Negi, Manali.

CONTENTS

Introduction x

This book does not include a chapter on **KASHMIR**, owing to the continuing political unrest in the region.

MAP SYMBOLS

REGIONAL MAPS

- ▬▬▬ Railway
- ═══ Main Road
- ── Minor Road
- ----- Track or Trail
- ·········· River
- ── ── Ferry
- ▬▬ ▬▬ International boundary
- ═══ State boundary
- --- --- Chapter division boundary
- ⌃⌃ Mountains
- ▲ Peak
-) (Pass
- ☆ Viewpoint
- ⸬ Marshland
- ⬚ Beach
- ● Town
- ◆ Place of interest
- ✕ Airport
- ⱦ Lighthouse
- ⬧ Hut
- ⸬ Glacier

STREET MAPS

- ▬▬▬ Railway
- ═══ Main Road
- ═══ Secondary Road
- ═══ Lane
- ===== Track
- ----- Path
- ── River
- ▪▪▪▪ Fortified wall
- ▨ Park
- ▬ Building
- ⊞ Church
- ⓘ Tourist Office
- ✉ Post Office
- Ⓐ❶ Hotel or Restaurant

COMMON SYMBOLS

- 🕌 Mosque or Muslim Monument
- ⌂ Buddhist Temple
- ▲ Hindu or Jain Temple
- ▤ Ghat

LIST OF MAPS

INTRODUCTION

The home of one of the world's oldest civilizations, and several of the world's great religions, India has been changing and re-shaping itself for as long as anywhere on earth, forever producing new forms of culture and absorbing new influences. Visiting the subcontinent, you'll see Kipling-esque visions of spectacular carved temples and gleaming marble palaces, lonely Himalayan lamaseries and far-flung dusty villages where council meetings are held under the shade of a *banyan* tree, plodding camels and man-eating tigers, holy cows, snake charmers and wild-haired *sadhus*; you'll also find a dynamic state racing towards the twenty-first century. The boundaries of modern India, fixed less than fifty years ago, are merely the latest in a four-thousand-year sequence of redefinitions that have produced one of the most heterogenous societies in the world. The land where the Buddha lived and preached, and where the Moghul Muslims erected the Taj Mahal, has recreated itself as both a majority Hindu nation and the world's largest secular democracy, home to over nine hundred million people.

Many first-time visitors cannot see past the grinding poverty of the country's most disadvantaged citizens. Others expect a timeless ascetic wonderland and are indignant to find that materialism has its place here too. Still more find themselves intimidated by what may seem, initially, an incomprehensible and bewildering continent.

This book sets out, chapter by chapter, to guide you through the states, cities and towns of India, offering historical, architectural and cultural information to enrich your trip, whether you intend to travel for a few weeks or several months. The work we've put in has been in the hope of sparing you the mistakes and anti-climaxes that can spoil the best-laid plans, and to direct you towards off-beat delights as well as world-famous landmarks. Each chapter covers a specific state, starting off by introducing its major sights, surveying its history, and summarizing its major travel routes. In each town we've detailed the best places to stay and eat, reviewing palace hotels of faded grandeur alongside inexpensive lodges and simple pilgrim guesthouses, and Mughlai

---

ROUGH GUIDE FAVOURITES

Wildlife Parks and Nature Reserves

Corbett (UP) Tiger sanctuary in the high Himalayan wilderness. p.266.

Gir Forest (Guj) The last refuge of the rare Asiatic lion, symbol of Buddhist emperor Ashoka. p.558.

Kanha (MP) Classic *Jungle Book* territory; probably the best chance to see a tiger. p.378.

Ranthambore (Raj) Jungle cats, paradise fly-catchers, a medieval fort, *chhatris* and palaces – and a Maharaja's hunting lodge to stay in. p.153.

The Sunderbans (WB) Where crocodiles and amphibious man-eating tigers lurk in the marshes of West Bengal. p.759.

Beaches

Arambol (Goa) Tranquil fishing village, popular with long-stay travellers, and hippies who bathe in the stinking sulphurous mud of the nearby hot springs. p.712.

Kovalam (Ker) Friendly hangout a stone's throw from the relaxed south Indian town of Thiruvananthapuram. More for seafood fans than ravers. p.992.

Mamallapuram (TN) Long, empty beaches overlooked by ancient shore temple. p.915.

Ozran Vagator (Goa) Relatively secluded Goa beach, with a freshwater spring and just enough shack cafes to cater for the young, hip crowd. p.708.

restaurants next to village food stalls that dish up spicy *dals* in spotless tin trays. We haven't set out to list the cheapest options everywhere, because here, as anywhere else, the cheapest can easily be the worst. As well as providing detailed accounts of all the major sights, we provide the information you need to search out performing arts, enjoy Indian cinema, explore ashrams and religious centres, and get swept away by the fervour of the great festivals.

The best Indian **itineraries** are the simplest. To imagine that there is some set list of places you must go, or things you must see, is a sure way to make your trip self-defeating. You couldn't see everything in one expedition, even if you spent a year trying. Far better then, to concentrate on one or two specific regions, and above all, to be flexible. Although it requires a deliberate change of pace to venture away from the cities, rural India has its own very distinct pleasures. In fact, while Indian cities are undoubtedly adrenalin-fuelled, upbeat places, it is possible – and certainly less stressful – to travel for months around the subcontinent and rarely have to set foot in one.

The **Basics** section, which takes up the first seventy pages of this book, provides an overview of the practical aspects of travelling in India. To put it simply, it's not as difficult as you may imagine, or may be told. Some travellers impose an exhausting sequence of long-distance journeys and other privations upon themselves that no Indian would dream of attempting, and then wonder why they're not enjoying their trip. Although becoming overtired is an almost inevitable part of travelling around India, getting ill – despite the interminable tales of Delhi-belly and associated hardships so proudly told by a certain type of India bore – certainly isn't. If you give yourself time to rest there's no reason why you should pick up anything worse than a headache. **Food** is generally extremely good, especially in south India, famed for its creative vegetarian cuisine; **water** can be bought in bottles, just like anywhere else in the world, and there are plenty of comfortable, inexpensive places to **stay**. Though the sheer size of the country means that **travel** is seldom straightforward, the extensive road, rail and air links ensure that few destinations are inaccessible, and fares are invariably cheap. Furthermore, the widespread use of English makes communication easy for the majority of western visitors. Journeys may be long – a four-hour bus ride is normal, and travelling constantly for thirty hours not uncommon – but they can provide some of the very best moments of a trip: punctuated with frequent food stops and memorable encounters, and passing through sleepy villages and an everchanging landscape. For

---

Monuments

Ajanta caves (M) Vibrant murals in caves chiselled into basalt cliffs. p.645.

Alchi gompa (L) Ancient Buddhist murals and wood sculpture, hidden away in a hamlet in the curve in the milky blue River Indus. p.483.

Darasuram (TN) Exquisite Chola temple near the holy city of Kumbakonam. p.940.

Ellora caves (M) Buddhist, Hindu and Jain caves, and the Hindu Kailash temple, carved from a single rock. p.638.

Khajuraho (MP) Superbly restored temples, famed for erotic carvings. p.360.

Konarak (Ori) Ruined temple – an enormous chariot dedicated to the sun god Surya – buried for centuries under the sand. p.865.

Mamallapuram (TN) Dazzlingly naturalistic bas-reliefs, man-made caves and south India's earliest stone-built temple, in a wonderful setting by the sea. p.915.

Orchha (MP) Deserted medieval city of palaces, finely carved *havelis*, temples and cenotaphs in peaceful riverbank setting. Wonderful place to kick back. p.356.

Sanchi (MP) Immaculate Buddhist *stupa*, one of India's earliest religious structures, surrounded by intricate sculpture. p.334.

Taj Mahal (UP) Simply the world's greatest monument: this anthem to romantic love fully matches all expectations. p.212.

Vijayanagar/Hampi (Kar) Deserted city of one of the greatest Hindu empires, scattered over a bizarre landscape of giant, dramatically balanced rocks. p.1066.

long hauls, much the best way to go is by **train**; with computerized booking now established almost everywhere, the Indian rail network is as efficient as almost any in the world. Rail journeys also offer the chance to meet other travellers and Indians from all walks of life, and a constant stream of activity as *chai*-wallahs, peanut-sellers, musicians, astrologers and mendicants wander through the carriages. The travel details in each chapter will help you decide on the most convenient transport, show you the best way to book tickets, and save a great deal of time and frustration.

Finally, the **Contexts** at the end of the book draw together the many facets of Indian life and culture discussed throughout the *Guide*, including summaries of the subcontinent's **history** and manifold **religions**, and overviews of Indian **music** and **cinema** – among the least understood art forms in the world. We also recommend further reading to enjoy before you go and as you travel.

When and Where to Go

Before you decide exactly **where** you go in India, you need to take into account **when** you're going. Broadly speaking, the **best time to visit** most of the country is after the monsoon, and before the summer heat returns – effectively, between October and March. At that time, conditions in the hottest regions, such as Rajasthan and Madhya Pradesh, are at their mildest, and major festivals are held all over the country, while the scenery of southern India is a delight. Between April and September, you should either expect to have to pace yourself even more slowly than at other times, or head for the high mountains, as this is the trekking season in the Himalayas. For more on the

Pilgrimage Sites

Amritsar (H&P) Site of the fabled Golden Temple, the holiest shrine of the Sikhs. p.505.

Bodh Gaya (B) Only last century did archeologists reveal that this was the site of the Buddha's last sermon; now pilgrims come from all over the world. p.789.

Gangotri (UP) Where the sacred Ganga springs from a Himalayan ice-cave; desolate, craggy scenery, a short walk to one of the most beautiful glaciers in the inner Himalayas. p.251.

Madurai (TN) Definitive south Indian temple city, centred on its vibrant, compelling medieval temple. p.954.

Puri (Ori) Gigantic pyramidal Jagannath Temple, one of the four Hindu "Abodes of the Divine", thronging with pilgrims year round. p.856.

Pushkar (Raj) Atmospheric desert town; *ghats* lead down to a shimmering lake, and boasts one of two temples in the world dedicated solely to Lord Brahma. p.157.

Sravanabelgola (Kar) Extraordinary hilltop naked Jain colossus. p.1057.

Varanasi (UP) City of Light, founded by Shiva, where the bathing *ghats* beside the Ganga teem with pilgrims. p.298.

Great Journeys

Camel treks (Raj) Wonderfully romantic way to experience the deserts of Rajasthan; sleep under the stars and visit desert villages. p.168.

Kalka–Shimla: The Viceroy's Toy Train (HP) Tiny blue-and-white diesel locomotive rattling up to the popular summer hill station, deep in the Himalayan foothills. p.408.

Kettuvallam backwaters (Ker) Long lazy boat trips through lush tropical waterways. p.1001.

The Manali–Leh Highway (HP/L) India's greatest high-Himalayan road trip, along the second highest road in the world. p.460.

Neral–Matheran (M) Train up to Maharashtra hill station along 20km of track with 281 sharp bends; hard wooden benches are the price you pay for extraordinary views. p.663.

The Palace on Wheels (Raj) India's answer to the *Orient Express*; one of the most magnificent, opulent train journeys in the world, taking travellers in one pampered week to Rajasthan's major cities and to Agra. p.128.

general topography of India, and the temperatures and rainfall to expect at different times of the year, see p.50.

The most-travelled circuit, combining spectacular monuments with the flat arid landscape that for many people is archetypally Indian, is the so-called "Golden Triangle" in the north – **Delhi** itself, the capital, and within easy reach of it **Agra**, the home of the Taj Mahal, and the Pink City of Rajasthan, **Jaipur**. **Rajasthan** is probably the single most popular state with travellers, who are drawn by its desert scenery, and the romantic Rajput past epitomized by the fort of Jaisalmer, the palaces of Udaipur, and the hilltop temples of Mount Abu.

North of Delhi stretch the mighty **Himalayas**. Kashmir was until the recent escalation of tensions the most touristed region of the mountains; as it was too dangerous to consider researching (and to venture into the Kashmir Valley at the moment, is, sadly, an exercise in pointless bravado) we do not include a chapter on the state in this book. We do however include very detailed accounts of the other Indian Himalayan regions, which partly as a result of government policy are rapidly developing their facilities for visitors. Both **Himachal Pradesh** – where Dharamsala is the home of a Tibetan community that includes the Dalai Lama himself – and **Uttar Pradesh** – where the glacial source of the sacred River Ganges has attracted pilgrims for over a thousand years – offer magnificent trekking, while deeper in the mountains, **Ladakh** and **Sikkim** are scattered with remote Buddhist monasteries.

East of Delhi, the Ganges meanders through some of India's most densely populated regions to reach the extraordinary holy Hindu city of **Varanasi** (also known as

Music and Festivals

Dussehra: Kullu (HP) Village deities brought to Kullu and led in procession by the master god of them all, Raghunathji. Folk music and funfairs. p.442.

Hemis Setchu (L) Two days in summer when this peaceful *gompa* comes alive, crowded with Ladakhi villagers: monks mime out ancient Buddhist texts, while children scamper to join them. p.480.

Khajuraho (MP) Springtime classical dance festival in the ancient city of the Chandellas. p.369.

Konarak (Ori) Odissi dance performances beside the Sun Temple. p.865.

Nizamuddin (D) Medieval district of Delhi, where you can catch hypnotic *qawwali* performances in the exquisite marble courtyard of a Sufi shrine. p.93.

Pushkar camel mela (Raj) The sacred desert city becomes a flurry of life, when camel traders flock from all over the state to race and sell their animals. p.160.

Shantiniketan (WB) Rabindranath Tagore's traditions continue, in the home of the itinerant Baul musicians. p.762.

Thrissur Puram (Ker) Spangled elephants and fireworks accompanied by ear-shattering south Indian drums. p.1022.

Palaces and Forts

Amber Palace (Raj) Breathtaking palace complex: ivory and sandalwood carvings, glittering mirror mosaics and best of all, elephant rides. p.138.

City palace, Jaipur (Raj) Resplendent Rajasthani palace in the wonderful Pink City. p.129.

Daulatabad (M) Imposing Muslim fort that briefly replaced Delhi as capital in the 1300s. p.634.

Golconda (AP). Resolutely elephant-proof stronghold of the Qutb Shahs. p.1082.

Jaisalmer (Raj) Honey-coloured fairytale fort, emerging from the desert sands. p.168.

Jai Vilas, Gwalior (MP) Shamelessly eccentric nineteenth-century palace crammed with fusty antiques. p.352.

Junagarh Fort, Bikaner (Raj) Behind a modest exterior, this sixteenth-century fort shelters magnificent murals and sculpture. p.174.

Padmanabhapuram (Ker) Archetypal south Indian tiled-roofed palace, notable for its religious murals. p.995.

Stok palace (L) Dignified residence of the Ladakhi royals. p.477.

Benares), where to witness the daily rituals of life and death focussed around the waterfront *ghats* (bathing places) is to glimpse the continuing practice of India's most ancient religious traditions. Further east still is the great city of **Calcutta**, the capital until early this century of the British Raj, and now a vibrant centre of Bengali culture that also epitomizes contemporary India's most pressing problems, poverty and over-population.

Heading south from Calcutta along the coast, you come first to **Orissa**, where Puri's Jugganath temple is the scene of one of India's greatest festivals, and the temple at Konarak has re-emerged from beneath the sands to re-state its claims as one of the most fabulous achievements of the medieval stone masons. **Tamil Nadu**, further south, has its own tradition of magnificent architecture, with towering *gopura* gateways dominating towns whose thriving temple complexes are still the focus of everyday life, scuttling with devotees, tourists, gaily painted elephants, and clattering musicians. **Kerala**, near the southernmost tip of the subcontinent on the western coast, is India at its most tropical, and relaxed, with lush backwaters teeming with simple wooden craft of all shapes and sizes, and red-roofed towns and villages all but invisible between the verdant canopy of palm trees. Here, in south India, you will dine on what is simply one of the finest cuisines on earth. Further up the coast is **Goa**, the former Portuguese colony whose 100km-coastline is fringed with beaches to suit all tastes and budgets, from upmarket package tourists to zonked-out ravers, and whose towns hold white-washed Christian churches that might have been transplanted from Europe.

Some of India's most memorable monuments lie far inland, on long-forgotten trading routes across the heart of the peninsula – the abandoned city of **Vijayanagar** (or **Hampi**) in **Karnataka**, whose ruins are scattered across a primeval boulder-strewn landscape; the painted and sculpted Buddhist caves of **Ajanta** and **Ellora** in Maharashtra; the deserted temples of **Khajuraho** and **palaces** of Orchha in Madhya Pradesh. Finally, there's much-maligned **Bombay**, an ungainly beast that has been the major focus of the nationwide drift to the big cities. Centre of the country's formidable film industry, it reels along on an undeniable energy that, after a few days of acclimatization, can prove compelling.

As we've said, however, to appreciate your travels to the full, you'll need to conserve your energies. On a long trip, it makes sense to pause and rest a while every few weeks. Certain places have fulfilled that function for generations. Dotted across the continent are the Victorian **hill stations**, resorts designed to escape the summer heat, created by the British towards the end of the last century wherever a suitable stretch of hills stood conveniently close to the workaday cities of the plains. Within the last thirty years, a network of "alternative" hang-outs for young budget travellers has also developed. These are often places where a tourist infrastructure had already been created, such as the beach resort of **Mamallapuram** in Tamil Nadu, which is also the site of some of India's earliest surviving experiments in temple architecture, or Hampi, mentioned above, or **Manali**, a former hill station in Himachal Pradesh. Elsewhere, the presence of sand and sea is enough, as with many of the beaches of Goa, or **Kovalam** in Kerala.

GETTING THERE FROM BRITAIN AND IRELAND

Direct flights to India from Britain – the quickest, if not necessarily the least expensive, way to reach the subcontinent – serve Delhi, Bombay, Madras and Calcutta. Although Delhi and Bombay are that bit nearer and that bit cheaper, exactly which city you choose to fly to will obviously depend on the area(s) of the country you're intending to explore. If cutting costs is a major priority, investigate the possibilities opened up by taking an indirect flight. As this involves a change of plane, it inevitably takes a few hours longer at the very least, though it may also allow you the option of a stopover on the way out or back. For short stays only, there are also ever-increasing numbers of charter flights to Goa.

Most days, around three direct flights leave **London** for **Delhi**, with *Air India, British Airways, Air Canada* and *Thai* among airlines flying the route. Discounted return fares on these vary from just under £400 return in low season (roughly Jan, Feb, March, May, June & Nov) to upwards of £550 in high season (July, Aug & Dec). *Air Canada* tend to be the cheapest, but *Air India* and *British Airways* sometimes have off-season special offers, which can drop as low as £350.

Cheaper fares – down to as little as £310 return out of season – can usually be found if you're prepared to take an indirect flight with an ex-Soviet Bloc airline such as *Aeroflot, Tarom* or *Air Uzbekistan*. However, there has been a lot of concern recently about the safety records of some of these (notably *Aeroflot*), they can involve

long late-night or multi-day stopovers in unlikely and inhospitable places, and they have been known to leave passengers stranded for weeks waiting for a seat on the return flight (this is especially liable to happen at peak periods; book your return flight as soon as possible). As a result, many agents refuse to deal with them. One more reliable alternative is an indirect flight via Paris with *Air France*, which may work out cheaper than direct-flight prices.

BA and *Air India* also fly direct every day from **London to Bombay** (*Air India's* Sunday flight has a connection to **Goa**), while *Singapore Airlines* cover the route twice weekly. Prices are much the same as those to Delhi. *Egyptair*, with a change in Cairo, charge one fare all year round, which usually makes them the cheapest option in high season.

BA's three weekly direct flights from **London to Madras** cost around £500 return in low season, £600 high season, sometimes reduced as low as £400. Going *Air India* and changing at Bombay may save a little, or you can fly *Air Lanka* and change at Colombo (£520–550; they also fly to Thiruvananthapuram and Tiruchirapalli).

Once again, only *BA* fly direct from **London to Calcutta**, twice weekly; fares with them and with *Air India* cost slightly less than to Madras. *Tarom* and *Aeroflot* are bargain-basement alternatives, at around £350–400 return.

There are no direct flights to India from any **other British cities**. You could fly *BA*, changing at London, but add-on fares are high, so that's not usually the most economical way. From Manchester, your best bet is with *Emirates* to Delhi or Bombay via Dubai for £420–520, depending on season. You can pick up *KLM* flights to India by flying first to Amsterdam, either with *KLM* from Manchester, Belfast, Birmingham, Bristol or Cardiff, or with *Air UK* from Edinburgh, Glasgow, Aberdeen, Humberside, Leeds/Bradford, Norwich, or Newcastle. Similarly, *Air France* fly to Paris from Birmingham, Bristol, Edinburgh and Glasgow; in general, both *KLM* and *Air France* beat *BA* by about £50–100. *Aeroflot* and *Gulf* are other alternatives.

British companies operating winter (Oct–May) **charters to Goa**, include *Hayes and Jarvis* from Gatwick, *Inspirations Holidays* and *Kuoni* from Gatwick and Manchester, and *Inspirations East* from Gatwick, Manchester and Glasgow (see box for addresses). These are usually for stays of two weeks, though one and up to six weeks are also possible. The fare varies from less than £400 out of season to over £650 at Christmas, sometimes including basic accommodation. Note that Indian passport holders cannot fly charter.

FLIGHTS FROM IRELAND

There are no direct flights to India **from Ireland**. Apart from *British Airways* via London, Dublin is also served by *Royal Jordanian* to Delhi, *Swissair* to Bombay or a combination of *Air Inter* and *Air France* to both. Of these, *Royal Jordanian* will be the cheapest in low season (discounted tickets

around I£510 return, rising to I£675 in high season), *Swissair* (around I£600 all year) in high. *Aeroflot*'s daily flight from Shannon is the rock-bottom alternative, at around I£500 all year round.

DISCOUNT AGENTS

The best deals on tickets to India are normally to be found through **discount agents**, who sell off excess seats for airlines at rock-bottom prices. Some of these specialize in youth and student travel, and often have cheap insurance packages on offer too. Try the agents listed on the following pages, or check the ads in the Sunday newspaper travel sections or weekly magazines.

AIRLINES AND AGENTS IN BRITAIN

Airlines

Aeroflot ☎0171/355 2233		**KLM** ☎0181/750 9000	
70 Piccadilly, London W1.		8 Hanover St, London W1.	
Air France ☎0181/742 6600		**Pakistan International Airways** ☎0171/734 5544	
Colet Court, Hammersmith Rd, London W6.		1–15 King St, London.	
Air India ☎0171/491 7979		**Qantas** ☎0345/747767	
17 New Bond St, London W1.		182 The Strand, London W1.	
Air Lanka ☎0171/930 4688		**Royal Jordanian** ☎0171/734 2557	
22 Regent St, London SW1.		177 Regent St, London W1.	
Air UK ☎0345/666777		**Singapore Airlines** ☎0181/747 0007	
Biman ☎0171/629 0252		143–147 Regent St, London W1.	
17 Conduit St, London W1.		**Swissair** ☎0171/434 7200	
British Airways ☎0181/897 4000		Swiss Centre, 3 New Coventry St, London W1.	
156 Regent St, London W1.		**Tarom Romanian Airline** ☎0171/224 3693	

Discount Flight Agents

27 New Cavendish St, London W1.

Campus Travel
52 Grosvenor Gardens, London SW1 ☎0171/730 3402
541 Bristol Rd, Birmingham ☎0121/414 1848
39 Queen's Rd, Clifton, Bristol ☎0117/929 2494
5 Emmanuel St, Cambridge ☎01223/324283
53 Forest Rd, Edinburgh ☎0131/668 3303
166 Deansgate, Manchester ☎0161/273 1721
13 High St, Oxford ☎01865/242067
Student/youth travel specialists, with branches also in YHA shops and on campuses all over Britain.

Flightfile ☎0171/323 4203
49 Tottenham Court Rd, London W1.
Recommended for budget flights.

Global Travel ☎0171/629 5123
10 Maddox St, London W1.

South Coast Student Travel ☎01273/570226
61 Ditchling Rd, Brighton.
Student experts; plenty to offer non-students as well.

STA Travel
74 Old Brompton Rd, London W7 ☎0171/937 9962
25 Queen's Rd, Bristol ☎0117/929 3399
38 Sidney St, Cambridge ☎01223/66966
75 Deansgate, Manchester ☎0161/834 0668
Discount fares, with particularly good deals for students and young people.

Trailfinders
42–48 Earls Court Rd, London W8 ☎0171/938 3366
194 Kensington High St, London W8 ☎0171/938 3939
58 Deansgate, Manchester ☎0161/839 6969
One of the best informed and most efficient agents dealing with Asia; good for RTW tickets, too.

Travel Bug ☎0161/721 4000
597 Cheetham Hill Rd, Manchester.

Union Travel ☎0171/493 4343
93 Piccadilly, Mayfair, London W1.
Competitive airfares and agents for Aeroflot.

USIT ☎01/679 8833
Aston Quay, O'Connell Bridge, Dublin 2, Ireland.

SPECIALIST TOUR OPERATORS IN BRITAIN

Abercrombie and Kent ☎0171/730 9600
Sloane Square House, Holbein Place, London SW1W
8NS. *Upmarket sightseeing and tailor-made holidays,
plus* ExplorAsia's *trekking and wildlife trips.*

Alfred Gregory Holidays ☎0114/272 9428
c/o *Woodcock Travel,* 25–31 Wicker, Sheffield S3
8HW. *Annual photographic trip from a firm founded by
Tensing and Hillary's official snapshot man.*

Asia Experience ☎0171/636 4343
83 Mortimer St, London W1N 7TB. *Tailor-made and
regular tours.*

Bales ☎01306/740048
Bales House, Junction Rd, Dorking, Surrey RH4 3EJ.
*Well-established India tour operator with a range of
sightseeing and wildlife trips.*

Butterfield's Indian Railway Tours ☎01262/470230
Burton Fleming, Driffield, Yorks YO25 0PQ. *Train tours
in the company's own special "bogie" (carriage).*

Coromandel ☎01572/821330
Andrew Brock Travel Ltd, 54 High St, Uppingham,
Rutland LE15 9PZ. *18-day car tours, textile tours to
village craft workshops, plus* David Sayers *botanical
and horticultural tours, and* Himalaya *treks.*

Cox & Kings ☎0171/931 9016
St James Ct, 45 Buckingham Gate, London SW1E 6AF.
Tour operators to India since the days of the Raj.

Cygnus Wildlife Worldwide ☎01548/856178
96 Fore St, Kingsbridge, Devon TQ7 1PY. *Birdwatching
and tiger-watching tours, usually in Feb/March.*

Discover India ☎0181/429 3300
29 Fairview Cres, Rayners Lane, Harrow, Middx HA2
9UB. *Tailor-made trips including tours arranged for
pilgrims and for football or cricket teams.*

Explore Worldwide ☎01252/319448
1 Frederick St, Aldershot, Hants GU11 1LQ. *Trekking,
walking and sightseeing.*

Global Link ☎0171/409 7766
Colette House, 52–55 Piccadilly, London W1V 9AA. *Run
a gourmet food tour as well as standard and tailor-
made sightseeing.*

Hayes and Jarvis ☎0181/748 5050
152 King St, London W6 0QU. *Charter flights, Goa
beach holidays.*

Highlife Holidays ☎0181/452 3388
79 Cricklewood Bdy, London NW2 3JR. *Sightseeing
tours with optional Goa beach extensions.*

High Places ☎0114/275 7500
The Globeworks, Penstone Rd, Sheffield S6 3AE.
*Specialists in trekking, hiking and mountaineering "by
outdoor people for outdoor people".*

Himalayan Folkways ☎01323/646604
c/o *Chandertal Tours,* 10 Station Parade, Eastbourne,
Sussex BN21 1BE. *Specialities include trekking, mountain biking, fishing and white-water rafting.*

Holt's Battlefield Tours ☎01304/612248
15 Market St, Sandwich, Kent. *Annual military history
tours – on the Mutiny, for example – usually in Jan.*

Indian Encounters ☎01929/480548
Creech Barrow, East Creech, Wareham, Dorset BH20
5AP. *Set tours including golf, painting, textiles, and
camelback safaris, plus tailor-made itineraries.*

Inspirations East ☎01753/830883
PO Box 990, Windsor, Berks SL4 3UW. *Charter flights
and beach holidays in Goa and Kovalam.*

Inspirations Holidays ☎01293/822244
Saxley Court, Horley, Surrey RH6 7AS. *Charter flights,
beach holidays in Goa and Lakshadweep. Also painting and photography specials.*

Interchurch Travel Ltd ☎0800/300444
Saga Building, Middleburg Sq, Folkestone, Kent CT20
1AZ. *Interdenominational religious-interest visits.*

Karakoram Experience ☎017687/73966
32 Lake Rd, Keswick, Cumbria CA12 5DQ. *High-
altitude trekking and mountaineering.*

Kuoni Travel ☎01306/740500
Kuoni House, Dorking, Surrey RH5 4AZ. *Charter flights
and a range of tours.*

Maxwell Scott Agency ☎01347/878566
Foss House, Strensall, York YO3 4TU. *Fishing, trekking
and other tailor-made tours.*

Munjeeta Travel ☎01483/773331
12 Cavendish Rd, Woking, Surrey GU22 0EP.
"Homestay" holidays, lodging with Indian families.

Pettits India ☎01892/515966
14 Lonsdale Gardens, Tunbridge Wells, Kent TN1
1NU. *Tailor-made holidays off the beaten track.*

The Romance of India by Rail ☎01232/329477
c/o *Williams Travel,* Whitehead, Co Antrim BT38 9PZ.
Set itineraries and tailor-made tours by train.

Sherpa Expeditions ☎0181/577 2717
131A Heston Rd, Hounslow, Middx TW5 0RD.
Trekking and hiking.

Somak Holidays ☎0181/423 3000
Somak House, Harrovian Village, Bessborough Rd,
Harrow-on-the-Hill, Middx HA1 3EX. *Goa beach holi-
days; optional sightseeing and wildlife extensions.*

Swan Hellenic ☎0171/831 1515
77 New Oxford St, London WC1A 1PP. *Art tours with
specialist guides.*

Trans Indus Travel ☎0181/566 2729
Northumberland House, 11 The Pavement, Popes
Lane, London W5 4NG. *Fixed and tailor-made tours.*

Travel Alternative ☎01865/791636
27 Park End St, Oxford OX1 1HU. *Textile and handicraft tour of Rajasthan and Gujarat every February.*

World Expeditions ☎01628/74174
8 College Rise, Maidenhead, Berks SL6 6BP. *Trekking,
Rajasthan by camel, North India by mountain bike.*

At certain times (Christmas for one), the best-value flights can get booked up weeks, even months, in advance, so plan ahead. If you're flying on to Southeast Asia or the Middle East, it may be possible – but is unlikely to be any cheaper – to get your onward ticket in India rather than at home.

PACKAGES

A large number of operators run **package holidays** to India, covering such activities as trekking and safaris as well as sightseeing and sunbathing. Specialist minority-interest tours range from steam locomotives and war history to religion and food.Even among straight sightseeing tours, most firms have a considerable range of options usually including the "Golden Triangle" of Delhi, Agra and Jaipur, or a tour of Rajasthan, or a southern tour taking in Bangalore, Hyderabad, Madras and Kochi. Some also offer wildlife tours, or the *Palace on Wheels* train journey (see p.29), take in Nepal or even Bhutan, and have various combinations of all these. In addition, many companies will now arrange **tailor-made tours**, where they help you plan your own itinerary.

Of course, any package holiday is a lot easier than going under your own steam, particularly if you only have a short time and don't want to use it up on making your own travel bookings. On the other hand, a typical sightseeing tour can rather isolate you from the country, shutting you off in air-conditioned hotels and buses. Specialist trips such as trekking and tailor-made tours will work out rather expensive, compared to what you'd pay if you organized everything independently, but they do cut out a lot of hassle. However, Goa beach holidays, particularly with charter operators, may even work out cheaper than a normal flight, and usually offer tour options as extras.

FLIGHTS FROM EUROPE

Direct flights connect Delhi and Bombay with Amsterdam, Paris, Rome, Frankfurt, Geneva, Zurich and Moscow. In addition, there are flights from Bucharest to Delhi with *Tarom*, and Athens to Bombay with *Biman*. There are no direct flights from Europe to Madras, and to Calcutta only one weekly (from Moscow with *Aeroflot*). Amsterdam and Athens have their own array of discount agents, but Europeans may find it worthwhile to get to London and buy tickets there: try calling the UK agents listed and comparing their prices to those available where you live.

ROUND THE WORLD

Other possibilities include taking in India as a stopover while flying, for example, between Britain and Australasia, or on a **round-the-world ticket**, which makes a lot of sense if you are planning a long trip with several stops in Asia. A typical one, open for a year, would depart and return to London, taking in Delhi, Bangkok, Sydney, Honolulu and LA; variations could include doing a leg from Delhi to Kathmandu overland.

OVERLAND ROUTES TO INDIA

The classic Asia **overland trip** is still alive and kicking, despite periodic re-routeings in the face of political circumstances. Leaving Europe behind at Istanbul, the usual route traverses Turkey, angles down through Iran, entering Pakistan via Quetta (Afghanistan, alas, is still off-limits), thence to Lahore and across into India at Amritsar, where in the days of Partition, half the population of the Punjab used the same route: Muslims one way, Hindus and Sikhs the other. Thanks to this, crossing the border is rather an abrupt exit from the austere world of Islam into the multi-coloured cacophony of India, as the all-concealing *burqa* suddenly gives way to the graceful *sari*.

Iran is still off-limits, however, to US passport holders, who must therefore find **another route**. One way might be on the trans-Siberian express to China, thence down the Karakoram Highway – if it's open – into Pakistan; another might be to negotiate a ride on a *dhow* from the Gulf to Karachi. It may just be possible to find a cargo ship or a private yacht to take you from the Red Sea or East Africa, but you shouldn't count on it: many travellers have tried and failed.

If you are considering coming by car, motorbike or bicycle, you'll find further information under "Driving" and "Cycling" in the "Getting Around" section on p.32.

The following **overland expedition** operators in the UK run 6- to 18-week trips in special vehicles along the overland trail, most finishing in Kathmandu, Nepal. Expect to pay £1300–2000 for the one-way trip from London, depending on the length of the journey (some detour around the Middle East) and the level of luxury.

Encounter Overland, 267 Old Brompton Rd, London SW5 9JA, ☎0171/370 6951. 11- or 16-week trips to Kathmandu including 1–3 weeks in India. No discount for getting off at Delhi (except perhaps on a last-minute deal). Also trips within India.

FLIGHTS PER WEEK BETWEEN INDIA AND SOUTHEAST ASIA

	Delhi	Bombay	Madras	Calcutta
Dhaka	Air India (2) Biman (1) US$240/£160	BA (2) Biman (1) US$240/£160	via Delhi	Indian Airlines (4) Biman (15) US$50/£35
Karachi	PIA (3) MAS (2) US$100/£65	PIA (5) Indian Airlines (2) Air Lanka (2) US$80/£55	via Bombay	via Delhi
Kathmandu	Royal Nepal (12) Indian Airlines (7) US$145/£95	Royal Nepal (2) US$235/£135	via Delhi	Indian Airlines (3) Royal Nepal (2) US$115/£75
Colombo	Air Lanka (2) US$240/£160	Air Lanka (2) US$150/£100	Air Lanka (7) Indian Airlines (7) US$65/£45	via Madras
Bangkok	Thai (5) Indian Airlines (2) Aeroflot (2) Air France (1) Air India (1) US$220/£150	Cathay (4) Air India (2) Air France (1) US$220/£150	via KL or Colombo	Indian Airlines (4) Thai (3) Air India (1) Druk Air (1) US$170/£115
Kuala Lumpur	MAS (2) Air India (1) US$255/£175	Air India (1) US$255/£175	MAS (6) Air India (2) US$255/£175	via Bangkok or Madras
Singapore	Air India (4) Singapore (3) Aeroflot (1) US$350/£230	Singapore (7) Air India (6) US$400/£270	Air India (8) Singapore (5) Indian Airlines (2) US$400/£270	Air India (2) Singapore (2) US$375/£250
Hong Kong	Air India (4) Air France (1) US$300/£200	Cathay (4) Air India (4) Swissair (3) Air France (1) US$300/£200	via Singapore or KL	via Bangkok

Chittagong (Bangladesh)–Calcutta	Biman (2); Indian Airlines (1)	US$95/£65
Lahore (Pakistan)–Delhi	PIA (4)	US$65/£45
Kathmandu–Varanasi	Indian Airlines (7)	US$80/£55
Colombo–Tiruchirappalli	Air Lanka (7)	US$45/£30
Colombo–Thiruvananthapuram	Air Lanka (5); Indian Airlines (1)	US$45/£30
Penang (Malaysia)–Madras	MAS (1)	US$255/£175
Malé (Maldives)–Thiruvananthapuram	Indian Airlines (7)	US$45/£30

There are no direct flights from **Rangoon** to India.

Not all these (one-way) **fares** are official; they are rough estimates of what you may expect to pay if you shop around.

Exodus Expeditions, 9 Weir Rd, London SW12 0LT, ☎0181/675 5550. 15 weeks to Kathmandu. Discount given if you get off at Islamabad (9 weeks), but not in India.

Hinterland Travel, 2 Ivy Mill Lane, Godstone, Surrey RH9 8NH, ☎01883/743584. London to Delhi almost entirely by train, and London to Kathmandu by bus (3 weeks in India, discount for getting off there).

Top Deck Travel, 131–135 Earls Court Rd, London SW5 9RH, ☎0171/370 4555. 11 weeks to Kathmandu by double-decker including 1–3 weeks in India. Discount if you get off there.

GETTING THERE FROM NORTH AMERICA

India is basically on the other side of the planet from North America. If you live on the East Coast it's somewhat shorter to go via Europe, and from the West Coast it's shorter via the Pacific; but either way it's a long haul, involving one or more intermediate stops, and you'll arrive fresher and less jet-lagged if you can manage to fit in a few days' layover somewhere en route.

Delhi and Bombay are the busiest – and, in general, the cheapest – air gateways to India, and either one makes a good starting/ending point for a tour of the whole country or of the popular north and west. Some airlines fly into Madras, the main port of entry for the south, and Calcutta, in the east; *Air India* also offers direct flights to Goa, on the west coast, and *Gulf Air* flies to Trivandrum in the south. You should be able to ticket a connecting internal flight on *Indian Airlines*, the domestic carrier, at the same time as your international flight. Some typical round-trip add-on fares: Agra, $46 from Delhi; Amritsar, $104 from Delhi; Bangalore, $176 from Bombay; Hyderabad, $118 from Bombay; Trivandrum, $104 from Madras; and Varanasi, $148 from Delhi. (*Indian Airlines'* unlimited-travel air passes can also be purchased in advance – see "Getting Around".)

Air fares from North America to India are highest from around early June to late August, which is fortunate since not too many travellers want to go then anyway. They drop during the "shoulder" seasons (September to early

December and during the last half of May), but you'll get the best deals during the low season (mid-December through mid-May, excluding Christmas). Note that flying on weekends ordinarily adds about $100 to the round-trip fare; price ranges quoted in the sections below assume midweek travel.

If India is only one stop on a longer journey, you might want to consider buying a **round-the-world ticket**. Some travel agents can sell you an "off-the-shelf" RTW ticket, touching down in about half a dozen cities (Delhi is on most itineraries); others will have to assemble one for you, which is apt to be more expensive. Figure on $2200 for a RTW ticket including India and Europe. (Note, however, that you can save quite a bit of money by not going all the way around: round-trip fare to India with multiple stopovers in Asia, but leaving Europe out, will cost less than $1800.)

SHOPPING FOR TICKETS

Airline tickets are sold through many channels, and there's no magic rule for predicting which will be cheapest. Whatever the airlines are offering, however, any number of specialist travel agents set out to beat it. These are the outfits you'll see advertising in the Sunday newspaper travel sections, and they come in several forms. **Consolidators** buy up large blocks of tickets to sell at a discount. Besides being cheap, they don't normally impose advance purchase requirements (although in busy times you'll want to book ahead to be sure of getting a seat), but they do often charge very stiff fees for date changes; note also that airlines generally won't alter tickets after they've gone to a consolidator, so you can only make changes through the consolidator. Also, as these companies' margins are pretty tiny, they make their money by dealing in volume – don't expect them to entertain lots of questions. **Discount agents** also wheel and deal in blocks of tickets offloaded by the airlines, but typically offer a range of other travel-related services such as insurance, youth and student ID cards, car rentals, tours and the like. They tend to be most worthwhile to students and under-26s. **Discount travel clubs**, offering money off air tickets, car rental and the like, are an option if you travel a lot. Most charge annual membership fees.

MAJOR AIRLINES IN NORTH AMERICA

Aeroflot ☎1-800/995 5555
Flights from several US cities and Montréal to Moscow; connections to Delhi and Bombay.

Air Canada call ☎1-800/555 1212 for local toll-free number
All major Canadian cities to London, and on to Delhi.

Air France ☎1-800/237 2747
Flies to Paris from several US cities, and Montréal and Toronto in Canada; connections to Delhi and Bombay.

Air India ☎1-800/223 7776
New York and Toronto to Delhi, Bombay, Madras and Calcutta; also New York to Goa.

British Airways ☎1-800/247 9297
Flies from major North American cities to London, and on to Delhi, Bombay, Madras and Calcutta.

Cathay Pacific ☎1-800/233 2742
LA to Hong Kong; connections to Bombay.

Egypt Air ☎1-800/334 6787
New York to Cairo and on to Bombay.

Gulf Air ☎1-800/553 2824
New York to various Gulf capitals; connections to Delhi, Bombay and Thiruvananthapuram.

KLM ☎1-800/374 7747 (US)
☎1-800/361 5073 (Canada)
Major US and Canadian cities to Amsterdam; connections to Delhi, Bombay and Calcutta.

Kuwait Airways ☎1-800/458 9248
New York to London, and on to Delhi and Bombay.

Lufthansa ☎1-800/645 3880
Many US and Canadian cities to Frankfurt; connections to Bombay, Delhi and Madras.

Northwest Airlines ☎1-800/225 2525
Offers flights from several US cities to India in cooperation with Air India.

PIA ☎1-800/221 2552
New York to Karachi/Lahore, on to Delhi and Bombay.

Singapore Airlines ☎1-800/742 3333
LA or Vancouver to Singapore; connections to Delhi, Bombay, Calcutta and Madras.

Thai International ☎1-800/426 5204
LA to Bangkok; connections to Delhi and Calcutta.

Tower Air ☎1-800/221 2500
New York to Delhi via London.

Don't automatically assume that tickets purchased through a travel specialist will be cheapest – once you get a quote, check with the airlines and you may turn up an even cheaper promotion. Be advised also that the pool of travel companies is swimming with sharks – exercise caution with any outfit that sounds shifty or impermanent (has the phone number changed? the address?), and *never* deal with a company that demands cash up front or refuses to accept payment by credit card.

FROM EASTERN AND CENTRAL USA

Flying eastwards, you'll stop over somewhere in Europe (usually London), and probably again somewhere in the Gulf. Figure on at least 18 hours' total travel time from the East Coast. *Air India* has the only direct flights to India (from New York); on all other airlines, you'll change planes in their hub city.

Air India and *PIA* discount their tickets heavily through a few specialist, understaffed New York consolidators (see box). Marked-down tickets on European carriers – notably *British Airways, Air France* and *Lufthansa* – are frequently sold by other discount agents. Other airlines flying between the eastern US and India include *KLM, Aeroflot, Gulf Air, Kuwait, Egypt Air* and *Tower Air.* Or you can simply hop on any of the dozens of airlines that fly to London and pick up a flight to India from there.

Prices are most competitive out of **New York**, where the cheapest low-season fares to Delhi or Bombay hover around $1250 ($1400 high season). From **Washington** or **Miami**, figure on $1300/ $1450; from **Chicago**, $1400/$1500; and from **Dallas/Ft Worth**, $1450/$1600. Fares to Madras, Calcutta or Goa run about $100 to $150 higher.

FROM THE WEST COAST

From the West Coast, it takes about as long to fly eastwards or westwards – a minimum of 22 hours' total travel time – and if you're booking through a consolidator there may not be much difference in price, either. *Thai, Cathay* and *Singapore* are the main carriers flying over the Pacific to India, via their respective hubs. *Air India* doesn't do the trans-Pacific route, but can book passengers on *Northwest* to any of several Asian capitals and then fly them the rest of the way. For eastbound routings, see above.

From **Los Angeles** or **San Francisco**, you're looking at a minimum of $1400 to fly to Delhi or Bombay in low season, or $1500 in high season. Flights to Madras, Calcutta or Goa cost about $50 more (Goa is only served by *Air India*, via London).

NORTH AMERICAN TOUR OPERATORS

Adventure Center ☎1-800/227 8747
1311 East 63rd St, Emeryville, CA 94608.
Trekking.

Cox & Kings ☎1-800/999 1758
511 Lexington Ave, Suite 355, New York, NY 10017.
Deluxe sightseeing.

Himalayan Travel ☎1-800/225 2380
112 Prospect St, Stamford, CT 06901.
Custom regional tours.

InnerAsia ☎1-800/777 8183
2627 Lombard St, San Francisco, CA 94123.
Unusual tours (eg, sea kayaking in the Andamans).

Journeyworld International ☎1-800/635 3900
119 West 57th St, Penthouse N, New York, NY 10019.
Regional tours.

Mercury Travels Limited ☎1-800/223 1474
820 2nd Ave, Suite 1302, New York, NY 10017.
Custom regional tours.

Mindful Journeys ☎1-800/654 7975
1242 24th St, Santa Monica, CA 90404.
"Appropriate tourism".

Mountain Travel/Sobek ☎1-800/227 2384
6420 Fairmount Ave, El Cerrito, CA 94530.
Trekking, camel safaris.

Nature Expeditions International ☎503/484 6529
474 Wilamette St, Eugene, OR 97440.
Wildlife tours.

Tours of Distinction ☎1-800/888 8634
141 East 44th St, New York, NY 10017.
Regional and all-India tours.

Wilderness Travel ☎1-800/368 2794
802 Allston Way, Berkeley, CA 94710.
Rajasthan camel safari.

Worldwide Adventures ☎1-800/387 1483
36 Finch Ave West, North York, ON M2N 2G9.
Sightseeing plus trekking, cycling and sailing.

DISCOUNT AGENTS, CONSOLIDATORS AND TRAVEL CLUBS

Air Brokers International ☎1-800/883 3273
323 Geary St, Suite 411, San Francisco, CA 94102.
Consolidator.

Council Travel ☎1-800/743 1823
Head Office: 205 E 42nd St, New York, NY 10017.
*Nationwide US student travel organization. Branches
(among others) in San Francisco, Washington DC,
Boston, Austin, Seattle, Chicago, Minneapolis.*

Discount Travel International ☎1-800/334 9294
Ives Bldg, 114 Forrest Ave, Suite 205, Narberth, PA
19072.
Discount travel club.

Fly Time ☎212/760 3737
45 West 34th St, Suite 305, New York, NY 10001.
Consolidator specializing in tickets to India.

Hariworld Travel ☎212/957 3000
30 Rockefeller Plaza, Shop 21, Mezzanine Floor, New
York, NY 10012.
Biggest Indian consolidator; agent for Indrail Passes.

HighTime Travel ☎212/684 7700
303 5th Ave, Suite 204, New York, NY 10016.
Consolidator specializing in tickets to India.

Moment's Notice ☎212/486 0503
425 Madison Ave, New York, NY 10017.
Discount travel club.

New Frontiers (US) ☎1-800/366 6387
Nouvelles Frontières (Canada) ☎514/526 8444
12 E 33rd St, New York, NY 10016.
1001 Sherbrook East, Suite 720, Montréal, H2L 1L3.
*French discount travel firm. Other branches in LA, San
Francisco and Québec City.*

STA Travel ☎1-800/777 0112
Head office: 48 East 11th St, New York, NY 10003.
*Worldwide specialist in independent travel with
offices in Los Angeles, San Francisco, Boston.*

Stand Buys ☎1-800/255 0200
311 W Superior St, Chicago, IL 60610.
Discount travel club.

Travel Cuts ☎416/979 2406
Head office: 187 College St, Toronto, ON M5T 1P7.
Nationwide Canadian student travel organization .

Unitravel ☎1-800/325 2222
1177 N Warson Rd, St Louis, MO 63132.
US consolidator.

FROM CANADA

At the time of writing, the only direct flights from
Canada to India were Toronto–Delhi on *Air India*
and Vancouver–Delhi on *Air Canada* (both via
London, and both taking under 20hr). All other
routings involve a plane change and more layover
time. *Air Canada* flies from all major Canadian
cities to London, where passengers can join the
Vancouver–Delhi flight. Other airlines offering

services to India, via their capitals, include *British
Airways, Air France, Lufthansa, KLM* and *Aeroflot*.
This list doesn't convey the full range of possibilities, however. A discount agent will probably
break the journey into two, using one of dozens of
carriers for the transatlantic (or trans-Pacific) leg.

Typical discounted low/high season fares to
Delhi or Bombay: from **Montréal** or **Toronto**,
CDN$1350/$1550; from **Vancouver**, CDN$1400/
$1600. Add $100 for Madras, Calcutta or Goa.

PACKAGES AND ORGANIZED TOURS

Wrapping India up into a tidy **package** makes it less daunting and more comprehensible to many first-time tourists, and this is not a bad thing. A tour company can also shield you from the subcontinent's many little frustrations, enabling you to cover more ground than if you were going it alone. Of course, you'll have to be prepared to forgo independence and spontaneity, and accept that there will be only fleeting and predominantly mercenary encounters with local people.

Tours of India work best when they focus on one region of the country, or when based on an activity or a special interest. A fairly standard best-seller list is offered by many companies: Rajasthan palaces, Rajasthan camel safaris (often timed to coincide with the Pushkar Camel Fair), Agra–Varanasi–Khajuraho (often packaged with a few days in Nepal), wildlife parks, Goa, temples and/or beaches of the south, and the *Palace on Wheels* railway. Quite a few companies specialize in trekking in the Himalaya, although they invariably offer many more itineraries in Nepal than in India.

Tour prices are always wildly out of line with the cost of living in India, and whether you take one will depend on which is tighter, your budget or your schedule. Excluding airfare, a two-week tour is likely to cost at least $1000, and a three-week trip with all the bells and whistles can cost $3000 or more. The *Palace on Wheels* is the ultimate in expense – $1850 for eight days. Your local travel agent should be able to book any tour for you at no additional cost.

GETTING THERE FROM AUSTRALASIA

One of the best-value air fares **from Australia** to India is on *Qantas* and *Air India* from the east coast, Perth and Darwin: flying via Singapore to Bombay or Delhi costs around Aus$1400, while via Kuala Lumpur to Madras or Calcutta is more like $1260. An *Indian Airlines* airpass (see p.31) can be added on for another US$400. For most of the year there are two flights weekly; in the peak season, from March onwards, that rises to around five.

Of possible alternatives, *Thai International* fly via Bangkok to Delhi from eastern Australia ($1320) and Perth ($1218), and to Calcutta ($1269/$1167). Also via Bangkok, *British Airways*

and *Air France* combine for Bombay ($1400). *Malaysian Airlines* fly twice weekly from eastern Australia via Kuala Lumpur to Madras or Delhi ($1300), and to Colombo or Karachi ($1390). *Singapore* fly to Bombay or Delhi for $1725 from eastern Australia, $1467 from Perth or Darwin, and to Calcutta ($1655/$1408) or Karachi ($1795/$1530). *Cathay Pacific* charge $1560 to Bombay via Hong Kong from the east coast or Perth. There's also a weekly *Qantas* and *Royal Nepal* deal to various destinations in India via Kathmandu ($1890).

Round-the-world fares from Australia using the above airlines can take in India; for example, *Thai* and *Air New Zealand*, flying Sydney–Kathmandu, making your own way to Delhi, then Delhi–Los Angeles–London is around $2160. If you want to **add on** to a round-the-world deal that doesn't include India – such as *Qantas* and *British Airways*' **Global Explorer** pass (from $2299 to six destinations) – it costs around $652 for a three-month excursion fare to Delhi from Kuala Lumpur, Singapore or Bangkok.

From New Zealand, *Malaysian Airlines* have the best deal, flying twice weekly to Delhi, Madras or Karachi via Kuala Lumpur from NZ$1770. *Air France* (via Bangkok), *Singapore*, *Korean*, *Cathay Pacific* (via Hong Kong), *Thai* and *Air India* fly to Delhi, Calcutta, and Bombay from around NZ$1800.

AIRLINES AND AGENTS IN AUSTRALASIA

Airlines

Aeroflot ☎02/233 7911
388 George St, Sydney

Air France
12 Castlereagh St, Sydney ☎02/233 3277
57 Fort St, Auckland ☎09/303 1229

Qantas
Hunter and Phillip St, Sydney ☎02/952 9555
154 Queen St, Auckland ☎09/303 2506

Singapore Airlines ☎02/231 6333
5 Elizabeth St, Sydney.

Specialist Agents

Flight Centres
Circular Quay, Sydney ☎02/241 2422
Bourke St, Melbourne ☎03/650 2899
205–225 Queen St, Auckland ☎09/309 6171
50–52 Willis St, Wellington ☎04/472 8101
Branches throughout Australia and New Zealand.

STA Travel
732 Harris St, Ultimo, Sydney ☎02/212 1255
256 Flinders St, Melbourne ☎03/347 4711
10 High St, Auckland ☎09/309 9995
233 Cuba St, Wellington ☎04/385 0561
223 High St, Christchurch ☎03/379 9098
Branches throughout Australia and New Zealand.

Adventure World ☎02/956 7766
73 Walker St, Sydney.

Budget Travel ☎09/309 4313
PO Box 505, Auckland.

Discover India Tours ☎03/654 2333
12 Southern Cross Hotel, Melbourne.

Harvey World Travel ☎02/570 5677
7 Frederick St, Oatley, NSW.

India-Ceylon Travel Service ☎02/264 5839
104 Bathurst Rd, Sydney.

India Information Centre ☎09/221 1207
Airways House, 195 Adelaide Terrace, Perth.

India/Nepal Adventure Travel ☎07/854 1022
1st Floor, 132 Wickham St, Brisbane.

India/Nepal Travel Centre ☎07/221 4788
262 Adelaide St, Brisbane.

Into India ☎02/328 1672
17 Knox Lane, Double Bay.

Nepal Trade and Travel ☎09/386 2102
16 Robinson St, Nedlands, Perth.

Peregrine ☎03/663 8611
258 Lonsdale St, Melbourne.

Summit Travel ☎09/321 1259
862 Hay St, Perth.

BY LAND AND SEA THROUGH SOUTHEAST ASIA

It's barely possible to get from Australasia to India without flying at least part of the way. Flights from Darwin to Timor or Bali can in any case be rather more convenient than the boat trip, but your real barrier is Burma, still impassable by land. With the return of the boat service between Penang (Malaysia) and Madras as yet still no more than a rumour, the only solution is to fly from Singapore, KL or Bangkok to Calcutta, Dhaka or Kathmandu.

VISAS AND RED TAPE

Gone are the days when Commonwealth nationals could stroll visa-less into India and stay for as long as they pleased: nowadays everybody needs a visa, except Nepalis and Bhutanis.

Tourist visas for all nationalities are issued either for one month from date of entry, with that entry having to be within a month of issue (£3/US$5/CDN$15; this visa not available by post), or for six months from the date of issue (*not* of entry; £16/US$24/CDN$35). As you're asked to specify whether you need a single-entry or a multiple-entry visa, and the same rates apply for both, it makes sense to ask for the latter, just in case you make a side trip to Nepal or another neighbouring country.

Much the best place to get a visa is in your country of residence, from the embassies and high commissions listed on p.14. Embassies in those countries that neighbour India often drag their feet, demand letters of recommendation from your embassy (expensive if you are, for example, British), or make you wait and pay for them to send your application to Delhi. Tourist visas are available by post in most countries, though in the US for example this takes a month as opposed to two days if you do it in person – check your nearest embassy, high commission or consulate to be sure.

It's also possible in many countries, and in most instances faster, to pay a **visa agency** to obtain them on your behalf. In Britain, *Worldwide Visas* are at 9 Adelaide St, London WC2; ☎0171/379 0419, fax 071/497 2590.

Tourist visas can be **extended** by three months at the foreigners' registration office in Delhi, Bombay, Calcutta and Madras (see the relevant chapters for addresses), or with the Superintendent of Police at any District Headquarters. Officially, this is free, but charges are sometimes made to oil the wheels of bureaucracy, and you'll also need four passport photos.

If you do stay more than 180 days, before you leave the country you are supposed to get a **tax clearance certificate**, available at the foreigners' section of the income tax department in every major city. They are free, but you should take bank receipts to show you have changed your money legally. In practice, tax clearance certificates are rarely demanded, but you never know.

For details of other visas – foreigners of Indian origin, business travellers, and even students of yoga, can get five-year visas – contact your nearest Indian embassy.

Duty-free allowances for travellers arriving in India are covered on p.66.

SPECIAL PERMITS

In addition to a visa, **special permits** may be required for travel to certain specific areas of the country, while others – such as parts of Sikkim and the northeast frontier states, and the far northeast of Himachal Pradesh near the Tibetan border – remain out of bounds altogether to foreign nationals. If you have some special reason for going to any of these, apply for a permit to the Ministry for Home Affairs Foreigners' Section, Lok Nayak Bhavan, Khan Market, New Delhi 110 003, at least four weeks in advance.

Permits for those areas of **Sikkim** that are open to tourists are easily available at all foreigners' registration offices, immigration officers at the main international airports, all Indian embassies, consulates and high commissions abroad, and at offices in nearby Darjeeling and Siliguri. Sikkim is the only place where you need a special **trekking permit**.

Certain parts of the northeastern hill states are sometimes open to visitors, often only on group tours. Assam permits are the easiest to get, and

For more details of **permit** requirements, see the relevant chapters of this book.

can be issued by all foreigners' registration offices and Indian diplomatic missions abroad. When available, permits for the other northeastern states are issued at the foreigners' registration offices in Calcutta, New Delhi, Bombay or Madras, or their state representatives' offices in Calcutta; you *may* be able to get some of them with your visa at Indian diplomatic missions abroad.

Should you get your hands on a visa for **Bhutan**, you'll also need a transit permit for the border area from the Ministry of External Affairs.

INDIAN DIPLOMATIC REPRESENTATIVES ABROAD

UK
Embassy: India House, Aldwych, London WC2B 4NA, ☎0171/836 8484.

Consulate: 82 New St, Birmingham B2 4BA, ☎0121/643 0366.

Ireland
6 Leeson Park, Dublin 6, ☎01/970843.

USA
Embassy of India (Consular Section): 2107 Massachusetts Ave NW, Washington DC 20008, ☎202/939 7000.

Consulates: 3 East 64th St, New York, NY 10021-7097, ☎212/879 7800; 540 Arguello Blvd, San Francisco, CA 94118, ☎415/668 0662; 150 N Michigan Ave, Suite 1100, Chicago, IL 60601, ☎312/781 6280; 201 St Charles Ave, New Orleans, LA 70170, ☎504/582 8106; 1100 Huntingdon Building, Cleveland, OH 44155, ☎216/696 1100; 2051 Young St (PO Box 15683), Honolulu, HI 96826, ☎808/947 2618.

Canada
High Commission: 10 Springfield Rd, Ottawa, ON K1M 1C9, ☎613/744 3751.

Consulates: 2 Bloor St W, #500, Toronto, ON M4W 3E2, ☎416/960 0751; 325 Howe St, 2nd Floor, Vancouver, BC V6C 1Z7, ☎604/662 8811.

Australia
Embassy: 3–5 Moonah Place, Yarralumla, Canberra, ACT 2600, ☎06/273 3999.

Consulates: 153 Walker St, 11th floor, North Sydney, NSW 2060, ☎02/955 7055; 13 Munro St, Coburg, Vic 3058, ☎03/384 0141; c/o *Magic Carpet Tours & Travels Ltd*, 4th floor, 195 Adelaide Terrace, East Perth, WA 6004, ☎09/221 1207.

New Zealand
10th floor, 180 Molesworth St (PO Box 4045), Wellington 1, ☎04/473 6390.

ASIA
Bangladesh House 120, Rd 2, Dhanmondi Residential Area, Dhaka, ☎02/503606; 1253–1256 OR Nizam Rd, Mehdi Bagh, Chittagong, ☎031/211007.

Burma (Myanmar) Oriental Assurance Building, 545-547 Merchant St (PO Box 751), Rangoon, ☎01/82550.

Japan 2-11, Kudan Minami 2-Chome, Chiyoda-ku, Tokyo 102, ☎03/3262 239.

Malaysia 2 Jalan Taman Dlita (off Jalan Duta), PO Box 10059, 50704 Kuala Lumpur, ☎03/253 3511.

Nepal Lainchaur (off Lazimpath), PO Box 292, Kathmandu, ☎01/410900. Mon–Fri 9.30–11am, allow a week – plus extra fee – to fax Delhi; Brits and some Europeans need letters of recommendation.

Pakistan G-5, Diplomatic enclave, Islamabad, ☎051/814371; India House, 3 Fatima Jinnah Rd (PO Box 8542), Karachi, ☎021/512542.

Singapore India House, 31 Grange Rd (PO Box 9123), Singapore 0923, ☎737 6777.

Sri Lanka 36-38 Galle Rd, Colombo 3, ☎01/421605; 31 Rajapihilla Mawatha, PO Box 47, Kandy, ☎08/24563.

Thailand 46 Soi 23 (Prasarn Mitr), Sukhumvit Rd, Bangkok 10110, ☎02/258 0300; 113 Bumruangrat Rd, Chiang Mai 50000, ☎053/243066. Visas may take as much as two weeks to issue, with letters of recommendation required.

OTHER EUROPEAN COUNTRIES
Austria Kärntner Ring 2, 1015 Wien, ☎01/505 8667.

Belgium 217 Chaussée de Vleurgat, 1050 Brussels, ☎02/640 9140.

Denmark Vangehusvej 15, 2100 København, ☎3118 2888.

France 15 Rue Alfred Dehodencq, 75016 Paris, ☎1/4050 7070.

Germany Adenauerallee 262-264, 53113 Bonn 1, ☎0228/54050; Majakowskiring, 13156 Berlin, ☎030/480 0178; Mittelweg 49, 60318 Frankfurt Main, ☎069/153 0050; Raboisen 6, 20095 Hamburg, ☎040/338036; Lenzhalde 65, 70192 Stuttgart, ☎0711/301 4266.

Italy Via XX Settembre 5, 00187 Roma, ☎06/488 4642; Via Larga 16, 20122 Milan, ☎02/869 0314.

Netherlands Buitenrustweg 2, 251 KD, Den Haag, ☎070/346 9771.

Norway Niels Juelsgaten 30, 0244 Oslo 2, ☎2255 2229.

Spain Av Pio XII 30–32, 28016 Madrid, ☎91/345 0406; C/T Roviralta 21–23, 08022 Barcelona, ☎93/212 0422.

Sweden Adolf Fredriks Kyrkogatan 12, Box 1340, 11183 Stockholm, ☎08/107008.

Switzerland Effingerstraße 45, 3008 Berne, ☎031/382 3111.

TRAVEL INSURANCE

In the light of the potential health risks involved in a trip to India – see p.17 – travel insurance is too important to ignore. In addition to covering medical expenses and emergency flights, it also insures your money and belongings against loss or theft.

Flights paid for with a major credit or charge card offer some automatic cover, but usually only while travelling to and from your destination. Some package tours too may include insurance, but package operators more commonly offer an insurance deal as an extra: it might be worth checking against alternative policies, though differences in price and cover are likely to be slight.

Always check the fine print of a policy. A 24-hour medical emergency contact number is a must, and one of the rare policies that pays your medical bills directly is better than one that reimburses you on your return home. The per-article limit for loss or theft should cover your most valuable possession (a camera for example) but, conversely, don't pay for cover you don't need – such as too much baggage or a huge sum for personal liability. Make sure, too, that you are covered for all the things you intend to do. Activities such as climbing are usually specifically excluded, but can be added for a supplement.

Frequent travellers may benefit from **annual** insurance policies, but these almost invariably put an upper limit on the duration of any single trip, likely to be ninety days at most.

Among **UK insurers**, *Endsleigh* are about the cheapest, offering a month's cover for around £45 (£36 for under-35s). Their policies are sold by most youth/student travel specialists, or direct from their offices at 97–107 Southampton Row, London WC1B 4AG (☎0171/436 4451). *Columbus Travel Insurance* (☎0171/375 0011) also offer low rates.

Travellers from the **US** should carefully check their current insurance policies before taking out a new one. You may discover that you are already covered for medical and other losses while abroad. Holders of ISIC cards are entitled to be reimbursed for $3000-worth of accident coverage and 60 days of in-patient benefits of up to $100 a day for the period the card is valid. If you do want a specific travel insurance policy, there are numerous kinds to choose from: short-term combination policies covering everything from baggage loss to broken legs are the best bet and cost around $25 for ten days, plus $1 per day for trips of 75 days or more. Companies you might try include *Travel Guard*, 110 Centrepoint Drive, Steven Point, WI 54480 (☎715/345 0505 or 1-800/826 1300), *Access America International*, 600 Third Ave, New York, NY 10163 (☎212/949 5960 or 1-800/284 8300), and *Travel Assistance International* (☎1-800/821 2828).

In **Australia**, *Cover-More* policies issued by *CIC Ltd* (☎02/202 8000) cater for the needs of travellers on all budgets.

If you need **to claim**, you *must* have a police report in the case of theft or loss, and supporting evidence of medical treatment in the form of bills, though with some policies, doctors and hospitals will be able to bill your insurers direct. Keep photocopies of everything you send to the insurer and don't allow months to elapse before informing them. Write immediately and tell them what's happened; you can usually claim later.

HEALTH

A lot of visitors get ill in India, and some of them get very ill. However, if you are careful, you should be able to get through the country with nothing worse than a dose of "Delhi belly". The important thing is to keep your resistance high and to be aware of health risks such as poor hygiene, untreated water, mosquito bites and undressed open cuts.

What you **eat** and **drink** is crucial: a poor diet lowers your resistance. Ensure you eat a balance of protein, energy, vitamins and minerals. Meat and fish are obvious sources of protein for non-vegetarians in the west, but not necessarily in India; eggs, pulses (lentils, peas and beans), rice and curd are all protein sources, as are nuts. Overcooked vegetables lose a lot of their vitamin content; eating plenty of peeled fresh fruit helps keep up your vitamin and mineral intake. With all that sweating, too, make sure you get enough salt (put a bit extra on your food) and drink enough water. It's also worth taking daily multi-vitamin and mineral tablets with you. Above all, make sure you eat *enough* – an unfamiliar diet may reduce the amount you eat – and **get enough sleep** and rest: it's easy to get run down if you're on the move a lot, especially in a hot climate.

In Britain, travellers who call the "**Health Line**" run by *Masta* – the Medical Advisory Service for Travellers Abroad – on ☎01891/224100 receive the latest detailed health advice by return post. *Masta* is based at the London School of Hygiene and Tropical Medicine, Keppel St, London WC1E 7HT (☎0171/631-4408).

PRECAUTIONS

The lack of sanitation in India can be exaggerated. It's not worth getting too worked up about or you'll never enjoy anything, but a few **common-sense precautions** are in order, bearing in mind that things such as bacteria multiply far more quickly in a tropical climate, and your foreign body will have little immunity to Indian germs.

For details on the **water**, see the box below. When it comes to **food**, it's every bit as likely that tourist restaurants and "western" dishes will bring you grief. Be particularly wary of prepared dishes that have to be reheated – ask yourself how long they've been on diplay in the heat and

the flies. Anything that is boiled or fried (and thus sterilized) in your presence is usually all right, though meat can sometimes be dodgy; anything that has been left out for any length of time is definitely suspect. Raw unpeeled fruit and vegetables should always be viewed with suspicion, and you should avoid salads unless you know they have been soaked in an iodine or potassium permanganate solution.

Be vigilant about **personal hygiene**. Wash your hands often, especially before eating, keep all cuts clean, treat them with iodine or antiseptic, and cover them to prevent infection. Be fussier about sharing things like drinks and cigarettes than you might be at home; never share a razor or toothbrush. It is also inadvisable to go around barefoot – and best to wear flip-flop sandals even in the shower.

Among items you might wish to carry with you – though all are available in India itself, at a fraction of what you might pay at home – are hypodermic needles and sterilized skin wipes (more for the security of knowing you have them with you, than any fear that an Indian hospital would fail to observe basic sanitary precautions), antiseptic cream, plasters, lints and sealed bandages, a course of Flagyl antibiotics, a box of Immodium (Lomotil) for emergency diarrhoea treatment, rehydration sachets, insect repellent and some thing such as *Anthisan* for soothing bites, and paracetamol or aspirin (useful for combating the effects of altitude).

Advice on avoiding **mosquitoes** is offered under "Malaria" below. If you do get bites or itches try not to scratch them: it's hard, but infection and tropical ulcers can result if you do. Tiger balm and even dried soap may relieve the itching.

Finally, especially if you are going on a long trip, have a **dental check-up** before you leave home – you don't want to go down with unexpected tooth trouble in India. If you do, and it feels serious, head for Delhi, Bombay or Calcutta, and ask a foreign consulate to recommend a dentist.

VACCINATIONS

No **innoculations** are legally required for entry into India, but meningitis, typhoid, and hepatitis A jabs are recommended, and it's worth ensuring that you are up to date with tetanus, polio and other boosters. All vaccinations can be obtained

WHAT ABOUT THE WATER ?

One of the chief concerns of many prospective visitors to India is whether the **water** is safe to drink. To put it simply, no, though your unfamiliarity with Indian micro-organisms is generally more of a problem rather than any great virulence in the water itself. The fact is, if you are in the country for a while, your stomach will have to get used to local bugs, and you will probably get diarrhoea a few times. By exercising reasonable caution, however, you can minimize the risk of going down with anything more serious.

It is generally not a good idea to drink **tap water**, although in big cities it is usually chlorinated. However, it is almost impossible in practice to avoid untreated tap water completely: it is used to make ice, which may appear in drinks without being asked for, *lassis* are made with it, utensils are washed up with it, and so on. **Bottled water** is widely available. Always check that the seal is intact, as refilling bottles is not uncommon. Carbonated water is generally safer, as it is more likely to be genuine.

If you plan to go somewhere with no access to bottled drinks – which really only applies to travellers venturing well off the beaten track – find an appropriate method of **treating water**, whether your source is tap water or natural groundwater such as a river or stream. **Boiling** it for a minimum of five minutes (longer at higher altitudes) is sufficient to kill micro-organisms, but is not always practical and does not remove unpleasant tastes. **Chemical sterilization** is cheap and convenient, but dirty water remains dirty, and still contains organic matter or other contamination. You can sterilize water using chlorine or iodine tablets, but these leave a nasty after-taste (which can be masked with lemon or lime juice) and are not effective in preventing such diseases as amoebic dysentery and giardia. Tincture of iodine is better; add a couple of drops to one litre of water and leave to stand for twenty minutes. Pregnant women, babies, and people with thyroid problems should avoid using iodine sterilizing tablets or iodine-based purifiers, or use an additional iodine-removal filter. The various kinds of **filter** only remove visible impurities and the larger pathogenic organisms (most bacteria and cysts). However fine the filter, it will not remove viruses, dissolved chemicals, pesticides, herbicides etc.

Purification, a two-stage process involving both filtration and sterilization, gives the most complete treatment. Portable water purifiers range from pocket-size units weighing 60 grams, up to 800 grams. Some of the best water purifiers on the market are made in Britain by **Pre-Mac**; for suppliers, contact:

Pre-Mac (Kent) Ltd ☎01892/534361 40 Holden Park Rd, Southborough, Tunbridge Wells, Kent TN4 0ER, England.	**Outbound Products** ☎800/663 9262 1580 Zephyr Ave, Box 56148, Hayward CA 9454, USA.
All Water Systems Ltd ☎01/456 4933 Unit 12, Western Parkway Business Centre, Lr. Ballymount Rd, Dublin 12, Ireland.	**Outbound Products** ☎604/321 5464 8585 Fraser St, Vancouver, BC V5X 3Y1, Canada.

in Delhi, Bombay and other major cities if necessary; just make sure the needle is new.

Hepatitis A is not the worst disease you can catch in India, but the frequency with which it strikes travellers makes a strong case for immunization. Transmitted through contaminated food and water, or through saliva, it can lay a victim low for several months with exhaustion, fever and diarrhoea – and may cause liver damage if mixed with alcohol. The new *Havrix* vaccine has been shown to be extremely effective; though expensive, it lasts for up to ten years. The protection given by gammaglobulin, the traditional serum of hepatitis antibodies, wears off quickly and the injection should therefore be as late as possible before departure: the longer your planned stay, the larger the dose.

Symptoms by which you can recognize hepatitis include a yellowing of the whites of the eyes, general malaise, orange urine (though dehydration could also cause that) and light-coloured stools. If you think you have it, avoid alcohol, try to avoid passing it on, and get lots of rest. More serious is **hepatitis B**, passed on like AIDS through blood or sexual contact. There is a vaccine, but it is only recommended for those planning to work in a medical environment. Otherwise, your chances of getting hepatitis B are low – assuming you take the precautions you should be taking to avoid AIDS.

Typhoid, also spread through contaminated food or water, is endemic in India, but rare outside the monsoon. It produces a persistent high fever with malaise, headaches and abdominal pains, followed by diarrhoea. Vaccination can be by injection (two shots are required, or one for a booster), giving three years' cover, or orally – tablets are more expensive but easier on the arm.

Cholera, spread the same way as hepatitis A and typhoid, causes sudden attacks of watery diarrhoea with cramps and debilitation. It is endemic in the Ganges basin, but only during periodic epidemics. If you get it, take copious amounts of water with rehydration salts and seek medical treatment. There is a vaccination but it offers very little protection (the vaccine used in India is usually stronger than at home, with longer-lasting after-effects).

Most medical authorities now recommend vaccination against **meningitis** too. Spread by airborne bacteria (through coughs and sneezes for example), it is a very unpleasant disease that attacks the lining of the brain and can be fatal.

You should have a **tetanus** booster every ten years whether you travel or not. Tetanus (or lock-jaw) is picked up through contaminated open wounds; if you cut yourself on something dirty and are not covered, get a booster as soon as you can.

Assuming that you were vaccinated against **polio** in childhood, only one (oral) booster is needed during your adult life. Immunizations against mumps, measles, TB, and rubella are a good idea for anyone who wasn't vaccinated as a child and hasn't had the diseases.

Although **rabies** is a problem in India, the best advice is to give dogs and monkeys a wide berth, and not to play with animals at all, no matter how cute they might look. A bite, a scratch or even a lick from an infected animal could spread the disease; wash any such wound immediately but gently with soap or detergent, and apply alcohol or iodine if possible. Find out what you can about the animal and swap addresses with the owner (if there is one) just in case. If the animal might be infected, act immediately to get treatment – rabies is invariably fatal once symptoms appear. There is a vaccine, but it is expensive, serves only to shorten the course of treatment you need anyway, and is only effective for a maximum of three months.

MALARIA

Protection against **malaria** is absolutely essential. The disease, caused by a parasite in the saliva of *Anopheles* mosquitoes, is endemic everywhere in India except high-altitude regions of Himachal Pradesh, Kashmir and Sikkim. It has a variable incubation period of a few days to several weeks, so you can become ill long after being bitten.

It is vital to take **preventative tablets** according to a strict routine, and to cover the period before and after your trip. The basic drug used is chloroquine (trade names include *Nivaquin*, *Avloclor* and *Resochin*), usually two tablets weekly, but India has chloro-quine-resistant strains, and you'll need to supplement it with daily proguanil (*Paludrine*) or weekly *Maloprim*. A new weekly drug, mefloquine (*Lariam*), is supposed to replace all these, but is not currently recommended for journeys of more than two months. Australian authorities are now prescribing the antibiotic tetracycline instead.

If you go down with malaria, you'll probably know. The fever, shivering and headaches are like severe flu and come in waves, usually beginning in the early evening. Malaria is not infectious, but can be dangerous and sometimes even fatal if not treated quickly. If you can, go to a doctor for a blood test to confirm the strain; if this isn't possible, take two 600mg quinine tablets three times daily for seven days, then three *Fansidar* tablets. If you can't get quinine, take ordinary chloroquine (10mg per kilo body weight up to 600mg maximum, usually four tablets), then half as much eight hours later. If you improve, repeat the second dose on the next two days; if not, your malaria is chloroquine-resistant, so see a doctor or obtain and take three *Fansidar*.

Side-effects of these drugs may include itching, rashes, hair loss and even sight problems, and it is probably not advisable to use them for prolonged periods, but on a three-month trip, it is just common sense. Chloroquine and quinine are safe during pregnancy, but *Maloprim*, *Fansidar*, mefloquine and tetracycline should be avoided then. Note that the doses we quote apply to adults: children will want lower ones.

The most important thing, however, is to **avoid mosquito bites**. Sleep under a net if possible – one which can hang from a single point is best (you can usually find a way to tie a string across your room to hang it from), burn mosquito coils (easily available, but easy to break in transit), or use repellent (an Indian brand called *Odomos* is widely available and very effective; Avon *Skin So Soft* bath oil is regarded by many as the best repellent of all). Mosquito "buzzers" are a lot less effective. Though active from dusk till dawn, female *Anopheles* mosquitoes prefer to bite in the evening, so be especially careful at that time. Wear long sleeves, skirts and trousers, avoid dark colours, which attract mosquitoes, and put repellent on all exposed skin.

Another illness spread by mosquito bites is **dengue fever**, whose symptoms are similar to those of malaria, plus a headache and aching bones. The only treatment is complete rest, with drugs to assuage the fever.

INTESTINAL TROUBLES

Diarrhoea is the most common bane of travellers. When mild and not accompanied by other major symptoms, it may just be your stomach reacting to unfamiliar food. Accompanied by cramps and vomiting, it could well be food poisoning. In either case, it will probably pass of its own accord in 24–48 hours without treatment. In the meantime, it is essential to replace the fluids and salts you're losing down the drain, so take lots of water with oral rehydration salts (commonly referred to as ORS, or called *Electrolyte* in India). If you can't get them, use half a teaspoon of salt and three of sugar in a litre of water. It's a good idea to avoid greasy food, heavy spices, caffeine and most fruit and dairy products; but some say bananas and pawpaws are good, as is coconut water, while curd or a soup made from *Marmite* or *Vegemite* (if you happen to have some with you) are forms of protein that can be easily absorbed by your body when you have the runs. We advise against drugs like *Lomotil* or *Immodium*, which simply plug you up – they undermine the body's efforts to rid itself of infection – but they can be a temporary stop-gap if you have to travel. If symptoms persist more than a few days, a course of antibiotics may be necessary; this should be seen as a last resort, following medical advice.

Sordid though it may seem, it's a good idea to look at what comes out when you go to the toilet (and it makes an endless topic of polite mealtime conversation with your fellow travellers). If your diarrhoea contains blood or mucus, the cause may be dysentery or giardia. With a fever, it could well be caused by **bacillic dysentery**, and may clear up without treatment. If you're sure you need it, a course of antibiotics such as tetracycline should sort you, but they also destroy "gut flora" in your intestines (which help protect you – curd can replenish them to some extent), and if you start a course, be sure to finish it, even after the symptoms have gone. Similar symptoms without fever indicate **amoebic dysentery**,

which is much more serious, and can damage your gut if untreated. The usual cure is a course of metronidazole (*Flagyl*), an antibiotic which may itself make you feel ill, and should not be taken with alcohol. Similar symptoms, plus rotten-egg belches and farts, indicate **giardia**, for which the treatment is again metronidazole. If you suspect that you have any of these, seek medical help, and only start on the metronidazole (750mg three times daily for a week for adults) if there is definitely blood in your diarrhoea and it is impossible to see a doctor.

Finally, bear in mind that oral drugs, such as malaria pills, and *the* pill, are likely to be largely ineffective if taken while suffering from diarrhoea.

BITES AND CREEPY CRAWLIES

Worms may enter your body through skin (especially the soles of your feet), or food. An itchy anus is a common symptom, and you may even see them in your stools. They are easy to treat: if you suspect you have them, get some worming tablets from any pharmacy.

Biting insects and similar animals other than mosquitoes may also aggravate you. The obvious ones are **bed bugs** – look for signs of squashed ones around cheap hotel beds. An infested mattress can be left in the hot sun all day to get rid of them, but they often live in the frame or even in walls or floors. Head and body **lice** can also be a nuisance but medicated soap and shampoo (preferably brought with you from home) usually see them off. Avoid scratching bites, which can lead to infection. Bites from ticks and lice can spread **typhus**, characterized by fever, muscle aches, headaches and eventually red eyes and a measles-like rash. If you think you have it, seek treatment (tetracycline is usually prescribed – for adults, a single 1g dose followed by 300mg four times daily for five days).

Snakes are unlikely to bite unless accidentally disturbed, and most are harmless in any case. To see one at all, you need to search stealthily – walk heavily and they usually oblige by disappearing. If you do get bitten, remember what the snake looked like (kill it if you can), try not to move the affected part, and seek medical help: anti-venoms are available in most hospitals. A few **spiders** have poisonous bites too. Remove **leeches**, which may attach themselves to you in jungle areas, with salt or a lit cigarette rather than just pulling them off.

HEAT TROUBLE

The sun and the heat can cause a few unexpected problems. Many people get a bout of **prickly heat** rash before they've acclimatized. It's an infection of the sweat ducts caused by excessive perspiration that doesn't dry off. A cool shower, zinc oxide powder (sold in India) and loose cotton clothes should help. **Dehydration** is another possible problem, so make sure you're drinking enough liquid, and drink rehydration salts frequently, especially when hot and/or tired. The main danger sign is irregular urination (only once a day for instance), but dark urine also probably means you should drink more, although it could indicate hepatitis.

The **sun** can burn, or even cause sunstroke, and a high-factor sun-block is vital on exposed skin, especially when you first arrive, and on areas newly exposed by haircuts or changes of clothes. A light hat is also a very good idea, especially if you're doing a lot of walking around in the sun.

Finally, be aware that overheating can cause **heat-stroke**, which is potentially fatal. Signs are a very high body temperature without a feeling of fever, but accompanied by headaches and disorientation. Irrational behaviour by your travelling companions may be down to this. Lowering body temperature (a tepid shower for example) is the first step in treatment.

ALTITUDE SICKNESS

At high altitudes, you may develop symptoms of **acute mountain sickness (AMS)**. Just about everyone who ascends to 4000m or more experiences mild symptoms, but serious cases are rare. The simple cure – descent – almost always brings immediate recovery, but never descend too quickly.

AMS is caused by the fact that at high elevations there is not only less oxygen, but also lower atmospheric pressure. This can have all sorts of weird effects on the body: it can cause the brain to swell and the lungs to fill with fluid, and even bring on uncontrollable farting. The syndrome varies from one person to the next, but common symptoms include breathlessness, headaches and dizziness, and nausea and appetite loss. More extreme cases may cause disorientation and loss of balance, and the coughing up of pink frothy phlegm.

AMS strikes without regard for fitness – in fact, young people seem to be more susceptible, possibly because they're more reluctant to admit they feel sick. Most people are capable of acclimatizing to very high elevations, but the process takes time and must be done in stages. The golden rule is not to go too high, too fast. Above 3000m, you should not ascend more than 500m per day; take mandatory acclimatization days at 3500m and 4000m – more if you feel unwell – and try to spend these days day-hiking higher. If you fly direct to a high-altitude destination such as Leh, be especially careful to acclimatize; you'll certainly want to avoid doing anything strenuous at first.

Other precautions to take at high altitudes include drinking more liquid, and protecting your skin against UV solar glare.

HIV AND AIDS

Aids is still an unknown quantity in India, and often regarded as a foreign problem, but indications are that HIV levels are already high among prostitutes, and the same presumably applies to intravenous drug users. You are also of course at risk from your fellow travellers. It is therefore extremely unwise to contemplate casual sex without a condom. Carry some with you (preferably brought from home as Indian ones may be less reliable; also, be aware that heat affects the durability of condoms), and insist on using them. They also protect you from other sexually transmitted diseases, and even work as a contraceptive.

Should you need an injection or a transfusion in India, make sure that new, sterile equipment is used; any blood you receive should be from voluntary rather than commercial donor banks. If you have a shave from a barber, make sure he uses a clean blade, and don't submit to processes such as ear-piercing, acupuncture or tattooing unless you can be sure that the equipment is sterile.

GETTING MEDICAL HELP

Pharmacies can usually advise on minor medical problems, and most doctors in India speak English. Basic medicaments are made to Indian Pharmacopoea (IP) standards, and most medicines are available without prescription (always check the sell-by date). Hospitals vary in standard. Private clinics and mission hospitals are

AYURVEDIC MEDICINE

Ayurved, a five-thousand-year-old holistic medical system, is widely practised in India. Ayurvedic doctors and clinics in large towns deal with foreigners as well as their usual patients, and some pharmacies specialize in Ayurvedic preparations, including toiletries such as soaps, shampoos and toothpastes.

The "knowledge of life" assumes the fundamental sameness of self and nature. Unlike the allopathic medicines of the west, which depend on finding out what's ailing you and then killing it, *ayurved* looks at the whole patient: disease is regarded as a symptom of imbalance, so it's the imbalance that's treated, not the disease. Ayurvedic theory holds that the body is controlled by three forces, which reflect the forces within the self: *pitta*, the force of the sun, is hot, and rules the digestive processes and metabolism; *kapha*, likened to the moon, the creator of tides and rhythms, has a cooling effect, and governs the body's organs; and *vata*, wind, relates to movement and the nervous system. The healthy body is one that has the three forces in balance. To diagnose an imbalance, the Ayurvedic doctor goes not only to the physical complaint but also family background, daily habits and emotional traits.

Imbalances are typically treated with herbal remedies designed to alter whichever of the three forces is out of whack. Made according to traditional formulae, using indigenous plants, Ayurvedic medicines are cheaper than branded or imported drugs. In addition, the doctor may prescribe various forms of yogic cleansing to rid the body of waste substances. To the uninitiated, these techniques will sound rather offputting – for instance, swallowing a long strip of cloth, a short section at a time, and then pulling it back up again to remove mucus from the stomach.

often better than state-run ones, but may not have the same facilities; hospitals in the big cities are generally pretty good, university or medical school hospitals best of all. Indian hospitals usually require patients (even emergency cases) to buy necessities such as plaster casts and vaccines, and to pay for X-rays, before procedures are carried out. However, charges are usually so low that for minor treatment the expense may well be lower than the initial "excess" on your insurance. Addresses of clinics and hospitals can be found in our "Listings" sections for major towns in this book.

Some of the illnesses and parasites you can pick up in India may not show themselves immediately. If you become ill within a year of returning home, tell whoever treats you where you have been.

INFORMATION AND MAPS

Inside India itself, both national and local governments run **tourist information offices**, providing general travel advice and handing out an array of printed material, from city maps to glossy leaflets on specific destinations. The Indian government's tourist department, whose main offices are on Janpath in New Delhi and opposite Churchgate railway station in Bombay, has branches in most regional capitals. These, however, operate independently of the information counters and bureaux run by the state tourism development corporations, usually referred to by their initials (eg MPTDC, RTDC, etc), who offer a wide range of travel facilities, including **guided tours**, **car rental**, and their own **hotels** (which we identify with the relevant acronyms throughout this book).

The Indian government maintains a number of tourist offices abroad, where you can pick up a range of pamphlets. Their main purpose is to advertise rather than inform, but they can be extremely helpful and knowledgeable.

Other sources of information include travel agents (who are in business for themselves, so their advice may not always be totally unbiased), and the *Indian Railways* representatives listed on p.30.

Just to confuse things even more, the Indian government tourist office has a go-ahead corporate wing too. **ITDC** (Indian Tourism Development Corporation), is responsible for the *Ashok* chain of hotels, and operates tour and travel services, frequently competing with its state counterparts.

For the latest up-to-the-minute information on hotels, restaurants, transport and problems on the road, however, your best source may well be your **fellow travellers**. Sometimes, you may

INDIAN GOVERNMENT TOURIST OFFICES ABROAD

Australia ☎02/232 1600 or 1796
Level 5, 65 Elizabeth St, Sydney NSW 2000.

Canada ☎416/ 962 3788
60 Bloor St West, #1003, Toronto, Ontario M4W 3B8.

France ☎1/ 4265 8386
8 Bd de la Madeleine, 75009 Paris.

Germany ☎069/ 235423 or 235424
Kaiserstraße 77–111, 6000 Frankfurt Main –1.

Italy ☎02/ 804952
Via Albricci 9, 21022 Milano.

Japan ☎03/571 5062 or 5063
Pearl Bldg, 9–8 Ginza, 7–Chome,
Chou-ku, Tokyo 104.

Malaysia ☎03/ 242 5285
2nd floor, Wisma HLA, Lot 203,
Jalan Raja Chulan 500200, Kuala Lumpur.

Netherlands ☎020/620 8991
Rokin 9–15, 1012 KK, Amsterdam.

Singapore ☎235 3800
20 Karamat Lane, 01–01A United House,
Singapore 0922.

Spain ☎91/345 7339
Av Pio XII 30, 3, 2, 28016 Madrid.

Sweden ☎08/918995
Sveavagen 9–11, S-11157, Stockholm.

Switzerland ☎022/732 1813
1–3 Rue de Chantepoulet, 1201 Geneva.

Thailand ☎02/ 235 2585
Singapore Airlines Bldg, 3rd floor,
62/5 Thaniya Rd, Bangkok.

UK ☎0171/ 437 3677
7 Cork St, London W1X 1PB.

USA
3550 Wiltshire Bd, Suite #204,
Los Angeles, CA 90010 ☎213/ 380 8855
30 Rockefeller Plaza, Room 15, North Mezzanine,
New York, NY 10020 ☎212/ 586 4901 or 4902

even find it worth staying in cheaper dormitory or guest-house accommodation simply in order to meet people and swap experiences.

MAPS

Getting good **maps** of India, in India, can be difficult; the government forbids the sale of detailed maps of border areas, which include the entire coastline. It makes sense to bring a basic one with you, such as *Bartholomew's* 1:4,000,000 map of South Asia, which has coloured contours and serves as a reliable **route map** of the whole country. *Lascelles* also produce one on the same scale, as do *Nelles Verlag*, who show good road detail but can be less accurate; *Nelles* also cover parts of the country with 1:1,500,000 regional maps. The ITDC does a very basic one for free.

If you need larger-scale **city maps** than the ones we provide in this book – which are keyed to show recommended hotels and restaurants – you can usually get them from tourist offices. The

TT company (328 GST Rd, Chromepet, Madras 600044) also publish state and city maps, while the *Survey of India* (Janpath Barracks A, New Delhi 110 001; ☎332 2288) have authoritative town plans at scales of 1:10,000 and 1:50,000 (whose export is illegal, so they may be unwilling to sell you them).

As for **trekking maps**, the US Army Map Service produced maps in the 1960s which remain superbly accurate on topography, but are of course out-dated on the latest road developments. Most other maps that you can buy are based on their work, and no single series is especially worth recommending above the others. The official Indian mapping organization, the *Survey of India* (based in Dehra Dun in Uttar Pradesh) has issued a rather poor new 1:250,000 series for trekkers in the UP Himalayas; they are simplified versions of their own infinitely more reliable maps, produced for the military, which it is absolutely impossible for an outsider to get hold of.

BOOK AND MAP OUTLETS

IN THE UK:

Books from India ☎0171/405 3784
45 Museum St, London WC1A 1LY.

John Smith and Sons ☎0141/221 7472
57–61 St Vincent St, Glasgow.

National Map Centre ☎0171/222 4945
22–24 Caxton St, London SW1.

Stanfords ☎0171/836 1321
12–14 Long Acre, London WC2. *Mail order service.*

Thomas Nelson and Sons Ltd ☎0131/557 3011
51 York Place, Edinburgh EH1 3JD.

The Travellers Bookshop ☎0171/836 9132
25 Cecil Court, London WC2.

IN AUSTRALASIA:

Bowyangs ☎03/670 4383
372 Little Bourke St, Melbourne, VIC 3000.

Hema ☎07/221 4330
239 George St, Brisbane, QLD 4000.

The Map Shop ☎08/231 2033
16a Peel St, Adelaide, SA 5000.

Perth Map Centre ☎09/322 5733
891 Hay St, Perth, WA 6000.

Travel Bookshop ☎02/241 3554
20 Bridge St, Sydney, NSW 2000.

IN NORTH AMERICA:

British Travel Bookshop ☎1-800/448-3039
551 5th Ave, New York NY 10176.

The Complete Traveler Bookstore ☎212/685-9007
199 Madison Ave, New York NY 10016.

The Complete Traveler Bookstore ☎415/923-1511
3207 Fillmore St, San Francisco CA 92123.

Elliot Bay Book Company ☎206/624-6600
101 South Main St, Seattle WA 98104.

Open Air Books and Maps ☎416/363-0719
25 Toronto St, Toronto M5R 2C1.

Rand McNally ☎312/321-1751
444 N Michigan Ave, Chicago IL 60611.

Rand McNally ☎212/758-7488
150 East 52nd St, New York NY 10022.

Rand McNally ☎415/777-3131
595 Market St, San Francisco CA 94105.

Rand McNally ☎202/223-6751
1201 Connecticut Ave NW, Washington DC 20036.

Traveler's Bookstore ☎212/664-0995
22 West 52nd St, New York NY 10019.

Ulysses Travel Bookshop ☎514/289-0993
4176 St-Denis, Montréal.

World Wide Books and Maps ☎604/687-3320
1247 Granville St, Vancouver.

COSTS, MONEY AND BANKS

India is, unquestionably, one of the least expensive countries for travellers in the world; a little foreign currency goes a long way. That means you can be confident of getting consistently good value for your money, whether you're setting out to keep your budget to a minimum or to enjoy the opportunities that spending a bit more will make possible.

While we attempt below to suggest the kind of sums you can expect to pay for varying degrees of comfort, it is vital not to make a rigid assumption at the outset of a long trip that whatever money you bring to India will last for a certain number of weeks or months. On any one day it may be possible to spend very little, but cumulatively you won't be doing yourself any favours if you don't make sure to keep yourself well rested and properly fed.

What you spend depends on you: where you go, where you stay, how you get around, what you eat and what you buy. On a budget of as little as US\$8/£5 per day, you'll manage if you stick to the cheapest of everything and don't move about too much; double that, and you can permit yourself the odd splurge meal, the occasional mid-range hotel, and of course a few souvenirs. If you're happy spending US\$20–30 (£15–20) per day, however, you can really pamper yourself; to spend much more than that, you'd have to be doing a lot of travelling, and consistently staying in the best hotel in town and eating in the top restaurant.

Accommodation ranges from US\$2/£1.50 per night upwards (see p.34), while a mid-range vegetarian **meal** in an ordinary restaurant is unlikely to cost even that much. Rice and *dal* can be had for well under 50¢, but you wouldn't want to live on that alone. Transport in town costs pennies (even by taxi or the most over-charging rickshaw), while a 12-hour train journey might cost \$3–4 (£2) in second class, \$15 (£10) in first.

Where you are makes a difference: Bombay is notoriously pricey, especially for accommodation, while tourist enclaves like the Goa beaches will not be cheap for things like food, and there will be more souvenirs on sale to tempt you. Delhi too is substantially more costly than most parts of the country. Out in the sticks, on the other hand, and particularly away from your fellow tourists, you will find things incredibly cheap, though your choice will obviously be more limited.

Some independent travellers tend to indulge in wild and highly competitive penny-pinching, which Indian people find rather pathetic – they know how much an air ticket to Delhi or Bombay costs, and they have a fair idea of what you can earn at home (not much? more than most Indians!). Bargain where appropriate, but don't begrudge a few *rupees* to someone who's worked hard for them: consider what their services would cost at home, and how much more valuable the money is to them than it is to you. Even if you get "ripped off" on every rickshaw journey you make, it will only add at most one percent to a \$1500/£1000 trip. Remember too, that every pound or dollar you spend in India goes that much further, and luxuries you can't afford at home become possible here: sometimes it's worth spending more simply because you get more for it. At the same time, don't pay well over the odds for something if you know what the going rate is. Thoughtless extravagance can, particularly in remote areas that see a disproportionate number of tourists (such as Ladakh), contribute to inflation, putting even basic goods and services beyond the reach of local people at certain times of year.

INDIAN MONEY

India's unit of currency is the **rupee**, usually abbreviated "Rs" and divided into a hundred *paise*. You may also hear the odd reference to an old unit, the *anna* (16 to a *rupee*, so four *annas* is 25 *paise*). Almost all money is paper, with notes of 1, 2, 5, 10, 20, 50, 100 and 500 *rupees*. Coins start at 1 *paisa* (for temple offerings), then range up through 5, 10, 20, 25 and 50 *paise*, and 1, 2 and 5 *rupees*.

Banknotes, especially lower denominations, can get into a terrible state, but don't accept **torn banknotes**; no-one else will be prepared to take them, so you will be left saddled with the things. You can change them at the *Reserve Bank of India* and large branches of other big banks, or slip them into the middle of a wad when paying for something (which is probably how they'll have been passed to you). Don't pass them on to beggars; they can't use them either, so it amounts to an insult.

Large denominations can also be a problem, as **change** is often in short supply, particularly in small towns. Many Indian people cannot afford to keep much lying around, and you shouldn't necessarily expect shopkeepers or rickshaw *wallah*s to have it (and they may – as may you – try to hold onto it if they do). Paying for your groceries with a Rs100 bill will probably entail waiting for the grocer's errand boy to go off on a quest around town trying to change it. Keeping a wad of Rs1 notes handy isn't a bad idea (you can get bundles of a hundred stapled together in banks; holes from the staples don't count as rips, so long as they don't reach the edge of the note).

TRAVELLERS' CHEQUES AND CREDIT CARDS

Carry a mixture of cash and travellers' cheques to cover all eventualities, with a few small denominations for the end of your trip, and for the odd foreign-currency purchase. US dollars are the easiest **currency** to convert, with pounds sterling a close second. Major hard currencies such as Australian dollars, Deutschmarks, yen or French francs can all be changed easily in tourist areas and big cities, less so elsewhere. If you enter the country with US$10,000 or the equivalent, you are supposed to fill in a currency declaration form.

Travellers' cheques aren't as liquid as cash, but obviously more secure (and you get a slightly better exchange rate for them at banks). Not all banks, however, accept them, and those that do can be quirky about exactly which ones they *will* change (well-known brands such as *Thomas Cook*, *American Express* or *Visa* are your best bet).

A **credit card** is a handy back-up, as an increasing number of hotels, restaurants, large shops and tourist emporia as well as airlines now take plastic, *American Express*, *Access/Mastercard*, *Visa* and *Diners Club* being the most commonly accepted brands. If you have a selection of cards, take them all; you'll get much the same exchange rate as you would in a bank, and bills can take a surprisingly long time to be charged to your account at home. The *Bank of Baroda* issues *rupees* against a *Visa* card at all its branches, while *Amex* will issue *rupees* or travellers' cheques to cardholders against a cheque at their offices.

It is illegal to carry *rupees* into or out of India, and you won't get them at a particularly good rate in the west anyhow (though you might in Thailand, Malaysia or Singapore).

BANKS

Changing money can be a time-consuming business, involving lots of form-filling and queuing at different counters, so change substantial amounts at any one time. Banks in main cities are likely to be most efficient; not all banks change

---

TRAVELLERS' CHEQUES AND CREDIT CARDS: ADDRESSES

American Express

Lost and stolen cards ☎687 5050

New Delhi ☎332 4119
Wenger House, "A" Block, Connaught Place

Bombay ☎204 8278
Oriental Building, 364 Dr DN Marg, Colaba

Calcutta ☎248 6281
21 Old Court House

Madras ☎825 6120
S-5/6, Spencer Plaza, 769 Anna Salai

Thomas Cook

New Delhi ☎374 7404
Rishya Mook Building, 84-A, Panchkuin Rd

Bangalore ☎587147
70 Mahatma Gandhi Rd

Bombay ☎204 8556
Dr DN Marg, Colaba

Calcutta ☎247 5378
Chitrakoot Building, 2nd Floor, AJ Chandra Bose Rd

Jaipur ☎60940
Jaipur Towers, 1st Floor, Mohammed Ismail Rd

Both *American Express* and *Thomas Cook* have offices in other major cities throughout India.

foreign currency, and some won't take travellers' cheques or currencies other than dollars or sterling. In small towns, the *State Bank of India* is your best bet. Note that if you arrive at small airports (Varanasi, Tiruchirapalli, or Thiruvananthapuram for example), you may not be able to change anything except cash US dollars or sterling.

Outside **banking hours** (Mon–Fri 10am–2pm, Sat 10am–noon), large hotels may change money, probably at a lower rate. Banks at Delhi, Bombay, Calcutta and Madras airports, and at the *Ashok Hotel* in Delhi and the *Air India* building in downtown Bombay, stay open **24 hours** per day but none of these is very conveniently located. Otherwise, there's always the black market.

Hold on to **exchange receipts** ("encashment certificates"); they will be required if you want to change back any excess *rupees* when you leave the country, or buy things like air tickets with *rupees*, and if you need a tax clearance form (see p.13). The *State Bank of India* now charges for these.

Wiring money to India is a lot easier than it used to be. Indian banks with branches abroad, such as the *State Bank of India* and the *Bank of Baroda*, can wire money by telex from those branches to large ones in India in two working days. *Western Union* (information on ☎1-800/325 6000 in the US or ☎0800/833833 in the UK) can transfer cash or banker's drafts paid into their overseas branches to any of 43 offices in India within fifteen minutes, for a typical fee of around 7.5 percent of the total amount, and similar services are offered by *American Express*, *Thomas Cook*, and foreign banks with branches in India such as *ANZ Grindlays* (who have the most).

THE BLACK MARKET

Whether the **black market** survives the transformation of the *rupee* to a convertible currency remains to be seen: it probably will, as its main *raison d'être* is to finance gold smuggling. It only offers a premium of five percent or so above the official rate in any case, if that, and only operates in the major tourist areas of the biggest cities. Small denominations are not popular, with the best rates given for bills of US$100, £50 or DM1000; you will, of course, have to haggle.

Always do this kind of business with shopkeepers rather than shady "hello my friend"-types on the street, and proceed with caution. Never hand over your pile until you have *yourself*

counted and checked the *rupees* and have them in your hand; make sure they really are the denominations you think. Unusually high rates suggest a con, as does any attempt to rush you, or sudden claims that the police are coming. Remember what you are doing is illegal; you can be arrested and you may be set up.

At one or two of India's land borders, unofficial money-changers may be your only option; as their rates will not be good, however, only change as much as you need to get you to a bank.

BAKSHEESH

As a presumed-rich *sahib* or *memsahib*, you will, like wealthy Indians, be expected to be liberal with the **baksheesh**, which takes three main forms.

The most common is **tipping**: a small reward for a small service, which can encompass anyone from a waiter or porter to someone who lifts your bags onto the roof of a bus or keeps an eye on your vehicle for you. Large amounts are not expected – five *rupees* should satisfy all the aforementioned. Taxi drivers and staff at cheaper hotels and restaurants do not necessarily expect tips, but always appreciate them, of course, and they can keep people sweet for the next time you call. Some may take liberties in demanding *baksheesh*, but it's often better just to acquiesce rather than spoil your mood and cause offence over trifling sums.

More expensive than plain tipping is paying people to **bend the rules**, many of which seem to have been invented for precisely that purpose. Examples might include letting you into a historical site after hours, finding you a seat or a sleeper on a train that is "full", or speeding up some bureaucratic process. This should not be confused with bribery, a more serious business with its own risks and etiquette, which is best not entered into.

The last kind of *baksheesh* is **alms giving**. In a country without social security, this is an important social custom. People with disabilities and mutilations are the traditional recipients, and it seems right to join local people in giving out small change to them. Kids demanding money, pens or the like are a different case, pressing their demands only on tourists. In return for a service it is fair enough, but to yield to any request encourages them to go and pester others. Think twice before you do.

GETTING AROUND

Inter-city transport in India may not be the fastest or the most comfortable in the world, but it's cheap, goes more or less everywhere, and generally gives you the option of train or bus, sometimes plane, and occasionally even boat. Transport around town comes in even more permutations, ranging in Calcutta for example from rickshaws still pulled by men on foot to a spanking new metro system.

Whether you're on road or rail, public transport or your own vehicle, India offers the chance to try out some classics: narrow-gauge railways, steam locomotives, the *Ambassador* car and the *Enfield Bullet* motorbike, they're all here. Some people come to India for these alone.

> At the start of each chapter in this book, you'll find a chart of "**Travel Details**" summarizing major transport connections in the relevant state. In addition, boxes at the end of each major city detail "**Moving On**" from that city.

BY TRAIN

Travelling by train is one of the great experiences of India. There may be railway systems that are faster, more punctual and more comfortable (though perhaps none cheaper), but nowhere will you find one that is more, well, Indian !

Indian railways are a frenetic, crowded, yet in some ways rather quaint world of "up" trains and "down" trains, carrying untold masses of people in barrack-like carriages, echoing to the ubiquitous cries of the *chai-wallahs* as they dispense tea in disposable clay cups, and food hawkers whose stalls spring into action on every railway platform as each train arrives and they jostle for

position with sellers of coconuts, *bidis*, newspapers and magazines. From tiny country stations where the daily train is the big event, to massive labyrinthine city terminals where families make their homes on the platforms as the new broom of computer technology sweeps through the dusty offices of railway functionaries and station officials, it's a system which looks like chaos, but it works, and well. Trains are often late of course, by hours rather than minutes, but they do run, and with amazing efficiency too: when the train you've been waiting for rolls into the station, the reservation you made halfway across the country several weeks ago will be on a list pasted to the side of your carriage, and when it's time to eat, the packed meal you ordered down the line will be ready at the next station, put on the train and delivered to your seat.

Once rolling, you can settle down to enjoy an excellent view of the countryside as it slips past, fall into conversation with your fellow passengers, enjoy a nice cup of *chai*, or relax with a book or newspaper. It's worth bearing in mind too, with journeys frequently lasting 12 hours or more, that an overnight train can save you a day's travelling and a night's hotel bill, assuming you sleep well on trains. While carriages can be jampacked during the day, between 9pm and 6am anyone with a bunk reservation is entitled to exclusive use of their bunk. When travelling overnight, always padlock your bag to your bunk.

ROUTES AND CLASSES

The railway network covers almost the entire country; only a few places (such as Sikkim, Ladakh, and most of Himachal Pradesh and Goa) are inaccessible by train. **Inter-city trains**, called "express" or "mail", vary a lot in the time taken to cover the same route. Slow by western standards, they're still much faster than **local "passenger" trains**, which you need only use to get right off the beaten track. There are also one or two special "super-fast" a/c trains, such as the Delhi–Bombay and Delhi–Calcutta *Rajdhani* expresses; these can cut journey times by as much as fifty percent.

Most lines are either metre-**gauge** or broadgauge (1.676m, or 4'6"), the latter being somewhat faster, but there are also a few narrow-gauge lines (often referred to as "toy trains"), notably to the hill stations of Darjeeling, Shimla, Matheran and Ootacamund. **Steam locomotives** are still used on the first and last (the latter on Sundays only) of these, as well as on some local lines and goods services, and you may well see some in use in shunting yards, but they are fast disappearing; almost all trains nowadays are diesel-hauled.

Mainline services usually carry three **classes**: first, second and air-conditioned first. First class, in compartments of two or four berths, is very comfortable and insulates you to a certain extent from the chaotic hustle and bustle – which you may or may not consider to be an advantage. It costs about three and a half times as much as second class, which can be unbearably crowded if you travel unreserved, but much less so if you reserve a seat, and quite comfy with a sleeper. Air-conditioned first class, at about two and a half times the price of ordinary first, has little extra to offer apart from the eponymous air-conditioning.

One or two services also have second-class air-conditioned "chair cars" with reclining seats, which cost about double the usual second-class fare, and second class air-conditioned sleepers at about five times more than normal second (and 25 percent more than non-a/c first). On special trains such as the *Rajdhani* expresses, only a/c accommodation is available. At the same time, some less celebrated services, and all local services, have second-class only, and no air-conditioning.

In general, most travellers (not just those on low budgets) choose to travel second class, and positively prefer not to be in a/c compartments; an open window keeps you cool enough, and brings you into contact with the world outside, while air-conditioning by definition involves being sealed away behind glass, often virtually opaque. Doing without a sleeper on an overnight journey is however a false economy. Bed rolls (sheet, blanket and pillow) are available in first class and a/c second for that extra bit of comfort – book these with your ticket, or before you board the train.

TIMETABLES AND TICKETS

Indian Railways publish an annual **timetable** of all mail and express trains – in effect, all the trains you are likely to use. Called *Trains at a Glance*, it is available from information counters and newsstands at all main stations, and from *IR* agents abroad. *Thomas Cook*'s *International Timetable Vol II* (the blue one) has a limited selection of timetables, while the elusive monthly *Indian Bradshaw* covers every scheduled train in the country. In theory, this is available at major termini, but it is often difficult to get hold of (Calcutta seems to be the best place); complete regional timetables are widely available however.

All rail **fares** are calculated according to the exact distance travelled; *Trains At A Glance* prints a chart of fares by kilometres, and also gives the distance in kilometres of stations along each route in the timetables, making it possible to calculate what the basic fare will be for any given journey. Endless poring over the columns reveals little more than that fares are very cheap indeed.

Each individual train has its own name and number, prominently displayed in station booking halls. When **buying a ticket**, it makes sense to pay the tiny extra fee to reserve a seat or sleeper (the fee is already included in the price of a first-class sleeper). To do so, you fill in a form specifying the train you intend to catch, its number, your date of travel, and the stations you are travelling to and from. Most stations these days have computerized booking counters, and you will be told immediately whether or not seats are available. In larger cities, the major stations have special **tourist sections** to cut the queues for foreigners buying tickets (Indian citizens resident abroad also count as tourists), with helpful English-speaking staff; however, you have to pay in pounds sterling or US dollars (travellers' cheques or cash). Elsewhere, buying a ticket can often involve a long wait, though women can cut this down immeasurably at those ticket counters which have "ladies' queues". Some stations also operate a number system of queuing, allowing you to repair to the *chai* stall or check the timetable until your number is called.

It's important to plan your train journeys in advance, as the demand frequently makes it impossible to buy a ticket on the same day that you want to travel. Travellers following tight itineraries tend to buy their departure tickets from particular towns the very moment they arrive, to avoid having to trek out to the station again. At most large stations it's possible to reserve tickets for journeys starting elsewhere in the country; whenever you've worked out your schedule a few days ahead, try to buy all the tickets you'll need

INDRAIL PASSES

Indrail **passes**, sold to foreigners and Indians resident abroad, cover all fares and reservation fees for periods ranging up to 90 days. Even if you travel a lot, this works out considerably more expensive than buying your tickets individually (especially in second class), but it will save you queuing for tickets, allow you to make and cancel reservations with impunity (and without charge), and generally smooth your way in for example finding a seat or berth on a "full" train: passholders, for example, get priority for tourist quota places. *Indrail* passes are available, for sterling or US dollars, at main station tourist counters, in India, and outside the country at *IR* agents (see p.30).

RATES IN US$

	A/c First Class		First Class, or A/c Sleeper, or A/c Chair car		Second Class	
	Adult	Child	Adult	Child	Adult	Child
1 day	78	39	35	18	15	8
7 days	270	135	135	68	70	35
15 days	330	165	165	83	80	40
21 days	400	200	100	100	90	45
30 days	500	250	250	125	110	55
60 days	720	360	360	180	165	83
90 days	960	480	480	240	210	105

in one of those places. In fact, you can even book tickets for specific journeys before you leave home, with *Indian Railways* representatives abroad (see box). They accept bookings up to six months in advance, with a minimum of one month for first class, and three months for second.

If you have to **cancel your ticket**, the fare is refunded up to a day before departure, minus a fee for the reservation (Rs10 in second class, Rs20 in first, Rs30 a/c first). Between a day and four hours before scheduled departure, you get 75 percent back; you can still claim a 50 percent refund if you present your ticket up to twelve hours after the train actually leaves on a journey of over 500km, or three hours after on a short journey.

If there are **no places available** on the train you want, you have a number of alternatives. First, some seats and berths are set aside as a "tourist quota" – ask at the tourist counter if you can get in on this, or else try the stationmaster. Failing that, other special quotas, such as one for VIPs, may remain unused – however, if you get a booking on the VIP quota and a *pukka* VIP turns up, you lose the reservation. Drawing a blank there, a "reservation against cancellation" (RAC) ticket will give you priority if sleepers do become available – the ticket clerk should be able to tell you your chances – or you could get a plain unreserved ticket, get on the train and go and see the

ticket inspector as soon as possible. You may be able to persuade them to find you a place if one is free: something usually is, but you'll be stuck in unreserved if it isn't. Alternatively, and especially if you get on where the train starts its journey, *baksheesh* may persuade a porter to "reserve" you an unreserved seat or, better still, a luggage rack where you can stretch out for the night. You *could* even fight your way on and grab one yourself, although we don't rate your chances. As for attempting to **travel unreserved**, for journeys of any length it's too uncomfortable to be worth seriously considering.

Ladies' compartments exist on all trains for women travelling unaccompanied; they are usually small and can be full of noisy kids, but can give untold relief to women travellers who otherwise have to endure incessant staring in the open section of the carriage. On the other hand, particularly if you like (or are with) children, they can be a good place to meet Indian women. Some stations also have ladies-only waiting rooms.

THE PALACE ON WHEELS

Should you fancy something a bit posher than a normal scheduled train, the Rajasthan Tourist Development Corporation (RTDC) run the *Palace on Wheels*, a luxury, refurbished, air-conditioned train that goes on weekly tours of Rajasthan, departing from Delhi Cantonment

INDIAN RAILWAYS SALES AGENTS ABROAD

UK: **SD Enterprises Ltd** ☎0181/903 3411
103 Wembley Park Drive, Wembley, Middx HA9 8HG.
(Mon–Fri 9am–5.30pm, Sat 9am–2pm).

USA: **Hariworld Travels Inc** ☎212/957 3000
30 Rockefeller Plaza, #21, New York, NY10112.

Australia: **Adventure World** ☎02/956 7766
73 Walker St (PO Box 480), North Sydney, NSW 2059.

France: **Le Monde de l'Inde et de l'Asie**
15 rue des Ecoles, 75005 Paris ☎1/4634 0320

Germany: **ASRA Orient** ☎069/253098
Kaiserstraße 50, 60329 Frankfurt Main.

Bangladesh: **Omnitrans Internat'l** ☎02/834401
70/1 Inner Circular Rd, Kakrail, Dhaka.

Japan: **Japan Travel Bureau** ☎031/284 7391
1-6-4 Marunouchi, Chiyoda-ku, Tokyo 100.

Malaysia: **East West Travels** ☎03/293 0569
Sdn Bhd No 135-A, Jalan Bunus, 50100 Kuala Lumpur.

Thailand: **SS Travels Service** ☎02/236 0557
10/12–13, SS Building, Convent Rd, Bangkok 10500.

station every Wednesday evening between September and April, and returning the following Wednesday morning, with accommodation on board. For more details see p.128. Bookings can be made through *Indian Railways* representatives abroad or RTDC, Bikaner House, Pandara Rd, New Delhi (☎011/381884 or 383837); rates start at US$175 per person per night. Some package operators include it in tours.

Such has been the success of the *Palace on Wheels* that seven similar (less expensive) train services are currently planned to start touring different regions of India. As this book went to press, a *Temple on Wheels* tour of Tamil Nadu had just been announced: others being set up will cover the Buddha trail in Uttar Pradesh (aimed primarily at East Asian tourists), and Gujarat.

As an alternative to these, British travel operators *Butterfields* (see p.5) run tours in their own specially converted carriages, which are attached to a series of scheduled trains and hauled around the country. These must be booked in the UK.

CLOAKROOMS

Most stations in India have "cloakrooms" (sometimes called "parcel offices") for passengers to leave their baggage. These can be extremely handy if you want to go sightseeing in a town and move on the same day. In theory, you need a train ticket or *Indrail* pass to deposit luggage, but they don't always ask; they may however refuse to take your bag if you can't lock it. Losing your reclaim ticket causes problems; the clerk will be assumed to have stolen the bag if he can't produce it, so there'll be untold running around to obtain clearance before you can get your bag without it. Make sure, when checking baggage in, that the cloakroom will be open when you need to pick it up.

BY AIR

Though obviously more expensive than train or bus, **flying** can save a lot of time: Delhi–Madras, for example, takes 36 hours' hard travelling by train, a mere 1hr 40min by plane. Delays and cancellations can whittle away the time advantage, especially over small distances, but if you're short of time and plan to cover a lot of ground, you should definitely consider a flight or two for longer journeys.

India now once again has just one national internal air carrier, **Indian Airlines**, which serves 147 routes, and also flies to the southeast Asian destinations listed on p.7. In addition, *Air India* runs shuttles between the four main cities (from the international, not the domestic, terminal), and there are one or two local operators such as *Jagson* and *Modiluft* out of Delhi, and *Jet* and *East-West* out of Bombay. (You may see references to *Vayudoot*, who disappeared in 1993; confusingly many of its offices remain open, selling tickets for former *Vayudoot* routes now taken over by *Indian Airlines*.) Short flights can be cheap, often less than US$50, but longer ones are hardly less than equivalent distances anywhere else: Delhi–Madras, again, is currently US$125.

One problem with flying is that you may have to spend a massive amount of time queuing at the airline office to get a reservation; you may prefer to book through a hotel or travel agent. If you haven't got a confirmed seat, be sure to get to the airport early and keep checking your position in the queue.

Airlines have offices or representatives in all the places they fly to; all are listed in this book in the relevant city sections. *Indian Airlines* tickets must be paid for in hard currency or with a credit card. Travellers under the age of 30 get a 25 percent youth reduction, children under 12 pay half fare, and under-twos (one per adult) pay ten percent. There are no cancellation charges if you paid in foreign currency, but tickets are not replaceable if lost, so look after them.

Indian Airlines do a few **multi-flight deals** which might be of interest, notably "Discover India", a rover ticket allowing unlimited travel (but not the same route twice) on all their internal flights for 21 days at US$400, and "India Wonderfares", covering one region of the country on selected routes for seven days at US$200 ($300 if Port Blair is included). Passengers who fly in from Colombo or the Maldives to Madras, Tiruchirapalli or Thiruvananthapuram are eligible for a thirty percent discount on south Indian journeys.

Timetables should be available at *Indian Airlines* offices; failing that, they are published in *Divan* and *Excel* magazines, and shown on tele-text if you can get access to that.

BY BUS

Although the railway is the definitive way to travel in India, and generally more comfortable than a **bus**, there are places (such as most Himalayan valleys) where trains don't go, where they are awkward and inconvenient, or where buses are simply faster (as in most of Rajasthan and other places without broad-gauge track). Alternatively, you might just fancy a change, or the train you want might be booked up. In that case, the bus is for you; and you'll be pleased to know that they go almost everywhere, more frequently than trains (though mostly in daylight hours), with state-government-operated services everywhere, and plenty of private firms besides.

Buses vary somewhat in price and standard of seating. In general, the longer the journey, the more comfortable the bus – local stopping services are usually ramshackle affairs, packed to the gunwales with people, livestock and luggage. Longer distance or express buses generally go faster (though with fairly frequent stops for food, tea and toilets), have softer seats, are less crowded and often play videos – usually high-volume *masalas*. Buses without videos will play *filmi* music, at least loud enough to distort on the speakers. Ear plugs may help. Avoid the back of the bus if possible, as it gets a bumpier ride than the front.

Luggage travels on the roof (you may be able to travel up there yourself if the bus is too crowded, though it's dangerous and illegal); check that it's well secured (ideally, lock it there) and not liable to get squashed. *Baksheesh* is in order for whoever puts it up there for you.

Buying a bus ticket is usually less of an ordeal than buying a train ticket. Women should be aware that, as at railway stations, there is usually a separate, quicker, ladies' queue, although the sign to indicate it may not be in English. Prior booking is usually necessary for express and private services, but often tickets are bought on the bus itself.

BY BOAT

Apart from river ferries, not many **boat services** run in India. The Bombay–Panjim boat has been out of action for years, though there are always rumours of its imminent reappearance.

The Andaman Islands are connected to Calcutta and Madras by boat – as well as to each other – and there are luxury services between Kochi and Lakshadweep, but the only part of mainland India with a regular passenger boat system is **Kerala**, where a number of services operate out of Alappuzha and Kollam, including the popular "backwater trip" between the two.

BY CAR OR MOTORBIKE

It is much more usual for tourists in India to be driven than it is for them to drive; car rental firms operate on the basis of supplying chauffeur-driven vehicles, and taxis are available at cheap daily rates. Arranged through tourist offices, local car rental firms, or branches of *Hertz*, *Budget* or *Europcar*, a chauffeur-driven car will run to about US$20 per day. The driver sleeps in the car. The big international chains are the best bet for self-drive car rental; in India they charge around thirty percent less than chauffeur-driven, with a Rs1000 deposit against damage, though if you pay in your home country it can cost a whole lot more. In one or two places, motorbikes or mopeds may be rented out for local use, but for biking around the country, it is a much better idea to buy (see below).

In any case, driving in India is not for beginners. If you do drive yourself, expect the unexpected, and expect other drivers to take whatever liberties they can get away with. Do not expect them to obey traffic regulations, use indicators, give way or observe lane discipline. Traffic in the cities is heavy and undisciplined; vehicles cut in and out without warning, and pedestrians, cyclists and cows wander nonchalantly down the middle of the road as if you didn't exist. In the country the roads are narrow, in terrible repair, and hogged by overloaded *Tata* trucks that move aside for nobody, while something slow-moving like a bullock cart or a herd of goats can easily take up the whole road. A huge number of potholes don't make for a smooth ride either. Furthermore, during the monsoon roads can become flooded and dangerous; rivers burst their banks and bridges get washed away. Ask local people before you set off, and proceed with caution, sticking to main highways if possible.

If you have a **driving licence** from home, you won't need an international one, but it helps if you do. Traffic circulates on the left. Insurance is compulsory, but not expensive. Car seat belts and motorcycle crash-helmets are not compulsory but very strongly recommended, and helmets are best brought from home. Accident rates are high, and you should be on your guard at all times, taking special care after dark – not everyone uses lights, and bullock-carts don't have any. If you have an **accident**, it might be an idea to leave the scene quickly and go straight to the police to report it; mobs can assemble fast, especially if pedestrians or cows are involved.

Fuel is reasonably cheap compared to home, but the state of the roads will take its toll, and mechanics are not always very reliable, so a knowledge of **vehicle maintenance** is a help, as is a check-over every so often to see what all those bone-shaking journeys are doing to your conveyance. Luckily, if you get a flat tyre, puncture-*wallahs*, as they're known, can easily be found almost everywhere.

To import a car or motorbike into India, you'll have to show a *carnet de passage*, a document intended to ensure that you don't sell the vehicle illegally. These are available from foreign motoring organizations such as the *AA*. It's also worth bringing a few basic spares, as spare parts for foreign makes can be hard to find in India, although low-quality imitations are more widely available. All in all, the route is arduous (see p.6), and bringing a vehicle to India something of a commitment.

The classic **Indian automobile** is the Hindustan *Ambassador* (basically a *Morris Oxford*), nowadays largely superceded by more modern vehicles such as the Japanese-style *Maruti*. Renting a car, you'll probably have a choice of these two or others. If you're interested in buying one, the *Ambassador* is not famed for its mod cons or low mpg, but has a certain style and historical interest, and later models make little sense as prices are higher and quality lower than in the west.

Buying a bike is a much more reasonable proposition, and again, if it's a classic you're after, an old British model, the *Enfield Bullet*, leads the field. If low price and practicality are your priorities, however, a smaller model, perhaps even a moped or a scooter, might better fit the bill. Many Japanese bikes are now made in India, as are *Vespas* and *Lambrettas*, and motorcycles of various sorts can easily be bought new or second-hand. Garages and repair shops are a good place to start; see Delhi "Listings" for details of the city's Karol Bagh area, renowned for its motorcycle shops. Obviously, you will have to haggle for the price, but you can expect to pay half to two-thirds the original price for a bike in reasonable condition. Given the right bargaining skills, you can sell it again later for a similar price – perhaps to another foreign traveller, by advertising it in hotels and restaurants. A certain amount of bureaucracy is involved in transferring vehicle ownership, but a garage should be able to put you on to a broker ("auto consultant") who, for a modest commission, will help you find a seller or a buyer, and do the necessary paperwork.

BY BICYCLE

Ever since Dervla Murphy's *Full Tilt*, a steady but increasing trickle of travellers have either themselves done the overland trip **by bicycle**, or else bought a bike in India and ridden it around the country. In many ways it is the ideal form of transport, offering total independence without loss of contact with local people. You can camp out, though there are cheap lodgings in almost every village – take the bike into your room with you – and, if you get tired of pedalling, you can put it on top of a bus as luggage, or transport it by train (it goes in the luggage van: get a form and pay a small fee at the station luggage office).

Bringing a bike from abroad requires no *carnet* or special paperwork, but spare parts and accessories may be of different sizes and standards in India, and you may have to improvise. Bring basic spares and tools, and a pump. Panniers are the obvious thing for carrying your gear, but fiendishly inconvenient when not attached to your bike, and you might consider sacrificing ideal load-bearing and streamlining technology for a backpack you can lash down on the rear carrier.

Buying a bike in India presents no great difficulty: most towns have cycle shops and even cycle markets (such as the one around Esplanade Rd in Delhi). The advantages of a local bike are that spare parts are easy to get, locally produced tools and parts will fit, and your vehicle will not draw a crowd every time you park it. Disadvantages are that Indian bikes tend to be heavier and less state-of-the-art than ones from abroad (bikes with gears, let alone mountain bikes, are unheard of). Selling should be quite easy: you won't get a tremendously good deal at a cycle market, but you may well be able to sell privately, or even to a rental shop.

Bicycles can be **rented** in most towns. Rs10–20 per day is the going rate, usually more in tourist centres, and you may have to leave a deposit, or even your passport as security. Most bicycle-rental firms rent bikes for in-town use only; they won't take too kindly to you disappearing round the country on them. If you want to do that, buying would be a much better option in any case.

IBT, 4887 Columbia Drive S, Seattle WA 98108-1919 (☎206/628 9314), publish information and offer advice on bicycle travel around the world. In India, the *Cycle Federation of India* (C-5A/262, DDA Flats, Janak Puri, New Delhi 110058; ☎553006) is the main cycle-sports organization.

CITY TRANSPORT

Transport around town takes various forms, with **buses** the most obvious. These are usually single-decker, though double-deckers (some articulated) exist in Bombay and elsewhere. City buses can get unbelievably crowded, and you'll want to beware of pickpockets and razor-armed pocket-slitters; the same applies to **suburban trains** in Bombay (Madras is about the only other place where you might want to use trains for local city transport).

You can also take **taxis**, usually rather battered *Ambassadors* (painted black and yellow in Delhi and Bombay). With luck, the driver will agree to use the meter; in theory you're within your rights to call the police if he doesn't, but the usual compromise is to agree a fare for the journey before you get in. Naturally, it helps to have

an idea in advance what the fare should be, though any figures quoted in this or any other book should be treated as being the broadest of guidelines only. From places such as main stations, you may be able to find other passengers to share a taxi to the town centre, while large airports operate pre-paid taxi schemes with set fares that you pay at the airport; more expensive pre-paid limousines are also available.

That most Indian of vehicles, the **auto-rickshaw** (as ridden by James Bond through the streets of Udaipur, in *Octopussy*), is the front half of a motor-scooter with a couple of seats mounted on the back. Cheaper than taxis, better at nipping in and out of traffic, and usually metered (again, you'll probably have to insist), auto-rickshaws are a little unstable and their drivers often rather reckless, but that's all part of the fun. Rickshaws can however be more trouble than they're worth: in many places they hassle you endlessly on the street, often shoving themselves right in your path to prevent you ignoring them. Moreover, agreeing a price before the journey, which you should always do, will not necessarily stop your rickshaw *wallah* reopening discussion when the journey is under way, or at its end. In general it is better to hail a rickshaw than to take one that's been following you.

One or two cities also have larger versions of auto-rickshaws known as **tempos**, with six or eight seats behind, which usually ply fixed routes at flat fares. In Delhi they are built onto old *Harley Davidson* motorbikes. Here and there you'll also come across horse-drawn carriages, or **tongas**.

Slower and cheaper still is the **cycle rickshaw** – basically a glorified tricycle. Foreign visitors often feel squeamish about travelling this way, and with good reason; except in the major tourist cities, cycle rickshaw *wallahs* are invariably emaciated pavement dwellers who earn only a pittance for their pains. In the end, though, to deny them your custom on those grounds is spurious logic; they'll earn even less if you don't use them. Only in Calcutta do the rickshaw *wallahs* continue to haul the city's *pukka* rickshaws on foot.

If you want to see a variety of places around town, consider hiring a taxi, rickshaw or auto-rickshaw for the day. Find a driver who speaks English reasonably well, and agree a price beforehand. You will probably find it a lot cheaper than you imagine.

ACCOMMODATION

There are far more Indians travelling around their own country at any one time – whether for holidays, on pilgrimages, or for business – than there are foreign tourists, and a vast infrastructure of hotels and guest houses caters for their needs. Only a very few luxury establishments are able to charge rates that even come close to what you might pay for an ordinary room in a typical western country, and that is for a very high standard of comfort and service; on the whole, accommodation, like so many other things in India, provides extremely good value for money.

Throughout this book we recommend places to stay in cities, towns and villages that range from lavish lakeside palaces to the most basic dormitory accommodation. Travellers on all budgets are looking to get the best return for what they're prepared to spend, and we set out to spotlight bargains in every category. However, we have not slavishly listed the very cheapest rooms, regardless of quality; there's usually a reason why specific hotels have much lower rates than the others, and part of the function of this book is to spare you from finding out what that reason is.

INEXPENSIVE HOTELS

Whether catering for backpacking tourists or less well-off Indians, you'll find **cheap hotels** charging less than Rs100 for a room ($3/£2) in almost every town in India. Budget accommodation varies from filthy fleapits to homely guest houses and, naturally, tends to be cheaper the further you get off the beaten track; it's most expensive in Bombay, where prices are at least double those for equivalent accommodation in most other cities.

Cold showers or "bucket baths" are the order of the day – not really a problem in most of India for most of the year – and it's always wise to check out the state of the bathrooms and toilets before taking a room. Bed bugs and mosquitoes are other things to check for – splotches of blood around the bed and on the walls where people have squashed them are tell-tale signs.

If a taxi driver or rickshaw *wallah* tells you that the place you ask for is full, closed or has moved, it's more than likely that it's because he wants to take you to a hotel that pays him commission – added, in some cases, to your bill.

ACCOMMODATION PRICE SYMBOLS

All **accommodation prices** in this book are coded using the symbols below. In principle the prices given are for the least expensive double rooms in each establishment, although where mid-range hotels have one or two budget options we've opted for the typical price of an a/c room. In addition, some hotels, usually in category ①, charge per bed rather than per room. Local taxes are not included unless specifically stated.

India doesn't have a "**tourist season**" as such, and most accommodation keeps the same prices throughout the year. Certain resorts however, and some spots on established tourist trails, do experience some variation and will be more expensive, or less negotiable, when demand is at its peak. For the hill stations, this will be in the summer (April–July); for Goa and other beach resorts in the south, it'll be the winter, especially around Christmas and New Year. We indicate such fluctuations where appropriate.

①	up to Rs100	④	Rs225–350	⑦	Rs750–1200
②	Rs100–150	⑤	Rs350–500	⑧	Rs1200–2200
③	Rs150–225	⑥	Rs500–750	⑨	Rs2200 and up

In some major tourist spots, hotel touts operate; they too work for commission from the hotels they take you to.

Finally, if you find yourself disagreeing with our review of a particular hotel, it was probably true when we wrote it; one unavoidable effect of books such as this is that the hotels we recommend may well change in character as a result. Many of the long-standing "backpackers' haunts" around the country are these days so inundated with foreign budget travellers as to have lost any sense of being in India – or even on this planet. To a lesser extent, they may also decide to raise their prices or lower their standards. And make sure you've got the right place; another spin-off is that imitators spring up to cash in on the popularity of well-known budget hotels. In Varanasi, for example, a *Jogi Lodge* and a *New Yogi Lodge* have sprung up to lure customers looking for the *Yogi Lodge*.

MID-RANGE HOTELS

Even if you value your **creature comforts**, you don't need to pay through the nose for them. A large clean room, freshly made bed, your own spotless (often sit-down) toilet, and hot and cold running water can still cost under Rs200 ($6/£4). Extras that bump up the price include TV, mosquito nets, a balcony, and, above all, **air-conditioning**. Abbreviated in this book and in India itself as **a/c**, air-conditioning is not necessarily the advantage you might expect – in some hotels you can find yourself paying double for a system that is so dust-choked, wheezy and noisy as to preclude any possibility of sleep – but providing it is what seems to entitle a hotel to consider itself mid-range. Some also offer a halfway-house option known as "air-cooled". Many medium-priced hotels also have attached restaurants, and even room service.

New hotels tend to be lined inside, on floors and walls, with marble (or an approximation thereof), which can make them feel totally characterless. They are however much cleaner than older hotels, where dirt and grime clings to cracks and crevices, and damp quickly devours paint.

Most state governments run their own "**tourist bungalows**", similar to mid-range hotels, but often also offering pricier a/c rooms and cheaper dormitories. They are usually good value, though they vary a lot from state to state (Rajasthan's, for example, tend to be rather run-down, whereas

Tamil Nadu's, all called *Hotel Tamil Nadu*, are as a rule very well kept), and even within states. If you're on a medium budget, it's not a bad idea to think first of staying in the state-run hotel in any town; to make that easier, we've consistently indicated such places through this guide by including the state acronym in the name – eg MPTDC *Palace*.

UPMARKET HOTELS

Most luxury hotels in India fall into one of two categories: old-fashioned institutions brimming with class, and modern jet-set chain hotels, largely confined to large cities and tourist resorts.

The faded grandeur of the **Raj** lingers on in the venerable edifices of British imperial hangouts such as Calcutta and the hill stations. These can be well worth seeking out for their olde-worlde charm, and their knack of being somehow more quintessentially British than the British ever manage. In addition, in states such as Rajasthan, UP and Madhya Pradesh, magnificent old forts and palaces (*thikanas*) from feudal estates, and *havelis*, the former homes of aristocratic families, have been designated "**heritage hotels.**"

Modern deluxe establishments – slicker, brighter, faster and far more businesslike – tend to belong to chains, as often Indian as international. The *Taj* in Bombay for example, the country's grandest hostelry, has a number of offshoots, including former palaces in Rajasthan. Other chains include *Oberoi*, *Holiday Inn*, *Meridien*, *Hyatt* and *Sheraton*, as well as ITDC's *Ashok* chain. You'll find such hotels in most state capitals and some resorts favoured by rich Indian and foreign tourists. Prices in them do begin to approach those of their counterparts back home, but only *begin* to.

Bookings for many of the larger hotel chains can be made in offices around the world. The *Taj*, *Oberoi* and *Sheraton* chains are among those with outlets in the UK and the US. Otherwise, bookings can be made by mail or fax to:

Ashok Group, Ashok Reservation Service, *Hotel Samrat*, Chanakyapuri, Delhi 110021; ☎011/603030, fax 011/687 3216.

Oberoi Group, *Oberoi Maidens*, 7 Sham Nath Marg, Delhi 110054; ☎011/252 5464, fax 011/292 9800.

Taj Group, *Taj Mahal Intercontinental*, Apollo Bunder, Bombay 400039; ☎022/202 3366, fax 022/287 2711.

Welcomgroup (Sheraton), *Maurya Sheraton*, Diplomatic Enclave, New Delhi; ☎011/303 0101, fax 011/301 2892.

YOUTH HOSTEL ASSOCIATIONS

Australia
Australian YHA ☎02/565 1325
Level 3, 10 Mallett St, Camperdown, NSW.

Canada
Canadian Hostelling Association ☎613/237-7884
#400, 205 Catherine St, Ottawa, Ontario K2P 1C3.

England and Wales
Youth Hostel Association (YHA) ☎017278/45047
8 St Stephen's Hill, St Alban's, Herts AL1.
London shop and information office ☎0171/836 1036
14 Southampton St, London WC2.

Ireland
An Oige ☎01/363111
39 Mountjoy Square, Dublin 1.

New Zealand
YHA of New Zealand ☎03/799970
PO Box 436, Christchurch 1.

Northern Ireland
YHA of Northern Ireland ☎0232/324733
56 Bradbury Place, Belfast, BT7.

Scotland
Scottish YHA ☎01786/511817
Glebe Crescent, Stirling, FK8 2JA.

USA
American Youth Hostels (AYH) ☎202/783-6161
733 15th St NW 840, PO Box 37613, Washington DC 20005.

Ys AND YHs

Official and non-official **youth hostels**, some run by state governments, are spread haphazardly across the country. Often run-down and often full (though on occasion completely empty), they'll give *IYHA* cardholders a discount, but rarely exclude non-holders, nor do they usually impose daytime closing or other silly rules. Prices match the cheapest hotels; where there is a youth hostel, it may well be the best budget accommodation available – which goes especially for the *Salvation Army* ones.

YMCAs and YWCAs, confined to big cities, are plusher and pricier, comparable to a mid-range hotel. They are usually good value, but often full, and sometimes only take members of one sex.

OTHER PLACES

Many railway stations have "**retiring rooms**" for passengers to sleep. These can be particularly handy if you're catching an early morning train, but tend to get booked up in advance. They vary in price, but generally charge roughly the same as a budget hotel; dormitories, where you can bank on being woken at the crack of dawn by a morning chorus of throat-clearing, are often available.

In one or two places, you can rent **rooms in people's homes**. In Rajasthan, the state tourist development corporation runs a "Paying Guest Scheme" to locate tourists with families offering lodging, while *Munjeeta Travel* in London (see p.5) organize "Homestay Tours" across India – an excellent way to get to know an Indian family and see how they live. **Houseboats** were the thing in

Srinagar, Kashmir, but going there is not a particularly good idea at present.

Camping is possible too, although in most of the country it's hard to see why you'd want to be cooped up in a tent overnight when you could be sleeping on a cool *charpoi* (a sort of basic bed) on a roof terrace for a handful of *rupees* – let alone why you'd choose to carry a tent around India in the first place. Except possibly on treks, it's not usual simply to pitch a tent in the countryside, but many hotels allow camping in their grounds. The *YMCA* run a few sites, as do state governments (Maharashtra in particular), and the scouts and guides.

Finally, some temples, particularly Sikh *gurudwaras*, offer accommodation for pilgrims and visitors, and may put up tourists. A donation is often expected, and certainly appreciated. Pilgrimage sites, especially those far from other accommodation, also have **dharamshalas** where visitors can stay.

PRACTICALITIES

Check-out time at most hotels is noon. Always confirm this when you arrive: some expect you out by 9am, while others operate a 24-hour system, under which you are simply obliged to leave by the same time as you arrived. Some places let you use their facilities after the official check-out time, sometimes for a small charge, others (notably the grotty group of budget guest houses around Delhi's Janpath) won't even let you leave your baggage after then unless you pay for another night.

In cheap hotels and hostels, you needn't expect any **additions to your basic bill**, but as you go up the scale, you'll find taxes and service charges creeping in, sometimes adding as much as a third on top of the original tariff. Service is generally 10 percent, but taxes are a matter for state governments and vary from state to state.

Like most other things in India, the price of a room may well be open to **negotiation**. If you think the price is too high, or if all the hotels in town are empty, try haggling. You may get nowhere – but nothing ventured, nothing gained.

EATING AND DRINKING

Indian food has a richly deserved reputation throughout the world for being aromatic and delicious. Visiting India, you should exercise a little caution as to where and what you eat, but most travellers develop a level of tolerance after a period of controlled exposure.

If you're a **vegetarian**, you've come to the right place. Indians are used to people having special dietary requirements: yours will be respected, and no-one will think you strange for having them. Most religious Hindus, and the majority of people in the south, do not consume the flesh of animals, while some orthodox Brahmins will not eat food cooked by anyone outside their household (or onions or garlic, as they inflame the baser instincts), and Jains are even stricter. Veganism as such is not common, however; if you're vegan, you'll have to keep your eyes open for eggs and dairy products.

Many eating places will state whether they are vegetarian or non-vegetarian ("veg" or "non-veg"); sometimes, as with station canteens, there are both, and on public transport, you always get the option of veg or non-veg food. Even when meat is available, especially in the larger towns,

its quality is not high (so health risks are greater) and you won't get much in a dish anyway – it's mainly there for flavouring. Hindus, of course, do not eat beef and Muslims shun pork, so you'll only find those in a few Christian enclaves such as the beach areas of Goa.

Broadly speaking, there are three types of eating establishments. *Bhojanalayas* or *dhabas* are **cheap Indian diners**, where food is basic but often good, consisting of vegetable curry, sometimes meat, *dal* (a lentil soup pronounced "da'al"), and rice or Indian bread (the latter more standard in the north). Diners can be grubby – look them over before you commit yourself – and they have a bit of a tendency to pile on the *garam masala* as a substitute for fresh and appropriate spices. They do, on the other hand, have the advantage of being dirt cheap.

Restaurants as such vary in price and quality, and can be veg or non-veg, offering a wide choice of dishes, much like Indian restaurants anywhere else in the world. If you're in a group, you can order a variety of dishes and sample each one. Deluxe restaurants such as those in five-star hotels can be very expensive by Indian standards, but they offer a chance to try classic Indian cooking of a very high standard: rich, subtle, mouthwatering, and still a fraction of the price you'd pay for such delights at home – assuming you could find Indian food that good. Try a meal in one at least once.

The third type of eating place caters specifically for foreign travellers with unadventurous tastebuds: the **tourist restaurant**, found in beach resorts, hill stations and travellers' meccas across India. Here you can get pancakes and fritters, omelettes and toast, chips, fried prawns, cereal, and fruit salad. The downside is that they can be a little bit pricey, some miss the mark by a long way, and they are not, of course, authentically Indian.

Finally, should you be lucky enough to be invited into someone's home, you will get to taste the most authentically Indian food of all.

For advice on **water** in India, see p.17.

Most Indian women are professional cooks and housewives, trained from childhood by mothers, grandmothers and aunties, and aided by daughters and nieces. They can quite easily spend a whole day cooking, grinding and mixing the spices themselves, and using only the freshest ingredients.

INDIAN FOOD

What westerners call a **curry** covers a variety of dishes, each made with a different *masala*, or mix of spices. Curry powder does not exist in India, the nearest equivalent being *garam masala* ("hot mix"), a combination of dried ground black pepper and other spices in theory added to a dish at the last stage of cooking to spice it up, but often used as a substitute for other aromatics. Commonly used **spices** include chilli, of course, and also turmeric, garlic, ginger, cinnamon, cardamom, cloves, coriander – both leaf and seed – cumin and saffron. These are not all added at the same time, and some are used whole, so beware of chewing on them. The spice that gives British and Caribbean curry powder its distinctive taste, fenugreek, is used much more sparingly in India.

It's the Indian penchant for **chilli** that alarms many western visitors. The majority of foreigners develop a tolerance for it; if you don't, you'll just have to stick to mild dishes such as *kurma* and *biryani* where meat or vegetables are cooked with rice, and eat plenty of *chapati*. Indians tend to assuage the effects of chilli with chutney, *dahi* (curd) or *raita* (curd with mint and cucumber, or other herbs and vegetables). Otherwise, **beer** is one of the best things for washing chilli out of your mouth; the essential oils that cause the burning sensation dissolve in alcohol, but not in water.

Vegetarian curries are usually identified (even on menus in English) by the Hindi names of their main ingredients. Terms like "curry" and "masala" don't really tell you what to expect; meat curries are more often given specific names such as *kurma* or *dopiaza*, to indicate the kind of *masala* used.

Regional variety is vast: the Bengalis love fish and cook a mean *mangsho* (meat) curry as well as exotic vegetable dishes such as *mo-cha* – cooked banana flower. They also like to include fish bones for added flavour in their vegetable curries – a nasty surprise for vegetarians. Biharis are known for their *satu* – a staple flour used

instead of rice. Tibetans and Bhotias from the Himalayas have a simple diet of *thukpa* (meat soup), and *momo* (meat dumplings), as well as a rancid salty tea. In Punjab and much of northern India, home cooking consists of *dal* and vegetables along with *roti* (bread) and less rice than the Bengalis. Food in Gujarat is often cooked with a bit of sugar.

In the north of India especially, but as far south as Hyderabad, the influence of the Moghuls lives on in the form of **Mughlai cooking**. Mostly non-veg, the food is extremely rich, using ingredients such as cream, almonds, sultanas and saffron. *Mughlai* as the name of a *masala* normally indicates a mild, creamy one. *Mughlai paratha* is spicy fried bread with egg.

The other big northern style is *tandoori*. The name refers to the deep clay oven (*tandoor*) in which the food is cooked. *Tandoori* chicken is marinated in yoghurt, herbs and spices before cooking. Boneless pieces of meat, marinated and cooked in the same way are known as *tikka*; they may be served in a medium-strength *masala* (*tikka masala*), one thickened with almonds (*pasanda*), or in a rich butter sauce (butter chicken). Breads such as *nan* and *roti* are also baked in the *tandoor*.

Certain combinations are traditional and seasonally repeated, such as *makki ki roti* (fried corn bread) with *sarson ka sag* (mustard-leaf greens) around Punjab and other parts of north India. *Baingan bharta* (puréed roast aubergine) is commonly eaten with plain yogurt and *roti* (plain bread). In good Muslim cooking from the north, delicately thin *rumali roti* (handkerchief bread) often accompanies rich meat and chicken dishes. *Dal* is a safe bet with almost any meat or vegetable dish, and easy to eat with rice or bread.

In the south, where fish is more abundant, meat much less so, and all food generally spicier, the most common meal is a mound of rice surrounded by various vegetable curries, *sambar dal*, chutney and curd, and usually accompanied by *poppadums* and *vadas*. Traditionally served on a round metal *thali* or tray (also found in north India), with each side dish in a separate metal bowl, it is sometimes dished out on a rectangle of banana leaf instead. In most places, you can eat as much as you want, and staff circulate with refills of everything. In the south even more than elsewhere, eating with your fingers is *de rigueur* (you want to feel the food as well as taste it) and cutlery may be unavailable.

Wherever you eat, remember to use only your right hand, and wash your hands before you start.

SNACKS AND STREET FOOD

Feeling peckish should never be a problem, with all sorts of snack meals and finger food to choose from. Of the sit-down variety, *chana puri*, a thin chick-pea curry with a *puri* (or sometimes other breads) to dunk, is a great favourite in the north of the country; *idli sambar* – lentil and vegetable sauce with rice cakes to dunk – is the southern equivalent. But the great snack meal of the south is *masala dosa*, a potato and vegetable curry wrapped in a crispy rice pancake.

Street finger food includes *bhel puris* (small vegetable-stuffed puris with tamarind sauce), *pani puris* (the same puris dunked in peppery and spicy water – only for the seasoned), *bhajis* (deep-fried cakes of vegetables in chick-pea flour), *samosas* (meat or vegetables in a pastry triangle, fried), and *pakoras* (vegetables in potato dipped in chick-pea flour batter and deep-fried). Kebabs are common in the north, most frequently *seekh kebab*, minced lamb grilled on a skewer, but also *shami kebab*, small minced lamb cutlets. Kebabs rolled into griddle-fried bread are popular in Calcutta, where they are known as *kathi rolls*. Food left lying around attracts germs – make sure it's freshly cooked.

You won't find anything called "Bombay mix" in India, but there's no shortage of dry spicy snack mixes, often refered to as *channa chur*. You'll also find the constituents on sale separately at shops and stalls. Jackfruit chips are sometimes sold as a savoury snack, though they are rather bland, and cashew nuts are a real bargain.

NON-INDIAN FOOD

Chinese food has become widespread in large towns, where it is cooked by local chefs and is not what you'd call authentic. Still, it can make a pleasant change, and dishes such as fried rice are safe options if you have an upset stomach. A few cities, like Calcutta, have large Chinese communities, and you can get very good Chinese cuisine indeed.

Western food is either dire or expensive, or often both. *McDonald's* has yet to reach India, but *Wimpy* in Delhi will do you a "lamburger" (what did you expect, beef?), or a plate of unlimited salad for a price high by local standards but cheap compared to elsewhere in the world. Delhi and Bombay also offer international cuisine such as Thai, Japanese, Italian and French, but it doesn't come cheap.

BREAKFAST

Unreconstructed westerners seem to get especially homesick around breakfast time; but getting your fry-ups and hash browns is likely to be a problem. *Chana puri* is an option in the north, if a little spicy for some, and *alu paratha* with *dahi* is another traditional start to the day. *Iddli sambar* and *masala dosa* is the most common equivalent in the south, where members of the *India Coffee House* chain can usually be depended upon for some decent coffee and toast.

In those towns which have established a reputation as hang-outs for "travellers", budget hotels and restaurants serve up the usual hippy fare – banana pancakes, muesli, etc – as well as omelettes, toast, porridge (not always oatmeal), cornflakes, and even bacon and eggs.

PAAN

You may be relieved to know that the red stuff people spit all over the streets isn't blood, but juice produced by chewing **paan** – a digestive, commonly taken after meals, and also a mild stimulant.

A *paan* consists of chopped or shredded nut (always referred to as betel nut, though in fact it comes from the areca palm), wrapped in a leaf (which *does* come from the betel tree) that is first prepared with ingredients such as *katha* (a red paste), *chuna* (slaked white lime), *mitha masala* (a mix of sweet spices, which can be ingested), and *zarda* (chewing tobacco, not to be swallowed on any account). The triangular package thus formed is wedged inside your cheek and chewed slowly, spitting out the juice as you go.

Paan, and *paan masala*, a mix of betel nut, fennel seeds, sweets and flavourings, are sold by *paan-wallahs*, often from tiny stalls squeezed between shops. *Paan-wallahs* develop big reputations; those in the tiny roads of Varanasi are the most renowned of all, asking astronomical prices for *paan* made to elaborate specifications including silver and even gold foil. *Paan* is an acquired taste; novices should start off, and preferably stick with, the sweet *mitha* variety.

A GLOSSARY OF FOOD TERMS

General Terms and Requests

bhat	cooked rice	*hath dhoney*	water for washing	*mehti*	spicy
chamach	spoon	*ka pani*	hands	*mirch*	pepper
chawal	uncooked rice	*jhal*	chilli hot	*murgi*	chicken
cheeni	sugar	*kala mirch*	black pepper	*namak*	salt
cheeni mat	do not put	*kam* or *kamti*	less – eg *jhal kam*	*pani*	water
dhalna	sugar (eg in tea)		(less hot)	*peeney ka*	drinking water (not
chhoori	knife	*kanta*	fork	*pani*	mineral water)
dudh	milk	*khaana*	food	*plate*	plate
garam	hot	*lal mirch*	red pepper	*tanda*	cold
gosht	meat	*macchi*	fish	*ziadah* or *awr*	more

Vegetables

adrak	ginger	*gaajar*	carrot	*paneer*	Indian cheese
alu	potatoes	*gobi*	cauliflower	*piaz*	onions
baingan	eggplant	*kadoo*	pumpkin	*sabzi*	literally greens; used
or *brinjal*	(aubergine)	*karela*	bitter gourd		for all vegetables
bhindi	okra or ladies finger	*lasoon*	garlic	*sag*	general term for
chana	chick peas (garbanzo beans)	*matter*	peas		green vegetables
dal	lentils	*palak* (or *sag*)	spinach	*tamatar*	tomato

Dishes and cooking terms

alu baingan	potato and aubergine; mild to medium	*karahi*	meat with dry *masala* in a cast-iron dish; medium-strength
alu methi	potato with fenugreek leaves; usually medium-hot	*keema*	minced lamb
bhindi bhaji	fried okra; gently spiced	*kofta*	balls of minced vegetables or meat in a curried sauce
bhuna	thickened-down medium-strength curry, usually tomato and onion	*kurma*	meat braised in yoghurt sauce, mild
biryani	rice with saffron or turmeric, whole spices, and meat (sometimes vegetables), and often hard-boiled egg; mild	*maacher jhol*	mild fish stew, often with the entire fish – a Bengali delicacy
		malai kofta	minced lamb kebabs in a rich cream sauce; medium-mild
Bombay duck	dried bummelo fish	*molee*	curry with coconut, usually fish, originally Malay (hence the name), now a speciality of Kerala; hot
chingri	prawns		
chop	minced meat or vegetable surrounded by breaded mashed potato	*mulligatawny*	curried vegetable soup, a classic Anglo-Indian dish; medium-strength
cutlet	cutlet – often minced meat or vegetable fried in the form of a flat cake	*pathia*	thickened curry with lemon juice; hot
		pomfret	a flatfish popular in Bombay
dahi maach	fish curry with yoghurt, ginger and turmeric; a mild Bengali dish	*pulau*	rice, gently spiced and prefried
dal gosht	meat cooked in lentils; hot	*rogan josh*	deep red lamb curry, a classic Mughlai dish; medium-hot
dhansak	meat and lentil curry, a Parsi speciality; medium-hot	*sambar*	soupy lentil and vegetable curry with asafoetida and tamarind
dopiaza	with onions added at two different stages of cooking; medium-mild	*subje*	white coconut chutney often served with *vada*
dum	steamed in a casserole		
jalfrezi	with tomatoes and green chilli; medium-hot	*tarka dal*	lentils with a *masala* of fried garlic, onions and spices
jeera	cumin; a *masala* so described will usually be medium-hot	*vindaloo*	Goan vinegared meat (sometimes fish) curry, originally pork; very hot (but not as hot as the kamikaze UK version)

Breads and Pancakes

appam*	rice pancake speckled with holes, soft in the middle	papad or poppadum	crisp, thin chick-pea flour cracker
batura	soft bread made of white flour and traditionally accompanying *chana* (chickpeas); common in Delhi	paratha	wholewheat bread made with butter, rolled thin and griddle-fried; a little bit like a chewy pancake, often stuffed with meat or vegetables
chapati	unleavened bread made of wholewheat flour and baked on a round griddle-dish	puri	crispy, puffed-up, deep fried wholewheat bread
dosa*	rice pancake; should be crispy		
iddli*	steamed rice cake, usually served with sambar	roti	loosely used term; often just another name for *chapati*, though it should be thicker, chewier, and baked in a tandoor
kachori	small thick cakes of salty deep fried bread especially good in Varanasi		
loochi	delicate *puri* often mixed with white flour; cooked in Bengal	uttapam*	thick rice pancake often cooked with onions
nan	white leavened bread baked in a tandoor	vada*	doughnut-shaped deep-fried lentil cake

*South Indian terminology; all other terms above, and opposite, are either in Hindi or refer to North Indian cuisine

SWEETS

Many Indians have rather a sweet tooth; Indian sweets can be very sweet. Of the more solid type, *barfi*, a kind of fudge made from milk which has been boiled down and condensed, varies from moist and delicious to dry and powdery. Its often sold covered with silver leaf (which you eat). Smoother-textured, round *penda* and thin diamonds of *kaju katri*, plus *sandesh* and the harder *paira*, both popular in Bengal, are among many other sweets made from *chhana* or boiled-down milk. Crunchier *mesur* is made with chick-peas; numerous types of *halwa*, not to be confused with the Middle Eastern variety, include the rich *gajar ka halwa* made from carrots and cream.

Getting softer and stickier, those circular orange tubes dripping syrup in sweet-shop windows, called *jalebis* and made of deep-fried treacle, are as sickly as they look. *Gulab jamuns*, deep-fried sponge balls soaked in syrup, are even sicklier. Common in both the north and the south, *ladu* consists of balls made from semolina flour with raisins and sugar, while among Bengali sweets, widely considered to be the best are *rasgullas*, rosewater-flavoured cream cheese balls floating in syrup. *Ras malai*, found throughout north India, is similar but soaked in cream instead of syrup.

Indian *Cadbury's* chocolate is not tremendously nice, but among the large ice-cream vendors, *Kwality*, *Gaylord* and *Dollops Bounty* bar (coconut choc-ice) stand out. Uniformed men push carts of ice cream around and the bigger companies have many imitators, usually quite obvious. Some have no scruples – stay away from water ices unless you have a seasoned constitution. Ice-cream parlours selling elaborate concoctions including sundaes have really taken off; Connaught Circus in Delhi has several. Be sure to try *kulfi*, a pistachio- and cardamom-flavoured frozen sweet which is India's answer to ice cream; *bhang kulfi*, not available everywhere, has an interesting kick to it.

FRUIT

What fruit is available varies with region and season, but there's always a fine choice. Ideally, you should peel all fruit, or soak it in strong iodine or potassium permanganate solution for half an hour. Roadside vendors sell fruit which they often cut up and serve sprinkled with salt and even *masala*.

Mangoes of various kinds are usually on offer, but not all are sweet for eating – some are used for pickles or curries. Indians are picky about their mangoes, which they feel and smell before buying; if you don't know the art of choosing the fruit, you could be sold the leftovers. Among the species appearing at different times in the season, which lasts from spring to summer, look out for *Alphonso* and *Langra*. Bananas of one sort or another are also on sale all year round, and oranges and tangerines are generally easy to come by, as are sweet melons and thirst-quenching watermelons.

Tropical fruits such as coconuts, *papaya* (pawpaws) and pineapples are more common in the south, while things such as lychees and pomegranates are very seasonal. In the north, temperate fruit from the mountains can be much like that in Europe, with strawberries, apricots and even rather soft apples available in season.

Among less familiar fruit, the *chiku*, which looks like a kiwi and tastes a bit like a pear, is worth a mention, as is the watermelon-sized jackfruit, whose spiny green exterior encloses sweet, slightly rubbery yellow segments, each containing a seed. Individual segments are sold at roadside stalls.

DRINKS

India sometimes seems to run on **tea** (**chai**), grown in Darjeeling, Assam and the Nilgiri Hills, and sold by *chai-wallahs* on just about every street corner. However, although it was introduced from China by the East India Company in 1838, its use was only popularized by a government campaign in the 1950s. Tea is usually made by putting tea dust, milk and water in a pan, boiling it all up, straining it into a cup or glass with lots of sugar and pouring back and forth from one cup to another to stir. Special *chai* might be made with ginger and/or cardamoms. If you're quick off the mark, you can get them to hold the sugar. English tea it isn't, but most travellers get used to it: "Just don't think of *chai* as tea," advise some. Occasionally, you might get a pot of European-style "tray" tea, generally consisting of a tea bag in lukewarm water – you'd do better to stick to the *pukka* Indian variety.

In the south, **coffee** (**kofi**) is more common than tea, and far better than it is in the north. One of the best places to get it is in outlets of the *India Coffee House* chain, found in every southern town, and apparently creeping ever northwards. A whole ritual is attached to the drinking of milky Keralan coffee in particular, poured in flamboyant sweeping motions between tall glasses to cool it down.

With **bottled water** so widely available, you may have no need of **soft drinks**. These have long been surprisingly controversial in India. *Coca Cola* and *Pepsi* have recently made comebacks, after being banned from the country for seventeen years. That policy was originally instigated by socialists in the Janata government, in part to prevent the expatriation of profits by foreign companies; since their return, militant Hindu groups such as the BJP and the RSS have threatened to make them the focus of a new boycott campaign against multinational consumer goods. The absence of *Coke* and *Pepsi* spawned a host of Indian colas such as *Campa Cola* (innocuous), *Thums Up* (not unpalatable), *Gold Spot* (fizzy orange), and *Limca* (rumoured to have dubious connections to Italian companies, and to contain additives banned there). All contain a lot of sugar but little else: adverts for Indian soft drinks have been known to boast "Absolutely no natural ingredients!". None will quench your thirst for long.

More recommendable are straight water (treated, boiled or bottled; see also p.17), and cartons of *Frooti* and similar brands of fruit juice drinks, which come in mango, guava, apple and lemon varieties. If the carton looks at all mangled it is best not to touch it as it may have been recycled. At larger stations, there will be a stall on the platform selling *Himachali* apple juice. Better still, green coconuts are cheaper than any of these, and sold on the street by vendors who will hack off the top for you with a machete and give you a straw to suck up the coconut water (you then scoop out the flesh and eat it). You will also find street stalls selling freshly made sugar-cane juice: delicious, and not in fact very sweet, but not always as safe healthwise as you might like.

India's greatest cold drink, *lassi*, is made with curd and drunk either sweetened with sugar, salted, or mixed with fruit. It varies widely from smooth and delicious to insipid and watery, and is sold at virtually every cafe, restaurant and canteen in the country. Freshly made milk shakes are also commonly available at establishments with blenders. They'll also sell you what they call a fruit juice, but which is usually fruit, water and sugar (or salt) liquidized and strained. With all such drinks, however appetizing they may seem, you should exercise great caution in deciding where to drink them; try to find out where the water came from.

ALCOHOL

Prohibition, once widespread in India, is now only fully enforced in Gujarat and some of the northeastern hill states, although Tamil Nadu and some other states, retain partial prohibition in the form of "dry" days, high taxes, restrictive licences, and health warnings on labels ("Liquor – ruins country, family and life," runs Tamil Nadu's). Prohibition rules have even been extended recently in Delhi, where the right-wing

Hindu BJP local government has introduced 48 dry days and extraordinary taxes.

Alcoholic enclaves in prohibition states can become major drinking centres: Daman and Diu in Gujarat, and Pondicherry and Karaikal in Tamil Nadu are the main ones. Goa, Sikkim and Mahé (Kerala) join them as places where the booze flows especially freely and cheaply. Interestingly, all were outside the British Raj. **Liquor permits** – available from Indian embassies, high commissions and tourist offices abroad, and from tourist offices in Delhi, Bombay, Calcutta and Madras – allow those travellers who bother to apply for one to evade certain restrictions in prohibition states.

Beer is widely available, if rather expensive by local standards. Price varies from state to state, but you can usually expect to pay Rs30–50 for a 650ml bottle. *Kingfisher* is the leading brand, but there are plenty of others. All lagers, they tend to contain chemical additives, but are usually pretty palatable if you can get them cold. In certain places, notably unlicensed restaurants in Tamil Nadu, beer comes in the form of "special tea" – a teapot of beer, which you pour into and drink from a teacup to disguise what it really is. A cheaper, and often delicious, alternative to beer in Kerala and one or two other places is *toddy* (palm wine). In Bengal a similar wine, found in rural areas and made from the date palm, is known as *tadd*. In the morning it's a mild and pleasant juice; by the evening, strong fermentation leaves it smelling like essence of old socks.

Spirits usually take the form of "Indian Made Foreign Liquor" (IMFL), local varieties of whisky, gin and brandy: pretty rough, but strong enough. In Goa, *fene* is a spirit distilled from coconut or cashew fruit. You are warned, however, to steer well clear of illegally distilled *arak*, which often contains methanol (wood alcohol) and other poisons. A look through the press, especially at festival times, will soon reveal numerous cases of blindness and death as a result of drinking bad hooch. Licensed country liquor, sold in several states under such names as *bangla*, is an acquired taste. In the Himalayas, the Bhotia people, of Tibetan stock, drink *chang*, a beer made from millet, and one of the nicest drinks of all – *tumba* where fermented millet is placed in a bamboo flask and topped with hot water, then sipped through a bamboo pipe.

MAIL, TELECOMMUNICATIONS AND MEDIA

There is no need to be out of touch with the rest of the world while you're in India. The mail service is pretty reliable if a little slow, international phone calls are surprisingly easy, there are a number of decent English-language newspapers, and more people and places than you might imagine have access to satellite TV in English too.

MAIL SERVICES

Mail can take anything from three days to four weeks to get to or from India, depending largely on where exactly you are; two weeks is about the norm. Stamps are not expensive, and aerogrammes and postcards cost the same to anywhere in the world. Ideally, you should have mail franked in front of you. Most post offices are open Mon–Fri 10am–5pm and Sat 10am–noon, but big city GPOs keep longer hours (Mon–Fri 9.30am–6pm, Sat 9.30am–1pm). You can also buy stamps at big hotels.

Poste Restante (General Delivery) services throughout the country are pretty reliable, though exactly how long individual offices hang on to letters is more or less at their own discretion; for periods of longer than a month, it makes sense to mark mail with your expected date of arrival. Letters are filed alphabetically; in larger offices, you sort through them yourself. To avoid misfiling, your name should be printed clearly, with the surname in large capitals and underlined, but it is still a good idea to check under your first name too, just in case. Have letters addressed to you c/o Poste Restante, GPO (if it's the main post office you want), and the name of the town and state. In Delhi, you will probably want to specify "GPO, New Delhi", since "GPO, Delhi" means Old Delhi GPO, a lot less convenient for most tourists. Sometimes too, as in Calcutta and Madras, local tourist offices might be more convenient than the GPO. Don't forget to take ID with you to claim your mail. *American Express* offices also keep mail for holders of their charge card or travellers' cheques.

Having parcels sent out to you in India is not such a good idea – chances are they'll go astray. If you do have a parcel sent, have it registered.

Sending a parcel out of India can be quite a performance. First you have it cleared by customs at the post office (they often don't bother, but check), then you take it to a tailor and agree a price to have it wrapped in cheap cotton cloth (which you may have to go and buy yourself), stitched up and sealed with wax. In big city GPOs, people offering this service will be at hand. Next, take it to the post office, fill in and attach the relevant customs forms (it's best to tick the box marked "gift" and give its value as less than Rs1000 or "no commercial value", to avoid bureaucratic entanglements), buy your stamps, see them franked, and dispatch it. Parcels should not be more than a metre long, nor weigh more than 20kg. Surface mail is incredibly cheap, and takes an average of six months to arrive – it may take half, or four times that, however. It's a good way to dump excess baggage and souvenirs, but don't send anything fragile this way.

As in Britain, North America and Australasia, books and magazines can be sent more cheaply, unsealed or wrapped around the middle, as **printed papers** ("book post"). Remember that all packages from India are likely to be suspect at home, and searched or X-rayed: don't send anything dodgy.

PHONES

Privately run **phone services** with international direct dialling facilities are very widespread. Advertising themselves with the acronyms **STD/ISD** (standard trunk dialling/international subscriber dialling), they are extremely quick and easy to use; some stay open 24 hours per day. Both national and international calls are dialled direct. To call abroad, dial the international

International Codes		
	From India:	To India:
UK	☎00 44	☎00 91
Irish Republic	☎00 353	☎00 91
US and Canada	☎00 1	☎011 91
Australia	☎00 61	☎0011 91
New Zealand	☎00 64	☎00 91

access code (00), the code for the country you want – 44 for the UK, for example – the appropriate area code (leaving out any initial zeros), and the number you want; then you speak, pay your bill, which is calculated in seconds, and leave. Prices are much the same at small private places as at official telecommunications offices; many have fax machines too. Calling from hotels is usually more expensive.

Home country direct services are now available from any phone to the UK, the USA, Canada, Ireland, Australia, New Zealand, and a growing number of other countries. These allow you to make a collect or telephone credit card call to that country via an operator there. If you can't find a phone with home country direct buttons, you can use any phone toll-free, by dialling 000, your country code, and 17 (except Canada which is 000-167).

To **call India** from abroad, dial the international access code, followed by 91 for India, the local code minus the initial zero, then the number you want.

THE MEDIA

India has a large number of **English-language daily newspapers**, usually either regional or in regional editions. The most prominent of the nationals are *The Hindu*, *The Statesman*, the *Times of India*, the *Independent*, the *Economic Times*, and the *Indian Express* (usually the most critical of the government). All are pretty dry and sober, and concentrate on Indian news; the *Independent* and the Calcutta *Telegraph* tend to have better coverage of world news than the rest. India's press is the freest in Asia and attacks on the government are often quite outspoken. However, as in the west, most papers can be seen as part of the political establishment, and are unlikely to print anything that might upset the "national consensus".

In recent years, a number of *Time/Newsweek*-style **news magazines** have hit the market. The first and best of these is *Frontline*, published by *The Hindu*. Others include *India Today*, *Sunday* and *The Week*. As they give more of an overview of stories and issues than the daily papers, you will probably get a better idea from them of what is going on in Indian politics, and most tend to have a higher proportion of international news too. *Business India* is more financially orientated, the *Illustrated Weekly of India* lighter and less political, and *The India Magazine* more cultural. Film fanzines and gossip mags are very popular (*Screen* is one of the best, though you'd have to be reasonably *au fait* with Indian movies to follow a lot of it), but magazines and periodicals in English cover all sorts of popular and minority interests, so it's worth having a look through what's available. One publication of special interest is *Amar Chitra Katha*'s series of Hindu legends, Indian history and folk tales in comic form for children.

Foreign publications such as the *International Herald Tribune, Time, Newsweek, The Economist* and the weekly edition of the British *Guardian* are all available in the main cities, and in the most upmarket hotels, but they are rather costly and often out of date. For a read through the British press, try the British Council in Delhi, Bombay, Calcutta and Madras.

BBC world service radio can be picked up on short wave on 15.31MHz (19.6m) between about 8.30am and 10.30pm (Indian time). Alternative frequencies if reception is poor include 17.79MHz (16.9m), 15.56MHz (19.3m) and 11.96MHz (25.1m).

The government-run **TV** company, *Doordarshan*, which broadcasts a sober diet of edifying programmes, has found itself totally unable to compete with the onslaught of mass access to **satellite TV**, with illegal use of cables ensuring that one satellite dish can serve dozens of homes at an affordable price. The main broadcaster in English is Rupert Murdoch's **Star TV** network, which incorporates the BBC World Service, *MTV*, the Hindi-film oriented *Zee TV*, and a couple of American soap and chat channels.

TREKKING

For many visitors, the opportunity to trek in the magnificent mountains is one of the main reasons to come to India. Well-tried routes can be found throughout the Himalayas, from Kashmir to Sikkim, as well as in other parts of the country, and are detailed at the appropriate points throughout this book. Trekking is less commercialized, but then again, less well organized than in neighbouring Nepal, and routes tend to be shorter.

One or two operators run package trekking holidays, and trekking agencies exist at such places as Manali, Darjeeling and Gangtok, but most people go under their own steam and organize guides, plus porters or ponies, privately. A trek normally lasts a week or two; the longer it is, in general, the more you'll get out of it.

Himachal Pradesh, which issues trekking maps, brochures and trekking guides, is the most efficient state in which to trek; the West Himalayan Mountain Institute is on hand in Manali to offer advice. Himalayan **Uttar Pradesh** sees fewer trekkers, but departments of the tourist corporation give out advice and information in Garhwal and Kumaon respectively, which see great crowds of pilgrims in summer. Kashmir itself is not the best place to venture at present, but there are exciting and exotic treks through the ancient Buddhist kingdoms of **Ladakh** and **Zanskar**. At the eastern end of the Himalaya, Darjeeling offers a good base from which to explore the surrounding mountains, while nine- and twelve-day treks in **Sikkim** require a permit issued by the Foreigners' Registration Office in Gangtok, and a guide from a recognized agency to be taken with you (the dollar fees are high). Shorter and less strenuous treks are available in the Ghats and the Nilgiri hills of **southern India**.

Having the right **equipment** for a trek is obviously important, but high-tech gear isn't essential – bring what you need to be comfortable but keep weight to a minimum. In some places, such as Darjeeling, you can rent equipment, but otherwise, you'll have to buy what you need or bring it with you. Make sure everything (zippers for example) is in working order before you set off. Clothes should be lightweight and versatile, especially considering the range of temperatures you might encounter: dress in layers for maximum flexibility.

CHECKLIST OF TREKKING EQUIPMENT

The checklist below is based on staying in rest houses or *chai* shops. This may not be possible, especially on treks lasting over 3–4 days. If you plan to **camp** (tents are easy to rent) or **climb** you'll need more.

Essentials
Backpack
Sleeping bag
Water bottle
Toiletries and toilet paper
Torch/Flashlight
Pocket knife
Sunglasses (UV protective)
Sunblock and lip balm
Compass and map

High-altitude gear
Gaiters
Down pants and booties
Telescopic ski poles (to help carry large loads over snow)
Ice axe (rarely needed on usual treks)
Crampons (ditto)

Clothes
Shirts/T-shirts
Trousers
Skirt/Dress (mid-calf length is best)
Thermal underwear
Woolly sweater
Parka (down or lightweight fibre)
Woolly hat/Balaclava (should cover ears)
Mittens or ski gloves
Rainproof plastic coat or poncho
Cotton hat with brim

Footwear
Trekking boots
Cotton and woollen socks

Other useful items
Plastic bag (to rainproof your pack)
Candles
Emergency snack food
Insect repellent
Spare bootlaces
Sewing kit
Small towel
Insulation mat
Large mug and spoon
Umbrella to keep off the sun

Health care equipment
Rehydration sachets
Water purification (see p.17)
Aspirin/Paracetamol
Plasters
Knee supports

Mountaineering is a more serious venture, requiring planning and organization; if you've never climbed, don't start in the Himalayas. Mountaineering institutes at Darjeeling, Uttarkashi (UP) and Dharamsala (HP), run training courses, though only the one at Dharamsala usually accepts foreigners; it also organizes high-altitude treks. Permission for mountaineering expeditions should be sought at least six months in advance from the *Indian Mountaineering Federation*, Anand Niketan, Benito Juarez Rd, New Delhi 110021, ☎011/671211. Peak fees range from US$600 to US$3000, according to height, and expeditions must be accompanied by an *IMF* liaison officer equipped to the same standard as the rest of the party. The *IMF* can also supply lists of local mountaineeering clubs; climbing with such clubs enables you to get to know local climbers, and obtain permits for otherwise restricted peaks.

For advice on the potential **health hazards** of mountain trekking, see p.20.

WILDLIFE VIEWING

With habitats running the gamut from high mountain to tropical jungle, there are all sorts of plants and animals to see in India. Tigers and elephants are just the two most obvious species. The **Indian elephant**, distinguished from its African cousin by its smaller ears, is still used as a beast of burden, and in temple processions and ceremonies. In the wild, it is not currently under threat.

The elephant's co-pachyderm, the one-horned **rhinoceros**, retains a foothold in the east of the country, but the tiger's fellow **big cats** have not fared so well. The cheetah is now extinct in India, while the Asiatic lion clings on in one tiny patch of Gujarat. The snow leopard is increasingly rare too, although the leopard (aka panther) of the plains can still be found in several places. Other indigenous felines include the jungle cat, the fishing cat of Bengal, and a kind of lynx called the caracal.

The larger cats' prey, deer and antelope, are much more abundant. The largest of the **deer** is the *sambar*, usually a solitary animal. Smaller and more gregarious are the spotted deer or *cheetal*, and others include the *muntjac* (barking deer) and *para* (hog deer). The smallest deer in India is the *chevrotain*, known from its size as the mouse deer. The swamp deer (*barasingha*) is rarer, while the *hangul* (Kashmiri red deer) is now an endangered species. **Antelopes** include the *nilgai* or bluebull, the black buck, the four-horned *chowsingha*, and the Indian gazelle known as the *chinkara*.

Among other animals you might hope or expect to see in India, **monkeys** (particularly macaques and langurs) are very common, as are the triple-striped palm squirrel. There are wild **buffalo**, and also *gaur*, the massive Indian bison. Indian wild dogs are called *dhole*, and there are also wolves and foxes. **Wild boar** are reasonably common too. Harder to spot are the shaggy sloth bear, and Asia's answer to the armadillo, a scaly anteater called a pangolin. **Reptiles** run from common-or-garden lizards to cobras, massive pythons, monitor lizards and crocodiles. In the Ganges, notably at Varanasi, river dolphins can be seen.

Among India's spectacular **birdlife**, both resident and migratory, waterfowl such as flamingoes, spoonbills and pelicans are the biggest draw, but eagles and peacocks are at least as spectacular, and herons, storks, ibises, hornbills and vultures are all there if you know where to look.

National Parks and **Wildlife Reserves** cover all of India's natural environments, and offer a chance to see a huge variety of birds, mammals and plants. Entrance fees and facilities vary, as do the seasons at which they are best visited, though October to June is usually the best time and most parks are closed during the monsoon. Since most visitors are Indian holidaymakers rather than foreign tourists, the more popular places can get quite packed at weekends, so it is usually better to visit them during the week.

Park accommodation, if it exists, is rather spartan and often full (book ahead if possible, especially for weekends), so you may well be staying at a town or village on the edge of the reserve rather than in the park itself. Park tours by jeep can generally be arranged with the park authorities, and boat trips, even elephant rides, are available at some parks too.

Corbett National Park (UP), is the country's first (it opened in 1935) and most popular. It was here that "Project Tiger" was launched in 1973 to protect the stripey felines, whose numbers had fallen to a low of 1830 across the country (see box p.381). Of the 19 reserves in the project, others where you might catch a glimpse of the elusive beasts include Dudhwa (UP), Kanha and Bandhavgarh (Madhya Pradesh), Ranthambhore (Rajasthan), Bandipur (Karnataka), and Manas and Kaziranga (Assam). Unfortunately, you are less likely to see tigers in their classic home, the **Sunderbans** of West Bengal – they are there, but considered too fierce to show the punters.

SELECTED INDIAN WILDLIFE PARKS

Park or Reserve	State	Terrain	Wildlife	Best Season
Bandhavgarh NP	Madhya Pradesh	hilly grassland	tiger, leopard, sloth bear, *sambar, chital, gaur, muntjac, nilgai, chinkara,* drongos	Feb–June (cl July–Oct)
Corbett NP	Uttar Pradesh	lake and forested foothills	tiger, leopard, elephant, sloth bear, *sambar, chital, muntjac*	Dec–May
Dudhwa NP	Uttar Pradesh	*sal* forest & marshland	tiger, leopard, sloth bear, *nilgai, barasingha*	Dec–May (cl June–Nov)
Flower Valley NP	Uttar Pradesh	alpine valley	mountain flowers	July & Aug
Hazaribagh NP	Bihar	*sal*-forested hills	tiger, leopard, *sambar, chital*	Feb–April
Jaldapara Wildlife Sanctuary	West Bengal	tropical forest & grassland	rhino, leopard, elephant, boar, *gaur*	Dec–May
Jawahar NP (Bandipur, Nagarhole, Mudumalai, Wayanda)	Karnataka, Kerala & Tamil Nadu	mixed forest	tiger, leopard, elephant, *sambar, chital, gaur, muntjac,* chowsingha, pangolin	Dec–June & Sept–Oct (open all year)
Kanha NP	Madhya Pradesh	*sal* forest & grassland	tiger, leopard, boar, *chital, gaur,* black buck, *barasingha, chowsingha, dhole,* birdlife	Feb–June (cl July–Oct)
Kaziranga NP	Assam	grassland, swamp and forest	rhino, tiger, leopard, elephant, bear, buffalo	Nov–March (cl April–Oct)
Keoladeo Bird Sanctuary	Rajasthan	marshland	resident & migratory water-fowl, pythons, deer	Oct–March
Krishnagiri Upavam NP	Maharashtra	marshland	water birds	Oct–June
Little Rann of Kutch Wildlife Sanctuary	Gujarat	desert	wild ass, wolf, caracal, desert wildlife	Oct–June
Manas Wildlife Sanctuary	Assam	rainforest & grassland	rhino, tiger, elephant, buffalo, golden langur, pygmy hog	Jan–March
Nal Sarovar Bird Sanctuary	Gujarat	lake	flamingoes, migratory water birds	Nov–Feb
Palama Tiger Reserve	Bihar	deciduous hilly forest	tiger, leopard, elephant, jungle cat, *sambar, chital,* wolf	Oct–April (open all year)
Periyar Wildlife Sanctuary	Kerala	forest with large (dam-created) lake	elephant, boar, *sambar, chital, gaur,* black langur	Dec–May
Point Kalimere Bird Sanctuary	Tamil Nadu	tidal mud flats	flamingoes, herons, teals, curlews, plovers	Nov–Feb (open all year)
Ranthambore NP	Rajasthan	deciduous forest	tiger, leopard, crocodile, sloth bear, *sambar, nilgai*	Nov–May (cl June–Sept)
Sariska NP	Rajasthan	deciduous forest	tiger, leopard, *sambar, chital, nilgai,* black buck	Nov–June (cl July & Aug)
Sasan Gir NP	Gujarat	forest & lake	Asiatic lion, leopard, *sambar, nilgai, chinkara, chowsingha*	Jan–May (cl May–Oct)
Shivpuri NP	Madhya Pradesh	deciduous forest with lake	tiger, leopard, *nilgai, chinkara, chowsingha*	Jan–May
Similipal Tiger Reserve	Orissa	*sal* forest	tiger, leopard, elephant, *sambar, chital, muntjac,* wolf	Nov–May (cl June–Oct)
Sunderbans Tiger Reserve	West Bengal	mangrove swamp & delta forest	crocodiles & other reptiles, Bengal tiger, fishing cat, boar, spotted deer, dolphin	Dec–March (cl July to mid-Sept)
Tadoba NP	Maharashtra	teak forest & lake	tiger, leopard, *sambar, chital, nilgai,* nocturnal life	March–May
Vedanthangal Water Bird Sanctuary	Tamil Nadu	forest & marshland	cormorants, herons, storks, pelicams, glebes, spoonbills	Oct–March
Velvadar	Gujarat	grassland	black buck	Oct–June

Elephants can most easily be seen at Periyar (Kerala), where you'd be lucky to spot a tiger, Similipal (Orissa), also a tiger reserve, and Manas (Assam). India's main **bird sanctuary** is at Keoladeo Ghana (Rajasthan), a monsoon wetland favoured by both resident and migratory waterfowl, but there are others at Govind Sagar (Himachal Pradesh), and Vedanthangal and Point Kalimere (Tamil Nadu). Two rather different parks are both to be found in Gujarat: Gir, last remaining home of the **Asiatic lion**, and the desert sanctuary of the Rann of Kutch, where wild asses may be seen.

As for **mountain flora**, the Valley of Flowers (UP) comes into stunning multicoloured bloom from June to September every year and, though sometimes closed, makes an excellent excursion from local trekking routes.

SPORTS

India is not perhaps a place that most people associate with sports, but cricket, hockey and football (soccer, that is) all have their place.

Cricket is the most popular of these, and a fine example of how something quintessentially British (well, English) has become something quintessentially Indian. International test matches in particular are followed avidly and you'll see games being played on open spaces around the country. Unless it's a special match, you'll probably be welcome to join in, provided you know how to play of course.

India was the first country outside the British Isles to have a **golf** course, at the Royal Calcutta Golf Club, opened in 1829. Other record-breaking courses include the world's highest at Gulmarg (Kashmir), and there are now so many courses that you can even go on golfing tours of the country.

Horseracing can be a good day out, especially if you enjoy a flutter. Calcutta's racecourse is the most popular, often attracting crowds of over 50,000, but there are several others around the country, mostly in larger cities such as Bombay, Pune, Hyderabad, Mysore and Bangalore. An exception is that of Darjeeling, the world's smallest course. Other (mainly) spectator sports include **polo**, originally from upper Kashmir, but taken up by the British to become one of the symbols of the Raj, and **hockey**, which regularly furnishes India with Olympic gold.

A massive variety of other sports are available in India, from **tennis** and squash, in private clubs and big hotels, to sea and river **fishing**, whitewater **rafting** in the mountains, and even **hanggliding**, for which several clubs exist around the country (the climate and landscape give excellent thermals).

One indigenous sport you're sure to see being played in north India is **kabaadi**, played formally at national level on a small (badminton-sized) court, and informally on any suitable open area. The game consists of a player from each team alternately attempting to "tag" as many members of the opposing team as possible in the space of a single breath (cheating is impossible; the player has to maintain a continuous chant of *kabaadikabaadikabaadikabaadi* etc), and getting back to his/her own side of the court without being tagged in return.

Finally, though India may be a far cry from Colorado or the Alps, you can **ski** here too. With the Kashmiri resort of Gulmarg currently out of action due to the political situation, skiing is still on at Narkanda and Manali in Himachal Pradesh, and Auli in Uttar Pradesh, at prices that are also a far cry from those of Europe or North America. The season is January through March.

CLIMATE AND GEOGRAPHY

India's range of climate and season is enormous. In the far north, the mountain valleys of the Himalayas experience the four seasons of northern temperate zones, while down at the other end of the country, the Deccan peninsula is tropical. With the northern Gangeatic plain, it shares a long dry season building up in heat and intensity until the monsoon douses it in massive quantities of rain.

THE LAY OF THE LAND

Sweeping across the top of India, the massive barrage of the **Himalayas**, backed by the plateau of Tibet, marks the country's northern boundary. The water that flows off these mountains feeds the basin of the **River Ganges**, which flows westwards across the plain of Uttar Pradesh into the Bay of Bengal. The mountains support a range of climates from barren and inhospitable at the highest altitudes to pleasantly alpine in the foothills, while the Ganges sustains a largely dry subtropical **plain** right across the north of the country. To its west is the valley of the Indus, which, though now in Pakistan, gives India its name. The watershed between the two river systems is the Thar Desert (**desert** characterizes much of the northwestern states of Rajasthan and Gujarat), which also separates India from Pakistan; to its north, the Punjab, split between the two countries, is irrigated by tributaries of the Indus. East of the Ganges basin, the River Brahmaputra waters the **jungles of Assam**. Beyond, the north–south line of the Naga Hills constitutes India's eastern boundary with Burma. The Brahmaputra and the Ganges join forces at their lower reaches to form the massive **delta** that is Bengal, the eastern half of which is Bangladesh.

South of the northern plain rise the Vindhya and Satpura hills of Madhya Pradesh, drained by the River Narmada, and behind them, the great southern plateau called the **Deccan** (also sometimes known as the Indian Peninsula). This is bounded on both sides by ranges of hills called the **Eastern** and **Western Ghats**. The Western Ghats being the higher of the two ranges, most Deccan rivers flow east. The other way, the coastal plane of the Western Ghats is the lush state of Kerala.

CLIMATE

The mountain valleys of the Himalayan foothills are usually snowed in in winter and pleasantly warm in summer. Some passes are closed in winter and places such as Ladakh and Zanskar (really part of the Tibetan plateau) extremely cold and hard to reach. Spring is very pleasant, with trees in blossom (avalanches are a danger at higher altitudes during the thaw), but the summer is the best time to visit, when the snows have melted and all the passes are open. Autumn brings the harvest, with fresh produce available in every mountain valley.

In the rest of India, the most important feature of the climate is the wet season, or **monsoon**. The main ("southwest") monsoon strikes the coast of Kerala at the very end of May, working its way northwest across the country over the next month and a half. While it lasts, expect rain every day – heavy tropical rain (as in rainforest). Most days, the rain will last a couple of hours, then the sun will come out and eveything will be steamy and flooded. At the height of the season, especially in jungle regions like Assam and Bengal, the rain may seem endless, and it certainly has a major impact on communications, disrupting road and rail services, causing floods, homelessness, death and destruction, but also bringing life to the parched land and putting a carpet of green on even desert areas like Rajasthan.

By September, the monsoon has started to recede, but it takes a good three months before it finally withdraws from the Deccan. The east of Tamil Nadu and southern Andhra Pradesh – the coastal plain of the Eastern Ghats – and the Andaman and Nicobar islands, are subject to a different monsoon (the "northeast") which begins in mid-October, ending around the new year.

Down on the plain, the heat begins to build up as the **dry season** gets under way. In the north, it is still tempered by the winter, and doesn't really get going until February, leaving a cool period in between. Delhi in particular can get quite surprisingly nippy at this time, especially at night. It is at this time of year that many travellers head south, before the heat there gets serious.

From February onwards, the temperature begins to rise, reaching its peak just before the monsoon. April and May can be unbearably hot

AVERAGE TEMPERATURES AND RAINFALL

		Jan	Feb	March	Apr	May	June	July	Aug	Sept	Oct	Nov	Dec
Agra	Av daily max (°C)	22	26	32	38	42	41	35	33	33	33	29	24
	Rainfall (mm)	16	9	11	5	10	60	210	263	151	23	2	4
Ahmedabad	Av daily max (°C)	29	31	36	40	41	38	33	32	33	36	33	30
	Rainfall (mm)	4	0	1	2	5	100	316	213	163	13	5	1
Bangalore	Av daily max (°C)	28	31	33	34	33	30	28	29	28	28	27	27
	Rainfall (mm)	4	14	6	37	119	65	93	95	129	195	46	16
Bombay	Av daily max (°C)	31	32	33	33	33	32	30	29	30	32	33	32
	Rainfall (mm)	0	1	0	0	20	647	945	660	309	17	7	1
Calcutta	Av daily max (°C)	26	29	34	36	36	34	32	32	32	31	29	27
	Rainfall (mm)	13	22	30	50	135	263	320	318	253	134	29	4
Darjeeling	Av daily max (°C)	9	11	15	18	19	19	20	20	20	19	15	12
	Rainfall (mm)	22	27	52	109	187	522	713	573	419	116	14	5
Delhi	Av daily max (°C)	21	24	30	36	41	40	35	34	34	35	29	23
	Rainfall (mm)	25	22	17	7	8	65	211	173	150	31	1	5
Gangtok	Av daily max (°C)	14	15	19	22	22	23	23	23	23	22	19	15
	Rainfall (mm)	44	56	142	222	493	644	663	588	476	152	35	15
Hyderabad	Av daily max (°C)	29	31	35	37	39	34	30	29	30	30	29	28
	Rainfall (mm)	2	11	13	24	30	107	165	147	163	71	25	5
Jaipur	Av daily max (°C)	22	25	31	37	41	39	34	32	33	33	29	24
	Rainfall (mm)	14	8	9	4	10	54	193	239	90	19	3	4
Jaisalmer	Av daily max (°C)	24	28	33	38	42	41	38	36	36	36	31	26
	Rainfall (mm)	2	1	3	1	5	7	89	86	14	1	5	2
Kochi	Av daily max (°C)	31	31	31	31	31	29	28	28	28	29	30	30
	Rainfall (mm)	9	34	50	139	364	756	572	386	235	333	184	37
Madras	Av daily max (°C)	29	31	33	35	38	37	35	35	34	32	29	28
	Rainfall (mm)	24	7	15	25	52	53	83	124	118	267	309	139
Madurai	Av daily max (°C)	30	32	35	36	37	37	36	35	35	33	31	30
	Rainfall (mm)	26	16	21	81	59	31	48	117	123	179	161	143
Nagpur	Av daily max (°C)	29	33	36	40	43	38	31	30	31	32	30	29
	Rainfall (mm)	15	2	25	20	10	174	351	277	181	62	9	2
Nainital	Av daily max (°C)	10	13	17	21	24	24	21	21	21	19	16	13
	Rainfall (mm)	117	44	54	25	75	273	769	561	331	305	7	35
Panjim (Goa)	Av daily max (°C)	31	32	32	33	33	31	29	29	29	31	33	33
	Rainfall (mm)	2	0	4	17	18	580	892	341	277	122	20	37
Pune	Av daily max (°C)	31	33	36	38	37	32	28	28	28	32	31	30
	Rainfall (mm)	2	0	3	18	35	103	187	106	127	92	37	5
Puri	Av daily max (°C)	27	28	30	31	32	31	31	31	31	31	29	27
	Rainfall (mm)	9	20	14	12	63	187	296	256	258	242	75	8
Shimla	Av daily max (°C)	9	10	14	19	23	24	21	20	20	18	15	11
	Rainfall (mm)	65	48	58	38	54	147	415	385	195	45	7	24
Varanasi	Av daily max (°C)	23	27	33	39	41	39	33	32	32	32	29	25
	Rainfall (mm)	23	8	14	1	8	102	346	240	261	38	15	2

and dusty, with a debilitating dry heat (temperatures over 40°C/100°F are quite normal) that saps you of energy and dehydrates you fast. Many head up to the mountains to escape it. The Raj used to move its capital yearly for this reason: originally from Calcutta to Darjeeling, later from Delhi to Shimla. In the south, travellers make for hill stations up in the Ghats. As the hot season draws on, everyone anxiously awaits the return of the monsoon. Finally, heralded by high clouds and electric storms, it is back and the cycle starts again.

The **best time** to see most of the country is between the monsoon and the height of the hot season, that is between about October and March, spending the mid-part of that time in the south. Come April or May, it makes sense to head up into the mountains.

Unfortunately, it is not always possible to fit the seasons in with your travel plans and sometimes you will have to visit places where the weather is not at its optimum. That is not the end of the world; so long as you are prepared for India's extremes of climate and the limits they may place on your movements and activities, anywhere can be rewarding all year round. What's more, visiting at the "wrong" time of year avoids the other tourists, while getting the best air fares (though it probably won't affect the price of accommodation). Nonetheless, it is a good idea to take weather conditions into account if possible when planning your trip.

CRIME AND PERSONAL SAFETY

In spite of the crushing poverty and the yawning gulf between rich and poor, India is on the whole a pretty safe country in which to travel. As a tourist, however, you are an obvious target for thieves (who may include some of your fellow travellers), and stand to face serious problems if you do lose your passport, money and ticket home. Common sense therefore suggests a few precautions.

Carry valuables in a money belt or a pouch around your neck at all times. If the latter, the cord should not be easy to cut through (a metal guitar string is good). Beware of crowded locations, such as packed buses or trains, in which it is easy for pickpockets to operate – slashing pockets with razor blades is quite a common method – and don't leave valuables unattended on the beach when you go for a swim. Backpacks in dormitory accommodation are also obvious targets.

Budget travellers would do well to carry a padlock, as these are usually used to secure the doors of cheap hotel rooms and it's reassuring to know you have the only key; strong combination locks are ideal. You can also lock your bag to seats or racks in trains. Don't put valuables in your luggage for bus or plane journeys: keep them with you. If your baggage is on the roof of a bus, make sure it is well secured. On trains and buses, the prime time for theft is just before you leave, so keep a particular eye on your gear then, beware of deliberate diversions, and don't put your belongings next to open windows. Remember that routes popular with tourists tend to be popular with thieves too.

However, don't get paranoid. Crime levels in India are a long way below those of western countries, and violent crime against tourists is extremely rare. Virtually none of the people who approach you on the street intend any harm: most want to sell you something, some want to practise their English, others (if you're a woman) to chat you up, while more than a few just want your address in their book. Anyone offering wonderful-sounding money-making schemes, however, is almost certain to be a con artist. Be wary of **credit card fraud**; a credit card can be used to make duplicate forms which your account

DRUGS

Future is black if sugar is brown – Bombay anti-drugs poster.

India is a centre for the production of **cannabis** and to a lesser extent **opium**, and derivatives of these drugs are widely available. *Charas* (hashish) is produced all along the Himalayas, where the harvest is around September. East of Kashmir, it is rubbed from the plant; westwards it is threshed. Kashmir itself produces both varieties: rubbed *attar*, and threshed *garda* (known as "twist"). The best-known growing area is Manali and the surrounding region, but Almora (UP) also produces a crop. *Ganja* (marijuana) is available in all these areas too, as well as Kerala (especially), West Bengal, Rajasthan and Orissa.

Charas and *ganja* are normally smoked in a *chillum*, originally the bowl of a hookah pipe, used by the poor, who would cup their hands around it to make a smoke-cooling chamber. Nowadays, *chillum*-making has become something of an art form, with centres at Pondicherry, Hampi and Pushkar.

The use of cannabis is frowned upon by respectable Indians – if you see anyone in a movie smoking a *chillum*, you can be sure it's the baddie. *Sadhus*, on the other hand, are allowed to smoke *ganja* legally as part of their religious devotion to Shiva, who is said to have originally discovered its narcotic properties.

Bhang (a preparation made from marijuana leaves) is legal and widely available in *bhang* shops: it is used to make sweets and drinks such as the notoriously potent *bhang lassis* which have waylaid many an unwary traveller. *Bhang* shops also frequently sell *ganja*, much weaker *charas*, and opium (*chandu*), mainly from Rajasthan. Its derivatives, morphine and heroin, are widespread too, with addiction an increasing problem among the urban poor; Varanasi is becoming notorious for its heroin problem. Use of LSD and other illegal drugs such as ecstasy and cocaine is confined to tourists.

All of these drugs except *bhang* are strictly controlled under Indian **law**, with a minimum sentence of ten years for possession. Anyone arrested with less than five grams of cannabis which they are able to *prove* is for their own use is liable to a six-month maximum, but cases can take years to come to trial (two is normal, and eight not unheard of). Police raids and searches are particularly common at the following places, where all foreign visitors are liable to be seen as potential drug users: Manali, the Kulu valley and Almora, and buses from those places to Delhi, especially at harvest time; budget hotels in Delhi's Paharganj; the beach areas of Goa; and the growing regions of Kerala. "Paying a fine now" *may* be possible with one or two officers on arrest, but once you are booked in at the station, your chances are slim.

Prison conditions in India are grim, and western prisoners always glad of a visit – your country's consul should be able to supply names, or you can go to the prison and ask. Some prisons are easier than others to visit. Inmates are likely to appreciate books, fresh fruit and vegetables, chocolate and cigarettes.

is then billed with for fictitious transactions, so don't let shops or restaurants take your card away to process – insist they do it in front of you. Even **monkeys** rate a mention here – it is not unknown for them to steal things from hotel rooms with open windows.

It's not a bad idea to keep US$100 or so separately from the rest of your cash, along with your travellers' cheque receipts, insurance policy number and phone number for claims, and a photocopy of the pages in your passport containing personal data and your Indian visa. This will cover you in case you do lose all your valuables.

If you get robbed, report it as soon as possible to the local **police**. They are very unlikely to recover your belongings, but you need a report from them in order to claim on your travel insurance. Dress smartly and expect an uphill battle – city cops in particular tend to be jaded from too many insurance and travellers' cheque scams. Police **corruption**, partly a consequence of low pay and delayed payment of salaries, is an increasing problem, especially in states such as Goa where drug use among tourists is widespread, and arrests may be followed by informal "out-of-court" settlements.

CULTURAL HINTS AND ETIQUETTE

Cultural differences extend to all sorts of little things. While allowances will usually be made for foreigners, visitors unacquainted with Indian customs may need a little preparation to avoid causing offence or making fools of themselves. The list of do's and don'ts here is hardly exhaustive: when in doubt, watch what the Indian people around you are doing.

EATING AND THE RIGHT HAND RULE

The biggest minefield of potential faux-pas has to do with **eating**. This is usually done with the fingers, and requires a bit of practice to get absolutely right. Rule one is: **eat with your right hand only**. In India, as right across Asia, the left hand is for wiping your bottom, cleaning your feet and other unsavoury functions (you also put on and take off your shoes with your left hand), while the right hand is for eating, shaking hands, and so on.

Quite how rigid individuals are about this tends to vary, with Brahmins (who at the top of the hierarchical ladder are one of the two "right-handed castes") and southerners likely to be the strictest. While you can hold a cup or utensil in your left hand, and you can usually get away with using it to help tear your *chapati*, you should not eat, pass food or wipe your mouth with your left hand. Best is to keep it out of sight below the table.

This rule extends beyond food too. In general, do not pass anything to anyone with your left hand, or point at anyone with it either; and Indians won't be impressed if you put it in your mouth. In general, you should accept things given to you with your right hand – though using both hands is a sign of respect.

The other rule to beware of when eating or drinking is that your lips should not touch other people's food – *jhuta* or sullied food is strictly taboo. Don't, for example, take a bite out of a *chapati* and pass it on. When drinking out of a cup or bottle to be shared with others, don't let it touch your lips, but rather pour it directly into your mouth. This custom also protects you from things like hepatitis. It is customary to wash your hands before and after eating.

TEMPLES AND RELIGION

Religion is taken very seriously in India; it's important always to show due respect to religious buildings, shrines, images, and people at prayer. When entering a temple or mosque, remove your shoes and leave them at the door (socks are OK and protect your feet from burning-hot stone ground). Some temples – Jain ones in particular – do not allow you to enter wearing or carrying leather articles. Dress conservatively (see below), and try not to be obtrusive. In a mosque, you'll not normally be allowed in at prayer time; in a Hindu temple, you are not usually allowed into the inner sanctum; and at a Buddhist *stupa* or monument, you should always walk round clockwise (ie, with the *stupa* on your right). Hindus are very superstitious about taking **photographs** of images of deities and inside temples; if in doubt, desist. Do not take photos of funerals or cremations.

DRESS

Indian people are very conservative about **dress**. Women are expected to dress modestly, with legs and shoulders covered. Trousers are acceptable, but shorts and short skirts are offensive to many. Men should always wear a shirt in public, and avoid shorts (a sign of low caste). These rules go double in temples and mosques.

Never mind sky-clad Jains or *naga sadhus*, **nudity** is not acceptable in India. The mild-mannered people of Goa may not say anything about nude bathing (though it is in theory prohibited), but you can be sure they don't like it. If you respect them, you will not bathe in the nude, and certainly not where there are Indian families.

In general, Indians find it hard to understand why rich Western *sahibs* should wander round in ragged clothes, dress shamelessly like prostitutes, or imitate the lowest ranks of Indian society, who would dearly love to have something more decent to wear. Staying well-groomed and dressing "respectably" (and you don't have to go over the top) vastly improves the impression you make on local people, and reduces sexual harassment too. Wearing Indian dress is practical, and fits in with most Indian values, though *lunghis* on western men are not regarded favourably away from beaches.

OTHER POSSIBLE GAFFES

Kissing and embracing are regarded in India as part of sex: do not do them in public. It is not even a good idea for couples to hold hands, though Indian men can sometimes be seen holding hands as a sign of "brotherliness". Be aware of your **feet**. When entering a private home, you should normally remove your shoes (follow your host's example); when sitting, avoid pointing the soles of your feet at anyone. Accidental contact with one's foot is always followed by an apology.

Indian English can be very formal and even ceremonious. Indian people may well call you "sir" or "madam", even "good lady" or "kind sir". At the same time, you should be aware that your English may seem rude to them. In particular, **swearing** is taken rather seriously in India, and casual use of the F-word is likely to shock.

MEETING PEOPLE

Westerners have an ambiguous status in Indian eyes. In one way, you represent the rich *sahib*, whose culture dominates the world, and the old colonial mentality has not completely disappeared: in that sense, some Indians may see you as "better" than them. On the other hand, as a non-Hindu, you are an outcaste, your presence in theory polluting to an orthodox or high-caste Hindu, while to members of all religions, your morals and your standards of spiritual and physical cleanliness are suspect: in that sense Indians may see themselves as "better" than you. Even if you are of Indian origin, you may be considered to suffer from western corruption, and people may test you out on that score.

Nonetheless, as a traveller in India, you will constantly come across Indian people who want to strike up a conversation. English not being their first language, they may not be familiar with the conventional ways of doing this, and thus their opening line may seem abrupt if at the same time very formal. "Excuse me good gentleman, what is your mother country?" is a typical one. It is also the first in a series of questions that Indian men seem sometimes to have learnt from a single book in order to ask western tourists.

Some of the questions may baffle at first ("What is your qualification?" "Are you in service?"), some may be queries about the ways of the west or the purpose of your trip, but mostly they will be about your family and your job.

You may find it baffling or even intrusive that Indian people should want to know that sort of thing, but bear in mind that their culture is different to yours and they do not see it the same way. For one thing, these are subjects which interest them (showing photos of your family always goes down well, especially between women). Secondly, they are considered polite conversation beween strangers in India, and help people place each other in terms of social position. Thirdly, your family, job, even income, are not considered "personal" subjects in India, and it is completely normal to ask people about them. Asking the same questions back will not be taken amiss – far from it. Being curious does not have the "nosey" stigma in India that it has in the west: taking an interest in other people's lives is totally up front and considered quite normal.

Things that Indian people are likely to find strange about *you* are lack of religion (you could adopt one), travelling alone, leaving your family to come to India, being an unmarried couple (letting people think you are married can make life easier), and travelling second class or staying in cheap hotels when, as a tourist, you are obviously rich. You will probably end up having to explain the same things many times to many different people; on the other hand, you can ask questions too, so you could take it as an opportunity to ask things you want to know about India. After all, many Indians are every bit as cosmopolitan as you. Members of the large and growing middle class in particular are usually extremely well informed and well educated, and you are likely to be drawn into conversations that are way out of your depth.

India can mean many things to many people, and visitors who come here searching can easily fall into the trap of imagining they have found the "real" India, one that the materialistic city-dwelling Indian has lost. This mixture of religion and fantasy is best kept under control by getting to know the people who actually live here.

SHOPPING

So many beautiful and exotic souvenirs are on sale in India, at such low prices, that it's sometimes hard to know what to buy first. On top of that, all sorts of things (such as made-to-measure clothes) that would be vastly expensive at home are much more reasonably priced in India. Even if you lose weight during your trip, your baggage might well put on quite a bit – unless of course you post some of it home.

WHERE TO SHOP

Quite a few items sold in tourist areas are made elsewhere and, needless to say, it's more fun (and cheaper) to pick them up at source. Best buys are noted in the relevant sections of the guide, along with a few specialities that can't be found outside their regions.

Virtually all the state governments in India run handicraft "**emporiums**", and most of them have branches in Delhi. There are also *Central Cottage Industries Emporiums* in Delhi, Calcutta and Bombay. Goods in these places are generally of a high quality, if their (fixed) prices are a little expensive, and they are worth a visit to get an idea of what crafts are available and how much they should cost.

BARGAINING

Whatever you buy (except food and cigarettes), you will almost always be expected to **haggle over the price**. Bargaining is very much a matter of personal style, but should always be light-hearted, never acrimonious. There are no hard and fast rules – it's really a question of how much something is worth to you. It's a good plan, however, to have an idea of how much you want, or ought, to pay.

Don't worry too much about initial prices. Some guidebooks suggest paying a third of the opening price, but it's a flexible guideline depending on the shop, the goods and the shopkeeper's impression of you. You may not be able to get the seller much below the first quote; on the other hand, you may end up paying as little as a tenth of it. If you bid too low, you may be hustled out of the shop for offering an "insulting" price, but this is all part of the game, and you will no doubt be welcomed as an old friend if you return next day.

Don't start haggling for something if in fact you know you don't want it, and never let any figure pass your lips that you are not prepared to pay. It's like bidding at an auction. Having mentioned a price, you are obliged to pay it. If the seller asks you how much you would pay for something, and you don't want it, say so. And never go shopping with a tout or rickshaw *wallah*, who will get a commission on anything you buy, which means a higher price to you.

METALWARE AND JEWELLERY

Artisans have been casting **bronze statues** of Hindu gods for over a thousand years. The images are produced by the lost-wax process, in which a model is first carved out of wax, then surrounded in clay, and finally fired. That melts the wax to leave a terracotta mould; small pieces can be cast from a single mould, but larger ones have to be assembled from up to a dozen pieces, the joins concealed by ornate ornamentation. The best-quality images will have carefully detailed fingers and eyes, and the metal should not have pits or spots. The south is one major area for them (dancing Shivas a favourite here – check out the quality in the palace art gallery at Thanjavur), the Himalayas another.

Brass and copperware can be very finely worked, with trays, plates, ashtrays, cups and bowls among products available. The best trays – which should be forty years old or more – are from Varanasi. In the north, particularly in Rajasthan, enamel inlays (*meenakari*) are common. **Bidri work**, named after Bidar (Karnataka), where it originated, is a method of inlaying a gunmetal alloy with fine designs in brass or silver, then blackening the gunmetal with sal-ammoniac, to leave the inlay work shining. *Bidri* jewellery boxes, dishes and *hookah* pipes, among other things, are widely sold, especially in Karnataka and Andhra Pradesh; while the Orissan filigree *tarakashi* is worth looking out for. **Stainless steel** is less decorative and more workaday: *thali* sets and spice tins are among the possible buys.

Among precious metals, silver is generally a better buy than **gold**. The latter is usually 22 carat and very yellow, but relatively expensive due to taxes (smuggling from the Gulf to evade them is rife) and to its popularity as a form of investment – women traditionally keep their wealth in this form, and a bride's jewellery is an important part of her dowry. Indian gold jewellery too is a little garish for western tastes. **Silver** varies in quality, but is usually reasonably priced, with silver jewellery generally heavier and rather more folksy than gold. Rajasthan and Bengal are its main centres, and Tibetan silver jewellery is also popular. Gold and silver are usually sold by weight, the workmanship costing very little. The *tola* – the weight of a silver *rupee*, 180 grains or roughly 11.6g – is the usual unit.

Gemstones can be something of a minefield; scams abound, and you would be most unwise to even consider buying gems for resale or as an investment without a basic knowledge of the trade. Having said that, however, some precious and semi-precious stones can be a good buy in India, particularly those which are indigenous, such as garnets, black stars and moonstones. Jaipur is a major centre for gems, while Hyderabad specializes in sorting **pearls**, which can therefore be picked up at low prices.

WOODWORK, CERAMICS AND STONE

Wooden furniture, if a little heavy to carry with you, can be a real bargain, and is especially good in the mountainous areas of the north. Carvings of gods (often in sandalwood) are particularly common in the south, and those of elephants are always a favourite. Old wooden carvings from houses or temples that are being refurbished are often available at reasonable prices, if sometimes a little weathered.

Terracotta figures are a speciality of Bengal and Bihar, but the finest **ceramic** work is the glazed pottery of Jaipur, Kurja, and Delhi. Brightly painted clay and plaster gods are another souvenir possibility, while marble and soapstone are both used for sculpture (though big pieces weigh a ton), and marble items inlaid in the style of the Taj Mahal are popular souvenirs in Agra. Somewhat less weighty than these are papier-mâché items sold in Kashmiri shops that have sprung up around the country (most of which seem to get their supplies in Delhi).

CARPETS AND RUGS

If you get dragged into a Kashmiri arts shop, chances are it's a **carpet** they really want to sell you. Kashmiri rugs are among the best in the world (up there with Iran) and, given a little bit of caution and scepticism, you can get yourself a bargain in India (though you can also get ripped off if you're not careful). A *pukka* Kashmiri carpet should have a label on the back stating that it is made in Kashmir, what it is made of (wool, silk, or "silk touch" – wool combined with a little cotton and silk to give it a sheen), its size, density of knots per square inch (the more the better), and the name of the design. To tell if it really is silk, scrape the carpet with a knife and burn the fluff – real silk shrivels to nothing and has a distinctive smell. Even producing the knife should cause the seller of a bogus silk carpet to demur. Carpets in styles such as Bokhara (Afghan) are now being produced in Rajasthan, but tend not to be as fine as the original.

The surest way to make sure a carpet reaches home is to take it away and post it yourself; a seller may offer to post it to you and bill you later, which is fair enough, but be aware that your carpet will be sent immediately, whatever you say (will you be there to receive it?), and if you use a credit card, your account will also be billed immediately, whatever is said.

Dhurries (woven carpets or kilims), traditionally made of wool, are an older art form, and a less expensive one. UP is the main centre for these, particularly Agra and Mirzapur, but they are made in Rajasthan, Gujarat and the Punjab too, and also in Andhra Pradesh. Tibetan rugs are available in areas with a large Tibetan community, such as Himachal Pradesh. Many foreigners prefer carpets in "tasteful" earthy colours, assuming them to be traditional and therefore "ethnic". In fact, Indian carpets traditionally come in bright colours, though the synthetic dyes used nowadays are of course new-fangled.

TEXTILES AND CLOTHING

Textiles are so much a part of Indian culture that Gandhi wanted a spinning wheel put on the flag. The kind of cloth he had in mind was the plain white homespun material worn by Nehru, whose hat, jacket and *dhoti* remain a mark of support for the Congress Party to this day. Homespun, hand-loom-woven hand-printed cloth is called **khadi**, and is sold in government shops called *Khadi Gramodyog* all over India. Methods of dyeing and printing this and other cloth vary from the tie-dyeing (*bhandani*) of Rajasthan to block printing and screen printing of calico (from Calicut – now Kozhikode, Kerala) cotton, and of silk.

Saris are normally made of cotton for everyday use, although **silk** is used for special occasions, and quite common in the south. Western women are notoriously inept at wearing this most elegant of garments – it takes years of practice to carry one properly – but silk is usually a good buy in India, provided you make sure it is the real thing (the old test was to see whether it was possible to pull the whole garment straight through a wedding ring; however, some synthetics apparently go through too, so burn a thread and sniff it to be sure). Varanasi silk is world famous, but the best nowadays comes from Kanchipuram and Madurai in Tamil Nadu.

Other popular fabrics include the heavy mirror-embroidered cloth of Rajasthan, Bengali *baluchari* brocade, and Indonesian-style ikat and batik from Orissa and Gujarat, while clothing to take home includes *lunghis* in the south (as much a sheet as a garment), thick Tibetan sweaters from Darjeeling, and *shalwa camise*, the elegant pyjama suits worn by Punjabi women, and, increasingly, by fashion-conscious "new women". Long loose shirts – preferably made of *khadi*, and known as *kurta* or *panjabi* – are practical in the heat of India, and traditionally worn with white pyjamas. Tourist shops sell versions in various fabrics and colours. Block-printed blankets, as well as being useful, make good wall-hangings, as do Punjabi *phulkari* (originally wedding sheets), but every region has its own fabrics and its own methods of colouring them and making them up – your choice is endless.

On top of this, with **tailoring** so cheap in India, you can choose the fabric you want, take it to a tailor, and have it made into whatever you fancy. For formal western-style clothes, you'll probably want to see quite a posh tailor in a big city (Calcutta is probably the best), but tailors in almost every village in the country can run you up a shirt or a pair of pyjama-type trousers in next to no time. Many tailors will also copy a garment you already have.

PAINTINGS AND ANTIQUES

Art and antiques are another field where only experts should look for an investment, but where a souvenir hunter is very likely to find a bargain. Silk and cotton paintings are popular in Rajasthan and the north, but vary vastly in quality, so check out a few before you buy. The village of Kishangarh (Rajasthan) is known for them.

Most Tibetan *thangkas* (Buddhist religious paintings mounted on brocaded silk) are mass produced (usually in Nepal) and modern, what-

ever the seller says, but even the cheapest can't hide the dense Buddhist symbolism inherent in the form. You'll find them in the north, where there are Tibetan communities, and a little investigation of the range of styles is well worthwhile if you are thinking of buying one.

Leaf skeleton paintings, originally from southern Kerala, are much cheaper and widely available, though they too vary somewhat in quality. **Miniatures** in the traditional style, often masquerading as antiques, are common in tourist shops too, but subject to the same provisos as *thangkas*.

When it comes to **antiques**, if they really are genuine – and, frankly, that is unlikely – you'll need a licence to export them, which is virtually impossible to get. The same applies to "art treasures". Age and status can be verified by the **Archaeological Survey of India** (Janpath, **New Delhi** 110011, ☎011/301 9451; Sion Fort, Sion, **Bombay** 400022, ☎022/407 1102; 27 Biplabi Trailokya Maharaj Sarani, Narayani Building, **Calcutta** 700001, ☎033/261933; Fort St George, **Madras** 600009, ☎044/560396; Old Town, **Bhubaneshwar** 751002, Orissa; ☎0674/56575; #364, 16th Main, 4th T Block, Jayanagar, **Bangalore** 560041, Karnataka, ☎080/645901), who also issue export clearance certificates.

ODDS AND SODS

Of course, not everything typically Indian is old or traditional. **Tapes or records** of classical, *bhangra, filmi*, and western music are very popular; the actual cassettes fall apart all too readily, so it's well worth copying any you buy once you get home. **Videos** too are widely available, though often bad quality, unsubtitled, and so ridden with adverts as to be almost unwatch-able. Insist on watching before you buy; southern films are more likely to be subtitled than Hindi ones.

Books are excellent buys in India, whether by Indian writers (see *Contexts*) or writers from the rest of the English-speaking world. They are likely to be much cheaper than at home, if not so well printed or bound.

Leatherware can be very cheap and well-made, though the leather doesn't normally come from cows, of course. Rajasthani camel-hide *mojadi* slippers go down well, as do distinctive *kholapuri* slippers, which need to be broken in, and *chappal* (sandals). Otherwise, buffalo-hide belts and bags can be very reasonable compared to similar items made of cowhide in the west;

Madras and Pondicherry are good places to go looking.

Bamboo flutes are incredibly cheap, while other **musical instruments** such as *tabla*, *sitar* and *sarod* are heavy to carry and available in the west anyway. The quality is crucial; there's no point going home with a *sitar* that is virtually untunable, even if it does look nice. Students of music purchase their instruments from master craftsmen or established shops; get advice before you buy, and never buy one from a tourist shop.

Other possibilities include kitchen implements, wind-up clockwork tin toys, film posters, tea (especially from Darjeeling, Assam and Nilgiri), coffee, spices, peacock feather fans (though these are considered unlucky), and really anything which reminds you of India – which needn't be expensive or arty after all.

Things not to bring home include ivory and anything made from a rare or protected species, including snakeskin and turtle products. As for drugs – don't even think about it.

FESTIVALS AND HOLIDAYS

Virtually every temple in every town or village across the country has its own festival. The biggest and most spectacular include Puri's Rath Yatra festival in June or July, Pushkar's camel fair in November, Kullu's Dussehra, and Madurai's three annual festivals. While mostly religious in nature, merrymaking rather than solemnity are generally the order of the day, and onlookers are usually welcome. Indeed, if you are lucky enough to coincide with a local festival, it may well prove to be the highlight of your trip.

Alas, we cannot list here every festival in every village across India, but local festivals are listed throughout the body of the guide. Below is a list of the main national and regional celebrations. It requires a little explanation. Hindu, Sikh, Buddhist and Jain festivals follow the Indian lunar **calendar** and their dates therefore vary from year to year against the plain old Gregorian

calendar. Determining them more than a year in advance is a highly complicated business best left to astrologers. Each lunar cycle is divided into two *paksa* (halves): "bright" (waxing) and "dark" (waning), each consisting of fifteen *tithis* ("days" – but a *tithi* might begin at any time of the solar day). The *paksa* start respectively with the new moon (*ama* or *bahula* – the first day of the month) and the full moon (*purnima*). Lunar festivals, then, are observed on a given day in the "light" or "dark" side of the month. The lunar calendar adds a leap month every two or three years to keep it in line with the seasons. Muslim festivals, however, follow the Islamic calendar, whose year is shorter and which thus loses about eleven days per annum against the Gregorian.

You may, while in India, have the privilege of being invited to a **wedding**. These are jubilant affairs with great feasting, always scheduled on auspicious days. A Hindu bride wears red for the ceremony, and puts a *bindi* on her forehead for the rest of her married life. Although the practice is officially illegal, large dowries change hands. These are usually paid by the bride's family to the groom, and can be contentious; poor families feel obliged to save for years to get their daughters married.

Funeral processions are much more sombre affairs, and should be left in peace. In Hindu funerals, the body is normally carried to the cremation site within hours of death by white-shrouded relatives (white is the colour of mourning). The eldest son is expected to shave his head and wear white following the death of a parent. At Varanasi and other places, you may see cremations; such occasions should be treated with respect, and photographs not taken.

PRINCIPAL INDIAN FESTIVALS

India has only four national public holidays as such: Jan 26 (Republic Day); Aug 15 (Independence Day); Oct 2 (Gandhi's birthday); and Dec 25 (Christmas Day). Each state, however, has its own calendar of public holidays, and you can expect most businesses to close on the major holidays of their own religion, marked with an asterisk below.

Although not all the festivals below are Hindu, we have divided them according to the Hindu calendar; most dates vary against the Gregorian calendar, as is explained on p.000.

Key: **B**=Buddhist; **C**=Christian; **H**=Hindu; **J**=Jain; **M**=Muslim; **N**=non-religious; **P**=Parsi; **S**=Sikh.

Magha (Jan–Feb)

H Pongal (1 Magha): Tamil harvest festival celebrated with decorated cows, processions and *rangolis* (chalk designs on the doorsteps of houses). *Pongal* is a sweet porridge made from newly harvested rice and eaten by all, including the cows. The festival is also known as Makar Sankranti, and celebrated in Karnataka, Andhra Pradesh and the east of India.

H Ganga Sagar: Pilgrims come from all over the country to Sagar Dwip, on the mouth of the Hooghly 150km south of Calcutta, to bathe during Makar Sankranti.

H Vasant Panchami (5 Magha): One-day spring festival in honour of Saraswati, the goddess of learning, celebrated with kite flying, yellow *saris*, and the blessing of schoolchildren's books and pens by the goddess.

N Republic Day (Jan 26)*: A military parade in Delhi typifies this state celebration of India's republic-hood, followed on Jan 29 by the "Beating the Retreat" ceremony outside the presidential palace in Delhi.

N International Kite Festival at Aurangabad (Maharashtra).

H Floating Festival (16 Magha) at Madurai (Tamil Nadu).

M Urs Ajmer Sharif: Festival in Rajasthan dedicated to a local Sufi.

M 1st Ramadan (Feb 1 1995; Jan 22 1996; Jan 10 1997; Dec 31 1997): The start of a month during which Muslims may not eat, drink or smoke from sunrise to sunset, and should abstain from sex. Towards the end of the month it takes its toll, so be gentle with Muslims you meet at this time.

Phalguna (Feb–March)

B Tibetan New Year (1 Phalguna): Celebrations among Tibetan communities, especially at Dharamsala.

H Shivratri (10 Phalguna): Anniversary of Shiva's *tandav* (creation) dance, and his wedding anniversary. A *sadhu* festival of pilgrimage and fasting, especially at important Shiva temples.

H Holi (15 Phalguna)*: Water festival held during Dol Purnima (full moon) to celebrate the beginning of spring, most popular in the north. Expect to be bombarded with water, paint, coloured powder and other mixtures; they can permanently stain clothing, so don't go out in your Sunday best.

M Id ul-Fitr (1 Shawwal)*: Feast to celebrate the end of Ramadan, after 28 days.

N Khajuraho (Madhya Pradesh) Dance Festival.

C Carnival (Mardi Gras): The last day before Lent, 40 days before Easter, is celebrated in Goa, as in the rest of the Catholic world.

Chaitra (March–April)

H Gangaur (3 Chaitra): Rajasthani festival (also celebrated in Bengal and Orissa) in honour of Parvati, marked with singing and dancing.

H Ramanavami (9 Chaitra)*: Birthday of Rama, the hero of the *Ramayana*, celebrated with readings of the epic and discourses on Rama's life and teachings.

C Easter (movable feast)*: Celebration of the resurrection of Christ. Good Friday in particular is a day of festivity.

P Pateti: Parsi new year, also known as No Ruz, celebrating the creation of fire. Feasting, services and present giving.

P Khorvad Sal (a week after Pateti): Birthday of Zarathustra (aka Zoroaster).

H Chittirai, Madurai (Tamil Nadu): elephant-led procession.

Vaisakha (April–May)

HS Baisakhi (1 Vaisakha): To the Hindus, it's the solar new year, celebrated with music and dancing; to the Sikhs, its the anniversary of the foundation of the *Khalsa* (Sikh brotherhood) by Guru Gobind Singh. Processions and feasting follow readings of the *Granth Sahib* scriptures.

J Mahavir Jayanti (13 Vaisakha)*: Birthday of Mahavira, the founder of Jainism. The main Jain festival of the year.

M Id uz-Zuha (10 Zoul Hagga)*: Pilgrimage festival to commemorate Abraham's preparedness to sacrifice his son Ismail. Celebrated with slaughtering and consumption of sheep.

H Puram Festival, Thrissur (Kerala): frenzied drumming and elephant parades.

B Buddha Jayanti (16 Vaisakha)*: Buddha's birthday. He achieved enlightenment and *nirvana* on the same date. Sarnath (UP) and Bodh Gaya (Bihar) are the main centres of celebration.

Jyaishtha (May–June)

H Ganga Dussehra (10 Jyaishtha): Bathing festival to celebrate the descent to earth of the goddess of the Ganges.

M Muharram: Festival to commemorate the martyrdom of the (Shi'ite) Imam, Prophet's grandson and popular saint, Hussain.

Ashadha (June–July)

H Rath Yatra (2 Ashadha): Festival held in Puri (and other places, especially in the south) to commemorate Krishna's (Lord Jaggernath's) journey to Mathura.

H Teej (3 Ashadha): Festival in honour of Parvati, to welcome the monsoon. Celebrated particularly in Rajasthan.

Shravana (July–Aug)

H Naag Panchami (3 Shravana): Snake festival in honour of the *naga* snake deities. Mainly celebrated in Rajasthan and Maharashtra.

H Raksha Bandhan/Narial Purnima (16 Shravana): Festival to honour the sea god Varuna. Brothers and sisters exchange gifts, the sister tying a thread known as a *rakhi* to her brother's wrist. Brahmins, after a day's fasting, change the sacred thread they wear.

B Hemis Festival, Leh (Ladakh).

N Independence Day (15 Aug)*: India's biggest secular celebration, on the anniversary of her Independence from Britain.

Bhadraparda (Aug–Sept)

H Ganesh Chaturthi (4 Bhadraparda): Festival dedicated to Ganesh, especially celebrated in Maharashtra. In Bombay, huge processions carry images of the god to immerse in the sea. 1995's festival is on Aug 29–Sept 8; in 1996, Sept 16–Sept 26; in 1997, Sept 6–Sept 15.

H Onam: Keralan harvest festival, celebrated with snake-boat races, especially at Alappuzha.

H Janmashtami (23 Bhadraparda)*: Krishna's birthday, an occasion for fasting and celebration, especially in Agra, Bombay, Mathura (UP) and Vrindaban (UP).

H Avani Mula festival, Madurai (Tamil Nadu): Celebration of the coronation of Shiva.

Ashvina (Sept–Oct)

H Dussehra (1–10 Ashvina)*: Ten-day festival (usually two days' public holiday) associated with vanquishing demons, in particular Rama's victory over Ravana in the *Ramayana*, and Durga's over the buffalo-headed Mahishasura (particularly in West Bengal, where it is called Durga Puja). Celebrations include performances of the *Ram Lila* (life of Rama). Best in Mysore (Karnataka), Ahmedabad (Gujarat) and Kullu (Himachal Pradesh).

N Mahatma Gandhi's Birthday (2 Oct)*: Rather solemn commemoration of Independent India's founding father.

Kartika (Oct–Nov)

H Diwali (Deepavali) (15 Kartika)*: Five-day festival of lights to celebrate Rama and Sita's homecoming in the *Ramayana*. Festivities include the lighting of oil lamps and firecrackers, and the giving and receiving of sweets.

J Jain New Year (15 Kartika): Coincides with Diwali, so Jains celebrate alongside Hindus.

S Nanak Jayanti (16 Kartika)*: Guru Nanak's birthday marked by prayer readings and processions, especially in Amritsar and the Punjab, and at Patna. Nov 7 1995.

Margashirsha, or Agrahayana (Nov–Dec)

H Sonepur Mela: World's largest cattle fair at Sonepur (Bihar).

N Pushkar (Rajasthan) Camel Fair.

Pausa (Dec–Jan)

CN Christmas (Dec 25)*: The Christian festival the whole world celebrates, popular in Christian areas of Goa and Kerala, and in big cities.

N Posh Mela (Dec 27): held in Shantiniketan near Calcutta, a festival renowned for *baul* music.

Movable

H Kumbh Mela: Major three-yearly festival held at one of four holy cities: Nasik (Maharashtra) in Shravana, Ujjain (Madhya Pradesh) in Kartika, Allahabad (UP) in Magha, or Haridwar (UP) in Chaitra. In 1995, it's at Ujjain, in 1998 at Hardwar.

WOMEN TRAVELLERS

India is not a country that provides huge obstacles to women travellers, petty annoyances being more the order of the day. In the days of the Raj, upper-class eccentrics started a tradition of lone women travellers, taken up enthusiastically by the flower children of the hippy era. People will no doubt think you a rare bird if you travel on your own, but obstacles will not be thrown in your way.

If you're travelling with a man, expect Indian men to approach your male companion (assumed, of course, to be your husband – an assumption it is sometimes advantageous to go along with) and talk to him about you quite happily as if you were not there. Beware, however, if you are (or look) Indian with a non-Indian male companion: this may well cause you grief and harassment, as you will be assumed to have brought shame on your poor family by adopting the loose morals of the west.

Sexual harassment, or "Eve teasing" as it is bizarrely known, is likely to be a nuisance, but not generally a threat. It is nowadays widely recognized as a social problem, which is a start, but it remains a daily fact of life for Indian women. Expect to get groped in crowds, and to have men "accidentally" squeeze past you at any opportunity. It tends to be worse in cities than in small towns and villages; in strongly Muslim areas, wandering around on your own may attract unwanted attention. Western women in general are seen as loose, "cheap" and "easy": "modest" dress (covering shoulders, arms and legs) may help, but don't count on it. Women who smoke are not looked upon favourably.

Violent sexual assaults on tourists are rare, but **rape** is not unknown as a form of political and sectarian violence. Most Indian women keep quiet about being raped – it is considered as much a disgrace to the victim as to the perpetrator – but you should not be afraid to call on passers-by (who will always help) or police if you feel threatened. Shouting, slapping or punching is often called for; a man transgressing social norms is out of line, and Indian women often become aggressive if offended. Taking off your left shoe and holding it in the face of a harassing man is very effective.

The role of women in Indian society is in theory very well-defined. It is to marry a man approved (if not chosen) by her parents, join his family, bear and bring up his children and look after their home. Before marriage, contact between the sexes is rigorously controlled: you don't want your daughter marrying into the wrong caste or, worse, the wrong religion, after all.

In spite of this, women are highly visible in everyday life and you will see women in India doing all sorts of jobs that you may not have expected, though they are unlikely to earn as much as men of the same social class. Fieldworkers and roadside labourers are often women, but most of them belong to the "scheduled castes" and are paid next to nothing. Women do have a lot of power and influence in Indian society, but it is through the family unit, not independently.

A small number of women belonging to the westernized elite are exceptions to this rule and have made great headway in the professions (Indira Gandhi, one of the modern world's first women political leaders, among them), but most women with such ambitions are held back by tradition, poverty or both. At the other end of the economic scale women have organized themselves with sometimes astounding success. One example is Ahmedabad's Self-Employed Women's Association (SEWA), a cooperative that has managed to rescue its low-caste low-income members from economic dependence on moneylenders, and act as a pressure group for their rights.

WOMEN'S ORGANIZATIONS IN INDIA

Centre for Women's Development Studies, B-43, Panchseel Enclave, New Delhi 110017 (☎643 8428).

Feminist Resource Centre (FRC), 13 Carol Mansion, 35 Sitladevi Temple Rd, Mahim, Bombay 400016. Feminist-perspective research on wide-ranging issues (eg, health, sexuality, violence against women, discrimination at work).

Forum against the Oppression of Women, c/o Vibhuti Patel, K8 Nensey Colony, Express Highway, Borivili East, Bombay 400066.

Indian Social Institute (ISI) Programme for Women's Development, Lodi Rd, New Delhi 110003 (☎622379).

Indian Council of Social Science Research (ICSSR), 3F Shah Rd, New Delhi 110001 (☎383186). Organize workshops and symposia on feminist themes and run a women's studies programme.

Kali for Women, N84 Panchshila Park, New Delhi 110017. Feminist publisher.

Self-Employed Women's Association (SEWA), Textile Workers' Union Building, Ahmedabad, Gujarat. Self-help union mentioned in text opposite.

Streelekha (International Feminist Bookshop and Information Centre), #67, 2nd floor, Blumoan Complex, MG Rd, Bangalore 560011, Karnataka. Stocks books, journals, posters; provides space for women to meet.

Women's Centre, 307 Yasmeen Apartments, Yashwant Nagar, Valoka, Santa Cruz East, Bombay.

Aside from these, however, tradition still rules. Dowries are illegal, but still demanded by prospective in-laws. Even *sati* (immolation of a widow on her husband's funeral pyre, banned by the British in 1829) is still not unheard of. Girls may be allowed an education, but this is to attract a husband, not to enter a career. Women's groups exist – mainly composed of educated middle-class women, but the network is widening. Main issues are dowries, discrimination, pay differentials and sexual harassment. They may not always see themselves as akin to Western feminists.

There is also an upside to all this: in India you are a "lady" and treated accordingly. Advantages include "ladies-only" queues at train and bus stations, ladies-only waiting rooms and ladies-only compartments on trains. These can be a very handy way to avoid queues, crowds and harassment, although they may be a mixed blessing if you don't like screaming kids.

Indian tampons are mostly prehistoric and not easy to find: take your own.

As for **publications** of interest to women, India has plenty of "women's magazines" along pre-Cosmo western lines. *Femina* is the best known, but has scores of imitators. They won't tell you how to pick up Indian men, but they might give you an idea of what interests Indian women are supposed to have. In addition, look out for the following:

Manushi, c/o 202 Lajpat Nagar, New Delhi 110024. Excellent Hindi and English journal of information and analysis on women's issues in India.

Newsletter of the Institute of Social Studies (ISS), 5 Deen Dayal Upadhyaya Marg, New Delhi 110002. Research on women's organizations, access to employment, role in development.

Quarterly Newsletter of the Research Unit on Women's Studies, SNDT, Women's University, 1 Nathibai Thackersey Rd, Bombay 400020.

GAY TRAVELLERS

Homosexuality is not generally open or accepted in India, and "carnal intercourse against the order of nature" (anal intercourse) is an offence under article 377 of the penal code, while laws against "obscene behaviour" are used to arrest gay men for cruising or liaising anywhere that could be considered a public place. The same law could in theory be used against lesbians, but that is unusual as lesbian liaisons are much more clandestine.

Physical contact between members of the same sex, such as holding hands, is commonplace in India and should not necessarily be taken as sexual. On the other hand, as in many countries where heterosexual contact outside of marriage is difficult, homosexual behaviour is frequent among people who do not consider themselves gay, and a surprising number of Indian men are bisexual. For this reason, however, one-offs are much more likely than long-term relationships.

For lesbians, **making contacts** will be rather difficult: the *Sakhi* resource centre in Delhi (details below) is the only public face of a very hidden scene. For gay men, a network exists in most big cities, especially Bombay, where gay parties are a regular event. Contact the *Khush Club*, PO Box 573551, Bombay 400058 – which does not have fixed premises – for details of forthcoming social activities in the city.

Cruising areas are strictly defined by time and place, with police harassment frequent and sometimes brutal. Male prostitution also exists, but robberies are common.

Some Indian gay male couples make their relationship acceptable by one of them becoming a **eunuch** (eunuchs are semi-accepted as a kind of "third sex"), but such a step would probably be a little drastic for most western visitors. Gay westerners contemplating a relationship should be aware that they will not be able to bring their lovers home with them.

Contacts (write in advance for information – most addresses are PO boxes):

Bombay Dost, 105A Veena-Beena Shopping Centre, Bandra Station Rd, Bandra (West), Bombay 400050. Publish a newsletter and have contacts nationwide.

Sakhi, PO Box 7032, Srinivas Puri, New Delhi 110065. Lesbian guest house and resource centre.

Arambh, c/o Aalok, PO Box 9522, New Delhi 110095.

The Council Club, PO Box 9612, Calcutta 700016.

Pravartak, PO Box 9087, Calcutta 700027. Publish a newsletter.

Friends of India, PO Box 59, Mahanagar, Lucknow 226006, ☎0522/247009.

Freedom, PO Box 5429, Bangalore 566001, Karnataka. Publish a newsletter.

Gay Info Centre, c/o Owais, PO Box 1662, Secunderabad HPO 500003, Andhra Pradesh.

Men India Movement, PO Box 866, Kochi 682005, Kerala.

DISABLED TRAVELLERS

Disability is common in India; many conditions that would be treatable in the west, such as cataracts, are permanent disabilities here because people can't afford the treatment. Disabled people are unlikely to get jobs (though there is a famous blind barber in Delhi), and the choice is usually between staying at home being looked after by your family, and going out on the street to beg for alms.

For the disabled traveller, this has its advantages: disability and disfigurement, for example, do not get the same embarrassed reaction from Indian people that they do from able-bodied westerners. On the other hand, you'll be lucky to see a wheelchair or a disabled loo (major airports usually have both, though the loo may not be in a usable state), and the streets are full of all sorts of obstacles that would be hard for a blind or wheelchair-bound tourist to negotiate independently. Kerbs are often high and ramps non-existent. There are potholes all over the place, open sewers and all sorts of unexpected obstacles from cows to heaps of rubbish to negotiate your way around. Some of the more expensive hotels have ramps for the movement of luggage and equipment, but if that makes them accessible to wheelchairs, it is by accident rather than design.

If you walk with difficulty, you will find street obstacles and steep stairs hard going. Another factor that can be a problem is the constant barrage of people proffering things at you (hard to wave aside if you are for instance on sticks or crutches), and all that queuing, not to mention heat, will take it out of you if you have a condition that makes you tire quickly. A light, folding camp-stool is one thing that could be invaluable if you have limited walking or standing power.

Then again, Indian people are likely to be very helpful if, for example, you need their help getting on and off buses or up stairs. Taxis and rickshaws are easily affordable and very adaptable; if you rent one for a day, the driver is certain to help you on and off, and perhaps even around the sites you visit. If you employ a guide, they may well also be prepared to help you with steps and obstacles.

If complete independence is out of the question, going with an able-bodied companion might be on the cards. In the UK, the *Holiday Care Service* (2 Old Bank Chambers, Station Rd, Horley, Surrey RH6 9HW, ☎0293/774535) may be able to help you get in touch with someone. Otherwise, some package tour operators try to cater for travellers with disabilities – *Bales*, *Butterfield's* and *Somak* among them – but you should always contact any operator and discuss your exact needs with them before making a booking. You should also make sure you are covered by any insurance policy you take out. Contacts for further information:

DISABLED ORGANIZATIONS

UK *RADAR*, 250 City Rd, London EC1V 8AS, ☎0171/250 3222.

Ireland *National Rehabilitation Board*, 25 Clyde Road, Ballsbridge, Dublin 4, ☎01/668 4181.

USA *SATH*, 347 Fifth Ave, Suite 610, New York NY10016, ☎212/447 7284.

Travel Information Center, Moss Rehab Hospital, 1200 West Tabor Rd, Philadelphia PA 19141-3099.

Canada *Canadian Rehabilitation Council for the Disabled*, 45 Sheppard Ave E, Toronto, Ontario M2N 5W9, ☎416/250 7490.

Australia *ACROD*, PO Box 60, Curtain, ACT 2605, ☎06/682 4333.

Barrier Free Travel, 36 Wheatley St, North Bellingen, NSW 2454, ☎066/551733.

New Zealand *Disabled Persons Assembly*, PO Box 10–138,The Terrace, Wellington, ☎04/472 2626.

India *Rehabilitation Co-ordination – India*, A–2 Rasadhara Co-operation Housing Society, 385 SVP Rd, Bombay 400004.

Rehabilitation Institute for the Disabled, WZ101 Nangal Rai Pankha Rd, Delhi 110046, ☎551062.

TRAVELLING WITH KIDS

Travelling with kids can be both challenging and rewarding. Indians are very tolerant of children so you can take them almost anywhere without restriction, and they always help break the ice with strangers.

The main problem with children, especially small children, is their extra vulnerability. Even more than their parents, they need protecting from the sun, unsafe drinking water, heat and unfamiliar food. All that chilli in particular may be a problem, even with older kids, if they're not used to it. Remember too, that diarrhoea, perhaps just a nuisance to you, could be dangerous for a child: rehydration salts (see under "Health", p.19) are vital if your child goes down with it. Make sure too, if possible, that your child is aware of the dangers of rabies; keep children away from animals, and consider a rabies jab.

For babies, nappies (diapers) and places to change them can be a problem. For a short visit, you could bring disposable ones with you; for longer journeys, consider going over to washables. A changing mat is another necessity. And if your baby is on powdered milk, it might be an idea to bring some of that: you can certainly get it in India, but will it taste the same? Dried baby food too could be worth taking – mix it with hot (boiled) water that any cafe or *chai wallah* should be able to supply you with.

For touring, hiking or walking, child-carrier backpacks such as the *Tommy Lightrider* are ideal, start at around $45/£30, and can weigh less than 2kg. If the child is small enough, a fold-up buggy is also well worth packing – especially if they will sleep on it (while you have a meal or a drink . . .).

DIRECTORY

Airport Departure Tax As you depart from any Indian airport, you are expected to pay a tax of either Rs300 – for most international flights – or Rs150, for domestic flights and flights to Pakistan, Bangladesh, Nepal, Sri Lanka, Burma, the Maldives and Afghanistan. Ideally you'd pay with left-over *rupees* kept for that purpose, but travellers' cheques (so hang on to some low-denomination ones) and credit cards are also acceptable. This tax also applies to international sea departures.

Cigarettes Various brands of cigarettes, included imported makes such as *Rothmans* and *Benson and Hedges*, are available in India, most of them tolerable to foreign smokers. One of the great smells of India is the *bidi*, the cheapest smoke, made of a single low-grade tobacco leaf. Roll-ups are also possible, though Indian *Capstan* cigarette papers are thick and don't stick very well.

Duty Free Allowance Anyone over 17 can bring in 1 US quart (0.95 litre – but nobody's going to quibble about the other 5ml) of spirits, or a bottle of wine and 250ml spirits; plus 200 cigarettes, or 50 cigars, or 250g tobacco. You may be required to register anything valuable on a Tourist Baggage Re-export Form to make sure you take it home with you, and to fill in a currency declaration form if carrying more than US$10,000 or the equivalent. There is a market for duty free spirits in big cities: small retailers are the best people to approach.

Electricity Generally 220V 50Hz AC, though direct current supplies also exist, so check before plugging in. Most sockets are European-style double round-pin but sizes vary. British, Irish and Australasian plugs will need an adaptor, preferably universal; American and Canadian appliances will need a transformer too, unless multivoltage. Power cuts and voltage variations are very common.

Initials and acronyms Widely used in Indian English. Thus, the Janata Party Prime Minister, VP Singh, was always "VP", and many middleclass Indian men bear similar monikers. The United Provinces, renamed Uttar Pradesh after independence, have always been UP. More recently, and less universally, Himachal Pradesh is HP, Madhya Pradesh MP, and Andhra Pradesh (not Arunchal Pradesh) AP. State and national organizations such as ITDC, RTDC and so on are always known by their acronyms. MG Road means Mahatma Gandhi Road, Victoria Terminus in Bombay is VT, and the only reason Calcutta has come to accept the new name for Dalhousie Square is because they can call it BBD Bagh (that's Benoy Badal Dinesh).

Laundry In India, no-one goes to the laundry: if they don't do their own, they send it out to a *dhobi-wallah*. Wherever you are staying, there will either be an in-house *dhobi-wallah*, or one very close by to call on. The *dhobi-wallah* will take your dirty washing to a *dhobi ghat*, a public clothes-washing area (the bank of a river for example), where it is shown some old-fashioned discipline: separated, soaped and given a damn good thrashing to beat the dirt out of it. Then it is hung out to dry in the sun and, once dried, taken to the ironing sheds where every garment is endowed with razor-sharp creases and then matched to its rightful owner by hidden cryptic markings. Your clothes will come back from the *dhobi-wallah* absolutely spotless, though this kind of violent treatment does take it out of them: buttons get lost and eventually the cloth starts to fray. For more on *dhobi-wallahs*, see our Bombay chapter; if you'd rather not entrust your Savile Row made-to-measure to their tender mercies, dry-cleaners do exist in large towns.

Meditation Meditation courses and retreats are on offer all over India, held by various schools and sects, and usually based on Buddhist practices. For Buddhist meditation, Bodh Gaya (Bihar) is an important centre, as is Dharamsala (HP), where there's a choice between Tibetan and Indian traditional teachings. *Vipassana* centres, which offer meditation courses of varying lengths, are dotted around the whole country; enquire through the *Vipassana Centre*,

Dharmaghetta, in Kusumnagar, Hyderabad (☎0842/530290), or by calling the *Vipassana International Academy* in Igatpuri, Maharashtra (☎0253/72592). In England, contact the *Vipassana Trust*, Dharmadipa, Harewood End, Hereford (☎01989/730234); in the US, *Dharmamahavana*, PO Box 1167, North Fork, CA 93643 (☎209/877 4386).

Numbers A hundred thousand is a *lakh* (written 1,00,000); ten million is a *crore* (1,00,00,000). Millions, billions and the like are not in common usage.

Opening Hours In theory, standard shop opening hours in India are Mon–Sat 9.30am–6pm. Most big stores, at any rate, keep those hours, while smaller shops vary from town to town, religion to religion, and one to another, but usually keep longer hours. Banks are open roughly Mon–Fri 10am–2pm and Sat 10am–noon, post offices Mon–Fri 10am–5pm and Sat 10am–noon (big city GPOs Mon–Fri 9.30am–6pm, Sat 9.30am–1pm). Government offices are open 9.30am–5pm during the week, closing at 1pm on Saturdays (and often open only every other Sat). Government tourist offices are open in principle Mon–Fri 9.30am–5pm, Sat 9.30am–1pm, though these may vary slightly; state-run tourist offices are likely to be open Mon–Fri 10am–5pm.

Photography Beware of pointing your camera at anything that might be considered "strategic", including airports and anything military, but even bridges, stations and main roads. Remember too that some people prefer not to be photographed, so it is wise to ask before you take a snapshot of them – and only common courtesy after all. Camera film is widely available in India (but check the date on the box), and it's pretty easy to get films developed, though they don't always come out as well as they might at home. Prices are broadly similar to those in the west, with the exception of slide film, which is considerably more expensive.

Time India is all in one time zone: GMT +5hr 30min all year round. In principle this makes it 5hr 30min ahead of London, 10hr 30min ahead of New York, 15hr 30min ahead of LA, and 4hr 30min behind Sydney; however, summer time in those places will vary the difference by an hour.

Toilets A visit to the loo is not one of India's more pleasant experiences: toilets are often filthy and stink. They are also, of course, major potential breeding grounds for disease. And then there is the squatting position to get used to; this is the natural position for defecation and once you get the hang of it, you may even prefer it, especially since it involves no physical contact with the toilet (you don't need loo-seat paranoia to prefer avoiding that!). Paper, if used, often goes in a bucket next to the loo rather than down it. Indians use instead a jug of water and their left hand, a method you may also come to prefer, but if you do use paper, keep some handy – it isn't usually supplied, and it might be an idea to stock up before going too far off the beaten track as it is not available everywhere.

Yoga One- or two-week yoga courses for visitors, involving physical and mental practices based on Hindu philosophy (usually the *Bhagavad Gita*), are run in major centres such as Varanasi (UP) and Rishikesh (UP). Most cities have their own yoga ashrams. Serious spiritual seekers can also go to the controversial Rajneeshi ashram in Pune (M), or The Mother's spiritual centre at Auroville (TN).

THINGS TO TAKE

Many things are of course easy to find in India and cheaper than at home, but here is a miscellaneous and rather random list of items you should consider taking to India with you:

A padlock (to lock rooms in budget hotels, and attach your bag to train fittings)

A universal electric plug adaptor and a universal sink plug (few sinks or bathtubs have them)

A mosquito net

A sheet sleeping bag (made by sewing up a sheet – so you don't have to worry about the state of the ones in your hotel room)

A small flashlight

Earplugs (for street noise in hotel rooms and music on buses)

High-factor sunblock

A pocket alarm clock (for those early morning departures)

An inflatable neck-rest, to help you sleep on long journeys

A multi-purpose penknife

A needle and some thread (but dental floss is better than cotton for holding baggage together)

Plastic bags (to sort your baggage, make it easier to pack and unpack, and keep out damp and dust)

Tampons (those available in India are not so wonderful)

Multi-vitamin and mineral tablets

Suggestions for a general **medical kit** are listed on p.17; details of **trekking** prerequisites are on p.46.

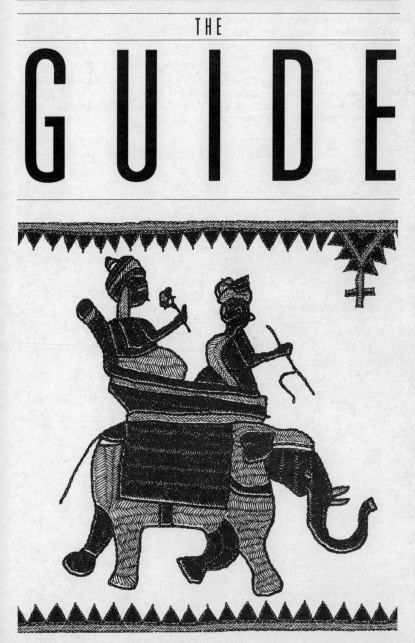

CHAPTER ONE

DELHI

Delhi is the symbol of old India and new . . . even the stones here whisper to our ears of the ages of long ago and the air we breathe is full of the dust and fragrances of the past, as also of the fresh and piercing winds of the present.

Jawaharlal Nehru

O n first impressions, **DELHI**, with its tower blocks and temples, forts, mosques and colonial mansions, and jam-packed streets, can be as disorienting as it is fascinating. It certainly takes a while to find your feet – literally – as you attempt to weave a path through buses, trucks, nippy modern cars, mopeds, rickshaws, nonchalant cows, bullock carts and hand-pulled trolleys. Unlikely juxtapositions are everywhere you look; suit-and-tie businessmen rub shoulders with traditionally dressed orthodox Hindus and Muslims, groups of young Delhi-ites wearing *Levi's* pile into burger-joints, bars and discos, turbaned snake charmers tease hypnotizing moans out of curved pipes, pundits pontificate while *sadhus* smoke their *chillums*, and ragged beggars clutching dusty children plead for a little help towards a meal.

The daunting scale of Delhi becomes more manageable as you start to appreciate that geographically as well as historically it consists of several distinct cities – if anything, more than the **Seven Cities** of tradition. The hub of the metropolis is Central **New Delhi**, an orderly plan of wide roads lined with sturdy colonial buildings which was established as the capital of British India in 1911. Most of the city's hotels are here, concentrated amid the columned facades of **Connaught Place**, as are the **parliamentary buildings**, the architectural jewels in the Imperial crown. **Old Delhi**, Shah Jahan's seventeenth-century capital, lies 2km or so further north. This is Delhi at its most quintessentially Indian, where the traditional lifestyle of its predominantly Muslim population has changed little over two hundred years. A visit to Old Delhi's mighty **Red Fort** and **Jami Masjid**, the largest mosque in India, is a must, and should be combined with a stroll through the old city's bazaars, a warren of clustered houses, buzzing with commotion, and infused with aromatic smells drifting from open-fronted restaurants, spice shops and temples.

DELHI: CONTENTS

The other five of Delhi's ex-capitals, further south, are today all but deserted, standing as impressive monuments to long-vanished dynasties. Among them you'll find the towering free-standing column, the **Qutb Minar** (twelfth century), that marks the first capital, Dhillika. Walls and dilapidated pillars survive from the fourteenth-century city of **Tughluqabad**, and **Purana Qila**, the sixth capital. Interspersed between these historic ruins are the grand **tombs** of Delhi's former rulers, plus a plethora of domed **mosques** and Hindu **temples**. The whole city can surprise visitors with its sheer greenness, dotted with open parks and a generous sprinkling of trees.

As befits a national capital, Delhi provides plenty of opportunities to learn about the rest of the country, not least in its admirable range of political, historical and art **museums**. **Shops** trade in goods from every corner of India, and with a little legwork you can find anything from Tibetan carpets, antiques, and jewellery to modern art and designer clothes. Unlike Bombay, Delhi has little nightlife to speak of – only a handful of discos and an assortment of more congenial bars – but its auditoria host a wide range of **national music** and **dance** events, featuring India's most accomplished performers.

Delhi's crowds and stifling, heavily polluted atmosphere soon become tiring, if not unbearable, and few tourists stay longer than a week. However, its long history and firmly rooted traditions ensure that the city never seems quite so much on the brink as Bombay, and many people grow to enjoy its diversity and vivacity.

History: The Seven Cities of Delhi

Growing popular belief has it that Delhi was the city of the Pandavas, the heroes of the *Mahabharata* – though as the Hindu epic is essentially mythology, any attempt to place it within a specific landscape has to be questionable. Nonetheless, the earliest known settlement in the Delhi area, thought to have stood close to the River Yamuna (near the Purana Qila) between 1000 BC and the fourth century AD, has been identified with the city of **Indraprastha**, mentioned in the *Mahabharata*. There's also evidence that Delhi lay on an important trunk route of the Mauryan period, and Ptolemy, who came here in the second century AD, mentions "Dilli".

However, modern Delhi is usually said to have come into being when the Tomara Rajputs founded **Lal Kot** in 736 AD. That was extended, and renamed **Qila Rai Pithora**, the first city of Delhi, in 1180, after a rival Rajput clan, the Chauhans, had ousted the Tomaras; only a few walls of Lal Kot now remain, at the Qutb Minar complex in southwest Delhi. Soon afterwards, in the two successive battles of Tarain in 1191, the Rajputs first managed to hold off an invading force from Afghanistan led by Muhammad Ghuri, and then succumbed to it a few months later.

Unlike other invaders from Central Asia who swept into the north Indian plains, Muhammad Ghuri had come to stay and not merely to plunder. He himself was assassinated in 1206, and his kingdom did not survive long in Afghanistan, but his Indian provinces remained more or less intact in the hands of his Turkish general, Qutb-ud-din Aibak. This ex-slave, who founded the **Delhi Sultanate** (or Slave Dynasty – the first major Muslim rulers of the subcontinent), established himself at the site of Lal Kot, and commenced the construction of the **Qutb Minar**. His successor, **Iltutmish** (1211–27), was arguably the greatest of the early Delhi Sultans.

In 1290, another group of Turks came to power – the Khaljis. Inspired by **Ala-ud-din-Khalji** (1296–1316), they extended their dominion to the Deccan in central India. His reign, the pinnacle of the Delhi Sultanate, was marked by agrarian reforms, and the establishment of **Siri**, the second city of Delhi in 1303. Near present-day Hauz Khas, it grew into a flourishing commercial centre. Ala-ud-din was to die a disappointed man, as cracks appeared in his dream of empire; the ensuing period of confusion only ended when **Ghiyas-ud-din Tughluq** proclaimed himself Sultan in 1320.

Ghiyas-ud-din in turn built a city fortress, at **Tughluqabad**, 8km east of Qutb, but Delhi's third city was occupied for just five years from 1321; apart from the ramparts encompassing the crumbling ruins, and the odd building and tomb, little of it now remains. It was replaced by the fourth, **Jahanpanah**, built between Lal Kot and Siri by the eccentric Muhammad bin Tughluq to protect the vulnerable open plain; that scheme also failed, and the capital was briefly and unsuccessfully transferred south 1100km to Daulatabad in the Deccan in 1328. Most of the energies of the next Sultan, **Firuz Shah**, were taken up with suppressing rebellion, as the Sultanate began to disintegrate, but his reputation as an iconoclast is belied by his keen interest in Indian culture and history. Fascinated by the Ashokan pillars of Meerut and Topra, he had them moved to the new capital, the fifth city of **Firozabad**, built beside the river in 1354.

The Tughluq line came to an end in 1398, when **Timur** (Tamerlane), a Central Asian Turk, sacked Delhi. His successors, the Sayyids (1414–50), were ousted by Buhlul **Lodi**, who established a dynasty that left behind the fine pieces of architecture still to be seen in the **Lodi Gardens**. Ibrahim Lodi made many enemies, and the governors of Punjab and Sind invited **Babur**, a descendant of Genghis Khan and Timur, who was seeking his fortune in Afghanistan, to come to their aid. Lodi died in battle, fighting the brilliant and enigmatic Babur on the plain of Panipat just north of Delhi in 1526. That heralded the start of Babur's new dynasty, the **Moghuls** (a derivative of Mongol), who eventually achieved the dream of an Indian empire that had eluded the Delhi Sultans. Babur's reign was brief, and he moved his capital to Agra not long after taking Delhi; his *Babarnama*, a chronicle of the times, makes fascinating reading.

Babur was succeeded in 1530 by his son, Humayun, who moved to Delhi in 1534. Here he built the fort, **Din-Panah**, or Asylum of Faith, which still stands on the banks of the Yamuna in the southwest of modern Delhi and is known as **Purana Qila**. All the signs indicated that Humayun's reign would be prosperous, but in 1540 the Afghan Sher Shah laid siege to Delhi and he fled to Persia. Sher Shah began the construction of a new citadel around Humayun's fort – the sixth city of **Shergarh** – but the string of bickering power-thirsty relatives who followed him were overcome when Humayun returned from Kabul to retake Delhi in 1555. When the scholar and astronomer Humayun died in a fall in 1556, his son **Akbar** (who could not read or write) took over as emperor, and the capital was moved once more to Agra.

Delhi once again became capital under Prince Khurrum in 1638, who assumed the title **Shah Jahan**, "Ruler of the Universe", and began a fruitful reign that oversaw the construction of some of the finest Moghul monuments, including the Taj Mahal in Agra. The new walled capital of **Shahjahanabad**, the seventh city, which is now Old Delhi, incorporated the mighty Red Fort with its opulent courts and the huge Jami Masjid mosque, fringed by bazaars. Shah Jahan was deposed (and imprisoned in Agra) by his ruthless son, **Aurangzeb**, who ruled from Delhi until 1681, when he transferred the capital to the Deccan.

For the next sixty years Delhi's government was controlled by courtiers, and the city fell victim to successive invasions. In 1739 Nadir Shah, the emperor of Persia, swept across north India and overcame Muhammad Shah in the Red Fort, taking away precious booty and wiping out much of the local population. Soon after, in 1760, the Hindu Marathas and Jats, unhappy with Moghul supremacy, combined forces against the rulers and besieged and looted the Red Fort, but did not take power.

The Moghul rulers were reduced to puppet kings, and the **British**, who had already gained footholds in Madras and Bengal under the guise of the East India Company, moved to Delhi in 1803 during the reign of the blind Moghul emperor, Bahadur Shah. They swiftly took control, leaving Bahadur with his palace and his pension, but no power. British forces fended off a number of Maratha attacks in the next decade, and faced determined opposition during 1857 when the Indian Mutiny (or "First War of Independence") broke out. Bahadur Shah was proclaimed Hindustani Emperor in the Red Fort, and it took much bloodshed before the British regained the city.

DELHI

HOTELS:
- Ⓐ Oberoi Maidens
- Ⓑ New Delhi Tourist Camp
- Ⓒ Holiday Inn
- Ⓓ Ashok Yatri Niwas
- Ⓔ Janpath
- Ⓕ ITDC Kanishka
- Ⓖ Le Meridien
- Ⓗ Taj Palace
- Ⓘ Maurya Sheraton & Towers
- Ⓙ Youth Hostel
- Ⓚ Ashok & Samrat
- Ⓛ Claridges
- Ⓜ Taj Mahal
- Ⓝ Ambassador
- Ⓞ Oberoi
- Ⓟ Maharani Guest House
- Ⓠ Lodhi
- Ⓡ Hyatt Regency
- Ⓢ Surya Sofitel
- Ⓣ Qutab

RESTAURANTS:
- ❶ Vig Coffee House
- ❷ Moti Mahal
- ❸ Basil & Thyme

△ Airport

Yamuna River

Humayun's
Tomb

Hazrat
Nizamuddin
Railway Station

Hazrat
Nizamuddin
Aulia

Golf
Club

Tibet
House

Lodi
Gardens

Safdarjang's
Tomb

Rail
Transport
Museum

All India Institute
of Medical Sciences
Hospital

Moth Ki
Masjid

Deer
Park

Hauz Khas

HAUZ KHAS
VILLAGE

Qutb Minar
Complex

Ashokan
Rock Edicts

Bahai
Temple

Kalkaji
Temple

Tughluqabad

Ghiyas Ud Din
Tughluq's Tomb

Adilabad

LALA LAJPAT RAI PATH

PANCHSHEEL MARG

MEHRAULI BADARPUR RD

SRI AUROBINDO MARG

RING RD

AFRICA AVE

VIKAS MARG

SHANTIPATH

OUTER RING RD

PARADE RD

MATHURA RD

MATHURA RD

LODI RD

THE SEVEN CITIES OF DELHI:

★ Qila Rai Pithora
★2 Siri
★3 Tughluqabad
★ Jahanpanah
★ Firozabad
★ Shergarh
★ Shahjahanabad

0   2 km

N

The British retained a hold on Delhi while administering affairs of state from their capital in Calcutta. When King George V came to India from England to be crowned as Emperor in 1911, it was decided to make Delhi India's new **capital**. Fervent construction of grand houses, parliamentary buildings and public offices followed, and in 1931 Delhi was officially inaugurated as the capital of Britain's largest colonial possession.

With India's declaration of **Independence** in 1947, the British, represented in Delhi by the Viceroy Lord Mountbatten, lost all authority, and the democratically elected Congress Government came to power with Nehru at its head. The recent history of Delhi is entwined with that of the country as a whole, and the capital continues to grow as a commercial and governmental centre.

Arrival

Delhi is India's main point of arrival for overseas visitors, and has two **airports**. **State buses** from all over the country pull into the Inter-state Bus Terminal in Old Delhi, while private buses stop in the more central location close to New Delhi Railway Station. **Trains** arrive at the railheads in Old or New Delhi, both well-connected to Connaught Circus, the commercial centre of the city, by rickshaws and taxis.

For a summary of the different kinds of accommodation available in different areas of the city, which may well determine where you head for first, see p.98. Basically **Connaught Circus**, the heart of New Delhi and packed with banks, restaurants and shops, can cater to all budgets, while there are cheaper options in **Paharganj**, close to New Delhi railway station, and **Old Delhi**.

By air

International flights land at **Indira Gandhi International Airport** (☎329 5126), 23km southwest of the centre (and formerly known as Palam airport). The *State Bank of India* in the airport is open 24 hours for changing money; make sure you get some small change for taxis and rickshaws. The **ITDC** desk in the departure hall has a list of ITDC hotels and will book accommodation on production of a deposit, but if you're after budget lodgings you should make your own way to a hotel. There's another small tourist office at the airport used by **domestic flights**, 15km southwest of town. Both airports have comfortable **retiring rooms** if you wish to stay overnight to make an early connection (④–⑤).

From the international airport, the least expensive way to get into Delhi is by **bus**. You can buy tickets for the *Ex-servicemen's* shuttle (*EATS*) in the departure hall, or board one of the State Transport buses that wait outside; both take roughly thirty minutes to reach the city centre. Expect to pay Rs20, plus an additional Rs5 for luggage. All buses go via the domestic terminal, from where it is a twenty-minute ride into the city (Rs12), and stop at Janpath, in New Delhi.

Taxis are faster (20min) and more comfortable, and should be booked at the pre-paid kiosk in the departure hall. Fixed rates (Rs200–250) apply, with a 25 percent surcharge between 11pm and 5am. Picking up a non-registered taxi near the bus rank is not recommended; they charge negotiable (usually higher) prices, and may refuse to take tourists to their chosen hotel. The **rickshaws** that wait in line at the departure gate are less expensive than taxis (Rs100–150), but constitute the most precarious and least reliable form of transport from the airport. Many tourists have complained of being taken to a hotel other than the one requested, and being hassled for more money on arrival. It makes sense to settle in for a while before you try using one.

For details of **onward transport connections** from Delhi, both international and domestic, and including specific train recommendations, see p.115 onwards.

The telephone **area code** for Delhi is ☎011.

By train

Delhi has two major **railway stations**. The **New Delhi Station** is east of Paharganj, and within walking distance of many of the area's hotels, though tourists burdened with luggage often prefer to hail an auto-rickshaw, which shouldn't cost more than Rs15 for the short ride to Paharganj – negotiate the fare in advance or insist the meter is turned on. If you're heading for hotels south of the station, don't take a cycle rickshaw as they cannot enter Connaught Place. Pre-paid taxis can be booked at the taxi rank. **Delhi Station** in Old Delhi, west of the Red Fort, receives most trains from Rajasthan. Both stations have **retiring rooms** (②–③), and are notorious for theft: don't take your eyes off your luggage for a moment. Lesser stations in the Delhi area include **Hizrat Nizamuddin**, south of the centre on the main line into New Delhi.

By bus

State buses terminate at the Inter-state Bus Terminal, north of the train station in Old Delhi. Auto-rickshaws to New Delhi or Paharganj take about fifteen minutes, cycle rickshaws twice that. **Private buses** from all over India terminate outside New Delhi train station; some will drop passengers in Connaught Place if they pass that way.

Information and communications

There are reasonably helpful tourist offices at the international and domestic airports, railway stations and bus terminals. However, much the best place to pick up information on Delhi's sites, city tours, shopping, cultural events and accommodation, and free maps – which are also sold at negotiable prices on the street – is the **Government of India tourist office** at 88 Janpath just south of Connaught Place (Mon–Fri 10am–5pm, Sat 10am–2pm; ☎332 0005).

Banks and currency exchange

There's a 24-hour branch of the **State Bank of India** at the international airport. Other banks (usually Mon–Fri 10am–2pm & Sat 10am–noon or 1pm) include *ANZ Grindlays*, 5 Kasturba Gandhi Marg; *Andhra Bank*, 35 M-Block, Connaught Place; *Bank of America* and *Banque Nationale de Paris*, Hansalaya Building, Barakhamba Rd; *Bank of Baroda* (for *Visa* encashments) and *State Bank of India*, Sansad Marg; *Deutsche Bank*, Tolstoy House, 15–17 Tolstoy Marg; and *Hong Kong Bank*, ECE House, 28 Kasturba Gandhi Marg. In addition, all major **hotels** offer exchange; the *Ashoka* in Chanakyapuri changes currency for non-residents even on Sundays. *Thomas Cook* are in the *Hotel Imperial*, Janpath, and *American Express* in A-Block, Connaught Place (Mon–Sat 9.30am–7pm).

Mail services

Delhi's **poste restante** is at the back of the **Foreign Post Office** (Mon–Sat 10am–5pm) on Bhai Vir Singh Marg (formerly Market Rd); to claim mail you must show your passport. Letters sent to "Poste Restante, Delhi", rather than to New Delhi, may end up in **Old Delhi GPO**, north of the railway line on Mahatma Gandhi Rd. You can also have mail sent to the **Government of India tourist office**, 88 Janpath, who pass any parcels to the Foreign Post Office.

Other **post offices** are on Janpath and on A-Block, Connaught Place; all have a **speed post** service, and you can guarantee next-day delivery of parcels and papers to all international destinations with *Overnite Express Pvt Ltd*, whose office is in Kanishka Shopping Plaza, Janpath.

Telephone and fax

Making international **telephone** calls from Delhi has become increasingly easy in recent years. STD booths, marked with yellow signs, have direct-dialling facilities and display the length and cost of each call. Several will allow you to receive incoming calls.

Fax machines are not so common, though some STD booths, easily identified by large advertisements, have them. You'll find a couple on Paharganj, one in the Post Office on Janpath, and a fax office in Kanishka Shopping Plaza on Janpath. Prices are usually by the page, and incoming faxes are stored until collected. Expensive hotels equipped with faxes let residents use them at inflated prices.

Publications

For details of exhibitions or cultural events in Delhi, pick up a local **magazine** from any bookstore or street stall (and see p.112). The excellent weekly *Delhi Diary* lists useful information on current events, lectures, exhibitions and films, and has a comprehensive directory; *First City* is packed with listings, articles and a city directory.

The pocket-sized *Genesis – The City Guide* also has articles and listings, plus a clear guide to what's on and a basic **map**. Travel tips, and train and airline timetables within Delhi and further afield, can be found in the monthly *Travel Links*. *City Scan* (monthly) has features on topical issues from sports and arts to politics and industry.

City transport

In the absence of the much-promised underground metro system, Delhi's **public transport** remains ill-equipped to cope with the city's size and ever-increasing complexity. Buses and a few suburban trains carry most of the burden, though many visitors prefer to pay more for auto-rickshaws and taxis.

Buses

Despite running over 300 different routes, the *Delhi Transport Corporation*'s vast centralized **bus network** can seem totally inadequate. Guides (in Hindi) to their own routes, and those run by other state transport corporations, are available from their office, near the tourist office at Scindia House, Janpath (☎251 9083; enquiries also on ☎331 9847). The first digit of each three-digit route number shows the direction of each bus – thus routes starting with "5" head south from the centre towards Mehrauli, and those starting with "4" travel southeast towards Kalkaji. Specific services useful for tourists include #454 between Connaught Place and Nizamuddin, #505 to Mehrauli and the Qutb Minar, #620 to Chanakyapuri, and #101 and #139 between the *Regal Cinema* bus stand and the Red Fort. **Night buses** start with the digit "0", such as #055 which passes Nizamuddin on its way to Connaught Circus. All buses are liable to get hid-eously overcrowded – **women** travellers will appreciate the row of seats on the left of each which is reserved exclusively for their use.

Minibuses and private buses, such as the "**Green**" and the slightly more expensive "**White**" lines ply many of the same routes, and are often less congested. A Ring Service runs around the Ring Road, both clockwise (marked with a "+") and anti-clockwise ("-"). **Railway Specials** connect outlying stations with the centre; #42 to Tughluqabad is handy for visitors to the ancient fort.

Auto-rickshaws and cycle rickshaws

Auto-rickshaws (or "autos", or even *fut-futs*) – scooters converted into three-wheeler taxis – can be extremely useful in Delhi's chaotic traffic. In theory they should charge what's shown on the meter, but even on the rare occasions when their meters are working, the rates tend to be out of date, and liable to supplements according to a table which drivers are required to carry but sometimes don't (saying "chart dekhao" – show me the chart – can help). For most journeys, it's simplest just to agree a price before you set out; by way of example, at the time this book went to press Delhi Gate to Connaught Place cost around Rs10, Red Fort to Connaught Place more like Rs20. Try to avoid catching the rickshaws that hang around major tourist centres.

Four- or six-seater autos also ply certain fixed routes for flat fees, some built on ancient but immaculately kept **Harley Davidsons**. **Cycle rickshaws** are not allowed in Connaught Place and parts of New Delhi, but are handy for short routes in outlying areas and around Old Delhi, as well as in Paharganj.

Taxis

Taxis, which charge around seventy percent more than auto-rickshaws – thus Red Fort to Connaught Circus costs in the region of Rs35 – are generally considered to be the most reliable mode of transport. Drivers belong to local taxi stands, which you can telephone; if you flag a taxi down on the street you're letting yourself in for some hectic haggling. Between 11pm and 5am at night, there is a surcharge of around 25 percent.

Car and cycle rental

The cheapest outlets for chauffeur-driven *Ambassador* cars, for local sightseeing and journeys beyond the city confines, are at the southern end of the Tibetan Market on Janpath; most are willing to negotiate a price. If you want the option of self-drive, and don't mind paying extra to brave Delhi's notoriously dangerous roads, try *Budget*, G3 Arunchal Building, Barakhamba Rd (☎331 8600), or *Hertz*, 4–5 Kanchenjunga Building, Barakhamba Rd (☎331 8695) and 32, M-Block, Middle Circle, Connaught Place.

Cycling in the large avenues of New Delhi takes some getting used to, but a bike can be handy for reaching the various sites. **Bicycle rental** is surprisingly difficult to come by; *Mehta Electricals*, on Rajguru Rd in Paharganj, charges around Rs15 per day.

City and regional tours

The **tourist office** at 88 Janpath organizes morning tours of New Delhi (daily 9am–2pm; Rs60) and afternoon tours of Old Delhi (daily 2.15pm–5.15pm; Rs60), plus a museum tour on Sundays only, and can supply guides if you prefer to travel under your own steam. Alternative city tours include those run by *American Express Travel Service*, A-Block, Connaught Place (☎332 4119), whose *Delhi Darbar* tour is good but expensive, and *Royal Express*, *Moghul Tours & Travels*, GL4 Ansal Bhavan, 16 K G Marg, Connaught Place (☎371 6611). All the five-star hotels offer their own, more expensive, tours. Longer trips to destinations such as Agra and Fatehpur Sikri can be arranged through *Royal Express* (above) or *Scenic Tours & Travels*, MB 23A Indraprakash, Barakhamba Rd (☎331 5320).

The City

Monuments in sandstone and marble, scattered throughout the city in assorted states of repair, make Delhi a veritable museum of Indo-Islamic architecture. Although it dates back as far 1000 BC, it was the advent of the Delhi Sultans, under Qutb-ud-din Aibak who erected the **Qutb Minar**, that signalled the development of the city that visitors see today. Simply by introducing the mosque, which uses a radically different approach to space for worship from indigenous temples, the Muslims broke the conventional mould of Indian cities; however, perhaps the finest expressions of their architectural genius were the grand *charbagh* (quartered garden) mausoleums of **Humayun's Tomb**, and, most famously, the Taj Mahal in Agra. The major monument of the great Moghul period is **Lal Qila**, the "Red Fort", in Shah Jahan's capital of

Shahjahanabad, now Old Delhi (which was built using the ruins of Firozabad and Shergarh for raw materials,so it's hardly surprising little remains at those two sites).

For all the achievements of the Moghuls, however, Delhi today, as experienced by its many thousands of visitors, centres very much around the imperial city built by the British from 1911 onwards. Most foreign travellers to India find it necessary to call in at some at least of the myriad administrative offices that fill the formal buildings of Connaught Place, the heart of the nation's capital.

Old Delhi (Shahjahanabad)

Alhough it's not in fact the oldest part of Delhi, the seventeenth-century city of **Shahjahanabad**, built by the Moghul emperor, Shah Jahan, is known as **OLD DELHI**. The original city walls spread for seven miles, enclosing the sprawling fort, **Lal Qila**, and the formidable **Jami Masjid**, or "Friday Mosque". Old Delhi's main thoroughfare, **Chandni Chowk**, a seething mass of hooting, pushing cars, tempos, cycle rickshaws and ox-carts, was once a sublime canal lined with trees and some of the most opulent bazaars of the east. Today the city walls have crumbled, and houses and shops have long since spilled beyond the fourteen old gates, only five of which remain.

On the banks of the River Yamuna northeast of the modern centre, Old Delhi resembles an overgrown village of tight-knit communities, alive with intriguing contradictions and contrasts. Photographers huddled at the east end of Chandni Chowk using rickety equipment left over from the days of the Raj are overlooked by garish film boards and advertisements for sex clinics, while the bazaars in the back alleys have changed little since the eighteenth and nineteenth centuries. It's a fascinating area, but you'll need stamina, patience and time to endure the crowds and traffic, and pursue a rewarding exploration of the city's streets, mosques, temples and *guradwaras*.

Lal Qila (Red Fort)

The largest of Old Delhi's monuments is **Lal Qila**, or Red Fort (daily dawn–dusk; Rs0.50), whose thick red sandstone walls, bulging with turrets and bastions, rise above a wide dry moat in the northeast corner of the original city of Shahjahanabad. The fort covers a semi-octagonal area of almost 2km, its longest walls facing the town in the west and the River Yamuna in the east. Work was started on the fort – modelled on the royal citadel in Agra – in 1639, and it was completed by 1648. It contains all the expected trappings of the centre of Moghul government: halls of public and private audience, domed and arched marble palaces, plush private apartments, a mosque, and elaborately designed gardens. Today the Yamuna no longer flows close to the east wall, the "Stream of Paradise" no longer trickles through each palace, copper-plated domes have been replaced with plainer marble domes, and there are few signs of the precious stones and gems once set into the marble walls. Nevertheless, the fort remains an impressive testimony to Moghul grandeur, despite being attacked and plundered by the Persian emperor Nadir Shah in 1739, and by British soldiers during the battles of 1857 – as well as being rubbed, touched and worn down by marvelling tourists.

Entrance to the fort is through the mighty three-storey **Lahori Gate** in the centre of the west wall. A booking office sells tickets just outside, and eager guides will offer their services at negotiable prices (Rs20–50) – generally more than twice the price that you'd pay within. The main entrance opens onto **Chatta Chowk**, a covered street flanked with arched cells that used to house Delhi's most talented jewellers, carpet makers, goldsmiths and silk weavers, but now stock the usual souvenirs: miniatures, *hookahs*, brass ornaments, stone and wood carvings and low-quality jewellery. Just beyond a small restaurant at the end of Chatta Chowk, the road stretches past the military colony into the heart of the fort, coming to an end at **Naubhat Khana**, the erstwhile "drum house", where music was once played five times a day and which now bears scant remains of its original painting.

From Naubhat Khana, a path runs east through wide lawns to the hall of public audience, the **Diwan-i-Am**. This lofty hall, with sturdy pillars supporting its roof and its floor raised on a high platform, was the scene of daily public appearances by the emperor until the custom was stopped by Aurangzeb. When in use it was laid with silk carpets and partitioned with hanging tapestries and curtains. Set against the west wall is "the seat of the shadow of God", a marble throne surrounded by twelve panels inlaid with precious stones. It was designed by an artist from Bordeaux, whose frieze of the Greek god Orpheus with his flute makes a surprising departure from the more usual floral designs of the Moghuls. Lord Curzon, Viceroy of India from 1898 to 1905, restored the hall and returned the emperors' seat from the British Museum in 1909.

The **palaces** in the fort along the east wall face spacious gardens in the west and overlook the banks of the Yamuna, once the scene of animal fights laid on to entertain the royal occupants. Immediately east of the Diwan-i-Am, **Rang Mahal**, the "Palace of Colour", housed the emperor's wives and mistresses. "The crowning jewel of Shah Jahan's seraglio" was crowned with gilded turrets, delicately painted and decorated with intricate mosaics of mirrors, and with a ceiling overlaid with gold and silver that was reflected in a central pool in the marble floor. Unfortunately, it was greatly defaced when the British used it as an Officers' Mess after the Mutiny, and today is a shadow of its former glory. The similar **Mumtaz Mahal**, south of the main *zenana*, or women's quarters, and probably used by princesses is now a **museum** (daily except Fri 10am–5pm) housing weaponry, textiles, carpets, ornate chess sets and *hookahs*.

On the northern side of Rang Mahal, the marble **Khas Mahal** was the personal palace of the emperor, divided into separate apartments for worship, sleeping and sitting. The southern chamber, **Tosh Khana** (robe room), has a stunning marble filigree screen on its north wall, carved with the scales of justice. Viewing the screen from the north you'll see suns surrounding the scales, but from the south these look more like moons. The octagonal tower projecting over the east wall of the Khas Mahal was used by the emperor, who would appear here daily before throngs gathered on the river banks below. In 1911, when Delhi was declared capital, King George V (Emperor of India) and Queen Mary sat here before the citizens of Delhi.

North of Khas Mahal, in the large **Diwan-i-Khas** (hall of private audience), the emperor would address the highest nobles of his court. Today it's the finest building in the fort, a marble pavilion shaded by a roof raised on stolid pillars embellished with amber, jade and gold, meeting in ornate scalloped arches. On the north and south walls you can still make out the Persian inscription attributed to Shah Jahan's prime minister:

Agar Firdaus bar ru-e-zamin ast
Hamin ast o hamin ast o hamin ast.

(If there be paradise on the face of earth,
It is this, Oh, it is this, Oh, it is this.)

A marble and gold Peacock Throne inlaid with rubies, sapphires and diamonds once stood on the central pedestal, bypassed by a stream that gurgled through the cool

SOUND AND LIGHT SHOWS

Each night a **Sound and Light show** takes place in the **Red Fort**: the palaces are dramatically lit, and an historical commentary blares from crackly loudspeakers. The show starts after sunset and lasts an hour (Rs5 and Rs10; in **Hindi** 7pm Feb–April & Sept–Oct, 7.30pm May–Aug, 6pm Nov–Jan; in **English** 8.30pm Feb–April & Sept–Oct, 9pm May–Aug, 7.30pm Nov–Jan; ☎60 0121).

Another nightly *son et lumière* show, at the **Nehru Museum** – see p.90 – tells the story of the Independence struggle (Rs2 and Rs5; English 7.15pm–8.15pm; ☎301 5026).

Both shows are subject to cancellation during the monsoons.

chamber. It took seven years to construct, and was the pride of the fort, but the Persian Nadir Shah took it back to his kingdom as booty after a raid in 1739.

A little further north are the **hammams**, or royal baths, sunken into the marble floor inlaid with delicate patterns of precious stones, and dappled in jewel-coloured light that filters through stained-glass windows. The western chamber contained hot baths while the eastern apartment, with fountains of rose water, was used as a dressing room.

West of the baths the tiny **Moti Masjid**, built by Aurangzeb, is beautifully proportioned, but desperately in need of maintenance. In the gardens beyond, pavilions stand among symmetrical flower beds and neat lawns intersected by stream-beds that once bubbled with water drawn from the Yamuna.

Jami Masjid

India's largest mosque, the red sandstone and marble **Jami Masjid**, 1km west of the fort, was Shah Jahan's last great work of architecture, built between 1644 and 1656 by five thousand artisans. Originally called *Masjid-i-Jahanuma*, or "mosque commanding a view of the world", this grand structure stands on Bho Jhala, one of Shahjahanabad's two hills, and looks east to the sprawling Lal Qila, and down on the seething streets of Old Delhi all around. Stairways lead to the south and north gateways: the main (eastern) entrance, which remains closed, was used only by emperors. There is no objection to non-Muslims entering the mosque, but all visitors must remove their shoes, and foreigners need to pay a Rs5 entrance fee (plus Rs5 for a camera). If you're wearing shorts, you'll have to rent a *lunghi* to wrap around your legs and hide your knees.

The **main prayer hall** on the west side (facing Mecca), fronted by a series of high cusped arches and topped with three bulbous marble domes, houses the *mihrab*, a niche in the west wall that shelters the prayer leader. Worshippers use the prayer hall on most days, but on Fridays and other holy days the vast **courtyard** is full of the bending bodies of up to 25,000 faithful. The pool in the centre is used for washing feet, hands and faces before prayer. At each corner of the square yard a slender minaret crowned with a marble dome rises to the sky, and it's well worth climbing the tower south of the main sanctuary (Rs5, plus Rs5 for camera) for an unrivalled view over Delhi, ancient and modern. By the north gate, a cupboard contains a collection of Muhammad's relics, watched over by keepers who are keen to reveal the contents: two Korans written on deerskin by relatives of the prophet, a red beard-hair of Muhammad's, his sandals, and his "footprint" embedded in a marble slab, decked with coins by the faithful.

Digambara Jain Temple and Jain Bird Hospital

The oldest Jain temple in Delhi, the **Digambara Jain Temple** at the east end of Chandni Chowk, was first built in 1526, but has been modified and added to ever since. A haven of tranquillity amid the noise and chaos of the main street, it is not as ornate as the fine temples in Gujarat and Rajasthan, but has detailed carvings, and gilded paint-work in the antechambers surrounding the main shrine to Parshvanath. You'll have to remove your shoes, and hand them over with your bags and all leather articles to a kiosk before entering.

The **Jain Bird Hospital** just south of the temple puts the Jain principle that all life is sacred into practice, admitting up to sixty sick birds per day. It serves as a rescue sanctuary for partridges, caught and wounded by fowlers and bought in bulk by Jain merchants who bring them here to recover, and there are separate wards for pigeons, parrots, sparrows (notoriously vulnerable to deadly whirring ceiling fans) and domestic fowl. Squirrels, who will not hurt the birds, are also treated here, but birds of prey are seen on a strictly out-patient basis, as they are not vegetarian. There's no entrance fee, but donations are appreciated. Recovered birds are set free each Sunday.

THE BAZAARS OF OLD DELHI

Old Delhi's trading is carried out in bustling **bazaars**, where shops huddle together in open houses or beneath makeshift awnings, and between them stock an incredible array of goods ranging from fish and spices to currency garlands and giant candles. If you take time to amble down side streets branching off **Chandni Chowk**, you'll come across lively markets of all kinds, each concentrating on one particular trade.

Chor Bazaar A curious bazaar behind the old ramparts of the Red Fort, which comes to life on Sundays to trade a mix of "secondhand" and allegedly stolen goods.

Kinari Bazaar A colourful street set behind the *guradwara* on Chandni Chowk, and connected to the main road by Dariba Kalan, "the street of incomparable pearl", which is the centre for jewellers. The shops in Kinari Bazaar overflow with bright wedding finery, including garlands made of *rupee* notes, grooms' turbans, rosettes and glistening tinsel used by Hindus, Christians and Muslims in vivid and noisy marriage ceremonies. In October (the month of Ram Lila) the shops stock props for the annual theatre productions – bows and arrows, cardboard swords and fake heads for the evil nine-headed King Ravana.

Naya Bazaar Spice market on Khari Baoli, near Fatehpuri Masjid, clouded with the fine dust of flour and spices, and heavy with rich aromas. The nuts, spices and dried fruits sold here are reputed to be the best in Delhi, and many are sold to wholesalers by the sack; weighed-down porters load their burdens onto ox-carts which trundle off to other parts of the city through the mass of motorized traffic. The covered **Gadodia Market**, just off Khari Baoli, is a gathering place for wholesalers who weigh their goods on huge old-fashioned scales. Among the spices and condiments you can find aniseed, turmeric, pomegranate, dried mangoes, ginger, saffron, *reetha* nuts (used for washing hair and cleaning silver), lotus seeds, pickles, sugars, chutneys and edible leaves of silver paper used to coat sweets and cakes.

Meena Bazaar A distinctively Islamic bazaar of cramped shops clustered around the base of the Jami Masjid, full of clothes, domestic implements and smells not found in Hindu regions of the city. Here you can buy *burquas*, *dupattas*, *topis*, caged chickens, bangles, kebabs, sticky sweetmeats and devotional pictures of shrines.

Car Parts Bazaar Also south of the Jami Masjid, it stocks, or rather piles high, new and secondhand automobile parts from all models, ranging from speedometers and the all-important horn to complete engines.

Chawri Bazaar Named for the Marathi word *chawri* (meeting place), a street running west from the Jami Masjid that was once flanked by huge mansions, destroyed by the British after the Mutiny. In the nineteenth century it was famous for its "dancing girls", who looked into the streets below from arched windows and balconies and beckoned men with enticing glances; they were moved out by the Delhi Municipal Corporation in the twentieth century. Today the shops specialize in copper and brass Buddhas, Vishnus, Krishnas, bells, lamps, ashtrays, masks and boxes. The long road, **Nai Sarak**, which connects Chawri Bazaar with Chandni Chowk, is lined with nineteenth- and twentieth-century buildings whose lower storeys are used for making and selling paper, and shops stocking educational books and stationery.

Kalan Mahal A small market street further south of the Jami Masjid near the Kalan Masjid, Kalan Mahal is the gathering place for brass polishers, and also has stalls displaying intricately carved bone necklaces.

Poultry and Fish Markets These markets fill a small area east of Kalan Mahal, opening onto **Netaji Subash Marg**, where hens are cooped up in cages, slaughtered and plucked, and fish from coastal areas further south are laid out on ice. The scene can be bloody, and the pungent smells will send all but the most hardy back to the main road for some fresher Delhi air.

Gauri Shankar Temple

Tucked behind the fragrant mounds of marigolds, roses and jasmine blossoms sold on Chandni Chowk just west of the Jain temple, the large marble **Gauri Shankar Temple**, dominated by its eight-hundred-year-old *lingam*, is Delhi's holiest Shiva temple. Devotees enter up a narrow flight of marble steps, flanked by pillars carved with chains and bells, that opens onto a spacious courtyard, always a scene of animated devotional activity. Inside, offerings for sale include *bilva* (wood apple) leaves, *chandan* (sandalwood paste), marigolds, red powder, rice, and cotton threads. The main sanctuary holds bejewelled statues of Gauri (Parvati) and Shankar (Shiva) standing beneath a silver canopy, and the ancient brown stone *lingam* resting on a marble *yoni* encased in silver and draped with silver serpents. Shrines to other deities line the south wall.

Raj Ghat

When Shah Jahan established his city in 1638, its eastern edges bordered the River Yamuna, and a line of *ghats*, or steps leading to the water, was installed along the river banks. *Ghats* have been used in India for centuries, primarily for worship, but also for washing clothes and bathing. After Mahatma Gandhi's death in 1948, he was cremated on **Raj Ghat**, roughly 1km south of the Red Fort, a short way east of Delhi Gate, where a solid black memorial stands in his memory. Prayers are held every Friday evening, and on his birth and death anniversaries (Sept 30 & Oct 2) hundreds gather to pay homage. The small **Gandhi Memorial Museum** (daily except Thurs 9.30am–5.30pm), one of many such in India, displays photographs and other items connected with Gandhi's life, and has an informative film show on Sundays (Hindi 6pm, English 7pm).

Firoz Shah Kotla

The prosperous fifth city of Delhi, **Firozabad**, was founded in 1354, and stretched from the north ridge to Hauz Khas in the south, but few traces survive save the remains of the palace of Firoz Shah Kotla, set amid ornamental gardens 500 metres east of Delhi Gate. Its most incongruous and yet distinctive element is the single polished sandstone **Ashokan Column** (third century BC), carried down the Yamuna by raft from Ambala to grace a palace that is now a crumbling ruin. The 14m-high column, the second brought to Delhi, continues to protrude above the surroundings, withstanding the ravages of time and dominating the (ill-kempt) gardens. Next to a *baoli* (step-well) lie the massive ruins of a mosque which once accommodated over 10,000 worshippers; Timur (Tamerlane) is said to have been so impressed by it that it served as the model for his great mosque in Samarkand. Today, surrounded by large and busy roads, the gardens and its monuments lie almost forgotten and few tourists stop by.

North of the Old City

Just north of Old Delhi, not far from the Inter-state bus terminal, the peaceful **Qudsia Gardens** are a fading reminder of the magnificent pleasure gardens commissioned by Queen Qudsia, favourite mistress of Muhammad Shah, and mother of Ahmed Shah, in the mid-eighteenth century. The original mosque still stands, but part of the park was taken over by the British Masons, who built a hall and banned Indians from entering the park in the afternoons. There's also a Hindu monument here; a mounted figure represents the valiant Pratap Singh who earned undying fame for his unfaltering defiance of Akbar. Close to the gardens is **Mother Theresa's orphanage**, "Little Sisters of the Poor", where voluntary help is always welcomed.

Just west of Qudsia Gardens, on Qudsia Road, Delhi's oldest burial ground, **Nicholson Cemetery**, is named after Brigadier General John Nicholson who led the attacks on Delhi in 1857 when the British were striving to regain the city from the Nationalists. The graveyard is still used, but most of the headstones show the names of British residents killed defending this outpost of the British Empire, or stricken as young children by fatal diseases at the start of the twentieth century.

If you're not wearying of trampling through Old Delhi, one last area is worth a visit: **Delhi Ridge**, a sharp outcrop northwest of the old city where the major monuments of British India were built before New Delhi was established. Few buildings remain, but the **Ashokan Pillar**, brought here from Topra by Firoz Shah Tughlak, stands heavily restored, still bearing imprints of the emperor Ashoka's edicts, close to the Gothic

Mutiny Memorial raised in memory of the bloody battles of 1857. The views south over Delhi from the ridge are superb.

Central New Delhi

The modern area of **CENTRAL NEW DELHI**, with its wide tree-lined avenues and solid colonial buildings, has been the seat of central government since 1931. At its hub, the royal mall, **Rajpath**, runs from the palatial **Rashtrapati Bhavan**, in the east, to **India Gate** war memorial, in the west. At the north edge of the new capital is the thriving business centre, **Connaught Place**, where neon advertisements for *Wimpy*, *American Express*, hotels and countless airline offices adorn the flat roofs and colonnaded verandahs of high white buildings that curve around a central park to form an almost perfect circle. Central New Delhi also has its fair share of more recent high-rise offices and hotels, standing close to pre-British constructions such as the open-air observatory, **Jantar Mantar**.

Rashtrapati Bhavan

After George V, king of England and emperor of British India, decreed in 1911 that Delhi should replace Calcutta as capital of India, the talented and ambitious English architect, **Edwin Lutyens**, was commissioned to plan the new governmental centre. **Rashtrapati Bhavan**, the official residence of the president of India, is one of the largest and most grandiose of the Raj constructions, built by Lutyens and Sir Herbert Baker between 1921 and 1929. Originally the Viceroy's House, this salmon-pink H-shaped structure on the gentle rise of Raisina Hill was built to dominate: a symbol asserting imperial power in the face of its doomed struggle against Indian Nationalism, it was home to Lord Mountbatten, Viceroy in the years leading up to Independence. Its grandeur was considered nothing more than "vulgar ostentation and wasteful extravagance" by Motilal Nehru, while Mahatma Gandhi claimed that the construction of such "architectural piles" was "in conflict with the best interests of the nation".

Despite its classical columns, Moghul-style domes and *chhatris*, and Indian filigree work, the whole building is unmistakeably British in character. The majestic proportions are best appreciated from India Gate to the east, from where you can see the perfectly balanced residence slightly raised on the hill, flanked in pleasing symmetry by the two Secretariat buildings below – though with increasing pollution, the view is often clouded by a smoggy haze. At closer quarters the height and multitude of pillars supporting the front verandahs are clearly seen, while the immensity of the central crowning copper dome, the dominating feature of the whole complex, is quite overwhelming. Between the entrance gates and the east side of the residence, the slender **Jaipur Column**, donated by the Maharaja of Jaipur, rises to a height of 145m, piercing the sky with a glass star balanced on a bronze lotus blossom. Close to its base an early plan of New Delhi is etched onto a square panel. Troops and guards parade before the iron-grille gates each Saturday (9.35–10.15am) in a ceremony that is Delhi's answer to London's Changing of the Guards.

The apartments inside are strictly private, but the **gardens** at the west side are open to the public each February. Modelled on Moghul pleasure parks, with a typically ordered square pattern of quadrants dissected by waterways and refreshed by fountains, Lutyens' gardens extend beyond the normal confines to include eight tennis courts, butterfly enclosures, vegetable and fruit patches and a swimming pool. The immaculate flowerbeds contain many English varieties, and trees lining walkways are trimmed into perfect oblongs. In 1947, 418 staff worked in the gardens, fifty of whom alone were employed to frighten away birds.

The **Secretariats** on the north and south side of Raisina Hill are an interesting synthesis of Moghul and colonial styles, topped with baroque domes overlaid with low-relief lotus motifs and elephants. Built by Baker, today they house the Home and Finance Ministries and the Ministry of Foreign Affairs.

Vijay Chowk, immediately in front of Rashtrapati Bhavan, leads into **Rajpath**, the wide straight road once known as King's Way, flanked with gardens and fountains that are floodlit at night, and the scene of annual **Republic Day** celebrations (Jan 26). Rajpath runs directly east to **India Gate**, the "All India War Memorial" designed by Lutyens in 1921. The high stolid arch, reminiscent of the Arc de Triomphe in Paris, commemorates the 90,000 Indian soldiers killed fighting for the British in World War I, and bears the names of over three thousand British and Indian soldiers who died on the Northwest frontier and in the Afghan War of 1919. The extra memorial beneath the arch honours the lives lost in the Indo-Pakistan War of 1971.

Parliament House

Northeast of Rashtrapati Bhavan at the end of Sansad Marg is **Parliament House**, now known as **Sansad Bhavan**. Planned by Lutyens and built under the supervision of Baker, the low circular structure covers more than five acres. Obliged to respond to complaints about its extravagant design and large costs, Baker himself referred to the unusual building as a "merrie-go-round", but successfully completed a momentous project. From outside, Parliament House presents an unbroken circle of high buff pillars, and a higher storey (not originally planned) that screens a central dome.

Inside, three semicircular chambers were built to house the Council of State, the Assembly Chamber and the Council of Princes. Today the latter, where leaders from

THE PARLIAMENT OF INDIA

The **Indian Parliament** in Delhi was formed under the British in 1931, and later tailored to the needs of the newly independent nation under the leadership of Jawaharlal Nehru. Today, Delhi's parliament closely follows the English model. It is made up of a politically neutral president, an Upper House, the **Rajya Sabha**, and a Lower House, the **Lok Sabha** (literally "People's House"). Members represent all India's seventeen states and ten Union Territories, in numbers proportionate to each district's population. Thanks in part to the influence of Mahatma Gandhi, a quota of seats is reserved for "untouchables", or *Harijans*. Members of the Lok Sabha are elected every five years, and every two years elections replace one-third of the Rajya Sabha. Communists and Hindu fundamentalists are gradually gaining more seats in central government, but Congress MPs still account for a majority, their party having remained nationally popular since 1947.

The Lok Sabha, the larger of the two houses, comprises up to 525 members, at least fifty of whom must be present to propose and pass bills. Only two or three times a year does the whole house attend. While bills may be put forward in either house, most originate in the Lok Sabha, and are passed to the Rajya Sabha for approval. Taxing, spending, budgets and government economy are discussed only in the Lower House. Each day in the Lok Sabha begins with an hour of questions to the speaker, when government policies are clarified, and opposition parties criticize and push for change.

The smaller Rajya Sabha, the "Council of States", with 250 members, serves as more of an advisory body. It does, however, have the power to create or abolish states and alter boundaries – issues that were of particular importance between 1953 and 1956, when 562 principalities acceded and the Congress demanded territories determined by common language. The more recent formation of Punjab and Nagaland states and the Union Territory of Himachal Pradesh was also determined by the Rajya Sabha.

Despite their separate roles, the two houses meet for collective votes on bills that have not been passed by a majority, and to elect the parliamentary president. While the large membership and exhaustive screening of bills ensures the fullest consideration of political issues, government critics argue that the two-house system wastes energy, and thickens India's already stifling web of bureaucratic confusion.

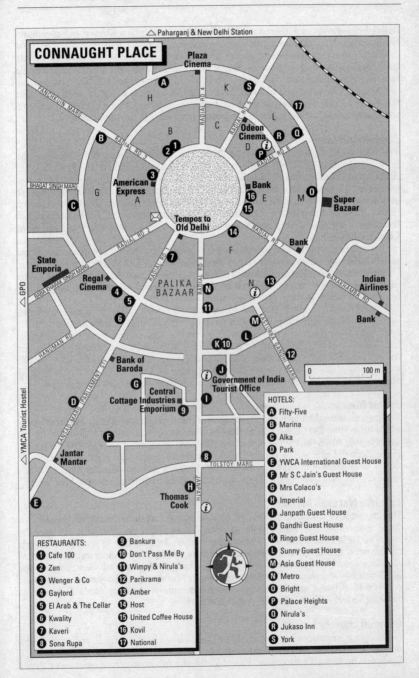

△ Paharganj & New Delhi Station

CONNAUGHT PLACE

Plaza Cinema

PANCHKUIN MARG

RADIAL RD 4

RADIAL RD 5

RADIAL RD 3

BHAGAT SINGH MARG

Odeon Cinema

RADIAL RD 6

American Express

Bank

RADIAL RD 2

Tempos to Old Delhi

Super Bazaar

RADIAL RD 1

RADIAL RD 8

RADIAL RD 7

Bank

State Emporia

BARA KHARAK SINGH MARG

Regal Cinema

PALIKA BAZAAR

BARAKHAMBA RD

Indian Airlines

Bank

HANUMAN RD

KASTURBA GANDHI MARG

GPO

Bank of Baroda

SANSAD MARG (PARLIAMENT ST)

Government of India Tourist Office

0   100 m

Central Cottage Industries Emporium

YMCA Tourist Hostel

Jantar Mantar

TOLSTOY MARG

JANPATH

Thomas Cook

N

RESTAURANTS:
1 Cafe 100
2 Zen
3 Wenger & Co
4 Gaylord
5 El Arab & The Cellar
6 Kwality
7 Kaveri
8 Sona Rupa
9 Bankura
10 Don't Pass Me By
11 Wimpy & Nirula's
12 Parikrama
13 Amber
14 Host
15 United Coffee House
16 Kovil
17 National

HOTELS:
A Fifty-Five
B Marina
C Alka
D Park
E YWCA International Guest House
F Mr S C Jain's Guest House
G Mrs Colaco's
H Imperial
I Janpath Guest House
J Gandhi Guest House
K Ringo Guest House
L Sunny Guest House
M Asia Guest House
N Metro
O Bright
P Palace Heights
Q Nirula's
R Jukaso Inn
S York

India's princely states gathered until Independence, contains a **library** with a comprehensive collection of books and records detailing political history from the 1920s onwards (Mon–Sat 10am–5pm; closed 2nd Sat of each month). It's suitably formal, stuffy even, its walls overlaid with convex teak panels positioned at a downward angle to improve acoustics, and the coats of arms of India's royal families. The **Lok Sabha**, or "People's House", meets today in the Assembly Chamber, and with permission from the reception office on Raisina Road (and a letter of introduction for foreigners from a relevant embassy), visitors can watch debates from seats in the public gallery.

Connaught Place

The hub of New Delhi, **Connaught Place** could not be more different from the crowded centre of Old Delhi that it replaced. Conceived by Robert Tor Russell, Chief Architect of the Government of India, it is one of the few areas of the new city that was not actually designed by Lutyens, though its lofty facades and classical columns are very derivative of the style he established with Rashtrapati Bhavan. Originally designed in the shape of a horseshoe, Connaught Place now forms a full circle, divided into blocks A–N by seven radial roads and rimmed by a busy outer ring road known as **Connaught Circus**.

It's rather grand for a commercial centre, with shops and offices housed in colonnaded buildings almost as splendid as the parliamentary headquarters further south. Unsurprisingly, considering its wealth of tourist facilities, including a glut of hotels and most of Delhi's restaurants, the area buzzes with touts and salesmen selling anything from airline tickets to five-metre-long leather whips.

From Connaught Place, **Sansad Marg** runs southwest to the parliamentary buildings, while southbound **Janpath**, with the busy Tibetan Market at its northern end, is lined with several modern hotels, Russell's majestic Eastern and Western Courts, and the Central Post and Telegraph Office. The park at the core of Connaught Place, and the grassy area over the underground Palika Bazaar, close to Janpath, offer respite from the busy streets, and provide the perfect arena for Delhi's ice-cream sellers, shoe-shiners, masseurs and flower-vendors, who peddle their wares from dawn to dusk.

Jantar Mantar

Between Connaught Place and Rashtrapati Bhavan on Sansad Marg, **Jantar Mantar** (daily 9am–7pm; Rs1) stands little changed since its construction in 1725 as the first of five open-air observatories designed by the ruler of Jaipur, Jai Singh II (see p.129). Huge deep-red and white slanting stone structures loom over palm trees and neat flower beds, giant sundials that cast shadows formerly used to calculate time, solar and lunar calendars and astrological movements, all with an admirable degree of accuracy.

Lakshmi Narayan Mandir

Directly west of Connaught Place on Mandir Marg, **Lakshmi Narayan Mandir** is a large modern temple also known as Birla Mandir after its sponsors, the wealthy Marwari Birla merchants. The extravagant temple, built mainly of marble on several raised tiers, lies in attractive gardens. In front of the main sanctuary, dedicated to Lakshmi (goddess of wealth), a large prayer hall is the scene of silent prayers and jovial singing accompanied by *tabla* and *bhaja*. Marble passages, stairways and open courtyards connect smaller shrines, which include a dazzling room dedicated to Krishna bedecked with coloured stones and mirrors.

Colonial churches

No British governmental centre could be complete without a church, and work began on the **Church of the Redemption**, directly east of Parliament House, in 1927. Designed by Russell's successor, Henry Medd, the robust structure owes more than a passing nod to Lutyens with its high curved vaults, and subtle yet dominant domed tower – it appealed so much to the then-Viceroy, Lord Irwin, that it became known as "Viceroy's Church". The exterior is plain and boldly linear, while within, high rounded arches and shafts of strong light streaming through crescent windows impart an over-whelming sense of space. A company of painted angels look down from the curved roof above the altar.

Further north, at the south end of Bhai Vir Singh Marg, is one of Medd's more ambitious projects, the Roman Catholic **Church of the Sacred Heart**. This betrays a strong Italianate influence, with a facade of white pillars supporting a canopy set against a dark brick background, and circular colonnaded turrets rising above the roof to each side of the entrance porch. The lofty interior has a towering curved roof, polished stone floors and broad arches set into smooth walls, and is far grander than would be expected from the largely stark and unadorned facade.

Paharganj

The bazaar of **Paharganj**, leading west from New Delhi railway station, lies a few minutes' walk north of Connaught Place. Renowned for its budget hotels (see p.100), it's also packed with restaurants, fruit and vegetable stalls, pharmacies, public phone booths, travel agents, and shops selling anything from brass bells, kettles and clothes to perfumed bath oil and wooden massage kits. Off the main thoroughfare tall houses teeter over winding alleys, where children play among chickens and pigs, and the commercial city seems miles away.

National Museum

Janpath. Tues–Sun 10am–5pm. Admission free.

Delhi's largest museum, providing the best general overview of Indian culture and history, is the **National Museum**, packed with exhibits ranging over five thousand years. It takes several hours to get around the whole thing, which follows a circular plan, with galleries arranged around a central yard. A small shop in the entrance hall sells postcards, books and souvenirs, and has details of daily film shows (2.30pm).

The ground floor is dominated by architectural displays, setting off with simple stone **Neolithic** tools (3000–1500 BC), and shell and bone jewellery excavated from **Indus Valley civilization** sites such as Mohenjo Daro and Harappa in Pakistan, Lothal (Gujarat) and Kalibangan (Rajasthan). Carved pillars and statues from the **Mauryan** empire (250 BC) feature typical designs such as the Emperor Ashoka's lion motif and common Buddha symbols: lotus blossoms, *bodhi* trees, *stupas*, footprints and wheels. An assortment of **Gupta** (400AD) terracottas includes imposing statues of the river goddesses, Ganga and Yamuna, who stand with water vessels in their hands, and can often be seen guarding temple sanctuaries. **South Indian** temple architecture is represented by a series of bold rounded sandstone figures from Pallava temples, dominated by Shiva and his consort, and some more intricate dark grey stone friezes from later Chola constructions. Stone and bronze **Buddhist** statues from India are set beside exquisitely designed Thai figurines, such as the elegant Tara (Goddess of Wisdom), fashioned in jade and crowned with a jewelled tiara. Take a little time to absorb the complexity of the Tibetan manuscripts, painted in sweeping black-ink characters and illustrated in extraordinarily minute detail.

Another gallery on the ground floor holds a superb collection of bejewelled clothes, dark-wood boxes inlaid with mother-of-pearl, fierce swords, daggers and spears, silk tapestries and ivory ornaments, all of which belonged to the powerful **Moghul** rulers who combined art forms from Persia, Afghanistan and India to create a unique and elaborate style. The Moghul theme is continued on the first floor, where Persian and Arabic manuscripts include the handwritten memoirs of Emperor Jahangir (1605–27). Other paintings on this floor show the work of several Indian schools, the most distinctive of which are the **Pahari** miniatures of the Himalayan regions of Gharwal and Kangra – simple yet striking scenes of courtly life and loving couples, whose fine lines were often drawn using a single hair. Continuing through the first-floor galleries you'll come across a section devoted entirely to models and masks made in **Nagaland**, whose long straight noses, square set faces and slanted eye-slits evoke Peruvian art: the assorted masks and religious statues from Morocco, Peru and Costa Rica on the second floor make for interesting comparison. Also tucked away on the upper floor are several thick-set and intricately carved wooden doors, lintels and window shutters, examples of the elaborate carpentry that remains a strong tradition in **Gujarat**. The three hundred musical instruments on display in the adjoining gallery represent only part of India's vast musical tradition – it's a good collection, but if you want an even better insight into Indian music, head for *Sangeet Natak Akademi* (see opposite).

Nehru Memorial Museum and Library

Teen Murti Marg. Tues–Sun 9.30am–5pm. Admission free.

Built in 1930 as the residence for the British Commander in Chief, the **Nehru Memorial Museum and Library** later became the home of India's first Prime Minister, Jawaharlal Nehru. Set amid formal gardens, the grand house faced in stone and stucco has a sombre feel that was originally meant to project power and position. Nehru's rooms are immaculately preserved; the personal effects in his bedroom provide a glimpse, through sheet-glass, into his life and times. Elsewhere, his role in the Independence struggle is related through photographs, letters and cuttings. Daily film shows are at 11am and 3pm; an adjoining planetarium proves just as popular.

National Gallery of Modern Art

Jaipur House, near India Gate. Daily 10am–5pm. Admission free. ☎382 5835.

Once the residence of the Maharaja of Jaipur, the extensive **National Gallery** is a rich showcase of Indian contemporary art. Its ground floor, focusing on post-1930s work, has many of the best exhibits, including pieces by the "Bengali Renaissance" artists Abanendranath Tagore and Nandalal Bose, the great poet and artist, Rabindranath Tagore, and Jamini Roy, whose work, reminiscent of Modigliani, reflects the influence of Indian folk art. Also on show are the romantic paintings and etchings of Thomas Daniell and his nephew William, British artists of the Bombay, or Company, School. An **Art Reference Library** has a large collection of art books, journals and periodicals.

Indira Gandhi Memorial

1 Safdarjung Rd. Daily 9.30am–5pm. Admission free. ☎301 0094.

Something of a shrine to the late Prime Minister, the **Indira Gandhi Memorial Museum** holds an assortment of her possessions, photographs and memorabilia. The *sari* she was wearing when she was assassinated, here in her home, by her own body-guards in the cause of Sikh separatism, has been encased for posterity in glass, with its bloodstains chemically preserved. The museum reflects the reverence in which Indira Gandhi was held by many Indians, and the psychological gap left by her demise.

National Museum of Natural History

FICCI Building, Tansen Marg. Mon–Sun 10am–5pm. Admission free. ☎331 4932.

Galleries at the **National Museum of Natural History** illustrate natural resources and ecology from all over the world, and especially India. Along with models of dinosaurs, stuffed animals and birds and fossils, there are supervised activity rooms in which children learn to model animals and handle specimens. Such appreciation of ecological issues is all too rare in India, where forests and natural habitat are fast disappearing, and the list of endangered species is growing rapidly.

National Philatelic Museum

Dak Bhavan, Sardar Patel Chowk, Sansad Marg. Mon–Fri 9am–4pm. Admission free.

The **National Philatelic Museum**, with its collection of rare stamps, first-day covers and special cancellations, is all but impossible to find. It's housed in the large post office on Sansad Marg (Parliament St), but no signs point the way and visitors have to rely on erratic directions. A counter sells stamps from all over the world.

Sangeet Natak Akademi

Rabindra Bhavan, Firoz Shah Rd. Mon–Fri 9.30am–6pm. Admission free. ☎38 7246.

India's premier institution for music (*sangeet*), dance (*natak*), and the performing arts, **Sangeet Natak Akademi** is more of a resource centre than a museum, with a large audio-visual archive, photographs and films.

A gallery displays an extensive collection of folk and classical musical instruments, masks and costumes, while its library holds all sorts of rare and otherwise unobtainable volumes.

Tibet House

1 Institutional Area, Lodi Rd. Mon–Sat 10am–1pm & 2–5pm. Rs1. ☎61 1515.

Tibet House, a cultural centre that organizes seminars, monthly lectures, and retreats, also has a small and somewhat limited museum of Tibetan art. Displays include *thangkas* (painted scrolls), old currency notes, costumes, objects of prayer and musical instruments, and a shop sells clothes, jewellery, medicines, incense and curios.

Crafts Museum

Pragati Maidan, Bhairon Rd. Daily 9.30am–5.30pm. Admission free. ☎331 8287 or 331 7641.

Immediately north of Purana Qila, the **Crafts Museum** is a uniquely dynamic exhibition of the rural arts and crafts of India. Its village complex displays an assortment of building traditions, bringing together cultures from throughout the subcontinent to provide a unique if artificial insight into rural life.

Authentically constructed mud huts are beautifully decorated with folk art, and exhibits include wood carvings, paintings, papier mache and pottery. Live demonstrations by the artisans themselves, and a well-stocked crafts shop, offer close-up glimpses of the folk arts that can be all too difficult to obtain as you travel elsewhere in the country.

South Delhi

Most of the early settlements of Delhi, including its first cities, are to be found not in "Old Delhi" but in **South Delhi**, the area south of Connaught Place. Although the rapid expansion of suburban Delhi is systematically swallowing up the countryside, it remains littered with monuments from the past, and pockets of almost untouched rural peace make it a fascinating blend of the contemporary, the pastoral and the historic. This mix of urban and rural is at its most startling in the housing enclaves and shopping precincts springing up throughout the vast area, such as the fashionable **Hauz Khas**.

Early Muslim kingdoms built their cities on the foundation of earlier settlements, creating the **Qutb Minar Complex**; the later developments of **Siri**, **Tughluqabad**, **Jahanpanah**; **Firozabad**, north along the river; and **Shergarh**, around the **Purana Qila**. **Humayun's Tomb**, which heralded the great Moghul period in architecture, is not far from the elegant **Lodi Gardens** and one of the holiest shrines of Sufism, **Hazrat Nizamuddin**. Development has been haphazard, so communications have not always kept pace, and access to sites is not always easy.

Purana Qila

Daily, dawn–dusk. Admission free. Served by buses between Delhi Gate and Sundernagar such as #423 and #438. The #411 continues to nearby Nizamuddin, and #482 goes on to Kalkaji.

The majestic fortress of **Purana Qila**, whose crumbling ramparts dominate the busy **Mathura Road**, 4km southeast of Connaught Circus, is often said to stand on the site of **Indraprastha**, the city of the Pandavas, of *Mahabharata* fame. More certainly, it was the centre of the sixth city of Delhi, created by Humayun, the second Moghul emperor, as **Din-Panah**, and renamed **Shergarh** by Sher Shah, who briefly displaced him.

Two principal buildings survive to hint at the former glories of the fortress. The **Qila-i-Kuhna Masjid** is one of Sher Shah's finest monuments. Constructed in 1541 in the Afghan style, influenced by Indo-Islamic architecture, it consists of five elegant arches, embellished with white and black marble to complement the red sandstone. The **Sher Mandal**, a red sandstone octagonal observatory and library, was the scene of the death of Humayun, just a year after he defeated Sher Shah and returned to power. He stumbled down its treacherously steep steps in 1556 as he answered the *muezzin*'s call to prayer; visitors today can climb to the top for panoramic views of Delhi and the River Yamuna to the east. The fortress is entered through the lofty south gate, **Lal Darwaza**, just inside which a small museum houses sculpture from the Mauryan era (daily 8am–6.30pm; free).

The few other remains of the once-extensive sixth city include the grey and red arch known as **Sher Shah's Gate**, and **Khair-ul-Manzil Masjid**, built in 1561 during the reign of Akbar for use as a *madrasa* or seminary, whose cloistered courtyard is reached via an elegant large sandstone gateway opposite Lal Darwaza and the zoo.

The Yamuna formerly flowed along the eastern base of Purana Qila; the moats it fed are now dry, save a lake to the west used for boating. During the painful Partition of India in 1947, hordes of Muslim refugees gathered within the confines of the fort, in extremely unhygienic conditions and amid great much trepidation, to await transportation to the newly-created nation of Pakistan.

Zoo

Daily except Fri; summer 8am–6pm, winter 9am–5pm. Admission Rs0.50.

Below the southern ramparts of the Purana Qila, the open-air enclosures and cages of **Delhi Zoo** cover an extensive area. Although it may look attractive, a visit may well severely disappoint anyone who loves animals. It does house some magnificent white tigers, but nothing is done to educate visitors, and as a result the disdainful creatures have to submit to prods and taunts all day long. Recent allegations of corruption against zoo officials regarding the sale of animals further taint the picture.

Lodi Gardens

The leafy, pleasant **Lodi Gardens** (previously Lady Willingdon Park; daily 5am–8pm; free) form part of a belt of fifteenth- and sixteenth-century monuments, 4km south of Connaught Circus, that now stand incongruously amid golf greens, large bungalows and privileged estates. The park is especially full in the early mornings and early evenings, when middle-class fitness enthusiasts come for brisk walks or to jog through the manicured gardens against a backdrop of much-graffitied medieval monuments.

Near the centre of the gardens is the imposing **Bara Gumbad** (Large Dome), a square late-fifteenth-century tomb capped by the eponymous dome. While its monotonous exterior is relieved by grey and black stones, the inside is adorned with painted stucco work. The mosque alongside was built in 1494, with a rectangular prayer hall faced by five arched openings. Heavily ornamented with coloured tiles, foliage and Koranic inscriptions, the tapering Tughluq-style minarets next to the *mihrab* seem to herald the octagonal towers of the coming Sur and Moghul period. **Shish Gumbad**

(Glazed Dome), a similar tomb 50m north, still bears a few traces of the blue tiles liberally used to form friezes below the cornice and above the entrance. Inside, plasterwork is inscribed with ornate Koranic inscriptions.

The octagonal **tomb of Muhammad Shah** (1434–44) of the Sayyid dynasty, stands 300m southwest of Bara Gumbad, surrounded by verandahs and pierced by arches and sloping buttresses. Accented by turrets at each corner, a sixteen-sided drum supports a majestic dome. Enclosed within high walls and a square garden, 300m north of Bara Gumbad, the **tomb of Sikandar Lodi's** (1517–18) repeats the octagonal theme, with a central chamber encircled by a verandah. **Athpula** (Eight Piers), a sixteenth-century ornamental bridge, lies just east, in the northwest corner of the park.

Nizamuddin

Now engulfed by a busy road network and plush suburbs, the *mahalla* (neighbourhood) of **Nizamuddin** is almost isolated from the rest of the city; to enter it is like passing through a time warp into the middle ages. The heart of the village is just off the busy Mathura Road, 6km south of Connaught Circus, and easily accessed by public transport such as the #454 bus, which passes Paharganj and Palika Bazaar.

Alleys lead past shops selling flowers and accoutrements of worship to the marble courtyard of one of Sufism's greatest shrines, **Hazrat Nizamuddin Dargah**. The tomb of the fourth saint of the Chishtia order, Sheikh Nizamuddin Aulia (1236–1325), was built the year he died, but has been through several renovations, and the present mausoleum dates from 1562. A distinctive white marble dome ornamented with vertical black lines, crowns its small square chamber surrounded by marble-faced verandahs. Lattice screen and arches in the inner sanctum surround the actual tomb, enclosed by a marble rail and a canopy of mother-of-pearl. Religious song and music play an important role among the Chishtias, and *qawwals* (bards) gather to sing in the evenings (especially on Thursdays and feast days). Sheikh Nizamuddin's disciple, the poet and chronicler **Amir Khusrau** – considered to be the first Urdu poet and the founder of *khyal*, the most common form of north Indian classical music – lies in a contrasting red sandstone tomb in front of his master's mausoleum.

Anyone entering either building – both are open to all – should cover their heads with a handkerchief or cap bought or borrowed from one of the stalls selling offerings.

QAWWALI

Of all Indian art forms, **qawwali** is among the most adaptable and versatile, appearing as popular entertainment at modern weddings and on concert platforms. Nonetheless, its prime purpose is to gain *hal* (spiritual ecstasy). Musically, *qawwali* is linked to the north Indian classical form of vocal music, *khyal*, deriving its melody from such sources as classic *ragas* (modal compositions) and its own forms based on central Asian roots. Comprising a chorus led by solo singing accompanied by the clapping of hands and usually a harmonium combined with *dholak* (double-membraned barrel drum) and *tabla* (paired hand-drums), the resulting hypnotic rhythm can inspire its audience into a state of *mast* (spiritual intoxication), manifested in wild swaying and swinging of the head. The various simple but effective drum patterns used include *qawwali tal*, *dadra*, and *keherwa* – respectively four-, six- and eight-beat rhythmic cycles.

Most *qawwals* (as the performers are called) are hereditary musicians who trace their lineage back to **Amir Khusrau**, to whom several songs are attributed. Some compositions have become universal hymns, such as the haunting *Dam-a-dam mast Qalandar* (constantly intoxicated Qalandar) and the robust *hamd* (a eulogy in praise of God, the Prophet, or a saint), *Allah Hu*. Musical gatherings, known as *Mehfil-e Sama*, are held regularly in *dargahs* such as Nizamuddin and in Ajmer, with especial poignancy during the *urs* (anniversary) of the saint in question.

Sheikhs hover about ready to assist and take donations off visitors. Twice a year, on the anniversaries of the deaths of Sheikh Nizamuddin and Amir Khusrau, an *urs* (religious fair) draws thousands of pilgrims, and Nizamuddin resounds to the sound of *qawwali*.

The oldest building in the area, the red sandstone mosque of **Jam-at Khana Masjid**, looms over the main *dargah* on its western side. It was built in 1325 by Khizr Khan, the son of Ala-ud-din-Khalji. Enclosed by marble lattice screens next to Amir Khusrau's mausoleum, the tomb of **Princess Jahanara**, the favourite daughter of Shah Jahan, is topped by a hollow filled with grass in compliance with her wish to have nothing but grass covering her grave. At the north gate of the *dargah's* compound is a holy *baoli* (step-well), next to the mosque **Chini-ka-Burj** (Tower of Tiles) named for its upper chamber profusely decorated with coloured tiles.

Prominent Muslims buried in Nizamuddin include **Mirza Ghalib**, the nineteenth-century poet whose work lives on in *ghazals* (devotional and love poetry, often set to music) popular throughout the Urdu-speaking world. Alongside is the elegant marble pavilion of **Chausath Khamba** (Sixty-Four Pillars), built in 1625.

Humayun's Tomb

Close to the medieval Muslim centre of **Nizamuddin**, 2km from Purana Qila and 500m from Nizamuddin railway station, **Humayun's Tomb** stands at the crossroads of the Lodi and Mathura roads. Delhi's first Moghul tomb, it was constructed from 1564 onwards, after the death of the second Moghul emperor, under the watchful eye of Haji Begum, Humayun's senior widow and mother of Akbar, who camped here for the duration. The grounds were later used to inter several prominent Moghuls, and served as a refuge for the last emperor, Bahadur Shah II, captured here by the British in 1857.

Though later eclipsed by the Jama Masjid and the Taj Mahal, its sombre elegance marks this as one of Delhi's finest historic sites. Constructed of red sandstone, inlaid with black and white marble, on a commanding podium looking towards the Yamuna, it stands in the centre of the formal *charbagh*, or quartered garden. The enclosure is dissected into quarters by causeways and channels, and each square is further quartered. Rising on an arcaded platform, the octagonal structure is crowned with a double dome that soars to a height of 38m – the inner shell forms the vaulted ceiling. Porches on each side rise to 12.2-metre-high pointed arches, flanked by outer bays and recessed windows with lattice screens of stone and marble. Below the cenotaph, inside the building, are the graves of Humayun and Haji Begum.

Among tombs of uncertain origin nearby is **Nila Gumbad** (Blue Dome), an octagonal tomb with a dome of blue tiles, to the southeast outside the enclosure. Nila Gumbad was supposedly built by one of Akbar's nobles to honour a faithful servant but may possibly predate Humayun's Tomb. Within the grounds southeast of the main mausoleum, another impressive square tomb has a double dome and two graves inscribed with verses from the Koran. It is tentatively considered to be that of **Babur**, the first Moghul Emperor and father of Humayun. Immediately south of Bu Halima's Garden (who exactly Bu Halima was remains a mystery), which marks the entrance to Humayun's Tomb, the central dome of the tomb of **Isa Khan**, a nobleman of Sher Shah, rises off a 32-sided drum.

Safdarjang's Tomb

The tomb of **Safdarjang**, the Moghul viceroy of Avadh under Muhammad Shah (1719–48), and the father of the Nawab of Avadh, Shuja-ud-Daula, stands at the end of the Lodi Road, 5km southwest of Connaught Place. Built between 1753 and 1774, it is one of the last in the tradition of Moghul garden tombs. At the centre of another *charbagh*, reached through a grand double-storeyed gateway off a busy main road to the east, the double-storeyed mausoleum, made of red and buff sandstone and relieved by marble, rises on a dramatic platform overlooking the adjacent airport of the *Delhi Flying Club*.

However, its inordinate height and bulbous dome somehow lack the grandeur of Humayun's Tomb. A single cenotaph in the square central hall marks the underground tombs of Safdarjang and his wife. Immediately to the south is the site of the battlefield upon which Timur (Tamerlane) routed Muhammad Shah Tughluq in 1398.

Hauz Khas

Hauz Khas, the Soho of Delhi, is a wealthy suburban development, packed with boutiques and restaurants, 12km southwest of Connaught Circus. The "village" is just off Aurobindo Marg (or the Delhi–Mehrauli Road), which leads from the centre to the Qutb Minar Complex, and adjacent to a pleasant deer park. From the shopping enclave, a small road leads to the ruins of Ala-ud-din-Khalji's large tank (enclosed reservoir), built early in the fourteenth century to supply the inhabitants of Siri, Delhi's second city. It was expanded almost fifty years later by Firoz Shah, who added a two-storey *madrasa* (seminary), and a mosque at its northern end. The entire complex was constructed in an L-shape, with latticed windows, and deep stone niches for books.

In among the anonymous tombs scattered throughout the area is that of Firoz Shah himself, next to the southeast corner of the *madrasa*. Its high walls, lofty dome, and doorway spanned by a lintel with a stone railing outside, are fine examples of Indian traditions effectively blended with Islamic architecture. Once the site of Timur's camp, the bed of the tank is used today to hold concerts and dance recitals for wealthy tourists who dine against this impressive backdrop (see p.106).

Moth-ki-Masjid

The **Moth-ki-Masjid** mosque, built during the reign of Sikandar Lodi (1488–1517), is now all but abandoned, isolated in a rural setting within the rapidly spreading suburbs of south Delhi, 2km from Hauz Khas off the Delhi–Mehrauli Road. A milestone in the evolution of the Moghul mosque, its three domes, ornate *mihrab* and arches stand on a raised plinth, enclosed by walls pierced by an elegant red sandstone gate to the east. Legend has it that Sikandar Lodi picked a grain of *moth* (a type of lentil), sown by his minister Miyan Bhuwa; doubled and sold again and again, it financed the construction of the mosque. Some houses in the village of the same name still have mangers.

Khirki-ki-Masjid

Firoz Shah's **Khirki-ki-Masjid**, "The Mosque of Windows", famous for its heavy stone lattice windows, lies close to the site of Jahanpanah, Delhi's fourth city, 4km east of Qutb Minar and 13km south of Connaught Circus. The battered bastions of the squat double-storeyed mosque, flanked by short minarets, give it a fortress-like aspect. Its unusual roof, consisting of 25 squares capped by domes and flat sections, is open at the centre to allow light into a dark pillared courtyard, plagued by bats.

Baha'i Temple and Kalkaji

Often compared to the Sydney Opera House, on open ground atop Kalkaji Hill 12km southeast of Connaught Place, Delhi's modern **Baha'i Temple** has become yet another symbol of the city. Dominating the haphazard suburban sprawl, giant white petals of Rajasthani Macrana marble in the shape of an unfolding lotus spring from nine pools and walkways, to symbolize the nine spiritual paths of the Baha'i faith. Inside uniformed tour guides lead you to the central hall, which rises to a height of 30.5m without the distraction of supporting columns. Set amid well-maintained gardens, the temple is at its most impressive when the rays of the setting sun catch the lotus petals. Remove your shoes on entering, and keep silence. Otherwise open from dawn to dusk, the temple is closed to tourists during morning and evening prayers, which last an hour (Tues–Sun 10am & 4pm).

The domed twelve-sided *shakti* **Kalkaji** temple (also known as Kalika or Kalka Devi) lies on the same hill as the Baha'i Temple. Though of no architectural significance, this popular Kali shrine is at the heart of a village that has somehow ignored the march of time, and the Hindu worship of its *mahants* (important *sadhus*) makes a fascinating contrast with the brash new faith of the Baha'is. Kalkaji is a major bus depot – among buses from the centre are #433 and #440 from Connaught Circus.

Ashoka's Rock Edict

Ashoka's Rock Edict was discovered in 1966, engraved on a rock overlooking the Yamuna near Srinivaspuri 11km southeast of Connaught Circus, not far from Kalkaji. A ten-line epigraph in the ancient Brahmi script, one of many such placed at important sites and crossroads throughout Ashoka's vast empire, the inscription proves that Delhi was occupied during the Mauryan period, prior to both Muslim and Rajput settlement. It states that the emperor's exertions in the cause of *dharma* had brought the people of India (*Jambudvipa*) closer to the gods; and that through their efforts, irrespective of their station, this attainment could be increased even further.

Tughluqabad

On a rocky escarpment, 8km east of Qutb Minar and 15km southeast of Connaught Place on the Mehrauli–Badarpur road, stand the crumbling 6.5-kilometre-long battlements of the third city of Delhi, **Tughluqabad**, built during the short reign of Ghiyas-ud-din Tughluq (1321–25). The huge ruins are almost entirely abandoned, overgrown with scrubland and home to nomadic Gujars and rhesus monkeys – which is seen by some as a fulfilment of a curse by the Sufi saint, Sheikh Nizamuddin Aulia (see p.93).

Divided into three main portions, Tughluqabad had its high walled citadel to the south near the present entrance off the main road; only a long underground passage, the ruins of several halls and a tower, now remain. The grid pattern of some of the city streets to the north is still traceable, while the palace area is to the southwest. The southernmost of its thirteen gates still looks down on a causeway, breached by the modern road, that rises above the flood-plain, to link the fortress with **Ghiyas-ud-din Tughluq's Tomb**. Itself resembling a small fortress, it has withstood the ravages of time, rising beyond a massive red sandstone gateway on a high plinth, surrounded by pentagonal stone walls. The distinctive mausoleum consists of sloping walls topped with a marble dome and contains the graves of Ghiyas-ud-din, his wife, their son Muhammad Shah II, and even what is purported to be Ghiyas-ud-din's favourite dog – although dogs are traditionally held to be unclean. The later fortress of **Adilabad**, built by Muhammad Shah II and now in ruins, can be seen on a hillock to the southeast.

Tughluqabad is awkward to get to by **bus**; either take #451 bus from Jantar Mantar to Badarpur, and change onto a Mehrauli-bound service, or take #505 to Mehrauli/Qutb Minar Complex, and catch a bus going east.

Qutb Minar Complex

Daily, dawn–dusk. Admission Rs3. On bus route #505 from Ajmeri Gate.

Above the foundations of **Lal Kot**, settled in the eighth century by the Tomara Rajputs and developed in the twelfth century by the Chauhans, the first monuments of Muslim India, now known as the **Qutb Minar Complex**, stand in well-tended grounds 13km south of Connaught Circus. One of Delhi's most famous landmarks, the fluted red sandstone tower of the **Qutb Minar**, tapers upwards from the ruins, covered with intricate carvings and deeply inscribed verses from the Koran, to a height of 72.5m.

Work on the Qutb Minar started in 1199 as Qutb-ud-din Aibak's victory tower, celebrating the advent of the Muslim dominance of Delhi (and much of the subcontinent) that was to endure until 1857. For Qutb-ud-din, who died four years after gaining power, it marked the eastern extremity of the Islamic faith, casting the shadow of God over east and west. It was also a minaret, from which the *muezzin* called the faithful to prayer. Only the first storey of the Qutb Minar has been ascribed to Qutb-ud-din's short reign; the rest were built by his successor Iltutmish, and the top was restored in 1369 by Firoz Shah, who used marble to face the red sandstone. Access to the balconies via the staircase inside has been closed after a spate of accidents and suicides.

Adjacent to the tower lie the ruins of India's first mosque, **Quwwat-ul-Islam** ("the might of Islam"), built by Qutb-ud-din using the remains of 27 Hindu and Jain temples and the help of Hindu artisans – their influence can be seen in the detail of the masonry and the indigenous corbelled arches. Steps lead to an impressive courtyard flanked by cloisters and supported by pillars unmistakeably taken from a Hindu temple, while especially fine ornamental arches, rising as high as 16m, remain of what was once the prayer hall. Beautifully carved sandstone screens, combining Koranic calligraphy with the Indian lotus, form a facade immediately to the west of the mosque, facing Mecca. Iltutmish and his successors extended the mosque, enlarging the prayer hall and the cloisters and introducing such Islamic architectural traditions as geometric designs, calligraphy, glazed tiles set in brick, and squinches (arches set diagonally to a square to support a dome).

In complete contrast to the predominant Islamic surroundings, an **Iron Pillar** bearing fourth-century inscriptions of the Gupta period, 7.2m high and 37cm in diameter, stands in the courtyard of the mosque. Once topped with an image of the Hindu bird god, Garuda, the extraordinary and virtually rust-free pillar, made of 98 percent pure iron, is a puzzle to metallurgists. It must have been transplanted here, but its origins remain hazy. Tradition has its that anyone who can encircle the column with their hands behind their back will have their wishes granted.

Ala-i-Darwaza, a mausoleum-like gateway with stone lattice screens, was added by Ala-ud-din Khalji (1296–1316). Its inlaid marble embellishments are owed to an influx of artisans from Byzantine Turkey, and the import of Seljuk influences – the true arches were the first in India. The south entrance to the complex is marked by yet another tower, **Alai Minar**. Planned as grander and larger than the Qutb Minar, it was left abandoned after the construction of its 24.5-metre-high first storey.

On a plinth west of Quwwat-ul-Islam, the **Tomb of Iltutmish**, built in 1235 by the ruler himself, was the first Muslim mausoleum in India – something new to the subcontinent, as Hindus cremate their dead rather than bury them. A relatively plain exterior blending Indian and Muslim styles, with three ornate arches, hides an interior nine metres square with geometric arabesque patterns combined with calligraphy and lotus and wheel motifs. The square red-sandstone chamber was once covered by the dome that now lies in pieces around the site; only its corbelled squinches bear witness to a flawed method of early Indo-Islamic building.

Ala-ud-din-Khalji's Tomb and Madrasa (theological college), lies on the southwest perimeter of Quwwat-ul-Islam, its L-shaped structure reflecting the Seljuk influence. To the southeast of the Ala-i-Darwaza is the small and attractive tomb of the Sufi saint Imam Muhammad Ali, better known as **Imam Zamin**, a native of Turkestan who came to India during the reign of Sikandar Lodi (1488–1517).

The octagonal Moghul tomb of Muhammad Quli Khan, one of Akbar's courtiers, 150m southeast of the Qutb Minar, was occupied and converted by **Charles Metcalfe**, Resident at the Moghul Court, into a country house but is now in ruins. Outside the complex, north of the Qutb Minar, **Adham Khan's Tomb** stands on the remains of the walls of Lal Kot. A general in Akbar's army, he was hurled from the ramparts of Agra Fort on the orders of the emperor after some murderous court feuding.

Cafes and a good restaurant at the complex offer refreshments, while Mehrauli, adjacent to it, is developing as a chic shopping centre.

Rail Transport Museum

Chanakyapuri. Tues–Sun 9.30am–5.30pm. Adults Rs2, children Rs1, plus Rs5 for cameras.

Venerable trains remain in use throughout the country, but to see the cream of India's royal coaches and her oldest engines, you should head for the **Rail Transport Museum** in Chanakyapuri. Outside, 27 locomotives and 17 carriages stand on short tracks in the open air. Look out for the ornate gold-painted saloon car of the Maharaja of Baroda (1886), the teak carriage of the Maharaja of Mysore, trimmed in gold and ivory, and the cabin used by the Prince of Wales in 1876. Steps beside each carriage enable visitors to peer in without damaging the well-preserved interiors.

The covered section of the museum is a delight for train buffs, with models of famous engines and coaches, explanations of the workings of narrow- and broad-gauge lines, displays of old tickets, and even the skull of an elephant hit by a train near Calcutta in 1894. The pride of the museum is a model of India's very first train, a steam engine which made its maiden voyage of 21 miles from Bombay to Thana in 1853. Train spotters who wish to delve deeper can ask the curators to open the library.

Accommodation

As befits a capital city, Delhi has a healthy mix of **places to stay**, and you'll have no difficulty finding anything from a dirt-cheap lodge to an extravagant international hotel. Bookings for upmarket hotels can be made at the tourist desks at the airports and railway stations, but budget travellers have to do their searching on their own.

The hotels of **Connaught Circus** cover all price ranges, are handy for banks, restaurants and shops, and have good transport connections to all the main sights. North of Connaught Circus, the busy market area of **Paharganj**, close to New Delhi railway station, has the best of the budget accommodation, and **Old Delhi** has some even cheaper hotels. The main youth hostel is in the **south**, otherwise very much the preserve of Delhi's top **luxury hotels**, most complete with bars, discos, swimming pools and health clubs.

Central Delhi

Staying in **central Delhi** makes sense if you want to take ITDC tours which start from Janpath, catch the airport bus, or get to Old Delhi on the cheap and bumpy *fut-futs* that gather near Palika Bazaar. The area is also somewhat quieter than Paharganj.

The circular **Connaught Circus**, Delhi's commercial hub, and the southbound radial road, **Janpath**, have between them a full cross-section of accommodation. The least expensive lodges, huddled around the north end of Janpath, near the Government of India tourist office, offer dorms as well as rooms, but are cramped, over-priced and often full. Within the curved colonial lanes of Connaught Circus you'll find moderately priced hotels of varying standards. Further south the upmarket towers on and around Janpath and along **Sansad Marg** cater mainly to business travellers and tourist groups. Most of these have plush restaurants, bars, and **American plan** rooms (which include meals), and some have pools – all add heavy taxes to their bills.

Inexpensive

Asia Guest House, 14 Scindia House (☎331 3393). Central a/c hotel, above the *Air France* office, with spartan, but spacious and clean, windowless rooms, and an amicable atmosphere. ③.

Mrs Colaco's, 3 Janpath Lane (☎332 8758). Another pleasant alternative to crowded lodges, in a quiet family house with basic rooms and dorms, and common bathrooms. ③.

Gandhi Guest House, 80 Tolstoy Lane, behind Scindia House (☎332 1113). Less cramped than the neighbouring lodges, with larger rooms and a tiny roof area. Standards of hygiene could improve, and the dorms leave much to be desired. All rooms have shared bath, hot water in winter. ③.

ACCOMMODATION PRICE CODES

All **accommodation prices** in this book have been coded using the symbols below. In principle the prices given are for the least expensive double rooms in each establishment; however, some hotels, usually in category ①, offer rates per bed rather than per room. Local taxes are not included unless specifically stated. For more details, see p.34.

①	up to Rs100	④	Rs225–350	⑦	Rs750–1200
②	Rs100–150	⑤	Rs350–500	⑧	Rs1200–2200
③	Rs150–225	⑥	Rs500–750	⑨	Rs2200 and up

Mr SC Jain's Guest House, 7 Pratap Singh Building, Janpath Lane. Large, plain rooms with shared bathrooms in a laid-back family bungalow, away from the noise and bustle of Janpath. Small front verandah with comfy wicker chairs. ②–③.

Janpath Guest House, 82–84 Janpath (☎332 1935). Spacious but stuffy carpeted rooms, all with private bath and some with a/c. ④.

Ringo Guest House, 17 Scindia House (☎331 0605). Cramped but friendly lodge, popular for its rooftop dorms. Individual rooms are poky and airless, but offer privacy and undisturbed sleep. ③.

Sunny Guest House, 152 Scindia House (☎331 2909). Also crowded but friendly, with rooms and dorms squeezed onto a tiny roof. No spaces between dorm beds, and noisy fans, but pleasant roof terrace, clean bathrooms, helpful management, and booking facilities for private buses. ③–④.

Moderate

Alka, 16/90 G-Block, Connaught Circus (☎34 4328). Stuffy but comfortable carpeted rooms, all with TV and a/c, few with windows. Excellent in-house veg restaurant. ⑦.

Bright, 85 M-Block, Connaught Place (☎332 1433). Dismal rooms and an uninspiring atmosphere. Rooms with or without bath, and some with air cooler and a/c. ④–⑤.

Hotel Fifty-Five, 55 H-Block, Connaught Place (☎332 1244). A moderate hotel that has definitely seen better and cleaner days. Reasonably sized rooms, bar and balcony terrace. ⑥.

ITDC Ashoka Yatri Niwas, 19 Ashoka Rd (☎332 4511). The airport bus stops here, but it really should be a last resort. Service is terrible, rooms damp, blankets rationed (and expensive), the plumbing atrocious and the lifts, to all fifteen storeys, slow. Check-in and -out can take an hour. ⑤.

Jukaso Inn, L-Block, Connaught Place (☎332 4977). Pristine but unimaginative marble-walled rooms with attached bath. No lift to higher floors, and small rooms that hardly justify the price. ⑦.

Metro, 49 N-Block, Connaught Place (☎331 3856). Despite visible ageing, and a severe lack of maintenance, the large shabby rooms of this once-grand hotel retain a little of their former charm. ⑥.

Nirula's, L-Block, Connaught Place (☎332 2419). Fairly smart hotel, with a handful of small, cosy rooms and a variety of restaurants. Often full. ⑦.

Palace Heights, D-Block, Connaught Place (☎332 1419). Very central. Small rooms, some with windows, some a/c, and a cosy atmosphere. Pleasant balcony terrace. ④–⑥.

YMCA Tourist Hostel, Jai Singh Rd (☎31 1915). Staid and sterile place with sermons played on loudspeakers. Good restaurants, swimming pool and attractive gardens. Ordinary and a/c rooms, and a reliable hot water suppply in both the common and private bathrooms. ⑥–⑦.

York, K-Block, Connaught Place (☎332 3069). Soulless place, with tatty a/c rooms. ⑦.

YWCA International Guest House, 10 Sansad Marg (☎31 1561). Clean and airy a/c rooms with private bathrooms, most, but not all, occupied by women. Set meals in the hostel's restaurant. Foreign currency preferred. ⑦.

Expensive

Holiday Inn, Barakhamba Rd (☎332 0101). American-style towers, extremely spacious, with efficient service, fussy decor and several good restaurants; some may find it a bit impersonal. ⑨.

The telephone **area code** for Delhi is ☎011.

Imperial, Janpath (☎332 5332). Plush, well-maintained rooms with an unmistakably European flavour. Swimming pool (Rs300 for non-residents), shops and beauty parlour, and several restaurants. Non-resident Indians must pay in foreign currency. ⑨.

ITDC Kanishka, 19 Ashoka Rd (☎332 4422). The best government-run hotel in the area. Comfortable but unimaginative rooms, on eighteen storeys, all with TV and clean bathrooms. Swimming pool, bars and food halls, including a rooftop restaurant. ⑧.

Janpath, Janpath (☎332 0070). Declining hotel with a stale moth-ball ambience and poor service, but some exceptionally good restaurants. ⑨.

Marina, 59 G-Block, Connaught Circus (☎332 4658). Old but refurbished hotel with sizeable rooms and good service, at inflated rates. Rooms facing the road are constantly invaded by traffic noise. The travel counter organizes tours, and books onward journeys. ⑨.

Le Meridien, Windsor Place (☎371 0101). Posh hotel, with all the frills and a tax on everything. Glitzy futuristic design, fourth-floor swimming pool, health club, restaurants, bars and disco. ⑨.

Park, 15 Sansad Marg (☎35 2477). Comfortable but soulless rooms with carpets, bathtubs, fridges, TV and room service, and views over Jantar Mantar from the front. Not the best of its category. ⑨.

Paharganj

The **Paharganj** area, just east of New Delhi railway station, a popular hunting ground for inexpensive and mid-range accommodation, is a lively scene of typical Indian city life – see p.89 – that you'll miss if you stay in Connaught Circus, just ten minutes' walk south. The railway station, for all onward rail bookings, is a stone's throw away, and it's also the kind of place where you can buy from other travellers things they no longer need: *Enfield* motor bikes, rucksacks, camping gear, malaria tablets and so forth.

Lodges at knock-down prices are invariably poky, stuffy and grubby, with rickety beds, moth-eaten mattresses and thin partition walls, but if you're intent on finding a budget room, there are exceptions in the alleys off the **Main Bazaar**, which runs west from New Delhi railway station for roughly 1km. The area lacks the space enjoyed by hotels further south, and the narrow main street is constantly blocked with cars, rickshaws, and mopeds billowing exhaust fumes into the air and fighting for space with cycles, carts and wandering bovines. Each day sees several crashes and mini pile-ups.

Note, too, that Paharganj is notorious for its hotel **touts**, and it's not uncommon for rickshaw drivers to announce that the hotel you're heading for has burnt down, gone bankrupt, changed its name, or simply never existed. Be firm and stand your ground.

Ajay Guest House, 5084-A Main Bazaar (☎777 7617). Marble decor and well-kept, clean, small rooms, most with baths but no outside windows. Good-value dorms and an airy roof terrace. ②–③.

Anand, 2537/48 Chuna Mandi (☎52 6911). A reasonably clean place close to *Imperial Cinema*, with long balconies on each floor. Some rooms with fridge, all with bath. ③.

Anoop, 1566 Main Bazaar (☎73 5219). Clean, modern lodge with a rooftop restaurant. ③.

Bright, 1089–1090 Main Bazaar (☎752 5852). Clean, inexpensive, and often full. Small rooms around a courtyard – extra charges for blankets and hot water. ①.

Camran Lodge, 1116 Main Bazaar (☎52 6053). Small lodge with an interesting carved facade and more character than the newer hotels, despite being dim and poky. ②.

Hare Rama Guest House, 298 Main Bazaar (☎752 9293). Popular, modern, marble-slab lodge. Poorly ventilated rooms, but good service, with left-luggage and airport taxis. ③.

Kanishta, 22 Main Bazaar (☎52 5365). Uninspiring place close to the railway station with cosy double rooms. Though some are airless, those with balconies are good value. ④.

Madan Guest House, 4362 Main Bazaar (☎73 9943). A smart hotel above *Madan's Store* not far from the railway station, with unremarkable decor but friendly service. ③.

Metropolis, 1634 Main Bazaar (☎52 5492). Paharganj's most upmarket and comfortable hotel, at the westernmost end of the Main Bazaar. Dorm beds are a bit pricier than elsewhere, but there are only four per dorm, and lockers are provided. Some double rooms have a/c, large windows, and a shower with constant hot water. A good restaurant on site. ④–⑥.

Mohit Guest House, 647 Mahalla Bowali, 6 Tooti Chowk (☎52 8592). Budget lodge in a quiet alley set back from the main road. Rarely cleaned – bring your own bedclothes. ①.

Navrang, 644-C Mahalla Bowali, 6 Tooti Chowk (☎52 1965). Adequate and inexpensive rooms, tucked off the main street. ①.

Payal, 1152 Main Bazaar (☎52 0867). Grim, cheap place off the main road, near the station. ②.

Shree Lodge, 2012–2015 Chuna Mandi (☎52 6864). In a quiet alley off Chuna Mandi, all the character of a family house. Simple cosy rooms, spacious great-value suites – and precarious stairs. ①.

Star Palace, 4590 Main Bazaar (☎752 4849). One of Paharganj's more salubrious hotels, with rooms around a central courtyard, TVs, and constant hot water in private bathrooms. The rooftop restaurant is overpriced, but the rooms are good value. ③.

Vijay Guest House, 4459 Katra Raiji, Main Bazaar (☎751 9611). Fresh, well-kept four-storey hotel with constant hot water, blankets, a pleasant roof terrace and friendly management. ③.

Vishal, 1600 Main Bazaar (☎753 2079). Unoriginal marble decor, but clean and comfortable, with a good restaurant. ③.

Vivek, 1534–1550 Main Bazaar (☎52 3015). Popular place, with a 24hr rooftop restaurant, and unremarkable rooms. Most have attached bath and hot water, and room service. The best rooms have windows facing the street, and some are a/c. ③.

Old Delhi and north of Connaught Circus

If you find Paharganj too much of a travellers' hangout, or Connaught Circus too impersonal, head for **Old Delhi**, where foreign tourists seldom stay. Here you'll find yourself swamped by the noise and smells of one of the most quintessentially *Indian* parts of Delhi. Prices are low and standards not very high, but the hotels are well-sited for visits to the Red Fort and Jami Masjid, and you can guarantee constant activity on the crowded streets, excellent meaty food and superb sweets from Muslim roadside stalls.

New Delhi Tourist Camp, Jawaharlal Nehru Marg (☎327 2898). Small bungalows, with cramped but clean single and double windowless rooms, that become fearful heat traps in summer. Plenty of room for camping, and ample parking space; for a minimal fee you can sleep in your vehicle on site. A restaurant serves western, Indian and Chinese food, and there's a laundry service, left-luggage facilities, trekking equipment for rent, a travel agency, and a daily airport bus. Reasonably clean communal washing blocks have hot showers. Good value, but far from Connaught Circus. ①–②.

New India Hotel, 172 Katra Bariyan, Fatehpuri (☎23 5117). Old house, opposite Fatehpuri mosque, where large simple rooms, steeped in the character of the old city, open onto a central courtyard: some double rooms have their own balcony. Basic communal washing facilities. ③.

Oberoi Maidens, 7 Sham Nath Marg (☎252 4422). Top-notch hotel in a colonial mansion north of Old Delhi, not far from the Inter-state Bus Terminal. The pleasant rooms aren't quite as smart as in equivalent hotels, but the location is good; leafy gardens, swimming pool and fine restaurant. ⑨.

Qudsia Gardens Tourist Camp, opposite the Inter-state Bus Terminal (☎252 3121). Camping facilities and dank huts. A feasible option only if you arrive late or need to leave early by bus. ①–③.

Rio Travel Lodge, 1490–1491 Kashmere Gate (☎252 1421). Dismal place, with shabby rooms over a noisy street; a last resort if you get stranded at the Inter-state Bus Terminal late at night. ③.

Sawan Guest House, 1481–1486, E5 Pyare Lal Building, Chandni Chowk (☎252 9515). Simple, small rooms, a minute's walk from the Red Fort. Excellent views over Old Delhi from the balcony. ②.

Star Guest House, 186 Katra Bariyan, Fatehpuri (☎292 1127). Poky, characterless rooms in a fairly new hotel. Worth considering if you can't get into *New India Hotel*. ③.

South Delhi

Most of the accommodation **south of Connaught Circus** lies firmly in the exclusive category, although there are a few guest houses in Sundernagar, the odd mid-range hotel is tucked away in a residential area, and the modern **youth hostel** is near the exclusive diplomatic enclave. The five-star hotels provide Delhi's best restaurants, bars, health centres, night clubs and most exclusive discos – facilities otherwise lacking in a town that dies early each evening. As a result, the city's high society uses them to entertain, be seen and hold lavish weddings, cocooned from the outside world.

Ambassador, Sujan Singh Park (☎463 2600). Next to Khan Market, recently acquired by the *Taj Group*. Comfortable and friendly; no frills and large old-fashioned rooms. Slightly showing its age. ⑧.

Centaur, Delhi Airport (☎548 1411). Serves transit passengers and airline crews. Large and comfortable, with airy rooms and all services, but otherwise characterless. ⑧.

Claridges, 12 Aurangzeb Rd (☎301 0211). An elegant Thirties-style facade leads into the marble foyer of one of Delhi's oldest and finest establishments. Tennis courts and swimming pool. ⑧–⑨.

Hyatt Regency, Bhikaiji Cama Place, Ring Rd (☎688 1234). Smart, elegant and not too brash, with all the comforts of this renowned chain. Excellent eating, plus a fitness and health centre. ⑨.

ITDC Ashok, Chanakyapuri (☎60 0121). A landmark in the grand pseudo-Moghul style, finished in red sandstone. One of Delhi's finest, but not as efficient as some of the new pretenders. ⑨.

ITDC Lodhi, Lala Lajpat Rai Marg (☎436 2422). Built in mock-Tughluq style but otherwise characterless and showing its age, though it does have an open-air swimming pool. ⑦.

Maharani Guest House, 3 Sundernagar (☎69 3128). A comfortable alternative to the usual hotels. Experience residential Delhi in a pleasantly sited, exclusive colony with a good shopping arcade. ⑦.

Maurya Sheraton and Towers, Diplomatic Enclave (☎301 0101). Extremely plush, exclusive and very grand, imposing and expensive. ⑨.

Oberoi, Dr Zakir Hussain Marg (☎436 3030). One of Delhi's first in the super league; manages to retain its elegance without being loud and brash. Highly recommended if you can afford it. ⑨.

Qutab, off Sri Aurobindo Marg (☎66 0060). Concrete and characterless, but otherwise comfortable. All mod cons including tennis courts, swimming pool and the only bowling alley in Delhi. ⑦–⑧.

Samrat, Chanakyapuri (☎60 3030). Comfortable place, behind the *Ashok*, with pretentious five-star treatment aimed at business users. Not very well maintained. ⑨.

Sartaj, A-3, Green Park (☎66 7759). An unusual location in a southern suburb, garish and essentially nouveau riche Indian in taste. ⑥–⑦.

Shyama, C 5/32, Safdarjang Development Area (☎66 5222). Small and friendly, away from the traditional tourist areas in a residential area near the Indian Institute of Technology in south Delhi. ⑥.

Surya Sofitel, Friends Colony (☎683 5070). The only five-star accommodation in this part of southeast Delhi; comfortable, but rather isolated. ⑨.

Taj Mahal, 1 Mansingh Rd (☎301 6162). Ornate and luxurious in the typical grand style of the *Taj Group*, with marble foyer and chandeliers, and an excellent choice of restaurants. ⑨.

Taj Palace, 1 Sardar Patel Marg (☎301 0404). Grand, imposing, very comfortable and exclusive, but otherwise lacking the character of the flagship *Taj Mahal*. ⑨.

Youth Hostel, 5 Naya Marg, Chanakyapuri (☎301 6285). Away from the hustle and bustle of the city centre, ultra-modern building in grey concrete, with dormitories and a limited number of family rooms. The showpiece-cum-administration centre of the Indian YHA. Non-members pay extra. ①.

Eating

Delhi's **restaurants** cater to floods of tourists and business travellers, and menus cover an exhaustive array of dishes from all over the world. There's something for every budget, from delicious Indian dishes served in roadside stalls, to well-made western food (French, English or Italian) in the five-star hotels where expert cooking and careful presentation is reflected by high prices. Makeshift **stalls** in Paharganj, Palika Bazaar and Janpath dish up wonderful fresh snacks; watch out for the cordials sold here, however, as Delhi's **water** is rarely clean enough for Western stomachs. Note that restaurants close early by western standards; if you're looking for a **late-night** meal, you'll either have to eat in a top hotel, or head to the markets of South Delhi.

Connaught Circus

Connaught Circus has snack bars for quick stops, and plenty of upmarket restaurants, as well as budget sit-down joints that attract a largely western clientele. Even if you can't afford a meal in an expensive restaurant, it's worth going into air-conditioned comfort and treating yourself to silver-service tea, filter coffee, or a cool milkshake. For patties, sandwiches and take-out meat and veg dishes, head behind the market at the top of Janpath, where you'll find great snacks at incredibly good value. Larger restaurants remain closed on Sunday mornings.

Amber, 19 N-Block, Connaught Circus (☎331 2092). Typical dimly lit, a/c restaurant catering to wealthy Indians and tourists. Refreshing chilled beer, and great food: veg and non-veg lightly spiced Indian and western choices. Pricey, but good value.

El Arab, Sansad Marg. Great place for Middle Eastern dishes on the corner of Sansad Marg and the outer ring of Connaught Circus, with prices ranging from medium to high. Tasty *hummus*, *baba ghanoush* and Lebanese salads.

Bankura, Janpath. Long-established cafe next to the *Central Cottage Industries Emporium*, with excellent fresh snacks, and imaginative main meals including tasty veg options and heaps of salad. Popular, especially for lunch, and moderately priced.

Cafe 100, B-Block, Connaught Place. Ice creams galore, plus pizzas, burgers, and fries to take away or eat in (standing). Long lunchtime queues; buy a meal ticket before you reach the counter.

The Cellar, beneath *El Arab*. Gastronomic delights for meat-eaters: unbeatable steaks, German salads, roasts and desserts – and outrageously filling bacon-sausage-egg breakfasts (from 10am).

Don't Pass Me By, Scindia House. Friendly, inexpensive Chinese restaurant just off Janpath, popular with travellers staying nearby. Opens early for breakfast – fresh juices, huge bowls of porridge, *corn flacks*, eggs, toast, and great Tibetan bread. Filling but unoriginal meals include noodles, rice and soup. Be prepared to come across the occasional cockroach.

Gaylord, Connaught Circus, off Sansad Marg. High-quality Indian cuisine in plush surroundings lit by glittering chandeliers. Fairly expensive, but good value.

Host, F-Block. A/c relief from the Indian heat, and a good place to sit with a beer, silver-service tea, or strong filter coffee, but the meals are overpriced, and the portions stingy.

Kaveri, Palika Parking Complex. Tasty veg snacks to take away.

Kovil, 2 E-Block, Connaught Place. Fresh, no-smoking restaurant serving exclusively south Indian veg dishes, with great *dosas*. Pricey.

Kwality, Regal Building, Sansad Marg. High standards of service and hygiene, with good but unspectacular international cuisine.

National, opposite L-Block, Connaught Circus. The best of a bunch of inexpensive sit-down restaurants, with great fiery curries, and an endless supply of *chapati*.

Nirula's, 135 L-Block, Connaught Circus. Quality food, including salads and pastries, in downstairs snack bar (serving packed lunches) and first-floor restaurant. The open ground-floor parlour serves over fifty flavours of Delhi's best ice cream. A second branch on N-Block, near the *Wimpy*, is a quick-snack bar, with wonderfully smooth ice-cream shakes.

Parikrama, Kasturba Gandhi Marg. Novel revolving restaurant at a height to beat most of New Delhi's modern buildings. Delicious Indian and western meals and snacks, including a truly spectacular cheese toast. Views over Delhi are superb; a single rotation takes 100 minutes. A great place for a splurge, particularly at sunset. Noon–3pm & 7–10.30pm.

Sona Rupa, 46 Janpath. Undoubtedly the best in the area for good north and south Indian and Chinese food, extremely popular with families. Unfussy surroundings, no-nonsense prices, great food and dramatic *dosa*-flinging in the open-fronted kitchen downstairs. Beer and north Indian food upstairs; buy a food ticket at the till and present it to the cooks.

Surang, *Alka Hotel*, P-Block, Connaught Circus. A minor treat – Tandoori and Mughlai specialities.

United Coffee House, 15 E-Block, Connaught Circus. Multi-cuisine, a/c, and high prices. Not bad for a splurge, but you could do better. Closed Sun.

Vega, *Alka Hotel*, P-Block, Connaught Circus. Delicious, varied pure veg dishes, and a terrace.

Wenger & Co, 16 A-Block, Connaught Circus. Mouthwatering patties, pasties, rolls, cutlets, sandwiches, sweet cream cakes and a variety of bread to take away. Great value.

Wimpy, 5 N-Block, Connaught Circus. American-style joint with burgers, fries, shakes and Chicken nuggets. Popular with students and tourists, but not that great, and pricey for what you get.

Zen, 25 B-Block, Connaught Circus. Excellent Chinese and Japanese meals served in traditional style, with chopsticks, and western snacks (3–7pm). Distinctly upper-class, with prices to match, and a selection of wines, spirits and beers. Noon–3pm & 7–11.30pm.

Paharganj

Food comes inexpensive and unelaborate in the lively market area of **Paharganj**. You can guarantee finding some excellent wholly Indian joints, particularly in the alleys opposite the railway station which waft with the aroma of pungent spices, and where hot *dhals*, meat and veg dishes are freshly cooked nearly all day. Restaurants geared to tourists offer typically poor western imitations and under-spiced "curries", but are popular hangouts, and good for a tame breakfast of toast, porridge, muesli or cereal if you can't stomach chillies too early. Look out too, for meat cuts hanging in shop fronts where you can choose a piece to be grilled or tandooried, and mobile stalls where fresh french fries seasoned with *masala*, salt, pepper and lemon juice, and served in a bowl made of dried leaves, will set you back only Rs5. Roadside juice stalls now stock *Mars Bars*, *Snickers*, *Yoplait* yoghurt, European cheeses, and all brands of international cigarettes.

Appetite, *Hotel Vishal*, 1600 Main Bazaar. Popular travellers' restaurant serving pizzas in addition to the usual Indo-western food. The cable TV is switched on during international sports matches.

Chat House, Main Bazaar. Noodles, soup, *samosas* and red-hot curries at knock-down prices in cramped but clean surroundings.

Khalsa Punjabi Hotel, Main Bazaar. Inexpensive and unelaborate open-fronted food house where the seating overflows onto the pavement. A good place to sit lazily and watch the chaos of the main street. Filling breakfasts and large cups of *chai*.

Lord's Cafe, *Hotel Vishal* , 1600 Main Bazaar. International cuisine, and pretty inexpensive steaks.

Metropolis, 1634 Main Bazaar. Cosy a/c ground-floor restaurant, with the priciest dishes in Paharganj, but great service and tasty food.

EATING IN THE TOP HOTELS OF DELHI

For superlative food, comfortable a/c surroundings, unbeatable service, and hefty bills, head for any of Delhi's luxury hotels. In some, you'll be expected to dress the part.

Ambassador, Sujan Singh Park. *Dasaprakash* is considered one of the best south Indian restaurants in Delhi.

Claridges Hotel, 12 Aurangzeb Rd. The Chinese *Jade Garden* complements the *Dhaba*, designed to look like a trucker's cafe, with a reconstructed truck to add atmosphere – for those who want to eat good *dhaba* cooking without having to go on to the streets.

Holiday Inn, Barakhamba Rd. *Grill Room* is strong on steak and seafood; *Baluchi* serves *tandoori* and food from the Northwest Frontier; the *Rendezvous* is a coffee shop and piano bar with an expensive, limited menu; *Silk Orchid* is a popular Thai restaurant.

Imperial, Janpath. The open-air *Garden Party Restaurant & Bar* has a pleasant atmosphere, and good food.

Janpath, Janpath. The *Mandarin Room* for excellent Chinese dishes, a 24-hr coffee shop, *The Gulnar* for Indian and Mughlai food with accompanying live music, and *The Orbit* for buffet spreads at lunch and dinner.

Kanishka, 19 Ashoka Rd. The *Dilkusha Restaurant*, with international food, plus a tea lounge, a cocktail bar, and a 24-hr coffee shop.

Le Meridien, Windsor Place. The *Pierre* and the nouvelle cuisine *Le Belvedere* are two very good French restaurants; also *Pakwan Restaurant* for tandoori and Mughlai, *Aloha Bar*, and *La Brasserie* coffee shop. All exceptionally high standard, and very expensive.

Oberoi, Dr Zakir Hussain Marg. Besides *La Rochelle*, specializing in French cuisine and the *Taipan* serving Chinese food, *Baan Thai* is Delhi's second and newest Thai restaurant with traditional floor seating known as *khuntoke* as well as contemporary tables and chairs in a teak-lined dining room.

Taj Mahal, 1 Mansingh Rd. A good choice includes the *Casa Medici*, primarily an Italian restaurant but also offering other cuisines at its lunch buffets; the exclusive Chinese *House of Ming*; and *Haveli*, serving Mughlai to the accompaniment of live Indian music and folk dances (try *karhai paneer* – cheese cubes cooked in a wok).

Taj Palace, 1 Sardar Patel Marg. *Tea House of the August Moon*, as featured in the Goon Show, serves excellent Chinese regional cooking; and *Handi* has Indian and Mughlai food.

Sim, *Vivek Hotel*, 1534–1550 Main Bazaar. The *Vivek* restaurant, on the ground floor, is losing business to the new airy rooftop *Sim* (climb the stairs to the fifth floor), lit with fairy lights and candles. Open 24hr for Indian, Chinese and western dishes. Uninspiring food and slow service, but a good atmosphere; bring your own cassettes to play.

Old Delhi

Among the shops, offices and houses in **Old Delhi**'s crowded streets, simple, grubby, unadvertised hole-in-the-wall food halls serve surprisingly good, and invariably fiery Indian dishes for less than Rs15. There are few upmarket places in the heart of Old Delhi, but a number of larger, cleaner restaurants on the outskirts offer surroundings more conducive to leisurely and relaxed eating.

Chor Bazaar, *Hotel Broadway*, Asif Ali Rd. Amusing decor, including a sports car-cum-salad bar, and reasonable, moderately priced food.

Karim's, Matya Mahal. Superb Mughlai cuisine and mouthwatering kebabs in traditional roadside eating house; another branch can be found in Nizamuddin.

Moti Mahal, Netaji Shubash Marg. The first restaurant in Delhi to offer meat and fish cooked in a *tandoor*. Has seen better days, but the food is as good as ever, and there's live *qawwali* singing from 8.30pm on Sat and Sun. Noon–3pm & 7–11pm, closed Tues.

Natraj Bhalla Corner, Chandni Chowk. Extremely busy at lunchtime, this popular snack bar, close to the Town Hall, has delicious Indian and western appetizers and prompt service.

Paratha Wali Gali, Chandni Chowk. A restaurant that's been established here for over a hundred years, with typical Islamic dishes and ageing decor.

Sonis, Nai Sarak. First-floor restaurant just off Chandni Chowk, close to Fatehpuri mosque. Great *thalis* in typically Indian unfussy surroundings.

Tandoor, *Hotel President*, Asif Ali Rd. Great traditional Indian food, plush decor, live Indian classical music and snappy service. Pricey.

Vig Coffee House, Chandni Chowk. A small snack stall just over from the Red Fort serving excellent coffee, cold drinks, *samosas*, toasties and veg burgers.

South Delhi

The enclaves and villages spread across the vast area of **South Delhi** offer countless eating alternatives. Trendy **Hauz Khas**, with its Village Bistro restaurant complex, is renowned as one of Delhi's best areas for dining out, where visitors can combine eating with shopping and sightseeing. The small, chic **Santoshi Shopping Complex** near the diplomatic enclave has one of Delhi's most raved-about restaurants – *Basil & Thyme* – while Chankyapuri, better known for its embassies and top hotels, holds a cluster of **Tibetan** *dhabas* selling *momos* (dumpling) and *thukpa* (soup). The alleys and lanes of the medieval village of **Nizamuddin** conceal cafes and restaurants of varying standards, with the extraordinarily rich Muslim cooking of *Karim's* as the real highlight. Part of the **Asiad Games Village**, built 5km south of Connaught Circus to house the mid-1980s Asian Games, has been converted into a small restaurant complex.

Finally, some **late-night** alternatives, if you need to eat late and don't want to pay five-star prices. The good and popular cafes of **Bengali Market** on Tansen Road, near Connaught Circus and New Delhi railway station, keep going until about 11pm, when much of Delhi has closed up, while the restaurants of **Pandara Road Market**, close to India Gate, are not especially good but they do stay open until 2am

Aangan, Asiad Games Village (☎644 1945). Smart and upmarket, serves Indian food.

Al Capone, the Village Bistro, Hauz Khas Village. Western cuisine.

American Pie, Asiad Games Village (☎644 7230). Fast-food outlet selling burgers etc.

Angeethi, Asiad Games Village (☎644 1945). Specializes in dishes from the Northwest Frontier.

Basil & Thyme, Santushti Shopping Complex. Popular with Delhi's jet set, serving western and Parsi food at very reasonable prices.

THE AWB FOOD BANK

Delhi may be one of the few centres in India to cater to international tourists and high-flying Indian businessmen in plush five-star hotels, but it also has a growing population problem, and a high level of poverty. The disparity between rich and poor has led one Indian man, Varinder Bhalla, to seek cooperation from the city's top hotels in his attempt to provide food for the hungry. Bhalla, a US-based engineer, together with his brother in Delhi, set up the **AWB (Agya Wanti Bhalla) Food Bank** in 1991, with financial aid from other non-resident Indians, and the help of volunteers to run the project. The organization started by collecting left-overs from Delhi's hotels, and distributing it to schools and organizations that care for the needy. Initially it provided one hundred meals a day to children of the Multipurpose Centre for the Deaf and Dumb at Jit Singh Marg in south Delhi, but after only two years the output of meals had increased to over a thousand a day and fed not only deaf and dumb children, but also children from the National Blind Institute, the Lepers' Colony, and those in poor urban housing areas.

With an estimated thirty or forty kilos of food being thrown out daily by each of Delhi's upmarket hotels, and more and more hotels wishing to participate in the project, it is likely that over three thousand meals will be given to Delhi's poor children every day by the end of 1995. The success of Delhi's food bank has led to plans for the establishment of similar projects in Bombay, Calcutta, Madras and Bangalore, which between them aim to give fifteen thousand meals a day to children who would otherwise live on minimal amounts of food or suffer from malnutrition.

Bengali Sweet House, Bengali Market. More than a sweet shop; busy cafe whose menu ranges from *dosas* to onion *kulcha* and *channa* (bread and chickpeas), plus ice creams and milk shakes. Also take-away *makki-ki-roti* (cornbread) with *sarson ka sag* (mustard-leaf spinach) and yogurt.

Chicken Inn, Pandara Rd Market (☎38 5553). Dimly lit but comfortable – the only restaurant in the market selling Chinese food.

Chopsticks, Asiad Games Village (☎644 1945). Airy and smart with excellent Chinese food.

Dakshin, the Village Bistro, Hauz Khas Village. A good south Indian restaurant.

Darbar, the Village Bistro, Hauz Khas Village. Mughlai cuisine, good views from atop Hauz Khas.

Ghalib's Kabab Corner, Nizamuddin. As its name suggests a budget cafe strong on kebabs in a strongly Muslim corner of New Delhi.

Great Wall of the Village, the Village Bistro, Hauz Khas Village. Great, pricey Chinese food.

Karim's, Nizamuddin. Legendary, unmissable Mughlai cooking, though the sumptuous food is very rich. Much-renowned specialities, plus kebabs, *korma* and *rumali roti* (super-thin bread).

Khas Bagh, the Village Bistro, Hauz Khas Village. Tandoori food specializing in kebabs.

Nathu's Sweets, Bengali Market. A busy, similar, rival to the *Bengali Sweet House* across the road.

Osaka, Main Square, Hauz Khas Village. Chinese and Japanese food with a pleasant ambience and gentle on the pocket.

Top of the Village, the Village Bistro, Hauz Khas Village. Popular *tawa* (griddle) and barbecues.

Triveni Kala Sangam, 205 Tansen Marg, near Bengali Market. Excellent little art-centre cafe serving Indian food. Go for lunch, but be prepared to share a table and put up with frantic service.

Shopping

Although the traditional places to shop in Delhi are around **Connaught Place** and **Chandni Chowk**, a number of the suburbs created by the rapid growth of the city are emerging as fashionable shopping districts. The best known of these is the "ethnic chic" shopping area of **Hauz Khas Village**, 12km southwest of Connaught Place, with its boutiques, excellent restaurants, jewellery shops and galleries, some pretentious and others well worth a browse. Well-heeled visitors to this leafy, exclusive residential area can also take in evening dance and music performances, set against the picturesque backdrop of the ruins of Ala-ud-din Khilji's fourteenth-century tank.

The garden complex of **Santoshi Shopping Arcade**, just inside Wellington Barracks next to the *Samrat Hotel* in Chanakyapuri, and run by Air Force officers' wives, is another trendy place, patronized by embassy officials. **Mehrauli**, a new precinct near the Qutb Minar, also holds boutiques and curio shops, as does **Greater Kailash**, a hot spot for "ethnic chic" designer clothes. Elsewhere, self-contained local precincts ranging from bookshops to European vegetables include **Khan Market**, 500m south of India Gate, and **Bengali Market**, off Barakhamba Road, which is especially renowned for its sweet shops and large bustling cafes.

For detailed accounts of the **markets of Old Delhi**, see p.83.

Art, antiques, crafts and jewellery

Much the best area to go shopping for **art and antiques** – even if sceptics do consider it vastly overpriced and rarely authentic – is the small **Sunder Nagar Market**, in a wealthy residential area near Purana Qila and the zoo. However, you shouldn't expect a bargain – the antique and art trade in India is a cut-throat business – and bear in mind that it is illegal to take art objects over 100 years old out of India.

Elsewhere, **curio shops** aimed at tourists sell everything from carpets and fabrics to handicrafts and collectors' items. Few locals bother to venture to the stretch of Janpath known as **Tibetan Market**, packed with vendors feeding off the tourist trade; in fact its shops have a fine assortment of **jewellery**, using semi-precious stone and even silver. Be sure you can tell the difference between silver and white metal.

Central Cottage Industries Emporium, Janpath. Popular and convenient government-run complex, with handicrafts, carpets, leather and reproduction miniatures at fixed (if fractionally high) rates. Jewellery ranges from tribal silver anklets to costume jewellery to precious stones.

Cottage of Arts and Jewels, 50 Hauz Khas Village (☎66 9150). Interesting, eccentric jewellery and papier-mâché. A sift through Mrs Jain's semi-precious stones and trinkets is highly recommended.

Ellora, Shop 9, Sundernagar (☎61 8557). Silver specialists; jewellery and Indian handicrafts.

Friends Electric Company, Shop 25, Sunder Nagar Market (☎61 8061). Makers and exporters of brassware and handicrafts. An interesting array of white metal furniture, plus brass, metal, trinkets, chandeliers and a few antique watches. You never know what you may find.

Jain Super Store, 172 Palika Bazaar, Gate #6. Perfumes, bottles, tea, incense, spices and the like at very reasonable prices.

Kumar Gallery, Sunder Nagar Market. Specializes in antique bronzes and paintings.

Lotus Eaters, Santoshi Shopping Complex. Fashion boutique stocking excellent silver jewellery.

M Zee Handicrafts, 48 Palika Bazaar, Gate 3, Connaught Place. Good for silver jewellery.

Nav-Rattan Arts, Shop 26, Sunder Nagar Market (☎61 6967). As the name ("nine gems") suggests, an emphasis on gems, with jewellery, silver, bronze and tapestries, plus antique perfume bottles.

Poonam Backliwal, Shop 5, Sunder Nagar Market (☎61 1835). Established in 1880, boasting exceptional original miniatures, bronze and stone sculptures, Tanjore glass paintings and medieval jewellery. You may find rare and exquisite Bundi drawings or a miniature of a Moghul emperor.

R-Expo, 1115 Main Bazaar, Paharganj. Aromatic oils, bath stuff, scented candles, sandalwood, massage implements, *chillums*, solid and liquid perfumes; dubious quality, but great presentation.

Works of Art, 1 Hauz Khas Village (☎66 2361). Upmarket gallery with an interesting collection of brass, papier-mâché and frames.

Books

Delhi has a wide selection of places to buy books and magazines. **Pavement vendors** around Connaught Circus will sell you anything from Sidney Sheldon to Vivekananda, as well as guidebooks. **Bookstores** generally lack the western trivia, but sell all kinds of publications in English, Hindi, and other European languages. You'll find books on all aspects of Indian history and culture, and an evergrowing supply of short works by Indian authors published by *Penguin India*. Upmarket **hotels** often have their own bookshops, which usually tend towards the coffee-table market; *Khazana*, at the *Taj Mahal*, and *Jainson's* at *Janpath Hotel*, are worth perusing. Several budget hotels have multi-lingual collections of **secondhand** books for sale, swap or part exchange.

Amrit Book Co, 21 N-Block, Connaught Circus. Vast stock of novels and books on history, philosophy and religion.

Book World, Shop #7, Palika Bazaar. A wealth of glossy hardbacks, architectural books, travelogues and novels. Credit cards accepted.

Moti Lal Benarsi Das, Nai Sarak, Chandni Chowk. One of India's premier publishing institutions, retailing as well as publishing academic books on India.

Oxford Book & Stationery Co, Scindia House. Old and new philosophy and history books, plus a few coffee-table copies, a bulging stock of British classics, and a hoard of language dictionaries.

People Tree, 8 Regal Buildings, Parliament St. Pamphlets and books covering poverty, environmental issues, women's issues and controversial politics, as well as students' art work, T-shirts and jewellery. Also details forthcoming films and lectures at centres such as the Max Mueller Bhavan.

Rajiv Book House, Shop #30, Palika Bazaar. Expensive photo-packed hardbacks, great for gifts and collections, and often reduced in price, as well as cheaper novels and paperbacks.

The Bookshop, Khan Market. One of the best of a few good bookshops in this popular market.

Fabrics and clothes

In Delhi you can buy anything from high-quality silks, homespun cottons, Kashmiri jackets and shawls, to traditional everyday wear and multi-coloured tie-dyed western-style outfits. Buyers are expected to **bargain** in most street-side stalls, which can make shopping all the more fun. Be wary of high prices – the same item is often available in different shops at varying rates. Shops with fixed prices should have a sign to prove it. For western-style trousers, skirts and shirts, try **Paharganj**, the **Tibetan Market** at the north end of Janpath, and **Palika Bazaar**. Beautiful silks and fine cotton are at their best in **government emporia**, most of which are on Baba Kharak Singh Marg.

Delhi also holds a few upmarket **boutiques**, trading in haute couture and furnishings; some, such as *Anokhi*, now have shops all around the world.

Anokhi, Santoshi Shopping Arcade. Clothes and soft furnishings; particularly renowned for handblock printed cottons combining traditional and contemporary designs.

Bata, 16 B-Block, Connaught Place. Reliable and hardy sandals, trainers and smarter leather shoes, that will survive in India much longer than flimsy leather flip-flops sold in most bazaars.

The Bina Ramani Collection: Twice Upon a Time, 12 Hauz Khas (☎686 2205) and H5/6 Mehrauli Rd (☎65 7537). One of India's leading designers, Ramani's clothes are very chic, very exclusive and very expensive (notice the play on *Armani*).

Cashmeir Galleri, 50 Hauz Khas Village (☎685 4503). Handmade oriental carpets in silk and wool, chain stitch rugs, shawls and papier-mâché.

Central Cottage Industries Emporium, Janpath. Tucked behind the Tibetan Market, this has one of the best ranges of raw silks and cottons in town, and stocks traditional Indian dress, silk ties and finely tailored jackets and suits.

Dastkar, 1A/1 Hauz Khas Village (☎65 7301). Reasonably priced terracotta, block prints, *saris*, patchwork, toys, leather, basketry, weaves, and beautiful folk-art Madhubani prints on cloth.

Handloom House, 9 A-Block, Connaught Circus. Exquisite silks; top quality, sky-high prices.

Khadi Gramodyog Bhavan, 24 Regal Building, corner of Sansad Marg and Connaught Circus. Great place to pick up hardy, lightweight travelling clothes. Reasonably priced, ready-made, traditional Indian garments include *shalwa camise* (trouser and shirt), woollen waistcoats, *kurta pygama*, shawls and caps, plus rugs, material by the metre, incense, cards and tablecloths.

New Kashmir Stores, 225B Village Lado Sarai, Mehrauli (☎66 5905). One of those places rental car drivers take you to against your will. The reward is a fine collection of carpets, some of which are antique – the problem is to guess which ones.

Shyam Ahuja, Santoshi Shopping Arcade. Exclusive rugs and *dhuris* by a world-famous rug designer, patronized by shops such as *Liberty* of London.

Tibetan Carpets and Handicrafts, HH the Dalai Lama's Charitable Trust Handicraft Exports, 16 Jor Bagh, Lodi Rd. Carpets of all sizes, seamless and runner, woollen pullovers, jackets, bags, *chuba* (Tibetan women's dress), incense and other gifts.

Vastra, 12 Hauz Khas Village (☎644 4307 or 644 4171). Essentially a clothes store, selling *shalwa camise*, some in antique silk – also sells frames and old photographs.

Musical instruments and cassettes

Delhi has a lively classical **Indian music** scene; the *Triveni* arts centre (see p.110) is a good place to catch live performances as well as to get information on instrument makers. Among classical recordings, the *Music Today* series has an excellent collection of both north and south Indian classical music.

Blue Bird & Co, 9 Regal Buildings, Sansad Marg. Cassettes, compact discs, videos and hi-fis.

Lahore Music House, Netaji Subhash Marg, Darya Ganj. North Indian musical instrument-makers who have a long reputation and have been exporting instruments for years.

Rangarsons, Outer Circle, Connaught Circus. Extraordinary shop that once boasted regiments of the British Indian army among its patrons. A collection of brass and other marching band instruments as well as contemporary *tablas* and *sitars*.

Rhythm Corner, 16 N-Block, Connaught Place. Much like *Blue Bird*; copious quantities of CDs, cassettes, and videos of contemporary and classical music, including international chart hits.

Ricki Ram, Outer Circle, Connaught Circus. Once *sitar*-makers to the likes of Ravi Shankar, they maintain their exclusive airs and produce quality instruments, but have lost the leading edge.

Nightlife and entertainment

There's surprisingly little to do after dark in Delhi; outside the city's restaurants, your best bet for a drink is in the **bars** of the upmarket hotels, where you can get shorts and often cocktails as well as the more easily available *Kingfisher* and *Eagle* beers. However, demands by BJP ministers in mid-1994 resulted in increased alcohol restrictions and much higher prices, and if the political climate doesn't change, you can expect to pay more than you would in a western bar. A sprinkling of **discos** in the five-star hotels cater to the city's yuppies, who can meet here outside family confines and dance the night away to western and Indian popular music.

The city fares much better on the cultural front. A few venues host performances of classical dance such as **Bharatnatyam** and **Kathakali**, and there are nightly shows at Hauz Khas in the south of the city. Check any of the listings magazines detailed on p.78 to see what's on at **India International Centre**, a good place to catch lectures and films on all aspects of Indian culture and environment, and the city's principal venue for musical performances.

Bars

Broadway, *Hotel Broadway*, Asif Ali Rd, New Delhi. Decked out in an attempt to recreate the New York scene in the 1960s. Beers and a variety of "American" cocktails.

Jazz Bar, *Maurya Sheraton Hotel*, Diplomatic Enclave. Live jazz of varying standards from Indian musicians. Serves beer in pitchers, and cocktails such as New Orleans Surprise and Cool Jazz.

Maikada, *Hotel Marina*, 59 G-Block, Connaught Circus. Comfortable bar with a small outside terrace and well-presented but pricey drinks.

Le Meridien, Windsor Place. Two exclusive bars with extortionate prices but nothing less than five-star treatment.

Saqi, *Hotel Alka*, G-Block, Connaught Circus. Very dimly lit bar that's a little sleazy, but you can take your drink out onto a small verandah.

Tavern, *Hotel Imperial*, Janpath. A restaurant-cum-bar, with tolerable live music and a moderate range of drinks.

Dance performances

Dances of India, Parsi Anjuman Hall, Bahadur Shah Zafar Marg (☎331 7831). Excellent classical, folk and tribal dance. Daily 7–8pm.

Hauz Khas. Lavish meals accompanied by open-air dance shows. US$10 a head.

India International Centre, 40 Lodi Estate (☎461 9431). Regular dance shows. Performances often repeated several nights in a row; enquire by phone.

Triveni Theatre, 205 Tansen Marg (☎371 8833). A popular venue for dance shows by professionals and highly talented student groups.

Cinemas

After gloriously hyped releases, Bollywood movies make their way to the capital where there is passionate enthusiasm for burly heroes and red-lipped maidens. If you're interested in enjoying a classic Indian experience, the best **cinemas** to head for are the *Odeon* and *Plaza* in Connaught Place. Both show popular films with the compulsory goodies and baddies, a generous dose of manly courage and shy love, much singing and dancing, and happy endings. In addition you may be able to see dubbed western classics such as *James Bond* and *Crocodile Dundee*. Films in several non-Indian languages are shown at many of the cultural centres listed below.

Auditoria and cultural centres

There is nearly always some cultural activity going on in Delhi – check at the tourist office, or get hold of local newspapers and publications like *City Scan* and *City Guide*.

THE FESTIVALS OF DELHI

India's annual **religious celebrations** are a large part of Delhi social life, and it's well worth trying to time your visit to enjoy their whirl of rowdy activity, traditional dances and vibrant costumes. In addition, several **secular festivals** are particular to the capital, and India's top performers gather for **music, dance and drama** festivals.

January

Lohri (Jan 13). The climax of winter is celebrated with bonfires and song.

Republic Day Parade (Jan 26). The first event in a week of celebrations. Soldiers, musicians and dancers from every state parade down Rajpath, salute the president, then pass India Gate, and head north to the Red Fort. Tickets (Rs100) for seats on Rajpath can be bought from travel agents and hotels – arrive early to get a good view. The "dress rehearsal" 2–3 days before the event is free and less crowded. Fanfares of "Beating the Retreat" in Vijay Chowk, close to Rashtrapati Bhavan, round things off on Jan 29.

Martyr's Day (Jan 30). Songs and prayers throughout the morning at Raj Ghat, which is surrounded by a guard of honour, to remember Mahatma Gandhi and others who lost their lives in the Independence struggle.

Delhi Rose Festival (end of Jan). Roses from all the world displayed at Safdarjang's tomb.

Shankarlal Sangeet Sammelan (end of Jan). A festival of Indian music with performances in several venues: check local magazines for details.

February

Basant Panchami (Feb 2). The official date of the first day of Spring, when the Moghul gardens behind Rashtrapati Bhavan are opened for the month, after a great deal of dedicated watering and pruning.

Delhi Flower Show. Held in the sublime Purana Qila grounds; horticulturalists exhibit flowers and hybrids from all over the world.

Thyagaraja Festival. An enthusiastic display of south Indian music and dance, opposite Nehru University in Vaikunthnath temple.

March

Holi. March, when spring reaches its height, is celebrated with the random flinging of coloured powder and squirting of coloured liquids. Great fun, but can be a little over the top, especially when drunk men are involved.

April

Amir Khusrau. Prayers and *qawwali* singing in Nizamuddin, on the anniversary of the birth of the famous musician.

Id-ul-Fitr (sometimes at the end of March). A day of Muslim feasting and celebrations at the end of the Ramadan fast. Thousands gather for prayers at Jami Masjid.

National Drama Festival. Classical and contemporary dance, music and drama, at Rabindra Bhavan.

May

Buddha Jayanti. The birth of the Buddha is celebrated on the first full moon night of the month with prayers at Ladakh Buddha Vihara, Ring Rd, and the Buddha Vihara next to Lakshmi Narayan Mandir on Mandir Marg.

July

Id-ul-Zuhr. Muslims recall the sacrifice of Ibrahim's son with animal sacrifice, feasting on mutton and sweet vermicelli, and prayers.

International Mango Festival. A peculiar event, with over 500 types of mango on show, usually in Talkatora Stadium. Free tastings.

August

Crafts Mela. Shops and stalls are set up at Suraj Kund just after the monsoon, to display handicrafts and fabrics from all over India.

Janmasthami. Krishna's birthday, celebrated throughout the city; festivities are grandest at Lakshmi Narayan Mandir.

Independence Day (15 Aug). Huge crowds gather to watch the Indian flag hoisted at the Red Fort amid cheering and singing.

October

Gandhi Jayanti (2 Oct). Mahatma Gandhi's birth; singing and prayers at Raj Ghat.

Dussehra. Celebrated in Delhi, and all India, with ten nights of festivities and stage plays of the *Ramayana*. Spectacular performances of the *Ramlila Ballet* at Delhi Gate (all month). The demon king Ravana is burnt in effigy on the ninth night of the festival.

Diwali. "Festival of lights", with funfairs in parks and in front of the Red Fort. Night skies are lit by dazzling firework displays.

December

Christmas and **New Year**. Although neither Hindu nor Muslim, Christmas is a public holiday, and a good excuse for parties, when many hotels lay on special buffet spreads.

Alliance Francaise, D13 NDSE Part II (☎644 0128). Hosts film shows and has an art gallery.

American Centre, 24 Kasturba Gandhi Marg (☎331 6841). Concerts, talks and films.

British Council, 17 Kasturba Gandhi Marg (☎371 0111). Talks, films shows and concerts, plus a good library and reading room.

India International Centre, 40 Lodi Estate, Max Mueller Marg (☎61 9431). Originally designed for academics but now an exclusive club. Regular concerts, lectures, seminars and film shows and a very good reading room.

Italian Culture Centre, 2 Golf Links (☎462 7808). Seminars and film shows, plus a library.

Japan Cultural Centre, 32 Firoz Shah Rd (☎332 9803). Lectures, seminars and exhibitions, and a library.

Kamani Auditorium, Copernicus Marg (☎38 8084). Concerts and theatre.

Lalit Kala Akademi, Rabindra Bhavan, 35 Firoz Shah Rd (☎38 7241). Delhi's premier art academy, with an extensive collection of paintings, sculpture, frescoes and drawings. Also hosts films and seminars, and has a photographic section and a sales counter.

Max Mueller Bhavan, 3 Kasturba Gandhi Marg (☎332 9506). Along with hosting concerts and exhibitions which include Indian artists, this German government cultural centre also has a library.

Russian Cultural Centre, 24 Firoz Shah Rd (☎332 9102). Holds exhibitions, talks and films and houses the *Eisenstein Film Club* and the *Botwinnik Chess Club*, which organizes chess competitions.

Sahitya Akademi, Rabindra Bhavan, Firoz Shah Rd (☎38 6088). An excellent library devoted to Indian literature through the ages, with some books and periodicals in English.

Sangeet Natak Akademi, Rabindra Bhavan, Firoz Shah Rd (☎38 7248). The premier performing arts institution with a large archive and collections (see p.91).

Siri Fort, Asian Village Complex (☎649 3370). Cultural programmes and film shows.

Triveni Kala Sangam, 205 Tansen Marg (☎371 9470). Two galleries devoted to dance and fine art, two theatres (one open-air), a bookshop, a good cafe, music archives, a sculpture park, and a collection of terracotta; and they also organize classes in art, classical music and dance.

Discotheques

Most, if not all, of the **discos** popular with elite Delhi-ites are in the luxury hotels; expect to pay around Rs250 for entrance and to follow some sort of dress code.

CJ's, *Le Meridien* (☎371 0101). Selective entry.

Ghungroo, *Maurya Sheraton* (☎301 0101). For residents only.

My Kind of Place, *Taj Palace* (☎301 0404). Nostalgia for the over 30s.

Number One, *Taj Mansingh* (☎301 6162). Young and flash local crowd.

Oasis, *Hyatt Regency* (☎688 1234). Flashy basement atmosphere; women-only night Wed.

Swimming, sports and outdoors activities

The recreational activity most likely to appeal to visitors in the pre-monsoon months has to be a dip in one of Delhi's **swimming pools**, but local diversions for the athletically minded include **bowling, golf**, and even **rock climbing** on crags on the outskirts of the city, during the cooler months.

Bowling Alley, *Qutb Hotel*, off Sri Aurobindo Marg (☎66 0060). Four-lane bowling alley.

Delhi Flying and Gliding Club, Safdarjang Airport (☎61 8271). Temporary membership available.

Delhi Golf Club, Dr Zakir Hussein Marg (☎69 9236). Busy and beautiful 220-acre golf course on the fifteenth-century estate of the Lodhi dynasty, planted with over 200 variety of trees, which also acts as a bird sanctuary. Monuments and mausoleums, such as the ruined *barakhamba* on a hillock next to the seventh green, dot the grounds. Temporary membership is available.

Delhi Lawn Tennis Association, Africa Ave, Asian Games Village (☎65 3955).

Delhi Polo Club, President's Estate, Rashtrapati Bhavan (☎37 5604). Temporary membership is available with prior arrangement through the Secretary, President's Body Guard.

Delhi Riding Club, Safdarjang Rd (☎301 1891). Morning rides start at 6.30am and afternoon rides at 2pm; open to the public but with prior arrangement through the Club Secretary.

Delhi Tourism, N-36 Bombay Life Building, Middle Circle, Connaught Place (☎331 5322). Local activities such as rock climbing, paragliding and water sports, plus treks as far afield as Sikkim.

Indian Mountaineering Foundation, Benito Juarez Marg (☎67 1211). Official organ governing mountaineering and permits throughout India, with a library and an outdoor climbing wall. Some equipment can be rented here, and you can get information on local crags and climbing groups.

Skating Rink, Pragati Maidan. Popular roller-skating rink with skate rental.

Swimming Pools *Hotel Imperial*, Janpath, Rs300 for non-residents; *Hotel Samrat*, Chanakyapuri, Rs150 per day. Other hotels, such as *Ashok*, *Maurya*, and *Claridges*, usually allow non-residents to swim in their pools, for around Rs200 per day, but they tend to alter their rules so check first. The city's main public swimming baths are the *NMDC Pools*, in Nehru Park, Chanakyapuri.

Listings

Ambulance ☎102.

Airport Enquiries International ☎301 7733; domestic ☎329 5434.

Bus Enquiries *Delhi Transport Corporation* is on ☎251 9083, and will provide enquiry numbers for buses run by other state transport corporations.

Churches *Church of the Redemption*, Church Rd; Sacred Heart *Free Church*, Parliament St.

Embassies & Consulates *Australia* 1/50-G Shantipath, Chanakyapuri (☎688 5673); *Bangladesh*, 56 Ring Rd, Lajpat Nagar III (☎683 4668); *Belgium*, 50-N Shantipath, Chanakyapuri (☎60 8295); *Bhutan*, Chandragupta Marg, Chanakyapuri (☎60 9217); *Canada*, 7/8 Shantipath, Chanakyapuri (☎687 6500); *China*, 50-D Shantipath, Chanakyapuri (☎60 0328); *Denmark*, 11 Aurangzeb Rd (☎301 0900); *Finland*, E3 Nyaya Marg, Chanakyapuri (☎60 5409); *France*, 2/50-E Shantipath, Chanakyapuri (☎60 4004); *Germany*, Plot 6 Block 50-G, Shantipath, Chanakyapuri (☎60 4861); *Greece*, 16 Sundernagar (☎61 7800); *Hungary*, 2/50M Niti Marg, Chanakyapuri (☎60 8414); *Indonesia*, 50A Chanakyapuri (☎60 2305); *Italy*, 50E Chandragupta Marg, Chanakyapuri (☎60 0071); *Japan*, 50-G Shantipath, Chanakyapuri (☎687 6564); *Kenya*, E66 Vasant Marg, Vasant Vihar (☎687 6538); *Malaysia*, 50M Satya Marg, Chanakyapuri (☎60 1291); *Mauritius*, 5 Kautilya Marg, Chanakyapuri (☎301 1112); *Nepal*, Barakhamba Rd (☎332 8191); *Netherlands*, 6/50-F Shantipath, Chanakyapuri (☎688 4951); *New Zealand*, 50-N Nyaya Marg (☎688 3170); *Nigeria*, 21 Olaf Palme Marg, Vasant Vihar (☎687 6228); *Norway*, 50-C Shantipath, Chanakyapuri (☎60 5982); *Pakistan*, 2/50G Shantipath, Chanakyapuri (☎60 0601); *Poland*, 50-M Shantipath, Chanakyapuri (☎60 8321); *Portugal*, B-76 Greater Kailash I (☎644 9648); *Romania*, A52 Vasant Vihar (☎67 0700); *Singapore*, E6 Chandragupta Marg, Chanakyapuri (☎60 4162); *Spain*, 12 Prithviraj Rd (☎301 5892); *Sri Lanka*, 27 Kautilya Marg, Chanakyapuri (☎301 0201); *Sweden*, Nyaya Marg, Chanakyapuri (☎60 4961); *Switzerland*, Nyaya Marg, Chanakyapuri (☎60 4225); *Thailand*, 56-N Nyaya Marg, Chanakyapuri (☎605679); *Trinidad & Tabago*, 131 Jor Bagh (☎61 8186); *Turkey*, 50-N Nyaya Marg, Chanakyapuri (☎60 1921); *Uganda*, C6/11, Vasant Vihar (☎687 7687); *United Kingdom*, Shantipath, Chanakyapuri (☎60 1371); *United States of America*, 28B Institutional Area, Chanakyapuri (☎60 0651); *Vietnam*, 17 Kautilya Marg, Chanakyapuri (☎301 8059); *Zimbabwe*, B8 Anand Niketan (☎688 5060).

Hospitals *All India Institute of Medical Sciences*, Ansari Nagar, Sri Aurobindo Marg (☎66 1123), 24hr emergency service and good treatment; *East West Medical Centre*, 38 Golf Links Rd (☎69 9229), good private clinic; *Dr Ram Manohar Lohia Hospital*, Baba Kharak Singh Marg (☎34 5525), also private; *Lok Nayak Jaya Prakash Hospital*, Jawaharlal Nehru Marg, Old Delhi, a government hospital opposite the *Tourist Camp*.

Immigration and Foreigners' Registration For visa renewal and permits for restricted states, go to the Foreigners' Registration office, Hans Bhavan, Mathura Rd, near Tilak Bridge railway station (10am–1pm & 1.30–5pm; ☎331 9489), with four passport photographs. Be sure to wait in the right line – to pay either in *rupees* (backed up by exchange certificates), or foreign currency – and take plenty of change. If you've been in India more than 90 days, you'll need to get a tax clearance certificate before you can leave, from the Foreign section of the Income Tax Dept (10am–1pm & 2–5pm; ☎331 7826) in the Central Revenue Building next to the FRO; bring bank certificates.

Left Luggage Left luggage counters at the railway stations are expensive. To deposit your bags long-term ask at your hotel; most charge Rs2–4 per day. Hotels *Hare Rama*, *Anoop*, and *Ajay* in Paharganj offer access to a 24-hr lock up, only Rs2 per day.

Libraries For a bit of hearty reading or access to foreign newspapers, try the *British Council*, 17 Kasturba Gandhi Marg, *India International Centre*, 40 Lodi Estate, or *Max Mueller Bhavan*, 3 Kasturba Gandhi Marg. *Sahitya Akademi*, Rabindra Bhavan, Firoz Shah Rd, stocks all genres of Indian literature, and a number of periodicals, many in English.

TRAVEL AGENTS IN DELHI

American Express, A Block, Connaught Place (☎332 4119).

Amber Tours, 606 Akash Deep, Barakhamba Rd (☎331 3229). Expensive adventure tours with rafting, trekking, wild-life safaris and fishing.

Ashoka Tours and Travels, Kanishka Shopping Plaza, 19 Ashoka Rd (☎332 4422). Package tours, car rental.

Balmer and Lawrie, 32–33 Nehru Place (☎641 9222).

Cox and Kings, Indra Palace, Connaught Place (☎332 0067). International operators.

Hans Travel Service, *Vishal Hotel*, Main Bazaar, Paharganj (☎52 7629).

Mackinnon, 16 Parliament St (☎332 3741).

Mercury, Jeevan Tara Building, Parliament Street (☎31 2008).

Nepal Travel Information Centre, 203-204 Adhanik Chambers, 13/29 East Patel Nagar (☎572 5770).

Peak Adventure Tours, B 29A, Kailash Colony (☎643 2894). Established tour and trekking agency.

Rajasthan Tourism Development Corporation, Bikaner House, Pandara Rd (☎38 3837). Package tours of Rajasthan by coach or car, including a wildlife tour of Sariska, Ranthambore and Bharatpur.

Shantum Seth, 309-B, Sector 15-A, Noida, UP 201301 (☎892 1520). Shantum operates a unique circuit of the Buddhist sites of UP, Bihar and Nepal.

Sita World Travel, F12 Connaught Place (☎331 1122). International and domestic flights and package tours.

STIC, *Hotel Imperial*, Janpath (☎332 7582). Agents for a number of international airlines.

Student Travel Information Centre, *Hotel Imperial*, Janpath (☎332 4788). Good for student cards, reliable if not always cheap.

Thomas Cook, *Hotel Imperial*, Janpath (☎332 8468).

Trade Wings, 60 Janpath (☎35 1638).

Travel Corporation of India, N49 Connaught Circus (☎332 7468). Established and efficient tour operators.

Tripsout Travels, Tolstoy Lane, 72/7 Janpath (behind tourist office) (☎332 0452). Popular and trustworthy travel service with international airlines and some discounts.

Y's Tours & Travels, YMCA, Jai Singh Rd (☎31 1915). Why queue up when you can get your train tickets from here.

Youth Hostelling International, 5 Nyaya Marg, Chanakyapuri (☎301 6250). Extremely good-value treks in the mountains of Himachal Pradesh.

Maps The *Survey of India Map Sales Office*, in *Central Cottage Industries Emporium*, Janpath, sells guide maps of various cities and states, some of which are grossly out of date; see *Basics*.

Mother Theresa Hostels The orphanage inspired by Mother Theresa close to Qudsia Gardens north of Old Delhi accepts voluntary help.

Motorcycles The Karol Bagh area is known for its many good motorcycle shops; new or second-hand *Enfields* can be bought here at the reliable *Inder Motors*, 1744/1755 Hari Singh Nalwa St, Abdul Aziz Rd (☎572 8579), while *Lucky Auto Accessories*, 53/1767 Shri Kishan Dass Rd (☎73 8815) offers excellent renovations of secondhand (ex-army) *Enfield Bullets*.

Opticians *Lawrence & Mayo*, 76 Janpath: good, expensive glasses and sunglasses; *Medikos Opticians*, 1588 Main Bazaar, Paharganj: cheap computerized eye-tests, prescription lenses and sunglasses made up in half a day; *Optical Corner of India*, 26 D-Block, Connaught Place (☎332 2709).

Pharmacies Nearly every market has at least one pharmacy. Those in *Super Bazaar*, Connaught Place, and the *All India Medical Institute*, Ansari Nagar, Sri Aurobindo Marg, are open 24 hours.

Photographic Studios *Delhi Photo Company*, 78 Janpath, for high-quality developing and printing, and slide processing. Also *Capital Studio* 5 B-Block, Connaught Place, and *Master Color*, 1484 Chandni Chowk, Old Delhi.

Police ☎100.

State Tourist Offices *Andaman and Nicobar Islands*, F105 Curzon Rd Hostel, Kasturba Gandhi Marg (☎38 7015); *Andhra Pradesh*, Andhra Bhavan, 1 Ashoka Rd (☎38 2013); *Arunachal Bhawan*, Kautilya Marg (☎301 3915); *Assam*, State Emporia Complex, Kharak Singh Marg (☎34 5897); *Bihar*, 216 Kanishka Shopping Plaza, 19 Ashoka Rd (☎332 4422); *Goa*, Goa Sadan, 8 Amrita Shergill Marg (☎69 2065); *Gujarat*, A6 State Emporia Building, Baba Kharak Singh Marg (☎34 3173); *Haryana*, Chandralok Building, 36 Janpath (☎332 4764); *Jammu & Kashmir*, 202 Kanishka

Shopping Plaza, 19 Ashoka Rd (☎332 5373); *Karnataka*, C4 State Emporia Building, Baba Kharak Singh Marg (☎34 3862); *Kerala*, Information Centre, 219 Kanishka Shopping Plaza (☎331 6191); *Madhya Pradesh*, 204–205 Kanishka Shopping Plaza (☎332 1187); *Maharashtra*, A8 State Emporia Building, Baba Kharak Singh Marg (☎34 3774); *Manipur*, C7 State Emporia Building, Baba Kharak Singh Marg (☎34 4026); *Meghalaya*, Meghalaya House, 9 Aurangzeb Rd (☎301 4417); *Mizoram*, Mizoram Bhawan, Circular Rd, Chanakyapuri (☎301 0548); *Nagaland*, Government of Nagaland, 29 Aurangzeb Rd (☎301 4289); *Orissa*, B4 State Emporia Building, Kharak Singh Marg (☎34 4580); *Punjab*, 214–215 Kanishka Shopping Plaza (☎332 3055); *Rajasthan*, B2 State Emporia Building, Kharak Singh Marg (☎332 2332); *Sikkim*, New Sikkim House, 14 Panch Sheel Marg, Chanakyapuri (☎301 5346); *Tamil Nadu*, C1 State Emporia Building, Kharak Singh Marg (☎34 4651); *Tripura*, Tripura Bhavan, Kautilya Marg, Chanakyapuri (☎301 5157); *Uttar Pradesh*, Chanderlok Building, 36 Janpath (☎332 2251); *West Bengal*, A/2 State Emporia Building, Kharak Singh Marg (☎35 3840).

Student Travel Information centre for students at *Hotel Imperial*, Janpath; issue and renewal of student cards and details of travel reductions.

Yoga Centres *Yoga Shakti Mission*, 14–20 Ajit Arcade, Kailash Colony (☎641 2379); *Yoga Vishwatayan*, Ashoka Rd (☎371 8866).

Onwards from Delhi

Delhi has good domestic and international travel connections. Anyone heading from the south to the western Himalayas (Himachal Pradesh, Kulu, Manali, Ladakh) will pass through Delhi; it seldom takes more than a day to arrange the onward journey. Scores of **travel agents** sell bus and air tickets; **touts**, concentrated at the top of Janpath, waylay tourists with promises of cheap fares, but can't always be trusted.

Travel within India

Whichever direction you're heading in, there'll be a plane, train or bus to get you there. Buses leave Delhi extremely frequently, and tourists are usually ensured places on trains in a reserved **tourist quota**. Flights should be booked as far in advance as possible, but since most routes are covered daily, nobody should have to wait too long.

FLIGHTS FROM DELHI

	Frequency	Time		Frequency	Time
Agra	1 daily	45min	**Indore**	1 daily	1hr 10min
Ahmedabad	2 daily	1hr 25min	**Jaipur**	2 daily	40min
Aurangabad	1 daily	3hr 35min	**Jammu**	1 daily‡	2hr 15min–3hr
Bangalore	2 daily	2hr 30min	**Jodhpur**	1 daily	2hr
Bhopal	1 daily	1hr 10min–2hr	**Kathmandu**	3 daily	1hr 45min
Bhubaneshwar	1 daily	3hr 20min	**Khajuraho**	1 daily	1hr 55min
Bombay	8 daily	2–4hr	**Kulu**	1 daily‡‡	1hr 45min
Calcutta	3/4 daily	2–5hr	**Leh**	4 wkly@	2hr 30min
Chandigarh	1 daily**	40min	**Madras**	2 daily	3hr 30min
Kochi	1 daily**	4hr	**Nagpur**	6 wkly+	1hr 25min
Dehra Dun	1 daily‡	50min	**Pune**	1 daily*	2hr
Dhaka	3 wkly§§	2hr 30min	**Srinagar**	1 daily§	1hr 15min–2hr 30min
Goa	1 daily**	2hr 25min	**Udaipur**	2 daily	2–3hr
Hyderabad	2 daily	2hr	**Varanasi**	2 daily	1hr 15min–3hr

Key: * not Sun ** not Mon § 2 on Sat @ Mon, Wed, Fri & Sun
‡ not Wed ‡‡ not Thurs §§ 2 on Sun, 1 on Thurs + 2 on Mon & Sat, 1 on Tues & Thurs

For details of flight connections between Delhi and **Southeast Asia**, see p.7.

By plane

Internal flights leave from the domestic terminal, 15km southwest of town, easily reached by the convenient *EATS* bus service (Rs12 plus charge for luggage; 20min) that departs from Palika Bazaar, just outside the *Wimpy*. Rickshaws and taxis are more expensive, but slightly quicker. Passengers on domestic flights must check in two hours prior to departure. A simple food counter sells tea, coffee, and snacks.

By train

Delhi's main railhead, **New Delhi Station** at the eastern end of Paharganj, less than 1km north of Connaught Circus, has regular departures to all corners of India, and a very efficient **booking office** for tourists on the first floor (Mon–Sat 8am–8pm). They'll give you advice on the fastest trains, and you should have little difficulty finding a seat or berth: **women** travelling alone in second class may prefer to ask for a berth in the ladies' carriage. Foreigners must show passports, and pay in foreign currency.

Southbound trains leave from New Delhi, many stopping also at **Old Delhi** station, where you can board the train if it's more convenient. All trains to **Rajasthan**, except

RAIL ROUTES FROM DELHI

To Rajasthan			To the Punjab and Himachal Pradesh		
Abu Road	4 daily	13hr 20min–19hr	Ambala Cantt	13 daily	2hr 20min–4hr
Ajmer	5 daily	10hr 20min–15hr	Amritsar	9 daily	7hr 20 min–12hr
Bharatpur	4 daily	4hr–5hr 10min	Chandigarh	3 daily	3hr–6hr 10min
Bikaner	3 daily	11hr–12hr 25min	Firozpur	2 daily	8hr 30min
Chittaurgarh	2 daily	12hr/16hr	Jalandhar	8 daily	6hr 20min–9hr
Jaipur	8 daily	5hr–13hr 25min	Jammu Tawai	3–4 daily	13hr 15min–15hr
Jhunjhunu	1 daily‡	5hr 50min	Kalka, for Shimla	2 daily	4hr–5hr 20min
Jodhpur	2 daily	12hr–14hr 35min	Ludhiana	6 daily	5hr 20min–8hr
Kota	6 daily	8hr–11hr 40min	Pathankot	3–4 daily	10hr 15min–12hr
Sawai Madhopur	4 daily	7–8hr			
Sikar	1 daily‡	8hr 25min	**To central India**		
Udaipur	2 daily	15hr 30min/20hr	Bhopal	14 daily	7hr 45min–15hr
			Gwalior	15 daily	3hr 15min–7hr
To Uttar Pradesh			Hyderabad	2–3 daily	24hr 25min–28hr
Agra	15 daily	2hr–4hr 15min	Indore	1 daily	27hr 40min
Allahabad	9 daily	7–14hr	Jhansi	15 daily	4hr 25min–9hr
Dehra Dun	1–2 daily	7hr 30min–10hr			
Gorakhpur	1 daily	13hr 20min	**To Gujarat and Bombay**		
Kanpur	15 daily	5–10hr	Ahmedabad	4 daily	17hr–24hr 30min
Lucknow	5–6 daily	6hr–9hr 45min	Bombay	8 daily	16hr 30min–29hr
Mathura	11 daily	2hr 50min			
Varanasi	6 daily	13–18hr	**To the south**		
			From New Delhi Station		
To the east			Bangalore	1 daily	40hr 35min
Bhubaneshwar	1 daily	29hr 35min–34hr	Ernakulam	1 daily+	48–50hr
Cuttack	1 daily	28hr 30min–33hr	Kanyakumari	1 on Mon	57hr 20min
Gaya	3 daily	15hr–17hr 20min	Madras	2–3 daily	33hr 20min–43hr
Guwahati	1 daily	36hr	Thiruvananthapuram	1 daily+	53–55hr
Howrah, Calcutta	1–2 daily§	18hr–34hr 15min	**From Hizrat Nizamuddin Station**		
Puri	1 daily	36hr 50min–38hr	Pune	1 daily	26hr 35min
Vijayawada	6 daily	27hr 30min–37hr	Vasco Da Gama*	1 daily	41hr 35min
			*change at Miraj		

Key: ‡ not Sun   § not Mon   + 2 on Mon

those to Bharatpur, Kota and Sawai Madhopur, begin their journey at Old Delhi. Bookings can be made at New Delhi. If you're going to Pune or Vasco da Gama, you'll have to start the journey at **Hizrat Nizamuddin station**, southeast of Purana Qila.

By bus

Delhi is at the centre of an extensive **bus** network covering much of the neighbouring states in north India. Buses can often be quicker than trains, but the long-distance ones especially tend to be pretty uncomfortable.

The vast majority of state-run buses depart from the **Inter-state Bus Terminal** near Kashmiri Gate in Old Delhi (☎251 9083), which has a cafe and left luggage counter. To be on the safe side, arrive at the terminal an hour or so before your bus leaves. You have to book seats before getting on the bus, which involves a frustrating search for the relevant counter (there are over thirty), where you may well be turned away, having arrived just when the attendant decides to take a break. Make sure you book yourself on the correct bus: most leave frequently and it's usual practice to take the next service. Ask for the registration number and departure platform. Besides *Delhi*

RECOMMENDED TRAINS FROM DELHI

Frequent trains connect Delhi with all parts of India; see the summary opposite. Those below are recommended as the fastest and/or most convenient for specific cities. All are daily if not otherwise marked.

	Name	No.	From	Departs	Total Time
Agra	Shatbadi Express*	2002	ND	6.15am	1hr 55min
	Taj Express	2180	ND	7.05am	2hr 45min
	Punjab Mail	1038	ND	7.15am	2hr 55min
	A.P. Express	2734	ND	5.55pm	2hr 30min
Ahmedabad	Ashram Express	2905	OD	6.10pm	17hr 5min
Ajmer	Pink City Express @	2901	OD	6am	8hr
	Delhi–Ahmedabad Mail	9901	OD	9.55pm	10hr 20min
Bombay	Rajdhani Express‡	2952	ND	4.05pm	16hr 30min
Calcutta	Shatbadi Express §	2004	ND	5.15pm	18hr
	Kalka–Howrah Mail	2312	OD	8am	24hr 30min
Jaipur	Pink City Express	2901	OD	6am	5hr 5min
	Ahmedabad Mail	9901	OD	9.55pm	6hr 35min
Jhansi	Shatbadi Express	2002	ND	6.15am	4hr 25min
	Punjab Mail	1038	ND	7.15am	6hr 10min
	Amritsar–Dadar Express	1058	ND	8.50pm	8hr 55min
Madras	Tamil Nadu Express	2622	ND	10.30pm	33hr 20min
Udaipur	Pink City Express @	2901	OD	6am	15hr 30min
	Chetak Express	9915	OD	1pm	20hr 15min
Varanasi	New Delhi–Howrah Express*	2382	ND	4pm	13hr 15min
Vasco da Gama	Karnataka Express+	2628	HN	12.25pm	17hr 35min

OD Old Delhi **ND** New Delhi **HN** Hizrat Nizamuddin
* a/c only + Change to connecting train at Miraj
§ Does not run Sat & Sun @ Does not run Sun ‡ Does not run Tues

Transport Corporation, the terminal holds offices of *Rajasthan Roadways* (☎251 4417), *Haryana Roadways* (☎252 1262), *Punjab Roadways* (☎251 7842), and *Himachal Pradesh Roadways* (☎251 6725), and is also used by *Jammu & Kashmir Roadways*, based at *Hotel Kanishka* (☎332 4422 ext 2243), and *UP Roadways*, at Ajmeri Gate (☎251 8709).

Both *UP* and *Haryana Roadways* run deluxe buses to **Agra** (5hr) every half-hour, but the train is much more convenient. 25 basic *Rajasthan Roadways* buses per day go to **Jaipur** (6hr; Rs37), as do a number of deluxe services (5 hr; Rs75). *Haryana Roadways* runs cheaper, less frequent buses, both deluxe and ordinary; one a/c deluxe bus leaves at 3pm (Rs100). Some *Rajasthan Roadways* deluxe buses also run to Jaipur from the more pleasant environs of Bikaner House, Pandara Rd near India Gate (☎38 3469). Other *Rajasthan Roadways* destinations include **Ajmer** (also served by *UP* and *Haryana Roadways*, **Alwar**, and **Bikaner** (1 daily, 6.20am; 11 hr).

Ordinary *HP* and *Haryana Roadways* buses leave for **Manali** (16hr) at 7.30am, 4pm, 4.30pm and 9.15pm; a deluxe *HP Roadways* service departs at 8.30pm for Kulu and Manali (14hr; Rs70). Regular basic *DTC*, *HP* and *Haryana Roadways* buses to **Shimla** (9–10hr) are supplemented by *HP*'s a/c service (Thurs & Sat only, 8am; Rs160), which leaves from their offices at Chanderlok Building, 36 Janpath. Both *DTC* and *HP Roadways* also run to **Dharamshala** (6.30am, 6.45am, 7.10am & 10pm; 12hr; Rs75).

UP Roadways buses into the mountains include frequent departures to **Haridwar** (5hr), and fewer to **Rishikesh** (6hr). Services to **Nainital** (8–9hr) range from the excruciating ordinary bus (Rs50) to the *Super Deluxe* (Rs90); avoid the *Video Coach*. There are also plenty of buses to **Dehra Dun** and **Mussoorie**, and three daily to **Almora** – an overnight deluxe bus leaves at 9.15pm (10hr; Rs90). To get to **Corbett National Park**, head for **Ramnagar** (7–8hr; Rs40); the buses are pretty basic but there's little alternative. *DTC*, *Punjab*, *Haryana* and *HP Roadways* buses to **Chandigarh** take 5 or 6 hours; an excellent a/c service costs around Rs120. *J&K Roadways* has a single deluxe bus leaving for **Srinagar** at 5pm (14hr; Rs20).

Private **deluxe buses**, in theory faster and more comfortable than state buses, usually depart from Chelmsford Road, opposite New Delhi train station, but some pick up passengers at hotels. They often delay departure to ensure a full quota, and many boast extremely loud video systems that blare throughout the night. Even so, the seats are soft, and usually recline, and some are air-conditioned. Popular destinations include Kulu, Manali, and Dharamsala, which are not accessible by train. Buy tickets a day or two ahead at the agencies on Chelmsford Road or Paharganj.

Leaving India

Delhi is well connected to neighbouring Asian countries, and to distant continents, and has no shortage of agents selling tickets. Most travellers leave India by **plane**, while the most likely overland destination from Delhi is Pakistan, and it's not uncommon to head straight for Nepal.

Anyone travelling to a country that requires a **visa** should get the necessary documentation from the embassy concerned (see "Listings"). Before going to the embassy, call to check opening hours, how many photos you'll need, and the likely waiting period.

By air

If you don't already have a ticket for a **flight** out of India, you'll have little trouble finding one, except between December and March when it may be difficult to get one at short notice. While you can buy tickets directly from the airlines, who all have offices around Connaught Place, it saves time and leg work to book through an **agency** (see p.114); reputable agents abound in Paharganj, and there are several on Janpath. The cheapest deals are to be had from touts on the street; make sure they're genuine by ringing the airline to check you have a seat. In any case, confirm your flight 72 hours before leaving.

AIRLINE OFFICES IN DELHI

International Airlines

Aeroflot, N-1 Connaught Place, Middle Circle, 1st Floor, BMC House (☎331 0426).

Air Canada, 105 Indra Prakash Building, 21 Barakhamba Rd (☎332 5876).

Air France, 7 Atma Ram Mansion, Connaught Circus (☎331 0407).

Air India, Jeevan Bharati Building, opposite Palika Bazaar, Connaught Circus (☎331 1225).

Air Lanka, Room 1, *Hotel Janpath*, Janpath (☎332 6843).

Alitalia, Surya Kiran Building, 19 Kasturba Gandhi Marg (☎331 1019).

American Airlines, 105 Indra Prakash Building, Barakhamba Rd (☎332 5876).

Bangladesh Biman, c/o *Jet Air*, N-40 Connaught Place (☎331 2119).

British Airways, DLF Centre, Parliament Street (☎332 7428).

Canadian Airlines, 66 Janpath (☎372 2162).

Cathay Pacific, Tolstoy House, Tolstoy Marg (☎332 1286).

Continental Airlines, *Hotel Janpath*, Janpath (☎372 2162).

Ethiopian Airlines, *Hotel Janpath*, Janpath (☎372 2162).

Gulf Air, G-12 Marina Arcade, Connaught Place (☎332 2018).

Japan Airlines, 36 Chandralok Building, Janpath (☎322 7724).

KLM, 7 Prakash Deep, Tolstoy Marg (☎331 1747).

Kuwait Airways, 2C, DCM Building, 16 Barakhamba Rd (☎331 0506).

Lufthansa, 56 Janpath (☎332 3310).

Malaysian Airlines, G-55 Connaught Place (☎332 1605).

North West Airlines, Indra Prakash Building, Barakhamba Rd (☎371 6006).

Qantas Airways, Mohandev Building, 13 Tostoy Marg (☎332 9732).

Royal Nepal Airlines, 44 Janpath (☎332 1575).

Sabena, Himalaya House, (☎331 2928).

SAS, B-1 Connaught Place (☎332 7503).

Saudi Arabian Airlines, Hansalaya Building, 15 Barakhamba Rd (☎331 0464).

Singapore Airlines, G-11 Connaught Circus (☎332 0145).

Swiss Airlines, 56 Janpath (☎332 5511).

Thai Airways, Ambadeep, Tolstoy Marg (☎332 3608).

United Airlines, 66 Janpath (☎371 2266).

US Air, 622 Indra Prakash Building, 21 Barakhamba Rd (☎371 4621).

Domestic Airlines

Indian Airlines main office, Safdarjang Airport (☎462 2220). Open around the clock.

General enquiries ☎141

Pre-recorded information ☎142

Departures ☎143

Indian Airlines Booking Offices: PTI Building, Sansand Marg (Mon–Sat 10am–5pm; ☎371 9168); Malhotra Building, Janpath (daily except Sat 10am–5pm); Kanchenjunga Building, Barakhamba Rd (Mon–Sat 10am–5pm; ☎331 3732).

Archana Airways, 41A Friends Colony East, Mathura Rd (☎684 2001).

Jagson Airlines, 12E Vandhana, 11 Tolstoy Marg (☎371 1069).

Modiluft, 2 Commercial Complex, Masjid Moth, Greater Kailash II (☎643 1128).

Trans Bharat Aviation, 201/72 Laxmi Bhawan, Nehru Place (☎641 9600). Flights to Kulu, daily except Sun.

Vayudoot, Malhotra Building, Janpath (☎331 2729). No longer flying, but sell tickets.

Airport buses to the international airport leave from opposite the Palika Bazaar *Wimpy* at the top of Janpath every half-hour from 5am to 10.30pm; they take about thirty minutes to cover the 23km. Make sure you arrive two hours prior to departure for all international flights, and put aside Rs300 for the obligatory **airport tax**. Most tourists taking night-time flights book a **taxi** in advance (Rs200–250) to avoid sleeping at the airport, where there's only a minimal food stall. It's a good idea to take a little food and drink in any case – delays are very common. If you're travelling on your own, you should have no difficulty finding someone who will share a taxi.

Overland travel

For journeys to neighbouring countries, there's always the alternative of **overland travel**, a long haul by train and/or bus. Crossings to **Pakistan** should be made from Amritsar, 10 hours by train from Delhi, where buses cross the border and head to Lahore (lifts with trucks are no longer easy to find). Those travelling overland to **Nepal** should make for **Gorakhpur**, to pick up a bus that crosses the border, and drives on to Kathmandu. In addition, several agencies now offer direct bus services to Kathmandu from Delhi – a gruelling two- or three-day journey that is convenient, but rarely comfortable. Connections east to **Bangladesh** can be made via Calcutta or Chittagong.

CHAPTER TWO

RAJASTHAN

Southwest of Delhi, fertile plains roll into the sharp tree-covered crags of the Aravalli mountains, which stretch from the northeastern corner of **RAJASTHAN** down to the south. They peter out in the west of the state, to give way to the parched, forbidding **Great Indian Desert**, whose sands extend west to Pakistan and north to Punjab and Harayana. By contrast, near its southern border with Gujarat, Rajasthan is characterized by verdant hills and fertile fields.

This diverse landscape, until recently a realm of kings, princes, heroic battles, and extravagant merchants, is littered with illustrious palaces, crumbling forts, and sprawling mansions, and emboldened with the vivid, almost luminous, hues of bulging turbans, flowing skirts and pleated scarves and veils. Outside the princely capitals, Rajasthan's vast rural population continues to live in close-knit communities, raising livestock and tending fields of wheat, sugar cane, castor, millet, pulses and rice.

Rajasthan is among India's most popular tourist destinations, with an abundance of palace-hotels that reaches the height of luxury in **Jaipur**, the capital, and **Udaipur**, where one of several palaces glistens white in the centre of a lake. Forts adorn almost every town and city, and range from modest bastions to immense citadels, such as that at **Chittaurgarh**. Thanks to the erstwhile rulers of the palaces and forts, who earmarked land for private hunting expeditions – and tribes such as the Bhils and Bishnois – the outlying countryside offers a rich assortment of wildlife. Tigers, leopards, and a host of other animals and birds, can be sought out in the grassy **Sariska National Park** not far from Delhi, and in **Ranthambore National Park** further south, where tawny-brown royal lodges provide perfect lookouts, with vistas over the lakes and forested hills beyond. The wetlands of **Keoladeo National Park** near Bharatpur boast India's densest concentration of migratory birds, and attract almost three hundred different species in the cool winter months.

Out of the major cities, where pushy touts and tradesmen can quickly become tiresome, visitors can enjoy quiet, leisurely towns and villages, where camels pad lazily through the streets, and few locals speak English. Many harbour spectacular temples, forgotten forts and beautiful mansions, such as the Marwari heartland of **Shekawati**, north of Jaipur, where painted houses, temples and palaces bring colour and life to the monotonous deserts.

Rajasthan's **climate** reaches the extremes common to desert regions. Temperatures can rise unbearably to over 45°C between May and June, before the heavy skies over central and east Rajasthan break with a fierce monsoon that revitalizes the arid land and fills empty river beds. The summer heat remains until mid-September or October, when night temperatures drop considerably and you'll need a shawl or thick jumper if you're outdoors, and a sleeping bag for night journeys and hotels that don't provide blankets. The best time to visit is between November and February, when daytime temperatures rarely exceed 30°C, and celebrations at fairs and festivals such as Gangaur and Holi bring swirls of colour to the streets.

Getting around Rajasthan is rarely problematic, though there's no avoiding some tedious long hauls. The efficient state-run road transport system has regular **bus** services between cities; routes via small towns and villages take longer, and breakdowns and delays are often due to the poor state of the roads rather than a failing in the vehicle. If you don't want to subject yourself to sleepless nights on buses and the din of video coaches, **trains** connect all major cities and many smaller towns – always book ahead for night journeys. Only Jaipur, Jodhpur and Udaipur have **airports**.

Some history

People of the Indus Valley Civilization are known to have spread into western India as far as the Gujarati coast, from their base of Mohenjo Daro in Pakistan, but few Rajasthani sites – such as Kali Bangan in the north, thought to have been settled by the **Harappans** before 2500 BC – have been discovered. Similarly, the Buddhist influence of the powerful Mauryan empire, who rose to prominence in Gujarat between 360 BC and 210 BC, touched only the southernmost districts of Rajasthan.

The turbulent history of Rajasthan, characterized by courtly intrigue and inter-state warfare, only really begins in the sixth and seventh centuries AD, with the emergence of warrior clans such as the Sisodias, Chauhans, Kuchwahas and Rathores – the **Rajputs** ("sons of princes"). These heroic fighters seem originally to have been denied positions of power by a rigid caste system, due to low social status or foreign birth, but claimed to be able to cleanse themselves of impurities by complex fire rituals. Never exceeding eight percent of the population, they were to rule the separate states of **Rajputana** for centuries. Their code of honour set them apart from the rest of society – as did the popular belief that they were descended from the sun and moon – but did not invite excessive hostility. Classic feudal leaders, the Rajputs provided land, employment and trading opportunities for their subjects, and are still praised as gods in some communities.

The Rajput codes of chivalry that lay behind endless clashes between clans and family feuds found their most savage expression in battles with Muslims. **Muhammad of Ghori**, the first to march his troops through Rajasthan, met with the fierce defiance of the Chauhan Rajputs at Ajmer; however, the success of his second onslaught gained him the foothold that enabled him to establish the **Sultanate** in Delhi. During the 350 years that followed, much of central, eastern and western India came under the control of the Sultans, but, despite all the Muslims' efforts and victories, Rajput resistance precluded them from ever undermining family solidarity and taking over Rajputana.

Ghori's successors were pushed out of Delhi in 1483 by the Mughal Babur, whose grandson **Akbar** came to power in 1556. Aware of the futility of using force against the Rajputs, Akbar chose instead to negotiate in friendship, and married Rani Jodha Bai, a princess from the Kuchwaha family of Amber. As a result, Rajputs entered the Mughal courts, and the influence of Mughal ideas on art and architecture remains evident in palaces, mosques, pleasure gardens and temples throughout Rajputana.

When the Mughal empire began to decline after the accession of Aurangzeb in 1658, so too did the power of the Rajputs. Aurangzeb sided with a new force, the **Marathas**,

FESTIVALS IN RAJASTHAN

Rajasthan's striking juxtaposition of vibrant local costumes against the arid sandscape is most dazzling during the state's **festivals**, that accompany cattle markets and celebrate nationwide religious events, local folk heroes and village deities. In addition to intoxicating blazes of colour, the festivals invariably feature traditional dancing, singing, and the music of pipes, drums and rickety stringed instruments. Some are geared particularly towards foreign visitors, and many of the most important celebrations fall in the tourist season (the cool months between November and March). For dates of specific events, ask at tourist offices; most festivals fall on days determined by the lunar calendar.

Most **weddings** are held between April and June; noisy, communal affairs when out-of-tune bands and dancing relatives jostle through the streets waving *rupee*-notes, and mobile strip lights illuminate dapper bridegrooms decked in turbans and tinsel.

Tilwara Cattle Fair (Jan). The small town of Barmer comes alive during Rajasthan's largest cattle market that draws traders from all over the state.

Nagaur Cattle Fair (Feb). Dancing, singing and sales of local handicrafts accompany the trading of cows, buffalo, donkeys and horses at Nagaur, 100km south of Bikaner.

Desert Festival (Feb). Jaisalmer's own two-day event when camel races, handicraft stalls, folk dances and competitions are laid on primarily to attract tourists, but also help sustain traditional arts and crafts.

Holi (Feb/March). A festival celebrating the end of winter and the destruction of evil demons, held throughout northern India. Dancing and drumming (especially good in Churu) continue for several days before the final day of manic coloured-powder throwing.

Elephant Festival (March). Parades of mounted elephants bedecked in jewels march through the streets of Jaipur and into the City Palace to the accompaniment of drums and trumpets.

Eid-ul-fitr (March). Muslims celebrate the end of Ramadan, a month of fasting, with special milk sweets, *sheer kurma*, and gather for prayers in the mosques.

Mewar Festival (March/April). The Ranas of Udaipur commemorate their long line of rulers with dance shows and music and a bellowing refrain from a bagpipe orchestra in the *Shiv Niwas Palace* hotel.

Gangaur (April). A festival unique to Rajasthan, when women pray for their husbands, and unmarried girls wish for good ones. Effigies of Gauri (Parvati) and Isa (Shiva) – the ideal couple – are carried through the streets along with potted rice and flowers which hark back to the days when this was primarily a harvest festival. Excellent in Jaisalmer, when the local Raja heads the procession amid an entourage of camels.

Urs Mela (April/May). Thousands of Muslims and Hindus converge on the Dargah in Ajmer to commemorate the life of the Sufi saint and teacher Muin-ud-din Chisti, who died here in 1236. Much drumming, praying and feasting.

Muharram (April/June). This Shi'a Muslim festival remembering the death of Hussain is concentrated in Muslim quarters of cities and in Fatehpur, Jhunjhunu and Churu. Models of saint's tombs are led through the streets in grand procession after a night of vigorous drumming, especially in Churu.

Rani Sati Mela (Aug). A day of prayers and dances in Jhunjhunu, in memory of a merchant's widow who committed *sati*, sacrificing her life on her husband's pyre, in 1595.

Gugaji Mela (Aug). A festival held in honour of the local goddess in Churu.

Dussehra (Oct). Nine days of dancing and singing dedicated to the goddess Durga. Scenes from the *Ramayana* are acted out on makeshift stages, but in Bissau (Shekawati) these are replaced by silent dances at dusk.

Diwali (Nov). A five-day festival of lights celebrated across India but of particular importance to the merchant community, especially in Shekawati, since it marks the start of the financial year and includes a day of praises to Lakshmi, goddess of wealth. Hundreds of delicious sweets are cooked and exchanged by families and friends.

Pushkar Camel Fair (Nov). Rajasthan's largest event, when traders of camels, oxen, buffaloes, cows and donkeys are joined by handicraft sellers and thousands of tourists who are accommodated in specially erected tent cities. Camel races, dances and fireworks continue for four days.

Chandrabhaga Fair (Nov). The full moon of Kartika is celebrated in Jhalawar at the temples on the banks of the Chandrabhaga, and devotees bathe in the river.

Govt of India Statement - The external boundaries of India are neither correct nor authenticated.

RAJASTHAN TRAVEL DETAILS

	Trains Frequency	Trains Time	Buses Frequency	Buses Time	Flights Frequency	Flights Time
To and From JAIPUR						
Agra Fort	3 daily	6hr	5 daily	5hr		
Ahmedabad	4 daily	11hr 30min–25hr				
Ajmer	6 daily	3hr 20min	every 15min	2hr 30min		
Alwar	6 daily	2hr 10min–3hr 45min	hourly	4hr		
Aurangabad					1 daily	2hr 25min
Bharatpur	4 daily	3–4hr	every 30min	4hr		
Bikaner	1 daily	10hr 20min	4 daily	7hr		
Bombay					2–3 daily	1hr 30min–4hr
Chittaurgarh	3 daily	7hr 45min	7 daily	8–9hr		
Churu	2 daily	5hr 30min	3 daily	5hr		
Delhi	6 daily	5hr 30min–13hr	every 15 min	5hr 30min	2 daily	40min
Indore	1 daily	16hr				
Jaisalmer			1 daily	13hr		
Jhunjhunu	3 daily	5hr	every 45min	4–5hr		
Jodhpur	1 daily	6hr	every 30min	7–8hr	1 daily	45min
Kota			8 daily	5–7hr		
Mount Abu*	4 daily	8–17hr	1 nightly	14hr		
Pushkar**			6 daily	3hr 30min		
Sawai Madhopur	2 daily	4hr 30min	2 daily	5hr		
Sikar	4 daily	3hr	hourly	3hr		
Udaipur			13 daily	10hr	2 daily	45min–2hr
To and From JODHPUR						
Ahmedabad	3 daily	8–13hr				
Ajmer			hourly	4hr		
Alwar	1 daily	9hr 15min				
Bharatpur	2 daily	12–19hr				
Bikaner	1 daily	10hr 15min	hourly	5hr		
Bombay					1 daily	2hr 20min
Delhi	2 daily	12–14hr			1 daily	50min
Jaipur	3 daily	6hr 25min–7hr 45min	hourly	7hr	1 daily	40min
Jaisalmer	2 daily	9–10hr	10 daily	6–8hr		
Mount Abu*	2 daily	3–5hr				
Osiyan			hourly	2hr		
Ranakpur			2 daily	5hr		
Udaipur			2 daily	11hr	1 daily	40min
To and From UDAIPUR						
Ahmedabad	1 daily	10hr	11 daily	7hr		
Ajmer	2 daily	8hr	7 daily	7hr		
Alwar	2 daily	14–16hr				
Aurangabad					1 daily	1hr 10min
Bombay					2 daily	1hr–2hr 35min
Chittaurgarh	2 daily	3hr 30min	7 daily	2hr 30min		
Delhi	2 daily	16hr 40min–20hr	2 daily	17hr	2 daily	2hr
Jaipur	2 daily	11hr	7 daily	10hr	2 daily	45min–2hr
Jaisalmer			2 daily	14hr		
Jodhpur			3 daily	8hr	1 daily	40min
Kota			7 daily	6hr		
Mount Abu*			4 daily	5hr		
Ranakpur			2 daily	4–6hr		

Note that no individual route appears more than once in this chart; for any specific journey, check against where you want to get to as well as where you're coming from.

	Trains		Buses		Flights	
	Frequency	Time	Frequency	Time	Frequency	Time
To and From Ajmer						
Ahmedabad	4 daily	12–21hr	1 daily	12hr		
Bharatpur	1 daily	9hr 20min	8 daily	6–8hr		
Bombay			1 daily	25–30hr		
Chittaurgarh	5 daily	3hr 40min–5hr	7 daily	5–6hr		
Delhi	4 daily	10–12hr	10 daily	9–12hr		
Jaisalmer			1 daily	12hr		
Kota			hourly	4hr		
Pushkar**			every 15min	40min		
To and From Alwar						
Agra			hourly	2hr		
Ajmer	5 daily	6–8hr	4 daily	6–7hr		
Bharatpur			every 30min	2hr 30min		
Chittaurgarh	2 daily	13–17hr				
Deeg			every 15min	1hr 30min		
Delhi	8 daily	3–4hr	15 daily	4–5hr		
To and From Bharatpur						
Agra	3 daily	2hr	hourly	2hr		
Bombay	4 daily	19hr 20min–27hr				
Delhi	4 daily	5–6hr	15 daily	4–5hr		
Mathura	4 daily	1hr				
Sawai Madhopur	5 daily	2hr 10min–4hr 35min				
To and From Bikaner						
Churu	2 daily	4hr 30min				
Delhi	2 daily	11hr 30min	3 daily	11hr		
Fatehpur			5 daily	5hr 30min		
Gajner			9 daily	1hr		
Jaisalmer			6 daily	6hr 30min		
Jhunjhunu			1 daily	7hr		
Mandawa			1 daily	6hr		
To and From Kota						
Ahmedabad	2 daily	10hr 10min				
Bombay	6 daily	11hr 30min–21hr				
Bundi			hourly	45min		
Chittaurgarh			6 daily	4–6hr		
Delhi	9 daily	5hr 30min–9hr 30min				
Jhalawar			hourly	2hr 30min		
Mathura	5 daily	5–7hr				
Sawai Madhopur	6 daily	1hr 40min–2hr 50min	7 daily	3–5hr		
Ujjain	1 daily	6hr	2 daily	5–6hr		
To and From Mount Abu*						
Ahmedabad	4 daily	4hr 25min–8hr	2 daily	6hr		
Ajmer	3 daily	7hr				
Alwar	1 daily	8hr 30min–16hr				
Bharatpur	1 daily	22hr				
Bhuj			1 daily	8hr		
Delhi	3 daily	18–20hr				
Jaisalmer			1 daily	12hr		
Ranakpur			1 daily	5hr		

* Trains for Mount Abu use the **Abu Road** station, 1hr away on regular buses; see p.191.
** Long-distance travel connections for **Pushkar** are best made via Ajmer; see p.157.

THE PALACE ON WHEELS

To enjoy the life of Rajasthan's former maharajas and maharanis, you have two options: either splash out and stay a night in one of the illustrious palace hotels, or go the whole hog and spend a week travelling like royalty between the state's finest cities on the **Palace on Wheels**. India's answer to the *Orient Express*, the *Palace on Wheels* is among the most luxurious trains in the world, and offers an unrivalled tour of beautiful countryside and stupendous monuments. In 1993 the maharajas' carriages were updated into modern coaches, still decorated with original designs. Within the air-conditioned train, twin bedrooms, spacious lounges, dining rooms and bars are all decked out in classic Rajput style, using local cloths and soft bolsters to complement the traditional carved wood and stone inlay designs that cover the walls. Each group of tourists is attended by hosts in full royal livery, often greeted with garlands and trumpets in the larger cities, and courteously guided around forts and palaces.

The whistle-stop tour starts each week in Delhi, with stops at Jaipur, Chittaurgarh, Udaipur, Jaisalmer, Jodhpur, Bharatpur and Agra. The price (Oct–March US$200 per person per day for double occupancy, US$350 for single occupancy; April–Sept US$175 for double occupancy, US$300 for single occupancy) includes all meals, buffet lunches at the palace hotels of Udaipur and Jaipur, and a camel ride and dance show in Jaisalmer. The trip is brief, and extortionately expensive, but it's a must for train buffs, upmarket travellers with limited time, and anyone who simply likes to be pampered.

Bookings can be made through RTDC offices, or in railway offices in the US, Australasia, Thailand, the UK and other European countries. Addresses are given in *Basics* on p.30; for details of plans for similar services elsewhere in India, see p.30.

who plundered Rajput lands and extorted huge sums of protection money from territories as strong as Mewar, whose capital was Udaipur, and Marwar, whose ruling family in Jodhpur had never submitted to any other power. The Rajputs eventually turned for help to the Marathas' chief rivals, the **British**, and signed formal treaties as to mutual allies and enemies. Although in theory the Residents who represented British authority in each state were supposed to be neutral communicators, they were soon wielding more power than the Rajput princes. However, the Rajputs were never denied their royal status, and relations were so amicable that few joined the Mutiny of 1857. Wealth from overland trade enabled the Rajputs to festoon their palaces with silks, carpets, jewels and furnishings far beyond the imagination of most Rajput citizens, while the prosperous **Marwari** merchants of the northwest built and decorated stylish mansions, temples and meeting halls. Murals depicting British ministers with Indians, British hunting parties, ladies, motor cars and black-capped bobbies are firm reminders of the strong alliance between the two ruling powers.

The nationwide clamour for Independence in the years up to 1947 eventually proved stronger in Rajasthan than Rajput loyalty; when British rule ended the Rajputs were left out on a limb. With persuasion from the new Indian government including the offer of "privy purses", they agreed one by one to join the Indian Union, and in March 1949 the 22 states of Rajputana finally merged to form the state of **Rajasthan**.

But for three brief years of Janata domination from 1977 onwards, the **Congress** has held sway over Rajasthan since its first democratic elections in 1952. Central control soon exposed the Rajputs' neglect of their subjects, whom they had entrusted to power-thirsty landowners (*jaghidars*), and village councils (*panchayats*) were set up to organize local affairs. Nonetheless, several princes still maintain splendid households amid great honour. Since 1947 the literacy rate has risen from 8.95 percent to 25 percent, and several universities have been established, though female illiteracy is still higher than elsewhere in India. New industries benefit from an increased electricity supply that once only met the needs of palaces, and now reaches most villages, while irrigation schemes such as the Indira Gandhi Canal, which brings water from Punjab across the northern deserts to Bikaner and Jaisalmer, have improved crop production, and provided relief in times of inadequate monsoon.

Jaipur

A flamboyant showcase of Rajasthani architecture and flair at its most irresistible, the **Pink City** of **JAIPUR** has long been established on tourist itineraries as the third corner of India's "Golden Triangle", just 300km southwest of Delhi and 200km west of Agra. Though the "Pink City" label itself applies specifically to the old walled quarter of the Rajasthani capital, in the northeast of town, glorious palaces and temples, in an assortment of styles that span the centuries, are scattered throughout the whole urban area. The walled city is suffused with a gentle pink light, flashed through by bright turbans and *saris*, while in the pink shops and houses that line its orderly streets, craftsmen create objects of delicate beauty with time-honoured traditional skills, in full view of the hectic swirl of shoppers and tourists outside.

Lying snugly on the bed of a long-dry lake, Jaipur laps against hills in the north, east and west, and rolls across the open plains to the south towards Bundi. Getting and keeping your bearings is simple; even if you can't see the high walls of the Pink City, the hills behind it in the northeast, topped by **Nahagarh Fort**, are always conspicuous.

The **Pink City** houses the principal tourist attractions – the Palace of Winds or **Hawa Mahal**, and Jai Singh's **City Palace** and **Observatory** – while the **Ram Niwas Garden**, zoo, **Albert Hall** (**Central Museum**) and **Modern Art Gallery** are a short way south of the walls, within easy walking distance of its gates.

Broad and widely spaced roads in the newer areas outside the walls accommodate the industries and businesses that underlie the economy of the modern city, as well as most of Jaipur's hotels. **Mirza Imail Road** is the main route from west to east (south of the old city), on which you'll find the GPO, hotels and restaurants and some of the larger boutiques and jewellery shops. **Station Road** runs from the railway station in the west, past the bus stand and on to Chand Pole, the westernmost gate of the old city.

For all its appeal, Jaipur's somewhat impersonal layout and heavy traffic, combined with the aggression of over-eager traders, tends to reduce the appeal of a long stay. Few travellers find it easy to relax here, though most spend a good few days visiting the sublime palaces, exploring the ruins and wandering through the bazaars, renowned for carpets, clothes, and the best selection of precious stones and metals in India.

If you're anywhere near Jaipur in March, don't miss the **Elephant Festival**, one of India's most flamboyant parades, celebrated with full Rajput pomp.

A brief history

Jaipur is one of Rajasthan's younger cities, founded in 1727. In 1700, **Jai Singh II** succeeded at the tender age of thirteen to the throne of the **Kuchwaha Rajputs** in Ajmer, inheriting a realm that encompassed Shekawati to the north, and spread east to the borders of the kingdom of the Jats at Bayana, south to Aligarh, and west to Kishangarh where its boundaries met the mighty kingdoms of the Mewars (Udaipur) and Marwars (Jodhpur). Although the Kuchwaha Rajputs had been the first to ally themselves with the Mughals, in 1561, thereby inviting contempt from other Rajput clans, the free flow of trade, art and ideas with their obliging overlords had by this time won them great prosperity. Jai Singh's sharp wit greatly impressed the Mughal emperor Aurangzeb, who bestowed upon him the title of "Sawai" (one and a quarter), to imply his superlative potential. Jai Singh proved his distinction, excelling in battle, politics and learning, and quickly showing an aptitude for astronomy and an extraordinary passion for symmetry.

When Jai Singh decided to move his capital south from the cramped hilly area of Amber, he drew up plans for the new city of Jaipur, named after himself, in accordance with the ancient Hindu treatise *Shilpa Sashtra*, a formal exposition on architecture written soon after the compilation of the *Vedas*. With the aid of the superb Bengali architect Vidyadhar Bhattacharaya, he had the city built in under eight years, following the sacred guidelines with unrivalled precision. The **City Palace** was also designed by him, as was **Jantar Mantar**, the largest stone-built observatory in the world.

After Jai Singh's fruitful 43-year reign came an inevitable battle for succession between the offspring he had fathered with 28 wives and four concubines, and the state was thrown into turmoil. Much of its territory was lost to Marathas and Jats, and the British quickly moved in to take advantage of Rajput infighting, gaining power for themselves while forming alliances with the Rajputs to avoid inconvenient conflict. Unlike their neighbours in Delhi and Agra, the rulers of Jaipur remained loyal to the British during the bloody uprisings of 1857. Following Independence in 1947, Jaipur merged with the states of Bikaner, Jodhpur and Jaisalmer; it became capital of Rajasthan in 1956. Today, with a population bordering on two million, the state's most advanced commercial and business centre remains as prosperous as ever.

Arrival and information

Jaipur's **airport**, 15km south of the main town, plays host to the internal flights of *Indian Airlines*. An airport bus into town costs Rs20; taxis charge more like Rs80–100.

The **railway station** is 1km west of the Pink City, very close to the main concentration of hotels, while ordinary and "deluxe" **buses** from all over Rajasthan and further afield arrive at the central **Inter-state bus terminal** on Station Road. Rickshaws at both stations will take you to your lodgings, invariably asking over the odds; for hotels along MI Road and Station Road the fare should be between Rs5 and Rs10.

Information

Tourist information offices in all the RTDC hotels (see p.136) provide information on Jaipur's sights and guided tours. The most efficient office, on Platform 1 of the railway station (☎69714), is open round the clock except on public holidays. They can help find accommodation, and have good local maps. The monthly **Jaipur Vision**, listing hotels, restaurants, sights, events, shopping hints and fair rickshaw prices, should be in stock in *Books Corner* on MI Rd, and costs Rs3.

Changing travellers' cheques is no problem, though it may be time-consuming. Most **banks** open on weekdays only, between 11am and 2pm; they include *Bank of Baroda*, Johari Bazaar; *State Bank of India*, Sanganeri Gate, MI Rd; *Punjab National Bank*, near Hawa Mahal; and *State Bank of Bikaner and Jaipur* (Mon–Fri noon–6pm). All upper-class hotels offer currency exchange, usually at poor rates.

For **poste restante** go to the GPO on MI Rd (Mon–Sat 9am–6pm). Parcels or registered mail should be picked up from the sorting office behind the main desks.

City transport

Jaipur's frenzied flow of vehicles is at its heaviest during the morning and evening peak periods; at other times the streets can be surprisingly quiet, and you can enjoy the sights and street activity without gripping your seat in fear. Jaipur is fairly spread out, and although it's pleasant to walk around the Pink City, you may well need some form of transport to get you there.

The telephone **area code** for Jaipur is ☎0141.

JAIPUR

△ Galta

RESTAURANTS:
1 Bismallah
2 Bamboo Hut
3 Annapurna
4 Natraj
5 Surya Mahal
6 Niro's

Suraipole Gate

Elephant Owners' Area

HOTELS:
A Jaipur Ashok
B Jaipur Inn
C Bissau Palace
D Khetri House
E RTDC Swagat
F RTDC Teej
G Jai Mangal Palace
H Mangal
I Arya Niwas
J Mansingh
K RTDC Gangaur
L Rajputana Palace

M Khasa Kothi
N Kaiser-I-Hind
O Jai Mahal
P RTDC Jaipur
Q Evergreen Guest House
R Rajmahal Palace Hotel
S Rambagh Palace
T Diggi Palace
U Narayan Vilas
V Sweet Dream
W L M B Hotel & Restaurant
X Kailash
Y Tourist Hotel

△ Gaitor & Amber

△ Nahargarh Fort

SURAJPOLE BAZAAR

GHORA NIKAS RD

MOTI KATRA BAZAAR

Talkatora Tank

Jantar Mantar

Govind Devji

RAM GANJ BAZAAR

HAWA MAHAL BAZAAR

City Palace & Museum

Hawa Mahal

Jami Masjid

Cycle Rental Shop

SIRE DEORHI BAZAAR

JOHARI BAZAAR

TRIPOLIA BAZAAR

INDRA BAZAAR

GANGAURI BAZAAR

CHANDPOLE BAZAAR

KISHAN POLE BAZAAR

GHAT DARWAZA RASTA

Ram Niwas Gardens & Zoo

New Gate

Central Museum

Museum of Indology

MOTI DOONGARI RD

JAWAHAR LAL NEHRU MARG

INDUSTRIAL RD

Ajmeri Gate

Rajmandir Cinema

MI RD

GOPI NATH MARG

BHAGWAN DAS RD

MAHAVIR MARG

HOSPITAL RD

SAWA RAM SINGH RD

RAM SINGH RD

Chand Pole

JHOTWARA RD

STATION RD

Bus Stand

Sita World Travels

TANK RD

GOVIND MARG

YANASAI MARG

MIRZA ISMAIL RD

ASHOK MARG

BRAHMPURI MARG

MALVIYA MARG

KAROLINI MARG

Police Station

KABIR MARG

SHIV MARG

TANTANDRA RD

STATION RD

MIRZA ISMAIL RD

SADAR PATEL MARG

Jaipur Railway Station

BHAWANI SINGH MARG

SARDAR PATEL MARG

PRITHVI RAJ RD

△ Airport

500 m

N

Unmetered yellow-top **taxis** have stands on MI Road. Precarious **tempos** can be hailed along all the main thoroughfares in and out of the Pink City; the flat rate is Rs2 or 3. Cheaper (and fuller) **minibuses**, some coloured light pink, ply the same routes, zig-zagging and jerking through the chaotic jumble of traffic. For a less hair-raising experience, try an **auto-rickshaw**, which should be metered, or a **cycle rickshaw**.

A stall on Kishan Pole Bazaar on the right, a little beyond Ajmeri Gate, rents out reliable **bicycles** for Rs10 per day (opens at 8am), or residents at the *Evergreen Hotel* can rent from there. The use of an RTDC **car** (with driver) costs from Rs100 for one hour to Rs500 for twelve; they can be picked up at the *Tourist Hotel*, MI Rd.

City tours

One efficient way to see Jaipur's main attractions is on a guided tour. The inexpensive RTDC tours can be a trifle rushed, but they are good value and the guides are very informative. **Half-day** tours take in Hawa Mahal, Observatory, City Palace and Museum, Amber Fort, Jaigarh Fort and Central Museum (daily, starting from the railway station and the RTDC *Tourist Hotel* on MI Rd at 8am, 11.30am & 1.30pm; 5hr, book the day before). The **full-day** tour (daily 9am–6pm) also includes the Dolls Museum, Birla Mandir and Nahagarh Fort – getting to the fort alone costs more than the tour itself, unless you walk. RTDC plans to make the morning and afternoon half-day tours different, so that you can see everything in two separate half days without exhausting yourself. ITDC *Ashok Travels and Tours* at the gates of the *Khasa Kothi* hotel offers full- and half-day tours of Jaipur and Amber.

The Pink City

For anyone familiar with other Indian cities, the rigorous geometry of Jaipur's **Pink City** may come as a surprise. High walls with ten gates enclose the old city, which is divided into seven sectors, with the City Palace at its heart. Maharaja Jai Singh clearly aimed for architectural perfection when he planned the city in 1727; instead of a maze of narrow winding alleys, the spacious streets are completely straight and laid out at right angles to each other, in accordance with calculations laid down in the *Shilpa Shastra*. All streets are of prescribed widths and the shops are equally proportioned; even the mosques and temples slot neatly into place between shops and houses. The only buildings to stray from the structural uniformity are the City Palace and the Hawa Mahal.

The single most striking feature of the old city, its **pink** colour, did not in fact form part of Jai Singh's plans. Although many people think the rosy hue is as old as the buildings themselves, they were in fact originally a sallow yellow. Pink is traditionally the colour of hospitality in Rajasthan, but the wash, now regularly reapplied, has only been compulsory since the city was spruced up in preparation for the visit of Prince Albert from England in 1856.

Each quarter in the Pink City is home to a particular centre of activity or commerce. **Surajpole Bazaar** in the southeast corner houses elephants and their owners; **Nehru Bazaar** (closed Tues) and **Bapu Bazaar** (closed Sun) are special centres for textiles, perfumes and locally styled camel skin shoes; shops in **Tripolia Bazaar** and **Chaura Rasta** sell textiles and household utensils. For Jaipur's much celebrated silver, sparkling gems and tie-dyed *saris*, go to **Johari Bazaar** (partly closed on Sun & Tues). Behind the City Palace, to the north, spacious gardens surround Govind Devji Temple and the vast Talkatora water tank.

Hawa Mahal

Jaipur's most acclaimed landmark, the tapering **Hawa Mahal**, or "Palace of Winds", stands to the west of the City Palace, where it exudes an orangey pink glow in the rays of the rising sun. Built in 1799 to enable the women of the court to watch street processions while remaining in a strict state of *purdah*, its five-storey facade, decked with no less than 593 finely screened windows and balconies, makes the building seem far larger than it really is; in fact it is little more than one room thick in most parts.

Though the primary source of its appeal is undoubtedly the fantastic honeycomb pink and white face, visitors can go inside to see exactly where the women sat and take a close look at the detailed stone work (enter from the back: daily 9am–4.30pm; Rs1).

City Palace

Daily 9am–4.30pm. Rs20; half-price on holy days. Cameras Rs10 extra, videos Rs35.

The magnificent **City Palace**, open to the public as the **Sawai Man Singh Museum**, stands enclosed by a high wall in the centre of the city amid fine gardens and courtyards. The royal family still occupies part of the palace, advancing in procession on formal occasions through the grand **Tripolia Gate** in the centre of the southern wall. Less regal visitors must enter through **Atish Gate** left of the main gate or **Nakkar Gate** in the west, passing the food stalls and souvenir shops in **Jalebi Chowk**.

The palace was conceived and built by Jai Singh, but many of the apartments and halls were added by his successors. The exhibits and interior design have lost none of the pomp and splendour of their glory days. Each door and gateway is heavily decorated, each chandelier intact and each hall guarded by sentinels decked in full royal livery, so that Jaipur's palace, unlike any other in Rajasthan, impresses upon the visitor the continuity of a living royal presence.

An ornate gateway in the southwest corner of the complex leads into the first courtyard, with the solid marble **Mubarak Mahal** in its centre. This elegant palace, built in 1890, holds the textile section of the museum, where stylish clothes include those worn by Madho Singh I (one of Jai Singh's sons) who stood a full two metres tall. Musical instruments used to entertain the rulers are also on display.

The first floor of the building next to the Mubarak Mahal houses the royal **arsenal**. Inside what was once the harem, with its delicate paintings on the walls and mirrors glittering on the ceilings, is laid out a menacing array of spears, swords, shields and daggers. The terrifying blades conjure up images of raging battles, but inscriptions and bejewelled decorations on handles and shields make them surprisingly attractive on purely aesthetic grounds.

As you enter the second courtyard you're confronted by the raised **Diwan-i-Khas**, the Hall of Private Audience, built in sandstone and marble. Open sided, with its roof raised on marble pillars, the hall contains two silver urns, reputedly the largest crafted silver objects in the world, each over five feet high. When Madho Singh II went to England to attend the coronation of King Edward VII in 1901, he was so reluctant to trust the water in the west that he had these urns filled with Ganges water and took them along with him.

In the centre of the compound, with balconies and windows studding its seven-storey facade, **Chandra Mahal** is the residence of the royal family. You can see it best from **Pritam Niwas Chowk**, known as Peacock Courtyard, to the west of the Diwan-i-Khas. Against the ochre walls of this court, four gateways provide a shock of dazzling colour, decorated with peacocks and regular patterns in red, green, blue and gold.

The last, and largest, section of the museum is housed in the **Diwan-i-Am**, once the Hall of Public Audience, where ornate pillars support the high ceilings. The walls, intricately painted with touches of deep red and gold, provide perfect mounts for immense medieval Afghan and Pakistani carpets. Miniatures from the Mughal and Jaipur schools, and Jai Singh's translations in Arabic and Sanskrit of the astronomical treatises of ancient scientists such as Euclid and Ptolemy, are displayed in glass cases, all under the breeze of huge fans and the shimmer of chandeliers.

Jantar Mantar

The incredible brick curves, slants, circles and pillars of Jai Singh's astronomical **observatory**, overlaid with sherbet-yellow gypsum, are solidly planted in the southern courtyard of the palace complex. A total of eighteen instruments were erected between 1728 and 1734 by Jai Singh; some are triangular, some are circular or semicircular, and all are very large. Although Jai Singh was influenced by the works of foreign astrologers and the advice of his teachers – one of whom was his mother – many of the devices were of his own invention.

Entrance to the observatory (same hours as the palace) is Rs5, though it's a good idea to pay Rs25–50 extra to get the services of a guide. The instruments are built so that shadows fall onto marked surfaces, identifying the position and movement of stars and planets, telling the time, and even predicting the intensity of the monsoon. The time calculated is unique to Jaipur, between ten and forty-one minutes (depending on the time of year) behind Indian standard time, but is used to calculate the Hindu (lunar) calendar. Probably the most impressive of Jai Singh's constructions is the sundial, **Samrat Yantra**. Its slanting centrepiece, or *gnomon*, reaches a height of ninety feet, casting shadows onto curved stone faces that are graduated in hours. Each hour is divided into thirty parts, so the time calculated is accurate to within two minutes. The smaller sundial has an accuracy of twenty minutes.

A more original device, the **Jaiprakash Yantra**, consists of two hemispheres laid in the ground, each composed of six curving marble slabs with a suspended ring in the centre whose shadow marks the day, time and zodiac symbol. The latter function is vital in calculations of auspicious days for marriage; when unfavourable planets are in influential positions, for example between August and October, marriages have always been avoided.

Outside the Pink City

Jaipur's attractions outside the Pink City include museums, temples and cenotaphs, which can be reached from the centre of town on foot or by rickshaw.

Ram Niwas Public Gardens

South of the Pink City, on the road leading out of New Gate, lie 36 acres of lush gardens, named **Ram Niwas Public Gardens** after the planner, Ram Singh, who ruled Jaipur from 1835 to 1880. The gardens represent but a small fraction of Ram Singh's successful efforts to improve public services, and originally covered 76 acres.

As well as providing parks for the citizens, the gardens now house a number of institutions, the most notable being the **Albert Hall**, in which you'll find the **Central Museum** (daily 9am–4.30pm; Rs1), designed by the British architect Sir Samuel Jacob. This remarkable stately construction, built over several years from 1867 onwards, drew heavily on contemporary British models, but its arched verandahs and rooftop domed pavilions hint at the Mughal background of its artisans. The exhibits within, including miniature paintings, rocks, clothes and ornamental wooden boxes, are not quite as inspiring as the building itself, but it's worth seeking out the highly original display of *yoga* postures demonstrated by tiny clay *sadhus*.

Other museums within the gardens include the **Museum of Indology**, **Gallery of Modern Art** (same hours as the Central Museum) and the **zoo** (same hours), which houses Indian wildlife in the usual poor conditions, and baby crocodiles in a small breeding farm.

Gaitor

A short distance north of the City Palace, and just over 6km from central Jaipur on the Amber road, the walled complex of **Gaitor** contains the stately marble *chhatris* of

Jaipur's ruling family. Built by Jai Singh II, the complex contains memorials to himself and his successors, including his son and grandson, with room set aside for a future memorial to the present head of the family.

Unless a ruler should happen to die an untimely death, the construction of his cenotaph is normally well under way during his lifetime, and traditionally each ruler takes exceptional pains to ensure that the marble carving on his own tomb is of an appropriately high standard. That of Jai Singh is inlaid with scenes from Hindu mythology, and processions from his reign, depicting among other things the Hawa Mahal.

Birla Mandir

One of Jaipur's newer temples, **Birla Mandir**, was built in the southeast of town in 1985, funded by the affluent Birla family. The large marble structure houses ornate statues of Lakshmi and Narayan dressed in gaudy robes, representing the Hindu vision of heavenly luxury. Carvings in the temple and on pillars supporting covered walkways include images of the Hindu pantheon and Jesus, Mary and St Francis of Assisi. The design leans towards the idea of universal religion, but architecturally its standard is nowhere near as high as India's ancient temples.

Accommodation

As a major centre for business and tourism, Jaipur has a wide selection of **hotels**. Dull but adequate options and elaborate old palaces share roads with hotels that wouldn't seem out of place in any western capital. Some have swimming pools, most have restaurants, and the more expensive hotels offer taxi services to and from the airport. At busy times of year, such as Christmas and the Elephant Festival (first half of March), it's prudent to book ahead.

Inexpensive

Diggi Palace, Diggi House, Shivaji Marg, Hospital Rd (☎374265). A welcome respite from the dust and noise. Clean and well-managed 200-year-old palace with accommodation for budget travellers as well as a/c rooms and cottages facing beautiful lawns. Excellent meals in terrace restaurant. Party in grand hall at Christmas. ①–⑤.

Evergreen Guest House, Chameliwala Mkt, MI Rd (☎363446). Crowded and shabby, but the best of the market's budget hotels, popular with young travellers. Exceptionally poor dorms and more agreeable rooms, many with private bathrooms. Pleasant garden area, mediocre restaurant and tiny swimming pool. Often full. ①–③.

Jaipur Inn, Shiv Marg, Bani Park (☎66057). A selection of rooms and an excellent dormitory, all spotlessly clean. Camping on the lawn at cheap rates. Tasty and filling evening meals. ①–②.

Kaiser-I-Hind, Palace Rd (☎74195). Just opposite the *Rajputana Palace*. An old house whose huge suites and musty dining hall still ring of the days of the Raj, and perhaps haven't been dusted since. Loads of character. Airy verandahs and garden. ②.

Tourist Hotel, MI Rd (☎360238). Large place with tatty, cheap rooms and vast lawns. ①–②.

<table>
<tr><td colspan="3">**ACCOMMODATION PRICE CODES**</td></tr>
<tr><td colspan="3">All **accommodation prices** in this book have been coded using the symbols below. In principle the prices given are for the least expensive double rooms in each establishment; however, some hotels, usually in category ①, offer rates per bed rather than per room. Local taxes are not included unless specifically stated. For more details, see p.34.</td></tr>
<tr><td>①   up to Rs100</td><td>④   Rs225–350</td><td>⑦   Rs750–1200</td></tr>
<tr><td>②   Rs100–150</td><td>⑤   Rs350–500</td><td>⑧   Rs1200–2200</td></tr>
<tr><td>③   Rs150–225</td><td>⑥   Rs500–750</td><td>⑨   Rs2200 and up</td></tr>
</table>

Moderate

Arya Niwas, behind Amber Complex, Sansar Chandra Rd (☎73456). Extremely clean, but lacking character and slightly impersonal. Large hotel; all rooms have private bathroom and running hot water. Restaurant and bar, overlooking front lawn. Tours and car rental. ②–④.

Jai Mangal Palace, Station Rd (☎62222). Directly opposite the bus stand. Simple but clean rooms, hot water in private bathrooms, TV and uninspired decor. Bar, restaurant and beauty parlour. ③–⑤.

Kailash, Johari Bazaar (☎565372). One of the few hotels in the heart of the Pink City, opposite the Jama Masjid. Though a little cramped, the rooms are OK; the most expensive have private bathrooms with showers, and windows overlooking the constantly active street. ③.

Khetri House, outside Chand Pole. Huge suites, complete with antique furniture, in an old house where you can feel the centuries. Not to all tastes, but some will love it. ③–⑤.

Mangal, Sansar Chandra Rd (☎75126). Good location near the bus stand, off the busy main road. The rooms, all with TV, are carpeted and stuffy. Good service, restaurant, but over-priced. ③–⑤.

RTDC Gangaur Tourist Bungalow, Sansar Chandra Rd (☎60231). Smart hotel. Comfortable, carpeted, tastefully furnished rooms; some deluxe, some a/c. Good restaurant and snack bar. ③.

RTDC Jaipur, MI Rd (☎60231). Rooms are spacious and well furnished but dull and unkempt; poor value. Snacks and vegetarian dishes in attached restaurant. ⑤.

RTDC Swagat Tourist Bungalow, Station Rd (☎67560). Moderately comfortable place, close to the train station. Uninspiring but clean rooms, and a dormitory. ③.

RTDC Teej, Collectorate Rd, Bani Park (☎74206). Extremely well-kept, clean and comfortable. Cheaper beds in spacious and fresh dorms. It also has a good restaurant. ④.

Sweet Dream, Nehru Bazaar (☎74409). Friendly lodge, just inside Ajmeri Gate in the Pink City. Clean rooms on several floors, some with balcony, some a/c, and a rooftop restaurant. ③–⑤.

Expensive

Bissau Palace, outside Chand Pole (☎74191). A 1920s building decorated with artefacts of the heroic fighting days before Independence. Tasteful rooms, some a/c, plus pleasant gardens, swimming pool, lawn tennis and badminton courts. Adequate parking space, and dining facilities. ⑤–⑥.

Jai Mahal, Jacob Rd, Civil Lines (☎371616). A plush hotel southwest of the railway station, a few kilometres from the Pink City. Regal atmosphere, swimming pool, gardens and restaurant. ⑥.

Jaipur Ashok, Jai Singh Circle, Bani Park (☎75121). Immaculate a/c rooms. En-suite bathrooms, luxurious swimming pool, bar, coffee shop and restaurant – plus resident astro-palmist. ⑧.

Khasa Kothi, just south of the junction of Station Rd and MI Rd (☎75151). Faded but comfortable, if a little expensive. Mediocre open-air restaurant amid spacious lawns. ⑤–⑦.

L M B, Johari Bazaar (☎565844). Plush a/c rooms, some with huge windows facing the road; much duller ones at the back. Foreigners pay in foreign currency. Excellent vegetarian restaurant. ⑥–⑦.

Mansingh, Sansar Chandra Rd (☎78771). Luxurious a/c twin and double rooms with large windows. Swimming pool, restaurant and bar. ⑧.

Narayan Vilas, Narayan Singh Circle (☎561291). Delightful old palace, almost 2km from the Pink City. Individually styled rooms feature original paintings on walls and ceilings, and classic furniture including four-poster beds. Very clean, with patios and shady gardens. Good food available. ⑥–⑦.

Rajmahal Palace, Sardar Patel Marg (☎521757). Stylish grand hotel, sensitively converted from the former British Residency. Swimming pool and bar. ⑨.

Rajputana Palace, Palace Rd (☎62030). A new high-standard, business-oriented *Welcome Group* hotel with high security, a fountained lobby, bar and restaurant. ⑨.

Rambagh Palace, Bhawani Singh Marg (☎381919). Spectacular palace hotel, popular with Indian movie stars, in fountained gardens. Super posh, with bar, restaurant, indoor swimming pool, tennis and squash courts, and nightly open-air folk music and dance performances. Foreigners pay in foreign currency. ⑨.

Eating and drinking

Jaipur's **restaurants** serve an assortment of Indian, Chinese and western cuisine. Plenty of sumptuous dishes are on offer in the top hotels, where you can relax in a bar before and after a meal. There are few street snack sellers, but inexpensive roadside

MOVING ON FROM JAIPUR

From Jaipur's **airport**, 15km south of town, the daily 9.40am flight to **Bombay** passes through **Aurangabad** (2hr 20min) and **Udaipur** (45min), and the daily 6.20pm departure goes via **Jodhpur** (45min) as well as Udaipur. There's an additional direct flight at 8pm on Mon, Wed, Fri & Sun (1hr 30min). Flights to **Delhi** (2 daily) take only 40min. Bookings can be made at *Indian Airlines* in Nehru Place (☎514500). Other airline offices include *Air India* (☎68569), *Delta Airlines* (☎62525), and *Thai Airways* (☎70062), all along MI Rd; *Air France* (☎77202), *Alitalia* (☎69120), and *Gulf Air* (☎577202) are in Jaipur Towers, also on MI Rd. *British Airways* is on Park St, off MI Rd (☎70734).

Train bookings should be made at least a day in advance. The fastest service to **Delhi**, the *Pink City Express* #2902, leaves daily at 5pm and arrives at 10.10pm. If you'd rather arrive in the morning, opt for the overnight *Jaipur–Delhi Shekawati Express* #9734, departing at 5.15pm (12hr). The *Bikaner Express* #4737 is the only train to **Bikaner** (10hr; overnight), while for **Shekawati**, the best bet is the 11.25am departure via Sikar (3hr 25min) and Jhunjhunu (5hr 35min). For Chittaurgarh (6hr 40min) and Udaipur (10hr 15min), take the day-time *Pink City Express* #2901, or the slower nightly *Chetak Express* #9615.

For destinations **south** of Rajasthan, good rail connections can be picked up at Ahmedabad, best reached on the 5.50pm *Ahmedabad Express* #9903 which arrives the next morning, having stopped at **Abu Road** at 4.55am. The fast *Express* #7569 to Andhra Pradesh departs daily at 1.40pm and arrives in Secunderabad the next day at 6.20am.

Shorter journeys to Agra, Ajmer, Pushkar and Bharatpur are best made on the frequent *Rajasthan State Transport* **buses** from the Inter-state bus stand. For longer routes, "deluxe" services guarantee seats, may be air-conditioned, and usually take less time than standard buses. Enquiries can be made by phone (☎75034), but it's less hassle in the long run to turn up at the Inter-state bus stand in person, and head for the relevant booking office (destinations are listed outside each cabin). **Udaipur** (10hr) is linked to Jaipur by three daily deluxe services, and ten leave each day for Jodhpur. Four deluxe buses make the seven-hour journey to Bikaner, and Delhi has 21 departures per day.

Some **travel agents** have their own services, or will book a seat for you, on desperately uncomfortable **video coaches** to Bombay, Lucknow, and even further afield.

eating-houses around the bus stand and on MI Rd, opposite Chameliwala Market, sell highly spiced and tasty *dhals* and sloppy curries.

For a cool refreshing drink, the *Milk Stop*, on Station Rd by the main crossroads, has velvety thick milkshakes, soft ice-cream and a genuine certificate to prove its ice and water are free from bacteria.

Annapurna, behind *Raj Mandir* cinema. Tasty Gujarati dishes and other veg food at low prices.

Ashiana, Nehru Bazaar. Small roof terrace above *Hotel Sweet Dream*, with views towards the Albert Hall, and good Indian food.

Bamboo Hut, MI Rd. Also called *Handi*, this open-air restaurant serves very good meat and vegetarian north Indian dishes at reasonable prices. Basic standards of hygiene.

Bismallah, Chandpole. One of a small group of restaurants bordering the busy meat and vegetable market, serving distinctly Islamic cuisine. Cheap meat dishes, a couple of vegetarian options.

Gauri, at *Gangaur Tourist Bungalow*, Sansar Chandra Rd. Fairly pricey snacks in a comfortable coffee shop.

L M B, Johari Bazaar (☎565844). A vegetarian restaurant of the purest and highest standards using special *deshi ghee*, but no garlic or onion. Outstandingly tasty food in comfortable a/c surroundings; dishes from south and north India. Very popular. Live classical music from 7pm onwards.

Natraj, MI Rd. Air-conditioned; good vegetarian food in the upper price bracket.

Niro's, MI Rd (☎374493). The vegetarian food here is superior, and so are the prices. Chinese, western and speciality Mughlai dishes.

Rambagh Palace Hotel, Bhawani Singh Marg (☎381919). Top-notch food from all over the world, at very steep prices. Beautiful gardens and an outdoor bar make a meal here a real treat.

Surya Mahal, MI Rd. Next to *Natraj* and *Niro's*, and very similar; its menu also offers pizza.

Listings

Bookstores *Books Corner* on MI Rd just past *Niro's* has up-to-date magazines, newspapers and books in all major European languages. Hotels *Evergreen* and *Jaipur Inn* have secondhand stalls.

Cinemas Jaipur is packed with picture palaces including the huge, famous and very plush *Raj Mandir* on Bhagwan Das Rd just off MI Rd. Four daily showings, and there's always a queue.

Cultural Entertainment *Panghat Theatre* at *Rambagh Palace Hotel* has nightly performances of Rajasthani dance and music, from 7pm.

Emergency Services Police ☎100; Ambulance ☎102; Fire ☎101.

Hospitals The most reliable is *SMS Hospital*, Jawaharlal Nehru Marg (☎560291 or 564222).

Opticians Many places in Kishan Pole Bazaar near Ajmeri Gate.

Phone Most hotels offer direct dialling to other states and abroad, but calls are cheaper in shops offering STD/ISD/PCO. Look for the yellow signs. Some such shops also offer fax facilities.

Photography *Fuji* outlet on Kishan Pole Bazaar, near Ajmeri Gate.

Police Stations The main station is on Station Rd opposite the railway station (☎74444).

Swimming Pools Non-residents can use the pool at *Hotel Jaipur Ashok* for Rs150, where lawns, deck chairs and poolside refreshments are available. *Evergreen Guest House* charges Rs40 for use of a small pool with a concrete surround. No other upper-class hotels allow non-residents to swim on their premises.

Travel Agents *GSA Janta Travels*, MI Rd (☎68569). *Sita World Travels*, Station Rd (☎66809 or 68226), an agent for *Indian Airlines*, deals with international and domestic flights very efficiently. The *Thomas Cook* office is in Jaipur Towers, MI Rd. *Rajasthan Tours*, at the *Rambagh Palace* (☎381041), is a reputable agent for excursions out of Jaipur.

Around Jaipur

Forts, palaces, temples and ruins from a thousand years of Kuchwaha history adorn the hills and valleys in the vicinity of Jaipur. The superb palaces of **Amber** provide the most obvious destination for a trip out of the main city, but you can also visit the forts of **Jaigarh** and **Nahagarh** that crown the hills to the north, the temples strewn in the valley east of Jaipur at **Galta**, or travel south to search out the traditional potters and dyers of **Sanganer**.

Organized tours go north and visit Amber, Jaigarh and Nahagarh in a day; only Amber is accessible by public transport, though minibuses run to Sanganer, and there's always the option of car rental for more leisurely excursions. Rickshaw *wallahs* who offer tours are likely to stop at shops and factories to get the commission vital to their livelihood. Although this can prove irritating, it enables you to watch Jaipur's artisans at work, probably see carpets in the making and stop wherever you want en route.

Amber

On the crest of a rocky hill behind Maota Lake, 11km north of Jaipur, the Rajput stronghold of **AMBER** was the capital of the Kuchwaha Rajputs from 1037 until 1728. Fortified by natural hills, high ramparts and a succession of gates along a cobbled road, Amber's magnificent palaces are distinctly Rajput, but it's clear that Mughal ideas crept in to influence the design. For instance, the practice of covering walls with mosaics of mirrors is purely Mughal, first introduced to India at Agra and Fatehpur Sikri.

It's worth visiting Amber independently, as there's so much to see; tour groups rarely get enough time to view the entire compound, let alone to scramble into the town behind it, dotted with fascinating temples and ruins. Regular public buses to Amber leave from outside Jaipur's Hawa Mahal, stopping on the main road below the palaces. From there you can either enjoy a pleasant twenty-minute (uphill) walk, take a jeep for Rs10, or waddle like the royals of yesteryear on an elephant for a steep Rs250 (per elephant).

Entering the palace complex (daily 9am–5pm; Rs2) from the east through Suraj Pole (Sun Gate), you step into the main courtyard, **Jaleb Chowk**, where there's another opportunity to ride an elephant, for Rs20. In its southwest corner, the Shri Sila Devi temple was the Kuchwaha shrine to the goddess of war, Sila, an aspect of Kali; the image inside was brought to Amber from Bengal in 1604. Next to this, at the head of a flight of steps, Singh Pole (Lion Gate) provides access to the palaces.

The lofty Hall of Public Audience, **Diwan-i-Am**, used by Raja Jai Singh I and his successors from 1639 onwards, stands in the entrance courtyard, while opposite in the south wall of the yard, the exquisitely painted **Ganesh Pole** leads through narrow passages into the charming royal apartments. Here, protruding from the east wall, the dazzling **Sheesh Mahal** houses what were the private chambers of the Maharaja and his queen. Shards of mirror and coloured glass form an intricate mosaic that entirely covers the inner and outer walls and ceilings of the rooms. From a distance they seem to be covered in jewels, tinted with pastel shafts of sunlight that seep through the stained-glass windows.

A fountained garden separates the mirrored palace from the "pleasure palace" opposite, **Sukh Mahal**, where marble rooms are cooled by water cascading through fine perforations in the centre of the wall – an early and very efficient system of air conditioning. The doors here are inlaid with ivory and sandalwood.

Above the Sheesh Mahal, the small chamber of the brilliant **Jas Mandir** radiates with the light and colour of similar mosaics. Guarded from the glare of the sun in the east by delicate marble screens, it served as a cool refuge in summer.

The oldest part of the complex, the **Palace of Man Singh I**, lies south of the main quadrangle. The pillared *biradiri* in the centre of the courtyard was once a meeting area for the maharanis, shrouded from men's eyes by flowing curtains. Narrow passages and stairwells connect small rooms and open balconies on all sides.

Walking down the hill behind the fort – via the elephant stable in the western corner of Jaleb Chowk – brings you to the temples and ruined mansions of **Amber town**.

Jaigarh

The mighty **Jaigarh**, or "Tiger Fort" (daily 9am–4.30pm; Rs10), built in 1600, stands high on the hill behind Amber. As the Kuchwahas were on friendly terms with the Mughals, the fort saw few battles, and its immense cannon – the largest in Asia, it needed a hundred kilos of gunpowder for one shot and could send a ball 27 miles – was never fired in anger. The small museum displaying artillery, old maps, coins and photographs is unspectacular, but has an interesting hand-drawn floor plan of the palaces at Amber. The fort's robust bastions command a view unrivalled in the whole of Rajasthan.

You can walk to Jaigarh from Amber, but it's a pretty long climb; the alternative is to descend to the valley and follow by vehicle the much longer road that leads to both Jaigarh and Nahagarh.

Nahagarh

Teetering on the edge of the hills northeast of Jaipur, **Nahagarh Fort** (entrance free) was built by Jai Singh II in 1734 as a retreat for his wives, the maharanis. Its unique design, regular and repetitive, stands in contrast to the other royal dwellings in Jaipur, and the views are breathtaking.

All the queens' apartments are identical, arranged around the central courtyard in perfect symmetry, each with a room for a personal maidservant. Ram Singh, who in 1868 built more apartments on the upper floor, continued Jai Singh's tradition of orderly design by constructing another set of identical rooms. These bear traces of paintings, and their stained-glass windows are slightly damaged but still quaint.

Vehicles of any kind can only get to the fort along a road that branches off Amber Road, a nine-kilometre journey from Jaipur. However, if you're feeling energetic, it's possible to **walk** there along a two-kilometre footpath that starts northwest of the City Palace. A very reasonably priced cafe by the fort serves meals and snacks.

If you want to **stay** somewhere a little out of the ordinary, the old buildings next to the fort hold one double room for rent (②; book at a tourist office in town): the room is simple but the views spectacular, with six windows facing west and south.

Galta

Nestling in a steep-sided valley 2km west of Jaipur, **GALTA** is a picturesque collection of temples, two hundred and fifty years old. Once again, you can either get there by road, following a route that winds around the hills for 16km, or take a fairly gruelling walk from town, leaving by **Suraj Pole** and climbing up to the Surya temple on the crest of the hill before dropping down into the valley below.

Galta owes its sacred status in large part to a freshwater spring that seeps constantly through the rocks in the otherwise dry valley, keeping two tanks fresh and full, and hordes of monkeys (associated with the monkey god Hanuman) happy. Humans bathe in the upper water tank, while monkeys jump and splash in the lower pool.

The temples themselves are intricately and vividly painted. Friezes around the top of pavilions that face the monkeys' tank show scenes from religious festivals and stately occasions; behind one procession the City Palace is sketched in dubious proportions. Inside the roofs, swirling red, yellow and blue clouds ring more of Michelangelo than of traditional Hindu style.

The long road to Galta passes **Sisodia Rani ka Bagh** (daily 8am–6pm; Rs1), 8km east of Jaipur. Landscaped with fountains and painted pavilions, these gardens are part of a palace complex built in the eighteenth century by Jai Singh II for the Udaipur princess he married to secure relations with his neighbouring Sisodia Rajputs. When the political alliance weakened, the queen lost favour with the Jaipur household and moved to a private palace with her son, Madho, who later succeeded his father.

Temples at the back of the gardens, coated with the sherbet-yellow wash that covers the whole compound – the original colour of the Pink City – and enhanced with naturalistic designs, are open midday and early evening for worship.

Sanganer

At **SANGANER**, 16km south of Jaipur and the busiest crafts centre in the region, you can visit artisans in their workshops and pick up bargains from the makers themselves. Block and screen printing are among the techniques used to adorn locally made cloth, while offcuts are recycled into paper.

Artists also decorate pottery in Jaipur's distinctive style; graceful floral designs in white or deep-sea green are painted over a traditional inky-blue glaze. Within the town there are ruined palaces and a handful of elegant Jain temples. Minibuses (Rs3) leave for Sanganer from Chand Pole.

Samode

SAMODE, 42km northwest of Jaipur on the outskirts of Shekawati but normally visited as a day trip from the city, is notable for a superb restored eighteenth-century **palace** with exquisite murals and delicate stonework. The centre of attention here is the main hall, **Sheesh Mahal**, or mirror palace, where the glasswork is even more stunning than at Amber. The Samode palace is now a heritage hotel, and its highly priced rooms offer the chance of a luxurious stop en route to Shekawati (②; bookings can be made at *Samode House*, Ganga Pole, Jaipur; ☎42407).

North of Jaipur: Shekawati

Beyond the last ripples of the Aravalli range, north of Jaipur, lies the easternmost extent of the Thar desert, where small towns rest between sand dunes and infertile expanses of dusty land in the area known as **Shekawati** (also spelt Shekavati). While the terrain is barren, dry and hostile, the architecture and painting of the region's buildings possess a beauty and richness unparalleled in all India. Mansions, palaces and cenotaphs in a succession of sleepy, semi-rural towns are decorated inside and out with detailed and vivid scenes of folk tales, religious stories, local merchants and cities, animals, local customs and even Europeans with their Victorian technology, each mural bordered with delightful floral designs. Most of the towns are so small that you can amble at whim without losing your bearings, and be sure of finding rich rewards on any path you follow.

As Shekawati has not yet become part of the well-trodden tourist trail in Rajasthan – few locals speak English, and there's little prospect of accommodation or western food – the region presents great scope for exploration. Only the main towns have been listed here, but – perhaps with the help of Ilay Cooper's *Guide to Painted Towns of Shekawati*, produced locally by *Shri Om Printers* in Jhunjhunu – you should be able to find exciting sites in any town or village you pass through. Many of the buildings are still privately owned; ask permission to enter any house, and respect the custom of removing your shoes before you do so.

A brief history of Shekawati

The first people to settle the lands north of Jaipur, Muslims of the Khaimkani clan, established two small states based at **Jhunjhunu** and **Fatehpur** in 1450. Their hold on the region was broken in 1730, when the Rajput **Sardul Singh** of the Shekawat clan took over Jhunjhunu. Two years later he consolidated Shekawati rule by helping his brother (already ruler of Sikar) to seize Fatehpur from its Muslim Nawab.

Although the area is known as Shekawati, the Shekawat Rajputs were only responsible for the construction of the forts in each town. The caravan route known as the "spice road" passed through the region on its way between China and the coast of Gujarat, and it was the local **merchants** – the Marwaris, Hindus of the *vaisya* caste, and Jains – who funded the building and painting of family houses (*havelis*), temples, wells and rest houses (*dharamshalas*). During the nineteenth century – when the devel-

THE HAVELIS OF SHEKAWATI

The magnificent houses built by the rich merchants of Shekawati were called **havelis** after the Persian word for "enclosed space". Each house, anything from one to four storeys high, incorporated at least one courtyard, which provided a space where the women of the family could live in *purdah*, shielded from the eyes of the street. More extravagant Marwari mansions might have up to four large courtyards, as well as grand domed facades and overhanging upper storeys supported on sturdy stone brackets. Huge arched entrance porches with carved brass or wooden doors would lead to the forecourt where guests were received, behind which the main courtyard was entered through the most ornate doorway of the house. The tradition of wood carving that produced the imposing doors and window shutters is still strong, particularly in Churu.

The meticulous painting of the interiors was executed by craftsmen from outside the region, using a vast array of intense hues, often highlighted with gold or silver leaf and mirrored designs. Religious themes, especially episodes from the life of Krishna, were common, and often feature along the lintels above the main doors. The outer walls were usually decorated by the masons who built the *haveli*, employing bolder designs and weather-hardy green, maroon and yellow ochres, with the occasional flash of blue.

opment of new ports and increased brigandry damaged overland trade – many Marwaris moved with British encouragement to Bombay, Madras and, especially, Calcutta. They continued, however, to send their profits back to Shekawati, erecting elaborate buildings either to prove their worth as prospective bridegrooms, or simply as aid projects during times of famine.

When the British left India a number of Marwaris purchased British industries, and such names as *Birla* and *Poddar* remain prominent in business today. However, many merchant families have now left Shekawati and settled more permanently in the major urban centres. The region's current inhabitants continue to rear goats and sheep for their wool, and reap what they can from the dry earth, while maintaining the traditional crafts: tie-and-dye, screen printing, lacquer work, wood carving and silverwork.

Arrival and local transport

Travelling to Shekawati from Jaipur, your most likely point of arrival is **Sikar**, two hours' journey by road (110km) or almost twice that by train (4 daily; 3hr 45min).

Although Sikar has many attractive buildings, it has now extended beyond the old city walls and lost much of its original charm. With only basic lodging available, it's best to limit your stay to a couple of hours and head northwest to **Nawalgarh**, where you'll find better hotels and a more relaxed, rural atmosphere.

From Bikaner to the west, a four- or five-hour journey brings you to **Fatehpur** (48km north of Sikar), which has some fair accommodation and is a convenient base for visiting the other Shekawati towns.

Fairly regular local **buses**, always overcrowded, usually stop on the outskirts of town; few operate after dark. Jeeps run from place to place according to demand, picking up as many passengers as physically possible. For less congested and precarious transport, you can rent a jeep in Jhunjhunu, but by far the most comfortable (and most costly) way to get round the area is by taxi from Jaipur.

Travelling around Shekawati by rail is far less convenient than by bus; slow and infrequent trains arrive at stations also on the outskirts of towns. The main line runs from Sikar to Churu (3hr) via Lakshmangarh (40min), Fatehpur (1hr 10min), Ramgarh (1hr 50min) and Bissau (2hr 20min). Three day time services run in each direction. Another line connects Sikar with Jhunjhunu (2hr) with two day time services each way.

Within the small towns the semi-rural life runs at a leisurely pace, and there is little traffic apart from the odd moped dodging between meandering donkey and camel carts. In the larger towns such as Churu, tempos and tongas cover the distance between the bus station and the centre of town.

Fatehpur

The charming, compact, and bustling market town of **FATEHPUR** has the feel of a crumbling open-air museum. In 1450 Fateh Khan, a Muslim Khaimkani Nawab, claimed leadership of the small settlement and held it until it passed into the hands of the Shekawats in the eighteenth century.

Fatehpur's merchant community left a rich legacy of remarkable buildings; almost every street is flanked with the painted outer walls of *havelis*, and their interiors are among the finest in Shekawati. A common theme for paintings is Lakshmi, the goddess of wealth, attended by mighty, regal elephants, and set against a rich azure background. Friezes in several temples depict scenes from the great Hindu epics.

The most celebrated of Fatehpur's *havelis* is the small but exquisite **Goenka Haveli**, built in the mid-nineteenth century by a Jain merchant, Mahavir Prasad, and reached by following the main road north from the bus stand and turning left at the first main crossroads. While the inner courtyard is beautifully painted, the first-floor room is dazzling, its walls and ceiling decorated in the finest detail with a myriad of colours, gold leaf and mirrors. Panels to either side of the door show Krishna riding an elephant (on the right) and a horse (on the left), each animal made up of contorted female figures. A smaller room next door shows further scenes from Krishna's life, and women spinning, churning butter and decorating each other's feet with spidery henna patterns. A later building to the left of Goenka Haveli has superb mirrorwork in the front porch.

If you rejoin the main northbound road at the crossroads, and turn right after twenty yards, you'll come to **Nand Lal Devra Haveli**, whose splendid ceiling panels in the reception area were copied by many other merchant families. The murals on the courtyard walls, and the complex carving of the wooden doors and shutters, are equally impressive.

To the north of town, some distinctive Shekawati **wells** stand raised on square platforms, with domed shelters on each corner. Once the lifeline of the community, and still common meeting places, these wells have not suffered the decay seen elsewhere since the advent of more sophisticated plumbing systems.

Practicalities

The bus stand (more of a crowded street than a formal station) is in the west of town on the main Sikar–Churu road. Five buses per day arrive from Bikaner (5hr 30min) and Jaipur (3hr 30min). Buses leave hourly for Jhunjhunu via Mandawa, and a little less frequently for Churu, via Ramgarh.

A little south of the bus stand, facing a yard set off the road, the clean and homely *Shanti Lodge* (①) is an old *haveli* where a few large rooms (with common bathrooms) still bear faded vestiges of murals. South of town on NH-11, the more modern RTDC *Hotel Ratangarh* (☎293; ③–④) has ordinary or air-cooled rooms as well as a cheap dorm. It's clean, comfortable and offers meals, beer and transport to other towns. If you don't eat at the *Ratangarh*, try any of the *dhabas* near the bus stand or *Shanti Lodge*; the food is good, but meals are only cooked around noon and after 6 or 7pm.

Ramgarh and Lakshmangarh

The two small towns of Ramgarh and Lakshmangarh, near Fatehpur, boast rich selections of *havelis*. Neither has any accommodation for visitors, but each can be easily visited in a day, using local buses or jeeps.

RAMGARH, 20km north of Fatehpur, was founded in 1791 and developed almost as a status symbol by the Poddar merchant family, who made every effort to make their new town outshine Churu. They were successful; there's hardly a bare wall in town, even among the shops in the bazaar. Most of the grand Poddar *chhatris* beside the main Churu–Sikar road preserve attractive murals within their domes, while the family *havelis* in the north of town, west of Churu Gate, are decorated with scenes from local folk stories, and a three-fish motif that is unique to Ramgarh. Temples such as Natwar Niketan, Ram Lakshman temple and Ganga temple cherish excellent depictions of scenes from the *Ramayana*, *Bhagavad Gita* and local legends, and the **Shani temple** in the northwest of town also holds some elaborate mirrorwork.

The most imposing feature of the quaint little desert town of **LAKSHMANGARH**, 20km south of Fatehpur, is the nineteenth-century **fort**, hewn from steep, smooth grey rocks, that dominates the west side of town. It is now empty and dim inside, though you can climb the ramp to the summit to enjoy a spectacular view.

Lakshmangarh is easy to explore, thanks to a symmetrical street grid inspired by that of Jaipur. It holds three principal squares, several wells and temples, and plenty of richly painted *havelis*. Just below the fort, near the bus stand with its snack stalls and fruit sellers, stands the huge **Char Chowk Haveli**. Built around four large courtyards (*chowks*), it remains in private ownership, and access is therefore restricted. In any case, it's best seen from the fort, from where its peculiar design can be appreciated.

Other excellent – and amusing – frescos in town include the heavily painted **Kyal** and **Naria** *havelis* in the southeast of town, the scenes of European women on walls near the clock tower, and **Sanganeeria Haveli**, east of the Radha Murlimanohar temple. In the far east of town, near a *chhatri* and a well, the bright but dilapidated **Pansari Haveli** shelters a semi-permanent settlement of *Lohars*, nomadic iron workers.

Mandawa

Small, attractive **MANDAWA**, 20km east of Fatehpur, was founded by the Shekawat family in 1760, though most of its paintwork dates from the early nineteenth century. The town's original **fort**, right in the centre, now houses the finest **hotel** in the region (see below), as well as a small museum of royal artefacts.

The outer walls, jutting balconies, alcoves and overhanging upper storeys of the **Goenka Double Haveli** in the west of town are replete with patterns and paintings, ranging from traditional Rajasthani women and religious motifs to Europeans in stylish hats and Victorian finery. In the **Nand Lal Murmuria Haveli** next door, paintings of trains, cars, George V, and Venice were executed during the 1930s by Balu Ram, one of the last working artists of the region. Murals in the **Thakurji Temple** opposite these two mansions include soldiers being shot off the mouths of cannons, a reflection of the horrors of the Mutiny. Further west are a couple of *chhatris*, and a step-well, still used today and still bearing paintings inside its decorative corner domes.

Another *haveli* worth asking for by name is **Gulab Rai Wadia Haveli**, south of the fort, where the decoration of the outer and inner walls is perhaps the finest in Shekawati. Blue washes here and there betray twentieth-century censorship of the erotic scenes that had been commonly acceptable in the nineteenth century.

Practicalities

Buses stop outside Sonthilia Gate in the west of town, arriving hourly from Fatehpur, Jhunjhunu and Nawalgarh, with less frequent services from Jaipur and Bikaner. The last bus out of Mandawa is no later than 5.30pm. Jeeps also pass through, and run later in the evening.

Mandawa has a tempting choice of **accommodation**. In the fort, *Hotel Castle Mandawa* (☎01592/89324; ⑦), with its authentically furnished rooms complete with original murals, is one of the most appealing luxury hotels in Rajasthan. If you can't budget for a night's stay, you can always pop in for a reasonably priced buffet dinner.

The less luxurious *Hotel Rath Mandawa* on the western outskirts of town (☎01592/89340; ⑤, reduced April–Sept), lacks the palatial atmosphere, but offers comfortable rooms with balconies and desert views. Bookings for the *Desert Camp* (④), a complex of huts south of town on the Mandawa–Nawalgarh road, can be made at *Castle Mandawa*.

Nawalgarh

NAWALGARH, 30km southeast of Fatehpur, came into its own in 1737, when the Shekawat Nawal Singh claimed what was then a small village as the site for a fort. Thick stone walls, pierced by four gateways, were erected to encircle the town; the fort still stands in its southern section, housing banks and offices around a central yard crowded with vegetable vendors.

The first of the *havelis* built by the merchants who thrived in the security of Nawalgarh, undisturbed by brigands, can be found south of the fort. Turning left before Nansa Gate, you enter a grid of streets that holds, among others, **Surajmal Chhauchharia Haveli**, where murals include a picture of Europeans floating past in a hot-air balloon. The painter was obviously unclear about the exact mechanics involved; the two passengers are blowing into the balloon to power their journey. Alternatively, if you go through Nansa Gate, past the colourful **Lakshminarayan temple**, turn right, and take a side street on the right after about 250m, you'll find yourself surrounded by painted walls, many of which form part of **Aath Haveli**, a complex of seven *havelis* (eight – *aath* – were planned). The murals here feature trains, carts, false windows (very common in Nawalgarh) and barbers at work. Other *havelis* in Nawalgarh include **Goenka Haveli**, in the north of town near Bowri Gate, and the magnificent **Anandi Lal Paddar Haveli**, east beyond Poddar Gate. Built in 1920 and now a school, it treasures some excellent paintwork, especially in the forecourt.

Practicalities

Nawalgarh's **bus** and **jeep** stand is about 1km west of town, served by frequent buses to Mandawa (until 5pm) and jeeps to other smaller towns.

Much the most comfortable **accommodation** in Nawalgarh is in the spacious, smart rooms of the *Roop Niwas Palace* (☎2008; ⑥), set in fresh and attractive gardens a kilometre or so east of town along the main road leading out of Poddar Gate, which provides a real taste of how Shekawati's ruling class lived in days gone by. Somewhat pricey meals are available in the plush dining room. The *Natraj Hotel* in Sabzi Mandi in the heart of town (☎3154; ①) is very cheap and very basic, while the pleasant *Nawal Hotel*, out by the bus stand on Mandawa Road (☎2155; ②), makes a good option if you arrive late. It has two rooms to each common bath, plus a couple of rooms with private bathrooms – rooms at the back are quieter – and prepares decent food.

It's also possible to stay in the much smaller town of **Dundlod**, 7km north of Nawalgarh, which has its own interesting murals. Although not as palatial as *Roop Niwas Palace* or *Castle Mandawa*, Dundlod's fort, *Dera Dundlod Qila* (☎98; ⑦), captures the Shekawat style with its own painted rooms and a grand diwan-i-khas.

Parasrampura

The life of **Sardul Singh**, the founder of Shekawati, is commemorated by further painted buildings in the quiet and unassuming village of **PARASRAMPURA**, just over 10km southeast of Nawalgarh, where he lived and died.

Murals in the **Gopinath temple**, built in 1742, include depictions of the terrible torments of hell (a common theme in the eighteenth century), and Sardul Singh with his five sons; flocks of Persian-style angels look down from the ceilings. However, these frescos are only half-completed, as the artists were diverted to decorate the **Chhatri of Sardul Singh** when he died that same year. The large dome of his cenotaph, supported by twelve pillars, contains a flourish of lively and well-preserved murals. Once again there are images of hell, and of Sardul Singh with his sons; this time he's also seen smoking a hookah and enjoying a tiger hunt. Parasrampura's modest **fort**, still in reasonable repair, is on the west bank of the dry river bed.

Jhunjhunu

The large settlement of **JHUNJHUNU**, taken over by the Shekawats in 1730 as the capital of their newly formed territory, has managed to retain much of the tranquillity and appeal of the regions' smaller towns. The quiet, narrow and dusty streets within its old boundaries hold a profusion of beautifully designed and painted buildings, spanning five centuries, and remain relatively unaffected by the twentieth-century accretions on the outskirts of town that have helped to make Jhunjhunu one of the major business centres of modern Shekawati.

The main bazaar in the south of town, not far north of the bus station, is sandwiched between the outer walls of two large private mansions, decorated with striding camel trains, elephants, women and religious scenes. The ornate gateway of **Modi Haveli**, the larger of the two, can be reached by a grand flight of steps from the shops built into the base of its walls. Inside, through an entrance porch embellished with scenes from the life of Krishna, the forecourt features more paintings of Krishna and several portraits of Europeans, while the pillared reception area or *baithak* has excellent murals on the ceiling and soft mattresses and bolsters on the floor. The door to the inner courtyard is lavishly carved, and bordered with exquisite designs including a scene of Jaipur. Opposite, the similar **Kaniram Narsinghdas Tibrewala Haveli** boasts coloured glass windows around the top of its *baithak*.

Further east, the unique **Khetri Mahal** palace, built in 1760, is ageing and empty, but there's no mistaking the originality of its design: marble pillars stand in place of walls wherever possible, and a covered ramp, wide enough for horses, winds up to the roof. Views over Jhunjhunu from here stretch to the old **Muslim sector** to the south, Pirzada Mahalla, where a grand mosque is surrounded by tombs dating back to 1500. Many of Jhunjhunu's Muslims – still an important sector of the population – were wealthy merchants who built painted *havelis* of their own. A wander through the

Muslim quarter leads past mosques, *dargahs* and meat markets, as well as neat rows of shops painted in pastel greens, blues and pinks unlike anywhere else in Shekawati.

In the northwest of town, at the foot of the conical Kana Pahar hill, are **Badalgarh** – the only remaining fort from the Nawab period – and the **Dargah of Kamaruddin Shah**, where a mosque, *madrasa* and collection of tombs stand in a small complex. Behind the *madrasa* stands a monument to the infant son of Henry Forster, who died in 1841. Forster was the head of the British-run Shekawati Brigade, set up in Jhunjhunu to suppress local brigandry.

Practicalities

Buses from the sprawling bus stand in the south of town run throughout Shekawati, and to Bikaner, Delhi and Jaipur. Three **train** services run from Jaipur to Jhunjhunu; the most useful is the *Fast Passenger* #205, which departs at 11.25am, stops at Sikar at 2.45pm, and arrives in Jhunjhunu at 4.30pm. Jhunjhunu is quite spread out, and walking around can be tiring, but many of the streets of the old town are too narrow for cars; rickshaws tend to operate as taxis, picking up as many passengers as they can. Bicycles can be rented from a small shop near the park in the south. Taxis to explore further afield gather at a rank outside the bus station, costing around Rs3 or 4 per kilometre.

The best bet for inexpensive **accommodation** nearby is the *Hotel Sangam* (☎2544; ①–④), which has clean and spacious rooms. It's set back from the bus station, so doesn't get the noise that infiltrates the hotels *Ashok* and *Kulhari*, both pretty grim and very basic (①). Further east, the *Shiv Shekawati Hotel* (☎2651; ③), is a smart and well-kept no-smoking lodge with a touch of Shekawati character. It has a **tourist office** and a restaurant, which is just as well as it's so far out of town. Numerous food stalls are concentrated around the bus stand, as well as basic sit-down joints such as *Nehru's Hotel* and *Amber Restaurant* in Gandhi Chowk.

North from Jhunjhunu

The first significant stop on the road northwest of Jhunjhunu, after 40km, is the small and atmospheric town of **BISSAU**, 10km northeast of Ramgarh (see p.144). Opposite the bus stand here, the **Chhatri of Hammir Singh** commemorates the son of Shyam Singh, a brigand leader. It's fenced in, but you can get the key from a barber shop just outside the gate. Several domes stand above a high basement structure, where decaying murals adorn the walls. Of the heavily painted *havelis* in town, **Kedia Haveli** in the west has some distinctive depictions of Europeans on elephants, a Gangaur procession and relaxed hookah-smoking. Nearby, the **Jhunjhunuwala Haveli**, currently used as a student hostel, holds wonderful detailed paintings, especially in its porticoed forecourt. During Dussehra (Oct), all-but-silent dances in Bissau's bazaar, to honour Durga, take the place of the more usual stage play.

The much larger town of **CHURU** is 10km further on, a three-kilometre tempo ride from the bus station. Though Churu has never been part of Shekawati, being officially in Bikaner territory, it too was home to many merchant families – including the Poddars, before they left for Ramgarh. Equally noteworthy (if rather scattered) buildings and murals here include some attractively decorated temples (open before 10am and after 5pm) around the clock tower in the central square. *Havelis* around the bazaar, just west, include **Kanhaiyal Baglia Haveli**, whose south wall is decorated with a grand frieze showing Dhola and Maru, lovers from local folklore, fleeing on camels, preceded by a couple from a Punjabi tale on horseback. The frieze is behind the compound wall; if you can get permission, you'll get an excellent view from the walls of the Jami Masjid nearby. Probably the best time to visit Churu is during the Shi'a festival of Muharram (April/June), when the local Muslim drummers come into their own.

East of Jaipur

The fertile area **east of Jaipur**, interspersed with the forested slopes of the Aravalli hills, holds an inviting mixture of historic towns and wildlife sanctuaries. The fortified town of **Alwar** to the northeast, fought over for centuries before its incorporation into Rajasthan in 1949, served as refuge for the exiled Pandava brothers of the *Mahabharata* during their thirteenth year of hiding, before Krishna helped them in the fierce battle against their cousins, the Kauravas, chronicled in the *Bhagavad Gita*.

Not far from Alwar, **Sariska Wildlife Sanctuary** is renowned for its tigers, while further east are the former princely capitals of **Deeg** and **Bharatpur**, and India's finest bird sanctuary, **Keoladeo National Park**. The wildlife sanctuary at **Ranthambore**, southeast of Jaipur, has lost most of its tigers to poachers, but the old palaces in its grounds, plus the rich vegetation and fauna, still attract many visitors.

Alwar

Roughly 140km northeast from Jaipur towards Delhi, **ALWAR** rests peacefully in a valley, overlooked by a fortress that stretches along a high craggy ridge to the northwest. Alwar was not always so calm; its strategic position on the Rajput border resulted in incessant warfare between the Jats of Bharatpur and the Kuchwahas of Amber, from the tenth to seventeenth centuries. It later fell first to the Marathas and then the British, before Pratap Singh, the shrewd Rana of Mewar, brought it under Hindu control. The fort, now a radio station, can only be visited with police permission; the buildings within are in any case unspectacular, though the views make the climb worthwhile.

Construction of Alwar's Indo-Islamic **Vinay Vilas Palace** began under the leadership of Bhaktawar Singh, Pratap Singh's successor. Although time has worn away much of its glory, it remains flamboyant, with domed roofs, lavish verandahs decorated in gold leaf, and delicate balconies facing a huge tank flanked by symmetrical *ghats* and pavilions. The stately sandstone and marble **Moosi Maharani Chhatri** here was built in memory of Bhaktawar Singh's mistress, who sacrificed her life on his funeral pyre. A **museum** on the top floor of the palace (daily except Fri 10am–5pm; Rs1) houses a collection of courtly memorabilia, including remarkable Arabic and Sanskrit manuscripts, tenth-century statues, ivory ornaments, fine embroidery and the inevitable weapons and stuffed animals.

Much of the palace is now taken up with government offices; in the main courtyard, used as the venue for the local courts, typists, lawyers and advisors huddle round rickety tables under banyan trees, drinking tea and filing through endless piles of paper.

Practicalities

The **bus stand** in the west of Alwar sees services to and from Deeg and Bharatpur every fifteen minutes, and Sariska every half hour or so. Frequent buses also run north to Delhi and south to Jaipur (both 2–3hr). Several food stalls at the bus stand sell drinks and fiery curries, and there's a **bike rental** shop near the exit. The **train station**, receiving trains from Delhi, Jaipur, Jodhpur and Ahmedabad, is a few kilometres away on the east side of town, and has retiring rooms.

The **tourist office** on Raghu Marg (Mon–Sat 10am–5pm) has dusty piles of aged leaflets about Rajasthan, and information on Alwar's **hotels**. Close to the bus stand on Manu Marg, the best for your money is *Ashoka Hotel* (☎21780; ①), which has basic rooms with or without bath, and better rooms upstairs. Within spitting distance are the noisy, dull but large *Imperial* (☎21430; ②), and the *Alankar* (②), with acceptable spacious rooms. Two hundred metres from the train station, the much smarter *Aravali Hotel* (☎70316; ①–⑤) offers cheap dorm beds, basic rooms and more expensive deluxe doubles. Its bar and good **restaurant** are useful, as Alwar has little else to offer a hungry traveller.

A journey of around 20km west – either by rickshaw, or on a Sariska-bound bus which can drop you off at a turning 3km short – the RTDC *Lake Castle Tourist Bungalow* in **Siliserh** (☎22991; ③, with a cheaper dorm) is housed in a former palace beside a lake. It's a great place to relax, complete with a restaurant, bar and boating facilities.

Sariska

Alwar is the jumping-off point for the beautiful wooded **Sariska Tiger Reserve and National Park**, surrounded by barren hills tipped with ancient temples, and under the charge of Project Tiger. Though the sanctuary has an abundance of **wildlife** – including *nilgai* (blue bulls), *sambar* (antelope), *chital* (spotted deer), wild boar, mongooses, monkeys, peacocks, parrots and other birds – poaching has regrettably decimated its population of **tigers**. The best prospect of seeing one is around the water holes that attract animals in the dry season when other sources of moisture dry up. Access to the park (closed altogether during July and August) is limited to daylight hours (dawn–dusk), to protect tigers from surreptitious night poaching.

Practicalities

The 37-kilometre journey by bus to Sariska from Alwar's bus stand (Rs5; 1hr) can be very crowded. Alternatively you can take a tour from the *Aravali Hotel* in Alwar, paying well over the odds for a trip in a packed minibus that rushes through the park, with a minimal chance of any sightings.

If you choose to stay overnight in Sariska there are two options. *Hotel Tiger Den* (☎2348; ⑤), set in peaceful gardens right next to the park entrance, offers well-kept spacious rooms and an inexpensive dorm, while the more extravagant *Sariska Palace* (☎222; bookings can be made in Jaipur on ☎66804; ⑦), one of the largest hunting lodges in India, has a total of 27 rooms, some a/c.

An **entrance fee** of Rs100 per jeep, and Rs25 per person is payable at the park gate. **Tours** around the 480-square-kilometre central area can be arranged at either of the two hotels. *Hotel Tiger Den* charges Rs300 or Rs400 per jeep (excluding entrance fee) for a three-hour tour, *Sariska Palace* is slightly more expensive. Drivers are usually prepared to slow down or stop on request.

Deeg

Few foreigners visit **DEEG** (also spelt *Dig*), around 50km east of Alwar, 30km northwest of Bharatpur, and only 95km from Agra. However, its sublime complex of summer palaces, intended to represent a "paradise on earth", really is worth seeing, perhaps as a pause for a few hours on a longer journey.

Construction of the royal retreat began in 1730, when the Jat ruler Badan Singh established Deeg as the second capital of Bharatpur state. There's a commanding view from the high fortified walls of his citadel, and you can still see some of the original cannons. The delicate design of the **palaces** or *bhawans* (daily 8am–noon & 1–7pm), with arches, pillars and domes reflected in surrounding water tanks, and the leafy gardens interspersed with two thousand fountains, is typical of the erstwhile rulers of Rajasthan. Most were built by the Jat king Surajmal in 1756, and even the oldest, **Purana Mahal**, still bears traces of wall paintings. The largest, **Gopal Bhawan**, near the entrance to the complex, was Surajmal's summer residence. Its spacious, plushly furnished hall is built in graceful proportion, with majestic archways, sculpted pillars and intricate balconies overlooking the tank **Gopal Sagar**. A pavilion stands on either side of the *bhawan*; the deliberate resemblance of the whole ensemble to a pleasure barge is best appreciated from the west.

In the east of the complex, overlooking Rup Sagar, **Kesav Bhawan** is an open-sided square pavilion, designed to recreate the freshness of monsoon. In Surajmal's time, fountains played within it, producing a shimmering rainbow in the sunshine, while cooling water showered from the roof to the accompaniment of artificial rolls of thunder. The reservoir for the fountains took a week to fill and only a matter of hours to empty, and nowadays they are only switched on during local festivals.

Practicalities

Deeg fell into decline along with the Jat rulership at the beginning of the nineteenth century, and remains very small, though it is served by bus. Permission to stay over night at the *Dak Bungalow* (①) must be obtained from the Overseer in the Public Works Department office, Kama Darwaja. The only place to eat is the *Tamolia Restaurant*, just past Lakshman Mandir.

Bharatpur and Keoladeo

The compact town of **BHARATPUR** is just a stone's throw from the border with Uttar Pradesh, 150km east of Jaipur, and a mere 18km from Fatehpur Sikri, Akbar's deserted citadel (see p.222). Though it may not hold any especially distinguished attractions, it's fun to explore by bike or foot, with traditional markets dotted with mosques and temples and a massive fort encircled by a wide and murky moat.

However, the real reason anyone comes here is to visit **KEOLADEO NATIONAL PARK**, a large expanse of wetland 7km south of town, which welcomes thousands of indigenous and migratory birds every year. Other common wildlife such as antelope and deer roam freely within the marshy sanctuary, and, even for the non-ornithologist, it's a place not to be missed.

Arrival and information

Bharatpur's **bus stand** is in the east of town near Anah Gate, just off NH11. Inter-state buses run to all major centres in Rajasthan and to Delhi, Agra and Fatehpur Sikri. Two kilometres northwest, the **train station** lies on the main Delhi–Bombay and Delhi–Udaipur routes, and is also connected to Ahmedabad in Gujarat. The town's **tourist office** (Mon–Sat 10am–5pm; ☎3700), where you can pick up good maps of Rajasthan and information on Bharatpur and the sanctuary, is nearer the park in the *Saras Tourist Bungalow*.

Cycle rickshaws are the main form of transport within the city, but rickshaw fares for the long haul in and out of town soon mount up, and it makes sense to rent a **bicycle**, either from your hotel (most have bikes for Rs20–25 per day) or the shop on NH11 outside the *Spoonbill Restaurant*. If you need to **change money**, head for the *State Bank of Bikaner and Jaipur*, Binarayan Gate (Mon–Fri 11am–3pm).

The City

Bharatpur itself was founded by the Jat leader Surajmal, who built the virtually impregnable **Lohagarh Fort** at its heart in 1732; known as the eastern gateway to Rajasthan, it soon developed into a busy market centre. Although the original moat, forty-five metres wide and up to fifteen metres deep, still encircles the town, little remains of the thick eleven-kilometre walls that protected it – the British spent four months in 1805 trying in vain to penetrate them, before suffering their heaviest defeat in Rajasthan.

The telephone **area code** for Bharatpur is ☎05644.

As you enter the fort from the north, through Assaldati Gate, you'll see a jumble of old and new buildings, among them the three palaces built by the Jats between 1730 and 1850. Of these, the **Maharaja's Palace** with its stone lattice windows, painted walls and a curious collection of *hamams* (sunken baths) on the ground floor, is the most aesthetically appealing. The **Kamra Palace** in the west of the fort now houses the government museum (daily except Fri 10.30am–5pm), with a well-stocked gallery of Jain sculptures, a copious assortment of weaponry and some graphic manuscripts in Arabic and Sanskrit. Among its collection of statues from the region is a figurine of a *yaksha* from the first century BC. From the shade of a lofty pavilion on the roof of the palace you can enjoy great views of the surrounding countryside.

South of the fort, in the main market area, lie the **Jama Masjid**, fronted by a magnificent arched portal, and **Ganga Mandir**, a large, elaborate temple of pure sandstone.

Keoladeo National Park

Keoladeo National Park, formerly known as Bharatpur Bird Sanctuary, was originally reserved by the royal family for hunting – despite sixty years of which, the avian population flourished. It became a sanctuary in 1956 and received total protection in 1981 on recognition as a national park. Keoladeo's 29 square kilometres of swamp and lakes constitute one of the most important **heronries** in the world, with such species as the dazzling purple heron, the common grey and the tiny brown pond heron. Other residents include orange-headed painted storks, snake-like darters, spoonbills, white ibis and grey pelicans. Some are vegetarian, but many feed on frogs, beetles and fish, and soon after the breeding season (July–Oct), birds of prey home in on the vulnerable fledglings to supplement their usual diet of rodents and fish.

Between October and March each year, the 120 species of Indian birds who live in the park year-round are joined by a further 130 species from as far afield as the Russian steppes and Central Asia. The finest and rarest of these migratory birds, all of whom spend the winter in Bharatpur building up reserves of fat before the long flights back to their breeding grounds, are the five pairs of Siberian cranes who nest in the south of the park each winter. Only 125 such cranes, pure white with crimson bills and facial patches, are estimated to survive in the entire world.

You may also glimpse wild boar, mongoose, *chital* (spotted deer), *nilgai* (blue bulls) and *sambar* (antelope) along the paths, and may spot jungle cats, hyenas, jackals, otters and Indian black buck. Languorous rock pythons sun themselves at Python Point, just past Keoladeo temple, and in the dry bush land off the main road close to the entrance barrier.

The park is at its most picturesque at dawn and dusk, and fullest between October and March. In summer months you miss the migratory flocks, but should catch some busy nesting activity. A single metalled road passes through the sanctuary; numerous small paths lined with *babul* trees cut across lakes and marshes and provide excellent cover for bird-watching. If you need help identifying the birds, or finding vantage points, you can hire a **guide** at the gate (Rs50 per hour for up to 10 people), who will probably have binoculars. The best way to get around is by bike – also available at the sanctuary gate – and cycle rickshaws, whose drivers are very clued up and know the main nesting areas, can be rented for Rs20 per hour (maximum two people). Tongas (Rs40 per hour) carry up to six people. During the winter, gondola-style **boats** provide a superb opportunity to get really close to the birds in the heart of the wetland (Rs15 per person per hour; minimum Rs50).

Accommodation and eating

Few people stay in Bharatpur proper – the entrance to the park is 7km south of the train station on the far side of town, and it makes more sense to spend the night in one of several assorted hotels along NH11, which passes by the northern edge of the park. The two hotels actually inside the park are quite upmarket, but most of the rest are inexpensive, and all offer snacks or full meals. The open-air *Spoonbill Restaurant* near the *Saras Tourist Bungalow* serves excellent Indian dishes at very low cost.

Bambino Guest House, NH11 (☎2902). Three cosy double rooms just outside the park, with private bathrooms and a collection of two-bedded canvas tents around a pleasant garden with camp fire. The imaginative menu (open-air dining) includes pizza. Extensions planned. ②–④.

Bharatpur Forest Lodge, inside the park (☎2722 or 2760). Immaculate a/c rooms with private balconies. Staying here, constantly surrounded by bird song and avian activity, is a real treat. Bar, banking facilities and post office counter (11am–1pm), and an excellent restaurant with sumptuous buffet spreads, open to non-residents when the hotel isn't full. Book in advance. ⑨.

Eagle's Nest, NH11 (☎3547). Situated at a noisy junction, but it's not far from the park, and the comfortable, carpeted rooms have hot water in their private bathrooms. ③.

Falcon. Small, quiet and clean place, set back from the main road near the park, with home cooking by friendly family. Bikes from shop opposite. ②.

Forest Rest House, inside the park (☎2777). Right in the thick of the forest, with shady gardens and a restaurant. Decent rooms with private bath. Often full, so book ahead. ⑤.

Keoladeo Resort, NH11 (☎2251). A tented compound with hot showers, garden and camp fire; the nearest lodging to the park entrance. ②.

Paradise, NH11 (☎3791). Smart rooms near the bus station in town, convenient if you're catching an early-morning bus. ⑤.

Pelican, NH11. Small, homely rooms near park entrance, with or without bathroom. ②.

RTDC Saras Tourist Bungalow, NH11 (☎3700). Poorly maintained, at junction of main road near the park, with many large, cleanish rooms and a dorm. Restaurant and bar for residents only. ④–⑥.

Sunbird, NH11. Three very clean rooms with attached bathrooms, convenient for the park. ③.

Tourist Complex, near Goverdhan Gate (☎3546). Basic rooms in the actual town, near the railway station, with a reasonable restaurant. ①.

Ranthambore National Park

One of Rajasthan's last sizable stretches of verdant bush land, **RANTHAMBORE NATIONAL PARK**, lies 10km east of **Sawai Madhopur**, a small junction town between Kota and Bharatpur, 180km north. Unlike Sariska to the north (see p.149), Ranthambore is fed by several perennial rivers, so the park never becomes a yellow expanse of dry grasses, and a number of lakes, haunted by crocodiles and attracting hundreds of water-birds, remain full all year round. The tenth-century Chauhan fort and quaint pavilions, palaces and *chhatris* give the hill-fringed sanctuary a unique charm, and it's possible to stay in the maharajas' former hunting lodge, the shady *Jogi Mahal*, over-looking a blue-green lily-covered lake.

Although the fort was conquered by Ala-ud-din-Khalji's army in 1031 AD, and Akbar in 1569, for most of its existence Ranthambore has been controlled by the Rajputs, and was set aside by the rulers of Jaipur for royal hunting jaunts. Soon after Independence the area was declared a sanctuary, becoming a national park under Project Tiger (see p.381) in 1972. Ranthambore used to be famous for its "friendly" tigers, who often hunted in full daylight, and rarely shied from cameras and jeep-loads of tourists. However, relentless poaching to satisfy Chinese demand for tiger bones and tiger-penis soup has decimated the tiger population, and made those who remain more elusive, and wary of human presence. There's every likelihood that less than ten survive today. However, Ranthambore is still home to *chital, nilgai*, jackals, panthers, jungle cats and a wide selection of birds, among which you may see crested serpent eagles, paradise fly-catchers and more common painted storks.

The park is open between October and May (daily 6.30–10am & 2.30–5pm). Most visitors see it from **jeeps**, which carry up to six passengers, and are available from most lodges (Rs600 for a morning or evening safari). Only 24 jeeps are allowed within the park at any one time, so in full tourist season (Dec–Feb), it's a good idea to get to the entrance well before opening time. A cheaper way to drive through is in one of RTDC's five-seater **minibuses** (Rs400). Skimping on price, however, means getting a raw deal, as they don't go as far into the park as the jeeps.

Arrival and information

Most tourists arrive at Sawai Madhopur by **train**, from either Bharatpur (5hr north) or Kota (1hr 50min south) on the Delhi–Bombay line. Another two-metre-gauge track meets the main line here, heading west to Jaipur (4hr 30min) and Bikaner.

The **tourist office** (☎2223) with details of up-to-date jeep prices and information on the park, is in the office of *Project Tiger* in Sawai Madhopur, a little south of the railway station, opposite the cinema.

Accommodation and eating

The range of **hotels** in Sawai Madhopur has something to appeal to all budgets; most lodges are in the town itself and along the **Ranthambore Road** leading to the park. Within the sanctuary, the only hotel is the idyllic converted *Jogi Mahal*, a former palace of the maharajas. Though the food isn't special in the cheaper lodges, you'll be glad it's there at all; there's precious little alternative.

Ankur Resort, Ranthambore Rd. A pleasant, modern complex of reasonable rooms with attached bath, 1.5km from Sawai Madhopur. Filling veg meals are served up in its dining room. ④–⑤.

Castle Jhoomar Baori (☎2495). In terms of location this is the best hotel outside the park, situated on a hillside well out of town (7km). Eleven comfortable rooms in the former hunting lodge of Jaipur's rulers, with exclusive suites, a plush lounge and airy roof terrace. Book ahead. ⑤–⑥.

The Cave, Ranthambore Rd. A tented compound for the outdoor sort, just outside town and a little overpriced considering its rough-and-ready standards. ②.

Jogi Mahal. Beautiful old hunting lodge in the thick of the park, with palatial rooms (only four) and meals included in the tariff. Book well ahead by contacting the director at *Castle Jhoomar Baori*. ⑥.

Pink Palace, Ranthambore Rd. Medium-range hotel in Sawai Madhopur, close to the fly-over. Fairly ordinary rooms, with attached bath. ③.

RTDC Kamdhenu, Ranthambore Rd (☎2334). Run-of-the-mill RTDC place, 3km out of town. Convenient rather than comfortable, but good inexpensive dorm beds, and a reasonable restaurant. ③–⑤.

Swagat, Ranthambore Rd. The cheapest and most basic hotel, roughly 500m from the train station. Each room has attached bath, but don't expect any hidden comforts. ①.

West of Jaipur

Heading west out of Jaipur towards Ajmer, National Highway 8 passes through an arid landscape that is largely barren for all but that fraction of the year when the rains tease growth out of the desert soils. As it approaches **Ajmer**, craggy ridges of the northern Aravalli range break out of the sandy plains to shelter larger settlements such as **Kishangarh**. This small and busy market town, 30km east of Ajmer, won fame for the miniature paintings produced in its fort during the seventeenth century. Decorated within by murals of the life of Krishna, the fort today stands almost empty just outside town, beside a lake that brims with lotus flowers during the monsoon.

Thousands of pilgrims converge on the area each year for its **festivals**. Muslims flock to Ajmer during Urs Mela (April/May), while Hindus and local traders commune in **Pushkar**, a little northwest, for Karttika Purnima, the **camel fair** (Oct/Nov). Not far from Pushkar, flashes of surprising colour in the desert sands, acres and acres of roses can be seen in full flower in April, before they are collected to be sprinkled by devotees over the Muslim saint's tomb in Ajmer. Carpets of dazzling pink cover the flat rooftops of Ajmer and Pushkar, where the roses are laid to dry before being packaged and sent to Mecca for use in worship, and made into incense.

Road and rail routes lead out of Ajmer to Jodhpur (west), Udaipur (southwest) and Kota and Bundi (south). Pushkar is a popular place for visitors to relax, particularly before flying out of Delhi, a night's train or bus journey away.

Ajmer

The unspectacular town of **AJMER** is famous throughout India as the former home of the Sufi **Khwaja Muin-ud-din Chisti**, founder of the Chistiya Order – still India's foremost Sufi order. He died here in 1236, at a time when Ajmer was under Muslim rule, the forces of the fearsome Muhammad of Ghori having successfully besieged what was previously a stronghold of the Rajput Chauhans in 1191. To this day, Chisti's tomb remains one of the most fascinating and holy Muslim shrines in the country.

Ajmer belonged to the Sultanate until 1326, but from then until the advent of the British, it was constantly fought over by neighbouring states, with just a century of peace under Akbar and Jahangir. Though its dusty main streets now burst with traffic, the narrow lanes of the bazaars and residential quarters are quieter and almost medieval, thronging with pedestrians. Near the Dargah, bazaar stalls overflow with offerings and souvenirs, while the streets of Nalla Bazaar are lined with shoe shops, clothes and sewing machines. **Ana Sagar**, a sprawling artificial lake west of town, freshens the desert, and the gardens on its southern edge are popular for picnics and evening strolls.

The telephone **area code** for Ajmer is ☎0145.

Arrival and information

Ajmer's **railway station** is in the centre of town, with regular services to the rest of Rajasthan, and points south; the main **bus stand**, with an exhaustive array of routes, is about 2km southwest. Frequent buses to **Pushkar**, however, leave from outside Gandhi Bhawan, a few hundred metres east of the railway station. Seats on private buses – many of which pick up tourists from Pushkar – can be reserved at Ajmer bus station, Pushkar hotels, or at any of the travel agents along Kutchery Road between the bus stand and railway station.

The efficient **tourist office** (Mon–Sat 8am–noon & 3–6pm) adjoins *Khadim Tourist Bungalow*, not far from the bus stand. **Banks** include *State Bank of Baroda*, Pushkar Rd (opposite the GPO) and *State Bank of Bikaner and Jaipur*, on Station Rd.

Ajmer's chief attractions lie within walking distance of each other, in the centre of town, and are easily visited in a day. To rent a **bike**, try the *Vijay Cycle Works* outside Delhi Gate (Rs8 per day, Rs1 per hour). Fares for cycle rickshaws, more popular here than auto-rickshaws, should be negotiated in advance. If you don't plan to stop for the night you can leave luggage at the railway station.

The Dargah

The revered Sufi, Khwaja Muin-ud-din Chisti, who died in Ajmer in 1236, was buried in a small brick tomb that is today engulfed by a large marble complex known as the **Dargah**. Erected by Humayun, the Dargah contains mosques built by rulers such as Shah Jahan, Jahangir and Akbar (who visited the shrine on numerous occasions and even walked twice from Agra).

The complex is entered from Dargah Bazaar, through a high gateway that leads into the first courtyard. Once inside, you'll see two immense cauldrons, known as *degs*, each 3m across. Donations are thrown in and later shared among the poor, continuing the tradition of giving succour to the needy that was so important to the saint. During the saint's Urs festival, the *degs* are filled with sweetened rice and sold to devotees by "looters" who receive the profits. To the right is the marble mosque donated by Akbar, and to the left stands an assembly hall for the homeless.

The tomb itself, surrounded by silver railings, is enshrined in a domed marble chamber in the centre of the second courtyard, near the magnificent mosque of Shah Jahan. Devotees file past, some sprinkling roses over the grave, others simply standing and praying. Visitors are asked for donations, offered blessings, lightly brushed with peacock feathers and given the chance to touch the cloth covering the tomb. The continual murmur of singing, praying, sobbing, laughter and music, the heady scent of flowers and the flurry of bright-robed women creates an unforgettable spectacle.

Islamic monuments

The **Adhai-din-ka-Jhonpra**, or "two-and-a-half-day mosque", slightly west of the Dargah, is the oldest survivor of Ajmer's days under Muslim rule; built in 1200 and now no longer in use, it remains one of the finest examples of medieval architecture in Rajasthan. Although probably named after a festival, tradition holds that the mosque was constructed as quickly as its name suggests. Its arched facade is covered with Islamic calligraphy, while many of its bricks and pillars were taken from nearby Hindu and Jain temples, considered of little worth by the new Muslim governors.

The most recent of Ajmer's Islamic relics is the squat sandstone **Daulat Khana** palace in the heart of the city, used by Akbar and his son Jahangir. Here, in 1616, Sir Thomas Roe became the first British ambassador to be given official audience. It now houses the government **museum** (daily except Fri 10am–4.30pm; Rs1), which displays Rajasthani statues dating back to the eighth century, and pieces excavated from Mohenjo Daro (second millennium BC). Exhibits in the Jain gallery include a beautiful statue of Saraswati from Banswara.

Other attractions

When Ajmer came under British control in 1818, it was one of the few cities in Rajputana outside the hegemony of the princely states. Monuments still standing as echoes of its colonial past include the **Jubilee Clock Tower** opposite the railway station, **Edward Memorial Hall** a little to the west and the famous **Mayo College**, originally built as a school for princes, and now a leading educational institution.

About 3km west of the Dargah, high above the city, the **Taragarh** or "Star Fort" was built in 1100 AD as one of India's first hill forts. It's now badly ruined, and the only reward for the steep climb to the crest of the hill is the panoramic view.

Perhaps the most bizarre sight in Ajmer is the mirrored **Soniji-ki-Nashiya** hall, which commemorates the life of Rishabdeo, the first Jain *tirthankara* (also known as Adinath), believed to have lived countless eons in the past (daily March–Aug 8am–5.30pm; Sept–Feb 8.30am–5pm; Rs2). From the uppermost of the three storeys that surround it you can look down on musicians flying above the sacred Mount Sumeru on swans, peacocks and elephants. The whole display is in gold, extravagantly detailed in fantastic proportions appropriate to the realm of legend. Admission to the Jain temple alongside, Nashiyan Mandir, is restricted to Jains.

Accommodation

Ajmer has many hotels to house the flow of pilgrims visiting the Dargah. Most are full during Urs Mela, but at other times rooms are in plentiful supply. A collection of modest rest houses stand opposite the railway station, and there are also a few hotels in the bazaar area. If you want to stay in style, try the grand *Mansingh Palace*.

Bhola, Agra Gate, Subzi Mandi (☎23844). The best value of the cheap hotels, kept very clean, with a good restaurant. ①.

Haji Guest House, Nala Bazaar (☎23835). Right next to the Dargah in lively bazaar area. All the rooms are spotless, some have balconies. ②.

Mansingh Palace, Ana Sagar Circular Rd (☎24702). Lavish but poorly maintained hotel in ideal surroundings, a few kilometres northwest of town. ⑦.

Nagpal Tourist, Station Rd (☎21603). Bright and breezy modern hotel, where the cheaper rooms have no hot water. ②–⑤.

Paramount, Station Rd (☎33737). Moderate and clean. ③–④.

Regency, Delhi Gate (☎31296). Smart air-cooled and a/c rooms with TVs. ④–⑤.

RTDC Hotel Khadim, (☎20490). Close to the bus stand. Good standard and reasonably priced, with cheap dormitory. ②–⑤.

Sobhraj, Delhi Gate (☎23488). A once-plush hotel on the decline, with some a/c rooms. ③–④.

Eating

In addition to the snack and fruit juice places around Dargah Bazaar and Delhi Gate, Ajmer has a handful of larger restaurants.

Bhola Hotel, Agra Gate, Subzi Mandi. Excellent pure vegetarian food, including good-value *thalis*.

Jai Hind Restaurant, Station Rd. Tucked behind the clock tower opposite the station. A range of very good vegetarian dishes, in smart surroundings.

Honey Dew Restaurant, Station Rd. A selection of vegetarian and meat dishes at middling prices, next to the King Edward Memorial. There's a garden, and a good selection of *Kwality* ice cream.

Mansingh Palace Hotel, Ana Sagar Circular Rd (☎24702). Pricey but delicious international cuisine in a clean and fresh dining hall.

Pushkar

With its smooth spread of white-domed houses and temples reflected in a tranquil lake, **PUSHKAR**, a mere 13km northwest of Ajmer, resembles nothing so much as a pearl dropped in the desert. Although during the annual **camel fair**, held during the full moon in October or November, Pushkar is transformed into a crowded hive of activity, for the rest of the year this profoundly peaceful and relaxing town makes a welcome respite from the din and hassle of the cities, and it's one of those places where travellers tend to stay considerably longer than they originally envisage.

No one knows quite how old **Pushkar** is: legend relates that at the beginning of time, Brahma dropped a lotus flower (*pushkara*) from the sky, declared the lake that sprang from the arid desert sands to be holy, and promised that anyone who bathed in it would be freed from their sins. As the site of one of only two temples in the world dedicated solely to the Lord Brahma, Pushkar attracts a constant flow of pilgrims to worship and bathe from its fifty-two lakeside *ghats*. Records of visits go back as far as the second century, when the Kshatrapa ruler of western India came to immerse himself and present gifts to the Brahmins.

The streets of Pushkar are too narrow for traffic, and there are no rickshaws; a lazy stroll around the shores of the lake and through the main bazaar takes little more than an hour. Shopping is the prime pastime for visitors; you're encouraged to take all the time you want browsing at the countless small roadside stalls, choosing from a vast assortment of clothes, jewellery and Rajasthani paintings.

Arrival and information

Most long-distance journeys to and from Pushkar have to be made via Ajmer; Pushkar does not have a railway station. The **Ajmer bus stand** in the west of town is served by buses from Ajmer and Jaipur, while travellers from further afield arrive in the north of town at **Marwar bus stand**, to be besieged by eager accommodation touts. The lack of rickshaws means that you'll have to walk to your hotel. Those buses that leave from Pushkar itself can be booked from most hotels; there are departures for Bombay, Delhi and Udaipur at 8.30pm, and for Jodhpur and Jaisalmer at 6am.

The management at *Peacock Hotel* will book onward **rail** journeys from Ajmer for a small charge (and book, cancel or change air tickets). Otherwise go to Ajmer to book for yourself well in advance; trains to Delhi in particular are often reserved days ahead.

There is no **tourist office** in Pushkar. The main **post office** for parcels and poste restante is in the north of town, but there's a smaller one on the market square. The *State Bank of Bikaner and Jaipur* (Mon–Fri 11am–3pm) in the square near Varaha Ghat is the best bet for currency exchange.

Temples

There are over four hundred temples in and around Pushkar; many had to be rebuilt after pillaging during the merciless rule of Emperor Aurangzeb (1656–1708), while others are recent additions. Some, like the splendid Vishnu temple, are out of bounds to non-Hindus.

Pushkar's most important temple, **Brahma Mandir**, may not be architecturally astounding, but its layout is superb. The main sanctuary, raised on a stepped platform in the centre of a courtyard, is surrounded on three sides by chambers and smaller shrines topped with flat roofs providing views across the desert west of Pushkar to **Saivitri Mandir** on the summit of a nearby hill. The two-hour climb to the top of that hill is rewarded by superb vistas over the town, surrounded on all sides by desert, and is best done in the evening, to reach the summit for sunset. **Gayitri Mandir**, on the other hand, set on a hill east of the town and named for the other of Brahma's wives (see box), faces east and should therefore ideally be visited at sunrise.

The ghats

The **ghats** of Pushkar – broad flights of steps leading down into the water – constitute a vital link between temple and lake, and are themselves sacred. Each is named after an event or person, and three in particular bear special significance. Primary among them is **Gau Ghat**, where visiting ministers and politicians come to worship, and from which ashes of Mahatma Gandhi, Jawaharlal Nehru and Shri Lal Bahadur Shastri were

---

BRAHMA

Brahma, revered as the Creator from later Vedic times onwards, was seen as one of the most important gods, together with Shiva (Destroyer) and Vishnu (Preserver). The three served in anthropomorphic terms to represent the powerful, non-conceptual Brahman – an unchanging and eternal force associated with cosmic unity. As the concept of *samsara* came to be at the heart of Hindu philosophy, however – and life was envisaged as endless transmigration with no beginning – Brahma's role as Creator was questioned by later philosophers. His importance as a cult god dwindled until it had almost ceased to exist by the nineteenth century, but he is still regarded as a major divinity.

Nevertheless, stories of Brahma's exploits are still told and retold in **Pushkar**, where a temple dedicated exclusively to Brahma still stands. One such tale reveals the significance of the temples named after Brahma's wives, **Saivitri** and **Gayitri**. According to this, Brahma was waiting on the ghats for his wife Saivitri, in order that he could perform *puja* at the appointed time. She did not arrive soon enough, and Brahma insisted that he perform the ritual accompanied by a wife. So an unmarried woman was found and bathed in cow's milk as a means of purification, and the ritual commenced. The woman was named after the sacred cow, *Gau*. Saivitri in her anger withdrew to the mountain in the west of town where a temple now stands in her honour, and Gayitri is remembered by the hill-top temple to the east.

△ Tourist Village at time of Camel Festival

PUSHKAR

Hospital
Marwar
Bus Stand
GPO
Ⓐ
Camel Market during Festival
N
Ⓑ
Ⓞ
Ⓟ
Ⓕ
Ⓝ
BADI BASTI (MAIN BAZAAR)
❸Ⓔ
Bank
Saivitri Temple
Ⓗ
Ⓒ
Ⓓ
Brahma
Temple
❷
Main
Ghat
Varah
Ghat
Ⓖ
Pushkar Lake
Ⓘ
Vishnu
Temple
Ajmer
Bus
Stand
Hanuman
Tower
Ⓑ
❺Ⓚ
AJMER RD
Ⓜ
❹
Ⓙ
Ⓗ
Ajmer
Ⓛ
0   300 m
Ⓖ

HOTELS:
Ⓐ Everest Guest House
Ⓑ Amar
Ⓒ Bharatpur Palace
Ⓓ Navratan Palace
Ⓔ Lake View
Ⓕ Payal Guest House
Ⓖ Lotus

Ⓗ RTDC Sarovar Tourist Bungalow
Ⓘ Pushkar Palace
Ⓙ Om
Ⓚ Oasis
Ⓛ Peacock
Ⓜ Chandra Palace
Ⓝ Siva
Ⓞ Sai Baba & Shanti Palace

Ⓟ Prince
RESTAURANTS:
❶ R S
❷ Rainbow & Krishna
❸ Sanjay
❹ Sunset Cafe
❺ Man Sarovar
❻ Venus

sprinkled into the lake. **Brahma Ghat** marks the spot where Brahma himself is said to have worshipped, while at the large **Varah Ghat**, just off the market square, Vishnu is believed to have appeared in the form of Varaha (a boar), one of his nine incarnations. At all the *ghats*, it is a respected and unspoken request that visitors should remove their shoes at a reverential distance from the lake, and refrain from smoking and taking photographs.

Indian and western tourists alike are urged by local Brahmin priests to worship at the lake, that is, to make **Pushkar Puja**. This involves the repetition of prayers while scattering rose petals into the lake, and then being asked for a donation which *usually* goes to temple funds, or to the priest who depends on such benefaction. On completion of the *puja*, a red thread taken from a temple is tied around your wrist. Labelled the "Pushkar Passport" by locals, this simple token means that you'll no longer attract pushy Pushkar priests, and can wander unhindered onto the ghats.

Accommodation

As with other holy centres, Pushkar has numerous *dharamshalas* for pilgrims. For the ever-growing influx of western tourists, there's a wide choice of **hotels**, many of them family homes where rooms are available to foreigners. Most are pretty basic, but they're comfortable, and a few are similar to hotels in larger towns, providing well-

KARTTIKA PURNIMA AND PUSHKAR CAMEL FAIR

Hindus visit Pushkar all year round to take a dip in the redemptory waters of the lake, but there is one day of the year when bathing here is believed to relieve devotees of all their sins, and ultimately free them from the bonds of *samsara*: the full moon (*purnima*) of the **Karttika** month (usually Nov). For five days leading up to and including the full moon, Pushkar hosts thousands of celebrating devotees, following prescribed rituals on the lakeside and in the Brahma temple. To add to the flurry of colour and festivity, a few days before the main religious festival a large **camel fair** is held in the sandy flats west of the town, when hordes of traders from all over Rajasthan gather to parade, race and trade their camels, horses and cattle. The transformation of Pushkar from a peaceful desert town is complete and overwhelming – the streets are packed with swarms of devotees, eager traders and hundreds of tourists; hotels and restaurants are choc-a-bloc, and prices soar. Families from all over Rajasthan struggle through the crowded lanes laden with children, blankets, food and makeshift tents, setting up camp west of town where night fires, delicious open-air cooking smells and harmonious tunes drifting through the starlit night create an unforgettable experience.

Once trading is under way camels and cattle are meticulously groomed, lined up and auctioned, while women dressed in mirrored skirts and vivid shawls lay out embroidered cloth, jewellery, pots and ornaments beside the herds, stopping trade occasionally to gather dung to fuel the evening fires. Cattle, poultry, sheep and goats are entered for competitions, and prizes given for the best displays of fruit and vegetables. Away from the main activity, the dusty ground is stirred up by vigorous **camel races**, noisily urged on by gamblers. Things become even more animated as acrobats balance precariously on tight ropes and cartwheel between the crowds, and insouciant jugglers toss fire batons before enthralled onlookers. Photo-opportunities are limitless, and anyone with a camera should definitely over-budget on films, which may not be on sale in Pushkar.

The fair attracts up to two hundred thousand people, many of whom are tourists. Hotels are usually full well before the start, but extra accommodation is provided by RTDC in tented compounds outside town where there's a choice between dormitory beds (①) or fully equipped rooms (②–⑧) and huts (⑨), complete with private bathrooms. Be sure to book ahead by contacting the RTDC office in Jaipur (☎60586 or 65076) or writing well in advance to the General Manager, RTDC, Usha Niwas, Kalyan Path, Jaipur. The tent village has an information counter (☎2074), foreign exchange facilities, safe deposits, shops and a medical centre. Not surprisingly, **food** stalls spring up everywhere, during the fair, serving freshly cooked regional specialities.

---

furnished rooms with private bathrooms. Views over the lake are rare, but many have rooftops looking across Pushkar to the distant hills. Some hotels operate 11pm curfews, and most are visited regularly by cheeky, inquisitive monkeys.

Amar. A delightful little place, set back from the main road in the centre of town, with ground-floor rooms facing a lush garden. Common bathrooms. ①.

Bharatpur Palace, Brahma Temple Rd. Large house bordering the lake with spacious roof area and simple but charming rooms; more expensive ones face the lake. Shared bathrooms. ①.

Chandra Palace, Ajmer Rd. Five expansive well-furnished rooms with private bathrooms (hot water) set amid peaceful rose gardens, a small way out of town. Excellent value. ①.

Everest Guest House, near the Marwar bus stand (☎2080). A cheap and popular place, though not as homely as some. ①.

Lake View, Sadar Bazaar (☎2106). Simple rooms with shared bathrooms on large roof top. Perfect situation on lakeside. ①.

Lotus, south shore of the lake. Set in quiet gardens that meet the southern edge of the lake, with cramped rooms in a welcoming environment. Popular for long stays, and often full. ①–②.

Navratan Palace, Brahma Temple Rd (☎2145). Very close to Brahma temple. A new but somewhat characterless place with large comfortable rooms, all with private bath; great views towards the hills. Swimming pool under construction. ③.

Oasis, Ajmer Rd (☎2100). Right next to the bus stand, but comfortable and cosy, with an interior courtyard and a wide roof area. Constant hot water on tap. ①.

Om, Ajmer Rd (☎2143). A ramshackle place with central courtyard. Basic rooms, with or without bathroom. Non-residents can use the small pool for Rs20. ①.

Payal Guest House, Sadar Bazaar. Small central hotel with rooms around a fresh and leafy courtyard. Good value and night curfew. ①.

Peacock, Ajmer Rd (☎2093). A little out of town past Ajmer bus stand, and popular mainly for its pool, which non-residents can pay Rs40 to use. Decent rooms but nothing special, plus cheap dorms and more expensive suites. Also has its own restaurant. ①–⑤.

Prince, on the road leading to Varah Ghat Mandir. A quiet place with unelaborate rooms set around a verdant courtyard; roof area and restaurant. ①.

Pushkar Palace (☎2001). On the east side of the lake, with panoramic views from a peaceful garden. Rooms range from tiny and basic to large and lavish. Cheaper dorm also available, though general atmosphere is somewhat upper class. Good restaurant. ④–⑤.

Sai Baba Guest House & **Shanti Palace**. Small neighbouring converted family homes with roof areas and basic facilities, up a winding street past the post office in the market square. ①.

RTDC Sarovar Tourist Bungalow, Ajmer Rd (☎2040). Entered at the end of Ajmer Rd, but set back from the street in peaceful gardens, just east of the lake. Pleasant and well maintained; rates include evening meal, but the food is notoriously poor. Dorms available. ③–④.

Siva, opposite the *Sai Baba Guest House*. Popular little place with a leafy courtyard and roof top. ①.

Eating

As Pushkar is sacred to Lord Brahma, all food is strictly vegetarian: meat, eggs and alcohol are banned (and taking drugs of any form is considered highly offensive). However, its **restaurants** cater to both Indian and western palates, offering national dishes as well as pizza, spaghetti and even apple pie. Be wary of the many buffets offering tempting all-you-can-eat menus; most are likely to consist of terribly unhealthy reheated food, and it's safer to stick to the more expensive places. If you fancy a change, stalls opposite *Gau Ghat* sell sumptuous freshly made sweets.

Garden Restaurant, Ram Ghat. Delicious Indian and western food of a standard rarely matched by other restaurants.

Krishna, Brahma temple Rd. Tasty Indian dishes, including south Indian *dosas* at breakfast.

Man Sarovar, Ajmer Rd. Good western and Indian food in pleasant garden surroundings, next to the Ajmer bus stand.

Pushkar Palace. One of the pricier but more reliable buffets. A menu of the evening meal is posted outside the restaurant each morning.

R S, opposite the Brahma temple. A long-standing favourite, with a small garden area and patio seating. Try some of its inexpensive but high-quality Indian dishes.

Rainbow, Brahma Temple Rd. Rooftop restaurant above the *Krishna*; good views but over-priced.

Sanjay, Sadar Bazaar. Rooftop seating overlooking the lake, but again the food is nothing special.

Sunset, on the southeast corner of the lake. The food is poor by any standards, and the service can be tedious, but the views from the garden are superb and there's often fresh bread in the mornings.

Venus. Set back from the lake, with a garden and a roof terrace. The Indian dishes are good, but they haven't quite got the hang of western cooking.

Jodhpur

On the eastern fringe of the Thar desert, the city of **JODHPUR** sprawls across the sandy terrain, watched over by a mighty walled fort that emerges from a high rocky outcrop. Jodhpur was once the centre of Marwar, the largest princely state in Rajputana, and today has a population close to half a million.

Most of the tourists that stop in Jodhpur only stay for a day, squeezing in a visit to the fort and palaces before heading west to Jaisalmer (300km) or east to Jaipur

(320km). It's a shame to rush the place though, and if you spend more time here you'll be able to explore the wonderful bazaars, search out puppeteers and dyers, and get a taste of rural Rajasthan by taking a trip to the surrounding villages.

A brief history

In 1459, Rao Jodha of the Rathore clan moved the capital of Marwar state several kilometres from the exposed site of **Mandore** to a massive steep-sided escarpment, where he named his new capital after himself. The high barricaded fort proved virtually impregnable, and the city soon amassed great wealth from trade en route to the ports of Gujarat. Not surprisingly, the Mughals were eager to take over Jodhpur, but realizing there was little prospect of that they presented treaties and riches to the Rathores in exchange for military aid in their onslaught on Gujarat. A marriage alliance between Udai Singh's sister and Akbar in 1561 ensured the most friendly of terms.

However, the tide turned in the mid-seventeenth century, after Jaswant Singh joined Shah Jahan's forces in an unsuccessful bid for power against his fellow Mughal Aurangzeb. Aurangzeb set out to purge his enemies, and demanded the death of Jaswant's young son, **Ajit Singh**. That demand was not satisfied, but Jodhpur was sacked in 1678 and its inhabitants forcibly converted to Islam. In the finest romantic tradition, Ajit Singh eventually recaptured his rightful kingdom after thirty years in hiding. The performance of *sati* on his funeral pyre by six wives and fifty-eight concubines in 1731 may seem shocking now, but at the time was testimony to his heroism.

The eighteenth century saw many bloody and violent battles between Jodhpur, Jaipur and Udaipur, despite their policy of unification against the Mughals. At its close, Jodhpur passed first into the hands of the Marathas and then the British; the signing of a friendship treaty with the East India Company in 1818 guaranteed its safety, albeit at great cost to Rathore honour.

The last Maharaja before Independence, **Umaid Singh**, is commemorated by his immense Umaid Bhawan Palace; he set three thousand citizens to work for sixteen years on its construction, in part to alleviate problems during a severe famine by creating employment. Jodhpur is now a democratic union within the independent India, but its social fabric remains tinged with feudalism and a medieval atmosphere prevails.

Arrival and information

Jodhpur's **railway station** is in the south of town, close to several basic hotels, and a couple of kilometres from the fort; it offers an efficient left-luggage service. **Tickets** for onward rail journeys must be reserved at the office next to the **post office** on Station Rd. The **bus stand**, past the courts on the eastern edge of town, is well connected with the rest of Rajasthan, Delhi, Gujarat and Uttar Pradesh.

Auto-rickshaws are the main form of city transport, supplemented by tempos and small minibuses that follow fixed routes along the main road. **Bicycles** can be rented from shops opposite the railway station (Rs7 per day), and **cars** from *Hotel Ardash Niwas*, Station Rd (☎26936). *Rajasthan Tours*, Hospital Rd (☎32694 or 36942) is a reliable agent for **tours** around the state.

The **tourist office** (Mon–Sat 10am–4.30pm; ☎44010), in the RTDC *Goomar Tourist Bungalow* on High Court Rd, has city maps and information on private bus services. A bus for Jaisalmer leaves from here at 6.30am, if there are enough passengers. The *State Bank of India* is behind the Collectorate, off High Court Rd (Mon–Fri 11am–3pm), and *Indian Airlines* have an office on Ajit Rd (☎28600).

The telephone **area code** for Jodhpur is ☎0291.

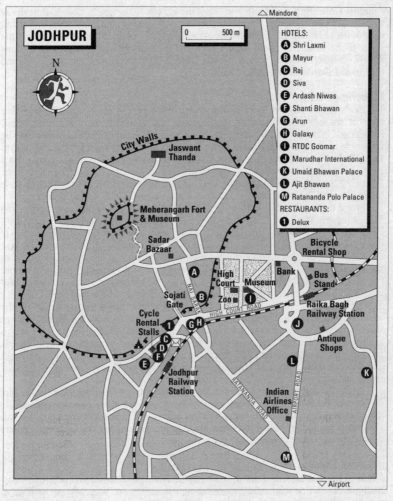

The City

Life in Jodhpur focuses very much around the fort, still almost completely encircled by the strong walls erected by Rao Maldeo in the sixteenth century. The precise significance of the blue wash so conspicuous on most of the city's houses is unclear; while the colour is alleged to deter mosquitoes, some say that blue indicates Brahmin families, and others that it's the traditional mark of Jains' houses. Everybody seems to have a different opinion.

The bazaars of the old city are gathered around the tall **clock tower**, with different areas assigned to different trades. Locally made goods include tie-and-dye material, puppets and lacquered jewellery.

Jalori Gate and **Sojati Gate** lead out of the old city to the south, close to the railway station, GPO and hospital. Beyond the walls, more modern buildings spread east and west of the old boundaries, the domes of the splendid **Umaid Bhawan** dominating the scene to the west. The grand **High Court**, and the **Government Museum** are immediately outside the old walls, near **Mertia Gate**. Behind the High Court is a library and the **Umaid Gardens**, which hold a zoo.

Meherangarh Fort

Jodhpur's **Meherangarh Fort** provides what must be the most authentic surviving taste of the ceaseless round of war, honour and extravagance that characterized Rajputana. Unlike the fort in Jaisalmer, it is now uninhabited, its paths trodden only by visitors to the temples and palaces within its high crenellated walls. On the wall next to **Loha Pole**, the sixth of seven gates designed to hinder the ascent of enemies up a steep winding cobbled road, are the handprints of Maharaja Man Singh's widows. Following the Rajput code of honour, they voluntarily ended their lives in 1843 on their husband's pyre, in defiance of the law against *sati* passed in 1829 by the British.

Beyond the massive **Suraj Pole**, the final gate, lie the palaces that now serve as the **Meherangarh Museum** (daily 9am–5pm; Rs30, plus Rs35 for camera, Rs75 for video). From the courtyards, you can see the fantastic *jali* (lattice) work that almost entirely covers their sandstone walls and balconies. The exotic names of the palaces evoke a courtly society that between violent battles loved to indulge in beauty and elegance. In the **Jhanki Mahal**, or "Queen's Palace", there's a colourful array of cradles of former rulers, while **Moti Mahal** (Pearl Palace) houses the majestic marble coronation seat upon which all the rulers apart from Jodha have been, and still are, crowned. One prize exhibit in the museum is a 250-year-old pure silk tent seized during a raid on the Mughal court in Delhi. The most elaborate of the apartments is **Phool Mahal** (Flower Palace), a dancing hall for the entertainment of the Maharaja and his guests. Pictures of dancers, deities and rulers look out from its walls and wooden ceilings, brightly painted with touches of gold. Other palaces have sandalwood ceilings, mirrored walls and decorated archways, and the last section displays solid silver *howdahs* (elephant seats) and palanquins, perfectly carved and very, very heavy.

The fascinating walk up to the fort from the old city passes through busy bazaars and communal living areas, where some of the streets are so narrow that pedestrians have to advance in single file, vying for right of way with goats and chickens. You can also reach the fort by taxi or rickshaw along the much longer road (5km) that enters the old city at Nagauri Gate.

Jaswant Thanda

North of the fort, and connected to it by road, **Jaswant Thanda** is a pillared marble memorial to the popular ruler Jaswant Singh II (1878–95), who purged Jodhpur of dacoits, initiated irrigation systems and boosted the economy. The cenotaphs of members of the royal family who have died since Jaswant are close by his memorial; those who preceded him are remembered by *chhatris* at **Mandor** (see p.166).

Accommodation

Hotels in Jodhpur are grouped in three main areas. Those along Station Road (a noisy area) are acceptable only to thick-skinned budget travellers, with the exception of the *Ardash Niwas*; the hotels on Nai Sarak (also called New Road) are a little less basic. The more costly are in the southwest of town. Rates for extremely simple rooms in Jodhpur are surprisingly high, and whatever budget you are on it's worth considering a night in the irresistible *Ajit Bhawan* on the eastern edge of town.

Ajit Bhawan, Ajit Colony (☎20409). Grand a/c suites in a palace, set in leafy gardens and still used by the royal family, plus spotless and characterful round huts for two; each is named and designed to a village theme. Regal treatment and a true taste of Rajasthani tradition; evening buffets (see below) feature performances by villagers. Also daily village excursions. ⑦–⑧.

Ardash Niwas, Station Rd (☎26936). Modern, clean, comfortable, and convenient for the station, but uninspiring. Marble decor and few windows. Hot water and TV in all rooms, some a/c. ④–⑦.

Arun, Sojati Gate (☎20238). A four-storey hotel, the best value of the cheap places; rooms are minimal, with or without bathroom, and there's a dorm. ①–②.

Galaxy, near Over Bridge, Nai Sarak (☎20796). Various standards of dingy rooms. ②–④.

Marudhar International, opposite KN Hall, Raikabagh (☎23208). Plain rooms (some a/c) a little out of the centre, set around a compact lawn. Clean and quiet, with a reasonable restaurant. ④.

Mayur, 10 Nai Sarak (☎27511). Simple rooms, quite clean; some have balconies. ②.

Raj, Station Rd (☎28447). Rooms with baths are spartan but sufficient, those without are airless cells. Pleasant sitting area on roof. Good value. ②.

Raj Basera, Residency Rd (☎31973). A little out of town, good for tour groups. Recently built village-style cottages with interesting decor; swimming pool and open-air restaurant. ⑦.

Ratanada Polo Palace, Residency Rd (☎31910). A plush but characterless hotel catering to the tastes of visiting western polo-players. Spacious carpeted rooms with TV. Large swimming pool, tennis courts, bar and restaurant. Poor value compared to its neighbours. ⑨.

RTDC Goomar, High Court Rd (☎44010). Fairly typical RTDC hotel with large and bare rooms in need of a spring clean. Cheap dorm, alcohol shop, restaurant and travel counter. ③–⑤.

Shanti Bhawan, Station Rd (☎21689). Right opposite the railway station; rooms range from bare and cramped to spacious and comfortable. Friendly management. ①–③.

Siva, Station Rd (☎24774). Clean rooms with private bath around small courtyard. A bit sterile. ②.

Shri Laxmi, 132–133 Nai Sarak (☎27511). Very near the Clock Tower. Rooms (with bath) are clean and adequate. ②.

Umaid Bhawan Palace (☎22516 or 22366). For those with extravagant tastes and bulging purses. The building is awesome and rooms are expansive, but some lack the style you'd expect for the price. Numerous bars, huge gardens and an underground swimming pool. ⑨.

Eating

Jodhpur's narrow range of **restaurants** caters for all tastes and all budgets, and you shouldn't have any difficulty finding a good meal. Directly opposite the railway station, beneath *Shanti Bhawan*, a collection of small dimly lit stalls serve surprisingly tasty dishes. Look out for *dhood fini*, a sweet mixture of wheat strands and milk.

Ajit Bhawan, Ajit Colony (☎20409). Delicious evening buffets with local meat and veg dishes, accompanied by folk music and dance. Book ahead. Breakfast and lunch don't need to be booked.

Delux, High Court Rd. Small drinks-store at the junction with Station Rd, serving excellent *Makhania lassi*, fresh fruit juice and milk shakes.

Kalinga, Station Rd (☎26936). Smart restaurant adjoining *Ardash Niwas,* with a wide choice of tasty Indian meat and veg dishes at very reasonable prices.

Punkhaj, Station Rd. Small and friendly, serving great vegetarian dishes and superb tandoori nans.

Shri Laxmi, 132–133 Nai Sarak (☎27511). Small, cheap vegetarian restaurant attached to the hotel.

Sharma Tandoori, Station Rd. Basic food stall with a few rickety tables, offering Indian and Chinese vegetarian dishes.

Umaid Bhawan Palace (☎22516 or 22366). Buffet spreads in the huge embellished dining hall are extremely expensive, with a cover charge demanded before you enter and hidden taxes, and the food leaves many disappointed. Booking advisable if you want to see what all the fuss is about.

Around Jodhpur

Should you stay in Jodhpur for longer than a day, and be tempted to see more than the fort and the medieval bazaars, you can visit the gardens in the old capital of **Mandor**

THE BISHNOIS

The **Bishnoi** people follow 29 principles laid down by Guru Jambhoji, who made environmental and wildlife protection a "religion" in the fifteenth century. Common throughout Rajasthan and Gujarat, they are renowned for a concern for nature, particularly for their refusal to harm the black buck, which now survives only in Bishnoi areas.

Bishnoi beliefs came to the political forefront in 1730, when the king of Jodhpur ordered his men to collect wood for a new palace. Despite the pleas of the Bishnois, felling commenced in the small village of Khejadali near Jodhpur. In desparation Amritdevi, a Bishnoi woman, hugged a tree. The fellers, assuming that the king's request was to be respected, ignored her plea. She and 362 of her fellow people lost their lives trying to protect the forests. On hearing the news the king recalled his men and accorded state sanction to the Bishnoi religion, a turning point in history remembered each September when thousands attend a festival at Khejadali.

---

on the outskirts of town, where former rulers are remembered by elaborate temple-like constructions, or a remarkable collection of early Jain and Hindu temples further afield at **Osiyan**, an hour's drive away.

Jodhpur's arid surroundings can also be explored on organized **village safaris**, which take small groups of tourists out into rural Rajasthan for a taste of traditional life. With several very dubious agencies around, much the most enlightening option is the half-day trip led by Maharaja Swaroop Singh of the *Ajit Bhawan Palace Hotel* (daily, book at least a day in advance; 8am–1 or 2pm; Rs250, including lunch). Each tour visits nearby villages, set in scrubland where the rare black buck, a beautiful indigenous antelope that is a menace to crops, is protected by the Bishnoi tribe. In desert dwellings, mostly circular thatched huts, you can taste traditional food, learn about herbal remedies, and watch crafts such as spinning and carpet making. The Maharaja, who receives an enthusiastic welcome from the villagers, encourages the fair sale of their handicrafts in the hope that they can thereby avoid emigration to the city, a sad necessity that has destroyed the traditional way of life of so much of India's rural population.

Mandor

Most of Jodhpur's minibuses head for the royal cenotaphs, or *dewals*, of the Maharajas in the fertile gardens 9km north of the city at **MANDOR**, the capital of the Parihar Rajputs between the sixth and fourteenth centuries. The Parihars were ousted when the Rathore Rao Chauhan in 1381 established the seat of government for his new kingdom at Mandor, and little remains of their fortified city. The dark red sandstone *chhatris*, memorials to Jodhpur's rulers, grew in size and grandeur as the Rathore kingdom prospered, culminating with the last and largest, that of Maharaja Dhiraj Ajit Singh (died 1763). It's Shaivite in style, fronted by a balustraded porch and topped with a towering roof crowned with four faces of Shiva.

By the *chhatris* you'll find the **Hall of Heroes**, a strange display of life-sized gods and Rajput fighters that were hewn out of the rock face early in the eighteenth century. The museum opposite is not worth a visit.

A path leads over the hill behind the gardens to another set of cenotaphs, seemingly neglected on a sandy slope among twisted cacti. These commemorate the ranis of Jodhpur and though smaller, are more stately than those of the men. The detailed carving on the pillars and domed roofs is exquisite.

Osiyan

Rajasthan's largest group of early Jain and Hindu temples lies on the outskirts of the small town of **OSIYAN**, 64km north of Jodhpur (hourly buses; 2hr). Sixteen Pratihara (eighth–eleventh centuries) temples are clustered south, west and north of the town.

The earliest **Harihara temples**, in the south, retain a considerable amount of decorative carving: twisted serpents coil around the doorways to the sanctuaries, and friezes on the outer walls include pictures of Krishna. The large **Mahavira temple** (late eighth-century) among the western group is richly decorated with an intricacy characteristic of Jain sculptors – notice the finely pierced stone screens beneath the domed ceilings. The gateway embellished with figurines was added in 1015. In the same area the **Surya temple** has splendid images of Durga, Surya and Ganesh. Among the temples to the north, the **Sachiya Mata temple**, still used for worship, has a grand domed roof supported by adorned brackets, seated porches adjoining the sanctuary, and some remarkable statues in the wall niches.

Jaisalmer

The westernmost town of Rajasthan, a good 100km beyond its closest neighbour Pokaran, **JAISALMER** is a desert city *par excellence*, its honey-coloured fort emerging from the flat dry sands like a fairy-tale kingdom, abounding in ancient palaces, temples and delicately sculpted houses. This is one of Rajasthan's most enchanting cities, tranquil and beautiful, its soft desert-yellow streets spiced with bright oranges, reds, yellows and blues of turbans, scarfs and skirts. As the sun sets the sandstone buildings emit the lustrous glow that make Jaisalmer the "Golden City".

After its foundation as a Rajput stronghold by Rawal Jaisal of the Bhatti clan in 1156, a turbulent and heroic history unfolded. Initially there were constant wars with the neighbouring Rajput states of Jodhpur and Bikaner; later, in 1294, Muslim invaders attacked and conquered Jaisalmer, inducing large-scale *johar* (voluntary death by sword and fire) by the warriors and their womenfolk. In the fourteenth century the Bhatti Rajputs retook the city, but provoked a second sacking when they challenged the Muslims at Ajmer. Relations with the Muslims improved, and in 1570 the ruler of Jaisalmer married one of his daughters to Akbar. From the seventeenth century the city prospered as a market centre for traders on the overland routes between India and Central Asia; the magnificent *havelis* of the merchants bear witness to those times. However, with the emergence of Bombay as a major port, overland trading diminished, and so did Jaisalmer's wealth. After Independence, the city was left almost stranded, but its location so close to the newly sensitive border lent it significance during the Indo-Pakistan wars of 1965 and 1971, and it is now a major military outpost.

Arrival and information

The main point of arrival, served by twice-daily trains to and from Jodhpur, is the **railway station**, 2km southeast of the city. Over-eager touts – supposedly kept at a safe distance by a "tourist rescue" police service – accost arriving passengers with offers of free taxi services to particular hotels. Either take one of these, or pay Rs3 to get into town by jeep and choose a hotel without hassle. Travellers arriving at the **bus stand** nearby face a less severe predicament, and it's easy to take a rickshaw or taxi into town. Buses come to Jaisalmer from as far afield as Ahmedabad. There are **bike rental** shops in the main street, and opposite *Fort View Hotel*.

The **tourist office** (Mon–Sat 8am–noon & 3–6pm) is in the *Tourist Bungalow* west of the city, but the office of *Thar Safari Excursion Agent* (☎2722) in Gandhi Chowk is equally good at providing information, with bus timetables, details of hotels and camel safaris, and tips on local sights and history. A **post office** stands shaded by a huge banyan tree in the main market square, but poste restante is at the main office in the west of the city. The *Bank of Baroda* in Gandhi Chowk changes money (Mon–Fri 11am–3pm; Sat 11am–1pm).

CAMEL SAFARIS

Few visitors who make it as far as Jaisalmer pass up the opportunity to go on a **camel trek**, which provides the wonderfully romantic chance to cross the barren sands on a sturdy ship of the desert, sleep under the stars, and sing traditional desert songs. Sandstorms and sore backsides aside, the safaris are usually great fun. Most hotels offer their own versions, as do agencies (see below) and freelance camel owners, working for extremely low prices, who may stop you in the street and offer their services.

Treks last for one, two, three or four days, at prices varying from Rs90 to Rs900 per night. In general the less you spend the less you get, in terms of food, blankets, fitness of camel etc; it pays to ask around to see who has just had a successful trek of the standard you're after. A lot depends on whether the guides are friendly, how big the group is, and what expectations you have. Things to make sure of are an adequate supply of blankets, to sleep on and under (it can get very cold at night), a quota of fruit if you're paying anything over the average, and whether there will be a camp fire. If you're only going for a day, none of this applies, but be sure to wear a hat and take high-factor sun-protection lotion.

Following government restrictions on routes, most safaris head west of Jaisalmer through places such as Sam sand dunes, Lodurva, Amar Sagar, Bada Bagh and assorted small villages. Some visitors feel this puts too much emphasis on sightseeing; it's possible to arrange a few days' amble through the desert without stopping at any monuments if you'd prefer to leave them out. Taking a jeep at the start or end of the trek enables you to go further in a short time. Longer safaris to Pokaran, Jodhpur or Bikaner can be arranged.

Thar Safari Excursion Agent (☎2722) in Gandhi Chowk is the most efficient agency offering a range of safaris, many with tents provided, and reliable guides. They will also arrange treks to Jaisalmer from Pokaran if given at least ten days' notice, and are among the few agents who genuinely take care to protect the desert environment. Less expensive agencies include *Sahara Travels* at First Fort Gate (☎2609) and *Shree Shive* on Kachari Rd.

Increased demand has resulted in higher prices, worse service, and attitude problems from some hotels, such as *Fort View*, but safaris organized by the *Paradise* have a good reputation. For alternative routes, try *Hotel Deepak* and *Sunil Bhatia Rest House*.

The City

Getting lost in the narrow winding streets of Jaisalmer is both easy and enjoyable, though the city is so small that it never takes long to find a familiar landmark. Main roads lead around the base of the fort from the central market square, east to **Gadi Sagar Tank**, and west to **Gandhi Chowk** where the banks are located.

Within the fort the streets are yet narrower, but orientation is simple: head west from the main *chowk* and **Maharawal's Palace** to reach the **Jain temples** and hotels nestled within the walls.

Jaisalmer's flourishing tourist trade has helped keep alive many local crafts; good buys include woven jackets, dyed cloth, wooden boxes and ornaments, and western-style clothes. An outlet of the *Khadi Gramdyog* chain, inspired by Gandhi's example of spinning, sells inexpensive rugs and clothing made from homespun cloth.

Jaisalmer fort

Every part of Jaisalmer **fort**, from its outer walls to the palace, temples and houses within, is made of soft yellow sandstone. The narrow winding streets are flanked with carved sandy facades, and from the bastions, some of which still bear cannons, you can see the thick walls that drop almost 100m to the town below. Today the fort stands strong, housing nearly a quarter of the town's population, and strict rules limit additional building.

JAISALMER

Railway Station △

HOTELS:
Ⓐ Narayan Vilas &
   Narayan Niwas
Ⓑ Pleasure
Ⓒ Pushkar Palace
Ⓓ Swastika
Ⓔ Jaisal Palace
Ⓕ Laxmi Niwas
Ⓖ Deepak Rest House
Ⓗ Jaisal Castle
Ⓘ Shrinath & Suraj
Ⓙ Paradise
Ⓚ Pooja
Ⓛ Fort View & Flamingo
Ⓜ Sunil Bhatia Rest House

RESTAURANTS:
❶ Kalpana
❷ Trio
❸ 8th July
❹ New Jaisal
❺ Moti Mahal
❻ Leo
❼ Natraj

0 _____ 200 m

N

Gadi Sagar Pole

Gadi Sagar Tank ▷

GADI SAGAR RD

Patwon-
Ki-Haveli

Nathmalji-
Ki-Haveli

Salim
Singh's
Haveli

FORT

Palace

MAIN
CHOWK

Amar
Sagar
Gate

GANDH
CHOWK

Royal
Palace

Local
Bus Stand

Private
Bus Stand

GPO

Hospital

AMAR SAGAR RD

A paved road punctuated by four huge gateways winds up to the fort, built when the city was founded in 1156. The fourth gateway leads into the main *chowk*, which these days becomes a crowded mass of colour and life during festive celebrations, but was once the scene of the gathering of troops, marriage parties and the terrible act of *johar* when women chose death above dishonour for themselves and their children after their husbands left for the battlefield. The *chowk* is dominated by the old palace of the Maharawal (daily 10am–3pm), whose five-storey facade of balconies and windows displays some of the finest masonry work in Jaisalmer, while the interior is painted and tiled in typical Rajput style. The monarch would address his troops and issue orders from the large ornate marble throne to the left of the palace entrance.

Although the fort holds temples dedicated to Surya, Lakshmi, Ganesh, Vishnu and Shiva, none is as impressive as the **Jain temples** (daily 9am–noon), built between the twelfth and fifteenth centuries in the familiar Jurassic sandstone, with their yellow and white marble shrines. Walls, ceilings and pillars bear exquisite sculpted motifs, and small corridors and stairways connect one temple to another. In a vault beneath the Sambhavnath temple, the **Gyan Bhandar** (daily 10–11am) contains Jain manuscripts, paintings and astrological charts dating back to the eleventh century.

The havelis

The streets of Jaisalmer are flanked with numerous honey-pale facades, covered with lattice work and floral designs, but the city's real showpieces are its **havelis**. Each of these extravagant mansions, comprising three or more storeys around a central courtyard, was commissioned by a wealthy merchant during the eighteenth or nineteenth century. Their stonework was the art of *silavats*, a community of masons responsible for much of Jaisalmer's unique sculpture.

The large **Patwon-ki-haveli** (daily 10.30am–5pm; free), not far from *Narayan Niwas* in the north of town, was constructed over fifty years by the Patwa merchants, traders in brocades. Five separate suites with individual entrances facing a narrow street are connected from within, and all have flat roof areas – the views are excellent. Traces of stylish wall paintings survive in some rooms.

Salim Singh's small *haveli* provides Jaisalmer's only favourable memory of the tyrannical Salim Singh Mohta, prime minister in 1800, who impoverished the citizens through vigorous taxation and extortion rackets. His curious family home is topped with small bluish domes; its upper floor, enclosed by a protruding balcony, is best seen from the roof of *Natraj Restaurant*. The house is still lived in, but you can go inside. On the road to Malka Pole, you pass the decorative facade of the late nineteenth-century **Nathmalji-ki-haveli**, also built for a prime minister of Jaisalmer. No visitors are allowed, so you won't be able to view the skilful paintings on the interior walls.

Gadi Sagar Tank and the Folklore Museum

South of the city through an imposing triple gateway, **Gadi Sagar Tank**, built in 1367, was once Jaisalmer's sole water supply. Its north and east banks are flanked with ghats and temples whose sandstone bricks glow with a warm deep ochre in the evening light. This peaceful place is the focus of the festival of Gangaur in March, when women fling flowers into the lake and pray for a good husband, and the Maharawal heads a procession to the tank amid a pomp and splendour unchanged for generations.

The delightful little **Folklore Museum** near the tank's main gate (daily 9am–noon & 3–6pm; Rs2) has some interesting displays of folk art, much of it religious. Locally styled wooden statues of Krishna and Radha, musical instruments, paintings and a travelling temple (*kavad*) are among its exhibits.

The telephone **area code** for Jaisalmer is ☎02992.

Desert festival

In January or February, depending on the lunar calendar, RTDC organizes a huge **desert festival**, more for the sake of tourists than out of tradition, which features camel racing, dances, music, puppet shows and moustache competitions. Accommodation is provided in a special "tourist village"; prices for rooms and food soar.

Accommodation

Jaisalmer has no shortage of hotels, most of them in the budget category. Almost all offer camel treks, which vary in standard and price, and some managers can be uncomfortably pushy if you don't want to arrange a safari through them. The *New Tourist Hotel* is one to avoid for this reason. Many visitors prefer the peaceful and atmospheric hotels among the jumble of sandstone houses and *havelis* within the fort, whose roofs offer splendid desert vistas. Below the fort in the town, the hotels generally have less character, but many are small and intimate with lovely roof terraces.

In the fort

Deepak Rest House (☎2665). In the south of the fort, beyond the Jain temples. Small and friendly with basic rooms, dormitory and a roof terrace. One more expensive room with balcony. ①.

Jaisal Castle (☎2362). An old *haveli* in the southern corner of the fort. Great views, but lacking general cleanliness. Dusty and overpriced. ⑧.

Laxmi Niwas (☎2758). Small and basic with mattresses on the floor, shared bathrooms and minimal roof terrace. ①.

Paradise (☎2674). Well-run, comfortable hotel with grassy courtyard, large roof area and some excellent rooms with balcony and private bath. Popular. ②–⑤.

Shrinath. Small stylish family home in an old *haveli* with large rooms, close to the Jain temples. Very basic toilet facilities. ④.

Suraj (☎3023). Superbly carved sandstone *haveli* with real style. Four spacious, comfortable rooms in family atmosphere. Excellent rooftop view. ⑤.

In the town

Flamingo, Central Mkt (☎2609). Small, windowless rooms around a courtyard in family house. ①.

Fort View, Central Mkt (☎2214). Large hotel, impersonal but clean enough. Roof restaurant. ①–②.

Jaisal Palace, behind Royal Palace (☎2717). Very clean modern hotel, a little sterile with tasteless decor. Large roof area. ④.

Jawahar Niwas Palace, Amar Sagar Rd (☎2208). An old palace less than 1km west of town with grand but musty rooms. Veg and non-veg restaurant. ⑦.

Madhuwan, Mainpura (☎3027). Reasonable basic rooms, friendly staff and good view from roof. ①.

Narayan Niwas, on the northern edge of town (☎2397). A/c rooms are clean but unimaginative and without windows. Large grass courtyard and pleasant bar area. Overpriced. ⑧.

Narayan Vilas, next to *Narayan Niwas* (☎2283). An old and characterful *haveli*. Comfortable and clean. ⑥.

Pleasure, Gandhi Chowk (☎2323). Average rooms in house with small courtyard and roof terrace. Common bathroom. ①.

Pooja, near Fort First Gate (☎2656). Beautiful old *haveli* in typically carved sandstone, with a small roof terrace. A few more pricey and atmospheric rooms. ①.

Pushkar Palace, Gandhi Chowk. Very small family house with comfortable basic rooms, shared bathrooms and large roof area. ①.

RTDC Moomal Tourist Bungalow, Amar Sagar Rd (☎2392). Clean and spacious rooms in well-run hotel. Round huts in the grounds, each with double room and bathroom, are less pricey and great value. Good restaurant, free outdoor dance programme on Sunday evenings. ②–⑤.

Sunil Bhatia Rest House, off Central Mkt (☎2533). Among the more basic hotels, but with great hot showers. ①.

MOVING ON FROM JAISALMER

Jaisalmer's only **rail** connection is to Jodhpur, over 250km east; the ten-hour journey is best done overnight, on the *JPJ Passenger* #3 which leaves at 9.15pm.

All other long-distance journeys involve tedious **bus** journeys. **"Deluxe"** buses are the best option, and leave from the crossroads just outside Amar Sagar Gate, where you'll find the booking office. Frequent but much slower local buses, which can't be booked, use the bus stand a little north of the crossroads.

The 4.30pm bus to **Bikaner** takes six hours, half the time of the other five daily departures. Nine daily buses go to **Jodhpur** (6–7hr), while the service to **Jaipur** (13hr) via **Ajmer** leaves at 4pm. Journeys southeast to **Udaipur** (14hr) can be made via **Barmer** (3hr; depart 6am), or **Jodhpur** (depart 2.30pm). Services to **Mount Abu** and **Ahmedabad** and **Bhuj** (all three take 12hr) leave at 5.30am.

Swastika, Mainpura (☎4152). Excellent cheap hotel, clean and cosy with free morning tea and hot showers. Great view from roof. ①.

Vrinda Palace, Shiv Marg (☎3025). One of the cleaner and more modern low-priced places. Rooms with attached bath and rooftop restaurant. Pay more for a western-style loo. ①.

Eating

Being so popular with foreign tourists, Jaisalmer offers many a western delight in its **restaurants**. Peanut butter, vegemite, pizzas, pancakes, apple pie and cakes feature on most menus alongside typical Indian dishes. The choice of places to eat is thin, however, and it only takes a day or two to find one you'll want to stick with.

8th July, in the fort. Restaurant overlooking the main square, where the extensive and imaginative menu include thick, milky smoothies. The other *8 July,* just off the market square, may serve vegemite, but it's dull and cramped with a less creative menu.

Fort View, Market Square. Rooftop hotel restaurant. Good food at reasonable prices, plus views over the market square.

Kalpana, Gandhi Chowk. Reasonable Punjabi dishes at low prices. Open-air seating.

Leo, Gadi Sagar Pole. A wide choice of fabulous, very affordable food.

Moti Mahal. Small ground-floor restaurant opposite Salim Singh's *haveli*. Excellent and inexpensive food. Some tables face the street from the front verandah.

Natraj. Pleasant rooftop restaurant facing the top floor of Salim Singh's *haveli*. The food is of a high standard and moderately priced.

New Jaisal. A tiny upper-storey place overlooking the market square that hasn't quite perfected the art of cooking, though it's OK for a drink and not expensive.

Trio, Gandhi Chowk. With sumptuous food, tasteful decor, snappy service and live folk music this is a wonderful place to dine, and you'll only pay a little over the average.

Around Jaisalmer

Although the countryside around Jaisalmer is sandy and barren, it does harbour some unexpected architectural sights which loom out of the sweeping sands. The best way to visit these places, and see villages and abandoned towns inaccessible by road, is on a camel trek (see p.168). It's also possible to rent a jeep (at greater cost), and there are buses, but they run very infrequently.

Amar Sagar

A short distance northwest of Jaisalmer, **AMAR SAGAR** is a small peaceful town set around a large lake (empty during the dry season). A former palace and large complex of Jain temples, currently being restored to their former magnificence, stand on the lake edges. Both are built out of sandstone.

Sam

The huge, rolling sand dunes 40km west of Jaisalmer are known as **SAM**, though strictly this is the name of a small village a bit further west. The dunes are so famous in Rajasthan that most tourists don't realize that there are others throughout the desert; consequently they have become a prime attraction. There's even a *Tourist Bungalow* here, though it only opens if you get permission in Jaisalmer, and given the inexorable rate of advance of the dunes it will more than likely be buried by sand within the next decade. Sunset at Sam can be breathtaking, though drink sellers, musicians and numerous camel trains somewhat dilute the romance. The undulating sandscape looks spectacular at sunrise, so it's worth sleeping the night here if you're on a camel safari.

A bus does run to Sam, but it doesn't return until the next day. Those visitors who aren't travelling on camels usually make the journey by jeep.

Bada Bagh and royal cenotaphs

Six kilometres north of Jaisalmer, in the fertile area of **BADA BAGH**, a collection of cenotaphs built in memory of Jaisalmer's rulers stand clustered on a hill. Domed roofs shade small marble or sandstone slabs bearing inscriptions and equestrian statues. The gardens below are where most of the fruit and vegetables of the region are grown, and the greenery seems almost unreal amid the hostile waste of sand and scrub.

Lodurva

Another 10km north of Bada Bagh, **lodurva** was the capital of the Bhatti rulers until the foundation of Jaisalmer in the twelfth century. Of the city's fine buildings, only a few Jain temples, rebuilt in the 1970s, remain (open all day; camera charge Rs15, video Rs35). The *toran* (archway) at the entrance to the temple compound is the most exquisite in the Jaisalmer district. The main temple has detailed tracery work in the stone walls and a finely carved exterior. A smaller temple, built on a series of diminishing square platforms, stands to its right.

Fossil park

The scattered remains of tree fossils up to 180 million years old in the **fossil park**, 14km south of Jaisalmer, are of interest only to the most avid paleobotanists. Permission to visit must be obtained from the collector's office, just outside town near the *Moomal Tourist Bungalow*. Buses to Barmer pass through, but for a quicker visit it's best to take a jeep, which will cost about Rs200 for the round trip.

Barmer

BARMER, 158km south of Jaisalmer, is another important desert outpost, but has little to offer tourists. It's usually a dusty backwater, where the manufacture of handicrafts, forming its main export, occupies much of the population. In January however, the place is transformed during the hectic **Tilwara Cattle Fair**, held on the banks of a saltwater river nearby. This is the largest cattle market held in Rajasthan, attended by villagers and traders from all over the state, and swirls with colour and activity.

One bus a day takes three hours to run between Barmer and Jaisalmer. The scarcity of accommodation and food stalls in Barmer leaves little room for choice; if you need to stay the night, try the basic *Krishna Hotel* (①) near the railway station.

Pokaran

POKARAN, with its red sandstone fort and superb *havelis*, is a quiet, seldom-visited desert town 110km east of Jaisalmer, situated at the road and rail junctions between Jodhpur, Bikaner and the west. Once included in the territory of Jodhpur, it passed into the huge state of Jaisalmer after Independence. The fort has a maze of passages behind its ornate facades, and you can stay within its walls in the charming *Hotel Pokaran*

(☎2274; ⑤). For a less expensive room try the *Monica* (☎2269; ①). Not far from Pokaran, in **Ramdevra**, a tiny town consisting mostly of *dharamshalas*, an old temple dedicated to Ram is the scene of celebrations on Ram's birthday (end of March or the start of April) and during a fifteen-day festival in October.

Bikaner

The commercial city of **BIKANER** may not quite possess the aesthetic attraction of its more venerable neighbour, Jaisalmer, over 200km southwest, but it does boast a spectacular fort and an old city dotted with *havelis* and surrounded by 7km of high walls. In addition, simply because Rajasthan's fourth largest city receives fewer visitors than other major settlements, it has a certain "unspoilt" feel.

The city was founded in 1486 as a link in the overland trading route, by **Bika**, one of fourteen sons of Rao Jodha, the Rathore king who established Jodhpur as the centre of the state of Marwar. Under Rai Singh, who came to the throne in 1573, **Junagarh Fort** was built and closer ties were forged with the Mughals; Rai Singh gave his daughter in marriage to one of Akbar's sons. Later, during the reign of Ganga Singh at the start of the twentieth century, new agricultural schemes, irrigation work, town planning and the construction of a rail link with Delhi helped Bikaner's economic advance; it has long since outgrown the confines of the city wall, and has tripled in size since 1947.

Arrival and information

Well connected to Jaisalmer, Jodhpur and Shekawati, Bikaner's **bus stand** is a few kilometres north of town, just opposite the Lalgarh Palace. Plenty of rickshaws ply the route to the south of town where the railway station and most hotels are found.

The **tourist information bureau** (daily 10am–5pm; ☎27445) is just inside the Fort gate. The *State Bank of Bikaner and Jaipur* (Mon–Fri 10am–2.30pm) opposite the fort entrance will change travellers' cheques.

For trips around town, use any of the cycle or auto-rickshaws, or rent a bike; you'll find two **bike rental shops** outside the **post office** on Station Road.

Camel treks are not as established in Bikaner as they are in Jaisalmer (see p.168), but the idea is catching on. *Desert Tours*, whose office is behind the GPO, arrange camel safaris in the Bikaner region and further afield – or you can take a leisurely tour of the city itself on a camel for Rs150.

The City

It's definitely worth spending a day or two simply wandering around Bikaner, watching dyers at work, visiting the ancient **Jain temples**, and discovering the delights of **Junagarh Fort**. Bikaner is also famous for its skilled lacquer work and attractive handicrafts, and the markets are full of good buys.

Junagarh Fort

Built on ground level, defended only by high walls and a wide moat, **Junagarh Fort** (daily except Fri 10am–4.30pm; Rs25, Rs5 for resident Indians; camera Rs10, video Rs25) is not as immediately imposing as the mighty hill forts elsewhere in Rajasthan. But the decorative interiors and sculpted stone of the palaces, temples and thirty-seven pavilions within its walls are almost unrivalled in their magnificence.

The telephone **area code** for Bikaner is ☎0151.

The fort was constructed between 1587 and 1593, during the rule of Rai Singh, and later rulers added their own palatial suites, temples and plush courtyards. The **Karan Mahal**, with gold-leaf paintings adorning its pillars and walls, was built in the seventeenth century to commemorate a victory over the Mughal emperor Aurangzeb, while the imaginatively painted **Chandra Mahal** and the dazzling **Phool Mahal** were erected by Gaj Singh, a hundred years later.

Stained-glass windows, finely carved stone and wood balconies, and brightly painted walls and ceilings throughout the fort leave no doubt as to the extravagant tastes of these rulers, or the skills of the artisans they employed. The **Anup Mahal** is perhaps the most opulent, with wooden ceilings inlaid with mirrors, Italian tiles and delicate lattice work on the windows and balconies. The huge carpet is one of many made by inmates of Bikaner jail, a manufacturing tradition that has only recently ceased.

Although it was never conquered, the fort was attacked – handprints set in stone near the second gate, **Daulat Pole**, bear witness to the voluntary deaths of royal women, remembered as *satis*, whose menfolk had lost their lives in battle.

Visitors are escorted through the fort by English- and Hindi-speaking guides, with the tour finishing in the huge **Ganga Singh Hall**. The most recent part of the fort, dating from 1937, it houses part of the **museum**, whose exhibits include the inevitable weaponry and an unexpected World War II aeroplane, still in tip-top condition.

The old city

Kote Gate at the west end of MG Road is the main entrance through the high city walls into the atmospheric **old city**, where the clashing and banging of metalworkers resonate through the winding streets tinted with the hues of local dyers. The main attractions here are the two **Jain temples** in the southwest corner (daily 6–11.30am & 6–8pm). Built by two merchant brothers, both are remarkable for the sheer mass of colour and intricate design of wall paintings, a rare feature in Rajasthan's Jain temples.

The ground floor of **Bhandreshwar temple** (1571) has a cluster of pillars; some are decorated with gilded floral designs known as *usta* typical of Muslim artisans, others with embossed male and female sculptures common in medieval India. A statue of Lord Suminath, the fifth *tirthankara*, stands on the second floor. **Sandeshwar temple**, dedicated to Neminath and dated to 1536, houses rows of saints shaped from solid marble, and has enamel and gold-leaf paintings on the walls.

The sixteenth-century **Laxminath temple** nearby was built by Lunkaran Singh, the third ruler of Bikaner, on the edge of the high city wall. It overlooks a Muslim community of dyers and screen printers, with the barren desert in the distance.

Lalgarh Palace

The sturdy red-sandstone **Lalgarh Palace** in the north of town is home to the royal family of Bikaner, although parts now serve as a hotel. It was built during the reign of Ganga Singh, who lived there from 1902, using the fort only for private business, and despite some detailed carving, its modern aspect makes it fairly dull in comparison to other Rajasthani palaces. The enormous collection of photographs of the golden days of the Raj in its **Shri Sadul Museum** (daily except Wed 10am–5pm) are boring in the extreme, and the stuffed animals offer little relief. However, the **Anup Sanskrit Library** (same hours) in the palace has some unique and well-preserved manuscripts, parchments and engraved copper, plus gold and silver plaques.

Ganga Golden Jubilee Museum

The small **Ganga Golden Jubilee Museum** (daily except Fri & Sat 10am–4.30pm) on NH 8 near the *Tourist Bungalow* contains a moderately interesting display of costumes, weapons, ornaments, ancient statues and paintings, one of which depicts the signing of the Versailles Treaty by Ganga Singh. Older exhibits include terracottas belonging to the Gupta period (fourth and fifth centuries).

Accommodation

The range of **hotels** in Bikaner is narrow. A group of cheap and dingy places stand opposite the station, with some slightly more acceptable ones lining Station Road. For more upmarket accommodation you'll have to go further afield to the *Tourist Bungalow* or the extremely posh *Hotel Lalgarh Palace*, the only option near the bus stand.

Amit, Station Rd (☎28064). A small but clean place set back a little from the noisy road. ②.

Delux, Station Rd (☎23292). Cramped shabby rooms, some with balcony facing the road. ①.

RTDC Dhola Maru Tourist Bungalow, Pooran Singh Circle (☎28621). Well-kept rooms ranging from ordinary to super deluxe with balconies, and a cheap dormitory. ②–⑦.

Green, Station Rd (☎23396). Run-down hotel in the same building as the *Delux*, with tiny airless rooms. ①.

Joshi, Station Rd (☎26123). The smartest hotel in the area. Clean carpeted rooms, some a/c. ④–⑥.

ABHIVYAKTI

The rulers of Bikaner have always objected to commercial exploitation of their heritage, and have therefore forbidden traders to set up shop in the fort. However, the royal principles have been relaxed for a good cause in the case of a handicrafts shop, **Abhivyakti**, inside the main fort gate, next to the tourist office. *Abhivyakti* was established with the aid of funding from the local *Urmul Trust* and from *Oxfam* in England. The high-quality rugs, bags, clothes, cushion covers, shawls and stools sold here are made in seventy villages around Bikaner. You can buy reasonably priced artefacts that are uniquely styled, safe in the knowledge that no middlemen will lap up the profits, and the artisans will reap full benefit from the sale of their work.

Lalgarh Palace (☎25963). Expansive richly furnished rooms. Swimming pool, tennis courts and restaurant for guests only. ⑨.

Shri Shanti Niwas. Directly opposite the station, but best avoided; grim and cheap. ①.

Eating

Bikaner has only a few **restaurants** outside the hotels, serving mostly vegetarian dishes. For quick, low-priced food try any of the open-air shacks on Station Road which always have several cauldrons of constantly warmed curries to choose from.

Amber, Station Rd. Tasty vegetarian Punjabi dishes at moderate prices and good simple breakfasts.

Annapurna, Mahatma Gandhi Rd. An inexpensive and unpretentious place serving south Indian and continental dishes. No smoking.

Chhotu Motu Joshi Restaurant, Station Rd. Mid-range restaurant attached to *Hotel Joshi*; very popular and always busy.

Delux, Station Rd. Both this and the *Green* hotel serve snacks and light south Indian meals.

Dhola Maru Tourist Bungalow, Pooran Singh Circle. The only place apart from roadside stalls that sells meat dishes. Good, inexpensive food.

Around Bikaner

Several places of interest close to Bikaner can be visited in a day. The most unusual sites are the **camel breeding farm** and **Karni Mata temple**, a scurrying mass of sacred rats. Memorials of the rulers of Bikaner stand at **Devi Kund Sagar**, and further out of town in **Gajner** their former royal hunting ground is now a wildlife reserve.

Devi Kund Sagar

The majestic cenotaphs or *chhatris* of sandstone and marble that commemorate the rulers of Bikaner stand around an artificial lake at **Devi Kund Sagar**, about 8km west of the city. The most recent cenotaph in the enclosure, which dates back to the eighteenth century, is that of Sadul Singh, the last Maharaja, who died in 1950.

Camel breeding farm

What is probably Asia's largest **camel breeding farm** (daily 3–5pm) lies out in the desert 10km south of Bikaner, an easy round trip by rickshaw that should cost around Rs50. Although Bikaner has long been renowned for its famously sturdy beasts, and the camel corps was a much-feared component of the imperial battle formation, the farm itself was only founded in 1975. Its propagation programme has been so successful that it now provides fifty percent of India's camels, hundreds of whom, young and old, can be seen strutting their knock-kneed way across the sands.

Karni Mata temple

Devotees at the unique **Karni Mata temple** in **Deshnok** – 30km south of Bikaner and served by hourly buses – believe that departing souls are saved from the wrath of Yama, the god of death, by being reincarnated as **rats**. Teeming hordes of free-roaming holy rodents, known as *kabas*, are accordingly worshipped and fed by visitors; the experience of having one run over your feet is considered a great privilege. It is also deemed auspicious to eat *prasad* (blessed food from the main shrine) after it has been nibbled by the *kabas*.

The large black-and-white-marble temple is named after the patron goddess of the Bikaner dynasty Karni Mata, an incarnation of the fearsome Durga, and features a stunning set of solid silver doors donated by Maharaja Ganga Singh. On the last night of the festival of Navratri (March), crowds from nearby villages and towns flock here to pay homage to the goddess.

Gajner sanctuary

Once the imperial hunting ground of Ganga Singh, the lake and wooded area in **Gajner**, 32km west of Bikaner, is now a protected sanctuary that shelters *nilgai*, black buck, *chinkara* and gazelles all year round. In winter it's a popular spot for migratory birds, particularly the Siberian grouse. Buses leave Bikaner every half hour for Gajner, where double **rooms** are available in the old palace on the shore of the lake (⑦).

Nearby, at the temple-studded pilgrimage centre of **Kolayat**, devotees and wandering *sadhus* worship and bathe in an artificial lake that never dries up.

Nagaur

The grand mosques and painted palaces of the heavily fortified little town of **NAGAUR**, 100km south of Bikaner, are testimony to years of both Hindu and Muslim sovereignty. Nagaur is famous for its stout breed of bullock, and holds a week-long **cattle fair** (late Jan–early Feb) that attracts camel, horse and bullock traders from all over Rajasthan. Festivities, races and dances precede the sales, and although prospects of accommodation in Nagaur are poor, it's worth visiting for a day – connections with Bikaner are straightforward by both road and rail.

Udaipur

> The valley of Oodipur, the most diversified and most romantic spot on the
> continent of India . . .
>
> James Tod, *Annals and Antiquities of Rajasthan* (1829)

Set around the vast Pichola Lake and dominated by dramatic palaces, **UDAIPUR** is Rajasthan's most atmospheric and picturesque city. High whitewashed houses and narrow winding alleys lend it an almost medieval charm, even if the newer quarters with their wide roads and squat buildings are less aesthetically pleasing. Prevailing over all else is the peaceful influence of the shimmering lake, and the joy of relaxing on a roof terrace in the cool of the evening tempts many travellers to forget their tight schedules. In any case, it takes a good week to explore the city's monuments, and the temples, forts, palaces and scenery of the hills and valleys nearby.

The smooth rolling hills that surround Udaipur like sleeping armadillos were once covered with forests. Widespread felling, instigated by the Indian government in the 1970s after it took possession of the Mewar lands, left them irreversibly barren and have added to the dry and dusty desert conditions of the Udaipur valley.

A brief history

Udaipur takes pride in having been the capital of the state of **Mewar**, the only one of the seven major Rajput states to uphold its Hindu allegiance in the face of Muslim invasions and political compromises. Its present ruler is the seventy-sixth in the unbroken line of Mewar suzerains, which makes the Mewar household the longest lasting of all ruling powers in Rajasthan, and perhaps the oldest surviving dynasty in the world.

The history of Udaipur itself stretches back far beyond its foundation in the sixteenth century, for the actions and policies of its Sisodia maharanas follow a code of honour laid down by the very first in line, **Guhil**, who established Mewar in 568 AD. Legend claims that Guhil was of local stock, but he seems at the time to have been fleeing south Gujarat during Muslim invasions. Either way, Guhil dwelt in the forest where he was trained in leadership and devotion by a hermit. His successors set up their capital at **Nagda**, which now stands in ruins just over 30km north of Udaipur. Chittaurgarh (also known as Chittor; see p.196) replaced Nagda as capital in the eighth century, and its hill-top fort protected the Sisodia Rajputs for almost 800 years.

By the time **Udai Singh II** inherited the throne of Mewar and the leadership of the Sisodia Rajputs in 1537, it was clear that the magnificent fortress of Chittor was doomed; his mother had sacrificed her life two years previously during its second major sacking. Udai scanned the surrounding countryside for a suitable site for a new capital, and settled for the area beside Lake Pichola, protected on all sides by outcrops of the Aravalli range. Having laid the foundation stones in 1559, he fled the battlefield when Chittor finally fell to the Mughals eight years later to his new city of **Udaipur**.

On his death in 1572 Udai was succeeded by his son **Pratap**, a legendary hero whose refusal to recognize the Mughal **Akbar** as emperor led to the battle of Haldi Ghati, in which Akbar's forces were outwitted and peace in Udaipur was guaranteed.

As the city prospered, the arts flourished; Mewar's superior school of miniature painting became firmly rooted and the awesome palaces on the lake and its shore were constructed. However, in 1736 Mewar was attacked by the destructive Marathas whose pillage had by the turn of the century reduced the city to poverty and ruin. The British, whose role in the East India Company had until then been purely commercial, stepped in to pick up the pieces, presenting the Maharana with a treaty of "perpetual alliance and friendship" in 1818. Guaranteeing protection from invaders and restoration of all its hereditary territories, this treaty and the support of the British helped to put Udaipur on the road to recovery. Yet the principle of refusing to bow down to a foreign power persisted and the maharanas never allowed the British to displace them.

The promises of "perpetual" protection had of course to be dissolved when Britain withdrew from India in 1947. The Maharana of Udaipur spearheaded the movement by the princely states to join the new democratic and independent India, and was later at the forefront of a campaign to persuade Indira Gandhi's Congress government to retain the privy purses that funded the upkeep of Rajputana's historic monuments. Congress was however determined to reduce the Rajput princes to the status of normal citizens, and political recognition of royalty came to an end.

Centuries of loyalty between rulers and subjects have been kept alive by songs, stories and paintings; the Maharana may now lack political power, but he remains as respected by the people of Udaipur as were his forefathers. His personal funding and income from tourism are invested in the *Maharana of Mewar Trust*, which subsidizes local hospitals and educational institutions, and supports environmental projects.

Arrival, information and city transport

Daily flights connect **Dabok Airport** (☎23011), 25km east of Udaipur, with Bombay, Delhi, Aurangabad, Jaipur and Jodhpur. Taxis and infrequent buses run to the city itself. **Trains** from Delhi and Ahmedabad pull in at **Udaipur City Station** a little to the south of the town centre (don't get off at Udaipur Station, much further north). The **bus stand** is a few hundred metres north of here, directly opposite **Udaipole**, the westernmost gate of the old city. The best way to get to a hotel from either point is to take a rickshaw: head for a particular area and check out the hotels yourself to avoid paying extra for the driver's commission. The moderately helpful **tourist information bureau** (daily 10am–5pm; ☎29535) in the grounds of RTDC *Kajri Hotel*, Shashtri Circle, has some useful literature. Most hotels offer maps and tips on local sightseeing.

Money can be changed at *State Bank of Bikaner and Jaipur*, Chetak Circle (Mon–Fri 11am–3pm), or *State Bank of India* and *Canara Bank*, Hospital Rd (same hours). For **poste restante**, go to the GPO on Chetak Circle (Mon–Sat 10am–3pm); there's also a City Post Office (Mon–Sat 10am–4pm) on Shastri Circle.

City transport

Rickshaws and **taxis** (available from any tour operator) are the usual means of transport. Rickshaw prices are relatively high and **bicycle rental** is well worth considering:

decent cycles can be had at very reasonable rates from *Shri Averi Cycle Works*, Lake Palace Rd, and a few stores near the clock tower.

RTDC, based at the tourist office, offers car rental and tours around the city and further afield. In addition, Udaipur's **travel agencies** – mostly located around Lalghat, Lake Palace Road and Chetak Circle, and listed on p.187 – offer city tours (daily 8am–1pm; Rs30–40), airport transfer (Rs125), private car rental, and booking services for trains and buses. All charge similar rates. Taxi tours include visits to Sajjangarh (2hr; Rs300), Nagda, Eklingji and Nathdwara (4hr; Rs450: 9hr, or Rs900 including Ranakpur). For longer hauls, charges per car are approximately Rs3 per kilometre.

The City

The original settlement of Udaipur focused around the grand **City Palace**, bordering the west shore of **Lake Pichola**. Immediately to the north is the maze of tightly winding streets that constitute the **old city**. It takes a few days of wandering before this labyrinth becomes intelligible; start by getting acquainted with the gates and circles that form traffic islands at the major crossroads. From the clock tower that marks the northern edge of the old city, roads lead east to the tourist information bureau and Ahar, west to the lake, and north to the GPO at Chetak Circle. Continuing north, the road passes the excellent folk art museum, Bharatiya Lok Kala, and heads to Sahelion-ki-Bari, the gardens of the royal ladies.

The road that encircles **Lake Fateh Sagar** north of Lake Pichola carries on west to the crafts village of **Shilpgram**, a showcase for all types of traditional Indian art. It's a good cycling route; you can stop off at **Pratap Memorial Gardens** on the eastern shore of the lake, visit **Nehru Park** in its centre and cool off with an ice cream or drink from mobile stands near the jetty. In the very west of the city, **Sajjangarh** – the "Monsoon Palace" – commands superb views across the plains, while to the east both the royal cenotaphs and **Ahar museum** with its fifth-century BC relics can be visited in a morning.

Lake Pichola

The serene lakeside location chosen by Udai for his new capital made a welcome change from the craggy heights of Chittaurgarh. He enlarged the lake, which drew water from mountains up to 160km away, and now covers eight square kilometres. Later rulers added dams and canals to prevent flooding during the monsoon.

The two islands in the lake, topped with the ivory-white domes and arches of private palaces, are the most familiar and photogenic features of Udaipur. **Jag Niwas**, now the **Lake Palace Hotel**, is the larger of the two, built as a summer palace during the reign of Jagat Singh (1628–52). Even if you aren't staying here, you can visit the palace for lunch, dinner or afternoon tea; the price includes the boat ride from the mainland (booking advisable; see p.186).

The smaller **Jag Mandir**, on the island to the south, has changed little since its construction by Karan Singh in 1615. It takes its name from Jagat Singh who added to the initial structure. Intended as a small Rajput palace, it was never used as such; Karan Singh offered refuge here to the Mughal prince Khurum (later Emperor Shah Jahan), exiled by his father, Emperor Jahangir, in the 1620s. Khurum succeeded his father while still in Udaipur, and the Mughal gathering for the occasion defied the established code of Rajput–Mughal enmity. During the Mutiny (1857) the island once again served as a safe haven, this time for European women and children.

The telephone **area code** for Udaipur is ☎0294.

UDAIPUR

N

Sahelion Ki Bari

Sukadia Circle

Moti Magri

Nehru Park

Jetty

Fateh Sagar

Lake Pichola

Gangaur Ghat

JAGDISH CHOWK

Jagdish Temple

GANGAUR GHAT MARG

NAVGHAT

LALGHAT

0   500 m

Shilpgram

RANI RD

FATEH SAGAR RD

Bhartiya Lok Kala

Chetak Circle

TANK FATEH RD

GPO

Bank

Swaroop Sagar

Bank

HOSPITAL RD

Hospital

Shashiri Circle

Indian Airlines

Ahar River

Raj Bridge

Rang Sagar

Chandpole

Hathipole

Delhi Gate

Clock Tower

Town Hall

Sajjangarh

Ahar Museum

Airport

see inset

City Palace

Surajpole

CITY STATION RD

Bus Stand

Udaipole

Lake Palace

Lake Pichola

Sajjan Niwas Garden & Zoo

Jag Mandir

Sunset Point

City Railway Station

HOTELS:

Ⓐ Siva Guest House
Ⓑ Sai Niwas
Ⓒ Jagat Niwas
Ⓓ Kallika
Ⓔ Evergreen
Ⓕ Lake Ghat
Ⓖ Lalghat Guest House
Ⓗ Lehar Guest House & Badi Haveli
Ⓘ Monalisa
Ⓙ Anand Bhawan
Ⓚ Laxmi Vilas Palace
Ⓛ Hilltop Palace
Ⓜ Lake End
Ⓝ Natural
Ⓞ Lake Shore
Ⓟ Lake Pichola
Ⓠ Lake Palace
Ⓡ Shiv Niwas & Fateh Pakash Palace
Ⓢ Rang Niwas Palace
Ⓣ Jhala Maan
Ⓤ Mahendra Prakash
Ⓥ Yatri
Ⓦ Apsara
Ⓧ International & Tourist

RESTAURANTS:

❶ Mayur Cafe
❷ Ganesh Lodge
❸ Park View

The main building facing the City Palace has detailed stone inlay work within its domed roof. In front of it a green marble *chhatri* carved with vines and flowers is the centrepiece of a garden guarded by stone elephants. The island's only inhabitants other than flocks of birds are three royal servants who tend the gardens and grow flowers for the Maharana's celebrations.

Half-hour **boat rides** around the lake depart from the jetty behind the City Palace (hourly 10am–5pm), while an hour's trip (Rs90) includes a stop at Jag Mandir. The view of the palaces and shoreline from the lake at sunset is one of the most memorable images of Rajput splendour.

The City Palace

Udaipur's fascinating **City Palace** stands moulded in soft yellow stone on a rocky promontory on the northwest shore of Lake Pichola, its thick windowless base crowned with ornate turrets and canopies. Eleven constituent *mahals* (palaces), constructed by successive maharanas during the three hundred years that followed the foundation of Udaipur in 1559, and characterized throughout by their exemplary workmanship, together form the largest royal complex in Rajasthan.

Part of the palace is now a museum (daily 10am–5pm; Rs7, camera Rs15, video Rs50), entered through **Toran Pole** from the massive courtyard where elephants once lined up for inspection before battle. Although **guided tours** (which cost from Rs30 for groups of up to five to Rs50 for over twenty; Rs15 extra for a non-Indian language) are not compulsory, they do serve to illuminate the chronology of the palaces, the significance of the paintings, and details of the lives of the maharanas.

Everywhere you look the marble and granite walls are laden with brilliant miniature paintings, decorated with tiles or overlaid with spangling mosaics of coloured glass and mirrors, and each room glows with sunlight filtering through stained-glass windows. Narrow low-roofed passages connect the different *mahals* and courtyards, creating a haphazard design and preventing surprise intrusion by armed enemies.

Each of the three large peacocks (*mor*) set into the walls of the seventeenth-century **Mor Chowk**, placed there by Sajjan Singh 200 years after the palace was built, is composed of 5000 pieces of glass, glittering in green, gold and blue. The pillared apartments that face Mor Chowk are adorned with scenes from Krishna legends, a favourite theme of the paintings in the **Zenana Mahal**, the women's quarters. With alcoves, balconies, coloured windows, tiled walls and floors, these are the most splendid rooms in the palace. Other chambers include **Kanchi-ki-Burj**, decorated throughout with a mosaic of mirrors, and **Chandra Chowk** (Moon Square) which although right at the top of the palace manages to enclose its own garden – it rests on the crest of a hill that rises in the heart of the palace. **Krishna Vilas**, an apartment full of miniatures, honours a nineteenth-century Udaipur princess who poisoned herself to avoid the dilemma of choosing a husband from the two rival households of Jodhpur and Jaipur.

Adjoining the palace, the **Government Museum** (daily 10am–4.30pm; Rs1) contains a dusty collection including clothes, unlabelled relics and a stuffed and decaying two-headed deer. It's worth passing through to the last room to see a good selection of temple statues, dating back to the eighth century, but otherwise the museum does not merit a detour.

Jagdish Temple

Raised above the main crossroads a little north of the City Palace, **Jagdish Temple** is a centre of constant activity. Built in 1652 and dedicated to Lord Jagannath, an aspect of Vishnu, its outer walls and towering *shikhara* are heavily carved with figures of Vishnu, scenes from the life of Krishna, and dancing *apsaras* (nymphs). The spacious *mandapa* leads to the sanctuary where a black stone image of Jagannath sits shrouded in flowers, while a small raised shrine in front of the temple protects a bronze Garuda, the

THE EUNUCHS OF INDIA

Every country in the world has its share of transvestites, hermaphrodites and sexual ambivalents, but rarely do they play such a prominent a social role as India's eunuchs – the **hijras**. Numbering well over 400,000, with 150,000 in Delhi alone, the *hijras* have been around for centuries; they are mentioned in the *Mahabharata*, and the *Kama Sutra* outlines the best ways to have sex with a eunuch.

The *hijras* gather in clans that supplant the ties of family and caste renounced at initiation, and usually live in well-defined territories within major cities. Most *hijras* are effeminate, since castration results in hormonal changes, but they are not by definition homosexual. They are easy to recognize, gaudily made-up, unusually tall and often making crude gestures, and their dances to harsh rhythmic music are unmistakeably sexual. Popularly despised for their abnormality and vulgar behaviour, they are also feared for the strange power implied by their ambiguity: their curses are dreaded. Some earn their living as temple beggars or prostitutes, but most dance and sing at weddings and births, being paid *badhai* (tips) either to pronounce blessings or simply to go away. Their presence at the birth of a child, especially a boy, is particularly auspicious – the *hijra* is believed to absorb any homosexual tendencies from the infant, and in certain towns any family that refuses to invite a eunuch to a birth risks gossip among the local community that they may be hiding a hermaphrodite child.

Each *hijra* clan has a guru, an older eunuch who presides over initiation ceremonies, protects the socially vulnerable group, and corners a high proportion of any money earned. Members of the **All India Hijra Kalyan Sabha**, a social-work group formed in 1984 to protect the rights of *hijras*, have recently revealed that at least a thousand young men each year – some homeless, some married with children – are kidnapped, pushed into prostitution and eventually forcibly gelded. The Hijra Kalyan Sabha believes that the gurus make much of their money by auctioning off fresh eunuchs, so it pays them to pick healthy and attractive men. Horrendous castrations, performed by ill-equipped backstreet doctors, are carried out on heavily drugged patients whose wounds are later tended with substances such as herbs, mustard oil and cow dung. No anaesthetic is used, more than a hundred stitches are often needed, and the death rate may be as high as seventy-five percent (though a "doctor" accused of performing castrations recently claimed that only one of the one thousand operations he had performed was fatal).

In 1993 the Hijra Kalyan Sabha backed up the claims of a number of eunuchs who courageously spoke out against those who forcibly castrated them. As *hijra* mafias compel silence with death threats, filing charges is no mean feat. Indian law does not recognize emasculation as an offence (the nearest equivalent listed under the penal code is "abduction and grievous injury with a sharp weapon"); police are reluctant to interfere, and providing conclusive evidence of abduction and castration is extremely difficult. Local courts have been more cooperative, and have begun to force police to complete efficient investigations, but few cases have resulted in conviction, and the victims continue to face a struggle in a society where they will never be fully accepted.

half-man, half-bird vehicle of Vishnu. Smaller shrines to Ganesh and Hanuman stand to either side of the main temple.

Bharatiya Lok Kala

Udaipur's folk museum, **Bharatiya Lok Kala** on Panch Vati Road just north of Chetak Circle (daily 9am–6pm; Rs3), provides an inspiring introduction to Rajasthani arts and folklore. Exhibits include village paintings, puppets of all descriptions, printing blocks, terracotta images, costumes, musical instruments, toys, jewellery and photographs of local Bhil and Garasia tribal people. Short amusing **puppet shows** (free of charge) continue throughout the day, and are easy to follow even if you don't understand Hindi; longer performances take place between 6pm and 7pm every evening. The museum also runs short courses in puppet making and theatre; call ☎24296 for details.

Sahelion-ki-Bari

The "garden of the maids of honour", **Sahelion-ki-Bari**, roughly 2km north of Hathi Pole (daily 9am–6pm; Rs1), was laid out by Sangram Singh early in the eighteenth century for the diversion and entertainment of the ladies of the royal household. Surrounding a shady courtyard, the fountained garden must once have made a delightful retreat, but today the fountains only play at the request of visitors, and the focus of attention is the wide range of indigenous trees and flowers. During the monsoon the lotus pond behind the courtyard is ablaze with colour.

Fateh Sagar

Not far west of Sahelion-ki-Bari is **Fateh Sagar**, a lake fringed by sharp hills and connected to Lake Pichola by a canal built shortly after the turn of the century. At the jetty on the western shore, you can rent pedal boats (daily 7.30am–6.30pm; Rs40 for 30min) or hop on the boat (Rs2) that ferries tourists across the water to **Nehru Park** in the centre of the lake. The park, constructed in 1937 as a famine relief project, had to be renovated in the 1980s. The gardens are rather unexciting, but pleasant enough if you want to get away from the bustle of the town.

A two-minute walk from the boat moorings towards Udaipur brings you to **Moti Magri** (daily 9am–6pm; Rs3). In theory, the gardens here preserve the memory of Maharana Pratap Singh, who denied Akbar control of Udaipur and is remembered for his courage in the battle of Haldi Ghati (see p.189). However, they are now in such a sorry state as to be barely worth a visit. A statue of Chetak, Pratap's faithful steed, stands at the top of the hill.

Shilpgram

The road running around the north of Fateh Sagar leads to the rural arts and crafts centre, **Shilpgram** (daily 9.30am–6pm; Rs3), near the village of Havala, 5km out from town and best reached by bike. Organized by the West Zone Cultural Centre, the crafts village was set up to promote and preserve the traditional architecture, music and crafts of the tribal people of western India, and holds rare displays of the diverse traditional lifestyles and customs of India's rural population.

Indian dwellings arranged in the compound include a solid two-storey wooden house from northern Gujarat, exquisitely carved throughout, circular painted huts from Kutch (Gujarat), thick-walled low-roofed houses from the Rajasthani deserts, and Goan potters' huts. All help to suggest itineraries of villages to visit once you move on from Udaipur. Musicians and dancers perform around the houses, while weaving, potting, puppetry and embroidery continue as they would in their original localities. *Hijras* (eunuchs) are often among the dancers. Allow at least an hour to walk round the compound; the best time to go is at weekends, when the centre is filled with artisans.

Sajjangarh

High on a hill 5km west of the city, the "Monsoon Palace", **Sajjangarh**, was abandoned by the royal family soon after its construction in 1880. It had been found to be impossible to pump water to the palace, which is now used as Udaipur's radio station and is closed to visitors. The views over Udaipur from the courtyards of the palace are unrivalled, however, especially if you can make it up there for sunrise, when the surrounding countryside looks its most magical. Getting up the hill requires a bit of effort, however, as the climb is too steep to tackle by bicycle. The journey takes a good fifteen minutes by rickshaw or taxi, and costs over Rs50 for the round trip.

Royal cenotaphs and Ahar museum

Across the narrow Ahar River, 2km east of Udaipur, domed cenotaphs huddle together on the site of the royal cremation ground. Raised on platforms, some of which are decorated with *shivalingams*, many of the *chhatris* are falling into disrepair, and the site is pretty dirty. Even so, it's a good place to pick up on local history, featuring an ornate memorial to the prodigious builder Jagat Singh (1628–52) and the cenotaph of Amar Singh (died 1620) who contributed so much to the City Palace, embellished with friezes depicting the immolation of his wives.

Less than 1km south of here, archeological exhibits at the **Ahar museum** (daily except Fri 10am–5pm; Rs2) include locally unearthed pottery from the first millennium BC. Among more recent statues is a handsome tenth-century Surya image.

Accommodation

Udaipur has literally hundreds of places to stay, ranging from simple lodges near the bus stand, unexciting but handy for early-morning departures, to extravagant palaces. Most hotels are sandwiched between the **City Palace** and **Jagdish Temple** on the east side of Lake Pichola; all offer excellent views over the lake to the west. Restaurants abound nearby, though you tend to get better value for money in less patronized areas. Hotels around the smaller lakes **Rang** and **Swaroop** are peaceful and homely, most only ten minutes' walk from Jagdish Temple. Behind the City Palace along Lake Palace Road, the hotels have larger rooms and gardens but lack views across the lake.

Near the bus stand

Apsara, City Station Rd (☎23400). Relatively quiet, set back a little from the road. Decent enough rooms. Car parking. ①.

International, City Station Rd (☎29479). Basic and uninviting. ①.

Tourist, City Station Rd (☎28055). Noisy and basic roadside hotel. ①.

Yatri, City Station Rd (☎27251). Convenient location opposite bus stand. Moderate standard, but a little musty. ①–②.

Jagdish Temple area/East side of Lake Pichola

Badi Haveli, 86 Gangaur Ghat Marg, Jagdish Chowk (☎25420). Delightful hotel in 350-year-old *haveli* with individually styled rooms and excellent views of lake and palace. ②.

Evergreen, 32 Lalghat. Popular lakeside place with basic rooms set around a grassy courtyard; very reasonable rates and a rooftop restaurant. ①.

Jagat Niwas, 25 Lalghat (☎29728). Right on the lakeside, entered down a narrow alley. Quiet, comfortable and relaxing, with shady courtyards, rooftop and restaurant. ③–⑤.

Kallika, 14 Lalghat. Family guest house with imaginative restaurant. One glass-fronted room has superb views. ②.

Lake Ghat, 4/13 Lalghat. Modern and smart, lacking character but with quite spacious rooms, and a dorm. ①–②.

Lalghat Guest House, 34 Lalghat. Popular and cheap, with a roof terrace overlooking the lake and cooking facilities for guests. ①.

Lehar Guest House, 86 Gangaur Ghat Marg. Basic but spacious rooms in an old house with plenty of character. Roof terrace and restaurant. ①.

Sai Niwas, 75 Navghat (☎24909). Beautiful rooms with hand-painted decorations and classic furniture. Some rooms have lake-facing balconies. Romantic atmosphere and excellent management. ⑤.

Siva Guest House, 74 Navghat. Small three-storey hotel with comfortable rooms, some with balcony; shared bathrooms (constant hot shower) and high roof terrace. ①.

Along Lake Palace Road

Jhala Maan, Lake Palace Rd (☎27235). Pleasant, good-value hotel surrounded by trees. Large fresh rooms with bathroom (hot water); the best has huge windows, bath tub and balcony. ①.

Mahendra Prakash, Lake Palace Rd (☎29370). All rooms are spacious, with bathroom (hot water). A large garden, central courtyard, roof terrace and parking facilities. ①.

Monalisa, 104 Bhatiyani Chohatta, Lake Palace Rd (☎26147). A comfortable option with small garden and sizeable rooms. ②.

Rang Niwas Palace, Lake Palace Rd (☎25091). Just opposite the gate leading to *Shiv Niwas*. Palatial old building offering cheap dorms, basic rooms and furnished suites. The large garden and welcoming atmosphere makes up for the lack of a view. ①–⑤.

West side of Lake Pichola, Rang Sagar and Swaroop Sagar

Lake Pichola, outside Chand Pole (☎29197). Lovely, stately place with superb lake-facing rooms and grand dining hall. ⑥.

Lake Shore, outside Chand Pole. Next to *Lake Pichola Hotel*. Small peaceful hotel; doubles have trellised windows overlooking the lake. Roof terrace with beautiful view. ①.

Natural, near Raj Bridge, Rang Sagar. Basic but large and clean rooms at knock-down prices, many with balconies over the lake. A beautiful and peaceful budget location. ①.

Around Fateh Sagar

Anand Bhawan, Fateh Sagar Rd (☎23256). Excellent hotel with carpeted rooms and commanding view. Good value. ⑤–⑥.

Hilltop Palace, Ambavgarh (☎28708). Smart hotel, high above Fateh Sagar, with all mod cons. ⑧.

Lake End, Rani Rd, Fateh Sagar (☎23891). A formerly top-notch lakeside hotel in considerable decline. Poor swimming pool. ⑧.

Laxmi Vilas Palace, Fateh Sagar Rd (☎29713). Expensive and comfortable. Snappy service, excellent view, luxurious swimming pool and good (but pricey) restaurant and bar. ⑧.

Luxury accommodation

Fateh Pakash Palace, City Palace (☎28239). True regal style in wonderfully decorated rooms; splendid yet homely. Four double and two single suites, slightly cheaper deluxe rooms. Guests enjoy breathtaking views from turrets, and use of the facilities at the *Shiv Niwas*. ⑨.

Lake Palace, Lake Pichola (☎23241). With its central swimming pool, royal suites and lakeside dining area this has to be the most romantic of the smart hotels, glittering in the heart of the lake. An opportunity not to miss if you have the money. Book ahead. ⑨.

Shiv Niwas, City Palace (☎28239; fax 23823). Live like a monarch in this architecturally perfect palace, still occupied in part by the royal family, and host to the regal Mewar festival every spring. An assortment of rooms and suites, all with their original interior design. All mod cons in traditional setting; pool, bar and restaurant. ⑧–⑨.

Eating

Eating prospects in Udaipur are gradually improving and some excellent **restaurants** have sprung up, most open all day and catering to all budgets. Many hotels offer food; the *Lake Palace* in particular tempts most travellers to drift over the lake for a rather extravagant meal on the terrace.

Evergreen, 32 Lalghat. Rooftop restaurant on the lakeside that serves excellent Indian and western dishes at very reasonable rates.

Ganesh Lodge, Jagdish Chowk. A small, cheap place that prepares the best *thalis* in town.

Jagat Niwas, 25 Lalghat. Charming restaurant jutting over the lake. Tasty Indian meals and great continental breakfasts at fairly high prices.

Kallika, 14 Lalghat. High rooftop restaurant that (eventually) serves up superb and inexpensive Mexican food as part of its imaginative spread.

Lake Palace Hotel (☎23241). For a hefty price you can wine and dine in this plush palace, but you may be disappointed by food that doesn't match the standard you might anticipate.

Mayur Cafe, Gangaur Ghat Marg. Indoor restaurant near Jagdish temple, serving excellent Indian dishes, spaghetti, pizza, and tasty sweets at bargain prices. TV dinners in a separate room are accompanied every night by James Bond's *Octopussy*, with its manic boat chase on Pichola Lake.

MOVING ON FROM UDAIPUR

Flights leave Udaipur daily for **Aurangabad** at 10.55am (1hr 10min), **Bombay** at 10.55am (2hr 35min) and 8.45pm (1hr 10min), **Delhi** at 10.15am (1hr 55min) and 7pm (3hr), **Jaipur** at 10.15am (45min) and 7pm (1hr 50min), and **Jodhpur** at 7pm (40min). *Indian Airlines*, is on Dhan Mandi, off Ashwani Rd (Mon–Fri 10am–5pm; ☎24433).

To go by **train** to **Ahmedabad**, take the #9643 *Udaipur-Ahmedabad Express* at 6.45pm (10hr). Both the #2916 *Garib Nawaz Express* (5.30am) and #9616 *Chetak Express* (6.15pm) go to **Delhi** (17hr) via **Chittaurgarh** (3hr 30min), **Ajmer** (8hr), **Jaipur** (11hr) and **Alwar** (14hr 30min).

Buses connect Udaipur with **Ahmedabad** (11 daily; 7hr), **Delhi** (daily 4pm & 7pm; 17hr), **Jaipur** (7 daily; 10hr), **Jodhpur** (3 daily; 8hr), **Kota** via **Chittaurgarh** (7 daily; 6hr), and **Mount Abu** (4 daily; 5hr). **Private companies** operate daily services to these destinations on fairly comfortable coaches that cover the distance in a shorter time.

Natural View, near Raj Bridge. Picturesque location overlooking Rang Sagar, but unexciting food.

Park View, Town Hall Rd, opposite the Town Hall. Medium-priced softly lit restaurant, popular with locals and offering a very high standard of Indian vegetarian and meat dishes.

Roof Garden Cafe, Lake Palace Rd. Bustling rooftop restaurant with a largely western clientele, bedecked with fairy lights at night.

Sai Niwas, 75 Navghat. Carefully prepared food on a lake-facing terrace. Pricey but very tasty.

Shri Nath Juice Centre, outside Hathi Pole. Convenient snack stop on the way to Chetak Circle. South Indian snacks, fresh fruit juices and hot drinks.

Listings

Cultural Entertainment Folk dance performances (daily 7pm) at *Meera Kala Mandir*, Meera Bhawan, Sector 11 (☎83176); puppet shows and folk dances (daily 6–7pm) at *Bharatiya Lok Kala Mandal*, Panch Vati Rd (☎24296).

Pharmacies *National Medical Store*, City Station Rd; *Vijay Medical Store*, Hospital Rd. *Laxmi General Store*, Lake Palace Rd, is a useful general chemist selling almost anything you could need.

Photographic Stores *Unique Camera Image*, 103 Bhattiyani Chohatta, is among many that sell good-quality films, take pictures and offer a developing service.

Travel Agents Tour operators to choose from include ITDC in *Hotel Kajri*, Shastri Circle (☎25122), the very efficient *Haveli Tours & Travels*, Lake Palace Rd (☎23500), who will also book and confirm flights, *Gangaur Tours & Travels*, Lake Palace Rd (☎27528) and *Taldar Travels*, Town Hall Rd (☎28160), next to the pick-up point for private buses. *Rajasthan Tours* (☎25777), is a reputable agency offering longer tours around Rajasthan.

Around Udaipur

You'd need to have a lot of time on your hands before you could hope to see more than a fraction of the ruins, palaces, temples, forts, lakes and wildlife sanctuaries that abound in the countryside around Udaipur.

Day trips northeast of the city can take in such destinations as **Nagda**, **Eklingji**, **Nathdwara**, and **Kankroli** along NH8 towards Bhilwara, or the peaceful wooded surroundings of **Ranakpur** and **Kumbalgarh**, which also make appealing stopovers before you join NH15 en route to Jodhpur. Renting a car saves time, but regular and efficient local buses, as well as private tour companies, serve both routes.

Southeast from Udaipur, an easy drive leads to **Jaisamand** lake and wildlife sanctuary and the ruined temples at **Jagat**. A poor road continues south to the palaces at **Dungarpur**, set on a high and rocky plateau and festooned with wall paintings.

Nagda

The ragged remnants of the ancient capital of Mewar, **NAGDA**, which date back to 626 AD, stand next to a lake 20km northeast of Udaipur, a couple of kilometres short of Eklingji. Buses from Udaipur set down passengers for Nagda shortly before the road drops into the valley that shelters the Eklingji temple, beside a *chai* stall and bicycle shop. Nagda itself is a short ride away, west of the lake.

Most of the buildings were either destroyed by Mughal zealots or submerged by the lake, which has naturally accumulated over the centuries. All that survives is a majestic pair of tenth-century Vaishnava temples, known as **Saas-Bahu** – literally "Mother-in-law" and "Daughter-in-law". Each has a main sanctuary fronted by a *mandapa* (pillared entrance hall) and topped by a pyramidal roof. The larger (Mother-in-law) has an astounding wealth of carving in its interior. Within the *mandapa*, a marriage area is marked by four pillars bearing images of the gods to which a couple must pay homage: Brahma, Vishnu, Shiva and Surya. On the northeast pillar you can make out representations of Sita's trial by fire, a favourite episode from the *Ramayana*, while scenes from the *Mahabharata* cover the ceilings. The outer walls of both temples display images of the entire Hindu pantheon, nubile *apsaras* (heavenly maidens), and even a few couples engaged in erotic acts.

The quickest route to Eklingji from the cycle shop is a path that leads behind the old protective walls and downhill, passing shaded tanks and half-preserved muddy brown temples.

Eklingji

The god **Eklingji**, a manifestation of Shiva, has been the protective deity of the rulers of Mewar ever since the eighth century, when Bappa Rawal was bestowed with the title *dawan* (servant) of Eklingji by his guru. To this day, the Maharana of Udaipur still visits his temples at the eponymous **EKLINGJI** every Monday evening – the day traditionally celebrated all over India as being sacred to Shiva. Lesser mortals can make the straightforward half-hour trip northeast of Udaipur by means of very frequent buses from the main bus stand, or taxis.

The milky-white marble main temple (daily 4.30–6.30am, 10.30am–1.30pm & 5.30–6.45pm), dominating the compound with an elaborate two-storey *mandapa* guarded by stone elephants, surrounds a four-faced black marble *lingam* that marks the precise spot where Bappa Rawal received his accolade. Images of Shiva and his fellow deities, *apsaras* and musicians are etched into the walls both outside and within, where silver doors, chests and lamps glint in the shady halls, and a solid silver (Nandi) bull faces the main sanctuary. The temple had to be rebuilt under Maharana Raimal at the end of the fifteenth century, and again two hundred years later after the ravages of Aurangzeb's iconoclastic forces. Numerous smaller shrines, some also composed of white marble, house images of deities such as Ganesh and Vishnu.

Behind the temple complex to the north, the temples of **Indra Lake**, bordered by *ghats* on its southern shore, resonate with drum beats and singing each Monday. *Kailash Guest House* near the bus stand has a few simple rooms on offer (①).

Nathdwara

The temple dedicated to Krishna – known also as **Nath**, the favourite *avatar* (incarnation) of Vishnu – at **NATHDWARA**, "Gateway to God", is a major goal for Vaishnavite pilgrims. Nathdwara was called Sihar until the moment in the seventeenth century when a chariot laden with an image of Krishna became stuck in the mud 26km north of Eklingji. The idol was being carried from Krishna's birthplace Mathura to Udaipur to

HALDIGHATI

At **Haldighati**, west of Nathdwara, Hindu pilgrims pause to pay homage to **Maharana Pratap Singh** at the site of the famous battle he fought with the forces of the Mughal emperor Akbar in 1576. Pratap epitomizes the role of the maharanas of Mewar as defenders of the Mewari people, sworn never to submit to foreign power.

Although wounded and obliged to withdraw, Pratap remained in hiding protected by Bhil tribesmen, and succeeded in preventing supplies from reaching the nominally victorious Mughal warriors. They were left with no choice but to surrender, an act which put an end to their arrogant certainty of sweeping all the Rajput states under Mughal suzerainty.

For the casual visitor, there's little to see except the dark yellow sands of the battlefield in a narrow pass between the hills, a cenotaph to Pratap's valiant horse, **Chetak**, and the tomb of **Hakim Khan Suri**, the leader of Pratap's forces.

spare it almost certain destruction by Aurangzeb; its bearers interpreted the event as a divine sign and established a new temple where it had stopped.

Nathdwara is on NH8, and welcomes a constant flow of buses en route north and south. Although the area around the bus stand is grim, a short ride on a rickshaw west brings you to narrow streets where stalls display incense, beads, perfumes and small Krishna statues, and blossom with the pinks, yellows and reds of temple decorations. In the centre of town the **Shri Nathji temple** opens for worship eight times daily, when the image is woken, dressed, washed, fed and put to bed. The most elaborate session, *aarti*, takes place between 5pm and 6pm. Don't miss the radiant *pichwai* paintings in the main sanctuary, made of handspun cloth and coloured with strong vegetable pigments: these original hangings possess a brilliance unmatched by the numerous copies available all over Rajasthan.

Rooms are at a real premium during the festivals of **Janmasthami** (Aug/Sept) and **Diwali** (Oct/Nov).

Accommodation

Hotels in Nathdwara and the surrounding valley, whose primary function is to serve the needs of pilgrims, include the RTDC *Hotel Gokul* (☎02953/2685; ③) in the north of town overlooking Lal Bagh, which offers reasonable deluxe and ordinary rooms and a cheap dormitory. In the central Naya Bazaar, *Hotel Vindra* (☎02953/2218; ③–⑤) has pleasant rooms and serves tasty meals in its own restaurant. Watch for the early 8am check-out time.

Kankroli and Rajsamand

Northeast of Nathdwara, NH8 winds through another 17km of undulating scrub before reaching **KANKROLI**, 65km from Udaipur. This small dusty market town stands on the shores of the vast deep blue **Rajsamand Lake**, whose construction was commissioned by Maharana Raj Singh in the seventeenth century when a terrible drought swept Rajasthan, leaving a trail of death and pestilence. He hoped the lake would prevent the recurrence of such large-scale disaster.

On the lake's western shore, a few kilometres out of town, is **Nauchowki**, a collection of nine *chowks* (pavilions), on platforms above the steps leading to the water. With carved pillars and ceilings showing scenes from the life of Krishna, these *chowks* were erected by Raj Singh to commemorate his marriage to Princess Charumati of Kishangarh, an act that saved her from the matrimonial clasp of Aurangzeb.

The **Dwarkadish temple** overlooking the southern shore houses an image of Krishna installed by Raj Singh in 1676, and has a sanctuary similar to that at Nathdwara. It forms part of an old palace whose passages wind through low-ceilinged rooms to covered walkways beside the lake. On steps descending to the water you can buy grain to feed the flocks of pigeons who survive on the charity of pilgrims.

The best views of the lake are to be had from the Digambara Jain temple, dedicated to Adinath, which crowns a steep hill between Nauchowki and the bus stand. From here you can see the Dwarkadish temple, Nauchowki, scattered old palaces on the nearby hills, and the Aravalli landscape rolling south as far as the eye can see.

J & K Guest House (①), east of the bus stand, has very basic **rooms**.

Ranakpur

Surprisingly few foreign visitors to Rajasthan take the time to venture out to the absolutely stupendous complex of **Jain temples** couched in the small wooded valley of **RANAKPUR**, 60km north of Udaipur. There is nothing else in this secluded spot except a small *chai* stall, and a tourist bungalow on a hill to the west.

The main temple (open daily for worship, noon–5pm) is dedicated to the first *tirthankara* **Adinath**, whose four-faced image is enshrined in its central sanctuary. Built in 1439 on land donated to the Jains by Rana Kumbha, the temple is two or three storeys high in parts, and its roof, topped with five large *shikharas*, undulates with tiny spires that crown the small shrines to Jain saints lining the temple walls. Within, 29 halls, some octagonal and many more than one storey high, are dissected by 1444 pillars, each sculpted with unique designs. The carving on the walls, columns and the domed ceilings is absolutely superb. Friezes depicting the life of the *tirthankara* are etched into the walls, while musicians and dancers have been modelled out of brackets between the pillars and the ceiling.

Two smaller temples dedicated to **Parshvanath** and **Neminath** nestle among the trees close by; the sculptures within are of a similarly high standard. Also in the compound is a contemporary Hindu temple dedicated to **Surya**, inside which carvings depict racing chariots commanded by the solar deities.

Practicalities

Ranakpur is a long day's journey out from Udaipur on the road towards Jodhpur, and can also be reached from Mount Abu. Its *dharamshala* asks overnight guests for donations, and provides lunch (noon–1pm) and dinner (5–6pm) for a small fixed price. The state-run *Hotel Shilpi* (②) has clean rooms, a cheap dorm and a restaurant serving acceptable if pricey food.

Private **buses** out of Ranakpur leave for Jodhpur and Jaipur at 8am, and there's a state bus to Jodhpur at 12.30pm.

Kumbalgarh

The remote and mighty hill-top fort of **KUMBALGARH**, 84km north of Udaipur, is perhaps the most formidable of the thirty-two constructed by Maharana Kumbha in the fifteenth century. Protected by a series of seven thick ramparts, it was only successfully besieged once, when Akbar poisoned the Sisodias' water supply – and he later returned it to them anyway.

Sandy brown crenellated walls encircle the crest of the hill to protect the palace on its summit. The crumbling Jain temples among the reservoirs and gardens within are said to have been erected in the second century; the tombs of Kumbha (murdered by his eldest son) and his grandson Prithviraj (poisoned by his brother-in-law) stand just to the east. A guide can show you the room where Udai Singh was raised by his nurse after fleeing Chittaurgarh in 1535, and the topmost Cloud Palace, restored and furnished by Udaipur's Fateh Singh early this century.

Practicalities

Kumbalgarh's new heritage hotel *Aodhi* (☎ Kelwara 222; April–July ⑤, otherwise ⑧) provides some relief after the long journey from Jodhpur or Udaipur. From the hotel you can take a horse (for a steep US$150) or jeep (Rs500) safari in the countryside, passing through a wildlife sanctuary which protects one of India's few families of wolves, as well as leopards and flying squirrels. Bookings for the safaris, and for the delightful palace hotel in the nearby town of **Ghanerao** (⑧), must be made through *Shiv Niwas Palace*, Udaipur (☎28239; fax 23823).

South of Udaipur

Asia's largest artificial lake, **Jaisamand**, created by Jai Singh as a summer retreat in the seventeenth century and measuring 10km by 15km, is 48km southeast of Udaipur. Apart from a few ruined palaces, there's not much to see, though a boat trip on the lake (Rs20), skirts a few islands inhabited by Bhil tribespeople. The surrounding area was declared a sanctuary in 1957, for *chital*, *chinkara* and the odd leopard.

Tucked away in the woods at **Jagat**, between Udaipur and Jaisamand, an elaborately carved tenth-century temple dedicated to Ambika Mata is crammed with images of Hindu goddesses.

NH8 leads directly south to the village of **Rishabdeo**, 40km from Udaipur, where a temple to the Jain *tirthankara* Rishabdeo attracts Jains, Vaishnavites (who worship him as an incarnation of Vishnu) and Bhils.

Dungarpur, which traces its roots back to a Sisodia Rajput who left Udaipur in the thirteenth century after a family dispute, is a further 30km south and connected to Udaipur and Ahmedabad by road and rail. However, you'll need your own transport to get to the old city, built on a rocky hill two kilometres above the forested plains. Its thirteenth-century palaces, built of grey-green granite and marble, are bedecked with arched windows, ornate balconies, and pillars twisted like barley sugar. Inside the walls are bright with remarkably well-preserved paintings, tiles and mirror mosaics.

Mount Abu

Set amid craggy outcrops on a high southwestern plateau, Rajasthan's only hill station, **MOUNT ABU**, is named for a mountain whose mythological past (if not its recorded history) is central to the development of the state. Mount Abu was long a favourite summer home for the rulers of Rajasthan and Gujarat, who built affluent summer palaces here, and for the British, who used it as a recuperation centre. These days, like many hill stations, it remains a popular resort for Indian honeymooners, although foreign tourists may feel it has little to offer beyond a welcome respite from the heat of the plains and the proximity of the spectacular Jain temples at Dilwara.

The focal point of Mount Abu is **Nakki Lake**, said to have been formed when the gods scratched away at the mountain with their fingernails (*nakh*). Legend tells of the powerful ceremony of *yagna agnikund* performed here after the fall of the Gupta Empire in the eighth century, on a spot now marked by a small temple at Gaumukh, 3km short of Mount Abu on the road up from the plains. Prayers in front of a sacred fire (*agni*) created the fighting clans that were later to rule large parts of India – the Solankis, the Chauhans, and the mighty Rajputs.

Arrival and information

Mount Abu itself is accessible only by road. Aim to spend as little time as you can in the uninspiring town of **Abu Road**, the nearest railhead, at the start of the one-hour ascent from the plains. It has a few typically Rajasthani bazaars, but very poor accommodation.

Passengers arriving at the main **bus stand** in the southeast of Mount Abu are swamped by hotel touts and would-be luggage porters pushing pram-like trolleys. Turn right to get to the more expensive hotels, the *Tourist Bungalow* and *Tourist Guest House*; left for the large central polo ground, most of the budget hotels, and the lake.

Some buses stop at the **taxi stand** at the south end of the polo ground. The road along the east side of the ground is the quickest route to Nakki Lake, the main bazaar and most of the restaurants.

Buses leave Mount Abu for Abu Road every half hour, **jeeps** leave when full (Rs10 per passenger), and **taxis** are available on request (Rs200–300 for a full car). If you plan to travel onwards by train, there's an information and booking office (Mon–Sat 9am–4pm) at the south end of Mount Abu next to the petrol pump.

Many small companies offer daily tours and buses to Abu Road and further afield, though not all are reliable. *Shobha Travels*, near *Samrat Hotel* (☎3302), run daily services, mostly overnight, to Udaipur, Ahmedabad, Jaipur, Ajmer, Surat and Baroda.

Information

Details on local sights and guide services are available at the **tourist office** (Mon–Sat 11am–1.30pm & 2–5pm), directly opposite the main bus stand.

The *Bank of Baroda* (Mon–Fri 10am–2pm, Sat 10am–noon) on the crossroads at the south end of the polo ground, changes travellers' cheques and offers *Visa* encashments. The *Chacha Museum*, a shop further along Nakki Lake Rd, has similar facilities but won't take *Visa*. Mount Abu's **post office** (Mon–Sat 10am–3pm) is in the bazaar, just past *Mount Hotel*. Inter-state and international **phone** connections can be made at a small cabin in the *Tourist Municipal* complex just north of the tourist office.

The Town

Mount Abu has a significant number of religious sites, whether Jain, Hindu or otherwise; but all are some way out of town. Nearer the centre, **Nakki Lake** is a pleasant spot for boat rides and the eucalyptus woods nearby are great for walks. Keep an eye out for strange granite outcrops around the lake such as the looming Toad Rock; Camel Rock and Nandi Rock are not so easily identified. Of several panoramic viewpoints on the fringes of town above the plains, **Sunset Point** is the favourite – which means that with its hordes of holidaymakers, peanut sellers, camel drivers, cart pushers and horse owners, it has to be the noisiest and least romantic place imaginable to watch the sun sink over the horizon.

Further out of town are several Hindu temples and the Jain **Dilwara Temples**, all of which can be seen by taking a half-day tour from the tourist office or any private operator (8.30am–1.30pm or 2–7pm; Rs30–40). However, if you're interested in architecture rather than pilgrimage sites, forget the rushed tour and make your own way to Achalgarh, and to the Dilwara Temples, allowing a good one or two hours to pick your way through the extraordinary wealth of intricate carving.

Dilwara Temples

As Jains consider temple building to be an act of devotion, their houses of worship are without fail intricately and lovingly adorned. The **Dilwara Temples** 5km northeast of Mount Abu (daily for non-Jains noon–6pm; no leather articles, no cameras, no transistors or tape recorders, and no entry to menstruating women), are probably the finest Jain structures in India, matched only by those at Ranakpur 200km northwest (see p.190). Each of the four main temples in the complex is made purely from marble. The oldest, **Vimala Vasahi**, named for the Gujarati minister who funded its construction in 1031 AD, is dedicated to Adinath, the first *tirthankara*, whose image sits cross-legged in the central sanctuary guarded by tall statues of Parshvanath. Although the exterior

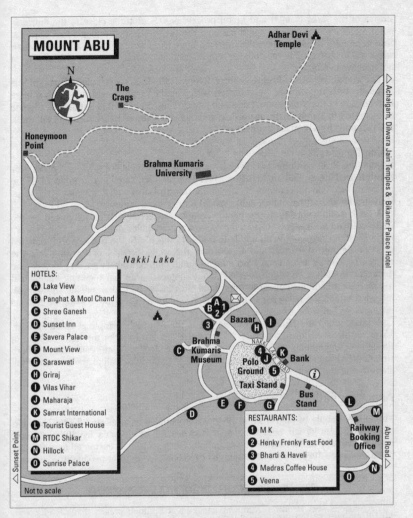

MOUNT ABU

N

Adhar Devi Temple

The Crags

Honeymoon Point

Brahma Kumaris University

Nakki Lake

▷ Achalgarh, Dilwara Jain Temples & Bikaner Palace Hotel

HOTELS:
- **A** Lake View
- **B** Panghat & Mool Chand
- **C** Shree Ganesh
- **D** Sunset Inn
- **E** Savera Palace
- **F** Mount View
- **G** Saraswati
- **H** Griraj
- **I** Vilas Vihar
- **J** Maharaja
- **K** Samrat International
- **L** Tourist Guest House
- **M** RTDC Shikar
- **N** Hillock
- **O** Sunrise Palace

Bazaar

Brahma Kumaris Museum

Polo Ground

Taxi Stand

Bank

Bus Stand

Railway Booking Office

◁ Sunset Point

Abu Road ▷

RESTAURANTS:
- **1** M K
- **2** Henky Frenky Fast Food
- **3** Bharti & Haveli
- **4** Madras Coffee House
- **5** Veena

Not to scale

of the temple is simple, once you go inside you'll see that not one wall, column or ceiling is left unadorned; the work, carried out by almost two thousand labourers and sculptors, took fourteen years to complete. Eight of the forty-eight pillars in the front hall form an octagon that supports a domed ceiling arranged in eleven concentric circles, alive with dancers, musicians, elephants and horses. Within the sanctuary and the cloisters that surround it, small shrines, countless pillars, brackets and wall niches are imaginatively decorated, and each section of the roof is adorned; deities among the lotus designs and dancing maidens include Saraswati, Ganesh and Krishna.

The later **Neminath Temple** (started 1230 AD) imitates that dedicated to Adinath, but its carvings are yet more precise and detailed. The large dome over the entrance hall is unprecedented. Friezes etched into the walls depict cosmological themes, stories of the *jinas* (saints) and grand processions. Sculptures close to the entrance porch commemorate the temple's patrons, the two brothers Vastupala and Tejapala. Said in popular legend to have discovered a huge treasure, they were advised by their wives – also portrayed here – to build temples, and also funded many on the holy hill of Shatrunjaya in Gujarat.

The remaining two fifteenth-century temples are less spectacular. Although the **Adinath Temple** – not to be confused with Vimala Vasahi – which houses a huge brass image of the *tirthankara*, has some fine carving, much of it is unfinished; the one consecrated to Parshvanath has ornate ceilings and *jinas* etched into the outer walls, and is topped by a high grey stone tower.

Hindu Temples

Beyond the Brahma Kumaris University, about 3km northeast of town, a flight of over four hundred steps climb up to **Adhar Devi Temple** (dedicated to Durga), cut into the rocky hill-top. The milk-coloured water of the **Doodh Baori** well at the foot of the steps is the traditional source of pure milk (*doodh*) for gods and sages.

A further 8km northeast, the temple complex at **Achalgarh** is dominated by the **Achaleshwar Mahadeo** (Shiva) temple. Its sanctuary holds neither an image of Shiva nor a *lingam*, only a *yoni* with a hole in it said to reach into the netherworld, watched over by figures of Parvati and Ganesh on the walls. Statues of Parvati flank the entrance, faced by an unusually large metal Nandi bull. Subsidiary shrines include one dedicated to Vishnu, in which detailed plaques depict the familiar reclining Vishnu and his nine incarnations. The large tank lined with stone buffaloes outside the temple, intended to contain purifying water, is the legendary scene of the slaying of demons disguised as buffaloes who stole purifying *ghee* from the tank.

Another important Hindu pilgrimage site is the Atri Rishi temple at **Guru Shikar**, 15km northeast of town, which at 1772m above sea level marks the highest point in Rajasthan. Depending on how energetic you're feeling, you can enjoy superb panoramic vistas either from the temple itself, or the drinks stall at the bottom of the steps that lead up to it.

Accommodation

The steady supply of pilgrims and honeymoon couples ensures that Mount Abu has plenty of hotels. A fair sprinkling offer luxuries for newly-weds in special "couple rooms"; the *Samrat International*, for example, takes pride in its curtained four- (or six-) poster beds and deep marble bathtubs, and even boasts swings for two in some rooms.

BRAHMA KUMARIS

The religious sect **Brahma Kumaris** (children of Brahma) preach that all religions reach for the same goal, but label it differently. At about two thousand centres around the world they teach Raja Yoga – meditation that directs people to knowledge of an inner light, the "divine spark" or soul, that is part of, and one with, the all-encompassing soul, Shiva. Belief in the five evils – anger, ego, attachment, greed and lust – is shared with Buddhism and Hinduism, with the ultimate goal being their elimination, and the advent of a **Golden Age** of peace, prosperity and purity.

The **Brahma Kumaris Spiritual University** aims to foster awareness, tolerance, love and "God-consciousness" in a meditative atmosphere where smoking, alcohol, meat and sex are avoided. Classes at **Om Shanti Bhawan**, the international headquarters just outside Mount Abu (☎3348), range from three-day Raja Yoga camps, to advanced six-month courses; lectures are translated into ten languages. The **Brahma Kumaris Museum** (daily 8am–8pm) beside the polo ground holds daily meditation classes.

Prices are variable and rocket in **high season** (April–June & Sept–Dec), reaching their peak during Diwali (Oct or Nov). During the **low season**, you can live in stylish comfort for little more than you might otherwise pay for rock-bottom accommodation. The codes below refer to low-season rates, unless otherwise indicated.

Check-out time is usually 9am, and the flow of hot water can be sporadic.

Inexpensive

Griraj (☎3501). Quiet, clean rooms with private bathrooms, near the main bazaar. Good value. ①.

Lake View, Nakki Lake (☎3590). Rooms are fresh and clean; the more expensive ones facing the lake have the best view in town. Roof terrace. ②–④; high season ⑤.

Maharaja (☎3561). Smart but impersonal rooms, some facing the polo ground. ③.

Mool Chand (☎3591). Very basic and very cheap rooms with tiny bathrooms. Two have lake-view balconies. ①.

Mount View (☎3320). Very pleasant rooms in a two-storey building opposite the polo ground, with central courtyard and front lawn. Hot water available in the morning. ②; high season ⑥–⑧.

Panghat (☎3386). Reasonable rooms with bathrooms, at the end of the road leading to Nakki Lake, Roof terrace overlooking the lake. ①; high season ②.

RTDC Shikar Tourist Bungalow (☎3219). Opposite the *Tourist Guest House*. Large impersonal rooms or cottages, all set in agreeable gardens. Restaurant. ①–③; high season ②–④.

Samrat International (☎3173). Clean and plush rooms with an imaginative touch. Bargain off-season prices. ②–④; high season ⑤–⑦.

Saraswati (☎3237). Large fresh rooms with bathroom and sitting area. Fine views from upper floors. Restaurant serving good vegetarian Gujarati and Punjabi food. ①–②; high season ④.

Shree Ganesh, near Sophia High School (☎3591). The cleanest and best value of the budget hotels, in a quiet location. ①; high season ①.

Tourist Guest House, near petrol pump (☎3200). Pleasant place, where rooms around the flowery courtyard are kept clean and fresh. ①; high season ④–⑦.

Vilas Vihar, Nakki Lake Rd, Shivaji Marg (☎3585). Quiet rooms with attached bathrooms and optional piped music. Running hot water and room service. ①.

Moderate to expensive

Hillock, Abu Rd (☎3467). Smart new high-rise hotel. Carpeted rooms are kept immaculately clean, and provide great views over the Abu hills. Restaurant and bar, plus parking facilities. ⑦.

Palace Hotel, Bikaner House (☎3121). Well out of town, a former summer palace equipped with private lawns and tennis courts, plus its own lake. A luxurious and peaceful treat. ⑤–⑥.

Savera Palace (☎3354). Modern bungalow with carpeted, dusty rooms offering steam baths and swimming – you may have to share the pool with several hundred midges. ④; high season ⑥.

Sunrise Palace, Bharatpur Kothi (☎3214). Huge and opulent rooms in a former palace, on the crest of a hill behind the *Hillock*. A glass-walled restaurant surveys the valley below. ⑥–⑦.

Sunset Inn, Sunset Rd, PO Box 24 (☎3194). Smart hotel, poorly serviced. Carpeted rooms with modern furnishings. ⑤–⑥; high season ⑥–⑦.

Eating and drinking

Nakki Lake Road, between the bus stand and the market, is lined with inexpensive **restaurants** with open-air seating, serving vegetarian dishes from Gujarat, Punjab and south India. You can breakfast on *samosas*, *dosas* or toast. Nearer the lake, ice cream stalls and "fast food" stops neighbour restaurants with indoor seating. Upper-class hotels serve **alcohol**; it is also available at the wine and beer shops near the crossroads at the bottom of town.

The telephone **area code** for Mount Abu is ☎029742.

Aangan, Nakki Lake Rd. Attached to the *Samrat International*. Well known for its very reasonably priced Gujarati *thalis* and comfortable atmosphere.

Ambika, Nakki Lake Rd. Primarily south Indian dishes, eaten outdoors. Inexpensive.

Bharti, Nakki Lake Rd. Tucked away off the main street at the top end of the polo ground, this modest place serves great Gujarati *thalis* for a mere Rs10.

Haveli, Nakki Lake Rd. A slightly more expensive option adjoining the *Bharti*, serving mainly Punjabi food. Very good quality.

Henky Frenky Fast Food, Nakki Lake Rd. On the right of the main road leading to the lake, an incongruous place serving good vegetarian south Indian dishes, cutlets and burgers.

Hotel Veena, Nakki Lake Rd. Open-air seating next to the main road. A high standard of inexpensive south Indian and Gujarati meals.

Madras Coffee House, Nakki Lake Rd. On the main road towards the market. Wide range of Indian coffees, fruit juices, shakes and an imaginative selection of ice cream.

MK Restaurant, Nakki Lake Rd. Good Chinese food at reasonable prices; indoor seating.

East of Udaipur

The belt of hilly land east of Udaipur is the most fertile in Rajasthan, watered by several perennial rivers; at the tail end of the monsoon cliffs and ravines resound with the rush of waterfalls. Although you need your own vehicle to penetrate the countryside, the historic town of **Chittaurgarh**, which preceded Udaipur as the seat of Mewar's rulers, is easily accessible.

Further east, clusters of time-worn temples mark the sites of ancient cities. In the far southeast, the heartland of the princely state of Kota, palaces and forts in **Kota** and **Bundi** stand sentinel over fields of wheat, groundnut, castor-oil plants and poppies.

Chittaurgarh

The colossal fort at **CHITTAURGARH**, also known as **Chittor**, sits on a rocky plateau high above the smooth plains of southern Rajasthan, 115km northeast of Udaipur. Steeped in the terrors and triumphs of Rajput battles, its crenellated walls and buildings are hewn from the same yellow-brown stone that comprises its rocky foundation. Seen from afar, only a few towers and turrets, protruding above the protective walls, betray its existence.

Below the fort, the town is severed by the River Ghambiri, alive with leaping fish, and decorated by bright *saris* laid out to dry on its banks. Apart from the usual turmoil of its crowded back streets, the **old city** east of the river has little to grab your attention. In fact, some tourists choose to squeeze a tour of Chittaurgarh into a day trip from Udaipur; a one-night stop leaves time for a more leisurely visit to the fort and a stroll through the town or along the river.

Some history

Of all the Rajput capitals, Chittaurgarh stands out as the strongest centre of Hindu resistance. The uncompromising policy of death before submission followed by its **Sisodia** overlords ensured that its history brims with tales of loyalty and terrible sacrifice. Its origins are however shrouded in legend; some claim that **Guhil**, the first of the Mewar leaders, founded the city in the sixth century, others favour the popular eighth-century **Bappa Rawal**, true forefather of the Sisodia Rajputs.

From a battle-scarred past, three devastating attacks are most remembered. The first, in 1303 during the reign of **Ratan Singh**, was launched by **Ala-ud-din-Khalji**, the fiercest of the Delhi Sultans. Having besieged the city, and all but starved the Rajputs out, he offered to withdraw – if he could take Ratan's queen, **Padmini**, with him. After being permitted to glimpse the queen's reflection in a mirror, the Sultan took Ratan prisoner. Padmini left the fort accompanied by an army of men disguised as maids of honour, but the Rajputs lost the ensuing battle. Thirteen thousand women, led by Padmini, committed *johar* by throwing themselves and their children onto a huge funeral pyre. The angry Sultan destroyed most of the fort's temples and palaces.

After returning to Rajput hands in 1326, Chittaurgarh saw two hundred years of prosperity. However, in 1535, an unexpected onslaught led by **Sultan Bahadur Shah** from Gujarat once again decimated the Rajput warriors, and the women surrendered their lives in another ghastly act of *johar*. The young heir, **Udai Singh**, who had been whisked away to safety by his nursemaid Panna Dai, returned to Chittaurgarh at the age of thirteen. Aware of its vulnerability, he searched for a new site for his capital, and in 1559 founded **Udaipur** on the shore of Lake Pichola. This proved to be a prescient decision. **Akbar** laid siege to Chittaurgarh in 1567. His forces killed 30,000 of the fort's inhabitants, the women once again sacrificed themselves in a raging pyre, and many of the buildings within the fort were devastated. Although Chittaurgarh was ceded back to the Rajputs in 1616, the royal family never resettled there.

Arrival and information

Chittaurgarh's **railway station**, in the western corner of the city, is served by two daily trains from Udaipur, two from Delhi via Jaipur, and one from Indore. From here it's about 2km to **Roadways bus stand** on the west bank of the Ghambiri.

For maps and information on accommodation and tours of the fort, head for the **tourist office** in the RTDC *Hotel Janta Avas Grah* opposite the train station on Station Rd. The GPO (Mon–Sat 8am–4pm) is on Shri Gurukul Rd near *Pratap Palace Hotel*.

Tours of the fort can be made by rickshaw (Rs45), complete with jangly pop music and silky curtains, or tonga (Rs25); either can be rented through the tourist office, with a driver who will act as guide. However, the drivers prefer to take in only the most famous monuments rather than the entire fort, which extends 5km long by 1km wide. To see the whole thing – which takes a good three hours – you'd do best to rent a **bike** from the shop next to *Hotel Janta Avas Grah*. The initial climb is steep, but most of the roads on the plateau itself are flat.

The fort

The ascent to the fort, protected by massive bastions, begins at **Padan Pole** in the east of town and winds upwards through a further six gateways (*pols*). Close to the second *pol* stand the *chhatris* of **Kalla** and **Jaimal**, heroic fighters who lost their lives in the final sacking of 1567. The houses of the small community that still inhabits the fort are huddled together near the final gate, **Rama Pole**.

As you enter the fort, you pass the fifteenth-century **Shingara Chauri Mandir**, a highly adorned Jain temple dedicated to Shantinath. Ahead of this, the slowly deteriorating fifteenth-century **Palace of Rana Kumbha** – built by the ruler who presided over the period of Mewar's greatest prosperity – remains a classic example of Rajput architecture, and is immortalized as one of the scenes of *johar*. Nearby the modern **Fateh Prakash Palace**, built for the Maharana in the 1920s, is the site of a small, dimly lit **archeological museum**, filled with weaponry (daily 10am–5pm; Rs1). Also in the palace compound is the **Kumbha Shyama Temple**, crowned by a pyramidal roof and lofty tower, whose eighth-century sanctuary enshrines an image of Varaha, the boar incarnation of Vishnu. A smaller temple slightly to the south with a delicate curved tower, again constructed by Rana Kumbha, is dedicated to **Meerabai**, a Jodhpur princess famed for her unrelenting devotion to Krishna and emotive poetry.

The main road within the fort continues south to its focal point, **Jaya Stambh**, the soaring "tower of victory", erected by Kumbha to commemorate the Rajput victory over the Muslim Sultan. This magnificent sand-coloured tower, whose nine storeys rise 120ft, took a decade to build; its walls are lavishly carved with mythological scenes and images from all Indian religions, including Arabic inscriptions in praise of Allah. You can climb the dark narrow stairs to the very summit for Rs0.50: watch for low ceilings. Kumbha himself wrote a detailed study of the style and purpose of the Jaya Stambh.

A path leads from the tower through more fine but ruined temples to **Gaumukh Kund**, a large reservoir fed by an underground stream that trickles through carved mouths (*mukh*) of cows (*gau*). This quiet spot, away from the main road, commands superb views across the plains.

Buildings further south include the **Kalika Mata Temple**, originally dedicated to **Surya** in the eighth century, but rededicated to the Mother Goddess afer renovations in 1568. Close inspection of the carvings on the outer wall reveals images of Surya, the guardians of the eight directions (such as Indra, Yama, Agni and Vayu), and friezes depicting the churning of the ocean by the gods and demons, a popular creation myth. An image of Surya guards the main entrance to the temple.

Padmini's Palace, now rather dilapidated, stands opposite in the centre of a pool. From a building on the shore, you can look into the mirror that revealed the queen to Ala-ud-din-Khalji.

The road continues south past the deer park to the point used for hurling traitors to their deaths, and returns north along the eastern ridge. Several temples line the route, but the most impressive monument is **Kirti Stambh**. The inspiration for the tower of victory, this smaller "tower of fame" was built by Digambaras as a monument to the Jain *tirthankara* Adinath, whose unclad image is repeated throughout its six storeys.

Accommodation and eating

All the **hotels** at the lower end of the price scale are pretty dingy; if you want a little comfort you'll have to spend more than elsewhere. *Padmini Palace*, the best of the bunch, makes a delightful refuge from the dusty streets. There's not much prospect of finding a tasty slap-up meal in Chittaurgarh's **restaurants**, as the only alternative to the hotels is the selection of roadside stalls around the bus station. The usual spicy vegetable dishes vary in standard from day to day.

Laxmi Lodge, Fort Rd (☎2266). Grey rooms with attached bathrooms, and hot water by the bucket. Unexciting food in restaurant. ①.

Natraj, City Rd (☎3009). Next to Roadways bus stand. Dull but passable, and very cheap. ①.

Padmini Palace, Chanderiya Rd, near Sainik School. A peaceful place overlooking the river with good views towards the fort and its own garden restaurant. ④–⑤.

Pratap Palace, Shri Gurukul Rd (☎2099). Opposite GPO. Fresh, expansive and attractive – but the food is terrible. Running hot water; some bath tubs. ③–⑤.

RTDC Janta Avas Grah, Station Rd (☎3238). Sub-standard poky rooms opposite train station. ①.

RTDC Panna, Station Rd (☎3238). Smarter RTDC option a short way from the station, with spacious and comfortable rooms and a cheap dorm. ⑤.

From Chittaurgarh to Kota

The stretch of countryside east of Chittaurgarh towards Kota harbours some interesting small places that can be reached by public transport, but are more easily visited if you rent your own vehicle. A turning at the small lakeside town of **Bassi**, 25km out of Chittaurgarh, leads to **Bijaipur**, a quaint village whose elegant 200-year-old **palace** now serves as an idyllic hotel (⑥; book through *Pratap Palace Hotel*, Chittaurgarh ☎2099). The walled palace, all domed ceilings, alcoves, and antique furniture, is wonderful; little but birdsong and distant voices disturb the peace, and the food is excellent.

On the edge of a deep gorge at **Menal**, which rumbles with the sound of vigorous waterfalls after the monsoon, a group of well-preserved twelfth-century temples surrounds a tank. They still bear many Shiva statues, and friezes showing Shiva cavorting with his consort, Parvati.

Bijolia, just east of Menal, was the centre of the Chauhan kingdom in the tenth century. It once had a hundred temples; those that survive are beautifully fashioned in a style common in central India at the time. Elaborate carving covers the towering roof and outer walls of the Undeshvara temple, dedicated to Shiva.

The main road from Bijolia continues northeast to **Bundi**, while a smaller route heads to **Kota**, 70km east. Both cities owe their origins to the thirteenth-century **Hadaoti** state, ruled by the Hadachauhan Rajputs from a hill-top stronghold at Bundi, although Kota became capital of its own princely state in 1625. Bundi is much the more attractive as a destination, but Kota is the usual base for visits not only to Bundi but also the imposing tenth-century temples in **Baroli** and **Jhalrapatan** to the south.

Kota

KOTA, 230km south of Jaipur on a fertile plain fed by Rajasthan's largest river, the Chambal, is one of the state's dirtier and less stimulating cities, and foreign visitors are sufficiently unusual to attract stares in the streets. But it does have some beautiful gardens, while its old **palaces** house the best museum in all Rajasthan.

In the seventeenth century, when Kota was declared capital of a newly independent princely state by the Mughal Emperor Jahangir, it was ruled by Rao Madho Singh of the Hadachauhan Rajputs. Today it is one of Rajasthan's major commercial and industrial cities, with hydro, atomic and thermal power stations along the banks of the Chambal, and Asia's largest fertilizer plant. The nuclear plant of Rawat Bhata, protected by stringent security 60km southwest, is notorious for its impact on local villagers.

Greatly prized *saris* from the village of **Kaithoon**, 20km southeast of Kota, are sold in all the bazaars. Made of tightly woven cotton or silk, and often highlighted with golden thread, they are known here as *masooria* and elsewhere as *Kota doria sari*.

Arrival and information

Kota's **railway station** is in the north of town, a few kilometres from the central **bus stand**. As well as the usual auto-rickshaws, an abundance of rather groovy tempos, plush with purple padded seats and tinsel, run throughout town collecting as many passengers as possible for Rs1 or 2 per head. They get unbearably crowded towards noon. Private **cars** (with drivers) can be rented from *Hotel Navrang* (☎23294), or, for guests only, *Brijraj Bhawan Palace Hotel* (☎25203).

For information on local sites, accommodation and transport head for the **tourist office** (Mon–Sat 8am–noon & 3–6pm; ☎27695) in *Chambal Tourist Bungalow*, Kshar Bagh, not far from the bus stand. Changing **money** is a tedious and time-consuming process. The *State Bank of India* on Aerodrome Circle will change travellers' cheques: other banks do not. The **post office** is on Station Rd (Mon–Sat 10am–4pm).

The City

The residential areas, bazaars, fort, City Palace and museum east of the Chambal face harsh buildings and factory smokestacks across the river. **Kishor Sagar**, an artificial lake built in 1346, gives picturesque relief. The red and white palace in its centre, **Jag Mandir**, was commissioned by the Maharani of Mewar in 1740 and can be visited only with permission from the Superintendent Engineer of Kota; ask at the tourist office. Gardens to the north of the tank are lush with viridescent mango trees, dahlias and palms, and crocodiles and gharial sun themselves in a shallow pond in the **Chambal Gardens** on the edge of the river a few kilometres south of the fort. Efforts are being made to increase their numbers after excessive hunting.

The telephone **area code** for Kota is ☎0744.

Kota's **fort**, raised above the flat bank of the Chambal 2km south of the bus stand, was built in 1264 by Rajkumar Jait Singh of Bundi. In a turret of the fort wall at the main gate, the **Government Museum** (daily except Fri 10am–4.30pm; Rs1) has a small collection of clothes, weapons and miniature paintings and a fascinating hand-drawn plan of Kota's manoeuvres during the Mutiny of 1857 that shows positions of defence and attack in minute detail.

Construction of the **City Palace** and offices of state within the fortifications began in 1625, and continued sporadically until the early years of this century. Although the older fort ramparts are falling into disrepair, the palaces are still in excellent condition. Apartments in the heart of the palaces house the excellent **Maharao Madho Singh Museum** (daily except Fri 11am–5pm; Rs5, camera Rs20 & video Rs35), approached through a brightly painted gateway flanked by elephants. Among a vast collection of carefully decorated weapons, the size and severity of which is almost out of this world, are spears, daggers, firearms, arrows in fine quivers and shields adorned with the solar symbol of the Hadachauhan Rajputs, large enough to protect an elephant. Solid silver artefacts and fading sepia photographs of viceroys, maharajas, polo teams and Queen Victoria record the extravagance of royalty, while the outstanding examples of *Kota Kamba*, miniatures from Kota's school of painting, are the best to be seen in India. A sickening array of stuffed animals in the basement is accompanied by photographs of proud hunters. The most spectacular apartment is **Raj Mahal**, which contains the royal throne. Its walls, decked with eighteenth-century paintings of the exploits of Krishna, hunting parties and Maharajas, glow with mosaics of gold and glass, while the ceiling glitters with silver and mirrors.

Accommodation and eating

Kota's **hotels** cater mainly for passing business travellers, and the cheaper rest houses reflect the dustiness and neglect that prevails in the town. Inexpensive dives are grouped around the railway station and the areas known as Civil Lines and Nayapura close to the bus stand and main market. If you don't **eat** in your hotel, you'll have to settle for a roadside stall – there are a couple of good places outside *Hotel Navrang*.

Brijraj Bhawan Palace (☎25203). Still home to the Maharaja of Kota; an oasis set in beautiful gardens on the banks of the Chambal. Lovely rooms and suites, plus a restaurant for residents. ⑦.

Chaman, Nayapura (☎23377). Reasonable accommodation; the surface dirt makes it look worse than it really is. Quieter rooms at the back, away from the road. ①.

Chambal Tourist Bungalow, Kshar Bagh (☎26527). Big place, with attractive gardens. Uninspiring but spacious clean rooms. ②–⑤.

Meghraj, Kota Junction (☎26870). Off the main street near the railway station. Average cramped three-storey hotel, quite clean. Rooms with bathroom and TV. ②.

Navrang, Civil Lines (☎23294). Spacious rooms with attached bathrooms and hot water. Above average. ④–⑦.

Samrat, Nayapura (☎22215). Next to the *Chaman*. Dirty cell-like rooms invaded by traffic noise. ②.

Shri Anand, Station Rd (☎21773). Small, clean, noisy rooms, not far from the station. ①.

Bundi

The walled town of **BUNDI**, 37km north of Kota, lies in the north of the former Hadaoti state, shielded on the north, east and west by jagged outcrops of the Vindhya range. Visible only from the south and guarded by the tremendous **Taragarh** or "star fort" high in the north of town, Bundi made a perfect capital for the Hadachauhans, perched in their immense turreted **palace**, beneath the highest walls of the fort. However, although settled in 1241, 25 years before Kota, Bundi never amounted to more than a modest market centre, and remains relatively untouched by modern developments.

From the **bus stand** in the south of town a short walk north through the central bazaar leads to the hillside **palace** at the base of the fort, built during the sixteenth and seventeenth centuries in authentic Rajput style, untainted by Mughal influence. Guides are available inside the palace, or from *Bundi Cafe & Crafts* (see below). A short steep path winds to the entrance, **Hathi Pole**, flanked by the elephants that are so common in the Hadaoti region. From the small courtyard within, steps lead to **Ratan Daulat**, the Diwan-i-Am or Hall of Public Audience, with its simple marble throne. Paintings from the *Bundi kalam* school of art adorn the walls of the **Chattra Mahal**, the royal living apartments, built entirely of green serpentine rock. Other paintings, though less well preserved, can be seen in **Chittra Shala**, a courtyard enclosed by cloisters vivid with blue, green, turquoise and white. Many of the palace apartments are closed, which helps to stoke rumours of a vast undiscovered treasure, said to be hidden far below in subterranean labyrinths. Views over Bundi from the palace take in the **Nawal Sagar** tank with its half-submerged temple.

A walk from the palace westwards through the walled bazaar and old gateways takes you to Rajasthan's most spectacular step-well, **Raniji-ki-Baori**, built in 1699 by Nathwati, wife of Rao Raja Singh. It lies deep beneath the surface of a small park, reached by a flight of steps punctuated by platforms and embellished pillars. Watch out for stones thrown from above by mischievous children.

East of town, a few kilometres by rickshaw, the beautiful **Sukh Niwas** – summer palace – on the northern shore of **Jait Sagar** tank cannot be visited, though ITDC plan to convert it into a hotel. You can however take a pleasant stroll in the adjoining gardens, and continue to a collection of cenotaphs at the far end of the lake.

Practicalities

Bundi is accessible only by road; **buses** travel between Kota and Bundi (1hr) every half-hour, and cover the six-hour journey to Chittaurgarh (143km) via Menal and Bijolia twice a day. A daily service also runs between Bundi and Ajmer (165km, 6hr), but for any longer distances it makes more sense to take a train from Kota (see p.199).

Although usually visited in a day from Kota, Bundi is a delightful place to stay. The 150-year-old rooms at *Bundi Cafe & Crafts* (☎0747-2755 or 3322; ⑨) below the palace are homely and full of character; the hotel provides good meals and has a shop selling local crafts. Simple and cheap lodgings can also be found at the *Bundi Tourist Palace* (①) facing Azad Park.

South of Kota

The inviting smaller towns of the former Kota state definitely merit a longer stay in the district. **Baroli**'s temples have been used for over a thousand years, and **Jhalrapatan**, near **Jhalawar**, abounds with the bustle of lively bazaars, and boasts some superbly ornate tenth-century temples.

Baroli

Local buses make the one-hour journey southwest from Kota to **BAROLI** (hourly; 40km), dropping passengers off a little short of the village beside a group of elaborate tenth-century temples on a small grassy patch surrounded by fields of wheat and castor-oil plants.

Though ruined, these temples are the finest to remain from the Pratihara period (*c.* 900 AD), and still shelter a resident priest – plus several hoopoes and jewel-coloured peacocks. The central, and best-preserved, **Ghateshvara Temple** has a high pyramidal roof and a columned porch leading to the main sanctuary. Within the doorway, decorated with dancing Shivas, Vishnus and river goddesses, five natural stones serve as *lingams*. A particularly exquisite statue of Chamunda is set in the north wall. Geometric and foliate designs cover the ceiling of the porch whose shafts are bursting with busty maidens. The other temples are in a state of disrepair, many of their better statues having been removed to the Kota museum, but doorways and walled shrines still display some magnificent carving. It's best to visit the temples early, when the reddish stone glows in the morning light. Buses for the return journey can be hailed as they pass along the road.

Alternatively, the **Darrah Wildlife Sanctuary** 10km beyond Baroli covers over 250 square kilometres of woodlands, peppered with ruins. Between February and May, visitors have a good chance of seeing the rare Indian wolf, leopard, sloth bear and chinkara. Enquire about availability of rooms at the *Forest Rest House* in the park (①).

Jhalawar and Jhalrapatan

Beyond the sanctuary, the southbound road arrives at **JHALAWAR**, 85km from Kota and a two-and-a-half-hour journey by hourly local buses. The medium-sized **fort** in the centre of town now houses government offices, which grant permission to visit the **Janana Khas** (daily except Fri 10am–4.30pm), a room in the fort decorated with coloured glass, mirrors and bright paintings of Jhalawar's turbaned rulers. In the winter months the fields are carpeted with opium poppies.

From Jhalawar, local buses or tempos continue 7km south to the walled town of **JHALRAPATAN**, alive with the hues of locally dyed turbans and skirts. Once evocatively and appropriately known as the "city of temple bells", Jhalrapatan may no longer have 108 temples, but many do survive. The most elaborate is the large sandy eleventh-century **Surya temple** in the main street, with a wide entrance hall dissected by sculpted pillars and crowned with domed pavilions in a style common in central India. Open for worship in the morning and evening, at other times it's a hectic meeting place. Other notable central temples include **Shantinath Jain Mandir**, displaying the typical Jain expertise of carving and, less typical, some unusual Jain painting, and **Dwarkadish temple** on the western edge of town, where images of Krishna attract devotees from all over India.

On the banks of the **River Chandrabagha**, 1km south, is a collection of temples dating from the seventh and eighth centuries. Time and battle have eroded many of the superb images lining its lintels and roofs, but resident priests still tend some of the temples by the small *ghats* on the river's edge. The simple beauty of the compound makes this among the most serene spots in Rajasthan – except during the festival of the **Karttika Purnima** (full moon Oct/Nov), when bathing in the Chanrabagha is considered especially auspicious.

CHAPTER THREE

UTTAR PRADESH

Although **UTTAR PRADESH** – "the Northern State", known as **UP** since the days of the United Provinces, under the Raj – is only the fourth largest state in India, it is the most varied and heavily populated, dominating the nation in culture, religion, language, and politics. Geographically, it has almost everything except the sea, stretching from the Himalayan snows in the northwest to the vast steamy Gangetic plains in the east.

The **history** of UP is very much the history of India, and its temples and monuments – Buddhist, Hindu and Muslim – are among the most impressive in the country. It holds some of Hinduism's most venerated sites, including, deep in the Himalayas, the source of the holy Ganga – the **River Ganges**. UP is also the heartland of **Hindi**, the principal indigenous language of India, and the official language of government.

Not far from Delhi, in the west of the state, **Agra**, home of the Taj Mahal, and deserted **Fatehpur Sikri**, stand as poignant reminders of the great Moghuls. Nearby, on the other hand, somehow sheltered from successive waves of Muslim conquest, the much-mythologized Hindu land of **Braj**, centered on **Mathura** and **Vrindavan**, was the childhood playground of the god Krishna.

Northeast of Delhi, on the borders with Nepal and Tibet, the mountains of **Garhwal** and **Kumaun** rise from the fertile sub-Himalayan plains. Every summer, pilgrims flock to the high temples known as the **Char Dham** – **Badrinath**, **Kedarnath**, **Yumnotri** and **Gangotri** – while trekkers and mountaineers explore newly de-restricted trails that lead to the glaciers of the inner Himalayas. Hill stations such as **Nainital** in Kumaun and **Mussoorie** in Garhwal retain their Victorian charm, their promenades thronging with refugees from the heat of the plains. At **Haridwar**, not far from the tiger-inhabited forests of **Corbett National Park**, the Ganga thunders out from the foothills on its

UTTAR PRADESH TRAVEL DETAILS

	Trains		Buses		Flights	
	Frequency	Time	Frequency	Time	Frequency	Time
To and From AGRA						
Ahmedabad	1 daily	24hr 15min				
Alwar			hourly	2hr		
Bhopal	16–19 daily	5hr 30min–9hr				
Bhubaneshwar	1 daily	39hr				
Bombay	2 daily	23hr 30min–27hr				
Calcutta	1 daily	30hr				
Delhi	15 daily	2hr–4hr 15min	hourly	5–6hr	1 daily	40min
Gwalior	15–19 daily	1hr 20min–2hr	hourly	3hr 30min		
Haridwar			5–6 daily	10hr		
Indore	1 daily	14hr 25min				
Jaipur	3 daily	6hr	20 daily	5hr		
Jalgaon	3–4 daily	14hr 20min–19hr				
Jhansi	15–19 daily	2hr 15min–5hr				
Kanpur	2 daily	7hr	1 daily	10hr		
Khajuraho			1 daily	11hr 30min	daily	45min
Lucknow	2 daily	7hr–8hr 30min	1 daily	9hr 30min		
Madras	1–2 daily	34–42hr				
Mathura	12 daily	1hr 30min–2hr	hourly	1hr 30min		
Nainital			3 daily	10hr		
Puri	1 daily	40hr				
Thiruv'puram	1–2 daily	50hr 30min–53hr				
Ujjain	1–2 daily	12hr 35min–16hr				
Varanasi	1 daily	10hr 30min			1 daily	2hr
To and From VARANASI						
Allahabad	5–8 daily	3–5hr	8–10 daily	3hr		
Ahmedabad	1 daily	43hr				
Bhubaneshwar	Tues, Fri & Sun	20hr 30min			4 weekly	1hr 15min
Bodhgaya	5–8 daily	4hr 30min–9hr	1 daily	6hr		
Bombay	4 daily	28–30hr			3 weekly	2hr 10min
Calcutta	5–8 daily	8hr 30min–20hr				
Dehra Dun	2 daily	20hr				
Delhi	6 daily	13–18hr			2 daily	1hr 15min–3hr
Gorakhpur	3 daily	6–10hr	8–12 daily	6hr		
Gwalior	1 daily	19hr 20min				
Haridwar	1 daily	20hr				
Jabalpur	7 daily	8hr 30min–11hr				
Jalgaon	4 daily	18hr–22hr 25min				
Jhansi	2 daily	17–19hr				
Kanpur	5–6 daily	8–9hr	2 daily	10hr		
Kathmandu					1 daily	1hr 10min
Khajuraho					1 daily	45min
Lucknow	8 daily	5–7hr	4 daily	8hr	4 weekly	45min
Madras	Mon & Wed	36hr				
Puri	3 weekly	22hr				
Ujjain	1 daily	33hr 25min				
To and From Haridwar						
Bombay	1 daily	40hr				
Calcutta	1 daily	28hr				
Dehra Dun	8 daily	2hr	hourly	1hr 15min		
Delhi	3 daily	7–10hr	4–6 daily	5–6hr		
Nainital			2 daily	9hr		
Rishikesh	2 daily	30min	25 daily	45min		

long journey to the sea. Nearby **Rishikesh** is familiar from one of the classic East-meets-West images of the 1960s; it was where the Beatles came to stay with the Maharishi.

Central UP, and especially **Lucknow**, the state capital, is redolent with memories of the lavish and ultimately decadent last days of the Moghuls, when the Kingdom of Avadh faded away before the advance of the British imperialists of the nineteenth century. The scars of the First War of Independence – the "Mutiny", a despairing reaction to the British usurpation of power – have in places yet to heal. To the east, **Allahabad** is the site of one of the world's largest religious fairs, when millions congregate at the confluence of the Ganga and the Yamuna to mark the auspicious occasion of **Kumbh Mela**. Along the southern borders of the state, the rugged Vindhya Mountains mark the end of the Deccan plateau. Once the domain of the Chandela Rajputs, the belt known as **Bundelkhand** harbours forgotten fortresses such as gigantic **Kalinjar**; the fort at **Jhansi** remains a symbol of the struggle for Independence.

The Ganga meanders across the vast plains of **Eastern UP** to the holiest Hindu city of all – the sacred *tirtha* (crossing-place) of **Varanasi**, where death transports the soul to final liberation. Even before Hinduism, this land was sacred; the Buddha himself,

	Trains		Buses		Flights	
	Frequency	Time	Frequency	Time	Frequency	Time
To and From Jhansi						
Bombay	4 daily	19–23hr				
Calcutta	3 weekly	23hr 25min				
Delhi	16–20 daily	4hr 25min–9hr				
Goa	1 daily	35hr				
Indore	1 daily	10hr 45min				
Khajuraho			3–5 daily	6hr		
Madras	2–4 daily	28–38hr				
Orchha			4 daily	1hr 30min		
Ujjain	2–3 daily	8–14hr				
To and From Lucknow						
Bombay	1 daily	30hr			4 weekly	2hr
Calcutta	5–6 daily	21hr 45min–28hr			3 weekly	3hr 20min
Dehra Dun	2 daily	14–18hr				
Delhi	5–6 daily	6hr–9hr 45min	2 daily	10hr		
Gorakhpur	3–5 daily	5hr	5 daily	6hr		
Haridwar	1 daily	11hr				
Kanpur	15 daily	1hr				
Nainital			1 daily	14hr		
Patna					3 weekly	1hr
Sonauli (for Nepal)			8 daily	11–12hr		
To and From Nainital						
Almora			4 daily	2hr 30min		
Dehra Dun			1 daily	10hr 30min		
Delhi			4 daily	8hr		
Kausani			4 daily	5hr		
Ramnagar			4 daily	3hr 30min		
Ranikhet			4 daily	3hr		
Rishikesh			1 daily	10hr		

Note that no individual route appears more than once in this chart. For any specific journey, check against where you want to get to as well as where you're coming from.

For details of connections with **Delhi** – especially services between Delhi and the UP Hills – see p.116 onwards.

and Mahavira, the founder of Jainism, frequented Varanasi, and the whole state, from Mathura to **Sarnath** on the outskirts of Varanasi, and beyond to the great schools of learning in Bihar, was long under the influence of Buddhism.

Although UP was once a thriving centre of Islamic jurisprudence and culture, many Muslims departed during the painful years after Independence, and the Muslim population is now just sixteen percent. In recent years, UP has become a major stronghold of the right-wing Hindu BJP, who for a brief period controlled its government. The state has acquired an unfortunate reputation as the focus of bitter communal tensions, most notoriously in the destruction in 1992 of the Babri Masjid mosque in **Ayodhya**.

With an efficient if basic state bus system and an excellent railway network, **travelling** around the state is generally straightforward (the one exception is Bundelkhand in the south). The main road from Delhi to Kathmandu passes through Gorakhpur, while Garhwal and Kumaun in the mountains are also well connected to the capital, and have local buses to penetrate the interior. The major tourist cities, **Agra** and **Varanasi**, have been coping with visitors and pilgrims for centuries; as well as good transport connections, they have all the facilities the traveller could require.

WESTERN UP

On the fringes of Delhi, and serving as the gateway to the heartland of the subcontinent, **Western Uttar Pradesh** has always been close to the centre of power in India. Once the Moghul capital, **Agra** is renowned for the most stunning mausoleum in the world – the **Taj Mahal** – as well as the stupendous battlements of the **Agra Fort**. Not far away, the beautiful sandstone pavilions of **Fatehpur Sikri**, built by the Moghul Akbar and abandoned after only fifteen years, remain perfectly preserved in the dry desert-like air.

The earliest records of the area date back 2500 years, when Gautama Buddha visited the city of **Mathura**, whose strategic position at the junction of several major trade routes had already earned it the prosperity that was to attract adventurers and conquerors. Later, Mathura was incorporated at the centre of the Hindu mythological landscape of **Braj**, associated with the childhood of Krishna.

Immediately north and east of Delhi, an industrial belt of commercial and administrative towns on busy road and railway networks includes **Meerut**, with its British-built Cantonment, the Mall and churches, which is only noteworthy as the place where the "Mutiny" of 1857 began.

Agra

The river Yamuna flows through it for five Kos, and on either bank are delightful villas and pleasant stretches of meadows. Filled with people from every country, Agra is the crossroads of the world. His majesty [Akbar] has built a fort of red sandstone, the like of which travellers have never recorded.

Court historian and chronicler, early eighteenth century

The splendour of **AGRA** – capital of all India under the Moghuls – remains undiminished, from the massive fort to the magnificent **Taj Mahal**. Along with Delhi, 204km northeast, and Jaipur in Rajasthan, Agra is the third apex of the "golden triangle", India's most popular tourist itinerary. It fully merits that status; the Taj effortlessly transcends all the frippery and commercialism that surrounds it, and continues to have a fresh and immediate impact on all who see it.

Most of Agra is on the west bank of the **River Yamuna**, with the fort and the Taj at its nucleus. The city radiates outwards from here, to the **Taj Ganj** area, directly south of the Taj, which holds the great preponderance of hotels and other amenities, and southwest to the commercial centre around the Sadar Bazaar and Cantonment areas. Of its monuments, **Agra Fort** provides an insight into the private lives of the Moghuls, its high ramparts crowded with exquisite pavilions, while the beautifully inlaid marble tomb of **Itmad-ud-daulah**, across the river, offers a refreshing tranquillity. **Akbar's Mausoleum** at Sikandra, 10km northwest, and the eerie abandoned city of **Fatehpur Sikri**, 32km west, are further unforgettable echoes of a grand and eloquent past. Although it is possible to see Agra in a day trip from Delhi, the Taj alone deserves so much more; a fleeting visit would miss the subtleties of its many moods, as the light changes from sunrise to sunset.

History

Little is known of the pre-Muslim history of Agra; one of the earliest chronicles, dated to the Afghan invasion under Ibrahim Ghaznavi in 1080 AD, describes a robust fort occupying a chain of hills, with a flourishing city strategically placed at the crossroads between the north and the centre of India. However, Agra remained a minor administrative centre until 1504, when the Sultan of Delhi, **Sikander Lodi**, moved his capital here, to keep a check on the warring factions of his empire. The ruins of the Lodis' great city can still be seen on the eastern bank of the Yamuna. After defeating the last Lodi Sultan, Ibrahim Lodi, at Panipat in 1526, **Babur**, the founder of the Moghul empire, sent his son **Humayun** ahead to capture Agra. In gratitude at their benevolent treatment at his hands, the family of the Raja of Gwalior rewarded the Moghul with jewellery and precious stones – among them the fabled **Kohinoor Diamond**, now among the crown jewels of England.

Agra's greatest days arrived during the reign of Humayun's son, **Akbar the Great** (1556–1605), with the construction of Agra Fort. The city maintained its position as the capital of the empire for over a century; even when **Shah Jahan**, Jahangir's son and successor, built a new city in Delhi, his heart remained in Agra. He pulled down many of the earlier red sandstone structures in the fort, replacing them with his hallmark – exquisite marble buildings. Although the empire flourished under his heir Aurangzeb (1658–1707), his intolerance towards non-Muslims stirred a hornets' nest. Agra was occupied successively by the Jats, the Marathas, and eventually the British.

After the uprising in 1857, the city lost the headquarters of the government of North-Western Provinces and the High Court to Allahabad. Agra began to decline, but its medieval treasures ensured its survival and the city is once again prospering, as an industrial and commercial centre, as well as a tourist destination.

Arrival and information

Daily *Indian Airlines* flights arrive from Delhi, Khajuraho and Varanasi at the **airport**, 7km southwest of the city. Accommodation can be booked on arrival, and taxis wait in line to carry passengers into town (Rs150–200).

Agra has no less than six **railway stations**. The best place to alight is **Agra Cantt Station**, in the southwest; this is convenient for most hotels, and has a tourist information counter. To get to a hotel, flag down one of the rickshaws (Rs15–20) or taxis (up to Rs60) that wait outside the station, or accept an offer from one of the drivers who dash onto the platform to find passengers. Trains from Rajasthan pull in close to the fort at **Agra Fort Station**, further from the main hub of hotels. Don't be persuaded to get off at Agra City Station, an expensive rickshaw ride away from town.

Buses usually stop at **Idgah bus stand** close to Agra Cantt Station, though services from Mathura arrive at **Agra Fort bus stand** just west of the fort. Some buses from Delhi stop outside the fort gate, where you'll have no trouble finding a rickshaw.

Information

Agra has two **tourist offices**, one run by the Government of India at 191 Mall Rd (Mon–Fri 9am–5.30pm, Sat 9am–1pm; ☎72377), and one run by UPTDC close to the *Clarks Shiraz* at 64 Taj Rd (same hours; ☎75034). Both are staffed by rather sleepy attendants, but they do have information on hotels and local sights, and details on **tours** that start and end at Agra Cantt railway station.

Banks, including the *Andhra* and the *Allahabad* (in the *Hotel Clarks Shiraz*), congregate on Taj Road; money transfers can also be arranged through *Sita World Travel*, also on Taj Rd (☎363013). The main **post office** is on the Mall (☎74000), near the Government of India Tourist Office.

City transport

You'd expect the local transport system in Agra to be geared towards getting as many tourists as possible around the city as fast as possible. However, the streets are surprisingly quiet; **cycle rickshaws** outnumber auto-rickshaws and taxis, pedalling slowly and noiselessly from place to place. Drivers often offer their services for day tours, and they'll more often than not have a book full of encouraging comments from delighted tourists. If you want to walk, expect an unending stream of offers from cycle-rickshaw *wallahs*. Early-morning rides to the Taj should be booked the night before. **Tongas**, horse-drawn carriages, are also common, and fairly cheap, but the sight of skinny near-lame horses, often covered in open sores, is enough to put most people off.

Auto-rickshaws provide a faster, and more expensive, alternative for short trips, and they're great value if rented for the day. Prices, including waiting time, are reasonable (upwards of Rs50), but rise sharply if you want to visit Akbar's tomb and other monuments on the outskirts of the city. **Taxis** are less popular, though very handy for trips to the airport or station – unlike rickshaws, they won't stop at jewellers, craft shops and the like to earn extra commission. Expensive hotels have their own fleet of taxis, and there are taxi ranks at the stations and airport. Whichever form of transport you choose, you'll be expected to **bargain**. Agra sees so many "fresh" tourists that the drivers will always quote high prices – if you object, the price falls. After dark, rickshaw *wallahs* converge in the centre of town, so if you want to get out of Taj Ganj after an evening meal, you may be faced with a long walk before you find a rickshaw.

To save the hassle of taking public transport, you can always rent a **bicycle**, and do everything at your own pace. Try the rental shop near *Taj View Hotel*, where charges are Rs3 per hour, and no more than Rs15 per day. **Car rental** is also an option, though cars are more useful for driving out of Agra than for getting around town. Chauffeur-driven cars can be rented from the reliable *Travel Corporation of India*, whose office is in *Hotel Clarks Shiraz* (☎361122). Self-drive cars are available from *Budget Rent a Car*, at *Mumtaz Hotel* on Fatehbad Rd (☎361771), though their prices are extremely high.

Tours

Agra's surprising lack of organized **tours** of the city is more than made up for by the cycle and auto-rickshaws who offer their services for a full day. For a more comfortable sightseeing jaunt, rent a taxi from a high-class hotel: expect to pay Rs300–500 for a full day. Coach tours in Agra cater more to long journeys: those run by *UPSRTC* include a morning excursion to Fatehpur Sikri (10.15am–2pm), a day tour of the Taj, Agra Fort and Fatehpur Sikri (10.15am–6.30pm) and another day trip adding Sikandra to the

---

The telephone **area code** for Agra is ☎0562.

AGRA

0   1 km

Chini Ka Rauza

RESTAURANTS:
❶ Dasaprakash
❷ Zorba the Buddha
❸ Ching Wah
❹ Hot Bite
❺ Prakash
❻ Kwality
❼ Sonam
❽ ITDC Cafeteria

St John's Church

Jami Masjid

Agra Fort

Yamuna River

Agra Fort Bus Stand

Taj Mahal

TAJ GANJ
(hotels listed on p. 218)

Idgah Bus Stand

GPO

THE MALL

Agra Cant Railway Station

HOTELS:
❹ Sakura
❷ Rose
❸ Lauries
❹ Major Bakshi Tourist Home
❺ Basera
❻ Tourist Rest House
❼ Agra
❽ Akbar Inn
❾ Taj Kheema
❿ Agra Ashok
Ⓚ Grand
Ⓛ Jaiwal
Ⓜ Clarks Shiraz
Ⓝ Amar
Ⓞ Taj View
Ⓟ Mayur Tourist Complex
Ⓠ Highway Inn
Ⓡ Akbar International
Ⓢ Safari
Ⓣ Novotel Agra

previous list (9am–7pm). The tours, invariably rushed, leave from *Taj Kheema Hotel*, next to the Taj Mahal. Similar tours are offered at higher prices by other agents, such as *Ashok Tours and Travels* at *Agra Ashok*, The Mall (☎361223), and *Mercury Travels* (☎360282) and *Travel Corporation of India* (☎361122), both at *Clarks Shiraz*.

The Town

Agra city centres on the **old town**, a sprawling web of alleys, bazaars, mosques and cramped houses, but its focal point is the mighty **fort** immediately to the south, rising above the River Yamuna at the sharp bend where it changes its course to flow past the **Taj Mahal**, two kilometres east. Although Agra stretches for ten kilometres north to south, most tourists concentrate their attention on the district south of the fort, where hotels, restaurants and offices are conveniently located for the main sights.

If you want to walk between the fort and the Taj, take the path that runs through **Shahjahan park**, with its lofty trees and well-tended flower beds.

The Taj Mahal

Daily, dawn–dusk. Admission Rs2 8am–5pm, Rs100 before 8am and after 5pm. Free on Friday.

Described by the Indian classical poet Tagore as a "tear on the face of eternity", the **Taj Mahal** is undoubtedly the zenith of Moghul architecture and quite simply one of the world's most marvellous buildings. Volumes have been written on its perfection, and its image adorns countless glossy brochures and guide books; nonetheless, the reality never fails to overwhelm all who see it, and few words can do it justice.

The glory of the monument is strangely undiminished by the crowds of tourists who visit each day, as small and insignificant as ants in the face of this immense and captivating monument. However, the Taj is undoubtedly at its most alluring in the relative quiet of early morning, shrouded in mists and bathed with a soft red glow. As its vast marble surfaces fall into shadow or reflect the sun, its colour changes, from soft grey and yellow to pearly cream and dazzling white; it's well worth visiting at different times. This play of light is an important decorative device, symbolically implying the presence of Allah, who is never represented in anthropomorphic form.

There's no time limit on visits to the Taj, and some people spend most of the day here, sitting, reading, dozing or picnicking in the beautifully kept gardens. Hawkers and salesmen are not allowed in, and guides are not available on site, but can usually be provided by hotels, and always accompany organized tours. The ticket office, just outside the western gate, is rarely blocked by long queues, except between 4 and 5pm before the admission fee increases; bring the right change to avoid delays.

Overlooking the River Yamuna, and visible from the fort in the west, the Taj Mahal stands at the northern end of vast gardens enclosed by walls. Though its layout follows a distinctly Islamic theme, representing Paradise, it is above all a monument to romantic love. **Shah Jahan** built the Taj to enshrine the body of his favourite wife, Arjumand Bann Begum, better known as Mumtaz Mahal ("Elect of the Palace"), who died shortly after giving birth to her fourteenth child in 1631. The Shah was devastated by her death, and set out to create an unsurpassed, eternal monument to her memory. Of all the Moghuls, only Shah Jahan, who had been designing palaces and forts since the age of sixteen, could have come up with such a magnificent design. The name of the chief architect is unknown, but Amanat Khan, who had previously worked on Akbar's tomb, was responsible for the calligraphic inscriptions that adorn the gateways, mosque and tomb. Construction by a workforce of some 20,000 men from all over Asia commenced in 1632, and the tomb was completed in 1653. Marble was brought from Makrana, near Jodhpur, in Rajasthan, and precious stones for decoration – onyx, amethyst, malachite, lapis lazuli, turquoise, jade, crystal, coral and mother-of-pearl were carried to Agra from Persia, Russia, Afghanistan, Tibet, China and the Indian Ocean.

The story is given an exquisite poignancy by the fate of Shah Jahan himself, who became a tragic and inconsolable figure. Eventually, his devout and austere son Aurangzeb seized power, and Shah Jahan was interned in Agra Fort, where he lived out his final years gazing wistfully at the Taj Mahal in the distance. He died there in January 1666, with his daughter, Jahanara Begum, at his side; his body was carried across the river to lie alongside his beloved wife in his peerless mausoleum.

The walled complex is approached from the south through a red sandstone forecourt, Chowk-i Jilo Khana, whose wide paths flanked by arched kiosks run to high gates in the east and west. The original entrance, a massive arched gateway topped with delicate domes and adorned with Koranic verses, stands at the northern edge of Chowk-i Jilo Khana, directly aligned with the Taj, but shielding it from the view of those who wait outside. Today's entrance, complete with security checks, is through a narrow archway in the southern wall to the right of the gate.

Once beyond the southern wall, you'll see the mighty marble tomb at the end of superb gardens designed in the *charbagh* style so fashionable among Moghul, Arabic and Persian architects. Dissected into four quadrants by waterways, they evoke the

Islamic image of the Gardens of Paradise, where rivers flow with water, milk, wine and honey. The "rivers" converge at a marble tank in the centre that corresponds to *al-Kawthar*, the celestial pool of abundance mentioned in the Koran. Today only the watercourse running from north to south is full, and its precise, glassy reflection of the Taj is a favourite photographic image. Views from the paths lining the east–west canal, lined with lofty trees, ferns and deep red and pink flowers, are equally sublime. To the west of the tomb is a domed red sandstone mosque, and to the east a replica (*jawab*), probably built to house visitors, and necessary to achieve perfect symmetry.

Essentially square in shape, with peaked arches cut into its sides, the Taj Mahal surmounts a square marble platform marked at each corner by a high minaret. Topped with a huge central dome, it rises for over 55m, its height accentuated by a crowning brass spire, itself almost 17m high. Steps lead to the platform, and visitors must remove their shoes before climbing to the tomb. The marble floor can be icy cool in the morning, but at midday it gets extremely hot – you may want to wear socks, or rent a cloth foot-cover from the shoe attendants. On approach, the tomb looms ever larger and grander, but not until you are close do you appreciate both its awesome magnitude and the extraordinarily fine detail of relief carving, highlighted by floral patterns of precious stones. Carved vases of flowers including roses, tulips and narcissi, rise subtly out of the marble base, a pattern repeated more colourfully and inlaid with precious stones around the four great arched recesses (*pishtaqs*) on each side. Arabic verses praising the glory of paradise fringe the archways, proportioned exactly so that each letter appears to be the same size when viewed from the ground.

The south face of the tomb is the main entrance to the interior: a high, echoing octagonal chamber flushed with pallid light reflected by yellowing marble surfaces. A marble screen, cut so finely that it seems almost translucent, and decorated with

---

POLLUTION THREATENING THE TAJ MAHAL

Although the Taj Mahal may appear to the untrained eye almost as perfect as the day it was completed, the marble is undeniably sullen and yellow in parts, and empty casings here and there betray lost precious stones. These are the early effects of the threat posed by environmental **pollution** from traffic and industry, and some 25,000 tourists who visit each day of the year. While marble is all but impervious to the onslaught of wind and rain that erodes softer sandstone, it has no natural defence against the sulphur dioxide that lingers in a dusty haze and shrouds the monument; sometimes the smog is so dense that the tomb cannot be seen from the fort. Sulphur dioxide mixes with atmospheric moisture and settles as sulphuric acid on the surface of the tomb, making the smooth white marble yellow and flaky, and forming a subtle fungus that experts have named **"marble cancer"**.

The main sources of pollution are the 1700 **factories** in and around Agra, and the continuous flow of vehicles along the national highways that skirt the city. Chemical effluents belched out of factory chimneys are well beyond safety limits laid down by environmental committees. Despite laws demanding the installation of pollution-control devices, and an exclusion zone marking 10,400 square kilometres around the Taj Mahal that should be free of any new industrial plants, pollutants in the atmosphere have continued to rise, and new factories have been set up illegally. In September 1993 the Supreme Court finally took action and ordered 212 plants to shut down until emissions fell to legal limits.

Cleaning work on the Taj Mahal rectifies the problem to some extent, but the chemicals used will themselves eventually affect the marble. Already attendants shine their torches on repaired sections of marble to demonstrate that they have lost their translucency. The doubtful methods of the Archaeological Survey of India, such as scrubbing with toothbrushes, may prove disastrous in the long term. Hopes for proper care of the Taj Mahal have been raised since the government turned its attention to the plight of India's greatest monument, and entry fees have been increased in an attempt to regulate the flow of tourists, but the fate of the Taj Mahal hangs in the balance.

precious stones, scatters dappled light over the cenotaph of Mumtaz Mahal in the centre of the tomb, and that of Shah Jahan next to it. Inlaid stones on the marble tombs are the finest in Agra; attendants gladly illuminate the decorations with torches. No pains were spared in perfecting the inlay work – each petal or leaf may comprise up to sixty separate stone fragments. Ninety-nine names of Allah adorn the top of Mumtaz's tomb, and set into Shah Jahan's is a pen box, the hallmark of a male ruler. These cenotaphs, in accordance with Moghul tradition, are only representations of the real coffins, which lie in the same positions in an unadorned and humid crypt below that's heavy with the scent of heady incense and rose petals. Have a few coins ready for a respectful donation to an attendant priest who will lay the offering on the graves.

If you're spending a full day at the Taj and want a break from the sun, make a small detour to the **museum** (daily 10am–5pm) in the western wall of the enclosure. The interior contains exquisite miniatures, two marble pillars believed to have come from the fort, and portraits of Moghul rulers including Shah Jahan and Mumtaz Mahal. Further into the building a gallery shelters architectural drawings of the Taj Mahal, a display of elaborate porcelains, seventeenth-century coins and examples of stone inlay work, though you'll more than likely have seen enough in the Taj.

Agra Fort

Daily 7am–6pm. Admission Rs2. Free on Friday.

The high red sandstone ramparts of **Agra Fort**, stretching for almost 2.5km, dominate a bend in the River Yamuna, 1.6km northwest of the Taj Mahal. Akbar laid the foundations of this majestic citadel, built between 1565 and 1573 in the form of a half moon, on the remains of earlier Rajput and Suri fortifications. Agra Fort developed as the seat and stronghold of the Moghul empire under successive generations: Akbar constructed the walls and gates, his grandson Shah Jahan had most of the principal buildings erected, and Aurangzeb, the last great emperor, was responsible for the ramparts.

The curved bastions of the sandstone ramparts are interrupted by impressive gates, of which only the **Amar Singh Gate** is open to the public. Ornamented with glazed tiles, and with impressive double walls and a forecourt, this gate was used by the victorious General Lake when he entered the fort in 1803. The original and grandest entrance was through the western **Delhi Gate**, leading to the inner portal, **Hathi Pol** or "Elephant Gate", now flanked by two red sandstone towers faced in marble, but once guarded by colossal stone elephants with riders – destroyed by Aurangzeb in 1668.

Access to much of the fort is restricted, so masterpieces of Moghul architecture such as Shah Jahan's beautiful **Moti Masjid** (Pearl Mosque) are out of bounds to visitors. Only those parts open to the public are described in detail below.

DIWAN-I-AM AND THE GREAT COURTYARD

The graceful **Diwan-i-Am** (Hall of Public Audience), open on three sides, stands immediately to the east as you approach from Amar Singh Gate. Replacing an earlier wooden structure, the sandstone building was constructed by Shah Jahan in 1628. After use as an arsenal by the British, it was restored in 1876 by Sir John Strachey. Three rows of white polished stucco pillars topped by peacock arches support the flat roof; the elegance of the setting would have been enhanced by the addition of brocade, carpets and satin canopies for audiences with the emperor. The ornate throne alcove is inlaid in marble decorated with flowers and foliage in bas-relief, and connects to the royal chambers within. Adjacent to the alcove, the Baithak, a small marble block, is where ministers would sit to deliver their petitions and receive commands.

An incongruous intrusion in the centre of the great courtyard is a gothic Christian tomb marking the **grave of John Russel Colvin**, the Lieutenant-Governor of the North-Western Provinces who died here during the rebellion of 1857.

THE ROYAL PAVILIONS

Clustered around a high terrace overlooking the river, the **royal pavilions** were designed to catch the cool breeze wafting across the Yamuna – and for ease of access to a water supply. The **Macchi Bhavan** (Fish Palace), approached through the alcove in the Diwan-i-Am, has suffered through the ages. During the period of Jat control, the Maharaja of Bharatpur removed some of its marble fixtures to his palace in Deeg; later, Lord William Bentinck auctioned off much of the original mosaic and fretwork, including parts of the **Hammam-i-Shahi**, the Royal Bath. The palace was once strewn with fountains and flower beds, interspersed with tanks and water channels stocked with fish for the angling pleasure of the emperor and courtiers. In the northwest corner of the enclosure, the exquisite little **Nagina Masjid** (Gem Mosque) is entirely made of marble. Capped with three domes and approached from a marble-paved courtyard, it was built by Shah Jahan for the ladies of the *zenana*. Below it, overlooked by a beautiful marble balcony with carved lattice screens and peacock arches, is the **Inner** or **Zenana Mina Bazaar,** where ladies of the court could browse through goods such as silk, jewellery and brocade offered by merchants, without being seen themselves.

The **Chitor Gate**, salvaged by Akbar as a trophy from the horrific sacking of the Rajput stronghold of Chitor and installed in 1568, leads to the **Mandir Raja Ratan**, erected in 1768 during the Jat occupation of the fort. Past this is the Hall of Private Audience, the **Diwan-i-Khas**, where the emperor would receive kings, dignitaries and ambassadors. Built in 1635, the building was badly damaged when it came under bombardment by General Lake in 1803, but the hall – with its ornate pillars and arches inlaid with lapis lazuli and jasper – survives. Two thrones adorn the large terrace in front of the Diwan-i-Khas, one of black slate and the other of white marble. Shah Jahan apparently took his evening repose in the white throne; from the black one, the emperor would amuse himself by watching elephant fights in the eastern enclosure. Tucked away by the west wall of the hall, approached by a staircase, is the tiny **Mina Masjid** (Heavenly Mosque), the emperor's personal mosque, where Shah Jahan prayed during his imprisonment.

A doorway from the rear of the Diwan-i-Khas leads to a two-storeyed pavilion or tower known as **Musamman Burj**, famous in Moghul legend as the spot where, in the open octagonal chamber atop the highest of the riverside bastions, Shah Jahan caught his last glimpse of the Taj Mahal before he died. Surrounded by a verandah, the elegant chamber has a lattice-screen balustrade with ornamental niches; exquisite inlay covers almost every surface, and a marble *chhatri* adds the finishing touch. In front of the tower a courtyard, paved with marble octagons, has a *pachisi* board at its centre, where the emperor played a rather bizarre version of the game (a form of backgammon) using dancing girls as pieces.

To the south of Musamman Burj lies the marble building known as **Khas Mahal** (Private Palace), possibly used as a drawing room or the emperor's sleeping chamber. Khas Mahal is designed for comfort, with cavities in its flat roofs to insulate against the searing heat of an Agra summer, and with soothing riverside and garden views. The palace is flanked by two **Golden Pavilions**, their curved roofs covered with gilded copper tiles, in a style similar to the thatched roofs of Bengali village huts. Stretching in front of the Khas Mahal to the west is **Anguri Bagh** (Grape Garden), a miniature *charbagh*, with its quarters delineated by wide marble pavements. In the northeast corner, the **Shish Mahal** (Palace of Mirrors) was where royal women bathed, steeped in the soft lamplight reflected from the mirrorwork mosaics that covered the walls and ceiling. Connected to the Khas Mahal by an extensive corridor, the **Shah Jahani Mahal** (Shah Jahan's Palace) is supported by wooden beams; its four chambers were originally painted in bright colours and embossed in gold.

THE PALACES OF JAHANGIR AND AKBAR

Immediately southwest of the Shah Jahani Mahal is the robust, square **Jahangiri Mahal**. This red sandstone palace, built either by Jahangir or by Akbar on his son's behalf, is almost entirely Hindu in its interior design. In the Assembly Hall, carved ornamental brackets support beams, wide eaves and ceilings with struts; the serpentine form being emitted from a dragon's mouth is reminiscent of a Gujarati temple.

Rooms to the west are thought to have been the temple and drawing room of Jahangir's Rajput wife Jodhbai. Below the palace, three storeys of basement chambers were used to escape the heat; this dark unpleasant labyrinth hides secrets of a long-forgotten harem and includes a guillotine. **Jahangir's Hauz** or cistern, a giant bowl made in 1611 from a single block of porphyry and inscribed in Persian, was unearthed in the nineteenth century and stands in the courtyard in front of the Jahangiri Mahal.

Returning towards Amar Singh Gate to the left, an assembly hall, a verandah overlooking the river and excavations are all that remain of the southernmost palace, the once extensive **Akbari Mahal**, built in 1571.

Jami Masjid

Opposite the fort and overlooking the railway station, the **Jami Masjid** was built by Shah Jahan in 1648 and dedicated to his favourite daughter, Jahanara Begum. Standing on a high plinth approached by stairs, and with five arched entrances to the courtyard, the mosque is crowned by three large sandstone domes distinguished by their zigzag bands of marble.

Itmad-ud-daulah

Dawn–dusk. Admission Rs2, free on Friday.

Itmad-ud-daulah, the beautiful tomb of Mirza Ghiyath Beg, an important member of Akbar's court and later *wazir* to Emperor Jahangir, stands amid gardens scampering with monkeys on the east bank of the Yamuna, less than three kilometres from the city. The first building to be constructed of pure marble in Moghul India, this charming two-storey mausoleum is small but perfectly executed, with translucent stones etched into its walls and tracery work adding a delicate finishing touch. It's unmistakably feminine, having been designed by Ghiyath Beg's daughter, the favourite queen of Jahangir, and the most powerful woman in Moghul history, named Nur Jahan, "Light of the world", by Jahangir. He respected her intellect and talent so much that he ordered coins to be minted in her name, and by the time of her father's death in 1622 she had substantial control over the empire.

The square mausoleum, with an octagonal turret at each corner, foreshadows the Taj Mahal in its exclusive use of marble, but is more daintily proportioned, and has a pavilion on its roof rather than a dome. Ghiyath Beg's grave is underground, next to his wife's sarcophagus, shrouded in flowers and sallow light. A pierced and intricately carved wall in front of the entrance to the grave casts a soft hazy light over paintings of flowers, cypresses, vases and wine vessels, all symbols of paradise, in the inner chamber. From the garden you can look over the Yamuna. Wide and vigorous during the monsoon, for most of the year it trickles in a shallow stream. *Saris* are laid to dry on its sandy bed and melancholy buffalo wallow in its waters.

Chini-ka-rauza

Less than 1km north of Itmad-ud-daulah is **Chini-ka-rauza**, built in 1635 and reputed to be the mausoleum of Afzal Khan, a Persian poet and Shah Jahan's prime minister. Neglected and decaying, its soft brown stone is victim to the elements and its eaves shelter pigeons. Topped with a bulbous dome the dull earth-coloured tomb is a far cry from Nur Jahan's delicate work, but is distinctive as Agra's sole Persian construction. Parts of the walls are still covered with the coloured enamel tiles (*chini*) that once enhanced the whole of the exterior and gave the tomb its name, while traces of paintings and Islamic calligraphy can still be made out on the high domed ceiling.

Ram Bagh

Ram Bagh, laid out by Babur in 1528 and probably the first pleasure garden of its kind, is only a few kilometres north of Chini-ka-rauza. Reputedly the resting place of Babur's body before it was taken to Kabul, the garden is now dilapidated and overgrown, and only a few tattered columns and walls remain of the stone pavilions that once sheltered the royal family. Its original name, Aram Bagh (garden of rest), was corrupted to Ram, after the Hindu god.

Akbar's mausoleum

Sikandra. Dawn–dusk. Admission Rs2, free on Friday.

Given the Moghul tradition of building magnificent tombs for men and women of high status, it comes as no surprise that the mausoleum of the most distinguished Moghul ruler was one of the finest and most ambitious structures of its time. **Akbar's mauso-**

leum, a majestic composition of deep-red sandstone and cool marble designed by Akbar and modified by his son, Jahangir, in 1605, borders the roadside at Sikandra, 10km northwest of Agra. Rickshaws charge at least Rs50 to make the round trip, or you could hop on any bus bound for Mathura from the Agra Fort bus stand.

The most overwhelming feature of the complex is its huge south gate, **Buland Darwaza**, "Gateway of Magnificence" – so high that it obstructs any view to the tomb beyond. Surmounted by four tapering marble minarets, and overlaid with marble and coloured tiles set in repetitive geometrical patterns, it bears the Koranic inscription "These are the gardens of Eden, enter them and live forever." Buy a ticket at the office set into the left face of the gate, then walk through to the gardens, divided by wide paved walkways into four equal quadrants in typical Moghul fashion, and enclosed by high walls. Along the paths friendly long-tailed langur monkeys laze in the sunshine and groom one another, and black buck roam through the tall grasses.

In the centre of the gardens, directly in front of Buland Darwaza, the broad-based square mausoleum has arcaded cloisters along each side and pavilions enhanced by delicate marble domes rising above its centre. A high marble gateway in the southern face draws attention to meticulous lattice screens shielding a small vestibule, once painted with rich sea-blue frescoes and Koranic verses. From here a ramp leads to a subterranean crypt, where Akbar's grave lies sprinkled with roses and bathed in a cool yellow light. Akbar's mausoleum may not be as grand nor as awesome as the indomitable Taj, but it possesses a serenity sometimes lost among the throngs of tourists at Agra's most visited monument. It also marks the important transition in Moghul design after Akbar's death, replacing his bold, masculine red stone monuments with more ethereal and sensuous marble buildings, epitomized and perfected in the Taj Mahal.

Accommodation

The cluster of narrow streets just south of the Taj Mahal is known as **Taj Ganj**. Away from the worst of the city's traffic, and with plenty of restaurants, shops and auto-rickshaws to hand, it's a great place to stay. However, its hotels only cater for budget travellers; if you're looking for greater comfort, most of the tourist-class hotels are dotted around in the more spacious locale to the south. Luxury hotels, as well as a few cheaper bargains, remain aloof in the **Cantonment**, near Agra Cantt railway station. **Sadar Bazaar**, around the commercial hub, has hotels in all price ranges.

Taj Ganj

Gulshan Lodge, South Gate. Dingy but passable low-priced rooms with attached bath. The restaurant here is popular. ①.

India Guest House, South Gate. Very simple rooms around the plant-filled courtyard of a family house; cosy but spartan. ①.

Jahangir Lodge, Taj Rd, Purani Mandi. Further from the Taj than most, but homely and clean. ①.

Kamal, Chowk Kagzi, South Gate (☎360926). Fresh and clean rooms in a new hotel with a great view from the roof-top and a good restaurant. ①.

Noorjahan, South Gate. Closest to the south gate of the Taj, the rooms here are plain and simple. To sample the acclaimed view, you'll have to climb a rickety ladder to the roof. The restaurant on the ground floor has good-value breakfasts. ①–②.

Pink, East Gate (☎360677). Painted entirely in pink, this hotel is friendly, has adequate rooms, some with attached bath, and a restaurant. ①.

Santi Lodge, Chowk Kagzi, South Gate (☎361644). Rooms of varying standards, most with smelly bathrooms hidden by thin partitions, some with balconies; one of the best views of the Taj. ①–②.

Shah Jahan, South Gate. A selection of clean rooms, the best of which are on the roof; one special suite decked out like a Swiss chalet, but musty and overpriced. ①–③.

Sheela, East Gate (☎361794). The best bet for budget travellers; no views, but only 200m from the east gate of the Taj. Ground-floor rooms with attached bath, amid colourful gardens. ①–②.

Siddartha, West Gate (☎360238). A homely and clean hotel with spacious rooms set around a leafy courtyard, all with attached baths and some with hot water. ①–②.

Sikander, 2/10 South Gate. Clean rooms, some carpeted with attached bath, and a spacious roof for excellent views. Great value. ①.

Taj Kheema, East Gate (☎360140). Uninspiring airless rooms, some a/c. Superb views of the Taj from a grassy mound in the parched gardens, but non-residents have to pay just to sit there. ②–④.

Taj View, Taj Rd, Purani Mandi. Not to be confused with the luxury hotel of the same name. Extremely spartan, fairly cheap, and absolutely no view of the Taj. ①.

Sadar Bazaar and Cantonment

Agra, F M Cariappa Rd (☎363331). Old-world atmosphere in a garden setting, with views of the Taj Mahal from the patio. Now showing their age, the rooms (some a/c) are dim and musty but spacious, with large bathrooms and hot showers. ②–⑤.

Agra Ashok, 6B The Mall (☎361223). Style and carpeted comfort, with large luxurious rooms arranged around gardens and a swimming pool; choice of high-standard expensive restaurants. ⑧.

Akbar Inn, 21 The Mall (☎363212). Reasonably priced with a garden and a small campsite; the annexe has cheap, basic rooms; pleasant open-air cafe. ①–②.

Basera, 19 Ajmer Rd, Baluganj (☎363641). In the busy bazaar area, small and well equipped, with a range of rooms. ③–⑤.

Clarks Shiraz, 54 Taj Rd (☎362421). Pleasant setting with extensive grounds, including swimming pools and golf; restaurants, bar, shopping arcade, banks and travel services on the premises. ⑧–⑨.

Deepak Lodge, 178 Ajmer Rd, Pratap Pura. Small but pleasant and popular, with a garden; close to all amenities. ①–③.

Grand, 147 Station Rd (☎364014). Extensive with a pleasant garden, restaurant and bar, but a bit tacky and expensive for what it is. ⑤–⑦.

Jai Hind, Sadar Bazaar (☎363503). Pokey and uninviting rooms, if clean; extensions planned. ①–②.

Jaiwal, Taj Rd, Sadar Bazaar (☎363716). Spotless but unimaginative rooms. ③–④.

Lauries, Mahatma Gandhi Rd (☎364536). One of Agra's legendary hotels, now undergoing major renovation. Open-air swimming pool and pleasant grounds and gardens; camping facilities. ⑤.

Major Bakshi Tourist Home, 33–38 Ajmer Rd (☎76828). Sikh-run and friendly, clean and pleasant, with a dormitory and good home cooking; recommended. ③–④.

Novotel Agra, Tajnagri Scheme, Fatehbad Rd (☎368282). Tasteful, efficient and comfortable, with good restaurant and swimming pool. Recommended, but far from central, and 3km from the Taj. ⑧.

Pawan, Taj Rd, Sadar Bazaar (☎363716). Roomy but expensive, in the heart of the busy restaurant belt of Sadar Bazaar. ④–⑥.

Rose, 21 Old Idgah Colony (☎367562). Mr Gulati goes out of his way to welcome foreigners – by far the best accommodation available in the Idgah Bus Stand area. The cheaper rooms are good value and there is also a dormitory. You can see the Taj Mahal from the rooftop cafe. ①–⑤.

Sakura, 49 Old Idgah Colony. Close to Idgah Bus Stand – Rajasthan buses leave from the forecourt. Some rooms are pokey, but it's handy and has a swimming pool. Pasta and Mexican food. ②–③.

Tourist Rest House, Baluganj (☎363961). Popular budget accommodation and a place to meet other travellers, but ageing rooms (some with private bathrooms) set around a cramped but green courtyard. Hot showers in common bathroom and dreary vegetarian food available. ①–③.

Agra is renowned for its marble table tops, plates, vases and trays, inlaid with semi-precious stones in lavish floral designs, in imitation of that found in the Taj Mahal. It is also an excellent place to buy **leather**: Agra's shoe industry supplies all India, and its tanneries export bags, briefcases and jackets. **Carpets** and **durries** are manufactured too, and traditional embroidery continues to thrive. *Zari* and *zardozi* both employ bright colours, the latter building up three-dimensional patterns with fantastic motifs; *chikan* uses more delicate overlay techniques.

Shopping or browsing around the Mall, MG Road, Munro Road, Kinari Bazaar, Sadar Bazaar and the Taj Complex is entertaining, but you need to know what you're buying and be prepared to haggle; you should also be wary of ordering anything to be sent overseas. Commission payable by shops to rickshaw- and taxi-drivers and tour guides can inflate prices. Shops in the big hotels may be more expensive, but their quality and service are usually more reliable. *UP Handicrafts Palace*, 49 Bansal Nagar, have a wide selection of marble; other state emporia round the Taj include UP's *Gangotri*, which has fixed prices. Close to the East Gate, *Shilpgram* is an extensive crafts village with arts and handicrafts from all over India, and occasional live music and dance performances.

South of Taj Ganj

Akbar International, near *Hotel Taj View*, Fatehbad Rd (☎360749). Away from it all in a quiet residential area off the main road, with a pleasant garden where concerts are occasionally held. Excellent value – the proprietor will arrange traditional Muslim cooking to order. ①–②.

Amar, Fatehbad Rd (☎360695). All mod cons including a health club and swimming pool, but unattractive and garish. ⑦.

Highway Inn, opposite radio station behind *Hotel Amar*, Vibhav Nagar (☎360458). Campsite-cum-motel being converted into a hotel; basic but friendly and relaxed. ①–③.

Mayur Tourist Complex, Fatehbad Rd (☎360302). Extraordinary pseudo-Moghul cottages. Facilities include restaurant, bar, camping and a swimming pool. ⑥–⑦.

Moghul Sheraton, Fatehbad Rd (☎361701). Opulent, lavish and expensive, the fake Moghul splendour feels overdone. Excellent restaurants, bar and a pleasant swimming pool. ⑨.

Safari, Shaheed Nagar, Shamsabad Rd (☎360013). Under the same management as the *Tourist Rest House*, the more expensive rooms represent good value. Close to the *Indian Airlines* office, and with views of the Taj Mahal from the rooftop cafe. ②–④.

Taj View, Fatehbad Rd, Taj Ganj (☎361171). All the hallmarks of the Taj Group – marble lobby, comfortable rooms – lavish and yet understated with all facilities. ⑨.

Eating

Some of the best eating to be had is in the luxury hotels, but at a price. Agra's speciality, Mughlai cuisine, imitated in Indian restaurants throughout the world, is known for its rich cream and curd-based sauces, kebabs, *naan* and tandoori breads roasted in earthen ovens, rice dishes and milky sweets such as *kheer*. A constant flow of tourists ensures that Agra has a wide choice to suit most budgets.

Sadar Bazaar

Ching Wah, Gopi Chand Shivare Rd (opposite *Zorba* – see below), Sadar Bazaar. Popular Chinese garden restaurant with thatched huts and a varied menu of reasonable Chinese food.

Dasaprakash, Meher Theatre Complex, 1 Gwalior Rd. Close to the *Hotel Agra Ashok*, large and bright with mid-priced south Indian food and an extensive ice-cream menu.

Garden Restaurant, Sadar Bazaar. Next to the *Lakshmi Villas*, with a range of food – the "garden" is a small forecourt.

Gaylords, Sadar Bazaar. Chinese and Indian food similar and close to *Kwality*.

Hot Bite, 7 Shopping Arcade, Sadar Bazaar. Smart and new place opposite *Kwality* with Indian, Chinese and international dishes, including a selection of pizzas and burgers.

Kwality, Sadar Bazaar. Renovated branch of the large chain, with predictable, mid-priced food.

Lakshmi Villas, Sadar Bazaar. Traditional south Indian cafe with an established reputation.

Prakash, 49 Taj Rd, Sadar Bazaar. A dimly lit restaurant serving south Indian dishes, Bengali cuisine, good *thalis* and non-veg alternatives.

Priya, 4/17A Baluganj. Near the *Tourist Rest House*; multi-cuisine, strongest on south Indian food.

Savitri, Gopi Chand Shivare Rd, Sadar Bazaar. Indian cuisine; speciality kebabs and chicken tikka.

Sonam, 51 Taj Rd. Mid-price garden restaurant and bar, one of the few in Agra to accept credit cards. The menu has Chinese and international dishes, buffets in winter, and a budget section featuring *thalis*, but is strongest on Indian cooking, attempting to recreate medieval Mughlai cuisine.

Zorba the Buddha, E-13 Shopping Arcade, Gopi Chand Shivare Rd, Sadar Bazaar. A quiet, no-smoking vegetarian restaurant whose staff are clearly enthused; delicious Indian and western food and perfect roux sauces – not the cheapest, but worth at least one visit. Open noon–3pm & 6–9pm.

Taj Ganj

Gulshan Lodge, South Gate. Roadside seating, bargain breakfasts and reasonable snack food, including crepes.

ITDC Cafeteria and Restaurant, Western Gate. Large government-sponsored restaurant and cafe serving Indian and international food, which can prove to be a bit expensive.

MOVING ON FROM AGRA

The two main daily **flights** from Agra are north to **Delhi** (5.45pm; 40min), and east to **Khajuraho** and on to **Varanasi** (9.25am); bookings can be made at the *Indian Airlines* office (☎360153) in the *Clarks Shiraz*, which also holds offices of *Jet Air* & *Lufthansa*.

If you're leaving Agra by **train**, book well in advance at Agra Cantt Station. A daily train leaves for **Calcutta** (30hr) via Patna, and the daily *Punjab Mail* #1038 passes through on its way from Delhi to **Bombay** via Gwalior, Jhansi and Bhopal. The fastest, and most expensive, train to **Delhi** is the fully a/c *Shatbadi Express* #2001 (8.18pm; 2hr). A convenient morning service to Delhi is the *A.P. Express* #2723 (5.40am; 3hr); the fastest midday train is the *Kerala–Mangala Express* #2625 (12.10pm; 3hr). You can also pick up trains to **Madras** (1–2 daily; 34–42hr) and **Thiruvananthapuram** (1–2 daily; 50hr 30min– 52hr 40min) from Agra Cantt.

Trains to **Rajasthan** depart from Agra Fort station – the starting point for services to Jaipur (*Agra Fort–Jaipur Express* #2921; 5pm; 5hr) and Jodhpur (22hr 45min) – as do trains destined for **Kathgodam**, the nearest railhead to **Nainital** hill station in northern Uttar Pradesh. Take the daily *Kumaon Express* #5311 (10pm; 12hr 10min).

Onward journeys by **bus** are best made on deluxe vehicles and *Rajasthan Roadways* buses that leave from **Idgah bus stand** in the southwest of town. Seats on *Rajasthan Roadways* buses should be booked at the bus stand: for any destinations further afield than Jaipur, take a bus to **Jaipur** (every 15min 6am–2pm, then every 2hr; via Bharatpur) and pick up a connecting service. Deluxe buses leave from the forecourt of *Shital Lodge* next to the bus stand. There's a booking office in the lodge for fast and direct coaches to **Delhi** (hourly; 5–6hr; via Mathura) and **Gwalior** (5 daily; 3hr 30min), and early morning departures for **Khajuraho** (12hr), **Lucknow** (9hr 30min) and **Nainital** (10hr). Additional buses to the same destinations leave from the tourist office on Taj Rd: book a day in advance at the office.

Agra Fort bus stand, chaotic, dusty and potholed, has extremely frequent services (several each hour) on rickety, often windowless, buses heading for Delhi, Mathura, Gwalior, Jhansi, Kanpur and as far afield as Indore. Here it's a case of locating the bus you want, jumping on, finding a seat, and then buying a ticket.

Unless you fly, getting to **Khajuraho** involves a 12hr bus journey (daily; 5am), or a train to Jhansi (2hr 45min–3hr 50min), and then a 4hr bus ride.

Joney's Place, South Gate. A tiny restaurant with a minute kitchen dishing up some unusually good vegetarian food, including spaghetti, aubergine bake and delicious *hummus*.

Pink, East Gate. Hearty Indian dishes and a few alternatives such as chips; good value.

Saeed's Place, South Gate. A simple but cosy restaurant specializing in Israeli food – and Israeli music. The menu includes falafel, *hummus*, pitta (and great chips).

Listings

Foreigner's Registration Office 16 Idgah Colony (☎72631).

Golf *Agra Club*, 191 The Mall (☎74084): apply directly to the Secretary or the Marker. Some of the exclusive hotels such as *Taj View* also keep clubs and arrange temporary membership for guests.

Hospitals *Lady Lyall Hospital*, Noori Gate Rd (☎74184); *S N Hospital*, Hospital Rd (☎72222).

Music and Dance *The Gallery*, Fatehbad Rd (☎365714), has daily folk and classical dance recitals at 7pm; tickets cost around Rs100. The *Akbar International*, off Fatehbad Rd (☎360749), hosts *mehfils* (private concerts), when there is enough demand. UP Tourism organizes an annual arts and crafts fair each February, the Taj Mahotsava, with cultural performances including dance and music.

Photographic Supplies *Agra Color Lab*, E6–7 Shopping Arcade, Sadar Bazaar (☎363221), and 34/2 Sanjay Place, opposite Soor Sadan, offers one-hour processing.

Swimming Agra's exclusive hotels sometimes let non-residents swim in their pools, for daily fees of up to Rs200. Try *Clarks Shiraz*; *Lauries*; *Mayur*; *Sakura*; or the *Taj View* on Fatehbad Rd.

Fatehpur Sikri

The ghost city of **FATEHPUR SIKRI** straddles the crest of a rocky ridge 37km southwest of Agra. Built between 1569 and 1585 by the great Moghul emperor Akbar, it has lain silent for almost four centuries; by 1600, its meagre water supply had proved incapable of sustaining the population. Now deserted, it is almost perfectly preserved – a masterpiece in sandstone, glowing in subtly changing shades of pink and red as the day progresses and the light fades. The very embodiment of Akbar's unorthodox court, the city fuses Hindu and Muslim artistic traditions; Hindu buildings such as **Birbal's Palace** and **Jodhbai's Palace** mingle with the pavilions and halls of the grand court, while the **Jami Masjid**, the only building of exclusively Muslim derivation, houses one of the most exquisite mausoleums of the Moghul period, the marble **Tomb of Sheikh Salim Chishti**.

Fatehpur Sikri was originally intended to be joint capital with Agra; although it receives only a fraction of the visitors of its rival, the stunning elegance of its palace and courts ensure that it remains as powerful a testimony to Moghul grandeur.

The Royal Palace

Sprawling along the crest of the hill for around 1km, the main **Royal Palace** and court complex (daily dawn–dusk; Rs0.50, free on Fri), unused and uninhabited since its abandonment but still more or less intact, is best entered via the **Shahi Darwaza**. As there are no signs within the compound, you may prefer to hire an official guide at the booking office, for around Rs10–15.

Inside the magnificent complex, whose layout was inspired by that of a Moghul camp, you wander into a world resonant with echoes of the forgotten palace. The spacious courtyard of the **Diwan-i-Am** (Hall of Public Audience) lies at its heart, surrounded by colonnades, with the emperor's platform at the western end. Adjacent to the Diwan-i-Am, west of the main imperial residence, the **Daulat Khana** (Abode of Fortune), comprises a series of buildings distinguished by exquisite stone screens, elaborate brackets, broad eaves, and columns mounted on carved bell-shaped pedestals. Behind the library, Akbar's beautiful sleeping chamber, the **Khwabgah** (House of Dreams), is decorated with faded inscriptions of Persian verse. Separating the Daulat Khana from buildings to the north is the **Pachisi Court**, a giant stone board for the game known as *pachisi* or *chawpai*, similar to ludo; Akbar is said to have indulged in the odd game, using slave girls dressed in colourful costumes as live pieces.

At the centre of the otherwise unremarkable **Diwan-i-Khas**, the Hall of Private Audience, an extraordinary carved column, the **Throne Pillar**, supports a large circular platform from which four balustraded bridges radiate outwards. From the central throne platform, the emperor would debate with representatives of diverse religions seated at the four corners, before an audience congregated on the floor below. Access to the pillar and balconies is via steps on the exterior of the building. Close by lies the three-roomed **Treasury**, its brackets embellished by mythical sea creatures, guardians of the treasures of the deep; it was apparently used to play the game of **Ankh Michauli** (Hide and Seek), the origin of the building's other name. Next to it is the Astrologer's Seat, a small pavilion with elaborate Jain carvings.

To the northeast of the Diwan-i-Khas, the **Anup Talao Pavilion,** also known as the **Turkish Sultana's House**, is thought to have been the palace of one of Akbar's favourite wives, the Sultana Ruqayya Begum. With balconies and Kashmiri-style wood-carvings, this exquisite building betrays Persian, Turkish and even Chinese influences, and may have been a *hammam* (bath) or pleasure pavilion. Legend has it that the great musician **Mian Tansen** once sang *Deepak*, the *rag* of fire, on its central dais. So effective was his performance that he grew hotter and hotter, until his daughter had to come to the rescue by performing the rain *rag*, *Malhar*. Understandably nervous at this onerous responsibility, she faltered on the seventh note of the scale, thereby creating one of the most famous and stirring *ragas* of north India – *Mian ki Malhar*. Happily, the *rag* had the desired effect; rain fell, and Tansen was saved. The southern aspect overlooks the Anup Talao or "Peerless Pool" where, on a central dais surrounded by perfumed water, Akbar is believed to have taken repose.

One of Fatehpur Sikri's most famous structures, the **Panch Mahal** or Five-Storeyed Palace, looms northwest of Anup Talao. The palace tapers to a final single kiosk and is supported by 176 columns of varying designs; the ground floor contains 84 pillars – an auspicious number in Hindu astrology. At one time, the Panch Mahal also had stone lattice screens, which would have been augmented by layers of dampened *khas*, a scented grass still harvested and used to cool verandahs throughout northern India.

The Women's Quarters

Next to the Daulat Khana, a courtyard garden reserved for the *zenana*, the ladies of the harem, signals the start of the women's area of the palace complex. The adjoining **Sunahra Makan** (Golden House) is variously thought to have been the home of the emperor's mother or the palace of one of Akbar's wives – hence its alternative names of the **Palace of the Christian Queen** and **Mariam's House** – although no record exists of Akbar's marriage to a Christian called Mariam. Once adorned with gilded murals, the only ornamentation that survives are some inscriptions of verse penned by Fazl, Akbar's court poet.

Solemnly presiding over the whole complex, the main harem, known as **Jodhbai's Palace**, blends elements of traditional Islamic architecture with influences from Gujarat and Gwalior, incorporating an elegant tulip motif characteristic of Fatehpur Sikri. The **Hawa Mahal** (Palace of the Winds), a small screened tower with a delicately carved chamber, was designed to catch the evening breeze, while a covered walkway gave the imperial ladies of the court access to the lake, now dry, to the north.

The third women's palace, part of the **Haram Sara** (Imperial Harem) is called **Birbal's Palace** – a misnomer, as Birbal, Akbar's favourite courtier, was a man and would have been most unwelcome in this area. It may in fact have been the residence of two of Akbar's senior wives. The palace's profuse carvings include a ceiling crafted to resemble a canopy of blossoms.

Jami Masjid

At the southwestern corner of the palace complex, with the village of Fatehpur Sikri nestling at its base, stands **Jami Masjid**, also known as Dargah Mosque. The alignment of the entire palace complex was determined by the orientation of the mosque's *mihrab* (prayer niche) towards Mecca. Housing the tomb of Sheikh Salim, the mosque is unusual in that it is also a living Sufi shrine.

The main approach is through the imposing **Buland Darwaza** (Great Gate), though you may choose to use the Shahi Darwaza once again to escape the attentions of touts and hawkers. Built around 1576, possibly to commemorate Akbar's brilliant campaign in Gujarat, the spectacular gate reaches a height of 54m and is scaled by an impressive flight of steps. Flanked by domed kiosks, the archway of the simple sandstone memorial is inscribed with a message from the Koran:

> Said Jesus Son of Mary (peace be on him): The world is but a bridge – pass over without building houses on it. He who hopes for an hour hopes for eternity; the world is an hour – spend it in prayer for the rest is unseen.

Before entering the mosque itself, visitors are required to remove their shoes, but cloth sandals can be borrowed for a small fee. The gate leads into a vast cloistered courtyard containing the **Zenana Rauza** (Tomb of the Royal Ladies), and the lattice-screen **Tomb of Islam Khan**, one of many nobles buried here. The focus of the Sufi shrine or *dargah* is the relatively small but exquisite **Tomb of Sheikh Salim Chishti**, much of which was originally crafted in red sandstone and only later faced in marble: the lattice screens are among the most intricate and beautiful in the world, with striking serpentine brackets supporting the eaves.

Sheikh Salim played a crucial role in the founding of Fatehpur Sikri: the site of the city was primarily determined by its connections with the saint, who had prophesied the birth of a son to the emperor. When one of Akbar's wives, Rani Jodh Bai, a Hindu Rajput princess from Amber, became pregnant she was sent here until the birth of her son Salim, who later became the emperor Jahangir. Fatehpur Sikri was constructed in the saint's honour and, some historians believe, abandoned when Akbar's faith changed. The *dargah* still attracts women who come here to pray for offspring, tying string onto the marble screen; when entering the main chamber, visitors cover their heads with cloth as a mark of respect. During Ramadan, an *urs* is held here, attracting *qawwals* (singers of Sufi songs; see p.93) from all over the country.

Practicalities

Buses to and from Agra run every half-hour from about 5.45am until 6.30pm, and take between forty minutes and one hour. Regular buses also leave for Bharatpur (30min).

Though well worth a day or two, Fatehpur Sikri has a limited choice of places to **stay**. About 1.5km from the Buland Darwaza, the *Gulistan Tourist Complex*, Agra Rd (☎05619/251; ④–⑥), is a comfortable if slightly impersonal state-run complex, with food at reasonable prices, and beer available. The small and homely *Maurya Rest House*, Buland Darwaza (☎05619/2348; ②–③), has an open leafy courtyard serving reasonable snacks, while *Shree Tourist Guest House & Restaurant*, Main Market, Dargah Gali (near the bus stand) (☎05619/2276; ①–②) is a no-frills lodge and cafe. *Dak Bungalow* (①), booked through the Archaeological Survey at 22 Mall Rd in Agra, is extremely good value and quite comfortable. Abdul Ghani Arif at the *Kallu Hotel*, next to the car park below the Buland Darwaza, is known for excellent Mughlai **cooking**, especially his *paratha*.

Braj: Mathura and Vrindavan

Although the holy land of **BRAJ** can be precisely located on the map – centred around the city of **Mathura**, it lies in the southwestern corner of the Gangetic valley, extending 75km north to south and 50km east to west, with its northern boundary roughly 80km south of Delhi – its prime significance is on a metaphysical plane, as the mythological backdrop to the idyllic childhood of **Krishna**.

Early texts only specifically mention Mathura itself – Krishna's birthplace – the forest tract of **Vrindavan**, the hill of **Govardhan**, and the **River Yamuna**. However, in the sixteenth century, Bhakti saints such as Chaitanya and Vallabha, "rediscovered" the area and identified it with "Braj", Krishna's legendary pastoral playground. By then Vrindavan had already been decimated by deforestation, but they gave the myths a new spatial reality by mapping out the sites of Krishna's youthful adventures, pinpointing twelve smaller "forests", various woods, and assorted lakes and ponds. The fact that Braj lay between Delhi and Agra, and thus had borne the brunt of the Muslim conquests, provided a historical explanation for the previous "loss" of these sacred sites.

Braj became, and remains, one of the most important pilgrimage centres for devotees of Krishna, who tour the twelve forests – now reduced to groves on the outskirts of towns and villages – on foot. This great circular pilgrimage, known as the **Ban Yatra** or "Forest Pilgrimage", or the **Chaurosi Kos Parikrama** (which refers to the circumambulatory distance of 84 *kos*, equivalent to 224km), can take several weeks. Less energetic or devout visitors may well prefer to explore the major sites by bus.

BRAJ:
MATHURA & VRINDAVAN

△ Delhi

N

0   10 km

Kosi

Shergarh

Chata

Nandagaon

Barsana

Mat

Vrindavan

Belban

Radhakulp

Yamuna River

Raya

△ Hathras

Govardhan

Jetipura

Mathura

Mahaban

Gokul

Baldevi

Sonkh

Kumher

▽ Bharatpur   ▽ Agra

Mathura

The city of **MATHURA**, 141km south of Delhi and 58km north of Agra, is celebrated above all as the place where Krishna was born, on the banks of the River Yamuna that features so prominently in tales of his boyhood. Hindu mythology claims that it was founded by Satrugna, the youngest brother of another incarnation of Vishnu, Rama – the king of Ayodhya, and hero of the *Ramayana*. However, Mathura's earliest historical records date back around 2500 years, before the conquests of Alexander. Buddha himself founded monasteries here, in what was known to later Greeks as *Madoura ton Theon* ("Mathura of the Gods"). The city reached an early peak under the Indo-Bactrian Kushan people, whose greatest ruler Kanishka came to power in 78 AD. Fa Hian, the Chinese pilgrim, reported that in 400 AD it held twenty Buddhist monasteries, with about three thousand resident monks.

The enduring prosperity and sophistication of Mathura, which lay on a busy trade route, attracted such adventurers as the Afghan Mahmud of Ghazni in 1017, whose plundering and destruction signalled the death knell of Buddhism. Sikander Lodi from Delhi wrought further havoc in 1500, as did Aurangzeb. Mathura has grown in recent years into a multi-faceted urban sprawl, incorporating the teeming **old city** with its many Krishna-associated sites, a vast British military cantonment to the south, known as the **Civil Lines**, and haphazard industrial development on the outskirts.

Arrival and information

The city's principal railway station, **Mathura Junction**, lies southwest of the centre, around 4km from Holi Gate and the old city. It's on the main Delhi–Agra line, 2hr 30min from Delhi on the fast *Taj Express* #2179 and only half an hour short of Agra, and also served by Delhi–Bombay trains, so services such as the *Bombay Express* #9020 and *Paschim Express* #2926 make it easy to get to Sawai Madhopur (if you're heading for the wildlife park of Ranthambore; see p153) and Kota.

Mathura has two bus stands; the **Old Bus Stand**, near Holi Gate, has hourly connections to Agra and serves **Govardhan**, 25km west, while the **New Bus Stand**, a little way west is used by Delhi and Jaipur buses as well as more Agra services.

Cycle and auto-rickshaws are always on hand for local journeys, and shared tempos and horse-drawn tongas are also available. The **tourist information** office (Mon–Sat 9.30am–5pm) at the Old Bus Stand organizes occasional **city tours**, and **foreign exchange** is handled by the *State Bank of India*, Railway Station Rd (☎405814).

The Town

The ornate sandstone **Holi Gate** at the entrance to the old city is Mathura's major landmark, now plastered with political and other posters as well as years of dust and grime. To the east, the riverfront is minute compared to Varanasi, the bathing *ghats* are much smaller, and the streets are not as interesting. Along the river towards the north lie the remains of **Kans Qila**, a fort built by Raja Man Singh of Amber and rebuilt by Akbar – little is left apart from the foundations, and no traces survive of the astronomical observatory constructed by Jai Singh (as seen in Jaipur, Delhi, and Varanasi).

To the south, the brightly coloured **Vishram Ghat** is the "*ghat* of rest" where Krishna is said to have recuperated after killing the evil Kamsa. Several shrines around its marble-paved courtyard include one in the corner to Krishna Balava, and another to the river goddess Yamuna in a small annexe. **Boats** for river excursions can be rented at the *ghat*. Just south, on the riverbank, the square red sandstone tower of **Sati Burj** is alleged to have been built in 1574 to commemorate the *sati* (self-immolation) of the wife of the Raja of Amber on her husband's funeral pyre. This unremarkable seventeen-metre-high edifice has been the subject of some abysmal repair work.

Heading through the network of narrow streets that radiates from Vishram Ghat brings you (by way of several bangle shops) to Radha Dhiraj Bazaar, and the large and ostentatious turn-of-the-century **Dwarkadhish** temple, approached by steep steps off the busy main road. The **Jami Masjid**, on a plinth raised above street level a little way north, was completed in 1661 by Aurangzeb's governor Abd-un-Nabi. It has long since lost its original vivid glazed tiles, but remains surrounded by four minarets and assorted outer pavilions. Around 500m west, stands another of Aurangzeb's mosques, the impressive red sandstone **Katra Masjid**. This was erected on the foundations of the once-famous Kesava Deo temple, destroyed by the Moghul emperor, which had itself been built on the ruins of a Buddhist monastery. Some traces of the Hindu temple can be seen around the back, where the **Shri Krishna Janamsthan** or Janambhoomi

The telephone **area code** for Mathura is ☎0565.

KRISHNA – THE MYTH

One of the most popular gods of the Hindu pantheon, appearing in numerous forms in a vast body of mythological literature, **Krishna** was probably originally a tribal chieftain who was later deified and came to be recognized as an *avatar* or incarnation of Vishnu. Although he is represented as a warrior hero in the *Mahabharata*, even that incorporates the Song of the Lord – the *Bhagavad Gita* – of which the Lord is Krishna. In the *Bhagavad Gita* he is seen initially as a profound seer, living in Dwarka, who teaches Arjuna about Ultimate Reality; however, Krishna later reveals himself to be not simply an incarnation of Vishnu, but the Supreme Lord of the Universe, and first propounds the **Bhakti** religion of selfless loving devotion to the Supreme Lord.

Legend tells how, over three thousand years ago, the throne of Mathura was usurped by Krishna's uncle, the tyrannical **Kamsa**. When Kamsa came upon a prophecy that he would meet his end at the hands of the son of his sister Devaki, he incarcerated Devaki and her husband Vasudev and set out to slaughter every newborn baby. However, under the cover of a stormy night, Vasudev managed to smuggle the infant Krishna across the River Yamuna.

Krishna grew up as an enchanting but mischievous boy in the nomadic encampment of the cowherders (*gopa*) of **Braj**, which as **Gokul** provided the setting of the childhood pranks during which he first revealed his divinity. Later, the nomads moved on to the mythical forest of **Vrindavan**, where he further demonstrated his omnipotence by defeating demons sent by the wicked Kamsa. Eventually, Kamsa found out about the remarkable boy, and realizing his identity invited him to match his skills at a tournament. Krishna won easily, killed Kamsa, and took his body to the banks of the Yamuna for cremation.

The image of the irresistibly charming adolescent Krishna, cavorting with the milk-maids (*gopi*) amid a verdant pastoral landscape, recurs throughout Hindu iconography and popular performing arts. It traditionally culminates in an autumnal moonlit tryst in the sacred basil groves, with Krishna captivating the *gopi* with his magical flute. Allegories of the human soul yearning for a selfless union with the Divine Lord, the *gopis* perform the **Maharasalila**, the Great Circular Dance. The divine Krishna multiplies himself so that each milkmaid, who has abandoned her husband to be with the Lord, imagines him to be dancing with herself alone.

complex now stands. Directly behind the mosque, approached through a corridor, a shrine marks Krishna's exact birthplace (*janamsthan*); its cage-like surround signifies that he was born in captivity, when his parents were prisoners of the tyrant king Kamsa. Inside the adjacent **Bhagwat Bhavan** – a modern, towering, flamboyant great hulk also known as **Gita Mandir** – a garishly painted ceiling depicts scenes from Krishna's life. No cameras are allowed into the complex, where although the shops and shrines combine to produce a park-like atmosphere, nothing obscures the heavy para-military presence – a reminder of underlying Hindu-Muslim tensions. Nearby, the impressive stepped sandstone tank of **Potara Kund** is believed to have been used to wash Krishna's baby clothes.

Close to the centre of Mathura in Dampier Park, the **archeological museum** (Tues–Sat 10.30am–4.30pm; free), places a particular emphasis on Buddhist and Jain sculpture, dating from the Kushan (first–third centuries AD) and Gupta periods (fourth–sixth centuries). Known collectively as the **Mathura school**, the sculpture, characterized by its spotted red sandstone, reflects in its fusion of styles the fluctuating history of the region. Building on the skill of earlier craftsmen, sculptors assimilated primitive cults within the Jain, Buddhist and Hindu pantheons. The museum's highlight, one of the finest examples of Gupta art, is a miraculously intact standing Buddha. Shown with a beautiful benign expression, an ornate halo, and delicate fluted robes, he is making the Abhaya *mudra* ("fearless") hand gesture. Both this and a seated Buddha, also in red sandstone and this time depicted as the Enlightened One, are thought to have been created by the monk Dinna around 434 AD. Kushana art on display includes a headless image of King Kanishka in a foreign-styled tunic and boots, and some exquisite railings carved with floral motifs and human figures, while contemporaneous pieces of Gandhara sculpture, originally from northwest Pakistan but discovered locally, prove early contact between the two centres of civilization. A well-presented **terracotta** gallery is built around the work of the German Archaeological Mission, which has been digging at **Sonkh**, 35km west of Mathura, since 1966.

Accommodation

Despite being not only an important pilgrimage centre but also a large industrial and military town, Mathura offers a very limited choice of **accommodation**, and none of its mid-range or luxury hotels is especially worthy of recommendation.

Agra, Bengali Ghat (☎403318). Small place, overlooking the river in the old city and redolent of the atmosphere of the *ghats*. Bengali food on request, and a wide choice of rooms. Recommended. ②–④.

Brijraj, opposite Shri Krishna Janamsthan (no phone). Reasonable budget accommodation, with some affordable a/c rooms, and a good cafe downstairs. ①–③.

International Guest House, Shri Krishna Janamsthan (☎405888). Large institution-like building beside the temple. Very affordable and clean, with a good *bhojanalaya*, or vegetarian cafe. ①.

Kwality, near Old Bus Stand (☎406195). Claims to be the oldest hotel in the city – and may well be, considering its dire need of refurbishment. The restaurant is good, however. ②–③.

Madhuvan (☎404064). Probably the best hotel Mathura has to offer, thanks only to the lack of competition. Plenty of facilities, including a swimming pool open to non-residents. ⑤–⑥.

Modern, Agra Rd (☎404747). Close to the town centre, opposite the New Bus Stand. Has a popular dimly-lit bar but is otherwise quite ordinary. ②.

Nepal, Delhi Rd (☎404308). A dull exterior and unflattering location hides some quite pleasant budget accommodation, with ordinary and air-cooled rooms set around a courtyard. ①–③.

Sanjay Palace, Sanjay Market, Arya Samaj Rd (☎407867). Run-of-the-mill accommodation above shops within a commercial precinct, near Holi Gate not far from the river. Some a/c rooms. ②–④.

Shri Yamuna Palace Guest House, Radha Dhiraj Bazaar (no phone). Dilapidated former property of the Maharajah of Bharatpur, near Vishram Ghat, set around a courtyard entered through magnificent old carved wooden gates. A couple of atmospheric roof-top rooms overlook the river. ①.

Eating

Due to the city's spiritual significance for Vaishnavas, restaurants and cafes in Mathura tend to serve **vegetarian** food only. As a result, many tourists restrict themselves to eating in their hotels, with perhaps the occasional foray into the numerous sweetshops.

Anupam, *Hotel Nepal*, Delhi Rd. Reasonable and standard Indian food, generally quite plain.

Brijraj, Shri Krishna Janamsthan. Hotel and cafe which serves *dosas* and snacks.

Brijwasi Mithai Wala, Shri Krishna Janamsthan. Appealing sweetshop opposite *International Guest House*.

Deepak, next to *Hotel Nepal*, Delhi Rd. One of Mathura's best restaurants, providing both south and north Indian food, from *dosas* to whole meals, at reasonable prices.

Kwality, near Old Bus Stand. Clean and comfortable place, serving good vegetarian food. Formerly part of the famous chain, and retaining much of its typical look and feel.

Around Mathura

At the very heart of Braj, Mathura is the obvious base for peregrinations in the pastoral landscape associated with the adolescent Krishna, where the sacred temple-crowned hills of **Govardhan**, **Barsana** and **Nandagaon** stand in striking contrast to the prevailing flatness. Very little survives of its idyllic legendary forests, and only serious pilgrims would choose to walk rather than catch local buses.

Mahaban and Gokul

Across the Yamuna from Mathura, 10km southeast of the city and reachable by boat or bus, **Mahaban** and **Gokul** are associated with Krishna's foster parents, Nanda and Yashoda. **MAHABAN**, "the Great Forest", was sacked by Mahmud of Ghazni at the beginning of the eleventh century, and a fort built in the fourteenth century was also soon occupied by the Muslims. Of temples here, the most interesting is **Nanda's Palace**, also known as **Assi Khamba** or "Eighty Pillars", an amalgam of several influences including Buddhist. Rebuilt as a mosque under Aurangzeb, the temple's pillars resemble the Qutb Minar in Delhi, and probably date back to the tenth century.

On a high bank overlooking the river 2km from Mahaban, **GOKUL**, the cowherd encampment to which the newborn Krishna was smuggled, is the headquarters of the followers of the sixteenth-century saint Vallabha. This is where Krishna first revealed his divinity to his foster mother Yashoda – she made him open his mouth after catching him eating earth, only to peer in and see the entire universe. All of Gokul's sixteenth- and seventeenth-century temples are in a very bad state of repair.

Govardhan

GOVARDHAN, 25km west of Mathura, is significant as the hill that Krishna is said to have lifted on the tip of one finger, to shelter the inhabitants of Braj from a deluge caused by the wrath of the god Indra. A popular Vaishnavite icon, the entire hill is circumambulated by thousands of pilgrims each year.

The eponymous town is clustered close to a masonry tank known as Mansi Ganga, in a gap towards the hill's northern end. Two impressive cenotaphs immediately opposite the tank commemorate Randhir Singh and Baladeva Singh, two of the Bharatpur rajas, while the temple of Hari Deva, founded during the reign of Akbar, lies nearby. At the northern extremity of the hill, the twin tanks of **Radhakund**, "rediscovered" by Chaitanya, are said to have been manifested for Krishna's expiatory ablutions after he had killed the demon bull, Arishta; on the hill's southern crest, above the village of Jatipura, the ruined temple of **Sri Nath** was founded by Vallabha in 1520.

Barsana and Nandagaon

The hill sites of Barsana and Nandagaon, 25km and 32km north of Govardhan respectively, were originally dedicated to Brahma and Shiva before being appropriated into the Krishna myth.

An impressive stone staircase leads from the town at the base of the hill at **BARSANA** to an extensive ridge, where temples include that of **Lali Ji**, a local name for Krishna's mistress, Radha. Priya Kund, on the outskirts of the town, is a sacred bathing tank. Similarly, the eighteenth-century temple of **Nand Rae** dominates the smaller hill and town of **NANDAGAON**, identified as the village of Krishna's foster father Nanda; it too can be reached by stairs, which also provide access to the sacred lake of Pan Sarovar nearby. A curious local ritual takes place each year during the spring festival of Holi. First the menfolk of Nandagaon invade Barsana, to taunt the women with lewd songs and be beaten with long wooden staffs for their pains; then on the next day the procedure is reversed, and the men of Barsana pay courting calls to the women of Nandagaon.

Vrindavan

The dusty little town of **VRINDAVAN**, on the banks of the Yamuna 11km north of Mathura, is among the most important pilgrimage sites in Braj, attracting an estimated 500,000 pilgrims each year. In practice, most of these come during the spring Holi festival, which in Braj is extended for up to a month, and during the two months of celebrations for the birthdays of Krishna and his mythical mistress, Radha, in the autumn.

Although Vrindavan is in theory a *tirtha* or holy crossing place on the Yamuna, in fact it has been progressively abandoned by the river, as it meanders away from the original two-kilometre-long waterfront, and all but five of its 38 *ghats* are now without water. Neither is there much trace of the forests of the Krishna legend, and only a few sacred basil groves remain at the spot where he cavorted with the *gopis*. Nevertheless, as a *tirtha*, the town attracts elderly Vaishnavas who believe that to die here earns instant *moksha* or liberation. Along with its many *dharamshalas*, Vrindavan holds several "widow houses", maintained by wealthy devotees, which provide food and shelter for the poor women who find solace in daily devotion to Krishna. Two thousand of them congregate in the **Mirabai Ashram** twice a day to sing *bhajans*, devotional songs.

If not exactly boasting the thousand temples of popular exaggeration, the town does hold numerous shrines, many of them now neglected and crumbling. Close to the centre, on the main Mathura–Vrindavan road, **Govinda Deva** is one of northern India's most impressive medieval Hindu edifices. Erected by Raja Man Singh in 1590, its main tower is said to have been seven storeys high; the three storeys that survived the depredations of Aurangzeb leave it with a squat and truncated look. An impressive *mandapa* (front hall), with open balconies on two floors, sports elaborate columns, brackets and overhanging eaves. Adopting traditions from mosque architecture, Govinda Deva's sharply cut mouldings and sculptured detail avoid depicting any human form, utilizing true arches and a domed interior (now housing a flock of bats).

At the western end of town, the temple of **Madan Mohan** overlooks the river from the small hill of Dwadashaditya Tila. Next to its octagonal *shikhara* (spire), adorned with square motifs, stands a smaller and much more recent, egg-shaped *shikhara*. Close to **Keshi Ghat** at the northern end of Vrindavan, the temple of **Jugal Kishor** is distinguished by a large *shikhara* capped with an *amalaka* – a flat cylindrical crown – and an entrance arch which has an image of Krishna holding up the hill of Govardhan.

Although of much later design, and rebuilt in the nineteenth century, **Banke Bihari**, off Purana Bazaar, is Vrindavan's most popular temple, renowned for impressive floral decorations of the deity. Banke Bihari's image was supposed to have been worshipped by the musician saint, Swami Hari Das, who as a musician was Tansen's guru, and who was visited by the emperor Akbar. Close by, the temple of **Radhavallabha**, founded by the followers of the medieval poet saint Hit Hari Vans, is hidden behind a nondescript exterior and entered via an impressive archway.

The small **Radha Damodar** temple, off Loi Bazaar, houses the tombs of Jiva, Rupa and Sanatan, followers of Chaitanya who were sent to establish Vrindavan as the spiritual centre for devotees of Krishna at the end of the sixteenth century. Approached via Loi Bazaar, **Nidhi Ban**, a walled garden associated with Swami Hari Das, is in reality a dust bowl, notorious for marauding monkeys, holding a few basil (*tulsi*) plants.

Opposite Govinda Deva, across the main road, lies the lavish new south-Indian-style temple of **Shri Ranganatha**, also known as **Rangaji Temple**, where ostentatious displays include the numerous gold-plated embellishments that crown its lofty *shikhara*, and the gold-plated **Dhwaja Stambha** column in the inner courtyard (no admittance to non-Hindus). An electronic puppet show enlivens the entrance gate, and a small museum inside houses processional images and chariots (Rs0.50). Also within the large courtyard, a subsidiary image of **Tirupathi Balaji** is bathed in milk every Friday. The ceremonial **Gajendra Muksh Kund** tank, adjacent to the temple, holds an image of an elephant and crocodile fighting; bathing is forbidden.

ISKCON, the International Society of Krishna Consciousness, has been building a lavish new temple complex around 2km west of Vrindavan, which will incorporate a marble mausoleum in honour of the society's founder, Swami Prabhupada. He passed away in 1977, and his private chambers have been made into a museum. ISKCON runs courses all year round, ranging from meditation to Ayurvedic medicine (☎82478).

Practicalities

Getting to Vrindavan from Mathura is straightforward; two local **trains** leave Mathura Junction each day (at 9am and 8pm) for the station in the south of Vrindavan (and return at 9.30am and 8.30pm), as do frequent **buses,** shared **tempos,** and **taxis**.

Besides the numerous *dharamshalas*, several **ashrams** offer reasonable accommodation at fixed rates, as well as food. The clean new *Krishna Sadhak Seva Ashram* on Gurukul Rd (①–②), which even has some comfortable suites; *Mor Bhavan*, in Ahir Para near Banke Bihari (①–②), and the nearby *Jaipuriya Bhavan* (①–②); and the *Yatrika*, Rangjika Bagicha (①–②), all represent good value. ISKCON's *Guest House* (①–②), west of town, offers rooms on a suggested donation system which works out a real bargain, and their vegetarian restaurant serves some of the best food in the region.

THE UP HILLS

Within easy access of Delhi, the **UP Hills** – also known as **Uttaranchal** – consist of the two regions of **GARHWAL** in the west and **KUMAUN** in the east. Both are progressively opening up to visitors, with the slow demilitarization of the Tibetan border regions to the north. Although not as high as the giants of Nepal, further east, or the Karakoram, the snow peaks here rank among the most beautiful mountains of the inner Himalayas, forming an almost continuous chain that culminates in Nanda Devi, at 7816m the highest complete mountain in India. Perhaps the single most enticing spot is **Gangotri Glacier** in north-central Garhwal – just a day's walk from the road, and revered as the source of the Ganges.

Rising from the steamy sub-Himalayan plains (*terai*) towards the permanent snows of Tibet, both Garhwal and Kumaun have preserved their own distinct languages and cultures. Successive deep river valleys shelter fascinating micro-civilizations, where Hinduism meets animism and the Buddhist influence is never too far away. The high alpine meadows known as **bugyals** – the summer pastures, where rivers are born and paths meet – play an important role in the life of the mountain communities. Local pilgrimages and shrines honour their spirits, and classic treks such as the Kuari Pass trail cross them through the heart of the mountains.

Every year the monsoons play havoc with the roads, causing giant landslides and avalanches. In 1992 the huge **Uttarkashi earthquake** devastated central Garhwal, and scientists predict another by the end of the century. Nonetheless, the government are going ahead with a plan to dam the River Bhagirathi at Tehri, with potentially disastrous consequences way beyond the evacuation of the fertile and well-populated valley.

A brief history of the mountains

The first known inhabitants of the Uttaranchal were the **Kuninda** in the second century BC, who seem to have had a close affinity with contemporary Indo-Greek civilization. Essentially a central Himalayan tribal people, practising an early form of Shaivism, they traded in salt with Tibet. A second-century Ashokan edict at Kalsi in western Garhwal shows that Buddhism made some inroads in the region, but Garhwal and Kumaun remained Brahmanical. The Kuninda eventually succumbed to the **Guptas** around the fourth century AD, who despite controlling much of the north Indian plains failed to make a lasting impact in the hills. Between the seventh and the fourteenth centuries, the Shaivite **Katyuri** dominated lands of varying extent from the Katyur-Baijnath valley in Kumaun, where their stone temples still stand. Under them **Jageshwar** was a major pilgrimage centre, and Brahmanical culture flourished. Eastern Kumaun prospered under the **Chandras**, from the thirteenth to the fifteenth centuries, when learning and art took on new forms and the Garhwal school of painting was developed. Later on, the westward expansion of the **Gurkha** empire was brought to an end by British annexation in the nineteenth century.

Garhwal

Garhwal, which holds the sources of the mighty Ganga and Yamuna rivers, is the holy land or **Uttarkhand**. In the wake of the decline of Buddhism in northern India, the ninth-century reformer Shankara incorporated many of the mountains' ancient shrines into the fold of Hinduism. He founded the four main **yatra** (pilgrimage) **temples**, deep within the Himalayas, known as the **Char Dham** – **Badrinath, Kedarnath**, and the less-visited pair of **Gangotri** and **Yumnotri**. Each year, between May and November, once the snows have melted, streams of pilgrims penetrate high into the mountains, passing by way of **Rishikesh**, the land of *yogis* and ashrams.

For over a millennium, the *yatris* (pilgrims) came on foot. However, the annual event has been transformed in the last few years; roads blasted by the military through the mountains during the war against China in the early 1960s are now the lifelines for a new form of motorized *yatra*. Eastern Garhwal in particular is getting rich, and the fabric of hill society is changing rapidly. Visitors hoping to experience the old Garhwal should spend at least part of their time well away from the principal *yatra* routes.

Many travellers from Delhi get their first sight of the snows at the hill station of **Mussoorie**. Just below that is the pleasant cantonment town of **Dehra Dun**, while further south, not far from Rishikesh, holy **Haridwar** marks where the Ganga emerges from the hills on to the Indian plains; technically the town is not actually in Garhwal or Kumaun, but its spiritual links are strong enough to include it here.

All the tourist bungalows in Garhwal are operated by Garhwal Mandal Vikas Nigam – **GMVN**. Most are concentrated along the pilgrimage routes, although their network has been expanding, and takes in the ski area at Auli. Standards vary widely, but the **food** tends to be particularly poor. GMVN also organize **tours** (often over-priced and inefficient), and offer expensive **car rental**.

Dehra Dun

The administrative centre of Garhwal and the UP Hills, **DEHRA DUN**, 255km north of Delhi, tends to be seen simply as a staging post on the way to the hill station of Mussoorie, 34km north, and the Garhwal interior. Pleasantly located at just below 700m, as the Himalayan foothills begin their dramatic rise, Dehra Dun never gets too hot in summer, and snows only rarely in winter. With its vast open spaces and colonies such as the Cantonment, this popular retirement spot is renowned for its elite public schools, and prestigious institutions. Although occupied in turn by Sikhs, Moghuls, and Gurkhas, it is clearly an overgrown British town, with its Raj roots always showing.

Dehra Dun stands at the centre of the 120-kilometre-long **Doon Valley** (*dun* or *doon* literally means "valley"), famous for its long grain rice – *basmati* – and unique in being hemmed in by the Yamuna to the west and the Ganga at Rishikesh to the east. Also in the east is Rajaji National Park, known for its wild elephants, while the low forested Shivalik hills separate the valley from the dusty plains to the south. The local administration is fighting back against devastating deforestation; the springs are returning to life and with them, the dry river beds that criss-cross the valley. Those tracts of forests that remain are best seen at its eastern and western extremities.

Arrival and information

Jolly Grant **airport**, 24km east of Dehra Dun, is a stop on the regular bus route to and from Rishikesh; if you do arrive on one of its rare and over-priced flights, you can also get to town by taxi. The **railway station** is on Gandhi Road, just south of the **City Bus Stand**, which is next to the Clock Tower in the centre of town. The *State Bank of India* (Mon–Fri 10am–2pm, Sat 10am–noon; ☎26643) and the **post office** are both right alongside.

GARHWAL & KUMAON

HIMACHAL PRADESH

Mana Pass

Kamet 7756m

Nil Par 647

Satopanth 7075m

Mar

Sudarshan 6507m

Gangotri Glacier

Badrinath

Lanka

Gomukh

Shivling 6543m

Bhagirathi 6856m

Nilkantha 6596m

Chaukhamba 7138m

Harsil

Gangotri

Kedarnath 6940m

Har-ki-Dun

Swargarohini 6252m

Jogin 6465m

Khatling Glacier

Kedarnath

Madhmaheshwa

Osla

Yamnotri

Bandarpunch 6316m

Khatling

Gaunkund

Rudrana Gopeshw

Janki Chatti

Dodi Tal Lake

Kalyani

Sonprayag

Okhimath

Hanuman Chatti

Uttarkashi

Gangi

GARHWAL

Chandras 3930m

Tunganath

Netwar

Ghuttu

Karnapra

Budha Kedar

Bhilangna

Barkot

Mandakini

Rudrapraya

Nowgaon

Bhagirathi

Ghamsali

Alakananda

Deoban

Tehri

Srinagar

Nag Tiba 3027m

Pauri

Chakrata

Tons

Mussoorie

Kunjapuri 2240m

Devaprayag

Kalsi

Dehra Dun

Narendranagar

Lansdow

Rishikesh

Chila

Rajaji National Park

Haridwar

Yamuna

Bijnor

Roorkee

Ganges

Yamunanagar

Saharanpur

▽ Delhi

IBET

Niti Pass

Lipu Lekh
Pass

Malari

Hathi
Parbat
6727m

Hemkund

hangaria

lukeshwar

oshimath

Lata

Auli

Tapovan

) (Kuari Pass

eshwar

Pipalkota

Rammani

ndaprayag

Ghat

Pindar

Debal

Gwaldam

Tharali

Kausani

Dwarahat

Ranikhet

Ramganga

Kosi

Dhikala

Corbett ♦
ional Park

Ramnagar

Milam Glacier

Milam

Dunagiri
7066m

Nanda Devi
7816m

Nanda Devi
East
7434m

Trishul
7120m

Pindari
Glacier

Puridya

Dwali

Khati

Loharkhet

Raglam

Martoli

Nanda Kot
6861m

Panchuli
6904m

Api
7132m

Lilam

Munsyari

Girgaon

Tejam

Didihat

Thal

NEPAL

Baijnath

Bageshwar

Chaukori

Barinag

Pithoragarh

Binsar
2412m

Jageshwar

KUMAON

Almora

Bhowali

Bhimtal

Naini Tal

Kathgodam

Tanakpur

Haldwani

0   50 km

Govt of India Statement - The external boundaries of India are neither correct nor authenticated.

▽ Delhi

> The telephone **area code** for Dehra Dun is ☎0135.

The **Tourist Information Bureau**, 9 Astley Hall (☎26508), focusses specifically on Dehra Dun, while the **Regional Tourist Office**, at the GMVN *Hotel Drona*, 45 Gandhi Rd (Mon–Sat 10am–5pm; ☎23217), covers all Garhwal, and books GMVN accommodation and tours. GMVN have another office at 74/1 Rajpur Rd (☎26817). The Director General of Tourism for the UP Hills is just off the main road at 75 Rajpur Rd (☎25121).

Abundant local transport includes cycle and auto-rickshaws and multi-seater *Vikrams*. Better-value **car rental** than that offered by GMVN is available through *Jaura Taxi Service*, 2 Krishna St (☎29176), or *Ventures Rent-a-car*, 87 Rajpur Rd (☎22724).

If you're looking to fix up a **trek** in the region, *Garhwal Tours & Trekking*, 151 Araghar (☎27769), is an established and experienced organization. The similar *Royale Expeditions*, Rajeev Bali, 75/2 Block II, Arya Nagar, Rajpur Rd, also arranges **rafting**.

The Town

Most of Dehra Dun's busy markets lie near the tall Victorian **Clock Tower**, from where Rajpur Road, the lifeline to Mussoorie, stretches northwards. Four kilometres along is the vast leafy colony occupied by the **Survey of India**, founded in 1767. Its greatest achievement was to determine the height of Mount Everest – and name it after the Surveyor General, Sir George Everest. Most of the stock in its **map shop** is old and out of date, and anything interesting you might pick up will almost certainly be stamped "Not For Export" if it includes such sensitive areas as any portion of India's coastline. Their new trekking series of the UP Himalayas is very poor (see p.23).

Crossing the rainy-season river bed of Bindal Rao, Kaulagarh Road progresses northwest past Dehra Dun's top private school, the Doon School, to the expansive grounds of the chateau-like **Forest Research Institute**, devoted to the preservation of India's much-threatened woodlands (Mon–Fri 10am–5pm; free). Along with a library and bookstore, there's a large and interesting museum, holding wood samples, insects, furniture, and wildlife – even a few stuffed animals. **Tapkeshwar Mahadev**, Dehra Dun's only significant temple, lies 2km further north, 6km from the centre. Steps lead down to a rocky and wooded river, beside which a cave with water dripping from its ceiling contains a Shiva shrine. According to the *Mahabharata,* Shiva made milk flow from this cave for Ashwathama, the son of the guru Dronacharya.

Accommodation

Dehra Dun has a good selection of mid-range **hotels**, many of them strung along Rajpur Rd as it heads north to Mussoorie. What little budget accommodation there is can be found near the town centre – or in the old-fashioned railway retiring rooms.

Chandra, Old Mussoorie Rd (☎(684/2360). Excellent, atmospheric place (if a bit damp), set in the hills 10km north of Dehra Dun. Nice garden. ②–④.

Dinex, 59 Gandhi Rd (☎28107). Reasonable, very central, budget lodging. ②.

Embassy, 18 Dhamawala (☎24439). Down a series of lanes, not far from the centre and well worth seeking out. A good range of rooms. ②–④.

GMVN Drona, 45 Gandhi Rd (☎24371). Central and close to all amenities, with tourist information and tour and travel operators on the premises; the range of rooms includes a dorm. ④–⑤.

Hilton, 54 Hardwar Rd (☎29591). Not related to the famous chain, but quite pleasant and new. ⑦.

Kwality, 19 Rajpur Rd (☎27001). A landmark near the centre of Dehra Dun, established in the motel-influenced 1960s, with large comfortable rooms, good restaurant and bar. Recommended. ⑤.

Madhuban, Rajpur Rd (☎24094). With two popular restaurants, a bar, travel desk and a swimming pool, this is one of Dehra Dun's best. A favourite with the few tour groups that come through. ⑦–⑧.

MOVING ON FROM DEHRA DUN

Occasional and unpredictable **flights** from Jolly Grant airport, 24km east of Dehra Dun, go to **Delhi** and **Lucknow**; the fare to Delhi for foreigners is around Rs2000.

Major **trains** back down to the plains include the *Doon Express* #3010, through Lucknow to Calcutta, the *Mussoorie Express* #4042 to **Delhi**, the *Dehra Dun–Varanasi Express* #4266, and the *Dehra Dun–Bombay Express* #9020. Hourly **buses** from the City Bus Stand head to **Mussoorie**, while buses to Delhi leave from the Gandhi Road Bus Stand; a deluxe bus costs around Rs100. You can also get buses to **Shimla**, **Dharamsala**, **Chandigarh**, **Kulu**, **Manali**, as well as **Rishikesh** and **Haridwar**, 43km and 54km southeast.

Tickets can be booked in the GMVN *Drona*, 45 Gandhi Rd (☎24371).

Osho Resorts, 111 Rajpur Rd (☎29544). Extraordinary place on the road to Mussoorie – part hotel, part restaurant and part ashram, with wooden cottages and a good multi-cuisine restaurant. The piped audio-visual channels include lectures by Osho, once known as Bhagwan Rajneesh. ⑤–⑥.

Shahinshah, 74C Rajpur Rd (☎28508). Clustered with a number of similar establishments, new, with friendly staff but suffering from some teething problems. ⑦–⑨.

Shipra, 74C Rajpur Rd (☎24611). Designed to catch the Mussoorie traffic. Comfortable option, with a good restaurant – especially at breakfast – and a bar. ⑥–⑦.

Victoria, near railway station, Gandhi Rd (☎623486). Simple, central, lodge, with a courtyard. ②.

Eating

Dehra Dun has several commendable mid-priced eating places, such as the *Kwality*, and also a bunch of adequate cheaper cafes around the bus and train stations.

Daddy's, 3 Astley Hall, Rajpur Rd. Above *The Vegetarian* but not vegetarian itself. Multi-cuisine from pizzas to *thalis* in a friendly atmosphere.

Heaven's Garden, Osho Resorts, 111 Rajpur Rd (☎29544). Part of the Bhagwan Rajneesh complex with Indian, Chinese and western. Bar-Be-Que, fast food counter and a roof-top restaurant.

Kumar Vegetarian, Astley Hall, Kwality Chowkh. Recommended mid-budget Indian vegetarian place.

Kundan Palace, opposite *Madhuban*, Rajpur Rd. Open-air multi-cuisine place, popular with locals.

Kwality, 19 Rajpur Rd. Good and reliable multi-cuisine chain restaurant with bar, next to the motel.

Pushp, 65 Gandhi Rd. A well-priced cafe offering a wide range from *dosas* to omelettes.

The Vegetarian, Astley Plaza, Rajpur Rd. South Indian and Punjabi cooking in a canteen-like atmosphere.

Mussoorie

Spreading for 15km along a high serrated ridge, **Mussoorie** is the closest hill station to Delhi, just 278km north of the capital, and 34km north of Dehra Dun (from where it is clearly visible). At an altitude of 2000m, it provides travellers from the plains with a long-awaited first glimpse of the snow-covered Himalayan peaks of western Garhwal, as well as dramatic views of the Dehra Dun Valley below. Established in 1823 by a certain Captain Young, Mussoorie soon became a typical Victorian resort, centering on its long promenade – **the Mall** – and boasting an Anglican church, library and club.

These days, Mussoorie is very popular with Indian tourists; although some of the old settlement can still be seen, much of the centre is now congested and unattractive. Dominated by the long Banderpunch massif (6316m), with Swargarohini (6252m) in the west and the Gangotri Group in the east, Mussoorie's mountain panorama may not be as dramatic as some other hill stations, but it forms a pleasant backdrop to rambling walks when you feel like escaping the busy holiday town.

The telephone **area code** for Mussoorie is ☎01362.

Arrival, transport and information

As Mussoorie's two-kilometre-long **Mall** is closed to motor vehicles during the tourist season, its two ends – the **Library** area at the west end, and the **Kulri** area in the east – serve as distinct transport hubs. Buses and shared taxis from Dehra Dun, the plains and the rest of Garhwal arrive either at the **Library Bus Stand** at Gandhi Chowkh, or the **Kulri** or **Masonic Lodge Bus Stand**, but not both. At the smaller **Tehri Bus Stand**, east of Landour 5km from the Mall, buses pull in from Tehri and points east. Shared taxis and cars are available at the bus stands, while ponies and hand-drawn carriages – glorified rickshaws – run along the Mall itself. Ponies can also carry you around the Camel's Back Rd, but cross-country pony trekking has yet to catch on. *Bertz* (no, not *Hertz*; ☎2930), near Darpan in Kulri and in London House on the Mall, rent 100cc **motorcycles** by the hour, half-day and full day.

Facilities along the Mall include the information-only **Tourist Bureau** (☎2863), the **post office** (at the Kulri end), and a GMVN office at the *Hotel Garhwal Terrace* (☎2984), which runs tours of town and further afield. *Ambica Travels* (☎2238) and *Kulwant Travels* (☎2717) are approved tour and car rental operators.

The Town

Surprisingly, the Mall and the main hub face away from the snows towards Dehra Dun; the distant peaks can best be seen from the flat summit of **Gun Hill**, which rises like a volcano from central Mussoorie. This can be ascended on foot or pony on a bridle path that forks up from the Kutcheri, or on the 400-metre "Ropeway" cable-car ride from the Mall. Alternative prospects of the mountains can be had on a peaceful stroll or ride around the three-kilometre-long **Camel's Back Road**, which girdles the northern base of Gun Hill, passing by the distinctive **Camel's Rock**. Another vantage point, the highest in the immediate vicinity, is **Childer's Lodge**, 5km east of the Mall above Landour.

Just below the Mall, beside the *Padmini Niwas* hotel, a **Tibetan street market** has become something of a fixture, with traders selling sweaters and woollens to unprepared tourists. The markets of Kulri and Landour provide more local colour.

Away from the noise and bustle, close to Convent Hill and 3km west of the Library, the substantial Tibetan settlement of **Happy Valley** holds a large school and the small but beautiful **Tchechen Choling** *gompa* (monastery), overlooking the Doon Valley and surrounded by gardens. It makes an enjoyable walk from the Mall along wooded roads, but you can also catch a taxi for around Rs60 return.

Somewhat further afield, **Kempty Falls**, 18km northwest on the road down to Yamuna Bridge, is served by regular buses from the Library stand. This local beauty spot has been all but ruined by its deluge of day-trippers. In theory they come to take a dip in the pool at the foot of the falls themselves, though there always seem to be a lot more people watching from the surrounding tea shops (which rent out towels and swimming costumes) than swimming. The steps down to the pool from the road lead past shops, beggars and snake charmers, while commercial photographers lie in wait at the bottom to capture holiday snaps.

Accommodation

Mussoorie is packed with **hotels** to suit all budgets – most of them clustered around the Mall. Room rates fluctuate between three rather vague **seasons**; lean (Jan–March & July–Sept, when the rains come), shoulder or mid-season (Christmas, April and the "Bengali season" of Oct & Nov), and peak (May–July), when prices can quadruple.

Carlton's Plaisance, Happy Valley Rd (☎2800). A rambling old block and a newer building, full of character, with pleasant garden. Threatened by the expansion of the adjacent civil service college. ⑥.

Darpan, near *Picture Palace*, Kulri (☎2483). Reasonable and clean with good mountain views from the rooms and a good vegetarian restaurant. ④.

GMVN Garhwal Terrace, The Mall (☎2682). Upmarket tourist lodge, with a popular restaurant, in the centre of the Mall close to the cable car. ⑤–⑦.

Hakmans Grand, The Mall (☎2159). Incredible old rambling Victorian structure, a landmark which once was the hub of activity but is now haunted by the ghosts of the past. ②–③.

Padmini Niwas, Library, The Mall (☎2793). Just below the Mall with beautiful grounds and garden, one of Mussoorie's better and more established addresses; the cottage is attractive. ⑤–⑧.

HAR-KI-DUN VALLEY TREKS

An undemanding but superb trek **from Mussoorie** takes four days (including one on the bus) to reach the sparsely populated "Valley of the Gods", **HAR-KI-DUN**, in the **Fateh Parvat** region of northwestern Garhwal. In the valley itself if not higher in the mountains, accommodation is widely available, and food can usually be bought.

The rivers and streams of Har-ki-Dun drain the glaciers and snowfields that cloak the peaks of Swargarohini (the "ascent to heaven"; 6252m) and Bandarpunch (the "monkey's tail"; 6316m). Local people trace their lineage to the *Mahabharata*, claiming descent from Duryodhana and his followers. Like the Pandavas of the epic, they practise a form of polyandry, and follow intriguing religious customs. Worship at Taluka's Duryodhana temple, for example, consists of throwing shoes at the idol, while at Pakola, the image has its back to the congregation. Their distinctive alpine buildings have beautifully carved wooden doors and windows, with the mortar construction punctuated by wooden slats.

The trek to Har-ki-Dun

Starting out from Mussoorie on **DAY 1**, catch a Yumnotri bus and change at Nowgaon to continue via **Netwar** (9km short of Barkot, from where a road climbs to Hanuman Chatti) to **Purola** – a total of 154km. You can stay in Purola at a PWD bungalow, set amid a patchwork of wheat and rice terraces, which is where to get permission to stay at the forest rest houses further on. Simple cafes can be found around the bus stand.

Early the next morning – **DAY 2** – take the bus to the roadhead at **Sankri**, which also has a bungalow. A gentle trail from here leads the 12km to **Taluka** (1900m) where there is another bungalow and simple food.

On **DAY 3**, the trail follows the River Tons through beautiful forests. Although you can get tea at the hamlet of Gangari, no food is available until you've walked the full 11km to **Osla** (2259m). Osla too has a *Forest Rest House*, where security is unfortunately doubtful; from here on you have to carry your food, so stock up.

A steep 14km climb from Osla on **DAY 4** brings you finally to the campground at **Har-ki-Dun** (3560m) – an excellent base from which to explore the *bugyals* below the Swargarohini to the east, and the Jaundhar Glacier (3910m) at the head of the valley.

Returning along the same route takes two days, or one if you're really fit.

Across Yumnotri Pass

From the head of Har-ki-Dun valley, a challenging trail – only to be tackled by fully equipped and acclimatized trekkers, with local guides – winds for 30km over the **Yumnotri Pass** (4890m). Take the trail that forks off above **Osla**, and head 10km east along the Ruinsar Nala gorge to the mountain lake of **Ruinsara Tal** (3350m). From here, it takes a full day to climb to a campsite just below the pass at 4135m; on the second day you cross the pass and camp on the far side at 4000m; the third ends at **Yumnotri** itself (see p.249).

From here, the gentle 14km trek outlined on p.249 leads down to **Hanuman Chatti** (2134m), from where you can either embark on the Dodi Tal trek to create a two-week expedition through stunning mountain scenery, or catch a bus out.

Peak View, opposite *State Bank of India*, Camel's Back Rd (☎2052). Close to amenities, good Punjabi cooking, comfortable with an open terrace and views of the snows. ④–⑦.

Priya, The Mall, Kulri (☎2477). Spacious good-value rooms with hot water; good views down to the market and the hills beyond but otherwise neglected and without food. ①–②.

Ratan, Gandhi Chowkh (☎2719). In the busy Library area, friendly, clean and excellent value with a terrace looking onto the snows. Recommended. ③–④.

Savoy, The Mall (☎2010). Above the Library, a driveway leads to pleasant grounds with large period buildings; captures all the ambience of Victorian Mussoorie. Recommended. ⑦–⑧.

Shalimar, Charliville Rd (☎2410). Good-value, old world, place, below the road to Kempty. ②–③.

Shilton, Library (☎2983). One of a small complex of hotels overlooking the Doon valley bang next to the Library; modern and comfortable with lots of facilities but expensive. ⑦–⑧.

Shining Star, opposite Vasu Theatre, Library, The Mall (☎2500). Glitzy but at a quiet spot above the Mall with all mod cons including a sauna. ⑦–⑨.

Valley View, The Mall (☎2324). Sunny disposition with terrace overlooking the Doon Valley and a good restaurant; clean and close to all amenities – recommended. ③–⑦.

Eating

Cafes and **restaurants** all along the Mall and around Kulri serve everything from hot dogs to Chinese specialities; we recommend several below, but there are more good restaurants in hotels such as the *Valley View* and the atmospheric *Savoy* (see above).

Clarks, The Mall, Kulri. Period atmosphere with a multi-cuisine restaurant and bar.

Coffee House, near *Carlton's*, Happy Valley Rd. Pleasant cafe away from the noise and bustle on the way to Happy Valley, with Chinese and Tibetan food.

Kwality, The Mall, Kulri. Part of the large chain; the usual good Indian, western and Chinese food.

Le Chef, The Mall, Kulri. Fast food, hot dogs, burgers, pizzas and piped MTV.

Mahaluxmi, The Mall, Kulri. On the corner near the GPO – nice place, with tasty vegetarian *thalis*.

Tavern, The Mall, Kulri. Near the Kulri bus stand, a multi-cuisine restaurant and bar with occasional live bands and dancing during the high season.

Whispering Windows, Gandhi Chowkh (☎2611). Also a hotel, one of Mussoorie's better restaurants – lively with piped music and a bar.

Haridwar

At **HARIDWAR** – the Gates (*dwar*) of God (*Hari*) – 214km northeast of Delhi, the **River Ganges** emerges from its final rapids past the Siwalik Hills, to commence the long slow journey across northern India to the Bay of Bengal. Stretching for roughly 3km along a narrow strip of land between the craggy wooded hills to the west and the river to the east, Haridwar is especially revered by Hindus, for whom its revered **Har-ki-Pairi** *ghat*, literally the "Footstep of God", marks the exact spot where the river leaves the mountains. Looking north along the vast Doon Valley, the faint lines of the Himalayan foothills can be discerned rising above Rishikesh in the distance, while Haridwar itself faces east across the river to the hills of the Rajaji National Park. A major road and rail junction, linking Delhi and the Gangetic plains with the mountains of Uttarkhand and their holy *yatra* network, Haridwar may not be administratively part of the mountain districts, but it posesses a crucial spiritual and geographical significance.

Along with Nasik, Ujjain, and the holiest of them all, Prayag in Allahabad, Haridwar is one of the four holy *tirthas* or "crossings" that serve as the focus of the massive **Kumbh Mela** festival. Every twelve years, thousands of pilgrims come to bathe at a pre-ordained moment in the turbulent waters of the channelled river around Har-ki-Pairi. The Kumbh Mela is next due to take place here in 1998. Busy at the best of times, Haridwar can become unbearably congested during the Mela, when surging crowds around the bathing areas can create stampedes.

Arrival and information

Haridwar's **railway station** and **Station Bus Stand**, southwest of the centre, face each other across the main thoroughfare that channels all traffic through to meet the river at Har-ki-Pairi. **Trains and buses** connect Haridwar with Rishikesh, Dehra Dun and the mountains, and run back down to Delhi. You can also get to Rishikesh in shared taxis, while *Vikrams* and tempos ply the few roads in town. To arrange a **tour** of Garhwal by bus or car, call in at *Konark Tourist Service*, Jasaram Rd (☎427210).

An information booth at the station operates at arrival times, and information is also available at the **Regional Tourist Office**, facing the Mal Godown warehouse on Upper Rd (Mon–Sat 10am–5pm; ☎427370), and the **UP Tourist Information Bureau**, near the bus stand at *Rahi Motel*, Station Rd (Mon–Sat 10am–5pm, closed 2nd Sat each month; ☎427370). There's a **post office** on Upper Rd, opposite *Ram Panjawani* (☎427266), the local agents for *Indian Airlines*. **Money** can be changed at the *State Bank of India*, near *Chitra Talkies* on Sadhu Bela Marg (☎426103).

The Town

Split by a barrage north of Haridwar, the Ganges flows in two principal channels, divided by a long sliver of land. The main natural stream lies to the east, while the embankment of the fast-flowing canal to the west holds *ghats*, ashrams and buildings that seem to emerge out of the water. Promenades, river channels and bridges create a pleasant riverfront ambience, with the major *ghats* and religious activity clustered around **Har-ki-Pairi**, which bears a distinct resemblance to a railway station. Bridges

---

---

and walkways connect the various islands, and metal chains are placed in the river to protect bathers from being swept away by ferocious currents. Non-Hindus are not allowed onto the actual Har-ki-Pairi *ghat*, where Vishnu left his footprints in stone, but the platform-like island opposite it, topped by a clocktower, provides an excellent vantage point, especially for evening worship. At dusk, the spectacular daily ceremony of **Ganga Arati** draws a crowd of thousands onto the islands and bridges. Lights float down the river, and priests perform elaborate choreographed movements, swinging torches in an ancient ritual to the accompaniment of gongs and music.

Near Vishnu Ghat in the centre of town, the uninspiring **Shri Mayadevi** temple, built on a site that dates back to the eleventh century, is dedicated to a form of Shakti. Further north along the Rishikesh road, the pool of **Bhimgoda** was gorged out by Bhima, one of the Pandava heroes of the *Mahabharata*. Haridwar's teeming network of **markets** are the main other focus of interest. **Bara Bazaar**, at the top of town, is strong on brass, cane and bamboo-ware – a good place to buy a *danda* (bamboo staff) for lengthy treks in the mountains. Stalls in the colourful **Moti Bazaar** on the Jawalapur road sell everything from clothes to spices.

High above Haridwar, ever conspicuous on the crest of a ridge, the gleaming white *shikhara* of the **Mansa Devi** temple dominates both town and valley. The temple is easily and enjoyably reached by **cable car**, from a base station off Upper Rd in the heart of town (daily 8am–noon & 2–5pm; Rs6), though the steep 1.5-kilometre walk is pleasant enough early in the mornings. None of the shrines and temples up top holds any great architectural interest, but you do get excellent views along the river. An elaborate queuing system leads pilgrims to *darshan* of the main image, showing Mansa Devi – a triple-headed image of Shakti as the goddess Durga. Photography is taboo.

The extraordinary modern seven-storeyed **Bharat Mata** temple, 5km north of Haridwar and reachable in shared *Vikrams* for around Rs3, is dedicated to "Mother India". A temple with a similar name and intent can be found in Varanasi, but this one is much newer, and much more garish – and is obviously doing very nicely. Each of its various floors – connected by elevators – is dedicated to a celestial or political theme, and populated by life-like images of heroes, heroines and Hindu deities.

The **Shri Dakheshwar** temple, also known as **Daksha Mahadev**, 6km south of Haridwar in Khankhal, is beautifully situated with large trees above a *ghat*. The new main temple contains a gilded image of a snake symbolizing Shiva; legend relates Shiva's wife Sati was so enraged when her father snubbed Shiva by failing to invite him to a sacrifice performed on this spot that she sacrificed herself by self-immolation. A few hundred metres away, within the impeccable retreat of **Anandamoyee Ma Ashram**, a marble mausoleum is dedicated to the recently deceased Bengali woman guru. An adjacent bookshop sells literature connected with her life and work.

Across the river 5km east of Haridwar, **Chandi Devi**, another Shakti *pith* (temple) on a high ridge, looks down on the valley; its final rise can only be negotiated on foot.

Accommodation

Although it has no luxury hotels, Haridwar has **accommodation** to suit most budgets and temperaments. It's a small place, so wherever you stay the river and the bazaars are never too far away. Most hotels are within a Rs5 rickshaw ride northeast of the station; some, like the *Rahi*, are in walking distance.

Aarti, Railway Rd (☎427456). Quite a reasonable hotel on a busy main road, convenient for the railway station and bus stand. ④–⑤.

Amba Niwas, Choti Sabzi Mandi, Vishnu Ghat (no phone). Small but new and clean hotel in a crowded bazaar, with hot and cold running water in attached bathrooms. ②–③.

GMVN Tourist Bungalow, Belwala (☎426379). One of the few places on the east bank, in a pleasant garden away from the noise, on the main island. Rooms range from a dorm to a/c. ①–④.

Inder Kutir Guest House, Sharwan Nath Nagar (☎426336). The comfortable Chaudhury family home, near the river; a highly recommended break from the usual seedy, characterless hotels. ②–③.

Kailash, Shiv Murti (☎427789). Central hotel near the railway station, with a handy counter for rail and bus tickets. Around 70 rooms, some air-cooled, and a vegetarian restaurant. ③–⑤.

Mansarover International, Upper Rd (☎426501). New hotel in the heart of the old town, comfortable and well equipped. ④–⑦.

Mayur, near Ropeway (☎427586). Ordinary place; good value during the lean season but overpriced during May and June. ①–④.

Raj Deluxe, Vishnu Ghat (☎427755). At the heart of a busy market, close to the river and bridge, but otherwise quite ordinary. ②.

Sahni, Niranjani Akhara Rd, Sharwan Nath Nagar (☎427906). In the congested part of the old town near the river. Small but reasonable, especially in the low season, when the rooms are half-price. ④.

Surprise, Jawalapur–Haridwar Rd, Jawalapur (☎427780). Sited on a busy thoroughfare 6km south of Haridwar, deliberately outside the restricted eating zone, so its restaurant can serve meat. Expensive option, with all mod cons including foreign exchange and a swimming pool. ⑦–⑧.

Suvidha, Sharwan Nath Nagar, behind *Chitra Talkies Cinema* (☎427423). Pleasant location, near the river but away from the bustle of the bazaars and main roads. Comfortable and plush. ⑤–⑥.

Tourist Villa, Himalaya Depot Gali, Sharwan Nath Nagar (no phone). Popular and quite new with a range of rooms. The ones at the top are less noisy. Food available as room service only. ②–④.

UP Tourism Rahi Motel, Station Rd (☎426430). Comfortable modern bungalow next to the bus stand, made of red brick, with a dormitory plus a restaurant set in pleasant gardens. ②–③.

Eating

Haridwar is a strictly **vegetarian** town; if you're happy with that, the food is very good, whether in the cafes around Har-ki-Pairi or the restaurants of Upper Rd. If you have to have meat, head for the cafes or the *Hotel Surprise* at **Jawalapur**, 6km south.

Ahaar, Railway Rd (☎427601). Excellent mid-range Sikh-run restaurant, with a wood-panelled ambience, and serving good *thalis*, Chinese food and superb Punjabi cuisine such as the traditional and seasonal *makki-ki-roti* (corn *paratha*) with *sarson ka saag* (mustard-leaf spinach).

Chotiwala, Lalta Rao Bridge, near *Big Town Hotel*, Upper Rd. Another top-notch restaurant, offering Indian food and good *thalis*. Established in 1937, and with a branch in Swarg Ashram, Rishikesh, it's still one of the best around. Its many imitators include one near Har-ki-Pairi.

Gazal, *Hotel Surprise*, Jawalapur–Haridwar Rd (☎427780). Multi-cuisine and quite expensive, but it does serve meat if you can't get by without it.

Satkar, Vishnu Ghat. Half-restaurant, half-*dhaba*, but quite pleasant, with Indian and Chinese food.

Shiwalik, Station Rd. One of a row of three good restaurants; tasty south Indian snacks like *dosas*.

MOVING ON FROM HARIDWAR

No scheduled buses connect Haridwar with Jolly Grant, the barely used **airport**, 22km northwest, it shares with Dehra Dun and Rishikesh (see p.233).

Major **trains** passing through include the excellent *Mussoorie Express* #4042 between Dehra Dun and **Delhi**, which leaves Haridwar around 10.50pm and takes 7hr to reach Delhi. Other trains to Delhi include the *Dehra Dun Express* and the *Bombay Express*, while the *Janata Express* covers the 850km to **Varanasi** in 20hr, and the *Doon Express* #3009, through **Lucknow** to **Calcutta**, can prove to be an even more epic journey. Local trains on the branch line to Rishikesh are barely useful in view of the excellent road connections.

Buses to **Delhi** leave from the **Station Bus Stand** almost every half-hour (5–6hr; fares from Rs40); a **taxi** to Delhi from the stand opposite costs more like Rs700. Five or six buses a day leave for **Agra**, 368km south (10hr; Rs80). Similarly, numerous buses go to **Rishikesh**, 24km north, and **Dehra Dun**, 57km northwest, as well as **Shimla**, **Nainital** and **Almora**. Travellers heading into the mountains should go to Rishikesh to pick up onwards transport.

Rajaji National Park

Around 830 square kilometres of the Himalayan foothills immediately east of Haridwar are taken up by **RAJAJI NATIONAL PARK**, which belongs to the same forest belt as Corbett National Park, 180km east. Although not geared for tourism to the same extent as Corbett, the park is absolutely beautiful, with a similar range of wildlife – most notably elephants, but also tigers and even a rare species of ant-eater.

The main gates of the national park are at **Chila**, 13km east of Haridwar by road, across the Ganges (early Nov to mid-June; Rs30 entry fee, plus Rs50 per vehicle, and camera fees). **Elephant rides** from here cost around Rs200 for two hours. However, visitors don't have to go into the core area to experience the jungles of Rajaji; it's also possible to venture in from Chila or Rishikesh, or from the road between the two, paralleling the canal that marks the western boundary of the huge fringe forest.

Chila

To get to **CHILA** from Haridwar, catch a Kandi- or Kandra-bound **bus** from the stand opposite the railway station, or a shared **jeep** from Chandi Ghat opposite Har-ki-Pairi. You could even **walk**; Chila is visible from Haridwar, and taking a short cut from Har-ki-Pairi via the riverbeds and a bridge makes it just four kilometres east.

The town itself is neither attractive nor interesting, located right beside the Ganges barrage and its massive electricity pylons. However, it makes a good base for explorations of the park, and **Chila Beach** – occasionally used by large river turtles – lies within walking distance through the woods, 1km north along the Ganges.

Managers can make or break tourist bungalows, and so it is with the GMVN *Chila Tourist Centre* (②–③), where Mr R B Raturi is always happy to share his enthusiasm for the forests of Rajaji. The bungalow has a dormitory, plus standard and a/c rooms, huts, and camping facilities.

Bindevasani and forest trails

Along the Kimsar road, which penetrates the deep *sal* forests northeast of Chila, visitors have a reasonable chance of glimpsing **wild elephant**. Elephant herds migrate here seasonally from as far away as Corbett, and can sometimes be seen in the forests behind Swarg Ashram in Rishikesh. The tiny hamlet of **BINDEVASANI**, 14km northeast of Chila and linked to both Chila and Haridwar by regular buses, stands at the foot of steep hills. Besides a small *dharamshala* and a tea shop, there's little here to detain travellers, but it's possible to camp in the covered forecourt of the small clifftop Durga temple, which affords dramatic views over the confluence of the Bindedhara and Nildhara rivers. For around 4km before Bindevasani, the road follows a vast riverbed, dry and extremely hot in summer, and still fordable during the rainy season.

A copious network of **trails** lace through the hills around Bindevasani. Possible routes include one to the village and temple of **Nilkantha** (14km north; see p.248); one to **Lakshmanjhula** (20km northwest; see p.247), the bridge and roadhead near Rishikesh; and one to the remote hamlet of **Yamkeshwar** (22km northeast), where a small Shiva temple on the banks of the Ravasan is surrounded by deep forest.

Rishikesh

RISHIKESH – forever famous as the spot where the Beatles met the Maharishi – is 238km northeast of Delhi and 24km north of Haridwar, at the point where the wooded mountains of Garhwal rise abruptly from the low valley floor, and the Ganges crashes onto the plains. Its many ashrams – some very clearly ascetic, some verging on the opulent – continue to draw devotees and followers of all sorts of weird and wonderful gurus, with the large **Shivananda Ashram** in particular renowned as a yoga centre.

Rishikesh has one or two ancient shrines, but its main role has always been as a way station for *sannyasin*, *yogis*, and *sadhus* heading for the high Himalayas. The arrival of the Beatles was one of the first manifestations of the lucrative expansion of the *yatra* pilgrimage circuit; these days it's all too easy to see why the perspicacious Ringo thought it was "just like Butlin's". By far the best time to visit is in winter, when the mountain temples are shut by the snows. In the absence of the *yatra* razzmatazz, you can get a sense of the tranquillity that was the original appeal of the place.

Confusingly, the name Rishikesh is applied to a loose association of five distinct sections, encompassing not only the town but also hamlets and settlements on both sides of the river – **Rishikesh** itself, the commercial and communications hub; sprawling suburban **Muni-ki-Reti**; **Shivananda Nagar**, just north; the multi-storeyed and multi-coloured temples of **Lakshmanjhula**, straddling the river a little further north; and the assorted ashrams around **Swarg Ashram** on the east bank.

Arrival, transport and information

Far more visitors arrive in Rishikesh by road or rail than at the airport, 18km west (see p.233). The **Main Bus Stand**, used by Haridwar and Dehra Dun services, as well as direct buses to and from Delhi (6hr), is on Bengali Mandir Rd, close to the centre; buses for the Garhwal hills use the **Yatra Bus Stand**, off the Dehra Dun Rd. Rishikesh is at the end of a small branch **railway** line, served by trains to and from Haridwar. Advance reservations can be made from the station, which only has a small quota.

The telephone **area code** for Rishikesh is ☎01364.

Local transport connecting the main areas includes cycle and auto-rickshaws and shared *Vikrams*. Some head south towards Haridwar, but few go all the way. **Cars** and **taxis** can be rented through *Ajay Travels*, at the *Hotel Nilkanth*, Haridwar Rd (☎30644), or *Neelam's* restaurant, just off Haridwar Rd. Long-distance journeys can be booked at *Triveni Travels*, Shop No 1, opposite *PNB*, Haridwar Rd (☎30989).

The **UPT Tourist Office**, Nehru Park, Railway Rd (Mon–Sat 10am–5pm; ☎30209), is friendly and helpful but provides information only. **GMVN** in theory help arrange trekking and mountaineering from their headquarters in Muni-ki-Reti (☎30372), but you may find the private *Tourist Information & Facilitation Desk*, opposite *PNB*, Muni-ki-Reti (☎31654), more use; they also organize **rafting** on the Ganges.

Banks in town include the *State Bank of India*, Railway Lok, near *Inderlok Hotel* (☎30114), and *Bank of Baroda*, Dehra Dun Rd (both Mon–Sat 10am–2pm).

The Town

Most of the pilgrims who pass through Rishikesh on their way to the Himalayan shrines of the Char Dham pause for a dip and *puja* at the large sandy expanse of **Triveni Ghat**, close to the centre of town. The *ghat* looks especially spectacular during *arati* (evening worship), when *diya* lights float on the river. Nearby, at **Bharat Mandir**, Rishikesh's oldest temple, a black stone image of Vishnu is supposed to have been consecrated by Shankara in the ninth century; the event is commemorated during Basant Panchami, to mark the first day of spring.

The dense-knit complex of cafes, shops and ashrams collectively known as **Swarg Ashram**, opposite Shivananda Nagar, is the most attractive part of Rishikesh, backing on to forest-covered hills where caves are still inhabited by *sadhus*. The river can be crossed at this point either on the new Ram Jhula footbridge, or more romantically on **ferries**, which operate between 8am and 7pm according to demand (Rs2.50 one-way, Rs4 round-trip). The eponymous **Swarg Ashram** itself, popularly referred to as Kale

---

ASHRAMS, YOGA AND MEDITATION

Due to an ongoing dispute with the government, Maharishi Mahesh Yogi's beautifully situated **Shankaracharya Nagar Transcendental Meditation Centre**, home to the Beatles in February 1968, is not presently functioning; it stands empty on a high forested bluff above the river. However, plenty of other ashrams in Rishikesh welcome students of yoga, and don't charge the US$350 per day John Lennon et al. had to pay.

Shivananda Ashram Large institution, with branches all over the world, run by the *Divine Life Society* and founded by the remarkable Swami Shivananda (who passed into what his followers refer to as *maha samadhi*, final liberation, in 1963). It places an emphasis on the philosophy of Advaitya Vedanta, based on the belief of non-dual Brahman, or godhead as the undivided self, and has a well-stocked library, a forest retreat, and a charitable hospital with allopathic, homeopathic and Ayurvedic treatment. Courses in meditation and other forms of yoga, plus other activities, are always going on. To arrange a long-term stay, write one month in advance to the Secretary.

Dayananda Vedanta Ashram Not far from Shivananda Ashram; lectures on Vedanta and yoga classes.

Omkarananda Ashram Above Yoga Niketan, and also known as Durga Mandir; kindergarten school, plus classes which include classical Indian music and dance.

Vanamli Gita Yogashram On an idyllic site overlooking the river at Tapovan near Lakshmanjhula and offering short courses on different aspects of yoga.

Ved Niketan Huge ashram, across the river south of Swarg Ashram. Yoga classes early in the mornings and evening lectures.

Yoga Niketan Meditation centre, reached by a path adjacent to Shivananda Ashram. Founded by the late Swami Yogeshwarananda, it offers a range of courses, with accommodation if necessary.

Yoga Study Centre Reputable school for the Iyengar form of Hatha Yoga, 1km south of central Rishikesh.

Kumbli Wale, was founded in honour of Swami Vishudhanand, who came here in 1884 and habitually wore a black (*kala*) blanket (*kumble*). The most conspicuous of the other ashram-temples is **Parmarth Niketan**, whose large courtyard is crammed with brightly-clad gods and goddesses. Gita Bhavan runs a free Ayurvedic dispensary here, as well as selling books and *khadi,* handloom cloth.

Around 2km north of Swarg Ashram, a path skirts the east bank of the river, and beautiful sandy beaches sheltered by large boulders, en route to **Lakshmanjhula**. A footbridge named after the brother of Ram spans the river here as it negotiates its final rocky course out of the mountains. Many of the temples and ashrams around both ends of the bridge – such as the extraordinary futuristic **Kailashananda Ashram**, with each of its thirteen storeys dedicated to a different deity – are complete eyesores.

Accommodation

Choosing a place to **stay** depends where you want to be – the hotels of Rishikesh are the nearest to the buses and general amenities, and Muni-ki-Reti is not too far either. Swarg Ashram and the east bank of the river, away from the noise and near the ashrams, are more pleasant, but quite a way from town; Lakshmanjhula is further still.

Arvind Lodge, Yatra Bus Stand. Simple budget accommodation; not too bad at all, and very handy for early-morning buses to the hills. ①

Banprast Ashram, next to Ved Niketan, Swarg Ashram. Comfortable, very well maintained bungalows at extraordinarily good rates, in attractive grounds within a walled enclosure. ①.

Baseraa, 1 Ghat Rd (☎30767). Comfortable modern hotel in the heart of the market area. ⑤–⑥.

Bhandari Swiss Cottage, Lakshmanjhula. Two secluded cottages with spacious pleasant rooms, in beautiful woodland above the main road. Not to be confused with the *Swiss Cottage*, below. ③.

Ganga Kinar, Barrage Rd (☎30566). Large and overpriced place, 2km south of Rishikesh near the Ganges Barrage. Hosts an International Yoga Week, and runs yoga classes. ⑦.

GMVN Tourist Complex, Rishilok, Rishikesh (☎30373). Pleasant setting with garden and cottages away from the main centres. Busy during the *yatra* season. ④–⑤.

Green, Swarg Ashram (☎31242). Justifiably popular little hotel tucked behind Gita Bhavan. All rooms have attached baths, and a restaurant serves under-spiced Indian and Chinese food. ①–②.

Inderlok, Railway Rd (☎30555). Long-established and recommended central hotel. Comfortable rooms opening onto an inner well, plus restaurant, roof garden, and foreign exchange. ④–⑤.

Saket, 154 Ashutosh Nagar (☎31776). Off the Dehra Dun Rd down a quiet lane opposite the Yatra Bus Stand, with a small restaurant. The ordinary rooms share bathrooms without hot water. ③–④.

Shikar, Lakshmanjhula. Small, new and quite pleasant on the west bank, 500m from the bridge. ①.

Surichi, Yatra Bus Stand (☎30356). Modern and highly recommended hotel, with good restaurant. Convenient for buses for the Char Dham, if a bit far from the centre. ④.

Swiss Cottage, Chandra Bhaga. Run by the affable Swami Brahmananda, once one of Swami Shivananda's inner group of disciples. Near the bridge and down unnamed lanes towards the river, a small but peaceful haven with nine rooms in a motley selection of huts and buildings. Not an ashram, but popular with long-term visitors, and extremely good value, so often booked up. ①.

Ved Niketan, Swarg Ashram. Enormous ashram, well south on the east bank of the river. Very popular with low-budget westerners, though it is definitely more of an ashram than a hotel. ①.

CHAR DHAM BUSES

During the April to November pilgrimage season, when the **Char Dham** temples are open in the Garhwal Hills, direct buses connect Rishikesh's Yatra Bus Stand with Badrinath (297km), Kedarnath (210km, via Gaurikund), Gangotri (250km), and Yumnotri (280km, via Hanuman Chatti). Buses leave around 4am and few complete the journey in a day; the roads are treacherous and tedious, so you might prefer to break the journey along the way.

GMVN in Muni-ki-Reti organize **package tours** (a four-day trip to Badrinath, including bus, food and lodging, costs around Rs450), as well as very expensive car rental.

Eating

In addition to the restaurants in the larger hotels, Rishikesh has plenty of cafes and *dhabas*. *Neelam's* is an all-time favourite with an almost exclusively western clientele.

Anjali, Railway Rd. Popular cross between a *dhaba* and a restaurant.

Chotiwala's, Swarg Ashram. *The* place to eat on this side of the river – large, busy and famous cafe that has spawned imitators throughout the region. An extensive menu including ice cream, sweets and cold drinks, while a special *thali* costs around Rs22. Years ago, customers were greeted by a rotund pink cherub in a *dhoti* and shaven except for a large knot of hair, a *choti*, on the crown.

Madras Cafe, Shivananda Nagar. Near the ferry, and strong on south Indian food.

Neelam's, off Haridwar Rd. Towards the bridge and Muni-ki-Reti, Sikh-run *dhaba* always filled with young foreign travellers. Even if you want to get away from it all, the food and prices are worth it.

Around Rishikesh: local treks

Although a road has now been blasted through the forest to the small Shiva shrine in the hamlet of **Nilkantha**, east of Rishikesh, it's still possible to walk there along the old pilgrim path. This beautiful forest track rises through the forests behind Swarg Ashram, passes Mahesh Yogi's ashram, and eventually crosses a spur before descending to Nilkantha. There's a chance you may encounter wildlife along the way; keep a safe distance from wild elephants. Nilkantha itself is changing with its ever-growing numbers of pilgrims. Its small bazaar and *dharamshala* become especially animated for around a month from mid-July, when pilgrims flock to the temple, which commemorates the time when the god drank the poison of creation and ended up with a blue (*nil*) throat (*kantha*).

Another hike leads high above Lakshmanjhula for ten kilometres to the small white Shakti temple of **Kunjapuri**, at the sharp point of an almost perfectly conical hill with stupendous views of the Himalayas to the north and towards Haridwar in the south. Try to catch the sunrise from the top, before the haze seeps into the atmosphere.

PANCH PRAYAG – THE FIVE HOLY CONFLUENCES

As **Ganga** descended to earth at the behest of the gods, she fell onto Shiva's head and flowed down his matted locks; these strands are the mountains, where the separate ribbons of rivers meet to form the holy river before she emerges onto the plains of northern India. Five sacred **confluences** mark successive stages on the journey.

The Alaknanda, which rises near Badrinath, meets the Dhauli Ganga 10km north of Joshimath at **Vishnuprayag**, in a deep valley hidden from the sun for most of the day. A few shrines are all that mark the dramatic, rocky confluence.

The next confluence, where the river is joined by the Nandakini, is at the small town of **Nandprayag**, on the road from Uttarkashi that descends alongside the Alaknanda.

A further 21km downstream, the Alaknanda meets the Pindar, dropping from Nanda Devi, at the market town of **Karnaprayag**, named after a character in the *Mahabharata*.

The Alaknanda continues on its turbulent way to join the Mandakini at **Rudraprayag**, 34km from Karnaprayag. Rudraprayag has expanded haphazardly over recent years; the plaque that marks the famous spot where Jim Corbett shot a man-eating leopard is today at the heart of the noisy and bustling commercial centre. Crossing the river, a road forks up the valley, towards the source of the beautiful deep-blue Mandakini at Kedarnath.

After Rudraprayag, the Alaknanda descends through the open valley of Srinagar before its final and most dramatic mountain confluence, **Deoprayag**. Here it meets the Bhagirathi, a river of equal importance, descending from Gomukh on the glacier above Gangotri, and the two become the Ganga as it heads first to Rishikesh, 68km away, and then Haridwar, where it emerges on to the northern plains. The two mighty rivers meet with great force at a promontory of rock, where temples and a *ghat* in the shape of India extend into the confluence.

The Trek to Yumnotri

Cradled in a deep cleft in the lap of Bandarpunch, and thus denied mountain vistas, the temple of **Yumnotri** (3291m), 223km northeast of Rishikesh, marks the source of the Yamuna, India's second holiest river after the Ganges. As the least dramatic of the four *dhams* of Garhwal, it's also the most unspoiled and the least commercial, and the undemanding fourteen-kilometre (5hr) trek up to it from **Hanuman Chatti** is one of the region's most popular short hikes. The trail leads through attractive countryside, following the turbulent river as it runs below terraced fields, with snowy peaks in the distance.

Hanuman Chatti

The roadhead for the Yumnotri trek, **HANUMAN CHATTI**, is connected by bus with Dehra Dun, Mussoorie, and Rishikesh. Some routes necessitate a change at **Barkot**, 29km short, which has a scattering of accommodation. Buses and shared taxis run the last leg up from there along a poor-condition road that is prone to landslides. Hanuman Chatti itself holds an over-priced GMVN *Tourist Bungalow* (②–③), between the bus stand and the river, and a couple of better-value basic hotels nearby. Food is available either at the bungalow or at cafes around the bus stand.

The path leads up across a bridge from Hanuman Chatti to meet the trail to Dodi Tal (see p.250), then veers left along the Yamuna for 6km, passing one or two small hamlets with tea shops, to **Phul Chatti**, where a couple more tea shops serve food. If you're planning any more ambitious trekking than the hike up to Yumnotri you're strongly advised to secure the aid of a local **guide**; Tota Ram and the older Shankar Singh are based in Phul Chatti, and others can be found in Hanuman Chatti.

Janki Chatti

The main trail from Phul Chatti continues along the river and over a bridge. A short and narrow section then traverses a landslide high above the river, before widening to reach **JANKI CHATTI**, 3km out of Phul Chatti. As the village gets a lot more sun then Yumnotri, just 5km further up, and is significantly larger and more hospitable, a lot of trekkers choose to stay here. Its GMVN *Tourist Bungalow* (②–③) is friendly, if a bit overpriced, and has its own cafe. GMVN also run a simpler hostel with dormitories (①), down by the river, and further along the main trail, the *Ganga Jamuna* (①–②) provides a new alternative, with a cafe.

While you're in Janki Chatti, it's worth making the one-kilometre detour across the river to the traditional Garhwali village of **Kharsali**, home to the *pandas* (pilgrim priests) of Yumnotri. Its dry stone buildings, with their beautifully carved wooden beams, contrast sharply with the characterless concrete structures cropping up all over the *yatra* trails of Garhwal. However, the unique three-storey Shiva temple – dedicated to Someshwar, lord of the mythical intoxicant Soma – has developed a slight tilt since the terrible earthquake of 1990. You can also hike to Kharsali direct from Phul Chatti.

Yumnotri

A short way beyond Janki Chatti, the trail begins to get really interesting. One especially hair-raising stretch involves negotiating a vertical cliff-face on a path 50 metres above the river, which when not hacked into the rock is built out over the abyss on concrete slabs. It's straightforward enough if you keep your head, but some of the path is in poor condition and the railings are often inadequate. You can only sympathize with the pilgrims who come this way mounted on ponies; as well having to duck to avoid the overhanging roof, they are under strict instructions never to look down.

After a final climb through some beautiful rocky forested crags, the path rounds a bend to offer the first glimpse of the small and dingy hamlet of **YUMNOTRI**, just a few hundred metres away. Sited near the river, around three piping-hot sulphur springs,

Yumnotri's **temple** is new and architecturally uninteresting; it has to be completely rebuilt every few years due to the impact of heavy winter snows and monsoon rains. Its main shrine – actually part of the top spring, worshipped as the source of the river – holds a small silver image of the goddess Yamuna, bedecked with garlands. The daughter of Surya, the sun, and Sangya, consciousness, Yamuna is the twin sister of Yama, the lord of death; all who bathe in her waters are spared a painful end, while food cooked in the water is considered to be *prasad* (divine offering).

Technically, the source of the Yamuna is the glacial lake of **Saptarishi Kund**. This is reached via a hard twelve-kilometre trek, which heads straight up the mountain alongside the river until finally easing towards the base of Kalinda Parbat. Both this trek, and the route over the challenging Yumnotri Pass to Har-ki-Dun (see p.239) necessitate at least one day's acclimatization, and the services of a guide.

If you choose to **stay** in Yumnotri, there's a simple dormitory at the GMVN *Tourist Bungalow* near the temple (①). Probably the best of the few *dharamshalas* is the *Ramananda Ashram* (①), commanding good views from the hill above the temple, and owned by the head priest. Simple food arrangements can be made through the ashrams and the bungalow. Below the temple, a bridge leads across the river to a small complex of tea stalls and shops selling paraphernalia for worship.

THE DODI TAL TREK

The relatively short **Dodi Tal trek**, which links the Gangotri and Yumnotri regions without straying into high glacial terrain, is one of Garhwal's all-time classics. It's not a difficult hike, but local villagers are keen to offer their services as porters or guides, and you should definitely avail yourself of their help if you want to wander off the beaten track. Carry as much of your own food as possible, and also your own tent.

The trek is described below from east to west, starting from **Uttarkashi** on the way to Gangotri, and ending at **Hanuman Chatti**, the roadhead for Yumnotri.

On **DAY 1**, catch one of the three daily buses from Uttarkashi to **Kalyani** via Gangotri (the first is at 7am, and takes 1hr). From Kalyani, a good but steep trail rises through open fields to **Agoda**, 7km on. Stop for the night at the basic *Tourist Bungalow* (①), at the far end of the village, however tempted you may be to press on. You'll need a carry-mat to sleep on.

On **DAY 2**, the trail from Agoda climbs beside a river and then zig-zags steadily upwards through lush pine and spruce forests, with a couple of *chai* shops en route. After 14km and a final undulation, it arrives at **Dodi Tal** (3024m), a lake set against a backdrop of thickly forested hills. The basic forest bungalow in the clearing here, severely damaged by the earthquake, has yet to be repaired, so there's just a *chai* shop and some simple accommodation, which can get cramped – you may prefer to use your own tent.

Some trekkers consider the full 18km from Dodi Tal to Shima on **DAY 3** to be too long and arduous, and prefer to split it into two days. Follow the well-marked path along (and often across) the stream that feeds Dodi Tal, which can get steep and entail scrambling; continue straight ahead, ignoring tracks that cross the trail, until you emerge above the treeline. After a further 1.5km the trail heads left to a small pass then zig-zags up scree to **Darwa Top** (4130m). This is the highest point of the trek, providing superb panoramas of the Srikanta range. If you're ready to rest here, a leftward path beyond the top leads to camping and water. The main route goes down to a valley and then climbs sharply again. **Shima**, where you re-join the treeline, has basic hut accommodation; bring your own food.

The beautiful 12km trail down from Shima on **DAY 4** kicks off with a steep 1.5km scramble alongside a stream, then eases past forest and *bugyal*, where shepherds have their huts. A well-defined rocky path drops steadily through two villages and zigzags down to the Hanuman Ganga river. It emerges at **Hanuman Chatti** (see p.249), from where buses run via Barkot to Uttarkashi, Mussoorie and other points in Garhwal.

The Dodi Tal trek can be easily be tied in with hikes in the **Har-ki-Dun** and **Yumnotri** areas; see also pages 239 and 249.

Uttarkashi

The largest town in the interior of Garhwal, **UTTARKASHI**, occupies the flat and fertile valley floor of the Bhagirathi. Most pilgrims pass through without bothering to stop, but it can make a warm and sunny break in the long journey between Rishikesh, 148km south, and Gangotri, 100km northeast. *Uttar* Kashi ("northern Kashi"), like Varanasi (also known as "Kashi"), centres around the Shiva temple of **Vishwanatha**, although the unassuming temple complex here, surrounded by large trees, has much less spiritual significance. In fact, Uttarkashi was little known to the outside world until it lent its name to the massive nearby earthquake in 1991.

Uttarkashi's busy and well-stocked market is ideal for stocking up on supplies before high-altitude treks, and the town is also a good place to contact experienced mountain **guides** – mostly graduates of its Nehru Institute of Mountaineering. The going rates stand at around Rs60 per porter and Rs100–150 for a guide. Specialist operators include *Mount Support*, PO Box 2, B D Nautial Bhawan, Bhatwari Rd (☎01374/2419), on the main road near the bus stand, who also have equipment for rent.

Practicalities

All **buses** to and from Uttarkashi – which has hourly services to both Gangotri and Rishikesh between May and November – stop on the main highway, near the bazaar between the road and the river. **Taxis** can be picked up in the market area; the round trip to Gangotri costs around Rs800. On the main drag, the information-only **Tourist Bureau** (☎01374/2290) is almost hidden behind the queues of noisy buses.

Good and reasonably priced **lodges** in the main bazaar include the *Hanslok* (②–④), and the *Meghdoot*, next door (②–④). Both have some a/c rooms. GMVN's poorly run *Tourist Bungalow* (③–④), around 1km away near the bridge, is a large faceless complex with a garden, where the spacious rooms have attached baths. Away from the bustle, in a pleasant location overlooking the valley 3km north of Uttarkashi just off the Gangotri road, the *Monal* (①–②) has cheap and comfortable rooms, but no restaurant.

Among the many *bhojanalaya* (vegetarian cafes) in central Uttarkashi, *Roopam* on the main road serves healthy local cuisine with *dhal* and fresh *roti*.

Gangotri and around

Set amid tall *deodar* pine forests at the head of the Bhagirathi gorge, 248km north of Rishikesh at 3140m, **Gangotri** is the most picturesque of the four *dhams* (pilgrimage sites) of Garhwal. Although the Alaknanda, which flows past Badrinath, has in some ways a better claim to be considered the main channel of the Ganges, Gangotri is for Hindus the spiritual source of the great river, while its physical source is the ice cave of **Gomukh** on the Gangotri Glacier, 14km further up the valley. From here, the **River Bhagirathi** begins its tempestuous descent through a series of mighty gorges, carving great channels and cauldrons in the rock and foaming in white-water pools.

The road up

Several daily buses run from **Uttarkashi** to Gangotri. The first significant town en route, **Gangnani**, has a welcome hot spring above the road and a temple, plus a couple of *dharamshalas*, *chai* shops and a simple GMVN *Tourist Bungalow* (②). An Italian "baba", or *sadhu*, and his family have taken up residence here, and have become a well-known curiosity throughout Garhwal.

Parts of the road beyond, where the vast and fertile Bhagirathi flood plain is famous for its apple orchards, were damaged by the earthquake; gigantic blocks of rock almost dammed the river and created a lake. **Harsil**, off the main road down a rough track 31km along, marks the bottom limit of the Gangotri gorge. The village itself is grubby and depressing, and harbours a large army base, but there's a new and very pleasant *Tourist Bungalow* (②–③) beside the river. A stone path leads along the valley floor and over a couple of bridges to an appealing Bhotia village. Prayer flags flutter over the small Buddhist temple of Vagori, standing amid the apple trees in a small garden.

Ten kilometres beyond Harsil, the road crosses the deep Bhagirathi gorge at **Lanka**, on a dramatic bridge said to be among the highest in the world. This is an army area, so don't take any photographs. At the hamlet of **Bhaironghati**, 3km further on and 11km short of Gangotri, the Rudragaira emerges from its own gorge to meet the Bhagirathi. A small temple stands in towering *deodar* forests, and there are a few tea shops as well as a barely used GMVN *Tourist Bungalow* (②–③).

Gangotri

Although most of the nearby snow peaks are obscured by the desolate craggy mountains looming immediately above **GANGOTRI** itself, the town itself is redolent of the atmosphere of the high Himalayas, populated by a mixed and ever-changing cast of Hindu pilgrims and foreign trekkers. Its unassuming **temple**, overlooking the river just beyond a small market on the left bank, was built early in the eighteenth century by the Gurkha general Amar Singh Thapa. Capped with a gilded roof, consisting of a squat *shikhara* surrounded by four smaller replicas, it commemorates the legend that the Ganga was enticed to earth by acts of penance performed by King Bhagirath, who wanted her to revitalize the ashes of his people. As she fell from heaven, Shiva braced the impact by entangling her in his locks; she was released by Brahma in answer to further prayers from the pious king. Inside the temple is a silver image to the goddess, while a slab of stone adjacent to the temple is venerated as **Bhagirath Shila**, the spot where the king meditated. Steps lead down to the main riverside *ghat*, where the devout bathe in order to cleanse their bodies and souls of sin.

Across the river, a loose development of ashrams and guest houses leads down to **Dev Ghat**, overlooking the confluence with the Kedar Ganga. Not far beyond, at the impressive waterfall-fed pool of **Gaurikund**, the 20-kilometre-long gorge starts to get into its stride. Beautiful forest paths lead through the dark *deodar* woods and past a bridge along the edge of the gorge to a flimsy rope-bridge, commanding great views of the ferocious river below.

Several **teashops** and **lodges**, whose rates rise wildly in high season, lie below the final carpark and bus stand at the Gangotri roadhead. Most of the nicer guest houses lie across the river from here, reachable either via a beautiful footbridge or the main cantilever bridge near the temple; this bank is leafier and more pleasant, even if it doesn't catch so much sun. GMVN's *Tourist Bungalow* (①–③), over the footbridge, has a reasonably cheap dorm. Nearer the main bridge, the large and popular *Ganga Niketan* (①–②) has a cafe overlooking the river, and *Birla Mangal Niketan* (①) is a large faceless block opposite the temple, where rates for the spacious rooms with attached baths remain fixed all season. The most attractive of the bungalows, the *Forest*

GANGOTRI ASHRAMS

Although most of the so-called "ashrams" in Gangotri are in reality boarding houses, a few *sadhus* offer rooms on a donation basis for visitors looking for a quiet retreat.

The simple, atmospheric **Kailash Ashram**, overlooking the confluence of the Kedar Ganga and the Bhagirathi, is run (along with a small Ayurvedic clinic) by the affable Bhim Yogi, who welcomes guests for medium- and long-term stays. Nearby, **Nani Mata's Ashram** belongs to an English *mataji* (woman *sadhu*), who has lived in Gangotri for many years and is held in high esteem. Above Kailash Ashram, the larger **Yoga Niketan** ashram, set in an attractive garden, operates along much more regimented lines, with fixed meal times and meditation periods, and a fixed though nominal fee.

Guest House (①), is a beautiful new log cabin in immaculate gardens; it can only be booked through the Forestry Department in Uttarkashi.

Meat is not available in Gangotri; the best places to eat are the large terrace at the *Ganga Niketan*, where the open-air seating comes with colourful umbrellas, and the *Manisha*, near the bus stand, which serves simple south and north Indian food.

Gomukh and Gangotri Glacier

A flight of steps alongside the temple at Gangotri leads up to join a large pony path that rises gently, providing stunning mountain vistas, towards the **Gangotri Glacier** – one of the most beautiful and accessible glaciers in the inner Himalayas, within 17km of the road. As the path emerges from the trees just beyond Gangotri, and the day progresses, you know you're in for a long hot climb in the high-altitude sun.

Approaching the oasis of **Chirbasa**, 7km out of Gangotri, the skyline is dominated by magnificent buttresses and glass-like walls, culminating in the sharp pinnacles of Bhagirathi 3 (6454m) and Bhagirathi 1 (6856m). Chirbasa amounts to no more than a few tea shops strung along the path for around 500m, as it winds through a rocky sheltered section. These provide basic meals and mattresses, or tents – the best are on the Gomukh path out of town – and there's also a basic forest lodge (①), below the road.

The path then climbs above the treeline, continuing along the widening valley to enter a high mountain desert. A number of accidents have been reported at the point just beyond Chirbasa where the trail across a cliff face has badly deteriorated, so great care is called for. Soon after crossing a stream, the path rounds a shoulder to offer a glimpse of the glacier's snout near Gomukh, the ever-present Bhagirathi peaks, and the huge expanse of the Gangotri Glacier – 24km long, and up to 4km wide – sweeping like a gigantic highway through the heart of the mountains.

Down below on the flat valley bottom, 5km from Chirbasa, is the cold grey hamlet of **Bhojbasa**, where most visitors spend the night before heading on to Gomukh. For once, the GMVN *Tourist Bungalow* here (①–③) comes out on top – even though mice run riot, and there's no electricity. As well as a dormitory and basic double rooms, some with attached bathrooms, there are some chilly but rodent-free tents. Guests huddle in the evening in the small but friendly cafe, which is where to arrange for a mountain **guide** if you plan to cross the glaciers. Accommodation in the only competitor, *Lal Baba's Ashram* (①), is even more basic – just mattresses on the floor.

A good track continues from Bhojbasa for 5km to **Gomukh** ("the Cow's Mouth"), where the river emerges with great force from a cavern in the glacier. As the ice is constantly in flux, the huge greyish-blue snout of the glacier continually changes in appearance, and chunks of ice tumble into the gushing water – be careful of standing above the cave. Two or three *chai* shops near here provide food and basic shelter.

Tapovan and Nandanvan

The campsites of **Tapovan** and **Nandanvan**, 6km beyond Gomukh on slightly divergent glacier-side routes, are popular objectives for lightweight trekking and mountaineering, as a rule best attempted using guides engaged from Gangotri or Bhojbasa.

A difficult track leads past the last tea shop at Gomukh to ascend the moraine on the left edge of the glacier, following it for 1km before crossing the glacier diagonally towards a high point in the middle, in line with Shivling. Depending on the season, this stage can be confusing and dangerous; heavy snow can conceal deep crevasses and the cairns that mark the way. From the high point, you should be able to see a stream coming down the high bank opposite. Use this as a marker; an extremely steep and strenuous climb up unstable ground runs to its left, to top out eventually on the peaceful grassy meadow of **TAPOVAN**, where you're greeted by the fantastic sight of Shivling (6543m) towering above. With its herds of grazing, almost tame *bharal* (mountain goats), and tranquil stream, the meadow makes a bizarre contrast to the sea of ice below.

TREKKING IN TEHRI GARWHAL: KHATLING GLACIER

The **Khatling Glacier**, source of the Bhilangana, lies at the head of a remote valley between the Gangotri and Kedarnath regions. It forms a huge watershed, with Jaonli (6632m) to the west, the Jogin group (6465m) to the north, and the striking peaks of Kirti Stambh (6270m) and Bharte Kunta (6578m) to the east. The upper Bhilangana valley is virtually unspoiled, with vast tracts of forest, beautiful waterfalls, and mountain streams descending from high *bugyals*.

Trails radiate from the nearest roadhead, **Ghuttu**, 147km north of Rishikesh, to the Bhagirathi to the west, and Sonprayag and the Mandakini valley to the east, while high mountain routes lead to Kedarnath via Khatling, and Uttarkashi via Gomukhi Tal.

Most long-distance bus journeys to Ghuttu involve a change at **Ghansyali** on the Uttarkashi–Rudraprayag road, three hours' drive west of Tehri (served by regular buses to and from Rishikesh). Simple hotels and cafes can be found at Ghansyali and Ghuttu.

The Khatling Glacier trail

DAY 1 of the moderately strenuous trail up to **Khatling Glacier** is a gentle introduction, with an ascent of just 650m in the 10km hike from Ghuttu to **Reeh**. You can stay above Reeh in the *Forest Rest House* (①) at Buranshchauri. An arduous trek of 10km on **DAY 2** brings you to the last inhabited village of the valley, **Gangi**. Continue 6km to camp at **Kalyani**, a village used by shepherds during the grazing season. **DAY 3** leads 14km from Kalyani, beyond Kharsoli, to **Bhelbagi** – at 3110m, the base camp for the glacier. On **DAY 4**, follow a rough trail up to Khatling Glacier (3658m), for a grand view (weather permitting) of the amphitheatre of snow peaks, and back to **Bhelbagi** – a 14km round trip.

On to Kedarnath

Using local guides, acclimatized and well-equipped trekkers can continue beyond Khetling Glacier to **Kedarnath** (see p.256), past a succession of mountain lakes. From **Bhelbagi**, a difficult track leads 7km to **Maser Tal** (4572m), where pilgrims bathe in the freezing waters. Camping here is recommended, as the icy conditions get extreme at the high **Pain Tal** (5629m), 7km further on. From there, a track descends rough terrain for 6km to **Vasuki Tal** (4328m); you could camp here, but if you're going well and are dying for a *chai* shop and a bed, Kedarnath is just 9km further along a well-marked pony track. However, the descent to 3584m can be hard on the legs. From **Kedarnath** a 14km pony track, often full of pilgrims, leads to the Sonprayag roadhead and a hot spring.

Sahastra Tal

The seven small lakes known as **Sahastra Tal** lie close to each other, high on the divide between the Bhilangana valley in Tehri Garhwal and the Philangana valley in Uttarkashi, and cradled within rough rocky ground, covered with snow for much of the year. The lakes are venerated by local people in the belief that the Pandavas of the *Mahabharata* inhabited their shores, and built the natural stone terraces to sow their grain. During the rainy season, villagers from both sides of the divide carry deities to the lakes in an annual pilgrimage and perform ceremonies for their dead ancestors.

Although the lakes can be reached along a 35km trek from Malla on the Uttarkashi–Gangotri road, via Shilla and the simple refuge of Dharmshala, the path from **Gangi** to the highest lake – **Gomukhi Tal**, on the Bhilangana side – is shorter, and can be combined with the trip to Khatling Glacier. From **Kalyani** (see above), a rough track that becomes progressively harder to discern rises for 8km to the campsite at Tari Udiyar.

The Sonprayag trail

The major pilgrim path that linked the Gangotri and Uttarkashi region with Kedarnath until the motor road opened leads east from Ghuttu to **Sonprayag** (see p.256), with simple shelter and food available along the way. The first stop is the village of Panwali Kanta, 10km out of Ghuttu. Maggu is 6km further on, and the popular temple village of **Triyugi Narayan**, with its eternal flame (see p.256), is 5km beyond that. A rough motor road connects Triyugi Narayan to the main road, and a trail of around 3km cuts through the forest to Sonprayag.

Many trekkers arrive in Tapovan without camping equipment, expecting to shelter in either of its two ashrams. However, although Mataji, a female *sadhu* who lives here throughout the year, and Shimla Baba do indeed have small hermitages with blankets, and are prepared to feed visitors, their resources are greatly stretched. Whether or not you stay with them, please carry supplies, which will always be welcome, and bring camping and cooking equipment if you plan to be here more than a day or two.

NANDANVAN lies on a similar but less frequented meadow below the Bhagirathi Peaks, at the junction of the glacier known as the Chaturang Bamak and the Gangotri Glacier. From here you get magnificent views of Bhagirathi, Shivling, and the huge snowy mass of **Kedar Dome** (6831m), hiding a steep sheer rocky face. The trail up follows the same path from Gomukh, but instead of the diagonal slant towards Tapovan continues across the Raktaban Glacier and follows the left bank of the Gangotri Glacier. If you do get confused and find yourself in Nandanvan by mistake, an indistinct 3km trail across Gangotri Glacier leads back to Tapovan.

Kedar Tal
Kedar Tal, the source of the Kedar Ganga – an emerald lake 5000m above sea level, surrounded by a grand amphitheatre of mountains – makes a challenging objective. Although it's only 17km from Gangotri, the 2000m climb to such an altitude means that trekkers should be well equipped and fully acclimatized to the height.

A steep rough trail through the forest from Dandi Chetra, near Gangotri's Dev Ghat, follows the right bank of the Kedar Ganga for 7.5km to the meadow of **Bhoj Kharak**. At this point – a good campground – the pine woods give way to *bhoj* (birch), whose bark was used to write on before the introduction of paper. Continuing along a stretch made treacherous by rockfall and avalanche, the path rises for 4km above the treeline to reach another *bugyal* (meadow) suitable for camping – **Kedar Kharak**.

From Kedar Kharak, the gruelling 5km ascent to Kedar Tal scrambles over difficult loose terrain directly towards the rocky pinnacle of Thalesagar. Surrounding the beautiful glacial lake at the head of the valley, the cirque of mountains include, from left to right, Bhrigupanth (6772m), Thalesagar (6904m) and the Jogin group.

The Route to Kedarnath

It's hard to imagine a more dramatic setting for a temple than **Kedarnath**, 223km north of Rishikesh, close to the source of the Mandakini at 3583m above sea level, and overlooked by tumbling glaciers and huge buttresses of ice, snow and rock.

Kedarnath – the "field" (*kedara*) where the crop of *moksha* (liberation) is sown – is the most important shrine in the Himalayas, and among the major Shiva temples of all India. According to the *Puranas*, when the Pandavas were searching for Shiva to grant them absolution, they succeeded in tracking him down to Kedarnath, where he disguised himself as a bull in a herd of cattle. One of the brothers, Bhim, then straddled the valley and allowed the herd to pass beneath him, reasoning that the only bull to refuse must be Shiva himself. When Shiva was unmasked, he dived into the ground; Bhim grabbed him from behind, and held on tight. However, all that remained of the god was his rear; his *lingam* appeared in Varanasi (Kashi), while assorted other pieces of his anatomy are commemorated by the Panch Kedar temples (see p.258).

As one of India's twelve *Jyotrilinga – lingams* of light – Kedarnath attracts hordes of pilgrims in summer, undeterred by the gruelling fourteen-kilometre trek up from the roadhead at **Gaurikund** that forms the final leg of the journey. So popular is it on the *yatra* trail that the path up has been all but stripped of vegetation, used for fuel and to feed the ponies that carry wealthier pilgrims. *Chai* shops set up to provide food and shelter all along the route, especially in the upper sections, add to the environmental damage.

The road up

The main road to Kedarnath heads north from Rudraprayag towards Sonprayag. Deep in the Mandakini valley, the temple of **Kalimath** is one of the few temples devoted to Kali in the region. Beyond it, on the road to Gopeshwar, is the pleasant town of **Okhimath**, to which the population of Kedarnath decamps in winter, to continue worship when the high temple is snowed in.

Larger **Sonprayag** was, until the road was pushed another 5km up to Gaurikund in the late 1970s, the transport junction for Kedarnath, which explains its sizeable bus stand and plentiful amenities, including a pretentious hotel-like *Tourist Lodge* (②–③). From Sonprayag, a rough but drivable road rises 3km to the temple of **Triyugi Narayan**, outside which an eternal flame burns on the spot where Shiva and Sati are said to have been married in the presence of Vishnu (also known as Narayan).

Gaurikund

GAURIKUND, formerly a charming village but since the advent of the motor road and the expansion of its *yatra* trade rapidly growing into a small ugly town, is for the moment the starting point of the trek up to Kedarnath (although there are plans to extend the road to Rambara). En route to or from chilly Kedarnath, a dip in its **Tapt Kund** hot springs can be very welcome, although sadly they are not well maintained. The small temple of Gauri Devi, adjacent to the pool, is dedicated to Parvati.

Direct buses run to Gaurikund all the way from Rishikesh, but most visitors arrive on local buses and taxis from the larger bus terminal at **Guptkashi**, 29km lower down. This receives services from Rudraprayag, 109km south on the busy main Rishikesh–Joshimath–Badrinath route, and Gopeshwar, 138km southeast.

Inexpensive *dharamshalas* and rest houses in Gaurikund itself include the large grey *Bharat Seva Ashram* (①), *Punjab Sindh* (①–②), where some rooms have attached baths, and the smaller *Sanjay Lodge* and *Sunil Lodge* (both ①–②). Rates for the very cosy rooms in the GMVN *Tourist Centre* (①–④) are pricier, but remain constant even in high season (when it's advisable to book in advance), and it also has a cheap dorm. The *Gauri's Grand* **restaurant** is a complete culture shock, with MTV piped through the sound system – however, it is comfortable and clean and its wide-ranging menu even extends as far as veggie burgers.

The trail from Gaurikund

A large pony track, dotted with *chai* shops, climbs from Gaurikund, traversing the hillside through the disappearing forests, to the village of **Rambara**, 7km up and halfway to Kedarnath. With its many cafes and rest houses (and open sewers), Rambara signals the end of the tree-line and the start of the alpine zone. Several conspicuous short cuts scar the hillside as the track rises steeply to Garur Chatti, then levels off roughly 1km short of Kedarnath. Suddenly, rounding a corner, you come face to face with the incredible south face of the peak of Kedarnath (6940m) at the end of the valley, with the temple town dwarfed beneath it and almost insignificant in the distance.

Kedarnath: town and treks

KEDARNATH is not in itself a very attractive town – in fact it's almost unbearable at the height of the pilgrimage season (May, June & Sept). It's a grey place, consisting of a central thoroughfare stretching for 500 metres between the temple and the bridge, lined with rest houses and *dharamshalas*, pilgrim shops, and administrative offices. However, the sheer power of its location tends to sweep away any negative impressions, and it's always possible to escape to explore the incredible high-altitude scenery.

At the head of the town, the imposing **temple** is constructed along simple lines in stone, with a large *mandapa* (fore-chamber) housing an impressive stone image of

SHANKARA IN GARWHAL

Immediately behind the temple at Kedarnath, towards the glacier, a gigantic hand holding an ascetic's staff protrudes from a marble wall. This newly-built monument – which, it has to be said, is a complete eyesore – commemorates the ninth-century Hindu philosopher and reformer, **Shankara**, who is said to have died here.

Shankara travelled through the region as the Buddhist era came to a close, introducing sweeping reforms that helped to create the order of *sanyas* (monkhood). In Garhwal, he converted fertility and animist cults into Shaivite and Vaishnavite shrines, and helped to establish the great pilgrimage centres such as Kedarnath. Today, the **Rawal** who heads both Badrinath and Kedarnath continues to be chosen from the same Nambudiri sect of Keralan *brahmins* that he belonged to. Among the four major seats of learning set up by Shankara in the four corners of India, each headed by a *Shankaracharya*, was one in Joshimath.

Shiva's bull, Nandi. Within the inner sanctum, open to all, *pandas* sit around a rock considered to be the hindquarters of Shiva, left as he plunged head-first into the ground. Mendicant *sadhus* congregate in the elevated courtyard in front of the temple.

A solid path from near the main bridge, before the town, crosses the Mandakini to the left of the valley, and ends 4km away at the **glacier**. At its edge, the **Chorabari Tal** lake is now known as **Gandhi Sarovar**, as some of Mahatma Gandhi's ashes were scattered here. Close by, around 800m before the lake, is the source of the Mandakini; it emerges from a hole in the moraine on extremely suspect ground, which should not be approached. You could also cross the river by the small bridge behind the temple, and scramble up the rough boulder-strewn moraine to meet the main track.

East of town, a well-marked path rises diagonally along the hillside to the prayer flags that mark a small shrine of the wrathful emanation of Shiva – **Bhairava**. The cliff known as **Bhairava Jhamp** is said to be somewhere nearby; until the British banned the practice in the nineteenth century, fanatical pilgrims used to leap to their deaths from it in the hope of gaining instant liberation.

The most challenging of all the Kedarnath excursions is the 9km trek to the lake of **Vasuki Tal** (4328m). From the *Tourist Bungalow*, a well-marked pony track zigzags in clear view of Kedarnath, heading up the hill for around 1km before negotiating scree and rough ground near the crest, and descending slightly to Vasuki Tal. Don't be surprised to find wealthier pilgrims being led most of the way on horseback. Beyond Vasuki Tal, a challenging trail – only to be attempted with full supplies, appropriate clothing and an experienced guide – continues to the **Khatling Glacier**, via the high lakes of Pain Tal and Maser Tal (see p. 254).

PRACTICALITIES

Kedarnath's GMVN *Tourist Bungalow* (①–④), standing like a disused railway station to the right of the path before the bridge that leads into town, has a cheap dorm and standard double rooms. Appealing alternatives include the clean and comfortable *Bharat Seva Ashram* (①), a large red building beyond the temple on the left; the pleasantly located bungalow of *Modi Bhavan* (②), behind and above the temple near the monument, which has large rooms and kitchenettes; and *Punjab Sindh* (①–②), next to the post office on the right of the main road.

Food in the cafes along Kedarnath's main street is simple but expensive, as all supplies have to be brought up from the valley on horseback. The canteen run by the temple committee, *Shri Badrinath Kedarnath Mandi Samiti*, behind the temple, serves meals and *alu paratha*. It is also a good place to contact a mountain **guide**, if you plan to attempt the Vasuki Tal and Khatling crossing.

Panch Kedar

Pilgrim trails cross the heart of Garhwal from Guptkashi in the west to Gopeshwar and the Alaknanda valley in the east, winding their way far above the steamy valleys and terraced fields, up through beautiful forests to the sharp grassy ridges that hold the widely scattered Shiva temples collectively known as **Panch Kedar**.

The Panch Kedar temples almost certainly started life as shrines to fertility gods, and had little to do with each other until the ninth-century reformer Shankara passed this way and incorporated them into the framework of Hindu mythology, saying that they represent the five (*panch*) parts of Shiva's body left protruding from the earth when he escaped the Pandavas by fleeing into the underworld (see p.255). Strictly speaking, the five include Kedarnath, but the term usually refers only to the other four, which have escaped the commercialism of the main *yatra* trails.

These four – **Madhmaheshwar** in the northwest; **Tunganath**, the highest temple in India, at 3680m, in the centre; and **Rudranath**, with **Kalpeshwar** below it, overlooking the Alaknanda valley in the east – can be taken in on a long circular trek. However, most visitors use vehicles along the Okhimath–Gopeshwar road to avoid the hike between the separate areas. Even if you do that, getting to the temples themselves involves a bit of trekking, although **Tunganath** is only 3km above Chopta on the main road. One daily **bus** leaves Gaurikund, near Kedarnath, at 5am, for Badrinath, and stops at access points for Panch Kedar en route; a local bus connects Gopeshwar and Guptkashi.

Madhmaheshwar

The most remote of the Panch Kedar temples, at **MADHMAHESHWAR**, north of **Okhimath**, is also the least visited. One of Garhwal's most beautiful roads climbs up from the Mandakini valley beyond Okhimath for 10km through dense forest to the tiny hamlet of **Sari**, the start of the 5km trail to the wooded lake of **Deoria Tal**.

Beyond Deoria Tal, the trail continues for 15km, through the village of Mansuna and across the Madhmaheshwar Ganga river, to Lank and Ransi. At this point, a poor trail, only to be attempted with a guide, branches left across the high ridges to Kedarnath. The main path from Ransi, however, continues 3km to Gondhar, crosses a river, then climbs 10km to the hamlet of Madhmaheshwar, set in pleasant meadows at 3497m. The small temple here, a simple stone structure with colourfully painted woodwork on the door and on the top of the *shikhara*, is dedicated to the middle (*madhya*) of the bull-Shiva. The village offers simple pilgrim shelter and food.

Chopta and Tunganath

The beautiful little village of **CHOPTA** is situated amid dark *deodar* forests and sweeping alpine meadows at the end of the road up from Okhimath (21km) and Gopeshwar (40km). This quiet and peaceful spot holds a few simple *chai* shops and the region's one – over-priced – GMVN *Tourist Bungalow* (①–④), where the rooms have attached baths, with hot water available by the bucket. They also run camping facilities and a rather poor roadside cafe.

A steep three-kilometre trail climbs up from Chopti, winding through a dense forest of pine and rhododendron before emerging onto open meadows along a well-marked pony track as the view towards the Yumnotri, Gangotri and Kedarnath peaks gradually unfolds. The virgin forests around teem with wildlife such as leopard and bear. As you approach, a tiny dot near the top of the ridge, reveals itself to be the stone temple of **Tunganath**, associated with Shiva's hand (*bahu*). Simple accommodation and food is available here; due to its exposed position, it can get very cold indeed, even in summer.

Beyond Tunganath, a well-marked path skirts the edge of the precipitous ridge, and zigzags for 1km up the steep *bugyal* to culminate at the grassy knoll of **Chandrashila Peak** (3930m), with an incredible 180° panorama of Himalayan snow peaks.

Kalpeshwar and Rudranath

The unspoiled temples of **Kalpeshwar** and **Rudranath** are most easily accessed from the Badrinath–Rishikesh highway as it runs through the Alaknanda valley, although tackling the route from the other end, starting at Mandal on the Chopta–Gopeshwar road, makes it easier to combine with Tunganath. Either way, the criss-crossing mountain paths can get very confusing, and enlisting the aid of a guide is advisable.

Buses along the Badrinath–Rishikesh highway serve the village of **Helang**, 14km south of Joshimath, from where a path sets off across a footbridge over the Alaknanda and winds for 9km to **Urgam**. As well as its own temple, Urgam has simple accommodation and food. A 1.5km side trail leads to the temple of **KALPESHWAR**, dedicated to the *jata* (hair) of the bull-Shiva, beside a cave with a beautiful waterfall.

A little further beyond, in **Dumak**, the last village before Rudranath, it's possible to stay in the postmaster's house. Several trails split off; but the main trail first rises, then descends to cross a river, and rises once more to the lake of **Toli**, after 9km. Used for pasture, this has no accommodation; continue to **Panar**, where a *sadhu* provides accommodation in a cave beyond two small Shiva temples, and there's also excellent camping, with a good supply of water. From here on you'll have to be self-sufficient.

Beyond Panar, the path follows the high ridge visible from Tunganath, sometimes left and sometimes right of the crest, to the junction of several trails. After 3km, you come to a col; the hamlet of **RUDRANATH** lies a short distance right of the crest, with some small stone shrines dedicated to the mouth of the bull-Shiva. There are a few houses up here, but the whole place closes during the long winters – check whether anyone will be around before you set off.

Back at the col on the ridge, you should be able to pick out the 16km track that descends to the Shakti temple of **Anasuya Devi**, set on a shelf in a spellbinding spot in the woods. Below Anasuya Devi and its few basic *dharam-shalas*, the path drops to a crystal-clear river, where you can bathe in the pools of a waterfall amid bamboo and dense forest. **Mandal** village, 6km below Anasuya Devi on the Chopta–Gopeshwar road, has a few *chai* shops and very basic rooms, and there's a *Forest Rest House* (①) at Pangar Basa 1km away. **Buses**, and the odd shared taxi, run to Gopeshwar, 11km east.

Joshimath and Auli

The scattered administrative town of **JOSHIMATH** clings to the side of a deep valley 250km northeast of Rishikesh, with tantalizing glimpses of the snow peaks high above, and the prospect far below of the road disappearing into a sunless canyon at Vishnu Prayag, the confluence with the Dhauli Ganga. Few of the thousands of pilgrims who pass through en route to Badrinath linger here, but Joshimath has close links with **Shankara**, the ninth-century reformer, who attained enlightenment here beneath a mulberry tree, before going on to establish **Jyotiramath**, one of the four centres of Hinduism (*dhams*) at the four cardinal points. In winter, when Badrinath is closed, the Rawal, the head priest of both Badrinath and Kedarnath, resides at Joshimath.

Joshimath consists of a long drawn-out upper bazaar, and, around 1km from the main square on the Badrinath road, a lower bazaar holds the colourful **Narsingh**, **Navadurga**, **Vasudev** and **Gauri Shankar** temples. Narsingh, dedicated to Vishnu as a lion, is the largest, with brightly painted woodwork reminiscent of Badrinath. In addition, **Tapovan**, 11km north of Joshimath along the Dhaul Ganga Valley and named after its hot springs, is the end of the **Curzon Trail** over Kuari Pass.

Practicalities

Most **buses** up to Joshimath stop in the upper bazaar. All motorized transport onwards to Badrinath – and there are plenty of buses during the *yatra* season – is obliged to move in **convoys**. A gate system controls traffic in each direction, in two equal 24-

kilometre stages – the first between Joshimath and Pandukeshwar, the second between Pandukeshwar and Badrinath. Several convoys leave Joshimath each day, forming around the Narsingh temple complex. At night the road remains closed.

Rooms at the GMVN *Tourist Rest House* (☎01389/2181; ②–④), at the north end of the upper bazaar, include a dormitory, and a cafe serves simple meals. The *Rest House* doubles as the local **tourist office** (Mon–Sat 10am–5pm), renting out basic Indian-made sleeping bags, tents and rucksacks for a nominal cost, and providing trekking guides. *Nanda Devi Mountain Travel*, *Hotel Nanda Devi*, Main Bazaar (☎01389/2170), organize treks and river rafting; they also have offices in New Delhi and Manali.

Small hotels around the main square include the basic *Kamet* (①–③), where the rooms facing the square are much cheaper than those on the other side, and the no-frills *Marwari* (①–③), above a good, busy vegetarian restaurant. A short way south, *Jyoti Lodge* (②–③) is excellent value, while the older *Neelkanth* (②–③) opposite has quiet pleasant rooms overlooking the valley. The *Paradise* cafe next to the *Tourist Rest House* has the best north and south Indian food in town, plus porridge for breakfast.

Auli

A rough road winds fifteen kilometres up through the *deodar* forest from Joshimath to **AULI**, which is being developed as a **ski** resort, partly in the hope of replacing the ski areas rendered inaccessible by the war in Kashmir. In the process, fundamental change is coming to the extensive meadows of **Auli Bugyal**. So far there's one chair lift, a new cable-car and a couple of tow lifts, and they don't reach the best of the ski runs, which lie towards the 24-kilometre trail to Kuari Pass. At present, all the pistes empty into one central run, arriving at the badly sited GMVN *Tourist Centre*, which faces the wrong way and has no views at all. Ski packages are available at very competitive rates, or you can ski on a day trip for around Rs100, including lift charges and the rental of (rather poor) equipment.

The *Tourist Centre* (①–⑤) has two large, good-value dormitories, and comfortable, if pricey, rooms and suites in its outbuildings. The friendly staff in the dining hall try their best, but don't expect any *après-ski* activity.

Badrinath

The most popular of the four main temples of Garhwal, 298km northeast of Rishikesh and just 40km south of Tibet, is that of **BADRINATH** – "Lord of the Berries". One of Hinduism's holiest sites, it was founded by Shankara in the ninth century, not far from the source of the Alaknanda, the main tributary of the holy Ganga. Although the temple has a stunning setting, beneath the sharp snowy pyramid of Nilkantha (6558m), the town that has grown up around it is grey, grubby and unattractive. Set in a deep valley, it remains in shade for most of each day.

Until a few years ago, Badrinath was a remote and evocative place, where legends spoke of mysterious *sadhus* such as the Englishman who lived high in the mountains amid the snow and ice. Now, however, it has grown out of all proportion to its infra-structure. The army-built road up from Joshimath, 48km south, brings endless convoys of buses and taxis, and the temple turns over astronomical amounts of money. Pilgrims crowd in, the streets are lined with mendicant *sadhus* and beggars, and roadside stalls sell all sorts of religious paraphernalia.

Badrinath is still presided over by a Nambudiri *brahmin* from Kerala – the Rawal, who also acts as the head priest for Kedarnath. According to myth, the two temples were once close enough together for the priest to worship at both on the same day. The **temple** itself, also known as Badri Narayan, is dedicated to Vishnu, who is said to have done penance in the mythical Badrivan ("Forest of Berries"), that once covered the mountains of Uttarkhand. Unusually, it is made of wood; the entire facade is repainted each May, once the snows have receded and the temple opens for the season. From a distance, its bright colours resemble a Tibetan *gompa*; there's some debate as to whether the temple was formerly a Buddhist shrine. Inside where photography is strictly taboo, the black stone image of **Badri Vishal** is seated like a *bodhisattva* in the lotus position (some Hindus regard the Buddha as an incarnation of Vishnu). *Pandas* (pilgrim priests) sit around the cloisters carrying on the business of worship and a booth enables visitors to pay in advance for rituals chosen from a long menu. This site, on the west bank of the turbulent Alaknanda, may well have been selected because of the sulphurous **Tapt Kund** hot springs on the embankment right beneath the temple, which is used for ritual bathing. Immediately south of the temple, the **old village** of Badrinath is still there, its traditional stone buildings and a small market seeming like relics from a bygone age. A sign on the main road north of Badrinath prohibits foreigners from proceeding further towards Tibet. However, visitors can normally – check the current situation – take local buses to the end of the road at the Bhotia village of **Mana**, 4km on, where a small army camp on the far side of the river effectively bars your way. It's also possible to walk this far along a footpath. The village itself consists of a warren of small lanes and buildings piled virtually on top of each other; the local Bhotia people, Buddhists of Tibetan origin who formerly traded across the high Mana Pass, now tend livestock and ponies. A path drops from the village to cross a bridge, then continues west along the side valley towards the mountain of Satopanth on the divide between the Mana and Gangotri regions, to the base of the impressive high waterfall of **Vasudhara**. Dropping from a hanging valley, this is considered to be the source of the Alaknanda, where it falls from heaven.

Practicalities

At the **Information Centre** run by Badrinath's **Temple Committee**, on the east bank opposite the temple, you can book rooms in the various pilgrim rest houses they manage, such as the nearby *Modi Bhavan* (②), and *Gujarat Bhavan* (③), next to the temple on the west bank. *Kale Kambli Wale's Ashram* (①), behind the temple, is also excellent value. The most comfortable option in town is the large GMVN *Devlok* (④) at the top car park; **GMVN** have another, simpler, lodge near the post office between the two car parks, with dorms as well as rooms (①–②). The most atmospheric area for cafes and *chai* shops is the old section close to the temple, but the more commercial east bank holds a few more upmarket neon-lit restaurants, such as *Kwality* and *Saket*.

Traffic back down to Joshimath, including the regular local buses, moves in the same convoy system as on the way up (see p.259). Long-distance buses run direct to Rishikesh – the nearest railway station – with an overnight halt en route, and to Gaurikund near Kedarnath (14hr), bookable at the bus stand office above the town.

Hemkund and the Valley of the Flowers

Starting from the hamlet of **Govind Ghat**, 28km south of Badrinath on the road to Joshimath (local buses will stop on request), an important pilgrim trail winds for 21 steep kilometres up to the snow-melt lake of **HEMKUND** (4329m). In the Sikh holy book, the *Guru Granth Sahib*, Govind Singh recalled meditating at a lake surrounded by seven high mountains; only this century was Hemkund discovered to be that lake. A large *gurudwara* (Sikh temple), and a small shrine to Lakshmana, the brother of Rama of *Ramayana* fame, now stand alongside. However, to protect the *deodar* forests along the trail, visitors can no longer spend the night.

Instead, the overgrown village of **Ghangaria**, 6km below Hemkund, serves as a base for day-hikes. It has several *chai* shops, basic lodges, *gurudwaras* and even a GMVN *Tourist Bungalow*, complete with dormitory (①–④; check it's open before hiking here out of season). Govind Ghat too has a large *gurudwara*, run on a donations system.

An alternative trail forks left from Ghangaria, climbing 5km to the mountain *bugyals* of the Bhyundar valley – the **VALLEY OF THE FLOWERS**. Starting at an altitude of 3352m, the valley was discovered by the visionary mountaineer, Frank Smythe, in 1931 who named it, not surprisingly, on account of its multitude of rare plants and beautiful flowers. The meadows are at their best towards the end of the monsoons, in early September; they too have suffered at the hands (or rather feet) of large numbers of visitors, and camping is not allowed here either. As a result, it is not possible to explore the ten-kilometre valley in its entirety, in the space of a day's hike from Ghangaria.

Nanda Devi Sanctuary

The majestic twin peaks of **Nanda Devi** – at 7816m, the highest complete mountain in India – dominate a large swathe of northeastern Garhwal and Kumaun. The eponymous goddess is the most important deity for all who live in her shadow, a fertility symbol also said to represent Durga, the virulent form of Shakti. Surrounded by an apparently impenetrable ring of mountains, the fastness of Nanda Devi was long considered inviolable; when mountaineers Eric Shipton and Bill Tilman finally traced a way through, along the difficult **Rishi Gorge**, in 1934, it was seen as a defilement of sacred ground. A string of catastrophes followed; as recently as 1976, an attempt on the mountain by the father and daughter team of Willi and Nanda Devi Unsoeld ended in tragedy, when Nanda Devi Unsoeld died below the summit for which she was named.

The beautiful wilderness around the mountain now forms the **Nanda Devi Sanctuary**. In theory, it's a magnificent place to camp, but it has been closed since 1983 for what are claimed to be environmental reasons. As the entire area lies comfortably in India, away from the Tibetan frontier, there is hope that the current easing of border tensions may soon lead to the reopening of the sanctuary; check with KMVN or GMVN, and don't try to go it alone. If the trail does reopen, be prepared for a gruelling sixty-kilometre haul from the village of **Lata**, on the Joshimath–Malari road.

Gwaldam

Straddling a pass between Garhwal and Kumaun, surrounded by pine forests 61km east of Karnprayag, the peaceful hamlet of **GWALDAM** looks down upon the beautiful valley of the Pindar, a world away from the hectic *yatra* trails. This picturesque spot used to be a tea plantation; now, thanks to its ease of access on the main road to Alomra, 90km southeast, it makes an ideal base for treks, especially following the ten-day **Curzon Trail** across the high mountain *bugyals* of northeastern Garhwal, over **Kuari Pass** to Tapovan and Joshimath.

The unassuming little Buddhist **Khamba Temple**, or **Drikung Kagyu Lhundrup Ling**, stands alongside orchards in the middle of a Tibetan settlement about 1.5km from Gwaldam's main crossroads. On the ridge above the village, the small shrine of **Badhangari**, dedicated to the goddess Durga and not far from the remnants of a Chand stone fort, commands superb views of the mountains of Kumaun and Garhwal. To reach it, take a bus for 4km to the village of **Tal**, then trek another 4km – some of which is quite steep – through rhododendron forests.

Practicalities

The exceptional GMVN *Tourist Rest House* (③–④), above the crossroads in Gwaldam, consists of an old cottage equipped with two comfortable suites, and a new block with dormitories; only limited food is available. This is the place to arrange guides for local treks. Alternative accommodation includes the good-value *Trishul* (①), where a pleasant little garden offers views of the snows.

Roop Kund: the mysterious lake

The high mountain lake of **Roop Kund**, a couple of days out of Gwaldam on the Curzon Trail, is never one of the most attractive spots in the mountains; during the short summer thaw, when the snow and ice on its surface melts, it reveals a grisly secret. Three hundred **skeletons**, thought to be six hundred years old, can be seen in the water. Some say that they are what remains of the army of a Dogra general, Zorawar Singh, who tried to invade Tibet, but they probably belonged to a party of royal pilgrims caught by bad weather while making the Nanda Jat pilgrimage to the lake of **Hom Kund**, 13km away, to propitiate the goddess Nanda Devi.

Kumaun

The Shaivite temples of **Kumaun**, such as **Jageshwar**, **Bhageshwar** and **Baijnath**, do not attract the same fervour as their equivalents in Garhwal. Instead they remain frozen in time, undisturbed by the throngs from the plains. Hill towns like **Almora**, **Ranikhet** and **Kausani** have a charm of their own, with views towards the snows, while in **Corbett National Park**, southeast of the resort of Nainital, vast jungles continue to protect tiger and huge herds of wild elephant. To the east, Kumaun's border with Nepal follows the Kali valley to its watershed with Tibet; threading through it is the holy trail (closed to foreigners) to the ultimate pilgrimage, Mount Kailash in Tibet, the abode of Shiva and his consort Parvati.

Kumaun Mandal Vikas Nigam, or **KMVN**, are in charge of tourism in Kumaun, providing a similar (and equally patchy) range of services to GMVN in Garhwal.

Nainital

The dramatic lake of **NAINITAL** (*tal* means lake), set in a mountain hollow at an altitude of 1938 metres, 277km north of Delhi, gives its name to the largest and most important town in Kumaun. Discovered for Europeans in 1841 by Mr Barron, a wealthy sugar merchant, Nainital swiftly became a popular escape from the summer heat of the lowlands, and continues to be one of India's main hill stations. Throughout the year, and especially between March and July, hordes of tourists and honeymooners pack the **Mall**, the promenade that links **Mallital** (head of the lake), the older colonial part of Nainital at the north end, with **Tallital** (foot of the lake).

Nainital's position within striking range of the inner Himalayas – visible from vantage points above town – makes it a good base for exploring Kumaun; Corbett National Park, Almora and Ranikhet are all within easy access. When the town's commercialism gets a bit much, it's always possible to escape into the beautiful surrounding country, to lakes such as **Sat Tal**, where the foothills begin their sudden drop towards the plains to the south, or to the forested ridges around **Kilbury**.

Arrival and information

Two main highways approach Nainital from opposite ends – one arrives from the north at Mallital, the other comes in at Tallital in the south. Buses and taxis from the main stands here connect with great frequency to the closest railhead at Haldwani, 35km south. **Delhi** is an eight-hour ride away with either *UPSRTC* buses (8am & 7pm) or the *Delhi Transport Corporation* (9am & 7pm), while **Almora**, 67km north, is served by buses (4 daily, 2hr 30min) and shared taxis from Bhowali, 11km from Nainital. To get to **Corbett National Park**, 113km southwest, take a bus for 66km to Ramnagar. The nearest airport, at **Pantnagar**, 72km south, is best reached by taxi.

Parvat Tours and Tourist Information Centre, Tallital (☎05942/2656), run by KMVN, organizes tours, car rental and books accommodation at all KMVN lodges. Cars can also be rented from agencies along the Mall, such as *Hina Tours & Travels* (☎05942/ 2860), though cycle rickshaws are the most convenient means of local transport. The **UP tourist office**, on the Mall towards Mallital (Mon–Sat 10am–5pm; ☎05942/2337), simply hands out leaflets. For specialist advice on **trekking** and **mountaineering**, call in at *Naini Tal Mountaineering Club*, CRST Inter College Building (☎05942/2051), or *Altitudes*, in the *Hotel Konark*, Bara Bazaar, Mallital (☎05942/2112). **Banks** in town include the *State Bank of India* and *Allahabad Bank*, on the Mall in Mallital.

The Town

Most of the activity around the crater lake of Nainital takes place along the 1.5-kilometre-long **Mall**. Basic **boat rental** starts at around Rs30 per hour out of season; dinghies, arranged at the boat club on the northwest corner of the lake in Mallital, cost more like Rs50. The large area known as the **Flats** here, now used as a play and meeting ground, was hit by a huge landslide in 1880, which buried the *Victoria Hotel* along with 150 people. Beside the boat club stand a large onion-domed *gurudwara* (Sikh temple), and an unremarkable new temple dedicated to one of Kumaun's most important deities, **Naina Devi**. This marks the spot where Sati's eyes (*naina*) fell as Shiva carried her disintegrating body; steps lead down from it to the water's edge. Also in Mallital, the **Tibetan Market** sells clothing to shivering tourists up from the plains.

A **ropeway** climbs from near the *Mayur* restaurant on the Mall to **Snow View**, 2270 metres up; the return ticket covers a one-hour stay (9.30am–1pm & 2–5pm; Rs30 return, Rs15 one way). Otherwise it's a two-kilometre hike, along a choice of steep trails, which can also be undertaken on ponies for a similar fee. At the top, which gets overcrowded in season, you'll find a promenade and cafes; views of the snow peaks are most assured early in the morning. Trails lead on for six kilometres to **Naina Peak**, at 2611 metres one of the best vantage points around, and to the isolated **China Peak** (pronounced "Cheena"), the craggy rise to the west.

About halfway up to Snow View, conspicuous thanks to its abundant prayer flags, lies the Tibetan *gompa* (monastery) of **Gadhan Kunkyop Ling**. The simple hut-like structure that has served as the main temple for the last thirty years is currently being replaced by a more permanent brick and mortar building in traditional *gompa* style.

Accommodation

As a holiday town, Nainital is full of **hotels**; however, budget accommodation is hard to come by. Prices are high between March and July, but you can normally find discounts at other times. On the whole, room rates are cheaper in Tallital than in Mallital.

Alka, The Mall (☎05942/2220). Large and comfortable place. The restaurant is strong on Gujarati and Punjabi food. Rates are lower in the pretty *Annexe* (☎2225), 300m towards Mallital. ③/⑤–⑦.

Arif Castles, above Mallital (☎05942/2801). An extraordinary affair, part Gothic, part space age. Well-furnished rooms, luxurious bathrooms and very reasonably priced food. Garden restaurant and coffee shop, plus a disco charging Rs100 for a couple – no single men allowed. ⑦–⑧.

Armadale, Waverly Rd, Mallital (☎05942/2855). Quiet location. Reasonably comfortable mid-range rooms, with free transport on arrival. ③–⑥.

Ashok, Tallital (☎05942/2721). A bit dark and musty, but otherwise quite clean. ②.

Basera, Mallital. Clean budget rooms next to the ropeway station; hot water by the bucket. ①–②.

City Heart, Mallital (☎05942/2228). Above the main drag on a road up from Mallital's rickshaw stand. Upper rooms have superb lake views. No food, but near amenities. Recommended. ③–⑤.

Evelyn, The Mall (☎05942/2457). Overlooking the lake, with excellent views from the large roof patio. Spacious and well kept. Recommended. ④–⑦.

Grand, The Mall (☎05942/2406). One of Nainital's oldest establishments, where time seems to stand still – period atmosphere but a bit musty. ④–⑥.

Himalaya, Tallital (☎05942/2258). Above the bus stand. Assorted rooms, some lake views. ①–④.

KMVN Tourist Bungalows, booked through *Parvat Tours*, The Mall (☎05942/2656). Identikit KMVN places, one in Tallital close to the bus stand, another on the outskirts of Mallital. ②–④.

Krishna, The Mall (☎05942/2662). The newer and more expensive lake-view rooms upstairs are comfortable and clean. ②–⑤.

Manu Maharani, Grasmere Estate (☎05942/2531). Nainital's finest, with all mod cons including the only bar in town,and good Szechuan food in the *Lotus Garden* restaurant. ⑧.

Savoy, Tallital (☎05942/2721). Next door to the *Ashok*, run by the same management, and a little better. No views, but hot water. ②–③.

Shervani Hilltop Inn, Mallital (☎05942/3304). Once a Maharajah's palace, below China Peak and next door to *Arif Castles*. Extensive gardens, and cottage accommodation as well. ⑦.

Swiss, Mallital (☎05942/3013). Justifiably popular family-run place. Spacious old-fashioned rooms and plenty of atmosphere, with food included. ⑥–⑦.

Vikram Vintage Inn, Mallital (☎05942/3177). Full-featured hotel; billiards and snooker and smart and comfortable rooms. No views, but surrounded by pines and away from the bustle. ⑦–⑨.

Youth Hostel, Mallital (☎05942/3353). 44 dorm beds and two double rooms, in charming secluded spot above Mallital. Slightly more expensive for non-YHA members. Excellent value. ①.

Eating

Nainital has plenty of places to **eat**, with restaurants and fast-food options along the Mall geared to tourists, in addition to everyday *dhabas* (local cafes) in the bazaars at either end.

Capri's, The Mall, Mallital. Popular mid-range restaurant.

Embassy, The Mall, Mallital. One of Nainital's better restaurants with wood-panelled interior; serves pizzas and baked dishes but strongest on Mughlai cooking.

Kwality, The Mall, Mallital. Lakeside restaurant; tables overlook the water. The usual multi-cuisine.

Marino, The Mall, Tallital. A very good selection of vegetarian *thalis*.

Rasoi, The Mall. Towards Mallital, mid-priced vegetarian cooking but otherwise unexceptional.

Sakley's, The Mall, Mallital. Versatile restaurant, with western food on the menu, plus a bakery and confectioners.

Sher-e-Punjab, The Mall. Good Indian food, halfway along between Mallital and Tallital. Another branch near the main bazaar of Mallital is just as good and a bit cheaper.

Shiva, Mallital. Cheap but good and popular *dhaba* in the bazaar.

Sonam Tea Stall, Tibetan Market, Mallital. Roadside cafe in the covered section of the market selling *momos* (steamed meat dumplings) and *thukpa* (soup).

Corbett National Park

Corbett National Park, based at **Ramnagar**, 250km northeast of Delhi and 63km southwest of Nainital, is one of India's premier wildlife reserves. Established by Jim Corbett among others as the Hailey National Park, India's first, in 1936, and later renamed in his honour, it is one of Himalayan India's last expanses of wilderness. Almost the entire 521-square-kilometre park, spread over the foothills of Kumaun, is sheltered by a buffer zone of mixed deciduous and giant *sal* forests, which provide impenetrable cover for wildlife. Most of the Core Area of 330 square kilometres at its heart remains out of bounds, and many visitors are disappointed to find that safaris on foot are strictly forbidden; they are only permissible in the fringe forests.

Corbett is most famous for its large cats, and in particular the **tiger** – this was the first designated Project Tiger Reserve, in 1973 – but its tigers are extremely elusive. Sightings are very far from guaranteed, and should be regarded as an unlikely bonus. Nonetheless, although there have been problems elsewhere with the project, and the very survival of the tiger in India is in serious jeopardy (see p.381), Corbett does at least seem to be prioritizing the needs of tigers over those of other wildlife – and of tourists – and claims to have poaching under control.

The park holds a great assortment of other animals. Large **elephant** herds have been confined within its boundaries since the construction of the Ramganga Reservoir blocked migratory routes that formerly ranged as far as Rajaji National Park, 200 kilometres west. The best place to see them is around the picturesque Dhikala camp near the reservoir, especially in spring, when the water level drops and the animals have more space to roam. The reservoir shelters populations of **gharial**, a long-snouted, fish-eating crocodile, and **maggar**, a large marsh crocodile, and other reptiles. **Jackal** are common, and **wild boar** run through the camps in the evenings. The grasslands around Dhikala are home to deer species such as the spotted deer known as **chital**, **hog deer** and the larger **sambar**. **Rhesus** and **common langur** are both abundant, representing the two main classes of Indian monkeys. Bird life ranges from water birds such as the **pied kingfisher** to birds of prey, including the **crested serpent eagle**, **Pallas's fishing eagle** and **Himalayan greyheaded fishing eagle**.

ENTRY INTO CORBETT NATIONAL PARK

All visitors to Corbett National Park have to obtain **permits** from the park administration centre at Ramnagar. Indians pay less than overseas visitors. Rates have shot up over the last few years, and no doubt will continue to do so, but as a rough idea the entrance fee for foreigners as this book goes to press is Rs100 for the first three days at Dhikala, excluding board and lodging. Each additional day is Rs50, use of a still camera costs Rs50 and a video camera is Rs500. Elephant rides are Rs50 per head or Rs200 per elephant.

Note that Corbett is closed between June and mid-November, when the monsoons flood the river beds and cut the fragile road links.

Getting to and from Corbett National Park

Ramnagar is served by frequent **buses** to and from Nainital and Ranikhet, 100km north. Buses arrive every half-hour or so after the eight-hour trip from **Delhi**; *Delhi Transport Corporation* run a semi-deluxe service (costing around Rs70), and most of the alternatives are pretty basic. The only direct **train** to Delhi leaves at 8pm and arrives at 6.30am, with interminable stops along the way. For faster trains and connections to other parts change at Moradabad. The nearest airport is at Pantnagar, 80km southeast.

The closest of the various **gates** into the park, 1km from central Ramnagar, is on the road to **Bijrani** camp, 11km away, a base for day trips. **Dhangarhi Gate**, 18km along the highway north to Ranikhet, provides access to the northern and northwestern portion of the park along the Ramganga river valley, and the main camp of **Dhikala**.

Jeeps, the most convenient way to travel within the park, can be rented for around Rs500 per day in Ramnagar from the KMVN *Tourist Lodge* and other agencies such as *Bharat Hotel* (☎05946/85775) near the bus stand. One bus each day goes to Dhikala from Ramnagar, stopping at the *Forest Rest Houses* en route.

Ramnagar

Situated in the rich farm-belt of the *terai*, on the southeastern fringes of the great forests, the busy market town of **RAMNAGAR** is the main administrative centre for Corbett National Park and Project Tiger. There's little to do around Ramnagar itself except go **fishing**. At Lohachaur, 15km north along the River Kosi, good anglers are in with a chance of landing the legendary mahseer, a redoubtable battling river carp. Permits to have a go must be sought from the Project Tiger office in Ramnagar; most resorts also arrange all-inclusive fishing trips.

Although most tourists head straight to Dhikala in the park as soon as they arrive, Ramnagar does have some **accommodation**. The KMVN *Tourist Lodge* (①–③), next to the Project Tiger offices, is not bad as such places go, with a dorm as well as basic

---

JIM CORBETT (1875–1955)

Jim Corbett – hunter of man-eating tigers, photographer, conservationist and author – was born in Nainital of English and Irish parentage. A childhood spent around the Corbett winter home of Kaladhungi (halfway between Nainital and Ramnagar, and now a rather disappointing memorial to him) brought young Jim into close communion with nature, and an instinctive understanding of jungle ways. After working in the railways, he joined the Indian Army in 1917 at the age of forty; he rose to the rank of Lieutenant Colonel, and saw action in Flanders at the head of the 70th Kumaun Company.

Known locally as "Carpet Sahib", a mispronunciation of his name, Jim Corbett was called upon time and time again to rid the hills of Kumaun of man-eating tigers and leopards. Normally shy of human contact, such animals turn man-eaters when infirmity brought upon by old age or wounds renders them unable to hunt their usual prey. Many of those killed by Corbett were found to have suppurating wounds caused by porcupine quills embedded deep in their paws; tigers always seem to fall for the porcupine's simple defensive trick of walking backwards in line with its lethal quills.

One of Corbett's most memorable exploits was the killing of the Rudraprayag leopard, which accounted for 125 human lives between 1918 and 1926, and was bold enough to steal its victims from the midst of human habitation; he also terminated the careers of the Chowgarh tigress, the Talla Des and the Mohan man-eaters. Corbett described his adventures in books such as *My India*, *Jungle Lore* and *Man-Eaters of Kumaun*; Martin Booth's *Carpet Sahib* is an excellent biography of a remarkable man. Awarded the Order of the British Empire in recognition of his lifelong work with nature, Jim Corbett was unhappy in post-Independence India, and left to settle in East Africa.

---

doubles, while the *Everest* at the bus stand (①), has decent budget rooms. On the main road opposite the bus stand, *Govindas* is a surprisingly good multi-cuisine **restaurant**, where Indian food is the best value. Across from the *Tourist Lodge*, *Corbett Jungle Bar & Restaurant*, a restaurant during the day, turns into a popular bar in the evenings.

Dhikala

Corbett's main camp, **DHIKALA**, is 40km northwest of Ramnagar. As you can only stray beyond the confines of the camp under armed guard, on elephant back or in a car or jeep, the whole place has something of the air of a military encampment, but it's beautifully situated, overlooking the Ramganga reservoir and the forested hills beyond. **Accommodation** ranges from the 24 bunk beds in the *Log Huts* (①), via the simple, overpriced *Green Hut* (③) and other assorted spartan huts (④), to more comfortable bungalows and cabins (⑤–⑥). **Food** is available either per day, with higher prices for western food, or on a *Janta* ("peoples") meal basis. There's also a library and reading room, and film shows on wildlife are arranged.

It's normally possible to see plenty of animals and birds from the **lookout tower** beside a waterhole 1km from the camp; bring binoculars, remain quiet, and don't wear loud colours or perfume. *Chital*, *sambar*, and various other deer species find refuge in the savannah grasslands known as the "maidan", behind the camp to the south, and tigers are occasionally drawn in looking for prey. Two-hour **elephant rides** (Rs50 per head, less for Indian citizens; in theory, rides are first-come-first-served) explore this sea of grass, rarely penetrating far into the deep jungles beyond; try to convince your *mahout* (elephant driver) to venture in, as they can be quite magical, concealing unexpected animals at every turn. Come at dusk or dawn; in the heat of the day you probably won't come across much more than deer among the tall grass. Tiger sightings are few and far between, but you may be rewarded with fresh pug marks.

On the way to Dhikala from the Dhangarhi gate, the road passes through magnificent forest – if you have your own transport, stop at the **High Bank** vantage point, and try to spot crocodile or even elephant on the river below. The **Sultan**, **Gairal** and **Sarapduli** forest rest houses on the road (all ③) are bookable through Project Tiger, but you have to make your own food arrangements and there is no electricity. The bungalows are surrounded by deep forest; as movement on foot is restricted, you'll only see such wild animals as stray close to or into the compound. The beautifully sited **Kanda** rest house stands on a hill above the Ramganga reservoir and Dhikala itself.

Resort accommodation around Corbett

A number of self-contained resorts are springing up on the fringes of Corbett, providing a higher standard of accommodation – at a price – as well as guides for expeditions in the forests, which can be as rich in wildlife as the park, without the restrictions.

Corbett Riverside Resort, Garija, Ramnagar; reservations through Delhi (☎011/660665). A picturesque setting, on the edge of Garija village 10km north of Ramnagar, looking across the River Kosi to forest-covered cliffs. Much of the complex was washed away not long ago, when the river dramatically changed course; it has now been rebuilt, with some buildings sited on a ledge above the extensive beach area, and a more rustic hut on the beach itself. Safaris arranged; full board. ⑧–⑨.

Quality Inn Corbett Jungle Resort, Kumeria Reserve Forest, Mohan (☎05946/85219). Wood-panelled stone cottages in a leafy mango orchard above the Kosi, 29km from Ramnagar on the road north to Ranikhet, 9km beyond the Dhangarhi gate. Elephant rides into the forest and safaris into the park itself. Full board; good off-season discounts from June to November. ⑧.

Tiger Tops Corbett Lodge, Dhikala, Ramnagar (☎05946/85279). Corbett's most ostentatious resort, overlooking the Kosi and the forested hills beyond. Large comfortable rooms, a library, a well-stocked bar and a swimming pool. Activities include nature trails with the resort's own naturalists, jungle rides, fishing, trekking and films. Not related to the famous *Tiger Tops* in Nepal. ⑨.

Ranikhet

The scattered and deliberately undeveloped town of **RANIKHET**, 50km west of Almora, is one of UP's pleasantest hill stations. Essentially, it's an army cantonment, the home of the Kumaun Rifles. New construction is confined to the hectic **Sadar Bazaar** area, while the rest of the town above it, climbing up towards the crest of the hill, retains pine woods that lend it a dark but leafy atmosphere. Beautiful forest trails abound, including short cuts from the bazaar to the Mall; leopards still roam some of the more remote areas within the town boundaries, despite efforts by army officers to prove their skill at hunting. Ranikhet is for some reason only marginally popular with Indian tourists, so its parade grounds, churches and beautifully maintained golf course, within sight of the snows, remain unspoiled, making it an ideal place for a quiet break.

Arrival and information

Buses from all over Kumaun including the railhead at Kathgodam, 84km away, arrive at the **bazaar**, at either of two bus stops. The **KMOU stand**, on the Haldwani road, is the base for buses to Haldwani (hourly; 4hr), the nearest town to Kathgodam; to get to Nainital, change at Bhowali, or take one of the three daily direct services (10am, 11am & 4pm; 3hr). The **Roadways (Almora) Bus Stand**, 500 metres on, is used by regular services to Almora (1hr 30min). Buses between the bazaar and the Mall, 3km away, run every ninety minutes, stopping outside the *Hotel Meghdoot*.

KMVN provide the usual Kumaun-wide services from their *Tourist Bungalow* on the Mall (☎05966/2297), while the UP Tourist Bureau, above the Almora Bus Stand, offers a haphazard assortment of leaflets. There's a *State Bank of India* on Gandhi Chowkh.

The Town

Although in India the word "Mall" normally conjures up images of a busy promenade with shops and joy-rides, visitors to Ranikhet will be pleasantly surprised; its Mall, running along on the wooded crest of the ridge, has few buildings apart from leafy officers' messes and a sprinkling of hotels. Parade grounds and the occasional sound of gunfire from the adjacent firing ranges are evidence of the strong military presence, which otherwise does not seem overbearing. Traces of the colonial past remain evident everywhere, in the form of large bungalows and church steeples.

At the **Shawl & Tweed Factory and Outlet**, above the Narsingh Stadium Parade Ground – an old church equipped with looms and wheels – you can buy herringbone and houndstooth tweed. Kumaun has a tradition of weaving, and the Gandhi Ashram in the bazaar, has a selection of local fabric including *pankhis*, plain shawls for men.

Local tourist authorities heavily promote the idea of a visit to the orchards of **Chaubatia**, 10km east beyond the Mall. It's a scenic enough spot, with good views of the snows, and a pleasant short walk leads along a lofty pine-covered ridge to the small lake of **Bhaludam**. On the way up to Chaubatia, the temple of Jhula Devi, dedicated to Shakti (here a sister of **Nanda Devi**), would be unremarkable but for the huge collection of **bells** fixed to the shrine as offerings – a custom found throughout Kumaun.

Accommodation and eating

Hotels in Ranikhet readily divide into two sections, clustered either around the busy bazaar, or in quieter locations along the Mall. The choice of **eating** is pretty limited; the best food is found in its better hotels, but there are a few simple cafes and *dhabas* in the market area, such as the *Mayur* by Almora Bus Stand, a good-value vegetarian place.

Meghdoot, The Mall (☎05966/2475). Comfortable suites with running hot water, parking and room service, plus a good mid-price restaurant. Recommended. ③.

Moon, Bazaar (☎05966/2258). Extensive place in the heart of the bazaar, with suites, two cottages and a multi-cuisine restaurant. ④–⑥.

Norton's, The Mall (☎05966/2377). Wooden family-run hotel, just down from the *Meghdoot*. ②–③.

Parwati Inn, Ratan Palace Compound (☎05966/2325). Large, new, unmistakeable edifice above the Almora road. The most positive feature are the balconied rooms looking onto the snows. ⑤–⑦.

Rajdeep, Bazaar (☎05966/2247). Nearly always busy, near the *Moon*. A bit noisy, but clean. ①–③.

Tourist Bungalow, the Mall (☎05966/2297). Cottages and dormitories, tucked away 4km from the bazaar in a beautiful wooded spot that enjoys the best of Ranikhet. ②–⑤.

West View, Mahatma Gandhi Rd (☎05966/2261). Grand old-world establishment in an idyllic spot among the pines on the outskirts of town. Spacious rooms, with fireplaces. ⑤–⑦.

Almora

ALMORA, 67km north of Nainital, is one of the rare Kumauni towns that conspicuously pre-dates the Raj, with its cobbled alleyways and wood and stone buildings. Founded by the Chand dynasty in 1560, and occupied successively by the Gurkhas and the British, it remains a major market town, and is considered the cultural capital of the region. Set at a pleasant altitude of 1646m on rambling ridges that look towards the inner Himalayan snows, Almora's peaceful environs have attracted an eclectic assortment of visitors over the years, such as Swami Vivekananda, Timothy Leary and the Tibetologist and author of *The Way of the White Clouds*, Lama Angarika Govinda.

Arrival and information

Almora has regular **bus** connections with Nainital (6 daily; 3hr), Ranikhet (2hr 30min), Kathgodam, the nearest railhead, and Kausani (2hr 30min). All buses use either of two adjacent stands on the Mall, which has a taxi stand close by if you're heading for distant accommodation, such as the *Tourist Bungalow* on the Mall (☎22250) – the local KMVN headquarters. However, most hotels are in walking distance. Access to much of the centre, including the market area above the Mall, is restricted to pedestrians.

UP Tourism maintain an information-only **tourist office**, next to the *Savoy Hotel*, above the HPO (Mon–Sat 10am–5pm; ☎22180), but the best place to find out about local **treks** is *Discover Himalaya*, opposite the main post office on the Mall, who can supply mountaineering guides and equipment. *Surya Travels* on the Mall (☎23445) can also arrange treks. The *State Bank of India* on the Mall provides an erratic service, sometimes confining itself to changing *American Express* cheques.

The Town

Although most of Almora's official business is conducted along the **Mall**, the **market area** immediately above and parallel to it along the crest of the saddle, holds much more of interest. Exploring its well-stocked bazaars, knitted together with lanes flanked by beautifully carved wooden facades, you feel as though you're drifting into the distant past. Among items you might want to buy are *khadi* (home-spun) cotton textiles and ready-mades from the Gandhi Ashram near the bus stands, and local woollens from *Garur Woollens* or *Kumaun Woollens* on the Mall. However, the great local tradition is the manufacture of **tamta**, beaten copper pots plated with silver, which are sold in the busy Lala Bazaar and the Chowk area at the northeast end of the market.

Towards the top of town, beyond Chowk, a compound holds a group of Chand-period stone **temples**. The main one, a squat single-storey structure, is dedicated to **Nanda Devi**, the goddess embodied in the region's highest mountain. More typical of Kumauni temple architecture are two larger Shaivite painted stone temples, capped with umbrella-like wooden roofs covering their stone *amalaka* (circular crowns). During Sravana (Jul/Aug), a large fair is held here in honour of Nanda Devi.

Enclosures amid the tall pine woods of **Deer Park**, a pleasant three-kilometre walk northeast of the Mall, house assorted deer, as well as Himalayan black bear and sorry-looking leopards. Following the Mall southwest for three kilometres, on the other hand, brings you to the hill called **Bright End Corner**, where you may, weather permitting, catch views of the hills and vales of Kumaun, and the distant snow peaks.

Accommodation

Accommodation in Almora itself is largely centered along the Mall. However, it is also possible to "go native" in village houses in the region around **Kasara Devi**, a small and unremarkable Durga temple 8km east of Almora above the Bhageshwar Road. Enquire about places to rent at the *chai* shops in Kalimath nearby.

Kailas, The Mall, above the HPO (☎22624). Quaint, brightly coloured and funky place, with an incredibly cheap dormitory, redolent of the eccentricities of its owner Mr Shah, a legend among travellers. Nothing has changed in years – some may like it, others may not. ①.

KMVN Tourist Bungalow, The Mall (☎22250). Large, characterless place, with a main building and cottages, and a good-value dormitory, set in a nice garden 2km from the busy centre. ②–③.

Renuka, The Mall (☎22860). Next to the GPO, new and slightly garish hotel, quite pleasant on the whole, with a good mid-range multi-cuisine restaurant. ③–④.

Savoy, Police Line, above the GPO. A quiet place, away from the noise of the Mall and the markets, but handy for all amenities. Spacious rooms, garden and verandah. ②–③.

Shikhar, The Mall (☎22253). Almora's central landmark. Don't be put off by the exterior or expensive reputation; a wide range of rooms, some at very reasonable prices, with common baths. ②–⑥.

Eating

Cafes and **restaurants** are strung along the Mall, especially around the bazaar area at its northern end. There should be something for everybody.

Glory, near *Shikhar*, The Mall. Multi-cuisine cafe-cum-restaurant, strong on north Indian cooking.

Madras Cafe, opposite the *Glory*, The Mall. The name is misleading, as the emphasis is, once again on good-value north Indian food. Tasty coffee, too.

Dhaba, The Mall bus stand. Excellent, nameless budget Sikh-run *dhaba* which can get crowded.

Swagat, next to the *Shikhar*, The Mall. Large cafe, with *dosas* and other snacks as well as meals.

Kausani

Spreading from east to west along a narrow pine-covered ridge, 52km northwest of Almora, the quiet hill resort of **KAUSANI** is more of a loose settlement than a town. It is at its most concentrated in the area around the Mall, where the Almora road crosses the lowest point in the ridge en route north to the Katyur valley and Baijnath.

A popular day trip from Almora, Kausani is renowned as an ideal place for a retreat, and holds several ashrams. Mahatma Gandhi walked here in 1929, thirty years before the road came through; Gandhi-ism continues to be a major influence in these hills and his symbol of self-reliance, the spinning wheel, is still used in homes around Kausani.

Practicalities

Kausani is well connected by bus to Almora and Ranikhet, and to Bageshwar and Gwaldam further north. Guests prepared to observe ashram rules, such as not smoking, are welcome to stay at Gandhi's pleasant but spartan former ashram, known as *Anashakti Ashram* (①), above the Mall. Further up, *Amar Holiday Home* (☎4115; ③–④) is a small family-run establishment close to forest walks with a beautiful garden and a panorama of the snows. The KMVN *Tourist Bungalow* (☎4106; ②–⑥), 2km west of the Mall, has the usual tourist lodge atmosphere but is at least secluded, and surrounded by pine forests. The fanciest place to eat is the *Hill Queen*, a mid-priced multi-cuisine restaurant below the *Anashakti Ashram*.

Around Kausani: Baijnath

Halfway between Kausani, 20km southeast, and Gwaldam to the west, the road (served by occasional buses) drops down to a broad valley and the eleventh-century stone temples of **BAIJNATH**, standing at a bend in a beautiful river. This was once an important town of the Katyurs, who ruled much of Garhwal and Kumaun; now it's more like a park, with intrusive lights placed between the temples. Unusually, the main temple is devoted to Parvati, the consort of Shiva, rather than Shiva himself; its 1.5-metre image of the goddess is one of the few in the complex to have withstood the ravages of time. Beside the river, a pristine pool teems with large carp; as they are considered holy, fishing is prohibited. Baijnath has no accommodation at present, but it does have a couple of simple cafes including the *Calcutta*.

Binsar

Known locally as **Jhandi Dhar**, the forest-clad hill of **BINSAR**, 34km north of Almora, rises in isolation to a commanding 2412 metres. A steep road leads 11km up from the main Almora–Bageshwar highway, to a tourist complex near the top of the hill. This was the summer capital of the Chands, but today little remains in the area, except the imposing stone Shiva temple of **Bineshwar** 3km below the summit. Most visitors come for the 300-kilometre panorama of Himalayan peaks along the northern horizon, including from west to east Kedarnath, Chaukhamba, Trishul, Nandaghunti, Nanda Devi, Nandakot, and Panchuli. Closer at hand, you can enjoy quiet forest walks through oak and rhododendron woods. Recently designated a nature reserve, Binsar is rich in alpine flora, ferns, hanging moss and innumerable species of wild flowers.

Practicalities

Binsar is only accessible by public transport if you are willing to walk from the main road; **taxis** from Almora charge from Rs200 for a one-way drop. Besides the poorly maintained KMVN *Tourist Bungalow* (②–③), the town's only accommodation is a beautifully situated but lonely *Forest Rest House* (①) above the tourist complex, booked through the department in Almora. There are no shops or cafes.

Jageshwar

Surrounded by giant ancient *deodars*, 1870m up, **JAGESHWAR**, 34km northeast of Almora, is the very heart of Kumaun, a place where language and customs have resisted change. An idyllic small river meanders through dark pines into this ancient world, 3km off the main road from Artola, stumbling onto a complex of 124 shrines and ornate stone temples whose construction continued for a thousand years, from the eighth century.

Jageshwar is one of India's twelve *Jyotrilinga*, where the luminous energy of Shiva is epitomized by a *lingam* of light, and was a medieval centre of Lakulisha Shaivism (Shiva with the Club). Its main temple, **Shri Jyotrilinga** or **Mahamrityunjaya**, has a short forechamber and a ten-metre-tall main temple with sculpted motifs on the sides and heavy lattice stone windows. The *dvarpalas* – sculpted stone doorkeepers – that protect the entrance are Nandi and Bhrangi, the wrathful bodyguards of Shiva.

Although ugly modern buildings are beginning to intrude, Jageshwar retains much of its traditional charm, with stone paved lanes and beautifully carved wooden doors and windows painted in turquoise and other striking colours. Good local **walks** include the steep three-kilometre ascent through beautiful pine forests to the small hamlet and stone temples of **Vriddha** or **Briddh Jageshwar** (Old Jageshwar), with an extensive panorama from the mountains of Garhwal to the massifs of western Nepal. A trail from here leads 12km along an undulating ridge to **Binsar** (see above); the trail finally emerges from the woods near the stone temple of **Bineshwar**.

Practicalities

Two **buses** each day connect Jageshwar with the railhead at Haldwani, via Almora, and buses to destinations all over Kumaun leave from Artola, 3km away on the main highway. The large, brash KMVN *Tourist Bungalow* (②–③) makes no attempt to blend in with its surroundings, but inside, it's comfortable and clean, and has dormitories; food is expensive. Next to the gate, a *dharamshala* in a traditional building is very basic but full of atmosphere (①). Accommodation in village houses can also be negotiated. *Rajmahal* opposite the temple gates is a refreshing little restaurant, with a good if limited selection, specializing in *khue – suji* (semolina) and banana fritters.

Bageshwar

In a steamy valley, 90km north of Almora, **BAGESHWAR** is one of Kumaun's most important pilgrimage towns. It's not a particularly attractive spot, despite its setting just before the final rise to the high Himalayas, but its market is a good opportunity to stock up on provisions for long treks.

Overlooking the confluence of the Gomti and Sarayu rivers, a large group of ancient temples and ashrams is dominated by the Shiva temple of **Baghnath** with its *amalaka* (ribbed circular crown) capped with an umbrella-like roof made of wood and slate. As in many Kumauni temples, the fabulous bronze bells at shrines throughout the complex are offerings from devotees. According to legend, Bageshwar was built here in the shadows of Mount Nila, the home of gods, *sadhus*, *gandharvas* and *apsaras* (celestial musicians), by a certain Chandisa for his master Shiva. When Shiva and Parvati arrived at the confluence they were welcomed by an *akashvani* (celestial song); hence the place was named Vagiswar (the lord of eloquent speech).

Practicalities

Bageshwar has good **bus** connections with Almora, Nainital (156km south), and Gwaldam (43km west); the longer of the two roads to Almora passes through Kausani. The large, ugly, KMVN *Tourist Bungalow* (③), 2km from the temples across a bridge, is the only hotel, though there are basic *dharamsalas* and *dhabas* around the temple.

THE TREK TO PINDARI GLACIER

One of the most accessible and varied treks into the heart of the Kumauni Himalayas leads from Bageshwar through forests, valleys and high *bugyals* right up to the Pindari Glacier, 3820 metres above sea level in the shadow of Nanda Devi. Unless you want to spend a night at the glacier itself, there's no need to carry a tent or stove, as the route is amply supplied with KMVN bungalows. These should be booked in advance through the bungalow in Bageshwar, which can also provide trekking equipment and information.

On **DAY 1**, take a local bus from Bageshwar either to **Bharari**, where there is a basic hotel and a PWD bungalow, and walk for 16km from there along the Sarayu valley to **Song**, or catch the bus all the way. From Song, continue for 3km on foot to **Loharkhet**, which has a basic KMVN *Tourist Bungalow* overlooking the village, and a PWD bungalow.

DAY 2 is considerably more gruelling, involving around 1000m of ascent along a good forest track for 11km over **Dhakuri Pass** (2835m), which has superb mountain views, before dropping 2km down to the KMVN *Tourist Bungalow* at **Dhakuri**.

DAY 3 consists of an 8km walk along the Pindar valley to **Khati**, where the Pindar and Sunderdhanga rivers meet. The last major village along the trail, Khati too has a bungalow.

Continuing beside the Pindar on **DAY 4**, you follow a forested trail past bamboo, fern and spectacular waterfalls, for 11km to **Dwali**, where there is more KMVN accommodation (a trail right from here, with no further facilities of any kind, leads 13km to Kafni Glacier, near the base of the elegant 6860m peak of Nanda Kot). For an early start for Pindari Glacier, head another 5km from Dwali to **Phurkia**, where the tree-line gives way to *bugyal*, used for summer pastures, and there's a KMVN *Tourist Bungalow*.

Although it's just 8km from Phurkia up to the glacier, **DAY 5** can prove long and exhausting, because if you don't have a tent you'll have to get back down to Phurkia by nightfall. **Zero Point**, at 3820 metres, marks the foot of the **Pindari Glacier**, which consists of two sections; the bottom is dry and crevassed, with a large rubble-strewn lateral moraine, while the top is a severely broken ice-fall, topped by a snowfield known as **Traill's Pass**. Some maps show a route up to the pass, but only expert mountaineers should attempt it.

Chaukori

KMVN are doing their utmost to promote **CHAUKORI**, 132km north of Almora and 48km east of Bageshwar, as a tourist destination in its own right, largely because it can boast UP's only, very dilapidated, tea estate. However, there's so little here that Chaukori is only of interest if you want to spend a day or two doing absolutely nothing – in which case rambling around the gentle local ridges will enable you to enjoy an impressive Himalayan panorama, centered on the twin peaks of Nanda Devi.

Practicalities

The road from Bageshwar to Chaukori, taken by regular **buses**, must be one of the most beautiful roads in Kumaun, following a pine-covered ridge for most of the way. Daily buses leave Chaukori for Almora at 7am and 2pm, and there are several services each morning to Pithoragarh (5hr). The sixteen-bed KMVN *Tourist Bungalow* (③), which has a dormitory and private rooms, is hopelessly inadequate to cope with the increasing number of visitors. Book in advance through KMVN if you plan to come.

Munsiyari

The sprawling and unattractive village of **MUNSIYARI** stands at the threshold of the inner Himalayas, 154km north of Pithoragarh, looking down on the Gori river gorge and deep valleys branching up into the high mountains. Vantage spots throughout the area offer breathtaking views of the five almost-symmetrical Panchuli peaks, which owe their name – the "five cooking pots" – to their plumes of wind-blown snow. These are notorious for their bad weather, but on clear days at Munsiyari, you feel you could almost reach out and touch them.

Among spectacular local high-mountain walks, which are being increasingly de-restricted, is the gentle 11km trek up to the **Kalika Pass** (2700m), where a small Shakti temple stands amid dark pines. More difficult trails lead via the small village of **Matkot**, 12km away, to the glaciers in the Panchuli group, and 30km to the large alpine meadows of **Chiplakot Bugyal**, dotted with tiny lakes, as well as up to the Johar Valley (see box). Many of the local people are Bhotias, of Tibetan stock, who have over the ages absorbed Indian religious and cultural practices, though their origins can still be seen in the Tibetan-style weaving of carpets, adorned with the ubiquitous dragon motif. These are sold in Munsiyari by *Pratpsing Pangtey*, an elderly gentleman who runs a small carpet factory just below the bus stand.

TREKKING: MILAM GLACIER AND THE JOHAR VALLEY

The **Milam** trail from **Munsiyari** sets out to explore the beautiful and remote Johar Valley, in the vicinity of the magnificent peak of Nanda Kot (6860m). Lying near the border with Tibet, and policed by the Indo-Tibetan Border Police, Milam has been closed to visitors until quite recently; check current regulations before you set out.

DAY 1 consists of a total walk of 12km. Follow the pony trail from Munsiyari down to Jemighat, and then along the River Gori until a final forested rise for 3km to **Lilam**, a village which has a PWD bungalow, plus a couple of tea shops and cafes.

Another 12km walk on **DAY 2** continues from Lilam beside the Gori along a forested trail for 8km to Railgari (whose unusual name means "railway train") where simple cafes offer very basic accommodation in season. **Bugdiar**, 4km further on, has a PWD guest house with a kitchen, a few very limited cafes – and an ITBP checkpost.

A steady but gentle rise from Bugdiar on **DAY 3** leads for 7km to mountain *bugyals* and the hamlet of Manpanga, which also has a seasonal tea shop. Press on for 5km to **Railkot**, where there is limited seasonal accommodation and food.

Set off from Railkot on **DAY 4** up a gentle path that reaches the tree-line after 6km at the large village of Burfu, where basic accommodation includes a hotel. From Burfu a gentle track leads for 4km to Bilju, with a tea shop and views of Nanda Kot. A further 3km brings you to the large village of **Milam**, home to the Rawats and other groups of Hindu Bhotias; Milam also has a large ITBP presence and a checkpost. Milam Glacier is 2km further on.

Practicalities

Munsiyari is at the end of the road, so few **buses** come this way and those that do are very basic; there are daily departures to Pithoragarh (5.30am; 8hr) and Almora (5am; 11hr). KMVN are about to open a tourist lodge, and further facilities for tourists are bound to appear soon; for the moment, the PWD *Bungalow* (①) has four very comfortable suites with hot water geysers at extremely cheap rates. Food is usually available, at a price. The bazaar has a couple of simple lodges and there are two simple cafes at the bus stop. Prem Ram, of Gram Bunga, Tala, Nayabasti, is a well-spoken guide who can organize treks including cooks and porters, for around Rs100 a day.

Pithoragarh

PITHORAGARH, the headquarters of the easternmost district of Kumaun, in the beautiful sprawling Sore Valley 188km northeast of Nainital, has recently become the site of the only airport in the UP hills. Combine that with the ongoing removal of restrictions on access to the interior (although foreigners will find it impossible to get permits to trek into Tibet), and the town seems certain to grow and change for the worse in years ahead. As it is, the location remains beautiful, fringed with terraced cultivation at an altitude of around 1650m and offering glimpses of Panchuli and the remote mountains of western Nepal.

Above Pithoragarh, in the pine-wooded slopes of the Leprosy Mission at **Chandag** 7km north, a large cross overlooks the valley in benediction, commanding views of the valley and of Saipal and Api in western Nepal. It makes a pleasant walk up from the *Tourist Bungalow*, or you can take local buses en route for Bans.

Practicalities

Pithoragarh's airport has had erratic connections to Lucknow and Delhi; check on the latest schedules. Private **bus** companies and *UPSRTC* buses connect the town with Nainital (8hr) and Almora (6hr), as well as the railheads of Tanakpur, 151km south, and Pilibhit, 215km southeast. Amenities in town remain extremely limited. **Hotel** accommodation is comparatively basic and for once, the KMVN *Tourist Lodge* (①–②), tucked away in the woods 1.5km above the bazaar on the Chandag Road, comes out tops. The more central *Ulka Priyadarshani* (☎2596; ①–②), in the bazaar close to the bus stand, and the less roomy *Trishul* nearby (①–②), are reasonable budget hotels. Simple cafes and *dhabas* are available in the bazaar area.

CENTRAL UP

Large tracts of **CENTRAL UP**, along the fertile flood-plains of the Doab, constituted the nineteenth-century **Kingdom of Avadh**. Eventually little more than puppets of the British, its wealthy Nawabs focussed their attentions on the arts, and created a unique civilization centred around **Lucknow**. Monuments from those days, and traces of the bitter fighting of the "Mutiny" that coincided with the final eclipse of Avadh, are scattered throughout both city and region. However, Lucknow is now the capital of a Hindu-controlled state far removed from the communal harmony of Avadh – named after the now-notorious holy town of **Ayodhya**, the recent flashpoint of right-wing Hindu militancy. Industrialized **Kanpur**, southwest of Lucknow, was as "Cawnpore" the scene of some of the bloodiest moments of the rebellion of 1857. It's now most worth visiting to explore its near-neighbour **Bithur**, a miniature and forgotten Varanasi beside the Ganges. Further east, the holy river flows towards **Allahabad**, and the sacred confluence at **Prayag**, where it meets the Yamuna and the mythical Saraswati that flows from heaven.

Kanpur

Although the teeming metropolis of **KANPUR**, 438km east of Delhi and 190km west of Allahabad, is among the most polluted cities in the world, it's not a particularly unpleasant place to visit. Its setting is certainly attractive, on a fertile escarpment on the south bank of the Ganges, 1.5km wide at this point, and in the leafy Civil Lines area you can remain happily oblivious of the tanneries, chemical works, engineering and industrial developments that belch on the outskirts. Kanpur has been a textile-manufacturing centre since its cotton mills were established in 1869, and together with its twin city, Lucknow, 76km northeast, it dominates the industrial heartland of Uttar Pradesh.

The problem with Kanpur as a tourist destination is simply that it's not all that interesting. Unlike other points along the Ganges, the riverside is of little significance; its *ghats* are run down, and only those at **Bithur**, 20km upstream, are worth exploring.

Arrival, transport and information

Trains on the main Delhi–Calcutta line pull in regularly at Kanpur Central, in the most congested part of the city. **Buses** from Lucknow and points east terminate at the **Collectorganj** Bus Stand (☎0512/63259) in Sadar Bazaar, a short way east, while services from Delhi, Agra, Haridwar and the west arrive at **Chunniganj** (☎0512/63603), 3km west of the Mall. Few people fly to Kanpur, as rail connections are more reliable, but there's an **airport** in the southeast, a Rs90 taxi-ride from the centre. *Indian Airlines* have offices opposite M G College, Civil Lines (☎0512/211430) and at the airport (☎0512/43042).

Local buses use stands such as Ghanta Ghar, near the Mall; **taxis** are plentiful near the station; **cars** can be rented through the larger hotels; and **cycle** and **auto**-rickshaws abound. Noisy diesel-powered *Vikrams* and tempos operate along fixed routes, and horse-drawn tongas can be rented on a shared or exclusive basis.

As the government does not consider Kanpur to be a tourist destination, the city has no official information centre. The main **post office** is the GPO, at Bara Chaurha on The Mall, and money can be changed nearby at *ANZ Grindlays* **bank**.

The Town

The focus of modern Kanpur is north of the station, where the large avenue known as **The Mall** threads east to west to form a hub for the more cosmopolitan sectors of the city. Further north and west, beyond the exclusive **Civil Lines** area, is the river.

"**Cawnpore**", among the most vital of the British East India Company's garrisons along the Ganges, was a major focus of the wild revolt of 1857 – what the British call the "**Indian Mutiny**" and Indians the "**First War of Independence**". One thousand or so British residents were besieged throughout June by the forces of Nana Sahib of Bithur, their numbers whittled away by disease, starvation and enemy sharp-shooting. Only a few hundred were still alive when Brigadier-General Wheeler finally managed to negotiate a truce. However, as they boarded boats at Satichaura Ghat, to carry them to Allahabad, they were mown down by gunfire, and any survivors put to the sword. When relief under Brigadier-General Havelock finally reached Kanpur a few days later, on 17 July, they found that two hundred imprisoned women and children had been butchered in revenge for previous British atrocities. Terrifying and equally brutal reprisals by the British included executions of innocent civilians, the razing of villages, and the shooting of captives spreadeagled across the mouths of cannons.

Around 1.5km east of the station, close to the run-down Kanpur Club, broad tree-lined streets lead to the red-brick **All Saints' Memorial Church**. Erected in 1875, near the site of General Wheeler's original entrenchment, it serves as a tribute to the British dead. A fine stained-glass window above the west door filters light into the spacious and cool interior, where marble tablets line the walls; the vestry holds a plan of the entrenchment. Outside, enclosed by iron railings, a tiled memorial marks the graves of officers and men, not far from a capped well where many died trying to draw water. Within an enclosure east of the church, the **Memorial Garden** has a Gothic screen designed by Sir Henry Yule, and a touching epitaph in stone by Baron Carlo Marochetti. The memorials originally stood over the site of the terrible Bibighat well in the centre of the city, where Havelock discovered the still-warm remains of the massacred women and children; they were relocated here after Independence.

Although **Kanpur Zoo**, an oasis amid the noisy urban sprawl at Allen Park 5km west of the Mall, might on first sight appear to be just another zoological park, it is far from ordinary (daily except Mon, dawn–dusk; Rs2). This vast area of woodland provides a surreal setting in which wild animals co-exist alongside others in open enclosures and cages. Along the southeast, extensive low-lying marshlands provide grazing for herds of wild deer, and sustain a mixed assortment of birds. During feeding time, in the early evenings, *nilgai* antelope ("blue bull") emerge from the dense surrounding woods to gorge on grain laid out close to their captive cousins.

The new, brash **JK Mandir**, in attractive gardens 4km west of the Mall, not far from the the zoo, has become one of Kanpur's principal temples – an object lesson as to where mass religion in India is heading. This extraordinary white marble and alabaster edifice was constructed by a local business family in a hybrid modern style that incorporates north and south Indian elements, capped by five *shikharas* (spires). In separate chapels inside the huge central hall, hung with chandeliers, numerous deities are represented in hyper-realistic detail. The large **Moti Jheel** tank nearby is popular with picnickers.

Accommodation

Several of Kanpur's better **hotels** can be found in and around the Mall, while cheaper accommodation is concentrated near the Central Railway Station – which itself has reasonable retiring rooms.

Attic, 15/198 Vikramjit Singh Rd, Civil Lines (☎0512/311691). Mysteriously misnamed Kanpur landmark, with a distinct whiff of the Raj. Comfortable bungalow and a garden, full of character. ⑤.

Bliss, near Gumti 5, Gurudwara, 11A/5 G T Rd (☎0512/291731). Sikh-run, clean and moderately comfortable with both air-cooled and a/c rooms. ③–④.

Ganges, 51 Nayaganj (☎0512/69185). Cheap and near the station, with reasonable veg food. ①–③.

Gaurav, 18/54 The Mall (☎0512/268616). Central hotel, four doors down from the better-known *Geet*, but not as loud and a lot more pleasant. ④–⑥.

Grand Trunk, 84/79 G T Rd (☎0512/245435). One of the city's more expensive hotels, with numerous facilities including a travel desk and a small swimming pool. ⑦.

The Landmark, 10 The Mall (☎0512/317601). Spanking new place behind Som Dutt Plaza; the closest Kanpur comes to luxury. Features include currency exchange. ⑦.

Meera Inn, The Mall (☎0512/319972). Friendly and comfortable place opposite *Reserve Bank* but showing its age. Despite lacking its own restaurant, it does offer room service. ④–⑤.

Meghdoot, The Mall (☎0512/311999). Large modern block opposite Company Bagh, with a small rooftop swimming pool, health club, several restaurants and a bar. ⑦.

Natraj, 71/150 Suterkhana (☎0512/366907). Reasonable budget accommodation close to the railway station. Some rooms with shared baths and some small a/c. ①–④.

Swagat, 80 Feet Rd, Brahm Nagar (☎0512/241923). Close to amenities, newish with comfortable rooms and several facilities including car rental. ④–⑤.

Yatrik, Lucknow Pathak, Suterkhana (☎0512/360373). Tacky and overlooking the tracks but very handy for the station. ②–④.

Eating

While few of the high street **eating places** can be recommended, several of Kanpur's better hotels such as the *Landmark* and the *Meghdoot* have good restaurants.

Kailash Mistha Bhandar, G T Rd, Gumti 5. The best of a couple of roadside cafes near Moti Jheel, serving snacks such as *dosas* to locals who come here to take the evening air.

Kwalitys, The Mall. Part of the national chain; predictable multi-cuisine food and a separate bar.

Little Chef, Vikramjit Singh Rd, Civil Lines. Modern fast-food place, next to the *Attic*. Burgers, ice cream, and Indian food, plus piped music. Attracts a well-heeled young crowd, but pleasant enough.

Shanghai, The Mall. Popular Chinese restaurant in the centre of town.

Yog, Moti Jheel. Multi-cuisine garden restaurant, often crowded although well out from the centre.

Bithur

Some Hindus consider the charming little town of **BITHUR**, set in rich farming country beside the Ganges 20km west of Kanpur, to be the centre of the world. However, few pilgrims, let alone tourists, come to this miniature Varanasi, where many of the *ghats* have been reclaimed by the river, since being devastated by the British bombardment that followed the uprising of 1857. Bithur's principal shrine, at the main *ghat*, is one of the few in the Hindu world to be dedicated to **Brahma**. The town is also connected to the *Ramayana*, and specifically with Rama's wife Sita – this is where her sons were born, and where she died when the earth opened and swallowed her.

Much the best way to enjoy the ambience of the place is to rent a **boat** at the main *ghat*. Most are owned by the *pandas* (pilgrim priests) whose houses are huddled together with the *dharamshalas* near the *ghat*'s dilapidated gate. Less than a kilometre upriver stands another of the many mosques built on the foundations of devastated Hindu temples during the reign of Aurangzeb. As in Ayodhya (see p.286), this mosque has attracted the attention of Hindu fundamentalists, but the local *pandas* proudly inform visitors that here Hindus and Muslims continue to co-exist in harmony.

Practicalities

Three local **trains** per day connect Bithur with Kanpur Central, while buses and shared auto-rickshaws travel between Kanpur and Mandhana, where local transport to Bithur can be picked up. For the moment, the only way to arrange food and lodging is through the *pandas*, who are generally pleasant and helpful. During the full moon of Karttika Purnima (Oct/Nov), Bithur plays host to a large and colourful rustic fair.

Lucknow

In the approximate centre of Uttar Pradesh, 570km east of Delhi, the state capital **LUCKNOW** is best remembered for the ordeal of its British residents during the five-month **siege** of 1857. However, the city had earlier witnessed the last days of Muslim rule in India, before the final capitulation to the British. In fact the summary British deposition of the incompetent last Nawab of **Avadh** – or Oudh as the British called it – Wajid Ali Shah, is usually numbered among the root causes of the "Mutiny". Many of Lucknow's fading nineteenth-century monuments bear the scars of the fighting, and of the destruction wrought by the British army when they eventually regained control.

The centre of Muslim power shifted gradually from Delhi to Avadh from the middle of the eighteenth century onwards, as the Moghul empire declined. The later Nawabs of Avadh are a byword in India for indolence and decadence, but it has to be acknowledged that under their rule the arts flourished, cocooned from the responsibilities of government. Avadh became a magnet for poets and artists, where Hindus and Muslims worked in harmony, fuelled by wealth and plentiful leisure time. Lucknow was also an important repository of Shi'a culture and Islamic jurisprudence, with its Farangi Mahal school of law attracting students from as far afield as China and Central Asia.

The patronage of the Shi'a Nawabs also produced new expressions of the faith – the annual **Muharram** processions, in memory of the martyrdom of Hussain and his two sons, developed into elaborate affairs with **tazia**, ornate reproductions in paper of the Shi'a Imam's shrine at Karbala in southern Iraq, being carried to the local Karbala for burial. In Lucknow, Muharram is often a time of great tension between the Shi'a and their rival Sunni Muslims. During the rest of the year the *tazia* images are kept in Imambara ("houses of the Imam"); these range from humble rooms in poor Shi'a households to the **Great Imambara** built by Asaf-ud-Daula in 1784.

Extraordinary sandstone monuments, now engulfed by modern Lucknow, still testify to the euphoric atmosphere of this unique culture. European edifices too are prominent on the skyline, often embellished with flying buttresses, turrets, cupolas and floral patterns, but the brick and mortar which which they were constructed means that they are not ageing as well as their Muslim counterparts.

The telephone **area code** for Lucknow is ☎0522.

Arrival, information and transport

From **Amausi Airport** (☎244030), 16km south on the Kanpur Road, a taxi to the centre of Lucknow costs around Rs120. Airport buses connect with flights, and charge Rs15 for the trip to the downtown *Hotel Clarks Avadh*.

Lucknow's main **Charbagh Railway Station**, 4km southwest of the central hub of Hazratganj, is itself a remarkable building, with prominent *chhatris* above the entrance arcade. Buses from Varanasi, Allahabad, Agra, Jhansi and Kanpur arrive at the **Charbagh** stand alongside, while buses from the Nepal border at Sonauli and from Gorakhpur, Faizabad and Ayodhya pull in at the **Kaisarbagh** stand, near Hazratganj.

City transport and guided tours

The fierce competition for space makes rush hours in Lucknow particularly interesting. Tempos and *Vikrams*, their diesel engines sounding like hundreds of loud rattles, have more or less taken over from city buses, plying regular routes such as from Charbagh to the GPO, with depots at Janpath Market, Clarks Avadh Crossing and the Chowk. Adding to the chaos are legions of reasonably priced cycle rickshaws, more common than auto-rickshaws and charging around Rs5 from the station to Hazratganj.

Cars can be rented from various operators, including *Hotel Clarks Avadh*, *UP Tours* at the *Hotel Gomti*, 6 Sapru Marg (☎232659), and *Transworld Travel & Tours*, 98 *Carlton Hotel*, Shah Najaf Rd (☎232145). Comprehensive daily **city tours**, which must be booked in advance through *UP Tours*, leave the *Hotel Gomti* at 9am and return at 1.30pm. They will also pick up clients from the station (at 7.45am) and assorted other hotels. Guide fees are included in the price of Rs45, but any entrance charges are not.

Information

The national government's **Regional Tourist Bureau**, down a side road close to the railway station at 10 Station Rd (Mon–Sat 10am–5pm, closed 2nd Sat of each month; ☎246205), provides information only; they also operate a stand at the railway station.

THE PERFORMING ARTS OF LUCKNOW

In the eighteenth and nineteenth centuries, Muslim Lucknow saw the emergence of an astounding range of music and dance forms that remain prominent in the performing arts of north India. The period is still considered as a Golden Age of artistic achievement.

Apart from the musicians of the court, and knowledgeable courtiers – among them some of the Nawabs themselves – **tawwaif** (courtesans) took on a vital role in the cultural life of the city, becoming highly proficient as poets and in dance and song. While *khyal* and *dhrupad* remained the mainstay of classical music, **thumri** – love songs amalgamating classical *ragas* and folk melodies – developed a high degree of sophistication, and forms such as *dadra*, *tappa* and *hori*, influenced by folk traditions, also became widely popular. Often referred to as "semi" or "light" classical music, these are fading from the repertoire of modern musicians.

Kathak, the main genre of north Indian classical dance, developed under Nawabs such as Shuja-ud-Daula (1756–75) and Asaf-ud-Daula (1775–97). The theme of Krishna cavorting with the milkmaids (*gopis*) became especially important within performances that otherwise rely on strong and energetic footwork around *laikari*, intricate rhythmic compositions accompanied by *tabla* or hand-drums. Some of Avadh's great **Gharana** (schools) of dance and music – including those at Lucknow, Farrakhabad, and Rampur – are gradually being assimilated into a new system of patronage, now dependent on the middle classes.

The **Lucknow Festival**, held during February, gives visitors an excellent opportunity to sample the city's vibrant traditions of music and dance. For information, contact UP Tourism.

Lucknow's main **post office** is the GPO on Vidhan Sabha Marg. Among **banks** for foreign exchange are *Punjab National Bank*, Ashok Marg, Hazratganj (☎231290), and *State Bank of India*, also on Ashok Marg (☎23341) and at Moti Mahal Marg (☎240186).

The Town

Most of Lucknow's monuments are spread along or near the southern bank of the Gomti, a sluggish weed-covered stream when the rains aren't falling. Close to the main central bridge lies the modern economic centre of **Hazratganj**, with the **Shah Najaf Imambara** to its north near the riverbank. Further west, beyond the ruins of the **Residency**, the road passes the majestic **Bara Imambara**, leading through the large gate of **Rumi Darwaza** to the **Hussainabad Imambara**. South of Hussainabad, between Hazratganj and Charbagh, the old city sector of Aminabad holds a maze of busy streets and fascinating markets.

Hussainabad

In the west of the city, in the vicinity of Hardinge Bridge around "old" Lucknow, lie several crumbling relics of the Nawabs of Avadh. Chief among them is the Great or **Bara Imambara**, which boasts one of the largest vaulted halls in the world – 50 metres long and 15 metres high. Flat on top, slightly arched inside, and built by Asaf-ud-Daula in 1784 without the aid of a single iron or wooden beam, the roof was constructed using a technique known as *kara dena*, in which bricks are broken and angled to form an interlocking section and then covered with concrete – here several feet thick. The arcaded structure is approached through what must have been an extravagant gate, now pockmarked and on the verge of collapse. Two successive court-yards lead from the gates to the Imambara itself, which unlike the sombre architecture of mosques is festive and loud. Steps lead up to a labyrinth of chambers known as *bhulbhulaiya* – the "maze". Adjacent to the Bara Imambara and overlooking it is **Asaf-ud-Daula's Mosque**, set upon a two-tiered arcaded plinth with two lofty minarets. Closed to non-Muslims, it can be readily viewed from the Victoria Gardens that adjoin it to the west (daily except Fri dawn–dusk; Rs6).

Straddling the main road west of the main gates, the colossal **Rumi Darwaza** is an ornamental victory arch modelled on one of the gates to Asia Minor at Istanbul (known to the Islamic world in Byzantine times as "Rumi"). Now decaying, it sports elaborate floral patterns and a few extraordinary trumpets. Steps lead up to open chambers that command a general prospect of the monuments of Hussainabad.

A short distance further west, the lavish **Hussainabad Imambara** is also known as the Chota ("small") Imambara, or the Palace of Lights, thanks to its fairy-tale appear-ance when decorated and illuminated for special occasions. The raised tank in front of it, which is approached via a spacious courtyard, adds to the overall festive atmos-phere. A central gilded dome dominates the whole ensemble, busy with minarets, small domes and arches and even a crude miniature Taj Mahal. Built in 1837 by Muhammad Ali Shah (1837–42), partly to provide famine relief through employment, the Imambara houses a silver-faced throne, plus the tombs of important Avadhi person-alities. The dummy gate opposite the main entrance was used by ceremonial musi-cians, while the unfinished watch-tower is known as the Satkhanda or "Seven Storeys", even though only four were ever constructed. West of the Imambara, and surrounded by ruins, are the two soaring minarets and three domes of the **Jami Masjid**, completed after the death of Muhammad Ali Shah, which does not admit non-Muslims.

Beyond the Hussainabad Tank, east of the Hussainabad Imambara, the isolated 67-metre-high **Hussainabad Clocktower**, an ambitious Gothic tower completed in 1887, carries the largest clock in India. Close to this bizarre monolith lies **Taluqdar's Hall**, built by Muhammad Ali Shah to house the offices of the Hussainabad Trust, and the **Picture Gallery**, also known as the **Muhammad Ali Shah Art Gallery** (Mon–Sun 6am–6pm; Rs1). Exhibits in its one large hall include old photographs and paintings including a famous portrait of the ineffectual and feeble last Nawab of Avadh, Wajid Ali Shah (1847–56), with his left nipple showing. Dusty and dank, the gallery nevertheless captures the spirit of Avadh – as indeed do the adjacent trust offices. **Aurangzeb's Mosque**, on the high ground towards Hardinge Bridge known as **Lakshman Tila**, was the site of Lucknow's original fifteenth-century settlement.

The Residency

The blasted **Residency** (daily dawn–dusk; Rs1, free on Fri) rests in peace amid land-scaped gardens southeast of Hardinge Bridge – a battle-scarred ruin left exactly as it stood when the siege was finally relieved by Sir Colin Campbell on 17 November 1857. Its shattered tower became a shrine to the tenacity of the British in India, and contin-ued to be maintained as such even after Independence.

During the siege, every building in the complex was utilized for the hard-fought defence of the compound. The **Treasury**, on the right through the **Baillie Guard Gate**, served as an arsenal, while the sumptuous **Banqueting Hall** immediately west was a makeshift hospital, and the extensive single-storey **Dr Fayrer's House** just south housed women and children. Most of the original structures, such as **Begum Kothi**, were left standing to impede direct fire from the enemy. On the lawn outside Begum Kothi, a large cross honours the astute but helpless Sir Henry Lawrence, responsible for building its defences, who died shortly after hostilities began.

The pockmarked **Residency** itself holds a small museum. Circular steps descend into its bowels, to the huge cellar known as the *tikhana* where many of the women and children took shelter. On the ground floor, the **Model Room** (daily 9am–4.30pm; Rs1),

THE SIEGE OF THE RESIDENCY OF LUCKNOW

The mutinous *sepoys* who poured across the River Gomti into Lucknow on 30 June 1857 found the city rife with resentment against the recent British takeover of the kingdom of Avadh. The tiny, isolated, **British garrison**, under the command of Sir Henry Lawrence, took refuge in the **Residency**, which became the focus of a fierce struggle for survival.

Less than a thousand of the three thousand British residents and loyal Indians who crammed into the Residency survived the relentless war of attrition. So unhygienic were their living conditions that those who failed to succumb to gangrenous and tetanus-infected wounds were liable to fall victim to cholera and scurvy. While a barrage of heavy artillery was maintained by both sides, a simultaneous **subterranean** battle was being fought. The *sepoys* pinned their hopes of breaching the defences on tunnelling and laying mines; but the British were far more adept at such methods. The skills of the ex-miners of the 32nd (Cornish) Regiment enabled them to follow the sounds of enemy chipping and defuse mines, and even to take the offensive and blow up several *sepoy*-controlled buildings on the peripheries of the complex.

Morale remained high among the 1400 **non-combatants**, who included fifty school-boys from La Martiniere, and class distinctions were upheld throughout. While the wives of European soldiers and non-commissioned officers, children and servants took refuge in the *tikhana* (cellar), the "Ladies" of the Residency occupied the higher and airier chambers, until the unfortunate loss of Miss Palmer's leg, carried off on 1 July, persuaded them of the gravity of their predicament. Sir Henry Lawrence was fatally wounded the next day.

The wealthier officers managed to maintain their own private hoard of supplies, living in much their usual style. Matters improved when after three months General Sir Henry Havelock arrived with reinforcements, and the normal round of visits and invitations to supper was resumed despite the inconvenient shortage of good food and wine.

Not until 17 November was the siege finally lifted, by the forces of Sir Colin Campbell. When the Highlanders liberated the Residency, their offers of tea were turned down by the women; they were used to taking milk in their tea, which the soldiers could not supply.

the only one with its roof intact, houses a large model of the defences and of the Residency, and a small but excellent collection of etchings and old photographs.

Several victims of the siege are buried in the **Cemetery** next to the ruined church west of the Residency. Not far away east, along the river, the rather dull **Shaheed Smarak** is a corresponding post-Independence memorial to the Indian martyrs who died here fighting the British in the "First War of Independence".

Kaisarbagh

Isolated by the noise and bustle of modern Lucknow, the nineteenth-century monuments around **Kaisarbagh**, south of the Residency, should ideally have been maintained in recognition of the vitality of Avadh; instead they stand forlorn and unattended. Large chunks of the rambling **Kaisarbagh Palace**, built in 1850 by Wajid Ali Shah and intended to be the eighth wonder of the world, have vanished, while the nearby **Chattar Manzil**, once the United Services Club, has lost most of its roof. Within the grounds of the Kaisarbagh, beside the smaller grave of his wife **Khurshid Zadi**, is the handsome tomb of **Saadat Ali Khan** (1798–1814). Now overgrown and often locked, it is distinguished by black-and-white marble paving, beneath which a dark narrow stairway drops down to the vault.

Kaisarbagh's **Folk Art Museum**, a large hall devoted to the contemporary arts of UP, is a disappointment. Nearby, the former coronation hall on Lal Baradari is now the **Lalit Kala Academy** (Mon–Fri 9am–5pm; free), the gallery for the government school of art. It too is dilapidated and poorly maintained.

Hazratganj

Along the river, opposite the fading *Carlton Hotel* on Rana Pratap Marg, squats the huge dome of the **Shah Najaf Imambara** (daily except Fri 8am–5pm; donations), named after the tomb of Ali in Iraq and at its best when adorned with lights during Muharram. Its musty interior holds some incredibly garish chandeliers used in processions, several *tazia*, and the silver-faced tomb of the decadent and profligate Ghazi-ud-din-Haidar (1814–27), buried with three of his queens.

The Imambara was commandeered as a *sepoy* stronghold in 1857, and the crucial battle that enabled the British to relieve the Residency was fought in the adjacent pleasure gardens of **Sikandrabagh** on 16 November. It took one and a half hours of bombardment for the soldiers of Sir Colin Campbell to breach the defences of the two thousand *sepoys*; then the Sikhs and 93rd Highlanders poured through, to embark on a rampage of slaughter. There was no escape for the terrified *sepoys*, some of whom are said to have believed the bloodstained, red-faced, kilted Scots to be the ghosts of the murdered European women of Kanpur. Driven against the north wall, they were either bayoneted or shot, and the dead and dying piled shoulder-high. Tranquil once again, Sikandrabagh is now home to the National Botanical Research Institute and the beautiful **Botanical Gardens** (daily 6am–5pm; free), with their conservatories, nurseries, herb, rose and bougainvillaea gardens, and manicured lawns.

Towards the east of Lucknow, an extraordinary chateau-like building has become almost a symbol of the city – **La Martiniere**, an exclusive public school in the finest colonial tradition. It was built as a country retreat by Major-General Claude Martin, a French soldier-adventurer taken prisoner by the British in Pondicherry in 1761. The enigmatic Martin later joined the East India Company, made his fortune in indigo, and served both the British and the Nawabs of Avadh. The building is an outrageous but intriguing amalgam, crowned by flying walkways; Greco-Roman figures on the parapets give it a busy silhouette, gigantic heraldic lions gaze across the grounds, and a large bronze cannon graces the front. Martin himself is buried in the basement. During the siege, La Martiniere was occupied by rebels, while its boys were evacuated to the Residency. Entry to the building is by prior arrangement with the Principal.

Close to the centre of Hazratganj, its grounds dotted with derelict Avadhi monuments, Lucknow's small **zoo** also serves as an amusement park with a miniature train to view the animals (daily except Mon 7.30am–5.30pm; Rs2). Head through the zoo to reach the **State Museum** (daily except Mon 10.30am–4.30pm; Rs0.50, cameras Rs2), with its delicate, speckled-red-sandstone sculpture from the Mathura school of the Kushana and Gupta periods (first–sixth centuries AD). Besides sculpture from Gandhara, Mahoba, Nalanda and Sravasti, it boasts a gallery of terracotta and even an Egyptian mummy. Musical instruments, paintings and costumes provide atmosphere in the Avadh Gallery; while the natural history section is a taxidermist's dream.

Shopping

Shops and showrooms in Janpath Market, Nazirabad and Aminabad, and at **Chikan Corner** outside the Chota Imambara in Hussainabad, sell *saris* and *kurtas* decorated with **chikan** embroidery. *Chikan* is a long-standing Lucknavi tradition, in which designs are built up to form delicate floral patterns along edges such as neck-lines and collars. Workshops can be found around the Chowk, the market area of old Lucknow. The fixed prices at **Gangotri**, the UP government emporium in Hazratganj, are more expensive than those prevailing in the markets, but the quality is assured and reticent souls may be glad to be spared the process of haggling.

Lucknow is also renowned for its **ittar** (or *attar*), concentrated perfume sold in small vials – an acquired (and expensive) taste. Small balls of cotton wool are daubed with the scent and placed neatly within the top folds of the ear; musicians believe that the aroma heightens their senses. Popular *ittar* are *ambar* from amber, *khus* from a flowering plant and *ghulab* from rose. The best place for *ittar* is *Asghar Ali Mohammad Ali*, Aminabad, who have their own factories in Kannauj 150km away.

Accommodation

Budget and mid-range **hotels** are concentrated in the **Charbagh** area, around the bus and train stations, and along Vidhan Sabha Marg, the main artery feeding into the city centre around the GPO. The more cosmopolitan **Hazratganj** district holds a few bargains. Top-range hotels under construction as this book went to press include the *Taj Palace* in Gomti Nagar and *Arif Castles*, 4 Rana Pratap Marg.

Amber, Naka Hindola (☎235658). Spacious air-cooled rooms, with clean Indian-style toilets. ②–④.

Avadh Lodge, 1 Ram Mohan Rai Marg (☎243821). A hall hung with hunting trophies captures the atmosphere of old Lucknow, but the place is a bit musty and showing its age. ④–⑤.

Baba Tourist Lodge, Charbagh Railway Station (☎54357). A stone's throw from the station, pleasant and quite clean Sikh-run option with a range of rooms from shared baths to a/c. ①–④.

Carlton, Shah Najaf Rd (☎244021). Fabled Lucknow address, a rambling *fin-de-siècle* Euro-Avadhi edifice. Large rooms, ancient plumbing and a pleasant garden with coffee shop and restaurant. ⑦.

Charans, 16 Vidhan Sabha Marg (☎247219). Mid-range and quiet, even though it lies just off the main road, with a choice of air-cooled or a/c rooms. ④–⑥.

MOVING ON FROM LUCKNOW

Indian Airlines **flights** from Lucknow include IC695 to **Bombay** (Mon, Tues, Thurs & Sat); IC409 to **Calcutta** via **Patna** (Mon, Wed & Fri), and several to **Delhi** – IC436 (daily), IC410 (Mon, Wed & Fri), and IC836 (Sat, Sun, Tues & Thurs). *Indian Airlines* have offices at *Hotel Clarks Avadh*, 8 Mahatma Gandhi Marg (☎240927), and at the airport at Amausi (☎51030).

By **rail**, the excellent a/c *Shatabdi Express* #2003 makes the journey on weekdays to **Delhi** (7hr); cheaper alternatives include the *Gomti Express* #2419 (daily except Tues; 8hr), and the slower overnight *Lucknow Mail* #4229. The best choice to **Agra** is the *Avadh Express* #5063 (daily 9.50pm; 7hr). The *Kushinagar Express* #1016 travels daily to **Bombay** (30hr). **Calcutta** is served by several trains, such as the *Amritsar–Howrah Mail* #3006 and the slower *Amritsar–Howrah Express* #3050, which both take over twenty hours. Alternatives to **Varanasi** include the fast evening *Lucknow–Varanasi Varuna Express* #2428 (7hr), and the overnight *Kashi–Vishwanath Express* #4058 (8hr). In the opposite direction, the *Varanasi–Dehra Dun Express* #4265 heads for **Dehra Dun** (14hr) via **Haridwar**.

Trains such as the *Vaishali, Kushinagar* and *Sabarmati Expresses* travel to **Gorakhpur** (5hr), where you can catch a bus to the **Nepal** border at **Sonauli** – the choice of buses to **Kathmandu** and **Pokhara** is better on the Nepalese side of the border. This may seem a convoluted way to get to Nepal, but is more comfortable than a long gruelling direct bus to the border. If you're content to make the 11- to 12-hour journey by road, several buses leave from **Kaisarbagh** bus stand, from where further buses also go to Gorakhpur and to Faizabad. Kaisarbagh also offers Delhi buses, and an efficient night service to Nainital.

Agents for air, rail and bus tickets include *Hollywood Travels*, Mayfair Building, 29 Hazratganj (☎246559); *Travel Corporation of India*, 3 Shah Najaf Marg (☎233212); and the efficient, friendly *UP Tours*, Hotel Gomti, 6 Sapru Marg (☎232659).

Finally, if you're heading for the UP hills, Lucknow holds offices of both **GMVN** (opposite Kalakakar House, Civil Lines, Old Hyderabad; ☎77585), and **KMVN** (near *Kirpa Automobiles*, Gopal Khera House, Sarojini Naidu Marg; ☎235903), who organize tours of, and accommodation in, **Garhwal** and **Kumaun** respectively. For more on both, see p.233 and p.263.

Chowdhury Lodge, 3 Vidhan Sabha Marg (☎241911). Close to the GPO, well priced, pleasant, friendly and justifiably popular. Bed tea in the mornings. ②–③.

Clarks Avadh, 8 Mahatma Gandhi Marg (☎240131). An imposing landmark, the best that Lucknow has to offer, even if it lacks the character of others in the chain (such as Varanasi). ⑨.

Deep Avadh, Naka Hindola, Aminabad Rd (☎236521). New place, with a good multi-cuisine restaurant and a travel desk, in a busy and interesting part of town close to the station. ③–⑤.

Elora, 3 Lalbagh (☎241100). Popular with travellers in the interesting and busy heart of Lucknow with air-cooled and a/c rooms. ③–⑥.

Hardik Guest House, 16 Rana Pratap Marg, near Jappling Road Crossing (☎231765). New and clean, a comfortable and recommended little guest house including air-conditioned rooms. ④–⑤.

Kohinoor, 6 Station Rd (☎232715). Set back from the main road close to the station – quite pleasant and clean with a nice 24hr coffee shop. ⑤–⑥.

Mayur, Charbagh (☎50464). Opposite the station, next to the Charbagh Bus Stand and above the *Bharat Restaurant*. The more expensive rooms are better value. ②–⑤.

UP Tourism Gomti, 6 Tej Bahadur Sapru Marg (☎232291). Showpiece establishment with large spacious rooms off the busy centre of Hazratganj; *UP Tours* is also housed here. ⑦.

Vaishali, Latouche Rd, Aminabad (☎244382). Simple budget rooms in the heart of the crowded and interesting old market area. ①.

Eating

The rich traditional Lucknavi **cuisine** – featuring such Mughlai dishes as *shami kebabs, mughlai parathas, sheekh kebabs*, chicken *musallam* and *boti kebab* – is available from food stalls throughout the city, in places such as Shami Avadh Bazaar near the K D Singh Babu Stadium, and behind the *Tulsi Theatre* in Hazratganj. Standard air-conditioned restaurants are found mostly in Hazratganj, while, of course, hotel restaurants such as the expensive *Clarks Avadh* serve excellent but pricey food.

Bharat Restaurant, Charbagh. One of several open-air cafes opposite the station. Good *dosas*.

Chef Restaurant, Vidhan Sabha Marg, near GPO (☎243313). Multi-cuisine restaurant with snacks and an ice cream parlour.

Hong Kong, Mahatma Gandhi Marg, Hazratganj. Popular Chinese restaurant with good food.

India Coffee House, Ashok Marg. Once a hotbed of Lucknow's intelligentsia; still popular with the faithful, but now dingy and a bit run down. South and north Indian snacks and coffee.

John Hing, opposite *Sahu Cinema*, Mahatma Gandhi Marg, Hazratganj. One of the few reasonable Chinese restaurants in Lucknow.

Kwalitys, Mayfair Building, Hazratganj. Dimly lit, a/c, the standard menu of this nationwide chain.

Mehman Fast Foods, Charbagh. Open station cafe; Chinese and north and south Indian food.

Royal Cafe, Hazratganj. Popular multi-cuisine a/c restaurant close to *Kwalitys*.

Ayodhya

As one of the seven holy cities of the Vaishnavites, the small town of **AYODHYA**, on the south bank of the River Ghaghara, 150km east of Lucknow and 6km east of Faizabad, attracts pilgrims from all over India. Even before the events of 1992 catapulted Ayodhya into world prominence, as the putative birthplace of Rama, it was renowned as a potential flashpoint for sectarian violence, and only the foolhardiest of foreign tourists venture out here. The town, and especially the area around the Babri Masjid mosque, remains highly volatile, and any disturbance should be avoided.

The embattled and guarded site of what was once Babri Masjid – the **Ram Janma Bhumi** – stands near the river, just south of the shrine known as **Janam Sthana**, the "birthplace", where Rama is said to have spent much of his early childhood. Other sites associated with specific events in the Rama legend include **Lakshmana Ghat**, a river landing near the bridge north of town, where Rama's brother Lakshmana is said to have committed suicide after breaking a vow. Not far away, on the banks of a rivulet, is the prominent and much-venerated temple of **Kala Rama**, while the nineteenth-century **Kanak Bhavan** temple in the centre of town is devoted to Rama and his wife Sita. Further south, towards the railway station a kilometre east of the Ram Janma Bhumi, the **Hanuman Gadhi** temple ("Hanuman's Fortress"), is enclosed within a quadrangle protected by massive white bastion-like walls. Embossed silver doorways lead to several shrines of Rama's monkey companion, Hanuman, and one of Sita.

Practicalities

Though Ayodhya has a small **railway station** of its own, south of town, most visitors come for the day from busy Faizabad (see below), on buses and auto-rickshaws from the station there. If you want to **stay** in Ayodhya, the *Pathik Niwas* (②–④), next to the station, has a dormitory and a wide range of rooms, as well as a decent restaurant. Due to its religious significance, Ayodhya is a **vegetarian** town.

Around Ayodhya: Faizabad

During the reign of Shuja-ud-Daula (1756–75), as the Moghul empire disintegrated, **FAIZABAD**, 6km southwest of Ayodhya, attracted craftsmen, artists and musicians from Delhi. However, the first capital of Avadh declined in tandem with the rise of Lucknow (see p.279). Among the few monuments to survive is the lofty white marble

---

BABRI MASJID AND RAM BHUMI

Although legend tells of Ayodhya as the birthplace of **Rama** – an incarnation of Vishnu and hero of the epic *Ramayana* – archeologists have found no proof of the existence of the king or his capital. They have however shown that Ayodhya was inhabited in the seventh century BC, and a Jain settlement dated to the fourth century BC is among the oldest known, said to be the home of the first and fourth Jain *tirthankaras*. The Buddha is also said to have visited the town, but there is little evidence that Ayodhya had any significance prior to the Muslim invasion in the fifteenth century. It can be argued that any earlier Hindu structures would have suffered from the usual practice of razing temples and replacing them with mosques, but the fact that the many shrines today crowded into the small town are relatively new is more likely to be simply because the re-emergence of Rama is a modern development.

Rama has been hijacked as the champion of fundamentalist Hindus, orchestrated by political parties such as the Vishwa Hindu Parishad (**VHP**) and the Bharatiya Janata Party (**BJP**) to advance their campaign against the "secularism" of the ruling Congress Party. They focussed attention on the quiet and barely used **Babri Masjid** mosque, constructed by the first Moghul emperor Babar in the fifteenth century, which had long co-existed alongside the shrine known as **Ram Janma Bhumi**, on what they consider to be the spot where Rama was born. After a few years of ugly confrontation, Babri Masjid was attacked in 1992 by thousands of Hindu fanatics, who tore it down with their bare hands. Television footage of the onslaught inspired "communalist" riots throughout India, especially in Bombay and Gujarat. Repercussions were felt wherever in the world Hindu and Muslim communities live side by side, including Britain, and there were violent demonstrations in Muslim countries. The central government of India, still at odds over the issue, has yet to carry out its declared intention of reconstructing the mosque alongside a Hindu shrine; meanwhile, in 1994, the egalitarian *purohit* (priest) of Ram Janma Bhumi – according to whom, Hindus and Muslims had shared the premises peacefully for years until the right-wing parties manipulated the issue – was murdered by persons unknown. A more encouraging development was the defeat of the BJP in state elections that year, when they lost Uttar Pradesh, Himachal Pradesh and Madhya Pradesh, but managed to hold on to Rajasthan and Delhi.

Tomb of Bahu Begum, the widow of Shuja-ud-Daula, close to the Nawab's own mausoleum. Faizabad's cantonment area is a legacy of British rule – caught up in the rebellion of 1857, it was thankfully spared the bloodshed seen in Kanpur and Lucknow.

Cheap central **accommodation** can be found near the *chowk* in the *Hotel Ambha* (①); the *Shan-e-Awadh* (②–④), in Rikabganj near the bus stand, has more comfortable a/c rooms. Faizabad is practically equidistant between Lucknow, Varanasi, Allahabad and Gorakhpur. Buses to all those cities take three to five hours, and there are regular trains to Lucknow and Varanasi.

Allahabad

The administrative and industrial city of **ALLAHABAD**, 135km west of Varanasi and 227km southeast of Lucknow, is also known as **Prayag** ("Confluence"), as the point where the rivers Yamuna and Ganga meet the mythical Saraswati. Sacred to all Hindus, the **Sangam** (which also means "confluence"), east of the city, is one of the great pilgrimage destinations of India. Allahabad comes alive during its *melas*; the annual **Magh Mela** (Jan/Feb), and the colossal **Maha Kumbh Mela**, held every 12 years.

Allahabad is a pleasant city to visit, with vast open riverside scenery and good amenities, but is without major temples or monuments – and there's little evidence that it had any before the Muslims arrived in 1194 either. At the junction of the fertile Doab, the "two-river" valley between the Yamuna and the Ganga, it did however possess a crucial strategic significance; its massive **fort**, built by the emperor Akbar in 1583, is still used by the military. Another Moghul, Jahangir's son Khusrau, was murdered here by his brother Shah Jahan, who went on to become emperor and build the Taj Mahal.

Allahabad played a vital role in the emergence of modern India. After the "Mutiny" of 1857, the British moved the headquarters of their North Western Provinces here from Agra, and the formal transfer of power from the East India Company to the crown took place here the following year. Well-preserved relics of the British impact include **Muir College** and **All Saints Cathedral**. The city also witnessed the first Indian National Congress in 1885, and the inauguration of Mahatma Gandhi's non-violent movement in 1920. **Anand Bhavan**, the home of Pandit Jawaharlal Nehru, is now a shrine to the Independence movement.

Arrival, information and transport

Allahabad has four **railway stations** (including Prayag, City and Daraganj), but major trains on the broad-gauge Delhi–Kanpur–Calcutta line arrive at the main **Allahabad Junction**. Most of the city's hotels are nearby; be sure to use the exit appropriate to the area where you plan to stay.

Leader Road bus stand, used by buses from western destinations such as Agra, Lucknow, Kanpur and Delhi, is just outside the station's south gates, while the smaller **Zero Road** bus stand, serving Mahoba and Satna to the south – the railheads for Khajuraho – is 1km southeast. Buses from points east, including Varanasi, arrive at the **MG Marg** bus stand, next to the *Tourist Bungalow*, about 1km east of the Civil Lines. For those few who arrive by **air**, from Delhi, Patna or Varanasi, no buses run to or from Bamrauli Airport, 15km west on the road to Kanpur; taxis charge around Rs100 for the journey. *Indian Airlines* have their office at Tashkent Marg, Civil Lines (☎624105).

Taxis are widely available around the station, but auto- and cycle rickshaws are the most common mode of transport; a trip to the Sangam from the Civil Lines crossing

The telephone **area code** for Allahabad is ☎0532.

THE KUMBH MELA

Hindus traditionally regard river confluences as auspicious places, and none more so than the **Sangam** at Allahabad, where the Yamuna and the Ganga meet the River of Enlightenment, the mythical Saraswati. According to legend, Vishnu was carrying a *kumbha* (pot) of *amrita* (nectar), when a scuffle broke out between the gods, and four drops were spilled. They fell to earth at the four *tirthas* of Prayag, Haridwar, Nasik, and Ujjain (*tirtha* means "ford of a river", a place where the devout can cross from this finite world into divine celestial realms; see Varanasi p.298). The event is commemorated every three years by the **Kumbh Mela**, held at each *tirtha* in turn; the Sangam is known as Tirtharaja, the "King of *Tirthas*", and its *mela*, once every twelve years, is the greatest and holiest of all.

The **Maha Kumbh Mela** – the "Great" Kumbh Mela – is the largest religious fair in India, attended by literally millions of rejoicing pilgrims. The vast floodplains and river banks adjacent to the confluence are overrun by tents, organized in almost military fashion by the government, the local authorities and the police. The *mela* is especially renowned for the presence of an extraordinary array of religious ascetics – *sadhus* and *mahants* – enticed from remote hideaways in forests, mountains and caves. Once astrologers have determined the propitious bathing time or *Kumbhayog*, the first to hit the water are legions of **Naga Sadhus** or **Naga Babas**, the ferocious-looking members of the "snake sect" who cover their naked bodies with ash, and wear their hair in long dreadlocks. The *sadhus*, who see themselves as guardians of the faith, approach the confluence at the appointed time with all the pomp and bravado of a charging army. The next Maha Kumbh Mela is due to take place in 2001.

costs around Rs12 (hang on to your vehicle for the return journey). **Car rental** through general travel agencies such as *Kant Travel* (☎605699) and *Krishna Travel* (☎605536), both at 936 Daraganj, costs in the region of Rs400 per day.

Information

The **Tourist Information Office**, at the *Tourist Bungalow*, 35 MG Marg, Civil Lines (Mon–Sat 10am–5pm; ☎601440), can provide useful information during the *melas* but otherwise has little to offer. Allahabad's **post office** (known as the GPO or HPO), is at Sarojini Naidu Marg, near All Saints Cathedral in the Civil Lines.

The Town

As the railway line crosses the centre, it splits Allahabad in two, with the chaotic and congested **old city** or **Chowk** south of the main station, and the well-defined grid of the **Civil Lines** to the north. Not far from the centre of the Civil Lines, around one kilometre north of the station, the yellow and red sandstone bulk of the Gothic **All Saints Cathedral** dominates the surrounding avenues. Designed by Sir William Emerson, architect of the Victoria Memorial in Calcutta, the cathedral retains much of its stained glass and an impressive altar of inlaid marble. Plaques provide interesting glimpses of Allahabad in the days of the Raj, while flying buttresses and snarling gargoyles on the exterior add to the effect of an English county town. Sunday services continue to attract large congregations; so too do masses at the flamboyant **St Joseph's Roman Catholic Cathedral**, a short distance west.

On the edge of the pleasant **Chander Shekhar Azad Park**, also in the Civil Lines, the grounds of the **Allahabad Museum** (daily except Mon 10am–5pm, closed 2nd Sat each month; Rs2) are dotted with pieces of ancient sculpture. Inside, you'll find early terracotta artefacts, eighth-century sculptures from the Buddhist site of Kaushambi, and a striking twelfth-century image from Khajuraho of Shiva and Parvati. A copious collection of modern Indian art includes work by Haldar, Sajit Khastgir and Rathin Mitra, as well as Jamini Roy, who was inspired by folk art. European paintings concentrate on spiritual themes, with sombre but naive canvasses by the Russian artist Nicholas Roerich, and further pieces by the Tibetologist Lama Angarika Govinda. A natural history section features stuffed animals and birds, and photographs and documents cover the Independence struggle.

North of the museum rise the nineteenth-century sandstone buildings of Allahabad University, and the Gothic **Muir College**, built in 1870. A 61-metre-high tower accompanies domes clad with blue and white glazed tiles (some of which are missing), and a quadrangle with tall and elegant arches. Just beyond the college, in beautiful grounds roughly 1km northeast of the museum, is **Anand Bhavan** (daily except Mon 9.30am–5pm; Rs2 allows entry to the first floor; planetarium Rs5). This ornate Victorian building, with Indo-Saracenic effects finished in grey and white trim and crowned by a *chattri*, was the boyhood home of the first prime minister of an independent India, Jawaharlal **Nehru**. It is now maintained as a museum, allowing queues of visitors to peer through plate glass into the opulent interior to see how the first family lived. Nehru was the father of one assassinated prime minister, Indira Gandhi, who was born here, and the grandfather of another, Rajiv Gandhi; Mahatma Gandhi (no relation of the family) stayed here when he visited the city. Also within the grounds, as at the Nehru Museum in Delhi (see p.90), is a **planetarium**, which puts on hourly shows.

Not far from Anand Bhavan, down a small road next to a children's park, the **Bharadwaj Ashram** is not an ashram as such but a collection of small temples. None is particularly old, but the ashram is named after the philosopher, scientist and ascetic Bharadwaj, said in the *Ramayana* to have had his hermitage here, and to have been visited by Rama. Legend relates that the ashram once had ten thousand students. Unusually, women are numbered among its *purohits* (priests), and act as caretakers.

A short way south of the main railway station, a lofty gateway leads to the attractive walled gardens of **Khusrau Bagh**, where the remains of Jahangir's tragic son Khusrau rest in a simple sandstone mausoleum, completed in 1622. Khusrau made an unsuccessful bid for power that ended in death at the hands of his brother Shah Jahan, and is buried far from the centre of Moghul power. His mother's two-storeyed mausoleum is a short way west, beyond a tomb reputed to be that of his sister. Once Jahangir's pleasure garden, today much of Khusrau Bagh has been made into an orchard, famous for its guavas, and a rose nursery, but parts are unkempt and overgrown.

Most of Allahabad's river frontage is along the Yamuna, to the south, where women perform *arati* or evening worship at **Saraswati Ghat** by floating *diya*, small oil-filled lamps, downstream. Immediately to the west, in **Minto Park**, a memorial marks the exact spot where the British Raj came into being, when India was taken away from the East India Company in 1858 and placed under the auspices of the crown.

East of Saraswati Ghat, close to the Sangam, loom the huge battlements of Akbar's **Fort** – best appreciated from boats on the river. Much of the fort remains in military occupation, and public access is restricted to the leafy corner around the **Patalpuri Temple**, approached through one of the three massive gates that puncture the fort's defences. The catacombs occupied by the temple have been converted into a sort of religious supermarket; its religious figures and deities are reminiscent of an extended Punch and Judy show. A sapling is said to be descended from the infamous **Akshaya Vata** or "Undying Tree", visited by the Chinese pilgrim Hiuen T'siang in the seventh century, from which desperate pilgrims threw themselves to their deaths in order to gain instant *moksha* (salvation). According to some reports the tree itself is bricked away beyond public access. Much of the superstructure of the fort is neglected; the **Zenana** with its columned hall does survive, but can only be viewed with prior permission. At the main gates to the fort stands a poorly restored polished stone **Ashoka Pillar**, inscribed with the emperor's edicts and dated to 242 BC.

THE SANGAM

Around seven kilometres from the centre of the Civil Lines, overlooked by the eastern ramparts of the fort, wide flood-plains and muddy banks protrude towards the sacred **Sangam**. At the point at which the brown Ganga meets the greenish Yamuna, *pandas* (priests) perch on small platforms to perform *puja* and assist the devout in their ritual ablutions in the shallow waters. Beaches and *ghats* are littered with the shorn hair of pilgrims who come to offer *pind* for their deceased parents.

Boats to the Sangam, used by pilgrims and tourists alike, can be rented at the *ghat* immediately east of the fort, for around Rs10 per head. Prices for a whole boat soar to Rs250 during peak seasons, but Rs60–80 is more normal. On the way to the Sangam, high-pressure aquatic salesmen loom up on the placid waters selling offerings such as five-*rupee* coconuts for pilgrims to discard at the confluence. Once abandoned, the offerings are fished up and sold on to other pilgrims – a blatant if efficient form of recycling.

Where the eastern battlements of the fort meet the river, a muddy *ghat* is busy with boatmen jostling for custom from the steady stream of pilgrims to the Sangam. Inland along the base of the fort, with the vast flood-plain of the Sangam to the right, a road leads past rows of stalls catering to pilgrims to the **Hanuman Temple**. What's unusual about this otherwise nondescript temple is that its large sunken image of the monkey god is reclining rather than standing erect; the story goes that during the annual floods the waters rise to touch his feet before once again receding.

Accommodation

Allahabad has **hotels** to suit most budgets and temperaments, with cheaper options generally in the old Chowk area to the south, and the mid-range and more expensive ones in the Civil Lines.

Allahabad Regency, 16 Tashkent Marg, Civil Lines (☎601519). Excellent value; clean, comfortable and tastefully furnished rooms, plus a sauna, jacuzzi, swimming pool and well-kitted gym. ⑥–⑦.

Milan, 46 Leader Rd (☎56021). Close to the station and south of the railway line in the busy bazaar area. Assorted reasonable rooms, with hot and cold running water and telephones. ③–⑤.

N C Continental, Katju Rd (☎56431). Good, clean accommodation south of the railway lines and very handy for the station. A bit more spacious than the *N Cee*. ②–④.

N Cee, Leader Rd. Sister to *Hotel N C Continental*, south of the railway line in the busy bazaar area. The rooms are small, but it's a pleasant and friendly place. ②.

Old Sangam, Johnstonganj Crossing. Basic, no-frills, budget accommodation in the old city. ①.

Presidency, 19D SN Marg, Civil Lines (☎623308). Plush, comfortable guest house in quiet residential area, run by an ex-MP, with swimming pool and foreign exchange. Book in advance. ⑤.

Raj Deluxe, 6 Johnstonganj (☎54684). Very cheap and basic budget accommodation. ①–③.

Royal, Civil Lines (☎604121). In the centre of the Civil Lines area, close to all amenities and equipped with western-style toilets, but otherwise nondescript. ②–④.

Tourist Bungalow, 35 MG Marg, Civil Lines (☎601440). The comfortable, cylindrical new block, built around a central well, overlooks the bus stand; choose your room carefully to avoid round-the-clock noise. The older block, now showing its age, is less noisy. Basic but friendly restaurant. ②–④.

Vilas, 22C Sardar Patel Marg, Civil Lines (☎604589). Moderately priced and central, but otherwise quite ordinary. ③–④.

Yatrik, 33 Sardar Patel Marg, Civil Lines (☎601713). Popular, and one can see why – well run and with a beautiful garden graced with elegant palms. ⑤–⑥.

Eating

Most of the better cafes and restaurants are in the Civil Lines area, within walking distance from each other close to the main crossing.

El Chico, MG Marg, Civil Lines. Smart high-street restaurant, close to *Kwalitys*. One of the city's best, with good Indian, Chinese and western cuisine. The adjacent pastry shop prepares sandwiches.

Hot Stuff, 15 Elgin Rd, Civil Lines. Popular hang-out for Allahabad's young and trendy, as well as the not-so-young. Burgers, shakes, Chinese food and ice creams.

Jade Garden, MG Marg, Civil Lines. Small thatched garden restaurant, strong on Chinese food.

Kwalitys, The Mall, MG Marg. In a corner of a small shopping centre, part of a once-formidable chain, predictable but good multi-cuisine restaurant now succumbing to the competition.

Shamiyana, Civil Lines. Cafe serving both north and south Indian food in the centre of town.

Tandoor, MG Marg. Tucked into a shopping precinct opposite *Kwalitys* and *El Chico*. Comfortable and upmarket, it preserves a reputation as one of the best places in the city for Indian food.

Around Allahabad

Allahabad makes a good base from which to venture into the remoter parts of Bundelkhand to the south. The pilgrimage town of **Chitrakut** (see p.297) is 132km south, and easily accessible by both train and bus; **Kalinjar** (see p.295) is 150km away.

Closer at hand, just 63km south on the banks of the Yamuna, are the extensive ruins of **Kausambi**, a major Buddhist centre where the Buddha himself came to preach. The city flourished between the eighth century BC and the sixth century AD; archeological evidence suggests even earlier habitation. According to legend, it was founded by descendants of the Pandavas, after floods destroyed their city of Hastinapur. Mud ramparts, originally faced with brick, tower over the fields, running along an irregular six-kilometre perimeter, and sections remain of a defensive moat. Within the complex, excavations have revealed a paved road, brick houses, wells, tanks and drains, a monastery with cloisters and a large *stupa*, and the remains of a palace in the southeast corner. The only standing feature is a damaged sandstone column ascribed to **Ashoka** – a second column, moved by the Moghuls, now graces the gates of the fort at Allahabad.

If you have your own vehicle, Kausambi is a straightforward day trip from Allahabad. Bus connections are a bit more tricky; head first to Serai Akil, from where several forms of local transport run the remaining 15km. The Buddhist pilgrimage circuit is developing rapidly, so it's worth consulting local tourist authorities to see if any direct services have been introduced since this book went to press.

SOUTHERN UP: BUNDELKHAND

BUNDELKHAND – the area defined by the craggy Vindhya Mountains, which stretch across southern UP – was carved by the ninth-century Chandella Rajputs into a mighty kingdom that included **Khajuraho** in Madhya Pradesh (see p.360). Today, it abounds in relics of the past – the colossal astrologically aligned fortress at **Kalinjar**, the Chandella capital of **Mahoba**, the Vaishnavite pilgrimage centre of **Chitrakut**, and the fortified town of **Jhansi**, scene of epic nineteenth-century resistance to the British. However, the sheer difficulty of the terrain, and the all but unbearable heat in the summer, make this the most difficult region of the state to explore.

In fact, the labyrinthine hills and valleys along the border with Madhya Pradesh are also the most difficult region to govern, and even today are home to infamous bands of outlaw **dacoits**. Many of these brigands have become folk-heroes among local villagers, who shelter them from the almost equally brutal police force. The most celebrated in recent years was **Phoolan Devi**, a woman dacoit who massacred the men of an entire village in 1981 in revenge for being raped, eventually surrendered to the police, and was released in 1994.

Jhansi

Unless you harbour a passion for seventeenth-century forts, you'll find the rail- and road-junction town of **JHANSI**, located in an anomalous promontory of UP that thrusts south into Madhya Pradesh, unremittingly dull. Most visitors only stop long enough to catch a connecting bus to **Khajuraho**, five-and-a-half hours further southeast in Madhya Pradesh.

Until 1742, Jhansi was a sleepy satellite village of the Bundela capital at nearby Orchha, 18km southeast. When the local Raja died without a male heir in 1853, the British enacted the controversial Principle of Lapse to wrest control of the town from his widow. Four years later, resentment at this colonial opportunism bubbled over into a full-blown **rebellion**, sparked off by the Mutiny at Kanpur (see p.276). Once the uprising had been put down by the British, they handed Jhansi over to Maharaja Scindia in exchange for Gwalior, in 1861, then reclaimed it 25 years later.

Arrival and information

Trains on both of the *Central Railway* branches that converge on Jhansi pull in at the station on the west side of town, near the Civil Lines area. Of the two state **tourist information** kiosks on platform one, MP Tourism's (✆442622) is more useful, as it sells tickets for the express coaches to **Khajuraho** (6am, 7am & 11am; Rs150). The **Regional Tourist Office**, *Hotel Veerangana* (✆44126), provides literature and information on Bundelkhand and the route to Khajuraho (Mon–Sat 10am–5pm, closed 2nd Sat).

If you miss the express bus to **Khajuraho**, much slower state buses also leave from the station in the morning, and, at 1pm, from the **Kanpur Road** bus stand, 4km away

> The telephone **area code** for Jhansi is ☎0517.

northeast of the main Sadar Bazaar. This is also the place to pick up buses for Datia and Gwalior; **tempos** for **Orchha** (faster than local buses, at 45min, and more frequent) wait alongside. **Car rental** is available through the larger hotels, as well as *Baghel Travels*, Nehru Market (☎441255), and *Ruby Travels*, near Elite Crossing (☎441136).

If you need to **change money**, the *State Bank of India* (Mon–Fri 10am–2pm, Sat 10am–noon; ☎440534) stands on Jhokan Bagh Road beside the busy intersection in the dead centre of town, exactly halfway between the railway station and the bus stand.

The Town

In common with many former British cities, Jhansi is divided into two distinct areas: the wide tree-lined avenues, leafy gardens and bungalows of the **Cantonment** and **Civil Lines** to the west, and the clutter of brick and concrete cubes, narrow lanes, minarets and *shikharas* of the **old town** to the east.

Dominating it all from a bare brown craggy hill, **Jhansi fort** (daily except Mon 10am–5pm; Rs0.50) is the obvious place to head if you've time to kill. Built in 1613 by one of the Orchha Rajas, Bir Singh Joo Deo, it's worth visiting primarily for the **views** from the lofty ramparts – down to the densely packed old town on one side, and out across a dusty *maidan* and the Cantonment to the other. The legendary Rani of Jhansi was supposed to have leapt over the west wall on horseback when she escaped from the British – if so, she must have had a pretty unusual horse. Inside the fort are a couple of unremarkable temples, plus an old cistern and the ruins of a palace. The only other attraction is the bizarre model of the 1857 siege of Jhansi fort recently installed beside the main road on the south slope of the hill. An accompanying interpretative panel recounts the story of the battle in very colourful English.

The new **archeological museum** (daily except Mon 10am–5pm) stands to the left of the road as you head back into town, with an unremarkable collection of Hindu **sculpture** saved from the area's many ruined medieval temples. Once the palace of the Rani of Jhansi, the **Rani Lakshmi Mahal** (daily except Mon 10am–5pm) is a small stately home in "Bundela style" (lots of ornate balconies and domed roofs), two minutes' walk from the roundabout directly below the fort. This was the scene of a brutal **massacre** in 1858, when British troops bayoneted all its occupants. These days, the building is a memorial-cum-museum-cum-archeological-warehouse, with unlabelled fragments of antique stone sculpture littered around its attractive interior courtyard. A couple of rooms upstairs, once the Rani's private quarters, harbour traces of seventeeth-century wall and ceiling paintings – now faded and flaking off in the heat.

The grounds of a pleasant seminary in the Cantonment area hold one of the most important Catholic pilgrimage sites in India, **St Jude's Shrine**. A bone belonging to Jude the Apostle, the patron saint of hopeless causes, is said to be buried in the foundations of the grey and white cathedral, with a simple but elegant dome. On his feast day, 28 October, thousands come to plead their own special causes.

Accommodation

With Orchha just down the road, it's hard to see why you might **stay** in Jhansi unless you arrive too late to move on. Most of its hotels are too far from the train and bus stations to be easily reached on foot. The cheaper ones operate 24-hour check-out times, as opposed to noon in the mid-price and more expensive hotels.

Jhansi, Shastri Marg (☎1360). Former haunt of British *burra-sahibs*. Comfortable rooms, some a/c, plus *Star TV*, verandahs, and a big garden. The over-priced but diverting bar-restaurant dishes up tasteless colonial food – roast chicken, steamed vegetables, and puddings. ⑤.

THE RANI OF JHANSI

Rani Lakshmi Bhai, better known as the **Rani**, or Queen, **of Jhansi**, was one of the great nationalist heroines of pre-Independence India. Born the daughter of a Benares *brahmin*, she was married off to Raja Gangadhar of Jhansi, but never bore him children – a fact exploited by the British to force her and her adopted baby son into retirement in 1853. The Rani retaliated in 1857, the year of the "Mutiny", by leading her personal bodyguard of five hundred Afghan-Pathan warriors to seize Jhansi fort. The British dispatched troops to see off the insurgents, but took seventeen days to blow a breach in the walls of the citadel. Three days of fierce hand-to-hand fighting ensued, in which five thousand soldiers were killed. With her son strapped tightly to her back, the Rani somehow managed to slip through the British net and rejoin the main rebel army at Gwalior, where she rode to her death, "dressed as a man ... using her sword with both hands and holding the reins of her horse in her mouth".

Statues of Rani Jhansi in this heroic pose stand all over northern India. For many in the Independence movement, she was India's Joan of Arc; a martyr and icon whose example set in motion the freedom struggle that eventually rid the subcontinent of its colonial rulers.

Prakash Guest House, Shri Sardari Lal Market (☎443133). Nothing special, but clean enough, and close to the fort and centre of town. *Star TV* and some a/c. ③–④.

Pujan, Gwalior Rd (☎1737). Close to *Prakash*. Cheap, airy double rooms are a very good deal. Single occupancy too. ②–③.

Raj Palace, near Head Post Office, Shastri Marg (☎442554). Clean, comfortable and handy for the bus stand. Rooms all have attached bathrooms and hot water. Some a/c. 24hr check-out. ③–⑤.

Sita, Shivpuri Rd (☎442956). New, immaculate western-style hotel close to the station, with well-appointed rooms and a good restaurant. Credit cards accepted. Some a/c. ④–⑥.

UPTDC Veeranganga, near Exhibition Ground, Shivpuri Rd (☎2402). Shabby hotel, five minutes by scooter from the station. Plain rooms, some a/c, plus rock-bottom dorms and a nice lawn. ①–④.

Eating

With the exception of the cheaper lodges, nearly all of Jhansi's hotels have their own restaurants. For a cheap alternative, try the *Railway Refreshment Rooms* in the station, which serve freshly cooked ten-*rupee thalis* and budget breakfasts.

Holiday, Shastri Marg. Posh but not all that expensive a/c restaurant east of the *Jhansi Hotel*. Low light, table cloths, attentive service and classy Indian and western food.

Nav Bharat, Shastri Marg. Western-style fast food and Indian snacks, behind the post office.

Sharma Sweets, Shastri Marg. Hygienic sweet shop selling delicious take-out *rasgulla, gulabjamun, jalebi* and *barfi*.

Sita, Shivpuri Rd. Spotlessly clean, upmarket hotel-restaurant with a wide selection of Indian (and some continental) dishes. The place for a splurge.

Veeranganga, Shivpuri Road. Standard inexpensive veg/non-veg menu served inside in hotel-restaurant or al fresco on the lawn (bring mosquito repellent).

Kalinjar

Deep in the heart of Bundelkhand, in a remote region 150km west of Allahabad and 53km south of Banda, the abandoned star-shaped fortress of **KALINJAR** looks down on the Gangetic Valley from the final escarpments of the craggy Vindhya Hills. Little remains of its huge fortifications, save sections of battlements around the rim of the high forested plateau, and much of the fort has been reclaimed by dry shrubby forest, populated by monkeys. Once-grand avenues are now rocky footpaths that wind through the few remaining dilapidated buildings.

Possibly one of the oldest forts in India, referred to by Ptolemy as Kanagora, Kalinjar may have started life as a hill shrine before it was converted into a fortress; now devoid of military significance, it is once again becoming a place of worship. Kalinjar is known to have been a stronghold of the Chandellas (ninth to twelfth centuries AD), the creators of Khajuraho, who left their mark in stone sculptures around the temple of Nilkantha, below the western battlements. This strategic location attracted repeated Muslim onslaughts; Mahmud of Ghazni laid unsuccessful siege in 1023, Qutb-ud-din-Aibak destroyed several temples in his conquest of 1202, and Humayun spent fifteen years trying to capture the fort. After Sher Shah Suri, who temporarily wrested power from the Moghuls, died when an exploding shell ignited gunpowder as he attacked Kalinjar in 1545, his son went on to take the fortress. Even the British occupied it for a while, before its strategic importance was finally exhausted, and it was left to decay.

The fortress

Each of the seven gates, sheltered by barbicans, that pierces the walls of Kalinjar symbolizes one of the seven planets. Steep steps lead straight up from **Kalinjar village**, in the valley at the northern base of the fort, to the main gate, known as the **Alam Darwaza**. To the southeast, an unkempt boulder-strewn road gradually climbs across the hillside to approach the southernmost **Panna Gate**, where rock carvings depict seven deer. Beyond Lal Darwaza to the east, the **Bara Darwaza** or "Large Gate" is flanked by two iron cannons. Beneath it, in the artificial cave of **Sita Sej**, a stone couch dated to the fourth century holds some of Kalinjar's earliest inscriptions.

Colossal rambling battlements provide sweeping views of the Gangetic plain to the north and the Vindhya hills to the south, hiding the crumbling remains of a fortress that is almost 1.5km long. Tracing the faint marks of the old avenues, you arrive at its heart, littered with roofless and devastated buildings. **Kot Tirth**, a ceremonial tank with stone steps, is the largest of several bodies of water on the plateau, and still in frequent use by villagers and pilgrims. Above it, beyond a small Hanuman shrine, stands the well-preserved palace-like **Raja Mansingh Mahal**. Further west, beside the bougainvillaea-fringed road that passes the PWD bungalow, the small British graveyard holds a monument to Andrew Wauchope, the first Commissioner of Bundelkhand. Paths through desultory woodland lead to a gate overlooking the western flank, where steep steps flanked by rock carvings wind down from the massive stone battlements to the temple of **Nilkantha** – the "Blue Throated One", an epithet of Shiva. Although the temple has lost its roof, its *mandapa* (forechamber) sports some beautifully carved stone pillars. Its main shrine is housed within a cave – a *lingam*, worn smooth over centuries. Trickles from the rocky hill drain out near the neck of the image, keeping it perpetually wet.

To the left of the main shrine, within the temple compound, a five-metre-high low-relief rock carving, of primeval intensity, portrays **Bhairava**, the wrathful emanation of Shiva as Destroyer, sporting four arms and brandishing weapons. A gap in the retaining wall provides access to the steps back down to the village. Above the pool of **Bhairan Kund**, adjoining the temple, a walkway leads along the face of the large stone buttresses that fall in tiers from the edge of a plateau to a point where rainwater seeps into a cave. Steps hewn into the rock allow bathers into the flooded interior, supported by carved pillars dated to the Chandella period. Although the cave is no longer than 10 metres, swimming in the deep water beneath its low roof is an eerie experience.

Practicalities

Kalinjar has no tourist facilities to speak of – accommodation or food is only available in absolutely basic fly-infested tea shops – and precious few tourists. Most of those who do come are either on day trips from Chitrakut or Allahabad, or stay in **Banda**, which is on major train and bus routes and is connected to Kalinjar by local buses.

However, the ruined **PWD bungalow**, looking across from the top of the fortress towards the interior of the Vindhyas, is gradually being rebuilt – check with UP tourist authorities before you set off to see if it's ready for guests.

Chitrakut

The large sprawling town of **CHITRAKUT** stands on the banks of the Mandakini, 128km southwest of Allahabad and 116km east of Mahoba. Together with its twin town of **Sitapur**, 8km east, Chitrakut is a major Vaishnavite pilgrimage centre. In the *Ramayana*, Rama, his wife Sita, and his brother Lakshmana, sought refuge in a forest that covered this entire area, after being banished from Ayodhya.

Most of Chitrakut's religious and leisure activity revolves around the small, charming, and very central **Ramghat**, where boats with electric-blue mattresses and pillows create a pretty picture against a backdrop of ashrams and *ghats* to either side of the narrow, slow-moving river. Half-hour boat trips cost around Rs10. Among the pilgrim shops and cafes nearby are several **temples**, such as the new **Tulsibedi**, dedicated to the poet saint (see p.308) who is said to have spent time here. This was built on the site of an earlier shrine, located in an extended cave up an alley off the *ghat*. Steps above the *ghat* lead to the **Math Gajendranath** Shiva temple, and its picturesque river views. Taking a rickshaw beside the Mandakini to **Sitapur** enables you to see several more riverside temples, as well as waterfront *ghats* much like Ramghat.

Pilgrims to Chitrakut traditionally perform the Parikrama, or ritual circumambulation of the wooded hill of **Kamedgiri**, 3km southwest of town. On its course around the base of the hill, the five-kilometre path passes numerous temples and shrines, including the big **Kantanath Swami** temple, which holds a modern image of Rama and Sita and a more venerated monolithic stone image, black and embellished with large eyes. A long flight of stairs at the **Hanumandhara** hill shrine, 3km east, leads up to a large image of the monkey god Hanuman, a companion of the trio from the *Ramayana*.

Practicalities

Long-distance transport connections are best made via **Sitapur**. From the main **Sitapur Bus Stand**, several daily buses run to Allahabad, passing through Serai Akil, 15km from the Buddhist ruins of Kausambi, and also to historic Mahoba, a possible stop-off en route to Khajuraho. The **railway station** too has services for Allahabad and Mahoba, as well as Varanasi (374km northeast, a nine-hour journey). From the **Satna Bus Stand** in Chitrakut, buses head south into Madhya Pradesh; connecting buses from Satna itself can also carry you to Khajuraho.

Unless you read Hindi, you may not find the **information** provided by the **UP Tourist Office**, at Karbi Rd, Sitapur (Mon–Sat 10am–5pm, closed 2nd Sat; ☎0519768/218), all that helpful. Despite the lack of competition, **rooms** and dorms at the UPTDC *Tourist Bungalow* alongside (☎0519768/219; ②–③) are not really to be recommended; it's drab and poorly maintained, and food is only provided to order. MP Tourism's old-fashioned *Tourist Bungalow*, at the Satna bus stand in Chitrakut (☎0519768/326; ②–③), is more comfortable, and serves basic Indian food.

Several simple **hotels**, *dharamshalas* and guest houses can be found around Ramghat; though the accommodation is basic at the *Vishram Grah* (①) on the *ghat* itself, it's full of atmosphere, with a lovely terrace overlooking the river, and the adjacent *bhojanalaya* – vegetarian cafes – serve simple but wholesome food.

South of Chitrakut

Several further shrines linked with the *Ramayana* are tucked away in the region **south of Chitrakut**. The major **Janki Kund** temple ("pool of Janki", Janki being another name for Sita) is just 2km south of Chitrakut on the Satna road, on the border with Madhya Pradesh. This rocky pool was where Rama's wife bathed in the Mandakini; a path above it leads through a complex of ashrams and shrines to a small footbridge that crosses the picturesque river to the wooded far bank.

Further down the main road, 1km south, a path through a similar complex of ashrams leads to the large flat rock of **Sphatekshila**, protruding onto the river, where Sita used to sit. It supposedly bears the impressions of the feet of Rama. This idyllic spot, with its beautifully kept *ghat* surrounded by large trees, and with more woods on the other side of the river, powerfully evokes the legend of the *vanvasi* – the forest dwellers that the exiled Rama, Lakshmana and Sita became.

EASTERN UP

Flowing beyond Allahabad across the plains of **EASTERN UP**, the Ganges turns sharply north at **Chunar** and traces a great arc through ancient **Varanasi**. Even before the Hindus declared this to be the most sacred spot on Earth, it stood at the centre of the Buddhist universe, linked by trading routes from Rajgir in Bihar to Mathura near Delhi. It was on the outskirts of Varanasi, at the deer park at **Sarnath**, that the Buddha delivered his first sermon. North of Varanasi, the much-travelled road to **Nepal** passes through the large administrative town of **Gorakhpur**, not far from **Kushinagar**, where the Buddha achieved final enlightenment.

Varanasi

> *Older than history, older than tradition, older even than legend, and looks twice as old as all of them put together.*
>
> Mark Twain

The great Hindu city of **VARANASI**, also known as **Banaras** or **Benares**, glows golden in the early morning sun. Stretched along the crescent of the holy river Ganga – born in heaven and descended to earth – Varanasi's waterfront is dominated by long flights of stone steps known as *ghats*, literally "landings", where thousands of pilgrims and residents come for their daily ritual ablutions. The *ghats* remain the single major attraction of Varanasi; it does not possess temples or monuments of any antiquity, thanks largely to the destruction wrought by the emperor Aurangzeb.

Known to the devout as **Kashi**, the Luminous – the City of Light, founded by Shiva – Varanasi is the one of the oldest living cities in the world. It has maintained its religious life since the sixth century BC in one continuous tradition, in part by remaining outside the mainstream of political activity and historical development of the subcontinent, and stands at the centre of the Hindu universe, the focus of a religious geography that reaches from the Himalayan cave of Amarnath in Kashmir, to Kanyakumari, the southern tip of India, Puri to the east, and Dwarka to the west. Located next to a ford on an ancient trade route, Varanasi is among the holiest of all *tirthas* – "crossing places", that allow the devotee access to the divine and enable gods and goddesses to come down to earth. It has attracted pilgrims, seekers, *sanyasins*, and students of the *Vedas* throughout its history, including sages such as the Buddha, Mahavira, the founder of the Jain faith, and the great Hindu reformer Shankara.

Life and death go hand in hand in Varanasi; in among the bathing *ghats*, smoke rising from the cremation grounds signals the final release of tormented souls from the earthly round of *samsara*, the unceasing cycles of death and rebirth. Anyone who dies in Varanasi, on the banks of the river of life, attains instant *moksha* or enlightenment. Widows and the elderly come here to seek refuge or to live out their final days, finding shelter in the temples assisted by alms gifted by the faithful.

NAMES OF THE CITY

Numerous names have been given to **Varanasi**, though its recently revived official appellation is mentioned in the *Mahabharata* and in the *Jataka* tales of Buddhism. It probably derives from the two rivers that flank the city, the Varana to the north and the Asi to the south. Many still use the anglicized forms of **Banaras** or **Benares**, while pilgrims refer to **Kashi**, first used three thousand years ago to describe the kingdom and the city outside which the Buddha preached his first sermon; the "City of Light" is also called Kashika, "the shining one", referring to the light of Shiva. Another epithet, **Avimukta**, meaning "Never Forsaken", refers to the city that Shiva never deserted, or that one should never leave. Further alternatives include **Anandavana**, the "forest of bliss", and **Rudravasa**, the place where Shiva (Rudra) resides.

Varanasi's associations with Shiva stretch back to the dawn of time: legends relate how, after his marriage to Parvati, Shiva left his inhospitable Himalayan abode and came to reside in Kashi with all the gods in attendance. Temporarily banished during the rule of the great king Divodasa, Shiva sent Brahma and Vishnu as his emissaries, but eventually returned to his rightful abode guarded by his faithful attendants Kalabhairav and Dandapani. Over 350 gods and goddesses, including a protective ring of Ganeshas form a *mandala* or sacred pattern with Shiva Vishwanatha at its centre.

Each name carries an additional meaning in terms of the sacred symbolism of the city, with each defining a progressively decreasing arc starting and ending on the west bank of the Ganges. While the boundary of **Kashi** is delimited by the circular Panchakroshi Road, **Varanasi** is the main city, extending from Asi Ghat and circling around to the confluence of the Ganges and the Varana. Yet a smaller area, defined as **Avimukta**, starts at Kedara Ghat in the south and ends at Trilochana Ghat. Most important of all is **Antargriha**, the "Inner Sanctum" around the Vishwanatha Temple, which encompasses Dashashwamedha Ghat, Surya Kund, the *lingam* of Bharabhuta, and Manikarnika Ghat. Another, later, interpretation suggests three sectors or *khandas* in the form of Shiva's trident, each centered around a temple – Omkara to the north, Vishwanatha in the centre and Kedara to the south.

Western visitors since the middle ages have marvelled at the strangeness of what is perhaps the most alien of Indian cities – at the tight mesh of alleys barely wide enough to accommodate a rickshaw, at the accoutrements of religion, the host of deities great and small, and at the proximity of death. At sunrise, flotillas of camera-clicking tourists peruse the *ghats* in amazement, while the pilgrims and people of Kashi continue their morning rituals without so much as a second glance.

Arrival, information and city transport

An airport bus (Rs20) connects with flights landing at **Babatpur Airport**, 22km northwest of the city and goes to the *Indian Airlines* office, via the Government of India tourist office, both in the Cantonment area. The main Delhi–Calcutta **railway** line bypasses Varanasi, but local buses and taxis regularly make the seventeen-kilometre trip from the station at Moghul Sarai. Some major trains do serve the **Varanasi Cantonment** station, which is convenient for the more luxurious hotels and the garden hotels to the north, while the old city and the *ghats* are two kilometres south – a Rs10 cycle rickshaw ride.

Most **buses** terminate in the vicinity of the station: the **Cantonment Bus Stand** tends to be used by services from Nepal and Gaya, while private operators and buses from Mirzapur and Chunar use the **Pilikothi Bus Stand**.

The telephone **area code** for Varanasi is ☎0542.

SARNATH

Damekh Stupa
Bo Tree
Sarnath Railway Station
Jain Temple
Monasteries
GPO
Archaeological Museum
Tourist Lodge
Tibetan Temple
Chaukhandi Stupa

Raj Ghat

Varana River

Bansghat Rd

City Railway Station

Grand Trunk Rd

Sanskrit University

Azamgarh Rd

Bus Stand

Mahbub Alam Rd

Lahurabazar Rd

GPO

State Bank of India A

India Airlines

CANTONMENT
Varanasi Cantt

Babatpur Airport

HOTELS:
- A Surya
- B Ideal Tops
- C Clarks
- D Ashok
- E de Paris
- F Tourist Dak Bungalow
- G Taj Ganges
- H Vaibhav
- I Temples Town
- J Shalimar
- K India
- L Relax
- M Tourist Bungalow
- N Pradeep
- O Gautam
- P G M Guest House
- Q Garden View
- R Hindusthan
- S Pallavi

RESTAURANTS:
- 1 Kemps
- 2 Mandarin
- 3 El Parador
- 4 Winfa
- 5 Sindhi

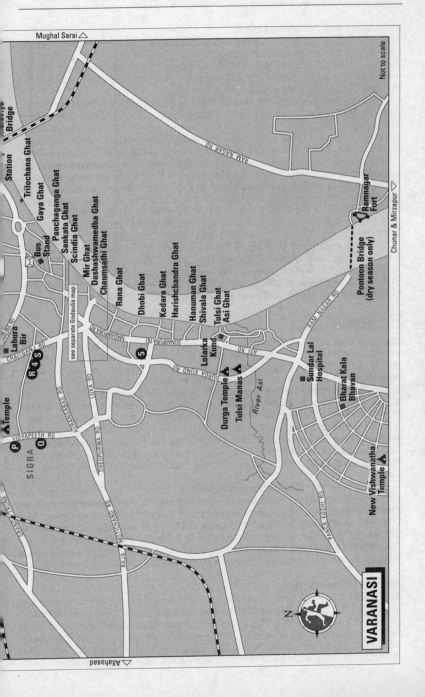

Mughal Sarai △

Not to scale

Station Bridge

Trilochana Ghat

Gaya Ghat

Panchaganga Ghat

Sankata Ghat

Scindia Ghat

Mir Ghat

Dashashwamedha Ghat

Chaumsathi Ghat

Rana Ghat

Dhobi Ghat

Kedara Ghat

Harishchandra Ghat

Hanuman Ghat

Shivala Ghat

Tulsi Ghat

Asi Ghat

Bus Stand

Lahura Bir

CHAITGANJ RD

KASHI RD

R 4 S

Temple

P

SIGRA

VIDYAPEETH RD

O

LUXA RD

AURANGABAD RD

SHEOPURWA RD

MADANPURA RD

SONARPURA RD

DURGA KUND RD

see separate Godaulia map

5

Lolarka Kund

Durga Temple

Tulsi Manas

ASI RD

River Asi

Sundar Lal Hospital

Bharat Kala Bhavan

New Vishwanatha Temple

RAM NAGAR RD

Pontoon Bridge (dry season only)

Ramnagar Fort

Chunar & Mirzapur ▽

RAM NAGAR RD

RAJA NOICHAND RD

GRAND TRUNK RD

Allahabad ▽

N

VARANASI

Information and communications

The **Government of India tourist office** languishes in the leafy suburbs of the Cantonment, a long way from the main attractions of the old city and the *ghats*, at 15B The Mall (Mon–Sat 9.30am–5pm; ☎43744). Its primary function is to dish out information on the whole of India, but the staff can assist with booking accommodation; they also maintain a booth at the airport during flight times.

The main **UP Government tourist office** is at their *Tourist Bungalow*, Parade Kothi (☎43413), though they also have an information counter (☎43486) at the railway station nearby. Both book accommodation, especially in the state-run tourist bungalows, and provide a useful free map. The **Bihar Government tourist office** on Englishia Line (☎43821) is useful if you're heading east towards the Buddhist centres.

Both the Indian Government and the UP tourist offices have information on half-day **conducted tours**, taking in either the *ghats* or Sarnath and Ramnagar for around Rs45. These can be unreliable and disorganized; to experience the *ghats* at sunrise, or the peace of Sarnath, you're better off making your own arrangements. **Car rental** is available from ITDC, in the *Hotel Varanasi Ashok*, the Mall (☎46032), which serves as a fully fledged tour agency, and from such agencies as *Khan Travels*, S20/52, 3A Nepali Kothi (☎46623), and *Travel Corporation (India)*, *Hotel Clarks*, the Mall (☎46209).

Most foreign-currency branches of the major **banks** are located in the Cantonment area: the *State Bank of India* is behind *Hotel Ideal Tops*, Varuna Bridge, The Mall (☎43445), and *Union Bank* is at the Sri Das Foundation, in front of the *Taj Ganges* (☎46733). The main **post offices** are in Cantonment and Bisweswarganj, with other offices throughout the city, and a convenient sub post office in *Hotel Clarks*.

The Ghats

The great river banks at Varanasi, built high with pavilions and palaces, temples and terraces, are lined with an endless chain of stone steps – the **ghats** – progressing along the whole of the waterfront, altering in appearance with the dramatic seasonal fluctuations of the river level. Each of the hundred *ghats*, big and small, is marked by a *lingam*, and occupies its own special place in the religious geography of the city. Some have crumbled over the years, others continue to thrive, with early-morning bathers, *brahmin* priests offering *puja*, and people practising meditation and yoga. Hindus regard the Ganga as *amrita*, the elixir of life, which brings purity to the living and salvation to the dead; sceptical outsiders tend to focus on the all-pervasive and extreme lack of hygiene. Ashes of the dead, emissions from open drains and the left-overs from religious rites float by the devout as they go about their bathing and ceremonial cleansing.

For centuries, pilgrims have traced the perimeter of the city by a ritual circumambulation, paying homage to shrines on the way. Among the most popular routes is the **Panchatirthi Yatra**, which takes in the Pancha (five) Tirthi (crossings) of Asi, Dashashwamedha, Adi Keshava, Panchganga and finally Manikarnika. To gain merit or appease the gods, the devotee, accompanied by a *panda* (priest), recites a *sankalpa* (statement of intent) and performs a ritual at each stage of the journey. For the casual visitor, however, the easiest way to see the *ghats* is to follow a south–north sequence.

Asi Ghat to Kedara Ghat

At the clay-banked **Asi Ghat**, the southernmost in the sacred city, at the confluence of the Asi and the Ganges, pilgrims bathe prior to worshipping at a huge *lingam* under a *peepal* tree. Another *lingam* visited is that of **Asisangameshvara**, the "Lord of the Confluence of the Asi", in a small marble temple just off the *ghat*. Traditionally, pilgrims continued to **Lolarka Kund**, the "Trembling Sun", a rectangular tank fifteen metres below ground level, approached by steep steps. Now almost abandoned, except during the Lolarka Mela fair (Aug/Sept), when thousands come to propitiate the gods and pray for the birth of a son, Lolarka Kund is among Varanasi's earliest sites, one of only two remaining Sun sites linked with the origins of Hinduism. Equated with the twelve *adityas* or divisions of the sun, which predate the great deities of modern Hinduism, it was attracting bathers in the days of the Buddha.

Much of the adjacent **Tulsi Ghat** – originally Lolarka Ghat, but renamed in honour of the poet Tulsi Das, who lived nearby in the sixteenth century – has crumbled. Continuing north, above **Shivala Ghat**, **Hanuman Ghat** is the site of a new temple built by the *ghat*'s large south Indian community. Considered by many to be the birthplace of the fifteenth-century Vaishnavite saint Vallabha, who was instrumental in the resurgence of the worship of Krishna, the *ghat* also features a striking image of **Ruru**, the dog **Bhairava**, a ferocious and early form of Shiva.

Named for a legendary king said to have almost lost everything in a fit of self-abnegation, **Harishchandra Ghat,** one of Varanasi's two cremation or burning *ghats*, is easily recognizable from the smoke of its funeral pyres.

Further north, the busy **Kedara Ghat** is ignored by pilgrims on the Panchatirthi Yatra. Above its steps, a red-and-white-striped temple houses the **Kedareshvara lingam**, an outcrop of black rock shot through with a vein of white. Mythologically related to Kedarnath in the Himalayas (see p.256), Kedara and its *ghat* become a hive of activity during the sacred month of Sravana (July/Aug), the month of the rains.

Chauki Ghat to Chaumsathi Ghat

Northwards along the river, **Chauki Ghat** is distinguished by an enormous tree that shelters small stone shrines to the *nagas*, water-snake deities, while at the unmistakable **Dhobi** (Laundrymen's) **Ghat** clothes are still rhythmically pulverized in the pursuit of purity. Past smaller *ghats* such as **Manasarovara Ghat**, named after the holy lake in Tibet, and **Narada Ghat**, honouring the divine musician and sage, lies **Chaumsathi Ghat**, where impressive stone steps lead up to the small temple of the **Chaumsathi** (64) **Yoginis**. Images of Kali and Durga in its inner sanctum represent a stage in the emergence of the great goddess as a single representation of a number of female divinities. Overlooking the *ghats* here is Peshwa Amrit Rao's majestic sandstone *haveli* (mansion), built in 1807 and currently used by *Hotel Clarks* as an auditorium for concerts and religious ceremonies.

Dashashwamedha Ghat

Dashashwamedha Ghat, the second and busiest of the five *tirthas* on the Panchatirthi Yatra, lies immediately ahead past the plain, flat-roofed building that houses the shrine of **Shitala**. Extremely popular, even in the rainy season when devotees have to wade to the temple or take a boat, Shitala represents both benign and malevolent aspects – ease and succour as well as disease, particularly smallpox.

Dashashwamedha is Varanasi's most popular and accessible bathing *ghat*, with rows of *pandas* sitting on wooden platforms under bamboo umbrellas, masseurs plying their trade and boatmen jostling for custom. Its name, "ten horse sacrifices", derives from a complex series of sacrifices performed by Brahma to test King Divodasa: Shiva and Parvati were sure the king's resolve would fail, and he would be compelled to leave Kashi, thereby allowing them to return to their city. However, the sacrifices were so perfect that Brahma established the **Brahmeshvara lingam** here. Since that time, Dashashwamedha has become one of the most celebrated *tirthas* on earth, where pilgrims can reap the benefits of the huge sacrifice merely by bathing.

Man Mandir Ghat to Lalita Ghat

Man Mandir Ghat is known primarily for its magnificent eighteenth-century observatory, equipped with ornate window casings, and built for the Maharajah of Jaipur.

Pilgrims pay homage to the important *lingam* of Someshvara, the lord of the moon, alongside, before crossing **Tripurabhairavi Ghat** to **Mir Ghat** and the **New Vishwanatha Temple**, built by conservative *brahmins* who claimed that the main Vishwanatha *lingam* was rendered impure when Harijans (untouchables) entered the sanctum in 1956. Mir Ghat also has a shrine to **Vishalakshi**, the Wide-Eyed Goddess, on an important *pitha* – a site marking the place where various parts of the disintegrating body of Shakti fell as it was carried by the grief-stricken Shiva. Also here is the **Dharma Kupa**, the Well of Dharma, surrounded by subsidiary shrines and the *lingam* of **Dharmesha**, where it is said that Yama, the Lord of Death, obtained his jurisdiction over all the dead of the world – except here in Varanasi.

Immediately to the north is **Lalita Ghat**, renowned for its **Ganga Keshava** shrine to Vishnu and the Nepali Temple, a typical Kathmandu-style wooden temple which houses an image of **Pashupateshvara** – Shiva's manifestation at Pashupatinath, in the Kathmandu Valley – and sports a small selection of erotic carvings.

Manikarnika Ghat

North of Lalita lies Varanasi's pre-eminent cremation ground, **Manikarnika Ghat**. Such grounds are usually held to be inauspicious, and located on the fringes of cities, but the entire city of Shiva is regarded as **Mahashmashana**, the Great Cremation Ground for the corpse of the entire universe. The *ghat* is perpetually crowded with funeral parties, as well as the **Doms**, its Untouchable guardians, busy and pre-occupied with facilitating final release for those lucky enough to pass away here. Seeing bodies being cremated so publicly has always exerted a great fascination for visitors to the city, but photography is strictly taboo; even having a camera visible may be construed as intent, and provoke hostility.

Lying at the centre of the five *tirthas*, **Manikarnika Ghat** symbolizes both creation and destruction, epitomized by the juxtaposition of the sacred well of **Manikarnika Kund**, said to have been dug by Vishnu at the time of creation, and the hot, sandy ash-infused soil of cremation grounds where time comes to an end. In Hindu mythology, Manikarnika Kund predates the arrival of the Ganga and has its source deep in the Himalayas. Vishnu carved the *kund* with his discus, and filled it with perspiration from his exertions in creating the world, at the behest of Shiva. When Shiva quivered with delight, his earring fell into this pool, which as Manikarnika – "Jewelled Earring" – became the first *tirtha* in the world. Every year, after the floodwaters of the river have receded to leave the pool caked in alluvial deposits, the *kund* is re-dug. Its surroundings are cleaned and painted with brightly coloured folk art, which depicts the presiding goddess, **Manikarni Devi**, inviting pilgrims to bathe and worship at its small Vishnu shrine, and at the *paduka* (footprint) of Vishnu set in marble on the embankment of the *ghat*. The most important of the *lingams* is the remains of **Tarakeshvara**, Shiva as Lord of the Taraka Mantra, a "prayer of the crossing" recited at death.

Strictly speaking, Manikarnika is the name given to the *kund* and to the *ghat*, while the constantly busy cremation ground is Jalasi Ghat, dominated by a dark smoke-stained temple built by Queen Ahalya Bai Holkar of Indore in the eighteenth century.

Scindia Ghat

Bordering Manikarnika to the north is the picturesque **Scindia Ghat**, with its tilted Shiva temple lying partially submerged in the river, having fallen in as a result of the sheer weight of the *ghat*'s construction around 150 years ago. Above the *ghat*, several of Kashi's most influential shrines are hidden within the tight maze of alleyways of the area known as **Siddha Kshetra** (the Field of Fulfilment). Vireshvara, the Lord of all Heroes, is especially propitiated in prayer for a son; the Lord of Fire, Agni, was supposed to have been born here.

BOAT TRIPS ON THE GANGES

All along the *ghats,* and especially at the main ones such as Dashashwamedha, the prices of **boat** (*bajra*) **rental** are highly inflated, with local boatmen under pressure to fleece tourists and pilgrims. There's a police counter on the square above Dashashwamedha, but the lack of government tourist assistance means that renting a boat to catch the dawn can be a bit of a free-for-all, and haggling is essential. A few boatmen operate on a fixed rate, determined in conjunction with UP Tourism, of about Rs25 per half-hour.

Panchganga Ghat to Adi Keshava Ghat

Beyond Lakshmanbala Ghat, with its commanding views of the river, lies one of the most dramatic and controversial *ghats,* **Panchganga Ghat,** dominated by Varanasi's largest riverside building, the great **Mosque of Alamgir,** known locally as Beni Madhav-ka-Darera. With its minarets now much shortened, the mosque stands on the ruins of what must have been one of the city's greatest temples, **Bindu Madhava,** a huge Vishnu temple that extended from Panchganga to Rama Ghat before it was destroyed by Aurangzeb and replaced by an impressive mosque. Panchganga also bears testimony to more favourable Hindu–Muslim relations, being the site of the initiation of the medieval saint of the Sufi-Sant tradition, Kabir, the son of a humble Muslim weaver who is venerated by Hindus and Muslims alike. Along the riverfront lies a curious array of three-sided cells, submerged during the rainy season, some with *lingams,* others with images of Vishnu, and some empty and used for meditation or the practice of yoga. One of these is a shrine to the Five (*panch*) Rivers (*ganga*) which, according to legend, have their confluence here: the two symbolic rivulets of Dhutapapa (Cleansed of Sin) and the Kirana (Sun's Ray), which join the mythical confluence of the Yamuna and the Sarasvati with the Ganga.

Above **Trilochana Ghat,** further north, is the holy ancient *lingam* of the Three (*tri*) Eye (*lochana*) Shiva. Beyond it, the river bypasses some of Varanasi's oldest precincts, now predominantly Muslim in character; the *ghats* themselves gradually become less impressive and are usually of the *kaccha* (clay-banked) variety.

At **Adi Keshava Ghat** (the "Original Vishnu"), on the outskirts of the city, the Varana flows into the Ganga. Unapproachable during the rainy season, when it is completely submerged, it marks the place where Vishnu first landed as an emissary of Shiva, and stands on the original site of the city before it spread southwards; around Adi Keshava are a number of Ganesha shrines.

Vishwanatha Khanda – the Old City

At the heart of Varanasi, between Dashashwamedha Ghat and Godaulia to the south and west and Manikarnika Ghat on the river to the north, lies **Vishwanatha Khanda,** sometimes referred to as the Old City. The whole area rewards exploration, with numerous shrines and *lingams* tucked into every corner, and buzzing with the activity of pilgrims, *pandas* and stalls selling offerings to the faithful.

Approached through a maze of narrow alleys and the **Vishwanatha Gali** (or Lane), the temple complex of **Vishwanatha** or **Visheshwara,** the "Lord of All", is popularly known as the **Golden Temple,** due to the massive gold plating on its *shikhara* (spire). Inside the compound – which is hidden behind a wall, and entered through an unassuming doorway – is one of India's most important *shivalingams,* made of smooth black stone and seated in a solid silver plinth, as well as shrines to the wrathful protectors **Mahakala** and **Dandapani,** and the *lingam* of **Avimukteshvara,** the Lord of the Unforsaken, which predates Vishwanatha and once held much greater significance. The current temple was built in 1777 by Queen Ahalya Bai Holkar of Indore, and is closed to non-Hindus, who have to make do with glimpses from adjacent buildings.

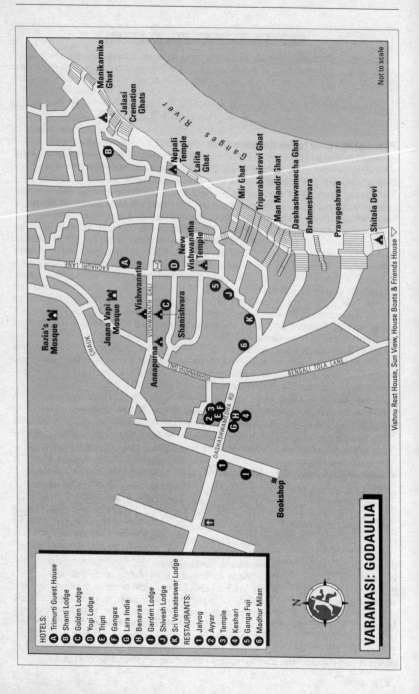

Vishnu Rest House, Sun View, House Boats & Friends House

Manikarnika Ghat

Jalasi Cremation Ghats

Ganges River

Nepali Temple

Lalita Ghat

Mir Ghat

Tripurabhairavi Ghat

Man Mandir Ghat

Dashashwamedha Ghat

Brahmeshvara

Prayageshvara

Shitala Devi

KACHAULI LANE

New Vishwanatha Temple

Vishwanatha

VISHWANATH GALI

Razia's Mosque

Jnana Vapi Mosque

Annapurna

Shanishvara

VISHWANATH GALI

CHAUK

BENGALI TOLA LANE

DASHASHWAMEDHA RD

Bookshop

VARANASI: GODAULIA

Not to scale

N

HOTELS:
A Trimurti Guest House
B Shanti Lodge
C Golden Lodge
D Yogi Lodge
E Tripti
F Ganges
G Lara India
H Banaras
I Garden Lodge
J Shivesh Lodge
K Sri Venkateswar Lodge

RESTAURANTS:
1 Jalyog
2 Ayyar
3 Temple
4 Keshari
5 Ganga Fuji
6 Madhur Milan

Vishwanatha's history has been fraught. Sacked by successive Muslim rulers, the temple was repeatedly rebuilt, until the grand edifice begun in 1585 by Todar Mal, a courtier of the tolerant Moghul Akbar, was finally destroyed by Aurangzeb. On its foundations, guarded by armed police to protect it from Hindu fanatics, stands the **Jnana Vapi Mosque**, also known as the Great Mosque of Aurangzeb. Its simple white domes tower over the **Jnana Vapi** (Wisdom Well), immediately north, housed in an open arcaded hall built in 1828, where Shiva cooled his *lingam* after the construction of Vishwanatha. Covered by a grate to prevent people jumping in in search of instant *moksha*, and covered with a cloth to stop coins being thrown in, only the presiding brahmins have access to its waters, considered to be liquid knowledge. Pilgrims offer their *sankalpa* or statement of intent here, before commencing the Panchatirthi Yatra. Slightly north, across the main road, the thirteenth-century **Razia's Mosque** stands atop the ruins of a still earlier Vishwanatha temple, destroyed under the Sultanate.

Close by, the temple of **Annapurna Bhavani** is dedicated to the supreme Shakti ("She, the Being of Plenteous Food"), the queen and divine mother also known in this benevolent form as Mother of the Three Worlds. As the provider of sustenance, she carries a cooking pot rather than the fearsome weapons borne by her horrific forms Durga and Kali; a subsidiary shrine opened only three days a year houses a solid gold image of Annapurna. Nearby is a stunning image, faced in silver against a black surround, of **Shani** or Saturn. Anyone whose fortunes fall under his shadow is stricken with bad luck – a fate devotees try to escape by worshipping here on Saturdays.

The rest of the city

Although it can take years to explore the *ghats* and the old city, Varanasi does hold a few other sites of interest, especially in the area south of Godaulia just beyond Asi Ghat. The **Durga Temple** here, and the Bharat Kala Bhavan museum of **Benares Hindu University** (BNU) are easily accessible, while just across the river, **Ramnagar** and its impressive fort continue to play an important role in the life of the city.

Bharat Mata

About three kilometres west of Godaulia, outside the old city, the modern temple of **Bharat Mata** (Mother India), inaugurated by Mahatma Gandhi, is unusual in that it has a huge relief map in marble of the whole of the Indian subcontinent and the Tibetan plateau, with mountains, rivers and the holy *tirthas* all clearly visible. Pilgrims circumambulate the map before viewing it in its entirety from the second floor. The temple can be reached by rickshaw from Godaulia for around Rs6.

South of the Old City: The Durga Temple and the Hindu University

The nineteenth-century **Durga Temple** – stained red with ochre, and known among foreign travellers as the Monkey Temple, thanks to the aggressive and irritable monkeys that occupy every nook and cranny – stands within a walled enclosure 8km south of Godaulia, not far from Asi Ghat. It was built in a common north Indian style, with an ornate *shikhara*, consisting of five segments symbolizing the elements, and supported by finely carved columns. The whole ensemble is best seen from across Durga Kund, the adjoining tank. Permeated by a stark primeval atmosphere, it is devoted to Durga, the terrifying aspect of Shiva's consort, Parvati, and the embodiment of *shakti* or female power. In contrast to the benevolent Annapurna, Durga, the Unassailable destroyer of demons, clad in red and riding a tiger, is fully armed with Shiva's trident, Vishnu's discus and a sword. A forked stake in the courtyard is used during festivals to behead sacrificial goats, in an early or pre-Hindu form of worship which has now generally been replaced by a symbolic mark in vermilion.

MUSIC IN VARANASI

Renowned as a centre for north Indian **classical music**, Varanasi attracts students from all over the world, and is famous for its exhilarating school (*gharana*) of *tabla* (paired hand-drum) playing. The city is home to such legendary figures as **Ustad Bismillah Khan** (*sehnai* – oboe) and **Pandit Shanto Prasad** (*tabla*), and **Pandit Ravi Shankar** (*sitar*) has also been based here. Small schools and instrument shops in the alleys off Dashashwamedha try to catch the transient tourist trade, but if you want to probe deeper, the traditional scene, based around student–teacher relationships, continues to thrive. Between Jangambali post office and Bengali Lane, the *International Music Centre*, D33/81 Khalishpura, holds concerts and organizes classes aimed at foreigners. **Asi Ghat** has always been known for its rapidly changing music scene, and there's a lively music department at BNU.

Varanasi is renowned for big music festivals, generally held around April. The **Dhrupad Mela** is devoted to *Dhrupad*, an archaic form in which the voice, treated as a musical instrument, is accompanied by the double-membrane barrel drum, *pakhawaj*. *Pakhawaj* solos are particularly vibrant; the drum has a deep and sonorous tone, and performances rise to energetic crescendoes. Varanasi's large Muslim community also makes its mark: there is an active Sufi tradition, and at *dargars* (shrines) you may chance upon a **qawwali** performance; these are often given on Thursdays at the Dargar of Chandan Sahid, Raj Ghat.

Most of the best instrument makers are tucked away in the alleys of the old city, known only to practitioners; some also supply the Dashashwamedha tourist shops, who then add on a hefty mark-up. For those in the know, much the best idea is to have an instrument made to order. The following places are worth a look if you're hooked:

Ankit Music House, D5/15 Tripura Bhairavi, Dashashwamedha, near Vishwanatha. Run by a young *tabla* player, Bablu, who offers classes and concerts and good-quality *tabla*, but at a premium designed to cash in on the tourist trade.

Imtiaz Ahmed, Laxa Road, Sidh Giri Bagh. Another master craftsman, offering made-to-order *tabla* at similar prices.

Baddaruddin, near Arya Samaj Temple, Lalapura. One of Varanasi's best craftsmen, *tabla*-maker to the professionals; you can expect to pay Rs1300 for a pair of made-to-order *tablas*.

Kesho Prasad, C K 38/5 Gyanwapi, near Dashashwamedha. Specializes in string instruments such as the *sitar* and *tanbura* (drone).

Non-Hindus are admitted to the courtyard, but not the inner sanctum, of the Durga temple, but access to the **Tulsi Manas Temple** alongside is unrestricted (daily 5am–noon & 3pm–midnight). Built in 1964 of white-streaked marble, its walls are inscribed with verses by the poet and author of the *Ramcharitmanas*, the Hindi equivalent of the great Sanskrit epic *Ramayana*. On the second floor, moving images bring to life episodes from the classics.

A little further south, the **Bharat Kala Bhavan** museum (daily except Sun; summer 8am–noon, winter 11am–4.30pm; free, Rs10 camera fee) has a fabulous collection of miniature paintings, sculpture, contemporary art and bronzes. Dedicated to the city of Varanasi, a gallery with a stunning nineteenth-century map has a display of the recent Raj Ghat excavations and old etchings of the city. Along with Buddhist and Hindu sculpture and Moghul glass, galleries are devoted to foreign artists who found inspiration in India, such as Nicholas Roerich and Alice Boner. Jamini Roy, the Bengali renaissance painter so influenced by folk art, is also well represented.

Bharat Kala Bhavan forms part of BNU, the campus of which also holds the **New Vishwanatha Temple** (daily 4am–noon & 1–9pm), distinguished by its lofty white marble *shikhara*. The brainchild of Pandit Malaviya, founder of the university and a great believer in an egalitarian and casteless Hindu revival, it was built by the Birlas, a wealthy Marwari industrial family. Although supposedly modelled on the original temple destroyed by Aurangzeb, the building displays characteristics of the new wave of temple architecture, amalgamating influences from various parts of India with a garish interior. Tea shops, flower sellers and other vendors in the small market outside the gates cater to a continuous flow of visitors.

Ramnagar

The residence of the Maharajah of Varanasi, **Ramnagar Fort**, looks down upon the Ganges not far south of the Asi Ghat. The best views of the fortifications – especially impressive in late afternoon – are to be had from the other side of the river, which is reached by a road heading south from the BHU area and over a rickety pontoon bridge. During the monsoon the bridge is dismantled and replaced by a ferry, still preferable to the long main road that crosses the main Malaviya bridge in the north before heading down the eastern bank of the river.

Inside, the fort bears testimony to the wealth of the Maharajah and his continuing influence. A dusty and poorly kept **museum** (daily 9am–noon & 2–5pm; Rs3) provides glimpses of a decadent past: horse-drawn carriages, old motor cars, palanquins, gilded and ornate silver *howdahs* (elephant seats), *hookahs*, costumes and old silk in a sorry state are all part of the collection, along with an armoury, a collection of minute ivory carvings, an astronomical clock and hunting trophies. Some visitors have reported having tea with the affable Maharajah after chance encounters.

Across the courtyard, a section is devoted to the **Ram Lila** procession and festivities, held during Dussehra (Oct). Varanasi is renowned for its Ram Lila, during which episodes from the *Ramayana* are re-enacted throughout the city and the Maharajah sponsors three weeks of elaborate celebrations.

Accommodation

Most of Varanasi's better and more expensive hotels lie on its peripheries, either in the **Cantonment** in the north or in the commercial belt in places like Sadar Bazaar, and staying away from the hustle is certainly conducive to a peaceful night's sleep. However, to experience the full ambience and mystery of the city, you have to stay close to the *ghats* and the lanes of **Vishwanatha**. Small lodges make this ideally suited for the budget-conscious traveller.

Old City

Banaras Lodge, Dashashwamedha Rd (☎321050). Large, rambling hotel in the thick of things, which has seen better days but is still good value. ①–②.

Friends House, Aliyabhai Ghat. Simple and basic with good views of the river. Best approached via Dashashwamedha Ghat past Shitala Devi to the right and up the next *ghat* to a lane. ①.

Ganges, Bank of Baroda Building, Dashashwamedha Rd (☎321097). Off the congested main thoroughfare, in its own yard, this guesthouse has an excellent reputation. Its bright new *Temple* restaurant, with piped music, has been an instant success with travellers. ②–④.

Garden Lodge, opposite *Sushil Cinema*, Godaulia. Simple budget accommodation, with shared baths, close to Dashashwamedha; pleasant rooftop cafe next door. ①.

Golden Lodge, D8/35 Kalika Lane (☎323832). Close to the *Yogi Lodge*, a pleasant guesthouse, popular with budget travellers, which boasts a rooftop patio and restaurant. ①.

House boats, Mansarovar Ghat. Quite basic and not particularly hygienic, but ideal for soaking up the ambience of life along the river. ①.

Lara India, Dashashwamedha Rd (☎320323). Small but with a good mid-range restaurant, strong on local Varanasi food, and smart a/c rooms in the heart of Godaulia. ④–⑤.

Shanti Lodge, Manikarnika Ghat (☎322568). A roof terrace close to the burning *ghats*, dormitory and budget accommodation popular with travellers. ①.

ACCOMMODATION PRICE CODES

All **accommodation prices** in this book have been coded using the symbols below. In principle the prices given are for the least expensive double rooms in each establishment; however, some hotels, usually in category ①, offer rates per bed rather than per room. Local taxes are not included unless specifically stated. For more details, see p.34.

①	up to Rs100	④	Rs225–350	⑦	Rs750–1200
②	Rs100–150	⑤	Rs350–500	⑧	Rs1200–2200
③	Rs150–225	⑥	Rs500–750	⑨	Rs2200 and up

Shivesh Lodge, D5/10 Meer Ghat. Tiny but extremely cheap lodge in the thick of the Dashaswamedha–Vishwanatha triangle. ①.

Sri Venkateswar Lodge, D5/64 Dashashwamedha Rd (☎322357). Simple but clean and close to the *ghats* and to Vishwanatha, capturing the ambience of the old city. ①.

Sun View Guest House, B6/105 Kedar Ghat (First Floor). Small lodge – a bit pokey, but with a garden overlooking the river. ①.

Trimurti Guest House, near Vishwanatha Temple (☎322616). Good range of rooms (some air-cooled), which can be on the small side. Extensive views from the terrace. ①–③.

Tripti, Dashashwamedha Rd (☎322346). Some reasonably priced rooms on the roof look down on the crowded and interesting thoroughfare. ②–③.

Vishnu Rest House, Pandey Ghat. One of the nicest of the riverside lodges with a lovely patio and cafe overlooking the Ganga, best approached via the *ghats* – turn right at Dashashwamedha. ①.

Yogi Lodge, D8/29 Kalika Gali (☎322588). An old favourite with budget travellers which still retains much of its charm and reputation. ①.

Cantonment and the peripheries

Clarks, The Mall, Cantt (☎46771). Plush and well presented, with all mod cons including swimming pool, the best that Varanasi has to offer. ⑧–⑨.

de Paris, 15 The Mall, Cantt (☎46601). Founded by a Frenchman at the turn of the century, and set in extensive gardens, capturing an old-world atmosphere with large comfortable rooms. ⑦.

Garden View, Vidyapeeth Rd, Sigra (☎360859). Pleasant enough, with a small garden set back from a busy main road, but away from the main hubs around the station and the old city. ②–③.

Gautam, Ramkatora (☎46239). Clean but mediocre and a bit expensive. ④–⑤.

GM Guest House, 1 Chandrika Colony, Sigra (☎361292). Away from the old town, but easy to reach. Excellent-value rooms, large and air-cooled with clean bathrooms, plus good food. ②–④.

Hindusthan International, C21/3 Maldahiya (☎57075). New and plush, with an atrium at its centre, good facilities including a swimming pool, but otherwise characterless. ⑧.

Ideal Tops, The Mall (☎42591). Brand new hotel next to *Clarks*, lacking in character. ⑦.

India, 59 Patel Nagar (☎45127). Best of a row of similar places, now overhauled and extended. ③–⑥.

ITDC Varanasi Ashok, The Mall (☎46020). Next to *Clarks* in the quiet leafy Cantonment; plush with all mod cons including a swimming pool – at a price. ⑧.

Pallavi International, Hathwa Place, Chetganj (☎56939). Extensive ex-maharajah's palace behind a busy shopping mall – ornate but a bit tacky; used for weddings. ④–⑥.

Pradeep, Jagatganj (☎44963). Newish, comfortable, quite smart and popular with tour groups; away from the *ghats* but within striking distance. Attractive multi-cuisine *Poonam* restaurant. ④–⑤.

Relax, Parade Kothi, Cantt (☎43503). Good-value budget option near the railway station, just outside the gates of the *Tourist Bungalow* and next to the *Mandarin* Chinese restaurant. ①.

Shalimar, Varuna Bridge, The Mall (☎46227). Close to the *India* in the quiet Cantonment area, pleasant but a little more simple. ③–⑤.

Surya, S20/51, A5 Varuna Bridge, Cantt (☎385930). Pleasant, comfortable, but ordinary. ②–④.

Taj Ganges, Nadesar Palace Grounds (☎42481). Top hotel, in the grand *Taj* style. Excellent facilities – two restaurants, a bar and a swimming pool – but lacking the character of *Clarks*. ⑧–⑨.

Temples Town, 53 Patel Nagar (☎46582). One of the cheapest in the Cantonment area. ②.

UPTDC Tourist Bungalow, Parade Kothi, Cantt (☎43413). Close to the bus and railway station, this large complex, with a range of rooms and a dorm, is trying to live down a poor reputation. The institutional atmosphere has been alleviated by the addition of a bar, restaurant and garden. ②–⑤.

UPTDC Tourist Dak Bungalow, 59 Cantt (☎42182). Friendly atmosphere and extensive grounds popular with overlanders and campers. Also has rooms and a cafe serving a full breakfast for around Rs40 – and hosts music performances in the evenings. ②–③.

Vaibhav, 56 Patel Nagar (☎46466). Quite a smart little establishment with moderate-sized rooms and the good *Palki* restaurant serving Indian, Chinese and western food. ④–⑤.

Eating

Most of the old city cafes are vegetarian, and alcohol is not tolerated, but the newer Cantonment area is less constrained by religious mores. Some of the more expensive hotels have bars, while a cold beer in cheaper places like the *Tourist Dak Bungalow* is not hard to find. After a trip on the boats in the early morning, try *kachori*, savoury deep-fried pastry bread, in the old city next to the *ghats* – a city tradition.

Ayyar's Cafe, next to *Banaras Lodge*, Dashashwamedha Rd. At the back of a shopping arcade, a small cafe serving south Indian food, including *masala dosas*, and filter coffee at reasonable prices.

El Parador, Maldahiya Roadways, near Pani Tanki (☎46555). Run by a Gurkha family from Darjeeling. Remarkable menu ranging from Mexican to Italian, with chocolate cake and pancakes.

Fagin's, D8/35 Kalika Lane, near Vishwanatha, Dashashwamedha (☎323832). An ideal travellers' haunt, with an extensive menu, reasonable prices, and (recorded) music. Part of *Golden Lodge*.

Ganga Fuji, D5/8 Kalika Gali, near Vishwanatha, Dashashwamedha. Odd name for a pleasant little cafe, serving assorted cuisine and with live music in the evenings.

Garden, opposite *Sushil Cinema*, Godaulia. Rooftop cafe, next to *Garden Lodge*. Good breakfasts.

Jalyog, Dashashwamedha Rd. Long-standing local cafe, serving vegetarian food strong on *puris* (deep fried puffed bread) and the legendary Varanasi *kachoris*.

Kemp's, Parade Kothi, Cantt. Good-value international restaurant, outside the *Tourist Bungalow*.

Keshari, lane opposite *Banaras Lodge*, Godaulia. *Paneer* (cheese) dishes, and good-value *thalis*.

Madhur Milan Cafe, Dashashwamedha Ghat. Good for *lassis*, sweets and *kachoris*.

Mandarin, Parade Kothi, Cantt. Reasonably priced and good Chinese food near the railway station and the cluster of hotels around the *Tourist Bungalow*.

Sindhi, Bhelupur Thana. One of Varanasi's most popular restaurants, 1.5km from Godaulia. The rickshaw ride will be rewarded with excellent vegetarian food.

Winfa, near *Prakash Cinema*, Lahurabir. Not much to look at, but the best Chinese food in town.

Listings

Astrologers *Dr Sidh Nath Srivastava*, Planet Guide Centre, *Tourist Dak Bungalow*, The Mall (☎42182). Palmist and astrologer.

Automobile Association *UP Automobile Association*, Bulanala (☎63500).

Bookshops *Universal Book Company*, Godaulia.

Foreigners Registration Office Srinagar Colony, Sigra (☎53968).

Hospitals *Sir Sunderlal Hospital*, BHU – Benares Hindu University (☎5583), *Birla Hospital*, Machhodari (☎56357), *SSPG Hospital* (government-run), Kabirchaura (☎62424).

Motorcycles Jagatganj, near the Sanskrit University. Mechanics and workshops specializing in *Enfields* are clustered in this area; you may be able to pick up a secondhand bike here by asking around.

Opticians *Gupta Optical*, Godaulia.

Pharmacies *Singh Medical*, near *Prakash Cinema*, Lahurabir, and near the main hospitals.

Photography *Bright Studio*, Godaulia; *Passi Studio*, Lahurabir; *Veer Studio*, Jagatganj, in front of Queen's College.

MOVING ON FROM VARANASI

A full summary of transport connections from Varanasi can be found on p.206.

Indian Airlines' daily **flight** IC252 to **Kathmandu** gets very heavily booked in winter; IC408 flies daily to **Delhi**, via Khajuraho and Agra. In addition four flights a week on IC497 link Varanasi to **Delhi** and **Bhubaneshwar** and three to **Bombay** and **Lucknow** on IC695. *Air India* are in *Hotel Clarks* (☎46326); *Indian Airlines* are behind *Hotel de Paris*, Cantt (Mon–Fri 10am–1pm & 2–5pm; ☎45959), and they also have an airport office (☎43742).

Some of the super-fast **trains** on the main east–west line bypass Varanasi: head by road for **Moghul Sarai** for a wider choice of expresses. All major trains depart from the Cantt station (reservations daily 8am–2pm & 2.30–7pm; ☎131 or 43404). The daily *Mahanagri Express* #1094 is the fastest service to **Bombay** (11.35am; 28hr). For **Calcutta** via **Gaya**, the daily choice lies between the *Amritsar–Howrah Express* #3050 (7.50pm, 20hr) and the *Amritsar–Howrah Mail* #3006 (5.25pm, 15hr). Two good trains run to **Delhi**: the *AC Express* #2381 (Tues, Thurs & Sat, 9.15pm; 14hr), and the *Neelachal Express* #8475 (Mon, Wed & Sun, 7.35am; 14hr). For the **mountains** of UP, the daily *Dehra Dun–Varanasi Express* #4265 (9.15am; 20hr) is a better bet than the *Doon Express* #3010 (7.45pm; 20hr), which is nearly always late. To get to Nepal via **Gorakhpur** (see p.317), three trains each day take 8–10hr; they're not mainline services, so they are subject to infuriating delays.

Avoid direct **buses** to Nepal: buses on the far side of the frontier are generally better. *UPSRTC* run buses, including overnight services, to the border at **Sonauli** (11hr) via **Gorakhpur** from the Cantt Bus Stand. A daily bus departs for Gaya, near **Bodh Gaya** (6hr) at around 6am. Regular services ply the Grand Trunk Road east to **Patna**, and there are good deluxe buses for **Allahabad**, which is also on an excellent rail link.

General **travel agencies**, selling tickets and offering car rental, include ITDC, at the *Ashok*, The Mall (☎46032); *Khan Travels*, S20/52, 3A Nepali Kothi (☎46623) and *Hotel de Paris*, The Mall; *Sita Tours and Travels* (☎43421) and *Travel Corporation India* (☎46209), both at *Hotel Clarks*; and *Varuna Travels*, Panday Haveli, near Durga Charan Girls School.

Shopping With hustlers and rickshaw drivers keen to drag tourists into shops offering commission, shopping in Varanasi can be a nightmare – but it's worth seeking out the city's rich silk-weaving and brasswork. The best areas to browse are the Thatheri Bazaar (for brass), or Jnana Vapi and the Vishwanatha Gali with its *Temple Bazaar* (for silk brocade and jewellery). State-run emporia in Godaulia, Lahurabir and the Chowk – the three *UP Handlooms* outlets at Lahurabir, Nadesar and Neechi Bag, and *Mahatex* in Godaulia – offer fixed prices and assured quality.

Silk Sales pitches tend to become more aggressive when it comes to silk, and you need to be wary of the hard-sell. *Qazi Sadullahpura*, near *Chhavi Mahal Cinema*, lies at the heart of a fascinating Muslim neighbourhood devoted to the production of silk. For tailoring, try *Paraslakshmi Exports*, 71 Chandrika Colony, Sigra (☎361496), a silk business providing a good and prompt service; they'll deliver to your hotel, and also offer ready-made waistcoats and boxer shorts.

Around Varanasi

Although the most obvious excursion from Varanasi is the ten-kilometre trip north to **Sarnath**, the site of the Buddha's first sermon – see p.314 – other possible attractions include Sher Shah's grand fortress at **Chunar**, and the great Muslim city of **Jaunpur**, with its beautiful and intriguing mosques, a long day trip to the northwest.

Chunar

From their vantage point at the northern extremity of the Kaimur Hills, the impressive sandstone battlements of **CHUNAR** command a meander in the Ganga before the river curves north to Varanasi 22km away. Evidence of the earliest occupation of the site dates it to Vikramaditya of Ujjain in 56 BC. Chunar sandstone has been used for centuries, most famously in Ashokan pillars – highly polished for sheen and longevity – and is still quarried, leaving the surrounding hills looking ravaged in places.

The almost impregnable citadel, protected by massive Moghul ramparts, looks down onto the river, graced by a beautiful beach of silver sand during the dry season; the views of the sunset are stunning. Akbar stormed the fortress in 1575, and it was presided over by the Nawabs of Avadh until the British took it in 1764. Chunar is also associated with Warren Hastings, who took refuge here from an uprising in 1781; a large British graveyard lies near the western gate by the river. The ramparts and huge gates aside, the buildings themselves are unremarkable, except for a picturesque pavilion, built during the reign of Sher Shah Suri (*c.*1538) as a gate house. Now a PWD bungalow, it makes an atmospheric and inexpensive stopover (①), bookable through the PWD at Mirzapur; food is available by arrangement with the caretaker.

On the banks of the river, the small, pleasant, traffic-free town of **Balu Ghat** has a small market and a few basic cafes; Chunar village, off the Ramnagar–Mirzapur highway and thronged with sandstone merchants, is a bit more animated.

The best way to get to Chunar is by local bus from Godaulia to Chunar Ghat, 22km south, from where a pontoon bridge crosses to Balu Ghat, at the base of the fortress. During the rainy season, the bridge is dismantled and a ferry takes its place.

Jaunpur

Few tourists visit the large dusty town of **JAUNPUR**, 65km northwest of Varanasi, and founded by Feroz Shah in 1360 to guard the eastern flank of the Delhi Sultanate. The city flourished until a ruthless onslaught by Sikander Lodi spared only its remarkable **mosques** – built in a unique hybrid style, using the plundered remains of previous Hindu and Buddhist structures – and later returned to prominence under the Moghuls.

The River Gomti, which bisects Jaunpur, is spanned by the massive sixteenth-century **Akbari Bridge**. Designed by an Afghan architect, the stone structure's fifteen arches have withstood floods and earthquakes; at its southern end, a large sculpture of a lion tussling with an elephant doubles as a provincial milestone.

The older sector, north of the river, is the site of Feroz Shah's original **Fort**, whose stone walls still show traces of coloured and glazed-brick cladding, and the remnants of masonry from an earlier Hindu temple. Little remains of its towers, blown up by the British in 1857. Around 350 metres north of the bridge, **Atala Masjid** is the earliest and finest example of the architecture of the independent Sharqi dynasty. Built by Sultan Ibrahim Sharqi in 1408, and incorporating the remains of the temple of Atala Devi, it holds two-storeyed cloisters, large arches and an open-pillared verandah. Along with three handsome gateways, the most impressive feature of the mosque is the prayer hall to the west: its huge central arch, composed of three pylons and flanked by two tapering towers, reaches a height of 23m.

Less than a kilometre north, the ambitious **Jami Masjid** mosque, built by Sultan Hussain Shah Sharqi (1458–79), sits on a high plinth. Approached by steep steps, its prayer hall has an imposing square chamber capped with a lofty dome; remnants of Hindu structures can be seen embedded in the cloisters and walls. Around six kilometres northwest of Akbari Bridge, the small **Lal Darwaza Mosque**, built around 1450 by Bibi Raji, the queen of Sultan Muhammad Shah (1436–58), is a cut-down version of Atala Masjid, with just one dome over its prayer hall and an almost square arch giving it a squat appearance.

What basic accommodation and food is available is concentrated around the Fort. Most visitors come from Varanasi for the day: both trains and buses take two hours.

Sarnath

SARNATH, 10km north of Varanasi, is a place of pilgrimage for Buddhists, and has also become popular with day-trippers, who picnic among its ruins and parklands. It was in a quiet grove here, in the sixth century BC, that Siddhartha Gautama – who came to be known as the **Buddha**, the "Awakened One" – gave his first sermon, and set in motion the Wheel of Law, the *Dharmachakra*. During the rainy season, when the Buddha and his followers sought respite from their round of itinerant teaching, they would retire to Sarnath. Also known as **Rishipatana**, the place of the *rishis* or sages, or **Mrigadaya**, the deer park, its name derives from *Saranganatha*, the Lord of the Deer.

Over the centuries, Sarnath flourished as a centre of Buddhist art and teaching, particularly for **Hinayana** Buddhism (the "Lesser Way"). In the seventh century, the Chinese pilgrim Hiuen T'siang recounted seeing 30 monasteries, supporting some 3000 monks, and a life-sized brass statue of the Buddha turning the Wheel of Law.

Buddhism in India floundered under the impact of Muslim invasions and the rise of Hinduism, and except for the vast bulk of the Dhamekh Stupa much of the site lay in ruins for almost a millennium. Prey to vandalism and pilfering, Sarnath remained abandoned until 1834, when Major General Sir Alexander Cunningham, the head of the Archaeological Survey, visited the site. Today it is once more an important Buddhist centre, and its avenues house missions from all over the Buddhist world.

The Main Site and the Dhamekh Stupa

Dominated by the huge bulk of the Dhamekh Stupa, the extensive archeological excavations of the main site of Sarnath are maintained within an immaculate park. Entering from the southwest, the pillaged remains of the **Dharmarajika Stupa** lie immediately to the north: within its core the *stupa* concealed a green marble casket full of human bones and precious objects, including decayed pearls and gold leaf. Commemorating the spot where the Buddha delivered his first sermon, the *stupa* is attributed to the reign of Ashoka in the third century BC, but was extended a further six times.

Adjacent to Dharmarajika Stupa are the ruins of the **Main Shrine**, where Ashoka is said to have meditated. To the west stands the lower portion of an **Ashokan Pillar** – minus its famous capital, now housed in the museum. The ruins of four monasteries, dating from the third to the twelfth centuries, are also contained within the compound; all bear the same hallmark of a central courtyard surrounded by monastic cells.

Most impressive of all is the **Dhamekh Stupa**, also known as the **Dharma Chakra Stupa**, which stakes a competing claim as the exact spot of the Buddha's first sermon. The *stupa* is composed of a cylindrical tower rising 33.5 metres from a stone drum, ornamented with bas-relief foliage and geometric patterns; the eight arched niches halfway up may once have held statues of the Buddha. It dates from the Gupta period, but with evidence of earlier Mauryan construction; some archeologists have conjectured that the *stupa*'s upper brickwork may originally have been plastered over.

The **Sri Digambar Jain Temple**, or **Shreyanshnath Temple**, is believed to mark the birthplace of Shreyanshnath, the eleventh *tirthankara*. Built in 1824, the interior houses a large image of the Jain saint, as well as attractive frescoes depicting the life of Lord Mahavira, the founder of the religion and contemporary of the Buddha.

Museum

Daily 10am–4.45pm. Rs0.50.

Opposite the gates to the main site, the **museum**, designed to look like a *vihara* (monastery), has a small but renowned collection of Buddhist and Brahmanist antiquities, consisting mostly of sculpture in the excellent medium of Chunar sandstone.

The most famous exhibit is the **lion capital**, removed here from the Ashokan column on the main site. Constructed by Ashoka (273–232 BC), the great Mauryan king and convert to the *dharma*, it has become the emblem of modern India: four alert and beautifully sculpted lions guard the four cardinal directions, atop a circular platform. Belonging to the first and second century AD are two impressive life-size standing *bodhisattvas* – one has a stone parasol with fine ornamentation and emblems of the faith. Among the large number of fifth-century figures is one of the **Buddha**, cross-legged and with his hands in the *mudra* gesture. Perfectly poised, with his eyes downcast in deep meditation, and a halo forming an exquisite nimbus behind his head, the Buddha is seated above six figures, possibly representing his companions, with the Wheel of Law in the middle, to signify his first sermon. Later sculptures, dating from the tenth to twelfth century, include an exceptionally delicate image of the deity **Avalokiteshvara** with a lotus, and another of **Lokeshvara** holding a bowl.

Chaukhandi Stupa

The dilapidated brick remains of the **Chaukhandi Stupa**, a kilometre south of the main site, date from the Gupta period (300–700 AD), and are said to mark the spot where the Buddha was reunited with the Panchavargiya Bikshus, his five ascetic companions who had previously deserted him. Standing on a terraced rectangular plinth, the *stupa* is capped by an incongruous octagonal Moghul tower, built by Akbar in 1589 AD to commemorate his father's visit to the site.

Mulagandha Kuti Vihara and modern sites

To the east of the Dhamekh Stupa, the lofty church-like **Mulagandha Kuti Vihara** was built in 1931 with donations from the international Buddhist community. Run by the Mahabodhi Society, it drew devotees from all over the world to witness its consecration, and has become one of Sarnath's greatest attractions for pilgrims and tourists alike. The entrance foyer is dominated by a huge bell – a gift from Japan – and the interior houses a gilded reproduction of the museum's famous image of the Buddha, surrounded by fresco-covered walls depicting scenes from the life of the Buddha.

A little way east, shielded by a small enclosure, Sarnath's **Bodhi Tree** is an offshoot of the tree at Bodh Gaya in Bihar under which the Buddha attained enlightenment. Sangamitta, Emperor Ashoka's daughter, took a branch from the original tree in 288 BC and planted it in Anuradhapura, in Sri Lanka, where its offshoots have been nurtured through the ages.

Buddhist communities from other parts of the world are well represented in Sarnath. In addition to the long-established **Mahabodhi Society**, the **Central Institute of Tibetan Studies**, founded in 1967, offers degree courses in Tibetan philosophy and the ancient language of Pali. Close to the *Tourist Bungalow* is the traditional-style **Tibetan Temple** with frescoes and a good collection of *thangkas* (Tibetan scroll paintings): its central image is a colossal Shakyamuni, or Buddha Calling the Earth to Witness (his enlightenment). The **Chinese Temple** lies 200 metres east of the main gates; to the west, the **Burmese Temple** houses a white marble image of the Buddha flanked by two disciples. Behind the *Tourist Bungalow* are the **Japanese Temple** and the **Thai Temple**, the latter run by the Mrigdayavana Mahavihara Society.

Practicalities

Sarnath is easily reached by road from Varanasi but, given the sporadic **bus** service, auto-rickshaws might be a better option at Rs25 one-way; shared autos are also available for around Rs5 per person from Godaulia in Varanasi. Sarnath is included in the afternoon **coach tour** (Rs45) departing from Varanasi's tourist office, but the frantic itinerary doesn't make for a relaxing visit. Sarnath **railway** station, served only by local trains, is around 1km to the east. The main sites can be quite easily – and pleasantly – explored on foot; the so-called guides who linger outside the main gates and near the museum aren't really necessary.

Close to the main gate, the UPTDC *Tourist Bungalow* (☎42002; ①–③) is a typical government-run affair, with a dormitory and private rooms. Some of the monasteries, such as the pleasant *Burmese Vihara*, north of the main site, have rooms where visitors can stay on payment of a donation (①). There are a few simple **cafes and restaurants** outside the main gates near the Mulagandha Kuti Vihara, and a rather institutional restaurant serves *thalis* at the *Tourist Bungalow*. Also at the *Tourist Bungalow* is the UP **Tourist Bureau** (Mon–Sat 10am–5pm), and the main **Post Office** is opposite.

Gorakhpur

GORAKHPUR, 230km north of Varanasi, which rose to prominence as a way station on a pilgrim route linking Kushinagar (the place of the Buddha's enlightenment) and Lumbini (his birthplace, across the border in Nepal), is now known primarily as a gateway to Nepal. It was named after the Shaivite yogi Gorakhnath, and holds a large ashram and temple dedicated to him. Tourists and pilgrims tend to hurry through, their departure hastened by the town's infamous flies and mosquitoes; if you do get stranded, there's a bustling bazaar, adequate amenities and a few passable hotels.

Around 5km northwest of the station, along the road to Nepal, the Gorakhnath ashram is an extensive complex of shrines, residences, and meeting halls, all rebuilt this century. On the site of an earlier temple, considered to be the traditional seat of the **Dharmanath** and **Ram Panths** (*panth* means branch or path) of the **Nath Yogi Sampradaya**, the ornate marble **Gorakhnath Temple** is decorated with images in the realistic style now popular throughout India. Surrounded by other shrines to Durga and Bhaironath, and a building that houses an eternal flame, the temple overlooks well-maintained grounds.

Arrival and information

There are three **bus** stands – the main Railway Station bus stand for buses to the Nepalese border at **Sonauli** and to **Kushinagar**; the Kacheri bus stand 1km southwest of the station has buses for **Allahabad**, **Lucknow** and a few for Varanasi, but the main bus stand for **Varanasi** (6hr) is at Pedleyganj, 2km southeast of the station. Buses on their way between Varanasi and Nepal often stop here, and some pause briefly opposite the station gates.

Major daily **trains** servicing Gorakhpur include the fast *Vaishali Express* #2553 to **Lucknow** (5.35pm) and the *Kushinagar Express* #1016 for **Bombay** via Lucknow (6am); among trains to **Varanasi** are a *Fast Passenger* (3am; 9hr), and the *Triveni Express* #5206 (7.20pm; 7hr). Station facilities include quite pleasant retiring rooms, a basic restaurant and a **tourist information** booth (daily except Sun 9am–5pm).

Rickshaws are the main means of **transport**, with few hotels more than one kilometre from the station. **Car rental** can be arranged through *Tours & Travels* (☎330915) in the Elora Building, opposite the railway station. The main **GPO** is in Golghar, to the southwest. The *State Bank of India* is on Bank Rd (☎334765); foreign-exchange facilities can also be found at some of the more expensive hotels.

Accommodation and eating

Surprisingly, Gorakhpur has a wide range of hotels from the budget-type near the station to mid-range accommodation in the dull commercial hub around Golghar, a kilometre southwest. During the hot months, air-cooled or the more expensive a/c rooms are welcome, especially if you have just come down from the mountains. Cheap *dhabas* can be found in the vicinity of the station; a row of them stand outside the station gates. Elsewhere, the best eating is in the more expensive hotels.

GETTING TO NEPAL

Gorakhpur is a convenient jumping-off point for western Nepal, offering access to Pokhara and even Kathmandu. Direct **buses** to **Kathmandu** and **Pokhara** are not a very good deal – your best bet is to enter Nepal at the 24-hour crossing at **Sonauli**, where there is a better choice of transport. Buses for Sonauli (3hr) depart from the bus stand near the railway station between 4.30am and 9pm; deluxe buses (Rs65) leave from in front of the railway station. Take one of the earliest if you want to get a connecting bus to Pokhara (10hr) or Kathmandu (14hr) in daylight, to enjoy the views; night buses also ply the routes. Private buses leave Sonauli almost hourly in the mornings, between 5am and 11am. The most popular service for Kathmandu, the government-run *Saja*, actually operates from **Bhairawa**, 4km away but still in India; the booking office is near Bhairawa's *Yeti Hotel*. Local buses cover the 24km from Bhairawa to Lumbini (Nepal), the birthplace of the Buddha.

If you want to **break your journey**, the pleasant *Hotel Niranjana* (①–③) in Sonauli, a kilometre short of the border, has a dorm and air-cooled rooms; in Bhairawa, the *Yeti* and the *Himalayan Inn* are popular. There's more choice over the border in Nepal.

Avantika, Kushinagar Rd, Mohaddipur (☎338765). On the outskirts, 4km from the (currently dormant) airport and 2.5km from the station; new, promising and well managed with a good mid-priced international restaurant. ③–⑤.

Bobina, Nepal Rd (☎336663). About 2km from the station; an extraordinary and now rather tacky building where facilities include foreign exchange, a garden, restaurant and bar. ④–⑤.

Elora, opposite Railway Station (☎330647). One of the best of the station hotels, with a range of rooms including a/c and air-cooled. ②–④.

Ganges, *Tarang Cinema* crossing, towards Gorakhnath Temple (☎333530). Pronounced *gang-ez*, one of Gorakhpur's best hotels. All mod cons, including two good restaurants. ⑤–⑥.

Marina, Golghar (☎337630). Tucked away behind the *President* in the same compound, this place is older, less ostentatious and more pleasant; room service but no restaurant. ③–④.

President, Golghar (☎337654). Off the main road, with a reputation as one of Gorakhpur's ritziest. A range of mid-priced rooms, plus the recommended *Queen's* restaurant. ③–⑤.

Raj, opposite Railway Station (☎336759). Quite basic accommodation, but with a more attractive annexe close by, and a cafe attached. ②.

Retiring Rooms, Railway Station. Good value; recommended if you need to catch an early train. ①.

Shalimar, Ghosh Company Chowkha (☎337502). Extensive and excellent-value budget accommodation in the centre of town, close to all amenities. ①.

Surya, Char Phatak, Railway Crossing, Mohaddipur (☎332210). One of the cheapest in the station area, with private bathrooms. ②.

Kushinagar

Set against a pastoral landscape, the small hamlet of **KUSHINAGAR**, 53km west of Gorakhpur, is revered as the site of the Buddha's **Mahaparinirvana**, his death and cremation that marked his final liberation from the cycles of death and rebirth. During the Buddha's lifetime, **Kushinara**, as it was then called, was a small town in the king-dom of the Mallas, surrounded by forest. It remained forgotten until the late nineteenth century when archeologists rediscovered the site, and began excavations – based on the writings of seventh-century Chinese pilgrims, including Hiuen T'siang.

Set in a leafy park at the heart of Kushinagar, the **Nirvana Stupa**, dated to the reign of Kumaragupta I (413–55 AD), was extensively rebuilt by Burmese Buddhists in 1927. Within the accompanying shrine lies a large gilded **reclining Buddha**, recon-structed from the remains of an earlier Malla image, and the surrounding area is strewn with *stupas* erected by pious pilgrims, and the ruins of four monasteries. At a crossing immediately southwest, excavations continued at the **Mathakunwar** shrine, where a stunning tenth-century blue schist Buddha has been unearthed. About 1.5km southeast of the main site – surrounded by fields of rice, wheat and cane – the crumbling bricks of the **Ramabhar Stupa** are thought to be the original **Mukutabandhana Stupa** erected to mark the spot of the Buddha's cremation.

Today, Kushinagar is rediscovering its roots as a centre for international Buddhism, and is home to many *viharas* (monasteries), including a Tibetan *gompa* devoted to Shakyamuni (the historical Buddha), a Burmese *vihara*, and temples from China and Japan. The strikingly simple **Japanese Temple**, built by the Atago Isshin World Buddhist Cultural Association, consists of a single circular chamber housing a golden image of the Buddha, softly lit through small, stained-glass windows.

Practicalities

Regular buses link Kushinagar with **Gorakhpur** and **Varanasi**, the journey taking up to two hours from Gorakhpur and around eight hours from Varanasi. Shared taxis and jeeps also travel to and from Gorakhpur, but are a lot less comfortable. **UP Tourism** maintains a low-key office and information desk in Kushinagar.

Accommodation options are limited: for a donation, you can stay in rooms for visiting pilgrims at one of the temples, or at the quiet and pleasant *International Buddhist Guest House* (①), opposite the Tibetan *gompa*. The relatively expensive state-run tourist bungalow, *Pathik Niwas* (☎05563/7138; ④–⑥), has a/c rooms, luxury cottages called "American Huts" and a canteen-like **restaurant**; food stalls at the Kasia crossing provide inexpensive snacks.

CHAPTER FOUR

MADHYA PRADESH

ot, dusty **MADHYA PRADESH**, India's largest state, is a vast landlocked expanse of scrub-covered hills and sun-parched plains, peppered with sprawling cities and a myriad of towns and tiny farming villages. Stretching from the headwaters of the mighty **River Narmada** at the borders of Orissa and Bihar to the fringes of the Western Ghats, it is a transitional zone between the Gangetic lowlands in the north and the high dry **Deccan plateau** to the south.

Despite its diverse array of exceptional attractions, ranging from ancient temples and hill-top forts to superb isolated wildlife reserves, Madhya Pradesh receives only a fraction of the tourist traffic that pours between Delhi, Agra and Varanasi, being bypassed by most tour operators on the grounds of the relative inaccessibility of major sites such as Khajuraho and Sanchi.

Any exploration of central India will be illuminated if you have a grasp of its long and turbulent **history**. Most of the marauding armies that have swept across the peninsula over the last two millennia passed along this crucial corridor, leaving in their wake a bumper crop of monuments. The very first traces of settlement in Madhya Pradesh are the ten-thousand-year-old paintings on the lonely hill-top of **Bhimbetka**, a day trip south of the capital **Bhopal**. Aboriginal rock art was still being created here during the Mauryan emperor Ashok's evangelical dissemination of Buddhism, in the second century BC. The immaculately restored *stupa* complex at **Sanchi**, not far away, is the most impressive relic of this era, among the finest early Buddhist remains in Asia. Nearby, the rock-cut Jain and Hindu caves at **Udaigiri** recall the dynasties that succeeded the Mauryans, from the Andhras to the Guptas in the fourth century.

By the end of the first millennium AD, central India was divided into several kingdoms: the Paramaras, whose ruler Raja Bhoj founded Bhopal, controlled the southern and central area, known as **Malwa**, while the **Chandellas**, responsible for some of the subcontinent's most exquisite temples, held sway in the north. Lost deep in the countryside, equidistant from Agra and Varanasi, their magnificent erotica-encrusted sandstone shrines at **Khajuraho** were erected sufficiently far from the main north–south route to have been overlooked by the iconoclastic warriors who marched past in the

MADHYA PRADESH TRAVEL DETAILS

	Trains		Buses		Flights	
	Frequency	Time	Frequency	Time	Frequency	Time
To and From Bhopal						
Agra	16–19 daily	5hr 30min–9hr				
Bombay	4 daily	14–17hr			daily	2hr 15min
Calcutta	2 weekly	29hr				
Delhi	16–19 daily	7hr 40min–15hr			5 weekly	1–2hr
Goa	1 daily	30hr				
Gwalior	16–19 daily	4hr 30min–7hr			2 weekly	1hr 45min
Indore	3–4 daily	6hr	hourly	5hr	5 weekly	35min
Jabalpur	1–2 daily	6hr–7hr 30min	2 daily	8hr		
Jalgaon	3 daily	7–9hr				
Jhansi	16–19 daily	3hr–5hr 40min				
Madras	2–3 daily	24–32hr				
Nagpur	6–9 daily	6hr 30min–10hr				
Pune	2 daily	17hr				
Raisen			5 daily	1hr		
Sanchi			hourly	2hr		
Ujjain	3–4 daily	4–6hr	2 daily	6hr		
Vidisha	8 daily	45min	hourly	3hr		
To and From Gwalior						
Agra	15–19 daily	1hr 20min–2hr	hourly	3hr		
Bombay	3 daily	20hr 15min			2 weekly	3hr 25min
Calcutta	3 weekly	25hr 30min				
Delhi	16–19 daily	3hr 25min–9hr			2 weekly	50min
Goa	1 daily	37hr				
Indore	1 daily	12hr 30min			2 weekly	1hr 50min
Jabalpur	1 daily	13hr				
Jalgaon	3 daily	12–17hr				
Jhansi	16–20 daily	1hr–2hr 45min	hourly	3hr		
Madras	2–4 daily	30–39hr				
Pune	2 daily	23hr 35min				
Puri	1 daily	39hr				
Shivpuri			2 daily	3hr		
Ujjain	1–2 daily	11–14hr	1 daily	14hr		
Varanasi	1 daily	19hr 20min				
Vidisha	8 daily	5–6hr 30min				
To and From Indore						
Agra	1 daily	14hr 25min				
Ajmer	3 daily	12hr–14hr 35min				
Aurangabad			1 nightly	8–10hr		
Bombay	1 daily	14hr 45min	1 nightly	12hr	daily	1hr 10min
Calcutta	2 weekly	36hr				
Chittaurgarh	3 daily	7–10hr 45min				
Delhi	2 daily	16hr–18hr 30min			5 weekly	2hr 15min
Dhar			hourly	2hr		
Jaipur	1 daily	15hr 35min	1 nightly	16hr		
Jhansi	1 daily	10hr 45min				
Kota	1 daily	7hr 45min				
Madras	1 weekly	25hr 30min				
Mandu			4 daily	5hr		
Nagpur	1 weekly	14hr 15min				
Omkareshwar			2 daily	2hr 30min		
Udaipur			2 daily	12–14hr		
Ujjain	3–4 daily	1hr 30min–2hr	hourly	1hr 30min		

	Trains		Buses		Flights	
	Frequency	Time	Frequency	Time	Frequency	Time
To and From Jabalpur						
Bombay	5 daily	18–20hr				
Calcutta	1 daily	23hr				
Delhi	1 daily	20hr				
Indore	1 daily	14hr 45min				
Jhansi	1 daily	11hr				
Madras	3 weekly	32hr 30min				
Nagpur	6 weekly	10hr	9 daily	7hr		
Patna	1–2 daily	12hr 30min–15hr				
Satna	8 daily	3hr				
Ujjain	1 daily	12hr 30min				
Varanasi	7 daily	8hr 30min–11hr				
To and From Khajuraho*						
Agra			1 daily	11hr 30min	daily	45min
Bhopal			1 nightly	12hr		
Delhi					daily	1hr 55min
Gwalior			1 daily	9hr		
Jabalpur			1 daily	11hr		
Jhansi			3–5 daily	6hr		
Mahoba			5 daily	3hr		
Satna			5 daily	4hr		
Varanasi					daily	45min
To and From Ujjain						
Ahmedabad	2–3 daily	9–10hr 30min				
Agra	1–2 daily	12hr 35min–16hr				
Calcutta	2 weekly	33hr 40min				
Delhi	2–3 daily	14hr–21hr 30min				
Jhansi	2–3 daily	8–14hr				
Kota	1 daily	2hr 50min				
Madras	1 weekly	33hr 15min				
Nagpur	1 weekly	12hr				
Varanasi	1 daily	33hr 25min				
Vidisha	1 daily	5hr				

* For connections to **Jhansi** in Uttar Pradesh, the major railhead for Khajuraho, see p.207.

Note that no individual route appears more than once in this chart; for any specific journey, check against where you want to get to as well as where you're coming from.

eleventh and twelfth centuries. Today, the site is as far off the beaten track as ever; its many visitors either fly in, or make the five- to six-hour bus journey from the nearest railheads at **Satna** (in the east) and **Jhansi** (to the west in Uttar Pradesh, see p.293).

Monuments associated with the long Muslim domination of the region, by contrast, are much easier to get to. The romantic ghost-town of **Mandu**, capital of the Malwa Sultans, can be reached in a day from the industrial city of **Indore**, in western Madhya Pradesh, while **Gwalior**, whose hill-top fort-palace was the lynchpin of both the Delhi Sultanate's and the Moghuls' southward expansion, straddles the main Delhi–Bombay railway in the far north. Finally, between Jhansi and Khajuraho, the atmospheric ruined capital of the Bundella rajas at **Orchha** merits a short detour from the highway.

Under the **British**, the middle of India was known as the "Central Provinces", and administered jointly from Nagpur (now in Maharashtra), and the summer capital, the hill-station of **Pachmarhi** near Bhopal. Madhya Pradesh, or "MP", only came into being after Independence, when the Central Provinces were amalgamated with a number of smaller princedoms. Since then, the 93 percent Hindu state has remained more stable than neighbouring Uttar Pradesh and Bihar. Major civil unrest was virtually unheard of until the Bhopal riots of 1992–93, sparked off by events in Ayodhya. As elsewhere in India, the upsurge in communal tension has been accompanied by a swing towards the fundamentalist BJP, who ousted Congress in the 1989 state legislature elections. Central rule was imposed by the Indian Prime Minister Narashima Rao in the heat of the crisis, but the BJP were re-elected once the dust settled.

In addition to its historic sites, Madhya Pradesh boasts the finest **wildlife reserves** on the subcontinent. In the sparsely populated east, remote savannah grasslands are an ideal habitat for deer and bison, while the shady *sal* forests and *tarai* swamplands that surround the *maidans* provide perfect cover for larger predators such as the **tiger**. Of the two **national parks** hidden away here, the more famous **Kanha** is deservedly popular, but if crowds bother you and you don't mind investing some extra time, check out **Bandhavgarh** northwest.

Getting around Madhya Pradesh without your own vehicle invariably involves a lot of bone-shaking bus journeys, usually under the auspices of MPSRTC, the state road transport authority. For longer distances, trains are the way to go. The *Central Railway*, the main broad-gauge line between Bombay and Calutta, scythes straight through the middle of the state between northern Maharashtra and southeast Uttar Pradesh, forking at **Itarsi** junction. One branch veers north towards Bhopal, Jhansi, Gwalior and Agra, while the other continues northeast to Varanasi and eastern India. In the far west, at Indore and the holy city of **Ujjain**, you can also pick up the *Western Railway*, which heads through eastern Rajasthan to Bharatpur and Delhi.

The **best time to visit** Madhya Pradesh is during the relatively cool winter months between November and February. In the hot season, in April, May and June, the region heats up like a furnace, and daytime temperatures frequently exceed 40°C. The rains finally sweep in from the southeast in late June or early July.

CENTRAL MADHYA PRADESH

All roads through the central regions of Madhya Pradesh lead to the state's capital, and its largest and fastest growing city – **Bhopal**. Although not the most attractive of cities – a perception not exactly improved by the appalling disaster of 1984 – it does make a reasonably interesting stopover, within easy access of the unmissable Buddhist *stupa* complex at **Sanchi**, and a number of even older sites. The prehistoric site of **Bhimbetka** is just 45km south of Bhopal, while at the attractive, but rarely visited hill station of **Pachmarhi**, further southeast, enjoyable hikes lead through craggy mountains and thick forests littered with more ancient rock-art sites.

Bhopal

With well over a million inhabitants, **BHOPAL**, the capital of Madhya Pradesh, consists of an amorphous mass of minarets, tightly packed streets and unfinished ferro-concrete suburbs, sprawling from the eastern shores of a huge artificial lake. Once, the gently sloping barren hills that rise from the southern and western sides of the old town centre lay well beyond its outer limits. Now these, together with acres of flat arid scrubland to the north, have been overtaken by creeping conurbation, industrial zones and miles of makeshift houses thrown up by Bhopal's beleaguered slum-dwellers. Aesthetically, it's far from being the most inspiring spectacle in central India. Nevertheless, if you're passing through on the main Delhi–Bombay railway, you could do a lot worse than break your journey here for a day.

In addition to the nineteenth-century **mosques** that bear witness to Bhopal's endur-ing Muslim legacy, the packed **bazaars** of the walled old city are well worth a visit. Elsewhere, excellent archeological **museums** house large hoards of ancient sculpture. **Bharat Bhavan**, on the lakeside, is one of India's premier centres for performing and visual arts, with an unrivalled collection of contemporary painting, sculpture and *adivasi* ("tribal") art, while the **Rashtriya Manav Sangrahalaya**, or "museum of man", is an open-air exhibition of *adivasi* houses and technology which aims to challenge prevailing stereotypes of the country's many indigenous groups.

History

Bhopal's name is said to derive from the eleventh-century **Raja Bhoj**, who was instructed by his court gurus to atone for the murder of his mother by linking up the nine rivers flowing through his kingdom. A dam, or *pal*, was built across one of them, and the ruler established a new capital around the two resultant lakes – **Bhojapal**. By the end of the seventeenth century, **Dost Muhammed**, an opportunistic ex-soldier of fortune and erstwhile general of Aurangzeb, had occupied the now-deserted site to carve out his own kingdom from the chaos left in the wake of the Moghul empire. The Muslim dynasty he established eventually became one of central India's leading royal families. Under the Raj, its members were among the select few to merit the accolade of a nineteen-gun salute from the British – a consequence of the help given to General Goddard in his march against the Maharathas in 1778. In the nineteenth century, Bhopal was presided over largely by women rulers. Holding court from behind the wicker screen of *purdah*, successive begums revamped the city with noble civic works, including the three sandstone **mosques** which still dominate the skyline.

Large areas of Bhopal have retained a distinctively Muslim feel. Communal unrest, however, was virtually unheard of here until December 1992, when rioting sparked off by the destruction of the Babri Masjid in Ayodhya led to the imposition of India's longest-ever curfew, lasting eleven days. Things have calmed down considerably since then, although the extreme-right Hindu fundamentalism of the BJP continues to cast its shadow over the mainly Muslim walled city.

Arrival, information and city transport

Bhopal's **airport**, served by daily *Indian Airlines* flights to and from Delhi and Bombay, is around a dozen kilometres by taxi or auto-rickshaw from the city. The main **railway station**, by contrast, is within easy walking distance of the centre; to reach the main hotel district, leave by the exit on platforms four or five, and head past the tonga rank until you reach the busy corner of **Hamidia Road**. Approaching Bhopal from the south, most trains also stop briefly at **Habibganj station**, a long way out – only get down here if you intend to stay in one of the expensive hotels in Shamla Hills or the New Market area. The **bus stand**, used by long-distance buses from Gwalior, Indore, Jabalpur, Pachmarhi, Sanchi and Ujjain is ten minutes' walk west of the railway station.

MPTDC, Madhya Pradesh's state tourist authority, have helpful **information** coun-ters in the arrivals hall at the station (platform one exit), and on the fourth floor of the Gangotri Building on TT Nagar, New Market (☎554340). They don't hand out street maps but are a useful source of travel information, and can pre-book accommodation if you plan to visit Pachmarhi or either of the national parks in eastern Madhya Pradesh.

There are two large **post offices**, one on TT Nagar in New Market and the other – the GPO, where **poste restante** letters end up – on Sultania Rd near the Taj-ul Masajid (Mon–Fri 10am–5pm, Sat 10am–noon). Two *State Banks of India* are currently the only places outside the top hotels to **change money** (Mon–Fri 10am–2pm, Sat 10am–12.30pm). One is opposite the bus stand, the other, inconveniently, is in the New Market district, ten minutes' by scooter south of the train station.

BHOPAL

RESTAURANTS:
① Manchar Ice Cream & Snack Bar
② Bagicha & Dragon Restaurants
③ Indian Coffee House

HOTELS:
Ⓐ Imperial Sabre
Ⓑ Shamla Palace
Ⓒ Lake View Ashok
Ⓓ Jehan Numa Palace
Ⓔ MPTDC Palash
Ⓕ Taj
Ⓖ Jyoti
Ⓗ Ramson's International

Ⓘ Richa
Ⓙ Gulshan
Ⓚ Ranjit
Ⓛ Rama International
Ⓜ Red Sea Plaza
Ⓝ Surya
Ⓞ Sangam
Ⓟ Deep
Ⓠ Shalimar Deluxe

Bhojpur, Bhimbetka & Itarsi △

△ Raisen

△ Sanchi & Delhi

△ Airport & Delhi

△ Indore & Ujjain

Habibganj Station

Arera Hill

Burla Mandir & Museum

Railway Station

Bus Stand

State Bank of India

CHOWK

Jama Masjid

Moti Masjid

Lower Lake

State Museum

British Library

New Market

ⓘ MPTDC Offices & Indian Airlines

GPO

Shaukat Mahal

Kilol Park

Bharat Bhavan

Ⓑ

Ⓓ

Ⓒ

Shamla Hills

Ⓔ

Taj-ul Masajid

Idgah Hills

Upper Lake

Museum of Man

Palace

Ⓐ

MP Emporium

Ⓜ Ⓝ

Ⓚ Ⓛ

③ Ⓞ

HAMIDIA RD

Ⓟ

Bus Stand

Ⓖ Ⓗ Ⓘ

Ⓕ ② Ⓙ

①

Chowk (bazaar)

City transport

Most of Bhopal's principal places of interest are so far apart (and frequently difficult to find) that the best way of **getting around** has to be by metered **auto-rickshaw**. The **tongas** parked up outside the train station might seem a less expensive option, but few of the emaciated horses look as though they'd make it out of the paddock. **Taxis** can be found outside all of the top hotels, or else arranged through MPTDC.

Tickets for MPTDC's **city tours** (Tues, Thurs & Sun, 9am–4pm) are available at the counter at the train station or the main office on TT Nagar. MPTDC also rent out *Ambassador* or *Maruti* **cars** and minibuses for around Rs1000 per day.

The City

Bhopal has two separate centres. Spread over the hill to the south of the lakes, the **New Market** area, as its name implies, is a recent extension of the city – a modest and largely uninteresting agglomeration of shopping arcades, ice-cream parlours, cinemas and modern office blocks. Once you've squeezed over the strip of land that divides the Upper and (smaller) Lower lakes, sweeping avenues, civic buildings and pleasure gardens quickly give way to the more heavily congested **old city**. Focused around the **Jama Masjid** mosque, or **Chowk** area, the **bazaar** occupies the dense grid of streets between **Moti Masjid Square** to the south and the most chaotic stretches of Hamidia Road to the north. The art **galleries** and **museums** are all well off the beaten track, tucked away down side-roads or on top of the hills that overlook the city.

Chowk

Bhopal's vibrant bazaar, situated in the old **Chowk** district, comes as a very welcome splash of colour after the dismal, traffic-filled streets around the train station. Famous for "*zarda*, *purdah*, *garda* and *namarda*" (tobacco, dust, veil, and eunuchs), its bustling back lanes have retained a Muslim ambience absent from most Indian cities. Many of the women only venture out in long black *burkhas*, while the older men, sporting *shalwa camises*, crocheted skull-caps and henna-ed beards, spend much of the day sitting cross-legged on their raised wooden shop-fronts or *haveli* balconies murmuring verses from the Koran. The bazaar is also a great place to shop for *tussar* silk, silver jewellery and the gaudily beaded women's purses for which Bhopal is renowned.

The most straightforward way to approach the northern – Hamidia Road – end of the bazaar is via the lane leading south off the busy crossroads by the main bus stand. Bear right at the bottom and you'll eventually come out near a large **fortified gateway** – one of the last remaining fragments of the walls that once encircled the Old City. At the very centre of the bazaar, the rich red sandstone walls and stumpy minarets of the **Jama Masjid** appear at the end of the street. Built in 1837 by Kudsia Begum, the mosque boasts neither age nor great architectural merit, but its whitewashed domes and gleaming gilded pinnacles lend an exotic air to proceedings in the square below. Most of the money that changes hands here does so in the dozens of open-fronted **silver shops** crouched around the base of the mosque itself. Pass through on any day except Friday or Monday (when most of Chowk Bazaar is closed) and you're sure to see large family groups huddled around sets of scales, scrutinizing the elaborate necklaces, belts, anklets and earrings worn by Muslim women on their wedding day.

Each of the narrow streets radiating from the square specializes in a different type of merchandise. One has a monopoly on brocaded "Chanderi" silk *saris*, another, west of the square, is given over to the bass-drums and wailing clarinets of Bhopali wedding bands, and others deal in brassware, film cassettes, spices or shoes.

The telephone **area code** for Bhopal is ☎0755.

THE BHOPAL GAS TRAGEDY

Bhopal is notorious as the site of the world's worst **industrial disaster**. In the early hours of December 2, 1984, a lethal cloud of methal icosynate, a toxic chemical used in the manufacture of pesticides, escaped from a tank at the huge Union Carbide plant on the northern edge of the city. The rapidly cooling air and a lack of wind that night kept the gas at ground level as it dispersed through the densely populated nearby residential districts and shanty settlements. By the end of the following day, the leak had left two thousand people dead and many times that number with chronic and incurable health problems.

Lax safety procedures were immediately blamed. Later, the decision by the then Chief Minister, Arjun Singh, not to evict the plant's low-paid workers from illegally built shacks along the perimeter of the factory compound was also singled out as having contributed to the high death toll. A decade on, however, with ultimate responsibility for the accident now admitted by Union Carbide, **compensation** for the victims has become the big issue. To date, $470 million has been handed over by the company; yet special courts set up to adjudicate the 659,000 claims have so far only managed to process a fraction of them – great for all the lawyers involved, but frustrating for the victims, who may have to wait for as long as twenty years before they see a *rupee* of what they are owed.

Imam Square to the Taj-ul Masajid

A short way southwest of the Chowk area, **Imam Square** was once the epicentre of royal Bhopal. Nowadays, it's little more than a glorified traffic island, only worth stopping at to admire the **Moti Masjid** on its eastern edge. The "Pearl Mosque", erected in 1860 by Sikander Begum, Kudsia's daughter, is a diminutive and much less imposing version of Shah Jahan's Jama Masjid in Old Delhi, notable more for its slender, gold-topped minarets and sandstone cupolas than its size.

Lining the opposite, northern side of the square near the ceremonial archway is a markedly more eccentric nineteenth-century building. The **Shaukat Mahal** palace was originally designed by a French architect (allegedly descended from the Bourbon kings) and is an unlikely fusion of Italian, Gothic and Islamic influences. Unfortunately, neither the palace nor the elegant **Sadar Manzil** ("Hall of Public Audience") nearby are officially open to visitors; both have been converted into government offices. No-one, however, is likely to stop you from having a quick look around.

Five minutes' walk west out of Imam Square (under the archway) brings you out at the foot of Bhopal's most impressive monument. With its matching pair of colossal pink minarets soaring high above the city skyline, the **Taj-ul Masajid** certainly lives up to its epithet (denoted by the extra "a" in its name) of "The Mother of All Mosques". Whether it also deserves to be dubbed the biggest in India, as locals claim, is rather less certain. The main **entrance**, on the south side at the end of a stretch of wasteland, opens onto a large walled courtyard and square *dukka* – the fountain and water tank used for ritual ablutions. From here, the bulbous white domes and multi-tiered towers flanking the facade are at their most imposing. Work on the building commenced under the auspices of Sultan Jehan Begum (1868–1901), the eighth ruler of Bhopal. After the death of her domineering husband, the Begum embarked on a spending spree that left the city with a postal system, new schools and a railway, but all but impoverished the royal family – the reason the Taj-ul Masajid was never completed.

The mosque is open to visitors every day except Friday, and during the Muslim festival of Id, which normally takes place in February. If you plan to venture inside, make sure you come suitably attired.

The state archeological museum

Hidden away near Raj Bhavan just south of Lower Lake, the modest, poorly labelled collection of ancient sculpture, bronzes and Moghul miniatures at the **Madhya**

Pradesh state archeological musem, or *Rajkiya Sangrahalaya* (Tues–Sat 10am–5pm), is only likely to inspire real enthusiasts. If you do end up here, among the more noteworthy exhibits in the main gallery are the second-century BC *yakshis* (female fertility figures), the standing Buddha in black granite and the fifth-century statue of Karttikeya, the Hindu god of war. The far wall in the last gallery holds a reproduction of the famous, now badly damaged, Bagh frescoes – contemporary with those at Ajanta in Maharashtra. On your way out through the main foyer, have a look at the plaster-cast souvenir copies of the exquisite *salabhanjika* figurine from Gyaraspur (see p.341). The original, one of India's most valuable pieces of stone sculpture, is locked away in the vaults of the Gwalior museum (see p.350).

The Birla Mandir museum

Much to the chagrin of the state museum, the **Birla Mandir** collection comprises some of the finest stone sculpture in Madhya Pradesh. It's also more informatively displayed, with explanatory panels in English in each of the main galleries. To get there, ask the rickshaw *wallah* for "Birla Mandir", the garish modern Hindu temple that stands high on the hill overlooking Lower Lake. The museum is in a large detached house a little further down the same side of the main road.

As usual, the exhibition is divided between Vishnu, the Mother Goddesses and Shiva. The **Vishnu** section contains some interesting representations of the god's diverse and frequently bizarre reincarnations (*avatars*), though the portly Rajnavahara – the wild boar whose form he adopted in order to rescue the Earth from the depths of the primordial ocean – hardly oozes with the panache one might expect of a cosmic super-hero. In the **Devi** gallery next door, a cadaverous Chamunda (the goddess Durga in her most terrifying aspect) stands incongruously amid a row of voluptuous maidens and fertility figures. Note the dying man writhing at her feet. The **Shiva** room, by contrast, is altogether more subdued. Many of the beautifully carved bas-reliefs show the god of preservation and destruction enjoying moments of marital bliss on Mount Kailash with his consort Parvati – an icon known as *Uma-Maheshwar*.

Finally, have a look at the replicas of the 3500-year-old **Harrapan** artefacts encased under the stairs. One of the seals bears an image of the pre-Aryan god Rudra, seated in the lotus position, who archeologists believe was the ancient forerunner of Shiva.

Bharat Bhavan

Inaugurated in 1982 as part of a national bid to promote visual and performing arts, **Bharat Bhavan** (daily; Feb–Oct 2–8pm, Nov–Jan 1–7pm) was originally intended as one of several such institutions set up in state capitals throughout the country. After Indira Gandhi's death, however, the initiative fizzled out, and Bhopal's contribution emerged as provincial India's most outstanding arts centre.

Once you're within range, the building isn't hard to find. Charles Correa's campus of concrete domes and dour brickwork was designed, apparently, to "merge in exquisite harmony with the landscape, creating a visual impact of spacious and natural elegance"; it might look less out of place on the Maginot Line. Fortunately, the prospect improves when you step inside. In addition to its large and sympathetically displayed collection of modern Indian painting, Bharat Bhavan has one gallery full of sculpture and another devoted exclusively to **adivasis art**. Talent scouts spent months roaming remote regions searching for artists to include. Among their more famous discoveries was the Gond painter **Jangarh Singh Shyam**, featured by veteran BBC correspondent Mark Tully in his recent book *No Full Stops In India*. A number of Jangarh's works are on display here, along with a colourful assemblage of masks, terracottas, wood-carvings and ritual paraphernalia. The absence of background information is intentional – the exhibition is intended to represent the objects as works of art in their own right, rather than merely anthropological curios.

If you're wondering how to spend an evening in Bhopal, scan the posters in the foyer for forthcoming **events** at Bharat Bhavan such as theatre productions and music and dance recitals. The pleasant cafe, to the right of the main building, is just the place to pen a couple of the tribal art **postcards** on sale in the office next to the gate.

Rashtriya Manav Sangrahalaya – the "Museum of Man"

The story of India's indigenous minorities – the *adivasis*, literally "original inhabitants" – is all too familiar. Dispossessed of their land by large-scale "development" projects or exploitative money-lenders, the "tribals" have seen a gradual erosion of their traditional culture – a process hastened by proselytizing missionaries and governments that tend at best to regard tribal people as anachronistic and, at worst, as an embarrassment. The **Rashtriya Manav Sangrahalaya** (daily 10am–6pm) is an enlightened attempt to redress the balance, setting out to provide genuine insights into ways of life few see at first hand. The aim is twofold: firstly to expose city people to the overall richness and ingenuity of India's tribal culture, and secondly to foster among the participants themselves a greater respect for their own heritage.

Overlooking the city on one side and the majestic sweep of Upper Lake on the other, the two-hundred-acre hill-top site includes a partially reconstructed "coastal village", a rock-art gallery, a research centre and, as its centrepiece, a permanent open-air exhibition of traditional *adivasis* dwellings and other structures collectively known as the "**tribal habitat**". Teams of *adivasis* building specialists and artisans from all over India were brought in to work on the project. Using only tools and materials available in their home environments, each group put together authentic replicas of its own highly distinctive houses, compounds, encampments, religious shrines and work-places.

Before tackling the exhibition proper, have a quick look at the **introductory gallery** in the small building opposite the main entrance. From here, a flight of steps leads underneath a thatched gateway (a structure adapted from the "youth dormitory" of the Ao-Naga from Nagaland) up to the top of the hill, where the seventeen or so dwelling complexes are scattered. On a quiet day, when hordes of noisy school children aren't scrambling around them, the empty mud huts, corrals and beaten-earth courtyards form a striking contrast with the teeming city below. Nearly all the **interiors** contain original tools, cooking utensils, baskets and musical instruments, while some are beautifully decorated with intricate **murals**, mouldings and carved beams. Of particular note are the multi-coloured paintings of horses adorning the walls of the Rathwa huts (look out for the picture of the train that carried the artists from their village in Gujarat); the ochre, red, black and yellow rectangular designs inside the Gadaba buildings (from Orissa); and the famous Warli wedding paintings of northern Maharashtra, which show the tribal fertility goddess Palghat framed by complex geometrical patterns. Other highlights include the giant votive terracotta statues of the tribal deities of Tamil Nadu's Ayyanar, and, both from Bastar in southeastern Madhya Pradesh, the wooden sculptures under the eaves of the Maria's shrine and the splendid twelve-metre-high chariot (*rath*) hauled by the Dashahana during their annual religious festival.

The only way of **getting to the museum** without your own vehicle is by auto-rickshaw; drivers are likely to insist on double the meter rate for the twenty-minute ride from the railway station, as they're unlikely to pick up a return fare, so negotiate a flat rate for the round trip, taking at least an hour's waiting time into consideration.

Accommodation

Visitors not too bothered by the roar of traffic and clouds of carbon monoxide shouldn't have to look much further than **Hamidia Road** for a **place to stay**. Bhopal's busy main thoroughfare, close to the train and bus stations, is crammed with hotels, ranging from grim "men-only" flea-pits to modern western-style establishments sporting bellboys and glitzy reception desks. Bargains are thin on the ground; all, even the dingiest dives, slap a ten percent "luxury" tax and an equally stiff "service charge" on to your bill. Most of Bhopal's **top hotels** eschew the noise and haste of the city centre in favour of more congenial locations close to **Upper Lake**, a ten-minute ride from the train station. Check-out time in all of the following is 24 hours unless otherwise stated.

Deep, behind *Sangam Cinema*, Hamidia Rd (☎545339). Basic but pleasant enough. Economy rooms are much the best value, but there are some with a/c. ③–④.

Gulshan, 3 Hamidia Rd (☎73506). Cavernous old building down a narrow back lane. Rooms are basic and cramped, but don't come much cheaper. ②.

Imperial Sabre, Palace Grounds (☎740542). Former Maharaja's lakeside guest house now gone to seed, with a/c rooms. Might appeal to die-hard Raj-ophiles. ⑤.

Jehan Numa Palace, 57 Shamla Hills (☎540107; fax 551992). Bhopal's most stylish and expensive hotel. Palazzo-style building around central courtyard, set in spacious grounds with top-notch restaurant, coffee shop, bar and foreign exchange, but no lake view. Noon check-out. ⑥–⑦.

Jyoti, 53 Hamidia Rd (☎76838). Small, respectable hotel with "non-alcoholic atmosphere", run by Gujarati family. Recommended for women travellers. Some a/c. ②–④.

Lake View Ashok, Shamla Hills (☎462013). Ugly building, but in a prime site overlooking the lake. All the usual facilities including money changing, swish restaurant and shops. ⑥–⑦.

MPTDC Palash, TT Nagar, near New Market (☎553006). Pleasant and popular, with 33 large rooms around a relaxing lawn. Good restaurant, cafe and bar. Book ahead. Noon check-out. ④–⑥.

Railway retiring rooms. Dorm beds and cheap rooms in train station. The cacophony of platform noises and nocturnal throat-clearing can be trying. Best avoided. ①–③.

Rama International, Hamidia Rd (☎543278). A shade more expensive than the *Gulshan*, but very much in the same mould. Some (cheap) a/c. ③.

Ramson's International, off Hamidia Rd (☎75299). Well appointed with satellite TV, restaurant, bar and verandah, though now over-priced and decidedly grubby. Noon check-out. ④.

Ranjit, Hamidia Rd (☎75211). Plain rooms (all with attached bathrooms), terrace bar and popular cheap restaurant downstairs. Good value. ②.

Red Sea Plaza, Hamidia Rd (☎75551). Large, functional hotel overlooking the train station. Handy for early-morning departures and weary travellers, but the tariffs are a little over the odds. ③–④.

Richa, 1 Hamidia Rd (☎76073). Clean and efficient, with satellite TV and hot water in all rooms. Good value. ③–⑤.

Sangam, Overbridge Rd (☎542328). Big building with variously priced, clean rooms on different floors. Fine for a night. ②–④.

Shalimar Deluxe, Hamidia Rd (☎77063). Nothing deluxe about it. Mentioned only because rock-bottom bathless singles are the cheapest in town. ②.

Shimla Palace, 31 Shimla Rd (☎540313). Very pleasant, family-run place in quiet suburban back-street overlooking the lake. Rooms, some with views, are neat and spacious. ⑤.

Surya, Hamidia Rd (☎76073). More upmarket than most, with facilities and prices to match. ④–⑥.

Taj, Hamidia Rd (☎73161). Poshest place in town centre. A bit boxed in, but rooms are fairly large, with satellite TV and some bath-tubs. Accepts most credit cards. Noon check-out. ③–⑥.

ACCOMMODATION PRICE CODES

All **accommodation prices** in this book have been coded using the symbols below. In principle the prices given are for the least expensive double rooms in each establishment; however, some hotels, usually in category ①, offer rates per bed rather than per room. Local taxes are not included unless specifically stated. For more details, see p.34.

①	up to Rs100	④	Rs225–350	⑦	Rs750–1200
②	Rs100–150	⑤	Rs350–500	⑧	Rs1200–2200
③	Rs150–225	⑥	Rs500–750	⑨	Rs2200 and up

Eating

Restaurants in Bhopal's larger hotels serve uniformly spicy north Indian food with a few Chinese dishes thrown in for good measure; the neon-strip-light-and-formica-furnishings cafes opposite the bus stand do *thalis* and hot platefuls of *subzi*, rice and *dal* for next to nothing. The Nepali-run *Manchar Ice-cream & Snack Bar*, a little further down the same side of Hamidia Rd (towards the train station), is just the place to soothe away the chilli-burn afterwards.

Bagicha Bar and Restaurant, Hamidia Rd. Mostly Moghul and Punjabi dishes served al fresco in courtyard. Pleasant but quite pricey.

Bharat Bhavan Cafe. Refreshingly mixed crowd of artists, workers and visitors lounge around on uncomfortable designer furniture. Tea, coffee and light snacks.

Dragon, Hamidia Rd. Noodle, stir-fry vegetable and meat dishes with distinctly Indian bias.

Indian Coffee Houses, New Market or next to *Sangam Cinema*. Bhopal's big breakfast venues offer tasty south Indian snacks, eggs and filter coffee served with great style. New Market branch is brighter and its popular "ladies room" is a haven for women travellers. Cheap.

Jehan Numa Palace, Shamla Hills. The best place to splash out on fine Moghul-style cuisine. Also has a good western menu.

Jyoti, 53 Hamidia Rd. Popular hotel-restaurant specializing in inexpensive traditional (mild, pure veg) Gujarati food. Lunchtime *thalis* particularly good value.

Kwality, New Market. A/c chain restaurant with varied menu and polished service. A little pricey.

Mehfil, below *Ranjit Hotel*, Hamidia Rd. Dingy-looking restaurant and bar serving up generous piles of no-nonsense Northern food to discerning office workers.

Palash, TT Nagar, New Market. Moderately priced, popular venue for business lunches and formal family dinners. Predictable but tasty food, with some Chinese and western options.

Listings

Airline Offices *Indian Airlines* have an office in the Gangotri complex on TT Nagar, New Market (☎61633), and a booking counter at the airport (☎8524).

Bookstores The two English language bookstores at the top of Bhadbada Rd in New Market stock a reasonable range of paperbacks (mostly popular fiction and Indian authors in translation). A more limited selection is available from the newsstand on platform one at the train station.

Hospital Bhopal's main Hamidia hospital (☎72222) is on Sultania Rd, between Imam Square and the Taj-ul Masajid. Doctors are best arranged through the top hotels.

Left Luggage Most hotels will look after your bags free of charge. If not, try the parcel office at the train station.

MOVING ON FROM BHOPAL

Bhopal is on one of the two broad-gauge **railway** lines between Delhi and Bombay. If you're heading **north** via Jhansi (for Orchha/Khajuraho), Gwalior or Agra, you have a choice between ten or so regular services and the superfast, completely a/c *Shatabdi Express*. India's answer to the bullet train leaves Bhopal daily at 1.40pm on the dot and arrives in **Delhi** a mere 7hr 40min later. The one train (apart from the passenger services) to avoid on this route is the super-slow *Amritsar-Dadar Express* #1058. In the other direction, the 5.52pm *Punjab Mail* #1037 is the best train for **Bombay**. For Jabalpur, Varanasi, Calcutta and all points **east**, you normally have to change at **Itarsi** junction, 92km south.

Most journeys from Bhopal are easier and quicker by train, but the city's good **bus** connections are especially useful for **Indore**, which can be reached either on frequent state buses or the daily MPSRTC superfast luxury coach service, which links with the arrival of the *Shatabdi Express* (for **Ujjain**, get off at Dewas and pick up a local bus for the remaining 37km). Tickets are sold at the MPTDC counter in the train station.

A daily train to **Sanchi** leaves Bhopal at 9.50am; there are also buses (see p.325).

Library The *British Council* have a library in the GTB Complex on Roshanpura Naka, New Market (Tues–Sat 11am–7pm; ☎553767). Non-members are welcome to peruse their collection of British newspapers, magazines and periodicals.

Shopping Chowk (closed Mon & Fri) is the best place for silk and silver; New Market (Tues–Sat) has some bigger stores – *Mrignayani* for handicrafts, men's calico shirts and trendy ethnic *shalwa camises*. The *MP State Emporium* on Hamidia Rd is the place to buy batiks, *dokra* metalwork, *khadi* clothes, bedspreads and silk *saris*..

Around Bhopal

A wealth of monuments scattered within a day's reach of Bhopal more than makes up for the state capital's own lack of sights. To the northeast, beyond **Raisen**'s dishevelled hill-top fort, the third-century BC *stupas* at **Sanchi** can be seen in a round trip from Bhopal, or as a stopover as you head north on the *Central Railway*. Sanchi's peaceful setting and good facilities make it an ideal base for visits to **Udaigiri**'s rock-cut caves, combined with a detour to the **Heliodorus pillar** – the last free-standing remains of the Mauryan city that paid for Sanchi. Avid templo-philes with the luxury of their own vehicle may also be enticed by the remote Gupta ruins at **Gyaraspur** and **Udayapur**.

Close to the main road south towards Hoshangabad and the Narmada Valley, the prehistoric cave paintings at **Bhimbetka** can be visited in a day by bus. If you rent a car, the eleventh-century Shiva temple at **Bhojpur**, with its monolithic *shivalingam*, is also worth checking out along the way.

Raisen

Resting on a sheer plateau, high above a sea of parched flat farmland 14km northeast of Bhopal, the ruined fort at **RAISEN** makes a nice break on a bus trip along the scenic back route to Sanchi, 23km further north. The citadel, erected by an independent local ruler around 1200 AD, became a stronghold of the Malwa Sultans two centuries later. The Rajput king Silhadi took over in 1520, but his rule was cut short after only twelve years by the Sultan of Gujarat, Bahadur Shah, who invaded on the pretext that the heathen Hindus had Muslim women locked up in their harem. It seems the rumour was ill-founded, for after the fort's male defenders had all been put to the sword, the seven hundred women inside threw themselves off the cliff rather than fall into the hands of the invaders. Raisen was repeatedly besieged in the years that followed, before being left to rot in the nineteenth century. Today, the once-grand complex of palaces, mosques, temples and tanks lies in ruins, inhabited only by troupes of mangy pink-bottomed monkeys and a lonely ASI caretaker who must be wondering what he did in a past life to deserve a posting in such a forlorn place.

The stony **path** up to the fort from the main road begins behind the improbably named "S & M Convent School", near a small Muslim *dargah*, or shrine-tomb – ask the **bus** between Bhopal and Vidisha to drop you off here and not in the town proper, another kilometre down the road. There is no clean drinking **water** on top of the hill, so take plenty with you – the stiff twenty-minute climb up the rocky hillside can be thirsty work. Beyond a series of fortified **gateways**, surmounted by crumbling pavilions, you come to the imposing battlements that encircle the fort. The main **ruins** are on the far northern end of the plateau, reached along the track to the right. En route to this clutter of tumbledown colonnaded courtyards, corridors and half-collapsed buildings, crowned with gently curving Afghan domes, you pass a couple of impressive **tanks**, lined with pond-weed and pools of stagnant green water. In the one wing of the old palace still in good shape, to the right of the main walkway, a courtyard strewn with rusting cannons is surrounded by arched cloisters, and the elegant projecting **balcony** from which Raisen's womenfolk committed suicide during the siege of 1532.

Sanchi

From a distance, the smooth-sided hemispherical object that appears on a hillock over-looking the main railway line at **SANCHI**, 46km northeast of Bhopal, has the surreal air of a space station or an upturned satellite dish. In fact, the giant stone mound stands as testimony to a much older means of communing with the cosmos. Quite apart from being India's finest surviving Buddhist monument, the **Great Stupa** is one of the earliest religious structures in the subcontinent. It presides over a complex of ruined temples and monasteries that collectively provide a rich and unbroken record of the development of Buddhist art and architecture from the faith's first emergence in central India during the third century BC, until it was eventually squeezed out by the resurgence of Brahmanism during the medieval era.

A visit to Sanchi, however, is no dry lesson in South Asian art history. The main *stupa* is surrounded by some of the richest and best-preserved ancient **sculpture** you're ever likely to see *in situ*, while the site itself, floating serenely above a vast expanse of open plains, has preserved the tranquillity that must have attracted its original occupants. Most visitors find a couple of hours more than sufficient to explore the ruins, although you could spend days poring over the four exquisite gateways, or **toranas**, that surround the Great Stupa. Paved walkways and steps lead around the hill-top enclosure (daily 8am–6pm), dotted with interpretative panels and shady trees to relax under if the heat gets the better of you.

The site is connected to the small village at the foot of the hill by a metalled road. Once you've bought a fifty-*paise* entrance ticket from the booth outside the **museum**, head up the stone steps on the right, past the welcoming posse of postcard-*wallahs*, to the main entrance. From here, the central walkway runs alongside the new Buddhist Vihara and a cold drink stall, before making straight for the Great Stupa.

History

Unlike the other famous Buddhist centres in eastern India and Nepal, Sanchi has no known connection with the life of Buddha himself. It first became a place of pilgrimage when the Mauryan emperor **Ashok**, who married a woman from nearby **Besnagar** (see p.340), erected a polished stone pillar and brick-and-mortar *stupa* here midway through the third century BC. The complex was enlarged by successive dynasties, but after the eclipse of Buddhism Sanchi lay deserted and overgrown until its rediscovery in 1818 by General Taylor of the Bengal Cavalry. In the years that followed, a swarm of heavy-handed treasure hunters invaded the site, eager to crack open the giant stone eggs and make off with what they pictured as their valuable contents. In fact, only *stupas* number three and four yielded anything more than rubble (a couple of soap-stone relic caskets, now in the British Museum). These amateur archeologists, however, left the ruins in a sorry state. Deep gouges gaped from the sides of *stupas* one and two, a couple of ceremonial gateways completely collapsed, and much of the masonry was plundered by the villagers for building materials (one local landlord is alleged to have carted off Ashok's pillar to use as a roller in his sugar cane press).

Restoration work made little impact until the archeologist John Marshall and the Buddhist scholar Albert Foucher took on the job in 1912. The jungle was hacked away, the main *stupas* and temples were rebuilt, lawns and trees planted and a museum erected to house what sculpture had not been shipped off to Delhi or London.

Stupa one

Stupa one, the "Great Stupa", stands on a stretch of level ground at the western edge of the plateau. Fragments of the original construction, a much smaller version built in the third century BC by Ashok, still lie entombed beneath the thick outer shell of concrete and lime plaster added a century later. The **Shungas** were also responsible for the raised processional balcony, and the two graceful staircases that curve gently around the sides of the drum from the paved walkway at ground level, as well as the aerial-like *chhattra* and its square enclosure which crown the top of the mound. Four elaborate gateways were added next by the **Satavahanas** in the first century BC, followed by the four serene **meditating Buddhas** that greet you as you pass through the main entrances. Carved out of local sandstone, these were installed during the Gupta era, around 450 AD, by which time figurative depictions of Buddha had become acceptable (elsewhere in Sanchi, the Master is euphemistically represented by an empty throne, a wheel, a pair of footprints or even a parasol).

As you move gradually closer to the *stupa*, the extraordinary wealth of sculpture plastered over the **toranas** slips slowly into focus. Staring up at these masterpieces from below, you can see why archeologists believe them to have been the work of ivory craftsmen. Every conceivable nook and cranny of the eight-metre upright posts and three curving cross-bars teems with delicate figures of humans, demi-gods and goddesses, birds, beasts and propitious symbols. Some of the larger reliefs depict narratives drawn from the lives of Gautama Buddha and his six predecessors, the Manushis, while others recount Ashok's dissemination of the faith. In between, there are plenty of purely decorative panels too, as well as illustrations of heaven intended to inspire worshippers to lead meritorious lives on earth. Start with the *torana* on the south side, which is the oldest, and proceed in a clockwise direction around the *stupa* – as is the custom at Buddhist monuments.

SOUTHERN TORANA

Opening directly onto the ceremonial staircase, the **southern torana** was the Great Stupa's principal entrance, as is borne out by the proximity of the stump of Ashok's original stone pillar. Over the years, some of the best sculpted panels have dropped off the gateway (and are now housed in the site museum), but those that remain on the three cross-beams are still in reasonable condition. A carved frieze on the middle architrave shows Ashok, complete with royal retinue, visiting a *stupa* (apparently to plunder its contents). On the reverse side, the scene switches to one of the Buddha's previous incarnations. For the **Chhaddanta Jataka**, the *bodhisattva* adopts the guise of an elephant who, in extreme selflessness, helps an ivory hunter saw off his own (six) tusks.

STUPAS

The hemispherical mounds known as **stupas** have been central to Buddhist worship since the sixth century BC, when Buddha himself modelled the first prototype. Asked by one of his disciples for a symbol to help disseminate his teachings after his death, the Master took his begging bowl, teaching staff and a length of cloth – his only worldly possessions – and arranged them into the form of a *stupa*, using the cloth as a base, the upturned bowl as the dome and the stick as the projecting finial, or spire.

Originally, *stupas* were simple burial mounds of compacted earth and stone containing relics of the Buddha and his followers. As the religion spread, however, the basic components multiplied and became imbued with **symbolic significance**. The main dome, or **anda** – representing the sacred mountain, or "divine axis" linking heaven and earth – grew larger, while the wooden railings, or **vedikas**, surrounding it were replaced by massive stone ones. A raised ambulatory terrace, or **medhi**, was added to the vertical sides of the drum, along with two flights of stairs and four ceremonial entrances, carefully aligned with the cardinal points. Finally, crowning the tip of the *stupa*, the single spike evolved into a three-tiered umbrella, or **chhattra**, standing for the Three Jewels of Buddhism: the Buddha, the Law and the community of monks, or Sangha.

The *chhattra*, usually enclosed within a low square stone railing, or **harmika** (a throwback to the days when sacred *bodhi* trees were surrounded by fences) formed the topmost point of the axis, directly above the reliquary in the heart of the *stupa*. Ranging from bits of bone wrapped in cloth, to fine caskets of precious metals, crystal and carved stone, the reliquaries were the "seeds" and their protective mounds the "egg". Excavations on the 84,000 *stupas* scattered around the subcontinent have shown that the solid interiors were also sometimes built as elaborate **mandalas** – invisible patterns that exerted a beneficial influence over the *stupa* and those who walked around it. The ritual of circumambulation, or **pradhakshina**, which enabled the worshipper to tap into a magical force-field and be transported from the mundane to the divine realms, was always carried out in a clockwise direction from the east, in imitation of the sun's passage across the heavens.

Of the half-dozen or so giant *stupa* sites dotted around ancient India, only **Sanchi** has survived to the present day. To see one in action, however, you have to follow in the footsteps of Ashok's missionaries southwards to Sri Lanka, northwards to the Himalayas and the Tibetan plateau, or across the Bay of Bengal to Southeast Asia, where, as "**dagobas**", "**chortens**" and "**chedis**", *stupas* are still revered as repositories of sacred energy.

WESTERN TORANA

The **western torana** collapsed during the depredations of the nineteenth century, but has been skilfully restored. Some of Sanchi's liveliest sculpture appears around its two square posts. In the top right panel, a troop of monkeys scurries across a bridge over the Ganges, made from his own body by the *bodhisattva*, their leader, to help them escape a gang of soldiers (below). According to the **Mahakapi Jataka**, the troops were dispatched by the local king to capture a coveted mango tree from which the monkeys had been feeding. You can also just about make out the final scene, where the repentant monarch gets a stern ticking-off from the *bodhisattva* under a *peepal* tree. Meanwhile, high on the top cross-beam, the eight Buddhas, including Maitreya, the Buddha-to-come, appear as a line of *bodhi* trees and *stupas*.

One of the most frequently represented episodes from the life of the Buddha features on the first two panels of the left-hand post facing the *stupa*. In the **Temptation of Mara**, the Buddha, who has vowed to remain under the *bodhi* tree until he attains enlightenment, heroically ignores the attempts of the evil demon Mara to distract him with threats of violence and seductive women (Mara's beautiful daughters). Notice the contrast at the end between Mara's agitated troops and the solemn-faced procession of angels who accompany Buddha after he has achieved his goal.

NORTHERN TORANA

Crowned with a fragmented Wheel of the Law and two tridents symbolizing the Buddhist trinity, the **northern torana** is the most elaborate and best preserved of the four gateways. Scenes crammed onto its two vertical posts include Buddha performing an aerial promenade – one of many stunts he pulled to impress a group of heretics – and a monkey presenting the Master with a bowl of honey. Straddling the two pillars, a bas-relief on both faces of the lowest cross-beam depicts the **Vessantara Jataka**, telling of a *bodhisattva*-prince banished by his father for giving away a magical rain-making elephant. During his exile, the over-generous Vessantara was persuaded to part with everything else that was dear to him, including his wife and kids, before finally being forgiven by the king. A better view of the inner, south-facing side of the plaque can be had from the balcony of the *stupa*'s raised terrace. Note the little tableau on the far right showing the royal family trudging through the jungle: the prince's son is holding his father's hand, while his daughter clings to her mother's hip. The four **elephants** sculpted from the capital supporting the architraves are also very realistic, as are other, smaller elephants, horses and female wood-nymphs separating the three beams.

EASTERN TORANA

Leaning languorously into space from the right capital of the **eastern torana** is Sanchi's most celebrated piece of sculpture, the sensuous **salabhanjika**, or wood-nymph. The full-breasted fertility goddess is one of several such figures that once blessed worshippers as they entered the Great Stupa. Only a few, however, still remain in place, others having been removed to Los Angeles and London. Her *tribhanga*, or hip-shot stance is a classical dance pose which, from this moment onwards, was to become a distinctive feature of all Indian religious sculpture.

Panels on the inner face of the pillar below the *salabhanjika* depict scenes from the life of the Buddha, including his conception when the *bodhisattva* entered the body of his mother, Maya, in the form of a white elephant, shown astride a crescent moon. The front face of the middle architrave picks up the tale some years later, when the young Buddha, represented by a riderless horse, makes his **Great Departure** from the palace where he grew up to begin the life of a wandering ascetic. The reverse side shows the fully enlightened Master, now symbolized by an empty throne, with a crowd of celestial beings and jungle animals paying their respects.

Elsewhere around the enclosure

Of the dozens of other numbered ruins around the 400-metre enclosure, only a handful are of more than passing interest. Smaller, plainer and graced with only one ceremonial gateway, the immaculately restored **stupa three**, immediately northeast of *stupa* one, is upstaged by its slightly older cousin in every way but one. In 1851, a pair of priceless reliquaries were discovered deep in the middle of the mound. Turned on a lathe from a fine marble-like soapstone called steatite, the caskets were found to contain relics belonging to two of Buddha's closest disciples. In one, fragments of bone were encased with beads made from pearls, crystal, amethyst, lapis lazuli and gypsum, while on the lid, the initial of the saint they are thought to have belonged to, Sariputra, was painted in ink. Both are now in the British Museum, along with several other treasures pilfered from Sanchi.

From *stupa* three, pick your way through the clutter of pillars, small *stupas* and exposed temple floors nearby to the large complex of interconnecting raised terraces at the far **eastern edge** of the site. The most intact monastery of the bunch, **vihara forty-five**, dates from the ninth and tenth centuries, and has the usual layout of cells ranged around a central courtyard. Originally, a colossal, richly decorated sanctuary tower also soared high above the complex, but this collapsed to leave the inner sanctum exposed. The river goddesses Ganga and Yamuna number among the skilfully sculpted figures flanking the entrance to the shrine itself – testimony to the mounting popularity of Brahminism at the start of the medieval era. Inside, however, Buddha still reigns supreme. Regally enthroned on a lotus bloom, his right hand touches the ground to call upon the earth goddess to witness the moment of his enlightenment.

The enclosure's tenth-century eastern **boundary wall** is the best place from which to enjoy Sanchi's serene **views**. To the northeast, a huge, sheer-sided rock rises from the midst of Vidisha, near the site of the ancient city that sponsored the monasteries here (traces of the **pilgrimage trail** between Besnagar and Sanchi can still be seen crossing the hillside below). South from the hill, a wide expanse of well-watered wheatfields, dotted with clumps of mango and palm trees, stretches off towards the angular sandstone ridges of the Raisen escarpment on the distant horizon.

THE SOUTHERN AREA

The **southern area** of the enclosure harbours some of Sanchi's most interesting **temples**. Pieces of burnt wood dug from the foundations of **temple forty** prove that the present apsidal-ended *chaitya* was built on top of an earlier structure contemporary with the Mauryan *stupa* one. **Temple seventeen** is a fine example of early Gupta architecture and the precursor of the classical Hindu design developed later in Orissa and Khajuraho. Its small, flat-roofed sanctum is entered via an open-sided porch held up by four finely carved pillars with lion capitals. Nearby, directly opposite the Great Stupa's southern entrance, the tall slender pillars of **temple eighteen** lend it a distinctly Greek air – a legacy of the lingering presence of Alexander the Great's descendants, the Bactrians, in northwest India at the time of its construction in the seventh century.

Before leaving the enclosure, hunt out the stump of Ashok's pillar (#10) to the right of *stupa* one's southern *torana*. Columns such as this were erected by the Mauryan emperor all over the empire to mark sacred sites and pilgrims' trails (see *Contexts*). Its finely polished shaft (made, like all Ashokan pillars, with a sandstone known as Chunar after a quarry on the Ganges near Varanasi) was originally crowned with the magnificent lion capital now housed in the site museum. The inscription etched around its base is in Pali, the forerunner of all Indian scripts.

The western slope

A flight of steps beside *stupa* one leads down the **western slope** of Sanchi hill to the village, passing two notable monuments. The bottom portions of **vihara fifty-one**'s thick stone walls have been carefully restored to show its floor-plan of 22 cells around a paved central courtyard. Further down, the second-century BC **stupa two** stands on an artificial ledge, well below the main enclosure – probably because its relics were less important than those of *stupas* one and three. The ornamental railings and gateways around it are certainly no match for those up the hill, although the carvings of lotus medallions and mythical beasts (including some bizarre horse-headed women) that decorate them are worth checking out. The straps that dangle from some of the horse-rider's saddles are believed to mark the first appearance in India of stirrups.

The archeological museum

Sanchi's small **archeological museum** (daily except Fri 10am–5pm; Rs0.50), just behind the admission kiosk to the left of the road up to the hill-top, houses a modest collection of artefacts, mostly fragments of sculpture recovered during successive excavations. Its **main hall** contains the most impressive pieces, including the famous Ashokan lion-capital (see above) and two damaged *salabhanjikas* from the gateways of *stupa* one. Also of note are the distinctive Mathuran red sandstone Buddhas, believed to have been sent to Sanchi from Gandhara in the far northwest of India – source of the first figurative representations of the Master. The best preserved of them dates from the Gupta period around the fourth century AD. Gallery one contains more large pieces of sculpture, while the remaining sections are devoted to smaller antiquities – votive terracotta figurines, stone plaques, jewellery, pottery, weapons and tools.

Sanchi practicalities

Although Sanchi is on the main Delhi–Bombay railway line, **getting there** by **train** can be a tricky and arcane business, as few services (mostly painfully slow passenger trains) make scheduled stops. One notable exception is the 9.50am departure from Bhopal, which takes only one hour to cover the 47km. First-class passengers who have come at least 161km can also arrange to make a "special halt" at Sanchi – except for some obscure reason on the "superfast" a/c chair services, like the *Shatabdi Express*, which only stop at Bhopal. The nearest mainline station is **Vidisha**, 10km northeast.

Buses from Bhopal to Sanchi depart from the main city bus stand more or less hourly, and ply two different routes. The longer and more scenic southern one takes two and a half hours, passing through Raisen on the way (68km), while the more direct northern road follows the *Central Railway* line, taking around an hour and a half.

Cheap **accommodation** can be found in the unusually good *Retiring Rooms* at the train station (①), or else at the nearby *Sri Lanka Mahabodhi Society Guest House* (☎239; ①), where a Rs30 donation is requested for a *charpoi* in a bare cell. Moving up the scale, the MPTDC *Tourist Cafeteria* (☎243; ③), next door to the museum, has two plain but clean rooms with attached shower-toilets. By far the most comfortable option in Sanchi, however, has to be the other MPTDC hotel, the *Tourist Lodge* (☎223; ④–⑤), five minutes' walk south of the crossroads. Their eight spacious and spotless rooms (including two a/c) are excellent value, but often fully booked; try to reserve at least five days in advance through any MPTDC office, or in Delhi (see p.115). If everywhere else turns out to be full when you arrive, the *Government Rest House* (①) behind the *Tourist Cafeteria* may have basic rooms free.

MPTDC also has the monopoly on good **places to eat** in Sanchi. The *Tourist Cafeteria* offers the usual range of over-priced snacks and drinks, while the *Tourist Lodge*'s menu of standard Indian and Chinese favourites is the better option for a more substantial evening meal. If you don't want to risk an omelette and a glass of *chai* at the stalls by the station, this is also the best venue for breakfast.

Finally, **bicycles** – good for trips to the nearby Udaigiri and Kandagiri caves (see p.340) – can be rented for next to nothing from the stand at the crossroads.

Vidisha

The main reason to call in at the gritty railroad and market town of **VIDISHA**, a straightforward 56-kilometre train or bus ride from Bhopal, and also served by buses from nearby Sanchi, is to hop on a tonga to the archeological sites at Udaigiri and Besnagar. However, if you're not pushed for time, the small **museum** (Tues–Sun 10am–5pm; Rs2), hidden away behind the train station in the east of town, is also worth a visit. The majority of its prize pieces, such as the three-metre fertility goddesses (*yakshi*) in the hallway, are second-century Hindu artefacts unearthed at Besnagar. Attractive Jain *tirthankaras* and lumps of masonry salvaged from the district's plethora of ruined Gupta temples litter the garden outside.

Vidisha is also known for having financed a prolific third-century BC spate of *stupa* construction, including much of the work at Sanchi. By the sixth century AD however, it lay deserted and in ruins, remaining so until the arrival of the Muslims three hundred years later when a settlement, called **Bhilsa**, was founded around the flat-topped hill in the centre of the modern town. Vidisha's other rather tenuous claim to fame is that the bricks of a nearby second-century BC Vishnu temple were stuck together with lime mortar, believed to be the world's oldest **cement**.

Udaigiri and Besnagar

The modest collection of rock-cut caves and ruined temples at **Udaigiri** lie 6km west of Vidisha, scattered around a long thin outcrop of sandstone that rises from the surrounding patchwork of yellow and green wheatfields. Much the most congenial way to explore the area is on one of the tongas that hang around outside Vidisha's bus stand (Rs20–30 round trip), though the site is also an easy cycle ride from Sanchi.

The road out from Vidisha crosses the **River Betwa** via an old stone bridge, shortly after emerging from the bazaar on the edge of town. The whitewashed temples and *ghats* on either side of the river mark a holy bathing spot. Several stone plaques carved with handprints commemorate acts of ritual self-immolation (*satis*), performed here in the past by newly widowed women.

Once across the river, either turn left to Udaigiri, or head straight on to the ruins of ancient **BESNAGAR**. During the time of the Mauryan and Shunga empires, between the third and first centuries BC, a thriving provincial capital overlooked the confluence of the Bes and Betwa rivers. The emperor **Ashok** himself was governor here at one time, and even married a local girl – the daughter of a Besnagar banker. Nowadays, a few mounds and some scattered pieces of masonry are all that remain of the houses, *stupas*, temples and streets. One small monument, however, makes the short detour worthwhile. According to the inscription etched around its base, the stone pillar over-looking the river bank, known as the **Column of Heliodorus**, was erected in 113 BC by a Bactrian-Greek envoy from Taxila, the capital city of Gandhara (now the northwest frontier region of Pakistan). The shaft, dedicated to Krishna's father Vasudeva, was originally crowned with a statue of Vishnu's vehicle Garuda. Heliodorus converted to the local Vaishnavite cult during his long diplomatic posting here. Most of the other archeological finds dug up on the site – including a colossal fertility goddess (*yakshi*) – have been removed to the museum in Vidisha.

UDAIGIRI lies at the end of a long tree-lined avenue from the Betwa bridge. Most of the hillside's twenty or so fifth-century Hindu and Jain caves are small single-celled sanctuaries scraped from the foot of its near-vertical, east-facing escarpment. The first one along the road, **cave nineteen** at the far northern end of the cliff, has worn but attractive reliefs of gods and demons above its doorways. The Nandi bull and *lingams* inside were later additions. From the right of the cave entrance, a path climbs steeply up to the top of the hill. Hunt out the fifth-century **Jain temple** carved into the rocks at the far end, then follow the path south, past the **hill-top ruins** of a large Hindu temple, until it drops down again through a gap between two bluffs.

The most interesting cluster of caves are opposite the tiny terracotta-roofed village on the roadside. An ASI *chowkidar* should be around to unlock the doors for you. The site's *pièce de résistance*, a four-metre image of the boar-headed hero Varaha, stands at the back of the verandah in **cave five**. Vishnu adopted the guise of this long-snouted monster to rescue the earth-goddess, Prithvi (perched on a lotus next to his right shoulder) from the churning primordial ocean – depicted by delicate wavy lines. Varaha's left foot rests on a Naga king wearing a hood of thirteen cobra heads, while the river goddesses Ganga and Yamuna hold water vessels on either side. In the background you can see Brahma and Agni, the Vedic fire-god, plus sundry sages and musicians. The scene, prominent in many contemporary Hindu monuments, has been interpreted as an allegory of the emperor Chandragupta II's conquest of northern India.

Other caves worth a quick look are number **four**, known as the "Veena cave" after the figure playing an Indian lute carved above its doorway, and number **one**, at the top of the southernmost hillock, which according to an inscription was excavated in 272 AD, making it the oldest at Udaigiri. The icon of the twenty-third Jain *tirthankara* Parshvanath that it now houses must have been placed there at a later date.

Gyaraspur

The middle-of-nowhere market town of **GYARASPUR** may have been an important provincial capital during the Pratihara era, a thousand or more years ago, but it now languishes in obscurity at the end of a sixty-minute ride down a pot-holed back-road from Vidisha, which is 35km southwest. Daily **buses** connect the two, although as there's nowhere to stay in Gyaraspur, trips from either Sanchi or Bhopal are not really feasible without your own vehicle. Friday, when all the local villagers pour in on their bullock carts for the weekly **market**, is the best day to visit.

The most interesting of the handful of dilapidated monuments that survive is the ninth-century **Maladevi Mandir**, clinging to the scarp-side of the steep narrow rocky spur behind the town. Reached via a motorable dirt track, the temple terrace looks over a sweeping vista of geometric farmland and a low, thinly wooded ridge of hills that tapers away southwest. Originally, the building's ornate sandstone surfaces would have included fine individual pieces of sculpture. Over the years, however, many of these have either crumbled away down the hill or, like the exquisite *salabhanjika* (wood nymph) now locked in the vaults of the Gwalior museum, been carried off somewhere else. Maladevi's cavernous interior, partially cut from the surrounding hillside, houses a small collection of Buddha-like Jain *tirthankaras* together with a few Hindu fertility goddesses encrusted with bat droppings. There's no need to slip your shoes off before stepping inside; the sanctum is no longer kept as a living shrine.

At the foot of the hill on the opposite side of town, 1500m west, a couple of stone posts and four small seated Buddha figures are all that's left of Gyaraspur's oldest monument, a sixth-century **stupa**. On the way over, look out for eight richly carved columns mounted on a raised plinth in a patch of open ground near the market place – the remains of another ninth-century Hindu temple, the **Atha Khamba**.

Udayapur

Remote, rural **UDAYAPUR**, 73km northeast of Bhopal, is the site of one of Madhya Pradesh's least-visited architectural gems. Unfortunately, to get there from Bhopal or Vidisha, you have to catch a train to **Basoda**, and then a local bus for the final 10km. Check the return times carefully before leaving, as there's nowhere to stay in the town, with the possible exception of the first-class waiting room at the train station.

The magnificent **Neelkantheswara temple**, built in 1080 AD by the Paramara king Udayadita, took 22 years to complete and is considered to be on a par with its illustrious cousins at Khajuraho, even if its sculpture is rather more restrained. Its sandstone *shikhara* soars high above the surrounding clutter of dusty streets. Some of the best stonework is to be found in the niches around the huge curvilinear sanctuary tower. A large panel on the front face frames a dancing Shiva, **Nataraj**, surmounted by a sea monster with bulging eyes and the seven mother goddesses, the Sapta Matrikas. The doorways of the three entrance porches of the pyramidal-roofed *mandapa* assembly hall, are also richly carved with demi-gods and goddesses, including several amorous couples. Inside, the pillars are encrusted with garlands of flowers and bells, in marked contrast to the bare shrine room, which still houses a living *shivalingam*.

Bhojpur

Raja Bhoj's legendary mania for hydraulic experiments was by no means confined to Bhopal. At **BHOJPUR**, 28km southeast of the capital (and devoid both of direct bus services and of any accommodation), the eleventh-century Paramara ruler created another enormous tank, this time from the waters of the River Betwa. Enclosed by a ridge of hills on one side and two enormous earth embankments on the other, the 400-

square-kilometre artificial lake was eventually destroyed by the second Sultan of Mandu, Hoshang Shah, when his invading army cut a breach through the smaller of the two dams. Legend has it that the water took three years to seep through the rupture, and that its eventual disappearance transformed the local climate.

With the lake long gone and its stone-lined dams supporting no more than a road to a nearby village, Bhojpur's only real attraction these days is its colossal **Shiva temple** – another of the Raja's large-scale projects. The **Bhojeshwar Mandir** rests unfinished and dishevelled, but not entirely forlorn, on a rocky bluff, amid a patchwork of fertile farmland and tiny hamlets stretching south towards the Vindhya hills. It's a pleasant spot, and one which sees little more than a trickle of visitors. The few who do venture out here come primarily to pay their respects to the temple's imposing centrepiece – a two-and-half-metre-tall polished limestone *shivalingam*, maintained as a living shrine. It rests on an even more enormous pedestal (*yonipatha*), from which the resident *pujari* dispenses smudges of vermillion powder to worshippers. High above his head, the domed ceiling of the sanctuary, though incomplete, is encrusted with some well-preserved sculpture and a couple of appropriately large beehives. A stone's throw away north, beyond a jumble of boulders and collapsed masonry, the ASI have fenced off a flat rock onto which the Raja's architects chiselled their original plans for the temple. This is also a good place to view the remnants of the earthen **ramp** they used to raise chunks of unworked stone up to the roof.

Look out for the yellow pennants of the **Jain shrine** directly behind the sanctuary, at the end of the dirt track up from the village. Its central icon is a giant stone image of **Mahavira**, the sixth-century founder of the faith, represented in the attitude of "immobile bodily discipline" (standing erect, with arms and hands held at the side) similar to the famous seventeen-metre statue of Gommateshvara in Karnataka. This one's a lot smaller than its southern cousin, but is still among the largest of its kind.

Bhimbetka

Shortly after NH12 peels away from the main Bhopal–Hoshangabad road, 45km southeast of the state capital, a long line of boulders appears high on a scrub-covered ridge to the west. The hollows, overhangs and crevices eroded over the millennia from the crags of this malleable sandstone outcrop harbour one of the world's largest collections of **prehistoric rock art**. Discovered in 1957 by the archeologist Dr VS Wankaner, **BHIMBETKA** is South Asia's equivalent of the cave complexes at Lascaux in southwest France and Altamira in Spain, or the rock paintings of aboriginal Australia. If you have your own transport, or are prepared to do a bit of walking to get here, this rarely visited site makes a fascinating day trip from Bhopal.

Of the thousand **shelters** so far catalogued along the ten-kilometre hill-top, around half contain rock paintings. These date from three different periods, each with its own distinctive style. The oldest fall into two categories: green outline drawings of human figures, and large red images of animals. Lumps of haematite (from which the red pigment was manufactured) unearthed amid the deepest excavations on the site have been carbon-dated to reveal origins in the upper-**paleolithic** era, around ten thousand years ago. The second, and more prolific phase accounts for the bulk of Bhimbetka's rock art, and took place in the late-**mesolithic** – the "stone age" – between 8000 and 5000 BC. These friezes depict dynamic hunting scenes full of rampaging animals, initiation ceremonies, burials, masked dances, sports, wars, pregnant women, an arsenal of different weapons, and even what seems to be a drinking party. No-one is sure why these sophisticated communities of hunter-gatherers decorated their temporary abodes in this way. One theory is that the cave art served the ritual or **magical** function of ensuring a plentiful supply of game; but while abundant depictions of bison, wild boar, antelope and deer lend credence to that notion, animals such as tigers and elephants also appear, that were not on the mesolithic menu.

Shards of pottery found amid the accumulated detritus on the rock-shelter floors show that Bhimbetka's third and final spate of cave painting took place during the early historic period, after its inhabitants had begun to trade with settled agriculturalists. Their stylized, geometric figures bear a strong resemblance to the art still produced by the region's *adivasi*, or tribal groups.

From the car park at the top of the hill, a paved pathway winds through the jumble of rocks containing the most striking and accessible of Bhimbetka's paintings. A *chowkidar* wielding a long stick will, for a bit of *baksheesh*, point out the highlights. As you wander around, look out for the paleolithic images in green, the wonderful "X-ray" animals in-filled with cross-hatching and complex geometric designs, and the recurrent image of a bull chasing a human figure and a crab – a motif believed to represent a struggle between the totemic heroes of three different tribes. At the bottom of the track, on the base of a tall column of sandstone not included in the guides' whistlestop tour, there's also a very fine wild boar in black and red.

Practicalities

Without your own vehicle, **getting to Bhimbetka** from Bhopal involves an 80-minute bus journey, with a change 10km short at the market town of **Obaidullaganj**. From there, hop on one of the frequent buses bound for **Hoshangabad** and get off after about 7km when you see a sign to the right in Hindi (with "3.2" written on it). The side road runs over a level crossing before starting the gradual three-kilometre climb up to the rocks.

There's nowhere to **eat** or **drink** for miles around Bhimbetka, so bring a day's supply of food and water with you.

Pachmarhi

Halfway between Bhopal and Jabalpur, a forbidding wall of weird sandstone peaks, precipitous ravines and impenetrable forest rears along the south side of the Narmada Valley. The **Mahadeo mountains** were among the last tracts of central India charted by the British. Not until 1857, the year of the Mutiny, did the first column of red-coated Bengal Lancers hack their way up from the sweltering plains. Led by the infamous explorer and big-game hunter Capt J Forsyth, the troops were astonished to discover, deep in this wilderness of *sal* trees and sheer red cliffs, an idyllic saucer-shaped plateau strewn with huge boulders and criss-crossed by perennial clear-water streams.

At over a thousand metres above sea level, **PACHMARHI** had one other quality that appealed to the sun-weary soldiers – deliciously cool air. Within five years Forsyth was back, this time with a gang of surveyors to push a road through the hills from the railhead at **Piparia**. A military sanitorium was established, quickly followed by bungalows, churches, club houses, a race-course, a polo pitch and a network of cart tracks through the woods. By the end of the century, India's newest hill station had become the summer capital of the entire Central Provinces.

The Pachmarhi plateau was, however, inhabited long before it became a fashionable retreat for Nagpur's homesick British contingent. Abundant **prehistoric rock art** scattered across a wide area of remote hills and valleys suggests that this northern spur of the Mahadeos, known as the **Satpuras**, harboured a population of hunter-gatherers as long ago as the late stone age. Finding "the paintings" can be difficult, but enjoyable, involving lots of scrambling through dense forest.

The majority of visitors who venture up to Pachmarhi are either honeymooners from the nearby cities, or elderly English-speaking Bengalis muffled in thick woollen hats and gloves to keep out the chilly morning air. Rarely do they manage much more than a sedate stroll or jeep excursion, and the only occasion the sleepy hill station sees any real

The telephone **area code** for Pachmarhi is ☎07578.

action is during the annual **Shivratri mela** (Jan/Feb), which draws *lakhs* of pilgrims to ancient shrines hidden in the gorges and on the peaks surrounding the plateau. The trail trodden by the exuberant crowds of ragged *yatris* winds through spectacular scenery to the top of **Chauragarh mountain**; out of season, it makes an excellent day-**hike** from the town. Less strenuous saunters along woodland tracks offer an equally rewarding way to sample the area's abundant flora and fauna. The **Satpura National Park** encompasses a 247-square-kilometre swathe of old-growth *sal* and teak forest, and supports a wide array of wildlife, including Indian bison (*gaur*), barking deer, sambar, *barasingha*, jackals, wild dogs and a handful of elusive tigers and leopards.

The best **time to visit** Pachmarhi is between September and May, when the cool, clear mountain air makes a refreshing change from the heat and dust at lower elevations. It's especially worth trying to be here for the *mela*, although the bus journeys up from the plains can be nightmarish when the festival is in full swing.

Arrival and information

The nearest railhead to Pachmarhi is the one-horse town of **Piparia**, 47km north. If you're unlucky enough to arrive there after the last bus up the mountain has left, the only decent place to stay is the MPTDC *Tourist Motel* (☎22299; ②), behind the train station. Regular buses also connect Pachmarhi with Bhopal and Hoshangabad to the north, and Nagpur and Chhindwara to the south. From Chhindwara, the 107-kilometre trip takes four hours, passing through the Mahadeo mountains en route, before crossing a vast, flat-bottomed valley to begin the climb into the Satpuras.

Buses from all destinations pull in at Pachmarhi's small bus stand, where you'll also find an MPTDC **information** counter (Mon–Sat 10am–5pm) which can book accommodation and hands out cheap, if wildly inaccurate, **maps**. Most of the private budget accommodation lies a short walk up the hill in the bazaar, but a few of the more comfortable MPTDC hotels are a five-minute rickshaw ride south on the far side of the lake. **Jeeps** and **cars** (with drivers) may be rented for excursions around the plateau through the main MPTDC office in the *Amaltas Hotel*, 1500m south of the bus stand.

Neither the *State Bank of India* nor any of the hotels have foreign exchange facilities. The nearest places to **change money** are in Bhopal, Jabalpur or Nagpur.

Pachmarhi: Town and Hikes

The **town** of Pachmarhi itself is clean, green and pleasant, with a very laid-back feel. Although nothing like India's larger and better-known hill stations, it retains a colonial ambiance, enhanced by the elegant British bungalows and Victorian church spires that nose incongruously above the tropical tree-line. The sprawling army training camp, though built after Independence, adds a further touch of the Raj. Military bands march across the spacious *maidans* to the strains of Colonel Bogey, while retired army officers with handlebar moustaches and tweed jackets still enjoy a game of snooker in the old-style gentleman's clubs.

The web of forest tracks and pilgrim trails that thread their way around Pachmarhi's widely dispersed archeological and religious sites make for excellent **walking**, but few, if any, routes are marked. The tourist office, and some hotels and restaurants, may be able to put you in touch with a **guide**, though some sites are known only to academics and the local tribal people. **Bikes**, rented for around Rs20 per day, from the repair shop just below the Government Gardens, are a handy way of getting to the trailheads.

Popular short hikes include the 45-minute trip up from the whitewashed Muslim shrine in the Babu Lines area of town (1km southwest of the bus stand) to the top of **Pachmarhi Hill**, from where you have a fine panoramic view over Pachmarhi town on one side, and the thickly forested ravine of Jambu Dwip on the other. The craggy cliffs lining the north side of the uninhabited gorge below you are riddled with hidden rock-shelters and caves.

Another 45-minute walk follows a well-beaten track from the bus stand, twisting north from the main bazaar into the hillside through a narrow steep-sided canyon to the sacred **Jatashankar cave**, a prominent point in the Shivratri *yatra*. En route, in a small cluster of prehistoric rock-shelters just off the path, **Harper's cave** is named for a seated figure of a man playing a harp, and also holds an unusual portrait, painted in white and outlined in red, of a man riding an X-shaped horse. From the clearing below Harper's cave, the path picks its way past small temples and an eerie blue effigy of Shiva emerging from a large wayside boulder, to the head of a dark chasm. The Jatashankar cave itself lies deep in the bowels of the mountain at the foot of a long flight of stone steps. Lord Shiva is said to have fled here through a secret passageway under the Mahadeo range to escape the evil demon Bhasmasur. The grotto's name, which literally means "Shiva's hair-style", derives from the rock formation overhead, supposed to resemble the god's matted dreadlocks. During the week of the *mela*, the claustrophobic cleft in the rock resounds with the ringing of *puja* bells and the raised voices of *yatris* and *sadhus*, whose fires and incense offerings have blackened the sides of the cliff. Off season, a lone *pujari* tends the *shivalingam* inside the tiny cave.

Pandav caves to Dhuandhar

A ninety-minute walk around the eastern fringes of the plateau strings together a small cluster of ancient rock-cut caves and a prehistoric rock-shelter. First head up to the *Panch Pandav*, or **Pandav caves**, which occupy a nobbly sandstone hillock just east of the road between the ATC cantonment and the petrol pump. Hindu mythology tells that these five simple cells, from which the name Pachmarhi derives, sheltered the infamous Pandava brothers during their thirteen-year exile. Archeologists however maintain that the bare stone chambers and pillared verandahs were excavated by a group of Buddhist monks around the first century BC.

Rejoin the metalled road in front of the caves and head around the back of the hill to the melancholy **British cemetery**. Beyond that, the road peters out into a dusty but jeepable dirt track leading to a small car park. Drop down the hill through the woods from here until you reach a "T" junction of trails, then turn right. At the fork a little further on, bear left and keep to the path as it winds steeply down the rocky sides of an overgrown gulley.

The **Dhuandhar rock-shelter** is formed by a fifteen-metre slab of sandstone overhanging a dusty, rubble-strewn ledge in the forest. Over the years, the site has suffered abuse at the hands of latter-day graffiti "artists", but plenty of lively prehistoric murals survive. Most of the white-painted forms plastered across the ochre, grey and sand-red surfaces are human figures engaged in warfare or hunting; their dangling loin-cloths, hooped earrings and top-knots suggest the work of the aboriginal **Gonds**, some time between 500 and 800 AD. Dhuandhar's real highlight, however, is considerably older. The red and white bull, or bison, towards the middle of the rock face is thought to date from the late stone age. Note the characteristic "X-ray" style, and the way the artist has rendered the animal's magnificent horns.

If you return from here to the "T" junction mentioned above, and instead of heading back the way you came carry straight on through the woods to the stream, you'll eventually arrive at the **Apsara Vihar**, or "Fairy's Pool" – an idyllic bathing place and picnic spot tucked at the foot of a small waterfall nearby. Troupes of black-faced langur monkeys crash through the canopy overhead as you approach the 150-metre **Rajat Prapat**, or "Big Falls", little more than a five-minute scramble over the boulders further downstream.

Chauragarh

The 23-kilometre climb to the sacred summit of **Chauragarh mountain**, on the south rim of the Pachmarhi plateau, follows the main *yatra* trail used by pilgrims during the Shivratri *mela*. A **bicycle** is definitely recommended, as the trailhead is approached along eight kilometres of surfaced road.

From the main bazaar and bus stand area at the top of town, head south across the lake towards the crossroads in front of the MPTDC *Amaltas Hotel* – a junction known to local people as the **Tehsil**. Heaped around the trunk of a mature mango tree nearby are a collection of spatula-shaped wooden memorial plaques placed here by members of the local Gond tribe. Beautifully carved with traditional designs, they are part of the Gond's ancestor-worship cult and should not be disturbed.

The road to Chauragarh runs due south into the woods beyond the MPTDC *New Block Hotel*. Bear left at the fork a few kilometres further on, and keep going until you see a sign on the left to **"Priyadarshini"**, or "Forsyth's Point". The spot from which the explorer first spied the Pachmarhi plateau also looks over the spectacular **Handi Khoh** ravine to the south, supposed to have been created by Lord Shiva as a prison for a giant serpent that once inhabited the nearby lake. The evil reptile had been hassling pilgrims; to punish it, Shiva drank the lake and forced it into a ravine gouged out with a mighty wallop of his trident. It is often suggested that this legend may be rooted in the events of the sixth and seventh centuries AD, when the plateau's Buddhist occupants, referred to by the *Vedas* as "Snakes", were ousted by Hindus.

After Priyadarshini, the going gets tougher as the road switchbacks up some steep thickly wooded hills. Eventually, it emerges at the head of a sweeping valley, with the striking profile of the Chauragarh peak rising high above the sea of tree-tops. At the height of the Shivratri *mela*, the bare conical summit that crowns the near-vertical flanks of the mountain shimmers and glints with immense crowds.

The **footpath** proper begins at the very bottom of the valley, after the road has plunged down another sequence of hairpin bends. Before setting off, make a brief diversion up the *khud* behind the modern **temple** to the **Mahadeo cave**, where pilgrims take a purifying dip in the cool perennial spring water that gushes through its pitch-black interior before the strenuous two-hour climb to the top of the holy mountain. The ancient trail passes several other sacred caves sheltering Shaivite *sadhus*, before reaching a knife-edge ridge, where it joins another pilgrim path that scales the mountain from the south. At the very summit, after a flight of concrete steps, a lurid blue statue of Shiva is surrounded by a thicket of orange tridents, and a temple houses the all-powerful Chauragarh *lingam*. The view over the verdant Satpuras, to the dusty scrubland and distant flat-topped mountains, is suitably sublime.

Accommodation

Finding **accommodation** in Pachmarhi is only a problem during May and June, when visitors flock to escape the heat of the plains. The tourist information counter in the bus stand can tell you which of the five MPTDC hotels have vacancies, and a handful of private places on or around the main street in the bazaar make good fall-backs.

MPTDC Amaltas, near Tehsil (☎2098). Small hotel with plain but clean rooms, fans, and a so-so bar-restaurant. ④.

MPTDC Holiday Homes, near SADA Barrier (☎2099). No-frills economy rooms close to bus stand. ②.

MPTDC Panchavati Cottages, near Tehsil (☎2079). Five pricey self-contained chalets in their own gardens, pitched mainly at honeymooners. ⑤.

MPTDC Panchavati Huts, near Tehsil (☎2079). Well-run mid-range hotel set in pleasant grounds with spacious rooms, attached shower-toilets, and on-site restaurant. Good value. ④.

MPTDC Satpura Retreat (☎2097). *Pukka* British bungalow with six comfortable, old-fashioned rooms, huge white-tiled bathrooms and views over an immaculate flower garden from easy chairs on the verandah. Well worth shelling out for. Some a/c. ⑤–⑥.

New Block, on the Chauragarh road, near the petrol pump. Rock-bottom, spartan rooms in large institutional hotel. A rickshaw ride south of the bazaar. ②.

Pachmarhi, Patel Marg (☎2170). One of a batch of budget hotels in the same road. Unexciting rooms at assorted prices, but clean enough. ③.

Saket, Patel Marg (☎2165). Close to *State Bank* in the heart of the bazaar, five minutes from bus stand. Very cheap and clean, with fans and attached bathrooms. Good value. ①.

Eating

All the most congenial **places to eat** in Pachmarhi are run by MPTDC. The best of the bunch, by a long chalk, is at the *Satpura Retreat*, although even there the food is of less note than the bungalow's faded charm. If you're on a tight budget, a couple of cheap little vegetarian cafes can be found in the small square above the bus stand.

Amaltas, near Tehsil. Quiet restaurant with predictable menu and the town's only bar.

China Bowl, near *Panchavati Huts*. Standard MPTDC restaurant, with a few extra soups, chop sueys and chow meins thrown in for form. Open for breakfast – mainly cutlets, eggs and *iddlis*.

Kalsa, bottom end of bazaar off the main road. Inexpensive, delicious Punjabi and Chinese dishes served inside under strip lights or in the garden. Beer available in side room. Recommended.

Mrignayani, Gandhi Chowk. The most hygenic of the cheap *thali* joints in the bazaar, serving no-nonsense, fiery, pure-veg curries and piping hot *rotis* from large vats.

Satpura Retreat. Regular MPTDC range of veg and non-veg food dished up in TV lounge or al fresco on the atmospheric verandah. A bit of a trek from town if you're not staying here. Moderate.

NORTHERN MADHYA PRADESH

The remoteness of the famous temples at **Khajuraho** means that you could well find yourself travelling through a large tract of **northern Madhya Pradesh**. Given the non-stop coach services and tight train connections from the main Delhi–Agra artery, not many visitors choose to linger in the region. Yet this much-trodden trail passes within striking distance of several sights that are well worth taking time out to see. Foremost among them is the hill-fort at **Gwalior**. In addition to the immaculately restored palaces and ancient Hindu temples within the fort itself, the city also boasts an extravagant European-style palace crammed with quirky art treasures and curios. Further south, **Jhansi** in UP (see p.293) is the main jumping-off point both for Khajuraho and the deserted medieval ghost-town of **Orchha**. Architecture enthusiasts may also want to visit one of the few Indian monuments admired by Lutyens, the brain behind imperial New Delhi. The multi-storey fort-palace at **Datia**, 27km north of Jhansi, stands within sight of an even more rarely visited monument, the Jain hill-top temple complex and pilgrimage site of **Sonagiri**.

The region's major rail and road routes arc north from Bhopal, passing through the jigsaw joint with neighbouring Uttar Pradesh at Jhansi, before heading north to Agra and Delhi. In the east, the *Central Railway* connects the state capital with **Satna**, the nearest railhead to Khajuraho, then veers northeast towards Varanasi and the Ganges basin. Cutting between the two on the busy backcountry road to Khajuraho enables you to take in Orchha on the way.

Gwalior

Straddling the main Delhi–Bombay railway line, **GWALIOR** is the largest city in north-ern Madhya Pradesh and the site of India's most spectacular hill-top **fort**. The old sand-stone citadel, with its temples and palaces, peers down from the edge of a sheer-sided plateau above a haze of petrol fumes, busy streets and cubic concrete houses. Once you've checked out the archeological **museum**, and the rock-cut Jain colossi at the foot of the cliff, the city's other unmissable attraction is the supremely kitsch **Jai Vilas palace** belonging to the local ruling family, the **Scindias**.

Despite its proximity to Agra, 119km north, Gwalior sees few foreigners; in truth, with its drab modern centre and gritty bazaar, it does lack the charm of its counterparts in nearby Rajasthan. Nevertheless, it can be a worthwhile place to pause for a day, particularly around late November and early December, when the old **Moghul tombs** in Gwalior's Muslim quarter host one of India's premier classical **music festivals**.

History

A donatory inscription unearthed in a now-defunct sun temple proves that Gwalior was first occupied in the sixth century BC by Hun invaders from the north. Local legend, however, attributes the founding of the fort to the Kuchwaha prince **Suraj Sen**, said to have been cured of leprosy during the tenth century by the hermit **Gwalipa** after whom the city is named. The water tank where the miracle took place, the Suraj Kund, remains intact, as do a pair of ornate temples, the Sasbahu Mandirs, erected by the Rajput clan. The Kuchwahas' successors, the Parihars, were brutally overthrown in 1232 by **Iltutmish**, following an eleven-month siege. Before the fort eventually fell to the Muslim army, the Rajput women trapped inside committed mass suicide by self-immolation. Afterwards, the Delhi Sultan added to the carnage by ordering the execu-tion, outside his tent, of all seven hundred prisoners taken in the battle.

A third Rajput dynasty, the **Tomars**, retook Gwalior in 1398, and ushered in the city's "golden age". Under **Man Singh**, who ascended to the Tomar *gadi* in 1486, the hill-top gained the magnificent palaces and fortifications that were to earn it the epithet "the pearl in the necklace of the castles of Hind". Skirmishes with neighbouring powers dogged the Rajputs' rule, however, culminating in 1517 when the **Lodis** from Delhi besieged the fort for the second time. On this occasion they were successful. Man Singh was slain, and his son, who managed to fend off the attackers for another twelve months, finally surrendered. Thereafter, Gwalior was ruled by a succession of Muslim overlords, including Babur, Humayun and Sher Shah, before falling to Akbar.

With the decline of the Moghuls, the **Marathas** – a confederacy of Hindu dynasties from the Deccan region – worked their way northwards into the power vacuum. Gwalior became the base of the most powerful of the four Maratha clans, the **Scindias**, in 1754. Twenty-six years later, wily British East India Company troops conquered the fort in an audacious night raid, using rope ladders and socks stuffed with cotton to muffle the sound of their approach. Within hours, the citadel was overrun, and Gwalior became a British feudatory state ruled by a succession of puppet rajas. The most famous of these, the immensely rich Jayaji Rao Scindia (1843–86), remained loyal to the British during the 1858 Mutiny, although 6500 of his troops joined the opposing forces led by Tantia Topia and the infamous **Rani Lakshmi Bai** of Jhansi (see p.295). Both rebel leaders were killed in the ensuing battle, and the Maharaja quickly resumed his role as host to some of the grandest viceregal dinners, royal visits and tiger hunts ever witnessed by the Raj. The Scindias remained influential after Independence, and still live in Gwalior; the Maharaja was until recently a high-ranking minister in the Congress government, while his aged mother is prominent in the far-right Hindu-revivalist BJP. Like their British counterparts, the royal family's political fortunes, quar-rels and marriages continue to provide fodder for voracious gossip columnists.

GWALIOR

Arrival and information

Gwalior's mainline **railway station** lies in the east of the city, just around the corner from the **government bus stand**. Apart from the handful of cheap lodges nearby, most of the accommodation is an auto-rickshaw ride away to the west, down the busy MLB (Maharani Lakshmi Bai) Road. If you're travelling light, you could save on the fare by squeezing into one of the inexpensive tempos that run along the main street outside the station. Gwalior **airport**, 9km to the northeast of the centre, is served by both taxis and auto-rickshaws. Finally, anyone arriving on private buses will find themselves on the southwest edge of town, at the inconveniently situated **private bus stand**.

MPTDC have a helpful **information** counter at their *Hotel Tansen* (☎21568), ten minutes' walk southeast of the train station on Gandhi Rd. If you need to **change money**, and are not staying in a hotel with a foreign exchange facility, the *State Bank of India* (Mon–Fri 10am–2pm, Sat 10am–noon) is at the heart of the bazaar district, on **Jayaji Chowk**, close to the **GPO**.

The telephone **area code** for Gwalior is ☎0751.

The fort

Gwalior's imposing **fort** (daily 8am–6pm) sprawls over a three-kilometre-long, narrow outcrop of sandstone to the north of the modern city. Its mighty turreted battlements encompass no less than six palaces, three temples, and several water tanks and cisterns, as well as a prestigious public school and a shiny new Sikh Gurudwara.

Two routes wind up the hill. In the west, a motorable track climbs the steep gorge of the **Urwahi valley**, passing a line of rock-cut Jain statues along the way. The other, more accessible entrance is on the northwest corner of the cliff, at the head of a long stepped ramp. The two can be combined by taking a rickshaw to the Urwahi side, then walking across the plateau and dropping down via the northeastern entrance to the museum and Jama Masjid, from where it's easier to pick up a rickshaw back into town.

The northeastern approach and museum

The **northeastern approach** to the fort leads under five successive fortified **gateways**. The first, the **Alamgiri gate**, was built by Matamad Khan in 1660 in honour of the Moghul emperor Aurangzeb. Beyond its small courtyard, the **Badalgarh gate**, named after Man Singh's uncle Badal (also known as the "**Hindola**" after the *hindol*, or "swing", that used to hang from it) is in the same Hindu style as the hill-top palace, with two round turrets raised above its doorway.

The small two-storeyed **Gujuri Mahal**, to the right of the Badalgarh gate, was built by Man Singh to woo his favourite Rani, Mrignayani, when she was still a peasant girl. According to legend, the Raja first became smitten with the "fawn-eyed" Gujur tribeswoman when he saw her wrestle apart a pair of water buffalo during an expedition in the forest; but she would not agree to marry him until he supplied the new palace with water from her village well – the source of her superhuman strength. The elegant sandstone palace now houses Gwalior's **archeological museum** (Tues–Sun 10am–5pm; Rs2), where the large exhibition of sculpture, inscriptions and painting is well worth a look, even if the labels are woefully uninformative. Highlights include the twin lion capitals from Vidisha in gallery two; the massive lintel carved with a depiction of "the humbling of Bali" in gallery seven; and gallery nine's erotic bas-relief, in which a prince is shown gently removing the top of his beloved's *sari*. Unfortunately, the real *pièce de résistance* is locked away in its vaults. The priceless **Salabhanjika** is a small, exquisitely carved female figurine found in the ruins of the temple at Gyaraspur (see p.341). Noted for her sensuous curves and sublime facial expression, the statue is often dubbed "India's Mona Lisa". Plaster casts and photographs are usually on display somewhere in the building.*

The next gateway up the hill, the **Ganesh gate**, dates from the mid-fifth century. Close by stand an old pigeon coop, or *kabutar khana*, and (on the far side of the arch) a modern Hindu shrine assembled from the ruins of an earlier one dedicated to the sage **Gwalipa**, which Mutamad Khan replaced with a mosque in 1664. Before arriving at the **Lakshman gate**, you pass a ninth-century Vishnu temple, the **Chatarbhunj** ("four-armed") **mandir**; a Muslim memorial to one of Ibrahin Lodi's nobles who died during the siege of Gwalior in 1518; and a flight of steps up to some unremarkable Jain rock-cut statues. The fifth and final gateway, the **Hathiya** ("Elephant") **Paur**, the most spectacular in the series, forms the entrance to the Man Mandir. Its twin turrets and ornate blue tilework are contiguous with the rest of the massive stone facade.

---

*If you're determined to see the real thing, write to the Commissioner of Archeology, State Archeological Museum, Bhopal, for permission, giving a sound reason for, and the precise dates of, your proposed visit.

The Man Mandir

Towering above the northeastern approach to the fort, the **Man Mandir** has to be one of the finest early Hindu palaces in India. Built between 1486 and 1517 by the Tomar ruler Man Singh, it's known as the "Chit Mandir", or "painted palace", for the rich ceramic **mosaics** that encrust its facade. The best preserved fragments of tilework, on its south side, can be seen from the bank left of the main Hathiya Paur gateway. Spread in luxurious bands of turquoise, emerald-green and yellow across the ornate stonework are tigers, elephants, peacocks, banana trees and crocodiles brandishing flowers.

By contrast, the **interior** of the four-storeyed palace is very plain. Some of the larger halls, however, do contain fine pierced-stone *jali* screens, behind which the women of the palace would assemble to receive instruction from Gwalior's great music gurus. The circular chambers in the lower storeys were formerly the palace dungeons. Prisoners incarcerated here in Moghul times were fed on a preparation made with boiled poppy heads called *poust* – a cruelly ingenious form of torture that ensured a protracted and painful death from malnourishment and drug addiction.

Around the Man Mandir

The **Vikram Mandir** (1516), next door to the Man Mandir, is joined to Man Singh's palace by a network of passages hidden in the thick outer walls. The **Karam Mandir**, a two-storeyed Hindu building with a long colonnaded hall at its centre, stands further to the north, a short walk from the remnants of the now-derelict Jehangiri and Shah Jehan palaces. In the far northwestern corner of the enclosure is the large **Jauhar Kund**, the water tank where, in 1232, the women of the Parihar court performed mass suicide by self-immolation, to avoid capture by Iltutmish's advancing army.

The Teli-ka-Mandir and Suraj Kund

The thirty-metre-tall **Teli-ka-Mandir**, on the south side of the plateau, is the oldest surviving monument in the fort. Dating from the mid-eighth century, it consists of a huge rectangular sanctuary tower capped with an unusual vaulted-arch roof, whose *peepal*-leaf shape derives from the *chaitya* windows of much earlier rock-cut Buddhist caves. In the aftermath of the Gwalior Mutiny in 1858, the temple, dedicated to Vishnu, was used by the blasphemous British as a soda factory. The ASI are now carrying out extensive restoration work.

Set back from the road at the head of the Urwahi ravine, just north of the Teli-ka-Mandir, the **Suraj Kund** is the hundred-metre-long tank whose magical waters are supposed to have cured the tenth-century ruler Suraj Sen, later Suraj Pal, of leprosy.

The Sasbahu Mandirs and Sikh Gurudwara

The **Sasbahu**, or "mother- and daughter-in-law", temples overlook the city from the eastern edge of the fort, near the unsightly TV mast. The larger of the pair has a three-storey *mandapa* (assembly hall), supported by four intricate pillars, while the smaller one consists of an open-sided porch with a pyramidal roof. Both were erected late in the eleventh century and are dedicated, like the Teli-ka-Mandir, to Vishnu.

The huge gold-domed marble building to the south is a modern **Sikh Gurudwara**. Built to commemorate a Sikh hero who was imprisoned in the fort, the temple attracts a constant stream of pilgrims, most of whom drive here in specially converted "Public Carrier" trucks from the Punjab. Along the road leading to it, you'll pass groups of men clad in the traditional garb of Sikh warriors – long blue *kurtas*, bulky turbans, daggers and spears held over their shoulders – filing along like foot-soldiers from a bygone era. The Gurudwara's cool marble courtyard, filled with the strains of devotional music, makes an atmospheric place to escape the heat. Before entering, make sure you cover your arms, legs and head, remove your socks and shoes, and wash your feet in the tank at the bottom of the steps. Tobacco is strictly prohibited inside the complex.

The rock-cut Jain sculptures

The sheer sandstone cliffs around the fort harbour some imposing **rock-cut Jain sculpture**. Carved between the seventh and fifteenth centuries, most of the figures are large honey-coloured icons of the twenty-four Jain Teacher-Saviours – the *tirthankaras*, or "Crossing Makers", depicted in the characteristic standing pose, their arms held stiffly at their sides, staring serenely into the distance. Many lost their faces and genitalia when Babur's iconoclastic army descended on the city in 1527.

The larger of the two main groups lines the southwestern approach to the fort, along the sides of the **Urwahi** ravine. Among the images are a huge nineteen-metre Adinath, and a row of 22 standing *tirthankaras* with inscriptions dating from the mid-fifteenth century. The other group stands on the southeast corner of the plateau, on a narrow ledge overlooking the city. To get there, follow the main road north along the foot of the cliff from Phool Bagh, near the **Rani Jhansi memorial**, until you see a paved path winding up the hill from behind a row of houses on the left. Once again, the *tirthankaras*, which are numbered, occupy deep recesses hewn from the rock wall. One of the few not defaced by the Muslim invaders, #10, is still used by Gwalior's small Jain community as a shrine. After bathing in the spring in cave #1, devotees leave offerings of flowers and rice at the *tirthankara*'s gigantic feet.

The old town

A number of interesting Islamic monuments are tucked away down the narrow, dusty back streets of Gwalior's predominantly Muslim **old town**, clustered around the north and northeast corners of the hill. The **Jama Masjid** stands close to the Gujuri Mahal, near the main entrance to the fort. Erected in 1661 by Mutamad Khan, using sandstone quarried from the plateau above, the beautifully preserved mosque has two slender minarets, and three bulbous onion domes crowned with golden spires.

The city's most famous Muslim building, however, is set amid balding lawns and unruly bougainvillea bushes 1km further east. The sixteenth-century **Tomb of Ghaus Muhammed**, an Afghan prince who helped Babur take Gwalior fort, is a fine specimen of early Moghul architecture and a popular local shrine. Elegant hexagonal pavilions stand at each of its four corners, surrounding a large central dome formerly plastered with blue-glazed tiles; its walls are inlaid with exquisite pierced-stone *jali* screens, whose complex geometric patterns are best admired from the incense-filled interior.

The second and smaller of the tombs in the gardens is that of the famous Moghul singer-musician **Tansen**, one of the "Nine Jewels" of emperor Akbar's court. Every year, performers and afficionados from all over India flock here for Gwalior's annual **music festival** (Nov–Dec). At other times, impromptu recitals of *Qawwaali*, Islamic devotional singing accompanied on the harmonium (see p.93), take place on the terrace outside. Local superstition holds that the leaves of the **tamarind tree** growing on the plinth nearby have a salutary effect on the singing voice, which explains why its bottom branches have been stripped bare.

The Jai Vilas palace

Due south of the fort, in the heart of Gwalior's upper-class neighbourhood, the **Jai Vilas palace** (Tues–Sun 9.30am–5pm; Rs20; no photos) is one of India's most grandiose and eccentric nineteenth-century relics. It was built in 1875 by Jayaji Rao Scindia. Wanting his residence to rival those of his colonial overlords in Britain, he dispatched his friend Colonel Michael Filose – "Mikul Sahib", the descendant of an Italian mercenary – on a grand tour of Europe to seek inspiration. A year or so later, Filose returned with a vast shipment of furniture, fabric, paintings, tapestries and cut-glass, together with the blueprints for a building that borrowed heavily from Buckingham Palace, Versailles, and a host of Greek ruins and Italian-Baroque stately homes. The result is an improbable blend of Doric, Tuscan and Corinthian architecture, with one of the most shamelessly over-the-top interiors you're likely to see outside Hollywood.

The Scindias, who still occupy parts of the palace, have opened two wings to the public. The one nearest the main entrance has been converted into a **museum** of the more valuable and extraordinary artefacts accumulated by the rulers of Gwalior. Collecting dust in the dozens of rooms and creaky wood-panelled corridors are countless Moghul paintings, Persian rugs, gold and silver ornaments, and pieces of antique furniture acquired by Filose when Louis XVI's estate was sold off piecemeal after the French Revolution. Elsewhere, you'll come across a swing made from Venetian cutglass which the royal family used to celebrate Krishna's birthday, and a room full of stuffed tigers and sepia photographs that show the Maharaja posing stiffly with rows of pipe-smoking pith-helmeted British guests. Finally, a room upstairs is given over to **erotica**. The *chowkidar* will gleefully point out its centrepiece: a life-size marble statue of a woman succumbing with some elan to the amorous advances of a swan.

The palace's most extravagant wing lies across the courtyard from the museum. The **Durbar hall** was where the Maharaja entertained important visitors, among them the Prince of Wales (later Edward VII), who descended on Gwalior in 1875 with an entourage of one thousand people. Displayed in the banquet hall on the ground floor is a silver toy-train used by Jayaji Rao Scindia to dispense brandy and cigars after dinner; the Maharaja would tease anyone he didn't like by not stopping the electric locomotive when it reached them. A sweeping Belgian glass staircase leads from the lobby to the gargantuan assembly hall upstairs. Suspended from its ceiling are the world's biggest **chandeliers**. At over three and a half tonnes apiece, they could not be installed until the strength of the roof had been tested with eight elephants – a feat that necessitated the construction of a 500-metre-long earth ramp. The rug lining the floor of the hall is equally enormous. Woven by inmates of Gwalior jail, it took twelve years to complete and, at over forty metres in length, is the largest handmade carpet in Asia.

Accommodation

Most of Gwalior's **hotels** are strung between the train station and Lashkar, the main bazaar area, along the hectic MLB Rd. Two notable exceptions are the MPTDC *Hotel Tansen*, around the corner from the train station, and the luxurious *Usha Kiran Palace*, tucked away in its own grounds south of the main thoroughfare, near the Jai Vilas palace. Standards at the cheaper end of the market are particularly low, with cramped windowless cells the norm.

Inexpensive

All of the following have hot and cold water, attached bathrooms, and 24-hour checkout times, and offer cheaper rates for single travellers.

Ambika, Tansen Rd, Padav (☎28761). Reasonably clean budget hotel within walking distance of the train station (take platform 2 exit). The rooms at the back escape the noise from the flyover. ②.

Bhagwati, Nai Sarak. Best of the budget bunch if you want to be near the bazaar. Rock-bottom rates, and fort views too. ②.

India, Station Rd (☎24983). No-frills lodge run by *Indian Coffee Workers' Co-op*; clean, but noisy rooms overlooking main street. Deluxe rate buys you a western toilet. Handy for the station. ③.

Man Mandir, High Court Lane (☎321442). Small, friendly, well maintained, and very good value, but hard to find. A rickshaw ride from the station. ②.

Regal, MLB Rd (☎22599). Used to be a nice place, but has become seedy of late. The fort views from the rooftop terrace are now its only attraction. ①–④.

Safari, Railway Station Market (☎24638). Identical to *India*, only marginally cheaper and with a more recent lick of paint. ③.

Moderate to expensive

Fort View, MLB Rd (☎23409). Plain but comfortable and well managed, with light rooms, *Star TV* and some a/c. "Regular" rooms are particularly good value. ②–⑤.

Meghdoot, MLB Rd (☎27374). Over-priced, mostly windowless rooms with air-coolers or a/c.

MPTDC Tansen, 6-A Gandhi Rd (☎21568). Large, efficient hotel in its own gardens near the station, with spacious rooms and a good restaurant. Popular with business travellers, so advance booking is recommended. Some a/c. ④–⑥.

Park View, near Rani Jhansi memorial, Phool Bagh Gate, MLB Rd (☎21323). In a dingy basement but clean enough. Some a/c rooms. ④–⑤.

Regency, near bus stand (☎29516). Modern, ritzy and near the station. Mod cons include *Star TV*, foreign exchange, health club (with jacuzzi) and a pool. ⑥.

Ushan Kiran Palace, Jayendraganj, Lakshar (☎323213). Former Maharaja's guest house now run by *Welcomgroup* as an opulent five-star. Period furnishings, large verandahs, and a lawn with wicker chairs preserve some of its original *fin de siècle* feel. ⑧–⑨.

Eating

With a couple of exceptions, all the best **places to eat** in Gwalior are in the mid- and top-of-the-range hotels, where main dishes set you back anywhere between thirty and a hundred *rupees*. More basic, and much **cheaper** *dal*, *subzi* and *roti* meals are doled up on stainless steel plates at the row of dodgy *dhabas* outside the train station. Look out too for the **juice bars** dotted around Jayaji Chowk, over in the west end of town, which serve glasses of refreshing, freshly squeezed fruit juice.

Indian Coffee House, Station Rd. Delicious *dosas* and other South Indian snacks, plain or with "special" nut and veg fillings. Opens 7.30am for breakfast – *iddlis* and eggs – and a read of the paper.

Kwality, MLB Rd. The usual tasty-but-pricey formula food in a/c comfort.

Tansen, Gandhi Rd. Run-of-the-mill menu includes several *tandoori* and vegetarian options at moderate prices, with some milder *chow meins* and *chop sueys*.

Ushan Kiran, Jayendraganj. Modest selection of (expensive) gourmet Indian and western food, with lots of mouthwatering Moghul-style dishes. The buffet lunches are good for a splurge.

Shivpuri

SHIVPURI, the former summer capital of the Scindias, lies 114km southwest of Gwalior, at a crossroads on the main Jhansi–Jaipur highway. Local rulers from the Moghuls onwards were drawn here by the abundance of game in the area's lush decid-uous forests. These days, however, all but a few fragments of woodland have disap-peared, and the small market town is now marooned in a landscape of shaley scrub, dried-up riverbeds and escarpments peppered with dusty brown trees. Apart from a couple of nineteenth-century cenotaphs and a minor-league national park, very little remains of Shivpuri's princely past, and the only plausible reason to call in here is to break a journey to Rajasthan's famous Ranthambore wildlife reserve, 180km northwest.

The town's main monuments, the **chhatris**, or tombs, of the Scindia family, stand a two-kilometre tonga ride from the bus stand, by the side of the road leading to the MPTDC *Tourist Village*. Facing each other across an ornamental garden, the brilliant white marble cenotaphs fuse Hindu and Islamic styles, juxtaposing slender temple *shik-haras* with Moghul domes and pavilions. The larger of the pair, dedicated to the dowa-ger queen Maharani Raje Scindia, boasts a grand double-storeyed facade that opens onto a water tank intersected by walkways. Her son Madho Rao Scindia's *chhatri* is even more ornate. Standing on a raised platform and flanked by ersatz Victorian street lamps, its intricately carved walls are inlaid with lapis lazuli and onyx stones. Both enshrine life-size effigies of the Scindias, which local musicians regale with devotional music during the evenings.

Note that the city of **JHANSI**, the major *Central Railway* junction used by travellers heading to the temples at **Khajuraho**, is in Uttar Pradesh state, and is thus covered on p.293.

Shivpuri's other attraction, the **Madhav national park**, is definitely not worth bothering with unless you have your own vehicle, as the most exciting animals you're likely to spot are run-of-the-mill Indian deer: *cheetal, chinkara, nilgai, sambar* and *chausingha*. Jeeps can be rented through MPTDC, at the reception desk of the *Tourist Village*, for full- or half-day tours, and the unexciting **tiger safari** (the animals are captive). Birdwatchers may find Madhav marginally more inspiring, however, as its large artificial (and crocodile-infested) lakes attract several species of migratory wildfowl during the winter. The rare Indian bustard also nests 40km away to the east, in the **Karera bird sanctuary**, which is only accessible by car.

Practicalities

Shivpuri can be reached by **bus** from both Gwalior and Jhansi, 84km east, as well as from Datia (with a change at Karera). Tongas and more expensive unmetered autorickshaws are on hand at the bus stand, in the middle of town, to ferry visitors out to Shivpuri's two best **hotels**, both run by MPTDC. The cheaper *Chinkara Motel* (☎2297; ④), on the main Bombay–Agra NH3, has four basic but clean non-a/c rooms; the lakeside *Tourist Village* (☎2600; ⑤), 3km from the bus stand, is more peaceful and comfortable. Its chalets are spacious and modern, with attached bathrooms, a/c on request, and a good licensed restaurant. Ideally, you should reserve at least five days in advance (through any MPTDC office), as the rooms are often block-booked for conferences.

The MPTDC hotels are also the best places to **eat**. If you're on a tight budget, there are a handful of grotty *dhabas* on the main street near the bus stand.

Datia

Constructed by Bir Singh Deo at the height of the Bundela's "golden age", the majestic multi-storeyed palace at **DATIA**, 30km northwest of Jhansi, is regarded as one of the finest Rajput buildings in India. Although few of the visitors who spy the exotic hulk of yellow-brown ramparts, cupolas and domed pavilions from the nearby railway line actually stop here, those that do are rarely disappointed. The palace presides from the top of a rocky outcrop at the edge of a busy market town over a mass of white- and blue-washed brick houses packed tightly onto a saucer-shaped depression in the plains.

The **Nrsing Dev Palace**, or "Govind Mandir" as it's sometimes known, stands in the north of town, separated from the train and bus stations by a tangle of narrow streets and lanes that are difficult to negotiate without the aid of a tonga *wallah*. Decorated with paintings and stone carving, the main entrance leads into the gloomy bowels of the building under a massive five-storey facade. Half the fun of the labyrinthine palace is trying to find a path from its pitch-black subterranean chambers, hewn out of the solid base of the hill for use during the hot season, to the Rani's airy apartment on the top floor. In between, a maze of cross-cutting corridors, flying walkways, walls encrusted with fragments of green, yellow and turquoise ceramic tiles, hidden passages, latticed screens and archways, pavilions, and suites of apartments lead you in ever-decreasing circles, until you eventually run out of staircases. The views from the upper storeys are breathtaking. Scattered around the town below are several other Rajput monuments, including a sprawling fort, the **Bharat Garh**, and the stately homes and well-watered gardens of Datia's present ruling family. Immediately to the north, a large tank, the **Karna Sagar**, stands amid *dhobi ghats* and the ruins of temples and *chhatris*. The white pinnacles of Sonagiri are also visible on the horizon.

Nearer the bus stand, the less impressive of Datia's two hill-top palaces, the **Raj Garh**, houses a small **museum** (Tues–Sat 10am–5pm; free), whose dull collection of sculpture and painting is far less inspiring than the views from its balcony.

Practicalities

Datia is on the main Delhi–Bombay railway line, and served by bus or train from both Jhansi and Gwalior. Tongas and auto-rickshaws ferry passengers into town from the small **railway station**, 2km southwest, while **buses** pull in at a lot on the south side of the centre. If you're coming from Shivpuri, 97km west, you'll have to change buses at Karera. There's no **accommodation** in town; the palace has to be visited as a day trip from Jhansi, or by breaking a journey to or from Gwalior, 71km northwest.

Sonagiri

SONAGIRI, 61km southeast of Gwalior, is among the more ethereal landmarks punctuating the Delhi–Bombay rail journey. Flowing down the east-facing slope of a solitary hillock, deep in the central Indian countryside, 84 gleaming white shrines mark the spot where the legendary King Nanganang Kumar, together with five-and-a-half *crore* of his followers, achieved liberation from the cycle of rebirth. Today the site, sacred to **Digambar** ("Sky-clad") **Jains**, makes an atmospheric pause for a couple of hours en route to one of the nearby cities.

Minibuses to Sonagiri from the mainline station pull in at the "manager's office" in a small **village square**, where you can check that it's OK to visit. From here, most pilgrims make for the "**mirror temple**", down the lane to the left, in which artists can be seen fashioning mosaics of *tirthankaras* from coloured glass and mirrors. More somber spiritual pursuits take place in the seminary at the back of the square, next to the main entrance. Old Digambar monks conduct religious discussions with pilgrims in the courtyard, their distinctive yellow wooden water pots (*dariyes*), and peacock-feather whisks beside them. For most of the year, these ascetics wander naked around the country, returning to monasteries for a few months to give and receive teachings. More secular Jains notch up credits on the cosmic balance sheet by making gifts to religious establishments instead – as evidenced by the dozens of donatory plaques set in the **marble walkway** leading up the hill. Crowning the summit of Sonagiri, the main **temple** houses a colossal *tirthankara* icon, while below it, a ceramic scale model of **Mount Meru**, the axial mountain said by Jains to support the cosmos, looks out over the cascade of whitewashed spires and fluttering yellow pennants to the plains in the distance.

Practicalities

Without your own vehicle, the only way to get to Sonagiri is by **train**. Check the timings of onward services carefully before leaving the station, as there's very little **accommodation**. If you get stuck, the office in the main square will fix you a dorm bed for a night in the Jain *dharamshala*. Pure vegetarian **food**, snacks, *chai* and cold drinks are available at the insanitary-looking stall opposite the bus stand.

Orchha

ORCHHA, literally "hidden place", certainly lives up to its name. Languishing amid a tangle of scrubby *dhak* forest, 18km southeast of Jhansi, the former capital of the **Bundela** dynasty siphons off only a fraction of the tourist traffic bound for Khajuraho on the nearby highway. The deserted medieval town is, nevertheless, an architectural gem, and the ideal place to break the long journey to the temples. Guano-splashed temple *shikharas*, derelict palaces, *havelis* and weed-choked sandstone cenotaphs lie neglected by the banks of the tranquil River Betwa – home to troupes of black-faced langurs, vultures, and wheeling flocks of bright green parakeets.

Clustered around the foot of the exotic ruins, a sleepy village of neatly painted houses, market stalls, and a couple of attractive government hotels provide most of the basic amenities. Orchha doesn't yet have a telephone link with the rest of India, and the electricity supply is intermittent, but it's a fine place to unwind. Apart from a couple of hours in the middle of the day, when coach parties swoop in for lunch and a break-neck tour of the monuments, you should have the place virtually to yourself.

History

According to one legend, the name of Orchha's founding dynasty, the **Bundelas**, derives from an eleventh-century ancestor who sacrificed five severed heads (or five drops of his own blood) to the mountain goddess Vindhyabatha – a deed that earned him the epithet of "Vindhyela", or "he who offered blood". Expelled by his brothers from their homeland near Varanasi, Vindhyela and his descendants roamed central India until finally settling at **Garkhundar**, the first capital of Bundelkhand. Pushed on by the Delhi Sultan Tuqluq late in the fifteenth century, the Bundelas decamped 45km to a more remote and defensible jungle site. The old Malwan outpost at **Orchha**, astride an island formed by a sharp bend in the River Betwa, proved an ideal platform from which to dominate the region when the Tuqluqs' power eventually declined.

Work on Orchha's magnificent fortifications, palaces and temples was started by Raja **Rudra Pratap** soon after the move, and continued after he was killed in 1531 trying to wrestle a cow from the clutches of a tiger. Thereafter, the dynasty's fortunes depended on the goodwill of their mighty neighbours, the **Moghuls**. After being defeated in battle by Akbar, the proud and pious **Madhukar Shah** nearly signed his clan's death warrant by showing up at the imperial court with a red *tilak* smeared on his forehead – a mark banned by the staunchly Muslim emperor. Luckily for the Bundelas, however, Madhukar's bold gesture earned Akbar's respect, and the two became friends – an alliance fostered in the years that followed by Orchha's most illus-trious Raja, **Bir Singh Deo**. Long before he acceded to the throne, the ambitious young Bundela saw the value of keeping on the right side of his counterpart in Delhi, Prince Salim. In 1601, he assassinated the latter's much-loathed adversary, **Abdul Fazl**, and sent Salim the decapitated head on a platter. The murder infuriated Akbar but was never forgotten by his son, who, when he became Emperor Jehangir in 1605, rewarded Bir Singh Deo's brutal act by helping him to seize the Bundela throne from his elder brother Ram Shah.

During his 22-year rule, Bir Singh Deo erected a total of 52 forts and palaces across the region, including the citadel at **Jhansi**, the rambling Nrsing Dev at **Datia** (see p.355), and many of Orchha's finest buildings. After he was killed by bandits while returning from the Deccan with a camel-train full of booty in 1627, however, Bundelkhand's relations with the Moghuls rapidly deteriorated. Attacks by the armies of Shah Jehan, Aurangzeb, and the Marathas ensued, and a spate of eighteenth-century Jat peasant uprisings finally forced the Bundelas to flee Orchha for the comparative safety of **Tikamgarh**. Apart from the Sheesh Mahal, now converted into a small hotel, the magnificent monuments have lain virtually deserted ever since.

Arrival and information

Tempos shuttle regularly between Orchha and Jhansi, pulling in on the south side of the village crossroads. Buses cost the same (Rs4) and tend to be marginally less of a crush, but take twice as long to make the eighteen-kilometre trip. Coming from **Khajuraho**, you can ask to be dropped at the Orchha turning on the main road, a seven-kilometre scooter ride from the village. If you're heading in the other direction, don't risk flagging the express MPSRTC coaches down on the highway, as they're often full. Instead, get to Jhansi early in the morning and arrange a ticket before the Delhi/Agra trains get in. Private **jeeps** (with drivers) do the round trip from Orchha to Khajuraho and back in a day, costing upwards of Rs600 – well worth it if you get a group together. The manager of the MPTDC *Sheesh Mahal* hotel can put you in touch with the owners.

Jhansi is the nearest place to **change money** and make STD **telephone calls**.

The monuments

All of the best preserved of Orchha's scattered palaces, temples, tombs and gardens lie within comfortable walking distance of the village and can easily be seen in a day. If you don't mind trailing wearing a headset, following arrows painted on the floors and courtyards, MPTDC's new **walkman tour** of the highlights (Rs25, plus Rs500 deposit), complete with dramatic voice-over and raucous medieval Indian music, can be quite entertaining. Ask at the reception desk in the Sheesh Mahal.

The Raj Mahal and the Rai Praveen Mahal

The first building you come to across Orchha's medieval granite **bridge**, the **Raj Mahal** (daily 10am–5pm) was started by Rudra Pratap, and completed by one of his successors, the indomitable Madhukar Shah. From the end of the bridge, bear left at the main entrance, and work your way through the dilapidated lower half of the palace to its better-preserved central section further up the slope. Of the two rectangular courtyards inside, the second, formerly used by the Bundela ranis, is the most dramatic. Opulent royal quarters, raised balconies and interlocking walkways rise in symmetrical tiers on all four sides, crowned by domed pavilions and turrets. Those apartments projecting into the quadrangle on the ground floor belonged to the most favoured queens. As you wander around, look out for the fragments of mirror-inlay and vibrant **painting** plastered over their walls and ceilings. Some of the friezes are still in remarkable condition, depicting Vishnu's various outlandish incarnations, court and hunting scenes, and lively festivals involving dancers, musicians and jugglers.

Reached via a path that leads from the Raj Mahal around the northern side of the hill, the **Rai Praveen Mahal** is a small, double-storeyed brick apartment built by Raja Indramani for his concubine in the mid-1670s. The gifted poetess, musician and dancer, Rai Praveen, beguiled the Moghul emperor Akbar when she was sent to him as a gift, but was eventually returned to Orchha to live out her remaining days. The small *mahal* is set amid the well-watered lawns of the **Anand Mahal gardens**, with a main assembly hall on the ground floor (used to host performances of music and dance) and the boudoirs upstairs.

The Jehangir Mahal

Orchha's single most admired palace, the **Jehangir Mahal**, was built by Bir Singh Deo as a monumental welcome present for the Moghul emperor when he paid a state visit here in the seventeenth century. Jehangir had come to invest his old ally with the sword of Abdul Fazl – the emperor's erstwhile enemy whom Bir Singh had murdered some years earlier. Entered through an ornate ceremonial gateway, the main, east-facing facade is still encrusted with turquoise tiles. Two stone elephants flank the stair-way, holding bells in their trunks to announce the arrival of the Raja. Once again, three storeys of elegant hanging balconies, terraces, apartments and onion domes are piled around a central courtyard. This palace, however, has a much lighter feel, with count-less windows and pierced stone screens looking out over the exotic Orchha skyline to the west, and a sea of treetops and ruined temples in the other direction.

The Sheesh Mahal

Built during the early eighteenth century, long after Orchha's demise, the **Sheesh Mahal** ("Palace of Mirrors") was originally intended as an exclusive country retreat for the local Raja, Udait Singh. Following Independence, however, the property was inherited by the state government, who now run it as a small hotel. The low, rather squat palace stands between the Raj Mahal and the Jehangir Mahal, at the far end of an open-sided courtyard. Covered in a coat of whitewash and stripped of most of its Persian rugs and antiques, the building retains little of its former splendour. The only rooms worth a peep – assuming they're not occupied (check with reception) – are numbers one and two upstairs, which contain some of the Raja's original furniture and bathroom fittings.

Around the village

Dotted **around the village** below the hill are several other interesting monuments. The **Ram Raja Mandir** stands at the end of the small bazaar, in a cool marble-tiled courtyard. Local legend has it that Madhukar Shah constructed the building as a palace for his wife, Rani Ganesha, and it only became a temple after a Rama icon, which the queen had dutifully carried all the way from her home town of Ayodhya, could not be lifted from the spot where she first set it down. The god, it seems, had only consented to the move on condition that he be immediately enshrined in his own purpose-built temple. When she got back to Orchha, however, the Rani was dismayed to find the Chatturbunj temple still unfinished. True to its word, when the time came to transport the deity over to the new shrine, it remained stuck to the floor, where it has stood ever since. Nowadays, the ochre-coloured Ram Raja Mandir is a popular pilgrimage site. During major Rama festivals, thousands of worshippers gather in front of its ornate silver doors to await *darshan* of the garlanded deity inside.

With its huge pointed *shikharas* soaring high above the village, the temple originally supposed to house Rani Ganesha's icon, **Chatturbunj Mandir**, seems on the face of it well worthy of that honour. Unusually for a Hindu temple, its interior is spacious, with high ceilings and large arched windows. One reason often advanced for this is that the Bundelas were followers of the **bhakti** cult – a form of worship involving large congregations of people rather than a small elite of priests. You can climb up to the temple's flat cruciform roof via spiral staircases off the main hall.

On the opposite side of the village, the **Phool Bagh** ornamental garden contains a now-defunct fountain and a small colonnaded pavilion. The rajas and their families would retreat here in summer to escape the fierce central Indian heat. The *haveli* overlooking it, the **Palkhi Mahal**, has been turned into a small budget hostel.

The Lakshminarayan Mandir

The lone **Lakshminarayan Mandir** (daily 10am–5pm) crowns a rocky hillock just under 1km west of Orchha village, at the end of a long paved pathway. From the square directly behind the Ram Raja temple, the leisurely fifteen-minute stroll is rewarded with more fine views, and excellent seventeenth- and nineteenth-century **paintings**. For a small tip, the resident *chowkidar* will lead you through the triangle of galleries inside the temple. Look out for the frieze depicting the battle of Jhansi, in which the Rani appears in an upper room of the fort next to her horse, while musket-bearing British troops scuttle about below. Another great battle scene is the epic encounter between the ten-headed, twenty-armed demon Ravana and Rama's army of monkey soldiers. Elsewhere, episodes from the much-loved Krishna story crop up regularly, as do portraits of the Bundela rajas and their military and architectural achievements. Finally, a side pillar bears a sketch of two very inebriated English soldiers – as much a parody of the colonials' curious customs as an invective against the evils of drink.

The Chhatris

Standing in a solemn row of pale brown weed-choked domes and spires, the riverside **Chhatris** are Orchha's most melancholy ruins and a fitting place to wind up a tour of the town. The fourteen cenotaphs, memorials to Bundelkhand's former rulers, are best viewed from the road bridge or, better still, from the boulders on the opposite bank, where you get the full effect of their reflection in the still waters of the Betwa.

Accommodation and eating

Orchha only has a few **places to stay**, though they seem able to cope with the demand. Most of the **cheap accommodation** is managed by the Special Area Development Authority, and located down in the village. Much the best deal in this category is the *Palkhi Mahal* (①), a beautiful old *haveli* overlooking the Phool Bagh, which has three simple but clean and characterful rooms opening on to a terrace. Rooms in the *Mansarovar* (①), just off the crossroads above a *chai* shop, are a bit pokey, and no place to hang around during the day, but they're fine for a night or two. As a fall-back, try the *Prayatak Dharamshala* (①), a real eyesore down by the moat. Its spartan rooms and huge dorm are meant for Hindu pilgrims, but foreign visitors are welcome if there are vacancies. In the unlikely event of these three places being full, Orchha's only other cheap rooms are to be found in SADA's inconveniently situated *Satar Yatri Niwas* (①), 2km north of the village on the main road.

The most atmospheric and stylish place to stay, by a long chalk, has to be a converted seventeenth-century palace, the MPTDC *Sheesh Mahal* (①–⑥). Formerly the local Raja's country bolt-hole, this small, very friendly hotel only has seven non-a/c double (④) and one single (①) rooms – all excellent value, with attached bathrooms, window shutters and superb views. If you can possibly afford it, treat yourself to a romantic night in the royal apartment, room #1 (⑥). Perks include having your evening meal served by candlelight on your own private verandah, a bath-tub, and the ultimate loo with a view. Advance booking is recommended.

At present, there are only two **places to eat** in Orchha. The *Betwa Tarang*, a small rooftop cafe on the right-hand side of the bazaar as you head towards the bridge, serves cheap, mostly vegetarian Indian food with a couple of less spicy Chinese dishes. Portions at the more expensive MPTDC restaurant, up in the *Sheesh Mahal*, are not particularly generous, but the food is tasty, and the colonnaded dining hall is an attractive and sociable place to hang out in the evenings.

Khajuraho

The resplendent Hindu temples of **KHAJURAHO**, immaculately restored after almost a millennium of abandonment and neglect, are despite their inaccessibility among the most essential stops on any itinerary of India's historic monuments. Famed above all for the delicate sensuality – and forthright **eroticism** – of their sculpture, they were built between the tenth and twelfth centuries AD as the greatest architectural achievement of the **Chandella** dynasty. Mysteriously, the Chandellas appear to have forgotten about the temples soon afterwards, and it took "re-discovery" by the British before these masterpieces were fully appreciated in India, let alone internationally.

Although Khajuraho might look central on maps of the subcontinent, 400km southeast of Agra and the same distance west of Varanasi, it remains as remote from the Indian mainstream as it was when the temples were built – which is presumably what spared them the depredations of marauders, invaders and zealots that devastated so many early Hindu sites. No train routes cross this extended flood plain, set against the backdrop of the jagged Dantla Hills, and visitors who don't fly straight here are faced with a long bus journey from either of the nearest railheads.

THE EROTIC ART OF KHAJURAHO

Prurient eyes have been hypnotized by the unabashed **erotica** of Khajuraho ever since the "re-discovery" of the site in February 1838. A young British officer of the Bengal Engineers, **TS Burt**, alerted by the talk of his *palki* (palanquin) bearers, had deviated from his official itinerary when he came upon the ancient temples all but engulfed by jungle – "They reared their sun-burnt tops above the huge trees by which they were surrounded, with all the pride of superior height and age. But the chances are, the trees (or jungle rather) will eventually have the best of it".

Frank representations of oral sex, masturbation, copulation with animals, and such acts may have fitted into the mores of the tenth-century Chandellas, but were hardly calculated to meet with the approval of the upstanding officers of Queen Victoria:

> *I found . . . seven Hindoo temples, most beautifully and exquisitely carved as to workmanship, but the sculptor had at times allowed his subject to grow a little warmer than there was any absolute necessity for his doing; indeed some of the sculptures here were extremely indecent and offensive, which I was at first much surprised to find in temples that are professed to be erected for good purposes, and on account of religion. But the religion of the ancient Hindoos can not have been very chaste, if it induced people under the cloak of religion, to design the most disgraceful representations to desecrate their ecclesiastical erections. The palki [palanquin] bearers, however, appeared to take great delight at those, to them, very agreeable novelties, which they took care to point out to all present.*

Burt found the inscription on the steps of the Vishvanatha temple that enabled historians to attribute the site to the Chandellas, and to piece together their genealogy, but it was several more years before Major General Sir Alexander Cunningham produced detailed plans of Khajuraho, drawing the distinction between "Western" and "Eastern" groups that is still applied today. For Cunningham, "all [the sculptures] are highly indecent, and most of them disgustingly obscene".

The erotic images remain the subject of a disproportionate amount of controversy and debate among academics and curious tourists alike. The task of explanation is made more difficult by the fact that even the Chandellas themselves barely mentioned the temples in their literature, and the very name "Khajuraho" may be misleading, simply taken from that of the nearby village.

Among attempts to account for the sexual content of the carvings have been suggestions of links with **tantric** cults, which use sex as a pivotal part of worship. Some claim that they were inspired by the **Kama Sutra**, and similarly intended to serve as a manual on love, while others argue that the sculptures were designed to entertain the gods, divert their wrath, and thus protect the temples against natural calamities. Alternatively, the geometric qualities of certain images have been put forward as evidence that each represents a *yantra*, a pictorial form of a *mantra*, for use in meditation.

The sixteen large panels depicting sexual union that appear along the northern and southern aspects of the three principal temples – Kandariya Mahadeva, Lakshmana and Vishvanatha – concentrate on the junction of the male and the female elements of the temples, the *mandapa* and the *garbha griha* (the "womb" – see p.365). They might therefore have been intended as a visual pun, elaborated by artistic licence.

A radical new approach that ties history and architecture with living traditions has been proposed by Shobita Punja, in her book *Divine Ecstasy* (Penguin, 1992). Citing certain historic references to Khajuraho under the name of *Shivpuri* – the "City of Shiva" – she uses ancient Sanskrit texts to suggest that the dramatic temples and their celestial hordes represent the **marriage party of Shiva and Parvati**, taking place in a mythical landscape that stretches along the Vindhya Hills all the way to Kalinjar in the east. Thus Punja argues that the lower panel on Vishvanatha's southern walls shows Shiva as a bridegroom accompanied by his faithful bull, Nandi, while the intertwined limbs of the panel above – the couple locked in *mithuna*, assisted by a maiden to either side – show the actual consummation, with the lustful Brahma depicted as a pot-bellied voyeur at their feet.

The exquisite intricacy of the **temples** themselves – of which the most spectacular are **Kandariya Mahadeva**, **Vishvanatha** and **Lakshmana**, all in the conglomeration known as the **Western Group** – was made possible by the soft buff-coloured sandstone used in their construction. Considering the propensity of such stone to crumble, they have withstood the ravages of time remarkably well (suggestions that the 25 temples seen today are all that remain of an original 85 can be discounted, in the face of the lack of debris in the vicinity). Much of the ornate **sculpture** that adorns their walls is in such high relief as to be virtually three-dimensional, with strains of pink in the stone helping to imbue the figures with gentle flesh-like tones. The incredible skill of the artisans is evident throughout, with friezes as little as 10cm wide crammed with naturalistic details of ornaments, jewellery, hairstyles and even manicured nails. A huge congregation of gods and goddesses are everywhere in attendance.

To add to the beauty of the whole ensemble, the temples subtly change hue as the day progresses, passing from a warm pink at sunrise, to white under the midday sun, and back to warm pink at sunset. Dramatic floodlights pick them out in the evening, and they glow white beneath a luminous moon.

Arrival, information and local transport

Much the easiest way to get to Khajuraho is on the daily **flights** from either Delhi via Agra, or Kathmandu via Varanasi. The local **airport** is 5km south of the main square of Khajuraho town; the taxi ride in costs Rs50. The two nearest railheads are at **Jhansi** to the northwest, covered on p.293 (6hr by bus; 3–5 daily), and **Satna** to the southeast (4hr by bus; 5 daily). Most luxury buses, including the one that meets the *Shatabdi Express* at Jhansi on its way from Delhi via Agra to Gwalior, arrive next to *Raja Cafe* on the main square, while local buses terminate less than 1km southeast at the Bus Stand, within walking distance of most central hotels.

Information

The Government of India **tourist office** beside the *Raja Cafe* provides information only (Mon–Fri 9am–5.30pm, Sat 8am–noon; ☎2047); a counter at the airport operates at flight times. Staff at the MPTDC counter at the bus stand can book rooms at any of their Khajuraho locations (Mon–Fri 9am–5.30pm, Sat 8am–noon); their main office is at the *Tourist Lodge*.

Money can be changed at the *Canara Bank* in the *Ashoka Hotel* (Mon–Fri 10am–2pm; ☎2071), or at the *State Bank of India*, Maqbara Building (Mon–Fri 10.45am–2.30pm & 4–5pm; ☎2029). Khajuraho's **post office** is near the bus stand.

Local transport

Khajuraho is no more than an overgrown cluster of villages, without public transport, and visitors are dependent on the various rented vehicles that thrive in competition with each other. **Taxis** and **rental cars** are available at the main square, through *Raja Cafe,* or through operators such as the reliable Sanjay Jain of the *Hotel Jain* (☎2052), or *Khajuraho Tours* (☎2033) and *Travel Bureau* (☎2054), both in the Maqbara Building in the main square. Typical costs are Rs100 for half a day of local sightseeing, and Rs150 plus Rs4 per kilometre for longer journeys. **Rickshaw** drivers ask around Rs15 per hour; trips to the Eastern or Southern groups from town work out around Rs20.

By far the most enjoyable form of transport, with virtually empty roads, is to rent a **bicycle**; both the *Assi Restaurant* on Jain Temple Rd and *Mohammad Bilal* next door rent machines by the day and half-day.

The telephone **area code** for Khajuraho is ☎076861.

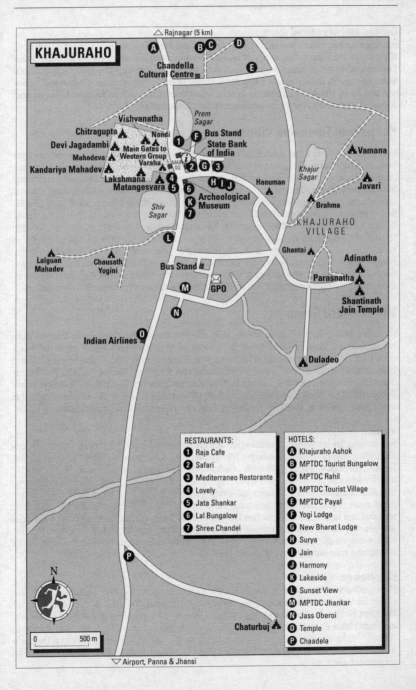

KHAJURAHO

△ Rajnagar (5 km)

Chandella
Cultural Centre

*Prem
Sagar*

Vishvanatha
Chitragupta
Nandi
Devi Jagadambi
Mahadeva
Main Gates to
Western Group
Kandariya Mahadev
Varaha
MAIN
SQ
Lakshmana
Matangesvara
Bus Stand
State Bank
of India

*Khajur
Sagar*

Vamana

Hanuman

Javari

Brahma

*Shiv
Sagar*

Archeological
Museum

KHAJURAHO
VILLAGE

Lalguan
Mahadev
Chausath
Yogini
Bus Stand
Ghantai

Adinatha
Parasnatha

GPO

Shantinath
Jain Temple

Indian Airlines

Duladeo

RESTAURANTS:
1 Raja Cafe
2 Safari
3 Mediterraneo Restorante
4 Lovely
5 Jata Shankar
6 Lal Bungalow
7 Shree Chandel

HOTELS:
A Khajuraho Ashok
B MPTDC Tourist Bungalow
C MPTDC Rahil
D MPTDC Tourist Village
E MPTDC Payal
F Yogi Lodge
G New Bharat Lodge
H Surya
I Jain
J Harmony
K Lakeside
L Sunset View
M MPTDC Jhankar
N Jass Oberoi
O Temple
P Chaadela

N

0   500 m

Chaturbuj

▽ Airport, Panna & Jhansi

Guides and organized tours

Among recommended and highly experienced **guides** who can help you make sense of Khajuraho are Ganga, the owner of *Hotel Harmony* (☎2135), and Brijendra Singh of the *Lal Bungalow* restaurant. Guides can also be contacted through the *Raja Cafe*; charges average around Rs80 for half a day for a group of up to four people. **Organized tours** are laid on by the more expensive hotels, while operators such as *Khajuraho Tours* and *Travel Bureau* (see above) can arrange explorations further afield.

Khajuraho: Town and Village

Facilities for visitors are concentrated in the uncluttered avenues of the small modern town of **Khajuraho**; the gates of the Western Group of temples open immediately onto its main square, which is surrounded by hotels and cafes. Curio shops sell everything from clothes, film and jewellery to Tibetan *thangkas*, but the sales pitch of their owners can be aggressive, and it makes sense to be wary of buying anything. Most local people live a pleasant 1.5-kilometre walk or cycle ride away to the east, in the more rustic setting of **Khajuraho Village**, near the **Eastern Group**. Two further temples, loosely termed the **Southern Group**, lie some distance out. Water is a prominent feature of the landscape, with the lake or tank of **Shivsagar** just south of the Western Group, **Khajursagar** to the east before the village, and the large **Premsagar** on the right to the north of the main square. Quite a few other villages are dotted within striking distance in the flat and rolling countryside; on the whole the inhabitants are pleased to see visitors.

The Western Group

Stranded like a fleet of stone ships, amid pristine lawns and flowerbeds fringed with bougainvillaea, Khajuraho's **Western Group** of temples seem oddly divorced from their past. With the exception of **Matangesvara**, just outside the main complex, all are now virtually devoid of religious significance, and they only spring back to life during Shivratri, the Shiva festival (Feb/March). The temples are open daily between dawn and dusk; the entrance fee (Rs0.50; Fri free) also grants access to the museum near the main gates. Visitors must remove their shoes before entering individual temples.

Varaha

Just inside the complex, a small open *mandapa* pavilion, built between the tenth and eleventh centuries, houses a huge, highly polished sandstone image of **Vishnu** as the Boar – **Varaha**. Carved in low relief on its body, 674 figures in neat rows represent the major gods and goddesses of the Hindu pantheon. Lord of the earth, water and heaven, the alert boar straddles Shesha the serpent, accompanied by what Burt conjectured must have been the most beautiful form of **Prithvi**, the earth goddess – all that remains are her feet and a hand on the neck of the boar. Above the image the lotus ceiling stands out in relief. Archeologists suggest that Varaha either belonged to the earlier Gupta period, and was brought here from elsewhere, or that the artisans of Khajuraho may simply have admired the Gupta style and chosen to emulate it.

Lakshmana

Beyond Varaha, adjacent to the Matangesvara temple across the boundary wall, the richly carved **Lakshmana** temple, dating from around 950 AD, is the oldest of the Western Group. It stands on a high plinth covered with processional friezes of horses, elephants and camels, as well as soldiers, domestic scenes, musicians and dancers. Among explicit sexual images is a man buggering a horse, flanked by shocked women onlookers. The sheer energy of the work gives the whole temple an astounding sense of movement and vitality.

THE BODY AND THE WOMB

The **Jangha**, or body, of each temple at Khajuraho – the walls between the base (*adisthana*) and the crowning spire (*shikhara*) – is the realm of the celestial. Their support and protection of the whole structure is symbolized by the strange composite animals, embodying strength and intelligence, depicted on two or three ornate encircling belts known as *bhandas*. Despite the popular belief that the copulating couples of Khajuraho represent the lives of ordinary people, according to Shobita Punja (see p.361) the *jangha* here in fact shows the marriage of Shiva and Parvati. She argues that the beautiful nymphs caught in naturalistic everyday poses are expressing surprise and wonder at seeing the god and the wedding party.

The construction of every temple echoes the creation of life itself, developing from a single seed (*bindu*) placed within its foundations. The central image of the temple, be it a *lingam* or a manifestation in human form, is positioned directly over this seed, and immediately under the highest point, the *shikhara*, in the sacred room known as the **Garbha Griha** – the womb. Though surrounded by the diverse manifestations and shapes of the world of matter – most obviously, on the external walls of the temple – the womb remains simple and without ornamentation, a representation of the dark generative nucleus of life.

While the plinth depicts the human world, the temple itself, the *adhisthana*, brings one into contact with the celestial realm. Two tiers of carved panels decorate its exterior, with gods and goddesses attended by *apsaras*, "celestial nymphs", and figures in complicated sexual acts on the lower tier and in the recesses. Fine detail includes a magnificent dancing Ganesh, the elephant god, on the south face, a master architect with his students on the east, and heavenly musicians and dancers.

Successive pyramidal roofs over the *mandapa* and the porch rise to a clustered tower made of identical superimposed elements. Small porches with sloping eaves project from the *mandapa* and passageway, with exquisite columns, each with eight figures, at each corner of the platform supported by superb brackets in the form of *apsaras*. The inner sanctum, the *garbha griha*, is reached through a door whose lintel shows Vishnu's consort **Lakshmi**, accompanied by **Brahma** and **Shiva**; a frieze depicts the **Navagraha**, the nine planets. Inside, the main image is of Vishnu as the triple-headed, four-armed Vaikuntha, attended by his incarnations of boar and lion.

Kandariya Mahadeva

Sharing a common platform with other temples to the rear of the enclosure, the majestic **Kandariya Mahadeva** temple, built between 1025 and 1050 AD, is the largest and most imposing of the Western Group. A perfect consummation of the five-part design instigated in Lakshmana and Vishvanatha, this Shiva temple represents the pinnacle of Chandellan art, its ornate roofs soaring dramatically to culminate 31m above the base in a *shikhara* that consists of 84 smaller replicas.

Kandariya Mahadeva is especially popular with visitors for the extraordinarily energetic and provocative **erotica** that ornaments its three tiers, covering almost every facet of the exterior. Admiring crowds can always be found in front of a particularly fine image of a couple locked in **mithuna**, sexual intercourse, assisted by a maiden to either side. One of Khajuraho's most familiar motifs, it seems to defy nature, with the male figure suspended upside down on his head; only when considered as though from overhead do the sinuous intertwined limbs begin to make sense.

An elaborate garland at the entrance to the temple, carved from a single stone, acts as a *torana*, the ritual gateway of a marriage procession. Both inside and out, lavish and intricate images of gods, goddesses, musicians and nymphs celebrate the occasion; within the sanctuary a dark passage leads to the *garbha griha*, and its central *shivalingam*. Niches along the exterior contain images of **Ganesh**, **Virabhadra** and the **Sapta**

Matrikas, the Seven Mothers responsible for dressing the bridegroom, Shiva. Wrathful deities and fearsome protectors, the seven consist of Brahmi seated on the swan of Brahma, a female counterpart of Shiva; a three-eyed Maheshvari on Shiva's bull Nandi; Kumari; Vaishnavi, seated on the bird Garuda; Varahi, the female form of Vishnu as the boar; Narasimhi, the female form of Vishnu as lion; and the terrifying Chamunda, the slayer of the *asuras* or "demons" Chanda and Munda, who is the only one of the Sapta Matrikas not a female representation of a major male god.

Devi Jagadambi

North of Kandariya Mahadeva along the platform, the earlier **Devi Jagadambi** temple is a simpler structure, whose outer walls lack projecting balconies. Originally dedicated to Vishnu, its prominent *mandapa* is capped by a massive pyramidal roof. Three *bhandas* (belts) bind the *jangha* (body), adorned with exquisite and sensuous carvings; the erotica on the third is arguably the finest in Khajuraho. Vishnu appears throughout the panels, all decorated with sinuous figures of nymphs, gods and goddesses, some in amorous embrace. Some consider the image in the temple sanctum to be a standing Parvati, others argue that it is the black goddess Kali, known here as Jagadambi.

Between Kandariya Mahadeva and Jagadambi, the remains of **Mahadeva** temple shelter a metre-high lion accompanied by a figure of indeterminate sex. Recurring throughout Khajuraho, the highly stylized lion motif, seen here rearing itself over a kneeling warrior with drawn sword, may have been an emblem of the Chandellas.

Chitragupta

Beyond the platform, and similar to its southern neighbour, Jagadambi, the heavily (and in places clumsily) restored **Chitragupta** temple is unusual in being dedicated to **Surya**, the sun god. Once again its design emphasizes the *mandapa*, which here has large projecting balconies, rather than the main temple. Ornate depictions of hunting scenes, nymphs and dancing girls accompany processional friezes, while on the southern aspect a particularly vigorous ten-headed Vishnu embodies all his ten incarnations. Within the inner chamber, the fiery Surya rides a chariot driven by seven horses.

The small and relatively insignificant temple in front of Chitragupta, also heavily restored and now known as **Parvati**, may originally have been a Vishnu temple, but holds an interesting image of the goddess Ganga riding on a crocodile.

Vishvanatha

Laid out along the same lines as Lakshmana, **Vishvanatha**, in the northeast corner of the enclosure – the third of the three main Western Group shrines – can be precisely dated to 1002 AD, as the work of the ruler Dhangadeva. Unlike some other temples at Khajuraho, which may have changed their presiding deities, Vishvanatha is most definitely a Shiva temple, as confirmed by the open *mandapa* pavilion in front of the main temple, where a monolithic seated **Nandi** waits obediently. Hundreds of small *shikharas* resembling miniature temples decorate the *mandapa* roof, sweeping up towards the climax of the main tower. Large panels between the balconies once more show *mithuna*, with amorous couples embracing among the sensuous nymphs. Idealized representations of the female form include women in such poses as writing letters, playing music and fondling babies. Decorative elephant motifs appear to the south of Vishvanatha, and lions guard its northern aspect.

Matangesvara

The simplicity of the **Matangesvara** temple, outside the complex gates, shows it to be one of Khajuraho's oldest structures; but although built early in the tenth century it remains in everyday use. Deep balconies project from the walls of its circular sanctuary, inside which a pillar-like *shivalingam* emerges from the pedestal *yoni*, the vulva – the recurring symbol of the union of Shiva. During the annual festival of Shivratri, the great wedding of Shiva and Parvati, the shrine becomes a hive of activity, drawing pilgrims for ceremonies that hark back to Khajuraho's distant past.

Shivsagar

A short way south of the complex, a few hundred metres from Matangesvara, the **Shivsagar** tank is surrounded by a motley assortment of buildings and open space. The steps down to it are animated with pilgrims bathing and collecting water from the "Ocean of Shiva". Cunningham's original map of the temples showed a body of water that ran north to divide the Western Group into two sections; crossing it to the temples may have represented a symbolic transition from the finite to the celestial.

Chausath Yogini

Beyond Shivsagar, to the southwest, lie the remains of the curious temple of **Chausath Yogini** – the "Sixty-Four Yoginis". Dated to the ninth century, Chausath Yogini consists of 35 small granite shrines clustered around a quadrangle; there were originally 64 shrines with the presiding goddess's temple at the centre. Only fourteen other temples, all in northern India, are known to have been dedicated to these wrathful and bloodthirsty female attendants of the goddess Kali; art historians surmise that the site was used by an esoteric tantric group. Around 1km further west are the ruins of **Lalguan Mahadev**, a small temple dedicated to Shiva.

The Eastern Group

The two separate networks of temples that make up Cunningham's "Eastern Group" are reached along the two forks of the road east of town. One is the tightly clustered **Jain Group**, while slightly north, scattered in the vicinity of Khajuraho Village, are a number of shrines and the two larger temples of Vamana and Javari.

Left of the road just beyond town, a comparatively new temple holds a 2.1-metre-high image of the monkey god **Hanuman** that may predate all of Khajuraho's temples and shrines. As the road forks left along the eastern shore of the murky Khajursagar lake, at the edge of Khajuraho Village, it passes the remains of a single-room temple erroneously referred to as the **Brahma** temple. Often considered to be a Vishnu temple, it is in fact a shrine to Shiva, as demonstrated by its *chaturmukha* – "four-faced" – *lingam*. While the eastern and western faces carry benign expressions, and the north face bears the gentler aspect of Uma, the female manifestation of Shiva, the ferocious southern face is surrounded by images of death and destruction. Crowning the *lingam* is the rounded form of **Sadashiva**, Shiva the Infinite at the centre of the cosmos.

The dirt road continues to the small **Javari** temple, set on a plain terrace and featuring a double porch and a slender *shikhara*, similar to Chaturbhuj of the Southern Group. Built late in the eleventh century, it may not have the exuberance seen elsewhere but nevertheless contains some fine sculpture, including alluring nymphets in classic Khajuraho style.

The largest of the Khajuraho Village temples, **Vamana**, stands alone in a field 200m further north. Built slightly earlier than Javari, in a fully evolved Chandella style, Vamana has a simple uncluttered *shikhara* that rises in bands covered with arch-like motifs. Figures including seductive celestial nymphs form two bands around the *jangha*, the body of the temple, while a superb doorway leads to the inner sanctum, which is dedicated to Vamana, an incarnation of Vishnu. On the way to the Jain Group, the road runs near what survives of a late tenth-century temple, known as **Ghantai** for its fine columns sporting bells (*ghantai*), garlands and other motifs.

The temple of **Parsvanatha**, dominating the walled enclosure of the **Jain Group**, is probably older than the main temples of Khajuraho, judging by its relatively simple ground plan. Its origins are a mystery; although officially classified as a Jain monument, and jointly administered by the Archaeological Survey and the Jain community, it may have been a Hindu temple that was gifted to the Jain community who settled here at a later date. Certainly, the animated sculpture of Khajuraho's other Hindu temples is well represented on the two horizontal bands around the walls, and the upper one is crowded with Hindu gods in intimate entanglements. Among Khajuraho's finest work, they include Brahma and his consort; a beautiful Vishnu; a rare image of the god of love, **Kama**, shown with his quiver of flower arrows embracing his consort **Rati**; and two graceful female figures, one applying *kohl* to her eyes and another removing a thorn from her foot. A narrow strip above the two main bands depicts celestial musicians (*gandharvas*) playing cymbals, drums, stringed instruments and flutes, some carrying garlands, cleverly caught in mid-flight with billowing robes. Inside, beyond an ornate hall, a black monolithic stone is dedicated to the Jain lord Parsvanath, inaugurated as recently as 1860 to replace an image of another *tirthankara*, Adinath.

Immediately south of Parsvanath, **Adinath**'s own temple, similar but smaller, has undergone drastic renovation. Three tiers of sculpture surround its original structure, of which only the sanctum, *shikhara* and vestibule survive; the incongruous *mandapa* is a much later addition. Inside the *garbha griha* stands the black image of the *tirthankara* Adinath himself. The huge 4.5-metre-high statue of the sixteenth *tirthankara*, **Shantinath**, in his newer temple, is the most important image in this working Jain complex. With its slender beehive *shikharas*, the temple attracts pilgrims from all over India, including naked *sadhus*.

The Southern Group

What is generally referred to as Khajuraho's **Southern Group** consists of two widely separated temples. The nearer to town, **Duladeo**, is down a dirt track south of the Jain Group, 1.5km from the main square – an isolation that stops it achieving the same impact as the great Western Group temples. Built early in the twelfth century, Duladeo in any case bears witness to the decline of temple architecture in the late Chandellan period, noticeable above all in sculpture that lacks the hallmark fluidity of Khajuraho. Nevertheless, its main hall does contain some exquisite carving, and the angular rippled exterior of the main temple is unique to Khajuraho. Rising on a star-shaped ground plan, on which the square inner sanctum dedicated to Shiva is extended by a multifaceted geometrical design, its complex architectural themes are developed only at the expense of becoming rather tediously repetitive. The entire structure, especially the *shikhara* and the pyramidal roof of the *mandapa*, has been extensively renovated.

Across the Khodar stream on the way south towards the airport, a road leads left along a dirt track to the disproportionately tall, tapering **Chaturbhuj**, around 5km south of Khajuraho – the *shikhara* is visible for miles above the trees. A forerunner to Duladeo, built around 1100 AD and bearing some resemblance to the Javari temple of the Eastern Group, Chaturbhuj is plainer than Duladeo and devoid of erotica. A remarkable 2.7-metre-high image of Vishnu graces its inner sanctum.

Museums

Opposite the Western Group, the small **Archeological Museum** is principally noteworthy for a remarkable sculpture of a pot-bellied dancing Ganesh, his trunk swinging with a vibrant sense of motion. Other assorted friezes, brackets and pieces of carving include a panel depicting the transportation and cutting of stone used to build the

THE KHAJURAHO FESTIVAL OF DANCE

The sleepy town of Khajuraho is transformed during the pleasant spring month of Phalguna (Feb/March), when the festival of **Maha Shivratri** draws pilgrims from all over the region to commemorate the marriage of Shiva.

Maha Shivratri also sees one of India's premier dance events – the **Khajuraho Festival of Dance**, a showcase for all forms of classical dance. The festival is typical of a new breed of event, sited at ornate ancient temples to attract visitors by combining tourism with culture (see also Konarak, in Orissa). However, although some performances are presented against the stunning backdrop of the Western Group, most take place in an outdoor arena, away from the temples at the Chandella Cultural Centre.

Precise dates for the festival, which is jointly organized by the Delhi-based Bharatiya Kala Kendra and MPTDC, tend to be confirmed late. Check with Government of India tourist authorities, and book early, as this is the one time of year when Khajuraho is certain to get busy. Tickets for specific events cost between Rs50 and Rs250, with foreigners expected to pay in US dollars.

temples; Vishnu reclining on the endless serpent, Anantha, with a lotus rising from his navel supporting Brahma the originator; a seated Buddha, the only one found in Khajuraho; and of course some erotica. Tickets for the Western Group entitle you to visit the museum for no extra charge, as many times as you like within a single day (daily 10am–5pm).

Sculpture in the small circular **Jain Museum**, at the entrance to the Jain temples, includes representations of all twenty-four *tirthankaras* (daily 7am–6pm; Rs1).

Accommodation

Khajuraho's more exclusive **hotels** are a bit secluded, but nearly all the mid-range and budget accommodation is close to the town centre, near the Western Group. Khajuraho can get very hot indeed, especially during the run-up to the monsoons, from February towards the end of June, and after the rains between August and November; air-cooled or air-conditioned rooms are a real boon at those times.

A good alternative to Khajuraho itself is *Gile's Tree House* in Madla, 24km southeast (see p.371), which can be booked through the two sisters who run the *Raja Cafe*.

Chandela (☎2054). Khajuraho's grandest address, with every amenity and all the hallmarks of the Taj Group, including a marble foyer and chandeliers. Non-residents can use the pool for Rs150. Puppet shows are held in the evenings. ⑨.

Harmony, Jain Temples Rd (☎2135). Neat and clean, with a restaurant. Ask for a room facing the small garden. Run by Ganga, an expert local guide. ③–④.

Jain, Jain Temples Rd (☎2052). Close to the heart of Khajuraho, near the *Harmony*. Reasonable air-cooled rooms and good vegetarian food. ②–③.

Jass Oberoi, By-Pass Rd (☎2085). Elegant but pleasantly understated. Top-of-the-range place where amenities include tennis courts, swimming pool and a good restaurant. ⑨.

Khajuraho Ashok (☎2024). Comfortable rooms and all conceivable facilities, such as a swimming pool (non-residents Rs75) and a bank. The helpful staff can arrange itineraries and car rental. ⑦–⑧.

Lakeside, opposite Shivasagar Lake (☎2120). Assorted rooms not far from the main square, including a dormitory. Popular with Japanese tourists. ②–⑤.

MPTDC Jhankar, near the *Oberoi* (☎2063). The best of Khajuraho's government-run accommodation; clean with a good restaurant but otherwise quite plain. ④–⑤.

MPTDC Payal (☎2076). Typical, rather charmless mid-range government place; but the rooms are spacious and quiet. The *Camp Ground* alongside can be booked through reception. ④–⑨.

MPTDC Rahil (☎2062). More government-run accommodation, once again soulless but in a leafy spot. Offers a dormitory and a canteen-like restaurant. ③–④.

MPTDC Tourist Bungalow (☎2064). Small, but having only six rooms seems to work to its advantage. ④.

MPTDC Tourist Village (☎2128). Modern mud huts spread across a few acres in imitation of a small village; the mock-rustic restaurant is also in a hut. ③.

New Bharat Lodge, Jain Temple Rd (☎2082). Cheap and basic, with its own cafe – clustered with other similar accommodation such as the *Sita* and *Yadav*. ①.

Sunset View, opposite Pahil Batika (☎2077). Quite ordinary, with a dormitory and budget accommodation as well as more expensive a/c rooms. ①–④.

Surya, Jain Temple Rd (☎2145). Clean, good-value place around a courtyard; does not give commissions to rickshaws. ②–③.

Temple, Airport Rd (☎2035). Low- to mid-budget rooms in a popular but quiet spot away from the centre. The arcade includes the *Indian Airlines* office. ②–④.

Yogi Lodge (☎2158). Behind the *Raja Cafe*, close to the Western Group. Excellent-value budget accommodation with a small courtyard. ①.

Eating

Khajuraho is surprisingly good for **food**; it even has an exciting new Italian place among its well-priced restaurants and cafes. The budget choices are not bad, and a cold beer never too far away, while the top hotels all provide reasonable to excellent eating.

Cafe Blue Sky, Airport Rd, Shivsagar. An open room overlooks the lake to lure in passers-by, but the food itself is disappointing.

Jass Oberoi, By-Pass Rd (☎2085). Elegant yet understated multi-cuisine restaurant in luxury hotel; works out as good value when paid for in foreign exchange. Highly recommended.

Jata Shankar, next to the Western Group gates, Main Square. Reasonable vegetarian *thalis*.

Lal Bungalow, next to the Museum. Very pleasant courtyard ambience with salads and Indian, Chinese and western cooking.

Lovely Restaurant, near the Western Group gates, Main Square. Quaintly named and reasonable Sikh-run *dhaba*.

Mediterraneo Ristorante Italiano, Jain Temple Rd. Excellent cafe with a pleasant roof terrace, run by an Indian-Italian couple. Fresh pasta makes a welcome change – you may miss the wine though.

MOVING ON FROM KHAJURAHO

Indian Airlines' IC407 **flight** leaves Khajuraho for Varanasi and Kathmandu at 12.25pm daily; the same plane returns in the afternoon as IC408, departing for Agra and Delhi at 5.45pm. Booking a flight at Khajuraho – *Indian Airlines* can be contacted at the *Temple* hotel (☎2035) or the airport (☎2036) – can be harrowing. Although you may be promised a confirmation, you can only be sure of a place on the flight at the airport, shortly before departure; allow a little leeway, and be prepared to be patient.

By far the easiest **road and rail** route out of Khajuraho is to take a bus to **Jhansi**, 175km east, and catch the a/c #2001 *Shatabdi Express* train via **Gwalior** and **Agra**, to **Delhi**. An express a/c tourist bus departs for Jhansi at noon, takes five hours, and costs around Rs200; much cheaper and much slower alternatives leave throughout the day (5.30am–4.45pm).

Between 6am and 3.30pm daily, buses set out on the four-hour journey to **Satna**, 125km east, which is served by trains on the **Bombay–Varanasi–Calcutta** network, as well as to **Gorakhpur**, from where buses head for the Nepal border.

To get to **Varanasi**, 415km northeast, take one of the many daily buses north to **Mahoba** (7.30am–4pm; 3hr; Rs20); the #1107 train to Varanasi departs at 8.50pm.

Finally, a single bus leaves Khajuraho at 9am for the long and gruelling 395-kilometre journey to **Agra**, arriving at 8.30pm, with a fare of under Rs100.

Raja Cafe, Main Square. Where it all happens in Khajuraho. The food might not be all that special, but you can pick up guides, information, and cold beers, and there's a bookstore and curio shop.

Safari, Jain Temple Rd. Popular among travellers, serving chicken and chips and salads.

Shree Chandel Vegetarian, Jain Temple Rd. Low-cost *thalis*, in simple cafe facing the bike shops.

Tourist Village (☎2128). Quite a nice place, despite the mock-rustic atmosphere, and the *thalis* are good. Not all that cheap, but recommended.

Panna National Park

The vast **Panna National Park**, known for its large cats (including tiger), deer and antelope (*nilgai*), lies a short way east of Khajuraho, spreading across a landscape of rocky hills and ravines covered mostly by scrubby deciduous forest. Access is easier than in some of India's better-known sanctuaries – you can even go in on foot if you take along an armed guide. It's best visited in winter, as the entire area gets extremely hot during summer – though there is a better chance then of seeing tigers as they emerge in search of water. Flowing north through the park towards the Ganges, the **River Ken**, whose rocky islands are bare during the lean seasons, harbours both the two major species of Indian crocodile, *magar* and the long-snouted *gharial*.

The exquisite lake of **Pandava Falls**, couched in a hollow and fed by a waterfall, is 11km east of Madla (see below). Legend has it that the Pandavas of *Mahabharata* fame spent time here. A short road leads left off the main road to a car park and tea shop that overlook a rocky escarpment and the lake. It's an idyllic spot, set within the deep emerald cover of the Panna forest, which offers a good chance of spotting wildlife – tigers are said to frequent the lake to drink. If you descend to the lake and follow a rough track, you'll emerge after a short distance beneath dripping cliffs, where caves have been hewn out of the rock to form shrines.

Park practicalities: Madla

The village of **MADLA**, 24km southeast of Khajuraho near a bridge across the picturesque River Ken, is the most convenient point of access to the park, and has the nearest accommodation. Two basic *Forest Rest Houses* can be booked through the Director, Panna National Park, Panna (☎52135); food arrangements must be made separately, which poses a problem in an area that offers only the occasional tea shop.

At *Gile's Tree House* (①), a beautiful open platform in the branches of a large tree on the riverbank, camping and sleeping out beneath the stars are free. Be prepared to be woken by the blaring of recorded opera to keep away tigers and other animals; the local crocodile was last seen slinking away to the south. Visitors should either bring food or make a donation towards their meals; a bar serving chilled beer is open long hours. The welcoming if eccentric Gile's previous *Tree House* was washed away a few years ago, when the Ken river dam was mistakenly opened and caused a devastating flood. Madla's more upmarket *Ken River Lodge* (⑦) consists of comfortable modern mud cottages overlooking the river near the bridge, with package deals including meals and a visit to the national park, or longer safaris.

Car rental for a comprehensive tour of the national park costs around Rs800, and is best booked at Khajuraho – facilities at Madla are extremely limited. To get to Madla by **bus**, take any Panna- or Chhatarpur-bound bus, then change at the T-junction 12km south of Khajuraho and pick up a jeep or a bus east. Allow plenty of time if you want to get from Khajuraho to Pandava Falls and back within a day; there's no accommodation near the falls apart from a friendly caretaker's lodge at the crossing on the main road.

En route to Madla, the Chhatarpur–Panna Road passes 1km north of the rambling white **Rajgarh Palace**, perched high on the commanding spur of a hill overlooking the valley, where visitors are allowed to wander the battlements.

EASTERN MADHYA PRADESH

The closest most visitors come to exploring **eastern Madhya Pradesh** is an occasional sleepy glance out of a train window during the interminable trip across the middle of India. Given the drabness of much of the landscape and the virtual absence of places worth breaking a long journey to see, this is hardly surprising. Nevertheless, the comparatively remote and sparsely populated east end of the state can still boast one attraction lost long ago by more heavily industrialized areas: an amazing abundance of **wildlife**. Far off the beaten track, though still accessible by public transport, two of the country's finest **national parks**, **Kanha** and **Bandhavgarh**, enable visitors to dip into some of the few remaining fragments of a forest that until 150 years ago extended right across central India. Both these reserves are among the last strongholds for many endangered species of birds and mammals, including the **tiger**.

Two major **rail networks** cut through the region. The *Central Railway* heads straight up the Narmada Valley to **Jabalpur**, the springboard for Kanha National Park, before veering north to Satna (4hr from Khajuraho) and the Gangetic Plains. The other main route, traced by the *Southeastern Railway*, skirts the top of Bastar (the remote and very poor southern extension of the state, dovetailing with Maharashtra, Andhra Pradesh and Orissa) and pushes on to the grim industrial cities of Raipur and Bilaspur at the head of the Chhattisgarh Valley. From here, the three big rivers that rise in the coal-rich hills to the north flow eastwards, while the railway makes for the Orissan border.

Jabalpur

After running in tandem across an endless expanse of wheat-fields and impoverished villages, the main Calcutta to Bombay road and railway lines converge on eastern Madhya Pradesh's largest city. Though an important provincial capital, **JABALPUR**, 330km east of Bhopal, harbours little of interest beyond a half-decent museum, some stalwart Raj-era buildings, and the **marble cliffs** gouged by the River Narmada out of some otherwise featureless countryside nearby. It's only really worth visiting en route to the national parks and tiger reserves, Kanha and Bandhavgarh, a day's journey east.

The city as it stands today is of comparatively recent origin. Formerly, access to the fertile Narmada Valley (and its lucrative trade routes) was controlled from the ancient capital at **Tripuri**, 9km west. The site, occupied from around 2000 BC onwards, rose to prominence under the Kushanas at the start of the Christian era. The Satavahanas (or "Andhras") followed, picking up what pieces their predecessors hadn't frittered away on court intrigues and unbridled debauchery. It was under the powerful and militaristic **Kalchuri** (or "Chedi") dynasty, however, that the city emerged as the region's dominant force. Pre-eminence on the battlefield enabled successive rulers to extend their borders westwards almost to within sight of the Arabian Sea before they were finally swept aside in the eleventh century by the **Gonds**, descendants of Tripuri's aboriginal inhabitants. Based at **Garha**, on the outskirts of modern Jabalpur, Gond rule gradually spread down the Narmada to Bhopal before it was challenged in 1564 by Asaf Khan, one of Akbar's more ambitious governors. Despite some brave resistance from **Rani Durgavati**, a sixteenth-century Rajput Boadicea, Gondwana was overwhelmed by the imperial army and Asaf Khan installed as its overlord. The **Garha-Mandla Gonds**, as the new ruling dynasty became known, were in turn ousted from their new capital at Mandla by the Marathas late in the eighteenth century, and they by the British, who established a military cantonment and administrative centre in Jabalpur in 1819.

Since then, the city has continued to prosper. Due largely to its location at the centre of India, Jabalpur these days is experiencing a period of intense and chaotic growth, driven by an influx of migrant workers from the poorer rural districts to the east.

Arrival, information and city transport

Central Railway **trains** arrive at the city's only **railway station**, 2km east of the centre. From here, it's a five-minute auto-rickshaw ride into town; less if you plan to stay in either of the slightly more expensive hotels at the top end of the cantonment district. The shambolic city **bus stand** is more in the thick of things, a short way south of the bazaar and west of Naudra Bridge, site of several cheaper hotels.

MPTDC has a friendly and efficient **tourist office** (Mon–Sat 10am–5pm; ☎22111) inside the main arrivals hall at the railway station. Apart from providing the usual range of hand-outs, they're also happy to give advice on travel arrangements, and can tell you if there are any vacancies in their hotels in Kanha or Bandhavgarh.

English-language newspapers and magazines are only available on the *Jackson's* hotel campus or from platform one in the railway station. The **Post Office** is a five-minute walk south of the railway station near the *Hotel Kalchuri*. If you need to **change money** (there are no foreign exchange facilities in either national park), the *State Bank of India* (Mon–Fri 10am–2pm, Sat 10am–noon) is a mile or so west of the railway station. The *Samdariya* or *Jackson's* hotels may also agree to help out in emergencies, though officially they're only supposed to change money for residents.

City transport

Jabalpur teems with both **auto-** and **cycle rickshaws**, while *Ambassador* **taxis**, more of a rarity, can usually be found in front of the *Samdariya*. Vehicles for day trips can be rented through the top hotels. Otherwise, **bicycles** make a good way to get about the city; ask in the repair shops opposite *Hotel Kalchuri*, or on Malvna Chowk in the main bazaar. The dilapidated **tempos** and **minibuses** that chug through the centre of town service outlying suburbs and are only useful for travelling out to the Marble Rocks.

The telephone **area code** for Jabalpur is ☎0761.

The City

With few real sights to speak of, the best way to kill time in Jabalpur **city** itself is a leisurely tour by bicycle or rickshaw. To the south of the railway line you'll find the remains of the former colonial enclave – now a peaceful suburb of leafy streets, bungalows, churches, British-style boarding schools and barracks. The underpass east of the station opens onto the far end of Collectorate Road. Head west from here, past Madhya Pradesh's Victorian **High Court** building, and you'll eventually arrive at the **clock tower** at the start of Jabalpur's large **bazaar** district. An intricate grid of long dusty streets lined with small shops, factories and disintegrating wooden buildings, the commercial hub is drab by Indian standards, and flooded with raucous traffic.

Due south of the bazaar, a short way down a side-road off Russel Chowk, the **Rani Durgavati Museum** (Tues–Sat 10am–5pm) preserves sculpture and inscriptions in the nineteenth-century home of the local Maharaja. The scruffy garden outside contains Hindu and Jain pieces, the finest being a partially damaged depiction of Shiva and Parvati (as Uma-Maheshwar), to the right of two large Jain statues. Inside, the ground-floor galleries are divided between Shiva (and Parvati), Vishnu and Jain *tirthankaras*, while the upstairs rooms are mostly devoted to bronze plates and seals recording regional dynastic histories. In the last room on the first floor, a small collection of female fertility figures includes a particularly striking *iskalitwashna*, or "naked courtesan bathing", which is a big hit with the bored museum attendants.

Three kilometres west of the centre, the main highway runs alongside a large tank lined with bathing *ghats*, banyan trees and a picturesque row of Hindu shrines crumbling into the water. Opposite, on top of a moraine of enormous granite boulders, stand the ruins of the **Madam Mahal** (pronounced *M'den Mel*) – a fortress-cum-pleasure-palace built by the Gond ruler Madan Shah in 1116. Nowadays, the stony slopes around the bottom of the hill also shelter a sprawl of ramshackle dwellings belonging

---

THUGS

With their pot-holes, unlit bullock carts, and suicidal drivers, trunk roads in Madhya Pradesh can be trying on the nerves at the best of times. For travellers in past centuries, however, a much more sinister threat to life lurked along the highways of central India. A secret sect of bandits and **Kali**-worshippers known as **Thugs** used to express their devotion to the jet-black four-armed goddess of death (usually shown splattered with blood, wearing a necklace of skulls and a belt of dead men's hands) by committing ritual murders on her behalf. The *thugs* would fall in with hapless travellers, gain their confidence, then summarily throttle them with silk scarves. Any pieces of the corpse not required for offerings were dumped in wells or buried in large pits.

Fear of retribution, and the belief among local rulers and village headmen that *thugee* was in some way the sacred will of the goddess herself, allowed the killing to continue unchecked for generations. Then, in 1830, the British dispatched the zealous sleuth Colonel – later Sir – **William Sleeman** to eradicate the sect. His tactics were ruthless and effective. Using promises of lenient prison sentences, Sleeman recruited a network of "super-grass" informers to expose the identities of the clandestine stranglers. In all, some four thousand *thugs* were captured during the twenty-year campaign, many of whom had notched up three hundred or more murders – one even confessed to killing 931 people in the course of his career. Special courts sent a total of four hundred convicted *thugs* to the gallows, and many more to jail or penal colonies in places such as the Andaman Islands. As for the informers, most ended up with their families in the purpose-built "School of Industry" (now a reform school) at **Jabalpur** where they were taught to turn their hand from silk scarves to carpet weaving. The word "thug" passed into common usage thanks to the characteristically macabre interest in the phenomenon shown by the British press.

to a community of potters (whose wares you can see piled up on the roadside), and a couple of immaculately whitewashed **Jain temples**.

The left fork in the main road 1km or so further on drops down to an impressive bridge spanning the River Narmada. Known locally as **Tilwara Ghat**, the handful of shrines near the water's edge below marks one of the sacred places where Mahatma Gandhi's ashes were scattered. The right fork takes you out towards the Marble Rocks.

Accommodation

The majority of Jabalpur's **hotels** are within easy reach of the bus stand – handy for early departures to Kanha or Bandhavgarh. Watch out for "luxury taxes" and "service charges" levied by the pricier places. If you're on a tight budget and don't fancy a seedy windowless cell (par for the course in the cheaper lodges) try the "economy" rooms in the mid-range hotels. The railway station has **retiring rooms** and cheap dorms.

Jackson's, Civil Lines (☎322320). This must have cut a fine dash in the Fifties, but it's now slipping into an advanced, if idiosyncratic, state of decay. A relaxing garden is some compensation for the rather inflated prices. Some a/c. ③–⑤.

Kanishka, Russel Chowk (☎29266). Nothing special, but the cheaper "standard" rooms are a good deal. Some a/c. ④–⑤.

Mayur, Malvna Chowk (☎31035). Large building on a hectic roundabout with dozens of very basic rooms, some without windows or bathrooms. Close to the bazaar. ①.

MPTDC Kalchuri, Civil Lines (☎321491). Immaculate and welcoming, though slightly character-less, hotel around the corner from the railway station. Rooms are spacious. Some a/c. ④–⑤.

Rahul, opposite *Jyoti Cinema*, Naudra Bridge (☎25570). A slight improvement on rock-bottom, but not much. Most of the cheaper rooms are windowless. Some a/c. ②–④.

Samdariya, off Russel Chowk (☎27580). Well run and central with simple, light, good-value "standard" rooms. Some a/c. ③–④.

Sawnhey, Naudra Bridge (☎31057). Basic and cheerless, but fine for a night. Avoid the back rooms. ①.

Sivalaya Lodge, opposite *Jyoti Cinema*, Naudra Bridge (☎21188). Currently the best-value budget place. Simple but clean rooms with hot water and attached bathrooms. Easy access to bus stand. ①.

Utsav, Russel Chowk (☎26038). An efficient, modern hotel smack in the centre of town. Rooms (all with satellite TV, attached bathrooms and hot water) range from excellent-value "economy" to ostentatious "super-deluxe" with bath-tubs. Mostly a/c. ②–⑥.

Eating

With a few exceptions, the best **places to eat** in Jabalpur are the hotels. Prices are reasonable and most menus varied, though not all of the restaurants serve alcohol.

The Grub Room, *Jackson's Hotel*, Civil Lines. Jaded and spartan decor, but the moderately priced veg and non-veg grub is good. Some Chinese and adventurous western options.

Indian Coffee Houses, both in the bazaar district (see map). Great for cheap *dosas, iddlis, utta-pams* and other light snacks. Also open early (8.30am) for breakfast.

Kalchuri, Civil Lines. Low light, starched table cloths and the usual MPTDC menu: a modest selection of tasty but rather over-priced meat, veg and Chinese dishes. Tandoori after 7.30pm only.

Samdariya, off Russel Chowk. The place to splash out on top-notch Indian, Chinese etc. Western-style coffee shop also does delicious south Indian snacks.

Satyam Shivam Sundaram, near *Jyoti Cinema*, Naudra Bridge. Don't be put off by the bizarre rococo interior. The strictly veg food, including *thalis* and some set menus, is excellent value and some tables overlook the street. Inexpensive.

Sawney, Naudra Bridge. Bustling, unpretentious and cheap. Generous heaps of spicy Punjabi food served mainly to an office crowd. The a/c family room (*Eskimo*) next door is alcohol-free.

Utsav, Russel Chowk. Studiously respectable vegetarian restaurant with an enormous and surprisingly inexpensive menu. The dingy dining room is better for evening meals.

MOVING ON FROM JABALPUR

Kanha National Park is most travellers' next move after Jabalpur. Direct *MPSRTC* services leave the central bus stand twice daily for the main gate at Kisli: the first, at 7am, is faster by one hour; the second leaves at 11am. **Bandhavgarh** is harder to reach; you have to catch a train out to Umaria (via Katni) and take a local bus from there.

To get to **Khajuraho**, catch one of the frequent early-morning trains as far as Satna (3hr), where you can pick up direct state buses. **Varanasi** is on the main Bombay–Calcutta line. Aim for the *Bombay–Ratnagiri Express* (#1065; Mon, Wed & Thurs at 10.45pm). Daily trains from Jabalpur to **Patna** help travellers en route to **Nepal**.

Of the five or six daily express trains to **Bombay**, the *Bombay Mail* #3003 is the most convenient. For **Delhi**, take the daily *Mahakosal Express* #1449 at 2.35pm, or travel down to Itarsi junction to pick up the more frequent northward services via Bhopal, Gwalior and Agra. There are also three weekly trains to **Madras** (Tues, Thurs & Sun, 3.15am).

The marble rocks

In a bustling, dusty, Oriental land, the charm of coolness and quiet belonging to these pure cold rocks, and deep and blue yet pellucid waters, is almost entrancing.

Capt J Forsyth, *The Highlands of Central India* (1889).

West of Jabalpur, the Narmada suddenly narrows, plunges over a series of dramatic waterfalls, then squeezes through a seam of milky-white marble before continuing on its westward course across the Deccan. The thirty-metre cliffs and globulous shapes worn by the water out of the rock may not exactly rank as one of the seven wonders of the natural world, but the **MARBLE ROCKS**, known locally as **Bheraghat**, are as good a place as any to while away an idle afternoon.

Bheraghat **village** itself, overlooking the gorge, is a sleepy little place, with few signs of activity beyond the ringing of chisels in the workshops of its many **marble-carvers**. Most pieces on display in the shop-fronts are heavy-duty Hanumans, *shivalingams* and other deities, destined for other parts of India – the local translucent white marble is much in demand for new temples and shrines.

From the main street, a flight of steps leads down to the river and the **ghats**, where **rowing boats** are on hand to ferry visitors up the gorge. Trips take thirty to forty minutes, depending on the water level (if the dams upstream are open, the current can be too strong for the boats to pass), though you're more than likely to spend at least that long waiting for the requisite fifteen passengers to show up. Once under way, the boatman begins his spiel, pointing out the more interesting **rock formations**. The most appreciative noises from the other passengers are not reserved for the "footprint of the celestial elephant", however, or even the "monkey's leap" (jumped over by Hanuman on his way to Lanka), but for the places where Hindi movie-stars posed in well-known films shot on location here. Look out for the enormous **bees' nests** dangling from the crevices in the rock. One nineteenth-century guidebook urged its readers to refrain from "smoking or firing guns" in the gorge, as an angry swarm once attacked a party of English army engineers who were carrying out survey work for a new railway here. A memorial plaque, still visible on top of the cliffs, was erected to one of their number who drowned trying to shake the bees off. During the evenings the formations are floodlit.

Not surprisingly, Bheraghat is also something of a religious site. From the fork in the river, 107 stone steps lead up to the tenth-century **Mandapur temple**, a circular building known for the 64 beautifully carved tantric goddesses, or **Chausath Yogini**, which stand in its enclosure.

Beyond the temple, at the far end of the gorge, the **Dhaundhar** or "Smoke Cascade" waterfall is particularly dramatic when shrouded in spray after the monsoons. It's reached either by following the main street out through the village, or else via the goat-track that twists along the top of the cliffs below the MPTDC *Motel*. Just above the waterfall, you pass a string of stalls loaded with locally carved marble goods – among them some fine pocket-size pieces of religious kitsch. Tempos back to Jabalpur start from the open space between the stalls and the village.

Practicalities

Getting to Bheraghat under your own steam from Jabalpur involves picking up a **tempo** from the bus stand next to the museum. Although the 45-minute stop-and-start trip can be excruciating, it's an improvement on the only alternative: a tedious bicycle ride along a busy main road. Clamber off the tempo when you see a row of cold drink and souvenir stalls lining a sharp left-hand bend in the main street.

Some **accommodation** is available in the village if you want to stay the night. Just off the road out to the falls, MPTDC have converted a colonial bungalow, complete with verandah, well-kept lawn and easy chairs, into a very pleasant *Motel* (☎83424; ④). The garden looks out over the gorge and a small **restaurant** serves a standard veg and non-veg menu. The only other option is the much cheaper, if less salubrious *Hotel Rahul Tourist Home* (☎83450; ①–②), opposite the brightly painted Jain temple on the main street (sign in Hindi). Prices start at rock-bottom and increase with the size of the rooms, which are basic but reasonably clean. There's also some common roof-space, and a small restaurant that knocks up simple vegetarian food if given a little warning.

From Jabalpur towards Kanha

From Jabalpur, the four-hour bone-shaking bus ride to Kanha takes you into some of eastern Madhya Pradesh's most isolated rural districts. When Capt J Forsyth and his Bengal Lancers pushed through en route to the uncharted interior at the end of the nineteenth century, this landscape was a virtually unbroken tract of *sal* forest teeming with Indian bison, deer and tigers. Since then, the local aboriginal hunter-gatherers have taken up the plough, and all but a few patches of forest clinging to the ridges of nearby hillsides have been logged, cleared for farmland or simply burnt as firewood by the burgeoning populations of share-croppers. A further scar on the land was inflicted more recently when several valleys were flooded as part of a large-scale **dam project**. During the short winter dry spell, you occasionally come across desolate stretches of mud and tree stumps where only a decade ago woodland and villages stood.

Shortly after **Narayanganj**, a junction where the bus halts for a ten-minute *chai* stop, the road rejoins the Narmada again, twisting through the patchwork of ripening wheat and sugar-cane planted in the well-watered alluvial soil that lines the river banks. Along the way, look out for the two-tiered terracotta roofs on the village huts – a local design inherited from earlier thatching techniques.

It was around these parts, in 1564, that **Rani Durgavati**, the warrior queen of Gondwana, was defeated in battle by Asaf Khan, one of Akbar's right-hand men. When she heard that the viceregal army was advancing on her kingdom, Durgavati rounded up her troops from the harvest, and marched north on elephant-back to waylay the attackers. Unable to hold off the better-armed Moghuls, the Gonds were soon forced to retreat to a place near Mandla where, with the swollen river blocking their only escape, they were finally routed. Asaf Khan allegedly captured 101 cooking pots full of gold and jewels, though not Durgavati, who stabbed herself through the heart to avoid the ignominy of being incarcerated in his harem.

Mandla

Three hours out of Jabalpur, the bus pulls into **MANDLA**, the district headquarters and last sizeable town before Kanha. Travellers rarely, if ever, venture further than the bus stand here, though it's perfectly possible to do so if you catch the early service from Jabalpur and pick up the later one when it arrives in Mandla at 2pm – leaving a more than adequate four hours in which to explore the town.

Mandla's easily defensible position, on a narrow tongue of land in the River Narmada, made it an obvious site for the new regional capital when the old one, Garh, was menaced from the north during the seventeenth century. In spite of its **fort** and walls, the Maharathas managed to overthrow the last Garha-Mandla king a hundred years later, torturing him to death in his own castle. A couple of crumbling old gateways are virtually all that's left of the original buildings, overlooking the picturesque **confluence** of the Banjar, Sarasvati and Narmada rivers.

From the bus stand, head straight down the main street, past the market (on the right), as far as the staggered crossroads. The narrow lane opposite takes you past rows of **silver** and "bell-metal" (brass) shops full of jewellery, cooking utensils and smiths bent over blow-torches in the half-light, to a stone bridge spanning an overgrown moat. Once across, you come out alongside the ruined fort – much less noteworthy nowadays than the shiny white temples in its midst. The fortified **gateway** at the far end, which you can climb inside, opens on to a strip of yellow sand from where the ferry-boats push off for the far bank (pay the *chowkidar* sitting under the arch).

Known since the ancient Hindu scriptures as **Trivendi Sangam**, the confluence, said to form the shape of the auspicious "Om" symbol, is a place of pilgrimage and the area's prime site for performing mortuary rituals. It's one of those magical little spots you sometimes come across in central India where the pace and tone of life seems to have changed very little for centuries: *pujaris* (priests) sit cross-legged under rickety bamboo sun-shades, pilgrims bathe in the river, and flat-bottomed canoes paddle past on their way to the market. Just up from the river are a couple of temples, one dedicated to Durga and the other, distinguished by its three oddly tapering towers, to Rama. Assorted ashrams and *mathas* (religious institutions), further around the river bend, can be reached by ferry from the eastern side of the town, where there are also more *ghats* and dilapidated seventeenth-century temples.

Practicalities

Bicycles can be rented, at the princely hourly rate of Rs1, from either of two shops opposite the bus stand. Finding somewhere sanitary to **eat** however is more of a problem, the only places being the grim sweet and snack stalls dotted around town.

If, for any reason, you want to **stay** the night, avoid the two filthy dives at the top of the main street and seek out the *PWD Inspection Bungalow* (①), close to the Kanha road up in the north side of the town. Permission normally has to be obtained in advance, though tourists are usually granted special dispensation. Mandla's *State Bank of India* (Mon–Fri 10am–2pm, Sat 10am–noon) exchanges cash but not travellers' cheques.

Kanha National Park

Often dubbed the greatest of all India's wildlife reserves, **KANHA NATIONAL PARK** rarely disappoints those travellers who make the arduous five- or six-hour haul over bumpy back-country roads to get there. Nearly two thousand square kilometres of deciduous forest, savannah grassland, hills and gently meandering rivers are encompassed within its borders – home to literally hundreds of species of animals and birds, including the declining population of **tigers** that are for most people the big attraction.

Central portions of the Kanha Valley were designated as a wildlife sanctuary as long ago as 1933. Prior to this, the whole area was one enormous viceregal hunting ground, its game the exclusive preserve of high-ranking British army officers and civil servants seeking trophies for their colonial bungalows. Not until the 1950s though, after a particularly voracious hunter bagged thirty tigers in a single shoot, did the Indian government declare Kanha a bona fide national park. Since then, animal numbers have recovered dramatically, and the park, one of the original participants in Indira Gandhi's **Project Tiger**, has expanded to encompass a large protective buffer zone – a move not without its opponents among the local tribal community, who depend on the surrounding forest for food and firewood. Over the years, the authorities have had a hard time reconciling the needs of the villagers with the demands of conservation and tourism; but for the time being at least, an equitable balance seems to have been struck. Kanha basks in its reputation as a model in wildlife management, and is a thoroughly congenial environment in which to enjoy some of central India's most beautiful, unspoiled, and quintessentially Kipling-esque countryside.

The Park

From the main gates, at **Kisli** in the west and **Mukki**, 35km away in the south, a complex network of motorable dirt-tracks fans out across the park, taking in a good cross-section of its diverse terrains. Which animals you see from your open-top jeep largely depends on where your guide decides to take you. Kanha is perhaps best known for the broad sweeps of grassy rolling meadows, or **maidans**, along its river valleys, which support large concentrations of **deer**. The park has several different species, including the rare "twelve-horned" **barasingha** (swamp deer), plucked from the verge of extinction in the 1960s; a handful of *hiran* (blackbuck), now perforce enclosed by tall jackal-proof fences; and the ubiquitous *chital* (spotted deer – the staple diet of Kanha's tigers), which congregate in especially large numbers during the rutting season in early July, when it's not uncommon to see four thousand at one time.

The **woodland** carpeting the spurs of the Maikal Ridge that taper into the core zone from the south, consists of *sal*, teak and moist deciduous forest oddly reminiscent of northern Europe. Troupes of black-faced langur monkeys crash through its canopy, while *gaur*, India's tallest wild buffalo, forage through the fallen leaves. Years of exposure to snap-happy humans seem to have left the awesome, hump-backed bulls impervious to camera flashes, but it's still wise to keep a safe distance. Higher up, you may catch sight of a spiky-horned *nilgai* (blue cow), a porcupine, python, sloth bear, wild boar, mouse deer or a secretive *sambar* – a favourite snack for the nocturnal predators that prowl through the trees. Sightings of **leopards** too are not an impossibility, although these shy animals tend to steer well clear of motor vehicles.

Kanha also boasts an exotic and colourful array of **birds**, including Indian rollers, bee-eaters, golden orioles, paradise fly-catchers, egrets, some outlandish **hornbills** and numerous kingfishers and birds of prey. Enthusiasts should try to stay at Mukki as it's closer to the **River Banjar** area with its many different water-birds.

As for **tigers**, with their prey consisting of virtually anything that bleeds, from river fish to *gaur*, you could easily stumble across one at any moment. Brakes of bamboo and the tall elephant-grass lining the banks of streams and water-holes are good places. Guides will also stop from time to time to point out pug-marks or "drag-tracks" left by tigers tugging their quarry to cover off the roadside. To be sure of seeing one in the flesh, reckon on spending at least two to three days in Kanha, going out for a few hours every morning and evening. Failing that, there's always the **"tiger show"**. At the end of each morning sortie, all the jeeps converge on the visitor centre in the middle of the park (7–10.30am & 4–6pm) where you're left to watch a twenty-minute audio-visual show, and to peruse a dry but informative exhibition on local flora and fauna. In the meantime, the *mahouts* are out with their elephants trying to run a well-fed female tiger to ground somewhere nearby. When they've found one, you're ferried off to the spot and, for a small sum, can then ride the short distance on elephant-back to where she's dozing apparently unperturbed in the long grass. Although this faintly ludicrous performance is no replacement for the elephant safaris they used to have at Kanha, it does allow you to get to within a few yards of a wild tiger – a somewhat disconcerting experience – and to take as many close-up photographs as you want. Incidentally, rumours that the animals are somehow drugged for the "show" are untrue; they're simply too full of food and too accustomed to all the attention to complain.

Park practicalities

Kanha is **open** from September 1 until the monsoon arrives at the end of June. During peak season, between November and February, the nights and early mornings can get very **cold**, and there are frequent frosts, so bring a jumper or shawl – without one, an open-top jeep safari quickly gets to be a real endurance test.

Getting there

The most straightforward way to **get to Kanha** is via Jabalpur, which is well connected by rail to most other parts of the country. If you're coming from **Orissa**, take a direct train to Katni on the main Bombay–Calcutta line and change there. The nearest airport with scheduled domestic flights is at Nagpur (226km).

Daily **buses** leave Jabalpur for Kisli (via Mandla) at 7am and 11am, the first taking five hours to cover the 176km and the second six hours. Both stop briefly at the barrier in **Khatia**, a bedraggled collection of *chai* stalls and lodges 4km down the road from Kisli, so you can register your arrival with the park office. **Mukki** can only be reached by the daily 12.30pm private bus from Mandla to Malakhand/Khatia.

Getting around

As **walking** inside the park is strictly forbidden, **jeeps**, which leave from Kisli every day at 6am and 6pm on the dot, are the only way to **get around**. The best way to arrange a seat for yourself is to have a word with one of the managers of the MPTDC hotels, preferably 24 hours beforehand. The fare, worked out according to distance and including the fee for the obligatory **guide**, is divided equally between however many passengers there happen to be (up to a maximum of six). Expect to pay Rs350–450 between you for a full session. Avoid the diesel jeeps if possible; these are noisier and tend to scare off the animals long before you get anywhere near them.

If you arrive on the early bus and feel up to an evening safari, try asking groups on their way through the main Kisli barrier if they have a spare place. Only parties on package deals from the upmarket hotels are likely to decline the offer, as they usually have their own *Landrovers* and can afford to shun hitch-hikers.

Food and accommodation

Kanha sees a lot more visitors than you might expect, and even outside high season it's wise to book **accommodation** in advance. Although MPTDC have a *Forest Lodge* at **Mukki** in the south, most of the "hotels" are in and around **Kisli** at the western entrance, which is easier to get to by public transport, and is situated in an altogether more atmospheric location inside the park proper. MPTDC recommend that you reserve your room at least five working days before arrival – either by calling into one of their regional tourist offices (in Delhi, Bombay, Calcutta, Jhansi, or Jabalpur, or most other major towns and cities in Madhya Pradesh) or by sending a fifty percent advance to: Central Reservations–Tours Division, *MPSTDC Ltd*, Fourth Floor Gangotri, TT Nagar, Bhopal 462 003 (☎0755/554340). If you turn up hoping to find somewhere on

THE INDIAN TIGER

Feared, adored, immortalized in myth and used to endorse everything from breakfast cereals to petrochemicals, few animals command such universal fascination as the **tiger**. Only in India, however – thanks to drastic conservation measures – can this rare and enigmatic big cat still be glimpsed in the wild, stalking through the teak forests and *terai* grass to which it is uniquely adapted. A solitary predator, at the apex of the food chain, it has no natural enemies save one.

As recently as the turn of the century, up to forty thousand tigers still roamed the subcontinent. However, **shirkar**, tiger hunting, had long been the "sport of kings"; an ancient dictum held it auspicious for a ruler to notch up a tally of 109 dead tigers, and nawabs, maharajas and Moghul emperors all indulged their prerogative to devastating effect. The trigger-happy British brought tiger hunting to its most gratuitous excesses. Photos of pith-helmeted, bare-kneed *burrasahibs* posing behind mountains of striped carcasses became a hackneyed image of the Raj. Even Prince Philip (now President of the World Fund for Nature) couldn't resist bagging one during a royal visit to India.

Poaching too has taken its toll. The black market has always paid high prices for live animals, and for pieces of them believed to hold magical or medicinal properties. Tiger meat is used in China to ward off snakes; its brain to cure acne; its spore for piles; and kidney fat, applied liberally to the afflicted organ, as an antidote to male impotence.

In the years following Independence, **demographic pressures** nudged the Indian tiger perilously close to the edge of extinction. As the human population increased in rural districts, more and more trees were cleared to open up new land for farming – thereby depriving large carnivores of their main source of game and of the cover they needed to hunt. Forced to turn on farm cattle as an alternative, tigers were drawn into direct conflict with man; some animals, out of sheer desperation, even turned **man-eater** and attacked human settlements.

By the time an all-India moratorium on tiger shooting was declared in 1972, numbers had plummeted to below two thousand. A radical response came the following year, with the inauguration of **Project Tiger**. At the personal behest of Indira Gandhi, nine areas of pristine forest were set aside for the last remaining tigers. Displaced farming communities were resettled and compensated, and armed rangers employed to discourage poachers. At first, the strategy seemed to work well. Using **pug marks** – like human fingerprints, unique to each individual animal – wardens monitored a steady recovery in the tiger population inside the reserves, from the low-point of 268 in 1973 to 1327 in 1992. Today, there are nineteen different Project Tiger sites, while a further 3000 tigers are thought to live in other areas of protected forest not incorporated into the scheme.

Nevertheless, the Indian tiger is still far from safe. Since 1988 the overall population should, through natural regeneration, have increased by well over a thousand; instead it has remained stagnant. The fate of the missing animals is no mystery. Tiger bone fetches around $300 per kilo, and most are packed into parcels, posted to remote border stations and smuggled off to the Far East to be turned into traditional medicine. In August 1993, undercover wildlife investigators recovered a 400kg-haul of tiger bones, together with forty fresh carcasses, from a team of Tibetan smugglers in Delhi who had promised to supply 1000kg more on demand. Sadly, much of the illegal trade seems to be centred on the very reserves set up to protect the animals in the first place. Well-organized guerrilla groups operate out of remote national parks, including Corbett, Dudhwa and Kanha, where inadequate numbers of poorly armed and poorly paid wardens offer little more than token resistance. You won't hear this from many Project Tiger people, park officials or guides (who are understandably reluctant to jeopardize lucrative tourist traffic by admitting that sightings are getting rarer), but the prognosis looks very gloomy indeed. Some experts even claim that at the present rate of destruction, India's most exotic animal could face extinction by the year 2000.

Poachers permitting, your best chances of seeing a wild tiger in India at the moment are at Kanha and Bandhavgarh (Madhya Pradesh), Ranthambhore (Rajasthan), Corbett and Dudhwa (Uttar Pradesh), Manas and Kaziranga (Assam) and Bandipur (Karnataka).

spec, your choice may at best be limited to a room in Khatia. This shouldn't, however, apply to budget travellers as the *Youth Hostel*, Kanha's best cheap deal, has 24 dorm beds and rarely fills to capacity. Everywhere listed below also serves food, and the MPTDC restaurants are open to non-residents if you give them some warning.

Wherever you stay, make sure you get off the bus at the right place, as the hotels at Khatia and the park gates are scattered along a six-kilometre stretch of road that sees very little traffic during the day.

Indian Adventures, Khatia (book through: *IAWR*, 257 SV Rd, Bandra, Bombay 400 050; ☎022/640 6399). A similar "all-in" package to *Kipling Camp*. Separate chalets overlooking river, library, resident experts and al fresco restaurant with occasional tribal cabaret. ⑨.

Kipling Camp, 4km from Khatia (book through: *Tollygunge Club Ltd*, 120 DP Sasmal Rd, Calcutta 700 033). British-owned and run cottage complex offering rustic comfort at absurd prices. "Ethnic" rooms, meals around the fire and pleasant forest location. Full board, safari and guides included. ⑧.

Moti Chandan, Khatia (☎07642/4252). Just before the barrier on the roadside. Very basic rooms with fans, old beds and bathrooms. Meals in rough and ready restaurant are part of the deal – the cheapest in Kanha. More expensive "VIP Deluxe" chalets have bath-tubs and air-coolers. ③–④.

MPTDC Baghira Log Huts, Kisli. Spacious but dark rooms in self-contained chalets in the heart of the forest. Good restaurant, with a varied menu, that also serves beer. ⑤.

MPTDC Jungle Camp, Khatia. The best-value cheap rooms if the *Youth Hostel* doesn't appeal. Surrounded by woodland, close to the main road, but a drive from the Kisli campus. ③.

MPTDC Kanha Safari Lodge, Mukki. Open all year round. 35km from Kisli at the southern entrance to park, with good access to more remote areas. The best place to get away from it all. Meals, jeeps, guides etc available on site. Some a/c. ④–⑤.

MPTDC Youth Hostel, opposite Kisli's "bus stand". Large rudimentary dorms and communal washrooms; rates include a relentless diet of *thalis* served in military-style canteen. Excellent value. ②.

Bandhavgarh National Park

Despite its claim to have the highest density of **tigers** of any reserve in India, **BANDHAVGARH** has never enjoyed the popularity of its southern cousin Kanha. Yet Madhya Pradesh's newest national park, lying amid the rugged western fringes of the Bhagelkhund Plateau 195km northeast of Jabalpur, packs the same wealth of wildlife into a smaller area, and also offers fine scenery and exotic ancient ruins. Unfortunately, it's also much harder to get to by public transport and has, as yet, made few concessions to budget travellers. If, however, you're determined to see a wild tiger and are prepared to spend a little more time and money to do so, a trip to Bandhavgarh is well worth considering.

Inscriptions in the rock-cut **caves** hewn from the cliffs that protect the northern approaches to Bandhavgarh **fort**, at the centre of the park, show a human presence since at least the first century BC. The **Chandellas**, responsible for the temples at Khajuraho, were among successive dynasties to establish power bases here before the twelfth century. Thereafter, the **Bhagels** took over – the first in a long and unbroken line of kings who ruled out of Bandhavgarh until the court decamped to Rewa in 1617. Like his forefathers, the present Maharaja of Rewa used the area as a hunting ground before handing it over to the government in 1968. In 1986, two more chunks of forest were added to the original core zone, giving the park a total of 437 square kilometres.

The park

An all-weather road cuts straight through Bandhavgarh at its narrowest point, connecting Umaria, the nearest town, and **Tala**, the park headquarters just beyond its northern limits. Most of the area north and west of the fort is covered by 32 craggy sandstone hills, separated by perennial streams, swamps, and grassy valleys. To the south, large tracts of *sal* and damp deciduous forest are interspersed with open *maidans* – perfect terrain for the sixty or so tigers who prey on the deer and antelope that browse on the park's abundant grassland. These include a shy but animated gazelle, the *chinkara*; the world's only four-horned deer, the *chausingha*; as well as the more common *nilgai* (blue cow) and *chital* (spotted deer). Hyenas, foxes and *dholes* (wild dogs) also appear occasionally in the open country.

Bandhavgarh's **forests** shelter a wide assortment of mammals and reptiles, among them muntjac, *gaur*, a few sloth bears, porcupines, *sambar*, pythons and a small but highly elusive population of leopards. Look out too for some very exotic **birds** – one hundred and fifty species at the last count, though no doubt you could add to the list if you stayed long enough. Regular stars include various drongos, fly-catchers, bee-eaters, rollers, parakeets, eagles, vultures and two kinds of rare **hornbills**.

The fort

According to the *Ramayana*, Bandhavgarh's ancient **fort** was built by the same monkey architects who erected the bridge used by Rama and Hanuman to invade Lanka. Today, it lies deserted and in ruins, towering 800m above the surrounding countryside atop a dramatic escarpment of sandstone.

Visits can be made either on foot or by jeep, though **permission** – a formality – must first be arranged through your hotel. The best way to approach the plateau is from the south side, starting at an 11-metre reclining Vishnu left by the Chandellas. From the **Shesh Saya**, a path leads past a small water-tank, the source of the River Charaganga, up towards the entrance to the fort. After passing through the main gateway, you emerge to a stretch of open ground strewn with chunks of masonry and sculpture – including a colossal Vishnu depicted in his fourth incarnation as the man-lion **Narashima**. The stunning **views** over the ramparts are well worth the steep climb.

Park practicalities

Bandhavgarh is **open** from November to June, the **best time to visit** being during the cool months of December through to March. Without your own vehicle, **getting there** can be tricky. From Jabalpur, catch a train up to Katni then head a short way down the *Southeast Railway* to Umaria, the nearest railhead to the park. Regular buses leave here for **Tala**, 33km northeast. Approaching from Varanasi or Khajuraho, the nearest **airport**, make your way to Satna on the main railway line and pick up a train to Katni/Umaria. The only alternative is a laborious stop-and-start trip on local buses via Amarpatan or Beohari. From Delhi (or Agra), the best train to catch is the *Utkal Express* #8479, which leaves Nizamuddin at 12.50pm and arrives in Umaria at 6am the next day. That leaves plenty of time to cover the remaining distance before nightfall.

Jeeps, arranged a day ahead through one of the hotels in Bandhavgarh, are the only means of **transport around the park**. Drivers charge by the kilometre, so the cost depends on the distance covered and the number of people in a group. **Guides** are part of the deal. Elephant safaris have been discontinued, but it's still possible to enjoy a quick jaunt on elephant-back at Bandhavgarh's morning "**tiger show**" (similar to the one at Kanha, see p.379), which also gives the chance to see at least one tiger.

Accommodation at Bandhavgarh is very limited, and should ideally be booked well in advance. The popular MPTDC *White Tiger Forest Lodge* (☎308; ④–⑤) at Tala has 26 rooms, two of them a/c, with a reasonable **restaurant** and bar set in a campus-style forest complex. They also provide jeeps and guides. Reservations can be made through any MPTDC office or by sending a fifty percent deposit to: Central Reservations-Tours Division, *MPSTDC Ltd*, Fourth Floor Gangotri, TT Nagar, Bhopal 462 003.

Also in Tala, the new *Chalukya Resort* specializes mainly in **luxury** packages. Rates depend on the size of your party, but expect to pay somewhere between Rs1600 and

2000 per person per day for a bed, full board, jeeps, guides and a tiger show. If all the rooms aren't full, you can rent one for as little as Rs180 per day (Rs120 single), much the **cheapest** option in Bandhavgarh. Bookings should be arranged by writing to: Mr SK Tiwari, PO Tala, Distt. Shahdol, Madhya Pradesh 484 661.

The third and final place to stay within striking distance of the park itself is the *Jungle Camp* – another hotel catering to wealthy foreign wildlife enthusiasts. Prices are comparable with those at *Chalukya*; reservations should be made through *Tiger Tops Mountain Travel*, 1/1 Rani Jhansi Rd, New Delhi.

WESTERN MADHYA PRADESH

The geography of **western Madhya Pradesh** is dominated by the River Narmada, which drains westwards through a wide alluvial valley, bounded in the south by the Satpura hills and the Maharashtran border, and in the north by the rugged Vindhya range. Forming the major trade corridor between the Ganges plains and the west coast, the region was for nearly a thousand years known as **Malwa** – an independent princely state ruled from the sprawling hill-top fort complex at **Mandu**. The former capital, now deserted, is, with its ruined mosques, tanks and palaces, and its spectacular panoramic views, the area's outstanding tourist attraction.

Most visitors travel to Mandu via the industrial city of **Indore**, then continue northeast to Bhopal, or south on the main Delhi–Bombay railway line towards the jumping-off point for the Ellora and Ajanta caves, Jalgaon. Alternatively, you could head off to the fascinating riverside Hindu pilgrimage centres of **Omkareshwar** and **Maheshwar** – looping east to Mandu, before rejoining the railway at Indore. The sacred city of **Ujjain**, 55km further north, boasts a bumper crop of modern Hindu temples, but little else. You could, nevertheless, choose to pause here on your way to or from southern Rajasthan on the *Western Railway*, the most direct land link with Delhi.

Indore

INDORE, the second largest city in Madhya Pradesh, is huge, modern, heavily industrialized, and generally dull. If you find yourself with time to kill en route to or from **Mandu**, 105km southwest, however, a couple of worthwhile sights lie hidden among its tangle of ferro-concrete flyovers, expressways and crowded bazaars.

Situated at the confluence of the Kham and Saraswati rivers, the city was for centuries an insignificant stopover on the pilgrimage trails to Omkareshwar and Ujjain, 55km north. In the eighteenth century, it became the capital of the **Holkar** dynasty, whose chief, Malhar Rao, had previously managed to scrounge several choice scraps from the Marathas during their northward advance against the Moghuls. Later, Rao's daughter-in-law, **Ahilya Bai**, took over control of the state, which at its height stretched as far as the Ganges and the Punjab. Described by a contemporary British diplomat as "the most exemplary ruler that ever lived", the Rani was a kind of central Indian Queen Victoria, who, in addition to founding the modern city of Indore, built palaces, temples, *dharamshalas* and charitable institutions all over the country. When she died in 1795, her four grandsons dragged the state into a bloody civil war. A series of skirmishes with the Marathas and East India Company followed, ending in the Treaty of 1818, which secured for the dynasty a small but rich dominion with Indore as the capital. The city's expansion gained momentum in the nineteenth century, fuelled by a lucrative trade in cotton and opium. Despite remaining loyal to the British in the Mutiny, however, the maverick Holkar Maharajas remained firmly under the thumb of their colonial overlords until Independence, when they were finally relieved of their powers by the Congress.

Indore, these days, is the region's biggest business and commercial centre. The nearby industrial estate of **Pithampur**, hyped as "the Detroit of India", hosts numerous giant steel and auto manufacturers, including *Honda, Bajaj, Hindustan Motors* and *Pratap Steel*. The resulting **affluence** has made a big impact; satellite dishes, luxury hotels and American-style shopping malls are popping up all over the place, while the *nouveaux riches* swan ostentatiously around town on brand-new Japanese scooters. Even the auto-rickshaws seem shinier.

Arrival and information

Trains arriving in Indore on the *Central Railway* pull in at the mainline station in the middle of the city. The principal **bus stand**, "Sarawate" (☎65788), is a short walk south from platform one, beyond the overpass. Most Mandu buses, however, use the less convenient "Gangawal" bus stand (☎65688), a three-kilometre auto-rickshaw ride west towards the domestic **airport**, 10km out.

The most convenient means of **getting around** is by metered auto-rickshaw; note that the tariffs increase by fifty percent after 10pm. Alternatively, you could brave the traffic yourself by renting a **bicycle** from one of the stalls opposite the train station.

MPTDC's helpful **information** office (10am–5pm; ☎38888), behind the Ravindra Natya Griha Exhibition Hall on RN Tagore Rd, hands out the usual glossy leaflets and a better-than-average city map. They also rent **cars** (with drivers), and run two-day **tours** to Mandu (Rs500), and a one-day tour to Omkareshwar and Maheshwar (Rs250).

The *State Bank of Indore* (Mon–Fri 10am–2pm, Sat 10am–noon) has a **foreign exchange** office opposite their main branch on Raj Wada. The *State Bank of India* (same opening hours) is across town on AB Rd, next door to the **GPO**. Finally, there's a 24-hour **pharmacy** (☎23021) in the MY Hospital compound, off AB Rd.

The City

With the exception of Indore's museum, over on AB Rd near the GPO, most of the city's sights lie west of the railway line, in and around the bazaar. Two broad thoroughfares, MG Marg and Jawahar Marg, form the north and south boundaries of this cluttered and chaotic district, which is interrupted in the east by the confluence of the Saraswati and Kham rivers – little more than trickles of black slime bordered by *bastees* and heaps of decomposing rubbish. The surrounding suburbs, by contrast, are a much more congenial prospect of detached houses, new apartment blocks and leafy gardens – home to Indore's managerial classes and a couple of old Holkar palaces.

The Lal Bagh palace

Set in its own grounds on the banks of the Kham, the **Lal Bagh palace** (Tues–Sun 10am–5pm) is another of those extravagant neo-classical creations so beloved of the ludicrously rich maharajas of the nineteenth and early twentieth centuries. The building took two generations of the Holkar family around thirty years to complete, and was, in its day, rivalled only by the Scindias' Jai Vilas palace in Gwalior. Granted carte blanche and a limitless budget, its British architects and interior decorators came up with a cross between Brideshead and Versailles – a vast stately home dripping with Doric columns, gilt stucco, crystal chandeliers, and piles of replica rococo furniture. In 1987, the property was inherited by the state government, who installed a small museum in the reception hall and renamed it the Nehru Centre.

Lal Bagh's main entrance is via a pair of grandiose wrought-iron **gates**, modelled on those at Buckingham Palace, which bear the Holkar family arms, with its motto "Success attends he who strives" inscribed in Hindi below. Note the wheat and poppies in the background, symbolizing the two main sources of the dynasty's prosperity. The ground floor of the palace consists of several large chambers: the Durbar Hall, used for royal assemblies, the state banquet hall, and the ballroom, with its specially sprung herring-bone dance floor. Hanging on the wall of the billiards room nearby, a fine picture of Tukoji Rao (1902–25) – the ruler responsible for completing the palace – is encrusted with precious stones. The Maharaja sent his own court artist to France to study European painting so that his portrait could be rendered in the "correct" style. The cherubs, flying nymphs, and Greek and Roman gods that adorn the ceilings of the adjacent rooms are equally convincing. Also worth checking out is the underground passage leading down to the kitchens. One of the rooms hidden away in this vault contains a modest but very colourful collection of **tribal artefacts**, including terracotta votive statues, clothes, jewellery, murals and brass sculpture.

The Raj Wada

The Holkars' Old Palace, the **Raj Wada**, is Indore's principal landmark, presiding over a palm-fringed square in the heart of the city. Built in the style of a western Indian town-house, the eighteenth-century mansion's most prominent feature is a lofty, seven-storey gateway. Its upper four floors were originally made of wood, which made it particularly prone to fire; most of the palace collapsed after the last one, in 1984. Only the facade and the family temple, immediately inside the main courtyard, survive.

The Kanch Mandir and bazaars

Tucked away deep in the bazaar district, ten minutes' walk west of Raj Wada, the Jain **Kanch Mandir**, or "Mirror Temple" (daily 10am–5pm), is one of the city's more eccentric religious monuments. Surprisingly for a faith renowned for its austerity, the interior of the temple is decked with multi-coloured glass **mosaics**. Vivid tableaux lining the sides of the entrance hall depict the horrors in store for sinners in the afterlife. Upstairs, mirrors in one chamber are supposed to multiply three statues of the prophet Mahavir inside it twenty-one times – the exact number of Jain *tirthankaras*.

The **bazaars** in the vicinity of the Kanch Mandir and Raj Wada are great for a stroll. Rows of stalls and open-fronted shops are jammed beneath picturesque four-storeyed houses with overhanging wooden balconies. The gold and silver jewellery market, Sarafa Bazaar, is Indore's most famous. You'll find it around the corner from the Mirror Temple, near the massive wholesale textile market, where cloth is still sold by weight. Also worth seeking out are shops on Bajaj Khana Chowk that specialize in traditional embroidered and beadwork costumes, and the atmospheric fruit and vegetable market on the river bank beneath the lime-green **Khala-Ma mosque**.

The Central Museum

Indore's **Central Museum** (Tues–Sun 10am–5pm) is located over in the southeast of the city, near the GPO. Its large collection includes finds from nearby prehistoric sites, as well as fine Jain and Hindu sculpture from the ruined eleventh- and twelfth-century temples at Hinlajgarh. The downstairs gallery boasts a handful of priceless **Harappan terracottas** unearthed at Mohenjo Daro, in southern Pakistan. None of the exhibits is adequately labelled, but the museum attendants are happy to show you around.

Elsewhere around the city

Several exotic onion-domed cenotaphs dotted around the city are dedicated to former Holkar rulers and their families. The two main concentrations of **chhatris** are near the riverside fruit and vegetable market, below the MG Road bridge, and southwest of the city centre near the Lal Bagh palace. The latter, **Chhatri Bagh**, consists of two weed-infested walled enclosures and can only be visited between 8am and 11am, when offerings are left at the tombs by *pujaris*.

A more state-of-the-art Hindu shrine stands 1km west of Raj Wada, off the busy MG Road. The **Bada Ganpati** temple houses a massive 11-metre seated icon of the elephant-headed god of prosperity, Ganesh. Painted bright orange and decked with sequins, tinsel and garlands of imitation flowers, the idol is made of such unlikely ingredients as cow dung, sugar cane extract, Ganges water, soil from India's seven holiest cities, and ground diamonds, emeralds, rubies, pearls and topaz.

Accommodation

The majority of Indore's **hotels** cater for business visitors, and are scattered around the prosperous suburb of **Tukoganj**, 1km east of the railway station. Competition here is stiff, so standards tend to be high, and prices reasonable. The same can not be said of the cheaper accommodation, most of which is in the noisy and polluted area between Sarawate and the railway station. Ignore the touts who try to drag you off to the dire lodges opposite the bus stand, and head instead for the more salubrious and much better-value budget hotels along **Chhoti Gwaltoli**, a lane beneath the big Patel flyover. All but the absolute rock-bottom lodges levy the mandatory state **luxury tax**.

Amrit, 25/6 Chhoti Gwaltoli (☎467054). No-frills lodge with clean, reasonably large rooms. "Deluxe" buys you a round bed and Alpine murals. Some a/c. ③–④.

Indotel Manor House, AB Rd (☎31645; Fax 492283). The city's top hotel. 4km outside the centre, and with all mod cons; gourmet restaurant, 24-hour coffee shop and exchange counter. ⑥–⑦.

MPTDC Tourist Bungalow, RN Tagore Rd (☎38888). Small, rather claustrophobic place tucked away behind the *Tagore Natya Griha* exhibition hall. No restaurant. Some a/c. ③–④.

Payal, 38 Chhoti Gwaltoli (☎463202). By far the best deal amoung the inexpensive hotels. Airy, clean rooms, with attached shower-toilets, *Star TV* and a musical lift. ③.

President, 163 RNT Rd (☎432858). Very glam, with turbanned doormen, central a/c, health club, excellent vegetarian restaurant and roof-top cafe. ⑤–⑥.

Purva, 1–4 Dhenu Market (☎38554). Small, friendly and spotlessly clean hotel five minutes from the station. Very good value. ③–⑤.

Railway Retiring Rooms, railway station. The recently renovated dorms are cleaner and slightly more expensive than usual. Handy for an early morning departure. ①.

Samrat, 18/5 MG Rd (☎37256). Large, modern, and well run, although its illegally built restaurant is regularly bulldozed by the Municipality.

Shreemaya, 12 RNT Rd (☎34151). Indore's largest hotel has all the usual facilities, including foreign exchange and a car park. ③–④.

Surya, 5/5 North Mandi Road (☎38465). A slick hotel pitched squarely at visiting businessmen, with an above-average restaurant. ③–⑤.

Yashoneel, 37/1 Chhoti Gwaltoli (☎465286). Very basic, but a good-value fall-back if the neighbours are full. Sign in Hindi. ②.

MOVING ON FROM INDORE

A full summary of Indore's transport connections appears on p.322.

Tickets for *Indian Airlines* **flights** from Indore airport (☎31244) can be booked at the office on Race Course Rd, 2km northeast of the station (☎7069). There is no airport bus.

As for **trains**, two broad-gauge branches of the *Western Railway* connect Indore to cities in northern India. The fastest service to **Delhi**, the daily *Indore–Nizamuddin Express* #9301, leaves at 9pm and heads north via Ujjain, Kota and Bharatpur, arriving in Delhi at 12.35pm the next day. The other branch, serviced by the daily *Malwa Express* #4068 (depart 3.05pm, arrive 9.35am) runs east to Bhopal, then north to Delhi on the *Central Railway* via Jhansi, Gwalior, and Agra.

Trains to **Rajasthan** leave three times daily on the metre-gauge line for Chittaurgarh, Ajmer and Jaipur. The quickest, by several hours, is the night service, *Express* #7570. Getting to **Ellora** and **Ajanta** involves a complicated rail journey to **Jalgaon**, via Khandwar and Bhusawal junctions; expect long waits for connecting trains at both.

Buses to **Mandu** from Indore leave the Gangawal bus stand (in the west of the city) every couple of hours from 8.30am onwards. There's also a mid-afternoon departure from Sarawate, the main bus stand near the train station. If you can't get on a direct service, head for Dhar (departures are hourly from Gangawal) and pick up a private bus there.

The state transport corporation, MPSRTC, operate a twice-daily luxury a/c coach (with pneumatic suspension) to **Bhopal** via Dewas, leaving the *Tourist Bungalow* at 8am and 3.15pm to meet the superfast *Shatabdi Express* train to and from Delhi. Tickets should be booked ahead through the tourist office (Rs160; ☎38888).

Reliable **travel agents** in town include: *Royal Travels*, 164 RNT Marg (☎5860); *Multani Sona Travels*, 15 Jhabua Tower, RNT Marg (☎31223); *Shatabdi Travels*, Jhabua Towers, 170 RNT Marg (☎23550); and *Vikrant Travels*, Chhoti Gwaltoli (☎67311).

Eating

Eating out is popular among Indore's middle classes, so there are plenty of quality restaurants around the city centre to choose from. Most are located in the larger hotels, such as the *Shreemaya*, *Surya*, and *President*, and serve the usual Indian and Chinese dishes. Thanks to the current "health food" craze, there are a couple of excellent pure-vegetarian places as well, the classiest being *Woodlands* in the *President*. Cheaper food is available at the dingy *dhabas* and canteens around Sarawate bus stand. Stick to the ones doing a brisk trade, and you shouldn't go far wrong.

Ding Dong, 18 MG Rd. Popular south Indian snack bar near the High Court, with tables on an outside terrace. Pleasant in the evenings.

Gypsy, MG Rd. American-style fast-food joint near Nath Mandir Crossing, serving lamb-burgers, pizzas and fries, and a range of ice creams, cakes and pastries at moderate prices.

Indian Coffee House, Rampura Building, off MG Rd. The usual south Indian snacks served by old-style waiters in turbans and cummerbunds. Opens at 7.30am for big breakfasts and the papers.

Siddarth, 564 MG Rd. Dim basement bar-restaurant (men only), with *al fresco* alcohol-free family terrace upstairs. Standard Indian/Chinese veg and non-veg menu. Inexpensive.

Status, below *Hotel Purva*, 565 MG Rd. Superb eat-till-you-burst Rajasthani lunch-time *thalis*, with varied vegetable dishes, *dals*, breads and chutneys – for under Rs30. Vegetarian *à la carte* later on.

Woodlands, 163 RNT Marg. *Hotel President*'s swanky pure-veg restaurant serves stylish, but pricey south Indian specialities. Good for a splurge.

Dewas

The dusty, fly-blown town of **DEWAS**, 35km northeast of Indore on NH3, is dominated by a large volcanic hillside that rises from its northern fringes. The site of several ancient rock-cut hermits' caves and a small temple dedicated to the fierce, skeletal goddess Chamunda, the hill inspired the title of EM Forster's autobiographical novel, *The Hill of Devi*. Forster lived in the nearby palace as personal secretary to the local Raja in the 1920s – a post he described as his "great opportunity". Many of the young author's experiences of life in this small central Indian town found their way into *A Passage to India*. The palace is still occupied and not open to visitors, but you can climb (or drive) to the top of the hill to visit its tiny temple, and to appreciate the views.

Although Dewas has no hotels, its frequent bus connections with Bhopal, Ujjain and Indore, mean that you can pause here briefly without running the risk of being stranded.

Dhar

DHAR, 65km west of Indore, was the capital of Malwa before Hoshang Shah moved the royal court to Mandu in 1405. Too little remains of this bygone era to warrant breaking a journey, but if you do find yourself here between buses, leave your bags in the managers' office at the bus stand and head through the bazaar to the north of town, where you'll find the ruins of an old mosque. Like its cousins at Mandu, the **Kamal Masjid** (1400) was built from fragments of much earlier Hindu temples. Its shallow domes and low colonnades were the prototype of an architectural style that reached its peak in the mid-fifteenth century. A second ruined mosque, the **Lal-ki-Masjid** (1405), built in a similar style but in much better condition, stands 1km south of the bus stand, at the end of a dirt track that leads south off the main Mandu road. All but a few small fragments of the elaborate tile work that decorated it have, however, disappeared.

Dhar's only other noteworthy monument is the sandstone **fort** that crowns the hill to the east of the bazaar. The scene of a British rearguard action during the Mutiny, the citadel stands on the site of a ruined Paramara palace, founded by Raja Bhoj in the tenth century. Now a prison, it is out of bounds to visitors.

Mandu

Set against the rugged backdrop of the Vindhya hills, the medieval ghost-town of **MANDU**, 98km from Indore, is one of central India's most atmospheric historical monuments. Come here at the height of the monsoons, when the rocky plateau and its steeply shelving sides are carpeted with green vegetation, and you'll see why the Malwa Sultans christened their capital **Shadiabad**, or "City of Joy". Even during the relentless heat of the dry season, the ruins make an exotic spectacle. Elegant Islamic palaces, mosques and onion-domed mausolea crumble beside large medieval reservoirs and precipitous ravines, while below, an endless vista of scorched plains and tiny villages stretches off to the horizon. Mandu can be visited as a day trip from Indore, but you'll enjoy it more if you spend a couple of nights. That not only gives you time to explore the ruins, but enables you to witness the memorable sight of the sun setting over the Narmada Valley.

History

Archeological evidence suggests that the remote hill-top was first fortified around the sixth century AD, when it was known as Mandapa-Durga, or "Durga's hall of worship" – in time corrupted to "Mandu". Four hundred years later, the site gained in strategic importance when the powerful **Paramaras** moved their capital from Ujjain to Dhar, 35km north. The plateau's natural defences, strengthened by Raja Bhoj (see p.325), proved, however, unable to withstand persistent attacks by the Muslim invaders during the twelfth century. The fort eventually fell to the Sultans of Delhi in 1305.

When the Sultanate had their hands full fending off the Mongols on their northern borders a century or so later, Malwa's Afghan governor, Dilawar Khan **Ghuri**, seized the chance to establish his own independent kingdom. He died after only four years on the throne, however, leaving his ambitious young son at the helm. During **Hoshang Shah**'s illustrious 27-year reign, Mandu was promoted from pleasure resort to royal capital, and aquired some of the finest Islamic monuments in Asia, including the Jama Masjid, Delhi Gate, and the Sultan's own tomb.

Mandu's golden age continued under the **Khalji**, who took over from the Ghuri dynasty in 1436, when Mahmud Shah Khalji poisoned Hoshang Shah's grandson. Another building boom and several protracted wars later, Malwa settled down to a lengthy period of peace and prosperity under **Ghiyath Shah** (1469–1500). Famous for his love of cooking and beautiful women, Ghiyath amassed a harem of 15,000 courtesans, and a bodyguard of a thousand Turkish and Abyssinian amazons, whom he accommodated in the appropriately lavish Jahaz Mahal. The sybaritic Sultan lived to a ripe old age, but was poisoned by his son shortly after his eightieth birthday. His successor, Nasir Shah, died of guilt ten years later and Malwa, dogged by feuds and the threat of rebellion, became an easy target for the militaristic Sultan of Gujarat, who invaded in 1526. In the centuries that followed, control over the fort and its rapidly decaying monuments passed between a succession of independent rulers and the Moghuls. It never regained its former prominence, however, and was deserted by the time the Marathas annexed the region in 1732. These days, Mandu is a tranquil backwater that sees far fewer visitors than it deserves. Apart from at weekends, when busloads of exuberant day-trippers breeze in from Indore, the only people you're likely to see picking through the ruins are the Bhil villagers who farm the surrounding fields.

The monuments

Mandu's **monuments** derive from a unique school of Islamic architecture that flourished here, and at the region's former capital, Dhar, between 1401 and 1516. Much admired for their elegant simplicity, the buildings are believed to have been a major influence on the Moghul architects responsible for the Taj Mahal in Agra.

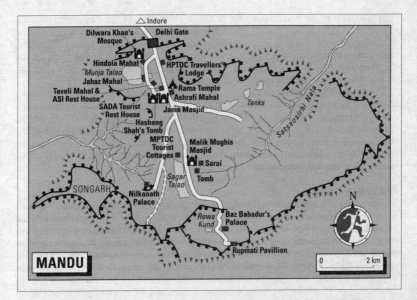

The 23km-square plateau is separated from the body of hills to the north by the **Kakra Khoh**, literally "deep ravine". A narrow causeway forms a natural bridge across the gorge, then climbs via a series of subsidiary gates to the fort's main entrance, the Delhi Gate. From here, the road runs south past the first and main concentration of monuments, the **Royal Enclave**, to the village square, which stands in the middle of the second, or **village group**. The remaining sites lie further to the south, east of the picturesque **Sagar Talao** tank, and in a fortified enclosure overlooking the Narmada Valley known as the **Rewa Kund group**.

If you don't have your own vehicle, the most pleasant way of **getting around** the fort and its widely dispersed monuments is to rent a bicycle from the *VIP Wine Shop*, just off the main square. Alternatively, the village's decrepit old tempo tours the highlights for around Rs100. Haggle hard, but remember to take waiting time into account.

The Royal Enclave

Reached via the lane that leads west off the village square, the **Royal Enclave** is dominated by Mandu's most photographed monument, Ghiyath Shah's majestic **Jahaz Mahal**, or "Ship Palace". The name derives from its unusual shape, and elevated situation on a narrow strip of land between two large water tanks. It originally housed the Sultan's huge harem, and the thousand-strong all-women guard that protected them. A breezy rooftop terrace, crowned with four domed pavilions, looks over **Munja Talao** lake to the west, and the square, stone-lined **Kapur Sagar** in the other direction. From the northern balcony, you also get a good view of the geometric sandstone bathing pools where the palace's inhabitants would have whiled away their long incarceration.

The next building along the lane is the **Hindola Mahal**, or "Swing Palace" – so-called because its distinctive sloping walls supposedly look as though they are swaying from side to side. The design was, in fact, purely functional, intended to buttress the graceful but heavy stone arches that support the ceiling inside. At the far end of the T-shaped assembly hall, a long stepped ramp allowed the Sultan and his retinue to reach the upper storey on elephant-back.

Sprawling over the northern shores of Munja Talao lake are the dilapidated remains of a second royal pleasure palace. The **Champa Baodi** boasts an ingeniously complex ventilation and water-supply system which kept its dozens of subterranean chambers, or *tykhanas*, cool during the long Malwan summers. Immediately to the north stands the venerable **Mosque of Dilawara Khan**, dating from 1405. The chunks of Hindu temple used to build its main doorway and colonnaded hall are still very evident.

The **Hathi Pol**, or "Elephant Gate", was the main entrance to the Royal Enclave. Once past its pair of colossal, half-decapitated elephant guardians, a dusty track heads north to the edge of the plateau and the grand **Alamgir**, or "Delhi" **Gate**. Built around the same time as Dilawara Khan's mosque, this imposing bastion is one of twelve that stud the battlements along the fort's 45-kilometre perimeter. The views from its ramparts over Kakra Khoh, the chasm through which invading armies invariably chose to attack Mandu, are spectacular.

The village group

Some of the fort's best-preserved buildings are clustered **around the village**. Work on the magnificent pink sandstone mosque on the west side of the main square, the **Jama Masjid**, commenced during the reign of Hoshang Shah and took three generations to complete. Said to be modelled on the Great Mosque at Damascus, it rests on a huge raised plinth pierced by rows of tiny arched chambers – once used as cells for visiting priests. A flight of steps leads up from the square to the large domed entrance porch. Beyond the ornate *jali* screens and bands of blue-glaze tiles that decorate the main doorway, you arrive in the Great Courtyard, enclosed by rows of pillars and small domes. The prayer hall, or Qibla, at the far end, is surmounted by three larger domes, and houses a small pulpit and some finely carved Koranic inscriptions.

Hoshang Shah's tomb (*c.* 1440), directly behind the Jama Masjid, is this group's real highlight. It stands on a low plinth at the centre of a square walled enclosure, and is crowned by a squat central dome and four small corner cupolas. Now streaked with mildew and mud washed down from the swallows' nests caked inside its eaves, the tomb is made entirely from milky white marble – the first of its kind in the subcontinent. An inscription on the right door jamb records the visit, in 1659, of the Moghul emperor Shah Jehan, who brought four of his architects to admire the building before they began work on the Taj Mahal. The interior of the tomb is very plain, except for the elaborate pierced-stone windows that illuminate Hoshang's sarcophagus.

On the opposite side of the square to the Great Mosque, the **Ashrafi Mahal**, or "Palace of Coins", was a theological college (*madarasa*) that the ruler Muhammad Shah later converted into a tomb. The complex included a giant marble mausoleum and seven-storey *minar*, or victory tower, of which only the base survives.

Around the Sagar Talao

En route to the Rewa Kund, a further handful of monuments are scattered around the fields east of Sagar Talao. Dating from the early fifteenth century, the **Mosque of Malik Mughis** is the oldest of the bunch, once again visibly constructed using ancient Hindu masonry. Note the turquoise tiles and fine Islamic calligraphy over the main doorway. The high-walled building opposite was a **caravansarai**, where merchants and their camel trains would rest during long treks across the subcontinent.

A short way south of the *sarai*, the octagonal tomb known as the **Dai-ki-Chhoti Bahan-ka-Mahal** looms above the surrounding fields from a raised plinth, still retaining large strips of the blue ceramic tiles that plastered most of Mandu's beautiful Afghan domes. Young couples from the nearby village creep off here during the evenings for a bit of privacy, so make plenty of noise as you approach.

The Rewa Kund group

The road to the **Rewa Kund group** heads past herds of water buffalo grazing on the muddy foreshores of the lake, then winds its way gently through a couple of Bhil villages towards the far southern edge of the plateau. Stately old baobabs line the roadside, like giant upturned root vegetables. The bulbous-bottomed trees, natives of the African Sahel, were introduced to India by Arab traders, and are now used by the local tribespeople for their many medicinal properties.

The **Rewa Kund** itself nestles behind a rise further up the hill. Noted for its curative powers, the old stone-lined reservoir is popular with bus parties of Indian visitors, who picnic under the trees by its banks. Water from the tank used to be pumped into the cistern in the nearby **Baz Bahadur Palace**. Bahadur, the last independent ruler of Malwa, retreated to Mandu to study music after being trounced in battle by Rani Durgavati (see p.377). Legend has it that he fell in love with a Hindu singer named Rupmati, whom he enticed to his hill-top home with an exquisite palace that she could admire from the window of her father's house on the Nirmar Plains below. The couple eventually married, but did not live happily ever after. When Akbar heard of Rupmati's beauty, he dispatched an army to Mandu to capture her and the long-coveted fort. Bahadur managed to slip away from the ensuing battle, but his bride, left behind in the palace, poisoned herself rather than fall into the clutches of the attackers.

The romantic **Rupmati Pavilion**, built by Bahadur for his bride-to-be, still rests on a ridge high above the Rewa Kund. Beneath its lofty terrace, the plateau plunges a sheer 300m to the gently undulating Narmada Valley. The view is breathtaking, especially on a clear day, when you can just about make out the sun-bleached banks of the sacred river as it winds west towards the Arabian Sea.

The Nil Kanth Palace

Another idyllic spot to watch the sun set over the plains is the **Nil Kanth Palace**, an old Shiva temple converted by the Moghuls into a water pavilion. It clings to the top of a steep cliff at the head of a rugged ravine on the western edge of the plateau, and was used by Akbar as royal retreat. Persian verses on the walls of one room record the emperor's military exploits in the Deccan, and, in a more philosophical vein, remind readers of the transience and futility of worldly achievement. It can be reached along a track that forks right off the main road, 500m south of Mandu village square.

Practicalities

Although *MPSRTC* operate direct **buses** to Mandu from Indore, it's quicker to travel to Dhar and pick up a local service to the fort from there – a 35-kilometre journey that takes upwards of ninety minutes. **Taxis** charge around Rs750 for the round trip from Indore, plus a hefty Rs250 waiting charge if you stay overnight – which still works out cheaper than the least expensive MPTDC rental car. MPTDC and a couple of private companies also run day-long guided **tours** of Mandu from Indore on weekends (and some weekdays in high season). Ask at the tourist office on RNT Rd in Indore, or in the travel agency across the street, for details. You can also get to Mandu by state bus from Bhopal, Ujjain and Maheshwar.

Most **places to stay** inside the fort are managed by MPTDC, who advise visitors to book a couple of days in advance. Their cheapest hotel, the *Travellers' Lodge* (☎224; ④), at the north end of the plateau near the SADA barrier, has scenic views, clean rooms with attached bathrooms and hot water, and very welcoming staff. It's a one-kilometre hike from the main square where the buses pull in, however, so ask to be dropped off en route. Cheaper accommodation is available in the centre of the village, where SADA's ultra-basic *Tourist Rest House* (①), opposite the Jama Masjid, has a few spartan rooms without running water for Rs40. If you're not on a die-hard budget, by far the best value are the two double rooms in the *Archeological Survey Rest House* (②) in the Taveli Mahal – a medieval mansion-cum-stables overlooking the Ship Palace which is almost invariably booked up. The MPTDC *Tourist Cottages* (☎3235; ④–⑤), 2km south of the square, is Mandu's most comfortable and expensive hotel. The campus of chalets overlooks the Sagar Talao tank, and boasts twenty large rooms with attached shower-toilets, hot water and some a/c.

The *Tourist Cottages'* pleasant semi-open-air restaurant is the best **place to eat** in the fort. Unlike the cafeteria in the *Tourist Lodge*, you don't have to order your evening meal a couple of hours in advance, and they serve beer in addition to the standard MPTDC menu of moderately priced Indian, Chinese and western food. Anyone lucky enough to get a room in the *Archeological Survey Rest House* can also eat there, providing they let the *chowkidar* know beforehand. Otherwise, the best cheap meals are the vegetarian *thalis*, *subzi* and *chappatis* in the orange-painted *Shivani Hotel*, halfway between the square and the SADA barrier. The *Relax Point*, on the square, also offers *chai*, cold drinks and greasy fried snacks. Avoid **meat** wherever you eat, though, as frequent power-cuts mean that even places with refrigerators can have problems keeping it fresh.

At present, there is nowhere to **change money**; the nearest bank is in Indore.

Ujjain

Situated on the banks of the sacred River Shipra, **UJJAIN**, 80km north of Indore, is one of India's seven holiest cities. Like Haridwar, Nasik and Prayag (near Allahabad), it plays host every twelve years to the country's largest religious gathering, the **Kumbh Mela** (see p.289), which in 1992 drew an estimated fifteen million pilgrims here to bathe. Outside festival times, however, Ujjain can be a dull destination for non-Hindus. Despite their manifold mythological associations, its temples are mostly ugly ferro-concrete affairs, while the fabled *ghats* resemble a run-of-the-mill municipal swimming pool. If you come expecting a mini-Varanasi, you'll be disappointed. On the plus side, the city is a good place to experience the more lurid side of modern Hinduism: Disney-style architecture, colourful *puja* stalls, and the electric devotional music that is nowadays broadcast from virtually every roadside shrine and temple courtyard.

History

Excavations north of Ujjain have yielded traces of settlement as far back as the eighth century BC. The ancient city was a major regional capital under the Mauryans (Ashok was governor here for a time during the reign of his father), when it was known as **Avantika** and lay on the main trade route that linked northern India with Mesopotamia and Egypt. According to Hindu mythology, Shiva later changed its name to **Ujjaiyini**, "He Who Conquers With Pride", to mark his victory over the demon king of Tripuri. Chandragupta II, renowned for his patronage of the arts, also ruled from here in the fourth and fifth centuries. Among the Nava Ratna, or "Nine Gems", of his court was the illustrious Sanskrit poet **Kalidasa**, whose much-loved narrative poem *Meghduta* ("Cloud Messenger") includes a lyrical evocation of the city and its inhabitants.

Ujjain was sacked in 1234 by Iltutmish, of the Delhi Slave Dynasty, who razed most of its temples. Thereafter, the Malwan capital was governed by Sultans of Mandu, the Moghuls, and by **Raja Jai Singh** from Jaipur, who among his many renovation projects was responsible for building the Vedha Shala observatory (Ujjain straddles the Hindu first meridian of longitude). Ujjain's fortunes declined from the early eighteenth century onwards, except for a sixty-year renaissance between the arrival of the Scindia dynasty in 1750 and their departure to Gwalior. These days, nearby Indore sees the lion's share of the region's industrial activity, leaving Ujjain's 367,000-strong population to make its living by more traditional means.

Arrival and information

Trains arriving in Ujjain on both broad-gauge branches of the *Western Railway* pull in at the station in the centre of town, two minutes' walk west of the state **bus** stand. The city is fairly spread out, so you'll need to **get around** by auto-rickshaw, or by renting a **bicycle** from the shop opposite the bus stand. **Taxis** hang around the MPTDC *Hotel Shipra* (☎25237), in the cantonment area, which, along with the tourist reception counter in the station (☎29240), is the best source of **information**. The *State Bank of India* (Mon–Fri 10.30am–2pm, Sat 10.30am–noon) is on Udwaria Rd, east of the main bazaar.

The City

The *Western Railway* cuts straight through the centre of **the city**, forming a neat divide between the spacious and affluent residential suburbs to the south, and the more interesting, densely packed streets northwest of the station. Unless you spend all day wandering through the bazaar, sightseeing in Ujjain usually means treading the temple trail, with a brief foray south of the *ghats* to visit the Vedha Shala observatory.

The Mahakaleshwar Mandir and the Harsiddhi Mandir

Ujjain's chief landmark, the **Mahakaleshwar Mandir**, crowns a rise above the river, and is the logical place to start a tour of the town. Its gigantic saffron-painted sanctuary tower, a modern replacement for the one destroyed by Iltutmish in 1234, soars high above a complex of marble courtyards, water tanks and fountains, advertising the presence below of one of India's most powerful *shivalingams*.

Housed in a claustrophobic subterranean chamber, the *lingam* is mounted on a solid silver base and piled high with floral offerings left by a constant stream of worshippers. It is one of India's twelve **Jyotrilinga** – *"lingams* of Light" – whose essential energy, or *shakti*, derives from the earth, rather than from the rituals performed around it. A narrow passage leads out of the sanctum to an adjacent courtyard, where several smaller accessory shrines are dedicated to Shiva's consort, Parvati, and his two sons, Ganesh, the elephant-headed god of prosperity, and Kartikeya, the god of war.

From the Mahakaleshwar Mandir, head west down the hill past the Rudra Sagar tank to another auspicious temple. Hindu mythology identifies the **Harsiddhi Mandir** as the spot where Parvati's elbow fell to earth while Shiva was carrying her burning body from the *sati* pyre. The temple has been a centre of Devi worship ever since. Its main shrine, erected by the Marathas in the eighteenth century, houses (from left to right) images of Mahalakshmi (the goddess of wealth), Annapurna (an incarnation of Durga), and Saraswati (the goddess of wisdom). The two odd-shaped pillars flanking the entrance to the courtyard also date from the Maratha era, and feature in the annual Dushhera festival, when the dozens of tiny butter lamps that encrust their soot-blackened surfaces are lit to celebrate Rama's victory over the demon Ravana.

Ram Ghat

A dip in the Shipra at **Ram Ghat** is the reason most devout pilgrims still travel to the city. During the 1992 Kumbh Mela, the waterfront was jammed solid with naked *sadhus* waiting to wash away several lifetimes of accumulated bad *karma*. Most days, however, very little of note happens here. Soapy kids splash in and out of the shallows, while sleepy *pujaris* ply their trade beneath the rows of orange- and whitewashed riverside shrines. The large ceremonial archway on the opposite (west) bank – writhing with multicoloured gods and goddesses – was erected as part of the *mela* celebrations.

The telephone **area code** for Ujjain is ☎0734.

UJJAIN

Bhopal / Dewas △

△ Kalideh Mahal, Siddavath & Bhartrihari Caves

Bhopal / Dewas ▷

Radam ▽

N

0   1 km

GOVINDPURA MARG (various street labels)

Govandhan Sagar

Ksheer Sagar

Surana Palace Hotel

New Raj Kumar Restaurant

Madav Clock Tower

Five Star Restaurant

Grand Hotel

MPTDC Hotel Shipra

GPO

Bus Stand

Chanakya Restaurant

Railway Station

Hotel Chandragupta

Hotel Rama Krishna

Girnar Hotel

Atlas Hotel

Chattri Chowk & Scindia Statue

Gopal Temple

Harsiddhi Temple

Ram Ghat

Mahakaleshwar Temple

River Shipra

foot bridge

River Shipra

Vedha Shala Observatory

JAI SINGH PURA MARG

AHILYA BHAI MARG

MAHAKALESHWAR MARG

TILAK MARG

MANDIR MARG

PATEL MARG

RAM GHAT MARG

CHANDRASHEKER AZAD MARG

ARYA SAMAJ MARG

ALA LAJPAT RAI MARG

ASHOK MARG

KAIDAS MARG

SAMYA RAJA MARG

TATA TOPE MARG

VIKRAM MARG

DHANVANTRI MARG

VISHWA VIDYALAYA

YANTRA MAHAL MARG 1

YANTRA MAHAL MARG 2

KHAWAYMAN MARG

SUBHAS MARG

209 RD

The Gopal Mandir and the Vedha Shala

Standing at the end of a chaotic market square, in the heart of the bazaar, the pictu-resque **Gopal Mandir** was erected by one of the Scindia Ranis in the early nineteenth century. With its distinctive blend of Moghul domes, Moorish arches and lofty Hindu sanctuary tower, the temple makes a fine example of late Maratha architecture. Inside, the sanctum's silver-plated doors were put here by Mahaji Scindia, who rescued them from Lahore after they had been carried off by Muslim looters. The shrine room itself, lined with marble, silver and mother-of-pearl, contains icons of the presiding deity, Gopal (Ganesh), together with his parents, Shiva and Parvati.

In addition to being a major religious centre, Ujjain was the birthplace of mathemati-cal astronomy in India. Research into the motion of the stars and planets has been carried out here since the time of Ashok. Later, Hindu astronomers fixed both the **first meridian** of longitude and the Tropic of Cancer in the city – the reason why Raja Jai Singh of Jaipur, governor of Malwa under the Moghul emperor Muhammed Shah, chose it as the site for another of his surreal open-air observatories. Built in 1725, the **Vedha Shala** lies 1km southwest of the train station, overlooking a bend in the River Shipra. The complex is nowhere near as large as its more famous cousins in Delhi and Jaipur, the Janta Mantars, but remains in excellent condition. Local astronomers continue to use its five instruments, or *yantras*, to formulate ephemerides (charts predicting the positions of the planets), which you can buy at the site.

The northern outskirts

The **Kalideh Mahal**, a summer retreat built in 1458 by the Sultans of Mandu, rests on an island in the Shipra, 9km north of the city centre. Though renovated by the Scindias early this century, the once-grand water palace and its adjacent tank are now derelict and boarded up. You might, however, choose to come out here simply to enjoy a ride through pleasant countryside, past some minor religious sites. **Siddavath**, a sacred banyan tree, stands beside the Shipra just north of the city limits. Shiva's consort, Parvati, is believed to have performed penances here, and during big *melas*, thousands of pilgrims hack through a thick layer of pond weed to bathe in holy water below.

Finally, the **Bhartrihari caves**, overlooking the east bank of the river near the Gadkalika temple, are definitely recommended for serious *sadhu* spotters. Local legend has it that King Vikramaditya's step-brother, the great poet and scholar Bhartrihari, lived here as a hermit in the fifth century. Today, the caves are home to a rare sect of *yogis*. The Kanphatas, or "Split-ears", are named after their arcane initiation rite, which involves cutting holes into the middle of novices' ears with a double-edged knife. You can tell a Kanphata-*yogi* by his large hooped earrings.

Accommodation

Most of Ujjain's limited **accommodation** is within easy walking distance of the railway station, so ignore the auto-rickshaw *wallahs* when you arrive unless you plan to stay in one of the two upmarket hotels, both 2km southeast in the cantonment area. Luxury tax of between ten and fifteen percent is charged on all rooms costing over Rs100.

Atlas, Station Rd, Indore Gate (☎25873). Respectable, well-managed hotel close to the station. All rooms have windows, attached bathrooms and comfortable beds. ②–④.

Chandragupta, Subhash Marg (☎25500). Cell-block-style lodge opposite the station, with passably clean, but small rooms. ①–④.

Girnar, Station Rd, Indore Gate (☎25873). Next door to the *Atlas*. Clean and quiet, with comforta-ble, good-sized rooms. Some attached shower-toilets. Recommended. ②–③.

Grand, Free Ganj, near Madhav Clock Tower (☎25742). Ex-Maharaja's palace, now run by munici-pality as budget hotel. The rooms are large, with huge tiled bathrooms attached, but very spartan and thick with grime and cobwebs. ①–②.

MPTDC Shipra, University Rd (☎29628). Immaculately tidy and peaceful, with relaxing inner courtyard-cum-garden, and a good licensed restaurant. Some a/c. ④–⑤.

Rama Krishna, Subhash Marg (☎25912). In the same mould as the *Chandragupta* next door, with identical prices and a vegetarian restaurant downstairs. ①–④.

Surana Palace, 23 GDC Rd, Dushera Maidan (☎25474). Large and comfortable, with spacious lawn. Like the *Shipra*, but *Star TV* in all rooms. Two luxurious suites, and bargain economy rooms. ③–⑦.

Eating

Ujjain suffers from a dearth of decent **places to eat**. Most visitors either stick to their hotel's restaurant, or else chance a plate of vegetable curry, rice and *chappatis* in one of the cheap places opposite the train station.

Chanakya, Subhash Marg. The best of several no-frills restaurants opposite the station. Spicy, inexpensive, vegetarian food, and chilled beer. The popular *Ankur* next door offers more of the same.

Five Star, Madhav Clock Tower Square. Inexpensive south Indian snack bar serving filling *dosas*, *iddlis* and *waddas* in cramped first-floor cafeteria, or on roof-top overlooking the square.

Navratna, *Shipra Hotel*, University Rd. Stylish MPTDC restaurant with the usual menu of tasty vegetarian, Moghlai, tandoori and Chinese dishes, plus some western options. Moderate.

New Raj Kumar, 20 Bhaktawar Ganj, Dushera Maidan. Low-priced and unpretentious strict vegetarian joint, tucked away down a suburban backstreet near *Surana Palace*.

Surana Palace, 23 GDC Rd. Wide range of carefully prepared Indian and Chinese dishes at moderate prices, served indoors or on the lawn. Well worth the rickshaw ride if you're not staying here.

Maheshwar

Overlooking the north bank of the mighty River Narmada, 91km southwest of Indore, **MAHESHWAR** has been identified as the site of King Kartvirajun's ancient capital, **Mahishmati**, a city mentioned in both the *Mahabharata* and *Ramayana*. In the eighteenth century, Maharani **Ahilya Bhai** (see p.384) built a palace and several temples here, giving the town a new lease of life. Today, it's a prominent port of call on the Narmada Hindu pilgrimage circuit, but well off the region's tourist trail.

The waterfront **ghats** that line the river below an old sandstone palace, however, make a quintessentially Indian spectacle. Parties of *yatris* take holy dips, drying their clothes in the breeze blowing off the river, while *pujaris* and groups of *sadhus* sit around murmuring prayers under raffia sun-shades. If you're not pushed for time, you could enjoy a fifteen-minute ferry trip across the river to the hamlet of **Navdatoli** on the far bank, where archeologists have uncovered evidence of settlement dating from the Lower Paleolithic era – not that there's much to see when you get there.

Once you've had a look at the whitewashed shrines and the **sati stones** dotted around the *ghats*, head for the flight of steps leading under the ornate sandstone facade of the palace to a raised courtyard, where you'll find a pair of eighteenth-century temples. The larger of the two, the Ahilya Bhai Mandir, has an overhanging balcony wrapped around its tower with a great bird's eye view over the waterfront.

The **palace** and **fort** complex itself, further up the steps, houses the workshops of the Rewa Society, established by the Maharani 250 years ago to promote the local handloom industry. Maheshwari **saris** are famous all over India for their distinctive patterns and superior quality; check out the designs for yourself by visiting the weavers' workshops (Mon–Fri 10am–5pm), which are sponsored by a German aid project. Though descendants of the old ruling family still occupy parts of the building, a couple of rooms around the entrance courtyard have been given over to a small **museum**. Exhibits include a life-size effigy of the devout Ahilya Bhai (shown seated on her throne, or *rajgadi*), a couple of moth-eaten palladins, old photographs of the Holkar dynasty, and the shrine from which Maheshwar's annual Dushhera festival begins.

Practicalities

Accommodation in Maheshwar is limited to the *Ahilya Trust Guest House* (①), a charitable institution near the palace, and the handful of rudimentary *dharamshalas* around the small square behind the *ghats*. This, in part, explains why many visitors prefer to visit on MPTDC guided tours, or as a day trip from Indore. **Buses** from Indore are fairly frequent, taking three and a half hours with a change at the market town of Dhamnod, 76km southwest of Indore on the NH3. The nearest rail-head is at **Barwaha**, 39km west. You can also call in at Maheshwar en route between the area's other religious centre, Omkareshwar, and Mandu, from where there are direct buses.

Places to eat are comparatively thin on the ground, as the majority of visitors to the town are pilgrims who cook their own food. Try a vegetarian meal in one of the *dhabas* on the square if your digestive system is up to it.

Omkareshwar

East of the main river crossing at Barhawa, the Narmada dips southwards, sweeps north again to form a wide bend, and then forks around a two-kilometre-long wedge-shaped outcrop of sandstone. Seen from above, the island, cut by several deep ravines, bears an uncanny resemblance to the "Om" symbol. This, coupled with the presence on its sheer south-facing side of a revered *shivalingam*, has made **OMKARESHWAR**, 77km south of Indore, one of the most sacred Hindu sites in central India.

Since ancient times, pilgrims have flocked here for *darshan* and a holy dip in the river. Until recently, however, few foreign visitors knew of the village's existence; but it is among the region's most atmospheric spots, and anyone who can survive for a couple of days without a comfortable hotel room is likely to enjoy it. Ruined temples, wayside shrines, bathing places, and caves inhabited by chillum-smoking Shaivite *sadhus* are dotted around the island, strung together by an old paved pilgrims' trail.

From the bus stand at the bottom of the village, Omkareshwar's only street runs 400m uphill to a ramshackle square, where you'll find most of the *dharamshalas, chai* shops, and a handful of stalls hawking lurid *puja* paraphernalia (including the excellent stylized **maps** taken home by pilgrims as souvenirs of their visits). The island itself is connected to the mainland by a high concrete footbridge, and by flat-bottomed ferries that shuttle between the *ghats* crouched at the foot of the river gorge. Once across, you're soon swallowed up by the narrow damp lane leading to the main temple.

The prominent white *shikhara* that now soars above the **Shri Omkar Mandhata Mandir** is a relatively new addition to the dense cluster of buildings on the south side of the island. Below it, the ornate pillars in the assembly hall, or *mandapa*, are more representative of the shrine's great antiquity. Myths relating to the origins of the deity in the low-ceilinged sanctum date back to the second century BC. Another of India's total of twelve **Jyotrilinga** ("*lingams* of Light"; see Ujjain), it is said by Hindus to have emerged spontaneously from the earth after a struggle between Brahma, Vishnu and Shiva.

Around the island

Traditionally, the *parikrama* (circular tour) of Omkareshwar begins at the *ghats* below Shri Mandhata and proceeds clockwise **around the island**. The walk takes at least a couple of hours, so carry plenty of water if you plan to do the whole thing at one go.

The first section of the trail is a leisurely half-hour stroll from the footbridge to the pebble-strewn western tip of the island, where you'll find a small *chai* stall and a couple of insignificant shrines. The **Trivendi Sangam**, or "Three-rivers confluence", is an especially propitious bathing place, where the Narmada forks as it merges with the Kaveri. From the confluence, the path climbs above the fringe of fine white sand lining the northern shore until it reaches level ground. The ruins of the **Gaudi Somnath**

temple stand in the middle of the plateau, surrounded by a sizeable collection of sculpture mounted on concrete plinths. The sanctuary houses a colossal *shivalingam*, attended by an equally huge Nandi bull. At this point, drop down a steep flight of steps to the village, or continue east, towards the old fortified town that crowned the top of the island before it was ransacked by Muslims in the medieval era. Numerous chunks of temple sculpture, lying discarded among the rubble, include a couple of finely carved gods and goddesses, used for shade by families of black-faced langur monkeys.

After scaling the sides of a gully, the trail leads under the large ornamental archway of the **Surajkund Gate**, flanked by three-metre figures of Arjun and Bheema, two of the illustrious Pandava brothers. The tenth-century **Siddhesvara temple** stands five minutes' walk away to the south, on a patch of flat ground overlooking the river. Raised on a large plinth decorated with rampaging elephants, it has some fine *apsaras*, or female fertility figures, carved over its southern doorway, and a donatory Sanskrit inscription that the resident *chowkidar* will, for some *baksheesh*, point out to you.

Of the two possible routes back to the village, one takes you along the top of the plateau, before dropping sharply down, via another ruined temple and the **Maharaja's palace**, to the Shri Mandhata temple. The other follows a flight of steps to the river bank, and then heads past a group of *sadhus*' caves to the main *ghats*.

Practicalities

Omkareshwar is connected by state **bus** to Khandwa (4 daily; 2hr), Maheshwar (1 daily; 2hr 30min), and Indore (2 daily; 2hr 30min). You can also get there by catching the Indore to Khandwa bus as far as **Omkareshwar Road**, a junction and *chai* stop on the NH3, from where a beaten-up local bus runs the remaining 15km. Omkareshwar Road is also the nearest railhead, but only slow passenger services stop here. Barhawa, on the north bank of the Narmada, is the closest mainline train station.

Finding **somewhere to stay** can be a problem if you're fussy about space and hygiene. The only inexpensive hotel-style place, the *Yatraki Niwas* (①) behind the bus stand, has spartan rooms, to say the least, but they're reasonably clean and some have bathrooms. Most visitors end up in the central *dharamshalas*, which are cheap, sociable and make a good way to experience pilgrim culture at close hand. On the down side, *dharamshala* rooms tend to be windowless cells, with washing facilities limited to a standpipe in the yard (to encourage people to use the river), and communal toilets. The cleanest are the *Ahilya Bhai* (①), left of the main square (look for the roof-top statue of the Queen on horseback); *Rewa Gauza* (①), west of the village *ghats* near the Mamaleshwara temple; and the *Shri Tirole Kumbhi* (①), which overlooks the river.

If you can't face a spell in a *dharamshala*, there are a couple of alternatives. Overhanging the steps leading to the *ghats* from the village square is an old building which the owner rents out to long-stay westerners. The rooms are very cheap, spacious and light, and the views over the waterfront are excellent. Unlike several other privately run places around the village, this one has both running water and electricity. Visitors with their own vehicle may also manage to talk their way into the large, pink, and very *pukka Irrigation Project Guest House* (④) at the top of the hill, whose clean comfortable rooms are normally reserved for visiting engineers. At the attractive *PWD Rest House* (③) nearby, once again, special permission to stay is normally required.

Unless you cook your own **food** (most *dharamshalas* provide pots and stoves), the only places to eat are the grungy *chai* stalls ranged around the square, which serve platefuls of fiery *dal*, *subzi* and rice. A small cafe down by the bus stand, just beyond the barrier, cooks fresh vegetables, eggs and *chappatis* to order. **Mineral water** is available at *Jain Cold Drinks*, 100m from the bus stand, on the left side of the main street.

Omkareshwar does not, at present, have an STD telephone link, nor money changing facilities. The nearest bank with a foreign exchnage counter is at Indore. A small **post office** on the main street, however, offers a reliable poste restante service.

CHAPTER FIVE

HIMACHAL PRADESH

R uffled by the lower ridges of the Shivalik Range in the far south, cut through by the Pir Panjal and Dhauladhar ranges in the northwest, and dominated by the great Himalaya in the north and east, **HIMACHAL PRADESH** (HP) is India's most popular and easily accessible hill state, sandwiched between the Punjab and Tibet. Lowland orchards, sub-tropical forests and maize fields peter out in the higher reaches where pines cling to the steep slopes of mountains whose inhospitable peaks soar in rocky crags and forbidding ice fields to heights of over 6000 metres.

Together with deep gorges cut by rivers crashing down from the Himalaya, these mountains form natural boundaries between the state's separate districts. Each has its own architecture, from rock-cut shrines and *shikhara* temples to colonial mansions and Buddhist monasteries. Roads struggle against the vagaries of the climate to connect the larger settlements, which are way outnumbered by remote villages, many of which are home to semi-nomadic **Gaddi** and **Gujjar** shepherds.

An obvious way to approach the state is to head north from Delhi to the state capital, **Shimla**, beyond the lush and temperate valleys of **Sirmaur**. The former summer location of the British government, Shimla is a curious, appealing mix of grand homes, churches and chaotic bazaars, with a favourable climate and breathtaking views. The main road **northeast** from Shimla tackles a pass just north of **Narkanda**, then follows the River Sutlej east to **Sarahan**, with its spectacular wooden temple, and enters the eastern district of **Kinnaur**, most of which is accessible only to those holding **Inner Line permits** (see p.457). Alpine and green in the west, Kinnaur becomes more austere and barren as it stretches east to the Tibetan plateau, its staggering beauty enhanced by delicate timber houses, temples, and fluttering prayer flags.

Another road from Shimla climbs slowly northwest to **Mandi**, a former market town that is still a major crossroads. To the north is Himachal's most popular tourist spot, the **Kullu Valley**, an undulating mass of terraced fields, orchards and forests overlooked by snowy peaks. Its epicentre is the tourist town of **Manali**, just sixteen hours by bus from Delhi. Long a favourite hang-out of western "hippies", Manali is set in idyllic mountain scenery, cloaked in apple orchards and murmuring with bubbling rivers. As well as being a perfect starting point for treks, Manali offers **white-water rafting** between May and June, and relaxing sulphurous springs in nearby **Vashisht**.

Beyond the Rohtang Pass in the far north of Kullu district, the valleys of **Lahaul and Spiti** stretch beneath mighty peaks in vast brown, bare expanses, where remote settle-

HIMACHAL PRADESH TRAVEL DETAILS

	Trains		Buses		Flights	
	Frequency	Time	Frequency	Time	Frequency	Time
To and From SHIMLA						
Ani			1 daily	8hr		
Chail			3 daily	2hr		
Chamba			3 daily	16hr		
Chandigarh			every 30min	3hr 30min		
Dalhousie			1 daily	16hr		
Dehra Dun			2 daily	9hr		
Delhi			hourly	10hr	daily	1hr 10min
Dharamsala			7 daily	9–10hr		
Haridwar			5 daily	9hr		
Jammu			1 daily	16hr		
Kalka	4–7 daily	5hr 30min–7hr				
Kangra			8 daily	10hr		
Kasauli	3 daily	4hr 30min–6hr	hourly	2hr 30min		
Kullu			5 daily	7–8hr		
Manali			5 daily	9–10hr		
Mandi			~5 daily	4hr 30min–5hr		
Nahan			6 daily	6hr		
Narkanda			5 daily	3hr		
Pathankot			5 daily	12hr		
Rampur			5 daily	6hr		
Rekong Peo			5 daily	8–10hr		
Sangla			2 daily	10hr		
Solan	3–6 daily	2hr 30min–3hr	every 30min	1hr 30min		

	Buses			Buses	
	Frequency	Time		Frequency	Time
To and From Chamba			**To and From Dharamsala** (continued)		
Brahmour	5 daily	3hr	Mcleodganj	every 20min	40min
Dalhousie	5 daily	2hr 30min	Nahan	1 daily	12hr
Delhi	1 nightly	18hr	Pathankot	12 daily	3hr 30min
Kangra	1 daily	6hr	Shimla	5 daily	10hr
Khajjiar	3 daily	1hr 30min	**To and From Kangra**		
Mandi	1 daily	15hr	Chamba	2 daily	6hr
Pathankot	hourly	5hr	Delhi	every 30min	12hr
To and From Dalhousie			Jawalamukhi	every 15min	1–2hr
Amritsar	2 daily	5hr 30min	Mandi	4 daily	6hr
Jammu	1 daily	6hr	Masrur	3 daily	2hr
Jullundhar	1 daily	6hr	Pathankot	10 daily	3–4hr
Khajjiar	2 daily	1hr	**To and From Kasauli**		
Pathankot	hourly	3hr 30min	Chandigarh	5 daily	2hr 30min
To and From Dharamsala			Delhi	3 daily	7hr 30min
Bir	1 daily	4hr	Kalka	3 daily	1hr 30min
Chamba	2 daily	9hr	Solan	5 daily	40min
Chandigarh	6–15 daily	7–8hr	**To and From Kullu**		
Dalhousie	1 daily	7hr 30min	Amritsar	1 daily	16hr
Delhi	7 daily	12hr	Chandigarh	8 daily	6hr 30min
Jawalamukhi	8 daily	2hr 30min	Dehra Dun	1 daily	14hr
Kangra	every 30min	1hr	Delhi	6 daily	12–14hr
Kullu	3 daily	8hr	Haridwar	1 daily	14hr
Manali	3 daily	11hr	Mandi	hourly	3hr
Mandi	5 daily	7hr	Manikaran	9 daily	2–3 hr
Masrur	2 daily	4hr	Nagar	hourly	1hr 30min–2hr

	Buses			**Buses**	
	Frequency	Time		Frequency	Time
To and From Manali			**To and From Manali** (continued)		
Amritsar	1 daily	16hr	Nagar	hourly	2hr
Chandigarh	8 daily	8–11hr	Nahan	1 daily	12hr
Darcha	1 daily	12hr	Pathankot	5 daily	12hr
Dehra Dun	1 daily	16hr	Udaipur, Lahaul	1 daily	7hr
Delhi	6 daily	14–17hr			
Haridwar	1 daily	16hr	**To and From Nahan**		
Jammu	1 daily	16hr	Ambala	1 daily	2hr 30min
Kangra	4 daily	12hr	Chandigarh	6 daily	2hr
Kaza	1 daily	12hr	Dehra Dun	6 daily	3hr
Keylong	8 daily	6hr	Delhi	3 daily	6hr
Kullu	every 15min	1hr 15min–2hr	Mandi	1 daily	8hr
Mandi	1 hourly	4hr	Mussourie	6 daily	5hr
Manikaran	9 daily	3hr 30min	Renuka	6 daily	2hr

For more details of transport connections from **Delhi**, see p.116 onwards; for **Pathankot** connections, see p.496.

Note that most individual routes appear only once in this chart; check against where you want to get to as well as where you're coming from.

ments are surveyed by stark *gompas*, or monasteries. Although **permits** are needed for trips into the far-flung regions of Lahaul and Spiti, without one you can follow unmatched trekking routes from **Kaza** or **Kibber**, or continue north on the road to Leh.

Visitors to the densely populated **Kangra Valley** invariably make a bee-line for **Dharamsala**, whose large community of Tibetan exiles includes the Dalai Lama himself. Trekking paths lead east from here to the tea-growing district of **Palampur**, and north across the treacherous passes of the Dhauladhar mountains into the **Chamba Valley**.

Finding guides and porters for **treks** is rarely difficult. The season begins as the monsoon washes away the snow in early June, and lasts until late November in the west, and late October in the north and east. In **winter**, heavy snows transform all but the far south of the state into a wonderland. The region north of Manali is accessible only from late June to early October when the roads are clear. Even in **summer**, when the days are hot and the sun strong, northern Himachal is beset with cold nights; always carry warm clothes, or pick up a locally made shawl.

Some history

The earliest known inhabitants of the area now known as Himachal Pradesh were the **Dasas**, who entered the hills from the Gangetic plain between the third and second millennium BC, having been pushed out of their homeland by the Indus Valley civilization that swept into India from the west. By 2000 BC the Dasas had been joined by the **Aryans**, and a number of tribal republics, known as *janapadas*, began to emerge in geographically separate regions, where they fostered separate cultural traditions.

The terrain made it impossible for one ruler to hold sway over the whole region. The **Guptas** forged inroads into the mountains between the second and fifth centuries AD, only to be ousted in turn by Vardhana rulers, then petty Rana and Thakhur chieftains, and ultimately the Hindu **Rajputs**. As early as 550 AD Rajput families had gained supremacy over the northwestern districts of Brahmour and Chamba, just two of the many princely states created between the sixth and sixteenth centuries. Of these, the most powerful was **Kangra**, where the Katoch Rajputs held off attacks on their treasure-stocked fort from the Sultans, Mahmud of Ghazni (1009 AD), and the Tughluqs (fourteenth century) before finally falling to the Moghuls in the sixteenth century.

Govt of India Statement – The external boundaries of India are neither correct nor authenticated.

50 km

0

N

During the medieval era, **Lahaul and Spiti** remained aloof, governed not by Rajputs, but by Jos of Tibetan origin, who introduced Tibetan customs and architecture, and profited from trade between India, Lhasa and Samarkand. After a period of submission to Ladakh, Lahaul and Spiti came under the Rajas of **Kullu**, a central princely state that reached its apogee in the seventeenth century. Further south, the region around **Shimla** and **Sirmaur** was divided into over thirty independently governed *thakurais*. In the late seventeenth century, the newly empowered **Sikh** community, based at **Paonta Sahib** (Sirmaur), added to the threat already posed by the Moghuls. By the eighteenth century, under **Maharaja Ranjit Singh**, the Sikhs had gained strongholds in much of western Himachal, and considerable power in both Kullu and Spiti.

Battling against Sikh expansion, Amar Singh Tapur, the leader of the **Gurkha** army set on extending his own Nepalese dominion, failed to take Kangra, but consolidated power in the southern Shimla hill states. The *thakurai* chiefs turned to the **British** for help, and forced the last of the Gurkhas back into Nepal in 1815. Predictably, the British assumed power over the south, thus tempting the Sikhs to battle in the **Anglo-Sikh War**. With the signing of a treaty in 1846 the British annexed most of the south and west of the state, and in 1864 pronounced Shimla, a cool retreat for British officers and their families, the summer government headquarters.

After Independence, the regions bordering present-day Punjab were integrated, named Himachal Pradesh ("Himalayan Provinces"), and administered by a Chief Commissioner. By 1956 HP was recognized as a Union Territory, and in 1966 the state as it exists today was formed, with Shimla as its capital.

Despite being a political unity, Himachal Pradesh is hardly culturally homogenous. With over ninety percent of the population living outside the main towns, and many areas remaining totally isolated during the long winter months, Himachal's separate districts maintain distinct customs, architecture, dress and agricultural methods. Though Hinduism dominates, there are substantial numbers of Sikhs, Muslims and Christians, and Lahaul, Spiti and Kinnaur have been home to Tibetan Buddhists since the tenth century. After the nationwide reactions to the demolition of Ayodhya's mosque in 1993 (see p.287), Himachali support for the BJP rose, particularly among the high-caste landowning Thakhurs, the informal alliance of apple growers whose wealth gives them considerable influence over Himachali politics. However, after a neck-and-neck race, the **Congress** came out on top in the 1993 autumn elections, placing Himachal Pradesh within the fold of the national Congress majority.

SHIMLA AND AROUND

Shimla, Himachal's capital, is India's largest and most famous hill station, in a region which holds several considerably lesser and duller rivals but a wealth of spectacular scenery. Probably the best way to enjoy it is to take a two- to three-day round-trip from the capital to the village of **Sarahan**, site of the famous Bhima Kali temple and gateway to the eastern district of Kinnaur. The 176-kilometre journey, which takes around eight hours by bus, winds over the heads of several scenic valleys. To make the most of the superb views of the northwest Himalaya, stay a night in **Narkanda**, a roadside settlement 65km northeast of Shimla.

Although most travellers from the south come straight from Delhi to Shimla, a possible detour from Ambala in Haryana, or the approach from Uttar Pradesh, involves crossing the low-lying district of **Sirmaur**, the southernmost area of the state, at the edge of the Haryana plains. Cut by the River Giri, on its way to join the Yamuna in the south, this is among the most fertile areas of the state, blessed with an unusually equitable climate. Near the border, the pretty little town of **Paonta Sahib**, where pastel-yellow houses are packed tightly into the cobbled streets, holds an important shrine dedicated to Guru Gobind Singh, the tenth Sikh guru, who lived here. From Punjab or Harayana, the first town on the road is **Nahan**, Sirmaur's capital, connected by bus to Ambala, 105km southwest, and the hill stations further north. Neither Nahan nor the surrounding forests merit more than a short amble, unless you arrive at the end of the rains and happen upon the **Bhawan Dwadashi** festival, when 52 deities are carried to the Jagannath temple, and floated in a pool until dark.

Six daily buses (2hr) make the journey 45km east of Nahan to **Dodahu**, 2km from the secluded lake at **Renuka**, where a **wildlife sanctuary** protects rare deer plus a magnificent pride of Asiatic lions, introduced here in the hope of creating a stable breeding population. Tropical forests flow down to the lake, along which trees and reeds shelter colonies of herons, kingfishers and bee-eaters. Bright carp and snub-nosed turtles flash by, free in this sacred enclave from the threat of poachers. Lilting devotional music and the toll of brass bells echo over the lake at sunrise and sunset from the Hindu temples. HPTDC *Hotel Renuka* (☎8339; ④–⑤), in sloping gardens on the western shore, has rooms opening onto a shady verandah, and serves good food; order in advance, and watch out for cheeky monkeys.

Shimla

Whether you travel by road or rail, the last stretch of the climb up to **SHIMLA** seems interminable. Deep in the foothills of the Himalayas, the hill station is approached via an unfeasibly sinuous route that winds from the plains at Kalka across nearly 100km of precipitous river valleys, pine forests, and mountainsides swathed in maize terraces and apple orchards. It's not hard to see why the British chose this inaccessible site as their summer capital. At an altitude of 2159m, the crescent-shaped ridge over which it spills is blessed with perennially cool air, crisp light, and superb **panoramas** across verdant, undulating country to the snowy peaks of the Great Himalayan range.

Named after its patron goddess, Shamla Devi (a manifestation of Kali), the tiny village that stood on this spot was "discovered" by a team of British surveyors in 1817. Shortly afterwards, groups of battle-weary army officers began to trickle up here between skirmishes with the Gurkhas in the Sutlej valley. Glowing reports of its beauty and climate gradually filtered to the imperial capital, Calcutta, and within a decade, the ridges around Shimla were peppered with bungalows and holiday cottages. The British finally persuaded the local Raja to part with the land in 1830, and the settlement became the subcontinent's most fashionable summer resort. Each year, long trains of packhorses and coolies picked their way up from the plains, bringing with them the Raj's top brass, and legions of grass-widows whose husbands were obliged to sweat it out at lower elevations. The annual migration was finally rubber-stamped in 1864, when Shimla – now an elegant town of mansions, churches and cricket pitches – was declared the Government of India's official hot-season HQ. The civil servants had to carry on business as usual, but for most of its temporary residents, the summer capital was an endless round of garden parties, formal dinners, high teas, balls, bridge games and evening promenades along the main street, the Mall. With the completion of the **Kalka–Shimla Railway** in 1904, Shimla lay only two days by train from Delhi. Its meteoric rise continued after Independence, when, following the reorganization of the Punjab in 1966, it became state capital.

Today, Shimla is still a major holiday resort, popular mainly with *nouveau riche* Punjabis and Delhites who flock here during the May–June run-up to the monsoons. Its jaded colonial charm also appeals to foreigners looking for a taste of the Raj. The *burra-* and *memsahibs* may have moved on, but Shimla retains a decidedly **British feel**: *pukka* Indian gentlemen in tweeds stroll along the Mall smoking pipes, while neatly

THE VICEROY'S "TOY TRAIN"

Until the construction of the **Kalka–Shimla railway**, the only way to get to the hill station was on the so-called **Cart Road** – a slow, winding trail trodden by lines of long-suffering porters and horse-drawn tongas. Plans for a narrow-gauge railway had been started as early as 1847, but it took the intervention of the Viceroy himself, **Lord Curzon**, to provide the impetus needed to get the massive undertaking off the ground.

By the time the 96-km line was completed in 1891, 103 tunnels, 24 bridges, and 18 stations had been built between Shimla and the railhead at Kalka, 26km northeast of Chandigarh. These days, buses may be quicker, but a ride on the "toy train" is far more memorable – especially if you travel first-class, in one of the glass-sided "rail cars". Hauled along by a tiny blue-and-white diesel locomotive, they rattle at a leisurely pace through stunning scenery, taking from five and a half to seven hours to reach Shimla.

Along the route, you'll notice the guards exchanging little leather pouches with staff strategically positioned on the station platforms. The bags they receive in return contain small brass discs, which the drivers slot into special machines to alert the signals ahead of their approach. **"Neal's Token System"**, in place since the line was first inaugurated, is a fail-safe means of ensuring that trains travelling in opposite directions never meet face-to-face on the single-track sections of the railway.

For information about train times and ticket booking, see p.414.

turned-out school children scuttle past mock-Tudor shop-fronts and houses with names like *Braeside*. At the same time, the dense, chaotic mass of corrugated iron roof-tops immediately below the ridge, Shimla's **bazaar**, lends an unmistakably Oriental aspect to the town, an active market and gateway for the northwestern Himalayan region.

The **best time to visit** is during October and November, before the Himachali winter sets in, when the days are still warm and dry, and the morning skies are clear. From December to late February, heavy snow is common, and temperatures hover around, or below zero. The spring brings with it unpredictability: warm blasts of air from the plains, and flurries of freezing rain from the mountains. Avoid **high season**, in May, June and July, when accommodation is scarce and expensive. Whenever you come, though, bring plenty of warm clothes as the nights can get surprisingly chilly.

Arrival and information

Buses arriving on the main Chandigarh and Manali highways approach Shimla from the west, via Cart Rd. Before pulling in to the chaotic main **bus stand**, halfway around the hill, they stop briefly outside HPTDC's helpful **tourist reception centre** (daily 10am–5pm), just above the **railway station** – the place to head for general advice on transport and trekking around the state. Unless you plan to stay in the bazaar, which sprawls above the bus stand, get off here; it's a far less strenuous walk away from the top of the town and most of the accommodation. Buses from Narkanda, Rampur and Kinnaur arrive at the **Rivoli**, or "Lakkar Bazaar" **bus stand** on the north side of the Ridge. Shimla's **airport** lies 21km north of town on the Mandi road. If your budget won't stretch to a Rs300 taxi ride, take the city bus (Rs35), which meets every flight.

HPTDC's main **tourist office** (daily 10am–5pm; ☎78311), on the Mall near Scandal Corner, hands out the usual glossy leaflets, and sells tickets for their sightseeing tours (see below) and daily luxury and deluxe coaches to Manali and Dharamsala. The green-painted, Swiss-chalet-style **GPO** (Mon–Sat 10am–7pm, Sun 11am–4pm), with its efficient poste restante counter, stands just off Scandal Corner on the Mall. Nearby, the *UCO* is the cheapest and most efficient bank in Shimla with a **foreign exchange facility**. Otherwise, try the *State Bank of India*, halfway between Scandal Corner and the train station; expect a long wait, and to be charged Rs20 for an encashment certificate.

SHIMLA

Kufri △

Jakhu Temple
2455m

△ Narkanda, Rampur & Kinnaur

HOTELS:
Ⓐ Classic
Ⓑ Dalziel
Ⓒ Basant
Ⓓ Surya
Ⓔ Thakur
Ⓕ Oberoi Clarke's
Ⓖ Sanjeet
Ⓗ YMCA
Ⓘ White
Ⓙ Dreamland
Ⓚ Uphar
Ⓛ Chanakya

Ⓙ Ⓚ
Ⓛ
LAKKAR BAZAAR
Ⓘ
Christ Church
Ⓗ
Taxi Rank
Lift
Ⓕ Ⓖ
THE RIDGE
7
HPTDC Tourist Office
Rivoli
Bus Stand
ANZ Grindlay's Bank
GPO
Gaiety Theatre
Town Hall
6 THE MALL
8
BAZAAR
UCO Bank
Ⓓ
SCANDAL CORNER
1 2 3 4
5
Main Bus Stand
Ⓒ
Ⓔ
CART RD
Railway Station
VICTORY TUNNEL
Ⓐ Ⓑ
THE MALL
State Bank
Taxi Rank
Tourist Reception Centre
Railway Station

△ Airport (21 km)

N

RESTAURANTS:
1 Indian Coffee House
2 Devico's
3 Baljee's
4 Choice
5 New Plaza
6 Himani
7 Ashiana & Goofa
8 Sheer-e-Punjabi

△ Museum, IIAS & Prospect Hill
△ Kalka, Chandigarh & Delhi

250 m
0

> The telephone **area code** for Shimla is ☎0177.

Local transport

Wherever you arrive in Shimla, you'll be mobbed by Kashmiri **porters**. Most of the town is pedestrianized, so you may be glad of one to lug your gear up the hill. Fix the fee in advance, and ignore claims that your chosen hotel is full. The tourist office keeps a list of "coolie rates for important places" such as Scandal Corner (20min; Rs15–20).

Taxis, which line up outside the tourist reception centre on Cart Rd, are the best way to get to the pricier hotels on the outskirts. The main *Taxi Drivers' Union* rank (☎77136) is 1km east of the bus stand, below the foot of the **elevator** that connects the east end of Cart Rd with the Mall. Their published list of set fares applies to high season; at other times, you should be able to negotiate considerable discounts.

HPTDC organizes whistlestop **sightseeing tours** to destinations around Shimla, including Kufri, Chail, Narkanda and Sarahan. For **trekking, mountaineering, and jeep safaris** to Kinnaur and Spiti, contact Mr Pramode Paul at *Ibex Adventures & Travels* – Shimla's most experienced and reliable adventure tourism outfit.

The Town

Although Shimla and its satellite districts sprawl over the flanks of five or more hills, the centre is fairly compact, on and immediately beneath a shoulder of high ground known as the "**Ridge**". From here, a tangle of roads and lanes tumbles down in stages, each layer connected to the next by precipitous stone steps. **The Mall**, the main pedestrian thoroughfare, curves around the south slope of the hill, high above the train line and **Cart Road**, the upper limit for motor traffic, which encircles the base of the town.

The Ridge

Shimla's busy social scene revolves around the broad and breezy piazza that straddles **the Ridge**, overlooking impressive rippling foothills with the jagged white peaks of the Pir Panjal and Great Himalayan ranges on the horizon. In the afternoon, when the mountains are enveloped in cloud, honeymooners have their photos taken in brilliantly patterned *puttoos* (homespun blankets), while vacationers stroll by, watched by rows of shoe-shine boys and Kashmiri porters, their arms tucked inside long woollen *pherans*.

The Victorian-Gothic spire of **Christ Church** in the square, for some reason recently painted a bright yellow, is Shimla's most prominent landmark. Built to accommodate the peak-season Europeans, it was never quite able to cope with the crush: on one occasion, the vicar complained to the assembled *memsahibs* that their copious crinolines took up too much space. The five **stained-glass windows**, the finest in British India, depict (from left to right) Faith, Hope, Charity, Fortitude, Patience and Humility.

At the other end of the square, **Scandal Corner** is the focus of Shimla's famous mid-afternoon *volta*, when crowds of locals gather in front of *ANZ Grindlay's* to gossip. Watched over by a statue of the Punjabi nationalist hero Lala Lajpat Rai, the intersection takes its name not from all this tongue-wagging, but from the elopement of a high-ranking British official's daughter with a handsome Indian prince that began here.

The Mall

At Scandal Corner, the road from the railway station finally arrives at **the Mall**, having run past ice cream parlours, shawl shops, and department stores stuffed with electronic gadgets. The *HP State Emporium* is worth a browse for its discounted woollen goods, which include Kullu shawls and dapper green-felt-fronted Kinnauri caps. Flanked by a long row of unmistakably British half-timbered buildings, Shimla's main shopping street was, until World War I, strictly out-of-bounds to all "natives" except royalty and rickshaw pullers. These days, rickshaws, man-powered or otherwise, are banned, and white faces are few. The quintessentially colonial **Gaiety Theatre**, however, looks exactly as it did in the heyday of the Raj. The *Shimla Amateur Dramatic Company* still performs here, while in the gentlemen's club next door, the talk continues to revolve around cricket and share prices.

The bazaar

Drop down any of the narrow lanes leading off the Mall, and you're plunged into a warren of twisting backstreets. Shimla's **bazaar** is the hill station at its most vibrant – a maze of dishevelled shacks, brightly lit stalls, and minarets, cascading in a clutter of corrugated iron and rotting timber to the edge of Cart Road. Little has changed since the nineteenth century, when Rudyard Kipling, in his novel *Kim*, said: "A man who knows his way there can defy all the police of India's summer capital, so cunningly does verandah communicate with verandah, alley-way with alley-way, and bolt-hole with bolt-hole." Apart from being a good place to shop for authentic souvenirs, this is also one of the few areas of town that feels Himalayan: multi-coloured Kullu caps (*topis*) bob about in the crowd, alongside the odd Lahauli, Kinnauri or Tibetan face.

The museum

Tucked away on the eastern edge of town, the HP state **museum** (Tues–Sat 10am–1.30pm & 2–5pm) is fiendishly difficult to find, but well worth the effort. Its diverse collection includes contemporary, as well as antique works of art, well displayed in an elegant colonial mansion. To get there, head east along the Mall towards the gigantic TV relay mast, and ask for directions when you arrive at the foot of the hill.

The ground floor is given over largely to temple sculpture, and a gallery of magnificent **Pahari miniatures** – examples of the last great Hindu art form to flourish in northern India before the deadening impact of western culture in the early nineteenth century. An offspring of the Moghul painting tradition, the Pahari or "Hill" school is renowned for subtle depictions of romantic love, inspired by scenes from Hindu epics.

THE HIKE TO THE JAKHU TEMPLE

The early-morning hike up to the **Jakhu**, or "monkey" **temple** is something of a tradition in Shimla. The top of the hill (2455m) on which it stands offers a superb panorama of the Himalaya – particularly breathtaking before the bubbles of cloud blister up later in the day. The relentlessly steep climb takes from twenty to forty minutes. Visitors with mobility problems may want to arrange a horse; a couple usually hang around in the main square opposite the Gandhi statue. The path starts just left of Christ Church. When you arrive at the *Dreamland Hotel*, turn right, follow the hand rail up the hill, then bear left five minutes later at a fork in the lane. The summit is another ten to fifteen minutes' walk through the woods, beyond a colourful shrine that blasts out electric devotional music.

After the hard hack up, the temple itself, a red-and-yellow brick affair crammed with fairy lights and tinsel, comes as something of an anticlimax – the resident *pujari* doubles as a telephone attendant. The shrine inside houses an image, and what are believed to be the footprints of **Hanuman**, commander-in-chief of the monkey army that helped Rama in his struggle against the arch-demon Ravana – the subject of the *Ramayana*. Legend has it that the monkey god, adored by Hindus for his strength and fidelity, rested on Jakhu after collecting healing Himalayan herbs for Rama's injured brother, Lakshmana. These mythological connections explain the troupes of mangy monkeys around the temple. Pampered by generations of pilgrims and tourists, they have become a real pest; hang on to your bags, and don't carry food or wear bright clothes.

Among the museum's **paintings** are dozens of Moghul miniatures and a couple of fine "Company" watercolours. Produced for souvenir-hunting colonials by the descendants of the Moghul and Pahari masters, the *fakirs*, itinerant *sadhus* and mendicants they depict could have leapt straight from the pages of Kipling. Also worth checking out are the striking contemporary oils of the Himalayas, a small collection of nineteenth- and twentieth-century deity masks from Kullu (see p.441) and Sarahan (see p.416), and an exhibition of Indian children's paintings that is as insightful as it is cute.

The Viceregal Lodge and Prospect Hill

Shimla's single most impressive colonial monument, the old **Viceregal Lodge** (daily 10am–4.30pm; Rs5), today a conference centre, is fifteen minutes' walk west of the museum, astride the flattened, wooded top of Observatory Hill. The location, a natural watershed, could not have been more apt for the high seat of imperial power in British India. From here, streams trickle into the Sutlej and Arabian Sea in one direction, and down to the Jamuna, the Ganges, and the Bay of Bengal in the other.

Set amid fragrant pine forests, landscaped gardens, and well-watered lawns, the Lodge is a shamelessly ostentatious mock-Tudor mansion conceived in pompous "Scottish-baronial" mould. Completed in 1888 for the Viceroy Lord Dufferin, it boasted a staff of eight hundred (including forty gardeners) and was mission control for the Raj.

The entrance ticket buys a breathless guided tour of the Lodge's **ground floor**, with its huge library (formerly the ballroom), impressive teak-panelled entrance hall, and the guest room, notable for its intricately carved walnut ceiling and period furniture. The **conference room**, hung with photos of Nehru, Jinnah and Gandhi, was the scene of crucial talks in the run-up to Independence. On the stone terrace to the rear of the building, a bronze plaque profiles and names the peaks visible in the distance.

The short hike up to **Prospect Hill** (2176m), a popular picnic spot, ties in nicely with a visit to the Lodge. By cutting through the woods to the west of the mansion, you can drop down to a busy intersection known as **Boileauganj**, from where a tarmac path climbs steeply up to the small shrine of Kamana Devi. The summit gives fine views across the entire south side of Shimla ridge, and over the hills and valleys of southern HP towards the plains of the Punjab – a murky brown haze on the horizon.

Accommodation

Most travellers only spend a couple of nights in Shimla – long enough to see the sights, and to book a ticket somewhere else. One reason for this is that **accommodation** is, in the main, phenomenally expensive. Between mid-April and mid-September, tariffs double; during May, June and July, finding anywhere at all to stay is impossible if you haven't booked in advance. At other times it's worth trying to negotiate a **discount**: a fifty percent reduction is the norm from October to early April.

Visitors on tight budgets tend to head straight for the *YMCA*, above Christ Church. Their stiff "temporary membership fee", however, means that you end up paying the same for a short stay as you would for a cleaner room, with bathroom, higher up the hill. Mid-range accommodation is scattered around the Mall, or on the edge of the bazaar near the bus stand, and there are also a couple of old-style **luxury hotels**.

Basant, Cart Rd, west of the bus stand. Best of the rock-bottom bunch in the bazaar area, with cleanish rooms (attached or common shower-toilets). The road can be noisy. Some singles. ①–②.

Chanakya, Lakkar Bazaar (☎3338). Cosy, clean and central. Cheapest rooms are a good deal. ④.

Chapslee (☎77319; fax 77567). Genteel old manor house in its own grounds on the edge of town, stuffed with antiques. Six luxurious suites, library, card room, tennis court, and a croquet lawn. ⑨.

Dalziel, The Mall (☎72691). Old wooden building five minutes' walk uphill from the train station. Spotless, tiled bathrooms, all with big geysers, and fine views from the back balconies. ④–⑤.

Dreamland, The Ridge, above the church (☎5057). One of the best-value, friendliest budget hotels, with clean rooms, most with geysers, *Star TV*, and superb morning views of the Himalaya. ③–④.

ACCOMMODATION PRICE CODES

All **accommodation prices** in this book have been coded using the symbols below. In principle the prices given are for the least expensive double rooms in each establishment; however, some hotels, usually in category ①, offer rates per bed rather than per room. Local taxes are not included unless specifically stated. For more details, see p.34.

①	up to Rs100	④	Rs225–350	⑦	Rs750–1200
②	Rs100–150	⑤	Rs350–500	⑧	Rs1200–2200
③	Rs150–225	⑥	Rs500–750	⑨	Rs2200 and up

Oberoi Clarks, The Mall (☎6091). Period building converted into posh, formula five-star. ⑨.

Sanjeet, The Mall (☎5823). Swanky modern hotel, a cut above others like it, and good value. ⑤.

Surya, Circular Rd (☎78191). Popular and comfortable mid-range hotel on the north side of the Victory tunnel. Room service, restaurant, and *Star TV*. ④–⑤.

Thakur, just above the bus stand (☎77545). Large, blue wooden building with some original fittings. Good if you can't face the climb up the hill from the bus stand. ③.

Uphar, The Ridge, near the *Dreamland* (☎77670). Basic, but sizeable, light and airy rooms. The pricier ones come with *Star TV*; all have geysers. ③–④.

White, Lakkar Bazaar (☎5276). Immaculate, light rooms, most with views, in centrally located, well-managed hotel. No off-season discount. Recommended. ⑤–⑥.

Woodville Palace, Raj Bhavan Rd (☎72763). Elegantly old-fashioned, 1930s mansion on the peaceful western side of town, with huge rooms, period furniture, lawns and a badminton court. Members of the former royal family still live upstairs. ⑦–⑧.

YMCA, The Ridge (☎72375). Large rooms (nearly all with shared bathrooms), dining hall, *Star TV*, snooker tables, and sun-terrace make this Shimla's most popular budget option – despite shabbiness, and high membership fee. Get a room in the more modern west wing, if possible. ②.

Eating

Few **restaurants** in Shimla retain the colonial ambience you might expect. Catering mainly for Indian visitors, they are heavily Punjabi-oriented, with rich, spicy, meat-based menus. If you're looking for a really cheap and filling meal, try a tin plate piled high with fried potato patties (*tikki*) or chick pea curry and *puris* (*channa batura*) at one of the snack bars that line the steps opposite the *Gaiety Theatre*. An ice cream or cake from one of the many **bakeries** along the Mall rounds off the evening nicely.

Ashiana, The Ridge. HPTDC-run restaurant in a converted bandstand offering mainly non-veg Indian food, including tasty chicken *makhanwalla*, pizzas, and a few Chinese dishes. Moderate.

Balijee's, 26 The Mall. A landmark on Shimla's culinary and social map, this hectic smart-set coffee house does a roaring trade in snacks, sweets, and non-alcoholic drinks, especially in the evenings. Try the piping hot *gulab jamuns*, served to after-dinner strollers at their take-away counter.

Choice, Middle Bazaar (follow the steps down the side of *Balijee's* and look for the sign on the left). Tiny, no-nonsense Chinese restaurant with an exhaustive menu of cheap and delicious dishes.

Devico's, The Mall. Impeccably clean, western-style fast food joint serving south Indian snacks, including delicious *rawa masala dosas*, as well as veggie-burgers, and shakes. Good views, too.

Fascination, 26 The Mall. *Balijee's* swish à la carte wing (upstairs) offers a good selection of Indian and Chinese dishes, including some very "non-veg" options such as "brains curry". Moderate.

Goofa, The Ridge. The *Ashiana's* dreary veg sibling – directly below in a cavernous basement – serves filling, moderately priced *thalis*.

Himani, 48 The Mall. *Balijee's* main rival has a lively (mostly male) bar downstairs, and a swanky restaurant on the top floor, whose menu includes tasty *tandoori* dishes.

Indian Coffee House, The Mall. Pleasant, slightly shabby cafe with colonial ambience, offering the usual *Coffee House* package of veg snacks, coffee, and attentive service from turbaned waiters.

New Plaza, 60/1 Middle Bazaar, down the steps opposite the *Gaiety*. Deservedly popular, unpretentious family restaurant. Drab decor, but the mostly Indian dishes are fresh, tasty and good value.

MOVING ON FROM SHIMLA

Most travellers bypass Shimla on their way between Delhi and Manali, but HP's capital is a perfect halfway house if you're heading up country into the Kullu Valley, or back in the other direction towards the plains of Haryana-Punjab.

The toy train leaves Shimla four to seven times daily for **Kalka** (5hr 30min–7hr), where you can change onto the main broad-gauge line for **Chandigarh**. The best connections for **Delhi** leave at 10.15am and 11.55am, which get you into Kalka in time to catch the 5.22pm *Himalayan Queen* #4096, arriving in New Delhi at about 10pm. **Reservations** for the following day's first-class seats can be made until 1pm at the *Northern Railway*'s out-office on the Mall, just below the *Indian Coffee House* (daily 10am–5pm). Second-class tickets should be bought at the station at least an hour before departure.

The Cart Rd **bus stand**, below the bazaar, handles services to Chandigarh, Delhi, Mandi, Kullu, Dharamsala, Manali, and elsewhere, while "Lakkar Bazaar" bus stand (reached via the path that drops behind *ANZ Grindlay's Bank* on Scandal Corner) is the place to pick up departures to Narkanda, Ani, Rampur, Sarahan, and Kalpa (for Kinnaur).

Passengers for **Manali**, **Chandigarh**, or **Delhi** can choose between "luxury" (a/c) and "deluxe" (non-a/c) services run by HPTDC and others, or *HPSTC*'s standard boneshaking "express" buses. Tickets for the former should be booked a day in advance at travel agents on the Mall, or through the tourist office on Scandal Corner, which also has a hatch (daily 10am–1pm & 2–4pm) to reserve seats on all state buses from Shimla (including regular expresses to **Dharamsala**, **Chandigarh** and **Delhi**). Alternatively, join the rucks at the reservation counters at the main bus stand on Cart Road.

Note, that the first leg of the journey to **Mandi** (for Kangra, Dharamsala and Manali) can be an ordeal if you suffer from **travel sickness**, as the bus drivers pelt down the switchbacks at incredible speeds. Keep nausea at bay by sitting at the front of the bus (another reason to book early), and by eating a large breakfast before you set off.

Jagson's Airlines operate daily **flights** on 18-seater planes from Shimla to Delhi. The trip takes 1hr 10min and costs around US$100, or the *rupee* equivalent. Seats are nearly always available, and can be booked through *Jagson's* main agent in Shimla, and a good all-round **travel agent**, *Ambassador Travels*, 58 The Mall (☎4662).

Permits for travel into the restricted **"Inner Line"** zone, the recently opened road loop through Kinnaur and Spiti, are issued at the District Commissioner's office below the Mall. Unless you're travelling in a group of four or more, under the auspices of a reputable travel agent, your chances of getting one are virtually nil.

Sher-e-Punjabi, Lower Bazaar. A string of rock-bottom *dhabas* just below the Mall. The veg branch dishes up hearty ladles of spicy bean, chickpea, and *dal* dishes, for next to nothing.

Kasauli

The small, slow-paced town of **KASAULI**, 77km southwest of Shimla and served by frequent **buses** (3hr), is ideal for a short lazy break. Raised high enough above the plains to afford good views south over the glinting lights of Chandigarh at night, as well as north to the Himalayas, it is still low enough to maintain a pleasant climate. Crisscrossed by spindly cobbled streets, spreading along low ridges carpeted with forests and flower-filled meadows, Kasauli abounds in gentle short **strolls**; the hike to the summit of nearby **Monkey Point** (4km) is as energetic as most tourists get.

When you're ready to move on, a neat way to turn a visit to Kasauli into a round-trip excursion is to trek an easy 12km south through the woods to **Kalka**, and catch the **toy railway** back to Shimla from there (trains also pass through the tattered and rather dismal would-be hill station of **Solan**, 15km north by bus). Details of the path to follow, plus train and bus times, are available at the small **tourist office** by the bus stand. You can **change money** at the *Bank of Baroda* (Mon–Fri 11am–3pm) on Lower Mall.

Accommodation and eating

The choice of **accommodation** in Kasauli is thin, but adequate for most visitors' needs. The only modern hotel is the *Hotel Ros Common*, though the older hotels, with large rooms, fireplaces and wooden balconies, are soaked in the character of Raj days. Few have built-in water heaters, and supply hot water in buckets. As for **food**, away from Kasauli's larger hotels you're likely to find it monotonous. *Dhabas* in Sadar Bazaar dish up standard *aloo mutter, aloo gobi* and *dal*, plus fresh *puris* in the morning, and there are a couple of good snack stops by the bus stand.

Alasia, Lower Mall (☎01793/2008). Musty Raj-era house, facing north to the distant mountains. Large rooms with balconies, plus a couple of special suites. ⑤.

Anchal, Post Office Rd (☎01793/1052). Good-value option. Some rooms are poky and dim, but others have balconies and views south over the lowlands. One room holds six people. ③.

Gian, Post Office Rd. Unremarkable, but homely. Common or private bathrooms, and balconies. ①.

HPTDC Ros Common, Lower Mall (☎01793/2005). Extremely smart hotel almost 1km east of town, where beautiful gardens offer silver-service tea and coffee all day. Six well-maintained and spotless rooms. Often full – call ahead or book through Shimla's *Hotel Holiday Home* (☎0177/212890). The restaurant, open to non-residents, has Kasauli's most expensive and extensive menu. ⑤–⑥.

Maurice, Lower Mall (☎01793/2974). Well-kept Raj house; towering ceilings and airy balconies. ④.

R Maidans, Lower Mall (☎01793/2128). Stylish but ageing Raj mansion with spacious rooms. Some have balconies, and some fireplaces. ④–⑥.

Narkanda

Comparatively few foreign visitors find their way out to **NARKANDA**, a scruffy collection of corrugated-iron and timber houses, *chai* stalls, and wayside *dhabas* 65km northeast of Shimla. This former staging post on the old Hindustan–Tibet caravan route became, during the Raj, a popular weekend retreat for sporting Shimla-*wallahs* who came to bag bears; you won't see many bears today (the surrounding forests have been mercilessly logged) but the **views** of the Himalayas, rising in snowy ranks from the far side of the valley to the north, are superlative.

Straddling the main Rampur road, NH22, just below the pass that leads from the foothills into the Sutlej Valley, the town is the road-head and market for the area's widely dispersed apple and potato growers. From December to February, it also functions as one of the state's few **skiing** resorts. HPTDC run inexpensive ten-day packages in the *Government Trekking & Ski Centre*, near the bus stand. The deal includes rental, tuition, and a room in HPTDC's dour *Hotel Himview* (③–④).

Most visitors come to Narkanda from Shimla on HPTDC's tour (leaves Rivoli bus stand 10am, returns 5pm; Rs100), or en route to Sarahan and Kinnaur, northeast. If you aren't in a hurry, though, the village is worth a longer visit. The best views are from **Hatu peak** (3143m), a seven-kilometre hike from the main road, crowned by a lonely hilltop **Durga temple**. To complete the three- to four-hour round trip in time to see the Himalayas in all their morning glory, you'll probably have to stay the night in Narkanda, arriving on one of the frequent Rampur-bound buses. *Hotel Snow View* (③), above the hospital, is the best-value **accommodation**, and the safest place to eat.

Rampur

Once over the pass at Narkanda, the highway winds steadily down the south side of the Sutlej Valley, passing through several fragrant stands of *deodar* and pine forest. As you approach the river, the trees thin out and the mountainside grows increasingly sunparched and bare, except for the rice terraces that swirl, in stripes of green and pale yellow, around the banks of the roaring milky-turquoise torrent below.

THE BASHLEO PASS TREK

The four- to five-day trek from Rampur over the **Bashleo Pass** to Banjar – one of the trails followed by Penelope Chetwode in her famous travelogue *Kullu: The End of the Habitable World* (*Time Books International*, Delhi 1989) – is a good alternative to the busier Ani–Jalori Pass route to the Kullu Valley, now somewhat spoiled for walkers by the introduction of a motorable road. The trail up to the pass is comparatively easy, and several forest rest-houses allow the luxury of hiking without a tent. A number of picturesque villages, clustered around old wooden tower temples, also lie at regular intervals along the route. The largest, **Sarahan** (not to be confused with the village of the same name on the opposite side of the Sutlej Valley; see p.421), is usually reached at the end of the second day. Stage three takes you over the pass and down the other side to **Bathad**. After passing through **Bandal** and **Gushaini** villages on the fourth or fifth days, you finally arrive at the main road, from where daily buses head south, via **Banjar** and the Jalori Pass, to **Luri**, on NH22, and northwards to **Larji** in the Kullu Valley.

The river – the border between Shimla and Kullu districts – can be crossed at this point. A fair-weather jeep track climbs up the *nala* to the north towards the village of **Ani** and the **Jalori Pass** – for centuries the principal route north to the Kullu Valley. The main road, meanwhile, veers east along the even floor of an increasingly grandiose, V-shaped defile towards **RAMPUR**, 132km northeast of Shimla. Formerly the capital of the princely state of Bhushar, the town was once a prosperous and picturesque settlement, thronging with merchants from China, Yarkhand, and Tibet. Today, however, it's a gritty and cheerless cluster of unfinished concrete houses hemmed in by a forbidding wall of rock. The only time you may want to stop is during the **Lavi mela**, November 11–14, when hill-folk from the remote interior gather in their finest garb to trade bundles of wool, homespun shawls, and sacks of dried fruit and nuts.

If you find yourself stuck in Rampur, check out the gabled **Padam Palace**, home of the local ruling family, the Bahadurs, who trace their lineage back 123 generations to Lord Krishna. Built in 1919, the palace encloses an older Moghul-style building and a grand *durbar* hall – complete with silver throne and slits in its wood-panelled walls to allow the women of the court to spy on proceedings within. Across the main road, and easily accessible from the bus stand, stands a small Buddhist **gompa**. Inside the dimly-lit *lakhang*, or main hall, you'll find a huge metal prayer wheel decorated with bronze friezes, a polished-brass Buddha, shelves stacked with dusty Tibetan books, and a rock bearing what the monk insists are ten million minute inscriptions of the *mantra* "Om Mane Padmi Hum". In the east of town near the bus stand, the *Rama Guest House* (②), which has poky, airless rooms and shared toilets, is the best budget **accommodation**; the *Hotel Bhagavati* (③), at the bottom of the bazaar, is marginally more comfortable.

Sarahan

Secluded **SARAHAN**, erstwhile summer capital of the Bhushar rajas, sits astride a 2000-metre ledge above the River Sutlej, near the Shimla–Kinnaur border. Set against a spectacular backdrop, the village harbours one of the northwestern Himalaya's most exotic spectacles – the twin wooden pagodas of the gilt-pinnacled **Bhima Kali temple**. Until the opening of the "Inner Line" to tourists in 1992, only die-hard architecture buffs and the odd Spiti-bound trekking party ever passed through here. Now, with the nearby road no longer a "dead end", and despite a trickle of jeep safaris, it remains an off-track destination, an excellent two-day foray from Shimla, 174km southwest.

With its two multi-tiered sanctuary towers, elegantly sloping slate-tiled roofs, and gleaming golden spires, **Bhima Kali** is the most majestic of the few early timber temples left in the Sutlej Valley – an area renowned for its unusual tradition of housing holy shrines on raised wooden platforms. Although most of the structure dates from early this century, parts are thought to be more than eight hundred years old. The same **construction technique**, of stacking dry stone blocks between logs, has been used throughout, giving the walls their distinctive brown-and-grey stripes.

The main entrance, through a pair of elaborately decorated metal doors in the west of the compound, opens onto a large courtyard flanked by rest rooms and a small carved-stone **Shiva shrine**. Leave shoes and any leather articles at the racks, and head up the steps to a second, smaller yard. Beyond another golden door, also richly embossed with mythical scenes, the innermost enclosure holds the two **sanctuary towers**. The one on the right houses musical instruments, flags, palladins and ceremonial weapons used in religious festivals, a selection of which is on show in the small "museum" in the corner of the courtyard. Non-Hindus who want to climb to the top of the other, more modern tower for *darshan*, a ritual viewing of the highly polished gold-faced deity, have to leave cameras with the *chowkidar*, and don a saffron cotton cap. On your way across the yard, note the delicate carving that surrounds the main tower's projecting wooden balconies, and the gargoyles that gape from the eaves of its gabled roof – crowned with crimson pennants to advertise the presence of the goddess within. **Bhima Kali** herself is enshrined on the top floor. Decked with garlands of flowers, she peers out from behind clouds of *dhoop* smoke, tended not by ordinary villagers, as is normally the case in Himachal, but by bona fide *brahmin* priests.

Practicalities

The most convenient of the direct **buses** from Shimla to **Jeori** (pronounced *Jew*ri), the jumping-off point for Sarahan, departs at 7.30am for Sangla, in the Baspar Valley (see p.421). Tickets can't be booked in advance, so get to the Rivoli bus stand in good time. You can also reach Jeori by catching a bus to Rampur, and changing buses there.

Three buses leave Jeori each day (noon, 4.30pm & 6.30pm; 45min) for the 18km trip up to **Ghart**, a hamlet just below Sarahan. Alternatively, you can **hike** up along a well-worn mule track. The stiff ninety-minute climb is hard work, but a far less daunting prospect than if you miss the last bus than a night in Jeori, whose only accommodation is a flea-infested room above a sweet shop.

Sarahan itself only has two **places to stay**. You can't miss the first, and more expensive: HPTDC's *Hotel Shirkhand* (④), a concrete monster in quasi-traditional Sutlej style. Rooms here are clean, comfortable, and come with hot-water geysers, and valley views. The small, moderately priced restaurant has a hit-and-miss veg menu, and a relaxing terrace commands fine views over the mountains to the north. If you're on a tighter budget, try one of *Temple Rest House*'s four clean pleasant rooms (②–③), inside

---

BLOOD SACRIFICE IN SARAHAN

The **Bhima Kali** deity, a local manifestation of the black-faced, bloodthirsty Hindu goddess Kali (Durga), has for centuries been associated with **human sacrifice**. Once every decade, until the disapproving British appeared on the scene in the 1800s, a man was killed here as an offering to the *devi*. Following a complex ceremony, his newly spilled blood was poured over the goddess's tongue for her to drink, after which his body was dumped in a deep well inside the temple compound. If no victim could be found, it is said that a voice used to bellow from the depths of the pit, which is now sealed up.

The tradition of blood sacrifice continues in Sarahan to this day, albeit in less extreme form. During the annual **Astomi** festival, two days before the culmination of **Dussehra** (see p.442), a veritable menagerie of birds and beasts are put to the knife, including a water-buffalo calf, a sheep, a goat, a fish, a chicken, a crab, and even a spider. The gory spectacle draws large crowds, and is a memorable alternative to the Dussehra procession in Kullu, which takes place at around the same time in mid-October.

the Bhima Kali's main courtyard. They also have a few dorm beds (①) in a room off the square outside the temple. This is a long, chilly walk from the nearest toilet, and has no bathroom, but the *chowkidar* will let you use one of the rooms around the corner if they are free. If the temple kitchens aren't dishing up their usual cheap, filling pilgrims' food, the only places to eat are the grubby *dhabas* ranged around the square outside.

KINNAUR

Before 1992, the remote backwater of **KINNAUR** was strictly off-limits to tourists. A rugged buffer zone between the Shimla foothills and the wild western extremity of Chinese-occupied Tibet, it was considered too sensitive for foreigners to wander around unsupervised. To some extent this still holds true. Although visitors are now allowed to travel through the "Restricted Area", and onwards to complete the loop through Spiti and Lahaul to the Kullu Valley, special permission must first be obtained. At present, "**Inner Line permits**", issued at Shimla, Kullu, Rampur, and the district headquarters, **Rekong Peo**, are only granted to groups of four or more who have organized their trip through government-approved tour operators – which effectively renders most of the region out of bounds to independent travellers. Even if you can't afford a "jeep safari", however, those areas of Kinnaur that lie outside the no-go zone still offer incentives to brave the region's minimal infrastructure – notably the **Baspar Valley**, and sacred **Kinner-Kailash** massif, visible from the mountain village of **Kalpa**.

Straddling the mighty River Sutlej, which rises on the southern slopes of Shiva's winter abode on the Tibetan plateau, Mount Kailash, Kinnaur has for centuries been a major trans-Himalayan corridor. Merchants travelling between China and the Punjabi plains passed through on the **Hindustan–Tibet caravan route**, stretches of which are still used by villagers and trekkers. The bulk of the traffic that lumbers east towards the frontier, however, uses the newer fair-weather road, veering north into Spiti just short of the ascent to Shipki La Pass, on the Chinese border, which remains closed.

In the well-watered, mainly Hindu west of the region, the scenery ranges from subtropical to almost alpine: wood-and-slate villages, surrounded by maize terraces and orchards, nestle beneath pine forests and vast blue-grey mountain peaks. Further east, beyond the reach of the monsoons, it grows more austere, and glaciers loom on all sides. The hospitable Buddhist inhabitants of middle and upper Kinnaur are descendants of aboriginal peoples pushed into the mountains by the Aryan invasions of the second millennium BC. **Buddhism** arrived thanks to the tenth-century kings of Guge, who ruled what is now southwestern Tibet. **Rinchen Zangpo** (958–1055), the "Great Translator" credited with the "Second Spreading" of the faith in Guge, passed through here on his way home from the plains, where he had been sent by the ruler Yeshod to absorb the traditions of Indian Buddhism. In his wake, he left behind several monasteries, and a devotion to a pure form of the Buddhist faith that has endured here for nearly one thousand years. In the sixteenth century, after Guge had fragmented into dozens of petty fiefdoms, the **Bhushar kings** took control of Kinnaur. They remained in power throughout the British Raj, when this was one of the battlegrounds of the espionage war played out between agents of the Chinese, Russian and British empires – the "Great Game" evocatively depicted in the novels of Rudyard Kipling.

Rekong Peo

East of Jeori, the road climbs high above the Sutlej, traversing the sheer ravines that run into the valley from the south by means of flimsy-looking *jhulas*, or cable bridges. Tiny wooden villages, each with a pagoda-roofed temple, cling to the mountainsides – many at gradients beyond which human habitation would seem impossible. At **Wangtu** bridge, the old Inner Line, and trailhead for the Kinnaur–Pin Valley–Kaza trek (see p.421), the highway switches to the north bank of the river before running due east to the dishevelled, claustrophobic village of **Tapri**. Travelling by bus, you'll probably have to stop here to catch onward transport to Rekong Peo, or to Sangla, in the Baspar Valley. It's no place to get stuck, however, as there's no accommodation.

The district headquarters of Kinnaur, **REKONG PEO**, lies ninety minutes further up the valley, 4km above the main road. A batch of hastily constructed concrete houses and government buildings around a small *maidan*, it has the air of a dismal frontier settlement – a nightmare posting for the junior officials that stroll dejectedly along the main street. The only reason to stop is to buy trekking supplies, or to pick up the trail to Kalpa. Peo's **bazaar** is, however, a good place for crowd-watching, particularly in late afternoon when it fills up with dusty villagers waiting for the bus home. Many of the women don traditional Kinnauri garb for their trip to town – green velvet jackets, heavy homespun blankets with intricate borders, raw-silk cummerbunds, stacks of elaborate silver jewellery, and caps set at at jaunty angles above their long black plaits.

Practicalities

Rekong Peo's **buses** are fairly frequent considering its relative isolation. Five daily services ply between here and Shimla; there's a 4.30am departure for Mandi, and a direct bus at 2pm to Sangla. With an Inner Line permit, you can flag down the Tapri–Kaza bus as it passes Poberi, the Rekong Peo turn-off on the main road, at around 7am.

Accommodation is very limited. If the PWD *Rest House* (④) near the *maidan* is full, the next best option is the *Hotel Fairyland* (③), above the main street where the buses pull in. Rooms here are clean and aired, with a choice of attached or shared baths, and views across to Kinner-Kailash. Avoid the grungy *Mayur Guest House* (①–②), just down the road. In between the two, the small *Chinese Restaurant* is the village's only decent **place to eat**, serving filling meat-based noodle dishes, spicy veg stews, and Tibetan salt-butter tea. You can't get mineral water or soft drinks this far up the valley.

Kalpa (Chini)

Almost 250km northeast of Shimla, **KALPA** – known, when it was the British district heaquarters, as **Chini** – can be reached by road, or on foot along the steep mule track up the mountain from behind Rekong Peo's small *gompa* (look for the large yellow standing Buddha). After a stiff hour's hike through *deodar* trees, orchards and farm terraces, you rejoin the road just before it reaches a bazaar. A scruffy collection of market stalls and slate-roofed farmhouses, Kalpa would not be worth the climb were it not for for its dramatic location, astride a rocky bluff high above the right bank of the Sutlej. Opposite, the magnificent **Kinner-Kailash** massif sweeps 4500m up from the valley floor – a rugged ridge of sharp grey peaks flecked with folds of ice and snow. The mountain in the middle, Jorkaden (6473m) is the highest, followed by the sacred summit of Kinner-Kailash (6050m) to the north, and the needle point of Raldang (5499m) in the south. Up the valley you'll see remains of the Hindustan–Tibet road.

Practicalities

Kalpa is a far more attractive place to stay than Rekong Peo, although finding **accommodation** can involve a lot of walking. The best place is the *Forest Rest House* (④), a splendid ex-British bungalow at the top of the village, with large rooms, superb views from its garden and a resident *chowkidar*-cum-cook. Head up the dirt track that turns right off the metalled road 400m below the bazaar, and follow the path past the school and Forest Department Office. On the way, you pass Kalpa's only budget option, the

Vicky Guest House (②), whose sole (four-bedded) room is tacked onto the side of a family house. In the unlikely event of both these places being full, you can find a cheap bed for the night by asking around the bazaar on the other side of the village.

Apart from the *Rest House*, the only **places to eat** in Kalpa are its grubby *chai* shops, or the stores on and around the square, where you can buy fresh fruit, biscuits, lentils and rice, but little else; a camping stove is useful.

The Baspar Valley

Hemmed in by the pinnacles of Kinner-Kailash to the north, and the high peaks of the Garhwal range to the south, the seventy-kilometre River Baspar rises in the mountain wilderness along the Indo-Tibetan border, to flow through one of Kinnaur's most beautiful, secluded areas. Despite its comparative accessibility, the **Baspar Valley** sees few visitors, as its remotest reaches lie beyond the Inner Line. Nevertheless, the picturesque villages lower down the valley merit a detour from the main Rampur–Spiti road.

The valley's largest settlement, **SANGLA**, overlooks the right bank of the Baspar from the lower slopes of Kinner-Kailash. Served by daily **buses** from Shimla and Tapri, its chief attractions are a small saffron farm, and the wood-and-stone, gable-roofed **Kamru fort**, a thirty- to forty-minute walk above the village. You can **stay the night** in what must be one of India's swankiest government bungalows, the *Electricity Rest House* (④). Trekkers and campers should, however, bring their own food and fuel with them, so as not to over-burden the village's subsistence-oriented economy.

Without an Inner Line permit, **CHITKUL**, a day's hike beyond Sangla, is as far up the valley as you can go. The tiny village, which has a *Rest House*, sits at the bottom of a sprawling glacial moraine, crossed by the trail that winds up to **Charang La Pass** – the route of the Kinner-Kailash *parikarma*, or pilgrimage circuit, described opposite.

Upper Kinnaur

Access to **upper Kinnaur**, the remote region east of Kalpa, is restricted. Only visitors with Inner Line permits can travel beyond the checkpoint at Khangi, and on towards the confluence of the Sutlej and Spiti rivers. Five to six hours by jeep from Rekong Peo, within a day's hike of the frontier, the tiny hamlet of **PEOH** (or **Puh**) is the area's main settlement, chosen by the Dalai Lama in summer 1992 as the venue for the rarely performed **Kalachakra ceremony**. Buddhists from all over the world – including Richard Gere and Cindy Crawford, whose arrival almost upstaged the great man himself – flocked here to listen to Tibet's leader-in-exile read from a secret and highly auspicious text, which is believed to divulge a super-fast short-cut to Enlightenment.

Beyond Peoh, the road bends north, crossing the Sutlej for the last time at **Khabo**, near the Spiti confluence. To the northeast, **Leo Pargial II** (6770m), Kinnaur's highest peak, rises in a near-vertical 4000-metre wall of cream-coloured buttresses and pinnacles to mark the international frontier. The mountain also overlooks the old Indo-Tibet road as it enters China via the **Shipki La pass** (5569m). The present road, meanwhile, winds north above the Spiti through the barren wastes of the Hanglang Valley. Within the rainshadow of the Himalayas, this far-eastern edge of Himachal Pradesh, with its deep blue skies, crisp clear light, and arid mountain scenery, closely resembles Ladakh. Its only settlements are small scatterings of cubic dry-stone houses piled high with fuel and fodder, and surrounded by thickets of shimmering poplars, apricot groves, and terraces of barley. **NAKO**, the largest village, nestles high above the east side of the river around the banks of a small circular **lake**. Its eleventh-century *gompa*, founded by Rinchen Zangpo, houses ancient Buddhist statues and paintings.

TREKKING IN KINNAUR

Unfrequented mountain trails criss-cross Kinnaur, offering **treks** ranging from gentle hikes to challenging climbs over high-altitude passes. The routes along the **Sutlej Valley**, punctuated with government rest houses and villages, are feasible without the aid of ponies, but away from the main road you need to be completely self-sufficient. **Porters** can usually be hired in Rampur and Rekong Peo for around Rs100–150 a day, except in early autumn (Sept/Oct), when they and their horses are in great demand for the apple harvest.

Sarahan to Wangtu

This sedate four- to five-day hike along the path of the old Hindustan–Tibet road is an ideal introduction to the scenery and culture of the Sutlej Valley. The trail begins just below **SARAHAN** (see p.421), peeling away to the right after a sharp switchback in the metalled road that leads down to Jeori. Beyond several kilometres of pine and oak forest, it crosses a couple of mountain streams lower down the valley, before continuing north-east towards the first night-halt, the rest house at **Chaura** village, site of the picturesque Hirmal Devi temple. The second day takes you as far as **Tranda** (8km), or onwards another 10km, via the steep-sided Solding *nala*, or stream-gorge, to the rest house at **Paunda**. The third/fourth stage is an easy 12km amble through the village of Sungra, with its ancient *devi* temple, to **Nechar Rest House**. From here, the track drops 5km to meet the main highway. At **Wangtu**, where it crosses the river, you can pick up transport back to Shimla, or further up the Sutlej to Rekong Peo and Kalpa.

The Kinner-Kailash circuit

The five- to seven-day circumambulation of the majestic **Kinner-Kailash** massif, a sacred pilgrimage trail, makes a spectacular trek, for which you need an **Inner Line permit** (see p.457). The circuit starts at the village of **MORANG**, on the left bank of the Sutlej, served by buses from Tapri or Rekong Peo. A jeepable track runs southeast from here alongside the Turung Gad torrent to **Thangi**, the trailhead. The first night-halt, a level patch of ground beside the confluence of two streams at **Rahtak**, lies 12km up the valley. The gruelling second stage takes in the stiff climb up to the **Charang La Pass** (5266m), after which the path plunges steeply through a glacial moraine to the village of **Chitkul** in the **Baspar Valley** (see opposite), where there's a small *Forest Rest House*. At this point, the Inner Line ends and the trail follows the river down to the beautiful village of **Sangla**. If you're not pushed for time, a number of worthwhile day hikes can be slotted in here: up to **Kamru fort** behind the village, or the steep ascent to the **Shivaling La Pass**, on the opposite (west) side of the valley to Sangla, from where there are superb views of Raldang (5499m), the southernmost peak on the Kinner-Kailash massif. The final stage of the circuit passes through the lower, greener end of the Baspar Valley, via Shang and Brua on the left bank of the river, to **Karcham**, which overlooks the main highway.

Wangtu to Kaza, via the Pin Valley

This challenging route across the Great Himalayan range, via the Kalang Setal glacier and the Shakarof La Pass, is a dramatic approach to Spiti and the **Pin Valley**. The trail, which is very steep, snow-covered, and hard to follow in places, should definitely not be attempted without ponies, porters, adequate gear, and a **guide** – preferably one arranged through a reputable trekking agency (for an address in Shimla, see p.410).

The first day, starting at **WANGTU** on the main highway, is an easy 8km hike up the valley to **Kafnoo** village. Stage two (12km) leads beyond the tree-line to a Gaddi grazing ground called **Mulling**, from where it's another 12km uphill through high pastures to **Phustirang** (3750m), the camp ground below the **Bhaba Pass** (4865m). Day four (or three if you're acclimatized) is a gruelling slog over the pass through eternal snowfields and down the other side into the beautiful and isolated **Pin Valley**. Kaza (see p.459), the district headquarters of Spiti, lies a further three or four days' hike to the north. On its way to the main road, the trail winds through remote settlements such as the village of **Kharo**, within striking distance of the ancient Buddhist *gompa* at **Khungri**.

NORTHWEST HIMACHAL

The riverside town of **Mandi**, 159km north of Shimla and more or less in the centre of HP, amounts to little more than a crossroads for travellers heading for the high mountains, though nearby **Rewalsar** makes a charming diversion. Northeast from Mandi lies the Kullu Valley, with Lahaul and ultimately Ladakh beyond. The section which follows traces the route from Mandi into **northwest Himachal**, initially following the River Beas and the NH21 as they weave into the gentle fertile hills of the **Kangra Valley**.

The valley's main settlement is the unspectacular market town of **Kangra**, whose ruined fort once tempted raids from Muslims and Sikhs, but its most popular tourist spot is lively **Dharamsala**, home to a thriving community of Tibetan refugees since the Chinese invasion of Tibet. This is a perfect place for setting off on treks over the soaring Dhauladhars to the **Chamba Valley**, where **Chamba** itself, and its predecessor as district capital **Brahmour**, are known for majestic temples. Close to the western state border, and well connected to Pathankot, the fading Raj outpost of **Dalhousie** entices visitors with its cool tree-clad heights, sublime views and nostalgic atmosphere.

Mandi to Dharamsala

The road northwest from Mandi skirts the edges of the hills, passing through thick pine forests and lush tea gardens. While most visitors make the six-hour journey to Dharamsala in one go, on one of the nine daily **buses**, those with more time can pause at the small towns of **Baijnath** and **Palampur**, or pick up the narrow-gauge train as it trundles slowly through the fertile valleys between **Jodindernagar** and **Kangra**.

Mandi

At the point where the southern plains meet the Kullu and Kangra valleys, 158km north of Shimla, **MANDI** straddles the River Beas, its houses clinging to the rising slopes of the gorge. For centuries a trading post for Ladakhis heading south – *mandi* means market – it boasts few sights, though **Tarna Hill**, 2km northwest of the centre, holds a fine collection of **temples**, built in sixteenth-century Nagari style and carved with a medley of deities. The gates and spire of the largest, dedicated to Bhutnatha (Shiva as lord of the Bhutas, or demons), are lavished in gold and silver.

Buses from north and south arrive at a **bus stand** on the east bank, where an excellent cafe cooks delicious veg food all day. Services to Rewalsar leave from here, and also from a smaller depot, exclusively dedicated to Rewalsar, near Guntur Ghar on the west bank. The town has plenty of **hotels**, most a rickshaw- or taxi-ride away from the main bus stand, across the river. Near the river on the east bank, the quiet family-run *Heritage Guest House* (☎01905/2284; ①–③) has assorted doubles and a comfortable dorm, while close to the central markets, the ramshackle *Raj Mahal* (☎01905/2041; ④) is a period-furnished palace set in shady gardens, with a good restaurant and the only bar in town. Less expensive options nearby include the simple *Standard* (☎01905/2948; ①), opposite the Rewalsar bus depot, and *Siva* (☎01905/4211; ②–④) on the main road by the town square. The cheapest accommodation of all is in the basic dorm of the HPTDC *Hotel Mandav* (☎01905/2123; ①–⑤), 1km behind the main bus stand, which also has poorly maintained and rather grubby rooms.

Rewalsar

If you've any interest in Buddhism it's worth taking a detour 24km southeast of Mandi to the **monasteries** of **REWALSAR**, which belong to the Nyingma sect, the original school of Tibetan Buddhism. The peaceful village comprises less than a hundred low slate-roofed houses, ranged around a lake. Red, yellow and white **Buddhist temples** crowned with gold-fringed pagodas, are reflected in pleasing symmetry in the waters. Monks and nuns circumambulate the sacred lake beneath fluttering prayer flags, and amble through lanes that echo with the clinks of stone cutters, the hum of hand-powered sewing machines and the toll of bells from Hindu and Buddhist temples.

According to Buddhist legend, the eighth-century monk Padmasambhava wanted to train the daughter of the local Hindu raja in meditation. Her incensed father struck Padmasambhava down in flames, but the powerful monk manifested himself as a lotus flower surrounded by water. Suitably impressed, the king allowed his daughter to train under Padmasambhava, who set up a Buddhist centre here before embarking on the pilgrimage during which he introduced the faith to Tibet.

For the Hindus, on the other hand, Rewalsar lake dates back to the post-Vedic era, and specifically the writing of the *Puranas* (possibly sixth-century), one of which refers to Rewalsar as the abode of the sage Lomas, for whose sake the lake was created with waters from the Ganga and Yamuna. Emerging from a canopy of trees on the west shore, the newer Sikh **gurudwara** attracts pilgrims who retrace the steps of Guru Gobind Singh; this is one of the few sites associated with his life in Himachal. To the south a small **sanctuary** protects deer and Himalayan black bears.

The HPTDC *Rewalsar Inn* (①–③), a short way back from the north shore, has comfortable **rooms**, each with bath and hot showers, and a small dorm; visitors who plan to stay for a while can also sleep in the Nyingma monastery (①). Opposite, a small Tibetan restaurant serves *thukpa*, *momo* and noodles, while standard greasy north Indian food is prepared at *dhabas* along the main road.

Jogindernagar and Bir

JOGINDERNAGAR, 63km northwest of Mandi, is an uninviting little town holding little more than two streets flanked by wooden-fronted houses, and a crowded, disorganized bus stand. The main reason to get off a bus here is to pick up one of the three daytime **trains** that make the slow journey through the Kangra valley to Baijnath and Kangra. Rickshaws near the bus stand cover the three-kilometre journey west to the station; train timetables and comfortable **accommodation** can be found at the smart HPTDC *Tourist Bungalow* (☎200; ③) at the eastern end of the main road.

Jogindernagar is the place to stay if you want to visit **BIR**, 15km west, where the community weave carpets, and grow potatoes, rice and apples in patchy fields dissected by trickling brooks. Below the village a Tibetan settlement supports a handicraft centre, a school and a community of monks who live in a grand temple. A couple of simple stalls brew acrid Tibetan butter tea and sweet *chai*, but nothing else. **Treks** from Bir over the Dhauladhars lead west to Chamba or east to Manali (see p.432).

Baijnath

BAIJNATH, 30km west of Jogindernagar, is an unattractive, cramped and dirty place, where the streets seem always to be blocked with traffic, and clusters of hanging electricity wires imperil passengers travelling on the roofs of buses. The town is only noteworthy for its grey stone **Vaidyanath temple**, dedicated to Shiva as Lord of Physicians, whose round-edged *shikhara* is easily visible from the main road, a few hundred metres from the bus stand. It stands in a walled compound set off by the distant backdrop of severe Dhauladhar slopes; niches at regular intervals in the outer walls shelter images of Hindu deities, and there's a stone *lingam* within. Carvings on the sides depict Surya (the sun-god), Karttikeya (the god of war, Shiva's second son), and an emaciated Chamunda (a terrible form of Durga), garlanded with skulls.

Palampur

Further into the Kangra valley, tree-clad slopes give way to rolling deep green fields, as the westbound road enters Himachal's prime tea-growing area, around the small town

TREKKING FROM PALAMPUR DISTRICT

Palampur is an ideal starting point for a **trek**; scenery nearby includes lush tea gardens, alpine meadows and the harsh and rocky crags of the Dhauladhar range. Passes north of the town offer unmatched views of the Kangra valley to the south.

One easy four-day hike leads **from PALAMPUR** over **Waru Pass** (3850m), the "gateway of wind", via Satchali, Thanetar and Dhog to **Holi**; continuing for two more testing days brings you to the sacred **Manimahesh Lake** near Brahmour. From Dhog it's possible to continue east to Barabhangal and as far as Manali.

A pleasant but difficult seven- or eight-day trek **from PALAMPUR** starts by crossing **Sunghar Pass** (4473m), then leads back across the Dhauladhars at **Jalsu Pass** (3600m), and south to Baijnath. In fact **Baijnath**, only 40km from Palampur by road, is itself a good trailhead for treks to Chamba or Bharabhangal, following paths that traverse glaciers, waterfalls, the high Thamsar Pass (4665m) and the River Ravi.

Further long-distance treks start north of the main road **at BIR**, half an hour on frequent buses from Baijnath or Jogindernagar. Once there, a 14km journey by jeep or foot brings you to **Billing**, 2600m up, from where a 12km track winds north to the potato farms at Rajgunda and on to Palachak, where a flat shady campground and a huddle of *dhabas* stay open all summer. A gentle track then ascends wooded paths for 9km to **Panihardu**, where you can rest before tackling the steeper route to Thansar Pass, which takes at least five hours. There's a campground at the snout of the glacier at **Marhu**, below the pass across tricky boulder fields. At this point green meadows and thin tree-cover replace rocky expanses on the route to **Bharanbhangal**, a knot of flat-roofed barns and wooden houses hemmed in by mountains and completely cut off in winter.

Routes head west **from MARHU** to **Chamba** (3 days) and **Manimahesh** (3 days), and southeast to **Manali** over Kalihan ("black ice") Pass. This latter, strenuous, route takes a further six days, and is suitable only for experienced trekkers. A gradual ascent through forests and over streams and frequent ridges leads to the lofty meadows of **Sukha Parao**, with views of snowy peaks on all sides. A 9km climb up the thin path to **Lama Parao** (3150m) brings you to the upper limit of the forests, before the track weaves across treeless hillsides to **Gwari** (3750m). This is the final stop before the pass, reached after a demanding ascent of 7km over boulders and the bed of a glacier. Once across, the descent traverses a snow field and drops to **Sanghor**, where small but flat fields are perfect for camping. The next leg crosses ridges and streams to **Railli** (9km), and continues through thick clusters of *deodar* and pine to **Sangchur** (22km). After three days' hard trekking, you'll be glad of the easy walk down through villages, bright valleys and pine woods along the River Beas for 12km to **Manali**.

of **PALAMPUR**, less than 30km northwest of Baijnath. This is the trailhead for walks to nearby hills, tea fields and gorges, and **treks** into the Kullu and Chamba valleys.

The best of Palampur's **hotels** is HPTDC *Hotel T-Bud* (π2081; ⑨), surrounded by lawns and pine trees 1km north of town, where the rooms are spacious and immaculate, and the restaurant serves excellent food. Options along the main road closer to the bus stop include the cheap and cheerful *Sahni* (①) and *Yamini* (①). A path heads 2km north of the *T-Bud* to the spectacular 300-metre-wide **Neugal Gorge**, which resounds with echoes of the River Bundla rushing through the deep valley and is overlooked by the HPTDC *Neugal Cafe*.

Kangra

KANGRA, above the valley of the Banganga and below the Dhauladhar hills, is usually just passed through by the passengers who get off trains from Pathankot or Jogindernagar on their way to Dharamsala, 18km north. **Buses** from all over Kangra valley, and further east and west, pull into the bus stand 1km north of the town centre.

Frequent services make the journey to Dharamsala (1hr). If you arrive by train, get off at **Kangra Mandir station**; as rickshaws don't usually wait here, you'll probably have to walk 3km over the river, and up the hill.

Before the creation of Himachal Pradesh state, Kangra was capital of a district of the same name; it fell prey for centuries to invasions of Sikhs and Muslims, before the British took control in 1847 and reinstated the Katoch rajas in the town that they had founded in the tenth century. Amid the crowded streets, the **central bazaar** brims with *puja* paraphernalia – red powder, coconuts, tinsel and sugar. Behind it, against the precipitous Dhauladhars, the **Bajreshwari Devi temple** dominates a courtyard chequered in marble and black stone. The temple's legendary wealth invited much Muslim interest between the twelfth and fifteenth centuries; Mahmud of Ghazni, Feroz Shah Tughluq and Sikander Lodi all took their turn sacking and looting. It was finally laid low by an earthquake in 1905; what you see today is the result of extensive rebuilding, and holds little architectural appeal. The only remaining valuable possessions are the silver parasols that shade the idol, though the site is still important to devotees of Shakti, the female embodiment of Shiva's energy.

Kangra's crumbling yet still sturdy **fort**, accessible by rickshaw, imperiously surveys the river valley from 4km south. It too was damaged by the earthquake, and is a shadow of its former self, overgrown and inhabited by screeching green parrots that flit through a few simple temples still tended by priests. High gates, some British-built, span a cobbled path to the deserted ramparts. It was the fort (*garh*), incidentally, supposedly built over the ear (*kan*) of Shiva, that gave the name to town and district.

You're not likely to want to spend more than a day in Kangra, but it does have a few unelaborate lodges. **Hotels** along Dharamsala Rd, which runs from the bus stand into town, include the simple *Ashoka* (☎5147; ①), the less clean *Gaurav* (☎5176; ①) and *Preet* (☎5260; ①), and the nicer *Maurya* (☎5244; ③) with airy rooms and private baths. In Nehru Bazaar near the temple, *Hotel Anand* (☎5243; ②–③), up a deceptively dirty flight of stairs at the top of a noisy shopping complex, has reasonably clean rooms. They also serve good **meals**, and several *dhabas* in the bazaar have an almost constant supply of spicy local dishes. The *State Bank of Patiala* (Mon–Fri 11am–2pm), next to the post office on Dharamsala Rd, handles **foreign exchange**.

Masrur

A narrow road leads 30km southwest from Kangra to the hamlet of **MASRUR**, clinging to the hillsides to offer some of the best views in the lower valley. This is the only place in the Himalayas to feature **rock-cut Hindu temples** like those found at Ellora in Maharashtra. These fifteen huge and badly eroded structures were built during the ninth and tenth centuries, with high pillars, curved towers and dimly lit inner sanctuaries. The central temple, denoted by its high-roofed sanctuary, was surrounded by twelve subsidiary shrines; all were hewn out of a single pale sandstone rock face, and topped with spires more akin to Dravidian *gopuras* than the regional Indo-Aryan *shikharas*. Most statues from the site have been removed to Shimla, but the larger temples hold well-preserved images of Shiva, Rama and Sita, still used in worship.

Jawalamukhi

One of north India's most important Hindu shrines is protected by a simple whitewashed temple in **JAWALAMUKHI**, 35km south of Kangra. The sanctuary, crowned with a squat golden spire, contains a blue gas flame, considered a manifestation of the goddess of fire, Jawalamukhi. Priests are eager to light emissions of gas in smaller chambers for expectant devotees, but only the main flame is kept alight continuously.

The HPTDC *Jawalaji Hotel* (☎2080; ③–⑤) offers smart a/c **rooms**, and a restaurant serving local and north Indian food.

Dharamsala

As the home of the Dalai Lama and the Tibetan government in exile, and the starting point for some exhilarating treks into the high Himalayas, **DHARAMSALA** is one of Himachal's most irresistible destinations. As well as playing host to casual tourists, it is a place of pilgrimage that attracts Buddhists and interested parties from all over the world, many of whom visit India specifically in order to come here.

Spread across wooded ridges, beneath the stark rock faces of the Dhauladhar range, 150km east of Pathankot and 160km northwest of Mandi, Dharamsala is divided into two distinct and widely separated sections, which differ in height by almost a thousand metres. Originally a British hill station, the town has been transformed by the influx of refugees fleeing Chinese oppression in Tibet. They have been arriving ever since 1960, when their welcome, here and elsewhere, by the Indian government owed much to their propaganda value at a time of great tension between India and China.

Most Tibetans now live in **McLeodganj**, the upper town and the real heart of Dharamsala, where monks and nuns can always be seen strolling through lanes lined with trading stalls and restaurants. Their achievements include the creation of temples, schools, monasteries, nunneries, and meditation centres, and an excellent library of Tibetan history and religion. However, some tourists arrive in McLeodganj anticipating a "little Lhasa", and are disappointed. The Tibetan influence is strong, but Dharamsala remains Indian, with a substantial community of Hindus and Sikhs.

Despite heavy snows and low temperatures between December and March, McLeodganj receives visitors year round. The summer brings torrential rains that linger in dribs and drabs for much of the year; even then, the days may be hot, but you'll need warm clothes for the chilly nights.

Arrival and information

Buses from Mandi, Pathankot, Kangra and Delhi pull into the bus stand in the very south of the lower town. The nearest point of arrival for **trains** from Delhi, Punjab and Jamu Tawai is Pathankot, while the narrow-gauge train up from Jogindernagar terminates at Kangra. It's also possible to get here by **air**: three weekly flights leave the airport, 11km south of town at Gaggal, for Delhi via Chandigarh.

The **tourist office** (Mon–Sat 10am–5pm; ☎2363), stocked with information on accommodation and transport, is at the foot of the main bazaar in the lower town, just a few minutes' walk from the bus stand. For enquiries about the Tibetan settlement, call in at the **Welfare Office** on Bhagsu Rd in McLeodganj, where donations of clothes, books, blankets and pens for new Tibetan arrivals are always gratefully accepted.

McLeodganj's **post office**, on Jogibara Rd (Mon–Fri 9am–5pm, Sat 9am–3.30pm), has a poste restante counter that holds letters for up to a month. Letters not addressed to McLeodganj end up in the **GPO** (same hours), a steep 1km out of the lower town. STD telephones are widely available. The *State Bank of India* in McLeodganj (Mon–Fri 10am–2pm) sometimes refuses to change particular travellers' cheques; the branch in lower Dharamsala is more co-operative (also open Sat 10am–noon). The *Bank of Baroda*, in the lower town, issues money to *Visa* card holders, with a few days' delay.

The lower town

It's easy to see why most visitors bypass Dharamsala's **lower town**, a haphazard jumble of shops, offices and houses. Although it holds the tourist office and banks, the only place of interest is the small **Museum of Kangra Art** (Tues–Sun 10am–5pm), and even that, with its scanty collection of Kangra miniatures, supplemented by some modern art, merits the briefest of visits.

△ Dal Lake & TCV

DHARAMSALA

DHARAMKOT

MCLEODGANJ

■ Tushita

Bus Stand ■

St John in the
Wilderness

Mountaineering
Institute

Temple &
Prayer
Wheels ▲

Handicrafts
Centre

Welfare
Office

FORSYTH
GANJ

M C L E O D G A N J

ⓕ

ⓘ

QUONIUM RD

BHAGSU RD

Namgyal
Monastery

Dalai Lama's
Residence

Tibetan Library
& Secretariat

ⓖ

⑤
⑥
⑦

Carpet
Centre

Bank

Kotwali
Bazaar

Bank

ⓘ

Taxi
Stand

Museum of
Kangra Art

Bus
Stand

GPO
✉

LOWER
TOWN

N

Tibetan Library
& Dharamsala

RESTAURANTS:
❶ McLlo
❷ Friends Corner
❸ Shambala
❹ Rasoi
❺ Gakyi
❻ Aroma
❼ Ashoka
❽ Chocolate Log
❾ Lazeez

Not to scale

HOTELS:
Ⓐ Paljor Gakyil Guest House
Ⓑ Kalsang Guest House
Ⓒ Lhasa Guest House
Ⓓ Tibet
Ⓔ Green
Ⓕ Om
Ⓖ Ashoka,
Loseling Guest House &
Tibetan Ashoka

Ⓗ Surya Resorts
Ⓘ Natraj
Ⓙ Him Queen
Ⓚ HPTDC Bhagsu
Ⓛ Ladies Venture
Ⓜ Rising Moon
Ⓝ Padmini
Ⓞ Basera Lodge
Ⓟ HPTDC Dhauladhar View

▽ Pathankot & Chandigarh

From the bus stand at the southern limit of the lower town, a road takes buses and cars north through the crowded bazaars and continues for ten kilometres of hairpin bends to the northern edge of McLeodganj. On foot, the quickest route is a shorter (3km) but much steeper track winding up to McLeodganj's southern end from behind the vegetable market, passing the Tibetan Library and the Dalai Lama's residence.

The telephone **area code** for Dharamsala is ☎01892.

McLeodganj

The tiny settlement of **Mcleodganj** extends along a slender high ridge that juts out over the valley below. Despite being named after David McLeod, the Lieutenant Governor of Punjab when the hill station was founded in 1848, it now shows little evidence of former British occupation. Intersected by two narrow potholed roads, the focal point of McLeodganj is its Buddhist **temple**, ringed with spinning red and gold prayer wheels. The ramshackle buildings of the town are decked with white, red, green, blue and yellow flags, printed with prayers, that flutter constantly in the wind, and the streets are dabbled with the ruby robes of monks and nuns. Today Indian residents are outnumbered by Tibetans, who still stream in after long journeys across Nepal from the Tibetan plateau. For them McLeodganj is not simply a haven, but also the home of their spiritual leader, the Dalai Lama, and a place where children are free to learn Tibetan language, history and religion without breaking the laws imposed by the Chinese in Tibet.

It's easy to find your way around McLeodganj. At its northern end, the road up from the lower town arrives at a small square that serves as the bus stand. Roads radiating from here head south to the Dalai Lama's residence, and the Library of Tibetan Works and Archives, north to the village of Dharamkot and Tushita Retreat Centre, which runs courses in meditation, and to the Tibetan Children's Village next to Dal Lake.

The Residence of the Dalai Lama

The Dalai Lama settled temporarily in McLeodganj in 1960; a third of a century later he's still there, and his **residence** on the south edge of town has become his permanent home in exile. His own quarters are modest, and most of the walled compound overhanging the valley is taken up by government offices. In front of the private enclosure Dharamsala's main Buddhist temple, **Tsuglagkhang**, shelters three images: Shakyamuni (the historical Buddha), Padmasambhava (who took Buddhism to Tibet) and Avalokitesvara (the Bodhisattva of compassion). The simple open-fronted temple, surrounded by shops and small markets, has a line of prayer wheels along its back wall. After paying homage to the Buddha, devotees tap the wheels, setting them turning to scatter their prayers with the wind. Always open for worship, it is also the scene of audiences given by the Dalai Lama. Each afternoon monks from the nearby Namgyal monastery hold fierce but disciplined debates in the courtyard opposite, amid shouts, claps and gestures that make up the traditional art of discussion.

Library of Tibetan Works and Archives

Dharamsala's **Library of Tibetan Works and Archives** (April–Sept Mon–Fri 9am–5.30pm; Oct–March Mon–Fri 9am–5pm) has one of the world's most extensive collections of original manuscripts, books on all aspects of Tibet, copious information on Indian culture and architecture, and a rich cache of old photos. Decorated on the exterior with bright Tibetan motifs, it is housed in the Tibetan Central Administration compound, below the southern end of McLeodganj. Its literature is not the only attraction – Tibetan language and philosophy **courses** are held each weekday, and usually run for a month. Classes on *dharma*, or Buddhist thought and precepts, are given by Tibetan monks and translated; rooms are crammed with eager listeners, and sessions continue long beyond their allotted time as questions lead to further discussion.

On the first floor of the library, a small **museum** displays Buddhist statues, finely moulded bronzes, and *mandalas* (symmetrical images, used in meditation to symbolize inner spiritual journeys and the pattern of the universe), among which is the only wooden *mandala* outside Tibet. In front of the library, a small cafe serves hot drinks and cakes. An information centre in the **Tibetan Secretariat** beside the entrance to the compound has recent news from Tibet. Just outside, the small **Astro Medical Institute** is staffed by monks who diagnose symptoms by examining the eyes and the pulse, and prescribe pills made of herbs, precious stones and sometimes animal products, some of which are mixed on particularly auspicious lunar dates.

North and east of McLeodganj

A minor road winds northwards from the McLeodganj bus stand to **Dharamkot**, a huddle of squat houses tucked between trees and rocks, passing the mountaineering institute and the **Tushita retreat centre**, which holds meditation courses throughout the year. Dharamkot is the starting point for short walks to the high plateau at **Triund** (2975m), or further over the high passes to the Chamba valley.

The small, murky **Dal Lake**, connected to Dharamkot by a path down through the wooded slopes, is the scene of an animal fair and Shaivite festival in September. Nearby, the **Tibetan Children's Village** (TCV) provides education and training in traditional handicrafts for around 2000 students, many of whom are orphaned or have been brought to safety by parents who have returned to Tibet.

Bhagsu road heads east from McLeodganj's main square, skirting the hillside for two kilometres before reaching **Bhagsu**, a village on the banks of a mountain stream. A path meanders up boulder-strewn slopes from here, through a slate quarry, to the **waterfall** that feeds the stream, where there's a small *chai* stall. Pilgrims come to bathe in the waters of the tank of Bhagsu's Shiva temple each September.

Accommodation

Most visitors stay in **McLeodganj**; it's only worth staying in the **lower town**, where the choice is smaller and the standards lower, if you have an early bus to catch, or arrive late. Hotels fill up between October and March, and especially at Tibetan New Year (Feb/March). Tourists planning long stays often head to **Bhagsu** or **Dharamkot**, where farmers let simple huts for a minimal sum; if you do stay out here, expect to cook your own meals, and to queue with the locals for a supply of kerosene at the beginning of each month (wood collecting is restricted). A handful of rooms in the Tibetan Library are available to students on courses, and for fervent Buddhists, there's always the possibility of staying at a monastery or nunnery.

The lower town

Basera Lodge, Kotwali Bazaar (☎2234). The best of the cheap lodges in the bazaar, with clean rooms, each with bathroom and TV. ②.

HPTDC Dhauladhar View, near bus stand (☎2889). Spacious rooms with private baths (constant hot water) and balconies giving superb views over the plains to the south. Cheap beds in a small dorm. Delicious medium-priced food in the hotel restaurant and a bar with garden terrace. ④–⑤.

Padmini, Kotwali Bazaar (☎2456). Four adequate rooms overlooking bazaar area, each with a bathroom and hot water. ②.

Rising Moon, Kotwali Bazaar (☎2635). The cheapest option in the lower town. Spartan accommodation and shared bathrooms, and a small restaurant serving low-priced Indian and Chinese food. ①.

McLeodganj

Ashoka, Jogibara Rd. Overpriced but clean, with no view to speak of. Not to be confused with the much better *Tibetan Ashoka Hotel* next door. ②–③.

Green, Bhagsu Rd. Well kept and comfortable, with good views over the valley. ①–③.

Him Queen, south end (☎4361). A selection of ordinary, deluxe and VIP rooms, all with balcony and TV, carpets and an air of freshness. ⑥–⑦.

HPTDC Bhagsu, at southern extremity (☎3191). Smart, well-run hotel. Comfortable carpeted rooms, small gardens. ⑤–⑦.

Kalsang Guest House, Quonium Rd (☎2609). Simple rooms and common bathrooms. Large roof with good views. ①.

Ladies Venture, Jogibara Rd. Homely place nestled among the trees near *Geden Choeling Nunnery*. Friendly owners keep it spick and span, and dish up Tibetan delicacies in the small restaurant. ②.

Lhasa Guest House, Bhagsu Rd. A large collection of simple rooms set off a warren of corridors. Adequate, but invaded by noise from the bus stop. ②.

Loseling Guest House, Jogibara Rd. Standard lodge, well maintained and unelaborate. Good views from an open roof terrace. Slightly overpriced. ②.

Natraj, south end (☎2375). Large characterless place next to *Him Queen*, slightly frayed at edges. Front rooms give excellent views, as does spacious roof terrace. ④ off-season, otherwise ⑤–⑥.

Om, near bus stand. Simple, quiet lodge on the west edge of town, with a few homely rooms on the upper terrace and a cosy restaurant. ①.

Paljor Gakyil Guest House, Quonium Rd (☎2571). Immaculate lodge with plain or carpeted rooms, dorm beds and great views. ①–④.

Surya Resorts, south end (☎2768). Big modern hotel, with some large glass-fronted rooms facing west. Carpets, low-level double beds and plush bathrooms. ⑥ off-season, otherwise ⑦–⑧.

Tibet, Bhagsu Rd (☎2587). Excellent hotel overlooking the valley, with superb restaurant. ⑤–⑥.

Tibetan Ashoka, Jogibara Rd. Friendly and congenial. Rooms vary from simple without bath to deluxe with bathroom and hot shower. Superb views from roof patio. ①–④.

Eating

With its ever-changing community of travellers, McLeodganj is one of those places where sitting and chatting in **restaurants** is a favourite activity; many have sound systems, and the food served is varied. Not surprisingly, Tibetan dishes are prominent, along with Chinese options such as egg noodles, drop soup, *chow chow*, *momo* and stir fry. Look out for the bakery opposite *Namtso Guest House* on Temple Rd, which sells fresh-baked Tibetan bread and cakes every morning. If you're yearning for western food you'll find fries, toast, veggie-burgers or even vegetable *au gratin* and roast chicken, and several restaurants specialize in Israeli food. In **lower Dharamsala** there's no shortage of snack stalls, but less choice of cuisine; your best bet is *Hotel Dhauladhar View* for Indian and western dishes, or *Lazeez Restaurant* in Kotwali Bazaar for spicy kebabs and curried vegetables. All the restaurants listed below are in **McLeodganj**.

Aroma, Jogibara Rd. Spicy Indian dishes, plus Israeli specialities at unbeatable prices. Great *hummus*, fresh salads, thick pitta breads and tasty schnitzel (breaded chicken pieces).

LHAMO – THE FOLK OPERA OF TIBET

Exiled Tibetan communities everywhere, and Dharamsala above all others, remain determined to keep alive their traditional arts and crafts, suppressed at home by the Chinese. The **Tibetan Institute of Performing Arts**, fifteen minutes' walk north of McLeodganj bus stop, especially nurtures **lhamo**, a form of folk opera so popular in nineteenth-century Tibet that each district had its own troupe.

In Dharamsala, open-air performances take place on national holidays throughout the year, and for a full week at the start of each April. Singers dress in exotic costumes, loosely modelled on the clothing of the Lhasa aristocracy, and wear elaborate hats and masks, either flat and made of cloth, or moulded as faces with caricatured expressions. Some are made by children at the Centre for Tibetan Arts and Crafts at the Tibetan Children's Village, who are also trained in *thangka* painting and wood carving.

Before each performance the stage – a flat piece of ground sheltered by a canopy – is purified. This complex procedure involves seven Ngonpa characters, dressed in black baggy trousers, white shirts with red sashes, and flat black masks, and six dancing fairies, or Ringas. They sing praises to Thangtong Gyalpo, the patron saint of *lhamo*, a statue of whom is always placed in the centre of the stage, often accompanied by a juniper branch and a bowl of *tsampa* (a staple food made from barley flour). The narrator, Shung Shangen, then enters the stage, which holds no other props, and offers a résumé of the opera in classical Tibetan (now understood by very few), culminating with a high shout.

The performers themselves enter to the sound of drums and cymbals. The main characters appear first: the **hero** (a prince or king), dressed in dragon-patterned brocade and a wide-brimmed hat; the **heroine**, draped in golden silk and wearing a hat of flowers; the **villain**, often a witch, dressed in black and hiding behind a black-and-white mask, followed by a retinue of ghoulish **demons** whose masks show wide staring eyes, blood-red lips and sharp fangs. Each character has a special dance, and sings in a drawn-out, droning manner known as *namthar*. The plots revolve around tales from early Buddhist texts, re-enactments of the Buddha's life and the deeds of great Tibetan saints, or stories from the courts of the emperor Songsten Gampo, under whom Buddhism was established in Tibet. Even if you don't know what's going on, you can spot the new drum beat and different dance steps that denote a change of scene.

Lhamo instructors from the institute carry the art to other Tibetan settlements in India and Nepal, and also teach non-Tibetan students. Other classes in traditional art forms, plus lectures and study courses, are held in the **Norbulingka Institute** in the valley below Dharamsala; enquire at the Department of Culture and Religion (☎2685).

Ashoka, Jogibara Rd. Friendly place; the town's best Indian food and beers, pricier than average.

Chocolate Log, Jogibara Rd. Delicious cakes, pies and truffles plus savouries such as spinach pizza. Eat inside or laze on deckchairs on an open roof terrace. Reasonably priced. Closes 6pm.

Friends' Corner, Temple Rd. Popular, comfortable place by the bus stop, with a tasty range of food and beers, but small portions. Excellent *chow chow*. Dimly lit and with a good sound system.

Gakyi, Jogibara Rd. Humble and homely, with great Tibetan and western veg dishes, and the town's best fruit muesli.

Hotel Tibet, Bhagsu Rd. Without doubt Dharamsala's best venue for Tibetan and Chinese food, veg and non-veg. High prices, but worth every *paise*.

Ladies Venture, Jogibara Rd. Tasty Chinese, Tibetan and western dishes, and great omelettes.

McLlo, Central Square. Comfortable first-floor seating overlooking the bus stop, and superb food. Unmatched selection of western dishes; hearty portions, fairly high prices, good service, lots of beer.

Om, *Om Hotel*. Friendly, comfortable restaurant jutting out over the hillside. Generous portions of good Tibetan and Chinese veg food and a few western-style snacks. Great value.

Rasoi, Temple Rd. A small unpretentious place with a wide balcony facing the plains. Specialities include filling *thalis* (standard or special) and pizzas.

Shambala, Jogibara Rd. Cramped seating but good veg food, with fresh cakes and filled pancakes.

TREKKING FROM DHARAMSALA

Dharamsala is one of the most popular starting points for **treks** over the rocky ridges of the Dhauladhar range, which rise steeply from the Kangra valley, surmounted by passes as high as 4600 metres. Most of the routes are used by **Gaddi shepherds**, who cross from north to south in the winter, cradling bundles of lambs and kids in their jackets, and return to the northern pastures in summer. Trails pass through forests of *deodar*, pine, oak and rhododendron, cross streams and rivers, and wind along vertiginous cliff tracks, passing the occasional lake, waterfall and glacier.

Villages en route, most of them temporary Gaddi settlements, are largely agricultural, growing rice, maize, potatoes and even apples; the gently slanting rooftops of the houses are often ablaze with the bright reds and yellows of chillies and maize laid out to dry in the midday sun.

Only attempt treks with the help of guides, cooks and porters. The **Mountaineering Institute**, on Dharamkot Rd, supplies guides, and rents equipment at very reasonable prices; you can pay per day, and buy food yourself in the bazaar before you set off. **Yeti Trekking** (☎2887), also on Dharamkot Rd, offers fixed-price treks (roughly US$18 per day) and has plenty of equipment. Meet your guide before you settle anything. Despite the availability of rough huts and caves, it's best to take a tent. For general advice on trekking, see p.45.

The best **season** to trek is from mid-August to late October. Trekking during the monsoon itself (June–Aug) is more difficult, as paths are frequently washed away and wet equipment gets very heavy, but at this time the fields and forests are at their freshest, and alpine meadows burst with colour. Winter climbing should only be attempted by experienced trekkers, comfortable using crampons and ice picks.

Dharamsala to Chamba over Indrahar Pass (4350m)

The most frequented route from Dharamsala to the Chamba valley, over the **Indrahar Pass** (4350m), is arduous in places, but most novice trekkers manage it in around five days. The first section, from Dharamkot, winds through thick forest and steep rocky terrain for 9km to a grassy plateau at **Triund**. To stay in the forest rest house, book at the forest office in Dharamsala.

From Triund, the path climbs less steeply to **Illaqa Got**, a grassy rise at the treeline, fed by glacial waters flowing from the ridge above. Staying a little higher, in the low-roofed but well-sheltered **Lahesh Cave**, saves time and effort before the ascent to the pass early the next day. This is a trying scramble over scattered boulders on ill-defined paths, but the view, south over the Kangra valley and north to the snowy Pir Panjal peaks, is breathtaking. From the pass the descent along the Ravi valley, through alpine meadows and pine woods, is difficult only where paths across sheer rock faces are all but worn away. After re-entering the forests and passing waterfalls, you reach the Gaddi village of **Kuarsi**, from where a 6hr walk along the steep river gorge drops to dusty **Macchetar**, connected to Brahmour and Chamba by road.

Other routes from Dharamsala to Chamba

Several **other routes** cross the Dhauladhar range. To head over **Toral Pass** (4575m), start from **Tang Narwana** (1150m), 10km from Dharamsala. A long ascent leads through scrub, pine and oak woods to **Guntu Got** (3385m), from where the demanding climb to the pass is more difficult during May and June when snow still covers the slopes, and during the monsoon when there's a risk of flash floods. The two-day descent from the pass traverses treacherous boulder fields before meeting a forest and reaching the verdant Gaddi pastures at Kuthehar, 6km from the nearest road, to Chamba and Brahmour.

The most difficult route north is the five- or six-day trek across **Bhimghasutri Pass** (4580m), covering near-vertical rocky ascents, sharp cliffs and dangerous gorges. A much easier four- or five-day trek from Dharamsala crosses **Bleni Pass** (3710m) in the milder ranges to the northwest, weaving through alpine pastures and woods and crossing a few streams, before terminating at **Dunali**, on the Chamba road.

△ Barabhangal & Manali

Not to scale

Dhog

Jalsu Pass
3600m

Bajinath

Thanetar

Satchali

Waru Pass
3850m

Deol

Palampur

Holi

Sunghar Pass
4473m

Harser

Brahmour

Kuthehar

Guntu Got

River Ravi

Toral
Pass
4575m

Tang
Narwana

Macchetar

Kundli Pass
4550m

Kuarsi

Indrahar Pass
4350m

Illaqa
Got · Lahesh
Cave

Triund

Dharamkot

McLeodganj

Gag Pass
4243m

Bhimghasutri
Pass
4580m

Minkiani Pass
4250m

Dharamsala

△ Chamba

Dunali

Bleni Pass
3710m

N

DHAULADHAR TREKS

Listings

Medical help Lower Dharamsala has the Zonal Hospital (☎2333), but most sick travellers head for the *Tibetan Medical and Astrological Institute* ten minutes from the library. A former physician of the Dalai Lama, Dr Yeshi Dhondhen, has a well-sign posted clinic off Jogibara Rd in the main bazaar.

Meditation Besides staying in a monastery, it's possible to take week- or month-long meditation courses, at the *Tushita Retreat Centre* (Tibetan Buddhism), a collection of simple wooden huts in a leafy enclosure near Dharamkot, north of McLeodganj, or the stricter *Vipassana Centre* (Indian Hinayana Buddhism). Check noticeboards in restaurants for dates, and details of yoga courses.

Publications Tibet-focussed magazines published in Dharamsala include *The Tibet Journal*, the glossy *Cho-Yang*, and the *Tibetan Bulletin*, published in Hindi, French and English.

Shopping Stalls and little shops along the main streets offer Tibetan trinkets, inexpensive warm clothing, incense, prayerbells, rugs and books. The large handicrafts shop on Jogibara Rd sells *thangkas* of all sizes, and prayer flags. *Nowrojee* store by the bus stand, unchanged since the nineteenth century, doles out sweets from ancient thick glass jars, along with its own bottled pop.

Train bookings Train journeys from Pathankot can be booked through travel agents, or by turning up at the office in the bus stand (10–11am), which has a meagre quota of two tickets per train.

Travel Agents The helpful *Himachal Travels*, a tiny office on TCV Rd (☎2723 or 2453), books local and private buses, trains from Pathankot, and domestic flights, and confirms or alters international flights. You can also rent taxis for journeys within HP or beyond, and enquire about treks.

Dalhousie and around

The quiet, relaxed hill station of **Dalhousie** spreads over five low-level hills at the western edge of the Dhauladhar range. While the town itself, interspersed with Raj-era buildings, low-roofed stalls and hotels, is unremarkable, the pine-covered slopes around it are intersected with paths and tracks ideal for short undemanding walks.

From Dalhousie the road east zigzags in and out of deep copses, skimming the hillsides. After 30km it arrives at sleepy **Chamba**, perched above the rushing River Rav. Though seldom visited, it's a good place to recuperate after a trek, with some fascinating temples, and a small art museum. **Brahmour**, three hours further east and the final settlement on the road into the mountains, holds more Hindu temples. Both towns make good bases for **treks** into the remote **Pangi Valley**.

Dalhousie

DALHOUSIE owes its name to Lord Dalhousie, Governor General of Punjab (1849–56), attracted by the cool climate to establish a sanitorium here for the many British, who, like himself, suffered ill health. Early in the twentieth century, it made a popular alternative to crowded, expensive Shimla, but thereafter it declined. A small population of Tibetans has grown up since the Chinese invaded Tibet in 1959; some have moved to Dharamsala, but many have stayed, selling sweaters, watches, bags and ornaments. Today Dalhousie receives only a handful of western tourists, and few stay longer than a day or two, though Punjabis come up to escape the heat of summer.

Dalhousie is most usually approached by **bus** from Pathankot in the Punjab, 80km southwest (see p.505); the tortuous bus journeys through the Himalayan foothills from Dharamsala (7hr 30min) and Shimla (18hr) are not recommended. The steep path that climbs the hill from the bus stand towards the Mall is the shortest route to the centre.

From the central **Gandhi Chowk**, narrow roads lead west to the bus stand and south to another crossroad, Subhash Chowk, as well as dropping southwest to the army cantonment. **The Mall**, in the north of town, affords splendid views to high snow-capped peaks. Forest tracks snake around the hillsides, linking the main roads. The one between Gandhi and Subhash *chowks* dips beneath overhanging pines, and passes rocks painted in bold bright colours with the Buddhist goddess Tara and short Tibetan prayers. Further south, a thin road leads to **Panch Pulla**, where five bridges span a rushing stream and a memorial commemorates the freedom fighter Ajit Singh, a firm supporter of the left-wing Congressman Subash Chandra Bose who raised the Indian National Army to fight alongside the Japanese during World War II. The road north out of Gandhi Chowk meanders up the hill to **Bakrota**, where a small community of weavers make traditional Tibetan carpets.

Accommodation

Numerous **hotels** cater to Dalhousie's summer visitors; in winter, when most lie empty, many offer substantial discounts, so beautiful suites cost little more than simple lodges in larger cities. *Maruti* vans ferry visitors to hotels that lie beyond walking distance from the bus stand.

Aroma & Claire's, Court Rd (☎018982/2199). Old house, sprawling over the hillside in the south of town and bursting with character. Leafy patios, a library, and spacious rooms, some heated by 1930s burners. Expensive, but reasonable value out of season. ④–⑤ off-season, otherwise ⑥–⑦.

Chaanakya, The Mall (☎018982/2670). Truly luxurious; carpets, cable TV and private bathrooms, and excellent views to the mountains from the front rooms. ⑤–⑥ off-season, otherwise ⑥–⑦.

Grand View, bus stand (☎018982/2623). Robust 1920s building with a selection of lofty suites opening onto north-facing verandahs. Prompt service in true Raj style, and a well-stocked bar. ⑥.

Green, between Gandhi and Subhash *chowks* (☎018982/2167). Old hotel, reminiscent of the Raj, and set on a quiet path. Homely rooms and covered verandahs. ② off-season, otherwise ⑤.

HPTDC Geetanjali, near bus stand (☎018982/2155). Ageing hotel with few mod cons, and huge rooms with incredibly high ceilings and attached baths. Overpriced, and no discounts. ④.

Moonlight, Panch Pulla Rd. Simple family-run guest house, a short walk from Gandhi Chowk. One of the cheapest hotels in the off-season; unelaborate but comfortable. ①–② off-season, otherwise ④.

Youth Hostel (☎2189). The cheapest option for YHA members – non-members must pay more. Dorms for Rs20 a head, but minimal comfort and washing facilities that are far from clean. ①.

Eating

Dalhousie's **veg** food is generally good, and prices reasonable, but this is no place to eat **meat** – the scrawny chickens yield little but skin and bone. The ever-busy Punjabi *dhabas* just off Subhash Chowk on Court Rd give the best value. Snack stops around the bus stand serve fresh *puris* for breakfast and fiery curries throughout the day.

Kwality, Gandhi Chowk. Tucked behind the GPO; high-standard Chinese and Indian dishes and ice cream, and crispy *dosas*. Cheap to moderate.

Milan, Gandhi Chowk. Small place, bedecked with pictures of Madonna and Indian pop stars, with views over the Mall to the hills beyond. Good, reasonably priced, meat and veg Indian dishes.

Moti Mahal, Subhash Chowk. Meat and veg Indian and Chinese food and light Indian beer.

Preet Palace, Subhash Chowk. Standard north and south Indian and Chinese cuisine.

Punjabi, Gandhi Chowk, on the lane leading to *Green Hotel*. Dim and uninviting haunt, but one of the few that promises a wide selection of meaty dishes in true Punjab style.

Khajjiar and Kalatope Wildlife Sanctuary

It's possible to trek 30km from Dalhousie to Chamba along the eastbound road from Gandhi Chowk. En route, in the flat Khajjiar valley, **Khajjiar** itself consists of a few single-storey houses overlooking a vast green, with a modest and grimy lake at its centre. HPTDC *Hotel Devdar* (☎33; ①–⑤), sheltered by pines and spruce on the edge of the green, has a six-bed dorm, comfortable double rooms with big windows, and good food. The ridge above the valley holds the **Kalatope wildlife sanctuary**, whose ibex, deer, bears and leopards rarely come out of hiding. The last 20km from Khajjiar to Chamba, across thickly wooded hillsides, can be walked in a day.

Chamba

Shielded on all sides by high mountains, and protected by forces in Kangra to the south, **Chamba** was ruled for over a millennium by kings descended from Raja Singh Varma, who founded it in 920 AD. Unlike Himachal states further south it was never formally under Moghul rule, and its distinct Hindu culture remained intact until the first roads were built to Dalhousie in 1870. When the state of Himachal Pradesh was formed in 1948, **CHAMBA** became the capital, and only large town, of Chamba district.

In summer, **Gujjars**, nomadic Muslim dairymen, wheel great urns of milk through the streets, and migratory Gaddi shepherds gather in Chamba before moving south to Kangra. The *chowgan*, a large green used for sports, evening strolls and festive celebrations, marks the centre of town, overlooked by the **Rang Mahal** palace, now a college.

Lakshmi Narayan temples

The intimate complex of **Lakshmi Narayan temples**, behind Dogra Bazaar west of the *chowgan*, is of a style found only in Chamba and Brahmour. Three of its six earth-brown temples are dedicated to Vishnu and three to Shiva, all with profusely carved outer walls and curious curved *shikharas* (spires), topped with overhanging wooden canopies and gold pinnacles added in 1678 in defiance of Aurangzeb's order to destroy all Hindu temples in the hill states. Niches in the walls contain images of deities, but many stand empty, some statues lost in the earthquake of 1905 and others looted more recently. The ensemble is roamed by friendly cats, and murmurs with the prayers of devotees and the laughter of children playing in the cool waters of the tank.

Entering the compound, you're confronted by the largest and oldest temple, built in the tenth century. It enshrines an idol of Lakshmi Narayan (Vishnu), sculpted in Rajasthani marble. Female deities flanking the entrance to the sanctuary, each holding a water vessel, represent the rivers Ganga and Yamuna, while the interior is decorated with scenes from the *Mahabharata* and *Ramayana*. One shows Vishnu with a lotus stem emerging from his navel that blooms with six flowers, each supporting a separate god. Temples dedicated to Shiva, watched over by a ferocious statue of half-man half-bird Garuda, the destroyer of obstacles who also serves as Vishnu's mount, fill the third courtyard. Among the images on the outer walls, Shiva's consort is depicted in her various forms as Parvati, Durga, Gauri and Uma. In the inner sanctuary, once your eyes are accustomed to the dim light, you'll see sturdy brass images of Shiva, Parvati and Nandi, inlaid with silver and copper brought from mines nearby.

Other temples

Of Chamba's other temples, the most intriguing is the tenth-century **Chamunda Devi temple** high above the town in the north, a steep half-hour climb up steps that begin near the bus stand. Decorated with hundreds of heavy brass bells and protecting a fearsome image of the blood-thirsty goddess Chamunda, the temple is built entirely of wood, and commands an excellent view up the Ravi gorge and to the hills in the north. Panels cut into the wooden ceiling depict such scenes as Krishna stealing butter, four-armed Shiva wearing a tiger's skin, and comely maidens surrounded by birds.

Back in town, south of the *chowgan* near the post office, the small, lavishly carved **Hariraya temple** contains a smooth brass image of Vaikuntha, the triple-headed aspect of Vishnu. Though often obscured by cloth and vermillion, it is a fine example of the excellent bronze work that has become Chamba's hallmark.

Bhuri Singh Museum

Although small and poorly maintained, the **Bhuri Singh museum** (daily except Mon 10am–5pm; free), opposite Sham Singh hospital at the south end of the *chowgan*, holds a reasonable display of local arts and crafts. Its eighteenth- and nineteenth-century **Kangra miniature paintings**, depicting court life and amorous meetings, and men and women smoking elaborate *hookahs*, are much bolder than their Moghul-influenced Rajasthani equivalents. Temple statues and sculptures, pillars and lintels are displayed alongside silver jewellery, heavy bronzes from Chamba, early coins, and murals taken from the palace. Inscribed copper plates record land and property grants and temple donations from the tenth to the eighteenth centuries.

The museum's best feature is its small cache of **rumals**. Made by women since the tenth century, used in ceremonial exchanges to cover gifts, *rumals* are like embroidered paintings, depicting scenes from popular myth rather than the geometric and floral patterns more common elsewhere in India. Today only a few women continue this tradition, but a weaving centre in the old palace is attempting to revitalize the art.

TREKS IN THE PANGI VALLEY TO LAHAUL

Few trekkers make it to the spectacular, all-but-inaccessible **Pangi valley**, sandwiched between the soaring Greater Himalayan Range in the north and the Outer Himalayan Range in the south. With its deep river gorges and barren mountain peaks, it offers a wide range of scenery and vegetation: cultivated fields give way to forests of pine, *deodar*, spruce and silver oak, and beyond that hardy shrubs. Inhabited by nomadic Gaddi shepherds, the valley maintains a unique village culture. Several peaks within it have never been climbed, and onward paths lead to Kashmir, Lahaul and Zanskar.

The valley itself starts 140km northeast of Chamba. The last villages accessible by road are **Trella**, 90km north of Chamba below **Sach Pass** (4390m; open May–Nov), and **Brahmour**, 80km east of Chamba, en route to the high passes of the **Pir Panjal**. Equipment, porters and guides can be obtained at Chamba and Brahmour.

From Chamba to Udaipur (Lahaul) over Sach Pass (4390m)

Trekkers already acclimatized can complete this moderately difficult trek in nine or ten days. After the 5hr bus ride to Trella, on a poor road that twists tightly up precipitous escarpments, the walk begins with a steep climb to the treeline at **Satrundhi** (3500m). This is the last stop before a tricky 3–4hr ascent to the high pass, across boulder fields that are covered with snow in May and June, and have no well-defined tracks. Flower meadows at **Dunai** below the pass make a perfect camping spot before you cross the fresh fast waters of the River Chenab, and gradually descend from the grasslands into forests for 14km east to **Killar**. The next section of the trek is a tiring walk of 12km up and down the steep sides of the Chandra Bhaga gorge, to **Sach Khas**, a campground with a small forest rest house where you can relax before heading east to Purthi (15km) through deep and humid jungle. The last stage follows an unnerving path that clings to almost vertical rock faces; a precarious ropeway spans the Chandra Bhaga before **Raoli**. It's possible to take a bus from here to Tindi, but the final hike is an undemanding and enjoyable amble along the river valley. Motorable roads link Tindi with Udaipur (25km), from where buses head over Rohtang Pass to Keylong and Manali.

Treks from Brahmour

Trekking routes lead north from Brahmour (2130m) across passes covered with snow for most of the year. The challenging trek over **Kalichho Pass** (4990m), aptly named "the abode of Kali" (the goddess of death), starts with a gradual ascent of 24km to **Badagram** (2325m). On the next stage you climb 900 metres through a lush stream-filled *deodar* forest to **Dhikla** (3300m). The next day's walk of 11km crosses steep ridges interspersed with rich forest along the Bana Diva gorge to a campground at **Bhansar Got**. From here a steep hike climbs to an inhospitable campground at **Alyas**, separated from Kalichho Pass by ice fields. The ascent to the pass is tiring and time-consuming – you have to cut steps as you go – but once over the summit it's not far to a suitable spot to pitch a tent. The last leg of the trek crosses stony ground and descends along the Kalichho valley to verdant pastures, with views over the Pattan valley, cut by the River Chandra Bhaga, and ahead to a panorama of high snow-capped mountains. The village at the end of the trail is **Triloknath**, whose ancient temple to three-faced Shiva is sacred to both Hindus and Buddhists. Buses run from here to Udaipur, and on to Keylong and Manali.

Another demanding route crosses the **Kugti Pass**, "that which makes one miserable to reach", at an awesome 5040m. From **Harsar**, an hour by bus from Brahmour, the path follows the River Budhil for 12km to **Kugti**, known for fine yak milk and curds. Rolling alpine meadows and terraced fields overshadowed by Kailash peak line the second day's route, culminating at **Kuddi Got**, a vast flower-filled meadow (4000m). The next stage, over the pass, requires crampons and ice axe for an incredibly taxing 6hr climb. Having enjoyed the views of the towering peaks of Lahaul and Zanskar from the summit, you plummet once again to the head of a glacier at **Khardu**. For the next 12km the track traverses loose scree, forging a couple of streams, before reaching the orchards and terraces of **Raape**, 7km from Shansha, which is linked to Udaipur and Keylong by road.

Practicalities

Buses from both north and south arrive at the cramped bus stand in the north of town, overlooked by *Thakur* and *Natraj* lodges (avoid at all costs, unless you enjoy sleeping with bugs), and the much better, though slightly shabby *Hotel Chamunda* (☎6267; ③–④). Chamba's best hotel is the HPTDC *Hotel Iravati* (☎2659; ④–⑤) on the northwest edge of the *chowgan*, where the spotless, carpeted rooms have private bathrooms with hot water. Budget options include the less salubrious but passable *Rishi* (☎4343; ①–②) opposite the Lakshmi Narayan temples. The best and most filling **meals** can be found at the *Iravati* or *Rishi*; both serve such specialities as *madhra*, a rich, oily, and slightly bitter mix of beans, curd and *ghee*, or *gucchi*, mushrooms served with fried rice. The string of *dhabas* south of the *chowgan* dish up cheaper north Indian and local dishes in less hygienic surroundings, as well as juicy kebabs and freshly puffed *puris*.

Brahmour

BRAHMOUR is a one-horse town of shiny slate-roofed houses, apple trees and small maize fields, shadowed on all sides by high snowy peaks. The **temples** whose curved *shikharas* dominate the large neatly paved central square are more dramatic and better preserved than their rivals at Chamba. The sanctuaries are unlocked only for *puja* in the mornings and evenings, permitting a glimpse of bold bronze images of Ganesh, Shiva and Parvati, unchanged since their installation in the seventh and eighth centuries when Brahmour was capital of the surrounding mountainous region.

The efficient **Mountaineering Institute** has details of local **treks**, reliable guides and porters, and equipment for rent. The most popular route begins at **Harsar**, a bumpy one-hour bus journey from Brahmour, and leads to **Manimahesh Lake**, high in the mountains one or two days' walk away. This tarn is held sacred by Shaivites who worship at its waters and follow the ritual circumambulatory path. Hundreds of pilgrims flock to its shores for the *mela* each August. Dharamsala lies five or six days' walk south, a fairly easy route that crosses the Dhauladhars at Indrahar pass (see p.432).

Practicalities

Rooms can be found at the *Mountaineering Institute* (①), north of town, and the congenial *Hotel Amit* (②) at the bottom of the only road, which runs from the square to the bus stand, where simple food stalls dish up hearty meals all day.

THE KULLU VALLEY

The majestic **KULLU VALLEY** is cradled by the Pir Panjal to the north, the Parvati Range to the east, and the Barabhangal Range to the west. This is Himachal at its most idyllic; roaring rivers, pretty mountain villages, orchards and terraced fields rising in fastidious steps to deep green pine forests and high snow-flecked ridges.

Known in the ancient Hindu scriptures as **Kulanthapitha**, or "End of the Habitable World", the Kullu Valley extends 80km north from the mouth of the perilously steep and narrow **Largi Gorge**, near Mandi, to the foot of the **Rohtang Pass** – gateway to the arid mountain wastes of Lahaul and Ladakh. For centuries, it formed one of the major **trade** corridors between Central Asia and the Gangetic plains. Local rulers, based first at **Jagatsukh** and later at **Nagar** and Sultanpur (now **Kullu**), were able to rake off handsome profits from the through-traffic, extending their kingdom as far south as Mandi, east to the Sutlej, and north into Lahaul and Spiti. This trade monopoly, however, also made it a prime target for invasion, and in the eighteenth and early nineteenth centuries, the Kullu rajas were forced to repulse attacks by both the Raja of Kangra, and by the Sikhs, before finally succumbing to the British in 1847.

KULLU VALLEY

Over the following years, colonial families crossed the Jalori Pass from Shimla, making the most of the valley's alpine climate to grow the **apples** that, along with **cannabis** cultivation, today form the mainstay of the rural economy. The first road, built to export the fruit, wriggled up to Kullu in 1927. Improved communications brought greater prosperity, but spelt the end of the peace and isolation, prompting many settlers to pack up and leave long before Independence. The population expanded again in the 1950s and 1960s, however, swollen by **Tibetan refugees**.

In spite of the changes wrought by roads, in-migration and, more recently, mass tourism, the Kullu Valley's way of life is maintained in countless timber and stone villages. Known as **paharis** ("hill people"), the locals – high-caste landowning Thakhurs, and their (low-caste) share-cropping tenant farmers – still sport the distinctive Kullu cap, or *topi*. The women, meanwhile, wear colourful headscarves, and *puttoos* fastened with silver pins and chains. Venture into the lush meadows above the treeline, and you'll cross paths with nomadic **Gaddi** shepherds who follow their flocks between pastures, invariably with an orphaned lamb muffled inside their long woollen coats.

Few of the tourists that pour in during the summer, however, bump into a bona-fide nomad. After a gruelling bus journey from Delhi or Leh, most make a bee-line for bed in **Manali**, where the closest you'll get to a Gaddi is a picture on a postcard. With its burgeoning hotels, restaurants, and travel agents, the area's chief resort, entrepot and trekking hub is a convenient base from which to explore India's most accessible and – since the outbreak of unrest in Kashmir – most frequented high-Himalayan valley.

North of the largely uninteresting district headquarters of Kullu, **Nagar**'s castle and ancient temples make a pleasant change from the claustrophobic concrete of modern Manali, as do **Manikaran**'s sacred hot springs, up the spectacular **Parvati Valley**. **Trekking** opportunities range from day-hikes up the Beas River's side valleys, or **nalas**, to challenging long hauls over high-altitude passes and glaciers. Away from the roads, you step into a medieval time warp little altered since the days when the Kullu Valley was one of the most remote places on earth.

Kullu

KULLU, the valley's capital since the mid-seventeenth century, became headquarters of Kullu district after Independence. Despite being the region's main market and transport hub, however, it is deservedly eclipsed as a tourist centre by Manali, 40km north. A dishevelled, lacklustre collection of shops and concrete houses stacked around the right bank of the Beas, Kullu is noisy, polluted, and grim: a world away from the tranquil villages that peer down from the surrounding hillsides.

Most travellers stay just long enough to pick up transport somewhere else. If you find yourself with time to kill, the old pilgrims' paths that lead to any of the unspectacular **temples** around the town provide an escape, and take in some fine valley views.

Arrival and information

Long-distance **buses** heading up and down the valley pull in at the **main bus stand**, on the north side of the Sarvari Nala, which flows through the town from the west. Local services heading north also drop and pick up passengers opposite the congested **Akhara Bazaar depot**, in the north end of town, and at the top of Dhalpur **maidan**. This is closer to most of the hotels and restaurants, and the District Commissioner's office – the place to apply for **Inner Line permits** for travel to Spiti and Kinnaur. HPTDC's **tourist office** (daily 9am–7pm) is on the west side of Dhalpur *maidan*, two minutes' walk from the *State Bank of India* (Mon–Fri 10am–2pm, Sat 10am–noon).

If you're travelling on to **Nagar**, catch one of the frequent Manali-bound buses that run north along the main road, on the west side of the valley, and jump off at **Patli**

Khul, 5km north of Katrain, where you can pick up a shared taxi or local bus for the remaining six kilometres. Buses also run direct to Manali via Nagar, from the end of the Tapu suspension bridge, across the river from the Akhara Bazaar bus depot. This service, which leaves more or less hourly, is slower, but far more scenic.

DUSSEHRA IN THE "VALLEY OF THE GODS"

In the Kullu region, often dubbed "**the Valley of the Gods**", the village deity reigns supreme. No one knows how many *devtas* and *devis* inhabit the hills south of the Rohtang Pass, but nearly every hamlet has one, each with its own history, foibles, and temple. Legend has it that they originally descended from the Chandrakani Pass. Jamlu, the maverick god of Malana (see p.455), lifted the lid of the chest in which they were all trapped, and a gust of wind scattered the small circular icons around the villages.

The part each one plays in village life depends on his or her particular **powers**; some heal, others protect the "parish" borders from evil spirits, summon the rains, or ensure the success of the harvest. Nearly all, however, communicate with their devotees by means of **oracles**. Drawn from the lower castes, the village shaman, or **gaur**, is subject to prohibitions that forbid him, among other things, to cut his hair, wear leather, or spread manure on his fields. When called upon to perform, he strips to the waist and, accompanied by the trumpets and drums of the temple band, enters a trance in which the *devta* uses his voice to speak to the congregation. The deity, carried out of the temple on a ceremonial palanquin, or *rath*, rocks back and forth on the shoulders of its bearers as the *gaur* speaks. His words are always heeded, and his decisions final; the *devta*-oracle decides the propitious dates for marriages, and for sowing crops, and arbitrates disputes.

The single most important outing for any village deity is **Dussehra**, which takes place in the town of **Kullu**, every October after the monsoons. Although the week-long festival ostensibly celebrates Rama's victory over the demon-king of Lanka, Ravana (in the local dialect, *dushet hera* means "the demon killed"), it is also an opportunity for the *devtas* to reaffirm their position in the grand pecking order that prevails among them – a rigid hierarchy in which the Kullu Raja's own tutelary deity Rama, alias **Raghunathji**, is king.

The Kullu Dussehra is though to date from the seventeenth century, when the valley's Hindu rulers set out to weaken the hold of indigenous "nature cults": the worship of animist spirits residing in mountain peaks, rocks, trees, streams, and caves. Judging by the turn-out for the festival, the Raja's ruse worked a treat. On the tenth day of the new, or "white" moon in October, between 150 and 200 *devtas* make their way to Kullu to pay homage to the Raghunathji. As befits a region that holds its elderly women in high esteem, the procession proper cannot begin until **Hadimba**, the grandmother of the royal family's chief god, arrives from the Dunghri temple in Manali. Like her underlings, she is borne on an elaborately carved wooden *rath* swathed in glittering silk and garlands, and surmounted by a richly embroidered parasol, or *chhatri*. Facing each of the four directions, eight or twelve gold and silver **masks** are strapped to the side of the deities, preceded by raucous trumpets, standard bearers, priests, and bare-chested *gaurs*.

Raghunathji leads the great **procession** in his six-wheeled *rath*. Hauled from the Rupi palace on long ropes by a team of 200 honoured devotees, the palanquin lurches to a halt in the middle of Kullu's dusty *maidan*, to be circumambulated by the Raja, his family, and retinue of priests. Thereafter, the festival's more secular aspect comes to the fore. **Folk dancers**, decked out in traditional Himachali dress, perform for the vast crowds; the *maidan* by this time has acquired all the trappings of an Indian fun-fair, with market stalls, sweet-sellers, itinerant snake charmers, astrologers, *sadhus* and tawdry circus acts, all serenaded by a deafening barrage of drumming and Hindi film music. The revelries finally draw to a close six days later on the full moon, when the customary **blood sacrifices** of a young buffalo, a goat, a cock, a fish and a crab are made to the god.

Kullu's Dussehra, now a major tourist attraction, has become increasingly staged and commercialized. Book accommodation in advance, and be prepared for a crush if you want to get anywhere near the *devtas*.

The temples

Kullu's most famous temple, the **Raghunathji mandir**, overlooks the Sarvari *nala* from the steep hillside to the north, in the **Sultanpur** district. To get there, cross the main road outside the bus stand and follow the lane up the hill opposite the *Kailash* cinema. The temple, a long low building tucked away behind the Kullu Raja's **Rupi Palace**, is surprisingly plain considering the pre-eminence of the deity behind its sanctum's iron grille. Lord Raghunathji, a manifestation of Rama, was brought to Kullu from Ayodhya in Oudh by Raja Jagat Singh in the mid-seventeenth century. The Raja had been advised by his priests to install the sacred icon here and crown it king in his place, as a penance for causing the death of a local *brahmin* (thereby ridding himself of a punitive curse that had been turning all his food into worms). To this day, the Kullu rajas consider themselves mere viceroys of Raghunathji, the most powerful *devta* in the valley and the focus of the Dussehra procession. Half an hour's walk further up the paved trail leads beyond Sultanpur to a high ridge, with excellent views over the Beas to the snow peaks in the east. **Vaishno Devi mandir**, a small cave-temple that houses an image of the goddess Kali (Durga), is a stiff three kilometres on.

Another important temple stands eight kilometres southeast of town, atop the bluff that overlooks the sacred confluence, or *sangam*, of the Beas and Parvati. Although it's far closer to Bhuntar than Kullu, you have to approach the **Bijli Mahadev mandir** via the Akhara Baza–Tapu suspension bridge and a well-worn track south along the left bank of the Beas. Bijli Mahadev is renowned for its extraordinary *lingam*. Bolts of lightning, conducted into the inner sanctum by means of the twenty-metre, trident-tipped pole, are said periodically to shatter the icon, which later, with the help of invocations from the resident *pujari*, magically reconstitutes itself.

Accommodation and eating

It's hard to think why, with Nagar and Manali just up the valley, anyone would choose to spend the night in Kullu, but – except during Dussehra – the town has a reasonable choice of **accommodation**. The rates quoted are for high season; at other times discounts of up to fifty percent are usually given. Most of the hotels have small, moderately priced **restaurants**. Otherwise, there are rock-bottom *dhabas* in the bazaar: the *Radha*, on the town side of the footbridge, is the cleanest. For a pit-stop between buses, try the *Kapoor Chinese Hut*'s tasty Tibetan food, in a shack on the bus stand square.

Bijleshwar View, behind the tourist office, Dhalpur. Quiet, clean, central and friendly, with baths and fireplaces in large rooms, and some dorm beds. Recommended. ①–③.

Daulat, Circuit House Rd, Dhalpur (☎01902/2358). Run-of-the-mill, recently renovated hotel, with en-suite rooms and good off-season discounts. ③.

HPTDC Hotel Sarvari, Dhalpur, off the *maidan*. Large, efficient hotel with some dorms. ①–④.

Madhu Chandrika, Lower Dhalpur, near the footbridge (☎01902/2771). Doubles with or without bathrooms, and clean dorm beds – Kullu's best budget option. Handy for the main bus stand. ①–②.

Shobla, Dhalpur (☎01902/2800). Kullu's top hotel, overlooking the river. Large, well-appointed rooms, a good mixed-cuisine restaurant – expensive by Kullu standards – and a relaxing lawn. ④–⑥.

The Parvati Valley

Hemmed in by giant-pinnacled mountain peaks, the **Parvati Valley**, which twists west from the glaciers and snowfields on the Spiti border to meet the Beas at Bhuntar, 8km south of Kullu, is the Kullu Valley's longest tributary. Picturesque hamlets perch precariously on its sides, amid lush terraces and old-growth pine forests. Only those along the road, however, see many visitors – an incongruous combination of western hippies and van-loads of Sikh pilgrims bound for the *gurudwara* at **Manikaran**, 32km northeast of the Beas-Parvati confluence. Crouched at the foot of a gloomy ravine, this ancient religious site, sacred to Hindus as well as Sikhs, is famous for the sulphurous **hot springs** that bubble out of its stony river banks.

To make the most of Parvati's stunning scenery you'll have to **hike**. Two popular trails thread their way up the valley: one heads north from **Jari**, over the Chandrakani Pass to Nagar, passing through the remote, fascinating hill village of **Malana** (see p.455); the other follows the River Parvati east to another sacred hot spring and *sadhu* hang-out, **Khiraganga**, and on to the pass that leads into Spiti's remote **Pin Valley**.

Jari

Spilling over the main road and down the south side of the Parvati Valley, **JARI**, 15km from Bhuntar, looks across to the precipitous Malana *nala* in the north, and to the snow-flecked needles of the Baranagh rangeon the eastern horizon. Like many of its lookalike cousins, the tatty settlement supports a transient population of stoned westerners, attracted by the village's *charas*, who spend much of the day in the dreary *Deepak Cafe* on the square where the buses pull in. If you're tempted to **stay**, the *Ratna Guest House* (①) above the square is the best budget bet. The newer *Krishna Guest House* (②), five minutes' walk back towards Bhuntar, overlooks the valley.

Manikaran

Beyond Jari, the road winds down towards the rushing grey-green Parvati, which it meets at **Kasol**. HPTDC's small *Tourist Hut* (③) stands in the centre of the village, and several small cafes and guest houses tucked away in the woods cater for the trickle of trekkers that plod through on their way to or from Rashol Jot (2440m). The pass, a hard day's climb up the north side of the valley, provides an alternative approach to Malana and the Chandrakani route to the Kullu Valley, described on p.455.

Clouds of pungent steam billowing from the rocky riverbank 10km upstream herald the Parvati Valley's chief attraction. Hindu mythology identifies **MANIKARAN** as the place where the serpent king Shesha stole Parvati's earrings, or *manikara*, while she and her husband Shiva were bathing in the river. When interrogated by the god of destruction, the snake, who had slithered away to hide in his subterranean kingdom, Patala, flew into a rage and snorted the earrings out of his nose. Ever since, boiling water has poured out of the ground. The site is also venerated by Sikhs, who have erected an onion-domed concrete *gurudwara* over the springs.

Boxed in at the bottom of a vast, sheer-sided chasm, Manikaran is a damp, dark and claustrophobic place where you're unlikely to want to spend more than a night – long enough for a soak in a hot tub, and a chat to the *babas* who congregate on the riverbank. Most of the action revolves around the springs themselves, reached via the lane that leads through the village from the footbridge: just follow the stench of sulphur. On the way, check out the finely carved pale-grey stone **Rama temple** in the main square, and the pans of rice and *dal* cooking in the steaming pools on the pavements. Down at the riverside **Shiva shrine**, a brightly painted concrete box whose accessory deities have also been left to stew in the hot springs, semi-naked *sadhus* sit in the sulphurous vapours smoking *chillums* and bumming cigarettes from the curious westerners who wander past. Sikh pilgrims, meanwhile, make their way to the nearby **gurudwara**, where they take a purifying dip in the underground pool, then congregate upstairs to listen to musical recitations from the Sikhs' holy book, the Guru Granth Sahib. If you visit, keep your arms, legs and head covered; tobacco is prohibited inside the complex.

Practicalities

Buses leave Bhuntar every couple of hours for Manikaran (1hr 30min), which is as far east as the road goes. The last bus for Kullu, via Bhuntar, leaves at 6pm. *Maruti*-van **taxis** are also available for the trip, costing Rs400, or less out of season.

Apart from in May and June, when Manikaran fills up with Punjabi visitors, **accommodation** is plentiful and inexpensive. All but the very cheapest guest houses are neat and clean; all those listed here have wonderful indoor **hot tubs**. The HPTDC *Hotel Parvati* (④), near the Raghunath temple on the main street, has large, well-furnished rooms, a restaurant, and a riverside lawn; opposite it, and at the other end of the scale, the *Sharma Sadan Guest House* (①) boasts four spotless en suite rooms overlooking the square. The clean, comfortable *Sharma Guest House* (②), near the *gurudwara*, has attached doubles; the *Paaha Family Guest House* (②), opposite, is similar, with rooms around a courtyard, but the noise of the river can keep you awake.

Places to eat range from the *Parvati*'s pricey Punjabi restaurant, to the no-frills makeshift *dhabas* along the main street. The best of the tourist cafes catering for trekkers and budget travellers is the Tibetan-run *Shiva Cafe*, near the springs, which serves Indian and Chinese food, plus brown bread, pizza, porridge, pancakes and apple pie. The dimly-lit *Holy Place*, back towards the square, is similar, with a juice bar next door selling *lassis* and glasses of freshly squeezed mangoes, oranges, and apples.

Nagar

Stacked up the lush terraced lower slopes of the valley as they sweep towards the tree-line from the left bank of the Beas, **NAGAR**, 6km from the main road, is the most scenic and accessible of the hill villages between Kullu and Manali. Clustered around an old **castle**, this was the regional capital before the local rajas decamped to Kullu in the mid-1800s. A century or so later, European settlers began to move in.

Seduced by the village's ancient **temples**, tranquil setting and unhurried pace, many visitors find themselves lingering in Nagar – a far less hippy-fied village than those further north – longer than they intended. Numerous tracks wind up the mountain to more remote settlements, providing a choice of strenuous, enjoyable **hikes**.

Arrival and information

Nagar is connected by regular **buses** to Kullu and Manali. The direct services that ply the left-bank road, on the eastern side of the valley, are slower (2hr from Manali, or 1hr 30min from Kullu), but more scenic and more straightforward than the more frequent services along the main highway on the opposite, west side. These drop at **Patlikuhl** (5km north of Katrain), from where hourly buses cross the Beas to climb up to Nagar (6km). If you arrive in daylight and are not weighed down with bags, you can also walk from Patlikuhl on the old mule track – a hike of up to an hour.

The castle, Roerich Gallery, temples, and most of Nagar's accommodation lie above the small bazaar where the buses pull in: head uphill on the metalled road for about a hundred metres, then turn right onto the steep concrete path. If you have your own vehicle, you can drive all the way up to the Roerich Gallery at the top of the village – the trailhead for the Nagar–Chandrakani Pass–Malana–Parvati Valley **trek** (see p.455).

The castle

Since it was erected by Raja Sidh Singh (*c.*1700), Nagar's central **castle**, astride a sheer-sided bluff, has served as palace, colonial mansion, court house and school. These days it houses a small state-run hotel; non-residents can wander in to admire the views from its balconies. Built in the traditional "earthquake-proof" *pahari* style (layers of stone bonded together with cedar logs), the castle surrounds a central courtyard, next to which stands a small museum, and an even smaller shrine. The **Jagti Patt temple**'s amorphous deity, a triangular slab of rock strewn with rose petals and *rupee* notes, is said to have been borne here from its home on the summit of Deo Tibba by a swarm of wild honey bees – the valley's *devtas* in disguise.

The Nicholas Roerich Gallery

Perched on the upper outskirts of the village, the **Nicholas Roerich Gallery** (daily 9am–1pm & 2–5pm; Rs10) houses an exhibition of paintings and photographs dedicated to the memory of its former occupier, the Russian artist, writer, philosopher, archeologist, explorer and mystic. Around the turn of the century, Roerich's atmospheric landscape paintings and esoteric philosophies – an arcane blend of eastern mysticism and *fin de siècle* humanist-idealism – inspired a cult-like following in France and the US. Financed by donations from devotees, Roerich, variously compared by his admirers to Leonardo and Buddha, was able to indulge his obsession with Himalayan travel in a series of lengthy expeditions to far-flung corners of Tibet and Central Asia. He finally retired to Nagar in 1929, living here until his death eighteen years later.

The exhibition, in a small room on the ground floor, comprises a dozen or so evocative oil paintings of the Himalayas, and a few old photos of the self-styled guru, pictured in Chinese silk robes, cossack boots and burly beard, posing on the front lawn with visiting dignitaries such as Jawaharlal Nehru.

The temples

The largest and most distinctive of Nagar's ancient Hindu **temples** and shrines, the wooden pagoda-style **Tripuri Sundri**, stands in a small enclosure at the top of the village, just below the road to the Roerich Gallery. Like the Dunghri temple in Manali, it is crowned with a three-tiered roof, whose top storey is circular. Animal carvings project from the eaves of the shrine, which houses an image of the Mother Goddess – "Beauty of the Triple World". Its *devta* is the focus of an annual *mela* (May 18–24) in which deities from local villages are brought in procession to pay their respects.

Ten minutes' walk further up the hill – follow the stone steps that lead right from the road – brings you to a clearing where the old stone **Murlidhar** (Krishna) **mandir** looks down on Nagar, with superb views up the valley to the snow peaks around Solan and the Rohtang Pass. Built on the ruins of the ancient town of Thawa, the shrine is strictly off-limits to non-Hindus.

Finally, on your way to or from the bus stand at the bottom of the village, look out for the finely carved stone *shikharas* of the **Gaurishankar mandir**. Set in its own paved courtyard below the castle, this Shiva temple, among the oldest of its kind in the valley, houses a living *lingam*, so slip off your shoes before approaching it.

Accommodation and eating

Nagar's most popular place to **stay**, the HPTDC *Hotel Castle* (①–⑤), offers well-furnished en-suite doubles (some with superb views from spacious wooden balconies), and cheap dorm beds. It's well worth booking in advance at any HPTDC tourist office to secure one of the more expensive rooms in the west wing – which is allegedly haunted by the **ghost** of a young rani, who threw herself off the balcony after her jealous husband had beheaded an itinerant musician whom she had complimented. Non-residents can eat in its small **restaurant**. A good fall-back is the *Sheetal Guest House* (⑤) around the corner, where rooms come with balconies, attached bathrooms and hot water, and there's a reasonable Indian-western-Chinese restaurant next door. The equally comfortable *Hotel Poonam* (④), also within easy walking distance, has a good non-veg restaurant, and a shady garden cafe serving strict veg food al fresco.

The rest of Nagar's accommodation is ten minutes away at the top of the village. The friendly *Snow View Guest House* (①–③), adjacent to the Tripuri Sundri temple, has doubles that open on to a pleasant garden, along with cheaper non-attached rooms, and a handful of clean dorm beds. You can eat here in their inexpensive rooftop cafe. By far the best budget option, however, has to be the *Alliance Guest House* (①–②), halfway between the Tripuri Sundri and the Roerich Gallery. Run by a Frenchman who settled here in the 1970s, the *Alliance* has simple, clean rooms (shared bathrooms), and a warm family atmosphere, with kids and dogs scampering around its airy terrace. Tasty, inexpensive food – generous breakfasts, *thalis* and western dishes – is also available.

Manali

Himachal's main tourist resort, **MANALI**, stands at the head of the Kullu Valley, 108km north of Mandi. Despite lying at the heart of the region's highest mountain ranges, it remains easily accessible by road from the plains; just sixteen hours after stepping on the night bus in Delhi, you could be staring from your hotel verandah across apple orchards and thick pine forests to the eternal snowfields of Solang Nala, which shine a tantalizing stone's throw away to the north. Set at the foot of the **Rohtang Pass**, gateway to the rugged regions of Lahaul and Spiti, the town is also the roadhead for the recently opened trans-Himalayan highway, and thus the best place to pick up transport for the near-legendary two-day journey to **Leh**, the capital of Ladakh.

Barely a century ago, Manali was little more than a desultory collection of remote hamlets and colonial hunting lodges grouped above the banks of the Beas. Known as **Dana**, literally "Fodder", its grassy meadows provided the last good grazing for pack-animals bound for the barren mountain wastes to the north. In the nineteenth century, Manali's abundant game attracted a steady trickle of British visitors, many of whom retired here to hunt and manage the orchards for which the town is today famous. A few married local women, and built broad-verandahed family homes that their descendants converted into stylish "paying guest houses".

Not until the early 1970s, however, did tourism really take off. Lured by the area's cheap and abundant *charas*, the first arrivals were *chillum*-smoking westerners who, each spring, decamped en masse from the beaches of Goa. Little has changed in the nearby village of **Vashisht**, visited by an annual exodus of "freaks" each June, but Manali is nothing like the mini-Kathmandu it used to be. A combination of the middle-class Indian penchant for hill-station holidays, coupled with the effective closure of Kashmir, have submerged the riverine meadows that once fortified mule trains under a hotch-potch of hastily erected hotels, restaurants, travel agencies and handicraft shops.

Manali may not be a textbook example of town planning, but it makes an ideal **trekking** base. Whether you're embarking on a short hike or a long expedition, you'll find the streets packed with potential companions, guides, porters, and provisions, as well as countless agencies keen to put a package together for you. The relaxing hotels in Manali's cleaner greener outskirts, and dozens of sociable cafes and restaurants, ranged around a well-stocked **bazaar**, provide a welcome antidote to the austerities of the mountain trails. For more on treks around Manali and the Kullu Valley, see p.454.

Arrival and information

All buses pull in to Manali's **bus stand** in the middle of the Mall, a short walk from the helpful HPTDC **tourist office** (daily 10am–5pm; ☎2325), where you can make reservations for the town's state-run hotels. If you need to **change money**, the *State Bank of India* (Mon–Fri 10am–2pm, Sat 10am–noon) is just off the square at the top of town. The main **post office**, off Model Town Rd, has a reliable poste restante counter (Mon–Sat 9am–5pm, Sun 9–10am & 2–3pm). **STD telephones** are still few in Manali. The best place to make long-distance and international calls is the phone booth next to the tourist office, which charges standard "government-approved" rates.

The **telephone** area code for Manali is ☎019 01.

TAXIS AND TOURS

Manali's *Taxi Operators' Union* kiosk (☎2450) stands on the east side of the square at the top of town, just up from the tourist office. Out of season you should be able to negotiate reductions on the normal "fixed" rates (around Rs900 for a full day) to local landmarks.

Weather and road conditions permitting, HPTDC run daily bus **tours** to the **Rohtang Pass** (leaves 9am, returns 4pm; Rs80). The trip, popular with domestic tourists eager to experience snow for the first time, provides a good opportunity to take in the views north over the Chenab Valley to the stark mountain scenery of Lahaul. Other daily tours include day trips to **Nagar**, via Jagatsukh (9am–4pm; Rs100), and **Manikaran** in the Parvati Valley (9am–6pm; Rs125). Tickets can be booked ahead at the tourist office.

If you're planning a **trekking or rafting** trip (see p.452), shop around to compare prices and packages; many agencies are fly-by-night operators who make their money from mark-ups on long-distance bus tickets to Delhi, Chandigarh and Leh. Long-established **reliable agents** include *Himalayan Adventurers*, opposite the tourist office (☎2182), *Ultimate Expeditions*, at the *Highland Hotel* (☎2399), and *Himalayan Journeys*, next to the *State Bank of India* (☎2365), who also have their own rafting gear.

The Town

Though lacking the space and gentility of its namesake in Shimla, Manali's main street, **the Mall**, must be one of the most cosmopolitan thoroughfares in Asia. Settle in to a window seat at one of its many glass-fronted cafes, and you'll be passed by Kulluis in brightly patterned *puttoos*, Tibetan women wearing ankle-length rainbow-striped pina-fores, Nepali porters, Buddhist monks, and even the odd party of Zanskaris swathed in fusty woollen *gonchas*. Rubbing shoulders with this varied assortment of Himalayan hillfolk is an equally mixed bag of tourists, ranging from dressed-up Delhi-ites to English "crusties" in quasi-tribal garb.

The Dunghri temple

Resting on a flat hilltop in a dense stand of old *deodar*, fifteen minutes' walk northwest of the bazaar, the **Dunghri temple** is Manali's oldest shrine and the seat of **Hadimba** (or "Hirma Devi"), the "grandmother" of the Kullu raja's tutelary deity, Raghunathji. Originally a beautiful *pahari* maiden, she became an incarnation of the demon-goddess Durga after marrying Bhima (one of the five Pandava brothers of the *Mahabharata*). Local villagers regard Hidamba as a powerful protectress and rain-maker, and worship her in times of adversity. She also plays a key role in the Dussehra festival (see p.442).

The **temple** itself, a giant triple-tiered wooden pagoda crowned by crimson pennants and a brass ball and trident (Shiva's *trichul*), dates from 1553, and is a replica of earlier ones that burned down in successive forest fires. Its facade writhes with wonderful wood carvings of elephants, crocodiles and folk deities, as well as scenes from a legend in which a raja chops the hands off the royal sculptor to prevent him from repeating his masterpiece elsewhere. Entered by a door surmounted by wild ibex horns, the gloomy **shrine** is dominated by several large boulders, one of which shelters the stone on which goats and buffalo are sacrificed during important rituals. The hollow in its middle, believed to be Vishnu's footprint, channels the blood to Hadimba's mouth.

The gompas

Manali harbours the highest concentration of **Tibetan refugees** in the Kullu valley, which accounts both for the abundance of *mani* poles and strings of bedraggled prayer flags fluttering over the approach roads to the town, and the presence, on its southern edge, of two shiny new **gompas**, or Buddhist monasteries.

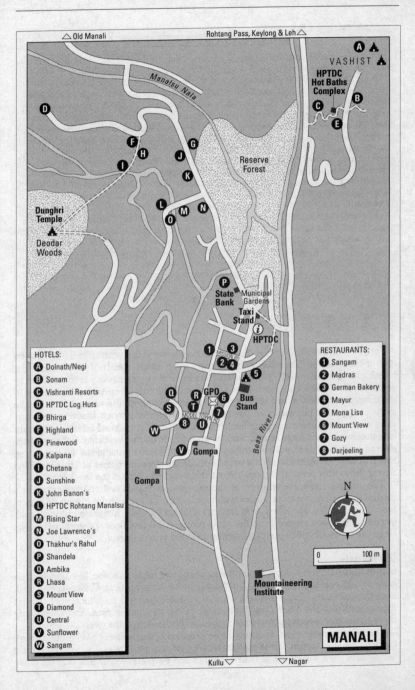

△ Old Manali
Rohtang Pass, Keylong & Leh △

VASHIST

Manalsu Nala

HPTDC
Hot Baths
Complex

Reserve
Forest

**Dunghri
Temple**

**Deodar
Woods**

**State
Bank**

Municipal
Gardens

**Taxi
Stand**

HPTDC

MISSION RD

GPO

**Bus
Stand**

MODEL TOWN RD

Gompa

Gompa

Beas River

N

**Mountaineering
Institute**

0   100 m

MANALI

HOTELS:

A Dolnath/Negi
B Sonam
C Vishranti Resorts
D HPTDC Log Huts
E Bhirga
F Highland
G Pinewood
H Kalpana
I Chetana
J Sunshine
K John Banon's
L HPTDC Rohtang Manalsu
M Rising Star
N Joe Lawrence's
O Thakhur's Rahul
P Shandela
Q Ambika
R Lhasa
S Mount View
T Diamond
U Central
V Sunflower
W Sangam

RESTAURANTS:

1 Sangam
2 Madras
3 German Bakery
4 Mayur
5 Mona Lisa
6 Mount View
7 Gozy
8 Darjeeling

Kullu ▽
▽ Nagar

SHOPPING IN MANALI

Manali's days as an "authentic" *pahari* bazaar ended when the mule trains were superseded by *Tata* trucks, but it is still an excellent place for souvenir **shopping**.

Woollen goods are the town's real forte, particularly the brilliantly patterned **shawls** for which Kullu Valley is famous. The NSC market near the bus stand sells a good selection. What you pay for a shawl depends on its size, age, the quality of the wool, the number of hours' work that have gone into its manufacture, and, most important of all, your ability to haggle. The cheapest, which can be bought from Tibetan street stalls for between Rs150–200, are machine-woven, thin, and neither warm nor durable. Genuine pure-wool handloom shawls with intricately embroidered borders start at around Rs500, but can cost up to Rs4000 if they are made from finest *pashima* – an exquisitely soft wool shorn from the underbelly of Himalayan goats. A good place to familiarize yourself with fair prices at the top of the range is the *Bodh Shawl Factory Shop*, just off the Mall south of the bus stand, which sells high-quality shawls at fixed rates. While there, try out the acid-test for *pashima*: if it creases when crumpled, it isn't pure.

Elsewhere around the bazaar innumerable stalls are stacked with hand-woven goods and pill-box Kullu *topis*. Those with gaudy multi-coloured up-turned flaps and gold piping are indigenous to the valley, but you can also pick up the plain-green velvet-fronted variety favoured by Kinnauris (and by the state's "men-of-the-people" politicians).

Manali's other speciality is Himalayan **handicrafts**: mainly assorted **Tibetan curios** such as prayer wheels, amulets, *dorjes* (thunderbolts), masks, musical instruments and *thangkas*. Few of the items hawked as antiques in the NSC market and the souvenir shops on or behind the Mall are genuine, but it takes an expert eye to spot a fake. The same applies to silver **jewellery** inlaid with turquoise and coral, which can nonetheless be attractive and relatively inexpensive.

Capped with polished golden finials, the distinctive yellow corrugated-iron pagoda roof of the **Gadhan Thekchhokling gompa** is an exotic splash of colour amid the ramshackle huts of the Tibetan quarter. Built in 1969, the monastery is maintained by donations from the local community and through the sale of **carpets** hand-woven in the temple workshop. When they are not manning the **shop**, the young *lamas* huddle in the courtyard to play *cholo* – a Tibetan dice game involving much shouting and slamming of wooden *tsampa* bowls on leather pads. The brightly painted *lakhang*, or prayer hall, dominated by a large seated Shakyamuni, stands on the west side of the quadrangle and is open to visitors. Photography is permitted; leave a donation in the box as you leave. Beside the main entrance a roll of honour recounts the names of Tibetans killed during the violent political demonstrations that wracked China in the late 1980s.

The smaller and more modern of the two *gompas* stands nearer the bazaar, in a garden that in late summer blazes with sunflowers. Its main shrine, lit by dozens of bare electric bulbs and filled with fragrant Tibetan incense, houses a colossal gold-faced Buddha, best viewed from the small room on the first floor. Downstairs, monks sit on the verandah block-printing brightly coloured prayer flags.

Old Manali

Old Manali, the village from which the modern town takes its name, lies 3km (half an hour's walk) north of the Mall, on the far side of the Manalsu *nala*. Unlike its crowded, unsightly offspring, the settlement retains an unhurried and traditional feel. To get there, head past the *State Bank*, bear right at the fork in the road, and keep going through the pine woods until you reach the iron bridge across the river.

The village proper, clustered on top of a steeply shelving ledge of level ground above the *nala*, is also known as **"Manaligarh"** after its ancient citadel – a now-ruined fort surrounded by a patchwork of maize terraces and deep-green orchards that fan down to the Beas. Built in the old *pahari* style, most of the houses have heavy stone roofs and wooden balconies hung with bushels of drying herbs and tobacco. Handlooms holding half-woven woollen shawls stand outside doorways whose lintels are painted with folk murals, while cows chew their way through bales of sweet-smelling hay scattered across smoky courtyards. The only indication that tourism has not entirely passed Old Manali by are the bands of scruffy kids that accost you in the damp cobbled lanes, thrusting lumps of *charas* and demanding *baksheesh*.

Accommodation

Manali's older, characterful hotels are dotted around the north and western outskirts of town. The only **budget** places of note are in **Old Manali**, where rough-and-ready family-run guest houses nestle amid the orchards. Although the *charas*-induced torpor that hangs over some of them (especially the dismal small hotels ranged along the stream near the bridge), and the trek to and from town, can pall, the peace and quiet, and views from their flower gardens, more than compensate. **Women** should be wary of walking along the lane from town to Old Manali after dark, which has been the scene of several attempted **rapes** in recent years.

Tariffs rocket in Manali during **high season**, from April until June, and from mid-September to late November. At other times, a fifty percent reduction on the advertised rates (listed below) is standard. The few hotels that stay open in **winter** cater mainly for skiing parties, and charge around Rs50 per day extra for heating.

Chetana, below the Dunghri temple, near *Log Huts* (☎2245). Spruce red and white building with large, neat rooms, lawns, verandahs, a boiler system and peaceful situation. ⑤.

Diplomat, Old Manali. Large modern building with spacious rooms and verandahs. ②.

Highland, north of town centre, on the ridge above Manalsu Nala (☎2399). Established upmarket hotel surrounded by orchards and lawns. Not outstanding value, but the old wing has character. ⑥.

HPTDC Log Huts, overlooking Manalsu Nala (☎2360). "Honeymoon Huts" and wooden holiday cottages tucked away in the woods. *Star TV*, and most comforts, but overpriced. ⑥–⑧.

HPTDC Hotel Rohtang Manalsu, north of town centre (☎2332). Large, comfortable, but overpriced hotel on the edge of town, with a flower garden and restaurant. ⑦.

Joe Lawrence's, Old Manali Rd. Five-star comfort with a difference: an old colonial campus converted into separate cottages. Stylish, but pricey. ⑦–⑧.

John Banon's, Old Manali Rd. Old guest house, something of an institution. Impeccable rooms, easy chairs, valley views, and a convivial host who keeps a fine table. "Strictly no riff-raff". ⑤.

Kalpna, near the *Chetana Hotel* (☎2413). Large, well-furnished, variously priced rooms ranged around a central lawn at the tranquil top end of town. ④.

Laxmi, Old Manali. Large, clean, and simple budget rooms ensconced amid shady flower gardens and orchards. Shared bathrooms only. Recommended. ②.

Pinewood, off Old Manali Rd (☎2118). Colonial building with furniture and garden to match. Popular with tour parties and trekking groups. Good value. ⑤.

MODEL TOWN HOTELS

As soon as you step off the bus in Manali, you'll be assailed by "card-*wallahs*" clamouring to drag you off to one of the **hotels** crammed into the grid of narrow streets immediately behind the Mall, the quarter known as **Model Town**. Though bland and boxed-in, these carbon-copy mid-range places make good bases from which to hunt around for more congenial better-value accommodation once you've found your feet. The majority offer generous off-season discounts, too; a little haggling should get you a clean room with extra blankets and a geyser for around Rs100. Recommended Model Town clones include: the *Central* (☎2319; ④), the *Diamond* (☎3058; ④), the *Lhasa* (☎2134; ④), the *Sangam* (☎3019; ⑤), the *Mount View* (☎2465; ④), and the *Ambika* (☎2203; ④).

Rising Star, near *Rohtang Manalsu* (☎2381). Budget back rooms boast big verandahs that overlook a leafy garden. Among the best deals in town. ③.

Shandela, near PSEB office (☎2426). Big, light rooms with views, baths and 24hr hot water. ④.

Sunflower, Tibetan quarter (☎2419). Friendly family-run hotel with en-suite rooms. ③–④.

Sunshine, off Old Manali Rd. The last word in understated colonial elegance: old double-storey wooden building with period furniture, fireplaces, and magnificent views from spacious balconies. Meals served on request in common dining room. ④.

Thakur's Rahul, opposite *Rohtang Manalsu* (☎2180). Modern building, with an old wing on the opposite side of a relaxing garden. The cheaper rooms are good value. ③–⑤.

Veer, Old Manali. The cheapest of the budget bunch and excellent value, with fine views down the valley from a lovely leafy garden. Some attached bathrooms, too. ①–②.

Eating

Manali's wide range of **restaurants** reflect the town's melting-pot credentials: Tibetan *thukpa* joints stand cheek-by-jowl with south Indian coffee houses, Gujarati *thali* bars, and Nepalese-run German pastry shops. Whatever their ostensible speciality, though, most offer mixed menus that include Chinese and western dishes alongside standard north Indian favourites. For rock-bottom budget food, head for one of the *dhabas* opposite the bus stand. The *Krishna* and *Lakshmi* both do a roaring trade in piping hot *parathas*, *channa batura*, *puris*, and other snacks spooned out of giant woks of bubbling oil.

Virtually every cafe in Manali also serves serious "tourist **breakfasts**" of porridge, pancakes, toast and jam; *chai* and omelette-*wallahs* appear on the Mall before dawn if you need to steel yourself for a long and bumpy bus journey.

Finally, stock up on energy-rich **trekking food** at the local produce stores and bakeries in the bazaar. The state-sponsored co-op, near the temple on the Mall, sells sacks of nuts, dried fruit and pots of pure honey at fixed prices, while *Superbake*, just up the road from the *State Bank*, is the place to binge on home-baked cookies, apple crumble and slabs of sticky chocolate cake.

Darjeeling, Model Town Rd. Popular backstreet cafe serving Tibetan and tourist-oriented food indoors or outside in small terrace garden, plus the definitive Manali breakfast.

German Bakery, Mission Rd and Old Manali. Both good places to buy trekking supplies, or simply to indulge a sweet tooth: apple pie, strudel, lemon cake, and western wholefood snacks.

Gozy, The Mall. Upscale all-rounder with tablecloths, low light, and an eclectic menu.

Madras, Mission Rd. Cheap and fiery south Indian food, and filling Rs25 *thalis*.

Mayur, Model Town. Dull decor, but the tasty Gujarati food is Manali's best pure-veg cuisine.

RAFTING AND SKIING IN MANALI

Considering the abundant white water that thrashes down the Kullu Valley during the spring snow melt, Manali's **rafting** scene is surprisingly low-key. Nevertheless, more companies are following the example of their Nepalese counterparts and investing in quality equipment. Raft trips down the River Beas occur between the end of May and early July, when water levels are highest, begining at Bhuntar (just south of Kullu) and ending 40km downstream at the mouth of the Larji gorge. The price for the day, around Rs600, should include meals, lifejackets, helmets, and return travel; check exactly what you're paying for, as some unscrupulous operators expect you to make your own way back to town after the trip. Reputable agents-cum-rafting outfits are listed on p.448.

If you're in Manali between December and June, you can sign up for one of the *Mountaineering Institute*'s popular five-day **ski** schools, run from their chalets in Solang Nala, 13km northwest of town. The cost (Rs300 per day) includes full board, equipment rental and instruction. Bookings should be made in advance by sending the full course fee to: The Director, *Mountaineering & Allied Sports*, Manali 175131.

MOVING ON FROM MANALI

Manali is well connected by **bus** to other Himachali towns, and major cities on the plains. Three types of services ply the more popular routes: "luxury" (a/c, reclining seats, videos, and limited stops), "deluxe" (non-a/c, less leg-room, no video), and "ordinary" (cramped, rock-hard seats and frequent stops). During the summmer demand invariably outstrips supply, particularly for the faster services, so book as far in advance as possible, and be prepared for regular and fruitless visits to the bus stand.

The luxury and deluxe buses to **Delhi** (2 daily, 1 nightly; 16hr), **Shimla** (1 daily, 1 nightly; 9hr), and **Chandigarh** (1 daily; 10hr), are all operated by HPTDC (who sell tickets), and depart from the tourist office in the centre of town. A handful of **private companies** also run deluxe coaches to Delhi (via Chandigarh), bookable through any of the agents along the Mall. Cheaper tickets for "express" services to **Shimla** (1 daily; 9hr) and **Dharamsala** (1 daily; 11hr) are sold by HPSRTC at Manali's main bus stand.

Transport to Leh

If you can afford the Rs8–10,000 fare, mini-van **taxis** are the most comfortable way to get to Ladakh from Manali. The vast majority of visitors, however, have to travel the 485km **to Leh** by **bus** – an arduous, but unforgettable two-day (28hr) trip that involves a night-halt under canvas along the route.

With its cushioned, well-spaced seats, HPTDC's daily "luxury" bus, bookable through the tourist office, is the least gruelling option. If your budget won't stretch to the Rs500 fare, their "deluxe" service is also worth considering. Otherwise, choice is limited to the beaten-up buses operated by HPSRTC and their Jammu & Kashmiri equivalents, or even dodgier private mini-buses that sell seats through the travel agents on the Mall.

Officially, the **Manali–Leh Highway** is open when the high passes open in mid-June until September 15, after which the state services are suspended. Many of the private companies, however, continue to operate well into October, when the inflated end-of-season prices they can charge encourage them to risk getting stuck in an early snowfall.

Whenever and however you travel, avoid the bumpy back seat of the bus, and take plenty of food, especially in autumn when *chai* stalls and *dhabas* are few and far between.

Mona Lisa, bazaar area. Cosy, sociable tourist cafe with a moderately priced menu of mainly Indian and Chinese dishes, desserts, soups and light snacks.

Moonlight Cafe, next to *Hotel Chetana*. Cheap garden cafe with resident masseur, dishing up indifferent food, mostly *momos* and noodles, to young *charas*-toking tourists.

Mount View, The Mall. Copious mouthwatering Chinese, Japanese, and authentic Tibetan food served under paper lanterns. Very popular, so arrive early or reserve a table. Moderate.

Sangam, Mission Rd. Good-value veg restaurant tucked away at the end of a narrow lane. Try their delicious mixed fruit and veg curries.

Shiva Cafe, Old Manali. Wicker chairs on a lazy balcony, an open fire most evenings, and Chinese, Indian and pasta dishes make this Old Manali's most popular budget travellers' joint.

Tasty, *Mount View Hotel*. Far and away the best western food in town: crepes, spaghetti, macaroni cheese, veg shepherd's pie, and very good pizza. Try their "hot'n'spicy" apple juice.

Vashisht

Famous for its sweeping valley views and sulphurous hot-water springs, the large settlement of **VASHIST** (formerly Bashist) is an amorphous jumble of traditional timber houses and modern concrete cubes, divided by paved courtyards and narrow muddy lanes. Only three kilometres from Manali, it is the epicentre of the local budget travellers' scene; tranquil and traditional, with a good choice of guest houses and cafes.

You can get to Vashisht either by road, or along the footpath that winds up from the main highway to its principal attraction. Supplied by water piped from underground springs, HPTDC's **Hot Bath Complex** (7am–1pm & 2–8pm; Rs24–60) is *the* perfect

TREKS AROUND MANALI AND THE KULLU VALLEY

The Kullu Valley's spectacular alpine scenery and proximity to some of HP's most dramatic and accessible peaks make it perfect **trekking** terrain. Ascending from a base altitude of 2000m to passes of 3500m and above, the trails are long and steep, but more than repay the effort with superb views, varied flora, and the chance to visit remote hill villages – an excellent introduction to Himalayan trekking, and the ideal way to acclimatize if you plan to attempt longer hikes at higher elevations in Lahaul or Zanskar.

Within striking distance of several major trailheads, **Manali** is the most popular place to begin and end treks. While the **package deals** offered by the town's many agencies can save time and energy, however, you can easily and safely keep costs to a minimum by organizing the trip yourself. The tourist office on the Mall, and the Mountaineering Institute at the bottom of town, are both good sources of advice, while porters and pack-horse-*wallahs* ply their trade in the square behind the main street. Guides are only hard to come by during September and October, when ponies are needed for the harvests.

However you decide to trek, always take a reliable **guide**, especially on less frequented routes. You cannot rely solely on **maps**, none of which, not even the *US Army Map Service U502* series map *#NI 43–16*, or *Leomann's* (less dependable) *Indian Himalayas Map Sheet #5*, is one hundred percent accurate. The *Survey of India's Kullu Valley Trekking Map*, available locally, helps you select a route, but little else.

The optimum **season** to trek is right after the monsoons, from mid-September to late October, when skies are clear and pass-crossings unproblematic. From June to August, you run the risk of sudden, potentially fatal snow, or view-obscuring cloud and rain.

Manali to Beas Kund

The relatively easy trek to **Beas Kund**, a glacial lake at the head of Solang *nala*, is the region's most popular short hike. Encircled by five- to six-thousand-metre peaks, the well-used campground beside the lake, accessible in two days from Manali, makes a good base for side-trips up to the surrounding ridges and passes.

Day 1 begins at the village of **Palchan**, a 30min bus-ride north of Manali on the main highway. From the road, a jeep track heads up the valley to **Solang**, site of a small ski station, rest house, and the *Mountaineering Institute's* log huts. The next two hours take you through pine forests, grassy meadows, and boulder chokes to the streamside campground at **Dhundi** (2743m), Gaddi grazing land dwarfed by the Hanuman Tibba massif (5928m) to the west. **Day 2**, when the trail becomes steeper and harder to follow, is more strenuous, winding across a huge moraine to reach **Beas Kund** after 5–6hr. The hike up to the Tentu La Pass (4996m) and back from here can be done in a day, as can the descent to Manali via Solang. Alternatively, head over Tentu La and down to Tantgari *nala*, to pick up a trail that climbs back into the Kullu Valley further south via the Manali Pass (4880m) – a tough ten-day round trip.

Jagatsukh to Deo Tibba

The base of **Deo Tibba** (6001m), is reached via the forests, alpine meadows, and high grazing pastures of the Jagatsukh *nala* – a return trip of between four and five days that is hard going in places. On **Day 1**, the path climbs from the trailhead at **Jagatsukh**, 11km south of Manali, through small villages and across a broad sweep of scree to a wooded ravine, beyond which lie a high glaciated valley and the campground of **Chikha**. **Day 2** is considerably shorter, taking you up to **Serai**, a lush grassy meadow where sheep graze in summer, from where you can trek further up the *nala* to the ridges that overlook the southwest face of Deo Tibba, and on to Chandra Tal lake (not the same as the one in Lahaul). Allow at least a day for the descent from Serai to Jagatsukh.

Manali to Lahaul, via the Hampta Pass

The trek from the Kullu Valley over the Hampta Pass to Lahaul, the old caravan route to Spiti, is a classic. Rising to 4330m, it is high by Kullu standards; do not undertake it without allowing good time for acclimatization along the way. **Day 1**, from the trailhead at

Prini (near Manali) to the campground above **Sethen**, via Hampta village, is an easy 4–5hr hike up the verdant, forested sides of the valley. **Day 2**, another 5hr, brings you to **Chikha**, a high Gaddi pasture below the pass; stay put for a day or so if you're feeling the effects of the altitude. **Day 3**'s ascent (700m) to the **Hampta Pass** (4330m) is gruelling, but the views from the top – of Indrasan and Deo Tibba to the south, and the endless moonscape of Lahaul to the north – are sublime recompense. It takes 6–7hr of relentless rock-hopping and stream crossings to reach **Chatru**, on the floor of the Chandra Valley. From here, you can turn east towards Koksar and the Rohtang Pass, or west past the world's largest glacier, Bara Shigri, to **Batal**, the trailhead for the Chandratal–Baralacha trek (see p.458).

Nagar to Jari, via the Chandrakani Pass and Malana

Combining grandiose scenery with varied landscapes and flora, the hike to Jari in the Parvati Valley from Nagar, 21km south of Manali, is quintessential Kullu Valley trekking. At a pinch, the round trip can be completed in three days, but you may be tempted to linger in Malana, to explore the roadless and rugged country to the northeast. A **guide** is essential for this trek, both because the first stage involves crossing a maze of grazing trails, and because Malana is a culturally sensitive spot requiring some familiarity with local customs. Note too that the descent to the Parvati Valley is too steep for pack ponies; porters are available in Nagar (through the *Alliance Guest House*), or in Manali.

Beginning at **Nagar**, **Day 1** is a gradual ascent through wonderful old-growth forests of mixed chestnut, walnuts, pines and huge *deodar* cedars. The open pasture just above the treeline makes ideal camping ground. **Day 2** starts with a 4km climb up to the **Chandrakani Pass** (3660m), which has fine views west over the top of the Kullu Valley to the peaks surrounding Solang Nala, and north to the Ghalpo mountains of Lahaul.

Reached after a steep 7km descent from the pass, **MALANA** comprises seventy or so double-storey timber and stone houses, in three separate areas according to caste. Its inhabitants, distinguished by their plain-black-fronted homespun caps and unique Tibetan-based dialect, are famed for their frostiness, and a staunchly traditional way of life, which remains as far from the mainstream as the village does from the nearest road. Although traditional notions of **caste pollution** (the root of the locals' legendary reluctance to interact with outsiders) are not as strictly adhered to as they once were, you should observe a few basic "**rules**" while in Malana: wait to be invited into the village before you enter; stick to the paths at all times; keep away from the temple; and don't, above all, touch anybody or anything, especially not children or houses. If you do commit a cultural blunder, you'll be expected to make amends: usually in the form of a cash payment for a compensatory sacrificial offering of a young sheep or goat to the village deity, **Jamlu**. One of the most powerful of all the Kullu Valley's gods, Malana's imageless deity is as xenophobic as his devotees. During Dussehra (see p.442), he alone is exempt from paying tribute to the omnipotent Raghunathji, remaining on the far bank of the Beas throughout the week's festivities. His **temple**, only open to high-caste Hindus, is decorated with lively folk carvings, among them images of soldiers – the villagers claim to be the area's sole remaining descendants of Alexander the Great's army. Jamlu also presides over Malana's council of elders, which convenes on the large flat slab of grey rock in the centre of the village; the smaller rock nearby is used exclusively by Jamlu's *gaur*.

In spite of Malana's inhospitable air, a couple of trekkers' **guest houses** have sprung up. *Santu Ram's* (①), in the middle of the Harijan quarter, is the most popular, as its owner is an authority on local trails. Or ask someone to show you to the Pradhan, or village headman's house, part of which has been converted into a small hostel (①). Both offer simple meals. The official campground lies 100m beyond the village spring.

The third and **final stage** of the trek takes you down the sheer limestone and scrub-strewn sides of Malana *nala* to the floor of the Parvati Valley – a precipitous 12km drop. From the hamlet of **Rashol** (or "Bashona"), you have a choice of three onward routes: either head east up the right bank of the river to **Manikaran** (see p.444); follow the trail southwest to the sacred **Bijli Mandir** (see p.443); or climb the remaining 3km up to the road at **Jari**, from where regular buses leave for Bhuntar, Kullu and Manali.

place to soak away the aches and pains of a long trek or bus journey. The tiled tubs come in two sizes: single and double. Clean towels and soap are available for a small extra charge, and you can sip delicious fresh apple juice on the sun terrace.

Vashisht also boasts a pair of old stone **temples**, opposite each other above the main square. Dedicated to the local patron saint Vashista (a deified sage and guru of Raghunathji), the smaller of the two opens on to a partially covered courtyard, and is adorned with elaborate wood carvings. Those lining the interior of the shrine, blackened by years of oil-lamp and *dhoop* smoke, are particularly fine. As you leave, check out the **temple tanks**, the free and communal equivalent of HPTDC's hot tubs. Divided into separate sections for men and women, they attract a decidedly mixed crowd of Hindu pilgrims, western hippies, semi-naked *sadhus*, and gangs of local kids that splash happily about in the pungent soapy water.

Accommodation

Vashisht is packed with budget **guest houses**, many of them old wooden buildings with broad verandahs and uninterrupted vistas up the valley. If you don't mind primitive plumbing, grungy beds and dope smoke, the only time you'll not be spoilt for choice is during high season, when even floor-space can be at a premium. On the outskirts, a couple of larger hotels offer good value, comfortable rooms.

Amrit, tucked away behind the temple. Turquoise-painted wooden house with basic amenities and lots of charm. ②.

Bhirga Hotel, below the village centre, on the roadside (☎8240). Large, slightly shabby hotel whose west-facing rooms all have attached bathrooms and superb views from balconies. ④.

Dharma, 15mins' walk up the lane behind the temples. Secluded guest house with rudimentary rooms, common toilets, and a south Indian snack annexe tacked on its first-storey verandah. ①–②.

Dolath/Negi, off the square. Incongruous modern buildings offering spartan, but clean accommodation at rock-bottom rates. Common toilets. ①–②.

Sonam, just down the road from the square. Cramped and dilapidated, but an old favourite. ①–②.

Vishranti Resorts, just above the main highway. A bright white building overlooking the footpath, with large, light, clean rooms, a sunny roof-terrace, and restaurant. The best value in its class. ③.

Eating

But for the *Superbake* store, behind the square, which has cornered the lucrative cake and bun market (try the wholewheat bread and apple crumble), most of the places to eat in Vashisht fall into the catch-all category: jacks of all trades, but masters of none.

Damrho, next to the *Sonam*. Poky "travellers" cafe with western breakfasts and basic veg dishes.

Dreamland, the square. Sociable restaurant serving the usual Indian, western, and Chinese.

Freedom, on the southern edge of the village. Worth the walk (10min) for its good attempts at Italian food, copious plates of *pulao*, breakfast menu, and *tandoor* oven, which fires up at 2pm.

Kanyakumari, on the main road below the square. Tourist-oriented breakfasts and snacks, and more authentic south Indian main meals, with classical Karnatic music in the background.

LAHAUL AND SPITI

Few places on earth can mark so dramatic a change in landscape as the **Rohtang Pass**. To one side, the lush green head of the Kullu Valley; to the other, an awesome vista of bare, chocolate-coloured mountains, hanging glaciers and snowfields that shine in the dazzlingly crisp light. The district of **Lahaul and Spiti**, Himachal's largest, is named after its two sub-divisions, which are, in spite of their numerous geographical and cultural similarities, distinct and separate regions.

Lahaul, sometimes referred to as the Chandra–Bhaga Valley, is the massive trough that divides the Great Himalaya and Pir Panjal ranges. Its principal river, the Chandra, rises deep in the barren wastes below the **Baralacha Pass**, a major landmark on the Manali–Leh road, from where it flows south, veering northwest around the base of the immense **Bara Shigri glacier** towards its confluence with the River Bhaga near Tandi. Here, the two rivers become the Chenab, and crash north out of Himachal to Kishtwar in Kashmir. Lahaul's **climate** is very similar to that of Ladakh and Zanskar, which border it to the north. Beyond the reach of the monsoon, the valley sees little rain in summer, when the sun is strong, and the nights cool. Between late October and late March, heavy snow closes the passes, and seal off the region. Even so, its inhabitants, a mixture of Buddhists and Hindus, enjoy one of the highest per capita incomes in the subcontinent. Using glacial water channelled down the mountains through ancient irrigation ducts, Lahauli farmers manage to coax a bumper crop of **seed potatoes** from their painstakingly fashioned terraces. The region is also the sole supplier of **hops** to India's breweries, and harvests prodigious quantities of wild herbs, used to make perfume and medicine. Much of the profit generated by these cash crops is spent on lavish jewellery, especially seed-pearl necklaces and coral and turquoise-inlaid silver plaques, worn by the women over ankle-length burgundy or fawn woollen dresses.

Lahaul's traditional costume and Buddhism are a legacy of the Tibetan influence that has permeated the region from the east, along the course of the River **Spiti**. From its headwaters below the **Kunzum Pass**, the Spiti drains 130km southeast to within a yak's cough of the border of Chinese-occupied Tibet, where it meets the Sutlej. The valley itself, surrounded by huge peaks and with a mean elevation of 4500m, is one of the highest and remotest inhabited places on earth – a desolate, barren tract scattered with tiny whitewashed mud-and-timber hamlets and lonely lamaseries.

Until 1992, Spiti in its entirety lay off-limits to foreign tourists. Now, only its far southeastern corner falls within the **"Inner Line"** – which leaves upper Spiti, including the district headquarters **Kaza**, freely accessible from the northwest via Lahaul. If you are really keen to complete the loop through the restricted area to or from Kinnaur (see p.421), you can do so with a **special permit**, issued only to groups of four or more organized through HPTDC, or a government-approved travel agent (see p.448).

One of the main incentives to splash out on a "jeep safari" through the restricted zone is the chance to visit **Tabo** *gompa*, which harbours some of the oldest and most exquisite Buddhist art in the world. It is one of several *gompas* in Spiti believed to have been founded by **Rinchen Zangpo**, the "Great Translator" who imported Buddhism to western Tibet (Guge) in the tenth and eleventh centuries. The others are even further off the beaten track, tucked away in side valleys. Getting to them is half the fun: footpaths and mule tracks to the more remote areas offer some of India's best **trekking**.

Getting around

State **buses** run from Manali up the Chandra and Bhaga Valleys to Keylong and Darcha from whenever the Rohtang Pass is cleared, usually in late June, until it snows up again in late October. You can also travel through Lahaul on private Leh-bound buses if there are free seats. Traffic to Kaza in Spiti is much lighter, although one bus leaves Manali each morning in summer while Kunzum La is open. The only other way to get around is on foot, or by renting a **jeep** from HPTDC or a reliable travel agency.

Keylong

Lahaul's largest settlement, **KEYLONG**, 114km north of Manali, is a good place to pause on the long road journey to Ladakh. Although of little interest in itself, the village lies amid superb scenery, within a day's climb of three large Buddhist **gompas**, visible on the opposite (south) side of the grandiose Bhaga Valley. A couple of basic **stores** sell trekking supplies if you are heading off towards Zanskar.

TREKKING IN LAHAUL AND SPITI

If you have come to the Himalayas to hike across high passes and vast scree-covered mountainsides, you'll be spoilt for choice in **Lahaul** and **Spiti**. The old trade routes to Ladakh and Tibet may have been tarmacked, but most of this remote and spectacular region is still only accessible on foot. Its trails, though well-frequented in high season, are long, hard and high, punctuated by few settlements, so you must be self-sufficient in food, fuel, ponies, and take along a guide. Packhorses and provisions are most readily available in **Manali**; or **Keylong** and **Darcha** (Lahaul) and **Kaza** (Spiti) if you can afford to wait around for a few days. A good rope for stream crossings is also essential on many of the routes, particularly in mid- and late summer after the snow bridges have melted.

The **best time** to trek is from July to early September, when brilliant blue skies make this an ideal alternative to the monsoon-prone Kullu Valley. By late September, the risk of snowfall deters many visitors from embarking on longer expeditions. Whenever you leave, allow enough time to acclimatize to the **altitude** before attempting any big passes: AMS (Acute Mountain Sickness) claims victims here every season (see *Basics*, p.20).

Altitude problems are common on the most popular route: from **DARCHA** in the Bhaga Valley over the **Shingo La** pass (5090m) to Zanskar. The trailhead, on the main highway, can be reached by bus from Manali, 145km south. The trail itself winds up the east bank of the Barai or Khade *nala* over the pass to **Kurgiakh**, the highest village in Zanskar. It can be completed in three stages, with a recommended extra day's acclimatization at Shingo La base camp if this is your first trek at altitude. From Kurgiakh, it takes seven more days to hike down the Tsarap Lingti Valley to **Padum**. Among the more amazing sights en route is the famous **Phuktal gompa**, a 4hr side trip from the main path. In recent years, a string of "hotels" (temporary *chai* stalls-cum-tent camps) have sprung up at one-day intervals along the well-marked path, making it possible to dispense with ponies and guides. This may be a safe way to trek in July and August, but you should definitely not bank on finding food and shelter here at the start or end of the season. In September 1988, a party of ten inexperienced trekkers travelled too light and were killed when a freak blizzard caught them on the notoriously snow-prone Shingo La.

Lahaul's other old-favourite trekking route, which follows the River Chandra north to its source at the **Baralacha Pass** (5100m), makes a good extension to the Hampta Pass hike described on p.454. Alternatively, catch the daily Kaza bus from Manali to the trailhead at **Batal**, a checkpoint and *chai* stop below Kunzum La. About 3km beyond the bridge, a track peels left off the main road to climb towards the beautiful milky-blue **Chandratal** ("Moon") **Lake**, a relentless 7hr slog from Batal. The ascent is enlivened by stunning views south across the world's longest glacier, **Bara Shigri**, and the forbidding north face of the **White Sail** massif (6446m). If you struggled for breath during the first stage, spend the second day acclimatizing with gentle side hikes around the lake before continuing up the valley to the next campground at **Tokping Yongma** torrent. Stage four of the trek takes 6–8hr, depending on how swollen the streams are: ask the Gaddis to show you the best crossing points, and always use a rope. **Tokpo Yongma**, the second of the two big side torrents, is particularly tricky. Most trekkers camp on its south bank and then ford it early in the morning of the final day, a steady climb up to the Baralacha Pass.

From **BARALACHA LA**, crossed by the Manali–Leh highway, catch a bus south to Keylong and the Kullu Valley, or continue north on foot to pick up the trail to Zanskar via the 5435m **Phirtse La** – a challenging alternative to the Darcha–Shingo La–Kurgiak route above. This 10-day trek involves lots of difficult stream crossings and strenuous climbing, and should only be attempted by experienced trekkers. If you travel direct to the trailhead from Manali, take acclimatization breaks after each ascent.

SPITI, a day's bus-ride east of the Rohtang Pass, offers fewer appealing long-distance routes. One exception is the **Pin Valley** trek. Starting 24km southeast of Kaza, a trail heads south along the right bank of the River Pin past a string of traditional settlements and monasteries to **Ghurguru**, where it forks in two; the northern path over the Pin-Parvati Pass (4802m) to **Manikaran** in the Parvati Valley (see p.444), and the southern one to Wangtu in **Kinnaur** via the Bhaba Pass (4865m). For more details, see p.421.

Lahauli Buddhists consider it auspicious to make a clockwise circumambulation – known as the **Rangcha Parikarma** – of the sacred **Rangcha** mountain (4565m), which soars above the confluence of the Bhaga and Chandra rivers. A well-worn trail that makes a long day-hike from Keylong, the route is highly scenic, and takes in the **Khardung gompa** along the way. Rising over 1000m from its base elevation (3348m), the trail is a hard slog if you haven't acclimatized, and should not be undertaken lightly. Carry plenty of food, water, and warm clothing, and be prepared to turn back if you start to feel dizzy and/or acutely short of breath.

Practicalities

Keylong is connected by regular state **buses** to Manali, and (in summer) by private buses to all points north and south along the main highway. Note that onward transport **to Leh** can be difficult to arrange in high season (July & Aug), as most buses are full by the time they get here. Travellers frequently find themselves having to ride on the roof, or hitch a lift on one of the trucks that stop at the *dhabas* on the roadside above the village: neither legal, nor particularly safe.

HPTDC's *Tourist Bungalow* (①–③) has three en-suite doubles, dorms, and tents. Among the numerous places around the bottom of the village, the *Gyespa Hotel*'s basic doubles (②) come with attached shower-toilets. Ten minutes further down the lane is the newer, posher *Dikyid Hotel* (④). All serve simple meals if given advance warning.

Kaza

KAZA, the sub-divisional headquarters of **Spiti**, lies 76km southeast of the Kunzum Pass, overlooking the left bank of the river. Accessible in summer by direct daily buses from Manali (leaving at 5am), 201km southwest, this is the region's main market and roadhead, and a good base from which to explore the remote settlements and monasteries nearby. If you plan to do any **trekking** in the region, Kaza is the place to pick up porters and ponymen: rates are comparable with Kullu. Of the **places to stay** in the old Spitian quarter, the best are *Milarepa's* (②), and *Sakya's Abode* (②) next door, both friendly family-run guest houses that offer modest, clean rooms, and meals. Also worth trying are the Electricity Board *Rest Houses* (④) in the newer part of town.

Kyi gompa

Set against a backdrop of snow-flecked mountains and ochre and brown cliffs, **KYI GOMPA**, whose white buildings stick limpet-like to the steep sides of a windswept conical hillock, is a picture-book example of Tibetan architecture, and one of Himachal's most exotic spectacles. Founded in the sixteenth century, Kyi (pronounced "Kee") is the largest **monastery** in the Spiti Valley, supporting a thriving community of *lamas* whose Rinpoche, Lo Chien Tulk from Nako village in Kinnaur (see p.420), is said to be the current incarnation of the "Great Translator" Rinchen Zangpo. His glass-fronted quarters crown the top of the complex, reached via crumbling stone steps that wind between the *lamas'* houses below. A monk carrying a bunch of old Tibetan-style keys will lead you around a labyrinth of dark passages and wooden staircases to the prayer and assembly halls, where you'll be shown collections of old *thangkas*, weapons, musical instruments, manuscripts, and devotional images.

Kyi lies 12km northwest of Kaza by road, and can be reached in summer by bus (every other day). To get the full force of its dramatic southern aspect, walk at least the last part of the trip, or better still **walk** all the way, along the nine-kilometre footpath.

Kibber

KIBBER (4205m) is reputedly the highest settlement in the world with a motorable road and electricity. Jeep tracks, satellite dishes and the odd tin-roofed government building aside, its smattering of a hundred or so old Spitian houses is very picturesque. Surrounded in summer by lush green barley fields, Kibber also stands at the head of a trail that picks its way north across the mountains, via the high **Parang La** pass (5578m) to Ladakh. Before the construction of roads into the Spiti Valley, locals used to lead ponies and yaks this way to trade in Leh bazaar. These days only the old folks in the village know the path, which is used by shepherds as a route to the pastures above.

Without your own vehicle, the only way to get to Kibber from Kaza, 16km southeast, is to catch the bus that lumbers up the mountain every two days during the summer, or to hike. There are no *pukka* guest houses in the village.

Tabo

If you are lucky enough to get your hands on an **Inner Line permit** for the journey through eastern Spiti and Kinnaur, don't miss **TABO gompa**, 46km east of Kaza. The mud and timber boxes that nestle on the steep north bank of the Spiti may look drab, but the multi-hued murals and stucco sculpture they contain are some of the world's richest and most important ancient Buddhist art treasures: the link between the cave paintings of Ajanta, and the more exuberant tantric art that flourished in Tibet five centuries or so later. According to an inscription in its main assembly hall, the monastery was established in 996 AD, when **Rinchen Zangpo**, an emissary of King Yeshe Od of Guge, was disseminating *dharma* across the northwestern Himalaya. In addition to the 158 Sanskrit Buddhist texts he personally transcribed, the "Great Translator" brought with him a retinue of Kashmiri artisans to decorate the temples. The only surviving examples of their exceptional work are here at Tabo, at Alchi in Ladakh, and Toling and Tsaparam *gompas* in Chinese-occupied western Tibet.

Enclosed within a mud-brick wall, Tabo's **Chogskhar**, or "sacred enclave", contains eight temples and a scattering of twenty-four *chortens* (*stupas*). The largest and oldest structure in the group, the **Sug Lhakhang**, stands opposite the main entrance. Erected at the end of the tenth century, the "Hall of the Enlightened Gods" was conceived in the form of a three-dimensional *mandala*, whose structure and elaborately decorated interior functions as a kind of magical diagram of the universe and its constituent deities. Scan the side walls with your flashlight (don't use a camera flash: they damage the murals), and you can make out three distinct bands of detail. The paintings on the lower level depict episodes in the life of the Buddha and his previous incarnations; above are stucco gods and goddesses, while strung around the top of the hall are lines of meditating Buddhas and *bodhisattvas*. The giant four-armed figure in front of the altar, lit by butter lamps, is **Vairacana**, a manifestation of the primordial Buddha.

The other temples, which the *lama* will unlock for you, date from the fifteenth and eighteenth centuries. Their contents illustrate the development of Buddhist iconography from its early Indian origins to the Chinese-influenced opulence of medieval Tibetan tantricism that still, in a more lurid form, predominates in modern *gompas*.

You can **stay** at Tabo in the *PWD Rest House* (③), or at the monastery, where the monks keep a couple of simple rooms for visitors (leave a donation). The new *gompa*, inaugurated by the Dalai Lama in 1983, houses thirty or so *lamas* and a handful of *chomos* (nuns), some of whom receive training in traditional painting techniques under a *geshe*, or teacher from eastern Tibet.

The Manali–Leh Highway

Since it opened to foreign tourists in 1989, the famous **Manali–Leh highway** has deservedly replaced the old Srinagar–Kargil route as the most popular approach to Ladakh. In summer, a stream of clapped-out government buses, private mini-buses and *Enfield* motorcycles set off from the Kullu Valley to travel along the second highest road in the world, which reaches a dizzying altitude of 5328m. Its surfaces vary wildly, from bumpy asphalt to dirt tracks sliced by glacial streams, running through a starkly beautiful lunar wilderness peopled only by nomadic shepherds, tar-covered road coolies, and the gloomy soldiers that man the isolated military checkpoints.

Depending on the road condition, the 485-kilometre journey can take anything from twenty-six to thirty hours. Bus drivers cover more distance on the first day than the second, stopping for a short and chilly night in one of the "tent camps" along the route. These, however, are few and far between after September 15, when the highway officially closes. In practice, all this means is that the Indian government won't airlift you out if you get trapped in snow; plenty of companies run regardless. For more details on **transport** between Manali and Leh, see p.453.

Manali to Keylong

Having made its way past the bleak military installations and wayside settlements above **Manali**, the road crosses the Beas to begin its long ascent of the **ROHTANG PASS** (3978m). The views over the eternal snows of Solang *nala* improve as you progress up the switchbacks, which emerge from the conifers to enter grassy mountain pastures strewn with glacial debris and grazed by herds of *dzos* and wild horses. Just below the pass proper, the buses pull in for breakfast at a row of makeshift *dhabas*. Nearby, a modern Hindu temple, reached via a flight of steps, crowns the top of a bluff from where you get a great panorama of the upper Beas Valley. Though not all that high by Himalayan standards, Rohtang itself, a U-shaped defile between two 5000-metre peaks, is one of the most treacherous passes in the region. Each year, Gaddis and mountaineers are caught unawares by sudden weather changes; hence the vultures wheeling overhead, and Rohtang's name, which literally means "piles of dead bodies". A road-builders' beacon tells you when you've reached the top, upstaged by the breathtaking vista of the dusty dark-brown mountains of **Lahaul** to the north.

The descent from Rohtang to the floor of the **Chandra Valley** affords tantalizing glimpses of the shining White Sail massif (6446m) in the east. **KOKSAR**, where the road finally reaches the river, is little more than a scruffy collection of *chai* stalls with a **checkpoint** where you have to enter your passport details in a ledger – one of many such stops on the road to Leh. At the height of the season in 1993, hundreds of tourists and truckers were trapped here when a freak snow storm blocked the highway: a sobering thought given the normally benign blue skies of the Lahauli summer.

The next few hours are some of the most memorable on the entire trip. Bus seats on the left are best, as the road runs across the northern slopes of the valley through the first Buddhist settlements, hemmed in by towering peaks and hanging glaciers. A sharp descent around the base of the sacred **Rangcha** mountain (see p.459) brings you to the Chandra–Bhaga confluence at **Tandi**, after which the road crosses the river on a Bailey bridge and veers north along the Bhaga Valley to **Keylong** (see p.457).

Keylong to Sarchu Serai

Beyond Keylong, the Bhaga valley broadens, but its bare sides support very few villages. By the time you reach **Darcha**, a lonely cluster of dry stone huts and tent camps on the edge of a vast pebbly river confluence, the landscape is utterly denuded. All buses stop here for passengers to grab a hot bowl of Tibetan *thukpa* from a wayside *dhaba*. There's little else to do in Darcha, which would be the definitive one-horse frontier post were it not for all the ponies hanging around on its outskirts near the Shingo La trailhead – the main trekking route north to Zanskar (see p.458).

From Darcha, the road climbs steadily northeast across mountainsides of wine-red and pale-green scree. **Zingzing Bar** must be the ultimate punishment posting for Indian soldiers, so be patient if they take their time perusing your passport. However, if you thought Zingzing Bar was desolate, **Baralacha La** will blow your mind. A windswept vale of red-brown rock and grit splashed with streaks of snow, the "four-roads" or "twelve-horned" pass forms the head of three valleys, the Bhaga, the Chandra, and the Yunan, which fall away from its sides in different directions. The only shelter for miles are a couple of corrugated-iron government huts.

By the time you get to **Sarchu Serai** you'll be more than ready for your bed, which is likely to be a piece of lumpy ground in a tent made from army-surplus parachutes. HPTDC's *Tent Camp* (①) serves steaming plates of *dal*, rice and *subzi*, in competition with a handful of similarly priced *dhabas* nearby.

Sarchu Serai to Tanglang La

After September 15, Sarchu Serai packs up for the season. Northbound buses have therefore to press on over **Langlacha La** (5059m), the second highest pass on the highway, to the tent camp at **Pang**, which stays open longer. Unfortunately, this means a drive through one of the most dramatic stretches of the route in darkness, arriving at the *serai*, a row of parachute *dhabas* beside a stream at the foot of parched yellow hills, late at night. Nor is the site, at just under 4500m, a sensible place to spend the night if you have come direct from Manali – a net elevation gain of around 2500m.

The army camp at Pang, 3km north of the *serai*, stands at the far southern end of the extraordinary **Moray Plains**: a 45-kilometre-long plateau encircled by rolling hills and, nosing up above them, brilliant white Himalayan peaks. This serene Tibetan landscape is the domain of nomadic *pashima*-rearing herdsmen who migrate here from Rupsu in eastern Ladakh each summer. Look out too for wild ass, po-faced marmots, and the elusive blue sheep (*nabu*) that graze the open grassland.

North of Moray is the dismal **Dibring Camp** where, when they are not bent over barrels of boiling tar, ragged gangs of Bihari roadworkers sit around sipping whisky tea. In a land of a million miserable occupations, theirs must surely rank among the very worst: maintaining a high-altitude highway that never recovers from the ravages of the previous winter. After Dibring, the road starts its ascent of the fourth and final pass. At a head-spinning 5328m, **Tanglang La** is the highest point on the Manali–Leh highway. Drivers pull in at the top for you to visit the "Government Urinals", and to have your photograph taken beside the beacon, whose run-down of Tanglang La's vital statistics ends with the exclamation: "Unbelievable! Is It Not". Staring north beyond the thicket of multicoloured prayer flags across Ladakh to the Karakoram range, just visible on the horizon, you may well agree.

CHAPTER SIX

LADAKH

L ADAKH, the far-flung eastern corner of troubled **Jammu and Kashmir** state, is India's most remote and sparsely populated region: a high-altitude snow desert cradled by the Karakoram and Great Himalaya ranges, and criss-crossed by a myriad razor-sharp peaks and ridges. To government servants and soldiers from the plains, charged with the unenviable task of guarding its fragile frontiers with China and Pakistan, this barren, breathless land is a punishment posting. For tourists, however, it offers the chance to experience at first hand a landscape and culture that, until 1974, had only been glimpsed by a few intrepid western travellers.

Far beyond the reach of the monsoons, Ladakh receives little snow, and less rain (the same amount as the Sahara). Only the most frugal methods enable its inhabitants to farm the thin sandy soil, frozen solid for eight months of the year and scorched by searing sun for the other four. Nourished by meltwater channelled through elaborate irrigation ditches, a single crop of barley (roasted to make the staple **ngamphe**) is sown and harvested between late June and the first October frosts. At lower elevations, where neat terraced fields are vivid green splashes against the bare rock and mica-flecked scree slopes, this is supplemented by fast-growing strains of wheat, garden vegetables, apricots and walnuts. Higher up, the relentless chill and steep gradients render agriculture impossible, and villagers depend on animals – yaks, goats, sheep and *dzos* (a hybrid of the yak and the domestic cow) – for wool, milk and butter to barter or sell for grain and fuel. Despite the harsh conditions, Ladakhis are unfailingly cheerful and courteous. Rarely do you pass villagers on a trail or working the fields without a chorus of "julay! julay!", the Ladakhi word for "hello" (or "goodbye").

Variously described as "Little Tibet" or "the last Shangri-La", **La-Dags** – "land of high mountain passes" – is one of the last enclaves of Mahayana **Buddhism**, Ladakh's principal religion for nearly a thousand years, now brutally suppressed by the Chinese in its native Tibet. Except near the Kashmiri border, the outward symbols of Buddhism are everywhere: strings of multicoloured prayer flags flutter from the roof-tops of houses, while bright prayer wheels and whitewashed *chortens* (the regional equivalent of *stupas*) guard the entrances to even the tiniest settlements. More impressive and mysterious still are Ladakh's medieval **monasteries**. Perched on rocky hilltops and clinging to sheer cliffs, **gompas** are both repositories of ancient wisdom and living centres of worship, whose gloomy prayer halls and ornate shrines harbour remarkable art treasures: giant brass Buddhas, *thangkas*, libraries of antique Tibetan manuscripts, weird musical instruments, and painted walls that writhe with fierce tantric divinities.

The highest concentration of monasteries is in the Indus Valley near **Leh**, the region's capital. Surrounded by sublime landscapes and crammed with hotels, guest houses, and restaurants, this atmospheric little town, a staging post on the old Silk Route, is most visitors' point of arrival and an ideal base for side trips. West of Leh, beyond the windswept **Fatu La** and **Namika La** passes, Buddhism peters out as you approach the predominantly Muslim district of **Kargil**. Ladakh's second largest town, at the mouth of the breathtakingly beautiful **Suru Valley**, marks the halfway stage of

Due to ongoing unrest in the region, this book does not include a chapter on **Kashmir**.

LADAKH TRAVEL DETAILS					
To and From Leh		**Flights**	**To and From Leh**	**Buses** (continued)	
Chandigarh	1 weekly	55min	Spitok	hourly	20min
Delhi	5 weekly	1hr 15min	Srinagar	1–2 daily	24hr
Jammu	1 weekly	1hr	Stok	2 daily	45min
Srinagar	1 weekly	50min	Temisgang	1 daily	5hr
To and From Leh		**Buses**	Thak Thok	3 daily	2hr 30min
Alchi	1 daily	3hr	Tikse	hourly	90min
Chemrey	3 daily	2hr			
Hemis	1–2 daily	1hr 45min	**To and From Kargil**		**Buses**
Lamayuru	1–2 daily	6hr 30min	Drass	2–3 daily	2hr
Likkir	1 daily	3hr	Mulbekh	2–3 daily	1hr 30min
Manali	6–8 daily	28hr	Padum	2 weekly	18hr
Matho	1 daily	1hr	Panikhar	2 daily	3hr
Phyang	3 daily	1hr 15min	Sankhu	3 daily	1hr 30min
Shey	hourly	1hr	Srinagar	1–2 daily	12hr

The bus details here apply between July 1 and September 15 only.

the journey to or from Srinagar, and is the jumping-off point for **Zanskar**, the vast and virtually road-free wilderness in the far south of the state that forms the border with Lahaul in Himachal Pradesh.

Two main "highways" connect Ladakh with the rest of India. Due to the unrest in Kashmir, the legendary Srinagar–Leh road now sees far less traffic than the route up from **Manali**, almost 500km south. These two, plus the dirt track from Kargil to Padum in Zanskar, also link the majority of Ladakh's larger settlements with the capital.

Bus services along the main Indus Valley highway are frequent and reliable, but grow less so the further you get from Leh. To get to and from off-track side valleys and villages within a single day, it is much easier to splash out on an *Ambassador* or a jeep **taxi**, available in Kargil and Leh. The alternative, and more traditional, way to get around the region, of course, is on foot. Popular **treks**, which you can organize yourself or through an agency, range from sedate two-day hikes through roadless villages, to gruelling long-distance routes across the mountains to Zanskar, and beyond.

Unless you fly direct to Leh (the world's highest airport), the decision of **when to visit** Ladakh is largely made for you: the passes into the region are only open between late June and late October, when the sun is at its strongest and the weather pleasantly warm. Even then, the nights can be chilly, so bring a sleeping bag. From November onwards, temperatures drop fast, often plummeting to -40°C between December and February, when the only way in and out of Zanskar is along the frozen surface of the river. Another reason to come in summer is to make arguably the most spectacular road journey in the world. The hour-long flight over the Himalayas may be memorable, but is no substitute for the two-day trip from Manali (see p.460) – a crash-course in just how remote and extraordinary this lonely mountain kingdom really is.

History
The first inhabitants of Ladakh are thought to have been a mixture of nomadic herdsmen from the Tibetan plateau and a small contingent of early Buddhist refugees from northern India called the Mons. Sometime in the fourth or fifth centuries, these two groups were joined by the **Dards**, a tribe of Indo-Aryan origin who migrated southeast along the Indus Valley, bringing with them irrigation and settled agriculture.

Details of **treks** in Ladakh and Zanskar appear on p.490–491.

The first independent kingdom in the region was established in the ninth century by the maverick nobleman Nyima Gon, taking advantage of the chaos after the collapse of the Tibetan empire of Guge. **Buddhism**, meanwhile, had also found its way across the Himalayas from India. Disseminated by the wandering sage-apostles Padma Sambhava (alias "Guru Rinpoche") and Milarespa, *dharma* gradually displaced the pantheistic shamanism of the **Bon-Cho** cult (which still holds sway in remote villages north of Khalsi, near Lamayuru). The eastward expansion of the faith towards the Tibetan plateau continued in the tenth and eleventh centuries – the period later dubbed the "**Second Spreading**". Among its key proselytizers was the "Great Translator" **Rinchen Zangpo**, a scholar and missionary associated with the foundation of numerous monasteries in Ladakh, including **Alchi** (see p.483).

Around the thirteenth century, Ladakh passed through a dark age during which, for reasons that remain unclear, its rulers switched allegiances from Indian to Tibetan Buddhism. Encouraged by royal patronage, the **Gelugpa** ("Yellow Hat") order established monasteries in the region, having espoused the more radical teachings of the **Vajrayana** school – an esoteric brand of Buddhism that fused elements of Hindu Tantra with the mysticism and arcane rituals of Bon-Cho. Under the **Tashi Namgyal** (1555–75), who re-unified the kingdom, Ladakh became a major Himalayan power, and the ascent to the throne of the "Lion", **Sengge Namgyal**, at the start of the seventeenth century signalled further territorial gains. After being routed by the Moghul-Balti army at Bodh Kharbu in 1639, he turned his energies to civil and religious matters, founding a new capital and palace at Leh, as well as a string of monasteries that included Hemis, seat of the newly arrived **Drugpa** ("Red Hat") sect.

Sengge's building spree created some fine monuments, but it also drained the kingdom's coffers, as did the hefty annual tribute paid to the Moghuls after the Bodh Kharbu debacle. Finances were further strained when Deldan, Sengge's successor, picked a quarrel with his ally, Tibet. The fifth Dalai Lama dispatched an army of Mongolian horsemen to teach him a lesson, and three years of conflict were only ended after the Moghul governor of Kashmir intervened on Ladakh's behalf. This help, however, came at a price: Aurangzeb demanded more tribute, ordered the construction of a mosque in Leh, and forced the Ladakhi king to convert to Islam.

Trade links with Tibet resumed in the eighteenth century, but Ladakh never regained its former status. Plagued by feuds and assassinations, the kingdom teetered into terminal decline, and was an easy target for the **Dogra** (Sikh) general Zorawar

---

SUMMER FESTIVALS IN LADAKH

Most of Ladakh's Buddhist **festivals**, in which masked dance dramas are performed by *lamas* in monastery courtyards, take place in January and February, when roads into the region are snow-bound. This works out well for the locals, for whom they relieve the tedium of the relentless winter, but it means that few outsiders get to experience some of the northern Himalayas' most vibrant and fascinating spectacles. Recently, however, a few of the larger *gompas* around Leh have followed the example of **Hemis** and switched their annual festivals to the summer, to attract tourists. Proceeds from ticket sales go towards maintenance and restoration work, and the construction of new shrines.

The following festivals are held in summer. Their precise dates, which vary according to the Tibetan lunar calendar, are available through the tourist office in Leh.

Hemis (late June). The largest event of its kind draws huge crowds, and is unmissable if you are within striking distance. See p.480.

The Festival of Ladakh (early Aug). A popular J&KTDC-sponsored event; archery contests, polo matches, and traditional Ladakhi dance.

Phyang (mid-Aug). Featuring the usual *cham* dances, and the ritual exposition of a giant *thangka*.

Tikse (late Aug). Put on primarily for tourists, but no less of a spectacle than its long-established winter counterpart, one of the most dramatic events of the Ladakhi year.

Singh, who annexed it for the Maharaja of Kashmir in 1834. The Ladakhi royal family were banished to Stok palace, where they reside to this day.

Ladakh became a part of independent India in 1948, following the first of the three Indo-Pak wars fought in the region. However, both the international frontier, and the so-called **"Cease Fire Line"** that scythes through the top of Jammu and Kashmir remain "unauthenticated": even today, the two armies take periodic pot-shots at each other across the disputed Siachen Glacier in the Karakorams, 100km north. When you consider the proximity of China, another old foe who annexed a large chunk of Ladakh in 1962, it is easy to see why this is India's most sensitive border zone – and why it remained off-limits to tourists until 1974. These days, the most pressing political issue is the region's relations with the state government. Many Ladakhis feel that they do not get a fair deal from Srinagar, and are lobbying for greater autonomy in the form of a separate legislature or **"Hill Council"**. Dissatisfaction with outside rule, and the increasing domination of Leh bazaar by Kashmiri traders, are also cited as reasons for the Buddhist–Muslim riots that have broken out in the capital over the past five years – the first communal violence ever seen in normally peaceful Ladakh.

Leh

As you approach **LEH** for the first time, via the sloping sweep of dust and pebbles that divide it from the floor of the Indus Valley, you'll have little difficulty imagining how the old trans-Himalayan traders must have felt as they plodded in on the caravan routes from Yarkhand and Tibet: a mixture of relief at having crossed the mountains in one piece, and anticipation of a relaxing spell in one of central Asia's most scenic and atmospheric towns. Spilling out of a side valley that tapers north towards eroded snow-capped peaks, the Ladakhi capital sprawls from the foot of a ruined Tibetan-style palace – a maze of mud-brick and concrete flanked on one side by cream-coloured desert, and on the other by a swathe of lush irrigated farmland.

Leh only became regional capital in the seventeenth century, when Sengge Namgyal shifted his court here from Shey, 15km southeast, to be closer to the head of the Khardung La–Karakoram corridor into China. The move paid off: within a generation, the town had blossomed into one of the busiest markets on the Silk Road. During the 1920s and 1930s, the broad bazaar that still forms its heart received more than a dozen pony- and camel-trains each day. Leh's prosperity, managed mainly by the Sunni **Muslim** merchants whose descendants live in its labyrinthine **old quarter**, came to an

---

HEALTH IN LEH: ALTITUDE SICKNESS AND DIRTY WATER

As Leh is 3505 metres above sea level, some travellers, and especially those who arrive by plane from Delhi or Chandigarh, experience mild **altitude sickness**. If you develop any of the symptoms – persistent headaches, dizziness, insomnia, nausea, loss of appetite or shortness of breath – your body has not yet acclimatized to the comparative lack of oxygen in the thin Ladakhi air; don't worry, it will, probably in as little as twenty-four hours. In the meantime, take it easy: drink plenty of fluids, lay off alcohol, and don't try to climb any hills for a couple of days. For more information, see p.20, or call the hospital's **AMS** (Acute Mountain Sickness) **hotline**: ☎560 (24hr), or ☎212 (daily 9am–5pm).

A health problem that affects far more travellers, however, is diarrhoea. **Dirty water** is invariably the culprit – a consequence of the grossly inadequate sewage system, which can't cope with the massive summer influx of visitors. Redouble your normal health precautions while you are here: take extra care over what you drink, and avoid salads and raw vegetables unless you know they have been cleaned in sterilized water. Meat of any kind is also a no-no; most of it travels up from Srinagar in unrefrigerated trucks.

abrupt end with the closure of the Chinese border in the 1950s. Only after the Indo-Pak wars of 1965 and 1971, when India rediscovered the hitherto forgotten capital's strategic value, did its fortunes begin to look up. Today, khaki-clad *jawans* (soldiers) and their families from the nearby military and air force bases are the mainstay of the local economy in winter, when foreign visitors are few and far between.

Undoubtedly the most radical shake-up, however, ensued from the Indian government's decision in 1974 to open Ladakh to foreign **tourists**. From the start, Leh bore the brunt of the annual invasion, as bus-loads of backpackers poured up the road from Srinagar. Twenty or so years on, though the main approach is now via Himachal Pradesh rather than Kashmir, the summer influx shows no sign of abating. Leh has doubled in size and is a far cry from the sleepy Himalayan town of the early 1970s. During July and August, tourists stroll shoulder to shoulder down its main street, most of whose old-style outfitters and provision stores have been squeezed out by Kashmiri handicraft shops, art emporiums, and Tibetan restaurants.

Leh has nonetheless retained a more tranquil side, and makes a pleasant place to unwind after a long bus journey. Attractions in and around the town itself include the former **palace** and **Namgyal Tsemo gompa**, perched amid strings of prayer flags above the narrow dusty streets of the **old quarter**. A short walk north across the fields, the small monastery at **Sankar** harbours accomplished modern tantric murals and a thousand-headed Avalokitesvara deity. Leh is also a good base for longer **day trips** out into the Indus Valley. Among the string of picturesque villages and *gompas* within reach by bus are **Shey**, site of a derelict seventeenth-century palace, and the spectacular **Tikse gompa**. Until you have adjusted to the altitude, however, the only sightseeing you'll probably feel up to will be from a guest-house roof terrace or garden, from where the snowy summits of the majestic **Stok-Kangri massif** (5508m), magnified in the crystal-clear Ladakhi sunshine, look close enough to touch.

Arrival and information

A taxi up the hill from in front of the terminal building at Leh **airport**, 5km southwest of town on the main Srinagar highway, will set you back a fixed fare of around Rs80. In theory, an airport bus should also meet incoming flights, but don't bank on it being there when you arrive.

State and private **buses** pull into the dusty town bus stand, five minutes' walk south of the bazaar. Himachal Tourism's Manali buses, however, drop passengers outside their office in Karzoo, close to most of the hotels.

J&KTDC's **tourist reception centre** (Mon–Sat 10am–4pm; ☎2497), recently relocated 3km from the bazaar on the airport road, is absurdly far out of town and only worth visiting to check out its travellers' notice board (good for finding trekking partners), or to rent trekking equipment. Next door is the **GPO** (Mon–Sat 10am–4.30pm), with an unreliable poste restante cupboard in a room around the back.

The **Taxi Operators' Union** rank (daily 7am–6pm) is tucked away behind the main street at the top of Fort Road. Each driver carries a list of fixed fares to just about everywhere you might want to visit in Ladakh, taking into account waiting time, *gompa* entrance fees, and night halt charges. However, these rates only apply to peak season; reductions of up to forty percent can be had at other times. Deal directly with the drivers, or their boss in the Union office will take a cut (passed on to you).

Money can be changed on the first floor of the painfully slow *State Bank of India* (Mon–Fri 10am–2pm, Sat 10am–noon), at the top of the bazaar, and in some of the upmarket hotels, although these tend to offer a poor rate of exchange.

Trunk and international **telephone** connections are poor: expect to be cut off at any moment. The *Artou* bookstore on the main street, and *Gypsy's World Treks and Tours* (July–Sept 8.30am–10pm; ☎2420, fax 3835), both have STD/IST and fax facilities; their exorbitant rates will no doubt come down as more lines appear in the town.

The telephone **area code** for Leh is ☎01982.

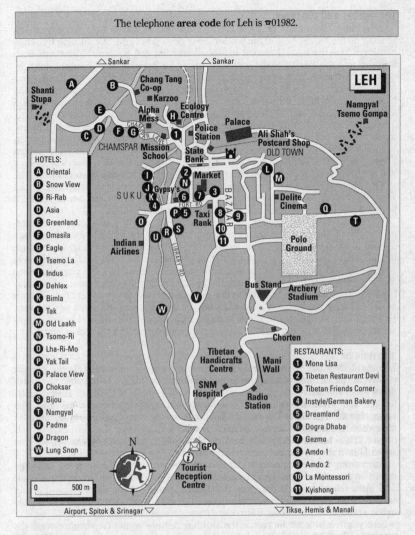

The Town

With the mighty hulk of the palace looming to the north, it is virtually impossible to lose your bearings in Leh. A mere five minutes' walk from the bus stand, the broad main bazaar runs north to south through the heart of town, dividing the labyrinthine old quarter and nearby polo ground from the greener and more spacious residential districts of **Karzoo** and **Suku** to the west. **Fort Road**, the other principal thoroughfare, turns west off the main street and then winds downhill past the taxi rank, the *Dreamland Restaurant*, and the arrival and departure point for Himachal Tourism's buses, towards the *Indian Airlines* office on the southern outskirts.

The bazaar and old town

After settling into a hotel or guest house, most visitors spend their first day in Leh soaking up the atmosphere of the **bazaar**. Sixty or so years ago, this bustling tree-lined boulevard was the busiest market between Yarkhand and Kashmir. Merchants from Srinagar and the Punjab would gather to barter for *pashima* wool brought down by nomadic herdsmen from western Tibet, or for raw silk hauled across the Karakorams on Bactrian camels. These days, though the street is awash with kitsch curio shops and handicraft emporiums, it retains a distinctly central Asian feel. Clean-shaven Ladakhi *lamas* in sneakers and shades rub shoulders with half-bearded Baltis and elderly Tibetan refugees whirring prayer wheels, while now and again, snatches of Chinese music crackle out of the shopkeepers' transistor radios. At the bottom of the bazaar, women from nearby villages, stovepipe hats perched jauntily on their heads, sit behind piles of vegetables, spinning wool and chatting as they appraise the passers-by. Even if you are not shopping for trekking supplies, check out the **provision stores** along the street, where bright pink, turquoise, and wine-red silk cummerbunds hang in the windows. Inside, sacks of aromatic spices, dried pulses, herbs and tea are stacked beside boxes of incense, soap, and spare parts for kerosene stoves.

When you have had enough of the bazaar, head past the new green-and-white-painted **Jama Masjid** at the top of the street, and follow one of the lanes that lead into the **old town**. Apart from the odd electric cable, nothing much has changed here since the warren of flat-roofed houses, crumbling *chortens*, *mani* walls, and narrow sandy streets was laid down late in the sixteenth century – least of all the plumbing. One place definitely worth picking through the putrid-smelling puddles to visit, however, is the **Chamba temple**. It's not easy to find on your own; ask at the second row of shops on the left after the big arch for the key-keeper (*gonyer*), who will show you the way. Hemmed in by dilapidated medieval mansions, the one-roomed shrine houses a colossal image of Maitreya, the Buddha to come, and some wonderful old wall paintings.

The palace

Lording it over the old town from the top of a craggy granite ridge is the derelict **palace** of the sixteenth-century ruler Sengge Namgyal (daily 7–9am; Rs5). A scaled-down version of the Potala in Lhasa, it is a text book example of medieval Tibetan architecture, with gigantic sloping buttressed walls and projecting wooden balconies that tower nine storeys above the surrounding houses. Since the Ladakhi royal family left the palace in the 1940s, damage inflicted by nineteenth-century Kashmiri cannons has caused large chunks of it to collapse. Bring a flashlight, and watch where you walk: in spite of restoration work, holes gape in the floors and dark staircases.

Apart from the flaking murals that decorate the ruined royal apartments and state rooms on the upper levels, very few remnants of the palace's former splendour survive. The main reason to pick your way through its gutted interior is to reach the **roof terrace**, which offers spectacular **views** over the mud-brown roof-tops of the old town to the wrinkled flanks and snow-covered ridges of the Stok-Kangri mountains.

Also worth a look as you pass is the **Dukhar temple** on the fourth storey (ask the monk to unlock it for you). The gloomy shrine, whose centrepiece is a thousand-armed image of the goddess Tara, houses eerie masks, musical instruments and weapons – props for the recitals and religious ceremonies once held in the courtyard outside.

Namgyal Tsemo gompa

Once you are acclimatized to the altitude, the stiff early-morning hike up to **Namgyal Tsemo gompa** (daily 7–9am), the monastery perched precariously on the shaley crag behind Leh palace, is a great way to start the day. Two trails lead up "the Hill of Victory", whose twin peaks are connected by giant strings of multicoloured prayer flags; the first and most popular zig-zags across its south side from the palace road, while a second scales the more gentle northern slope via the village of Chubi (the route followed by the *lama* from Sankar *gompa* who tends to the shrine each morning and evening). Alternatively, you could drive there along the dirt track that turns left off the main Khardung La highway, 2km north of the bus stand.

Approaching the *gompa* from the south, the first building you come to is the red-painted **Maitreya temple**. Thought to date from the fourteenth century, the shrine houses a giant Buddha statue flanked by *bodhisattvas*. However, its wall paintings are modern and of less interest than those in the **Gon-khang** up the hill. Most famous of these are the four-hundred-year-old "twin" portraits of Tashi Namgyal, the temple's founder, in the Persian-style court scene on the left wall (look for the big turbans). The veiled central deity itself sports a shiny phallus, believed to cure infertility in women.

The Shanti Stupa

A relatively new addition to the rocky skyline around Leh is the toothpaste-white **Shanti Stupa** above Chamspar village, 3km west of the bazaar. Inaugurated in 1983 by the Dalai Lama, the "Peace Pagoda", whose sides are decorated with gilt panels depicting episodes from the life of the Buddha, is one of several such monuments erected around India by an order of Japanese Shinto Buddhists. It can be reached by car, or on foot via a steep flight of five hundred steps, which winds up the ridge from the end of Chamspar Lane. When you get there, try a pot of *chai* at *Heaven's Tea Room*, whose terrace takes in a sweeping panoramic view of Leh and its environs.

The Ecology Centre

Five minutes' walk north of the main bazaar (next to the *Tsemo-La Hotel*), the **Ecology Centre** is the headquarters of LEDeG (the Ladakh Ecological Development Group) – a local non-governmental organization that aims to counter the negative impact of western-style "development" by fostering economic independence and respect for traditional culture. This involves promoting "appropriate" technologies such as solar energy, encouraging organic farming and cottage industries, and providing education on environmental and social issues through village drama, workshops and seminars. A garden hosts an open-air exhibition of solar gadgets, hydraulic pumps, water mills and other ingenious energy-saving devices, and there's a small **library**, and a **handicraft shop**, selling locally made clothes, *thangkas*, T-shirts, books and postcards.

Try to catch a screening of LEDeG's short **video** *Ancient Futures: Learning From Ladakh* (Mon, Wed & Fri, 3pm), which gives an insightful account of Ladakhi culture and the sweeping changes of the past thirty years, many of them direct results of tourism. Helena Norberg Hodge, the Swedish-born founder of LEDeG who appears in the film, has written an excellent book on Ladakh called *Ancient Futures* (*Sierra Club Books* US; *Rider* UK), available at the handicraft shop.

SECMOL

SECMOL (the Students' Educational and Cultural Movement of Ladakh) was founded in 1988 to involve young people in development issues and to lobby for changes in the region's educational system. Less than ten percent of Ladakhi students graduate from state high schools; even fewer go on to further studies in college. Besides underfunding, this is in part because the curriculum, devised in Srinagar and taught in Hindi or Urdu, has little or no relevance to local needs. In the hope of getting more Ladakhis through college, to become the next generation of teachers, SECMOL encourage foreign visitors to help local students practise their English (the language used in the state exams). They really appreciate formal lessons from trained EFL teachers; if you think you can help, or would just like to meet members of SECMOL, drop into their office on the northern outskirts of Leh (☎3585), ten minutes' walk up the hill from *Ali Shah's Postcard Shop*. SECMOL also arrange family stays ("**solidarity tours**") for tourists in local villages, both as a means of "promoting inter-cultural understanding", and to raise funds for their educational projects: ask at the office for more information.

Sankar gompa

Nestled amid the shimmering poplar coppices and terraced fields of barley that extend up the valley behind Leh, **Sankar gompa**, 3km north of the town centre, is among the most accessible monasteries in central Ladakh – hence its restricted visiting hours for tourists (daily 7–10am & 5–7pm; Rs10). You can get there either by car, or on foot: turn left at the junction above *Ali Shah's Postcard Shop*, and then right onto the concrete path that runs alongside the stream. Sankar appears after about twenty minutes' walk, surrounded by sun-bleached *chortens* and a high mud wall.

The monastery, a small under-*gompa* of Spitok, is staffed by twenty monks, and is the official residence of the **Kushok Bakul**, head of the Gelugpa ("yellow hat") sect. Appropriately for such a high-ranking *rinpoche*, his glass-fronted penthouse enjoys pride of place on top of the main building, crowned with a golden spire and a *dharma chakra* flanked by two deer (symbolizing the Buddha's first sermon in Sarnath). A flight of steps leads from the courtyard to the **Du-khang**. Beyond the Lords of the Four Quarters and Wheel of Life *mandala* that adorn the verandah, you enter a high-ceilinged hall whose walls writhe with lustrous multicoloured murals. Those on either side of the doorway are the most amazing: many-armed pot-bellied bovine monsters drink blood from skull cups, while the copulating *yab-yum* couples to the right are garlanded with severed heads and engulfed in swirling red and yellow flames.

The *gompa*'s principal deity, a thousand-armed, hundred-headed **Avalokitesvara**, is directly above the *Du-khang*. The turquoise-studded *bodhisattva* of Compassion presides over a light, airy shrine room, whose walls are adorned with a Tibetan calendar and tableaux depicting "dos and don'ts" for monks – some very arcane indeed. Yet another flight of steps leads to the *gompa* **library** and, eventually, a roof terrace with fine views over the north side of Namgyal Tsemo hill and the valley to the south.

CHORTENS AND MANI WALLS

Among the more visible expressions of Buddhism in Ladakh are the chess-pawn-shaped **chortens** at the entrance to villages and monasteries. These are the Tibetan equivalent of the Indian *stupa* (see p.336) – large hemispherical burial mounds-cum-devotional objects, prominent in Buddhist ritual since the third century BC. Like their southern cousins, they are imbued with mystical powers and **symbolic significance**: the tall tapering spire, normally divided into thirteen sections, represents the soul's progression towards *nirvana*, while the sun cradled by the crescent moon at the top stands for the unity of opposites, and the oneness of existence and the universe. Made of mud and stone (now also concrete), many *chortens* were erected as acts of piety by Ladakhi nobles. Those enshrined in monasteries, however, generally made of solid silver and encrusted with semi-precious stones, contain the ashes or relics of revered *rinpoches* (incarnate *lamas*). Always pass a *chorten* in a clockwise direction: the ritual of circumambulation mimics the passage of the planets through the heavens, and is believed to ward off evil spirits. The largest array is to be found in the desert east of **Shey** (see p.478), the former capital, but look out for the giant, brightly painted specimen on the way into Leh, whose red spire stands out against the snowy Stok-Kangri mountains to the south.

A short way downhill from the big *chorten*, near the radio station, stands an even more monumental symbol of devotion. The 500-metre **Mani wall**, erected by King Deldan Namgyal in 1635, is one of several at important religious sites around Ladakh. Ranging from a couple of metres to over a kilometre in length, the walls are made of hundreds of thousands of stones, each inscribed with prayers or sacred *mantras* – usually the invocation *Om Mani Padme Hum*: "Hail to the Jewel in the Lotus". It goes without saying that such stones should never be removed.

Accommodation

Leh is absolutely glutted with **accommodation**, most of it refreshingly neat, clean and excellent value for money. Budget travellers in particular are in for a treat. Gone are the days of bedding down on dusty, tick-infested roof-tops. Now most of the town's **cheap guest houses** are immaculately whitewashed traditional houses, set on the leafy outskirts, with sociable garden-terraces that look onto green fields. Simple double rooms go for under Rs100, even in high season. For a little more, you can often find a sunny en-suite "glass room" with a view all to yourself. Breakfasts are usually included in the tariff, served at low Tibetan tables (*chogtse*) in the family kitchen, surrounded by chests full of shiny copper pots, plates and brass and wooden tea urns (*gur-gurs*).

Rooms in Leh's **mid-range hotels** come with en-suite shower-toilets and piped hot water, while **upscale** accommodation is very poor value for money by Indian standards – unless you see wall-to-wall carpets, room service and (ecologically unsound) bath-tubs as a must. The rates below are for the high season, when they tend to be block-booked by package tour groups, and include both the ten percent state **luxury tax**, and the extra ten percent "**service charge**" levied by the pricier places, where appropriate.

Inexpensive

Rooms in family houses, grouped in three main areas, account for the bulk of Leh's plentiful **budget accommodation**. **Karzoo** and **Suku**, northwest of the main street, are very central but become tourist ghettos during high season; head for **Chamspar** village, fifteen minutes' walk west of the bazaar, if you're after peace, quiet, idyllic countryside and mountain views. More in the thick of things are the mainly Muslim houses of the **old town**. Crouched in the shadow of Leh palace, these are cheap and full of atmosphere, but the district's dodgy plumbing means that finding your way home after dark through the maze of narrow unlit lanes can be a trial (especially in flip flops).

Asia, Chamspar. Large, secluded riverside guest house. Sociable terrace-cum-cafe, but no views. ②.

Bimla, Suku (☎3854). Central, though secluded, with nice rooms and plenty of space outside to lounge around. ②.

Dehlex, Karzoo. An old favourite, now popular with long-stay foreign anthropologists. Run-of-the-mill rooms, bucket hot water on request, and a large awning in the garden. ②.

Eagle, opposite the army mess, Chamspar Lane, Chamspar. Plain, but clean and old-established, with a good-sized terrace around the back and valley views. ②.

Greenland, Chamspar. Spacious glass rooms or smaller singles downstairs, and a cosy garden. ②.

Indus, Karzoo. Cheap singles and a few doubles, with some attached bathrooms, solar-heated water on tap, and great views from the first floor. ②.

Lung Snon, 1km south of the centre past the *Indian Airlines* office. Old-style, friendly family guest house in a serene setting. Recommended, but a bit of a walk. ②.

Namgyal, old town. Mud-and-timber town house hemmed in by crumbling *chortens* on the edge of the old town, with basic rooms in a newer concrete annexe. ①.

Old Ladakh, old town. Ladakh's first-ever guest house is homely and central, and offers a choice of different rooms: the kitsch "deluxe" one (pink pillows and Tibetan rugs) is a real winner. ①–③.

Oriental, below the Shanti Stupa, Chamspar Lane, Chamspar. Congenial guest house with the best of everything: spotless rooms, solar-heated water, superb views, nourishing home-cooked meals, and a warm welcome. Recommended. ②.

Padma, off Fort Rd. Very traditional by Leh standards: immaculate rooms, a beautiful kitchen, a garden, and mountain views. ②.

Palace View, old town. The cleanest of the local rock-bottom bunch. Some en-suite rooms. ①–②.

Tak, old town. Another old favourite, but boxed in beneath the palace and very grubby. Again, its (cheap) glass rooms are by far the best deal. ①–②.

Moderate

Bijou, Library Rd (☎2331). Spacious, comfortable rooms in large Ladakhi house, five minutes' walk from the centre. Breakfasts served on secluded back terrace. Good value. ④.

Choksar, Library Rd (☎3626). A traditional timber-frame building whose bright and airy glass rooms are an excellent deal. ③.

Ri-Rab, Chamspar Lane. Stolid modern hotel with crisp cotton sheets and roof-top views. ⑤.

Snow View, Karzoo Lane. New, purpose-built hotel on the western outskirts, with superlative views from its large first-floor rooms. Parking and road access not a problem. ⑤.

Yak Tail (☎2318). Slap in the centre of town, and with most amenities, including money changing and a pricey restaurant that hosts weekly culture shows. ⑥.

Expensive

Dragon, south of the bazaar (☎339). An ersatz traditional building close to the centre, with plush western-style rooms ranged around a central courtyard, and a good restaurant. Recommended. ⑦.

Lha-Ri-Mo, south Leh (☎2377). Tasteful, palatial, repro mansion on the outskirts. Very swish. ⑦.

Omasila, Chamspar Lane (☎2319). Another (unconvincing) mock-up of an old-style Ladakhi house, with all the usual amenities, and good views. ⑦.

Tsemo La, near the Ecology Centre (☎2281). A rambling "A"-class hotel: comfortable rooms, lots of garden space, and directors' chairs on a scruffy lawn. ⑦.

Tsomo-Ri, Fort Rd (☎2471). Big and bland, but very central, and with its own generator and reliable water supply. Also recommended. ⑦.

Eating

As Leh's thriving restaurant and cafe scene has been cornered by the refugee community, **Tibetan food** has a high profile, alongside tourist-oriented Chinese and European dishes. The most popular Tibetan dish is *momos* – crescent-shaped pasta shells, stuffed with meat, cheese, or vegetables, and (if you're lucky) ginger, then steamed and served with hot soup and spicy sauce. Fried *momos* are called *kothays*. *Thukpa*, another wholesome favourite, is broth made from fresh pasta strips, meat and vegetables. These, and dozens of variations, are dished up in swanky tourist restaurants such as the now-legendary *Dreamland*, but you can tuck into bigger portions of the same stuff (for a fraction of the price) at modest backstreet "*momo* kitchens".

Most visitors have **breakfast** in their hotel or guest house, where the host family cook small round loaves of Ladakhi wheat-flour bread (*tagi shamos*), eaten piping hot with honey, or jam, and butter. For a truly authentic Leh breakfast, grab a couple of flat-breads from the clay-oven bakeries on the narrow lane at the top of the bazaar; the Tibetan restaurateurs don't mind you turning up with your own. If you fancy a change, apple-pie-and-chocolate-brownie **pastry shops** are dotted all over town.

Finally, the **liquor store** opposite the taxi stand sells take-out beers. **Chang**, a local barley brew, is harder to come by: ask at your guest house if they can get some in for you. Failing that, the *Mona Lisa* bar sells the stuff by the glass, albeit at an extortionate price. If you're desperate, you might manage to find your way to one or other of the illegal hole-in-the-wall *chang* bars tucked away in the backstreets behind the bazaar – not recommended for sensitive stomachs.

SHOPPING IN LEH

Between June and September, Leh is swamped by almost as many transient Tibetan and Kashmiri traders as souvenir-hungry tourists. Most of the merchandise hawked in their temporary boutiques and stalls comes from outside the region too: papier-mâché bowls, shawls and carpets from Srinagar, jewellery and miniature paintings from Jaipur, and "Himalayan" handicrafts churned out by Tibetan refugees in Old Delhi. Prices tend to be high, so haggle hard, and don't be conned into shelling out for cleverly faked "antiques".

Tibetan and Ladakhi **curios** account for the bulk of the goods on sale in Leh's emporiums. Of these, the *Ladakh Art Palace* off the main bazaar, one of only two locally owned and run souvenir stores, is the least pushy, and a good place to browse. Among its vast array of articles are Tibetan trumpets (*thumpchen*), cymbals, brass and copper *chang* kettles, prayer wheels, thunderbolts (*dorjes*), *gur-gur* tea churners, *cham* dance masks, *thangkas*, and coral and seed-pearl necklaces, to name but a few. If money is no object, you could even splash out on a **perak**; the long Ladakhi headdresses, encrusted with turquoises, cost upwards of Rs4000. Stocking fillers such as amulets, butter lamps, beads, and cheaper silver jewellery inlaid with semi-precious stones are sold from stalls outside the fresh produce market south of **Fort Road**. However, the best place to head for **thangkas** and hand-woven **Tibetan carpets** is the *Tibetan Children's Village Handicraft Centre*, up the hill from the GPO, which also has racks of cheap woollen Nepali-style jackets, waistcoats, and the whole gamut of "Free Tibet" stickers and posters.

For more **authentic Ladakhi souvenirs**, try the outfitters and provision stores dotted along the main bazaar. The Lahauli-run *Sonambongo Barongpa & Sons*, at the top-right end of the street, sells traditional costume and religious paraphernalia at fixed prices. If you've been wondering where to find those dapper stovepipe hats (*tibi*), hand-dyed *gonchas*, raw silk cummerbunds, tie-dyed rope-soled shoes (*pabbu*), Bhutanese cross-button shirts, prayer flags, real Ladakhi incense, or even monks' robes, look no further.

The **Ecology Centre**'s handicraft shop is another source of good-quality traditional clothing, including hand-knitted woollen jumpers, hats and socks. Genuine **pashima shawls**, however, are hard to come by; start looking in *Chang Tang Co-operative* in Karzoo, five minutes' walk up the lane past the Ecology Centre. Run by five local women who buy wool direct from nomadic herdsmen in eastern Ladakh, the co-op was set up to break the Kashmiri's traditional monopoly on the *pashima* business. Even if you are not in the market for a shawl – they start at around Rs3500 – the workshop is well worth a visit.

Easily the best **bookstore** in Leh is *Artou's*, who have two branches: one on the main bazaar, and another between *Tibetan Restaurant Devi* and the Ecology Centre. Both stock a fair selection of Indian *Penguin* classics, plus dozens of more expensive titles on Ladakh and the Himalayas. Secondhand paperbacks are sold or part-exchanged at the stationer's opposite the vegetable market. Finally, for **postcards**, black-and-white photographs of Ladakh, and stationery, visit *Ali Shah's Postcard Shop* above the main bazaar.

Amdo, Main Bazaar. Two Tibetan restaurants overlooking the main street. The one on the east side catches the morning sun, and serves hearty *tsampa* porridge for breakfast.

Dogra Dhaba, Fort Rd (opposite *Dreamland*). Spicy vegetarian Punjabi food at low prices, including beans, *dal*-fry, hot *rotis*, and tasty *tikkis* (potato patties), served up on tin plates.

Dreamland, Fort Rd. A perennial favourite and easily Leh's most popular all-rounder, even though the food is so-so, and pricey.

German Bakery, Karzoo. Sister business to its Manali namesake, equally well stocked with home-baked chocolate cakes, apple strudel, and wholewheat bread. Tell yourself you need it for the trek.

Gezmo, Fort Rd. Inexpensive street-side cafe popular with postcard and diary scribblers, mainly for its coffee and European breakfasts.

Instyle, Karzoo. Laid-back terrace restaurant. Wholefood breakfasts (muesli, curd, honey), passable espresso, and Chinese meals (tasty garlic-fried noodles) served to tourists under an old parachute.

Kyishong, south of the main bazaar. Arguably the best cheap Tibetan joint in town is run by a smiling old chap and his teenage side-kick. Groaning portions of freshly cooked food, and as much jasmine tea as you can drink for free. Recommended.

La Montessori, Main Bazaar. Choir mats and minimal decor, but mouth-watering cheese *kothays* figures among the many inexpensive Tibetan dishes.

Mona Lisa, off Chamspar Lane, near the Ecology Centre. A Ladakhi-run restaurant serving all the usual stuff, and some ambitious international alternatives (such as Swiss cream cheese, and felafels) indoors or *al fresco* on a sociable terrace. A popular bar, too. Moderate prices.

Tibetan Friends Corner, opposite the Taxi Stand. A bit dingy, but the food is filling and cheap, and a big hit with local *thukpa*-slurping Tibetans.

Tibetan Restaurant Devi, at the top of the bazaar. Cosy and sociable budget travellers' hang-out, with a run-of-the-mill menu of mostly vegetarian soups and noodle dishes.

MOVING ON FROM LEH

As befits India's remotest Himalayan town, Leh is singularly hard to get to, and even harder to leave. Fragile road and air links mean visitors all too often find themselves stranded waiting for passes to open, or planes to appear. Wherever and however you travel, book your onward ticket as far in advance as possible, be prepared for delays if the weather changes, and allow plenty of time to connect with onward flights.

The quickest way out of Leh is **by plane**. *Indian Airlines* fly 737s to and from **Chandigarh** (Mon; 55min; Rs1100), **Delhi** (Mon, Wed, Fri, Sat & Sun; 1hr 15min; Rs687), **Jammu** (Sun; 1hr; Rs962), and **Srinagar** (Wed; 50min; Rs830). Tickets can be booked and confirmed at the *Indian Airlines/Tushita Travels* office beyond *Hotel Lha-Ri-Mo* on Fort Rd (Mon–Fri 10am–5.30pm, Sat 10am–noon; ☎2276), but you may have to wait: the new computer is "down" a lot more than it's "up". Excessive demand for seats also contributes to the queues, which are worst at the start and end of the tourist season before the passes open. In addition, due to the altitude of Leh airport (the highest served by jet aircraft in the world), planes arriving here full have to leave with a lighter load (ie empty seats), so some people inevitably get stuck. Even confirmed tickets on outward-bound flights offer no guarantee of a prompt departure. Because the runway is surrounded by high mountains, the approach requires near-perfect visibility. The slightest scrap of cloud in the wrong place can result in the last-minute cancellation of the flight, whose passengers are then dumped on to "will-I-won't-I" waiting lists.

Since the Kashmir crisis took a turn for the worse, most **overland** travellers have been reaching Leh via **Manali** in Himachal Pradesh (see p.447). The 485-kilometre journey across the Himalaya takes two days, with a night halt in a tent camp en route. Tickets for HPTDC's comfortable daily "luxury" (a/c) and "deluxe" (non-a/c) coaches can be booked in advance (until Sept 15, when they are suspended) at the HPTDC office opposite the *Dreamland* on Fort Rd. Cheaper options include the ramshackle buses run by the *HPSRTC* and *J&KSRTC* state transport corporations, bookable the day before departure at the town bus stand. This is also the place to pick up seats on the many private minibuses. Don't underestimate the Manali–Leh highway. Even when the road is in good shape, it can be a long hard haul. Many passengers suffer **altitude problems** on the first day during the ascent of Tanglang La – at 5328m, the second highest motorable pass in the world (the highest, 5578-metre Khardung La, is just north of Leh on the Nubra Valley road). A full account of the route, starting at Manali, is given on p.460.

J&KSRTC buses to **Srinagar** still run throughout the summer (mid-June to late Oct), albeit carrying far fewer tourists than in past years. The two-day, 434-kilometre trip is broken by an overnight stop in Kargil (see p.486), and long waits at road blocks while interminable military and civil truck convoys lumber up the one-way sections of the road. Tickets go on sale between 4pm and 5pm of the day before departure (after they know how many buses have made it through) at *J&KSRTC*'s office in the town bus stand.

If you want to **hitch** to either Manali or Srinagar, the truck park in Leh is between the bus stand and the polo ground. Bear in mind you'll be expected to pay your way (around two thirds of the current bus fare), and that trucks break down (and go over the edge) far more often than buses.

For information regarding **local bus services** to destinations in Ladakh, see the relevant account, or consult the "Travel Details" on p.465.

Listings

Emergencies For police, ☎2218. There are no ambulances in Leh (see Hospital, below).

Hospital Leh's overstretched, poorly equipped *SNM Hospital* (☎2360) is 1km south of the centre on the main road. For urgent medical treatment, contact a doctor through any upscale hotel.

Laundry If your hotel or guest house doesn't take laundry, try the *Snow White Dry Cleaners* opposite the *Dreamland Restaurant*, or the street stall in front of the J&KTDC *Tourist Bungalow*. Avoid the *Ladakh Dry Cleaners* off Chamspar Lane, which leaves your clothes stinking of kerosene.

Libraries The Ecology Centre's excellent library (Mon–Fri 10am–1.30pm & 2–4.30pm) keeps books on everything from agriculture to Zen Buddhism, as well as periodicals, magazines, and files of articles on Ladakh and development issues. Serious students of Buddhism should check out the CIBS library in Choglamsar (daily 10am–1pm & 2–4pm), where the helpful librarians speak English.

Mountain bikes Mountain bikes may be rented through *Highland Adventures* in the *Hotel Ibex* complex. Rates are high, but they offer good discounts for longer periods.

Photography *Ali Shah's Postcard Shop*, two minutes' walk north of the main bazaar, stocks fresh film of all kinds, including slide film. If it's closed, try *ND Dijoo & Sons* on the main street.

Travel agents Reliable travel agents, recommended as trekking operators, include *Adventure North*, *Hotel Dragon* (☎339); *Gypsy's World Treks and Tours*, Fort Rd (☎2420); *Ladakh Adventure Travels*, *Hotel Ibex* (☎458); *Highland Adventures*, *Hotel Ibex* complex (Delhi ☎11/578 6116).

Yoga Small classes for all levels are run by a western teacher in Chamspar (Mon–Fri 10.30am–noon). Ask around Chamspar Lane for Thaganj House, or look for posters pinned up in local cafes.

Southeast of Leh

Southeast of Leh, the Indus Valley broadens to form a fertile river basin whose lush geometrical barley fields, interspersed with a tangle of turquoise streams, contrast sharply with the bare brown snow-capped mountains that sweep up from its sides. Among the spectacular Buddhist monuments that crown the rocky knolls and razor-back ridges at the edge of the flat valley floor, and make good **day trips from Leh**, are **Shey**, site of a ruined palace and giant brass Buddha, and the stunning monastery of **Tikse**. Both overlook the main highway and are thus served by regular buses.

With the exception of **Stok Palace**, home of the Ladakhi queen, sights on the opposite (south) side of the Indus, linked to the main road by a relatively unfrequented dirt track, are generally harder to reach by public transport. South of Stok, **Matho** *gompa* is more famous for its bi-annual winter oracle festivals than its art treasures, but is well worth a visit, if only for the superb views from its roof terrace. Further south still, either cross the Indus and rejoin the highway, calling in at **Stakna** *gompa* en route, or continue down the left bank to **Hemis**, Ladakh's wealthiest monastery and the venue for one of the few religious festivals held in summer. Finally, if you want to side-step your fellow tourists without spending a night away from Leh, head up the austerely beautiful tributary valley opposite Hemis to **Chemrey** and **Thak Thok** *gompas*. The latter, built around a fabled meditation cave, presides over a tiny village that sees only a trickle of the traffic that rumbles past on the main highway below.

Stok

Just beyond the Tibetan refugee camp at **Choglamsar**, a side road turns left off the highway to cross the Indus on an iron bridge plastered with prayer flags. Visible in the distance, at the top of a huge moraine of pebbles swept down from the mountains, the elegant four-storey **STOK Palace** stands above barley terraces studded with threshing circles and whitewashed farmhouses. Built early in the nineteenth century by the last ruler of independent Ladakh, it has been the official residence of the Ladakhi royal family since they were ousted from Leh and Shey two hundred years ago.

The present *Gyalmo* or "Queen", Deskit Angmo, a former member of parliament and friend of Indira Gandhi, still lives here during the summer, but has converted one wing of her 77-roomed palace into a small **museum** (daily 7am–7pm; Rs20). The fascinating collection comprises some of the family's most precious heirlooms, including antique ritual objects, ceremonial tea paraphernalia, and exquisite sixteenth-century **thangkas** illuminated with paint made from crushed rubies, emeralds and sapphires. The *pièces de résistance*, however, are the *Gyalmo*'s **peraks**. Still worn on important occasions, the ancient headdresses, thought to have originated in Tibet, are encrusted with slabs of flawless turquoise, polished coral, lapis lazuli and nuggets of pure gold. Also of interest are a couple of swords whose blades were allegedly tied in knots as a demonstration of strength by King Tashi Namgyal, and several sacred **dzi stones** – "pearls of pure happiness", said to have dropped from heaven, and worn to ward off evil spirits.

Stok gompa, five minutes' walk up the valley, boasts a collection of dance-drama masks, and some lurid modern murals painted by *lamas* from Lingshot *gompa* in Zanskar – the artists responsible for the Maitreya statue in Tikse (see opposite).

Buses leave Leh for Stok at 8.30am and 9am every morning, returning at 3pm and 6pm. This allows more than enough time to do the museum and the *gompa* justice, and to explore the beautiful side valley behind the village – trailhead for the Markha Valley trek (see p.490). If you are tempted to stay, **accommodation** is limited to the pricey *Hotel Highland* (⑤), a palatial two-storey house with fine views from its well-furnished en-suite rooms, and the grubby nameless guest house (①) just above it.

Shey

SHEY, 15km southeast of Leh and once the capital of Ladakh, is now all but deserted, the royal family having been forced to abandon it by the Dogras midway through the last century. Only a semi-derelict palace, a small *gompa*, and a profusion of *chortens* remain, clustered around a bleached spur of rock that juts into the fertile floor of the Indus Valley. The ruins overlook the main highway, and can be reached on the frequent minibuses between Leh bus stand and Tikse. There is nowhere to stay in the village.

The **palace**, a smaller and more dilapidated version of the one in Leh, sits astride the ridge below an ancient fort. Crowned by a golden *chorten* spire, its pride and joy is the colossal metal Buddha housed in its ruined temple (daily 6–9am). Installed at the behest of Sengge Namgyal's widow, Skalzang Dolni (1647–49), the twelve-metre blue-

---

RAFTING ON THE RIVER INDUS

While water levels are high, between the end of June and late August, Leh's more entrepreneurial travel agents operate **rafting** trips on the River Indus. The scene is still in its infancy, and the routes tame by comparison with Nepal's, but floating downstream in a twelve-seater rubber inflatable is a hugely enjoyable way to experience the valley's most rugged and beautiful landscape. Two different stretches of the river are used: from **Spitok** to the Indus-Zanskar confluence at **Nimmu** (3hr; Rs650), and from Nimmu to the ancient temple complex at **Alchi** (2hr 30min; Rs850). Experienced rafters may also want to try the more challenging route between Alchi and Khalsi, which takes in the kilometre-long series of rapids at **Nurla**. The cost of this option is negotiable, as it is rarely undertaken and involves considerably more travelling than either of the other two.

Tickets should be booked at least a day in advance, preferably through the operators themselves to avoid paying an agent's commission. The three best-established and most reliable companies in Leh are: *Ri-Mo Rafting*, who work from the *Hotel Kang-La-Chen* near the Ecology Centre, *Highland Adventures*, on the ground floor of the *Hotel Ibex* complex, and *Indus Himalaya*, opposite the *Hotel Yak Tail* on Fort Road. Make sure when you book that the price includes transport to and from the river, rental of life vests and helmets and meals, and that the raft has a waterproof strong box for valuables.

haired icon allegedly contains a horde of precious stones, *mandalas*, and powerful charms. The temple's recently restored **wall paintings**, preserved for hundreds of years under a layer of sticky black butter-lamp soot, are among the finest in the valley.

Five minutes' walk across the fields from the palace, and looking more like a mansion than a monastery, Shey **gompa** (daily 7–9am & 5–6pm) enshrines another massive Shakyamuni statue. Best viewed from the mezzanine verandah on the first floor, it is slightly older than its cousin up the hill. The descendants of the Nepali metal-workers who made it, brought here by Sengge Namgyal's mother, still live and work in the isolated village of **Chilling**, famous for its traditional silverware. Downstairs, the *gompa*'s main assembly hall (*Du-khang*) contains dusty old *thangkas* and manuscripts.

Easily missed as you whizz past on the road is Shey's most ancient monument. The **rock carving** of the five Dyani Buddhas, distinguished by their respective vehicles (*vahanas*) and hand positions (*mudras*), appears on a smooth slab of stone on the edge of the highway, and is believed to date from the eleventh century. The old reliquaries in the *chorten*-strewn strip of grey desert to the east, erected by the generations of Ladakhi kings and queens, form a striking and surreal spectacle.

Tikse

Ladakh's most photographed and architecturally impressive *gompa* is at **TIKSE**, 19km southeast of Leh. Founded in the fifteenth century, its whitewashed *chortens* and cubic monks' quarters rise in ranks up the sides of a craggy sun-bleached bluff, crowned by an imposing ochre- and red-painted temple complex whose gleaming golden finials are visible for miles in every direction.

A metalled road cuts up the empty west side of the hill from the main highway to the monastery's small car park. If you arrive by mini-bus from Leh (hourly, from the town bus stand), pick your way across the wasteground below the *gompa* and follow the foot-path up through its lower buildings to the main entrance, where monks issue tickets (Rs15). Tikse's reincarnation as a major tourist attraction has brought it mixed blessings: its constant stream of summer visitors spoils the peace and quiet necessary for meditation, but the income they generate has enabled the monks to invest in major refurbishments, among them the spanking new **Maitreya temple** immediately above the main courtyard. Inaugurated in 1980 by the Dalai Lama, the spacious shrine is built around a gigantic gold-faced Buddha-to-come, seated not on a throne as is normally the case, but in the lotus position. The Disney-bright murals on the wall behind, painted by monks from Lingshet *gompa* in Zanskar, depict scenes from Maitreya's life.

Tikse's garish modern temple may have had hours of work lavished upon it, but its dingy **Du-khang**, at the far end of the courtyard up a steep flight of steps, hasn't seen a lick of paint in centuries. Faded murals of ghoulish tantric deities peer out of the gloom of the old prayer hall, which contrary to appearances is still in everyday use. The key-keeper will show you around the tiny chapels behind the head *lama*'s throne, pointing out the ancient cloth-bound manuscripts stacked in wooden racks against the side walls. Before you leave the *Du-khang*, check out the enormous *thangkas* stored on the shelf opposite the main doorway. These are unrolled once each year during the annual *chaam* dance festival, Tikse Gostor. For most foreign visitors, however, the highlight of a trip to Tikse is the view from its lofty **roof terrace**. A swirling patchwork of barley fields stretches across the floor of the valley, fringed by rippling snow-flecked desert mountains and a string of Tolkien-esque monasteries, palaces, and Ladakhi villages: Shey and Stok to the northwest, Matho on the far side of the Indus, and Stakna crown-ing a knoll to the south. Come here early enough in the morning, and you'll be able to enjoy this impressive panorama accompanied by primeval groans from the *gompa*'s gargantuan Tibetan trumpets – played on the rooftop at *puja* time.

The village's *Skalzang Chamba Hotel* (③) offers basic **food** and **accommodation**.

Matho

MATHO, 27km south of Leh, straddles a spur at the mouth of an idyllic side valley that runs deep into the heart of the Stok-Kangri massif. Though no less interesting or scenically situated than its neighbours, the *gompa*, the only representative in Ladakh of the Saskyapa sect, sees comparatively few visitors. Unlike Tikse, across the Indus, it does not lie on the main highway, so it is far less accessible by bus: only one service a day runs to the nearby village, leaving Leh at around 9am and returning at 2.30pm. If you are travelling by car, Matho also makes an ideal half-way halt on the bumpy journey along the unsurfaced left-bank road between Stok and Hemis.

Despite its collection of four-hundred-year-old *thangkas*, the monastery is best known for its **oracle festivals**, held around the Tibetan New Year (Feb/March). The two oracles, known as *rongzam*, are elected by lot every three years from among the sixty or so resident *lamas*. During the run-up to the big days, the pair fast and meditate in readiness for the moment when they are possessed by the spirit of the deity. Watched by crowds of rapt onlookers, they then perform all manner of death-defying stunts that include leaping blindfold around the *gompa*'s precipitous parapets while slurping kettle-fulls of *chang*, and slashing themselves with razor-sharp sabres without drawing blood. The events are rounded off with colourful *chaam* dances in the monastery courtyard, and a question-and-answer session in which the *rongzam*, still under the influence of the deity, make prophecies about the coming year.

You can check out the costumes and masks worn by the monks during the festivals in Matho's small **museum**, tucked away behind the *Du-khang*. Men are also permitted to visit the eerie **Gon-khang** on the roof (strictly no photography), where the oracles' weapons and ritual garb are stored. The floor of the tiny temple lies under a deep layer of barley brought as harvest offerings by local villagers.

Hemis

Thanks to the **Hemis Setchu** festival – one of the few held in summer, when the passes are open – **HEMIS**, 45km southeast of Leh, must be the most famous *gompa* in Ladakh. Every year in late June/early July, hundreds of foreign visitors join the huge crowds of locals, dressed up in their finest traditional garb, that flock to watch the colourful two-day pageant. However, at other times, the rambling seventeenth-century monastery can be disappointingly dull and scant reward for the hassle of getting here by public transport. Only a skeleton staff of monks and novices are resident off-season, giving the impression that the *gompa* is now run largely for the benefit of tourists.

Crouched at the foot of a narrow sinuous ravine, amid a leafy oasis of poplar and willow trees, Hemis stays hidden from view until you are virtually beside it. The only signs of the *gompa*'s existence from the valley are the immense *mani* walls stretching over the rock outflow above you, pointing like giant arrows to the mouth of the gorge.

The main entrance, reached via a long flight of steps, opens onto the large rectangular courtyard where the festival **chaam dances** are performed. Accompanied by cymbal crashes, drum rolls and periodic groans from the temple trumpets, *lamas* dressed in opulently brocaded silk costumes and ghoulish masks mime episodes from Buddhist mythology. Now and again, young novices scamper on to the stage to caricature the stylized gestures of the baddies, egged on by a delighted crowd. The show culminates on the second day with a frenzied dismemberment of a dummy, symbolizing the destruction of the human ego, and thus the triumph of Buddhism over ignorance and evil. As well as illustrating the basic teachings of Mahayana Buddhism, the dramas are also a form of popular entertainment, eagerly anticipated by Ladakhi villagers.

Once every twelve years, the Hemis festival also hosts the ritual unrolling of a giant *thangka*. The *gompa*'s prize possession, which covers the entire facade of the building, was embroidered by women whose hands are now revered as holy relics. Decorated with pearls and precious stones, it will not now be on show again until 2004. Among the treasures on permanent display is an exquisite Buddha Shakyamuni, also inlaid with jewels. The serene-faced colossus sits in the *Cho-khang* at the far end of the courtyard, along with a couple of richly inlaid silver *chortens*.

Practicalities

By car, Hemis is a possible day trip from Leh. **Bus** services are only at all frequent during the festival, and those buses that do come don't hang around long enough for you to look around all of the monastery. You can spend the night here, either in a small tent camp in the woods below the *gompa*, where you can rent mattresses and blankets, or, if you have your own tent, in one of the many secluded camping sites beside the stream. Simple **food** is available at the parachute *dhaba* near the car park.

Chemrey

Clinging like a swallow's nest to the sides of a shaley conical hill, the magnificent *gompa* of **CHEMREY** sees very few visitors because of its location – tucked up the side valley that runs from Karu, below Hemis, to the Chang La pass into Nubra. If you don't have your own vehicle, you'll have to be prepared to do some walking to get here. It takes around fifty minutes to follow the dirt track down to the river and up to the monastery after the Leh–Thak Thok bus drops you off beside the main road.

Founded in 1664 as a memorial to King Sengge Namgyal, the monastery is staffed by a dwindling community of around twenty *Drugpa* monks and their young novices. Its main **Du-khang**, off the courtyard on the lower level, boasts a fine silver *chorten* and a set of ancient Tibetan texts whose title pages are illuminated with opulent gold and silver calligraphy. Upstairs in the revamped **Guru-Lakhang**, reached via several flights of rickety wooden steps, sits a giant brass statue of the sage Padma Sambhava, swathed in silk brocade and encrusted with semi-precious stones. Its exuberant murals, painted in the early 1980s, are the work of an artist from Nimmu village.

Thak Thok

Clustered around a lumpy outcrop of eroded rocks, 4km up the valley from Chemrey, the small *gompa* of **THAK THOK** (pronounced *Tak-Tak*) is the sole representative in Ladakh of the ancient Nyingmapa order. The main shrine of the "place with a mountain ceiling" is a cave, in which the apostle Padma Sambhava is said to have meditated during his epic seventh-century journey to Tibet. Blackened by years of sticky butter-lamp and incense smoke, the dark and mysterious grotto is now somewhat upstaged by the monastery's more modern wings nearby. As well as some spectacular thirty-year-old wall paintings, the **Urgyan Photan Du-khang** harbours a collection of multi-coloured yak-butter candle-sculptures made by the head *lama* of Thak Thok.

For a glimpse of "state-of-the-art" Buddhist iconography, head to the top of Thak Thok village, where a shiny new temple houses a row of huge gleaming Buddhas, decked out in silk robes and surrounded by garish modern murals.

Apart from during the annual **festivals** of Thak Thok Tse Chu (9th–11th of the 6th Tibetan month) and Viz Thak Thok Manchog (20th–29th of the 9th Tibetan month), the village itself is a tranquil place, blessed with serene views south over the snowy mountains behind Hemis. If you want to stay, **accommodation** is available in the new J&KTDC *Tourist Bungalow* (①–②). There are also plenty of ideal camping spots beside the river, although as ever you should seek permission before putting up a tent on someone's field. Three **buses** a day leave Leh for Thak Thok: the first and most convenient at 10.30am, and the last at 4pm, returning three hours later.

West of Leh

Of the many *gompas* accessible by road **west of Leh**, only **Spitok**, piled on a hilltop at the end of the airport runway, and **Phyang**, which presides over one of Ladakh's most picturesque villages, can be comfortably visited as day trips from the capital. The rest, including the unmissable temple complex at **Alchi**, with its wonderfully preserved tenth-century murals, are usually seen en route to or from **Kargil**. The 231-kilometre journey, taking in a couple of high passes and some mind-blowing scenery, can be completed in a single twelve-hour haul. To do this remarkable stretch of road justice, however, spend at least a week making short forays up side valleys, where idyllic settlements and *gompas* nestle amid swathes of barley fields and stark, shattered mountains.

Among landmarks punctuating the former caravan route is the photogenic monastery of **Lamayuru**. Reached via a nail-biting sequence of hairpin bends as the highway climbs out of the Indus Valley to begin its windy ascent of **Fatu La**, it lies within walking distance of some extraordinary lunar-like rock formations, at the start of the main trekking route south to Padum in Zanskar. Further west still, beyond the dramatic **Namika La** pass, **Mulbekh** is the last Buddhist village on the highway. From here on, *gompas* and *gonchas* give way to onion-domed mosques and flowing *shalwa camises*.

Transport along the main highway is straightforward in summer, when ramshackle state and private buses ply between Leh and Kargil. Getting to more remote spots, however, can be hard. Many travellers resort to paying for a ride on one of the countless *Tata* trucks that lumber past in long convoys; which may save time, but is a far more dangerous way to travel this hair-raising road than by bus.

Spitok

SPITOK gompa, rising incongruously from the end of the airport runway, makes a good half-day foray from Leh, 10km up the north side of the Indus Valley. If you can't afford the taxi fare, the easiest way to **get there** is to stroll down to the crossroads above the GPO and J&KTDC's tourist reception centre, and then flag down any of the buses heading west along the main Srinagar highway. Travellers who walk the whole way invariably regret it, as the route is relentlessly dull, passing through a string of unsightly military installations hemmed in by barbed-wire fences.

By contrast, the fifteenth-century monastery, which tumbles down the sides of a steep knoll to a tight cluster of farmhouses and well-watered fields, is altogether more picturesque. Approached by road from the north, or from the south along a footpath that winds through Spitok village, its spacious roof-tops command superb views.

The main complex, a typical mixture of dusty, dimly lit old prayer halls and vivid modern shrine rooms, is of less interest than **Paldan Lumo** chapel, perched on a ridge above. A sign outside warns visitors not to "deliberately mistake" the *Gon-khang* for a Kali temple. Offerings made to the black-faced and bloodthirsty Hindu goddess of death and destruction are, it insists, "not acceptable". The confusion no doubt arose because of the shrine's distinctly spooky feel. Lit by flickering butter lamps, the cluttered and cobwebbed chamber houses a row of veiled guardian deities whose ferocious faces are only unveiled once a year. After waving incense smoke before them and muttering a few *mantras*, the key-keeper *lama* will pass around handfuls of sweets newly infused with protective power. If you have a flashlight, check out the 600-year-old paintings on the rear wall of the chapel, which is Spitok's oldest building.

Phyang

A mere 24km west of Leh, **PHYANG gompa** looms large at the head of a secluded side valley that tapers north into the rugged Ladakh range from the Srinagar highway.

Of the three daily buses that run here from the capital, the 8am departure is the most convenient as it allows you plenty of time to explore the monastery and the pretty nearby village. When the expected slackening of the Inner Line restrictions comes, it may also be possible to hike 4km further up the valley to Phyang **lake**; check at the tourist office in Leh to see if access is allowed.

The *gompa* itself, a tall buttress-walled building, houses a fifty-strong community of Drigungpa *lamas*, but few antique murals of note, most having recently been painted over with new, brighter colours. Its only real treasures are a small collection of fourteenth-century Kashmiri bronzes (locked behind glass in the garishly modern **Guru-Padmasambhava temple**), and the light and airy main **Du-khang**'s three silver *chortens*, one of which is decorated with a seven-eyed coffee-coloured **dzi stone**. The gem, considered to be highly auspicious, was brought to Phyang from Tibet by the monastery's former head-*lama*, whose ashes the *chorten* encases.

Tucked away around the side, the shrine in the *gompa*'s gloomily atmospheric **Gon-khang**, lit by a single beam of dusty sunlight, houses a ferocious veiled Kali deity and an amazing collection of weapons and armour plundered during the Mongol invasions of the fourteenth century. Also dangling from the cobweb-covered rafters are various bits of dead animals, including most of a vulture, an ibex skull, and several sets of yak horns, believed to be nine-hundred-year-old relics of the Bon-Cho cult (see p.466).

Phyang's annual **festival**, formerly held during the winter but recently switched to summer in order to coincide with the tourist season, is the second largest in Ladakh (after Hemis). Celebrated with the usual masked *chaam* dances, the event is marked with a ritual exposition of a giant ten-metre brocaded silk *thangka*.

Alchi

Driving past on the nearby Srinagar–Leh highway, you'd never guess that the cluster of low pagoda-roofed cubes 3km across the Indus from **Saspol**, dwarfed by a spectacular sweep of pale-brown and wine-coloured scree, was one of the most significant historical sites in Asia. Yet the *Chos-khor*, or "religious enclave", at **ALCHI**, 70km west of Leh, harbours an extraordinary wealth of ancient wall paintings and wood sculpture, miraculously preserved for over eight centuries inside five tiny mud-walled temples. Art historians rave about the site because its earliest murals are the finest surviving examples of a style that flourished in Kashmir during the "Second Spreading", as Buddhism began to diffuse across the Himalayas from India into Tibet. Barely a handful of the monasteries founded during this era escaped the Muslim depredations of the fourteenth century. Of them all, Alchi is the most impressive, the least remote and the only one you don't need a special permit to visit. Nestled beside a bend in the milky blue River Indus, amid some dramatic scenery, it's also a serene spot and the perfect place to break a long journey to or from the Ladakhi capital.

The *Chos-khor* consists of five separate temples, various residential buildings and a scattering of large *chortens*, surrounded by a mud-and-stone wall and a curtain of tall poplar trees. If you are pushed for time, concentrate on the two oldest buildings, the **Du-khang** and the **Sumtsek**, both in the middle of the enclosure. Entrance tickets (Rs15) are issued by a pair of elderly *lamas* from nearby Likkir *gompa*, who shuffle around to unlock the doors. To make the most of the paintings' vibrant colours, you'll need a strong flashlight; but don't under any circumstances use a camera flash as it will irreparably damage the murals, last restored in the sixteenth century.

The Du-khang

An inscription records that Alchi's oldest structure, the **Du-khang** or main prayer hall, was erected late in the eleventh century by Kaldan Shesrab, a graduate of the now-ruined Nyarma *gompa* near Tikse, itself founded by the Great Translator Rinchen

Zangpo (see p.466). Approached via a walled courtyard and a path that runs under a hollow *chorten*, the temple's wooden doorway is richly carved with meditating *bodhisattvas*. Once your eyes adjust to the gloom inside, check out the niche in the rear wall where Vairocana, the "Buddha Resplendent", is flanked by two attendants. The other walls are decorated with six elaborate *mandalas*, interspersed with intricate friezes.

The Sumtsek

Standing to the left of the *Du-khang*, the **Sumtsek** is Alchi's most celebrated temple, and the highest achievement of early-medieval Indian-Buddhist art. Its paintings, dominated by rich reds and blues, are almost as fresh and vibrant today as they were nine hundred years ago, when the squat triple-storeyed structure was built.

The resident *lama* leads visitors under a delicate wooden facade to the interior of the shrine, shrouded in a womb-like darkness broken only by flickering butter lamps. Scan the walls with a flashlight and you'll see why scholars have filled volumes on this chamber alone. Surrounded by a swirling mass of *mandalas*, Buddhas, demi-gods and sundry other celestials stand three colossal **bodhisattvas**, their legs and bodies filling the niches on the ground floor, while their heads peer serenely down through gaps in the ceiling. Each of these four-metre-high stucco statues wears a figure-clinging *dhoti*, adorned with different, meticulously detailed motifs. Avalokitesvara, the *bodhisattva* of Compassion to the right, has pilgrimage sites, court vignettes and battle scenes on his robe, while that of Maitreya, the Buddha-to-come (in the middle), is decorated with episodes from the life of Gautama Buddha. Finally, to the right, the robe of Manjushri, Destroyer of Falsehood, shows the 84 Masters of Tantra adopting arcane yogic poses.

Among exquisite **murals** is the famous six-armed green goddess Tara, heavily bejewelled and seated on a lotus next to Avalokitesvara's right leg. Amazingly, this, and the multitude of other images that plaster the interior of the Sumtsek, resolve, when viewed from the centre of the shrine, into a harmonious whole.

Other temples

The *Chos-khor*'s three **other temples** all date from the twelfth and thirteenth centuries, but are nowhere near as impressive as their predecessors. Tucked away at the far river end of the enclosure, the **Manjushri Lakhang** is noteworthy only for its relatively recent "Thousand Buddha" paintings and gilded presiding icon, mirrored in the murals behind. The **Lotsawa Lakhang** next door, is one of a handful of temples dedicated to Rinchen Zangpo, the "Great Translator" whose missionary work inspired the foundation of Alchi. Finally, the *lama* may need to be cajoled into unlocking the **Lakhang Soma**, the small square shrine just above the Sumtsek, which is decorated with three large *mandalas* and various figures that include an accomplished *yab-yum*: the tantric image of the copulating deities symbolizes the interpenetration of cosmic opposites.

Practicalities

One **bus** per day leaves Leh for Alchi in summer (around mid-afternoon), taking three hours to cover the 70km and returning early the next day. Alternatively, flag down any of the long-distance buses on the Srinagar–Leh road and get off at **Saspol**, to walk the remaining 2.5km via the motorable suspension bridge west of the village.

Of the two very rudimentary **guest houses** in Alchi, the *Lotsav* (①), left of the main road as you approach the *Chos-khor*, is the most pleasant. Simple rooms with beaten earth floors and *charpois* cost Rs50, and the landlady serves cheap and filling breakfasts and evening meals in the small garden if you give her enough warning. The only other place to stay is the *Zimsgang Hotel* (③), just above the temples, which is an OK place to eat but whose rooms are grungy and overpriced. In the unlikely event of these two being full, return to Saspol and try the four-roomed J&KTDC *Tourist Bungalow* (③), at the top of the lane that leads from the main road past the army depot.

Lamayuru

If one sight could be said to sum up Ladakh, it would have to be **LAMAYURU gompa**, 130km west of Leh. Hemmed in by soaring scree-covered mountains, the whitewashed medieval monastery towers above a scruffy cluster of tumbledown mud-brick houses from the top of a near-vertical, weirdly eroded cliff. A major landmark on the old silk route, the *gompa* numbers among the 108 founded by the Great Translator, Rinchen Zangpo, in the tenth and eleventh centuries. However, its craggy seat, believed to have sheltered Milarespa during his religious odyssey across the Himalayas, was probably sacred long before the advent of Buddhism, when local people followed the shamanical Bon-Cho cult (see p.466). Just twenty yellow-hat *lamas* are left now, as opposed to the four hundred that lived here a century or so ago. Nor does Lamayuru harbour much in the way of art treasures. The main reason visitors make the short detour from the nearby Srinagar–Leh road are to photograph the *gompa* from the valley floor, or to pick up the trail to the Prikiti La pass – gateway to Zanskar – which begins here.

The footpath from the highway brings you out near the main entrance to the monastery, where you should be able to find the *lama* responsible for issuing entrance tickets (Rs5), and unlocking the door to the **Du-khang**. Lamayuru's newly renovated prayer hall houses little of note other than a **cave** where Milarespa meditated, and a rancid collection of yak-butter sculptures. If you're lucky, you'll be shown through the tangle of narrow lanes below the *gompa* to a tiny **chapel**, whose badly damaged murals of *mandalas* and the Dhyani Buddhas are contemporary with those at Alchi (see above).

Practicalities

Lamayuru lies too far from either Leh or Kargil, 107km west, to be visited in a day trip, so you either have to call in en route between the two, or else spend the night at the monastery itself – not advisable for anyone fussy about hygiene. Buses stop opposite the *Dehung Labrang Restaurant*, which serves simple meals and offers a very grubby room for around Rs100. Unfortunately, the *gompa*'s squalid rest house (①), next to the main entrance, is no better, with filthy cells, broken *charpois*, and no running water. A couple of young *lamas* also dish up *dal* and rice downstairs from an insanitary kitchen, eaten crouched over kerosene lamps in a tiny dining room-cum-trekkers tea shop. Unless you're really on a tight budget, head instead for the considerably more salubrious family-run *Dragon Guest House* (①–②) below the monastery. The newly opened *Meditation Centre*, above the monastery, also has a couple of pleasant rooms (②).

Mulbekh

West of Lamayuru, the main road crawls to the top of **Fatu La** (4091m), the highest pass between Srinagar and Leh, then ascends **Namika** ("Sky-Pillar") **La**, so called because of the jagged pinnacle of rock that looms above it to the south. Once across the windswept ridge, it drops through an Arizona-esque landscape of disintegrating desert cliffs and pebbly ravines to the wayside village of **MULBEKH**. The last sizeable Buddhist settlement along the road is scattered around the banks of the River Wakha, whose glacial waters flow through a lush carpet of barley fields peppered with poplars and orchards of walnut and apricot trees.

Formerly an outpost of the Zangla kingdom of western Ladakh (the deposed monarchs, King Nyima Norbu Namgyal Dey and his Queen, Tashi Deskit Angmo, still live in a dilapidated four-storeyed mansion on the western outskirts of the village), Mulbekh would be a sleepy hamlet were it not for the endless convoys of trucks and tourist buses that thunder through while the passes are open. Those visitors who stop at all tend only to stay long enough to grab a *chai* at a roadside *dhaba*, and to have a quick look at the seven-metre-high **Maitreya** ("Chamba" in Tibetan) **statue** carved from the face of a gigantic boulder nearby. The precise origins of the shapely four-armed Buddha-to-be are not known, but an ancient inscription on its side records that it was carved between the seventh and eighth centuries, well before Buddhism reached Tibet. The best place from which to view the bas-relief is the flat roof of the small *gompa* that partially obscures it. No entrance fee is charged, but the *lamas* appreciate a small donation for showing you their brightly painted twenty-year-old shrine.

Another incentive to prolong your stay in Mulbekh are the village's two **gompas**, perched atop a smooth two-hundred-metre rock 1km west of the Chamba statue. A steep flight of steps winds up to the whitewashed temples, one of which is occupied by a small community of young *chomos* (nuns). Neither houses any great treasures, but the views down the Warkha Valley from their terraces make the climb (a very stiff one if you're not yet acclimatized to the altitude) well worth while.

Accommodation in Mulbekh is limited to shabby rooms above the tea shops on the main road opposite the Chamba statue. The one at the end of the row, nearest the temple, is the cleanest and also serves the best *dal*, rice and omelettes.

Kargil

Even though it is surrounded by utterly awe-inspiring scenery, few travellers find anything positive to say about **KARGIL**, capital of the area dubbed "**Little Baltistan**", which rises in a clutter of corrugated iron roof-tops from the confluence of the Suru and Dras rivers. Ladakh's second largest town is largely seen as a charmless rite of passage en route to somewhere more appealing. That reputation, a legacy of the days when tourists poured through in their thousands en route to or from Kashmir, derives from the generally low standard of its budget accommodation, and the fact that the main street doubles as a highway, jammed all summer with cacophonic convoys of *Tata* trucks and buses. If you're overnighting on the way between Leh and Srinagar, this hardly matters. Virtually all you'll see of the town between the time the bus pulls in (around 7pm) and leaves (5am the next morning) is the grim bus stand and, as likely as not, the inside of an equally grotty hotel. If, on the other hand, you're bound for Padum in Zanskar, an eighteen-hour journey south down the Suru Valley, two or three days waiting for a bus is par for the course, allowing plenty of time to sample Kargil's dubious charms.

Unusually for Ladakh, the majority of Kargil's 5500 inhabitants are strict **Muslims**. Unlike their Sunni cousins in Kashmir, however, the locals here are ultra-orthodox **Shias**, which not only explains the ubiquitous Iranian Ayatollah photographs, but also the conspicuous absence of women from the bazaar. Descendants of settlers and Muslim merchants from Kashmir and Yarkhand, Kargilis speak a dialect called **Purig** – a mixture of Ladakhi and Balti. Indeed, had it not been for the daring reconquest of the region by India during the 1948 Indo–Pak war (the Indian army forced their Pakistani adversaries out of town after transporting an entire tank division over the Zoji La pass), Kargil would today be part of Baltistan, the region across the nearby Cease Fire Line which it closely resembles. Prevailing Islamic laws make it strongly advisable to **dress conservatively**. Women especially should not wander around in shorts, sleeveless tops, or even knee-length skirts (without trousers on underneath): wear a *shalwa camise* and a headscarf if you have one.

Once you've found somewhere to stay, there's little to do in Kargil beyond a stroll along the main street. Formerly a major market on the old Samarkhand–Srinagar cara-van route, the busy **bazaar** is nowadays a run-of-the-mill string of provision stores, iron-mongers, hole-in-the-wall cafes, and fly-blown butchers whose windows are hung with gruesome sheep carcasses. Here and there, stall-holders sit cross-legged on their raised shop fronts smoking *hookahs*, or murmuring verses from the Koran. Among the bearded and woolly-hatted passers-by you'll also come across the odd white turban of an **Agha**. Kargil's puritanical spiritual leaders, who have banned polo and dancing in the town, still travel to Iraq to receive religious training, which they follow up with bouts of study at the famously austere **Imambaras** – Shi'ite theological colleges – at the east end of the main thoroughfare.

Also worth considering if you have time is the short hike up to the picturesque village of **Goma** (Upper) **Kargil**, site of a Shi'ite shrine and a hot spring. From the top of Hospital Road (turn left up the hill at the end of the bazaar), the trail takes you through a tract of woodland to an open stretch of terraced mountainside, with fine views of the snow peaks to the north. Alternatively, cross the river via the footbridge below the bazaar and follow the track to **Poyen**. The town's oldest satellite settlement, a tumbledown cluster of flat-roofed houses grouped around a small silver-domed mosque, is renowned for its apricots, sold by the sack-load in the bazaar.

Arrival and information

Buses arriving in Kargil from Leh, Srinagar, and Padum either pull in to the main bus stand, immediately below the top (west) end of the bazaar, or at the truck park above the river, two minutes' walk downhill from the main street. If you plan to head off early in the morning, check when you buy your ticket where the bus leaves from.

J&KTDC's **tourist reception centre** (July–Aug Mon–Sat 10am–7pm, Sept–June Mon–Sat 10am–4pm) is on the east side of town, around the corner from the **taxi stand** and most of the hotels. As well as handing out the usual leaflets on Ladakh and Kashmir, they have a well-used travellers' notice board, and rent quality Norwegian **trekking equipment**, including four-season sleeping bags, tents, coats, and boots.

If you need to **change money** (or travellers' cheques), the *State Bank of India* (Mon–Fri 10am–2pm, Sat 10am–noon) is located in the middle of the main street. Its rates are poor, but better than the *Siachen Hotel*'s, whose small foreign exchange counter is the only place to cash currency outside bank hours.

At present, Kargil has just one STD **telephone** booth – located 1.5km east of the bazaar near the Zanskar road-bridge/military checkpoint.

Accommodation

If you've heard anything about Kargil, it is probably that its **hotels** are dreadful – which may be unfair on the few upscale places, and the J&KTDC *Tourist Bungalows*, but is certainly true of the rock-bottom "guest houses" around the bazaar. The Kashmir crisis, which reduced tourist traffic to a trickle, has aggravated the problem by squeezing half the hotels out of business. Those that remain are either geared towards tour groups, or else are total dives. What's more, room tariffs soar in July and August, when a flea-infested windowless hovel without running water can cost as much as Rs200. The rates quoted below apply to peak season; discounts are usually available at other times.

D'Zoji La, Lankore (☎01985/336). Kargil's top hotel, 2km east of town, offers upmarket accommodation for wealthy trekkers. Phone on arrival for a courtesy coach. ⑥.

Evergreen, below the taxi stand. A good fall-back, but common shower-toilets only. ②.

Greenland, at the end of the lane leading off the east side of the taxi stand. A notch above rock-bottom, with reasonable rooms (some attached bathrooms), and a reliable water supply. ③.

J&KTDC Tourist Bungalow #1, five minutes' walk uphill from the crossroads just above the bus stand. Clean rooms, clean sheets, and peaceful, with a small dining room. By far the best budget deal in town. If the *chowkidar* says it's full, get a "chit" from the tourist office. ①.

J&KTDC Tourist Bungalow #2, behind the truck park above the river. Not a patch on its namesake across town, but still good value and convenient for early departures. ①.

Marjina, behind the *State Bank of India*. Shabby and functional, but OK, with a busy dining hall. ①.

Siachen, below (the west side of) the taxi stand (☎01985/221). Large and comfortable, with immaculate en-suite rooms, own generator, STD phones, and foreign exchange. Book ahead in July and Aug. ⑤.

Eating

Unless you stay in one of the upscale hotels, finding somewhere to **eat** in Kargil is a toss-up between the small tourist-oriented cafes on the lane from the truck park to the bazaar, or a *dhaba* on the main street. Choice is even more limited for **breakfast**; all the restaurants are closed, but hot *chapatis* and omelettes are served from 7am onwards at the *chai* stall just up from the *Nuktal* (take your own plate). If you are leaving at the crack of dawn, a couple of *chai-wallahs* also hang around the bus stand.

Nuktal, between the truck park and the bazaar. Pink net curtains and fierce "Ayatollah" decor, but the food – basic Chinese ("spring rods") and some bland western alternatives (best avoided) – is fine. Generous portions and cheap, too. Try the delicious (bottled) apple juice. Recommended.

Popular Chacha, main bazaar. One of several pokey cafes on the high street serving piles of unremarkable-but-safe Chindian food, mostly to men.

Punjabi Jananta & Ruby, east end of main street. Two of a kind: spicy Indian sauces spooned on to groaning platefuls of rice. The cleanest *dhabas* in town. Cheap.

Shashila Chinese, main bazaar. *Nuktal*'s main rival, with a flashy exterior, but run-of-the-mill food.

The Suru Valley

A spellbinding divide between two of the world's most formidable mountain ranges, the **SURU VALLEY** winds south from Kargil to the desolate Pensi La pass – principal entrepot for Zanskar. Since a fair-weather road was bulldozed all the way to Padum, you can travel to the heart of this remote region by bus (albeit a clapped-out J&K state one), in a single haul of around eighteen hours. The first leg, usually undertaken in the pre-dawn darkness, leads through the broad lower reaches of the Suru Valley, whose fertile floor is strewn with Muslim villages, clustered around gleaming metal mosque domes. By the time the first rays of daylight appear in the east, the surrounding mountains have grown vast, bare and brown, only cultivated along the narrow strip lining the river. Gradually, the pristine white ice-fields and rocky pinnacles of **Nun-Kun** (7077m) nose over the horizon. Apart from a brief disappearance behind the steep sides of the valley at **Panikhar**, this awesome massif dominates the landscape all the way to Zanskar.

Shortly after Panikhar, the Suru veers east around the base of Nun-Kun, passing within a stone's throw of the magnificent **Gangri Glacier**. Having wound across a seemingly endless boulder choke, closed in on both sides by sheer mountain walls, the road emerges to a marshy open plain surrounded by snow peaks and swathes of near-vertical strata. **Juldo**, a tiny settlement whose fodder-stacked roof-tops are strung with fluttering prayer flags, marks the beginning of Buddhist **Suru**.

The climb to the pass from **Rangdum gompa**, across the flat river basin from Juldo, is absolutely breathtaking. One glistening 6000-metre peak after another appears atop a series of side valleys, many lined with gigantic folds of rock and ice. The real high point occurs shortly beyond **Pensi La** (4401m), as the road, swinging around dizzying switchbacks, overlooks the colossal S-shaped **Darung Drung Glacier**, whose milky green melt-waters drain southeast into the Stod Valley, visible below.

Panikhar

Although by no means the largest settlement in the Suru Valley, **PANIKHAR**, three hours' bus ride south of Kargil, is a good place to break the long journey to Padum. Before the Kashmir troubles, it was a minor trekking centre, at the start of the Lonvilad Gali–Pahalgum trail. These days, the scruffy collection of roadside stalls and poor mud-brick farm houses sees very few tourists, even in high season.

The main reason to stop is to hike to nearby **Parkachik La**, for panoramic views of the glacier-gouged north face of the mighty **Nun-Kun massif**. The **trail** up to the pass, known locally as Largo ("Nothing") La, begins on the far side of the Suru, crossed via a suspension bridge thirty minutes south of the village. It may look straightforward from Panikhar, but the four-hour round-trip climb to the ridge gets very tough indeed towards the top, especially for those not used to the altitude. However, even seasoned trekkers gasp in awe at the sight that greets them when they finally arrive at the cairns. Capped with a plume of cloud and snow streaming from its huge pyramidal peak, Nun sails 3500 metres above the valley floor, draped with heavily crevassed hanging glaciers and flanked by its sisters, multi-pinnacled Kun and saddle-topped Barmal.

There are only two **places to stay** in Panikhar. The *Kayoul Hotel & Restaurant* (①), directly opposite the bus stop, has a couple of very basic rooms with fold-away *charpois* and shared "earth" latrines, plus the only place to **eat**, a ramshackle roadside cafe where the affable owner serves freshly cooked veg-noodles and omelettes. For a bit more comfort, try the modest J&KTDC *Tourist Bungalow* (①), 100m further down the road on the left, where a large en-suite room with running water and a western toilet sets you back a mere Rs40. **Buses** to Kargil leave from the *Kayoul* at 7am and 11am. If you're looking for a lift to Padum, collar the truckers as they leave the *dhaba* after their lunch; the one-way fare costs around the same as the bus (Rs100).

Zanskar

Until the Indian government drops restrictions on travel to Rupsu and the Nubra Valley, mountain-locked **ZANSKAR**, literally "Land of White Copper", remains the most remote corner of Ladakh accessible by road *and* open to tourists. Hemmed in by the Zanskar range and the Great Himalayan divide, the nucleus of the region is a Y-shaped glacial valley system drained by three main rivers. The **Stod** (or Doda) rises above the Pensi La pass to flow southeast into a wide triangular plain at **Padum**, the district headquarters, where it merges with the **Lungdok** (or Tsarap) to form the River **Zanskar** (or Cham). From here, the fast-flowing milky turquoise torrent surges northeast to meet the Indus, gouging a chasm through the jagged mountains en route.

Lying to the leeward side of the Himalayan watershed, Zanskar sees a lot more snow than central Ladakh. Even its lowest passes remain blocked for six or seven months of the year, while average mid-winter temperatures drop to a bone-numbing -40°C. Ten thousand or so tenacious souls subsist in this bleak and treeless terrain – among the coldest inhabited places on the planet – muffled up for half the year inside their smoke-filled whitewashed crofts, a winter's-worth of fodder piled on the roof.

A little over a decade ago, anything the resourceful Zanskaris could not produce for themselves (including timber for building) had to be packed into the region over four-to five-thousand-metre passes, or, in mid-winter, carried along the frozen surface of the Zanskar from its confluence with the Indus at Nimmu – a twelve-day round-trip that is still the quickest route to the Srinagar–Leh road from Padum. Finally, in 1980, a motorable dirt track was blasted down the Suru and over Pensi La into the Stod Valley. Landslides and freak blizzards permitting (Pensi La can be snow-bound even in August), the bumpy journey from Kargil to Padum can now be completed in as little as fifteen hours. Improved communications may yet turn out to be a mixed blessing for Zanskar. For while it has undoubtedly brought a degree of prosperity to Padum, the new road has already forced significant changes upon the rest of the valley – most noticeably a sharp increase in tourist traffic – whose long-term impact on the region's fragile ecology and traditional culture has yet to be fully realized.

Most visitors come to Zanskar to **trek**. Numerous trails wind their way northwards from Padum to central Ladakh, west to Kishtwar, and south to neighbouring Lahaul – all long hard hikes that involve strenuous ups and downs (see p.490). If, on the other hand, you travel down here hoping to use the district headquarters as a comfortable base from which to make short day trips, you'll be disappointed. Only a handful of

TREKKING IN LADAKH AND ZANSKAR

The ancient footpaths that criss-cross **Ladakh** and **Zanskar** provide some of the most inspiring **trekking** in all the Himalayas. Threading together remote Buddhist villages and monasteries, cut off in winter behind high passes whose rocky tops bristle with windswept thickets of prayer flags, nearly all are long, hard, and high – but they are rarely dull.

Whether you make all the necessary preparations yourself, or pay a specialist agency to do it for you, **Leh** is the best place to plan a trek. **Equipment**, including high-quality tents, sleeping bags, karrimats, boots and duck-down jackets, can be rented through J&KTDC's tourist reception centre at the bottom of town, or (more cheaply) at *Himalayan Adventures* in the *Hotel Ibex*, Fort Rd. Alternatively, buy your own Indian-made kit in the bazaar and re-sell it again afterwards. To find **ponies** and **guides**, essential for all the routes outlined below, head for the Tibetan refugee camp at **Choglamsar**, 3km south of Leh.

Trekking is undoubtedly the most rewarding way to explore the region, but it can also be highly disruptive. Minimize your impact in culturally and ecologically sensitive areas by respecting the following "golden rules", set out in LEDeG's *Guidelines For Visitors To Ladakh* (see p.471). First and foremost, be as **self-reliant** as possible, especially with food and fuel. Buying provisions along the way puts an unnecessary burden on the villages' subsistence-oriented economies, and encourages strings of unsightly "tea shops" (invari-ably run by outsiders) to sprout along the trails. Always burn kerosene, never wood – a scarce and valuable resource. Refuse should be packed out, not disposed of along the route, no matter how far from the nearest town you are. Always bury your faeces and, if you can't convert to water, burn your toilet paper afterwards. Finally, do not defecate in the dry stone huts along the trails; local shepherds use them for shelter during snow storms.

Spitok to Hemis via the Markha Valley

The beautiful **Markha Valley** runs parallel with the Indus on the far southern side of the snowy Stok-Kangri massif, visible from Leh. Passing through cultivated valley floors, undu-lating high-altitude grassland, and snow-prone passes, the winding trail along it enables trekkers to experience life in a roadless region without having to hike for weeks into the wilderness – as a result, it has become the most frequented route in Ladakh. Do not attempt this trek without adequate wet- and cold-weather gear: snow flurries sweep across the higher reaches of the Markha Valley even in August.

The circuit takes six to eight days to complete, and is usually followed anti-clockwise, starting from the village of **Spitok** (see p.482), 10km south of Leh. A more dramatic approach, via **Stok** (see p.477), affords matchless views over the Indus Valley to the Ladakh and Karakoram ranges, but involves a sharp ascent of **Stok La** (4848m) on only the second day; don't try it unless you are already well acclimatized to the altitude.

From Spitok, the trail crosses the Indus via an iron footbridge, then follows the south bank of the river 7km west to the narrow mouth of the tree-lined Jingchen Valley. Camp beside the stream at **Jingchen** village, 4km further on, or higher up the valley near **Rumbak**. Day 2 takes you 5hr south down a side valley, via the picturesque village of **Yurutse**, to a camp at the foot of **Kunda La** (4907m), crossed after a long climb on Day 3. **Shingo**, the first settlement below the pass, is a pleasant spot to set up camp if you are doing the trek in short stages. Otherwise, press on 6km down a wild-rose- and willow-lined stream gorge to the **River Markha**. A boggy campsite below the village of **Skiu**, hidden in a side valley 2km further upstream from the confluence, marks the end of this stage.

The next two days' walking are relatively easy, winding west along the river via a series of footbridges and small villages such as **Markha**, where you can visit a ruined fort and small *gompa*. Beyond **Umling**, 3km east, the valley widens, and the peak of **Kang Yurze** (6400m) rears up to the south. **Hankar** stands at the mouth of a side valley which you follow up to the **Nimaling plain**, a rolling pasture criss-crossed by gurgling streams and grazed by the yaks, *dzos*, sheep and horses of nearby villages. The ascent of **Kongmaru La** (5274m), the highest pass on the route, begins shortly after Nimaling on the penultimate leg. It takes 2hr if you are properly acclimatized, and is rewarded with fine views north across the Indus Valley. By the time you reach **Chogdo** after the steep and zig-zagging descent from the ridge, you may well be more than ready to call it a day; if not, carry on through **Sumda** to **Martselang** on the main Indus Valley highway, from where a dusty trail winds up to **Hemis** *gompa* (see p.480). The campsite in the woods below the monastery, serviced by a couple of *chai* stalls, marks the end of the trek.

Likkir to Temisgang

Plans are afoot to bulldoze a motorable road along the old caravan route through the hills between **Likkir** and **Temisgang**, north of the main Indus Valley. For the moment, this leisurely 2-day hike, which takes in three major monasteries (Likkir, Ridzong and Temisgang) and a string of idyllic villages, is a great introduction to trekking in Ladakh, the perfect acclimatizer if you plan to attempt any longer and more demanding routes. Ponies and guides for the trip may be arranged on spec at either Likkir or Temisgang villages, both of which have small guest houses and are connected by regular buses to Leh.

Lamayuru to Alchi

Albeit short by Ladakhi standards, the five-day trek from **Lamayuru** to **Alchi** is one of the toughest in the region, winding across high passes and a tangle of isolated valleys, past a couple of ancient *gompas*, and offering superb panoramic views of the wilderness north of the Indus Valley. It's very hard to follow in places, so don't attempt it without an experienced guide, ponies, and enough provisions to tide you over if you lose your way.

Day 1 follows the main Zanskar traverse (outlined below) southeast from **Lamayuru** (see p.485), to **Wanla** via the Prikit La pass (3810m). Shortly after the campground at **Phanjila**, 3hr beyond Wanla at the confluence of the Spong and Ripchar *nalas*, the trail peels away from the Padum route and heads east up Ripchar Nala to **Hinju**, at the foot of **Konki La** (4905m). Take time out here before the strenuous climb up to the pass. Once across, a zig-zagging descent winds down to the head of Sumdah Chu stream gorge, and thence through the tiny hamlets collectively known as **Sumdah Chunoon**, where there is a small *gompa* and plenty of space to camp. Stage four, to the bottom of the high **Stakspi La** pass (5180m), takes you north up a side valley and can be completed in 8hr. If you are fully acclimatized, the ensuing 3hr ascent should present no problems, although the steep 1000-metre drop down the other side to **Alchi** (see p.483) is tricky in places.

Padum to Lamayuru

The trek across the rugged Zanskar range from **Padum** to **Lamayuru** on the Srinagar–Leh highway, usually completed in ten to twelve days, is a hugely popular but very demanding long-distance route, not to be attempted as a first-time trek, nor without adequate preparation, ponies and a guide. We describe the route from south to north here, but there is no reason not to follow it in the opposite direction, from Lamayuru.

Two trails from **Padum** (see p.492) cover the first half of the trek. The slightly easier one winds along the east bank of the Zanskar via **Thonde** and **Zangla** (where you can detour up to an old palace and monastery), to **Honia**. Then the route ascends **Namtse La** pass (4446m), crossed halfway through the third stage. Day 4 involves a long hard slog over **Nerag La** (4850m) and a steep drop to cross the Zanskar at **Nerag** village. An hour or so north of the river, you meet up near **Yelchang** village with the other path which, after following the Zanskar's west bank to **Karsha** (see p.493), has wriggled over four passes, including the 5000-metre **Hanuma La**. This second and longer route allows you to visit the spectacular **Lingshet gompa**, famous for its *thangka* artists.

From Yelchang, a single track picks its way across a sheer wall of scree to **Sengge La** (the "Lion Pass"; 5000m). **Photokasar** above the River Photang, normally reached on Day 6 or 7, marks the start of the climb up a side valley to **Sisir La** (4990m), after which you drop sharply down to Spong Nala, thence to the campground at **Honupatta** village. Two relatively easy stages round off the trek. The trail follows the river 4km downstream to **Wanla**, and then up the Shilakung Valley and through a rocky gorge to **Prikit La**. **Lamayuru** (see p.485) nestles on the narrow floor of the Sangeluma gorge, 1hr 30min below the pass.

For an outline of the two main approach routes to Zanskar from the south, see "Trekking in Lahaul and Spiti", p.458.

Zanskar's widely scattered *gompas* and settlements lie within striking distance of the road. The rest are hidden away in remote valleys, reached after days or weeks of walking and surrounded by a shattered wilderness of mountains, where life has altered little since Buddhism first crossed the Himalayas from Kashmir nine hundred years ago.

Padum

After a memorable trek or bus ride, **PADUM** comes as an anticlimax. Instead of the picturesque Zanskari village you might expect, the region's administrative headquarters and principal roadhead turns out to be a desultory collection of crumbling mud and concrete cubes, oily truck parks, and incongruous tin-roofed government buildings, scattered around the sides of a stony hillock. The settlement's only real appeal lies in its superb location. Nestled at the southernmost tip of a broad, fertile river basin, Padum presides over a flat patchwork of farm land fringed with grey-pebble river beds and enclosed on three sides by colossal walls of scree and snow-capped mountains.

Straddling a nexus of several long-distance trails, Padum is also an important **trekking hub** and the only place in Zanskar where tourism has thus far made much of an impression. During the short summer season, you'll see almost as many weather-beaten westerners wandering around its sandy lanes as locals – a mixture of indigenous Buddhists and *shalwa-camise*-clad Sunni Muslims descended from the Dogra troops posted here by the Zorawar Singh in the 1840s. Even so, facilities remain very basic, limited to a small tourist office, a handful of temporary tea shops and guest houses, as well as the inevitable rash of Kashmiri handicraft stalls. Nor is there much to see while you are waiting for your blisters to heal or your bum to recover from the bus journey down here. Apart from a small **mosque**, the Jama Masjid, whose plate-metal roof and multicoloured minarets are Padum's most prominent feature, the only noteworthy sight within easy walking distance is a small **gompa**, ensconced amid the poplar trees fifteen minutes' walk south down the Tsarap Valley.

Arrival and Information

Arriving in Padum by bus (twice weekly; 18hr), you'll be dropped in the dusty square at the far south end of the village, close to the old quarter and a couple of the cheaper guest houses. Tickets for the eighteen-hour trip (Rs100) go on sale around 2pm the day before departure at Kargil bus stand, or on the bus itself if you are already in Padum. J&KTDC's **tourist reception centre** (July–Sept Mon–Sat 10am–7pm) lies 1km north of the square on the side of the main road, two minutes' walk from the other main concentration of guest houses. Unlike their branches in Leh and Kargil, this one doesn't rent out trekking gear, but it is a good place to go for general advice.

As yet, there is nowhere in Padum to change money or make telephone calls, although you can post letters at the GPO next door to the tourist complex.

Basic **trekking supplies** are sold at the two hole-in-the-wall stores above the bus stand. Prices are much higher than elsewhere, so it pays to bring your own provisions with you from Kargil. By mid-October, imported food of any kind is hard to come by.

Most trekkers arrange **horses** through the tourist office or guest house owners. Either way, expect to pay from Rs100 to Rs250 per horse per day, depending on the time of year (ponies transport grain during the harvest, so they're more expensive in October). If you are having trouble finding a horse-*wallah*, ask around Pibling village, thirty minutes' walk north across the fields from Padum, where most of them hang out.

Accommodation

Accommodation in Padum is limited to a handful of grotty guest houses and rooms in private family homes. In both cases, bathrooms are usually shared, and toilets of the "long-drop" variety. One exception is the simple but comfortable J&KTDC *Tourist*

Bungalow (②), whose well-maintained en-suite double rooms have running water. A more authentic option is the double-storey farm house nearby, the *Ibex Guest House* (①); its rooms are nothing special, but its very welcoming owners serve breakfast, evening meals, and endless rounds of butter-and-salt tea to guests in their traditional kitchen. By 1995, a large purpose-built tourist hotel should be up and running on the roadside to the west. While it promises to be a real eyesore, the *New Ibex* (③), with its thirty en-suite rooms, will relieve the congestion in the village proper, where at present the least shambolic of the budget guest houses is the *Greenland* (①), which boasts a couple of light and airy glass rooms.

If you have your own tent and would prefer to **camp**, pitches at the J&KTDC site, up near the tourist reception centre, cost Rs15 per night. Trekkers arriving from Shingo La also sometimes camp beside the stream in the Tsarap Valley; ask before you do.

Eating

Finding **food** in Padum only tends to be a problem towards the end of the trekking season; by mid-October, stocks of imported goods (virtually everything except barley flour and yak butter) are low, and even a fresh egg can be a cause for celebration. Earlier in the year, temporary tea-shops and cafes ensure a supply of filling and fairly inexpensive meals. Among the few of these rough-and-ready joints to reappear every year is the popular *Ibex Restaurant*, just south of the tourist office, which dishes up the usual (packet) soups, *dal* and rice, stringy chicken or mutton stew, and "potato *halwa*" (spuds mashed with onions and tomatoes). For cheap Chinese and Tibetan food, try the *Changtang* near the *Tourist Bungalow*, or *Babu Chinese*, back towards the village. Most guest houses also serve half-board if given enough warning.

Around Padum

Public transport around the Zanskar Valley is virtually non-existent, so unless you can afford the vastly inflated fares demanded by Padum's two or three taxi-*wallahs*, you can only get as far into the sweeping plains **around Padum** as you can hike in a day. For all but the most athletic and determined, this leaves just two possible excursions, of which the hike across the fields to **KARSHA** *gompa* is easily the most rewarding. From a distance, this cluster of whitewashed mud cubes clinging to the rocky lower slopes of the mountain north of Padum looks like some strange geological formation. Only close up is it possible to pick out the individual monk's quarters and temples, which date from the tenth to the fourteenth centuries. Of the prayer halls, the *Du-khang* and recently renovated *Gon-khang* at the top of the complex are the most impressive, while the small *Chukshok-jal*, set apart from the *gompa* below a ruined fort on the far side of a gully, contains Karsha's oldest wall paintings, contemporary with those at Alchi (see p.483).

The quickest way to **get to Karsha** on foot is to head north from Padum to the new cable bridge across the Stod, immediately below the monastery. Set off early in the morning; the violent icy storms that blow in from the south across the Great Himalayan range around mid-afternoon make the ninety-minute hike across the exposed river basin something of an endurance test.

Karsha can also be reached by road, via the bridge at **Tungri**, 8km northwest of Padum. En route, you pass another large *gompa*, **SANI**, the oldest in Zanskar, and one of the few built on the valley floor. Local legend attributes its foundation to the itinerant Padma Sambhava ("Guru Rinpoche"), but the name of a large *chorten* beside the main temple – the **Kanishka chorten** – suggests that it may have been established by the Kushan king Kanishka in the first or second century AD – a thousand years before the "Second Spreading" of Buddhism from India over the Himalayas to Tibet. Among Sani's more unusual features is the Naropa *Lakhang*'s painted stucco bas-reliefs, whose deep niches enshrine dusty gold-faced icons and other votive objects.

CHAPTER SEVEN

HARYANA AND PUNJAB

The prosperous, but politically unstable state of **HARYANA AND PUNJAB** – the flat, fertile tract of Gangetic Plain that extends northwest from Delhi to the Pakistan border – came into being after the cataclysmic **Partition** of August 1947. Crossed by the five major tributaries of the **Indus**, the former British-administered region of Punjab ("Land of Five Rivers") was split down the middle at Independence. Indian Muslims fled west into Pakistan, and Hindus east, in an exodus accompanied by horrific massacres. The Sikhs, meanwhile, threw their lot in with India, which they considered a safer option than the homeland of their Muslim arch-enemies. In 1966, prime minister Indira Gandhi, in response to Sikh pressure, divided the state into two semi-autonomous districts: predominantly Sikh Punjab, and ninety-six percent Hindu Haryana, both governed from the newly built capital of **Chandigarh**.

The protracted and violent campaign for Sikh self-rule, together with the fact that there's not much to see at the best of times, mean that Haryana and Punjab sees comparatively few foreign visitors. Nevertheless, the "bread basket of the nation" plays a hugely important part in the Indian **economy**. Modern crop technology and irrigation canals, introduced during the "**Green Revolution**" of the 1960s, enable Punjabi farmers to produce nearly a quarter of India's wheat, and one third of its milk and dairy foods, while the cities are major industrial centres. **Ludhiana** churns out ninety percent of the country's woollen goods, and the *Hero* factory in **Jalandhar** manufactures the world's best-selling bicycle. Helped by remittance cheques from millions of expatriates in the UK and US (and the cheap migrant labour of Bihari *bhaiyas* who took their place), the state's per capita income is nowadays double the national average.

Much of the credit for this has to go to the **Sikhs**. Recognizable by their beards and bulky turbans (or, in the case of women, flowing *shalwa camises*), India's most distinctive minority are fiercely independent and proud: their faith explicitly encourages economic self-reliance, family ties, and a readiness to fight for the mother country. Their military tradition, which dates from the days of resistance against the Moghuls, served the Sikhs well during the Raj, when they formed the backbone of the British-Indian army. The eldest sons, however, invariably stayed home to work the land, and Punjabi **Jat** farmers are now the most affluent peasant class in India: nearly every field has a small diesel pump house, while tractors, a rarity elsewhere, are a common sight. In the cities, Sikhs are better known as mechanics, or truck, taxi and auto rickshaw *wallahs*, particularly in Delhi, where many Punjabi refugees settled after Partition.

Despite the full-bearded fundamentalists you'll see strolling around the **Golden Temple** in the holy city of **Amritsar**, most Sikhs today are non-orthodox. Known as **sahajdharis**, less devout members of the faith are frequently stereotyped as *bon viveurs*, and with some justification: Punjab boasts both India's richest regional cuisine, and its highest per capita consumption of **alcohol**.

Most travellers simply pass through – perhaps with a detour to the beautiful **Golden Temple** – en route to Himachal Pradesh, or to the Indo-Pak border at **Wagha**, near Amritsar. However, if you linger long enough to check out Le Corbusier's experimental city of Chandigarh, the Moghul monuments at **Sirhind** and **Pinjore**, or the countless brick villages that stud the monotonous plains, you'll find its inhabitants, all of whom seem to have a cousin in Toronto or Southall, extremely garrulous and hospitable.

Govt of India Statement - The external boundaries of India are neither correct nor authenticated.

HARYANA AND PUNJAB TRAVEL DETAILS

	Trains		Buses		Flights	
	Frequency	Time	Frequency	Time	Frequency	Time
To and From Amritsar						
Agra	1 daily	15hr 30min				
Allahabad	1 daily	21hr 30min				
Bombay	3 daily	31hr 25min–44hr				
Calcutta	2 daily	38hr 10min–47hr				
Dehra Dun			1 daily	10hr		
Delhi	9 daily	7hr 20min–12hr	8 daily	10hr	4 weekly	55min
Dharamsala			1 daily	7hr		
Ganganagar			2 daily	8hr		
Gwalior	1 daily	18hr 20min				
Jammu			every 30min	5hr		
Jhansi	1 daily	20hr 35min				
Kullu			1 daily	16hr		
Lahore	1 daily	4hr				
Srinagar					4 weekly	50min
Varanasi	2 daily	23hr 15min–26hr				
Wagha			2 daily	45min		
To and From Chandigarh						
Agra			1 daily	10hr		
Amritsar			every 30min	5hr 30min–6hr		
Dehra Dun			14 daily	5hr		
Delhi	3 daily	3hr 10min–6hr	every 5min	5hr 30min–6hr	1 daily	40min
Dharamsala			6–15 daily	7–8hr		
Haridwar			14 daily	6hr		
Jaipur			7 daily	11hr		
Jammu			8 daily	10hr		
Kalka	5 daily	50min	every 30min	30min		
Kasauli			5 daily	2hr 30min		
Kullu			8 daily	6hr 30min		
Leh					1 weekly	1hr 25min
Manali			8 daily	8hr		
Shimla			every 30min		3hr 30min–4hr	
Sirhind			every 20min	1hr 30min		
To and From Pathankot						
Agra	1–2 daily	15hr 38min–19hr				
Ambala	1 daily	7hr 10min	every 20min	7hr		
Amritsar	1 daily	2hr	every 5min	3hr		
Chamba			hourly	5hr		
Dalhousie			hourly	3hr 30min		
Delhi	2–3 daily	11hr 35min–15hr	every 20min	11hr		
Dharamsala			12 daily	3hr 30min		
Gwalior	1–2 daily	17hr 30min–22hr				
Jammu	4 daily	2hr 40min–4hr	every 5min	3hr		
Jogindernagar	3 daily	8hr				
Jullundhar	2 daily	3hr	hourly	3hr		
Kangra	1 daily	3hr 25min	10 daily	3–4hr		
Manali			5 daily	12hr		
Mandi			5 daily	8hr		
Shimla			5 daily	12hr		
Varanasi	2 daily	28–31hr				

Note that no individual route appears more than once in this chart; for any specific journey, check against where you want to get to as well as where you're coming from.

THE GRAND TRUNK ROAD

Crossing Haryana and Punjab en route to or from Delhi, you're bound at some stage to travel along part of the longest, oldest, and most famous highway in India. Stretching two thousand kilometres from Peshawar near the rugged Afghan–Pakistan frontier to Calcutta on the River Hooghly, NH1, alias the **Grand Trunk Road**, was described by Kipling in his novel *Kim*, whose hero and his Tibetan *lama* companion set off along it in search of "The River of Arrows", as "the Big Road", and "the Backbone of all Hind".

The first recorded mention of this ancient trade corridor dates from the fourth century BC, when it was known as the **Uttar Path**, or "High Way". The emperor Ashoka upgraded it with paving stones and watchtowers a century later, placing edict pillars at intervals along the route. Midway through the tenth century, the ruthless Afghan warlord Sher Khan Sur added several *sarais*, or staging posts for caravan trains, including **Sirhind** near modern Chandigarh. He also stamped out highway robbery by holding village headmen personally accountable for crimes committed on their stretch of the road.

In the years to come, the Moghuls sank wells along the Grand Trunk Road, and the British covered it in asphalt. More recently, several sections were converted into four-lane highways, complete with crash-barriers and neat white lines that everyone ignores. However, the streams of *Tata* trucks and overloaded buses that nowadays tear along NH1 have done little to deter more traditional traffic: donkey carts (*ekkas*), rickshaws, cyclists, and barefoot pilgrims still plod along the hard shoulder, watched by imperious holy cows. The *sarais*, meanwhile, have been overtaken by their twentieth-century counterpart, the roadside *dhaba*, where Sikh truckers in singlets and shorts can wash their long black locks under stand-pipes, tuck into a plate-full of chicken and *chana dal*, and crash out on a *charpoi*. As Kipling put it, "such a river of life . . . exists nowhere in the world."

Some history

Punjab's arid Chaggar Valley, stretching south from the Shivalik Hills on the HP border to the deserts of Rajasthan, witnessed the rise of urban settlement as early as 3000 BC. Later labelled the **Harappan** civilization, this string of fortified towns was invaded by the Aryans around 1700 BC. Among the Sanskrit scriptures set down in the ensuing "Vedic" age was the **Mahabharata**, whose epic battles drew on real-life encounters between the ancient kings of Punjab at **Karnal**, 118km north of Delhi. Conquered by the Mauryans in the third century BC, this became the classic route for Muslim invaders marching on Delhi through the Khyber Pass. These included the mighty Moghul army of Babur, who routed Ibrahim Lodi at **Panipat**, beside the Jamuna, in 1526.

Further north, meanwhile, **Sikhism** was beginning to establish itself under the tutelage of Guru Nanak (1469–1539). Based on the notion of a single Formless God, the Guru's vision of a caste-less egalitarian society found favour both with Hindus and Muslims, in spite of Moghul emperor Aurangzeb's concerted attempts to stamp it out. Suppression actually strengthened the Sikh faith in the long run, inspiring the militaristic and confrontational tenth Guru **Gobind** Singh to introduce the Five Ks: part of a rigorous new orthodoxy called the **Khalsa**, or "Community of the Pure" (see *Contexts*).

Having survived repeated seventeenth-century Aghan invasions, the Sikh nation emerged to fill the power vacuum left by the collapse of the Moghuls. Only in the 1840s, after two bloody wars with the British, was the Khalsa army finally defeated. Thereafter, the Sikhs played a vital role in the Raj, helping to quash the Mutiny of 1857. The relationship only soured after the **Jallianwalla Bagh massacre** of 1919 (see p.510), which also ensured that the Punjab's puppet leaders (who hailed the general responsible as a hero) were discredited, leaving the way open for the rise of radicalism.

After the bloody **Partition** era, things calmed down enough after Independence for the new state to grow wealthy on its prodigious agricultural output. As it did, militant Sikhs began to press for the creation of the separate Punjabi-speaking state they called Khalistan. A compromise of sorts was reached in 1966, when the Hindu district of

Haryana and the Sikh-majority Punjab were nominally divided. However, the move did not silence the separatists, and in 1977 Indira Gandhi's Congress was trounced in state elections by a coalition that included the Sikh religious party, the **Akali Dal**.

A more sinister element entered the volatile equation with the emergence of an ultra-radical separatist movement led by **Sant Jaranil Singh Bhindranwale**. Covertly supported by the national government (who saw the group as a way to defeat the Akali Dal), Bhindranwale and his band waged a ruthless campaign of sectarian terror in the Punjab which came to a head in 1984, when they occupied the Golden Temple; Indira's brutal response, **Operation Blue Star** (see p.506), plunged the Punjab into yet another ugly bout of communal violence. Four years later, history repeated itself when a less threatening occupation of the Temple was crushed by **Operation Black Thunder**. Since then, the Punjabi police have gone on to make considerable advances against the terrorists – helped, for the first time, by the Punjabi peasant farmers, the Jats, who had grown tired of the inexorable slaughter. These days, the situation is calm, and Haryana and Punjab, previously a no-go zone for tourists, is safe to travel in once again.

Chandigarh

After the traumatic Partition of India in 1947, when Punjab's principal city Lahore was claimed by Pakistan, the new state of Haryana and Punjab found itself without a capital. Premier Jawaharlal Nehru saw this as a golden opportunity to realize his vision of a city "symbolic of the future of India, unfettered by the traditions of the past, [and] an expression of the nation's faith in the future", and dispatched scouts to Europe to search for designers. When their original choice, Polish-born Mathew Nowicki, was killed in a plane crash in 1950, the controversial Swiss-French architect Charles-Edouard Jeanneret, alias **Le Corbusier** (1887–1965), was offered the job.

Begun in 1952, **CHANDIGARH** was to be a ground-breaking experiment in town planning. Instead of the usual amorphous tangle, Le Corbusier's blueprints were for an orderly grid of sweeping boulevards, divided into 29 neat blocks, or **Sectors**, and interspersed with extensive stretches of green: a fusion of "sun, space and verdure". However, far from promoting harmony and accord, the resulting city – situated within sight of the Himalayan foothills between two seasonal rivers – has been a source of heated controversy since it was completed in the 1960s. Specialists applaud Le Corbusier's brainchild as "the greatest architectural achievement of the twentieth century", while detractors complain that the design was flawed, self-indulgent, and "un-Indian": in a country where only a tiny number of people own cars, Le Corbusier created a city for fast-flowing traffic, complete with dozens of enormous roundabouts and parking lots. Nor did he and his team pay much heed to the climate. During the summer, Chandigarh's unfinished concrete office and apartment blocks are like ovens, uninhabitable without expensive air-conditioning. After three decades, many are also showing signs of terminal decay, as weeds grow through the cracks in their mildewing walls.

In spite of Chandigarh's infrastructural and aesthetic shortcomings, its 650,000 inhabitants are very proud of their capital, which is cleaner, greener, and more affluent than other Indian cities of comparable size: a sort of south Delhi without the slums. Nor has the orderly American-style street plan entirely eradicated all signs of "Indian-ness", as its critics claim; cycle rickshaw *wallahs* and turbanned *sahajdharis* on scooters routinely take short-cuts the wrong way around traffic islands, while palmist-astrologers ply their trade under the trees on broken sidewalks.

As a tourist destination, though, Chandigarh is a dud, despite its recent application for UNESCO "World Heritage City" status. Unless you have a penchant for twentieth-century architecture, you'll probably only stay long enough to change buses between Delhi and Himachal Pradesh, or to pick up transport to Amritsar, 240km northwest.

Arrival and information

Chandigarh **airport** lies 11km south of the city centre. Facilities in the terminal building include a small *Indian Airlines* office (☎44304), a sub-branch of the *State Bank of Patiala* (Mon–Fri 7.30–11.30am, Sat 7.30–9.30am), and a Chandigarh Industry and Tourism Development Corporation (CITCO) information counter which hands out maps and leaflets, and will make phone bookings for government-approved hotels. Mini-van taxis and auto-rickshaws line up outside the airport to whisk you downtown; passengers invariably get a group together to split the Rs100 fare.

Arriving by train, you'll find yourself an inconvenient 8km southeast of the centre. Either hop in an (un-metered) auto-rickshaw, or wait for one of the half-hourly *CTU* (*Chandigarh Transport Undertaking*) buses that stop outside the station.

Buses from Delhi, HP and Amritsar pull in to the frenetic **Inter-State Bus Terminus** (aka the **ISBT**), on the south edge of the main commercial and shopping district, Sector 17. Only a short walk from most of the hotels, the bus stand also houses CITCO's very helpful **tourist office** (Mon–Sat 9am–1pm & 1.30–6pm; ☎5446145), situated on the first floor of the building and a good place to check bus and train times. *Northern Railway*'s computerized **reservation counter** (Mon–Sat 9am–1pm & 1.30–4pm; ☎32696) is on the next floor up. Other regional tourist corporations with offices in Chandigarh (all open Mon–Fri 10am–5pm) include Haryana, Sector 17 (☎21955); HP, Sector 22 (☎26494); UP (☎41649); and Punjab, Sector 22 (☎20869).

Several of the banks ranged around the square on the northwest side of Sector 17 **change money**, including the *Andhra Bank*, which also handles *Visa*.

Finally, the 24-hour cloakroom in the bus stand charges Rs1 per article per day for **left luggage**, but will only accept rucksacks if they are securely locked.

City transport

As Chandigarh is too spread out to explore on foot, the most convenient way of **getting around** is to flag down one of its many un-metered blue **auto-rickshaws**: the main rank is beside the bus terminus. **Cycle rickshaws** are almost as ubiquitous, and much cheaper, but find the long haul up to the north end of town very tough going. *Ambassador* **cars** (with drivers) can be rented for half- or full-day sightseeing excursions through the tourist office, or from in front of upscale hotels such as the *Piccadilly*, *Shivalik View*, and *Mount View*. Expect to pay around Rs500–600 per day.

The City

Chandigarh is made up of 47 numbered **sectors**, subdivided into lettered blocks. Le Corbusier conceived of the city plan as a living organism, with the imposing **Capital Complex** to the north as a "head", the shopping precinct, **Sector 17**, a "heart", the green open spaces as lungs, and the cross-cutting network of roads, separated into eight different grades for use by various types of vehicles (in theory only), a "circulatory system". A rickshaw can get around the few noteworthy sights in two to three hours.

The museum and art gallery

Chandigarh's large **museum and art gallery** (Tues–Sat 10am–4.30pm; camera permits Rs5), five minutes by rickshaw north of the city centre in Sector 10, houses a sizeable and informatively displayed collection of ancient sculpture, miniature paintings and contemporary Indian art. Among prize pieces on the first floor are a dozen or so standing Buddhas from Gandhara, noted for their delicately carved "wet-look" *lunghis*

The telephone **area code** for Chandigarh is ☎0172.

and distinctly Hellenic features – a legacy of Alexander the Great's conquests. Also Greek-influenced are the beautiful terracotta heads mounted in glass cases at the top of the main staircase; like the Buddhas, they date from the first and second centuries BC.

Art enthusiasts will find plenty to pore over in the adjacent gallery, where abundant exquisite Moghul, Kangra, and Rajasthani miniatures are accompanied by interpretive panels outlining the main features of the respective schools. Modern works featured in the end room include a couple of AN Tagore's atmospheric watercolours, five original Roerichs, and several over-the-top patriotic and devotional Sikh canvasses.

The Capital Complex

Three blocks north of downtown, in the shadow of the Shivalik Hills, the **Capital Complex**, Sector 1, is the site of some of Le Corbusier's most ambitious experiments. The concrete campus, set amid balding sun-parched lawns, was originally designed to express the strength and unity of independent India. Ironically, the whole area is now surrounded by barbed wire and patrolled by armed guards for fear of terrorist attacks, but it is still worth checking out, if only to see what inspired all those ferro-concrete university campuses that mushroomed across Europe and the US during the 1960s. Guided **tours** are run by CITCO from the reception desk of the Legislature Assembly (daily 10.30am–12.30pm & 2.30–4.30pm).

The complex's three most impressive edifices stand to the sides of its giant main piazza. One eminent architect, a fan of Le Corbusier but not of Chandigarh, said that he could see "no possible physical relation between [them]". They were meant to blend together to form a harmonious whole, based on the proportions of the human body (Le Corbusier's "**Le Modulor**" theory); that they don't is largely because the Municipality ran out of money before realizing the plans – hence all the yawning open spaces.

The most imposing edifice in the group is the eight-storey **Secretariat**, Chandigarh's highest building, which houses Haryana and Punjab's ministerial offices, and has a roof garden with good views over the city. The resemblance of the **Legislature Assembly**, or Vidhan Sabha, just north, to a power station is no coincidence: Le Corbusier was allegedly inspired by a stack of cooling towers he saw in Ahmedabad. The most colourful of the three buildings stands opposite the Secretariat. Said to incorporate elements of the Buland Darwaza in Fatehpur Sikri, the **High Court**, whose double roof symbolizes the protective power of the law, is decorated inside with huge woollen tapestries.

Before leaving the Capital Complex, head north from the High Court for a look at the black **Open Hand** monument. Chandigarh's adopted emblem, which revolves on ball-bearings like a weather vane, stands for "post-colonial harmony and peace" – the reason why the army consider it a potential target for Sikh militants.

The rock garden

Close to the Capital Complex, and a refreshing counterpoint to Le Corbusier's drab concrete cityscape, is the bizarre **Rock Garden** (daily, April–Sept 9am–1pm & 3–7pm, Oct–March 9am–1pm & 2–6pm; Rs1) – a surreal fantasyland fashioned from fragments of shattered plates, neon strip lights, pots, pebbles, broken bangles and assorted urban-industrial junk. The open-air exhibition is the lifelong labour of retired Public Works Department road inspector, **Nek Chand**. Inspired by a recurrent childhood dream, he spent seven years scouring the stream beds of the Shivalik Hills for materials, and another nine on site before his vision was revealed to the public in 1976. CITCO's leaflet gives a wonderfully romantic rendition of Chand's toils: "Sitting by his hut, under the star-spangled Chandigarh sky, he used to burn cycle and auto-tires to provide him spotlight and, while his eyes profusely watered in the acrid smoke of the improvised fire . . . would patiently shape, stone by stone, an enchanted kingdom of his dreams."

Nearly forty years on, Nek Chand is still hard at work. His Rock Garden has expanded into a labyrinthine four-acre site that comprises more than a dozen different enclosures, interconnected by narrow passages, arched walkways, streams, and tiny bridges. Teeming on weekends with excited children and their parents, the complex also features several sculptural set-pieces: mostly birds, animals, and human figures, whose rigid stance and transfixed facial expressions take their cue from Indian *adivasi* (tribal) art. Stick to the path, or you could end up wandering the maze of pebble palaces and mock-Moghul ramparts until the *chowkidar* finds you at closing time.

Accommodation

Chandigarh's sky-high realty prices make its **accommodation** among the most expensive in India. Tariffs at the bottom end are particularly inflated, with no improvement in standards. If you want to spend less than Rs150, choice is limited to the train and bus stations' grim and noisy **retiring rooms** (①), or an airless cell in one of the many unlicensed budget guest houses (alias "tourist bungalows"), tucked away in quiet suburbs or backstreets, which the Municipality are forever trying to close down. Otherwise, try for an economy room in one of the mid-range hotels opposite the ISBT, or look for a vacancy in the cramped modern "motels" along the lane immediately behind these (in Sector 22): the best are the *Surya* (☎21037; ③) and the *Peeush* (☎20683; ③).

Luxury tax is not levied in Chandigarh, but several of the pricier places slap ten percent **service charges** on top of the bill. **Check-out time** for all the following is noon.

Alankar, Sector 22-A (☎21303). Modern, clean, and close to the bus stand. Some a/c. ④–⑤.

Amar, 806–6 Udyog Path, Sector 22-A (☎26608). The cheapest of three identikit hotels in this block (opposite the ISBT) has simple, tidy en-suite rooms with air-coolers, but no single occupancy. ③.

Aroma, Himalaya Marg, Sector 22-C (☎44463). Reasonably priced two-star with restaurant, lawn, pastry/coffee shop, and some good value non-a/c rooms. ④–⑤.

Baliji Tourist Bungalow, 534 Sector 36-B (☎536534). Small guesthouse in quiet suburb, 10min by rickshaw from Sector 17. All rooms have bathrooms, air-coolers, and hot water. Some a/c. ③–④.

MOVING ON FROM CHANDIGARH

Chandigarh's long-distance transport connections are summarized on p.496. As the train station is 8km from downtown, most travellers **move on** from the city by **bus**. Ordinary state buses operate out of the Inter-State Bus Terminus (ISBT) in Sector 17, as do additional tourist development corporation a/c, deluxe, and semi-deluxe services to destinations such as Delhi, Manali, and Amritsar. Buses run every five minutes to **Delhi** (248km; 5hr 30min–6hr), a journey which can be made in as little as 3hr 10min by train on the superfast a/c #2006 *Shatabdi Express* (depart 6.50am).

The quickest way to get to **Shimla** is by bus – direct *Himachal-* or *Haryana-SRTC* "express" services leave every 20–30min from the ISBT (3hr 30min–4hr). You can also get there on the slower but more congenial Viceroys' "Toy Train" (see p.408), but you have to catch a bus 26km northeast to **Kalka** first. For details of connecting services, see p.496.

Tickets for a/c, deluxe, and semi-deluxe bus services have to be pre-booked at the reservation hatches on the ground floor of the ISBT. For ordinary express buses, you can either buy your ticket at the booths on the platform, or pay the conductor. CITCO's tourist office in the ISBT has departure times and booking information.

Finally, *Indian Airlines* fly direct from Chandigarh to **Leh**, once a week (#IC481; Mon 9.35am; 1hr 30min). The flight tends to be less heavily booked than the more frequent Delhi–Leh service, and is thus worth considering if you want to get to Ladakh quickly but can't get a seat on a plane from the capital.

Airline offices in Chandigarh include *Air India*, #124, Sector 17 (Mon–Fri 9.30am–1pm & 2–5.30pm, Sat 9.30am–1pm; ☎544834); *Indian Airlines*, #171–2, Sector 17-C (Mon–Fri 10am–1pm & 2–5pm; ☎544539); *Japan Airlines*, Onkar Travels, Sector 17-B (☎32630); *Kuwait Airlines*, Trans Air Travels, Sector 17 (☎28333); *Lufthansa*, Bird Travels, Sector 17-C (☎29337); *Vayudoot*, Shivalik Travellers, Mini Hall, *Hotel Piccadilly*, Sector 22-B (Mon–Fri 10.30am–5.30pm; ☎32222 up to 32227).

ACCOMMODATION PRICE CODES

All **accommodation prices** in this book have been coded using the symbols below. In principle the prices given are for the least expensive double rooms in each establishment; however, some hotels, usually in category ①, offer rates per bed rather than per room. Local taxes are not included unless specifically stated. For more details, see p.34.

①	up to Rs100	④	Rs225–350	⑦	Rs750–1200
②	Rs100–150	⑤	Rs350–500	⑧	Rs1200–2200
③	Rs150–225	⑥	Rs500–750	⑨	Rs2200 and up

Chandigarh Tourist Bungalow, 97 Sector 21-A (☎23321). The best of the unlicensed "bungalows". Cleaner than average en-suite rooms (with windows), near the bus stand. Some a/c. ②–④.

Chandigarh Yatri Niwas, Sector 24 (☎24540). Municipal hostel, well out of centre. Very spartan, shared shower-toilets only, but clean and popular; call to see if it has vacancies. Some a/c. ②–④.

Mount View, Sector 10 (☎67146, fax 42111). Chandigarh's top hotel, in its own grounds 2km from downtown. Most amenities, including multi-cuisine restaurant, foreign exchange, and a pool. ⑥–⑦.

Piccadilly, Himalaya Marg, Sector 22-B (☎32223). Upmarket business-oriented hotel smack in the heart of the city with central a/c, classy restaurant, bar, coffee shop, and in-house travel agent. ⑥.

Shivalik View, Sector 17 (☎61731). The largest and swankiest hotel in the centre boasts a roof-top Chinese restaurant, 24hr cafe, and shopping arcade. ⑦.

Sunbeam, Udyog Path, Sector 22-B (☎41335). Top-notch hotel with swish marble lobby and most comforts: central a/c, coffee shop, foreign exchange. Good value for its class. ⑥–⑦.

Eating

Chandigarh has no shortage of **places to eat**, whether you just want to grab a quick snack between buses from a rough-and-ready roadside *dhaba*, or splash out on a classy Punjabi meal. Alcohol is widely available.

Amrit, Punjabi & Vinee, opposite the bus stand. Identical rock-bottom but hygienic *dhabas*; spicy piles of no-nonsense south Indian, Punjabi *tandoori*, and filling *chana batura* from formica tables.

Bhoj, #1090–1, Sector 22-B. Classy pure-veg *thali* joint run by Sai Baba devotees. Recommended.

Chopsticks, near *Hotel Piccadilly*, Himalaya Marg. Air-con Chinese restaurant with tinted windows and an impressive menu that includes some Indian options. Moderate.

Mehfil, Sector 17 (☎544224). The exclusive preserve of Chandigarh's smart set, *the* place to splurge on rich Mughlai and Punjabi cuisine in a/c comfort. Reservations for dinner.

Nikaha Chicken Corner, Udyog Path, Sector 22-B. No-frills *dhaba* serving large portions of cheap, spicy, and delicious chicken (*tandoori*, barbeque or freshly fried) to a beer-swilling male clientele.

Tasty Bite, Himalaya Marg. Snazzy south Indian fast food that specializes in veggie burgers, *dosas*, shakes and other light snacks. Moderate.

Listings

Emergency Police station ☎25600; for an ambulance, ☎44697.

Foreigners' Regional Registration Office Visas may be extended at the FRRO in the Town Hall Building, Sector 17 (Mon–Fri 10am–5pm).

Hospital Chandigarh's General Hospital is located in Sector 16 (☎44697).

Shopping Several states run handicraft emporiums in the Sector 17 shopping complex, among them Haryana, whose *Phulkari* store stocks a good range of embroidered silk, woodwork, and traditional pointy Punjabi shoes (*phulkari*). For quality handloom products, try the nearby UP emporium, or the *Khadi Gramodyog* in the *Shivalik View*'s small arcade: both are strong on block-printed calico garments, especially women's *shalwa camises*. Business hours are 10am–7.45pm.

Sport Rowing boats and pedalos can be rented on Sukhna Lake, in the north of the city. There are swimming pools in Sectors 14 (the University campus) & 23, 5min by rickshaw from the centre.

Sirhind

Close to the Grand Trunk Road (NH1) and *Northern Railway*, **SIRHIND**, 48km south-west of Chandigarh, was the capital of the Pathan Suri Sultans, and the site of an important *caravansarai* (the name derives from *Sir-i-Hind*, "Frontier of Hind"). Today, only a couple of minor-league Moghul palaces, hot baths, and pleasure pavilions remain from the illustrious past, but it is still a pleasant overnight stop between Delhi and Amritsar, just as it was when the emperors and their entourages passed through. Punjab Tourism (PTDC) have converted one building into a small **hotel**, where you can while away an evening on the verandah watching parakeets careening through the gardens, while devotional music drifts across the fields from the *gurudwara* (founded in memory of Guru Gobind Singh's two sons, stoned to death for not embracing Islam).

Sirhind's best-preserved **monuments** lie within walking distance of the hotel, encircled by the high walls of Sher Shah Sur's sixteenth-century **fort**. Approached via a tree- and fountain-lined walkway, the ruins of the old baths, or **hammam**, enclose a giant circular well whose water used to be hauled up by hand using pulleys, and channelled into geometric bathing pools outside. Nearby, the shell of emperor Shah Jahan's double-storey residence overlooks the leafy gardens and farmland. Originally decorated with ceramic tiles and elaborate stucco, only a few traces of painted plaster still cling to the exposed brickwork on the roof. Immediately behind PTDC's hotel, and in much better shape than the ruins at the opposite end of the garden, is the seventeenth-century **Sheesh Mahal**. The elegant "Palace of Mirrors", now an Archaeological Survey office, presides over a large tank whose ramparts you can walk around.

Practicalities

Regular **buses** run between Chandigarh and Sirhind (every 20min; 1hr 30min). The Moghul ruins and PTDC's *Maulsarai Tourist Complex* (④), known collectively as **Aam-Khas-Bagh**, lie 2.5km north of the town proper, 5km from a railway station served by trains from Delhi and Amritsar. Cycle rickshaws will ferry you out to the hotel for Rs20, but it is easier to jump off the bus as it passes the turn-off on the main road. Buses from Amritsar, usually drop passengers at the Grand Trunk Road intersection, 7km south of Aam-Khas-Bagh; catch a local bus into town to pick up a cycle rickshaw for the last leg.

The **hotel** itself, a small eighteenth-century summer palace, overlooks a well-watered garden on one side, and the old tank and Sheesh Mahal on the other. At Rs200 per night, its four large shabby rooms are overpriced, but full of character, with high ceilings and lots of peeling plaster. Inexpensive **food**, chilled beers, and cold drinks are served in the dining room, or *al fresco* on the tank-side terrace. **Mosquitoes** can be a problem, so if you do eat outside, slap on plenty of insect repellent.

Pinjore

Known in Aryan times as Panchpura, the walled **Yadavindra Gardens** at **PINJORE**, 22km north of Chandigarh on the Shimla road, is one of many sites associated with the exile of the Pandavas, chronicled in the *Mahabharata*. The well-watered beauty spot, at the foot of the Shivalik Hills 4km south of Kalka, originally belonged to the rajas of Sirmaur. Under the Moghuls, it was taken over by Aurangzeb's foster brother, Fidai Khan, who erected three pleasure palaces for his wife amid the cypress trees and lush *maidans*. Legend has it that the Raja reclaimed his summer retreat by sending a female fruit-seller with goitre as a present to the imposters. On being told that the woman's unsightly swelling was caused by the local water, the Begum and her entourage fled.

These days, the walled gardens harbour a small **otter sanctuary**, **aviary**, and **zoo**, and are a popular picnic spot. One of three attractive Moghul summer palaces has been converted by Haryana Tourism into a hotel, the bizarrely named *Budgerigar Motel* (④), which boasts half a dozen a/c rooms and is a convenient place to break a car journey between Delhi and Shimla. Local **buses** connect Pinjore with Kalka and Chandigarh.

Pathankot

The dusty town of **PATHANKOT**, at the end of the northbound railway line from Delhi near the border with Himachal Pradesh, is only worth passing through to pick up bus connections to Dharamsala, Dalhousie, Chamba and Kashmir, or to take the slow train east across the Kangra Valley. If you're stuck in town waiting for a connection, you can make a short excursion to the pale sandstone fort of **Shahpur Kandi**, 13km north. Now empty, this was in the sixteenth century a stronghold of the rajas of Pathan.

Practicalities

Pathankot can rustle up a few **hotels**, should you need to spend the night. *Hotel Airlines* on Post Office Chowk (☎20505; ①–②) has unspectacular but reasonable rooms, and a restaurant-cum-bar; the *Tourist Hotel and Restaurant* (☎20660; ②) on Railway Rd has unelaborate, fairly clean rooms with attached bath but little ventilation. The best bet, if you're lucky enough to find space, are the well-kept *Railway Retiring Rooms* (①–②); in addition to the usual basic ones, a couple of comfortable a/c rooms provide sofa and chairs, carpets, and a private bathroom with hot water.

Amritsar

The Sikh's holy city of **AMRITSAR**, site of the fabled **Golden Temple**, is the largest city in Punjab, an inevitable port of call for travellers heading to or from the Pakistani frontier crossing at Wagha, 35km west. If you are arriving from Lahore, you may find it a vibrant yet relaxed place, full of well-stocked bazaars and courteous people. Visitors bound for the border, however, tend to remember Amritsar as a run-of-the-mill Indian city: noisy, dirty, dusty, and hopelessly congested. Its one saving grace, and incentive enough to make a special trip out west, is the Golden Temple, which rises above the mêlée like an eye in a storm of teeming streets and tenement blocks.

Some history

Amritsar was founded in 1577 by **Ram Das**, the fourth Sikh Guru, beside a bathing pool famed for its healing powers. The land around the tank was granted in perpetuity by the Moghul Akbar to the Sikhs (who paid off the local Jat farmers regardless to avoid any future dispute over ownership). When merchants moved in to take advantage of the strategic location on the Silk Route, Amritsar expanded rapidly, gaining a grand new temple under Ram Das' son and heir, **Guru Arjan Singh**. Sacked by marauding Afghans in 1761, the shrine was eventually rebuilt by the Sikhs' greatest secular leader, **Maharajah Ranjit Singh**, who donated the gold top for which the temple would henceforth be renowned.

Amritsar's history in the **twentieth century** has been blighted by a series of appalling **massacres**. The first occurred in 1919, when thousands of unarmed civilian demonstrators were gunned down without warning by British troops in **Jallianwalla Bagh** – an atrocity that inspired Gandhi's Non-Cooperation Movement. Following the collapse of the Raj, Amritsar experienced some of the worst communal blood-letting ever seen in the subcontinent. The Golden Temple, however, remained unaffected by the volatile politics of post-Independence Punjab until the 1980s. As part of a protracted and bloody campaign for the setting up of a Sikh homeland, heavily armed fundamentalists under the charismatic preacher-warrior, Sant Jaranil Singh **Bhindranwale**, occupied the Akal Takht, symbol of Sikh militancy. The siege was brought to an end in early June 1984, when prime minister Indira Gandhi ordered an inept paramilitary attack on the temple, code-named **Operation Blue Star**. An estimated two hundred soldiers, and two thousand others (mostly pilgrims trapped in the *gurudwaras*), died.

Widely regarded as an unmitigated disaster, Blue Star led directly to the assassination of Indira Gandhi by her Sikh bodyguards just four months later, and provoked the worst riots in the city since Partition. Nevertheless, the Congress government seemed to learn little from its mistakes. In 1987, Indira's son, Rajiv Gandhi, reneged on an important accord with the Sikhs' main religious party, the Akali Dal, thereby strengthening the hand of the separatists, who retaliated by occupying the temple for a second time. This time, the army responded with greater restraint, leaving **Operation Black Thunder** to the Punjab police. Neither as well-provisioned nor as well-motivated as Bhindranwale's martyrs, the fundamentalists eventually surrendered. The defeat proved a major set-back for their cause, and today, Amritsar is no more unstable than most other north Indian cities with a culturally mixed population of more than 700,000.

Arrival and information

Amritsar's quiet domestic **airport**, arrival point for *Indian Airlines* flights from Delhi and Srinagar, lies 12km northwest of the city. **Trains** pull in at the railway station on the northern edge of the centre, 2km west of the inter-state bus stand, and a ten-minute auto-rickshaw ride from PTDC's **tourist office** (Mon–Fri 9am–5pm; ☎231452). It is hard to think of any reason why you might want to call in here, but the staff are helpful. To obtain reliable bus and train information, join the rucks at the respective stations.

If you are not staying in one of Amritsar's few hotels with a foreign exchange facility, **changing money** can be a time-consuming business. The easiest bank to find, if not the most efficient, is the *State Bank of India* (Mon–Fri 10am–2pm, Sat 10am–noon), halfway between the bus stand and the Golden Temple.

Luggage can be left for short periods at the Golden Temple's *gurudwaras* (see below), or, provided it is securely locked, at the railway station cloakroom.

City transport

Amritsar is too large and labyrinthine to negotiate on foot. If you are crossing town or in a hurry, flag down an (un-metered) **auto-rickshaw**. Otherwise, stick to **cycle rickshaws**, which are the best way to get around the narrow, packed streets of the old quarter. **Taxi** *wallahs* tout for trade outside the train station (northern exit, turn left), and the *Ritz Hotel* in the north of the city. Alternatively, rent a **bicycle** from one of the stalls lined up on the main road outside the bus stand.

The City

The Golden Temple stands in the heart of the **old town**: a disorientating maze of narrow lanes and bazaars encircled by a broad thoroughfare. Eighteen fortified **gateways** punctuate the aptly named **Circular Rd**, of which only one (to the north) is original. Skirting the edge of the old quarter, the railway line, crossed by a series of chaotic road bridges, forms a sharp divide between the bazaar and the more spacious British-built side of the city. Most of the hotels and restaurants are located in this district, around the Maginot-Line-style **railway station**. Further north, long straight tree-lined streets full of fast-moving traffic eventually peter out into leafy residential suburbs,

The telephone **area code** for Amritsar is ☎0183.

△ Delhi

i HPTDC

CIRCULAR RD

H **I**

Jallianwala Bagh

RAMGHARIA BAZAAR

Bus Stand

CHITTI WIND BAZAAR

MUKHRIAN BAZAAR

Golden Temple

J

BOHRI BAZAAR

SHIWALLA BHALAN RD

HALL BAZAAR

SHAROPA NAND BAZAAR

NIMAK MANDI

LAHORI BAZAAR

HUKMA SINGH RD

Ram Bagh

2

F **G**

DELHI RD (NH1)

CIRCULAR RD

KHAZANA BAZAAR

Cole Bagh

DELI RAM BAZAAR

1

TAYLOR RD

C Indian Airlines

MALL RD

A

GPO

D **E**

QUEENS RD

LINKS RD

ALBERT RD

St Paul's

Railway Station

▲ Durgiana

Fort

COURT RD

GOBINDGARH RD

ISLAMABAD RD

RAM TIRATH RD

B

△ Airport

N

0   500 m

AMRITSAR

HOTELS:
A Mohan International
B Mrs Bhandari's Guest House
C Ritz
D Pegasus Palace
E Grand
F Airlines
G Tourist Guest House
H Dhabas
I PTDC Amritsar International
J Sita Niwas

RESTAURANTS:
1 Kwality
2 Sindhi Kitchen

peppered with run-down churches and colonial bungalows. The fastidiously neat military barracks of the **cantonment** form the northwestern limits of the city.

The Golden Temple

Even visitors without a religious bone in their bodies cannot fail to be moved by Amritsar's resplendent **Golden Temple**, spiritual centre of the Sikh faith. Built by Guru **Arjan Singh** in the late sixteenth century, the richly gilded **Hari Mandir** rises from the middle of a rectangular artificial lake, connected to the toothpaste-white marble complex that surrounds it by a narrow causeway. For Sikhs, this serene spectacle is as sacred as the Ka'aba and Mecca are for Muslims. Every devout member of the faith tries to make at least one pilgrimage here in their lifetime for *darshan* of the original Sikh holy book, the *Adi Granth*, and to bathe in the purifying waters of the temple tank, known since the time of the fourth Guru, **Ram Das** (1574–81), as the **Amrit Sarovar**: "Pool of Immortality-Giving Nectar".

The Golden Temple is also renowned for the two bloody battles waged in the 1980s between Sikh militants and the Indian army and police. However, since Operations **Blue Star** and **Black Thunder**, things have calmed down considerably, and life inside the complex has returned to normal. Ugly scars remain, but most of the bullet-holes and shell craters have been patched up, and the once-conspicuous military presence in the surrounding alleys and squares is now very low-key.

The best time to visit the temple is on a weekday morning before it is swamped by crowds. Get here early enough, and you'll catch the first rays of sunlight gleaming on the shrine's bulbous golden domes, whose shimmering reflection in the water of the Amrit Sarovar, enlivened by devotional songs (**kirtans**) emanating from the inner sanctum, is something to savour.

THE PARIKRAMA

The principal north entrance to the temple, the **Darshini Darwaza**, leads under a Victorian **clock tower**, which caught fire during Operation Black Thunder, to the head of a flight of steps, from where you catch your first glimpse of the majestic Hari Mandir, floating serenely above the glassy surface of the Amrit Sarovar. Dropping down as a reminder of the humility necessary to approach God, the steps end at the polished marble **Parikrama** that surrounds the tank, its smooth white stones set with the names of Sikh worthies who contributed to the temple's construction. A long colonnaded verandah opens onto the sacred pavement, always circled in a clockwise direction.

The shrines on the north edge of the enclosure are known as the **68 Holy Places**. Arun Singh, the fifth Guru, told his followers that a visit to these was equivalent to a pilgrimage around all 68 of India's most sacred Hindu sites. Several have been converted into a **Gallery of Martyrs** in which paintings of glorious but very gory episodes from Sikh history are displayed.

Four glass-fronted booths punctuate the Parikrama. Seated in each is a priest, or **granthi**, intoning verses from the *Adi Granth*. The continuous readings take 48 hours to complete and are performed in three-hour shifts; passing pilgrims touch the steps in front of the booths with their heads and leave offerings of money.

GOLDEN RULES

Visitors of all nationalities and religions are allowed into the Golden Temple provided they respect a few basic **rules**, enforced by patrolling guards. Firstly, tobacco, alcohol, and drugs of any kind are forbidden. Before entering, you should also leave your shoes at the free cloakrooms, cover your head with some kind of cloth (cotton scarves are sold for Rs5 at the shops right of the main entrance), and wash your feet in the pool below the steps. **Photography** is permitted on the *parikrama*, but not inside any of the shrines.

At the east end of the Parikrama, the two truncated **Ramgarhia Minars** – brick watchtowers whose tops were blasted off during Operation Blue Star – overlook the Guru-ka-Langar and the main bathing **ghats**. Hang around here long enough, and you'll see a fair cross-section of modern Sikh society parade past: families of Jat farmers, NRIs (Non-Resident Indians) on holiday from Britain and North America flaunting flash video cameras, and the odd group of fierce-looking warriors carrying lances, sabres and long curved daggers. Distinguished by their deep-blue knee-length robes and saffron turbans, the ultra-orthodox **nihangs** (literally "crocodiles") are devotees of the militaristic tenth Guru Gobind Singh.

THE GURU-KA-LANGAR

For Sikhs, no pilgrimage to the Golden Temple is considered complete without a visit to the **Guru-ka-Langar**. The giant communal canteen, which overlooks the eastern entrance to the temple complex, provides **free food** to all-comers, regardless of creed, colour, caste or gender. Sharing meals with strangers in this way is intended to reinforce one of the central tenets of the Sikh faith, the **principle of equality**, instigated by the third Guru, **Amar Das**, in the sixteenth century to break down caste barriers.

The tradition of commensality is still practised in *gurudwaras* all over India, but nowhere more forcefully reaffirmed than here at the Langar. Some ten thousand *chapati* and black *dal* dinners are dished up each day in an operation of typical Sikh efficiency, which you can witness for yourself by joining the queues that form outside the hall at meal times (daily 11am–3pm & 7–9pm). When the doors open, up to three thousand pilgrims at a time pile in to take their places on the long coir floor mats. The meal begins only after grace has been sung with great solemnity by one of the Langar's volunteers, or *sevaks*, and continues until everyone has eaten their fill. By the time the tin trays have been collected up and the floors swept for the next sitting, another crowd of hungry pilgrims has gathered at the gates, and the cycle starts again. Although the meals are paid for out of the temple's coffers, most visitors leave a small donation in the boxes in the yard outside.

THE AKAL TAKHT

Directly opposite the ceremonial entrance to the Hari Mandir, the **Akal Takht** is the second most sacred shrine in the Golden Temple complex. A symbol of God's authority on earth, it was built by Gobind Singh in the seventeenth century to house the *Shiroman Gurudwara Parbandhak* committee, the religious and political governing body of the Sikh faith, which he founded.

During the 1984 siege, **Bhindranwale** and his army used the golden-domed building as a headquarters, fortifying it with sandbags and machine-gun posts. When Indian paratroopers tried to storm the shrine, they were mown down in their hundreds while crossing the courtyard in front of it: the reason why the army ultimately resorted to much heavier-handed tactics to end the siege. Positioned at the opposite end of the Amrit Sarovar, tanks pumped a salvo of high-explosive squash-head shells into the delicate facade, reducing it to rubble within seconds. The destruction of the Akal Takht offended Sikh sensibilities more than any other aspect of the operation.

The shrine has largely been rebuilt and now looks almost the same as it did before June 6, 1984. Decorated with elaborate inlay, its ground floor is where the *Adi Granth* is brought each evening from the Hari Mandir, borne in a gold and silver *palladin*.

THE JUBI TREE

The gnarled old **Jubi Tree** in the northwest corner of the compound was planted 450 years ago by the Golden Temple's first High Priest, or *Babba Buddhaya*, and is believed to have special powers. Barren women wanting a son hang strips of cloth from its branches, while marriage deals are traditionally struck in its shade for good luck – a practice frowned upon by the modern temple administration. Most days, Sikh *sevaks*, or religious volunteers, can also be seen beneath the tree polishing blocks of marble for use in the reconstruction of the Akal Takht.

THE HARI MANDIR

Likened by one Guru to "a ship crossing the ocean of ignorance", the triple-storeyed **Hari Mandir**, the "Golden Temple of God" from which the complex takes its name, was built by Arjan Singh to house the *Adi Granth*, or "Original Book", which he compiled, and which still forms the lynchpin of the Sikh faith. Instead of the usual single door, the temple has four to indicate that it is open to all four caste divisions of Hindu society. The large dome on its gilded roof, decked with 100kg of gold leaf, is in the form of an inverted lotus, symbolizing the Sikhs' concern for temporal as well as spiritual matters.

The long causeway, or **"Guru's Bridge"**, which joins the Mandir to the west side of the Sarovar, is approached via an ornate archway, the **Darshani Deorhi**, where worshippers collect dollops of sticky sweet wheaten porridge on a leaf: **prasad** that will later be placed as an offering in the shrine itself. As you approach the sanctum, check out the amazing Moghul-style marble inlay on its sides, and the beautiful floral gilt above the doors and windows.

The **interior** of the temple, dripping in yet more gold and silver, and adorned with ivory mosaics and intricately carved wood panels, is dominated by the enormous **Adi Granth**, which rests on a sumptuous throne beneath a jewel-encrusted silk canopy. Before his death in 1708, Guru Gobind Singh, who revised the "Original Book", declared that he was to be the last living Guru, and that the tome would take over after

---

THE JALLIANWALLA BAGH MASSACRE

Only 100m northeast of the Golden Temple, a narrow lane leads between two tall buildings to **Jallianwalla Bagh** memorial park (winter 10am–4pm, summer 9am–5pm), site of one of the bloodiest atrocities committed in the history of the British Raj.

In 1919, a series of one-day strikes, or *hartals*, was staged in Amritsar in protest against the recent **Rowlatt Act**, which enabled the British to imprison without trial any Indian suspected of sedition. When the peaceful demonstrations escalated into sporadic looting, the Lieutenant Governor of Punjab declared martial law and called for reinforcements from Jalandhar. A platoon of infantry arrived soon after, led by **General REH Dyer**.

Despite a ban on public meetings, a mass demonstration was called by Mahatma Gandhi for April 13, the Sikh holiday of Bhaisakhi. The venue was to be a round-bottomed stretch of waste ground in the heart of the city, hemmed in by high brick walls and with only a couple of alleys for access. An estimated 20,000 people gathered in Jallianwalla Bagh for the meeting. However, before any speakers could address the crowd, Dwyer and his 150 troops, stationed on a patch of high ground in front of the main exit, opened fire without warning. By the time they had finished firing, ten to fifteen minutes later, thousands of unarmed demonstrators lay dead and dying, many of them shot in the back while trying to clamber over the walls. Others perished after diving for cover into the well that still stands in the middle of the *bagh*.

No one knows exactly how many people were killed. Official estimates put the death toll at 372, with 1200 injured, although the final figure may well have been three to four times higher. Hushed up for over six months in Britain, the Jallianwalla Bagh massacre caused an international outcry when the story finally broke. It also proved seminal in the independence struggle, prompting Gandhi to initiate the widespread civil disobedience campaign that played such a significant part in ridding India of its colonial overlords.

Moving first-hand accounts of the horrific events of April 13, 1919, together with contemporary pictures and newspaper reports, are displayed in Jallianwalla Bagh's small **martyrs gallery**. The **well**, complete with chilling bullet holes, has been turned into a memorial to the victims.

him: hence its full title, the *Guru Granth Sahib*. *Granthis* intone continuous readings from the text as the worshippers file past, accompanied by singers and musicians, whose ethereal performance is relayed by loudspeakers around the complex.

Accommodation

Amritsar's numerous **hotels** are spread out all over the city. While mid-range and upscale accommodation is plentiful, budget options are few and far between, limited to the Golden Temple's rudimentary *gurudwaras* (see below), or the *Tourist Guest House*, on the main road between the bus stand and the train station, which commission-hungry rickshaw *wallahs* will try to tell you is full.

Airlines, Queens Rd. Solid mid-price hotel near the train station. All en-suite rooms, with TVs, carpets, some a/c, and swings, believe it or not. ④–⑥.

Grand, opposite the railway station (☎62977). Neat, clean, convenient and central: the best deal in its category in the city centre. ③–④.

Mohan International, Albert Rd (☎27801). Amritsar's top hotel has all the trimmings, including central a/c, swish restaurant, coffee shop, bathtubs, and a pool, but is looking a touch run-down. ⑦.

Mrs Bhandari's Guest House, 10 Cantonment (☎64247). Separate chalets in *pukka* colonial home, complete with original 1950s fittings, furniture, and feel. Camping/parking space in the garden popular with overlanders. Not cheap, but worth the extra for the novelty. Recommended. ⑤.

Pegasus Palace, opposite the train station (☎65111). Unappealing, but the cleanest of the dives around the station, and a good fall-back if the *Tourist Guest House* is full. ②.

PTDC Amritsar International, off Delhi Rd (☎31991). Modern, bland government-run hotel near the bus stand, with a restaurant, and some a/c. ④–⑤.

Ritz, 45 The Mall (☎226606). Stylish, slightly old-fashioned hotel in quiet suburb just north of city centre, with lawns, gym, and a pool. Recommended. ⑦.

Sita Niwas, near *Guru Ram Das Niwas* and Golden Temple (☎43092). A good budget option if the *gurudwara* doesn't appeal. Variously priced rooms, all with windows and a recent lick of paint. 24hr hot water and some attached bathrooms also available. ②–③.

Tourist Guest House, Hide Market, near Bhandari Bridge, GT Rd (☎33130). The one place pitched at budget travellers; a shabby vestige of the "hippy trail" days, run by a retired army officer. Avoid the rooms at the back next to the railway, and the absurdly overpriced food, served on a verandah. ②.

Eating

Amritsar boasts a clutch of swish air-conditioned **restaurants**, most of them located in the modern end of town north of the railway. For cheaper food, try the no-nonsense

---

THE GURUDWARAS

Undoubtedly the most authentic places to stay in Amritsar are the Golden Temple's two **gurudwaras**. Intended for use by Sikh pilgrims, these charitable institutions also open their doors to foreign tourists, who can stay for a maximum of three nights. Lodging is free, as is the Sikh custom, but donations are gratefully accepted. Of the pair, the *Sri Guru Ram Das Niwas* is the larger, while the neighbouring *Sri Guru Nanak Niwas* (where Bhindranwale and his men holed up prior to the Golden Temple siege in 1984) also offers a limited number of double rooms with attached shower-toilets. A charge is made for these, but they're still a bargain at only Rs15 per night.

Apart from the inevitable dawn chorus of throat-clearing, the downside of staying in a *gurudwara* is that facilities are very basic (*charpoi* beds and communal wash basins in the central courtyard), and **security** a real problem: mug shots of thieves caught stealing pilgrims' possessions are displayed at the main entrance. If space is limited, as it nearly always is during temple festivals, tourists tend to be rounded up and crammed into a bed-less, airless dorm, prompting most to decamp for more congenial quarters elsewhere.

vegetarian **dhabas** opposite the Golden Temple, or the bus stand, where a pile of hot *puris* and spicy *chana dal* will set you back less than Rs20.

Kwality, Mall Rd. Inexpensive, hygienic south Indian snack bar-cum-ice-cream parlour, in addition to the usual dimly lit a/c restaurant.

Mrs Bhandari's, 10 Cantonment (☎64247). Homely "British-style" 3-course meals (pudding and custard for afters) cooked in Mrs B's "Commando Bridge" kitchen. Reservations essential for non-residents. Moderate to expensive.

Palace, ground floor, *Hotel Pegasus Palace*, opposite railway station. A jumped-up *dhaba* serving generous piles of non-veg Indian food, mainly *biryanis* and chicken dishes. Cheap, but low on atmosphere.

Sindhi Kitchen, opposite Ram Bagh. Tinted windows and table cloths, and an exhaustive mixed-cuisine menu that includes several Sindhi specialities. Moderate to expensive.

Listings

Church St Paul's Catholic Church on Albert Rd opposite the train station holds mass daily at 8am during the summer, or 8.30am in winter.

Hospital Amritsar's Kakkar House Hospital, on Mall Rd near Customs House Chowk (☎62063) is the best in the city. For an ambulance, ☎24060.

Shopping *Tablas* (hand-drums), harmonia and other musical instruments are available at the shops outside the Golden Temple, where you can also buy cheap cassettes of the beautiful *kirtans* played in the shrine itself. Other possible souvenirs of Amritsar include a pair of traditional *Arabian Nights*-style Punjabi leather slippers – sold at stalls east of the temple's main entrance. While you are there, keep an eye out for the man who distributes religious pamphlets that include: *Cleaning Up The Ganges*, *The Cow and Peace*, and, most intriguingly of all, *Human Hair; A Factory Of Vital Energy*.

Swimming Pools Both the *Mohan International* and *Ritz* hotels charge non-residents Rs50 to use their outdoor pools (towels not included).

MOVING ON FROM AMRITSAR

Amritsar is a major hub for traffic heading northeast to Jammu & Kashmir, southeast towards Delhi via Chandigarh (the main jumping-off place for Shimla and central HP), and westwards to India's only land-border crossing point with Pakistan at Wagha.

Buses to **Delhi** (9 daily; 10hr) are considerably less comfortable and slower than travelling by rail. The best trains (7hr 30min) to aim for are the #2460 *Amritsar–New Delhi Express* (departs 6.20am) or the #2498 *Shane–Punjab Express* (2.30pm). *Indian Airlines* also fly four times each week between Amritsar and Delhi (55min). Tickets cost Rs1256 and can be booked or reconfirmed at the computerized *IA* office at 16 The Mall, near the *Ritz Hotel* (Mon–Fri 10am–1pm & 2–5pm; ☎66433).

Heading for **Pakistan**, you're better off taking the bus. Two services each day, at 10.30am and 11.30am, leave Amritsar for **Wagha**, 35km west (45min). Before you get on, make sure the bus goes all the way to Wagha and not just to **Atari**, several kilometres east of the border (open daily 9am–4pm). Basic accommodation in PTDC's *Neem Chameli Tourist Complex* (③) is available at Wagha if you get stuck; onward connections to Lahore from the Pakistani side of the frontier are generally good. The same trip by train, however, invariably takes longer than the scheduled four hours, as the daily *Indo–Pak Express* (#4607; departs 9.30am) tends to get fouled up at customs; delays occasionally run into the night. Foreign travellers coming from Lahore should also avoid this train, which, if it happens to be carrying a large contingent of Pakistanis (who are not officially allowed to alight in the Punjab), won't stop in Amritsar.

For a full rundown of destinations reachable by train and bus from Amritsar, see p.496.

CHAPTER EIGHT

GUJARAT

The western state of **GUJARAT** – the wealthiest in India – sees relatively few tourists, but it rewards those who do come not only with important temple cities, forts and palaces, but also the chance to search out unique crafts made in tribal communities whose vivid costumes, dances and music remain little affected by modern innovations. Gujarat's foreign trade, started by the **Harappans** in the third millennium BC, was based on the export of goods such as shell jewellery and textiles, many of which still provide major sources of income for the state.

As so often in India, Gujarat's **architectural diversity** reflects the influences of its many different rulers – the Buddhist Mauryans, who also supported the Jain faith, Hindu rajas, and Muslim emperors who combined their skills and tastes with Hindu craftsmanship to produce remarkable mosques, tombs and palaces. **Ahmedabad**, state capital until 1970 and the obvious place to begin a tour, harbours the first mosques to be built in the curious **Indo-Islamic** style, plus richly carved temples and step-wells dating to the eleventh century. Fascinating residential areas are lined with tall wooden residential *havelis*, carved in finest detail by prosperous merchants from the eighteenth century onwards. From Ahmedabad it's an easy trip north to the ancient capital of **Patan** and the Solanki sun temple at **Modhera**, or south to the excavated Harappan site at **Lothal**. Continuing south, the thin coastal strip, followed by the main railway line from Ahmedabad to Bombay, features a few towns of lesser interest, among them the old Portuguese port of **Daman** in the far south.

The Kathiawar peninsula, also known as **Saurashtra**, is the true heartland of Gujarat, liberally scattered with temples, mosques, forts and palaces that bear testimony to centuries of rule by Buddhists, Hindus and Muslims. Architectural highlights here include the superb Jain temples on the hills of **Shatrunjaya**, near Bhavnagar, and **Girnar** close to Junagadh. The coastal temple at **Somnath** is said to have witnessed the dawn of time, and that at **Dwarka** to be built on the site of Krishna's ancient capital. At **Junagadh**, rocks bearing two-thousand-year-old inscriptions from the reign of Ashoka stand a stone's throw from curious mausolea and Gothic mansions built by the Muslims in the nineteenth century. There's plenty of scope for spotting **wildlife**, too, in

GUJARAT TRAVEL DETAILS

	Trains		Buses		Flights	
	Frequency	Time	Frequency	Time	Frequency	Time
To and From AHMEDABAD						
Abu Road	6 daily	3hr 20min–6hr	2 daily	7hr		
Agra	1 daily	24hr 15min				
Ajmer	5 daily	8hr 30min–20hr				
Bangalore					3 weekly	2hr
Bhavnagar	1 daily	6hr	10 daily	5–6hr		
Bhuj	1 daily	16hr 45min	3 daily	8hr		
Bombay	8 daily	7hr 30min–11hr	3 daily	11hr	2 daily	1hr
Calcutta	1 daily	44hr				
Delhi	6 daily	16–25hr			2 daily	1hr 25min
Diu			1 daily	8hr		
Dwarka	1 daily	10hr				
Indore			1 nightly	10–11hr		
Jaipur	5 daily	11hr 25min–25hr				
Jamnagar	2 daily	7hr	4 daily	9hr		
Jodhpur	3 daily	9–13hr	2 daily	10–12hr		
Junagadh	2 daily	10hr 25min	4 daily	6–8hr		
Madras	4 weekly	35hr			3 weekly	2hr 15min
Palitana			10 daily	4hr 30min		
Porbandar	1 daily	10hr	1 daily	9hr		
Rajkot	4 daily	4–6hr	4 daily	6–7hr		
Surat	1 daily	4hr	5 daily	6–7hr		
Udaipur	1 daily	9hr	6 daily	6hr		
Ujjain	3 daily	9hr				
Una			6 daily	8hr		
Vadodara	5 daily	1hr 30min	8 daily	3–4hr	1 daily	30min
Varanasi	1 daily	43hr				
Veraval	2 daily	13hr				
To and From Bhavnagar						
Bhuj			16 daily	12hr		
Bombay					4 weekly	50min
Junagadh			4 daily	6–7hr		
Palitana			16 daily	1hr 30min		
Rajkot			10 daily	4hr		
Una			12 daily	5hr 30min		
To and From Bhuj						
Bombay					Mon & Sun	1hr
Gandhidham	3 daily	2hr	3 daily	1hr		
Junagadh			3 daily	9hr		
Palanpur	2 daily	12hr				
Rajkot			3 daily	5–6hr		
To and From Diu						
Bombay					3 weekly	1hr 10min
Rajkot			1 daily	6hr 30min	3 weekly	1hr 50min
Una			8 daily	40min		
Veraval			2 daily	2–3hr		
To and From Dwarka						
Bombay	1 daily	20hr				
Jamnagar	1 daily	2hr 30min	2 daily	3hr		
Junagadh			4 daily	4hr 30min		
Porbandar			10 daily	3hr		
Rajkot	1 daily	5hr				
Veraval			hourly	5–6hr		

	Trains		Buses		Flights	
	Frequency	Time	Frequency	Time	Frequency	Time
To and From Junagadh						
Jamnagar			1 daily	3hr		
Palitana			1 daily	3hr 50min		
Porbandar			16 daily	1hr 45min		
Rajkot	1 daily	3hr 30min	16 daily	2hr		
Sasan Gir	1 daily	2hr 30min	4 daily	2hr		
Una	1 daily	5hr 40min	3 daily	2–4hr		
Veraval	3 daily	2hr 30min	5 daily	2–3hr		
To and From Porbandar						
Bombay					4 weekly	1hr 30min
Jamnagar	1 daily	2hr 45min				
Rajkot	1 daily	4hr 20min	5 daily	5hr		
Una			2 daily	4–5hr		
Veraval			15 daily	2hr 40min		
To and From Rajkot						
Bhuj					Mon & Sun	35min
Bombay	3 daily	15–18hr			Mon & Sun	2hr 10min
Jamnagar	2 daily	2hr 40min	16 daily	2hr		
Una			6 daily	6hr		
Vadodara	1–2 daily	7hr				
Veraval	1 daily	4hr	16 daily	5–6hr		
To and From Una						
Palitana			1 daily	8hr		
Sasan Gir	1 daily	3hr 30min	5 daily	1–2hr		
Veraval			hourly	2–3hr		
To and From Vadodara						
Baruch			hourly	1hr 30min		
Bombay					1 daily	55min
Calcutta	1 daily	40hr 40min				
Delhi	4 daily	12hr 30min–23hr			1 daily	1hr 25min
Gandhidham	1 daily	8hr				
Indore	3 daily	8–10hr				
Pune	2 weekly	10hr 30min				
Surat	2 weekly	2hr	hourly	2–3hr		

Note that no individual route appears more than once in this chart; check against where you want to get to as well as where you're coming from.

particular the lions in **Gir Forest** and herds of strutting black buck at **Velavadar**. Separated from the south coast by a thin sliver of the Arabian Sea, the island of **Diu**, fringed with beaches, leafy palm groves and the whitewashed spires of Portuguese churches, provides an idyllic setting for lazy sun-kissed days.

In the northwest, the largely barren region of **Kutch** – often cut off from the rest of the state by vast tracts of flooded marshland – was bypassed by Gujarat's successive waves of foreign invaders. Consequently, this intriguing area preserves a village culture where crafts long forgotten elsewhere are practised with age-old skill.

Geographically Gujarat takes a little from each of its neighbours: with forested hilly tracts and fertile plains in the south and east, dry desert sands in the northwest, and a wide stretch of coast, in parts sandy, and in parts rocky and barren, that includes the coral enriched shoreline close to **Jamnagar**. It can become unbearably hot in summer, though a cool sea breeze does relieve the tension of heavy pre-monsoon days along the coast. The **best time to visit** is in the warm pleasant months between October and

February, when you may also encounter traditional music and dances at numerous festivals. Thanks to extensive road and train links, **travel** within Gujarat presents few problems, but communication barriers do require a little effort to overcome (few timetables are written in English). You'll also need stamina to negotiate the booking requirements for slow train journeys and to endure long rides on rickety local buses that are supplemented by newer private vehicles in only a few larger towns.

You'll be hard pushed to find a luxury **hotel** outside Ahmedabad, and many places hold little choice of accommodation beyond spartan lodges. As for **food**, which is predominantly vegetarian, Gujarat's good-value *thalis* are renowned for their size and sweetness. Note that the state operates severe **alcohol restrictions**: to enjoy a cold beer, you'll have to head to the Union Territory enclaves of Daman and Diu.

Some history

The first known settlers in what is now Gujarat were the **Harappans**, who appeared from Punjab in around 2500 BC and established over a hundred towns and cities. Their skilful craftsmanship, combined with important trade links with Africans, Arabs, Persians and Europeans, won them prosperity; despite this, the civilization fell into decline in 1900 BC, largely because of severe flooding around the Indus delta. From 1500 to 500 BC the **Yadavas**, the clan that had Krishna among its ranks, held sway over much of Gujarat, with their capital at Dwarka on the western tip of Saurashtra.

Gujarat's political history begins in earnest with the powerful **Mauryan empire**, established by Chandragupta with its capital at Junagadh, then known as Girinagar, and reaching its peak under Ashoka. After his death in 226 BC, Mauryan power dwindled; the last significant Mauryan ruler was Samprati, Ashoka's grandson, a Jain who built fabulous temples at *tirthas* – pilgrimage sites – such as Girnar and Palitana.

In the first century AD the Western **Satraps**, members of the Saka, or Scythian, tribes, gained control over Saurashtra. They ruled it until soon after 388 AD, before being supplanted first by the **Guptas** and then by the **Maitrakas**, who established their capital at Valabhi. The ensuing centuries saw the arrival of the northern Gurjar tribes, who were to give the state its name, and the Kathi tribespeople from the northwest, who established several independent petty states in Saurashtra. The rulers of Sind (now in Pakistan) meanwhile dominated western Gujarat, including Kutch.

In the eleventh and twelfth centuries Saurashtra came under the sway of the **Solanki** (or Chauhan) dynasty; their splendid Jain temples suffered during the raids of Mahmud of Ghazni in 1027. The advent of Muslim rule under the Khaljis in the thirteenth century marked the beginning of over two centuries of Islamic government in Gujarat, for the most part controlled from Ahmedabad. In this period Muslim taste and Jain and Hindu styles were melded to produce remarkable Indo-Islamic mosques and tombs, characterized by the elaborate carvings found in Jain temples, and intersected in Hindu fashion by slender pillars meeting in delicate arches. Contrary to impressions encouraged by recent sectarian violence, particularly in Ahmedabad, Islam never eclipsed Hinduism or Jainism, and the three have lived side by side for centuries.

In the sixteenth century, the **Portuguese**, already settled in Goa, turned their attention to the Gujarati coast, aware of the excellent potential of its ports and its long history of trade. Having captured Daman (1531), they took Diu (1535), building forts and typically European towns and coming to dominate the oceans with the imposition of high taxes and import duties. Fending off Arab and Muslim attacks, the Portuguese governed the ports until they were subsumed by the Indian Union in the 1960s.

The **British East India Company** set up its original Indian headquarters in Surat in 1613, and soon established their first "factory", a self-contained village for labourers' and merchants' houses and warehouses, sowing the seeds of a prospering textile industry. When British sovereignty was established in 1818 governor-generals moved into some of Gujarat's main cities, though the peninsula of Saurashtra never passed

A GUJARATI GLOSSARY

Although **Gujarati** takes some words from Hindi, and follows the same grammatical rules, it is a distinct language and sounds very different. Only in the largest towns can you make yourself understood in Hindi: a little knowledge of Gujarati can go a very long way. Note that the final "e" in words such as *mane* is pronounced "eh", a softer form of the English "ai", as in "tail". The "u" is pronounced in roughly the same way as in "pull".

Traditional greeting (hello)	*kemcho*	I am unwell	*Mane saru nati*
Traditional reply	*majama*	How much is this?	*A ketla nu che?*
Goodbye	*alljo*	What time is it?	*Ketla wai ga?*
What is your name?	*Tamaru naam su che?*	When does the train leave?	*Gadi ketla waige jawanni?*
My name is (Indira)	*Maru naam (Indira) che*	When does the train arrive?	*Gadi ketla waige awanni?*
Where are you from?	*Tame kya tin aiwa?*	Food	*khouwa/jahmawu*
I am from (Ireland)	*Hu (Ireland) tin aiwa chu*	Rice	*bhat*
Please	*maafkaro*	Salt	*mithu*
Thank you	*abar/abarho*	Sugar	*khan*
Yes	*ha*	Tea	*char*
No	*na*	Water	*paani*
Where is the doctor's?	*Doctor-ni syrgery kya che?*	Milk	*dhood*
Where is the chemist?	*Chemist-ni kya che?*	Vegetables	*sakbhaji*
Where is the railway station?	*Railway station kya che?*	Bag	*baggage*
Where is (Raja Lodge)?	*(Raja Lodge) kya che?*	Temple	*mandir*
Do you have any rooms?	*Tumari pass ke camera che?*	Brother	*bhai*
What food do you have?	*Aya khouwa ma su che?*	Sister	*bhen*
		Husband	*dhani*
How are you?	*tam eh kemcho*	Wife	*bhairi*
I am fine	*tik che*	Friend	*doorst* (male), *bhen pani* (female)

into British control and remained an amalgamation of over two hundred petty states until Independence. British rule brought mixed results; while machinery upgraded textile manufacture and brought substantial wealth to the region, many manual labourers were put out of business. Their cause was valiantly fought by Gujarat-born **Mahatma Gandhi**, whose campaigns for Independence and social equity brought international attention to his ashram in Ahmedabad. After Partition, due to its position bordering the new Muslim state of Pakistan, Gujarat received an influx of Hindus from Sind and witnessed terrible sectarian fighting as Muslims fled to their new homeland.

Gujarat state was formed in 1960, incorporating much of what, after Independence, had been Bombay state; the Portuguese enclaves, along with Goa, were forcibly annexed by the Indian government in 1961. Since Independence Gujarat has been a Congress stronghold, with temporary losses to the Janata party in 1977 and the BJP in 1991. Today Gujarat's textile industry is still the largest in India, with the trading of the business-minded Jain community helping to maintain its wealth.

Ahmedabad

AHMEDABAD, a mass of factories, mosques, temples and high-rise offices, sprawls along the banks of the River Sabarmati some 90km from its mouth in the Bay of Cambay. First impressions can be poor: Gujarat's largest city is a dirty, polluted place,

TATTOOS

If you spend any time in the rural areas of Gujarat, or come across tribal people in the cities, you'll notice the heavy blues and blacks of tattoos that cover the arms, hands, faces and torsos of most tribal women and many tribal men. This art, **chhundana padavava**, has been practised for centuries, and like *mehandi* – rich red henna patterns stencilled onto hands and feet – is a traditional form of beautification and identification.

For women, the typical rows and symmetrical designs of dots and simple shapes around necks, wrists and earlobes are endowed with the power to attract men and increase chances of love at first sight, as well as inducing fidelity in a spouse. In some regions, a woman without *chhundana* is thought to have less chance of bearing children, and runs the risk of reincarnation as a camel. Tattoos of scorpions and serpents are believed to protect from bites and stings, while images of churning masts, *ravaiyo*, guarantee a continuous flow of milk from the family cattle. Men who are initiated into the occult and practise "black magic" bear a *narmund*, a human skull, on their chest, while a weighing scale on the palm of a woman's hand indicates that she has been offered in marriage without a dowry demanded from her parents. The actual process of tattooing is often carried out amid dancing, singing and the pulsating beat of *dhola* drums.

noisy with a grumbling flow of traffic. Give it a little time, however, and the mix of ancient and modern – along with the combination of thriving Hindu, Muslim and Jain communities – lends the city an undeniable character that can be hard to resist.

Ahmedabad is packed with a pungent diversity of architectural styles: over fifty mosques and tombs, as well as Hindu and Jain temples and grand step-wells (*vavs*). A wander through the bazaars and *pols* (residential areas) of the bustling **old city** is rewarding enough, but the outstanding monuments must be **Sidi Sayyid's Mosque**, **Bhadra citadel** – the site of the original city – the step-well **Dada Harini Vav**, and the hybrid **Jami Masjid** mosque. In addition, assorted **museums** provide a good introduction to Gujarati culture; the extensive **Calico Museum of Textiles** in the northern district of Shahi Bagh rates as one of the world's finest, and Mahatma Gandhi's **Sabarmati Ashram** has an exhibition on his life and the Indian Freedom Movement.

A brief history

When **Ahmed Shah** inherited the leadership of Gujarat in 1411, he chose to move his capital from Patan to the site of Asawal village, a small settlement on the east bank of the Sabarmati, renaming it after himself. The city quickly grew, welcoming skilled artisans and traders who were invited to settle. Its splendid mosques were clearly intended to assert Muslim supremacy, and heralded the new **Indo-Islamic** style of architecture, which though best displayed here, is a marked feature of many Gujarati cities.

In 1572, Ahmedabad became part of the growing Moghul empire, regarded as India's most handsome city and profiting from a flourishing trade in textiles that exported velvets, silks and shimmering brocades as far afield as Europe. But after a devastating famine in 1630 and a period of political instability when government passed to and fro between the Muslims and the Hindu Marathas, the city declined. Another famine in 1812 left it almost crippled, but five years later the British arrived, lowering taxes to encourage the return of merchants and traders who had left under Maratha rule. Trade in opium grew – the British needed something to offer the Chinese in return for silk and tea – and the introduction of modern machinery re-established Ahmedabad as a textile exporter that came to be known as "Manchester of the East".

When Mahatma Gandhi entered Indian politics in the early 1900s, as a Gujarati and an advocate of self-sufficiency, he was welcomed by Ahmedabad's manual labourers, who under his guidance revitalized their textile production and eventually formed protective trade unions. With the formation of national political parties and the imminence of India's release from British governance, the city became an important seat of political power, and a hotbed for communal tension as parties vied for popularity. Riots instigated by political and religious differences in recent years have sullied Ahmedabad's reputation, but have done little lasting damage to the city's communities.

Arrival, information and city transport

Ahmedabad's **airport** (☎67195) is linked to the city, 10km south, by taxis (Rs200–300) and frequent buses that terminate in the west of the old city at **Lal Darwaja**, the station for local buses. Long-distance buses arrive at the **Central Bus Stand** in the southeast of the old city, a few kilometres from any accommodation, while the **train station** is to the east. Both have taxi stands, and rickshaws are constantly available.

The telephone **area code** for Ahmedabad is ☎0272.

Information

Most of the action in Ahmedabad is on the east bank of the Sabarmati; however, the main **tourist office**, providing an efficient information service and inexpensive, accurate maps, is across the river in HK House, just off Ashram Rd (Mon–Sat 10am–5pm; ☎449683). It operates a reliable car rental and tour service and stocks the free monthly *The Choice Is Yours*, detailing useful addresses and forthcoming events. Smaller but more central is the office at the Ahmedabad Municipal Corporation near Sadar Patel Rd in the old city (Mon–Sat 10am–5pm; ☎365611). Offices at the airport and the train station have general information, and help book accommodation; the branch at Lal Darwaja bus stand is less helpful. There's also a Rajasthan Government tourist office on Ashram Rd, Usmanpura (Mon–Sat 10am–5pm; ☎450289). **Exchange facilities** are available in the *Bank of Baroda*, Relief Rd, Lal Darwaja (no *Visa* encashments); *Bank of India*, Bhadra; and *Central Bank of India*, Lal Darwaja (all Mon–Fri 11am–3pm, Sat 11am–1pm). The main **post office** is on Salapose Rd (Mon–Sat 10am–6pm).

City transport

It can be fun to amble the narrow backstreets of the old city on foot, but to cover wider distances and avoid the noise and chaos of walking along the main roads you'll need to take public transport. This can be stressful, as the overloaded **buses** which race round town have their destination written in Gujarati, and few bus stops are marked. All buses are numbered, however: #82 and #84 cross to the west bank and follow Ashram Road to Gandhi's ashram; #32 runs from Lal Darwaja to the Central Bus Stand and on to **Kankaria Lake**, and #31 is convenient for visits to **Sarkhej**, southeast of Ahmedabad. Fares are minimal; **for information** call ☎352911.

Metered **taxis** can be hailed or picked up at the airport, the train station and both bus stands, and cycle and auto **rickshaws** are abundant. *The Choice Is Yours* features a conversion table to convert rickshaw meter readings to *rupees*.

Car rental, with driver, is available from the travel agents mentioned on p.530.

The City

The historic heart of Ahmedabad is the **old city**, an area of about three square kilometres on the east bank of the river, dissected by the main thoroughfares Relief Road and Gandhi Road and reaching its northern limits at **Delhi Gate**. It's the best place to start any exploration, taking in the squat buildings of the original citadel, **Bhadra**, the **mosques** and tombs of Ahmedabad's Muslim rulers, vibrant bazaars and *pols*, labyrinths of high wooden *havelis* and narrow cul-de-sacs that still house families of common caste or trade.

Bhadra and Sidi Sayyid's mosque

The solid fortified citadel, **Bhadra**, built of deep red stone in 1411 as Ahmedabad's first Muslim structure, is relatively plain in comparison to later mosques. The palace inside, now occupied by offices, is off-limits to tourists, but you can climb to its roof via a winding staircase just inside the main gateway and survey the streets below from behind its weathered bastions. In front of the citadel is a small public garden and **Alif Shah's mosque**, gaily painted in green and white. Further east, beyond the odoriferous meat market in **Khas Bazaar**, is **Teen Darwaja**, a thick-set triple gateway built during Ahmed Shah's reign, that once led to the outer court of the royal citadel. A trio of pointed arches, engraved with Islamic inscriptions and detailed carving, span the busy road below and shelter shoemenders and peddlers.

CENTRAL AHMEDABAD

HOTELS:
- **A** Cama
- **B** Stay Inn
- **C** Alif International
- **D** Ambassador
- **E** Bombay
- **F** Gujarat
- **G** Esquire, Goodnight & Gulmarg
- **H** Balwas
- **I** Cadillac
- **J** Relax & Sahil
- **K** Alka Guest House & Ashiana
- **L** Natraj
- **M** Embassy
- **N** Surya
- **O** A-One Guest House
- **P** Moti Mahal Guest House
- **Q** Manila

RESTAURANTS:
- **1** Kalapi
- **2** Hotel Paramount
- **3** Sanman
- **4** Anand
- **5** Chetna
- **6** Bellur

A prominent feature on the front of glossy city brochures, **Sidi Sayyid's mosque** (1573), famed for the ten magnificent *jali* (lattice work) screens lining its upper walls, sits in the centre of a busy traffic circle in the northwest corner of Bhadra. The two semicircular screens high on the western wall are the most spectacular, with floral designs exquisitely carved out of the yellow stone so common in Ahmedabad's mosques. The eastern face is open, revealing a host of pillars that divide the hall into fifteen areas, each with skilfully carved domed ceilings. Carvings within depict heroes and animals from popular Hindu myths – one effect of Hindu and Jain craftsmanship on an Islamic tradition that rarely allowed the depiction of living beings in its mosques. Women cannot enter, but the gardens around it afford good views of the screens.

Ahmed Shah's mosque

South of Bhadra citadel, not far from Victoria Gardens, **Ahmed Shah's** small and attractively simple **mosque** was the private place of worship for the royal household. Sections of an old Hindu temple, perhaps dating back to 1250 AD, were used in its construction – hence the incongruous Sanskrit inscriptions on some of the pillars in the sanctuary. The *mihrabs*, recesses in the west wall indicating the direction of prayer, are particularly ornate, the central one carved in white and black marble. Hidden behind pierced stone screens above the sanctuary in the northeast corner, the *zenana*, or women's chamber, is entered by steps from outside the main wall.

Jami Masjid

A short walk from Teen Darwaja along Gandhi Road leads to the spectacular **Jami Masjid**, or "Friday Mosque". Completed in 1424, it stands today in its entirety, except for two minarets destroyed by an earthquake in 1957. Always buzzing with people, the mosque is fullest on Friday when thousands converge to worship.

A wide flight of steps leads to a vast marble courtyard surrounded on three sides by shady arched cloisters, known as *dalans*. A meeting place as well as an area for prayer, the courtyard has a water tank used for ablutions in its centre, and at the west end, facing Mecca, is the sandstone *qibla*, the main prayer hall, crowned with three rows of five domes. The 260 elegant pillars supporting its roof are covered with profuse, unmistakably Hindu carvings, while close to the sanctuary's principal arch a large black slab is said to be the base of a Jain idol inverted and buried as a sign of Muslim supremacy. The *zenana* is behind finely perforated stone screens above the main sanctuary.

Manek Chowk and the Tomb of Ahmed Shah

East of the Jami Masjid, the jewellers' market, **Manek Chowk**, is a bustling hive of colour where jewellers work in narrow alleys amid newly dyed and tailored cloths. Immediately outside the east entrance of the mosque the square **Tomb of Ahmed Shah I**, who died in 1442, stands surrounded by pillared verandahs. Women are not permitted to enter the central chamber, where his grave, plus those of his son and grandson, lies shrouded in cloth.

Further into the market area, you'll find the mausoleum of Ahmed Shah's queens, **Rani-ka-Hazira**, surrounded by the dyers' colourful stalls. Its plan is identical to Shah's own tomb, with pillared verandahs clearly inspired by Hindu architectural tastes. Inside, the graves are elaborately decorated with metal inlay and mother-of-pearl, now a little faded and worn.

Swaminarayan temple

North from Rani-ka-Hazira through a narrow street of material shops, and across Relief Road, the **Swaminarayan temple** stands behind huge gates and brightly painted walls. Forming a delicate contrast to the many hard stone mosques in the city, both the temple and the houses in the courtyard surrounding it are of finely carved wood, with elaborate and intricate patterns typical of the style of the *havelis* of north and west Gujarat. The temple's main sanctuary is given over to Vishnu and his consort Lakshmi.

Mosque and Tomb of Rani Sipri

Near Astodia Darwaja in the south of the city, the small, elegant **mosque of Rani Sipri** was built in 1514 at the queen's orders. Her grave lies in front, sheltered by a pillared mausoleum. The stylish mosque shows more Hindu influence than any other in Ahmedabad, with several Hindu carvings and an absence of arches. Its pillared sanctuary has an open facade to the east and fine tracery work on the west wall.

THE KITES OF AHMEDABAD

In mid-January, when Gujarat celebrates **Makar Sankrati** to mark the last harvest of winter, Ahmedabad hosts the **International Kite Festival**, the largest of its kind in the world. For weeks in advance shops brim with a splendid assortment of kites of strange and original designs, many painted with animals or the faces of gods and heroes.

India has a long tradition of kite-flying, and during the festival the city comes alive with diving and darting kites flitting through the clear blue skies as families join with enthusiasts from all over Asia and as far afield as America and Japan. On the first day of the festival, crowds of kite-flyers gather in Patang Nagar, a "kite town" – usually in the police stadium – to display models of all sizes, made of paper, cloth, bamboo and fibre glass. There's a carnival atmosphere, with food and crafts stalls and performances of dance and music late into the night. On the second day you can follow the experts to the city's roof terraces and learn to fly kites, and after dark the night sky is ablaze with *tukal* kites strung with coloured lights. The climax of the festival comes on the third day, when kite strings are coated with a lethal mixture of ground glass, egg yolk and boiled rice, and kites are played off against one another in fierce combat. Cries of "kata!" (I've cut!) fill the air as slashed kites fall stricken from the skies and come to rest limply on telegraph wires and trees.

Sidi Bashir's minars

South of the train station, opposite Sarangpur Darwaja, **Sidi Bashir's minars** are all that remain of the mosque popularly named after one of Ahmed Shah's favourite slaves. Over 21m high, these are the best existing example of the "shaking minarets" – built on a foundation of flexible sandstone, probably to protect them from earthquake damage – that were once common to Ahmedabad's skyline. At least two European visitors, Robert Grindlay (1826) and Henry Cousens (1905), reported climbing to the top storey of one minaret, shaking it hard, and causing its twin to shake, but as entry is restricted you'll be lucky to be able to try this yourself, or even to get into the modern mosque beneath the minars.

Dada Harini Vav

Northern Gujarat abounds in remarkable step-wells – deep wells with elaborately carved walls and broad flights of covered steps leading to the shaft – but **Dada Harini Vav**, in the northwest of the city, just outside the old boundaries, is among the very finest. It can be reached by taking bus #111 to Asarwa; ask to be dropped nearby, and take a short rickshaw ride to the well. While it's a Muslim construction, built in 1500 for Bai Harir Sultani, superintendent of the royal harem, the craftsmen were Hindu, and their influence is clear in the lavish and sensuous carvings on the walls and pillars. The best time to visit is an hour or so before noon when the sculpted floral patterns and shapely figurines on the walls descending to the water level are bathed in the light of the sun. Bai Harir's lofty mosque and lattice-walled tomb stand west of the well.

A couple of hundred metres north, the neglected **Mata Bhavani Vav** was probably constructed in the eleventh century, before Ahmedabad was founded. It's profoundly Hindu in character, and dedicated to Bhavani, an aspect of Shiva's consort Parvati, whose modest shrine is set in the back wall of the well shaft.

Hathi Singh temple

The Svetambara **Hathi Singh temple** (daily 10am–noon & 4–7.30pm), less than 1km north of Delhi Gate, is easily distinguished by its high carved column, visible from the road. Built entirely of white marble embossed with smooth carvings of dancers, musicians, animals and flowers, this serene temple is dedicated to Dharamnath, whose statue stands in the main sanctuary. He is the fifteenth *tirthankara*, or "ford-maker", one of twenty-four great teachers sanctified by the Jains. Other *tirthankaras* peer out with jewelled eyes from smaller shrines in the pillared cloisters around the courtyard.

Calico Museum of Textiles

Nobody should leave Ahmedabad without visiting the **Calico Museum of Textiles** (daily except Wed, 10.30am–12.30pm & 2.45–5pm; free), in the Sarabhai Foundation, Shahi Bagh, 3km north of Delhi Gate; it's simply the finest collection of textiles, clothes, furniture, temple artefacts and crafts in the country. It's best to arrive early so you can take your time; once inside, you'll be shown round by a guide. Colourful embroidered wall-hangings depicting Krishna legends hang from the second floor right down to ground level. Cloth decorated with tie-dye (*bandhani*), glinting mirror work, screen prints, block prints and intricate embroidery include exquisite pieces made for the British and Portuguese and exported to Bali, while from India's royal households there's an embroidered tent and the robes of Shah Jahan, along with elaborate carpets and plump cushions that furnished Muslim palaces.

The collection also includes some of the best examples anywhere of the *patola saris* woven in Patan (see p.534), as well as the extravagant *zari* work that gilds *saris* in heavy gold stitching, and can bring their weight to almost nine kilos. The Jain section features statues housed in a replica *haveli* temple, along with centuries-old manuscripts

---

SEWA

Of the female workers in India, 89 percent are self-employed. They are particularly subject to exploitation, existing outside the protection of labour laws and national standards of minimum wage. The slide into debt is always a real threat, with all that entails for their children and families. Ahmedabad, however, has since the days of Gandhi maintained a tradition of self-help, and has achieved world recognition as the home base of the ground-breaking **Self-Employed Womens' Association**, or SEWA, founded in the early 1970s by Ela Bhatt. Its original remit, to offer legal advice, training and child care for women, negotiating with police and local government for vendors' licences, and education for the members' children, soon mushroomed. To enable the women of Ahmedabad to buy basic materials and tools, and use their income to live on rather than to pay off loan sharks, SEWA opened its own cooperative *Mahila Bank*, the first to give low interest loans to women, offer savings and deposit accounts and insurance.

In 1984 a major textile industry slump affected 35,000 families, most of them Harijans and Muslims. Many had to resort to rag and paper picking, collecting grimy scraps of paper, polythene and broken glass for recycling, a task which threatened their health and brought in pathetic wages. Setting up training centres in weaving, sewing, dyeing and printing, and providing efficient machinery, SEWA helped to re-establish many women in the textile labour force, and provided an outlet for their products. Contracts with government institutions guarantee a place of work for cleaners and vendors; members now provide vegetables, fruit and eggs to all government hospitals, jails and municipal schools.

SEWA also trained its members in accountancy, management and office skills, and its management committee includes farmers, rag pickers and *bidi*-makers. By the 1980s, members felt confident enough to bring their personal grievances to this approachable team, voicing complaints of verbal and sexual assault in the workplace and at home. Two thousand women registered a protest against *sati* (widow burning) in 1987. A committee was formed to investigate crimes against Muslim women, particularly *talak*, a practice sanctioned by the Koran that allows a man to divorce his wife by uttering the words "I divorce you" three times, often leaving them destitute. Verbal divorce and polygamy, still common elsewhere in India, was banned in Gujarat in 1988. SEWA also strongly opposes sex determination tests that lead to female foeticide, a widespread practice in Gujarat, and its work has now spread to nine other Indian cities.

GANDHI'S SALT MARCH

Probably the most famous single act of civil disobedience in India's history, the great **salt march** was organized in Ahmedabad by Mahatma Gandhi as part of his campaign of non-violent passive resistance (*satyagraha*). Protesting against the British government monopoly on the production and sale of **salt**, Gandhi and almost eighty followers from around the country – among them Hindus, Muslims, and Harijans – set off on foot from the Sabarmati Ashram on March 12, 1930.

Gandhi's rousing speeches advocating *swaraj*, or Independence, and the distribution of clothing to the poor, brought the protesters enormous support and international attention. When, after a full month, they finally reached the coastal town of **Dandi**, some 386km south in the Gulf of Cambay, the *satyagrahis*, surrounded by followers who formed a wall against the police, courted arrest by collecting seawater and boiling it to produce salt. They had planned to seize natural deposits from the mudflats, but the police ground the salt back into the sand; the Mahatma did manage, however, to hold a mock-auction, selling off a tiny fragment of salt for Rs1600.

The effects of the salt *satyagraha* were widespread; salt was made illegally and government salt works raided, while in Gujarat government servants resigned and refused to pay land revenues. The government responded with repression; picketing was made illegal, and peaceful protests were frequently met with police brutality. Gandhi was arrested on May 5, under an 1827 regulation that required neither a trial nor a sentence. Even behind bars, he exerted considerable influence, advising colleagues and holding meetings. Soon after his release, in January 1931, he met the British Viceroy, Lord Irwin, in Delhi, to sign the Gandhi–Irwin Pact, agreeing to a cessation of civil disobedience, the release of civil disobedience prisoners, restoration of lands to those who had refused to pay increased rates, and reinstatement of village officers. This led directly to the Round Table Conference in London, where Gandhi was to join in discussions on India's future.

and *mandalas* painted on palm leaves; note the traditional symbols such as the snake-and-ladder motif representing rebirth and *karma*. Among exhibits from elsewhere in India are Kashmiri shawls, Kulu embroidery, glittering silk brocades from Varanasi, *Phulkari* folk art from the Punjab and masks and temple cars from Tamil Nadu.

Tribal crafts such as Kutchi silk-and-cotton *mushroo* weaving are displayed in spectacular wooden *havelis* from Patan and Siddhpur in north Gujarat. Clearly labelled models and diagrams explain the weaving, dyeing and embroidery processes.

Gandhi Smarak

At the northern end of Ashram Road, set by the sublime gardens of Gandhi's **Sabarmati Ashram**, the **Gandhi Smarak** (daily, April–Sept 8.30am–6.30pm, Oct–March 8.30am–6pm; free) displays the Mahatma's letters and possessions, along with a powerful collection of photographs of his years of fighting for freedom. It was here that Gandhi lived in humble apartments from 1917 until 1930 and held meetings with weavers and Harijans as he helped them find security and re-establish the manual textile industry in Ahmedabad. In keeping with the man's uncluttered lifestyle, the collection of his personal property is modest but poignant – wooden shoes, white seamless clothes and a pair of round spectacles. A **Sound and Light show** telling his life story runs in Gujarati (daily 7pm), Hindi (Mon, Tues, Thurs & Sat 8.30pm) and English (Sun, Wed & Fri 8pm), costs Rs15 and lasts 65 minutes. Tickets are sold at the museum, during opening hours. The ashram itself is no longer operating, but many people come here simply to sit and meditate.

Other museums

Ahmedabad's museums are especially strong in arts and crafts. Among them, the **Shreyas Folk Art Museum** (Tues–Sat 3–6pm, Sun 10am–noon & 3–6pm), way out to the west near the city boundary (bus #41 from Lal Darwaja), displays the traditional work of Gujarat's many tribes. The **Tribal Museum** (Mon–Fri noon–5pm) in Gujarat Vidyapith at the north end of Ashram Rd is equally informative, detailing the various peoples of the state and their customs, such as the painting of "magical" pictures by Bhils to ward off disaster. **MC Mehta Gallery** (Tues–Sun 11am–noon & 3–5pm) in **Sanskar Kendra** on Bhagtacharya Rd, west of the river, has a superb collection of miniature paintings from all over India.

Parks and gardens

Ahmedabad's quieter spots and open spaces provide welcome relief from the chaos of the busy streets. Just south of Bhadra the **Victoria Gardens** are suitably formal, with spacious lawns and treelined promenades around a pompous statue of Queen Victoria. Southwest of the old city, more picturesque gardens surround the artificial 34-sided **Kankaria Lake**. Dating from 1451, the lake has a fascinating ornate sluice gate on its eastern edge, a collection of Dutch and Armenian tombs on the west bank, and an island in the centre. The typically Indian **zoo** is not far north. It's best to visit in the cool of the evening; bus #32 runs frequently between Kankaria and Lal Darwaja.

Vishalla village

If you're not going to get the chance to make it to any genuine Gujarati villages, don't turn your nose up at **Vishalla village** (daily 5–10pm), out on Sarkhej Rd, 4km south of town (bus #31). Designed this century by Surendra Patel, Vishalla is an admirably authentic collection of traditionally decorated mud huts where potters, weavers and *paan*-makers demonstrate their skills. The **Vechaar Utensils Museum** (Mon–Sat 5–11pm, Sun 5–10pm) houses a vast collection of Gujarati metalware, including jewellery, knives and forks and odd-looking machinery for milking camels.

The village atmosphere can also be taken in during a leisurely evening trip, when dinner is served (arrive before 8pm to book) to the accompaniment of local dance, music or puppet shows; the menu includes Gujarati dishes, super-sweet deserts and mugs of buttermilk. Lunch is served from 11am until 1pm.

Accommodation

Ahmedabad's **hotels** range from grubby adequacy to polished luxury. Most are conveniently located in the west end of the old city, within walking distance of the bazaars, the local bus station, banks, the GPO and many of the sights. Cheaper places to stay cluster around the train station, while north of Nehru Bridge on the east bank, in the rather classy Khanpur area, the hotels are smarter, if not luxurious.

In the west end of the old city

Alka Guest House, Shreenath Chamber, Salapose Rd (☎20830). The least expensive option in this area with adequate facilities, clean rooms and a dormitory for men. ①.

ACCOMMODATION PRICE CODES

All **accommodation prices** in this book have been coded using the symbols below. In principle the prices given are for the least expensive double rooms in each establishment; however, some hotels, usually in category ①, offer rates per bed rather than per room. Local taxes are not included unless specifically stated. For more details, see p.34.

①	up to Rs100	④	Rs225–350	⑦	Rs750–1200
②	Rs100–150	⑤	Rs350–500	⑧	Rs1200–2200
③	Rs150–225	⑥	Rs500–750	⑨	Rs2200 and up

Ashiana, Murtuza Manzil, Salapose Rd, Khas Bazaar (☎351114). Simple, tidy rooms with little ventilation. No singles. ②.

Balwas, 6751 Relief Rd (☎351135). A modern, well-kept place. Most rooms have a/c; all have clean private bathrooms with constant hot water. ④–⑤.

Bombay, KB Commercial Centre, near Dinbai Tower, Lal Darwaja (☎351746). Cramped, and not as clean as it might at first seem; but at least there's constant hot water. Some a/c rooms. ②–④.

Cadillac, Dr Tankaria Rd, Lal Darwaja (☎351481). Small, colourful and inexpensive rooms, some with private bath. Dormitory for men. ①.

Embassy, behind *Bank of Maharashtra*, Lal Darwaja. Excellent, comfortable hotel in a modern building with all amenities. Good value. ⑤–⑥.

Esquire, Lal Darwaja (☎352840). Opposite Sidi Sayyid's mosque. Rooms here are nothing special, though they are clean. Often full. ③.

Goodnight, Dr Tankaria Rd, Lal Darwaja (☎351997). Spick and span modern hotel opposite Sidi Sayyid's mosque. Rooms with TV and private bathroom. ④.

Gujarat, Third Floor, Sneha Complex, Dr Tankaria Rd, Lal Darwaja (☎356627). North of the clock tower. Attractive, modern and spotlessly clean with swinging cane chairs on a leafy roof terrace. ④.

Gulmarg, Lal Darwaja (☎354202). Opposite Dinbai Tower. Basic, reasonably clean rooms, some with balcony, some with a/c. ②–③.

Natraj, Dada Mavlankar Rd, Bhadra (☎350048). In a quiet area near Victoria Gardens. Cosy rooms with private bathrooms (bucket of hot water), some with large balconies. ②.

Relax, Dr Tankaria Rd, Lal Darwaja (☎354301). A modern, clean place in a noisy side street opposite *Advance Cinema*, with room service and constant hot water in private bathrooms. ③–④.

Sahil, Dr Tankaria Rd, Lal Darwaja (☎353265). Friendly place next to *Relax Hotel*. Ordinary and a/c rooms, with carpets and private bathrooms. ④–⑤.

Around the railway station

A-One Guest House, Station Rd (☎349823). Directly opposite the station, this offers very basic rooms and a dormitory for men, and is rarely cleaned. ①.

Manila, Lalbhai Chambers, Kapasia Bazaar, Kalupur (☎38586). Clean place with standard marble decor and some a/c rooms. ④–⑤.

Moti Mahal Guest House, Kapasia Bazaar (☎339091). Very well-kept, clean hotel offering rooms with bathroom and TV, some a/c. ④.

Shakunt, HK Bhavan Reid Rd (☎344615). Set back a little from Station Rd. Smart reception area but the rooms are on the grubby side and have poor ventilation. ④–⑥.

Surya, Extra Commercial Complex, Sarangpur Kotri Rang, Panchkuva Sindhi Mkt (☎344151). Clean and homely carpeted rooms. ④.

Khanpur district

Alif International, opposite *Bombay Mercantile Bank* (☎359440). Immaculate, some a/c. ⑤–⑥.

Ambassador, Lady Vidyagauri Rd (☎353244). Large and modern with little character. Rooms without a/c are the least expensive. ④–⑤.

Cama, Lady Vidyagauri Rd (☎25281). Luxurious rooms overlook River Sabarmati and a garden terrace with swimming pool. All mod cons, restaurant, bar and coffee shop. Lower rates for Indian nationals, foreigners must pay in foreign currency. ⑧.

Stay Inn, Lady Vidyagauri Rd, Khanpur Gate (☎354127). Smart and comfy with partial a/c. ④–⑥.

Eating

Ahmedabad's **restaurants** are clustered around Salapose Road and Relief Road, with good mobile stalls in Khas Bazaar serving kebabs and fresh, gloopy *dal*. Restaurants in Navrangpura, near the university 2km west of the river, offer Indian and western dishes. For a cool **drink**, try the juice centre on Dr Tankaria Rd north of Sidi Sayyid's mosque.

Anand Dining Hall, Salapose Rd, off Relief Rd. Small, inexpensive place for average veg food.

Balwas Restaurant, Relief Rd. Comfortable, a/c restaurant serving reasonably priced meat and vegetarian Indian dishes, and a variety of desserts including jelly and ice cream.

Bellur, Station Rd. Low-priced south Indian dishes in simple surroundings with a/c upstairs.

Chetna Dining Hall, Relief Rd. A popular place serving excellent south Indian dishes, and sumptuous Gujarati *thalis* for Rs15. Opens for dinner at 6.30pm.

Food Inn, in the basement of *Hotel Goodnight*, Dr Tankaria Rd. Smart, a/c restaurant with a wide variety of medium-priced Indian dishes.

Gandhi Cold Drinks House, Khas Bazaar, Bhadra. Interesting milk and ice cream concoctions, unique to Ahmedabad. A good place to sit with a refreshing drink.

Gopi Dining Hall, Pritamrai Rd (☎76388). Excellent no-smoking veg place on the west side of Ellis Bridge. Gujarati and Punjabi *thalis* at unbeatable prices. Very popular, so reserve. Closed 3–6pm.

Kalapi, Dr Tankaria Rd. An a/c no-smoking restaurant opposite *Advance Cinema*. The best veg food in Bhadra at easily affordable prices.

Moti Mahal, Kapasia Bazaar. A stone's throw from the railway station, this restaurant and sweet centre is renowned for its service and quality.

Nishat, Khas Bazaar, Bhadra. Very inexpensive, unelaborate place with a selection of meat dishes.

Hotel Paramount, Bhadra. Despite its drab appearance, this a/c restaurant dishes up a wide selection of excellent Indian dishes and desserts at very affordable prices. Great for breakfast.

Sanman, Gandhi Rd, opposite the Jami Masjid. Gujarati and Punjabi dishes and filling inexpensive *thalis*. Open all day for snacks, meals and drinks – the *lassis* are excellent.

Toran Tourist Restaurant, Gandhi Ashram, Ashram Rd. Punjabi meals and snacks, fixed *thalis* for under Rs25. Reasonable but not worth going out of your way for.

Listings

Bookstores For maps, guides and books try *People's Book House* and *Sastu Kitab Ghar* on Relief Rd. *H Patel & Co Book Company*, Ellis Bridge, sells books on Indian philosophy, architecture and crafts. Stalls under Fernandes Bridge on Relief Rd stock tatty US and British paperback classics.

Cinemas *Advance Cinema* on Salapose Rd and *Krishna Cinema* on Relief Rd are very popular.

Emergency Services Police ☎100; Ambulance ☎101 or 102.

Hospitals *VS General*, Ellis Bridge (☎77620); *Akhhandanand Ayurvedic*, Akhandanand Rd (☎834170).

■ MOVING ON FROM AHMEDABAD

Indian Airlines **fly** twice daily to **Bombay** (7.35am & 7.50pm; 1hr) and **Delhi** (8.35am & 8.25pm; 1hr 25min), as well as to Bangalore (2hr) and Madras (3hr 15min) on Wed, Fri and Sun; they have an office on Lal Darwaja (☎353333). Other **airline offices** in town include *Air France* (☎442391), *British Airways* (☎465621), *Delta* (☎448143), and *KLM* (☎77875), all on Ashram Rd; *Air India*, near High Court, Nehru Bridge (☎425644), and *Ethiopian Airlines*, just behind High Court (☎404056); and *Swiss Air*, Relief Rd (☎449149).

For most destinations in Gujarat, there's only one **train** from Ahmedabad Junction each day; that goes for **Bhavnagar** (daily 4.45pm; 6hr) and **Bhuj** (*Fast Passenger Express* #65; daily 8.25pm; 16hr). For **Junagadh**, the best of two services is the *Girnar Express* #9846 (daily 8.45pm; 13hr). The best service to **Delhi** is the *Ashram Express* #2906 (daily 5pm; 17hr); for **Jaipur** it's the *Delhi Express* #9904 (daily 6pm; 16hr 20min). Several trains leave daily for **Bombay**; to arrive early in the morning, catch one of the evening departures, the #9008 or #9018: both take just over 9hr. A 6.25am train leaves for **Madras** (35hr) every Mon, Tues, Fri and Sat.

For journeys within Gujarat, it can be less hassle to opt for a bus, which at least travel at sociable hours. However, the confusing Central Bus Stand is spread across two sides of a busy road, with poorly marked ticket and information offices. If you arrive by rickshaw, ask the driver to drop you on the appropriate side; you are often expected simply to find your bus and jump on. Tickets are sold in advance for less crowded buses from stalls lining the road outside. More comfortable and expensive buses to Gujarati towns run from *Punjab Travels*, 3 Embassy Mkt, Ashram Rd (☎449777). *Shrinath Travel Agency* (☎44345), next door, organizes services to Rajasthan, and a night bus to Jaisalmer.

Motorbikes Buy an *Enfield* or have one repaired at *Shaik & Co Agency*, Swastik Supermarket, Ashram Rd (☎449522).

Photographic Equipment *Panubhair Shah Photo Goods*, next to GPO, Salapose Rd (☎25421); *Scanner Fotoshop*, Padshah Pol, Relief Rd (☎357125).

Visa Extensions Go to the Police Station in Shahi Bagh (☎333999), or phone Gandhinagar (☎9220388).

Around Ahmedabad

The most obvious day trip from Ahmedabad is north to **Adalaj**, with its impressive step-well, and perhaps on a little further to the new capital of **Gandhinagar**, and its amazing Swaminarayan complex. South of town lie the lake, pavilions and mausoleums of **Sarkhej**. If you're in the region between November and February, **Nal Sarovar** bird sanctuary is an ideal place to spot migratory birds. Further south is **Lothal**, and the excavation of an ancient Harappan site dating back four thousand years; the mosques in **Dholka** en route date back to the fourteenth century.

Adalaj Vav

One of Gujarat's most spectacular step-wells, or *vavs*, **Adalaj Vav** (daily; free), stands in lovingly tended gardens about 1km from a bus stop on the route between Ahmedabad (19km) and Gandhinagar. Once a Hindu sanctuary, the well is now totally out of use; modern water taps nearby enable local women to wash clothes and cooking utensils.

The monument is best seen around noon, when sunlight penetrates to the bottom of the five-storey octagonal wellshaft. Steps lead down to the cool depths through a series of platforms raised on pillars. Alive with exquisite sculptures, the walls, pillars, cornices and niches portray erotica, dancing maidens, musicians, animals and images of Shiva in his terrible aspect, Bhairava. Stone elephants, horses and mythical animals parade around the sides of the shaft, where green parrots swoop down from outside to rest out of the glaring sun. Before descending you'll see several Sanskrit inscriptions etched into the walls just above eye level, one of which records the building of the well by Ruda, wife of a local chief, in 1498.

Gandhinagar

The second state capital after Chandigarh to be built from scratch since Independence, the uninspiring city of **GANDHINAGAR** is laid out in thirty residential sectors, in an ordered style influenced by the work of **Le Corbusier**, who designed Chandigarh, and had a hand in conceiving the layout of New Delhi. Its near-symmetrical numbered streets are wide and strangely quiet, lined with a total of 16 *lakh* trees – that's 26 per head of the city's population. There's little to warrant spending much time here, but the headquarters of the Swaminarayan sect, **Akshardam**, is worth a look. This vivacious Hindu revival movement, established in 1907 by Brahmaswarup Shastriji Maharaja, promotes Vedic ideals pronounced by Lord Swaminarayan (1781–1830). Born in Uttar Pradesh, the saint settled in Gujarat where he built six temples, wrote religious discourses and proclaimed that his presence would continue through a succession of saints, the most recent of whom is a Gujarati named Pramukh Swami Maharaja.

The Akshardam may advocate simplicity and poverty, but the colossal **Swaminarayan complex** on J Rd, Sector 20 (daily except Mon, 7am–10pm), a centre for representing the precepts and practices of the sect, is hugely extravagant. Built of pink sandstone, all six thousand tonnes of it brought from Rajasthan, with domed roofs raised on almost one hundred profusely carved pillars, it's furnished inside with Karnataka rosewood, and the statues of Swaminarayan and two other prominent gurus shimmer with a gold leaf coating. The Hall of Holy Relics, containing possessions of Swaminarayan, also has a state-of-the-art display of images projected onto fourteen screens. In Nityanand Hall, fair-complexioned figures represent themes from the great Hindu epics, while the works of Indian mystical poets such as Tulsidas and Kabir are shown in Premanand Hall. Models of *sadhus* in Nijnanad Hall tolerantly "discuss" world religions with a view to attaining universal harmony, and there's a Centre for Applied Research in Social Harmony under construction in the landscaped gardens.

Should you want to **stay** in Gandhinagar, try the *Youth Hostel* (①) or *Hotel Purnima* (③) both in Sector 16, or the a/c *Hotel Haveli* (⑦) in Sector 11, near the bus stand.

Sarkhej

Just under 10km southwest of Ahmedabad (bus #31 from Lal Darwaja) in the suburb of **Sarkhej** is a complex of beautifully fashioned monuments arranged around an artificial lake. The square tomb of the revered saint Sheikh Ahmed Khattu, the spiritual mentor of Ahmed Shah, who died in 1445, is the largest mausoleum in Gujarat, with scores of pillars inside supporting the domed roof, tracery work and inlaid marble on the upper walls and rows of arched wooden doors and brass screens on the outer wall. The mausoleum was constructed by Ahmed Shah's successor, Muhammad Shah, in 1446, and the later Sultan Muhammad Beghada (died 1511) so deeply admired Sheikh Ahmed that he built palaces, a harem and a vast lake at the site, and chose to have his own tomb here. Sarkhej became a retreat of Gujarati Sultans, who added gardens, pavilions and tombs to the elaborate complex. While some of the buildings are falling into ruin, it remains a charming place, usually teeming with brightly dressed Gujarati holidaymakers, and has a serene beauty comparable to that of Udaipur in Rajasthan.

Nal Sarovar

A visit to **Nal Sarovar**, a reserve set in 121 square kilometres of wet grasslands 50km or so southwest of Ahmedabad is best between November and February, when it attracts colonies of flamingoes, cranes, storks, pelicans, ducks and geese. Nal Sarovar is seen as a valuable asset by conservationists campaigning for the reduction of road building and industrial pollution, both fast drying out Gujarat's remaining expanses of wetland. **Rooms** at the Forest Department's *Holiday Home* (③) can be booked on arrival, or in advance from the tourist office in Ahmedabad.

Dholka

A 35-kilometre journey southwest of Ahmedabad by bus or train brings you to **DHOLKA**, and its three majestic ruined mosques. The modestly proportioned **Masjid of Hilal Khan Qazi** (1333), featuring detailed tracery work, and the **Tanka Masjid** (1361), decorated with elaborate Hindu carvings, are both unaffected by Islamic design. More dilapidated, the **Mosque of Alif Khan** (1453) is distinctively Persian, dominated by solid square towers on either side of the facade. Dholka village is famous for its pomegranate and guava orchards, and also has a stunning wooden *haveli* temple.

Lothal

Remains of the **Harappan** (Indus Valley) civilization that spread across what are now western India and eastern Pakistan have been discovered in over fifty places in Gujarat. The largest excavated site is at **Lothal** (daily dawn–dusk), close to the mouth of the River Sabarmati, roughly 100km south of Ahmedabad, and an easy journey by bus (change at Dholka), or train. Foundations, platforms, crumbling walls and paved floors are all that remain of the prosperous sea-trading community that dwelt here between 2400 and 1900 BC, when a flood all but destroyed the settlement.

A walk around the **central mound** reveals the old roads that ran past ministers' houses and through the acropolis, where you can see remains of twelve baths and a

THE INDUS VALLEY CIVILIZATION

Before the Mauryan empire took hold in the fourth century BC, the greatest empire in India was the **Indus Valley civilization**. Well-planned, sophisticated settlements dating back to 2500 BC were first discovered in 1924 on the banks of the River Indus in present-day Sind, Pakistan, at **Mohenjo Daro** (which means "mound of the dead" in Sindi). Further excavations in 1946 on the banks of the River Ravi in Punjab revealed the city of **Harappa**, dating from the same era, which became a prototype of the entire Indus Valley civilization for archeologists. In its prime, this great society spread from the present borders of Iran and Afghanistan to Kashmir, Delhi and southern Gujarat, covering an area larger than the Egyptian and Syrian dominions put together. It lasted until 1900 BC when a series of heavy floods swept away the towns and villages in the delta regions of major rivers in Sind, Saurashtra and south Gujarat.

A prosperous and literate society, importing raw materials from regions as far west as Egypt, and trading ornaments, jewellery and cotton cultivated in the fertile delta plains, it also had a remarkable, centrally controlled political system. Each town was almost identical, with separate areas for the ruling elite and the "workers", and all buildings built with bricks measured according to a system distinctly similar to that laid out in the Vedic *Shastras*, the earliest Hindu treatises. A uniform system of weights and measures, corresponding almost exactly to modern ounces, was used, and the complex, efficient drainage systems remained unmatched by any other pre-Roman civilization.

Towns established on river deltas were perfectly placed for trade. **Lothal**, close to the Gulf of Cambay in south Gujarat, was a major port, and also the source of shells which the Harappans made into jewellery. Some four thousand years later, Cambay is still the largest producer of shell jewellery in India, and south Gujarati artisans make their wonderful beadwork using barely altered materials and techniques.

Although much about this complex society remains unknown – including their impenetrable script – similarities do exist between the Indus Valley civilization and present-day India. While their most important deity appears to have been a horned god, there was also a strong custom of worshipping a mother goddess, in the same way as the Hindus. The *peepal* tree was revered as it is by Buddhists today, and there is evidence, too, of phallic worship, still strong among Shaivites. In Lothal, altars bearing the remains of animal sacrifice have been discovered, and in every settlement large baths suggest a belief in the purifying quality of water.

For more about the Indus Valley Civilization and its significance in Indian history, see *Contexts*.

sewer. The lower town, evident today from a scattering of fragmented bricks and foundations, comprised a bazaar, workshops for coppersmiths, beadmakers and potters, and residential quarters. On the eastern edge of the site, shattered walls enclosing a rectangle indicate the existence of a dock – the only one discovered of its kind, suggesting that Lothal was probably a port serving a number of Harappan towns.

Evidence has been found here of an even older culture, perhaps dating to the fourth millennium BC, known from its red pottery as the **Red Ware Culture**. You can see remains from this period and from the Indus Valley civilization in the illuminating site **museum** (daily except Fri 10am–5pm). Among the jewellery collection, a necklace made from gold beads, each a mere 25mm in diameter, provides evidence of sophisticated skills and great wealth. Seals, delicately carved with animal motifs, were used by the Harappans to mark packages; one from Bahrain, imprinted with a dragon and gazelle, is testimony to the extent of their trading links. A range of accurate weights and compasses testify to the Harappans' knowledge of geometry and astronomy. From the Red Ware Culture, the museum displays bowls, jars, ceramic and terracotta pots and toys – including touchingly familiar spinning tops and marbles.

Northern Gujarat

North of Gandhinagar, the district of Mehsana was the Solankis' seat of government between the eleventh and thirteenth centuries. Some remains of their old capital – including the extraordinary **Rani-ki-Vav** step-well – still stand at **Anhilawada Patan**, just outside the modern city of **Patan**, which is home to Gujarat's last remaining *patola* weavers. From the city of **Mehsana**, at the province's centre, it's easy to get to the ancient and well-preserved sun temple at **Modhera**, or visit spectacular *havelis* in the small town of **Siddhpur**. Jain temples in the hills at **Taranga** and **Idar** can be reached from Mehsana, or directly from Ahmedabad.

Mehsana

The crowded residential city of **MEHSANA**, less than 100km north of Ahmedabad, doesn't merit a visit for its tourist sights – the one building of any interest is the old **Rajmahal** palace, now used as government offices. As the only place in the area to offer reasonable **accommodation**, it does, however, make an obvious base for visiting any of the towns in north Gujarat. The best bet is *Hotel Apsara* (☎02762/20027; ①–④) in Janta Supermarket on Rajmahal Rd, close to the bus station. It has clean and simple ordinary and air-conditioned rooms, some with balconies and all with private bath, and a food hall selling excellent *thalis*. Opposite the railway station, the smaller *Bombay Guest House* (☎02762/24025; ①) has modest, homely rooms and a basic Punjabi restaurant on the ground floor. Staff at Mehsana's **information centre** (no phone), across the road from the *Apsara*, can help you book accommodation elsewhere in the region.

Modhera

If you visit only one town in northern Gujarat, it should be **MODHERA**, where the eleventh-century **sun temple** (daily 8am–6pm) is the best example of Solanki temple architecture in the state. Almost a thousand years old, the temple has survived Muslim iconoclasm and nineteenth-century earthquakes; apart from a missing *shikhara* and slightly worn carvings, it remains largely intact.

The Solanki kings numbered Jains among their courtly advisors, and were probably influenced in their temple design by Jain traditions; deities and their vehicles, animals, full-breasted maidens and complex friezes adorn the sandy brown walls and pillars. Within the *mandapa*, or pillared entrance hall, twelve *adityas* set into niches in the wall portray the transformations of the sun in each month of the year – representations found only in sun temples. According to Indian convention, Modhera's sun temple is positioned so that at the equinoxes the rising sun strikes the images in the sanctuary, which at other times languish in a dim half-light. In front of the temple, a large tank with staggered steps and small shrines set into its four sides lies dry for most of the year. During the monsoon, however, it gives freshness to the temple, and the gardens around bloom with colour.

Modhera is linked by road to Mehsana (40min) and Ahmedabad (2–3hr). There are no **hotels**, but the state-run *Toran Cafeteria* in the temple grounds sells *thalis*, snacks and ice cream.

Patan and Anhilawada Patan

Modern, bustling **PATAN**, roughly 70km northwest of Mehsana, was founded in 1796. It has few monuments to speak of, but the streets of its older quarters are interesting enough, overlooked by the carved balconies and lintels of Muslim *havelis* and the marble domes and canopies of Jain temples. In an area called **Sadvi Wada** you can watch the complex weaving of silk *patola saris*, once the preferred garment of queens and aristocrats, and now made by just one family. Each *sari* takes from four to six months to produce, and is sold for up to seventy thousand *rupees* (more than US$2000). Silk threads are dyed in a set pattern before being woven on a complex loom, and the utmost care is taken to ensure completely even tension throughout the cloth.

The big-city bustle of Patan is a far cry from the old Gujarati capital at **Anhilawada Patan**, 2km northwest. The original city served several Rajput dynasties, including the Solankis, between the eighth and the twelfth centuries, before being annexed by the Moghuls. It fell into decline when Ahmed Shah moved the capital to Ahmedabad in 1411. Little remains now except traces of fortifications scattered in the surrounding fields, and the stunning step-well, **Rani-ki-Vav**, built for the Solanki queen Udaimati in 1050 and extensively restored during the 1980s. The recent restorations, unlike those at the sun temple in Somnath (see p.553), are not obtrusively modern, and recreate as perfectly as possible the original carving.

Rani-ki-Vav is undoubtedly Gujarat's greatest step-well, with a deep octagonal shaft, wide flights of steps, and exquisite figures and foliate designs etched into dark grey stone walls and pillars. The well shaft, now home to a colony of particularly large bees, boasts most of its original decoration, and not one tiny area of stone has been missed by the *silavat* masons whose penchant for sculpting voluptuous and shapely maidens has left Rani-ki-Vav with almost as many round bosoms and tilted hips as Hindu friezes. Several sun motifs adorn the well shaft, dating from the era of pre-Hindu sun worship, but these are far outnumbered by sculptures of Vishnu and his various *avatars*, or incarnations. Look out for elephant-headed Ganesh figures.

Not far from the well is **Sashtraling Talou**, the "Thousand-*lingam* Tank" built at the turn of the twelfth century, but razed during Moghul raids. Only a few pillars remain of the Shiva temples that surrounded the tank. Sparse ruins of Rani Udaimati's house crumble nearby, on a hill that affords excellent views over the surrounding plains. The mosques and tombs that you see are within easy walking distance, and make for interesting exploration; many were constructed using pillars from Hindu temples.

Siddhpur

Roughly 40km north of Mehsana, the small town of **SIDDHPUR** is known for its **Rudramala Temple**, built with delicate stone work and golden domes in the twelfth century and destroyed by Ala-ud-din Shah in 1297. The temple itself is not that impressive – sorry ruins fenced off from the town and guarded by uniformed caretakers – but Siddhpur's architecture is more interesting. Neat *pols* feature wooden *havelis* and grand pillared mansions, built in imitation of the European structures in Bombay and Surat by Muslim merchants in the nineteenth century. For **accommodation**, the small *Ambaji Guest House* (①) offers cramped and dirty rooms; the charming spacious *Government Guest House* (②) on the main Mehsana Rd is usually reserved for government officials, but if you ask at Mehsana's information office you may strike lucky.

The Jain temples at Taranga and Idar

Although some way off the tourist trail, the hilltop temples at **Taranga** and **Idar** are not hard to get to: 60km or so from Mehsana, both can be reached by bus, and Taranga is on the railway line (though the train chugs up from Mehsana at a snail's pace, taking almost three hours). Idar is also connected to Ahmedabad, over 100km south, by road.

Built during the Solanki period, the **Taranga** temples are particularly striking, and better preserved than more famous sites such as Mount Abu, Girnar and Shatrunjaya. Pilgrims and white-clad monks and nuns gather here year round to take blessings and pray at its shrines. The main temple, built of durable sandstone, is dedicated to Ajitanath, the second of twenty-four *tirthankaras* who represent the great teachers of Jainism. His image, complete with the jewelled eyes that adorn all Jain statues, gazes out from the main sanctuary, sturdy and still, while the rest of the temple is alive with a frenzied tangle of voluptuous maidens and musicians in smooth carved stone round the walls, pillars and ceilings, interspersed with rollicking animals and floral patterns.

The temples at **Idar** are less interesting, though they too are etched with numerous carvings. A plaque states that the larger Svetambara temple was built in 242 BC – it's more likely to date from the eleventh century, though the site itself may well have been a pilgrimage centre for centuries before. Most of what you see today is the result of recent renovation. Beside it, the Digambara temple is less ornate and more peaceful, decked with pictures of naked saints and ascetics who were shunned by the Svetambaras when the two sects formed. Used by Hindu and Jain meditators, the caves cut into the hills nearby are said to be sources of great spiritual power.

The town below the hill has a distinctly medieval feel, with few modern buildings and an abundance of delicately carved *havelis*. Now a quiet market town, it was once the home of the Maharaja of Idar and the capital of a large province; remnants of its rich past include an eerie ruined palace, twelfth-century Shiva temples overlooking a dry lake, a small dirty step-well and grand arched city gates. The basic *Hotel Dreamland* on Highway Rd (☎50597; ①), has slightly grubby but adequate rooms.

Southeastern Gujarat

The seldom visited **southeastern** corner of Gujarat, sandwiched between Maharashtra and the Arabian Sea, harbours few attractions likely to entice you off the road or railway line to or from Bombay. There's little to recommend **Vadodara** (Baroda), former capital of the Gaekwad rajas, but its proximity to the old Muslim town of **Champaner**, and the ruined forts and exotic Jain and Hindu temples that encrust **Pavagadh Hill**. Further south, the dairy pastures around **Anand** gradually give way to a swampy, malaria-infested coastal strip of banana plantations and shimmering salt pans that are cut by silty, sinuous rivers and peppered with mango trees and brick villages. The area's largest city is **Surat**, a sprawling modern industrial centre whose handful of colonial monuments are engulfed by some of the most chronically congested streets in South Asia. The historic port of **Bharuch**, overlooking the River Narmada, 66km north of Surat, is neither picturesque nor evocative; the only place of real interest in the far south of the state is the former Portuguese territory of **Daman**. Although nowhere near as appealing as its colonial cousins Goa and Diu, the twelve-kilometre-long enclave, whose main *raison d'être* is as a watering hole for alcohol-starved Gujarati men, does boast some impressive colonial architecture, and a couple of so-so beaches.

The west coast's main **transport** arteries, the NH8 and *Western Railway*, wind in tandem between Bombay and Ahmedabad. Even if you are only making short hops, stick to the trains: the highway, a graveyard of overturned buses and *Tata* trucks, is one of the most nail-bitingly terrifying roads in India.

Vadodara

The area between Ahmedabad and **VADODARA** (previously known as **Baroda**) is lush and fertile, but Vadodara itself is a heavily congested, noisy industrial city. Though the old city does retain some interest, with its beautiful ancient *havelis* and various bazaars, Vadodara has few tourist attractions. However, it does make the most convenient place to stay for trips to the ruined cities of **Champaner** and **Dabhoi**.

The telephone **area code** for Vadodara is ☎0265.

VADODARA

△ Ahmedabad   Airport △

RESTAURANTS:
❶ Kalyan Hotel
❷ Hotel Gokul
❸ Satkar

Baroda Museum

Long Distance Bus Stand

Sayaji Bagh ■ Planetarium

Railway Station   Local Bus Stand

TILAK RD

Kirti Mandir

R C DUTT RD

River

Sursagar

HOTELS:
Ⓐ Baroda Municipal Corporation
Ⓑ Welcomgroup Vadodara
Ⓒ Green
Ⓓ Delux
Ⓔ Rama Inn
Ⓕ Chandan Mahal & Ambassador
Ⓖ Laxmi Lodge
Ⓗ Surya
Ⓘ Aditi

N

Vishwamitri

NEHRU RD

Laxmi Vilas Palace

0   500 m

■ Maharaja Fateh Singh Museum

Prior to Independence, Vadodara was ruled by the Gaekwad Rajputs. Unlike their Rajasthani counterparts, they were little affected by the Indian government's withdrawal of privy purses, and continue to live in lavish palaces.

Arrival and information

Daily flights from Delhi and Bombay arrive at the **airport**, 6km northeast of town; tickets can be booked at *Umiya Travels Service*, Koti Char Rasta, Anandpura (☎558118). Vadodara **railway station**, close to most hotels and the main bus station, is the main railhead, welcoming trains from Ahmedabad, Bombay, and further afield. The station is constantly crowded and lines for tickets are long; bypass the hassle and buy a ticket from *Yogikrupa Travel Service* opposite (☎327677). The **bus stand** on Tilak Road, a little north, has regular, state-run services to other Gujarati towns. Stalls selling tickets for **private buses** (to Bombay, Rajasthan and Madhya Pradesh) line Tilak Road.

The moderately helpful **tourist office** (☎329656) opposite the railway station arranges city tours (Tues, Wed & Fri, 2pm), if there is enough demand.

The City

Vadodara's chief tourist attractions are in **Sayaji Bagh**, the large green park whose main entrance is on Tilak Road. It takes one or two hours to get round the large Indo-Saracenic **Baroda Museum and Picture Gallery** (Sun–Fri 9.30am–4.45pm, Sat 10am–4.45pm; Rs1), reached from University Road, which holds art and textiles from all over the world, Gujarati archeological remains, an ethnology section, and the inevitable stuffed animals. Among its best exhibits are carved doors and lintels taken from

Gujarat's *havelis*, and some fine fifth-century Jain bronzes excavated near Vadodara. Moghul miniatures and minor European works are stocked in the Picture Gallery. As well as the museum, Sayaji Bagh contains a **Planetarium** (shows in Gujarati, 4pm; English, 5pm; Hindi, 6pm; Rs3), a pitiful **zoo** and a small **Health Museum**.

Of Vadodara's palaces (all closed to the public), **Laxmi Vilas Palace** in the south of town is the most extravagant. Glimpse it from the road, or from the dull **Maharaja Fateh Singh Museum** (Mon–Fri 9am–1pm & 3–6pm) in the Palace grounds.

The old part of the city is in the east; ask for **Nyaya Mandir**, literally "New Temple", and walk past Sursagar tank through the narrow streets lined with wooden *havelis*. The tourist office will give directions to the **Sureshwar Desai Haveli** and **Mairal Mandir** – both difficult to find but worth searching out – and the elaborate **Tambekarwada Haveli** in Dandia bazaar in the south of the old city. Tilak Road connects the old and the new city, passing **Kirti Mandir**, the mausoleum of Baroda's rulers.

Accommodation

Vadodara's **hotels** are designed with business visitors in mind; there are several medium and high-class places, and just a handful of inexpensive lodges which could all do with improved maintenance. Most of the hotels are grouped in the **Sayaji Gunj** area just south of the railway station.

Aditi, Sayaji Gunj (☎336402). A tall building just behind *Kwality Restaurant*. Carpeted rooms with fridge, room service and TV, and clean bathrooms. ⑤–⑥.

Ambassador, Sayaji Gunj (☎327417). Clean and spacious rooms with TV and bath. A good mid-range option. Arranges air and railway reservations. ④–⑤.

Baroda Municipal Corporation, Pravasi Gruh (☎329656). Dim, spartan place opposite the railway station that proudly denies room service and can't guarantee running water, which may – if you're lucky – come for an hour each day. Unsurprisingly, the cheapest in town. ①.

Chandan Mahal, Sayaji Gunj (☎331822). Small, reasonably clean rooms in a pleasant old house with a central courtyard. Most rooms a little dusty, some have a/c. Overpriced. ③.

Delux, Kadak Bazaar (☎329604). A small and clean hotel in the heart of a lively bazaar just south of the railway station. ①.

Green Hotel, RC Dutt Rd (also called Racecourse Rd) (☎323111). The best low-budget option; rooms in a 100-year-old house with period furniture. Lacks a modern touch, but real character. ②.

Laxmi Lodge, Sayaji Gunj. Spacious rooms with wooden beds in a rarely cleaned old house. Cheap open-air dorm for men. ①.

Rama Inn, Sayaji Gunj (☎330131; fax 331133). Smart sizeable rooms in this plush modern hotel with restaurants, health club, swimming pool and wine shop. Credit cards accepted. ⑥–⑧.

Surya, Sayaji Gunj (☎336500; fax 336504). Smart, but less upmarket than the *Rama*; no pool. ⑤–⑦.

Welcomgroup Vadodara, RC Dutt Rd (☎323232). Gujarat's only five-star hotel, with predictably swanky and well-maintained rooms. ⑧.

Eating

With a large student population and a constant influx of business people, Vadodara has a choice of **restaurants** ranging from cheap and cheerful to plush and expensive, with a good selection of Indian, western and Chinese food. Several upmarket hotels lay on buffet spreads; for fast food and snack stops, head for the bus and railway stations.

Hotel Gokul, Koti Char Rasta. Just past Kirti Mandir, this small snack bar serves excellent south Indian, Punjabi and Gujarati *thalis* and ice cream at very low prices.

Kalyan Hotel, Sayaji Gunj. The hotel has a veg canteen extremely popular with students, a coffee shop specializing in Mexican snacks, and a restaurant; all are reasonably priced.

Kwality, Tilak Rd. White tablecloths, folded napkins and padded seats, and western, Chinese and Indian dishes of a high standard typical of the *Kwality* chain.

Maharaja, on the top floor of *Hotel Aditi*, Tilak Rd. Medium-priced restaurant with a great view, unmatched by the uninspiring cuisine.

Myra, *Hotel Surya*, Sayaji Gunj. Uniquely Gujarati food; delicious *thalis* cost around Rs50.

Oriental Spice, Tilak Rd. A rather plush restaurant turning out some very good Chinese food.
Satkar, Tilak Rd. One of the best, least expensive options. Excellent Gujarati *thalis* and desserts.
Vega, *Hotel Surya*, Sayaji Gunj. Another *Hotel Surya* restaurant, offering filling buffets with dishes from all over the world.

Around Vadodara

The Solanki kings, and later Muslim rulers, who between them held sway over Baroda for several centuries, left behind some fine architecture. A small town full of cloth and tailors' shops, **Dabhoi**, 24km southeast of Vadodara (1hr by bus), has four magnificent gateways. These, the only remnants of the thirteenth-century Solanki fortifications, are finely sculpted with gods, nymphs, animals and plants. The Kalika Mata temple next to the northern Mori Gate, though worn by time, features some excellent friezes.

Pavagadh and Champaner

The hill of **Pavagadh**, 45km northeast of Vadodara, rises 820m above the plains, overlooking the almost forgotten **Muslim city** of **CHAMPANER**. Take a jeep from Champaner, or walk up the path that ascends through battered gates and past the old walls of the Solanki fortress, to a mid-point where you can get snacks, souvenirs and a welcome cup of sweet *chai*. From here you can proceed by chairlift (7min) – or on foot up a well-trodden path – to the summit, where a number of Jain temples lie below a Hindu temple dedicated to Mataji, with a shrine to the Muslim saint Sadan Shah on its roof. The view stretches for miles over the patchwork plains of south Gujarat, and you can spot concrete barricades under construction along the Narmada canal.

In 1297 the Chauhan Rajputs made Pavagadh their stronghold, and fended off three attacks by the Muslims before eventually losing to Muhammad Begada in 1484: all the women and children committed *johar*, and the men who survived the battle were slain when they refused to embrace Islam. After his conquest, Muhammad Begada set to work on building Champaner, which took 23 years. The town was the political capital of Gujarat until the death of Bahadur Shah in 1536, when the courts moved to Ahmedabad and Champaner fell into decline.

Champaner today has a strange, time-warped atmosphere. The massive city walls with inscribed gateways still stand, encompassing several houses, exquisite mosques, Muslim funerary monuments, and newer Jain *dharamshalas* to accommodate and feed pilgrims visiting Pavagadh. Champaner's largest mosque, the exuberant **Jami Masjid**, is east of the walls. Towering *minars* stand either side of the main entrance, and the prayer halls are dissected by almost two hundred pillars supporting a splendid carved roof raised in a series of domes. The central dome, three times the height of the others, shelters an octagonal shaft trimmed with richly carved balconies. The *zenana*, or women's prayer section, is in the northwest corner behind perforated stone walls.

Buses from Vadodara leave hourly (via Halol; 1hr 30min) for Champaner, where you can get refreshment at the modest *chai* stall. There's also a direct service from Ahmedabad, every three hours. The state-run *Hotel Champaner* (☎41; ②–③; hot water only 7–7.30am) halfway up Pavagadh, has adequate **rooms** with magnificent views over the vast plains of south Gujarat. The **restaurant** serves veg *thalis*.

Bharuch

The rarely visited provincial backwater of **BHARUCH** (formerly Broach), halfway between Vadodara and Surat, stands on the marshy north bank of the Narmada, 48km short of the Arabian Sea. A thriving port and mercantile capital since the first millennium AD, its heyday was during the seventeenth century, when its ships sailed for Southeast Asia, to fetch spices to trade at its now-ruined British and Dutch factories.

Today, the coastal trade hurtles past on the NH8, and only if you have a penchant for jaded colonial trading posts will you find the tumbledown European houses and forlorn old quarter worth an hour or so out of a long train journey.

Clustered onto the two-kilometre-long narrow ridge that separates the bustling modern end of Bharuch from the sleepy right bank of the Narmada, the **old quarter** lies a ten-minute ride west of the railway station and bus stand: ask the rickshaw *wallah* to head for the **Jama Masjid**, a fourteenth-century mosque hemmed in by wooden balconies and flaking colour-washed walls. Its colonnaded courtyard, pierced by three doorways and crowned with a row of thirteen shallow domes, is a giant jigsaw puzzle of intricately carved masonry plundered from a Jain temple that formerly stood on the spot. Once you've checked out the richly decorated ceilings in the sanctuary hall, head downhill until you reach the town **walls**, erected by Shivaji to replace those destroyed by Aurangzeb in 1660. A walkway runs along the top of the ramparts, giving good views over marshy mud-flats, grazed by sleek grey water buffalo, to the river.

The walls veer north when they arrive at the edge of a dried-up creek, near a pale-blue Victorian clocktower, and the large colonial-style palace of an ex-nawab who frittered away his inheritance on opium. Drop down from here, and follow the river bank west through a putrid-smelling *basti*, to come out eventually at the old **quay**, now a fishing dock. Apart from their triangular sails (a legacy of Bharuch's trading links with the Arabian Gulf), the ramshackle flat-bottomed inshore fishing *dhows* here, built in the roadside carpenters' yards at the top of the hill, are identical to those that still fish the saltwater lagoons of central Portugal, whence their distinctive design.

Practicalities

Luggage can be left at the railway station parcel office, right of the main exit, while you explore the town. If you intend to stay, most of the **accommodation** is near the train station. The best budget option is the *Hotel Classic* (☎02642/32264; ②–③), tucked away behind the tall buildings on the south side of Station Rd, which offers en-suite doubles with carpets, *Star TV*, and balconies, or clean, windowless wood-partition cells. The *Hotel Palmland* (☎02642/33788; ④), around the corner from the bus stand, is nothing to write home about, but has clean and well-furnished rooms, some a/c, while the nearby *Hotel Plaza* (☎02642/30922; ⑤–⑥) offers central a/c and a posh restaurant.

The *Hotel Palmland*'s institutional *thali* joint is a reassuringly hygienic **place to eat**. Otherwise, take your pick from the lookalike veg cafes along Station Rd, a little west of the *Plaza*. Drinks and ice creams are sold at the stalls outside the railway station.

Surat

Packed around a tight bend in the River Tapti, 19km before it dumps its silty waters into the Gulf of Cambay, sprawling **SURAT** was the west coast's principal port before the meteoric rise of Bombay. These days, it is one of India's fastest growing industrial centres, but of no real interest to visitors, other than business travellers or die-hard colonial history buffs. Apart from a couple of melancholic European cemeteries, Surat's most memorable feature is its **traffic**, which, even by Indian standards, is appalling.

Founded by Parsi refugees in the twelfth century, Surat emerged as a minor trading post during the 1500s, when it was plundered and razed numerous times by the Portuguese. In 1592, after a protracted siege, the town fell to Akbar, under whose patronage it became one of India's most prosperous mercantile capitals, as well as a key embarkation point for Muslims heading to Mecca. The **British** first appeared on the scene in 1612, after being granted permission by the Moghuls to trade in the area. Three years later, they routed the Portuguese in a navy battle off "Bloody Point", mouth of the nearby Swally estuary, opening a trading "**factory**" soon after. The Dutch and French followed, but saw their *godowns*, or warehouses, sacked by Shivaji's

Marathas in 1664. The British, however, came through unscathed. By the end of the eighteenth century, their hold over the town and its shipyard was finally secure. Surat might eventually have become west India's number one city had it not been devastated by fire and floods in 1837. Many of the Jain and Parsi merchants fled south to Bombay, precipitating a decline from which Surat has only recently recovered.

Over the past decade, the city's booming textile, chemical and diamond-cutting businesses (a legacy of the Dutch trade-links) have generated a sixty percent growth in population. The resultant overcrowding and pressures on an already over-taxed infrastructure, however, are all too evident. In the winter of 1992–93, the packed commercial and Muslim districts around the main bazaar finally burst at the seams, erupting into some of the worst communal riots the state has ever seen.

Arrival and information

Surat's mainline **railway station**, used by all trains that run between Delhi and Bombay via Ahmedabad, stands on the eastern edge of the city centre, directly opposite the inter-state **bus terminus**. Although making a reservation can be a major hassle, trains are still more convenient than buses to get to or from Ahmedabad, Vadodara (Baroda), Bharuch (Broach), Daman, and Bombay.

GTDC's **tourist office** (daily 10.30am–6pm; ☎0261/26586), hidden on the opposite side of the city centre in Napura (Rs15 by rickshaw from the train station), has city maps and can arrange visits to **diamond-cutting workshops**. The *State Bank of India* (Mon–Fri 10am–2pm, Sat 10am–noon) is nearby.

The City

Surat's few sights are very spread out, but can be seen in an hour if you take a rickshaw between them. A good spot to start is **Chowk**, the busy riverside intersection at the foot of Nehru Bridge. Facing the old British High Court building on one side, and the incongruous steeple of an Anglican church on the other, the **castle** is the city's oldest monument, erected in 1540 on the banks of the Tapti by the Sultan of Gujarat in an attempt to curtail the trading activities of the Portuguese. Although equipped with top-notch Turkish cannons (now removed), and protected on its landward side by a huge ditch (now filled in), the fort fell both to the Moghuls and the British. These days the bastion houses government offices, and is far from the imposing edifice it must have been when General Sir George Oxinden, erstwhile President of Surat and Bombay saw off the Marathas from its battlements. You can wander in and scale the ramparts, from where there are views upriver and over the old walled town to the east.

The only other of Surat's historic sites worth hunting out lies fifteen minutes' northeast across town beside Kataragama Road, beyond the fortified gateway of the same name. Buzzing past in a rickshaw, you could easily mistake the domed mausolea of the weed-choked **English cemetery** for an oriental tomb garden. Now in a sorry state, the graveyard is locked and enclosed behind a low wall, which you can hop over behind the *peepal* tree on the pavement. Its most impressive sepulchre, a mildewing collection of pillars and arches crowned with crossed cupolas, is that of General Oxinden and his brother Christopher. The smaller of the two large tombs, on the left, is believed to be the final resting place of Gerald Aungier, of Bombay fame. Elsewhere in the cemetery, some four hundred more modest graves belong to young colonial officers and their families who succumbed to fever in what was, in the seventeenth century, a lonely, malaria-infested trading post.

If you are not yet tombed out, head 500m back towards the centre, turn left, and keep going for 100m until you reach the **Dutch cemetery**. The grandest of the mausolea here, that of Baron Adriaan van Rede (1691), bears a telling inscription in which "Souratta" merits a capital letter, but "bombai" appears in lower case. The **Armenian cemetery** next door is also worth a look.

Accommodation

Although you are unlikely to choose to stay in Surat, there is plenty of **accommodation** within easy distance of the train station. Finding a room is only a problem towards the end of weekday afternoons, by which time most places are booked by visiting businessmen. Avoid a protracted room hunt in the heat by telephoning ahead: there are a couple of STD booths opposite the station.

Alfa, opposite the railway station, near the Jain *dharamshala* (☎0261/36839). Neat, clean and respectable, with *Star TV*, and some a/c. ④–⑥.

Omkar, Eighth Floor, Omkar Chambers (☎0261/39329). Small rooms on the top storey of a skyscraper, with attached or shared shower-toilets, a busy room-service kitchen, views and optional *Star TV*. A good budget deal. *Vaibhav*, in the same building, is identical. Both ②–③.

Rama Regency, Bharti Park, Athwa Lines (☎0261/666 565). Surat's only five-star, 5km out in a peaceful residential suburb, has luxurious rooms and all the trimmings, including a pool. ⑦.

Sarvajanik, opposite the train station (☎0261/26434). Spotless en-suite singles, doubles, and hot water until 9am. Recommended. ③.

Simla, Station Rd. One of several rock-bottom lodges lining the road that runs west from the station. This one has mostly shared bathrooms and cramped rooms, but is cleaner than most. ②–③.

Yuvraj, near the *Alfa* (☎0261/53621; fax 652 177). A slick three-star boasting bath-tubs, central a/c, terrace garden and two good restaurants. The best in its bracket. ⑥.

Eating

Most of Surat's **restaurants** are in the better hotels, while many of the cheaper lodges offer basic room-service menus. If you're passing through and want a good, inexpensive meal near the station, you won't do better than the *Sheetal*'s tasty lunchtime *thalis*.

Ashoka, Station Rd. Filling, spicy veg and non-veg food served in clean, Punjabi-run restaurant.

Sheer-e-Punjabi, below Omkar Chambers. Swanky *tandoori* house with marble floors, table cloths and a varied non-veg menu. Moderate to expensive.

Sheetal, opposite the railway station. Excellent set *thalis* and pure-veg Gujarati dishes served at speed in a first floor restaurant.

Tex Palazzo, *Hotel Tex Palazzo*. India's first revolving restaurant offers superb views, but less than inspiring food. Moderate.

Yuvraj, opposite the railway station. Stylish Gujarati cooking in sophisticated surroundings. Pricey, but good for a splurge.

Daman

Ask any Gujarati what they know about **DAMAN** and they'll probably say "liquor". Thanks to its semi-independent status, the former Portuguese enclave enjoys more liberal alcohol laws than the dry state that surrounds it – a fact the town has turned to its advantage. Most weekends, the otherwise sleepy fishing port is swamped by buses of men who drink themselves senseless, sway up and down the main street, and then crash out in a cheap hotel room for the night. If all this sounds like hell (it *is* for most women travellers), Daman's other attractions – immaculate Portuguese churches, houses and forts, and a couple of uninspiring beaches – may seem a poor pay-off.

Straddling the mouth of the **Damanganga River**, which rises in the Sayadhri range on the Deccan plateau, Daman made an obvious target for the Portuguese, who took it in 1531 from the Abyssinian chief Siddu Bapita. The governor of Goa, Dom Constantino de Braganza, cajoled the Sultan of Gujarat into ceding the territory 28 years later, after which it became the hub of the Portuguese trans-Arabian Sea trade with East Africa. The town's economic decline was precipitated by the British occupation of Sind in the 1830s, which effectively strangled its **opium** business. Colonial rule, however, survived until 1961, when Nehru lost patience with the Portuguese president Salazar's refusal to negotiate a peaceful handover of the enclave, and sent in the troops.

Today, Daman is administered from New Delhi as a Union Territory, along with India's other two ex-Portuguese colonies, Goa and Diu. Apart from alcohol production and sales, its chief sources of income are coconuts, salt production, and smuggling. In recent years, the local tourist office has also been trying to promote the area as a mini-Goa. Don't be taken in: the unbroken stretch of palm-fringed sand that runs along its twelve-kilometre coastline may look idyllic in the brochures, but on closer inspection turns out to be a grubby fishing beach, used as a toilet by the locals.

Daman is made up of two separate districts. On the north side of the Damanganga River is **Nani**, or "Little" **Daman**, where you'll find most of the hotels, restaurants, bars and markets; **Moti**, or "Great" **Daman**, the old Portuguese quarter, lies to the south, its baroque churches and Latinate mansions encircled by imposing stone battlements.

Arrival and information

The nearest railhead to Daman is 12km east at **Vapi**. Check when you make your reservation that your train stops here. Rickshaws will run you to town from the square in front of the station, but it is far cheaper to squeeze into a shared *Ambassador* **taxi**, which will drop you on Seaface Rd, a five-minute walk east from most of the hotels.

The **tourist office** (Mon–Fri 10am–5pm; ☎02636/2014), just north of the covered market on Devka Rd, hands out a glossy brochure that, along with lots of gushing prose, contains a useful **map** of the town and its environs. **Money** can be changed at the *State Bank of India* (Mon–Fri 10am–2pm, Sat 10am–noon) on Kabi Kabarda Rd, a short walk north of the **GPO**, which stands at the foot of the Damanganga road bridge.

Nani Daman

Most of the action in **Nani Daman** centres on **Seaface Road**, which runs west from the market past rows of hotels, seedy bars and IMFL (Indian Made Foreign Liquor) stores to the **beach**. Too polluted for a comfortable swim or sunbathe, Daman's dismal strand is only worth visiting around sunset, when the local fisherwomen hang strips of filleted pomfret on wooden racks to dry. At the opposite (east) end of Seaface Road, the Portuguese **covered market** has a reputation as a purveyor of exotic contraband, although you won't find many packets of the fabled foreign cigarettes or bottles of Scotch whisky among the Hindi film cassettes and cheap cotton clothes. More picturesque is the open-air **farmers' market** around the corner where, on weekday mornings, local women squat beside piles of fresh flowers, whole spices, fruit, vegetables and terracotta pots full of *papri*, the local palm wine.

Daman's noisiest trading, however, takes place at the riverfront. Head down here in the morning and you'll see scores of fishing boats moored at the quayside, their bows hung with garlands of marigolds for good luck. While the night's catch is being landed, coolies haul heavy blocks of ice up the gangplanks to be hacked into pieces over baskets full of glistening fish that the fisherwomen, gathered on the beach below, then sell to the assembled housewives and restaurateurs. A good place from which to watch it all are the ramparts of **St Jerome's Fort**, directly behind the quay. Erected in the early seventeenth century to counter the threat of Moghul invasion, the citadel encircles a small *maidan*, a Catholic church, and a well-kept walled Portuguese graveyard.

Moti Daman

The town's most impressive monuments are all across the river in the leafy colonial compound of **Moti Daman**, 2km south of Seaface Road. Once inside the huge, heavily fortified walls that surround the quarter, you're worlds away from the sandy cluttered streets of the new town: elegant double-storeyed mansions with sweeping staircases, wooden shutters, verandahs and colour-washed facades stand on sun-dappled courtyards. Now used as government offices, these grand residences were originally the homes of Portuguese nobles or *hidalgos* – the only people allowed to live inside the fort.

Moti Daman's highlights, however, are its **churches**, which rank among the oldest and best-preserved Christian monuments in Asia. Grandest of all is the the the **Sé Cathedral** (Church of Bom Jesus) on the main piazza. Built in 1603, its gigantic gabled baroque facade opens on to a lofty vaulted hall, at the end of which stands a gilded altar watched over by six statues of saints and a benign Madonna. On the opposite side of the square, the **Church of Our Lady of the Rosary** is crammed with ornate woodwork, and strings of fragrant jasmine and rose petals festoon its ceilings. Further south, distinguished by its buttressed walls, **Our Lady of Remedios** (1607) houses five altars, and a small collection of seventeenth-century paintings and engravings.

Beaches

If you crave a beach, but are turned off by Nani Daman's drab sands, there are a couple of more appealing spots outside town. **Devka** (or Dwarka beach), backed by coconut plantations and a string of large resort hotels, can be reached in fifteen minutes by rickshaw, or by bus from the stop on the main road near the market. At the far southern end of the territory, also fifteen minutes' rickshaw ride from Nani Daman, **Jeypore** is cleaner and less frequented, but no good for swimming as the tide recedes too far.

Accommodation

Most of Daman's **hotels** are in and around the grid of streets between the market and the beach. Aim for a first floor, west-facing room if you can, as these catch the best of the welcome sea breezes that blow in during the evenings.

Brighton, Seaface Rd (☎02636/2922). Rock-bottom prices, standards to match. A last resort. ①.

Diamond, near old taxi stand (☎02636/2938). Neat rooms in solid respectable hotel. Some a/c. ④.

Gurukripa, Seaface Rd (☎02636/2846). The poshest place to stay in town: spacious en-suite rooms, all with *Star TV*, and a roof garden, bar, and quality restaurant. Good value. ④–⑤.

Marina, behind the Police Station (☎02636/2420). Simple rooms with period furniture in stylish, tatty colonial house. A bargain if you don't mind peeling plaster, dodgy plumbing and old beds. ①–②.

Sovereign, Seaface Rd (☎02636/2823). Large, well-maintained hotel near the beach. Economy rooms have attached shower-toilets, fans and balconies, and are Daman's best budget deal. ②–④.

Sun'n'Sea, opposite the Municipal Library (☎02636/32506). Overlooking the river, but shambolic and overpriced. ③–⑤.

Sweet Mary, opposite the bus stand (☎02636/2869). Newly decorated and very spruce, with large, clean, and comfortable en-suite rooms: the ones on the top floor are best. ③.

Eating and drinking

Daman's disproportionately large number of **places to eat** is due to the town's liquor laws, which oblige all bars to serve food with alcohol. Most of the "bar-restaurants" along Seaface Rd are restaurants in name only, and best avoided. **Seafood**, on offer all year (except during the monsoons), is especially good from late September to early November, when the fish market is glutted with fresh crabs, prawns and lobsters.

Darshan, Seaface Rd. Best of the dingy men-only beer bars on the main road. This one serves cheap and filling fish dishes as well as drinks, and has a small terrace out back.

Gurukripa, opposite the *Darshan*, Seaface Rd. The place for a slap-up meal: veg and non-veg *tandoori*, seafood (tiger prawns, stuffed pomfret, and grilled fish), with a good selection of Chinese dishes, and Goan *fenni* nips. Pricey, but not prohibitively so.

Samrat, Seaface Rd. Spotless roadside restaurant that specializes in inexpensive, eat-till-you-burst Gujarati *thalis* that come with *namkeens*, a couple of different *dals*, and mouthwateringly mild veg dishes. Strictly "pure-veg" (read "no alcohol") , and excellent value.

Sovereign, Seaface Rd. South Indian snacks, side dishes, and a range of beers served indoors or *al fresco* on a breezy balcony. Inexpensive to moderate.

Saurashtra

SAURASHTRA, also known as the **Kathiawar Peninsula**, forms the bulk of Gujarat state, a large knob of land spreading south from the hills and marshes of the north out to the Arabian Sea, cut into by the Gulf of Cambay and the Gulf of Kutch on the east and west. This is Gujarat at its most diverse, with Hindu, Jain, Buddhist and Muslim architecture, modern urban centres and traditional bazaars, populated by cattle-rearing tribes and industrialists. Saurashtra boasts India's finest Jain temple city at **Shatrunjaya** near **Palitana**, Krishna temples at **Dwarka** and **Somnath** and Ashoka's Buddhist capital, **Junagadh**. Lions thrive in **Gir Forest**, while in the flat yellow grassland northeast of Bhavnagar India's largest herd of black buck live in a protected sanctuary at **Velavadar**. Gandhi's birthplace is still honoured in **Porbandar**; he is also remembered by a museum in **Rajkot** where he spent some years. The best place to head for to enjoy sun, sea and beaches is the island of **Diu**, just off the south coast.

Bhavnagar

The coastal port of **BHAVNAGAR**, founded in 1723 by the Gohil Rajput Bhavsinghji, whose ancestors came to Gujarat from Marwar (Rajasthan) in the twelfth century, is an important trading centre whose principal export is cotton. With few sights of its own, Bhavnagar does, however, boast a fascinating bazaar in the old city, and is the obvious place to stay before heading southwest to the wonderful Jain temples of Palitana (see p.548). It also has a curious public transport system – double-decker buses precariously hinged onto truck engines – and is one of the few places (Ahmedabad is another) where you'll see hand-carts being pulled by man and wife, or women alone.

Arrival and information

Flights connect Bhavnagar with Bombay (Mon, Tues, Thurs & Sat; 50min). The airport lies 5km southeast of town; *Indian Airlines* (Mon–Fri 9am–1pm & 2–4.30pm; ☎0278/24745) is on Diwanpara Rd near the *Life Insurance* building.

Bhavnagar can also be reached by **hovercraft** from Surat across the Gulf of Cambay (1 daily; 2hr 30min). *Sita Ram Travels*, Kala Nala, opposite the Madhadeep complex (☎0278/20466 or 28224), sells tickets: book in advance but remember that crossings are not always guaranteed. Coming by **bus**, you'll pull in to the station on ST Station Rd, west of the centre. **Trains** arrive from Ahmedabad at the north end of Station Rd, which runs south into town. For **Diu**, take a bus to Una (12 daily; 5hr 30min).

The City

The focus of interest in Bhavnagar is the **old city**, alive with character and charm, its vibrant markets overlooked by delicate wooden balconies and the plush pillared fronts of former merchants' houses. Sections of the old city are reserved for specific trades; there's a silver bazaar, a street lined with rope and tool stalls, a cloth bazaar where tailors perch like birds in tiny cubby holes above the shops, and a gold bazaar full of watchmakers and menders. Local handicrafts to look out for include *bhandani* and the elaborate beadwork characteristic of the region.

Bhavnagar has only a couple of formal attractions. The marble temple, **Ganga Devi Mandir**, by the dry tank in the centre of town has a large dome and intricate lattice work in its walls, while the otherwise unspectacular **Takhteshwar temple**, raised on a hill in the south of town, at least affords a good view over the city to the Gulf of Cambay in the east. Southwest of the town centre on Diamond Chowk is the **Gandhi Smriti Museum** (Mon–Sat 8.30am–12.30pm & 2.30–6pm; free). Labelled mostly in Gujarati, the exhibits include Buddhist, Jain and Hindu statues, medieval bronzes, Harappan terracottas and a fossil display flanked by the four-metre jaw bones of a sperm whale. Upstairs is a display devoted to Gandhi's life, and a *Khadi Gramodyog* shop (3–6pm).

Accommodation

Bhavnagar has a reasonable choice of **places to stay**. There are a few budget hotels near the railway station, which also has retiring rooms; the more upmarket options are in Darbargadh, towards the bus stand, and around the bus stand itself.

Apollo, ST Station Rd, opposite the bus stand (☎0278/25251). Carpeted, clean rooms with TV, some a/c. ④.

Blue Hill, opposite Pil Gardens (☎0278/26951). Modern, well-maintained five-storey hotel with all mod cons, views over the gardens from front rooms, and a roof terrace. ⑥.

Jubilee, opposite Pil Gardens (☎0278/20045). Similar to the *Blue Hill*, but a little less smart. ⑤.

Mini, Station Rd (☎0278/24415). Clean, well-kept rooms (doubles only), some without windows. ①.

Nilambagh Palace, ST Station Rd (☎0278/24241 or 21337). The classiest hotel in Bhavnagar; an old palace set in vast gardens west of the bus stand. Large luxurious rooms. ⑦.

Paradise, Station Rd. Very inexpensive; not that clean, but each room has its own bathroom. ①.

Shital, Darbargadh (☎0278/28773). Small hotel; basic accommodation and a men's dormitory. ①.

Vrindavan, Darbargadh (☎0278/27391). Immaculately clean but unelaborate rooms set in part of an old palace in the centre of town. The best value for budget travellers. ①.

Eating

Most of Bhavnagar's **restaurants** adjoin the main hotels, and offer local, national and international cuisine; the most extravagant is in the *Nilambagh Palace Hotel*. An excellent unnamed place behind the Police Chowk on Gandhi Rd stays open all day for low-priced local *thalis*. Look out for good juice centres in the jewellery bazaar.

Blue Hill, opposite Pil Gardens. Two restaurants – *Nilgiri* (Indian, Chinese and western) and *Gokul* (Gujarati *thali*) – both vegetarian, of a high standard, and moderately priced.

JK Restaurant & Pan House, High Court Rd. A cheap place for traditional Gujarati food.

Jubilee, opposite Pil Gardens. Two good veg restaurants: *Ankur* for Indian, western and Chinese, and *Girnar* for south Indian and Gujarati dishes. Prices are lower than at the *Blue Hill*.

Manali, *Apollo Hotel*, ST Station Rd. Excellent meat and vegetarian dishes, served in a clean and fresh restaurant. Good breakfasts at medium prices from 10am.

Mini Dining Hall, *Hotel Mini*, Station Rd. Simple local dishes at low prices.

Natraj, near Ganga Devi Mandir. Popular mid-range place, north of the crossroads of Gandhi Rd and High Court Rd. Tasty veg south Indian and Punjabi food, and a great ice cream selection.

Velavadar Black Buck Sanctuary

Outside the tiny village of **Velavadar**, 65km north of Bhavnagar, the **Black Buck Sanctuary** (best Nov–May) shelters the highest concentration of this Indian antelope anywhere in India. Although the area was officially declared a sanctuary in 1969, the buck were always protected by the Bishnoi tribe (see p.166). You can see the elegant black-and-white males strutting, chasing and jousting with their magnificent curved horns to define and defend their territories, each accompanied by a group of light-coloured females. It is also possible to walk in the park, and watch for wolves, now rare in India, who visit the water holes betwen dawn and dusk.

Buses leave Bhavnagar for Valabhipur (40km; 50min) eight times daily, but as the only connecting service to Velavadar is at 3.15pm, a visit to the sanctuary entails at least one night's **stay** at the small, perfectly located *Kaliyar Bhavan Forest Lodge* (①). **Permission** must be sought from Bhavnagar's Forest Office, Multi Storeyed Building, Annexe F/10, just west of the bus stand. Remember to ask about the availability of food – if the lodge is empty, you may have to take your own supply. Buses return to Valabhipur from Velavadar at 7 and 9am, and 7pm.

Palitana

For many visitors, the highlight of a trip to Saurashtra is a climb up the holy hill of **Shatrunjaya** (accessible from 7am–7pm), India's principal Jain pilgrimage site, just outside **PALITANA**, 50km southwest of Bhavnagar. Almost nine hundred temples – many made of marble – crown this hill, said in legend to be a chunk of the mighty Himalayas where the Jains' first *tirthankara*, Adinath, and his chief disciple gained enlightenment. While records show that the hill was a *tirtha* as far back as the fifth century, the existing temples date only to the sixteenth century, anything earlier having been lost in the iconoclastic Muslim raids of the 1500s and 1600s.

Climbing the wide steps up Shatrunjaya takes roughly two hours, though as with all hilltop pilgrimage centres, *dholis* (seats on poles held by four bearers) are available for those unable, or unwilling, to walk. The view as you approach is magnificent, with spires and towers swooping upwards, hemmed in by mighty protective walls. Once there, allow at least two more hours to see even half the temples.

The individual *tuks* – temple enclosures – are named after the merchants who funded them. Together they create a formidable city, fortified by the thick walls and laid over the two summits of Shatrunjaya. Each *tuk* comprises courtyards within court-yards, chequered in black-and-white marble, and several temples, their walls exqui-sitely and profusely carved with saints, birds, animals, buxom maidens, musicians and dancers. Many temples are two, or even three storeys high, with perfectly proportioned pavilions crowning balconies, looming conical *shikharas* (spires), and within, ceilings rising to the highest point, swarming with carved figures that flow in concentric circles outwards from a central lotus blossom.

The largest temple, dedicated to **Adinath**, in the Khartaravasi *tuk* on the northern ridge, constantly hums with murmured prayers and blessings, and is usually full of masked nuns and monks, dressed in white and carrying white fly-whisks. The southern ridge, and the spectacular **Adishvara** temple in its western corner, is reached by taking the right-hand fork at the top of the path. On a clear day, the view from the summit takes in the Gulf of Cambay to the south, Bhavnagar to the north and the mountain range which includes Mount Girnar in the west.

The **museum** close to the bottom of the hill displays a collection of Jain artefacts, labelled in Gujarati but well worth seeing, and an ancient clock that invites much atten-tion every hour when a model man emerges from a hole to hit a bell.

A path along the ridge and into the valley of Adipur, 13km away, is open for one day only, on the festival **Falgun Suth Tera** in celebration of Adinath, during the light half of the lunar month Falgun (Feb/March). Up to fifty thousand pilgrims come to Shatrunjaya for this unique display of devotion, and are welcomed at the end of their *yatra* in a tented compound at Adipur with food and drink donated by Jain merchants.

Practicalities
Buses arrive from, and leave for, Bhavnagar (1hr–1hr 30min) every fifteen minutes. A slow **train** service connects Palitana with Bhavnagar and Ahmedabad, via Sihor.

There is no **accommodation** on Shatrunjaya, so you'll have to stay in Palitana, either at one of many Jain *dharamshalas* in the old part of town that oblige guests to observe strict vegetarianism, or in a hotel nearer the bus stand. The comfortable GTDC *Hotel Sumeru* (☎2327; ①/④–⑤) on Station Rd, between the bus stand and the train station, has ordinary and a/c rooms, and inexpensive dorms. Its restaurant serves lunchtime *thalis*, evening buffets and simple breakfasts. Accommodation at the *Hotel Shavrak* (☎2428; ①/②), opposite the bus stand, is adequate, though less spacious; it also has inexpensive men-only dorms. In the narrow alley next to it, the basic *Jagurti Restaurant* serves excellent Gujarati meals and snacks, and is always busy.

Diu

Set a little off the southern tip of Gujarat, the island of **DIU**, less than 12km long and only 3km wide, was until thirty years ago under Portuguese control. Today, governed from Delhi along with Goa and Daman, it stands apart, and has a relaxed atmosphere quite different from anywhere in central Saurashtra. Though its smallish beaches are nowhere near as idyllic as in Goa, most visitors stay longer than intended, idling in cafes, cycling around the island, or strolling along the cliffs. The leisurely pace is also due in part to the lack of alcohol restrictions: the island's many bars can ply you with a vast array of beers and several good whiskies.

Diu island is easy to explore by bike. Diu Town in the northeast is the focus, where a maze of alleys lined with distinctive Portuguese buildings form the hub of the **old town**, while the **fort** covers the eastern tip of the island and looks out to the Gulf of Cambay and the Arabian Sea. Along the northern coast the island's main road runs past salt pans that give way to mud-flats sheltering flocks of water birds, including flamingoes that stop to feed in early spring. The route skirting the south coast passes rocky cliffs and beaches, the largest of which is **Nagoa Beach**, before reaching the tiny fishing village of **Vanakbara** in the very west of the island.

A brief history
The earliest records of Diu date from 1298, when it was controlled by the Chudasana dynasty. Soon after, like most of Gujarat, it fell into the hands of invading Muslims, and by 1349 was ruled by Muhammad bin Tughluq who successfully boosted the shipbuilding industry. Diu prospered as a Gujarati harbour, and in 1510 came under the government of the Ottoman Malik Ayaz, who repelled besieging Portuguese forces in 1520 and 1521. Well aware of Diu's strategic position for trade with Arabia and the Persian Gulf, and having already gained a toehold in Daman on the eastern edge of the Gulf of Cambay, the Portuguese did not relent. Under the leadership of Nuno da Cunha, they tried again, but failed, to take the island in 1531. In 1535 Sultan Bahadur of Gujarat agreed to sign a peace accord with Nuno da Cunha, but when the two leaders met, Bahadur was murdered and the Portuguese took control of Diu, immediately building the fort and a strong wall around the town.

While local traders and merchants thrived under the new rule, many resented paying taxes to boost Portuguese coffers already full with profits from customs duties levied on all vessels using the port. In defiance, local seamen made a series of unsuccessful raids on Portuguese ships. Moghul and Arab attacks were courageously resisted, too, but the Portuguese were finally forced out in 1961 by the Indian government, who after a swift bombing campaign declared Diu part of the Union Territory.

Arrival and information

The usual point of entry to Diu island is by road, via **Goghla**, the small fishing village on the mainland that forms the northern edge of Diu territory. The *Ahmedpur Mandvi Beach Resort* (☎2212; ③) here is nothing special, with a poor restaurant that doesn't serve beer, and most people head straight on to the island. All foreigners must show passports and visas at a checkpoint before crossing the new bridge that meets the island at the northwestern edge of Diu Town. **Buses** usually pull in to the town's bus stand in front of the main square in the north, close to most of the hotels, but if you're unlucky you may be dropped at the old bus stand by the bridge, from where you'll have to walk 1km to the town centre. **Trains** to the Saurashtran coast reach the end of the line at **Delwada**, connected to Diu Town by hourly buses.

Diu's **airport**, 5km west of Diu Town near the south coast, claims to connect Diu to Bombay and Ahmedabad (Mon, Wed & Fri), but the service is not guaranteed: check with *Reshma Travels* opposite *Nilesh Hotel* in town. The **tourist office** (Mon–Sat 9.30am–6pm), 300m west of the main square on the north coast road, has maps and information on buses from Diu and Una (on the mainland) to the rest of Saurashtra.

The most common way to get around is by **bike**, rented from shops near the main square, or close to the gate on the town's western edge. Rickshaws are available, but if you're staying at Nagoa and want to get back from town at night expect high charges.

Diu Town

Cosy little **Diu Town** is protected by the fort in the east and a wall in the west. **Nagar Seth's Haveli**, one of the grandest of the town's distinctive Portuguese mansions, is on Makata Rd, hidden in the web of narrow streets that wind through the residential Old Portuguese District. Fishers make daily trips from the north coast in wooden boats; women lay the silvery catch out on rugs to sell in the market near the mosque.

Although the Christian population is dwindling, along with the old language, a few **churches** built by the former European inhabitants are still used. Portuguese mass is celebrated beneath the high ceilings and painted arches of **St Paul's**, while the church of **St Francis of Assisi** further south is now a museum, with an art gallery upstairs.

Diu's serene **fort** (daily 9am–6pm) still stands robust, resisting the battering of the sea on three sides and sheltering birds, jackals and the town jail. Its wide moat and coastal position enabled the fort to withhold attack by land and sea, but there are obvious scars from the Indian government's airstrikes in 1961 – notice the hole above the altar of the church in the southwest corner. Now abandoned almost completely to nature, and littered with centuries-old cannon balls, it commands excellent views out to sea and over the island; it's a great place simply to while away the hours.

Around the island

Cliffs and rocky pools make up much of the southern coast of the island, giving way to the occasional sandy stretch. South of Diu Town is the small **Jallandhar Beach**, and the larger **Chakratirth Beach** overlooked by a high mound, is a little to the west. By far the longest and most attractive beach, however, is at **Nagoa**, 7km west of town, where a single hotel offers simple facilities. Naturally, sunbathing is tempting on these sun-kissed sands, but many women visitors have reported hassle from local men. **Buses** from Diu to Nagoa beach leave infrequently from the old bus stand at the end of the bridge (Diu–Nagoa daily 7am, 9am, 10am, 4pm, 4.30pm; Nagoa–Diu 8am, 10.45am, 11.30am, 12.30pm, 3.30pm, 4.30pm, 5pm). If you spend the day at Nagoa, or are staying at Nagoa and want to come into town, keep an eye on the time – missing the last bus leaves you with little choice but to walk.

Not far out of town, a turning off the Nagoa Road leads to **FUDAM**, an attractive village of Portuguese houses washed in pale yellow and sky-grey, dominated by the smooth white bell towers of its church. One small outdoor **bar**, shaded by twisted palm fronds, stands in the centre of the village.

Accommodation and eating

The atmosphere of Diu's **hotels**, concentrated in Diu Town, around the central open-air markets and along Fort Road on the northeast coast, is in keeping with the leisurely pace of the island. Most are low-priced with their own **restaurant**, and a bar serving cold Indian beers. Small restaurant-bars around the main square offer basic Indian dishes, and fresh seafood; the clean and airy *Deepee Restaurant* next to the GPO serves superb south Indian and Gujarati food and ice-cream desserts.

Alishan, Fort Rd (☎028758/2340). Clean rooms with or without bathrooms; those with balconies and good views are a little more expensive. ②–③.

Apana, Fort Rd (☎028758/2112). Spacious rooms; the priciest have sea-facing balconies. ①–⑤.

Gangar Sagar Rest House, Nagoa Beach (☎028758/2249). The only hotel (and restaurant) on the island with a beachfront location. Very mellow, with a courtyard facing the sea. With prior permission, non-residents can enjoy great views and eat decidedly average food at the restaurant. ②.

Hare Krishna Guest House, a little west of the centre, past the fish market (☎028758/2113). Small, cosy place; cheap, basic rooms, some with balcony, and a restaurant. ①.

Jay Shankar, Jallandhar Beach. A restaurant-cum-bar serving delicious food (particularly good fresh seafood), with rooms available in a tiny family house. Peaceful, homely, simple and cheap. ①.

Mozambique, Market Square (☎028758/2223). A good choice. Clean and airy rooms in a Portuguese building with balconies overlooking the vegetable market and beyond to the sea. Hot water constantly available. Pleasant bar on verandah and an unreliable restaurant. ①.

Nilesh, set back from the fish market (☎028758/2189). Large and small plain rooms with or without bathroom, a few rodents, a constantly full bar and a limited menu of fish and Indian dishes. ①.

Prince, Main Bazaar (☎028758/2265). Large clean rooms with balconies (but not much of a view). Lacks character, though, and its restaurant only serves omelettes and bread. ①–③.

Samrat, Collectorate Rd (☎028758/2354). Diu island's one "upmarket" hotel. Comfortable, carpeted a/c rooms with balconies, attached bathroom and constant hot water. The restaurant dishes up tasty meals at prices a little higher than elsewhere. ③–⑤.

MOVING ON FROM DIU

The most convenient way to head on from Diu is by **bus**. Long-distance buses usually leave from the main square, but may depart from the stand near the end of the bridge: check with the tourist office. One daily bus goes to Ahmedabad (8hr), another to Rajkot (6hr 30min) and two to Veraval (2–3hr); the later service (1pm) continues to Porbandar.

For long journeys it may be more convenient to leave from **Una**, 10km away on the mainland, and served by hourly buses from Diu (40min). Una's large central bus stand is well connected to such Gujarati destinations as Ahmedabad (6 daily; 8hr), Bhavnagar (12 daily; 5hr 30min), Junagadh (9 daily; 5hr), Rajkot (6 daily; 6hr) and Veraval (hourly; 2hr).

The slow **train** for Junagadh (6hr 50min), via Sasan Gir (3hr 30min), leaves daily from Una (12.20pm) and Delwada (12.45pm). Buses may be quicker, but this is a pleasant and quiet way to travel through the fields and forests of south Saurashtra. The trains are often delayed; check exact departure times at the Diu tourist office.

Sanman (*Fun Club*), Fort Rd (☎028758/2273). Popular place facing the sea with a good verandah restaurant serving a varied menu. Large rooms with locally made rugs and high ceilings. ②.
Tourist Cottages, Jallandhar Beach. Charming cottages for two, three or four people on the coast overlooking the Arabian Sea, and a small but imaginative restaurant. ③–⑤.

Veraval and Somnath

On the Saurashtran coast, midway between Diu and Porbandar, the most lingering impression of the port of **VERAVAL** is its fishy stench. There's little to do here, unless you can endure the smells to watch the *dhow*-building in the docks, but Veraval is the jumping-off point for trips to **Somnath**, 5km east, whose temple is one of the twelve *jyotirlingas* of Shiva (see *Contexts*). Its shrines to Vishnu and connection with Krishna – who with the Yadavas possibly lived here during the time of the *Mahabharata* – make it equally important for Vaishnavites.

Somnath

SOMNATH consists of only a few streets and a bus station – even its famed sea-facing **temple** is little to look at, despite its many layered history. Legend has it that the site, formerly known as **Prabhas Patan**, was dedicated to Soma, the juice of a plant used in rituals and greatly praised for its enlightening and strengthening powers (and hallucinogenic influence) in the *Rig Veda*. The temple of Somnath itself is believed to have appeared first in gold, at the behest of the moon-god, next in silver, created by the sun-god, a third time in wood at the command of Krishna, and finally in stone, built by Bhimdeva, the strongest of the five Pandava brothers (from the *Mahabharata*).

The earliest definite record, however, dates the temple to the tenth century, when, rich from devotees' donations, it spilled over with precious stones and gold and rang to the sounds of musicians and dancing girls. Not surprisingly, such wealth came to the attention of the brutal iconoclast Mahmud of Ghazni, who captured and plundered so many of western India's cities (997–1030); the temple was battered and pillaged, and its riches taken to Afghanistan. The next seven centuries saw a cycle of rebuilding and sacking, though the temple lay in ruins for over two hundred years after a final sacking by Aurangzeb before the most recent reconstruction in 1950, funded by the wealthy Sardar Vallabhai Patel. Very little of the original structure remains, and although planned in the style of the Solanki period, the temple is built from unattractive modern stone. It's just possible, however, to imagine its former glory, from the height of the pillars supporting the towering *mandapa* and the fervour of the stream of devotees who pray in its airy halls. The main *pujas* are held at 7am, noon and 7pm.

In the small yard a little to the north, Somnath's fascinating **museum** (daily except Wed, 9am–noon & 3–6pm) contains most of the architectural treasures saved from the temple – statues, lintels, sections of the roof pillars, friezes and *toranas* from the tenth to twelfth centuries. At present it's all a bit cramped, but plans to move the collection to a new building opposite the bus stand will no doubt improve matters, and perhaps encourage the curators to invest in more explanatory labels.

Tongas and rickshaws gather outside the bus station, ready to take pilgrims to **temple sites east of Somnath**. Most important of these is **Triveni Tirth**, at the confluence of the Hiran, Saraswati and Kapil rivers as they flow into the sea: a peaceful place with a couple of new unspectacular temples. Before reaching the confluence, the road passes the ancient **Surya Mandir**, probably built during the Solanki period, and now cramped by a newer temple and concrete houses built almost against its walls. Close to the sea, **Triveni Ghat** marks the place where Krishna's body was supposedly cremated after he was killed by a hunter who mistook him for a deer.

Practicalities

Veraval is well-connected by road to Junagadh, Porbandar, Diu and Dwarka; the bus stand is west of town. **Trains** pull in north of town, from Junagadh (2hr 30min), Rajkot (4hr) and Ahmedabad (13hr). For long journeys by train from Veraval it's best to go to Rajkot and change. To get to Somnath take the **bus** from Veraval (Rs2; every 15min) – it stops a few hundred metres east of the Shiva temple. **Rickshaws** are also available (roughly Rs15 one-way, or Rs40 round-trip).

Veraval has a wider choice of **accommodation** than Somnath, but its smell and dirt is enough to dissuade anyone from staying here. If you do, the *Tourist Bungalow* on College Rd (☎20488; ①/③), on the outskirts near the shore and the lighthouse, offers cheap dorms and spacious rooms, and has a modest restaurant. Other places include the smarter *Hotel Kasturi* (②), tucked away in a narrow street south of the bus stand, and the rapidly declining *Hotel Satkar* (☎20120; ②–⑤), which has a good restaurant, but overlooks the noisy street directly opposite the bus stand. In Somnath, *Sri Somnath Guest House* (①), on Triveni Rd opposite the bus station, has inexpensive and very simple rooms, while the modern *Mayuram* (①–②), almost immediately next door, has less spartan, cleaner rooms. Twenty kilometres north along the coast, the old **summer palace** of the Junagadh nawabs at **Chorwad** is now a pleasant seaside hotel (book ahead at any tourist office; ☎96; ③–⑤), with separate cottages in well-tended gardens. There's nothing else to see or do here, which is a great part of its charm.

Food in Veraval and Somnath is unremarkable but easy to come by, usually in simple form in hotels or unelaborate roadside stalls.

Junagadh

The friendly small town of **JUNAGADH** (also spelt Junagarh), less than 100km inland from Diu, is an intriguing place, with a skyline broken by domes and minarets and narrow streets whose shopfronts brim with spices piled in high powdery pyramids. It's fun to amble through the town's lively bazaars, and with a mixture of Buddhist monuments, Hindu temples, mosques, bold gothic archways and mansions – not to mention the magnificent Jain temples on **Mount Girnar** – Junagadh is an exciting city to explore for anyone with an interest in architecture and a taste for history.

From the fourth century BC to the death of the mighty Ashoka (*c.* 232 BC), Junagadh was the capital of Gujarat under the Buddhist Mauryas. The short reigns of the Kshatrapas and the Guptas came to an end when the town passed into the hands of the Hindu Chudasanas, who in turn soon lost out to Muslim invaders. Muslim sovereignty lasted until Independence when, although the leaders planned to unite Junagadh with Pakistan, local pressure ensured that it became part of the Indian Union.

Because of the sanctity of Mount Girnar, the Shivratri festival (Feb/March) assumes particular importance in Junagadh, when thousands of saffron-clad *sadhus* come to camp around the town and in the surrounding hills. Fireworks, processions, chanting, *chillum*-smoking and demonstrations of body-torturing ascetic practices continue for nine days and nights. Tourists arriving in Junagadh at this time are in for a memorable experience, but rooms are at a premium; book well in advance.

Arrival and information

Trains to Rajkot, Ahmedabad and the south coast call at Junagadh's station, a little north of the town centre. The *Down* #352 leaves for Sasan Gir and Delwada (for Diu) at 6.10am daily. **Buses** pull into the central bus stand just west of Chittakhana Chowk from Rajkot, Jamnagar, and points south, while Girnar services use the local depot a short way south of Chittakhana Chowk.

JUNAGADH

Zoo & Sakar Bagh

Mejwadi Gate

STATION RD

Ⓐ

Junagadh Railway Station

Maqbara

Long Distance Bus Stand

Chittakhana Chowk

Ⓒ Hospital Ⓑ Circle Chowk

DHAL RD

Bank

Durbar Hall Museum

MAHATMA GANDHI RD

Ⓘ Local Bus Stand

Ⓔ Ⓕ

Ⓓ Kalwa Chowk

Lal Bagh

HOTELS:
Ⓐ GTDC Girnar
Ⓑ Relief
Ⓒ Anand
Ⓓ Jai Shree Guest House
  & Lake Guest House
Ⓔ National
Ⓕ Capital
RESTAURANTS:
Ⓘ Santoor

Caves

UPERKOT

Tank Girnar

GIRNAR RD

Ashokan Edicts

N

0   1km

GPO ▽   Willingdon Dam ▽

Local transport is provided by **rickshaws**, though **bicycles** are great for getting around; with a bit of leg-work you can even cycle to the foot of Mount Girnar. Run-of-the-mill bikes can be had from a shop just west of Chittakhana Chowk, or *Relief Hotel*.

The seldom enlightening **tourist office** is in the GTDC *Girnar Hotel*, but you'll get better information on the town's sites and the religious significance of Girnar from the *National* or *Relief* hotels. The **GPO** (poste restante) is 2km south of town; a smaller branch next to the local bus depot sells stamps and aerograms. You can change foreign currency at the *State Bank of India* (Mon–Fri 11am–3pm) on Mahatma Gandhi Rd.

The City

The town is fairly compact, focusing around **Chittakhana Chowk** and **Kalwa Chowk** 1km further south. **Durbar Hall** with its modest museum is in the centre of town, where **New Bazaar** fills a fine classical terrace between towering Gothic gateways.

The imposing fortified citadel of **Uperkot** (daily 6am–7pm) on a thickly walled mound in the northeast of Junagadh, is a peaceful place with a rich history, colonized today by eagles, egrets and squirrels. Legend dates the fort's origins to the time of the Yadavas (Krishna's clan) who fled Mathura to settle in Dwarka, but historians believe it was built by Chandragupta the Mauryan in 319 BC. Rediscovered and repaired in 976 AD by Muslim conquerors, it regained importance as a defence, withstanding sixteen sieges in the next eight hundred years.

A grand set of three high gateways cut into solid rock during the Muslim occupation stands at the entrance, spanning a cobbled walkway that winds upwards past a *kund* (small pool) and some modern Hindu temples, to the summit of the raised fort, where the **Jami Masjid** stands abandoned to nature. Supporting the high roof, many of its 140 pillars were taken from the Chudasana palace and feature common Hindu motifs. The two fierce cannons opposite the mosque were used at Diu fort in defence against the Portuguese in 1530 and brought here in 1538.

Heading north from the Jami Masjid, you come to a complex of small cells arranged around courtyards cut down into the rock. These **"Buddhist Caves"** were built in the third or fourth century AD – much worn traces of figurines and foliage can still be made out on the columns in the lower level. Nearby, over 170 steps descend to the well **Adi Chadi Vav**, believed to have been built as the bequest of two maidservants of the royal household in the fifteenth century. The more impressive eleventh-century **Navghan Kuva**, in the southeast of the citadel, consists of a superb staircase that winds around the well shaft to the dimly lit water level over 52m below. A large tank nearby collects water from the surrounding hills to supply the town.

Below the southern wall of the fort, the **Babupyara Caves**, hewn from the rock between 200 BC and 200 AD, were used by Buddhists until the time of Ashoka, and then by Jains. A little to the north of Uperkot, the slightly later, plainer **Khapra Kodia caves** remain in good condition, intersected with staircases, colonnades and passages.

East of the main entrance to Uperkot, in Diwan Chowk, the **Durbar Hall Museum** (daily except Wed, 9am–12.15pm & 3–6pm; Rs0.50; closed 2nd & 4th Sat of each month) takes up part of the former palace of the nawabs. Silver chairs in the great hall stand in regal splendour around a large carpet, valuable silver clocks encase scruffy stuffed birds, and huge coloured chandeliers hang from the ceiling. Surrounding rooms contain silver *howdahs* (elephant seats), weaponry, portraits, and a collection of textiles including 400-year-old cloth embroidered with gold thread, displayed alongside royal parasols overlaid with intricate needlework.

Junagadh's chief Muslim monuments are the boldly decorated **muqbara** – quite unlike any other in Gujarat – on Mahatma Gandhi Rd opposite the High Courts. Built for Muslim rulers in the nineteenth century, the mausolea, squat and square, are crowned with a multitude of bulbous domes, and smaller domes fronting balconies that overhang high curved arches cut into the tombs' sides. The most opulent is the sepulchre of Mahabat Khan I, but more outstanding, for its complex design, is that of Vizir Sahib Baka-ud-din Bhar, flanked on each corner by tall minarets hugged with spiral staircases. Next to the *muqbara* is a mosque whose multi-coloured pillars and gaily painted walls are oddly reminiscent of *Alice In Wonderland*.

A group of smaller memorials to earlier nawabs stand in a peaceful graveyard, shielded by shops on Chittakhana Chowk and overgrown with coarse yellow grass. Delicate in both size and design, they boast fine carving on the eaves and stone lattice work cut from the walls. You'll have to scramble around the back of the shops to find the entrance: the rooftop of the *Relief Hotel* opposite gives good aerial views.

Ashokan edicts

East of town on the road to Girnar a granite rock engraved with the Buddhist **edicts of Ashoka**, Junagadh's most famous monarch (daily except Wed, 8.30–11am & 2–6pm), remains where it was placed in the third century BC, its impact somewhat dampened by the modern shelter and crude concrete platform surround. Written in the Prakrit dialect, the worn verses etched into the stone encourage the practice of *dharma* and equality, beseech different religious sects to live in harmony, and repent the evils of war (see *Contexts*). Situated on the route taken by pilgrims to the sacred hill of Girnar, the influence of Ashoka's edicts was strong; even as late as the seventh century AD there were about 3000 monks in Junagadh, and over 50 convents. Sanskrit inscriptions on the same rock were added during the reigns of King Rudraman (150 AD) and Skandagupta (455 AD).

Mount Girnar

Rising to a height of over 1100m, **Mount Girnar**, a steep-sided extinct volcano 4km east of Junagadh, is a major pilgrimage centre for both Jains and Hindus, and has been considered sacred since before the third century BC. Buses leave from Junagadh's local depot hourly, dropping passengers at the mountain base, from where five thousand irregular steps lead to the summit. It's best to start the ascent, which takes at least two hours, well before 7am, when the scorching sun rises from behind the peak. The path climbs through eucalyptus forests before zig-zagging across the sheer rock face, and there's a ready supply of *chai* and biscuits at stalls along the way.

On a plateau below the summit, roughly ninety minutes' climb from the base of the steps, the picturesque huddle of Jain temples has been slightly renovated since its erection between 1128 and 1500. **Neminath**, the 22nd *tirthankara*, said to have died on Mount Girnar after 700 years of meditation and asceticism, is depicted as a black figure sitting in the lotus position holding a conch in the marble **Neminath Temple**, the first on the left as you enter the "temple city". The temple comprises a vast complex of courtyards, cloisters and lesser shrines, and has exquisite carving on its pillars and within the domed roofs, decorated outside with unusual coloured mosaic. Opposite, the **Mallinath Temple** was built by the brothers Vastupal and Tejapala who also funded temples in Mount Abu and Shatrunjaya. Chequered black-and-white marble floors run through the three sanctuaries off the entrance porch. Carved musicians and dancers adorn the ceiling of the main shrine, and two smaller shrines feature images of *tirthankaras* raised on marble platforms.

It's well worth making the effort to climb the final two thousand steps to the summit of Mount Girnar. The views on the way are breathtaking. At the top, a temple dedicated to the Hindu goddess **Amba Mata** attracts both Hindu and Jain pilgrims, particularly newlyweds who come here to be blessed by the mother goddess, and pray for a happy marriage. Steps lead down from this temple and then up again along a narrow ridge towards **Gorakhnath Peak**, where a small shrine covers what are supposedly the footprints of the pilgrim Gorakhnath, and further to a third peak where the imprints of Neminath's feet are sheltered by a small canopy. At the most distant point of the ridge, a shrine dedicated to the fierce Hindu goddess **Kalika**, the eternal aspect of Durga, is a haunt for near-naked **Aghora ascetics** who express their absolute renunciation of the world by ritually enacting their own funerals, living among corpses on burial grounds, and smearing themselves with ash from funeral pyres.

Sakar Bagh

The pleasant flower-filled Sakar Bagh, 3.5km north of Junagadh, encloses the **zoo** and the small **Junagadh Museum** (daily except Wed, 9am–12.15pm & 3–6.15pm), which houses an assortment of pre- and proto-historic implements, medieval statues, manuscripts, ornaments and stuffed animals. The zoo, renowned for the successful breeding of endangered Asiatic lions, houses wolves, tigers, birds and bears, all a little cramped in treeless cages, and a dim aquarium boasting nothing more impressive than goldfish.

Accommodation and eating

Junagadh offers average, simple **accommodation**: a decent choice for budget travellers, but little with any claim to comfort and mod-cons. Hotel food halls are supplemented by small streetside stalls, and one or two **restaurants**; *Chai Thali Dukhan*, opposite the museum, is a great place for *thalis*, tea and coffee, while *Santoor Restaurant*, south of Chittakhana Chowk on Mahatma Gandhi Rd serves excellent south Indian and Punjabi dishes at very reasonable prices.

Anand, Bus Station Rd (☎22657). Clean and fresh with some a/c rooms. ②–⑤.

Capital, Kalwa Chowk. Similar to the neighbouring *Lake* and *Jai Shree* Guest Houses – all are cheap and low-standard, adequate for the more hardy budget traveller. ①.

GTDC Girnar, Mejwadi Gate (☎21201). Government-run hotel in the quiet outskirts of town: clean but impersonal with a reasonable restaurant that serves dinner from 6pm. ③–④.

National, Kalwa Chowk (☎27891). Carpeted, clean and comfy, and very good value. Delicious food in downstairs restaurant. ②–⑤.

Relief, Chittakhana Chowk (☎20280). Small, homely rooms, some with private bathrooms. Average restaurant that will serve breakfast as early as 5am. ②.

Gir National Park

The **Asiatic lion**, which thanks to hunting, forest-cutting and poaching has been extinct in the rest of India since the 1880s, now survives in the wild in just 1150 square kilometres of the gently undulating Gir Forest. **Gir National Park** (Nov–May, daily 9am–6pm), entered from **Sasan Gir**, 60km southeast of Junagadh and 45km northeast of Veraval, holds almost 300 Asiatic lions in its 260 square kilometres. They share the land with Maldhari cattle breeders, whose main source of income is buffalo milk. Many families have been relocated outside the sanctuary, but those who remain are paid compensation by the government for the inevitable loss of buffalo to marauding lions. Gir also shelters 200 **panthers**, more visible here than in any other Indian park.

Permits covering entry for up to three days can be obtained at the **park information centre** in the *Sinh Sadan Guest House* in Sasan Gir (Rs15 for foreigners plus Rs8 for camera, or Rs15 for video; Indian residents pay less). You must enter the park in a jeep (Rs6 per km, plus Rs8 for a guide, and a tip) and can stay for a maximum of three hours on any one visit. Guides, although lethargic and downright unenthusiastic at times, should know likely spots for sightings, and may be flexible enough to follow any

---

THE ASIATIC LION

The rare **Asiatic lion** (*panthera leo persica*) is paler and shaggier than the more common African breed, with longer tail tassles, more prominent elbow tufts and a larger belly fold. Probably introduced to India from Persia, the lions were widespread in the Indo-Gangetic plains at the time of the Buddha, and in 300 BC Kautilya, the minister of Chandragupta Maurya, offered them protection by declaring certain areas *abharaya aranyas*, "forests free from fear". Later, in his rock-inscribed edicts, **Ashoka** admonished those who hunted the majestic animals – the emblem of Ashoka, printed on all Indian currency notes, shows four Asiatic lions standing back to back.

Such a symbol of potency was favourite game for India's nineteenth-century rulers, and by 1913, not long after it had been declared a protected species by the Nawab of Junagadh, the Asiatic lion population was reduced to twenty. Since then, Gir Forest has been recognized as a sanctuary (1969), and a national park (1975), and their number has swelled to over 250. While this is good news for the lions, they are starting to stray from the sanctuary, and recent attacks on humans and their livestock have caused justifiable concern. If plans to create a new sanctuary near Porbandar come to fruition, the lions should be assured security in their natural habitat.

route you wish to take (maps are available at the information centre). Two good tracks are "Deva Danga" and "Riley's", or out to the lake near Kamelshwar, just west of the park boundary, where there's a good chance of glimpsing a marsh crocodile.

The lions are used to human noise, and seem not to be disturbed by jeeps, so if you do see one – and you probably will – you should be able to watch it for a while. For a failsafe guarantee, head for **Dewaliya** (daily except Wed, 9am–noon & 3–6pm; Rs70), a small fenced-off area of the park known as the "interpretation centre". Buses leave Sasan Gir for Dewaliya at 9am and noon, and in the centre visitors are driven in a mini-bus past docile lions. It's certainly not *wild*, but you'll see them very close up.

Practicalities

Sasan Gir village is connected by **train** to Junagadh and Veraval, and by **bus** to Junagadh, Veraval and Una. The railway station, which also serves as a bus stand, is set back from the one main road that bisects the tiny town.

There are only two **hotels**. The Forest Department's *Sinh Sadan Guest House* (☎40; ①–⑤) on the main road has large attractive rooms, all with mosquito nets, in an old house amid well kept gardens. It's a delightful place to stay, but should be booked ahead by phone, or at a tourist office. Reasonably priced meals are available for residents, and the **park information centre** is in the grounds.

Off the main road, past a small crocodile farm, the GTDC *Lion Safari Lodge* (☎21 or 28; ①/④–⑤) is shabbier, but the rooms are comfortable, each with private bath and towels provided. They also have four-bed dorms, and a dining hall serves great meals which should be ordered in advance. Another good place to **eat** is the stall at the station end of the main road.

Porbandar

Once an international port and state capital, **PORBANDAR**, smack in the middle of the 200km of coastline between Veraval and Dwarka, is inextricably associated with the **Gandhis**. Most famously it's the birthplace of Mahatma Gandhi, just one in an important political line – his uncle, father and grandfather all served as prime minister to the Maharaja of the Jethwa Rajput state. In addition, and in common with much of the southwest coast of Saurashtra, Porbandar is linked with the legends of **Krishna** – in ancient times the settlement was called Sudampuri, after one of Krishna's comrades.

Today, shrouded in a dim haze of smokey excretions from the cement and chemical factories on its outskirts, Porbandar has little to attract tourists, save, of course, Gandhi's house. Nevertheless, it's a relaxing place to pass some time, and a stroll through the characterful back streets, flanked with neatly carved wooden balconies, is pleasant enough. The town is bunched between the coast and a freshwater creek that curves around the north to meet the sea at the harbour – usually busy with shipbuilders and fishermen – in the west. A path follows the coast from east to west but the beaches in between, used as public toilets, are rather unpleasant.

Arrival and information

State buses pull in south of town, a few minutes' walk from the coast; the **railway** station is further north (daily trains to and from Bombay via Jamnagar, Rajkot, Ahmedabad, Vadodara and Surat). There are no private bus services. In town **rickshaws** are the commonest form of transport, but since Porbandar is almost completely flat it's easy to cycle. A shop opposite the bus stand rents **bikes** at low hourly rates.

The **tourist office** (☎22745), often unmanned, is five minutes' walk from the bus stand in *Toran Tourist Bungalow*, which has a large map of Porbandar in the front hall. There's a **GPO** (Mon–Sat 8am–6pm) close to the bus stand, and **banks** along Mahatma Gandhi Rd that accept travellers' cheques.

The Town

Mohandas Karamchand Gandhi was born in Porbandar in October 1869 and lived here until he was twelve. **Gandhi's birthplace** (free, but the guide will expect a donation) stands in the corner of a large courtyard in the west of town, in a narrow street entered through a large triple gateway and lined with carved wooden houses. There's barely anything to see inside the small three-storey structure; it is little changed since the family left in 1881, save for some fresh green paint on the wooden stairs and doorways. The whole place is empty, though some of the walls in the reading and prayer rooms on the upper floors bear faded traces of paintings.

The modern temple next to the house, **Kirti Mandir** (*kirti* means age), was donated to the city in 1950 by the industrialist Nanjibhai Kalidas, to commemorate Gandhi's 79 years of life; note the 79 lamps adorning its 79-foot-high spire. Upstairs, a **museum** has a display of photographs, hand-made Gujarati crafts and a bizarre collection of bottled seeds and oils – perhaps something to do with Gandhi's belief in self-sufficiency – while downstairs there's a small **bookstore**.

Mahatma Gandhi Road begins a little south of the triple gateway and runs east through the centre of town. To the north of the gateway, past **Jubilee Bridge** and fronted by a highly revered statue of Nehru, is the desperately old-fashioned **Planetarium** (shows in Gujarati 9.30am, 11.30am, 3.30pm & 5.30pm; Rs2; men and women must queue and enter separately). Directly opposite, set in a verdant garden, the airy pillared hall **Bharat Mandir** – another Kalidas benefaction – was built in memory of popular Hindi heroes. The divine, godly bodies of mythical figures are bright and distinct on the walls, and in the centre of the floor there's a large relief map of India.

Accommodation and eating

Porbandar has just enough **hotels** to cater to its few visitors. Those on the coast are the best, with sea views; places in town are more cramped, and invaded by traffic noise. Outside the hotel restaurants, there's a fairly uninspiring choice of **places to eat**; many seem to serve only one or two of the dishes listed on the menus. The *Samrat* on MG Rd is the best restaurant in town, serving excellent, medium-priced Punjabi and south Indian veg dishes in a softly lit environment, while the *National* is the best of a bunch near the main square.

Flamingo, MG Rd (☎23123). Comfortable, clean hotel with ordinary inexpensive rooms and luxurious a/c suites. ①/⑤.

New Oceanic Hotel, Villa No 8, Seaface Chowpatty (☎20217). Cosy rooms, some a/c, in a modern sea-facing house. The pleasant garden terrace holds a good, if pricey, restaurant. ⑤.

Rajkamal Guest House, MG Rd (☎20374). Cheap and cheerful hotel next to the *Flamingo*. ①.

Rupalee, Rupalee Corner (☎22873). A clean and basic lodge with an upstairs dining hall, opposite *Harish Talkies*. The restaurant serves filling all-you-can-eat *thalis* at extremely low prices. ①.

Sheetal, Junagadh Rd (☎23596). Curious, plush lodge opposite the GPO: all rooms have bathrooms. Those with a/c offer a real treat – padded wardrobes and bath tubs. ③–⑤.

Toran Tourist Bungalow, Chowpatty (☎22745). Large, clean rooms with sea-facing balconies. Two excellent cheap six-bed dorms, and bathrooms with constant hot water. A simple indoor restaurant facing the sea serves tasty but unimaginative dishes, if you order in advance. ①/④.

Vaibhav Guest House, MG Rd (☎23686). Opposite *State Bank of India*. Small but clean rooms and larger deluxe suites with or without a/c. ③–⑤.

Around Porbandar

Inland from Porbandar, a scattering of ancient temples are easily visited in a day. **Bileshwar**, an hour north (4 buses daily from the bus stand), is a small village built round an early seventh-century Shiva temple. Though the temple's exterior is of little interest, coated in modern plaster, the inner sanctuary has a large monument dating from the Maitraka period (sixth to seventh centuries). Twenty kilometres further, in a serene wooded valley, **Ghumli** boasts one of Gujarat's largest step-wells. Dating from the early twelfth century, **Vikai Vav** is superb, with richly carved pillars and pavilions topped by peaked pyramidal roofs; at the more dilapidated (thirteenth-century) **Naulakha temple** you can still see elaborate decorations beneath the collapsed roof. It's best to visit Ghumli early in the morning, as bus services back to Porbandar are infrequent.

Dwarka

In the very west of the peninsula, fertile wheat, groundnut and cotton fields, lightly ruffled by a cool sea breeze, emerge in vivid contrast to the arid expanses further inland. According to popular Hindu legend, Krishna fled Mathura (see p.228) to this coastal region, declaring **DWARKA** his capital. A labyrinth of narrow winding streets cluttered with temples, today the town resonates with the bustle of eager saffron-clad pilgrims and the clatter of celebratory drums. Dwarka really comes to life during the major Hindu festivals; the most fervent are Maha-Shivratri, dedicated to Shiva (Feb/March) and Janmashtami, Krishna's birthday (Aug/Sept).

The elaborately carved tower of **Dwarkadish temple** (daily 6am–12.30pm & 5–9pm) looms proudly 50m above the town. Inside, the sixteenth-century sanctuary, voluptuously sculpted and spilling out swirls of incense and murmured prayers, is surrounded by smaller shrines nestling in chiselled corners beneath sturdy pillars. Non-Hindus can enter only on signing a form declaring, at the very least, respect for religion. Get small change for donations from the change-*wallahs* at the east entrance.

When Krishna came to Dwarka with the Yadava clan, he eloped with Princess Rukmini. One kilometre east of town, the small **Rukmini temple** – which local priests may tell you is 1500 years old, but in fact dates from the twelfth century – is, if anything, more architecturally impressive than the Dwarkadish temple, with carvings of elephants, flowers, dancers and Shiva in several of his aspects covering every wall.

Practicalities

Trains from Jamnagar (2 daily; 3–4 hr) arrive at the station north of town from where tongas ferry visitors to hotels and the temple. The **bus stand** on the road to Okha has regular services to and from Jamnagar, three daily to Porbandar and two to Somnath.

Accommodation in Dwarka is, for the most part, cheap and unelaborate. The well-kept *Toran Tourist House* (☎313; ①), out of town near the coast, offers dorms and double rooms, all with mosquito nets. Both the *Radhika* (☎454; ④), opposite the bus stand (which has a disappointing restaurant), and the *Guruprena* (☎385; ④), closer to the town centre, have a/c and non-a/c rooms, but neither is in tip-top condition. Very near Dwarkadish temple, *Uttam Guest House* (☎234; ①) is homely enough, while towards the railway station *Vanda Guest House* (☎440; ①) and *Hotel Meera* (☎331; ①) are both clean and comfortable.The latter serves undoubtedly the best **food** in town, with splendid, limitless, lunch and dinner *thalis* for under Rs15.

Bet Dwarka

A day trip to the tiny island of **Bet Dwarka**, also closely associated with the Krishna legend, is a must for any pilgrim to Dwarka, as its (architecturally uninspiring) temple is said to stand on the spot where Krishna died. Small, precariously full wooden dinghies transport pilgrims from the port of **OKHA**, on the westernmost point of the peninsula, to the island, where devotees scatter *rupees* and flowers towards Krishna's shrine and wait eagerly for the appearance of the priest who hands out *prasad* (blessed food). Not surprisingly, fishing is a big source of income around here, but due to pollution, salt production and the destruction of mangroves, the quantity of fish is dangerously declining.

State **buses** run from Dwarka to Okha (1hr) every thirty minutes; private buses leave from the vegetable market at 8am and 2pm; and there are frequent jeeps.

Jamnagar

Close to the northwest coast of Saurashtra, the busy, noisy city of **JAMNAGAR** preserves at its heart some fabulous architectural surprises. Founded in the sixteenth century, the walled city was built to the east of Ranmal Lake, centering on the circular Lakhota Fort. **KS Ranjitsinjhi**, the famously elegant cricketer who played for England alongside WG Grace, ruled Jamnagar for several years at the turn of the century, improving commercial contacts and replacing run-down buildings with attractive constructions that remain as testimony to a prosperous and efficient rule. The city is renowned for excellent *bandhani* (tie-dye), sold in its markets.

Arrival

Buses from Rajkot, Junagadh and Dwarka arrive at the bus station (known as ST stand), a few kilometres west of town on a standard rickshaw route, at the far end of Ranmal Lake. Detailed and up-to-date timetables are available from the *Hotel Punit*. The **railway station** is northwest of town, beyond India's best Ayurvedic university.

The City

The most remarkable of Ranjitsinjhi's constructions is **Willingdon Crescent**, the swooping arches of its curved facade overlooking the wide streets of Chelmsford Market. In the heart of town, just off the road west from Bedi Gate, stands a sturdy domed mansion – now a school. It faces a wide street with Jamnagar's late nineteenth-century Friday Mosque, **Jami Masjid**, at its head. This grand domed prayer hall, its sandalwood doors inlaid with mother-of-pearl, is the unlikely neighbour to a magnificent pair of **Jain temples**, one dedicated to Adinath (the first *tirthankara*) and one built to honour Shantinath (the sixteenth). The quality and quantity of the **murals** on the walls, ceilings and pillars of the temples is extraordinary. Hazy yellows, greens, pinks, oranges and blues depict a riot of flowers, people, gods and domestic objects, while tableaux tell the life stories of Jain saints. The most spectacular of the two, **Shantinath Mandir**, is a maze of brightly coloured columns, each section of roof between them highlighted with individual designs; the marble floor beneath is emblazoned with distinctive Jain patterns in yellow, black, white and red. Above the main sanctuary, an enormous dome rises in a series of concentric circles glinting with gold. The outer side of the large dome over **Adinath Mandir** is inlaid with gold and coloured mosaic, and both temples have cupolas enriched with a design of mirrors above the entrance porch.

The temples form the hub of **Chandni Chowk**, an almost circular market area enhanced by doorways edged with mosaic panels. Small lanes flanked with the meticulously carved wooden doors and balconies of ancient homes lead off the *chowk*.

Stretching west, far out of town, Ranmal Lake acts as a wide moat and defence for **Lakhota Fort** (daily except Wed, 9am–noon & 3–6pm), connected to solid land by a causeway guarded by the stolid Bhirbhunjan Gate. Thick circular walls studded with gun-holes protect the inner building. On entering you'll pass a guardroom still containing muskets, swords and powder flasks; the **museum** on the upper floor holds a mediocre display of paintings, sculpture, folk art and coins.

Accommodation

Acceptable **accommodation** is very limited in Jamnagar. If you're on a low budget you'll have to grit your teeth and face the bedbugs, or dive into your pocket and pay a little more than normal. Only those worth considering are listed below. Most of the cheap places are in and around **New Super Market**, a three-storey complex at Bedi Gate, humming with the murmur of offices and daily trading in clothes shops. The more expensive hotels are good, though there aren't many to choose from.

Anand, First Floor, New Super Market, Bedi Gate (☎78983). Rooms with bath are comfortable enough, but have little more than basic standards of hygiene. ①.

Aram, Nand Niwas, Pandit Nehru Marg (☎78521). Palatial old house with a garden restaurant a 20min walk towards the railway station from New Super Market. The large rooms, nostalgic for the days of the Raj and filled with European antiques, have a faded charm. Some a/c options. ⑤–⑥.

Ashiana, 3rd Floor, New Super Market, Bedi Gate (☎76525). Carpeted deluxe rooms and grubbier doubles; all have TV and bathroom with hot water. The best option in the New Super Market. ①–③.

Janki, Third Floor, Anjaria Chamber, KV Rd (☎72908). Clean and spacious, this is the best bet for those on low and medium budgets. Hot water and TV in all rooms, and a/c for a little extra. ①.

President, Teen Bati (☎70516 or 70253). Very clean, well-managed hotel offering parking facilities, bar, restaurant and currency exchange. Credit cards accepted. ⑤.

Punit, Pandit Nehru Marg. Only a few minutes' walk from New Super Market. Friendly, clean and popular, with a small roof terrace. More expensive a/c rooms. ③.

Shital, opposite New Super Market (☎79579). Cheap, with basic amenities. ①.

Eating

A fairly wide choice of good inexpensive **restaurants**, mostly cluttered at the top end of Pandit Nehru Marg, serve veg dishes; the *Vishnu Halwa House* nearby is an excellent sweet shop. Most places close at 10pm.

Amiras, *Hotel Ashiana*, New Super Market. Very tasty Punjabi and Gujarati dishes in humble surroundings. It's surprisingly cheap and opens early for breakfast.

Kalpana, Pandit Nehru Marg. Ageing decor but great food: south Indian, Punjabi, ice cream, fruit juice and milkshakes. Opens 9am.

Rangoli, between *Kalpana* and New Super Market. South Indian and Punjabi dishes at prices that are a little above average. Closes 11pm.

Seven Seas, *Hotel President*. A/c and dimly lit with comfortable seats. Indian, Chinese and western dishes at medium prices. Good if you fancy a meat feast.

The marine national park

The northwest coast of Saurashtra, bordering the heavily tidal Gulf of Kutch, is fringed with more than forty small islands, whose ever depleting mangrove population gives rise to some of the richest marine life off mainland India. In 1980, 295 square kilometres of the gulf was declared a marine sanctuary, and in 1982, over half of this was officially recognized as a **marine national park**.

The coast off Jamnagar has always been exploited for pearl fishing, and still supports a small population of pearl oysters. Permission to take a boat from Jamnagar to **Pirotan Island** – where the coral is particularly rich – can be sought from the Chief Conservator of Forests and Wildlife, Koti Annexe, Vadodara (see p.536); don't, however, count on them allowing you to make the trip. Besides abundant coral, the Gulf of Kutch shelters sea-turtles, snakes, dolphins, sharks and octopuses and attracts thousands of birds such as flamingoes, pelicans, harriers, cormorants, ibises and oyster-catchers.

Despite pressure from conservationists, the mangroves are still cut for firewood, and industries along the west coast of Saurashtra continue to pollute the sea with effluents. As the mangroves disappear, so does the aquatic life they support; mud from the coastline, no longer anchored by tree roots, is pushed from the shore to smother the coral reefs, thus denying fish their natural habitat.

Rajkot

Founded in the sixteenth century, **RAJKOT** was ruled by the Jadeja Rajputs until merging with the Union of Saurashtra after Independence, since when it has become a successful industrial centre. Best known for its associations with **Mahatma Gandhi**, who lived and worked here for some time, this quiet city has little to attract tourists except a museum and Gandhi's family home. Its central position, however, makes it a good base for trips to nearby Morvi, Wankaner and Whadwan, and parts of the old city, at least, do have a certain charm.

Arrival and information

Indian Airlines services from Bombay land at Rajkot's **airport**, 4km northwest of town (Wed, Fri & Sat). The airline office (Mon–Sat 10am–1pm & 2pm–5pm; ☎27916) is on Station Rd. There are two **railway** stations; you should get off at **Rajkot Junction**, just over 2km north of Jubilee Bagh (Gardens). Frequent **buses** from the State Bus Terminal connect Rajkot with other Gujarati towns; private buses offer faster services for long-distance journeys, but are invariably as full as the state buses. Bookings can be made at *Shree Sadguru Travels* behind the bus station.

Rajkot's modest **tourist office** (☎31616) is on Jawahar Rd, behind the *State Bank of Saurashtra*.

The Town

In the most appealing area of Rajkot, the **old city**, typical Gujarati wooden-fronted houses, with intricately carved shutters veiling stained-glass windows, stand among more modern, faceless constructions. The Gandhis moved here from Porbandar in 1881; tucked away in the narrow streets, on Ghitaka Rd, the family house **Kaba Gandhi no Delo** (Mon–Sat 9am–noon & 3–6pm) has a small display of artefacts and photographs from the Mahatma's life.

Rajkot's chief tourist attraction, however, is the **Watson Museum** (daily except Wed, 9am–12.30pm & 2.30–6pm, closed 2nd & 4th Sat of each month; Rs1), in a robust nineteenth-century building in Jubilee Bagh. The museum, named after Colonel Watson, British Political Agent from 1886 to 1893, displays relics from 2000 BC to the nineteenth century, including findings from Indus Valley sites, medieval statues, manuscripts, miniature paintings and Rajput bronzes. On the ground floor a vast collection of portraits of Gujarat's rulers surrounds a staunch Queen Victoria, fashioned in 1899 by Alfred Gilbert who modelled Eros in London's Piccadilly Circus. On the upper gallery, dioramas portray Gujarati tribal groups and their crafts and instruments. The **Lang Library** (daily except Wed, 9–10.50am & 5–6.50pm) next to the museum is a grand but seldom used cobwebbed reading room, flanked with dusty English-language books that seem to be less attractive to the locals than the daily Gujarati newspapers.

Accommodation

Rajkot's inexpensive **hotels** leave much to be desired, but a few are adequate. It's worth spending a little more to find welcome relief from the noise and dirt of the city.

Babha Guest House, Panchnath Rd (☎32187). The cleanest budget hotel. Small rooms. ①–②.

Galaxy, Jawahar Rd (☎31781). Forty-two spacious rooms – some a/c – on the third floor of a shopping complex. High standard of hygiene and service. ④–⑥.

Himalaya Guest House, Lakhajiraj Rd, Sanganwa Chowk (☎31736). A large place with reasonably clean rooms, all with private bathrooms; bucket hot water. ①.

Jay Kishan Guest House, Sanganwa Chowk. Clean but tiny rooms in a place where, according to their advertising, "all staff is good 4 reliable". ①.

Jyoti Guest House, Kanak Rd (☎25271). Behind the bus stand, with fairly pleasant, low-priced rooms. The sign's in Gujarati. ①.

Kavrey, Kanak Rd (☎34942). Upmarket place set off a noisy road offering good comfortable rooms, some a/c, and suites. ⑤–⑦.

Milan, Shri Sadguru Complex, 30/37 Karanpara (☎27462). A large hotel behind the bus stand with relatively clean and airy rooms and hot water round the clock. ①.

Samrat International, 37 Karanpara (☎22269). A little south of the bus stand on a quieter road. Clean and well-managed, but not as good value as the *Galaxy*. ④–⑥.

Eating

Most **restaurants** in Rajkot serve unfailingly good Gujarati *thalis* with a wide range of sweet and sour tastes and often in unending supplies. Western food is only found in a few places in the more upmarket hotels. All the restaurants open at 10.30am; early risers will have to survive on a cup of sweet tea until then.

Havmor, Jawahar Rd (☎22728). A/c restaurant with comfortable furnishing and good Chinese, western and north Indian food, plus their own selection of ice creams. Medium-priced tariff.

Laxmi Lodge, Sanganwa Chowk. Popular dining hall serving Gujarati *thalis* at competitive prices.

Rainbow, Sanganwa Chowk. Small place for south Indian veg snacks, pizzas and ice cream (no hot drinks) below the *Himalaya Guest House*.

Samarkand, *Hotel Samrat International*, 37 Karanpara. A good selection of international cuisine in comfortable a/c restaurant. Middle of the range prices.

Vrindavan, *Hotel Kavrey*. Excellent veg restaurant decorated in traditional Gujarati village style, offering Gujarati and Punjabi dishes as well as macaroni and pizza. Good service and low prices.

Around Rajkot

The princes of Rajkot district left a rich legacy of elaborate residences whose architectural styles range from the delicate detail of the seventeenth century to bold 1930s Art Deco. The palaces at **Wankaner** and **Morvi** are easily seen in a day, while the older palace at **Halvad** a little further out can be combined with a trip to the wild ass sanctuary in the Little Rann of Kutch, accessible from **Dhrangadhra**.

Morvi

The delightful little town of **MORVI** (also spelt Morbi) two hours north from Rajkot on the banks of the River Machhu, once commanded a strategic defensive position, guarding against intrusions into the Kathiawar Peninsula from the Rann of Kutch in the north. Instability among neighbouring petty states left Morvi insecure until the mid-nineteenth century when the political climate changed and the town prospered. The

---

DHRANGADHRA AND THE WILD ASS SANCTUARY

The unassuming town of **Dhrangadhra**, over 100km northeast of Rajkot, has little to detain visitors, but is the starting point for a visit to the **wild ass sanctuary** in the flat saline wilderness of the Little Rann of Kutch. The wild ass is distinguished from a common ass by the dark brown stripe down its back; you'll almost certainly see herds of them, dainty and small but very fast when they sprint over the dusty mud-flats.

Permission to visit the sanctuary should be sought from the Sanctuary Superintendent in Dhrangadhra; **jeeps** can be rented for Rs300 for a maximum period of five hours. It's possible to **stay** in the *Government Rest House* (①), which can be booked in advance from Ahmedabad by calling ☎445068 or 448499.

eclectic **Mani Mandir**, built in 1880, marries conflicting Venetian Gothic, Rajput and Saracenic styles, to produce a surprisingly fine and extremely unusual result. A suspension bridge, built in 1882, spans the river to the entrance of the palace. Closer to the main road, the later Art Deco **New Palace** (1931–44) is more imaginatively decorated than its plain two-storey granite exterior suggests. One of its fourteen bedrooms, embellished with erotic murals, lies underground, and there is a bathroom completely covered in sea shells. There are no fixed **visiting hours** for either building; Mani Mandir is now used as offices and only the courtyards are open to visitors. If you catch the caretaker of the New Palace on a good day you may be lucky enough to be permitted to see all the fascinating interior.

Wankaner

The flamboyant Ranjit Vilas Palace at **WANKANER**, 39km northeast of Rajkot, is still home to the family who once ruled the old state of the same name. Built between 1899 and 1914, the symmetrical building can be seen from far across the flat Saurashtran plains. Up close, its fancy arched facade shows a frenzy of Moghul, Italianate and Victorian Gothic styles, with large windows and domed towers, and scores of hunting trophies looming from the walls. You can **stay** here, in buildings separate from the palace, one of which is an Art Deco structure with a swimming pool and a preserved step-well (☎02828/324; ⑦). Meals, taken in the palace, are included in the room rate.

Halvad

The seventeenth-century lakeside **palace** (Rs10) at **HALVAD**, 20km west of Dhrangadhra (see box), features some superb wooden carvings and, nearby, a number of intriguing **tombstone monuments** (*pallias*) commemorating acts of bravery and heroism. Certain images recur; the symbol of a raised hand or arm indicates the death of a woman who has committed *sati* or self-immolation, while a mounted spear-bearing bard records the death of a courtly poet, offered by his lord as surety for a loan, and driven to suicide in the case of default. Halvad's *Rest House* (①) has simple **rooms**.

Kutch

Bounded on the north and east by marshy flats and on the south and west by the Gulf of Kutch and the Arabian Sea, the province of **Kutch** (also spelt Kuchchh or Kachchha) is a place apart. All but isolated from neighbouring Saurasthra and Sind, Kutch's largely arid landscape is shot through with the colour from heavily embroidered local dress. It's a land of legends recorded in stone statues, and folk customs reflected in popular craft and jewellery designs. Few tourists make it out to this beautiful region, much of which is off-limits to visitors without official permits, but those who do are invariably enchanted. With a little effort, you can head out from the central city of **Bhuj** to villages, ancient fortresses, medieval ports and isolated monasteries.

The treeless marshes to the north and east, known as the Great and Little **Ranns of Kutch**, can flood completely during a heavy monsoon, effectively transforming Kutch into an island. Home to the rare wild ass (see opposite), the Ranns are also the only region in India where flamingoes breed successfully, during July and August, out of reach of any but the most determined bird watchers who can cross the marshes by camel. The southern district, known as **Banni**, was once among India's most fertile areas, and though drier today, still supports crops of cotton, castor-oil plants, sunflowers, wheat and groundnuts. Northern Kutch, on the other hand, is semi-desert, with dry shifting sands and no perennial rivers; villagers rely on income drawn from traditional crafts.

When **visiting Kutchi villages**, it goes without saying that you should be sensitive to their customs, removing your shoes before entering houses, and only taking photos with permission. Only the larger settlements are covered below; if you want to really get off the track, ask at the Bhuj tourist office.

Some history

Remains from the third millennium BC in eastern Kutch suggest that migrating Indus Valley communities crossed the Ranns from Mohenjo Daro in modern Pakistan to Lothal in eastern Gujarat. Traditional history recounts that Kutch belonged to the Yadavas, when it was known for rich grasses that flourished on ash-manure that fell from heaven at the request of a wandering sage. Despite being so cut off, Kutch felt the effect of the Buddhist Mauryan empire, and later came under the control of Greek Bactrians, the Western Satraps and the powerful Guptas. The Arab invasion of Sind in 720 AD pushed refugees into Kutch's western regions, and tribes from Rajputana and Gujarat crossed its eastern borders. Later in the eighth century the region fell under the sway of the Gujarati capital Anhilawada (modern-day Patan), and by the tenth century the Samma Rajputs, later known as the Jadejas, had infiltrated Kutch from the

KUTCHI HANDICRAFTS

Kutch has long been known for its distinctive traditional crafts, from embroidery to jewellery making and carving. The northern villages of Dhordo, Khavda and Hodko are home to the few remaining communities of **leather embroiderers** who soak hide in a solution of water, latex and lime in an underground earthen pot before stitching it with flower, peacock and fish motifs. The finished bags, fans, horse belts, wallets, cushion covers and mirror frames are sold in villages all through Kutch. Dhordo is also known for its **woodcarving**, while Khavda is one of the last villages to continue the printing method known as **ajrakh**. Cloth is dyed with natural pigments in a lengthy process similar to batik, but instead of wax, a mixture of lime and gum is used to resist the dye in certain parts of the cloth when new colours are added. Women in Khavda **paint terracotta** pots with dusky whites, reds and blacks, using cotton rags, and brushes made from bamboo leaves.

Rogan painting is now practised only in Biber in northern Kutch. A complex process turns hand-pounded castor oil into coloured dyes which are used to decorate cushion covers, bedspreads and curtains with simple geometric patterns. Craftsmen also make melodic **bells** coated in intricate designs of copper and brass, once used for communication among shepherds.

Kutchi **silver engraving** is a dwindling art form, practised mainly in Bhuj. Molten silver is poured into a mold, and, when dry, engraved by gentle taps with fine, sharp tools and small hammers. The final products, such as trays, pots, cups, pens and picture frames, are smoothed down and polished in an acid solution. Silver jewellery is common, featuring in most traditional Kutchi costumes. The anklets, earrings, noserings, bangles and necklaces are similar to those seen in Rajasthan, since much of it is made by the Ahir and Rabari communities who live in both areas. In Kutch, the silver is mixed with zinc to make it more malleable, and converted into wires and sheets. The main centres for silver are Anjar, Bhuj, Mandiri and Mundra.

The most common form of **cloth** printing is **bandhani**, or tie-dye, practised in most villages, but concentrated in Mandvi and Anjar. Kutchi clothes are distinctive for their fine embroidery and bold designs; one design unique to the area is *mushroo*-weaving (*ilacha*), a skill practised today by less than twenty artisans. The yarn used is silk, carefully dyed before it is woven in a basic striped pattern, with a complex design woven over the top in such fine detail that it seems to be embroidered. *Ilacha* cloth, made into *cholis* (blouses) and dresses, is hard to buy now; the best place to see it is Mandvi, or in the Calico Museum in Ahmedabad (see p.526).

west, and established themselves as rulers. Their line continued until Kutch was absorbed into the Indian Union in 1948.

When the Muslim Sultans ruled Gujarat, they made repeated unsuccessful attempts to cross into Kutch. It remained separate, with its own customs, laws and a thriving maritime tradition, while trade with Malabar, Mocha, Muscat and the African coast brought in spices, drugs, silks, rhino hides and elephant tusks. Connections with Africa also encouraged the slave trade, already common among the Portuguese in south Saurashtra. Africans deck-hands and slaves arrived with merchants and sailors, and after the abolition of slavery in 1834 a small African community settled in north Bhuj. Their crafts, dances and music have been integrated into the region's tradtional arts.

Bhuj

Set in the heart of Kutch, the narrow streets and old bazaars of the walled town of **BHUJ** retain a medieval flavour unlike any other Gujarati city. Bhuj was established as the capital of Kutch in the mid-sixteenth century by Rao Khengarji, a Jadeja Rajput. The one interruption before 1948 in his family's continuous rule of the city was a brief period of British domination early in the nineteenth century. When the governance of the state was handed back to the rightful ruler, Maharao Desal, in 1834, the import of slaves from Africa was banned and Africans were given homes in the north of the city. With the establishment of the city of Gandhidham and the port of Kandla east of the capital, the economic centre of gravity shifted away from Bhuj, leaving it to carry on its traditions little affected by the modernizations of the twentieth century.

> The telephone **area code** for Bhuj is ☎02832.

Arrival and information

Two flights a week from Bombay (via Jamnagar) land at Bhuj **airport**, 5km north of town. *Indian Airlines* lays on a minibus into the centre, and rickshaws offer their services. Trains from south Rajasthan and east Gujarat, via Palanpur or Gandhidham, arrive at the **railway station** a little over 1km north of town, from where a rickshaw to a hotel costs roughly Rs15. The **bus station** is on ST Station Road on the southern edge of the old city; bookings for onward journeys by road or rail can be made at any of the travel agents nearby. There's a branch of the **State Bank of India** in Aina Mahal (Mon–Fri 11am–3pm, Sat 11am–12.30pm), and the **GPO** (Mon–Sat 9am–4pm) is just past Waniawad Gate in the south of town.

Bhuj is a useful base for visits to outlying **villages**, whether by **bus** or the **taxis** that gather outside the ST stand. The **tourist office** (daily except Thurs 9am–noon & 3–6pm; ☎20004) in Aina Mahal in the old city has a wealth of information on Bhuj and Kutchi villages, and details of **permits** required to travel north, east and west (see p.572).

The Town

Bhuj is overlooked from the east by the old and crumbling fort on Bhujia Hill, while the vast **Hamirsar Tank**, with a small park on an island in its centre, stands on the western edge of town. The original city walls, built in 1715, were demolished in 1948, though parts remain in the north, near Bhid Gate. In the maze of winding streets that make up the **old city**, the **palace** of the Jadeja maharaos houses a fine **museum**. Further out, on the southeastern edge of the tank, the newer, less elaborate **Sadar Bagh Palace** lies amid well-kept gardens, west of the **government museum**.

In Bhuj's **old city** the pace of life is in tune with the plod of camels that amble through the streets, past old vegetable markets and countless cloth stalls, mingling with the region's notoriously resilient cows and the Kutchi people dressed in heavily embroidered traditional clothes. Only some of the buildings of the beautifully preserved **palace complex**, guarded by sturdy walls and high heavy gates, are open to the public. Its most dazzling section, **Aina Mahal**, is now **Maharao Madansinji Museum** (daily except Sat, 9am–noon & 3–6pm; Rs2). Built in the eighteenth century during the reign of Maharao Lakho, fondly known as Lakhpatji, Aina Mahal is a superb feat of architecture, its stunning interior designed by the Saurashtran, Ram Singh, who incorporated techniques picked up from as far afield as Europe. As a result, Lakhpatji's palace was decorated with a style unknown elsewhere in western India, a riot of finely blown glass lanterns, exquisite tile-work and detailed enamel designs.

The first hall of the museum is given over to historical artefacts, including letters between Viceroy Mountbatten and the Maharao of Kutch in the final years of the Raj. You can also see sequined royal robes, classic Kutchi embroidery, and a painted scroll over 20m long depicting Maharao Pragmalji with an entourage of courtiers, cavalry and elephants, celebrating victory over the Moghuls in the 1850s.

Built of marble and decked with an exquisite mirrored design, the **Hall of Mirrors** is the most elaborate of the palace apartments. Next door is **Fuvara Mahal**, Lakhpatji's music room, lit by Venetian glass lanterns. The huge pool was once alive with the spray of fountains (*fuvara*), and dancers and bards performed before the king; note the musical instruments around the platform from where he watched all the fun. The coins on show beneath Kutchi paintings in the adjoining chamber are the *kori, dhingla* and *dokda* that were Kutch's currency from 1617 to 1948.

Lakhpatji's private room, **Hira Mahal**, contains his gilded bed, chiming clocks, glass ornaments and mechanical toys made by Ram Singh, along with remarkable Kutchi carpets. In the picture gallery, subjects include a very relaxed Lakphatji smoking a *hookah*, attended by tiny African slaves; in another he is adorned with real pearls luxuriantly studded onto the surface of the portrait. The fabulous wooden door inlaid with ivory has been in the palace since 1708, despite more than one request by the British who wanted to add it to collections of Indian crafts in their own museums.

On the upper floor of the museum, Maharao Pragmalji's hand-drawn horoscope shows – not surprisingly – influential planetary positions, and there's a selection of illustrated manuscripts, as well as the (reconstructed) marriage room of Maharao Khengarji (1884). The throne for the betrothed couple is sheltered by a canopy of leaves and jewels, and flanked with towers of clay water pots.

The later **Prag Mahal** (same hours; Rs4), built nearby in the 1860s, is unmistakably more modern, combining Moghul, British, Kutchi and Italian architectural styles. A bemused-looking stuffed hippo stands at the entrance, and the main hall, used for *durbars* (state meetings) until 1948, holds a sad display of the spoils of royal hunts: scores of deer and blue bulls, 7 cheetahs, 7 tigers, 2 bears and 21 sets of deer horns, all killed in a single year. Climb to the top of the clock tower for views over Bhuj.

The plain building on the southeastern edge of Hamirsar Tank houses the **Kutch museum** (daily 9am–noon, closed 2nd & 4th Sat of each month; Rs0.50), not a patch on the Aina Mahal, but giving a more general overview of Kutchi culture. Archeological finds from Harappan times and ancient brass figures include Buddhas sitting with their hands poised in the *mudra* representing "no fear". A silver padlock in the shape of India is among the collection of gold and silver ornaments on the ground floor, most made in the nineteenth century and heavily influenced by European designs. A display of turbans on the upper floor explains the particular types worn by each tribe, albeit a little confusedly, and an impressive collection of musical instruments includes a *surando* (stringed instrument), a *transa* (drum) and a curious snake-like horn called a *nagfan*. The inevitable collection of stuffed animals includes, of course, the wild ass. If you're lucky you'll see craftsmen stone-sculpting in the museum forecourt.

The road that skirts the southern edge of Hamirsar Tank leads to **Sharad Bagh Palace** (daily except Fri 9am–noon & 3–6pm), built in 1867 and the retreat of the last Maharao. The small porticoed buildings are delicately proportioned and include the

---

FESTIVALS IN AND AROUND BHUJ

Bhuj's **Tourist Festival**, held over five days in January or February, hosts a wide selection of traditional music – from religious and maritime songs to African drums – as well as tribal and religious dance from Kutch and other parts of Gujarat. Stalls sell shoes, clothes and embroidered cloth.

Further afield in **Nakhatrana**, 50km west of Bhuj, a festival on the first Monday of Bhadrapada (Aug/Sept) commemorates the **Jakhs**, a mysterious horse-riding clan of 71 men and one lone woman who came to Kutch in the eleventh century. Their origins are unclear, though tales of their fair skin and medical skills could link them with the Zoroastrians from northern Iran who settled in Gujarat in the tenth century, and later formed communities in Bombay where they are known as Parsis. In Kutch they are worshipped as demi-gods and remembered as miracle workers able to cure barren women. During the festival bards and singers retell stories of their miraculous feats, and offerings are laid before equestrian images in hilltop temples.

plush drawing room, decked with hunting trophies, photographs and old clocks, and the dining room which contains Maharao Madansinjhi's coffin, which was shipped over from England after his death in 1991. The palace's most appealing feature, however, is its well-tended gardens, complete with pretty flower beds, giant bamboo trees, lofty palms and tennis courts.

In a cluster of shops and houses just south of the museum at Bhuj's southern edge, the 250-year-old **Ramkund** tank is made of hard grey stone and shaded by trees. Decorated with skilfully crafted images of Kali, Vishnu, Nag and Ganesh, the tank also has small niches in the walls where oil lamps would glitter in the dusk as devotees prayed at the evening *puja*. Nearby is a set of sixteenth-century *sati* stones.

On the road that runs parallel to the east side of Hamirsar Tank, the gaily painted and lively **Swaminarayan Temple** belongs to the oldest of the three Hindu revivalist sects inspired by the spiritual guru Swaminarayan. Its decorative bold pinks, yellows, greens and soft blues are particularly vivid here in the sandy surroundings of Bhuj. Devotees gather and chat in the courtyard, and to one side gaudily dressed Hindu deities peer out from shrines shielded by silver grilles unlocked only during *pujas*. The temple is home to *sadhus* who follow the precepts of Vedic study, vegetarianism, chastity and moderation laid down by Swaminarayan, the "God Supreme", and grow vegetables in the private gardens behind the temple.

Accommodation

Bhuj's **hotels and lodges** cater almost exclusively to the budget traveller, though a couple offer a/c and carpets for extra cash. The grottier places around the bus station, such as *Nityanand Lodge* and *Jay Bharat Lodge* are not recommended.

Anam, New Station Rd (☎23397). Fresh, comfortable rooms, all with private bath, though most are invaded by traffic noise. "Deluxe" rooms have a hot shower and a/c, and the popular veg restaurant on the ground floor serves high standard Gujarati *thalis* at easily affordable prices. ④–⑤.

Annapurna, Bhid Gate (☎20831). A small, friendly place with clean, homely rooms (bucket of hot water). Delicious Kutchi veg *thalis* are served in the inexpensive restaurant downstairs. ①.

City Guest House, Langa St (☎21067). Popular choice in the centre of the old town. Clean, simple rooms around a small courtyard, some with private bath. Snacks and breakfast available. Hidden in a confusing warren of alleys; take a rickshaw. ①–②.

Janta Ghar, New Station Rd, Waniawad Gate (☎20068). Dim, cell-like rooms on the ground floor, but some reasonable options with attached bath and hot shower, fan and window. ①.

Neelkanth Guest House, New Station Rd, Jantagarh (☎22538). A modern building; clean rooms with attached bath, and a dorm for men. ①.

Prince, New Station Rd (☎20370). Bhuj's one upmarket hotel. A/c, TV and private bath. Pay in foreign currency. The smart, expensive restaurant serves inviting Indian and western food. ⑦–⑧.

Ratrani, New Station Rd (☎22388). Impersonal place next to the main road with passable rooms. ②.

VRP Guest House, ST Station Rd (☎21388). Basic rooms in a three-storey complex opposite the taxi stand. The *Green Rock* restaurant is reasonable, serving north Indian dishes and a few western options, but no hot drinks. ①.

Eating

Many of the best **places to eat** in Bhuj are in the hotels (see above); elsewhere, food is basic but adequate. You won't be disappointed by the all-you-can-eat local *thalis* which may have up to ten separate veg curries.

Bharat Juice and Vadilal Ice-cream, ST Station Rd. A wide selection of ice cream and a variety of *lassis*, cold coffees and creamy milkshakes in a spotlessly clean open-fronted stall.

Green Hotel, Shroff Bazaar. Close to the old vegetable market, serving good, inexpensive Punjabi and south Indian food as well as milkshakes and ice cream.

Noorani, Dada Bazaar. One of the few non-veg restaurants in the old city. Good, inexpensive food.

Omlet Centre, ST Station Rd. A tiny, dim stall serving great eggy breakfasts with a choice between farm (free range) and *deshi* (battery) eggs.

Tickets for **flights** to Bombay (Mon & Sat, 4.25pm; 1hr 5min) can be booked through *Indian Airlines*, New Station Rd (Mon–Sat 10am–1pm & 1.45–5pm; ☎20204).

Buses link Bhuj with main towns and villages, but you have to do some walking to reach many of the most interesting Kutchi settlements, which lie a few kilometres from the nearest roads. Five daily **trains** from Bhuj run to Gandhidham, for connections for Rajasthan and Gujarat, and one daily direct train goes to Ahmedabad (1.30pm; 16hr 15min). The best route to Rajasthan is to travel to Palanpur and change (2 daily; 12hr; best train leaves at 10.35pm); trains continue to Mount Abu, Ajmer, Jaipur and Delhi.

Travel agents include: *Hali Travels*, ST Station Rd, selling tickets for deluxe buses to Rajkot; *Patel Travels*, ST Station Rd, for private bus services to Ahmedabad and Jamnagar; and *Shree Sahjanand Travels*, near Chhathi Bari, opposite the ST Station, for night buses to Ahmedabad and Bombay (2 weekly; 24hr). You can book train tickets to Abu Road, Ahmedabad and Delhi at *Panchtirth Tourists*, first on the left at the entrance to the bus stand, for a Rs15 surcharge.

Getting the free **permits** you need for each specific village you intend to visit, in all but the southern region of Kutch, is a time-consuming business: first take your passport and tourist visa to the Collector's Office on College Rd, south of the city (Mon–Sat 11am–2.30pm & 3–6pm; except for the 2nd & 4th Sat of the month), then go to the police station, and then return to the Collector's Office. Trips to **northern Kutch** are best made by taxi as accommodation cannot be guaranteed, and bus services are infrequent.

Mandvi

The compact town of **MANDVI**, on the west bank of a wide tidal estuary 60km south of Bhuj, faces the Arabian Sea to the south and supports a dwindling *dhow*-building industry. In the late eighteenth century it was the docking point for a fleet of four hundred vessels exporting goods from a hinterland that encompassed Gujarat and the lands to the north as far as Jaisalmer. Merchants, seamen, and later the British, were all keen to settle in this flourishing port; few remained, but they left behind grand mansions, imaginatively painted and carved in a style clearly influenced by European tastes.

Mandvi's **markets** are stocked with *bandhani* and silver, and one street crashes and clanks with the noise from the iron forgers' blackened stalls. It's a leisurely place, with several *chai* stalls set among old houses and cluttered shops that stretch west of the estuary, blocked in the south by the shifting sands of a long beach that's seldom used for swimming, but supports the tall windmills that power an electricity plant supplying the town. Beside the estuary you can see mighty Noah's Ark-style ships being hand-built from long wooden planks, with nails up to 1m long forged by local blacksmiths. Fifty men spend two years building each ship, many of which still make the long journey to ports in the west, often carrying Muslims to Mecca for the *haj* pilgrimage.

Mandvi's neglected and little-visited **Vijay Vilas Palace**, 6km west of town (daily; Rs5 plus fees for parking and camera), is a sandy-white domed building set in almost 700 acres of land, built as a summer retreat by Kutch's Maharao in the 1940s. Inside, Belgian, British and Italian furniture fills the high-ceilinged carpeted rooms, and hunting trophies deck the walls. A grand stairway leads to the ladies' quarters on the first floor; small apartments and cool marble courtyards open to the sky. A pavilion projecting from the roof catches fresh sea breezes and commands excellent views.

Practicalities

Buses run between Bhuj and Mandvi (1hr 30min) every half hour; **taxis** crammed with as many people as possible make the journey when full, for Rs15 a head. There's little

KUTCHI TRIBES

Kutch has the most significant and conspicuous population of tribal comunities in Gujarat, most of whom migrated from east and west from the seventh century onwards. Each tribe can be identified from its costume, and gains its income from pastoral farming or crafts such as weaving, painting, wood-carving and dyeing. Traditionally, each has concentrated on different crafts; the distinctions today are far less clear-cut.

The **Rabari** is the largest group in the Kutchi pastoral community, with three main tribes hailing from Marwad in Rajasthan. They rear cattle, buffalo, goats, sheep and camels, sell *ghee*, and weave, and are also known for fine **embroidery**. The men, most of whom sport a white turban, wear white cotton trousers tight at the ankle and in baggy pleats above the knee, a white jacket (*kehdiyun*) with multiple folds tucked around chest level and overlong sleeves, and a blanket thrown over one shoulder. Rabari women dress in black pleated jackets or open-backed blouses, full black skirts and tie-dyed head cloths, usually black and red, and always deck themselves with heavy silver jewellery and ivory bangles around the upper arms. Typical houses, made of mud or brick, are decorated inside with *gargomati* – a raised pattern of whitewashed mud and dung, inlaid with mirrors. Child marriages, customary among the Rabari, are performed over a four- or five-day period in the summer; immediately upon the birth of a daughter, a mother starts embroidering cloth to form the most valuable basis of her dowry. In **Bhujodi**, near Bhuj, the Rabari weave camel wool on pit looms into blankets and shawls.

Claiming descent from Krishna, the **Bharvad** tribes infiltrated Gujarat from Vrindavan, close to Mathura in Uttar Pradesh. Their dress is similar to that of the Rabaris, though the men are distinguishable from the peacock, parrot and flower motifs sewn into their *khediyun*, and the women by their bright backless shirts, *kapadun*, rarely covered by veils. Both men and women wear a thick *bori* cloth around the waist. Mass marriages take place among the Bharvad every few years; a custom originating as a form of protection in the Muslim period when single girls were frequently victims of abduction (the kidnapping of married girls was heavily punished). In the first week of each September the Bharvads gather at the Trinetresvar temple in **Tarnetar**, 65km from Rajkot, celebrating with dances and singing, sheltered under the shade of embroidered umbrellas made especially for the occasion.

The wandering **Ahir** cattle-breeders came to Gujarat from Sind, and settled as farmers in Kutch, and at Morvi in Saurashtra where they mixed with other tribes. Baggy trousers and *khediyun* are worn by the men, together with a white loosely wound head-cloth, and the women dress like the Rabaris, with additional heavy silver nose rings. The children's bright *topis*, or skull-caps, overlaid with neat fragments of mirrors, are like those common in Pakistan. During Diwali, Ahirs lead their cattle through the streets to be fed by other local communities, which bestows merit on the giver and is good for *karma*.

The **Charans**, the long-established bards of Gujarat, encompass in their clans the Maldharis who raise prize cattle in southern Kutch and the Gir Forest, and the leather-workers known as Meghavals. They claim descent from a celestial union between Charan and a maiden created by Parvati, and many gain almost divine status after death. The women are often worshipped by other tribes, since their connection with Parvati links them closely to the mother goddess, Ashpura, who is popular in Kutch, and the men's curses were once considered so powerful that they drove their opponents to kill themselves in the hope that the curse would be deflected upon the Charans: such "heroes" are remembered by stone monuments around Kutch depicting a man piercing his neck with a dagger.

Said to have migrated from Pakistan, the Kutchi **Jats** can be identified by their black dress. Young Jat girls have dainty plaits curving round the sides of their faces, and wear heavy nose rings. Traditionally semi-nomadic camel- and cattle-rearers, with houses made of reed (*pakha*) that are easily folded and carried from place to place, they have recently begun to settle more permanently.

choice of **accommodation**. *Veena Guest House* (①) is part of a family home next to the cinema north of the bus depot and has spartan rooms. The *Agency Bungalow*, out of town on the east bank of the estuary, has pleasant seafacing rooms (②), but bookings must be made at the Public Works Department office in Bhuj. You can also stay in the guest house at *Vijay Vilas Palace* (③) where the three furnished double rooms are far from luxurious, but full of character; meals (Rs50) are served in the aristocratic dining room. Otherwise the best bet for **food** is *Zorba the Buddha Restaurant* on KT Shah Rd, west of the bus stand behind an old town-gate. Wonderful *thalis* are served from 11am, with over ten dishes, plus fresh chutneys, pickles and sweets, all for less than Rs15.

Mundra

The small fishing port of **MUNDRA**, east of Mandvi, is best reached by bus (12 daily) direct from Bhuj, 30km away. The road to Mundra runs through a dry red-brown rocky landscape, past broad fields of wheat and sunflowers, before approaching the thick walls that circle the town. Local crafts include batik prints, heavy silver jewellery and unusual woollen *namadas*; floor coverings, wall-hangings and camel saddles dyed in earthy maroons, blues, yellows and black. Several small Rabari and Jat villages lie a bus ride and a short walk from Mundra, and to the east, the Jain temples at **Bhadresar** are a focus for pilgrims from all over Gujarat.

Southeast to Kandla

The 50-kilometre journey southeast from Bhuj to **KANDLA**, Kutch's main port, takes you past dry scrubland dotted with road signs proclaiming "Growing tree is symbol of living nation". In the small village of **Bhujodi**, less than 10km out of Bhuj, Rabari men weave thick shawls and blankets on pit looms dug into the floors of squat mud houses decorated with *gargomati*. You can buy their products from a small shop run by the Bhujodi Handweaving Co-op Society.

The first main town beyond Bhuj, **ANJAR** was the capital of Kutch until 1548. It's an important centre of bright and intricate Ahir embroidery, *bandhani*, batik, and nutcracker making, and holds busy markets once or twice a week. Further east is **GANDHIDHAM**, the city planned for Sind refugees who came to Kutch after Partition. An industrial centre, supporting the modern port of Kandla at the mouth of the Gulf of Kutch, Gandhidam holds little attraction for tourists, though it's convenient for road and rail connections to Rajasthan and Gujarat.

North of Bhuj

One bus a day from Bhuj makes the journey to northern Kutch, where the dry and barren terrain gives way to black mountain ranges that loom over the craft centres of **Khavda**, **Hodko** and **Dhordo**. Clusters of grass-roofed mud huts here are decorated with traditional clay and whitewash patterns. West of Khavda the village of **THAN** is home to a small community of Hindu *sadhus* known as *Khanpata* ("split-ear") because of the heavy ornaments they wear in their ears. The order was founded by the twelfth-century saint, Dharamnath, who travelled to Kutch from Saurashtra and practised severe austerities for years on a nearby hill. A temple marking the spot is visited by *sadhus* all year round, and may have been converted from an earlier sun temple by the Kathi tribe.

Near Than, the village of **BIBER** has a temple to Rama decorated with friezes depicting scenes from the *Ramayana*, executed using a long-forgotten technique known as *kamagar*. At neighbouring **NIRONA** you can see cloth painted in the ancient *rogan* style.

CHAPTER NINE

BOMBAY

Young, brash, and oozing with the cock-sure self-confidence of a maverick money-maker, **BOMBAY** revels in its reputation as India's most dynamic and westernized city. Behind the hype, however, intractable problems threaten the Maharashtran capital; foremost among them, a chronic shortage of **space**. Crammed onto a narrow spit of land that curls from the swamp-ridden coast into the Arabian Sea, Bombay has, in less than five hundred years since its "discovery" by the Portuguese, metamorphosed from an aboriginal fishing settlement into a sprawling megalopolis of thirteen million people. Whether you are being swept along broad boulevards by endless streams of commuters, or jostled by coolies and hand-cart pullers in the teeming bazaars, Bombay always feels like it is about to burst at the seams.

The roots of the population problem lie, paradoxically, in the city's enduring ability to create **wealth**. Bombay alone generates thirty-five percent of India's GNP, its port handles half the country's foreign trade, and its movie industry is the biggest in the world. Symbols of prosperity are everywhere: from the phalanx of office blocks clustered onto Nariman Point, Maharashtra's Manhattan, to the yuppie couples nipping around town in their shiny new *Maruti* hatchbacks. The flip-side to the success story, of course, is the city's much chronicled **poverty**. Each day, hundreds of economic refugees pour into Bombay from the Maharashtran hinterland. Some find jobs and secure accommodation; many more (around a third of the total population) end up living on the already overcrowded streets, or amid the appalling squalor of Asia's largest slums, reduced to rag-picking and begging from cars at traffic lights.

However, while it would definitely be misleading to downplay its difficulties, Bombay is far from the ordeal some travellers make it out to be. Once you've overcome the major hurdle of finding somewhere to stay, you may even begin to enjoy its frenzied pace and crowded, cosmopolitan feel.

Conventional **sights** are thin on the ground. After a visit to the most famous colonial monument, the **Gateway of India**, and a look at the antiquities in the **Prince of Wales**

Museum, the most rewarding way to spend time is simply to wander the city's atmospheric streets. **Downtown**, beneath the rows of exuberant **Victorian-Gothic** buildings, the pavements are full of noisy vendors and office-*wallahs* hurrying through clouds of wood-smoke from the *gram*-sellers' braziers. In the eye of the storm, encircled by the roaring traffic of beaten-up red double-decker buses, lie other vestiges of the Raj, the **maidans**. Depending on the time of day, these central parks are peppered with cricketers in white flannels, or the bare bums of squatting pavement-dwellers easing themselves on the parched brown grass. North of the city centre, the broad thoroughfares splinter into a maze of chaotic streets. The **central bazaar** districts afford glimpses of the sprawling Muslim neighbourhoods, as well as exotic **shopping** possibilities, while Bombay is at its most exuberant along **Chowpatty Beach**, which laps against exclusive **Malabar Hill**. Finally, when you've had enough of the mayhem, the beautiful rock-cut Shiva temple on **Elephanta Island** – a short trip by launch across the harbour from the promenade, **Apollo Bunder** – offers a welcome half-day escape.

If you're heading for Goa or south India, you'll have to pass through Bombay at some stage. Its international airport, **Sahar**, is the busiest in the country; the **airline offices** downtown are handy for confirming onward flights, and all the region's principal air, road and rail networks originate here. Whether or not you choose to stay for more time than it takes to jump on a train or plane to somewhere else, however, depends on how well you handle the burning sun, humid atmosphere and perma-fog of petrol fumes; and how seriously you want to get to grips with India of the 1990s.

History

Bombay originally consisted of seven **islands**, inhabited by small Koli fishing communities. At different times, various dynasties held this insignificant outlying district; the city of Puri on **Elephanta** is thought to have been the major settlement in the region, until King Bimba, or Bhima, built the town of Mahim, on one island, at the end of the thirteenth century. Hindus controlled the area until it was captured in the fourteenth century by the Muslim Gujarat Sultanate. In 1534 Sultan Bahadur of Ahmedabad ceded Bombay to the **Portuguese**, who felt the land to be of little importance, and concentrated development in the areas around Mahim and Bassein. They handed over the largest island to the English in 1661, as part of the dowry when the Portuguese Infanta Catherine Braganza married Charles II; four years later Charles received the remaining islands and the port. This was the first part of India that could properly be termed a colony; elsewhere on the subcontinent the English had merely been granted the right to set up "factories", or trading posts. Because of its natural safe harbour and strategic position for trade, the **East India Company**, based at Surat, wanted to buy the land; in 1668 a deal was struck, and Charles leased Bombay to them for a pittance.

The English set about an ambitious programme of fortifying their outpost, living in the area known today as Fort. However, life was not easy. There was a fast turnover of governors, and malaria and cholera culled many of the first settlers. A chaplain of the East India Company, Revd Ovington, wrote at the end of the seventeenth century: "One of the pleasantest spots in India seemed no more than a parish graveyard, a charnel house . . . Which common fatality has created a Proverb among the English there, that two monsoons are the age of a man". **Gerald Aungier**, the fourth governor (1672–77), set out to plan "the city which by God's assistance is intended to be built", and by the start of the eighteenth century the town was the capital of the East India Company. The "father of Bombay" is credited with encouraging the mix that still contributes to the city's success, welcoming Hindu traders, Goans (escaping Jesuit persecution), Muslim weavers, and most visibly, the business-minded Zoroastrian **Parsis**.

Much of the British settlement in the old Fort area was destroyed by a devastating fire in 1803, and the European population remained comparatively low well into the 1800s. The arrival of the **Great Indian Peninsular Railway** in the 1850s improved

THE DONS AND THE BOMBS

For many years, despite intense competition for jobs and living space among its diverse ethnic and social groups, Bombay boasted of being one of India's most stable cities. While Delhi and Calcutta reeled under communal riots and terrorist attacks in the early 1980s, the great Maharashtran melting-pot remained outwardly calm.

However, as early as 1982, Bombay's infra-structure was starting to buckle under the tensions of over-population. A bitter and protracted **textile strike**, or *bandh*, had impoverished tens of thousands of industrial workers, unemployment and crime were spiralling, and the influx of immigrants into the city showed no signs of abating. Among the few beneficiaries of mounting discontent was the extreme right-wing Maharashtran party, the **Shiv Sena**. Founded in 1966 by Bal "the Saheb" Thackery, a self-confessed admirer of Hitler, the Sena's uncompromising stand on immigration and employment (jobs for "Sons of the Soil" first), found favour with the disenchanted mass of lower-middle-class Hindus in the poorer suburbs. The party's venom, at first focussed on the city's sizeable south Indian community, soon shifted to its fifteen-percent Muslim minority. Communal antagonism flared briefly in 1984, when ninety people died in riots, and again in 1985 when the Shiv Sena routed the Congress party in municipal elections, thereby sweeping into the mainstream.

The rise of the right coincided with an intensification of **organized crime**. Previously, the city's gangsters had confined their activities to small-scale racketeering in poor neighbourhoods. After the post-1970s real estate boom, however, many petty "landsharks" became powerful godfather figures, or **"dons"**, with multi-*crore* drug- and gold-smuggling businesses. Moreover, the corrupt politicians who had employed the gangs' muscle-power to rig elections, were now highly placed political puppets with debts to pay – a phenomenon dubbed as **"criminalization"**. The dividing line between the underworld and politics grew increasingly blurred as the decade progressed: in 1992, no less than forty candidates in the municipal elections had criminal records. Meanwhile, Shiv Sena had consolidated its support, or **"vote banks"**, by striking up an alliance with the up-and-coming, and equally extreme-right Hindu party, the BJP.

Even to those who had been charting the communal situation, the events that followed the destruction by Hindu extremists of the **Babri Masjid** mosque in Ayodhya (see p.286) came as a shock. Between December 1992 and late January 1993 came two waves of **rioting**, affecting not only the Muslim ghettos and poor industrial suburbs, but, for the first time, much of downtown too. 150,000 citizens fled for the countryside, while 100,000 more moved into refugee camps. According to (conservative) official statistics, 784 people died, and around 5000 were injured – seventy percent of them Muslim. Although a great deal of blame for the madness must accrue to right-wing Hindu political groups such as Shiv Sena, some commentators believe other factions stood to gain from the situation, notably slum landlords whose tenants are protected under rent freezes imposed by the Bombay Rent Act. The thousands of slum dwellers who fled Bombay and their burning homes following the riots conveniently cleared the way, it is suggested, for property development.

Just as Bombay was regaining its composure, disaster struck again. Around mid-afternoon on 12 March 1993, ten massive **bomb blasts** ripped through the heart of the city, killing 317 people and gutting the Stock Exchange, the *Air India* building, the passport office and three swanky hotels near the airports. No one claimed responsibility, but the involvement of "foreign hands" (ie Pakistan) was suspected. Investigators claimed the bombs had been smuggled into India and planted by Muslim mobsters. The name of India's most wanted criminal, the *don* Dawood Ibrahim (presently exiled in Dubai), was bandied about in the press, although as yet neither he nor anyone else has been charged.

The city recovered from the explosions with astonishing speed. Most banks and offices reopened the next day, and slowly the paranoia, or "fear psychosis", subsided. It would, however, take more than the hoardings erected beside the freeways ("Bombay Bounces Back!", "It's My Bombay", "Bombay, I Love You") fully to restore the pride and ebullience with which India's most confident city had formerly gone about its business.

0   1 km

HOTELS:
- Ⓐ YMCA
- Ⓑ Bombay Palace
- Ⓒ Sahil
- Ⓓ Balwas International
- Ⓔ Bentley
- Ⓕ Norman's
- Ⓖ Oasis
- Ⓗ Welcome
- Ⓘ Grand
- Ⓙ Victoria
- Ⓚ Lord's
- Ⓛ Chateau Windsor
- Ⓜ Ambassador
- Ⓝ Sea Green Hotels
- Ⓞ Nataraj
- Ⓟ Oberoi/Oberoi Towers
- Ⓠ Ritz
- Ⓡ President

RESTAURANTS:
- ① China Town
- ② China Garden
- ③ Landmark
- ④ Bhaishankar's
- ⑤ London Pub & Revival
- ⑥ Badsha Juice & Snack Bar
- ⑦ Gulshan-e-Iran
- ⑧ Britania & Co
- ⑨ Modern Lunch Home
- ⑩ Satkar
- ⑪ Gaylord
- ⑫ Croissants Etc
- ⑬ Piccolo

communications, encouraging yet more immigration from elsewhere in India. In 1862 the first of many land-reclamation projects (still on-going) fused the seven islands; just a year later the rail link between Bombay and the cotton-growing areas of the Deccan plateau opened. **Sir Bartle Frere**, governor from 1862 until 1867, oversaw the construction of the city's distinctive colonial-Gothic buildings; the most extravagant of all, Victoria Terminus railway station, known simply as **VT**, is a fitting testimony to this extraordinary age of expansion. After the American Civil War, India replaced America as supplier of **cotton** to England, exporting the bulk of it via Bombay, and with the opening of the Suez Canal in 1869, and the construction of enormous docks, Bombay's access to European markets improved further.

Not all Bombay's grandest architecture is owed to the Raj; wealthy Jains and Parsis have also left their mark throughout the downtown area. As the most prosperous city in the nation, Bombay was at the forefront of the Independence struggle; Mahatma Gandhi used a house here, now a museum, to co-ordinate the struggle through three decades. Fittingly, the first British colony took pleasure in waving the final goodbye to the Raj, when the last contingent of British troops passed through the Gateway of India in February 1948. Despite its recent communal tensions, and growing crime-related violence, Bombay approaches the twenty-first century as the financial and commercial centre of India, with a cost of living almost equal to that in the US, and, in Malabar Hill in particular, some of the most expensive real estate in the world.

Arrival

Unless you arrive in Bombay by train at Victoria Terminus, be prepared for a long slog into the centre. Both the international and domestic airports are north of the city, way off the map overleaf and an hour and a half or more by road from the main hotel areas, while from Bombay Central train or bus station, you face a laborious trip across town. **Finding a place to stay** can be even more of a hassle; phone around from the STD telephone booths at all the main arrival points before you set off into the traffic.

By air

For many visitors, **Sahar**, Bombay's busy **international airport** (☎836 6767), provides their first experience of India. Once through customs and the lengthy immigration formalities, you'll find a 24-hour *State Bank of India* exchange facility, government and state (MTDC) tourist information counters, car rental kiosks, cafes and a pre-paid taxi stand in the chaotic arrivals concourse. If you're on one of the few flights to land in the afternoon or early evening – by which time most hotels tend to be full – it's worth paying on the spot for a room at the **accommodation booking desk** in the lobby.

The "ex-servicemen's" *EAT* **bus**, which leaves Sahar more or less hourly (except 1–4am) is a cheap and convenient way to travel the 26km into the city. It heads down the west side of the peninsula past Haji Ali's tomb, Chowpatty beach, and the *Air India* building at Nariman Point (the main drop) to the Gateway of India in Colaba. Tickets, bought on the bus, cost around Rs40. Many of the more upmarket hotels, particularly those near the airport, send out **courtesy coaches** to pick up their guests.

Taxis are more comfortable and not too extravagant. To avoid haggling over the fare, pay in advance at the taxi desk in the arrivals hall. The price of the chit, which you hand to the driver on arrival at your destination, is slightly more than the normal meter rate, but at least you can be sure you'll be taken by the most direct route. Taxi *wallahs* invariably try to persuade you to stay at a different hotel to the one you ask for. Don't agree; their commission will end up added on to the price of your room.

For **onward transport** from Bombay, including routes to **Goa**, see p.617 onwards.

Internal flights land at Bombay's **domestic airport, Santa Cruz** (☎611 6133 or 4433). If you're transferring directly from here to an international flight at Sahar, 3km northeast, either take the *EAT* bus (Rs20), or the special "fly-bus" that shuttles every fifteen minutes between the two. The brand new terminal building is more user-friendly than most Indian airports. The Indian government and MTDC both have 24-hour information counters in the arrivals hall, but there's no foreign exchange. Once again, the hourly *EAT* bus, which calls at Santa Cruz after leaving Sahar, is the cheapest way to get to the centre.

Don't be persuaded to use the **auto-rickshaws** that buzz around outside the airport; they aren't allowed downtown and will leave you at the mercy of unscrupulous taxi drivers on the edge of Mahim Creek, the southernmost limit of their permitted area.

By train

Trains to Bombay from most central, southern and eastern regions arrive at **Victoria Terminus** (aka "VT"), the main railway station at the end of the *Central Railway* line. From here it's a ten- or fifteen-minute ride to Colaba; either pick up a taxi at the busy rank outside the south exit, opposite the new reservation hall, or make your way to the main road and catch one of the innumerable buses.

Bombay Central, the terminus for *Western Railway* trains from northern India, is much further from the centre; take a taxi from the main forecourt, or cross the hectic road junction next to the station and catch a *BEST* bus from the top of Dr DN Marg (Lamington Rd); #66 and #71 run to VT, #70 to Colaba Causeway. An equally cheap option is to hop on a suburban train from Bombay Central's local platform, across the footbridge. Four stops on is **Churchgate** station, the end of the line, a short taxi ride from Colaba (Rs10).

Some trains from south India arrive at more obscure stations. If you find yourself at **Dadar**, way up in the industrial suburbs, and can't afford a taxi, cross the Tilak Marg

VICTORIA TERMINUS

Inspired by St Pancras station in London, FW Stevens designed **Victoria Terminus**, the most barmy of Bombay buildings, as a paean to "progress". **VT**, as it is known, is huge, built in 1887 as the largest British edifice in India; its extraordinary amalgam of domes, spires, Corinthian columns and minarets was succinctly defined by the journalist James Cameron as "Victorian-Gothic-Saracenic-Italianate-Oriental-St Pancras-Baroque".

Few of the two million or so passengers who fill almost a thousand trains every day notice VT's mass of decorative detail. A "British" lion and Indian tiger stand guard at the entrance, and the exterior is festooned with sculptures executed at the Bombay Art School by the Indian students of John Lockwood Kipling, Rudyard's father. Among them are grotesque mythical beasts, monkeys and plants and medallions of important personages. To minimize the sun's impact stained glass was employed, some designed with locomotives and elephant images. Above it all, "Progress" stands atop the massive central dome.

An endless frenzy of activity goes on inside, scuttling with passengers, hundreds of porters in red with impossibly oversize headloads, TTEs (Travelling Ticket Examiners) in black jackets and white trousers clasping clipboards detailing reservations, *chai-wallahs* with trays of tea, trundling magazine stands, crowds of bored soldiers smoking *bidis*, and the inexorable progress across the station of sweepers bent double. Amid it all, whole families spread out on the floor, eating, sleeping or just waiting and waiting.

road bridge onto the *Western Railway* and catch a suburban train into town, or take *BEST* bus #70 to Colaba. **Kurla** station, where a few Bangalore trains pull in, is even further out, just south of Santa Cruz airport. The only alternative to a cab from here is to catch bus #91 to Bombay Central Station and change there to #70 for Colaba or a suburban train for Churchgate. Trying anything so complicated during a rush hour, however – especially if you're carrying heavy luggage – is more trouble than it's worth.

By bus

Nearly all inter-state **buses** arrive at **Bombay Central** bus stand, a stone's throw from the railway station of the same name. Again, you have a choice between municipal black and yellow taxis, the *BEST* buses (#66, #70 & #71) which run straight into town from the stop on Dr DN Marg (Lamington Rd), two minutes' walk west from the bus station, or a suburban train from Bombay Central's local platform over the footbridge.

Most Maharashtran state buses terminate at the **ASIAD** bus stand, a glorified parking lot beside the main street in **Dadar**. Taxis are on hand for the thirty- to sixty-minute trip down to Colaba, or you can make your way over Tilak Marg road bridge to Dadar railway station and pick up a local train to Churchgate.

Buses from Goa drop off at various points between central and downtown Bombay. Most of the private companies currently work out of **Ballard Pier** in the Fort area, while *Kadamba* (the Goan state transport corporation) buses stop on MG Rd near the *Metro* cinema. Both places are an inexpensive taxi ride from the main hotel district.

Information and communications

The best source of **information** in Bombay is the excellent **India Government Tourist Office** (Mon–Fri 8.30am–6pm, Sat 8.30am–2pm; ☎203 3144) at 123 M Karve Rd, opposite Churchgate station's east exit. The staff here are exceptionally helpful and hand out a wide range of leaflets, maps and brochures both on Bombay and the rest of the country. There are also 24-hour tourist information counters at Sahar (☎632 5331) and Santa Cruz (☎614 9200) airports.

Maharashtra State Tourism Development Corporation's (**MTDC**) main office, on Madam Cama Rd (☎202 7762), opposite the LIC Building in Nariman Point, sells tickets for city sightseeing tours, and long-distance "luxury" buses (see p.621), and can reserve rooms in MTDC hotels. They too have information counters at Sahar (☎636 6700) and Santa Cruz (☎611 4788), as well as at VT railway station (☎262 2859) and on CS Marg, near the Gateway of India (☎241877).

Local publications

For detailed information about **what's on** in Bombay, ask at the government tourist office for a fortnightly listings pamphlet, or check out the "Entertainments" page in the *Times of India*, whose city edition, and that of the *Times of India*, is available from street vendors around Colaba and the downtown area.

If you need a detailed **map** of Bombay, look for *Karmarkar Enterprise*'s "*Most Exhaustive A–Z*" street plan (Rs60). It's fiendishly hard to find in bookstores, but the pavement guidebook- and magazine-*wallahs* along VN Rd, between Churchgate and Flora Fountain, may have copies.

> The telephone **area code** for Bombay is ☎022.

Banks

The logical place to change money when you arrive in Bombay is at the *State Bank of India*'s 24-hour counter in Sahar airport. Rates here are standard but you'll have to pay for an encashment certificate – essential if you intend to buy tourist quota railway tickets or an *Indrail* pass at the special counters in Churchgate or VT stations. The only bank open around the clock is at the *Air India* building on Nariman Point.

All the major **banks** downtown change foreign currency (Mon–Fri 11am–3pm, Sat 11am–1pm); some also handle **credit cards**. The *Andhra Bank* (☎218 3506), 18 Homi Modi St (near Flora Fountain), takes *Visa*, and the *Bank of America* (☎287 4959), in the Express Towers building, Nariman Point, deals with *Mastercard*. The *American Express* office (☎204 8278), in the Oriental Building, 364 Dr DN Marg, around the corner from the *Regal* cinema in Colaba, offers all the regular services (including poste restante) to travellers' cheque and card holders and is open to anyone wishing to change cash. The same applies to *Thomas Cook* (Mon–Fri 9.30am–6.30pm, Sat 9.30am–4.30pm; ☎204 8556), whose big branch on Dr DN Marg, between the *Khadi* shop and Flora Fountain, can also arrange money transfers from overseas. *Credit Lyonnais* (☎261 2313) has a branch on the first floor of Scindia House, NM Marg, Ballard Estate. *Eurocheques* are accepted at the *Deutsche Bank* (☎221250), Tulsiani Chambers, in Nariman Point.

Mail and telecommunications

The **GPO** (Mon–Sat 9am–8pm, Sun 9am–4pm) is around the corner from VT Station, off Nagar Chowk. Its **poste restante** counter (Mon–Sat 9am–6pm, Sun 9am–3pm) is among the most reliable in India, although they trash the letters after four weeks. The much less efficient parcel office (10am–4.30pm) is behind the main building on the first floor. Packing-*wallahs* hang around on the sidewalk outside.

STD booths abound in Bombay. For rock-bottom **phone** and **fax** rates however, head for Videsh Sanchar Bhavan, the swanky new government telecom building on MG Marg, where you can make **collect calls** to destinations such as the UK, US, and Australia. Receiving incoming calls costs a nominal Rs5.

City transport

Only a masochist would travel on Bombay's hopelessly overtaxed public **transport** for fun. For much of the day, traffic on the main roads crawls along at little more than walking speed, or grinds to a halt in endless jams at road junctions. On the plus side, it might take forever to ride across town on a dusty red double-decker **bus**, but it will never set you back more than a few *rupees*. Local **trains** get there faster, but are a real endurance test even outside rush hours. **Rickshaws** do not run downtown.

USEFUL BOMBAY BUS ROUTES

#1/3/6(Ltd)/11(Ltd)/16(Ltd)/19(Ltd)/ 103/124 Colaba bus station to Mahatma Phule (Crawford) Market, via VT (Nagar Chowk).

#43 Colaba bus station to GPO.

#70 Colaba to Dadar Station (W), via Bombay Central.

#103/106/107 Colaba to Kamala Nehru Park, via Chowpatty Beach.

#124 Colaba to Vatsalabai Desai Chowk, via Bombay Central.

#132 Colaba to Breach Candy, via Vatsalabai Desai Chowk.

#81 Churchgate to Santa Cruz, via Vatsalabai Desai Chowk (for Haji Ali's tomb and Mahalakshmi temple).

#66/71 Bombay Central to VT.

#91 Bombay Central to Kurla station.

Buses

BEST (*Bombay Electric Supply and Transport*; enquiries ☎414 3611 or 882 8737) operates a **bus** network of labyrinthine complexity, extending to the furthest-flung corners of the city. Unfortunately, neither the route booklets, maps nor "*Point to Point*" guides (which you can consult at the tourist office or at news stands) make things any clearer. Finding out which bus you need is difficult enough. Recognizing it in the street can be even more problematic, as the numbers are written in Hindi. Aim, wherever possible, for the "Limited" services, which stop less frequently, and avoid rush hours at all costs. Tickets should be bought from the conductor on the bus.

Trains

Bombay would be paralyzed without its local **trains**, which carry millions of commuters each day between downtown and the sprawling suburbs in the north. One line begins at VT, running up the east side of the city as far as Thane. The other leaves Churchgate, hugging the curve of Back Bay as far as Chowpatty Beach, where it veers north towards Bombay Central, Dadar, Santa Cruz and Vasai, beyond the city limits. Services depart every few minutes from 5am until midnight, stopping at dozens of small stations. Carriages remain packed solid virtually the whole time, with passengers dangling precariously out of open doors to escape the crush, so start to make your way to the exit at least three stops before your destination. The apocalyptic peak hours are worst of all. Women are marginally better off in the "ladies carriages"; look for the crowd of *saris* and *shalwa camises* grouped at the end of the platform.

Taxis

With rickshaws banished to the suburbs, Bombay's ubiquitous black-and-yellow **taxis** are the quickest and most convenient way to nip around the city centre. In theory, all should have meters and a current rate card (to convert the amount shown on the meter to the correct fare); in practice, particularly at night or early in the morning, many drivers refuse to use them. If this happens, either flag down another or haggle out a fare. As a rule of thumb, expect to be charged Rs5 per kilometre after the minimum fare of around Rs10, together with a small sum for heavy luggage (officially Rs1 per article).

Boats

Ferry-boats regularly chug out of Bombay harbour, connecting the city with the far shore and some of the larger islands in between. The most popular with visitors is the **Elephanta Island** launch (see p.598) which departs hourly (9am–12.15am; Rs40) from the Gateway of India. Boats to **Rewas**, the jetty across the bay which is the transport hub for Chaul, Murud-Janjira and the rarely used coastal route south, leave from Ferry Wharf, 4.5km north of Colaba up AS D'Mello (Frere) Rd.

Tours

Of MTDC's sightseeing **tours** around Bombay, the "City" tour (Tues–Sun 9am–1pm & 2–6pm; Rs60) manages to cram Colaba, Marine Drive, Jehangir Art Gallery, the Hanging Gardens, Kamla Nehru Park and Mani Bhavan into half a day; the "Suburban" tour (Tues–Sun 9.15am–6.15pm; Rs90) takes in Kanheri caves, Krishnagiri Upavan National Park, a lion safari and Juhu in a full day. Tickets should be booked in advance from the MTDC office on Madam Cama Rd (the departure point), or from the government tourist office.

MTDC also run four-day "outstation tours" to the caves at **Ellora**, **Ajanta** and **Aurangabad**. Either book all-in tickets, which include the cost of accommodation, for a stiff Rs1000, or else pay the one-way fare of Rs140.

Car rental

Cars with drivers can be rented per day (around Rs600 for a non-a/c *Ambassador*, upwards of Rs1000 for more luxurious a/c cars), or per kilometre, from ITDC's counter at the government tourist office, or through most good travel agents (see p.616).

Self-drive is also now available in Bombay, though the service seems to be intended more for middle-class Indians out to impress their friends ("They'll never know it's rented!"), than tourists. You will, in any case, be a lot safer if you leave the driving to someone more at home with the city's racetrack rules of the road. If you're willing to risk it, try *Budget Rent-a-Car*, 462 Phoenix Mill Compound, Senapati Bapat Marg, Lower Parel (☎494 2644); or the *Transport Corporation of India* (in collaboration with *Hertz*), 16th Floor, Nariman Building, Nariman Point (☎202 3734 or 202 3343).

The City

Between the airports to the north and the southern tip of Bombay lies a thirty-kilometre-long, seething mass of streets, suburbs and relentless traffic. Even during the relatively cool winter months, exploring it can be hard work, requiring plenty of pit-stops at cold drink stalls along the way. The best place to start is down at the far south end of the peninsula in **Colaba**, home to most of the hotels, restaurants and best-known sights, including the **Gateway of India**. Fifteen minutes' walk north takes you past the **Prince of Wales Museum** to the **Fort** area, home of all the banks and big stores, plus the cream of Bombay's ostentatious Raj-era buildings. The extravagant **Victoria Terminus** overlooks its northern limits, close to the impressive onion-dome of the **GPO**. The hub of the suburban train network, **Churchgate station**, stands 4km west, across the big *maidans* that scythe through the centre of town. Churchgate, and the **tourist office**, is a stone's throw from the sweeping curve of **Back Bay**. With **Nariman Point**'s skyscrapers at one end, lively **Chowpatty Beach** and the affluent apartment blocks of **Malabar Hill** at the other, the Bay is Bombay at its snazziest. The area immediately north and east, by contrast, is ramshackle and densely populated. The **central bazaars** extend from **Crawford Market**, beyond Victoria Terminus, right up to **J Boman (JB) Behram Marg**, opposite the other mainline train station, **Bombay Central**.

Colaba

At the end of the seventeenth century, **Colaba** was little more than the last in a straggling line of rocky islands extending to the lighthouse that stood on Bombay's southernmost point. Today, the original outlines of the promontory (whose name derives from the **Koli** who first lived here) have been submerged under a mass of dilapidated colonial tenements, hotels, bars, restaurants and handicraft shops. If you never venture beyond the district, you'll get a very distorted picture of Bombay. In spite of being the main tourist enclave and a trendy hang-out for the city's rich young things, Colaba has retained the distinctly sleazy feel of the bustling port it used to be, with dodgy money-changers, dealers and pimps hissing at passers-by from doorways.

The Gateway of India

Bombay's most famous landmark, the **Gateway of India**, was built in 1924 by George Wittet, responsible for many of the city's grandest constructions. Commemorating the visit of King George V and Queen Mary in 1913, India's own honey-coloured Arc de Triomphe was originally envisaged as a ceremonial disembarkation point for passengers alighting from the *P&O* steamers. Ironically, it is today more often remembered as the place the British chose to stage their final departure from the country – on 28 February 1948, the last detachment of troops remaining on Indian soil set sail from

COLABA

Rhythm House

SUBHASH CHOWK

Jahangir Art Gallery

Prince of Wales Museum

K DUBASH MARG

MAHATMA GANDHI RD

HOPE ST

N

0   100 m

MADAM CAMA RD

Wellington Circle

COOPERAGE MARG

Phillip's Antiques

American Express

Cottage Industries Emporium

Shakhari Bunder

Regal Cinema

SHIVAJI MARG

NATHALAL PAREKH MARG

RAJKAV GHUSHAN MARG

TULLOCH RD

Bombay Yacht Club

Police Station

ORMISTON RD

MANDLIK MARG

ORMISTON RD

Bus Depot

BARROW RD

HENRY RD

MERLEWEATHER RD

SHAHID BHAGAT SINGH MARG (COLABA CAUSEWAY)

Gateway of India

ARABIAN SEA

WALTON RD

GARDEN RD

P J RAMCHANDANI MARG (APOLLO BUNDER)

ARTHUR BUNDER RD

STRAND RD

Strand Cinema

HOTELS:

Ⓐ Lawrence
Ⓑ YWCA
Ⓒ Regency
Ⓓ Taj Mahal Intercontinental
Ⓔ Carlton
Ⓕ Diplomat
Ⓖ Regent
Ⓗ Salvation Army
Ⓘ Prosser's
Ⓙ Whalley's
Ⓚ Oliver Guest House
Ⓛ Cowie's
Ⓜ Kishan
Ⓝ Apollo Guest House
Ⓞ Sea Palace
Ⓟ Ascot
Ⓠ Goodwin
Ⓡ Garden
Ⓢ Shelley's
Ⓣ Gulf
Ⓤ Sea Shore & India
Ⓥ Fariyas
Ⓦ Strand & Kerawala Chambers

RESTAURANTS:

❶ Khyber
❷ Wayside
❸ Chetana
❹ Samovar
❺ Copper Chimney
❻ Golden Gate
❼ Ling's Pavillion
❽ Nanking
❾ Majestic
❿ Cafe Mondegar
⓫ Delhi Darbar
⓬ Bade Mian Kebab-wallah
⓭ Baghdadi
⓮ Alps
⓯ Leopold's
⓰ Olympic Coffee House
⓱ Light of Asia
⓲ New Martin
⓳ Fab Bistro
⓴ Kailash Parbat
㉑ Himroo Kebab-wallah

here. Nowadays, the only boats bobbing about at the bottom of its stone staircase are the launches that ferry tourists across the harbour to Elephanta Island (see p.598).

During the evenings, the recently spruced-up square surrounding the Gateway is a popular place for a stroll. At one end, an equestrian statue of **Shivaji**, the Maratha military adventurer who dogged the last years of the Moghul emperor Aurangzeb, looks sternly on. Shivaji has been appropriated as a nationalist symbol (the prototypical "Son of the Soil") by the extreme right-wing Shiv Sena, which explains the garland of marigolds often draped around the statue's neck.

Behind the Gateway

Directly behind the Gateway of India, the older hotel in the **Taj Mahal Intercontinental Hotel** complex stands as a monument to native hubris in the face of colonial oppression. Its patron, the Parsi industrialist JN Tata, is said to have built the old *Taj* as an act of revenge against what was then the best hotel in town, the "whites only" *Watson's*, for having refused him entry. The oversight proved their undoing. *Watson's* long ago disappeared, but the *Taj*, with its grand grey and white stone facade and red-domed roof, still presides imperiously over the seafront, the preserve of visiting diplomats, sheikhs and Bombay's jet-set. Lesser mortals are allowed in to sample the opulent tea-shops and restaurants.

From the *Taj*, you can head down the promenade, PJ Ramchandani Marg, better known as **Apollo Bunder** (nothing to do with the Greek sun god, the name is a colonial corruption of the Koli words for a local fish, *palav*, and quay, *bunda*), taking in the sea breezes and views over the busy harbour. Alternatively, Shivaji Marg heads north-west towards **Wellington Circle** (SPM Chowk), the hectic roundabout in front of the *Regal* cinema. The latter route takes you past the old **Bombay Yacht Club**, another idiosyncratic vestige of the Raj. Very little seems to have changed here since its smoky common rooms were a bolt-hole for the city's *burrasahibs*. Dusty sporting trophies and models of clippers and steamships stand in glass cases lining its corridors, polished from time to time by bearers in cotton tunics and cummerbunds.

Southwards along Colaba Causeway

To walk from Wellington Circle to the far south of the peninsula, you have first to run the gauntlet of street-vendors and hustlers who crowd the claustrophobic pavements of **Colaba Causeway** (this stretch of Shahid Bhagat Singh Marg). It's hard to believe that such a chaotic city thoroughfare, with its hole-in-the-wall cafes, clothes stores and incense stalls, once lay beneath the sea. By the time you reach the tall wooden-galleried houses of **Arthur Bunder Road**, however, even the Muslim perfumeries can barely smother the smell of fish wafting up the main street. The wholesale seafood market at **Sassoon Docks**, a kilometre or so south of central Colaba, provides an unexpected splash of rustic colour amid the drab urban surroundings. Koli fisherwomen, their cotton *saris* hitched *dhoti*-style, squat beside baskets of glistening pomfret, while coolies haul hand-carts and heavy blocks of ice over rickety gangplanks from the boats moored at the quay. The stench, as overpowering as the noise, comes mostly from the bundles of dried fish that are sold in bulk. "**Bombay duck**", the salty local snack, has found its way to many a far shore, but you'll be hard pushed to find any in Colaba's own restaurants. **Photography** is forbidden, as the market is close to a sensitive military area.

From the docks, a fair hike down Colaba Causeway leads to the **Afghan Memorial Church of St John the Baptist**. Hemmed in by the Cantonment area, the pale yellow church, with its tall steeple and tower, would look more at home beside the playing fields of Eton than the sultry waters of the Arabian Sea. It was built between 1847 and 1854 as a memorial to the British victims of the First Afghan War. If the door is unlocked, take a peek at the marble plaques and fine stained-glass windows inside.

Dr N Moos Marg passes the Navy hospital and Roman Catholic church (on your right), before eventually arriving at the southernmost tip of the Bombay mainland. The now-defunct Colaba **lighthouse** (the present one stands on a rock just off shore) commands a fine view over the harbour. Year round, dozens of heavy container vessels wait patiently in line to dock alongside Bombay's overtaxed wharves, as a flotilla of launches, tugs and triangular-sailed *dhows* tack between them. Directly behind the lighthouse, in the weed-infested old British **cemetery**, you might find the tomb of the 184 people drowned when the *Castlereagh* sank nearby in the mid-eighteenth century.

Downtown Bombay

Aldous Huxley described Bombay as "one of the most appalling cities of either hemisphere", with its "lavatory bricks and Gothic spires". The critic Robert Byron, a whole-hearted fan of New Delhi, was equally unenthusiastic, feeling moved to refer to **downtown Bombay** in 1931 as "that architectural Sodom", claiming that "the nineteenth century devised nothing lower than the municipal buildings of British India. Their ugliness is positive, daemonic." Today, however, the massive erections of Empire and Indian free enterprise appear not ugly, but intriguing.

Prince of Wales Museum and Jehangir Art Gallery

Tues–Sun 10.15am–6pm. Rs3, students free on Tues; photos without flash or tripod Rs15.

Set back from Mahatma Gandhi (MG) Rd in a pretty garden, the **Prince of Wales Museum** holds a superb collection of Indian paintings and sculpture. You'll need several hours, or a couple of visits, to get the most out of it. Its foundation stone was laid in 1905 by the future King George V, then Prince of Wales; the architect responsible, George Wittet, went on to design the Gateway of India and the Institute of Science, nearby. The museum is undoubtedly the finest example of his work; the epitome of the hybrid **Indo-Saracenic** style, it is said to be an "educated" interpretation of fifteenth- and sixteenth-century Gujarati architecture, mixing Islamic touches such as the arches and massive white tiled concrete dome, with typically English municipal brickwork.

The **central hall**, crowned by a dome and overlooked by a carved wooden balcony, provides a snapshot of the collection with a few choice Moghul paintings, jade work, weapons and miniature clay and terracotta figures from the Mauryan (third century BC) and Kushana (first to second century AD) periods. From Bengal (first century BC) are horrible-looking *yakshis* (godlings or sprites) devouring lizards. Sculpture galleries on either side of the hall open onto the front garden. The one to the right brings you to the museum's **natural history** section, which contains a fascinating and well-kept – if somewhat unfashionable – collection of stuffed birds, fish and animals.

The main **sculpture room** on the ground floor displays some excellent Gandharan (fourth to fifth century AD) heads and figures. Rosettes, an elephant head, a damaged *yakshi* and part of a Jataka scene were recovered from the *stupa* at Bharhut. Important Hindu sculptures include Gupta-period *ganas* from Gujarat, a seventh-century Chalukyan bas-relief from Aihole depicting Brahma seated on a lotus, and another Brahma image from Elephanta (see p.599). On the way up to the **first floor** a display on the astonishingly urban **Indus Valley civilization** (3500–1500 BC) incorporates models of typical settlements, mysterious seal moulds in an as-yet-undeciphered script, and jewellery. The main attraction on the first floor has to be the superb collection of **Indian painting**, including illustrations and illustrated manuscripts, and erotic Gita Govinda paintings in the pre-Moghul Sultanate style. **Moghul schools** are well represented, too, with fine portraits and folios from the reign of Akbar (1556–1605), and sublime drawings of animals and birds from the Jehangir (1605–28) school. The well-known portrait of the emperor Shah Jehan (1628–58) and his forefathers is also on display. A large part of the collection is devoted to **Rajasthan**, particularly the seventeenth-century Mewar, Malwa and Bundi schools and eighteenth-century Kishangarh and Bundi. The **Nepal and Tibet Gallery** features a collection of Buddhist *thangkas*, painted or embroidered cloth hangings, with elaborate *mandala* designs.

Jade, porcelain and ivory can be seen on the **second floor**, along with a collection of **European art** that includes a minor Titian and a Constable. Among the weapon collection are swords belonging to emperors Shah Jehan and Aurangzeb, a shield of Akbar ornamented with the zodiac, and various fearsome daggers, maces and guns. The **Indian textiles room** showcases eighteenth- and nineteenth-century Kashmiri shawls, patterned with flowers, birds, animals and abstract designs. Here also are two unusual late-eighteenth-century Kulu shawls decorated with hunting scenes, fine tie-dye silk wedding *patola saris* from Gujarat, and wax- or block-printed *kalamkari saris*.

The **publications counter** (10.15am–1.30pm & 2–6pm) next to the entrance sells a good selection of reasonably priced postcards, a guide to Indian art (with some references to the collection), and excellent folio reproductions of miniature paintings.

Technically in the same compound as the Prince of Wales Museum, though approached from further up MG Rd, the **Jehangir Art Gallery** (Mon–Fri 10am–5pm) is Bombay's best-known venue for contemporary art, with five small galleries specializing in twentieth-century arts and crafts from around the world. You never know what you're going to find – most exhibitions last only a week and exhibits are often for sale.

Madam Cama Road

On the eastern side of Madam Cama Rd, the cavernous **CJ Hall** was named after the Parsi businessman Sir Cowasjee Jehangir (1812–78), who started out as a *godown* (warehouse) keeper. Known for his philanthropy, Jehangir publicly donated at least Rs1,500,000 over the years, earning himself the nickname "Readymoney". After he donated the sum of £200 to some institution or other the English humour magazine, *Punch*, had its readers in stitches with the quip: "Is Mr Readymoney a Parsi? At any rate, he is the reverse of parsimonious." Financed largely by Parsi benefactors, CJ Hall is actually part of the Renaissance-style yellow basalt **Institute of Science**, which fills the rest of the block and curves into Karmaveer Bhaurao Patil Marg (Mayo Rd).

Around Oval Maidan

Karmaveer Bhaurao Patil Marg's southern edge holds a statue of Dr BR Ambedkar (1891–1956), born into a Hindu outcast community, who converted to Buddhism. A great number of "untouchables" followed suit; many are now part of a militant movement calling themselves *dalits*, "the oppressed", eschewing Gandhi's reconstructed name of *Harijans*, "god's people". Some of Bombay's most important Victorian buildings line the eastern side of the vast green **Oval Maidan**, behind the statue, a cricket ground where official or impromptu matches take place almost every day.

Partially obscured by police huts, the dull yellow **Old Secretariat** now serves as the City Civil and Sessions Court. Indian civil servant GW Forrest described it in 1903 as "a massive pile whose main features have been brought from Venice, but all the beauty has vanished in transhipment." Inside, you can only imagine the originally highly polished interior, which no longer shines. It does, however, buzz with activity. Lawyers in black gowns, striped trousers and white tabs bustle up and down the staircases, whose corners are emblazoned with expectorated *paan* juice, and offices with perforated swing-doors give glimpses of text-book images of Indian bureaucracy – peons at desks piled high with dusty be-ribboned document bundles.

Across AS D'Mello Rd from the Old Secretariat, two major buildings belonging to **Bombay University** (established 1857) were both designed in England by Sir Gilbert Scott, who had already given the world the Gothic extravaganza of St Pancras railway station in London. Access through the main gates is monitored by caretakers who only allow you in if you say you're using the library. Funded again by Mr "Readymoney", the **Convocation Hall** greatly resembles a church. Above the entrance a huge circular stained-glass window features a wheel with spokes of Greek pilasters that separate signs of the zodiac, while the 79.2-metre-high Rajabhai clock tower, over the **Library** (daily 10am–10pm), is said to be modelled on Giotto's campanile in Florence. Until 1931 it chimed tunes such as *Rule Britannia* and *Home Sweet Home*. It's worth applying for a visitors ticket (Rs5 a day, Rs10 for 3 days) just to see the interior. The magnificent vaulted wooden ceiling of the reading room, high Gothic windows and stained glass evoke a reverential approach to learning that seems thoroughly old-fashioned today.

Hutama Chowk (Flora Fountain)

A busy five-point intersection in the heart of the Fort area, **Flora Fountain** has been renamed **Hutama Chowk** ("Martyr's Square") to commemorate the freedom fighters who died to establish the state of Maharashtra in the Indian Union. The *chowk* centres on a statue of the Roman goddess **Flora**, erected in 1869 to commemorate Sir Bartle Frere. It's hard to see quite why – the Raj architecture expert, Philip Davies, was not being unkind when he said "The fountain was designed by a committee, and it shows."

Facing the Flora Fountain, a **statue of Dadabhai Naoroji** (1812–1917) shows the first Indian member of the British parliament (1892–95). You may want to tarry here a while to consult Machindra Govind Pawar, who for years has sat next to the statue daily except Sunday between 8am and 8pm. Signs explain his business, offering cures

---

DABAWALLAHS

Bombay's size and inconvenient shape create all kind of hassles for its working population – not least having to stew for upwards of four hours each day in slow municipal transport. One thing the daily tidal wave of commuters do not have to worry about, however, is finding an inexpensive and wholesome home-cooked lunch. In a city with a *wallah* for everything, it will find them. The members of the **Bombay Tiffin Box Suppliers Association**, known colloquially, and with no little affection, as "**dabawallahs**", see to that.

Every day, around four thousand *dabawallahs* deliver freshly cooked food from 125,000 suburban kitchens to offices in the downtown area. Each lunch is prepared early in the morning by a devoted wife or mother while her husband or son is enduring the crush on the train. She arranges the rice, *dhal*, *subzi*, curd and *parathas* into cylindrical aluminium trays, stacks them on top of one another and clips them together with a neat little handle. This **tiffin box**, not unlike a slim paint tin, is the lynchpin of the whole operation. When the runner calls to collect it in the morning, he uses a special colour code on the lid to tell him where the lunch has to go. At the end of his round, he carries all the boxes to the nearest train station and hands them over to other *dabawallahs* for the trip into town. Between leaving the wife and reaching its final destination, the tiffin box will pass through at least half a dozen different pairs of hands, carried on heads, shoulder-poles, bicycle handlebars and in the brightly decorated handcarts that plough with such insouciance through the midday traffic. Tins are rarely, if ever, lost, and always find their way home again (before the husband returns from work) to be washed up for the next day's lunch.

To catch *dabawallahs* in action, head for **VT** or **Churchgate** stations around late morning time, when the tiffin boxes arrive in the city centre. The event is accompanied by a chorus of "lafka! lafka!" – "hurry! hurry!" – as the *dabawallahs*, recognizable in their white Nehru caps and baggy khaki shorts, rush to make their lunch-hour deadlines. Most collect about one *rupee* for each tin they handle, netting around Rs1000 per month in total. *Daba* lunches still work out a good deal cheaper than meals taken in the city restaurants, saving precious *paise* for the middle-income workers who use the system, and providing a livelihood for the legions of poorer immigrants from the Pune area who operate it.

for "rheumatism, hair falling, piles, fistula and sex weakness". Sri Pawar, who hails from Pune, says he is a practitioner of *ayurveda* and operates on a basis that sounds like commercial suicide: he accepts no payment until his patients are cured.

Horniman (Elphinstone) Circle and the Town Hall

Elphinstone Circle, renamed **Horniman Circle** after a pro-Independence newspaper editor, was conceived in 1860 as a centrepiece of a newly planned Bombay by the then Municipal Commissioner, Charles Forjett, on the site of Bombay "Green". Forjett, a Eurasian, had something of a peculiar reputation. He was fond of disguising himself in "native" dress and prowling about certain districts of the city to listen out for seditious talk. In 1857, at the time of the First War of Independence (as it is now known by Indians; the British call it the Indian Mutiny), Forjett fired two suspected revolutionaries from a cannon on the Esplanade (roughly the site of the modern *maidans*).

It is often said that the design of Elphinstone Circle was based on Tunbridge Wells or Leamington Spa in England, with elegant Neoclassical buildings centering on a garden with a fountain. East of the square, the impressive Doric **Town Hall** on SBS Marg houses the vast collection of the **Asiatic Library** (see p.617).

St Thomas' Cathedral

The small, simple **St Thomas' Cathedral** (daily 6.30am–6pm), on Tamarind St, is reckoned to be the oldest English building in Bombay, blending Classical and Gothic styles. Governor Aungier self-righteously envisaged it with "the main design of inviting the natives to repair thereunto, and observe the gravity and purity of our own devotions". After his death, the project was abandoned; the walls stood five metres high for forty-odd years until enthusiasm was rekindled by Richard Cobbe, a chaplain to the East India Company in the second decade of the eighteenth century. He believed the church's unfinished walls represented "a mark of derision for the natives for whose conversion they were partly raised [and] a reproach and a scandal to the English in Bombay". It was finally opened on Christmas Day 1718, complete with the essential "cannon-ball-proof roof". In those days the seating was divided into useful sections for those who should know their place, including one for "Inferior Women".

St Thomas' whitewashed and polished brass-and-wood interior looks much the same as when the staff of the East India Company worshipped here in the eighteenth century. Lining the walls are memorial tablets to English parishioners, many of whom died young, either from disease or in battle. Incidentally, the fountain facing the entrance to the cathedral is yet another donation from "Readymoney".

Marine Drive and Chowpatty Beach

Netaji Subhash Chandra Marg, better known as **Marine Drive**, is Bombay's seaside prom, an eight-lane highway with a wide pavement built in the 1920s on reclaimed land. Sweeping in an arc from the skyscrapers at Nariman Point in the south, Marine Drive ends at the foot of Malabar Hill and the old **Chowpatty Beach**. The whole stretch is a favourite place for a stroll; the promenade next to the sea has uninterrupted views virtually the whole way along, while the apartment blocks on the land side – most of which are ugly unpainted concrete and called something-or-other Mahal – are some of the most desirable and expensive addresses in the city.

It's a great place for people-watching. Early in the morning yuppies in shorts speed-walk or jog before breakfast while street kids, mother-and-babies and limbless beggars take up position at the traffic lights at major junctions to petition drivers and passengers for a *rupee*. Those one rung further up the social ladder have something to sell: twisted fun balloons or a newspaper. Some kids perfunctorily wipe a rag over the bodywork and do their best to wrest a few coins from momentarily captive people, 90 percent of whom stare resolutely ahead.

Evening sees servants walking their bosses' pekinese or poodles and children playing under the supervision of their *ayahs* (nannies). Sometime after 6pm the place magically transforms; the British called it the "Queen's Necklace". The massive red sun disappears into the sea, street lights snap on, five-star hotels glow and neon lights blink. Innumerable couples materialize to take romantic strolls down to the beach, stopping on the way to buy from a peanut vendor or to pay off a *hijra*, eunuch (see p.183), threatening to lift up his *sari* and reveal all.

Just beyond the huge flyover, B Bridge, are a series of cricket pitches known as **gymkhanas**, where there's a good chance of catching a match any day of the week. A number are exclusive to particular religious communities. The first doubles as a swanky outdoors wedding venue for Parsi marriage functions; others include the Catholic, Islam and Hindu pitches, the last of which has a classic colonial-style pavilion.

At the northern end of the gymkhanas, the **Tarporevala Aquarium** (Tues–Sat 10am–7pm, Sun & hols 10am–8pm) is less notable for its sea snakes, vibrant green and yellow trigger fish, glinting tin foil fish, and turtles, than its two aquatic miracles: the "Quran fish", inscribed with a line from the Koran, and the "Christ Crab" which has a holy cross on his back. No photography is allowed.

Chowpatty Beach

Chowpatty Beach is a Bombay institution, which really comes to life at night and on Saturday. People do not come here to swim (the sea is foul) but to wander, sit on the beach, let the kids ride a pony or rusty Ferris wheel, have a massage, get ears cleaned or hair cut, listen to musicians, buy drugs, have a go on a rifle range, consult an astrologer, watch dreadlocked ascetics perform public austerities, get conned, and most importantly picnic on *bhel puri* and cups of *kulfi*. There are plenty of good ice cream bars and restaurants across Marine Drive, opposite the beach (see p.610), where you'll also find *Wagh's Fine Art Studio*, whose curious collection of plaster figures in the window includes a much larger than life Gandhi plus alsatian dog.

Amazingly enough, Chowpatty Beach is still home to a small fishing village that carries on as if the vast city of Bombay doesn't exist. Once a year in September the **Ganesh Chathurthi** festival (see p.614) draws gigantic crowds to participate in the immersion of idols, both huge and small, of the elephant-headed god Ganesh.

Mani Bhavan Mahatma Gandhi Museum

Mani Bhavan, 19 Laburnum Rd (daily 9.30am–6pm), was Gandhi's Bombay base between 1917 and 1934. Set in a leafy upper-middle-class road, the house is now a permanent memorial to the Mahatma with an extensive research library. Within the lovingly maintained polished wood interior, the walls are covered with photos of historic events and artefacts from the man's extraordinary life – the most disarming of which is a friendly letter to Hitler suggesting world peace. Gandhi's predictably simple sitting-cum-bedroom is preserved behind glass. Laburnum Road is a few streets along from the *Bharatiya Vidya Bhavan* music venue on KM Munshi Marg (see p.614) – if coming by taxi ask for the nearby Gamdevi Police Station.

Malabar Hill

Malabar Hill, the long, steep-sided promontory enfolding Chowpatty Beach at the north end of Back Bay, is Bombay's ritziest neighbourhood. Since the eighteenth century, its lush forests, fresh sea breezes and panoramic views have made the hill an attractive location for the grand mansions and bungalows of the city's merchants and governors. These days however, high-rise, high-rent apartment blocks have squeezed out all but a handful of the old colonial buildings to make way for Bombay's "new money" set – the in-crowd of politicians, millionaires, film stars and gangsters who flit across the glossy pages and gossip columns of India's popular magazines. Somehow, a few jaded remnants of the city's past have managed to weather the changes.

Before heading up the hill from the busy roundabout at the far end of Chowpatty Beach, make a short diversion through the narrow backlanes to **Bubulnath Mandir**, one of Bombay's most important Hindu temples. You'll have no trouble finding the entrance: just look for the melee of saffron-clad *sadhus*, stray cattle and flower-sellers that forms here around *puja* times. The building itself, a clumsy modern agglomeration of towers, turquoise arches and staircases, makes a much less interesting spectacle than the stream of *pujaris* (priests) and pilgrims on the greasy stone steps leading to it.

The municipal parks and the Jain temple

From the Bubulnath temple, the most pleasant and direct route up to Malabar Hill's main thoroughfare, **Ridge Road** (now re-named Bal Gangadhar, or BG, Kher Marg), is via the tangle of crumbling concrete paths through the woods below it. The trail emerges near a pair of dull but popular public parks. The larger, known as the "**Hanging Gardens**" (but recently renamed "Pherozeshah Mehta Gardens") is full of loving couples smooching ostentatiously around its gravel paths and manicured flower-beds. By contrast, the smaller **Kamla Nehru Children's Park** (across the road) is unlikely to appeal to anyone over the age of seven. The views of Back Bay are, in any case, better admired from the congenial terrace bars of the *Naaz Cafe* nearby.

A kilometre or so straight down the ridge from the parks stands Malabar Hill's **Jain temple**. Bombay's Jains originally came from Gujarat in the late seventeenth century to escape persecution by the Hindu Marathas. Since then, their legendarily sharp business sense has helped make these ultra-strict vegetarians one of the city's most prosperous minorities. According to an ancient dictum, Jains should, every day after bathing, walk barefoot to their local temple in a length of stitchless cloth to pray, a gesture of humility and renunciation that contrasts with the lavish decoration of the temples themselves. This temple, though on the small side, is no exception. Mirrors and colourful paintings cover the walls surrounding the approach to the central chamber, where the polished marble image of **Adinath**, the first of the twenty-four Jain teacher-prophets, or *tirthankaras*, is enshrined. In front of the image, devotees make

THE TOWERS OF SILENCE

High on the top of Malabar Hill, screened from prying eyes by an imposing wall and a dense curtain of vegetation, stand the seven Parsi **Towers of Silence**, or *Dokhmas*. If you know only one thing about the Parsis, it is probably that they dispose of their dead by leaving the corpses on top of tall cylindrical enclosures for their bones to be picked clean by vultures. This ancient mortuary ritual, thought to predate the 2500-year-old faith, was advocated by the prophet Zoroaster as a means of avoiding pollution of the four sacred elements (air, water, earth, and the holiest of all, fire). Recently, Parsis have been debating whether to switch to electric cremation as a sound, and more sanitary, alternative – supposedly because scraps of human flesh discarded by the over-fed vultures have been appearing on balconies, roof-tops and gardens near the Towers. Whatever they decide, none will thank you for trying to peep at the *Dokhmas* themselves, which are off-limits to all living people other than the pall-bearers who put the corpses in place. Not to be put off, *Time-Life* once published a colour photograph of a funeral taken from the buildings overlooking the site. Enraged Parsis retorted by asking how the photographer would feel if he saw pictures of *his* mother's body being pecked to bits by birds?

rice patterns as offerings. The temple also runs a stall selling freshly baked pure-veg biscuits, sweets and cakes. It's to the left of the main entrance, near the racks where shoes and leather articles have to be deposited.

Walukeshwar Mandir and Banganga Tank

Beyond the Jain temple, Malabar Hill tapers off to a narrow spit that shelves steeply down to Back Bay on one side, and the rocky sea shore on the other. **Walukeshwar Mandir**, among the few of Bombay's ancient Hindu sites not buried under layers of conurbation, can be reached via a lane left off the main road. According to the *Ramayana*, Rama paused here during his journey south to rescue Sita from the clutches of the evil Ravana, and fashioned a *lingam* out of sand to worship Shiva. Over time, the Walukeshwar, or "Sand-Lord" shrine, became one of the western Indian coast's most important religious centres, venerated even by the marauding Malabar pirates who menaced the islands. Today's temple, erected in 1715 after the original had been destroyed by the Portuguese, is unremarkable and best bypassed in favour of the more impressive **Banganga tank**, below it. Hemmed in by a towering wall of apartment blocks, the spring that feeds the tank is believed to have been created by an arrow fired from Rama's own fabled bow. Today, it's a minor pilgrimage site, busy only on "white" (full-) or "black" (no-) moon days of the month. At other times, Banganga's stone *ghats*, numerous subsidiary shrines, and scum-covered greenish waters see little more than a trickle of bathers, drawn mostly from the slum encampments which have sprung up on the broken land lining the shore. A path picks its way past these shacks, and the washing lines of the *dhobis* who live in them, to the **cremation ghats** nearby.

North of Malabar Hill

Two of Bombay's most popular religious sites, one Hindu, the other Muslim, can be reached by following Bhulabhai Desai Rd **north from Malabar Hill** as far as Prabhu Chowk, through the exclusive suburb of **Breach Candy** (bus #132 from Colaba). Alternatively, make for Bombay Central and head due west to **Vatsalabai Desai Chowk** (also bus #132 from Colaba).

Mahalakshmi Mandir is joined to Bhulabhai Desai Road by an alley lined with stalls selling *puja* offerings and devotional pictures. Bombay's favourite *devi*, **Lakshmi**, goddess of beauty and prosperity – the city's most sought-after attributes – is here propitiated with coconuts, sweets, lengths of shimmering silk and giant lotus blooms. At weekends, queues for *darshan* extend right the way across the courtyard and down the main steps beyond. Gifts pile so high that the temple *pujaris* run a money-spinning sideline reselling them. Their little shop, to the left of the entrance, is a good place to

---

THE MUNICIPAL DHOBI GHATS

On the face of it, the idea of going out of your way to ogle Bombay's dirty washing sounds like a very perverse pastime. If you're passing however, the **municipal dhobi ghats**, near Mahalakshmi suburban railway station, are well worth hopping off the train to see. This huge open-air laundry is the centre of one of those miraculous Indian institutions which, like the *dabawallah*'s operation (see p590), is usually regarded by westerners with disbelief. Each morning, washing from all over Bombay is brought here to be thrown into soapy piles and thumped by the resident *dhobiwallahs* in the countless concrete tanks, barrels and shanty shacks inside the compound. The next day, after being aired, pressed, folded in newspaper and bound with cotton thread, the bundles are returned to whence they came. The bird's-eye view over the V-shaped rows of *dhobi ghats* from Mahalakshmi road bridge is one of Bombay's most bizarre photo opportunities.

buy cut-price *saris* and brocades infused with lucky Lakshmi-energy. While you're here, find out what your future holds by joining the huddle of devotees pressing *rupees* onto the rear wall of the shrine room. If your coin sticks, you'll be rich.

A temple has stood on this rocky outcrop for well over a thousand years. Not until the eighteenth century however, when the hitherto swampy western edge of the city was drained, was the present building erected. Legend has it that the goddess herself told a contractor working on the project that unless her icon – which she said would soon reappear from the sea where it had been cast by Muslim invaders – was reinstated in a temple on the site, the breach-wall would not hold back the waves. Sure enough, the next day a Lakshmi deity was indeed fished out of the silt by workmen, to be installed on this small headland, where it has remained to the present day.

Another site shrouded in myth is the mausoleum of the Muslim saint, **Haji Ali**, occupying a small islet in the bay just north of the Mahalakshmi temple. Islamic lore says that the Afghan mystic lived and meditated on this spot, or, more picturesquely, that Haji Ali's coffin was washed ashore on these rocks after it had, on strict instructions from the saint, been cast into the sea off the coast of what is now Pakistan. The tomb is connected to the mainland by a narrow concrete **causeway**, only passable at low tide. When not immersed in water, its entire length is lined with beggars who change one-*rupee* pieces into ten-*paise* coins for pilgrims. The prime sites, closer to the snack bars that flank the main entrance, near the small mosque, and the gateway to the tomb itself, are allocated in a strict pecking order. If you want to make a donation, spare a thought for the unfortunates in the middle. After all the commotion, the **tomb** itself comes as something of a disappointment. Its white Moghul domes and minarets look a lot less exotic close up than when viewed from the shore, silhouetted against the sun as it drops into the Arabian Sea.

A couple of kilometres further up the coast, the densely packed districts of central Bombay are broken by a huge, empty expanse of dusty brown grass. The optimistically named **Mahalakshmi racecourse**, founded in 1879, is the home of the *Bombay Turf Club* and a bastion of the city's Anglophile elite. Regular meetings take place here on weekends between November and March. If you fancy a hack yourself, the *Amateur Riding Club* also rents out horses during the week (except Wednesdays).

The central bazaars

Lining the anarchic jumble of streets north of Lokmanya Tilak (formerly Carnac) Road, Bombay's teeming **central bazaars** are India at its most intense. You could wander around here for months without seeing the same shop-front twice. In practice, most visitors find a couple of hours mingling with the crowds in the heat and din quite enough. Nevertheless, the market districts form a fascinating counterpoint to the wide and westernized streets of downtown, even if you're not buying.

In keeping with traditional divisions of guild, caste and religion, most streets specialize in one or two types of merchandise – a pain if you want to see a smattering of all the goods on offer in a relatively short time. If you lose your bearings, the best way out is to ask someone to wave you in the direction of **Abdul Rehman Street**, the busy road through the heart of the district, from where you can hail a cab.

Crawford Market

Crawford (aka Mahatma Phule) **Market**, ten minutes' walk north of VT station, is an old British-style covered market dealing in just about every kind of fresh food and domestic animal imaginable. When Bombayites crave a *bhaji* or a budgie, this is the first place they'll head for. Thanks to its pompous Norman-Gothic tower and prominent position at the corner of Carnac Rd and Dr DN Marg, the Crawford Market is also a useful landmark and a good place to begin a foray into the bazaars.

Before venturing inside, check out the **friezes** wrapped around its exterior – a Victorian vision of sturdy-limbed peasants toiling in the fields designed by Rudyard Kipling's father, Lockwood, as principal of the Bombay School of Art in 1865. Apart from the bare electric bulbs and fans dangling from the iron ribs of its high ceiling, the market itself must look much the same now as it did in Kipling's day. The **main hall** is still divided into different sections: pyramids of polished fruit and vegetables down one aisle; sacks of nuts or oil-tins full of herbs and spices down another. Sitting crosslegged on a raised platform in front of each stall, is its eagle-eyed owner, wearing starched *khadi* pyjamas and a Nehru cap, with a fresh red *tilak* smeared on his forehead.

Around the back of the market, in the atmospheric **wholesale wing**, the pace of life is more hectic. Here, noisy crowds of coolies mill about with large reed-baskets held high in the air (if they are looking for work) or on their heads (if they've found some). Underfoot, a messy compost of rotting vegetables, litter and straw accumulates as the day wears on, while clouds of dust, kicked up by all the commotion, catch beams of sunlight streaming through the tarpaulins and corrugated-iron roof.

At the epicentre of all this atmospheric mayhem stands another of Lockwood Kipling's creations. Barely recognizable under a pile of empty boxes and hessian sacks, the **market fountain** was originally intended as a symbol of India's four great rivers. Its spouts, however, have long since run dry, much to the chagrin of the sparrows and swallows flitting around.

One place animal lovers should definitely steer clear of is Crawford Market's **pet** and **poultry** section, on the east side of the building. You never quite know what creatures will turn up here, cringing in rank-smelling, undersized cages. The **tobacco** market, by contrast, is altogether more fragrant. Look out for the Muslim *hookah* merchants selling picturesque smoking paraphernalia.

When you've had enough of Crawford Market, head past the shiny brass and hardware sections, and the stalls selling implausible wigs and false moustaches, to the west exits on Carnac Road. Across the street, the famous *Badshah Juice and Snack Bar*'s **faloodas** (see p.610) and milkshakes make a great pick-me-up.

North of Crawford Market

The streets immediately **north of Crawford Market** and west of **Mohammed Ali Road**, the main drag through Bombay's Muslim ghettoes, form one vast bazaar area. Ranged along both sides of narrow **Mangaldas Lane**, the cloth bazaar, are small shops draped with lengths of bright silk and cotton. Low doorways on the left open on to a colourful **covered market** area, packed with tiny stalls where you'll be badgered to sit and take tea while the merchants tempt you with dozens of different *saris* and scarves.

At the far end of Mangaldas Lane from Carnac Road, the pale green-washed domes, arches and minarets of the **Jama Masjid**, or "Friday Mosque" (1800), mark the start of the Muslim neighbourhoods. Hang around at this heaving crossroads for more than a few seconds and you'll be jostled and hissed by coolies and hand-cart pullers barging their way through dense crowds of shoppers. **Memon Street**, cutting north from the mosque, is the site of the **Zaveri Bazaar**, the jewellery market. Its rows of bright, air-conditioned shops, their windows glittering with gold and silver necklaces, rings and anklets, attract well-heeled family groups preparing for their daughters' weddings.

By the time the gleaming golden spire that crowns the **Mumba Devi temple**'s cream and turquoise tower appears at the end of the street, you're deep in a maze of twisting lanes hemmed in by tall, wooden-balconied buildings. The temple is one of the most important centres of Devi-worship in India. Reached via a tiny courtyard where *pujaris* regale devotees with religious songs, its shrine houses a particularly revered, and unusual, deity. The mouthless "Maha-amba-aiee" (Mumba for short) is believed to have started her life as an obscure aboriginal earth goddess. Her present resting place was built early in the nineteenth century, when she was relocated from her former home to make way for VT Station. Mumba Devi's other claim to fame is that her name is the original root of the word "Bombay", as well as the newer, and more politically correct, Maharashtran version, "**Mumbai**", which the government has been trying so unsuccessfully to institute in recent years.

The streets radiating off **Baiduni Chowk**, a short way northeast, are the place to shop for attractive hand-beaten **copper**- and **brass**-ware. Alternatively, jump in a taxi on the main road nearby for the two-kilometre trip north to the other concentration of markets around **Johar Chowk**. The most famous of these, **Chor** (literally "thieves") **Bazaar** (where vendors peevishly insist the name is a corruption of the Urdu *shor*, meaning "noisy"), is the city's largest **antiques**-cum-flea-market. Friday, the Muslim sabbath, is the best day to be here. From 9am onwards, the neighbourhood is cluttered with hawkers and hand-carts piled high with bric-a-brac and assorted junk being eagerly rummaged by men in skull-caps. At other times, the antique shops down on **Mutton Road** are the main attraction. Once, you could hope to unearth real gems in these dark, fusty stores, but your chances of finding a genuine bargain nowadays are minimal. Most of the stuff is pricey Victoriana – old gramophones, chamber pots, chipped china – salvaged from the homes of Parsi families on the decline. The place is also awash with **fakes**, mainly small bronze votive statues, which make good souvenirs if you can knock the price down.

Press on north through Chor Bazaar and you'll eventually come out on **Grant Road** (Maulana Shaukatali Rd). Further north and west, in the warren of lanes below JB Behram Marg, lies the city's infamous **red-light district**. **Kamathipura**'s rows of luridly lit, barred shop-fronts, from where an estimated 25,000 prostitutes ply their trade, are one of Bombay's more degrading and unpleasant spectacles. Many of these so-called "**cage girls**" are young teenagers from poor tribal areas who have been sold by desperate parents into **bonded slavery** until they can earn the money to pay off family debts – just one subject of Mira Nair's film *Salaam Bombay*. The area is definitely no place to wander around alone or on foot.

Bhuleshwar Market, Panjrapole Goshala and Flower Lane

Bhuleshwar Market, little visited by tourists, draws thousands of Bombayites for vegetables in the early morning or clothes bargains later in the day. The area is easiest approached from Charni Road railway station (two stops from Churchgate). Make for CP Tank Circle (a crossroads on Cowasji Patel Tank Rd also served by buses #68, #103 and #107 from Flora Fountain), a short walk from the junction locally known as Kumbhar Tukda. By the afternoon this area is jam-packed; the following places are close together, but keep asking for directions. As you weave your way through you may notice the *Maganlal Dresswalla* shop, which supplies costumes for Hindi movies.

Walking along Bhuleshwar from *Hiralal Kashiram Bhajiawala* (see p.610) the first junction you come to is Panjrapole Corner. Panjrapole Road, to the left, is full of **steel kitchen utensil shops**. At no. 200, *Mathalal Moortiwala & Sons* sells religious idols, to individuals and to temples. The best figures are made of white marble from Makrana in Rajasthan, and painted in bright colours. Back at the corner, *Maganlal Kedarlal & Co* sells soapstone and cheaper small figures plus white and black marble.

Compared to other Indian cities, the streets of Bombay are relatively cow-free. One contributory factor is the **Panjrapole Goshala**, or cow shelter, and animal sanctuary (daily 7am–6.30pm). It's a little tricky to find, tucked away on the other side of Panjrapole Rd, down a small lane, but any local will direct you if you ask for **Madhavbaug Temple**, with which it is associated. A regular stream of devotees find their way to this little-known and, to the outsider, decidedly fun spot where you can gain religious merit by feeding the animals. At a counter inside the shelter, on the right-hand side of the courtyard filled with animal sheds, you exchange your ticket (Rs5 or Rs10) for a big plate of feed. You're then free to wander round and feed any of the 400 raspy-tongued residents, improving your *karma* as you go. The district also boasts a few good eating houses where you gain no merit at all by feeding yourself.

Back in Bhuleshwar, continue to the next junction, where another small turning to the left is **Phool Galli**, or **"Flower Lane"**, a short, narrow street devoted to supplying elaborate flower arrangements to temples and wedding functions. The skilled artists use jasmine, spider lilies, roses, hibiscus, ladies lace, a rare flower known as "snake champa" and blue, purple, orange and yellow marigolds, along with banana, *tulsi* and *gol pada* ("round foot") leaves. When admiring the blooms remember that to smell or touch them will render them useless for a temple and will lead to them being discarded. It is for the god to smell them first.

Not all the shops in the lane sell flowers; *Mota Brothers* (their sign is in Marathi), on the corner, where the lane curves to the left, stocks a fascinating old-fashioned selection of items, many closely associated with the temple and family ceremonies. Dishes made from cashewnut leaves, and bowls of dried betelnut leaves fastened together with thorns have since the advent of stainless steel become a rare sight; some are even moulded with compartments like their steel cousins. Other items include oil lamp wicks, *neem* (margosa) stalks for toothbrushes, cow-dung cakes for cooking fires, and wood apples. Dried green coconuts wrapped in coloured thread are bought as offerings to the gods, and red earth known as *mitti* is used for *rangoli* floor designs.

Nearby, **Third Lane Bhoiwada**, which doesn't get going until 11am, is known for specialities such as the expensive *jari* (silver thread) and *bandhani* (fine quality tie-dye) *saris* from Gujarat and Rajasthan, and **glass bangle wholesalers**. The first turning on the left is a lane full of silver and pearl shops; a Sri Nathji temple a little way down on the left and another Krishna temple at the bottom of the lane cater to the many Gujaratis and Rajasthanis who live in the area. Through the gate of the temple you can see typical murals found on Rajasthani *havelis*.

Elephanta

An hour's boat ride from Colaba, the tranquil, forested island of **ELEPHANTA** is one of the most atmospheric places in Bombay. Populated only by a small fishing community, it makes a wonderful contrast to the seething claustrophobia of the city, even when crowded with day-trippers at weekends. Originally known as **Gharapuri**, the "city of Ghara priests", the island was renamed in the sixteenth century by the Portuguese in honour of the carved elephant they found at the port (see p.600). Its chief attraction is its unique **cave temple**, whose massive **Trimurti** (three-faced) **Shiva sculpture** is as fine an example of Hindu architecture as you'll find anywhere.

Luxury boats set off from the Gateway of India hourly from 8.45am to 2pm (Rs50, including guide; book through MTDC on Madam Cama Rd). Three leave with a cave guide on board (8.45am, 11am & 2pm); if you take any of the others you can claim your guide from the ticket office on arrival. Luxury boats do not run during monsoon (June–Sept). **Ordinary ferries**, also from the Gateway of India, cost Rs35, do not include guides, and are usually packed. The journey takes about an hour.

Cool drinks and souvenir stalls line the way up the hill, and at the top, the MTDC *Chalukya* restaurant offers a reasonably priced menu including beer. Their terrace gives good views out to sea. Their two clean double bedrooms, bookable through MTDC, are available for the day only (9am–5pm, ③).

There's more primitive **accommodation** in the *Forest Bungalows* (②), in Raj Bunder village, one of three on the island. In a delightful spot overlooking the sea and forest, fifteen minutes' walk (right) from the caves, the cottages are extremely basic, with three beds each, and lovely gardens. Contact the Range Forest Officer, Alibag Range, Forest Dept, Panvel (☎745 2759).

The Cave

Elephanta's impressive excavated **cave** (eighth century), covering an area of approximately 5000 square metres, is reached by climbing more than one hundred steps to the top of the hill. Inside, the massive columns, carved from solid rock, give the deceptive impression of being structural. To the right, as you enter, note the panel of **Nataraj**, Shiva as the cosmic dancer. Though spoiled by the Portuguese who, it is said, used it for target practice, the panel remains magnificent; Shiva's face is rapt, and in one of his left hands he removes the veil of ignorance. Opposite is a badly damaged panel of Lakulisha, Shiva with a club (*lakula*).

Each of the four entrances to the simple square main **shrine** – unusually, it has one on each side – is flanked by a pair of huge fanged *dvarapala* guardians (only those to the back have survived undamaged), while inside a large *lingam* is surrounded by coins and smouldering joss left by devotees. Facing the northern wall of the shrine another panel shows Shiva impaling the demon **Andhaka**, who wandered around as though blind, symbolizing his spiritual blindness. Shiva killed him as he attempted to steal a divine tree from heaven. The panel behind the shrine on the back wall portrays the marriage of **Shiva and Parvati**. Moving east, the next panel shows **Ganghadaran**, Shiva receiving the descending river Ganga, his lover, to live in his hair, while Parvati, his wife, looks on. A powerful six-metre-high bust of **Trimurti**, the three-faced Shiva, who embodies the powers of creator, preserver and destroyer, stands nearby, and to the west a sculpture shows Shiva as **Ardhanarishvara**, half male and half female. Close to the second entrance on the east, another panel shows Shiva and Parvati on **Mount Kailasha** with Ravana about to lift the mountain. His curved spine shows the strain.

Uptown and the outskirts

Greater Bombay has crept inexorably northwards to engulf villages and swampland in a pall of chimneys, expressways and slums. These grim industrial areas hold few attractions, but possibilities for full- or half-day excursions include the quirky **Victoria and Albert museum** and **botanical gardens** in Byculla, **Mount Mary**'s miracle-working Madonna in Bandra, and the beach at **Juhu**. All lie within reach of a suburban train station, although you will, in most cases, have to take a rickshaw or taxi for the last few kilometres. Beyond them to the north lie the Buddhist caves chiselled out of the hillside at **Kanheri**, and the crumbling Portuguese fort at **Bassein**.

Byculla and the Veermata Jeejamata (Victoria and Albert) museum

As the bedrock of Bombay's once-gigantic weaving industry, **Byculla**, immediately north of the central bazaar, epitomizes the grim legacy of nineteenth-century industrialization: idle chimney stacks, overcrowded *chawls* and pavements strewn with ragged, sleeping bodies. The cotton-mills and sweat-shops are still here, churning out cheap clothes for the massive domestic market, but few can claim the turnovers they enjoyed a hundred years ago. Today, eclipsed by their old Gujarati rivals in Surat and Ahmedabad, all but the larger nationalized mills teeter on the brink of bankruptcy.

Although visitors are generally welcome to look around the few of Byculla's cotton-mills still in business, a more common reason to come up here is to see the **Victoria and Albert museum** (now renamed the **Veermata Jeejamata museum**) on Dr Babasaheb Ambedkhar Marg (daily except Wed 10am–5pm; free). Inspired by its namesake in London, this grand Victorian-Gothic building was built in 1871 to house artefacts relating to Bombay's history and development. Old maps, engravings and photographs are displayed in a small gallery on the first floor, along with sundry objets d'art. Downstairs in the main hall, the exhibits are more eclectic. Among the Victorian china and modest assortment of south Indian bronzes, are cases filled with papier-mâché parakeets, pick-axe heads and plastic models of vegetables. More instructive, if a little prurient, is the scale model of a Parsi Tower of Silence (see p.593), complete with a gruesome description of the mortuary rituals performed in the real ones on Malabar Hill.

The museum's oldest and most famous exhibit, however, is the stone **elephant** in the small garden to the rear of the building. Now somewhat forlorn and neglected in the shadows, this was the very beast that inspired the Portuguese to name the island in Bombay harbour "Elephanta" (see p.600). The crumbling figure was brought here for safe-keeping in 1863 from its original, and more fittingly prominent site alongside the landing stage that leads up to the cave temple.

A wrought-iron gateway beyond the elephant opens onto one of Bombay's most popular venues for an old-fashioned family day out. The peaceful and green **botanical gardens** (daily except Wed 8am–6pm) hold a huge collection of South Asian flora, plus Bombay's only **zoo**, where, after a trip around the predictably small and smelly cages, kids can enjoy an elephant or camel ride.

Both museum and botanical gardens can be reached either by *BEST* **bus** (#3 or #11(Ltd) from Colaba; #19 from Flora Fountain and Crawford Market) or by suburban **train** to Byculla station, on the opposite (western) side of the expressway.

Bandra

North of Mahim Creek, the suburb of **Bandra** is one of the most desirable districts for Bombay's elite, a haunt of film stars. The main shopping area, **Vithalbhai Patel Road** (Linking Road) is full of clothes boutiques, jewellers and shoe-stalls.

A 5km auto-rickshaw ride from Bandra railway station, past swanky high-rise apartment blocks and a few old mansions with carved wooden verandahs, brings you to the black stone **church of St Mary** at the top of St Mary's Hill. Before entering the church, devotees buy wax effigies of all manner of things – eyes, babies, aeroplanes, heads, cars and houses – that require the blessing of the saint. Inside, a gold-robed Madonna and Child stands on a tiered marble dais beneath a double dome.

Juhu Beach

With its palm trees, glamorous seaside apartment blocks and designer clothes stores, **Juhu**, 30km north of downtown, is Bombay's answer to Sunset Boulevard. Unless you're staying in one of the many **five-star hotels** lining its five-kilometre strip of white sand, however, this affluent suburb holds little appeal. The **beach** itself is certainly no great shakes – thanks to an oily slick of raw sewage that seeps into the Arabian Sea from the slum *bastis* surrounding Mahim Creek to the south, sunbathing and swimming are out of the question. A more salubrious way to enjoy Juhu is to walk along the strand after office hours, when young families turn out in droves to enjoy the sunsets and sea breezes, attracting a bevy of *bhel puri-wallahs* and lads hawking cheap Taiwanese toys.

Further north up Juhu Road, the headquarters of the *International Society for Krishna Consciousness* (**ISKCON**) deals with matters more spiritual. Its richly appointed **Krishna temple** (daily 4am–1pm & 4–9pm) draws local Hindus in their Sunday-best shirtings and *saris*, and well-heeled westerners wearing kaftans, *kurtas* and *dhotis*. Rich visitors get to stay in what must surely rank as the world's most glamorous *dharamshala* – a modern, multi-storeyed hotel complex with its own veg restaurant, conference hall and theatre. The temple itself is entered via a large white-marble courtyard next to the road. An open-sided porch with stucco Moghul arches then leads into the main **assembly hall**. At the far end, flanked by lines of scale models depicting morally uplifting tales and episodes from the Hindu scriptures, stand a life-size mannequin of the late AC Bhaktividenta, *ISKCON*'s founder, and the two deities of Radha and Krishna. Books and cassettes are sold at the stalls outside in the courtyard, and delicious pure-*ghee* sweets are available from the snack counter.

Kanheri Caves

The chief reason to make the day's excursion to the suburb of Borivli, 42km out at the northern limits of Bombay's sprawl, is to visit the Buddhist caves of **Kanheri** (daily 9am–5.30pm), ranged over the hills in virtually unspoilt forest. It's an interminable journey by road, so catch one of the many **trains** (50min) on the suburban line from Churchgate (marked "BO" on the departure boards; "limited stop" trains knock 15min off the journey time). When you arrive, take the Borivli East exit, and pick up an **auto-rickshaw** as far as the bottom of the hill near the caves, 3km along a wooded road from the entrance. Bring water and food, as the stalls here only sell cool drinks.

Kanheri may not be as spectacular as other cave sites, but some of its sculpture is superb – though to enjoy the peace and quiet that attracted its original occupants you should avoid the weekend and the crowds of daytrippers. Most of the caves, which date from the second to the ninth centuries AD, were used simply for accommodation (*viharas*) during the four months of the monsoon, when an itinerant life was impractical – the season when the forest is at its most beautiful. They are connected by steep winding paths and steps; engage one of the friendly local guides at the entrance to find your way about, but don't expect any sort of lecture as their English is limited.

In **Cave 1**, an incomplete *chaitya* hall (a hall with a *stupa* at one end, an aisle and row of columns at either side), you can see where the rock was left cut, but unfinished. Two *stupas* from the Hinayana period stand in **Cave 2**; one was vandalized by a certain N Christian, whose carefully incised Times-Roman graffiti bears the date 1810. A panel shows seated Buddhas, portrayed as a teacher. Behind, and to the side, is the *bodhisattva* of compassion, Padmapani, while to the right the *viharas* feature rock-cut beds.

Huge Buddhas, with serenely joyful expressions and unfeasibly large shoulders, stand on either side of the porch to the spectacular **Cave 3**. Between them, you'll see the panels of "donor couples", thought to have been foreigners that patronized the community. Inside, leading to a *stupa* at the back, octagonal columns in two rows, some decorated with animal motifs, line the magnificent **Hinayana chaitya** hall.

The sixth-century **Cave 11** is a large assembly hall, where two long "tables" of rock were used for the study of manuscripts. Seated at the back, in the centre, is a figure of the Buddha as teacher, an image repeated in the entrance, to the left, with a wonderful flight of accompanying celestials. Just before the entrance to a small cell in **Cave 34**, flanked by two standing Buddhas, an unfinished ceiling painting shows the Buddha touching the earth. There must be at least a hundred more Buddha images on panels in **Cave 67**, a large hall. On the left side, and outside in the entrance, these figures are supported by *nagas* (snakes representing *kundalini*, yogic power).

Not far from the caves, a portion of **Krishnagiri Upavan National Park** (formerly Borivli National Park) has been turned into a **Lion Safari Park** (Tues–Sun 9am–5pm; open on Mon when it is a public holiday,and then closed Tues). The easiest way to see it is on a **tour** (see p.584), but, on Sundays only, **bus** #188 runs here from the station (10km).

Bassein

Trundling over the rickety iron bridge that joins the northern fringes of Bombay to the Maharashtran mainland, you could easily fail to notice the ruined fort at **Bassein** (or Vasai), 61km north of the city centre. Yet these mouldy stone walls, obscured by a carpet of palms and lush tropical foliage at the mouth of the milky-blue River Ulhas, once encompassed India's most powerful and prosperous colonial settlement. It was ceded to the Portuguese by Sultan Bahadur of Gujarat in 1534, in return for help in the Gujarati struggle against the Moghuls, and quickly became the hub of the region's maritime trade, "The Court of the North" from which the Portuguese territories at Goa, Daman and Diu were administered. In 1739, however, the **Marathas** laid siege to the city for three months, eventually wiping out the garrison, and a final death blow was dealt in 1780 by the cannons of the **British**. Bassein's crumbling remnants were left to be carried off for raw building material or reclaimed by the coastal jungle, and only a handful of weed-infested buildings still stand today.

If you don't mind spending hours in a crowded suburban train (around 1hr 15min from Churchgate, and no fun at all in rush hours), Bassein makes an atmospheric day trip from the city. Only a few express trains stop at the nearest mainline station, Vasai Road, from where the onward trip (11km) involves jumping in and out of **shared auto-rickshaws**. These stop halfway at a busy market crossroads, where you catch another ride for the last stretch from a stand 100m up a road left from the crossroads. Ask for the "*kila*", the Marathi word for "fort". Stock up on food and drink at Vasai Road; there's nowhere very sanitary to eat in Bassein.

The **fort** is entered through a large gateway in its slanting stone battlements. Once inside, the road runs past a modern monument to the Maratha leader, Shivaji, before heading towards the woods and the old Portuguese town. The ruins are a melancholy sight: *peepal* and tall palm trees poke through the chancels of churches and convents, while water buffalo plod listlessly past piles of rubble, and monkeys leap and crash through the canopy overhead.

By contrast, the small **fishing village**, under the archway from the rickshaw stand, is thriving. The spiritual legacy of the Portuguese has endured here longer than their architectural one, as shown by the painted Madonna shrines tucked into wall-niches and crucifixes gleaming on the singlets of the fishermen lounging in the local bar. On the **beach**, a short way down the narrow sandy footpath through the main cluster of huts, large wooden frames are hung with pungent-smelling strips of dried pomfret, while nearby, fishing boats bob around in the silt-laden estuary water.

Accommodation

Even though Bombay offers all kinds of **accommodation**, finding a room at the right price when you arrive can be a real problem. Budget travellers, in particular, can expect a hard time; standards at the bottom of the range are grim and room rates exorbitant. A windowless cell, with wood-partition walls and no running water can cost Rs300 and above, while a comfortable room in the centre of town, with an attached toilet and shower, and a window, may set you back the best part of Rs1000. The best of the relatively inexpensive places tend to fill up by noon, which can often mean a long trudge in the heat with only an overpriced flea-pit at the end of it, so you should really phone ahead as soon as (or preferably well before) you arrive. Prices in upmarket places are further inflated by the state-imposed "**luxury tax**" (between five and thirty percent depending on how expensive the room is), and "**service-charges**" levied by the hotel itself; such charges are included in the price symbols shown below.

Colaba, down in the far, southern end of the city, has dozens of possibilities in each price range and is where the majority of foreign visitors head first. A short way across the city centre, **Marine Drive**'s accommodation is generally a little more expensive, but more salubrious, with Back Bay and the promenade right on the doorstep. If you're

The telephone **area code** for Bombay is ☎022.

ACCOMMODATION PRICE CODES

All **accommodation prices** in this book have been coded using the symbols below. In principle the prices given are for the least expensive double rooms in each establishment; however, some hotels, usually in category ①, offer rates per bed rather than per room. Bombay's "luxury taxes" have been incorporated here. For more details, see p.34.

①	up to Rs100	④	Rs225–350	⑦	Rs750–1200
②	Rs100–150	⑤	Rs350–500	⑧	Rs1200–2200
③	Rs150–225	⑥	Rs500–750	⑨	Rs2200 and up

arriving by train and plan to make a quick getaway, a room closer to **VT** or **Bombay Central** stations is worth considering. Alternatively, **Juhu**, way to the north near the airports, boasts a string of flashy four- and five-stars, with a handful of less expensive places behind the beach. And for those who just want to crawl off the plane and straight into bed, there are plenty of options in the suburbs around Sahar and Santa Cruz **airports**, a short taxi ride from the main terminal buildings.

Finally, details of the new **"paying guests"** scheme for foreign visitors are available from the main tourist office on M Karve Rd, Churchgate (☎203 3144).

Colaba

A short ride from the city's main commercial districts, railway stations and tourist office, **Colaba** is a handy base. It also offers more in the way of food and entertainment than neighbouring districts, especially along its busy main thoroughfare, "Colaba Causeway" (Shahid Bhagat Singh – SBS – Marg). The streets immediately south and west of the **Gateway of India** are chock-full of accommodation, ranging from grungy guest houses to India's most famous five-star hotel, the *Taj Mahal Intercontinental*. Avoid at all costs the nameless lodges lurking on the top storeys of wooden-fronted houses along **Arthur Bunder Road** – the haunts of not-so-oil-rich Gulf Arabs and touts who depend on commission from these rock-bottom hostels to finance their heroin habits. If, like many, you find all this sleaze a turn-off, Colaba's quieter, leafier backstreets harbour plenty of respectable, mid-range hotels. You're less likely to have your stuff stolen in these places, but will have to pay more for the peace of mind.

INEXPENSIVE

Carlton, 12 Mereweather Rd (☎202 0259). Reasonable-value budget hotel in advanced state of decrepitude. Pricier rooms have attached baths. Common verandah. ④–⑤.

India, 4th Floor, 1/39 Kamal Mansion, Arthur Bunder Rd (☎283 3769). Ceilingless, partitioned rooms, no windows and common baths, but OK for a night and cheaper than *Sea Shore* upstairs. ④.

Kishan, Ground Floor, Shirin Manzil, Walton Rd (☎283 2515). Scruffy, but fairly clean and cool, and good for the price. Cheapest a/c option in the area. ④–⑤.

Lawrence, 3rd Floor, 33 Rope Walk Lane, off K Dubash Marg, opposite *Jehangir Art Gallery* (☎243618). Far and away Bombay's best-value cheap hotel. Six immaculate double rooms (1 single) with fans, common shower-toilet and breakfast included. Advance telephone bookings essential. ③.

Oliver Guest House, 6 Walton Rd (☎240291). Grubby and semi-derelict lodge, with slummy toilets and mattresses. Mentioned only because it's the cheapest in Colaba – a dubious distinction. ①.

Prosser's, PJ Ramchandani Marg (☎241715). Noisy, with mostly wood-partition rooms. ④.

Salvation Army, Red Shield House, 30 Mereweather Rd, directly behind *Taj* (☎241824). Rock-bottom bunk beds in cramped, stuffy dorms (lockers available), good-value doubles (some a/c), and a sociable travellers' scene. Cheap canteen food. Priority given to women. ①–⑤.

Hotels and restaurants in the **Colaba** area are shown in the **map** on p.586.

Sea Shore, 4th Floor, 1/49 Kamal Mansion, Arthur Bunder Rd (☎287 4237). Above *India*. Recently revamped and a reasonable deal, if the standards are maintained. The sea-facing rooms with windows are much better than airless cells on the other side. Common baths only. ④.

YWCA, 18 Madam Cama Rd (☎202 0445). Relaxing, secure and quiet hostel with spotless dorms, doubles or family rooms. Rate includes membership, breakfast and filling buffet dinner. One month's advance booking (by money order) advisable. ③–⑥.

MODERATE

Apollo Guest House, Dhun Mahal, Garden Rd (☎240121). Grotty and overpriced, boxed into dingy ground floor flat. Avoid its namesake on Colaba Causeway – no connection – at all costs. ⑤.

Cowie's, 15 Walton Rd (☎24032). Promising facade, but rooms are windowless, and non-a/c. ⑤–⑥.

Gulf, 4/36 Kamal Mansion, Arthur Bunder Rd (☎283 3742). Seedy surroundings, but respectable and recently redecorated, with clean, modern rooms. ④–⑥.

Kerawala Chambers, 3rd and 4th Floors, 25 PJ Ramchandani Marg (☎241197). Decent hotel tucked away above *Strand*, boasting the cheapest sea-facing rooms in Colaba. Good value. ⑤–⑥.

Regency, 18 Lansdowne House, Mahakari Bhusan Marg, behind *Regal* cinema (☎202 0292). Well-appointed rooms, some on the cramped side, and cheaper attic garrets with character. ⑥–⑦.

Strand, 30 PJ Ramchandani Marg (☎241624). Simple, spacious and reasonably comfortable rooms, although the sea-facing ones are way overpriced. Common or attached bathrooms. ⑤–⑦.

Whalley's, Jaiji Mansion, 41 Mereweather Rd (☎283 1802). Well-established, popular hotel on third floor of rambling colonial building, with 26 rooms (some very small), common or attached shower-toilets, pleasant verandah and some a/c. Reasonable value. ④–⑥.

EXPENSIVE

Ascot, 38 Garden Rd (☎287 2105; fax 287 1765). One of Bombay's oldest hotels. Comfortable, spacious rooms, with *Star TV*, room service etc. ⑦.

Diplomat, 24–26 PK Boman Behram Marg (☎202 1661). Hemmed in by the *Taj* across the road and in need of face-lift, but the rooms are pleasant enough. ⑦.

Fariyas, 35 Arthur Rd (☎204 2911). Next on the scale down from the *Taj*. Relaxing roof-garden, luxurious decor, pool, central a/c and all the trimmings. ⑧–⑨.

Garden, 42 Garden Rd (☎241476). Rather bland option, with no single occupancy rates for its comfortable a/c rooms, but a reasonable restaurant and bar. ⑦.

Goodwin, Jasmine Building, Garden Rd (☎287 2050). Top class three-star with glamorous rooftop restaurant, bar and 24hr room service. ⑦.

Regent, 8 Best Rd (☎287 1854; fax 287 2765). Luxurious, international-standard hotel on smaller scale, with all mod cons but smallish rooms. ⑦.

Sea Palace, 26 PJ Ramchandani Marg (☎285 4404). A touch shabby from the outside, but rooms are well-furnished and have bath tubs. Sea views at a premium. ⑦.

Shelley's, 30 PJ Ramchandani Marg (☎241624). Charmingly old-fashioned hotel in colonial mould. Period furniture, *pukka* dining hall and some (more expensive) sea views. ⑥–⑦.

Taj Mahal and Taj Mahal Intercontinental, PJ Ramchandani Marg (☎202 3366; fax 287 2711). The stately home among India's top hotels, and the haunt of Bombay's *beau monde*. Opulent suites in old wing or modern skyscraper; shopping arcades, outdoor pool, swish bars and restaurants. ⑧–⑨.

Marine Drive and Nariman Point

At the western edge of the downtown area, Netaji Subhash Chandra Marg, or "**Marine Drive**", sweeps from the skyscrapers of **Nariman Point** in the south to Chowpatty Beach in the north. Along the way, four- and five-star hotels take advantage of the panoramic views over **Back Bay** and the easy access to the city's commercial heart , while a couple of inexpensive guest houses have hung on in there and are worth trying if Colaba's cheap lodges don't appeal. Compared to Colaba, Marine Drive, and the arterial

Hotels and restaurants in **downtown Bombay** are shown in the **map** on p.578.

Veer Nariman (VN) **Road** that connects it with Churchgate, are more open and relaxed. Families and office cronies plod along the promenade in the evening, approached more often by *gram-* and balloon-*wallahs* than junkies and money-changers.

Ambassador, VN Rd (☎204 1131; fax 204 0004). Luxurious four-star with excellent views from upper front-side rooms and revolving rooftop restaurant. No pool. ⑨.

Bentley, 3rd Floor, Krishna Mahal, Marine Drive (☎203 1244). Run-down hotel on corner of D Rd. No lift, no a/c, no attached bathrooms and no frills (except windows). ③–④.

Chateau Windsor, 86 VN Rd (☎204 3676; fax 285 1415). Spotless single, double or group rooms (some on the small side), shared or attached bathrooms, optional a/c and self-catering for vegetarians. Very popular, so reservations recommended. ⑥–⑦.

Nataraj, 135 Marine Drive (☎204 4161; fax 204 3864). Swish four-star overlooking Back Bay. ⑨.

Norman's, 127 Marine Drive (☎203 4234). Small, moderately priced ground-floor guest house, with neat, clean rooms, some attached shower-toilets and a/c. ④–⑤.

Oberoi/Oberoi Towers, Nariman Point (☎202 4343). The *Taj*'s main competitor – India's most expensive hotel – is glitteringly opulent, with a pool and Polynesian restaurant. ⑨.

President, 90 Cuffe Parade (☎215 0808). Formula five-star boasting a pool, shopping mall, beauty parlour and good Italian restaurant. ⑨.

Ritz, 5 Jamshedji Tata Rd (☎285 0497). Another plush, western-style four-star with bars, restaurants and piped music but no pool. ⑧–⑨.

Sea Green, 145 Marine Drive (☎222284). Reasonable-value, efficient and clean hotel pitched at businessmen. *Star TV* in all rooms. 24hr check-out (8am for advance reservations). ③–⑥.

Sea Green South, 145-A Marine Drive (☎221613). Clone of *Sea Green* next door. ③–⑥.

Around Victoria Terminus

Arriving in Bombay after a long train journey at **Victoria Terminus**, you may not feel like embarking on a room-hunt around Colaba. Unfortunately, the area around the station and the nearby **GPO**, though fairly central and well-placed for bus departures to Goa from **Ballard Pier**, has little to recommend it. The majority of places worth trying are grouped around the crossroads of **P D'Mello** (Frere) **Rd**, **St George's Rd** and **Shahid Bhagat Singh** (SBS) **Marg**, immediately southeast of the post office, five minutes on foot from the station. The station itself has **retiring rooms**.

Grand, 17 Sprott Rd, Ballard Estate (☎261 1821; fax 262 6581). Solid, very comfortable hotel with faintly 1930s feel left by the British. *Star TV*, central a/c and foreign exchange. ⑧.

Lord's, 301 Adi Mazban Path (Mangalore St) (☎261 0077). Above *City Kitchen* restaurant. Drab, but reasonably clean and cheap for the area. Mostly common bathrooms. ③–④.

Oasis, 272 SBS Marg (☎261 7886). Small, well-maintained hotel close to VT. Few frills except 24hr running water. Good value. Some a/c. ④–⑤.

Victoria, 255 SBS Marg (☎261 1642). Noisy, crowded lodge with wooden partitions. Mostly men. ③.

Welcome, 257 SBS Marg (☎261 2196). A notch above the *Victoria*, with marble reception and better furniture, but way overpriced. ⑤–⑥.

Around Bombay Central

Unless you plan to catch an early morning bus or train, you're unlikely to want to stay near **Bombay Central** train or bus stations. Accommodation here is limited to a handful of grubby lodges on the crossroads opposite the train station, a couple of upmarket hotels along the busy **Dr J Boham Behram (JB Behram) Marg** and a "Y" which is invariably booked up months in advance. The roads, lanes and bazaars leading south, towards the notorious red light district around Grant Road, are, however, quintessential Bombay and will certainly appeal to those looking to escape the tourist scene. Bombay Central Railway Station has **retiring rooms**.

Balwas International, 265 E Bellasis Rd, opposite *BEST* bus depot (☎308 1481). Unpretentious mid-range hotel with *Star TV*, bathrooms and STD phones in all rooms. Also left-luggage. ⑤–⑦.

Bombay Palace, Syed Villa, off YMCA Rd (☎308 6118). Largish, comfortable rooms overlooking Muslim suburb and local cricket *maidan*. Discounts negotiable. All a/c. ⑥.

Sahil, 292 JB Behram Marg (☎308 1421). Sizeable, modern hotel with most amenities, including restaurant, central a/c and 24hr coffee shop. Most credit cards accepted. ⑦.

YMCA, 18 YMCA Rd (☎307 0601). Popular hostel; immaculate rooms, TV lounge, STD phone and dining hall. Tariff includes breakfast, dinner and membership. Reservations (paid) essential. ⑥.

Juhu Beach

Since the early 1970s, a crop of exclusive **resort-hotels** has been creeping steadily down the road that runs behind **Juhu Beach**, twenty minutes' drive from Santa Cruz airport. Most offer the predictable hermetically sealed five-star package, with bars, restaurants and a pool to lounge beside. It's hard to believe that anyone would come to India expressly for this sort of thing, but if money's no object and you want to keep well away from all the hustle, bustle and poverty, you'll be spoiled for choice.

Vile Parle (pronounced *Vee*lay *Par*lay) is the nearest suburban train station to Juhu. All the hotels below lay on courtesy coaches from the airports, unless stated otherwise.

Ajanta, 8 Juhu Rd (☎612 4890). No airport coach, pool or sea views, but comfortable enough. ⑥.

Centaur Juhu Beach, Juhu Tara Rd (☎611 3090). Gigantic five-star with palatial foyer, sea views, pool, jogging track and "Tex-Mex" restaurant (among others). The full works. ⑨.

Citizen, 960 Juhu Beach (☎611 7273; fax 611 7170). Behind the Mahatma Gandhi statue. Backs on to the beach, with pleasant restaurant and views but no pool. ⑦.

Holiday Inn, Balraj Sahani Marg (☎620 4444; fax 620 4452). Two pools, terrace garden, shops, bars and formula furnishings. ⑨.

Horizon, 37 Juhu Beach (☎611 7979; fax 611 6715). Swish restaurant, English-style pub, disco and pool, but past its prime and far from the best deal in its category. ⑧–⑨.

King's, Juhu Tara Rd (☎614 9775). Cheaper than most, but very shabby and way overpriced. ⑥.

Sands, 39/2 Juhu Beach (☎620 4511). Plush four-star (no pool). ⑧–⑨.

Sea Princess, Juhu Beach (☎612 2661; fax 611 3973). Five stars and a pool, smack on the beach. ⑧.

Seaside, 39/2 Juhu Beach (☎620 0293). Pleasant three-star next to *Sun-n-Sand*. No pool. ⑥–⑦.

Sun-n-Sand, 39 Juhu Beach (☎620 1811; fax 620 4821). Longest established of the big five-stars, with all amenities, including a pool. ⑧.

Around the airports

Hotels near Sahar and Santa Cruz **airports** cater predominantly for transit passengers and flight crews, at premium rates. If you're picking up your own tab, and arrive in Bombay at an inconvenient hour when most of the hotels in the city proper are closed or full, you may want to arrange less expensive accommodation in the nearby suburbs of **Santa Cruz**, **Vile Parle** or **Andheri**. **Bookings** can be made through the accommodation desk in the arrivals concourse at Sahar, or by phone.

Nearly all the "moderate to expensive" hotels below have **courtesy buses** to the terminal building.

INEXPENSIVE

Air View, 12 Nehru Rd, Santa Cruz East, behind Vile Parle railway station (☎612 0060). Very basic, but clean. Some a/c. ④–⑤.

Airlines International, Plot #111, Fourth Rd, Prabhat Colony, Santa Cruz East (☎614 3069). Unremarkable economy hotel near domestic airport. Separate baths, single rates available. ④–⑤.

Airport Palace, Vakola Bridge, Bull's Royce Colony Rd (☎614 0057). Small, airless rooms, but all with fresh bed linen and lockable doors. ④.

Highway Inn, Vishal Shopping Centre, Andheri Kurla Rd, Andheri East (☎832 0021). The best-value inexpensive hotel in the area, 3km from Sahar (aim for Andheri railway station). Clean rooms at assorted prices, with or without bathrooms and a/c. ③–⑤.

Rang Mahal, Station Rd, Santa Cruz West (☎490303). Tucked away down lane behind (west of) Santa Cruz railway station. Cramped and stuffy, but fairly clean. No single rooms. ⑤.

MODERATE TO EXPENSIVE

Airport Plaza, 70-C Nehru Rd, Vile Parle (☎612 3390). Plush four-star with a pool. ⑧–⑨.

Ashwin, near Marol Fire Station, Andheri Kurla Rd, Andheri East (☎830 0485). Medium-sized, international-standard hotel right outside Sahar. ⑦–⑧.

Centaur, Western Express Highway, Santa Cruz (☎612 6660). Circular building directly outside the domestic airport, with five stars, three restaurants, two bars and one pool. ⑨.

Columbus, 344 Nanda Patkar Rd, Vile Parle East (☎614 5717). Popular upscale place near posh suburban main street, with a/c rooms and restaurant. ⑦.

Galaxy, 113 Prabhat Colony, Santa Cruz East (☎612 5223). Clean and safe, but nothing special. ⑥.

Host Inn, opposite Marol Fire Station, Andheri Kurla Rd, Andheri East (☎836 0105). In same mould as *Ashwin*, with identical prices. ⑦–⑧.

Kumaria Presidency, Andheri Kurla Rd (☎604 2025). Facing the international airport. One of a string of three-stars bookable through the accommodation desk in the airport arrivals hall. ⑦–⑧.

Leela Kempinski, Sahar (☎636 3636). Ultra-luxurious. Best for sports. ⑨.

Samrat, Seventh Rd, Khar, Santa Cruz East, near Khar railway station (☎649 6806). Another comfortable transit hotel in quiet suburban backstreet. No courtesy bus. ⑤–⑥.

Satellite, 213/214 Dixit Rd, Vile Parle East (☎611742). Similar to the *Samrat*, but closer to domestic airport and with courtesy bus. All a/c. ⑥.

Sea Rock Sheraton, Bandra (☎642 5454). Now recovered from 1993 bombing and much the most congenial five-star in the north of the city. Dramatic seaside location and views from six revolving restaurants, excellent sports facilities, pool and courtesy bus. ⑨.

Yatri, behind *BEST* bus terminus, Santa Cruz East (☎612 3072). Run of the mill, but comfortable and quiet. No courtesy bus. ⑥–⑦.

Eating

In keeping with its cosmopolitan credentials, Bombay, and Colaba above all, is crammed with interesting **places to eat**, whether you fancy splashing out on a buffet lunch-with-a-view from a flashy five-star revolving restaurant, or simply tucking into piping-hot *roti kebab* by gaslight in the street.

Restaurants and cafes are listed below on a district-by-district basis. Most expensive restaurants, particularly in the top hotels, will levy "**service charges**" that can add thirty percent to the price of your meal. Phone numbers have been given where we recommend you reserve a table for dinner.

Colaba

Colaba has even more places to eat than it does hotels. In the space of little over one kilometre, you can sample the gamut of regional cuisines. Pure-**vegetarian** "Hindu hotels" serving delicious **Gujarati** and **south Indian** food stand cheek-by-jowl with **Muslim** cafes whose menus delight die-hard carnivores. Nearby, within a stone's

---

STREET FOOD

Bombay is renowned for distinctive **street foods** – and especially **bhel puri**, a quintessentially Bombay *masala* mixture of puffed-rice, deep-fried vermicelli, potato, crunchy *puri* pieces, chilli paste, tamarind water, chopped onions and coriander. More hygienic, but no less ubiquitous, is **pao bhaji**, a round slab of flat-bread stuffed with meat or vegetables and simmered in a vat of hot oil, and **kanji vada**, savoury doughnuts soaked in fermented mustard and chilli sauce. Even if all that doesn't appeal, a pit-stop at one of the city's hundreds of **juice bars** probably will. There's no better way to beat the sticky heat than with a glass of cool milk shaken with fresh pineapple, mango, banana, *chikoo*, or custard apple. Just make sure they hold the **ice** – made, of course, with untreated water.

throw of the *Taj* and its outrageously expensive gourmet restaurants, are Bombay's oldest and best-loved **Chinese** joints. Other than during the monsoons (when choppy seas keep the fishing fleet in the polluted waters of the harbour), these offer fresh, safe **seafood** dishes made from tiger prawns, crab or delicate white pomfret. Still in Colaba, traditional **Irani** restaurants serve minced lamb and mutton specialities, while revamped cafe-bars turn out reasonable pastiches of western food for tourists and local yuppies. Non-vegetarians will enjoy the succulent meats, smothered in the split lentil stew known as *dhansak*, in the **Parsi** restaurants, while **Goan** and **Mangalorean** "lunch-homes" crop up everywhere too – good for a pork *vindaloo* or a fiery fish curry.

The majority of Colaba's best cafes, bars and restaurants are up at the north end of the Causeway. Those below are divided into price categories based on the cost of a main dish: inexpensive (below Rs50), moderate (Rs50–100), and expensive (above Rs100).

INEXPENSIVE

Bade Mian, behind the *Taj* on Nawroji Fardunji Rd. Legendary Colaba kebab-*wallah*; delicious flame-grilled chicken, mutton and fish steaks, in hot *tandoori rotis*, from benches on the sidewalk.

Cafe Royal, opposite *Regal* cinema. Clean, cheap cafe with fans and a cosmopolitan menu of standard Indian favourites, Chinese, and English egg and chip options. Draught beer too.

Himroo Kabawallah, opposite *Strand* cinema. Cheap and popular sidewalk stall, serving up mouthwatering Sindhi *kofta* and *sheesh kebab* with chutney, chopped mint salad and freshly baked bread.

Kailash Parbat, 1 Pasta Lane, near *Strand* cinema. The outside doesn't look much, but the pure veg nibbles, hot snacks and sweets are worth the walk. Try their famous *makai-ka* (corn) *rotis*.

Light of Asia, near *Strand* cinema. Clean and crowded Muslim restaurant offering predictable range of pure meat dishes. "Brains and eggs" not for the squeamish.

Majestic, near *Regal* cinema, Colaba Causeway. Large, traditional south Indian joint patronized by off-duty taxi-*wallahs*, junior office staff and backpackers. Among the best value in this price range.

New Martin, near *Strand* cinema, Strand Rd. Unpromising formica booths, but famed for delicious Goan dishes such as prawn *pulao*, sausages, pork *vindaloo* and spicy fish curry. Also does take-outs.

Olympic Coffee House, 1 Colaba Causeway. Old-fashioned, *fin-de-siècle* Irani cafe with marble table tops, wooden wall panels and a mezzanine floor for "ladies". Decor more alluring than the menu of greasy meat dishes, but nonetheless, a good place for a coffee break.

MODERATE

Alps, Nawroji Fardunji Rd. Trendy, ersatz American restaurant serving lamb-burgers, fries, sizzling steaks and copious "mixed-grills".

Baghdadi, Tulloch Rd. Male-dominated place famous for its meat: mostly mutton and chicken steeped in spicy garlic sauce. Chauffeurs pick up take-aways for their bosses in the *Taj* from here.

Delhi Darbar, Colaba Causeway (☎202 0235). Popular branch of reputed Grant Rd restaurant specializing in classic Mughlai food with some vegetarian and Chinese alternatives. *Biriyanis* still cooked in traditional way – slowly over charcoal fire. Very reasonable prices.

Fab Bistro, 2/5 Kamal Mansion, Arthur Bunder Rd (☎241459). Former seedy bar, now reopened as suave family restaurant (a/c) serving sizzlers, steaks, seafood, Chinese and western dishes.

Nanking, Shivaji Marg (☎202 0594). One of Bombay's oldest and most authentic Chinese restaurants – delicious Cantonese dishes with lots of seafood options. The house speciality, beef in watercress, is widely rated but must be ordered in advance.

EXPENSIVE

Golden Gate, Madam Cama Rd, next to *YWCA* (☎202 6306). Classy a/c restaurant, best known for its buffet salad lunches. Also North Indian dishes, plus seafood and Chinese.

Lings Pavillion, 19/21 Landsdowne Rd, behind *Regal* cinema (☎285 0023). Swanky Chinese restaurant; soft lighting, marble floors and gourmet Cantonese cuisine.

Restaurant locations are marked on the maps on p.586 (Colaba) and p.578 (Downtown).

Menage à Trois, *Taj Hotel* (☎202 3366). Fussy French (nouvelle) cuisine – hors d'oeuvres and desserts only. Very expensive.

Palkhi, Walton Rd (☎240079). Over-the-top, quasi-medieval decor and traditional Mughlai cooking for the health-conscious (lighter on oil and spices). Lots of veg options too. Very reasonable.

Tanjore, *Taj Hotel* (☎202 3366). Opulent interior, rich Mughlai cuisine and classical Indian music and dance in the evening. Expense account prices.

Trattoria, *Hotel President*, 90 Cuffe Parade (☎495 0808). Surprisingly authentic Italian cuisine. Pizza and pasta with fresh herbs, real parmesan, and a big buffet lunch on Sundays (noon–3pm).

Downtown

Britania & Co, opposite the GPO, Sprott Rd, Ballard Estate. Definitive Irani/Parsi food and decor. Try their special "berry pulao" or Bombay duck dishes. A real find, and cheap too.

Chetana, 34 K Dubash Marg (☎244968). Painstakingly prepared Rajasthani/Gujarati food, including set *thalis* and numerous à la carte dishes – absolutely the last word in fine veg cuisine. Expensive, but not extravagant. Reserve for dinner.

City Kitchen, 301 SBS Marg. Venerable, highly rated Goan restaurant. Serves all the usual dishes – mostly fish and meat simmered in coconut milk and fiery spices. Inexpensive.

Copper Chimney, K Dubash Marg (☎204 1661). Renowned *tandoori* house; stylish renditions of standard north Indian dishes. Superb but expensive. Reservations essential.

Khyber, opposite *Jehangir Art Gallery*, Kala Ghoda (☎273227). Ultra-fashionable, with opulent Arabian Nights interior and uncompromisingly rich Mughlai/Punjabi cuisine. The chicken *makhanwallah* is legendary. Reservations essential.

Modern Lunch Home, Sidhwa Marg. Inexpensive Keralan restaurant serving veg *thalis* and delicious non-veg options – chicken fried in ginger or fish *masala* on groaning platefuls of rice.

Piccolo, Homi Mody St (☎274537). Authentic Parsi menu includes real *dhansak* and delicious *patra ni machhi* (fresh fish stuffed with chutney and steamed in banana leaves). Inexpensive.

Samovar, *Jehangir Art Gallery*, MG Rd. Very pleasant, peaceful semi-open-air cafe, with varying menu: *roti kebabs*, prawn curry, fresh salads and *dhansak* – and beer. Tues–Sat 10.30am–7.30pm.

Wayside Inn, opposite *Jehangir Art Gallery*, K Dubash Marg. Upmarket Parsi cafe, with red-chequered table cloths and solid English cooking. Nice place for a coffee after visiting the museum.

Churchgate and Nariman Point

Chopsticks, 90a VN Rd (☎204 9842). Wide choice of pricey meat, seafood and veg in fiery Szechuan and milder Cantonese style. Try the excellent *dim sum* or "ant climbing up the tree".

Croissants Etc, Industrial Insurance Building, opposite Churchgate station (☎221066). Filled croissants, pricey pastries and other western food.

Gaylord, VN Rd (☎221259). Surreal, Parisian-style terrace cafe in the heart of Bombay. Tandoori, sizzlers and some western food. Wholewheat bread, baguettes and sticky buns in the patisserie.

Kamling, VN Rd (☎204 2618). Favourite for the title of oldest, best and most authentic Chinese in town. Southeast Asian flight crews and well-heeled locals tuck into delicious Cantonese dishes – try the mouthwatering "chimney soup" or the (expensive) seafood specialities.

The Outrigger, *Oberoi Hotel*, Nariman Point (☎202 3577). Polynesian specialities (Chinese with more fruit thrown in), tribal masks and a full-size canoe. Expensive.

Purohit's, VN Rd (☎204 6241). Justly popular traditional restaurant and coffee house serving good range of inexpensive *thalis*, main dishes and snacks. Recommended.

Rangoli, Nehru Centre, Nariman Point (☎233211). Excellent-value buffet lunches its forte, but the à la carte menu (including fish and strict Jain veg dishes) is gourmet standard and reasonably priced.

Satkar, opposite Churchgate station's western exit. Excellent-value pure veg restaurant. Busy terrace for Indian "fast food" (*dosas*, *vadas* etc) and crowd-watching.

Talk of the Town, 143 Marine Drive (☎285 1876). Ostentatiously French, expensive restaurant with cut-glass candlesticks, linen tablecloths and an enormous gourmet menu. Jewish wedding band plays most nights, believe it or not. Reserve for dinner.

The Top, *Ambassador Hotel*, VN Rd (☎291131). Revolving restaurant in glam four-star hotel with panoramic views. Excellent lunch buffets are just the thing for a splurge. Reserve for dinner.

Crawford Market and the central bazaars

Badshah Juice and Snack Bar, opposite Crawford Market, Lokmanya Tilak Rd. Bombay's most famous *falooda* joint also serves delicious *kulfi*, ice-creams and dozens of freshly squeezed fruit juices. The ideal place to round off a trip to the market.

Bhaishankar's, near Bhuleshwar Market, CP Tank Circle. One of Bombay's oldest and most respected sweet shops. Try their Bengali *barfi*, cashew *kalingar* or *masala* milk (made with pistachio, almonds, saffron and nutmeg). Savouries include *bhel puri*, *dahi vada* and *canari sev*.

Gulshan-e-Iran, Palton Rd (☎265183). Popular Muslim breakfast venue on main road does inexpensive *biryanis*, kebabs, chutneys and fresh bread. Open all day.

Hiralal Kashiram Bhajiwala, Kumbhar Tukda, Bhuleshwar Market. Cheap restaurant serving great *farsan* savouries, including *ponk vadas* (millet and garlic balls), *batata vadas* (made with sweet potatoes) and *kand bhajis* (deep-fried purple-yam), all with a tasty, fiery chutney.

Rajdhani, Mangaldas Rd (in the silk bazaar opposite Crawford market). Outstanding, eat-till-you-burst Gujarati *thalis* dished up by barefoot waiters to discerning aficionados. A little more expensive than usual, but well worth it.

Chowpatty Beach and Kemp's Corner

Chowpatty Beach is a popular venue for a picnic, crowded with vendors selling *kulfi* in clay cups and *bhel puri*, *kanji vada* and *pao bhaji* (see p.607). **Kemp's Corner**, crouched under the hectic G Deshmukh flyover, fifteen minutes' walk north, boasts a clutch of very good places to eat – handy for visitors to Malabar Hill.

Cafe Mondegar, 5a Colaba Causeway, next to the *Regal* cinema. Small, western-style cafe-bar. Draught beer, by the pitcher or glass, loud juke box and murals by a famous Goan cartoonist are the main attractions, though the small tables can make life difficult for women on their own.

China Garden, Om Chambers, 123 August Kranti Marg (☎828 0841). Malabar Hill's glitterati don their finest for this place, offering expensive, authentic Chinese, Korean, Thai and Japanese food.

China Town, 99 August Kranti Marg (☎822 7147). A more down-to-earth, cheaper alternative to *China Garden*, with varied menu of Cantonese, Szechuan and plenty of veg options.

Landmark, opposite the *RTI* Building, 35 S Patkar Marg (Hughes Rd) (☎822 6077). Bigger branch of *Piccolo* (see p.609) and *the* place to sample traditional Parsi food. *Lagansara* stew, served at weddings, is a wholesome veg alternative to the usual mutton and chicken. Delicious desserts too.

Leopold's Cafe and Stores, Colaba Causeway. Colaba's perennially popular cafe-bar is determinedly western with a clientele to match. Four hundred items on the menu from scrambled eggs on toast to "drunken chicken", all washed down with cold beer. Overpriced.

New Yorker, Fulchand Niwas, 25 Chowpatty Seaface. Western food, such as baked potatoes, pizzas and burgers.

Paramount Restaurant, Marine Drive, near the aquarium. Small Irani cafe, which while it has a certain charm, with marble-top tables, wood-panelled and mirrored walls, applies strict rules. Signs request that you "Do not spit", "Do not comb your hair", "Do not stretch legs on other pieces of furniture" and, most advisedly, "Do not sit unnecessarily a long time".

Revival, above *London Pub*, Chowpatty Seaface. Fairly pricey 1930s retro-decor restaurant serving imaginative and tasty western and Indian dishes.

Sadar Refreshments, opposite bus depot, Tardeo Junction. The city's definitive *pao bhaji*. Cheap, filling and delicious.

Shopping

Bombay is a great place to shop, whether for last-minute souvenirs, or essentials for the long journeys ahead. Locally produced **textiles** and export-surplus **clothing** are among the best buys, as are **handicrafts** from far-flung corners of the country. With the exception of the swish arcades in the five-star hotels, **prices** compare surprisingly well with other Indian cities. In the larger shops, rates are fixed and **credit cards** are often accepted; elsewhere, particularly dealing with street-vendors, it pays to **haggle**. Uptown, the **central bazaars** – see p.595 – are better for spectating than serious shopping, although the **antiques** and Friday **flea-market** in the **Chor**, or "thieves" bazaar, can sometimes yield the odd bargain. The **Zaveri** (goldsmiths') bazaar opposite Crawford Market is the place to head for new gold and silver **jewellery**.

Opening hours in the city centre are Monday to Saturday, 10am to 7pm. The Muslim bazaars, quiet on Friday, the Sabbath, are otherwise open until around 9pm.

Antiques

The **Chor Bazaar** area, and Mutton Street in particular, is the centre of Bombay's **antique** trade – even if it is no longer highly regarded by serious collectors. For a full account, see p.597. Another good, if much more expensive, place to sift through bric-a-brac is *Phillip's* famous antique shop (Mon–Sat 9am–1pm & 2.30–6.30pm; ☎202564), on the corner of Madam Cama Rd, opposite the *Regal* cinema in Colaba. This fascinating, old-fashioned store has changed little since it opened in 1860. Innumerable glass lamps and chandeliers hang from the ceiling, while antique display cases are stuffed with miniature brass, bronze and wood Hindu sculpture, silver jewellery, old prints and aquatints. Most of the stuff on sale dates from the twilight of the Raj – a result of the Indian government's ban on the export by foreigners of items more than a century old.

In the *Jehangir Art Gallery* basement, a branch of the antiques chain *Natesan's Antiqarts* (☎285 2700; fax 285 2121) offers a tempting selection of antique (and reproduction) sculpture, furniture, paintings and bronzes.

Clothes and textiles

Bombay produces the bulk of India's clothes, mostly the lightweight, light-coloured "shirtings and suitings" favoured by droves of uniformly attired office-*wallahs*. For cheaper western clothing, you can't beat the long row of stalls on the pavement of MG Road, opposite the Bombay Gymkhana. "**Fashion Street**" specializes in reject and export-surplus goods ditched by big manufacturers, selling off T-shirts, jeans, leggings, summer dresses, and trendy sweatshirts. Better quality cotton clothes (often stylish designer-label rip-offs) are available in shops along **Colaba Causeway**, such as *Cotton World*, down Mandlik Marg. Nearby, clothes-racks along the main road are loaded with multi-coloured New Age Goa-rave gear.

If you're looking for more traditional **Indian clothes**, head for the **Khadi Village Industries Emporium** at 286 Dr DN Marg (☎204 3288), near the *Thomas Cook* office. As *Whiteaway & Laidlaw*, this rambling Victorian department store used to kit all the newly arrived *burra-sahibs* out with pith helmets, khaki shorts and quinine tablets. These days, its old wooden counters, shirt and sock drawers stock dozens of different hand-spun cottons and silks, sold by the metre or made up as vests, *kurtas* or block-printed *shalwa camises*. Other items – possible souvenirs – are the ubiquitous white Nehru caps, *dhotis*, Madras-check *lunghis* and fine brocaded silk *saris*. Actually buying the stuff requires four separate manoeuvres: you select an item, get a chit, go to the cash desk, pay for the goods, get a receipt, and go to the collection point, where your goods will be beautifully wrapped in paper bags just bursting to fall apart.

If you can't find the stylish "ethnic" *shalwa camise* you're looking for in the *Central Cottage Industries Emporium* (see below under "Handicrafts"), try the exclusive *Nayaab* boutique in the World Trade Centre, Cuffe Parade, or *Bibas* in the Whitehall Building, Kemp's Corner. Cheaper variations on a similar theme are to be found in the more authentic cloth bazaar on **Mangaldas Lane**, opposite Crawford Market, where touts lead you through a maze of stalls to backstreet shops crammed with inexpensive Indian clothes, silk scarves, embroidered Kashmiri shawls and Gujarati tie-dye wall-hangings.

Handicrafts

Regionally produced **handicrafts** are marketed in assorted state-run emporia at the World Trade Centre, down on Cuffe Parade, and along Sir PM Road, Fort. The quality is consistently high – as are the prices, if you miss out on the periodic holiday discounts. The same goes for the **Central Cottage Industries Emporium**, 34 Shivaji Marg, near the Gateway of India in Colaba (☎202 6564), whose size and central location make it the single best all-round place to hunt for souvenirs. Downstairs you'll find inlaid furniture, wood- and metal-work, miniature paintings and jewellery, while upstairs specializes in toys, clothing and textiles – Gujarati appliqué bedspreads, hand-painted pillowcases and Rajasthani mirror-work, plus silk ties and Noel Coward dressing-gowns. **Mereweather Road**, directly behind the *Taj*, is awash with Kashmiri handicraft stores stocking overpriced papier-mâché pots and bowls, silver jewellery, woollen shawls and rugs. Avoid them if you find it hard to shrug off aggressive sales pitches.

Colaba is also the best area for **leather** goods. Muslim leather-*wallahs* on and around the Causeway include the reliable *Shabir Boutique* factory outlet behind the *Taj*, where you can buy jackets, handbags and wallets at only a little above wholesale rates. They'll also manufacture your own designs if you give them enough warning.

Perfume is another Muslim preserve. Down at the south end of Colaba Causeway, around Arthur Bunder Road, shops with mirrored walls and shelves are stacked with cut-glass carafes full of syrupy, fragrant essential oils. **Incense** is hawked in sticks, cones and slabs of sticky *dhoop* on the sidewalk nearby (check that the boxes haven't already been opened and their contents sold off piecemeal). For bulk buying, the hand-rolled, cottage-made bundles of incense sold in the *Khadi Emporium* on Dr DN Marg (see above) are a better deal; it also has a handicraft department where, in addition to furniture, paintings and ornaments, you can pick up glass bangles, block-printed and calico bedspreads, and wooden votive statues produced in Maharashtran craft villages.

Books

Bombay's excellent English-language **bookstores** are well stocked with everything to do with India, and a good selection of general classics, pulp fiction and travel writing. Indian editions of popular titles cost a fraction of what they do abroad and include lots of interesting works by lesser-known local authors. If you don't mind picking through dozens of trigonometry textbooks, back issues of *National Geographic* and salacious 1960s paperbacks, the street-stalls between Flora Fountain and Churchgate station can also be good places to hunt for **secondhand books**.

Chetana, 34 Dubash Rd (formerly Rampart Row). Exclusively religion and philosophy.

Crossword, Mahalakshmi Chambers, 22 Bhulabhai Desai Rd, Breach Candy (☎492 2458). Bombay's largest and most reputed retailer, a bus ride (#132) from the downtown area.

Nalanda, Ground Floor, *Taj* (☎202 2514). An exhaustive range of coffee-table tomes and paperback literature, with a rack of quality postcards.

Pustak Bharati, *Bharatiya Vidhya Bhavan*, KM Munshi Marg (☎363 4462). Excellent small bookshop; Hindu philosophy and literature, plus details of *Bhavan*'s cultural programmes.

Shankar Book-Stand, outside the *Cafe Mondegar*, Colaba Causeway. Piles of easy-reads, guidebooks, classic fiction, and most of the old favourites on India.

Strand, near *HMV*, off PM Rd, Fort. The best bookstore in the city centre, with the full gamut of *Penguins* and Indian literature.

Music

The most famous of Bombay's many good **music shops** are near the *Moti* cinema along **SV Patel Road**, in the central bazaar district. *Haribhai Vishwanath*, *Ram Singh* and *RS Mayeka* are all government-approved retailers of traditional Indian instruments, including *sitars*, *sarods*, *tablas* and flutes.

The best place to shop for **cassettes** and **CDs** is on Subhash Chowk, next to the *Jehangir Art Gallery*. *Rhythm House* here is a veritable Aladdin's cave of classical, devotional and popular Indian music, with a reasonable selection of western rock, pop and jazz stocked in the back room.

BOLLYWOOD: THE CAPITAL OF THE HINDI FILM

For anyone brought up on TV, it's hard to imagine the power that **films** continue to wield in India. Every village has a cinema within walking distance, and with a potential audience in the hundreds of millions, film companies seem to have virtually cast-iron guarantees of vast profits. The Indian film industry is the largest in the world, producing around 750 full-length features each year. Regional cinema, catering for different language groups (in particular the Tamil cinema of Madras), though popular locally, has little national impact. Only the **Hindi film** – one-fifth of films made in India – has crossed regional boundaries to great effect, most particularly in the north. The home of the Hindi blockbuster, the "all-India film", is Bombay, famously known as **Bollywood**.

To cross boundaries of language and religion, the Bollywood movie follows rigid conventions and genres; as in myth, its characters have predetermined actions and destinies. Knowing a plot need not detract from the drama, and indeed, it is not uncommon for Indian audiences to watch films numerous times. Unlike the Hollywood formula, which tends to classify each film under one genre, the Hindi film follows what is known as a **masala** format, including during its luxurious three hours a little bit of everything: especially romance, violence and comedy. Frequently the stories feature dispossessed male heroes fighting evil against all odds with love interest thrown in. The sexual element is repressed, with numerous wet *saris* and dance routines featuring the tensest pelvic thrusts in the world. Other typical themes include male bonding and betrayal, family melodrama, separation and reunion and religious piety. Dream sequences are almost obligatory, along with a festival or celebration scene – typically Holi, when people shower each other with colour – a comic character passing through, and a depraved, alcoholic and most western "cabaret", filled with strutting villains and lewd dancing. One way in which Bollywood has moved closer to Hollywood in recent years, however, has been the development, alarming to traditionalists, of films in which the "hero" is no longer necessarily a moral exemplar, violence can be fun, and good does not always triumph.

Film song is the most popular form of music in India; an average of six songs play an essential part in the narrative of each film. A song can transcend its filmic context, remaining popular years after the film it was composed for has been forgotten. However, the apposite marriage of film and song, through **picturization**, means the story lives on in the mind of the listener. Equally, a good song, released before the film, acts as a trailer to help fill the theatres. The songs are created through the artistic collaboration of a film director, lyricist, music composer, arranger, studio instrumentalists, the "playback" singers (the most famous, Lata Mangeshkar, is in the *Guinness Book of Records* for the number of songs she has recorded), and finally the actor who mimes the song on screen.

The exploits of Bombay's **film stars** – on and off screen – and their lavish lifestyles in the city's clubs and millionaires' ghetto of Malabar Hill, are the subject of endless titillating gossip. Fanzines such as *Stardust, Star and Style, Film World* and *Cine Blitz* are snaffled up by millions, while the industry looks to the more sober *Screen*. Following the careers of the stars requires dedication; each may work on up to ten movies at once.

At one time specially arranged tours made it easy to get into a **film studio** to see a movie being made, but those days are gone. If you're very keen, try contacting *Mehboob Studios*, Hill Rd, Bandra West (☎642 8045); *Natraj Studios*, Western Express Highway, Andheri East (☎834 2371); or *Film City*, Goregaon East, Bombay 65 (☎840 1533).

Visitors to Bombay should have ample opportunity to sample the delights of a movie. To make an educated choice, buy *Bombay* magazine, which contains extensive listings and reviews. Otherwise, look for the biggest, brightest hoarding, and join the queue.

Of the two hundred or so cinemas, only eight regularly screen **English-language** films. The most central and convenient are the *Regal*, in Colaba, the *Eros*, opposite Churchgate, and the *Sterling*, the *New Excelsior*, and the *New Empire*, all within a few blocks two minutes' walk west of Victoria Terminus.

THE FESTIVALS OF BOMBAY

Bombay has its own versions of all the major Hindu and Muslim **festivals**, plus a host of smaller neighbourhood celebrations imported by its immigrant communities. Exact dates vary from year to year; check in advance at the government tourist office.

Elephanta Music and Dance Festival (Feb). MTDC-organized cultural event including floodlit performances by classical artists with the Shiva cave temple as back-drop.

Gokhulashtami (July/Aug). Riotous commemoration of Krishna's birthday; terracotta pots filled with curd, milk-sweets and cash are strung from tenement balconies and grabbed by human-pyramids of young boys.

No Ruz (July/Aug). The Parsi New Year is celebrated with special ceremonies in the Fire Temples and feasting at home.

Ganesh Chathurthi (Aug/Sept). Huge effigies of Ganesh, the elephant-headed god of prosperity and wisdom, are immersed in the sea at Chowpatty Beach in a ritual originally promoted by freedom-fighters to circumvent British anti-assembly legislation. Recently it has seemed in danger of being hijacked by Hindu extremists such as the Shiv Sena, tinging it more with chauvinism than celebration.

Nariel Purnima (Sept). Koli fishermen launch brightly decorated boats to mark the end of the monsoon.

Ramadan (varies according to the Muslim calendar). Annual bout of Muslim fasting and feasting; all-night food stalls in the bazaars, processions of Shi'ite flagellants commemorating the martyrdom of the Prophet's grandson at the battle of the Karbala.

Dusshera (Oct). Rama's victory over the evil king of Lanka, Ravana, is marked in Bombay by re-enactments of scenes from the *Ramayana* on Chowpatty Beach.

Nightlife and entertainment

As many have observed, Bombay never sleeps. No matter what time of night you venture out, there are bound to be others going about some business or other. However, like other parts of India, **nightlife** as westerners know it is not that developed. A few **bars** cater to young Westerners and Bombayites alike, and **discos**, usually in the swanky hotels, are something of a growth industry.

Of course, Bombay is also a cultural centre attracting the finest Indian **classical music** and **dance** artists from both north and south India. Venues such as *Bharatiya Vidya Bhavan*, K M Munshi Marg (☎363 1261) – the headquarters of the international cultural (Hindu) organization – *Cowasjee Jehangir (CJ) Hall, Birla Matushri, Tejpal Auditorium, Shanmukhananda Hall* and the *National Centre for the Performing Arts (NCPA) Auditorium* frequently present concerts and recitals. *NCPA* also offers contemporary Gujarati, Hindi, Marathi and English-language plays as well as western chamber music, while quite a smattering of platinum-selling western rock artists appear at Bombay stadia.

Bars and cabarets

Bombay has an unusually easy-going attitude to **alcohol**; popping into a bar for a beer is very much accepted (for men at least) even at lunchtime. Chowpatty Beach and Colaba Causeway are the main alternatives to the five-star hotels.

However, there is also a seamier side to the city's nightlife, concentrated around (illegal) late-night **cabarets** in the Grant Road area. These dens of iniquity, where women dance before men-only crowds in clothes that might in the west be considered Victorian in their propriety but would be unheard-of anywhere else in India, are not places the casual visitor should dream of venturing into.

Leopold Pub, 1st Floor, *Leopold's*, Colaba Causeway. Swanky, self-consciously western-style bar-nightclub, with bouncers, serving expensive beers to Bombay's smart set. No single men admitted.

London Pub, 39D Chowpatty Seaface. Designer frosted-glass bar with prog-rock murals and quality sound system. Uncomfortable bar stools.

The Tavern, *Fariyas Hotel*, Colaba. Ersatz English pub, complete with wooden beams and loud music.

Tiger Tim's, near the Stockmarket, Fort. Trendy bar with MTV sounds and clientele to match.

Discos

India has a long history of folk, classical and *filmi* dance, but people in general remain uncomfortable with free-style public frugging. The popularity of the bump'n'grind physicality of Apache Indian and the perennial "MJ", Michael Jackson may free up the scene, but don't expect wild-abandon rave culture. Many clubs operate a "couples-only" entrance policy, and even those that don't may prohibit "stag" dancing (a male on his own). Most discos are seriously expensive and the clientele reflects this. Since the 1993 bombings, many have been winding down by midnight, but opening hours are likely to edge back up again. Discos in the five-star hotels in the centre are frequently members-only; for a less intimidating scene, head to suburbs like Juhu and Santa Cruz.

The Cellar, *The Oberoi*. Hotel disco open to non-members as long as they're in a couple.

Go Bananas, Kamat's Plaza near Santa Cruz airport. Plays hit records and, on certain nights, allows singles onto its small dance floor.

The 1900s, *Taj Mahal*. Pounding disco, free to guests but otherwise for members only – a year's membership is a snip at Rs25,000.

Razzberry Rhinoceros, *Juhu Hotel*, Juhu Beach. A good size dance floor. Entrance is for couples only and they serve fairly pricey Chinese, western and Indian food.

RG's, *Natraj*. Members and their guests only.

Sheetal Again, Juhu. Small pub with an enthusiastic crowd, tiny dance floor, loud sound system and DJs playing international dance hits. The barmen dress in denim dungarees and confederate caps. Although singles are allowed in, the comfortable seating is reserved for the paired-up. Woe betide any man who tries to dance on his own; the DJ will call for him to leave.

The Wild Orchid, Chembur. Open until 4am – again couples only – with a rowdy late-night crowd.

Listings

Ambulance ☎102, 534 1552 or 768 1010.

Ashrams *Aurobindo*, B Rd, Churchgate (☎203 3076); *Satya Sai Baba*, Dharma Kshetra, Mahakali Caves, Andheri East (☎637 7999); *Vipassana*, c/o 2nd Floor, Sylvester Building, 10 Colaba Causeway (☎286 3637).

Ayurvedic Medicine *Yogayurveda Kendra*, Dr Shri Patel's Nursing Home, opposite Chowpatty bus stand.

Churches Protestant: St Thomas' Cathedral, Tamarind St, Fort (☎261 1275) or St John's Afghan Church, Colaba (☎215 0198); Wesley Methodist (British): opposite Electric House, Colaba (☎218 1565); Bowen Methodist (American): Landsdowne Rd, Fort (☎202 0372).

Consulates and High Commissions Although the many consulates and High Commissions in Bombay can be useful for replacing lost travel documents or obtaining visas, most of India's neighbour states, including Bangladesh, Bhutan, Burma, Nepal and Pakistan, only have embassies in New Delhi and/or Calcutta. *Australia*, 16th Floor, Maker Tower "E", Cuffe Parade (☎218 1071); *Belgium*, Morena, 11 ML Dahanukar Marg (☎493 9261); *Canada*, 41/42 Maker Chambers VI, Nariman Point (☎287 6028); *Denmark*, L & T House, Narottam Moraji Marg, Ballard Estate (☎261 8181); *France*, NG Cross Rd, off Peddar Rd (☎494 9808); *Germany*, 10th Floor, Hoechst House, Nariman Point (☎232422); *Ireland*, 7th Floor, *Thomas Cook*, Dr DN Marg (☎285 0330); *Israel*, Kailash Peddar Rd (☎386 2794); *Italy*, Kanchanjunga, 72 G Deshmukh Rd (☎387 2341); *Japan*, 1 Babasaheb Dahanukar Marg, Cumballa Hill (☎494 4310); *Netherlands*, 16 Queen's Rd (☎203 6840); *Norway*, Navroji Mansion, 31 Nathelal Parekh Marg (☎242042); *Philippines*, 116 Free Press House, Nariman Point (☎202 0375); *Singapore*, 9th Floor, 941 Sakhar Bhavan, 230 Nariman Point (☎204 3209); *Spain*, Ador House, 6 K Dubash Marg (☎287 4797); *Sri Lanka*, Sri Lanka House, 34 Homi Modi St, Fort (☎204 5861); *Sweden*, 85 Sayani Rd, Subash Gupta Bhavan, Prabhadevi (☎436 0493); *Switzerland*, 7th Floor, Manekh Mahal, 90 VN Rd (☎204 2003); *Thailand*, 2nd Floor, Krishna Bagh,

43 Bhulabhai Desai Rd (☎363 6404); *Turkey*, 25 Mistry Court, 208 Dr DN Marg (☎202 7246); *United Kingdom*, 2nd Floor, Maker Chamber IV, Nariman Point (☎283 0517); *USA*, Lincoln House, 78 Bhulabhai Desai Rd (☎363 3611).

Hindi Lessons *Kalina University*, in north Bombay, and a number of private academies run short courses. Ask at the tourist office in Churchgate (☎203 3144) for more details.

Hospitals The best hospital in the centre is the private *Bombay Hospital* (☎266 3343), New Marine Lines, just north of the government tourist office on M Karve Rd. *Breach Candy Hospital* on Bhulabhai Desai Rd, near the swimming pool, is also recommended by foreign embassies.

Left Luggage If your hotel won't let you store bags with them, try the cloakroom in VT station. Anything left here, even rucksacks, must be securely fastened with a padlock, or they'll refuse it. Luggage can be left for a maximum of 12 weeks, and don't, whatever you do, lose the receipt.

Libraries *Asiatic Society*, SBS Marg, Horniman Circle, Ballard Estate (Mon–Sat 10am–5.30pm; ☎266 0956); *British Council* (for British newspapers), "A" Wing, Mittal Towers, Nariman Point (☎223560); *Alliance Francaise*, Theosophy Hall, 40 New Marine Lines (☎203 1867); *Max Mueller Bhavan*, Prince of Wales Annexe, off MG Rd (☎202 7542). The *KR Cama Oriental Institute*, 136 Bombay Samachar Marg (Mon–Fri 10am–5pm, Sat 10am–1pm; ☎243893), specializing in Zoroastrian and Iranian studies has a public collection of 22,000 volumes in European and Asian languages. *Bombay Natural History Society*, Hornbill House (Mon–Fri 10am–5pm, Sat 10am–1pm, closed 1st & 3rd Sat of the month; ☎243421), has an international reputation for the study of wildlife in India. Visitors may become temporary members which allows them access to the library, natural history collection, occasional talks and the opportunity to join organized walks and field trips.

Mother Theresa's Asha Daan Hindustan Lever Compound, Sankli St, Byculla (☎897700).

Pharmacies *Real Chemist*, 1/51 Kaka Arcade (☎258972) and *Royal Chemists*, M Karve Rd (☎308 8401), both close to *Bombay Hospital*, are open 24hr. *Kemps* in the *Taj* hotel also opens late.

Photographic Studios and Equipment The *Javeri Colour Lab*, opposite the *Regal* cinema in Colaba, stocks colour-print and slide film, as do most of the big hotels. A small boutique behind the florists in the *Shakhari Bunder* covered market does instant *Polaroid* passport photographs.

Police The main police station in Colaba (☎202 1122) is on the west side of Colaba Causeway, near the crossroads with Ormiston Road. For emergencies call ☎100.

State tourist offices in Bombay include: *Delhi*, c/o MTDC, CDO Hutments, Madam Cama Rd, Nariman Point (☎285 5736); *Gujarat*, Dhanraj Mahal, PJ Ramchandani Marg (Mon–Sat 10am– 5pm; ☎202 2945); *Himachal Pradesh*, World Trade Centre, Cuffe Parade (Mon–Sat 10am–5pm; ☎218 1123); *Jammu and Kashmir*, also in the World Trade Centre (Mon–Fri 10am–3pm; ☎218 6249); *Kerala*, c/o Kairali, Nirmal Building, Nariman Point (Mon–Sat 10am–5pm; ☎202 6817); *Madhya Pradesh*, World Trade Centre (Mon–Sat 10am–5pm; ☎218 7603); *Rajasthan*, 230 Dr DN Marg (☎204 4162); *Tamil Nadu*, c/o *Peerless Hotels and Travels Ltd*, Ground Floor, Churchgate Chambers, New Marine Lines (Mon–Sat 9am–6pm; ☎262 4811); and *Uttar Pradesh*, World Trade Centre (Mon–Sat 10.30am–5.30pm, closed 2nd Sat of each month; ☎218 5458).

Swimming Pools The snooty expat sports club at Breach Candy, north of Malabar Hill, is a popular place to beat the heat. A day's membership costs around Rs50.

Synagogue Synagogues belonging to Bombay's vestigial Jewish community include *Shaar Harahamim*, Gate of Mercy, 254 Samuel St. A "Jewish Club" is based at 137 MG Rd (☎262 1628).

RECOMMENDED TRAVEL AGENTS IN BOMBAY

Agarwal Bros Travels, 24-D Krishna Building, Shop 3, SS Gaikwad Rd, Dhobi Talao Market, near *Metro* (☎206 0766).

Cox & Kings India Ltd, Grindlay's Bank Building, 270/272 Dr DN Marg(☎204 3066).

Designer Holidays, 6 Shanti Building, 19 Peddar Rd (☎492 4415).

Peerless Hotels & Travels Ltd, Ground Floor, Churchgate Chambers, 5 New Marine Lines (☎262 4811).

Sita Travels Pvt Ltd, 8 Atlanta Building, Nariman Point (☎240666).

Space Travels, 4th Floor, Nanabhoy Mansion, Pherozshah Mehta Marg, Fort (☎266 4749).

Travel Corporation of India, Chandramukhi, Nariman Point (☎202 1881).

Travelera Pvt Ltd, 4/5 Oberoi Shopping Centre, *The Oberoi*, Nariman Point (☎202 6228).

Visa Extensions Contact *Foreigner's Registration Office*, Office of the Police Commissioner, opposite Crawford Market (Mon–Fri 10am–1pm; ☎261 0446).

Yoga Centres *Kailvalyadham Ishwardas Chunilal Yoga Health Centre*, 43 Marine Drive (Mon–Sat 6.30–9.30am & 3.30–7pm; ☎201 0494); *Mani Umrolia*, Second Floor, Chateau Windsor, VN Rd (☎204 3376); *Yoga International Centre*, New Shelter, B Rd, Churchgate (☎201 0081).

Onwards from Bombay

Most visitors feel like getting out of Bombay as soon as they can. Fortunately, this is less of a chore than in many other Indian cities; Bombay is equipped with "super-fast" services to arrange or confirm **onward travel**. All the major international and domestic airlines have offices in the city, the train networks operate special, hassle-free tourist counters in the main reservation halls, and dozens of travel agents and road transport companies are eager to help you on your way by bus. Even so, a wait of at least a couple of days for a seat on the train or plane you want is still par for the course.

TRANSPORT SERVICES FROM BOMBAY

	Trains		Buses		Flights	
	Frequency	Time	Frequency	Time	Frequency	Time
Agra	2 daily	23hr 30min–27hr				
Ahmedabad	7 daily	9–12hr				
Aurangabad	1 daily	10hr	2 daily*	12hr	2 daily	45–65min
Bangalore	2 daily	24hr	3 daily*	24hr	4–5 daily	1hr 30min
Bhopal	4–5 daily	12–17hr			1 daily	2hr 10min
Bijapur			3 daily*	12hr		
Calcutta	4 daily	33–42hr			6–7 daily	2–3hr
Calicut	1–2 daily	34–39hr			4 daily	1hr 45min
Coimbatore	1–2 daily	30–35hr			3 daily	1hr 50min–3hr
Delhi	6–8 daily	17–33hr			12 daily	1hr 55min
Goa	2 daily	23–24hr	2 daily*	16–18hr	5 daily	1hr
Hyderabad	2 daily	14hr 20min–18hr	8 daily*	18hr	5 daily	1hr 15min
Indore	1 daily	14hr	2 daily*	16hr	6 weekly	55min
Jaipur	1 daily	22hr 30min			2–4 daily	1hr 30min–4hr
Jodhpur	1 daily	21hr 10min			1–2 daily	1hr 25min–2hr
Kochi	1–2 daily	35–60hr			4–5 daily	1hr 45min
Kolhapur	3 daily	11–13hr	hourly**	10hr		
Madras	3 daily	24–31hr			4–5 daily	1hr 45min
Madurai					1–2 daily	2–3hr
Mangalore	1–2 daily	40–46hr	4 daily*	24hr	2 daily	1hr 15min
Nagpur	5 daily	14–17hr			1 daily	1hr 15min
Nasik	16 daily	4hr	6 daily**	4hr		
Pune	18 daily	3hr 30min–5hr	hourly**	4hr 30min	2–3 daily	30–75min
Surat	24 daily	3hr 30min–6hr	1 daily*	7hr		
Thiruv'puram	1 daily	44hr 20min			2 daily	2–3hr
Udaipur	1 daily	24hr 30min	1 daily*	24hr		
Ujjain	1 daily	14hr	1 daily*	17hr	2 daily	2hr 20min
Varanasi	4 daily	27hr 30min–30hr			4 weekly	2hr 10min

* Buses from Bombay Central; ** Buses from ASIAD Dadar.   All flights from Santa Cruz.

Only **direct** trains are listed. For more details on transport to **Goa** – and a "stop press" – see p.619.

RECOMMENDED TRAINS FROM BOMBAY

The trains below are recommended as the **fastest** and/or **most convenient** services from Bombay. Most destinations are also accessible on other, slower trains – see p.617.

	Name	No.	From	Frequency	Departs	Total Time
Agra	Punjab Mail	1037	VT	daily	7.10pm	23hr 30min
Aurangabad	Bombay–Aurangabad Express	1003	VT	daily	10.30pm	10hr
Bangalore	Udyan Express	6529	VT	daily	7.55am	23hr 45min
Bhopal	Pushpak Express	2133	VT	daily	8.10am	12hr 10min
Calcutta	Gitanjali Express	2859	VT	daily	6.05am	33hr 10min
	Bombay–Howrah Mail	8001	VT	daily	7.35pm	36hr 35min
Delhi	Rajdhani Express*	2951	BC	Tues–Sun	4.55pm	17hr
	Bombay–New Delhi A/C Express*	2953	BC	Mon, Wed, Sat	5.40pm	17hr 10min
	Frontier Mail	2903	BC	daily	9.10pm	21hr 50min
	Paschim Express	2925	BC	daily	11.25am	23hr
	Punjab Mail	1037	VT	daily	7.10pm	25hr
Gorakhpur	Kushi Nagar Express	1015	VT	daily	9.20pm	34hr 45min
Hyderabad	Minar Express	2101	VT	daily	9.55pm	14hr 20min
Jaipur	Gujarat Express**	9011	BC	daily	5.45am	22hr 30min
Jodhpur	Saurashtra Mail**	9005	BC	daily	7.45am	21hr 10min
Kochi	Netravati Express	2135	VT	Tues, Thurs, Sun	8.15pm	35hr 25min
Madras	Dadar–Madras Chennai Express	6063	Dadar	Tues, Fri, Sun	8pm	24hr 10min
Nasik	Bombay–Ratnagiri Express	1065	VT	daily	5am	4hr
Pune	Indrayani Express	2113	VT	daily	6am	3hr 30min
Thiruv'puram	Kanniya Kumari Express	1081	VT	daily	3.35pm	44hr 20min
Udaipur	Saurashtra Express**	9012	BC	daily	7.45am	24hr 30min
Varanasi	Bombay–Varanasi Ratnagiri Express	1065	VT	daily	5am	27hr 30min

VT = Victoria Terminus. BC = Bombay Central.
* = A/c only. ** = Change to connecting train at Ahmedabad.

Travel within India

Bombay is the nexus of several major internal flight routes, train networks and highways, and is the main transport hub for traffic heading towards south India. The most-travelled trails lead north up the Gujarati coast to **Rajasthan** and **Delhi**; northwest into **the Deccan** via Aurangabad and the caves at Ellora and Ajanta; and south, through Pune and the hills of Western Ghats towards **Goa** and the Malabar Coast. Public transport, though cheap and frequent, never quite manages to keep pace with the ever increasing demand, so book as far in advance as possible and be prepared for delays.

By plane

Indian Airlines and several other domestic carriers operate **flights** out of Santa Cruz to destinations all over India. Computer-booking has made booking less of a lottery than it used to be, but availability on popular routes (such as Bombay–Goa–Bombay) should never be taken for granted. Check with the airlines as soon as you arrive; **tickets** can be bought directly from their offices, or through any reputable travel agent.

GETTING TO GOA

Many travellers only come to Bombay to pick up **transport to Goa**, 600km south. Since the suspension of the steamer service in 1987 (the Indian army commandeered the old boat to carry troops to Sri Lanka), there have been three main ways to make the journey. Going by **bus** – which entails a sleepless night of bumping on rock-hard seats – has long been more popular than the cheaper, more comfortable train (when running; see below).

By plane
At present, five domestic airline companies operate daily services to Goa – *Air India*, *Damania, East–West, Jet*, and *Modiluft* (see p.620). If you can afford it, this is the most painless way to go, but competition for seats is fierce and you may well have to wait several days. Only passengers who fly to India on *Air India* can book one of these flights before arriving in the country. The journey takes an hour and costs around Rs1300.

By train: STOP PRESS
As this book went to press, in Oct 1994, reports reached the *Rough Guides* office that **all train services within Goa were suspended** during the change-over from broad- to metre-gauge track beyond **Miraj**, 472km south of Bombay. The following are broad guidelines as to what the situation *may* be like once services return to normal.

The new, faster coastal route of the *Konkan Railway*, scheduled (optimistically) for completion in 1995, will make the **train** journey to Goa by far the best-value option. Until now, however, the prospect of a 24-hour trip through the Ghats has been enough to put most visitors off what, by Indian standards, is a perfectly manageable journey.

When this book was researched, two services left **Victoria Terminus** every day for **Vasco da Gama** station, Goa. The *Konya Express* (#7303) departed at 8.45am to meet the *Link Express* (#7838) at Miraj, for its 8.45pm onward departure, and arrived in Vasco at 9am the next day. The *Sahyadri Express* (#7203) left Bombay at 5.50pm, arriving at Miraj 11hr 30min later to connect with the 7am *Mandovi Express* , which reached Vasco around 5pm. The first-class fare was around Rs470; second class cost Rs130.

By bus
The Bombay–Goa **bus** journey ranks among the very worst in India. Don't believe travel agents who assure you it takes thirteen hours. Clapped-out coaches, and appalling road surfaces along the sinuous coastal route, make eighteen hours a more realistic estimate.

Bus tickets start at around Rs200 for a push-back seat on a beaten-up *Kadamba* (Goan government) or *MSRTC* coach. Tickets for these services are in great demand in season, so book in advance at Bombay Central or *Kadamba*'s kiosks on the side of Mahapalika Marg, just up from VT station. More and more **private** overnight buses also run to Goa, costing from around Rs250 for a noisy front-engine *Tata* bus, to Rs500 for a place on a top-of-the-range imported a/c coach with pneumatic suspension, video, and on-board toilet. Tickets should be booked at least a day in advance through a reputable travel agent (see p.616), though it's sometimes worth turning up at Walchand Hirachand Marg, Ballard Pier (opposite the *Grand Hotel*), where most buses leave from, on the off chance of a last-minute cancellation. Make sure, in any case, that you are given both your seat and the bus registration numbers, and that you confirm the exact time and place of departure with the travel agent, as these frequently vary between companies.

By boat
Ever since the old steamer service ended, the powerful Goan bus lobby has managed to block any comeback by the Bombay–Goa passenger ferry. However, one contender may well soon succeed in breaking the deadlock. *Nomad Travels Ltd*, Sharda House, A Road, Churchgate (☎202 1503), plan to launch a luxury liner, complete with a/c restaurants, sun-deck and a pool, which they hope will sail three times each week between Bombay and Panjim. The journey will take around eighteen hours and cost Rs5000 one way for a cabin, or Rs850 for deck passengers. Ask any good travel agent for the latest details.

AIRLINE OFFICES IN BOMBAY

International Airlines

Aeroflot, Ground Floor, 241/242 Nirmal Building, Nariman Point (☎221682).

Air France, 1st Floor, Maker Chambers VI, Nariman Point (☎202 5021).

Air India, Nariman Point (☎202 4142).

Air Lanka, Ground Floor, Mittal Tower, C Wing, Nariman Point (☎223299).

Air Mauritius, Ground Floor, Air India Building, Nariman Point (☎202 8474).

Alitalia, Industrial Insurance Building,VN Rd, Churchgate (☎222144).

British Airways, 202-B, Valcan Insurance Building,VN Rd, Churchgate (☎220888).

Canadian Airlines International, Podar House, 10 Marine Drive (☎204 2174).

Cathay Pacific, Ground Floor, old *Taj* hotel, Colaba (☎202 9112).

Continental Airlines (USA), Ground Floor, 6 Maker Arcade, Cuffe Parade (☎218 1440).

Delta, *Taj Hotel*, Colaba (☎202 9020).

Emirates, 228 Mittal Chambers, Nariman Point (☎287 1645).

Gulf Air, Maker Chamber VI, Nariman Point (☎202 4065).

Japan Airlines, 2 Raheja Centre, Nariman Point (☎287 4036).

KLM, Khaitan Bhavan, 198 J Tata Rd, Churchgate (☎221185).

Lufthansa, 4th Floor, Express Towers, Nariman Point (☎202 3430).

Pakistan International Airlines, 7 Brabourne Stadium, VN Rd, Churchgate (☎202 1598).

Qantas Airways, 42 Sakhar Bhavan, Nariman Point (☎202 0343).

Royal Nepal Airlines, Sherbanoo, 111 Maharishi Karve Rd (☎206 9365).

Saudia, Ground Floor, Express Towers, Nariman Point (☎202 0181).

Scandinavian Airlines, Ground Floor, Podar House, 10 Marine Drive, Churchgate (☎202 7083).

Swissair, Maker Chamber VI, 220 Nariman Point (☎287 2210).

Syrian Arab Airlines, 7 Stadium House, VN Rd, Churchgate (☎283 2996).

Thai Airways, Ground Floor, Podar House, 10 Marine Drive (☎202 3284).

Domestic Airlines

Indian Airlines, Air India Building, Nariman Point (Mon–Sat 10am–5pm; ☎202 3131); counters at the airport (☎611 6633), and in the receptions of the *Taj* (☎202 3366) and *Centaur Juhu Beach* (☎614 7461) hotels.

Damania, Terminal B, Santa Cruz (☎610 2345).

East-West, 18 New Kantwadi Rd (☎643 6678).

Jet, Amarchand Mansion, Madam Cama Rd (☎285 5788).

Modiluft, 89 Bhulabhai Desai Rd (☎363 1921).

By train

Two main rail networks converge on Bombay: the *Western Railway* runs to north and western India; while the *Central Railway* connects Bombay to central, eastern and southern regions.

Nearly all services to Gujarat, Rajasthan, Delhi and the far north leave from **Bombay Central** station, in the mid-town area. Second-class tickets can be booked here through the normal channels, but the quickest place for foreign nationals to make **reservations** is the efficient tourist counter on the first floor of the *Western Railway*'s main booking hall, opposite Churchgate station (Mon–Fri 9.30am–4.30pm, Sat 9.30am–2.30pm; ☎203 8016 ext 4577). This counter (#22) also has access to special "**tourist quotas**" on certain trains which aren't generally available in other stations. The one catch is that you have to pay in foreign currency (travellers' cheques will do), unless you have a recent encashment certificate. Change is always given in *rupees*. The same applies if you want to buy or book tourist quota tickets with *Indrail* passes. If the quota is "closed" or already used up, and you can't access the "**VIP quota**" (always worth a try), you may have to travel up to Bombay Central yourself to book a ticket.

Bombay's other "Tourist Guide Facility" is located in the snazzy new air-conditioned *Central Railway* booking office (daily 9am–1pm & 1.30–4pm; ☎204 3535) to the rear of **Victoria Terminus**, the departure point for most trains heading east and south. *Indrail* passes can also be bought here, and there's a tourist information kiosk over in the main hall if you need any help filling in your reservation slips.

Just to complicate matters, some *Central Railway* trains to south India, including the fast *Dadar–Madras Chennai Express* #6063 to Madras, do not depart from VT at all, but from **Dadar** station, way north of Bombay Central. Seats and berths for these trains are reserved at VT. Finally, if you're booking tickets to Calcutta, make sure your train doesn't leave from **Kurla** station, which is even more inconvenient, up near the airports. Getting to either of these stations on public transport can be a major struggle.

By bus

The main departure point for long-distance **buses** leaving Bombay is the frenetic **State Transport Terminal** on JB Behram Marg, opposite Bombay Central railway station. State bus companies with counters here (daily 8am–8pm), include Maharashtra, Karnataka, Madhya Pradesh, Goa and Gujarat. Few of their services compare favourably with train travel on the same routes. Reliable timetable information can be difficult to obtain, reservations are not available on standard buses, and most long-haul journeys are gruelling overnighters. Among the exceptions are the **deluxe buses** run by MSRTC to Pune, Nasik and Kolhapur; the small extra cost buys you more leg-room, fewer stops and the option of advance booking. The only problem is, most leave from the **ASIAD** bus stand in Dadar, half an hour or so by road north of Bombay Central.

Other possibilities for road travel include the "super-fast" **luxury coaches** touted around Colaba. Most are run by private companies, guaranteeing breakneck speeds and a constant barrage of noisy Hindi film videos along the way. MTDC and ITDC also operate similarly priced, video-less services to the same destinations, which you can book direct from their main offices downtown or through the more conveniently situated India Government tourist office, 123 M Karve Rd, Churchgate. Two night buses leave Nariman Point every evening for the twelve-hour trip to **Aurangabad** (Rs140), and there are morning departures to **Nasik** (Rs100) and **Mahabaleshwar** (Rs140), which take six and seven hours respectively.

Leaving India

In spite of its prominence on trans-Asian flight routes (as detailed in the box on p.7), Bombay is no longer the bargain basement for **international air tickets** it used to be. Discounted fares are very hard to come by – a legacy of Rajiv Gandhi's economic reforms of the 1980s. If you do need to book a ticket, stick to one of the tried and tested agents listed on p.616.

All the major airlines operating out of Bombay have offices downtown where you can buy scheduled tickets or confirm your flight. The majority are grouped around Veer Nariman Road, opposite the *Ambassador Hotel*, or else on Nariman Point, a short taxi ride west of Colaba.

CHAPTER TEN

MAHARASHTRA

V ast and rugged, the modern state of **MAHARASHTRA**, the third largest in India, was created in 1960, from the Marathi-speaking regions of what was previously Bombay State. As soon as you leave its seething port capital, **Bombay**, developed by Europeans, and now the epitome of modern, cosmopolitan, polyglot India – which as a law unto itself has its own chapter in this book – you enter a different world with a different history.

Undoubtedly, Maharashtra's greatest treasures are its extraordinary **cave temples** and **monasteries**. The finest of all are to be found near **Aurangabad**, renamed for the Moghul emperor Aurangzeb and still home to a sizeable Muslim population (as well as the "poor man's Taj Mahal", Bibi-Ka-Maqbara). The busy commercial city is the obvious base for visits to the caves at **Ajanta**, with their fabulous and still-vibrant murals, and the monolithic temples of **Ellora**, where the Hindu **Kailash temple** may look like a structural building but was carved in its entirety from the rock. From the second century BC, this region was an important centre of Buddhism; artificial caves were excavated to shelter monks, and the finest artists sculpted magnificent cathedral-like halls for congregational worship.

Away from the cities, the most characteristic feature of the landscape is a plenitude of **forts** – as the western borderland between north and south India, Maharashtra's trade routes were always important, but could also bring trouble. **Inland**, parallel to the sea, and never further than 100km from it, the mighty Western Ghats rise abruptly. The areas of level ground that crowned them, endowed with fresh water, were easily converted into forts where small forces could withstand protracted sieges by large armies. Less aggressive modern visitors can scale such windswept fortified heights at Sinhagad, Pratapgarh, and **Daulatabad** – which briefly, bizarrely and disastrously replaced Delhi as capital in the fourteenth century.

During the last century, the mountains found another use. When the summer proved too much for the British in Bombay, they sought refuge in nearby **hill stations**, the most popular of which, such as **Mahabaleshwar**, now serve Indian holidaymakers. **Matheran**, 170km due east, and 800 metres up, has a special attraction, apart from a cool climate, superb views and wooded paths – it is closed to all motorized road traffic. Instead, visitors board a miniature train that scales the hill via 281 curves. Beyond the

Ghats, Maharashtra extends 900km eastwards across the Deccan plateau to the geographical centre of the subcontinent, an area largely populated by tribal groups.

To the west, Maharashtra occupies 500km of the Konkan **coast** on the Arabian Sea, from Gujarat to Goa; travelling has always been circuitous, as the coast winds back and forth with countless inlets, ridges and valleys, again peppered with forts. In the absence of its former seaborne traffic, this region of picturesque ports and deserted beaches cannot provide enough work for its young people, who are forced to move to Bombay, though the imminent advent of the controversial **Konkan Railway**, connecting Bombay with Goa and southern Karnataka, may well open it up to new opportunities. Close to Bombay, sleepy, old-fashioned **Murud-Janjira** has splendid beaches and an extraordinary island fort. More determined travellers with time to zigzag their way around will find more, all the way to Goa; places such as Jaigarh, Ratnagiri, Vijaydurg, Malwan, and Sindhudurg, each with its own history and a battle-scarred fort to prove it.

For all the efforts of the Moghuls, Islam has made little impact on Maharashtra; eighty percent of the population is Hindu. **Nasik**, 187km northeast of Bombay, balances modern industry alongside ancient associations with the *Ramayana*; one of the four sites of the Kumbh Mela, when up to four million devotees bathe in the holy River Godavari, even during less auspicious times it is a magnet for pilgrims. A short distance west, one of India's most sacred Shiva shrines lies close to the source of the Godavari, reached by a short trek from **Trimbak**. In the south lie the Maratha cities of **Pune**, known to many foreigners solely for its connections with the new-age guru, Bhagwan Rajneesh, but still with its thriving old quarter to recommend it, and **Kolhapur**, almost at the Karnataka border, which has retained even more old-fashioned character.

MTDC, the efficient and go-ahead Maharashtra Tourism Development Corporation, are based in Bombay; their main office, on Madam Cama Rd (☎202 7762), can supply

MAHARASHTRA TRAVEL DETAILS

	Trains		Buses		Flights	
	Frequency	Time	Frequency	Time	Frequency	Time
To and From AURANGABAD						
Ahmedabad			1 nightly	14hr		
Ajanta			hourly	3hr		
Bombay	1 daily	10hr	6 nightly	10–12hr	2 daily	40min
Delhi					daily	3hr 30min
Ellora			every 30min	45min		
Indore			2 daily	12hr		
Jaipur					daily	2hr 20min
Jalgaon			hourly	90min		
Nagpur			4 daily	12hr		
Nasik	1 daily	5hr	8 daily	5hr		
Pune			7 daily	5hr		
Udaipur					daily	1hr 5min
To and From JALGAON						
Agra	3–4 daily	14hr 20min–19hr				
Ajanta			hourly	1hr 40min		
Bangalore	Sun only	24hr 25min				
Bhopal	3–4 daily	6hr–9hr 45min				
Bombay	11 daily	8–9hr				
Calcutta	4 daily	29hr–34hr 35min				
Delhi	3 daily	18–25hr				
Gwalior	3–4 daily	13hr				
Jhansi	3–4 daily	9hr 45min–12hr				
Madras	4 weekly	24hr				
Nagpur	5–6 daily	8hr–9hr 45min	1 daily	10hr		
Pune	1 daily	9hr 20min	5 daily	8hr		
Varanasi	4 daily	18hr–22hr 25min				
Wardha	5–7 daily	8hr–9hr 45min				
To and From NAGPUR						
Bhopal	13 daily	6hr 30min–9hr	1 daily	7hr		
Bhubaneshwar					3 weekly	1hr 15min
Bombay	4–5 daily	14hr–17hr 25min			1 daily	1hr 15min
Calcutta	4 daily	19–25hr			3 weekly	2hr 40min
Delhi	9 daily	16hr 25min–22hr				
Hyderabad	2–3 daily	11hr–12hr 35min			3 weekly	1hr 15min
Indore	1 daily	12hr	4 daily	11hr		
Jabalpur	6 weekly	10hr	9 daily	7hr		
Madras	3 daily	17hr 15min–24hr				
Pune	1 daily	18hr 20min	5 daily	16hr		
Ramtek			hourly	1hr 30min		
Varanasi	6 weekly	19hr 30min–22hr				
Wardha			hourly	2hr 30min		
To and From NASIK						
Agra	2–3 daily	17hr 30min–23hr				
Bhopal	3 daily	10–13hr				
Bombay	10–12 daily	4–6hr	6 daily	4hr		
Calcutta	3 daily	32–36hr				
Delhi	2 daily	21–29hr				
Jabalpur	7 daily	14hr 30min				
Nagpur	3 daily	11hr 30min–13hr				
Trimbak			hourly	45min		

To and From PUNE

Ahmedabad	1 weekly	12hr 35min				
Bangalore	1 daily	18hr 10min			3 weekly	45min
Bombay	18 daily	3hr 30min–5hr	hourly	4hr 30min	1–3 daily	35–45min
Delhi	1 daily	27hr 25min			6 weekly	2hr
Goa	2 daily	18hr	4 daily	15hr		
Hyderabad	1 daily	13hr 15min			3 weekly	1hr 30min
Kolhapur	3 daily	9hr	4 daily	12hr		
Madras	1 daily	22hr			3 weekly	3hr
Mahabaleshwar			4 daily	3hr		

For transport connections **from Bombay**, see p.617 onwards.

Note that most individual routes appear only once in this chart; check against where you want to get to as well as where you're coming from.

copious information, while their budget to mid-price hotels offer acceptable accommodation in many out-of-the-way places. Plans to open up the region to foreign visitors include promoting "adventure tourism" by supplying camper buses and drivers.

History

Although some paleolithic remains have been discovered, Maharashtra enters recorded history in the second century BC, with the construction of its first Buddhist caves. These lay, and still lie, in peaceful places of great natural beauty, but could never have been created without the wealth generated by the nearby caravan trade routes between north and south India.

The region's first Hindu rulers, based in Badami, appeared during the sixth century, but the eighth-century Rashtrakutas achieved a greater authority. Buddhism was almost entirely supplanted throughout the entire country by the twelfth century, in what has been characterized as a peaceful popular revolution attributable largely to the popular songs of poet-saints. Maharashtra was one of the main channels that helped the emotional and devotional *bhakti* school of Hinduism spread from southern to northern India, thanks here to the work of Jnanesvara (1271–96) whose commentary on the *Bhagavad Gita*, the *Jnanesvari*, was significantly written in the day-to-day spoken language, Marathi, as opposed to classical Sanskrit. The most famous of his contemporary poet-saints was the tailor Namdev (1270–1350), whose passionate devotional hymns caught the popular imagination. The tradition they established continued to flourish, even when forced underground by Islam, reaching its zenith in the simple faith of the anguished Tukaram (1598–1650), whose wife and son died in a famine, and Ramdas, the "Servant of Rama" (1608–81).

Ramdas, both ascetic and political activist, provided the philosophical underpinning behind the campaigns of Maharashtra's greatest warrior, **Shivaji** (1627–80). The fiercely independent Maratha chieftain united local forces to place insurmountable obstacles in the way of any prospective invader; so effective were their guerrilla tactics that he could even face the mighty Moghuls. Shivaji progressively fought his way northwards, at a time when the Moghuls, who had got as far as capturing Daulatabad in 1633, were preoccupied by family feuds. A year after he succeeded in sacking the great port of Surat (Gujarat), in 1664, he was defeated in battle and imprisoned by Aurangzeb in Agra. He is said to have escaped by hiding in a package which the prison guards imagined was an innocent present intended for local Brahmins; once outside, he simply walked away disguised as a religious mendicant. By the time he died, in 1680, Shivaji had managed to unite the Marathas into a stable and secure state, funded by the plunder gained through guerrilla raids as far afield as Andhra Pradesh.

Back at the Moghul court, the next year, Aurangzeb's son Akbar rebelled briefly against his father, then fled to Maharashtra, where he sought protection from Shivaji's son Shambhuji, before going into exile in Iran. That was the trigger for Aurangzeb to move his operations south; Bijapur (1686) and Golconda (1687) fell, and Shambhuji was captured and summarily executed in 1689. Aurangzeb must have thought that the way was now clear, but the Marathas proved impossible to subdue; he was to spend 25 years in the region, unable to leave, fighting a long series of inconclusive battles until his death at the age of 89. The Marathas had meanwhile become a confederacy whose dominion extended as far east as Orissa; but by the end of the eighteenth century, their power had weakened and the British took full control.

Maharashtra claims a crucial role in the development of a nationalist consciousness. An organization known as the Indian National Union, originally convened in Pune, held a conference in Bombay in 1885 which it named the **Indian National Congress**. This loose aggregate of key figures from local politics around the country was to change the face of Indian politics. At first, its aim was limited to establishing a national platform to raise the status of Indians, and it remained loyal to the British; in the long term, of course, it was instrumental in the achievement of Independence 62 years later. Many of Congress's factional leaders over the years were Maharashtran, notably **GK Gokhale**, and **Bal Gangadhar Tilak** (1856–1920), bitter enemies who were both Brahmins from the same town of Ratnagiri.

With Independence, the Bombay Presidency, to which most of Maharashtra belonged, became known as Bombay State; Maharashtra as such was created in 1960. Its manufacturing industries, centered on Bombay and to a lesser extent cities such as Nagpur, Nasik, Aurangabad, Sholapur and Kolhapur, now represent a quarter of the nation's output. Textiles have long been important, but this is now also the premier region for electronics. However, the majority of Maharashtra's 79 million people are engaged in **agriculture**; main crops include sugarcane, cotton, peanuts, sunflowers, tobacco, pulses, fruit and vegetables. The western edge of the Deccan plateau has uncertain rainfall, and cultivation is concentrated close to rivers, while the southwestern monsoon sometimes halts in the mountains, leaving the rocky land to the east unwatered. Here, farmers rely on hardy staples such as millet and maize.

NORTHERN MAHARASHTRA

Beyond the seemingly endless concrete housing projects, petrochemical works and mosquito-infested swamplands of Greater Bombay, a wall of bare bluish-brown hills dominates the horizon. The **Western Ghats** form a series of huge steps that march from the narrow, humid coastal strip to the edge of the **Deccan** plateau – a vast, dry tableland punctuated with ridges of flat-topped hills and scruffy villages and market towns. **Northern Maharashtra**'s main transport arteries, the NH3 and *Central Railway* line, wind in tandem through this stark landscape, following an ancient trade route that once linked the western ports with the prosperous cities further north. Over the centuries, a number of pilgrimage sites sprang up to take advantage of the lucrative through-traffic, and these form the principal points of interest in the region today.

The holy city of **Nasik** is a handy place to break journeys to or from Bombay, four hours away by road. Amid impressive scenery, 10km west at the start of a steep half-day hike to the source of the sacred River Godavari, the town of **Trimbak**, makes a more relaxing overnight stop. Most foreign visitors, however, head straight for the regional capital, **Aurangabad**, the jumping-off point for the rock-cut **caves** at **Ellora** and **Ajanta**. Among **Muslim monuments** to seek out here are Aurangabad's answer to the Taj Mahal, the **Bibi-Ka-Maqbara**, the dramatic hill-top fort at **Daulatabad**, and the tiny tomb town of **Rauza**, 5km from Ellora, where emperor Aurangzeb is buried.

From Aurangabad, a well-beaten track cuts through the middle of Madhya Pradesh, via **Jalgaon**, towards Varanasi and Nepal. Alternatively, you could head across central India to **Wardha** and **Nagpur**, in the far northeastern corner of the state, where a couple of **Gandhi ashrams**, and the picturesque whitewashed Hindu temple complex at **Ramtek** make pleasant pauses on long cross-country hauls.

Aurangabad

It's easy to see why many travellers regard **AURANGABAD** as little more than a convenient, though largely uninteresting, place in which to kill time on the way to Ellora and Ajanta. First impressions seem to confirm its dull reputation: wide streets, fast traffic, ugly building sites, and gaping patches of urban wasteland merge into a featureless ferro-concrete sprawl. Yet, given a little effort, northern Maharashtra's largest city can yield compensations for its architectural shortcomings. Scattered around its ragged fringes, the dilapidated remains of fortifications, gateways, domes and minarets – including those of the most ambitious Moghul tomb garden in western India, the **Bibi-Ka-Maqbara** – bear witness to an illustrious imperial past; the small but fascinating crop of **rock-cut Buddhist caves**, huddled along the flanks of the flat-topped, sandy yellow hills to the north, are remnants of even more ancient occupation.

The city, originally called **Khadke**, or "Big Rock", was founded in the early sixteenth century by **Malik Amber**, an ex-Abyssinian slave and prime minister of the independent Muslim kingdom of the Nizam Shahis, based at Ahmadnagar, 112km southwest. It was a perfect spot for a provincial capital: on the banks of the **Kham River**, in a broad valley separating the then-forested Sahyadri range to the north from the Satharas to the south, and at a crossroads of the region's key trade routes. Many of the **mosques** and palaces erected by Malik Amber still endure, albeit in ruins.

In 1629, Shah Jahan's redoubtable army swept south across the Deccan to usher in **Moghul** rule. As **Fatehnagar**, Aurangabad became the centre of operations for their protracted military campaign. It really rose to prominence, however, towards the end of the seventeenth century, when **Aurangzeb** decamped here from Delhi to supervise the subjugation of his troublesome enemies in the region. At his behest, the impressive city walls and gates were raised in 1682 to withstand the persistent Maratha attacks that bedevilled his later years. Following his death in 1707, the city – renamed in his honour – changed hands once again. The new rulers, the **Nizam of Hyderabad**, somehow staved off the Marathas for the greater part of 250 years, until the city finally merged with Maharashtra in 1956. Today Aurangabad is one of India's fastest growing commercial and industrial centres, manufacturing anything from pharmaceuticals to auto-rickshaws for a voracious Bombay market. It's a decidely upbeat kind of place, and a peaceful one which, despite the potentially uneasy combination of a local council dominated by the far-right Shiv Sena party, and a sizeable Muslim minority, has avoided the recent communal violence elsewhere in the region.

Arrival and information

Daily flights from Delhi and Bombay arrive at Aurangabad's only **airport**, Chikal Thana, 8km west of the city. Metered taxis and auto-rickshaws are on hand for the trip into town, and courtesy minibuses whisk away guests booked into the nearby five-stars. The mainline **railway station** stands on the southern edge of the city centre, within easy reach of most hotels, and 1500m ride south down Station Road from the **bus stand** – the hectic arrival point for all state, inter-state and private buses.

MTDC have helpful **tourist information** counters at the airport – open at flight times only – and in its *Holiday Resort* hotel (daily 10am–5pm; ☎24713). There's also an excellent government **tourist office** on Station Rd (Mon–Fri 8.30am–6pm, Sat 8.30am–12.30pm; ☎29817). All hand out leaflets on local attractions, and can book you on to their respective **guided tours** of the city and Ellora and Ajanta caves. The Station Rd branch can also arrange approved guides. Their maps, however, aren't up to much.

The most central place to **change money** is the *State Bank of India* (Mon–Fri 10am–2pm, Sat 10am–noon) on Kranti Chowk. The *Ashok* also has a foreign exchange facility, open to non-residents between 5pm and 10pm, and a counter at the aiport opens to coincide with the main flight times. The **GPO**, and efficient poste restante counter, are at Juna Bazaar Chowk, on the north side of the old city. A sealing wax and sewing service is available outside, and stationery is on sale in the shop opposite.

> The telephone **area code** for Aurangabad is ☎02432.

City transport

Most of Aurangabad's sights lie too far apart to take in on foot. The city is, however, buzzing with **auto-rickshaws**, which, on the whole, will happily flag their meters – longer sightseeing trips work out much cheaper if you settle on a fare in advance (taking waiting time into account). **Taxis** hang around outside the five-star hotels, and **cars** (with or without drivers) can be rented through travel agents such as *TPH Tours and Travels* (at the *Rajdhani* hotel); *Budget* (☎84441) and *Hertz* (☎82211) in the lobbies of *Rama* and *Ambassador* hotels; and at the airport. Expect to pay around Rs600 per day, or slightly more if the driver is included.

Much the cheapest and most satisfying way to get around the city, however, is by **bicycle**. While the busy main streets and market can be hair-raising at times, a ride out to the sights in the north of town makes an enjoyable alternative to public transport – although women are rarely, if ever, seen cycling in Aurangabad. Two stalls just up the road from the bus stand have the best bikes, hourly rental, and require no deposit.

Tours

Various companies run daily guided **tours** of the area, all operating to the same itineraries and departure times; only the prices vary. The popular **"Ellora and City"** tour (depart 9.30am, return 6pm; around Rs70) takes in the Bibi-Ka-Maqbara, Panchakki, Daulatabad fort, Aurangzeb's tomb at Rauza, and the Ellora caves (but not the Aurangabad ones), and is ridiculously rushed. The **Ajanta** tour (depart 8am, return 5.30pm; around Rs100) goes to the caves only, and is a long round-trip to make in a day. If you want to spend more time at the site, either stay in Ajanta or Fardapur (see p.651), or travel on to Jalgaon (see p.652).

The departure point for the ITDC tour is the *Ashok Hotel* (book in advance from the tourist office on Station Rd, or *Ashok Tours and Travel* in the hotel lobby); MTDC leave from outside the *Holiday Resort*, and the (cheaper) *State Transport Corporation* tours start at the railway station (book at the ticket office at the city bus stand).

The City

Captains of industry and five-star hotels may have surplanted Moghul emperors and palaces, but Aurangabad has retained much of its Islamic feel. Head for the Muslim quarter around the **Chowk** area of the city and you'll see women veiled in long black *burkhas*, as well as **mosques** that continue to draw large crowds on Fridays. The old walled city, laid out on a grid by Malik Amber in the sixteenth century, still forms the

AURANGABAD

N

△ Bibi-Ka-Maqbara & Aurangabad Caves   △ Ajanta, Jalgaon & Taj Hotel

Delhi Gate

Shivaji Maidan

KILA ARAK

Makai Gate

Jama Masjid

Town Hall

Purwar Museum

Dargah & Pan Chakki

Juna Bazaar Chowk

GPO

B A Z A A R

Shah Ganj Masjid

Police Station

Bicycle Rental

Weekly Market Ground

Bicycle Rental

Gulmandi Square

Bus Stand Ⓐ

Paithan Gate

DR AMBEDKAR RD

Kham River

△ Ellora, Rauza & Daulatabad

Ⓑ
②
Ⓒ
Ⓓ
Ⓖ
Ⓗ

Indian Airlines Office

Ⓔ

DR RAJENDRA PRASAD MARG

State Bank

Kranti Chowk

JALNA RD

P NEHRU MARG

Ⓕ

③

①

▷ Ajanta Ambassador & Rama International Hotels & Airport

STATION RD

Ⓙ
ⓘ
Ⓚ
Ⓛ
ⓘ
Ⓝ
Ⓞ
Ⓜ

Ⓟ

⑤ ④
①

STATION RD

Railway Station

RESTAURANTS:
① Agran Mistan
② Foodwala's Bhoj
③ Mingling
④ Rajdhika
⑤ Chanakya
⑥ Foodwala's Tandoori

HOTELS:
Ⓐ Green Palace
Ⓑ Devpriya
Ⓒ Printravel
Ⓓ Raviraj
Ⓔ ITDC Aurangabad Ashok
Ⓕ Amarpreet
Ⓖ Youth Hostel
Ⓗ Panchavati
ⓘ Rajdhani
Ⓙ Ashiyana
Ⓚ Tourist Home
Ⓛ Natraj
Ⓜ Vedant
Ⓝ MTDC Holiday Resort
Ⓞ Great Punjab
Ⓟ New Punjab

0 ———— 500 m

▽ Paithon

core of Aurangabad's large **bazaar** area. It's best approached via **Gulmandi Square** to the south, along any of several streets lined with colourful shops and stalls. The bazaar lacks the character and intensity of those in larger Indian cities, but has a pleasant, workaday feel, and you'll not be approached by too many zealous salesmen.

Keep walking north, and you'll come out at a chaotic east–west thoroughfare. Close by, in a tiny backroom behind a shop on the north side of the main street, 100m east of the busy Chowk crossroads, stands the **Purwar Museum**. This private collection of antiquities boasts a seventeenth-century Koran handpainted by Aurangzeb, superb **bronzes**, and a host of other wonderful objects accumulated by a retired doctor. At present, only a small part of his hoard is housed here, but if you have a specialist interest the proprietor, Mr Purwar, will do his best to fetch pieces from other caches in town. Look for the sign above a doorway, and ask at the handicraft shop next door to be let in.

The unremarkable (*c.* 1720) **Shah Ganj Masjid** mosque that presides over the nearby main square is surrounded on three sides by small shops and a congested roundabout-cum-racetrack. Anyone keen to see other remnants of Aurangabad's Moghul splendour should make for the city's largest and most impressive mosque, the **Jama Masjid**, 1km north. The present building is considerably older than its recent coat of pale-purple colourwash suggests; it's really an amalgam of parts begun by Malik Amber in 1612 and added to by Aurangzeb nearly a century later.

The ruins of Aurangzeb's former imperial headquarters, the **Kila Arak**, lie across the road from the Jama Masjid, scattered around a boulder-strewn wasteland. Once this complex of palaces, battlements, gateways, tanks and gardens stretched all the way from Delhi Gate in the northeast of the city, to Mecca Gate on the west side of the river, and housed three princes and a retinue of thousands. Sadly, precious little of it is left, and only die-hard rubble fans are likely to enjoy a visit.

Finally, every Thursday, an excellent **weekly market** is held just west of the bus stand. Villagers from outlying areas pour in all morning on bullock-carts, the women to set up eye-catching vegetable and spice stalls, the men to stand around in their best *dhotis* and Nehru caps while goats and glistening buffalo are put through their paces in the auction. The market gets into its stride around noon, winding up at about 5pm.

The Dargah and Pan Chakki

On the left bank of the River Kham, near Begampura Bridge, the **Dargah of Baba Shah Muzaffar** is a religious compound built by Aurangzeb as a memorial to his spiritual mentor, a *chisti* mystic. The principal point of interest is not so much the mosque, the modest tomb or ornamental gardens nearby, pleasant though these are, as the unusual adjoining **watermill** known as the **Pan Chakki**. Water pumped underground from a reservoir in the hills 6km away collects in a tank, now teeming with enormous *khol* fish, to drive a small grindstone once used to mill flour for the members of the *madrasa*, or theological college, next door. Directly beneath the fish tank, sealed behind a wall at ground level by the river, is a large assembly hall supported by four rows of enormous pillars. The whole complex was an impressive engineering feat for its time, although visitors from wetter climes may regard Pan Chakki's charms with rather less enthusiasm than the water-crazy locals.

HIMROO

Marco Polo wrote of some fabric he was given in the Deccan region that it was "as fine as a spider's web, and Kings and Queens of any country will take pride in wearing it". The material in question could well have been woven in Aurangabad. Since well before the arrival of the Muslims in the thirteenth century, the region's weavers have skilfully combined local silk with gold thread to produce some of the most opulent and sought-after brocades in India. However, following the decline in the city's fortunes after the departure of the Moghuls few could afford this extravagant mixture, or **kamkhab**. Cotton was therefore blended with silk to create a cheaper alternative – **Himroo**, literally "similar".

At one time Aurangabad held hundreds of Himroo handlooms. Today, only one family continues to produce the fabric in the traditional way. You can see them in action on their special double-sided looms in a tiny **factory** buried deep in the narrow back-streets of the Nawabpura district, north of Shah Ganj. It's not easy to find, but the rickshaw *wallahs* know the way. If you feel like buying some fabric as a souvenir (not an obligation), the weavers keep a counter stocked with shawls for sale at fixed prices.

The Bibi-Ka-Maqbara

Were it not so flagrantly a (cheap) imitation of the Taj, Aurangabad's much maligned Moghul tomb-garden would probably attract a great many more admirers. In spite of being one of India's most impressive Islamic monuments, however, the **Bibi-Ka-Maqbara** (daily 8am–8pm; Rs 1) is widely regarded as the definitive "also ran".

The mausoleum, completed in 1678, was dedicated to the memory of **Begum Rabi'a Daurani**, Aurangzeb's wife, by her son **Prince Azam Shah**. Originally intended by its designers to rival the Taj Mahal, lack of resources dogged the 25-year project, and the end result fell far short of expectations. The entrance to the complex is through an enormous brass-inlaid **door**, decorated with an elaborate geometric pattern said to be of Persian origin. An inscription around its edge names the maker, the year of its installation and the chief architect, **Ata Ullah**. Looking at the mausoleum from beyond the ornamental gardens and redundant fountains in front of it, you can see why commentators have been so ungenerous. The truncated minarets and ungainly entrance arch make the Bibi-Ka-Maqbara seem squat and ill-proportioned compared with the elegant height and symmetry of the Taj. The impression is not enhanced by the abrupt discontinuation of marble after the first 2m – a cost-saving measure.

Of the two entrances to the main tomb, one provides access to the inner balcony while the second leads down through another beautiful door to the **vault** itself (since a suicidal student jumped from a minaret, visitors may no longer climb them). Be sure to remove your shoes at the steps. Inside, an exquisite octagonal **lattice-screen** of white marble surrounds the raised plinth supporting Rabi'a Daurani's grave – like her husband's in nearby Rauza, "open" as a sign of humility. The unmarked grave beside it is said to be that of the empress' nurse. Through a slanted window on the back wall, the rays of the rising sun illuminate the tomb for three minutes each morning.

The caves

Carved out of a steep-sided spur of the Sahyadri range, directly overlooking the Bibi-Ka-Maqbara, Aurangabad's own **caves** bear no comparison to their cousins in nearby Ellora and Ajanta, but their fine **sculpture** makes a worthwhile introduction to rock-cut architecture. In addition, the infrequently visited site is peaceful and pleasant in itself, with commanding views over the city and surrounding countryside.

The caves themselves, all Buddhist, consist of two groups, eastern and western, numbered 1 to 9 by the ASI. The majority were excavated between the fourth and eighth centuries, under the patronage of two successive dynasties: the **Vakatkas**, who ruled the western Deccan from Nasik, and the **Chalukyas**, a powerful Mysore family who emerged during the sixth century. All except the much earlier cave 4, which is a *chaitya* hall, are of the *vihara* type, belonging to the Mahayana school of Buddhism.

Unless you cycle, the only practical way of **getting to the caves** is by auto-rickshaw or taxi; you'll be expected to shell out for waiting time, or the return fare. You could also, drop down on foot to the Bibi-Ka-Maqbara to pick up a scooter back into town.

The western group

The **western**, and oldest, group of caves is reached via a long flight of steps leading left off the main road. The first of interest, **Cave 2**, is a sixth-century *vihara*, with a columned verandah and a doorway flanked by two *bodhisattvas*. Inside, a small shrine containing a seated Buddha is surrounded by an unusual passage. **Cave 3** is a remarkably elaborate seventh-century *vihara*. Its most vivid friezes, depicting scenes from the lives of the Buddha, adorn the stone "beams" above the pillars in the main chamber.

Cave 4, the oldest at Aurangabad, may date from the first century AD, and is the only representative of the earlier and more austere Hinayana phase of architecture.

Unlike its neighbours, the cave is a rectangular apsidal-ended *chaitya* hall, with a mono-lithic *stupa* as its focal point. The characteristic timber-style ceiling is thought to have been an imitation of earlier free-standing wooden structures.

The eastern group

If you only have time to visit one group, it should be the **eastern**, 1km further along the hillside. **Cave 6** contains some finely carved *bodhisattvas*, together with traces of painting on the ceiling of its porch, but the sculpture in **cave 7** is the real highlight. Its verandah has columned shrines to either side, with a lotus-holding Padmapani (surrounded by six goddesses) and Shakyamuni to the left; Panchika (guardian of the earth's treasures) and Hariti (goddess of prosperity) stand to the right. The panel on the left of the doorway shows the *bodhisattva* Avalokitesvara (lord of compassion) encircled by the eight mortal fears: fire, the sword, chains (imprisonment), shipwreck, lions, snakes, rampant elephants and the Demon of Death. Nearby, a couple of heavy-breasted *tara* figures bear witness to the increasing preoccupation with female creative energy – *shakti* – cults during the latter part of the Buddhist epoch. Finally, to the left of the preaching Buddha in the sanctuary is Aurangabad's most celebrated panel: a frieze showing a dancer in a classical pose accompanied by six female musicians.

A small unnumbered cave next to cave 6 has intrigued archeologists since its redis-covery in 1961. Unusually, the central deity here is the Hindu god **Ganesh**, while on the mural to its right an image of the Buddha provides graphic evidence of the overlap of Buddhism and Brahmanism in the eighth century.

Accommodation

Aurangabad's proximity to some of India's most important monuments, together with its new "boom-city" status, ensures a profusion of **hotels**. On the whole, standards tend to be high and prices very reasonable, particularly in the **budget** places, most of which are strung along the road between the bus stand and the train station, and range from extremely basic Indian lodges to more pleasant travellers' hostels. All have 24-hour check-out unless otherwise stated. All the hotels in our "moderate to expensive" cate-gory, have noon check-out times, some a/c rooms, and charge luxury tax.

Inexpensive

Devpriya, near Sidharth Gardens, Bus Stand Rd (☎27558). Neat, clean and efficiently run family hotel. Doubles are good value, and there's a (reputable) massage parlour and steam bath. ②.

Green Palace, opposite the bus stand (☎29501). Spartan but clean. Handy if you've just crawled off a bus and can't face a room hunt. ②.

Natraj, Station Rd (☎24260). Very traditional lodge run by two elderly Gujarati brothers. Spacious, clean, good-value rooms with shared bathrooms. No left luggage, and strictly no alcohol. ①.

New Punjab, opposite the train station (☎21391). A large, functional though clean lodge with good-sized rooms, some with attached baths. Mostly men. ①.

Panchavati, Padampura, off Station Rd (☎28755). In a similar vein to the *New Punjab*, though with a popular restaurant. A convenient option if the nearby *Youth Hostel* is full. ①–②.

Tourist Home, Station Rd (☎24212). Congenial travellers' hostel with neat rooms, attached shower-toilet, and a sociable terrace where evening *thalis* are served. Excellent value. ①.

Youth Hostel, Padampura, off Station Rd (☎29801). Segregated dorms, and reasonable private rooms, often booked in advance. Full board too. The cheapest option in town. Check-out 9am. ①.

Moderate to expensive

Amarpreet, P Nehru Marg (☎24615; fax 02438/2792). Central, well-appointed Punjabi-run hotel on airport road. Two restaurants, coffee shop, bar and foreign exchange. Some non-a/c rooms. ④/⑥.

Ambassador Ajanta, Chikalthana (☎82211; fax 84367). Luxurious five-star near the airport, with over-the-top ersatz traditional interior. Excellent sports facilities. ⑧.

Ashiyana, Bansilal Nagar (☎29322). Immaculate if unexciting new hotel just off Station Rd, near the tourist office. Peaceful and good value. ③.

Great Punjab, Station Rd (☎21388). Brand-new business-oriented hotel very near the train station. All 42 rooms have bathrooms, balconies and TVs. Bland but very good value. ③.

ITDC Aurangabad Ashok, Dr Rajendra Prasad Rd (☎24520). Austere building in its own gardens. Pool, shops, travel counter, bar and 24hr coffee shop. Popular with western tour groups. ⑦.

MTDC Holiday Resort, Station Rd (☎23298). Spacious, comfortable rooms, if a tad shabby. Mosquito nets over beds. Good restaurant and garden. ④.

Printravel, Station Rd (☎29707). Faintly 1950s-style building near city centre. Common balcony with easy chairs and a good restaurant. Huge rooms (some a/c). ③.

Rajdhani, Railway Station Rd (☎27562). Comfortable but rather pricey, with room service, *Star TV* and carpets. Some a/c. ⑤.

Rama International, Chikalthana (☎82241). *Welcomgroup*'s plush five-star, near the airport, with absolutely all the trimmings including shopping arcades, tennis courts and acres of marble. ⑧.

Raviraj, Dr Rajendra Prasad Rd (☎27501). Classy, central chain hotel, with all amenities. ⑤.

Vedant, Station Rd (☎24329). A newly-opened American-style four-star with palatial lobby, 24hr coffee shop, beauty parlour, gym and pool. Very central. ⑦.

Eating and drinking

Food in Aurangabad tends to be an incongruous mixture of strictly vegetarian **Gujarati** and meat-centered Muslim dishes. Typically, "non-veg" is synonymous with dim lights, drawn curtains and a male clientele, while the veg restaurants attract families, and are particulary popular on Sunday evenings, when booking is recommended. Aurangabad has a conservative attitude to **alcohol**; on the whole, drinking is a male preserve, carried out in specially segregated bars (or **permit rooms**), with the exception of the larger and more tourist-oriented hotels and restaurants.

Agran Mistan, Aurangpura. Clean, no-nonsense restaurant on the southern edge of the old town, serving authentic Gujarati food, mainly to visiting business people. Moderate.

Chanakya, Dwarkapuri Rd. A big hit with the city's nouveau riche. Pretentious, but the food is excellent. Veg and non-veg (including fish) and alcohol served al fresco (bring mosquito repellent).

MOVING ON FROM AURANGABAD

Daily **flights** from Aurangabad to **Bombay** (40min) are operated by *Indian Airlines* (10am) and *East-West* (7.30pm). *Indian Airlines* also fly daily to **Delhi** (9.15am), calling at **Udaipur**, and **Jaipur**. Their office is on Jalna Rd (☎24864).

Both the state transport corporation (*MSRTC*; ☎23247) and MTDC run good-value "luxury" night-**buses** to **Bombay** (Rs120). If you feel like a little more comfort, the *Royal Coach Company* also has an a/c coach; tickets, booked through *Gulliver's Travels* on Adalat Rd (☎24151), cost Rs150. Getting to **Pune** is easy, on *MSRTC*'s "express" buses (7 daily; 5hr; the 7.30am bus is the only morning one). **Nasik** buses are less frequent (5 daily; 3hr). Both *MSRTC* and *Royal* run buses to **Indore**, one at 5.30am, the other at 9pm. Anyone heading up to **Udaipur** will need to take this, the first of two arduous twelve-hour journeys. The *MSRTC* bus to **Ahmedabad** is another gruelling overnighter.

Trains to and from Aurangabad are very limited, as the city is not on the main line. The one useful service is the heavily booked direct express #1003 to **Bombay**, which leaves at 7.30pm, arriving at VT ten hours later. Otherwise, the nearest mainline station, at **Jalgaon**, 108km north, is served by trains to Delhi, Agra, Bhopal, Calcutta, Madras, Secunderabad, and Udaipur and Varanasi. For **train enquiries**, call ☎24515.

Foodwala's Bhoj, near Baba Petrol Pump. An old favourite, pure-veg restaurant at shiny new premises. Renowned for its meticulously prepared, good-value lunchtime Gujarati *thalis*. Moderate.

Foodwala's Tandoori, Shyam Chambers, Station Rd. Upmarket a/c bar-restaurant with numerous à la carte chicken and mutton dishes. Pricey but worth it.

Kailash, MTDC *Holiday Resort*. Standard veg and non-veg menu, with some Indian-style Chinese. Generous portions at reasonable prices.

Mingling, *Rajdoot Hotel*, Jalna Rd. Best Chinese in town, though a tad ostentatious and over-priced.

Panchavati, Padampur, off Station Rd. Cheap, spicy food in "non-veg" atmosphere. Good value.

Radhika, *Hotel Nandanvan*. Justly popular, serving large selection of inexpensive veg dishes (mainly south Indian) in garden. *Rathi* next door is equally good non-veg version, with cold beer, but dingy surroundings. Both are excellent value.

Daulatabad

Northwest of Aurangabad, the main Ellora road runs through fertile Deccani farmland punctuated by the occasional red-brick village or Muslim tomb crumbling in shady evergreen glades. Looming on the horizon of this serene and prosperous countryside is the stark profile of one of India's most imposing fortresses. Invading armies must have stopped dead when confronted with **DAULATABAD**, 13km northwest of Aurangabad. The awesome hill-top citadel crowns a massive conical volcanic outcrop whose sides have been shaped into a sheer sixty-metre wall of granite. The fort's forbidding appearance is further accentuated by the slender victory **minaret** rising out of the ruins of the city that once sprawled from its base, like a pink finger in the face of the approaching enemy. If only for the panoramic **views** from its summit, Daulatabad makes an excellent pause en route to or from the caves at Ellora, 17km northwest.

Aside from the inevitable Buddhist and Jain hermits, occupation of the site – then known as **Deogiri**, "Hill of the Gods" – dates from its ninth-century role as bastion and capital of a confederacy of Hindu tribes. The **Yadavas** were responsible for scraping away the jagged lower slopes of the mount to form its vertical-cliff base, as well as the fifteen-metre deep moat that still encircles the upper portion of the citadel. Their prosperity eventually aroused the interest of the acquisitive Delhi Sultans, who stormed the fortress in 1294 and carried off a raja's ransom in gold, silver and precious stones.

Muslim occupation of Deogiri, however, began in earnest with the arrival in 1327 of Ghiyas-ud-din **Tughluq**. Convinced that the fort was the perfect base for campaigns further south, the Sultan decreed that his entire court should decamp here from Tughluqabad, the "third city" of Delhi (see p.73). The epic 1100-kilometre march cost thousands of lives, the Sultan's underfed and exhausted subjects dropping like flies by the wayside. Life in the new capital – which Tughluq prematurely renamed Daulatabad, or "Abode of Good Fortune" – was not much of an improvement. Within seventeen years, drought, famine and the growing threat of a full-scale Moghul invasion on his northern borders forced the beleaguered ruler to concede defeat and return to

Tughluqabad. His audacious governor, Zafar Khan, seized the moment, and in 1327 mounted a rebellion to establish the **Bahmani** dynasty. Thereafter, the fortress fell to a succession of different regimes, including Shah Jahan's **Moghuls** in 1633, before it was finally taken by the **Marathas** midway through the eighteenth century.

The fortress

Daulatabad's labyrinthine **fortress** incorporates so many ingenious ways to snuff out unwanted intruders that it's almost inconceivable anyone ever managed to penetrate the formidable outer defences, let alone fight their way up the 183 metres of ramparts, moats and dark passages to the citadel at the top. The tone is set by the vicious, elephant-proof spikes that stick menacingly out of the main gates. Once inside, three **cannons** (two Persian and one Dutch – look for the engraving of a European sailing ship) lie discarded in the first of several claustrophobic courtyards – reminders of the aerial bombardment which by this stage would have been raining down upon the attackers. The proud **Chandminar**, or "Victory Tower", further along, was more of a psychological than a military deterrent. Soaring above the heart of the old town, of which only the scantest traces now remain, the majestic pink minaret was erected by Ala-ud-din Bahmani to celebrate his conquest of the fort in 1435. The Persian blue and turquoise tiles that once plastered it in complex geometric patterns have disappeared.

The **Jama Masjid**, directly opposite the Chandminar, is Daulatabad's oldest Islamic monument. Built by the Delhi Sultans in 1318, to chastise Deogiri's Hindu occupants for their refusal to pay annual tribute, the well-preserved mosque comprises 106 pillars plundered from the Hindu and Jain temples which previously stood on the site. Recently, the *masjid* was converted into a Bharatmata temple – much to the chagrin of local Muslims. Nearby, the large stone-lined "Elephant" **tank** was once a central component in the fort's extensive water-supply system. Two giant terracotta pipes channelled water from the hills into the Deogiri's legendary fruit and vegetable gardens.

Once beyond the open ground surrounding the tower, the main walkway heads through a series of interlocking bastions, fortified walls, moats and drawbridges before emerging from under the third gateway to the **Chini Mahal**, or "Chinese Palace", where the last Galconda ruler Abdul Hasan Tana Shah was imprisoned in 1687 by the Moghul emperor Aurangzeb. Following thirteen years of torture at the hands of his sadistic captors, Tana Shah is said to have begged, of all things, for a pot of curd which, once eaten, caused his head to explode. His corpse was then dragged behind an elephant to Rauza where it was finally entombed. The impressive ram-headed **Kila Shikan** ("Fort Breaker") cannon, inscribed with its name in Persian, rests on a stone platform nearby. From here onwards, a sequence of macabre traps lay in wait for the unwary intruder. First, a moat infested with man-eating crocodiles had to be crossed in order to reach the foot of the citadel, or **Bala Kot**. Next, the attackers had to crawl through a maze of pitch-black passageways cut from the fort's solid-rock foundations. At one point, these fork and rejoin again to dupe enemy soldiers into fighting each other in the darkness. If they survived that ruse, the suffocating toxic fumes emanating from the red-hot iron cover that sealed the only exit to the underground tunnel would probably finish them off. Their bodies would then be dumped down the slanting chutes in the side-walls, to be devoured by the voracious crocs waiting in the moat below.

At the end of the tunnel, a broad flight of rock-cut steps climbs to an attractive twelve-pillared pavilion. The **Baradi** is thought to have been the residence of a Yadavi queen, though it was later used by emperor Shah Jahan during his visits to Daulatabad. The **views** from the flat roof of the building are superb. Note the tombs clinging to the foot of the barren brown hills to the east, and the street plan of the old town below, just discernible through the rubble-strewn wasteground beside the Jama Masjid. An even more impressive panorama is to be had from the **look-out post** perched on the summit of the hill, where you'll find another old cannon (the "Storm Creator") and an ancient rock-cut cave, home during the Moghul period to a renowned Hindu ascetic.

Practicalities

Although Daulatabad features on the MTDC guided **tour** of Ellora from Aurangabad (see p.628), you'll have more time to enjoy it if you travel there on one of the hourly shuttle **buses** between Aurangabad and the caves. The stop is directly opposite the main entrance to the fort, beside the string of *chai* and souvenir stalls and the good, small MTDC-run **restaurant**. Daulatabad holds no **accommodation** for visitors.

Rauza

As the silhouette of Daulatabad fort recedes into the haze on the horizon, the Ellora–Aurangabad road climbs a sun-bleached ridge of hills known as **Peepal Ghat**. Nestled on this saddle of high ground, 22km from Aurangabad and a five-kilometre ride from the caves, **RAUZA** is an old walled town famous for a bumper crop of tumbledown onion-domed **tombs**. Among the Muslim notables deemed worthy of a patch of earth in this most hallowed of burial grounds, also known as "**Khauldabad**" or "Heavenly Abode", were the emperor Aurangzeb, a couple of Nizams, and a fair few of the town's *chisti* founding fathers – the seven hundred mystic missionaries dispatched by the saint Nizam-ud-din Aulia to soften up local Hindus ahead of the Sultanate's invasion in the fourteenth century. Rauza's monuments are nowhere near as impressive as those in Delhi or Agra, but a couple harbour important **relics** and are still venerated for their miraculous properties. While they see a steady trickle of visitors, and even large crowds on festival days, the lesser mausoleums on the outskirts of the sleepy Muslim town lie deserted and all but forgotten, their old stone pavilions, bulbous domes and walled enclosures choked with weeds and grazed by herds of scruffy goats.

The Dargah of Sayeed Zain-ud-din

Rauza is encircled by tall granite battlements and seven fortified **gateways** raised by Aurangzeb before his death in 1707. The last of the great Moghuls is buried inside the town's most famous **dargah**, or shrine-tomb, midway between the North and South gates. Steps lead up from the main thoroughfare through a domed porch into a peaceful courtyard surrounded by whitewashed cloisters and minarets. **Aurangzeb's tomb** lies under the arch to the left. In keeping with the teachings of Islam, the grave itself is a humble affair, open to the elements instead of sealed in stone. The devout emperor insisted that it be paid for not out of the royal coffers, but with the money he had raised in the last years of his life by selling his own hand-quilted white skull-caps. The pierced-marble **screen** and walls that now surround the spot were erected much later by the British Viceroy, Lord Curzon, and the Nizam of Hyderabad.

Aurangzeb chose this as his final resting place primarily because of the presence, next door, of Sayeed **Zain-ud-din**'s tomb. The mausoleum of the Muslim saint, or *pir*, occupies a quadrangle separating Aurangzeb's grave from those of his wife and second son, Azam Shah. Its doors are beautifully inlaid with slabs of silver, brass and bronze, while the steps leading to it are encrusted with highly polished semi-precious stones donated by the wandering Muslim ascetics, or *fakirs*, who formerly came here on pilgrimages. Locked away behind a small door is Rauza's most jealously guarded relic. The **Robe of the Prophet** is revealed to the public once a year, on the twelfth day of the Islamic month of Rabi-ul-Awwal (usually around November), when the tomb becomes the focus of a festival attracting crowds of worshippers from all over India.

The other buildings in this *dargah* are a small **mosque** (on the west side of the main courtyard) and the **Nakkar Khanna**, or Music Hall, which, on high days and holy days, hosts performances of *qawwali*.

The Dargah of Sayeed Burhan-ud-din

Directly opposite Zain-ud-din's tomb is the **Dargah of Sayeed Burhan-ud-din**, a *chisti* missionary buried here in 1334. The shrine is said to contain hairs from the Prophet's beard which magically increase in number when they are counted each year. At the end of the fourteenth century, when a cash crisis had left the saint's disciples unable to provide for either themselves or the upkeep of the beloved *dargah*, a pair of "**silver trees**" miraculously sprouted in its central courtyard. These days, the only precious metal to be found in the tomb are the panels set into the doors of the shrine, although for a small donation the attendant will point out the two innocuous-looking lumps in the pavement nearby where the fabled trees once stood, and which are still said to secrete the odd drop of silver.

Around the town

Most of the other tombs on the outskirts of Rauza are difficult to locate without the help of a rickshaw *wallah*. Half a kilometre west of the two main *dargahs*, you'll find the *maqbara* of **Bani Begum**, the mistress of one of Aurangzeb's sons. This large walled garden tomb encloses some well-preserved Moghul-domed pavilions, pillars and arches set amid balding lawns and flower beds. The *dargah* of the Abyssinian ex-slave and founder of Aurangabad, **Malik Ambar**, is tucked away to the northwest, close to the whitewashed tomb of **Abdul Hasan Tana Shah**, the unfortunate ruler of Galconda who died after thirteen years of incarceration inside Daulatabad fort.

On the road down to the Ellora caves, you pass one of Rauza's few empty tombs. Commissioned by a foreign ambassador who fell ill here in the eighteenth century, this modest mausoleum was never occupied. Shortly after it was completed, the diplomat recovered from his supposdly terminal illness and limped home to Persia, where he eventually died, leaving his tomb to lie forever idle on this peaceful, west-facing ridge.

Practicalities

MSRTC **buses** pull in every half-hour or so at Rauza's small bus stand, a short walk west of the walls, en route between Aurangabad and the Ellora caves just down the hill. The only **place to stay** nearby is the *Government Rest House* (③) – a wonderful *dak* bungalow converted by the British from the tomb of Nizam Shah Bhairi. Rooms are reserved for government servants or guests, and normally booked up well in advance, but there's no harm in trying to persuade the *chowkidar* to squeeze you in if he has a vacancy. If the prospect of **eating** in one of the insanitary sweet shops and *chai* stalls in Rauza's main bazaar doesn't appeal, you'll have to wait until you get to Ellora.

Ellora

> *Palaces will decay, bridges will fall, and the noblest structures must give way to the corroding tooth of time; whilst the caverned temples of Ellora shall rear their indestructible and hoary heads in stern loneliness, the glory of past ages, and the admiration of ages yet to come.*
> Captain Seely, *The Wonders of Ellora*

Maharashtra's most visited ancient monument, the **ELLORA caves**, 29km northwest of Aurangabad, may not enjoy as grand a setting as their elder cousins at Ajanta (see p.645), but the amazing wealth of **sculpture** they contain more than compensates, and this is an unmissable port of call if you're heading to or from Bombay 400km south-west. In all, thirty-four Buddhist, Hindu and Jain caves – some excavated simultaneously, in competition – line the foot of the two-kilometre-long Chamadiri escarpment as it tumbles down to meet the open plains. The site's principal attraction, the gargantuan **Kailash temple**, rears from a huge, sheer-sided cavity cut from the hillside. The world's largest monolith, this vast lump of solid basalt is fashioned into a spectacular agglomeration of interconnecting colonnaded halls, galleries, and sacred shrines.

The original reason why this apparently remote spot became the focus of so much religious and artistic activity was the busy **caravan route** that cut through here on its way between the prosperous cities to the north and the ports of the west coast. Profits from the lucrative overland trade fuelled a five-hundred-year spate of excavation, beginning midway through the sixth century AD at around the same time that Ajanta, 100km northeast, was abandoned. This was the twilight of the Buddhist era in central India; by the end of the seventh century, **Hinduism** had begun to reassert itself. The Brahmanical resurgence gathered momentum over the next three hundred years under the patronage of the Chalukya and Rashtrakuta kings – the two powerful dynasties responsible for the bulk of the work carried out at Ellora, including the eighth-century Kailash temple. A third and final flourish of activity on the site took place towards the end of the first millennium AD, after the local rulers had switched allegiances from Shaivism to the Digambara sect of the **Jain** faith. A small cluster of more subdued caves to the north of the main group stand as reminders of this age.

Unlike the isolated site of Ajanta, Ellora did not escape the iconoclasm that accompanied the arrival of the **Muslims** in the thirteenth century. The worst excesses were committed during the reign of **Aurangzeb** who, in a fit of piety, ordered the systematic destruction of the site's "heathen idols". Although Ellora still bears the scars from this time, most of its best pieces of sculpture have remained miraculously intact. The fact that they were cut from hard rock, beyond the reach of the monsoon downpours, has preserved the caves in remarkable condition.

The caves

All the **caves** are numbered, following a roughly chronological plan. Numbers 1 to 12, at the south end of the site, are the oldest, from the Vajrayana Buddhist era (500–750 AD). The Hindu caves, 17 to 29, overlap with the later Buddhist ones and date from between 600 and 870 AD. Further north, the Jain caves – 30 to 34 – were excavated from 800 AD until the late eleventh century. Because of the sloping hillside, most of the cave entrances are set back from the level ground behind open courtyards and large colonnaded verandahs or porches. **Admission** to all but the Kailash temple is free.

To see the oldest caves first, turn right from the car park where the buses pull in and follow the main pathway down to cave 1. From here, work your way gradually northwards again, avoiding the temptation to look around cave 16, the Kailash temple, which is best saved until late afternoon when the bus parties have all left, and the long shadows cast by the setting sun bring its extraordinary stonework to life.

The Buddhist group

The **Buddhist caves** line the sides of a gentle recess in the Chamadiri escarpment. All except number 10 are *viharas*, or monastery-halls, which the monks would originally have used for study, solitary meditation and communal worship, as well as the mundane business of eating and sleeping. As you progress through them, notice how the chambers grow steadily more impressive in scale and tone. Scholars attribute this to the rise of Hinduism and the need to compete for patronage with the more overtly awe-inspiring Shaivite cave-temples being excavated so close at hand.

ROCK-CUT CAVES OF THE NORTHWESTERN DECCAN

The **rock-cut caves** scattered across the volcanic hills of the northwestern Deccan rank among the most extraordinary religious monuments in Asia, if not the world. Ranging from tiny monastic cells to colossal, elaborately carved temples, they are remarkable for having been hewn by hand from solid rock. Their third-century BC origins seem to have been as temporary shelters for Buddhist monks when heavy monsoon rains made their normal itinerant lifestyle impossible. Modelled on earlier wooden structures, most were sponsored by **merchants**, for whom the casteless new faith offered an attractive alternative to the old, discriminatory social order. Gradually, encouraged by the example of the Mauryan emperor Ashok, the local ruling dynasties also began to embrace Buddhism. Under their patronage, during the second century BC, the first large-scale monastery-caves were created at **Karle, Bhaja** and **Ajanta**.

Around this time, the austere **Hinayana**, or "Lesser Vehicle", school of Buddhism predominated in India. In keeping with the original teachings of the Buddha, closed communities of monks had little or no interaction with the outside world. Caves cut in this era were mostly simple "worship halls", or **chaityas** – long, rectangular apsed chambers with barrel-vaulted roofs, and two narrow colonnaded aisles curving gently around the back of a monolithic **stupa** (see p.336). Symbols of the Buddha's Enlightenment, these hemispherical burial mounds provided the principal focus for worship and meditation, circumambulated by the monks during their communal rituals.

The **methods** employed to excavate the caves altered little over the centuries. First, the basic dimensions of the ornamental facade were sketched onto the cliff face. Next, gangs of stonemasons hacked out a rough hole (later to become the *chaitya's* graceful horseshoe-shaped window), through which they chiselled deep into the rock. As they worked their way down to floor level, using heavy iron picks, the labourers left chunks of raw rock for skilled sculptors to transform into pillars, devotional friezes and *stupas*.

By the fourth century AD, the Hinayana school was losing ground to the more exuberant **Mahayana**, or "Greater Vehicle", school. Its emphasis on an ever-enlarging pantheon of deities and **bodhisattvas** (merciful saints who postponed their accession to *nirvana* to help mankind towards Enlightenment) was accompanied by a transformation in architectural styles. *Chaityas* were superseded by lavish monastery-halls, or **viharas**, in which the monks both lived and worshipped, and the once-prohibited image of the Buddha became far more prominent. Occupying the circumambulatory recess at the end of the hall, where the *stupa* formerly stood, the colossal **icon** acquired the thirty-two characteristic attributes, or **lakshanas** (including the long dangling ear-lobes, cranial protuberance, short curls, robe and halo) by which the Buddha was distinguished from lesser divinities. The highwater mark of Mahayanan art came towards the end of the Buddhist age. Drawing on the rich catalogue of themes and images contained in ancient scriptures such as the **Jatakas** (legends relating to the Buddha's previous incarnations), Ajanta's exquisite and awe-inspiring wall **painting** may, in part, have been designed to rekindle enthusiasm for the faith, which was, by this point, already starting to wane in the region.

Attempts to compete with the resurgence of **Hinduism**, from the sixth century onwards, eventually led to the evolution of another, more esoteric religious movement. The **Vajrayana**, or "Thunderbolt" sect stressed the female creative principle, **shakti**, with arcane rituals combining spells and magic formulas. Ultimately, however, such modifications were to prove powerless against the growing allure of Brahmanism.

The ensuing shift in royal and popular patronage is best exemplified by **Ellora**, where during the eighth century, many of the old *viharas* were converted into temples, their shrines housing polished *shivalingams* instead of *stupas* and Buddhas. Hindu cave architecture, with its predilection for dramatic mythological **sculpture**, culminated in the tenth century with the magnificent **Kailash temple**, a giant replica of the free-standing structures that had already begun to replace rock-cut caves. It was Hinduism that bore the brunt of the iconoclastic medieval descent of Islam on the Deccan, Buddhism having long since fled to the comparative safety of the Himalayas, where it flourishes to this day.

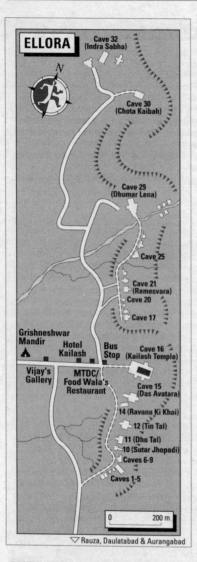

ELLORA

Cave 32
(Indra Sabha)

N

Cave 30
(Chota Kailah)

Cave 29
(Dhumar Lena)

Cave 25

Cave 21
(Ramesvara)
Cave 20

Cave 17

Grishneshwar
Mandir
Hotel   Bus   Cave 16
Kailash   Stop   (Kailash Temple)
Vijay's   MTDC/
Gallery   Food Wala's
Restaurant
Cave 15
(Das Avatara)

14 (Ravana Ki Khai)

12 (Tin Tal)

11 (Dho Tal)
10 (Sutar Jhopadi)
Caves 6-9

Caves 1-5

0   200 m

▽ Rauza, Daulatabad & Aurangabad

CAVES 1 TO 5

Cave 1 is a plain, bare *vihara* containing eight small cells and very little sculpture, which may have been a granary for the larger halls. In the much more impressive **cave 2**, a large central chamber is supported by twelve massive, square-based pillars while the side walls are lined with seated Buddhas. Both the main entrance and the doorway into the shrine room are flanked by two giant *dvarpalas*, or guardian figures: an unusually muscular **Padmapani**, the lotus-holding *bodhisattva* of compassion, on the left, and an opulent bejewelled **Maitreya**, the "Buddha-to-come", on the right. Both are accompanied by their consorts. Inside the sanctum itself, a stately Buddha is seated on a lion throne, looking stronger and more determined than his serene forerunners in Ajanta. **Caves 3** and **4**, slightly older and similar in design to cave 2, are in poor condition.

Known as the "**Maharwada**" cave because it was used by local Mahar tribespeople as a shelter during the monsoon, **cave 5** is the grandest single-storeyed *vihara* in Ellora. Its enormous thirty-six-metre-long rectangular assembly hall is thought to have been used by the monks as a refectory (note the two rows of **benches** carved out of the stone floor). At the far end, the entrance to the central shrine is guarded by two fine *bodhisattva* figures of Padmapani and Vajrapani – the "Thunderbolt Holder". The Buddha inside is seated, this time on a stool; his right hand touches the ground in the *mudra* denoting the "Miracle of a Thousand Buddhas", performed by the Master to confound a gang of heretics. Notice the delicate rendition of his long, flowing robe.

CAVES 6 TO 9

The next four caves were all excavated at roughly the same time in the seventh century. On the walls of the antechamber at the far end of the central hall in **cave 6**, are two of Ellora's most famous and finely executed figures. **Tara**, the female consort of the *bodhisattva* Avalokitesvara, stands to the left, with superbly supple limbs and an intense but kindly expression. To her right, the Buddhist goddess of learning, Mahamayuri, is depicted with her emblem the peacock, while a diligent student sets a good example at his desk below. The parallels with Mahayuri's Hindu counterpart, Saraswati, are obvious (the latter's mythological vehicle is also a peacock), and show the extent to which seventh-century Indian Buddhism incorporated elements from its rival faith in an attempt to rekindle its rapidly waning popularity. In the panel to the right of the sanctum door, the thunderbolt (*vajra*) of the *bodhisattva* Vajrapani is depicted (to his left) in human form instead of the more conventional trident, which makes a less conspicuous appearance on the front of his headgear instead.

The only other cave in this group worthy of note is **cave 9**, reached via the hall of its neighbour, cave 6. Carved across the facade, a splendid Tara stands guard over a snake, a sword, an elephant, a shipwreck and fire – symbols for five of the mortal perils faced by man on his passage through the world.

CAVES 10, 11 AND 12

Excavated during the first quarter of the eighth century, **cave 10** is one of the last and most magnificent of the Deccan's rock-cut *chaitya* halls. Steps lead from the left of its large verandah to an upper balcony, where a trefoil doorway flanked by heavenly nymphs, a frieze of playful dwarves, snake deities and flying amorous couples passes beneath an ornate facade to an interior balcony. From here, you have a good view down into the long apsed hall, with its octagonal pillars and vaulted roof. The stone "rafters" carved out of the ceiling, imitations of the beams that would have appeared in earlier free-standing wooden structures, are the source of this cave's popular name, the **Sutar Jhopadi**, or "Carpenter's Workshop". At the far end, a life-size seated Buddha is enthroned in front of a votive **stupa** – the hall's devotional centre-piece.

In spite of the rediscovery in 1876 of its hitherto hidden basement, **cave 11** continues to be known as the **Dho Tal**, or "two floors" cave. Its top storey is a long columned assembly hall housing a Buddha shrine and, on its rear wall, images of Durga and Ganesh, the elephant-headed son of Shiva – evidence that the cave was converted into a Hindu temple after being abandoned by the Buddhists.

Cave 12 next door – the **Tin Tal**, or "three floors" – is another triple-storeyed *vihara* approached via a large open courtyard. Again, the main highlights are on the uppermost level, used for teaching and meditation. The shrine room at the end of the hall, whose walls are lined with five large *bodhisattvas*, is flanked on both sides by seven Buddhas – one for each of the Master's previous incarnations. Those on the left are shown in deep meditation, while those to the right are once more depicted in the *mudra* taht signifies the "Miracle of a Thousand Buddhas".

The Hindu group

Ellora's seventeen **Hindu caves** are grouped around the middle of the escarpment, to either side of the majestic Kailash temple. Excavated at the start of the Brahmanical revival in the Deccan, during a time of relative stability, the cave-temples throb with a vitality absent from their restrained Buddhist predecessors. Gone are the rows of heavy-eyed, benign-faced Buddhas and *bodhisattvas*. In their place, huge **bas-reliefs** line the walls, writhing with dynamic scenes from the Hindu scriptures. Most are connected with **Shiva**, the god of destruction and regeneration (and the presiding deity in all of the Hindu caves on the site), although you'll also come across numerous images of Vishnu, the Preserver, and his various incarnations.

The same tableaux crop up time and again, a repetition that gave Ellora's craftsmen ample opportunity to refine their technique over the years leading up to their greatest achievement, the **Kailash temple** (cave 16). Covered separately on p.643, the temple is the highlight of any visit to Ellora, but you'll appreciate its beautiful sculpture all the more if you check out the earlier Hindu caves first. Numbers 14 and 15, immediately south, are the best of the bunch if you're pushed for time.

CAVE 14
Dating from the start of the seventh century AD, and among the last of the early excavations, **cave 14** was a Buddhist *vihara* that the Hindus later converted into a temple.
Its layout is very similar to that of cave 8, with the shrine room set back from the wall
and surrounded by a circumambulatory passage. The entrance to the sanctum is
guarded by two impressive river goddesses, Ganga and Yamuna, while in an alcove
behind, seven heavy-breasted fertility goddesses, the **Sapta Matrikas**, dandle chubby
babies on their laps. The female aspect of Shiva's elephant-headed son, Ganesha, sits
immediately to their right beside two cadaverous apparitions, Kala and Kali, the
goddesses of death. Superb **friezes** adorn the cave's long side walls. Starting at the
front, those on the left (as you face the shrine) show Durga slaying the demon buffalo
Mahisa; Lakshmi, the goddess of wealth, enthroned on a lotus as her elephant attendants shower her with water; Vishnu, in the form of the boar, Vahara, rescuing the
earth goddess Prithvi from the primordial flood; and finally Vishnu, shown with his two
wives. On the opposite wall, the panels are devoted exclusively to Shiva. The second
from the front shows him playing dice with his wife Parvati; then doing the dance of
death as Nataraja; and in the fourth frieze, blithely ignoring the demon Ravana's futile
attempts to shake him and his consort off their heavenly abode, Mount Kailash.

CAVE 15
Like its neighbour, the two-storeyed **cave 15** began life as a Buddhist *vihara* but was
hijacked by the Hindus and became a Shiva shrine. Skip the largely uninteresting
ground floor, and make for the upper level to find some of Ellora's most magnificent
sculpture. The cave's name, **Das Avatara**, is derived from the sequence of panels
along the right wall, which show five of **Vishnu**'s ten incarnations (*avatars*). In the
second frieze, the Preserver appears as the "**Primordial Dreamer**", reclining on the
coils of Anantha, the cosmic serpent of Infinity. His navel is about to sprout a lotus
flower from which Brahma will emerge to begin the creation of the world. The last
panel shows Vishnu in his fourth manifestation as the Man-Lion, **Narashima**, which he
adopted to slay a demon that could not be killed "by man nor beast, by day or night,
inside or outside a palace" (Vishnu got him by lying in wait at dawn inside the entrance
hall to his palace). Notice the demon's serene expression as he prepares to die, confident in the knowledge that he will attain salvation having been killed by a god.

A carved panel in a recess to the right of the antechamber shows Shiva emerging
from a *lingam*. His rivals, Brahma and Vishnu, kneel before the apparition in humility
and supplication – symbolizing the supremacy of Shaivism in the region at the time the
conversion work was carried out. Finally, halfway down the left wall of the chamber, as
you're facing the shrine, the cave's most elegant piece of sculpture shows Shiva, as
Nataraja, poised in a classical dance pose.

CAVES 17 TO 29
Only three of the Hindu caves strung along the hillside north of the Kailash temple are
worth making the effort to visit. **Cave 21** – the **Ramesvara** – was excavated late in the
sixth century. Thought to be the oldest Hindu cave at Ellora, it harbours some well-
executed sculpture, including a large Nandi bull (facing the central shrine), a fine pair
of river goddesses on either side of the verandah, and some sensuous loving couples,
or *mithunas*, dotted around the walls of the balcony. **Cave 25**, further along, contains a
striking image of the sun-god **Surya** speeding in his chariot towards the dawn.

From here, the path picks its way past two more excavations, then drops steeply
down the side of a sheer cliff, via rough-cut stone steps, to the bottom of a small river
gorge. Once under the seasonal **waterfall**, the trail climbs the other side of the gulley,
to emerge beside **cave 29**, the **Dhumar Lena**. Dating from the late sixth century, the

cave boasts an unusual cross-shaped floor plan similar to the Elephanta cave in Bombay harbour (see p.598). Pairs of lions guard its three staircases, while inside, the walls are covered with huge **friezes**. Left of the entrance, Shiva skewers the Andhaka demon, while in the adjacent wall panel he foils the many-armed Ravana's attempts to shake him and Parvati off the top of Mount Kailash (look for the cheeky dwarf baring his bum to taunt the evil demon). On the south side, a dice-playing scene shows Shiva teasing Parvati by holding her arm back as she prepares to throw.

The Kailash temple (cave 16)

Cave 16, the colossal **Kailash temple** (daily 6am–6pm; Rs2), is Ellora's masterpiece. Here, the term "cave" is not only a gross understatement, but a complete misnomer. For although the temple was, like the other excavations, hewn from solid rock, it bears a striking resemblance to the free-standing structures – at Pattadakal and Kanchipuram (see p.922) in south India – on which it was modelled. The monolith is believed to have been the brainchild of the Rashtrakuta ruler **Krishna I** (756–73). One hundred years and four generations of kings, architects and craftsmen elapsed, however, before the ambitious project was finally completed. Climb up the track leading along the lip of the compound's north-facing cliff, to the ledge overlooking the squat main tower, and you'll see why.

The sheer scale is staggering. Work began by digging three deep trenches into the top of the hill using pickaxes and lengths of wood which, soaked with water and stuffed into narrow cracks, expanded to crumble the basalt. Once a huge chunk of raw rock had been exposed in this way, the royal sculptors set to work. In all, a quarter of a million tonnes of chippings and debris are estimated to have been cut from the hillside, with no room for improvisation or error. The temple was conceived as a giant replica of Shiva and Parvati's Himalayan abode, the pyramidal **Mount Kailash** – a Tibetan peak, said to be the "divine axis" between heaven and earth. Today, all but a few fragments of the thick coat of white-lime plaster that gave the temple the appearance of a snowy mountain have flaked off, to expose elaborately carved surfaces of grey-brown stone beneath. Around the rear of the tower, these have been bleached and blurred by centuries of erosion, as if the giant sculpture is slowly melting in the fierce Deccani heat.

THE TEMPLE

The main **entrance** to the temple is through a tall stone screen, intended to mark the transition from the profane to the sacred realms. After passing between two guardian river goddesses, Ganga and Yamuna, you enter a narrow passage whose walls are carved with images of **Vyasa**, author of the *Mahabharata* (left), and **Valmiki**, the legendary sage who penned the *Ramayana* (right). The porch then opens on to the main forecourt, opposite a panel showing **Lakshmi**, the goddess of wealth, being lustrated by a pair of elephants – the scene known to Hindus as "Gajalakshmi". Custom requires pilgrims to circumambulate clockwise around Mount Kailash, so drop down the steps to your left and head across the front of the courtyard towards the near corner.

From here, all three principal sections of the complex are visible. First, the shrine housing Shiva's vehicle **Nandi**, the bull; next, the intricate recessed walls of the main assembly hall, or **mandapa**; and finally, the sanctuary itself, surmounted by the stumpy, 29-metre pyramidal tower, or **shikhara**. These three components rest on an appropriately huge raised platform, borne by dozens of lotus-gathering elephants. As well as symbolizing Shiva's sacred mountain, the temple also represented a giant **chariot**. The transepts protruding from the side of the main hall are its wheels, the Nandi shrine its yoke, and the two life-sized trunkless elephants in the front of the courtyard (disfigured by marauding Muslims) are the beasts of burden. Before leaving the corner, look for the **river goddess shrine** set in the north wall of the cliff. Originally, the two figures of Ganga and Yamuna were probably accompanied by Saraswati, to embody the three cardinal virtues of purity, devotion and wisdom respectively. Some scholars also say they stand for the domains conquered by the Rashtrakutans.

Most of the main highlights of the temple itself are confined to its side walls, which are plastered with vibrant **sculpture**. Lining the staircase that leads up to the *mandapa*, a long, lively narrative panel depicts scenes from the *Mahabharata*. Below this, you may recognize episodes from the life of **Krishna**, including one in which the young god suckled the poisoned breast of a wet nurse sent to kill him by his evil uncle. Krishna survived, but the poison dyed his skin its characteristic blue. The majority of the remaining panels around the lower sections of the temple are devoted to **Shiva**. On the south side of the *mandapa*, in an alcove carved out of the most prominent projection, you'll find the relief widely held to be the finest piece of sculpture in the compound. It shows Shiva and Parvati being disturbed by the arch-demon **Ravana**, who has been incarcerated inside the sacred mountain and is now shaking the walls of his prison with his many arms. Shiva is about to assert his supremacy by calming the earthquake with a prod of his left toe. Parvati, meanwhile, looks nonchalantly on, reclining on her elbow as one of her handmaidens flees in panic.

At this point, either call in at the **"Hall of Sacrifices"** in the bottom (southwest) corner of the courtyard to pay your respects to the seven mother goddesses, the **Sapta Matrikas**, and their ghoulish companions Kala and Kali (shown astride a heap of corpses), or head straight up the stairs, past the animated battle scenes in the dramatic **Ramayana frieze**, to the **mandapa**. The sixteen-columned assembly hall is shrouded in a gloomy half-light designed to focus worshippers on the presence of the deity within. Overhead, Shiva, as **Nataraja**, performs the dance of death, surrounded by patches of plaster and paintwork left over from the temple's original coat of stucco. The sanctum itself is no longer a living **shrine**, although it still houses a large stone *lingam* mounted on a *yoni* pedestal, symbolizing the dual aspects of Shiva's procreative energy.

The Jain group

Ellora's small cluster of four **Jain caves** is north of the main group, at the end of a curving asphalt road. They can be reached either from cave 29, by dropping down to the T-junction and bearing right, or directly from the Kailash temple. Either way, the two-kilometre round-trip is quite a hike in the heat, and you may feel like flagging down a rickshaw.

Excavated in the late ninth and tenth centuries, after the Hindu phase had petered out, the Jain caves are Ellora's swansong. After the exuberance of the Kailash temple, their modest scale and subdued interiors lack vitality and inspiration, although some of the decorative carving is very fine. Only one of the group is of any real note. **Cave 32**, the **Indra Sabha** ("Indra's assembly hall"), is a miniature version of the Kailash temple. The lower of its two levels is plain and incomplete, but the upper storey is crammed with elaborate stonework, notably the ornate **pillars** and the two *tirthanka-ras* guarding the entrance to the central shrine. The naked figure of **Gomatesvara**, on the right, is fulfilling a vow of silence in the forest. He is so deeply immersed in meditation that creepers have grown up his legs and animals, snakes and scorpions crawl around his feet. Opposite, **Parasnath's** protective coat of cobra heads is another mark of a spiritual superman. Note the massive lotus carved on the ceiling, and the traces of the original blue **painting** that survive around it. The shrine houses a Buddha-like icon **Mahavira**, the twenty-fourth *tirthankara* and founder of the Jain faith.

The Grishneshwar mandir

Rising above the small village west of the caves, the cream-coloured *shikhara* of the eighteenth-century **Grishneshwar mandir** pinpoints the location of one of India's oldest and most sacred deities. The *lingam* enshrined inside the temple's cavernous inner sanctum is one of the twelve "self-born" **Jyotirlinga** ("*lingams* of light"), thought to date back to the second century BC. Non-Hindus are allowed to join the queue for *darshan*, but men have to remove their shirts before entering the shrine itself.

Ellora practicalities

Most visitors use Aurangabad as a base for day trips to the caves, **getting to Ellora** either via the half-hourly *MSRTC* buses or one of MTDC's popular guided **tours** (daily depart 9.30am, return 5.30pm; Rs65). These latter are very rushed, however; if you want to take in the caves at a more leisurely pace and climb Daulatabad Hill, either spend the night at Ellora or leave Aurangabad early in the morning.

Ellora does offer a couple of decent **places to stay**. The new *Hotel Kailas* (☎43; ⑤) is a small campus of self-contained chalets insensitively positioned opposite the caves, but with good facilities, including a restaurant and bar. They also have a limited number of **dorm beds** in an adjacent wing, the *Nataraj* (①). The only other budget accommodation is *Vijay's Rock Art Gallery and Restaurant* (①–②), a little down the road from the *Kailas*. The rooms and washing facilities here are very basic, but the congenial guest house, run by a local painter for "visiting artists, writers and thinkers", is a nice place to stay if you've come to study the caves in any detail.

Tasty, moderately priced **food** is available at MTDC/*Food-Wallah*'s restaurant opposite the main bus stop. In addition to the usual veg and non-veg Indian dishes, they serve Chinese, good-value lunchtime *thalis* and cold beer – indoors under the fan or al fresco on the shady terrace. You can also order meals and filled rolls in the *Kailas*' slightly pricier *Caveman* restaurant, but their turnover is sluggish, especially during the week. Roadside stalls sell *bhajis*, *pakoras* and other greasy snacks.

Ajanta

Hewn from the near-vertical sides of a horseshoe-shaped ravine, deep in the semi-arid hills of the Deccan, the rock-cut caves at **AJANTA** occupy a site worthy of the spectacular ancient art they contain. Less than two centuries ago, this remote spot was known only to the local Bhil tribespeople – the shadowy entrances to its abandoned stone chambers lay buried deep under a thick blanket of creepers and jungle. The chance arrival in 1819, of a small detachment of scarlet-coated East India Company troops, however, brought the caves' obscurity to an abrupt end. The **rediscovery** reads like an *Indiana Jones* screenplay. Led to the top of the precipitous bluff that overlooks the gorge by a young "half-wild" aboriginal scout, the tiger-hunters spied, far below, what has now been identified as the facade of cave 10 protruding through the dense foliage.

The gung-ho British soldiers had made one of the most sensational archeological finds of all time. Further exploration revealed a total of twenty-eight colonnaded caves chiselled out of the chocolate-brown and grey basalt cliffs lining the River Waghora. More remarkable still were the exquisite and immaculately preserved **paintings** writhing over their interior surfaces. For in addition to the phalanxes of stone Buddhas and other **sculpture** enshrined within them, Ajanta's excavations are adorned with a swirling profusion of multicoloured murals, depicting everything from battlefields to boudoirs, sailing ships to city streets and teeming animal-filled forests to snow capped mountains. Even if you aren't wholly au fait with the narratives they portray, it's easy to see why these paintings rank among India's most beautiful treasures.

In spite of its comparative remoteness, Ajanta receives an extraordinary number of visitors. If you want to enjoy the site in anything close to its original serenity, try not to come on a weekend or public holiday – it takes a fertile imagination indeed to picture Buddhist monks filing softly around the rough stone steps, when riotous packs of school kids and holidaymakers are clambering over them. The best **seasons to visit** are either during the monsoon, when the river is swollen and the gorge reverberates with the sound of the crashing waterfalls, or during the cooler winter months between October and March. At other times, the relentless Deccan sun beating down on the bare south-facing rock can make a trip around Ajanta a real endurance test. Whenever you come, bring a hat, some shades, a strong **flashlight** and plenty of drinking water.

Some history

Located close enough to the major trans-Deccan trade routes to ensure a steady supply of alms, yet far enough from civilization to preserve the peace and tranquillity necessary for meditation and prayer, Ajanta was an ideal location for the region's itinerant Buddhist monks to found their first permanent monasteries. Donative inscriptions indicate that its earliest cave excavations took place in the second century BC.

In its heyday, Ajanta sheltered upwards of two hundred monks, as well as a sizeable community of painters, sculptors and labourers employed in excavating and decorating the cells and sanctuaries. Some time in the seventh century, however, the site was abandoned – whether because of the growing popularity of nearby Ellora, or the threat posed by the resurgence of Hinduism, no one knows. By the eighth century, the complex lay deserted and forgotten, overlooked even by the Muslim iconoclasts who wrought such damage to the area's other sacred sites during the medieval era.

Had the fateful tiger-hunting expedition not appeared over the horizon in 1819, Ajanta might have languished under a shroud of vegetation to this day. Instead, its wonders have been pored over by more prying eyes than just about any other Indian monument outside the "golden triangle" of Delhi, Agra and Jaipur. Early attempts to document the amazing discovery, however, met with such little success that Ajanta has been associated with a sinister **curse**. In 1866, after spending 27 years faithfully copying the paintings from his field-camp nearby, the artist **Robert Gill** lost his entire collection when London's Crystal Palace burned to the ground. The same fate befell another batch of facsimiles in the 1870s, which went up in smoke with London's Victoria and Albert Museum, while the efforts of a Japanese team were dramatically foiled when their rice-paper impressions of Ajanta's sculpture were crushed in an earthquake. Even **restoration** work has been dogged with misfortune. In 1920, the Nizam of Hyderabad (who then ruled the region) employed a pair of Italian experts to patch up some of the more badly damaged paintings. Unfortunately, the varnish they used to seal the flakier fragments of plaster to the cave walls darkened and cracked over time, causing further irreparable deterioration.

Nowadays, the job of restoration has fallen to the *ASI*. Among measures to minimize the impact of the hundreds of visitors who daily trudge through are a total ban on **flash photography**, and strict limits on the numbers allowed into a single cave at any given time – another good reason to avoid weekends. Recently, there has also been talk of a two-million-*rupee* investment to develop tourism. MTDC boldly boast of the snazzy new visitor centre, three-star hotels and craft village that they hope to build nearby. So far though, the only commercialism to have hit Ajanta is the mushrooming collection of postcard and souvenir stalls around the bus stand below the main entrance.

For more information on **rock-cut caves of the northwestern Deccan**, see p.639.

The caves

On arrival at the Ajanta **caves**, head straight through the pack of postcard- and gem-*wallahs* in the small bazaar-cum-bus stand, to the admissions kiosk on the other side of the rise (daily 9am–5.30pm; Rs0.50), to buy your entrance and all-important Rs5 **light-tickets**. An obvious path leads from there to the grand **Mahayana** *viharas*; if you'd prefer to see the caves in chronological order, however, start with the smaller

CAVE PAINTING TECHNIQUES

The basic **painting techniques** used by the artists of Ajanta to transform the dull rock walls into lustrous kaleidoscopes of colour changed surprisingly little over the eight centuries the site was in use, from 200 BC to 650 AD. First, the rough-stone surfaces were primed with a six- to seven-centimetre coating of paste made from clay, cow-dung, and animal hair, strengthened with vegetable fibre. Next, a finer layer of smooth white lime was applied. Before this was dry, the artists quickly sketched the outlines of their pictures using red cinnabar, which they then filled in with a coating of *terre verte*. The **pigments**, all derived from natural water-soluble substances (kaolin chalk for white, lamp soot for black, glauconite for green, ochre for yellow and imported lapis lazuli for blue), were thickened with glue and added only after the undercoat was completely dry. Thus the Ajanta paintings are not, strictly speaking, frescoes (always executed on damp surfaces), but **tempera**. Finally, after they had been left to dry, the murals were painstakingly polished with a smooth stone to bring out their natural sheen.

The artists' only sources of **light** were oil-lamps and sunshine reflected into the caves by metal mirrors and pools of water (the external courtyards were flooded expressly for the purpose). Ironically, many of them were not even Buddhists, but Hindus employed by the royal courts of the day. Nevertheless, their extraordinary mastery of line, perspective and shading, which endows Ajanta's paintings with their characteristic other-worldly light, resulted in one of the great technical landmarks in Indian-Buddhist art history.

Hinayana group of *chaitya* halls at the bottom of the river-bend (nos. 12, 10, 9 & 26), then work your way back up, via cave 17. If you need help getting up the steps, sedan chair-porters, or *dhooli-wallahs*, stand in front of the stalls below. Official **guides** can be arranged through the ticket office; most have an interesting enough spiel, but you may well feel like taking in the sights again afterwards, at a more leisurely pace.

Cave 1

Cave 1 contains some of the finest and stylistically most evolved paintings on the site. By the time work on it began, late in the fifth century, *viharas* served not only to shelter and feed the monks, but also as places of worship in their own right – hence the addition to the rows of cells lining the front- and side-walls of a central **shrine room**. Before entering the cave, check out the snake deities carved around the three main doorways. Formerly venerated by the local aboriginal population, these *nagarajas*, intertwined with musicians and amorous couples, demonstrate how Buddhism incorporated elements of the indigenous earth cults that it superseded. Once inside, the **murals** plastered across the walls and ceilings are the cave's most extraordinary feature. In common with most Mahayana *viharas*, these vibrant friezes depict episodes from the birth-story and former lives of the Buddha, the *Jatakas*. One of the most elaborate is the **Mahanjanaka**, which extends most of the way along the left-hand wall. This tells of a shipwrecked king who meets a solitary ascetic and decides to renounce all worldly attachments. On his return to his palace, his queen, with the help of a bevy of alluring dancing girls, unsuccessfully attempts to dissuade him. The last scene shows her husband leaving on horseback, with a crowd of wailing courtesans in his wake.

Immediately beyond the Mahanjanaka, left of the doorway into the main shrine, stands another masterpiece. **Padmapani**, the lotus-holding form of Avalokitesvara, is surrounded by an entourage of smaller attendants, divine musicians, lovers, monkeys and peacocks – his heavy almond eyes and languid hip-shot *tribhanga* (or "three-bend") pose exuding a distant and sublime calm. Opposite, flanking the right side of the doorway, is his counterpart, **Vajrapani**, the thunderbolt holder. Between them, these two *bodhisattvas* represent the dual aspects of Mahayana Buddhism, compassion and knowledge.

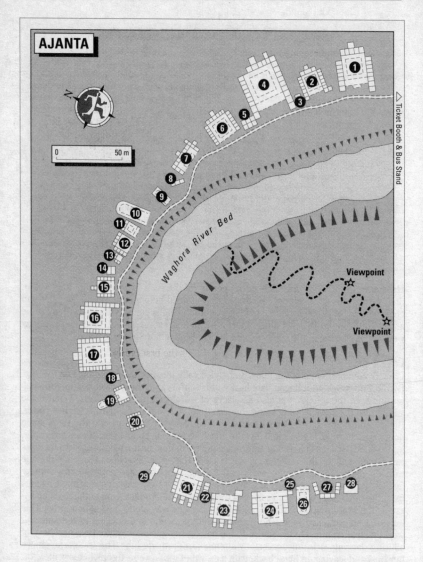

The real focal point of cave 1, however, is the gigantic sculpted Buddha seated in the shrine room – the finest such figure in Ajanta. Using portable electric spotlights, guides love to demonstrate how the expression on the Buddha's exquisitely carved face changes according to where the light is held: sombre to the left, blissful to the right, and serene when the light source is shone from below. On the pedestal below the statue, look for the wheel, symbolizing *dharma*, Buddha's teachings, and the deer which stands for the sermon he preached at Sarnath (see p.789).

On the way out, you may be able to spot this cave's other famous *trompe l'oeil*, crowning one of the pillars (to the right as you face the shrine): the figures of four, apparently separate stags which, on closer inspection, all share the same head.

Cave 2

Cave 2 is another, similarly impressive, Mahayana *vihara*, dating from the sixth century. Here the ceiling, which seems to sag like a tent roof, is decorated with complex geometric patterns, including lotus and medallion motifs. The design clearly takes its cue from ancient Greek art – a legacy of Alexander the Great's foray into the subcontinent half a millennium earlier. Friezes in the small subsidiary shrine to the right of the main chapel centre on a well-endowed fertility goddess, **Hariti**, the infamous child-eating ogress. When the Buddha threatened to give her a taste of her own medicine by kidnapping *her* child, Hariti flew into a frenzy (upper left), but was subdued by the Buddha's teachings of compassion (upper right). Below, a faded schoolroom scene shows a teacher waving a cane at a class of unruly pupils.

The side walls teem with lively **paintings** of the *Jatakas* and other mythological episodes. A frieze on the left verandah shows the apparently painless birth of the Buddha, emerging from under his mother's arm, and his conception when a six-tusked elephant appeared to her in a dream. Nearby, is one of several scenes portraying the "miracle of a thousand Buddhas", in which the Buddha, to confound a party of heretics, is said to have multiplied himself a thousand times.

Caves 3 to 9

Caves 3, 4, and 7 hold little of interest, but take a quick look into **cave 6**, a double-storeyed *vihara* with a finely carved door-jamb above its shrine room, a handful of octagonal pillars, and some peeling paintings above the entrances to its cells. Cave 8 is always closed; it contains the generator for the lights.

Cave 9, which dates from the first century BC, is the first *chaitya* you come to along the walkway. Resting in the half-light shed by a characteristic *peepal*-leaf-shaped window in the sculpted facade, the hemispherical **stupa**, with its inverted pyramidal reliquary, forms the devotional centrepiece of the fourteen-metre-long hall. The fragments of painting that remain, including the procession scene on the left wall, are mostly superimpositions over the top of earlier snake-deities (*nagarajas*).

Cave 10

Though partially collapsed, and marred by the unsightly wire meshing erected by the ASI to keep out bats, the facade of **cave 10**, a second-century BC *chaitya* hall – the oldest and most impressive of its kind in the ravine – is still a grand sight. The cave's main highlights, however, are far smaller and more subdued. With the help of sunlight reflected from a mirror held by an attendant, you may be able to pick out the fading traces of painting along the left wall. The scene in which a raja and his retinue approach a group of dancers and musicians surrounding a garlanded *bodhi* tree – a symbol of the Buddha (the Hinayanas preferred not to depict him figuratively) – is believed to be the earliest surviving Buddhist mural in India. Elsewhere on the same wall is graffiti scrawled by the British soldiers who rediscovered the caves in 1819.

The apsidal-ended hall itself, divided by three rows of painted octagonal pillars, is dominated by a huge monolithic **stupa** at its far end. If there's no-one else around, try out the *chaitya*'s amazing acoustics.

Cave 16

The next cave of interest, **cave 16**, is another spectacular fifth-century *vihara*, with the famous painting known as the "**Dying Princess**" near the front of its left wall. The "princess" was actually a queen named **Sundari**, and she isn't dying, but fainting after hearing the news that her husband, King Nanda (Buddha's cousin), is about to renounce his throne to take up monastic orders. The opposite walls show events from Buddha's early life as **Siddhartha**, while to the right of the main doorway Buddha appears again, as an elephant who hurls himself over a cliff to feed a band of hungry travellers.

Cave 17

Cave 17, dating from between the mid-fifth and early sixth centuries, boasts the best preserved and most varied paintings in Ajanta. As with caves 1 and 2, only a limited number of visitors are allowed in at any one time. While you wait, have a look at the frescoes on the **verandah**. Above the door, eight seated Buddhas, including Maitreya, the Buddha to come, look down; to the left, an amorous princely couple share a last glass of wine before giving their worldly wealth away to the poor. The wall that forms the far left side of the verandah features fragments of an elaborate "Wheel of Life".

Inside the cave, the murals are, once more, dominated by the illustrations of the *Jatakas*, particularly those in which the Buddha takes the form of an animal to illustrate certain virtues. Running in a continuous frieze down the left aisle, the **Vishvantara Jataka** tells the story of a prince who was banished from the court by his father for giving away a magic rain-making elephant. Among the more poignant and erotic scenes in this long narrative is one where Vishvantara bids farewell to his queen in their four-poster bed before heading off to a hermitage in the forest. Nearby, on the wall to the left of the main shrine, is one of Ajanta's more gruesome highlights. In the **Sudasa Jataka**, a *bodhisattva* adopts the guise of a lioness to talk a prince out of eating his subjects. The artists have spared no detail, with gory illustrations of the cooking pots and chunks of human flesh being chopped up to put in them. Cannibalism is also the theme of the great **Simhala** frieze on the right-hand side of the cave. This relates the story of a merchant-adventurer and his band of mariners who, after being shipwrecked and washed ashore on a desert island, find themselves surrounded by voluptuous maidens. In a cruel twist (which would no doubt have Freud chuckling into his beard), these beautiful women turn, by night, into a horde of blood-crazed, man-eating ogresses. Luckily for the castaways, a *bodhisattva* appears in the form of a horse to lead them into a victorious battle against the evil she-demons.

The pillar separating the *Simhala Jataka* from a smaller frieze, which shows how the Buddha tore out his eyes to give to a blind *brahmin*, holds an exquisite and much-celebrated portrait of a sultry, dark-skinned princess admiring herself in a mirror while her handmaidens and a female dwarf look on. The *chowkidars* will demonstrate how, when illuminated from the side, her iridescent eyes and jewellery glow like pearls against the brooding dark background.

Cave 19

Excavated during the mid-fifth century, when the age of Mahayana Buddhism was in full swing, **cave 19** is indisputably Ajanta's most magnificent *chaitya* hall, its **facade** teeming with elaborate sculpture. On the columns flanking the walls, benign *bodhisattvas* in translucent robes are interspersed with meditating Buddhas, while on either side of the gracefully arched and pointed window, two pot-bellied, double-chinned demi-gods look smugly down. The penchant of the Mahayanas for theatrical luxuriance has been interpreted as a response to the concurrent rise of Brahmanism. This Hindu influence is even more manifest in the friezes that line the interior of the **porch**. On the left wall, crowned with a halo of cobra heads, the snake-king Nagaraja and his queen sit in a relaxed pose – reminiscent of the many Shiva and Parvati panels at Ellora, and of the indigenous snake-cult that formerly held sway here in the Waghora gorge.

Inside the hall, the faded frescoes are of less note than the sculpture around the tops of the pillars. The standing Buddha at the far end, another Mahayana innovation, is even more remarkable. Note the development from the stumpier *stupas* enshrined within the early *chaityas* (caves 9 & 10) to this more elongated version. Its umbrellas, supported by angels and a vase of divine nectar, reach right up to the vaulted roof.

Caves 21 to 26

Caves 21 to 26 date from the seventh century, a couple of hundred years after the others, and form a separate group at the far end of the cliff. Apart from the unfinished **cave 24**, whose roughly hacked trenches and pillars give an idea of how the original excavation was carried out here, the only one worth a close look is **cave 26**. Envisaged on a similarly grand scale to the other large *chaitya*, cave 19, this impressive hall was never completed. Nevertheless, the sculpture which the artisans had chiselled out here before they inexplicably downed tools is among the most vivid and dramatic at Ajanta. In the gloomy apse at the far end, the Buddha sits in front of large cylindrical *stupa* ringed with *bodhisattvas*. In the "**Temptation of Mara**" frieze to his left, he appears again, this time impassively ensconced under a *peepal* tree as seven tantalizing sisters try to seduce him. Their father, the satanic Mara, watches from astride an elephant in the top left corner. The ruse to lead the Buddha astray fails, of course, eventually forcing the evil adversary and his daughters to retreat (bottom right). In contrast, the colossal image of **Parinirvarna**, Siddhartha reclining on his death bed, along the opposite wall is a veritable pool of tranquillity. Check out the weeping and wailing mourners below, and the flying angels and musicians above, preparing to greet the sage as he drifts into *nirvana*. The soft sunlight diffusing gently from the doorway over Buddha's fine sensuously carved features completes the appropriately transcendent effect.

The view point

The stiff thirty- to forty-minute climb to the "**view point**" from where the British hunting party first spotted the Ajanta caves requires plenty of stamina and bottles of water, but is worth the effort – the panorama over the Waghora ravine and its surrounding walls of bare, flat-topped mountains is stunning. To pick up the trail, drop down from cave 16 to the gardens lining the river bed, where a twisty path strikes up the steepest part of the ridge to the edge of the plateau. The view point is clearly visible from below.

Ajanta practicalities

The only way of **getting to Ajanta**, unless you have your own transport, is by **bus**. An hourly service makes the 100-minute climb into the hills from the nearest railhead at **Jalgaon**, 58km north. If you're coming from **Aurangabad** to the southwest, the 108-kilometre road trip takes a little over three hours, with a pit stop at the market town of **Shillod** en route. The last buses leave Ajanta for Jalgaon at 6.50pm, and for Aurangabad at 5.40pm. Provided you catch an early enough bus up here, it's possible to see the caves, grab a bite, and then head off again in either direction. Alternatively, you could do the round trip from Aurangabad on one of MTDC's rushed **tours** (daily depart 8am, return 5.30pm; Rs100). Tickets can be booked from any MTDC office.

Accommodation within striking distance is limited to two mediocre MTDC hotels. Most visitors stay in Aurangabad, which has a broader range of accommodation, or Jalgaon, to catch a train away early the following day. The *Traveller's Lodge* (☎26; ④), directly opposite the main entrance to the caves, has a poor reputation but was being revamped as this book went to press. Its rooms are all self-contained, with en suite shower-toilets, clean sheets and fans. The only place serving decent **food** in Ajanta is *Food-Wallah's* very ordinary restaurant, next to the bus stand, though cold drinks and insanitary snacks are available at the stalls around the foot of the steps.

The other lodging option is the *Holiday Resort* (☎30; ②) in the one-horse village of **Fardapur**, a few kilometres down the Jalgaon road, where the rooms are reasonably clean, with fans and tatty mosquito nets, and there's a rock-bottom dorm (①) if you don't mind sleeping on the floor. A small cafeteria serves unadventurous Indian and Chinese meals; a couple of hours' advance warning is strongly recommended.

Jalgaon

Straddling an important junction in the *Central* and *Western Railway* networks, as well as the main trans-Deccan trunk road, NH6, **JALGAON** is a busy market town for the region's cotton and banana growers, and a key jumping-off point for travellers heading to or from the Ajanta caves, 58km south. Even though the town holds nothing of interest, you may find yourself obliged to hole up here to be well placed for a morning departure. If so, an early night with a good book should appeal considerably more than the dismal cafes and seedy permit-rooms (bars) outside the train station.

Practicalities

Jalgaon is well-served by mainline **trains** between Delhi and Bombay, 420km southwest, and convenient for most cities to the north on the *Central Railway*. Express services also pass through en route to join the *Southeastern Railway* at **Nagpur**.

Buses to Indore (257km north) and Pune (336km) leave from the busy bus stand, a ten-minute rickshaw ride across town from the train station. If you're heading to **Ajanta**, the fastest bus is the hourly service to **Aurangabad**, 108km south. Before buying your ticket, make sure that the bus does stop at the caves, or you might find yourself marooned at **Fardapur** (see above), fifteen minutes north of Ajanta.

You shouldn't have any difficulty finding **accommodation**. If you're not too squeamish about dirty toilets and a dawn chorus of throat-clearing, you could try the **retiring rooms** above platform 1 at the train station (①–②). As well as the usual four-to six-bed dorms, some more expensive, but good-value rooms are tacked on the side. The rest of Jalgaon's places to stay are within easy walking distance. Among the cheap and grotty lodges around the station square and main street, *Amram Guest House* (①–②; ☎6549) is the most comfortable, with reasonably clean singles and doubles, fresh sheets, fans and some attached shower-toilets. The similar *Hotel Dhahashree* (①–②) is left off the main road down a little side street. Directly opposite, the a/c *Hotel Chandan* (②–③) offers plain, clean rooms. The best mid-range option, however, has to be the new, very spruce, *Hotel Plaza* on Station Rd (②–③). Its economy rooms are particularly good, with immaculate bathrooms, fans and 24-hour checkout; pricier rooms offer *Star TV*.

There's no better place to **eat** than the *Hotel Anjali*, immediately outside the station on the right. This small, spotless Gujarati restaurant opens early for breakfast and does a good range of pure-veg snacks and main meals, including copious *thalis*, at other times of the day. Beer and other alcoholic drinks are available in the low-lit, curtained booths of the (men-only) permit-rooms nearby.

Nasik

Lying at the head of the main pass through the dark eroded hills of the Western Ghats, **NASIK** makes an interesting stopover on the lengthy journey to or from Bombay, 187km southwest. From the grim barrage of industrial estates, hoardings, *dhabas* and general conurbation creeping along its ring-road, you'd be forgiven for thinking the city holds no interest for anyone other than truckers or travelling salesmen. However, this is one of the four sites of the world's largest religious gatherings, the triennial **Kumbh Mela** (see p.289). Every twelve years – next due in 2003 – millions of pilgrims descend on the temple and *ghat*-lined banks of the **River Godavari**, to take a purifying dip at one of the most auspicious moments in the Hindu calendar.

Even outside festival times, the riverside sees plenty of action. According to the *Ramayana*, Nasik was where Rama – Vishnu in human form – his brother Lakshmana, and wife Sita lived during their exile from Ayodhya, and the arch-demon Ravana carried off Sita from here in an aerial chariot to his kingdom, Lanka, in the far south. The scene of such episodes forms the core of the busy pilgrimage circuit – a vibrant enclave packed with religious specialists, beggars, *sadhus* and street vendors touting *puja* paraphernalia. However, Nasik has a surprising dearth of historical monuments – even the famous temples beside the Godavari only date from the **Maratha era** of the eighteenth century. However, the rock-cut caves at nearby **Pandav Lena**, excavated at the highwater-mark of Buddhist achievement on the Deccan, hark back to the days when, as capital of the powerful **Satavahana** dynasty, Nasik dominated the all-important trade routes linking the Ganges Plains with the ports to the west.

Today, the city continues to prosper, though the high profile of recently relocated Bombay businesses has done little to dampen its religious fervour. If anything, the extra cash has come as a boon for the local *pujaris*. Newly inaugurated temples, dripping with fairy lights and equipped with powerful hi-fi systems, stand cheek by jowl with glitzy *sari* emporia, shopping arcades and ice-cream parlours.

Arrival and information

Buses from Bombay pull in at the **Mahamarga Bus Stand**, a ten-minute rickshaw ride from the city centre. Aurangabad buses terminate at the chaotic central **City Bus Stand**, an easy walk from several cheap hotels and restaurants. Arrival by train is more problematic, as the **railway station**, Nasik Road, lies 8km southeast. In theory, buses meet incoming trains, but they tend to be sporadic or packed. Luckily, there's no shortage of shared auto-rickshaws. If you plan to leave Nasik by train, particularly on a weekend when the city booking counter, off MG Rd (Mon–Fri 10am–5pm) is closed, reserve your outward ticket on arrival to avoid having to make the trip out here again.

Predictably for a city that sees virtually no foreign visitors, the MTDC **tourist office**, out near the golf course on Old Agra Rd (✆0752/70059), is welcoming, but not worth the trouble to find. Their daily "Darshan Tour" of the city and its environs is only likely to appeal to people with a passion for ferro-concrete temple architecture. If you need to **change money**, the *State Bank of India* (Mon–Fri 10am–2pm, Sat 10am–noon) is just up from the City Bus Stand on Swami Vivekanand Road. The General Post Office is around the corner on Trimbak Rd. Anyone wishing to use the (unreliable) poste restante facility here should ask for the "Postmaster's letters".

The City

After the hectic main streets of Nasik's commercial centre, the more colourful **riverbank** area comes as something of a surprise. Turn down any of the narrow back lanes behind MG Road and you'll emerge eventually from the maze of dilapidated wooden houses and balconies of the old quarter at the open ground lining the Godavari (pronounced God*a*vri). The small stretch on the opposite bank, between the Holkar and Santar Gardi Mahara bridges, is the focal point. In 1991, during the Kumbh Mela, an estimated three and a half million devotees converged here to bathe; usually the site plays host to more secular pursuits. The salary-men's wives may have acquired twin-tubs, but most of Nasik still gathers here on the *dhobi ghats* each morning to thump away at soapy bundles, or to haggle over the farm produce piled neatly under rows of raffia sun-shades at the **riverside market**.

South of the market, below Ram Situ footbridge, lies the eighteenth-century **Naro Sankar Mandir**. Built by the Marathas, this distinctive dark-stoned Shiva temple has some lively sculpture on the roof of its *mandapa*, and a bustling *devi* shrine. Originally, it was known as the Rameshvara Mandir; the name was changed when a local warrior, Sardar Naroshakar, installed an enormous church bell which he'd plundered from the Portuguese after their defeat at the battle of Vasai (Bassein) in 1739. The now clapper-less bell is housed in a pavilion set in the wall of the western enclosure.

Ram Kund

A hundred metres further along the river bank, past the market and a lurid sky-blue and orange eight-metre-tall Hanuman, the **Ram Kund** is the reason most people come to Nasik. Surrounded by concrete viewing towers (built to alleviate the crush at the big *melas*), it looks more like an overcrowded municipal swimming pool than one of India's most ancient sacred places. Yet for the thousands of devout Hindus who avail themselves of its purifying properties each day, these murky waters are the holiest of holies.

Ram Kund's sacred powers were first discovered when Shiva overheard a **bull-calf** telling its mother that the water there could wash away even the most deadly of sins. This was music to Shiva's ears. Not long before, in yet another of his metaphysical tiffs with Brahma, he had lopped off one of his rival's five heads. To Shiva's mortification, the severed head remained stuck to his trident, which he then had to carry around with him, proclaiming his guilt of that most heinous sin, *Brahma hatya*, or "Brahmin-murder". Shiva tried all kinds of atonement rituals in many sacred places, but only after a dip in the calf's pond at Nasik did the head finally budge. Apart from accounting for the great sanctity of the tank, this story also explains the unusual absence of a Nandi statue in the nearby **Kapeleshvara Mandir**. For here, and only here, Shiva's vehicle, the bull, momentarily became his guru.

Among the Ram Kund's more arcane attributes is its capacity to dissolve bones – a trick that has earned it the epithet of "**Astivilaya Tirth**" or "Bone Immersion Tank". Some of the more celebrated remains said to have ended up here are those of King Dasharatha of Ayodhya (Rama's father), Jawaharlal Nehru, his daughter Indira Gandhi, her son Rajiv, and a host of saints, musicians and movie stars. The tank continues to be used for mortuary rites, and most days you can see young men with shaven heads – the deceased's eldest sons – sitting in front of a *pujari* and eleven small balls of specially rolled *ghee* and flour, performing the ritual to mark the end of mourning.

Kala Ram Mandir

Follow the street opposite Ram Kund up the hill, past assorted *ashrams* and *dharam-shalas*, to arrive at the city's second most important sacred site, the area around the Kala Ram Mandir, or "Black Rama Temple". Among well-known episodes from the *Ramayana* to occur here was the event that lead to Sita's abduction, when Lakshmana sliced off the nose of Ravana's sister after she had tried to seduce Rama in the form of a voluptuous princess. Sita's cave, or **Gumpha**, a tiny grotto known in the *Ramayana* as *Parnakuti* ("Smallest Hut"), is just off the square. On removal of shoes and payment of a small donation, you can squeeze into it to see where Sita spent all those lonesome hours while the boys were off doing battle with the forces of darkness and destruction.

The **Kala Ram temple** itself, at the bottom of the square, houses unusual jet-black deities of Rama, Sita and Lakshmana; these are very popular with visiting pilgrims, as access is free from all caste restrictions. The best time to visit is around sunset, after evening *puja*, when a crowd, mostly of women, gathers in the courtyard to listen to a traditional story-teller recounting tales from the *Ramayana* and other epics.

Pandav Lena

Halfway up one of the precipitous conical hills that overlook the Bombay–Agra Road, 8km southwest of Nasik, is a small group of 24 rock-cut caves, some dating from the first century BC. The **Pandav Lena** site is famous for its well-preserved inscriptions in the ancient Pali language, and fine ancient stone sculpture.

Access to Pandav Lena is via a steep and uneven path which could prove prohibitive for elderly or disabled visitors. To see the caves themselves, numbered from right to left in chronological order, start with **cave 18**, left of the entrance. This small *chaitya* hall has a striking facade, with two leaf-shaped arches encasing auspicious Buddhist symbols. The two monastery caves, *viharas*, to either side, reached by flights of stone steps complete with their original railings, contain carved Buddhas – later additions made during the sixth century. Two further noteworthy caves are over on the other side of the group. **Caves 3 and 10**, both *viharas* dating from the second century AD, have superb stone carvings, as well as the famed **Pali inscriptions** above their doorways. These set out in elaborate detail the caves' benefactors (among them dynastic rulers, wealthy landowners, a writer and even a local Hindu worthy), as well as the complex financial provisions made for the monks who lived here.

The most straightforward way of **getting to Pandav Lena** without your own vehicle is by auto-rickshaw, though infrequent and crowded municipal buses also pass them. You can catch the buses in town from the second stop on the right, heading north away from the City Bus Stand on the main road (called the "Old Highway").

Accommodation

Most of Nasik's hotels are pitched at middle-class Bombay business travellers. The few noteworthy exceptions are the lodge-style budget places around the City Bus Stand *chowk*. These, however, tend to fill up early, soon after their noon check-out times.

Basera, Sivaji Rd (☎0752/75616). Very close to the City Bus Stand. Airy, comfortable rooms, some a/c, all with hot water and windows. Extra mattresses only Rs40. Excellent value. ③.

Holiday Plaza, Sivaji Rd (☎0752/73521). Central, plush and popular with a business clientele. ④.

Padma, Sharampur Rd (☎0752/76837). Directly opposite the City Bus Stand. Safe, clean and convenient. All rooms have attached bathrooms and hot water. ③.

Panchavati, 430 Vakil Wadi (☎0752/75771). Nasik's largest hotel, right in the middle of town. Two restaurants, "Mexican-style" bar, foreign exchange and 24hr room-service; some a/c rooms. ⑤–⑥.

Panchavati Yatri, 430 Vakil Wadi (☎0752/71273). The *Panchavati*'s good-value cheaper wing, with money exchange, 24hr coffee shop, bar and an excellent veg restaurant. Some a/c rooms. ④.

Pathik, opposite Nehru Gardens (☎0752/71884). Modern Gujarati-run hotel. Clean if unexciting. ④.

Raj Mahal Lodge, Sharampur Rd (☎0752/72880). Across the road from the bus stand. Very basic, though neat and clean. All rooms have hot water and *Star TV*. The best-value budget hotel. ②.

Samrat, Swami Vivekanand Rd (☎0752/77211). Pleasant enough, with well-maintained rooms (some a/c) and a very popular restaurant. A touch overpriced. ⑤.

Eating

By and large, Nasik's best-value **meals** are to be had in its traditional "keep it coming" *thali* restaurants. While they may not always be the cheapest option, for less than the price of a beer you can enjoy carefully prepared and freshly cooked food, often includ-

MOVING ON FROM NASIK

Nasik has frequent **buses** down the trans-Ghat NH3 to **Bombay**. The regular state buses are painfully slow, but four daily "luxury" services from Mahamarga Bus Stand, also run by *MSRTC*, take only four hours to reach Dadar Station. Tickets must be booked in advance from the reservation counter in the City Bus Stand. If the state buses are all full you could try the more expensive twice-daily private minibus service. One leaves at 7am and can be booked at the travel agency in the *Holiday Plaza*; the other at 5.15pm, with tickets from *Rahul Travel Agency* on Sivaji Rd. Both can also be booked at a little travel agency opposite the *Hotel Panchavati*. Hourly buses leave the City Bus Stand for the five-hour journeys to **Aurangabad** and **Pune**; buy tickets in advance or on the bus.

Much the fastest of the ten or twelve daily **trains** to **Bombay** is the *Panchavati Express* #1002 (7.22am; 4hr). It's also very popular, so reserve early. The *Punjab Mail* #1037, which leaves Nasik at 11.06pm, is the best service for **Agra** (17hr 30min) and **Delhi** (21hr). Forget trains to **Aurangabad**; the only one leaves at 3.13am. The other main cities served by daily, direct express services from Nasik are Bhopal, Jabalpur, Varanasi and Calcutta (Howrah). Most other places can be reached via Jalgaon or Itarsi.

ing such regional specialities as *bajra* (wholewheat *rotis*) and *bakri* (hot oatmeal biscuits), together with a plethora of tasty vegetable, pulse and lentil dishes. The city's religious associations tend to mean that meat and alcohol are rarer than elsewhere, but plenty of the larger hotels have bars and restaurants with permits.

Chaat, *Holiday Plaza*, Sivaji Rd. The best Chinese menu in town, very expensive. Serves alcohol.

Dhaba, *Panchavati*, Vakil Wadi. Classy Rajasthani-style *thalis*. Popular with families.

Khyber, *Panchavati*, Vakil Wadi. Standard north Indian, with some veg alternatives and a bar.

Pangat, *Panchavati Yatri*, Vakil Wadi. Mild but mouthwatering veg *thalis* at reasonable prices in pseudo-traditional Maharashtran ambience (mud walls and murals). Very good value.

Samrat, Swami Vivekanand Rd. Well-known *thali* joint, five minutes from the bus stand, doing a brisk trade in moderately priced, quality Gujarati food.

Suruchi, under *Basera*, Sivaji Rd. Clean, no-nonsense, south Indian fast-food cafe. Very spicy snacks and drinks at rock-bottom prices. Crowds of office workers at lunch. Family/ladies room upstairs.

Trimbak

Crouched in the shadow of the Western Ghats, 10km west of Nasik, **TRIMBAK** – literally "Three-Eyed" in Marathi, another name for Lord Shiva – is yet another place of great significance for Hindus. This was the exact spot where one of the four infamous drops of immortality-giving *amrit*-nectar fell to earth from the *kumbh* vessel during the struggle between Vishnu's vehicle Garuda and the Demons – the mythological origin of the Kumbh Mela (see p.289). Trimbak is also near the source of one of India's longest and most sacred rivers, the **Godavari**. The spring rises in a magical spot – a wind-blown ledge high on one of the barren mountains that encircle the village – and can be reached via an ancient pilgrim-trail that cuts through a cleft in an awesome, guano-splashed cliff face. En route you pass colourful wayside shrines and a ruined **fort**, getting splendid views of the sparsely populated and mountainous country to the west.

Hourly buses from Nasik pull in to Trimbak's little bus stand at the top end of the village. Make your way from there down the main street, past ramshackle shops selling vermilion powder and strings of wooden beads, to the entrance of the **Trimbakeshwar Mandir**. Numbering among India's most sacred centres for Shiva worship (it houses one of the twelve "self-born" *Jyotirlinga* – see p.645), the temple is unfortunately closed to non-Hindus. Its impressive eighteenth-century *shikhara* (tower), however, can also be glimpsed from the back streets nearby. Close to the temple, the **Kushawarth Tirth** is a small, stone-lined tank said to contain Ganges water. Its name is thought to derive from the *kush* grass used in *puja* ceremonies that once grew in profusion around it. Although the present *ghats* and temple date from 1750, myths relating to the Kushawarth Tirth occur in the *Puranas*, so it may have been used for 2500 years.

The Brahmagiri hike

The round-trip to **Brahmagiri**, the source of the Godavari, takes between two and three hours. It's a strenuous walk, particularly in the heat, so make sure you take adequate water. From the trailhead at the bottom of the village, the way is paved and stepped as far as the first level outcrop, where there are some welcome *chai* stalls and a small hamlet. Beyond that, either turn left after the last group of huts and follow the dirt trail through the woods to the foot of the **rock-cut steps** (20min), or continue straight on, to the three **shrines** clinging to the base of the cliff above. The first is dedicated to the goddess Ganga, the second – a cave containing 108 *lingams* – to Shankar (Shiva), and the third to the sage Gautama Rishi, whose hermitage this once was.

The steps climb 550 metres above Trimbak to the remains of **Anjeri Fort** – a site that was, over the years, roughed up by the armies of both Shah Jahan and Aurangzeb before it fell into the hands of Shaha-ji Raj (father of the legendary rebel-leader Sivaji). The **source** itself is another twenty minutes further on, across **Brahmagiri Hill**, in the otherwise unremarkable Gaumukhu ("Mouth of the Cow") temple. From its rather unimpressive origins this paltry trickle somehow gathers sufficient momentum to flow for nearly 1000km east across the entire Deccan plateau to the Bay of Bengal.

Practicalities

Getting to Trimbak is easy. Hourly **buses** leave Nasik's City Bus Stand (45min). To return you can catch a bus (until around 8pm), or one of the shared **taxis** that wait outside Trimbak bus stand; there's no difference in price as long as the car is full.

Although Trimbak makes an easy day trip from Nasik, it's a peaceful and atmospheric place to spend a night, with plenty of basic **accommodation**. The MTDC *Tourist Bungalow* (①/④) at the bottom of the village is the nicest option, with scruffy doubles with attached bathrooms, cheap dorm beds, and even tents pitched in the garden. In the unlikely event of it being full, head for *Alpobatchet Bhavan Rest House* (②) opposite the start of the Brahmagiri path, where the rooms are also pretty grubby.

For **food**, the only alternative to the grimy sweet-stalls around the bus stand is the small restaurant in the *Tourist Bungalow*. Given a little advance warning, they'll prepare basic veg and rice dishes for non-guests.

Nagpur

Geographically at the virtual centre of India, **NAGPUR** is the focus of government attempts to develop the remote northeastern corner of Maharashtra. It has no real sights to speak of, though its proximity to the Gandhian ashrams at **Sevagram** and **Paunar**, near **Wardha**, 77km southwest, and the hill-top temple complex at **Ramtek**, a 90-minute bus ride northeast, make it a good stop on a long cross-country journey.

This site on the banks of the River Nag was first occupied in the tenth century by aboriginal Gonds, but Nagpur itself was founded by a family of militaristic local Hindu rulers, the Bhonslas, midway through the eighteenth century. In 1853, the Bhonslas fell foul of Lord Dalhousie's "Principle of Lapse" (a grossly iniquitous law which gave the British the right to take over any native state whose ruler died without a male heir), and Nagpur became the capital of the Central Provinces. Today, it's a thriving industrial and commercial centre, with a surprisingly affluent, easygoing and uncongested feel for a city of more than a million people. Ice-cream parlours line up alongside ritzy hotels and shopping malls, while "new-women" students in *shalwa camises* whizz around town on scooters – a far cry from the *khadi dhotis*, bullock-carts, and mud and thatched villages of the surrounding countryside.

Arrival and information

Nagpur's busy downtown mainline **train station**, Nagpur Junction, is a short auto-rickshaw ride from the main hotel and market districts. *MSRTC* **buses** pull in at the state bus stand, 1500m southeast. Buses to and from Madhya Pradesh use the smaller *MPSRTC* bus stand, five minutes' walk south down the main road outside the station.

At the helpful MPTDC **tourist office**, on the fourth floor of the Lokmat Building, Wardha Rd (Mon–Fri 10am–5pm; ☎0712/523374), you can book accommodation for Pachmarhi or Kanha National Park. The **GPO** is on Palm Rd, in the Civil Lines, 4km west of the centre. Large **banks** near the train station include the *State Bank of India* (Mon–Fri 10.30am–2.30pm, Sat 10.30am–12.30pm) on Kingsway.

The City

Nagpur's most prominent landmark, the **Sitabuldi Fort**, stands in the heart of the city, on a saddle between two low hills above the railway station. Strengthened by the British in the wake of the 1857 Mutiny, its ramparts and monuments have been annexed by the Indian territorial army and are closed to the public. Further reminders of Nagpur's colonial days survive in the **Civil Lines** area, immediately north and west of Sitabuldi Hill. The grand civic buildings and bungalows from which the British Commissioner administered the vast Central Provinces region (except in mid-summer, when he and his legions of *burrasahibs* decamped to Pachmarhi – see p.343) today house the university and government offices. Among the leafy avenues and lawns of the old cantonment area, you'll come across a couple of dilapidated Victorian-Gothic **churches**. The ornate white pavilion in the middle of the dusty central **maidan**, by contrast, is unmistakably oriental. It's a good place for a snooze in the shade, along with the gaggle of students and office-*wallahs* for whom its cool stone floor is a regular lunchtime spot.

If you have an evening to fill, you could take an auto-rickshaw out to the **Ambazari Bagh**, the large artificial lake and gardens 5km southwest of the railway station, for a row and a *chai* at its waterside cafes. Otherwise, the city **markets** are good places to kill time. The main bazaar areas lie southwest of Sitabuldi (off Central Bazaar Rd), and across town, on the opposite side of the railway tracks, at the far end of Central Avenue in the **Itwari** neighbourhood. Nagpur's most famous export, **oranges**, are sold whole-sale at the hectic Santara bazaar nearby, together with glistening green, tightly bound bundles of the region's other main produce, betel leaves.

Accommodation

Most of Nagpur's **places to stay** are either across the big railway bridge east of the train station, along **Central Avenue**; or southwest of the fort around **Sitabuldi**, in the central bazaar (women especially should avoid the **cheap** lodges in the unlit back-streets nearby). Economy rooms in mid-range hotels are a much better deal.

Blue Diamond, 113 Central Ave, Dosar Chowk (☎0712/727461). Tatty, cheap and near the station. Good facilities; *Star TV*, a/c, attached bathrooms and "peep-out" balconies. 24hr check-out. ②–④.

Centre Point, 24 Central Bazaar Rd (☎0712/523093; fax 524279). The most established of Nagpur's top hotels, with all the trimmings, including a pool. ⑦.

Hardeo, Dr Munje Margi Marg, Sitabuldi (☎0712/531526). A new, well-appointed 3-star-deluxe hotel in city centre. All a/c rooms, quality restaurant, bar and 24hr coffee shop. Recommended. ⑥.

Jagson's Regency, Wardha Rd (☎0712/528100). Brand-new luxury hotel, next to the airport, boasting a roof-top restaurant, shopping arcade, gym and pool. 24hr check-out. ⑦–⑧.

Pal Palace, 25 Central Ave (☎0712/724724). Clean, comfortable and spacious rooms, some a/c, in slick and central 3-star. Foreign exchange facility. ④–⑦.

Retiring rooms, Nagpur Junction Railway Station. Dorms for around Rs30, plus some self-contained rooms. Good if you're overnighting, but noisy, and usually full by late afternoon. ①–③.

Shri Gujrat Lodge, Modi Lane #3, off Sitabuldi Main Rd (☎0712/525791). Grimy walls, dogs fighting outside small, barred windows, but central, with all-attached bathrooms, and cheap. ①.

Skylark, 119 Central Ave (☎0712/724654). Close to railway station and best value in its class, with *Star TV* in all rooms and a good restaurant. Some credit cards accepted. ③–⑥.

Eating

While Nagpur's swish hotels, such as the *Hardeo* and *Jagson's Regency*, boast the majority of its top gourmet restaurants, a number of smaller, privately run and less pretentious **places to eat** offer excellent food at a fraction of the cost.

Ashoka, near Sadar Bazaar. Upmarket restaurant near the station, renowned for its exhaustive a la carte menu of "Chindian" and Mughlai-style dishes. Expensive.

Continental, Central Ave, opposite *Hotel Blue Moon*. Low light, lurid decor, and a good selection of spicy Indian food and chilled beer. Some veg options too. Inexpensive.

Kwality, Wardha Rd, near Rani Jhansi Chowk. Tasty but pricey food in dull a/c surroundings.

Naivedhyam, off Rani Jhansi Chowk, Sitabuldi. Respectable first-floor family restaurant serving delicious veg food to a background of Hindi-Hawaiian music and fish tanks. Moderate.

Parnakuti, Ambazari Rd, on the outskirts near the lake. Attractive restaurant noted for rustic decor and authentic, mouthwatering Maharashtran cooking. Hard to find but well worth it. Moderate.

Ramtek

The picturesque cluster of whitewashed hill-top temples and shrines at **RAMTEK**, 40km northeast of Nagpur on the main Jabalpur road (NH7), is one of those mysterious, alluring apparitions, espied from afar on long journeys through central India, which few travellers take the trouble to visit. According to the *Ramayana*, this craggy, scrub-strewn outcrop, marooned in a sea of yellowing wheat-fields, was yet another spot where Rama, Sita and Lakshmana paused on their way back from Lanka. It is also allegedly the place where the greatest-ever Sanskrit poet and playwright, **Kalidasa**, penned the fifth-century *Meghdoota*, "the Cloud Messenger". Although few traces of these ancient times have survived (most of Ramtek's temples date from the eighteenth century), the site's old paved pilgrim trails, sacred lake, tumbledown shrines and fine views across the endless plains more than live up to its distant promise.

From Nagpur, NH7 runs through the northern Harijan quarters, with their bespectacled blue icons of the "Untouchable" leader Dr Ambedkhar standing stiffly at the roadside, to the open countryside beyond. Ramtek appears on the horizon after an hour or so. The town's shabby bus stand is 2km from the central market square, **Gandhi Chowk**, which is most easily reached in a shared auto-rickshaw. Once in the small bazaar, head past the sweet stalls to the lane leading out of its top right-hand corner. At the T-junction, bear right and follow the track through the houses until it reaches open grazing land, on the far side of which a flight of whitewashed stone steps climbs steeply up the rocky, south-facing side of Ramtek hill.

The pathway, which breaches the imposing sandstone walls of the citadel via a narrow gateway, brings you out, puffing and panting, at a raised **courtyard** in front of the main entrance to the temple. Built in 1740 by Raghoji I, the Bhonsla ruler of Nagpur, the complex rests on the site of an earlier structure erected between the fourth and fifth centuries, of which only three small sandstone shrines remain. After depositing your shoes, head through the ornate entrance porch, with its old photographs of saints and benefactors, to the inner courtyard. Ahead of you, the subsidiary **Hanuman shrine** on the right is less grand than that dedicated to Rama's brother, Lakshmana, nearby. Having been smudged with red *tilak*, given a slurp of Ganga water and a handful of sugary bonbons for an offering, or *prashad*, you'll be ushered into the main **shrine-room** for *darshan* of the Rama and Sita deities. The pair peer from behind an ornate brass door and a backdrop of a solid-silver wall. The interior of the assembly hall, or *mandapa*, which is now completely enclosed, is also decorated with fading photographs and paintings of sages and gods, together with antique Maratha weapons.

The best **views** from the temple are from the small onion-domed belvederes and whitewashed pavilions that surmount the flat roofs and battlements encircling the inner courtyard. To the southwest, you look out over the cluttered jumble of Ramtek town to the shining blue irrigation tanks on its outskirts, while the panorama in the other direction takes in a vast expanse of dead-flat and dusty wheat fields peppered with the occasional coppice of trees. At *puja* times, this is a good vantage point from which to watch the temple *pujaris* doing their rounds of the various shrines, ringing bells and waving smoky oil lamps before the deities.

Ambala Lake

Another of Ramtek's sacred sites is **Ambala Lake**, a holy bathing tank 1500m on foot from the hilltop. To pick up the flagstone pathway that leads down to it, head along the concourse opposite the temple's main entrance-porch, past the women selling coconuts and sacks of crimson, orange and pink vermilion powder, to the edge of the plateau. From here, either turn left towards the small **Trivikarma** Krishna **temple**, clinging to the north slope of the hill, or continue down the main pilgrims' trail to the lake. Along the way, you pass three fifth-century sandstone **shrines** dedicated to different incarnations of Vishnu. A large banyan tree, also sacred to Vishnu, shelters a couple of amorphous orange-painted gods tended by a palmist-astrologer.

The lake itself lies at the bottom of the gulley, enfolded by a spur of parched brown hills. Its main attractions, at least for the shaven-headed pilgrims who make their way here in rented mini-vans for a *dhoti*-soaking dip in its holy waters, are the temples and *ghats* clinging to its muddy banks. More energetic visitors may wish to combine a look with a *parikama*, or circular **tour** of the tank, taking in the semi-derelict cenotaphs and weed-choked shrines that litter its more tranquil north and western shores.

Practicalities

Direct buses leave **Nagpur** (*MSRTC* stand) every hour for the hour-long trip to Ramtek. Long-distance *MPSRTC* buses also pass by en route to and from **Jabalpur**, although these will dump you on the main road, 3km from town. If you don't feel like hiking up to the temple, **auto-rickshaws** will whisk you up from the town bus stand, or from Gandhi Chowk (via Ambala Lake) for around Rs50.

The only **place to stay** in Ramtek, apart for the pilgrims' *dharamshalas* and ashrams around Ambala Lake, is the new MTDC *Holiday Resort* (☎255213; ①–③) on the hill beside the main temple complex. This offers cheap dorm beds and a couple of simple but clean self-contained rooms. **Food** can also be prepared here, though if you want anything more adventurous than *dhal*, *subzi*-of-the-day and rice, you should phone ahead or, better still, book in advance through any MTDC tourist office. Finally, the **PWD Rest House** in Ambala, opposite the big, red-and-white-painted fortified archway on the south bank of the lake, is also worth a try if you're stuck (②).

Sevagram

SEVAGRAM, Gandhi's model "Village of Service", is set deep in the serene Maharashtran countryside, 9km from the railroad town of **Wardha**. The Mahatma moved here from his former ashram at Sabarmati in Gujarat during the monsoon of 1936, on the invitation of his friend Seth Jamnalal Bajaj. Right at the centre of the subcontinent, within easy reach of the *Central Railway*, it made an ideal headquarters for the *Satyagraha* movement, combining seclusion with easy access to other parts of the country Gandhi needed in order to carry out his political activities.

These days, the small settlement is a cross between a museum and living centre for the promulgation of Gandhian philosophies. Interested visitors are welcome to spend a couple of days here, helping in the fields, attending discussions and prayer meetings, and learning the dying art of hand-spinning. The older ashramites, or **sadhaks**, are veritable fonts of wisdom when it comes to the words of their guru, Gandhiji.

The ashram

Buses to Sevagram from Wardha stop at a small crossroads half a kilometre from the village. Named after the Mahatma's wife, the **Kasturba Gandhi Hospital** on the corner of the main road was set up by the ashram to provide cut-price health care for local farming communities – hence the crush on the bus out here. From the hospital, a short walk down the lane to the right takes you past fields and farmland to the **visitors' centre** (daily 10am–6pm), with its photos and documents relating to Gandhi's life.

The real focal point of the ashram is the main **compound** on the left side of the lane. These modest rustic huts, with their two-tiered terracotta roofs, smooth mud walls and shady courtyards, are little altered since Gandhi and his disciples lived out the last years of the Independence struggle. Men and women in simple handmade cotton clothes sit crosslegged on the wide verandahs, spinning thread and singing devotional songs, to the mild amusement of visitors from the city who look on with a peculiar mixture of respect for Mahatma's memory and disdain for those who keep it alive. The first hut along the path has been converted into a small shop selling *khadi* goods and books about Gandhi. Nearby, the **Adi Niwas** was the Mahatma's first home in Sevagram. The sandy plot in front of it is today used by the *sadhaks* for prayer gatherings. The interior of the **Bapu Kuti** opposite, Gandhi's main residence, has been kept exactly as it was in the 1930s, complete with its original bed, massage table and the few "luxuries" which Gandhi permitted himself: a foot-cleaner, the famous pair of tiny round specs, a spittoon and his beloved three brass monkeys.

Elsewhere, the compound holds the Mahatma's **secretariat**, or correspondence room, which enshrines a phone installed by the British as a pre-Independence "hotline"; the **Ba-Kuti**, where Kasturba lived; the **Parchure Kuti**, home of the Sanskrit scholar Shri Parchure Shashtri (the Mahatma's devotion to this close friend, a leprosy sufferer, did much to de-stigmatize the disease in India); and the **Akiri Niwas**, or "Final Home", where Gandhi stayed before leaving Sevagram for the last time.

Practicalities

Half-hourly, jam-packed local **buses** run from **Wardha** – on the *Central Railway* and accessible from Bombay (759km) – to the crossroads outside the Kasturba Gandhi Hospital. Frequent "express" buses from Nagpur's *MSRTC* bus stand, 77km northeast, take around two and a half hours to reach Wardha.

Accommodation is limited to the ashram's own *Yatri Niwas* (①) – a basic but spotless hostel. Simple and filling veg meals are shared with the *sadhaks* on a verandah in the main compound and, like the rooms, cost a nominal sum. Donations, which finance the ashram's adult education programme, are gratefully accepted. Occasionally, the rooms fill up with people attending conferences, so seek out the person in charge of bookings as soon as you arrive. The only other place to stay nearby, MTDC's **hotel** in Wardha (☎2172; ①–③), has 28 dorm beds and a dozen more costly self-contained rooms. Check-out time is 8am; reserve in advance through any MTDC office.

Paunar

Crowning a low hillock overlooking a rocky river bank at **PAUNAR**, 10km north of Wardha on the Nagpur road, Vinoba Bhave's ashram has an altogether more dynamic feel to it than its more famous cousin at Sevagram. Bhave, a close friend and disciple of Gandhi, best remembered for his successful Bhoondan or **"land gift"** campaign to persuade wealthy landowners to hand over farmland to the poor, founded the ashram in 1938 to develop the concept of **swarajya**, or "self-sufficiency". Consequently, organic gardening, milk-production, spinning and weaving have an even higher profile here than the regular meditation, prayer and yoga sessions. Another difference between this institution and the one up the road is that the *sadhaks* here are almost all female.

The ashram's living quarters, painted the pale blue worn by most of its inhabitants, are ranged like cloisters around an attractive square courtyard. At the far end, Vinoba's old **room** is now a shrine, its bare interior enlivened by fresh marigolds and incense. Stone steps lead down from the upper level to a small terrace looking out over the **ghats** where two small memorials mark the spots where a handful of Gandhi's, and later Vinoba's, ashes were scattered onto the river: Gandhi's is the circular plinth at the end of the long, narrow jetty, Bhave's the brass urn on the small *stupa*-shaped dome to the right. Every year on February 12, the *ghats*, which are immersed by floods for four months during the monsoon, are inundated with half a million people who come here to mark the anniversary of Gandhi's death.

Fragments of ancient **sculpture** on show in the main building have, over the years, been unearthed by *sadhaks* digging in the ashram's fields and gardens. One of the best pieces, discovered by Vinoba himself in 1938 and housed in the small temple near his former room, depicts the scene from the end of the *Ramayana* where Rama, Sita and Lakshmana are re-united with Baratiya after the battle at the gates of Ayodhya. Note also the exquisite black stone Vishnu mounted in a glass case on the wall nearby – a relic of the Warkatak dynasty whose capital dominated the banks of the River Dhama not far from here between eight hundred and a thousand years ago.

Practicalities

Paunar can be reached by **bus** from either Nagpur (67km) or Wardha (10km) by jumping off at the old stone bridge across the river below it. Alternatively, you can **walk** the

3km from Sevagram. The path, a cart-track that runs over the hill opposite the hospital crossroads, comes out in the roadside village 1km west of the Paunar ashram.

As with Sevagram, it is possible to **stay** at Paunar in one of the visitors' rooms or dormitories. Again, these are frequently booked up during conferences or seminars, so check when you arrive. Women are given preference if space is short. **Meals**, made from organic, home-grown produce, are also available on request.

SOUTHERN MAHARASHTRA

Most tourists heading south from Bombay skip southern Maharashtra, but if you have a little time you can break up the journey profitably and ease the burden of covering vast distances in one go. **Pune** retains its Maratha character, in the old quarter at least, and also boasts a unique museum; some may also be attracted by its much-derided Osho Commune. Hill stations such as **Matheran** provide coolness, wooded walks and fine views, while **Murud-Janjira** has little-visited beaches, a picturesque old-fashioned town and a sea fort. From **Lonavala**, you can get to see the earliest Buddhist rock-cut art in the western Deccan, sometimes even in peaceful solitude, and **Kolhapur**, the last major city before Karnataka to the south, or Goa to the southwest, is a characterful place with a strange blend of Maratha and so-called Indo-Saracenic architecture.

Matheran

The little hill station of **MATHERAN**, 170km east of Bombay, is set on a narrow north–south ridge, 800m up in the Sahyadri Range. From viewpoints with such names as Porcupine, Monkey and Echo, at the edge of virtually perpendicular cliffs that plunge into steep ravines, you can see way across the hazy plains – on a good day, so they say, as far as Bombay. The town itself has for the moment one unique attribute; cars, buses motorbikes and auto-rickshaws are prohibited. That, added to the journey up, on a **miniature train** that chugs its way through spectacular scenery to the crest of the hill, gives the town an agreeably quaint, time-warped feel.

Since the mid-nineteenth century, Matheran ("mother forest") has been popular as a refreshing retreat from the heat of Bombay. The season is between mid-September and mid-June (at other times it's raining or misty); the most crowded times are during April and May, or virtually any weekend. There's really nothing to do but relax, wander the woods on foot or horseback, and enjoy the fresh air and views.

As the crow flies, Matheran is only 6.5km from Neral on the plain below, but the train climbs up on 20km of track with no less than 281 curves, said to be among the sharpest on any railway in the world. From 1907, the demanding haul was handled by four complex steam engines. Sadly, they puffed their last in 1980 and were replaced by cast-off diesels from Darjeeling, Shimla and Ooty. The two-hour ride is a treat, especially if you can get a window seat; but be prepared for a squash and hard benches.

In 1974, the All India Rail Strike cut Matheran off; only hand-pulled rickshaws and six-man palanquins, *dandis*, made the climb up from Neral. To combat the situation, the track was made passable for jeeps and finally in 1984 was tarred, up to Dasturi Naka, 2km from the town. A strong lobby wants to extend it to the centre, which if successful will undoubtedly destroy Matheran's character.

Arrival and information

To reach Matheran by **train**, you must first get to Neral Junction; the daily *Deccan Express* #1007 from **Bombay** VT (6.45am) stops here, but most express trains don't stop until Karjat (2–3hr), beyond Neral, so you may have to take one of the dozen daily passenger trains. From **Pune** (2–3hr), all expresses stop at Karjat; if the one you're on isn't stopping at Neral, change there. Trains up from Neral to Matheran depart at 8.40am, 11am and 5pm (also 4.15pm, April & May) and take about two hours. Matheran station is in the centre of town on MG Rd, which runs roughly north–south.

All **motor vehicles**, including shared taxis and minibuses from Neral, have to park at the taxi stand next to the MTDC *Holiday Camp* at Dasturi Naka, 2km north of the town centre, from where you can walk, rent an aged horse (its keeper walks with you) or take a labour-intensive cycle rickshaw. There is a little halt on the miniature railway nearby, but unless you've already booked a seat, you won't be allowed on. However you arrive, you must pay a **toll** to enter the town (Rs10). A small **tourist information** booth (daily 10am–6pm) opposite the railway station has maps and can help you get your bearings. There is nowhere to **change money** except the bigger hotels.

Accommodation and eating

Matheran has plenty of **hotels**; though there are no luxury ones, few could be termed cheap. Most are close to the railway station on MG Rd and the road behind it, Kasturba Bhavan. Reduced rates may apply for midweek or long stays, and during the rainy off-season (when many hotels are closed altogether). Virtually all the hotels cater for **full** or **half board**, and there are standard "meals" restaurants around MG Road.

Alexander, near Alexander Point, 2km south of the railway station (☎021483/251 or Bombay 492 6610). Pleasant wooded location with rooms, cottages (some a/c) and good restaurant. ⑦.

Gujarat Bhavan, Maulana Azad Rd (☎021483/278 or Bombay 388 1998). Clean and comfortable veg hotel with range of rooms and cottages (some a/c with TV). Full board. ⑤.

Hope Hall, MG Rd, opp. *Lord's Central* (☎021483/253). Bottom of the range, but not bad. ②.

Lord's Central, MG Rd (☎021483/228 or Bombay 201 8008). Matheran's most characterful hotel (often full), ten minutes from the railway station. Charming Raj (non-a/c) cottages with terraces, some with superb views across the valley. Excellent veg and non-veg food including Parsi dishes. ⑦.

Meghdoot, 9 Kasturba Bhavan (☎021483/266). Popular and average, with full board. ④.

MTDC Tourist Camp, Dasturi Naka (☎021483/277 or Bombay 202 6713). Good option, a forty-minute walk or horse ride from town, at the end of the road up. Bookable through MTDC offices in Bombay. Assorted cottages (nothing grand) and dorm, with a simple open-air restaurant. ①–④.

Prasanna, MG Rd, opposite the railway station (☎021483/258). Fairly basic full-board lodge. ③.

Royal, Kasturba Bhavan. Popular, with comfortable rooms (some a/c with TV). Full board. ⑤.

Rugby, Vithalrao Kotwal Marg (☎021483/291 or Bombay 221721). Two minutes' walk up the road opposite the railway station. One of the oldest hotels, now expanded, offering a range of accommodation, set around a garden. Twelve non-a/c rooms, 33 a/c doubles, suites and duplexes for couples. ⑧.

Murud-Janjira

The unspoilt, old-fashioned and quiet little coastal town of **MURUD**, 165km south of Bombay, was once part of the little-known state belonging to the **Siddis** of Janjira, descendants of Abyssinian sailor-adventurers. Modern development seems to have passed this quiet backwater by, and many of its characterful houses are largely of wood, some brightly painted, fronted by pillared verandahs with built-in benches and gates. Nearing Murud, the undulating coast road from Bombay passes through attractive countryside with the sea slipping in and out of view, its shore lined with casuarinas, coconut and betel palms; inland is agricultural land used to cultivate rice and string-beans, and beyond lie forested hills, prowling, according to locals, with leopards.

The imposing fort of **Janjira** (2km south), which until the 1970s was inhabited by descendants of the Siddis, was built on an island in the Rajpuri creek in 1515. Even the Marathas, fort fanatics as they were, failed to penetrate its 15-metre-high walls. Shivaji attacked in 1659, followed by his son Shambhuji, who tried digging a tunnel and even attempted to fill the channel out to the island. The trip out by local *hodka* boat (around Rs50), from the jetty at the southern end of town, makes an excellent excursion.

You can get fine views of the bay and surrounding countryside by climbing more than 200 steps up to the small hilltop **Dattatreya Temple**, dedicated to the triple-headed deity comprising Vishnu, Shiva and Brahma. It's a simple structure, with an Islamic-style tower; inside, decorative tiles cover the floor of the wood-and-brick *mandapa* with flower and peacock designs, while European-looking angelic figures and landscapes adorn the ceiling. Left of the cell holding a Dattatreya image is a portrait of the nineteenth-century Maharashtran saint, **Gajanan Maharaj**, smoking *ganja*. The temple's main **festival** is Dattanjayanthi (Dec), which lasts three days and nights.

The dilapidated eighteenth-century **Nawab's Palace** – which bears more than a passing resemblance to the Addams Family residence – overlooks Janjira, 2km north of Murud. It was opened in 1991 as a museum, but soon closed due to vandalism, and today its present owner, the erstwhile Nawab Shah Siddi Mahmood Khan, lives elsewhere. If you find the caretaker, however, and ask him nicely enough, he may permit you to look around the hauntingly abandoned interior. Inside, the Durbar Hall, illuminated by a stained-glass ceiling of nine domes, is littered with furniture of marble and finely carved wood, interspersed with stuffed tigers, leopards and lions. Living quarters contain nineteenth-century western furniture, badly in need of repair, and ancient, dusty, evocative photos, including a signed one of England's Queen Mary, and another showing the household in the days when the palace employed 350 servants.

Practicalities

Most **buses** from Bombay Central take five hours; there are two faster *Asiad* services (5.45am & 11am; 3hr 30min), which must be booked in advance. All stop on Murud's main street, Durbar Rd, parallel to the coast, where you'll find the post office, covered market, a few basic restaurants and the town's two **hotels**. Officially you're supposed to give fifteen days' notice to stay at the *Government Rest House* (①), but there's no harm in asking if one of their comfortable rooms is available (two have balconies overlooking the sea). Food is only cooked for groups, but you may be allowed to use the kitchen. The run-down concrete bungalows of the *Murud Beach Resort* (☎278; ②) have been taken over by MTDC, who plan to refurbish them. For now the place is gratifyingly quiet, inches from the virtually deserted beach, with a simple canteen-style restaurant.

Many visitors prefer to base themselves at **Kashid**, 15km north, where there's a fine beach, water sports, and an upmarket hotel, the *Kashid Beach Resort* (☎8262; ⑥), which offers 17 very comfortable split-level rooms with balconies looking down on the sea, a good restaurant and swimming pool. The three-kilometre stretch of unspoilt beach, where you can rent a variety of water sports equipment, is a stone's throw away. Rooms can be booked in advance in Bombay at *Beacon Marketing & Reservation Services*, Munshaw House, 22 Rustom Sidhwa Marg (☎262 5406). All buses from Bombay to Murud go via Kashid, but you may have to ask the driver to stop.

Lonavala and the Buddhist caves of Karle, Bhaja and Bedsa

Just thirty years ago, the town of **LONAVALA**, 100km southeast of Bombay and 62km northwest of Pune, was a quiet retreat in the Sahyadri Hills. Since then, the place has mushroomed to cope with hordes of holidaymakers from the state capital, and is now only of interest as a base for the magnificent **Buddhist caves** of **Karle**, **Bhaja** and **Bedsa**, some of which date from the Satavahana period (second century BC), and were on major trade routes to sites such as Ellora and Ajanta.

MTDC organizes **rock climbing** trips around Lonavala. Contact their Bombay office, or the MTDC *Karle Resort* (Bombay–Pune Rd; ☎Karle 30).

Arrival and getting around

Frequent buses arrive at Lonavala's central **bus station**, on the Bombay–Pune Road (NH4), but the train is infinitely preferable. Lonavala is on the main railway line between Bombay (3hr) and Pune (1hr 15min), and all express trains stop here. The **railway station** is on the south side of town, close to the centre. With a car, or by taking an early train, it's just about possible to make a day trip from Bombay, but it's better to allow yourself a full day to get around. At weekends it can be very crowded.

The three cave sites are some way from each other, all to the east of town. Covering Karle and Bhaja under your own steam by bus and or train, if you're prepared for a good walk, is manageable in a day, but if you want to get out to Bedsa too, and you can afford it, the easiest option is undoubtedly to **rent an auto-rickshaw or car for the day** (usually found at the railway station). A car is likely to charge a standard rate of around Rs400 for four hours and Rs800 for eight. Auto-rickshaw rates are negotiable, especially to Bedsa, as hardly anybody ever goes there; as a general rule of thumb you can expect to pay at least Rs200 for a round trip to Karle and Bhaja.

Karle

KARLE (also spelt Karla and Karli) lies 3km north of the town of Karle Caves Junction, 11km from Lonavala on NH4. Five buses a day (6am, 9am, 12.30pm, 3pm & 6.30pm) call at the MTDC *Karle Resort*; the last bus back to Lonavala leaves Karle at 7pm.

The rock-cut Buddhist *chaitya* hall at Karle, reached by steps that climb 110 metres, is the largest and best preserved in India, dating from the first century AD. As you approach across a large courtyard, itself hewn from the rock, the enormous fourteen-metre-high facade of the hall towers above, topped by a horseshoe-shaped window and with three entrances below, one for the priest and the others for devotees. To the left of the entrance stands a *simhastambha*, a tall monolithic column capped with four lions.

In the porch of the cave, dividing the three doorways, are panels of figures in six couples, presumed to have been the wealthy patrons of the hall. Two rows of octagonal columns with pot-shaped bases divide the interior into three, forming a wide central aisle and, on the outside, a hall that allowed devotees to circumambulate the monolithic *stupa* at the back. Above each pillar's fluted capital kneels a finely carved elephant mounted by two riders, one with arms draped over the other's shoulders. Amazingly, perishable remnants survive from the time when the hall was in use; teak ribs on the vaulted ceiling show that the stone was carved to resemble a wooden structural model. Surmounting the *stupa* are the remains of a carved wooden umbrella.

Full views of the main entrance are obscured by the much later accretion, to the right, of a Hindu shrine to **Ekviri**, a goddess-oracle revered by Koli fishing communities. Fences are often erected outside it, to regulate the flow of worshippers who seek *darshan* or to consult the goddess. When questions are addressed to Ekviri, areca nuts are placed on silver discs above the head of the image. Depending on which nut falls to the ground, right or left, the answer is "yes" or "no". Tuesdays and Fridays are the busiest times, but Karle is at its most frenetic during the annual Chaitra (March/April) festival, when the blood of sacrificed chickens is smeared on the steps up the hill.

Bhaja

Although the eighteen caves at **BHAJA** may not be as elaborate as those at Karle, they're more atmospheric, giving visitors a much clearer sense of their original tranquillity (particularly during the rainy season, when monks traditionally ceased their wanderings). They lie 3km south of Karle Caves Junction, reached by following a path up from the village square near the railway station at Malavli, just 1km away.

These caves are among the oldest in India, dating from the late second to early first centuries BC, during the earliest, Hinayana, phase of Buddhism. Most consist of simple halls (*viharas*) with adjoining cells that contain plain shelf-like beds; many are fronted by rough verandahs. Bhaja's apsidal *chaitya* hall (**#12**), which contains a *stupa*, but no figures, has 27 plain bevelled pillars, which lean inwards, mimicking the style of wooden buildings. Sockets in the stone of the exterior *chaitya* arch reveal that it once contained a wooden gate or facade. Further south, the last cave (**#19**), a *vihara*, is decorated with superb carvings. Mysteriously, scholars identify the figures as the Hindu gods, **Surya** and **Indra**, who figure prominently in the *Rig Veda* (*c*. 1000 BC). In Vedic mythology Surya, the sun god, is conventionally described flying through the sky as he banishes darkness; here, left of the entrance, he rides a chariot pulled by four horses and accompanied by two women who carry a parasol and fly-whisk. The chariot crushes the bodies of naked demonesses, who appear to float in the air. The panel to the right is thought to show Indra, who in the *Vedas* represents power, particularly lightning, thunder and rain, and thanks to the quantity of sacred *soma* drink that he quaffs, frequently becomes huge. In this striking sculpture, two figures are shown riding an elephant (Indra's vehicle), all gigantic in relation to the landscape. The elephant grasps what appears to be a little tree in his trunk.

Bedsa

It's quite possible you will not meet anyone else visiting the caves at **BEDSA**, which is one of its great attractions. Once you reach the village, which is 12km beyond Bhaja along NH4 or a three-kilometre bus ride from Kamshet, the nearest railway station, you'll have to ask the way to the unsigned path. If you're lucky, village kids hanging around will scramble up the steep hillside with you, for a fee.

Bedsa's **chaitya hall**, excavated later than that at Karle, is far less sophisticated. The entrance is extremely narrow, leading from a porch which appears to be supported, though of course it is not, by four octagonal pillars over 7m high, with pot-shaped bases and bell capitals; bulls, horses and elephants rest on inverted, stepped slabs on top. Inside, 26 plain octagonal columns lead to an unadorned monolithic *stupa*.

Lonavala: accommodation and eating

Lonavala has a wide range of **accommodation**, from very cheap to five-star; many of its hotels lower their rates out of season (Oct–March) or for longer stays. Budget and mid-range hotels are concentrated in the centre, on the Bombay–Pune Road, by the bus station and the railway station. Many offer good, reasonably priced food. For a **snack**, try the local *chikki* – delicious, dentally challenging, nut-and-honey sweets.

Adarsh, Shivaji Rd (☎021147/2353). Spotless rooms, some a/c, near the (noisy) bus stand, overlooking pleasant central courtyard. Jain-run restaurant with excellent pure veg Gujarati *thalis*. ②–⑤.

Chandralok, Shivaji Rd (☎021147/2294). Good-value, clean, comfortable and well-maintained rooms (deluxe with *Star TV*). Breakfast in room only. Restaurant open for lunch. ②–④.

Dukes Retreat, Pune–Bombay Rd, Khandala (☎021147/3826). Superb position overlooking ravine, with prize-winning garden and pool (open to non-residents, Rs100). Comfortable rooms and cottages; weekend packages include breakfast and dinner. Open-air cafe, a/c restaurant and bar. ⑧.

Matruchaya, Telang Rd, off Bombay–Pune Rd (☎021147/2875). Popular, decrepit old house. ②.

MTDC Karle Resort, Bombay–Pune Rd (☎Karle 30). On the Lonavala–Karle bus route, 2km from Malavli railway station. Wide range of comfortable accommodation (some a/c) in cottages, doubles and suites. Good restaurant (6am–10.30pm) and bar. Reserve from any MTDC office. ③–⑥.

Oriental, 158/159 Bombay–Pune Rd, opposite Power Station (☎021147/2552). Ten minutes' walk from the bus stand, with a certain eccentric charm. Don't be misled by the sign proclaiming "Luxury rooms available"; it's an old house with verandahs (one has a swing), ancient furniture and basic rooms (the cheapest is nothing more than a single bed by the stairs). Food can be arranged. ①–④.

Pitale Lodge, Bombay–Pune Rd (☎021147/2657). Seven rooms in an old bungalow. Characterful, friendly, basic and inexpensive. Bar and restaurant. ②.

Pune (Poona)

At an altitude of 598m, **PUNE**, Maharashtra's second city, lies close to the Western Ghat mountains (known here as the Sahyadri Hills), on the edge of the Deccan plains as they stretch away to the east. The British chose Pune in 1820 as an alternative head-quarters for the Bombay Presidency, to escape the summer heat and the monsoon deluge of the capital. Their military cantonment in the northwest of town is still used by the Indian army, and a number of British buildings, such as the Council Hall and Deccan College, survive.

Settlement on the site is thought to date back two thousand years, when Kasba, a fortified town, lay between the River Mula to the northwest and the Nagzari Nala creek to the east. Occupying a strategic position on trade routes between the Deccan and the Arabian Sea, the town prospered during the early Hindu period. Under the sixteenth-century Marathas, Pune became the capital and military headquarters of a sovereign state, until its rulers were deposed by the Brahmin Peshwa family. They dominated Pune during the eighteenth century, before the arrival of the British.

Since colonial days, Pune has continued to develop as a major industrial city and a centre for higher education. But to most outsiders, it is notorious as the home of the **Osho Commune International**, founded in 1970 by the charismatic Bhagwan Rajneesh, or Osho (1931–90), whose syncretic and, to many Indians, scandalous philosophy of life lured thousands of neo-hippies from Europe and America.

> The telephone **area code** for Pune is ☎0212.

Arrival and information

From Pune's **airport**, 10km northeast of the centre, taxis, auto-rickshaws and a regular ("Ex-Servicemen") bus service run into the city. Pune is an important point on the southern express train routes from Bombay (3hr 30min–4hr 30min); the **railway station** is in the centre of town, south of the River Mula. Auto-rickshaws and tourist taxis wait outside the station – locals often use the shared long-distance taxis to get to Bombay. Of the three main **bus stands**, that next to the railway station serves the city itself (though all the signs and timetables are in Marathi) and some destinations south, including Goa and Bombay. **Swargate**, about 3km south, close to Nehru Stadium, has services to Karnataka, while **Shivaji Nagar**, 3km west of the centre, has services from towns in the north, including Aurangabad and Lonavala.

Enkay Car Rentals, 307 MPJ Chambers, Wakdewadi, Bombay–Pune Rd (☎52487), and *Sawhney Services*, 18 Dr Coyaji Rd (☎666366), both offer reasonable **car rental**.

Information

You can book MTDC long-distance buses and guided city tours, and seek advice about other bus services at the **MTDC Tourist Information Counter** (Mon–Fri 10am–6pm & Sat 10am–1pm), opposite the railway station's First Class booking office. Like most government-run efforts, their three-hour **tour** of Pune (daily 8am & 3pm; Rs50) is too rushed. The other MTDC office, in the Central Office Building, Sassoon Hospital Rd (☎66697), is of little use. The easiest place to **change money** is *Thomas Cook,* halfway along Gen Thimmaya Rd, which runs between MG Rd and East St (Mon–Fri 10am–6pm, Sat 10am–12.30pm; ☎667188); they can also make airline and hotel reservations.

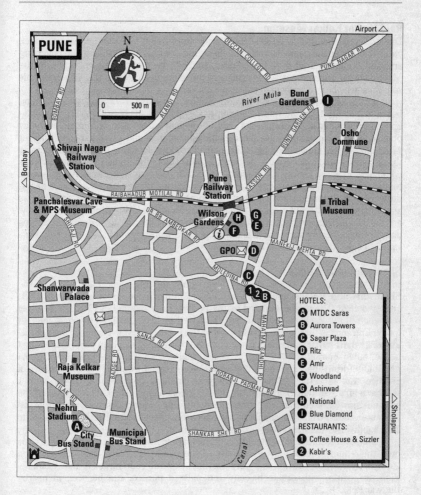

PUNE

N

0 500 m

Airport △

Bombay △

△ Bombay

River Mula

Bund Gardens

I Blue Diamond

Osho Commune

Shivaji Nagar Railway Station

Pune Railway Station

Panchalesvar Cave & MPS Museum

RAJBAHADUR MOTILAL RD

Wilson Gardens

H National

G Ashirwad

E Amir

F Woodland

Tribal Museum

GPO

D Ritz

C Sagar Plaza

1 **2** **B**

Shanwarwada Palace

Raja Kelkar Museum

Nehru Stadium

A MTDC Saras

City Bus Stand

Municipal Bus Stand

SHANKAR SHET RD

Canal

△ Sholapur

HOTELS:
A MTDC Saras
B Aurora Towers
C Sagar Plaza
D Ritz
E Amir
F Woodland
G Ashirwad
H National
I Blue Diamond
RESTAURANTS:
1 Coffee House & Sizzler
2 Kabir's

The City

Pune centre is bordered on the north by the River Mula and to the west by the River Mutha – the two join in the northwest to form the Mutha-Mula, at Sangam Bridge (previously Wellesley Bridge). The principal shopping area, and the greatest concentration of restaurants and hotels, is in the streets south of the railway station, particularly Connaught Road and further south, MG Road. The old **Peshwa** part of town, by far the most interesting to explore, is towards the west, between the fortified **Shaniwarwada Palace** and fascinating **Raja Dinkar Kelkar Museum**; old wooden *wadas*, palatial city homes, survive on these narrow, busy streets, and the Victorian, circular **Phule Market** is always a hive of activity.

Raja Dinkar Kelkar Museum

Dinkar Gangadhar Kelkar (1896–1990), aside from being a celebrated Marathi poet, published under the name Adnyatwass, spent much of his life travelling and collecting arts and crafts from all over the country. In 1975, he donated his collection to the Maharashtran government, as a permanent museum, dedicated to the memory of his son, Raja, who had recently died at the age of twelve.

In a huge old house, the **Raja Dinkar Kelkar Museum**, 1378 Shukrawar Peth, on buses #72 or #74 from the railway station to City Market (daily 8.30am–12.30pm & 3–6pm), is a wonderful pot-pourri, not only of objets d'art but also of humble everyday objects. Kitchen utensils include a camelskin oil container and a wooden noodle-maker which, like other Indian cooking tools such as coconut scrapers, requires its operator to sit astride it. Paraphernalia associated with *paan,* the Indian passion, includes containers in every conceivable design, made from silk, wood, brass and silver; some mimic animals or fish, or are egg-shaped and in delicate filigree, others are solid heavy-duty boxes built to withstand constant use. Lime applicators, nut-holders, and mortars are equally elaborate; nut-crackers often take the form of a loving couple. Also on show are musical instruments, superb Marathi textiles and costumes, toys, domestic shrines and furniture, beauty accessories and a model of Shaniwarwada Palace. Lavishly illustrated booklets (Rs75) are sold at the entrance.

Shaniwarwada Palace

In the centre of the oldest part of town, only the imposing high walls of the **Shaniwarwada Palace** (daily 8am–noon & 2–6pm) survive, following fires in 1791, 1812 and 1828. The palace, founded by the Peshwa ruler Bajrao I in 1730 and the chief residence of the Peshwas until the British arrived in 1817, has little to excite interest today. Entrance is through the Delhi gate on the north, one of five set into the perimeter wall, whose huge teak doors come complete with nasty elephant-proof spikes. Just inside, faded murals show Ganapati, Vishnu and scenes from the *Ramayana.* Court musicians (drums and double-reed wind *shehnais*) played from the balconies above, a practice that is revived three times a year: January 26 (Republic Day), May 1 (Maharashtra Workers Day) and August 15 (Independence Day). The interior of the palace is now grassed over, the seven-storey building entirely absent. Only one of the available guides, usually available in the afternoons, speaks English. Bus #3 runs the 2km southwest from the railway station to the palace.

In the seventeenth and eighteenth centuries, aristocrats and the upper middle class built their homes, *wadas,* in the vicinity of the palace. Typically they centred on a courtyard or, if the owner was very wealthy, several courtyards. A fine example, **Vishram wada**, with ornate balcony and pillared portico, can be seen in nearby Budwar Peth.

Panchalesvara Cave and Mahatma Phule Sangrahalaya Museum

The **Panchalesvara** (aka Pataleshvar) **Cave**, on the west of town, just across the Mula River, lies in a rather surprising urban setting at the northern end of busy Jungli Maharaj Rd (bus #4 or #98). Hewn from rock in the same manner as the more elaborate examples elsewhere in Maharashtra, the cave dates from the Rashtrakuta period (eighth–ninth centuries). Steps lead from the pavement to a path which ends in a square courtyard and a circular roofed Nandi enclosure. Beyond it, the roughly excavated cave, with broad, square, plain pillars, remains unfinished, bearing numerous chisel marks, and yet appears to have been in continuous use for a thousand years. Locals can be seen at prayer at most times of the day. The central shrine contains a *shivalingam,* while to either side subsidiary cells hold figures of Lakshmi, Ganesh, Rama, his wife Sita and brother Lakshmana.

Nearby, the **Mahatma Phule Vastu Sangrahalaya** (daily 8am–5.30pm) is a dusty, poorly labelled hotchpotch of handicrafts, mangy stuffed animals, shells, contemporary painting and dull irrigation displays. The high point is probably the piece donated by the man who is commemorated in the *Guinness Book of World Records* for inscribing 5151 characters onto a single grain of rice; here you can see a lesser work, a tiny piece of ivory engraved with a mere 5000 letters.

Aga Khan Palace and Gandhi Memorial

In 1942, Mahatma Gandhi, his wife Kasturba and other key figures of the freedom movement were interned at the **Aga Khan Palace** (daily 9am–12.30pm & 1.30–6pm), which is set in quiet leafy gardens, across the River Mula, 5km northeast of the centre

BHAGWAN RAJNEESH

It is twenty-five years or so since the first disciple was initiated into the **Bhagwan Rajneesh** cult, latterly renamed Osho Commune International, a gradually evolving philosophy involving Buddhism, Sufism, Sexual Liberationism, Zen, Yoga, Hypnosis, Tibetan Pulsing, Disco, Video and unabashed materialism. The first Rajneesh ashram (the name for a hermitage more usually associated with Hindus who have foregone worldly attachments for a life of meditation) was founded in Pune in 1974. It rapidly attracted droves of westerners and some Indians, who adopted new Sanskrit names and a uniform of orange or maroon cottons and bead necklace, attached to which was always a photo of the enlightened guru who, in classic style, sported long white hair and a beard. This costume immediately identified the wearer as a Rajneesh *sannyasin* (another term borrowed from Hinduism, particularly Shaivism, usually used to describe a renunciating mendicant who has attained a state of holiness).

Few early adherents denied that part of the attraction lay in Rajneesh's fun approach to fulfilment. His unapologetic dismissal of Christianity (dubbed "Crosstianity") as a miserably oppressive obsession with guilt, sin and the death of Jesus struck a chord with many, as did the espousal of liberation through sex. Within a few years, satellite ashrams were popping up throughout western Europe, most notably in Germany. Rajneesh assured his devotees that material comfort was not to be shunned and making money, at least for the ashram, was no bad thing. By 1980, outsiders and devotees alike could liberate themselves in plush Rajneesh discos with wacky names like *Zorba the Buddha* in big cities all over Europe.

Meanwhile, conscious of such potential threats to peace as pollution, nuclear war or accidents, AIDS and negative vibes, the Rajneesh organization was galvanized into action, pouring money and human energy into the Utopian project, **Rajneeshpuram**, on 64,000 acres of agricultural land in Oregon, USA – much to the dismay of their American neighbours. It was at this point that the tabloids and TV documentary teams really got interested in Rajneesh, who by now was said to be a multi-millionaire. His predilection for Rolls-Royces was big news; the fact that he couldn't drive and yet owned ninety of them was perfect grist to the mill. Baffled viewers watched as hordes of tambourine-banging, ecstatic devotees lined Main Street Rajneeshpuram, in order to catch a glimpse of the guru, bestowing beatific smiles as he swished by in decidedly non-ascetic transport.

Infiltrators leaked stories of the strange goings-on at Rajneeshpuram and before long his inner circle of high-powered female devotees/executives became the subject of police interest. Charges relating to tax evasion, drugs, fraud, arson and even a conspiracy to poison the population of the neighbouring town in order to sway the vote in local elections were all reported. Apparently unaware of such heinous crimes, Rajneesh nevertheless pleaded guilty to breaches of US immigration laws and was deported in 1985. Following protracted, futile attempts to gain permission to settle in up to 21 different countries, Rajneesh came home to India and finally back to Pune where, against all odds his commune has flourished, even since his death in 1990, at the age of 59.

(bus #1, #158 & #156). The Aga Khan donated the palace to the state in 1969, and it is now a small Gandhi museum, typical of many all over India, with captioned photos and simple rooms unchanged since they were occupied by the freedom fighters. A memorial behind the house commemorates Kasturba, who died during their imprisonment. A small *Khadi* shop sells handloom cloth and products made by village co-operatives.

Osho Commune International

Pune is the headquarters of the Bhagwan Rajneesh's avowedly non-religious **Osho Commune International**, 17 Koregaon Park (☎660963), 2km east of the railway station. Calling itself a "tasteful and classy resort" and claiming to attract more visitors than the Taj Mahal, the commune seems impervious to the sniping of cynical critics, quoting with pride the *Wall Street Journal*'s description of it as a "spiritual Disneyland for disaffected First World yuppies".

With a daily income of perhaps £40,000 during the peak season (Dec–March) and the dedicated toil of 700 volunteers, the Commune has transformed its twenty acres into an exclusive playground with cafes, swimming pool, sauna, clinics and a shop selling Osho's 650 books, videos and cassettes. They have erected space-age, air-conditioned buildings, landscaped gardens, bored tube wells for water and planted trees to improve the air and organic vegetables to escape insecticide poisoning. Courses at the Multiversity (US$1000 per month) are offered in countless New Age and traditional techniques. Osho's own brand of jargon is extensive; tennis, for example, has been reborn as Zennis, which helps you to "get out of your body's way, bring the outer and the inner together" in "a unique synthesis of tennis and meditation". However, this eco-friendly environment-bubble also proudly follows a door policy worthy of a fascist regime. Visitors who wish to spend longer in the Commune than the daily hour-long guided tours must produce an HIV-negative certificate no less than thirty days old.

Tribal Museum

The Tribal Research and Training Institute, which runs the **Tribal Museum** (daily 10am–5pm), 2km east of the railway station at 28 Queen's Garden, is dedicated to the protection and documentation of the surviving culture of Maharashtra's numerous tribal groups, such as the Wagdheo, Bahiram, Danteshwari and Marai, who number more than five million. The museum's photos, costumes and artefacts serve as an excellent introduction to this little-known world.

Parvati Hill

A ninety-step climb to the top of **Parvati Hill**, 4km south of the railway station (bus #4 and #99) and near Swargate bus stand, brings you to the small **Peshwa Museum** (daily 8am–noon & 3–6pm) dedicated to Pune's rulers, and an eighteenth-century **Ganapati temple**, built by the Peshwa ruler Balaji Baji Rao. There are good views over the city from here, the spot where Rao is said to have watched the British defeat his army at the battle of Kirkee.

Accommodation

Pune is well endowed with **hotels**, though in keeping with most big cities, prices are quite high for what you get. Most of the budget accommodation can be found in the area south of the railway station around Connaught Road.

Ajit, 775/2 Deccan Gymkhana (☎339076). Decent, small, mid-range place, 2km southwest of centre, with 20 rooms (some a/c), restaurant and bar. ④.

Amir, 15 Connaught Rd (☎661840). Good range of comfortable rooms and facilities. Coffee shop, bar, health club, shops and three restaurants (veg and non-veg). ⑤–⑦.

Ashirwad, 16 Connaught Rd (☎666142). Newish hotel near the railway station. Some a/c rooms with balconies and TV. Good veg restaurant. 24hr room service, exchange and travel desk. ④–⑤.

Ashiyana, 1198 FC Rd, Shivajinagar, 3km west of the railway station (☎321064). Reasonable hotel with 36 rooms (a few a/c), *Star TV*, Punjabi veg restaurant and ice cream parlour. ④.

Aurora Towers, 9 Moledina Rd (☎641818). Upper-range place 2km from railway station, with 68 rooms, 24hr room service and coffee shop, two good restaurants, shops and swimming pool. ⑦.

Blue Diamond, 11 Koregaon Rd (☎663775). 5-star hotel, 2km northeast of railway station. Posh Indian and Chinese restaurants, with lunch buffets, 24hr coffee shop, swimming pool, and shops. ⑧.

ITDC Executive Ashok, 5 University Rd, Shivajinagar (☎57391). Government-run upper-range business-style hotel. Comfortable modern a/c rooms with *Star TV*, pricey multi-cuisine *Golden Arch* restaurant, with buffet lunches, plus bar and coffee shop. ⑦–⑧.

MTDC Saras, Nehru Stadium, Swargate (☎430499). Semi-modern soulless concrete building with big, fairly comfortable rooms. ④.

National, 14 Sassoon Rd (☎68054). Rooms (some with verandahs and attached bathroom) in a dilapidated, characterful old building or in basic "cottages", two minutes' walk from the railway station. Friendly staff and popular with budget travellers. ②–③.

Ritz, Connaught Rd (☎62995). Inexpensive, good-sized rooms in a decrepit old building fairly near the railway station and opposite the GPO. Popular with backpackers. ②.

Sagar Plaza, 1 Bund Garden Rd (☎661880). Medium-sized (76 rooms), modern, a/c four-star, 1km from railway station, with restaurant, 24hr coffee shop, bar, bookshop and swimming pool. ⑦.

Span Executive, Revenue Colony, Shivajinagar, behind telephone exchange (☎59192). Comfortable businessman's hotel, 3km east from the centre, which has 38 rooms (some a/c), restaurant, coffee shop, 24hr room service and travel counter. 20 percent discounts off-season. ④–⑤.

Woodland, Sadhu Vaswani Circle (☎661111). Variety of rooms, most with a/c, ten minutes' walk from the railway station. Veg restaurant, travel desk and foreign exchange. ④–⑤.

Eating

In addition to the hotel restaurants described above, there are numerous reasonably priced cafes and fast-food outlets around **Connaught and Moledina Roads**, always busy in the evening. Authentic **Maharashtran food** is a little harder to find, but a couple of places over to the west on Apte Rd are worth trying.

Asha Dining Hall, 1224 Apte Rd, Deccan Gymkhana. Tucked away about 1.5km southwest of the Panchalesvara cave temple; take a rickshaw. Delicious home-cooked veg *thalis*. The kitchen is open for all to see. Excellent, inexpensive, and very popular with locals. 10am–noon & 7–10pm.

PUNE'S GANESH FESTIVAL

Pune's major festival, **Ganapati Chaturthi**, is dedicated to the elephant-headed Hindu deity Ganesh, the remover of obstacles and the most auspicious god for embarking on new endeavours. Once a domestic ritual, Ganesh Chaturthi was turned into a public rallying point for Hindus by the freedom fighter Bal Gangadhar Tilak in the late nineteenth century; both Pune and Bombay celebrate it in extravagant style each year.

On the first day, images of Ganesh, some gigantic, are erected in homes and public places, decorated with flower and food, and worshipped. Over the next ten days or so events include arts and crafts displays, a village fair, sports competitions and a food festival, as well as Indian classical music and dance performances, usually featuring the most illustrious names in the country. On the last day the Ganesh images are taken in procession and immersed in water, the streets teeming with singing and dancing devotees.

Needless to say, Pune is very crowded at this time. The Bombay MTDC, under whose auspices many of the events take place, are very well organized and can offer advice and even all-in packages for the festival. In **1995** the festival will be held on Aug 29–Sept 8; in **1996**, Sept 16–Sept 26; in **1997**, Sept 6–Sept 15.

MOVING ON FROM PUNE

Pune's **airport** (☎667538) sees regular *Indian Airlines* flights to **Delhi** (Mon–Sat 8.05pm; 2hr), and **Madras** (Mon, Wed & Fri 2pm; 3hr) via **Bangalore** (45min); their office is on Connaught Rd (☎664189; reservations ☎659939). There are also direct flights to **Bombay** (35–45min) on *East–West* (Hotel Amir Bldg, Sadhu Vaswani Rd; ☎665862; daily 6pm), and *Damania Airways* (17 MG Rd; ☎640814; Mon–Sat 8.30am). The existence of new *Raj Aviation* services to Bombay (Mon, Wed & Fri 3pm) and **Hyderabad** (Tues, Thurs & Sat noon; 1hr 30min) should be checked with the airport.

As Pune is one of the last stops for around twenty long-distance trains on their way to Bombay, **rail services** are excellent. Many depart at unpleasant hours of the morning, however, and some terminate at Dadar, so always check. The most convenient, if crowded, options for **Bombay VT** (3hr 30min–4hr 30min) are *Deccan Queen Express* #2124 (7.15am), *Pragati Express* #2126 (7.30am) and *Sahyadri Express* #7304 (7.35am). Daily trains from Pune also run to Hyderabad, New Delhi, Madras, Bangalore and Thiruvananthapuram. The daily (3pm) service to Vasco da Gama, *Goa Express* #2702/2704, requires a change at Miraj at 8pm; you arrive at 9am. The weekly *Cochin–Ahmedabad Express* #2638 goes up to Ahmedabad (Fri 3.05am; 12hr 35min).

Before travelling on the uncomfortable and crowded **state buses**, seek advice from the **MTDC Tourist Information Counter** at the railway station; the bus stands display no information in English. Buses from the stand next to the station head south, to Mahabaleshwar (3hr), Goa (15hr), Kolhapur (12hr). *Asiad* buses to Bombay (4hr) leave every 15 minutes between 5.30am and 11.30pm, but must be booked in advance.

Private luxury buses to Goa, Bangalore, Mangalore and Hyderabad can be booked through *Bright Star Tours & Travels*, 13 Connaught Rd, opposite Parmar Chambers (☎669647); to Ahmedabad, Vadodara, Indore, Surat and Goa from *Karan Travels*, 7 Konark Park, Dhole Patil Rd (☎663850); and for Aurangabad, Goa, Ahmedabad and Vadodara from *Prasanna Tours & Travels*, 396 Shaniwar Peth (☎431892) .

Coffee House, 2 Moledina Rd. Big a/c restaurant for reasonably priced veg Indian (both north and south), some Chinese and western food.

Kabir's, 6 Moledina Rd. Good selection of north Indian dishes including *tandoori*. Try to get a table outside. Serves beer.

Shreyas, 1242B Apte Rd. Maharashtran dishes with an outside terrace, pleasant in the evenings.

Sizzler, 7 Moledina Rd. Good fast food and variety of north Indian dishes. Very popular.

Venky's, 2 Wellesley Rd (☎27924). Popular fast food such as pizzas, burgers, fried chicken and milkshakes. Another branch on FC Road, opposite Ferguson College.

Sinhagad

The windswept, ruined fort of **SINHAGAD** (originally known as Kandana), 26km southwest of Pune at the top of an almost perpendicular cliff in the Bhuleshwar mountains, can easily be visited in a day trip from Pune by catching a bus (40min) from Swargate stand. This involves a stiff two-hour climb from the foot of the hill; if you have your own transport, you can drive a great deal closer. In 1647 Shivaji, the greatest chief of the Marathas, on hearing that his general Tanaji had died capturing the fort, lamented "I have won the fort, but lost the lion". To commemorate Tanaji's achievement, it was renamed Sinhagad, "lion fort". Tanaji had attacked on a moonless night, on the western side; the sheer size of the cliff was seen as such a deterrent that the fort was left undefended by the forces of Udai Bhan who were celebrating a wedding. However, according to legend, Tanaji had in his service the old campaigner Yashwanti, an iguana, which with a rope ladder tied to its tail was thrown onto the cliff face and, after three attempts, stuck securely. So strong was its grip that, before the night was out, three hundred of Tanaji's men had climbed into the fort.

Surprisingly, a few families live in simple houses within its twelve-metre-high walls. Some can serve you a cup of tea; other villagers from the plain are poor enough to climb up every day in the hope of selling pots of yoghurt to daytrippers.

Mahabaleshwar

MAHABALESHWAR, 250km southeast of Bombay and the most visited hill resort in Maharashtra, is most easily reached from Pune (120km northeast). The highest point in the Western Ghats, 1372 metres up, it is subject to extraordinarily extreme **weather** conditions. The start of June brings heavy mists and a dramatic drop in temperature, followed by a deluge of Biblical proportions; up to seven metres of rain can fall in the hundred days up to the end of September. As a result, tourists only come here between November and May; during April and May, at the height of summer, the place is packed. The main appeal is to enjoy a network of clearly marked **hiking trails** through the woods, leading to waterfalls and assorted vantage points with views over the peaks and down to the plains. You can also take boats out on the central **Yenna Lake**, and shop for strawberries, raspberries, locally made jams and honey in the market.

Arrival and information

The central **State bus stand**, has daily services to and from **Pune** (3hr), the most convenient railhead, as well as **Kolhapur** (7hr) and **Satara** (1hr). Satara is 17km from Satara Road railway station, connected to Bombay via Pune and Miraj (for Goa). To get here from **Bombay**, much the best option is to catch the *MSRTC* luxury bus which departs each morning at 7am (7hr); the bus back is less inconvenient, leaving at 3pm.

In season, MTDC run three daily **bus tours**, bookable through their *Holiday Resort*: Mahabaleshwar itself (2.15pm), Pratapgadh (7am), and Panchgani (11am).

Accommodation and eating

As in many hill-stations, despite an abundance of hotels prices in Mahabaleshwar are well above average. Many hotels close during the monsoon (mid-June to mid-Sept). Apart from a few basic places near the bus stand, such as the vegetarian *Shreyas* and non-veg *Sher-e-Punjab*, you're most likely to eat in the bigger hotels.

Dreamland (☎021686/228). Behind the bus stand. Decent mid-range hotel with 50 doubles (some with a/c and *Star TV*). The only outdoor restaurant in town, serving veg Mexican food. ⑤–⑥.

Fountain, opposite Koyna Valley (☎021686/227; bookable in Bombay through *Fountain's Fast Food Restaurant*; ☎367 7182). Close to the downtown area. Mid-range to expensive hotel with 50 double rooms (some a/c with TV). Pure veg restaurant; Indian, western and Chinese dishes. ⑤–⑥.

Frederick's (☎021686/240). Older hotel, near the bus stand, with 26 double rooms. ⑤.

Grand, Woodlawn Rd (☎021686/310). Simpler than its name would suggest, but decent rooms with verandah and very pleasant garden. ④.

MTDC Holiday Camp (☎021686/318 or ☎Bombay 2026713) Wide range of good-value accommodation, 2km from the centre, including cottages to sleep four, 50 doubles, a dorm and a hall where you can sleep on the floor. Simple restaurant and beer bar. ①–⑤.

Ripon, opposite IOC Holiday Home (☎291). Friendly, family run with lake view. ②.

Vyankatesh Lodge, Main Rd (☎245). Budget lodge, near the centre. ②.

Pratapgarh

An hour's bus ride away from Mahabaleshwar, or a 24-kilometre hike, the seventeenth-century fort of **PRATAPGARH** stretches the full length of a high ridge. Reached by means of five hundred steps, it is famously associated with the Maratha chieftain, **Shivaji**, who lured the Moghul general Afzal Khan here from Bijapur to discuss a possible truce. Neither, it would seem, intended to keep to the condition that they should come unarmed. Khan attempted to knife Shivaji, who responded by killing him with the gruesome *wagnakh*, a set of metal claws worn on the hand. Modern visitors can see Afzal Khan's tomb, a memorial to Shivaji, and views of the surrounding hills.

Kolhapur

KOLHAPUR, on the banks of the River Panchaganga 225km south of Pune, is thought to have been since ancient times an important centre of the tantric cult associated with Shakti worship. The town probably grew up around the sacred site of the present-day **Mahalakshmi temple**, still important in the life of the city, although there are said to be up to 250 other temples in the area. With a population of over 500,000, Kolhapur has become a major industrial centre, but the city has retained enough Maharashtran character to make it worthy of a stopover.

Between the tenth and thirteenth centuries the city was ruled by the Yadavas; later it came under the Moghuls, and in 1675 it was conquered by the Maratha chief Shivaji. His descendants, the Chhatrapatis, ruled until Independence, having shifted their provincial capital here from Panhala (18km northwest) in 1708. In the late nineteenth century, Kolhapur played an important role in the development of the so-called **Indo-Saracenic** style of architecture. The architect Major Charles Mant, under the auspices of the Maharajah, blended western styles with Muslim, Jain and Hindu, resulting in buildings that profoundly affected the evolution of colonial architecture. Mant's work, which can be seen all over the city, includes the **High School** and **Town Hall**; the **General Library**; the **Albert Edward Hospital**; and the **New Palace**, now a museum. Despite this prolific output, Mant lived in constant (unfounded) terror that his buildings would collapse; he commited suicide at the age of 42 in 1881.

Arrival and information

Two daily express **trains** from Bombay VT (13hr) via Pune (9hr) arrive at Kolhapur's **railway station**, 500m from the **bus stand** on Station Rd, near the centre of town. A five-minute walk from the station (turn right) brings you to the **MTDC Tourist Office**, in the Kedar Complex, Station Rd (Mon–Sat 8.30am–6.30pm). They organize a guided **tour** of Kolhapur and Panhala (Mon–Sat 10am–5.30pm; Rs50).

Mahalakshmi temple

The **Mahalakshmi temple**, near the centre of town, is thought to have been founded in the seventh century by the Chalukyan king Karnadeva; following damage inflicted during the Moghul period, however, what you see today probably dates from the early eighteenth century. It is built from bluish basalt on the plan of a cross, with the image of the goddess Mahalakshmi beneath the eastern and largest of five domed towers. The *mandapa* hallways leading to the main shrine hold figures of Garuda, Vishnu's bird vehicle, and Ganapati, which devotees circumambulate prior to approaching the goddess, flanked by the goddesses Mahakali and Saraswati. Four-armed Mahalakshmi, in black stone, holds a mace and shield, fruit and a cup. Her head is crowned with a cobra whose hood stands over a *shivalingam*. A second storey above contains another *shivalingam*, Nandi and a *yantra*, or sacred diagram, intimately associated with the tantric rituals of the goddess cult. On Fridays the goddess is brought out from the sanctum, seated in a palanquin, to process around the temple precincts.

Rajwada and the wrestling ground

Not far from the Mahalakshmi temple, the **Rajwada**, or Old Palace, is still occupied by members of the Chhatrapati family. Visitors can see the entrance hall (daily 10am–6pm), entered by passing under a porch which extends out into the town square and was once used for wedding ceremonies for the poor, financed by the Maharajah. Inside, overlooked by the private apartments, a large courtyard contains a shrine to the family deity, Bhavana. Among curious artefacts on display are sundry stuffed creatures and a statue of the late Maharajah, Shri Shahu Chhatrapati – still so revered by some locals that they bow when they pass it.

Kolhapur is famous as a centre for the traditional wrestling style, *kusti*. On leaving the palace, two right turns bring you to the sunken *motibaug*, or **wrestling ground**, where you can watch training sessions at 5.30am and 5.30pm. The main season is between June and September, the coolest part of the year, but you may find them working out at other times. Both Hindus and Muslims train together.

New Palace

The Maharajah's **New Palace** (Tues–Sun 9.30am–12.30pm & 2.30–5pm), 2km north of the centre, was built in 1884, following a fire at the Rajwada. Designed by Major Mant, its style fuses Jain and Hindu influences from Gujarat and Rajasthan, and local touches from the Rajwada, while remaining indomitably Victorian, with a prominent clock tower. The present Maharajah lives on the first floor, while the ground floor holds an absorbing collection of costumes, weapons, games, jewellery, embroidery and paraphernalia such as silver elephant saddles. Other memorabilia includes a letter from 1900 from the British Viceroy and Governor General of India, who writes "to his highness Sir Shahu Chattrapati Maharaj GCSF of Kolhapur government. I hereby confer upon you the title of Maharajah as an hereditary distinction."

The taxidermist in the employ of Shahaji – the present Maharajah's grandfather – must have been kept very busy indeed. In a single room you'll find ten stuffed tigers, six tiger heads, wild dog, sloth bear, staring wild buffalo, lion, *dik dik* (tiny deer), black panther, wild boar, black buck, any number of other deer varieties, and a Himalyan black bear. Photos include one of the Maharajah with his hundredth dead tiger, elephant hunts and a series detailing how to train a cheetah.

Panhala fort

Regular buses (30min) run between Kolhapur and **Panhala fort,** 18km northwest. Although it has legendary connections with the god Parashurama (Rama with the axe), the fort was probably founded by King Raja Bhoja in the late twelfth century. It covers a vast area, with massive perimeter walls over 7km in length and a steep slope beneath. Nevertheless, Panhala could not reasonably be described as impregnable. Over the years it has fallen to the Devagiri Yadavas, various Maratha chieftains, and, in 1489, the Adil Shahi dynasty of Bijapur, who erected the ramparts that still stand. Shivaji took Panhala in 1659, only just managing to escape with his life a year later when it was retaken by the Bijapur army. According to tradition, he was saved because one of his lieutenants posed as the leader and was killed, allowing Shivaji to make a quick exit, and regain it later. After this, the fort fell to the Moghul Aurangzeb (1700), became Maratha state capital under Tarabai until 1782, and went to the British in 1827.

The Teen Darwaza "three door" gate meant successive doors could only be approached at an awkward angle, trapping troops in the inner courtyard and making it impossible to charge. A well in the corner was used to send word to allies; lemons with incised messages were dropped into the water, and would float to a lake outside.

A number of modern buildings have been erected within the fort, some of them palatial homes belonging, it is said, to wealthy personages such as "sugar barons" and the famous Hindi film song artist, Lata Mangeshkar. There are also a couple of **hotels**.

Accommodation and eating

Most of Kolhapur's **hotels** are central, around **Station Rd**, while there are two good options further out in the **Panhala fort**. Outside the hotels, the best **food** is to be had at *Diners*, Vishal Chambers, Sambhaji Bridge, Venus Corner; a comfortable, modern a/c restaurant, with a varied menu including good Maharashtran *thalis*.

Hilltop Hotel, Panhala fort (☎Panhala 5054). Slightly kitsch, with comfortable, spotless, and over-decorated rooms, and a pleasant and simple outdoor garden restaurant. ③–④.

Maharaja, 514 Station Rd (☎29025). Basic lodge with veg restaurant, opposite the bus stand. ②.

MTDC Panhala, in a corner of the Panhala fort (☎Panhala 5048). Old-fashioned and slightly drab, but good value and comfortable, with a little courtyard and a tree. No restaurant, but meals are available through room service. ②–③.

Opal, 2104 E Poona–Bangalore Rd (☎23622). Small hotel with 9 non-a/c rooms with TV, 1.5km from railway with good restaurant specializing in Kolhapuri non-veg dishes. ③.

Shalini Palace, Rankala, A Ward (☎28915). Dilapidated but characterful old palace, in peaceful gardens next to lake, 5km from the centre. Designed by Mant, with central a/c . ⑥.

Tourist, 204 E New Shahupuri, Station Rd (☎20421). Mid-range hotel near the railway. 29 rooms (some a/c) with *Star TV*. Veg and non-veg Indian, Chinese and western restaurant, and a bar. ③–④.

Woodlands, 204E, Tarabai Park (☎20941). 500m from railway. Range of a/c and non-a/c rooms with TV, 24hr coffee shop, tri-cuisine restaurant, garden and bar.

CHAPTER ELEVEN

GOA

F amous for its soft white sand beaches, mesmeric sunsets, and laissez-faire attitude, the state of **GOA** has been renowned as one of India's most irresistible destinations ever since the Portuguese navigator Vasco da Gama sailed down the Malabar coast in 1498, in search of "Christians and spices". He found neither, but his favourable report resulted, twelve years later, in the erstwhile Muslim port and its hinterland becoming a **Portuguese colony**, which it remained until 1961. These days, the region's easygoing ambience, good food, and salubrious winter climate make it an ideal spot to unwind and enjoy simple, undemanding pleasures.

The very word "Goa" may be synonymous in some circles with hedonistic hippy holidays, but in reality, each of the countless beaches of this one-hundred-kilometre-long state seems to attract its own different kind of tourists, from Bombayites on weekend breaks, to fortnighting European holiday-makers, as well as long-stay shoestring travellers. Moreover, the fabled palm-fringed coastline, lapped by the warm waters of the Arabian Sea, is only part of the picture. Separated from the rest of India by the jungle-covered hills of the Western Ghats, Goa's heartland and most densely populated area is the alluvial strip **inland** from the beaches – a lush patchwork of paddyfields, coconut plantations, whitewashed churches, and gently meandering rivers.

Goa's 450 years under Portuguese domination produced a unique, syncretic blend of east and west that is at once exotic and strangely familiar: Christmas and Carnival are celebrated as enthusiastically as the thirty percent Christian minority as Diwali and Durga *puja* are by the mainly Konkani-speaking Hindus. The state's separate identity is discernible in numerous other ways too, most visibly in its Latin-influenced architecture, but also in a fish- and meat-rich cuisine that would be anathema to most Indians. Another marked difference is the prevalence of **alcohol**. Beer is cheap, and six thousand or more bars around the state are licensed to serve it, along with the more traditional tipples of *feni*, the local hootch, and *toddy*, a derivative of palm sap.

Thanks to a fecund tropical climate, and the well-watered soil of its seaward side, Goan (as against "Goanese", which has undesirable colonial connotations) farmers grow a wide array of **crops**, ranging from rice, the main staple, to cashew, areca (the source of betel nuts), and fruits for export. On the coast itself, coconut cultivation and **fishing** (both in-shore, with small boats, canoes, and hand-nets, and off-shore, with modern trawlers) are still the main sources of income. The recent discovery of **iron** in the hills to the east has also generated considerable revenue, and the economy is

GOA TRAVEL DETAILS

	Trains		Buses		Flights	
	Frequency	Time	Frequency	Time	Frequency	Time
To and from Vasco da Gama						
Agra	1 daily	39hr				
Bangalore	1 daily	20hr	1 daily	16hr	6 weekly	1hr
Belgaum			5 daily	6hr		
Bhopal	1 daily	31hr 20min				
Bogmalo			hourly	20min		
Bombay	2 daily	24hr			4–5 daily	1hr
Delhi	1 daily	42hr 15min			2 daily	2hr 30min
Gwalior	1 daily	37hr 20min				
Hubli	1 daily	6hr 50min				
Hyderabad					4 weekly	2hr 55min
Kochi					daily	1hr 10min
Kolhapur	2 daily	10hr 45min–11hr				
Madras					3 weekly	2hr 30min
Mangalore			2 daily	11hr		
Margao			every 15min	1hr		
Panjim			every 15min	45min		
Pune	3 daily	16hr–19hr 25min				
Thiruvan'puram					1 daily	2hr 15min
To and From Margao						
Belgaum			3 daily	5hr 30min		
Bombay	2 daily	23hr	2 daily	16hr		
Canacona / Chaudi			20 daily	1hr 40min		
Cavelossim			8 daily	30min		
Colva			12 daily	20–30min		
Gokarna			1 daily	4hr 30min		
Hubli	1 daily	5hr 50min	2 daily	6hr		
Karwar			20 daily	2hr		
Mangalore			2 daily	7hr		
Mapusa			10 daily	3hr		
Panjim			every 30min	1hr 30min		
Pune	3 daily	15hr–18hr 25min	1 daily	12hr		

Note that the same **trains** operate from Margao as from Vasco, usually leaving approximately one hour later.

	By Bus			By Bus	
To and From Panjim			**To and From Panjim** (continued)		
Anjuna	4 daily	1hr	Pune	8 daily	12hr
Arambol	12 daily	2hr 25min	Terekol	2 daily	2hr 30min
Baga	every 30min	50min	Vagator	every 15min	55min
Bangalore	6 daily	14hr	Velha Goa	every 30min	30min
Belgaum	11 daily	5hr			
Bombay	24 daily	15–18hr	**To and From Mapusa**		
Calangute	every 30min	45min	Anjuna	hourly	30min
Chapora	4 daily	1hr	Arambol	12 daily	1hr 45min
Hubli	8 daily	6hr	Baga	hourly	30min
Kolhapur	2 daily	9hr	Bombay	24 daily	14–17hr
Mangalore	5 daily	10–11hr	Calangute	hourly	45min
Mapusa	every 30min	35min	Chapora	every 15min	30–40min
Miraj	2 daily	9hr	Querim	4 daily	1hr
Mysore	1 daily	14–16hr	Vagator	every 15min	25min–35min

As this book went to press, all **rail** services to, from and within Goa were **suspended**; see p.619 and p.683. Note that no individual route appears more than once in this chart; for any specific journey, check against where you want to get to as well as where you're coming from. For more detail on **onwards travel** from Goa, see p.691.

further fuelled by the stream of remittance cheques sent home by expatriate Goans working in Bombay and the Gulf states. The consequent higher standard of living has, inevitably, in turn stimulated a massive influx of **immigrants** from elsewhere in India, who comprise around a third of the total population.

Goa's other big money-spinner, of course, is **tourism**. Lured here in the 1960s by the locals' apparently permissive stance on drink, drugs and nudity – not to mention abundant cheap food and accommodation – the first foreigners to take advantage of the new state's pristine beaches were the "**hippies**". As the region's fame spread, however, the marginal minority was gradually squeezed out, leaving the more accessible stretches of coastline near Panjim free for development as **mainstream resorts**. Today, budget travellers taking time out from trips around the subcontinent, and package tourists over for a dose of winter sun, flock here in roughly equal numbers. The "alternative" contingent, meanwhile, has fled up the coast, ditching Pink Floyd along the way in favour of hard-edged, chest-thumping techno music. The legendary **full-moon parties** have also survived, despite numerous police crackdowns, and continue to attract thousands of revellers, especially around the Christmas–New Year period.

Which beach you opt for when you arrive largely depends on what sort of holiday you have in mind. Heavily developed resorts such as **Calangute** and **Baga**, in the north, and **Colva** (and to a lesser extent **Benaulim**), in the south, offer more "walk-in" accommodation, shopping and tourist facilites than elsewhere. Even if you don't fancy crowded bars and purpose-built hotels, it can be worth heading for these centres at first, as finding places to stay in less commercialized corners is often difficult. **Anjuna**, **Vagator**, and **Chapora**, where accommodation is generally more basic and harder to come by, are the beaches to aim for if you've come to Goa to party. To get a taste of what most of the state must have been like twenty or thirty years ago, however, you'll have to travel further afield – to **Arambol**, a sleepy fishing-village-cum-hippy-hang-out in the far north; to **Betul**, at the far end of Colva beach; or to **Agonda** and **Palolem**, near the Karnatakan border, where, as yet, tourism has made very little impact.

Foremost among worthwhile attractions away from the coast are the ruins of the Portuguese capital at **Old Goa**, nine kilometres from Panjim – a sprawl of Catholic cathedrals, convents and churches that draws crowds of Christian pilgrims from all over India. Another popular day excursion is to Anjuna's Wednesday **flea-market**, a sociable place to shop for souvenirs and the latest rave gear. Further inland, the thickly wooded countryside around **Ponda** harbours numerous temples, where you can check out Goa's peculiar brand of Hindu architecture. The *taluka* (district) of Salcete, and its main market town, **Margao**, is also littered with wonderful Portuguese mansions, churches and seminaries, whose gabled baroque facades nose tantalizingly above the tropical treeline. Finally, wildlife enthusiasts may be tempted into the interior to visit the nature reserves at **Bondla**, and the Bhagwan Mahaveer sanctuary, near **Molem**.

The best **time to come** to Goa is during the dry, relatively cool winter months between late September and early March. At other times, either the sun is too hot for comfort, or the monsoon rains make life miserable for everyone except the fishers and hoteliers, who get to sit around all day snoozing and playing backgammon. During peak season, from mid-December to the end of January, the weather is perfect, with the temperature gauge rarely nudging above a manageable 32°C. Finding a room or a house to rent at that time, however – particularly over the Christmas and New Year fortnight when the tariffs double, or triple – can be a real hassle.

Some history

The sheer inaccessibility of Goa by land has always kept it out of the mainstream of Indian history; on the other hand, its control of the seas, and above all the lucrative spice trade, made it a much-coveted prize for rival colonial powers. Until a century before the arrival of the Portuguese adventurer **Vasco da Gama**, who landed near Kozhikode in Kerala in 1498, Goa had belonged for over a thousand years to the kingdom of Kadamba. In the interim it had been successively conquered by the Karnatakan Vijayanagars, the Muslim Bahmanis, and Yusuf Adil Shah of Bijapur, but the capture of the fort at Panjim by **Afonso de Albuquerque** in 1510 signalled the start of a Portuguese occupation that was to last for 450 years.

As Goa expanded, its splendid capital (now Old Goa) came to hold a larger population than either Paris or London. Though Ismail Adil Shah laid siege for ten months in 1570, and the Marathas under Shivaji and later chiefs came nail-bitingly close to seizing the region, the greatest threat was from other European maritime nations. While the

GETTING AROUND GOA

Before Independence, the many rivers that drain across Goa made **getting around** a problem. Nowadays, however, thanks to a network of road bridges, life is a lot easier. Of the **car ferries** still operating along the coast, the busier crossings are: Aldona to Corjuem – the main route between Mapusa and Bicholim (every 15min; 5min); Old Goa to Divar Island (every 30min; 10min); Dona Paula to Mormugao (Sept–May; 6–8 daily; 30–45min); and Siolim to Chopdem, for Arambol and Pernem *taluka* (every 20min; 10min). **Launches** also leave Panjim for pleasure cruises along the Mandovi, up the Mapusa, and down the coast (see p.687).

As elsewhere in India, **cars** and **taxis** can be rented by the hour, or by the kilometre for excursions. Details of rates, rental companies, and conditions are listed on p.687.

By train

As this book went to press, in Oct 1994, reports reached the *Rough Guides* office that all train services within Goa had been suspended while its slow metre-gauge track was converted to broad gauge. It is impossible to predict when the situation will return to normal. **Vasco da Gama** and **Margao** will no doubt remain major stations, but the effects of speeding up long-distance connections, combined with the long-promised opening of the *Konkan Railway*, running south from Panjim (via Colva and Benaulim) to Mangalore, and north to Bombay, will transform travel within Goa and to and from the rest of India.

By bus

The Goan transport corporation, **Kadamba**, runs services throughout the state from the main stands at Panjim, Mapusa and Margao. Buses to all the major resorts are cheap, frequent, and more relaxing than many in India. Details on how to get between specific destinations by bus are given in the relevant accounts, and on p.680.

By motorcycle taxi

Goa's unique pillion-passenger **motorcycle taxis** are ideal for nipping between beaches or into town from the resorts. Bona fide operators ride black bikes (usually *Enfields*) with yellow mudguards and white number plates. Fares, which should be settled in advance, are comparable with auto-rickshaw rates: roughly Rs2–3 per km.

By rented motorcycle

Renting a motorcycle in Goa gives a lot of freedom but can be perilous. In 1993–94, one person a day died on the roads; many were tourists on two-wheelers. Make sure the lights and brakes are in good shape, and be especially vigilant at night: many Goan roads are poor and unlit, and stray cows and bullock carts can appear from nowhere.

Officially, you need an **international drivers' licence** to rent, and ride, anything more powerful than a 25cc moped. Owners and rental companies rarely enforce this, but some local **police** use the rule to extract exorbitant *baksheesh* from tourists. If you don't have a licence with you, the only way around the problem is to avoid big towns such as Panjim, Margao and Mapusa (or Anjuna on market day), and only to carry small sums of money when driving. If you are arrested for not having the right papers, it's no big deal, though police officers may try to convince you otherwise; keep cool, and be prepared to negotiate. Some unlicensed operators attempt to rent out machines to unwary visitors; always make sure you get some evidence of rental and insurance.

Rates vary according to both season and vehicle; most owners insist on a hefty deposit and/or passport as **security**. The range is pretty standard. The cheapest, a 50cc **moped**, costs Rs50–100 per day. These are fine for buzzing to the beach and back, but to travel further you need gears and a bit more power. Options include, in descending price order (high-season rates): **Enfield Bullet 350cc**, popular mainly for its pose value; **Honda Kinetic 100cc**, a reliable bike, with automatic gears, which is a good first-time choice; the **Yamaha RD 100cc** is well-suited to Goan roads: light, fast enough, reliable, economical, and with manual gears. The unreliable Indian-made **Rajdoots** are best avoided.

Dutch made several unsuccessful attacks, the British at first preferred the avenue of diplomacy. Their **East India Company** signed the **Convention of Goa** in 1642, granting them the right to trade with the colony, and use its harbours.

Meanwhile, conversions to **Christianity**, started by the Franciscans, gathered pace when St Francis Xavier founded the **Jesuit** mission in 1542. With the advent of the Inquisition soon afterwards, laws were introduced censoring literature and banning any faith other than Catholicism – even the long-established Syrian Christian community were branded heretics. Hindu temples were destroyed, and converted Hindus adopted Portuguese names, such as da Silva, Correa and de Sousa, which remain common in the region. The trans-national influence of the Jesuits eventually alarmed the Portuguese government; the Jesuits were expelled in 1749, which made it possible for Indian Goans to take up the priesthood. However, standards of education suffered, and Goa entered a period of decline. The Portuguese were not preapred to help, but neither would they allow native Goans equal rights. An abortive attempt to establish a Goan Republic was quelled with the execution of fifteen Goan conspirators.

A spin-off of the British conflict with Tipu Sultan of Mysore (an ally of the French) at the end of the eighteenth century, was the **British occupation** of Goa, a little-known period of the region's history, which lasted sixteen years from 1797. The occupation was solely military; the Goan authorities never gave up their administration. Despite a certain liberalization, such as the restoration of Hindus' right to worship, the nineteenth century saw widespread civil unrest. During British occupation many Goans moved to Bombay to find work; now still more left for British India.

The success of the post-Independence Goan struggle for freedom from Portugal owed as much to the efforts of the Indian government, who cut off diplomatic ties with Portugal, as to the work of freedom fighters such as **Menezes Braganza** and **Dr Cunha**. After a "liberation march" in 1955 resulted in a number of deaths, the state was blockaded. Trade with Bombay ceased, and the railway was cut off, so Goa set out to

POLICE, TROUBLE AND NUDISM

While the vast majority of visitors to Goa never encounter any **trouble**, tourism-related crime is definitely more prevalent than in other parts of the country. **Theft** is the most common problem – usually of articles left unattended on the beach. Don't assume your valuables are safe in a padlocked house or hotel room, either. Break-ins, particularly on party nights, are on the increase. The most secure solution is to rent a deposit box in a bank, which costs around Rs50, or to opt for one of the few guest houses with lockers.

The other eventuality to avoid, at all costs, is getting on the wrong side of the law. **Drugs** are the most common cause of serious trouble. Many travellers imagine that, because of Goa's free-and-easy reputation, drug-use is legal: it isn't. Possession of even a small amount of cannabis is a criminal offence, punishable by large fines or prison sentences of up to ten years. Arrests, however, rarely result in court appearances. The Goan police like to ensure that offenders are given the opportunity of leaving the country first, having relieved them of nearly all their spare cash and valuables.

Though violent crime is rare, women should think twice before wandering down deserted beaches on their own. **Sexual harassment** usually takes the form of a bit of unsubtle ogling, but there have also been several incidents of rape in recent years.

Finally, remember that **nudism** is prohibited. Visitors in the past all too often rode roughshod over local sensibilities, forgetting or wilfully ignoring the fact that Goa is part of India, and still predominantly Hindu. In case tourists miss the "NO NUDISM" signs posted at the entrances to most beaches, police regularly patrol the busier resorts to ensure that decorum is maintained. If you are tempted to drop your togs, check that there are no families within eye-shot. No-one is likely to object openly, but when you consider that wet Y-fronts and *saris* are about as risqué as beachwear gets for most Indians, you'll see why men in G-strings and topless women cause such a stir.

forge international links, particularly with Pakistan and Sri Lanka. That led to the building of Dabolim airport, and a determination to improve local agricultural output. In 1961, the Indian army moved in. Along with Daman and Diu, Goa became part of India as a self-governing **Union Territory**, with minimum interference from Delhi.

Panjim

Take any mid-sized Portuguese town, add a sprinkling of banana trees, auto-rickshaws and a dash of *garam masala*, drench annually with torrential tropical rain, and leave to simmer in fierce humid sunshine for at least one hundred and fifty years, and you'll end up with something similar to **PANJIM** (or Panaji – "land that does not flood"). The Goan capital has a completely different feel to any other Indian city. Stacked around the sides of a lush terraced hillside at the mouth of the River Mandovi, its skyline of red-tiled roofs, whitewashed churches, and mildewing concrete apartment blocks has more in common with Lisbon than Lucknow. The lingering European influence is most evident in the small squares and cobbled lanes of the town's old Latin quarter, **Fontainhas**. Here, Portuguese is still very much the lingua franca, the shopfronts sport names like *Jose Pinto* and *de Souza*, and the women wear knee-length dresses that would turn heads anywhere else in the country.

For centuries, Panjim was little more than a minor landing stage and customs house, protected by a hill-top fort, and surrounded by stagnant swampland. It became capital in 1843, after the port at Old Goa had silted up, and its rulers and impoverished inhabitants had fled the plague. Although the last Portuguese viceroy managed to drain many of the nearby marshes, and erect imposing public buildings on the new site, the town never emulated the grandeur of its predecessor upriver – a result, in part, of the Portuguese nobles' predilection for erecting their mansions in the countryside rather than the city. Panjim expanded rapidly in the 1960s and 1970s, without reaching the unmanageable proportions of other Indian state capitals. After Bombay, or even Bangalore, its uncongested streets seem easygoing, and pleasantly parochial. Sights are thin on the ground, but the palm-lined squares and atmospheric Latin quarter, with its picturesque Neoclassical houses and Catholic churches, are good for a stroll.

Some travellers see no more of Panjim than its noisy bus terminal – which is a pity. Although you can completely bypass the town when you arrive in Goa, either by jumping off the train or coach at Margao (for the south), or Mapusa (for the northern beach resorts), or by heading straight off on a local bus, it's definitely worth spending time here – if only a couple of hours en route to the ruined former capital at **Old Goa**, nine kilometres east, or the Hindu temples, rare in Goa, further east at **Mardol** and **Ponda**.

Arrival and information

Domestic flights from Bombay and European charter planes arrive at Goa's **Dabolim airport**, 29km south of Panjim on the outskirts of Vasco da Gama (see p.714). Taxis into town (45min; Rs250) can be shared by up to five people. *Kadamba* buses (Rs20) meet *Indian Airlines* flights, dropping passengers at the main bus stand, and outside the *Indian Airlines* office on Dr D Bandodkar Rd, in the northwest of town. The least expensive way to get from the airport is to take a **motorcycle taxi** to the roundabout on the nearby main road, and then pick up a local bus into Vasco or Panjim – though this is more hassle than it's worth if you're weighed down with luggage.

Long-distance **buses** pull in to Panjim at the town's busy **Kadamba bus terminal**, one kilometre east of the centre, in the district known as Pato. It takes around ten minutes to walk from here across Ourem Creek to Fontainhas, where most of the budget accommodation is located. If you plan to stay in the more modern west end of

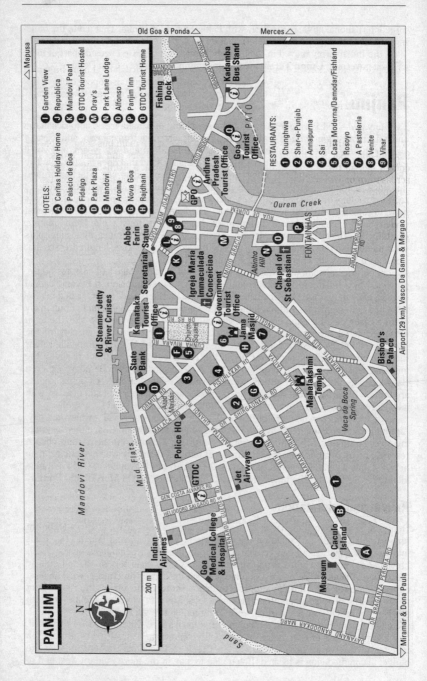

PANJIM

Mapusa △

△ **Old Goa & Ponda** △ **Merces** △

HOTELS:
- ❶ Garden View
- ❿ Republica
- ❹ Mandovi Pearl
- ❶ GTDC Tourist Hostel
- ❿ Orav's
- ❿ Park Lane Lodge
- ❿ Alfonso
- ❿ Panjim Inn
- ❿ GTDC Tourist Home
- Ⓐ Caritas Holiday Home
- Ⓑ Palacio de Goa
- Ⓒ Fidalgo
- Ⓓ Park Plaza
- Ⓔ Mandovi
- Ⓕ Aroma
- Ⓖ Nova Goa
- Ⓗ Rajdhani

RESTAURANTS:
- ❶ Chunghwa
- ❷ Sher-e-Punjab
- ❸ Annapurna
- ❹ Sai
- ❺ Casa Moderna/Damodar/Fishland
- ❻ Rosoyo
- ❼ A Pasteleria
- ❽ Venite
- ❾ Vihar

Kadamba Bus Stand

Fishing Dock

MANDOVI BRIDGE

Goa Tourist Office

PATO

Andhra Pradesh Tourist Office

Ourem Creek

GPO

Abbe Farin Secretariat Statue

Igreja Maria Immaculada Conceiçao

Government Tourist Office

Karnataka Tourist Office

Church Square

State Bank

Jama Masjid

Police HQ

GTDC

Jet Airways

Chapel of St Sebastian

Atinho Hill

FONTAINHAS

Mahalakshmi Temple

Vaca da Boca Spring

Bishop's Palace

Caculo Island

Museum

Goa Medical College & Hospital

Indian Airlines

Mandovi River

Mud Flats

Sand

Miramar & Dona Paula

Airport (29 km), Vasco Da Gama & Margao ▷

△ Vasco Da Gama & Margao ▷

DAYANAND BANDODKAR MARG

N

200 m

The telephone **area code** for Panjim is ☎0832.

---

town, flag down a motorcycle taxi or an (unmetered) auto-rickshaw. **Local buses** to Calangute, Baga, Anjuna, Chapora, Mapusa, Margao and Vasco also operate out of the main inter-state bus stand. Destinations are written above the relevant platform, and called out with machine-gun rapidity by the conductors.

Information

GTDC's handy **information** counter, in the concourse at the main bus stand (Mon–Fri 9.30am–6pm, Sat 9.15am–1pm; ☎225620), has details of bus and train times. The equally helpful **India Government tourist office** (Mon–Sat 9.30am–5pm; ☎223412) is across town on Church Square. Both sell good state maps – invaluable if you plan to do any motorcycling. Panjim also has tourist offices for **Andhra Pradesh**, Rua de Ourem (near *Sona Hotel*), Pato; **Karnataka**, 2nd Floor, Velo Building, Church Square (☎224110); and **Maharashtra**, *Tourist Hostel*, Swanpathra Rd (☎227103).

Banks with foreign exchange facilities include the *State Bank of India*, opposite the *Hotel Mandovi*, Avda Dom Joao Castro; the *Bank of Baroda* (also good for drawing money on *Visa* cards), on Azad Maidan; and the *Corporation Bank* on Church Square, around the corner from the GTDC tourist office. The *Pheroze Framroze & Co Exchange Bureau*, Room #119, *Hotel Fidalgo*, 18 June Rd (Mon–Sat 9.30am–7pm, Sun 9.30am–3pm), also changes currency and travellers' cheques at standard bank rates.

Panjim's highly efficient **poste restante** counter (Mon–Sat 9.30am–1pm & 2–5.30pm) is next door to the **GPO**, 200 metres west of Pato Bridge.

CITY TOURS AND CAR RENTAL

GTDC and several private companies run **tours** out of Panjim to destinations elsewhere in the state. Most are either whistlestop temple tours, or so-called "Beach Specials" – basically an excuse for large groups of lads to get drunk and eye up semi-naked women lying on the beach. Among the few itineraries likely to appeal are: the "Pilgrim Special", which takes in Old Goa and several Hindu temples (daily; 9.30am–1pm; Rs30); the "Holiday Special" to Ponda and the inaccessible Bondla wildlife sanctuary (daily; 9.30am–6pm; Rs50); and the "Island Special", to Durar Island, the Sri Saptakosteshwar temple, and Mayhem Lake and bird reserve (daily; 9.30am–6pm; Rs50). Tickets can be booked in advance at the GTDC *Tourist Hostel* , or *Tourist Home* in Pato – the main departure point.

GTDC's popular evening **cruises** along the River Mandovi are a pleasant way to idle away an hour. Two round trips leave every day from the old steamer jetty: the first at 6pm, and the second at 7.15pm. Aim for the earlier one if you can, as it usually catches the last of the sunset. Snacks and drinks, including beer, are available, and the price (Rs50) includes a "cultural programme" of Konkani and Portuguese folk singing, and Hindi cover artistes. Two-hour "Full Moon" cruises also leave daily (regardless of the lunar phase) at 8.30pm. Finally, GTDC have introduced a couple of good-value "Day Cruises". The more scenic cruise #1 (1–3.30pm; Rs150) runs in a circuit around Cabo Raj Bhavan, down the Zuari estuary, north up the Cambarjua Canal, and then west along the Mandovi, with a quick stop at Old Goa. Cruise #2 (2.30–5pm; Rs100) heads up the Mapusa to Aldona, via Britona, Pomburpa and Calvim. Bookings for cruises can be made through *Goa Sea Travels*, opposite the *Tourist Hostel*.

Cars with drivers can be rented for local sightseeing through GTDC, Trionora Apartments (☎3396), and the India Government tourist office on Church Square, from Rs300–550 for a half-day (4hr), and Rs475–950 for a full day (8hr), or Rs4.30–9.50 per km for longer hauls. Waiting charges and night-halts cost extra. Self-drive is available from *Budget Rent-a-Car* (aka *Sai Service*), Mapusa Rd, Pororim (☎217755); and *Hertz*, opposite Don Bosco School, Market Area (☎220304 or 223758).

The Town

Until recently, most visitors' first glimpse of Panjim was from the greasy decks of the old Bombay steamer as it chugged in to dock at the now-defunct ferry ramp. These days, the town is usually approached from the north, via the huge ferro-concrete road bridge that spans the Mandovi estuary, or from the south, on the recently revamped NH7, which links the capital with the airport and railhead at Vasco da Gama. Either way, you'll have to pass through the suburb of **Pato**, home to the main Kadamba bus terminal, before crossing Ourem Creek to arrive in Panjim proper. West of **Fontainhas**, the picturesque Portuguese quarter, lies the commercial centre's grid of long straight streets fanning out west from Panjim's principal landmark, **Church Square**; the two districts are separated by the steep **Altinho** hill. Further north, the main thoroughfare, Avenida Dom Joao Castro, sweeps past the post office and Secretariat building, before bending west along the waterfront down towards the nearby beach resort of **Miramar**.

Fontainhas

Panjim's oldest and most interesting district, **Fontainhas**, lies immediately west of Pato, overlooking the banks of the oily grey Ourem Creek. From the footbridge that cuts between the bus stand and town centre, a dozen or so blocks of Neoclassical houses rise in a tangle of terracotta roof-tops up the sides of Altinho hill. At siesta time, *Vespas* stand idle on deserted cobbled street corners, while women in western clothes exchange pleasantries with their neighbours from open windows and leafy verandahs. Many buildings have retained their traditional coat of ochre, pale-yellow, green or blue – a legacy of the Portuguese insistence that every Goan building (except the churches, which had to be kept white) should be colour-washed after the monsoons.

At the southern end of the neighbourhood, the pristine **Chapel of St Sebastian** is one of many Goan *igrejas* to remain faithful to the old colonial decree. It stands at the end of a small square where, in mid-November, Fontainhas' fair-skinned Portuguese-speaking locals hold a lively annual street *festa* to celebrate the Patron Saint's Day. The eerily life-like crucifix inside the chapel formerly hung in the Palace of the Inquisition in Old Goa.

Igreja Maria Immaculada Conceicao

Emidio Gracia Road cuts from the footbridge to the far side of Altinho hill, where Panjim's biggest church, the **Igreja Maria Immaculada Conceicao** (Mon–Sat 9am–1pm & 3.30–6pm, Sun 10.30am–1pm & 6.15–7pm) is flanked by clusters of slender palm trees and reached via a flight of criss-crossing laterite steps. The church, with its brilliantly whitewashed baroque facade, was built in 1541 for the benefit of sailors arriving in Panjim from Lisbon. The weary mariners would stagger up from the quay to give thanks for their safe passage, before proceeding to the capital at Old Goa – the original home of the over-sized bell that hangs from the central gable.

The commercial centre

The road **north from Church Square** skirts the edge of Fontainhas before emerging at the waterfront near the old **Secretariat**. Formerly known as the "Adi Shah Idhalçaon Palace", this splendid colonial mansion, with its carved stone doorway and cool interior courtyard, was built in 1615 on the foundations of the erstwhile Muslim rulers' residence. Now the town hall, it originally accommodated viceroys arriving from, or departing for Portugal, and became the official viceregal seat after Old Goa was abandoned. A hundred metres east, a peculiar statue of a man holding his hands over the body of an entranced reclining woman shows **Abbé Farin** (1755–1819), a Goan priest who emigrated to France to become one of the world's first professional hypnotists.

THE FESTIVALS OF GOA

Some of Goa's **festivals** are on fixed dates each year; ask at a tourist office for dates of the others. The biggest celebrations take place at Panjim and Margao.

Reis Magos (Jan 6). Epiphany celebrations include a procession to the Franciscan chapel of Reis Magos, near Panjim on the north bank of the Mandovi, 3km east of Fort Aguada. Other processions are held at Cansaulim and Chandor.

Carnival (Feb/March). For the last three days before Lent – a month of fasting and sobriety – processions take place all over the region with floats, music, dancing and entertainments with fancy dress and general, often *feni*-induced, mayhem.

Shigmo (Feb/March). The Goan version of Holi is celebrated with big parades and crowds; drum and dance groups compete and huge floats that threaten to bring down telegraph wires trundle through the streets.

All Saints (March). On the fifth Monday in Lent, statues of the saints are taken by the friars of the Third Order of Franciscans through Old Goa. A fair also takes place. The only other such festival is in Rome, Italy.

Pop, Beat and Jazz Music Festival (May). Local bands strut their stuff at the Kala Academy in Panjim.

Janmashtami (Aug). Ritual bathing in the River Mandovi, off Diwadi Island, to celebrate the birth of Krishna.

Dussehra (Sept/Oct). Nine days of festivities.

Diwali (Oct/Nov). Processions all over the region, often accompanied by fireworks.

Feast of St Francis Xavier (Dec 3). Large festival at Old Goa's Bom Jesus church.

Christmas (Dec 24/25). Celebrated everywhere in Goa. Late-night mass is usually followed by music and folk dance.

South of Church Square, the only landmark in a featureless jumble of concrete is the multicoloured **Mahalakshmi temple**. Behind it, a flight of stone steps climbs through shady woods to the top of Altinho hill, where the grandest of Panjim's old colonial houses languish in overgrown gardens. Among the few not suffering from terminal neglect is the **Bishop's Palace**, where the Pope stayed during his 1989 visit to Goa. Its owners have clearly deemed it holy enough to merit a coat of whitewash.

The museum

Moves are afoot to shift Panjim's small **museum** (Tues–Sat 9.30am–1.15pm & 2–5.30pm) to a purpose-built complex across town. For the time being, however, it occupies the dingy first floor of an office block at the far west end of the centre, near the Caculo Island intersection. The collection consists mostly of pre-colonial artefacts, including village deities, *puja* utensils, a handful of *sati* and hero stones, fragments of temple sculpture, and some fine **Jain bronzes** rescued by Customs and Excise officers from smugglers. Also of interest are **photographs** taken by a Portuguese colonial official around the turn of the century; among them are striking portraits of the contemporary rebel leader Dada Rane, and his heavily armed band of Goan freedom fighters.

Accommodation

With several well-known beach resorts a short bus ride up the coast, most travellers only stay long enough to catch a plane or train from Vasco the next morning. The town centre is, nevertheless, well stocked with **accommodation**. Finding a place to stay at the right price is only a problem during the festival of St Francis (early Dec), and at peak season, when tariffs double. At other times, hotels try to fill rooms by offering substantial discounts. The best inexpensive options are in **Fontainhas**, down by Ourem Creek, and in the backstreets behind the ferry jetty. Standards are generally good; even the cheapest rooms should have a window, a fan, running water, and clean sheets. The rest of the hotels are mostly bland places in the western, more modern, end of town.

Finally, **check-out times** in Panjim vary wildly. Find out what yours is as soon as you arrive, or your hard-earned lie-in could end up costing you an extra day's room rental. The rates quoted below apply to peak season.

Inexpensive

Alfonso, St Sebastian Chapel Square, Fontainhas. Modest family house in picturesque backstreet, with large rooms (all attached bathrooms), and some self-catering facilities. ③.

GTDC Tourist Home, around the corner from the bus stand, Pato (☎225715). Government-run hostel with run-of-the-mill dorm beds – fine for a night if you can't face hunting around town. ①.

Mandovi Pearl, PO Box #329, behind GTDC *Tourist Hostel* (☎226852). Idiosyncratic lodge run by garrulous landlord for salesmen and budget travellers. The rooms are roughish, but good value. ②.

Orav's, 31 Janeiro Rd (☎226128). Modern building in the old quarter with good-sized, comfortable rooms, but tiny balconies. ③.

Park Lane Lodge, near Chapel of St Sebastian (☎227154). Spotless, but cramped, family guest house in old colonial villa. Pot plants, parrots, and relaxed, friendly atmosphere. ②–③.

Republica, near GTDC *Tourist Hostel* (☎224630). Revamped, central, budget travellers' lodge with clean rooms, attached shower-toilets, large wooden verandah and river views. Very good value. ②.

Moderate to expensive

Aroma, Cunha Rivara Rd (☎223519). Very central, long-established hotel with popular *tandoori* restaurant. Rooms at various prices, some looking on to Church Square. ④–⑤.

Caritas Holiday Home, Caculo Island, St Inez. Shiny new place west of the town centre (near the museum), with spotless rooms, but little character. ③–④.

Fidalgo, 18 June Rd (☎226291). Large, well established, and with all mod cons, including central a/c, exchange, *Star TV* in all rooms, health club, shopping arcade, in-house travel agent etc. ⑦.

Garden View Hotel, opposite Municipal Gardens (☎223731). Large, modern, impeccably clean and well managed. More expensive front rooms overlook the square. Good value. ④–⑤.

GTDC Tourist Hostel, Avda Dom Joao Castro (☎227103). Very popular government-run hotel overlooking busy thoroughfare and the river. The rooms are large and pleasant enough, but no longer the bargain they used to be. Shops, hair salon, and tourist information in the lobby. ④–⑤.

Mandovi, Dr D Bandodkar Rd (☎226270). Grand waterfront hotel with river views from front rooms, central a/c, shops, in-house travel agent, and a pool. ⑦–⑧.

Nova Goa, Dr Atmaram Borkar Rd (☎226231; fax 224090). Panjim's newest and least expensive top hotel. In the heart of the shopping area, with the usual comforts, plus bath tubs, and a pool. ⑦.

Palacio de Goa, Gama Pinto Rd (☎22289). Kitsch, five-storey Neoclassical facade, and pleasant, plain rooms. *Star TV*, balconies, and a pure-veg restaurant. ④.

Panjim Inn, E-212, 31 Janeiro Rd, Fontainhas (☎226523). Grand old Portuguese town house, now managed by Tibetan family as an upmarket, but homely hotel. Period furniture, individual balconies, common verandah. Some rooms are better than others. Easily the best place in its class. ④–⑤.

Park Plaza, Azad Maidan (☎222601). New hotel on quiet square near the river. Close to commercial centre, and with all the usual amenities. ④–⑤.

Rajdhani, Dr Atmaram Borkar Rd (☎225362). Central, efficient and clean; with good veg food. ④–⑤.

ACCOMMODATION PRICE CODES

All **accommodation prices** in this book have been coded using the symbols below. In principle the prices given are for the least expensive double rooms in each establishment; however, some hotels, usually in category ①, offer rates per bed rather than per room. For more details, see p.34. In Goa, a **government-imposed luxury tax** of five percent is levied on all rooms over Rs100, raised to ten percent if the tariff exceeds Rs500.

①	up to Rs100	④	Rs225–350	⑦	Rs750–1200
②	Rs100–150	⑤	Rs350–500	⑧	Rs1200–2200
③	Rs150–225	⑥	Rs500–750	⑨	Rs2200 and up

Eating

Panjim is packed with good **places to eat**. Most are connected to a hotel, and there are plenty of smaller family-run establishments. Foreign visitors tend to stick to the perennially popular restaurant at the *Hotel Venite*, which offers a wide range of tasty Goan specialities, as well as more familiar western favourites, such as fresh fish and chips. Vegetarians will do better at the numerous south Indian-style cafeterias that have sprung up in recent years. Beer is available in all but the purest "pure veg" places.

MOVING ON FROM GOA

A full summary of rail, road and air routes from Goa to the rest of India appears on p.680. As you will see from p.619 and p.683, all **rail** services within Goa were **suspended** as this book went to press; the details below, and on p.680, may well no longer be accurate.

Unless you pick up onward transport in Mapusa or Margao, you'll probably pass through Panjim before you head off; its bus terminus is the state's largest, and both the airport and railhead at **Vasco da Gama** are only an hour's journey by road to the south.

Getting to **Bombay** is easy. Four or five **planes** per day leave **Dabolim** airport, on the outskirts of Vasco da Gama (see p.714), for Santa Cruz (1hr; Rs1200/US$50, 25 percent student discount). The same journey by **train** is ten times cheaper, but lasts 24 times as long, and involves a change at Miraj, in Maharashtra. Of the two daily services from Vasco station, aim for the *Gomanatak Express* #7806/*Konya Express* #7307, which leaves at 9am and gets into VT early the next morning. The *Mandovi Express* #7898/*Shayadri Express* #7303 leaves at 5pm. *Kadamba* and dozens of private companies operate bone-shaking night **buses** to Bombay (14–18hr; Rs200–450), which you can catch at Panjim or Mapusa. For more on the different ways to travel between Goa and Bombay, see p.619.

If you're heading to **Bangalore**, either catch a plane (6 weekly; 1hr; Rs1350), a bus (6 daily; 14hr), or the once-daily train (*Vasco–Bangalore Mail* #6202) that leaves Vasco at 10am. A couple of carriages on this twenty-four-hour trip get uncoupled at **Arsikere**, and continue to **Mysore**. Regular buses also run from Panjim to **Londa**, in Karnataka, where you can pick up more frequent trains to Mysore, and to **Hubli** junction,which has services on the main Bombay–Bangalore line to **Badami** and **Bijapur** (via Gadag), and **Hospet**, the jumping-off place for **Hampi**. Another, more straightforward way to get to Hampi is to take the *Gomanatak Express* (#7805) from Vasco at 9.15am, which connects with the *Link Express* (#7838) at Londa, arriving in Hubli at 6.15am the next day.

Unless you fly, the most direct way to get to **Delhi** is to hop on the daily *Goa Express* (#2703/#2701) from Vasco, which takes 42hr 15min to cover the 2400km.

Reservations, tickets and information

Airline offices include: *Air India, Hotel Fidalgo*, 18 June Rd (☎226291); *British Airways*, 2 Excelsior Chambers, MG Rd (☎/fax 224336); *Damania* (also *Gulf Air, Air France*, and *Air Canada*), Bernard Guedes Rd (☎223730); *East-West, Hotel Fidalgo*, 18 June Rd (Mon–Sat 9.30am–6pm, Sun 9.30am–2pm; ☎224108); *Indian Airlines*, Dempo Building, Dr D Bandodkar Rd (Mon–Fri 10am–1pm & 2–4.30pm; ☎224067); *Jet*, Rizvi Chambers, office #102, Caetano Albuquerque Rd (☎226154); *KLM* (also *PIA*), B-24 Triomora Apts (☎226190); *Modiluft*, Praca do Commercio, Dr Atmaram Borkar Rd (☎229524).

The **South Central Railway's** Out Agency reservation counter (daily 10am–1pm & 2.30–5pm) is on Platform #5 of Panjim bus stand. The quota here is very limited, but it's worth trying, as the main booking office is at Vasco station – the only place to make reservations on *Indrail* passes, and on the elusive tourist quota. Book *Kadamba* **bus tickets** in advance at their offices in Panjim and Mapusa bus stands (daily 9–11am & 2–5pm); private companies sell theirs through the many travel agents immediately outside the bus stand in Panjim, and at the bottom of the square in Mapusa. **Information** on all departures and fares is available from Goa Tourism's counter inside Panjim's bus stand (Mon–Fri 9.30am–6pm, Sat 9.15am–1pm; ☎225620). Reliable Panjim **travel agents** include: *AERO Mundial*, Ground Floor, *Hotel Mandovi*, Dr D Bandodkar Rd (☎223773); *Menezes Air Travel*, Rua de Ourem, near Pato Bridge (☎225081); and *Rauraje Deshprabhu*, Cunha Rivara Rd (☎225763).

A Pasteleria, Dr Dada Vaidya Rd. Panjim's best bakery does dozens of western cakes, cookies and sticky buns, including florentines, brownies, and fruit loaves. Take away only. Moderate.

Annapurna, Ormuz Rd. Traditional south Indian *thalis* and snacks dished up by cotton-clad waiters in a large, clean, and cool first-floor dining hall. Inexpensive.

Bem Vindo, GTDC *Tourist Home*, Pato. Inexpensive Indian dishes, including fiery fish curry and rice, and chilled beer, served in a bustling bar-restaurant, or on a more relaxing outdoor terrace.

Casa Moderna/Damodar/Fishland, off Ormuz Rd. Three jointly owned and run seafood joints serving copious platefuls of down-to-earth, spicy Goan fish dishes to local clientele.

Chunghwa, *Hotel Samrat*, Dr Dada Vaidya Rd (☎224318). Authentic, upscale Cantonese restaurant with a/c, attentive service, and a wide selection of moderately priced seafood, meat and veg dishes.

Rosoyo, behind the *Modiluft* office, Dr Atmaram Borkar Rd. Pure veg restaurant in the town centre, popular with Gujarati visitors for its cheap and tasty *thalis*. No alcohol.

Sai, 18 June Rd. Tiny hole-in-the-wall street cafe, three blocks east of *Sher-e-Punjab*, serving cheap and delicious Goan fish *thalis*, with piles of rice and hot *rotis*.

Sher-e-Punjab, 18 June Rd. North Indian food served up in crowded city-centre restaurant. Their speciality – butter chicken – is delicious, and there's a reasonable veg menu.

Tandoor, *Hotel Aroma*, Cunha Rivara Rd. Inexpensive first-floor restaurant, overlooking the main square, serves the town's best *tandoori* meat and fish, with some veg and Chinese alternatives.

Venite, 31 Janeiro Rd. Deservedly popular, serving great fresh seafood, including affordable lobster and crab, along with western dishes, desserts, *feni* "nips", and cold beers. Wooden floors, balcony seats, candles, and cassette collection add to the ambience. Good breakfasts too. Closed Sun.

Vihar, near *Venite*, 31 Janeiro Rd. Very popular Indian fast-food cafeteria with formica booths and barefoot waiters. Great *puri bhajis*, *dosas*, *wadas* and other snacks.

Listings

American Express *Menezes Air Travel*, Rua de Ourem, near Pato Bridge (☎225081).

Bookstores There are reasonable bookstores in both the *Hotel Fidalgo* and the *Hotel Mandovi*.

Hospital Panjim's largest hospital, the Goa Medical College, is in the west of town, at the far end of Avda Dom Joao Castro. For an **ambulance**, call ☎226300 or 224566.

Pharmacy *Hindu Pharma* (☎223176), near the tourist office on Church Square, for Ayurvedic, homeopathic and alopathic medecines.

Police The Police Headquarters is on Malaca Rd, central Panjim. In emergencies, call ☎100.

Visa Extensions The Foreigners' Registration Office is at the Police Headquarters (Mon–Fri 9.30am–1pm; ☎225360). If you're unsuccessful here, try Bombay or Bangalore.

Miramar

West of Panjim, the coast road passes through the swish suburb of Campal, with its grand colonial residences (and their modern concrete counterparts), before swinging south towards the beach at **MIRAMAR**. Anywhere else but Goa, you might be tempted to spend an afternoon here, enjoying the two-kilometre sweep of dark sand and the views across Aguada Bay. As it is, the beach's dodgy undercurrents, noisy bus parties, and over-zealous peanut-*wallahs*, make it far less attractive than most other resorts within easy reach of the capital. If all you want is a quick escape from Panjim to watch the sunset, however, Miramar, fifteen minutes' walk from the bus park, will do fine. At this time of day the only people you see are fishermen fixing their nets under the palm trees, and the odd cafe owner staring hopefully up the beach from an empty terrace.

Practicalities

Should you choose to **stay** in Miramar, the best option, by far, is GTDC's *Yatri Niwas* (☎227754; ③), a campus of double-storey chalets set in a sandy garden directly behind the beach. The rooms are spacious, breezy and clean, and very good value if you don't mind being so far out of Panjim. A short way back up the main road towards Panjim, tucked down a suburban backstreet, the *Youth Hostel* (☎225432; ③) offers much cheaper accommodation. Its rock-bottom dormitories are large, but get horrendously cramped and stuffy when there's a big block-booking of students.

Buses to Miramar leave every fifteen minutes from Panjim's Kadamba stand. You can also pick them up from the steamer jetty, and at various points along the waterfront. Travelling in the other direction, they stop just off Miramar's main roundabout, in front of the *Yatri Niwas*.

Dona Paula

Nestled on the south side of the rocky, hammer-shaped headland that divides the Zuari and Mandovi estuaries, **DONA PAULA**, 9km southwest of Panjim, is both small fishing village and upmarket beach resort. The views from the top of the peninsula over Miramar beach and Mormugao Bay are pleasant enough, but the village itself is characterless and commercialized, and not somewhere you'd choose to spend much time – unless you find yourself staying in one of the many five-star campus hotels that have mushroomed here in recent years.

Standing on the westernmost tip of the headland, known as **Cabo Raj Bhavan**, is the official residence of the Chief Minister of Goa, Daman and Diu. The site was originally occupied by a Portuguese fort, erected in 1540 to guard the entrance to Goa harbour, whose cannons crossed fire with those of Aguada to the north, and Mormugao to the south. These days, nothing remains of the old citadel. From the road beyond the *Institute of Oceanography*, you can, however, see the ruins of the small military **cemetery** the British built at the time of their brief occupation of the Cabo during the Napoleonic wars – a move intended to deter the French from invading Goa.

Velha Goa (Old Goa)

At one time a byword for splendour, with a population of several hundred thousand, Goa's erstwhile capital, **VELHA GOA** (Old Goa), was virtually abandoned following malaria and cholera epidemics that plagued the city from the seventeenth century onwards. Today you need considerable imagination to picture the once-great capital. The secular buildings have gone, and all that remains are a score of extraordinarily grandiose churches, seminaries and convents, some maintained by the *Archaeological Survey of India*, and some still used by the local population.

On the south bank of the River Mandovi, 8km east of Panjim, Velha Goa is reached acros the 1.5-kilometre-long Linhares Causeway. Regular buses run from Panjim, though if you don't feel the need to see each and every monument, Old Goa's main sights are taken in on the "Pilgrims Special" **bus tour** (see p.687). During certain festivals you can also get there by **boat**.

Arch of the Viceroys

Upon arriving at the river landing stage to the north, seventeenth-century visitors passed through the **Arch of the Viceroys** (1597) constructed to commemorate Vasco da Gama's arrival in India and built from the same porous red laterite as virtually all Old Goa's buildings. Above it a bible-toting figure rests his foot on the crouched figure of a "native", while its granite facade, facing the river, holds a statue of da Gama himself. It is hard to imagine today that these overgrown fields, and simple streets with a few cool drinks stands, were once the focus of a lively market, busy with silk and gem merchants, horse dealers and carpet weavers. The one surviving monument, known as the **Adil Shah Gate**, predates the Portuguese, and possibly the Muslim, period. Hindu in style, it consists simply of a lintel supported by two columns in black basalt, to which are attached the remains of perforated screens.

St Catherine Cathedral

The Portuguese Viceroy Redondo (1561–64) commissioned the See, or **St Catherine Cathedral**, southwest of the Arch, to be "a grandiose church worthy of the wealth, power and fame of the Portuguese who dominated the seas from the Atlantic to the Pacific". Today it stands larger than any church in Portugal, although it was beset by problems, not least a lack of funds and Portugal's temporary loss of independence to Spain. It took eighty years to build and was not consecrated until 1640.

On the Tuscan-style exterior, the one tower to survive houses the **Golden Bell**, cast in Cuncolim (south Goa) in the seventeenth century. Reconstruction of parts of the roof, which once had overhanging eaves, has damaged some paintings inside. The scale and detail of the Corinthian-style interior is overwhelming; huge pillars divide the central nave from the side aisles, and no less than fifteen altars are arranged around the walls, dedicated among others to Our Ladies of Hope, Anguish and Three Needs. An altar to St Anne treasures the relics of the **Blessed Martyrs of Cuncolim**, whose failed mission to convert the Moghul emperor Akbar culminated in their murder by Muslims, while a chapel behind a highly detailed screen holds the **Miraculous Cross**, which stood in a Goan village until a vision of Christ appeared on it. Said to heal the sick, it is kept in a box; a small opening on the side allows devotees to touch it. The staggeringly ornate gilded main **altar** comprises nine carved frames and a splendid crucifix. Panels depict episodes from the life of St Catherine of Alexandria (died 307 AD), including an interchange of ideas with the pagan Roman emperor Maxim, who wished to marry her, and her subsequent flogging and martyrdom.

Convent and church of St Francis of Assisi and Archeological Museum

Southwest of the Cathedral is the ruined **Palace of the Inquisition**, in operation up until 1774, while to the west stands the **Convent of St Francis of Assisi**, built by Franciscan monks in 1517 and restored in the mid-eighteenth century. Today, the core of its **Archeological Museum** (daily except Fri 10am–5pm) is a gallery of portraits of Portuguese viceroys, painted by local artists under Italian supervision. The grandees' stuffy costumes must have been intolerable in Goan weather. Other exhibits include coins, domestic Christian wooden sculpture, and downstairs in the cloister, pre-Portuguese Hindu sculpture. Next door, the **Church of St Francis** (1521), features fine decorative frescoes and paintings on wood showing the life of St Francis of Assisi.

Basilica of Bom Jesus

Close to the convent of St Francis, the 1605 church of **Bom Jesus**, "Good" or "Infant" Jesus (Mon–Sat 9am–6.30pm, Sun 10am–6.30pm), is known principally for the **tomb of St Francis Xavier**. In 1946, it became the first church in India to be elevated to the status of Minor Basilica. On the west, the three-storey Renaissance facade encompasses Corinthian, Doric, Ionic and Composite styles.

The interior is entered beneath the choir, supported by columns. On the northern wall, in the centre of the nave, is a cenotaph in gilded bronze to **Dom Jeronimo Mascaranhas**, the Captain of Cochin and benefactor of the church. The main altar, extravagantly decorated in gold, depicts the infant Jesus under the protection of St Ignatius Loyola; to each side are subsidiary altars to Our Lady of Hope and St Michael. In the southern transept, lavishly decorated with twisted gilded columns and floriate carvings, stands the **Chapel and Tomb of St Francis Xavier**. Constructed of marble and jasper in 1696, it was the gift of the Medici, Cosimo III, the Grand Duke of Tuscany; the middle tier contains panels detailing the saint's life. An ornate domed reliquary in silver contains his remains; on his feast day, December 3, each year, the saint's finger is displayed to devotees. Once a decade – most recently in 1994 – the entire remains are on show; in centuries gone by, various body parts are said to have gone missing, departed with fervent admirers to Italy, Portugal and Japan.

ST FRANCIS XAVIER

Francis Xavier (1506–52) was born in the old kingdom of Navarre, now part of Spain. Having taken a masters degree in philosophy and theology at the University of Paris, where he studied for the priesthood until 1535, he was ordained two years later in Venice. He was then recruited by (Saint) **Ignatius Loyola** (1491–1556) along with five other priests into the new "Society of Jesus", which later came to be known as the **Jesuits**.

When the Portuguese king, Dom Joao III (1521–57), received reports of corruption and dissolute behaviour among the Portuguese in Goa, particularly under the second governor, Lope Soares de Albergaria (1515–18), he asked Ignatius Loyola to despatch a priest who could influence the moral climate for the better. In 1541 Xavier was sent to work in the diocese of Goa, constituted seven years before, and comprising all regions east of the Cape of Good Hope. Arriving after a year-long journey, he embarked on a busy programme throughout south India. Despite frequent obstruction from Portuguese officials, he founded numerous churches, and is credited with converting thirty thousand people and performing such miracles as raising the dead and curing the sick with a touch of his beads. Subsequently he took his mission further afield to Sri Lanka, Malacca (Malaysia), China and Japan where he was less successful. In Japan he narrowly escaped a stoning for what, to Buddhists, amounted to sedition.

When Xavier left Goa for the last time, it was with the ambition of evangelizing in China; however, he contracted dysentery aboard ship and died on the island of San Chuan (Sancian), off the Chinese coast, where he was buried. On hearing of his death, a group of Christians from Malacca went and exhumed his body – which, although the grave had been filled with lime, they found to be in a perfect state of preservation. They reburied it in Malacca, but it was later removed and taken to Old Goa, where it has remained ever since. Francis Xavier was canonized by Pope Gregory XV in 1621.

Church of St Catejan

Opposite the Cathedral, the **Church of St Catejan** (1651) was modelled on St Peter's in Rome by monks from the Theatine order, who believed in Divine Providence; they never sought charity, but simply expected it. While it does boast a Corinthian exterior, you can also spot certain non-European elements in the decoration, such as the cashew-nut designs in the carving of the pulpit.

Holy Hill

A number of other important religious builidings, some in ruins, stand opposite Bom Jesus on **Holy Hill**. The **convent of St Monica**, constructed in 1627, destroyed by fire in 1636 and rebuilt the following year, was the only Goan convent at the time and the largest in Asia. It housed around a hundred nuns, the Daughters of St Monica, and also offered accommodation to women whose husbands were called away to other parts of the empire. The **church** adjoins the convent on the south. As they had to remain away from the public gaze, the nuns attended mass in the choir loft and looked down upon the congregation.

Inside, a **Miraculous Cross** rises above the figure of St Monica at the altar. In 1636, it was reported that the figure of Christ had opened his eyes, motioned as if to speak and blood had flowed from the wounds made by the crown of thorns. The last Daughter of St Monica died in 1885, and since 1964 the convent has been occupied by the Mater Dei Institute for nuns.

Nearby, the **Convent of St John of God**, built in 1685 by the Order of Hospitallers of St John of God to tend to the sick, was rebuilt in 1953. At the top of the hill, the **Chapel of Our Lady of the Rosary**, built in 1526 in the Manueline style (after the Portuguese king Manuel I, 1495–1521), features Ionic plasterwork with a double-storey portico, cylindrical turrets and a tower that commands fine views across the river.

Hindu temples of Mardol and Ponda

Due to the ravages of the Inquisition, **Hindu temples** of any age are rare in Goa. Not until the introduction of parliamentary government in Portugal in 1821 were Hindus permitted to follow their faith. Now three modest and predominantly eighteenth-century temples in **Mardol** (22km southeast of Panjim, 13km beyond Old Goa) and **Ponda** (29km) are popular places of pilgrimage. Regular **buses** run from Panjim to Ponda via Old Goa and Mardol, and the Sri Manguesh and Shantadurga temples are on the "South Goa", "Pilgrim Special" and "Goa Darshan" **tours** from Panjim (see p.687).

Mardol

Although the **Sri Manguesh** temple originally stood in a secret location in Cortalim, and was brought to **MARDOL** during the sixteenth century, what visitors see today dates from the 1700s. A gateway at the roadside leads to a paved path and courtyard that gives on to a water tank, overlooked by the white temple building, raised on a plinth. Also in the courtyard is a seven-storey *deepmal*, a tower for oil lamps. Inside, the floor is paved with marble, and bands of decorative tiles emblazon the white walls. Flanked by large *dvarpala* guardians, embossed silver doorways with floriate designs lead to the sanctum, which houses a *shivalingam*.

Two kilometres away, the **Mahalasa Narayani** temple was also transferred from its original site, in this case Salcete *taluka* further south, in the seventeenth century. Here, the *deepmal* is exceptionally tall, with twenty-one tiers rising from a figure of Kurma, the tortoise incarnation of Vishnu. Original features include a marble-floored wooden *mandapa* with carved pillars, ceiling panels of parakeets and, in the eaves, sculptures of the incarnations of Vishnu. The sanctuary, behind embossed silver doors, contains an image of Narayani, the consort of Vishnu, who is usually equated with Lakshmi.

Ponda

PONDA's temple is dedicated to **Shanta Durga**, the goddess credited with pacifying the warring Vishnu and Shiva. In a pleasant wooded setting 2km west of the town, the entrance is dominated by a sunken water tank. A gabled *mandapa* hallway adjoins the sanctuary, topped by a domed octagonal tower. Inside the marble-floored *mandapa,* glass chandeliers hang from the wooden ceiling. Embossed silver doors and door-frames open on to the sanctuary, which houses a small figure of the goddess, also made of silver. Unlike in the other temples, there is a circumambulatory passage with a subsidiary shrine to the left which serves as a bedchamber for the goddess.

North of Panjim

Beyond the mouth of the Mandovi estuary, the Goan coast sweeps **north** in a near-continuous string of beaches, broken only by the odd salt-water creek, rocky headland, and three tidal rivers – two of which, the Chapora and Arondem, have to be crossed by ferry. The most developed resorts, **Calangute** and **Baga**, occupy the middle and north-ern part of the seven-kilometre strip of pearl-white sand that stretches from the Aguada peninsula in the south to a sheer laterite promontory in the north. Formerly, the infa-mous colonies of Goa hippies gathered in these two villages during their annual winter migration; now both are glutted with hotels and restaurants. The "scene", meanwhile, has shifted northwards, to the beaches around Anjuna, Vagator, and Chapora, where most of the Christmas–New Year parties take place.

Most of the tourist traffic **arriving in north Goa** from Bombay is syphoned off towards the coast through **Mapusa**, the area's main market town. For short hops between towns and resorts, **motorcycle taxis** are the quickest and most convenient way to get around, but **buses** also run to all the villages along the coast, via the **ferry crossings** at Siolim, 7km north of Anjuna, and Querim (for Terekol).

Mapusa

The ramshackle market town of **MAPUSA** (pronounced *Map*sa) is the district head-quarters of Bardez *taluka*. If you arrive by road from Bombay and plan to stay in one of the north Goan resorts, you can jump off the bus here and pick up a local service straight to the coast, rather than continue on to Panjim, 13km further south. A dusty collection of dilapidated modern buildings scattered around the west-facing slope of a low hill, the town is of little more than passing interest in itself, although on Fridays it hosts a lively **market** (Calangute and Anjuna may be better stocked with souvenirs, but Mapusa's is more authentic). Visitors who have flown straight to Goa, and have yet to experience the rest of India, wander in on Friday mornings to enjoy the pungent aromas of fish, incense, spices and exotic fruit stacked in colourful heaps on the side-walks. The covered arcades around the municipal market are good places to stock up on cheap T-shirts and beachwear, and innumerable places to change money, official or otherwise, line the streets surrounding the main square.

Getting around

Other than to shop, the only reason you may want to visit Mapusa is to arrange **onward transport**. All buses between Goa and Maharashtra pass through here, so you don't need to travel to Panjim to book a ticket to Bombay or Pune. Reservations for private buses can be made at the numerous agents' stalls at the bottom of the square, next to where the buses pull in; the **Kadamba terminal** – the departure point for both long-distance state buses, and local services to Calangute, Baga, Anjuna, Vagator, Chapora, and Arambol – is five minutes' walk down the main road, on the southwest edge of town. You can also get to the coast from Mapusa on one of the **motorcycle taxis** that wait in line at the bottom of the square. Rides to Calangute and Anjuna take twenty minutes, and costs Rs25 to Rs30. **Taxis** charge considerably more, but you can split the fare with up to five people.

As soon as you step off the bus, you'll be pestered by touts trying to get you to rent a motorbike. They'll tell you that rates here are lower than on the coast – they're not. Another reason to wait a while is that Mapusa is effectively a "no-go zone" for rented motorbikes, especially on Friday, when the police set up road-blocks on the outskirts of town to collar tourists without international licences (see p.683).

Accommodation and eating

Nearly all long-distance buses pull in to Mapusa in the morning, leaving plenty of time to find **accommodation** in the coastal resorts nearby. If you have to spend the night here, plenty of places to stay lie within easy walking distance of the bus stand. The best deal is GTDC's *Tourist Resort* (☎083226/2794; ②–④), on the roundabout below the square, where the rooms are nothing special, but clean, and some have a/c. It also has an **information** counter. *Hotel Trishul* (②–③), a large, no-frills lodge tucked away in the back streets above the main square, is a good fall-back. To find it, head along the lane up the hill past the Maruti (Hanuman) temple, and take the second turning on the right. For a little luxury, the *Hotel Satyaheera* (☎083226/2849; ②–⑥), at the top of the square opposite the temple, offers comfortable rooms with bathrooms and hot water.

The *Satyaheera* also boasts Mapusa's best **restaurant**, offering a standard Indian menu with Goan and Chinese alternatives, and cold beers too. Apart from the excellent fresh fruit and juice bars dotted around the market, the only other commendable place to eat and drink is the inexpensive dining hall at the *Tourist Resort*. Any number of less salubrious Goan *thali* joints can be found in the streets east of the main square.

Candolim and Aguada

Considering the peak-season clamour at Calangute, 3km north along the beach, **CANDOLIM** is surprisingly sedate, appealing to an odd mixture of middle-class Bombayites, and burgundy-clad *sanyasins* taking a break from the Rajneesh ashram at Pune. This looks set to change with the encroachment of package holiday complexes, but for the time being, the village remains little more than a ribbon development of small hotels and cafes, with a few sandy jeep tracks leading through the dunes and palm groves to the sea. If you can afford a bit of comfort, and want to stay somewhere relatively peaceful, but not too far from the action, hop off the Panjim bus when it turns onto the main road, and have a look around before heading further up the coast. Only five minutes by scooter from Calangute market, Candolim also boasts a couple of banks, a post office, and several tourist shops, as well as a rapidly proliferating crop of bars and small seafood restaurants; the beach tends to be a lot less crowded, too.

Immediately south of Candolim, a long peninsula extends into the sea, bringing the seven-kilometre white sandy beach to an abrupt end. **AGUADA fort**, which crowns the rocky flattened top of the headland, is the best-preserved Portuguese bastion in Goa. Built in 1612 to protect the northern shores of the Mandovi estuary, its name derives from the presence inside of several fresh water springs – the first source of drinking water available to ships arriving in Goa after the long sea voyage from Lisbon. On the north side of the fort, a rampart of red-brown laterite juts into the bay to form a jetty between two small sandy coves. This picturesque spot, known as **Sinquerim Beach**, was among the first places in Goa to be singled out for upmarket tourism. *Taj Group*'s *Fort Aguada* resort lords over the beach from the lower slopes of the steep-sided peninsula, and is among the most expensive hotels in India, a swanky arrangement of concrete chalets, swimming pools and well-watered lawns.

The ruins of the **fort** can be reached by road; head through the *Taj* village, and turn right when you see the sign. Nowadays, much of the site serves as a prison, and is therefore closed to visitors. It's worth a visit, though, if only for the superb views from the top of the hill from the **lighthouse**: down over the vast expanse of sea, sand and palm trees of Calangute beach on one side, and across the mouth of the Mandovi to Cabo Raj Bhavan, and the tip of the Mormugao peninsula, on the other.

Accommodation and eating

The best place to start hunting for **accommodation** in Candolim is at the end of the lane that leads to the sea opposite the *Canara Bank*, at the north side of the village. The purpose-built concrete hotels here are the preserve of predominantly young package tourists, but accept "walk-ins" if they have vacancies – a rarity in high season. **Restaurants** in all but a few serve usual seafood and western dishes. The *Successo Bar*, just south of the Panjim turn-off, is also a popular place to eat and drink.

Alexandra Tourist Home, down the lane opposite *Canara Bank*. Increasingly package-tour-oriented, with restaurant, STD telephone, money-changing facilities and comfortable rooms. ④.

Altrude Villa, down the lane opposite *Canara Bank*. New, airy rooms with tiled attached bathrooms, and verandahs. *Monte Villa*, next door, is an older version in family house. Good value. ③.

Fort Aguada Beach Resort, including *Aguada Hermitage*, and *Taj Holiday Village*, Sinquerim Beach (☎7501). Five-star opulence in hermetically sealed, immaculately manicured vacation campus. Pools, but no private beach. ⑨.

Holiday Beach Resort, down the lane opposite *Canara Bank* (☎6088). Larger version of the *Alexandra*, with similar facilities and prices. ④.

Sea Shell Inn, Fort Aguada Rd, opposite the *Canara Bank* (☎6131). Homely, comfortable hotel on the roadside. Advance booking recommended for Dec–Jan. The congenial terrace restaurant cooks meals to order – good for vegetarians and anyone fed up with spicy Indian food. ⑤.

Xavier Beach Resort, Fort Aguada Rd, opposite the *State Bank of India*. Peaceful, with luxurious rooms, large verandahs, and views from sea-facing windows. ⑥.

Calangute

A mere 45-minute bus ride up the coast from the capital, **CALANGUTE** is Goa's busiest and most commercialized resort, and the flagship of the state government's recent bid for a bigger slice of India's package-tourist pie. In the 1970s and early 1980s, this once-peaceful fishing village epitomized Goa's popular reputation as a safe haven for hedonistic hippies. Indian visitors flocked by the bus-load from Bombay and Bangalore to giggle at the tribes of dreadlocked westerners lying naked on the vast white sandy beach, stoned out of their brains on local *feni* and cheap *charas*. The odd party of prurient day-trippers still arrives from time to time, but invariably leaves disappointed; Calangute has cleaned up its act. Apart from the handful of stalwart budget travellers' bars and guest houses on the edges of the town, the "scene" has been almost entirely squeezed out by more mainstream holiday culture. Hoteliers today joke about the old days, when they used to rent out makeshift shacks on the beach to backpackers. Now many of them manage tailor-made tourist settlements, complete with air-conditioned rooms, swimming pools and plush lawns, for groups of suitcase-carrying fortnighters.

Though heavily developed by Goan standards, Calangute is still a long way from the high-rise hell that many Asian resorts have become in recent years. Away from the narrow congested main road that runs from the bustling central market square to nearby Baga, most hotels are small, double-storeyed buildings, hidden among the dunes behind a noise-proof curtain of coconut trees.

The road from the village to the beach is lined with Kashmiri-run handicraft boutiques, and Tibetan street stalls selling Himalayan curios and jewellery. The quality of the goods on offer, mainly Rajasthani, Gujarati, and Karnatakan textiles, is generally high, but so are the prices. Haggle hard, and don't be afraid to walk away from a heavy sales pitch – the same stuff crops up every Wednesday at Anjuna's flea market (see p.706). The **beach** itself is nothing special – its sand is discoloured in places, and steeply shelving – but more than large enough to accommodate its huge numbers of high-season visitors. Most of the action centres on the beachfront below GTDC's unsightly *Tourist Resort*, where crowds of Indian women in *saris* and straw hats stand around watching their sons and husbands frolic in the surf. Nearby, stray cows nose through the rubbish left by the previous bus party, while an endless stream of ice cream and fruit sellers, *lungi*-wallahs, ear cleaners, and masseurs, work their way through the ranks of western sun-worshippers.

To escape the melee, head fifteen minutes or so south of the main beachfront area, towards the rows of old wooden boats parked below the dunes. In this virtually hawker-free zone, you'll only come across teams of villagers hauling in hand-nets at high tide, or fishermen fixing their tack under bamboo sun shades. Wherever you hang out, though, remember that Calangute's "**no nudism**" rule is for real, and enforced by special police patrols; this includes topless bathing. In addition, several incidents of **sexual harassment** and attempted rape have occurred here in recent years.

Arrival and information

Buses from Mapusa and Panjim pull in at the small bus stand-cum-market square in the centre of Calangute. Some continue to Baga, stopping at the crossroads behind the beach en route. Get off here if you can (as the main road veers sharply to the right); it's closer to most of the hotels. **Motorcycle taxis** hang around the little sandy square behind GTDC's *Tourist Resort*, next to the steps that drop down to the beachfront itself. Ask around here if you want to rent a **motorcycle**. Rates are standard; the nearest **gas station** is five minutes' walk from the beach, back towards the market on the right-hand side of the main road. **Bicycles** are also widely available for Rs20 to Rs25 per day.

If you need to **change money**, the *State Bank of India* is on the main street, midway between the beach and the market square. Finally, the *Shyam* secondhand **book-**

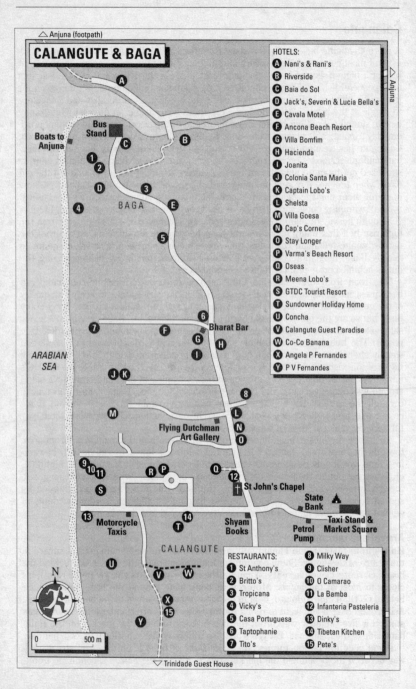

△ Anjuna (footpath)

CALANGUTE & BAGA

△ Anjuna

Boats to Anjuna

Bus Stand

BAGA

ARABIAN SEA

Bharat Bar

Flying Dutchman Art Gallery

St John's Chapel

State Bank

Motorcycle Taxis

Shyam Books

Petrol Pump

Taxi Stand & Market Square

CALANGUTE

N

0   500 m

HOTELS:

- **A** Nani's & Rani's
- **B** Riverside
- **C** Baia do Sol
- **D** Jack's, Severin & Lucia Bella's
- **E** Cavala Motel
- **F** Ancona Beach Resort
- **G** Villa Bomfim
- **H** Hacienda
- **I** Joanita
- **J** Colonia Santa Maria
- **K** Captain Lobo's
- **L** Shelsta
- **M** Villa Goesa
- **N** Cap's Corner
- **O** Stay Longer
- **P** Varma's Beach Resort
- **Q** Oseas
- **R** Meena Lobo's
- **S** GTDC Tourist Resort
- **T** Sundowner Holiday Home
- **U** Concha
- **V** Calangute Guest Paradise
- **W** Co-Co Banana
- **X** Angela P Fernandes
- **Y** P V Fernandes

RESTAURANTS:

- **1** St Anthony's
- **2** Britto's
- **3** Tropicana
- **4** Vicky's
- **5** Casa Portuguesa
- **6** Taptophanie
- **7** Tito's
- **8** Milky Way
- **9** Clisher
- **10** O Camarao
- **11** La Bamba
- **12** Infanteria Pasteleria
- **13** Dinky's
- **14** Tibetan Kitchen
- **15** Pete's

▽ Trinidade Guest House

store, where the main Baga road bends north, stocks a vast range of paperbacks in several languages, including English, French, German, Dutch, Swedish, and Japanese.

Accommodation

Calangute is chock-full of **places to stay**. Demand only outstrips supply in the Christmas–New Year high season; at other times, haggle a little over the tariff, especially if the place looks empty. Most of the **inexpensive accommodation** consists of small rooms in family homes, or in concrete annexes tacked onto the backs of houses. Though bare and basic, these usually have running water and fans. For a little extra, you can get a verandah or a balcony, and an attached bathroom; nowhere is far from the shore, but sea views are more of a rarity. The **top hotels** are nearly all gleaming white, exclusive villa complexes with pools, and direct beach access. High-season rates in such places are staggeringly steep, as they cater almost solely for package tourists.

INEXPENSIVE

Ancona Beach Resort, Baga side, near *Tito's*. Popular backpackers' hostel with dingy doubles and a restaurant next door. Close to the busy Baga end of the beach. ③.

Angela P Fernandes, Calangute's most popular budget travellers' hang out. Basic, but fairly clean, with reliable water supply, fans, and psychedelic murals. Cheaper rooms around the back. ①–②.

Calangute Guest Paradise, near *Angela P Fernandes*. Large and cheap, but charmless. ①–②.

Joanita, Baga Rd. Clean, airy rooms, with attached baths and some double beds, ranged around quiet garden. A bargain. ①.

NV's, Maddo Vaddo. Clean, friendly family guest house, a ten-minute walk down the beach. Rooms (some single) with separate bathrooms, 24hr water, fresh linen, and fans. Communal verandah, and an excellent restaurant. ②.

O Camarao, just north of GTDC *Tourist Resort* (☎6229). Spruce, blue-and-white painted bungalow, with immaculate rooms, verandahs, and a restaurant. Good value. ②.

Oseas Tourist Home, St John's Chapel, Umtavaddo (☎6065). Established guest house in rambling old Portuguese-style home. Attached or non-attached rooms, with wood partition walls. ①.

PV Fernandes, near *Angela P Fernandes*. Old-fashioned Portuguese bungalow threatened by advancing dunes. Bare rooms with old beds and common shower-toilets. A little overpriced. ②–③.

Sundowner Holiday Home, off beach road, behind *Tibetan Kitchen*. Large, good-value rooms, some with windows on two walls, fans and attached bathrooms. ③.

Trinidade, beyond *Angela P Fernandes*. Plain rooms in new extension block. Cheaper and quieter than places further up the lane. ①–②.

MODERATE

La Bamba, next to GTDC *Tourist Resort* (☎6108). Small, cosy and well-maintained guest house close to the beach. Some sea-facing rooms. ④.

Cap's Corner, Baga Rd, Cobravaddo. Dull concrete building, but the rooms are very clean and comfortable, if overpriced. ⑤.

Co-Co Banana, down the lane past *Meena Lobo's* restaurant. Very comfortable chalets, all with bathrooms, balconies and sea breezes, grouped around central garden. Good value. ④.

Concha, Umtavaddo (☎6506). Stylish old colonial villa, with banana plants in the garden, mosquito nets, verandahs, and well-furnished rooms. Worth the extra. ④–⑤.

GTDC Tourist Resort, overlooking the steps to the beach (☎6024). More like the *Last Resort*; grim concrete block, with marginally less hideous cottages adjacent. The rates aren't bad, though. ④.

Hacienda, Baga Rd. Nothing special, but popular, with big, airy rooms, balconies and a garden. ④.

Shelsta, Baga Rd (☎6069). Best of the ugly roadside hotels. Nice garden and rooms, but noisy. ④.

Stay Longer, Baga Rd, Cobra Vaddo. One of numerous unattractive, run-of-the-mill hotels on the main road. This one has spacious rooms, and is good value. ④.

The telephone **area code** for Calangute is ☎0832 27.

EXPENSIVE

Captain Lobo's, Cobravaddo (☎6103). A dozen or so luxuriously furnished, self-contained apartments, with a pool, and top restaurant, crammed on to small campus near the beach. ⑦.

Colonia Santa Maria (☎2571). *Lobo's* lookalike, in the heart of the exclusive package tour enclave. Two restaurants, a pool, and shops. Popular with 18–30s. ⑧.

Varma's Beach Resort, two minutes' east of GTDC *Tourist Resort* (☎6077). Attractive a/c rooms, with balconies overlooking a leafy garden. Secluded, but close to the centre of the village. ⑦.

Villa Bomfim, Baga Rd (☎6105). Long-established resort hotel, now given over to package tourists, with pleasant open-air restaurant, beauty parlour, safe deposit, money changing and so on. ⑤–⑦.

Villa Goesa, Cobravaddo (☎6182). A stone's throw from the beach and very swish. Occasional live music, and a cocktail bar. ⑥.

Eating

Calangute's bars and restaurants are mainly grouped around the entrance to the beach, and along the Baga road. As with most Goan resorts, the accent is firmly on **seafood**, though many places tack a few token veg dishes on to their menus. Western budget travellers' **breakfasts** (pancakes, porridge, muesli, eggs etc) are also popular.

Mr Cater's, GTDC *Tourist Resort*. Bustling terrace restaurant overlooking the beach, serves moderately priced *tandoori* seafood, meat sizzlers, *xacuti*, *cafreal*, and a range of Indian veg dishes.

Clisher, north of GTDC *Tourist Resort*, behind the beach. Best of the beach-side bar-restaurants, with the usual fresh seafood, good breakfasts, cold beer, and sea views. Inexpensive to moderate.

Dinky, beside the steps to the beach. Standard seafood and beer bar, with pleasant verandah for crowd watching. Popular with budget travellers.

Infantaria Pastelaria, near St John's Chapel, Baga Rd. Small roadside terrace packed out for breakfast. It may well not be what you came to India for, but there are few more irresistible ways to kick off a hard day by the sea than with a piping hot croissant, or a slice of freshly baked apple pie.

Meena Lobo, near *Varma's*. Tacky decor, but a good all-rounder.

Milky Way, midway between Calangute and Baga. Indian filter coffee, filled rolls (including delicious garlic cottage cheese), and other moderately priced snacks served in a shady garden.

NV's, south Calangute. A ten-minute trek down the beach, but well worth it for no-nonsense, hearty platefuls of grilled fish, calamari and crab, all fresh from the family boat.

Taptophanie, Baga Rd. Laid back, German-run terrace cafe-cum-clothes store, strong on western food: brown bread, apple pie, muesli, cakes, light meals, and excellent espresso. Moderate.

Tibetan Kitchen, off beach road. Filling, delicious Tibetan food, with western and Chinese options, full breakfasts, floaty New Age music, and chess sets. Tasty cheese-fried *momo*, homemade cakes.

Nightlife

Thanks to a concerted crackdown by the Goan police on beach parties and loud music, Calangute's **nightlife** is surprisingly tame. All but a handful of the bars wind up by 10pm, leaving punters to prolong the short evenings back at their hotels. One notable exception is *Tito's*, at the Baga end of the beach, which stays open until 11pm off season, and into the small hours in late December and January. Owned by rock star and local hero Remo Fernandes, Calangute's trendiest (and priciest) nightspot boasts a large sandy terrace overlooking the beach, a small dance floor, and a powerful techno sound system. The only other places that consistently open late are a couple of dull hippy hangouts in the woods to the south of the beach road. *Pete's Bar*, a perennial favourite next door to *Angela P Fernandes*, is generally the most lively, offering cheap drinks, backgammon sets, and relentless reggae.

Further afield, *Bob's Inn*, between Calangute and Candolim, is another popular bar, famous as much for its lasagne as its easy social scene. Also worth checking out while you're down that way is the *Golden Eye*, on the north side of Candolim beach, which draws crowds of young, well-heeled punters from the nearby package tour hotels.

Baga

BAGA, 10km west of Mapusa, is basically an extension of Calangute; not even the locals agree where one ends and the other begins. Lying in the lee of an eroded headland, the only real difference between this far northern end of the beach and its congested centre is that its scenery is marginally more varied and picturesque. A small river flows into the sea at the top of the village, below a broad spur of soft white sand, from where a dirt track strikes across an open expanse of rice paddy towards Anjuna. The old red-tiled fishers' houses behind the dunes have long been swamped by bars, restaurants, handicraft shops and guest houses, but you don't feel quite so boxed in as at Calangute. The river also marks the northernmost limits of mass tourism in Goa. Across the hideous cubic concrete bridge that links Baga with the far bank, you enter a tranquil hinterland of coconut plantations, peppered with tiny Hindu farming hamlets.

Most of the action in Baga revolves around the sandy square-cum-coach park at the top of the village, where the main metalled road from Calangute peters out, and the buses roll in from Mapusa and Panjim, 18km southeast. The restaurants nearby do a brisk trade during the day, and open late in the evening, when they fill up with punters from the nearby resort hotels. Further south, a row of lookalike bamboo beach bars compete for custom with uniformly raucous techno music systems. For some reason *Vicky's* draws a bigger crowd than the others, but they all charge the same for a beer, and swing well into the night during the season.

Accommodation

Accommodation is harder to find in Baga than in Calangute; places tend to be booked up well before the season gets under way. If you're keen to stay, you may well have to hole up further down the beach for a night while you hunt around for a vacancy. The rough-and-ready guest houses dotted around the fishing village usually have space; look for signs outside restaurants on the main square. The cheap houses and rooms for rent on the quieter north side of the river, are like gold-dust in December and January.

Baia do Sol, on the square (☎6084). Baga's best (2-star) hotel is modern, immaculate, and surrounded by a well-kept garden. No single occupancy in high season. Some a/c. ⑤–⑥.

Cavala Motel, down the Calangute road (☎2290). Modern building, with simple rooms, en suite bathrooms, and separate balconies. ④–⑤.

Jack's, in the village. Fourteen small and basic rooms, all with attached bathrooms and fans, behind restaurant of the same name. ②.

Lucia Bella's, in the village. Cramped, and not really pleasant enough for a lengthy stay, but OK as a stopover until you find your feet. ②.

Nani's & Rani's, north of the river. A handful of red-tiled, whitewashed cottages in a secluded back garden, popular with long-staying guests. Fans, common toilets, well water, and outdoor shower. ①.

Riverside, overlooking the square (☎6062). New, tasteful hotel with large comfy rooms, a good restaurant, and river views. Moving into the package bracket, but the best value at this price. ⑤.

Severin, in the village. Cramped and noisy, but cheap, and clean enough for a night. ②.

BOATS TO THE ANJUNA FLEA MARKET

Every Wednesday, **boats** leave Baga beach for the flea market at Anjuna, from around 9am until just before sunset. How much you pay for the twenty-minute trip depends on how many passengers the fishermen manage to cram on board, but it usually works out the same as a motorcycle taxi. If you go, pack your cameras and any valuables in a plastic bag. Accidents can happen when the fishermen load their vessels to the gunwhales, and then try to save time, and gas, by cutting through a narrow channel between two rocks – straightforward enough on calm days, but a hair-raising stunt when the sea is choppy.

Eating

Food options in Baga are confined to the open-air seafood restaurants clustered around the square at the top end of the village, and the no-frills cafes behind the beach. For a splurge, splash out on a candlelit dinner in the *Casa Portuguesa*. *Tito's*, Calangute's most popular nightspot, is just around the corner.

Britto's, on the square. Currently the most popular restaurant in the village, with a predictable menu of reasonably priced seafood and western dishes, and some Goan specialities.

Casa Portuguesa, Baga Rd. Portuguese and Goan food served by candle light inside romantic old colonial villa, or al fresco on a leafy lawn. The gregarious owner serenades diners with Amelia Rodrigues *fados* most evenings. Overpriced, but worth it for the atmosphere.

Jack's, in the village. No-nonsense, inexpensive seafood joint also serves Goan-fried (read "spicy") vegetables, and less than inspiring Chinese.

Nani's & Rani's, north side of the river. Friendly family-run restaurant serving unremarkable but inexpensive food on sociable verandah overlooking the river. Popular with budget travellers.

St Anthony's, off the square. *The* place to watch the sunset, accompanied by an icy beer and Indian classical music on a better-than-average sound system. The main meals are a touch pricey, though.

Tropicana, Baga Rd. Small roadside restaurant dishing up cheap snacks, shakes, and passable espresso coffee under a palm-leaf roof.

Valerios, next door to *Hotel Baia do Sol*. Sophisticated bar-restaurant with good sea and river views from a pleasant first-floor terrace. Live music on Weds after the flea-market. Moderate to expensive.

Anjuna

With its fluorescent-painted palm trees and infamous full-moon parties, **ANJUNA**, 8km west of Mapusa, is Goa at its most "alternative". Designer leather and lycra may have superseded cotton kaftans, but most people's reasons for coming are the same as they were in the 1970s: drugs, dancing, and lying on the beach slurping tropical fruit. Depending on your point of view, you'll find the headlong hedonism a total turn-off, or heaven-on-sea. Either way, the scene looks here to stay, despite government attempts to stamp it out, so you might as well get a taste of it while you're in the area – if only from the wings, with a day trip to the famous **flea-market**.

One of the main sources of Anjuna's enduring popularity as a hippy hang-out is its superb **beach**. Fringed by groves of swaying coconut palms, the classical curve of soft white sand conforms almost exactly to the archetypal vision of paradise. Bathing is generally safer than at most of the nearby resorts, especially at the more peaceful southern end, where a rocky headland keeps the sea calm, and the undertow to a minimum. North of the market ground, the beach broadens, running in an uninter-rupted kilometre-long stretch of steeply shelving sand to a low red cliff. The village bus park lies on top of this high ground, near small cafes, bars, and Kashmiri handi-craft stalls. Every lunchtime, tour parties from Panjim pull in here for a beer, before heading home again, leaving the ragged army of sun-weary westerners to enjoy the sunset.

The season in Anjuna gets under way earlier than at most other Goan resorts, start-ing in early November, when most of the long-staying regulars show up, and petering out in late March, when they drift off again. During the Christmas and New Year rush, the village is inundated with a mixed crowd of round-the-world backpackers, refugees from the English club scene, and revellers from all over India, lured by the promise of the big beach parties. The rest of the time, Anjuna has a surprisingly simple, unhurried atmosphere – due, in no small part, to the shortage of places to stay. Most visitors who come here on market day, or for the raves, travel in from other resorts.

Whenever you come, keep a close eye on your valuables. **Theft**, particularly from the beach, is a big problem. Party nights are the worst; if you stay out late, make sure you keep your money and papers on you, or lock them somewhere secure (see below). Thieves have even been known to break into local houses by lifting tiles off the roof.

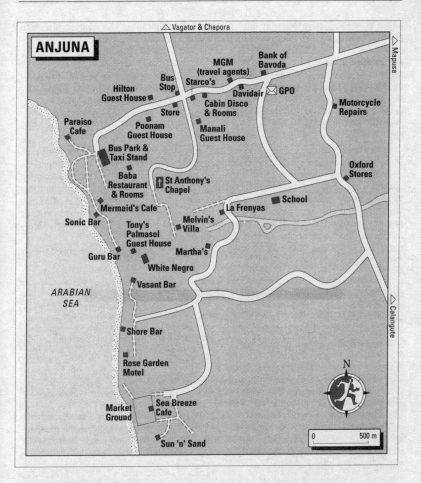

ANJUNA

△ Vagator & Chapora

▷ Mapusa

Bus Stop
MGM (travel agents)
Bank of Bavoda
Starco's
Hilton Guest House
Davidair ✉ GPO
Cabin Disco & Rooms
Store
Motorcycle Repairs
Paraiso Cafe
Poonam Guest House
Manali Guest House
Bus Park & Taxi Stand
Oxford Stores
Baba Restaurant & Rooms
† St Anthony's Chapel
Mermaid's Cafe
La Frenyas
School
Sonic Bar
Tony's Palmasol Guest House
Melvin's Villa
Guru Bar
Martha's
White Negro
ARABIAN SEA
Vasant Bar
Shore Bar
Rose Garden Motel
▷ Calangute
Market Ground
Sea Breeze Cafe
Sun 'n' Sand

N

0   500 m

Arrival and information

Anjuna is scattered over a wide area of paddy fields and coconut plantations, from the woods behind the southern end of the beach, to the sun-baked sides of Vagator hill in the north. **Buses** arriving from Mapusa and Panjim drop passengers at various points along the tarmac road across the top of the village, which turns right towards Chapora at the main "Starco's" crossroads. If you're looking for somewhere to stay, get off here as it's close to most of the guest houses. The crossroads has a couple of small stores, a **motorcycle taxi** rank, and functions as a de facto village square-cum-bus stand.

The other main agglomeration of buildings is a kilometre further inland, along the Mapusa road, where you'll find the **post office**, with its efficient poste restante counter, as well as several travel agents, restaurants and the **Oxford Stores**, which sells an amazing range of imported food and drink, including Swiss chocolate, German biscuits, and even champagne and caviar. The *Bank of Baroda* (Mon–Wed 9.30am–1.30pm, Fri 9.30am–1.30pm, Sat 9.30–11.30am) on the Mapusa road in the north of the village, doesn't do foreign exchange, but is a good place to leave **valuables**. Their safe deposit boxes cost Rs50, payable each time you make a withdrawal. The nearest places to **change money** are two kilometres up the road in Vagator (see p.700).

Accommodation

Most of Anjuna's very limited **accommodation** consists of small unfurnished houses. Finding one is a problem at the best of times; in peak season it's virtually impossible. By then, all but a handful have been let to long-staying regulars who book by post several months in advance. If you arrive hoping to sort something out on spec, you'll probably have to make do with a room in a guest house at first. Even this can be difficult, as most guest house owners are reluctant to rent out rooms for only one or two days at a time. Basically, unless you mean to stay for at least a couple of months, you'll be better off looking for a room in Calangute, Baga, or nearby Vagator and Chapora.

Something else to bear in mind is that Anjuna has, thanks to the extra inhabitants it attracts over the winter, become particularly prone to **water shortages**. These tend not to affect many visitors, as the drought only begins to bite towards the end of March when the majority have already left. For the villagers, however, the problem causes genuine hardship. Use well water very sparingly, and avoid water toilets if possible – traditional "dry" ones are far more ecologically sound.

Cabin Disco, next door to *Starco's*, on "Starco's" crossroads. Unappealing cells with common bathrooms. OK for a night or two, though. ②.

THE ANJUNA FLEA MARKET

Anjuna's Wednesday **flea market** is the hub of Goa's alternative scene, and *the* place to indulge in a spot of souvenir **shopping**. A few years back, the weekly event was the exclusive preserve of backpackers and the area's semi-permanent freak population, who gathered here to smoke *chillums*, and to buy and sell clothes and jewellery they probably wouldn't have had the nerve to wear anywhere else: something like a small pop festival without the stage. These days, however, everything is a lot more organized and mainstream. The pitches are rented out by the metre, drugs are banned, and the approach roads to the village are choked solid all day with air-conditioned coaches and *Ambassador* cars ferrying in package tourists from the resorts further down the coast.

The range of goods on sale has broadened, too, thanks to the high profile of migrant hawkers and stallholders from other parts of India. Each region, or culture, tends to stick to its own corner. At one end, westerners congregate around racks of New Age rave gear, Balinese batiks, and designer beachwear. Nearby, hawk-eyed Kashmiris sit crosslegged beside trays of silver jewellery and papier-mâché boxes, while the Tibetans, wearing jeans and T-shirts, preside over orderly rows of prayer wheels, turquoise bracelets, and sundry Himalayan curios. Most distinctive of all are the Karnatakan *adivasi* women who prowl the beaches. Decked from head to toe in traditional tribal garb, their speciality is elaborately woven multicoloured cloth, which they fashion into everything from jackets to money-belts, and which makes even the westerners' party gear look positively funereal. Elsewhere around the ground, you'll come across dazzling Rajasthani mirrorwork and block-printed bedspreads, Keralan wood carvings, and a scattering of Gujarati appliqué. One old man even sells anklets and armbands made from peacock feathers.

What you end up paying for this exotic merchandise largely depends on your ability to **haggle**. Lately, prices have been inflated because some tourists not used to dealing in *rupees* are prepared to part with almost anything. Be persistent, though, and you can usually pick things up for a reasonable rate.

Even if you're not spending, the flea market is a great place just to sit and watch the world go by. Mingling with the sun-tanned masses are bands of strolling musicians, itinerant beggars, performing monkey acts and snake charmers, as well as the inevitable hippy jugglers, clad in regulation waistcoats and billowing pyjama trousers. One wonders what the Indian visitors who bus in here for the day must make of it all.

Hilton, near the coach park. Rooms in characterless concrete out-building, 500m behind the beach. Some attached bathrooms. ②–③.

Manali, south from *Starco's*. Anjuna's best budget guest house has simple rooms around a yard, fans, safe-deposit, sociable terrace-restaurant, and shared bathrooms. Book in advance. ①–②.

Martha's, 907 Montero Vaddo. Three well-kept rooms run by warm family. Basic amenities include kitchen space and running water. ②.

Mermaid's, near the *Sonic Bar*. Bare and basic, with common bathrooms and dry toilets. Virtually on the beach. ②.

Poonam, east of the bus park. Double-storey purpose-built guest house with a leafy garden, and a cafe. The rooms are clean, but rudimentary and somewhat overpriced. ④.

Starco's, "Starco's" crossroads. Fusty, dark, cramped rooms around a yard. Good restaurant. ③.

Tamarind, 5km from the beach on the Mapusa road. Upmarket resort hotel pitched at package tourists, with lush garden, pool, wet-bar, restaurant, swish rooms, and resident fish-eagle. ⑦.

Tony's Palmasol Guest House, north of *Vasant Bar*, behind the middle of the beach. Large, comfortable rooms very near the beach, with running water, verandahs and a relaxing garden. ④.

White Negro, south of the village, behind *Guru Bar*. Pleasant chalets catching sea breezes, all with attached bathrooms, 24hr running water, and a lively restaurant. Friendly management. ③–④.

Eating

Both the beachfront and village at Anjuna are awash with good **places to eat and drink**. Most are simple semi-open-air, thatched palm-leaf affairs, specializing in fish and western food. All serve cold beer, invariably with thumping techno music in the background. On the beach, you'll be approached every ten minutes by women selling fresh fruit, including watermelons, pineapples, and locally grown coconuts.

Martha's Breakfast Home, near *La Frenyas*, off the road to the market. Secluded breakfast garden serving fresh Indian coffee, crepes, and American waffles, in addition to regular menu.

Rose Garden Motel, on the beach south of the *Shore Bar*. Not to be confused with the *Rose Garden Restaurant* in the village. The exhaustive menu here includes superb, reasonably priced seafood sizzlers and plenty of vegetarian options.

Sea Breeze, market ground. Does a roaring trade in cold beer and snacks on Wednesdays. At other times the vast *tandoori* fish are tasty and good value, especially for groups. Order in advance.

Shore Bar, in the middle of the beach. Draws a crowd for sunset after the flea market, and most Saturdays, with the best sound system in Anjuna. Light and main meals served as well as drinks.

Starco's, "Starco's" crossroads. Slightly more sophisticated bar-restaurant, serving tasty *tandoori* seafood, and western dishes, inside or on the roadside terrace.

Sun'n'Sand, market ground. Renowned for its whopping fresh-fruit salads served with crumbled coconut and curd. Great for inexpensive, healthy breakfasts.

White Negro, behind the *Guru Bar*. Conventional semi-open-air holiday restaurant offering a predictable selection of Indian, Goan and western dishes. Popular with liberal Bombayites.

Nightlife

Anjuna has become a popular **rave** venue in recent years, attracting partygoers from all over the world. Most of the big events take place around the Christmas–New Year full-moon period, although smaller parties happen whenever their organizers manage to muster the increasingly large pay-offs demanded by the local police. At other times **nightlife** centres on the *Shore Bar*, in the middle of the beach, which has a pounding sound system. The biggest crowds show up on Wednesdays after the market, to watch the sunset from the steps in front of the bar, accompanied by the latest ambient trance mixes from London. The music gains pace as the evening wears on, winding up around 11pm, when there's a general exodus over to the *Guru Bar*, further up the beach, or to the *Primrose Cafe* in Vagator, both of which stay open until after midnight. If, at this stage, you're still hankering after some action, and there isn't a rave in the offing, wander along the beach to see if you can find an impromptu party.

Listings

Boats Fishing boats shuttle between Anjuna and Baga beach every Wednesday from just below the market ground. You can catch a boat back to Arambol from here in the evening: see p.703.

Library The *Oceanic* circulating library, near the *White Negro Bar*, stocks a good selection of quality fiction and non-fiction. A labour of love run by a retired local woman, this place is a worthy recipient of any cast-off novels you might want to ditch before leaving.

Motorcycle Repairs Anjuna's two motorcycle repair workshops are both up the road from the *Oxford Stores*. The smaller one, further back from the roadside, is more helpful. Gas and some spares, such as inner tubes and spark plugs, can be bought from the store on "Starco's" crossroads.

Travel Agents *MGM* and *Davidair* (☎083227/6060; fax 6248), on the Mapusa road; *Speedy* (☎083227/3266), between the post office and *Rose Garden Restaurant*, is also reputable.

Vagator

Barely a couple of kilometres of cliff tops and parched grassland separate Anjuna from the southern fringes of its nearest neighbour, **VAGATOR**. A desultory collection of ramshackle farmhouses and picturesque old Portuguese bungalows scattered around a network of leafy lanes, the village is entered in the east via a branch off the Mapusa road, which passes a few small guest houses and restaurants, before running gently down through a thick carpet of tropical trees to the sea. Dominated by the red ramparts of Chapora fort, Vagator's broad white sandy beach is undeniably beautiful – only spoiled by the daily deluge of whisky-swilling, snap-happy coach parties that spill across it at lunch times.

Far better then to head down to the next cove south. Backed by a steep wall of crumbling palm-fringed laterite, **Ozran**, or "Little", **Vagator** is more secluded and much less accessible than either of its neighbours. To get there, walk ten minutes from "Big Vagator", or drive to the end of the lane off the main Chapora–Anjuna road, from where a footpath drops sharply down to a wide stretch of level white sand (look for the mopeds and bikes parked at the top of the cliff). At this southern end of the beach, a row of identikit makeshift cafes provides shade and sustenance for the predominantly young, hip crowd that hangs out here during the day. Nearby, someone has sculpted a contemplative face out of a rock, and a freshwater spring trickles through a lush tangle of vegetation into a shady pool at the foot of the cliff – ideal for washing off the salt after swimming. In spite of the Goan nudism laws, topless bathing is very much the norm; not that the locals, nor the odd groups of inebriated men from out of state that file past around mid-afternoon, seem in the least bit perturbed.

Like Anjuna, Vagator is a relaxed, comparatively undeveloped resort that appeals, in the main, to travellers on tight budgets with time on their hands. Accommodation is limited, however, and visitors for whom Ozran beach and the village's lively **cafe scene** hold a particularly strong appeal frequently find themselves travelling to and from Baga every day until a vacancy turns up in one of the guest houses.

Arrival and information

Buses from Panjim and Mapusa, 9km east, pull in every fifteen minutes or so at the crossroads on the far northeastern edge of Vagator, near where the main road peels away towards Chapora. From here, it's a one-kilometre walk over the hill and down the other side to the beach, where you'll find most of the village's accommodation, restaurants and cafes. The *Corporation Bank* (Mon–Wed & Fri 10am–2pm, Sat 10am–noon) is 200 metres south of the main crossroads, on the Anjuna road. The only other official place in Vagator to **change money** (both cash and travellers' cheques) is the *Primrose Cafe*, in the south (Anjuna) side of the village; they charge at bank rates and hand out encashment certificates free of charge. If you want to rent a **motorcycle**, *Prakash Auto Service* (☎083226/3214), near the *Sea Green Chinese Restaurant*, has the usual gamut of *Yamahas*, *Honda Kinetics*, *Enfields* and clapped-out *Rajdoots*.

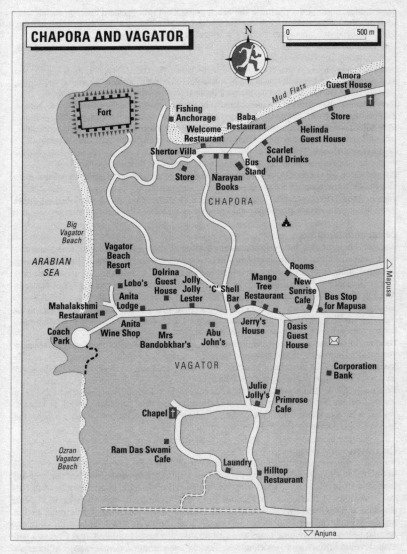

CHAPORA AND VAGATOR

N

0   500 m

Amora Guest House

Mud Flats

Fort

Fishing Anchorage

Baba Restaurant

Store

Welcome Restaurant

Helinda Guest House

Shertor Villa

Scarlet Cold Drinks

Bus Stand

Store

Narayan Books

CHAPORA

Big Vagator Beach

ARABIAN SEA

Vagator Beach Resort

Rooms

Dolrina Guest House

Jolly Jolly Lester

'C' Shell Bar

Mango Tree Restaurant

New Sunrise Cafe

Lobo's

Anita Lodge

Bus Stop for Mapusa

▷ Mapusa

Mahalakshmi Restaurant

Jerry's House

Coach Park

Anita Wine Shop

Mrs Bandobkhar's

Abu John's

Oasis Guest House

VAGATOR

Corporation Bank

Julie Jolly's

Primrose Cafe

Chapel

Ram Das Swami Cafe

Ozran Vagator Beach

Laundry

Hilltop Restaurant

▽ Anjuna

Accommodation

Accommodation in Vagator is limited to a few family-run budget guest houses, and dozens of small private properties rented out for long periods. The usual charge for a houses is between Rs200 and Rs450 per month; ask around the cafes and back lanes south of the main road. **Water** is also very short here, and should be used frugally at all times (see p.706).

Abu John's, halfway between the crossroads and the beach. Comfortable self-contained chalets in quiet garden; all with bathrooms and running water. ④.

Anita Lodge, north of the road near the beach (☎083226/4348). Standard concrete rooms, with western water toilets, and small balconies, in modern roadside bungalow. See the manager of *Anita Wine Shop* opposite for bookings, money changing, and STD telephone. ③.

Mrs Bandobkhar's, next to the *Anita Wine Shop*. Flats, or five rooms, in brand new building. Running water. Good value. ①–②.

Dolrina Guest House, north of the road near the beach (☎083226/4347). Vagator's largest, and most popular, budget guest house is run by a friendly Goan family; attached or shared bathrooms, hot water, a sociable common verandah, and individual safe deposits. Breakfasts available. ③.

Jerry's House, 100m west of the crossroads. Very cheap and basic rooms in family house. No use of the bathroom or toilet during the evenings, believe it or not. Only for emergencies. ①.

Jolly Jolly Lester, halfway between the crossroads and Big Vagator beach. Four pleasant doubles, with tiled bathrooms, in attractive woodland, plus small restaurant. Single occupancy possible. ③.

Oasis Guest House, 100m west of the crossroads, near *Jerry's*. Concrete house, surrounded by trees, with largish rooms, attached bathrooms and running water. Nothing special. ③–④.

Royal Resort, east of the bus stop. Recently opened, swanky hotel at the top of the village. Posh rooms, 24hr coffee shop and a pool. ⑦.

Vagator Beach Resort, behind Big Vagator beach (☎083226/4341). Well-established upmarket resort hotel, with cottages grouped around a central restaurant, in a dense palm grove. ⑥.

Eating and nightlife

Vagator's many cafes and restaurants are scattered along the main road, and along the back lanes that lead to Ozran beach. There are also several seafood joints behind "Big Vagator", one or two of which serve Indian dishes in addition to the usual fish-rich Goan specialities. **Nightlife** revolves squarely around the *Primrose Cafe*, out towards Anjuna, which boasts a beefier-than-average sound system, and a late bar.

Jolly Jolly Lester, half way between the village crossroads and Big Vagator beach. Not to be confused with *Julie Jolly's*, near the *Primrose*. This one's smaller, friendlier, and offers a better selection of inexpensive seasonal seafood, salads, and tasty western-style veg dishes.

Lobo's. The best of the batch behind the beach. Mostly Goan-style seafood, with some unadventurous western and vegetarian alternatives. Inexpensive.

Mango Tree, near the crossroads/bus stop. Moderately priced sizzlers, seafood, and delicious stir-fries prepared in front of you by resident Chinese chef.

Primrose Cafe & Restaurant, on the southern edge of the village. Goa's posiest cafe-bar livens up around 8-ish, and serves tasty German wholefood snacks, light meals and cakes, as well as drinks.

Ram Das Swami, above Ozran Vagator beach. Terrible service, but the portions are generous, the food tasty, and the sea views superb. Inexpensive.

Chapora

Crouched in the shadow of an old Portuguese fort on the opposite, northern side of the headland from Vagator, **CHAPORA**, 10km from Mapusa, feels busier than most north-coast villages. Dependent on fishing and boat-building, it has, to a great extent, retained a life of its own independent of tourism. The workaday indifference to the annual invasion of westerners is most evident on the main street, lined with as many regular stores as travellers' cafes and restaurants. It's highly unlikely that Chapora will ever develop into a major resort, either. Tucked away under a dense canopy of trees on the muddy southern shore of a river estuary, it lacks both the space and the white sand that have pulled the crowds to Calangute and Colva.

If you have your own transport, Chapora is however a good base from which to explore the region: Vagator is on the doorstep, Anjuna is a short ride to the south, and the ferry crossing at Siolim – gateway to the remote north of the state – is barely fifteen minutes away by road. The village is also well connected by bus to Mapusa, and there are plenty of sociable bars and cafes to hang out in during the evenings. The only drawback is that accommodation tends, once again, to be thin on the ground. Apart from the guest houses along the main road, most of the places to stay are little houses in the woods – invariably rented out for winter to long-stayers.

Once you're settled in, there's very little within walking distance to see or do; most visitors spend all day at Ozran Vagator beach. The only real sight, the **fort**, is most easily reached from the Vagator side of the hill. At low tide, you can walk around the bottom of the headland, via the anchorage, and the secluded coves beyond it, to Big Vagator beach, then head up the path to the fort. The **views** from the top – north to Morgim and Mandarem beaches, and south towards Anjuna – are well worth the climb.

Practicalities

Direct **buses** leave Chapora three times daily for Panjim, and every fifteen minutes for the half-hour trip to Mapusa; the last departs at 7pm. **Motorcycle taxis** hang around the old banyan tree at the far end of the main street, near where the buses pull in.

If you want a guest house while you sort out more permanent **accommodation**, try the popular *Shertor Villa* (①–②) off the west side of the main street. Nearly all its rooms, ranged around a sheltered back yard, come with fans and running water. If it's full, try the *Helinda* (①–③), at the far end of the village, which has rock-bottom options and more comfortable rooms with attached shower toilets, as well as a good restaurant. As a last resort, the dilapidated *Amora* (①), between the *Helinda* and the chapel down the lane, has grotty rooms in an extension to the local fishing tackle shop.

Finding somewhere to **eat** is more straightforward: take your pick from the crop of uniformly inexpensive little cafes and restaurants along the main street. The *Welcome*, halfway down, offers a reasonable selection of cheap and filling seafood, western, and veg dishes, plus relentless reggae and techno music, and backgammon. The *Preyanka*, nearby, is much the same, but has a few more Indian and Chinese options. If you're suffering from chilli-burn afterwards, *Scarlet Cold Drinks*, a short way east of the main street, knocks up deliciously cool fresh-fruit milkshakes.

Pernem and the far north

Sandwiched between the Chapora and Arondem (or "Tiracol") rivers, the predominantly Hindu *taluka* of **Pernem** – in the Novas Conquistas area – is Goa's northernmost district, and one of its least explored regions. Apart from the fishing village of **Arambol** (also known as **Harmal**), which since the 1970s has been attracting a trickle of backpackers seeking a peaceful and rustic alternative to the resorts south of the River Chapora, its beautiful coastline of long sandy beaches, coconut plantations, and salt-water lagoons is punctuated with few settlements equipped to cope with visitors. However, the picturesque, if bumpy, journey north from Arambol to **Terekol fort**, on the Maharashtra border, provides ample incentive to spend a day away from the beach. GTDC have converted the fort into a small rest house, providing the only **accommodation** in the region outside Arambol.

Heading to Pernem from Anjuna, Vagator, or Chapora, you have to travel a few kilometres inland to pick up the main Calangute road, as it runs north, over a low ridge of laterite hills, to the river crossing at **Siolim**. Boatmen sometimes paddle tourists over the estuary from Chapora, too, although their dug-outs are unstable when laden with passengers (they can't, in any case, carry motorbikes). The two car **ferries** that chug back and forth across the river from the ramp at Siolim begin at 6.30am, and continue until around 9.30pm. The ten-minute trip only costs a couple of *rupees*, but is one of the high points of the journey north. Fisherwomen, their gaily coloured cotton *saris* tied tightly around their legs, charge on and off the boats carrying baskets full of mackerel on their heads, while nearby, canoes stacked with fruit and vegetables bob about at the water-borne fresh produce market that is held here most mornings.

Once across, bear right until you reach a fork in the road, where a sign to "Harmal/Terekol" marks the quick route to Arambol. Alternatively, head left from the ferry dock, and follow the scenic back road along the north bank of the Chapora, past a crumbling old Catholic church, as far as a deserted beach, called **Morgim** (or Morji). A seemingly endless expanse of soft white sand stretches north from here, rounding a rocky headland where the local fishing fleet is beached, after which it widens, and empties completely. If you really want to get away from everything, **Mandarem**, with its palm-fringed dunes and acres of space, is perfect. Apart from the odd fisherman or tourist buzzing along the hard sand at low tide, the only signs of life are a couple of makeshift cafes serving tea, soft drinks, fish-*dal* and rice.

The easiest way to **get to Mandarem** is to follow the road that cuts north along the coast from Morgim towards Davanvado; park your bike when you see a cafe on the left.

Arambol (Harmal)

Of the fishing settlements dotted along the north coast, only **ARAMBOL**, 32km north-west of Mapusa, is remotely geared for tourism – albeit in a very low-key, low-impact fashion. If you're happy with basic amenities, the village offers two very fine beaches and a healthy dose of peace and quiet. Parties are occasionally held here, drawing revellers across the river from Anjuna and Vagator, but these are rare intrusions into an otherwise tranquil, out-of-the-way corner of the state.

Modern Arambol is scattered around an area of high ground west of the main coast road, where most of the buses pull in. From here, a bumpy lane runs downhill, past a large secondary school and the village church, to the more traditional end of the village, clustered under a canopy of widely spaced palm trees. The main **beach** lies 200 metres further along the lane. Strewn with dozens of old wooden fishing boats and a line of tourist cafe-bars, the gently curving bay is good for bathing, but much less picturesque than its neighbour around the corner.

The smaller, and less frequented of Arambol's two beaches can only be reached on foot, by following the stony track over the headland to the north. Beyond an idyllic, rocky-bottomed cove, the trail emerges to a broad strip of soft white sand hemmed in on both sides by steep cliffs. Behind it, a small freshwater lake extends along the bottom of the valley into a thick jungle. Hang around the banks of this murky green pond for long enough, and you'll probably see a fluorescent-yellow human figure or two appear from the bushes at its far end. Fed by boiling **hot springs**, the lake is lined with sulphurous mud, which, when smeared over the body, dries to form a surreal, butter-coloured shell. The resident hippies swear it's good for you, and spend much of the day tiptoeing naked around the shallows like refugees from some obscure tribal initiation ceremony – much to the amusement of Arambol's Indian visitors. Nearby, in the woods immediately behind the lake, other members of the lunatic fringe have taken to living in the branches of an old tree. The scene resembles nothing so much as a cross between *Lord of the Flies* and *Apocalypse Now* (minus the severed heads).

Anyone pining for a coastal walk will enjoy the trail that scales the headland at the northern edge of the beach. Keep walking along this path for long enough, and you'll eventually drop down to **Terekol beach** – another spectacular stretch of white sand, fringed with fir trees, which you'll probably have all to yourself.

Practicalities

Buses to and from Panjim (via Mapusa) pull in to Arambol every half hour until noon, and every ninety minutes thereafter, at the small bus stop on the main road. A faster private **mini-bus** service to Panjim departs daily at 2.30pm from opposite the *chai* stalls at the beach end of the village. **Boats** leave here every Wednesday morning for the ninety-minute trip to the flea market at Anjuna. Book tickets in advance from the *Welcome Restaurant* by the beach (Sun–Tues 8–9am & 8–9pm; Rs100), which also rents **motorcycles** (*Enfields* and *Yamaha* 100cc). The **post office**, next to the church, has a poste restante box; to change money, however, you'll have to head for Vagator, as Arambol's *State Bank of India* has no foreign exchange facility.

Apart from a couple of purpose-built chalets on the edge of the village, most of Arambol's **accommodation** consists of simple houses in the woods behind the beach. Some of the more expensive places have fully equipped kitchens, and showers, but the vast majority are standard-issue bare huts, with "pig" toilets and a well in the back garden. Long-stay visitors either bring their own bedding and cooking stuff, or kit themselves out at Mapusa market. The best place to stay if you only have a couple of days, however, is the *Ganesh Bar* (①–③), in the cove between the two main beaches. Scattered over the hillside directly above the cafe, a handful of small, new chalets have clean outhouses, and superb sea views from their verandahs. The bar is debatably the best place in Arambol from which to enjoy the sunset over a chilled beer.

Finding a **place to eat** is, as ever, less problematic than finding a bed. The *Welcome Restaurant*, next to the main entrance to the beach, is a popular and sociable cafe, serving a good range of locally caught seafood, and *toddy* to order. The palm-leaf bar-restaurants on the beach itself are slightly pricier, but still good value. For inexpensive, filling food, though, you can't beat the no-nonsense *chai* stalls at the bottom of the village. *Sheila's* and *Siddi's* cheap and tasty *thalis* both come with *puris*, and they have a good "travellers" breakfast menu of pancakes, eggs and curd. *Dominico's*, also at the bottom of the village (near where the road makes a sharp ninety-degree bend), is renowned for its generous tropical fruit salads and milkshakes.

Terekol

North of Arambol, the sinuous coast road climbs to the top of a rocky, undulating plateau, then winds down through a swathe of thick woodland to join the River Arondem, which it then follows for four kilometres through a landscape of vivid paddy fields, coconut plantations, and temple towers protruding from scruffy red-brick villages. The tiny enclave of **TEREKOL**, the northernmost tip of Goa, is reached via a clapped-out car **ferry** (half-hourly; 5min) from the hamlet of **Querim**, 42km from Panjim. After the long and scenic drive, the old **fort** that dominates the estuary from the north is a bit of an anti-climax. Hyped as one of the state's most atmospheric historic monuments, it turns out to be little more than a down-at-heel country house marooned on a lonely, sun-parched hillside. The bastion's forlorn appearance is helped neither by the presence, in the background, of an unsightly open-cast iron-ore mine, nor by the stark profile of the concrete water tower looming on the horizon. The view in the other direction is considerably more inspiring: an unblemished vista of blue sea and palm-fringed beach.

Terekol fort was built by the Marathas at the start of the eighteenth century, but taken soon after by the Portuguese, who held on to it more or less continuously until they were kicked out by Nehru in 1961. Nothing much of any importance ever happened here, except in 1825, when the Goan Governor General, Dr Bernado Peres da Silva, used it as a base for an armed insurrection against the Portuguese – the first of several such rebellions. The Governor's own troops mutinied at the eleventh hour, however, and were massacred by their colonial overlords. Thereafter, Terekol disappeared into obscurity until 1954, when a band of Goan Gandhi-ites (*satyagrahas*) hoisted an Indian tricolour over the ramparts in defiance of Portuguese rule.

If your visit coincides with the arrival of a guided tour (see below), you may well get a chance to look around the gloomy interior of the **Chapel of St Anthony**, in the fort's claustrophobic cobbled square; at other times it's kept firmly locked.

Practicalities

The few visitors that venture up to Terekol tend to do so by **motorbike**, heading back at the end of the day to the relative comfort of Calangute or Baga. If you run out of **gas**, the nearest service station is at Arambol. One of GTDC's daily **tours** from Panjim (see p.687) comes up here, as does one daily *Kadamba* **bus** from the capital; alternatively, the 7am bus from Siolim, on the Chapora, pulls in at the Querim ferry an hour later.

Accommodation is limited to the GTDC *Tourist Rest House* in the fort (☎248; ③–④), where the standard rooms are nothing special, but the "deluxe" suite, with its fantastic sea views and big double bed, is worth shelling out for. The inexpensive **restaurant** downstairs, kept busy in the daytime by coach parties, offers the usual seafood, Indian and Chinese dishes, as well as beer and soft drinks. Evening meals should be ordered a couple of hours in advance.

South Goa

At present, tourism is a good deal less developed in **south Goa** than in the north. However, beyond the unattractive port city of Vasco da Gama, and its nearby airport, the southern reaches of the state holds some of its best **beaches**, with little Portuguese villages nestled in its hilly interior.

Many visitors base themselves initially at **Colva**, 6km west of Goa's second city, **Margao**. The best known resort in the area, Colva stands at the head of a superb beach that stretches south for mile after mile, dotted with hotels and guest houses to suit all pockets. Budget travellers tend to settle down for long stays in **Sernabatim** and **Benaulim**, a few kilometres along. Goa's **deep south**, towards Karnataka, is at present sleepy and quiet, but change is bound to come with the advent of the *Konkan Railway*.

Vasco da Gama

The drab industrial town of **VASCO DA GAMA**, 29km by road southwest of Panjim, sits on the narrow western tip of the Mormugao peninsula, overlooking the mouth of the Zuari estuary. It's dominated by an unsightly oil refinery and container port, and the only reasons you might want to come are to book a ticket or to catch a **train**, or if you arrive at the nearby **Dabolim airport** too late at night to go anywhere else. Apart from the weekly street market, held on Sundays, there's absolutely nothing to see or do in Vasco. If you've time to kill, hop in a taxi, or rent a bicycle from the stall on the main square, and head off to **Bogmalo Beach**, 8km southeast.

Dabolim airport

Dabolim, Goa's only **airport**, lies on top of a rocky plateau 4km east of Vasco da Gama. Facilities in the terminal building include a *State Bank of India* exchange counter (Mon, Tues, Thurs & Fri 10.30am–1.30pm, Sat 10.30am–noon), a sub-post office, and several domestic airlines: *Indian Airlines* (7.15am–2pm; ☎512788), *Damania* (9.30am–5pm; ☎513987), *East-West* (9am–4pm) and *Jet* (9.30am–5pm: ☎511005). For details on how to **get from the airport** into Panjim, see p.685.

Practicalities

From Vasco's town **bus stand**, three blocks north of the train station, at the far side of the square, buses leave every fifteen minutes for Panjim and Margao, and every hour or so for Bogmalo. Long-distance services to Mangalore and Bangalore, however, often depart from the **inter-state bus terminal**, in the east end of town. **Taxis** wait opposite the **train station**, which is served by daily trains for Bangalore, Bombay, and other destinations via the broad-gauge junction at Miraj (but see the "stop press" on p.619).

There are plenty of **hotels** within walking distance of the train station. The best inexpensive accommodation is GTDC's large *Tourist Hotel*, on Swanpathra Rd (☎3119; ②), which has basic, clean doubles, all with fans and attached bathrooms. In the lobby there's a helpful **tourist information** counter (daily 9.30am–5pm; ☎512673), a laundry, photography shop, and a *Damania Airlines* office (Mon–Sat 9am–1pm & 2–5.30pm, Sun 2–5.30pm). Moving upscale, the *Maharaja*, opposite *Hindustan Petroleum*, west of the station (☎512559; ②–⑤), is a comfortable mid-range hotel with dismal views over the nearby refinery. All rooms have STD telephones and *Star TV*, and some are a/c. The "studio rooms" are the best value. The *Westend* around the corner (☎2288; ②–④) is a safe fall-back, with Vasco's cheapest a/c rooms, and a reasonable restaurant. Directly opposite, on Dattatreya Deshpande Rd, the posher *Nagina* (☎513674; ③–④) is a bit pricier, but still good value, with plush furnishings and an a/c restaurant. Finally, if you're really stuck, the *Tel-Jose-Mar Tourist Rest House* (☎513628; ①–②) on the western edge of town, has poky, lodge-style accommodation.

In general, the best **places to eat** are the à la carte restaurants attached to Vasco's better hotels. If you're on a tight budget, the *Nanking Restaurant*, three minutes' walk east of the train station, serves tasty, inexpensive Chinese food. GTDC's *Tradition Restaurant*, on the first floor of the *Tourist Hostel*, also offers a good selection of snacks and main meals, mostly Punjabi-style meat dishes, with some spicy "Chindian" alternatives, and has tables outside on a balcony if the barrage of Hindi videos gets too much.

Bogmalo beach

Immediately south of the airport, the Mormugao peninsula's sun-parched central plateau tumbles to a flat-bottomed valley lined with coconut trees and red-brick huts. The white sandy beach at the end of the cove would be even more picturesque if not for the monstrous multi-storey edifice perched above it. Until *Oberoi* dumped a huge five-star hotel here, **BOGMALO** was just another sleepy fishing village, hemmed in by a pair of palm-fringed headlands at the far northern end of Colva bay. The village is still here, complete with tiny whitewashed chapel and gangs of hogs nosing through the trash, but its environs have been transformed. Pricey cafe-bars blaring western music have crept up the beach, while the clearing below the hotel is prowled by Kashmiri handicraft vendors eager to relieve hapless tourists of their *Monopoly* money.

Even so, compared with Calangute or Colva, Bogmalo is still a small-scale resort. If you're staying at the *Oberoi*, and haven't come to Goa to get away from it all, nor yet to party, then you'll find it congenial enough. The beach is clean and not too crowded, the water reasonably safe for swimming, and there are plenty of places to eat, drink and shop. If, on the other hand, you're looking for somewhere not yet on the package tourist map, you'll be better off further south, at the far end of Colva beach, or beyond.

Practicalities

Bogmalo can be reached by **bus** or **taxi** from Vasco da Gama, 8km northwest. It's also near enough to the airport for a last-minute dip before catching the plane. If you're thinking of staying, **accommodation** is very limited and best booked ahead. The *Oberoi Bogmalo Beach* (☎0834/52191, fax 2150; ⑧) offers formula five-star luxury, with all the trimmings, including a pool, central a/c, and a sun terrace. The *El Mar Beach Resort* (☎0834/221274; ②), on the opposite side of the village, is altogether more humble, with plain, newly renovated rooms, attached bathrooms, and a small covered verandah-cum-restaurant. It's slap on the beach, friendly, and very good value.

What Bogmalo lacks in places to stay it makes up for in **bars** and **restaurants**. Most of the places dotted along the beach depend on a steady trickle of refugees from the *Oberoi*, and have whacked up their prices accordingly. The *Full Moon Kneipe*, outside the main entrance to the hotel, takes the lion's share of the overspill. Its menu of mainly seafood and chicken dishes, including locally caught tiger prawns and lobster, is predictably expensive, and the portions are not overly generous, but no one seems to mind. The *Sea Cuisine* opposite offers identical dishes, and prices, but tends to be less crowded at lunchtimes. Further up the beach, all the cafe-bars are in much the same rough-and-ready mould; only the music changes.

Margao (Madgaon)

Goa's second city, **MARGAO**, 30km southwest of Vasco da Gama, is a busy commercial centre where many visitors are bound to spend time, if only in transit. On the railway line, it makes an infinitely more congenial place to disembark than Vasco at the end of the line; in addition, bus connections to major destinations are plentiful. The approach from Vasco on NH17 passes the unpromising looking laterite scrub of the headland, dotted with naval-base buildings, power plants and factories, and a barrage of huge advertising hoardings before dipping down into the woody shaded villages of **Nagoa** and **Verna**, where the old Goan houses have two-tiered tiled roofs and pillared verandahs. **Nuvem**, the next village along, boasts the huge sparkling-white Holy Family church, whose yard is the venue for impromptu soccer and cricket matches.

Arrival and information

Margao's **Kadamba bus stand** is 1.5km north of the town centre on the Panjim road. Low-ceilinged minibuses hover at the exit, and when well and truly packed, run into Margao centre, with Goan pop-music tapes blaring. Auto-rickshaws are also available. All **trains** from Vasco stop at Margao an hour or so later. The **railway station**, which has a left luggage office and retiring rooms, is at the opposite end of town from the bus stand, five minutes' walk from the centre.The **train enquiry and reservation** counter (daily 8.30am–12.30pm & 2–5pm; ☎0834/22252) is on the left of the entrance hall as you go out; note that *Indrail Pass* reservations can only be made at Vasco da Gama.

The **Municipal Gardens** (Praca Dr George Baretto) lie at the centre of Margao, flanked by the **post office** to the north and the Municipal Building or **Secretariat** to the south. This latter is the place to book out-of-state buses when **leaving Margao**. **Taxis** park in front of it, while the **auto-rickshaw rank** is on the far side of the gardens, a few metres up a side turning to the east.

You can **change money** at the *State Bank of India* on the west side of the Gardens; for *Visa* cash withdrawals go to the *Bank of Baroda* (Mon–Fri 10am–noon) in the Marchon building, behind Grace Church on a road that leads from the east side of the Gardens. The small friendly **tourist office** (☎0834/22513), in the lobby of the GTDC *Tourist Hostel*, only stocks a few pamphlets, but can offer advice about travel.

The Town

For most visitors, any appeal Margao may have is eclipsed by the miles of magnificent beach that stretch southwards from Colva, 6km west, or the wooded hills, shady country roads, and sleepy villages of the interior. However, the town is not unpleasant; the streets that surround the leafy **Municipal Gardens** are packed with old Portuguese and Hindu houses, though they are so narrow as to necessitate a one-way system that forms a noisy racetrack.

Ten minutes' walk northeast, the old square, **Largo de Igreja**, centres on a mango tree and a large white crucifix. Once upon a time this was probably a peaceful enclave; today, however, the incoming traffic from the bus stand side crashes through, belching fumes and making a colossal din. Dominating its east side is Margao's most important church, **Holy Spirit**, built in 1564, and rebuilt in 1675. Its imposing four-tiered gleaming white facade is only slightly compromised by an ugly corrugated iron shelter tacked onto the front; on the side walls, the bright-red laterite brickwork has been left untreated. The interior is more impressive, with an elaborate Rococo carved altar and gold pulpit, twinkling chandeliers and ornate stucco on the ceiling.

The remaining three sides of the square hold some of the city's oldest **houses**. One curious example (now a surgery) has a double balustrade and a conical projecting eave above the entrance, with a little sculpted figure appearing from the top. In the south of town are two crowded **markets**, one of which is the biggest covered market in Goa.

Accommodation

The only reason you'd want to stay in Margao is if you've arrived late or you need an early start. As elsewhere in Goa, you've got to get in early or book ahead at Christmas.

Goa Woodlands, Miguel Loyola Furtado Rd (☎0834/221121). Tucked away around the corner on the road leading west from the GTDC *Tourist Hostel*. Very popular mid-range hotel, some a/c rooms with TV. Bar and decent restaurants (one a/c). No seasonal tariff changes. ③–④.

GTDC Tourist Hostel, behind Municipal Building (☎0834/221966). Good-value government block with 69 fair-sized rooms with balcony, within sniffing distance of fish market. The restaurant serves veg and non-veg food. Tourist office and handicrafts shop in lobby. ③.

Metropole, Avda Concessao (☎0834/221169). Ten minutes' walk north from the Municipal Gardens. Reasonable rooms, bar, restaurant and roof garden. ④.

Milan Kamat, Station Rd (☎0834/221715). Basic lodge, two minutes' from the railway station. ②.

Railway Retiring Rooms. Cheapest place in town, with three big but pretty grotty doubles and a six-bed dorm. Contact the ticket collector's office on platform 1. ①.

Rukrish, Station Rd (☎0834/221709). Acceptable low-end lodge, near the Municipal Building. ②.

Sanrit, opposite the railway station (☎0834/221226). Noisy place with some rooms with attached bathroom. The location is its main plus point. ①–②.

Eating

Eating in Margao, compared to Panjim, is not exactly a gourmet's delight, but there are a few adequate places in the town centre.

Bombay, Station Rd. Basic "meals" restaurant on the way out to the station.

Longuinhos, opposite GTDC *Tourist Hostel*. Popular venue for meaty, fishy repasts.

Meghdoot Kamat, Praca Dr George Baretto. On the eastern side of Municipal Gardens, close to Colva bus stop. Fast, cheap and busy veg restaurant serving tasty *dosa*, patties, sweets and drinks.

Chandor

Long before the advent of the Portuguese, the village of **CHANDOR**, 20km east of Margao, was as Chandrapur the capital of the Kadambas between the eleventh and the fourteenth centuries. The remains of a **fort** date from this time. Today Chandor is of interest for the superb European-style **mansions** that crowd its quiet streets. Built in the seventeenth century and expanded in the eighteenth, the magnificent **Menezes Braganza** house, opposite the village church, is a feast of tiled airy rooms crammed with antiques. Among them are a chandeliered ballroom, reception rooms with elaborate easy chairs, and a beautiful Baroque family chapel. Braganza de Pereia, the great-grandfather of the present owner, was the last knight of the king of Portugal; more recently, Menezes Braganza was a leader of the Goan freedom movement. Forced to leave Chandor in 1950, the family returned in 1962 to find their house, amazingly, untouched. To make an appointment to see the house, contact the family business, *Agua de Fonte*, opposite the *Blue Pearl Cinema* in Margao (☎0834/23754).

Beaches from Colva to Mabor

COLVA, 6km west of Margao, in itself little more than a cluster of houses and shops with a church, is the gateway to mile after mile of palm-fringed white sandy beach that runs south past the much smaller villages of **Sernabatim**, **Benaulim**, **Varca** and

Cavelossim, to end at **Mabor**. To the north, the beach extends almost as far as Bogmalo, passing places like **Majorda** and **Betalbatim**, but is far less attractive, an open and windswept stretch with limited facilities.

Inevitably, Colva's reputation as "unspoilt" has drawn droves of visitors spurning the developed beaches of the north, and today the place is in transition. As you face the sea (reached by a curved bridge), a fairly ratty-looking, but perfectly serviceable collection of restaurants is set back to the left; to the right are a few fruit stalls, craft shops and the ugly concrete GTDC *Tourist Cottages*, which has an **STD** telephone booth.

The further south you walk along the beach from Colva towards Benaulim or Sernabatim, the rarer the shack restaurants become, and you can wander next to the crystalline waters in semi-deserted hawker-free zones.

Arrival and local transport

Buses run from Margao to Colva (20–30min), approximately once an hour until about 7pm; some continue south to Cavelossim. Along with taxis, motorbikes, and auto-rickshaws, they stop in Colva at a large featureless square, from where they return when they've filled to capacity. Auto-rickshaws and motorbike-taxis only operate from Margao, though you may pick one up as it drops off someone else.

The lure of renting a **motorbike** in this virtually traffic-free area is very strong, tempting you to explore the deserted beaches and village churches, and the undulating hills of the interior. Along with bicycles and scooters, motorbikes are widely available in Colva and Benaulim, and in the larger beach hotels. For more advice on motorbikes, see p.683.

Unless your hotel will **change money**, you'll have to go into Margao to do it. The *Bank of Baroda* at Maria Hall Junction, Benaulim, handles *Visa* transactions.

Around Colva

The village of **BENAULIM**, 2km south of Colva, is centred around Maria Hall Junction, which holds some shops and a bank, ten minutes' walk from the beach. Further south, the resorts begin to take over. A shady road leads to **CAVELOSSIM**, 14km south, centering on a peaceful square with a white cross and a statue of Jesus standing in front of the **Santa Cruz church**. The road winds round the square and continues south towards **Mabor**, while almost immediately a turning to the left leads after 3km to the jetty for the **ferries** (half-hourly 6.15am–7.45pm) that ply back and forth for the five-minute trip to the sleepy village of **Assolna**.

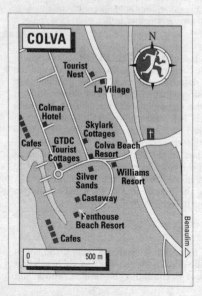

Ten kilometres further south, at the seaside village of **BETUL**, the road climbs steeply inland into the hills, giving magnificent views of densely wooded country. A left turn at the T-junction on the plateau at the top leads to the Shantadurga temple, near Fatorpa, and eventually **Quepem**. If you turn right, however, the road leads past the turning for **CANAGUINIM**, another rarely visited beach.

Continuing on this road through Cola, you eventually come to the turning for the quiet little village of **AGONDA**, which boasts a two-kilometre stretch of unspoilt, frequently deserted, and as yet unexploited beach, between wooded promontories. At the edge of the sands stands the impressive blue-and-white **church of St Anne**. To visit, call on the priest at the adjoining bougainvillaea-covered house. A door carved with images of St Bartholomew carrying a sword opens into the cool simple interior, where the only sounds are likely to come from the school next door. Agonda boasts just one **cafe**, for simple meals, tea and coffee.

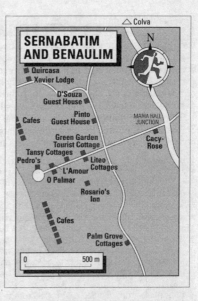

Accommodation

Many visitors searching for **accommodation** in this area first find somewhere at **Colva,** then set out unencumbered with luggage either by foot south along the beach, or on bike or scooter. Competition for rooms is fierce, and prices rise considerably in peak season (mid-Dec to mid-Jan). Some places, however, operate up to four separate seasons, so tariffs vary considerably. With smaller places, particularly for long stays, negotiation is often possible.

Colva offers nothing very grand, but prices in mid-range hotels don't reflect this. All the hotels listed are within ten minutes' walk of the centre. **Sernabatim** and **Benaulim** are quiet, something like Colva used to be; more **upmarket hotels**, mainly for tour groups, can be found further south at Varca and Cavelossim, on the main road that ends at Mabor and the hyper-luxurious *Leela Beach*. **North of Colva**, there's very little choice of places to stay or eat in Majorda and Betalbatim.

COLVA

Colmar, very close to beach, on the north (☎21253). Assorted cottages, and rooms, plus a bar and restaurant. ③–⑤.

Colva Beach Resort, first road north up from the centre (☎21975). Good rooms, some a/c. Terrace restaurant. ④–⑤.

GTDC Tourist Cottages, next to the bus stop (☎22287). "Modern" concrete place, good value and popular, with large rooms (some a/c) overlooking beach and sea, and a cheap dorm. Rather uninspiring restaurant. ①–④.

La Village, north of centre, fairly close to the beach. Basic rooms with shared bathroom. ②.

Penthouse Beach Resort, a little south of the village (☎21077). Package tour hotel set in its own private compound, with cottages and rooms (some non-a/c) in main building. Swimming pool, and good, pricey outdoor restaurant and bar in garden. ⑥–⑦.

Silver Sands, near the centre on the main road (☎21645). Gloomy corridors and average rooms (some a/c) which overlook decent little pool (open to non-residents) and outdoor cafe. Good restaurant indoors. Free airport transfer bus. Popular with package tours and often full. ⑤–⑦.

Skylark Cottages. Comfortable rooms, some a/c. Fairly recently built. ④–⑤.

Tourist Nest, north of the centre. Simple rooms with bathroom. ②.

Williams Resort, 5min from the beach on the main road into Colva (☎21077). Range of rooms (some a/c with TV and balcony) with the cheapest at the back. New swimming pool, and indoor and outdoor restaurant; pleasant, if overpriced. ②–⑥.

GOAN FOOD AND DRINK

Goa has few of the dietary restrictions or taboos that apply in other regions of India, both Hindu and Muslim. Here the idea of vegetarianism is probably more equated with poverty than purity, and drinking alcohol is not the shameful activity it is elsewhere. The Goan palate relishes meat, especially pork, and all kinds of fresh seafood.

Not unnaturally, after 450 years of colonization, Goan cooking has absorbed a strong Portuguese influence. **Palm vinegar** (unknown elsewhere in India), copious amounts of **coconut**, **garlic**, tangy **tamarind** and fierce local **chillies** all play their part. Goa is the home of the famous **vindaloo**, originally an extra-hot and sour pork curry, but now made with a variety of meat and fish. If you like to pig-out on pork, try **chourisso** red sausages, **sarpotel**, a hot curry made from pickled pig's liver and heart, or **suckling pig** or **balchaon**, pork in a rich brown sauce. Delicious alternatives include vinegar chicken, spicy chicken or mutton **xacutti**, made with a sauce of lemon juice, peanuts, coconut, chillies and spices. The choice of seafood, often cooked in fragrant *masalas*, is excellent – clams, mussels, crab, lobster, giant prawns – while fish, depending on the type, is either cooked in wet curries, grilled, or baked in *tandoor* clay ovens. Try **apa de camarao**, a spicy prawn pie with a rice and semolina crust. **Sannam**, like the south Indian *iddli*, is a steamed cake of fermented rice flour, but here fermented with palm toddy. Sweet tooths will adore **bebinca**, a rich, delicious solid egg custard with coconut.

As for **drinks**, locally produced wine, spirits and beer are cheaper than anywhere in the country. Red wine tends to be sweet, not unlike port; white, both still and sparkling, is considered an unpretentious tipple. Whisky, brandy, rum, gin and vodka come in a variety of brand names for less than Rs10 a shot, but at half the price, local speciality **feni**, made from distilled cashew or from the sap of coconut palm, offers strong competition. Cashew *feni* is usually drunk after the first distillation, but you can also find it double-distilled, flavoured with ginger, cumin or sasparilla to produce a smooth liqueur.

SERNABATIM AND BENAULIM

L'Amour, Benaulim. Very popular place with a variety of rooms set back from the beach: some basic with Indian toilet, others better with western, and a few pleasant cottages. Good shady restaurant and little bits of landscaped garden. Foreign exchange (residents only), and travel agent. ③–④.

Cacy-Rose, Benaulim. Two minutes down on the left side of the road that leads to beach from Maria Hall Junction. Six simple rooms, restaurant and bar. ②.

D'Souza Guesthouse, between Sernabatim and Benaulim. Spotless rooms, some attached bathrooms. Family-run and friendly, with home cooking. Travellers' cheques taken. Superb value. ②–③.

Green Garden Tourist Cottage, Benaulim. Two very basic rooms in private house on the right-hand side on the way to Benaulim from Maria Hall. Common bathroom, separate piggy toilet. ①.

Liteo Cottages, Benaulim, a short way down from Maria Junction; enquire at *Maxhouse Villa* opposite. New place, 5min from beach. Eight huge doubles with balcony. No restaurant. ③.

O Palmar, Benaulim, opposite *L'Amour*. Largish doubles in cottages, one minute from beach. The trick is finding the manager. No restaurant. ③.

Palm Grove Cottages, 10min walk from Benaulim. Doubles with fan (one a/c) and bathroom, some with balcony. Very pleasant and quiet with beautiful garden, where there's a restaurant. ④.

Pinto Guest House, off Benaulim's main road. Basic doubles with bathroom. Not that friendly. ②.

Quircasa Bar & Restaurant, aka *Camilson's Beach Resorts*, Sernabatim, south Colva. Close to beach. Simple good-value rooms (16 doubles with fan), some with sit-out balconies, set back from the beach in pleasant little garden, plus an attractive four-bed villa for around Rs1000. ②.

Rosario's Inn, Benaulim. Double rooms with fan and bathroom, some in family house, others in separate building (downstairs cheaper). Friendly and good value. ②.

Tansy Cottages, a few minutes from Benaulim beach. Four basic rooms with fan and bathroom. ②.

Xavier Lodge, Sernabatim, south Colva. Close to beach. Sixteen rooms with balcony, and simple good-value restaurant. ②.

VARCA, CAVELOSSIM AND MABOR

Dona Sylvia, Cavelossim (☎0834/46321). Attractive tour group hotel with cottage accommodation in gardens leading to beach. Swimming pool. ⑧.

Leela Beach, Mabor Cavelossim (☎0834/46263). Hyper-luxurious resort with restaurants, shops, artificial lake, swimming pool, water- and other sports, large gardens which lead to public beach. ⑨.

Old Anchor, Cavelossim (☎0834/46337). Five minutes' walk from beach. Big package tour family-style accommodation with absurd ship-shaped reception. Several restaurants and bar. ⑧.

Ramada Renaissance Resort, Varca (☎0834/23611). Stylish new five-star complex with two restaurants, all sea-facing rooms, pool, watersports and golf course. ⑨.

Resorte de Goa, Fatrade Rd, Varca (☎0834/45066). Thirty well-appointed doubles and fifteen suites with garden, restaurant and swimming pool. ⑦–⑧.

Eating

Finding somewhere to **eat** is hardly a problem in this area. Innumerable shack restaurants along the beach offer a wide range of fresh seafood, snacks and western dishes – in general what they lack in decor they make up for in good food. As elsewhere in Goa, however, vegetarians don't get much of a look-in. For more upmarket meals, the larger **hotels**, such as *Penthouse* and *Silver Sands* in Colva, are good; at Varca, the *Ramada Renaissance* offers a good range of Goan specialities.

Castaway Party House, Colva. Big, friendly restaurant with excellent food. After 10pm, loud music blasts from the *MTV* screen. Open most of the night if there are customers.

Pedro's Bar and Restaurant, Benaulim. Always busy, serving good-value seafood and snacks.

Shangrila, 5min from Majorda Beach (☎0834/223937). Mixed veg and non-veg hotel restaurant.

The far south

A beautiful forty-kilometre drive south from Margao, the NH17 runs west of Sahyadri Ghat through pleasantly wooded country, and across Karmali Ghat to arrive near the Karnataka border at the little town of **Chaudi** (aka Chauri, or Canacona). The town itself is of minimal interest, but is the transportation hub for anyone wanting to get to Goa's southernmost **beaches**, the **Mallikarjun temple** and **Cotigao Wildlife Sanctuary**. Few visitors make it this far south, but the area is virtually sure to develop rapidly with the forthcoming opening of the controversial Konkan Railway. At present, if you want to explore these tranquil hills and forests, it's best to have your own transport. Accommodation is available at Palolem and Kindlebag.

Frequent **buses** run between Margao and Karwar (in Karnataka), via Chaudi. To reach Palolem or Kindlebag (for Rajbag) either get down a kilometre before Chaudi at the four-way "Cha Rostay" junction and walk (2km to Palolem, further to Kindlebag) or go on to Chaudi and get an auto-rickshaw (around Rs20 to Palolem or Kindlebag) or taxi (Rs50). Only two buses each day go all the way to Palolem from Margao.

Palolem beach

PALOLEM, a stunning and sheltered crescent-shaped bay, studded with massive rocks, is a restful spot which has only recently made it onto the backpackers' map. It has a few beachside restaurants and a couple of places to stay right next to the sea; arrive early in the day to avoid disappointment. Local boats will take you out from Palolem to go **dolphin spotting** (Rs400).

At present the main place to **stay and eat** is the beachside *Palolem Beach Resort* (☎0834/643054; ①–③) which offers three simple, clean rooms with shared bathroom and six with bathroom attached, all set back from the beach. In season (Nov–Jan) they also erect a number of two-bed tents, each with a locker. The pleasant open-air restaurant serves the usual toast, omelettes and sandwiches, plus chicken, seafood and booze. STD phone calls can be made from the office. A little way along the beach, the

Fifth August Bar & Lodge (☎0834/643173; ①) has four basic sea-facing rooms and four at the back, all with bathroom attached. Their open-air cafe serves simple chicken and fish meals. Other places to eat include *Fernandes Bar & Restaurant*, the friendly *Sunset Bar & Restaurant,* good for veg food, and the veg and non-veg *Dropadi Restaurant.*

Palolem has a small post office, but is devoid of auto-rickshaws; *Palolem Beach Resort* has the only taxi (Rs300 to Margao, the nearest place to change money).

Rajbag

The long stretch of beach at **RAJBAG** village, a little south of Palolem, remains virtually undisturbed, enjoying a fabulous backdrop of the Ghats. There's very little shade on the beach though, with great areas of sand dunes – which shelter a small Vishnu shrine – instead of palm trees. On the southern edge of the village, the tranquil River Tari feeds into the deserted bay. Between Rajbag and Palolem, **Colomb** is a tiny, extremely rocky, double cove where a palm-shaded village extends to the water's edge. It's pleasant enough to visit, if not suitable for bathing.

Accommodation can be found at **Kindlebag**, 3km south. The *Molyma Hotel* (☎0834/643028, fax 643081; ③), in a quiet spot surrounded by woods, has a slightly forlorn atmosphere, but its rooms (none a/c) are good value, clean, and rarely booked up, a barn-like veg and non-veg **restaurant** serves fresh seafood, and there's even a bar too. Bikes and motorbikes are available for rent.

Mallikarjun temple

In a tranquil setting in the wooded hills, the simple **Mallikarjun Temple**, 5km northeast of Chaudi, is one of Goa's few temples to have escaped modernization on any grievous scale. A typically Goan tall *deepmal*, oil-lamp tower, stands in the courtyard. The Department of Archaeology has prevented any alterations to the interior, whose massive pillars are ornately carved with musicians, dancers and floriate designs, for some reason painted brown. A small Nandi (Shiva's bull vehicle) stands before the inner shrine, which contains a clothed *lingam* with a metal face attached; the embossed silver doorway is ringed by oil lamps. Carved wooden panels surround the outer entrance, while panels close to the ceiling relate stories from the epics.

Important **festivals** at the temple include the five-day Ratasaptami (Feb), when dramas are staged at night, and a chariot bearing the deity is taken out in procession. On two nights during Shivratri (March), Shiva is taken on a silver palanquin to Rajbag beach for a bath. The biggest crowds of all are drawn during Shigmotsava (Holi; Feb/March), when processions include colourful ornamental umbrellas and the most auspicious blessed food offering (*prasad*) is given to the devotees.

Cotigao Wildlife Sanctuary

Established in 1968, the **COTIGAO WILDLIFE SANCTUARY**, 10km east of Chaudi, covers 86 square kilometres of undulating hills, forest, teak, cashew, eucalyptus and rubber plantations. Wildlife includes about half a dozen leopards and tigers, many wild boar, two antelope, white monkey, sloth bear, bison, panther, Indian gazelle, porcupine, striped hyena, giant Indian squirrel and cobra; there are no elephants.

Though visitors are welcome (the best time to come is Oct–March), and it makes a relaxing day out, you're unlikely to see many animals. Guides, free of charge from the Forest Warden's Office, can show you to a 25-metre-high treetop watchtower, overlooking a watering hole that at dawn and dusk does attract the odd animal. Permission to stay **overnight,** in the watchtower or in the *Rest House* (①), must be sought from the Deputy Conservator of Forests, 1st Floor, Junta House, Panjim.

CHAPTER TWELVE

CALCUTTA AND WEST BENGAL

U nique among Indian states in stretching all the way from the Himalayas to the sea, **WEST BENGAL** is nonetheless explored in depth by few travellers. That may have something to do with the exaggerated reputation of its capital, **CALCUTTA**, which is actually a sophisticated and friendly city that belies its popular image as poverty-stricken and chaotic. Certainly the rest of Bengal holds an extraordinary assortment of landscapes and cultures, ranging from the dramatic hill station of **Darjeeling**, within sight of some of the highest mountains in the world, to the vast mangrove swamps of the **Sunderbans**, prowled by man-eating Royal Bengal tigers who share the seas with sharks and crocodiles. The narrow central band of the state is cut across by the huge River Ganges as it pours from Bihar into Bangladesh; its waters would virtually ignore West Bengal were it not for the **Farrakha Barrage**, which feeds south-flowing channels such as the River Hooghly, the lifeline of Calcutta.

At the height of British rule, in the nineteenth and early twentieth centuries, Bengal flourished both culturally and materially, nurturing a vibrant creative blend of west and east. The **Bengali Renaissance** produced thinkers, writers and artists such as Raja Ram Mohan Roy, Bankim Chandra Chatterjee, and above all **Rabindranath Tagore**, whose collective influence still permeates Bengali society a century later.

Not all of Bengal, however, is Bengali; the recent Nepalese-led separatist movement for the creation of a semi-autonomous "Gurkhaland" in the Darjeeling area has highlighted sharp differences in culture. Although the Hindu Nepalese largely displaced the indigenous tribal groups of the north during the nineteenth century, a new influx of Tibetans has revitalized the traditions of *lama*-ism. In the southwest, on the other

Govt of India Statement - The external boundaries of India are neither correct nor authenticated.

▽ Cuttack, Bhubaneshwar & Puri

WEST BENGAL TRAVEL DETAILS

	Trains		Buses		Flights	
	Frequency	Time	Frequency	Time	Frequency	Time
To and From Calcutta						
Agra	1 daily	30hr				
Ahmedabad	1 daily	44hr				
Bhopal	2 weekly	29hr				
Bhubaneshwar	9 daily	7hr 30min–12hr	4 nightly	8–10hr	5 weekly	55min
Bombay	4 daily	33–42hr			6–7 daily	2–3hr
Delhi	1–2 daily	18hr–34hr 15min			3–4 daily	2–5hr
Gwalior	3 weekly	25hr 30min				
Haridwar	1 daily	28hr				
Indore	2 weekly	36hr				
Jabalpur	1 daily	23hr				
Jalgaon	4 daily	29hr–34hr 35min				
Jhansi	3 weekly	23hr 25min				
Lucknow	5–6 daily	21hr 45min–28hr			3 weekly	3hr 20min
Nagpur	4 daily	19–25hr			3 weekly	2hr 40min
Nasik	3 daily	32–36hr				
Puri	2 nightly	11hr 30min	2 daily	12hr		
Siliguri	5 daily	12hr	8 daily	12hr	1–2 daily	1hr
Thiruv'puram	1 weekly	49hr				
Ujjain	2 weekly	33hr 40min				
Vadodara	1 daily	40hr 40min				
Varanasi	5–8 daily	8hr 30min–20hr				

For more details on routes to and from **Siliguri** and **Darjeeling**, see pages 767 and 773 respectively.

hand, tribal groups such as the Santals and the Mundas still maintain a presence, and itinerant Baul **musicians** epitomize the region's traditions of song and dance. The Bauls are most often heard around Tagore's university at **Shantiniketan**, where his own musical form, *Rabindra Sangeet*, is a popular amalgam of influences including folk and classical. Other historical specialities of Bengal include the erection of ornate and delicate **terracotta temples**, as seen at Bishnupur, and the manufacture of **silk**, concentrated around Murshidabad, the last independent capital of Bengal.

Bengal's own brand of Hinduism emphasizes the mother goddess, who appears in such guises as the fearful Kali and Durga, the benign Saraswati, goddess of learning, and Lakshmi the goddess of wealth. The most mysterious of all is Tara, an echo of medieval links with Buddhism; her temple at **Tarapith** is perhaps the greatest centre of tantricism in the entire country. In recent years, however, the prayer flags have given way to red flags, and the new religion of politics.

A brief history of West Bengal

Although Bengal was part of the Mauryan empire during the third century BC, it first came to prominence in its own right under the Guptas, in the fourth century AD. So dependent was it on trade with the Mediterranean that the fall of Rome caused a sharp decline, only reversed with the rise of the Pala dynasty in the eighth century.

After a short-lived period of rule by the highly cultured Senas, based at **Gaur**, Bengal was brought under Muslim rule at the end of the twelfth century by the first Sultan of Delhi, Qutb-ud-din-Aibak. Sher Shah Suri, who usurped power from the Moghuls in the mid-sixteenth century, achieved much in Bengal; it was thanks to him that the Grand Trunk Road took its most developed form, running all the way to the Northwest Province on the borders of his native Afghanistan. Akbar took back the territory in 1574, just in time to face the advent of the Europeans.

The Portuguese, who were the first to set up a trading community beside the Hooghly, were soon joined by the British, Dutch and French and many others. Rivalry between them – all received some degree of sanction from the Moghul court – eventually resulted in the ascendancy of the **British**, with the only serious indigenous resistance coming from the tutelary kingdom of **Murshidabad**, led by the young Siraj-ud-Daula. His attack on the fledgeling British community of Calcutta in 1756 culminated in the infamous **Black Hole** incident, when British prisoners, possibly in error (and possibly in fiction, for that matter) were incarcerated in a tiny space that caused many to suffocate to death. Vengeance, in the form of a British army from Madras under **Robert Clive**, arrived a year later. The defeat of Siraj-ud-Daula at the Battle of Plassey heralded the start of British domination of the entire subcontinent. Bengal became the mainstay of the British East India Company, and its lucrative trading empire, until the company handed over control to the Crown in 1854.

Until 1905, Bengal encompassed Orissa and Bihar; then it was split down the middle by Lord Curzon, leaving East Bengal and Assam on one side and Orissa, Bihar and West Bengal on the other. That aroused bitter resentment, and the rift it created between Hindus and Muslims was a direct cause of the second Partition, in 1947, when East Bengal became East Pakistan. During the war with Pakistan in the early 1970s that resulted in the creation of an independent **Bangladesh**, up to ten million refugees fled into West Bengal; most have now returned. Shorn of its provinces, and with its capital Calcutta replaced by Delhi in 1911, the story of West Bengal in the twentieth century has largely been a chronicle of decline.

Economically, the **rice** grown in the paddy fields of the lowlands remains West Bengal's most important cash crop, though **tea** is a close second. The introduction of tea was largely the work of the British, who cleared the forests of the Himalayan foothills; they brought tea plants from China, but local Darjeeling tea soon developed a reputation of its own. The other great nineteenth-century industry, **jute**, has not fared so well. Most was grown in East Bengal – now Bangladesh – while the mills themselves were located along the River Hooghly around Calcutta. As a result, after 1947, the mills found it hard to obtain supplies; however, new jute-growing regions have since been developed.

Politics permeates almost every aspect of life in West Bengal today, which has largely returned to stability after several troubled decades. The state was all but brought to its knees in the 1960s and 1970s, when the **Naxalites** (Communist Party of India – Marxist-Leninists) launched an abortive but bloody attempt at revolution. After a bitter three-way struggle between the Communist Party of India (Marxists), the Congress and the Naxalites, the CPI(M) finally emerged victorious. Since 1977, under the enigmatic leadership of Jyoti Basu, they have somehow succeeded in balancing rhetoric and old-fashioned socialism with a prudent practicality – and their strong rural base has enabled them to weather the collapse of world communism. Capitalism is allowed to survive, but made to support the political infrastructure.

CALCUTTA

One of the four great urban centres of India, Calcutta is to its proud citizens the equal of any city in the country in charm, variety and interest. Like Bombay and Madras, it is not an ancient city; its roots lie in the European expansion of the seventeenth century. The showpiece capital of the British Raj, this was the greatest colonial city of the Orient. Descendants of the fortune-seekers who flocked from across the globe to participate in Calcutta's eighteenth- and nineteenth-century trading boom remain conspicuous in its cosmopolitan blend of communities.

However, mass migrations of dispossessed refugees, occasioned by twentieth-century upheavals within the subcontinent, have tested the city's infrastructure to the limit. The resultant suffering – and the work of Mother Teresa in drawing attention to its most pathetic victims – has given Calcutta a reputation for **poverty** that its residents consider ill-founded. They argue that the city's problems are no longer as acute as those of Bombay or other cities across the world, and that the slum scenes familiar from the book and film *City of Joy* are distortions of the truth. In fact, though Calcutta's mighty Victorian buildings lie peeling and decaying, and its avenues have long been choked by its inability to expand any further, the image of a city struggling for survival belies a recent upsurge in its fortunes. Calcutta exudes a warmth that leaves few visitors unmoved, and with the return of political calm and the pragmatism of the Bengali government is buoyant with fresh optimism. The opening of India's first subway system in 1984 was seen as the first portent of a new beginning.

The Bengalis of Calcutta like to see themselves as the **intelligentsia** of India; a long-standing maxim states that "what Bengal does today, India will do tomorrow." This is a city where artistic endeavour is held in higher esteem than political and economic success, home to a multitude of **galleries** and huge Indian classical **music** festivals, with a thriving Bengali-language **theatre** scene and a tradition of **cinema** brought world renown by Satyajit Ray (see *Contexts*). Adding to the chaos and colour, Calcutta has a wonderful tradition of political posters and graffiti. Witty and flamboyant slogans compete with a forest of advertising hoardings to festoon every available surface.

Though Marxists may rule from the chief bastion of imperialism, the **Writers Building**, and the site of the notorious **Black Hole of Calcutta** is now obscured by the main post office, visitors still experience Calcutta first and foremost as a colonial city. Grand edifices in a profusion of styles include the imposing **Victoria Memorial** and the gothic **St Paul's Cathedral**, while the eclectic **Indian Museum**, one of the largest museums in Asia, ranges from natural history to art and archeology. Among numerous venerable Raj institutions to have survived are the race course, the polo ground, the reverence for cricket, and several exclusive gentlemen's clubs.

In terms of **climate**, Calcutta is at its best during its short winter, when the daily maximum temperature hovers around 27°C, and the markets are filled with vegetables and flowers. Before the monsoons, the heat hangs unbearably heavy; the arrival of the rains in late June brings relief, but usually also heavy floods that turn the streets into a quagmire. After a brief period of post-monsoon heat, October and November are quite pleasant; this is the time of the city's biggest festival, **Durga Puja**.

A history of Calcutta

By the time the remarkable **Job Charnock** established the headquarters of the **East India Company** at **Sutanuti** on the east bank of the Hooghly, in 1690, the riverside was already dotted with trading communities from European countries. Besides the British, previously based at Hooghly on the west bank, there were the French at Chandernagore, the Dutch and Armenians at Chinsurah, the Danes at Serampore, the Portuguese at Bandel, and even Greeks at Rishra and Prussians at Bhadeshwar.

Supported by Armenian funds, the East India Company bought land around Sutanuti, and in 1699 completed their first fort in the area – **Fort William**. A few years later the East India Company amalgamated Sutanuti and two other villages to form the town of **Calcutta**. The name may well derive from *Kalikutir*, the house or temple of Kali – a reference to the temple of **Kalighat**. Job Charnock, its first Governor, married an Indian wife who had been rescued from committing *sati* on her first husband's funeral pyre. With trading success came ambitious plans for development; in 1715 a delegation to the Moghul court in Delhi negotiated trading rights, along with several villages and towns on both banks of the Hooghly, to create a territory that was around fifteen kilometres long. The company built a moat around the perimeter to ward off possible Maratha attacks; known as the **Maratha Ditch**, it is marked by today's Circular Road. Later, the company entangled itself in the web of local power politics, with consequences both unforeseen – as with the Black Hole (see p.738) – and most assiduously desired – as when the Battle of Plassey in 1758 made the British masters of Bengal. Recognized by Parliament in London in 1773, the company's trading monopoly led it to shift the capital of Bengal here from Murshidabad, and Calcutta became a clearing house for a vast range of commerce, including the lucrative exportation of opium to China.

At first, the East India Company brought young bachelors out from Britain to work as servants. Referred to as "writers", they lived in spartan conditions in communal mud huts, until the **Writers' Building** was eventually erected for their convenience. As they took to indigenous ways, and cohabited with local women, they were responsible for the emergence of the new **Eurasian** community. In time, Parliament rescinded the company's monopoly; when the doors of trade were thrown open, merchants and adventurers flocked in from far and wide, including Parsis, Baghdadi Jews, Afghans and Indians from other parts of the country. By 1857, such splendid buildings as the Court House, Government House, and St Paul's Cathedral, had earned Calcutta the soubriquet "City of Palaces". In truth, the humid and uncomfortable climate, putrefying salt marshes and the hovels that grew haphazardly around the city created unhygienic conditions that were a constant source of misery and disease.

The city's affluent elite – Bengali merchants included – came to be known as the "**bhadra log**", the good people. Although the term was lampooned by Kipling in *The Jungle Book*, in his depiction of the *Bandar Log*, the Monkey People, they were respon-

THE BENGALI RENAISSANCE

Although a rich tradition of poetry existed in India long before the arrival of the Europeans – even scientific manuscripts were written in rhyming couplets – **prose** was all but unknown. Thus the foundation by the British of **Fort William College** in 1800 – primarily intended to assist administrators to learn Indian languages by commissioning prose in Bengali, Urdu and Hindi – had the unexpected side effect of helping to create a vital new genre in indigenous literature. Bankim Chandra **Chatterjee** (1838–99), a senior civil servant who wrote novels of everyday life, became known as the father of Bengali literature, while Michael Madhusudan **Dutt** (1829–73) introduced European poetic conventions into Bengali poetry. Simultaneously, westernization began to sweep Bengali middle-class society, as Bengalis grew disenchanted with their culture and religion.

A leading figure in the new intelligentsia was Raja Ram Mohan **Roy** (1774–1833), born an orthodox Hindu, who travelled in Tibet before joining the East India Company, and eventually died in England as the ambassador of the Moghuls. Roy founded the **Brahmo Samaj**, a socio-religious movement that believed in a single god and set out to purge Hinduism of its idol worship and rituals, advocating the abolition of *sati* and child-marriage. Keshab Chandra **Sen's Navabidhan** (New Dispensation), a synthesis of all the world's major religions, created a split in 1866 over its downplaying of the role of Hinduism. A renowned orator, Keshab Sen travelled to Britain to lecture, but actions such as marrying off two of his very young daughters – one to the Maharajah of Cooch Behar and the other to the Maharajah of Mayurbhanj – lost him much support.

The intellectual and cultural freedom of the Brahmo Samaj earned it an important influence over the Bengali upper classes that endures to this day. No single figure epitomized the **Bengali Renaissance** more than **Rabindranath Tagore**, a giant of Bengali art, culture and letters, who received the Nobel Prize for Literature in 1913. As well as writing several hymns, he set out the principles of the movement in *The Religion of Man*.

During and following the period of the Renaissance, several other religious leaders emerged in Calcutta. **Ramkrishna** (1836–86) was a great Kali devotee whose message was carried as far as North America by **Vivekananda**. **Paramhansa Yogananda** wrote the renowned *Autobiography of a Yogi*, and **Sri Aurobindo** (1872–1950) was a student in London before becoming a freedom fighter and later a philosopher. Preaching a return to a reformed esoteric Hinduism, he went on to establish his own ashram in Pondicherry.

sible for the great flowering of cultural and artistic expression known as the **Bengali Renaissance** (see box). The decline of Calcutta as an international port came with the opening of the Suez Canal in 1869, the emergence of Bombay, and the end of the opium trade. In 1911, the days of glory came to a definitive end; the imperial capital of India was transferred to Delhi.

Arrival

Calcutta's **airport**, 20km north of the city centre, is served by international flights from east and west – although only a small proportion of visitors actually enter India here – as well as services from throughout the country. Officially simply "Calcutta Airport", it is still universally known by its old name of **Dum Dum** – a name that became infamous during the Boer War, when the notorious (and now banned) exploding bullet was manufactured in a nearby factory. The international terminal has money-changing facilities, while the **domestic terminal**, reached by heading left through the main hall after you pass through customs, holds a counter that can book rooms in a limited selection of hotels, and a **pre-paid taxi** booth. Booked here, a taxi to the central Sudder Street area costs around Rs70; you'll pay more if you attempt to make your own arrangements. Alternatively, an airport **bus** (Rs17) passes the western end of Chowringhee.

Of Calcutta's two main **railway stations**, neither of which is on the Metro system, **Howrah Station** – the point of arrival for major trains from the south and west, such as the *Rajdhani Express* from Delhi – stands near the far bank of the Hooghly a couple of kilometres west of the centre. To reach the central downtown area, traffic has to negotiate Howrah Bridge – a definitive introduction to the chaos of the city, especially during rush hours, which start late in the mornings. Long queues form at Howrah's **taxi rank** when main trains pull in – it works on a metered system, whereas touts and taxis who break the rank ask astronomical prices. **Minibuses** and **buses** (#5 and #6) also operate from Howrah for a *rupee* or two, but tend to be far too crowded for comfort; the **trams** across town are a bit more bearable, if very slow. Probably the best alternative is to take a 1-*rupee* **ferry** ride to Babu Ghat, or the adjacent Chandpal Ghat, close to BBD Bagh, and pick up a taxi, bus or minibus from there.

Sealdah Station, used by trains from the north, is on the eastern edge of the centre, and much more convenient as you don't have to get across the river. It's served by an equivalent assortment of taxis and buses.

Long-distance **buses** from the south terminate at **Babu Ghat Bus Stand**, not far from Fort William on the east bank, while some luxury buses, such as the *Bullet* from Darjeeling, arrive at **Esplanade Bus Stand**, under a kilometre north of Sudder Street.

Information and communications

The **Government of West Bengal Tourist Bureau**, 3-2 BBD Bagh East (☎248 8271), arranges tours of Calcutta and package trips around West Bengal, and in theory books accommodation in tourist bungalows all over the state, though communications are too poor for that service to be reliable. They also provide permits and passes for the Marble Palace in Calcutta and the Sunderbans and Jaldapara wildlife parks, and maintain **tourist information counters** at the airport and at Howrah Station.

The **Government of India Tourist Office**, 4 Shakespeare Sarani (☎22 1402), is probably easier to deal with, maintaining a useful if rather outdated database on sites and amenities throughout the region. Although their main task is to supply information, they too provide passes for Marble Palace and assist in booking tours; and they too have a counter at Howrah Station.

△ Airport

M Dum Dum

Digambar
Jain Temple

BELGACHIA RD

M Belgachia

BIDHAN SISHU UDYAN SARANI

BARRACKPORE TRUNK RD

KOSIPORE RD

Shyambazaar

M

Shoba Bazaar

Sitalnath
Jain Temple

A P CHANDRA RD

Railway
Station

Dakhineshwar

Hooghly River

M Girish Park

Marble
Palace

MOHAN AVE

M M G Road

M Nakhoda
Mosque

Belur Math

Rabindra
Bharati

Church of
Our Lady of
the Rosary

Nimtola
Ghat

Howrah
Bridge

Armenian
Ghat

Armenian
Church

Synagogue

Chandpal

GRAND TRUNK RD

Howrah
Station
(Main) A

N

0   1 km

HOTELS:
Ⓐ Yatri Niwas
Ⓑ Great Eastern
Ⓒ Central Guest House
Ⓓ Grand
Ⓔ YWCA
Ⓕ Kenilworth
Ⓖ Hindusthan
Ⓗ Taj Bengal
RESTAURANTS:
① Royal
② India Coffee House
③ Scoop
④ Jimmy's Kitchen
⑤ Kim Fa
⑥ Tibetan Delights & Hamro Momo
⑦ The Dhaba
⑧ Kwality

CALCUTTA

The telephone **area code** for Calcutta is ☎033.

English-language **newspapers** such as the *Statesman, Telegraph, Amrita Bazaar Patrika* and the *Hindusthan Standard* remain the primary source for information on **what's on**, and WB Tourism produce an occasional leaflet, *Calcutta This Fortnight*.

Banks and currency exchange

Calcutta Airport has a 24-hour branch of the *State Bank of India*, as well as the *RN Dutta* bureau de change in the international departure lounge. Major **banks**, concentrated either in the vicinity of BBD Bagh or scattered around Jawaharlal Nehru Rd (Chowringhee Rd), include *Algemeene Bank Nederlands*, 18A Brabourne Rd; *American Express*, 21 Old Court House St; *Banque National de Paris*, 4a BBD Bagh East; *Bank of America*, 8 India Exchange Place; *Bank of Tokyo*, 2 Brabourne Rd; *Citibank*, 43 Jawaharlal Nehru Rd; *Grindlays*, 41 Jawaharlal Nehru Rd & 19 Netaji Subhas Rd; *Hong Kong & Shangai*, 8 Netaji Subhas Rd (24-hour teller); *Standard Chartered*, 4 Netaji Subhas Rd; *State Bank of India*, 1 Strand Rd & 43 Jawaharlal Nehru Rd.

Among licensed brokers, whose exchange facilities are useful outside normal banking hours, are *RN Dutta*, Stephen House, 4-5 BBD Bagh East, 5&7 Kidderpore Dock and at the airport; *Maneek Lal Sen*, New Market; and *RR Sen*, 18 Jawaharlal Nehru Rd.

Mail services

Calcutta's imposing **General Post Office**, on the west side of BBD Bagh, houses the **poste restante** and has a philatelic department. The **Central Telegraph Exchange** is nearby at 8 Red Cross Place, close to Telephone Bhavan, the headquarters for Calcutta Telephones. If you're staying in the Sudder Street area, the **New Market Post Office**, Mirza Ghalib St, is much more convenient; from another large post office, on **Park Street**, you can send parcels or have them made up by enterprising individuals.

Telephone and fax

Overseas phone calls can easily be made from STD and ISD booths all over the city, or the International Telephone Exchange on Wood Street. The best booths have LED

NEW AND OLD ROAD NAMES

Although many of Calcutta's old colonial **street names** have officially been changed over the last three decades, the original names continue to be widely used by Calcuttans.

Old Name	New Name	Old Name	New Name
Bowbazar Street	Bepin Bihari Ganguly Street	Lower Circular Road	AJC Bose Road
Camac Street	Abanindranath Tagore Street	Moria Street	Rev Martin Luther King Street
Chitpore Road	Rabindra Sarani	Red Road	Indira Gandhi Road
Chowringhee	Jawaharlal Nehru Road	Ripon Street	Muzaffar Ahmed Street
Dalhousie Square	BBD Bagh		
Dharamtala Street	Lenin Sarani	Theatre Road	Shakespeare Sarani
Free School Street	Mirza Ghalib Street	Upper Lower	Acharya Prafulla
Harrington Street	Ho Chi Minh Sarani	Circular Road	Chandra Road
Kyd Street	Dr Mohammed Ishaque Road	Wellesley Street	Rafi Ahmed Kidwai Street
Landsdowne Road	Sarat Bose Road	Wellington Square	Raja Subodh Mallick Square

monitors showing the exact duration of each call, and the number dialled; many also have fax machines. Trying to put through **internal calls** can be frustrating in the extreme, though conditions are not as farcical as they were, when it was said to be easier to pass messages via relatives on the other side of the world. As digital technology is introduced, the city's telephone numbers are being progressively altered – which explains why some numbers have six digits and some seven.

City transport

Virtually all the different modes of transport that clog the streets of Calcutta – trams, buses, human rickshaws, auto-rickshaws, metered taxis, and minibuses – add to the problem of congestion rather than providing a solution. Only the city's pride and joy, India's first and only **Metro**, comes close to being an efficient way to get around.

Increasingly, the **river** is being used for transport, with the *ghats* near Eden Gardens at the hub of a **ferry** system. The most pleasant way to beat the traffic is to take one of the very regular Rs1 ferries from Chandpal Ghat to Howrah Station, while other sailings head downriver from Chandpal or Babu Ghats to the Botanical Gardens.

The Metro

Calcutta's Russian-designed **Metro**, inaugurated in 1984, is every bit as good as its inhabitants proudly claim, a spotless contrast to the streets above, with trains operating punctually every few minutes, and videos on the platforms to keep passengers amused while they wait. Services get off to a slow start each day, beginning at 8am (and 3pm on Sun) and running until 8.30pm, with a standard ticket price of Rs3 whatever distance you travel.

At present, the single south–north line follows Chowringhee – known as Jawaharlal Nehru Rd for part of the way – from Tollygunge to Esplanade. Stations include Park St, Kalighat, and Rabindra Sadan, which is decorated with poems by Rabindranath Tagore. In due course the Metro will extend to Dum Dum near the airport in the north, though construction is advancing at a snail's pace, thanks to the nature of the soil and the heavy monsoons. A walk north of Esplanade towards Shambazaar reveals huge gaps in the road, and great mounds of excavated earth.

Buses and minibuses

Calcutta supports a vast and complicated **bus** network, in operation each day between roughly 5am and 9.30pm, and subject to hideous overcrowding and attendant pickpocketing problems. Red double-deckers and elongated trailer buses belonging to the *Calcutta Transport Corporation* – **CTC** – run much the same routes, for much the same minimal fares, as a horde of private companies. Among potentially useful routes are **#10**, between Esplanade and Gariahat; **#8** , from Howrah via Esplanade and Gariahat Rd to Gol Park; **#17**, from Chetla near Kalighat via Esplanade; and **#5** and **#6**, which both travel via Howrah and the Esplanade-Chowringhee area, and stop at the Indian Museum at the head of Sudder Street.

In addition, private brown-and-yellow **minibuses** travel at inordinate speeds on ad-hoc routes; their destinations are usually painted boldly in Bengali and English on their sides, and conductors shout them out at bus stops or major junctions. Originally intended as fast seating-only commuter services, they now take on standing passengers; an incredibly uncomfortable way to travel, as unless you're absolutely tiny, you have to crouch. An empty minibus at Howrah may look like an attractive option, but will almost certainly soon be packed.

CITY TOURS

City tours, run by West Bengal Tourism and Government of India Tourism (see p.729) can involve more time contemplating heavy traffic than the sites themselves. Advance booking is necessary. They operate daily (except for holidays; and note that most museums close on Mon), costing around Rs60 for a full day and less for half a day.

WB Tourism's tours start from their office in BBD Bagh East. The morning one (lasting from 7.30–11.40am) packs in Eden Gardens, Writers' Building, Botanical Gardens, Belur Math, Dakshineshwar, and the Sitalnath Jain Temple, then returns via the Esplanade. The afternoon tour (12.40–5pm) covers the Indian Museum, Nehru Children's Museum, Victoria Memorial, the zoo, the lakes and Birla Academy. The all-day Government of India tours follow a similar itinerary, leaving their office at 4 Shakespeare Sarani at 8am.

Taxis

Taxis in Calcutta are extremely good value. Most have working meters; those few taxi drivers who refuse to use them should be avoided. However, what you pay is not the price actually shown on the meter, but a figure produced with the help of a fare conversion table, which drivers are required to carry; these are updated to keep up with the spiralling costs of diesel and petrol. A small additional charge is made for luggage in the "dicky" (the boot or trunk).

Trams

Calcutta's cumbersome **trams**, barely changed since they started operating in 1873, are on their way out; their inability to deviate from fixed rails to cope with the city's crazy traffic makes them more of a nuisance than anything else. However, for all their grime and general dilapidation, they do have an odd quirky charm, and women travellers may well be glad of the rush-hour women-only coaches. Routes include #25, Sealdah to Ballygunge; #35, Sealdah via Esplanade to Behala; #32 and #21, Howrah via Esplanade and Rashbehari to Ballygunge; and #24, Kalighat via Esplanade to Sealdah.

Rickshaws, auto-rickshaws and cycle rickshaws

Calcutta shares with Hong Kong the dubious honour of being the only cities in the world to have **human-drawn rickshaws**, which are only available in the central areas of the city, especially around New Market. These come into their own during the monsoons, when the streets get flooded to hip height and the rickshaw-men can extract healthy amounts of money for their pains. If you take one, take care not to lean back; the superior weight of a westerner can launch the poor fellow into the air, with his legs cycling in space. Most of the rickshaw-pullers are Bihari pavement-dwellers, who live a short and difficult life; you'd have to be a strange sort of person to resent the fact that they invariably charge tourists extra.

Auto-rickshaws, rare in the centre of town, are often used as shared taxis to link with Metro stations in suburbs such as Rashbehari and Gariahat. **Cycle rickshaws**, banned from much of the city, are only available in outlying suburbs.

Car rentals

Among **car rental** companies, charging around Rs400 per day, are *Ashai International*, 12-12 Hungerford St (☎44 1987); *Car Rent Services*, 233-4A AJC Bose Rd (☎44 1285); *Durgapur Automobiles*, 113 Park St (☎29 4044); *New Lakshmi Travels*, 296 Rashbehari Ave (☎40 5317); and *Rent-a-Car Service*, 1-5 Dover Lane (☎46 7186). Cars can also be rented through most large hotels.

The City

Calcutta's crumbling weatherbeaten buildings and anarchic streets can create an intimidating first impression. Given a little time and patience, however, the huge metropolis starts to resolve itself into a fascinating conglomerate of styles and influences, with an uncontrollable profusion of buildings jockeying for attention.

The **River Hooghly**, which was until recently only spanned by the remarkable cantilever Howrah Bridge, is not all that prominent in the life of the city. Instead its heart is the green expanse of the **Maidan**, which attracts Calcuttans from all walks of life for recreation, sports, exhibitions and political rallies. Next to the busy **New Market** area alongside looms the all-embracing **Indian Museum**. Further north, the district centered on BBD Bagh is filled with reminders of the heyday of the East India Company, including the **Writers' Building** and **St Paul's Cathedral**, while the major temple of **Kalighat** is away to the south, in one of the city's most congested areas.

The Maidan, New Market and the Park Street area

The **Maidan** – literally "field" – which stretches from Esplanade in the north to the race course in the south, and is bordered by Jawaharlal Nehru Rd (**Chowringhee**) to the east and the Strand and the river to the west, is one of the largest city parks in the world. This vast area of open space stands in utter contrast to the chaotic streets of the city that surrounds it, big enough to swallow up several clubs, including the *Calcutta Ladies Golf Club*, and the immaculate greens of the *Calcutta Bowling Club*. It was created when the now-inconspicuous **Fort William** was laid out near the river in 1758, and Robert Clive cleared tracts of forest to give its guns a clear line of fire. Originally it was a haven for the elite, with a strictly enforced dress code. Now, early each morning, ordinary citizens come to exercise, shepherds graze their flocks, and riders on horseback canter along the old bridleways. In the late afternoons, it plays host to scores of impromptu cricket and football matches, as well as games of *kabaadi* (see p.49).

Esplanade

The 46-metre-tall vaguely Greek-style column of **Shahid Minar** (Martyrs' Memorial) towers over busy tram and bus terminals and market stalls at the northeast corner of the Maidan, known as Esplanade. As the **Ochterlony Monument**, it was built in 1828 to commemorate the memory of David Ochterlony, who led the East India Company troops to victory in the Nepalese Wars of 1814–16. Further northeast, in the small **Curzon Park** among the trees and fenced-off patches of greenery beyond the tram terminus, a colony of rats has burrowed a warren of holes. Local office workers spend their lunch hours feeding the fat and complacent rodents.

New Market and Chowringhee

Beneath its Gothic red brick clock tower, the single-storey **New Market**, in the centre of cosmopolitan Calcutta, can have changed little since it opened in 1874. Its real name is Sir Stuart Hogg Market; supposedly, the ghost of Sir Stuart haunts the market, roaming the corridors at night crying out for peace. It would be easier to imagine that he was bemoaning the antics of its coolies, who drag willing and unwilling customers into the various shops in search of commission, and also double as black-market touts. At the north end of the market, a characterless multi-storey building has been erected to replace sections gutted by a fire in 1985. Many of the shops were housed in a temporary market on the Maidan, opposite the Indian Museum, before being rehoused here; that area is now something of an ugly shanty town.

The market itself stocks a vast array of household goods, luggage, ready-made garments, jewellery, curio shops, book shops, textiles, and kitchenware, as well as meat, vegetables and fruit. Among shops that stand out from the rest, *Chamba Lama* sells Tibetan curios and antique items such as cosmetic and silver jewellery, and new bronzes. The *Symphony* music store has a good selection of classical and popular Indian music, while *Sujata's* is known for its silk, and *Nahoum & Sons* is a Jewish bakery (see p.748). Further up the corridor, condiment stalls offer cheese from Kalimpong, miniature rounds of salty Bandel cheese, and *amshat*, blocks made up of sheets of dried mango. *Dey Bros* is one of many bookshops in the southeastern part.

The formerly elegant colonnaded front of Chowringhee east of Esplanade, now in a sorry state of decay, is perpetually crowded with hawkers and shoppers. The only one of its grand institutions to survive relatively unscathed is the Victorian **Grand Hotel**, which after endless renovations and changes of management remains a haven of colonialism, with its palm court inspired by the famous *Raffles* of Singapore.

Indian Museum

27 J Nehru Rd (☎29 9853). Daily, March–Nov 10am–5pm, Dec–Feb 10am–4.30pm. Rs1; Fri free.

At the corner of Chowringhee and Sudder St, a few metres south of the *Grand*, the stately **Indian Museum** is the oldest museum in India, founded in 1814. Built around a central courtyard, the present high-ceilinged building was opened to the public in 1878, and is probably the largest museum in Asia, ranging across a huge spectrum of exhibits from sculpture to natural history.

Visitors come to the museum in their thousands, many of them villagers who bring offerings to the "house of magic". Its real showpiece is a collection of **stone and metal sculptures** obtained from sites all over India, which centres on a superb Mauryan polished sandstone **lion capital**, dated to the third century BC. One gallery houses the impressive remains of the second-century BC Buddhist *stupa* from Bharhut in Madhya Pradesh, partly re-assembled to display posts, capping stones, railings and gateways all made from red sandstone. Carvings depict human and animal figures, as well as scenes from the *Jataka* tales of the Buddha's many incarnations. There is also a huge collection of schist sculptures, dating from the first to the third-centuries from the Gandhara region; themes include scenes from Buddha's life and a host of other Buddhist divinities. You'll also see stone sculpture from **Khajuraho** and Pala bronzes, plus copper artefacts, stone-age tools and terracotta figures from different sites.

Along with an excellent exhibit of Tibetan *thangkas*, the museum holds Kalighat *pats* (see p.745) and paintings by the **Company School**, a group of mid-nineteenth-century Indian artists who emulated western themes and techniques for European patrons. Finally, there's a spectacular array of fossils and stuffed animals, most of which look in dire need of a decent burial.

Park Street

Just around the corner from the museum, the **Asiatic Society** at 1 Park St, established in 1784 by orientalists including Sir William Jones, has a members-only library with a huge selection of books and manuscripts, and a reading room open to the public (Mon–Fri 10am–8pm, Sat & Sun 10am–5pm; free). Its gallery of art and antiquities preserves paintings by Rubens and Reynolds and a large collection of coins.

Around two kilometres along Park Street from the Maidan, the disused but recently restored **Park Street Cemetery** is one of the city's most haunting memorials to its imperial past. Inaugurated in 1767, it is the oldest in Calcutta, holding a wonderful concentration of pyramids, obelisks, pavilions, urns and headstones, under which many well-known British personalities lie buried.

Fort William

A road leads west through the Maidan from the top of Park Street to the gates of **Fort William**. As the military headquarters of eastern command, this allows entry only to those who have sought permission in advance, although the public are allowed into certain sections on special occasions. Built on the site of the old village of Govindapur, and commissioned by the British after their defeat in 1756, the fort was completed in 1781 and named after King William III. A rough octagon, about five hundred metres in diameter, whose massive but low bunker-like battlements are punctuated by six main gates, the fort was designed to hold all the city's Europeans in the event of attack. To one side it commanded a view of the Maidan; to the other it dominated the river and its crucial shipping lanes. Water from the river was diverted to fill its surrounding moat. Eighteenth- and nineteenth-century structures inside include the Church of St Peter's (now a library), barracks and stables, an arsenal, strong rooms and a prison.

Victoria Memorial and the Calcutta Gallery

Daily except Mon, March–Oct 10am–3.30pm, Nov–Feb 10am–4.30pm. Rs2. Cameras must be deposited at the entrance. Sound and Light show held in English at 8.15pm; Rs5.

The dramatic white marble **Victoria Memorial** at the southern end of the Maidan, with its formal gardens and water courses, continues to be Calcutta's pride and joy. Other colonial monuments and statues throughout the city have been renamed or demolished, but the popularity of Queen Victoria seems to endure for ever; thirty years of attempts to change the name of the "VM" have come to nothing.

This extraordinary hybrid building, with Italianate statues over its entrances, Moghul domes in its corners, and tall elegant open colonnades along its sides, was conceived by Lord Curzon to commemorate the empire at its peak. Designed by Sir William Emerson, it was completed in 1921. Flanked by two ornamental tanks, a sombre statue of Queen Victoria gazes out towards the Maidan from a pedestal lined with bronze panels and friezes. Faced with Makrana marble from Jodhpur, the building itself is capped by a dome bearing a revolving five-metre-tall bronze figure of *Victory*.

The main entrance, at the Maidan end, leads into a tall chamber beneath the dome. The 25 galleries inside burst with mementoes of British imperialism – statues and busts of Queen Mary, King George V and Queen Victoria; paintings of Robert Clive and the Queen (again); a huge canvas of the future Edward VII entering Jaipur in 1876; French guns captured at the Battle of Plassey in 1758; and the black marble throne of a nawab defeated by Robert Clive. One air-conditioned chamber, converted and renamed the **Calcutta Gallery**, is dedicated to the Indians of the city and the Independence struggle. The evening **Sound and Light** show concentrates on the same theme.

Admission to the Victoria Memorial's popular gardens is free during the day. After they close at dusk, the Maidan in front of the gates is transformed. A seething mass of people come to enjoy the breeze, roadside snacks, and pony and *tikka* (open carriage) rides, and to watch the garish musical fountains.

St Paul's Cathedral and around

The gothic **St Paul's Cathedral**, a little way along from the Victoria Memorial, was erected by Major WN Forbes in 1847. Measuring 75 metres by 24 metres, its iron trussed roof was then the longest span in existence. For improved ventilation, the lancet windows inside extend to plinth level, and tall fans hang from the ceiling. The most outstanding of the many well-preserved memorials and plaques to long-perished imperialists is the stained glass of the west window, designed by Sir Edward Burne-Jones in 1880 to honour Lord Mayo, assassinated in the Andaman Islands. The original steeple was destroyed in the 1897 earthquake; after a second earthquake in 1934 it was remodelled on the Bell Harry Tower at Canterbury Cathedral.

Between the cathedral and the Victoria Memorial, the **Birla Planetarium**, one of the largest in the world, holds several shows every day, some in English (Rs8).

South of the cathedral, the **Academy of Fine Arts** on Cathedral Rd is a showcase for Bengali contemporary arts (daily except Mon 3–6pm; Rs1). As well as temporary exhibitions, it holds permanent displays of the work of artists such as Jamini Roy and Rabindranath Tagore. A cafe and pleasant grounds add to the appealing ambience.

Not far away on Chowringhee, the small **Nehru Children's Museum**, 94/1 J Nehru Rd (daily except Mon noon–8pm; Rs2, under-12s Rs1), places a strong emphasis on the Hindu classics, illustrating the *Ramayana* and the *Mahabharata* with toys, puppets and picture shows.

Central Calcutta

The commercial and administrative hub of both Calcutta and West Bengal is **BBD Bagh**, which die-hard Calcuttans still insist on referring to as **Dalhousie Square**. The new official name, in a fine piece of official rhetoric, commemorates three revolutionaries hanged for trying to kill Lieutenant-Governor General Lord Dalhousie. In the centre of the square is the large Lal Dighi tank, or artificial pond.

Built in 1868 on the site of the original Fort William – destroyed by Siraj-ud-Daula in 1756 – the **GPO** on the west of the square hides the supposed site of the **Black Hole of Calcutta**. Quite what the truth of that much-mythologized incident may have been remains a matter for debate, but an indignant British public was told that 146 English prisoners were forced on a hot June night in 1756 into a tiny chamber with only the smallest of windows for ventilation, and that most suffocated to death by the next morning. A memorial to the victims that formerly stood in front of Writers' Building was removed in 1940 to the grounds of St John's Church south of the GPO. When Robert Clive regained control of Calcutta, he had learned his lesson. Fort William was not rebuilt in this virtually undefendable location in a built-up area, but in its current location on the Maidan, with clear visibility in all directions.

Now the seat of the West Bengal Government, **Writers' Building** to the north of the square was built in 1780 to replace the original structure used to house the clerks or "writers" of the East India Company. No official tours take in the building, but wandering in to any department reveals a world of endless corridors and vast chambers, where desks are piled high with dusty old files and clerks seem to exude apathy.

West of Writers' Building, beyond the headquarters of Eastern Railways on Netaji Subhash Rd, you come to the heart of Calcutta's **commercial district**, clustered around the Royal Stock Exchange at the corner of Lyon's Range. The warren of buildings, erected along the same lines as the contemporary business districts of Shanghai, houses all sorts of old colonial trading companies; Scottish names in particular still seem to be very much in evidence. One of its most extraordinary sights is **Exchange Lane**, where stockbrokers sit in brightly painted wooden cubicles armed with telephones and carry on business with punters on the street. Not far away, around the corner on the pavement but hard to find in the confusion of vendors and pedestrians, lies a small "tomb" known as the **Memorial to the Dead Telephone**, built in 1984 by the Telephone Consumers Guidance Society of India.

A further symbol of Calcutta's Scottish traditions is the grey spire of **St Andrew's Kirk**, which rises in the middle of the road at the northeast end of BBD Bagh. This Scottish church was built in 1818, in the face of intense opposition from Church of England representatives. To the east, the oldest street in the city, formerly known as Mission Row but now called RN Mukherjee Rd, holds the **Old Mission Church**, founded in 1770 by the Swedish missionary Johann Kiernander. South of the GPO, **St John's Church** was erected in 1787. Inside, along with memorials to British residents and to the first Bishop of Calcutta, Bishop Middleton, hangs an impressive painting by Johann Zoffany of The Last Supper, in which prominent Calcuttans are depicted as apostles. In the grounds, Calcutta's first graveyard holds the tomb of Job Charnock.

Dominating this area south of BBD Bagh, **Government House** (only open to the public with prior permission) overlooks the north end of the Maidan and the ceremo-

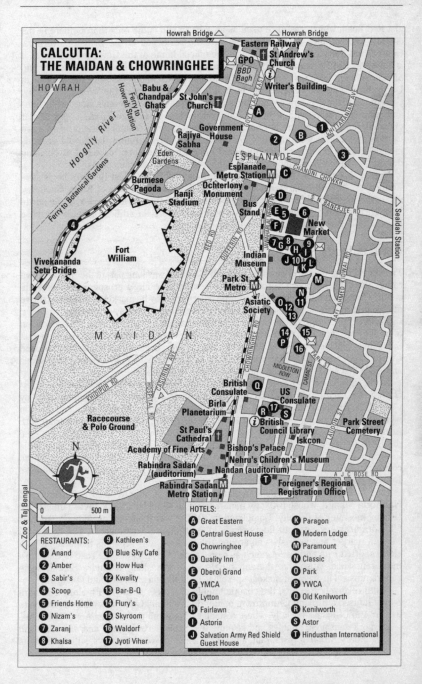

CALCUTTA: THE MAIDAN & CHOWRINGHEE

Howrah Bridge △ △ Howrah Bridge

Eastern Railway
St Andrew's Church
GPO
BBD Bagh
Writer's Building

HOWRAH

Babu & Chandpal Ghats
St John's Church
Government House
Rajiya Sabha
Eden Gardens

Ferry to Howrah Station
Hooghly River

Ferry to Botanical Gardens
Burmese Pagoda
Ranji Stadium

ESPLANADE
Esplanade Metro Station
Ochterlony Monument
Bus Stand

STRAND

Vivekananda Setu Bridge

Fort William

Indian Museum
Park St Metro
Asiatic Society

New Market

S N BANERJEE RD
CHANDNI CHOWK

M A I D A N

RED RD

British Consulate
Birla Planetarium
St Paul's Cathedral
Academy of Fine Arts
Rabindra Sadan (auditorium)
Rabindra Sadan Metro Station

US Consulate
British Council Library
Iskcon
Bishop's Palace
Nehru's Children's Museum
Nandan (auditorium)
Foreigner's Regional Registration Office

Racecourse & Polo Ground

MIDDLETON ROW

PARK ST
Park Street Cemetery

A J C BOSE RD

CASANOVA AVE
HOSPITAL RD
KHIDIRPUR RD

△ Sealdah Station

△ Zoo & Taj Bengal

N

0   500 m

RESTAURANTS:

1. Anand
2. Amber
3. Sabir's
4. Scoop
5. Friends Home
6. Nizam's
7. Zaranj
8. Khalsa
9. Kathleen's
10. Blue Sky Cafe
11. How Hua
12. Kwality
13. Bar-B-Q
14. Flury's
15. Skyroom
16. Waldorf
17. Jyoti Vihar

HOTELS:

- A Great Eastern
- B Central Guest House
- C Chowringhee
- D Quality Inn
- E Oberoi Grand
- F YMCA
- G Lytton
- H Fairlawn
- I Astoria
- J Salvation Army Red Shield Guest House
- K Paragon
- L Modern Lodge
- M Paramount
- N Classic
- O Park
- P YWCA
- Q Old Kenilworth
- R Kenilworth
- S Astor
- T Hindusthan International

nial Red Road, which was once used as an airstrip and is the only thoroughfare in the city without potholes. Until 1911, this was the residence of the British Governors-General and the Viceroys of India; now the official home of the Governor of Bengal, it is known as **Raj Bhavan**, which amounts to the same thing. When built at the very end of the eighteenth century, it was intended to be a palace, modelled on Kedleston Hall in Derbyshire, England. Sealed off by tall iron fencing from the rest of the city, Government House is approached through four ornamental gateways guarded by lions and sphinxes. Along with a throne room once used by George V, and a spectacular chandeliered ballroom, the interior holds Calcutta's first elevator introduced by Lord Curzon and still in working condition. Trophies littered around the formal grounds include a large bronze cannon mounted on a winged dragon, captured at Nanking during the Opium Wars, and brass cannons from the Afghan campaigns.

Nearby, opposite the **Assembly House** (Rajya Sabha) of West Bengal's Legislative Council, are the All India Radio building, and the sports complex of **Eden Gardens**, site of the huge world-famous cricket ground. West of the sports complex, at the northwest corner of the Maidan, an ornamental park offers an artificial lake, a Burmese Pagoda, and pleasant walks along palm-strewn paths.

North Calcutta

The sprawling and amorphous area of **north Calcutta** was long part of the "native" town rather than the European sectors, and was where the city's prosperous nineteenth-century Bengali families created their little palaces. Today its markets continue to thrive unchanged, and the occasional church stands as a reminder of days gone by.

North of BBD Bagh, the area known as **Barabazaar** has played host to a succession of trading communities; the Portuguese were here even before Job Charnock landed at the fishing village that stood close by, and it later became home to Marwari and Gujarati merchants. The small and hectic lanes south of MG Road are lined with shops and stalls that sell everything from glass bangles to textiles.

At the northwest corner of Barabazaar, near Howrah Bridge, is Calcutta's oldest church, the **Armenian Church of Our Lady of Nazareth**. Founded in 1724 by Cavond, an Armenian from Persia, it was built on the site of an Armenian cemetery in which the oldest tombstone dates to 1630. The Armenian community, drawn from both Armenia and Persia, was already highly influential at the courts of Bengal by the time the British arrived, and played an important role in the early history of the East India Company. Later they went on to help start the lucrative jute industry. Just around the corner on MG Road at Murghihatta, the "Chicken Market", stands the Portuguese **Roman Catholic Cathedral**, built in 1797.

East of Barabazaar on Rabindra Sarani (formerly Chitpore Road), the huge red **Nakhoda Masjid**, whose two lofty minarets rise to 46 metres, is the great Jami Masjid (Friday mosque) of the city. Completed in 1942, it was modelled on Akbar's Tomb at Sikandra near Agra; its four floors can hold ten thousand worshippers. The traditional Muslim market that flourishes all around the mosque sells religious items along with clothes, dried fruit and sweets such as *firni*, made of rice. Down the road is Calcutta's most renowned Muslim restaurant, the *Royal*. North along Rabindra Sarani, some superb musical instrument makers specialize in *sitars*, harmoniums and *tanburas*.

Until relatively recently, the chaotic jumble of streets to the south along Rabindra Sarani housed a thriving **Chinatown**, opium dens and all. Chinese families continue to live around Chhatawala Gully, where a small early-morning street market offers homemade pork sausages, noodles and jasmine tea. Stalls serve *wonton* and *dim sum*, and the legendary *Nanking* restaurant, albeit now a shadow of better days, still dusts off its broken china and silverware for the few visitors who wander in.

North of MG Road, on the tiny Muktaram Babu Street off Chittaranjan Avenue, the controversial **Marble Palace** preserves its lavish, sensuous and sometimes tasteless treasures in less than satisfactory conditions (Tues–Wed & Fri–Sun; free). Visitors are supposed to obtain passes from the main tourist offices at BBD Bagh or Shakespeare Sarani, but a little *baksheesh* to the caretaker has not been unheard of; photography is forbidden. Built in 1835 by Raja Rajendro Mullick Bahadur, a wealthy *zamindar* educated by an English tutor, the colonnaded mansion epitomizes the incredible profusion of influences of the period, and is still maintained by the Raja's descendants, who live here. The palace earns its name from its ornate marble-paved chambers, which hold statues, European antiques, Venetian glass, chandeliers, mirrors and Ming vases. There are paintings by Rubens, Titian, Sir Joshua Reynolds and Gainsborough; supposedly there's even a statue by Michelangelo. At the centre of the building, part of an Italian courtyard is taken up by an aviary, while the grounds hold a small zoo.

North of Marble Palace is the city's main red-light area, **Sonagachi**. This is not a district into which travellers are advised to venture; those who do invariably come to harm, at the very least through finding themselves arrested by the police.

On Dwarkanath Tagore Lane, a short walk northeast of the Marble Palace, the small campus of Rabindranath Tagore's liberal arts university, **Rabindra Bharati**, preserves the house where he was born and died. Now the **Rabindra Bharati Museum**, it holds a huge collection of his paintings (Mon–Fri 10am–5pm, Sat 10am–1.30pm; free). Next door, Bichitra Bhavan is used, as it was by Tagore himself, to stage theatrical performances. In September, it is the scene of a festival commemorating the Nobel Laureate.

Further east, **College Street** stretches along the edge of Calcutta University. Established in 1857 as the pride of Bengali learning, it still has one of the largest student bodies in the world. Senate House, one of its earliest buildings, was gutted during the turbulent days of the early Seventies. College Street deals exclusively in books and supplies for students; its pavement stalls and shops are an excellent hunting ground for secondhand books, if not genuine antiques. Adjoining Albert Street's famous **India Coffee House** remains at the centre of student life. The small **Ashutosh Museum of Indian History** at the Centenary Building on College Street has a good collection of Bengali art, handicrafts and fabrics as well as rare Buddhist manuscripts and statues (Mon–Fri 10.30am–3.30pm; free).

North Calcutta has two large **Jain temples**. One, in **Belgachia** next to the bridge and the Metro station, is a simple red sandstone structure, dedicated to the Digambara sect. The other, at **Manicktolla**, consists of a group of temples set in an ornate garden which holds ponds full of carp. It honours **Sitalnath**, the lord of water and the tenth in the line of twenty-four *tirthankaras* (crossing-makers) that culimnated with Mahavira,

---

POLLUTION AND FLOODS

With no controls on the emissions of its armada of diesel-engined vehicles, Calcutta is cursed with lethal atmospheric **pollution** – as any visitor to the city soon learns. For its residents, lung problems are part of everyday life. Rush hours are especially noxious, with grey fumes frequently obscuring the sunset. During the long months when the city holds its breath and waits for the monsoons to hit, the still and heavy air can be unbearable; and when the rains finally roll in at the end of June, Calcutta becomes a swamp. Being obliged to wade thigh-deep through filthy water, along roads riddled with pot-holes and open man-holes, contributes to further health problems. Calcutta's **water table** is contaminated to a depth of over 20 feet, and gastric disease is endemic. Anyone who can afford it equips their home with its own purification systems or tube well. On top of all that, the Calcutta Corporation is hopelessly unequal to the task of keeping the city clean; streets are strewn with litter, and rubbish tips pile shoulder high.

born in Vaishali in 599 BC. Neoclassical marble and alabaster statues grace the grounds, while the main temple, another architectural hybrid, is crowned by an ornate cupola. Inside the chamber the image of Sitalnath is surrounded by gaudy marble-work studded with silver. An odd mixture of Venetian and post-Moghul, its assorted multi-hued chandeliers are offset by the surrounding glass and mirrors. Along with an information centre, the temple area has several Jain shrines and boarding houses.

Howrah and the River Hooghly

Although **Howrah** is technically a separate town, as the home of much of Calcutta's industry, as well as Howrah Station, it forms an integral part of the city. Until recently the antiquated **Howrah Bridge** was the only road link across the River Hooghly; since the opening of the tall and elegant **Vivekananda Setu**, the second Hooghly bridge, a few years ago, the west bank of the river is changing rapidly. Vivekananda Setu provides easy access to Shibpur and the beautiful **Botanical Gardens**, and onwards southwest to the open highways towards Orissa.

Howrah Station, across the river from central Calcutta, is a truly remarkable railway station, used by millions of passengers each day. Built in 1906, it's a striking red-brick building, topped by eight square towers. During the war in Bangladesh, in the early seventies, it found itself sheltering thousands of refugees in horrific conditions.

Until silting rendered it impractical for large ships, the **River Hooghly**, a distributary of the Ganges, was responsible for making Calcutta a bustling port. Unlike those at Varanasi, the *ghats* that line its east (Calcutta) bank have no great esoteric significance; they simply serve as real landings and places for ritual ablutions. Around 1.5km north of Howrah Bridge, **Nimtolla Ghat**, one of the city's main cremation grounds, is sealed off from the public gaze. The large steps alongside, and a Shiva temple, attract strange *sadhus* as they head through the city on their way to January's Ganga Sagar Mela (see p.751). A little further north, behind **Kumartuli Ghat**, a warren of lanes is home to a community of artisans who specialize in making the clay, straw and pith images of deities used for the major festivals. In the days leading up to the great *pujas*, especially that of Durga, **Kumartuli** is a fascinating hive of activity. As you walk north, you come next to **Baghbazaar Ghat**, where overloaded barges of straw arrive for the craftsmen of Kumartuli. Baghbazaar, the Garden Market, stands on the original site of Sutanuti, its grand but decaying turn-of-the-century mansions epitomizing the long-vanished lifestyle of the Bengali gentry, the *bhadra log*.

South of Howrah Bridge, but right in its shadow, the large **Armenian Ghat** is at its most animated soon after dawn, when traditional gymnasts and wrestlers, devotees of

---

HOWRAH BRIDGE

One of Calcutta's most famous landmarks, **Howrah Bridge** – now also known by the new name of Rabindra Setu – is 97 metres high and 705 metres long, spanning the river in a single giant leap to make it the world's largest cantilever bridge. It was erected during World War II in 1943 to give Allied troops access to the Burmese front, replacing an earlier pontoon bridge that opened to let river traffic through. Looking like a giant version of something a child might make using a construction set, it's the world's busiest bridge, used by millions of commuters daily. Its eight lanes are perpetually clogged with vehicles, and it's so worn out that a man pushing his broken-down car is said to have fallen through a hole and disappeared. Don't let that put you off; joining the streams of perspiring pedestrians who walk across the bridge each day is a memorable experience.

Vivekananda Setu, the second Hooghly bridge, built three kilometres south to relieve the strain, was 22 years in the making. It's a vast toll bridge, high enough to let ships pass below, and with spaghetti-junction-style approaches.

Hanuman the monkey god, do their morning practice, and a flower market is in full swing. Nearby, vehicles from trams to handcarts battle inch by inch to gain access to the Howrah Bridge. As the cobbled and much-potholed Strand heads south, it passes several warehouses on the way beyond Fairly Place to another cluster of *ghats*. **Babu Ghat** here, identified by its crumbling colonnade, is used for early-morning bathing, attended by *pujaris* (priests) and nimble-fingered masseurs. Nearby, Babu Ghat's Bus Stand is one of Calcutta's main cross-country terminuses, while ferries from **Chandpal Ghat** a couple of hundred metres north provide an easy alternative to Howrah Bridge.

Further south, past Eden Gardens, the Strand opens out into the promenades near Fort William, where the people of the city come to enjoy the cool evening river breezes. An ice-cream parlour overlooks the river and snack vendors are everywhere. A short boat-trip to the new bridge and back costs around Rs30.

Botanical Gardens

The **Botanical Gardens** at Shibpur lie ten kilometres south of Howrah Station on the west bank of the Hooghly. Although they were created in 1786, to develop strains of Indian tea, only since the opening of the second bridge have Calcuttans started to appreciate these 109 hectares once again. Populated by countless bird species, such as waders, cranes, and storks, the huge gardens are best seen early in the mornings, when they're free from the grime of the metropolis. Their single most famous feature is the **world's largest banyan tree**, reaching up 24.5 metres high and embracing an astonishing circumference of 420 metres. Now over 240 years old, a survivor of cyclones in 1864 and 1867 that eventually caused it to lose its main trunk, its 1825 aerial roots drop from the overhead branches to create the effect of a small forest. Elsewhere, palm trees abound around the lakes, ponds and ornamental footbridges, and especially the brooding, atmospheric Palm House. The Orchid House, the Herbarium and the Fern Houses are also worth seeing, and there's an attractive riverside promenade.

As a rule, the gardens are empty during the week and packed at weekends. Much the nicest way to get here is by ferry from Babu Ghat or Chandpal Ghat, which costs a mere Rs1.25, though it's also accessible as a tedious road trip from Esplanade, by mini-bus (#6) or ordinary bus. Cafes within the gardens are open unpredictable hours.

South Calcutta

South of the Maidan and Park Street, Calcutta spreads towards boroughs such as **Alipore** and **Ballygunge**, both within easy distance of the centre. The thoroughfare that starts life as Jawaharlal Nehru Rd (Chowringhee) proceeds south from Esplanade past **Kalighat** to **Tollygunge**, following the Metro line which terminates near the luxurious *Tollygunge Club*, the mansion of an indigo merchant now surrounded by immaculate golfing fairways and bridle paths. Northeast of Tollygunge, beyond a white-tiled mosque built in 1835 by descendants of Tipu Sultan, the vast open area of the **Dhakuria Lakes** leads to **Ballygunge**, the home of Calcutta's Bengali middle classes.

Alipore

Around three kilometres south of Park Street, the crumbling nineteenth-century splendour of **Alipore** is slowly being engulfed by a forest of multi-storey buildings. Not far from the race course, opposite the luxury *Taj Bengal* hotel, the extremely popular **Calcutta Zoo** (daily 6am–5pm; Rs1) houses such weird and wonderful animals as a tigon, a cross between a lion and a tiger; a litigon, a cross between a tigon and a lion; a litatitigon . . . and so forth. It also has white tigers from Rewa; a reptile house; an aquarium; a children's zoo; and four restaurants. The only real drawback is that many of the cages are cleaner than their litter-strewn surroundings.

Elegant triple-arched gates just south of the zoo lead to **Belvedere**, the former residence of the Lieutenant-Governor of Bengal, now the **National Library** (Mon–Fri 10am–6pm; separate Reading Room on Esplanade Mon–Fri 9am–2pm, Sat & Sun 10am–6pm; free). Presented to Warren Hastings by Mir Jafar, the building's original simplicity was enhanced by double columns and the sweeping staircase that leads to the Durbar Hall. When the capital shifted to Delhi, this library was left behind; today it houses a huge and extensive collection of books, periodicals and reference material, as well as rare documents in an air-conditioned chamber.

Half a kilometre south, Alipore's immaculate **Horticultural Gardens** cherish a wide assortment of plants and flowers (Sun–Tues 6–10am & 2–5pm; Rs0.50). The flower show here at the start of February is well worth a visit.

Kalighat

Calcutta's most important temple, **Kalighat**, stands at the centre of a congested area 5km south of Park Street along Ashutosh Mukherjee Rd, an extension of Jawaharlal Nehru Rd. This plain but typically Bengali structure, built of brick and mortar in 1809 but capturing the sweeping curves of a thatched roof, is dedicated to Kali, the black goddess and form of Shakti. According to legend, Shiva went into a frenzy after the death of his wife Sati, dancing with her dead body and making the whole world tremble. The gods had attempted to stop him in various ways before Vishnu took his solar discus and chopped the disintegrating corpse into 51 bits. The spot where each piece fell became a *pitha*, or pilgrimage site, for worshippers of the female principle of divinity – Shakti. The shrine here marks where her little toe fell.

The temple is open all hours, and always a frenzied hive of activity. Unless you manage to leave your shoes yourself at the entrance, priests grab hold of them and whisk you downstairs to confront the dramatic monolithic image of the terrible goddess in the basement, with her huge eyes and bloody tongue.

The courtyard beyond the main congregational hall is used for sacrificing goats, especially during festivals such as Durga Puja and Kali Puja; supposedly, humans were formerly sacrificed here to appease the fertility goddess. To the north of the compound, a *lingam* is worshipped by women praying for children, while shops all around cater to pilgrims. Nirmal Hriday, Mother Teresa's home for the destitute and dying, is nearby.

MOTHER TERESA

Mother Teresa, Calcutta's most famous citizen, was born Agnes Gonxha Bojaxhiu to Albanian parents in 1910, and grew up in Skopje in Yugoslavia. After joining the Sisters of Loreto, an Irish order, she was sent as a teacher to Darjeeling, where she took her vows in May 1931 and became Teresa. In her work at St Mary's School in Calcutta, she became aware of the incredible poverty around her; in 1948, with permission from Rome, she put aside her nun's habit to clothe herself in the simple blue-bordered white *sari* that became the uniform of the **Missionaries of Charity**.

The best known of their many homes and clinics is Nirmal Hriday, a hospice for destitutes. In the face of local resistance, Mother Teresa chose its site at Kalighat – Calcutta's most important centre of Hinduism – in the knowledge that many of the poor specifically come here to die, next to a holy *tirtha* or crossing-place. Mother Teresa's simple piety and single-minded devotion to the poor, have won her international acclaim, including the Nobel Peace Prize in 1979.

In principle Mother Teresa relies on charity and voluntary work. If you're interested, contact the Missionaries of Charity at Mother House, 54A Lower Circular Rd. However, they do occasionally have to turn casual volunteers away; it's not always possible to make constructive use of all the would-be helpers who arrive unannounced.

KALIGHAT PAINTINGS

Early in the nineteenth century, Kalighat was in its heyday, drawing pilgrims, merchants and artisans from all over the country. Among them were the **scroll painters** from elsewhere in Bengal, who developed the distinctive style now known as **Kalighat Pats** (paintings). Adapting western techniques, they used paper and water-based paints instead of tempera, and gradually moved away from religious themes to depict contemporary subjects. By 1850, Kalighat *pats* had taken on a dynamic new direction, satirizing the middle classes in much the same way as today's political cartoons. As a result, their work serves as a witty record of the period, filled with images of everyday life. Kalighat *pats* can now be found in galleries and museums around the world, and in the Birla Academy here in Calcutta (see below).

Ballygunge and the Lakes

At the junction of Gurusaday Rd and Gariahat Rd, 4km southeast of Park St, the **Birla Industrial and Technological Museum** (daily except Mon; Rs1) is dedicated to Indian technology. Its large pleasant galleries set out to attract children in particular, with working models such as miniature mining scenes.

Turning left from Gurusaday Rd on to Gariahat Rd, past Calcutta Cricket Club, brings you to the huge unfinished **Lakshmi Narayan Temple**, also known as the Birla temple after its benefactors. Covered with bamboo scaffolding, the temple is designed on the model of the Lingaraj Temple at Bhubaneshwar in Orissa. Work has continued for over twenty years; it is said that according to a prophesy, the Birla family will meet with disaster if the air-conditioned monstrosity is ever finished.

Three kilometres south are the Bengali market of **Gariahat** and the **Gariahat Mor** intersection, whose pavement stalls are packed with shoppers in the evenings browsing through piles of *kurta pyjama*, traditional Bengali cotton *saris*, and contemporary clothing. The road to grassy **Gol Park**, set in the middle of the road 400m further south, is lined with vendors selling secondhand books and comics. From here, a road branches southeast to Dhakuria, and the tree-lined Southern Avenue leads along the side of the **Dhakuria Lakes**, now also known as **Rabindra Sarobar**. These man-made lakes, with their tree-lined walkways, are the base of Calcutta's flourishing rowing clubs. There's a rather dirty open-air public swimming area.

A multi-storeyed building on Southern Avenue houses the **Birla Academy of Art and Culture**, also funded by the industrial Birla family (daily except Mon 3.30pm–8pm; Rs0.50). Its small auditorium puts on concerts and theatre, while galleries hold exhibitions of contemporary art, plus an eclectic collection of Indian art through the ages covering folk art, bronzes, stone sculptures, terracotta, miniatures, textiles and Kalighat paintings. Among artists of the Bengali Renaissance represented here are the trio of Tagores – Rabindranath, Abanindranath and Gaganendranath. In addition, there are Indian classical dance classes and art classes. The **Lake Kali Bari** alongside has grown in three decades from a small Kali shrine to a major temple.

Accommodation

As soon as you arrive in Calcutta, taxi and rickshaw drivers are likely to assume that you'll be heading for the central **Sudder Street** area, next to New Market, which abounds in small and mid-sized hotels to suit short-stay overseas travellers. In fact, many visitors spend all their time in this one enclave. However, the city's very top hotels are slightly further afield; the beautifully maintained *Oberoi Grand*, Calcutta's answer to the *Raffles* of Singapore, is around the corner on Chowringhee, and the luxurious *Taj Bengal* is in Alipore to the south.

ACCOMMODATION PRICE CODES

All **accommodation prices** in this book have been coded using the symbols below. In principle the prices given are for the least expensive double rooms in each establishment; however, some hotels, usually in category ①, offer rates per bed rather than per room. Local taxes are not included unless specifically stated. For more details, see p.34.

①	up to Rs100	④	Rs225–350	⑦	Rs750–1200
②	Rs100–150	⑤	Rs350–500	⑧	Rs1200–2200
③	Rs150–225	⑥	Rs500–750	⑨	Rs2200 and up

The many **guest houses** now on offer all over Calcutta – usually comfortable private houses or flats, with the use of a "cook-cum-bearer" – provide mid-budget travellers with an alternative to Sudder Street. Be sure to clarify the food arrangements and all costs at the start of your stay. *The Guest* agency, a division of *Travel & Cargo Service*, 23 Shakespeare Sarani (☎47 9991), represents guest houses throughout the city.

Finally, well-heeled travellers might like to consider a stay in one of Calcutta's exclusive **clubs**. The only one to accept paying guests without a vetting procedure is the *Tollygunge Club*, at the southern end of the Metro line at 120 Deshapran Sasmal Rd (postcode Calcutta 700033; ☎46 3141; fax 74 1923; ⑥–⑧). Temporary membership gets you the use of an eighteen-hole golf course, plus riding, swimming, tennis and squash facilities, as well as open-air and indoor restaurants and a good bar. Contact the Secretary well in advance to reserve a room. If you're the kind of person who knows how to pull a few strings, you could also try the *Bengal Club*, 1-1 Russel St (☎29 9233; ⑧), still the meeting place for Calcutta's elite with its strict dress codes. Comfortable with an exclusive dining room, a Chinese restaurant and pastry shop.

Sudder Street area

Astoria, 6-2-3 Sudder St (☎244 9679). Rambling old hotel with large rooms tucked away in the crowded eastern end of the street. Facilities include inexpensive room service. ⑥–⑦.

Classic, 6-1A Kyd St, beside Dunlop House (☎29 7390). A stop-gap hotel, where the rooms tend to be quite small with low ceilings, but are moderately clean. ③–④.

Fairlawn, 13A Sudder St (☎43 1510). Landmark hotel, thankfully back on its feet again, and exuding all the charm of the Raj under the watchful eyes of Mr & Mrs Smith. If you enjoy old-world ambience and tea on the lawn, this is Sudder St's best place to stay. Room rates include meals. ⑦.

Hilson, 4 Sudder St (☎44 1864). One of several similar run-of-the-mill places on the street. ③.

Lytton, 14 Sudder St (☎29 1872). Completely re-built into a large modern and comfortable hotel with central a/c, TV etc. Facilities include a bar and restaurants. ⑦.

Modern Lodge, 1 Stuart Lane (☎247 4960). Cramped but reasonably priced accommodation, popular with budget travellers since the Sixties. The roof terrace gets lively in the evenings. ①–②.

Palace, 13 Chowringhee Lane (☎244 6214). Old dilapidated building in need of a spring clean, but a reliable fall-back if everywhere else is booked up. ②.

Paragon, 2 Stuart Lane (☎ 247 2445). Justifiably popular with budget travellers, it includes a dormitory and a pleasant courtyard cafe. Rooms downstairs languish in darkness. ②.

Paramount, 33-4 Free School St (☎29 4295). Close to Sudder St, reasonable and clean rooms all with attached baths and hot water by the bucket. A restaurant serves Indian and Chinese food. ③.

Salvation Army Red Shield Guest House, 2 Sudder St (☎24 2895). Good budget option, near the Museum, which is often booked up and has changed little over the years. Dorms and a few double rooms; passing through its large gate is a welcome relief from the noise and pollution outside. ①.

Shilton, 5A Sudder St (☎245 1512). Large old building set behind a gateway. The rooms are pleasant enough. Breakfast is available, and food can be arranged but no restaurant as such. ②.

Times Guest House, Sudder St, near *Blue Sky Cafe*. Small, friendly Sikh-run place with a dorm and a few double rooms. ①–③.

YMCA, 25 J Nehru Rd (☎29 2192). Large, rambling, depressing establishment near the Indian Museum – popular for long-term stays, with table tennis and a well-kept snooker table. ③–⑤.

YMCA, opposite *Lotus Cinema*, 42 SN Banerjee Rd (☎244 3814). Cheap rooms and a dorm. ②.

Elsewhere in the city

Astor, 15 Shakespeare Sarani (☎242 9950). Large Victorian house converted into a hotel, with popular garden restaurant and bar. ⑦.

Central Guest House, 18 Prafulla Sarkar St (☎27 4876). Assorted reasonable rooms near BBD Bagh. ③–④.

Chowringhee, 1 J Nehru Rd (☎28 7905). At the heart of the action, at the busy Esplanade-Dharamtala crossing. Moderate-sized and reasonably comfortable rooms, and a restaurant. ②–③.

Eastern Railway Yatri Niwas, Howrah Station (☎60 1742). New place ranging from dorms to a/c suites, for travellers with valid long-distance or upper-class rail tickets only. 1-night maximum. ①–④.

Great Eastern, 1-3 Old Court House St (☎28 2311). Famous old hotel near BBD Bagh – as used by Mark Twain – where the marble floors and wood-panelled corridors have seen better days. ⑤–⑧.

Hindusthan International, 235-1 AJC Bose Rd (☎247 2394). Comfortable business hotel with indifferent service. An arcade with shops and travel services, plus an *Indian Airlines* office, restaurants and a swimming pool open to the public for a fee. Vastly overpriced in dollars. ⑧.

ITDC Airport Ashok, Calcutta Airport (☎57 5111). Handy for the airport but not the town; large featureless government-run luxury hotel with a health club and swimming pool. ⑧.

Kenilworth, 1 & 2 Little Russel St (☎22 8394). Comfortable and plush place, consisting of an overpriced old block and a better-value new one, plus a bar, a restaurant and a pleasant garden. ⑧.

Oberoi Grand, 15 J Nehru Rd (☎29 2323). Completely revamped central hotel, part of the fabric of the city, whose white Victorian facade harks right back to the Raj. Very luxurious. ⑨.

Old Kenilworth, 7 Little Russel St (☎242 5325). Rambling and somewhat run-down old-world hotel – the original *Kenilworth*. Run by the eccentric Mrs Purdy. Full of character but overpriced. ⑦.

Park, 17 Park St (☎29 7336). Undistinguished modern hotel in a good location at the head of a cosmopolitan street, with all amenities and good food at hand. Comfortable but overpriced. ⑧.

Quality Inn, 12 J Nehru Rd (☎243 0222). Once the *Ritz*, now reopened after a strike closed it for years. Its shiny granite and marble interior has a very upmarket Bengali feel. ⑧.

Ramakrishna Mission Institute Guest House, Gol Park. Beautifully maintained high-ceilinged rooms overlooking a courtyard – comfortable if not luxurious, and intended for visiting scholars on medium-term lets. This is a religious institution, so smoking, alcohol and noise are not tolerated. ③.

Taj Bengal, 24B Belvedere Rd, Alipore (☎28 3939). New showpiece hotel, attempting to amalgamate Bengali culture with the usual *Taj* grandeur. Excellent Chinese and Indian restaurants. ⑨.

Youth Hostel, 10 Ananda Dutta Lane, near *Shamasri Cinema*, Howrah (☎67 2869). Dingy dorms. ①.

YWCA, Middleton Row (☎29 0260). For women who plan to stay in town a while, there is no better place. Just off Park St, it is built around a pleasant courtyard with an immaculate tennis court. Minimum stay is one week and meals are included. Under Rs1000 per week! ②.

Eating and drinking

Although Calcuttans love to **dine out**, they don't as a rule go out to eat their own food, so traditional Bengali cooking is generally restricted to the home. Chinese cuisine, available in areas such as Tangra on the road to the airport, is much the most popular option, though rich Muslim cooking can be sampled at places like the *Royal*, and Tibetan cafes fill the area around the Rabindra Sadan Metro. The most cosmopolitan strip of the city for bars and restaurants is the western end of **Park Street**, where incongruous names such as *Blue Fox* and *Moulin Rouge* date back to the street's role in the 1960s and 1970s as host to a small but thriving pop and jazz scene. Restaurants and cafes around Sudder Street cater to western travellers staying in the local hotels.

New Market and Sudder Street

Abdul Khalique, Marquis St. Cheap Muslim cafe near the corner of Stuart Lane, serving good *kati* and egg rolls.

Blue Sky Cafe, Sudder St. Halfway down the strip, a haunt of budget travellers who stumble in for breakfasts of curd and fruit, porridge, burgers and milk shakes.

Friends Home, Chowringhee Centre, opposite *Lighthouse Cinema*. Indian food and sweets.

How Hua, 10 Mirza Ghalib St. Good Chinese food with an interesting regional menu. Closed Tues.

Kathleen's, 12 Mirza Ghalib St. Around the corner from Sudder St – good for *tandoori* food, ice creams, teas and cold beer. They also have a popular bakery and patisserie. Closed Thurs.

Khalsa, Madge Lane. Simple but long-popular *dhaba* serving basic cheap food.

Nahoum & Sons, F20 New Market (☎44 3033). Fruitcake, *chola* (Jewish braided bread), cheese straws, chicken patties, bagels and cream cheese – evidence of the dwindling Jewish presence.

Nizam's, 22–25 Hogg Market. Legendary if somewhat faded place behind New Market to the north, which specializes in the *kati roll*. These spicey *sheekh kebabs*, rolled into a *paratha* of white flour, are now sold throughout the city. Take away or eat in cubicles around the central halls.

Oasis, 2 Madge Lane. Small a/c multi-cuisine restaurant between Sudder St and New Market. A good breakfast menu includes sausage and mash. Closed Thurs.

Ruchika's, Chowringhee Centre, opposite *New Empire Cinema*. Snacks and ice cream, as well as south Indian food.

Zaranj, 26 J Nehru Rd (at Sudder St) (☎29 9744). Part of the same excellent chain as the *Amber*, some feel it is even better. Upmarket and plush, specializing in North West Frontier food.

Around Park Street

Bar-B-Q, 43 Park St. Good Chinese food in nice surroundings, and a bar downstairs. Closed Thurs.

Blue Fox, 55 Park St. Once the leading jazz venue in town, it now keeps changing identity. Currently it's a restaurant-cum-bar serving a range of cuisine.

Flury's, 18 Park St. Calcutta landmark, on the corner with Middleton Row. Good for tea, cakes and Swiss pastries – try the rum balls. They also make their own chocolates. Closed Mon.

Guptas, 18B Park St, on the corner with Mirza Ghalib St. Highly recommended Indian food.

Kwality, 17 Park St. Comfortable, plush and airy, one of Park St's best restaurants, with a range of food as well as ice creams. Also serves alcohol. Closed Thurs.

Oasis, 33 Park St (☎44 6424). Similar to the 2 Madge Lane branch; see above. Closed Thurs.

Olympia, 21 Park St. A legend as a bar, it also serves good steak in the family restaurant upstairs.

Skyroom, 57 Park St. Cramped but pleasant place, retains the reputation for fine western cuisine that once made it the best "east of Suez". Look for the prawn cocktails, chicken kiev or smoked local fish. No alcohol served – a plus point in this often rowdy street. Book in advance. Closed Tues.

Tandoor, 43 Park St. As the name suggests, it specializes in *tandoori* food, but it isn't in the same league as *Amber*. Closed Wed.

Trinca's, 17B Park St. Multi-cuisine restaurant, strong on western food, with a bar. Once a popular night spot, it's now a bit faded, but still puts on occasional live music at a premium.

South Calcutta

The Dhaba, Ballygunge Phari. Sikh-run cafe, where the core menu of good Punjabi cooking in the mid-range restaurant upstairs has been extended to cover middle-class tastes. Recommended.

Hamro Momo, Suburban Hospital Rd (lane off Chowringhee, opposite Rabindra Sadan Metro). One of a handful of good Tibetan food cafes on this street.

Kim Wah, Garcha Rd, Ballygunge. Small but good Chinese restaurant.

Lazeez, Shambhu Nath Pandit St, Bhowanipur. Comfortable if pricey, and good for both Indian and western cooking.

Momo Plaza, 2A Suburban Hospital Rd (☎247 8250). One of a handful of good Tibetan cafes, this one specializes in *shyabhaley* – large flat *momos*.

Prema Villas, Lake Market, off Rashbehari Ave. Genuine south Indian local cafe near the Lakes, serving excellent milky coffee.

Radhu's, Lake Market. Snack bar serving fried fish and Bengali *alu dam* (steamed spicy potatoes).

Tibetan Delights, Suburban Hospital Rd. Down a lane just off the road, similar to *Momo Plaza* but with better ambience. Chicken *momos* are popular.

Elsewhere in the city

Amber, 11 Waterloo St (☎28 3477). Legendary restaurant serving absolutely superb Mughlai and *tandoori* cooking. Plush and dimly lit, it covers three floors, and has a bar downstairs.

Anand, 19 Chittaranjan Ave. South Indian snacks as well as veggie burgers and milk shakes.

Chung Wah, Chittaranjan Ave. Chinese food in authentic but faded splendour.

India Coffee House, College St. Atmospheric historic cafe in the heart of the university area where students and intellectuals continue to meet and debate in faded surroundings.

Jimmy's Kitchen, AJC Bose Rd and Shakespeare Sarani crossing. Justifiably popular Chinese restaurant with specialities like mandarin fish.

Jyoti Vihar, 3A Ho Chi Minh Sarani. Inexpensive and deservedly popular a/c south Indian cafe near the US consulate, which gets packed at lunch time.

Kim Fa, 9 South Tangra Rd. One of Tangra's best Chinese cafes – Thai soup and chili king prawns.

Kim Ling, South Tangra Rd. Good family-run restaurant – try the honey chicken, or the chicken with black mushrooms and baby corn.

Mandarin, 217 Lansdowne Rd. Popular and dimly lit Chinese restaurant with reasonable food.

Royal, near Nakhoda Masjid, Rabindra Sarani. Legendary restaurant serving excellent Muslim cuisine. Renowned for its *chanp* – a derivative of chop but cooked with spices and delicious with *rumali roti*, the super thin "kerchief" bread. The *biryanis* are highly recommended.

Sabir's, Chandni Chowk. Traditional, tasty but very rich Muslim restaurant behind the market. Try their *razala* – an aromatic meat curry.

Scoop, 71 Strand Rd, Man-o-War Jetty. Pleasant riverside location which gets crowded in the evenings. Renowned for its ice creams, it also serves pizzas.

Sin Fa, South Tangra Rd. Another recommended family-run Chinese restaurant.

Suruchi, 89 Elliot Rd. Run by a charity – the All Bengal Women's Union – and one of the few places you can sample authentic Bengali cooking. Unpretentious atmosphere, and very reasonable prices. Look out for *macher jhol* (fish stew). Highly recommended. Closed Sat and Sun pm.

Vineet, 1 Shakespeare Sarani. In the basement of the AC Market shopping complex – mid-priced vegetarian food plus snacks and ice cream. Occasional live Hindi popular music.

Hotel restaurants

Astor, 15 Shakespeare Sarani (☎242 9950). This small hotel has a bar and several restaurants including the multi-cuisine *Serai* and the *Banyan Tree* serving Bengali food, but the best is *Kebab-e-Que* in the garden, which serves excellent *tandoori* food.

Fairlawn, 13A Sudder St (☎43 1510). Soak in the fossilized Raj atmosphere with tea on the lawn.

Lytton, 14 Sudder St (☎29 1872). Along with a bar, the hotel has two good restaurants including the *Dynasty* serving Chinese food and *Gaylords* serving Indian and western.

Oberoi Grand, 15 J Nehru Rd (☎29 2323). *La Rotisserie* offers western cuisine, there's *tandoori* and Mughlai cooking in the *Moghul Room*, and the *Ming Court* for Chinese food.

Park, 17 Park St (☎29 7336). The new *Zen* is an "oriental" restaurant serving dishes from China, Burma, Thailand and Indonesia.

Quality Inn, 12 J Nehru Rd (☎243 0222). Among its eating and drinking places is *Ahdee*, one of the few restaurants in town to serve genuine Bengali cuisine.

Taj Bengal, 24B Belvedere Rd, Alipore (☎28 3939). Smart and beautifully presented, the *Chinoiserie* offers some of Calcutta's best Chinese food; *Sonargaon* (Bengali for Golden Town) serves local delicacies and north Indian food; the *Coffee Shop* is open all hours and also serves meals; and the pool-side barbecue prepares kebabs and griddle-based dishes.

Sweet shops

Milk-based sweets such as the small and dry *sandesh* are the speciality of Bengal. Though confections such as the white *rosogulla*, the brown (deep-fried) *pantua* and the distinctive black *kalojam*, all in syrup, are found elsewhere in north India, they are nowhere as good as in Calcutta. Try also *lal doi* – a delicious red yoghurt made with jaggery – or plain white *mishti doi* made with sugar. Sweet shops often serve savoury snacks in the afternoons such as *nimki* (literally salty), deep-fried light pastry strips, *shingara*, a delicate Bengali *samosa*, and *dal puri*, *paratha*-like bread made with lentils.

Ganguram, 46C J Nehru Rd. Legendary sweet shop near Victoria Memorial.

Girish Chandra Dey, 167N Rashbehari Ave. One of several good shops in the Gariahat area.

Jadav Chandra Das, 127A Rashbehari Ave. Another popular outlet in Gariahat.

KC Das, 11 Esplanade East and 1/433 Gariahat Rd. One of the city's most famous sweet shops.

Sen Mahasay, 171H Rashbehari Ave. Next to Gariahat Market, renowned for its *sandesh*.

Bars

Most of Calcutta's **bars** exude a tense all-male atmosphere; only the *Olympia* is a bit more welcoming. The obvious places to escape all that are the big hotels.

Amber, 11 Waterloo St. On the ground floor of a superb restaurant, with strong a/c and low lights.

Ashoka, 3B J Nehru Rd. Adjacent to Esplanade, and good for a cold beer.

Chowringhee Bar, *Oberoi Grand*, J Nehru Rd. Plush and well presented but pricey.

Esplanade, *Taj Bengal*, Alipore. Luxurious surroundings and an escape from the noise and grime of the city, but expensive.

New Central, 99 Chittaranjan Ave. Dour central Calcutta bar – good for a cold beer.

Olympia, 21 Park St. Renowned address, with a legendary (albeit dead) clientele. Basic marble-floored downstairs bar, more comfortable "family room" upstairs. Also renowned for its steaks.

Peter Cat, 18 Park St. Bar attached to a good kebab restaurant. Closed Thurs.

Shenaz, 2A Middleton Row. Plush, dimly lit a/c place just off Park St.

Tippu Sultan Bar, Tollygunge Club. Grand colonial atmosphere, in the shade of large trees and surrounded by a golf course. For temporary membership contact the Secretary (see p.746).

Culture and entertainment

Calcutta's lively arts scene is especially well known for its **music** and Bengali **theatre**. A handful of galleries hold regular exhibitions of fine art, and the cultural centres of the various consulates (listed on p.755) also play an important role in the life of the city. Of the many non-religious festivals each year, the new **Ganga Utsav**, held over a few weeks around the end of January at Diamond Harbour, involves music, dance and theatrical events.

Music

Calcuttan **music** audiences have a reputation as the most discerning in the country. The main concert season is winter and spring, with the huge week-long **Dover Lane Music Festival**, held under a marquee in south Calcutta around the end of January and early February, attracting many of India's best musicians. Other festivals to look out for include the **Hafiz Ali Khan Music Festival** and the **Sadarang Music Conference**, usually held indoors in halls such as *Kala Bhavan* or *Rabindra Sadan* which also host regular performances of both north Indian and Karnatik (south Indian) classical music and dance.

Sangeet Research Academy, near Tollygunge Metro Station, is one of India's leading north Indian classical music research institutes. It offers long-term courses in various music forms and holds free Wednesday-evening concerts. **All India Radio Calcutta** is a good source for Indian classical music, folk music and Rabindra Sangit, the songs of Rabindranath Tagore. There is also a small but thriving western classical music scene, with concerts at the **Calcutta Music School**, in Sunny Park, and the **Calcutta Jazz Festival** held sometimes in spring has been known to attract big names.

THE FESTIVALS OF CALCUTTA

Most of Calcutta's Hindu **festivals** are devoted to forms of the mother goddess, **Shakti**. As one of the last centres of north Indian Buddhism, Bengal reflects a unique blend of traditions; **tantric** Hinduism, closely related to Mahayana Buddhism, continues to be evident in the devotion to mysterious deities such as **Tara** (see p.725 and p.764). Calcutta's own deity, the black goddess **Kali**, is an emanation of **Durga**, the consort of Shiva. Kali is depicted with four arms, standing on the prostrate Shiva after killing the demon Raktviya. This gory image conveys a simple truth. Her left top hand holds a bloody sickle, and the bottom a severed head; together they signify complete self-sacrifice to the truth; her right top hand, raised with its palm open, signifies fearlessness, which leads to deliverance shown by the bottom hand. Kali stands on Shiva, the female upon the male.

The two-week **Durga Puja** (Oct/Nov) is the most lavish festival of all. A symbol of victory, **Durga**, wife of Shiva, is shown with ten arms slaying the demon Mahisasura, who assumed the shape of a buffalo and threatened the gods. Durga either sits on a lion, or is accompanied by one. Other *pujas* honour **Lakshmi**, the goddess of wealth, whose festival falls in autumn, and **Saraswati**, the goddess of the arts and learning, who is shown as a beautiful fair woman sitting on a lotus playing a *sitar*.

During the festivals, images of straw, papier-mâché, or *sola pith*, originally moulded as voluptuous women with large rounded breasts and physical detail, then clothed and deco- rated, are carried in noisy procession to makeshift altars called *pandals*. Supported by donations from businesses and local residents, *pandals* often block off small streets and blare popular music through distorting loudspeakers. Competition between *pandals* can lead to street fights, when the image is taken for immersion to the river after *puja*.

Ganga Sagar (mid-Jan) During the winter solstice of Makar Sankranti, hundreds of thousands of Hindu pilgrims travel through Calcutta for a 3-day festival at Sagar Dwip, 150km south at the mouth of the Hooghly where the Ganga meets the sea. Many of the *sadhus* drawn to the *mela* stay at the Shiva temple at Nimtolla Ghat, north of Howrah Bridge. After the *mela* is over, wandering Baul minstrels meet to make music in the Baul Mela at Joydeb near Shantiniketan.

Saraswati Puja (Jan/Feb) Important *pandal* festival to the goddess of learning, celebrated throughout the city.

Chinese New Year (Jan/Feb) Celebrated with a week-long festival of dragon dances, firecrackers and fine food, concentrated around the borough of Tangrak.

Shivratri (late Feb) The nationwide Shiva festival is celebrated all over the city.

Bakrid (Feb/March) Large parts of the Maidan are converted into a gigantic prayer ground when thousands of Muslims pray at the end of Ramadan. Id ul-Fitr is celebrated with feasting in Muslim restaurants.

Dol Purnima or **Holi** (Feb/March) The spring festival, when anyone foolhardy enough to venture is liable to be splashed and powdered in bright colours, is especially popular with Calcutta's Biharis.

Muharram (May/June) Shi'ite Muslims mark the anniversary of the martyrdom of Hussein by severe penance including proces- sions where they flagellate themselves.

Rath Yatra (June/July) The chariot festival, heralding the monsoon, honours Jagganath, the Lord of the World. In Calcutta, festivities are organized by ISKCON.

Vishvakarma Puja (Sept) Dedicated to the God of Creation; craftsmen and artists deco- rate their tools with images of the deity.

Durga Puja (Oct/Nov) At the onset of winter, Durga Puja is very much the Bengali equivalent of Christmas. It climaxes on Mahadashami, the tenth day, when images are taken to the river for immersion. Elsewhere, the festival is known as Dussehra.

Lakshmi Puja (Oct/Nov) Held five days after Mahadashami on the full moon, to honour the goddess of wealth.

Kali Puja (Oct/Nov) Two weeks after Lakshmi Puja, Kali Puja is held on a moonless night when goats are sacrificed. Kali Puja coincides with Diwali, the festival of light.

Christmas (Dec 25) Confined to the more cosmopolitan districts and Christian areas. Park Street and the New Market are adorned with fairy lights and the odd Christmas tree. Plum pudding is sold at confectioners, and midnight mass is well attended.

Posh Mela (late Dec) Held in Shantiniketan just after Christmas, the *mela* attracts Bauls, the wandering minstrels who perform to large audiences (too large for some tastes).

Cinemas

Cinemas that show English-language films three or four times each day can be found along Jawaharlal Nehru Road near Esplanade and New Market. All are air-conditioned; some, like the *Lighthouse* on Humayan Place, are fine examples of art deco.Names to look for include *Elite*, SN Banerjee Rd; *Globe*, Lindsay St; *Metro*, J Nehru Rd; and *Minerva*, Chowringhee Place. *Nandan*, behind Rabindra Sadan on AJC Bose Rd, is the city's leading "art-house" cinema.

Galleries

Bengal has a proud and lively tradition of contemporary art, with its few galleries showing a high standard of work.

Academy of Fine Arts, Cathedral Rd. Showplace for local artists and venue for international exhibitions of contemporary art.

Arts Acre, Kaikhali, Dum Dum (City office: 37C College Row (☎31 1372). A bit far from the centre, but a new and exciting venue for exhibitions on themesranging from pottery to painting.

Birla Academy of Art & Culture, Southern Ave (☎46 7843). Exhibitions of visiting artists.

CIMA (Centre of International Modern Art), 2nd Floor, Sunny Towers, 43 Ashutosh Chowdhury Ave. New and prestigious Ballygunge gallery, showing work by contemporary artists.

Gallery Katayun, Jassal House, Auckland Square. Close to Lower Circular Rd and the Rawdon St crossing with frequent exhibitions of contemporary artists.

Sports and swimming

Calcuttans are keenly interested in sports. **Football** matches, especially those between the two leading clubs, Mohan Bagan and East Bengal, and **cricket** test matches draw huge crowds. There are two major stadium complexes, the **Ranji Stadium** at Eden Gardens and the new **Salt Lake Stadium** on the edge of the city.

The **Maidan**, home to the *Calcutta Bowling Club* and the *Ladies Golf Club*, is a favourite venue for impromptu cricket and football matches, and the scene in winter and spring of regular race meetings. These are run by the *Calcutta Turf Club*, and bets can also be placed at their premises on Russell Street. Also in winter, army teams play **polo** at the grounds at the centre of the race course.

The easiest **swimming pool** for visitors to use is at the *Hindusthan Hotel*, 235-1 AJC Bose Rd (☎247 2394), which charges non-residents around Rs60 per day .

Across the road from the superbly equipped **Tollygunge Club**, where with the right connections you might get to use the pool and tennis courts, the elite *Royal Calcutta Golf Club* is the world's second oldest **golf** club, after St Andrews in Scotland.

Shopping

Unlike Delhi, Calcutta is not geared towards tourism – a fact which is reflected, with one or two exceptions, by its **shops**. However, it does hold many characterful **markets**, including the wide-ranging New Market (see p.735), and local institutions such as Gariahat in the south (see p.745) and Barabazaar to the north (see p.740).

Among typical Bengali handicrafts to look out for are metal *dokra* items from the Shantiniketan region northwest of the city, in which objects such as animals and birds are roughly cast by a lost-wax process to give them a rough, wiry look. Long-necked, pointy-eared terracotta horses from Bankura, in all sizes, have become something of a cliché. *Kantha* fabrics display delicate line stitching in decorative patterns, while Bengali **leatherwork** features simple patterns dyed in subtle colours.

Emporia

Good selections of most handicrafts, including lace, can be found in various **state emporia**, many of which are located in the large **Dakhsinapan** shopping complex south of Dhakuria Bridge near Gol Park. Offering fixed (if slightly high) prices, these are the simplest places to start shopping.

Aavishkar, 20K Park St (☎29 6294). Popular shop on the corner with Middleton Row, stocking stationery and cards, music, pottery by local artists, and garden-fresh Darjeeling and Assam teas.

Assam, 8 Russell St. As part of Assam House, the emporium sells handicraft and textiles from Assam including fabrics in *pat* and *moga*, two techniques of silk manufacturing.

Bengal Home Industries, officially 57 J Nehru Rd but just around the corner on AJC Bose Rd. Very strong on furnishings and fabrics, plus Bengali handicrafts including terracotta.

Central Cottage Industries, 7 J Nehru Rd, Esplanade. Part of the national chain, selling handicrafts from all over India. Along with fabrics, leather, papier-mâché from Kashmir and furnishings, there is a small but interesting collection of silver jewellery, with some tribal bracelets.

Gujari, Dakhsinapan complex, near Gol Park. A stand-out selection of Gujarati textiles, including handloom and mirrored cushion covers.

Kashmir Art, 12 J Nehru Rd. The usual Kashmiri handicrafts, including carpets and rugs.

Nagaland, 13 Shakespeare Sarani. A fine assortment of Naga shawls, with red bands and white and blue stripes on black backgrounds. As with Scots tartan, certain patterns denote particular tribes.

Orissa Handicrafts, Dakhsinapan complex, near Gol Park. Very strong on silk.

Books

College Street with its street vendors and small bookshops has long been the prime hunting ground for book collectors. The month-long **Calcutta Book Fair**, held on the Maidan near Park Street in January and February, is now among the biggest of its kind in the country, and provides a good opportunity to pick up books at a discount.

Bookmark, 56D Mirza Ghalib St. A selection of books upstairs.

Cambridge Book & Stationery, 20D Park St, Calcutta 700 016 (☎29 9017). Similar to the *Oxford Book & Stationery* and just as good.

Classical Books, Middleton Row. Small, friendly and well worth a browse.

Dey Bros, B47 New Market. One of several bookshops in this part of the market.

W Newman & Company, 3 Old Court House St, Calcutta 700 069 (☎28 9436). Bookshop and stationers neard BBD Bagh, which has been around for a long time – and it shows.

Oxford Book & Stationery, 17 Park St, Calcutta 700 016 (☎29 8509). A small but always interesting collection of maps, guides, fiction, stationery and postcards, plus coffee table books.

Objets d'art and antiques

Although Calcutta has surprisingly few antique shops, auction houses around Park Street deal with furniture and other objects. Along with the curios common to Tibetan shops, *Chamba Lama* in New Market occasionally has some interesting pieces.

Saroj, 3A Camac St, near Middleton Row (☎29 1002). Serious collectors' shop, with an interesting mixture of antique furniture and objets d'art, old prints, good reproductions and jewellery.

Terra-Cottal, 158/2A Prince Anwar Shah Rd. Art gallery and boutique near the lakes in south Calcutta. Jewellery, sculpted panels and terracotta tiles made; expensive but well worth seeking out.

Fabrics and clothing

Calcutta's dress sense, in general, is conservative, and the choice of ready-made garments is not very exciting. However, a wide range of fabrics is available, and all outlets should be able to point you towards a very good (and very cheap) **tailor**. At the Chinese-run shoe-shops along Chittaranjan Avenue, **shoes** can still be made to order.

Benetton, Park Mansions, 43 Park St. Although made in India, the standard *Benetton* line is good value, with jeans at a quarter of the price they sell for abroad.

Burlingtons, Park Mansions, 43 Park St. Long-established clothing boutique, specializing in up-market tailoring, supplying a range of fabrics. Ready-made garments are sold through a catalogue.

Good Companions, 13C Russell St. Upmarket fabric and clothes shop just off Park St.

Handloom House, 2 Lindsay St. Near New Market, a government-run shop with a wide range of textiles including cotton and raw silks at reasonable prices.

INTERNATIONAL AIRLINE OFFICES IN CALCUTTA

Aeroflot, 58 J Nehru Rd (☎242 3765).

Air Canada, 230A AJC Bose Rd (☎247 7783).

Air France, 41 J Nehru Rd (☎242 6161).

Air India, 50 J Nehru Rd (☎242 2356).

Air Lanka, 230A AJC Bose Rd (☎247 7783).

Alitalia, c/o *Jet Air*, 230A AJC Bose Rd (☎247 7394).

American Airlines, 2-7 Sarat Bose Rd, Vasundhara Building (☎75 1261).

Austria Airlines, c/o *Jet Air*, 230A AJC Bose Rd, (☎247 7783).

Balkan Airlines, *Stic Travels*, East Anglia House, 3C Camac St (☎29 4464).

Bangladesh Biman, 30A AJC Bose Rd (☎29 2844).

British Airways, 41 J Nehru Rd (☎29 3453).

Balkan Airlines, East Anglia House, 3C Camac St (☎29 2092).

Canadian Airlines, *IGAT*, Vasundhara, 2-7 Sarat Bose Rd (☎74 7622).

Canadian Pacific, *IGAT*, Vasundhara, 2-7 Sarat Bose Rd (☎75 0226).

Cathay Pacific, 1 Middleton St (☎40 32112).

Continental Airlines, 3C Camac St (☎29 2092).

Delta, 42 J Nehru Rd (☎247 5008).

Druk Air, 1A Ballygunge Circular Rd, 51 Tivoli Court (☎40 2090).

East West Airlines, 43 Park Mansions, Park St (☎29 9257).

Ethiopia Airlines, 230A A J C Bose Rd (☎247 5576).

Gulf Air, 230A AJC Bose Rd (☎247 7783).

Iberia Airlines, 230A AJC Bose Rd (☎247 4495).

Japan Airlines, 35A J Nehru Rd (☎29 8370).

KLM Royal Dutch Airlines, 1 Middleton St, Jeevan Deep (☎247 4593).

Kuwait Airlines, 230A AJC Bose Rd (☎247 7783).

Lot Polish, 230A AJC Bose Rd (☎247 4495).

Lufthansa Airlines, 30A/B J Nehru Rd (☎29 9365).

Malaysian Airlines, 3C Camac St (☎29 2092).

North West Airlines, 75C Park St (☎29 9218).

Qantas, *Hotel Hindustan International*, 235-1 Lower Circular Rd (☎247 0718).

Royal Jordanian Airlines, Vasundhara Building, 2-7 Sarat Bose Rd (☎75 1272).

Royal Nepal Airlines, 41 J Nehru Rd (☎29 8534).

SAS, 2-7 Sarat Bose Rd (☎74 7622-3).

Singapore Airlines, 18D Park St (☎29 9297).

Swiss Air, 46C J Nehru Rd (☎242 4643).

TWA, 230A A J C Bose Rd (☎247 5576).

Thai Airways International, 18G Park St (☎29 9846).

United Airlines, 2-7 Sarat Bose Rd (☎74 7622).

DOMESTIC AIRLINE OFFICES IN CALCUTTA

Indian Airlines, 39 Chittaranjan Ave, 012 (☎26 0730 or 26 3135).

Also at *Hotel Hindustan International*, 235/1 Lower Circular Rd, 020 (☎247 6606).

Citylink Airways, Suite 308, *Park Hotel*, 17 Park St (☎29 8254, 29 7337/8).

Damania Airways, 2-5 Sarat Bose Rd (☎475 6356).

Modiluft, Russell St (☎29 8437).

Sahara Indian Airlines, 227/2 AJC Bose Rd, Mangal Jyoti (☎247 2795).

Vayudoot, 28D Shakespeare Sarani (☎247 7062, or 40 5316).

Indian Silk House, AC Market, 1 Shakespeare Sarani. Lots of printed silks.

Karma Kutir, 32 Ballygunge Place. A good place to pick up traditional decorative *kantha* work.

Khadi Gramodyog, 28 Chittaranjan Ave. Huge warehouse-like shop selling handloom fabric; supposedly in the tradition of Mahatma Gandhi, but poorly kept and a real disappointment.

Kolhapuri Centre, Gariahat Rd, Ballygunge Phari. Dedicated to selling Kolhapuri sandals and shoes – painful at first, but very comfortable if you persist.

Louis Philippe, 33–34 Park Mansions, Park St. Manufactured in India under licence, a range of men's shirts from the international clothier.

Smartwear, Gariahat Rd, Gariahat Mor, Ballygunge. A long tradition of formal men's tailoring.

Musical instruments

In addition to having pieces for quick sale, master instrument-makers in Calcutta specialize in making instruments to order. Indian instruments bought in shops around the centre are invariably of inferior quality and may be beyond tuning; the shops along **Rabindra Sarani** (Chitpore Rd) are particularly mediocre. Calcutta must produce more *tabla* players than any other city; *tabla*-makers can be found at **Kalighat**, next to Kalighat Bridge and at **Keshab Sen St** off College St.

Braganza & Sons, 2A Marquis St. One of the best shops in the city for western instruments.

Hemen Roy & Sons, Rashbehari Ave, Triangular Park. Master *sarod*-makers, now manufacturing *sitars* and *tanburas* as well.

Hiren Roy & Sons, Rashbehari Ave, Gariahat. Hiren Roy, *sitar*-maker to Imrat Khan, Vilayat Khan, Ravi Shankar, and Nikhil Bannerjee, passed away recently, but his sons continue the tradition.

Listings

Ambulance Ambulance services are provided by *Dhanwantary Clinic*, 1 National Library Ave (☎45 6265) and *Emergency Doctors' Service*, A 165 Lake Gardens (☎46 6770).

Consulates *Bangladesh*, 9 Circus Ave (☎75 2795); *Britain*, 1 Ho Chi Minh Sarani (☎22 5171); *Czech Republic*, 7 Pretoria St (☎22 9419); *Denmark*, McLeod House, 3 Netaji Subhas Rd; *Finland*, Chitrakoot, 6th Floor, 230A A J C Bose Rd (☎247 4757); *France*, 26 Park Mansions (☎29 0978); *Germany*, 1 Hastings Park Rd (☎71 1141); *Greece*, c/o Stewarts & Lloyds of India, 41 J Nehru Rd (☎29 8104); *Indonesia*, 128 Rash Behari Ave (☎76 2297); *Italy*, 3 Raja Santosh Rd, Alipore (☎71 2426); *Japan*, 12 Pretoria St (☎22 2241); *Nepal*, 19 Woodlands, Sterndale Rd, Alipore (☎71 1117); *Netherlands*, 18A Brabourne Rd (☎25 1032); *Norway*, Chitrakoot, 6th Floor, 230A AJC Bose Rd (☎247 4757); *Philippines*, 14 Government Place East (☎428 1507); *Russian Federation*, 7 Alipore Ave (☎79 9973); *Singapore*, DBS Centre, Circular Court, 8 AJC Bose Rd (☎247 4990); *Spain*, c/o TIL Limited, 1 Taratolla Rd, Garden Reach (☎79 5954); *Sri Lanka*, Nicco House, 2 Hare St (☎28 5102); *Sweden*, 6 Poonam Building, 5/2 Russell St (☎29 3639); *Thailand*, 18B Mandeville Gardens (☎40 7836); *USA*, 5/1 Ho Chi Minh Sarani (☎22 3611).

Cultural centres Cultural representatives of overseas countries in Calcutta, typically with reading rooms and facilities for performances and film shows, include *Alliance Francaise*, 24 Park Mansions, Park St (☎29 8793); the *British Council*, 5 Shakespeare Sarani (☎22 5370); the Russian *Gorky Sadan*, Gorky Terrace, near Minto Park; and the German *Max Mueller Bhavan*, 8 Pramathesh Barua Sarani (☎75 9398). Similar facilities can be found at the *Ramakrishna Mission Institute of Culture* in Gol Park, and *USIS*, near Tata Building, J Nehru Rd. *Arts Acre*, 37C College Row at Kaikhali, near the airport (☎31 1372), is an artist's centre with studios, guest rooms and regular events.

Foreigners Registration & Income Tax *Foreigners Registration Office*, 237 AJC Bose Rd (☎47 3301). Apply here for visa extensions, as well as permits if you plan to go to the Andaman Islands by boat. *Tax Clearance*, Room 11, Income Tax Building, Bentinck St.

Government Hospitals Although cheap, government-run hospitals are notoriously mismanaged. *Calcutta Hospital & Medical Research Institute*, 7-2 Diamond Harbour Rd (☎45 3921); *Calcutta National Medical College & Hospital*, 24 Gorachand Rd (☎44 1012); *Medical College Hospital*, 88 College St (☎35 9252); *N R S Medical College & Hospital*, 138 Acharya JC Bose Rd (☎24 3213); *R G Kar Medical College & Hospital*, 1 Belgachia Rd (☎55 4311); *SSKM Hospital*, 244 Lower Circular Rd (☎44 9753).

Opticians *RC Ghose & Grandsons*, Gariahat Rd; *Himalaya Opticals*, 25 Camac St (☎40 2743); *Lawrence & Mayo*, 20E Park St (☎29 8310) and 11 Government Place East (☎248 1818; same-day delivery service); *Stephens Opticians*, 23 J Nehru Rd (☎29 1895).

Pharmacies *Blue Print*, 1 Old Court House St; *Dey's Medical Stores*, 20A Nelly Sengupta Sarani & 55 Gariahat Rd; *King & Co* (Homeopath), 29 Shyama Prasad Mukerjee Rd; *Singh & Roy*, 4-1 Sambhunath Pandit St (open daily, 24hr Wed–Sun); *Sterling & Co* (Homeopath), 91-C Elliot Rd; *Welmed*, 4-1 Sambhunath Pandit St (open daily, 24hr Mon & Tues).

For details of **flights** between Calcutta and **southeast Asia**, see p.7.

MOVING ON FROM CALCUTTA

By air

There is no central information system for flights from **Calcutta Airport** (see p.729); call the individual airlines listed on p.754 to confirm departure and arrival. Major domestic routes from Calcutta are summarized in the "West Bengal Travel Details" on p.725.

By rail

Ten 24hr numbers provide information on **train** connections: ☎20 3535 to 20 3544.

Making **reservations** to leave Calcutta by train is easy, with computerized booking offices throughout the city. Unless you really need to get on the tourist quota, have an Indrail Pass or want to pre-book tickets from other stations, you may well prefer not to brave the *Eastern Railways* office, off the northwest corner of BBD Bagh at 6 Fairlie Place (Mon–Sat 9am–1pm & 1.30–4pm, Sun & hols 9am–2pm; ☎22 2789 & 20 4025). The **Tourist Counter**, which gets very busy, is through the large gates next door to the main computerized booking counter. Reservations up to 60 days in advance, can be made for most trains out of the city and also for trains from other destinations; these latter should be confirmed as soon as possible after you get to the relevant city.

Other booking offices (same hours) include the *South Eastern Railway Booking & Information Centre*, Esplanade Mansions (opposite Raj Bhavan) (☎28 9530); *Booking Office for Eastern and South Eastern Railways*, Alexandra Court, 61 J Nehru Rd, Rabindra Sadan; *Howrah Station*, 1st Floor; *Computerized Booking Office*, 3 Koilaghat St (☎28 9494); *New Koilaghat*, 14 Strand Rd (☎23 4676); *Sealdah Station*, 1st Floor.

Among major trains departing from hectic **Howrah Station** are the a/c *Rajdhani Express* #2301 which covers the 1145km to **Delhi** in under 18hr, stopping at **Mughal Serai** (change for **Varanasi**), **Allahabad** and **Kanpur** en route. The *AC Express* #2381 (Tues, Wed & Sat) stops at **Gaya** and **Varanasi** on the way to Delhi; the *Kalka Mail* #2311 stops at Old Delhi before proceeding on to **Kalka** in Himachal Pradesh; and the *Doon Express* #3009 travels via Gaya, Varanasi and **Lucknow** to **Dehra Dun** and the UP Hills but is nearly always late. Trains through **Patna** include the *Amritsar Mail* #3005. For **Bombay**, 1968km southwest, the best trains are the *Gitanjali Express* #2860 which takes over 33hr and the slightly slower early-morning *Ispat Express* #8011. Going south, the *Puri Express* #8007 leaves in the evening and heads via **Bhubaneshwar** to arrive at **Puri** early in the morning; the *Howrah–Bhubaneshwar Dhauli Express* #2821 departs early in the morning and gets to Bhubaneshwar around 1.30pm; the *Coromandal Express* #2841 departs early afternoon and takes around 28hr to cover the 1663km to **Madras** via Bhubaneshwar.

Trains from **Sealdah** towards **Darjeeling** include the early-morning *Kanchenjunga Express* #2557, which pulls into **New Jalpaiguri** just too late in the evening to get by road to **Darjeeling** or **Gangtok**; it continues to **Guwahati**. The slower *Darjeeling Mail* #3143 leaves Sealdah at 7pm and arrives at NJP at 8.30am, to connect with the "Toy Train" to Darjeeling. It has a/c coaches, but its chair-car is uncomfortable.

By road

The most famous of the main roads leading out of the city are the **Grand Trunk Road** (see p.497), which runs via Varanasi and Delhi all the way to Peshawar in Pakistan, and the **Bombay Trunk Road**.

Normally, you have to reckon on an average speed on Bengal's notoriously poor highways of around 30kph, but the *Rocket Bus* to **Siliguri** – handy for **Darjeeling** and **Sikkim** – covers the 560km journey overnight, if not in any great comfort (departs 8pm; Rs115). *Rocket Bus* is one of several companies based at the **Esplanade Bus Stand**.

Frequent buses for **Bhubaneshwar** and **Puri** in Orissa leave the **Babu Ghat Bus Stand**, where *Orissa Roadways* and *West Bengal State Transport* have booths. Buses from Babu Ghat also head to **Namkhana**, en route to **Bakkhali**, and there's an early-morning local service for **Basanti** and the **Sunderbans**. Buses leave both Babu Ghat and Esplanade for the beach at **Digha**.

For details on getting to the **Andaman Islands** from Calcutta, by air or sea, see p.886.

Photography *Bombay Photo Stores*, 33-34 Park Mansions, Park St; *Narains's Photo Cine Centre*, 20H Park St; *North East Colour Photo*, 14 Sudder St near New Market, offers 1-hour processing.

Private Hospitals, Nursing Homes & Clinics Private medical care, if expensive by comparison, is infinitely superior to government hospitals. *Belle Vue Clinic*, 9 Dr UN Brahmachari St (☎44 2321); *Centre for Tibetan Herbal Medicine*, 400 Jodhpur Park; *Metropolitan Laboratory and Nursing Home*, 18 Shakespeare Sarani (☎43 2487); *Park Nursing Home*, 4 Victoria Terrace (☎44 3586); *Woodlands Nursing Home*, 8/6 Alipore Rd (☎45 3951).

State Tourist Offices The most useful of the many tourist offices representing other states in Calcutta are those that cover the northeastern hill states, and issue whatever permits may be necessary (details of permit requirements can be found on p.811), and that of the Andaman and Nicobar islands. *Andaman & Nicobar*, 3A Auckland Place (☎22 2604); *Arunachal Pradesh*, 4B Chowringhee Place (☎28 6500); *Assam*, 8 Russell St (☎29 8331); *Manipur*, 25 Ashutosh Shastri Rd (☎35 6943); *Mizoram*, 24 Old Ballygunge Rd (☎47 7034); *Nagaland*, 13 Shakespeare Sarani (☎22 5269); *Sikkim*, 5 Russell St (☎29 7516); *Tripura*, 1 Pretoria St (☎22 3836).

Travel Agents *American Express Travel Related Services*, 21 Court House St (☎28 9471); inbound tours and international flights. *Seagull Travels*, opposite *Blue Sky Cafe*, 2-1 Sudder St (☎44 9908); domestic and international flights. *Star Travels*, 10 Sudder St (☎43 1655); domestic and international flights. *Thomas Cook*, Chitrakoot Building, 230 AJC Bose Rd (☎47 5378); international flights and inbound tours. *Travel and Cargo Service*, 23 Shakespeare Sarani (☎247 5739); general travel services and also runs a number of guest houses. *Travel Media*, 40H Free School St (☎245 1985); multi-purpose shop selling international and domestic airline tickets as well as railway bookings. *Warren Travels*, 31 J Nehru Rd (☎29 6611); well-established service including international and domestic airlines, hotel bookings, group tours, and travel documents wherever possible.

Around Calcutta

The River Hooghly served for centuries as a lifeline for foreign traders; north of Calcutta, its banks are dotted with the remains of tiny European settlements. All these sites, together with the Hindu temples of **Dakshineshwar**, **Belur Math** and **Kalna**, and even the great Vaishnavite centre of **Nabadip** further north, can be taken in as day trips on local trains from Calcutta's Sealdah and Howrah stations. Some of the towns also offer limited accommodation in simple hotels.

Serampore

In 1799, the Englishman William Carey set up a press in Danish **SERAMPORE**, 25km north of Calcutta, and began to produce Bengali and Sanskrit bibles. He also pioneered Indian-language dictionaries, and established the Serampore College in 1819, which later became Asia's first modern university. Built on a high bank overlooking the river, the large Neoclassical building houses a small museum dedicated to Carey's life and work. Books in the accompanying library date back to the eighteenth century.

Dakshineshwar and Belur Math

At the outermost edge of Calcutta, 20km north of Esplanade on the east bank of the river, the popular temple of **DAKSHINESHWAR** (pronounced *Daukhineshwar*) stands in the shadow of Bally Bridge. Built in 1855 by Rani Rashmoni, a wealthy widow, it was a product of the Bengali Renaissance, consecrated at a time when growing numbers of middle-class Hindus were rejecting their faith. As the Rani was not a *brahmin*, she found it hard to employ a priest, but one of those she eventually contracted became renowned as the saint Ramakrishna. Set on a plinth in a vast courtyard, and ringed by a band of blood-red paint, the whitewashed main Kali temple is an ornate variation on the typical

Bengali hut design, with a curved roof and second storey capped by nine *chhatris*, each with a beehive cupola, in the *nava-rattan* ("nine-jewelled") style. Ramakrishna's former room, beside the main gate, now preserves his personal effects.

Along the riverfront, perched above the *ghats*, twelve identical small temples contain *shivalingams*, while another temple houses images of Radha and Krishna. In the small park outside the complex, visitors feed herds of rhesus monkeys.

Also in Dakshineshwar, not far from the main temple, **Yogoday Satsanga Math** is the headquarters of the Self-Realisation Fellowship, founded in California in 1925 by the author of *Autobiography of a Yogi*, Paramahansa Yogananda.

Across Bally Bridge from Dakshineshwar, 3km south along the west bank of the Hooghly, the massive riverfront temple at **BELUR MATH** was erected by a disciple of Ramakrishna, Swami Vivekananda, in 1938. A symbol of the resurgence in Bengali Hinduism, it incorporates elements from several world religions; the gate is inspired by early Buddhist sculpture, the windows by Islamic architecture, and the ground plan is based on the Christian cross.

Local trains run from Sealdah to Dakshineshwar, and from Howrah to Belur Math.

Chandernagore

Around 35km north of Howrah, the former French outpost of **CHANDERNAGORE** still bears traces of its colonial masters, who left in 1949 and officially seceded the town to India in 1952. Crumbling buildings along its grand riverside promenade, formerly the Quai Dupleix and now **the Strand**, include what was once the Hotel de Paris, while the Eglise du Sacré Coeur, set back from the river, houses an image of Joan of Arc. Nearby, the eighteenth-century mansion of the French administrator serves as the **Institut de Chandernagore**, with a library, a French-language school, and an interesting museum of documents, antiques, art and sculpture (Mon–Wed & Fri–Sat 4–6.30pm, Sun 11am–5pm; free).

Hooghly and Bandel

The next significant community as you continue north from Chandernagore is the former Armenian township of **Chinsurah**. A kilometre beyond that, **HOOGHLY** was a major East India Company trading post. Packed with Islamic monuments, it was devastated in turn by the Moghuls and the Marathas before being retaken by Robert Clive.

Eight kilometres out of Chandernagore, the grounds of the **Church of Our Lady of the Bandel**, one of eastern India's oldest churches and still a major centre of Catholic pilgrimage, sweep down to the river. Consecrated by Portuguese Augustan friars in 1599, it was destroyed by the Moghuls in 1640. A cross marks the spot where an image known as Our Lady of Happy Voyages, which had been lost in the river during the siege, miraculously re-appeared some years later. The church was rebuilt around 1660; it has now been faced with polished granite, so lacks any great aesthetic value. Along with a cloistered courtyard, it holds a grotto and a large hall devoted to St Augustine.

The old cemetery next to the church, where the mast of a boat stands as a flagstaff, are a popular picnic spot, offering boat rides on the river. Trains from both Howrah and Sealdah call at a station 2km away, from where cycle rickshaws are available.

Kalna

The small town of **KALNA**, just over 82km north of Howrah, is centered around a varied group of eighteenth- and nineteenth- century **terracotta temples**, built and still maintained by the family of the Maharajah of Burdwan. Its most unusual feature is a complex of 108 Shiva shrines, arranged in a *mandala* of two concentric circles, constructed by Maharajah Tek Chand in 1809; 108 is the holy number found on a *jap mala* or rosary. Opposite the shrines, gates lead into the main compound, where buildings in all states of repair include some that are still in use. Among them are the small

Pratapesvara (1849), the *jor-bangla* (twin-roofed) Siddheshwari (1740), Ananta Vasudeva, which has superb detail on its facade (1754), the large Krishnachandra, which has a porch on three sides (1755), and the massive Lalji (1739).

Also at Kalna, **Gauridas Mandir** is related to Sri Chaitanya (see below) and his disciple Pandit Gauridas. Still maintained by a descendant of Gauridas, it houses an ancient manuscript and a paddle said to belong to the saint. ISKCON (see below) want to buy the site, but the local community seem determined to hang on to their heritage.

Kalna's not very busy railway station is around 3km from the temples; you can also get here by bus from Bandel.

Nabadip and Mayapur

Pilgrims come in their thousands to the pleasant little town of **NABADIP** (also known as Nawadip), on the west bank of the Hooghly, 20km north of Kalna. However, although this was the eleventh-century capital of Bengal under the Sen dynasty, and later became famous as the home of **Sri Chaitanya** (1486–1533), one of the main inspirations behind the medieval Hindu revival, few of the many temples clustered around its Mayapur Ghat are of any great antiquity. The most important of these are **Gauranga Mahapur** and **Sonar Gauranga**, but the courtyards of virtually all are alive with devotees singing *kirtan* (devotional song). Especially enthusiastic worshippers perform the full fifty-kilometre *padakrama*, a foot pilgrimage around sites connected with Chaitanya that spread across the nine nearby islands. The conspicuous white temple on one of these, **MAYAPUR**, is a symbol of the contemporary face of Vaishnavism; it belongs to ISKCON, the "Hare Krishna" sect familiar the world over. A more relaxing way to enjoy Nabadip's waterfront is on a boat trip from the *ghat*.

Trains from Howrah run to Nabadip itself, while trains from Sealdah serve Nabadip Ghat on the river's east bank. The reasonable **rooms** of *Nabadip Lodge* (②–④) at the main *ghat* command good views across the water, and there are simple cafes nearby. ISKCON's comfortable *Guest House* (①) is bookable through their temple in Calcutta, at 3C Albert Rd (off Shakespeare Sarani); they also organize day trips by coach.

COASTAL BENGAL

The coast of West Bengal consists of two very distinct sections, to either side of the **River Hooghly**. To the east are the **Sunderbans**, one of the largest estuarine deltas in the world, where a group of mangrove-covered islands large and small shelter the **Sunderbans Tiger Reserve**. This area is not all tigers and forest, however; it also includes the seaside resort of **Bakkhali**. West of the Hooghly, the unbroken beaches of the Bay of Bengal curve south towards Orissa, taking in **Digha** along the way.

Sajnekhali and the Sunderbans Tiger Reserve

The cluster of islands known as the **Sunderbans**, or "beautiful forest", lie in the Gangetic Delta, stretching east from the mouth of the Hooghly to Bangladesh. Incredibly, they are home to the legendary **Royal Bengal tiger**, a ferocious man-eater which has adapted remarkably well to this watery environment, and swims from island to island – as much as 40km in one go, if the locals are to be believed. Among the people who find themselves sharing this delicate ecosystem with the mighty cats are honey collectors, woodcutters and fisherfolk. All, regardless of their official religion, worship Banbibi, the goddess of the forest; their occupations are so hazardous that wives take off all their married ornaments when their husbands go out to the forest, becoming widows until they return. As the tigers like to creep up from behind, the honey collectors and woodcutters wear masks at the back of their heads. Meanwhile, the women and children drag nets along the estuary shores to catch prawn – no less hazardous, considering they have to deal with crocodiles and sharks as well as tigers.

The headquarters of the **Sunderbans Tiger Reserve**, at **SAJNEKHALI**, is sealed off from the jungle by wire fencing (though tigers still occasionally stray into the compound); permits (see below) are meticulously checked as you pass through. Guests stay in the *Sajnekhali Tourist Lodge* (②), a large ramshackle forest lodge built on stilts. The Project Tiger complex has a mini zoo, a small museum and a watchtower. Food is left out for the wild animals in the late afternoons, which invariably attracts deer and monkeys but only rarely tigers. Other Sunderbans watchtowers stand at Sudhannyakhali, Haldi, and Netidhopani, near the ruins of a 400-year-old temple.

All transport within the reserve is by **boat**; country boats can be rented with the help of the staff at the lodge for around Rs60 an hour. You have to take along a Project Tiger guide. The loud diesel motors of the boats tend to scare wildlife away, but when they cut their engines the silence is awesome.

Getting to and from the Sunderbans

Getting to the Sunderbans **from Calcutta** is a laborious process. First of all, would-be foreign visitors to the game sanctuary have to pick up special **permits** from the Government of West Bengal. As these are now issued at the main tourist office in BBD Bagh East (see p.729), you might well want to reserve **accommodation** in Sajnekhali at the same time, or just sign up for one of their two-day **tours** by bus and launch. These cost Rs500 if you sleep on the launch, Rs550 if you stay at Sajnekhali, or more for a cabin on a luxurious yacht. The main disadvantage of a group tour is that the general noise of other people can all but preclude seeing any animals.

Whether you travel by **train** (from Sealdah; the route is outlined in reverse, below) or by **bus**, the journey from Calcutta to the Sunderbans by public transport is equally convoluted. To go by road, you start by catching a bus from Babu Ghat to **Basanti** (4 daily; 3hr; Rs15); aim for the 7am one. From Basanti, you cross by ferry to **Gosaba** (Rs3), an hour-long trip through the delta rendered far more pleasant if you sit well away from the belching diesel engines. **Sajnekhali,** which comprises a Government Guest House (closed to the public) and a Forest Department complex but little else, is a six-kilometre cycle rickshaw ride from Gosaba, along a road that passes through some lovely flower-bedecked villages. Finally, to reach the Project Tiger compound itself, and the *Tourist Lodge*, you have to cross the estuary again, on a country boat from the further back and less likely looking of the two *ghats*, or jetties. There isn't usually a lot of traffic around here, so you may well have to wait.

When you go **back to Calcutta**, allow plenty of time to make all the connections; the last bus leaves Basanti around 4pm. Alternatively, shared auto-scooters from Basanti can take you to **Docghat** (Rs6; 30min), to pick up a boat across the river to **Canning**, and then a local train to Sealdah via Ballygunge station. If you're unlucky enough to find that the tide is out when you get to Canning, you're faced with a laborious 500-metre wade through calf-deep squelchy mud. The faster you try to get out, the dirtier you get; the locals of course are well used to it, neatly roll up their trousers, and get through without a splash. A short walk through the town brings you to the station, where there are taps to wash the mud off. Your reward is the train ride itself, infinitely faster and more comfortable than the bus.

Along the Hooghly to the sea

As the Hooghly bends south on its way to the sea, it becomes larger and larger; when it reaches the Bay of Bengal at **Diamond Harbour**, 50km south of Calcutta, it is very wide indeed. The harbour was used by the East India Company, and a ruined fort is said to date back to Portuguese pirates. The trip down here from the city, by bus or train, is a popular day's excursion for Calcuttans, though it's also possible to stay the night at a *Tourist Lodge* (②–⑤), which has some a/c rooms. Book through the tourist office on BBD Bagh.

Sagardwip, at the mouth of the Hooghly and accessible by ferry or bus from Diamond Harbour, is revered by Hindus as the point where the Ganga meets the sea. The actual confluence is venerated at the **Kapil Muni Temple**, on an island that bears the brunt of the savage Bay of Bengal cyclones and is gradually being submerged. On Makar Sankranti (mid-Jan), during the **Sagar Mela**, hundreds of thousands of pilgrims from all over India descend on the island, cramming into the water to bathe. A number of *dharamshalas* and ashrams offer cheap lodging, and a *Youth Hostel* can be booked through *Youth Services*, 32/1 BBD Bagh South, Calcutta 700 001 (☎248 0626).

The beach resorts

DIGHA, 175km southwest of Calcutta and almost halfway to Puri in Orissa, was originally conceived as a health sanatorium. Now it's a popular and somewhat polluted seaside resort, with a beach of hard silt. The continental shelf is very shallow here, so the tide goes out a long long way. You can get to Digha from Calcutta by bus from the Esplanade Terminus, by train to Kharagpur and then a bus, or one of the daily coach tours organized by the main tourist office. They can also reserve accommodation here, ot you can just pick one of the many small hotels when you arrive.

If anything, the casuarina-lined beach at **BAKKHALI**, 80km south of Diamond Harbour on the east side of the Hooghly, is even harder than the one at Digha. However, it's much less developed and far more attractive, and at high tide gets some impressive surf. The journey here is an adventure in itself; from Calcutta, head first to **Namkhana**, either on an early bus from Babu Ghat or by train to Diamond Harbour and then a bus. From Namkhana take a country ferry, which can be alarmingly crowded, and then a bus on to Bakkhali via Fraserganj. The *Tourist Lodge*, behind the tree-lined dunes at Bakkhali (②–④), has recently been privatized, but can still be booked through Calcutta's tourist office, on BBD Bagh.

CENTRAL BENGAL

Central Bengal may now seem quiet, rural, and a long way from anywhere, but it was the site of the region's great early capitals. **Gaur**, on the outskirts of **Malda**, was the mightiest of all, until its glory passed, it began to sink back into the fields, and its building materials were plundered for use elsewhere. In **Bishnupur**, in its turn the capital of the Mallas, a cluster of exquisite terracotta temples now provide evidence of a forgotten art, while **Murshidabad**, north of Calcutta, was the capital of Bengal's last independent dynasty, supplanted by the British. Finally, the university of **Shantiniketan**, founded this century by Tagore, epitomizes the values of the Bengali Renaissance.

Bishnupur

The tranquil and attractive backwater of **BISHNUPUR**, just over 100km northwest of Calcutta, is a famous centre of Bengali learning, renowned above all for its exquisite **terracotta temples**. It was for centuries the capital of the Malla rajas, under whose patronage one of India's greatest (and still-flourishing) schools of **music** developed. Largely beyond the sphere of Muslim influence in Bengal, Bishnupur's long tradition of temple building had its roots in the basic form of the domestic hut, which in East Bengal consisted of a bamboo frame supporting jute or reed woven walls, and a thatched roof curved along the eaves and ridge. Translated into temple architecture, built of brick as stone was rarely available, and faced with finely carved terracotta decoration (often depicting scenes from the *Ramayana*), the temples combine a striking simplicity of form with a vibrant texture. The harmonious colouring of the terracotta blends with the surrounding earth.

Several temples stand within the enclosure of the later Muslim fort. **Raas Mancha**, built around 1600 by Bir Hambir in a unique pyramidal style, is used to display the images of Krishna and Radha during the annual Raas festival. The tenth-century **Mrinmoyee Temple** encloses the auspicious *nababriksha*, nine trees growing as one. An early example of the *pancharatna* design, **Shyam Rai** was built in 1643, with five (*panch*) brick spires and extensive decoration, even in the interior. The **Madan Mohan**, with its domed central tower, is one of the largest, dating from the late seventeenth century. Its facade panels depict scenes from the life of Krishna. The remains of the **Pathar Darwaza**, the laterite gate to the old Malla fort, can be seen, along with the remains of the strategically placed *bundhs* or reservoirs that doubled as moats.

Buses run to Bishnupur from **Tarakeshwar**, which is linked to Howrah Station, Calcutta, on the local *EMU* railway network. There's one direct train each day, while others travel to the main junction of **Kharagpur** on the Howrah–Jamshedpur–Puri line. **Accommodation** options in Bishnupur are restricted. Satyepirtola, the central market area, holds the basic *Tarama* and *Rangini* lodges (both ①), while the small, pleasant *Tourist Lodge* (②–③) is well situated, near a large tank close to the temples.

Shantiniketan

Far from the clamour and grime of Calcutta, **SHANTINIKETAN** is another peaceful haven, 136km northwest of the city. Founded by Rabindranath Tagore in 1921 on the site of his father's ashram, both the settlement, and its liberal arts university **Vishwa Bharati**, were designed to promote the best of Bengali culture. Towards the end of the Bengali Renaissance, Tagore's vision and immense talent inspired a whole way of life and art; the university and school continue to operate under this momentum, still holding classes under the trees in the open air in accordance with his original plan.

Centred around the **Uttarayan** complex of buildings, designed by Tagore, the university remains in perfect harmony with its surroundings, despite its recent growth as Calcuttans have settled or built holiday homes. Well-known graduates include Indira Gandhi, and departments such as **Kala Bhavan** (art) and **Shangeet Bhavan** (music) are still attracting students from all over the world. **Chini Bhavan** – the China Department – is the largest of its kind in India; its superb collection of manuscripts was for years locked away due to tensions between India and China.

RABINDRANATH TAGORE

The Bengali poet and literary giant, **Rabindranath Tagore** (1861–1941), has inspired generations of artists, poets and musicians. He developed an early interest in theatre, and set his poems to music – now, as *Rabindra Sangeet*, one of the most popular musical traditions in Bengal. Introduced to England and the west by the painter William Rothenstein and WB Yeats, Tagore had his collection of poems *Gitanjali* first published in translation in 1912, and the following year was awarded the Nobel Prize for literature. Though he preferred to write in Bengali, and encouraged authors in other Indian languages, he was also a master of English prose. Not until he was in his seventies did his talent as an artist and painter emerge, developed from scribblings on the borders of his manuscripts. Among his many illustrious students were the painter Nandalal Bose, whose family continue to be associated with Shantiniketan, and the film-maker Satyajit Ray, who based several of his films on the works of Tagore.

The centre of **Surul**, a village 4km from Shantiniketan (a 20-min cycle-rickshaw ride), holds several small but delightful **terracotta temples**. These are scattered near the Rajbari, or "the house of the *zamindar*" – a sort of manor house, which with its large courtyard feels very much like a relic of nineteenth-century Bengal.

The large fair of **Posh Mela** (also known as Posh Utsav), is held between 22 and 25 December to commemorate the initiation of Rabindranath Tagore's father, Maharshi Debendranath Tagore, into the Brahmo Samaj (see p.728). Posh Mela features sports, dances and music, all with a strong Shantal and folk influence, but is most renowned for the Bauls who come to perform. In recent years culture-vultures from Calcutta have descended upon the *mela* with their tape recorders and cameras.

Arrival and information

Bolpur, 3km south of Shantiniketan, is the nearest **railway** station, on the main line between Calcutta and Darjeeling and also served by local trains between Burddhaman (or Burdwan) and Rampurhat. The best train to get to Bolpur **from Calcutta** is the *Shantiniketan Express* #3015, which leaves Howrah at 9.55am and terminates at Bolpur at 12.30pm. It can get quite crowded, but the atmosphere is great. Sometimes a fancy first-class lounge-coach, decorated with terracotta, is attached, but even then it's more fun to travel second-class, as Baul singers get on and busk.

If you're heading on from Shantiniketan **to Darjeeling**, your best option is the *Darjeeling Mail*, which leaves at 10.28pm – or frequently later – and arrives in New Jalpaiguri at 8.30am the next morning in time to catch the 9am Toy Train into the hills (see p.766). Alternatively, the *Kanchenjunga* departs at 9.35am and arrives at NJP at 6.10pm, which means a night's stay in the Siliguri area before moving on to Darjeeling. Reservation quotas from Bolpur are tiny, so book early; there's another reservations counter near the post office in Shantiniketan.

Information is available at the Tourist Lodge, Bolpur although the Public Relations Office at Vishwa Bharati is of more use, especially regarding the university.

Local **buses** from Bolpur use either the Bolpur Bus Stand, next to the station, or the Shantiniketan Bus Stand, 2km west towards Surul. Cycle rickshaws are the chief means of transport in the area; the ride from Bolpur to Shantiniketan costs around Rs10.

Accommodation

The Shantiniketan area holds a reasonable amount of accommodation, with the university's *International Guest Houses* ideal if you're planning a medium- or long-term stay.

Bolpur Lodge, Bolpur (☎52662). Although it may look a bit like a hostel, the large lodge set off the main road has a pleasant leafy courtyard and a wide range from a dormitory to air-conditioned rooms and a large restaurant. ①–④.

Bolpur Railway Station Retiring Rooms. Very good value, if removed from the Shantiniketan ambience. The station restaurant is quite good, and the a/c room is less than Rs100 per night! ①.

Chhuti, 241 Charu Palli, Jamboni. New-style "resort" – a bit ostentatious but comfortable and well laid out, with ethnic-look thatched cottages, some a/c, and a good restaurant. Also booked through Ilaco House, 1/3 Brabourne Rd, Calcutta 700 001 (☎20 8305). ⑤–⑥.

International Guest House, Shantiniketan. The university runs two of these large guest houses – *Old* and *New* – although the old one looks newer. Large simple rooms and a cheap restaurant. ①.

Mayurakshi, Prantik (☎52958). Sticking up like the obelisk in *2001*, a new and very incongruous concrete and glass monstrosity near Prantik station. Worryingly, it may well herald the end of the rural idyll, but it is very comfortable, with all facilities, and accepts all credit cards. ⑤.

Nirala Lodge, Bolpur Tourist Lodge Rd. Simple accommodation at dirt cheap prices. ①.

Tourist Lodge, Bolpur Tourist Lodge Rd. Large and rather institutional, but otherwise not too bad. A/c rooms, dorm, and a decent restaurant. ②–⑤.

Around Shantiniketan

The gentle rolling countryside that surrounds Shantiniketan is home to the **Shantal** people. Though now obliged to co-exist with Bengalis, they somehow manage to maintain their separate animist traditions. In the evenings, the country resounds with the sound of distant Shantal drums, used to accompany song and dance. The many **Bauls** – the legendary itinerant folk singers of Bengal, pronounced *ba'ul* – concentrated in this area can often be heard singing on the streets, on trains or busking from door to door.

Kankalitala
Across the railway track, roughly 9km south of Shantiniketan via Bolpur, the small Kali temple of **Kankalitala** is unusual in having an oil painting of Kali as its central image. With its magnificent banyan tree, it makes a relaxing and attractive day trip. Behind the temple there's a *smashana* – cremation ground – used by tantrics (see below).

Tarapith
One of the most important centres of tantric Hinduism, **TARAPITH**, lies 8km from Ramparhat Railway Station, served by auto-rickshaws (Rs40 if you want one for yourself), cycle rickshaws, and buses. There is a Tarapith station, but it is not connected by surfaced road to Tarapith itself. The temple and cremation ground, in a grove beside the river, are popular with tantric *sadhus*, and it is not uncommon to witness rituals involving skulls and cremation ashes. The temple itself is a simple building in the *bankura* style dedicated to *shakti* as Tara (the image has a silver face and large eyes); shrines litter the area, and the grove is populated by vociferous monkeys. Tarapith has various simple lodges and rest houses, with a very clean *dharamshala* near the temple.

Kendubilwa
The rural site of **KENDUBILWA**, also known as Kenduli, on the bank of a wide shallow river 42km from Shantiniketan, is the birthplace of Jaidev, the author of *Gita Govinda*, and the spiritual home of the Bauls. Its small terracotta temple, complete with sheltering banyan tree, is engulfed each year during the January *mela*, when hundreds of pilgrims, *yogis* and *sadhus* gather to hear the Bauls perform throughout the night. At that time, special buses leave from Bolpur (2hr) and Calcutta.

Murshidabad

Set in the brilliant green landscape of rural Bengal, historic **MURSHIDABAD** lies close to the commercial town of **Behrampur**. Several eighteenth-century monuments along the banks of the Hooghly stand as reminders of its days as the last independent capital of Bengal. Established early in the eighteenth century by the **Nawab Murshid Quli Khan**, Murshidabad was soon eclipsed when the forces of Siraj-ud-Daula were defeated by Robert Clive at the Battle of Plassey in 1757, as a result of which the British came to dominate Bengal, from the new city of Calcutta. Clive described Murshidabad as equal to London, with several palaces and seven hundred mosques; now it's not even a city at all, though it does remain renowned today for such traditional crafts as silk weaving, hand-block printing, ivory carving and bell-metal ware.

Murshidabad's intriguing mixture of cultures is reflected in its architectural styles, which range from the Italianate **Hazarduari**, the Nawab's palace, designed by General Duncan Macleod of the Bengal Engineers, to the **Katra Mosque**, built by Murshid Quli Khan in the style of the mosque at Mecca. The palace, with its mirrored banqueting hall, circular Durbar room, armoury, and library of fine manuscripts is now an impressive museum. Its gardens and riverside promenade are a popular recreational area, with shops nearby catering to tourists.

A large ox-bow lake, the **Moti Jheel** or **Pearl Lake**, guards the desolate ruins of the palace where Siraj-ud-Daulah reigned before his defeat, subsequently occupied for a while by Clive. To the south, across the river, **Khushbag**, the **Garden of Delight**, holds the tombs of many of the Nawabs, including Alivardi Khan and Siraj-ud-Daulah. Bengal's unique style of temple building, with its exquisite terracotta surface decoration, is also represented, in the **Rani Bhawani Temple** at Baranagar.

All travel to Murshidabad has to be via **Behrampur**, which is a five-hour bus ride from Calcutta and is also served by trains from Calcutta's Sealdah Station. Behrampur's *Tourist Lodge* (②–④) has some a/c rooms and a small dorm; the comfortable *Samrat* (③–⑤) is on the main highway around 5km south of the centre.

Malda, Gaur and Pandua

The unattractive commercial town of **MALDA**, 340km north of Calcutta, is renowned for its local mango harvest. A natural port, at the confluence of two rivers, it was a prosperous trading post for silk and cotton; in the seventeenth and eighteenth centuries it housed Dutch, French and English factories. Little has survived of interest from that period, but Malda makes a good base to explore the historic sites of **Gaur** and **Pandua**, both earlier capitals of Bengal.

Malda is on the main line between Calcutta and Darjeeling, served by trains such as the *Gaur Express* and the *Darjeeling Mail*. **Accommodation** includes the old-fashioned rooms leading off the central courtyard of the *Malda Tourist Lodge*, Rathbari, English Bazaar (☎6123; ①–③), which doubles as the local tourist office. *Meghdoot Lodge*, nearby (②–④), has a range of pleasant rooms, both a/c and non-a/c.

Gaur

Spread across a landscape of lush paddy fields, 16km south of Malda on the border with Bangladesh, **GAUR** was the seventh-century capital of King Sasanka, and then successively belonged to the Buddhist Pals and the Senas. The latter, the last Hindu kings of Bengal, were violently displaced by the Muslims at the start of the thirteenth century. The city was eventually sacked in 1537 by Sher Shah Suri, and its remaining inhabitants were wiped out by plague in 1575.

Deserted and overgrown, Gaur today is hard to relate to the city of one million inhabitants described by the Portuguese historian, Faria-y-Souza. He said it was so crowded during religious festivals that people were crushed to death; now it is only visited by Hindu pilgrims, performing rites at Sadulapur *ghat*. Nothing remains of the pre-Muslim period apart from large tanks, such as the **Sagar Dighi**, built in 1126 and almost 1500 metres long, and the embankments of the old city, which extend for several kilometres through the verdant rural landscape. **Dakhil Darwaza**, an impressive gateway built in 1425 of small red bricks, leads through the embankments surrounding the **Fort**, in the southeast corner of which a colossal 20-metre-high wall encloses the ruins of the old palace. Nearby are the **Qadam Rasul Mosque**, built in 1531 to contain the Prophet's footprint in stone, and the seventeenth-century tomb of Fateh Khan, one of Aurangzeb's generals, in Bengali hut style. Other remains of interest include the elegant **Tantipara Mosque**, with its finely detailed terracotta decoration, the Lattan or **Painted Mosque** where traces remain visible of the enamelled bricks that gave it its name, and the massive **Bara Sona Masjid**, "Great Golden Mosque", northeast of the Fort.

Pandua

In the opposite direction, 18km north of Malda, the remains of Fakhr-ud-Din's capital at **PANDUA** are also struggling to survive. The splendid **Adina Masjid**, built by Sikander Shah around 1370, and in its day the largest mosque in the subcontinent, now lies in ruins. These betray the origin of much of the building materials – carved basalt masonry from earlier Hindu temples was used to support 88 brick-built arches and 378 identical small domes, the orthodox design following that of the great eighth-century mosque of Damascus.

Most of the monuments of interest lie on or around the ten-kilometre length of the old brick paved road that runs through the town. These include the **Eklakhi mausoleum** – one of the first square brick tombs in Bengal, it is the tomb of the convert son of a Hindu Raja, with a carved Ganesh on the doorway. **Qutb Shahi Masjid**, called the Golden Mosque after the original yellow glazing on its minarets, was built to honour Saint Nur Qutb-ul-Alam. His ruined shrine is nearby, with that of saint **Hazrat Shah Jalal Tabrizi**, known collectively as **Choti** and **Bari Dargah**.

NORTH BENGAL

NORTH BENGAL, where the Himalayas soar from the flat alluvial plains towards Nepal, Sikkim and Bhutan, holds some magnificent mountain panoramas, and also some of India's best **hill stations**. Most visitors pass as quickly as possible through **Siliguri** en route to **Darjeeling**, **Kalimpong**, and Sikkim itself.

Further northeast, nearer Assam, the sub-Himalayan Duar Hills have much in common with the Brahmaputra Valley – not only climate, but also wildlife such as the one-horned rhino, sheltered in the **Jaldapara Wildlife Sanctuary**.

Siliguri and New Jalpaiguri

The dull tea-auction centre of **SILIGURI** serves as the gateway to Darjeeling, Kalimpong, Sikkim and Bhutan. Together with its main railway station, **NEW JALPAIGURI** – commonly referred to as NJP – it forms an unavoidable link between the rail and air connections to Calcutta and Delhi, and the roads up into the mountains. The border with Nepal at **Kakarbitta** nearby is open to tourists.

Arrival and information

Bagdogra airport, 12km west of Siliguri and served (supposedly) by flights from Delhi and Calcutta, is connected by bus and taxis not only with Siliguri itself, but also directly to Darjeeling – much the best alternative.

THE TOY TRAIN

Completed in 1889, the small-gauge **Toy Train** was designed as an extension of the *North Bengal State Railway*, climbing from **New Jalpaiguri**, via **Siliguri**, for a tortuous ninety kilometres up to **Darjeeling**. Pulled by ancient little steam engines, the train follows the Hill Cart Road, which was designed so that even bullock carts could travel up its gradual incline from the plains, crossing it at regular intervals and even sharing it with traffic. First-class coaches with large viewing windows provide magnificent views.

As the nine-hour journey progresses the scenery gradually unfolds; at the high pass at Ghoom, 7km short of Darjeeling, the magnificent High Himalayan panorama suddenly unfolds. Just beyond Ghoom, the train does a complete circle at the **Batasia Loop** – the most dramatic of five such loops along the way.

No longer an essential mode of transport, the Toy Train has fallen on hard times. The service has become unreliable, and there's even been talk of axing it completely.

At present, two trains leave NJP each day, at 7.15am and 9am; they return, considerably quicker, in the late afternoon. If you don't have the (considerable) patience required for the full trip, it's possible to do a round trip between Darjeeling and Ghoom.

All **buses** arriving at Siliguri terminate in or around the **Tenzing Norgay Bus Terminal** or the **Sikkim National Transport Bus Stand** on Hill Cart Road, the road which runs all the way to Darjeeling. Recently renamed Tenzing Norgay Road, Hill Cart Road is Siliguri's central artery.

Siliguri does have its own railway station, used by the Toy Train, but the **New Jalpaiguri** (NJP) station, 4km east, is the largest railway junction in the region with trains to and from Calcutta, Delhi and Assam (Indian nationals only). Rickshaws into Siliguri from NJP cost around Rs12, auto-rickshaws more like Rs35; taxis are more expensive and take longer, as they can't take short cuts on the narrow lanes.

A **Tourist Bureau** on Hill Cart Rd (☎21632) provides information and organizes weekend excursions to Jaldapara. Nearby, the *Sikkim Tourist Information Centre*, SNT Colony (☎24602), in the same compound as the *Sikkim Nationalised Transport* stand, provides information and permits for Gangtok. Additional information counters are located at Bagdogra airport and the stations at NJP and Siliguri. There's a *State Bank of India* beside the *Air View Hotel* on Hill Cart Rd (☎22274), and **post offices** located on Bidhan Rd, near the *Central Railway Booking Office*, and Pradhan Nagar, near the Tenzing Norgay Bus Terminal.

Accommodation and eating

You might not actually choose to stay a night in Siliguri, but you may well have to anyway. The best of its **restaurants** can be found in its hotels.

Chancellor, Sevoke Mor (corner of Sevoke and Hill Cart roads) (☎24248). Tibetan-run and friendly with airy rooms with attached baths and balconies. Tibetan, Chinese and Indian food. ③–④.

Embassy, George Mehbert Rd (☎25251). Located behind bustling Bidhan Market, this business hotel is surprisingly pleasant. ④–⑤.

MOVING ON FROM SILIGURI

Bagdogra Airport is in theory served by daily *Indian Airlines* flights to Calcutta (IC722, plus an extra flight in high season) and Delhi and Guwahati (IC879); however, you'll have to check on the current situation. An airport bus leaves from Siliguri's *Indian Airlines* office, near *Hotel Sinclairs*, Pradhan Nagar (☎26689).

All major **trains** use NJP station, not Siliguri. To reserve tickets to **Calcutta** – on for example the *Kanchenjunga Express* #2557/2558, *Darjeeling Mail* #3143/3144, or the *Kamrup Express* #5659/5660 – or to **Delhi** – both the *North East Express* #2521/2522 and *Brahmaputra Mail* #2455/2456 also pass through **Patna** – go to the **Central Railway Booking Office**, Bidhan Rd (daily 8am–4pm).

To get to **Darjeeling**, either catch the Toy Train (see opposite), or take a bus from Siliguri's Tenzing Norgay Bus Terminal, or a shared taxi from the stand on Hill Cart Road (3–4hr, usually with a break in Kurseong). Regular buses also run to **Kalimpong**.

Overnight buses to **Calcutta** (12hr), such as the *Rocket Bus*, are much cheaper than the train, and have the advantage of depositing you in Esplanade in Calcutta, near the Sudder Street area. Whatever you're promised, be it "luxury bus" or "two by two", be prepared for a severe rattling.

If you're heading for **Kathmandu** in Nepal, you can catch a bus to the border at **Kakarbitta** (where it's possible to pick up a Nepalese visa) and make your own arrangements there, or you can book a ticket all the way (for around Rs210) through at various agencies at Siliguri including *Tourist Service Agency*, c/o *Overnight Express*, Pradhan Nagar (☎26547). The advantage of a pause in Kakarbitta is that it has a greater choice of onwards buses; overnight buses (Rs250) leave Kakarbitta around 4pm each day, arriving in Kathmandu around 9am the next morning.

Sikkim Nationalised Transport, Pradhan Nagar, Hill Cart Rd (☎20528) and Booking Office (☎21496) run a good service to **Gangtok** and various other points in Sikkim.

Hindusthan, Hill Cart Rd, Pradhan Nagar (☎26571). Opposite the Tenzing Norgay Bus Terminal, with a range of rooms. ①–⑤.

Mayor, Sevoke Rd (☎23939). On a main road, but nice large rooms, all with attached baths. Bar and restaurant serving Indian and Chinese food. ③–⑤.

Ranjit, Hill Cart Rd (☎22056). Clean Sikh-run hotel in a courtyard off the main drag with a good vegetarian restaurant and a range of prices – the cheaper rooms tend not to have windows. ②–④.

Sikkim, George Manbert Rd, behind Bidhan Market (☎23448). Simple budget hotel in a busy part of town with a cafe serving *momos* and the usual Chinese and Indian food. ②.

Sinclairs Siliguri, behind *Indian Airlines* office, Pradhan Nagar (☎22674). Siliguri's most prestigious hotel, with a swimming pool and full facilities. ⑦–⑧.

Tourist Service Agency Guest House, Pradhan Nagar (☎22387). A quaint bungalow on a quiet street. Good budget value, but often full as it only has a handful of rooms. ②–③.

WBTD Mainak Tourist Lodge, Pradhan Nagar (☎22018). Set in large grounds with comfortable rooms; facilities include car rental, restaurant and bar. Friendly and welcoming staff. ③–⑥.

Jaldapara Wildlife Sanctuary

Apart from Darjeeling and the hills, most of North Bengal is far off the beaten track; few travellers venture off the Darjeeling–Sikkim–Nepal road. Probably the best reason to do so is to visit the small **Jaldapara Wildlife Sanctuary**, roughly 140km east of Siliguri. The sanctuary was established in 1943 to help protect wildlife against the encroachment of tea cultivation. Consisting of tracts of tall elephant grass on the banks of the River Torsa, and set against the backdrop of forested foothills, it now shelters around fifty highly endangered greater **one-horned rhinoceroses**, as well as tiger, leopard, wild elephant, *sambar*, and hog deer.

Jaldapara is open from November to the end of April, with March being the best month to view animals, as they graze on new shoots. Much the best way to explore it is on elephant back. The easiest way to get here is on one of the tours organized by the *Tourist Bureau* of West Bengal in Siliguri (☎21632), bookable in Siliguri or Calcutta, though it is possible to travel by train or bus from Siliguri to the town of **Madarihat**, 7km from the sanctuary. Accommodation and food are available at the *Madarihat Tourist Lodge* (which can be booked throug the WBTDC in Calcutta; ☎28 5917; ③–⑥), or at the *Hollong Forest Lodge* (③) in the heart of the forest.

Darjeeling

Part Victorian holiday resort, part major tea-growing centre, **DARJEELING** (from *Dorje Ling*, "the place of the thunderbolt") straddles a ridge 2200m up in the Himalayas and almost 600km north of Calcutta. Fifty years after the British departed, the town remains as popular as ever with holiday-makers from the plains, and promenades such as the Mall and the Chowrasta still burst with life. Although the infrastructure created under the Raj is now struggling to cope, and Darjeeling is plagued by acute shortages of water and electricity, it's a fascinating and cosmopolitan place. Above all (literally), the greatest appeal for visitors has to be its stupendous mountain vistas – the equal of any hill station in India, with Kanchendzonga (also spelt Kanchenjunga), the third highest mountain in the world, dominating the northern horizon. The best seasons to come – and to attempt the magnificent trek to Sandakphu, to see Everest – are after the monsoons and before winter (late Sept to late Nov), and spring (mid-Feb to May).

Until the nineteenth century, Darjeeling belonged to **Sikkim**. However, in 1817, after a disastrous war with Nepal, Sikkim was forced to concede the right to use the site as a health sanatorium to the **British**, who had helped to broker a peace settlement. Darjeeling soon became the most popular of all hill resorts, especially after the Hill Cart Road was built in 1839 to link it with Siliguri. **Tea** arrived a few years later, and with it an influx of Nepalese labourers, and the virtual disappearance of the forests that previously carpeted the hillsides. The town's growing economic significance led Britain to force a treaty on the Sikkimese in 1861, thereby annexing Darjeeling and Kalimpong. (Part of the aim was to develop trade via the two towns with Tibet; when the Tibetans demurred, Colonel Younghusband was despatched into the mountains, where his troops pulverized the ill-equipped and archaic Tibetan army at Gyantse in 1904.) In the early 1900s, Darjeeling had a reputation of being one of the most glamorous and far-flung outposts of the British empire, attracting socialites and adventurers in equal numbers.

Meanwhile, the advent of the **Nepalese** had changed the face of the hills, so that its main language is now Nepali. After Independence the region joined West Bengal, administered from Calcutta, but calls for autonomy grew, taking shape in the **Gurkhaland** movement of the 1980s. Led by the Gurkha National Liberation Front (GNLF) under the leadership of Subhash Ghising, a long and frequently very violent campaign has recently ended in what some see as a compromise, and others as a sell-out. The GNLF now controls the Darjeeling Hill Council, still under the aegis of the West Bengal government, but running vital services such as tourism and transport.

Arrival, information and transport

Virtually all travellers arriving in Darjeeling from the plains come via Siliguri (and Bagdogra, its airport; see p.766), whether by the "toy train", shared taxi or bus. Taxis and buses draw in at the **Bus Stand** in the bottom half of the town. Those taxis which aren't continuing anyway up to the **Clubside** taxi stand at the top of town – a lot nearer most of the hotels – can usually be persuaded to do so for around Rs15.

The town itself is best explored on foot – in fact much of it, such as the Mall and the Chowrasta, is closed to all vehicles, but shared taxis, buses and jeeps are available for journeys away from the centre. In particular, if you want to get to Tiger Hill for the sunrise (see p.776), jeeps wait at Clubside for the 4am run. This is also the place to arrange **car rental**.

Staff at Darjeeling's **Tourist Bureau**, 1 The Mall, on the **Chowrasta** above the *Indian Airlines* office, can fix up accommodation and transport for local sightseeing, and sell tickets for *DGHC* buses to Siliguri and Bagdogra. Indira Gongba of *Trek-Mate*, who runs a little stall at Ajit Mansions, opposite the Tourist Bureau, is an invaluable source of sound advice and information. **Banks** such as the *State Bank of India* and *ANZ Grindlays* can be found on Laden La Rd, as can the main **post office**.

If you're planning to head on to **Sikkim**, you'll have to get yourself a **permit** in Darjeeling. First pick up a form from the Deputy Commissioner's Office (Mon–Fri 9am–5pm), below the Gymkhana Club; take it to be be okayed by the **Foreigners Registration Office** on Laden La Rd; then return to the DC's office for the final stamp. That may all sound complicated, but it only takes around an hour. You have to specify where you intend to go; you can choose to go direct to western Sikkim.

The Town

The heart of Victorian Darjeeling, the **Chowrasta** – the word means "crossroads", and it's a large flat promenade where locals and tourists alike take the air – stands above the hectic bazaar on Hill Cart Road. A small group of interesting shops line one side, with a bandstand at the northern end and a line of stables to the south, offering pony rides to tourists who often outweigh the emaciated beasts. One of the four roads that meet at the Chowrasta is **the Mall**, recently renamed **Nehru Road**. This extension of the promenade descends gradually to Clubside, below the prestigious **Planters' Club**. Established in 1868, and otherwise known as the Darjeeling Club, this venerable institution was once the centre of Darjeeling high society. Not much seems to have changed since the days when tea planters from all over the territory rode here to attend social occasions, but visitors who take temporary membership are welcome to stay, and facilities such as the snooker room are available for a day-use fee.

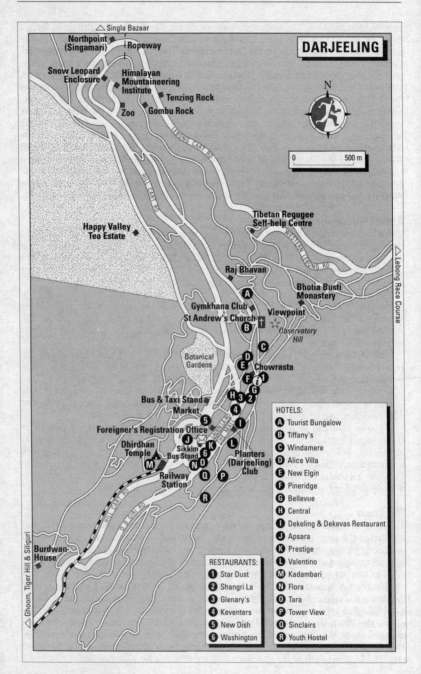

DARImage | DARJEELING

△ Singla Bazaar

Northpoint (Singamari) | Ropeway

Snow Leopard Enclosure

Himalayan Mountaineering Institute

Tenzing Rock
Gombu Rock
Zoo

N

0 ——— 500 m

Tibetan Regugee Self-help Centre

Happy Valley Tea Estate

Raj Bhavan

Bhotia Busti Monastery

△ Lebong Race Course

Ⓐ

Gymkhana Club
St Andrew's Church

Viewpoint

Ⓑ

Observatory Hill

Ⓒ

Ⓓ

Botanical Gardens

Ⓔ Chowrasta

Ⓕ Ⓘ❶
Ⓖ

Bus & Taxi Stand
Market

Ⓗ ❸ ❷
❹

Ⓘ

❺

Foreigner's Registration Office

Dhirdhan Temple

Ⓙ Ⓚ
❻
Ⓝ Ⓞ

Ⓛ

Sikkim Bus Stand

Planters (Darjeeling) Club

Ⓜ

Ⓠ Ⓟ

Railway Station

Ⓡ

Burdwan House

△ Ghoom, Tiger Hill & Siliguri

HOTELS:
Ⓐ Tourist Bungalow
Ⓑ Tiffany's
Ⓒ Windamere
Ⓓ Alice Villa
Ⓔ New Elgin
Ⓕ Pineridge
Ⓖ Bellevue
Ⓗ Central
Ⓘ Dekeling & Dekevas Restaurant
Ⓙ Apsara
Ⓚ Prestige
Ⓛ Valentino
Ⓜ Kadambari
Ⓝ Flora
Ⓞ Tara
Ⓟ Tower View
Ⓠ Sinclairs
Ⓡ Youth Hostel

RESTAURANTS:
❶ Star Dust
❷ Shangri La
❸ Glenary's
❹ Keventers
❺ New Dish
❻ Washington

Taking the right fork from the northern end of the Chowrasta, near the bandstand, brings you to a viewpoint where you can survey the Kanchendzonga massif and almost the entire state of Sikkim. From near the exclusive *Windermere Hotel* steps ascend the pine-covered hillside to **Observatory Hill** and another viewpoint. A steep road leads down from the summit, where a shrine to the Hindu goddess Kali is accompanied by streams of Buddhist prayer flags, to **Bhotia Busti**, the focus of Darjeeling's community of Bhotias, a people of Tibetan origin. Amid a warren of lanes stands the **Bhotia Busti Monastery**, with its beautifully painted facade. This small *gompa* was founded at the end of the nineteenth century, but is now almost empty.

Another Raj-era institution, now in sad decline, stands near Observatory Hill. The **Gymkhana Club** (☎55305) hit rock bottom during the Gurkhaland movement when a para-military outfit set up camp in its skating hall. It's now once again possible for visitors to drop in and play billiards, snooker, badminton, table tennis, tennis, squash and even roller skate. Below the club, a dreary **Natural History Museum** holds a huge but somewhat faded assortment of stuffed animals and birds (Thurs–Tues 10am–4pm & Wed 10am–1pm; Rs1). Further away from the Chowrasta, and a steep drop down from Government House, the extensive **Tibetan Self-Help Centre** stands above the road to the disused Lebong race course. Founded in 1959, it houses around 700 refugees, most of whom make carpets or Tibetan handicrafts. Tourists are welcome to wander through and watch the activity in the workshops; among items on sale are clothes, hats and leather items, and Tibetan boots made of embroidered cloth and leather soles. Whether ready-made or made to order, the carpets themselves are far from cheap.

A kilometre further on, north towards the high mountains and just above the gothic **St Joseph's College** (or Northpoint), the **Passenger Ropeway** is a cable car that in theory provides access to the tea gardens and Singla Bazaar in the Rangit Valley far below. Unfortunately, these days it never seems to be working. On the way there, however, Darjeeling's **Zoo** (daily 8am–4pm; Rs1) is worth a visit, not so much for its tigers, bears and wolves as for the enclosure of precious **snow leopards**, tucked away in the woods and reached by a separate entrance. Snow leopards are fluffier than ordinary leopards, with large bushy tails, and far more approachable, even playful. Officially an endangered species, they rarely breed in captivity; a breeding programme here is having mixed success.

Nearby Birch Hill is the home of the **Himalayan Mountaineering Institute**, reached via the zoo and covered by the same ticket. This is possibly India's most important training centre for climbers, holding countless courses (for Indians only) all year round. Its first Director was **Sherpa Tenzing Norgay**, the conqueror of Everest, who lived and died in Darjeeling; his nephew Nawang Gombu is now the Director. All the instructors are Sherpas or Bhotia mountain men, but the Principal is a representative of the armed forces, for whom the HMI plays a vital role. In the heart of the beautiful leafy complex are two fascinating exhibition halls (daily 9am–1pm & 2–4pm; additional Rs1). The **HMI Museum** is dedicated to the history of mountaineering, with equipment old and new, a relief map of the Himalayas, and a collection of costumes of different hill people, while the **Everest Museum** tells the story of the conquest of the highest mountain in the world. Photographs from early expeditions culminate with Tenzing and Hillary's successful climb in 1953. A huge telescope pointing at Kanchendzonga, known as "Hitler's telescope" because it was given by Hitler to a Nepalese general, provides remarkable views on a clear day.

Back in town, a road winds down from the bus stand in the bazaar to enter the **Botanical Gardens** (Mon–Sat 8am–6pm; free), where pines, willows and maples cover the hillside and pleasant walks zigzag down to the dilapidated central greenhouses, filled with ferns and orchids. One final prominent sight you're bound to notice is the multi-roofed **Dhirdham Temple** below the train station; built as a replica of the great Shiva temple of Pashupatinath, on the outskirts of Kathmandu, it is otherwise entirely lacking in significance.

DARJEELING TEA

Although the original appeal of Darjeeling for the British was as a hill resort with easy access from the heat of the plains, they soon realized its potential for growing **tea**. As they cleared the forests to introduce Chinese tea, they discovered that some of the plants they were discarding were indigenous strains of tea. Today, with the British long gone but the tea industry still going strong, the dominant strain grown here is Orange Pekoe, while China bushes also yield copious quantities.

If you're interested in learning at first hand just how tea is dried and processed, call in at the **Happy Valley Tea Estate** beyond the Botanical Gardens (Tues–Sat 8am–noon & 1–4.30pm, Sun 8am–noon; free). There are three separate plucking seasons each year; each is said to produce a "flush", with the first in the year considered to be the best.

As for **buying tea**, vendors with good reputations include *RN Agarwal*, who have a stall on the Mall, and *Nathmull's* on Laden La Rd, a large shop where they are only too happy to sit and explain the virtues, vices and vicissitudes of various teas. Such vendors usually trade in unblended tea, bought directly from tea gardens. Being independent, they are able to pick and choose according to quality and do not necessarily stock tea from the same garden every year. The typical cost of a kilo of good middle-grade tea is around Rs500. *Nathmull's* are happy to ship tea home for you.

Accommodation

One thing Darjeeling doesn't have a shortage of is **hotels**; in fact new ones spring up all the time, to place further strains upon the infrastructure. The main thing to establish before you check in anywhere is the **water** situation; many of the cheaper places only provide water in buckets, and charge extra if you like it hot.

Alice Villa, 41 HD Lama Rd (☎2381). Charming Victorian hotel at crossroads near Chowrasta. ⑥.

Apsara, 61 Laden La Rd (☎2983). Not far from the station; a modern building with reasonable rooms, but poorly located. ④–⑦.

Bellevue, The Mall (☎2129). Above the Tourist Bureau, and dominating the Chowrasta with very pleasant rooms, a bar and a restaurant. ⑥–⑦.

Central, Robertson Rd (☎2033). An old and prestigious establishment which captures the charm of Darjeeling and has a good restaurant. ⑧.

Chancellor, 5 Dr SM Das Rd (☎2956). A new hotel with good facilities including a restaurant and a pastry shop. Although comfortable it is poorly located, but the rooftop terrace makes up for it. ⑦.

Dekeling, 51 Gandhi Rd (☎3459). Well situated, with comfortable rooms and running hot water. Above *Dekevas* restaurant and owned by the same management. ③–④.

Flora, 7 Dr SM Das Rd (☎3458). Tibetan-run establishment offering simple budget rooms. ①–③.

High Land Inn, 176 Hill Cart Rd, below Railway Station. Near the Dhirdham Temple, convenient for late train arrivals. ③–④.

Kadambari, 15 Goodi Rd, near Railway Station (☎3064). Although friendly, this budget hotel does not feel geared up for foreign visitors, but may be handy for late arrivals. ①.

New Elgin, Robertson Rd (☎3314). Comfortable and well-maintained old-world atmosphere. Probably the second best after the *Windermere*; rates include all meals. ⑦–⑧.

Pagoda, 1 Upper Beechwood Rd. Close to Laden La Rd but surprisingly quiet, with reasonably priced rooms and a fire in the lounge. ②–③.

Pineridge, The Mall. Well situated next to the Chowrasta and part of a large mansion with spacious old-fashioned rooms. ③–④.

Planters' Club, also known as the *Darjeeling Club* (☎3400). Guests have to take out temporary membership; Rs50 for the first three days, reduced thereafter. Facilities include a billiard room, bar, restaurant and library. See also p.769. ⑥–⑦.

Prestige, above GPO, Laden La Rd (☎3199). Running hot water, good discounts and reasonable rooms makes this a popular place for travellers, on the steep steps leading up to Gandhi Rd. ④–⑤.

Rockville, 4 Rockville Rd (☎2513). New place with running hot water, electric and coal fires. ③–⑤.

Shamrock, Upper Beechwood Rd. Near the *Prestige* – an atmospheric and friendly Bhutanese-run establishment with a cosy kitchen. Popular with travellers for some years. ②–③.

Shangrila, The Mall (☎3349). Spacious old-world wood-lined rooms with fireplaces above a popular family restaurant that serves good Indian, Chinese and Tibetan dishes. ⑤–⑥.

Sinclairs, Gandhi Rd (☎54355). Large and insensitive newish building; one of the more expensive in town, but unremarkable and overpriced. ⑧.

Springburn, 70 Gandhi Rd (☎2054). Close to the similar *Tara*, with spacious rooms but no view. ②.

Tara, 125 Gandhi Rd (☎3060). Reasonable but otherwise unremarkable rooms and a restaurant with Indian and Tibetan food. ③–④.

Tiffany's, 4 Franklyn Prestage Rd, below *Gymkhana Club* (☎2840). Rambling old building and a bit dusty and decayed. Large rooms have fireplaces with a fire costing around Rs35; there is running water, but hot water comes in a bucket. Quiet, friendly and atmospheric. ⑤–⑥.

Tourist Lodge, Bhanu Sarani (☎2611). Tucked away behind the *Gymkhana*, a large and characterless establishment where rates include full board. ⑤–⑥.

Tower View, 8/1 Dr Zakir Hussein Rd, Rockville. Near the TV tower with good views, friendly and away from the noise with small rooms and a cosy Tibetan restaurant. ①.

Valentino, 6 Rockville Rd (☎2228). Situated in a warren of hotels above the telephone exchange, the Chinese-run *Valentino* is modern, well run, and clean for those on a mid-budget. ⑥–⑦.

Windermere, Observatory Hill (☎2397). The most celebrated of Darjeeling's hotels, which has accommodated a pantheon of rich and famous guests. Wonderful old-world atmosphere. ⑧–⑨.

MOVING ON FROM DARJEELING

The nearest **airport** to Darjeeling is Bagdogra,100km south (see p.766), with an utterly undependable service to **Calcutta, Delhi** and **Guwahati**. A *DGHC* bus leaves the *Tourist Lodge* and Clubside around 8am each day to connect with flights; book at the Tourist Bureau. *Indian Airlines* have an office on the Mall, at Chowrasta (☎2355).

To get to **Siliguri**, take a bus (Rs35) from the Bus Stand at the bazaar, or a shared taxi (Rs60) from the bazaar or Clubside. Taxis also head to **Kalimpong** (Rs30).

Two buses each day run to **Gangtok**; an ordinary one from the Sikkim Nationalised Transport Office, below the GPO on Laden La Rd, and an express from the Bus Stand.

The **Toy Train** (see p.766 for more detail) departs twice a day for **Siliguri** and **New Jalpaiguri** (8.30am & 10am), and an afternoon train travels to Kurseong. Reservations for mainline trains out of NJP can be made at Darjeeling's railway station.

Although it's possible to buy bus tickets for **Kathmandu**, you still have to change buses at Siliguri; it can be easier to make your own arrangements there (see p.766).

TREK AND TOUR OPERATORS

Greenland Tours & Travels, 21 Beechwood, Laden La Rd (☎2976). Tour and coach operators.

Himalayan Adventures, 15 The Mall (☎2204). Upmarket tour and trekking operation, run by Sheila Pradhan of *Das Studios* in conjunction with *The Trekking Company*, 37 Torrens St, Braddon ACT 2601, Australia (☎06/2576494).

Himalayan Nature & Adventure Foundation, 3 Belomber Rd, opposite Dhirdham Temple (☎2237). Run by Nima Tashi, Field Director of the HMI, a good organizer used to working with large expeditions. Singalila, Dzongri and Teesta valley treks.

Moktan Mountain Treks & Tours, c/o *Youth Hostel*, Dr Zakir Hussein Rd (☎2023). Friendly family-run concern, arranging treks to the Sandakphu and Sikkim.

Sherpa Adventure Foundation, NB Singh Rd. Rafting on the Teesta and Rangit rivers.

Shikhar Trekking, PO Maneybhanjan, Via Sukhia Pokhari, Darjeeling District, DGHC. Conveniently based for the Sandakphu trek.

Trek-Mate, Pine Ridge, Ajit Mansions, opposite Tourist Bureau, The Mall. Indira Gongba arranges tailor-made tours as well as treks to Sandakphu and western Sikkim. She can provide guides and porters and rents sleeping bags, down jackets and day packs.

SINGALILA TREKS

The single ridge of the **Singalila Range** rises near Darjeeling and extends all the way to the summit of Kanchendzonga. Relatively easy trails along its initial sections, to **Sandakphu** (3636m) and **Phalut** (3600m), do not stray onto glacial terrain, and provide magnificent views of the higher ranges. Lightweight expeditions are made possible by the existence of trekking huts (where the quilts are inadequate when it gets cold) and simple food stalls along the way. Several organizations in Darjeeling can arrange itineraries and guides, which are not absolutely essential for experienced trekkers, and rent equipment (see p.773). If you do plan to venture out alone, be sure to call in at the *Youth Hostel* in Darjeeling, where an incredibly useful log book records comments and descriptions from those who have done various treks and combinations of treks in the area.

Views from the Sandakphu–Phalut trail include four of the five highest mountains in the world – Everest, Kanchendzonga, Makalu and Lhotse. If you want to keep the panorama in sight rather than behind you, trek northwards from Sandakphu towards Phalut. The best time to trek is after the monsoons, in October and November, and during spring, February to May. It does get hot at the end of April and into May, but this is an especially beautiful season, with the rhododendrons in bloom.

Maneybhanjan, a small town and roadhead 27km from Darjeeling, is the most usual starting point for the route. Taking an early-morning bus (1hr 30min; Rs15) or taxi here from Darjeeling enables you to start the trek the same day, or you can stay here in basic accommodation such as the *Goperna Lodge* (②), or the simple but comfortable rooms above *Wangdi Tibetan Restaurant* (①). As far as Sandakphu, the steep trail is accompanied by a rough jeep track; if you're desperate, you can take a jeep all the way from Darjeeling to Sandakphu for Rs1200.

Assuming you start from Maneybhanjan, **DAY 1** begins with a sharp climb to **Meghma**, then eases to the hut at **Tonglu** (3070m). Most trekkers continue from Meghma to the small town of **Jaubari** in Nepal, with its handful of small cheap lodges such as the *Everest Lodge* (①), and places to eat. Officials, well used to trekkers passing through, look the other way. On **DAY 2**, the Jaubari trail rejoins the main one at **Gairibas**, continues to **Kalipokhari** and **Bikhaybhanjan**, then rises steeply to **Sandakphu** (3636m), which has a trekkers' hut and a couple of PWD bungalows.

The panorama opens out as you leave Sandakphu on **DAY 3**, and the trek follows the ridge to **Sabarkum**. There's no shelter or food there, but you can find both by dropping down to the right for half an hour to **Molley**. On **DAY 4**, retrace your steps to Sabarkum and continue along the ridge to **Phalut** (3600m) where there is a simple trekkers' lodge but nothing else. The panorama from here is particularly impressive. Either retrace your steps to Sandakphu on **DAY 5**, or follow the trail from Phalut via **Gorkhey** to **Rammam** (2560m), home of the *Sherpa Lodge* (①).

The final day, **DAY 6**, leads to **Rimbik** (2286m) where accommodation options include the *Shiva Pradhan* (①) which has hot water, and the warm and cosy *Sherpa Lodge* (①). Rimbik is a roadhead served by buses and taxis for Darjeeling, or you can walk for another (long) day's walk to Bijanbari, which also has transport to Darjeeling.

Youth Hostel, Zakir Hussein Rd (☎2290). On top of the ridge with wonderful views. Although a bit run down, it continues to be popular and the management are friendly. Dorms and a couple of double rooms. They also organize treks to Sandakphu. ①.

Eating

Darjeeling has plenty of choice for **eating out**; the more touristy of its restaurants are around the top of town. Many of the hotels reviewed above, such as the *Windermere*, *Central* and *New Elgin*, have very good multi-cuisine restaurants, and the *Windermere* also has a cosy bar.

Ailment, Zakir Hussein Rd. Close to the *Youth Hostel*, with good-value Chinese and Tibetan food.

Amigos, Chowrasta. Brash new fast-food restaurant; burgers, pizzas and south Indian food.

△ Legship & Pemayengtse

SIKKIM

Raman River

Phalut 3600m

Sabarkum

Molley

Raman

Naya Bazaar

Jorethang

0   5 km

N

Rimbik

Lodoma

Singla Bazaar

Sandakphu 3636m

Rangit River

△ Gangtok

Kalipokhari

Gairibas

WEST BENGAL

Lebong

Jaubari

Tonglu

Bijanbari

Little Rangit River

Darjeeling

△ Kalimpong

Meghma

Manaybhanjang

Ghoom

Tiger Hill 2590m

SINGALILA TREKS

Mirik ▽   Siliguri ▽

Glenary's, The Mall. Darjeeling's most reputable restaurant, with a Victorian tea-room atmosphere. A good place for tea, it also serves Indian and Chinese food and has a bar, bakery and patisserie.

Keventers, Clubside. Snack bar serving hearty ham-and-bacon breakfasts. The terrace above the crossroads is excellent for people-watching, even if the service is poor.

New Dish, JP Sharma Rd. Excellent Chinese food, prepared by Suyan, the former chef to the Bhutan royal family. A favourite with the local Chinese community, it was rebuilt after a fire in 1992.

Orient, NB Singh Rd. Close to the *New Dish* but nowhere near as good. Indian and Chinese.

Star Dust, Chowrasta. Open-air restaurant serving coffee and snacks, and strong on Indian food.

Listings

Bookshops *Oxford Books & Stationery*, Chowrasta.

Hospitals *Planters' Hospital*, Planter's Club, The Mall.

Pharmacies *Puri & Co*, The Mall.

Photography *Das Studios*, The Mall; *Darjeeling Photo Stores*, The Mall.

Shopping Apart from tea, Darjeeling is a good place to buy curios, semi-precious stones and Tibetan costumes and jewellery. The best shops in which to browse include *Lhasa Curio*, on Gandhi Rd near the *Hotel Tara*, and the confusing but potentially rewarding *Habib Mullick's* on the Chowrasta.

Around Darjeeling

One really unmissable part of the Darjeeling experience is the early-morning mass exodus to **Tiger Hill**, to watch the sunrise. That readily combines with a visit to the old monastery of **Ghoom**, and there's another huge monastery at **Sonada** on the Hill Cart Road towards Siliguri. The picturesque lake at **Mirik** near the Nepal border attracts weekend crowds.

Tiger Hill

Jeeps and taxis packed with tourists leave Darjeeling around 4am each morning, careering 12km through Ghoom and the woodlands to catch the sunrise at **TIGER HILL**. Tickets are required to enter either of the two floors of the **viewing tower** at the top of the hill; the top floor costs Rs7, the lower one Rs2, and both rates include tea and biscuits. This incredible viewpoint, at an altitude of 2585m, provides an unparalleled 360° Himalayan panorama, with the steamy plains bordering Bangladesh to the south, the Singalila range with Everest beyond to the west, Kanchendzonga and Sikkim to the north, and the Bhutanese and Assam Himalayas trailing into the distance to the north-east. From left to right, the peaks around Everest include Lhotse (which actually looks larger than Everest), Everest itself, and Makalu, then after a long gap the rocky summit of Kang on the Sikkim–Nepal divide, Jannu in Nepal, Rathong, Kabru South, Kabru North, Talung, Kanchendzonga Main, Central, South, Pandim, Simvo, Narsing and the fluted pyramid of Siniolchu. As the sun rises from the plains, it lights each in turn; not yet obscured by the haze of the day, they are bathed in pastel hues.

It's also possible to walk up during the day and camp for the night near the top. A *Tourist Bungalow* stands on the plain below the summit, but has been closed for some years; check in Darjeeling to see if it has re-opened. Night treks to Tiger Hill used to be popular, but are no longer recommended; if the bandits don't get you the dogs will.

Ghoom and other monasteries

Although one of the many monasteries along Hill Cart Road announces itself on a billboard as the "Ghoom Monastery", it isn't; it is in fact the new monastery of **Samten Choling**, beautifully sited looking over the mountains but otherwise unimportant.

Yiga Choling, the real **GHOOM MONASTERY**, is hidden above the road, reached via a side road that rises two hundred metres beyond Ghoom railway station towards Darjeeling, passes through a small market, then winds up to end at the monastery. Built by Sharap Gyatso in 1850, a renowned astrologer, the monastery comprises a single chambered temple, with a few residential buildings and an outhouse. Inside the prayer hall stands a huge image of Maitreya, the Buddha of the future. Adorned with *katas* (ceremonial scarves), he is unusally depicted seated on a chair; his eyes are blue, as according to one belief he will appear from the west. A beautiful painting of the demonic Mahakala is always covered with red cloth; he is considered too fierce to be looked at directly. At the entrance is a donation box with a suggested charge per photograph. Buses, shared taxis and trucks connect Ghoom with Darjeeling, but the pleasantest ways to travel have to be walking the 8km, or catching the Toy Train.

A bit further towards Darjeeling, the vast **Thupten Sanga Choeling** towers above the main road. The adjacent **Dali Gompa** was built by the Bhutanese monk Drukchen Rinpoche, a follower of the poet-saint Milarepa, to welcome the Dalai Lama in 1993.

In the small hamlet of Rongbul, south of Ghoom and below the Hill Cart Road, the small Nyingmapa **Gonjan Monastery** holds a stunning collection of *thangkas*, Tibetan painted scrolls. Alongside it, the *School of Tibetan Thangka Painting* is run by the artist Lama Tsondu Sangpo, whose work, sometimes for sale, displays a distinctive fluid style. Further down Hill Cart Road, the huge **Sonada Monastery**, founded in the 1960s, was the seat of Kalu Rinpoche who developed a large American and French following. It has just been extensively renovated, to house Kalu Rinpoche's *tulku* or re-incarnation, who has been recently discovered. Rooms are available for retreat.

Mirik

MIRIK, 45km southwest of Darjeeling near the border with Nepal, before the initial rise of the Singalila Range, is being promoted as a new resort, but for the moment it remains quiet and low-key except on weekends. Surrounded by huge tea estates, it's a nice place to come and enjoy a walk through the surrounding pine forests.

The two distinct settlements of Mirik offer a small choice of **accommodation**. The reasonable clean *Chinari*, Krishan Nagar (②), stands beside the picturesque central lake; the wooden *Prem Deep Lodge* (①) nearby is friendly if primitive; and the *Tourist Lodge* (①–③) has a dorm, double rooms and a cottage suite with good views of the lake. Restaurants and cafes in the vicinity include the *Chinari*, which serves Indian, Nepalese and Chinese food. Buses and shared taxis run to and from Darjeeling.

Kalimpong

Though it may seem quite grubby at first, the hill station of **KALIMPONG** – a sort of small sister to Darjeeling – has a lot to offer anyone who cares to explore, including an extraordinary profusion of spectacular flowers and orchids. Unlike Darjeeling, this was never a tea town or resort; it was a trading town on the vital route to Tibet, and may indeed be so again one day. Tensions between India and China over the last few decades have meant that local roads were also strategic military lifelines, and the whole region was closed to foreign tourists, but Kalimpong itself, and the hills around it, are now once more opening up. For the present it lies somewhat dormant, having suffered during the political upheavals of the Gurkhaland movement, and prone to severe water shortages as a result of the total neglect of its infrastructure – although the army is still here, remaining aloof in the cantonment area.

Kalimpong spreads along a curving ridge to either side of its main **market area**, known as **Tenth Mile**. Though this lacks the curio and tourist shops so common in Darjeeling and Gangtok, it remains worth investigating, especially on Wednesdays and Sundays when villagers flock in from the surrounding areas for the principal weekly markets. A few Tibetan stalls sell food as well as bags and jewellery.

Rinkingpong Hill, which looms above town to the southwest, was once a surveying point; hence the local name *Durpin Dara*, which means "binocular ridge". It is now firmly in the hands of the army, who allow tourists through in taxis but occasionally stop those on foot. At its highest point, entirely surrounded by the army, is the **Zong Dog Palri Fobrang Monastery**, consecrated by the Dalai Lama in 1976. As well as a large image of Guru Rinpoche, also known as Padma Sambhava, the patron saint and founder of the Nyingmapa order – it holds some impressive frescoes, and an excellent collection of *thangkas* (not always on display). Upstairs there's an image of the thousand-armed Chenrazee, or Avalokitesvara, and an ornate wooden model of heaven.

At the other end of town, half an hour's walk up Deolo Hill brings you to the **Tharpa Choling Gompa**, a Gelugpa or "Yellow Hat" monastery, founded in 1892 and now being completely rebuilt, as the original structure had cracked. Nearby is the **Thongsa Gompa**, a small Bhutanese monastery built in 1692. The strong impact of Christian missionaries on the area is evident in **Dr Graham's Home**, further up the hill. Founded in 1900 by the Scotsman, Rev Dr John Anderson Graham, as a home for six orphans, this famous school today has around 900 students, and has inspired several similar schools for the destitute and the handicapped. It also runs its own dairy. Kalimpong used to be known for its **cheese**, manufactured by a Swiss dairy; production is only now starting to pick up again after disruption during the Gurkhaland movement. Above Dr Graham's Home, **Deolo View Point** offers superb views of the town, the Teesta Valley below, and even, on a clear day, the snows and the passes of Nathula and Jelepla into Tibet. Nearby **Deolo Lake** is the town's inadequate reservoir.

Arrival and information

Kalimpong is only accessible by **road**, and served by regular buses, taxis and jeeps from Darjeeling (3hr 30min) and Siliguri (2hr 30min). Coming from Gangtok, you may have to change buses at Teesta Bazaar, on the River Teesta. Although as soon as you cross the river (no photos as you go over the bridge), at a sweltering 300m, you're confronted by a sign welcoming you to Kalimpong, the town itself is 15km further on, and over 1000m higher up.

Most transport pulls in at the **Motor Stand** in the central market area. This is the place to pick up buses to Darjeeling (run by the *Kalimpong Motor Syndicate* and the *Darjeeling Gurkha Hill Council*), Gangtok (*Sikkim Nationalised Transport;* ☎0352/319), and Siliguri (*North Bengal State Transport* among others). The last buses each day usually leave in early afternoon.

As Kalimpong is not in the mainstream of tourism, it has no tourist information bureau. However, a number of organizations arrange **walking** and **cycling** tours and assorted activities in the area, prime among them the highly efficient *Bike & Trek Himalayas*, Main Rd (☎0352/304). The head office of the Darjeeling Gurkha Hill Council, Silver Fir Building, The Mall, Darjeeling, can advise on the latest situation.

The main **post office** is close to the centre of town, above the bazaar area near the police station, and there's a *State Bank of India* (☎0352/310) a little further up.

Accommodation and eating

Kalimpong's acute **water** problems are likely to influence your choice of **accommodation** – few of the lower-range options have running water. Both the market area and the Motor Stand are centres for budget hotels. The Victorian **youth hostel**, set in what must have been lovely grounds, is sadly in a terrible state. Most of the best **restaurants** are in the hotels – especially the *Kalimpong Park* – but alternatives to look out for include the *Myal Lyang*, a very good Chinese restaurant on Rishi Road.

Chimal, Rinkingpong Rd (☎0352/776). New hotel, with a nice terrace on road level, a dining hall and tour services, and boasting attached baths with hot and cold running water. ③–⑤.

Cosy Nook, Motor Stand (☎0352/541). Family hotel, run by Anil Pradhan. Rooms with attached baths, handy for buses and taxis and recommended if you're on a tight budget. ①–③.

Deke Lodge, Tripai Rd, 10th Mile. Set in a quiet spot around ten minutes' walk uphill from the Motor Stand, and marked *T Temba Cottage*. Only a few rooms, but there's running water and meals are provided to order. Clean, friendly and recommended for the budget traveller. ①–②.

Gompu's, Dambar Chowk (☎0352/818). Landmark hotel in the heart of the market area, with atmospheric wooden rooms – the bar and restaurant downstairs are straight out of a film set for *Shanghai* or *Casablanca*. *Gompu's* has been plagued by water problems and is now very much the haunt of budget travellers. Proprietor Sonam Gompu is helpful and friendly. ②–④.

Himalayan (☎0352/248). Historic hotel, set amid exquisite gardens in the former residence of David Macdonald, an interpreter with the Younghusband Mission to Lhasa in 1904 who helped the 13th Dalai Lama to escape Tibet in 1910. The Macdonald family still run the hotel, which boasts oak ceilings, teak pillars and fireplaces in most rooms and is filled with memorabilia. ⑥.

Kalimpong Park (☎0352/304). Three-star family-run hotel with a bit of a split personality; the main building is old and quaint, but most guest rooms are in the spacious but characterless modern block behind. A helpful travel counter and a good restaurant; credit cards accepted. ⑤–⑥.

Myal Lyang Lodge, Rishi Rd (☎0352/333). Modern Chinese-run block not far from the Motor Stand. Double rooms with attached baths are quite cheap and reasonable, so long as you don't mind getting water by the bucket – they suffer from the usual water problems. ①–③.

Sherpa Lodge, Dr Ongden Rd (☎0352/572). Basic no-frills hotel, above the playground near the Motor Stand. ①.

Silver Oaks (☎0352/296 or 368). Comfortable and plush, Kalimpong's premier (four-star) hotel has a rather drab grey brick and glass exterior and generally lacks character. 20 rooms with telephones, and all amenities including currency exchange. ⑦–⑧.

WBTDC Hill Top Tourist Lodge, Hill Top (☎0352/384). Large and reasonably pleasant Victorian lodge. In the middle price range, but with a dorm. ①–⑤.

WBTDC Shangrila Tourist Lodge, near *Novelty Cinema* (☎0352/230). WBTDC's budget lodge, offering double rooms as well as a dorm. ①.

WBTDC Singamare Tourist Lodge, Durpin Hill (☎0352/384). Grand grey lodge, set in fabulous gardens and built for a British jute merchant. The equally beautiful annexe, the *Tashiding Tourist Lodge*, belonged to Jigme Dorji, a premier of Bhutan who was mysteriously murdered. ⑤–⑥.

CHAPTER THIRTEEN

BIHAR

One of India's poorest states, **BIHAR** occupies the flat eastern Gangetic basin, south of Nepal between Uttar Pradesh and West Bengal. The land of the Buddha – born in Lumbini in Nepal, he spent much of his life wandering through the kingdoms of the Ganges – Bihar's very name comes from *"vihara"*, monastery. In his quest for truth during the sixth century BC, Prince Gautama visited **Vaishali** and **Rajgir**, before moving on to **Bodh Gaya** and gaining enlightenment under the Bodhi Tree. Only during the nineteenth century was it demonstrated that the major events of the Buddha's life took place in identifiable sites here in north India, but the region now draws Buddhist pilgrims from all over the world. As well as being the first centre of Buddhism in north India, Bihar was its last bastion; the university of **Nalanda** stands as a poignant reminder of the extent of the faith. In addition, the state capital **Patna** (ancient Pataliputra) is sacred to Sikhs as the birthplace of Guru Gobind Singh, the tenth guru; **Gaya** is holy to Hindus; and the founder of Jainism, Mahavira, a contemporary of the Buddha who also lived and taught around Bihar, gained enlightenment at **Pawapuri** close to Nalanda.

Historically, Bihar's greatest moments came early. During the sixth century BC, this was the heartland of the **Magadhas**, whose King Bimbisara was converted by the Buddha at his capital of Rajagriha (now Rajgir). Shortly after the Magadhas shifted their capital to Patna, they were overthrown around 321 BC by the dynamic **Chandragupta Maurya**, said to have met Alexander the Great. The next major dynasty to rule Bihar were the **Guptas**, around the fourth century AD, whose advent marked the return of Hinduism. Extraordinarily, even after the Muslim Sultanate swept the region at the end of the twelfth century, and the Moghuls came to rule all northern India from Delhi three hundred years later, the Buddhist centre of Bodh Gaya continued to thrive. Bihar was incorporated into Bengal in 1764, soon fell under British jurisdiction, and eventually became a province and finally a state of modern India.

Thanks to intense poverty, inter-caste violence and general lawlessness, Bihar today has a reputation as one of the worst-run states in the country. The best that can be said for it is that its government (a coalition under the Janata Party, led by Lalu Prasad Yadav) is at least committed to secularism, even though it is virtually controlled by the Thakurs, a clan of caste-based landlords. During the traumatic aftermath of events in Ayodhya in late 1992, Bihar was one of the few north Indian states to escape violence. However, it is characterized by an almost complete absence of law and order – kidnappings, banditry and rape are commonplace – and agitation for independence among the tribes of the Chotanagpur plateau. Although the ordinary visitor or Buddhist pilgrim is usually unaffected, no one chooses to travel the roads of Bihar at night.

After the torrential monsoons hit the Himalayas, large tracts of the plains of Bihar are annually submerged by floods; rivers like the Kosi burst their banks, and the Ganges is in spate. At other times, the Gangetic basin is racked by drought; lacking the right alluvial deposits, its soil never manages to yield enough food. Only far to the south does the land become greener, where the slightly higher elevations of the Chotanagpur plateau, around industrial **Ranchi** and **Jamshedpur**, are still covered by forest. This remote southwestern region, hard against Madhya Pradesh, holds the wildlife sanctuary of **Palamau National Park**.

Govt of India Statement -
The external boundaries of India are neither correct nor authenticated.

Patna

The capital of Bihar, **PATNA**, dates back to the sixth century BC, which makes it one of the very oldest cities in India. Today, it's a nice enough place, but one which holds only the barest of indications of its former glory, as the centre of the Magadhan and Mauryan empires. The sprawling metropolis hugs the south bank of the Ganges, stretching for around 15km in a shape that has changed little since Ajatasatru (491–459 BC) shifted the Magadhan capital here from Rajgir.

The first Mauryan emperor, **Chandragupta**, established himself in what was then **Pataliputra**, in 321 BC, and pushed the limits of his empire as far as the Indus; his grandson **Ashoka** (274–237 BC), among the greatest of all Indian rulers, held sway over even greater domains. To facilitate Indo-Hellenic trade, the Mauryans built a Royal Highway from Pataliputra to Taxila, which later became the Grand Trunk Road, and similar highways reached towards the Bay of Bengal and along the east coast. The city experienced two later revivals. The first Gupta emperor, also named **Chandra Gupta**, made Patna his capital early in the fourth century AD, and a thousand years later it was rebuilt by the brilliant Afghan ruler Sher Shah Suri (1540–45), who constructed the Sher Shahi Mosque in the east of the city. Nearby, the beautiful *gurudwara* of **Har Mandir** was built to honour the birthplace of the tenth and most militant Sikh Guru – Guru Gobind Singh. In his honour, Patna is often referred to as Patna Sahib.

Arrival, transport and information

Patna has three railway stations, but all mainline services arrive at **Patna Junction**, in the west of the city in the Bankipur area. Frazer Road (now officially Mazharul-Raq Path) is the main drag, immediately north of the station. Patna's **airport** is a mere 5km west of here (a Rs18 cycle-rickshaw ride into town, or Rs70 by taxi), while a few hundred metres west of the station, the main **Harding Park Bus Stand** offers connections to Gaya, Varanasi, and the Nepal border at Raxaul. North of Frazer Road, on the northern (river) side of the large oval Gandhi Maidan, the **Gandhi Maidan Bus Stand** is a *Bihar Roadways* terminal serving destinations throughout the state.

Cycle rickshaws and auto-rickshaws are the most common means of transport; shared *Vikram* auto-rickshaws cross the city east to west for around Rs6.

The inadequate **Bihar Tourist Office**, Frazer Rd (☎25295), provides information and organizes tours at weekends, taking in Patna, Nalanda, Rajgir and Pawapur. The **Government of India Tourist Office**, Beer Chand Patel Path (☎26721), is a little brighter, but doesn't do much better. *Ashok Travels, TCI* and *Patna Tours* (see p.784) also organize tours and arrange **car rental**. The *State Bank of India*, on West Gandhi Maidan (☎226134), handles **foreign exchange**, and the GPO is on Buddha Marg.

The Town

In the most interesting area of Patna – the older part of town, 10km east of the centre – tiny congested lanes, crammed with vehicles of all kinds, lead to **Har Mandir Sahib**, the second holiest of the four great Sikh shrines known as *takhts* (thrones), and dedicated to Guru Gobind Singh, born in Patna in 1660. Visitors are obliged to remove their shoes and cover their heads before entering the central onion-domed marble temple, set in an expansive courtyard off the main road. Stairs lead up to a small museum containing relics from the Guru's life; one room focusses on the theme of martyrdom.

A little way north, the private **Qila House** (or Jalan Museum), on Jalan Ave, holds a fine collection of art including Chinese paintings and Moghul filigree work in jade and silver (call ahead for permission from the Jalan family; ☎42354). Among the antiques are porcelain that once belonged to Marie Antoinette, and Napoleon's four-poster bed. Further east, close to the river, the **Old Opium Warehouse** at **Gulzaribagh**, now a printing press, allows visitors to view the East India Company halls. Beyond it lies a small mosque known as **Saif Khan's Mosque** or the "mosque of stone".

A few fragments of a Mauryan hall, and a single highly polished sandstone pillar, stand at **Kumrahar** in south Patna, between Patna Junction and Rajendranagar stations, as the most significant surviving relics of the golden days of Pataliputra (daily except

The telephone **area code** for Patna is ☎0612.

PATNA

Sonepur, Vaishali, Muzaffarpur & Nepal

Nalanda & Rajgir

1 km

0

N

River Ganges

Mahatma Gandhi Bridge

Qila House

Har Mandir Sahib

Sher Shahi Mosque

ASHOK RAJ PATH

Old Opium Warehouse

Catholic Church

Rajendranagar Railway Station

Saif Khan's Mosque

Kumrahar Excavations

OLD BYPASS RD

NEW BYPASS RD

Khuda Baksh Oriental Library

BARI RD

ASHOK RAJ PATH

Mahendra Ghat Ferry Terminal

Khapi Emporium

Bus Stand

Golghar

Gandhi Maidan

Indian Airlines

British Library

State Bank of India

EXHIBITION RD

Patna Junction Railway Station

Patna Museum

BAILEY RD

DINAPORE RD

GPO

Bus Stand

Gaya

Airport

Muner & Varansi

HOTELS:
A Maurya Patna
B Rajasthan
C Rajdhani
D Pataliputra Ashok
E Samrat
F Indrasan
G Tourist Bungalow

RESTAURANTS:
1 Coffee Corner
2 Ashoka
3 Annapurna
4 Mayfair
5 Bansi Vihar

Mon 9am–5pm; Rs0.50). This is hardly the most dramatic of sites, though the surrounding gardens are attractive, and a small museum displays assorted finds. The massive hall once covered 77 square metres and was built on three storeys; most of it was made of wood, which may explain why it did not endure. The Chinese traveller Fa Hien, who came here in the fifth century AD, reported that it had already stood for 700 years.

Perhaps Patna's most remarkable monument – if in a sense also oddly mundane – dates from the British era. This huge grain storage house known as **Golghar**, the "round house" – now a symbol of the city – was built in 1786 by John Garstin at the behest of the then administrator, Warren Hastings, in the hope of avoiding a repetition of the terrible famine in 1770. Mercifully it never needed to be used. Overlooking the river and the *maidan*, it looks like the upper half of a gigantic off-white Easter egg, decorated with two sets of stairs that spiral their way to the summit, 29m above the road. These were designed so that coolies could carry grain up one flight, deliver their load through a hole at the top, and descend the other stairs. Constructed with stone slabs, the base of the structure is 125 metres wide, with 3.6-metre-thick walls. Sightseers now clamber up for views of the mighty river and the town itself.

Within walking distance, the **Patna Museum**, though faded and run-down, has an excellent collection of sculpture (daily except Mon 10am–4.30pm; Rs0.50). Among its most famous pieces is a polished sandstone female attendant or *yakshi*, holding a flywhisk, found at Didarganj and dated to the third century BC. Some Jain images from the Kushana period, and a group of Buddhist *bodhisattvas* from the Gandhara region (northwest Pakistan), belong to the second and third centuries AD. Natural history exhibits feature several stuffed animals, including a few freaks, and a gigantic fossilized tree thought to be 200 million years old. The museum also houses Chinese art, and some superb Tibetan *thangkas* (scroll paintings), albeit not in the best of conditions.

Founded in 1900, the **Khuda Bhaksh Oriental Library**, east of Gandhi Maidan, has a remarkable selection of books from all over the Islamic world, all gathered by one man. Besides rare Persian and Arabic manuscripts, it houses Moghul and Rajput miniatures, and manuscripts rescued from the Moorish University at Cordoba in Spain. One of its more unusual exhibits is a tiny Koran measuring just 25mm wide.

Accommodation and eating

Patna has an ample choice of **accommodation**. Cheaper hotels can be found around the station end of Frazer Road, while the top end can offer the *Maurya Patna* and the more affordable *Pataliputra Ashok*. Apart from those in the upmarket hotels, Frazer Rd holds several good **restaurants**, such as the *Annapurna*, which serves north and south Indian food, and the *Bansi Vihar*, a good-value south Indian vegetarian place.

Chanakya, Beer Chand Patel Marg (☎223141). A comfortable new hotel which has quickly found favour with visiting businessmen. ⑤–⑥.

Indrasan, Frazer Rd (☎226872). Good budget value, close to all amenities. ①.

Magada, Hotel Lane, off Frazer Rd. One of several hotels crowded into this lane, near the station with reasonable budget rooms. ①.

Maurya Patna, Frazer Rd, South Gandhi Maidan (☎222060). The only luxury hotel in town with numerous facilities and a nice location. The bar and restaurant are quite pleasant. ⑨.

Mayur, Frazer Rd (☎224149). Affordable rooms with running hot water. ③.

Pataliputra Ashok, Beer Chand Patel Path (☎226270). Friendly staff make up for this large rambling hotel which is now looking frayed at the edges. The restaurant is quite pleasant. ⑦–⑧.

President, off Frazer Rd (☎220600). Reasonable rooms, including some a/c. ③–④.

Rajasthan, Frazer Rd (☎225102). An old Indian-style hotel, with some air-cooled rooms and a good vegetarian restaurant. ③–④.

Samrat International, Frazer Rd (☎220560). Close to all amenities, with a choice of restaurants and reasonably comfortable a/c and non-a/c rooms. ⑥–⑦.

Tourist Bungalow, Tourist Bhavan, Beer Chand Patel Path (☎2254110). Next to the Tourist Office, with a dorm and good-value rooms with running hot water. ②.

MOVING ON FROM PATNA

Patna Junction is the most important **railway** station in the region, connected to **Gaya**, **Delhi**, **Varanasi**, **Darjeeling** (NJP), **Calcutta**, **Bombay** and **Madras**. Principal trains to Calcutta are the *AC Express* #2304 and the *Amritsar Mail* #3006, which in the other direction travels via Varanasi. The *AC Express* #2303 travels to Delhi and *Chapra Bombay Express* #5114 to Bombay. **Patna Airport** is linked by *Indian Airlines* (City Office, South Gandhi Maidan; ☎222554) to **Calcutta**, **Ranchi**, **Delhi**, **Bombay** and **Lucknow** but flights to **Kathmandu** have been suspended for the time being. Although it is just as easy to make your own arrangements, travel companies offer bus tickets to Kathmandu, with a voucher for the bus across the border. Buses for the Nepal border at **Raxaul** (5hr; Rs40; see p.786) depart from the main Harding Road Bus Stand, as do buses to **Gaya**, **Vaishali**, and via **Muner** to **Varanasi**. Buses to Vaishali also leave from the Gandhi Maidan Bus Stand.

Reliable **travel agents** in town include *Ashok Travel & Tours*, in the *Hotel Pataliputra Ashok*; *Inter Travel Shop*, Frazer Rd (☎221337); and *Travel Corporation of India*, Maurya Patna Complex (☎221699).

Around Patna

Patna makes a popular base for exploring Nalanda and Rajgir, as well as Vaishali to the north, but there are also places of interest closer at hand. The fabulous *dargah* – Sufi mausoleum – at **Muner**, on the road to Varanasi, is the prime attraction, but if you're in the area in October, don't miss the enormous month-long **cattle fair** at **Sonepur**, across the huge Gandhi Bridge 25km north of Patna, at the confluence of the Gandak and Ganges. Cattle, elephants, parakeets and other animals are brought for sale and barter, pilgrims combine business with a dip in the Ganga, *sadhus* congregate, and festivities include live song and dance performance.

Muner

The imposing but somewhat neglected red sandstone mausoleum of the Sufi saint Yahia Muneri overlooks a lake 27km west of Patna on the busy Varanasi road, 1km west of **MUNER**. It's an easy bus ride from the city, and the excursion is well worth while; however, the Bihar government seems to have given up its attempts to promote the site in the face of a lack of tourist interest. The shrine itself, built in 1605 by Ibrahim Khan, the governor of Gujarat under Jahangir, stands atop a hillock; the beautifully maintained gardens below are the responsibility of Sufi caretakers, whose timeless lifestyle provides an intriguing glimpse of days gone by. Every year, around February, a three-day *Urs* or festival in the saint's honour attracts pilgrims from far and wide, including *qawwals*, the renowned Sufi minstrels of the Chistia orders of Delhi and Ajmer. If you do come to Muner, it's worth knowing that the town is famous for its **sweets**, and especially *ladoos*, made of lentils.

North Bihar

The one area of Bihar capable of growing crops is the fertile agricultural belt along the Himalayan foothills north of the Ganges. Other than passing through en route to Nepal via the large town of **Muzaffarpur**, most visitors only pause to explore the remains of the abandoned Buddhist city of **Vaishali**, although the region also holds a handful of shrines and temple towns associated with the *Ramayana*.

MADHUBANI PAINTINGS

The small town of Madhuban, in the district of Mithila in north Bihar, is the home of a vibrant tradition of Indian folk art. **Madhubani paintings** started out as decorations for the outside of village huts, executed by the women using natural dyes. Illustrations of mythological themes, incorporating images of local deities as well as Hindu gods and goddesses, the paintings were eventually transferred onto hand-made paper, often using bright synthetic primary colours, mixed in unique ways, to fill the strong black line drawings. You do see plain black and white pictures, but more familiar now are paintings dominated by reds and blues and offset by yellow, on a white background.

Fabrics printed with Madhubani designs have become very chic; usually in one colour only, these days they tend to be professionally made elsewhere, and are sold in the expensive boutiques of India's major cities.

Vaishali

Set amid the paddy fields, 55km north of Patna, the quiet hamlet of **VAISHALI** is significant to both Buddhists and Jains. Archeological excavations are still in progress, and only a fraction of this ancient city, buried deep in the silted floodplains on the banks of the River Gandak and dating from the sixth century BC, has yet been unearthed. This was where the Buddha preached his last sermon, before he died in Kushinagara around 483 BC, and a silver urn containing ashes found in a *stupa* close to the Coronation Tank is said to contain his remains.

Named after King Visala, who is mentioned in the *Ramayana*, some historians believe Vaishali to have been the first city state in the world to practise a democratic, republican form of government. Prince Gautama, after leaving Nepal and renouncing the world and his family, studied here, then rejected his master's teachings to continue on the path which eventually led to his becoming the Buddha. He returned on three occasions; on his last visit, he announced his final liberation – *Mahaparinirvana* – and departure from the world. One hundred years later, in 383 BC, the Second Buddhist Council was held in Vaishali, and two *stupas* were erected. For a further thousand years, under Pataliputra (Patna) as capital, Vaishali continued to prosper.

At the quiet centre of the main site, surrounded by trees, the rectangular **Coronation Tank** (or Abhishekh Pushkarni) bears little evidence of its past; considered holy, its waters were used to anoint the leaders of the city. On one side of the tank, near the visitors' centre, a small but well-presented **archeological museum** is dedicated to the local excavations. Along with terracotta, seals, pottery, coins and sculpture from elsewhere, it provides a fascinating picture of the ancient Buddhist world (daily except Fri 10am–5pm; free). A short path next to the tank leads off to the remains of the *stupa*, now covered by a roof, where the supposed ashes of the Buddha were found.

Two kilometres north at **Kolhua**, reached via the left fork of the main road, stands the remarkably well-preserved **Ashokan Pillar**, erected by the Mauryan emperor (273–232 BC) to commemorate the site of the Buddha's last sermon. Out of the thirty such pillars throughout his immense kingdom, this is one of only two still on its original site. Known locally as Bhimsen-ki-lathi (Bhimsen's staff), the 18.3-metre-high pillar is made of highly polished red sandstone, and is crowned by a lion, sitting on an inverted lotus, which faces north towards Kushinagara. Alongside, near the remains of a large *stupa*, the elaborate remains of the brick-built **Monkey Tank** are gradually being excavated. According to legend, it was built by monkeys as an offering to the Buddha, after he was given honey by a monkey who was later re-incarnated as his disciple.

Jains of the Svetambara sect, who believe that the last *tirthankara*, Mahavira, was born in Vaishali in 599 BC, have erected a shrine in the fields 1km east of Kolhua.

Practicalities

Vaishali is near enough to Patna that most visitors come on day trips. Companies such as the *Travel Corporation of India* can arrange transport, or you can make your own way by bus as far as Sonepur or Hajipur, and change there onto one of the phenomenally crowded local shared taxis, to the roofs and even windscreens of which Biharis cling with remarkable adhesive powers.

The village does offer limited facilities if you want to stay a night or two. The small *Tourist Lodge* (①) on the main road has simple but reasonable rooms, and there's a pleasant and superbly located *Rest House* (①) at the Coronation Tank. At the other end of the same small strip the *Youth Hostel* (①) has a dormitory and canteen, where the welcoming staff prepare simple Indian food.

The road to Nepal

Travellers heading from Patna towards **Nepal** have to cross the border at **Raxaul**, which can be reached either by one of the few direct buses, which take five hours and can be very cramped, or by train or bus with a change at Muzaffarpur.

The largest town in northern Bihar, **Muzaffarpur** is set in a flourishing fruit-growing region. It holds minimal interest for the ordinary visitor, but has a reasonable range of accommodation, including the mid-priced *Ambassador* (③) and *Midway* (③) hotels at Nagataol, and several cheaper options in the town centre.

Raxaul itself is an unattractive, grubby town. If you need to stay, the *Railway Retiring Rooms* at the station are moderately clean (①), but guests have to have a rail ticket. Among budget alternatives nearby are the *Paris Lodge* at the main crossroads (①), and the *Taj*, Main Rd (①). The *Ajanta* on Ashram Rd (①–②) is surprisingly pleasant, with attached baths and meals prepared to order. Cafes along the main road include one at the cinema hall serving a local delicacy of kebab and *muri* (puffed rice).

The border itself, between Raxaul and the Nepalese town of **Birganj**, 5km away (a Rs20 rickshaw-ride), is open 24 hours for foreigners. Those who do not already have visas are expected to pay in cash dollars, so make sure you have the change. Early-morning buses run from Birganj – which has a greater selection of hotels than Raxaul – to Kathmandu (12hr; Rs120) and Pokhara.

Central Bihar

South of the Ganges, and north of the hills of the Chotanagpur plateau, **CENTRAL BIHAR** contains some of north India's most important Buddhist sites. The greatest shrine of all, a focus for Buddhists from around the world, is the Bodhi Tree at **Bodh Gaya** where the Buddha gained enlightenment. His contemporary Mahavira, the Jain patriarch, achieved *his* final liberation at **Pawapuri**, where a beautiful shrine marks his passing, not far from the ancient Buddhist university of **Nalanda**. In addition, the auspicious and holy city of **Gaya** attracts Hindus from all over India who come to make offerings for their deceased ancestors.

Rajgir

Twelve kilometres south of Nalanda, the small town of **RAJGIR** nestles in the rocky hills that witnessed the meditations and teachings of both the Buddha and Mahavira. The capital of the Magadha kingdom before Pataliputra, this was where King Bimbisara converted to Buddhism. Today it's a picturesque and quiet place, visited by international pilgrims but also enjoyed as a health resort because of its **hot springs**. The pools are always open, but can get unpleasantly crowded.

Several sites bear witness to the Buddha's many visits. A Japanese shrine at **Venuvana Vihara** marks the spot where a monastery was built for the Buddha to live in, while it was at **Griddhakuta** (Vulture's Peak) that the Buddha set in motion his second Wheel of Law. Each year, during the three-month rainy season, he preached to his disciples here. The massive modern *stupa* that now dominates the hill can be reached by a chairlift, a fifteen-minute round trip offering wonderful views. Look out for the 26 Jain temples on top of these hills, reachable by a challenging trek attempted almost solely by Jain devotees. On an adjacent hill, in the **Saptaparni cave**, the first Buddhist council met to record the teachings of the Buddha after his death.

Rajgir is connected by **bus** to both Gaya and Patna, and also features with Nalanda and Pawapuri on the itineraries of several **tours** from Patna. **Kund Market**, near the main hot springs (Brahma Kund), holds a number of cheap cafes such as the *Green Hotel*, while the nearby *Siddharta Hotel* (①–②) has reasonable budget rooms. Bihar Tourism run three lodges – *Gautam Vihar*, *Tathagat Vihar* and *Ajatshatra Vihar* (①–⑤). *Centaur Hokke* (⑥–⑧) is an impressive Japanese luxury hotel, serving Japanese and Indian cuisine in its air-conditioned restaurants.

Nalanda

The richly adorned towers and the fairy-like turrets, like the pointed hill-tops, are congregated together. The observations seem to be lost in the vapours of the morning, and the upper rooms tower above the sky . . . All outside courts, in which are the priests' chambers, are of four stages. The stages have dragon projections and coloured eaves, the pearl-red pillars carved and ornamented, the richly adorned balustrades, and the roofs covered with tiles that reflect the light in a thousand shades. These things add to the beauty of the place.
                    Hiuen Tsang, who spent twelve years at Nalanda as student and teacher.

Founded in the fifth century AD by the Guptas, the great monastic **Buddhist university** of **NALANDA** flourished, with thousands of international students and teachers, until it was sacked by the Afghan invader Bhaktiar Khilji in the twelfth century. Excavations have revealed nine levels of occupation on the site, dating right back to the time of the Buddha and the Jain founder Mahavira, in the sixth century BC. Most of it is now in ruins, but the orderliness and scale of what remains is staggering evidence of the strength of Buddhist civilization in its prime. Nalanda is now part of the modern Buddhist pilgrimage circuit, but even the casual tourist will appreciate taking the time to walk through the extensive site, or climb its massive *stupa* for commanding views.

Courses taught at Nalanda included the study of scriptures of both the Mahayana and Hinayana Schools of Buddhism, Brahmanical and Vedic texts, philosophy, logic, theology, grammar, astronomy, mathematics and medicine. Education was provided free, supported by the revenue from surrounding villages, and by benefactors such as the eighth-century King of Sumatra, who requested permission to endow a monastery.

The site includes the remains of *stupas*, temples, and eleven monasteries, most aligned north to south. Most of the monasteries consist of small cells leading off a verandah, surrounding an open central courtyard, with a guarded entrance to the west, and a shrine room to the east. Evidence has been found that the **great stupa**, more than 31 metres high, is built above seven previous structures. Smaller *stupas* surround it, with plaster *bodhisattvas* and seated Buddhas set into the walls.

Nalanda Museum houses antiquities found here and at Rajgir, including Buddhist and Hindu bronzes and a number of undamaged statues of the Buddha (daily except Fri 10am–5pm; free with ticket to the site). Other sculptures produced here during the eighth- to tenth-century Pala period are displayed at the Indian Museum, Calcutta, the National Museum, New Delhi and the Patna Museum. **Nava Nalanda Mahavihara**, the Pali post-graduate research institute, houses many rare Buddhist manuscripts, and is devoted to study and research in Pali literature and Buddhism.

Pawapuri

Pawapuri, 38km from Rajgir and 26km from Nalanda, is where Mahavira, founder of the Jain religion, gained enlightenment, and also where he died and was cremated on the bank of a large lake overflowing with lotus flowers. Today, however, its stunning beauty is unfortunately offset by clouds of mosquitoes. **Jalmandir**, the white marble temple in the centre of the lake is a centre of Jain pilgrimage, along with **Samosharan**, another temple nearby. Pawapuri lies 1km off the main road; buses from Nalanda and Rajgir serve the nearby town of Bihar Sharif.

Barabar and Nagarjuna caves

The mysterious caves of **Barabar** and **Nagarjuna**, which provided the inspiration for EM Foster's *A Passage to India*, are set in wild and inhospitable bandit country, 35km north of Gaya. Few travellers pass this way, and those who do make sure they get away again on the same day; travel in the evenings is not recommended. Probably the safest option if you do want to come is to arrange a tour through operators such as *Shiva Travels* in Bodh Gaya (see p.790); solitary visitors may even want to take the precaution of hiring a policeman from a local police station, which costs around Rs30 for the day.

The caves lie at the end of a 15-kilometre detour along a narrow and dreadfully potholed road that leads to the right off the main Gaya–Patna road just beyond **Bela**, 18km north of Gaya. They date back to the third century BC, when the emperor Ashoka, who despite his embrace of Buddhism allowed non-Buddhists to practise their faith, helped establish this as a centre for alternative religion.

The **BARABAR CAVES** consist of temples and sanctuaries hacked out of huge granite outcrops. Inspired by ordinary huts, they are designed to look as if they're made out of wood; the facade of the **Lomas Rishi** cave is sculpted to resemble lattice screens. Their interior surfaces are remarkably smooth, and some are thought to have served as retreats for Jain monks. The three smaller caves at **NAGARJUNA**, 1km northeast, bear inscriptions that date them to around fifty years later.

Gaya

The fly-blown and densely packed town of **GAYA**, 100km south of Patna, serves as an essential transit point for visitors to **Bodh Gaya** 13km away. Far from appealing in itself, it is however of great significance to Hindus, who traditionally come here to honour their parents a year after death by offering *pind* – a gift of funeral cakes. Legend has it that a good demon called Gaya, appalled by the sorrow caused by death, complained to Vishnu, and as a protest died for the world. Impressed by his resolve, Vishnu blessed Gaya with the power to absolve sinners. Like Varanasi, and many other riverside towns, Gaya is said to be a *tirtha* – a crossing across the celestial divide.

On the banks of the River Phalgu, the massive **Vishnupad Temple** is believed to have been built over Vishnu's footstep (*pad*); its main image is a footprint imprinted in a rock and surrounded by a silver basin. What you see today – and if you're not a Hindu, you'll only be able to get a glimpse from an adjacent building within the complex – was entirely rebuilt in 1787 by Rani Ahalyabai of Indore. Final rites for the dead are held beneath the **Akshayabat**, the immortal banyan tree that stands in the courtyard, under which the Buddha is said to have meditated.

After the monsoons, when the river is in spate, pilgrims bathe in the river and present their offerings. During the dry season, they have to content themselves with holes dug into the river bed, which resemble barrels of water.

Practicalities

Gaya is a major junction on the main railway line between **Calcutta**, **Varanasi** and **New Delhi**, served by trains such as the *Rajdhani Express* #2302, the *Howrah Kalka Mail* #2312, *New Delhi–Howrah Poorva Express* #2382, and the *Patna-Hatia Express* #8621 between **Patna** to the north and **Ranchi** to the south. *Bihar Roadways* run buses from the **Gandhi Maidan Bus Stand** to points such as **Patna** and **Ranchi**, while buses for **Rajgir** leave from the **Gaurakshini Bus Stand** on the outskirts of town. Cycle and auto-rickshaws are available for transport around town.

If you're heading onto Bodh Gaya, there's only any point **staying** at Gaya if you arrive after dark. However, there are clean *Railway Retiring Rooms* at the station (①–②), with a dorm as well as good-value a/c rooms, while in the *Ajatsatru*, opposite on Station Rd (①), the rooms have attached baths, and a comfortable restaurant serves an extensive menu of spicy dishes. Gaya's most comfortable and expensive hotel, the *Siddharta International*, hidden in its own compound on Station Rd (☎21254), has good a/c rooms and a plush multi-cuisine restaurant, and handles foreign exchange (④–⑥). Finally, there's a friendly budget establishment next door, also called the *Siddharta* (①).

Bodh Gaya

BODH GAYA, sacred to Buddhists as the place where the Buddha gained enlighten-ment after years of penance, lies 13km south of Gaya beside the River Phalgu. A small market town has grown along the approach to its majestic **Mahabodhi Temple**, and a shopping precinct caters to the constant flow of pilgrims, while the **Bodhi Tree** along-side is an offshoot of the original *peepal* tree under which the Buddha sat.

Although the site dates back to the period immediately following the Buddha's pass-ing, the temple complex probably began to take its present shape in the seventh century AD, around the time it was visited by the Chinese pilgrim Hiuen Tsang. Even after the sack of Nalanda and the virtual demise of Buddhism in north India, it contin-ued to flourish during the Muslim period. After the sixteenth century, it declined to such an extent that it fell into the hands of *brahmin* Hindu priests, who professed them-selves to be baffled by its origins when the first British archeologists turned up here early in the nineteenth century. Once excavations had shown the site's true prove-nance, it was rejuvenated by overseas Buddhists, and is now the most important pilgrimage site of international Buddhism, with all Buddhist nations represented in its many scattered monasteries, temples and shrines.

From November to February, Bodh Gaya is the home of an animated community of exiled **Tibetans**, usually including the Dalai Lama himself, as well as a stream of shaven-headed international Tibetophiles. In summer, long after the Dalai Lama's official and unofficial entourage has left for the hills, the region becomes oppressively hot, and Bodh Gaya returns once again to its quiet ways.

Unfortunately all is not right at this holiest of holy shrines. The Mahabodhi Temple is also sacred to Hindus, who see the Buddha as an incarnation of Vishnu, and, incred-ibly, the committee that looks after it is controlled by a Hindu majority, despite strong protests from the Buddhist world. The resultant unhappiness can be all too apparent, and is exacerbated by contrasting forms of worship – while the Buddhists continue a solitary inward approach, Hindus tend towards spectacle and bright, noisy ceremony.

Arrival and information

Several government-run *Nagar Seva* **buses** each day run to Bodh Gaya from the station in **Gaya** (last service 6.30pm; Rs3), as do private buses from the **Zila School Bus Stand**, 1km south of the station. Auto-rickshaws cost around Rs40, while some cycle rickshaws attempt the journey during the day for just over half that. Do not travel at night; after 7pm very little traffic moves along the route.

All buses – including the few direct services from Patna and Rajgir – stop in Bodh Gaya on the main road north of the Mahabodhi Temple. Most sites are within walking distance, but **bicycles** can be rented for Rs10 per day from the *Root Institute* (see "Accommodation"), and cars through *ITDC* at the *Ashok Hotel*. *Shiva Travel and Consultancy*, in the small commercial precinct opposite the Mahabodhi Temple also arrange car rental and tours, including trips to the Mahakala Cave and the Barabar Caves. The same Mahabodhi Temple Market Complex houses the local **Tourist Office** (daily except Sun 10am–5pm), which provides information on the area and assistance with tours. The *Bodhi News* is a local broadsheet useful for finding out about current activities such as meditation courses. Money can be changed at the *State Bank of India* in the shopping precinct or at the *Bank of India* near the *Tourist Lodge*.

The Mahabodhi Temple and the Bodhi Tree

The elegant single spire of the **Mahabodhi Temple**, rising to the lofty height of 55 metres above the trees of its leafy compound at the centre of Bodh Gaya, is visible from all over the surrounding countryside. Within the temple complex, which is liberally sprinkled with small *stupas* and shrines, the main brick temple stands in a hollow encircled by a stone railing dating from the second century BC. Only three quarters of the railing remains in place, other sections are in the site museum (see below) and museums in Calcutta and London.

Unlike most popular temples in India, the Mahabodhi Temple exudes an atmosphere of peace and tranquillity, albeit occasionally broken by the noise of Hindu religious ceremonies. Extensively renovated during the nineteenth century, it is supposed to be a replica of the seventh-century structure that in turn stood on the site of Ashoka's original third-century shrine. Its busy detail includes niches and short towers on all four corners. Inside the temple a single chamber holds a large gilded image of the Buddha, while upstairs are a balcony and a small plain meditation chamber.

At the rear of the temple to the west, the large **Bodhi Tree** grows out of an expansive base, in pleasant grounds that attract scholars and meditators. For all its holiness, this is in fact only a distant offshoot of the original tree beneath which the Buddha gained *nirvana*, which legend relates was destroyed by Ashoka before his conversion to the faith. His daughter Sanghamitta took a sapling to Sri Lanka, and planted it at Anuradhapura, where its offshoots were nurtured, and a sapling was brought back and

---

MEDITATION COURSES IN BODH GAYA

A visit to the Bodhi Tree is enough to inspire most visitors to meditate. Especially during the high season, in winter, short- and long-term **meditation courses** are available in either of two distinct traditions of Buddhism – Mahayana (the Great Vehicle), epitomized by the various forms of Tibetan Buddhism, and Hinayana (the Lesser Vehicle), as practised in Sri Lanka, Thailand and other parts of southeast Asia. During the winter check noticeboards in places such as the *Om Cafe*, and the pages of the *Bodhi News*.

Along with seminars and talks, the **Root Institute for Wisdom Culture**, in a rural setting 1.5km west of the main temple, organizes week-long residential courses, mostly focussing on the Mahayana tradition. The institute does not belong to any religious order, and has a low-key approach, working with the local community on education and health projects. Mud huts are available for retreats, and guests who simply appreciate a quiet environment are also welcome.

Two ten-day courses in the Hinayana tradition, run by Christopher Titmus, a western Buddhist, are held each winter at the **Thai Temple**; the cost of Rs50 per day includes food and lodging. The new **International Meditation Centre**, opposite, runs ten-day beginners' courses, based on Hinayana principles, and thirty-day courses for the more experienced. Donations are accepted, as there are no fixed fees.

BODH GAYA

N

0   250 m

◁ Magadha University

Gaya △

Burmese Vihara
(Monastery)

Ⓐ

▽ Mahakala Caves

Tibetan Market
(Winter & Spring)

Gelugpa Tibetan
Monastery

Chinese
Monastery

Main
Market

Bus &
Autorickshaw
Stand

ⓘ

Mahabodhi
Society

Animesh
Lochana

Mahabodhi
Temple

Bodhi
Tree

River Phalgu

Vietnamese
■ Monastery

Deer Park

Thai Temple
& Monastery

Ⓒ Ⓓ

Archaeological
Museum

Ⓑ

Lotus
Tank

Tamang
Monastery

Root
Institute

Karmapa Tibetan
Monastery ■

■ Bhutan
Monastery

Ⓔ ⚲ Daijokyo Japanese
Temple

Large Statue
of Buddha

Sakyapa Tibetan
■ Monastery

HOTELS:
Ⓐ Amar
Ⓑ Bodhgaya Ashok
Ⓒ Siddharth Vihar
Ⓓ Buddha Vihar
Ⓔ Daijokyo Buddhist Guest House

replanted here. Pilgrims tie coloured thread to its far-reaching branches, decorated by prayer flags, and Tibetans accompany their rituals with long lines of butter lamps. A sandstone slab with carved sides next to the tree is believed to be the **Vajrasana** or "thunder-seat" upon which the Buddha sat facing east (towards the temple).

The small white **Animeshlochana Temple** to the right of the compound entrance – a miniature version of the main one – marks the spot where the Buddha stood and gazed upon the Bodhi Tree in gratitude. It now obscures the view of the tree, but not the long raised platform known as the **Chankramana** along the northern wall where the Buddha paced in meditation. Remains of a row of columns suggest that it may once have been covered. Numerous ornate *stupas* from the Pala period (seventh–twelfth centuries AD) are littered around the grounds. Next to the temple compound to the south is the rectangular Lotus Pool where the Buddha may have bathed.

Entry to the temple compound is from the east (daily 6am–noon & 2–6.30pm; Rs1, cameras Rs10); shoes are tolerated within the grounds but not inside the temple, and can be left here. The west gate, leading straight to the Bodhi Tree, is sometimes open.

Temples and monasteries

Numerous monasteries and temples are located around Bodh Gaya, some simple and others, like the Thai Temple, elaborate reproductions. The **Tibetan Temple**, a monastery belonging to the Gelugpa (Yellow Hat) sect, is located within the Tibetan quarter northwest of the main shrine. Built over the last four decades in the style of a traditional *gompa*, the complex includes a central prayer hall, a large prayer wheel and residential buildings. Each winter, this area of Bodh Gaya is transformed by its annual influx of Tibetans, who erect a small market and open restaurants and cafes. The bigger of the two other Tibetan monasteries further west belongs to the **Karmapa** sect; its spacious main prayer hall is decorated with beautiful modern murals, Buddha images and a large *Dharma Chakra* or Wheel of Law.

Next to the Karmapa monastery, the **Daijokyo Japanese Monastery** captures in concrete some elements of a traditional Japanese temple. Opposite that, the **Indosan Nipponji Temple** has an elegant and simple hut-like roof and a beautiful image of Buddha inside its main hall. Further north, at the junction with the main road, the unmistakable **Thai Temple** is built as a typical *wat* with a terracotta roof of overlapping eaves. In a decorative garden at the end of a short road, the 25-metre-tall Japanese-style **Giant Buddha Statue** was consecrated by the Dalai Lama in 1989. The Sri-Lankan-based **Mahabodhi Society**, responsible for reviving Bodh Gaya in the nineteenth century, maintain a small complex northwest of the Mahabodhi Temple.

Bodh Gaya's **archeological museum**, a short way west of the Deer Park near the *Ashok Hotel,* holds a collection of locally discovered sculpture, and ninth-century Pala bronzes of Hindu and Buddhist deities (daily except Fri 10am–5pm; free).

Accommodation and eating

Most pilgrims to Bodh Gaya stay in their respective temples and monasteries; the casual visitor is left to choose between a couple of cheap hotels, two tourist lodges and a slightly upmarket government-run hotel – the ITDC *Bodhgaya Ashok*. If you do find a room in a monastery or a pilgrim rest house, you are expected to abide by the rules and respect the environment. As for food, there are several cafes in the Mahabodhi Temple Market Complex north of the temple, and Tibetan cafes, such as the *Om Cafe*, in the temporary tented market around the Tibetan Temple provide a popular alternative in winter.

Amar, near *BuddhaVihar*. One of a small cluster of cheap budget lodges. ①.

Buddha Vihar, near the Thai Temple. Tourist lodge with basic dorm accommodation. ①.

Burmese Vihar, Gaya Rd. Set in a pleasant garden. Run on a donations system, and very spartan. Popular with westerners, some of whom have difficulty following its no-smoking policy. ①.

Daijokyo Buddhist House, near Giant Buddha Statue (☎063181/747). Beautifully maintained for visiting Japanese pilgrims; others are allowed to stay on discretion, but they have had problems in the past with visiting westerners. An excellent kitchen specializes in Japanese cuisine. ⑥.

ITDC Bodhgaya Ashok, near the Museum (☎063181/725). The only hotel as such – comfortable and pleasant with a good upmarket restaurant and several facilities including a travel desk. ⑦–⑧.

Mahabodhi Society Pilgrim Rest House (*Sri Lanka Guest House*). Popular and often full. A dormitory and a handful of rooms, plus a reasonable vegetarian canteen. ①–②.

Root Institute, past Thai Temple. Really a meditation centre, which offers reasonably priced huts for retreats and accommodation including a dormitory in the main building. A pleasant rustic environment with a community spirit. Meals are provided and cycles are available for rent. ①–③.

Siddharth Vihar, near the Thai Temple. The second and more expensive tourist lodge. Spacious rooms and attached baths but otherwise poorly run and without character. ②–③.

Around Bodh Gaya: Mahakala Caves

The **Mahakala** (or Dungeshwari) **Caves**, in remote, almost desert-like surroundings on the far side of the Phalgu 18km northeast of Bodh Gaya, are the site where the Buddha did the severe penance that resulted in the familiar image of him as a skeletal, emaciated figure. After years of extreme self-denial at Mahakala, he realized its futility and walked down to Bodh Gaya, where he received rice as a gift. A short time later, after a final battle with temptation, he achieved *nirvana* under the Bodhi Tree.

During the dry season, a turn-off to the right from the Gaya road, 9km out of Bodh Gaya, leads across the large dry river bed and winds its way through three villages including Khiriyama. This walk should only be attempted in winter; at other times it gets far too hot. Wild dogs along the way, and desperately poor and deprived villagers, provide additional obstacles, making it advisable not to travel alone.

If you do make it to the base of the impressive cliff, a short climb leads to a Tibetan monastery and the small caves themselves. A Buddhist shrine inside the main cave is run by Tibetans, although a Hindu priest has recently set himself up in competition. Very few visit this place, and the occasional car or bus that does arrive gets mobbed by urchins and beggars. Offers by international Buddhist communities to help build roads and some sort of infrastructure have been rejected by the Bihar government.

Sasaram

Dreary, unattractive **SASARAM**, 17km west of the main railway junction of Dehri-on-Sone and the three-kilometre-long Sone River Bridge, is noteworthy as the site of the impressive **mausoleum of Sher Shah Suri**. It is one of two majestic Muslim monuments built by the same master architect, Aliwal Khan, which bear the distinctive heavy lines of the early Lodi monuments of Delhi. Of Afghan extraction, Sher Shah briefly interrupted the Moghul domination of India in 1540 by his displacement of Humayun (see p.73). In his brief reign he created the efficient system of government and administration that was adapted so successfully by Humayun's son Akbar.

The well-maintained five-storey sandstone mausoleum, capped by a massive dome, stands in the middle of a 430-square-metre artificial lake, beside the Grand Trunk Road around 1km west of the railway station. Originally approached by boat, it was later connected to the north shore of the lake by the still-existing causeway, entered through the gatehouse. Close inspection of this plain building reveals that it was once adorned by red, white, blue and yellow geometrical designs, and the dome, once white, topped with a golden lotus. A curious re-alignment means that the mausoleum is now at an angle of 8° to its base, to orient it with the points of the compass. At its centre, a large octagonal chamber contains the tomb itself, while pavilions mark each corner of the plinth, and steps lead down to the water.

Around 500m east, visible from the upper storeys of Sher Shah's mausoleum, is the tomb of his father, **Hasan Sur Khan**. Built in 1535 within a walled enclosure, and lacking a plinth let alone a lake, it has been engulfed by the rustic town of Sasaram and is in a somewhat dilapidated condition. Despite its status as a protected monument, some of the flag stones are being removed. Local people do not always take kindly to visitors.

Practicalities

Sasaram is halfway between **Varanasi** and **Gaya** (both 3 hours away) on the main railway line. Few expresses stop here apart from the *Doon Express* #3009, and the *Howrah–Bombay Mail* #3003 (which stops at Mughal Serai rather than Varanasi itself), but several passenger trains do – check the timetables carefully, for what they're worth – so it's probably best to think of it as a day trip not an overnight stop. Cycle rickshaws provide the main means of local transport.

The *Retiring Rooms* at the railway station have a double room for just Rs20 per head, there are plenty of simple hotels and restaurants on the main road nearby, and the basic *Tourist Lodge* (①) has some extremely good-value air-cooled rooms.

South Bihar: Chotanagpur

On the eastern extremities of the Vindhya Hills, at the northern fringes of the Deccan, lie the forested hills and escarpments of the rugged **Chotanagpur plateau**. Its largest town is **Ranchi**, although **Jamshedpur** in the southeast corner is one of eastern India's most important industrial towns, the headquarters of the steel conglomerate *TISCO*. The forests that surround Jamshedpur, at the edge of the plateau, are home to aboriginal tribes such as the Santals, Oraon and Munda, who amount to around sixty percent of the region's population. Christian missionaries have had a strong impact here, and some Munda villages display shrines to the Virgin, but much of the area is unsafe for travellers, thanks to the struggle of the Jharkand Movement for tribal autonomy.

This area was formerly renowned for its **wildlife**. Sadly, however, the beautiful forests of the **Palamau** or **Betla National Park** on the southwest edge of Chotanagpur have been damaged by years of drought. Its tigers are now severely endangered species, and the situation is even worse at the **Hazaribagh Wildlife Sanctuary**, north of Ranchi near the town of **Hazaribagh**, whose name means "a thousand tigers".

Ranchi

Industrial **RANCHI**, at the heart of the Chotanagpur plateau over 300km south of Gaya, is hardly a major-league tourist destination, but it does make a good base from which to explore some attractive rolling countryside, thick with lakes and waterfalls. This was once the summer capital of Bihar, but its tea-gardens have long since been abandoned in favour of heavy industry. The climate remains pleasant, however, which may explain the presence of ashrams such as the central **Yogoda Math Ashram**.

The **Ranchi Museum** on Morabadi Rd has an interesting ethnographic collection of tribal artefacts, costumes, implements and earthenware objects (daily except Fri 10.30am–5pm; free). A smaller replica of the temple at Puri, the **Jaganath Temple**, 6km southwest, is the scene of an annual Rath (chariot) festival.

Arrival and information

Several major **trains** either call at Ranchi station, near the southern end of the Main Road, or terminate at Hatia, 7km away. The *Hatia–Ranchi–Howrah Express* #8105 is a convenient overnight train to and from Calcutta while the *Patna–Hatia Express* #8623 leaves Patna in the evening and travels via Gaya to Ranchi. The *Bokaro–Aleppey Express* #8689 connects Ranchi with Tatanagar, the station for Jamshedpur, and points south.

From the **Main Bus Stand** near the station, regular *Nagar Seva* buses travel to **Gaya** (last one at 6.30pm; 7hr), Hazaribagh, Netarhat, Jamshedpur, and to **Daltonganj**, headquarters of the Palamau (Betla) National Park 160km west. Ranchi's **airport**, 5km east of the centre, is connected by *Indian Airlines* flights IC809 to Calcutta, and IC810 to Patna and Delhi. The *Indian Airlines* office is on Main Rd (☎408739).

Ranchi's main **tourist office**, on Circular Rd (☎20426), organizes tours of the region and maintains an information booth at the railway station during train times. The main forms of local transport are cycle and auto-rickshaws.

Accommodation and eating

Most of Ranchi's **hotels** are to be found along, or just off, the long Main Road. If you'd rather not eat in your hotel, *Friends Restaurant*, Station Rd, is a basic cafe serving south Indian snacks, and *Kwalitys*, Main Rd, is a reliable multi-cuisine restaurant.

Ashok, Station Rd. Basic and very cheap, with attached baths. ①.

Embassy, Station Rd (☎302717). Handily located; good budget rooms with attached baths. ①–③.

Highlands, Main Rd. Simple budget accommodation next to the Bus Stand. ②.

Hindustan, Makhija Towers, Main Rd (☎303988). At the centre of the busy strip, built over a shopping complex. Assorted rooms, and a range of facilities including a good restaurant. ④–⑦.

Kwality Inns, Station Rd (☎302083). Centrally a/c and smart with comfortable rooms in walking distance of the station. ⑥–⑦.

Ranchi Ashok, Doranda (☎30037). One of Ranchi's finest with central air-conditioning and all facilities including a good restaurant. ⑦–⑧.

South Eastern Railway, Station Rd. Capturing an old-world atmosphere, with pleasant gardens and cottages with sizeable rooms. ⑥–⑦.

Yuvraj, Main Rd, Doranda (☎300403). Some of the cheapest a/c rooms in town; not to be confused with the more expensive *Yuvraj Palace*, not far away. ③.

Around Ranchi

Macluskieganj, 40km northwest of Ranchi, was originally designed as a haven for Anglo-Indians. These days it's in a peculiar state of limbo, with most of its original community having long since left. Some of its garden cottages are dilapidated, others house retired urbanites and army officers. A few visitors make their way here to savour its vaguely Victorian ambience, and to enjoy pleasant walks along wooded paths, through flower gardens and orchards separated by large tracts of tall *sal* trees.

Perhaps the most picturesque of the many waterfalls near Ranchi, all at their most dramatic towards the end of the monsoons, are the **Hundru Falls**, 45km northeast off the Purulia road. They're not on a bus route, but *Bihar Tourism* occasionally run tours out here. A small single-track road bears left from the highway, heading past the beautiful lake of Getalsud set against a backdrop of red, wooded hills. Negotiating the edge of the plateau, the road passes through densely forested tribal country then disintegrates as it approaches the small complex above the falls. A couple of tea shops and a haunted-looking *Forest Bungalow* (①) look down on the 100-metre-high falls, created by the River Subarnarekha as it drops from the plateau along great rocky steps. A staircase descends to the bottom of the falls, where several pools are good for swimming.

Palamau (Betla) National Park

In a remote corner of the state, 170km west of Ranchi, the beautiful forests of the **PALAMAU NATIONAL PARK** (also known as Betla), cover around 1000 square kilometres of hilly terrain rising south towards Madhya Pradesh. Part of the **Project Tiger** scheme (see p.381), Palamau has been hard hit by drought, and even optimistic estimates of its tiger population stand at a mere sixty. Tiger sightings, more common in the hot season, are proudly announced on a noticeboard at the park offices.

Like many national parks, Palamau consists of a buffer zone, open to visitors, surrounding a core area which is not; the tigers are known to roam around 20km a day, but tend to concentrate in the core area. The fact that several villages are located within the park boundaries has not helped the protection of animals, despite a scheme of compensation for owners of cattle killed by tigers. Other animals found in the park include wild elephants, best seen after the monsoons, *nilgai* (antelope), leopard, *gaur* (bison), Indian wolf, wild boar and wild dogs.

Passing through the main gates at **Betla** brings you into a slightly surreal area, where a picturesque and well-maintained road leads through avenues of great trees. Deer that have grown used to human presence wander peacefully nearby, perhaps to escape predators in the deep jungles. The road soon descends into thick forest along ravines rich in bamboo; its total 25-kilometre circuit seems to be over all too quickly.

Much the best way to see the park is from the back of an **elephant**, and the earlier in the morning you go the more animals you're likely to spot. Elephant rides set out from Betla each morning at 5.30am and 7.00am; they last one hour and cost Rs40. Cars and jeeps (both of which cost Rs40), minibuses, buses and even trucks are allowed in, accompanied by a guide (Rs15 per hour); they penetrate further, but animals usually shy away from the noise and smell of their engines. Night tours also go into the park, using spotlights to dazzle the animals; a highly efficient way to spot different creatures, if one that many visitors find objectionable.

Practicalities

The official headquarters of the park, **Daltonganj**, 25km from Betla, is served by both direct buses and a branch railway line from Ranchi. Five buses each morning and three each afternoon (first at 7.30am; last at 4.30pm) run from Daltonganj to Betla, which is

6km off the main Ranchi–Daltonganj road. If you're coming from Ranchi, you could try to change buses at the turn-off and get to Betla without going through Daltonganj.

Next to the **Betla** gates, the main park entrance, a small complex holds administration offices, rest houses and an **information centre**, where entry tickets, elephant rides, and accommodation in any of the Forest Department's rest houses can be arranged. All arrangements, including car or jeep rental and accommodation, can also be made at Daltonganj through the Director, Project Tiger, Jail Compound.

Forest Department Rest Houses in Betla itself include the main one (②), which prioritizes visiting civil servants but is comfortable and offers attached baths, and the very cheap and basic *Janata* and *Shyama* lodges (①). Others not far away include the small and cheap one at Kechki (①), near the bridge over the River Koel close to the main highway, and one at Kehr, between Kechki and Betla (①). A slightly more expensive *Tourist Lodge* near the park gates is reasonably comfortable (②).

There are also a couple of new **hotels**. The privately-run *Naihar* (☎504; ①–④), 300m from the park gates, has a nice garden, a dorm, and a/c rooms, as well as a reasonable restaurant serving Chinese and Indian food, while the grand-looking *Van Vihar* (③–④), recently opened by *Bihar Tourism*, offers spacious ordinary and a/c rooms, and also has a restaurant. Simple cafes can be found opposite the gates at Betla.

Netarhat

The popular but undeveloped hill station of **NETARHAT** – the only one in Bihar, and known as "the Queen of Chotanagpur" – occupies the crest of a high ridge 120km south of the Palamau park, and served by direct buses from both Betla and Ranchi, 156km east (4hr; Rs40). Set at a pleasant altitude of 1138m, Netarhat is comfortable throughout the year, despite the occasional touch of frost in winter. Rambling walks through the hills around town offer superb views, especially at sunrise and sunset; Magnolia Point, 10km away, looks out to the Palamau plateau to the north, while the cascading Burhaghagh Falls are right on the edge of town. Of **accommodation** options in Netarhat, probably the best is the *Prabhat Vihar*, the tourist bungalow (③–④), which has its own restaurant. The *Palamau Dak Bungalow* (①) is comfortable and has a resident cook but needs to be booked through the District Board at Daltonganj, and there's also a *Youth Hostel* (①).

Parasnath

Towering 1000m above the plains, beside the Calcutta–Gaya railway line 30km west of Dhanbad, the crag of **PARASNATH** is rendered holy to Jains by its associations with the life of Mahavira. It is covered with dense forests, where Jain belief has it that even the tigers are vegetarian. Twenty-four shrines – one per *tirthankara* – are sprinkled along its lofty crest, including the main **Parasnath Temple** on the westernmost and highest summit. Pilgrims, on foot or carried on palanquins, follow a trail that winds its way up from the village of **Madhuban** (not to be confused with Madhubani, in North Bihar). Most come back down on the same day, as the facilities on top are limited. The final rise to the main temple is along a marble staircase, which echoes to the sound of bare feet. Sited on a rocky pinnacle, the pristine white temple, where tiny marble feet represent the footprints of the saint, repays the effort with superb views.

Just below the temple, a *Forest Bungalow* provides basic accommodation and beautiful sunsets (①), while Madhuban itself has a **Tourist Reception Centre** and several Jain *dharamshalas*. Cycle rickshaws and buses connect the village with **Parasnath Railway Station**, served by local trains to the major junctions of Dhanbad and Gaya. The town of Parasnath lies on National Highway 2, a major east–west bus route.

CHAPTER FOURTEEN

SIKKIM

The tiny but beautiful land of **SIKKIM** lies just south of Tibet, sandwiched between Nepal to the west and Bhutan to the east. Though measuring just 65 kilometres by 115 kilometres – the size of Switzerland – it ranges from sweltering deep valleys a mere three hundred metres above sea level to lofty snow peaks such as Kanchendzonga (or Kanchenjunga; 8586m), the third highest mountain in the world. Few roads penetrate this rugged Himalayan wilderness; most of those that do are in the eastern part of the state, around its capital **Gangtok**.

For many centuries, until war with China in the early 1960s led the Indian government to see it as a crucial corridor between Tibet and Bangladesh, Sikkim was an isolated, independent Buddhist kingdom. As a result of its annexation by India in 1975, it has experienced dramatic changes. Now a fully-fledged Indian state, it is predominantly Hindu, with a population made up of seventy-five percent **Nepalese** Gurungs, and less than twenty percent **Lepchas**, its former rulers. Even smaller proportions survive of **Bhotias**, of Tibetan stock, and **Limbus**, also possibly of Tibetan origin, who gave the state its name – *sukh-im*, "happy homeland". Nepali is now the lingua franca, and the Chief Minister, Mr Bhandari, who has been in power for over 15 years without serious opposition, is Nepalese. The ruling minority in neighbouring Bhutan, having observed this transition with alarm, has adopted an aggressive stance towards the Nepalese, and there has been ugly violence on both sides.

Sikkim holds a special status within the Indian union, exempt from income tax and attracting government subsidy. Only Sikkimese can hold major shares in property and

PERMITS AND RESTRICTIONS

Until recently, it was virtually impossible for visitors to enter Sikkim; now, though much of the north and east remains closed or restricted, getting hold of a **permit** to visit Gangtok and the west is a mere formality. These are initially issued for either ten or fifteen days; you have to specify in advance exactly which areas you intend to visit. Extensions and permits for specific areas are available at Gangtok – see p.800 – but as you might otherwise not go there, it's worth arranging whatever permissions you need before you arrive.

Permitted Areas

Central and Eastern Sikkim: Gangtok (including Rumtek), Tsangu Lake, Phodong.

North Sikkim: Mangan, Chungthang, Lachung and Yumthang.

Western Sikkim: Jorethang, Naya Bazaar, Pemayengtse and Pelling, Tashiding and Yuksom; Dzongri and Gocha La by special arrangement.

Offices issuing Permits

Indian High Commissions all over the world, when applying for a visa.

Airport immigration at the four main entry points – Delhi, Bombay, Calcutta, Madras.

Foreigners' Regional Registration Offices in Delhi, Bombay, Calcutta and Madras.

Resident Commissioner, Sikkim House, 14 Pancsheel Marg, New Delhi.

Sikkim Tourist Centre, SNT Bus Stand, Siliguri.

Deputy Commissioner, below the Gymkhana Club, Darjeeling.

Deputy Secretary, Home Dept, Writers' Building, BBD Bagh, Calcutta.

Assistant Resident Commissioner, Sikkim Govt, 4C Poonam, 5 Russell St, Calcutta.

businesses. The resultant prosperity is evident as soon as you cross the border from West Bengal – the roads in particular are very good, though this of course is largely the work of the Indian Army, for its own ends. Few maps may show them, but several of the old trade routes in northern Sikkim are now rough but motorable roads.

Culturally, historically and spiritually, Sikkim's strongest links are with **Tibet**. For those visitors who now make their way here, the main reasons to come – apart from the lure of the mountains themselves – are its **Buddhist monasteries**. There are over 250 of these, mostly belonging to the ancient Nyingmapa sect. Some, such as **Pemayengtse** in the west, are all but deserted except for special occasions, but others like **Tashiding** and **Rumtek** are thriving centres of Mahayana Buddhism.

Sikkim is where the monsoons that rush in off the Bay of Bengal hit the Himalayas; its gigantic mountain walls and steep wooded hillsides, drained by torrential rivers such as the **Teesta** and the **Rangit**, are a botanist's dream. The lower slopes abound in **orchids**; sprays of cardamom carpet the forest floor, and the land is rich with apple orchards, orange groves, and terraced paddy fields (to the Tibetans, this was **Denzong**, "the land of rice"). At higher altitudes, monsoon mists cling to huge tracts of lichen-covered forests, where every conceivable species of rhododendron and giant magnolia trees punctuate the deep cover. Higher still, approaching the Tibetan plateau, dwarf rhododendron provide vital fuel for yak herders. All over Sikkim, forests and wilderness areas are inhabited by snow leopard, *tahr*, wild ass on the Tibet plateau, *bharal* or blue sheep, and the symbol of Sikkim – the endangered **red panda**.

The best **time to visit** Sikkim is at the very end of April and, especially, May, when the rhododendrons and orchids bloom – although temperatures can be high, especially in the valleys. Any earlier than that, and the lingering winter snow makes trekking too difficult. During the monsoons, from the end of June until early September, rivers and roads become impassable, though plants nurtured by the incessant rain erupt again into bloom towards the end of August. October and November tend to have the clearest weather of all. As December approaches, it gets bitterly cold at altitude, and remains that way until early March, despite long periods of clear weather.

A brief history

No one knows quite when or how the **Lepchas** – or the Rong, as they call themselves – came to Sikkim, but their roots can be traced back to the animist Nagas of the Indo-Burmese border. **Buddhism,** which arrived from Tibet in the thirteenth century, took its distinctive Sikkimese form four centuries later, when three Tibetan monks of the old Nyingmapa order, disenchanted with the rise of the reformist Gelugpas, migrated

---

TREKKING IN SIKKIM

Trekking in Sikkim is confined to the western part of the state, and severely restricted. The fact that trekking permits do not extend your total stay in Sikkim places great strain on time, while high charges, payable in US dollars, ensure that only the rich or the very curious get to see certain areas. In addition, most Sikkimese trekking operators and guides are not as yet of a very high calibre, and there have been a number of complaints.

Trekking permits are usually available from the Foreigners' Regional Registration Office, Special Branch, Yangthang Building, Kazi Rd, Gangtok. Trekking or tour operators, listed on p.804, can make the necessary arrangements; if they do, check the papers before you set off, as the slightest error can lead to problems later on. Trekking parties have to consist of at least four people – numbers are usually made up by operators.

The only high-altitude trek currently on offer is the **Dzongri–Gocha La** route, detailed on p.808. However, mountains such as Thingchen Khang (5818m) and Jopuno (5805m) have also recently been designated as "trekking peaks", where officially sanctioned organizations are allowed to take clients.

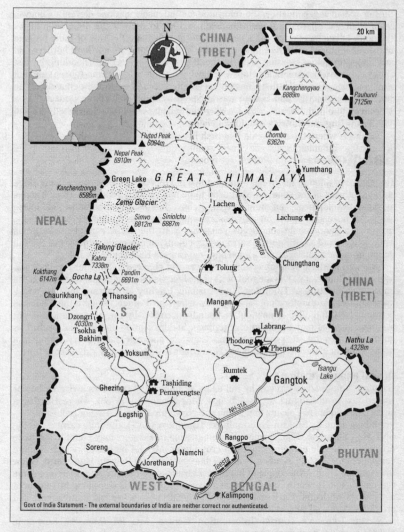

Govt of India Statement - The external boundaries of India are neither correct nor authenticated.

south and gathered at Yuksom in western Sikkim. Having consulted the oracle, they sent to Gangtok for a certain Phuntsog Namgyal, whom they crowned as the first **Chogyal** or "Righteous King" of Denzong in 1642. Both secular and religious head, he was soon recognized by Tibet, and set about sweeping reforms. His domain was far larger than today's Sikkim, taking in Kalimpong and parts of western Bhutan. Over the centuries, territory was lost to the Bhutanese, the Nepalese, and the British. Sikkim originally deeded Darjeeling to the East India Company as a spa in 1817, but were forced to give up all claims to it in 1861. The British set out to diminish the strong Tibetan influence by importing workers from Nepal to work in the tea plantations of Sikkim, Darjeeling and Kalimpong; they soon outnumbered the indigenous population.

After Indian Independence, the reforming and intensely spiritual eleventh Chogyal, Tashi Namgyal, strove hard until his death in 1962 to prevent the dissolution of his kingdom. Officially Sikkim was a protectorate of India, and the role of India became increasingly crucial with the Chinese military build-up along the northern borders that culminated in actual invasion early in the 1960s. His son Palden Thondup, the last Chogyal, married an American, Hope Cook, whose reforms as Gyalmo (queen), did not prove popular. The embattled Chogyal eventually succumbed to the demands of the the Nepalese majority, and Sikkim was annexed by India in 1975; he remained as a figurehead until his death in 1981, by which time Hope Cook had abandoned him and returned to the United States with their children.

Gangtok

The capital of Sikkim, the overgrown hill town of **GANGTOK**, occupies a rising ridge in the southeast of the state, on what used to be a busy trade route into Tibet. Thanks to rapid development and new wealth, it now retains few traditional Sikkimese elements; instead it sports an ugly assortment of concrete multi-storeyed buildings. However, a short amble soon leads you away from the hectic central market area, while longer walks out into the surrounding countryside provide glimpses of the full grandeur of the Himalayas. On a good day, you can see Kanchendzonga.

Although modern Gangtok epitomizes the recent changes in Sikkimese culture and politics, its Buddhist past is the root of its appeal for visitors, and remains evident at the impressive **Institute of Tibetology**, the charming **Enchey Monastery** and the marvellous **Rumtek monastery** not faraway. However, the **Palace** used by the Chogyals between 1894 and 1975 is now out of bounds, occupied by the new regime and not acknowledged as part of Sikkimese heritage. Sikkim's pride and joy, the **orchid**, is nurtured at several sites in and around Gangtok, and celebrated every spring in a flower show held near **White Hall**, the Governor's residence on the ridge above town.

Arrival and information

Gangtok is not served directly by rail or by air; almost all travellers arrive by bus or shared taxi from **Siliguri** in West Bengal (4hr 30min; see p.766), where **Bagdogra** airport, has flights to Calcutta and Delhi, and **New Jalpaiguri** is a major railhead.

All buses run by **Sikkim Nationalised Transport** (*SNT*), the state carrier, use the **SNT Bus Stand** on Paljor Stadium Rd, but arriving passengers may prefer to ask to be dropped off a little earlier at the main crossing on MG Rd higher up, which is more convenient for the tourist office. Non-*SNT* buses stop at the **Private Bus Stand**, below the National Highway a couple of hundred metres before the crossing; there are some reasonable hotels nearby, but it's not an interesting area. Taxis stop along MG Rd, or at a stand at **Childrens' Park** just above it. For details of buses to and from Siliguri, and around Sikkim – all subject to disruption during the monsoons – see p.804.

Sikkim Tourism's **Tourist Information Centre**, MG Rd (Mon–Sat 8am–4pm; ☎2064), provides poor-quality maps, arranges transport and organizes city tours (separate morning and afternoon tours can be combined, for a total cost of Rs95) and further afield, such as to Tsangu Lake, and to Yumthang in north Sikkim. The tourist office is also the place to pick up **west Sikkim permits** to cover Jorethang, Pemayengtse, Pelling, Kacheoperi and Yuksom. For details of **trekking permits**, see p.798.

There's a *State Bank of India*, near the tourist office, while the main **post office**, on Paljor Stadium Rd, has long-distance dialling facilities.

The telephone **area code** for Gangtok is ☎03592.

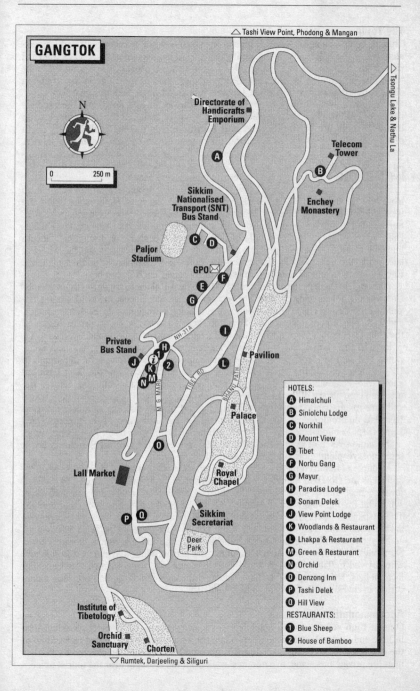

GANGTOK

△ Tashi View Point, Phodong & Mangan

△ Tsongu Lake & Nathu La

N

0   250 m

Directorate of
Handicrafts
Emporium

Telecom
Tower

Enchey
Monastery

Sikkim
Nationalised
Transport (SNT)
Bus Stand

Paljor
Stadium

GPO

NH-31A

Private
Bus Stand

Pavilion

TIBET RD

BHANU PATH

Palace

M G MARG

Royal
Chapel

Lall Market

Sikkim
Secretariat

Deer
Park

Institute of
Tibetology

Orchid
Sanctuary

Chorten

▽ Rumtek, Darjeeling & Siliguri

HOTELS:

A Himalchuli
B Siniolchu Lodge
C Norkhill
D Mount View
E Tibet
F Norbu Gang
G Mayur
H Paradise Lodge
I Sonam Delek
J View Point Lodge
K Woodlands & Restaurant
L Lhakpa & Restaurant
M Green & Restaurant
N Orchid
O Denzong Inn
P Tashi Delek
Q Hill View

RESTAURANTS:

1 Blue Sheep
2 House of Bamboo

The Town

Though central Gangtok – which means "the flattened hill" – is concentrated immediately below the Palace, its unchecked urban sprawl begins almost as soon as the road rises from the valley floor at Ranipool, 10km southwest. Most of the town itself looks west; one explanation for the lack of development east of the ridge is that tradition dictates that houses face northwest, towards Kanchendzonga, Sikkim's guardian.

The town's liveliest markets are the **New Market** on MG Road, and the produce bazaar of **Lall Market**, but few places sell souvenirs or crafts. At the huge complex run by the **Directorate of Handicrafts and Handloom**, on the National Highway north of the centre, visitors can watch rural Sikkimese create carpets, handloom fabrics, *thangka* paintings and wooden objects, and buy their work in a showroom. Curio shops on MG Rd and near the *Tibet* hotel on Paljor Stadium Rd sell turquoise and coral jewellery, and religious objects such as silver ritual bowls and beads.

Right at the top of town, just below a colossal and hideous telecom tower, 3km up from MG Rd and reached by several roads, of which the most picturesque follow the west side of the ridge, **Enchey Monastery** is a small two-storey Nyingmapa *gompa*. Surrounded by tall pines, and housing around ninety monks, it's a real gem of a place. Built by the Chogyal in the middle of the nineteenth century, on traditional Tibetan lines, its beautifully painted porch holds murals of protective deities and the wheel of law, while the conch shells that grace the doors are auspicious Buddhist symbols. Enchey holds an annual *chaam,* or masked *lama* dance, each December.

Although in theory guards deny entry to the **Royal Palace** to anyone without permission, visitors not carrying cameras are occasionally granted access to **Tsuklakhang**, the yellow-roofed royal chapel at its far end, to see its impressive murals, Buddhist images, and vast collection of manuscripts. Here too there's a *lama* dance, known as *kagyat*, at the end of December, during which the main gates are open to the public.

Beyond the chapel, the small **Deer Park** shelters not only deer, but also some caged **red panda** (Mon–Sat 8–11am & Sun 8am–5pm; free). In an echo of Sarnath in UP, an image of Buddha lends a little religious significance. Below the Deer Park but above the National Highway, set in wooded grounds 3km from the centre, the museum-cum-library of the **Institute of Tibetology** houses a huge collection of books and rare manuscripts, as well as religious and art objects such as exquisite *thangkas* (scrolls), embroidered in silk, commissioned for the ordination of the present Dalai Lama (Sept to mid-Dec & Jan–June only, Mon–Sat 10am–4pm; free). Past the Institute, in the same stretch of woods, the two hundred species at the **Orchid Sanctuary** are at their most resplendent in April and May (daily 8am–4pm).

A couple of hundred metres beyond, an imposing white-washed *chorten* (see p.472), known as the **Do-Drul Chorten**, stands on the prow of the hill. It is capped by a gilded tower, whose rising steps signify the thirteen steps to *nirvana*; the sun and moon symbol at the top stands for the union of opposites and the elements of ether and air. The auspicious 108 prayer-wheels that surround it – each with the universal prayer *Om mani padme hum*, "Hail to the Jewel in the Lotus" – are rotated clockwise by devotees as they circumambulate the *stupa*. Nearby, two large images commemorate Padma Sambhava, also known as **Guru Rinpoche**, the patron saint of Nyingmapa Buddhism, who arrived in Tibet in 747 AD and founded *lama*-ism, which incorporated existing local beliefs. He is supposed to have travelled through Sikkim hiding precious manuscripts in caves, for discovery at some future date.

Accommodation and eating

Outside **high season** – each hotel defines its own seasons, but broadly speaking April to June and September to November – Gangtok's hotels offer discounted rates. Most of the hotels we list as being on National Highway 31-A are clustered close to each other near the private bus stand, five minutes' walk from the crossing near the tourist office.

On the whole, the best places to **eat** are the hotel restaurants, although the inexpensive *Blue Sheep*, next to the tourist office on MG Rd, and the *House of Bamboo* opposite, provide good opportunities to sample authentic local specialities. **Sikkimese food** is a melange of Nepalese, Tibetan and Indian influences; rice is a staple, and *dal* is readily available, while *gyakho* is a traditional soup served on special occasions.

Most restaurants serve alcohol. "Foreign" liquor such as brandy and beer is cheap enough, but look out for **tomba**, a traditional drink consisting largely of fermented millet, with a few grains of rice for flavour, served in a wooden or bamboo mug, and sipped through a bamboo straw. The mug is occasionally topped-up with hot water; once it's been allowed to sit for a few minutes, you're left with a pleasant milky beer.

Denzong Inn, Lall Bazaar Rd, New Market (☎22692). Flashy new establishment in the middle of the bazaar, with about 20 comfortable rooms and a good restaurant. ④–⑤.

Dewachen, NH 31-A (☎23753). Clean new place with a bar and Tibetan restaurant. ③–④.

Gangtok Lodge, near Tourist Office, MG Rd. Friendly but basic, with a dorm, restaurant and travel and tour operators. ①–②.

Green Hotel, MG Rd (☎23354). Friendly budget accommodation; not all that clean, but known for the Chinese, Indian and Tibetan food of its legendary restaurant. ②–④.

Hill View, MG Rd (☎23545). Opposite *Tashi Delek*. Quietly situated in a charming little garden compound above the road. Airy rooms with high ceilings, friendly staff. Recommended. ③–⑤.

Himalchuli, NH 31-A (☎22714). North of the centre, a quiet location with friendly management, a range of rooms including a dorm and a pleasant roof-top restaurant with excellent views. Highly recommended, and well worth the ten-minute uphill walk. ②–④.

Karma, MG Rd, New Market. Budget accommodation with cheap single rooms, doubles and dormitories. Good off-season discounts but no food. ②.

Lhakpa, Tibet Rd (☎3002). Cheap, atmospheric hotel-restaurant above the main bazaar. As much of a bar (with *tomba*, see above) as a restaurant, it serves Sikkimese food with prior notice. ①–②.

Mayur, Paljor Stadium Rd (☎22825). A Sikkim Tourism establishment that has been recently privatized. A bit like the *Tibet* next door, without the charm, though its popular *Shaepi* restaurant has a pleasant ambience and serves reasonable *tandoori*, Chinese and Sikkimese cuisine. ④–⑤.

Mount View, Paljor Stadium Rd, near SNT Bus Terminus (☎23647). On the way down the hill past the GPO. Pleasant rooms and a good restaurant, but a bit expensive for what it is. ⑤–⑥.

Norkhill, Paljor Stadium Rd (☎3187). Luxurious former guest house of the Chogyal. All facilities including a good restaurant, but pricey, and an unfortunate location right next to the stadium. ⑧–⑨.

Orchid, NH 31-A (☎3151). An old favourite with budget travellers. Nice enough rooms especially those that face outwards. The restaurant is good for Chinese and Tibetan food. ②–③.

Paradise Lodge, NH 31-A (☎22710). Next to the footbridge by the tourist office – small dark rooms and simple Indian-style attached bathrooms. ②–③.

Siniolchu Lodge, Enchey. Situated above Gangtok near the prison and Enchey *gompa*. Extremely good value, except that it is a Rs15 taxi-ride up from the bazaar, and a brisk twenty-minute walk back again. Recommended if you want to get away from it all. ①.

Sonam Delek, Tibet Rd (☎22566). High above the bazaar, a promising hotel with a range of comfortable rooms. The best provide fine views of the snows. ②–④.

Stay Well, Arithang Rd (☎22963). Off the National Highway; new and comfortable, but overpriced. The food – Indian, Chinese, Sikkimese and *momos* – is better than the accommodation. ④–⑤.

Sunny Guest House, near Private Bus Stand, NH 31-A (☎22179). A relatively new establishment where all the rooms come as double; the restaurant does good *tandoori* food. ③–④.

Tashi Delek, MG Rd, New Market, Gangtok 737 101 (☎22038). An easily missed entrance off the market area hides one of Gangtok's most prestigious addresses – a plush, extensive but not especially remarkable complex. Full board only; the multi-cuisine *Blue Poppy* restaurant and adjoining roof-top cafe serve Sikkimese and Tibetan dishes, as well as club sandwiches. ⑧.

Tibet, Paljor Stadium Rd (☎22523 or 23468). Linked to the Dalai Lama's trust – mid-priced and popular with visiting western Buddhists. Friendly and comfortable, though some rooms are a bit small. The *Snow Lion* restaurant serves Chinese, Indian and Japanese food, but excels in Tibetan dishes. ⑤–⑥.

View Point Lodge, Arithang Rd (☎22449). Just off the National Highway, below the *Orchid*. Clean mid-range establishment with good views. Rooms on the higher floors are more expensive. ③–④.

MOVING ON FROM GANGTOK

Much the busiest route in and out of Sikkim is the road between Gangtok and **Siliguri** in West Bengal, site of the nearest airport and railway station (see p.766). Flights from Bagdogra can be booked at the *Indian Airlines* office on Tibet Rd in Gangtok (☎3099), trains from New Jalpaiguri at the *SNT Out Agency* near the tourist office (☎2016).

As outlined on p.800, *SNT* state **buses** use a different stand to the assorted private operators. *SNT* run several ordinary buses each day to Siliguri (7am–12.15pm; Rs40); the super deluxe *Sikkim Queen* leaves at 7am (Rs75), and there's also one *SNT* bus straight to Bagdogra airport (7am; Rs65). Private companies such as *Aspara*, *Sikkim Beauty* and *Sikkim Glory* travel the same route, departing in early and mid-afternoon (Rs21). Cramped shared taxis – mainly jeeps – leave regularly for Siliguri from the Children's Park taxi stand above MG Rd (Rs75); ordinary rental cars charge more like Rs100.

Both **Kalimpong** (8.30am; Rs23) and **Darjeeling** (7am; Rs65) are served by one *SNT* bus per day; private buses to Kalimpong (Rs20) include *Sangam* and *Crown*, which depart early in the afternoons, and *Jaishree* (7.30am). You can also get to Darjeeling or Kalimpong by taking any Siliguri bus and changing at Teesta Bazaar.

Apart from tour buses, only one *SNT* bus leaves for **Rumtek** each day (4pm; under Rs10). *SNT* buses for western Sikkim include those to **Ghezing** via **Rabangla** (7am & 11am; Rs35), and several services to **Jorethang**, where you can pick up connections to Ghezing and **Pemayengtse** via **Legship**. Buses to **Mangan** and **Singhik**, north of Gangtok, leave at 8am and 1pm.

Trekking and Tour Operators

Bayyul Tours and Travels, 27 Super Market (☎737101). Treks to Dzongri, Chaurikhang, Bikbari and Goechala.

Bigfoot, Paljor Stadium Rd (☎23574). Treks to Dzongri.

Hangsu Travels, MG Rd (☎23517). Treks and tours of Sikkim, Darjeeling, Nepal and Bhutan, plus domestic airline tickets, entry permits into Sikkim, and foreign exchange.

Mountain Adventure, 31 Super Market (☎22454). Treks to Dzongri and car tours; trekking equipment for rent; and will arrange permits for US$10–12 per day.

Shangrila Tours and Travels, above General Store, MG Rd (☎737101). Affiliated to *Gangtok Lodge*. Dzongri treks, package and customized tours, and a "hot-spring" tour.

Tashila Tours and Travels, NH 31-A (☎22979). Trekking; river rafting from Singtam to Rangpo (US $40 or Rs1000); yak safaris; angling; cultural and monastery tours.

Yak & Yeti Travels, *Hotel Himalchuli*, NH 31-A (☎22714). Treks and other activities.

Yuksom Tours and Treks, Borong House, above Thakurbari (☎23473). Treks to Dzongri and Goechala from US$45 per day.

Around Gangtok

The most obvious destinations for day trips from Gangtok are the great Buddhist monasteries of **Rumtek** to the southwest, and **Phodong** to the north. On the road to Phodong, **Tashi View Point**, 8km out of Gangtok, provides views of the eastern aspects of Kanchendzonga, whose tent-like appearance here is radically different to the way it looks from Darjeeling, and the snowy pyramid of Siniolchu (6888m), which the pioneering mountaineer Eric Shipton ranked among the most beautiful in the world.

Several operators, including Sikkim Tourism, *Hangsu*, and *Bayyul*, run excursions to snowy **Tsangu Lake**, 35km northeast of Gangtok on the military road to Nathu La. Recently opened to foreign tourists, this has long been popular with Indian visitors as an accessible opportunity to sample the high mountain environment.

Rumtek

Visible from Gangtok, a 24-kilometre road-trip southwest of the capital, the large *gompa* (monastery) of **RUMTEK** is the headquarters of the Karmapa branch of the reformist

Kargyudpa sect. Familiarly known as the **"Black Hats"**, Karmapa was founded during the twelfth century by Karmapa Ranchun Dorje, as a reversion to the old magical ways of the Nyingmapa, the original school of Tibetan Buddhism. According to legend, hordes of celestial maidens descended upon the first Karmapa Rinpoche, and a crown was woven using a single hair from each one. That crown is invisible to the common person, but the Empress of China later presented a black hat which all could see. Unless the Rinpoche holds onto the hat whenever he wears it, its magical powers will cause it to fly away.

Rumtek monastery was founded in 1740, but had to be rebuilt during the 1960s after an earthquake. Construction of the lavish four-level complex was made possible by international funding attracted by the sixteenth Karmapa Rinpoche, who established around 200 Karmapa centres all over the world. His death in 1981 was followed by a bitter struggle over the choice of a replacement *tulku* or incarnate *lama*; eventually the Dalai Lama came to Sikkim in 1993, performed the Kalachakra (Wheel of Time) ceremony at Gangtok, and resolved the conflict in favour of a Tibetan boy.

Rumtek's ornate facade is covered with intricate brightly-painted wooden lattice work. Large red columns support the high roof of the **prayer hall**, where the walls are decorated with beautiful murals and *thangkas*. Visitors are welcome to attend daily rituals, when lines of monks sit chanting. A chamber off the hall, used for tantric rituals, is painted with gold against a black background and depicts wrathful protective deities (which may not be photographed).

Behind the main temple is the most ornate of all the buildings, built in 1984 along Tibetan lines. Monks spend a minimum of nine years studying at the *Karma Shri Nalanda Institute of Buddhist Studies*, followed by an optional three-year period of isolated meditation. The main hall on the third floor is decorated with magnificent murals all over its walls, and holds images including the Buddha Shakyamuni – the historic Buddha – and the sixteenth Karmapa Rinpoche. His remains are contained in a gilded *chorten* or *stupa*, studded with semi-precious stones, opposite the institute.

At Lohsar, the Tibetan New Year (Feb), the main courtyard stages *chaam* dance spectacles, in which Black Hat ceremonial dancers in colourful costumes spin and move to the magical and ponderous sounds of horns, drums and clashing cymbals.

Below the new monastery and Rumtek village, a path leads to the simple original Rumtek *gompa*, in an attractive wooded clearing and surrounded by empty outbuildings in traditional Sikkimese alpine style, with latticed wooden windows.

The one-day city tours run by the tourist office in Gangtok (see p.800) include an hour in Rumtek, which is not nearly long enough. There's also one *SNT* bus from Gangtok each day, which leaves at 4pm and returns the next morning. **Rooms** of a pretty low standard are available opposite the main gates of the *gompa* (①), and a couple of *chai* shops next door serve basic meals. The *Sangay Hotel* (①), a couple of hundred metres down the Gangtok road, is more salubrious, and it too has an adjacent tea shop. Further towards Rumtek, the incongruous new *Shambala Resort* (⑥) so far has eight cottages and a main building, and plans to open a swimming pool; for reservations, contact *Shambala Lodge*, Nam Nang Rd, Gangtok (☎23020).

Phodong

PHODONG, 38km north of Gangtok on the Mangan road, is another living monastery, but a far less ostentatious one. Lying on a spur of the hill 1km above the main road, and commanding superb views, it consists of a simple square main temple, plus several outhouses and residential quarters. Also built in 1740, this was Sikkim's pre-eminent Kargyudpa monastery until the growth of Rumtek in the 1960s. It too hosts colourful *lama* dances, like the *chaam* of Rumtek, each December. A rough road leads for 4km up to another old monastery – the unusual octagonal **Labrang** – which has been recently renovated.

Sikkim Tourism run a **Tourist Lodge** near the *gompa*, which is clean and excellent value and prepares meals to order (①); rooms can be booked through the tourist office in Gangtok. Two kilometres beyond the Phodong monastery turn-off, the *Yak & Yeti Hotel* (②), in the hamlet on the main road, has a basic restaurant and reasonable budget rooms. The bus to Gangtok stops here around 4pm.

Western Sikkim

All trekking in Sikkim is currently confined to the area west of the River Teesta. On the far west, along the border with Nepal, the watershed of the Singalila range rises along a single ridge, with giants such as Rathong and Kabru culminating in Kanchendzonga itself. This beautiful land, characterized by great tracts of virgin forests and deep river valleys, holds ancient monasteries such as **Pemayengtse** and **Tashiding**; the old capital, **Yuksom**, lies at the start of the trail towards Dzongri and Kanchendzonga.

Permit restrictions (see p.798) mean that trekkers can only follow well-beaten trails within a limited period of time; as western Sikkim is nearer Darjeeling than Gangtok, it makes sense to arrange permits before you enter the state. Although only one high-altitude trail is currently available, several low-altitude treks, free from trekking restrictions, provide pleasant and undemanding walking through relatively unspoilt terrain.

Jorethang and Legship

The most important town in western Sikkim, **JORETHANG**, lies in the very south of the state, just across the River Rangit from Singla Bazaar in West Bengal and a mere 30km north of Darjeeling, barely visible across the tea plantations. Set on an extensive shelf, which makes it feel oddly flat despite the huge hills that rise in every direction, it's a surprisingly pleasant and well-ordered place, with a good market; at the time this book went to press, it looked as if a couple of small hotels were about to open, so there may by now by adequate accommodation if you need to break a journey here.

Although Jorethang is well connected by bus with the rest of Sikkim, and there is a direct bus to Siliguri, no buses cross the border due south into West Bengal. The territory south of the river from Naya Bazaar, Jorethang's twin town, is notorious bandit country, where vehicles are often held up and forced to pay money. Shared taxis, however, do venture along the perilous and poor-quality road to Darjeeling in daylight hours, charging around Rs45 – none leaves Jorethang after 1pm.

LEGSHIP, in the deep Rangit Valley 26km north of Jorethang, is the first town you come to if you approach western Sikkim from Gangtok, just under 100km east. It's an important regional road junction, but not an interesting destination. A police checkpoint near its main crossroads checks all permits, and the nearby *Hotel Trishna* (①), the only local restaurant, has a few basic rooms. Buses and shared taxis connect Legship with Gangtok, Ghezing, and Yuksom via Tashiding, and also with Jorethang.

Ghezing

Although of no great appeal in itself, the unattractive market town of **GHEZING**, 110km west of Gangtok, is the transportation hub of western Sikkim, with a major *SNT* bus terminal. It's a good place to stock up on provisions, and has a limited choice of accommodation if you're forced to stay overnight – but there's no earthly reason why you'd choose to. The handful of basic hotels around the main square include the *Mayalu* (①), the *West End* (①), and the *No Name* (①); the latter has a restaurant and bar serving Chinese and Indian food. By far the most pleasant address is the *PWD Bungalow* above town, which has to be booked through the department at Gangtok.

An *SNT* bus to Ghezing (5hr) leaves Gangtok at 7am, and arrives at noon, in time to catch the 2.30pm bus (one of several daily services) to **Pelling**, 9km north (see below), or walk to **Pemayengtse**. Going back to Gangtok, the bus leaves around 8.30am. There are also two daily buses to **Yoksum** (1pm, and, via Tashiding, 4pm), a direct service to **Siliguri** (7am), and shared taxis run to Legship among other destinations.

Pemayengtse and Pelling

Perched at the end of a ridge parallel to (and visible from) that of Darjeeling, the haunting monastery of **PEMAYENGTSE**, 118km from Gangtok, is poised high above the River Rangit as it snakes towards its confluence with the Teesta on the West Bengal border. The main road from Ghezing takes nine kilometres to wind up there, but a steep two-kilometre short cut through the woods leads past a line of *chortens* and the otherwise uninteresting ruins of Sikkim's second capital, **Rabdentse**.

"Perfect Sublime Lotus", founded in the seventeeth century by Lhatsun Chempo, one of the three *lamas* of Yuksom, and extended in 1705 by his re-incarnation, is the most important *gompa* of the Red Hat sect. A place of impressive solitude, it now has few resident monks; though used daily for morning and evening worship, it is generally quiet. Surrounded by exquisite outhouses, with intricate woodwork on the beams, lattice windows and doors, the main *gompa* itself is plain in comparison. Built on three floors, it centres around a large hall which contains images of Guru Rinpoche and Lhatsun Chempo, and an exquisite display of *thangkas* and murals. Upstairs, one of several ritual chambers holds a magnificent model of paradise, protected in a large glass case. Carved in wood and painted by Dungzin Rinpoche, a former abbot of Pemayengtse, it depicts Zandogpalr, the celestial abode of Guru Rinpoche, rising above the carnage of hell. Detail includes demons, animals, birds, Buddhas and *bodhisattvas*, *chortens* and flying dragons. An annual *chaam* – masked dance – is held here during the Tibetan New Year (Feb), and attracts visitors from all over Sikkim.

Both Pemayengtse and the small town of **PELLING**, 1.5km beyond, look north towards the glaciers and peaks of Kanchendzonga. High above the forest-covered hills, in an amphitheatre of cloud, snow and rock, the route to the Rathong Glacier over Dzongri La is displayed in near entirety, from its start at the great shelf at Yoksum.

A trail rises westwards for around 4km from Pelling through some important sites associated with Guru Rinpoche to reach the small monastery of **Sange Choling**. One of Sikkim's oldest *gompas*, built in 1697, this is another of Lhatsun Chempo's creations, and is highly venerated among the Nyingmapa. Gutted by fire, it has been recently rebuilt and houses some of the original clay statues.

Practicalities

The large *Mount Pandim* hotel just below the monastery in Pemayengtse offers by far the smartest and most comfortable accommodation in the whole of western Sikkim (☎03593/256; ⑤–⑥), with magnificent views, friendly staff, and a good restaurant serving cold beers. Next door, the *Trekkers Hut* (①) may seem an attractive proposition, but it is poorly run and not particularly clean.

The loose collection of buildings at the crossroads in Pelling includes a handful of small hotels and lodges such as the *Garuda* (☎03593/737113; ①). Run by the friendly Wangdi family, this typical travellers' hang-out has small but clean budget rooms and shared bathrooms, and a roof-top cafe. They will look after equipment while you trek, and the log book filled by previous guests is informative about local treks and conditions. *Kabur Lodge and Restaurant*, 300 metres away, is slightly more comfortable but less atmospheric, and its multi-cuisine restaurant next door is not as good, though it does offer the chance to sample *tomba* (see p.803). Also in Pelling, a Tibetan-run handicrafts centre manufactures furniture and carpets.

Some of the frequent buses from Pelling to Ghezing continue to Jorethang, on the main route to Darjeeling; there's also a daily direct service to **Yuksom** (7.30am).

Yoksum

The sleepy, spread-out hamlet of **YOKSUM**, which occupies a large shelf at the entrance to the Rathong Chu gorge, 40km north of Pemayengtse at the end of the motor road, holds a special place in Sikkimese history. This was the spot where the three *lamas*, including Lhatsun Chempo, arrived across high and difficult passes to establish Tibetan Buddhism in Sikkim, in the form of the **Red Hat** or Nyingmapa sect. However, although Yoksum was once the capital of the state, and the first Chogyal was crowned here, little evidence of its past remains. Abandoned by modern Sikkim, its main role these days is as the start of the **Dzongri Trail**.

Lhatsun Chempo is supposed to have buried offerings in Yoksum's large white **Norbugang Chorten** after the enthronement of the first Chogyal, Phuntsog Namgyal. Nearby, past the *Trekkers Hut*, a path branches left through a traditional part of the village to a small grove where the simple stone throne of the first Chogyal stands in front of a *chorten* built with stones and earth from different parts of Sikkim.

High above the town, prayer flags announce the site of the **Dubdi Monastery**, built in 1701. From the end of the road at the hospital, a path threads past water-wheels and a small river and rises through the forest to arrive at the dramatically situated *gompa*,

THE DZONGRI TRAIL

The one **high-altitude trek** currently allowed in Sikkim, from **Yoksum** to **Dzongri**, in the very shadow of Kanchendzonga, passes through huge tracts of forest and provides incredible mountain vistas. Would-be trekkers have to have special **permits** (see p.798), travel in groups organized by authorized agencies (see p.804), complete with largely superfluous guides and a liaison officer, and pay a daily rate of around US$35. You need to sort out food arrangements before you set off, and bring adequate clothing – including protective headgear to cope with the heat of the river valleys – boots, and sleeping bags. For general advice on trekking equipment and health issues, see *Basics*.

Although Dzongri is the junction of several trails, the prescribed route onwards leads to **Gocha La** via Zemanthang and Samiti Lake. Though yak herders also use the trail, it can at times seem too narrow for man or beast, but it penetrates surprisingly high into the mountains considering its brevity. Well marked, and dotted with basic accommodation, the trail is at its best in May, when the rhododendrons bloom.

DAY 1 consists of getting to **Yoksum**, either by bus or, more enjoyably, walking 18km from **Pelling** (see p.807). The route from Pelling starts by dropping down to a footbridge across a mountain river. Then you ascend diagonally to the right to join the motor road, and follow it past a tea shop and a small hamlet to pick up another trail which leads down again to a precarious bamboo bridge over the turbulent Rathong Chu. Beyond the white sandy beach and boulders, a steep trail climbs to a motor road and a tiny hamlet, then rises to catch the same road again. Turn left and follow this all the way past the school at **Yoksum** to the police station, near the end of the motor road.

DAY 2 takes 7hr to climb 18km from **Yoksum** to **Tsokha**. You begin by crossing the cultivated mountainside almost horizontally; then the trail reaches deep forest cover, to undulate past waterfalls and across minor bridges before arriving at the Parekh Chu above its confluence with the Rathong. The next 3 or 4km involve a knee-grinding ascent past the rambling *Forest Rest House* at **Bakhim**. You have now entered the lichen zone and cloud forests. **Tsokha**, 1.5km further on, and at 3048m around 300m higher, is settled by Tibetan yak herders. It has a *Trekkers Hut* and several rustic houses, where guests are offered Tibetan tea – a salty brew made with rancid butter – sitting in the kitchen beneath rafters blackened by smoke and hung with slowly curing chunks of yak meat.

looking out over Yoksum and Pemayengtse. Unless you've made prior arrangements, there's unlikely to be anyone around to let you have a look inside.

Visitors with west Sikkim permits are welcome in Yoksum, but unless you have a Dzongri Trek permit you're not supposed to venture any further. The police are quite vigilant, so there's not much chance of a surreptitious high-mountain trek, but so long as you're not carrying a backpack they may allow a day trip along the main trail to the Parekh Chu and its confluence with the Rathong Chu – a 28-kilometre round trip. You won't see the high Himalaya, but you do pass through some beautiful forest scenery (visibly being eroded to feed the increasing demands of the trekking industry). Yaks – or rather *dzo*, a more manageable cross between yak and domestic cattle – travel this route, with supplies for trekking parties and isolated communities.

Practicalities

The *Demazong* (①–②) at the bus stop in Yoksum is the newest, cleanest and most comfortable **hotel** in town, with reasonable rooms and a restaurant serving basic meals. Behind it, in the middle of a field, the chalet-like *Trekkers Hut* has primitive rooms (①), and out-house toilets, and allows camping. The best of the few rudimentary cafes is the friendly *Dzongrila*, opposite the *Demazong*. There are also two good *Forest Rest Houses* (①), bookable in Gangtok; *#1* is approached through gates near the police station, *#2* is about 1km beyond the Trekkers Hut on the Dzongri trail. A **bus** to Tashiding, Legship and Ghezing leaves from in front of the *Dzongrila* at around 7am.

It makes good sense to spend **DAY 3** acclimatizing yourself to the altitude at Tsokha, perhaps with a short trek of around 5km towards Dzongri, to a watchtower which (weather permitting) has superb views of Kanchendzonga.

The hike from **Tsokha** to **Dzongri** on **DAY 4** takes 5hr to cover 16km. The trail rises through beautiful pine and rhododendron forests before a final steep and gruelling ascent brings you out suddenly at the tracts of dwarf rhododendron of Phedang Meadows, before dipping down to the hut at desolate, snow-covered **Dzongri** (4030m).

Once again, it's worth staying around Dzongri on **DAY 5** for further acclimatization. That gives you the opportunity to climb Dzongri Hill above the hut, for early-morning and early-evening views of Kanchendzonga's rocky triple-buttressed South Summit. Also look out for the black tooth of Kabur, a forbidding-looking holy mountain that towers above Dzongri La. Several trails meet at the meadows at Dzongri – one descends to cross the Rathong Chu and rises again to the demanding pass of Kang La into Nepal; another crosses Dzongri La (4800m), descends around 450m and rises again to Chaurikhang.

On **DAY 6**, the trek from **Dzongri** to **Thangsing** (4hr; 14km) descends against an incredible backdrop of peaks to a rhododendron forest, crosses a bridge, and continues through woods to the *Trekkers Hut* at **Thangsing** (3800m), at the end of a glacial valley.

DAY 7's route crosses varied terrain from **Thangsing** to **Samiti Lake** (4hr; 10km). First the trail follows a stream and alpine meadows past a yak-herders' hut, then it traverses glacial moraine before again crossing meadows and a rocky landscape before arriving at the emerald-green **Samiti Lake** (4060m). The campsite here is next to a giant boulder, which provides some shelter from cold winds or storms.

DAY 8, very much the climax of the trek, is also by far its most difficult section – not because of any technicalities, but simply due to its high altitude. In a round-trip of 14km, you climb from **Samiti Lake** up to **Gocha La** (4hr) and back down again (2hr 30min). Leaving Samiti Lake, the trail follows glacial moraine, drops to a dry lake at Zemanthang, then makes a final grinding rise alongside cairns decorated with the occasional prayer flag to the defile at **Gocha La** (4940m). Kanchendzonga South is clearly visible above the pass, while to the left glaciers tumble off Kabru Dome.

Most of **DAY 9**'s long hike, from **Samiti Lake** back to **Tsokha** (8hr; 24km) is downhill, taking a short cut to avoid Dzongri. Crossing the bridge and following the path to a junction signed to the left puts you back above **Tsokha**, to rejoin the trail to Yoksum.

Tashiding

The beautiful *gompa* of **TASHIDING** – not strictly accessible on a west Sikkim permit – occupies the point of a conical hill 19km south of Yoksum, high above the confluence of the Rangit and the Rathong. "The Devoted Central Glory" was built in 1717, after a rainbow was seen to connect the site to Kanchendzonga. A wide path, lined with tall fluttering prayer flags, leads to the monastery complex, where traditional buildings, *chortens* and an impressive *mani* wall (inscribed with the mantra *Om mani padme hum*) are located around the unassuming main temple, which was recently rebuilt using some of the features and wooden beams of the original. Around February, on the fifteenth day of the first month of the Tibetan lunar calendar, devotees from all over Sikkim gather in Tashiding for the **Nyingmapa Bhumchu festival**. They are blessed by the holy water from an ancient bowl said by legend never to dry up; oracles consult the water's level to determine the future. The two hundred resident monks and acolytes are friendly, and often invite visitors to share Tibetan tea.

Around two kilometres below the *gompa*, Tashiding's tiny bazaar is situated near a saddle that separates the mountainside from the monastery hill. The *Gupta Tea Shop* (①) here has very cheap basic accommodation, and there's a small *Tourist Lodge* (①) higher up on the Yoksum Road. One daily **bus** goes to Yoksum (3pm), and two run down to Legship (18km); one leaves at 7am, the other passes through on its way from Yoksum at 8.30am. On foot, short-cuts through the forests lead to Pemayengtse, a difficult and confusing climb up on the far side of the Rathong (ask for directions), or to Legship, over the Rangit.

North Sikkim

Most of spectacular **north Sikkim** is closed to visitors. However, although up to 1993 no one was allowed to venture past Phodong, now groups armed with special permits who make arrangements through travel and tour operators in Gangtok are allowed as far as **Yumthang**, at the edge of the Tibetan plateau.

The road north of Gangtok follows the deep Teesta gorge past Phodong (see p.805), across what is said to be the highest bridge in the world (no photographs), before reaching the quiet little town of **Mangan**, after 60km. The administration centre for north Sikkim, it has a couple of basic hotels and cafes on the main road. A small and unremarkable *gompa* above the road around 5km north provides incredible views, especially early in the morning, of the huge east face of Kanchendzonga. Although a magnificent valley branches northwest from Mangan towards Kanchendzonga, this area is reserved as the Lepcha heartland and is closed to all non-Lepchas.

A further 40km north lies **Chungthang**, a dark and grubby town, set in a deep valley at the confluence of the Lachen and Lachung rivers, with a large military presence. There is a large PWD bungalow here as well as a couple of basic hotels on the main road, one of which has quite a decent but simple restaurant.

Beyond Chumthang, the valleys fork; these are border areas and the military who maintain the rough roads are very sensitive – photography, even of harmless monasteries, is not tolerated. The road to the right climbs rapidly to the small settlement of **Lachung**, the "big pass", a mere 15km west of Tibet. Across the river, **Lachung Monastery** is a two-storey Tibetan-style *gompa* belonging to the Nyingmapa sect. As the area opens up to tourism, one or two lodges are under construction.

Fifteen kilometres further north, the valley becomes ever more spectacular. Craggy snow-bound peaks rise as high as 6000m to either side, and there are large tracts of rhododendron and pine forests around **Yumthang**, which has hot sulphur springs and a small *Tourist Lodge* (②).

CHAPTER FIFTEEN

THE NORTHEASTERN HILL STATES

Certainly the most mysterious, and arguably the most beautiful region of India, the **NORTHEASTERN HILL STATES** have long been all but sealed off from the outside world. Only now, as government restrictions are gradually eased, do they appear to be on the point of opening up to travellers. Although the entire region was until the 1960s encompassed by the single state of **ASSAM**, separatist pressures since then have meant that it has been progressively split up into seven distinct states. Assam itself now consists of the low-lying valley of the **Brahmaputra**, while the others occupy the hills on all sides. In **ARUNACHAL PRADESH** to the north, the Himalayas rise to 6500m; to the south, the ancient rocks of the **Shillong Plateau** hold **MEGHALAYA**. To the east, on the border with Burma, the Arakans run south for 800km from Arunachal through **NAGALAND**, **MANIPUR** and **MIZORAM**, while **TRIPURA** nestles against Bangladesh west of Mizoram. The capital of Assam, **Guwahati**, is by far the most important city; the fact that foreigners can only arrive in

ACCESS AND PERMITS

Although the long-standing **restrictions** governing entry to the northeast for foreign and Indian visitors seem at present to be being eased, they are not being removed altogether, and the situation remains confusing. In the hope that more areas will soon be accessible to travellers, we have in this chapter covered some destinations which at present are not open to foreigners, and can only advise would-be visitors to check the current situation when they arrive in India. Interestingly, much of the pressure to lift restrictions comes from the states themselves; it's the central government of India that appears keen to keep the lid on what it regards as highly sensitive border areas.

At present, Indian citizens do not require **permits** to enter Assam, Manipur, Meghalaya and Tripura, but they do for Arunachal, Nagaland and Mizoram. In broad terms, this means that foreign visitors are unlikely to get into the latter three states (apart from on the hugely expensive group tours arranged by Arunachal Pradesh state), but may succeed in obtaining **Restricted Area Permits** for Assam, Manipur, Meghalaya and Tripura, either by applying to The Secretary, Ministry of Home Affairs, Government of India, N Block, New Delhi 110001, at least four weeks in advance, or through Indian consulates overseas at the same time as visa applications. **Foreigners Registration Offices** in the four major cities of Bombay, Calcutta, Delhi and Madras are authorized to issue permits for overseas visitors to access certain areas, and specific **State Tourist Departments** in the same cities can also help with permits and travel arrangements.

Logistically, there's no point having permits to enter certain states unless you have permits for appropriate neighbours. The entire northeastern area can at present only be entered **by air**, to **Guwahati** in Assam, and so a permit for Assam is crucial to entry to all the other states. Similarly, Imphal in Manipur can only be reached by road via Dimapur and Kohima in Nagaland. Foreigners are not permitted to access the region by road or rail.

Govt of India Statement -
The external boundaries of India are neither correct nor authenticated.

the region by **air** makes it the gateway to the entire northeast, and all the other states depend heavily on the transport routes of the Assam Valley.

The main appeals of visiting the northeast are its extraordinary diversity of **peoples** – ranging from tribes such as the Nagas and the Mizos to descendants of the Rajputs, and from animists and Buddhists, to Christians, Hindus, and Muslims – and its spectacular **landscapes**. One of the wettest monsoon belts in the world, most of the region was, until recently, rich in teak forests and wild elephants. Although elephant stockades are now rare, the lower-lying forests are being rapidly depleted, and many ecosystems are under severe strain, it still holds large tracts of bamboo, mixed deciduous and evergreen forests, and an astounding array of flora and fauna. Of its many **wildlife sanctuaries**, the most famous is **Kaziranga** in Assam, home of the Indian one-horned rhino; others, such as **Namdapha** in the farthest corner of Arunachal, remain miles off any normal tourist circuit. The recommended **time to visit** any part of the northeast is in winter and spring, when the sanctuaries are open. It rains heavily from May to the end of September, and you have to be prepared for rain at any time of year.

There are two major reasons why the Indian government is wary of encouraging tourism to the northeast. Firstly, ever since Indian Independence in 1947, tribal groups such as the Nagas, the United Liberation Front of Assam (ULFA), and the Bodos of north Assam have been engaged in a series of bitter independence struggles that have kept the entire region on the brink of political chaos. As recently as 1993, conflicts between southern Naga communities and the Kukis of Manipur left many dead.

Secondly, Indian military thinking sees the northeast as extremely vulnerable, being connected to the rest of the country by the slenderest of necks between the Himalayas and Bangladesh. That vulnerability was made cruelly apparent by the **Chinese**, who in a lightning invasion in 1962 succeeded in penetrating as far as the outskirts of Tezpur in the Brahmaputra Valley.

Assam

The state of **ASSAM** is dominated by the mighty **River Brahmaputra**, whose lush 700-kilometre valley is sandwiched between the Himalayan foothills to the north and the hills and plateau of Meghalaya to the south. Although much of the valley is under cultivation, large tracts of woodland make this one of the most forested states in India.

Assam produces more than half of India's **tea**. Most of its 800 tea estates were laid down by the British, who created a basic infrastructure of roads, as well as one golf club for every fifteen estates, to relieve the tedium and loneliness of the planters. Though most of the estates are now owned by large Indian companies, their managers are still known as "tea planters". The state also holds some of India's few **oil** fields; **Digboi** in Upper Assam (the northeast) was the first oil refinery in Asia. However, the earthquake-prone region has been unable to develop its hydro-electric potential. Bamboo and forestry are other major resources, and still use working **elephants**.

Political violence has wracked Assam over the last two decades, with the Marxist United Liberation Front of Assam (ULFA) fighting for independence. Kidnappings and murders generated an atmosphere of terror that threatened to close the tea industry, but in the early 1990s the Indian Army managed to bring about a degree of law and order. Issues have however been left simmering rather than resolved.

The capital of Assam, **Guwahati**, which once controlled a far greater area, is a busy town that continues to provide the key to the entire northeast region, with its vital air, rail and road connections. It is also the site of one of India's most important Kali temples, the *shaktipith* of **Kamakhya**, and the temple of **Navagraha**, once a great centre of astrology and astronomy. Within easy access of Guwahati, the bountiful grasslands of the wildlife sanctuary at **Kaziranga** are renowned for their one-horned **rhinoceroses** – the state symbol.

AHOMS AND BODOS

Migration of people has played a major role in the history of the northeast. Originally called the Shan, the **Ahom**, Buddhists from Thailand, invaded in 1228 and settled in the northeast corner of the valley of the Brahmaputra. Establishing their capital at Sibsagar, they named the region *Assam*, "undulating land". By the end of the sixteenth century the fiery and tenacious Ahoms had displaced the Kacharis and Koche of northeast Bengal and west Assam, and they later repelled several Muslim invasions from Bengal.

Intermingling with the mostly Bengali Aryans of the lowlands, they became accomplished cultivators; as they adopted Hindu socio-religious traditions, a new Assamese identity emerged. In the eighteenth century, the formal conversion of the Ahom chief to Hinduism prompted a rebellion, which was quelled with the help of the Burmese. The Burmese then absorbed the entire kingdom, which marked the end of Ahom rule, and it was united with India when they eventually ceded it to the British in 1826.

The term **Bodo**, derived from *Bhotia* (ie people from Bhot – another name for Tibet), serves to describe several trans-Himalayan tribes, including the Monpas, Daflas and Mishmis of Arunachal Pradesh, groups in the Cachar Hills of Tripura, and the Garos of Meghalaya. The Bodos have recently come to be regarded as a distinct socio-political entity, and a campaign for Bodo self-rule has grown over the last decade.

Guwahati

The most striking feature of **GUWAHATI**, the capital of Assam and gateway to the northeastern hill states, is the **Brahmaputra**, whose muddy swollen channel is so vast that the far shore is often invisible. Guwahati lies at the point where the wooded hills at the edge of the Shillong Plateau touch the southern banks of the river, with the flat alluvial plains of the Assam valley stretching away to the north. Busy and interesting markets occupy the town centre, while avenues radiate away to suburbs that nestle in the foothills. Of its many mysterious temples, **Kamakhya** and **Navagraha** overlook the river, while **Umananda** sits marooned on an island crag.

Guwahati's main business, **tea**, is booming, with the new *Assam Tea Auction Centre* holding auctions of the *CTC (Crush, Tear and Curl)* variety that previously took place as far away as Calcutta and London. In addition, Noonmati, on the northern outskirts, is the region's largest oil refinery. Despite Guwahati's recent prosperity and rapid growth, however, the town retains an appealing old-world atmosphere.

Arrival, information and public transport

As foreigners are obliged to fly to Assam, you're almost certain to arrive at the **airport**, 18km east of the centre. Taxis into town cost around Rs150, coaches more like Rs20; one, run by *Indian Airlines*, goes to their office in the central Paltan Bazaar.

The Assamese government's **tourist office** shares premises with the *Tourist Lodge* on Station Rd (Mon–Fri 10am–5pm, Sat 10am–1pm; ☎47012). They organize local and longer tours, with those to Kaziranga being particularly good value. The **Government of India Tourist Information**, BK Kakati Rd, Ulubari (☎31381), can provide information on the entire northeast (Mon–Fri 9.30am–5pm). *Grindlays Bank* and the *State Bank of India*, both in Fancy Bazaar, handle foreign exchange.

Guwahati has an efficient and extensive system of minibuses, known as **Canters**; routes are displayed at a few major stops. Cycle rickshaws tend to stay close to the centre, while auto-rickshaws cover a wider area but are expensive in comparison. Meters are ignored; agree a fare before you set off, at around Rs15 per kilometre. The main terminal for river **ferries**, used by operators like *Blue Hill*, is at **Sukreswar Ghat**.

The Town

Although strictly speaking Guwahati is split in two by the Brahmaputra – only crossed by the **Saraighat Bridge** and the ferries – "Guwahati" is taken to refer to the main town south of the river, while **North Guwahati** is virtually a separate town.

Paltan Bazaar and **Fancy Bazaar**, Guwahati's main bazaar areas, are bunched in the centre just south of the railway, with the older residential areas across the tracks. Most of the bazaars deal simply in provisions; if you're looking to buy **silk**, or other Assamese crafts, head for the *Assam Co-Op Silk House* or *Purbashree*, both on GNB Rd, or the *Pragjyotika Assam Emporium* in Ambari.

Archeological and ethnographic displays in Assam's **State Museum**, near the centre of town, include stone and copper plate inscriptions dating from the fifth century, a twelfth-century sculpture of Surya, terracotta and costumes (Tues–Sat 10am–4.30pm, Sun 8am–noon; 25p).

The Shiva temple of **Umananda**, reached by motor launches (Rs40) and public ferries (Rs3) from **Umananda Ghat**, stands on an island bluff in the middle of the Brahmaputra. Its location, at the top of a flight of steep steps up from the jetty, is more dramatic than the unassuming and unremarkable temple itself. One or two shops sell offerings at the temple gates, and the trees house beautiful golden langur, well used to being fed by passing pilgrims and happy to pose for a close-up.

On the commanding Nilachal Hill, overlooking the river 8km west of the centre, the important Kali temple of **Kamakhya**, with its beehive-shaped spire (*shikhara*), is a fine

example of the distinctive Assamese style of architecture. Said to occupy the site of a Khasi sacrificial ground, and to mark the place where Shakti's *yoni* (vulva) fell when her body disintegrated into 108 pieces, it has a somewhat eerie atmosphere, despite having been rebuilt in 1665 after a priest who converted to Islam burned down the original structure.

Small shops selling offerings crowd its main entrance, which throngs in the morning with priests clad in tantric red and saffron awaiting their clients. Myriads of pilgrims come up the hill by bus or car, while the poor and devout trudge up on foot. Animal sacrifice is a standard part of ritual; kid goats are bathed in the ceremonial tank and then led to their slaughter behind the temple hall. Non-Hindus are allowed to enter the inner sanctum, which involves walking barefoot on a floor sprinkled lightly with sacrificial blood. The queue, while orderly, can take a long time; another entrance leads to a subsidiary shrine if you don't want to wait. The priests get a good income from blessing and releasing ceremonial pigeons on behalf of pilgrims, then catching them and re-selling them to the next customers. A short walk up the hill brings you to a smaller and emptier temple, with great views of the Brahmaputra and Guwahati.

Another hill in east Guwahati holds the atmospheric **Navagraha** temple – the "temple of the nine planets", an ancient seat of astrology and astronomy – surrounded by large trees that shelter tribes of monkeys. Housed in a single red dome, again in the beehive style, the central *lingam* is encircled by a further nine representing the planets. Although limited by the lack of telescopes, Indian astronomers managed to discern seven planets (*graha*) – Sun (Surya, Ravi), Moon (Chandra, Soma), Mercury (Buddha), Venus (Sukra), Mars (Mangala), Jupiter (Brhaspati) and Saturn (Sani). Two more were added, Rahu and Ketu, the dragon's head and the dragon's tail, or the ascending and descending nodes of the moon. Hence *Navagraha*, meaning the nine planets.

At the base of a wooded hill, 5km east of the centre, Guwahati's leafy and well-managed **Zoo** consists of a lot of cages interspersed with a few open-air compounds. Among its prize animals are clouded leopards – a small leopard with a large bushy tail and strikingly beautiful markings – while in one dramatic enclosure a catwalk (literally) looks down from a height of ten metres on a white tiger languishing in a pool below, ignoring all comments from above with disdain. At the far end, the zoo blends into the ornamental **Botanical Gardens**, accessed by the same ticket (daily except Mon, Sept–March 7am–4pm, April–Oct 8am–5.30pm; Rs2).

Accommodation

Guwahati has a strong selection of **hotels**. In addition to the budget options in Paltan Bazaar, several new hotels compete for the business market.

Ananda Lodge, MN Rd, Pan Bazaar (☎44832). A very good value budget lodge, with a clean courtyard atmosphere but dingy rooms. Food is available; veg meals cost around Rs10. ①–②.

Belle Vue, MG Rd, opposite Raj Bhavan (☎40847 or 35448). On a wooded hill overlooking the river, away from the noise of the bazaars. Although showing its age, it still has some charm. ⑥.

Chilarai Regency, HP Brahmachari Rd, Paltan Bazaar (☎41530 or 43437). Near the *Indian Airlines* office, another luxury hotel with 44 rooms, restaurant and bar. ⑤.

Dynasty, SS Rd (☎43322 or 43330). Right in the heart of the market area; unlike many of the smart new hotels, the decor is pleasantly understated. Popular with package tours. Good Chinese food. ⑦.

ITDC Brahmaputra Ashok, MG Rd (☎41064 or 35310). The best hotel in Guwahati, near the river and 1km from the railway station, with a restaurant serving Indian, Chinese and European food. Bar and exchange and shopping facilities. *Ashok Travels* arranges transport and tours. ⑦.

Kuber International, Hem Barua Rd (☎32601). Guwahati landmark, right in the centre of Fancy Bazaar. Comfortable hotel with a unique revolving restaurant, serving excellent Indian food. ④–⑤.

Nandan, GS Rd (☎40855 or 43531). Opposite the *Indian Airlines* office, a large hotel, offering a modified American plan – breakfast and one meal. ⑤–⑥.

New Strand, GNB Rd, Pan Bazaar. Close to the railway station – clean and pleasant for a simple budget hotel and very competitively priced. ②–③.

Railway Retiring Rooms. One room and a small dorm, booked at the enquiry counter. ①–②.

Raj Mahal, AT Rd, Paltan Bazaar (☎32797). Garish three-star place with all mod cons. ④–⑤.

Tourist Lodge, Station Rd. Recently opened, in the same complex as the tourist office, not far from the railway station. A few a/c rooms available. Handy and quite clean, but unremarkable. ①–②.

Urvashi, Airport (☎28893). Comfortable hotel, well out of town but very convenient for catching flights – complimentary transfers. ⑤–⑦.

Eating

Most of Guwahati's middle and more expensive hotels have multi-cuisine **restaurants** and bars, concentrating on Mughlai and Chinese food. Some specialize in Assamese food – pleasantly underspiced, and reminiscent of Bengali food in its emphasis on fish.

Dynasty, SS Rd. A roof-top barbeque and a multi-cuisine restaurant serving good Chinese food.

Golden Dragon, GNB Rd, Pan Bazaar close to Station Rd. Quite a decent Chinese restaurant.

Ming Room, near the flyover, Ulubari. A bit far from the centre but the best Chinese food in town.

Paradise, MD Rd, Sangamari. Excellent Assamese restaurant, especially good for lunch.

Silver Tulips, GNB Rd, Silpukhuri (☎31535). Traditional Assamese decor of cane and bamboo. Recommended for its Mughlai cuisine, which is not over-spiced. Chicken mughlai Rs40.

Woodlands, GS Rd, Ulubari. Great north and south Indian veg restaurant; *thalis* and *masala dosas*.

Listings

Medical *Guwahati Medical College Hospital*, Bhangagarh (☎62159); *Life Pharmacy*, GS Rd, Ulubari is open 24 hours a day.

Photography *New Frontier Colour Lab*, SS Rd, Lakhtokia, near the Pan Bazaar Over Bridge (☎34686); *S Ghoshal*, HB Rd.

Travel Agents *Ashok Travel*, based at the *Hotel Brahmaputra Ashok*, is run by ITDC and is a comprehensive tour and travel agency with car rental and arrangements for airline tickets; *Rhino Travels*, ML Nehru Rd, Pan Bazaar (☎40666 or 40061) are recognized agents for *Indian Airlines*.

MOVING ON FROM GUWAHATI

Indian Airlines **flights** from Guwahati include services to **Delhi** (2 daily, IC890 and IC879); **Calcutta** (2 daily, including IC712, IC230 & IC258); **Dimapur** (2 weekly, IC257); and **Imphal** (2 weekly, IC209). *Indian Airlines* are based at Paltan Bazaar (enquiries ☎40355; bookings ☎40398).

Among **bus** companies that connect Guwahati with Siliguri, other parts of Assam, Arunachal Pradesh, Meghalaya, Manipur, Nagaland and Tripura are *Assam Valley*, Paltan Bazaar (☎46133); *Green Valley*, Paltan Bazaar (☎45289); *Blue Hill*, Paltan Bazaar (☎31427 or 43059); *Assam State Transport Corporation*, Paltan Bazaar (☎40208 or 47941). On the whole, buses leave from in front of each company's own office. The *ASTC* buses are very basic; *Blue Hill* run some very comfortable coaches along more popular routes, such as to Shillong, but they sub-contract lesser routes, and some of these can be a bit rough.

Around Guwahati

Guwahati is well placed for excursions to Kaziranga and Manas, as well as day and weekend breaks to the cooler climes of Shillong in Meghalaya. Closer to hand are the temples of **Basistha**, and, across the Brahmaputra, **Hajo**, while more distant **Tezpur** makes a convenient base for the small wildlife sanctuary of **Orang**.

Basistha

Beside a picturesque waterfall, 11km southeast of Guwahati, two small red-domed temples at **BASISTHA**, in Assamese beehive style, commemorate Vasistha Muni, the author of the *Ramayana* and the guru of Rama. Nestling within an impressive copse of trees, with rock carvings in the stream to add to the air of antiquity, Basistha is popular with pilgrims and picnickers alike. Regular minibuses run to and from the city.

Hajo

The small town of **HAJO**, 32km northeast of Guwahati, has a special place in Assamese culture, having been sacred even before the Ahom arrived as Buddhists, let alone their conversion to Hinduism. Now holy to Buddhists, Hindus and Muslims, it attracts pilgrims from all the faiths, in apparent harmony. A long palm-tree-lined stone staircase climbs a hill to the small Hindu temple of **Haigriba Madhab** where, some say, the Buddha gained *nirvana*. Praying at the mosque of **Pao Mecca** nearby grants Muslims a quarter (*pao*) of the spiritual benefit of Mecca. Hajo is easily accessible from Guwahati by *ASTC* buses (Rs4). Tours run by Guwahati's tourist office also take in the nearby village of **Sualkuchi**, where every household is engaged in producing silk.

Tezpur

Amid tea gardens and military cantonments on the north bank of the Brahmaputra, 181km east of Guwahati, the administrative town of **TEZPUR** stands on the site of **Sonitpur** (City of Blood), scene of a terrible mythological battle. As recently as 1962, it was almost captured by the Chinese. Centred on a large lake, Tezpur is an ideal base for visits to the wildlife sanctuary of **Orang**, 32km away, and to the beautiful nature reserve of **Bhalukpung**, 22km north on the road towards **Bomdila**, **Tawang**, and Arunachal Pradesh, where the River Jia Bharali emerges from the hills.

Tezpur is connected to Guwahati by bus, train, and even air, via the airport at Saloni, 10km away. Besides a number of simple hotels in the central bazaar at the centre of town, it has a couple of middle-grade hotels such as the *Luit*, near the bus stand (③–⑤). The *Tourist Lodge*, nearby (☎1016; ②), doubles as a **tourist office**.

The Wildlife Sanctuaries

Most of Assam's magnificent **wildlife sanctuaries** are located in the Brahmaputra Valley, where the large tracts of grasslands on the flood plains are home to the Indian one-horned rhino and other animals. The great advantage for travellers of such terrain, as compared to the thick jungle cover of most other Indian parks is that sightings of animals are all but assured.

Kaziranga, the greatest park of all, is renowned for its elephant grass and rhino, but it does also incorporate a certain amount of forest; the rarely visited, smaller, but no less beautiful **Orang** nearby occupies a similar habitat north of the Brahmaputra, near Tezpur. **Manas**, also known for its rhinos, extends over varied territory, taking in hills and river valleys on the border with Bhutan. The **Nambor Reserve Forest** in upper Assam, not far from Jorhat, consists of hill country away from the flood plains and grasslands.

Kaziranga

Covering an area of 430 square kilometres on the southern bank of the Brahmaputra, **KAZIRANGA NATIONAL PARK**, 217km east of Guwahati, occupies the vast valley floor against a backdrop of the forest-covered Karbi Anglong Hills. Rivulets and *bhils* (shallow lakes), and the semi-evergreen forested "Highlands", just out of reach of the Brahmaputra's annual floods, blend into marshes and flood plains covered with tall elephant grass. Animal sightings are guaranteed, with rhinos, deer and herds of wild buffalo grazing close to the park entrance not far from the administrative centre of **Kohora**. Rich birdlife includes egrets, herons, storks, fish-eating eagles and a grey pelican colony settled among the red cotton trees. However, few tracks penetrate this sea of grass, and the wild elephants seldom venture into it anyway, preferring to remain in the forested Highlands, while tigers are incredibly elusive. In addition, with the grasslands bordering onto cultivated fields and domestic cattle encroaching into the sanctuary and introducing epidemics, the wild animals are under increasing threat – poaching is rife, with rhino horns fetching astronomical prices as aphrodisiacs.

Kaziranga's large concentration of one-horned **rhino** – at over a thousand, the most in the subcontinent – are best seen from the back of an elephant, early on a winter's morning. Each of the three daily **elephant rides** lasts around one hour (5am, 6.30am & 3.30pm; Rs50); book in advance at the park offices at Kohora. The first is by far the best. Although the elephants do not penetrate far into the sanctuary, merely travelling in a circle of three or four kilometres, it is incredible how much wildlife can be seen in this small area. The mild-mannered rhinos seem oblivious to camera-clicking tourists – unlike the unpredictable wild buffalo, equipped with lethal horns and potentially ferocious. Although **jeeps** (arranged through the Deputy Director of Tourism at Kohora, or *Wild Grass*; see below) penetrate the forest to much greater depths, they do not allow you to approach wild animals anything like as closely.

Kaziranga is open during winter and spring only (mid-November to early April). During the monsoons, between June and September, the Brahmaputra bursts its banks, flooding the low-lying grasslands and causing animals to migrate from one area to another within the park. Deer and even leopard often cross the main road, heading for the hills until the waters recede.

KAZIRANGA PRACTICALITIES

Kohora, the administrative centre and main gate for Kaziranga, lies on National Highway 37, which follows the south bank of the Brahmaputra from Guwahati to Dibrugarh in north Assam. Although **bus** companies such as *Blue Hill* ply this route, the most convenient way to come is on the daily tourist bus from the *Guwahati Tourist Lodge* (see p.817), who also arrange complete package tours, including a night's accommodation and elephant ride, from Rs300.

The main crossing at Kohora, where through buses stop, consists of a handful of cafes and a small local market. The tourist bus from Guwahati turns right here and travels for a few hundred metres to *Bonani Lodge*, where the **Directorate of Tourism** (☎423) has its offices. All visitors have to sign in here, alongside the **park headquarters**, where you can book elephant and jeep rides, and accommodation in the lodges in the immediate vicinity. *Aranya* (⑤; ☎429) is the largest and most comfortable of these, with a/c and non-a/c rooms with attached baths, private balconies, room service, and the best restaurant; *Bonani* is smaller, with five a/c rooms and a restaurant (④–⑤). *Bonoshree* (②) has eight double rooms and a four-bedded room, all with attached baths, while the budget option, *Kunjaban* (①), has a dormitory but provides no linen.

Around 7km east of Kohora, *Wild Grass* (④–⑥) is a highly recommended **luxury resort** at the foot of the Karbi Hills on the River Diring. Endorsed by the World Wildlife Fund and Project Tiger, it organizes car safaris and elephant rides in the park and even arranges **fishing trips** to **Bhalukpung** on the River Jia Bharali, to catch the legendary *mahseer*, a pike-like game fish renowned as a fighter. In summer, when the park is closed, they offer swimming pool facilities, tours to view wildlife from the park's boundary, rafting and elephant rides. *Wild Grass* have a thatched lodge 6.5km inside the park, and can pick you up from Guwahati airport and even arrange your entire itinerary in Assam. Reserve through *Wild Grass*, PO Kaziranga, Dist Golaghat 785109 (☎037762/ 81437), or Barua Bhavan, 1st Floor, 107 MC Rd, Uzanbazar, Guwahati.

Manas

Bordering Bhutan, on the banks of the River Manas 176km west of Guwahati, **MANAS**, Assam's only **Project Tiger** sanctuary, is an absolutely spellbinding place, which has been closed to all visitors for the last few years thanks to the activities of the Bodo autonomous movement. Plans are afoot to re-open it soon, though by then its seriously endangered tiger population may have been wiped out. As it emerges from the jungle-covered Himalayan foothills, the snow-fed river has a reputation as one of the best fishing grounds for *mahseer*. Lying along a similar sub-Himalayan belt as Royal Chitwan in Nepal, Manas also has rhino, wild elephant, the rare hispid hare and the pigmy hog.

The Forest Department's two very basic bungalows at **Mathanguri** can be reserved through the Field Director, Tiger Project, Barpeta Rd (①). Eating arrangements are inadequate and food should be brought in. When it's safe to do so, conducted tours are arranged by Guwahati's *Tourist Lodge* (see p.817; Fri 8am–Sat 6pm).

East Assam

Stretching northeast from Guwahati along the valley, Assam penetrates the complex Brahmaputra watersheds at the eastern extremity of the Himalayas, in the area known as **Upper Assam**. Road and rail networks provide access to the mountainous interiors of Arunachal Pradesh and Nagaland, and vital communications to the most industrialized region of the northeastern hill states.

Jorhat, 310km east of Guwahati, holds research establishments dedicated to the tea industry, and plays host to an annual tea festival. Ferries run from **Neemati Ghat** here to **Majuli**, the largest river island in the world, which holds several *satras* or Vaishnavite monasteries. Upper Majuli is inhabited by the Mising and Deori tribes. Further south, the low-key hill-resort of **Haflong** lies near the border of Nagaland and Manipur.

Sibsagar

The former capital of the Ahoms, one of the oldest towns in Assam, **SIBSAGAR** – "The Ocean of Shiva" – lies 60km east of Jorhat and 369km from Guwahati. Now at the centre of an important tea- and oil-producing district, its cluster of monuments from six centuries of Ahom rule still holds cultural and historic resonance for modern Assam. A huge artificial tank, constructed by Queen Madambika in 1734, lies at the heart of the complex. Of the three temples that rise from its banks, the massive but plain 32-metre-high **Shivadol** is claimed to be the tallest in India. Temples and palaces in varying degrees of abandonment dot the area, including the **Rang Ghar**, a two-storey oval pavilion built by King Pramatta Singha in the eighteenth century to stage elephant fights and other sporting events; close by, isolated against a flat and bare countryside, are the ruined eighteenth-century palaces of the **Kareng Ghar** and the **Talatal Ghar**.

Buses run to Sibsagar from Guwahati and Jorhat, as well as from the nearest train station, 20km east at **Simaluguri**. Accommodation and food is available at the *Sibsagar Tourist Lodge* near Sibsagar Tank (☎2394; ①-②), which also serves as an information centre. Once again, Guwahati's *Tourist Lodge* (see p.817) arranges guided tours, this time on alternate Saturdays.

Meghalaya

Created in 1972 out of a section of Assam, **MEGHALAYA**, one of the smallest states in India, occupies the plateau and rolling hills between Assam and Bangladesh. Catching the main force of the monsoon-laden winds off the Bay of Bengal, much of Meghalaya, "the land of the rain-clouds", is covered with lush forests, rich in orchids. These "blue hills" are among the wettest places on earth; stupendous waterfalls can be seen near the capital, **Shillong**, but the most dramatic of all plummet from the plateau to the south, around **Cherrapunjee**. The hills of Meghalaya rise to just under 2000 metres, which makes for a pleasant year-round climate; Shillong, surrounded by tall elegant pines and rhododendron, is a welcome refuge from the steamy valleys of Assam.

Shillong

With its rolling hills and tall pines, **SHILLONG** has often been called "the Scotland of the east"; the impression is first brought to mind by **Barapani**, the loch-like (if monster-less) reservoir on its fringes. At an altitude of around 1500m, Shillong was a favourite holiday resort for the British, who built it on the site of a thousand-year-old Khasi settlement and made it the capital of Assam in 1874. Much of the original Victorian town is still evident; the large gardens around **Ward Lake** at its centre conjure up images of colonial masters hungering for a home far away. However, political uncertainty throughout the northeast, and violent unrest in Meghalaya, have left Shillong all but abandoned, with its Golf Club and Polo Ground gradually falling into decay.

Away from the centre, post-colonial Shillong hasn't worn well. An acute water shortage and a general lack of planning have resulted in haphazard growth, and the surrounding hills have been subjected to severe deforestation. Migration has created intense communal pressures over the years, with the Khasi population reacting with hostility to the influx of Bengalis and other outside groups.

Arrival and information

Shillong is connected by road to Guwahati, 103km south, a route served by **buses** – run by *Blue Hill* (4 daily; Rs35) and *Meghalaya Transport Corporation* – and taxis. Until recently *Vayudoot* **flew** to Umroi airport, 32km northwest, from Guwahati and Calcutta. If *Vayudoot* has emerged from its latest bankruptcy by the time you read this, the service may have resumed; check with *Sheba Travels*, Police Bazaar Point (☎23015).

KHASIS, GAROS AND JAINTIAS

The most prominent of the three main hill peoples of Meghalaya, the **Khasis**, belong to the Mon-Khmer group. Their origins go back to southern China, and they are related to the Mundas of north central India, who also erect stone monuments to their dead ancestors. Curiously, the Khasi word for "stone" is *men*, as in the ancient European words *dolmen* and *menhir*. The **Garos**, many of whom migrated to the hills of Meghalaya from East Pakistan (now Bangladesh) in 1964, are said to have Tibetan origins; certainly, their language belongs to the Tibeto-Burman linguistic group. Until the coming of the British in the last century, they were animists who practised human sacrifice; thanks to the missionaries, Christianity is now the dominant religion among the Garos just as it is with all the other groups. The **Jaintias** are of Mongolian origin, related, like the Mizos, to the Shans of Burma. The Khasis and Garos have matrilineal, strictly exogamous clans, said to be descended from the mythical "mother of the root". Though private land can be acquired by both sexes, the property of a woman is inherited by her daughter, while that of a man is inherited by his mother's family.

Buses and taxis pull in at the **Police Bazaar** area at the heart of town, opposite the state **Tourist Information Centre** (Mon–Sat 9.30am–5pm; ☎26220). This is the place to book places on guided tours of Shillong, or out to Cherrapunjee. The **Government of India Tourist Office** nearby, GS Rd, Police Bazaar (Mon–Sat 9.30am–5pm) provides a hotel reservation service. City buses are run by *Meghalaya State Transport*, and shared taxis ply major routes. The *State Bank of India* is opposite the Shillong Club, Kacheri (☎24998 or 23203).

The Town

Decorative, serpentine **Ward Lak**e, set in poorly maintained gardens, serves as the hub around which life in Shillong revolves. In the exclusive European Ward next to it, the large bungalows set in generous pine-shadowed gardens include Government House, the official residence of the governor.

The atmosphere in the heart of the colonial town is seemingly unaffected by the chaos around **Police Bazaar**, where emporia of the various northeastern states sell cane furniture, handicrafts, shawls and textiles. Khasi women wear the *jainsem*, which looks a bit like a toga worn over a dress; you often see it in checked patterns, with gingham being very popular, and even in tartans, a reflection of the Scottish influence. Khasi men smoke rough chiselled pipes, which resemble briars but have a home-made look about them. **Bara Bazaar** further west, is even more hectic, attracting locals and tribals from the hills to its warren of stalls and shops. Primarily, it is a produce and provisions market, but you may come across interesting jewellery and handicrafts.

Meghalaya's **State Museum**, Lachumiere, near Ward Lake, has some fascinating ethnographical exhibits depicting tribal customs, as well as a weaker collection of ancient sculptures from elsewhere in India (Mon–Sat 10am–4pm, closed 2nd Sat of each month; free). The small museum at the **Tribal Research Institute**, Mawlai, also holds tribal costumes and implements (Mon–Sat 10am–4pm; free). More unusual is the tiny and very hard to find **Meghalaya Museum of Entomology**, based in the home of Mr Wankhar, in the Riatsamthiah area, which holds an extensive collection of rare butterflies and moths (Mon–Fri 10am–5pm; Rs2; ☎23411). Since 1939, Mr Wankhar has run a breeding farm in the Khasi Hills to the south, shipping eggs and cocoons all over the world.

Although Shillong's **Botanical Gardens**, below the lake, across a viaduct, are not really worth a visit, **Lady Hydari Park**, about 1km away, is an attractive ornamental park, modelled on a Japanese garden. A small forestry museum, a mini zoo and a deer enclosure are tucked away among the pines. At the **Crinoline Falls**, next to Lady Hydari Park, a garden holds bonsai and orchids and also a swimming pool, which charges a nominal fee for membership and may ask for a health report before admitting you (women only Fri 6–8am). The actual flow of water at the falls, however, is

---

THE ARCHERY STAKES

Shillong's unique **Archery Stakes** started out as a genuine archery competition, which became such a focus of illegal gambling that the Stakes were eventually legalized by the state, in order to levy taxes on winnings. On most days of the year, two of the many clubs in the *Khasi Archers' Association* repeatedly shoot a set amount of arrows in four-minute bursts at a cylindrical bamboo target in a corner of the Polo Ground. The object of the game is to predict the last two digits of the number of arrows that stick – a matter of luck not judgement. The results of each competition are relayed throughout Shillong. If you expect a colourful pageant, you may be disappointed; the whole affair is geared specifically towards gambling, and the actual shooting of arrows is over relatively quickly. The archers squat in a semicircle; as the day progresses, most of them tend to become a little inebriated from imbibing local liquor in the bookmakers and refreshment stalls.

unreliable; dependable alternatives include **Beadon Bishop Falls**, off the Guwahati road at **Mawlai**, 3km north, where two falls drop over a hundred metres, and **Elephant Falls**, set amid fern-covered rocks 15km south, which have been turned into a picnic site, with walkways leading down to the lowest pool. Both are accessible by taxi.

Accommodation

Shillong has a healthy range of **accommodation**, with traditional old hotels clustered near and around Ward Lake, newer ones springing up in the congested Police Bazaar area, and a number of basic options along Quinton Road, behind Police Bazaar.

Alpine Continental, Quinton Rd (☎25361 or 23617). New three-star hotel behind the Police Bazaar. Comfortable rooms with room service, restaurant and bar, hot and cold water. ⑤–⑦.

Anand, Quinton Rd. A simple but clean vegetarian hotel with basic restaurant. ①.

Centre Point, Police Bazaar (☎25210). Plush new hotel in the heart of town; a good range of facilities, and all mod cons including a good restaurant. ⑤–⑥.

Monsoon, GS Rd (☎27106). Opposite the Government of India Tourist Office. Simple hotel with attached bathrooms, solar-heated water, the usual mid-budget rooms, and a reasonable dorm. ①–③.

Peak, Kacheri Rd (☎25445 or 26130). Old hotel, frozen in time, where the old colonial wooden rooms, complete with fireplaces, ooze character. Lacks the grounds and opulence of the *Pinewood*, but also its pretensions. A veg restaurant serves traditional Assamese food. Recommended. ④.

Pine Borough, Police Bazaar (☎27523 or 24435). In the middle of Police Bazaar, this friendly hotel has adequate rooms with attached baths, restaurant and bar, and a good tour and travel service. ④.

Pinewood Ashok, European Ward (☎23116 or 23765). Grand old hotel, straight out of the Raj, built in 1917 for British tea planters. Dotted around the landscaped grounds are cottages with Burma teak panels, carpeted wooden floors and fireplaces. The hotel arranges golfing facilities at nearby *Shillong Golf Club*, and has a billiards and snooker room. ⑥–⑦.

Polo Towers, Polo Rd (☎22863). Recently opened modern hotel, with comfortable rooms. ⑥–⑦.

Shillong Club, Kacheri Rd (☎26938). One of India's famous old clubs, offering accommodation along with temporary membership. Book ahead, or through the Tourist Bureau on GS Rd; the Secretary seems suspicious of tourists who turn up unannounced. ③–④.

YMCA, Mawkhar Main Rd, Lachumiere (☎25461). Opposite the Foreigners' Registration Office, the Y occupies part of a rambling old complex of buildings. ①.

Eating

Eating places in Police Bazaar include a popular South Indian cafe at Centre Point; Bara Bazaar too has a few simple restaurants and cafes. Otherwise, the obvious place to eat is in your hotel.

Abba, Main Rd, Malki Point, Lachumiere (☎25685). The best Chinese restaurant in Shillong, with chow mein at around Rs28. They have opened another, more central, branch on GS Rd.

La Galarie, *Hotel Centre Point*, Police Bazaar. One of Shillong's plushest restaurants; expensive but not exorbitant Indian and Chinese food. Good chicken in oyster sauce and wun tun soup.

Ming Restaurant, Bara Bazaar. Close to the *New Lhasa*; similar and a little cleaner.

New Lhasa, Bara Bazaar. Large cafe with Chinese and Tibetan food – egg chow mein and *momos*.

Around Shillong: Cherrapunjee

The important market town of **CHERRAPUNJEE**, 56km south of Shillong, was considered until recently to be the wettest place in the world. The greatest amount of rainfall ever recorded in a single day fell here in 1876 – an unbelievable 41 inches in 24 hours. Cherrapunjee has now lost its crown to nearby **Mawsynram**, but impressive waterfalls south of the town still plunge down the high escarpments on the edge of the plateau. Deep wooded ravines amid the lush rain-fed vegetation conceal a network of large caves. Once the administrative centre of the Khasis, the bustling market of **Cherra Bazaar** is famous for its honey and tribal jewellery. A popular day trip, Cherrapunjee is easily accessible from Shillong by bus, and the *Meghalaya Tourist Development Corporation* and a number of hotels organize tours.

Arunachal Pradesh

ARUNACHAL PRADESH, "the land of the dawn-lit-mountains", is one of the last unspoilt wilderness areas in India, dropping eastwards from the high Himalaya near Bhutan towards Burma, with the mountains of Tibet away to the north. Scarcely any roads penetrate this vast state, whose new capital, **Itanagar**, is only just across the border from Assam. As soon as it enters Arunachal, the road to **Tawang** runs through rugged hills, engulfed by virgin forests, with silver ribbons of rivers far below; a complete contrast to the denuded paddy bowls of Assam, though most of the Himalayan foothills must once have looked like this.

Only very recently have foreign tourists been permitted to visit Arunachal. This long-standing isolation is partly due to cultural considerations, and partly to political factors, as the border with the Chinese is still under dispute. The big attraction is the state's dazzling array of flora and fauna, in a habitat that combines glacial terrain, alpine meadows and sub-tropical rain forests. **Namdapha National Park**, in the northeast, is home to the rare Hoolock gibbon; other animals include the legendary snow-leopard, tigers, musk deer, bears, panda and elephant, while Arunachal also abounds in bamboo and cherishes over 500 species of orchids.

Itanagar

The new town of **ITANAGAR**, just under 400km northeast of Guwahati, has been developed as the capital of the state largely because of its convenient location, and holds little to interest visitors. Archeological evidence connects the site with the

---

THE TRIBES OF ARUNACHAL

The successive river valleys of Arunachal, separated by forbidding north–south ridges, enable distinct micro-cultures to flourish in what can be very small areas. The **Monpas**, who have a strong affinity with the Bhutanese, occupy the valleys north of Bomdila; their largest town, Dirang, with its *dzong* (fort), is just before the pass at Sela. Although they practise Buddhism, focussed around the great monastery of Tawang, they retain many of their original animist-shamanist beliefs. They are easily recognized by their dress – a *chuba* or short cloak, made of coarse wool dyed red with madder.

The **Sherdukpens** live south of the Bomdila Range, in the valleys of the Tengapani, and have close affinities with their Monpa neighbours. They wear distinctive *gurdams*, or yak's hair skull-caps, from which jut tassel-like projections that serve as guttering – this part of Arunachal sees very heavy rainfall. Traditionally Sherdukpen men wear a sword in a scabbard tucked into their waist or on a strap. Although they have a reverence for *lama*-ism, their religious beliefs are a curious blend of Buddhism and shamanism, with *jijis*, or priests, practising witchcraft to counteract malevolent spirits.

Further southeast are the **Akas**, literally "painted", who paint their faces with resin and charcoal. East of Kameng, the menfolk of the sturdy hill people known as the **Daflas** wear a distinctive wicker helmet surmounted by the red-dyed beak of a hornbill. Protruding in front of their foreheads is a bun of plaited hair called *podum*, skewered horizontally with a large brass pin. The Daflas trace their descent from Abo Teni, a mythical primeval man, as do the neighbouring **Apa Tanis**, who thanks to the work of European anthropologists are the best known of all the tribal groups. Occupying a 26-square-kilometre stretch of hanging valley in the central region of Subansiri, the Apa Tanis are experts at terraced rice cultivation. They too wear a hat and *podum* on their foreheads but do not sport the distinguishing yellow ribbon of the Daflas; both men and women tattoo their faces.

eleventh-century capital, Mayapur, but Itanagar remains essentially rural and low-key. It is built on a saddle overlooked by two hills, one occupied by the Governor's house and the other by a new Buddhist Temple; new light-weight earthquake-proof houses mingle with older traditional houses, a market and administrative offices. Facilities are shared with its twin town, **Naharlagun**, 10km away in the Assam Valley.

Recently consecrated by the Dalai Lama, the **Buddhist Temple** reflects the extensive Tibetan influence in this frontier land, and provides good views of Itanagar and the surrounding countryside. An extensive ethnographic collection devoted to local tribes in the **Jawaharlal Nehru State Museum** includes wood carvings, musical instruments, textiles, handicrafts as well as archeological finds (daily except Mon 10am– 5pm; Rs1), while a workshop in the *Handicrafts Centre* specializes in traditional cane manufacturing. The adjacent salesroom sells tribal handicrafts including shawls, carpets, cane and bamboo items, and *thangkas*, or scroll paintings. The emerald **Gyaker Sinyi** (Ganga Lake), 6km away, is surrounded by primeval vegetation, providing a small taste of the magnificent forests of the state.

Practicalities

The nearest **airport** to Itanagar, at **Lilabari** in Assam, 67km away, and served by connecting buses, is used by flights to and from Guwahati, Calcutta, Tezpur, and Ziro. *Arunachal Travels* (☎4411) are the agents for *Indian Airlines* in Itanagar. Fast passenger **trains** from Guwahati run as far as Harmuty, also in Assam but just 33km distant. Overnight *Blue Hill* buses connect Naharlagun with Guwahati, and *Arunachal State Transport* run an extensive if basic service throughout the state, as well as to Assam and Meghalaya.

Information is available from the **Tourist Department** at Naharlagun (☎4371), who also arrange transport. Un-metered taxis are available and shared taxis ply regularly between the two towns; cycle rickshaws are common in Naharlagun.

Limited accommodation can be found in both Itanagar and Naharlagun. The *Donyi-Polo Ashok* (☎2626; ⑤–⑦) is Itanagar's prime address, with comfortable rooms and a restaurant. Otherwise, simple options in Itanagar's Ganga Market include the *Ganga* (②–④) and the *Himalaya* (☎2210; ②). Rooms at the *Hornbill* in Naharlagun (☎4419; ②–④), range from the basic to the reasonably comfortable.

West Arunachal

Hemmed in by Bhutan and Tibet, the isolated hills and valleys of western Arunachal climb to some of the remotest glaciers and peaks in the Himalayas. Besides named peaks such as Gori Chen (6858m) and Nyegi Kangsang (7047m), around twenty mountains of above 6000m remain completely unknown. Cut off from the rest of Arunachal by a high ridge breached by the inhospitable and dramatic Sela Pass, the great monastery of **Tawang** dominates the land of the Monpas. On a spur of the Thagla Ridge, quiet **Bomdila** marks the dividing line between the rain forests to the south and the sub-alpine valleys to the north. The great River **Jia Bharali** drains the watersheds of the north, then meanders through deep forested valleys to emerge at **Tipi**, near Assam, where an orchid house nurtures several indigenous species. The swift Bharali, sweeping past boulder-filled shores, is renowned for its fish (see p.820).

The one highway that winds up through the forests to Bomdila sees little traffic beyond the occasional military convoy. During the Sino-Indian War of 1962, this was the scene of heavy fighting, when the Chinese took the Indians by surprise and reached the outskirts of Tezpur. The Indian army gradually fought their way back, and the road is littered with memorials to fallen comrades. Somehow, thankfully, the forests here have survived the large military concentrations further up.

Bomdila

With its apple orchards and tranquil walks along pine-forested ridges, **BOMDILA**, the headquarters of the West Kameng district, is an excellent place to break the journey between Tawang and Tezpur. Spread thinly over a hillside at around 2500m, it is a peaceful unspoilt town whose silence is only broken by the odd army convoy thundering through. **Bomdila peak**, 300m above the top of the town and an hour's walk away, provides a view of the not-so-distant snows.

Bomdila is split in two; the lower bazaar, site of the bus stand and petrol pump, is a few hundred metres below the upper town, and the main market – really just a few shops selling provisions – lies in between the two. There are two small **Buddhist monasteries**, one surrounded by apple orchards above the Circuit House and the other off the main road towards the lower town. A small museum in the upper town is devoted to local tribal costumes and customs (Mon–Fri 10am–4pm; free).

Of the limited **accommodation** on offer, the *Tourist Lodge* in the upper town (☎22049; ①–④) is most likely to be available, with eight rooms, a dormitory, and one suite kept in reserve for "genuine tourists", and equipped with the luxury of running hot water. The **tourist officer** based here is welcoming to the few tourists who come this way and is trying to pioneer trekking and other activities in the area. Nearby, the *Circuit House* (☎22028; ①–②) is more comfortable and very reasonably priced, but prioritizes visiting civil servants. More basic hotels include the *La* (②), at the top of the town, and the *Dawa* at the bottom (①).

Sela

Approaching the long narrow defile of **SELA PASS** – snowbound for six months in the year, 4215 metres up in the Himalayas – along treacherous hairpin bends is an unforgettable experience. High snow peaks rise on all sides of this gateway between the inner and outer Himalayas, where the Indian army maintains a large presence. They were completely outflanked by the Chinese in 1962, and caught with their guns facing the wrong way; the warren of pill-boxes below the pass on the Tawang side remains a memorial to that defeat. Beneath the towering crags, Sela has a trout farm and a lake.

Tawang

Like so many Tibetan Buddhist monasteries, **TAWANG**, 240km from Tezpur, has a superb setting. Perched at the end of a high ridge at over 3000m above deep valleys, the largest Buddhist monastery in India looks out onto a semicircle of snow-capped peaks that seem close enough to touch. The birthplace of the sixth Dalai Lama, Tawang was established in the seventeenth century. A large ceremonial gate leads to a small town of residential buildings, clustered around the main temple. Capable of housing five hundred *lamas*, the scholastic monastery has a renowned collection of manuscripts and *thangkas*. Unfortunately, it recently had to be rebuilt, after a crack threatened the original wood temple. The whole town, Buddhist, non-Buddhist, and even the Chief of Police, worked to construct the new temple, which follows traditional lines but is made of stone.

Tawang has very little **accommodation**; the *Circuit House*, above the bus stand (①–②), is badly run and poorly looked after, while the basic hotels on the short main drag, such as the *Siddharta* (①), suffer from a marked lack of sanitation. The *Samjhana Restaurant* beside the bus stand serves Tibetan food such as *momos* and *thukpa*.

Just two *Arunachal Pradesh State Transport* **buses** leave Tawang: a "Night Special" to Tezpur, and a stopping day-time service to Bomdila, which pauses in mountain hamlets for meals. Both are extremely uncomfortable; the word "special" begins to seem a misnomer in a remarkably short period of time. One or two marginally more comfortable private buses also ply the route. **Tezpur** (see p.818) is the nearest major railhead, with easy connections to points in the northeast, and is also connected by bus to Guwahati and Itanagar, and daily by air to Calcutta and Guwahati.

East Arunachal

In eastern Arunachal, the remote valleys of **Dibang** and **Lohit**, inhabited by tribes such as the Mishmis, descend from snow-covered passes to sub-tropical forests, where the rivers draining the east Himalayas flow into the Brahmaputra. The sacred Hindu sites of **Parasuramkund** and **Brahmakund**, on the banks of the River Lohit, are associated in myth with the birth of the River Brahmaputra.

Further south, the huge **Namdapha National Park** ranges from altitudes of 200 to 4500 metres along the border with Burma. The park headquarters are at **Miao**, where a *Tourist Lodge* can provide rental cars. At present, foreigners are only allowed to visit in groups of not less than four persons, accompanied by recognized tour operators, at the astonishing charge of US$200 per day.

Buses to and from Miao pass through **Margherita**, the nearest railhead, 64km west, **Tinsukhia**, another railhead 40km further on, and **Dibrugarh**, where an airport receives *Indian Airlines* flights from Calcutta via Guwahati.

Nagaland

On the border with Burma, south of Arunachal Pradesh and east of Assam, **NAGALAND** is physically and conceptually at the very extremitiy of the subcontinent. Many of its hills and valleys, home to the fiercely independent Nagas, were uncharted until recently, and the eastern regions, near Burma, remain far beyond the reach of the skeletal road system, despite the fact that the forested mountains rarely exceed 3000m in height. Entry to Nagaland involves braving a lot of red tape, usually with the help of well-organized itineraries and assisted by invitations. Much of the state has a heavy army presence, and travel remains restricted to places such as **Kohima**, the capital.

The British administrators of Nagaland who arrived at a truce with the Nagas towards the end of the nineteenth century, agreed not to penetrate beyond certain boundaries, so their maps left numerous blank areas. Based in the Angami village of Kohima, the Deputy Commissioner occasionally toured the territories to collect taxes and administer justice and came to hold a certain authority among the various tribes. Some developed a loyalty to the British, others saw them as intruders. In 1879 the **Khonoma Angami** rebellion against Kohima was relieved through assistance by loyal Kohima Angamis who helped to smuggle a message through to British lines in the Assam Valley. When the Indian flag replaced the Union Jack in 1947, it was promptly removed by Nagas, who had come to accept the British presence but did not want to join India. A Chinese-supported independence struggle became particularly bitter in the 1960s, since when the Indian army has managed to retain superiority. Although the Naga independence movement was officially abandoned in 1975, pockets of resistance endure. Armed patrols through the streets of Kohima are common, and the volatility of the border with Burma means that the state is still considered unstable.

Kohima

Although the capital of Nagaland, **KOHIMA**, 74km east of Dimapur in the Assam Valley, was built by the British in the nineteenth century, it was never a hill station, and lacks Victorian promenades, villas and public gardens. It was founded here – alongside the large Angami village known as **Kohima Village**, or in the adopted Hindusthani as **Bara Basti** (the large village) – strictly for the purposes of administration, and continues in much the same vein under a new regime. Kohima has grown rapidly, and now sprawls with little cohesion over a wide area, but still maintains a quiet, pleasant ambience. A walk up to Bara Basti, or the short trip to **Khonoma**, 20km beyond Kohima,

THE NAGAS

From villages perched high on the mountain ridges to either side of the valleys of Nagaland, **Naga** tribespeople survey their separate domains. Headhunters until not so long ago, the Nagas have long been feared and respected throughout the northeast, although in truth they are a warm and welcoming people. They seem originally to have lived in northeast Tibet, then moved through southwest China into Burma, Malaya and the Indonesian islands, as well as eastern Assam. In Nagaland, they can be divided into sixteen main groups, including the **Angamis** around Kohima, the **Konyaks**, **Ao**, **Kukis**, **Lothas**, **Semas** and **Wanchus**. Despite their fierce reputation, all are essentially farmers who cultivate terraced fields and tend cattle.

Traditionally, Nagas differentiated between the soul, a celestial body, and the spirit, a supernatural being, believing that the human soul resided in the nape of the neck and could only be set free by beheading, while the spiritual being, in the head, brought good fortune. Heads of enemies and fallen comrades were collected to add to those of the community's own ancestors. Some tribes decorated their faces with tattoos of swirling horns to mark success in headhunting. Trophies were hoarded in each village in the men's meeting house, or **morung**, which also served as the boys' dormitory. This large open hall was decorated with fantastic carvings of animals, elephant heads and tusks. Constructed of wood and bamboo, *morungs* were frequently destroyed by fire, along with the precious collection of heads; however, the benevolent spirits were retained by the re-creation of the lost collection in carved wood. In addition, the Naga still construct **megalithic monuments**, which line the approaches to villages, and come to personify those who erect them after death. Menhirs stand in pairs or in long double rows, to honour fame and generosity or enhance the fertility of a field. The Angamis were never ruled by chiefs; the closest equivalent is the *Tevo*, a descendant of the founder of the village and mediator between the community and the supernatural world. Each village is sub-divided into *khel*, which in the past often had independent inter-tribal policies, and who settled their own disputes by bloody fights. Relations between the sexes traditionally were conducted with great openness and equality. Few first marriages led to a permanent union, and in spite of the Christian influence divorce remains common.

Although each tribe has its own dialect, a pidgin drawn from various Naga languages, Assamese, and even Nepalese, has developed into the common **Nagamese** tongue. As the Nagas have been integrated into the modern world, their traditions are under threat. In an effort to realign society along so-called civilized lines, boys are encouraged to live at home with their parents, and *morungs* are discouraged and left to fall into ruin.

offers an intimate glimpse of traditional Naga life. Being invited to a Naga house and imbibing some of the local rice beer (technically illegal in this dry state), under rafters hung with drying and smoked meat, is a privilege not to be forgotten.

Arrival, information and public transport

Kohima lies on the Dimapur–Imphal road, three or four hours by road from the railhead and airport of **Dimapur**, in the Assam valley to the west (see p.830), and six hours from Imphal in Manipur to the south. *Nagaland State Transport* **buses** from Dimapur terminate in the market area in the centre of town; *Blue Hill* "luxury" services from Guwahati (18hr) stop at their office (☎548 or 594), 2km uphill beyond the *Japfu Ashok*; you may prefer to ask to be dropped at the cemetery. Taxis and minibuses are the main forms of public transport, though the central area is small enough to explore on foot.

The low-key but welcoming **Directorate of Tourism**, which can arrange transport and organize tours (Mon–Fri 10am–4pm; ☎607), is on the National Highway south, beyond the *Japfu* and below the Cathedral. There's a *State Bank of India* nearby (☎683).

The Town

Spread loosely over a saddle joining two large hills, Kohima forms a pass that played a strategic role during World War II. The highway from Imphal to Dimapur – the route along which the Japanese hoped to reach the plains of India – crosses the saddle at the foot of the **Second World War Cemetery**, which dominates the town. These immaculate gardens stand as a memorial to the Allies who died on this very spot during the three-month **Battle of Kohima**, which ended in April 1944. Two huge crosses, at the lowest and the highest parts of the cemetery, overlook Kohima. Each of 1200 neat markers, rising up steps lined with pristine lawns and flowerbeds, holds a bronze plaque with a single name. The ferocity of the battle is evident from the astonishingly close proximity in which it was fought – the apex of the struggle was the Deputy Commissioner's tennis court, where the lines have been preserved in concrete just a few metres apart.

Alongside the cemetery, central Kohima consists of busy markets and shopping precincts. Shawls, bags, decorative spears and other handicrafts are available at the *Nagaland Sales Emporium* near the bus stand at the centre of town. Weaving is a tradition passed on from generation to generation; each Naga tribe has its own distinctive design on its shawls such as the red, black and white *Tsungkotepsu* of the Ao Nagas.

The large Naga settlement of **Bara Basti**, or **Kohima Village**, is set on a high hill overlooking Kohima itself. Few of its buildings are now in traditional Naga style, with pitched roof and crossed "house-horns" on the gable, but with its tightly knit lanes and labyrinth of small houses the village maintains a definite Naga feel. Carved heads to signify family status, a huge grain basket in front of the house, and a trough used to make rice beer are among distinctive features. Many of the villagers are still farmers. On the way up to Bara Basti, you pass a ceremonial gate of the Angami Nagas, carved with motifs of warriors, guns and symbols of prosperity, while a large concrete Christian mission and school straddles the ridge at its heart.

The **State Museum**, 1.5km north of Kohima and a nice walk or easy minibus trip, provides a fascinating examination of the rich heritage of the Nagas (Mon–Fri 10am–4pm; Rs1). The real highlight is a small but stunning collection of Naga jewellery, dominated by yellow, red and dark blue beads, while along with costumes and weapons, surprisingly effective life-size exhibits depict the ways of the various Naga tribes. One recurring motif, a wooden war canoe that is too large for the rivers of Nagaland, reflects the belief that the Nagas may have originated from Sumatra. An art gallery upstairs displays and sells work by contemporary Naga artists.

The unmistakeable **Catholic Cathedral** on Aradura Hill is a landmark on the southeastern extremity of the town, below the *Tourist Lodge* and above National Highway 39 – "The Burma Road" – as it winds south towards Imphal.

Accommodation

Not surprisingly, in view of the restrictions on visitors, Kohima has a limited choice for **accommodation**.

Ambassador, D-Block (☎444). Nice airy rooms looking over to Kohima Village on the hill above town. The attached bathrooms have running hot water and there is limited room service. ④.

Capital, near *NST* bus stand. Simple, central rooms with attached baths; board only. ②–③.

Japfu Ashok, PR Hill (☎2721–6). Kohima and Nagaland's showpiece hotel; spacious rooms and restaurants. Credit cards accepted, foreign exchange, and transport can be arranged. ⑤–⑦.

Pine, Midland, Phool Bazaar (☎2234). Close to the cemetery and the market; popular low midranged hotel with clean rooms and attached baths. ③.

Tourist Lodge, Ministers Hill (☎2417). The large, concrete tourist lodge above the Cathedral is in a state of disrepair and a bit far from the main town, but suitable for those who would like some peace and quiet. Reasonably priced and airy rooms which aren't too uncomfortable. ①–②.

Valley View, Bus Station (☎2738). Moderately clean, central, budget to mid-range hotel. ②–③.

Eating

With a handful of small cafes in the market area, a couple of mid-range restaurants and the upmarket but ordinary *Japfu*, there are few options for **eating out**. Naga food is refreshingly simple and under-spiced, with boiled vegetables, chicken and ginger stew, pork, and in season, frogs.

ABC Hotel, Main Bazaar. Basic cafe serving chow mein at Rs20 and a plate of *momos* at Rs6.

Embassy Hotel, Supermarket, near the Art College, Main Bazaar. Chow mein and *momos* served in a dimly lit atmosphere, and rumour has it, one can get alcohol here.

Naga Japanese Hotel, near Secretariat. Curiously named restaurant, up the hill from the main market above the *Nagaland Emporium*, and definitely worth a visit. Along with standard Chinese dishes, the restaurant will, with prior notice, arrange Naga food. Very friendly service and a good place to meet young cosmopolitan Kohimans.

Tibet, Main Bazaar, 100 yards from the *NST* stand. Quite a pleasant cafe serving chow mein and *momos*.

Dimapur

DIMAPUR, the "City of the River People", 74km west of Kohima, is Nagaland's largest and most industrialized town – and the only one not in the hills. In fact, its vital communications may explain why it was included within the state, for it has absolutely no resemblance and affinity with the rest of Nagaland. An unlikely tourist destination in itself, it serves as the main entry point into Nagaland.

Dimapur was established by the **Kachari**, a Tibeto-Burmese people who erected huge carved fertility symbols. This was at a time when Hinduism had not conquered the Assam Valley, and these symbols are not directly connected to the Shaivite *lingam*. After the power of the Kachari kings had been shattered by attack from the **Ahoms** during the sixteenth century, they migrated southwest and set up their own kingdoms, which lasted until the British occupation in 1830. Dimapur today is a fly-blown and unattractive place which has pushed back the forest, polluted the river and encroached on the numerous large water-tanks.

Practicalities

The main railhead for Kohima, Dimapur is served by **trains** to Tinsukhia in Upper Assam, from where connections are available for Guwahati and the main railway network. In addition, it holds Nagaland's only **airport**, used by *Indian Airlines* flights to Calcutta and Delhi on alternate days. **Buses** run to Guwahati and towns throughout the northeast; several *Nagaland State Transport* services go to and from Kohima each day, as does the *Blue Hill* "luxury" bus.

Accommodation in Dimapur includes a *Tourist Lodge* (☎2147; ②), *PWD Bungalow* (☎2097; ①), and a basic *Youth Hostel* (①); a new tourist complex with board and lodging is being built at **Ruzaphema**, 5km out on the road to Kohima.

Manipur

The state of **MANIPUR**, stretching along the Burmese border, centres on a vast lowland area watered by the lake system south of its capital **Imphal**. This almost forgotten region is home to the **Meitheis** (originally Burmese, and also known as the Kukis), who have created in isolation their own fascinating version of Hinduism. Though the area around Imphal is now all but devoid of trees, the outlying hills are still forested, and shelter such exotic birds and animals as the spotted linshang, Blyths tragopan, the curiously named Mrs Hume's bar-backed pheasant, slow loris, Burmese peafowl and the beautifully marked clouded leopard, as well as numerous unclassified varieties of orchids. Probably its most unusual natural habitat is the floating mass of vegetation on **Loktak lake**, south of Imphal, inhabited by the unique *sangai* deer.

Manipur's history can be traced back to the foundation of Imphal in the first century AD. Despite periodic invasions from Burma, it has also had long periods of independent and stable government. Manipur was first incorporated into India at the end of the Indo-Burmese war in 1826, but only came under British rule in 1891 as a result of the Battle of Kangla. During World War II, most of Manipur was occupied by the Japanese, who used it as a base from which to strike towards the Assam Valley. Having been part of Assam, and later a Union Territory, Manipur became a fully fledged Indian state within the union in 1972. Since then it has been subjected to waves of violent unrest, initially as a result of self-rule campaigns and more recently through a brutal war between the Meitheis and their northern neighbours, the Nagas; inter-communal hostilities came to a head in 1993, when several villages were destroyed and many innocent people brutally slaughtered.

Imphal

Overlooked by a circle of distant hills, the capital of Manipur, **IMPHAL**, lies in an almost completely flat basin at an altitude of around 785m. Though devoid of dramatic monuments, it is at least given a sense of openness by its large avenues; but even the rivers and canals that run through the town are unable to give it any visual appeal. Instead, the real interest in Imphal is supplied by its people, whose handsome Meithei faces are adorned with the long and distinctive *tikki* (forehead mark) of Vishnu. Even though the valley is predominantly Hindu, Imphal feels more like southeast Asia than the rest of India, and visitors tend to be confronted by a language barrier. The ordinary person on the street understands neither English nor Hindusthani.

Arrival and information

In theory, Imphal's **airport**, 10km south of town, is connected to Calcutta via Silchar by daily *Indian Airlines* **flights**, but the schedule has been so disrupted of late that we can only advise you to check either in Calcutta, or once you're in Imphal at the *Indian Airlines* office on MG Rd (☎22099); flights to Guwahati in Assam are more reliable.

THE FESTIVALS AND PERFORMING ARTS OF MANIPUR

Manipuri dance, like the associated colourful traditions of Burma, Indonesia, and Thailand, is replete with Hindu themes and influences. Considered one of India's main classical dance forms, it centres around the story of Krishna cavorting with the *gopis* (milkmaids), a theme repeated throughout northern India (see p.228). Here the *gopis* are dressed in elaborate crinoline-like skirts, while the accompanying music includes energetic group drumming, with large barrel drums suspended across the shoulders. The *Jawaharlal Nehru Manipur Dance Academy*, North AOC, Imphal, Manipur's premier dance institution, arranges occasional recitals and hosts an annual dance festival.

The **martial arts** of Manipur are currently going through something of a revival with performances by men and women being choreographed for the stage. **Thang-Ta** is a dynamic form utilizing *thang*, the sword and *ta*, the spear. Fast, furious and seemingly extremely dangerous, performances take place each May during **Lai Haraoba**, a ritual dance festival held at Moirang. In Imphal, the *Huyel Lallong Manipur Thang-Ta Cultural Association* at Irilbung, puts on frequent ferocious performances of *Thang-Ta*.

Finally, the annual **Heikru Hitongba Boat Race** is held every September as part of a celebration to commemorate the founding of the two major Vaishnavite temples of Imphal, Bijoy Govinda and Govindjee. Two teams of rowers, standing in long dug-out canoes race on the Thangapat moat near the Bijoy Govinda temple.

State transport **buses** arrive at the Bus Stand next to the Polo Ground and private buses at their individual offices. Bus connections with **Guwahati** are good, but the 579-kilometre journey takes around twenty hours. *Manipur Golden Travels*, based on MG Rd (☎221332), provides by far the best service; *Blue Hill*, excellent elsewhere in the northeast, sub-contract this route and standards are low. National Highway 39 – "The Burma Road" – links Imphal with the closest railhead at **Dimapur**, 215km away, via Kohima in Nagaland; you need a permit for Nagaland to travel this way. The 200-kilometre bus ride to **Silchar** with *Kangleipak Tours & Travels*, MG Rd (☎222911), may look tempting, but ten anti-smuggling checkpoints along the way make it a bit of a nightmare, which can take up to fourteen hours.

With prior notice, Manipur's **Directorate of Tourism**, based at *Hotel Imphal* (☎224603), organizes conducted tours of Imphal and the surrounding area, including Sendra Island on Loktak Lake. The **Tourist Office of the Government of India**, on Jail Rd, provides information only (Mon–Fri 10am–5pm; ☎221131). There's a *State Bank of India* on MG Rd, and the main **post office** is on Secretariat Rd.

Auto and cycle rickshaws are the main means of transport within Imphal, and taxis and rental cars can be booked through hotels. Rather intimidatingly, and of no great help in bridging the language barrier, the cycle-rickshaw men of Imphal wear water-proof straw caps, and wrap their faces in cloth to keep out dust and fumes.

The Town

Imphal's small and congested centre is sandwiched between the stately avenue of Kanglapat on the east and the somewhat stagnant River Nambu on the west. The town's **Polo Ground** dominates the area; according to popular legend, the Manipuri game of *Sagol Kangjei* is the original form of the modern game of polo. In one corner, the Shaheed Minar commemorates the Meithei revolt in 1891 against British occupation, while just southeast, the **Manipur State Museum** focusses on tribal costumes, jewellery and weapons along with geological, archeological and natural history displays (Mon–Fri 10am–4.30pm; Rs1).

The fascinating market of **Khwairamband**, right at the heart of Imphal and also known as *Nupi Keithel* and *Ima Bazaar* or "Mothers' Market", is run solely by Meithei women, making it one of India's largest women's markets. One of its two sections is devoted to textiles, selling shawls and fabrics including the *moirangphee*, the traditional dress of Meithei women. This distinctive striped skirt comes in two pieces; for a small fee, women with sewing machines will stitch them together with amazing speed. Across the road, the other half of the market sells all sorts of local fish and vegetables, along with basic provisions, while smaller markets in the surrounding area include one dedicated to cane and wicker ware. If you prefer not to bargain, fixed-price shops selling handloom and handicrafts include *Sangai Handloom and Handicrafts*, at GM Hall, near the clock tower, and the *Handloom House* in Paona Bazaar.

Next to the ruins of the **Old Palace**, 2km east, is **Shri Govindjee**, Manipur's pre-eminent Vaishnavite temple. Otherwise a disappointing mix of twentieth-century buildings, Shri Govindjee is crowned by two gold domes and has an impressive large prayer hall preceding the courtyard and main temple. Covering around 200 acres with over a hundred species of orchids, the **Khonghampat Orchidarium**, the orchid centre of the Forest Department, lies 12km from Imphal on National Highway 39 and is best visited in April and May when the orchids are in bloom.

Accommodation and eating

Imphal has just a few simple **hotels** in the market area, and a handful of mid-range ones scattered all over town. Similarly the choice of **restaurants** is restricted – the best bets apart from the hotels are the *Airlines Hotel*, opposite *Indian Airlines* on MG Rd, and the more local *Meitei Hotel*, on Kangla Pat. There are certainly no **bars** – this is a dry state.

Centre Point, MG Rd. Conveniently placed opposite *Indian Airlines*, this small unfinished-looking hotel is reasonably clean. ②.

Excellency, Airport Rd (☎223231). A new hotel near the airport; the best that Imphal has to offer with all mod cons including a popular multi-cuisine restaurant. ④–⑤.

Imphal, North AOC Point, Imphal Dimapur Rd (☎220459). The rather resplendent Government-run hotel-cum-tourist lodge has nice large rooms, and a canteen-like restaurant. ③–⑥.

Pintu, North AOC, National Highway 39 (☎224172). Away from the noise and dust of the centre, a large, clean and friendly hotel with a multi-cuisine restaurant open to non-residents. ③.

Thampa, North AOC, National Highway 39 (☎221486). Cheap and simple hotel, with no restaurant but conveniently placed near small *dhabas* (cafes) and the bus stands. ①–②.

White Palace, 113 MG Rd (☎220599). In the centre of the busy commercial district, this newish hotel suffers from not having a restaurant. ②–④.

Around Imphal – Loktak Lake

South of Imphal, the huge and complex body of water known as **LOKTAK LAKE**, fed by numerous rivers and dotted with islands, is home to a unique community of fishermen, who live on large floating rafts made of reeds. Rare and endangered dancing *sangai*, brow-antlered deer, live on the floating vegetation that covers much of the lake, sharing their habitat with other species including the hog deer. Much of the lake is taken up by the **Keibul Lamjao National Park**, 53km from Imphal, which attracts a host of waterfowl and migratory birds between November and March. A hill-top *Tourist Bungalow* on **Sendra Island**, 48km from Imphal, provides a good vantage point from which to view the wildlife, and can be booked through the Deputy Director of Tourism, Government of Manipur, Imphal (☎20802; ①–②). The department also arranges transport, with tourist buses costing Rs45 for the return journey.

On the more populated western shore of Loktak, 45km south of Imphal, the small town of **Moirang** is the traditional centre of Meithei culture, with a temple devoted to the pre-Hindu deity **Thangjing**. In May each year, a large festival here includes performances of ritual dance and martial art. The Indian National Army, which fought for Independence alongside the Japanese, against the British Indian Army, during World War II, first unfurled its flag on Indian soil here at Moirang; a memorial and museum commemorates the event. Accommodation is available at the *Tourist Bungalow* (①–②), also booked through the Director of Tourism, Imphal. Guided tours of Loktak sometimes take in Moirang, and regular buses from the private bus stand at Keishampat, near the centre of Imphal, also run here, taking around an hour.

Mizoram

As you head south from the Assam Valley into the hills of **MIZORAM**, "the Land of the Highlanders", the change is instantaneous – from green paddy fields and tea estates to forests and bamboo-covered hills. Despite the difficult terrain, Mizoram is a gentle pastoral land, and the **Mizos** a friendly and welcoming people. Whitewashed Christian churches dot the landscape, making the region feel more like Central America than a state squeezed between Burma and the Chittagong Hill Tracts of Bangladesh.

Even as late as the end of the last century, the Mizos, who had migrated to the area in the eighteenth century from the Chin Hills in Burma, were regularly raiding tea plantations in the Assam Valley; only in 1924 did the British administration finally manage to bring about some semblance of control. They opened the doors of what were then the **Lushai Hills** to missionaries, who were so successful that now just a handful of animists remain, along with pockets of Buddhists in the west. Mizoram only became a state in 1987, after a violent twenty-year struggle to secede from India altogether.

Mizoram is now one of the most peaceful states in the country, with an optimism epitomized by **Aizawl**, its busy and cosmopolitan capital. Here in the heart of the state, traditional Mizo communities occupy the crests of a series of ridges, each village still dominated by its chief's house and *zawlbuk*, or bachelor's dormitory. An egalitarian people, without sex and class distinction, the Mizos remain justifiably proud of their age-old custom of *Tlawmgaihna*, a code of ethics which governs hospitality. Among surviving traditions are the **Cheraw**, "bamboo dance", performed for mothers who die in childbirth to welcome them to *Pialral*, the realm of the dead, and the weaving of local costumes such as the *puan*, characterized by white, black and red stripes.

The Mizo villages now look down on hillsides that are all but denuded of trees by the effects of *jhum* (slash and burn agriculture), and planted instead with large tracts of bamboo. Most of the untouched forests lie further south and east. Apart from Aizawl itself, the most likely destination to benefit if tourism opens up is the **Blue Mountain National Park** near **Phawngpui**, close to the southern border with Burma and rich in orchids and butterflies.

Aizawl

One of India's remotest state capitals, the picturesque and pleasant town of **AIZAWL** perches precariously on the steep slopes of a sharp ridge, straddling the watershed between the Tlawng and the Tuirial river valleys and given a comfortable year-round climate by its altitude of 1100m. Although it may lack snowy Himalayan backdrop, it has something of the feel of a Himalayan hill station, without the tourists on one hand but also largely without the infrastructure to cope with visitors. There isn't very much to see, but the markets are interesting enough, and the whole place is small enough that you can easily walk out to its very rural surrounds.

The road from the north makes a dramatic entrance through a deep cleft in the rocky ridge, emerging from the shadows, to provide a first glimpse of Aizawl. A huge white cross stands guard at the entrance of the pass.

Arrival, information and transport

Virtually all visitors to Aizawl arrive by **bus** from **Silchar**, 180km north in Assam. Most Aizawl to Silchar services run overnight, except for *Mizoram State Transport*'s two basic (and heavily over-subscribed) morning buses. Allow plenty of time to book tickets at *MST*'s chaotic office, near the GPO and below Zodin Square, where you can also arrange **rail** tickets for use on the network in Assam; the nearest major junction is at Lumding, a further 180km north of Silchar. Companies operating deluxe buses to and from Silchar, as well as Shillong and Guwahati, include *Capital Travels* and *Barak Travels*, both based at the other end of town in **Zarkawt**. Aizawl does have a small **airport**, 27km northeast and served by taxis and buses, but its supposed connections with Calcutta and Silchar are very unreliable.

Of the minibuses that run between central Aizawl and the suburbs, the most useful head from the top of town near the GPO and Zodin Square to Chandmari in the north – a tiring two-kilometre walk. One curious local means of transport, not available to the public but popular on the outskirts, is a rough wooden cart; carried uphill, sometimes by bus, it is then used to descend the steep windy roads. Many can only be brought to a halt by steering into the ditch.

The friendly and hospitable staff of the Mizoram government's **Directorate of Tourism**, Chandmari (Mon–Fri 10am–5pm; ☎3162), provide advice, information and transport, and can book tourist lodges throughout Mizoram – including the one here in Aizawl. The landmark **post office** is on Treasury Square (☎2348), near the main branch of the *State Bank of India*, which handles foreign exchange.

The Town

Thanks to its precipitous setting, much of Aizawl does not see the sun for significant parts of the day, and the new multi-storey concrete edifices clinging to the hillsides add to the overall greyness. The only relief from its monotonous sprawl is the Assam Rifles sports ground at the top of town, but thanks to its size the countryside is never too far away. **Chaltlang Hill**, high above Chandmari in the north, with an approach road rising on stilts, provides an excellent overall viewpoint.

Busy central markets include **Bara Bazaar**, which ranges from recordings of Mizo music to Chinese shoeshops which still make shoes to measure. Further up the hill, Solomon's Cave in **Zodin Square** is an indoor market selling fabrics, garments and music, but traditional items are notably absent. The *District Industries Centre* in Upper Bazaar stocks local handicrafts such as shawls and bags. The new and still developing **Mizoram State Museum**, rehoused in an unsuitable building on MacDonald Hill (Mon–Fri 10am–4pm; free), has a small but interesting collection of Mizo costumes and implements, and a few stuffed animals. The staff are welcoming and only too happy to guide you around.

Accommodation and eating

Several **hotels** in Aizawl are geared towards low- and mid-budget travellers, and its simple cafes, especially around Bara Bazaar, serve **Mizo food**. Lentils, fish, rice and bamboo shoots are popular; the under-spiced dishes can be a welcome change from most north Indian cooking.

Ahimsa, Zarkawt (☎3453). One of Aizawl's better hotels. Very centrally located and equipped with a popular restaurant serving a good multi-cuisine range. ③.

Chawlhna, Zarkawt (☎2292). Budget hotel. Quite dingy but with a busy canteen-like restaurant. ①.

Embassy, Chandmari (☎2570). Competitively priced and conveniently situated at the northern end of town, near the tourist office. Boasts one of Aizawl's best multi-cuisine restaurants. ②.

Moonlight, Bawngkawn (☎2647). Aizawl's most prestigious hotel, with all mod cons and a restaurant with a good reputation for Indian and Chinese cooking. ③–④.

Rajdoot, Treasury Square (☎532). Good value and convenient location. ②.

Ritz, Bara Bazaar (☎3358). Friendly, comfortable, and popular with business travellers. Singles with shared baths, and mid-range suites. Well-furnished, recommended, multi-cuisine restaurant. ③.

Tourist Lodge, Chaltlang (☎3526). Beautifully situated, perched on a sharp hill with a terrace providing dramatic views. Large comfortable rooms and a restaurant serving Mizo food with prior notice. The long steep walk from the centre can be an effort, but you can always get a taxi. ②–③.

Around Aizawl: Luangmual

The **Durtlang Hills** constitute a natural barrier immediately south of Aizawl, their high ridges punctuated by Mizo villages and Christian missions, and provide pleasant rambling country. In **LUANGMUAL**, dramatically poised on a high spur 7km west of Aizawl, the *Luangmual Handicrafts Centre* is a low-key institution which sets out to revive Mizoram's ailing indigenous crafts. Workers weave traditional water-resistant "khumbou" hats – very reminiscent of straw baseball hats – out of *h'manthial* leaves.

Luangmual has a basic *Youth Hostel* (①) and a large, modern, and often deserted *Tourist Lodge* (②), bookable through the tourist office in Aizawl.

Tripura

Tucked away in a corner of the northeast, surrounded by Bangladesh on three sides, the wooded hills and lowlands of **TRIPURA** have long served as a meeting place for a huge assortment of peoples and races. Over the last few centuries, however, its closest ties have been with Bengal, and the events of the last fifty years, with the Partition of

India and the subsequent creation of Bangladesh, have left it somewhat stranded away from the heartland of Bengali culture.

The **history** of the kingdom of Tripura, and its Manikya rulers, who claimed descent from far-off Rajput *kshatryas*, is presented in a curious Bengali poem of uncertain age, the *Rajmala*. Udai Manikya (1585–96), who founded the city of **Udaipur** on the site of the old capital of Rangamati, adorned it with beautiful tanks, buildings and temples. The **Tripura Sundari Temple** here is one of India's most important *shaktipiths*, or centres of female power. After staving off the Muslim rulers of Bengal, the Manikyas finally submitted to the Moghuls, but continued to rule over their states until they were eventually swallowed into British India. Maharaja Birchandra Manikya, who came to the throne in 1870 and was heavily influenced both culturally and spiritually by Bengal – and especially his close relationship with Rabindranath Tagore, the Bengali poet, author and painter – established Bengali as the language of the court. This century, migrations of Hindus and Muslims from Bangladesh, has meant that the Bengali influence has come to predominate, although tribal independence struggles continue in the hills of northeast Tripura.

Tripura's forests were once famed for their **elephants**, praised by the Moghul chronicler Abu Fazal in his *Ain-e-Akbari*. Sadly, due to the widespread and uncontrolled practice of slash and burn agriculture, and general pressure on the land, wildlife has come under severe threat. A handful of wildlife sanctuaries such as **Gumti**, **Rowa**, **Trishna**, and **Sepahijala** strive, largely in vain, to protect the few forests that remain.

Agartala

AGARTALA, the capital of Tripura, is a nondescript administrative and commercial town just two kilometres from the Bangladesh border, which lies within walking distance along Akhaura Road. Its only monument of any interest is the gleaming white **Ujjayanta Palace**, completed in 1901, which forms the hub around which most of the town revolves. Set amid formal gardens and artificial lakes, this huge building, whose main block now houses the State Legislative Assembly, covers an area of around 800 acres. One of the many temples located within its grounds, the **Jaganath** temple, an orange tower rising from an octagonal plinth, allows access to the public.

Most of Agartala's amenities, bazaars, bus stands and civil administration are concentrated in the centre, immediately south of the palace. Although the **markets** are hectic, almost all sell provisions and supplies rather than interesting artefacts of any kind; if you're looking for souvenirs, head to either of the two branches of *Purbasha*, the Tripura Government Emporium. One is on Jail Road, the other at *Hotel Kakali*, Mantri Bari Rd.

At Post Office Chowmuhani (the word *chowmuhani*, used in many addresses, means "crossing" or "four roads"), the **State Museum** displays interesting ethnographical and archeological exhibits (Mon–Fri 10am–1pm & 2–5pm; free). One gallery is devoted to the excavations at Unakoti in the forests of northern Tripura (see p.838).

Arrival, information and transport

Agartala's **airport**, 10km north of the centre, is connected by *Indian Airlines* (Palace Compound; ☎5470) with Calcutta, Silchar, and Guwahati. The nearest railhead is **Dharmanagar**, 200km northeast, and served by trains to Lumding, which has connections to Guwahati and the main railway network.

It makes more sense to travel by **bus**; long-distance services, mostly overnight, go to Guwahati (600km), Shillong (500km) and Silchar (300km). Buses either stop at the **Motor Stand** close to the Palace, or at their company offices; *Blue Hill*, LN Bari Rd, *Capital*, Durgabari, and *Assam Valley*, near *Surjaghar Cinema*, Surja Rd, are the most reliable companies. The bus stand at **Bartali Market** is the place to catch buses to other towns in Tripura, such as Udaipur.

The local **tourist office** (☎5930) is in a wing of the palace – in fact, it's the only part of the building a tourist is likely to see. It organizes tours and arranges transport for sightseeing. The main **bank** is the *State Bank of India* on HGB Rd, Melarmath, Bartala (☎5809), and the **post office**, logically enough, is at Post Office Chowmuhani.

Cycle rickshaws, whose rates are exceptionally low by any standards, and auto-rickshaws are plentiful, and cars can be rented for longer journeys either through the hotels or at the tourist office.

Accommodation and eating

Agartala has a small but good selection of **hotels** – nothing really fancy, perhaps, but something for everyone – and several cheap guest houses, such as *Gitanjalee* on Office Lane (①), and the *Tripura* (①) and *Indian* (①) on Chittaranjan Rd. The choice of **eating places** is rather more restricted, though the Mughlai cooking at the **Ambar** on Shakuntala Rd is something special. Agartala, like the rest of Tripura, is dry.

Ambar, SD Barman Sarani (☎3587). Close to all amenities, with reasonably priced a/c rooms. ③–④.

Janata Hotel, Motor Stand Rd (☎3853). Quite basic, as implied by its name, and very central, but a pleasant option with an enjoyable local ambience. ②.

Kakali, PO Chowmuhani, Mantri Bari Rd (☎3234). New landmark hotel near the centre of town and close to the museum, with a sales emporium on the ground floor. ③–④.

Minakshi, Khosh Bagan, Hawkers' Corner Rd (☎3430). Situated in a quiet spot, but handy for the bazaar area. A good range, from budget cubby holes to a/c rooms,. ②–④.

Rajarshi Yatri Niwas, Kunjaban, Near Circuit House (☎3837). Showpiece government hotel, with comfortable and clean rooms and well-kept grounds, but a bit far from the centre of town. Two restaurants, including the pleasant multi-cuisine *Atithi*. ④–⑤.

Rajdhani, BK Rd, near *Indian Airlines* office (☎3387). Newish mid-range hotel, away from the market but within walking distance of the palace. Comfortable but without much character. The *Panchali* restaurant, which serves Indian and Chinese food, should be booked in advance. ③–⑤.

Royal Guest House, Palace Compound (☎5652). Tucked away down a side street near the palace. Roomy and quite comfortable, with a good restaurant preparing Chinese and Indian dishes. ④–⑤.

Around Agartala

Old Agartala, or Puran Haveli, the previous capital of Tripura 5km east of the modern town, holds the unusual **Chaturdas Devata** or "fourteen deities" temple. This otherwise unassuming temple's tribal roots are revealed in July every year, when the festival of Karchi Puja draws people from all over the region.

The crumbling fairy-tale water palace of **Neermahal**, 55km south of Agartala, was built early in the twentieth century onto **Rudrasagar Lake**. Inspired by Moghul architecture, its bridges, moats, towers and pavilions stretch over the lake in prolific confusion. Now abandoned and left to the elements, Neermahal makes a picturesque backdrop for picnics; boats can be rented to explore the lake. Buses run from Agartala to Sonamura, the nearest town, and the tourist office occasionally arranges tours.

On the border with Bangladesh, 27km south of Agartala, the large lake of **Kamala Sagar** is overlooked by a small but important Kali Temple. Its twelfth-century sandstone image of Mahisa-Mardini, a form of Durga, has a *shivalingam* in front of it.

Udaipur

The former capital of the Manikyas, **UDAIPUR**, retains an atmosphere of antiquity not found in the metropolis of Agartala 52km north. Now an important market town, it nestles among paddy fields and low forested hills. On the southwest bank of the artificial lake **Jaganath Dighi**, the dome and vaulted roof of the ruined **Jaganath** temple reflect its strong Muslim influence, while the seventeenth-century **Moghul Masjid** shows that Udaipur was the very furthest outpost of the Moghul empire.

Otherwise known as **Matabari** or "mother's [Kali's] house", **Tripura Sundari**, the most important temple in the area, stands 5km outside Udaipur, on a small hillock in front of a holy lake which is teeming with carp. Built in typical Bengali-hut style with a square sanctum and large meeting hall in front, this is one of the 51 *pithasthan* sacred to the Tantras, and celebrates the spot where a leg of the disintegrating Shakti is supposed to have fallen. It is appropriately painted blood red.

Unakoti

In the dangerous northeastern corner of Tripura, 20km from Dharmanagar and 180km from Agartala, **UNAKOTI** is one of the most intriguing archeological sites in the northeast. The site consists of several gigantic rock-cut images scattered across a hillside, so vast that they remain relatively unscarred after a thousand years or more of neglect.

Most of the images are as yet unexplained; this is considered to be an eighth-century Shaivite site, and certainly Shiva, Durga and Vishnu, as well as a particularly enormous Ganesh, can be discerned, but there is also strong evidence of Buddhist occupation. At **Kailashahar**, the District Headquarters for North Tripura, 10km away, a *Forest Rest House* (①) and *Dak Bungalow* (①) provide accommodation. Kailashahar is connected to Agartala by bus, and even, intermittently, by plane.

CHAPTER SIXTEEN

ORISSA

D espite being one of India's poorest regions, **ORISSA** is among its most distinctive and vibrant. Protected by the thickly forested mountains of the Eastern
Ghats to the west and open to the Bay of Bengal on the east, the strip of fertile
alluvial plains lining the coast forms a long, low-lying delta, across which the
mighty Mahanandi and Brahmani rivers meander towards the sea. Thanks to its location, Orissa's densely populated "rice-bowl" heartland has historically been ravaged
less often by malevolent invaders than by floods and famine. Nor has the recent advent
of dams and weather satellites entirely insulated rural communities from the notorious
tropical climate. A heavier than average monsoon or, even worse, a cyclone sweeping
in from the sea can still rupture river banks and irrigation channels to spoil the crops.
Most of the time however, the Orissan countryside looks deceptively prosperous and
picturesque. The extreme brevity of the dry season (it can rain here any time between
March and December) means that whenever you visit the state, its countless thatched
villages, with their water tanks, palm-groves and whitewashed temple towers, are likely
to be surrounded by a patchwork of vivid green and mud-brown paddy fields.

The coastal plains also claim the highest concentration of historical and religious
monuments – Orissa's principal tourist attractions. **Puri**, site of the famous Jagannath
temple and venue for one of the world's most spectacular devotional processions, the
Rath Yatra, combines the heady intensity of a Hindu pilgrimage centre with the less
demanding pleasures of the beach. Only a short hop off the main Calcutta–Madras
road and railway, the town has in recent years become something of a backpackers'
hang-out, with a good crop of budget accommodation and an easy social scene.
Konarak, just up the coast, has the ruins of Orissa's most ambitious medieval temple.
Hidden for years under a gigantic sand dune, its surfaces writhe with exquisitely
preserved sculpture, including some eyebrow-raising erotica. The ancient rock-cut
caves and ornate sandstone temples of **Bhubaneshwar**, the state capital – all too often
skipped by travellers – hark back to the era when it ruled a kingdom stretching from
the Ganges delta to the mouth of the River Godavari.

Away from the central "golden triangle" of sights, tourism has yet to make much of
an impact. In these outlying districts, **wildlife reserves** are the main incentive to brave
the rigours of minimal infrastructure and over-taxed public transport. The **Simlipal
National Park**, deep in the *sal* forests of the far northeast, boasts some spectacular
scenery, wild tigers and elephants, and hundreds of other species of animals, birds and
reptiles that have all but disappeared from more populated areas. In winter, the small
islands dotted around **Chilka Lake**, a huge salt-water lagoon south of Bhubaneshwar,
become a bird spotter's paradise, while in the **Bhita Kanika Sanctuary** at the end of
Orissa's river delta, a remote stretch of beach is the nesting site for a school of giant
marine turtles that migrate here every year from the South American coast.

From the number of temples, pilgrims and wayside shrines in Orissa, you'd be
forgiven for thinking Hinduism was its sole religion. In fact, nearly twenty-five percent
of the population are **adivasis**, or "tribal" (literally "first-") people, thought to be
descended from the area's pre-Aryan aboriginal inhabitants. In the more inaccessible
corners of the state, such as the tract of near-impenetrable hill country running the
length of the interior, many of these groups have retained unique cultural traditions
and languages. Thus far, the scourge of "ethnic" tourism – so destructive elsewhere in

Asia – has been less of a threat to the Adivasis' way of life than encroachments by dam builders, missionaries and "advancement programmes" of the state government.

Orissa enjoys a fairly congenial **climate** for most of the year, with average temperatures ranging from 17°C between November and March, to a bearable-if-humid 32° during the summer. The monsoon blows in around mid-June, just in time for Rath Yatra. The cool winter months are the **best time to visit**, particularly around Makar Sankranti, in January, when Orissan villages celebrate the conclusion of the harvest with colourful festivals.

Getting around the state presents few practical problems if you stick to the more populated areas. National Highway 5 and the Southeast Railway, which cut in tandem down the coastal plain via Bhubaneshwar, are the main arteries of the region. A metre-gauge branch line also runs as far as Puri, connecting it by frequent, direct express **trains** to Delhi, Calcutta and Madras. Elsewhere, **buses** are the way to go. Regular government (OSTC) and private services cover all the main routes and most of the more remote stretches.

History

Other than scattered fragmentary remains of prehistoric settlement, Orissa's earliest archeological finds date from the fifth century BC and the appearance at **Sisupalgarh**, near modern Bhubaneshwar, of a fortified city. Little is known about the **Kalinga** dynasty, whose capital this was, except that its power was founded on domination of the lucrative land and maritime trade routes leading south. The existence of such rich pickings so close to his frontiers was too strong an enticement for the ambitious Mauryan emperor **Ashok**. In the third century BC, he descended on ancient Kalinga with his imperial army, and routed the kingdom in a battle so bloody that the carnage

ORISSA TRAVEL DETAILS

	Trains		Buses		Flights	
	Frequency	Time	Frequency	Time	Frequency	Time
To and From BHUBANESHWAR						
Agra	daily	39hr				
Balasore	12 daily	4hr	hourly	4hr		
Bangalore	Wed & Thurs	22hr				
Baripada			6 daily	7–8hr		
Berhampur	8 daily	2hr 20min–3hr	hourly	4–5hr		
Bombay					3 weekly	2hr 15min
Calcutta	9 daily	7hr 30min–12hr	4 nightly	8–10hr	5 weekly	55min
Cuttack			every 15min	45min		
Delhi	2 daily	30–34hr 30min			daily	2hr 10min
Hyderabad	2 daily	20–23hr 30min			5 weekly	3hr 10min
Kochi	4 weekly	36hr				
Konarak			1 daily	1hr 30min		
Madras	daily	22hr			2 weekly	2hr 40min
Pipli			every 15min	20min		
Puri	5 daily	2hr	every 15min	1hr		
Thiruvananthapuram	Tues	40hr				
Varanasi	Tues, Fri & Sun	20hr 30min				
To and From PURI						
Agra	1 daily	40hr				
Balasore	5 daily	5hr 30min				
Calcutta	2 nightly	11hr 30min	2 daily	12hr		
Chilka Lake			1 daily	3hr 30min		
Delhi	2 daily	32–36hr				
Konarak			every 30min	1hr		
Varanasi	3 weekly	22hr				
To and From BALASORE						
Baripada			hourly	1hr 15min		
To and From BERHAMPUR						
Gopalpur-on-Sea			every 30min	30min		
Koraput			1 daily	13hr		
Rayagada			1 daily	3hr		
Taptapani			hourly	1hr 15min		

Note that no individual route appears more than once in this chart; check against where you want to get to as well as where you're coming from.

was supposed to have inspired his legendary conversion to **Buddhism**. Rock edicts erected around the empire extol the virtues of the new faith, *dharma*, as well as the principles that Ashok hoped to instil in his vanquished subjects. With the demise of the Mauryans, Kalinga enjoyed something of a resurgence. Under the imperialistic **Chedi** dynasty, followers of the Jain faith, vast sums were spent expanding the capital and on carving elaborate monastery caves into the nearby hills of **Khandagiri** and **Udaigiri**. In the course of the second century BC however, the kingdom gradually splintered into warring factions and entered a kind of dark age. The influence of Buddhism waned, Jainism all but vanished, and **Brahmanism**, disseminated by the teachings of the Shaivite zealot Lakulisa, started to resurface as the dominant religion.

By the seventh century, Orissa's rise to prominence was well under way. Over the next five hundred years, a succession of powerful and prosperous Hindu dynasties ruled the region, creating some of the finest artistic and architectural achievements in the history of South Asia. When the **Eastern Gangas** took control early in the twelfth century, this "golden age" reached its zenith. Fuelled by the gains from a thriving trade network (extending as far east as Indonesia), the Ganga kings erected magnificent **temples** at Bhubaneshwar, Puri, and Konarak, in which the Shiva worship and arcane tantric practices espoused by earlier Orissan rulers were replaced by new forms of devotion to Vishnu. The shrine of the most popular royal deity of all, Lord Jagannath at Puri, was by now one of the four most hallowed religious centres in India.

With the exception of a brief incursion by Firuz Sultan in the fourteenth century, Hinduism in Orissa came through the Muslim occupation of Bihar and Bengal comparatively unscathed. Such good fortune, however, was not to last. In the fifteenth century, the **Afghans of Bengal** swept south to annexe the region, with Man Singh's **Moghul** army hot on their heels in 1592. That even a few medieval Hindu monuments escaped the excesses of iconoclasm that ensued is miraculous; thankfully some did, though ever since non-Hindus have never been allowed to enter the most holy temples in Puri and Bhubaneshwar (Indira Gandhi was refused entry to the Jagannath temple because of her marriage to a Parsi). In 1751 the **Maharathas** from Western India ousted the Moghuls as the dominant regional power. The East India Company, meanwhile, was also making inroads along the coast, and 28 years after Clive's victory at Plassey in 1765, Orissa finally came under **British rule**.

Since **Independence**, the state has sustained rapid **development** without the accompanying political instability which has dogged some of its neighbours. Discoveries of coal, bauxite, iron ore and other minerals have stimulated considerable industrial growth and infrastructural improvements. German-backed steel works and townships have been created at Rourkela in the north and new high-grade roads built to transport goods to and from the main port at Paradwip. Nevertheless, Orissa has remained, first and foremost, a poor rural state, heavily dependent on agriculture to provide for the basic needs of its 32 million inhabitants.

Bhubaneshwar

At first impression, **BHUBANESHWAR** may strike you as surprisingly dull for a city with a population approaching half a million and a history of settlement stretching back over two thousand years. Featureless Fifties architecture and rows of rapidly decaying concrete shopping arcades stand where you might expect exotic bazaars, while long tree-lined avenues diffuse the usual intensity of a busy state capital. Beyond the confines of the modern planned city, however, things improve considerably. Hidden away among the backstreets and wastegrounds of the messier southern suburbs are the remnants of some of India's finest medieval **temples**, evidence of a much earlier and infinitely more inspired building boom than the one that followed Independence.

The Bhubaneshwar area first appears in history during the fourth century BC, as the capital of ancient **Kalinga**. It was soon to be the target of Ashok's ferocious onslaught, which was responsible for the introduction of Buddhism, and the erection of one of the subcontinent's best preserved rock edicts – still in place near the site of the campaign's decisive battle at **Dhauli**, 5km south of the present city. Under the **Chedis**, who succeeded the Mauryans a century or so later, ancient Kalinga gained control over the region's thriving mercantile trade, and became the northeast seaboard's most formidable power. The elaborate sculpture adorning a complex of Jain caves cut from the hillsides of **Khandagiri** and **Udaigiri**, which overlook the capital, provides a taste of the military might and opulent royal lifestyles enjoyed by its rulers.

Not until the fifth century AD, long after the Chedis had disappeared, did Bhubaneshwar re-emerge as a regional force. As home to the revolutionary Pasupata sect, the city, known by this time as **Ekamrakshetra**, became a key centre for the promulgation of Shaivism – worship of the Brahmanical god Shiva and his female coun-

ORISSAN FESTIVALS

Your chances of coinciding with a festival while in Orissa are good, since the region celebrates many of its own as well as all the usual Hindu *pujas*. See p.875 for additional details of Mayurbhunj festivals.

Makar Mela (mid-Jan). Pilgrims descend on a tiny island in Chilka Lake to leave votive offerings in a cave for the goddess Kali.

Adivasis Mela (Jan 26–Feb 1). Bhubaneshwar's "tribal" fair is a disappointing cross between Coney Island and an agricultural show, with good live music and dance.

Magha Saptami (Jan/Feb). A small pool at Chandrabhaga beach, near Konarak, is swamped by thousands of worshippers during the white moon phase of Magha in honour of Surya, the sun god and curer of skin ailments.

Panashankanti (early April). On the first day of Vaisakha, saffron-clad penitents carrying peacock feathers enter trances and walk on hot coals. Various regions.

Chaitra Parba (mid-April). Santals perform Chhou dances at Baripada in Mayurbhunj district, northern Orissa. Some fishing castes also hold "horse-dances" involving wooden horse costumes, drumming and processions through the streets.

Ashokastami (April/May). Bhubaneshwar's own Car Festival, when the Lingaraj deity goes for a dip in the Bindu Sagar tank.

terpart Shakti. When the **Sailodbhavas** made it their capital in the seventh century, wealth and power were coupled with the mounting religious fervour and Bhubaneshwar embarked in earnest upon its "golden age". Nothing is so expressive of the prosperity and self-confidence of this era as its religious architecture. Between the seventh and twelfth centuries some seven thousand sandstone temples are said to have been erected around the **Bindu Sagar**, or "Ocean Drop Tank". Intended both as offerings to the gods and as symbols of authority, the temples evolved from the relatively modest proportions favoured by the Bhauma-Karas and Somavamsis, to the Gangas' gigantic creation, the **Lingaraj** – home of Tribhubaneshwara, or "Lord of Three Worlds" from which the city eventually took its name. Their passion for architecture did not however prevent Bhubaneshwar's medieval rulers from retaining an army strong enough to hold off the eastward advance of Islam until the end of the fifteenth century. When the Moghuls did eventually take the city, they made up for lost time by razing all but a few of the temples. Thereafter, Bhubaneshwar was consigned to relative obscurity. Only after Independence, when Cuttack had reached bursting point, was it officially declared the new state capital.

These days, Bhubaneshwar is easygoing by Indian standards, with enough of interest to warrant at least a day trip if you're in the area. Its monuments are indisputably the main attractions, with visits made all the more atmospheric by the animated religious life that continues to revolve around them, particularly at festival times.

Arrival and information

There's no regular bus service into the centre of Bhubaneshwar from its domestic **airport** on the southwest outskirts, but unmetered taxis and auto-rickshaws queue to meet incoming flights. Long-distance **buses** terminate at the inconveniently situated Baramunda Bus Stand, 5km out on the northwestern edge of town, though not before making a whistlestop tour of the centre. Ask to be dropped at **Station Square** (look for a statue of a horse in the middle of a large roundabout), which is close to most hotels. If you miss the stop, frequent local buses head back to the city bus stand on Raj Path.

The **railway station** is right in the centre of town close to many of the mid-range hotels. For **cheaper rooms**, leave the station via platorm four and catch a rickshaw from there down to Kalpana Square, a kilometre further south.

BHUBANESHWAR

Ⓐ

Ⓑ

N

NH-5

PATEL MARG

Tribal
Research
Institute

AZAD MARG

Baramunda
Bus Stand

Khandagiri & Udaigiri Caves

MADHUSUDAN
MARG

Shri Ram
Temple

Ⓒ

JAN PATH

GOPABANDHU
MARG

Secretariat

GPO

Ⓖ
ⒻⒾⒹ 1 2 ⒽⒺ
Ⓙ Ⓚ
Ⓓ

RAJ PATH

MAHATMA
GANDHI MARG

Old
Bus
Stand

Capital
Market

Railway
Station

STATION
SQUARE

State Bank
of India

Indian
Airlines

RAJ PATH

CUTTACK RD

Forest
Park

GAUTAM
NAGAR

EKAMRA MARG

UDYAN MARG

ⓁⓂ
Ⓝ

KALPANA
SQUARE

State
Museum

Ⓞ

ⓘ
ITDC

Rameswara

Ⓟ

Ⓞ OTDC

Airport

Muktesvara

ⓘ India Government
Tourist Office

Bhaskaresvara

Vital
Deul

Parasumaresvara

EKAMRA MARG

MAHATAB RD

Bindu
Sagar

Ⓡ Raj Rani

PURI RD

Brahmesvara

Lingaraj

Ⓒ

SISUPALGARH

0   1 km

HOTELS:
Ⓐ Oberoi Bhubaneshwar
Ⓑ Meghdoot
Ⓒ Prachi
Ⓓ Yatri Niwas
Ⓔ Bhubaneshwar
Ⓕ Jajati
Ⓖ Swosti
Ⓗ Nandan
Ⓘ Keshari
Ⓙ Anarkali
Ⓚ Richi
Ⓛ Bhagwat Niwas
Ⓜ Padma
Ⓝ Pushpak
Ⓞ New Kenilworth
Ⓟ Kalinga Ashok
Ⓠ OTDC Panthaniwas
Ⓡ Rajrani

RESTAURANTS:
❶ Hare Krishna
❷ Vineeth
❸ Athiti Bhavan

Information

Both the **Orissa Tourism Development Corporation** (OTDC) office on Jayadev
Nagar (Lewis Rd), near the *Panthaniwas* (Mon–Sat 10am–5pm; ☎50099), and the counter at the railway station hand out useful free maps of Orissa and can arrange taxis for
local sightseeing. The helpful India Government tourist office around the corner from
the *Panthaniwas* on BJB Nagar (Mon–Fri 10am–5pm; ☎54203) has a large selection of
leaflets and city plans for other parts of the country.

The **post office** is on the corner of Mahatma Gandhi Marg and Sachivalaya Marg.
For poste restante ask at "enquiries" on the middle counter. A *pan wallah* left of the
main entrance packs and seals parcels. The best place to **change money**, if you're not
staying in a hotel with a foreign exchange counter, is the *State Bank of India* (Mon–Fri
10am–2pm, Sat 10am–noon) on Raj Path, opposite New Market.

City transport

Modern Bhubaneshwar is too spread out to explore on foot, so **getting around** is basically a choice between **auto-** or **cyclerickshaws**. Sights outside the city, such as

Dhauli or the Udaigiri and Khandagiri caves, can reached by local **buses** from the bus stand near Capital Market, by auto-rickshaw or on one of OTDC's **luxury coach tours** (see below). Private *Ambassador* **taxis** can also be arranged for local sightseeing trips through most travel agents (see listings), the OTDC office on Jayadev Nagar, or at large hotels such as the *Swosti*, the *Kenilworth* or the *Ashok*. Expect to pay anywhere between Rs600 and 800 for a full day.

Tours

OTDC **tours** take in most of Bhubaneshwar's attractions (Tues–Sun 9am–5pm; Rs80), but are too rushed for most visitors. Tickets are available through the OTDC office on Jayadev Nagar and the bus leaves from in front of the *Panthaniwas*. Visits to *Mahila Vikash Samabaya Niga*, a government-run women's development co-operative set up to promote cottage industries, may be arranged by telephoning ☎401852.

It's also possible to visit **Puri** and **Konarak** on an OTDC tour from here (Mon–Sat 8.30am–6pm; Rs75 or a/c Rs100), though this again involves too much time on the bus and not enough looking around the sights. More upmarket **package tours** of Bhubaneshwar, Puri and Konarak, with four-star accommodation, transport in an a/c car, and guides, can be arranged through *Swosti Travel*, 103 Janpath (☎54178).

The temples

Of the five hundred or so **temples** that remain in Bhubaneshwar, only a handful are of interest to any but the most ardent templo-phile. These are grouped into three widely separated areas, but thanks to the city's ubiquitous rickshaw *wallahs*, who will find you long before you need them, it's possible to see most of the highlights in a full morning.

Most visitors see the temples in more or less chronological order. Apart from giving a sense of the development of Orissan architecture over the years, this also delays the onset of temple fatigue by leaving the most impressive monuments until last. The majority are active places of worship, so dress appropriately, remove your shoes (and any leather items) at the entrance and seek permission before taking photographs, particularly inside the buildings. The resident *brahmin* will expect a donation if he's shown you around, of course, but don't necessarily believe the astronomical amounts recorded in the ledgers you'll be shown.

The central group

The compact **central group**, just off Lewis Road beyond the museum and *Panthaniwas*, includes some of Bhubaneshwar's most celebrated temples. In order to see the oldest first, follow the footpath from the main road past the more recent Muktesvara and its adjacent water tank, as far as a small square lined with cold drink stalls and souvenir shops.

PARASUMARESVARA MANDIR

The best preserved and most beautiful of Bhubaneshwar's early temples, the lavishly decorated **Parasumaresvara Mandir**, stands in the shade of a large *banyan* tree just beyond the square. Art historians rave about this temple, which with its plain, rectangular assembly hall (*jagamohana*), simple stepped roof and squat beehive-shaped tower (*deul*), typifies the predominant style of late seventh-century Orissa. In addition to the sheer quality of its exterior sculpture, Parasumaresvara is significant in marking the then-recent transition from Buddhism to Hinduism. The *brahmin* may, for example, point out panels depicting **Lakulisha**, the proselytizing Shaivite whose sect was largely responsible for the Hinduization of Orissa in the fifth century. On the east side of the tower he appears with four disciples at his feet, while on the west, above the relief showing Siva as Nataraj, Lord of the Dance, he adopts the full-blown lotus position, looking every bit the meditating Buddha. Around the corners of the *deul* are even more blatant assertions of Hindu supremacy. Look for the **rampant lions** with their heads thrown back, crouched or standing above elephants, symbols of the beleaguered Buddhist faith.

Elsewhere the sculpture concentrates mainly on the Hindu pantheon and scenes from mythological narratives. Highlights include the marriage of Shiva and Parvati on the east side of the sanctuary tower, and the intricate friezes that line the north wall of the assembly hall. Among these stands a row of seven Mother Goddesses (*Sapta Matrikas*), with the emaciated Chamunda (Shiva's consort Durga in her terrifying aspect) to the right; an unusual depiction of Ganesh, Shiva's other (elephant-headed) son, here shown with a human face and a trunk growing from his chin; and further to the left, a dreadlocked *rishi*, or saint, counting on his rosary while strapped into an uncomfortable looking yogic pose. In the far corner of the courtyard, an intriguing *lingam*, the **Sahasralingam**, is decorated with a thousand miniature versions of itself.

MUKTESVARA MANDIR

Back towards the main road, the **Muktesvara Mandir**, set in its own low-walled courtyard, is often described as the "gem" of Orissan architecture. During the two hundred years after the Parasumaresvara was constructed, a new, more elaborate style evolved in Bhubaneshwar. The assembly hall (*jagamohana*) here has the complex pyramidal roof normally associated with Orissan temples, while the sanctuary tower (*deul*), though similar in shape to its predecessor, places more emphasis on vertical than horizontal lines. Once again, the sandstone **sculpture** is the most striking feature. Directly in front of the main entrance, the ornamental **gateway** (*torana*), topped by two reclining female figures, is the Muktesvara's masterpiece. The grinning lions and dwarves around the windows on the side of the porch, known as the *bho* motif, come a close second. Witty touches include the lice-picking monkeys around the latticed windows, and the little panel hidden amid the ornamentation along the side walls, whose geometric pattern, when partially covered, reveals two separate dancing nymphs.

Between the Muktesvara and the road, the murky green waters of the small **Marichi Kund** tank are believed to cure infertility in women – which doesn't altogether explain its popularity with noisy adolescent boys. Still, the *ghats* surrounding the tank are a pleasant place to sit and enjoy the temple. Around the frame of the door leading to it Lakulisha crops up again, this time encircled by students and ascetics reading books.

Finally, on the edge of Muktesvara's terrace stands an example of the mature phase of Orissan temple building. The unfinished **Siddhesvara** was erected at more or less the same time as the Lingaraj, in the eleventh century, but is nowhere near as impressive. The lesser deities around the tower, Ganesh and Karttikeya (Shiva's sons), are about its only remarkable points.

The eastern group

To reach the first of the more scattered **eastern group** of temples, ten to fifteen minutes' walk from Muktesvara, head back up Lewis Road as far as the crossroads, turn right down Tankapani Road, and keep going until you reach the park on the right.

RAJRANI MANDIR

Even though it was never completed, the majestic eleventh-century **Rajrani Mandir** is among the very finest of Bhubaneshwar's later temples. From the far end of the well-watered gardens in which it stands, the profile of the **sanctuary** (*deul*), with its successive tiers of projections rising to form an elegant eighteen-metre tower, is the building's most unusual feature. Closer to, you can make out the profusion of sculpted figures for which Rajrani is equally famous. The best are about three metres off the ground surrounding the sides of the tower. The **Dikpalas**, or Guardians of the Eight Directions, are the deities who "protect" the main shrine. Identifiable by their respective vehicles and attributes, they form a marked contrast to the languid and alluring poses of the exquisite female figures (*nayikas*) that stand between them. Among the more distinctive of the Dikpalas are (moving clockwise) Yama (south), the Judge of the Dead, with his club and noose; Nritti (southwest), the God of Misery holding a severed head;

ORISSAN TEMPLES

Orissan temples constitute one of the most distinctive regional styles of religious architecture in South Asia. To make sense of the buildings, you need to be able to identify their common features. Many of these conventions have endured for thousands of years, and are recorded in the **Shilpa Shastras** – Sanskrit canonical texts that set out, in meticulous detail, ancient building specifications and their symbolic significance. Exactitude was a hallmark of ancient architecture; as one of the *Shastras* says: " . . . if the measurements are perfect, there will be perfection in the Universe."

Unlike Christian churches or Muslim mosques, Hindu temples are not simply places of worship, but are *objects* of worship in themselves – recreations of the "Divine Cosmic Creator-Being" or the particular deity enshrined within them. For a Hindu, to move through a temple is akin to entering the very body of the God to be glimpsed in the shrine-room during the moment of *darshan*, or ritual viewing of the deity – the culmination of an act of worship. In Orissa, this concept also finds expression in the technical terms used in the *Shastras* to designate the different parts of the structure: the foot (*pabhaga*), shin (*jangha*), torso (*gandi*), neck (*kantha*), head (*mastaka*) and so forth . . .

Most temples are made up of two main sections. The first and most impressive of these is the **deul**, or sanctuary tower. A soaring, curvilinear spire with a square base and rounded top, the *deul* symbolizes the Divine Mountain from which the sacred Ganges flows into the world. Its intricately ribbed sides, which in later buildings were divided into rectangular projections known as *raths*, usually house images of the accessory deities, while its top supports a lotus-shaped, spherical *amla* (a motif derived from an auspicious fruit used in Ayurvedic medicine as a purifying agent). Above that, the vessel of immortality, the *kalasha*, is crowned by the presiding deity's sacred weapon, a wheel (Vishnu's *chakra*) or trident (Shiva's *trichul*). The actual deity occupies a chamber inside the *deul*. Known in Oriya as the **garbha griyha**, or inner sanctum, the shrine is shrouded in a womb-like darkness intended to focus the mind of the worshipper on the image of God.

The **jagamohana**, or "World Delighter", which adjoins the sanctuary tower, is a lighter porch where the congregation gathers for readings of religious texts and other important ceremonies. Its pyramidal roof, made up of layers of receding steps, contrasts sharply with the gently curving lines of the tower. Larger temples, such as the Lingaraj in Bhubaneshwar and the Jagannath in Puri, also have additional structures that were tacked on to the main porch when music and dance were more commonly performed as part of temple rituals. Like the *jagamohana*, the roofs of the **nata mandir**, the dancing hall, and **bhoga-mandapa**, the hall of offerings, are pyramidal. The whole structure, along with any smaller subsidiary shrines (often earlier temples erected on the same site), is usually enclosed in a walled courtyard.

Over the centuries, as construction techniques and skills improved, Orissan temples became progressively grander and more elaborate. It's fascinating to chart this transformation as you move from the earlier buildings in Bhubaneshwar to the acme of the region's architectural achievement, the stunning Sun temple at Konarak. Towers grow taller, roofs gain extra layers, and the **sculpture**, for which the temples are now famous all over the world, attains a level of complexity and refinement unrivalled before or since.

Varuna (west), the serene God of Light, shown standing on his vehicle, a sea monster; Kubera (north), God of Prosperity, complete with pot-belly and jar full of gem stones; Ishana (northeast), a form of Shiva whose erect phallus has seen an untimely end; and next to him Indra (east), the Storm God with his corn-on-the-cob-like thunderbolt.

Compared to the sanctuary tower, the Rajrani's porch looks plain and unfinished. Of considerably more interest to some may be the palm-leaf manuscripts being hawked in the temple gardens. Spurred on no doubt by Khajuraho's money-spinning example, enterprising local artists have tried to make up for Bhubaneshwar's comparative lack of erotic sculpture by applying this most ancient of Orissan skills to illustrating the *Kama Sutra*. The results sometimes verge on the surreal.

BRAHMESVARA MANDIR

From Rajrani, a fair walk leads up Tankapani Road to the turn off for the **Brahmesvara Mandir**, five hundred metres on your right. Along the way you cross a canal, originally dug by King Kharavela in the first century BC, and an open stretch of ground to the left of the road with an odd-shaped temple in the middle. The **Bhaskaresvara** is unfinished, but has an interesting three-metre *lingam*, or phallus, enshrined in its double-storeyed interior which archeologists claim was formerly a Mauryan column.

Unlike most of its neighbours, the eleventh-century Brahmesvara temple itself, at the end of the dirt lane opposite the entrance to the Bhaskaresvara, still houses a living deity, as indicated by the saffron pennant flying from the top of the sanctuary. The gateway in the high enclosure wall brings you out opposite a small cloth-covered image of Lakshmi. Here too you can see guardian figures (Dikpalas) on the corners, and a fierce-looking Chamunda on the western facade (shown astride a corpse and holding a trident and severed head), as well as curvaceous maidens admiring themselves in mirrors or, in the panels around the tower, responding with some abandon to the advances of their male consorts. An inscription, now lost, records that one Queen Kovalavati once made a donation of "many beautiful women" to this temple – proof perhaps that **devadasis**, the dancers-cum-prostitutes who were to become a prominent feature of Orissan temple life in later years, made an early appearance here. Unfortunately, the temple *brahmins* are reluctant to allow non-Hindus into the strongly atmospheric shrine room for *darshan*, or a view of the *shivalingam*. There's a majestic Nandi, Shiva's bull, with testicles polished by years of worshippers giving them a propitious rub on the way in; and an inner sanctum, richly carved and lit by butter lamps, which is filled with incense smoke and the scent of oil-soaked flowers left as *puja* offerings.

The Bindu Sagar group

By far the largest group of temples in Bhubaneshwar is clustered around the **Bindu Sagar**, or "Ocean Drop Tank", two kilometres due south of the city centre. This small artificial lake, mentioned in the *Puranas*, is itself a place of great religious importance. Said to contain nectar, wine and water drawn from all of the world's most sacred rivers, the tank is the main bathing place both for pilgrims visiting the city and for the Lingaraj deity, who is taken to the pavilion in the middle once every year during Bhubaneshwar's annual **Car Festival** (Ashokastami) for his ritual purificatory dip. The hours around sunrise and sunset are the most evocative time for a stroll here, when the residents of the nearby *dharamshalas* file through the smokey lanes and groups of stray cattle to the *ghats* to pray.

LINGARAJ MANDIR

Immediately south of the Bindu Sagar stands the most stylistically evolved temple in all Orissa. Built early in the eleventh century by the Ganga Kings, one hundred years before the Jagannath temple at Puri, the mighty **Lingaraj Mandir** has remained very much a "living" shrine. The small square in front of the main gateway still throngs with pilgrims clutching bananas and coconuts, bought at the colourful stalls nearby, to be offered as *prashad* to Tibhuvaneshwar, the "Lord of Three Worlds". Unfortunately, the square is about as close to the inside as most foreign visitors are allowed. Although the temple is open to all castes, non-Hindus (in practise non-Asians) have to be content with a peep from the top of the **viewing platform** overlooking the north wall, around the corner to the main entrance. From this vantage point you can still see all four of the principal sections of the building. The two nearest the entrance, the *bhoga-mandapa* (the Hall of Offering) and the *nata mandir* (the Hall of Dance, associated with the rise of the *devadasi* system – see p.868) are both later additions to the complex. If you have binoculars you may just be able to pick out some of the beautiful **sculpture**, depicting the music and dance rituals that would once have taken place inside.

Even more than the huge porch (*jagamohana*), loaded with fancy stonework and the characteristic pyramidal roof, the immense forty-five-metre sanctuary **tower** (*deul*) is the literal and aesthetic high point of the Lingaraj. Notice the rampant lion projecting from the gently curved sides of the tower, and the downtrodden elephant beneath him – once again symbolizing the triumph of Hinduism over Buddhism. On the top, the typical Orissan motif of the flattened, ribbed sphere (*amla*) supported by gryphons, is crowned with Shiva's trident (*trichul*). As in the Brahmesvara temple, the long saffron pennant announces the living presence of the deity below.

The **shrine** inside is very unusual. The powerful two-and-a-half-metre-thick Svayambhu (literally "self-born") *lingam* that it contains, one of the twelve *jyotirlinga* in India, is known as "Hari-Hara" because it is considered to be half Shiva, half Vishnu – an extraordinary amalgam that is thought to have resulted from the ascendancy of Vishnaivism over Shaivism in the twelfth and thirteenth centuries. Unlike other *lingams*, which are bathed every day in a concoction prepared from hemlock, Svayambhu is offered a libation of rice, milk and *bhang* by the *brahmins*. Another peculiar feature of the shrine room is that it lacks a ceiling. Instead, the roof reaches right to the top of the tower.

VITAL DEUL MANDIR

Anyone not totally templed-out by this stage should head left from the Lingaraj viewing platform and up the main street to the fascinating **Vital Deul**, one of the group's oldest buildings and a real feast of tantric art. The temple was built around 800 AD in a markedly different style from most of its contemporaries in Bhubaneshwar, drawing heavily on earlier Buddhist influences (the south Indian style tower, called *kakhara* after an Orissan pumpkin, resembles the distinctive *chaitya* arches found in rock-cut caves). The Vital Deul also boasts some very accomplished stonework. Among the panels of Hindu deities encrusting its outer walls, you may occasionally come across examples of some of India's earliest **erotic sculpture**, thought to catalogue positions exploited in the tantric rituals that took place inside.

Once your eyes adjust to the darkness of the **interior**, you swiftly realize that this was no ordinary temple. Even if you missed the tell-tale post outside the entrance (a four-faced *lingam* used for tethering the sacrificial offerings) the grotesque images adorning the walls of the *jagamohana* graphically convey the macabre nature of the esoteric rites once performed here. Durga, in her most terrifying aspect as **Chamunda**, peers out of the half-light from behind the grille at the far end of the hall – her withered body, garlanded with skulls and flanked by an owl and a jackal, stands upon a rotting corpse. In front of her, to the right of the door, an even more nightmarish figure of a man picks himself up from the floor, apparently after filling his skull-cup with blood from the decapitated body nearby. The whole gruesome frieze is littered with severed heads and jackals gnawing away at corpses, but you'll need a torch to see it properly.

Orissa State Museum

Tues–Sun 10am–1.30pm & 2.30–5pm; Rs2.

Bhubaneshwar's **museum**, a port of call on the OTDC tour, is housed in a large modern building at the top of Gautam Nagar (Lewis Road), a little way down from the *Hotel Ashok*. Its collection of "tribal" artefacts, illuminated manuscripts and various archeological finds are worth an hour or so en route to the temples.

On display in the downstairs galleries are pieces of religious sculpture, coins and donative inscriptions on stone and copper plates salvaged from the city's temples. The upstairs rooms feature ethnographic material from indigenous Orissan societies. As well as heavy jewellery, musical instruments, weapons, tools and moth-eaten traditional costumes, there are reproductions of **chitra muriya**, the folk murals seen on walls and floors in village houses around Puri. The museum's real highlight however has to be its collection of antique **painting** and illuminated **palm-leaf manuscripts** (see p.870), kept in the small room at the end of the corridor on the first floor. Only the National Museum in New Delhi holds finer examples of this traditional Orissan art form.

The Tribal Research Institute or "Museum of Man"

Hidden away on the northwestern edge of town, close to Baramunda bus stand, the *Tribal Research Institute*'s anthropological **Museum of Man** (Mon–Sat 10am–5pm) is given over solely to "tribal" art and culture. Material collected from across the state is exhibited in the garden, in traditional-style huts built and decorated by *adivasis* specialists. While most of the buildings are evidently idealized versions of the real thing, some of the **murals** decorating their walls are more authentic.

Accommodation

As state capital, Bhubaneshwar has a disproportionate number of hotels for its size, ranging from luxurious five-stars to the filthiest of lodges. While the better-class hotels are spread out all over the city, the inexpensive places tend to be grouped around the railway station, or a five-minute rickshaw ride away near the busy Kalpana Square junction at the bottom of Bhubaneshwar Road. Many of these can be pretty dreadful, but paying just a fraction more will get you clean sheets, a fan that works and a private bathroom. By far the best deals are the budget-price rooms offered by some mid-range hotels. The railway station also has **retiring rooms** if you're really stuck. Reservations must be made in advance at the counter in the main hall.

Inexpensive

Bhagwat Niwas, 9 Buddha Nagar (☎51808). Right behind the *Pushpak*. A cheap and cheerful hotel managed by an Aurobindo devotee. Basic but clean and good value. ①–②.

Nandan, 27a Station Square. Just behind the *Richi* and very much in the same mould. ②.

ACCOMMODATION PRICE CODES

All **accommodation prices** in this book have been coded using the symbols below. In principle the prices given are for the least expensive double rooms in each establishment; however, some hotels, usually in category ①, offer rates per bed rather than per room. Local taxes are not included unless specifically stated. For more details, see p.34.

①	up to Rs100	④	Rs225–350	⑦	Rs750–1200
②	Rs100–150	⑤	Rs350–500	⑧	Rs1200–2200
③	Rs150–225	⑥	Rs500–750	⑨	Rs2200 and up

Padma, Kalpana Square (☎51198). Next to the *Pushpak*. Not as neat and clean inside as out, with mostly windowless singles, shared bathrooms and a couple of marginally brighter doubles. ①.

Pushpak, Kalpana Square (☎50545). A popular budget hotel with fairly clean, large rooms, attached bathrooms, balconies and a small restaurant downstairs. Good value. ①.

Rajrani, Jayadev Nagar (☎51264). No-frills budget hotel with rock-bottom dorms and front rooms. The only redeeming feature is that it overlooks the Muktesvara temple. ①.

Richi, 12a New Station Square (☎406619). Opposite the railway station. A large, functional though well-run place with hot water in all the rooms, a fish tank in reception and a back-up generator. ②.

Yatri Niwas, Cuttack Rd. Institutional hostel run by the local authority, with cheap beds in large dorms or smaller rooms. ①.

Moderate

Anarkali, 110 Kharvel Nagar (☎404031). Two minutes from the station. Recently moved upmarket and now somewhat pretentious, though well appointed with all mod-cons including *Star TV*, bar and a/c restaurant. Some good-value budget rooms too. ③–⑤.

Bhubaneshwar, Cuttack Rd (☎51977). Very clean and comfortable with attached bathrooms, 24-hour hot water, balconies, a generator and pleasant little restaurant. Some a/c. Excellent value. ②–⑤.

Jajati, Kharvela Nagar (☎400352). Modern chain hotel at the top of Station Square. A little frayed around the edges, but very reasonably priced. Budget and more comfortable a/c rooms. ③–⑤.

Meghdoot, 5-B Sahid Nagar (☎55802). Rooms from basic non-a/c "coir-rugs" variety to luxurious suites with wall-to-wall carpets, bath tubs and colour TV. Also quality restaurant, coffee shop and foreign exchange. The best value in its class, but way up the top of town. ④–⑦.

OTDC Panthaniwas, Jayadev Nagar (☎54515). Government hotel close to museum and temples. Nothing fancy, but comfortable with three restaurants and satellite TV in reception. Some a/c. ③.

Expensive

Kalinga Ashok, Gautam Nagar (☎5318). Typically austere building set in its own grounds, with all the usual five-star facilities except a pool. Popular with tour groups and business travellers. ⑦.

Keshari, 113 Station Rd (☎408801). The full works from in-house movies to a craft shop in the lobby. A bar, plus a restaurant serving local specialities. Some cheaper non-a/c rooms. ⑤–⑦.

New Kenilworth, 86/A-1 Gautam Nagar (☎543300). A plush five-star in the centre of town with an excellent restaurant, bar, pool and tempting pastry shop. ⑦.

Oberoi Bhubaneshwar, Nayapalli (☎56116; fax 0675/56269). Indisputably the city's top hotel. A modern building, exquisitely furnished using antique textiles, stone and metal-work. Two restaurants with international menus, 24-hour coffee shop and a pool. Way out to the north of town. ⑧.

Prachi, 6 Janpath (☎751001). The longest established upmarket hotel in the city. Central a/c, pool, beauty parlour, money changing and travel agent. Also two good restaurants, one serving (almost) authentic Chinese food. ⑦.

Swosti, 103 Janpath (☎404178; fax 0675/407524). Award-winning, central, American-style four-star. Luxurious rooms, all with *Star TV*, two top-class restaurants and bar. Highly recommended. ⑦.

Eating

Eating out in Bhubaneshwar is usually a simple matter of choosing between the predictable five-star food dished up in the air-conditioned comfort of places such as the *Ashok* or *New Kenilworth*, or cheap and chilli-ful south Indian dishes served in rather less salubrious surroundings. The one or two restaurants that make an effort to include traditional **Orissan cuisine** on their menus are worth seeking out; seafood dishes combining prawns or delicate white "pomfret" fish with rice, fresh vegetables, yoghurt and spices may be common in the coastal villages, but you rarely see them in the city. One traditional delicacy you're sure to come across however is the **coconut milk** sold by street vendors – just make sure the straws are as fresh as the fruit.

Athiti Bhavan, Lingaraj Rd. A short way down the lane opposite the temple. A wide range of veg, non-veg, tandoori and Chinese dishes, plus superb Bengali *thalis* and cold beers. Very reasonable.

Fahien, OTDC *Panthaniwas*, Jayadev Nagar. A good selection of tasty vegetable and meat dishes, though ask them to hold the *masala* if you're after something mild.

Hare Krishna, Janpath. Waiters in dinner jackets not *dhotis*, but the food is strictly *ISKON*-style vegetarian and delicious. A/c and quite expensive.

Mohanty, OTDC *Panthaniwas*, Jayadev (Lewis) Rd. Copious portions of reasonably priced veg and non-veg food, mostly north Indian style (spicy), in spartan surroundings. Moderate.

Padma, Kalpana Square, under *Pushpak Hotel*. The best of the cheap south Indian restaurants. Does a roaring trade in unfeasibly large *dosas* and opens early for breakfast.

Swosti, 103 Janpath. Absolutely the best restaurant for a slap-up meal. Authentic Orissan dishes, such as mouth-watering *dahi machho* (river fish in yoghurt sauce), served with advance warning.

Vineeth, off Station Square. Dingy interior, but the pure vegetarian snacks and main meals are tasty, fresh and cheap. Popular with families.

Listings

Airlines *Indian Airlines* main booking office is on Raj Path, near New Market (Mon–Fri 10am–5.30pm; booking ends 4.15pm; ☎400533).

Ambulance (Red Cross) ☎50389.

Ayurvedic Hospital Between the *Panthaniwas* and the Ramesvara temple (☎51347).

Bookstores The *Modern Bookshop* at the top of Station Square has a rack of pulp fiction. The *Bookshop*, across the square in Ashoka Market, stocks a much more eclectic range with titles from Harold Robbins to Indian literature in translation. Also lots on politics, religion and history.

Bus Enquiries Baramunda bus stand ☎400540.

Dance Visits or lessons can be arranged through the *Odissi Dance Academy*, Plot #459/4962, near Airport Chowk (☎406797). For more on Odissi dance see p.868.

Hospital The Capital Hospital (and homeopathic clinic) is near the airport. Casualty is on ☎400688.

Music The only venue staging regular performances of Indian classical music and *ghazaals* is the *New Kenilworth Hotel* (☎54330). The *Meghdoot* (☎55802) also advertises recitals.

Photography Film and colour processing available from *Neel Kamal*, 29 West Market Building (☎401491) or from *Photomakers*, 28 West Tower, New Market (☎400700).

Police Station Near the *State Bank of India* (☎401232).

Railway Enquiries Best to go in person or ask at a travel agency; otherwise call ☎402233.

Travel agents The *Keshari*, *New Kenilworth*, *Meghdoot*, *Oberoi* and *Prachi* hotels all have in-house travel agents. *Swosti Travels* at 103 Janpath (☎54178) has a good reputation and in addition to the usual services runs specialist "wildlife", "tribal" and "architectural" tours. *Prime Tours and Travels* in the Pushpak Complex on Kalpana Square do car rental, tickets and sort out train reservations.

Around Bhubaneshwar

A number of interesting places around Bhubaneshwar are worth combining with a day trip to the city. Fifteen minutes by rickshaw out of the centre, the second-century BC caves at **Khandagiri** and **Udaigiri** offer a glimpse of the region's past prior to the rise of Hinduism. **Dhauli**, just off the main road to Puri, boasts an even older monument: a rock edict dating from the Mauryan era, commemorating the battle of circa 260BC that gave the emperor Ashok control of the eastern seaports, and thus enabled his missionaries to export the state religion across Asia.

Udaigiri and Khandagiri caves

Six kilometres west of Bhubaneshwar, beyond the leafy avenues of its exclusive neighbourhoods and the point where the green belt is broken by the busy Calcutta–Madras highway, a pair of low bony hills rise from the coastal plain. More than two thousand years ago, caves chiselled out of their malleable yellow sandstone were home to a community of **Jain monks**. Nowadays, they lie virtually deserted, left for troupes of black-faced langur monkeys and occasional parties of tourists to clamber over. Though by no means in the same league as the caves of the Deccan, **Udaigiri** and **Khandagiri** (daily 8am–6pm) rank, nevertheless, among Orissa's foremost historical monuments.

Inscriptions show that the **Chedi** dynasty, which ruled ancient Kalinga from the first century BC, was responsible for the bulk of the work. Apart from providing the monks with cells for meditation and prayer, the excavations enabled the rulers to show off their wealth and worldly achievements. Hallways, verandahs and facades outside several caves are encrusted with **sculpture** depicting court scenes, lavish processions, hunting expeditions, battles, dances and a host of more mundane details drawn from the daily life of Kalinga's cool set. The later additions, by contrast (made during medieval times, when Jainism no longer enjoyed royal patronage in the region), tend to be more austere, showing images of the twenty-four heroic Jain prophet-teachers known as *tirthankaras* ("crossing-makers").

Every year, Udaigiri and Khandagiri also play host to a **sadhu convention**. For a week or so in late January, the caves and surrounding woodland are claimed by dozens of itinerant holy men, resplendent in their saffron robes and coiled dreadlocks, who gather on the hillside to intone verses from the *Gita* into crackly PA systems. Predictably, the event has grown into something of a funfair. Crowds of exuberant day-trippers pour in on coaches to enjoy the religious spectacle and the many market traders, travelling theatre groups and circus acts who set up along the roadside.

From Bhubaneshwar, the caves are approached via a road that follows the route of an ancient **pilgrimage path** (leading, archeologists believe, to a now-defunct *stupa*). As you face the hills with the highway behind you, Khandagiri ("Broken Hill") is on your left and Udaigiri ("Sunrise Hill") on your right. Best to begin with the latter, which has the finest of the early stonework.

Udaigiri

The **Udaigiri** caves occupy a fairly compact area around the south slope of the hill. To reach the largest and most impressive in the group, walk up the main pathway and take the track off to the right. Cave **One**, the **Rani Gumpha** or "Queen's Cave", is tucked away around the corner. Its best sculpture is to be found over the pillars, arches and to the rear of the courtyard on the lower level, and across the back wall of the upper storey, where a long frieze shows rampaging elephants, panicking monkeys, sword fights and the abduction of a woman. Nobody, as yet, has managed to string all these scenes into a coherent narrative, though some are thought to illustrate episodes from the life of Kalinga's King Kharavela. Returning along the same path, the first caves of interest are numbers **three** and **four** – a double-storeyed cave containing sculptures of a lion holding its prey, elephants with snakes wrapped around them and pillars topped by pairs of peculiar winged animals. Cave **nine**, up the hill and around to the right, also has two storeys. Inside the lower, between the second and third doors, a badly damaged relief shows figures worshipping a long-vanished Jain symbol. The one wearing what looks like a crown (second from the left) is thought to be the Chedi king, Vakradeva, whose donative inscription can still be made out near the roof.

To reach cave **ten**, return to the main steps and climb towards the top of the hill. Its popular name, Ganesh Gumpha, is not derived from the elephants in front of the cave, but from the appearance on the rear wall of the cell on the right of the elephant-headed Ganesh. From here, follow the path up to the ledge at the very top of Udaigiri hill for good views and the ruins of an old **chaitya hall**. This was probably the main place of worship for the Jain monks who lived below and may even once have housed the legendary **Kalinga Jina**, a kind of votive cult object-cum-Holy Grail which Kharavela recovered after it had been removed by the King of Magadha (south Bihar).

Below the ruins are cave **twelve**, shaped like the head of a tiger, and cave **fourteen**, the Hathi Gumpha known for the long **inscription** in ancient Magadhi carved onto its overhang. This relates in glowing terms the life history of King Kharavela, whose exploits, both on and off the battlefield, brought in the fortune needed to finance the cave excavation. Guides take great delight in pointing out the hole in the rear wall that they insist was "the Queen's shitting place" – scatological conjecture perhaps, but the channels next to it do seem to lead from ruined reservoirs on the hill above.

Khandagiri

The caves on the opposite hill, **Khandagiri**, can be reached either by the long flight of steps leading from the road, just up from the main entrance to the Udaigiri caves, or else by cutting directly across from Hathi Gumpha via the steps that drop down from cave seventeen. The latter route brings you out at caves **one** and **two**, known as the "Parrot Caves" for the carvings of birds on their doorway-arches. Cave two, excavated in the first century BC, is the larger and more interesting. On the back wall of one of its cells, a few faint lines in red *brahmini* script are thought to have been scrawled two thousand years ago by a monk practising his handwriting. The reliefs in cave **three**, the Ananta Gumpha or "Snake Cave" – named after the serpents decorating the door-ways – contain the best of the sculpture on Khandagiri hill, albeit badly vandalized in places. Caves **seven** and **eight**, just left of the main steps, were former sleeping quarters, remodelled in the eleventh century as sanctuaries. Both house reliefs of *tirthankaras* on their walls as well as Hindu deities which had, by the time conversion work was done here, become part of the Jain pantheon. Cave **nine**, the last of any real note, was also reconverted in medieval times. It too contains *tirthankaras*, though only the three standing images of Rishabanatha (in black chlorite stone) are any good.

The best place to wind up a visit to Khandagiri is the modern **Jain temple** at the top of the hill. Aside from some old *tirthankaras* in the shrine room, the building itself, erected during the nineteenth century on the site of a much earlier structure, is rather less inspiring than the **view** across the plains from its terrace. The Jain monks who lived here would have been able to look out over the ancient city at Sisupalgarh, 9km southeast, on which they depended for alms. Today, the ruins are upstaged by the white peace pagoda at Dhauli and by the Lingaraj temple – Bhubaneshwar's most prominent feature, despite competition from an unsightly water-tower nearby.

Nandankanan Botanical Gardens and Zoo

April–Sept, Tues–Sun 7am–6pm; Oct–March, Tues–Sun 7.30am–5pm.

Set amid the open grassland and natural forest on the banks of Kanjia Lake, 20km north of Bhubaneshwar, is **Nandankandan** ("Garden of Pleasure"), India's largest **zoo**. While the enclosures are certainly luxurious and well maintained by Indian standards, wildlife enthusiasts will find the sight of animals in captivity no less depressing here than anywhere else. Kids, however, should enjoy the place enormously. Novelty attractions include a rare albino crocodile and the world's only **white tigers** to have bred successfully in captivity. Apparently, one mated with a wild tigress who scaled the perimeter fence in 1967 and then stayed on to give birth to her cubs. If you get fed up with the zoo, try a trip across the lake by pedalo or rowing boat to the peaceful **botanical gardens**. Failing that, there's always the toy-train ride, to the left of the main entrance, or a popular **lion safari** by minibus around an enormous fifty-acre reserve.

The simplest way to **get to** Nandankanan, apart from the OTDC **tour**, is to catch one of the hourly state transport **buses** from the bus stand in town. Otherwise, it's a pleasant 90-minute trip by **bicycle**, though finding a bike to rent in Bhubaneshwar isn't easy.

Sisupalgarh and Dhauli

Emerging from the ramshackle fringes of southern Bhubaneshwar, the Puri road crosses an old canal, then heads into open farmland towards the confluence of the Bhargubi and Daya rivers. The kilometre-long bank of earth to the left of the road at **SISUPALGARH** is a section of the ramparts that surrounded ancient **Kalinganagara**. Founded by the Kalingas in the fourth century BC, the city is thought to have been the region's capital until it was mysteriously deserted by the Chedis seven hundred years later. These days, all that's left are overgrown fortifications, a couple of gateways and the occasional patch of decaying brickwork – hardly worth getting off a bus to see.

Across the Daya, the stark profile of the Shanti Stupa at **DHAULI**, standing on top of a lone sandstone outcrop like something out of a Spielberg movie, is the flat riverine countryside's most dominant feature. The *stupa* overlooks the spot where the Mauryan emperor **Ashok** defeated the Kalingas in the decisive battle of 265 BC. Apart from bringing the prosperous Orissan kingdom to its knees, the victory also led the emperor, allegedly overcome by remorse at having slain 150,000 people, to renounce the path of violent conquest in favour of the spiritual one preached by Gautama Buddha. Thereafter, he set about promoting the maxims of his new-found faith in **rock edicts** installed at key sites around the empire (see *Contexts*). One such inscription, in ancient **Brahmi**, the ancestor of all non-Islamic Indian scripts, still stands on the roadside at the foot of Dhauli hill. A translation erected by the ASI nearby gives some idea of its contents: a typically colourful mixture of rambling philosophical asides, discourses on animal rights and tips on how to treat your slaves. The Dhauli edict also includes the famous "All men are my children . . ." line, but diplomatically omits the account that crops up elsewhere describing how many poor Kalingas Ashok had to put to the sword before he finally "saw the light".

Carved out of the rock directly above the inscription is a very life-like, frontal view of an **elephant**. Among the oldest of its kind on the subcontinent, the sculpture is thought to represent *dharma*, Ashok's name for Buddhism, and was probably placed here to announce the location of the edict to passersby. Nowadays, the gleaming white **Shanti Stupa** on top of Dhauli Hill does a much better job. Built by an order of Japanese Buddhists in 1972, the "peace pagoda" stands as a memorial both to the battle that prompted Ashok's legendary change of heart and to the zealous dissemination of *dharma* across Asia that ensued. Panels around the sides illustrate episodes from the life of the emperor (below) and the Buddha (above), while the umbrella-like projections on the top symbolize the five cardinal Buddhist virtues of faith, hope, compassion, forgiveness and non-violence. Alongside the *stupa*, somewhat eclipsed by its futuristic neighbour, there's also a recently renovated Shiva temple – the **Dhabaleshwara Mandir**. From the terrace on top of Dhauligiri, the **views** over the surrounding geometrically patterned rice fields are serene. Arrive here early enough and you might just catch the last of the morning mist hanging over the tiny hamlets and gently meandering water courses that line the bend in the River Daya nearby.

Getting to Dhauli

If you don't have your own vehicle and are not on a tour, **getting to Dhauli** involves a bit of a walk. Ask to be dropped off the bus at **Dhauli Chowk**, the junction on the main Puri–Bhubaneshwar road, and make your way along the avenue of cashew trees to the rock-edict. The road to the *stupa* begins its short climb up the hill here, ending at a small car-park surrounded by postcard and *chai* stalls – two kilometres in all.

Pipli

Fifteen minutes or so beyond Dhauli on the Puri road, splashes of bright colour in the shop fronts ranged alongside the main street announce your arrival in **PIPLI**, Orissa's

appliqué capital (see p.871). Much of what the artisans produce here nowadays on their hand-powered sewing machines is shoddy kitsch compared with the painstaking work traditionally undertaken for the Jagannath temple. Express enough interest, though, and you'll be shown some of the better-quality pieces for which Pipli is justly famed. Bedspreads, wall-hangings and small awnings, or *chhatris*, normally hung above household and temple shrines, are about the most authentic goods on offer – though who's to say Lord Jagannath doesn't use napkins.

Puri

A true-hearted pilgrim does not fear to measure kingdoms with his feeble footsteps.

Old Hindu saying

Whenever you approach the Orissan coast through its hinterland of lush green palm-groves and paddy fields, it's hard not to feel a sense of expectation. Never is this more true than upon arrival at **PURI** – the state's premier temple town and tourist resort. As the site of the famous **Jagannath temple** – which soars out of the narrow packed streets and colonial suburbs like some kind of misplaced space rocket – as well as the location of one of India's most spectacular religious festivals, the annual **Rath Yatra**, Puri has been attracting visitors in their thousands since long before the hippy trail found its way here in the early 1970s.

Three distinct contingents come to Puri: middle-class Bengalis lured by the combined pleasures of the promenade and a *puja* in the nearby temple; young western and Japanese visitors, for whom Puri's small **travellers' scene** offers a sociable retreat from the travails of exploring India; and the thousands of pilgrims who flock in every day to see Lord Jagannath. Over the years the three have staked out their respective ends of town and stuck to them. It all makes for a rather bizarre, but not unpleasant atmosphere, where you can be transported from the maelstrom of religious devotion, to the sea, and back again to the relative calm of your hotel verandah at the turn of a bicycle wheel.

History

The early history of Puri before its rise to prominence as a Hindu religious centre is rather obscure. It's known that the surrounding forests were once the territory of the Sabaras, a pre-Aryan group, and that the sacred Buddhist site of **Dantapura** ("Town of the Tooth"), where one of the Buddha's teeth was enshrined, may also have been here, but few traces of these ancient times have survived.

Until the seventh and eighth centuries Puri was little more than a provincial outpost along the coastal trade route linking eastern India with the south. Then, thanks to its association with the Hindu reformer **Shankaracharya**, the town began to feature on the religious map. Shankara made Puri one of his four *mathas*, or centres for the practice of a radically new, and more ascetic form of Hinduism. Holy men from across the whole subcontinent came here to debate the new philosophies – a tradition carried on in the town's temple courtyards to this day. With the arrival of the **Gangas** at the beginning of the twelfth century this religious and political importance was further consolidated. In 1135 Anantavarman Chodaganga founded the great temple in Puri, and dedicated it to **Purushottama**, one of the thousand names of Vishnu – an ambitious attempt to integrate the many feudal kingdoms recently conquered by the Gangas. Under the Gajapati dynasty in the fifteenth century Purushottama's name changed to Jagannath, "Lord of the Universe". Henceforth **Vishnaivism** and the devotional

---

The telephone **area code** for Puri is ☎06752.

worship of Krishna, an incarnation of Vishnu, was to hold sway as the predominant religious influence in the temple. Puri is nowadays one of the four most auspicious pilgrimage centres, or *Dhams*, in India. It's impossible to estimate the exact number of people who travel here each year, but in high season as many as five thousand pour daily through the bus and train stations, while during the annual Rath Yatra or "Car Festival", the population temporarily swells to nearly a million.

By comparison, western-style leisure **tourism**, centred firmly on the town's long sandy beach, is a new phenomenon. The British were the first to spot Puri's potential as a resort. When they left, the Bengalis took over their bungalows, only to find themselves sharing the beach with an annual migration of young, *chillum*-smoking western-ers attracted to the town by its freely available hashish. Today, few vestiges of this era remain. Thanks to a concerted campaign by the municipality to clean up Puri's image, the "scene" has dwindled to little more than a handful of rather dismal cafes, and is a far cry from the swinging hippy paradise some still arrive here hoping to find.

Arrival and information

The none-too-welcome sight of rickshaw *wallahs* sprinting alongside incoming **buses** to grab a fare is most visitors' first experience of Puri. This little ritual takes place at the Hospital Road–Grand Avenue crossroads, close to the Jagannath temple in the heart of town, where buses drop their passengers before heading off to the main bus stand, a mile or so east. Get off here and brave the melee – it's closer to the hotel district. Arriving by **train** is marginally more sedate. Puri's end-of-the-line railway station lies on the eastern edge of town, again a short ride from the beach and the hotels.

Puri is reasonably compact and flat, so **cycle rickshaws** are the best way to **get around**, at least when you first arrive – once you've got your bearings, you can rent a **bicycle** from any of the numerous stalls in the travellers' enclave. **Auto-rickshaws** are thin on the ground, though one or two are always hanging around the railway station. Keep an eye out too for **Enfield motorcycles**, rented out by a couple of travel agents for full or half days and useful for trips up the coast to Konarak. In-house **travel agents** at the larger hotels can help with all transport arrangements, though the most reliable all-round place for ticket booking, flights, car/motorcycle/bike rental and so on is *Heritage Tours*, currently based at the *Mayfair Beach Resort* (☎3656).

Information

Unless you collect outdated leaflets on Orissa, the OTDC **tourist office** (Mon–Sat 10am–5pm; ☎3464) on Station Road and the 24-hour counter at the railway station are a waste of time. Travel arrangements are best made or checked directly with the station itself or else through a travel agent (see listings).

Puri's main **post office** is on Temple Rd (Mon–Fri 10am–5pm, Sat 10am–noon); for poste restante, use the side door on the left side of the building. If you need to **change money**, the *State Bank of India* (Mon–Fri 10am–2pm, Sat 10am–noon, Sun 11.30am–1.30pm) is on Dig Barani Chowk, just up the road from the *Ashok Hotel*.

The Jagannath temple

The mighty **Jagannath temple** in Puri is for Hindus one of the four holy *Dhams*, or "Abodes of the Divine". Every year millions of pilgrims, or *yatris*, make their way here to spend three auspicious days and nights near Lord Jagannath, the presiding deity. Non-Hindu visitors, obliged despite the temple's long-standing "caste no bar" rule to observe proceedings from a nearby roof-top, will find the spectacle of the gigantic tower and surrounding compound thronging with devotees absolutely extraordinary.

PURI

△ Bhubaneshwar 60km △ Konark 33km

HOTELS:
- **A** Nilachal Ashok
- **B** OTDC Panthaniwas
- **C** Mayfair
- **D** Vijoya International
- **E** Youth Hostel
- **F** South East Railway
- **G** Holiday Resort
- **H** Love & Life
- **I** Dreamland Cottage
- **J** Ghandara
- **K** Paul International
- **L** Sea Foam
- **M** Shankar International
- **N** Holiday Inn
- **O** Travellers' Inn
- **P** Z

RESTAURANTS:
- **1** Chung Wah
- **2** Brady's
- **3** Peace
- **4** Harry's
- **5** Mickey Mouse

Markandeswara Tank

Jagannath Temple

Narendra Sagar

Hospital

Police Station

Raghunandan Library

Gundicha Ghar

Bus Stand

GARANTI RD

LOCKNATH RD

AKHRA NALA RD

GRAND AVENUE

HOSPITAL ROAD

TEMPLE RD

VIP RD

GPO

Utkalika Emporium

Chandra Bose Statue

State Bank of India

Puri Hotel

GOPAL BALLABH RD

DIG BARANI CHOWK

HARE KRSHNA RD

MARINE PARADE

SWARGADWAR RD

Municipal Park

Sudarshan Workshop

OTDC ℹ

STATION RD

ARMSTRONG RD

Railway Station

Hanuman Temple

Peter's Pan Shop

Chakra Tirtha Temple

CHAKRA TIRTHA (CT) RD

Bay of Bengal

N

0   200 m

The present structure, modelled on the older Lingaraj temple in Bhubaneshwar, was erected by the Ganga ruler Anantavarman Chodaganga, at the start of the twelfth century. The best place to see it from is the flat roof of the **Raghunandan Library** (Mon–Sat 10am–noon & 4–8pm) directly opposite the main gate. One of the librarians, wielding a long stick to fend off the monkeys, will show you up the stairs via their collection of dusty tomes and **palm-leaf manuscripts**, to the vantage point overlooking the East Gate. From here you have a fine view of the immense **sanctuary tower** (*deul*), at sixty-five metres by far the loftiest building in the entire region. To the Dutch sailors passing the Orissan coast three hundred or more years ago the tower was known as "the White Pagoda". More recently, archeologists chipping away at its distinctively plastered surface have begun to expose elaborate **carving** simular to that on the Lingaraj. The work being carried out at present is intended to restore this sculpture to its original state. Crowning the very top, a long scarlet pennant and the eight-spoked wheel(*chakra*) of Vishnu announce the presence of Lord Jagannath within.

In imitation of a ridge of mountain peaks, the pyramidal roofs of the temples' adjoining halls, or *mandapas*, rise in steps toward the tower. The one nearest the sanctuary, the *jagamohana* (assembly hall), is part of the original building, but the other two, the smaller *nata mandir* (dance hall) and the *bhoga-mandapa* (hall of offerings) nearest the entrance, were added in the fifteenth and sixteenth centuries. These halls still see a lot of action during the day as worshippers file through for *darshan*, while late every night they become the venue for devotional music and dance performances. Women and transvestite dancers (*maharis* and *gotipuras*) perform episodes for the amusement of the Lord Jagannath and his "brother" and "sister" from Jayadev's *Gita Govinda*, the much-loved story of the life of Krishna.

Outside the main building, in the walled compound surrounding the temple, stand dozens of subsidiary shrines that the pilgrims are supposed to honour during their visit. Nearby, on the left of the enclosure, are the **kitchens**. The food prepared here, known as *mahaprashad*, is blessed by Lord Jagannath himself before being eaten. It's said to be so pure that even a morsel of rice taken from the mouth of a dog and fed to a *brahmin* by a *harijan* (an "untouchable") will cleanse the body of sin. Among the ten thousand or so daily recipients of the *mahaprashad* are the six thousand employees of the temple itself. These **servants** are divided into ninety-six hereditary and hierarchical orders known as *chhatisha niyoga*, and include the priests who minister to the

---

PANDAS

Few non-Hindu visitors to Puri are aware of the world of the **yatri panda**, or pilgrimage priests. The *panda*'s job is basically to "look after" the pilgrims during their stay: to fix them up with board and lodging, to make sure they take in all the sites in the correct order, and, as *brahmins*, to offer prayers for them at the temple. In return, the pilgrims are expected to leave a generous goodbye tip, or **bidagi**, when they leave. Apart from bringing "good luck" in the next life, the *bidagi* system is also, needless to say, highly lucrative for the *pandas*.

No surprise then that each one, and the *dharamshalas* to which they are connected, has his own exclusive rights to the rich pickings. Every town and village in the country is carved up according to long-established links recorded in special **ledgers**. The first thing the *pandas* have to ascertain from the new arrivals therefore, is their place of birth, family name and caste. Once these are established, the pilgrims are ushered from the station back to the appropriate *dharamshala* and shown the records of visits made by previous generations from their village or family. Woe betide anyone who tries to poach clients either. When they're not relieving hapless *yatris* of their *rupees* or indulging in that time-honoured Puri tradition of drinking *bhangas* (a sugar and milk-based preparation containing ground cannabis leaves), *pandas* spend their days **wrestling** in Puri's old-style gyms.

THE JAGANNATH DEITIES AND RATH YATRA

Stand on any street corner in Orissa and you'd be hard pushed not to spot at least one image of the black-faced **Jagannath deity**, with his brother **Balabhadra** and sister **Subhadra**. This faintly grotesque family trio, with glaring eyes, stumpy legless bodies, and undersized arms protruding menacingly from heavily garlanded heads, seems to crop up everywhere – from buses and cycle *rickshaws*, to *beedee* wrappers and bags of nuts.

The origins of this peculiar national symbol are shrouded in **legend**. One version relates that the image of Lord Jagannath looks the way it does because it was never actually finished. King Indramena, a ruler of ancient Orissa, once found the god Vishnu in the form of a tree stump washed up on Puri beach. After performing all the necessary prostrations, he carried the lump of wood to the temple and, following instructions from Brahma, called the court carpenter Visvakarma to carve out the image. Visvakarma agreed to perform the task on condition that no-one so much as set eyes on the deity until it was completed. The King, however, unable to contain his excitement, peeped through a crack in the door of the carpenter's workshop during the night to see how the job was progressing. Visvakarma spotted him, downed tools just as he had promised and cast a spell on the deity so that no-one else could finish it.

These days, new versions have to be produced about every twelve years (they rot in the humidity) by specially trained temple priests in a sacred ceremony known as **Nava Kalebara**, literally "new embodiment". The culmination of highly secret, nocturnal ritual takes place when the "divine essence" of the old Lord Jagannath is removed from his hollowed-out chest and placed inside that of the new incumbent.

The Jagannath deities are also the chief focus of Puri's annual "Car Festival", the **Rath Yatra**. For a couple of weeks in midsummer, the town is saturated with visitors who come to witness the procession of the colossal Jagannath chariots, or *raths*, down Puri's Grand Avenue. Rath Yatra is just one episode in a long cycle of rituals that begins in the full moon phase of the Oriya month of Djesto (June/July). In the first of these, the **Chandan Yatra**, special replicas of the three temple deities are taken to the **Narendra Tank** where for twenty-one consecutive days they are smeared with *chandan* (sandalwood paste) and rowed around in a ceremonial, swan-shaped boat. At the end of this period, in a ceremony known as **Snana Yatra**, the three go for a dip in the tank, after which they head off for fifteen days of secluded preparation for Rath Yatra.

The Car Festival proper takes place during the full moon of the following month, Asadho (July/Aug). Lord Jagannath and his brother and sister are placed in their chariots and dragged by 4200 honoured devotees through the assembled multitudes to their summer home, the **Gundicha Ghar** ("Garden House"), a mile away. If you can find a secure vantage point and escape the crush, it's an amazing sight. The immense chariots are draped with brightly coloured cloth and accompanied down Grand Avenue by elephants, the local Raja (who sweeps the chariots as a gesture of humility and equality with all castes), and a cacophony of music and percussion. Each has a different name and a different colour cover, and is built anew every year to rigid specifications laid down in the temple's ancient manuals. Balabhadra's *rath*, the green one, leads; Subhadra is next, in black; and lastly, in the thirteen-metre-tall chariot with eighteen wheels and a vivid red and yellow drape, sits Lord Jagannath himself. It takes eight hours or more to haul the *raths* to their resting place. Then, after a nine-day holiday, the sequence is performed in reverse, and the three deities return to the temple to resume their normal lives.

Conventional wisdom has it that the procession commemorates Krishna's journey from Gokhul to Matheran; historians cite the similarity between the *raths* and temple towers to claim it's a hangover from the time when temples were made of wood. Whatever the reason for the Car Festival, its devotees take it very seriously indeed. Early travellers spoke of fanatics throwing themselves under the gigantic wheels as a short cut to eternal bliss (whence the English word **"Juggernaut"**, meaning an "irresistible, destructive force"). Contemporary enthusiasts are marginally more restrained, but like most mass gatherings in India the whole event teeters at times on the brink of complete mayhem.

needs of the deities (teeth cleaning, dressing, feeding, getting them ready for after-noon siesta, and so forth), as well as the teams of craftspeople who produce all the materials required for the daily round of rituals.

A good place to sample the atmosphere of the temple is in front of its main (East) Gate. The elaborate doorway is usually jammed with groups of *yatris*, some newly alighted from special buses, others making their way barefoot through the crowds from the nearby *dharamshalas* where they put up during their stay in Puri. In front of the gateway, its base splashed with vermillion and flowers, is a **column** that once stood before the Surya temple in Konarak. It was brought here in the eighteenth century by the Maharathas and is topped by a figure of Aruna, the charioteer of the sun god.

Around the Temple

The crowded streets **around the Jagannath temple** are buzzing with activity – commercial as much as religious. **Grand Avenue**, Puri's broad main street, is lined with a frenetic **bazaar**, many of its stalls specializing in *rudrat* and sandalwood beads, Ayurvedic cures and the ubiquitous images of Lord Jagannath. Look out too for the wonderful "religious maps" of Puri. Hindu mythology traditionally represents the pilgrimage site in the form of a conch-shell made up of seven concentric layers, with the deities' platform as the innermost core and the outer third under the sea. The maps may not be much help for finding your way around, but they make good souvenirs.

Leading south from the main square, the dingy **Swargadwar** ("Cremation") **Road** plunges you into a world of acrid smells, tea stalls and heaps of oily sweets swarming with flies. For most of the day the entire length of the lane is lined with beggars sitting in front of rice and ten-*paise* coins tossed by passing pilgrims. You're also likely to see bare-chested *brahmins* from the temple performing their ablutions, sacred threads tucked safely over their ears to preserve purity (the ear is the purest part of the body in Hinduism, being associated with the source of the Ganges). Keep going down Swargadwar Road for long enough and you eventually surface to the glaring sunshine and sea-breezes of the main promenade. The cremation ground itself, situated well beyond the south corner of the beach, is among India's most auspicious mortuary sites. Inquisitive tourists, especially those wielding cameras, are definitely not welcome.

A more enjoyable foray from the main square is the trip up to the **sacred tanks** in the north of town (best attempted on bicycles). Follow the north wall of the Jagannath temple up to the little road junction in the far corner, then turn right and stick to the same narrow twisting backstreet for about five minutes until you arrive at the **Markandesvara tank**. This large, steep-sided bathing place is said to have been the spot where Vishnu once resided in the form of a *neem* tree, while his temple, the precursor of the current one in Puri, was buried deep under a sand-dune. There's no sign of the tree, but the temples on the south side are worth a look, particularly the smaller of the group which contains images of the Jagannath trio.

If you retrace your route from here back down the lane as far as the first road junc-tion, then bear left and continue another mile or so, you'll emerge at the **Narendra Sagar** – Puri's most holy tank. In the middle stands a small temple, joined to the *ghats* by a narrow footbridge. During the annual **Chandan Yatra**, or "Swimming Festival", a replica deity of Lord Jagannath, Mandan Mohan, is brought here every day for his dip. The temple itself is plastered with vivid **murals** that you can photograph on payment of the set fee listed nearby. The list also advertises the range of services offered by the temple *pujaris*, including the unlikely sounding "Throw of Bone" and "Throw of Hair" – references to the tank's role as another one of Puri's famous mortuary ritual sites.

Museum and Sudarshan workshop

Puri's small **museum** (Tues–Sun 10am–5pm), tucked away above the tourist office on Station Road, houses tacky reproductions of the Jagannath deities' ceremonial garb, along with scale models of the *raths* used in the Car Festival. You won't find much information here, but the handful of items on display are clearly labelled and accompanied by lots of photographs.

Further down the road towards the station, close to the Shinto shrine, the **Sudarshan workshop** is one of the few traditional stone carvers' yards left in Puri. For once, the sculptors and their apprentices seem more interested in pursuing their art than selling it to tourists, but gladly point potential customers in the direction of the factory **shop** next door. Most of the pieces here are large religious icons beautifully carved out of khondalite – the multi-coloured stone used in the Sun temple at Konarak.

The beach

If a peaceful swim and a lie in the sun are your top priorities, you may be disappointed with **Puri beach**. It's not just the constant stream of hawkers that's the problem. Thanks to a combination of an open **sewer** trickling into the sea slap in the middle of the beach, and a stiff on-shore breeze to spread the contents around the shallows, bathing, at least along certain stretches, can be something of a health risk. So long as you keep to the area south of the *Mayfair Hotel*, well away from the outlet, you should be fine.

Pollution aside, Puri's strand makes an excellent place for a stroll. The bottom end is traditionally the preserve of Calcutta's salary men and their families. While the higher-ranking among them enjoy the use of company bungalows in the suburbs, the majority squeeze into rooms on the beach-front hotels overlooking the promenade – with its knick-knack stalls and cafes, faintly reminiscent of a shabby British seaside resort.

Local fishermen patrol the beach as **lifeguards**; recognizable more by their triangular straw hats and *dhotis* than their strapping physiques, they wade with their punters into the surf and literally hold their hands to keep them on their feet. This may seem a little excessive to anyone used to choppier water, but the **undertow** claims victims every year, so weak swimmers should be careful. When not saving lives, the fishermen are busy at the other end of the beach, engaged in the more traditional industries of mending nets and boats. The **fishing village** is one of the biggest in Orissa, with dozens of tiny triangular sails tacking to and fro off the coast during the day. Once landed, the catch is transferred to baskets for women to carry to the **fish market** in the village, and the heavy collapsible boats are split in two and dragged up the beach. The best time to see all this is around dawn, when the sight of the little fleet putting out towards the sun rising over the sea can make Puri seem truly exotic after all.

Accommodation

Virtually all Puri's **hotels** stand on or near the beach – a five-minute ride from the train station through the bumpy back streets. A strict distinction is observed between hotels pitched at domestic tourists – lined up behind the promenade, Marine Drive, on the west end of the beach – and those oriented towards budget-conscious westerners, sandwiched further east between the high-rise, upmarket resort hotels and the fishing *bastee*. This latter district around Chakratirtha (CT) Rd, known as **Pentakunta**, has become a real tourist enclave, and for many foreign visitors counts as Puri's main attraction. Literally dozens of places are tucked away down lookalike sandy lanes, most offering basic concrete-walled rooms, some dorm beds, lockers, fans and hot water. If you find the smaller lodges too cramped, the slightly decaying colonial buildings on the main street tends to be more comfortable. Many have wide verandahs, balconies, and courtyards full of potted plants, where you can relax during the hot afternoons.

The less expensive hotels are quiet during the summer months, but the **pricier accommodation** tends to be booked solid well in advance over Rath Yatra, which coincides with the Bengali holiday season – make your reservations as early as possible.

Inexpensive

Dreamland Cottage, off CT Rd (☎4122). Not exactly roses around the door, but homely and relaxed with a leafy, secluded garden. ①.

Ghandara International, CT Rd (☎4117). Considerately managed for the budget traveller, with rock-bottom, clean rooms around a courtyard, roof space, lock-up, generator, free washing machine and drinking water in the fridge. Some dorm beds. Excellent value. ①.

Love and Life, CT Rd (☎2513). Very popular with the many young Japanese visitors to Puri. Easy-going atmosphere, relaxing garden and a good restaurant. ②.

Paul International, CT Rd. Spacious, airy double rooms overlooking the street. Hardly a bargain though. ③.

Sea Foam, CT Rd (☎3226). Another old favourite, offering very basic creature comforts including hot water and safe deposit. A new extension promises more of the same with less grime. ②.

Traveller's Lodge, CT Rd. Cells with no common space. Nothing special, but clean enough and inexpensive. ①–②.

Youth Hostel, off CT Rd. Stuffy, segregated dorms and a 10pm curfew. Not a place to hang around during the evenings, but cheap and convenient if everywhere else is full. ①.

Z, CT Rd (☎2554). Now something of an institution, the "Z" (pronounced *jed*) made its name for providing inexpensive, clean and comfortable rooms in congenial surroundings. The prices have been hiked accordingly, but the rooms are still pleasant and there's a common room with scatter cushions and satellite TV. Some dorm beds. ①–②.

Moderate and Expensive

Holiday Inn, CT Rd (☎3782). Clinical but comfortable western-style hotel with simple, pleasant rooms, some overlooking the beach. ④.

Holiday Resort, CT Rd (☎2440). A monstrous and anonymous edifice. Ultra-modern with all the trimmings, including *Star TV* and foreign exchange. ④–⑦.

Mayfair Beach Resort, CT Rd (☎4041). Puri's newest and most fashionable hotel. Luxury chalets, backing on to a pool and the beach. Five-star facilities, excellent restaurant. Recommended. ⑧.

Nilachal Ashok, Raj Bhavan, VIP Rd (☎3639). Typically austere modern building set in its own grounds. Formulaic furnishings, now a touch jaded. All the usual comforts, except satellite TV. ⑦.

OTDC Panthaniwas, off CT Rd (☎2562). Impersonal hotel, where some of the plain but spacious rooms catch sea breezes, some are a/c. Bar, restaurant and coffee shop. Good value. ③–④.

Shankar International, CT Rd (☎2696). Slightly old-fashioned, though well-run, with rooms at assorted prices on three floors, sea views and a lawn with wicker chairs. ③–④.

South East Railway Hotel, CT Rd (☎2063). Turbaned bearers with big belts pad barefoot around the verandahs. Nothing has changed here since it was the premier bolt-hole for Calcutta's *burra-* and *mem-sahibs*. A must for Raj-ophiles. ⑥–⑦.

Toshali Sands, Konarak Rd (☎2888). Self-styled "ethnic village" 9km north of town. Cottages grouped around a garden and pool, with good restaurant, gym and sauna. Ideal for families. ⑧.

Vijoya International, CT Rd (☎2702). Another faceless giant, with all the usual facilities including central a/c, exchange, restaurant and "unending comforts". Also direct access to the beach. ④–⑥.

Eating

Inexpensive eating options around Pentakunta are limited to the handful of cafes along CT Road, most of which are of the "write your own order" ilk and seem to be staffed by twelve-year-olds. The food they dish up rarely amounts to anything more exciting than copious bland platefuls with a western bias – though the Chinese and Indian dishes are sometimes passable. In season, fresh **seafood** features prominently, as do puddings steeped in that great Indian-English tedium reliever, known here as "caustered".

Better food is to be found in the restaurants at the nearby resort hotels. Most serve a reasonable range of veg and non-veg Indian dishes, including fish, with a few Chinese alternatives thrown in for form. After the rough-and-ready style of the CT Road coffee houses, the middle-class Bengali atmosphere in these places can seem rather stilted.

Brady's, CT Rd. A good meeting place, with standard budget travellers' menu.

Chung Wah, Armstrong Rd, off Marine Drive. Hard to find, but worth the effort. Popular, family-run restaurant serving authentic and inexpensive Chinese food.

Harry's, CT Rd. The most popular place for a budget breakfast. Opens early.

Holiday Inn, CT Rd. Characterless surroundings, but the mostly Indian food is carefully prepared, delicious and not too pricey.

Holiday Resort, CT Rd. Classy a/c restaurant in the basement of a large hotel. The upmarket western decor is much less appealing than the food, which includes superb Bengali *thalis* (lunchtimes only). Fairly expensive, but not prohibitively so.

Love and Life, CT Rd. In addition to the staple travellers' favourites, this recently renovated roadside joint serves more costly Japanese dishes with an accent on fresh fish.

Mayfair, CT Rd. Sophisticated and expensive. A top-class resident Chinese chef and an unusually adventurous menu make this the best place for an extravagant evening away from *dal* and rice.

Mickey Mouse, CT Rd. The loudest music and the most original lampshades. Very laid-back service too, though chess sets are considerably provided.

Om, *Shankar International*, CT Rd. Small, unpretentious restaurant serving all the usual stuff at reasonable prices.

MOVING ON FROM PURI

Puri is joined to the main Calcutta–Madras routes by a branch line of the busy South East Railway network and a good metalled road through Bhubaneshwar, so it's well connected with most other major Indian cities. Travel agents at major hotels, especially the *Mayfair Beach Resort*, can book tickets.

By train

A couple of direct express trains take 32–36hr to link Puri with **Delhi**, some calling at **Varanasi** and **Agra** en route. Avoid the evening *Kalinga–Utkal Express*; it's much slower and frequently late. The quickest and most convenient train to **Calcutta** is the *Jagannath Express* #8410, which leaves Puri at 9.10pm for the 11-hour overnight trip.

If you're heading for **South India**, either pass through Bhubaneshwar or change at Khurda Road, 44km from Puri, to pick up daily trains to **Madras** (22hr). Two of these (*Howrah/Guwahati–Bangalore Express* #2611/2674) carry on to Bangalore on Wed and Thurs, while on Fri, Sat, Sun and Mon there's a direct service to Kochi. On Tues you can even go all the way to Thiruvananthapuram on the *Guwahati–Trivandrum Express* #2602.

Getting to **Bombay** is slightly trickier. First, you have to take the Delhi train as far as Kharagpur junction, just north of the Orissa border, then wait four and a half hours for the *Bombay Mail* coming from Calcutta. The total travelling time, all being well, is 46hr 30min. For **Central Indian** destinations such as Jabalpur or Nagpur, take the *Kalinga–Utkal Express* #8477 as far as Bilaspur and change there.

Computerized reservations can be made at the main station or, for second class tickets only, at the city booking office on Grand Avenue (opposite the police station).

By bus

Minibuses are definitely the easiest way to travel between Puri and **Bhubaneshwar**. Services are fast (1hr) and frequent until 5pm, but make sure that it's "non-stop" before you get on. The same applies to **Konarak** buses, which also leave more or less hourly from the main city bus stand in the east of town, near the Gundicha Ghar.

If you plan to head south by road along the Orissan coast, OTDC run a direct, non-stop "luxury" coach to the *Panthaniwas* at Balugaon on **Chilka Lake**. It leaves from the Puri *Panthaniwas* on Mon, Wed and Fri mornings, and costs Rs80.

South East Railway Hotel, CT Rd. Non-residents can sample the hotel's idiosyncratic colonial charm in its restaurant (with a couple of hours' advance warning). Checked table cloths, silver butter dishes and waiters in *pukka* turbans and belts. The poor-value set menus are less memorable.

Peace, CT Rd. Unremarkable if inexpensive food, served to an exclusively international clientele. Currently the most popular of the batch.

Listings

Medical Help Puri's main "HQ" hospital (☎2062) is well outside the town centre. Hotels such as the *Panthaniwas*, or *Heritage Tours* at the *Mayfair*, can help find a doctor in an emergency.

Shopping *Utkalika* and the other handloom emporiums, just up from the GPO on Temple Rd, stock a good range of local handicrafts at fixed prices. *Surdarshan* on Station Rd (close to the OTDC tourist office) is the best place to buy traditional stone sculpture. *Holiday Inn* and *Brady's* cafe have some jewellery, textiles and filigree, but are not the cheapest places in town. For reproductions of the Jagannath deity look in the bazaar around the temple.

Telephone An STD/IST phone at *Hotel Ghandara* on CT Rd is open for non-residents.

Tours OTDC run tour buses from in front of the *Panthaniwas* to nearby attractions including **Bhubaneshwar** and environs (Rs70), and **Chilka Lake** (Mon, Wed & Fri; Rs80).

Konarak

> *Time runs like a horse with seven reins,*
> *Thousand-eyed, unageing, possessing much seed.*
> *Him the poets mount; His wheels are all beings.*
> The *Artharva Veda*

If you visit only one temple in Orissa, it should be **KONARAK**. Standing imperiously in its compound of lawns and casuarina trees, 35km north of Puri on the coast road, this majestic pile of oxidizing sandstone is considered to be the apogee of Orissan architecture and one of the finest religious buildings anywhere in the world.

The temple is all the more remarkable for having languished under a huge mound of sand since it fell into neglect three hundred or so years ago. Not until early this century, when the dune and heaps of collapsed masonry were cleared away from the sides, did the full extent of its ambitious design become apparent. A team of seven galloping horses and twenty-four exquisitely carved wheels found lining the flanks of a raised platform showed that the temple had been conceived in the form of a colossal chariot for the sun god **Surya**, its presiding deity. Equally as sensational was the rediscovery among the ruins of some extraordinary **erotic sculpture**. Konarak, like Khajuraho (see p.360), is plastered with loving couples locked in ingenious amatory postures drawn from the *Kama Sutra* – a feature that may well explain the comment made by one of Akbar's emissaries, Abdul Fazl, in the sixteenth century: "Even those who are difficult to please," he enthused, "stand astonished at its sight."

Apart from the temple, a small **museum** and a fishing **beach**, Konarak **village** has little going for it. In recent years, cafes and hotels have mushroomed around its dusty bus stand to service the stream of coach parties that buzz in and out during the day. The crowds of daytrippers clambering over the ruins in their best silk *saris* and shirtings can be a diverting side-show, but Sundays and public holidays in particular are best avoided if you're hoping for some peace and quiet. In any case, aim to be around at sunset after most of the tour groups have left, when the rich evening light works wonders on the natural colours in the khondalite sandstone.

History

In common with all important temples, Konarak has its own popular **origin myth**. Samba, one of Krishna's sons, was once caught spying on his step-mothers while they were bathing in the river. Enraged by his son's prurience, Krishna is said to have cursed Samba with leprosy and expelled him from the palace. Twelve years of penances later, Surya (who doubles up as the divine healer of skin complaints) took pity on the boy and cured him of the disease, in return for which Samba built a temple dedicated to the sun god nearby.

History, as ever, has a different version of events. Inscription plates attribute the founding of the temple to the thirteenth-century Ganga monarch **Narashimadeva**, possibly to commemorate his military successes against the Muslim invaders. The mighty sun temple, with its 70-metre tower, was a landmark for European mariners sailing off the shallow Orissan coast (who knew it as the **"Black Pagoda"**; see p.859) as well as an obvious target for raids on the region. In the fifteenth century Konarak was sacked by the Yavana army. Though unable to raze the temple or destroy its deity, which had been smuggled away by the priests to Puri, the marauding Muslims nevertheless managed to damage it sufficiently to allow the elements get a foothold. As the sea receded, sand slowly engulfed the building and salty breezes set to work on the spongy khondalite, eroding the exposed surfaces and weakening the superstructure. By the end of the nineteenth century, the tower had disintegrated completely, and the porch lay buried up to its waist, prompting one art historian of the day to describe it as " an enormous mass of stones studded with a few peepal trees here and there".

Restoration work only really began in earnest at the start of this century. After putting an end to the activities of the local Raja, who had been plundering the ruins for masonry and sculpture to use on his own temple, government archeologists set about unearthing the immaculately preserved hidden sections of the building and salvaging what they could from the rest of the rubble. The porch was shored up with rocks and sand, large chunks of the walls were rebuilt, and chemicals applied to the stonework to prevent further deterioration. Finally, trees were planted to shelter the compound from the corrosive winds, and a museum opened to house what sculpture was not shipped off to Delhi, Calcutta and London. Today, Konarak is one of India's most visited ancient monuments, and the flagship of OTDC's bid to promote the region as an alternative to the "golden triangle" of Delhi, Agra and Jaipur.

The temple

The main entrance to the **temple** complex on its eastern, sea-facing side brings you out directly in front of the **bhoga-mandapa**, or "hall of offerings". Ornate carvings of amorous couples, musicians and dancers decorating the sides of its platform and stocky pillars suggest that the now roofless pavilion, which was a later addition to the temple, must originally have been used for ritual dance performances.

To get a sense of the overall scale and design, stroll along the low wall that bounds the south side of the enclosure before you tackle the ruins proper. As a giant model of Surya's war chariot, the temple was intended both as an offering to the Vedic sun god and as a symbol for the passage of time itself – believed to lie in his control. The seven **horses** straining to haul the sun eastwards in the direction of the dawn (only one is still intact) represent the days of the week, while the **wheels** ranged along the base stand for the twelve months. Originally, a **stone pillar** crowned with an image of Aruna, Surya's charioteer, also stood in front of the main door, though this has since been moved to the eastern gateway of the Jagannath temple in Puri.

With the once-lofty **sanctuary tower** now reduced to little more than a clutter of sandstone slabs tumbling from the western wing, the **porch**, or *jagomohana*, has become Konarak's real centrepiece. Its impressive pyramidal roof, rising to a height of 38m, is divided into three tiers by rows of uncannily life-like statues – mostly musicians and dancers serenading the sun god on his passage through the heavens. Among the figures on the bottom platform are a four-headed, six-armed Shiva, garlanded with severed heads and performing the dance of death. Though now blocked up, the huge cubic **interior** of the porch was a marvel of medieval architecture. The original builders ran into problems installing its heavy ornamental ceiling, and had to forge ten-metre iron beams as support – a considerable engineering feat for the time.

Amazingly elaborate **sculpture** embellishes every conceivable nook and cranny of the outside of the porch – and most other parts of the temple – in a bewildering profusion of deities, animals, floral patterns, mythical beasts and aquatic monsters. This is what attracts the majority of visitors to Konarak – above all, the infamous **erotica**. Look at any carved surface for long enough and you're sure to come across a voluptuous maiden striking an alluring pose or a richly bejewelled couple sharing a tender moment. Some of Konarak's most beautiful erotic pieces are to be found in the niches halfway up the walls of the porch, where a keen eye may be able to spot the tell-tale pointed beards of *sadhus*, clearly making the most of a lapse in their vows of chastity. Bawdier scenes also appear in miniature along the sides of the platform and around the two remaining intricate door-frames on the main building – just look for the groups of tittering teenagers. Though sculpture of this kind is not uncommon in India, only rarely does it run to such rampant excesses. Many theories have been advanced over the years to explain the phenomenon. In Konarak's case, it seems likely that the erotic art was meant as a kind of metaphor for the ecstatic bliss experienced by the soul when it fuses with the divine cosmos – a notion central to **tantra** and the related worship of the female principle, **shakti**, which were prevalent throughout medieval Orissa.

Moving clockwise around the temple from the south side of the main staircase, the intricately worked faces of the **platform** are what first grab most people's attention. Check out the detail on the **wheels**, and the extraordinary **friezes** that run in narrow bands above and below them. These depict military processions (inspired by King Narashimadeva's tussles with the Muslims) and hunting scenes, and feature literally thousands of rampaging **elephants**. If you want to keep any children busy for a while, tell them to find the **giraffe** which crops up somewhere on the top frieze (south side) – proof that trade with Africa took place during the thirteenth century.

Once past the porch you arrive at a double staircase that leads up to a shrine containing a **statue of Surya** himself. Carved out of top-quality green chlorite stone, this serene image – one of three around the base of the ruined sanctuary tower – is a real masterpiece. Notice his characteristic tall riding boots and the little figure of Aruna, the charioteer, holding the reins of the seven horses at his feet. The other two statues in the series are also worth a look, if only to compare their facial expressions which, following the progress of the sun around the temple, change from wakefulness in the morning (south) to heavy-eyed weariness at the end of the day (north). Before working your way around the far side of the porch, you can also climb down into the remains of the **sanctum sanctorum** where the deity was once enshrined. At the foot of the western wall there's an altar-like platform covered with carving: the kneeling figure in its central panel is thought to be King Narashimadeva, the donor of the temple.

Elsewhere in the compound

Dotted around the grounds are some other sites of relatively minor importance. The first and largest of the two small **shrines** in the southwest corner, the **Mayadevi temple** (formerly dedicated to Surya's wife, the shadow goddess), is the most interesting. Positioned at the north and south ends of the compound, now occupying their own separate pedestals, are the impressive animal **colossi** that once guarded the entrances to the temple: harnessed elephants to the north and rearing war-horses led by soldiers to the south. The lions that used to flank the eastern gateway have been moved to a spot near the "hall of offerings".

Some way outside the compound near the *Yatri Niwas*, the **archeological museum**'s (daily 9am–5pm) collection of sculpture is neither particularly inspiring nor informatively displayed, most of the juicy pieces having been taken off to Delhi. Of more interest is the small shed in the northeast corner of the enclosure. The stone architrave inside it, bearing images of **nine planet deities**, the Navagrahas, originally sat above one of the temple's ornamental doorways and is now kept as a living shrine.

Practicalities

The easiest way to get to Konarak from Puri, 33km down the coast, is by **bus**. There are regular services in both directions and the journey only takes an hour or so, which makes it perfectly possible to do the round trip in a day. Buses from Bhubaneshwar are much less frequent and take between two and four hours to cover the 65km (with a change at Pipli), depending on whether you catch the one direct express "tourist" coach, which leaves from the town bus stand at 10am. Alternatively, you could join one

---

ODISSI DANCE

Even visitors who don't normally enjoy classical dance cannot fail to be seduced by the elegance and poise of Orissa's own regional style, **Odissi**. Friezes in the Rani Gumpha at Udaigiri (see p.853) attest to the popularity of dance in the Orissan courts as far back as the second century BC. By the time the region's Hindu "golden age" was in full swing, it had become an integral part of religious ritual, with purpose-built dance halls, or *nata mandapas*, being added to existing temples and corps of dancing girls employed to perform in them. **Devadasis**, literally "wives (or slaves)" of the god, were handed over by their parents at an early age and symbolically "married" to the deity. They were trained to read, sing and dance and, as one disapproving early nineteenth-century chronicler put it, to "make public traffic of their charms" with male visitors to the temple. Gradually, ritual intercourse (a legacy of the tantric influence on medieval Hinduism) degenerated into pure prostitution, and dance, formerly an act of worship, grew to become little more than a form of commercial entertainment. By the colonial era, Odissi was all but lost, its secrets frozen in ancient sculpture or absorbed into the popular traditions of musical plays that toured provincial towns and villages.

This would probably have heralded the end of Odissi altogether, had it not been for the rediscovery in the 1950s of the **Abhinaya Chandrika**, a fifteenth-century manual on classical Orissan dance. Like Bharatiya Natyam, India's most popular dance style, Odissi has its own highly complex language of poses and steps. Based on the *tribhanga* "hip-shot" stance, movements of the body, hands and eyes convey specific emotions and enact episodes from well-known religious texts – most commonly the **Gita Govinda** (the Krishna story). Using the *Abhinaya* and temple sculpture, dancers and choreographers were able to reconstruct this grammar into a coherent form and within a decade Odissi was a thriving performance art once again. Today, dance lessons with a reputed guru have become de rigueur for the young daughters of Orissa's middle classes – an ironic reversal of its earlier associations.

Few types of dance match Odissi for sheer style. The dancers deck themselves out in extravagant costumes of pleated silk brocades, silver jewellery, bells, jasmin flowers and distinctive *dhotis*, while in front of the stage, musicians and singers recite hypnotic *talas* – cycles of devotional poetry set to music. Unfortunately, catching a **live performance** is largely a matter of being in the right place at the right time. The only regular recitals take place in the Jagannath temple. If, however, you're not a Hindu, the annual **festival of dance** at Konarak, which takes place in the last week of November, is your best chance of seeing Orissa's top performers. While the atmosphere might not be as authentic as in the temple, the dancing is superb and the flood-lit backdrop spectacular. Failing that, the state television station broadcasts Odissi quite regularly, especially on public holidays. If you're keen to learn, a number of dance academies in Bhubaneshwar run intensive **courses** for beginners (see p.852).

of OTDC's whistlestop **tours**, though as these combine Konarak with a string of other attractions they don't leave you nearly enough time to do the temple justice. The tour from Puri (Tues–Sat depart 6.30am, return 6.30pm; Rs70) takes in Bhubaneshwar and environs, while the one from Bhubaneshwar (Tues–Sat depart 8.30am, return 6pm; Rs75) includes Dhauli, Pipli and Puri. Both leave from in front of the *Panthaniwas*.

With Puri only an hour down the road, few people end up staying in Konarak. If, however, you want to enjoy the temple at a more leisurely pace or just fancy spending the night somewhere a little more peaceful, there's plenty of **accommodation** in the village. Not far from the main entrance to the monuments, the OTDC *Panthaniwas* (☎223; ②–③) is nothing special but has clean and reasonably priced rooms, some a/c; the nearby government-run *Ashok Travellers' Lodge* (☎231; ②–③) is similar. Much the best deal however is the *Yatri Niwas* (☎220; ②), up past the main bus stand a short way before the museum. The rooms are neat and pleasant, and unlike the other two hotels cost less if you're travelling alone. In the unlikely event of these three being full, there are also a couple of shabbier places out towards the beach. The *Labanya Lodge* (①) is the best of these, with clean rooms and communal roof-space.

For **food** you have a choice between the row of snack and tea stalls opposite the temple or a more substantial meal in one of the hotel restaurants. The *Panthaniwas'* very popular and inexpensive *Gitanjali* cafeteria serves the usual range of mostly vegetable and rice dishes. Further afield, the *Yatri Niwas* is also open to non-residents and less likely to be packed out at lunchtime with tour parties.

Power cuts permitting, the sun temple is **floodlit** most evenings (May–Sept 7–10pm, Oct–April 5.30–9.30pm). In early November it also hosts one of India's premier **dance festivals**, drawing an impressive cast of both classical and folk/"tribal" dance groups from all over the country. For the exact dates, line-up and advance bookings, contact OTDC in Bhubaneshwar (☎0675/54727) or Delhi (☎01/344580).

Around Konarak

Unless you like beaches, few attractions **around Konarak** are likely to tempt you to prolong your stay. Konarak's own **beach**, 3km from the temple along the Puri road, is very picturesque and a good place to watch the local fishing fleet at work, but far from an ideal place to swim or sunbathe. For more privacy, catch a local bus heading south and jump off after a couple of miles when you see a track leading from the main road through the woods and dunes to the sea. Chances are you'll have miles of white sand to yourself. To get back again, flag down a bus or jeep from the roadside.

A stone's throw away from Konarak beach lies the sacred pond where Krishna's son Samba was cured of leprosy – the miracle that allegedly inspired the founding of the sun temple. For a couple of days every year during the full or "white" moon phase of Magha (January/February), **CHANDRABHAGA** is also the site of a big religious festival, the **Magha Saptami mela**. Thousands of pilgrims converge on the pool during the small hours to take a holy dip in its curative waters, then shuffle off to the beach where, in accordance with an age-old custom mentioned in the *Puranas*, they watch the sun rise over the sea. The event is followed by a *puja* at the Navagrahas.

Cuttack

After the comparative serenity of the surrounding countryside, **CUTTACK** comes as something of a shock. Orissa's former capital and most densely populated city is packed onto a narrow island amid a tangle of tributaries and sandbanks in the River Mahanandi. Without the benefit of suburbs to break you in gently, its noisy, traffic-filled streets can seem all the more claustrophobic. Nevertheless, if you're not in a hurry and like ambling around crowded, old-fashioned bazaars, Cuttack has its enjoyable aspects.

The site has possessed great strategic importance since the war-like Keshari ("Lion") dynasty founded a *kataka*, or "military camp", here in 989 AD. As the major river crossing for the busy north–south land trade route, as well as a nexus for the canals that connect the Orissan interior with the sea, the island proved an ideal platform from which to dominate the region's economy. It was the Kesharis, in the eleventh century, who were responsible for building the impressive granite **embankment** still visible along the south of the island. Apart from making the site less vulnerable to attack, the walls also strengthened it against the ravages of Cuttack's other perennial threat – the annual monsoon floods. In the fourteenth century, the **Barbati Fort** was added on the north bank. Two hundred years later, Orissa's last independent Hindu ruler, Mukunda Harichandan, built a much grander, nine-storeyed palace on the same site. The Raja

ORISSAN ART AND ARTISTS

Few regions of India retain as rich a diversity of **traditional art forms** as Orissa. While a browse through the bazaars and emporia in Puri and Bhubaneshwar provides a good idea of local styles and techniques, a trip out to the **villages** where the work is actually produced is a much more memorable way to shop. On the whole, different villages specialize in different crafts – a division that harks back to the origins of the caste system in Orissa. Patronage from the nobility and wealthy temples during medieval times allowed local artisans, or *shilpins*, to refine their skills over generations. As the market for arts and crafts expanded, notably with the rise of **Puri** as a pilgrimage centre, **guilds** were formed to control the handing down of specialist knowledge and separate communities established to carry out the work. Today, the demand for **souvenirs**, particularly easily transportable ones, has given many old art forms a new lease of life.

Stone sculpture With modern temples increasingly being built out of reinforced concrete, life for Orissa's **stone sculptors** is getting tougher. Nevertheless, the work of a few small communities remains on a par with that of their illustrious forebears at Konarak and Bhubaneshwar. At **Lalitgiri**, the Buddhist monument northeast of Cuttack, families of sculptors claim to own tools used by their ancestors to build the eighth- and ninth-century monasteries nearby; the Santal villages near **Lulung**, in the Simlipal National Park, have lately had to diversify from stone phalluses to pressure cookers to stay in business; while in Pathuria Sahi ("Stonecarvers' Lane") and the famous *Sudarshan Workshop* in **Puri**, mastercraftsmen and apprentices still fashion Hindu deities and other votive objects according to specifications laid down in ancient manuals.

Painting *Patta chitra*, classical Orissan **painting**, is closely connected with the Jagannath cult. Traditionally, artists were employed to decorate the inside of the temples in Puri and to paint the deities and chariots used in the Rath Yatra. Later, the same vibrant colour schemes and motifs were transferred to laquered cloth or palm-leaves and sold as sacred souvenirs to visiting pilgrims. In the village of **Raghurajpur** near Puri, where the majority of the remaining artists, or *chitrakaras*, now live, business is still booming. Specialities include devotional images of Lord Jagannath, scenes from the *Gita Govinda* and sets of **ganjiffa** – small round cards used to play a trick-taking game based on the struggle between Rama and the demon Ravana, as told in the *Ramayana*.

Palm-leaf manuscripts Palm-leaves, or *chitra pothi*, have been used as writing material in Orissa for centuries, and the basic techniques have changed little. Using a sharp stylus called a *lohankantaka*, the artist first scratches the text or design on to the surface of palm-leaves, then applies a paste of turmeric, dried leaves, oil and charcoal. When the residue is rubbed off, the etching stands out more clearly. Some scholars claim that the rounded Oriya script may have developed to cope with the problems of writing on palm-never had much of a chance to enjoy it however, as only eight years after his succession the Moghuls and, soon after them, the Afghans of Bengal annexed the city.

Under the Maharathas, who took over in the eighteenth century, Cuttack expanded still further. Lucrative trade with the British on the coast financed the construction of new temples and, thanks to a particularly liberal administration, of **mosques** for the city's sizeable Muslim minority. When the British finally merged the region's twenty-six princedoms, Cuttack was a logical choice as state capital. Its prominence however was shortlived; constant floods and chronic overcrowding ensured that the capital had, eventually, to be moved to the drier and far less constricted site at Bhubaneshwar.

Apart from some big cricket matches played in the Barbati stadium, Cuttack only tends to hit the news nowadays in conjunction with the infamous **"hootch scandal"** of 1992, when 170 people died after drinking (poisonous) illegal liquor. The tragedy made national headlines and cost a number of prominent government ministers their jobs.

leaves, the straight lines of other Indian languages being more likely to pierce their surface. Today, *Patta chitra* artists in **Raghurajpur** bind strips of palm-leaves together to make canvases, and in the **Raghunandan library** in Puri, students diligently copy old manuscripts to sell to tourists. The best places to see genuine **antique books** however are the national museum in New Delhi or the state musuem in Bhubaneshwar.

Textiles Distinctive **textiles** woven on hand-looms are produced throughout Orissa. Silk *saris* from **Berhampur** and **Sambalpur** are the most famous, combining bands of rich colours and brocade with traditional geometric and figurative designs, though **ikat**, which originally came to Orissa via the ancient trade links with southeast Asia, is also typical. It is created using a "tie-dye", or *bandha*, technique in which bundles of thread are wrapped and dyed in different colours, and the pattern emerges automatically when they are woven together. The same principle is employed by weavers from the village of **Nuapatna**, 70km from Bhubaneshwar, who produce silk *ikats* covered in verses from the scriptures for use in the Jagannath temple.

Appliqué The village of **Pipli** (see p.856), between Bhubaneshwar and Puri, has the monopoly on **appliqué**, another craft rooted in the Jagannath cult. Geometric motifs and stylized birds, animals and flowers are cut out of brightly coloured cloth and sewn on to black backgrounds. Pipli artists are responsible for the chariot covers used in the Rath Yatra as well as for the small canopies, or *chhatris*, suspended above the presiding deity in Orissan temples. These days, the more entrepreneurial among them are turning their hands to garish secular goods, with wall-hangings, bedspreads, lampshades, handbags, beach-brollies and heart-shaped shields(*tarasa*) among the current favourites.

Metalwork *Tarakashi*, silver filigree, is Orissa's best known **metalwork** technique (*tara* = woven; *kashi* = wire). Using lengths of wire made by drawing strips of silver alloy through small holes, the smiths create distinctive ornaments, jewellery and utensils for use in rituals and celebrations. The **designs** are thought to have come to India from Persia with the Moghuls, though the existence of an identical art form in Indonesia, with whom the ancient Orissan kingdoms used to trade, suggests that the technique itself may be even older. *Tarakashi* is now only produced in any quantity in Cuttack (see p.872); thanks to a preference among Hindus for golden jewellery rather than silver, the gradual take-over of the trade by rip-off middle men, and a reluctance on the part of the artisans to change their designs with the times, it's becoming a dying art form.

Dhokra The "lost-wax" *dhokra* metal-casting technique practised by *adivasi* ("tribal") communities in Mayurbhunj and Keonjhar districts has done very well out of the recent revival of interest in "ethnic" art. You can spot *dhokra* objects – usually figurines depicting animals or tribal deities – by the distinctive woven-wire patterns that used to decorate them. The effect is achieved by adding threads to the original wax image, before it is covered with a clay mould which is filled with molten metal.

The City

Congestion, as you'll quickly discover, is Cuttack's big problem. The main arterial route between Calcutta and Madras scythes straight through the middle of the island, making the centre little short of chaotic, and your first priority should be to work your way east, away from the mayhem outside the bus stand, towards the more atmospheric **old quarter**.

Dozens of small jewellers' shops line the bustling main streets of **Nayasarak** and **Balu bazaars**, close to the incongruous British High Court building. They're loaded with glittering *tarakashi* **filigree** work (see p.871), unique to Cuttack and practised here for many centuries. Only a few elderly artisans survive; you're unlikely to see them in action, unless you ask one of the shopkeepers to take you to meet their suppliers.

A stone's throw away from the silver bazaar, the **Kadam-i-Rasul** is one of the few interesting buildings in Cuttack. A complex of domed mosques and shrines, it houses among other things a round stone carved with the footprints of the Prophet. The spirit of religious tolerance symbolized by the Kadam-i-Rasul – its construction was sponsored by the Hindu Maharathas – has fallen foul of the recent wave of communalism, and non-Muslims are no longer allowed to enter.

Towards the northwest corner of the city, the twisting, crowded streets of the bazaar peter out into the leafier and more spacious district around the Barbati stadium. The ruins of Barbati **fort**, Cuttack's only real monument, lie on the opposite side of the nearby *maidan*. Apart from the moats, a lone-standing gateway and an unimpressive mosque, most of this once grand complex, likened by one eighteenth-century traveller to Windsor Castle, has been reduced to rubble. The citadel in the middle looks slightly more promising, but is currently under excavation and is not accessible to visitors.

After Barbati, the road follows the river bank out as far as **Chahata Ghat**, on the westernmost point of the island. Ferries cross the Mahanandi from here to the picturesque local pilgrimage spot of **Dhabaleshwar**, where there's a small Shiva temple and an OTDC *Panathasala*. The accommodation, which is cheap and very rudimentary, should be arranged through the tourist office in advance so that they can warn the poor unfortunate who's posted there to expect you.

Practicalities

Cuttack's **railway station** lies east of the city centre, in the middle of the island. **Buses** in both directions turn west off NH5, which runs parallel with the railway line, toward the city bus stand, 2km further up Link Rd. Halfway between the two, the Arunodhya Market building is site of the ineffectual state government **tourist office** (daily 10am–5pm; ☎0671/23525), which also has a counter at the railway station (☎0671/25107).

If you choose to stay in Cuttack rather than nearby Bhubaneshwar, **accommodation** isn't a problem. The majority of the cheap hotels are to be found in the silver bazaar. The *Adarsa* (☎0671/25498; ①) on Chandi Chowk and the *Veena* (☎0671/24326; ②) in the same road are the best of a generally bad bunch. The OTDC *Panthaniwas* (☎0671/23867; ④–⑤) on Buxa Bazaar is a little more expensive but a much better deal. It has a range of simple but clean rooms, all with hot water, and a reasonable restaurant. The two most **expensive** hotels in town are the *Akbari Continental* on Haripur Rd (☎0671/25242; ④–⑤) which has central a/c, a restaurant, bar and foreign exchange counter, and the similar *Ashoka* on Ice Factory Rd, near College Square (☎0671/25708; ③–⑤). These two and the *Panthaniwas* are also by far the best **places to eat** in Cuttack.

Ratnagiri, Udayagiri and Lalitgiri

Hidden away in the well-watered backcountry south of the River Brahmani, 65km north-east of Cuttack, lie the remains of three ancient Buddhist universities, **Ratnagiri**, **Udayagiri** and **Lalitgiri**. Although interesting in themselves and very scenically situated, they're as yet virtually inaccessible by public transport. **Getting there** involves catching a bus north up NH5 from Bhubaneshwar or Cuttack as far as the **Chandikohl crossroads** and then picking up an auto-rickshaw for the (costly) 60-kilometre round trip. Alternatively, you can wait for a bus heading from Chandikohl to Paradwip, on the coast, and get down at Patharajpur – the turn-off for two of the three sites. It's a long hike from there however, and unless you're able to hitch a ride you'll find it impossible to see the ruins and return to Bhubaneshwar in a day. Luckily, there's a small OTDC hostel (*Panthasala*; ①), a short way east of the Ratnagiri turn-off on the main road, if you get caught out and need somewhere to stay. The warden will also arrange food when given warning. If all else fails, male visitors can find a freshly cooked meal and a *charpoi* to sleep on at one of the *dhabas* clustered around the busy Chadikohl road junction.

Ratnagiri

RATNAGIRI, the most impressive of the three sites, lies 20km from the main road (the last 10 along a dirt track), on the top of a hill overlooking the River Keluo. When the Chinese chronicler Hiuen T'sang visited the university in 639 AD, it had already been a major Buddhist centre for at least two hundred years. In those days the sea reached much further inland, and would have been visible from this point – which may in part account for the choice of location. **Missionaries** were trained in such places before being sent abroad to spread the Buddha's message in China and southeast Asia.

The focal point of the site is the enormous **stupa** at the top of the hill. A stone casket containing gold and silver artefacts, believed to be actual relics of the Buddha, was found inside it during excavations in the 1970s. Nearby, just below the *stupa*, lie two well-preserved **monasteries**. The larger of the pair, dating from the seventh century, has a paved courtyard surrounded by cells and a beautifully carved doorway made from local blue-green chlorite stone. Inside the shrine there's a large seated Buddha.

Udayagiri

Five kilometres back down the track towards the main road, at the point where the asphalt starts, stands a signpost for the smallest and most recently discovered site in the complex, **UDAYAGIRI**. The main highlights here are a gigantic seated Buddha figure halfway up the hill, and some rock-cut sculpture nearer the top. Like Ratnagiri, the whole place is littered with masonry and bricks from collapsed structures.

Lalitgiri

The turning for **LALITGIRI**, the most accessible of the three Buddhist sites, is 5km further along the mainroad towards Paradwip. The Archeological Survey of India are still carrying out excavation work here, so officially you're not allowed to take photographs. Most of the ruins on the two adjacent hills are thought to date from the ninth century, though an inscription in the ancient *brahmini* script has recently come to light which suggests that it may have been occupied seven hundred years earlier. Though the best of the sculpture has been placed in a small **museum** (Tues–Sun 10am–5pm), or incorporated into the modern Hindu temple up on Parabhadi hill, some pretty impressive chunks are still lying around the place – most notably the huge head of a Buddha which has become emblematic in OTDC's attempts to promote the site. The small community of **stone carvers** who live at the foot of the hill claim to be descended from the craftsmen who worked on the original Buddhist buildings (see p.870).

North from Cuttack

As you head **north from Cuttack** and the Mahanandi, the profile of the Eastern Ghats recedes temporarily into the haze on the horizon leaving a flat expanse of paddy fields, palm trees and mud-walled villages. The main railway line, and NH5 that twists alongside it, follow the path of the famous **pilgrim trail**, the *Jagannath Sadak*, that once led from Calcutta to Puri. Until the end of the nineteenth century this now-hectic route was no more than a mud track. Then, following the 1865 famine that wiped out nearly a quarter of Orissa's population, the British were pressured into completing a road and rail link with more prosperous parts of the country. With the addition of iron bridges in the 1960s, the highway became the stream of trucks, ramshackle old buses, *dhabas* and *chai*-stalls it is today.

Balasore

The first town of any note along the way, **BALASORE** (literally "Town of the Young Lord" – Krishna) was one of the earliest English outposts in India. In 1636 it was given by the emperor Shah Jahan to a British surgeon, Mr Gabriel Broughton, after he had successfully cured the Moghul princess of burns (her clothes had caught fire during a sea voyage). If the port hadn't silted up in the eighteenth century, Balasore might well have become Calcutta. As it is, the sea is now 13km away, and the town is little more than a collection of market stalls grouped around a crossroads and a railway station.

Practicalities

The chances are that if you end up in Balasore it'll only be a pit-stop en route to somewhere else. The mainline **railway station** is a short way off the main street. From here it's a ten-minute cycle-rickshaw ride over the railway bridge to the **bus stand** where you can catch regular buses to Baripada, Bhubaneshwar, Cuttack and Chandipur. **Accommodation** is not hard to come by. Unless you're catching an early morning train, avoid the dives around the station. The hotels on Sahadevkhunta Rd, just up from the bus stand on the other side of the tracks, are a much better deal. *Hotel Swarnachuda* (☎06782/756001; ①–⑤) has a range of rooms to suit most pockets (including some a/c) and is well run with a small restaurant and a bar. Further down, the *Suraj* (☎06782/2657; ①–②) only has cheaper rooms, none of them a/c, and a small restaurant. If you've got your own vehicle and are looking for something a little more comfortable, you couldn't do better than the *Hotel Torrento* (☎06782/3481; ④–⑥), three kilometres further out of town near NH5. It has large rooms, most with central a/c, a

---

SUBAI ROPE

Drive along any of Mayurbhunj's country roads while the sun is shining and you're sure at some point to see villagers laying out strips of what look like jungle creepers on the asphalt. It's all part of the region's principal cottage industry, the production of **subai rope**. With the depletion of forest resources, many local people have had to turn to less traditional sources of subsistence; for villagers in areas where the soil is too poor to grow rice, *baliba* grass has proved a literal lifeline. This hardy, indigenous plant stands up well to the Orissan sun, and helps prevent soil erosion during the monsoon. After harvesting, the *baliba* is twisted to make *subai* rope and sun-dried on the nearest road. Then it's rubbed against tree trunks or telegraph poles to make it smooth, bound into one-kilogram bundles, and finally taken to Baripada market on the back of a bicycle to be sold to buyers from the city.

spacious garden and a superb restaurant serving a la carte tandoori, mughlai, vegetarian and Chinese dishes.

There's nowhere in Balasore to **change money**, although the manager of the *Torrento* may be able to help you out if you're desperate.

Chandipur

From the main market square in Balasore, a narrow, surfaced road winds its way out through the remnants of the old town to the open fields and picturesque villages beyond. After running along 16km of flood-proof embankment it eventually arrives at the nearest seaside settlement, **CHANDIPUR**. The village has two claims to fame, neither likely to inspire much enthusiasm among foreign visitors. The first is that at low tide the sea here retreats five kilometres away from Chandipur's white sandy **beach**. This has proved something of a god-send for the locals who, with their dug-outs and hand nets, are able to fish the parts the big fleets down the coast fear to reach. The second is the presence just outside the village of a test-firing range for the Indian army's infamous Agni rockets. Periodically, the army turfs out the disgruntled villagers so that they can take pot-shots at targets positioned on Chandipur's famous sand-flats – the cause of a protracted controversy in the Orissan government and media.

Apart from the occasional rocket launches, and limitless possibilities for paddling in miles of silty sea water, there's not a great deal to do in Chandipur. It's a relaxing enough place though, and one which rarely attracts more than a handful of visitors.

Practicalities

Getting to Chandipur is straightforward: hop on one of the hourly buses from Balasore, which you can pick up at the crossroads near the railway station. Auto-rickshaws will also do the trip, though expect to have to pay the return fare.

Apart from during public holidays, when Chandipur is swamped with trippers from Calcutta, finding somewhere to **stay** is also relatively easy. The *Yarica Yatri Niwas* (☎06782/2374; ①–③) has modern rooms around a courtyard and some cheaper dorms. They also serve food, though there isn't a proper restaurant. Nearer the beach the OTDC *Panthaniwas* (③–④) is housed in a more old-fashioned colonial building and has a good restaurant serving up fresh fish (if given a couple of hours' notice).

Tours of the area's attractions, including some off-the-beaten-track **temples** that are hard to visit without your own transport, are supposed to depart twice daily (at 7.30am & 1.30pm; Rs42) from here too. Unfortunately, OTDC tend to be reluctant to leave unless the minibus is full, which it rarely (if ever) is outside holiday times. *Maharaja Tours*, a private company based in the village, also run sightseeing trips from Chandipur.

Baripada and Mayurbhunj

A little way north of Balasore, the highway crosses the River Burhabalanga and splits in two, the right fork towards the Bengal border and the left towards the hills of the Orissan interior. Further inland, the intensively cultivated alluvial plains of the coastal strip gradually give way to patches of deciduous forest and red-laterite soil, punctuated by termite mounds and neatly thatched villages. **BARIPADA**, headquarters of **Mayurbhunj** district (pronounced *marvunj*) and gateway to the nearby **Simlipal National Park**, appears after about an hour and a half.

As the main **market** town for some widely scattered farming communities, Baripada is unexpectedly busy. There are no real sights to speak of, but if you're not in a hurry it's a good place to get an idea of small-town Orissan life. The district is also the traditional home of the **Santal** tribe. Comprising around seventy percent of the local *adivasis* (tribal) population, the Santals are predominantly settled agriculturalists who practise a blend of ancestor worship and Hinduism. They're known for having developed a written form of their tribal language, Olchikki, and for their festivals and dances.

The **town** itself is a typically Indian mixture of tumbledown shops and houses, quietly decaying bungalows and grand, but time-worn civic buildings erected by the local Maharaja during the days of the Raj. Mayurbhunj was among the last of the princely states to join independent India. For centuries it remained under the **Bhanja** kings, a reputedly "progressive" ruling family favoured by the British, whose present incumbent still lives in an incongrous neo-classical mansion overlooking the river in the north of town. The older **palace**, now a college on the main street, was an even more ostentatious affair. Among its more extravagant features is a swimming-pool which the local council have converted into a library.

Apart from the whitewashed **Jagannath temple**, a miniature of Puri's, the one note-worthy place to seek out is Baripada's small **museum** (Tues–Sun 10am–5pm). Awkwardly situated in the backstreets to the east of town, it houses a dusty collection of sculpture, coins, pottery and inscriptions that once belonged to the Maharaja.

Practicalities

Arriving in Baripada, **buses** pass the temple at the bottom of the broad main street and then head up the hill to the bus stand and market. From here it's a short ride to the only central **accommodation**, the *Hotel Ambika* (☎06792/2557; ①–②), a shabby but adequate place with variously priced rooms, all with attached baths and frames over the beds for the much-needed mosquito nets. Downstairs is Baripada's best **restaurant**. The surroundings look none too salubrious but they serve mountainous portions of reasonably tasty vegetarian food and some passable Chinese dishes.

In the rare event of the *Ambika* being full, try the *Durga* (☎06792/2338; ①–②), in an old British-style building 3km out of town past the temple. The OTDC **tourist office** (Mon–Fri 10am–5pm), five minutes' walk from the bus stand in the other direction, is not worth the trouble to find. If you want to arrange transport to Simlipal, rent a bicycle, or need travel information, the manager at the *Ambika* is much more helpful.

Simlipal National Park

West of Baripada, the landscape changes suddenly from open fields to the thickly wooded slopes and ridges of the Eastern Ghats. At over a thousand metres in height, **Khairbhuru**, the peak visible from the outskirts of town, is the highest in the region and one of the last true wildernesses in eastern India. The mixed deciduous forests, perennial streams and glades of savannah grasslands draped around its flanks have allowed for an uncommonly rich diversity of flora and fauna.

In 1957 the whole area around the mountain was declared a wildlife sanctuary – primarily in an attempt to revive its dwindling population of **tigers** (see p.381). Prior to this it had been the exclusive preserve of the Maharaja of Mayurbhunj, who used the woods as a private hunting ground and source of timber (the narrow-gauge railway running from Baripada to the main line on the coast was built to carry the lumber out). Fifteen years later **SIMLIPAL** was officially designated a national park, and the following year became the site of one of India's first Project Tiger reserves.

Simlipal deserves be one of eastern India's major attractions. The fact it isn't has less to do with the amount of wildlife within its borders – abundant by any standards – than with its comparative **inaccessibility**. Unlike its counterparts in neighbouring states, transport to and around the park is a real problem, accommodation is rudimentary and advance permits (essential for overnight stays) difficult to arrange. If you overcome all these obstacles, the rewards more than compensate. Apart from the elusive tigers – park rangers, perhaps a touch optimistically, claim they number almost one hundred – the reserve boasts leopards, langurs, barking and spotted deer, gaur, sloth bears, mongoose, flying squirrels, porcupines, turtles, monitor lizards, pythons and the very rare (and ominous-sounding) **mugger crocodile**. Herds of wild **elephant** are also common (too common for the unfortunate villagers, who have to spend the night in tree houses in order to scare rampaging elephants away from their crops) and there are reportedly 231 species of **birds** flying around. All this to a backdrop of some beautiful granite hills and as tranquil and pristine an old-growth forest as you're likely to find anywhere. If nothing else, it's a perfect antidote to the frenzy of the coastal cities.

Park practicalities

The first major obstacle to be negotiated before you arrive in Simlipal (which is open only from mid-Oct to mid-June) is to obtain a **permit**. Officially, anyone intending to spend a night in the park (essential if you want to see any animals) must reserve accommodation, at least one month in advance, by writing to the Field Director of Project Tiger, Baripada 757002, Mayurbhunj District, Orissa (☎06792/2593). Include the exact dates of your visit and the names of the lodges you'd like to stay in. Before you set off, it's also important to confirm the reservation with the office in Baripada, up near the big radio transmitter at the top of town (when it's closed, call ☎06792/2773).

Much the easiest way to visit Simlipal is to book onto an organized **tour**. *Swosti Travel* in Bhubaneshwar (☎0674/54178), and *Heritage Tours* in Puri (☎06752/3656) are both reputable. They will arrange permits, transport, accommodation and guides at very short notice and charge reasonable rates. Without your own vehicle, the only alternative way to **get around** the park is to rent a **jeep** or an *Ambassador* **car**. This can be arranged through the manager at the *Ambika* in Baripada, or through the less reliable taxi *wallahs* hanging around the bus stand. In any case, expect to pay at least Rs1000 per day. If you're on a budget, you may be able to cushion the blow by getting a group together, though the chances of meeting people on arrival at Baripada are at best slim and this should be organized well in advance.

The park itself covers a total area of 2750 square kilometres, but the majority of the tigers are supposed to hang out in the 845-acre "core zone", which for the most part is out of bounds. There are two main **entrances**: one at Joshipur in the west (convenient if you're driving from Calcutta, and close to most of the lodges), and one near Baripada on the eastern side. You have to pay a small entry fee at the ranger's barrier and obtain more expensive camera permits if you intend to take photographs or film inside the park. From here, unsurfaced but motorable roads link up the lodges with the numerous waterfalls, panoramas, grazing areas and water holes in the buffer zone.

Where to go in Simlipal is largely dictated by the location of the lodges. There are six dotted around the park, but the best from the point of view of spotting wildlife is **Chahala** (83km from Baripada) – one of the Maharaja's former hunting lodges, just inside the core zone near a salt-lick where lots of animals congregate in the evenings. As with all **accommodation**, facilities there are very basic. You have to take in your own food (which the *chowkida* will cook for you) and bedding. The other lodges are Barheipani (73km), near a waterfall with impressive views; Newana (60km), believe it or not a "frost-prone area"; Gudugudia (25km from Joshipur) said to be particularly good for birdwatching; and Joranda (64km from Baripada) which has a bit of everything. The only lodge not requiring advance permission is the *Aranya Niwas* at **Lulung**, on the Baripada side. You're unlikely to see much wildlife here, but the rooms are pleasant and inexpensive, there's cheap dormitory accommodation and a restaurant, and the compound, surrounded by an elephant-proof ditch, is right in the heart of the forest. They even have **solar panels** to provide electricity.

Southern Orissa

Few places along the south coast are likely to inspire more than a cursory glance out of a bus or train window. Between the miles of dishevelled roadside settlements and rural stations, however, a couple of minor resorts may tempt you to break a long journey. Three hours' south of the capital, at the foot of a barren, sea-facing spur of the Eastern Ghats – which here creep almost up to the coast – is India's largest salt-water lake. **Chilka**'s main attractions are the flocks of migratory birds that nest here during the winter and leisurely boat trips to the islands dotted around the lagoon. Seventy or so kilometres further down the road, **Gopalpur-on-Sea** is sufficiently remote to have remained a decidedly low-key beach town. Out of season, the only crowds along the shore are families from the local fishing community. **Berhampur**, 16km inland from Gopalpur, is southern Orissa's biggest market-town, and the main transport hub for the sinuous route west through the hills to the tribal districts of **Koraput** and **Jeypore**.

Chilka Lake

Were it not for its glass-like surface, **CHILKA LAKE**, Asia's largest lagoon, could easily be mistaken for the sea. From its mud-fringed foreshore you can barely make out the narrow strip of marshy islands and sand-flats that separate the 1100-square-kilometre expanse of brackish water from the Bay of Bengal. The thousands of **migratory birds** that descend on the lake between December and February can certainly tell the difference though. Come here in the short nesting season and you'll see dozens of species from as far afield as Persia and Siberia, including avocets, ruffs, pelicans, ospreys, flamingoes and some rare cranes. *Chital* and black buck can also sometimes be spotted on the shore.

Elsewhere around the lake, several **islands** (some inhabited by small subsistence fishing communities) are popular destinations for daily **boat trips**. By and large, the fishing villages and fabled island "kingdom" of **Parikud** on the eastern side of the lake, home to one of India's whackier maharajas, are passed up in favour of the *devi* shrine on **Kalijai** island. Legend has it that a local girl once drowned here on the way to her marriage ceremony across the lake. Since no suitable male member of the family could be found to accompany the girl on the journey, her father stepped in at the last minute – a serious breach of Hindu custom. En route, a retributory storm blew in from the sea and overturned the boat. When they had all but given up the search for survivors, some fishermen claimed to have heard the girl's voice calling from under the water to say that she had become a goddess and that a shrine should be inaugurated in her name. Over the years the miracle has become associated with **Kali** (Shiva's consort Durga in her terrifying aspect) and the place it occurred something of a sacred site. Every year at *makar sankrati*, after the harvest, pilgrims flock to the tiny island from all over Orissa and West Bengal to leave votive offerings in the cave where the deity was enshrined.

Practicalities

Neither of the two **places to stay** on the lake are at all attractive, although the OTDC *Panthaniwas* (③) at **Balugaon** is passable. The rooms are shabby and over-priced, but all have attached bathrooms and mosquito nets (you wouldn't get a wink of sleep without one). A verandah downstairs overlooks an unkempt garden where **food** is served. The restaurant's menu is standard government issue but everything is freshly cooked and they offer reasonable vegetarian dishes. **Getting there** involves taking the bus as far as **Barkul**, 7km away, and then finding a rickshaw to do the last leg. Coming from Puri, a direct OTDC **tour bus** (Mon, Wed & Fri; Rs80) leaves from in front of the *Panthaniwas*. Barkul also has a couple of cheaper hotels, but they're right on the highway which rather defeats the object of coming to Chilka in the first place.

Though considerably cheaper and more accessible, the other *Panthaniwas* (②), near the railway station at **Rumbha** 34km further south, is an even more lacklustre affair and best avoided. All it has going for it is that it's better placed for walks around the more scenic southern corner of the lake.

A couple of OTDC motor launches, and rowing boats manned by local villagers, operate **boat trips** from the jetty below the Balugaon *Panthaniwas*. Both charge an hourly rate, so the amount you pay ultimately depends on the number of passengers. The round trip to **Kalijai island**, the most popular option with domestic tourists, takes around two hours, while the bird sanctuary of **Nalabana island** takes four. The manager at the *Panthaniwas* can arrange seats.

Rowing boats also depart from Rumbha, though the fishermen who run them seem to be more intent on attending to their nets than ferrying passengers to the islands.

Gopalpur-on-Sea

Two thousand or more years ago, when the Kalingas were piling up wealth from the pearl and silk trade with southeast Asia, **GOPALPUR-ON-SEA**, formerly the ancient port of Paloura, must have been a swinging place. Today, the only time you're likely to encounter much action here is during the monsoon, when the village is temporarily inundated with promenading Bengali holiday-makers. For the rest of the year, its desultory collection of crumbling bungalows and seafront hotels stands idle, left to the odd backpacker blown off-course by the promise of an undiscovered beach paradise, and the armies of industrious fishermen hauling in hand-nets on Gopalpur's endless empty shoreline. Paradise it certainly isn't, but if you're looking for a spot along the coast to unwind and enjoy the warm sea breezes, this could be just the place.

The village has plenty of accommodation, much of it heavily discounted in the off-season, and there's a reasonable choice of places to eat. Despite appearances to the contrary however, Gopalpur's long white sandy **beach** is far from an ideal place to swim and sunbathe. For the local fishing community (*katias*), the rare spectacle of a white (read "rich and apparently insane") person strolling half-naked through their workplace is a major distraction; a swim in the sea, let alone a discrete doze in the sun, is a veritable crowd-puller. Still, if you don't mind being the centre of attention and are content to watch the locals fish (they're certainly picturesque enough in their traditional pointy straw bonnets and bright *saris*), the beach is an enjoyable place to while away a few hours.

Getting there is most easily accomplished via Berhampur, from where frequent minibuses and jeeps depart for the 16-kilometre trip. These leave from the central bus stand in the middle of town. On **arrival** you'll be dumped at the top of Gopalpur's "main street", ten minutes' walk from the seafront and most of the hotels.

Accommodation

Gopalpur's many **rooms** tend to cost considerably more than elsewhere, and you may well feel inclined to haggle. Only during high summer, however, are they liable to be booked up in advance. The rates below all refer to the off-season period.

Holiday Home. A rambling wedding-cake of a building, right on the seafront. Overpriced rooms and surly management. ①–④.

Holiday Inn, near the lighthouse. Couldn't be less like its American namesake – a handful of very basic rooms around a yard with bucket baths and no running water. The friendly family allow guests to use their kitchen. ①.

Mermaid (☎0681250). On the north side of the beach. A plain, upmarket place pitched at wealthy Calcuttans. Tariffs include full board. ④–⑤.

Oberoi Palm Beach (☎068121). A cosy, characterful self-contained five-star. Chalets around central lawn, snazzy restaurant, bar, jogging track, lots of palm trees and easy access to beach. ⑧.

Rosalin (☎0681271). On the seafront. A chaotic, family-run establishment with cells around a small garden-cum-courtyard and a very informal restaurant. Cheap and cheerful. ①–②.

Sea Side Breeze (☎0681275). A simple but pleasant enough place to the north side of the beach. Rooms are spacious and neat, some opening on to the sea. Good value. ③.

Tourist Home "Lobo". Just off the bottom of the main street. Basic but clean rooms, all with attached bathrooms, and a pleasant verandah, garden and restaurant. ②.

SEA TURTLES

Every year around February and March, a strip of beach at the end of Orissa's central river delta witnesses what must surely be one of the world's most extraordinary natural spectacles. Having swum right across the Pacific and Indian oceans, two hundred thousand female **olive ridley marine turtles** crawl onto the sand; each looks for a safe spot, then sets about digging a hole with its hind flippers in which to lay its annual batch of eggs. Twenty minutes later, after a quick breather, they're off again into the surf, to begin the journey back to their mating grounds on the other side of the world.

No one knows quite why they travel such distances, but for the local villagers the arrival of the giant turtles has traditionally been something of a boon. Turtle soup for breakfast, lunch and tea . . . and extra cash from market sales. The trouble was, over the years the annual slaughter began to turn into something of a green gold rush and turtle numbers plummeted drastically. At the personal behest of Indira Gandhi, a special wildlife reserve was set up to protect them. Today, the *Bhita Kanika Sanctuary* on **Gahirmatha beach**, 130km from Bhubaneshwar, is a safe haven for the ridleys. Weeks before the big three-or-four-day invasion, coastguards monitor the progress of the schools of turtles as they approach the Orissan shoreline and armed rangers ensure that poachers are kept at bay. For wildlife enthusiasts it's a field day. Thanks to the fact that during their labour the preoccupied turtles are, not surprisingly, oblivious to the presence of humans you can watch the whole sequence at close range.

Visits to Gahirmatha are allowed, though you should ask at the OTDC tourist office in Bhubaneshwar to find out exactly when the turtles are expected. **Transport, food** and **accommodation** can be a problem unless you are prepared to rough it or to pay through the nose for a rental car, as the sanctuary is well off the beaten track.

Eating

Considering the amount of fish pulled out of the sea, there's a surprising dearth of **seafood** in Gopalpur. Some restaurant owners can however be cajoled into cooking you the odd "pomfret", given sufficient warning (the fish has to be bought in the morning market). Otherwise, your choice is limited to the usual range of spicy Indian dishes served in a couple of grim cafes, or the shamelessly expensive *Oberoi*.

Ajanta, *Hotel Rosalin*. Standard omelette, tea and toast breakfasts or *dal*, veg and rice dinners served on tables in the reception. Inexpensive.

Mermaid, *Hotel Mermaid*. Homely, carefully prepared Bengali *thalis* plus numerous veg and non-veg options. Advance notice for non-residents (dinner served at 8.30pm sharp). Moderate to pricey.

Naz Snack Bar, overlooking the beach. Hot drinks, fresh *samosas*, *pakoras* and other nibbles on rickety old furniture. Open until 10pm.

Oberoi. Luxurious surroundings and an extensive and expensive menu geared towards rich European and American palates.

Rohini, halfway up main street on left. Boasts adventurous-sounding Chinese dishes but is more of a cafe-bar. Inexpensive.

Berhampur

Having squeezed around the narrow strip of flat land at the southern fringes of the lake, the railway line skirts the bottom of an eroded hillside, then heads out across a fertile river basin towards **BERHAMPUR**, the last major town before Andhra Pradesh. A bustling provincial market, with noisy streets crammed full of trucks and little shops serenading passers-by with film music, the only real reason you might conceivably want to stop here is to catch a bus or train somewhere else. Sights are non-existent, except perhaps the **weavers' quarter** around the temple where Berhampur's famous silk *saris* are still produced using traditional handlooms.

Moving on is most people's first priority. From Berhampur it's possible to catch **buses** up the coast to Bhubaneshwar; north to Sambalpur and the Hirakud Dam; west past Taptapani towards Rayagada and Koraput; and east to Gopalpur-on-Sea. Private buses leave from the new bus stand, some way across town, while the state transport company works out of the more central bus stand in the square. The mainline **railway station** is ten minutes' rickshaw ride to the south.

If you need to spend the night in Berhampur there are only two decent **places to stay**. Much the best value is the *Government Rest House* (☎06812/4911; ①) opposite the cricket stadium; most rooms are pretty grungy but it's very cheap and central. Otherwise the more upmarket *Hotel Moti* (☎06812/72386; ②–⑤), just around the corner from the *Rest House*, is a pleasant alternative with some a/c rooms and a restaurant. If all else fails the **railway retiring rooms** at the station will do for a night. For **budget food**, the *Hotel Poonam* on bus stand square is a safe bet, though it doesn't open for breakfast.

Taptapani

One possible foray from Berhampur, if you're tempted by the lure of the nearby hills, is the trip up to **TAPTAPANI**, a spa village nestled in the Ghats 51km to the west. The road leads out through Berhampur's hectic commercial district to a broad, flat-bottomed river valley strewn with huge black granite boulders and poor-looking villages. Along the way, patches of rice paddy and red-brown soil are enlivened by glimpses of local women hard at work in their blue and green cotton *saris*. An hour or so out, the increasingly bumpy road gradually narrows and loses most of its traffic. The hills and *sal* forest begin to close in and the bus, stuffed full with villagers heading up-country, starts to crawl around the hairpins towards the pass. Among the passengers you're likely to see a number of **Tibetans** from the Chandragiri refugee camp, 45km off the main road beyond Taptapani. Following the Chinese invasion in 1957 the refugees were given land by the Orissan government on which to settle and have lived there ever since, weaving carpets and breeding ferocious guard dogs for a living.

After the journey up the valley, Taptapani itself comes as a marked disappointment. Little more than a line of dingy snack-stalls and mildewed bungalows deep within dense forest, it's the kind of place to which government servants pray not to be posted. Even the legendary **hot springs**, believed to cure infertility in women, look jaded. The boiling sulphurous water bubbles listlessly out of a cleft in the mountainside and is piped into a small tank set just below the road. Women seeking to avail themselves of its curative effects are supposed to grope under the surface for seeds that fall off the tree overhanging the pond – an act of endurance that can take days to accomplish.

If you choose to stay in Taptapani, you can enjoy the water in the privacy of your own hotel; it's pumped into capacious bathtubs in some rooms at the atmospheric OTDC *Panthaniwas* (③–⑤), a short distance down the hill from the springs and commanding fine views over the tree-tops and valley to the hills in the distance. Although the *Panthaniwas* is rarely full, there's absolutely nowhere else to stay for miles around, so it's safer to reserve a room through an OTDC office in advance.

Beyond Taptapani

Beyond Taptapani, you're soon worlds away from the congested roads and towns of Orissa's coastal plains. Traffic dries up, villages become even poorer and less frequent and rice cultivation is squeezed out by thick forest. The appearance of pots attached to sago palms and windowless mud huts with low thatched roofs also indicate that you've arrived in Orissa's *adivasis* (tribal) homeland. The pass above Taptapani is the start of the **Saora**'s traditional land. Further west around the Koraput and Jeypore area live the **Dongria Kondh**, the **Koya** and the **Bondas**.

Officially, you're not allowed into the district without first obtaining a **permit** from the state government. Paranoia about **naxalites** hiding out in the forests along the Andhran border, coupled with a marked reluctance to allow foreigners into tribal zones, make these notoriously difficult to obtain. Theoretically it's still possible to move freely around the various towns and villages in Orissa's wild west, though in practice it's hard to know which, if any, are worth the hassle of minimal infrastructure, rudimentary accommodation and infrequent transport. If you're really keen to visit *adivasis* villages, the best, though far from the cheapest, way is to arrange a trip through a specialist **travel agent** in Bhubaneshwar or Puri. They'll take care of the necessary permits, sort out food and accommodation when you arrive and, if they're any good, have local contacts to make sure you behave appropriately in the villages and markets. Whichever way you look at it though, turning up in an isolated and culturally sensitive place with an *Ambassador* car and a camera has got to be a pretty unsound way of "meeting" the locals.

CHAPTER SEVENTEEN

THE ANDAMAN AND NICOBAR ISLANDS

T he **ANDAMAN AND NICOBAR ISLANDS** lie in the Bay of Bengal, over 1000km off the east coast of India and accessible from either Calcutta or Madras. The islands themselves are thickly covered by deep green jungle – inhabited by unique bird species – and fringed with clean sandy beaches, but the real attraction for tourists lies offshore, in crystal-clear seas that harbour some of the world's richest and least spoilt marine reserves. Filled with dazzling fish and kaleidoscopic corals, and roamed by schools of dolphins and sharks, the waters are perfect for **snorkelling** and **scuba diving**.

The two groups comprise over 300 islands, summits of a submarine mountain range that stretches for 755km from north to south, populated in parts by indigenous tribes whose numbers have been slashed dramatically by the effects of nineteenth-century European settlement and rampant deforestation. Today felling is restricted, and eighty-six percent of the islands' forest is protected – nevertheless, *padauk* and teak are still used for building materials and made into furniture and tourist knick-knacks. Foreign tourists are only permitted to visit parts of the **Andaman** group, over 200 islands separated by the deep Ten Degree Channel from the nineteen islands further south that constitute the **Nicobars**, access to which is at present restricted to Indians.

The main island of the Andamans, and the point of arrival for boats and planes, is **South Andaman**, where the Indian and Burmese community in the small but busy capital, **Port Blair**, accounts for almost half the total population. **Permits** obtainable on the mainland or on arrival are initially granted for a stay of fifteen days, which allows just enough time to explore a few islands, or take a scuba-diving course; this can be extended to a maximum of one month. The most beautiful beaches and coral reefs are found on outlying islands. A healthy get-up-and-go spirit is essential if you plan to explore these, as you're likely to need your own transport, and on smaller islands your own supplies for camping, eating and drinking.

The **climate** remains tropical throughout the year, with temperatures between 24° and 35°C. By far the best time to visit is between November and May. From mid-May to October, heavy rains flush the islands, often bringing violent cyclones that leave west-coast beaches strewn with fallen trees, and in November and December less severe rains arrive with the northeast monsoon. Dense tree cover, marshy swamps, humidity and high rainfall combine to provide perfect breeding ground for mosquitoes, and **malaria** is very common. Despite being so far east, the islands run on Indian time, so the sun rises at 4am and darkness falls soon after 5pm.

A little history

The earliest mention of the Andaman and Nicobar Islands is found in **Ptolemy**'s geographical treatises (second century AD). Other records from the Chinese Buddhist monk I'Tsing (seventh century) and Arabian travellers who passed by in the ninth

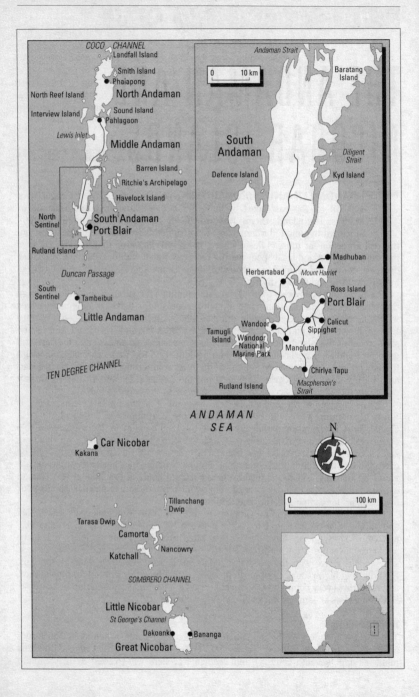

century, depict the inhabitants as fierce and cannibalistic. **Marco Polo** arrived in the islands in the thirteenth century and could offer no more favourable description of the natives: "The people are without a king and are idolaters no better than wild beasts. All the men of the island of Angamanian have heads like dogs . . . they are a most cruel generation, and eat everybody they catch . . ." It is unlikely, however, that the Andamanese were cannibals, as the most vivid reports of their ferocity were propagated by Malay pirates who held sway over the surrounding seas, and needed to keep looters well away from trade ships that passed between India, China and the Far East.

NATIVE PEOPLE OF THE ANDAMAN AND NICOBAR ISLANDS

Quite where the indigenous population of the Andaman and Nicobar Islands came from is uncertain. Negrito communities may have migrated here from the east and north when the islands were connected to Burma, or the sea was sufficiently shallow to allow transport by canoe. Their survival has been threatened by traders and colonizers, who introduced disease and destroyed their territories by widespread felling. Of perhaps 5000 aborigines in 1858, only five percent remain, from six of the twelve native tribal groups.

On the Nicobar Islands, the Mongoloid **Nicobarese**, who claim descent from a Burmese prince and were identified as *lojenke* (naked people) by I'Tsing, have integrated to some extent with recent settlers, and while they continue to live in small communities of grass huts raised on stilts, have adopted modern agricultural methods, raising pigs rather than hunting. The **Shompen** of Great Nicobar have not assimilated, however, and less than 200 remain, living on the coast, where they barter in honey, cane and nuts with the Nicobarese, and in isolated pockets further inland.

The Andaman communities, divided into *eramtaga* (jungle-dwellers), and *ar-yuato* (coast dwellers), subsist on fish, turtles, turtle eggs, pigs, fruits, honey and roots. They acknowledge an anthropomorphic deity, Phalgun, who is feared for his wrath in the form of storms, but do not worship him. Dreams are considered significant, and ancestors said to be able to influence events and cause earthquakes when angry. Daily ritual dances, central to communal life, are held on land enclosed by huts. Most tribes affix great importance to trees in their territory, and each male marks a tree as his own.

Less than twenty **Great Andamanese** remain, settled today on Strait Island, north of South Andaman. In the 1860s, Rev H Corbyn set up a "home" for them to learn English on Ross Island, insisting that they wear clothes and abandon body-painting. From the settlers the Andamanese contracted diseases such as syphilis, measles, mumps and influenza, and within three years almost the entire population had died.

The **Jarawas**, who shifted from their original homes when land was cleared to build Port Blair, now live on the western coasts of Middle and South Andaman, hemmed in by the Andaman Trunk Road which has since the 1970s cut them off from hunting grounds and fresh water supplies. Some contact with settlers has been made through gift-exchange at each full moon when the Jarawas sing and dance, and in apparent friendliness fart in the face of the visitors. Nevertheless, they remain unwilling to mix, and are determined to retain their land, firing arrows at settlers whose cattle and fields encroach upon vital resources.

Once used by the Chinese and Japanese to dive for valuable shells in exchange for alcohol and opium, the **Onges** are today the largest tribe on the Andaman Islands, living on Little Andaman and Rutland Island. Unlike other tribes, the Onges do not practice tattooing, but they paint their bodies with white clay and ochre, and the women smear themselves with yellow dye from orchids. They live in communal shelters (*bera*) and construct temporary thatched huts (*korale*) where they live for forty or fifty days at a time before moving on. In areas on Little Andaman, wooden huts have been built for the Onges by Indians, in an attempt to compensate for loss of land.

The most elusive tribe of all, the **Sentinelese**, live on North Sentinel Island west of South Andaman. Some contact was made with them in 1991, after a team put together by the local administration had left gifts on the beaches each month for two years.

During the eighteenth and nineteenth centuries **European missionaries** and trading companies turned their attention to the islands with a view to colonization. A string of unsuccessful attempts to convert the Nicobarese to Christianity was made by the French, Dutch and Danish, all of whom were forced to abandon their plans in the face of hideous diseases and a severe lack of food and water. Though the missionaries seldom met with any hostility, several fleets of trading ships that tried to dock on the islands were captured, and their crews murdered, by Nicobar people.

In 1777 the British Lieutenant Blair chose the South Andaman harbour now known as **Port Blair** as the site for a penal colony, based on the deportation of criminals that had proved successful in Sumatra, Singapore and Penang. Both this scheme, and an attempt to settle the Nicobar Islands in 1867, were thwarted by adverse conditions. However, the third go at colonization was more successful, and in 1858 **Port Blair** finally did become a penal settlement, where political activists who had fuelled the Mutiny in 1857 were made to clear land and build their own prison. Out of 773 prisoners, 292 died, escaped or were hanged in the first two months. Many lost their lives in attacks from Andamanese tribes who objected to forest clearance, but the settlement continued to fill with people from mainland India, and by 1864 the number of convicts had grown to three thousand. In 1896 work began on a jail made up of hundreds of tiny solitary cells, which was used to confine political prisoners until 1945. The prison still stands, one of Port Blair's few "tourist attractions".

In 1919, the British government in India decided to close down the penal settlement, but it was subsequently used to incarcerate a new generation of freedom fighters from India, Malabar and Burma. During World War II the islands were occupied by the **Japanese**, who tortured and murdered hundreds suspected of collaborating with the British, and bombed homes of the Jarawa tribes. British forces moved back in 1945, and at last abolished the penal settlement. After Partition, refugees, mostly Hindus from Bangladesh and Bengal, were given land in Port Blair and on the Nicobar Islands, where yet more woodland was cleared and new industries established. This replanted population, which has mixed with ex-convicts who chose to stay, now greatly outnumbers the indigenous people; contact between the two societies is limited, and not always friendly.

Getting to the Andaman Islands

Port Blair, on South Andaman, is served by flights from **Calcutta** (Tues, Thurs & Sat) and **Madras** (Wed & Fri); both outward and return journeys should be booked well in advance, through any *Indian Airlines* office.

It's also possible to get to Port Blair by **ship**; irregular sailings leave both Calcutta and Madras every one or two weeks. Although far cheaper than flying, the crossings are long (3–4 days), uncomfortable and often delayed by bad conditions. **Tickets** cost Rs300–500 for a simple bunk with little privacy, Rs800–1000 for a place in a four- or six-bed second-class cabin, Rs1100–1200 in a two- or four-berth first-class cabin, and Rs1300–1500 for a deluxe a/c two-bunk room. Meals of *dhal*, rice and vegetables are served for just under Rs100 per day, but vary little, so take some supplementary snacks and a good supply of fruit. It's best to arrange the outward and return journeys ahead, through the Shipping Corporation of India (**SCI**) offices at First Floor, 13 Strand Rd, Calcutta (☎284456) or Jawahar Building, near Customs House, Rajaji Rd, Madras (☎524950). There's also an information centre for the islands at F 104 *Curzon Road Hostel*, Kasturba Gandhi Marg, New Delhi (☎387015). You'll need a passport photo, and should confirm your place on the boat 48 hours before leaving.

Tourists arriving by plane can pick up the **permit** necessary to visit the islands on arrival at the airport; ship passengers should obtain one at a shipping office or Foreigners' Registration office before leaving India. The superintendent of police in Port Blair's Aberdeen Bazaar can **extend** your stay beyond the initial fifteen days.

South Andaman Island

South Andaman is today the most heavily populated of the Andaman Islands – particularly around the capital, Port Blair – thanks in part to the drastic thinning of the tree cover to make way for settlement. Foreign tourists can only visit its southern reaches – including the beaches at **Corbyn's Cove** and **Chirya Tapu**, and the fine reefs on the western shores at **Wandoor**, 35km southwest of Port Blair – and stretches of the northern region near **Mount Harriet** and **Madhuban** on the east coast, where elephants are trained for felling.

With your own transport it's easy to find your way along the narrow bumpy roads that connect small villages, weaving through forests and coconut fields, and skirting the swamps and rocky outcrops that form the coastline.

Port Blair

PORT BLAIR, a characterless cluster of tin-roofed houses, shops, restaurants and offices, meeting the sea in the north, east and west and fields and forests in the south, merits only a short stay. There's little here to see – just the **Cellular Jail** and a few small **museums** – but as the point of arrival for the islands, and the only place with a bank, tourist offices, hotels, and decent restaurants, it can't be avoided.

Arrival and information

Taxis wait at **Phoenix Bay Jetty**, where the **boats** come in, to cover the two-kilometre drive south to the town centre. The Marine Department at the jetty (☎20725) has the latest information on boats and ferries to other islands. The **airport** is 5km south of Port Blair; unless you're staying at the *Andaman Beach Resort*, which lays on a free airport shuttle bus, you'll have to rely on taxis (Rs30–40) to get to a hotel.

A counter at the airport has leaflets listing accommodation and sights around South Andaman Island, while the **Government of India tourist office** is in Super Shoppe complex, Junglighat, near the airport (Mon–Fri 10am–5pm; ☎21006). The **Andaman and Nicobar tourist office**, next to the Secretariat on the southern edges of the town itself (Mon–Fri 10am–5pm; ☎20694), is far more informative and efficient, and will tell you all you need to know about tours (see below) and ferry crossings to other islands. For information on island wildlife and forest tracks in areas such as Mount Harriet and Chirya Tapu, head for the **chief wildlife warden**'s office in Haddo, west of Phoenix Bay Jetty (☎20816). Government-run hotels can also help with maps and information.

Port Blair's main road is **Aberdeen Bazaar**, where you'll find the superintendent of police (for permit extensions), the SCI office (☎213470) for onward bookings by sea, and the *State Bank of India* (Mon–Fri 1–4.30pm). Some hotels will change travellers' cheques. Flights can be reserved at *Indian Airlines*, Middle Point (Mon–Fri 10am–4pm; ☎2205).

Local transport and tours

Walking is tiring and time-consuming in hilly Port Blair, even taking into account the minimal amount of sightseeing the place offers – and transport to get from place to place is essential. No rickshaws, auto or otherwise, operate on the island, but yellow-top **taxis** gather at the west end of Gandhi Rd, opposite the bus stand (see below). They all have meters, but negotiating the price before leaving is usual practice. Expect to pay Rs35–50 for a trip from the centre of town to Corbyn's Cove.

The telephone **area code** for Port Blair is ☎03192.

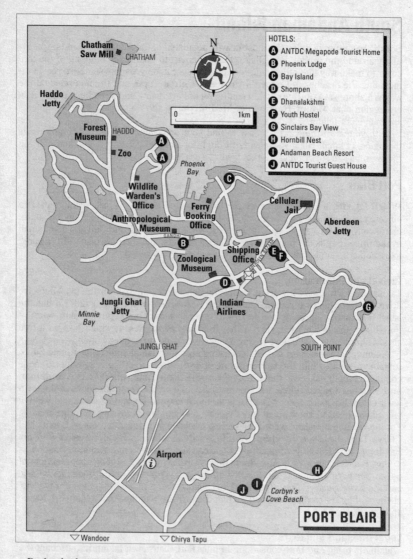

HOTELS:
- **A** ANTDC Megapode Tourist Home
- **B** Phoenix Lodge
- **C** Bay Island
- **D** Shompen
- **E** Dhanalakshmi
- **F** Youth Hostel
- **G** Sinclairs Bay View
- **H** Hornbill Nest
- **I** Andaman Beach Resort
- **J** ANTDC Tourist Guest House

PORT BLAIR

By far the best way to see Port Blair is on a **tour**. Good-value half-day taxi tours to the jail, museums and sawmill are organized by the Andaman and Nicobar Tourist office (Wed–Sun; Rs50), *Shompen Travels* in *Shompen Hotel* (on demand; Rs100) and *Andaman Beach Resort* (daily; Rs100). **Harbour cruises** (Tues, Thurs & Sat; book at the Marine Dept, ☎20725) depart from Phoenix Bay Jetty, drift around the floating docks, and make a fleeting visit to **Viper Island** (see p.892).

Local **buses** run infrequently from the bus stand in central Port Blair to Wandoor and Chirya Tapu, but are completely impractical for day trips. To get around South

Andaman, it's best to rely on your own transport. **Bicycles** can be rented from Aberdeen Bazaar, but the hilly roads to the coasts are most easily covered on a **Vespa** or **motorcycle**, both available for rent at *TSG Travels* (Mon–Sat 9am–5pm; ☎20894) on Babu Lane in the centre of town, at Rs120–200 per day. The petrol pump is on the crossroads west of the bus stand.

The Town

Port Blair's only firm reminder of its gloomy past, the sturdy brick **Cellular Jail** (Mon–Sat 9am–noon & 2–7pm), overlooks the sea from a small rise in the northeast of town. Built between 1896 and 1905, its tiny solitary cells were quite different and far worse than the dormitories in other prison blocks erected earlier. Only three of the seven wings that originally radiated from the central tower now remain; visitors can peer into the 13m-by-7m cells, and imagine the grim conditions under which the prisoners existed. Cells were dirty and ill-ventilated, drinking water was limited to two glasses per day, and the convicts were expected to wash in the rain as they worked clearing forests and building prison quarters. Food, brought from the mainland, was stored in vats where the rice and pulses became infested with worms; more than half the prison population died long before their twenty years' detention was up. Protests against conditions led to hunger strikes in 1932, 1933 and 1937, resulting in yet more deaths, and frequent executions took place in full view of the cells, at the gallows that still stand in squat wooden shelters in the courtyards. The **sound and light show** (in English Wed, Sat & Sun 7.15pm; in Hindi daily 6pm) outlines the history of the prison, and a small **museum** by the entrance gate (same hours as prison) exhibits lists of convicts, photographs and grim torture devices.

South of the jail, you can see tanks brimming with exotic fish and coral from the islands' reefs at the **marine museum** (daily 8.30am–12.30pm & 1.30–5pm), which includes a salt-water crocodile farm that breeds and releases crocodiles into the coastal mangrove swamps. In the Haddo area in the west of town, the **anthropological museum** (Mon–Sat 9am–noon & 1–4pm) illustrates the lives of Andaman and Nicobar tribes with photographs and miniature models.

Further north, on the knobby peninsula that marks the northernmost edge of Port Blair, **Chatham sawmill** (daily 7am–2.30pm) is one of the oldest and largest timber processing plants on Indian territory. The seasoning of beautiful and rare woods taken from various islands is sad testimony to continuing felling; photography is prohibited. Lumbering methods are clearly explained in the adjoining **forest museum** (Mon–Sat 9am–noon & 2–4pm), which also displays local types of wood used in the timber industry such as *padauk*, rosewood and marble wood. The **zoo** nearby (Mon–Sat 7am–noon & 2–5pm; Rs1) is small, but gives an impression of the rich variety of animals and reptiles on the islands, many of which, like the agile luminous-green Andaman gekko, are seen nowhere else in the world.

Accommodation

Port Blair's **hotels** offer something to suit every pocket. Budget accommodation is concentrated in the centre of town – spend a little more and you can stay in secluded lodges with gardens and views over the sea. As darkness falls at around 5pm it's a good idea to find a hotel that has verandahs and a bar where you can while away the evening.

Andaman Beach Resort, Corbyn's Cove (☎21463). Perfect setting amid gardens of palms, jasmine and bougainvillea, opposite a white sandy beach. Balconied a/c rooms, intimate cottages, bar, and a medium-priced restaurant where the evening buffet doesn't always match up to what is served in simpler places elsewhere. Table tennis and TV hall upstairs. Ideal for families. ⑦.

ANTDC Megapode Tourist Home, Haddo (☎20207). Well-maintained rooms, and wonderful a/c cottages set in leafy gardens with views over the sea. Good value, and a wide menu. ②–③.

ANTDC Tourist Guest House, Corbyn's Cove (☎20211). Four comfortable rooms with balconies, sheltered by heavy tree cover a stone's throw from the beach. Book at the tourist office in town. ①.

Bay Island, Marine Hill, Port Blair (☎20881). Port Blair's best hotel by far; elegant, airy, and finished with polished dark wood. All rooms have carpets, en suite bathrooms and balconies overlooking Phoenix Bay and the seas, but the less expensive ones are a little cramped. The restaurant is superb for a splurge, with unfailingly good Indian specialities and seafood, a well-stocked bar and beautiful views. Lush gardens and open-air seawater swimming pool. ⑧–⑨.

Dhanalakshmi, Aberdeen Bazaar, Port Blair (☎21953). Friendly hotel with dim but spacious rooms, and an excellent restaurant, preparing Indian dishes and seafood to order. ②–④.

Hornbill Nest, 1km from Corbyn's Cove (☎20018). Great value. Clean, roomy cottages on a hill by the coast. Good food available if you order well in advance. ①.

Phoenix Lodge, Manlana Rd (☎21820). Nothing to write home about, but adequate for a short stay, perhaps before catching a plane from the nearby airport. ①.

Shompen, Middle Point, Port Blair (☎20360). Unjustified prices for stuffy, tatty rooms, but you can negotiate rates. Travel counter and good seafood in rooftop restaurant. ⑤–⑥.

Sinclairs Bay View, on the coast road to Corbyn's Cove (☎21159). Clifftop hotel with spotless carpeted rooms, balconies and en suite bathrooms. Dramatic views, bar and restaurant. ⑤–⑥.

Youth Hostel, eastern edge of town (☎20459). Small lodge with basic facilities at very low rates. ①.

Eating

It's can be well worth forfeiting the convenience of the hotel restaurants reviewed above, and trying something a little different; between them, Port Blair's restaurants offer dishes from north and south India, Burmese specialities, and a wide variety of seafood. Don't miss the local **spiced fish** – the heads are considered to be the most delicious part. Roadside stalls sell plates of grilled fish for less than Rs20.

Avanti, opposite bus stand. Popular place for fixed meals, *dosas*, and northern dishes such as *chola bathura* (spicy chickpeas served with huge crispy *puris*). Good food, but dim surroundings.

China Room, near Phoenix Bay Jetty. By booking well in advance at this small family-run restaurant you can guarantee some superb Burmese-style seafood dishes at very reasonable prices.

Hotel Ashoka, Gandhi Rd. Small hole-in-the-wall joint not far from the bus stand, with only six tables. Tiffins, coffee, *lassis* and an assortment of breads all day long; inexpensive, hearty south Indian meals at lunchtime and in the evening.

Around the island

South Andaman's best spot for swimming and sunbathing is 10km southeast of Port Blair at **Corbyn's Cove**, a small stretch of smooth white sand fringed with palms. Bear in mind, though, that lying on the beach scantily clothed will bring you considerable attention from crowds of local workers. The long white beach at **Wandoor** is littered with the dry, twisted trunks of trees torn up and flung down by annual cyclones, and fringed not with palms, but with dense forest teeming with birdlife. You should only snorkel here at high tide. Boats leave Wandoor jetty, sailing through wide creeks that lap against mangrove swamps and out to nearby islands that constitute a **national park**, boasting exquisite coral and fish colonies.

At the southern tip of South Andaman, an hour's drive from Port Blair, is the tiny hook of **Chirya Tapu**, or Bird Island, where swamps give way to shell-strewn beaches, sharp rocks and vast coral reefs. The path from Chirya Tapu's small fishing village to its beach leads through thick humid jungle overhung with twisting creepers, echoing with bird calls and the shrill hum of insects, and passes massive termite mounds and streams trickling through deep red soil – don't return to the village too late, as walking through this looming jungle in semi-darkness can be pretty eerie.

Ferries from Phoenix Bay Jetty also make the short trip (30min) to **Madhuban**, a felling area where elephants work alongside men. Not far from Madhuban, **Mount Harriet**, at 400m, is one of the highest points on South Andaman. Permission to climb the nature trails that weave through dense forest to its summit must be obtained from the chief wildlife warden in Haddo. Although in theory Madhuban and Mount Harriet can only be visited as day trips from Port Blair, the warden might also give you permission to stay in the **forest rest house** at Mount Harriet, which technically is reserved for VIPs and visiting wildlife officers; the same goes for another rest house at Chirya Tapu.

Other islands

After a short stay in South Andaman, most visitors, tempted to search out more attractive beaches and richer coral reefs, head for one of the smaller islands nearby.

Havelock, **Cinque**, **Neil** and **Long islands** are all accessible by ferry from Phoenix Bay Jetty. It's possible to charter a boat from here or from *Shompen Travels* at *Shompen Hotel* (☎20721), which saves time, but is extremely expensive at around Rs10,000 per day per boat. Havelock has tourist facilities; on all other islands you'll have to take a tent (ask about rental at tourist offices or the Marine Department), food, and drinking water. Always carry lots of anti-bite cream to protect against sand flies and mosquitoes.

Day trips (only) can be made from Port Blair to **Ross** and **Viper islands**, north of the harbour. Travel agents also organize daily trips to **Red Skin** and **Jolly Buoy**, which are part of the Wandoor national park.

Havelock and Neil islands

Havelock Island, the largest of a scattering of islets northeast of Port Blair, can be reached by ferry (Fri & Tues, departs 6.30am; book at the Marine Department; ☎20725), on a four-hour route that passes colonies of playful dolphins.

SCUBA DIVING IN THE ANDAMAN ISLANDS

The seas around the Andaman and Nicobar Islands are some of the world's finest, relatively unexplored, unspoilt and dazzlingly colourful. Many species of fish and coral are unique to the area and fascinating life systems exist in ash beds and cooled lava around the eastern volcanic island of Barren.

For a quick taste of marine life, you could start by **snorkelling**; most hotels can supply masks and snorkels, though some equipment is in dire need of replacement. However, the only way to get really close, and venture out into deeper waters, is to **scuba dive**. The experience of weaving in and out of coral beds, coming eye to eye with fish or swimming with dolphins and barracudas is unforgettable, and at prices that are among the lowest in the world, it's an opportunity not to be missed.

The recently established **Andaman and Nicobar Scuba Diving Society** is run by Mr Chowdhary, a highly experienced and very competent instructor whose office is in *Bay Island Hotel* on Marine Hill, Port Blair (☎20881; fax 03192/21389). If you're a qualified diver with a valid certificate, you can rent equipment and make two dives with an instructor for Rs1500 per day. **Courses** for learners that result in PADI (Professional Association of Diving Instructors) certificates vary from one to four days (Rs500–6500); training in advance open water diving and rescue are also on offer (2–3 days; Rs4500). Gaining the certificate of Dive Master requires a three-week course (Rs15,500).

It's not uncommon to come across schools of sharks, which rarely turn hostile, but one thing to watch out for and avoid is the **black-and-white sea snake**. Though the snakes seldom attack – and, since their fangs are at the back of their mouths, would find it difficult to get a grip on any human – their bite is more deadly than that of the cobra.

It's essential to respect your environment when diving and snorkelling. Increased tourism inevitably puts pressure on the delicate marine eco-system, and poorly funded wildlife organizations can do little to prevent damage from insensitive visitors. Divers and snorkellers should never touch or pick coral; most of the reefs remain undamaged, but the dead coral in the shallow waters on the shores at Wandoor is an early sign of what happens if coral is walked on or picked.

The island, popular for its long white beaches, is slightly hilly and very fertile – much of the forest has been cleared so that fruit and vegetables can be grown for sale on South Andaman. **Accommodation** is available in clean double rooms at the new *Tourist Guest House* (①–③) by the jetty (book at the Andaman and Nicobar tourist office in Port Blair), where you can also get reasonable but unexciting food. The wide beach close to the hotel is good for sunbathing, and the sea is very shallow, but the best waters for swimming lie off the beach at **Radhnagar**, 10km from the jetty at the end of a narrow and poorly surfaced road; watch for pesky sandflies, especially in the evenings. There's no guaranteeing transport to Radhnagar – the best thing to do is to bring a moped (plus fuel) or bicycle with you from Port Blair.

Neil Island

The ferry from Port Blair to Havelock continues south to the smaller and more densely populated **Neil Island**, settled by Bengalis in the years following Partition. The largest of Neil's wide and deserted beaches is at Sitapur, on the east coast. You'll have to sleep in a tent, and bring food and water; you can supplement this with coconuts growing along the coast, and snacks from the bazaar further inland.

Cinque Island

South of Chirya Tapu, uninhabited **Cinque Island** emerges from some of the finest coral reefs open to tourists, and is shrouded in jungle. Until the proposed tourist rest house is built, visitors to Cinque will have to provide their own shelter in tents, and stock up with plenty of food – ferries between Phoenix Bay and the island run only once a week (3hr), though it is sometimes possible to get a ride on a fishing boat from Chirya Tapu.

Viper and Ross islands

Viper and Ross islands, northeast and west of Port Blair, are closely associated with the British. Harbour cruises from Port Blair (Tues, Thurs & Sat) include a short stop on **Viper Island**, where convicts were made to stay for a month to deter them from breaking prison discipline. Gallows, whipping posts and crumbling walls remain as relics of a punishment area.

A short boat tour from Phoenix Bay Jetty (daily except Wed, 8.30am, 10.30am, 12.15pm & 2pm) allows an hour on **Ross Island**, where Revd Corbyn established his home for the Andamanese and the British set up their administrative headquarters. It's interesting to see how quickly nature has regained its hold – the semi-ruined buildings are today withdrawing into the tangled branches and vines of trees and creepers, that will eventually hide some of the last monuments to British occupation of the islands.

Red Skin and Jolly Buoy islands

Part of the Wandoor national park, **Red Skin** and **Jolly Buoy islands** boast a stunning array of coral and fish. Travel agents organize daily trips to these uninhabited islands (departures from Wandoor jetty, daily except Mon, 10am; 90min; Rs100 for foreigners, Rs35 for Indians). Food and drink are usually provided on the organized tours, which also provide transport from Port Blair to Wandoor. If you don't arrange a trip through an agent or your hotel, it's possible to buy a ticket at the jetty and board the 10am launch, though you'll have to bring your own food and snorkelling equipment. Although the trips give less than three hours to explore fabulous reefs, they are still well worthwhile.

CHAPTER EIGHTEEN

TAMIL NADU

AMIL NADU, the cradle of south Indian temple architecture, is a living museum of styles that originated in the seventh century and matured in the huge temple complexes studded with towering gateways – *gopuras* – that soar above the markets of almost every town. Physically the state brims with green paddies and palm fields on its eastern edge, where flat alluvial plains roll to the **Coromandel Coast** to meet the Bay of Bengal, while in the west and north high rocky hills, in parts shrouded in forest, border Kerala, Karnataka and Andhra Pradesh. Apart from the **Kaveri**, the state has few perennial rivers: complex irrigation systems and tanks, often connected to temples, help maintain a water supply.

Despite its bold seafront fort, grand mansions, and excellence as a centre for the performing arts, the state capital **Madras** is probably its least interesting destination; a scruffy, dusty, noisy city with faint echoes of the British past. Much the best place to start a **temple tour** is nearby **Mamallapuram**, a sleepy seaside village that, quite apart from some exquisite Pallava rock-cut architecture (fifth–ninth centuries), boasts a long stretch of glorious beach. Not far inland, the pilgrimage city of **Kanchipuram** is filled with reminders of an illustrious past under successive dynastic rulers, while further down the coast is one of India's rare French colonial possessions, **Pondicherry**, where Auroville has found a new role in the "New Age".

The road south from Pondicherry puts you back on the temple trail, leading to the tenth-century **Chola kingdom** and the extraordinary architecture of **Chidambaram**, **Gangaikondacholapuram**, **Kumbakonam** and **Darasuram**. For the best Chola bronzes, however, and a glimpse of the magnificent paintings that flourished under Maratha rajas in the eighteenth century, travellers should head for **Thanjavur**. Chola capital for four centuries, the city boasts almost a hundred temples and was the birthplace of **Bharatanatyam** dance, famous throughout Tamil Nadu.

In the very centre of Tamil Nadu, **Tiruchirapalli**, a commercial town just northwest of Thanjavur, held some interest for the Cholas, but reached its heyday under later dynasties, when the temple complex in neighbouring **Srirangam** became one of south India's largest. Among its patrons were the Nayaks of **Madurai**, whose erstwhile capital further south, bustling with pilgrims, priests, peddlers, tailors and tourists, is an unforgettable destination. Here south India's most profusely carved temple dapples with light that seeps through countless pillared halls, and reflects from shimmering oil lamps onto gods, saints and maidens peering from every wall, column and gateway.

Rameshwaram, on the long spit of land reaching towards Sri Lanka, and **Kannyakumari**, at India's southern tip (the auspicious meeting point of the Bay of Bengal, the Indian Ocean and the Arabian Sea) are both important pilgrimage centres, with the added attraction of welcome cool breezes and vistas over the sea.

While Tamil Nadu's temples are undeniably its major attraction, it would take months to see them all, and there is plenty else to distract even the most ardent architecture buff. In the northwest of the state, where the hill stations of **Kodaikanal** and **Ooty** are the premier attractions, verdant hills offer mountain views and a network of trails wind through forests and tea and coffee plantations. **Mudumalai Wildlife Sanctuary**, a vast spread of deciduous forest dominated by teak, offers a good chance of spotting elephants and *dholes*, wild pack-hunting dogs, and you might even see tigers and leopards. **Anamalai sanctuary**, closer to Kodaikanal in the Palani hills, is better known for its lion-tailed macaques (black-maned monkeys). The wetlands of the coast provide perfect resting places for migratory birds, whose numbers soar during the winter monsoon at **Vedanthangal**, near Madras, and **Point Calimere**.

Temperatures in Tamil Nadu, which usually hover around 30°C, peak in May and June, when they often soar above 40°, and the overpowering heat makes all but sitting in a shaded cafe exhausting. The state is barely affected by the southwest monsoon that pounds much of India from June to September: it receives most of its **rain** between October and January. Cooler, rainy days bring their own problems; widescale flooding can disrupt road and rail links, and imbue everything with an all-pervasive dampness.

Tamil Nadu's **accommodation** prospects are good; all but the smallest towns and villages have something for all budgets. Most hotels offer their own dining halls which, together with local restaurants, sometimes offer sumptious *thalis*, tinged with tamarind and served on banana leaves. Indigenous dishes are almost exclusively vegetarian; for north Indian dishes or western alternatives, you'll have to head for five-star hotels.

Some history

Since the fourth century BC, Tamil Nadu has been shaped by its majority **Dravidian** population, of uncertain origins but physically quite different from north Indians. Their language developed separately, as did their social organization; the difference between high-caste *brahmins* and low-caste workers has always been more pronounced here than in the north. The influence of the powerful *janapadas*, established in the north by the fourth and third centuries BC, extended as far south as the Deccan, but they made few incursions into **Dravidadesa** (Tamil country). Incorporating what are now Kerala and Tamil Nadu, it was ruled by three dynasties: the **Cheras**, who held sway over much of the Malabar coast (Kerala), the **Pandyas**, in the far south, and the **Cholas**, whose realm stretched along the eastern Coromandel coast. Indo-Roman trade in spices, precious stones and metals flourished at the start of the Christian era, when **St Thomas** arrived in the south, but dwindled when trade links arose with southeast Asia.

The prosperity of the early kingdoms having faded by the fourth century AD, the way was clear for the **Pallavas**, who emerged in the sixth century as leaders of a kingdom centred around **Kanchipuram**. By the seventh century the successors of the first Pallava king, Simhavishnu, were engaged in battles with the southern Pandyas and the forces of the Chalukyas, based further west in Karnataka. However, the centuries of Pallava dominion are not marked simply by battles and territorial expansion; this was also an era of social development. **Brahmins** became the dominant community, responsible for lands and riches donated to temples. The emergence of *bhakti*, devotional worship, placed temples firmly at the centre of religious life (see p.935), and the inspirational *Sangam* literature of saint-poets fostered a tradition of dance and music that has become Tamil Nadu's cultural hallmark.

The **Vijayanagars**, who gained a firm footing in Hampi (Karnataka) in the fourteenth century, resisted Muslim incursions from the north and spread to cover most of south India by the sixteenth century, heralding a new phase of architectural development by building new temples, expanding older ones, and introducing colossal *gopuras*, or towers. In **Madurai** Vijayanagar governors, **Nayaks**, set up an independent kingdom whose impact spread as far as **Tiruchirapalli**. For a short period (1740–48)

TAMIL NADU TRAVEL DETAILS

	Trains		Buses		Flights	
	Frequency	Time	Frequency	Time	Frequency	Time
To and from MADRAS						
Bangalore	4–5 daily	5hr 30min–7hr	32 daily	9–11hr	4–6 daily	45min
Bhubaneshwar	7 daily	20hr–23hr 30min				
Bombay	1 daily	36hr 30min			3–5 daily	1hr 50min
Calcutta	6 daily	28hr–32hr 30min			3 weekly	3hr
Chengalpattu	10 daily*	1hr 10min	10 daily	1hr 30min–2hr		
Chidambaram	4 daily*	5hr 30min	20 daily	5–7hr		
Coimbatore	6 daily	8–9hr	7 daily	11–13hr	4 weekly	1hr 55min
Delhi	3 daily	33hr 45min–48hr			2–3 daily	2hr 30min–4hr
Dindigul	5 daily*	6hr 30min–12hr	9 daily	10–11hr		
Hyderabad	2 daily	14–15hr	1 daily	18–20hr	1–2 daily	1hr
Kanchipuram			46 daily	1hr 30min–2hr		
Kanniyakumari			7 daily	16–18hr		
Kochi	3 daily	13–14hr			1 daily	2hr
Kodaikanal	3 daily*	10–13hr	1 daily	14–15hr		
Kumbakonam	3 daily*	7hr 20min	5 daily	7–8hr		
Madurai	6 daily*	7hr 40min–14hr	20 daily	10hr	4 weekly	1hr 45min
Mamallapuram			53 daily	2hr–2hr 30min		
Mysore			1 daily	15hr 30min		
Pondicherry			70 daily	4–5hr		
Port Blair					Wed & Fri	2hr 5min
Pune	5 weekly	20–26hr			3 weekly	2hr 40min
Rameshwaram	2–3 daily*	14hr 30min–24hr	1 daily	14hr		
Salem	10 daily	4–5hr	4 daily	7–9hr		
Thanjavur	3 daily*	8–9hr	12 daily	8hr 30min		
Thiruv'puram	Sun only	18hr 10min	3 daily	16–18hr	4 weekly	45min
Tindivanam			40 daily	3–4hr		
Tiruch'palli	11 daily*	5hr 30min–11hr	35 daily	8–9hr	4 weekly	45min
Tirupati	2 daily	3hr	14 daily	3–4hr		
Tiruvannamalai			23 daily	4–6hr		
Udhagamandalam			1 daily	16hr		
Vedanthangal			3 daily	2–3hr		
Vellore			30 daily	3–4hr		
Vijayawada	13 daily	7–11hr	1 daily	13–16hr		
* Trains from Egmore; all others from Central						
To and from Chengalpattu						
Kanchipuram			20 daily	40min		
Kodaikanal	3 daily	9–12hr	1 daily	14hr		
Kumbakonam	3 daily	6hr–6hr 30min	3 daily	6–7hr		
Mamallapuram			40 daily	40min–1hr		
Rameshwaram	2 daily	13–15hr				
Thanjavur	3 daily	7–8hr				
Vedanthangal			8 daily	1hr		
To and from Chidambaram						
Chengalpattu	3 daily	4hr 10min–5hr				
Kodaikanal	1 daily	7hr 10min				
Kumbakonam	4 daily	1hr 40min				
Rameshwaram	1 daily	11hr				
Thanjavur	4 daily	2hr 30min–3hr	3 daily	8–9hr		
Tiruch'palli	4 daily	4hr				
Tirupati	2 daily	3hr				
Tiruvannamalai	1 daily	4hr 50min				
Vellore	1 daily	7hr				

To and from Coimbatore

Bangalore	1 daily	9hr 30min			4 weekly	50min
Bombay	1–2 daily	9hr 50min–11hr			3 weekly	1hr 45min
Calcutta	Tues & Thurs	39hr 30min			3 weekly	3hr
Delhi	1–2 daily	35–43hr				
Hyderabad	1 daily	20hr 50min				
Kanniyakumari	2 daily	12hr 35min–14hr				
Kochi	2 daily	5hr 30min				
Kodaikanal			2 daily	6hr		
Rameshwaram	1 daily	12hr 20min				
Salem	4 daily	3hr				
Thiruv'puram	4 daily	9hr 50min–11hr				
Tiruch'palli	1 daily	5hr				

To and from Kanchipuram

Tiruvannamalai	8 daily	2–3hr
Vellore	10 daily	2hr 30min

To and from Kanniyakumari

Bombay	1 daily	48hr
Delhi	Fri only	58hr
Kochi	2–3 daily	7hr 30min–9hr
Salem	1 daily	15hr
Thiruv'puram	2–3 daily	2hr–2hr 30min

To and from Madurai

Bangalore			21 daily	8–9hr
Chengalpattu	5 daily	10hr–12hr 40min	8 daily	8–9hr
Chidambaram	2 daily	8hr–9hr 30min		
Coimbatore	1 daily	5hr 50min	40 daily	10hr
Kochi			5 daily	10hr
Kodaikanal	6 daily	40min–1hr	10 daily	3hr 30min
Pondicherry			1 daily	8hr
Rameshwaram	5 daily	6hr 15min–7hr	20 daily	4hr
Thanjavur	2 daily	4hr 35min–6hr	8 daily	6hr
Thiruv'puram			10 daily	7hr
Tiruch'palli	8 daily	2hr 20min–8hr	15 daily	2–3hr
Tirupati	1 daily	18hr 20min		
Tiruvannamalai	1 daily	12hr 20min		
Vellore	1 daily	14hr 30min		

To and from Pondicherry

Bangalore	4 daily	7hr 30min
Kanchipuram	5 daily	2hr 30min–3hr
Mamallapuram	9 daily	2hr 30min
Thanjavur	2 daily	6hr
Tiruch'palli	6 daily	6hr
Udhagamandalam	1 daily	12hr

To and from Tiruchirapalli

Chengalpattu	9 daily	6hr 30min–9hr 20min		
Kanchipuram			3 daily	6–7hr
Kodaikanal	5 daily	2hr 40min	2 daily	5hr
Thanjavur	4 daily	1hr 40min	10 daily	1hr 30min
Tiruvannamalai			9 daily	4–5hr

Note that no individual route appears more than once in this chart; for any specific journey, check against where you want to get to as well as where you're coming from. Bear in mind, also, that there is only room here for a general summary; see the "Moving On" sections for specific cities for more details.

the **Marathas**, a strong force further north, took power in Madurai, Thanjavur and Tiruchirapalli, but they made little impact on the south's development.

Much more significant was the arrival of **Europeans**. First came the Portuguese, who landed in Kerala and monopolized Indian trade for about a century before they were joined by the British, Dutch and French. Though mostly on cordial terms with the Indians, the western powers soon found themselves engaged in territorial disputes. The most marked were between the French, based in **Pondicherry**, and the British, whose stronghold since 1640 had been Fort St George in **Madras**. After battles at sea and on land, the French were confined to Pondicherry, while British ambitions reached their apex in the eighteenth century, when the East India Company occupied Bengal (1757) and made firm its bases in Bombay and Madras.

As well as rebellions against colonial rule, Tamil Nadu also saw anti-*brahmin* protests, in particular those led by the Justice Party in the 1920s and 1930s. Independence in 1947 signalled the need to reorganize state boundaries, and by 1956 areas had been demarcated on a linguistic basis. Andhra Pradesh and Kerala were formed, along with Mysore state (later Karnataka) and **Madras Presidency**, a slightly smaller area than that governed from Madras by the British, where Tamil was the predominant language. In 1965 Madras Presidency became Tamil Nadu, the latter part of its name coming from the Chola agrarian administrative units known as *nadus*.

Since Independence, Tamil Nadu's industrial sector has mushroomed. Initially the state was led by Congress, but in 1967 the **DMK** (Dravida Munnetra Kazhagam), championing the lower castes and reasserting Tamil identity, won a landslide victory. Anti-Hindi and anti-centre, the DMK flourished until the film star "**MGR**" (MG Ramachandran) broke away to form the **All India Anna Dravida Munnetra Kazhagam** (AIADMK), and won an easy victory in the 1977 elections. Virtually deified by his fans-turned-supporters, MGR remained successful, promoting welfare schemes but rejecting industrial development, until his death in 1988, when the Tamil government fell back into the hands of the DMK. Soon after, the AIADMK were reinstated, led by **Sri Jayalalitha Jayaram**, an ex-film star and dancer once on close terms with MGR. Still in power as this book went to press, her policies of increasing low-caste reservations in jobs and education, and showering gifts upon poor communities, win her popular acclaim, but attract the criticism that she is simply buying votes.

Madras

In the northeastern corner of Tamil Nadu on the Bay of Bengal, **MADRAS** is India's fourth largest city, with a population nudging five and a half million. Hot, congested, and noisy, it is the major transportation hub of the south – the international airport makes a marginally less stressful entry point to the subcontinent than Bombay or Delhi – but most travellers stay just long enough to book a ticket somewhere else. The attractions of the city itself are decidedly sparse – some fine specimens of Raj architecture, pilgrimage sites connected with the apostle "Doubting Thomas", superb Chola bronzes at its chief museum, and plentiful music and dance performances.

The **capital** of Tamil Nadu, Madras is, like Bombay and Calcutta, a comparatively modern creation. It was founded by the **British East India Company** in 1639, on a narrow five-kilometre strip of land between the Cooum and Adyar rivers, a few kilometres north of the ancient Tamil port of **Mylapore** and the Portuguese settlement of San Thome, established in 1522. The site had no natural harbour; it was selected by Francis Day, the East India Company agent, in part because he enjoyed good relations with the Nayak governor Dharmala Ayyappa, who could intercede with the Vijayanagar Raja of Chandragiri, to whom the territory belonged. In addition, the land was protected by water on the east, south and west; cotton could be bought here twenty percent cheaper than elsewhere; and, apparently, Day had acquired a mistress in San Thomé. A fortified trading post, completed on St George's Day (April 23) 1640, was named **Fort St George**. By 1700, the British had acquired neighbouring territory including Triplicane and Egmore, while over the course of the next century, as capital of the **Madras Presidency**, which covered most of south India, the city mushroomed to include many surrounding villages. The British were repeatedly challenged by the French who, in 1746, destroyed much of the city. **Robert Clive** ("Clive of India"), then a clerk, was taken prisoner, an experience said to have inspired him to become a campaigner. Clive was among the first to re-enter Madras when it was retaken three years later, and continued to use it as his base. Following this, fortifications were strengthened and the British survived a year-long French siege (1759), completing the work in 1783. By this time, however, Calcutta was in the ascendancy and Madras lost its national importance.

Visitors to Madras should use **water** as sparingly as possible; the city's drastic shortage explains the water carriers trundling along its congested streets. Watch out for unofficial ones as you cross the road; tractors pulling tankers so heavy that they either topple over or fail to stop when brakes are applied, causing fatal accidents.

Arrival

Madras Meenambakkam airport is comprehensively served by international and domestic flights; the two terminals are a minute's walk from each other, 16km south-west of the city centre on National Highway 45. Out in the main hall of the international terminal, you'll find a 24-hour post office, several STD telephones, and a couple of snack bars. It's by no means certain that anyone will be staffing the **Government of Tamil Nadu Tourist Information Centre** booth at the arrivals exit, but if you're lucky you may be able to fix up accommodation in advance from here.

To **get away from the airport**, there are pre-paid minibus and taxi counters at the international arrivals exit. **Buses** (Rs40) include #1J and #21J (to Parry's Corner), and #18RR, #RR18 and #52J (to Broadway bus stand); the half-hour **taxi** ride to most of the bigger hotels costs Rs150, and to the railway stations Rs175; and **rickshaws** are slightly less expensive. A taxi all the way to Mamallapuram costs around Rs600. **Trains** run every 15 or 20 minutes (4.30am–11pm) from **Trisulam** station, 500m from the airport on the far side of the road, to Central, Egmore and North Beach stations, taking roughly 45 minutes.

Arriving in Madras by train, you come in at one of two **long-distance railway stations**, 1.5km apart on Periyar EVR High Rd, towards the north of the city. **Egmore Station**, in the heart of the busy commercial Egmore district, is the arrival point for most trains from Tamil Nadu and Kerala; on the whole, others pull in at **Central Station**, further east, on the edge of George Town, which has a 24-hour left luggage office, and STD phone booths outside the exit. Information booths at both stations are poorly staffed and badly equipped, but both have plentiful taxis and auto-rickshaws.

Buses from elsewhere in Tamil Nadu arrive at two bus stands, **Thiruvalluvar** and **Broadway** (also known as Express), opposite each other in George Town, near the

---

ROAD NAMES IN MADRAS

The names of several roads in Madras have recently changed; confusingly, both old and new names remain in use. What was **Mount Road** is now **Anna Salai**; **North Beach Road**, along the western edge of George Town, is now **Rajaji Salai**; and the east–west road across the north of the city, formerly **Poonamallee High Road**, has been renamed **Periyar EVR High Road**. **South Beach Road** has become **Kamaraj Salai**, and **Edward Elliot's Road** further south is now **Dr Radha Krishnan Salai**. We have used the new names throughout the chapter.

MADRAS

HOTELS:
Ⓐ Ranjit
Ⓑ Welcomgroup Park Sheraton
Ⓒ Savera
Ⓓ New Woodlands

RESTAURANTS:
❶ Taj Coromandel
❷ Palmgrove
❸ Palimar
❹ Saravana Bhavan
❺ Woodlands Drive-in
❻ Welcomgroup Chola Sheraton
❼ Amaravati

High Court complex off NSC Bose Rd. Though both stations are unbearably crowded and confusing, Broadway, which also sees services from Karnataka and Andhra Pradesh, is marginally worse: little more than a dirty, chaotic, pot-holed yard, and a nightmare to negotiate with luggage. It can also be a real problem to pick up a rickshaw. For details of buses to **Mamallapuram** from Broadway, see p.913.

Information and communications

At the highly efficient and very helpful **Government of India Tourist Office** (GITO) at 154 Anna Salai (Mon–Fri 9.15am–5.15pm, Sat 9.15am–1pm; ☎869695 or 869685), you can pick up leaflets, arrange accommodation and organize tours by rented car. They also supply approved **guides** by the day (Rs50–80) or half-day (Rs35–65).

Not far north, the **Tamil Nadu Tourism Development Corporation** (TTDC), 143 Anna Salai (Mon–Fri 10am–5.30pm; ☎830498 or 830390), has plenty of information on Madras, and organizes its own tours of the city. Advance bookings for Indian Tourism Development Corporation hotels can be made, and tours of the city arranged, at the ITDC office at 29 Victor Crescent, C-in-C Rd (Mon–Fri 6am–8pm, Sat & Sun 6am–2pm; ☎478884). Tourist offices for **other states**, including Himachal Pradesh, Kerala, Rajasthan and Uttar Pradesh, are at 28 C-in-C Rd (☎812955; Mon–Fri 10.30am–5pm).

Banks

Tourists rarely have any difficulties **changing money** in Madras: there are plenty of banks, and the major **hotels** offer exchange facilities to residents. The following places provide efficient service: *American Express*, G-17, Spencer Plaza, 769 Anna Salai (Mon–Sat 9.30am–5.30pm); *Bank of Baroda*, opposite GITO (for *Visa* encashments and travellers' cheques); *Central Bank of India*, Anna Salai; *Indian Overseas Bank*, 32 Dr Radhakrishnan Rd; and *Thomas Cook*, Rajaji Salai (Mon–Fri 10am–5pm).

Post and telephone

The **GPO**, with a poste restante counter, is just past Parry's Corner on Rajaji Salai (daily 8am–8pm; ☎512011). Madras' other main post office, **Mount Road Post Office** (same hours) at the northern end of Anna Salai, also has a poste restante, but only holds letters addressed to Mount Road PO. The post office on Triplicane High Rd (Mon–Sat 7am–3pm) is convenient if you're staying at *Broadlands* or *Himalaya Hotel*.

Telegram and **telephone** services are most efficient at the GPO. Trying to make a local or international call from Mount Rd Post Office requires tiresome form-filling, queuing and deposits – if you're in the area head for a phone booth advertising STD/PCO/ISD on a yellow sign, where you'll rarely have to wait in line.

THE VOICE OF SHANKARA

In April 1993, *Beta Byte Technologies* of Madras, expounding the importance of religious reassurance in today's climate of communal tension, opened a new phone-in service, the **Voice of Shankara**. Offering softly-spoken spiritual solace in both Hindi and Tamil, ranging from *bhajan* singing and the recital of the *Bhagavad Gita* to the daily almanac, the Voice of Shankara is on line to anyone willing to pay an enrolment fee of Rs12500, and an annual subscription of Rs1000. Callers can pose questions through the phone; each query, limited to three minutes so that the lines don't become blocked, is transmitted through a voice mail box to Kanchipuram. Acting as a kind of quasi-guru, within reach at any time of day or night, the Voice of Shankara is used by thousands of people, many of whom have come to see a call to the spiritual hot-line as a daily routine. The popularity of the service keeps two hundred staff working flat out, and plans are already afoot to set up similar lines in Hyderabad and Coimbatore.

The telephone **area code** for Madras is ☎44.

Publications

The long-established *Hallo! Madras* (monthly; Rs5, free in some tourist offices) is an accurate directory to all the city's services, with full moon dates (useful for estimating temple festivals), a guide to Tamil for tourists, and an outline of Madras bus timetables. *Variety Travel and Shopping Guide* (monthly; Rs15) is packed with travel details and comprehensive listings. Neither guide has a "What's On" section: for forthcoming music and dance performances, contact the venues or ask at the tourist office.

City transport

The offices, sights, railway stations and bus stands of Madras are spread over such a wide area that it's impossible to get around without using some form of **public transport**. Much the best way is by **bus**, a network relieved by an efficient **train** system that operates like an above-ground metro.

Buses

To ride the bus in most Indian cities you need to be incredibly resilient, a master of the art of hanging onto open doorways with two fingers. Buses in Madras, on the other hand, are regular, reliable, inexpensive, well-labelled, and only cramped during rush-hours. On Anna Salai, they have special stops – on smaller streets, flag them down, or wait with the obvious crowd. Buses in Egmore accumulate opposite the railway station.

USEFUL BUS ROUTES IN MADRAS

From Broadway Bus Station

#18A, #52B, D, E, F, #54T, #60A Broadway Bus St – Guindy – St Thomas Mt

#88 Broadway – Egmore RS

#18RR, #RR18 Broadway – Guindy – Airport

#19R Broadway – VGP Golden Beach

#52J Broadway – Little Mount – Guindy – Airport

From Egmore Railway Station

#22A, #27, #27B, #27H, #29A Egmore RS –Triplicane – Anna Square

#M4 Egmore RS – Periyar EVR High Rd – Central RS

#1JJ Egmore RS – Rajaji Salai – Parry's – Anna Salai – Triplicane

#23J & #29R Egmore RS – Anna Salai – Adyar

Northbound

#7J, #31, #32 & #32A Triplicane – Anna Square – Chepauk – Secretariat – Parry's

#18C St Thomas Mt – Guindy

#23A & B Adyar Bus Station – Egmore RS

From George Town

#9, #9B, #17D, E, K & T Parry's – Central RS – Egmore RS

#9A Parry's – Egmore RS – Nungambakkam (Income Tax Office and Foreigners' Registration Office)

#18E, T & G Parry's – Central RS – Guindy

#21E, #51R Parry's – Secretariat – Adyar – Guindy RS – St Thomas Mount

#1J Parry's – Anna Salai – Guindy – National Airport

#6JJ Beach Station – Parry's – Triplicane – St Thome

#1, #45J Parry's – Secretariat – Triplicane

#R18, #36R Beach Station – Anna Salai – Guindy

#19RR High Court – Anna Salai PO – Mylapore – Adyar – VGP Golden Beach

#21J High Court – Secretariat – Chepauk – Adyar – Guindy – National Airport

From Anna Salai

#40 Anna Square – Triplicane – Egmore RS

#45B Anna Square – Triplicane – Anna Salai – Guindy RS – Butt Rd (St Thomas Mount)

Trains

If you want to travel south from central Madras to Guindy (Deer Park), St Thomas Mount, or the airport, the easiest way to go is by **train**. Services run every 15 minutes (on average) between 4.30am and 11pm, prices are minimal, and you can guarantee a seat at any time except rush hour (9am & 5pm). First-class carriages substitute padded seats for wooden slatted benches, and are a little cleaner. Buy a ticket before boarding.

City trains follow the route: North Beach (opposite the GPO), Fort, Egmore, Nungambakkam, Kodambakkam, Mambalam (for T Nagar and silk shops), Saidapet (for Little Mount Church), Guindy, St Thomas Mount, and Trisulam (for the airport).

Taxis and rickshaws

Madras' yellow-top *Ambassador* **taxis** gather outside Egmore and Central railway stations, and at the airport. All have meters, but they often prefer to set a fixed price before leaving. Expect to pay Rs25–35 from either station to Anna Salai.

Flocks of auto- and cycle rickshaws wait patiently outside tourist hotels, and not so patiently outside railway stations. **Auto-rickshaw** drivers in Madras are notorious for their demand for high fares from city-dwellers and tourists alike. All rickshaws have meters; a few drivers use them if asked, but in many cases you'll save a lot of frustrating bargaining by offering a small sub above the meter-reading. If you need to get to the airport or station early in the morning, you can book a rickshaw, and negotiate the price, the night before (the driver may well sleep in his rickshaw outside your hotel).

Only take **cycle rickshaws** on the smaller roads; riding amid Madras traffic on a fragile tricycle seat can be extremely hair-raising.

Car and bike rental

Car rental, with driver, is available from tourist offices, and many of the upmarket hotels. It's a great, relatively stress-free way to get about if you can afford it (roughly Rs600 per day in Madras, Rs1000 per day outside Madras).

Anyone interested in renting a **moped** or **motorcycle** for short rides around the city, or tours of Tamil Nadu, should head for the *U-Rent Services* offices at 36 2nd Main Rd, Gandhi Nagar, Adyar (Mon–Sat 8am–8pm; ☎410544), or *Picnic Hotel*, 1132 Periyar EVR High Rd (Mon–Sat 6am–10pm; ☎588828). You'll need an international driving licence. Prices range from Rs60 to Rs200 per day.

TOURS IN MADRAS AND TAMIL NADU

One good way to get around the sights of Madras is on an ITDC or TTDC **bus tour**: bookings are taken in the relevant offices. Albeit inevitably rushed, they're good value, and the guides can be very helpful. On full-day tours, meals are included in the price.

ITDC tours from their office at 26 C-in-C Rd (daily 1.30–6pm; Rs30) visit Fort St George and the fort museum, St Mary's Church, the Government Museum and art gallery, memorials to Gandhi, Rajaji and Kamaraj, the children's park and Snake Park, Kapalishvara temple and Marina beach.

The **TTDC half-day tour** (daily: 7.30am–1.30pm; Rs55 or 1.30–6.30pm; Rs45) starts at 143 Anna Salai, and picks up passengers at the Express bus stand near the High Court in George Town. It takes in Fort St George, the Government Museum, the Snake Park, Kapalishvara temple and Elliot's Beach, and drives past the Marina. The **full-day** tours (daily 8am–7pm) add St Mary's Church, Birla Planetarium and VGP Golden beach resort.

Among longer TTDC tours are good-value **day-trips** to Mamallapuram (daily 7.30am–7pm; Rs90) and Kanchipuram (daily 6.20am–7pm; Rs105, Rs135 for an a/c bus). The **8-day Tamil Nadu tour** whistles through twelve towns that deserve more time: among them Chidambaram, Thanjavur, Rameshwaram, Kodaikanal, Pondicherry, Kannyakumari, Thiruvananthapuram, Madurai, and Trichy (dep Sat 7am; Rs1300–2000).

The City

Madras city divides into three main areas. The northern district, separated from the rest by the River Cooum, is the site of the first British outpost in India, **Fort St George**, and the commercial centre, **George Town**, that grew up during British occupation. At the southern end of Rajaji Salai, **Parry's Corner**, George Town's principal landmark – look for the tall grey building labelled *Parry's* – is a major bus stop.

Central Madras, sandwiched between the Cooum and Adyar rivers, and crossed diagonally by the city's main thoroughfare, **Anna Salai**, is dominated by modern commercial and residential areas, and gives way in the east to a long straight **coastline** where fishermen mend nets and set small boats out to sea, and tourists hitch up *saris* and trousers for a quick paddle. South of here, near the coast, **Mylapore**, inhabited in the sixteenth century by the Portuguese, boasts **Kapalishvara temple** and **San Thome Church**, both tourist attractions and places of pilgrimage. Further out, south of the Adyar, the Portuguese church on **St Thomas Mount** overlooks the green spaces of **Guindy National Park**, the only city national park in India.

Fort St George

Quite unlike any other fort in India, **Fort St George** stands amid state offices facing the sea in the east of the city, just south of George Town on Kamaraj Salai. It looks more like a complex of well-maintained colonial mansions than a fort; indeed many of its buildings are used today as offices, roamed during the week by businessmen passing between the Secretariat and State Legislature.

The fort was the first structure of Madras city, and the first territorial possession of the British in India. Construction began in 1640, but most of the original buildings had to be replaced later that century, after being damaged during French sieges. The most imposing structure is the eighteenth-century colonnaded **Fort House**, coated in deep slate grey and white paint. Next door, in the more modestly proportioned **Exchange Building** – site of Madras' first bank – is the fort **museum** (daily except Fri 10am–5pm). The collection within faithfully records the central events of the British occupation of Madras with portraits, regimental flags, weapons, coins minted by the East India Company, medals, stamps and letters written by figures such as Robert Clive. The squat cast-iron cage on the ground floor was brought to Madras from China, where for more than a year in the nineteenth century it had been used as a particularly sadistic form of imprisonment for a British captain. The upper floor, once the Public Exchange Hall where merchants met to gossip and trade, is now an **art gallery**, where portraits of prim officials and their wives sit side-by-side with finely sketched pictures of the British embarking at Madras in aristocratic finery, attended by Indians in loin cloths.

South of the museum, past the State Legislature, is the oldest surviving Anglican church in Asia, **St Mary's Church**, built in 1678, and partly renovated after the battle of 1759. The church, built with thick walls and a strong vaulted roof to withstand the city's many sieges, served as a store and shelter in times of war. It's distinctly English in style, crammed with plaques and statues in memory of British soldiers, politicians and their wives. The grandest plaque, made of pure silver, was presented by Elihu Yale, former Governor of Fort St George (1687–96), and founder of Yale University in the US. A collection of photographs of visiting dignitaries, including Queen Elizabeth II, is on display in the entrance porch, while the ageing mural of the Last Supper above the altar in the eastern wing, probably painted by a student of Raphael, was looted from the French headquarters in Pondicherry. The cemetery outside contains the graves of yet more soldiers, and smaller headstones commemorating young children struck down by disease. Nearby, **Robert Clive's house** and a tiny museum in his honour occupy a small office building with unpredictable opening hours.

George Town

North of Fort St George, the former British trading centre of **George Town** remains a focus for banks, offices and shipping companies. This confusing – if well-ordered – grid of streets harbours a fascinating medley of architecture: eighteenth- and nine-teenth-century churches, Hindu and Jain temples, and a scattering of mosques, inter-spersed with grand mansions. However, despite its potential charm, this is Madras' most chaotic and crowded area, a dirty and uninviting warren of streets clogged by particularly persistent hawkers and thick traffic. Probably the best way to appreciate the area is from its edges. In the east, on Rajaji Salai, the **GPO** occupies a robust earth-red Indo-Saracenic building, constructed in 1884. George Town's southern extent is marked by the bulbous white domes and sandstone towers of the **High Court**, and the even more opulent towers of the **Law College**, both displaying strong Islamic influence.

It can be fun to take a quick root around George Town's **bazaars**, lines of rickety stalls selling clothes, bags, umbrellas, watches, shoes and perfume, concentrated along Rajaji Salai and NSC Bose Rd. Further south, the pavements are crowded by stalls sell-ing balloons, fruit, flowers and lottery tickets.

Government Museum

Pantheon Rd, south of Egmore Railway Station. Daily except Fri 9am–5pm. Rs2, Rs12 camera fee.

It's well worth setting aside at least half a day to explore the Madras **Government Museum** for its remarkable archeological finds from south India and the Deccan, stone sculptures from major temples, and unsurpassed collection of Chola bronzes.

A deep red circular structure, fronted by Italian-style pillars and built in 1851, the **main building** stands opposite the entrance and ticket office. Inside, the first gallery is devoted to archeology and geology, with tools, pots, jewellery and weapons from the Stone and Iron ages, and maps of principal excavations. Later exhibits include a substantial assortment of dismantled panels, railings and statues from Amaravati (see p.1089), carved with episodes from the Buddha's life and scenes from the *Jataka* stories from early Hinayana Buddhist texts. To the left of this gallery, high arcaded halls full of stuffed animals and the like lead to the **ethnology gallery**, where models, clothes and weapons, along with photographs of expressionless faces in orderly lines, illustrate local tribal societies, some long since wiped out. A fascinating display of wind and string instruments, drums and percussion includes the large predecessor to today's *sitar* and several very old *tabla*. Nearby, a group of wooden doors, lintels and window frames from Chettinad, a region near Madurai, are exquisitely carved with floral and geometric designs much like those found in Gujarati *havelis*.

The museum's real treasure, however, is the modern, well-lit gallery, left of the main building, which contains the world's most complete and impressive selection of **Chola bronzes** (see p.945). Large statues of Shiva, Vishnu and Parvati stand in the centre, flanked by glass cases containing smaller figurines, including several sculp-tures of Shiva as **Nataraja**, the Lord of the Dance, encircled by a ring of fire, and standing with his arms and legs poised and head provocatively cocked. One of the finest models is **Ardhanari**, the androgynous form of Shiva (united with Shakti in transcendence of duality) familiar from Chola temples. The left side of the body is female and the right male, and the intimacy of detail is astounding. A rounded breast, a delicate hand and tender bejewelled foot are counterpoints to the harsher sinewy limbs and torso, and the male side of the head is crowned with a mass of matted hair and serpents.

A **childrens' museum** demonstrates the principles of electricity and irrigation with marginally diverting, semi-functional models, while the magnificent Indo-Saracenic **art gallery** houses old British portraits of figures such as Clive and Hastings, Rajput and Moghul miniatures, and a small display of ivory carvings.

EGMORE & ANNA SALAI

RESTAURANTS:
1 Ramprasad
2 Aavin
3 Maharaja
4 Buhari
5 Inland

Egmore Railway Station

CHINTADRIPET

EGMORE HIGH RD

Museum

PUDAPET

Indian Airlines

River Cooum

TRIPLICANE

Spencers

N

0   500 m

HOTELS:
A New Victoria
B People's Lodge
C Imperial
D Impala Continental
E YWCA International Guest House
F Tourist Home
G Vee Yes
H Udipi
I Diplomat
J Kanchi
K Connemara
L Madras International
M Vijaya Lodge
N Broadlands
O Himalaya

Central Station & George Town

Marina

One of the longest city beaches in the world, the **Marina** (Kamaraj Salai, aka South Beach Rd) stretches 5km from the harbour at the southeastern corner of George Town, to San Thome Cathedral. The impulse to transform Madras' "rather dismal beach" into a Marina, styled "from old Sicilian recollections" which would function as a "lung" for the city, was conceived by Mountstuart Elphinstone Grant-Duff (Governor 1881–86) who had otherwise won himself the reputation for being "feeble, sickly" and a "failure". Over the years, numerous buildings, some of which undoubtedly would not have figured in memories of Sicily, have sprung up.

The **beach** itself is a sociable stretch, peopled by idle paddlers, picnickers and pony-riders; on Sunday afternoons crowds gather for a market. Swimming and sunbathing are neither recommended nor approved – if you're desperate, however, you could try one of the shabby swimming pools. There's also a rather neglected aquarium, and two parks at the northern end, the **Anna Park** and **MG Ramachandran Samadhi**. The **landward** side reveals a wealth of colonial architecture; at the north, one of the oldest of the city's University buildings is the **Senate House** (1879), an uncharacteristically Byzantine-influenced design by Robert Fellowes Chisholm (1840–1915). He was one of the British leaders in developing the Indo-Saracenic hybrid style, incorporating Hindu, Jain and Muslim elements along with solid Victorian British brickwork.

Continuing south, past the Indo-Saracenic **Presidency College** (1865–71), a number of stolid Victorian University buildings include the **Lady Willingdon Teacher Training College**. Next door, the college's hostel, a huge lump of a building with a semicircular frontage painted white and yellow, was until 1870 Madras' Ice House, storing huge blocks of ice imported from New England.

Mylapore

Long before Madras came into existence, **Mylapore**, south of the Marina, was an important settlement; the Greek geographer Ptolemy mentioned it in the second century AD as a thriving port. During the Pallava period (fifth–ninth centuries) it was second only to Mamallapuram (see p.915).

An important stop – with Little Mount and St Thomas Mount – on the St Thomas pilgrimage trail, **San Thome Cathedral** (daily 6am–8pm) marks the eastern boundary of Mylapore, lying close to the sea at the southern end of the Marina. Although the present neo-Gothic structure dates from 1896, San Thome stands on the site of two earlier churches (the first possibly erected by Nestorian Christians from Persia during the tenth century) built over the tomb of St Thomas; his relics are kept inside. Behind the church, a small **museum** houses stone medallions, stones inscribed in Tamil, Sanskrit (twelfth-century Chola) and early Portuguese, and a map of India dated 1519.

The **Kapalishvara**, less than 1km west, is the most famous temple in Madras, its principal shrine to Shiva. Seventh-century Tamil poet-saints sang its praises, but the present temple probably dates from the sixteenth century. Until then, the temple is thought to have occupied a site on the shore; sea erosion or demolition at the hands of the Portuguese led it to be rebuilt inland. Dominating the eastern and main entrance, the huge (40m) *gopura* tower, covered in stucco figures, is comparatively recent (1906). Non-Hindus, denied access to the shrines, can enter the courtyard, where beneath an old tree a small shrine to Shiva's consort, Parvati, shows her in the form of a peahen worshipping a *lingam*. This commemorates the legend that she was momentarily distracted from concentrating on her Lord by the enchanting dance of a peacock. Shiva, miffed at this dereliction of wifely duty, cursed her, whereupon she turned into a peahen (*mayil*). To expiate the sin, Parvati took off to a place called Kapalinagar, and embarked upon rigorous austerities. To commemorate her success, the town came to be known as Mayilapore or **Mylapore**.

The oldest artefacts in the Kapalishvara temple are the movable bronze images of deities and the 63 Shaivite Nayanmar poet-saints, two of whom came from Mylapore. Unusually, the main shrine faces west, towards a space that appears vast in this cramped suburban district, and is dominated by a eighteenth-century waterlily tank.

Important **festivals** held here include Tai Pusham (Jan/Feb), when the bronze images of Shiva and Parvati are pulled around the temple tank in a decorated boat to the accompaniment of music. Brahmotsava (March/April) celebrates the marriage of Shiva and Parvati; on the eighth day, in the afternoon, all 63 bronze images of the Nayanmar saints are clothed and garlanded and taken out in palanquins along the streets to meet the bejewelled images of Shiva and Parvati. Vasantha (May/June), the summer festival, is marked by music concerts.

In the busy **market streets** that surround the temple, amid stalls selling pots and pans, flowers, religious paraphernalia and vegetables, glittering shops spill over with gold wedding-jewellery. Exquisite *saris* are unfolded for scrutiny in silk emporia; the finest quality comes from Kanchi, delicately embroidered with gold and silver thread that can add as much as Rs30,000 to the cost of a wedding.

A little further west, before you come to TTK Road (previously Mowbray Rd), the **Luz Church**, on Luz Church Rd, is thought to be the earliest in Madras, built by the Portuguese in the sixteenth century. Its founding is associated with a miracle; Portuguese sailors in difficulties at sea were once guided to land and safety by a light which, when they tried to find its source, disappeared. The church, dedicated to Our Lady of Light, was erected where the light left them.

Little Mount

St Thomas is said to have sought refuge from persecution in the **Little Mount caves**, 8km south of the city centre, now 200m off the road between the Maraimalai Adigal Bridge and the Residence of the Governor of Tamil Nadu. Entrance to the cave is beside steps leading to a statue of Our Lady of Health (see p.948). Inside, next to a small natural window in the rock, are impressions of what are believed to be St Thomas' handprints, made when he made his escape through this tiny opening.

Behind the new circular church of Our Lady of Health, together with brightly painted replicas of the Pietà and Holy Sepulchre, is a natural **spring**. Tradition has it that this was created when Thomas struck the rock, so the crowds that came to hear him preach could quench their thirst; samples of its holy water are on sale.

St Thomas Mount

Tradition has it that St Thomas was speared to death (or struck by a hunter's stray arrow), while praying before a stone cross on **St Thomas Mount**, 11km south of the city centre, close to the airport. **Our Lady of Expectation church** (1523) is reached by 134 granite steps marked at intervals with the fourteen stations of the cross. At the top of the steps, a huge old banyan tree provides shade for devotees who come to fast, pray and sing. Inside the church, St Thomas' cross is said to have bled in 1558; above the altar which marks the spot of the Apostle's death, a painting of the Madonna and Child is credited to St Luke. A memento stall stands nearby and cool drinks are available in the adjacent Holy Apostle's Convent.

The Theosophical Society Headquarters

The **Theosophical Society** was established in New York in 1875 by Colonel Olcott and the eccentric Madame Petrovna Blavatsky, who claimed occult powers and telepathic links with "Mahatmas" in Tibet. Claiming to believe in the equality and truth of all religions, the society in fact propagated a modern Hinduism, praising all things Indian and shunning Christian missionaries – so its two founders were greeted enthusiastically when they transferred their operations to Madras in 1882, establishing their headquarters near Elliot's Beach in the south. Even after Madame Blavatsky's psychic powers were proved to be bogus, the society continued to attract Hindus and western visitors, and its buildings still stand today, sheltering several shrines and an excellent library of books on religion and philosophy (Tues–Sun 8–11am & 1.30–5pm; ☎413528). A vast **banyan tree** in the gardens, a tangle of wide branches and hanging roots that form subsidiary trunks, is said to be the second largest in the world.

Guindy National Park

South of Elliot Beach Road, not far from Guindy railway station, the peaceful **Guindy National Park** is home to a healthy community of **black buck**, **chital** (spotted deer), mongooses and monkeys. However, it's rather neglected, and many visitors leave disappointed, without spotting any animals. One section is fenced off as a **Snake Park** (daily 9am–5.30pm), but its reptilian residents are neither unusual nor plentiful.

Accommodation

Finding a **place to stay** in Madras can be a problem, as the hotels are all too often full. Demand for lodgings has pushed prices up, so only a couple of hotels offer anything for less than Rs100. Standards in the less expensive places are not high – in contrast Madras' top-notch hotels are truly palatial, immaculately clean and very well run.

The main concentration of mid-range and inexpensive hotels is in **Egmore**, around the railway station. Head for the places listed below first; if they're full, a little bit of hunting around should turn up a reasonable fall-back. Other popular areas include **Anna Salai**, which tends to be more expensive, and Triplicane, further east. The bulk of the top hotels are in the south of the city; several offer buses to and from the airport.

Egmore

Diplomat, 38–39 Halls Rd (☎8253 728). Small, quiet place opposite the Children's Hospital. Not bad rooms with attached bath and a slight cockroach problem. Best rooms on the first floor. ③.

Impala Continental, 12 Gandhi Irwin Rd (☎8250 484). Large hotel with impersonal but clean rooms, all with attached bath and some with hot water. Good value and often full. ③–⑤.

Imperial, 6 Gandhi Irwin Rd (☎8250 376). Set back from the road. Assorted rooms, comfortable a/c suites. Restaurant, nightclub and travel services. The *Chandra*, in the forecourt, is cheaper. ⑤–⑦.

Majestic, 20 Kennet's Lane (☎8250 679). Very central, with grimy, smelly rooms for those who really want to spend less. Overpriced as it is. ①–②.

New Victoria, 3 Kennet's Lane (☎8253 638). Smart, modern and clean. All rooms with hot shower and some with balconies. ⑦–⑧.

People's Lodge, off Gandhi Irwin Rd (☎8359 380). Basic and grubby, but cheap. ①–②.

Sri Laxmi Lodge, 16 Kennet's Lane (☎8254 576). Standard non-a/c rooms opening onto dim corridors; clean and functional. ③.

Tourist Home, 21 Gandhi Irwin Rd (☎8250 079). Popular hotel directly opposite the railway station: fresher and better ventilated than many. Rooms (some a/c) with showers, telephones, clean sheets and towels. Good value and often full. ④–⑤.

Udipi Home, 34 Police Commissioner's Office Rd (☎8251 515). Clean, fresh rooms, and excellent service. ④–⑥.

Vee Yes, 35 Gandhi Irwin Rd (☎8252 547). Average small hotel, badly ventilated but clean enough. Carpeted, a/c rooms with hot showers. ④–⑤.

YWCA International Guest House, 1086 Periyar EVR High Rd (☎5324 234). Attractive hotel in quiet gardens. Spotless rooms and a good restaurant. ⑤–⑥.

Anna Salai and Triplicane

Broadlands, 16 Vallabha Agraham St, Triplicane (☎845573 or 848131). Whitewashed old house, around a leafy courtyard; the kind of budget travellers' enclave you either love or loathe. Large roof

---

ACCOMMODATION PRICE CODES

All **accommodation prices** in this book have been coded using the symbols below. In principle the prices given are for the least expensive double rooms in each establishment; however, some hotels, usually in category ①, offer rates per bed rather than per room. Local taxes are not included unless specifically stated. For more details, see p.34.

①	up to Rs100	④	Rs225–350	⑦	Rs750–1200
②	Rs100–150	⑤	Rs350–500	⑧	Rs1200–2200
③	Rs150–225	⑥	Rs500–750	⑨	Rs2200 and up

terrace and clean rooms, a few with private shower and balcony. Left-luggage facilities, and snacks, drinks and beer to order. The in-house masseur is not recommended. ④–⑤.

Himalaya, 54 Triplicane High Rd (☎847568). Clean, spacious rooms and efficient service. TV, table and chair, hot shower and balcony in all rooms; some a/c. ④–⑤.

Kanchi, 28 C-in-C Rd (☎471100). Good-value mid-priced hotel with non- and a/c rooms, two restaurants (one rooftop) and bar. ④–⑤.

Madras International, 693 Anna Salai (☎861811). Reasonable hotel with range of rooms, shops, veg and non-veg restaurant and bar. ⑦.

Taj Connemara, Binny Rd (☎860123; fax 860193). Close to Anna Salai but a world away from its tiresome traffic. A Madras institution, now immaculately kept by the *Taj Group*. The best rooms are the bigger, characterful old ones, complete with dressing room and conservatory-like verandah overlooking the swimming pool. Excellent service, restaurants and all expected facilities. ⑨.

Outside the centre

New Woodlands Hotel, 72–75 Dr Radha Krishnan Salai (☎473111). Clean, spacious rooms with hot showers. ⑥.

Ranjit, 9 Nungambakkam High Rd (☎8270 521). Spotless rooms (some a/c) with *Star TV*. Veg and non-veg restaurants. ⑥.

Savera, 69 Dr Radha Krishnan Salai (☎8274 700). Modern hotel boasting all mod-cons and a swimming pool, bar and restaurant. Smart rooms, including huge deluxe suites. ⑧.

Trident, 1/24 GST Rd (☎2344 747; fax 2346 699). Comfortable 5-star hotel set in pleasant gardens with swimming pool. Very convenient for the airport (3km), but long (albeit complimentary) drive into town (12km). Good restaurants, one of which serves Thai cuisine. ⑨.

Welcomgroup Park Sheraton, TTK Rd (☎452525; fax 455913). Last word in American-inspired, executive luxury, with bow-tied valets and in-room fax machines. Three excellent restaurants (see below), 24hr coffee shop and other 5-star facilities. ⑨.

Eating

Madras is jam-packed with **restaurants**, from the predictable range of standard "meals" joints, to places where you can sample the very best in south Indian cuisine. For budget experimentation you can't beat *Saravana Bhavan* in the T Nagar market area; with a fistful of cash, head for the luxurious *Park Sheraton* and *Connemara*.

Aavin, Anna Salai. Blissfully cooling milk and ice cream parlour, a few steps north of the Government Tourist Office. Takeaway only.

Amaravati, Cathedral Rd. Excellent, inexpensive Andhra food, with particularly good *biryanis*.

Buhari, 83 Anna Salai. A/c and non-a/c dining rooms and open-air terrace with a homely atmosphere, veg and non-veg south and north Indian food, plus freshly baked cakes.

Connemara, Binny Rd (☎860123). Irresistible buffet lunches at the *Verandah* coffee shop, albeit costing around Rs200. Excellent veg and non-veg Indian and western dishes, with wicked desserts. Breakfast is just as good. In the evening, the outdoor *Rain Tree* specializes in spicy dishes from Chettinad; live Carnatic classical music and Bharatanatyam performances add to the atmosphere.

Impala Continental, 12 Gandhi Irwin Rd, Egmore. Plain and simple restaurant in hotel complex. A variety of north Indian dishes; tasty but unspectacular.

Imperial, 6 Gandhi Irwin Rd, Egmore. Imaginative menu, featuring superb steaks, served at indoor and outdoor tables in an enjoyable family atmosphere.

Inland, Anna Salai. Cosy, with small rooftop terrace and a/c room serving reasonably priced variety of Indian snacks and meals.

Maharaja, 307 Triplicane High Rd. Simple restaurant, popular with budget travellers. Those who opt for the pricier "tourist" dishes (north Indian specialities) at the front miss out on the better-value set meals served at the back. Small ante-room for north Indian food open until midnight.

Other Room, *Ambassador Pallava Hotel*, 53 Monteith Rd. North Indian cuisine with live bands and dance floor in the evening; lunchtime buffet for less than Rs 200.

Palimar, 48 Ground Floor, Parsn Manere, 602 Anna Salai. Snack-oriented dishes (mostly south Indian, some *tandoori*) in modern smart a/c rooms, plus daily specials noon–3pm. Good value.

THE MADRAS FESTIVAL AND THE SABHAS

The **sabhas** of Madras – the city's arts societies and venues, of which the most illustrious is the *Madras Music Academy* – stage regular public performances of Carnatic classical music and Bharatanatyam dance, where ambitious artists have to undergo the scrutiny of an often fanatical audience and a less-than-generous bevy of newspaper critics, whose reviews can make or break a career.

Musicians are expected correctly to interpret the subtleties of any given composition, *raga* or *tala*. The sets of notes that make up a *raga* occupy a place midway between melody and scale; they must be played imaginatively in improvisation, but in strict sequences and with correct emphasis. The worst crime, the sign of an amateur, is to slip accidentally into a different *raga* that might share the same scale. *Tala*, the rhythmic cycle and bedrock of the music, will often be demonstrated by someone on stage, and consists of a series of claps and waves; unlike in north India, this element is overt in the south and the audience delights in clapping along to keep the often-complex time signatures. The pleasure is heightened during percussion improvisations on the barrel-shaped *mridangam* drum or *ghatam* clay pot that accompany many performances.

During the second half of December and early January, the two- to three-week **Madras Festival** stages up to 500 events in an orgy of classical music and dance recitals, during which many of India's greatest artistes – from both north and south – can be seen at work.

Female vocalists to look out for include MS Subbulakshmi, Mani Krishnaswamy, Charumathi Ramachandran, Sudha Raghunathan and Bombay Jayashree; duos such as the Bombay and Hyderabad Sisters are also popular. Top-ranking **male singers**, KV Narayanaswamy, Thanjavur M Thiagarajan, B Rajam Iyer and younger artists like Thrissur Ramachandran and TN Seshagopalan should not be missed. Among the best of the **instrumentalists** are Balachandar, Kalyana Krishna Bhavatar, E Gayatri and Rama Varma on the gentle melodic *vina*, a stringed instrument unique to the south; Ramani on flute; violinists such as TN Krishnan, D Ananda Raman; and N Ravikiran on *gottuvadyam*, a rare member of the *vina* family, laid flat on the floor and played much like a slide guitar.

The predominant **dance** style is Bharatanatyam, as performed by stars such as Alarmail Valli, and the Dhananjayans. Dance dramas are also staged by the *Kalakshetra Academy*, a school of dance and music set in a beautiful 100-acre compound near the sea in Tiruvanmiyur, on the southern outskirts of the city.

Outside the festival, to find out about **performances of music and dance**, ask at tourist offices, consult local papers, or contact the following *sabhas* and dance halls:

Indian Fine Arts Society, 15 Stringers St, Madras 18 (☎20661).

Kalaivanar Arangam, Govt Estate, Wallajah Rd (☎565669).

Kamaraj Memorial Hall, Anna Salai (☎451355).

Music Academy, 115E TTK Rd, Madras 14 (☎475619 or 472651).

Mylapore Fine Arts Club, 16 Oliver Rd, Madras 4 (☎72660).

Naranda Gana Sabha, 254 TTK Rd, Madras 18 (☎453201).

Rani Seethai Hall, 603 Anna Salai (☎8274 863).

Sri Krishna Gana Sabha, 8 Griffin Rd, T Nagar, Madras 17 (☎442806).

Sri Thyaga Brahma Gana Sabha, Vani Bhavan, 50 GN Chetty Rd, Madras 17.

Tamil Issai Sangam, Raja Annamalai, Esplanade (☎23425).

Palmgrove, 5 Kodambakkam High Rd (☎8271 881). Two veg restaurants: *Oorvasi*, with *tandoori* dishes and "meals"; the cheaper *Menaka* has south Indian snacks and good lunch *thalis*.

Ramprasad, 22 Gandhi Irwin Rd, Egmore. Small, simple dining hall attached to hotel. Standard south Indian dishes, fresh chutneys, and strong hot coffees. Great for breakfast.

Saravana Bhavan, Thanigai Murugan Rathinavel Hall, 77 Usman Rd, T Nagar. Off the tourist trail, near Ranganathan St Market (Mambalam railway station), but an excellent and very crowded place to eat authentic, inexpensive south Indian veg food. For tasty curries, and all the trimmings, try the deluxe "Tamil Nadu meal". The a/c first floor is more expensive than the hectic "leaf meals" canteen on the top floor, while the ground floor serves south Indian snacks, ice creams and sweets.

MOVING ON FROM MADRAS

Transport connections between Madras and the rest of India are summarized on p.897; flights between Madras and **southeast Asia** are listed on p.7; and details on how to get to the **Andaman islands** by sea or air are given on p.886.

By air

Cities served by daily **flights** from Madras include **Bangalore** (6 daily; 5 Fri; 4 Wed & Sun; 45min), **Bombay** (5 Mon, Tues & Sat; 4 Thurs; 3 Wed, Fri & Sun; 1hr 50min), and **Delhi** (2 daily, 3 on Wed & Sun; 2hr 30min–3hr 50min) and Hyderabad (1 daily, 2 Wed, Fri & Sun; 1hr); **Thiruvananthapuram** (2hr 40min) is served every day except Wed & Sun; **Madurai** (1hr 45min), **Tiruchirapalli** (45min), and **Coimbatore** (1hr 55min) are served on Mon, Tues, Thurs & Sat; **Pune** (2hr 40min) and **Calcutta** (3hr) are served on Mon, Wed & Fri only; and **Port Blair** (2hr 5min) on Wed & Fri only.

   Airline offices, mostly open Mon–Fri 10am–5am, Sat 10am–1pm, include: *Air India*, 19 Marshalls Rd (☎474477, airport ☎474484); *Air France*, 769 Anna Salai (☎88377); *Air Lanka*, 758 Mount Chambers, Anna Salai (☎8265 301); *British Airways*, Fagun Mansions, 26 C-in-C Rd (☎477388); *Gulf Air*, 52 Montieth Rd (☎87872); *Indian Airlines*, 19 Marshalls Rd (Mon–Sat 10am–1pm & 1.45–5pm; ☎8279 799 or 8277 900); *Lufthansa*, 171 Anna Salai (☎81483); *Qantas*, Eldorado Building, Nungambakkam High Rd (☎478649); *Swiss Air*, 40 Anna Salai (☎82583); *Thai International*, Aarti Buildings, 189 Anna Salai (☎89151).

By train

Trains to Trichy, Thanjavur, Pudukottai, Rameswaram, Kodaikanal Road, Madurai and Kollam leave from **Egmore Station**. All other departures are from **Central**. Left of the main building, on the first floor of the Moore Market Complex, the efficient **tourist reservation counter** (Mon–Sat 8am–8pm, Sun 8am–2pm) sells tickets for trains from either station. The booking office at Egmore, up the stairs left of the main entrance, has no tourist counter, and is open sporadic hours. You can also buy tickets through *Southern Railway* booking offices on Anna Salai (☎849642) and in Triplicane (☎842529).

   Most destinations are served by more than one daily train. For the long haul to **Delhi** the best service is the *Tamil Nadu Express* #2621 (daily 9pm; 33hr 45min). To save time on a journey to **Madurai**, opt for the fastest of six daily trains, the *Vaigai Express* #2635 (12.25pm; 7hr 40min) – all the other servies run overnight, arriving early in the morning. The *Madras–Trivandrum Mail* #6319 runs daily to **Thiruvananthapuram** (6.55pm; 17hr), supplemented by an additional service on Sundays. The closest railhead to **Ooty** is Mettupalayam, served by the nightly *Nilgiri Express* #6005 (9.05pm; 10hr 15min). For **Kodaikanal**, take a train to Kodaikanal Road (3 daily) or Dindigul (5 daily).

By bus

Getting away from **Thiruvalluvar** or **Broadway** bus stands can be confusing: few of the buses, run by several different operators, are marked in English. Both serve other towns in Tamil Nadu, but only Broadway serves Karnataka and Andhra Pradesh. Thiruvallavur operates a reasonably efficient booking system, but Broadway is far more chaotic. Here you'll have to rely on asking others, or accept the help offered by gangs of children (who expect tips) to find the bus you want. Buses to **Mamallapuram** leave from Broadway. The fastest services are #118, #118 A/B/D/K (2hr); #19, #119 and #108 take a little longer.

   In theory, you can pick up most buses at Parry's Corner, Anna Salai and Adyar, but the struggle to hail the right one, get through the crowds, and find a seat is best avoided.

Travel agents

Most travel agents book bus, train and air tickets for a small fee. Reliable operators include *American Express*, G-17 Spencer Plaza, 768/769 Anna Salai (☎8257 640); *Asian Travels*, 39 Anna Salai (☎476451); *Popular Travels*, Hotel Imperial, 6 Gandhi Irwin Rd, Egmore (☎8258 601); *Sita World Travels*, Fagun Mansion, 26 C-in-C Rd (☎8861); *Thomas Cook*, Eldorado Buildings, 112/G/4 Nungambakkam High Rd (☎473092).

Taj Coromandel, 17 Nungambakkam High Rd (☎8272 827). Two main restaurants: *Mysore* for a variety of Indian dishes and *Golden Dragon* for excellent Chinese. The basement *Pavilion Coffee Shop* is good for blow-out buffet breakfasts.

Welcomgroup Chola Sheraton, 10 Cathedral Rd (☎8280 101). Upmarket hotel with two good restaurants; the *Peshawari* serves lavish (and expensive) northwestern frontier food, while the excellent rooftop *Sagari* specializes in Chinese.

Welcomgroup Park Sheraton, 132 TTK Rd (☎452525). More – extremely good – upmarket hotel restaurants. The *Residency* serves Indian, western and Chinese, the *Khyber* is a meaty poolside barbecue, but the best of all is the south Indian *Dakshin*. Excellent choice of unusual veg dishes, seafood and fish in marinaded spices, plus spicy chicken from Andhra, Karnataka mutton *biryani*, and *meen moilee*. Piping-hot *idiappam* and *appam* made on the spot. Live Carnatic music.

Woodlands Drive-In, 30 Cathedral Rd. Pure veg tiffin joint, in garden setting, popular with young people on scooters and families in cars. Transport, however, is not compulsory. Best for breakfast.

Listings

Bookstores *Higginbothams* on Anna Salai is Madras' largest bookshop, with a vast assortment of books at reasonable prices. The hole-in-the-wall *Giggles Bookshop* in the *Connemara Hotel* has an excellent collection of novels and coffee-table books; *Giggles & Scribbles*, Wellingdon Estate, 24 C-in-C Rd (Mon–Sat 9.30am–7.30pm) is a larger branch, set back 50m from the road, selling rare reprints of historical books on India and Indian music cassettes, and with an efficient mail-order system. *Karnatic Music Book Centre*, 14 Sripuram First St, Royapettah, Madras 14 (☎860147) is an excellent bookshop for Carnatic classical music and Indian dance fanatics, with mail-order service.

Cinemas Cinemas such as *Abhirami* and *Lakshmi* along Anna Salai show English-language films.

Consulates *Germany*, 22 C-in-C Rd (☎471747; 9am–noon); *Sri Lanka*, 9-D Nawab Habibullah Rd (☎470831); *Sweden*, 71 First Main Rd, Raja Annamalaipuram (☎75133; 9.30am–1pm); *UK*, 24 Anderson Rd, Nungambakkam (☎473136); *USA*, 220 Anna Salai (☎473040; Mon–Fri 8am–5.15pm).

Cultural Institutions *Alliance Française*, 40 College Rd (☎472650); *British Council*, 737 Anna Salai (☎82857; Mon–Fri 10am–5pm); *Max Mueller Bhavan*, Express Estates, Club House Rd (☎811315).

Hospitals *Apollo Hospital* (private), 21/22 Greams Rd (☎471268); *KJ Hospital*, 496 Periyar EVR High Rd (☎664513).

Left Luggage Counters at Egmore and Central railway stations store bags for Rs2–4 per day, and usually require proof of train-booking. Some hotels also guard luggage at a daily rate.

Music Stores *Musee Musical*, 67 Anna Salai (☎849380), stocks *sitars*, percussion, flutes and poor-quality guitars. *Audiocon*, 10 Plaza Centre, 3 Anna Salai, has a wide selection of cassettes.

Opticians Eye tests, glasses, and contact lenses are available at *Lawrence and Mayo*, 68 Anna Salai.

Pharmacy *Lalitha's Medical and General Store*, 11 Gandhi Irwin Rd.

Photographic Equipment *Photo Emporium*, 46 Anna Salai, for film and developing. For camera repair try one of the string of shops on Meeran Sahib St, off Anna Salai near the *Casino Theatre*.

Tax Clearance To get a tax clearance certificate (see *Basics*) take exchange documents and passport to 121 Nungambakkam High Rd, and allow for 3–4 hours of tedious form-filling.

Visa Extension and Permits Foreigners Registration Office, 9 Village Rd (☎475424; Mon–Fri 9.15am–5.15pm, Sat 9.15am–1pm).

Yoga *Prof T Krishnamacharya's Yoga Mandiram*, 103 St Mary's Rd (☎77602); *International Shivananda Yoga Centre*, Vedanta Centre, 2 Ranjith Rd, Kottapuram (☎418431).

The northeast

Most visitors get out of Madras as fast as they can, heading for the extraordinary rock sculptures and shore temple of **Mamallapuram**, a sleepy town just a couple of hours south along the coast. Further inland, in **Kanchipuram**, the Pallava capital, early structures are set beside later, larger temples that totally dominate the town, for centuries a place of pilgrimage. **Pondicherry**, the former **French** capital of India and today a Union Territory, expounds a spirituality of a different kind at its Sri Aurobindo Ashram and "new age" village, **Auroville**.

Mamallapuram (Mahabalipuram)

The tiny seaside village of **MAMALLAPURAM** (aka Mahabalipuram) is set in a boulder-strewn landscape, 58km south of Madras on the Bay of Bengal. Although a perfectly feasible day trip from Madras, it has become in the last couple of decades a magnet for long-stay travellers. Many are drawn solely by the miles of unspoilt **beach**, but Mamallapuram was once a major port of the Pallavas, who ruled south India between the fifth and ninth centuries, and it boasts some of India's most sublime **rock-cut art**, for which it has been declared a World Heritage Site by UNESCO.

Little is known about life in the ancient port, and it is only possible to speculate about the purpose of much of the boulder sculpture littering the area. It does appear, however, that the community has always been a centre for sculpture, and that some of the temples were not made for worship at all, but rather as a showcase for the talents of local artists. Due in no small part to the maritime activities of the Pallavas, their style of art and architecture had wide-ranging influence, spreading from south India as far north as Ellora (see p.638), as well as to southeast Asia.

Mamallapuram art divides into four categories: open-air **bas-reliefs**, structured **temples**, man-made **caves** and **rathas** ("chariots", carved in situ from single boulders, to resemble temples or the chariots used in temple processions). The famous bas-reliefs, **Arjuna's Penance** and the **Krishna mandapa**, adorn massive rocks near the centre of the village, while the beautiful **Shore Temple** towers over the waves behind a protective breakwater. Sixteen man-made **caves**, in different stages of completion, are scattered through the area, but the most complete of the nine *rathas* are in a group, named for the five Pandava brothers of the *Mahabharata*.

Arrival and getting around

Numerous daily **buses** ply to and from Madras, along three different routes: via Kovalam, aka Covelong (#19c & #119a), Thirupperur (#19a & #119) and Madras airport (49km north; #108b). About a dozen run to Kanchipuram (2hr), and nine express buses run south to Pondicherry (2hr 30min; #188a/b/d/k). The bus stand is in the centre of the village. The nearest **railway station**, at Chengalpattu (Chingleput), 29km northeast on the bus route to Kanchipuram, is on the main north–south line, but not really a convenient access point. A **taxi** from Madras costs around Rs600.

Mamallapuram itself is little more than a few dusty roads. By far the best way to get to the important sites, if you're up to it, is by **bicycle**, which you can rent from shops on E Raja St, on Kovalam Rd opposite the entrance to the *Temple Bay Ashok Beach Resort*, or through many of the hotels. **Scooters** and *Enfield* motorbikes are also available (for around Rs200 a day), from *Indhu Motor Works*, opposite the Township Office. Government-approved guides must be arranged from Madras, at either of the tourist offices on Anna Salai. **Taxis** and **auto-rickshaws** gather by the bus stand.

Information

The **Government of Tamil Nadu Tourist Office** (Mon–Sat 10am–5.45pm; ☎2232) is one of the first buildings you see in the village, next to a smelly fish market, as you come in from Madras. You can **change money** at the bigger hotels or the *Canara* and *Indian Overseas* banks on E Raja St, and make **STD** calls from booths on E Raja St.

The Krishna mandapa and Arjuna's Penance

At the very heart of the village, the enormous bas-relief known as the **Krishna mandapa** shows Krishna raising Mount Govardhana aloft in one hand. The sculptor's

The telephone **area code** for Mamallapuram is ☎04113.

MAMALLAPURAM

△ Madras & Ⓐ

Ⓟ Pondicherry

ℹ
✉
Ⓘ ①

Ⓑ

Ⓒ ②
OTTAVADAI ST
③

Ⓓ Ⓔ
Ⓖ

Ⓕ

Ⓗ

④

⑤
BEACH RD

Pidari
Ratha

Krishna's
Butter Ball

Ganesha
Ratha

Koneri
Mandapam

Valayankuttai
Ratha

Varaha
Cave

Dharmaraja
Lion Throne

Talasayana
Peruni
Temple

Arjuna's
Penance

Shore
Temple ⑥

Rayala
Gopuram

Bus
Stand

SHORE TEMPLE RD

⑦

Ramanuja
Mandapam

Ⓘ

N

Shiva
Temple

Mahishamardini
Mandapam

Adivaraha
Temple

0   200 m

KIVALAM RD
E RAJA ST

HOTELS:
Ⓐ Silversands,
TTDC Tamil Nadu
Beach Resort,
Temple Bay Ashok,
& other beach hotels
Ⓑ Uma
Ⓒ Uma Lodge
Ⓓ Magesh
Ⓔ Ramakrishna Lodge
Ⓕ Tina Blue View
Ⓖ Surya
Ⓗ Mamalla Bhavan Annexe
Ⓘ TTDC Tamil Nadu
Unit II Camping Site

RESTAURANTS:
① Bamboo Hut Meeting Place
② Curiosity
③ Seashore
④ Gazebo
⑤ Sunrise
⑥ Honey Falls
⑦ Mamalla Bhavan

▽ Panch Pandava Rathas

original intention must have been for the rock above Krishna to represent the mountain, but the seventeenth-century Vijayanagar addition of a columned *mandapa*, or entrance hall, prevents a clear view of the carving. Krishna is also depicted seated, milking a cow, and standing, playing the flute. Other figures are *gopas* and *gopis*, the cowboys and girls of his pastoral youth. Lions sit to the left, one with a human face, and above them a bull.

Another bas-relief, **Arjuna's Penance** – also referred to as the "Descent of the Ganges" – is a few metres north, opposite the modern Talasayana Perumal temple. The surface of this rock erupts with detailed carving, most notably the endearing and natu-ralistic renditions of animals. A family of elephants dominates the right side, with tiny offspring asleep beneath a great tusker. Further still to the right, separate from the great rock, is a free-standing sculpture of an adult monkey grooming its young.

On the left-hand side, Arjuna, one of the Pandava brothers and a consummate archer, is shown standing on one leg. He is looking at the midday sun through a prism formed by his hands, meditating on Shiva, who is nearby represented by a statue, fash-ioned by Arjuna himself. The *Shiva Purana* tells that Arjuna made the journey to a forest on the banks of the Ganges to do penance, in the hope that Shiva would part with his favourite weapon, the *pashupatashastra*, a magic staff or arrow. Shiva eventu-ally materialized in the guise of Kirata, a wild forest-dweller, and picked a fight with Arjuna over a boar they both claimed to have shot. Arjuna only realized he was dealing with the deity after his attempts to drub the wildman proved futile; narrowly escaping death at the playful hand of Shiva, he was finally rewarded with the weapon. Not far away, mimicking Arjuna's devout pose, an emaciated (presumably ascetic) cat stands on hind legs, surrounded by mice.

THE TEMPLES OF TAMIL NADU

No Indian state is more dominated by its **temples** than Tamil Nadu, where temple architecture catalogues the tastes of successive dynasties, and testifies to the centrality of religion in everyday life. Most temples are built in honour of Shiva and Vishnu and their consorts; all are characterized not only by their design and sculptures, but by constant activity – devotion, dancing, singing, *pujas*, festivals and feasts. Each is tended by *brahmin* priests, recognizable by their *dhotis* (loincloths), a sacred thread draped over the right shoulder, and marks on the forehead. One to three horizontal (usually white) lines distinguish Shaivites; vertical lines (yellow or red) are common among Vaishnavites.

Dravida, the temple architecture of Tamil Nadu, first took form in the **Pallava** port of **Mamallapuram**. A step up from the cave retreats of Hindu and Jain ascetics, the earliest Pallava monuments were **mandapas**, shrines cut into rock faces and fronted by columns. The magnificent **bas-relief** at Mamallapuram, Arjuna's Penance, shows the fluid carving of the Pallavas at its most exquisite. This sculptural skill was transferred to free-standing temples, **rathas**, carved out of single rocks and incorporating the essential elements of Hindu temples: the dim inner sanctuary, the *garbhagriha*, capped with a modest tapering spire featuring repetitive architectural motifs. In turn, the Shore Temple was built with three shrines, topped by a *vimana* similar to the towering roofs of the *rathas*; statues of Nandi, Shiva's bull, later to receive pride of place, surmount its low walls. In the finest structural Pallava temple, the Kailasanatha temple at **Kanchipuram**, the sanctuary, again crowned with a pyramidal *vimana*, stands within a courtyard enclosed by high walls. The projecting and recessing bays of the walls, carved with images of Shiva, his consort and ghoulish mythical lions, *yalis*, were the prototype for later styles.

Pallava themes were developed in Karnataka by the Chalukyas and Rashtrakutas, but it was the Shaivite **Cholas** who spearheaded Tamil Nadu's next architectural phase, in the tenth century. In **Thanjavur**, Rajaraja I created the Brihadeshvara temple principally as a status symbol. Its proportions far exceed any attempted by the Pallavas; set within a vast walled courtyard, the sanctuary, fronted by a small pillared hall (*mandapa*), stands beneath a sculpted *vimana* that soars over 60 metres high. Most sculptures once again feature Shiva, but the *gopuras*, or towers, each side of the eastern gateway to the courtyard, were a new innovation, as were the lions carved into the base of the sanctuary walls, and the pavilion erected over Nandi in front of the sanctuary. The second great Chola temple was built in **Gangaikondacholapuram** by Rajendra I. Instead of a mighty *vimana*, he brought new elements, adding subsidiary shrines and placing an extended *mandapa* in front of the central sanctuary, its pillars writhing with dancers and deities.

By the time of the thirteenth-century **Vijayanagar** kings, the temple was central to city life, the focus for civic meetings, education, dance and theatre. The Vijayanagars extended earlier structures, adding enclosing walls around a series of *prakaras*, or courtyards, and erecting free-standing *mandapas* for use as meeting halls, elephant stables, stages for music and dance, and ceremonial marriage halls (*kalyan mandapas*). Raised on superbly decorated columns, these *mandapas* became known as **thousand-pillared halls**. **Tanks** were added, doubling as water stores and washing areas, and used for festivals when deities were set afloat in boats surrounded by glimmering oil lamps.

Under the Vijayanagars, the *gopuras* were enlarged and set at the cardinal points over the high gateways to each *prakara*, to become the dominant feature. Rectangular in plan, and embellished with images of animals and local saints or rulers as well as deities, *gopuras* are periodically repainted in pinks, blues, whites and yellows, a sharp and joyous contrast with the earthy browns and greys of halls and sanctuaries beyond. **Madurai** is *the* place to check out Vijayanagar architecture, and experience the timeless temple rituals. Dimly-lit halls and sun-drenched courtyards hum with murmured prayers, and regularly come alive for festivals in which Shiva and his "fish-eyed" consort are hauled through town on mighty wooden chariots tugged by hordes of devotees. Outside Tiruchirapalli, the temple at **Srirangam** was extended by the Vijayanagar Nayaks to become south India's largest. Unlike that in Madurai, it incorporates earlier Chola foundations, but the ornamentation, with pillars formed into rearing horses, is superb.

To the right of Arjuna, a natural cleft represents the **Ganges**, complete with *nagas*, water spirits in the form of cobras. Near the bottom, a fault in the rock that broke a *naga* received a quick-fix of cement in the 1920s. Evidence of a cistern and channels can be seen at the top, which at one time must have carried water to flow down the cleft, simulating the great river. It's not known if there was some ritual purpose to all this, or whether it was simply an elaborate spectacle to impress visitors. You may see sudden movements among the carved animals; lazing goats often join the permanent features.

A little way north of Arjuna's Penance, precipitously balanced on the top of a ridge, is a massive, natural, almost spherical boulder called **Krishna's Butterball**. Picnickers and goats often rest in its perilous-looking shade.

Ganesha ratha and Varaha cave

Just north of Arjuna's Penance a path leads west to a single monolith, the **Ganesha ratha**. Its image of Ganesh dates from this century; some say it was installed at the instigation of England's King George V. An interesting sculpture at one end, of a protecting demon with a tri-corn headdress, is reminiscent of the Indus Valley civilization's 4000-year-old horned figure known as the "proto-Shiva" (see *Contexts*).

Behind Arjuna's Penance, southwest of the Ganesha *ratha*, is the **Varaha-mandapa II** cave, whose entrance hall has two pillars with horned lion-bases and a cell flanked by two *dvarpalas*, or guardians. One of four **panels** shows the boar-incarnation of Vishnu, who stands with one foot resting on the *naga* snake-king as he lifts a diminutive Prithvi, the earth, from the primordial ocean; another is of Gajalakshmi, the goddess Lakshmi seated on a lotus being bathed by a pair of elephants. Trivikrama, the dwarf *brahmin* who becomes huge and bestrides the world in three steps to defeat the demon king Bali, is shown in another panel, and the fourth depicts a four-armed Durga.

The Shore Temple

East of the village, a distinctive silhouette above the crashing ocean, Mamallapuram's **Shore Temple** dates from the early eighth century and is considered to be the earliest stone-built temple in south India. The design of its two finely carved towers was profoundly influential; today, due to the combined forces of wind, salt and sand, much of the detailed carving has eroded, giving the whole a soft, rounded appearance.

The taller of the towers is raised above a cell that faces out to sea – don't be surprised to see mischievous monkeys crouching inside. Approached from the west through two low-walled enclosures lined with small Nandi (bull) figures, the temple comprises two *lingam* shrines (one facing east, the other west), and a third shrine between them housing an image of the reclining Vishnu. Recent excavations, revealing a tank containing a structured stone column thought to have been a lantern, and a large Varaha (boar-incarnation of Vishnu) aligned with the Vishnu shrine, suggest that the area was sacred long before the Pallavas chose it as a temple site.

The Lighthouses and the Mahishasuramardini Cave

At the highest point in an area of steep paths, unfinished temples, ruins, scampering monkeys and massive rocks, south of Arjuna's Penance, the **New Lighthouse** (daily 2–4pm) affords fine views east to the Shore Temple, and west across paddy fields and flat lands littered with rocks. Next to it, the **Olakanesvara** ("flame-eyed" Shiva), or **Old Lighthouse Temple**, used as a lighthouse until the start of the twentieth century, dates from the Rajasimha period (674–800 AD) and contains no image.

Nestling between the two lighthouses is the **Mahishasuramardini Cave**, whose central image portrays Shiva and Parvati with the child Murugan seated on Parvati's lap. Shiva's right foot rests on the back of the bull Nandi, and Parvati sits casually, leaning on her left hand. On the left wall, beyond an empty cell, a panel depicts Vishnu reclining on the serpent, his attitude of repose contrasted with the weapon-brandishing demons, Madhu and Kaithaba. Other figures seek Vishnu's permission to chase them.

Opposite, in one of the most celebrated sculptures in Indian art, a carved panel shows the eight-armed goddess **Durga** as Mahishasuramardini, the "crusher" of the buffalo demon **Mahishasura**. The story goes that Mahishasura became so powerful that he took possession of heaven, causing great misery to its inhabitants. To deal with such a dangerous foe, Vishnu and Shiva hit upon the idea of combining all the gods' powers into a single entity. This done, fiery jets appeared, from which emerged the terrifying "mother of the universe", Durga. In the ensuing battle, Durga caught Mahishasura with a noose, and he changed into a lion; she beheaded the lion, and he transformed into a human wielding a sword; she fired off a flight of arrows, only to see him turn into a huge trumpeting elephant; and she cut off his trunk, whereupon the buffalo returned. Now furious, Durga partook of her favourite beverage – blood, "the supreme wine". Climbing on top of the buffalo, she kicked him about the neck and stabbed him with her trident. The impact of her foot forced him halfway out of his own mouth, only to be beheaded by his own sword, at which point he fell. The panel shows Durga riding a lion, in the midst of the struggle. Accompanied by dwarf *ganas*, she wields a bow and other weapons; Mahishasura equipped with a club, can be seen to the right, in flight with fellow demons.

The tiny **Archaeological Survey Of India Museum** (daily 9am–1pm & 2–5pm) on W Raja St, near the Lighthouse, has a collection of Pallava sculpture found in and around Mamallapuram, and sells quality postcards at low prices.

Pancha Pandava rathas

In a sandy compound 1.5km south of the village centre stands the stunning group of monoliths known for no historical reason as the **Pancha Pandava** *rathas*, the five chariots of the Pandavas. Dating from the period of Narasimhavarman I (*c.*630–70 AD), and consisting of five separate free-standing sculptures that imitate structured temples plus some beautifully carved life-size animals, they were either carved from a single gigantic sloping boulder, or from as many as three distinct rocks.

The "architecture" of the *rathas* reflects the variety of styles employed in temple building of the time, and stands almost as a model for much subsequent development in the **Dravida**, or southern, style. The Arjuna, Bhima and Dharmaraja *rathas* show strong affinities with the Dravidian temples at Pattadakal in Karnataka and caves 32 and 16 at Ellora in Maharashtra. Carving was always executed from top to bottom, enabling the artists to work on the upper parts with no fear of damaging anything below. Thus any unfinished elements there may be are always in the lower areas.

Intriguingly, it is thought that the *rathas* were never used for worship. A Hindu temple is only complete when the essential pot-shaped finial, the *kalasha*, is put in place – which would have presented a physical impossibility for the artisans, as the *kalasha* would have had to have been sculpted first. *Kalashas* can be seen next to two of the *rathas* (Dharmaraja and Arjuna), but as part of the base, as if they were perhaps to be put in place at a later date.

The southernmost and tallest of the *rathas*, named after the eldest of the Pandavas, is the pyramidal **Dharmaraja**. Set on a square base, the upper part comprises a series of diminishing storeys, each with a row of pavilions. Four corner blocks, each with two panels and standing figures, are broken up by two pillars and pilasters supported by squatting lions. Figures on panels include Ardhanarishvara (Shiva and female consort in one figure), Brahma, the king Narasimhavarman I, and Harihara (Shiva and Vishnu combined). The central tier includes sculptures of Shiva Gangadhara holding a rosary with the adoring river goddess Ganga by his side and one of the earliest representations in Tamil Nadu of the dancing Shiva, Nataraja, who became all-important in the region. Alongside, the **Bhima** *ratha*, the largest of the group, is the least complete, with tooling marks all over its surface. Devoid of carved figures, the upper storeys, like in the Dharmaraja, feature false windows and repeated pavilion-shaped ornamentation. Its oblong base is very rare for a shrine.

The Arjuna and Draupadi *rathas* share a base. Behind the **Arjuna,** the most complete of the entire group and very similar to the Dharmaraja, stands a superb unfinished sculpture of Shiva's bull Nandi. **Draupadi** is unique in terms of rock-cut architecture, with a roof that appears to be based on a straw thatched hut (a design later copied at Chidambaram; see p.933). There's an image of Durga inside, but the figure of her lion vehicle outside is aligned side-on and not facing the image, a convincing reason to suppose this was not a real temple. To the west, close to a life-size carving of an elephant, the *ratha* named after the twin brothers **Nakula** and **Sahadeva** is, unusually, apsidal ended. The elephant may be a visual pun on this, as the Sanskrit technical name for a curved ended building is *gajaprstika*, "elephant's backside".

The road out to the *rathas* resounds with incessant chiselling from sculptors' workshops. Much of their work is excellent, and well worth a browse – it's unlikely you'll leave without at least a small memento at a very competitive price. The sculptors produce statues for temples all over the world and are used to shipping large-scale pieces. Some of the artists are horrifyingly young; children often do the donkey work on large pieces, which are then completed by master craftsmen.

Government College of Sculpture

A visit to the **Government College of Sculpture**, 3km from Mamallapuram on the Kovalam (Covelong) Rd, gives a fascinating insight into the processes of training. You can watch anything from preliminary drawing, with its strict rules regarding proportion and iconography, through to the execution of sculpture, both in wood and stone, in the classical Hindu tradition. Contact the college office (π2261) to make an appointment.

Tiger Cave

Set amid groves close to the sea, 5km north from Mamallapuram on the Kovalam (Covelong) Rd, the extraordinary **Tiger Cave** contains a shrine to Durga, approached by a flight of steps that passes two subsidiary cells. Following the line of an irregularly shaped rock, the cave is remarkable for the elaborate exterior, which features multiple lion heads surrounding the entrance to the main cell.

Tirukalikundram

The village of **TIRUKALIKUNDRAM**, 16km east on the road to Kanchipuram, is locally famous for its hilltop Shiva temple where two Neophran vultures swoop down from Varanasi daily at noon to be fed by the priests. Be prepared, however, after climbing more than 400 red-hot stone steps at the appointed time, for the fact that the vultures may decide not to call after all. Added to that, any interest you may have had in looking at the temple could well evaporate in the effort required to disabuse various individuals, including the priests, of the impression that you need their multifarious services and paid company. Visits to the village are made more worthwhile if you take the time to explore the vast Vijayanagar temple at its heart.

Crocodile Bank

The **Crocodile Bank** (daily 8am–5.30pm) at Vadanemmeli, 15km north of town on the road to Madras, was set up in 1976 by the American zoologist Romulus Whittaker, to protect and breed indigenous crocodiles. The bank has been so successful (fifteen crocs to five thousand in the first fifteen years) that its remit now extends to saving endangered species, such as turtles and lizards, from around the world.

Low-walled enclosures in its garden compound house hundreds of inscrutable crocodiles, soaking in ponds or sunning themselves on the banks. Breeds include the fish-eating, knobbly-nosed gharial, India's most common mugger, and the world's largest species, the saltwater *crocodylus porosus*, which can grow to 8 metres in length. You can watch feeding time at about 4.30pm each Wednesday. The temptation to take photos is tempered by the sight of those hungry saurians clambering over each other to chomp the chopped flesh, within inches of the top of the wall. Not surprisingly, excited kids ignore the sage advice not to lean over the walls.

Another important field of work is conducted with the collaboration of local Irula people, whose traditional expertise is with snakes. Cobras are brought to the bank for **venom collection**, to be used in the treatment of snakebites. Elsewhere, snakes are repeatedly "milked" until they die, but here at the bank only a limited amount is taken from each snake, enabling them to return to the wild.

Accommodation

With more than twenty years' experience of tourism, Mamallapuram is not short on **accommodation**. The bulk of cheap to **mid-range** lodges are concentrated within the village, some distance from the **beach**, which is the preserve of the more expensive places. Large hotels of varying standards sit side by side along a six-kilometre stretch of coast. Without a bike, getting to these can prove a bit of a hassle; it's easy enough to take a rickshaw out there from the village, but not in the other direction. However, the walk back into Mamallapuram, either along the beach or the Kovalam Rd (to which they are all connected by long driveways) is pleasant if you're not carrying luggage.

Golden Sun, 59 Kovalam Rd (☎2245; fax 944444). In an attractive garden compound 3km out on the coast road. Sea-facing rooms are the best value. Health club and good pool. ⑥.

Ideal Beach Resort, 3.5km from town, Kovalam Rd (☎2240). A little way before the Tiger Cave, these are possibly the most attractive cottages on this stretch. ⑤.

Magesh, E Raja St (☎2201). Basic and clean rooms in the centre of the village. No restaurant. ①.

Hotel Mamalla Bhavan, opposite the bus stand. Basic, very Indian rooms above a restaurant. ①.

Mamalla Bhavan Annexe, E Raja St (☎2260). Right in the centre of the village; 12 carpeted a/c rooms with *Star TV*, in immaculate condition – functional, not luxurious – overlooking a courtyard. Non-a/c rooms with mosquito nets. Room service. ③–④.

Pallava Seaside, Kovalam Rd, 2.5km from town (☎2273 or 2583). Pretty setting in a grove by the sea. The 8 rooms are not that great though, and there's no restaurant. ④.

Ramakrishna Lodge, 8 Ottavadai St (☎2331 or 2431). In the village, next to a lake. Clean, well-maintained rooms, all with bathroom but no a/c, set round a pretty courtyard. Sea views from the terrace on top floor. No restaurant, but room service. ②.

Silversands, Kovalam Rd (☎228). Huge luxury complex of cottages between the road and beach. Several craft shops. Splendid restaurant on the sand. Non-a/c and a/c; the priciest rooms have swings, balconies and private bathroom. Tariff includes breakfast. ⑤–⑥.

Surya, off Ottavadai St (☎2239). Lakeside hotel set in a tranquil leafy compound dotted with sculptures (including a replica Buddhist gateway). Simple, well-maintained rooms (some a/c); mosquito nets are available and, considering the proximity of the lake, essential. ④.

Taj Fisherman's Cove, Covelong Beach, 30mins' drive north from Mamallapuram (☎04128 2304). Four-star hotel, with bar and restaurants. Rooms in main building overlook a beachside garden, while circular cottages stand at the ocean's edge. ⑨.

Temple Bay Ashok (ITDC) Beach Resort (☎2251; fax 2257). Excellent location, on the beach but near the village, with views of the Shore Temple. Luxurious cottages on the beach all have sea-facing balconies, and there are huge rooms in the main building. Swimming pool and restaurant. ⑦.

Tina Blue View Restaurant and Lodge, 152 Ottavadai St (☎2319). Cheap rooms with bathrooms – no view, but sit-outs in leafy courtyard. One, more expensive, 4-bedded room faces the sea. ②.

TTDC Hotel Tamil Nadu Beach Resort, Kovalam Rd (☎2235). Huge split-level cottages (some non-a/c) with sea-facing sit-outs. Excellent value. Lovely swimming pool, and restaurants. ⑤.

TTDC Hotel Tamil Nadu Unit II Camping Site (☎2287). Eighteen non-a/c rooms; the sea-facing options (the sea is some distance away) are slightly more expensive. TV, but not *Star*. ③–④.

Uma, 138 E Raja St (☎2422). Basic but fair-sized rooms in newish building. Non-veg restaurant. ③.

Uma Lodge, 15 Ottavadai St (☎2322). Close to the main road, acceptable for the price. ①.

Eating

The village is full of cheap, shack-style restaurants, specializing in seafood. Prices are higher at the **beach hotels**, but the atmosphere, and often the food, is worth it.

Bamboo Hut Meeting Place, Kovalam Rd, just past the tourist office. Friendly, inexpensive little place, where only one table is reached by a fan, serving seafood, chicken, snacks, and omelettes.

Curiosity, Ottavadai St. Popular with westerners, for its breakfasts and selection of fresh fish. The little patio out front is a gathering spot for local children.

Gazebo, 101 E Raja St. Very friendly restaurant in a pleasant airy room. Fresh seafood, such as tiger prawns and lobster, cooked on a charcoal grill or barbecue. Open 6am–midnight.

Honey Falls, Shore Temple Rd. Tiny little place specializing in grilled fish and lobster.

Ideal Beach Resort, 3.5km from town, Kovalam Rd. Sri Lankan, Chinese, Indian and western food in a great location.

Mamalla Bhavan, opposite the bus stand. Superb, inexpensive Indian "meals" and good *tandoori*.

Mamalla Bhavan Annexe, E Raja St. Plush cafe, much the best source of veg food in the village, and also recommended for its ice cream sundaes.

Seashore Restaurant, on the beach, at the end of Ottavadai St. Great seafood, but dubious western dishes. Airy, though, and with a good view.

Silversands, Kovalam Rd. Wonderful restaurant on the sand serving good Indian, western and Chinese dishes, and some of the best south Indian seafood you're likely to taste.

Sunrise, Beach Rd. Specialists in *masala*-fried fish, shark steak and tiger prawns. Fresh lobster feast for Rs350!

Tina Blue View, 152 Ottavadai St. Breakfasts, seafood, Chinese and steaks. Nice rooftop location, with a gaudy mural, and views of the sea in the distance, but slow service and ordinary food.

TTDC Hotel Tamil Nadu Beach Resort, Kovalam Rd. The utilitarian restaurant next to the reception has a fair mixed menu; the thatched hut on the beach, serving basic Chinese food, is in a much better location, but be prepared for a long wait.

Kanchipuram

Once protected by robust walls, the modest-sized fly-blown city of **KANCHIPURAM** was for thousands of years a major arena for artistic and architectural achievement; the temple *gopuras* that soar above its narrow streets can be seen from far across the vast plains. Today, as the holiest Hindu city in south India – the only such site to be sacred to both Shaivites and Vaishnavites – it is a busy pilgrimage centre, buzzing with activity around its extraordinary temple precincts.

Established by the **Pallava** kings in the fourth century AD, Kanchipuram served as their capital for five hundred years, and continued to flourish throughout the Chola, Pandya and Vijayanagar eras. Under the Pallavas, it was an important scholastic forum, and a meeting point for Jain, Buddhist and Hindu cultures; today Hindu **temples** alone dominate the town, spanning the years from the peak of Pallava construction to the seventeenth century, when the ornamentation of the *gopuras* and pillared halls was at its most elaborate. All can be easily reached by foot, bicycle or rickshaw, and all close between noon and 4pm. You'll be offered a panoply of services – from sanctuary priests, shoe bearers, guides, women giving out food for fish in the temple tanks, and well-trained temple elephants that bless you with their trunks – so be prepared with a pocketful of change. Always animated, they really come alive during major festivals such as the **Car Festival** (May) and **Navaratri** (Oct/Nov).

Arrival and information

Flanked on the south by the River Vagavathi, Kanchipuram lies 70km southwest of Madras, and about as far from the coast. A potholed and chaotic **bus stand** in the centre is used by services from Madras (1hr 30min), Mamallapuram (1–2hr), and Chengalpattu (40min). Infrequent **trains** from Madras pull in at a station on the northwest edge of town, having taken twice as long as buses to make the journey.

There's no official **tourist office** in Kanchipuram, but you can glean a little information from the detailed map at the TTDC *Tamil Nadu Hotel*. The easiest way to **get around** town is by **bicycle** – available for minimal daily rates at stalls west and northeast of the bus stand. Kanchipuram's vegetable markets, hotels, restaurants and bazaars are concentrated in the centre of town, near the bus stand.

Ekambareshvara temple

Kanchipuram's largest temple and most important Shiva shrine, the **Ekambareshvara temple** in the north of town, is easily identified by its colossal whitewashed *gopuras*, which rise almost 60 metres. They're a dazzling sight, with gold-painted tops, and a riot of blue, pink and yellow figures and faces carved into the side. The main temple contains some Pallava work, but was mostly constructed between the sixteenth and seventeenth centuries, and stands within a vast walled enclosure beside some smaller shrines and a large fish-filled water tank.

Entrance, through a high arched passageway beneath an elaborate *gopura* in the south wall, leads to an open courtyard and a majestic "thousand-pillared hall", *kalyan mandapa*, whose slightly decaying grey stone columns are modelled as nubile maidens, animals, and deities. This hall faces the tank in the north and the sanctuary (inaccessible to non-Hindus) in the west that protects the emblem of Shiva (here in his form as **Kameshvara**, Lord of Desire), an "earth" *lingam* that is one of five *linga* in Tamil Nadu that represent the elements. Legend connects it with the goddess **Kamakshi** (Shiva's consort, "having eyes of desire"), who angered Shiva by playfully covering his eyes and plunging the world into darkness. Shiva reprimanded her by sending her to fashion a *lingam* from the earth in his honour; once it was completed, Kamakshi found she could not move it. Local myths tell of a great flood that swept over Kanchipuram and destroyed the temples, but did not move the *lingam*, to which Kamakshi clung so fiercely that marks of her breasts and bangles were imprinted upon it.

Behind the sanctum, an eerie bare hall lies beneath another profusely carved *gopura*, and in the courtyard a venerable mango tree represents the tree under which Shiva and Kamakshi were married. This union is celebrated during a festival each April, when many couples are married in the *kalyan mandapa*.

The somewhat neglected twelfth-century **Jvaraheshvari temple**, in leafy gardens to the south, is the only Chola (tenth–twelfth centuries) structure in Kanchipuram not to have been modified and overshadowed by later buildings. Unlike the Pallava constructions, it is built of hard grey stone; its sculpted pyramidal roof is an early form of the *gopuras* used extensively by the Pandyas.

Kailasanatha temple

The **Kailasanatha temple**, the oldest structure in Kanchipuram and the finest example of Pallava architecture in south India, is situated among several low-roofed houses just over 1km west of the town centre. Built by the Pallava king Rajasimha early in the eighth century, its intimate size and simple carving distinguish it from the town's later temples. Usually quieter than its neighbours, it becomes the focus of vigorous celebrations during the **Mahashivratri festival** each March. Like the contemporaneous Shore Temple at Mamallapuram, it is built of soft sandstone, but its sheltered position has spared it from wind and sand erosion, and it remains remarkably intact.

Topped with a modest pyramidal spire, the small temple stands within a rectangular courtyard, enclosed by a wall inlaid with tiny meditation chambers and sculpted with images of Shiva, Parvati and their sons, as well as rearing mythical lions (*yalis*). On the south side of the spire Shiva is depicted as a begging ascetic (Bhikshatana); on the north he's in the pose of the dance of destruction (Samhara-Tandava). Walls in the dim interior bear traces of frescoes, and the ceilings are etched with religious verses written in Pali. The sanctum (inaccessible to non-Hindus) shelters a sturdy sixteen-sided black *lingam,* guarded by elephant-headed Ganesh and Shiva's other son, Skanda, the god of war, with whom the king Rajasimha was closely associated. Double walls were built round the sanctuary to support the weighty tower above, and the passage between the walls is used as a circumambulatory path as part of the ritual worship of Shiva.

Vaikuntha Perumal temple

Built shortly after the Kailasanatha temple at the end of the eighth century, the smaller **Vaikuntha Perumal temple**, a few hundred metres west of the train station, is dedicated to Vishnu. Its lofty carved *vimana* (towered sanctuary) crowns three shrines containing images of Vishnu, stacked one on top of the other. Unusual scenes carved in the walls enclosing the temple yard depict events central to Pallava history, among them coronations, court gatherings, and battles with the Chalukyas who ruled the regions to the northwest. The temple's pillared entrance hall was added by Vijayanagar rulers five hundred years subsequently, and is clearly different in style, with much more ornate sculpting.

Kamakshi Amman temple

Built during Pallava supremacy and modified in the fourteenth and seventeenth centuries, the **Kamakshi Amman temple**, northwest of the bus stand, combines several styles, with an ancient central shrine, gates from the Vijayanagar period, and high *gopuras* set above the gateways much later. This is one of India's three holiest shrines to Shakti, Shiva's cosmic energy depicted in female form, usually as his consort. The goddess Kamakshi, a local form of Parvati, shown with a sugarcane bow and arrows of flowers, is honoured as having lured Shiva to Kanchipuram, where they were married, and thus having forged the connection between the local community and the god. In February or March deities are wheeled to the temple in huge wooden "cars", decked with robed statues and swaying plantain leaves. For the rest of the year the bulky but delicately carved temple cars, balanced on colossal wheels, are kept on Gandhi Road.

Varadarajaperumal temple

The Vaishnavite **Varadarajaperumal temple** stands within a huge walled complex in the far southeast of town, guarded by high gates topped with *gopuras*. The inner sanctuary boasts superb carving and well-preserved paintings, but non-Hindus only have access to the outer courtyards, and the elaborate sixteenth-century pillared hall close to the western entrance gate. The outer columns of this *mandapa* are sculpted as lions, and warriors on rearing horses, to celebrate the military vigour of the Vijayanagars, who believed their prowess was inspired by the power of Shakti.

Shopping

Kanchipuram has long been renowned for the superb quality of its hand-produced **silk**; *saris* are still made using methods little changed since Pallava times, when the industry supplied kings and queens with splendid fabrics. The high prices charged by its large specialist shops, south of the centre along Thirukatchininambi Koli Rd, are determined by weight. The most expensive, and spectacular, are fringed with borders of pure gold or silver thread. The silk is dyed with natural pigments and woven with complex but subtle patterns, which usually feature peacock, parrot or fruit motifs. You can see the weaving process at the *Weavers' Service Centre* (Sun–Thurs 10am–5pm), 20 Station Rd.

Accommodation and eating

There's not a great choice of **accommodation** in Kanchipuram, but its hotels are sufficient for a short stay, and all except *Hotel Tamil Nadu* are right in the centre. The less expensive lodges offer minimal comfort, while the pricier places, if not exactly elaborate, are clean and comfortable and serve generally good south Indian dishes in their own **restaurants**. If you don't want to eat in your hotel, you can guarantee a hearty meal at any of the **thali dhabas** lining Kamaraj Rd just west of the bus stand.

Baboo Surya, 85 E Raja Veethi St (☎04112/3575). Large, modern hotel with immaculate a/c and non-a/c rooms and a very good restaurant. Car rental and exchange facilities. ⑤.

Raja's Lodge, 20 Nellukkara St (☎04112/2603). Very cheap and very basic; small rooms. ①.

Sri Krishna Lodge, 68A Nellukkara St (☎04112/2831). Grotty hotel whose cell-like rooms are dim and cramped, but clean enough. ①.

Sri Rama Lodge, 21 Nellukkara St (☎04112/3995). More presentable than the other inexpensive lodges, and fairly clean. Attached bathrooms and some a/c rooms. ①–④.

TTDC Tamil Nadu, Railway Station Rd (☎04112/2561). State-run hotel near the train station. Comfortable, spacious rooms, some a/c, and a small restaurant serving uninspired food. ③.

Vellore

The uninspiring city of **VELLORE**, close to the River Palar just under 150km west of Madras, is dominated by towering granite fort walls that enclose government offices and a stunning sixteenth-century **temple**. There are no other buildings of interest to tourists in this confusion of dusty, crowded markets and streets; for most Indians, Vellore is significant only as the home of an excellent hospital for tropical diseases.

The approach to the **fort** (daily 8am–8pm) is from the east, over a modern bridge that straddles the wide moat, once filled with crocodiles. Headquarters in the fourteenth century of the Vijayanagar governor Chinna Bomma Reddi, and enclosed by two thick walls, the fort held off attacks until it fell to the Muslim Adi Shahis of Bijapur in the seventeenth century. Later the Marathas ousted their Muslim enemies, only to be overthrown in turn by Daud Khan of Delhi early in the eighteenth century. British officers took control in 1768, and remained overlords until Independence.

Close to the northern wall, the magnificent *kalyan mandapa* (pillared hall) in the outer courtyard of the **Jalakanteshvara Temple** boasts a vitality and richness of carving matched only at Srirangam (see p.952). The outer pillars depict rearing steeds, mythical dragons and warriors, while the central columns support sculptures of *yalis*, mythical lions prominent in much earlier Pallava temples. The temple shrine is dedicated to Shiva, represented by a *lingam*, and guarded by Nandi, the god's bull.

A cemetery to the right of the fort entrance holds the graves of the British soldiers who died during a swiftly defeated mutiny in 1806, when *sepoys* rose in protest against demands for them to shave their beards and adopt a common dress code.

Practicalities

Regular **buses**, from the bus stand just east of the fort, connect Vellore to Madras (half-hourly; 3–4hr), Kanchipuram (hourly; 2hr 30min) and Bangalore (10 daily; 5–6hr). **Trains** from Tirupati and Tiruvannamalai arrive at Vellore Station in the south; Katpadi Station, thirty minutes' north of the city, is on the Madras–Bangalore line.

Vellore is best visited as a day trip from Kanchipuram, but if you're looking for inexpensive **lodgings**, head for the eastern area of town, where the clean and basic *VDM Lodge* (☎24008; ①), with some a/c rooms, and *Srinivasa Lodge* (☎26389; ①), are both on Beri Bakkali St close to the hospital. On Babu Rao St, a little further south, the hotels *Balaram* (☎22476; ①) and *Mayura* (☎25488; ①) offer similar standards in well-kept, simple rooms. The modern and comfortable, partly a/c *Hotel River View* (☎25768; ③) on Katpadi Rd north of the city, is the town's most upmarket hotel.

Hotel River View has three **restaurants**, but you can get good south Indian meals and tiffins in restaurants closer to the fort on Ida Scudder Road. The reasonably priced *Susil* has a roof terrace and a broad menu of Indian dishes, while nearby the *Geetha* and *Best* specialize in south Indian food. *Chinatown*, a small, friendly place with excellent Chinese dishes, is on Gandhi Rd, which runs south of Ida Scudder Rd.

Vedanthangal

One of India's most spectacular mixed heronries lies roughly 1km east of the village of **VEDANTHANGAL**, a cluster of squat brown houses set in a patchwork of vivid green paddy fields 30km from the east coast and 86km southwest of Madras. It's a tiny, relaxed place, bisected by one road and boasting only two *chai* stalls.

The **sanctuary** (daily, dawn–dusk; Rs 1) a low-lying area less than half a kilometre square, is at its fullest between December and February, when it is totally flooded. The rains of the northeast monsoon, sweeping through in October or November, bring indigenous water birds ready to nest and settle until the dry season (usually April), when they leave for wetter areas. Abundant trees on mounds above the water level provide perfect nesting spots, alive by January with chirping fledglings, some of which fall prey to kites, eagles, scavenger vultures or migratory harriers that swoop when the parents are away from the nest. Visitors can watch the goings-on from a path at the water's edge, or from a watchtower; binoculars make a big difference, and try to come at sunset, when the birds return from feeding. Common Indian species to look out for are openbill storks, spoonbill pelicans, black cormorants, and **herons** of several types: the eastern grey heron, the smaller, duller night heron that nests in low branches, and the spritely pond heron whose wings flash white in flight against an unremarkable brown plumage. You may also see ibises, robust grey pelicans, migrant cuckoos and sand pipers, egrets, which paddle in the rice fields, and tiny, darting bee-eaters. Some migrant birds pass through and rest on their way between more permanent sites; swallows, terns and redshanks are common, while peregrine falcons, wigeons and doves are less regularly spotted.

Practicalities

Getting to Vedanthangal can present a few problems. The nearest town is Maduranthakam, 8km east, on NH45 between Chengalpattu and Tindivanam. Head here to wait for the hourly buses to the sanctuary, or catch one of the less frequent services from Chengalpattu. Taxis make the journey from Maduranthakam for Rs150–240, but cannot be booked from Vedanthangal, so visitors have to leave by bus.

Vedanthangal's only accommodation is at the three-roomed **forest lodge** (①) near the bus stop, school, and *chai* stall. Rooms, spacious and comfortable with attached bath, must be booked through the Wildlife Warden, 49 Fourth Main Rd, Adyar, Madras (☎413947). They'll prepare excellent home-cooked food if given enough notice.

Tiruvannamalai

Set in arid plains beneath a high conical hill at the northern end of the Shevaroy range, just over 100km south of Kanchipuram, **TIRUVANNAMALAI** is a small, quiet town dominated by the grand **Arunchaleshvara temple**. This is one of the most important Shaivite towns in south India, focused on its *agnilingam*, or fire-*lingam*, one of the five in Tamil Nadu associated with the elements. Smaller temples in town are dedicated to Ganesh and Shiva's consort, Parvati, often depicted in her wrathful form as **Durga**.

Tiruvannamalai's calendar is punctuated with festivals, when Shiva and his accompanying deities (Parvati, plus Ganesh and Subrahmanya, their two sons) are wheeled through town on huge wooden temple cars, or floated upon tanks dedicated to three of the guardians of the directions: Agni, Indra and Ishana. The largest celebrations are for **Karttigai**, the festival of fire, in December. For ten days, the town's population doubles as devotees gather to witness the lighting of a column of fire on the summit of the hill (this, rather than the image in the temple, is technically the fire-*lingam* to which the town is devoted), and circumambulate its base in a procession led by images of Shiva. Devotees also walk around the hill during the curious two-day festival (end of Jan) that re-enacts *tiruvudal*, the holy love-quarrel, a popular theme in Tamil literature, normally involving Nataraja (Shiva as Lord of the Dance) and his consort. The quarrel is mimed in the temples, and acted with vigour by temple singers in the streets.

Arunchaleshvara temple

The **Arunchaleshvara temple**, built over a period of almost a thousand years, and incorporating several distinct styles, consists of four courtyards whose gateways are topped by tapering *gopuras*, the largest of which cover the east and north gates. On the way to the main gate in the east wall, you pass through a covered bazaar that resonates with the bangs and clashes of metal being coaxed into shape. The shops here are full of shiny brass, iron and copper pots, trunks, bells, horns and cooking utensils piled in perilous metallic pyramids and weighed on immense scales.

The eastern gateway leads through the thick outer wall, carved with images of deities, local saints and teachers, and opens into a large courtyard. The large stepped Shivaganga tank to the left originally lay outside the temple precincts; on the right stands a vast "thousand-pillared" *mandapa*, where the temple elephant lives when not taking part in rituals. This outer courtyard usually presents a lively scene: fruit and nut sellers shaded by black umbrellas share space with *sadhus* and dozing devotees, while young boys swim in the tank and children gape at the elephant.

The second enclosure, built a couple of centuries earlier, around the thirteenth century, is much smaller, with a large Nandi bull facing the sanctuary and a shrine to the goddess (Shiva's consort) on its northern edge. In the temple kitchens, in its southeastern corner, food is prepared for the gods. A nineteenth-century roof shelters the central courtyard, surveyed by numerous deities etched into its outer walls, among them Shiva, Parvati, Venugopala (Krishna), Lakshmi, Ganesh and Subrahmanya. In the dim interior, arcaded cloisters supported by magnificently carved columns lead to the main shrine to Shiva, the only part strictly off-limits to non-Hindus: a *lingam* raised on a platform bearing inscriptions from the tenth century. This is the location of six daily *pujas*, or worships, when the *lingam* is bathed, clothed and strewn in flower garlands amid the heady smell of incense and camphor and the sound of bells and steady chanting.

Practicalities

Most visitors arrive in Tiruvannamalai by **bus** at the stand roughly 2km north of the temple on the main road to Gingee, though drivers often drop passengers much closer to the temple. Tiruvannamalai's **train station**, 500m north of the bus stand, is on the line between Tirupati and Madurai, with a daily service in each direction. A sprinkling of **rickshaws** gather at the bus and train stations.

Tiruvannamalai can be visited as a day trip, but two **lodges** offer simple accommodation if you're seduced by the peace and quiet. The most basic is *Aruna Lodge*, 82 Kosamadam St, just 200m east of the temple entrance (☎2757; ①). To the south, at 57-A Car St, *Udipi Brindhavan Hotel* (☎2693; ①) has spartan rooms with private bathrooms, and an excellent *thali* hall, where meals are filling and cheap.

Gingee

West of the outskirts of **GINGEE**, the eighteenth-century capital of a Maratha kingdom whose boundaries spread east to Pondicherry and west to Tiruvannamalai, **Gingee** fort (daily 9am–5pm; Rs0.50, free on Fri) covers the crests of three hills. Now deserted, with the plains grasses creeping into nooks and crevices of grey-brown crumbling walls and forgotten temples, its ramparts offer outstanding views, and the peaceful location makes a relaxing change from the bustle of temple cloisters. A narrow path to the fort passes a shrine to **Komalakanni Amman**, one of the seven guardian deities of Gingee, who is still worshipped today, and offered animal sacrifices on festival days. Other temples enclosed within the crenellated ramparts lie still and empty beside the remains of granaries, a palace and harem, a dilapidated mosque and an audience hall. Most of the fort was built by the Vijayanagars (sixteenth century), and modified by later occupants: Marathas, Moghuls, the French and British.

Gingee is served by hourly buses from Tiruvannamalai, 40km east (in which case you come to the fort before you reach the town; ask the bus driver to drop you off), and Pondicherry, 70km southeast; there's no accommodation, but a few hours is adequate for a leisurely perusal. Arrive early to avoid having to make the twenty-minute climb to the fort in the burning midday sun.

Pondicherry

PONDICHERRY, on the Bay of Bengal 160km south of Madras, lies amid flat scrubland, dotted with low thatched huts, tall palmyra palms, bamboo, casuarina and tamarind trees. Relatively few visitors make it down here from Madras, though that may change with the completion of the new coastal highway, partly financed by the World Bank. Once the capital of French India, it became in 1954 the headquarters of the **Union Territory of Pondicherry**, administering former French enclaves scattered over south India. For anyone more familiar with the British colonial imprint, it can induce culture shock to encounter French-speaking young Pondicherriens.

Set on either side of a canal, Pondicherry splits neatly into two parts. To the west is a bustling Indian market town; to the east, towards the sea, the streets are emptier, cleaner and decidedly European. The seaside promenade, **Goubert Salai** (formerly Beach Road), has the forlorn look of an out-of-season French resort, complete with its own white Hôtel de Ville. Tanned sun-worshippers share space with grave Europeans in white Indian costume, busy about their spiritual quest; **Sri Aurobindo Ghose** (1872–1950), a leading figure in the freedom struggle in Bengal, was given shelter here after it became unwise to live close to the British in Calcutta, and his **ashram** attracts thousands of devotees from all around the world, most particularly from Bengal.

Ten kilometres north, the Utopian experiment-in-living **Auroville** was inspired by Aurobindo's disciple, the charismatic Mirra Alfassa, a Parisian painter, musician and mystic better known as "The Mother". Today this slightly surreal place is populated by numbers of expats and visited by long-stay Europeans eager to find inner peace.

More dissolute visitors find solace in the fact that Pondicherry levies no tax on alcohol. **Beer** is extremely cheap.

Arrival and information

The two main **bus** stands, **Thiruvalluvar** (state buses), and **New Moffussil** (state and private), are near each other in the southwest of town on Maraimalai Adigal Salai (NH45a), a continuation of Lal Bahadur Sastri St. Both serve substantially the same destinations; for a summary of routes, see the "Travel Details" on p.896. Pondicherry's **railway station** is in the south, five minutes' walk from the sea; on a branch line, it's connected by two daily trains to the main line at Villupuram (departures 8.05am & 9pm; 2hr). For the latest information on **flights** from Madras and Bangalore to the airport 7km from the city (☎0413/33178) – not operating as this book went to press – contact *Souvenir Travels* on Mission St or *Auro Travels*, Nehru St (☎0413/25128).

The friendly staff at the tiny **Pondicherry Tourism Development Corporation** office on Goubert Salai (daily 8am–1pm & 2–7pm; ☎0413/39497) can give you their leaflet, arrange **city tours** (half-day from 8.30am; Rs25) or **car rental** (Rs160–560).

You can **change money** (except *Thomas Cook's* travellers' cheques) at branches of the *Indian Overseas Bank*, inside the Hôtel de Ville compound, Goubert Salai and on Nehru St. The **post office** is in the northwest corner of Government Place.

The Town

Pondicherry's beachside promenade, **Goubert Salai**, is a favourite place for a stroll, with cafes and bars to idle in and cooling breezes coming in off the sea. There's little to see, other than the world go by, but Hôtel de Ville, today housing the Municipal Offices building, is still impressive, and a four-metre statue of Gandhi, surrounded by ancient columns, dominates the northern end. Nearby, on the land side, a French memorial commemorates French Indians who lost their lives in World War I.

Just north of the Hôtel de Ville, a couple of streets back from the promenade, is the leafy old French-provincial-style square now named **Government Place**. A fountain stands at the centre, and among its paths and lawns are a number of sculptures carved in nearby Gingee. On its northern side, guarded by policemen in red *képis*, the impressive, gleaming white **Raj Nivas**, official home to the present Lieutenant Governor of Pondicherry Territory, was built late in the eighteenth century for Joseph Francis Dupleix, who became governor of French India. Bibliophiles and research scholars need special permission to examine the historical French collection of the ugly concrete **Romain Rolland Library** next door.

On the south side of Government Place in rue Romain Rolland, the **Pondicherry Museum** (daily except Mon 10am–5pm) holds Neolithic and 2000-year-old remains from Arikamedu, a few Pallava (sixth–eighth centuries) and Buddhist (tenth-century) stone sculptures, bronzes, weapons and paintings. Perhaps most intriguing, however, is the bizarre assembly of French salon furniture and bric-a-brac from Pondicherry

△ Auroville & Madras

PONDICHERRY

N

0   500 m

SARDAR VALLABHAI PATEL SALAI (NORTH BLVD)
THIYAGA RAJA ST
K KOIL ST
MA KOIL ST
TD KOIL ST
KA COVIL ST
L THOLLANDAL ST
SRI AUROBINDO ST
B DERICHEMONT ST
SUPHAYA CHETTIAR ST
OUPUY ST
C KOIL ST
A MADAM ST

Sri Aurobindo
Ashram

RUE NEHRU

❶

Market

❷

Ranga
Pillai House ■

RANGA PILLAI ST

VELLAJA ST

Ⓗ GPO

Raj
Nivas

Romain
Roland
Library

Ⓘ

Ⓖ

NIDARAJAPAYER ST

GOVERNMENT
PLACE

Old
Lighthouse

ST THERESA ST

Gandhi
Memorial Pier

❺

SINNA PAPPARA ST

Museum

LAPPORTH ST

Hôtel
de Ville

MONTHORSIER ST

C MUDHALIAR ST

Ⓘ

LAL BAHADUR SASTRI ST

Ⓕ

Botanical
Gardens

❹

Ⓔ

Alliance
Française

SUBBAIYAH SALAI (SOUTH BLVD)

Water
Tower

❸

Railway
Station

Ⓓ

AMBEDKAR AVE

△ Bus Stations, Villupuram, Cuddalore & **Ⓒ**

HOTELS:
Ⓐ Surguru
Ⓑ Victoria Lodge
Ⓒ Mass
Ⓓ Government Tourist Home
Ⓔ Ajantha Beach Guest Suite
Ⓕ Grand Hotel D'Europe
Ⓖ Kanchi
Ⓗ International Guest House
Ⓘ Sea Side Guest House

RESTAURANTS:
❶ Aristo
❷ Indian Coffee House
❸ Seagull Restaurant & Bar
❹ Chez Mathieu
❺ Le Cafe

houses, including a velvet S-shaped "conversation seat", piano, drinks cabinet, tables, carved cupboards, beds, lacquer boxes, long-case clock and plates.

Ananda Ranga Pillai (1709–61) was *dubash*, or close advisor, and translator to Joseph Francis Dupleix. The **Ranga Pillai house**, built in the 1740s, at 109 Ranga Pillai St, is one of the highlights of any visit to Pondicherry, but as his descendants still live here, viewing is by appointment only (enquiries to Mr Ananda Ravichandra; ☎0413/605001). Born in Madras into a wealthy merchant family, Pillai is principally known for his twelve-volumes diaries, an unparalleled source of social and political information about life in French India from 1736 onwards. As a trusted friend to Dupleix, he was accorded the highest status under the French regime, with his own palanquin, flag and other honours. The house is unmarked and indistinguishable from others in this busy market area; however, anyone in the vicinity can direct you. Entrance is through a courtyard surrounded by a raised platform with twelve tapering wooden columns. Rooms on the **first floor**, reached up steep wooden stairs, are very French, filled with extraordinary antiques, some in very poor shape. One bedroom, with a patterned tile floor, is dominated by Pillai's bed of carved ivory. Against the wall, the two almirah cupboards have secret drawers, made of Burma teak and delicate ivory inlay, while in a corner is a child's ivory swing-cradle which once hung from the ceiling. A miniature antique palanquin stands on the landing outside, used for transporting the deity in temple festivals.

Focus of the Aurobindo Society, the **Sri Aurobindo Ashram** on rue de la Marine (daily 8am–6pm, no children under 3yrs; photography with permission) is one of the best-known and wealthiest ashrams in India, founded in 1926. A beautifully maintained small rockery, cactus and flower garden greets you as you enter the compound. The **samadhi**, or mausoleum, of Sri Aurobindo and The Mother is daily covered with flowers and usually surrounded by supplicating devotees with their hands and heads placed on the tomb. Inside the main building, an incongruous and very bourgeois-looking western-style room complete with three-piece suite, is where The Mother and Sri Aurobindo chilled out. Make sure not to tread on the Persian carpet on the floor, as devotees prostrate here also. A bookshop in the next room sells tracts, and frequent cultural programmes are presented in the building opposite.

Pondicherry's shady **Botanical Gardens** in the southwest of town, established in 1826, offer many quiet paths to wander, and enough to see to pass a peaceful hour or two (daily 8.45am–5.45pm). The French planted nine hundred species here, experimenting to see how they would perform in Indian conditions; one, the *khaya senegalensis* from Senegal, has grown to a height of 25 metres, and you can also see an extraordinary fossilized tree found about 25km away in Tiravakarai.

Auroville

The most New Age place anywhere in India must surely be **AUROVILLE**, the planned "City of Dawn", 10km north of Pondicherry, just outside the Union Territory in Tamil Nadu. Founded in 1968, Auroville was inspired by The Mother, the spiritual successor of Sri Aurobindo. Around 800 families live in communes with such names as Fertile, Certitude, Sincerity, Revelation and Transformation, in what it is hoped will eventually be an ideal city for a population of 50,000. Architecturally experimental buildings, combining modern western and traditional Indian elements, are set in a rural landscape of narrow lanes, deep red earth and lush greenery. Income comes from agriculture, handicrafts, alternative technology, educational and development projects and *Aurolec*, a computer company. Although the avowed aim is to live in harmony, a life made meaningful through hard physical work backed up by spiritual discipline, the place has had its ups and downs, not least of which have been the disputes between the community and the Sri Aurobindo Society over ownership ever since The Mother's death in 1973. In addition, although Auroville is supposedly an international community, with lots of well-off westerners buzzing around on mopeds and motorbikes, Pondicherriens tend to assert that most of the Indians involved today are delegated to the status of labourers.

Still under construction, the **Matri Mandir** is a gigantic, costly, almost-spherical, hi-tech meditation centre intended as the focal point of Auroville (daily, temple 4–5pm, grounds 8am–5pm). In 1970 it was stated that "The Matri Mandir wants to be a symbol of the Divine's answer to man's inspiration for perfection. Union with the Divine manifesting in a progressive unity". Earth from 124 countries was symbolically placed in an urn, and is kept in the building. The **Boutique d'Auroville** (daily except Sun 9am–1pm & 2–5.30pm) nearby sells New Age souvenirs, books, Mother postcards, healing gems and joss sticks. Next to it is a smart, modern, vegetarian cafe and another building housing an exhibition on The Mother's philosophy.

Auroville does not actively encourage sightseeing, although the PTDC city tour (see p.929) calls at Matri Mandir. If you have a genuine interest, contact either the *Boutique d'Auroville* in Nehru St, Pondicherry, or the Information Centre, opposite the south-west entrance to Matri Mandir. As Auroville is so spread out, covering fifty square kilometres, it's best to come with your own transport – at the very least a bike. Buses only run as far as the villages of Periyamudaliarchavadi and Chinnamudaliarchavadi on the coastal road, and an auto-rickshaw trip to Matri Mandir from town costs around Rs100.

Accommodation

Pondicherry's **basic lodges** are concentrated around the main market area, Ranga Pillai and Nehru streets. Guest houses belonging to the **Sri Aurobindo Ashram** come with a lot of baggage apart from your own (regulations, curfews and overpowering "philosophy of life" notices). Although supposedly open to all, they are not keen on advertising, or on attracting misguided individuals indulging in "spiritual tourism". Travellers on a tight budget can try the Railway Retiring Rooms.

If you want to stay in **Auroville**, where accommodation ranges from the most basic to reasonably comfortable, contact the *Boutique d'Auroville* in Nehru St, Pondicherry; they too do not encourage common or garden tourists.

Ajantha Beach Guest Suite, southern end of Goubert Salai (☎0413/38898). Some a/c rooms but often full. On the seafront, but only three rooms face the sea. Restaurant and bar. ④.

Government Tourist Home, Ambedkar Ave, Uppalam, near the railway station (☎0413/36376). Spartan, clean place not far from the sea. 42 rooms (8 a/c), but often full. Snacks-only restaurant. ①.

Grand Hotel d'Europe, 12 rue Suffren, off Lal Bahadur St. Six rooms in elegant old hotel run by an octogenarian Pondicherrien Frenchman who doesn't expect the place to remain open for long. The restaurant, in verandah/entrance hall, serves French cuisine; rates include one meal a day. ⑤.

International Guest House, Gingee Salai, near the Post Office (☎0413/26699). An Aurobindo establishment with a range of rooms, some a/c. ③–④.

Kanchi, Mission St (☎0413/25540). Rather run down, but large rooms, some with balcony. ④.

Mass, Maraimalai Adigal Salai (☎0413/27221). Near the bus stands and the Botanical Gardens, in the southeast of town. All rooms a/c with *Star TV*. Veg and non-veg restaurants. ⑤.

Palms Beach Cottage Centre, Chinnamudaliarchavadi bus stop, 9km from Pondicherry on the old coastal road to Mamallapuram, near Auroville. Two double and four single cottages, all with shared bathroom, in a beautiful little garden. A real hippy hideaway. ①.

Pondicherry Ashok, Chinnakalapet, 12km from Pondicherry on the old coastal road to Mamallapuram, near Auroville (☎0413/854160). Twenty comfortable rooms in a quiet, breezy location on the seashore. *Star TV*, children's park, restaurant, barbeque and bar. ⑦.

Sea Side Guest House, 10 Goubert Salai (☎0413/26494). Aurobindo guest house in an old, converted house. Often full as there are only eight, good-size rooms (2 a/c). ④.

Surguru, 104 Sardar Vallabhai Patel Salai (North Blvd) (☎0413/33886; fax 34377). Clean, modern place some way from the sea on very busy road. 57 rooms (some very good value non-a/c). 24hr room service, travel agents, car rental. ④.

Victoria Lodge, 79 rue Nehru (☎0413/26366). Drab, but serviceable. ②.

Eating

Pondicherry has several places where you can eat by the waves, in the open air. Add a couple of genuinely good French restaurants, the sound of European voices, and a judicious amount of beer, and you can imagine yourself by the Mediterranean.

Ajantha, Goubert Salai. Restaurant on the land side overlooking the sea and promenade. Tables outside are quite pleasant, but the north Indian menu is fairly uninspiring. Best to go for a cool drink, tea or a snack. Alcohol is served only downstairs in the ground floor bar.

Anugraha, *Hotel Surguru*, 104 Sardar Vallabhai Patel Salai (North Blvd). Good pure veg, north Indian, Chinese and western dishes. Snacks served after 4pm.

Aristo, rue Nehru. Delightful rooftop restaurant below plant-filled arbour, filled with the twittering of budgies in cages. Good north Indian, western non-veg and some veg dishes.

Le Café, Goubert Salai. A balcony café which at high tide is only inches from the sea; selling drinks and snack food, *dosas*, omelettes and ice cream. Popular with students. Open 6am–9pm.

Chez Mathieu, 30 rue Suffren (☎0413/39132). A real French restaurant, run by emigrés with a bias towards southern French cuisine. *Coq au vin*, rabbit and seafood are standard, but the chef is determined to keep the menu changing. The *epicerie* next door serves real patisserie.

Indian Coffee House, rue Nehru. Not their cleanest branch, but the coffee is as good as usual.

Seagull Restaurant and Bar, rue Damas (☎0413/38643). Very friendly, reasonably priced, open-air rooftop restaurant in breezy spot right next to the sea, new pier and cargo harbour. Huge menu, with veg dishes, meat, seafood, Indian, Chinese and even some Italian (pizza, risotto, spaghetti).

The Chola heartland

Continuing south of Pondicherry along the Coromandel coast, you enter the flat landscape of the Kaveri (aka Cauvery) Delta. This was the very heartland of the mighty **Chola** empire, which was at its peak in the tenth century AD (see p.917). Much as the Cholas originally intended, every visitor is immediately awed by their huge temples, not only at cities such as **Chidambaram**, **Kumbakonam** and **Thanjavur**, but also out in the countryside at places like **Gangaikondacholapuram**, where the temple is all that is left of a once-great city. However, exploring the area for a few days will also bring you into contact with the more delicate side of Chola artistic expression, such as the magnificent **bronzes** of Thanjavur.

Chidambaram

CHIDAMBARAM, 58km south of Pondicherry, is so steeped in myth that its history is hard to unravel. As the site of the *tandava*, the cosmic dance of Shiva as **Nataraja**, king of the dance, it is one of the holiest sites in south India. A visit to the **Sabhanayaka temple** affords a fascinating glimpse into ancient Tamil religious practice and belief. The legendary king **Hiranyavarman** is said to have made a pilgrimage here from Kashmir, seeking to rid himself of leprosy by bathing in the temple's Shivaganga tank. In thanks for a successful cure, he enlarged the temple. He also brought three thousand *brahmins*, of the Dikshitar caste, whose descendants are to this day the ritual specialists of the temple, distinguishable by top-knots of hair at the front of their heads.

Few of the fifty *maths*, or monasteries, that once stood here remain, but the temple itself is still a hive of activity and plays host to numerous **festivals**. The two most important are ten-day affairs, building up to spectacular finales: on the ninth day of each, temple chariots process through the four Car streets (**"Car Festival"**), while on the tenth, **Abhishekham**, the principal deities in the Raja Sabha are anointed. For exact dates (one is in May/June, the other in Dec/Jan), contact any TTDC tourist office; plan well ahead, as they are very popular. Other local festivals include fire-walking and Kavadi folk dance (dancing with decorated wooden frames on the head) at the Thillaiamman Kali (April/May) and Keelatheru Mariamman (July/Aug) temples.

The town also has a hectic market, and a large student population, based at Annamalai University to the east, a centre of Tamil studies. Among the simple thatched huts in the local flat, sparsely populated countryside, which becomes very dry and dusty in summer, the only solid-looking structures are small roadside temples. Many honour Aiyannar, the village deity who protects borders, and are accompanied by *kudirais*, brightly painted terracotta or wooden figures of horses.

Arrival and information

The town revolves around the Sabhanayaka temple and the busy market area that surrounds it, along North, East, South and West Car streets. Though little more than a country halt, the **railway station**, 2km southeast of the centre, has good connections both north and south, and boasts retiring rooms and, on platform one, a **post office** (Mon–Sat 9am–1pm & 1.30–5pm). Buses from Madras, Thanjavur, Pichavaram, Mamallapuram, Nagapattinam and Madurai pull in at the **bus stand**, also in the southeast, but nearer the centre, about 1km from the temple.

Staff at the TTDC **tourist office**, next to TTDC *Hotel Tamil Nadu* on Railway Feeder Rd, are charming and helpful, but only have a small pamphlet to give visitors. You can **change money** at the *State Bank of India*, Pava Mudali St, *Central Bank*, 62 Bazaar St, and *Indian Bank*, 64 S Car St. North Car St hosts the **main post office**.

Sabhanayaka Nataraja Temple

The **Sabhanayaka Nataraja Temple** complex (daily 4am–noon & 4.30–9pm) covers about 55 acres, divided by four concentric walls. The oldest parts now standing were built under the Cholas, who adopted Nataraja as their chosen deity and crowned several kings here. The rectangular outermost wall, of little interest in itself, affords entry on all four sides, so if you have the time the best way to tackle the complex is to work slowly inwards from the third enclosure in clockwise circles. **Guides** are readily available but tend to shepherd visitors towards the central shrine too quickly. Frequent **ceremonies** take place at the innermost sanctum, the most popular being at 5pm. On Friday nights before the temple closes, during a particularly elaborate *puja*, Nataraja is carried on a palanquin accompanied by music and attendants carrying flaming torches and tridents. At other times, ancient devotional hymns from the *Tevaram* are sung.

THE THIRD ENCLOSURE

Four gigantic *gopura* towers rise out of the irregular third wall, each with a granite base and a brick-built superstructure of diminishing storeys covered in a profusion of carved figures. The western *gopura* is the most popular entrance, as well as being the most elaborately carved and probably the earliest (*c*.1150 AD). Turning north (left) from here, you come to the colonnaded **Shivaganga tank**, the site of seven natural springs. From the broken pillar at the tank's edge, all four *gopuras* are visible.

Facing the tank, on the left side, is the **Shivakamasundari temple**, devoted to Parvati, consort of Shiva. Step inside to see the Nayak (sixteenth-century) ceiling paintings arranged in cartoon-like frames in muted browns and greens, outlined in black. On the right as you enter, the story of the leper king Hiranyavarman (see above) is illustrated, and, at the back, some frames form a map of the temple complex. Next door, in the northwest corner, a shrine to Subrahmanya, the son of Shiva, is adorned with paintings illustrating stories from the *Skanda Purana*. Beyond this, in front of the northern *gopura*, stands a small shrine to the Navagraha (nine planets).

In the northeast corner, the largest building in the complex, the **Raja Sabha** (fourteenth to fifteenth century) is also known as "the thousand-pillared hall"; tradition holds that there are only nine hundred and ninety-nine actual pillars, the thousandth being Shiva's leg. During festivals the deities Nataraja and Shivakamasundari are brought here and mounted on a dais for the anointing ceremony, *abhishekha*.

BHAKTI AND THE TAMIL POETS

From the eighth century onwards, the devotional form of Hinduism known as **bhakti**, which blossomed in Tamil Nadu, spread north into the rest of India to become, as it still is, the dominant strain of Hinduism throughout the country. It was essentially a popular movement, whose emphasis that each individual devotee could form a personalized, emotionally charged relationship with a chosen god (*ishtadevata*) revolutionized Hindu practice by offering a religious path and goal open to all castes.

The great champions of *bhakti* were the **poet-saints** of Tamil Nadu, often said to have "sung" the religions of Jainism and Buddhism out of south India. Although in practice a variety of deities were worshipped, the movement had two strands – the **Nayanmars**, devoted to Shiva, and the **Alvars**, centred on Vishnu. Collections of their poetry, the greatest literary legacy of south India, remain popular today, and the poets themselves are almost deified, featuring on carvings in many temples.

The four most prominent of the 63 Nayanmar poet-saints were **Campantar**, who converted the king of Madurai from Jainism and had a great cult centre at Chidambaram; **Cuntarar**, a *brahmin* who had two low-caste wives; **Appar**, himself a convert from Jainism; and **Manikkavachakar**, whose mystical poems are still sung in homes and temples throughout Tamil Nadu. The Vaishnavite movement centred on Srirangam (near Trichy), its poets including men and women of all social classes. The most celebrated Alvar was **Nammalvar**, a *shudra* who spent his life in fasting and meditation. **Antal**, the most popular female Alvar, who is said to have married Vishnu's statue at Srirangam, was thereafter regarded as an incarnation of Vishnu's consort, Shri.

All the poems tell of the ecstatic response to intense experiences of divine favour, an emotion frequently described in terms of conjugal love, and expressed in verses of great tenderness and beauty. They stress selfless love between man and god, claiming that such love alone can lead to everlasting union with the divine. Devotees travelled the south, singing, dancing and challenging opponents to public debates.

By the tenth century the **Srivaishnava** sect had been formed around Alvar teachers. The most famous of these, **Ramanuja** (traditionally dated 1017–1137), was for a time head teacher at Srirangam. His works include philosophical treatises, commentaries on the *Bhagavad Gita* and the *Brahmasutra*, devotional poems and a manual of daily practice, written in Sanskrit to reach a wider audience. His new philosophical school, **Visishtadvaita**, proposed God (Vishnu) as the source of all created things and the ruler of the universe. Rejecting Shankara's concept that all except God is illusion, or *maya*, Ramanuja upheld the reality of God, souls and the world, stressing the *dependence* of all on Vishnu, whom he called Narayana, and envisioning the final "union" of the soul with God as an eternal relationship between two distinct entities. God was seen as desiring to offer his grace to all who made themsleves open to it. Ramanuja emphasized ritual as the first step to surrender (*prapatti*), and the increased participation of worshippers at all levels spread from Srirangam to Vaishnavite centres all over the south.

Out of Nayanmar poetry a parallel movement arose among Shaivites who, in the tenth century, developed the **Shaiva Siddhanta** system with the compilation of their poems in the **Tirumurai**. Focusing on ultimate union with Shiva, the Shaiva Siddhanta stresses that the human soul is sunk in evil, and can only obtain release through knowledge of God, initiated by Shiva's grace and the soul's love for him. Shiva is thought to appear as a guru, to entice the devotee.

The final major works of the Shaiva teachers were the **Umapati**, supposedly written by a Vaishnavite-turned-Shaivite at Chidambaram. In these, Shiva as Lord of the Dance, **Nataraja**, dances through the world in ceaseless activity to liberate souls. Though Shiva is transcendent, he is made imminent on earth through his power, or *shakti*, personified in iconography by his female consort. Temple festivals mark marriage, quarrels and other exploits of the couple. The Shaiva Siddhanta became firmly established at teaching centres in the south, based on *brahmin* institutions known as *maths*, but led by non-*brahmin* gurus, whose presence strengthened the position of *shudras*, not in a rejection of caste distinction, but in an assertion that the teachings were open to all.

The importance of dance at Chidambaram is underlined by the reliefs of dancing figures inside the east *gopura* demonstrating 108 *karanas* (a similar set is to be found in the west *gopura*). A *karana* (or *adavu*, in Tamil) is a specific point in a phase of movement prescribed by the extraordinarily comprehensive Sanskrit treatise on the performing arts, the *Natya Shastra* (*c.*200 BC–200 AD) – the basis of all Indian classical dance, music and theatre. A caption from the *Natya Shastra* surmounts each *karana* niche. Four other niches are filled with images of patrons and *stahapatis* – the sculptors and designers responsible for the iconography and positioning of deities.

A pavilion at the south *gopura* houses an image of Nandi, Shiva's bull. Although not accessible from here, the central Nataraja shrine faces south; as with all Shiva temples, Nandi sits opposite the god. In the southwest corner, a shrine contains one of the largest images in India of the elephant-headed son of Shiva, Ganapati (Ganesh). If you stand inside the entrance *mandapa* with your back to Ganapati, you'll see at the base of the two pillars nearest the shrine carvings of the two important devotees of Nataraja at Chidambaram (see below). To the right is the sage Patanjali, with a snake's body, and on the left Vyaghrapada, with a human body but tiger's feet.

THE SECOND ENCLOSURE

To get into the square second enclosure, head for its **western entrance** (just north of the west *gopura* in the third wall), which leads into a circumambulatory passageway. Once beyond this second wall it's easy to become disorientated as the roofed inner enclosures see little light and are supported by a maze of colonnades. The atmosphere is immediately more charged, reaching its peak at the very centre.

On the north side, the **Mulasthana** houses the *svayambhulingam* worshipped by Patanjali and Vyaghrapada. The **Devasabha**, or "hall of the gods", on the east, shelters as many as a hundred bronze images used in processions, and is a meeting place for members of the three hundred Dikshitar *brahmin* families who own and maintain the temple. Beyond it lies the other, eastern entrance to the second enclosure.

The **Nritta Sabha**, or dance hall, stands on the site where Shiva outdanced Kali (see below), now the southwest corner of the second enclosure. Probably the oldest surviving structure of the two inner areas, its raised platform was fashioned in stone to resemble a wooden temple chariot, or *ratha*. Before they were inexplicably concreted over in the mid-1950s, the east and west sides of the base were each adorned with a wheel and a horse; all that can be seen now are fragments.

THE DANCE COMPETITION BETWEEN SHIVA AND KALI

The thousand-headed cosmic serpent, **Adisesha**, upon whose coiled body Vishnu reclines in the primordial ocean, once expressed a wish to see Shiva's famed dance. Having arranged time off from his normal duties with Vishnu, Adisesha prayed to Shiva, who was so impressed by the serpent's entreaties that he promised to dance in the forest of Tillai (the site of Chidambaram). Adisesha was reborn as the human sage **Patanjali** (represented as half-man, half-snake) and made straight for Tillai. There he met another sage, **Vyaghrapada** – "Tiger Feet", who had been granted the claws of a tiger to help him climb trees and pluck the best flowers to offer Shiva – who shared his wish to see Shiva dance. Together, they worshipped a *svayambhulingam*, a *shivalingam* which had "self-manifested" in the forest, now housed in the Mulasthana shrine of Sabhanayaka temple. However, the guardian of the forest, who turned out to be the goddess **Kali**, refused to allow Shiva to dance when he arrived. In response, he challenged her to a **dance competition** for possession of the forest. Kali agreed but, perhaps due to modesty, could not match a pose of Shiva's which involved raising the right foot above the head. Defeated, Kali was forced to move off a little way north, where a temple now stands in her honour.

THE INNERMOST ENCLOSURE

Passing through the southern entrance (marked by a gold flagstaff) to the **innermost enclosure** brings you immediately into a hallway, which leads west to the nearby **Govindaraja shrine**, dedicated to Vishnu – a surprise in this most Shaivite of environments. Govindaraja is attended by non-Dikshitar *brahmins*, who, it is said, don't always get along with the Dikshitars. From outside the shrine, non-Hindus can see through to the most sacred part of the temple, the **Kanaka Sabha** and the **Chit Sabha**, adjoining raised structures, roofed with copper and gold plate and linked by a hallway. Two huge bells and extremely loud *nagaswarams* (double-reed wind instruments), *tavils* (drums) and *nattuvangams* (cymbals) call worshippers for ceremonies. The only entrance – closed to non-Hindus – is up five silver-plated steps into the Chit Sabha, guarded by the devotees Vyaghrapada and Patanjali and lit by an arc of flickering oil lamps.

The Chit Sabha houses bronze images of Nataraja and his consort Shivakamasundari. Behind and to the left of Nataraja, a curtain, sacred to Shiva and strung with rows of leaves from the bilva tree, demarcates the most potent area of all. Within it lies the **Akashalingam**, known as the Rahasya, or "secret", of Chidambaram: made of the most subtle of the elements, Ether (*akasha*), from which Air, Fire, Water and Earth are born, the *lingam* is invisible.

A crystal *lingam*, said to have emanated from the light of the crescent moon on Shiva's brow, and a small ruby Nataraja are worshipped in the Kanaka Sabha. They are ritually bathed in the flames of the priests' camphor fire or oil lamps six times a day.

Accommodation and eating

To cope with the influx of tourists and pilgrims, Chidambaram abounds in budget **accommodation**, but there are no upper-bracket options. If you'd prefer not to **eat** in the hotel restaurants, there are basic "meals" places on and around the Car streets, the *Get In*, opposite the TTDC tourist office, is a favourite with the Chidambaram student set, and there's an *Indian Coffee House*, on Venugopal Pillai St.

Akshaya, 17/18 E Car St (☎0416/22181). Modern hotel, backing onto the temple wall, with 30 rooms (3 a/c; non-a/c is better value). Of its three restaurants, the *Aswini* serves veg Chinese and Indian dishes (cheaper at lunchtime), you can eat non-veg dishes on the lawn next to the temple, and the best bet in the evening is the veg rooftop restaurant, with views of the *gopuras*. ②–④.

Railway Retiring Rooms, enquire at the Station Master's Office, platform 1. The best deal in town – huge clean rooms, though the bathrooms are a little dilapidated. ①.

Raja Rajan, 162 W Car St (☎0416/22690). Clean rooms, a bit cramped. ①.

Saradharam, 19 Venugopal Pillai St, opposite the bus stand (☎0416/22966). Large, clean and well-kept rooms (a/c ones have *Star TV*) in modern buildings, with small garden. There's a bar, and the a/c restaurant serves chicken and mutton dishes as well as veg items. ③.

Star Lodge, 101 S Car St (☎0416/22743). In a noisy part of town, but good value. A few scattered plants stave off grimness. Good, inexpensive veg meals in the *Babu* restaurant. Hot water at 6am. ①.

TTDC Hotel Tamil Nadu, Railway Feeder Rd, between railway station and bus stand (☎0416/23223). Friendly, but some rooms are woefully neglected: check bedding, and if the a/c works. Also hostel lodging, and decent, reasonably priced veg and non-veg south Indian snacks and meals. ①–⑤.

Gangaikondacholapuram

Devised as the centrepiece of a city built by the Chola king Rajendra I (1014–42) to celebrate his conquests, the magnificent **Brihadishwara Temple** stands in the tiny village of **GANGAIKONDACHOLAPURAM**, in Trichy District, 35km northeast of Kumbakonam. The tongue-twisting name means "the town of the Chola who took the Ganges"; under Rajendra I, the Chola empire did indeed stretch as far as the great river of the north, an unprecedented achievement for a southern dynasty. Aside from the temple, nothing of the city remains, although the site of Rajendra's palace, 2km east at Tamalikaimedu, long a source of bricks for local villagers, is being excavated.

Frequent **buses** run here from Kumbakonam, and it is also served by some between Trichy and Chidambaram. Facilities are minimal, little more than a few cool drinks stands, so be sure not to get stuck here between noon and 4pm when the temple is closed. Parts of the interior are extremely dark, and a torch is useful.

Brihadishwara Temple

The **Brihadishwara Temple** (daily 6am–noon & 4–8pm) is enclosed by a rectangular wall; visitors enter through a gateway on the north, separated from the main road by a car park. From here you arrive at a well-maintained, grassy courtyard, flanked by the closed *mandapa* hallway of the temple. Over the sanctuary, to the right, a massive pyramidal tower (*vimana*) rises 55 metres in nine diminishing storeys. Though smaller than the one at Thanjavur, the tower's graceful curve gives it an impressive refinement.

Turning left (east) inside the courtyard, you pass a small shrine to the goddess **Durga**, containing an image of Mahishasuramardini (see p.919). Just beyond, steps climb from a large seated lion, known as Simha-kinaru and made from plastered brickwork, to a well. King Rajendra is said to have had Ganges water placed in it to be used for the ritual anointing (*abhishekha*) of the *lingam* in the main temple.

Set into the east wall, the remains of a *gopura* entranceway lead directly to a large water tank. Directly in front, before the eastern entrance to the temple, stands a small altar for offerings (*bali-pitha*) and a huge Nandi bull. Two flights of steps on the north and south ascend to a porch, the *mukhamandapa*, where a large pair of *dvarpala*s flank the entrance to the long pillared *mahamandapa* hallway. Here you're likely to meet the ASI caretakers, who are worth taking as guides, especially if you'd like to climb up onto the roof for views of the vicinity and of the tower. Access is from within the temple, up steep steps. Immediately inside, on either side of the doorway, sculptures of Shiva in his various benevolent (*anugraha*) manifestations include him blessing Vishnu, Devi, Ravana and the saint Chandesha (see p.941). In the northeast corner an unusual square stone block features carvings of the nine planets (*navagraha*). A number of **Chola bronzes** (see p.945) stand on the platform.; the figure of Karttikeya, the war god, carrying a club and a shield, is thought to have had particular significance.

The *mahamandapa* leads to the small pillared antechamber (*ardhamandapa*) which has an entrance and stairway at the north and south. Beyond it, the square sanctum sanctorum (*garbha griha*) houses a massive *shivalingam*. Back outside, turning right from the *mukhamandapa* to the southern side of the temple you pass the staircase to the *ardhamandapa*, protected by a pair of *dvarpala* door guardians. In the southwest corner of the courtyard are two **shrines**. The first is to Shiva as Kailasanatha; the other contains a large image of Ganesh, his trunk gleefully curling around a glut of sweets, his favourite food.

The base of the main temple sanctuary is decorated with lions and scrollwork. Above, running from the southern to the northern entrance of the *ardhamandapa*, a series of sculpted figures in pilastered niches portray different images of Shiva. The most famous is at the northern entrance, showing Shiva and Parvati garlanding the saint Chandesha, who here is sometimes identified as Rajendra I.

Two minutes' walk east along the main road (turn right from the car park), the tiny **Archeological Museum** (daily except Fri 10am–1pm & 2–5.45pm) contains Chola odds and ends, discovered locally. The finds include terracotta lamps, coins, weapons, tiles, bronze, bangle pieces, palm-leaf manuscripts and an old Chinese pot.

Kumbakonam

The Cholas are said to have kept a high-security treasury in **KUMBAKONAM**, on the River Kaveri (Cauvery) 74km southwest of Chidambaram and 38km northeast of Thanjavur. Long a sacred site, it still boasts eighteen **temples** and numerous water

tanks, but it's now also the chief commercial centre for the Thanjavur region. The main bazaar, **Big Street**, sells cotton, plantains, brassware and quality costume jewellery. Quite apart from its own attractions, the town is within easy reach of the magnificent examples of **Chola architecture** at Darasuram and Gangaikondacholapuram nearby; if time is short, make them your priority.

Arrival and information

Kumbakonam's small **railway station**, in the southeast, 2km from the main bazaar, is well served by trains both north and south, and has a left luggage office (24hr) and decent **retiring rooms** (①). The busy and dusty **Moffussil** (local) and **Aringannar** (long-distance) bus stands are opposite each other in the southeast of town, just north of Mahamakham tank. All the timetables are in Tamil, but there's a 24-hour enquiry office. Buses leave for **Gangaikondacholapuram** and **Thanjavur** every few minutes, many via Darasuram, and daily services run to Madras, Bangalore and Pondicherry.

The *State Bank* and *Indian Bank* are opposite each other on TSR Big St.

The Town

According to legend, Kumbakonam's seventeenth-century **Kumbareshwara temple** centres on a *lingam* fashioned by Shiva himself. Apparently, a pot (*kumba*) of **amrita**, the beverage of immortality, was washed by a great deluge from atop sacred Mount Meru in the Himalayas, and carried all the way here. Shiva, who happened to be passing in the guise of a wild forest-dwelling hunter, for some reason fired an arrow at the pot, causing it to break. From the broken pieces, he made this very *lingam*.

The temple's east entrance is approached via a covered market selling a huge assortment of cooking pots, a local speciality, as well as the usual glass bangles and trinkets. As you enter, you pass the temple elephant, with painted forehead and necklace of bells. Beyond the flagstaff, a *mandapa* hallway, whose columns feature painted *yali* (mythical beast) brackets, leads to the principal *gopura* entranceway. A figure of Shiva's bull-vehicle, Nandi, faces the main sanctuary. There's also a fine collection of silver *vahanas*, vehicles of the deities, used in festivals, and *pancha loham* (compound of silver, gold, brass, iron and tin) figures of the 63 Nayanmar poet-saints (see p.935).

The principal and largest of the Vishnu temples in Kumbakonam is the thirteenth-century **Sarangapani Temple**. Entry, into a hundred-pillar hallway from the seventeenth century (Nayak period), is through a ten-storey pyramidal *gopura* gate, over 40 metres high. Passing through a smaller *gopura* leads into a second courtyard, containing another columned *mandapa* and to the right, a shrine to Lakshmi. The **central shrine** dates from the late Chola period with many later accretions. Its entrance, within the innermost court, is guarded by huge *dvarpalas*, identical to Vishnu whom they protect. Between them are carved stone *jali* screens, each different, and in front of them stands the sacred, square *homam* fireplace. During the day, pinpoints of light from ceiling windows penetrate the darkness around the sanctum, designed to resemble a chariot with reliefs of horses, elephants and wheels. A painted cupboard contains a mirror for Vishnu to see himself when he leaves the sanctum sanctorum.

Possibly the oldest in Kumbakonam, the small **Nageshwara Swami Shiva Temple**, one of the finest early Chola temples, noted for the quality of its sculpture, is thought to have been completed a few years into the reign of Parantaka I (907–*c*.940). Standing in a courtyard, the principal shrine to Shiva is connected to a columned *mandapa*. Both share a base carved with scenes from the epics and lotus petals. The main niches on the sanctum wall contain **sculptures**; on the north, Dakshinamurti ("south-facing" Shiva as teacher), on the west Ardhanarishvara (male Shiva and female Shakti in one figure) and Brahma on the south. Joining them are high-relief near-life-size sculptures of unidentified figures, perhaps worshippers, donors or royalty. Within the courtyard, a shrine to **Nataraja** features rearing horses and wheels, with tiny figures as spokes.

The most famous and revered of many *tirthas*, sacred **water tanks**, in Kumbakonam, the **Mahamakham** in the southeast of town, is said to have filled with ambrosia collected from the pot broken by Shiva. Every twelve years, when Jupiter passes the constellation of Leo, it is believed that water from the Ganges and eight other holy rivers flows into the tank. At this auspicious time as many as two million pilgrims come here to take an absolving bathe; in 1992, sixty people died in an accident variously ascribed to a collapsing wall or to general mayhem. During a lesser annual festival (Feb/March) the deity from the Kumbareshwara temple is taken to Mahamakham in procession.

Accommodation

Kumbakonam is not a major tourist location, and has a limited range of **accommodation**, with upper-range hotels entirely absent; the good news is that most places are clean and well-maintained. There's nothing very exciting about **eating out;** your best bet is to eat in the dining halls linked to the hotels.

ARR, 21 TSR Big St (☎21234). Reasonable rooms, some a/c, all with *Star TV*. Veg restaurant serves south Indian snacks in the evening and "leaf-meals" at lunchtime. ④.

New Diamond Lodge, 93 Nageswaram N St (☎20870). Inexpensive and clean. ①.

Pandiyan Lodge, 52 Sarangapani E St (☎20397). Clean rooms; some cheaper ones are windowless. Cheap veg and "deluxe" meals (with mutton); the *Arul Restaurant* opposite is also good. ②.

PRV Lodge, 32 Head Post Office Rd (☎21820). Basic lodge with veg restaurant. ②.

Raya's, 28–29 Head Post Office Rd (☎22545). Smallish, but very clean a/c and non-a/c rooms. *Star TV*. Veg and non-veg restaurants. ④–⑤.

Siva, 104 TSR Big St (☎21045). Non-a/c rooms; the deluxe options are large, but featureless. ②–④.

VPR Lodge, 105 TSR Big St (☎21045). Shares a reception desk with *Siva*; similar, but with a/c rooms with *Star TV*. ④.

Darasuram

The **Airavateshwara Temple**, built by King Rajaraja II (*c.*1146–73), stands in the village of **DARASURAM**, an easy five-kilometre bus trip (on the Thanjavur route) or bike ride southwest of Kumbakonam. This superb if little-visited Chola monument ranks alongside those at Thanjavur and Gangaikondacholapuram; but while they are grandiose, emphasizing heroism and conquest, it is far smaller, exquisite in proportion and detail and said to have been decorated with *nitya-vinoda*, "perpetual entertainment", in mind. Shiva is here known as Airavateshwara, because he was worshipped at this temple by Airavata, the white elephant of the king of the gods, Indra.

Entrance is through a large *gopura* gateway, a metre below ground level, in the main wall, which is topped with small reclining bull figures. Inside, the main building is set in a spacious courtyard. A prodigiously well-informed priest, Shri Pichai, is usually on hand to guide visitors. Next to the inner sanctuary, fronted by an open porch, the steps of the closed *mandapa* feature elegant curled balustrades decorated with elephants and *makaras* (mythical crocodiles with floriate tails). At the corners, rearing horses and wheels make the whole into a chariot. Elsewhere, clever sculptural puns include the head of an elephant merging with that of a bull.

Fine Chola black basalt images in wall niches in the *mandapa* and the inner shrine include **Nagaraja**, the snake-king, with a hood of cobras, and **Dakshinamurti**, the "south-facing" Shiva as teacher, expounding under a banyan tree. One rare image shows Shiva as **Sharabha**, part man, beast and bird, destroying the man-lion incarnation of Vishnu, Narasimha – indicative of the animosity between the Shaivite and Vaishnavite cults. Sharabha, in his own separate small *mandapa*, is approached by a flight of steps. Fanged *dvarpala* door guardians in *raudra* (furious) mood flank the shrine entrance. Each possesses a club, their four hands in an attitude denoting threat (*tarjani*) with Shiva's trident, the *trishula,* wound into their hair.

Outside, a unique series of somewhat gruesome panels, hard to see without climbing on to the base, form a band along the top of the basement of the closed *mandapa* and the sanctum sanctorum. They illustrate scenes from Sekkilar's **Periya Purana**, one of the great works of Tamil literature. The poem tells the stories of the Tamil Shaivite saints, the Nayanmars, and was commissioned by King Kulottunga II, after the poet criticized him for a preoccupation with erotic, albeit religious, literature. Sekkilar is said to have composed it in the Raja Sabha at Chidambaram; when it was completed the king sat every day for a year to hear him recite it.

Each panel illustrates the lengths to which the saints were prepared to go to demonstrate devotion to Shiva. The boy **Chandesha**, for example, whose job it was to tend the village cows, discovered one day that they were involuntarily producing milk. He decided to bathe a *lingam* with the milk as part of his daily worship. Appalled by this apparent waste, the villagers complained to his father, who went to the field, cursed the boy, and kicked the *lingam* over. At this affront to Shiva, Chandesha cut off his father's leg with an axe; Chandesha is shown at the feet of Shiva and Parvati, who have garlanded him. Another panel shows a man who frequently gave food to Shiva devotees. When his wife was reluctant to welcome and wash the feet of a mendicant who had previously been their servant, he cut off her hands. Elsewhere, a Pallava queen has her nose cut off for inadvertently smelling a flower, rendering it useless as an offering to Shiva. The last panel shows the saint **Sundara** who, by singing a hymn to Shiva, rescued a child who had been swallowed by a crocodile.

On the lowest portions of the base, rows of *yali* mythical beasts and *ganas*, the dwarf attendants of Shiva, dance and play musical instruments. Surrounding the main shrine, a four-metre-wide channel, created by a very low wall, is decorated with lotus patterns and badly damaged Nandis. At one time, this was filled with water, so the temple appeared to float in a pool.

Thanjavur

Although its history and treasures give it a crucial significance to south Indian culture, the bustling country town of **THANJAVUR** (aka Tanjore), 55km east of Tiruchirapalli and 35km southwest of Kumbakonam in one of the main rice-growing regions of the Kaveri (Cauvery) Delta, is often overlooked by travellers.

Thanjavur is roughly split in two by the east–west **Grand Anicut Canal**. The **old town**, north of the canal and once entirely enclosed by a fortified wall, was between the ninth and the end of the thirteenth centuries chosen as the capital of their extensive empire by all the Chola kings save one. None of their secular buildings survives, but you can still see as many as ninety temples – notably the magnificent **Brihadishwara temple**, an eloquent statement of the power and patronage of Rajaraja I (985–1014). Under the Cholas, as well as the later Nayaks and Marathas, literature, painting, sculpture, Carnatic classical music and Bharatanatyam dance all thrived here; quite apart from its own intrinsic interest, the Nayak **royal palace complex** houses an important library and museums including a superb collection of Chola bronzes.

Of major local **festivals,** the most lavish celebrations at the Brihadishwara temple are associated with the birthday of King Rajaraja, in October. An eight-day celebration of **Carnatic classical music** is held each January at the Panchanateshwara temple at **Thiruvaiyaru**, 13km away, to honour the great Carnatic composer-saint, Thyagaraja.

Arrival and information

Thanjavur's **airport** is no longer operative, and the nearest airlink is at Tiruchirapalli (64km). The two busy **bus stands** are close together, off Hospital Road in the south of the old town; the **long-distance one** sees frequent buses to and from Tiruchirapalli and Madurai, plus services for Madras and Pondicherry that can be booked in advance, while the **local** stand is used by Kumbakonam buses and also some for Tiruchirapalli.

The **railway station**, on the southern limits of town, has a uniquely barmy **reservation office** (daily 9am–1pm & 2–5pm); one of its two counters handles odd dates, the other even. Two daily trains run north to Madras (the *Cholan Express* #6154 leaves 8.40am); two go south to Madurai; four go to Tiruchirapalli; and there are services to Nagapattinam (11am) and Rameshwaram (5am). The red-and-cream station itself has an antiquated air, with its decorated columns in the main hall, and sculptures of dancers and musicians. Luggage can be left in the Parcel Office in a separate building.

Local transport consists of the usual cycle and auto-rickshaws and unmetered taxis. The Post Office and most of the hotels and restaurants lie on or around **Gandhiji Road** (aka Railway Station Rd), which crosses the canal and leads to the railway station in the south. The small **TTDC Tourist Office** in the compound of TTDC *Hotel Tamil Nadu I* on Gandhiji Rd, has a few leaflets (Tues–Sun 8–11am & 4–8pm).

You can **change money** at *Canara Bank* on South Main St, the *State Bank of India*, Hospital Rd, and *Hotel Parishutham* – useful out of banking hours. The Government **Hospital** is on Hospital Rd, and there are plenty of chemists on Gandhiji Rd. At #162, opposite Irattai Mastan Dharga mosque, *National Studio & Video* sells film.

Brihadishwara temple

Thanjavur's skyline is dominated by the huge tower of the **Brihadishwara temple**, which for all its size lacks the grandiose excesses of later periods. The site has no great significance; the temple was constructed as much to reflect the power of its patron, King Rajaraja I, as to facilitate the worship of Shiva. Profuse **inscriptions** on the base of the main shrine provide incredibly detailed information about the organization of the temple. They show it to have been rich, both in financial terms and in ritual activity. Among recorded gifts from Rajaraja, from booty acquired in conquest, are the equivalent of 600lbs of silver, 500lbs of gold, and 250lbs of assorted jewels, plus income from agricultural land throughout the Chola empire, set aside for the purpose. No less than four hundred female dancers, **devadasis** (literally "slaves to the gods", married off to the deity), were employed, and each provided with a house. Other occupations, forming a staff of another two hundred, included dance teachers, musicians, tailors, potters, laundrymen, goldsmiths, carpenters, astrologers, accountants and specialist attendants for all manner of rituals and processions.

Entrance to the complex is on the east, through two **gopura** gateways some way apart. Although the outer one is the larger, both are of the same pattern: massive rectangular bases topped by pyramidal towers with carved figures and vaulted roofs. At the core of each is a monolithic sandstone lintel, said to have been brought from Tiruchirapalli, over 50km away. The outer facade of the inner *gopura* features mighty fanged *dvarpala* door guardians, mirror images of each other, and thought to be the largest monolithic sculptures in any Indian temple. Panels illustrating scenes from the *Skanda Purana* decorate the base, including the marriage of Shiva and Parvati.

Once inside, the gigantic **courtyard** gives plenty of space to appreciate the temple buildings. A sixteenth-century pavilion, fronted by a tall lamp column and facing the main temple, holds the third largest Nandi (Shiva's bull-vehicle) in India.

The **main temple**, constructed of granite, consists of a long pillared *mandapa* hallway, followed by the *ardhamandapa*, or "half-hall" which in turn leads to the inner sanctum, the *garbha griha*. The plinth of the central shrine measures 46 square metres; above it, the pyramidal *vimana* tower (at just under 61 metres high, the largest and tallest in India) rises in thirteen diminishing storeys, the apex being exactly one third of the size of the base. Such a design is quite different from later temples, where the *vimanas* become smaller as the *gopura* entranceways increasingly dominate – a desire to protect the sanctum sanctorum from the polluting gaze of outsiders.

The long pillared *mandapa* from the Vijayanagar period (sixteenth century) has been roughly adjoined to the *ardhamandapa*; you can see the mouldings do not match. Inside, the walls are decorated with eighteenth-century Maratha portraits. The *vimana* is an example of a "structured monolith", a stage removed from the earlier rock-cut architecture of the Pallavas, whereby blocks of stone are assembled and then carved. The profusion of carvings, aside from the inscriptions, include *dvarpala* door guardians, Shiva, Vishnu, Durga, Ganapati (Ganesh), Bhu-devi (the female goddess Earth) and Lakshmi, arranged on three sides in two rows.

As the stone that surmounts the *vimana* is said to weigh eighty tons, there is considerable speculation as to how it got up there; the most popular theory is that it was hauled up a four-mile-long ramp. Others have suggested the use of a method comparable to the Sumer Ziggurat style of building, whereby logs were placed in gaps in the masonry and the stone raised by leverage. The simplest answer, of course, is that perhaps it's not a single stone at all.

You can enter the *vimana* tower at the north and south by large stairs leading to the **ardhamandapa**, where Chola bronzes include one of Rajaraja himself. The black *shivalingam,* over 3.5 metres high, in the inner sanctum is called Adavallan, "the one who can dance well" – a reference to Shiva as Nataraja, "the King of the Dance" who resides at Chidambaram and was the *ishtadevata*, chosen deity, of the king. The *lingam* is not always on view, but during *puja* ceremonies (8 & 11am, noon & 7.30pm), to the accompaniment of clanging bells, a curtain is pulled revealing the god to the devotees.

Surrounding the *garbha griha*, an **ambulatory passage** contains three massive sculptures of Shiva on the south, west and north sides. Along the upper register, a sculpted series of 108 classical dance poses predates the famous sets at Chidambaram (see p.933), though here Nataraja is depicted as the dancer. Paintings on the ceiling and walls, currently being restored, are the oldest to survive from the Chola period.

Outside, the walls of the courtyard are lined with **colonnaded passageways** – the one along the northern wall is said to be the longest in India. That on the west, behind the temple, contains 108 *lingams* from Varanasi and painted panels from the Maratha period. At the centre stands a small shrine to Varuna (the Vedic god, associated with water and the sea), next to an image of goddess Durga, usually kept clothed.

Other **shrines** inside the enclosure include one behind the main temple to a devotee-saint, Karuvurar, supposedly able to cure barrenness. To the northwest, a seventeenth-century temple to Subrahmanya (a son of Shiva) has a base finely decorated with sculptures of dancers and musicians. Close to the figure of Nandi is a thirteenth-century Devi shrine; in the northeast corner, a *mandapa* houses images of Nataraja, his consort, and a devotee, and is also used for decorating icons prior to processions.

In the southwest corner of the courtyard, the small **Archeological Museum** (daily 9am–noon & 4–8pm) houses an interesting collection of sculpture, including an extremely tubby, damaged Ganesh, before-and-after photos detailing restoration work to the temple in the 1940s and displays about the Cholas. You can also buy the excellent ASI booklet *Chola Temples*, which gives detailed accounts of Brihadishwara and the temples at Gangaikondacholapuram and Darasuram.

A path leads from between the two *gopuras* the length of the main wall where, behind the temple, the well-manicured lawn lined with benches is a haven of peace and quiet. The huge temple water tank lies just beyond, next to the northwest corner.

The Royal Palace compound

The poorly signposted **Royal Palace** compound, where members of the erstwhile royal family are still resident, is on E Main St (a continuation of Gandhiji Rd), 2km northeast of Brihadishwara temple. Dotted around the compound are several reminders of Thanjavur's past under the Nayaks and the Marathas, including an exhibition of oriental manuscripts and a superlative museum of Chola bronzes. The dusty and run-down **Tamil University Museum** contains coins and musical instruments.

The palace buildings have been in a sorry state for years; hopes were raised for their preservation when the responsibility for maintenance passed in 1993 to the Indian National Trust for Cultural Heritage (INTACH), but almost immediately some suffered extensive damage in storms. The Sarja Madi, "seven-storey" bell tower, built by Serfoji II in 1800, has been closed to the public due to its unsafe condition.

Work on the palace began in the mid-sixteenth century under Sevappa Nayak, the founder of the Nayak kingdom of Thanjavur; additions were made by the Marathas from the end of the seventeenth century onwards. Remodelled by Shaji II in 1684, the **Durbar Hall**, or hall of audience, houses a throne canopy decorated with the mirrored glass distinctive to Thanjavur. Although damaged, the ceiling and walls are elaborately

---

CHOLA BRONZES

Originally sacred temple objects, **Chola bronzes** are the only art form from Tamil Nadu to have penetrated the world art market. The most memorable bronze icons are the **Natarajas**, or dancing Shivas. The image, standing on one leg, encircled by flames, with wild locks caught in mid-motion, has become almost as recognizably Indian as the Taj Mahal, and few Indian millionaires would feel their sitting rooms complete without one.

The principal icons of a temple are usually stationary and made of stone. Frequently, however, ceremonies require an image of the god to be led in procession outside the inner sanctum, and even through the streets. According to the canonical texts known as *Agamas*, these moving images should be made of metal. Indian bronzes are made by the **cire-perdu**, "lost-wax", process. Three layers of clay mixed with burnt grain husks, salt and ground cotton are applied to a figure crafted in wax, with a stem left protruding at each end. When that is heated, the wax melts and flows out, creating a hollow mould into which molten metal can be poured through the stems. After the metal has cooled, the clay shell is destroyed, and the stems filed off, leaving a unique completed figure.

Knowledge of bronze-casting in India goes back at least as far as the Indus Valley civilization (3000–1500 BC), and the famous **"Dancing Girl"** from Mohenjo Daro. The earliest produced in the south were made by the Andhras, whose techniques were continued by the Pallavas, the immediate antecedents of the Cholas. The few surviving **Pallava** bronzes show a sophisticated handling of the form; figures are characterized by broad shoulders, thick-set features and an overall simplicity that suggests all the detail was completed at the wax stage. The finest bronzes of all are from the **Chola** period, in the late ninth to the early eleventh centuries. As the Cholas were predominantly Shaivite, Nataraja, Shiva and his consort Parvati (frequently in a family group with son Skanda) and the 63 Nayanmar poet-saints are the most popular subjects. Chola bronzes display more detail than their predecessors. Human figures are invariably slim-waisted and elegant, with the male form robust and muscular and the female graceful and delicate.

The design, iconography and proportions of each figure are governed by the strict rules laid down in the **shilpa shastras**, which draw no real distinction between art, science and religion. Measurement always begins with the proportions of the artist's own hand and the image's resultant face-length as the basic unit. Then follows a scheme which is allied to the equally scientific rules applied to classical music, and specifically *tala* or rhythm. Human figures total eight face-lengths, eight being the most basic of rhythmic measures. Figures of deities are *nava-tala*, nine face-lengths.

Those bronzes produced by the few artists practising today invariably follow the Chola model; the chief centre is now **Swamimalai**, 8km west of Kumbakonam. Original Chola bronzes are kept in many Tamil temples, but as temple interiors are often dark it's not always possible to see them properly. Important **public collections** include the Nayak Durbar Hall Art Museum at Thanjavur, the Government State Museum at Madras, and the National Museum, New Delhi.

---

painted. Five domes are striped red, green and yellow, and on the walls, friezes of leaf and pineapple designs, and trumpeting angels in a night sky show European influence.

Niches in the walls hold sculptures of deities, and figures including the Shiva devotee Patanjali (see p.936), with a snake winding around his leg, and an Englishman said to be in the unlikely situation of learning classical dance from a young woman, to whom he is presenting a gift. Visible on the left wall, as you face the throne, are traces of a Nayak mural of deer in a forest. Next to this, two holes in the floor, once entrances to a secret passageway, are now home to cobras and not recommended for exploration. Some of the later paintings portray the entertainers who revelled in the now overgrown square outside as recently as the 1960s – fighters, circus performers and wrestlers. A dilapidated columned passageway with Islamic arches runs the length of the square.

SARASWATI MAHAL LIBRARY MUSEUM

The **Saraswati Mahal Library**, one of the most important oriental manuscript collections in India, is closed to the public, but used by scholars from all over the world. Over eighty percent of its 44,000 manuscripts are in Sanskrit, many on palm-leafs, and some very rare or even unique. The Tamil works include treatises on medicine and commentaries on works from the Sangam period, the earliest literature of the south.

A small **museum** (daily except Wed 10am–1pm & 1.30–5.30pm) displays a bizarre array of books and pictures from the collection. Among the palm-leaf manuscripts is a calligrapher's tour-de-force, in the form of a visual mantra, where each letter in the inscription "Shiva" comprises the god's name repeated in microscopically small handwriting. Most of the Maratha manuscripts, produced from the end of the seventeenth century, are on paper; they include a superbly illustrated edition of the *Mahabharata*. Sadists will be delighted to see the library managed to hang on to their copy of the explicitly illustrated **Punishments in China**, published in 1804. Next to it, full reign is given to the imagination of French artist, **Charles Le Brun** (1619–90), in a series of pictures on the subject of physiognomy. Animals such as the horse, bullock, wolf, bear, rabbit and camel are drawn in painstaking care above a series of human faces which bear an uncanny, if unlikely, resemblance to them. You can buy postcards of this scientific study and exhibits from the other palace museums in the **shop** next door.

NAYAK DURBAR HALL ART MUSEUM AND RAJARAJA CHOLAN MUSEUM

A magnificent collection of **Chola bronzes** – all discovered locally – fills the **Nayak Durbar Hall Art Museum** (daily 9am–1pm & 3–5.45pm), a high-ceilinged audience hall with massive pillars, dating from 1600. The elegance of the figures and delicacy of detail is exquisite. A tenth-century statue of Kannappa Nayannar, a hunter-devotee, shows minutiae right down to his embroidered clothing, fingernails and the fine lines on his fingers. The oldest bronze shows Vinadhra Dakshinamurti ("south-facing Shiva") who, with a deer on one left hand, would have originally been playing the *vina* – the musical instrument has long since gone. Along with several dynamic examples of Nataraja, Shiva as the "King of the Dance", there's a fine Kalyanasundaramurti, where Shiva, with his arm draped around the shy Parvati, is about to be married.

Next door, the **Rajaraja Cholan Museum** (same hours) houses Chola stone sculpture and small objects excavated at Gangaikondacholapuram (see p.937) such as tiny marbles, gamesboards, bangles and terracotta pieces. Two illuminated maps show the remarkable extent of the Chola empire under the great kings Rajaraja I and his son, Rajendra I. Towering over these buildings is the Nayak-period **arsenal**, cunningly designed to resemble a temple *gopura*. Climb to the top for fine views of Thanjavur.

Shopping

In an old house in the suburb of Karanthattangudi, ten minutes by auto-rickshaw from the centre, *V R Govindarajan*'s shop at 31 Kuthirakkatti St (☎04362/0282) contains an amazing array of **antiques**, including brass pots, betelnut boxes, oil lamps, old coins and Tanjore paintings. Small, modern and simple examples cost around Rs500, while large, recently made pictures with twenty-four-carat gold decoration may cost as much as Rs20,000, and for a fine hundred-year-old painting you can expect to part with Rs80,000 or more. Upstairs, seven artists work amid a chaotic collection of clocks and bric-a-brac, and you can watch the various stages in the process of Tanjore painting.

The owner of the small craft shop at *Hotel Parishutham*, 55 Grand Anicut Canal Rd, is very knowledgeable about local craftsmen producing Tanjore paintings, copper "art plates" and musical instruments like the classical *vina*. A branch of the government chain, *Poompuhar Handicrafts*, on Gandhiji Rd (next to TTDC *Hotel Tamil Nadu*), stocks copper Thanjavur "art plates", brass oil lamps and sandalwood carvings.

TANJORE (THANJAVUR) PAINTING

The name **Tanjore painting** is given to a distinctive form of southern picture-making that came to prominence in the eighteenth century, encouraged by the Maratha Raja of Thanjavur, Serfoji. The term "painting", however, is misleading, and inadequate to describe work of the Tanjore school. It is distinctive because, aside from a painted image, details such as clothing, ornaments, and any (typically baroque) architectural elements are raised in low plaster relief from the surface, which is then decorated by the sumptuous addition of glass pieces, pearls, semi-precious or precious stones and elaborate gold leaf work. Other variations include pictures on mica, ivory and glass.

Figures are delineated with simple outlines; unmixed primary colours are used in a strict symbolic code, similar to that found in the make-up used in the classical dramas of Kerala, where each colour indicates qualities of character. Other schools of painting normally show Krishna with blue-black skin; in the Tanjore style, he is white.

Traditionally, most depicted Vaishnavite deities, with the most popular single image probably that of **Balakrishna**, the chubby baby Krishna (see p.228). In the tenth-century Sanskrit *Bhagavata Purana*, Balakrishna was portrayed as a rascal who delighted in stealing and consuming milk, butter balls, and curd. Despite his naughtiness, all women who came into contact with him were seized with an overflowing of maternal affection, to the extent that their breasts spontaneously oozed milk. Thanks to such stories, Krishna as a child became the chosen deity par excellence of mothers and grandmothers. Tanjore paintings typically show him eating, accompanied by adoring women.

Although Tanjore painting went into decline after the eighteenth and nineteenth centuries, in recent years there has been a new demand for domestic, rather than temple, shrines. High-quality work is produced in Thanjavur, Kumbakonam and Tiruchirapalli.

Accommodation and eating

Most of Thanjavur's **hotels**, which as a rule charge higher rates than you'd pay elsewhere, are concentrated in the area between the railway station and bus stands. There are plenty of straightforward **restaurants** around Gandhiji Rd; the roof-top *Golden Restaurant*, just around the corner on Hospital Rd has good veg food.

Karthik, 73 S Rampart St, near the bus stand (☎04362/2116). Very overpriced a/c rooms with windows opening onto a wall, torn curtains, and threadbare bedding. However, a popular restaurant serves low-priced veg "meals" at lunchtime, and south Indian snacks at night. ③–⑤.

Pandiyar Residency, Cutchery Rd, on the corner with Gandhiji Rd (☎04362/0574). Central, recently opened, all rooms (six a/c) have *Star TV*, and deluxe ones have views of the temple. ③–④.

Parishutham, 55 Grand Anicut Canal Rd (☎04362/1466). Comfortable, clean but expensive rooms with balcony, cable and *Star TV*. Craft shop, pool and foreign exchange. Cheap veg and non-veg restaurants where the varied menus include barely-warmed soups "from the boiling kettle". ⑧.

Railway Retiring Rooms, contact Matron on the first floor of railway station. Six big, clean double rooms opening out onto a large communal verandah, overlooking station approach. ①.

Rajarajan Lodge, Gandhiji Rd (☎04362/1730). Very basic rooms, and simple meals and snacks. ①.

TTDC Tamil Nadu (1), Gandhiji Rd, 10min from the bus and railway stands (☎04362/1421). Once the Raja's guest house; good value, good service. Large, comfortable carpeted rooms (a few more expensive with a/c and *Star TV*), set around a pleasant garden. Restaurant serving veg and non-veg "meals" and south Indian snack food, including tasty onion *utthapam* (thick pancakes), and a bar. ③.

Valli, 2948 MKM Rd (☎04362/21584). In a cul-de-sac near the railway station, alongside the car mechanics of Thanjavur. All the not-so-clean rooms have cable TV, and there's a veg restaurant. ③.

Nagapattinam and around

NAGAPATTINAM, 170km south of Pondicherry and 90km east of Thanjavur at the mouth of the Kaveri, was the key port of the Chola empire. Nowadays unprepossessing, it warrants little more than an overnight stop on the way to the pilgrimage sites of **Nagur** and **Velankanni**, where devotees of all faiths testify to the region's tradition of religious tolerance. In the flat **Kaveri Delta**, paddy fields stretch as far as the eye can see, broken up by tamarind, palmyra and coconut trees, and occasional fields of maize. Roads pick their way through a tangle of rivers, which most of the year are more sand than water. In December, however, destructive **cyclonic storms** render the area extremely dangerous, when the already poor roads become rivers with potholes of depths best left unplumbed. The surrounding villages, clusters of thatched huts with long sloping roofs, are largely Muslim, but the nearer you get to Nagapattinam the more red flags and hammer-and-sickle symbols you see. Here too are tight-knit, impoverished fishing communities which frequently come under suspicion for harbouring Tamils who arrive under cover of night from Sri Lanka.

Nagur

In the village of **NAGUR**, 10km north of Nagapattinam, the 500-year-old **dargah** of the Muslim saint Hazrat Mian Sahib comprises five golden-domed mosques set in a warren of paths, open courtyards and hallways teeming with pilgrims. Elaborately embossed silver steps decorate the shrines, while the paths and walls are covered in white tiles with patterned friezes. At the back of the mosques, people bathe in the large **Pirkulam** tank in the hope of being granted good health. In a little shelter at the water's edge, barbers busily shave the heads of children and adults who dispense with their hair as a form of penance. Stalls throughout the complex sell the blue, black or gold hats, similar to Nehru caps, worn by many male visitors, colourful Mecca and Koranic verse pictures, and *bhartia*: little baskets of sugar, joss and *shambrani* incense for offerings.

Velankanni

At **VELANKANNI**, 11km south of Nagapattinam, a strong atmosphere of devotion pervades the white, spired Roman Catholic church of **Our Lady of Good Health**, the Lourdes of south India. Families hold lighted candles, up to a metre tall, in front of the altar, while officials wave their carrier bags of offerings in front of the image of the Virgin. Rows of display cases in the **museum** (daily 9am–6pm) contain silver and gold models of multifarious parts of the body – arms, legs, feet, livers, hearts – and of objects such as cars, cows, stethoscopes and houses. Each is accompanied by a testimonial and photograph of the person whom Our Lady has helped. Also on show is a case of various gold jewellery stated to have been stolen on November 20 1987, and recovered by police "with miraculous help of Our Lady" on November 20 1988, as well as hundreds of notes, in Tamil and English, thanking Her for enabling couples to have children (especially the male variety) and students to pass their exams. Next door to the museum a shop sells plastic finger rings, postcards and novelty picture key-rings that flash between images of Our Lord and Our Lady. Close by are several simple "meals" **restaurants**.

Nagapattinam practicalities

Nagapattinam is connected by **train** to Thanjavur and Madras, and frequent **buses** from Nagur and Velankanni (both 20min), Madras, Thanjavur and Trichy call at the Thiruvalluvar bus stand. The only decent **accommodation** in the village is at *Hotel Tamil Nadu*, Thonitthurai Salai, near the railway station (☎04365/22389; ③). The rooms, some of which are a/c, lack charm but staff are friendly and the basic restaurant is a little more attractive than the "meals" places elsewhere. The only STD phone is at the **post office**, ten minutes' walk away in the centre of town.

Kodikkarai (Point Calimere)

On a small knob of land jutting out into the sea, 65km south of Nagapattinam and 80km southeast of Thanjavur, **KODIKKARAI BIRD SANCTUARY** plays host to around 250 species in an area of swampland, known as "the great swamp", and dry evergreen forest. On the way to the sanctuary, you pass through fifty thousand acres of salt marshes around **Vedaranyam**, the nearest town, 11km north – vast salt fields, traditionally the mainstay of the local economy, line the road, the salt drying in thatched mounds. During the Independence struggle this was an important site for demonstrations in sympathy with Gandhi's famous salt protest (see p.527). Over the last few years, however, salt has been pushed into second place by prawn cultivation, which brings a good income, but has necessitated widespread forest clearance and has reduced the numbers of birds visiting Kodikkarai.

The **best time** to visit the sanctuary is between November and February, when migratory birds come, mostly from Iran, Russia and Poland, to spend the winter. The rarest species include black bittern, barheaded goose, ruddy shelduck, Indian black-crested baza and eastern steppe eagle. During December and January the swamps play host to spotted billed pelicans and around ten thousand flamingoes – who live on tiny shrimp (the source of the lurid pink colouring of their plumage), and whose numbers have dropped from the thirty thousand that wintered here in the days before prawn production took off. The deep forest is the home of one of the most colourful birds in the world, the Indian pitta (*pitta brachyura*), which, though little bigger than a sparrow, sports a black, orange and white head, orange and yellow stomach, brown, blue, black, light and dark green wings each with a white spot and a tail of red, blue and black.

Prodigiously well informed local **guides**, equipped with powerful binoculars, can take you to key wildlife haunts. The Forest Department works with the Bombay Natural History Society to ring birds and trace their migrating patterns, and occasionally the BNHS organizes **field trips** around the area.

From the jetty, you might be lucky enough to spot a school of **dolphins**. To do so, however, you need to seek permission from the Navy Command – Kodikkarai is only 40km across the Palk Strait from Jaffna, and from the grounds of the *Rest House* (see below) the navy monitors all seaborne activity between Sri Lanka and the Indian coast.

Practicalities

Kodikkarai can only be reached (by regular bus) via Vedaranyam, connected by **bus** to Nagapattinam, Thanjavur, Trichy, Madras and Ramanathapuram (for Rameshwaram). Madras buses can be booked in advance in a house next door to *Shitharthan Medical Stores* on Vedaranyam's E Main St (over the road from the bus stand). The nearest **train** station is 30km away at Tiruthuraipondi.

The only **accommodation** in the area, the Forest Department's exceptionally inexpensive *Poonarai Rest House* (☎0436972/24; ①), has ten plain, spacious rooms, each with chairs, desk, fan, bedding, bathroom and balcony. Apart from in January, when the rest house is invariably full, it's usually possible to turn up without a reservation. **Food** is available only from a couple of *chai* shops outside the gate, although staff will bring it in if asked. If you need to eat in **Vedaranyam** turn left out of the bus stand, and again at a T-junction, into the main bazaar, Melai St. The best place is the simple *Karaivani*, on the left-hand side, which serves veg "leaf" meals.

Tiruchirapalli

TIRUCHIRAPALLI – more commonly referred to as **Trichy** – stands in the plains between the Shevaroy and Palani hills, just under 100km north of Madurai. Dominated by the dramatic Rock Fort, it's a sprawling commercial centre with a modern feel; the town itself holds little attraction, but pilgrims flock to **temples** such as the spectacular **Ranganathaswamy temple** in **Srirangam**, 6km north. You'll need at least a day to make the most of a visit to this structure, taking time to meander through cloisters and open courtyards and to discover some of the finest masonry in the south.

The precise date of Trichy's foundation is uncertain, but though little early architecture remains it is clear that between 200 and 1000 AD control of the city passed between the Pallavas and Pandyas. The Chola kings who gained supremacy in the eleventh century embarked upon ambitious building projects, reaching a zenith with the Ranganathaswamy temple. In the twelfth century, the Cholas were subverted by the Vijayanagar kings of Hampi, who stood proudly against invading Muslims until they were eventually overcome in 1565 by the Sultans of the Deccan. Less than fifty years later the Nayaks of Madurai came to power, constructing the fort and firmly establishing Trichy as a trading city. After almost a century of struggle against the French and British, who both sought lands in southeast Tamil Nadu, the town came under British control until it was declared part of Tamil Nadu state in 1947.

Arrival and information

Flights from Trichy's airport, 8km south of the centre, go four times weekly (Mon, Tues, Thurs & Sat) to Madras (45min) and Madurai (30min). The journey into town, by taxi or bus (#7, #63, #122 or #128) takes half an hour; for enquiries and bookings go to *Indian Airlines* on Dindigul Rd (☎23116). There are also two weekly flights to and from **Colombo** on *Air Lanka* (based in the *Hotel Lakshmi*, 3A Alexandria Rd; ☎27952).

Trichy's main train station, **Trichy Junction** – which has given its name to the southern district of town – provides frequent rail links with Madras, Madurai and the east coast. From here you're within easy reach of most hotels, restaurants and banks, as well as the **bus stands**. State transport and Thiruvalluvar buses run frequently to major towns such as Madurai; the efficient local service (#1) is the most convenient way of getting to the Rock Fort and Srirangam. **Rickshaws** are also widely available.

The **tourist office** (daily except Fri 10.30am–5.30pm), stocked with maps and information, is opposite the State bus stand in Trichy Junction just outside *Hotel Tamil Nadu*. **Banks** for foreign exchange include the *State Bank of India* on Dindigul Rd.

The Town

Although Trichy conducts most of its business in **Trichy Junction**, the southern district, all the main sights are at least 4km north. The **bazaars** immediately north heave with locally made cigars, textiles, and fake diamonds made into inexpensive jewellery and used for dance costumes. As you follow the northbound Big Bazaar Road, you're confronted by a looming solid stone hill, **Rock Fort**, an unexpected vision in the otherwise flat town, topped by a seventeenth-century Vinayaka (Ganesh) temple.

North of the fort, the wide River Kaveri marks the boundary between Trichy's crowded streets and its more serene temples; the **Ranganathaswamy temple** is so large it holds much of the village of Srirangam within its courtyards. Also north of the Kaveri are the elaborate **Shri Jambukeshwara temple**, while several British **churches** in Trichy town make for an interesting contrast.

The Rock Fort

The **Rock Fort** (daily 6am–8pm; Rs1 plus Rs10 for camera), looming over the bazaars and a rectangular water tank in the north of town, is Trichy's most dramatic and downright incongruous sight. The massive sand-coloured rock towers to a height of over 80 metres, its irregular sides smoothed by wind and rain. The Pallavas were the first to cut into it, building temples in cool recesses, but it was the Nayaks who grasped the site's potential as a fort, adding only a few walls and bastions as fortifications.

The telephone **area code** for Trichy is ☎0431.

△ Srirangam △ Jambukeshwara Temple

River Kaveri

NAYAR ST

KARUR RD

MADURA RD

Trichy Town Railway Station

Rock Fort

SALAI RD

CHINA BAZAAR

SHASTRI RD

MADRAS TRUNK RD

WEST BOULEVARD RD

BIG BAZAAR RD

EAST BOULEVARD RD

THANJAVUR RD

N

0   500 m

Woyakondan Channel

HEBER RD

DINDIGUL RD

MADURAI RD

see Inset

Indian Airlines

Trichy Junction Railway Station

HOTELS:
- Ⓐ Femina
- Ⓑ TTDC Tamil Nadu
- Ⓒ Vijey Lodge
- Ⓓ Rajasugam
- Ⓔ Abhirami
- Ⓕ Kalpana
- Ⓖ Anand
- Ⓗ Ashby
- Ⓘ Arun
- Ⓙ Sarada Lodge
- Ⓚ Jenney's Residency

TIRUCHIRAPALLI (TRICHY)

COLLECTOR'S OFFICE RD

ROYAL RD

WILLIAMS RD

BIRDS RD

GPO ⊠

Ⓐ

Ⓓ Ⓒ

ⓘ Ⓑ

State Bus Stand

Ⓔ

Ⓚ **Bank**

McDONALD RD

MADURAI RD

Ⓕ

Ⓙ

Ⓖ **Thiruvalluvar Bus Stand**

DINDIGUL RD

Ⓘ

0   250 m

Ⓗ

JUNCTION RD

Trichy Junction Railway Station

TRICHY JUNCTION

▽ Airport

Once you've craned your neck up to look at the Rock Fort from the outside, a walk through China Bazaar leads past shops and stalls overflowing with jewellery, clothes, imitation designer perfumes, films, transistors and clocks, to the fort's entrance, just beyond a pair of whitewashed Jain temples. At the entrance, where a weary elephant gives blessings in exchange for a few coins, the atmosphere becomes cool and clammy, and the passageway leads to a shrine at the base of the rock. A broad flight of painted steps ascends from here, passing Pallava and Pandya rock-cut temples, notable for their simple design, and closed to non-Hindus.

Near the top, you emerge into daylight to join a sloping path up to the simple rectangular **Ganesh temple** on the very summit. The temple is closed to non-Hindus, but anyone can enjoy the **views**, which take in the Ranganathaswamy and Jambukeshwara temples to the north, their *gopuras* rising from a sea of palms; to the south, red-brown tiled roofs and yellow-washed houses stretch as far as the eye can see.

Jambukeshwara temple

By the side of the Madras-bound road north out of Trichy, the **Jambukeshwara temple**, dedicated to Shiva, is smaller and later than the Ranganathaswamy temple. Much of it is closed to non-Hindus, but the sculptures that adorn the walls in its outer courts, of an extravagance typical of the seventeenth-century Nayak architects, are worth the short detour.

Srirangam: Ranganathaswamy temple

The **Ranganathaswamy temple** at **Srirangam**, 6km north of the city, is among the most revered shrines to Vishnu in south India, and also one of the largest and liveliest, engulfing within its outer walls homes, shops and markets. Enclosed by seven rectangular walled courtyards and covering over sixty hectares, it stands on an island defined by a tributary of the River Kaveri. This location symbolizes the transcendence of Vishnu, housed in the sanctuary reclining on the coils of the snake Adisesha, who in legend formed an island for the god, resting on the primordial Ocean of Chaos. **Buses** from Trichy frequently pull in and leave from outside the southern gate.

The temple is approached from the south. A gateway topped with an immense and heavily carved *gopura*, plastered and painted in bright pinks, blues and yellows, and completed as recently as 1987, leads to the outermost courtyard, the latest of seven courtyards built between the fifth and seventeenth centuries. Most of the present structure dates from the end of the fourteenth century, when the temple was renovated and enlarged after a disastrous sacking by the Delhi armies in 1313. The outer three courtyards, or *prakaras*, form the hub of the temple community, with houses of ascetics, priests, and musicians, and the streets are lined with food stalls and shops selling souvenirs, ritual offerings and plump fresh flower garlands to be presented to Vishnu in the inner sanctuary.

At the fourth wall, the entrance to the temple proper, visitors remove footwear before passing through a high gateway, topped by a magnificent *gopura* and lined with small shrines to teachers, hymn-singers and sages. In earlier days, this fourth *prakara* would have formed the outermost limit of the temple, and was the closest members of the lowest castes could get to the sanctuary. It contains some of the finest and oldest buildings of the complex, including a temple to the goddess **Ranganayaki** in the northwest corner where devotees should worship before approaching Vishnu's shrine. On the east side of the *prakara*, the heavily carved "thousand pillared" *mandapa*, or hall, was constructed in the late Chola period. During the month of Margali (Dec/Jan) Tamil hymns are recited from its southern steps as part of the Vaikuntha Ekadasi festival.

The pillars of the outstanding **Sheshagiriraya Mandapa**, south of the *mandapa*, are decorated with rearing steeds and hunters armed with spears. These are splendid examples of **Vijayanagar** style, which depicts chivalry defending their temple against

Muslim invaders, and represents the triumph of good over evil. On the southern side of the *prakara*, the Venugopala shrine, dedicated to Krishna, probably dates from the Nayak period (late sixteenth century). Its pillars are carved with beautiful maidens leaning on trees, playing musical instruments and looking into mirrors. Inside the porch, paintings show Krishna playfully courting his *gopis* (cowgirls). The western side of the courtyard is taken up by a large pond, which blossoms with lotus flowers in spring, when Vishnu is laid upon its waters in a barge at the height of a three-day festival. To the right of the gateway into the fourth courtyard, a small **museum** (daily 10am–noon & 3–5pm) contains a modest collection of stone and bronze sculptures, and some delicate ivory plaques. For a small fee you can climb to the roof of the fourth wall and take in the view over the temple rooftops and *gopuras*, which increase in size from the centre outwards. The central tower, crowning the holy sanctuary, is coated in gold and carved with images of Vishnu's *avatars*, or incarnations, on each of its four sides.

Inside the gate to the third courtyard – the final section of the temple open to non-Hindus – is another pillared hall, the **Garuda Mandapa**, carved throughout in typical Nayak style. Maidens, courtly donors and Nayak rulers feature on the pillars that surround the central shrine to Garuda, the man-eagle vehicle of Vishnu. Other buildings in the third courtyard include the vast kitchens, which emanate delicious smells as *dosas* and *vadas* are prepared for the deity, while devotees ritually bathe in the tanks of the moon and the sun in the northeast and southeast corners.

Chola structures and more recent shrines added by Vijayanagar and Nayak donors fill the second courtyard, while the dimly lit innermost courtyard, the most sacred part of the temple, shelters the image of Vishnu in his aspect of Ranganatha, reclining on the serpent Adisesha. The shrine is usually entered from the south, but for one day each year, during the **Vaikuntha Ekadasi festival**, the north portal is opened; those who pass through this "doorway to heaven" can anticipate great merit. Most of the temple's daily festivals take place in the courtyard, beginning each morning with *vina*-playing and hymn-singing as Vishnu is awakened in the presence of a cow and an elephant, and ending just after 9pm with similar ceremonies.

Accommodation and eating

Trichy has no shortage of **hotels** to accommodate the thousands of pilgrims that visit the town. Close to the bus stand you'll find an assortment of basic inexpensive lodges and some characterless but comfortable more upmarket hotels. If you want to stay in **Srirangam** the only option is the simple, minimally clean *Dandayuthapani Lodge* (①).

For **eating**, your best bet is the hotels, most of which serve good, reasonably priced south Indian food that is of a higher standard than in the town's basic "meals' houses. Most places have at least some Chinese dishes on the menu.

Abhirami, 10 McDonald's Rd (☎40001). A high tower block opposite the State bus stand. Clean but anonymous rooms, and one of the best restaurants in town. ③–⑤.

Anand, 1 Raquet Court Lane (☎40545). Very clean sizeable rooms with attached bath and towels provided. Some a/c rooms and a good restaurant serving standard south Indian dishes. ③–⑤.

Arun, 24 State Bank Rd (Dindigul Rd) (☎41421). Large hotel near the Thiruvalluvar bus stand. Impersonal, but clean enough. Restaurant and travel counter. ③–④.

Ashby, 17A Junction Rd (☎40652). Pleasant place facing Thiruvalluvar bus stand. Dim, big rooms (some a/c) with arched verandahs around a leafy courtyard. Small bar and restaurant, serving north and south Indian dishes and a few Chinese options; very slow service, western clientele. ②–④.

Femina, 14C Williams Rd, Cantt (☎41551). Well maintained place east of the State bus stand. Rooms and suites, some with balconies looking to the Rock Fort. Plush restaurants, 24hr coffee bar. ⑤–⑥.

Jenney's Residency, 3/14 McDonald's Rd (☎41302). Smart, homely carpeted a/c and non-a/c rooms; some family suites. Three very good restaurants – including an upmarket Chinese place – cocktail bar and a swimming pool, open to non-residents for Rs50. ⑥–⑦.

Kalpana, 9A Rockins Rd (☎40011). Simple and comfortable lodge with spartan rooms. ①.
Rajasugam, 13-B/1 Royal Rd (☎40636). Clean rooms, and a popular open-air veg restaurant. ①.
Sarada Lodge, McDonald's Rd (☎40216). Comfortable, quiet place, set off the road. ①.
Tamil Nadu, McDonald's Rd (☎40383). Good, well-kept rooms with large clean bathrooms overlooking a quiet gardened compound. ③.
Vijey Lodge, 13B Royal Rd (☎40511). A run-of-the-mill lodge opposite the State bus stand. The simple rooms here are clean enough, though a little stuffy, and some have private bathrooms. ①.

Madurai

One of the oldest cities in south India, the seat of power for the ancient Pandya dynasty, **MADURAI**, on the banks of the River Vaigai, is an archetypal Hindu city, a swirl of life revolving around its mighty **Meenakshi-Sundareshwarar temple**. Any day of the week no less than fifteen thousand people pass through its gates; on Friday, sacred to the fish-eyed Meenakshi (see p.957), that number increases by ten thousand. The temple's ritual life spills out into the streets in an almost ceaseless round of festivals and processions.

Madurai is the subject of an extraordinary number of myths. Its origins stem from a *sthala* (a holy site where legendary events have taken place) where Indra, the king of the gods, bathed in a holy tank and worshipped Shiva. Hearing of this, the Pandyan king Kulashekhara built a temple on the site and installed a *shivalingam*, around which the city grew. The name Madurai is popularly derived from the Tamil word *madhuram*, meaning "sweetness"; according to legend, Shiva shook his matted locks over the city, coating it with a fine sprinkling of *amrita*, the nectar of immortality.

Madurai's urban and suburban sprawl creates traffic jams to rival India's very worst. Chaos on the narrow potholed streets is exacerbated by demonstrations and processions, wandering cows – demanding right of way with a peremptory nudge of the haunch – and put-upon pedestrians forced onto the road by ever-increasing numbers of street traders. Open-air kitchens extend from tea shops, where competing *paratha-wallahs* literally drum up custom for their fresh breads with a tattoo of spoon-on-skillet signals. Given the traffic problems, it's just as well that Madurai, with a profusion of markets and intriguing corners, is an absorbing city to walk around. When some respite from the clamour of the city is required, the River Vaigai is close by.

A little history

Although invariably interwoven with myth, the traceable history and fame of Madurai stretches back well over two thousand years. Numerous natural **caves** in local hills and boulders, often modified by the addition of simple rock-cut beds, were used both in prehistoric times and by ascetics, such as the Ajivikas and Jains, who practised withdrawal and penance. In the third century BC, the Greek ambassador **Megasthenes** told of the city's splendour, and of its queen, Pandai, "a daughter of Herakles".

Madurai appears to have been the capital of the Pandyan empire without interruption for at least a thousand years. It became a major commercial city, trading with Greece, Rome and China; *yavanas* (a generic term for foreigners), frequent visitors to Pandyan seaports, were employed as palace guards and policemen. Long a seat of Tamil culture, under the Pandyas Madurai is credited with being the site of three literary **sangams**, "academies", said to have lasted ten thousand years and supported some eight thousand poets. Despite this fanciful reckoning, the most recent of these academies does have an historical basis; the "Sangam period" is generally taken to mean the first three to four centuries of the Christian era.

The Pandyas' capital fell, in the tenth century, when the **Chola** King Parantaka took the city; they briefly regained power in the thirteenth century, but early in the

HOTELS:
- **A** Duke
- **B** Gangai, Grand Central, International, Keerthi, Prem Nivas, Supreme, Thilaga & TM Lodge
- **C** Sree Devi
- **D** Aarathy
- **E** TTDC Tamil Nadu 1 (Star)
- **F** Madurai Ashok
- **G** TTDC Tamil Nadu
- **H** Pandiyan

MADURAI

River Vaigai

Railway Station

TTC Bus Stand

Shri Meenakshi

Thirumalai Nayak Palace

Palankanathan Bus Stand

0   500 m

▽ Airport

fourteenth century the notorious **Malik Kafur**, the Delhi Sultanate's "favourite slave", made an unprovoked attack on Madurai during a plunder-and-desecration tour of the south, and destroyed much of the city. Forewarned of the raid, the Pandya king, Sundara, fled with his immediate family and treasure, leaving his uncle and rival, Vikrama Pandya, to repel Kafur. Nevertheless, the latter returned to Delhi with booty said to consist of "six hundred and twelve elephants, ninety-six thousand *mans* of gold, several boxes of jewels and pearls and twenty thousand horses".

Shortly after this raid Madurai became an independent Sultanate; in 1364, it joined the Hindu **Vijayanagar** empire, ruled from Vijayanagar/Hampi (see p.1066) and administered by governors, the **Nayaks**. In 1565, the Nayaks asserted their own independence. Under their supervision and patronage, Madurai enjoyed a renaissance, being rebuilt on the pattern of a lotus with the Meenakshi temple at the centre. Part of the palace of the most illustrious of the Nayaks, **Thirumalai** (1623–55), survives today.

> The telephone **area code** for Madurai is ☎0452.

The city remained under Nayak control until the mid-eighteenth century when the **British** gradually took over. A hundred years later the British de-fortified Madurai, filling its moat to create the four Veli Streets that today mark the boundary of the old city.

Arrival and information

Madurai's small **airport**, 16km south of the city limits, is served by flights to and from Madras, Bombay and Thiruvananthapuram. Theoretically you should be able to get information at the **Government of Tamil Nadu Tourist Information Centre** booth by the exit, but it's not always open to meet flights. Very simple snack meals ("bread-omelette") are served at the **restaurant** (daily 9am–5pm). There's also a bookshop and a branch of *Indian Bank*, but they can't change money. **Taxis** into the city charge a fixed rate of around Rs100. Airport buses leave hourly either from near the exit or to the left, near the staff canteen. There is no STD telephone, only a local phone box.

Arriving by **bus**, you come in at one of four bus stands, all served by both long-distance and city buses. The largest, and nearest to the centre, is the **TTC stand** (buses from Madras, Kerala, Karnataka and Andhra Pradesh) on West Veli Street in the west of the old city, close to the railway station and most accommodation. **Arapalayam stand** (some services within the state, and Kerala) is in the northwest, close to the south bank of the river, about 2km from the railway station. **Palankanathan stand** (also written as Pazhanganatham; south Tamil Nadu and south Kerala) is in the southwest, 5km from the centre, and **Anna stand** (points north, such as the Chola cities) is 5km out in the northeast, north of the Vaigai.

The **railway station** is just west of the centre on W Veli St. You can leave your luggage at the office (24hr) next to the **reservations office** in the main hall where you'll also find a *Higginbothams* bookstall, STD telephone and a branch of the **Tourism Department Information Centre** (daily 6.30am–8.30pm; ☎33888), where you can make onward reservations (see p.963). There's a veg **canteen** on Platform 1, and, unusually, a **pre-paid auto-rickshaw booth** outside the main entrance, open to coincide with train arrivals. There are no pre-paid taxis. *SV*, W Tower St, near the west entrance to the temple, rents **bicycles** at low rates.

Information

In addition to the offices at the train station and airport (see above), the **Tourist Dept Main Office**, W Veli St (Mon–Fri 10am–5.45pm, Sat 10am–1pm; ☎22957), provides useful information about Madurai and surrounding areas. They have details of **car rental** and will also arrange, with a little notice, **city tours** with one of the Government-approved guides, who can usually be found at the southern entrance to the temple. Find out their names first at the tourist office as they're a much better bet than the other guys hanging around; the latter, however well-meaning, may be ill-informed and more than likely will want to get you into a shop double-quick. Official guides, for one to four visitors, cost around Rs80 for a half-day, Rs100 for an eight-hour city tour and Rs150 for trips outside the city. The fee for a temple tour is negotiable.

Madurai's **post office** is at the corner of Scott Rd and N Veli St. For stamps and parcels, enter on the Scott Rd side (Mon–Sat 11am–7pm, Sun & hols 10am–4pm); for speedpost and fax, go in by the N Veli St side (8am–8pm). You can **change money** at the *State Bank of India*, 6 W Veli St, and the *Central Bank of India*, 15 Meenakshi Koil St. *Mastercard* and *Visa* are accepted at the *Andhra Bank* on W Chitrai St, but no currency or travellers' cheques. For **visa extensions**, call at the Foreigners Regional Registration Office, Commissioner of Police, S Chithirai St (☎37379).

The City

The **old city** of Madurai, south of the River Vaigai and centered on the Meenakshi temple, is where you'll find the main markets, tourist office, post office, railway station, three of four main bus stands, and all the budget and mid-range accommodation. Principal streets are laid out concentrically around the temple and prefixed North, South, East or West, which helps somewhat with orientation. **North of the river** are a number of expensive hotels, the Gandhi Museum and the Anna bus stand.

Shri Meenakshi-Sundareshwarar Temple

Enclosed by a roughly rectangular six-metre-high wall, in the manner of a fortified palace, the **Meenakshi-Sundareshwarar** (daily 5am–12.30pm & 4–9.30pm) is one of the largest temple complexes in India. Much of it was constructed during the Nayak period between the sixteenth and eighteenth centuries, but certain parts are very much older. The principal shrines (closed to non-Hindus) are those to Sundareshwar (Shiva) and his consort Meenakshi; unusually, the goddess takes precedence. One part of the temple is given over to a small art museum.

For the first-time visitor, confronted with a confusing maze of shrines, sculptures and colonnades, and unaware of the logic employed in their arrangement, it's very easy to get disorientated. However, if you're not in a hurry, this should not deter you.

Quite apart from the estimated thirty-three million sculptures to arrest your attention, the life of the temple is absolutely absorbing, and many visitors find themselves drawn back at several different times of the day. Whether it be the endless round of *puja* ceremonies, loud *nagaswaram* and *tavil* music, weddings, *brahmin* boys under religious instruction in the *Vedas*, the prostrations of countless devotees, the busy glittering market stalls inside the east entrance, or, best of all, a festival procession, something is always going on.

Approximately fifty priests work in the temple, and live in houses close to the north entrance. They are easily identified – each wears a white *dhoti* (*veshti* in Tamil) tied between the legs; on top of this, around the waist, is a second, coloured cloth, usually of silk. Folded into the cloth, a small bag contains holy white ash. The bare-chested priests invariably carry a small towel over the shoulder. Most wear earrings and necklaces including *rudraksha* beads, sacred to Shiva. As Shaivite priests, they place three horizontal stripes of white ash on the forehead, arms, shoulders and chest and a red powder dot, sacred to the goddess, above the bridge of the nose. The majority wear

---

MEENAKSHI, THE FISH-EYED GODDESS

The goddess **Meenakshi** of Madurai emerged from the flames of a sacrificial fire as a three-year-old child, in answer to the Pandyan king Malayadvaja's prayer for a son. The king, not only surprised to see a female, was also horrified that she had three breasts. In every other respect, she was beautiful, as her name, Meenakshi ("fish-eyed"), suggests – fish-shaped eyes are classic images of desirability in Indian love poetry. Dispelling his concern, a mysterious voice told the king that Meenakshi would lose the third breast on meeting her future husband.

In the absence of a son, the adult Meenakshi succeeded her father as Pandyan monarch. With the aim of world domination, she then embarked on a series of successful battles, culminating in the defeat of Shiva's armies at the god's Himalayan abode, Mount Kailasa. Shiva then appeared at the battlefield; on seeing him, Meenakshi immediately lost her third breast. Fulfilling the prophecy, Shiva and Meenakshi travelled to Madurai, where they were married. The two then assumed a dual role, firstly as king and queen of the Pandya kingdom, with Shiva assuming the title Sundara Pandya, and secondly as the presiding deities of the Madurai temple, into which they subsequently disappeared.

their long hair tied into a knot, with the forehead shaved. Inside the temple they also carry brass trays holding offerings of camphor and ash.

Madurai takes the **gopura** so prominent in other southern temples to its ultimate extreme. The entire complex has no less than twelve such towers; set into the outer walls, the four largest rise to a height of around 46 metres, and are visible for miles outside the city. Each is covered, on each diminishing storey, with a profusion of gaily painted stucco images of gods and demons, with the occasional live monkey scampering and chattering among the divine images. It is sometimes possible, for a small fee, to climb the southern and tallest tower, to enjoy superb views over the town.

The most popular **entrance** is on the east side, where the actual *gopura* gateway has remained closed since the inauspicious suicide of a temple employee who jumped from the top. Nowadays, you enter nearby through a towerless gate which is directly in line with the Meenakshi shrine deep inside. In the **Ashta Shakti Mandapa** ("Eight Goddesses Hallway") just inside, a sparkling market sells *puja* offerings and souvenirs, from fat garlands of flowers to rough-hewn sky-blue plaster Ganeshes. Sculpted pillars illustrate different aspects of the goddess Shakti, and Shiva's sixty-four miracles at Madurai. Behind this hall, to the south, are stables for elephants and camels.

If you continue straight on from here, cross E Ati St, and go through the seven-storey **Chitrai gopura**, you enter a passageway leading to the eastern end of the **Pottamarai Kulam** (Tank of Golden Lotuses), where Indra bathed before worshipping the *shivalingam*. From the east side of the tank you can see the glistening gold of the Meenakshi and Sundareshwarar *vimana* towers. Steps lead down to the water from the surrounding colonnades, and in the centre stands a brass lamp column. People bathe here, prior to entering the inner shrines, or just sit, talk and rest awhile on the steps.

The ceiling paintings in the corridors are modern, but Nayak murals around the tank illustrate scenes from the *Gurur Vilayadal Puranam* which describes Shiva's Madurai miracles. Of the two figures located halfway towards the Meenakshi shrine on the north side, one is the eighth-century king Kulashekhara Pandyan, said to have founded the temple; opposite him is a wealthy merchant patron.

On the west side of the tank is the entrance to the **Meenakshi shrine** (closed to non-Hindus), popularly known as **Amman Koyil**, literally the "mother temple". The immoveable green stone image of the goddess is contained within two further enclosures that form two ambulatories. Facing Meenakshi, just past the first entrance and in front of the sanctum sanctorum, stands Shiva's bull-vehicle, Nandi. At around 9pm, the moveable images of the god and goddess are carried to the **bed chamber**. Here the final *puja* ceremony of the day, the **lalipuja**, is performed, when for thirty minutes or so the priests sing lullabies (*lali*), before closing the temple for the night.

The corridor outside Meenakshi's shrine is known as the **Kilikkutu Mandapa** or Parrot Cage Hallway. Parrots used to be kept just south of the shrine as offerings to Meenakshi; a practice discontinued in the mid-1980s, as the birds suffered due to "lack of maintenance". Sundareshwarar and Meenakshi are brought every Friday (6–7pm) to the sixteenth-century **Oonjal Mandapa** further along, where they are placed on a swing (*oonjal*) and serenaded by members of a special caste, the Oduvars. The black and gold, almost fairground-like decoration of the *mandapa* dates from 1985.

Across the corridor, the small **Rani Mangammal Mandapa**, next to the tank, has a detailed eighteenth-century ceiling painting of the marriage of Meenakshi and Sundara, surrounded by lions and elephants against a blue background. Sculptures in the hallway portray characters such as the warring monkey kings from the *Ramayana*, the brothers Sugriva (Sukreeva) and Bali (Vahli), and the indomitable Pandava prince, Bhima, from the *Mahabharata*, who was so strong that he uprooted a tree to use as a club.

Walking back north, past the Meenakshi shrine, through a towered entrance, leads you to the area of the Sundareshwarar shrine. Just inside, the huge monolithic figure of Ganesh, **Mukkuruni Vinayaka**, is said to have been found during the excavation of the Mariamman Teppakulam tank (see p.960). Chubby Ganesh is well-known for his love of sweets, and during his annual **Vinayaka Chathurti festival** (Sept), a special *prasad* (gift offering of food) is concocted from ingredients including three hundred kilos of rice, ten kilos of sugar and one hundred and ten coconuts.

Around a corner, a small image of the monkey god **Hanuman**, covered with *ghee* and red powder, stands on a pillar. Devotees take a little with their finger for a *tillak*, to mark the forehead. A figure of Nandi and two gold-plated copper flagstaffs face the entrance to

TEMPLE FESTIVALS AT MADURAI

Date	Name	No. of days	Date	Name	No. of days
Jan/Feb	**Teppa**	12	July/Aug	**Ati Mulaikkottu**	10
Feb/March	**Machi Mantala**	10	Aug/Sept	**Avani Mula**	12
March/April	**Kotaivasanta**	9	Sept/Oct	**Navaratri**	9
April/May	**Chittirai**	12	Oct/Nov	**Kolatta**	6
May/June	**Vasanta**	10	Nov/Dec	**Tirukkarttikai**	10
June/July	**Unchal**	10	Dec/Jan	**Ennai Kappu**	9

The date of each of the Madurai temple's **annual festivals** varies each year; check with a tourist office when you plan your visit. The principal and most exciting component of most of them is the **procession**, (*purappatu*, or "setting forth"), held on the morning and evening of every day. Each procession is accompanied by officiating *brahmins*, temple employees bearing royal insignia, umbrellas, silver staffs and, at night, flaming torches. The entourage is invariably preceded by the penetrating orchestra of *tavil* (barrel drum), hand cymbals, and the distinctive **nagaswaram** (double-reed oboe-like wind instrument), for which the Madurai area is particularly famous.

Processions circumambulate clockwise inside the temple, and many leave its precincts, starting from the east entrance, passing along the Chittirai, Avani Mula or Masi streets and, on special occasions such as the **floating festival** (days ten and eleven of the Teppa ceremonies), leave the centre of the city altogether. Locals and visiting pilgrims crowd the streets for *darshan*, a view of the deities. The evening processions, weaving through the starlit night, are undoubtedly the most atmospheric.

Icons from the temple, special movable images, are taken out, lavishly clothed in silk and ornaments of rubies, sapphires, pearls, silver and gold. When the festival celebrates both Meenakshi and Sundareshwara, the contingent is usually led by Vinayaka (Ganesh, son of Shiva), as the "remover of obstacles", followed in succession by Subrahmanya (another son of Shiva), Sundareshwara (a multiple image of the marriage of Shiva), Meenakshi and Chandeshwara (another form of Shiva). On some occasions, the deities are enshrined by simple canopies, but on others they ride on silver or gold vehicles (*vahanas*) such as horses, elephants or, most auspiciously, huge silver bulls.

At the **Avani Mula** festival, the coronation of Shiva is celebrated and his Madurain miracles are enacted in a series of plays (*lilas*). During the greatest festival of all, **Chittirai**, more plays are staged, telling the story of Meenakshi. The eighth day sees the goddess crowned as queen of the Pandyas, and, on the tenth, her marriage to Shiva draws as many as fifty thousand people to the temple. Out in the streets the next morning, mayhem ensues when the most elaborate transport is brought into use for procession. The god and goddess travel in fifteen-metre-high chariots, with giant wooden wheels, hauled through the streets by hundreds of devotees, all pulling on long ropes. Rising from a wooden platform, the massive pyramidal bamboo superstructures are decorated in colourful appliqué and fronted by a row of rearing wooden horses.

The god and goddess are taken to the banks of the River Vaigai, to meet Meenakshi's brother who, in southern mythology, is Lord Kallalagar (Vishnu). The icon of Vishnu is brought from the forested hilltop temple at Alagarkovil, 20km northeast of Madurai. Vishnu travelled to Madurai to give his sister away at the marriage ceremony, only to find on reaching the river that the ceremony had already occurred. Because of this, the festivities take place on the northern bank of the river.

the **Sundareshwarar shrine** (closed to non-Hindus). From here, outsiders can just about see the *shivalingam* beyond a blue and red neon sign that reads "*om*" in Tamil.

Causing a certain amount of fun, north of the flagstaffs are figures of Urdhva Thandavar and Bhadrakali, Shiva and Kali, in the throes of their dance competition (see p.936). A stall nearby sells tiny **butter balls** from a bowl of water, which visitors throw at the god and goddess "to cool them down".

If you leave through the gateway here, on the east, you'll find in the northeast corner the fifteenth-century **Ayirakkal Mandapa**, or thousand-pillared hall, now transformed into the temple **Art Museum**. In some ways it is a great shame, as screens have been erected and dusty educational displays replace a clear view of this gigantic hall. However, there's a fine, if rather dishevelled, collection of wood, copper, bronze and stone sculpture, an old nine-metre-high teak temple door and general miscellanea.

Vandiyur Mariamman Teppakulam tank and the floating festival

At one time, the huge **Vandiyur Mariamman Teppakulam** tank in the southeast of town (bus #4 or #4a; 15min) was full with a constant supply of water, flowing via underground channels from the Vaigai. Nowadays, thanks to a number of accidents, it is only filled during the spectacular Teppa **floating festival** (Jan/Feb), when pilgrims take boats out to the goddess shrine in the centre. Before their marriage ceremony, Shiva and Meenakshi are brought in procession to the tank, where they are floated on a raft, decorated with lights, which devotees pull by rope, three times encircling the shrine.

During the rest of the year the tank and the central shrine remain empty. Accessible by steps, the tank is most often used as an impromptu cricket green, and the shade of the nearby trees makes a popular gathering place. Tradition states that the huge image of Ganesh, Mukkuruni Vinayaka, in the Meenakshi temple, was uncovered here when the area was originally excavated to provide bricks for the Thirumalai Nayak Palace.

Thirumalai Nayak Palace

Roughly a quarter survives of the seventeenth-century **Thirumalai Nayak Palace** (daily 9am–1pm & 2–5pm), 2km southeast of the Meenakshi temple. Much of it was dismantled by Thirumalai's grandson, Chockkanatha Nayak, and used for a new palace at Tiruchirapalli. What remains was renovated in 1858 by the Governor of Madras, Lord Napier, and again in 1971 for the Tamil World Conference, held every fifty years. The palace originally consisted of two residential sections, plus a theatre, private temple, harem, royal bandstand, armoury, and gardens.

The surviving building, the **Swargavilasa** ("Heavenly Pavilion"), is a rectangular courtyard, flanked by 18-metre-tall colonnades. As well as occasional live performances of music and dance, the Tourism Department arranges a nightly **Sound and Light Show** (in English 6.45–7.45pm), which relates the story of the Tamil epic, *Shilipaddikaram*, and the history of the Nayaks. Some find the spectacle edifying, and others soporific – especially when the quality of the tape is poor. In an adjoining hall, the palace **museum** (same hours) includes Pandyan, Jain and Buddhist sculpture, terracottas and an eighteenth-century print showing the palace in a dilapidated state.

All that remains of the **Rangavilasa**, the palace where Thirumalai's brother Muthialu lived, are just ten pillars, wedged in a tiny back street. Take Old Kudiralayam St, right of the palace as you face it, pass the Archaeological Department Office and turn right into Mahal Vadam Pokki St. The third turning on the left (opposite the *New India Textile Shop*) is the unmarked Ten Pillars South Lane. One pillar contains a **shivalingam** which is worshipped by passers-by.

Tamukkam Palace – the Gandhi and Government museums

Across the Vaigai, 5km northeast of the centre near the Central Telegraph Office, stands **Tamukkam**, the seventeenth-century multi-pillared and arched palace of Queen

Rani Mangammal. Built to accommodate such regal entertainments as elephant fights, Tamukkam was taken over by the British, used as a courthouse and collector's office, and in 1955 became home to the Gandhi and Government museums.

Madurai's **Gandhi Museum** (daily 10am–1pm & 2–5.30pm), far better laid out than most of the species, charts the history of India since the landing of the first Europeans, viewed in terms of the freedom struggle. Generally the perspective is national, but where appropriate reference is made to the role played by Tamils. Wholeheartedly critical of the British, it states its case clearly and simply, quoting the Englishman, John Sullivan: "We have denied to the people of the country all that could raise them in society, all that could elevate them as men; we have insulted their caste; we have abrogated their laws of inheritance; we have seized the possessions of their native princes and confiscated the estates of their nobles; we have unsettled the country by our exactions, and collected the revenue by means of torture." One chilling artefact, kept in a room painted black, is the bloodstained *dhoti* the Mahatma was wearing when he was assassinated. Next door to the museum, the **Gandhi Memorial Museum Library** (daily except Wed 10am–1pm & 2–5.30pm) houses a reference collection, open to all, of 15,000 books, periodicals, letters and microfilms of material by and about Gandhi.

Opposite, the small **Government Museum** (daily except Fri 9am–5pm; closed 2nd Sat each month) displays stone and bronze sculptures, musical instruments, paintings (including examples of Tanjore and Kangra styles) and folk art such as painted terracotta animals, festival costumes and hobby horses. There's also a fine collection of shadow puppets, said to have originated in the Thanjavur area and probably exported to southeast Asia during the Chola period. A small house in which **Gandhi** once lived stands in a garden within the compound. Beside it, a number of unfinished latrines may have been intended as an exhibit, or a public amenity. It's rather hard to tell.

SHOPPING AND MARKETS IN MADURAI

Old Madurai is crowded with **textile and tailors' shops**, particularly in W Veli, Avani Moola and Chitrai streets and Town Hall Road. Take up the offers you're bound to receive to go into the shops near the temple, where locally produced textiles are generally good value. Many shops in the immediate vicinity also offer an incentive by allowing visitors to climb up to their roofs for views over the temple. Local tailors pride themselves on turning out faithful copies of favourite clothes in a matter of hours. South Avani Moola St is packed with **jewellery**, particularly gold, shops, while at 10 N Avani Moola St, you can plan for the future at the *Life & Lucky Number Numerology Centre*.

Madurai is also a great place to pick up south Indian **crafts**. Among the best outlets are *All India Handicrafts Emporium*, 39–41 Town Hall Rd; *Co-optex*, W Tower St, and *Pandiyan Co-op Supermarket*, Palace Rd, for handwoven textiles; and *Surabhi*, W Veli St, for Keralan handicrafts. For souvenirs such as sandalwood, temple-models, carved boxes and oil lamps head for *Poompuhar*, 12 W Veli St (☎25517), or *Tamilnad Gandhi Smarak Nidhi Khadi Gramodyog Bhavan*, W Veli St, opposite the railway station, which sells crafts, oil lamps, Meenakshi sculptures and *khadi* cloth and shirts.

The old purpose-built, wooden-pillared fruit and vegetable market, between N Chitrai and Avani Moola streets, provides a slice of Madurai life that can't have changed for centuries; beyond it, on the first floor of the concrete building at the back, the **flower market** (24hr) is a riot of colour and fragrance. Weighing scales spill with tiny white petals and fat pink garlands hang in rows. Varieties such as orange, yellow or white marigolds (*samandi*), pink jasmine (*arelli*), tiny purple spherical *vanameli* and holy *tulsi* plants come from hill areas such as Kodaikanal and Kumili. These are bought in bulk and distributed for use in temples, or to wear in the hair; some are made into elaborate wedding garlands (*kalyanam mala*). The very friendly traders will show you each and every flower, and if you've got a camera will more than likely expect to be recorded for posterity. It's a nice idea to offer to send them a copy of any photograph you take.

Kochadai Aiyannar Temple

The village of **Kochadai**, a northwestern suburb of Madurai, has a beautifully maintained temple dedicated to **Aiyannar**, the Tamil village deity and guardian of the borders. Travelling in Tamil Nadu, you often see such shrines from the road, but it may not always be possible, or appropriate, to investigate them. Here, however, they are accustomed to visitors. Flanked by two huge garish *dvarpalas* (doorkeepers), the entrance opens directly onto two gigantic horses with riders and furious-looking armed attendants. The shrine on the left houses the god Rama and his brother Lakshmana and, facing the entrance, is the shrine to Aiyannar. To the right, the *alamaram* tree, also a shrine, apparently houses a **cobra**, fed with eggs and milk. According to the priests he only comes out during full moon.

During a big **festival** in the Tamil month of Panguni (March/April), Aiyannar is taken around the village to the accompaniment of music and fireworks. Kochadai is served by frequent buses (#68 or #54) en route to Solavandan.

Accommodation

Madurai has a wide range of **accommodation**, from rock-bottom lodges to good, clean mid-range places that cater for the flocks of pilgrims and tourists. The upmarket options lie a few kilometres out of the town centre, north of the Vaigai.

Aarathy, 9 Perumalkoil, W Mada St (☎31571). Close to TTC bus stand. Good mid-range hotel, all rooms with TV, some with a/c and balcony. The open-air restaurant is popular, especially when the temple elephant is led through each morning. ③.

Arima, 4 TB Rd (☎23261). Adequate rooms, some a/c with balcony. Restaurant. ③.

Duke, 6 N Veli St close to the junction with W Veli St (☎26314). Modern hotel, a 10min walk from railway. Every surface is clean, but you may need to ask for acceptable bedsheets. Hot water, *Star TV* and room service, but no restaurant. Non-a/c options are the best value. ③–⑤.

Gangai, 41 W Perumal Maistry St (☎36211). Shabby, but will do as a last resort. ①.

Grand Central, 47–48 W Perumal Maistry St (☎36311). Non-a/c rooms, in need of a lick of paint. ②.

International, 46 W Perumal Maistry St (☎31552). Standard and deluxe doubles with *Star TV* and balconies overlooking the street. No restaurant. ③.

Keerthi, 40 W Perumal Maistry St (☎31501). Cramped little rooms (some a/c with *Star TV*) with views onto walls or the roof if you're lucky. A/c veg restaurant. ③.

Madurai Ashok, Alagarkoil Rd (☎43531). Plush hotel with 24hr room service, bar, currency exchange, craft shops and a swimming pool that costs Rs70 per day for non-residents. ⑦.

Pandiyan, Race Course, north of the river (☎42471). Comfortable hotel with a good restaurant, bar, exchange facilities, travel agency, bookstores and several craft shops. Nice garden, too. ⑥.

Prem Nivas, 102 W Perumal Maistry St (☎37531). Fairly small, clean rooms, all with *Star TV*. Some a/c options and a veg restaurant. ③.

Railway Retiring Rooms, first floor, stairway on platform 1 (turn right from the main entrance hall). Huge, clean rooms (some a/c) in this busy station. Often full. ①–②.

Sree Devi, 20 W Avani Moola St (☎36743). Good-value rooms (some a/c). No TV, or restaurant, but room service will send out for food. Great view over temple from the roof. ③.

Supreme, 110 W Perumal Maistry St (☎36331). Large hotel; all rooms with *Star TV*, and deluxe options with balcony and temple view. A duplex gives views of Yanna Malai hill range and railway line. Rooftop and vegetarian restaurants. ④.

Taj Garden Retreat, Pasumalai Hills (☎88256). Madurai's most exclusive hotel; a fine refurbished colonial house in the hills over the city, 6km out. Fifteen a/c rooms, restaurant, pool and bar. ⑨.

Thilaga, 111 W Perumal Maistry St (☎30762). Small, clean rooms with fan, in new building. ②.

TM Lodge, 50 W Perumal Maistry St (☎37481; fax 43682). Fair-sized rooms, but make sure you're not near the very noisy electricity generator. Non-a/c rooms upstairs are good value. ③.

TTDC Tamil Nadu I (Star), Alagarkoil Rd (☎42462). The posher of Madurai's two government hotels, north of the river, 5km from the centre. Good-sized rooms (some a/c) and restaurant. ④.

TTDC Hotel Tamil Nadu I, W Veli St (☎37470). Very busy, but comfortable, with some a/c rooms and a restaurant. ③.

MOVING ON FROM MADURAI

By Plane

Indian Airlines, 7a W Veli St (☎22957) operates flights to **Madras** (Mon, Thurs, Sat & Sun; 50min) and **Bombay** (Wed, Fri & Sun; 1hr 50min). Daily flights to **Bombay** via **Thiruvananthapuram** are operated by *East-West* (☎30833). Check in advance, as all flights are very much subject to change.

By Train

To make onward train reservations, the **Tourism Department Information Centre** (daily 6.30am–8.30pm; ☎33888) in the entrance hall of the station is particularly helpful; with a member of staff, foreign visitors can shamelessly jump the long queue.

Madurai is well connected to destinations in the south, but there are no direct trains to Bombay or Delhi. The fastest of the four daily services to **Madras**, the *Vaigai Express* #2636 (6.50am), calls at Trichy (2hr 20min), Villupuram (5hr) and Madras Egmore (7hr 40min). Slower Madras trains take 15hr, going via Thanjavur (5hr 10min), Kumbakonam (6hr), Chidambaram (8hr), Villupuram (11hr) and Chengalpattu (13hr 10min).

The three daily trains to **Rameshwaram** (4.45am, 2pm & 11.30pm; 5hr 30min–6hr 30min) call at Ramanathapuram (3hr–4hr15min). For **Ooty** and the **Nilgiris**, you have to take one of the two daily services to Coimbatore, and change there. The better of the two is the sleeper *Coimbatore Express* #6116 (10.05pm; 7hr). One train daily, at an ungodly hour, runs to **Kanniyakumari** – the *Madras–Kanniyakumari Express* #6019 (4.10am; 6hr). From Kanniyakumari it's a 2hr hop to **Thiruvananthapuram**; otherwise, the daily *Madurai–Quilon Express* #6161 stops at Kollam (7.10pm; 10hr 40min), where you can change for Kottayam, Kochi and Thiruvananthapuram. There is one daily service each to **Bangalore** (*Madurai–Bangalore Express* #6531; 8.10pm; 12hr 30min) and express to **Tirupati** in Andhra Pradesh (*Madurai–Tirupati Express* #6800; 10.30am; 18hr 30min).

By Bus

At the last count, four different stations operated long-distance **buses** from Madurai (see p.956); check on the current situation with the tourist office, to avoid unscrupulous hustlers who may take you under their wing and charge inflated prices.

From the TTC stand, numerous *TTC* buses leave day and night to **Madras** (11hr). Destinations in **Karnataka** include Bangalore, of which there are nineteen *TTC* (first 6am, last 11pm) and two *KSRTC* (7.45am & 10.30pm) buses. There's one a day to both Mysore (9.45pm) and Mangalore (6.30pm).

For **Kerala** there are three *TTC* and two *PRC* buses a day to Kozhikode (Calicut; 12hr) via Palakaad (Palghat), and the same number to Ernakulam (10hr), for Kochi, via Kottayam. Five *TTC* buses daily run to Tirupati (14hr) in Andhra Pradesh.

Buses to **Coimbatore** (10hr) leave from the **Arapalayam** stand every 15min during the day and every 30min during the night. There are nine a day to Kodaikanal (4hr). You can also get buses to Kumily (for Periyar Wildlife Sanctuary) every 30min, and one a day to Palakaad (9hr). The **Anna** stand offers regular buses to destinations north such as Thanjavur, Tiruchirapalli and Kumbakonam. Long-distance buses from **Palankanathan** stand include hourly services to both Kanniyakumari and Thiruvananthapuram.

Eating

As with accommodation, the range of places to eat in Madurai is gratifyingly wide, and standards are high, whether you're eating at one of the many utilitarian-looking "meals" places around the temple, or in a swanky hotel.

Amutham, Town Hall Rd. Western, Chinese and Indian non-veg snacks and "meals".

Chettinad, Chitraikara St. A local favourite for country-style cooking.

Jaya Vilas Mess, E Avani Moola St. Popular with visitors from surrounding villages, in for a day's shopping. Non-veg meals at ridiculously low prices; a little extra for chicken and mutton gravy.

Madurai Ashok, Alagarkoil Rd (☎43531). Smart hotel restaurant serving Indian, Chinese and western food (including "good ol' fish 'n' chips"). Open 6am–11pm.

Mahal, Town Hall Rd. Acceptable a/c veg and non-veg restaurant; popular with backpackers.

Pandiyan, Race Course (☎42471). Hotel restaurant with a reasonably priced lunchtime buffet and a varied evening menu; mostly Chinese and north Indian, with a few south Indian options.

Prem Nivas, 102 W Perumal Maistry St (☎37531). A/c veg restaurant, serving the usual Indian and Chinese dishes.

Supreme, 110 W Perumal Maistry St (☎36331). Mid-priced rooftop hotel restaurant with views of the temple, serving Indian, western and Chinese veg and non-veg dishes. Pleasant in the evening. Downstairs is the pure veg *Surya*.

Rameshwaram

The sacred island of **RAMESHWARAM**, 163km southeast of Madurai and less than 20km from Sri Lanka across the Gulf of Mannar, is a major Hindu pilgrimage site. Hindus tend to be followers of either Vishnu or Shiva, but Rameshwaram brings them together, being where the god Rama, an incarnation of Vishnu, worshipped Shiva in the *Ramayana*. The **Ramalingeshwara temple** complex, with its magnificent pillared walkways, is the most famous on the island, but there are several other small temples of interest, such as the **Gandhamadana Parvatam**, sheltering Rama's footprints, and the **Nambunayagi Amman Kali temple**, frequented for its curative properties. **Danushkodi**, "Rama's bow", at the eastern end of the peninsula, is where Rama is said to have bathed, and the boulders that pepper the sea between here and Sri Lanka, known as "Adam's Bridge", are the stepping stones used by Hanuman in his search for Rama's wife, Sita, after her abduction by Ravana, the demon king of Lanka. The ferry service to Sri Lanka has been suspended since 1984, due to the troubles there.

Rameshwaram is always crowded with daytrippers, and ragged mendicants who camp outside the Ramalingeshwara and the **Ujainimahamariamman**, the small goddess shore temple. An important part of their pilgrimage is to bathe in the main temple's sacred tanks and in the sea; the narrow strip of beach is shared by groups of bathers, relaxing cows and *mantra*-reciting *swamis* sitting next to sand *lingams*. As well as fishing – prawns and lobsters for packaging and export to Japan – shells are a big source of income in the coastal villages.

Arrival and information

NH49, the main road from Madurai, connects Rameshwaram with Mandapam on the mainland via the impressive two-kilometre-long Indira Gandhi Bridge, opened by Rajiv Gandhi in 1988. Armed guards at checkposts at either end keep a watchful eye on travellers. **Buses** from Madurai (via Ramnad), Trichy, Thanjavur, Kanniyakumari and Madras terminate at the bus stand, 2km northwest from the centre. The relatively quiet **railway station**, 1km southwest of the centre, is the end of the line for trains from Madras, Coimbatore, Madurai and Ramnad, and boasts decent **retiring rooms**, a veg refreshment room and a left luggage office (5.30am–9.30pm).

Red and white city buses run every ten minutes from the stand to the main temple; otherwise, **local transport** consists of unmetered cycle and auto-rickshaws that gather outside the bus stand. Jeeps are available for rent near the railway station, and bicycles can be rented from shops in the four Car streets around the temple.

The tiny TTDC **tourist office**, 14 E Car St (Mon–Fri 10am–5pm; ☎04573/371), dispenses information about guides, accommodation and boat trips to a nearby coral reef. TTDC also have an information counter at the railway station (daily 7–8.30am, 10.30am–1pm, 3–4.15pm, 7–8pm, to coincide with arriving trains; ☎04573/373). The **post office** (☎04573/230) is on Pamban Rd, the road to the bus stand.

Ramalingeshwara Temple

If a man goes with an impure mind into a temple he adds to the sins that he had already and goes home a worse man than when he left it . . . If sin is committed in any ordinary place it can easily be removed; but sin in a Tirtha [place of pilgrimage] cannot be removed . . . He who sees Shiva in the poor, in the weak and the diseased, really worships Shiva; and if he sees Shiva only in the image his worship is only preliminary. He who has served and helped one poor man seeing Shiva in him, without thinking of his caste or creed or race, Shiva is more pleased with him than with the man who sees Him only in temples . . . Unselfishness is the test of religion. And if a man is selfish, even though he has visited all the temples, seen all the places of pilgrimage and painted himself like a leopard, he is still further off from Shiva.

From a speech by Swami Vivekananda at Ramalingeshwara, inscribed in stone at the temple.

The core of the **Ramalingeshwara** (or Ramanathaswamy) **temple** was built by the Cholas in the twelfth century to house two much-venerated **shivalingams** associated with the *Ramayana*. After rescuing his wife Sita from the clutches of Ravana, Rama was advised to atone for the killing of the demon king – a *brahmin* – by worshipping Shiva. Rama's monkey lieutenant, Hanuman, was despatched to the Himalayas to fetch a *shivalingam*, but when he failed to return by the appointed day, Sita fashioned a *lingam* from sand (the *Ramanathalingam*) so the ceremony could proceed. When Hanuman eventually showed up with his *lingam*, in order to assuage the monkey's guilt Rama decreed that in future, of the two, Hanuman's should be worshipped first. The *lingams* are now housed in the inner section of the Ramalingeshwara, not usually open to non-Hindus. Much of what can be visited dates from the seventeenth century, when the temple received generous endowments from the Sethupathi rajas of Ramnad (see p.966).

High walls enclose the temple, forming a rectangle with huge pyramidal *gopura* entrances on each side. The gateways lead to a spacious closed ambulatory, flanked to either side by continuous platforms with massive pillars set on their edges. These **corridors** are the most famous attribute of the temple, their extreme length – 205 metres, with 1212 pillars on the north and south sides – giving a remarkable impression of receding perspective. Delicate scrollwork and brackets of pendant lotuses supported by *yalis*, mythical lion-like beasts, adorn the pillars.

Before entering the inner sections, pilgrims are expected to bathe in water from each of the twenty-two **tirthas** (tanks) in the temple; hence the groups of dripping wet pilgrims, most of them fully clothed, making their way from one tank to the next to be doused in a bucket of water by a temple attendant. Each tank is said to have special benefits: the Rama Vimosana Tirtha provides relief from debt, the Sukreeva Tirtha gives "complete wisdom" and the attainment of *Surya Loka*, the realm of the Sun, and the Draupadi Tirtha ensures long life for women and "the love of their spouses".

Monday is Rama's auspicious day, when the Padilingam *puja* takes place. **Festivals** of particular importance at the temple include **Mahashivaratri** (ten days during Feb/March), **Brahmotsavam** (ten days during March/April), and **Thirukalyanam** (July/Aug), celebrating the marriage of Shiva to Parvati.

Minor temples

The **Gandhamadana Parvatam** (daily 6–11am & 3.30–6.30pm), on a hill 2km north of Rameshwaram town centre, is a venerable shrine housing Rama's footprints. On some days, ceremonies are conducted here after the 5.30am *puja* at the Ramalingeshwara temple, encouraging pilgrims to climb the hill to continue their devotions. From the rooftop fine views extend over the surrounding country; on clear nights you can see the lights of Jaffna.

Three kilometres east of town towards the old fishing village of Dhanushkodi, the small **Nambunayagi Amman Kali temple**, set in a quiet sandy grove 200m off the main road, attracts people in search of cures for illnesses. Inside a banyan tree next to it is a shrine dedicated to the spirit Retatalai, "the two-headed". A pair of wooden sandals with spikes, said to belong to the spirit, is left in the shrine and locals say they can hear them clip-clopping at night when Retatalai chooses to wander. Pieces of cloth are tied to the branches of the tree to mark thanks for such boons as pregnancy after barrenness and the healing of family feuds.

Accommodation

Apart from the TTDC hotels, **accommodation** in Rameshwaram is restricted to basic lodges, mostly in the Car streets around the temple. The temple authorities have a range of rooms for pilgrims; ask at the Devasthanam Office, E Car St (☎04573/241).

Lodge Santhya, 1 W Car St (☎04573/329). Very inexpensive, passable double rooms. ①.

Maharaja's, 7 Middle St (☎04573/271). Good clean rooms next to the temple's west gate, two with a/c and TV. Temple views from balconies. No restaurant, but management will bring food in. ②.

Railway Retiring Rooms. Six large double and three triple rooms, generally cleaner (and quieter) than town lodges for the same price, plus a dorm. ①.

Santhana Lodge, S Car St. Basic en-suite rooms. ①.

Santhiya Lodge, W Car St (☎04573/329). 22 rooms, some a/c; reasonable for the price. ②.

Swami Ramanatha Tourist Home, W Car St (☎04573/217). Acceptable basic lodge. ①.

TTDC Hotel Tamil Nadu, near the beach (☎04573/277). The best place in Rameshwaram, in a pleasant location and with bar and restaurant. Comfortable rooms, some a/c, all sea-facing. Cheaper dorm and youth hostel beds. Often full – book in advance from another TTDC hotel or office. ①–③.

TTDC Hotel Tamil Nadu, 13km away in Mandapam, close to the mainland side of the Indira Gandhi bridge (☎04573/512). 12 double cottages on the beach, in a bay harbouring fishing boats. Primarily used by tour groups, so quite likely to be full. ②.

Venkatesh, Sithi Vinayagar Kovil St (☎04573/296). Fairly clean, darkish rooms, including 2 with a/c. No restaurant, but room service with buzzer. ②–④.

Eating

Eating in Rameshwaram is more about survival than delighting the taste buds. Most places serve up fairly unexciting "meals".

Arya Bhavan and **Kumbakonam**, W Car St. Both run by the same family; standard veg "meals".

Ashok Bhavan, W Car St. Regional varieties of *thalis*.

Devasthanam, on the left as you come out of the east gateway of the Ramalingeshwara temple. Temple-owned canteen serving good-quality and very cheap veg food.

TTDC Hotel Tamil Nadu, near the beach. Gigantic, noisy, high-ceilinged glasshouse near the sea, serving decent south Indian snack food and "meals", some non-veg.

Around Rameshwaram: Ramnad (Ramanathapuram)

RAMNAD offers a possible break on the bus or train between Madurai (120km northwest) and Rameshwaram (36km east). It's worth stopping here to see the neglected but atmospheric **Ramalinga Vilas**, palace of the Sethupati rajas, who by tradition were guardians of the mythical Sethu bridge built by Rama to cross to Lanka.

The entrance to the palace (daily except Fri 9am–1pm & 2–5pm; Rs2), 2km from the bus stand, takes you into the big and dusty **Durbar Hall**, whose central aisle is hung with oil portraits of the rajas of the last few hundred years. Ceilings and walls throughout the building are decorated with early eighteenth-century murals depicting subjects such as business meetings with the English and battles with the Maratha king Sarabhoji, as well as scenes from the epics. One battle scene shows soldiers fighting with boomerangs, and there's a real Indian boomerang on display. Also on show are palm-leaf manuscripts, a Ravi Varma painting with appliquéd brocade, and sculptures of Vishnu from the eighth and thirteenth centuries. From the **throne room**, a secret passageway once gave an escape route to a local temple. The Raja's throne, supported on carved elephant legs, is decorated with a coat of arms, given by the British, featuring a lion and unicorn. As further proof of the royal family's compliance with the foreign power, the Raja, at the end of the eighteenth century, allowed them to use the bedchambers upstairs – decorated with erotic murals – as a meeting hall. This cosy relationship did not find unanimous approval among his subjects. Influential local land-owners showed their contempt for the British by responding to tax demands with bags of stones and, in 1798 and 1801, rebellions took place, sometimes dubbed the "South Indian War of Independence". In 1803, at the request of the British, the Ramnad Raja was obliged to accept the lesser rank of Zamindar (feudatory chieftain).

On the roof is a stone bed on which the Raja would lounge in the evenings to enjoy panoramic views of the town and surrounding country. The buildings immediately below were royal guest houses, in one of which a descendant of the rajas now lives.

Kanniyakumari

KANNIYAKUMARI, at the southernmost extremity of India, is almost as compelling for Hindus as Rameshwaram. It is significant, not only for its association with a virgin goddess, Kanya Devi, but also as the meeting point of the Bay of Bengal, Indian Ocean and Arabian Sea. Watching the sun rise and set is the big attraction, especially on full moon day in April, when it's possible to see both the setting sun and rising moon on the same horizon. Although Kanniyakumari is in the state of Tamil Nadu, most foreign visitors arrive on day trips from Thiruvananthapuram, 86km northwest, the capital of Kerala. While the place is of enduring appeal to pilgrims, others may find it bereft of atmosphere, with nature's power to engender wonder in the human spirit obliterated by ugly buildings and hawkers selling shells and trinkets.

Arrival and local transport

Trains from Thiruvananthapuram, New Delhi, Bombay, Bangalore and even Jammu – at 86hr, the longest rail journey in India – stop at the **railway station** in the north of town, 2km from the seafront. The new Thiruvalluvar **bus stand**, near the lighthouse west of town, is served by buses from Thiruvananthapuram, Kovalam, Madurai, Rameshwaram (change at Madurai during the rainy season in Nov and Dec) and Madras. Taxis and auto-rickshaws provide **local transport**.

The Town

The seashore **Kumari Amman temple** (daily 4.30–11.30am & 5.30–8.30pm) is dedi-cated to the virgin goddess **Kanya Devi**, who may originally have been the local guar-dian deity of the shoreline, but was later absorbed into the figure of Devi, or Parvati, consort of Shiva. One version of Kanya Devi's story relates how she did penance to win the hand of Shiva. The god was all in favour and set out from Suchindram for the wedding, due to take place at midnight. The celestial *devas*, however, wanted Kanya Devi to remain a virgin, so that she could retain her full quota of *shakti* or divine power, and hatched a plot. Narada the sage assumed the form of a cock and crowed; on hearing this, Shiva, thinking that it was dawn and that he had missed the auspicious time for the ceremony, went home. The image of Kanya Devi inside the temple wears a diamond nose stud of such brilliance that it's said to be visible from the sea. Male visitors must be shirtless and wear a *dhoti* before entering the temple; non-Hindus are not allowed in the inner sanctum. It is especially auspicious for pilgrims to wash at the bathing *ghat* here.

The **Gandhi mandapam**, 300m northwest of the Kumari Amman temple, is a curi-ous modern imitation of an Orissan temple, so designed that the sun strikes the auspi-cious spot where the ashes of Mahatma Gandhi were laid, prior to their immersion in the sea, at noon on his birthday, October 2.

Possibly the original sacred focus of Kanniyakumari are two rocks, about 60m apart, half-submerged in the sea 500m off the coast, which came to be known as the Pitru and Matru *tirthas*. In 1892 they attracted the attention of the Hindu reformer Vivekananda, who swam out to the rocks to meditate. Incorporating elements of architecture from around the country, the 1970 **Vivekananda Memorial** (daily except Tues 7–11am & 2–5pm), reached by the Poompuhar ferry service from the jetty on the east side of town (every 30min; same hours), houses a statue of the saint. The footprints of Kanya Devi can also be seen here, at the spot where she performed her penance.

Accommodation and eating

As Kanniyakumari is a "must see" for Indian tourists and pilgrims, **hotels** can fill up early. Most of the accommodation is of a fairly low standard and overpriced. The better places, *Kerala House* and the TTDC hotel, are close to the sea, but there's stiff competition for space. Aside from the usual "meals" places, there are a few popular non-veg **restaurants** in the centre of town near the main shopping area, such as *Chicken Corner* and *Manikam Tourist Home*.

Kerala House, Seafront (☎04653/71229). Institutional-looking place whose cavernous doubles (2 a/c) have dressing rooms and bathrooms, and some sea views. Food can be ordered in advance. ⑤.
Kumari Bhavan (☎04653/71289). Cheap lodge very close to the bus stand. ①.
Sangam, Main Rd (☎04653/71351). Fairly grubby furnishings, but otherwise clean. Half of the 25 rooms have balconies; those at the front are noisy. ④.
Township Rest House, Main Rd (☎04653/71279). Reasonable double rooms with bathrooms. ①.
TTDC Hotel Tamil Nadu, Seafront (☎04653/71257). Cottages (some a/c) and clean rooms (a/c first floor), most with sea view. Cheaper "mini" doubles at the back and a youth hostel dorm. Good square meals served in functional surroundings. ①–⑤.

Suchindram

Construction of the **Stanunathaswami temple** at **SUCHINDRAM** (12km northwest of Kanniyakumari) extended over a period of at least six hundred years. Parts date back as far as the ninth or tenth century, others from the fifteenth century, and a huge seven-storey pyramidal *gopura* was erected during the sixteenth. Although its main sanctuary houses a *shivalingam*, the temple is jointly dedicated to Brahma, Vishnu and Shiva. Its proudest boasts are "musical" pillars, which emit a chime when struck, and an extraordinarily tall (3m) figure of Hanuman. A special *puja* takes place at sunset (around 6pm) every Friday, with music and a procession. Male visitors are required to wear a *dhoti* to enter, easily available from many willing guides who hover outside.

The Ghats

The Eastern and Western Ghats, which separate Tamil Nadu from Karnataka and Kerala, may not exactly rival the Himalayas, but like their counterparts further north they were much appreciated in the days of the Raj as escapes from the blast of the summer sun. Much the best known of the **hill stations** – in fact better known, and more visited, than it deserves – is **Udhagamandalam** (formerly Ootacamund, still often "Ooty"), in the **Nilgiris** (from *nila-giri*, "blue mountains"). The ride up to Ooty, on the **miniature railway** via Coonoor, is fun, and the views incredible, but in general, unless you can afford to stay in the best hotels, the town itself comes as a rude shock.

The other main hill resorts are **Kodaikanal**, further south not far from Madurai, and **Yercaud**, a low-key alternative within easy reach of Madras.

Salem and Yercaud

Situated in the low western ranges of the Shevaroy Hills, 100km northwest of Trichy, the busy industrial town of **SALEM** spreads over gently undulating hills at the base of the road that snakes 33km up to the peaceful hill station of **Yercaud**. Most of Salem's temples, and its fort, are badly ruined, and overshadowed by modern concrete buildings; all it really has to offer is a small **museum** (daily except Fri 9am–12.30pm & 1–5pm) on Omalur Rd, with an uninspiring display of long-dead animals and a small collection of Chola bronzes. Every Tuesday, hundreds of traders converge in the **bazaar** near Salem Market Station to sell locally made textiles in makeshift stalls.

Few tourists make the detour to **YERCAUD**, but in contrast to the congestion and clamour of Salem, this quiet, undisturbed town is a perfect spot to unwind and a convenient stop-off between Madras and Madurai or Coimbatore. Lower than Tamil Nadu's other hill stations, at just 1515m, Yercaud more than makes up for its lack of views by a picturesque setting among coffee plantations and thickly forested slopes, and supports a wide variety of flowers in its nurseries, parks and orchid house. Like any true hill station, it also has a small artificial **lake**, fed by waters that flow from the higher hills, forming a 300-metre waterfall just 3km away.

Practicalities

Salem is connected to Coimbatore, Cuddalore, Vellore and Madras by **train**; daily **buses** include two or three from Trichy, Pondicherry and Coimbatore, and one from Madras. A frequent bus service from Salem to Yercaud takes just under an hour.

What little **accommodation** there is in **Yercaud**, is of a high standard. *Shevaroys* on Hospital Rd (⑤–⑦), near the lake, is the best hotel, with several cottages, well-maintained rooms, private bathrooms, a good restaurant and bar. The smaller, reasonably comfortable TTDC *Hotel Tamil Nadu* (☎2273; ③–④) on Ghat Rd is typical of the chain, with some a/c rooms and an inexpensive restaurant. Cheapest of all is the simple TTDC *Youth Hostel* (①), not far from *Hotel Tamil Nadu*.

Hotels in **Salem** are more expensive, and less ideally located. The best of its dim, grotty and inexpensive lodges is *Coimbatore Lodge* (☎63649; ①) on Venkatroa St, where rooms, with common bathrooms, are small and spartan. The *National* (☎54100; ④–⑥) on Bangalore Rd is smart but unimaginative, with a restaurant and bar, and cottage accommodation in the grounds. Salem's grandest hotel is the modern *Salem Castle* (☎48702; ⑥–⑦) at A/4 Bharathi St, Swarnapuri; it has mirrored marble halls, spotless rooms with TV and big bathrooms, and a swimming pool, bar and restaurant.

Coimbatore

Visitors tend only to use the busy textile city of **COIMBATORE** as a stop-off on the way to Ooty, 90km northwest. There's little to do here, but you could weave your way along the cacophonous shopping area near the bus stand, crowded with what seem like hundreds of tailors' shops, traders plying garlands of flowers piled on blankets on the ground, and shoeshine boys clamouring for your trade.

Arrival and moving on

Coimbatore's two **bus stands**, Central and Thiruvalluvar, are close together towards the north of the city centre. From Central stand, on Dr Nanjappa Rd, buses leave for Ooty every thirty minutes. Buses to Bangalore and Mysore can be booked in advance at the **reservation office** (9am–noon & 1–8pm). There's also a frequent service to Ooty from the Thiruvalluvar stand on Cross Cut Rd, as well as regular buses to Madurai, Madras and Tiruchirapalli (Trichy).

The **railway station**, 2km south of the bus stands, is well connected to major southern destinations. To meet up with the *Nilgiri Blue Mountain Railway* to Ooty (see p.972), join the *Nilgiri Express* from Madras, which calls at Coimbatore at 6.20am, and change onto the narrow-gauge railway at Mettupalayam (7.50am). If you're catching this early train, try to stay near the railway station, or arrange transport the night before, as auto-rickshaws are few and far between at this hour of the morning.

Several overnight services leave for **Madras**, including *Nilgiri Express* #6006 (8pm) and *Cochin–Guwahati Express* #2649 (10.10pm). The daily *Rameshwaram Express* goes to Rameshwaram via Madurai; other daily trains are *Nagercoil–Bangalore Express* #6525 for Bangalore (8.55pm; 9hr30min); *Trichy–Cochin Express* #6365 for Kochi (12.45am; 5hr 30min); and the *Mangala Link Express* #2625 for Delhi (7.25pm; 43hr).

From Coimbatore **airport**, 11km northeast and served by buses to and from the Central bus stand, *Indian Airlines* fly daily to Bombay, Bangalore and Madras. They have an office (☎0422/22743) on Trichy Rd, 1km or so from the railway station. At the time of writing there was also a daily *East-West* (☎0422/217751) flight to Bombay.

Accommodation and eating

Most of Coimbatore's **accommodation** is around the bus stations. The cheapest places line Nehru St and Sastri Rd. As for **eating**, your best bets are the bigger hotels, many of which serve splendid south Indian food to a predominantly business clientele.

Alankar, 10 Sivasamy Rd, Ram Nagar (☎0422/26293). Government-approved, fairly gloomy place in need of decoration. Some a/c rooms. Veg restaurant and bar. ③–⑤.

Blue Star, 369 Nehru St (☎0422/37635). Highly designed interiors, some without windows (non-a/c half the price of a/c). Veg and non-veg restaurant. ③–④.

City Tower, just off Dr Nanjappa Rd, 2min walk south of the Central bus stand (☎0422/230681). Modern interiors, heavy on leatherette and various vinyls, but clean and decent (some a/c) with balconies. Excellent veg and non-veg restaurants. ④–⑤.

Sree Shakti, 11/148 Sastri Rd (☎0422/34225). A decent budget option near the bus stands. ②.

Sri Aarvee, 311a Gandhipuram (☎0422/43677). Clean business-style hotel, opposite the City bus stand. A/c and cheaper non-a/c rooms (all with *Star TV*). Good Andhra restaurant. ④–⑤.

Srinivasa, 365 Nehru St (☎0422/30116). Near the bus stands and just about OK for the price. ①.

TTDC Tamil Nadu, Dr Nanjappa Rd (☎0422/36311). Opposite Central bus stand. Convenient clean and reliable; many rooms with *Star TV*. Light and airy veg and non-veg restaurant. ④.

Coonoor

COONOOR, a busy Indian town on the *Nilgiri Blue Mountain Railway* (see p.972) lies at the head of the Hulikal ravine, 27km north of Mettupalayam and 19km south of Ooty, at an altitude of 1858m, on the southeastern side of the Dodabetta mountains. Often considered to be second best to its more famous neighbour, Coonoor has avoided Ooty's over-commercialization, and can make a pleasant place for a short stop.

The steep hills and valleys surrounding Coonoor are carpeted with tea bushes, interspersed with eucalyptus and silver oak. **Tea-pickers** work the slopes, carrying wicker baskets of fresh leaves and bamboo rods which they use like rulers to ensure that each plant is evenly plucked. Once the leaves reach the factory, they're processed within a day, producing seven grades of tea. Orange Pekoe is the best and most expensive; the seventh and lowest grade, a dry dust of stalks and leaf swept up at the end of the process will be sold on to make instant tea. To visit a tea or coffee plantation, contact *UPASI* (United Planters' Association of Southern India), "Glenview", Coonoor.

Coonoor loosely divides into two sections, with the bus stand (regular services to Mettupalayam, Coimbatore, and elsewhere in the Nilgiris), railway station and market huddled together in **Lower Coonoor**. In Upper Coonoor, **Sim's Park** is a fine botanical garden on the slopes of a ravine, with hundreds of rose varieties. Nearby **viewpoints** include Lamb's Rock (5km), overlooking Mettupalayam far away on the plains, and Dolphin's Nose (9km) which has spectacular views onto St Catherine's Falls on one side and Coonoor and Kotagiri streams, tributaries of the Bhavani, on the other.

Accommodation and eating

When it comes to finding somewhere to stay or eat, there's not a lot of choice in Coonoor. It's not a good idea to leave it too late in the day to be looking for a hotel. By and large the hotels are dotted around Upper Coonoor within around 4km of the station; you'll need an auto-rickshaw to find most of them.

Blue Hills, Mount Rd (☎04264/20103). Standard, clean doubles with soulless formica furnishing. "Blue Hills" bus stop outside; 1km from central bus stand. Good non-veg restaurant. ④.

Monarch Ritz, Ritz Rd (☎04264/620084). Russian-designed building in Upper Coonoor, near Sim's Park. Needs refurbishment, but the pleasant garden has a reasonable restaurant and bar. ⑤.

Sri Lakshmi Tourist Home, Kamrajpuram, Rockby (☎04264/7022). Basic lodge with plain restaurant. ②.

Taj Garden Retreat, Hampton Manor (☎04264/219241). Excellent, expensive old hotel with cottage accommodation and real character, run by the *Taj* group. The restaurant, overlooking the pretty garden, is the best place to eat in town – try the spectacular lunchtime buffet. ⑨.

Venkateswara Lodge, Cash Bazaar (☎04264/6740). Very basic option near the bus stand. ②.

Vivek Tourist Home, Figure of Eight Rd, Rockby (☎04264/7022). Standard lodge with reasonable rooms and a restaurant. ③.

YWCA Guest House, Wyoming, near the hospital (☎04264/20326). Beautiful old building in peaceful garden, with bags of character. Five clean doubles and seven cheaper singles with iron hospital-style beds. Dining hall serves wholesome food. Very small and often full, so try phoning ahead. ④.

Udhagamandalam (Ootacamund)

Originally a Toda village, **UDHAGAMANDALAM**, established by the British in the nineteenth century as a retreat from the heat of the plains below, continues to be known as **"Ooty"**, the "Queen of Hill Stations". Until the mid-1970s "Snooty Ooty" was home to English bungalows, schools, shops and churches and to the last colonial inhabitants who chose to "stay on", living out their last days on tiny pensions which only here would allow them to keep a lifestyle to which they had become accustomed.

Since Independence, travellers have continued to be attracted by Ooty's cool climate and peaceful green hills, forest and grassland. However, if you come in the hope of finding quaint vestiges of the Raj, you're likely to be disappointed; what with indiscriminate development and a deluge of holidaymakers, they're few and far between.

The **best time to come** is between January and March, avoiding the high-season crowds (April–June & Sept–Oct). In May, the summer festival brings huge numbers of people and a barrage of amplified noise; worlds away from the peaceful retreat envisaged by the *sahibs*. From June to September, and during November, it'll be raining, misty and quite cold, which appeals to some.

Arrival

Most visitors arrive in Ooty either by bus from Mysore in Karnataka (the more scenic, if steeper, route goes via Masinagudi), or on the **miniature mountain railway** from Coonoor and Mettupalayam. The bus and train stations are fairly close together, at the western end of the big bazaar and racecourse.

Local transport consists of auto-rickshaws and taxis, which meet incoming trains and gather outside the bus stand and on Commercial Road around Charing Cross. It's possible to **rent bicycles** but the steep hills make cycling very hard work.

Information

The **TTDC tourist office** (☎3964) in Super Market Building, Charing Cross, is of little use unless you want to book a **tour**. There are two to choose from: "Ooty and Mudumalai" (daily 8.30am–8pm) calls at Ooty Lake, Dodabetta Peak, the Botanical Gardens and Mudumalai Wildlife Sanctuary, making for a long day. Few people get to see any wildlife at the sanctuary on such a whistle-stop excursion. "Kotagiri and Coonoor" (daily 8.30am–6.30pm) goes to Kotagiri, Kodanad Viewpoint, Lamb's Rock, Dolphin's Nose and Sim's Park.

THE NILGIRI BLUE MOUNTAIN RAILWAY

The famous **narrow-gauge Mountain Railway** climbs up from Mettupalayam on the plains, via Hillgrove (17km) and Coonoor (27km) to Udhagamandalam, a journey of 46km through forest, tea plantations, sixteen tunnels and more than 250 bridges. It's a slow journey of four-and-a-half to five hours – sometimes the train moves little faster than walking pace – but the views are absolutely magnificent.

In theory, trains up from Mettupalayam set off at 7.50am, but this depends on what time the *Nilgiri Express* (an overnight service leaving Madras at 9.15pm) arrives. If you're in Coimbatore, you can pick up the *Nilgiri Express* there, ostensibly at 6.20am. Some visitors prefer to come by shared taxi or bus from Mettupalayam, and take the train from Ooty to Coonoor as an excursion later on. During the peak season (April & May) there are four trains a day downs from Ooty; the 8.55am and 6.05pm terminate at Coonoor, the 2pm and 2.50pm go through to Mettupalayam where you can pick up regular trains to Coimbatore and beyond. The popular *Nilgiri Express* to Madras departs at 7.15pm.

Ooty's **post office**, northwest of Charing Cross at Town West Circle, off Spencers Rd and near St Stephen's Church, has a poste restante counter (enquiries and stamps Mon–Fri 9am–5pm; parcels Mon–Fri 9am–3pm & Sat 9am–2pm). A central STD phone booth, close to Charing Cross, is at *K Gopalan*, Commercial Rd (Mon–Fri 6.30am–11.30pm, Sun 8.30am–3pm & 5–9pm).

To arrange elephant rides, transport and accommodation at Mudumalai Wildlife Sanctuary, see the **Wildlife Officer**, in the Mahalingam & Co Building on Coonoor Rd. It's almost inevitable that you'll need to book well in advance to get in.

The Town

Ooty sprawls over a large area of winding roads and steep climbs. The obvious focal point is **Charing Cross**, a busy junction on **Commercial Road**, the main, relatively flat, shopping street that runs south to the big bazaar and vegetable market. A little way northeast of Charing Cross, the **Botanical Gardens** (daily 8am–6.30pm; Rs1, camera Rs5, video Rs25), laid out in 1847 by gardeners from London's Kew Gardens, consist of twenty hectares of immaculate lawns, lily ponds and beds, with over a thousand varieties of shrubs, flowers and trees. There's a refreshment stand in the centre and shops outside sell candy floss, peanuts and snacks.

Northwest of Charing Cross, the small gothic-style **St Stephen's Church** was one of Ooty's first colonial structures, built in the 1820s on the site of a Toda temple; timber for its bowed teak roof was taken from Tipu Sultan's Palace at Srirangapatnam and hauled up here by elephant. The area around the church gives some idea of what the hill station must have looked like in the days of the Raj; on the way up to it you'll pass **Spencer's** store on Church Hill, opened in 1909, which still serves from old wooden counters. Over the road from the church, tucked away, the charming little branch of **Higginbotham's** is still the best place to buy books. Nearby, in the same compound as the post office, gowned lawyers buzz around the red-brick **Civil Court**, a quasi-gothic structure with leaded diamond-shaped windows, corrugated iron roofs and a clock tower capped with a weather vane. Over the next hill (west), the most snooty of Ooty institutions, the **Club**, dates from 1830. Originally the house of Sir William Rumbold, it became a club in 1843 and expanded thereafter. Entry is strictly restricted to members and their guests or members of affiliated clubs.

Local goods on sale along **Commercial Road** range from jewellery to fat plastic bags of cardamom tea, and special presentation packs of eucalyptus oil. West of the

The telephone **area code** for Udhagamandalam (Ooty) is ☎0423.

UDHAGAMANDALAM (OOTY)

HOTELS:
- Ⓐ Savoy
- Ⓑ Garden View
- Ⓒ Fernhill Palace
- Ⓓ Dasaprakash
- Ⓔ Nilgiri Woodlands
- Ⓕ YWCA
- Ⓖ Nahar
- Ⓗ TTDC Tamil Nadu
- Ⓘ Gangothri
- Ⓙ Weston

RESTAURANTS:
- ❶ Shinkow's
- ❷ Kurunji
- ❸ Tandoor Mahal

500 m

Botanical Gardens

KODAPPAMUND RD

WOODHOUSE RD

HAVELOCK RD

HAVELOCK RD

WESTBURY RD

OMUND RD

WOODCOCK RD

KANDAL BAZAAR RD

TIMSORE-OOTY RD

St Stephen's Church

GPO

BANK RD

CHARING CROSS

KELSO RD

COONOOR RD

THALAYATIMUND RD

COMMERCIAL RD

ETTINES RD

STD

Ooty Club

HOSPITAL RD

Railway Station

BIG BAZAAR

Bus Stand

Lake

NORTH LAKE RD

SOUTH LAKE RD

HIGH LEVEL RD

LOVE RD

Racecourse

BISHOP'S DOWN LANE

GODAVARI HOUSE RD

OSWION'S RD

Coonoor ▷

△ Mysore

TREKKING IN THE NILGIRIS

The best way to appreciate the Nilgiri Hills is to get well away from the towns by **trekking**; assorted routes, dotted with basic accommodation, wind through the local Reserved Forest. None is particularly difficult, but many lead through remote areas where help in an emergency is difficult to come by, and access is restricted to protect the environment.

If you arrive on spec, it can take up to a week to get the necessary permission from the relevant District Forest Officer (there are North and South divisions) at the **Nilgiri Wildlife and Environment Association**, based opposite *Higginbotham's* bookstore in Ooty (Mon–Fri 9am–5pm; ☎3968; postal address: Udhagamandalam, Nilgiris 643001). They can also advise about routes and guides.

Treks in the west of the region (best Dec–May) take you through largely uninhabited country with spectacular views, springs, rivers and rivulets, grassland, natural forest (*shola*) where wild flowers include rhododendron and orchids, and man-made forest of eucalyptus, wattle and pine. On the far west, at the edge of the escarpment that forms the western border of Mukurti Sanctuary, 1000-metre drops plummet to the heavy evergreen rainforest of Kerala. **Animals** include Nilgiri *tahr* and *sambar* (deer), wild dog, elephant, and even panther and tiger. The bird population is small: grey jungle fowl, hawks and harriers. At higher altitudes, bright daytime sunshine with temperatures of around 20°C is followed by a dramatic cooling to freezing point at night; warm clothing is essential.

The lower areas in the **north** and **east** are completely different; a dry, rough, rocky terrain with patches of dense thorny scrub, populated by diverse wildlife, including *sambar*, sloth bear and some *gaur* (Indian bison). Trekking is possible all year round, but the intense heat between March and May is not conducive to long walks.

railway station and racecourse (races mid-April to mid-June), the **Lake**, constructed in the early 1800s, is now one of Ooty's main tourist attractions, despite being heavily polluted. Honeymoon couples in particular go boating (8am–6pm; rowing, paddle and motor Rs20–100) and horseriding (short rides Rs10–40, or Rs75 per hour).

Fernhill Palace, close to the southeast end of the Lake and once the summer residence of the Maharaja of Mysore, is now run as a hotel (see below). It's an extraordinary pile, built in the fullest expression of Ooty's characteristic Swiss-chalet style, with carved wooden bargeboards and ornamental cast-iron balustrades. Among the compound of firs, cedars and monkey puzzle trees, a bizarre church-like building was erected as an indoor badminton court.

Local walks along the leafy lanes around Ooty are not what they once were, due to the volume of traffic, but it is still possible, at least out of the main seasons, to get some peace and magnificent views on parts of Wenlock Downs (8km on the Gudalur Rd), Dodabetta Peak (10km east, off the road to Kotagiri), Avalanche (24km) which is part of the *shola* forest with wild flowers and Pykara Dam (19km).

Accommodation

Ooty is a lot more expensive than many places in India; during April and May the prices shown below can double. It also gets very crowded, so you may have to hunt around to find what you want. The best by far are the grand old Raj-era places; otherwise, the choice is largely down to average hotels at above-average prices. In winter (Oct–Dec), when it can get pretty cold, most hotels provide heating at extra cost.

Dasaprakash, near the railway station and bus stand, south of racecourse (☎2434). Old-style Indian hotel, clean and reasonably quiet. No TV in standard rooms; Rs50 extra for heating. Two veg restaurants. Travel agent. ⑤.

Fernhill Palace (☎3910). Characterful old place, set in 40 acres of garden and woodland. Built by the British in the mid-1800s, it was sold to the Maharajah of Mysore soon afterwards, and only fell into the hands of the *Taj* group in 1991. It has yet to be refurbished, and its unique suites, antique furniture, carved teak details, ballroom and "Hunt Bar" give it a gloriously faded charm. ⑧–⑨.

Gangothri, Ooty–Mysore Rd (Club Rd) (☎3226). Spotless rooms in ugly modern building on a main road, a 15min walk from station. ⑤–⑥.

Garden View, opposite bus stand and next to the railway station (☎3349). Manky rooms, over-priced, with good views of Ooty's public transport facilities. ⑤.

Nahar, Charing Cross (☎2163). Decent rooms (best in the modern building at the back) with *Star TV*. Tariff halves in winter; Rs75 extra for heater. Two veg restaurants. ⑥.

Nilgiri Woodlands, Racecourse Rd, 1km from bus stand and railway station (☎2551). Arrange to be collected from the station. Raj-era building, with wood-panelled lobby and bare, clean rooms (phone and TV; Rs75 extra for heating). Dorm accommodation available. Restaurant. ①/⑤.

THE TODAS AND THE THREAT TO THE NILGIRIS

Until the arrival of the British, the **Todas** of the Nilgiri Hills maintained their own language and customs in villages (*munds*) of wagon-shaped huts of bamboo, thatch and reeds. Today the Toda tribal community still exists, albeit in depleted numbers. Some wear traditional costume; plain white waist-cloths under thick white woven cloaks striped with red and black. Once, all adult women had their upper body tattooed, their hair oiled and curled into long ringlets at the front; feminine beauty is judged by the narrowness of the feet and facial hair is admired. Men keep their hair and beards long.

Toda culture centres around the **buffalo**, held sacred; the only product they use is its milk, consuming it in vast quantities. Toda temples are dairies, off-limits to everyone save the officiating priests. The community is divided into fourteen patriarchal clans, though its polyandrous social system is fast breaking down. "Marriages" were arranged at birth with partners from another clan; at the age of fifteen the female moved in with the husband's family and automatically became the wife of his younger brothers too. She could also seek further partners from other families, with the permission of her principal partner, who would generally assume the paternal role for any resultant offspring.

The Todas lived in interdependence with three other tribal groups, based on a barter system under which their main responsibility was to supply the others with dairy products; the **Kotas** were ironsmiths and potters, and provided music for rituals, while jungle-dwelling **Kurumbas**, known for their aptitude in magic, also gathered honey and wood. The **Badagas**, who arrived in the fourteenth century, kept the others in grain and beans.

At present there are about 1500 Todas, of whom a quarter are Christian. Due to high infant mortality and the introduction of life-threatening diseases by the British, by the 1940s their population had dwindled to little more than 600. This alarming situation was dramatically reversed, largely through the efforts of an exceptional Toda woman, **Evam Piljain-Wiedemann**, who trained as a nurse in England, and succeeded in winning the confidence of other Todas to take advantage of a mobile medical clinic. She continues to work to secure rights for the Todas, and to protect the natural environment.

Blame for the threat to the Nilgiris cannot simply be laid at the door of colonial exploitation, though the story does begin with the arrival of the British in 1821. Despite their penchant for hunting (panther, tiger and deer) and fishing, the British were acutely aware, within the vision of the time, of protecting the natural landscape. The worst came after Independence. From 1952, a series of "five-year plans" towards "development" were implemented. Widespread planting of exotic trees, principally eucalyptus, wattle and pine, provided a generous income for the government, but had far-reaching effects on local ecology. A new synthetic fibre industry, established in the foothills, requires huge amounts of pulp to make fibre. Despite local fears and protests, including a *satyagraha*-style public fast, more and more acreage is cleared in order to feed factories.

Traditional *shola* forest, once destroyed, takes thousands of years to replace, while the newly planted eucalyptus draws water from miles around. For the first time in its history, this once swampy region suffers from **water shortages**. The Todas can no longer get enough thatching grass to build houses and temples, and their traditional homes are being replaced by concrete. Nothing grows under eucalyptus and pine, and the sacred buffalo have nowhere to graze. Many Todas have been forced to sell their stock, and barely enough are left to perform the ceremonies at the heart of Toda life.

Sabari, near Mariamman temple (☎2735). Large rooms, shabby but reasonably clean. ③.

Savoy, 77 Sylkes Rd (☎4142). Long-established *pukka* hotel, now run by the *Taj* group, with mani-cured lawns and bushes (quiet classical music seeps from the leaves). Immaculate and chintzy old-world cottages with working fireplaces, wood and brass fittings. Restaurant, bar, travel agent. ⑨.

Surya Holiday Inn, 11 Upper Bazaar (☎2567). Smallish, but clean rooms (heater Rs25 extra) in fairly recent and central hotel. ⑤.

TTDC Hotel Tamil Nadu (☎4010). Above the tourist office, reached by steps to the side. Good value, with decent, clean rooms and dorm accommodation. Restaurant. ①/④.

Weston, Ooty–Mysore Rd (Club Rd) (☎3500). Comfortable rooms (all with hot water, telephone and *Star TV*) in characterless concrete building between St Stephen's Church and Ooty Club. Heater Rs50 extra. Travel counter, veg and non-veg restaurants. Tariff halved in winter. ⑦.

YWCA, Ettines Rd. Very popular place tucked behind the eastern end of the racecourse, with a range of accommodation including double rooms with bathroom and dorms. Restaurant. ①–④.

Eating

Many of the mid-range hotels serve up good south Indian food, but Ooty has yet to offer a gourmet restaurant. The *Savoy* and *Fernhill Palace*, however, are well worth checking out for the colonial ambience.

Fernhill Palace. Unexciting restaurant with average mid-range food. Still, you get to see the palace, and Nilgiri mushrooms on fried bread with fresh hot "finger chips" is a great lunch snack.

Kurinji Snack Bar, Commercial Rd. Fast food outlet, open to the street; popular with Ooty youth.

Nahar, Charing Cross (☎2163). Two good veg restaurants, and a snack bar serving milk shakes, *dosa*, *aloo chaat* and the like, with some tables set outside.

Nilgiri Woodlands, Racecourse Rd (☎2551). The speciality is beef steak, but the inexpensive *thalis* are good too. Checked table-cloths and cane chairs give it the look of a village hall. No alcohol.

Sabari, near Mariamman temple and vegetable market. Basic budget veg snacks and "meals".

Savoy, 77 Sylkes Rd (☎4142). Not the cheapest, but the best of the old colonial places. The food is good with a mixed menu of Indian, Chinese and western; and the verandah overlooking the garden is a pleasant place for an alcoholic drink or a tray of tea.

Shinkows, 42 Commissioners Rd (☎2811). Good value, authentic Chinese food.

Tandoor Mahal, Commercial Rd. Central, very good value non-veg restaurant; serves beer too.

Weston, Ooty–Mysore Rd (Club Rd; ☎3500). Non-veg restaurant plus Gujarati pure veg.

Mudumalai Wildlife Sanctuary

Set 1140 metres up in the Nilgiri Hills, **MUDUMALAI WILDLIFE SANCTUARY** covers 322 square kilometres of deciduous forest, split by the main road from Ooty (64km) to Mysore (97km). The approach from Ooty is spectacular, twisting and turn-ing down thirty-six hairpin bends, through wooded hills and past waterfalls (in season). Monkeys dart and play in the trees, and you may glimpse a tethered elephant from the camp at **Kargudi**, where wild elephants are tamed for work in the timber industry.

MOVING ON FROM OOTY

Ooty **train** station has a reservation counter (10am–noon & 3.30–4.30pm) and a booking office (6.30am–7pm). For details of services on the narrow-gauge railway, see p.972.

You can also book **buses** in advance, at reservation offices for both state buses (daily 9am–12.30pm & 1.30–5.30pm) and the local company, *Cheran Transport* (daily 9am–1pm & 1.30–5.30pm). Towns served include Bangalore and Mysore (buses to both pass through Mudumalai), Kodaikanal, Thanjavur, Thiruvananthapuram and Kanniyakumari, as well as Kotagiri, Coonoor, and Coimbatore nearer to hand. **Private buses** to Mysore, Bangalore and Kodaikanal can be booked at hotels, or agents in Charing Cross; even when advertised as "super-deluxe", many turn out to be cramped minibuses.

Mudumalai has one of the largest populations of elephants in India, along with wild dogs, *gaur* (Indian bison), common and Nilgiri langur and bonnet macaque (monkeys), jackal, hyena and sloth bear – even a few tigers and panther. To make the most of a visit, you'll need to stay overnight, and trek out into the park. On a brief foray, such as the organized tour from Ooty (see p.971), you're not likely to see much wildlife.

Arrival and information

You can only get to Mudumalai by road. Regular buses from Ooty (2hr 30min) to Mysore and Bangalore pass through **Masinagudi**, the main village, and **Theppakkadu**, an access point 8km further on, the location of the **Wildlife Sanctuary Reception and Administration Centre** (☎0423/235). Here you can book conducted tours in a Forest Department van (Rs20 per hour) or by elephant (daily 6.30am & 4.30pm; Rs100 per hour; booked well ahead). Calling in at the sanctuary on spec without your own transport is not made easy.

Accommodation and eating

Accommodation standards in Mudumalai are high, often in gorgeous, peaceful settings. The best places are up to 5km off the main road from Masinagudi. Book in advance, and arrange for them to pick you up from the bus stop – taxis or jeeps are rare in the village. Most places expect guests for full board, as Masinagudi only has a few simple restaurants, and will arrange tours of the park for residents.

There is also basic **dorm accommodation** in the park. To make sure of securing a place you should book well in advance, at the Wildlife Office in Ooty (see p.972), but you can always ask Forest Department officials at Theppakkadu on the off-chance.

Bamboo Banks Guest House, 2km from the main road, Masinagudi (☎0423/222 or 211). Two rooms, and four styled cottages, in a very attractive setting. Excellent food served outdoors. ⑥.

Blue Valley Resort, 1km off the main road, Masinagudi (☎0423/244). Comfortable rooms, two restaurants. Will collect from the village, and can arrange trekking and jeep tours (Rs5 per km). ⑤.

Jungle Hut, 5km from the road, Bokkapuram, Masinagudi (☎0423/240). Twelve comfortable cottages, and a swimming pool. Excellent food, including barbecues. Will arrange trekking, elephant rides and pick-up from Theppakkadu. ⑤.

Monarch Safari Park, Bokkapuram, Masinagudi (☎0423/243 or 251). Fourteen rooms in *machans* (cottages on stilts) with *Star TV*; full and half board. Open restaurant, also on stilts. Safari rides, riding, cycling, trekking, golf, indoor games and meditation centre. ⑤–⑦.

Mountania Lodge, Masinagudi (☎0423/237). Cabins in Masinagudi's only roadside lodge. ④.

TTDC Youth Hostel, Theppakkadu (☎0423/249). Functional and clean dorms. Meals by arrangement, 7-night max stay. Book at the TTDC office in Ooty, but you may be lucky if they're not full. ①.

Kodaikanal

High on the southern ridges of the Palani hills, just over 100km northwest of Madurai, **KODAIKANAL**, also known as **Kodai**, is one of the south's more popular hill stations, but even so, like the others, it seldom detains tourists for more than a day or two. Kodai's greatest plus is its hilltop position, which affords views south over the plains and north to the smooth blue-green reaches of the Palani range. Raj-era houses and gardens flooded with the hues of flowers from all over the world add atmosphere, while short walks out of the centre lead to rocky outcrops, waterfalls and dense forest.

Kodaikanal's history, with an absence of wars, battles for leadership and princely dominion, is uneventful, and the only monuments to its past are the neat British bungalows that overlook the lake and Law's Ghat Road on the eastern edge of town. The British first moved here in 1845, to be joined later by members of the American Mission who set up schools for European children. One remains as Kodai International School; despite the name, it has an almost exclusively Indian student population. The school lays a strong emphasis on music, particularly guitar playing, and occasionally holds workshops, and concerts on the green just east of the lake.

After a while in the plains of south India a retreat to Kodai's cool heights is more than welcome. However, in the height of summer (June–Aug), when temperatures compete with those in the lowlands, it's not worth the trip – nor is it a good idea to come during the monsoon (Oct–Dec), when the town is shrouded in mists and drenched by heavy downpours. In late February and early March the nights are chilly; the busiest tourist season is from April to June, when prices soar.

Arrival, information and getting around

The **buses** from Madurai and Dindigul that climb the spectacular road up the steep hillside to Kodai from the plains pull in at the bus stand in the centre of town. The nearest **railhead**, Kodaikanal Road, is also connected to Dindigul (30min) and Madurai (50min); unless you're coming from as far as Madras or Tiruchirapalli, taking a bus is much more convenient. Rail tickets for onward journeys from Kodaikanal Road can be booked at an office on Woodville Rd, just south of the main bazaar (Mon–Sat 9.30am–12.30pm & 2.30–4.30pm), or at *King Tours and Travels* nearby, which will also reserve seats on buses and planes within south India. Kodaikanal's **tourist office** (Mon–Fri 10am–5pm), by the bus stand, offers little except unclear sketch maps of the area.

Four-hour **tours** are run twice daily by *Hotel Tamil Nadu*, taking in all the town's sights and most of the viewpoints. Alternatively, **taxis** line the main road, Anna Salai (Bazaar Road), in the centre of town, offering sightseeing tours at high but fixed rates. Most tourists prefer to amble around the town at their own pace. Compact and hilly as it is, Kodaikanal is best explored on foot, or you could rent a **bicycle** from a stall on Anna Salai for Rs15–20 per day; it may be fun to freewheel *down* hills, but most journeys will involve a hefty push.

If you need to **change money**, head for the *State Bank of India* on Bazaar Rd.

The Town

Kodai's focal point is its **lake**, sprawling like a giant amoeba over a full 24 hectares just west of the town centre. This is a popular place for strolls, or bike rides along the five-kilometre path that fringes the water's edge (a booth rents out bikes at low rates), and pedal- or rowboats can be rented on the eastern shore (Rs10–25 for 30min). Shops, restaurants and hotels are concentrated in a rather congested area of brick, wood and corrugated iron buildings east and downhill from the lake. To the south is **Byrant's Park**, with tiered flower beds and a backdrop of pine, eucalyptus, rhododendron and wattle, which stretches southwards to Shola Road, less than 1km from the point where the hillside drops abruptly to the plains. A path, known as **Coaker's walk**, skirts the hill, winding from *Taj Lodge* to *Greenland's Youth Hostel* (10min), offering remarkable views that on a clear day stretch as far as Madurai.

Once you've spent a little time in the town, and visited the lake and gardens, you'll probably be tempted to seek out a bit of peace and quiet in the less built-up areas. One of Kodai's most popular natural attractions is **Pillar Rocks**, a series of granite cliffs rising more than 100 metres above the hillside, 7km south of town. To get there, follow the westbound Observatory Road from the northernmost point of the lake (a moderate uphill slope) for roughly 4km, until you come to a crossroads. The southbound road passes the gentle **Fairy Falls** on the way to Pillar Rocks.

Observatory Road continues west to the **Astrophysical Observatory**, perched at Kodai's highest point (2347m). Visitors cannot go in, but a small **museum** (Fri only, 10am–noon) displays assorted instruments. Closer to the north shore of the lake, **Bear Shola Falls** are at their strongest early in the year, just after the monsoon.

East of the town centre, about 3km south down Law's Ghat Rd (towards the plains), the **Flora and Fauna Museum** (daily except Sun 10–11.30am & 3.30–5pm) has a far from inviting collection of stuffed animals. However, the orchid house is spectacular, and well worth a look on the way to **Silver Cascade** waterfalls a further 2km along.

Chettiar Park, on the very northwest edge of town, around 3km from the lake at the end of a winding uphill road, flourishes with trees and flowers all year round, and every twelve years is flushed with a haze of pale-blue **Kurinji blossoms** (next flowering 2006). These unusual flowers are associated with the god Murugan, the Tamil form of Karttikeya (Shiva's second son), and god of Kurinji, one of five ancient divisions of the Tamil country. A temple in his honour stands just outside the park.

Accommodation

Kodaikanal's inexpensive **lodges** are grouped at the lower end of Bazaar Rd. Many are dim and poky, however, so hunt around. Always ask whether blankets and hot water are provided. **Mid-range hotels** are usually good value, especially if you get a room with a view, but hike their prices to ridiculous levels during the high season.

Astoria, Anna Salai (☎04542/40525). Well-kept hotel opposite the bus stand, with homely rooms and a good, medium-priced restaurant. ⑤.

Carlton, Lake Rd (☎04542/40056). The most luxurious hotel in Kodaikanal. Spacious, tastefully renovated and well-maintained colonial house overlooking the lake, with a bar and comfortable lounge. Cottages within the grounds are available at higher prices; all rates include meals. ⑨.

Greenland's Youth Hostel, St Mary's Rd. Attractive old stone house offering unrivalled views, simple rooms and a cosy bunk-bed dorm. One of the best inexpensive options. ①–③.

Hilltop Towers, Club Rd (☎04542/40413). Modern rooms and excellent service. Only two minutes' walk from the lake. ⑥.

International Guest House, Anna Salai (☎04542/45420). One of the better low-priced lodges, with clean small rooms, some with attached bath, and hot water available by the bucket. ①–②.

Kodai International, Law's Ghat Rd (☎04542/43767). Modern and comfortable, with a bar, but poor service and an inconvenient location, more than 2km northwest of town. ⑤–⑦.

Mayura Lodge, Anna Salai. Friendly lodge with spartan washing facilities and simple rooms. ①.

Sangeeth, Anna Salai, opposite the bus stand (☎04542/40456). Reasonably sized and comfortable rooms, each with attached bath. Central, but with no views over the plains. Pay extra for a TV. ③.

Suhag, Woodville Rd (☎04542/41143). Large, comfortable rooms with TV; though the place has little character and unappealing views. ⑤.

Sunrise, Post Office Rd. Good-value lodge with great views from the front rooms, and attached baths with water heaters. ②.

Taj Lodge, off Club Rd. Cosy hotel set in pleasant gardens with excellent views. All rooms have attached bathrooms, but you'll have to get hot water by the bucket. ②–③.

TTDC Tamil Nadu, Fern Hill Rd (☎04542/41336). Large hotel northwest of town. Some of the deluxe rooms are in a tatty state, but there are smarter cottages and an inexpensive dorm. ①–⑦.

Eating

If you choose not to eat in any of the **hotel restaurants**, head for the food stalls along **Hospital Rd** just west of the bus stand. Menus include Indian, Chinese, western and Tibetan dishes, and some cater specifically to vegetarians. Look out, too, for the bakeries, with their wonderful fresh, warm bread and cakes each morning.

Apna Punjab, Hospital Rd. Great Indian cuisine and reasonably priced *tandoori* specialities.

Carlton, *Carlton Hotel*, Lake Rd. Expensive, tasty food. A buffet spread is laid out each evening and there's a well-stocked bar.

Chefmaster, Hospital Rd. The best place for Keralan dishes, including unbeatable *thalis*. Reasonable Chinese food and western-style snacks are also served.

Manna Bakery, Bear Shola Rd. Fresh doughnuts, bread, rolls, cakes and pizza, all in a very friendly atmosphere.

Silver Inn, Hospital Rd. Exclusively western menu; reasonable rates. Often full.

Tibetan Restaurant, Hospital Rd. Tibetan dishes ranging from thick bread to *momos* and noodles.

Palani

Few visitors venture further into the Palani hills than Kodaikanal, but in April it's worth making the bumpy bus journey (2 daily; 1hr) to **PALANI**, roughly 30km north. Usually a quiet little town, fringed by tea gardens, Palani comes alive at this time when it hosts a festival in honour of **Murugan**, Shiva's son (also known as Skanda), in its modern hilltop **Shri Dandayudhapani temple**. Hundreds of devotees, mostly male and clad in black *dhotis*, trudge up a winding flight of over 600 steps to worship the image, said to be formed from an aggregate of poisonous minerals, that, if mixed with coconut milk, fruits and flowers, produce medicinal herbs. A smaller festival takes place in February/March – check the date in Kodaikanal.

Palani, which has sparse accommodation in a simple *dharamshala*, is the jumping-off point for road or rail journeys to **Anamalai wildlife sanctuary**, in the southern reaches of the Cardamom hills, south of **Pollachi**, a busy junction 60km west. Though the sanctuary, a spread of mixed deciduous forest interspersed with teak and rosewood, is known for its lion-tailed **macaque** (black-maned monkeys), wild elephants, deer, *chital* and *sambar*, those visitors who come on short jaunts tend to leave disappointed.

Pollachi is connected to Anamalai by an infrequent **bus** service. Information and bookings for rooms in unelaborate **forest rest houses** (①) can be made through the Chief Wildlife Warden, 5 Round Rd, in Pollachi, where you can also check out the possibility of transport by elephant or jeep.

CHAPTER NINETEEN

KERALA

T hanks to its isolated position at the southwestern tip of India, sandwiched between the Arabian Sea and the forested Western Ghat mountains, the state of **KERALA** is blessed with unique geographical and cultural features. Its overpowering tropical greenness, with 41 rivers and countless waterways, fed by two annual monsoons, intoxicates every newcomer. Equally, Kerala's arcane rituals and spectacular festivals stimulate even the most jaded imagination, connecting spectators to centuries of unbroken tradition that has never strayed far from the realms of magic.

Travellers weary of daunting metropolises find no such problems here. Kerala's cities are small-scale, relaxed and generally a good deal less expensive than elsewhere. For visitors, the most popular is undoubtedly the great port of **Kochi** (Cochin), where Kerala's extensive history of peaceable foreign contact is evocatively evident in the tranquil old quarters of Mattancherry and Fort Cochin. The capital, **Thiruvananthapuram** (Trivandrum), almost as far south as you can go and a gateway to the nearby palm-fringed beaches of **Kovalam**, is a pleasant city in itself, providing visitors with varied opportunities to sample Kerala's rich cultural and artistic life.

However, more so than anywhere in India, the greatest joy of exploring Kerala is the actual travelling – above all, by **boat**, in the spell-binding Kuttanad region, near historic **Kollam** (Quilon) and **Alappuzha** (Alleppey). Vessels from cruisers to wooden longboats ply the **backwaters** in day-long voyages, well worth taking for the chance of a close-up view of village life in India's most densely populated state. Furthermore, it's always easy to escape the heat of the lowlands by taking off to the **hills**. Roads through a landscape dotted with churches and temples pass spice, teak and rubber plantations, and natural forest, en route to wildlife reserves such as **Peppara** or **Periyar**.

Kerala is short on the historic monuments prevalent elsewhere in India, mainly because wood is the building material of choice. Moreover, what ancient temples there are remain in use, more often than not closed to non-Hindus. Nonetheless, distinctive buildings throughout the state eschew grandiosity in favour of elegant understatement. Typical features of both domestic and temple architecture include long, sloping tiled and gabled roofs to minimize the excesses of both rain and sunshine, and pillared verandahs; the definitive example is **Padmanabhapuram Palace**. The elaborate *gopura* entrance towers seen in Tamil Nadu are almost entirely absent in Kerala.

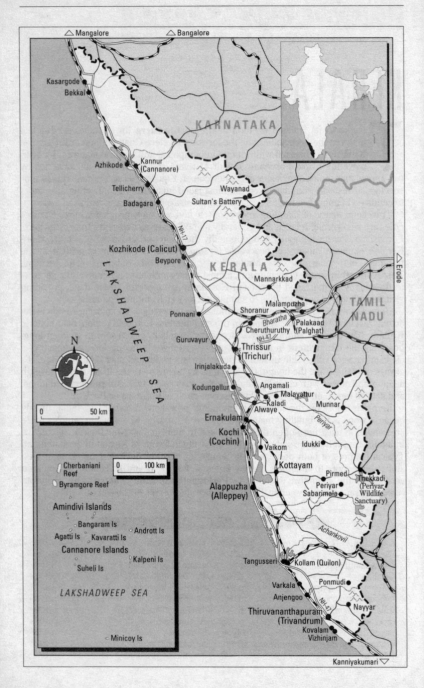

Kasargode
Bekkal

KARNATAKA

Azhikode
Kannur
(Cannanore)

Tellicherry
Wayanad
Badagara
Sultan's Battery

NH-17

Kozhikode (Calicut)
Beypore

KERALA

Mannarkkad

TAMIL
NADU

Malampuzha
Shoranur
Ponnani
Bharatha
Palakaad
Cheruthuruthy
(Palghat)
Guruvayur
NH-47

Thrissur
(Trichur)

Irinjalakuda

Kodungallur
Angamali
Malayattur
Kaladi
Munnar
Alwaye

Ernakulam
Periyar
Kochi
(Cochin)
Vaikom
Idukki
Kottayam
Pirmed
Thekkadi
(Periyar
Wildlife
Sanctuary)
Alappuzha
Periyar
(Alleppey)
Sabarimala

Achankovil

Tangusseri
Kollam (Quilon)
Varkala
Ponmudi
Anjengoo
NH-47
Nayyar
Thiruvananthapuram
(Trivandrum)
Kovalam
Vizhinjam

LAKSHADWEEP SEA

N

0   50 km

△ Erode

Cherbaniani
Reef
0   100 km
Byramgore Reef

Amindivi Islands

Bangaram Is
Andrott Is
Agatti Is
Kavaratti Is
Cannanore Islands
Kalpeni Is
Suheli Is

LAKSHADWEEP SEA

Minicoy Is

KERALA TRAVEL DETAILS

	Trains		Buses		Flights	
	Frequency	Time	Frequency	Time	Frequency	Time
To and From THIRUVANANTHAPURAM						
Alappuzha			15 daily	3hr 30min–5hr		
Bangalore	1 daily	19hr 20min			1 daily	1hr
Bombay	1 daily	45hr 15min			2–3 daily	2hr
Calcutta	1 weekly	49hr				
Colombo					1 daily	45min
Delhi	1 daily	53–55hr			1 daily	4hr 30min
Goa					1 daily	1hr
Kanniyakumari			12 daily	2hr		
Kochi	5 daily	5hr 20min	20 daily	5–6hr	1 daily	30min
Kollam	5 daily	1hr 35min	15 daily	1hr 30min		
Kottayam			5 daily	4hr		
Kozhikode	5 daily	10hr			1 daily	1hr 30min
Madras	1 daily	18hr	4 daily	17hr	1 daily	1hr 30min
Madurai			10 daily	7hr		
Malé (Maldives)					4 weekly	30min
Periyar			3 daily	8hr		
Ponmudi			6 daily	2hr 30min		
Thrissur	5 daily	7hr 20min				
To and From KOCHI/ERNAKULAM						
Ahmedabad	1 weekly	45hr 20min				
Alappuzha	2 daily	1hr 20min	15 daily	1hr 30min		
Angamali	3 daily	1hr				
Bangalore					4 weekly	1hr
Bombay	1–2 daily	41–60hr			4–5 daily	1hr 45min
Coimbatore	5 daily	4hr 45min			3 weekly	30min
Delhi	2 daily	49hr			6 weekly	4hr
Goa					6 weekly	1hr
Kollam	5 daily	3–4hr	15 daily	4hr		
Kottayam	5 daily	1hr 5min	15 daily	1hr 30min		
Kozhikode	5 daily	5hr			1 daily	30min
Lakshadweep					3 weekly	1hr 30min
Madras	3 daily	13–14hr			1 daily	2hr
Palakaad	5 daily	3hr 20min				
Periyar			10 daily	6hr		
Pune	1–2 daily	32–34hr				
Shoranur	5 daily	2hr 30min				
Thiruvananthapuram	5 daily	4hr 20min–5hr	20 daily	5–6hr		
Thrissur	5 daily	1hr 30min–2hr	7 daily	2hr		
To and From Periyar						
Kottayam			every 30min	3–4hr		
Kozhikode			every 30min	6hr		
To and From Thrissur						
Guruvayur			10 daily	40min		
Madras	3 daily	11hr 30min	1 daily	14hr		
Mysore			2 daily	10hr		
Palakaad			6 daily	2hr		

For details of **ferry** services on the **backwaters** – primarily between Allappuzha and Kollam – see p.1001.

Note that most individual routes appear only once in this chart; check against where you want to get to as well as where you're coming from.

In the last twenty years or so, a new (and highly competitive) style of extravagant domestic architecture has become evident, largely financed by petro-dollars earned by Keralans working in the Gulf. However, following an unwritten law, few buildings, whether houses or temples, are higher than the surrounding trees. From high ground in urban areas this can create the miraculous illusion that you're surrounded by forest.

Phenomenal amounts of money are lavished upon many, varied, and often all-night **entertainments** associated with Kerala's temples. Fireworks that might be mistaken for bombs rent the air, while processions of gold-bedecked elephants are accompanied by some of the loudest (and deftest) drum orchestras in the world. The famous **Puram** festival in Thrissur is the most astonishing, but smaller events take place throughout the state – often outdoors, with all welcome to attend.

No visitor could fail to notice the preponderance of **theatre** and **dance** styles in Kerala; not only the region's own female classical dance form, **Mohiniattam** ("dance of the enchantress"), but also the martial-art-influenced **Kathakali** dance drama, which has for four centuries brought gods and demons from the *Mahabharata* and *Ramayana* to Keralan villages. If Kathakali whets your appetite, its 2000-year-old predecessor, the Sanskrit drama Kutiyattam, is still performed by a handful of artists, while localized rituals known as Teyyam continue to be a potent ingredient of village life in the north.

History

The god Parashurama, "Rama with the battle axe", the sixth incarnation of Vishnu, is credited with creating Kerala. Born a brahmin, he set out to re-establish the supremacy of the priestly class, whose position had been usurped by arrogant *kshatryas*, the martial aristocracy. Brahmins were forbidden to engage in warfare, but he embarked upon a campaign of carnage, which only ended when Varuna, the all-seeing god of the sea, gave him the chance to create a new land from the ocean, for brahmins to live in peace. Its limits were defined by the distance Parashurama could throw his axe; the waves duly receded up to the point where it fell. Fossil evidence suggests that the sea once extended to the Western Ghats, so the legend reflects a geological truth.

Ancient Kerala is mentioned as the land of the Cheras in a third-century BC Ashokan edict, and also in the *Ramayana* (the monkey king Sugriva sent emissaries here in search of Sita), and the *Mahabharata* (a Chera king sent soldiers to the Kurukshetra war), while the Tamil *Silappadikaram* ("The Jewelled Anklet") was composed here and provides a valuable picture of life around the time of Christ. Early foreign accounts, such as in Pliny and Ptolemy, testify to thriving trade between the ancient port of Muziris (now known as Kodungallur) and the Roman Empire.

Little is known about the early history of the Cheras; their dominion covered a large area, but their capital Vanji has not been identified. Other contemporary rulers included the Nannanas in the north and the Ay chieftains in the south, who fought wars with the Pandyas from Tamil Nadu, in the eighth century. At the start of the ninth century, the Chera king Kulashekhara Alvar – a poet-saint of the Vaishnavite *bhakti* movement known as the *alvars* – established his own dynasty. His son and successor, Rajashekharavarman, is thought to have been a saint of the parallel Shaivite movement, the *nayannars*. The great Keralan philosopher Shankaracharya, whose *advaita* ("non-dualist") philosophy influenced the whole of Hindu India, lived at this time.

Eventually, the prosperity acquired by the Cheras through trade with China and the Arab world proved too much of an attraction for the neighbouring **Chola** empire, who embarked upon a hundred years of sporadic warfare with the Cheras at the end of the tenth century. Around 1100, the Cheras lost their capital at Mahodayapuram in the north, and shifted south to establish a new capital at Kollam (Quilon).

When the **Portuguese** ambassador/general Vasco da Gama first arrived in India in 1498, people were as much astounded by their recklessness in sailing close to Calicut during monsoon, as by their physical and sartorial strangeness. Crowds filled the streets of Calicut to see them, and a Moroccan found a way to communicate. Eager to meet the king, whom they believed to be a Christian, the Portuguese were escorted eighteen miles in torrential rain to his palace. However, da Gama soon discovered that the gifts he had brought from the King of Portugal had not made a good impression. The Zamorin (Raja) wanted silver and gold, not a few silk clothes and a sack of sugar.

Vasco da Gama, after such diplomatic initiatives as the kidnapping, mutilation and murder of assorted locals, nevertheless came to an agreement of sorts with the Zamorin, then pressed on to demand exclusive rights to the spice trade. He was determined to squeeze out the Keralan Muslim (Mappila) traders who for centuries had been a respected section of the community, acting as middlemen between local producers and traders in the Middle East. Exploiting an already existing enmity between the royal families of Cochin and Calicut, da Gama turned to Cochin, which became the site of India's first Portuguese fortress in 1503. The city's strategic position enabled the Portuguese to break the Middle Eastern monopoly of trade with western India; unlike previous visitors, they introduced new agricultural products such as cashew and tobacco, and for the first time turned coconut into a cash crop, having recognized the value of its by-products, coir rope and matting.

The rivalry between Cochin and Calicut allowed other colonial powers to move in; both the Dutch, who forcibly expelled the Portuguese from their forts, and the British, in the shape of the East India Company, established themselves early in the seventeenth century. During the eighteenth century, first Raja Martanda Varma, and then Tipu Sultan of Mysore, carved out independent territories, but the defeat of Tipu Sultan by the British in 1792 left the British in control right up until Independence.

Kerala today can claim some of the most startling **radical** credentials in India. In 1957 it was the first state in the world democratically to elect a communist government and despite having one of the lowest per capita incomes in the country it has the most equitable land distribution, due to uncompromising reforms during the 1960s and 1970s. Poverty is not absent, but it appears far less acute than in other parts of India.

Kerala is also justly proud of its reputation for health care and education, with a literacy rate that stands, officially at least, at one hundred percent. However, industrial development is negligible, with potential investors from outside tending to fight shy of dealing with a politicized workforce. Many Keralans find themselves obliged to leave home to seek work, especially in the Gulf. The resultant influx of petro-dollars seems only to have the negative effect of increasing inflation.

Thiruvananthapuram

Kerala's capital, the coastal city of **THIRUVANANTHAPURAM** (still widely known as **Trivandrum**), is set on seven low hills, 87km from the southern tip of India. Despite its administrative importance, demonstrated by wide roads and gleaming white colonial buildings, it retains the character of a Keralan country town. An attractive mixture of narrow backstreets, traditional red-tiled gabled houses, acres of palm trees and parks, and the constant proximity of the sea, make for a remarkably easygoing city.

Although it has few monuments as such, Thiruvananthapuram is an ideal first stop in the state, as a window on Keralan culture. The oldest, most interesting, part of town is the **Fort** area in the south, around the **Shri Padmanabhaswamy temple**, while important showcases for painting, crafts and sculpture, the **Shri Chitra Art Gallery** and **Napier Museum**, stand together in a park in the north. Schools specializing in the martial art Kalarippayat, and the dance/theatre forms of Kathakali and Kutiyattam, offer visitors an insight into the Keralan obsession with physical training and skill.

The telephone **area code** for Thiruvananthapuram is ☎0471.

HOTELS:

A Swapna Tourist Home
Swaraj Lodge &
Shaji Tourist Home

B Pankaj

C South Park

D Luciya Continental

E Swaraj Lodge
Udupi Sreenivas Tourist Home
& Arulakam

F KTDC Chaitram

G Yatri Niwas

H KTDC Mascot

RESTAURANTS:

1 Indian Coffee House

2 Azad

3 Anand Bhawan

Indian Airlines

Sri Chitra Art Gallery

Kanakunna Palace

MUSEUM RD

Museum of Science & Technology

MAIN CENTRAL RD

Napier Museum, Open Air Theatre & Natural History Museum

Library

Connemara Market

Forest Museum

STD

Telegraph Office

Secretariat

MAHATMA GANDHI (MG) RD

VANCHIYUR

PRESS RD

THYCAUD

Children's Museum

PAIKKAD HOSPITAL RD

GPO

MANJALIKULAM RD

SCHOOL RD

CHETTIKULANGARA RD

KTDC Tourist Reception Centre

KSRTC Bus Stand

STATION RD

Railway Station

THAMPANOOR

THAKARAPARAMBU RD

FORT

POWER HOUSE RD

Tank

City Bus Stand

CHENTITTA

N

Sri Padmanabhaswamy Temple

Bhajanapura Palace

CHALI BAZAR RD

CHALAI

Airport (6 km)

0   250 m

Bus Stand

THIRUVANANTHAPURAM

▽ Kovalam

THE CITY OF THE SNAKE ANANTHA

Thiruvananthapuram was the capital of the kingdom of Travancore from 1750 until 1956, when the state of Kerala was created. Its name (formally re-adopted to replace "Trivandrum"), derives from *thiru-anantha-puram* – "the holy city of Anantha", the coiled snake on which the god Vishnu reclines in the midst of the cosmic ocean.

Vishnu is given a special name for this non-activity – *Padma-nabha*, "lotus-navel" – and is invariably depicted lying on the sacred snake with a lotus growing umbilically from his navel. The god Brahma sits inside the lotus, which represents the beginning of a new world age. Padmanabha is the principal deity of the royal family of Travancore, and of Thiruvananthapuram's **Shri Padmanabhaswamy temple**.

Many travellers choose to pass straight through Thiruvananthapuram, hotfooting it to nearby **Kovalam**, a twenty-minute bus ride south. Particularly popular with long-stay European beach bums, it's close enough to use as a base to see the city.

Arrival and information

The **airport** (served by flights to and from most major Indian cities, as well as Sri Lanka, the Maldives, and the Middle East) is 6km southwest of town, connected by bus #14, auto-rickshaws and taxis. The long-distance KSRTC **bus** (☎71029) and **railway** (☎64585) stations face each other across Station Road in Thampanoor in the southeast of the city, a short walk east of Overbridge Junction, where Thiruvananthapuram is bisected by the long north–south **MG Road**.

Local buses (to Kovalam for example) are five minutes' walk from the stations, at the City bus stand, East Fort. **Rickshaws** are more useful within the city, and happy to run out to Kovalam for around Rs50. **Cars** can be rented from *Best Travels*, Pandit's Building, Palayam (☎61616); *Inter-Car*, Ayswarya Buildings, Press Rd (☎67964); *Nataraj Travels*, Thampanoor (☎63064); or *Travel India*, Convent Rd (☎78208).

Information and communications

Tourist offices at the airport (daily 8am–8pm; ☎71085), and the train station, platform 1 (daily 8am–8pm; ☎67224), can book accommodation and give information about trains. Another branch, near the museums at Park View in the northeast (☎61132), has the best selection of literature on the region.

Thiruvananthapuram's **GPO**, with poste restante (daily 8am–6pm), is in Palayam, a short distance west of MG Rd. The **Telegraph Office**, opposite the Secretariat on MG Rd, is open around the clock. Kerala's best STD **telephone** is at *Tandem Communications,* at the MG Rd end of Statue Rd, where the private booths have their own dials and charge meters. **Money** can be changed at the *State Bank of India*, near the Secretariat on MG Rd (Mon–Fri 10am–2pm, Sat 10am–noon), and major hotels.

The City

The historical and spiritual heart of Thiruvananthapuram is in the **Fort area**, at the southern end of **MG Road**, which encloses the Shri Padmanabhaswamy Vishnu temple. Following MG Road north leads through the main shopping district, busy all day, and especially choked when one of the frequent, but generally orderly, political demonstrations converges on the grand colonial **Secretariat** building halfway along. The whole centre can be explored easily on foot, though you might be glad of a rickshaw ride back from the museums and parks, close to the top end of the road.

Fort area

A solid but unremarkable fort gateway leads from near the Kovalam bus stand at East Fort to the **Shri Padmanabhaswamy Temple**, which is still under the control of the Travancore royal family. Unusually for Kerala it is in the Dravidian style of Tamil Nadu, with a tall *gopura* gateway, but it's surrounded by high fortress-like walls, and is closed to non-Hindus; little can be seen from outside, apart from the seven-storey *gopura*.

Most of the temple buildings date from the eighteenth century, added by Raja Marthanda Varma to a much older shrine. According to legend, the temple was founded after Vishnu, disguised as a beautiful child, merged into a huge tree in the forest, which immediately crashed to the ground. There it transformed into an image of the reclining Vishnu, a full 13km long. Divakara, a sage who witnessed this, was frustrated by his limited human vision, and prayed to Vishnu to assume a form that he could see in its entirety. Vishnu complied, and the temple appeared. The shrine at the centre of the complex now houses a large stone image, where three doors open to reveal parts of the god. The first shows Vishnu's head and characteristically limp right arm, the second his navel, and the last his feet.

The area in front of the temple, where devotees bathe in a huge tank, is thronged with stalls selling religious souvenirs, shell necklaces, *puja* offerings, jasmine and marigolds. As you approach, the *CVN Kalari Sangam*, a **martial arts** gymnasium, is on the left. A path along the north side of the tank leads past the north, west and southern entrances, all guarded by doormen armed with sticks, apparently to keep dogs away. It's an atmospheric walk, particularly in the early morning and at dusk, when devotees make their way to and from prayer (a closed iron gate bars the northern side, but everybody climbs through the gap). These neat little streets, in the old days of Kerala's extraordinary caste system, would have been a "no go" area, possibly on pain of death, to some members of the community. The palace near the temple is private.

Behind the temple at West Fort, set back from the road across open ground, the *Margi* school of **Kathakali** dance drama and **Kutiyattam** theatre (see p.1029) is housed in Fort High School. With prior notice you can watch classes; this is the place to ask about authentic Kathakali performances. One of *Margi*'s teachers, Nelliode, is famous for "red beards" – vile vicious types, and other unusual and humorous characters.

MG Road: markets and shopping

An assortment of craft shops along **MG Road** north of Station Road sell sandalwood, brass and Keralan bell-metal oil lamps (see p.1024). The Gandhian *Khadi Gramodyog*, between Pazhavangadi and Overbridge junctions, stocks handloom cloth (be prepared to dig around to find the best stuff), plus radios and cassette machines manufactured by the Women's Federation. *Natesan Antique Arts*, further up, is part of a chain of art shops that specialize in paintings, temple wood carvings and so forth. The prices are far from cheap, but they usually have some beautiful pieces. Most of the bookstores in the area are somewhat disappointing, largely intended for exam entrants; *Higginbothams* is probably the best for paperbacks. Two more handicraft shops stand near the Secretariat; *SMSM* behind it, and *Kairali* opposite it.

Almost at the top, just off the road on the right hand side, the excellent little **Connemara Market** is just the place to pick up essentials like plastic buckets, dried fish, fruit, vegetables, coconut scrapers, crude wooden toys, coir, woven winnowing baskets and Christmas decorations. It also holds the workshops of several **tailors**.

Public Gardens, Zoo and museums

A minute's walk east from the north end of MG Rd, opposite the Information Centre, you come to the entrance to Thiruvananthapuram's **Public Gardens**. As well as serving as a welcome refuge from the noise of the city – its lawns usually filled with courting couples, students and picnicking families – the park holds the city's best museums. However, while the **Zoo** is in a nice enough setting, just inside the gate on the left, the depressing state of the inmates, and the propensity of some visitors to get their kicks by taunting them, makes it eminently missable (daily except Mon 9am–4.45pm).

The extraordinary **Government (Napier) Museum** of arts and crafts (Tues & Thurs–Sun 9am–5pm, Wed 1–5pm), has a definite touch of Disney. Completed in 1880, it was an early experiment in what became known as the "Indo-Saracenic" style, with tiled double-storey gabled roofs, garish red-black-and-salmon-patterned brickwork, tall slender towers, and, above the main entrance, a series of pilasters forming Islamic arches. The spectacular interior boasts stained-glass windows, a wooden ceiling and eye-catchingly loud stripes painted in turquoise, pink, red and yellow. The architect responsible, Robert Fellowes Chisolm (1840–1915), set out to incorporate Keralan elements into colonial architecture; the museum was named after his employer, Lord Napier, the Governor of the Madras Presidency. Highlights of the collection include fifteenth-century Keralan woodcarvings from Kulathupuzha and Thiruvattar, gold necklaces and belts, minutely detailed ivory work, a carved temple chariot (*rath*), wooden models of Guruvayur temple and an oval temple theatre (*kuttambalam*), plus twelfth-century Chola and fourteenth-century Vijayanagar bronzes.

The attractive **Shri Chitra Art Gallery** (same hours), with its curved verandah and tiled roof, houses some splendid paintings from the Rajput, Moghul and Tanjore schools, as well as China, Tibet and Japan. The oil paintings by Raja Ravi Varma (1848–1906) have been criticized for their sentimentality and western influence, but his treatment of Hindu mythological themes is both dramatic and beautiful.

In the ethnographic collection at the **Natural History Museum** (same hours), there's a model of a Nayar *taravad* (manor house). Kerala is littered with traditional houses that follow this *nalekettu* ("four-sided") design, built around an open courtyard. Grander ones can have as many as four such courtyards – all hidden from prying eyes.

Away from the centre

The **Chachu Nehru Children's Museum** (Mon–Fri 10am–5pm), in Thycaud in the east of the city, serves as a rather dusty testament to the enthusiasm of some anonymous donor, presumably back in the 1960s. One room contains ritual masks, probably from Bengal, Rajasthan and Orissa, but the rest of the place is taken up with stamps,

FESTIVALS OF THIRUVANANTHAPURAM

The **Arat** festival, centered around the Shri Padmanabhaswamy temple, takes place twice each year, in Meenam (March/April) and Thulam (Oct/Nov). Each time, ten days of festivities inside the temple (open to Hindus only) culminate in a procession through the streets of the city, taking the deity, Padmanabhaswamy, to the sea for ritual immersion. Five caparisoned elephants, armed guards, a *nagasvaram* (double-reed wind instrument) and *tavil* drum group are led by the Maharaja of Travancore, in his symbolic role as *kshatrya*, the servant of the god. Instead of the richly apparelled figure that might be anticipated, the Maharaja, who is no longer officially recognized, wears a simple white *dhoti*, with his chest bare save for the sacred thread. Rather than riding, he walks the whole way, bearing a sword. To the accompaniment of a 21-gun salute and music, the procession sets off from the east gate of the temple at around 5pm, moving at a brisk pace to reach Shankhumukham Beach at sunset, about an hour later. The route is lined with devotees, many of whom honour both the god and the Maharaja. After the seashore ceremonies, the whole cavalcade returns to the temple at about 9pm, to be greeted by another gun salute. An extremely loud firework display rounds the day off.

For ten days in March, Muslims celebrate **Chandanakuamat** at the Beemapalli mosque, 5km southwest of the city on the coastal road towards the airport. The Hindu-influenced festival commemorates the anniversary of the death of Beema Beevi, a woman revered for her piety. On the first, most important, day, pilgrims converge on the mosque carrying earthenware pots decorated with flowers and containing money offerings. Activities such as the sword-form of *daharamuttu* take place inside the mosque, while outside there is dance and music. In the early hours of the morning, a flag is brought out from Beema Beevi's tomb and taken on a procession, accompanied by a *panchavadyam* drum-and-horn orchestra and caparisoned elephants, practices normally associated with Hindu festivals. Once more, the rest of the night is taken up with fireworks.

health education displays, and over 2000 dolls featuring figures in Indian costume, American presidents, gonks, Disney characters and British Beefeaters. The museum is really intended for school groups, for whom workshops are run in toy-making from recycled materials. Donations to the doll collection are welcomed.

Also on the eastern side of town, visitors can by prior arrangement watch classes at the *PS Balachandran Nair Kalari* **martial arts gymnasium** (daily, 6–8am & 6–7.30pm; Kalariyil, TC 15/854, Cotton Hill; ☎65140). Built in 1992 along traditional lines, in stone, the *kalari* fighting pit is overlooked from a height of 4m by a viewing gallery. The students, some as young as eight, train both in unarmed combat and in the use of weapons. Traditionally, the art of battle with long razorblade-like *urumi* is only taught to the teacher's successor. The school arranges short courses in kalarippayat for visitors, and can also provide guides for forest trekking. Like many kalarippayat gurus Mr Nair also works as a doctor, treating patients with herbal medicine and massage.

Accommodation

Thiruvananthapuram's mid-range and expensive **hotels** are, in general, more reasonably priced than in most state capitals, but are not concentrated in any one district. The area around **Station Road** is full of budget accommodation, which tends to get full later in the day; similarly priced and less busy alternatives can be found on **Statue Road**, which leads west from the Secretariat (halfway along MG Rd).

Arulakam, Station Rd (☎79788). Popular middle-class Indian-style hotel, close to the railway station, with some a/c rooms. ②/④.

KTDC Chaithram, Station Rd (☎75777). Modern block opposite the railway station, where the spacious rooms don't quite match the semi-swank of the lobby. A/c veg restaurant, bank, travel agent, car rental, beauty parlour, bookshop and bar. Some a/c rooms. ④.

ACCOMMODATION PRICE CODES

All **accommodation prices** in this book have been coded using the symbols below. In principle the prices given are for the least expensive double rooms in each establishment; however, some hotels, usually in category ①, offer rates per bed rather than per room. Local taxes are not included unless specifically stated. For more details, see p.34.

①	up to Rs100	④	Rs225–350	⑦	Rs750–1200
②	Rs100–150	⑤	Rs350–500	⑧	Rs1200–2200
③	Rs150–225	⑥	Rs500–750	⑨	Rs2200 and up

KTDC Mascot, Mascot Junction (☎68990). Dull modern hotel, expensive by KTDC standards, west of the north end of MG Rd. Restaurant, coffee shop, bar and swimming pool. All rooms a/c. ⑥–⑦.

Luciya Continental, East Fort (☎73443). Large modern hotel, a 10-min walk south of the railway station. 104 rooms plus "fantasy suites", restaurant, coffee shop, travel agent and shop. ⑥–⑦.

Pankaj, opposite Secretariat, MG Rd (☎76667). Very well maintained, modern hotel. Some rooms have beautiful views over trees, so too does the fifth-floor restaurant. Not all rooms are a/c. ④/⑥.

Shaji Tourist Home, Statue Rd (☎75982). Clean and cheap option, west of the Secretariat. ①.

South Park, MG Rd (☎65666). Comfortable, efficient, and geared towards business guests. Central reservation through other *Welcomgroup* hotels. Restaurant and 24-hr coffee shop. All rooms a/c. ⑦.

Swapna Tourist Home, Statue Rd (☎76891 or 76894). Popular budget lodge with no restaurant. ①.

Swaraj Lodge, Station Rd (no phone). Basic lodge, some rooms without bath. ①.

Udupi Sreenivas Tourist Home, Station Rd (☎79644). Shabby, spartan and respectable, with a useful list in the lobby of what's on at Thiruvananthapuram's 18 cinemas. ①.

Yatri Niwas, KTDC hostel, Thycaud (☎64462). In a residential area on the east of the city, 3km from Station Rd. Built in 1992, primarily for Indian students, it is the cleanest low-budget option in town. Some rooms can be shared. Cheap canteen food can be ordered in advance. ①.

YHA, near Boat Club, Veli (☎71364). Out-of-the-way hostel near the Veli bus stand, 13km from the City (East Fort) bus station. Dorm rooms plus morning and evening meals. ①.

Eating

Thiruvananthapuram is crying out for a **restaurant** specializing in delicious Keralan home-cooking. The top-range hotels maintain a good standard, but few do more than offer generalized Indian and western cuisine; the budget places are hurried and basic.

Anand Bhawan, opposite Secretariat, MG Rd. Cheap, simple restaurant near the *Pankaj*, some regional veg "meals".

Azad, MG Rd. Busy, cheap, get-it-down-quick, non-veg "meals" restaurant.

Indian Coffee House, Spencer Junction, MG Rd. Small colonial-style building, set back from the road and a good place to meet local students with good-value snack meals and coffee. There's another branch, in a bizarre spiral brick structure, near the station at East Fort.

Pankaj Hotel, opposite Secretariat, MG Rd. The fifth-floor restaurant is relaxing (see above), with a mixed menu and good-value lunch buffet; only the ground-floor restaurant is open for breakfast.

Listings

Bookstores The three main bookstores are on MG Rd: *Higginbothams* (☎79122), *Pai & Co* (☎75116), and the *India Book House* (☎75443).

Dance and Drama For Kathakali and Kutiyattam performances check with the *Margi School*, Fort High School, West Fort, or ask at the Tourist Information Centre, Park View (☎61132). This office organizes short dance performances every Saturday between September and the end of March, at the open-air *Nishagandhi Auditorium* (6.45pm, admission free).

Hospitals General Hospital, Vanchiyur; Ramakrishna Mission Hospital, Sastamangalam.

Visa Extension City Police Commissioner (☎60555), Residency Rd, near the Women's College, Thycaud (10am–5pm).

Daily domestic services from Thiruvananthapuram's **airport** include **Bombay** (2hr) on *Indian Airlines* (3pm) or *East-West* (12.15pm). *Air India*'s six weekly flights to Bombay (Sun, Mon, Tues, Thurs, & 2 on Fri) only accept passengers connecting with international flights. *Indian Airlines* fly daily to Bangalore (1hr), Kochi (30min), Goa (1hr), Madras (1hr 30min) and Delhi (4hr 30min). International flights go to **Colombo** in Sri Lanka (45min) on *Indian Airlines* (Mon, Thurs & Sat; 7.50pm) and *Air Lanka* (Tues, Wed, Fri & Sun), and **Malé** in the Maldives (30min) on *Indian Airlines* (Mon, Tues, Thurs & Sat).

Air India have offices at Museum Rd, Velayambalam Circle (☎64837), and the airport (☎71426); *Indian Airlines* are at *Air Centre*, Mascot Jctn (☎66370), and the airport (☎72228). *Air Lanka* are at Geethanjali Building, Geethanjali Hospital Rd, Vazhuthacaud (☎66475 or 63267); *Gulf Air* are c/o *Jet Air Travels*, Panavila Jctn (☎67514); and *Maldives Airways*, c/o *S&J Sales Corporation*, Glass House Building, Panavila Jctn (☎66105).

Daily northward **trains** through Kerala, taking 1hr 35min to Kollam, 3hr 40min to Kottayam, 5hr 20min to Kochi and 7hr 20min to Thrissur, include the *Kanniyakumari Express* #1082 (departs 7.25am; 45hr 15min to Bombay) – which enables you to connect with the backwater ferry from Kollam to Alappuzha – the *Trivandrum–Madras Mail* #6320 (1.30pm; 18hr to Madras), the *Kerala–Mangala Link Express* #2625 (9.40am; 53hr to Delhi), the *Kanniyakumari–Bangalore Express* #6525 (10.25am; 19hr 20min to Bangalore), and the *Malabar Express* #6029 (5.40pm; 16hr to Mangalore). The weekly *Trivandrum–Guwahati Express* #2601 (Thurs 12.50pm) goes to Madras and Calcutta (49hr).

Reserve tickets in advance from the **booking office** at the railway station (Mon–Sat 7am–1pm & 1.30–7.30pm, Sun 9am–5pm; ☎62966, ☎63066 after 6pm). Sleepers are sold throughout Kerala on a first-come, first-served basis, not on local stations' quotas.

From the long-distance KSRTC Thampanoor **bus stand** (☎71029), frequent services run to Kollam (1hr 30min) and Kochi (5hr) via Alappuzha (3hr 30min). Three buses a day go up to Kumily (Periyar Wildlife Reserve; 8hr), and one an hour to Kanniyakumari (2hr). Thiruvallar buses include Madurai (10 daily; 7hr) and Madras (4 daily; 17hr).

Travel agents include *Airtravel Enterprises*, LMS Jctn (☎60690); *Chanakya Group Travels*, St Joseph Press Building, Cotton Hill (☎65498); *Jaihind Travels*, *Hotel Magnet*, Thycaud (☎64454); *Kerala Travels*, MG Rd (☎62320); and *Tourindia*, MG Rd (☎79407).

Around Thiruvananthapuram

Although for virtually its entire 600-kilometre length the **Keralan coast** is lined with sandy beaches, rocky promontories and coconut palms, **Kovalam** is the only rural location where swimming in the sea is not considered eccentric by locals, and which offers accommodation to suit all budgets. When it gets too hot at sea level, **Ponmudi**, a bus ride away in the Cardamom hills through forest, spice and tea plantations, makes a refreshing break. Another easy excursion from Thiruvananthapuram is its predecessor as capital of Travancore, **Padmanabhapuram**, site of a magnificent palace.

Kovalam

The fishing village of **KOVALAM** may lie just 10km south from Thiruvananthapuram along the coast, but as Kerala's only **beach resort** it's becoming ever more distanced from the rest of the state. Each year greater numbers of western visitors – budget travellers and jet-setters alike – arrive in search of sun, sand and palm-fringed beaches. For many travellers it has become, with Goa (see p.679) and Mamallapuram (p.915), the third essential stop on a triangular tour of tropical south Indian paradises – or indeed just another leg of the trail along the coasts of South Asia.

Europeans have been visiting Kovalam since the 1930s, but not until hippies started to colonize the place some thirty years later were any hotels built. Even today development is relatively small-scale, the prices remain low, and it's still possible to walk for a few minutes away from the beach into village India. Slowly but surely, however, the paddy-fields back from the sea are being filled in and built over, and the current widening of the main road out from Thiruvananthapuram, lined now with advertising hoardings rather than trees, presumably heralds major changes.

Kovalam consists of three successive small crescent beaches; the southernmost, known for obvious reasons as **Lighthouse Beach**, is where most visitors spend their time. Roughly five minutes' trudge through the sand from end to end (none of it is paved), it's bordered with cheek-to-cheek low-rise lodging houses and restaurants, many of which offer only the most minimal facilities, but are constantly full with long-stay young travellers. The **lighthouse** (daily 2–4pm; max stay 15min) on the promontory at the southern end of the beach gives superb views across to Vizhinjam mosque. Semi-nude visitors are not welcome, and photography is forbidden.

The middle beach, overlooked from a rocky headland by the five-star **Ashok Radisson** resort, functions each morning as a base for local fishers, who drag a massive net through the shallows to scoop up thrashing multi-hued minnows, coiling endless piles of coir rope as they work. North of the *Ashok*, though in full view of its distinctive sloping terraces, the final beach is the least affected of all by the changing times, dotted with a few rudimentary wooden fishing vessels.

Swimming from the beaches is not always safe, as the undertow can be very strong; it's essential to follow the warnings of the safety flags. Even when the sea is calm, it's not necessarily hygienic; however, long days spent sprawling on the searing sands, or retreating under the awnings of the beach cafes, pass easily enough. Itinerant vendors wander back and forth, dangling assorted goodies under sun-burned noses; even if you resist the heavy fabrics from north India, you're bound to succumb to the blandishments of the village women who sell fresh fruits, always happy to lop the top off a cool green coconut with a deft machete-swipe.

Arrival and information

The frequent #111 **bus** from Thiruvananthapuram (East Fort; 20min) loops through Kovalam, and stops at the gates to the *Ashok Radisson* complex, at the northern end of the middle bay, where it picks up passengers for the return journey. Anyone carrying heavy bags who wants to stay by the sea (and not at the *Ashok*), should get down earlier, either at the road to the lighthouse, or at another one that leads down to the *Sea Rock* hotel. It's also possible to take an auto-rickshaw (Rs50) or taxi all the way from Thiruvananthapuram. The only **bank** is the *State Bank of India* (Mon–Fri 10.30am–2pm, Sat 10.30am–noon) at the *Ashok Radisson*.

> The long-distance **area code** for Kovalam is ☎04723; the code for **local** calls (ie from Thiruvananthapuram) is ☎54.

Accommodation

All the seafront **hotels** crammed along Lighthouse Beach fall into the budget category. There's little to choose between them, but you might as well check them out yourself because you'll pay a surcharge if you let a tout direct you to one. Rates given below are for the **high season**, generally considered as November to March; prices at other times can drop by fifty percent. Discounts are usually given for long-term stays.

Achutha and **Sumangali Lodges**, Lighthouse Beach (no phone). Five rooms in the older building at the front, and 15 better and more expensive ones in the newer two-storey building behind. ②–④.

Ashok Radisson Beach Resort (☎68010). Exclusive 5-star complex, belonging to the Govt ITDC chain. Charles Correa's sloping design has been much imitated elsewhere in India. Sea views, swimming pool, coffee shop, restaurant and shops, plus foreign exchange open to non-residents. ⑧.

Dwaraka Lodge, Lighthouse Beach (☎411). Ten decent rooms – those upstairs are more expensive – with western-style toilets. ③.

Eve's Beach, Lighthouse Beach (☎672). Cheap and basic. Six doubles, four 5-bedded rooms. Travel agent at entrance. ①–②.

Hawah Beach, Lighthouse Beach (☎431). Behind a restaurant, with free video shows. ②.

Palm Beach, Lighthouse Beach (no phone). Set back from the beach, after a row of shops. Eight rooms with fans, two face the sea. Enquire at beachside restaurant. ②/④.

Santana, Lighthouse Beach (☎234). Eight darkish but not bad rooms at ground level with shared verandah. The restaurant is often open until 3am, so you'd better enjoy a "party atmosphere". ②.

Sea Rock (☎422). The best of the beach hotels, around the headland from Lighthouse Beach. Plum rooms are the 11 sea-facing ones, with balconies. Terrace cafe and restaurant, where you can breakfast while watching the fishers haul in their nets, or feast upon seafood barbecue at night. ⑥.

Seaside Cottages, Lighthouse Beach (no phone). Eight simple cheap and clean rooms. ①.

Seaweed, Lighthouse Rd (☎391). "Away from the madness", near the lighthouse. Assorted comfortable rooms, set around a courtyard, and a pleasant rooftop restaurant. ③– ⑤.

Sunset, Lighthouse Beach (☎661). Five modern, rather kitsch sea-facing rooms above a cafe. ⑤.

Eating

Lighthouse Beach has a wide selection of **restaurants**; visitors choose either by inspecting the fresh lobster, tiger prawns, crab, squid and mussels laid out on steel trays at beach level, or simply on the basis of the music playing at each (Pink Floyd predominate; the rave scene has yet to hit Kovalam). Many places also offer "travellers" food such as banana pancakes, brown bread, peanut butter etc.

Sea Rock, *Velvet Dawn* and *Sheelas* are probably the best for open-air fish barbecues, while *Santana* offers a wide range of snacks and stays open late, with loud music. The *Seaweed*, set back a little from the beach, has a pleasant terrace restaurant and average food. The *Ashok Radisson* has an expensive coffee shop serving western-style snacks and south Indian food, and a much more expensive restaurant, specializing in elaborate fish dishes (some Keralan) and the usual upper-range hotel food.

Vizhinjam (Vilinjam)

The unassuming village of **VIZHINJAM** (pronounced *Virinyam*), 3km south along the coast from Kovalam, was once the capital of the Ay kings, the earliest dynasty in south Kerala. During the ninth century the Pandyans intermittently took control, and it was the scene of major Chola–Chera battles in the eleventh century. A number of small simple shrines survive from those times, and can be made the focus of a pleasant afternoon's stroll along quiet paths. They're best approached from the village centre, beyond a fishing community, rather than via the coast road. However, if you do walk along the coast road from Kovalam to the north side of Vizhinjam, you can't fail to be struck by the contrast; from the conspicuous consumption of a tourist resort you find yourself in a poor fishing village, where a huge modern pink mosque on the promontory overlooks a bay of tightly packed thatched huts.

For centuries, the fishermen here were kept at arm's length by the Hindu orthodox, perpetually forced into debt by the combination of low prices for their produce with the exorbitant interest charged by moneylenders on loans for boats and nets (as much as ten percent per day). However, cooperatives have recently started to arrange interest-free loans and sell fish on behalf of individuals. Without proper contact with the locals, you're not likely to be popular if you use Vizhinjam as a photo opportunity.

On the far side of the fishing bay, in the village centre, 50m down a road opposite the police station, a small unfinished eighth-century rock shrine features a carved figure of Shiva with a weapon. The **Tali Shiva** temple, reached by a narrow path from behind the Govt primary school, may mark the original centre of Vizhinjam. The simple shrine is accompanied by a group of *naga* snake statues, a reminder of Kerala's continuing cult of snake worship that survives from pre-Brahmanical times.

The grove known as **Kovil Kadu** ("temple forest") lies near the sea, ten minutes' walk from the main road in the village along Hidyatnagara Rd. Here a small enclosure contains a square Shiva shrine and a rectangular one dedicated to the goddess **Bhagavati**. Thought to date from the ninth century, these are probably the earliest structural temples in Kerala, although the Bhagavati shrine has been renovated.

Ponmudi and Peppara Wildlife Sanctuary

In the tea-growing region of the **Cardamom** (or Ponmudi) **Hills**, about 60km northeast of Thiruvananthapuram at an altitude of 1066m, the hill station of **PONMUDI** – not a town, or even a village, but merely some accommodation of a pretty minimal standard – commands breathtaking views out across the range as far as the sea.

The main reason anyone comes up here is that it serves as the only practical base for visits to the 53 square kilometres of forest set aside as **Peppara Wildlife Sanctuary**, which protects elephants, *sambar*, lion-tailed macaques, leopard, and assorted birds. Although Peppara is theoretically open all year, the main season is from January until May; check before you go with the District Forest Officer, Thiruvananthapuram Forest Division, Thiruvananthapuram (☎60637).

The beautiful drive up, via the small towns of Nedumangad and Vithura, runs along very narrow roads past areca nut, clove, rubber and cashew plantations, with first the Kavakulam and then the Kallar river close at hand. The bridge at **Kallar Junction** marks the start of the real climb. Twenty-two hairpin bends (numbered at the roadside) lead slowly up, firstly in the foothills, past great lumps of black rock and thick clumps of bamboo (*iramula*), then through the Kallar teak forest. You finally emerge into tea plantations; the temperature is noticeably cooler and, once out of the forest, the views across the hills and the plains below become truly spectacular.

Practicalities

Six daily **buses** make the 2hr 30min trip from Thiruvananthapuram to Ponmudi, via Vithura; the first is at 9.30am and the last at 3.30pm. The first bus back leaves Ponmudi at 12.30pm, and the last at 6.30pm. In 1992, the River Kallar broke its banks in freak December rains, killing a number of people, and the havoc caused may still be evident. Check that the road is safe before attempting the journey in your own vehicle.

The KTDC *Ponmudi Guest House* (☎Vithura 30; closed June & July; ①–②) has 24 rooms, a dorm, and seven cottages. Meals have to be ordered in advance, so it's worth having some provisions with you before you set out. The main building, which originally belonged to the Raja of Travancore, has pretty much lost any charm it may once have possessed, and the huge plate-glass windows of its empty canteen-like restaurant rattle disconcertingly in the wind, but views from the terrace make up for all that. Weekends tend to get lively, thanks to the beer parlour in one of the cottages.

There is also accommodation of a sort at Kallar Junction, but the four filthy double rooms at the *Golden Valley Tourist Home* (☎Vithura 494; ①) are hardly ideal.

Padmanabhapuram

Although now officially in Tamil Nadu, **PADMANABHAPURAM**, 63km southeast of Thiruvananthapuram, was the capital of Travancore between 1550 and 1750, and therefore has a far more intimate connection with the history of Kerala. For anyone with even a minor interest in Keralan painting, the **murals** of its small palace are an irresistible attraction, on a par with those at the Dutch Palace in Kochi (see p.1011).

Set in neat gravelled grounds in a quiet location away from the main road, the predominantly wooden **Padmanabhapuram Palace** (daily except Mon 9am–4.30pm) epitomizes the elegant, understated Keralan style of architecture. It is reached by crossing the main road from the bus station (see below), turning left, and then following a road on the right for a pleasant 10- or 15-minute walk through the paddy fields. The substantial walls of the palace compound serve to delimit a small village.

Against a backdrop of low hills and trees, the exterior of the palace – parts of which date back to the town's earliest days – displays a perfect combination of clean lines and gentle angles, with the sloping tiled roofs of its various interconnecting buildings broken by triangular projecting gables enclosing delicately carved screens. The whole ensemble is excellently maintained by the Archaeological Survey of India; all visitors have to be shown around by **guides**, who fortunately are very informative.

In the **entrance hall**, a verandah, a brass oil lamp hangs from an ornate ceiling carved with ninety different flowers. Shaped like a rearing horse and rider, the lamp stays inexplicably balanced, seeming to defy gravity. The Raja rested from the summer heat on the cool polished granite bed that stands in the corner. On the wall is a collection of *onamvillu*, ceremonial bows, painted with reclining Vishnus (or more properly Padmanabha), which local chieftains would present to him during the Onam festival.

Directly above the entrance, on the first floor, is the **mantrasala** or council chamber, gently illuminated through panes of coloured mica. Herbs soaking in water were put into the boxed bench seats along the front wall, as natural air-conditioning. The highly polished black floor was made from a now-lost technique using burnt coconut, egg whites, lime and sand.

The oldest part of the complex is the **Ekandamandapam** – "the lonely place". Built in 1550, it was used for rituals for the goddess Durga which typically employed *kalam ezhuttu*, elaborate floor paintings (see p.1013). A loose ring attached to a column is a tour de force of the carpenter: both ring and column are carved from a single piece of jackwood. Nearby is a *nalekettu*, the four-sided courtyard found in many Keralan houses, open to the sky and surrounded by a pillared walkway. A trapdoor once served as the entrance to a secret passageway leading to another palace, since destroyed.

The Pandya-style stone-columned **dance hall** stands directly in front of a shrine to the goddess of learning, Saraswati. The women of the royal household had to watch performances through screens on the side, and the staff, through holes in the wall from the gallery above – hardly very appealing for a night's entertainment. Steep wooden ladder-like steps, ending in trapdoors, connect the floors; a typical feature of old country houses. Belgian mirrors and Tanjore miniatures of Krishna adorn the chamber forming part of the **women's quarters**, where a swing hangs on plaited iron ropes. A four-poster bed, made from sixteen kinds of medicinal wood, dominates the **Raja's bedroom**. Its elaborate carvings depict a mass of vegetation, human figures, birds and as the central motif, the snake symbol of medicine, associated with the Greek physician Asclepius. Although the bed was presented to the Raja by the Dutch, the craftsmanship is Indian.

The **murals** for which the palace is famous – alive with detail, colour, graceful form and religious fervour – adorn the walls of the **meditation room**, used by the Raja and the heirs apparent, directly above the bedroom. Two lamps have been kept alight perpetually since the construction of the room; currently two elderly women are in charge of the flames. In recent years, the parlous state of some of the paintings has aroused concern; generations of visitors trailing their hands along the walls have clearly erased certain sections. If planned precautions have not yet been taken, it may be that the meditation room will be closed when you plan to come; when that has happened in the past, would-be visitors have had to seek special permission from the Cultural Minister or Cultural Secretary at the Govt Secretariat in Thiruvananthapuram.

Further points of interest in the palace include a **dining hall** intended for the free feeding of up to 2000 brahmins, and a 38-kilo stone which, it is said, every new recruit to the Raja's army had to raise above his head 101 times.

> ### TRAVANCORE AND THE SERVANTS OF VISNHU
>
> In front of a depiction of the god in the meditation, or prayer room, at Padmanabhapuram
> Palace lies a sword. In 1750, **Raja Marthanda Varma** symbolically presented this
> weapon to Padmanabha, the god Vishnu, who reclines on the sacred serpent Anantha in
> the midst of the cosmic ocean, and thereby dedicated the kingdom of Travancore to
> Vishnu. From that day, the Raja took the title of Padmanabhadasa ("servant of
> Padmanabha"), and ruled as a servant of the god.
>
> Thus Travancore belonged to Vishnu, and the Raja was merely its custodian – a spiri-
> tual, and presumably legal, loophole which is said to have proved invaluable in restricting
> the power of the British in Travancore to the installation of a British Resident.

Practicalities

Frequent **buses** run to Padmanabhapuram (heading for Nagercoil and Kanyakumari)
from Thiruvananthapuram's Thampanur station. If you're determined to see
Padmanabhapuram, Kanyakumari and Suchindram in one day, leave the city early to
arrive when the palace opens at 9am. Seats are harder to come by on the way back, but
with luck not all the passengers will be going right the way to Thiruvananthapuram.

The area around the bus station, being on the NH47, is noisy and dirty. It's better to
get **refreshment** from the *chaiya*-cum-food and "cool drinks" shops inside the outer
walls of the palace. Just outside the inner gate you can usually find tender **coconuts**.

Kollam (Quilon)

One of the oldest ports of the Malabar coast, **KOLLAM** (pronounced *Koillam*, and
previously known as Quilon), 74km northwest of Thiruvananthapuram and 85km south
of Alappuzha, was once at the centre of the international spice trade. The sixteenth-
century Portuguese writer Duarte Barbossa described it as a "very great city with a
right good haven", which was visited by "Moors, Heathen and Christians in great
numbers", and stated that "a great store" of pepper was to be found there. In fact, the
port flourished from the very earliest times, trading amicably with the Phoenicians,
Arabs, Persians, Greeks, Romans and Chinese. Its importance is demonstrated by the
fact that Kerala's modern calendar is associated with the town, measuring from 825
AD, the beginning of the "Kollamera" (although no one knows quite why).

Nowadays, Kollam is chiefly of interest as one of the entry or exit points to the backwaters of Kerala (see p.1001), and most travellers simply stay overnight en route to or
from Alappuzha. The **town** itself, sandwiched between the sea and the Ashtamudi
("eight inlets") lake, is less exciting than its history might suggest. It's a typically
sprawling Keralan market community, with a few characterful old tiled wooden houses
and winding backstreets, kept busy with the commercial interests of coir, cashew nuts
(a good local buy), pottery, aluminium and fishery industries. The missable ruins of
Tangasseri fort (3km from the centre) are the last vestiges of colonial occupation.

Arrival and information

The **boat jetty** (for ferry details, see p.1001) and **bus stand** are close together on the
edge of Ashtamudi Lake. Bookable express buses are available south to
Thiruvananthapuram (3hr 30min) and north to Kochi (3hr 30min) via Alappuzha (2hr).

The **railway station** is on the east of town, a three-kilometre auto-rickshaw ride
from the jetty. Three daily trains each way run to Ernakulam (3hr 30min) and
Thiruvananthapuram (1hr 30min) and beyond. On platform 4, the tiny **Tourist
Information Counter** (Mon–Sat 9am–12.30pm & 1.30–5pm; ☎0474/72558) offers an

excellent service. They will book hotels for travellers even outside the state; you have to pay one night in advance, but the only extra charge is for the phone calls.

Accommodation and eating

The most congenial **places to stay** are outside the town, across Ashtamudi Lake from the main jetty (easy enough to get to by auto-rickshaw, but more difficult to return). The old British Residency, now a Government Guest House, is the best of the bunch; when that's full, the KTDC is a less characterful but well-situated alternative, with a good restaurant. Other places to **eat** include the reasonable *Indian Coffee House* on Main Road, and *Guru Prasad*, a little way along, which serves decent veg "meals".

Govt Guest House, 3km out, by Ashtamudi Lake (☎0474/70356). Characterful Euro-Keralan building, with curved tiled roof and verandahs, in a vast compound. Ye olde British furniture in cavernous spaces, but only 5 rooms. Boats are available for rent on the lake. Only breakfast served. ①.

Karthika, Chinnakkada, 1.5km from bus and train (☎0474/76240). Eighty rooms, restaurant, bar. Acceptable for a night. ②.

KTDC Yatri Nivas, across from the jetty (☎0474/78638). Modern, clean rooms (2 a/c) overlooking the lake. Good restaurant with south Indian snacks and, as always with KTDC, a beer parlour. ②.

Lakeview, Mulankadakam, Thirumullavaram, 3km northwest on the Alappuzha road (☎0474/4669). New, but already crumbling at the edges – a shame, as the grounds are pleasantly sited next to the lake and colourful fishing boats. Some a/c rooms, restaurant. ②–④.

Railway Retiring Rooms, first floor of railway station. Spacious, clean, and very cheap. ①.

Sea Bee, Jetty Rd (☎0474/75371). Big hotel, close to the bus station and jetty, but poorly maintained. Some a/c rooms, restaurant, bar. ②.

Sudarsan, Parameswar Nagar (☎0474/75322). Central and popular. Rooms of different standards, some with a/c and TV. Busy, dark a/c restaurant with a white plaster *Last Supper* at one end and a TV at the other. Large Indian and Chinese menu, though not all is necessarily available, bar. ②–④.

Varkala

Long known to Keralans as a place of pilgrimage, **VARKALA**, 20km southeast of Kollam and 54km northwest of Thiruvananthapuram, is these days drawing more and more foreign visitors, who see the splendid **beach** and cliffs 1.5km beyond the town as a quiet, unspoiled alternative to Kovalam.

Papa Nashini ("sin destroyer") beach is associated with ancestor worship. Devotees come here after praying at Varkala's **Janardhana Swamy** temple (said to be over 2000 years old) to bring the ashes of departed relatives for "final rest". A small government Nature Cure Hospital, at its north end, was set up to benefit from three **natural springs**, and take advantage of the sea air, said to boost the health of asthma sufferers.

An **ashram** on Sivagiri Hill at the eastern end of Varkala attracts pilgrim devotees of Shri Narayana Guru, a saint who died here in 1922. Born into the low *ezhava* caste, he fought orthodoxy with a philosophy of social reform ("one caste, one religion, one God for man"), which included the consecration of temples with an open-door policy to all castes, and had a profound effect on the "upliftment" of the untouchables.

Practicalities

Regular **buses** run to Varkala from Thiruvananthapuram's Thampanoor stand (1hr 30min) and Kollam (40min). Some buses go to the beach, others only as far as the town, a five-minute auto-rickshaw ride away. There are few **accommodation** options, though the scheduled new five-star *Taj Group* hotel is bound to encourage more building. The *Govt Guest House* (☎Varkala 2227; ①), near the beach bus stop, has seven simple rooms. Food must be ordered in advance; the staff don't speak English, so any Malayalam you know will help. Nearby, the *J A Tourist Home* (①) offers basic rooms, a restaurant and bar. Some visitors also rent space in private houses. Two beach shack **cafes** serve simple Keralan food, one charmingly called the *Seaview Restorunt*.

Kayamkulam

The town of **KAYAMKULAM**, served by (non-express) buses running north from Kollam to Alappuzha, was once the centre of its own small kingdom, which after a battle in 1746 came under the control of Travancore's king Marthanda Varma. In the eighteenth century the area was famous for its spices, particularly pepper and cinnamon. The Abbé Reynal claimed that the Dutch exported some two million pounds of pepper each year, one-fifth of it from Kayamkulam. At this time, the kingdom was known also for the skill of its army, fifteen thousand Nayars (Kerala's martial caste).

Set in a tranquil garden, the dilapidated eighteenth-century **Krishnapuram Palace** (Tues–Sat 10am–4.30pm) is imbued with Keralan grace, constructed largely of wood, with gabled roofs and rooms opening out onto internal courtyards. It's now a museum, but unlike the palace at Padmanabhapuram (see p.995), with which it shares some similarities, the whole place is in great need of restoration. So few visitors ever find their way here that the motivation for upkeep must be minimal.

The collection inside is dusty, poorly labelled and neglected. A display case contains *puja* ceremony utensils and oil lamps, some of which are arranged in an arc known as a *prabhu*, placed behind a temple deity to provide a halo of light. Fine miniature *panchaloha* ("five-metal" bronze alloy, with gold as one ingredient) figures include the water god Varuna, several Vishnus, and a minuscule worshipping devotee. Small stone columns carved with serpent deities were recovered from local houses.

The prize exhibit is a huge **mural** of the classical Keralan school, in muted ochrereds and blue-greens, measuring over fourteen square metres, which depicts **Gajendra Moksha** – the salvation of Gajendra, king of the elephants. In the tenth-century Sanskrit *Bhagavata Purana*, the story is told of a Pandyan king, Indrayumna, a devotee of Vishnu cursed by the sage Agastya to be born again as an elephant. One day, while sporting with his wives at the edge of a lake, his leg was seized by a crocodile whose grip was so tight that Gajendra was held captive for years. Finally, in desperation the elephant called upon his chosen deity (*ishtadevata*) Vishnu, who immediately appeared, riding his celestial bird/man vehicle, Garuda, and destroyed the crocodile.

The centre of the painting is dominated by a dynamic portrayal of Garuda about to land, with huge spread wings and a facial expression denoting *raudra* (fury); the compassionate features of the multi-armed Vishnu are in stark contrast. Smaller figures of Gajendra, in mid-trumpet, and his assailant are shown to the right. As with all paintings in the Kerala style, every inch is packed with detail. Bearded sages, animals, mythical beasts and forest plants surround the main figures. The outer edges are decorated with floriate borders which, at the bottom, form a separate triptych-like panel showing Balakrishna, the child Krishna, attended by adoring females.

Rooms upstairs, reached via trapdoor stairs, are empty save for a display case of swords and shields. From here it's possible to gain access to the surrounding balconies, although they're probably not very safe. In the garden, beneath a small *mandapa* enclosure, is a stone Buddha figure recovered from a well at Karunagapalli. Other such finds have led scholars to believe that the area was once an important Buddhist centre.

Karunagapalli

At a quiet spot just outside the small town of **KARUNAGAPALLI**, 23km north of Kollam on the NH47 towards Alappuzha, it's possible to watch the construction of traditional **kettu vallam** ("tied boats"). These long cargo boats, a familiar sight on the backwaters, are built entirely without the use of nails. Each jackwood plank is **sewn** to the next with coir rope, and then the whole is coated with a caustic black resin made from boiled cashew kernels. With careful maintenance they last for generations.

Karunagapalli is best visited independently as a day trip from Kollam; regular **buses** pass through on the way to Alappuzha. One daytime **train**, #6525, leaves Kollam at

VALLAM CRUISES AND THE HOUSEBOAT AT KARUNAGAPALLI

Groups of up to ten people can charter a *vallam* moored at **Karunagapalli** for a day's **cruise** on the backwaters (see p.1001). The boat is simply furnished, with comfortable cane chairs and a raised central platform where passengers can laze on cushions. There is a toilet on board and cool drinks can be made available. Sections of the curved roof of wood and plaited palms open out to provide shade and allow uninterrupted views. Whether powered by local gondoliers or by sail, the trip is as quiet and restful (at least for the passenger) as you could possibly want. If not cheap, at around Rs3000 for the day, the luxury is well worth experiencing.

A second *vallam* was at the time of writing being converted into a houseboat for longer trips, equipped with two bedrooms. A kitchen and cook will also be provided.

For bookings, call *Tourindia*, MG Rd, Thiruvananthapuram (☎0471/79407 or 79437).

11.55am, arriving at Karunagapalli at 12.30, but you'd have to get a bus back. On reaching the bus stand or train station, ask an auto-rickshaw to take you to the boatyard of the *vallam asharis*, the boat carpenters. The boatbuilders are friendly and willing to let visitors watch them work. In the shade of palm trees at the edge of the water, some weave palm leaves, others twist coir strands into rope, and craftsmen repair the boats. Soaking in the shallows nearby are palm leaves, to use for thatch, and coconut husks for coir rope. If you want to buy a *vallam* you'll need more than *lakh* (100,000) *rupees*.

Accommodation is available, but not recommended, at *Achutha Lodge* (☎7203; ①) on the NH47. Close to the boatyard is a small, plain and simple "meals" restaurant.

Alappuzha

Under its former appellation of Alleppey, **ALAPPUZHA**, roughly midway between Kollam (85km south) and Kochi (64km north), is another romantic and historic name from Kerala's past. It was one of the best-known ports along the coast of Malabar, and tourist literature is fond of referring to it as "Venice of the East", but while it may be full of interconnecting **canals**, there the resemblance ends. Alappuzha is in reality a bustling town, chiefly significant in the coir (coconut fibre) industry, which accounts for much of the traffic on its waterways.

Alappuzha remains prominent on the tourist trail as one of the major centres for **backwater boat trips**, served by ferries to Kollam and Kottayam in particular. Most visitors stay just one night – but there's no reason why that shouldn't be enjoyable enough. No special sights demand attention, but the town is pleasant to stroll around, sufficiently small for exploration of its main street to take around twenty minutes, and with plenty of activity to watch on the canals.

Alappuzha really comes alive on the second Saturday of August, in the depths of the rainy season, when it serves as the venue for one of Kerala's major spectacles – the Nehru Trophy **snakeboat race**. This event, first held in 1952, is based on the traditional Keralan enthusiasm for racing magnificently decorated long boats, with raised rears designed to resemble the hood of a cobra. More than enthusiastically powered by up to 150 singing and shouting oarsmen, scores of boats take part, and Alappuzha is packed with thousands of spectators. A similar race can be seen at Aranmula (p.1003).

Arrival and information

The KSRTC **bus stand**, on the east of town, is served by half-hourly buses to Kollam (3hr) and Thiruvananthapuram (5hr), and to Ernakulam (2hr); less frequent buses run to Kottayam, Thrissur and Palakaad. The **boat jetty** is just one minute's walk west from the bus stand; backwater ferries are detailed opposite.

KUTTANAD: THE BACKWATERS OF KERALA

One of the most memorable experiences available to travellers in India – even those on the lowest of budgets – is the opportunity to take a boat journey on the **backwaters of Kerala**. The area known as **KUTTANAD** stretches for 75km from Kollam (Quilon) in the south to Kochi (Cochin) in the north, sandwiched between the sea and the hills. This bewildering labyrinth of shimmering waterways, composed of lakes, canals, rivers and rivulets, is lined with dense tropical greenery, and preserves rural Keralan lifestyles that are completely hidden from the road.

The views change from narrow canals and dense vegetation to open vistas and dazzling green paddy fields. Homes, farms, churches, mosques and temples can be glimpsed among the trees, and every so often you might catch the blue flash of a king-fisher, or the green of a parakeet. If you're lucky enough to be in a boat without a motor, at times the peace will be broken only by the squawking of crows and the occasional film song from a distant radio. Day-to-day life is lived on and beside the water. Some families live on tiny pockets of land, with just enough room for a simple house, yard and their own boat. They bathe and wash their clothes – sometimes their buffaloes too, muddy from ploughing the fields – at the water's edge, while you often pass villagers standing up to their necks in water, far from the banks and busy with impenetrable sub-aquatic chores.

Traditional Keralan longboats, *kettu vallam*, glide past, powered both by gondolier-like boatmen with poles and by sail. Often they look on the point of sinking, laden with heavy-weight cargo with water lapping perilously over the edge. Fishermen work from rowing boats or operate massive Chinese nets on the shore.

Coconut trees at improbable angles form shady canopies, and occasionally you pass under simple curved bridges. Here and there basic drawbridges can be raised on ropes, but major bridges are few and far between; most people rely on boatmen to ferry them across the water to connect with roads and bus services, a constant criss-crossing of the waters from dawn until dusk (a way of life beautifully represented in the visually stunning film *Piravi*, by Keralan director Shaji). The boatmen weave between poles sticking out of the water to indicate dangerous shallows. The **African moss** that often carpets the surface of the narrower waterways, incidentally, may look attractive to the visitor, but is a menace to small craft traffic and starves underwater life of light.

Routes and Practicalities

There are numerous backwater routes to choose from, while vessels range from local ferries, through chauffeur-driven speedboats offered by upmarket hotels such as the *Malabar* in Kochi, to customized *kettu vallam*. Much the most popular excursion is the full-day journey from **Kollam** (Quilon) to **Alappuzha** (Alleppey) or vice versa. All sorts of private hustlers may offer you their services, but the basic choice lies between boats run by the Alleppey Tourism Development Co-op Society, which go every other day, and the State Water Transport Department, whose "commuter" boats in theory operate daily but have recently become less dependable. ATDC charge Rs100 for their 8hr 30min trip through the more picturesque narrow canals, and make five stops; SWTD charge Rs56 for 8hr trips through broader waterways, making just two stops – at Ayiramthang near Kayamkulam, 3hr 30min out of Kollam, and Tontapally, 2hr further on. Both services are the equivalent of local buses; don't assume that you'll necessarily have a seat all the way, or that you'll be able to buy anything other than the most basic food and drink.

From Alappuzha, ATDC (based at *Karthika Tourist Home*; ☎0477/3462) depart on Mon, Wed and Fri at 9.45am, while SWTD (whose office is on Jetty Rd) are scheduled to leave daily at 10am. There are also 11 daily departures to **Kottayam** (Rs5; 2hr 30min), one every other day to **Kochi** (noon; 6hr), and one daily to Kumarakom (3pm; 2hr 30min). Noisy speedboats can be rented for Rs300 per hour.

From Kollam, the ATDC boat departs at 9.45am on Tues, Thurs and Sat only, while SWTD supposedly leave daily at 10am. Shorter trips are available to Kapapuzha and Guhanandapuram (2hr), if you don't have time for a full-day excursion.

From Kottayam, there are 11 daily boats to Alappuzha (2hr 30min, Rs5; first at 7.30am, last 8.30pm). The journey includes 21 stops.

As the backwaters prevent **trains** from continuing south beyond Alappuzha, only two major daily services depart from the **railway station**, 3km southwest of the jetty – the *Steel City Express* #8690 to Ernakulam Junction, at 5.35am, and the *Alleppey–Madras Express* #6042, to Ernakulam Junction and Thrissur, at 3.15pm.

Of the town's two **tourist information offices**, the ATDC office (☎0477/3462) at the *Karthika Tourist Home* across the canal from the jetty is probably the better, as it sells tickets for their ferries and rents out boats. The Alappuzha Tourism Promotion Council (☎0477/62308) on Jetty Rd next to the boat jetty is rather lackadaisical.

Accommodation and eating

Alappuzha's choice of **accommodation** is uninspiring – the cheapest lodges seem to regard the fact that most visitors stay only a single night as a disincentive to raise standards. If you're on a budget you might prefer to pass through without stopping at all. Fine dining is pretty much restricted to the better hotels. There is an *Indian Coffee House*, 2km south of the jetty near the railway station, but apart from the coffee itself it's not one of the better branches.

Alleppey Prince, AS Rd (☎0477/3752). The poshest option, 2km north of the jetty. All rooms a/c. Private backwater trips are organized, and occasional Kathakali dance performances staged. Reasonable, varied restaurant, and a pool. ⑥.

Karthika Tourist Home, Kathiyani Rd (☎0477/5524). Just across the canal, opposite the jetty. 20 non-a/c rooms, some with bath, and fairly decent for the price. ①–②.

Kuttanad Tourist Home, by the KSRTC bus station (☎0477/61354). Clean, basic rooms (some a/c). Roof restaurant, serving south Indian, western and Chinese dishes, and bar. Very good value. ②.

Sheeba Lodge, near Municipal Maidan (☎0477/4871). North of jetty canal. 20 rooms, all non-a/c. Reasonable for the price. ①.

Kottayam

The busy commercial centre of **KOTTAYAM** is strategically located between the backwaters to the west and the spice, tea and rubber plantations, forests, and the mountains of the Western Ghats to the east, 76km southeast of Kochi and 37km northwest of Alappuzha. Most visitors come here on the way somewhere else – foreigners take short backwater trips to Alappuzha or set off to **Periyar Wildlife Sanctuary**, while Ayappa devotees pass through en route to the forest temple at Sabarimala (see p.1007).

Kottayam's long history of **Syrian Christian** settlement is reflected by the presence of two thirteenth-century churches on a hill 5km northwest of the centre. Two eighth-century Nestorian stone crosses with Pahlavi and Syriac inscriptions, installed on either side of the elaborately decorated altar of the **Valliapalli** ("big") church, are probably the earliest solid evidence of Christianity in India. The interior of the nearby **Cheriapalli** ("small") church, in contrast, is covered with lively, naive paintings, thought to have been executed by a Portuguese artist.

Arrival and information

Kottayam's central **bus stand** is an important stop on routes to major towns. Four of the frequent buses to Periyar (3–4hr) each day go on to Madurai, in Tamil Nadu (7hr). The railway station (2km from the centre) sees a constant flow of traffic between Thiruvananthapuram and points north. For details of backwater trips, see p.1001.

You are defied to get any useful information from the booth that serves as the **Tourist Information Office**, Central Junction, but you may want to use their STD phone. Tourism enquiries get a more sympathetic ear at the *Hotel Aiswarya*; see below.

Accommodation and eating

Kottayam has a good choice of mid-range **hotels**. If you're not pressed for time, stay on the outskirts away from the noise. Two new (expensive) hotels in the backwaters near Kumarakom make appealing alternatives (see below). There are basic "meals" **restaurants** in the centre, such as the *Black Stone*, close to the bus station on TB Rd, and there's a fairly dingy *Indian Coffee House* on TB Rd, but for an evening out, the lovely lakeside *Vembanad Lake Resort* definitely wins.

Aida, MC Rd, 5km from the centre, 2km from train station (☎0481/61391). Forty clean, decent-sized rooms (8 a/c), some with TV. Roadside rooms are noisy. ③–④.

Anjali, KK Rd, 2km from train station, close to the square, downtown (☎0481/3661). Comfortable *Casino* group hotel with international and Chinese restaurants and bar. All 27 rooms are a/c. ④–⑤.

Green Park, Kurian Uthup Rd, Nagampadam (☎0481/563331 or 563243). Modern hotel, near train station and centre; more geared to businessmen than tourists but good value with decent rooms, a bar and two restaurants. Non-a/c: ②, a/c: ③.

KTDC Aiswarya, Thirunakkara (☎0481/61256). Near bus stand and jetty. Simply furnished modern block; lacks character, but the staff are friendly and the rooms, both a/c and non-a/c, good (deluxe rooms with TV are very spacious). Restaurant, beer parlour, 24hr room service. ②–③.

Vembanad Lake Resort, Kodimatha (☎0481/564866). Large, simply furnished modern cottages (4 a/c) in pleasant gardens beside Lake Vembanad, 2km from town and bus station. The restaurant has a good selection of Indian, western and Chinese dishes, including seafood. Tables are set outside in a lakeside garden as well as on a moored *kettu vallam* long boat – gorgeous at night. ④–⑤.

Around Kottayam

Some of Kerala's most attractive scenery lies within easy access of Kottayam. Probably the ideal destination for a day trip – it also has some wonderful accommodation – is the **Kumarakom** bird sanctuary, in the backwaters to the west. **Aranmula** to the south is one of the last villages still making *kannady* metal mirrors, and has a Krishna temple that organizes a ritual "non-competitive" boat race. The Mahadeva temple at **Ettumanur**, a short way north of Kottayam, is known to devotees as the home of a dangerous and wrathful Shiva, and to art lovers as a sublime example of temple architecture, adorned with wood carvings and murals.

Kumarakom

KUMARAKOM, 15km west of Kottayam, is technically an island on Vembanad Lake. Right in the thick of a tangle of lush tropical waterways, it can be enjoyably reached on a once-daily ferry from Alappuzha (see p.1001), but most people find it more convenient to come by bus from Kottayam (every 10min). The peak time to visit the **Kumarakom Bird Sanctuary** (daily 10am–6pm) is between November and March, when it serves as a winter home for a wide range of migratory birds, most of them from Siberia. Noteworthy species include the darter or snake bird, little cormorant, night heron, golden-backed woodpecker, crow pheasant, white-breasted water hen and tree pie.

Next to the sanctuary, set in lovely waterside gardens, a refurbished colonial bungalow that once belonged to a family of Christian missionaries and rubber planters is now a superb little luxury hotel. *The Taj Garden Retreat* (☎048192/377; ⑦) has just five rooms, plus a restaurant that given advance notice can be very good indeed. At the time this book went press, the *Casino Group* (☎048192/491) was due to open an attractive upper-range hotel nearby, built in traditional Keralan style beside the water.

Aranmula

The village of **ARANMULA** is another appealing day trip – so long as you start early – from Kottayam, 30km south of the town and 10km beyond Chengannur. Its ancient temple is dedicated to Parthasarathy, which was the name under which Krishna acted

---

CHRISTIANITY IN KERALA

The history of Kerala's **Christians** – who today represent twenty-one percent of the population – is said to date back to the first century AD, some three centuries before Christianity received official recognition in Europe. These days, the five main branches among a bewildering assortment of churches are the **Nestorians** (confined mainly to Thrissur and Ernakulam), **Roman Catholics** (found throughout Kerala), **Syrian Orthodox Church** (previously known as the Jacobite Syrians), **Marthoma Syrians** (a splinter group of the Syrian Orthodox), and the Anglican **Church of South India**.

A legend, widely believed in Kerala but the object of academic scepticism, states that **St Thomas** the Apostle – "Doubting Thomas" – landed on the Malabar coast in AD 52, where he converted several Brahmins and others, and founded seven churches. Muziris, his first port of call, has been identified as Kodungallur (see p.1025); the traditional accounts of Jews who arrived there in AD 68 state that they encountered a Christian community. Their number was augmented in the fourth century by an influx of Syrians belonging to seven tribes from Baghdad, Nineveh and Jerusalem, under the leadership of the merchant Knayi Thoma (Thomas of Cana).

Christians gradually came to the forefront as traders, and eventually gained special privileges from the local rulers. The early communities followed a liturgy in the **Syriac language** (a dialect of Aramaic). Latin was introduced by missionaries who visited Kollam in the Middle Ages; once the Portuguese turned up, in 1498, a large community of **Latin Christians** developed, particularly on the coast, and came under the jurisdiction of the Pope. In the middle of the seventeenth century, with the ascendancy of the Dutch, part of the church broke away from Rome, and local bishops were appointed through the offices of the Jacobite Patriarch in Antioch.

During the nineteenth century, the Anglican church amalgamated with certain "free" churches, to form the Church of South India. At the same time, elements in the Syrian church advocated the replacement of Syriac with the local language of Malayalam. The resultant schism led to the creation of the new Marthoma Syrian Church.

Christmas is an important festival in Kerala; during the weeks leading up to Dec 25, innumerable star-shaped lamps are put up outside shops and houses, illuminating the night and identifying followers of the faith.

---

as Arjuna's charioteer during the bloody Kurekshetra war recorded in the *Mahabharata*, and the guise in which he expounded the *Bhagavad Gita*. Each year towards the end of the Onam festival (Aug/Sept), when a **Snakeboat Regatta** is celebrated as part of the temple rituals, crowds line the banks of the River Pampa to cheer on the thrusting longboats (similar to those seen at Alappuzha; see p.1000).

Aranmula is also known for manufacturing extraordinary *kannady* **metal mirrors**, produced, using the lost wax technique, with an alloy of copper, silver, brass, lead and bronze. Once a prerequisite of royal households, these ornamental mirrors are now exceedingly rare; only two master craftsmen, Subramanian and Arjun Asary, and their families, still make them. The most modest models cost in the region of Rs300, while custom-made mirrors can cost as much as Rs 50,000. Enquiries should be made at the *Vishwasarthy Handicrafts Centre*, Aranmula.

The **Vijana Kala Vedi Cultural Centre**, at Tarayil Mukku Junction in Aranmula, offers visitors ways of "experiencing traditional India through the study of art and village life." Introductory courses are offered in Kathakali, Mohiniattam, Bharatanatyam dances, woodcarving and mural painting.

Ettumanur

The magnificent Mahadeva temple at **ETTUMANUR**, 12km north of Kottayam on the road to Ernakulam, features a circular shrine, fine woodcarving and one of the earliest (sixteenth-century) and most celebrated of Keralan murals. Although the shrine is open to Hindus only, foreigners may be allowed to see the painting – a 4m by 3m panel on its west, main, *gopura* entranceway. It depicts Nataraja – Shiva – executing a cosmic *tandava* dance, trampling evil underfoot in the form of a demon. Swathed in cobras, he stands on one leg in a wheel of gold, with his matted locks fanning out amid a mass of flowers and snakes. Outside the wheel, a crowd of celestials are in attitudes of devotion. Musical accompaniment is courtesy of Krishna on flute, three-headed Brahma on cymbals, and, playing the copper *mizhavu*, the holiest and most ancient of Keralan drums, Shiva's special rhythm expert Nandikesvara.

The deity of this temple is Shiva in one of his most terrible aspects, described as *vaddikasula vada*, "one who takes his dues with interest" and is "difficult to please". His predominant mood is *raudra* (fury) and it might be worth remembering as you inspect the gateway that Mahadeva faces west, in your direction . . .

Ettumanur's ten-day **annual festival** (Feb/March) reflects the wealth of the temple, with elaborate celebrations including music. On the most important days, the eighth and tenth, priests bring out figures of elephants, fashioned from 210 pounds of gold, presented in the eighteenth century by Marthanda Varma, the Raja of Travancore.

Periyar Wildlife Sanctuary

One of the largest wildlife reserves in India, the **Periyar Wildlife Sanctuary** occupies 777 square kilometres of the Cardamom Hills region of the Western Ghats. The majority of its many visitors come in the hope of seeing **tigers** and **leopards** – and are disappointed, as the few that remain very wisely keep their distance, and there's only a slight chance of a glimpse even at the height of the dry season (April/May). However, there are plenty of other animals: elephant, *sambar*, wild pig, Malabar flying squirrel, *gaur*, stripe-necked mongoose and over 260 species of birds including Nilgiri wood pigeon, blue-winged parakeet, white-bellied tree pie, laughing thrushes and flycatchers.

Periyar lies at cool altitudes ranging from 750 to 1500 metres, just over 100km east of Kottayam, and centres on a vast artificial **lake**, created by the British in 1895 to supply water to the drier parts of neighbouring Tamil Nadu, around Madurai. The royal family of Travancore, anxious to preserve favourite hunting grounds from the encroachment of tea plantations, declared it to be a Reserve Forest, and built the Edapalayam Lake Palace to accommodate their guests in 1899. It expanded as a wildlife reserve in 1933, and once again when it became part of **Project Tiger** in 1979.

Seventy percent of the protected area, which is divided into Core, Buffer and Tourist zones, is covered with evergreen and semi-evergreen forest. The **Tourist zone** – logically enough, the part accessible to casual visitors – surrounds the lake, and consists mostly of semi-evergreen and deciduous woodland interspersed with grassland, both on hilltops and in the valleys. Although excursions on the lake are the standard way to experience the park, you can get much more out of a visit by walking with a local guide in a small group, or, especially, staying in basic accommodation away from the crowd.

Getting to Periyar

Travellers heading for the sanctuary have first to make their way to the small tea and spice market village of **Kumily**, 4km short of the park entrance at **Thekkady**, on the northwest of the reserve. Kumily is served by **buses** from **Kottayam** (every 30 min; 3–4hr), **Ernakulam** (10 daily; 6hr), and **Madurai** in Tamil Nadu (frequent service; 5hr 30min); most of these terminate at *Aranya Nivas*, inside the sanctuary.

The pothole-filled road that winds through the undulating hills up to Periyar from Ernakulam and Kottayam makes for a very long slow drive, but it gives wonderful views across the Ghats, and is blissfully quiet when you stop. The whole route is dotted with grand churches among the trees, while the numerous jazzy roadside shrines to St Francis or the Virgin Mary could have been designed for 1950s sci-fi movies – a charming Keralan blend of ancient and modern. Once you've climbed into Idukki District, the mountains get truly spectacular.

KTDC runs hectic and uncomfortable **weekend tours** to Periyar from Kochi, calling at Kadamattom and Idukki Dam en route (see p.1010; Sat 7.30am–Sun 8pm).

Boat trips and walking

All boat and guide services are organized by the **Forest Department**, whose office (daily 9am–5pm) stands close to the shore of the lake. Tickets for **boat trips** on the lake (7am–4pm; Rs50 for open upper deck, Rs25 enclosed lower deck), however, are sold on the jetty close by. Although it would be unusual to see many animals from the boat – engine noise, and the presence of a hundred other people, make sure of that – you might spot a family group of elephants by the water's edge. To maximize your chances, take the earliest boat at 7am (wear something warm). At this hour, the mist rises over the lake and hills as you chug past dead trees, now bird perches, that were never cleared when the valley was flooded. You could also consider renting your own boat (Rs300 for 6 passengers, again at the jetty).

Group trekking is available between 9am and noon for Rs12 per head, but it's more enjoyable by far to rent a **private guide** to take you walking in the forest. This costs under Rs100 for three hours for two or three people; longer trips are negotiable. The guides go out of their way to point out anything of interest, and will reassure you that the fresh elephant dung on the path is really nothing to worry about.

Accommodation and eating inside the sanctuary

For adventurous travellers, the star attraction of Periyar has to be the prospect of staying in the Forest Department **watchtowers** (①) at Edappalayam and Manakkavala, or in the *Rest House* (②) at Edappalayam, all of which are reached by boat across the lake. On the far side, it takes 25 minutes to walk to Edappalayam from the shore, and 40 minutes to Manakkavala. The *Rest House* has one double room (bring food for the watchman to cook), while to each of the two-person watchtowers guests need to bring sleeping bags, plus food, water, matches, and candles. This accommodation (intended for forest employees) is often occupied, but those visitors staying in the area for more than a couple of days can often make an advance booking, by contacting the lakeside Forest Department office (daily 9am–5pm).

Also in the park, KTDC *Periyar House* (☎04869/2026; ①–④), five minutes before the lake on the way in, has single rooms and pricier doubles – ask for one facing the lake – plus a restaurant and bar. Its common balcony overlooks the monkey-filled woods that lead down to the lakeside. Nearer the lake, the much more upmarket KTDC *Aranya Nivas* (☎04869/2023; ⑧) offers comfortable rooms, not all a/c, a fine multi-cuisine restaurant and bar, and a pretty garden. It also offers two luxury suites in its *Lake Palace* annexe (⑧–⑨), a boat ride away in the forest. If you're booked here you must arrive by 4pm to catch the boat. You are unlikely to get into any of the KTDC hotels without prior reservation – they should be bookable through their offices elsewhere.

Accommodation outside the sanctuary; Kumily

Budget travellers in **KUMILY** can choose from the basic *Lake Queen Tourist Home*, Thekkady Junction (☎2086; ①), the rooms and dorm of the popular *Holiday Home* (①), and the wider range at the *Mukkumkal Tourist Home* (☎2070; ①–③).

More comfortable places to stay can be found on the Kumily–Thekkady road. The trendy new (terrifically eco-conscious) *Spice Village* (☎2314; ⑧) has smart and comfortable rooms in thatched huts, staff in quasi-local dress, and a swimming pool, shop and restaurant. Accommodation in the less swish *Ambadi* (☎2011; ①–⑤) includes pleasant cottages and a cheap dorm, and it has a good restaurant. The friendly *Coffee Inn*, on the Thekkady Rd, has a little garden, serves "travellers-style" food (mashed potato, peanut butter, brown bread, toast etc), and is often crowded.

Kumily is also a good place to buy **spices**; at the *Kerala Spices Centre*, a small, wonderfully smelly shop on Thekkady Rd, you might even be offered a delicious cup of cardamom tea. Shops and some hotels organize excursions to spice plantations and, unhappily, to local Mannan and Palayan tribal villages, a practice that only further demeans an already disenfranchized group.

Kochi (Cochin) and Ernakulam

The venerable city of **KOCHI** (long known as Cochin), Kerala's prime tourist destination, spreads across islands and promontories in a stunning location between the Arabian Sea and backwaters. Its main sections – modern **Ernakulam**, in the east, and the old districts of **Mattancherry** and **Fort Cochin** on a peninsula in the west – are linked by a complex system of ferries, and distinctly less romantic bridges.

Although most visitors end up staying in Ernakulam, Fort Cochin and Mattancherry are very much the focus of interest, where the city's extraordinary history of foreign influence and settlement is reflected in an assortment of architectural styles. During a wander through their narrow lanes, you'll stumble upon spice markets, Chinese fishing nets, a synagogue, a Portuguese palace, India's first European church, Dutch homes, and a village green that could have been transported from England's Home Counties.

Kochi sprang into being in 1341, when a flood created a natural safe port that swiftly replaced Muziris (Kodungallur, 50km north) as the chief harbour on the Malabar coast. The royal family transferred here from Muziris in 1405, after which the city grew rapidly, attracting Christian, Arab and Jewish settlers from the Middle East. Its name probably derives from *kocchazhi*, meaning the new, or small, harbour.

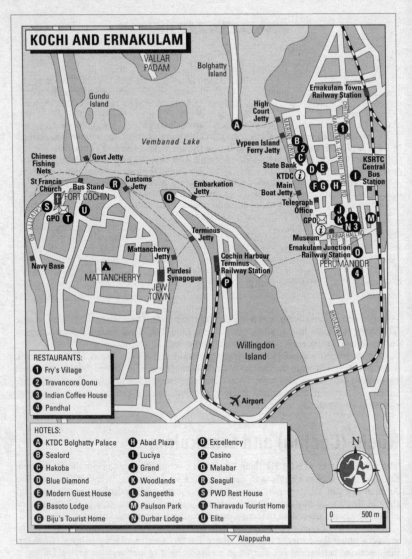

KOCHI AND ERNAKULAM

VALLAR PADAM

Bolghatty Island

Gundu Island

Ernakulam Town Railway Station

High Court Jetty

Vembanad Lake

Vypeen Island Ferry Jetty

A

B
2
C

State Bank

KTDC **i**

KSRTC Central Bus Station

D **E**

I

F **G** **H**

Chinese Fishing Nets

Govt Jetty

Customs Jetty

St Francis Church

Bus Stand

R

FORT COCHIN

Embarkation Jetty

Main Boat Jetty

Telegraph Office

GPO

Q

J **K**
L
N **3**
M

S

GPO **T** **U**

Museum

i DURBAR HALL RD

Ernakulam Junction Railway Station

O

PERUMANOOR

4

Navy Base

MATTANCHERRY

Mattancherry Jetty

Terminus Jetty

Purdesi Synagogue

JEW TOWN

Cochin Harbour Terminus Railway Station

P

Willingdon Island

X Airport

N

RESTAURANTS:
1 Fry's Village
2 Travancore Oonu
3 Indian Coffee House
4 Pandhal

HOTELS:
A KTDC Bolghatty Palace   **H** Abad Plaza   **O** Excellency
B Sealord   **I** Luciya   **P** Casino
C Hakoba   **J** Grand   **Q** Malabar
D Blue Diamond   **K** Woodlands   **R** Seagull
E Modern Guest House   **L** Sangeetha   **S** PWD Rest House
F Basoto Lodge   **M** Paulson Park   **T** Tharavadu Tourist Home
G Biju's Tourist Home   **N** Durbar Lodge   **U** Elite

0   500 m

▽ Alappuzha

The history of European involvement in Kochi, from the early sixteenth century onwards, is dominated by the aggression of, successively, the Portuguese, Dutch and British, competing in their desire to control the port and its lucrative spice trade. From 1800, the state of Cochin was part of the British Madras Presidency; from 1812 until Independence in 1947, its administration was made the responsibility of a series of *diwans*, or financial ministers. In the 1920s, the British expanded the port to make it suitable for modern ocean-going ships; extensive dredging created Willingdon Island, between Ernakulam and Fort Cochin.

Arrival and local transport

Kochi's busy **airport** – served by several flights daily from **Bombay**, one each from **Kozhikode** and **Madras**, and most days of the week from **Delhi** and **Madras** – is at the southern end of Willingdon Island, connected to Ernakulam (5km) by buses, taxis and auto-rickshaws. There are three **railway stations** – **Ernakulam Junction** (☎353100), closest to the centre, is the most important; Ernakulam Town (☎353920) lies 4km to the north. No trains run to Fort Cochin or Mattancherry. The Cochin Harbour Terminus (☎6050), on Willingdon Island, is useful only for people using the airport or staying in one of the swanky hotels on the island.

The KSRTC **Central bus station** (☎352033), beside the rail line a short way east of MG Rd and north of Ernakulam Junction, is the principal and most convenient station for long-distance buses. There are two private bus stands; **Kaloor stand** (rural destinations to the south and east) is across the bridge from Ernakulam Town railway station on the Alwaye Rd, and **Ernakulam South stand** (buses to Kumily, for Periyar Wildlife Reserve, and north to Trichur, Guruvayur and Kodungallur).

Although **auto-rickshaws** are plentiful in Ernakulam, and to a slightly lesser extent across the water in Mattancherry and Fort Cochin, everyone uses Kochi's **ferry system** whenever possible. **Bicycles** for exploring Mattancherry and the rest of old Kochi can be rented from a small shop on Bazar Rd between *Hotel Seagull* and Fort Cochin, while agencies supplying **cars** for longer journeys include *Petite Travels* (☎362792) and *Tom's Cabs* (☎351643) in the AR-Rahiman Complex, on MG Rd in Ernakulam, and *Royal Tours & Travels*, Lissy Junction (☎361770).

KOCHI BY BOAT

Half the fun of visiting Kochi is getting about on the cheap **local ferries**. When it's not downright impossible, catching a bus, rickshaw or taxi the long way round to most parts of the city takes much longer and is far less interesting.

KTDC's half-day **Kochi Boat Cruise** (daily 9.30am–1pm & 1.30–5pm; Rs40) makes an excellent way to orientate yourself. Departing from the High Court Jetty on Shanmugham Rd, Ernakulam, it calls at the Synagogue, Mattancherry Dutch Palace, St Francis Church, Chinese fishing nets, and Bolghatty Island. Book in advance at the KTDC Reception Centre, also on Shanmugham Rd (☎353234).

The map opposite shows Ernakulam's four jetties. Theoretically, the routes below should work in reverse. However, play safe, and don't rely on getting the last boat.

Ernakulam to Mattancherry
From Ernakulam (Main Jetty), via **Fort Cochin** (Customs Jetty), for Chinese fishing nets, St Francis Church, Dutch Cemetery; Willingdon Island (Terminus Jetty); and **Mattancherry Jetty** for Jewish Synagogue and Dutch Palace. Journey time 25min. First boat 7am, last 9.30pm.

Ernakulam to Vypeen
From Ernakulam (Main Jetty). This service has two routes: one via Willingdon Island (Embarkation Jetty; 25min), and a fast to Vypeen (Govt Jetty; 15min). First boat 7am, every 30min until 9.30pm.

Fort Cochin to Vypeen
Privately operated service, intended mainly for locals. Journey time 10min. First boat 6.30am, every 30min until 9pm.

Willingdon Island to Fort Cochin
From the Tourist Office Jetty (Willingdon Island) to Customs Jetty (Fort Cochin). Journey time 10min. First boat 6.30am, every 30min until 6.15pm.

Ernakulam (High Court Jetty) to Bolghatty Island
Journey time 10min. First boat 6.30am, last 6pm.

Ernakulam to Varapuzha
Local ferry service that provides a chance to see the **backwaters** (see p.1001) if you can't travel further south than Kochi. First boat 7.40am, last 6.45pm; 2hr each way. There's little to see at Varapuzha, apart from paddy fields and coconuts, so it makes sense to take the 2.30pm boat and stay on it, returning to Ernakulam just after dusk at 6.30pm.

> The telephone **area code** for Kochi and Ernakulam is ☎0484.

Information and communications

The helpful Government of India **Tourist Office** (☎340352), between the *Malabar Hotel* and Tourist Office Jetty on Willingdon Island, offers information on Kerala and elsewhere in India, and can provide guides for exploring locally and further afield. KTDC's **Reception Centre**, on Shanmugham Rd, Ernakulam (☎353234), will book hotels in their chain and runs a few sightseeing tours (to Periyar, for example; see p.1006). Further Kerala Tourism information counters can be found at the Old Collectorate, Park Ave, Ernakulam, and at the airport. The tiny independent **Tourist Desk**, at the entrance to the Main Boat Jetty in Ernakulam, is very helpful and friendly.

Two small cheap **publications** are widely available. *Jaico Timetable* sticks mainly to travel information, while *Hello Cochin* is an extremely condensed Yellow-Pages style magazine with listings from astrologers and banks to "Women's Finishing Institutes".

Banks and post offices

Banks along MG Rd in Ernakulam include *ANZ Grindlays* (☎361301), *State Bank of India* (☎366376) and *State Bank of Travancore* (☎352309). The **Head Post Office** is on Hospital Rd, not far from the Main Jetty (Mon–Fri 8.30am–8pm, Sat 9.30am–2.30pm & 4–8pm, Sun 10am–4pm, public hols 2–5pm), while a branch behind St Francis Church on Fort Cochin also handles poste restante.The **Central Telegraph Office** is at Jose Junction, MG Rd (24hr; fax & telex Mon–Sat 8am–8pm except public hols).

Mattancherry

With high-rise development restricted to Ernakulam, across the water, the old-fashioned character of **Mattancherry** and **Fort Cochin** remains intact. Within an area small enough to cover on foot, bicycle or auto-rickshaw, glimpses of Kochi's variegated history greet the visitor virtually at every turn. As you approach by ferry (get down at Mattancherry jetty), the shoreline is crowded with tiled buildings painted in pastel colours – a view that can't have changed for centuries.

Despite the large number of tourists visiting every day, trade is still the most important activity here. The air is filled with the pungent smell of spices. Many of the streets are busy with barrows loaded with sacks of produce trundling between *godowns* (warehouses) and little shops where dealers do business in tea, jute, rubber, chillies, turmeric, cashew, ginger, cardamom and pepper.

Jew Town

The road heading left from Mattancherry Jetty leads into the district known for obvious reasons as **Jew Town**, where *NX Jacob's* tailor shop and the offices of *JE Cohen*, advocate and tax consultant, serve to remind visitors of a once-thriving community. Nowadays many of the shops sell antiques, crammed with Hindu and Christian woodcarvings, oil lamps, wooden jewellery boxes and other bric-à-brac. Turning right at the India Pepper & Spice Trade Building, usually resounding with the racket of dealers shouting the latest spice prices, and then right again, brings you into Synagogue Lane.

The **Pardesi (White Jew) Synagogue** (daily except Sat 10am–noon & 3–5pm) was founded in 1568, and rebuilt in 1664. Its interior is an attractive, if slightly incongruous, hotchpotch; note the floor, paved with hand-painted eighteenth-century blue and white tiles from Canton, each unique, depicting a love affair between a mandarin's daughter and a commoner. The nineteenth-century glass oil-burning chandeliers suspended from the ceiling were imported from Belgium. Above the entrance, a gallery supported by slender gilt columns was reserved for female members of the congregation. The wooden seats, around the walls and surrounding the brass *teba* (pulpit) in the centre of the room, have a homely appearance, covered in chintz fabric with crimson frills.

On the opposite wall to the entrance, an elaborately carved Ark houses four scrolls of the *Torah* (the first five books of the Old Testament) encased in silver and gold, on which are placed gold crowns presented by the maharajas of Travancore and Cochin. The synagogue's oldest artefact is a fourth-century copperplate inscription from the Raja of Cochin, testifying to good relations with the Jewish community.

An attendant is usually available to show visitors around, and answer questions; his introductory talk features as part of the KTDC guided tour (see p.1010).

Mattancherry Palace

The **Mattancherry Palace** (daily except Fri 10am–5pm) stands on the left side of the road a short walk from the Mattancherry Jetty in the opposite direction to Jew Town. The gateway on the road is, in fact, its back entrance; although the most sensible side to approach from the ferry, it inexplicably remains locked with a loose chain. Visitors slim enough can, and do, enter through the gap, saving the walk around the block. In the walled grounds stands a circular, tiled Krishna temple (closed to non-Hindus).

Although known locally as the **Dutch Palace**, the two-storey palace was built by the Portuguese as a gift to the Cochin Raja, Vira Keralavarma (1537–61), and the Dutch were responsible for subsequent additions. While its appearance is not particularly striking, squat with whitewashed walls and tiled roof, the interior is captivating.

The **murals** that adorn some of its rooms are among the finest examples of Kerala's much underrated school of painting; friezes illustrating stories from the *Ramayana*, on the first floor, date from the sixteenth century. Packed with detail and gloriously rich colour, they manage to retain a uniform clarity in the depiction of human figures. The style is never strictly naturalistic; the treatment of facial features is pared down to the simplest of lines for the mouth, and characteristically aquiline noses. Female figures sport impossibly full, almost spherical breasts.

Downstairs, the women's bedchamber holds several less complex paintings, possibly dating from the eighteenth century. One shows Shiva in dalliance with Vishnu

KERALAN MURALS

The quality and unique style of the murals at **Mattancherry Palace** in old Kochi (see p.1011), along with those in as many as sixty other locations in Kerala, are probably the best kept secrets in Indian art. Most are on the walls of functioning temples, not marketable, transportable, or indeed even *seen* by many non-Hindus. Few date from before the sixteenth century, depriving them of the aura of extreme antiquity; their origins may go back to the seventh century, probably influenced by the Pallava style of Tamil Nadu, but only traces in one tenth-century cave temple survive from the earliest period. The traveller Castaneda, who accompanied Vasco da Gama on the first Portuguese landing in India, described how he strayed into a temple, supposing it to be a church, and saw "monstrous looking images with two inch fangs" painted on the walls, causing one of the party to fall to his knees exclaiming, "if this be the devil, I worship God".

Technically classified as **Fresco-Secco**, Kerala murals employ vegetable and mineral colours, predominantly ochre reds and yellows, white and blue-green, and are coated with a protective sheen of pine resin and oil. Their ingenious design, strongly influenced by the canonical text, *Shilparatna*, incorporates intense detail with clarity and dynamism in the portrayal of human (and celestial) figures; subtle facial expressions are captured with the simplest of lines, while narrative elements are always bold and arresting. In common with all great Indian art, they share a complex iconography and symbolism.

Non-Hindus can see fine examples in Kochi, Padmanabhapuram (see p.995), Ettumanur (see p.1004) and Kayamkulam (see p.999). Visitors interested in how they are made should head for the *Mural Painting Institute* at Guruvayur (see p.1026). A paperback book, *Murals of Kerala*, by MG Shashi Bhooshan (Kerala Govt Dept of Public Relations) serves as an excellent introduction to the field.

having adopted his female form, the divine enchantress Mohini; a second portrays Krishna holding aloft the Mountain Govardhana; another features a reclining Krishna surrounded by *gopis*, female cowherds. His apparently languid pose belies the activity of his six hands and two feet, intimately caressing adoring admirers.

While the paintings are undoubtedly the highlight of the palace, the collection also includes interesting Dutch maps of old Cochin, coronation robes belonging to past maharajas, royal palanquins, weapons and furniture. Useful postcards of locations thousands of miles away are available, but none of the palace. Without permission from the Archaeological Survey of India, photography is strictly prohibited.

Fort Cochin

Moving northwest from Mattancherry Palace along Bazar Road, you pass numerous wholesale emporia where the owners, sitting behind scales and surrounded by sacks of spices, may well be prepared to talk about their wares. After about half an hour's leisurely walk, cross the canal and find yourself in **Fort Cochin**.

The architecture of the quiet streets in this enclave is very definitely European, with some fine houses built by wealthy British traders, and even a few Dutch cottages with split farmhouse doors. At the water's edge there's a bus stand, boat jetty and numerous food and cool drinks stalls. This area, and nearby Princess Street (which holds a few budget hotels) attracts backpackers and the consequent local hustlers.

Chinese fishing nets

The huge, elegant **Chinese fishing nets** that line the northern shore of Fort Cochin – adding grace to an already characterful waterside view, and probably the single most familiar photographic image of Kerala – are said to have been introduced to the region by traders from the court of Kublai Khan. They can also be seen throughout the backwaters further south. Suspended from arced poles, and operated by levers and weights, they require at least four men to control. You can buy fresh fish from the tiny market here and have it grilled on the spot at one of the ramshackle stalls.

St Francis Church

Walking on from the Chinese fishing nets brings you to a typically English village green. In one corner stands the church of **St Francis**, the first European church in India. Originally built in wood and named Santo Antonio, it was probably associated with Franciscan friars from Portugal. Exactly when it was founded is not known, but the stone structure is likely to date from the early sixteenth century. The facade, with multi-curved sides, became the model for most Christian churches in India. Vasco da Gama was buried here in 1524, but his body was later removed to Portugal.

Under the Dutch, the church was renovated and became Protestant in 1663, then Anglican with the advent of the British in 1795 and since 1949 has been attached to the Church of South India. Inside, various tombstone inscriptions have been placed in the walls, the earliest of which is from 1562. Copies of baptism and marriage registers from 1751 to 1804 may be seen in the vestry. One hangover from British days is the continued use of *punkahs*, large swinging cloth fans on frames suspended above the congregation; these are operated by people sitting outside pulling on cords.

On the far side of the green, Dutch Cemetery Road winds left, parallel to the sea, past the *PWD Rest House*, to end at the evocatively abandoned and overgrown Dutch Cemetery. Beware of snakes!

The interior of the twentieth-century **Santa Cruz Cathedral**, south of St Francis church, will delight fans of the colourful – verging on the downright gaudy – Indo-Romano-Rococo school of decoration.

KALAM EZHUTTU

The tradition of *kalam ezhuttu* – detailed and beautiful ritual drawings in coloured powder, of deities and geometric patterns (*mandalas*) – is very much alive all over Kerala. The designs usually cover an area of around thirty square metres, often outdoors and under a *pandal*, a temporary shelter made from bamboo and palm fronds. Each colour, made from rice flour, turmeric, ground leaves and burnt paddy husk, is painstakingly applied using the thumb and forefinger as a funnel. Three communities produce *kalams*; two come from the temple servant (*amblavasi*) castes, whose rituals are associated with the god Ayappa (see p.1007) or the goddess Bhagavati; the third, the *pullavans*, specializes in serpent worship. Iconographic designs emerge gradually from the initial grid lines and turn into startling figures, many of terrible aspect, with wide eyes and fangs. Noses and breasts are raised, giving the whole a three-dimensional effect. As part of the ritual, the significant moment when the powder is added for the iris or pupil, "opening" the eyes, may well be marked by the accompaniment of *chenda* drums and *elatalam* hand-cymbals.

Witnessing the often day-long ritual is an unforgettable experience. The effort expended by the artist is made all the more remarkable by the inevitable destruction of the picture shortly after its completion; this truly ephemeral art cannot be divorced from its ritual context. In some cases, the image is destroyed by a fierce-looking **Vellichapad** ("light-bringer"), a village oracle who can be recognized by shoulder-length hair, a red *dhoti*, heavy brass anklets and the hooked sword he brandishes either while jumping up and down on the spot (a common sight), or marching purposefully about to control the spectators. At the end of the ritual, the powder, invested with divine power, is thrown over the onlookers. *Kalam ezhuttu* rituals are not widely advertised, but tourist offices may be able to put you in touch with someone who knows where one is to take place.

Ernakulam

ERNAKULAM presents the modern face of Kerala, possessing more of a city feel than the capital Thiruvananthapuram, while still remaining small enough not to be daunting. There's nothing in the way of sights, but it's a pleasant enough place to wander around. Along the busy, long, straight **Mahatma Gandhi (MG) Road**, which more or less divides Ernakulam in half 500m back from the sea, shopping, eating and movie-going are the main activities. Here you can fax and phone to your heart's content, and choose from an assortment of great places to eat Keralan food. This area is particularly good for cloth, with a seemingly infinite selection of colours. If there's a jazzy style in *lunghis* this year, you'll get it on MG Rd.

Many visitors get their first opportunity to see the extraordinary **Kathakali** dance drama in Ernakulam (see p.1028); hour-long tourist performances are staged most evenings, with an introductory talk about, and demonstration of, the art. You can watch the make-up process too. While informative, and convenient if you're in a hurry, they unavoidably lack the spirit of traditional performances.

An eight-day annual **festival** at the Shiva temple in Ernakulam (Jan/Feb) features elephant processions and *panchavadyam* (drum and trumpet group) out in the street. As part of the festival, there are usually performances of Kathakali at night, and the temple is decorated with an amazing array of electric lights: banks of coloured tubes and sequenced bulbs imitating shooting stars.

The **Parishath Thamburan Museum** (daily except Mon 9.30am–noon & 3–5.30pm) in Darbar Hall Rd houses a fairly unexciting collection of coins, nineteenth-century oil paintings, Hindu sculpture and memorabilia from the Cochin royal family.

Thripunitra

The small suburban town of **THRIPUNITRA**, 12km southeast of Ernakulam, is worth a visit for its dilapidated colonial-style **Hill Palace** (daily except Mon 10am–4pm), now an eclectic museum a short auto-rickshaw ride from the busy bus stand. The royal family of Cochin ("Honour is our family treasure") at one time maintained around forty palaces. All the Rajas, who bore the surname Varma, appear to have adopted one of only three first names, Rama, Kerala or Ravi; Rama Varma the last died in 1964.

One of the museum's finest exhibits is an early seventeenth-century wooden *mandapa* removed from a temple in Pathanamthitta, featuring excellent carvings of the coronation of the monkey king Sugriva and other themes from the *Ramayana*. Of interest too are silver filigree jewel boxes, gold and silver ornaments, and ritual objects associated with grand ceremonies. The **epigraphy** gallery contains an eighth-century Jewish *Torah*, and Keralan stone and copperplate inscriptions. Sculpture, ornaments and weapons in the **bronze** gallery include a *kingini katti* knife, whose playful decorative little bells belie the fact that it was used for beheading. Providing the place isn't crowded with noisy school groups here to see the nearby deer park, the **garden** with cashew trees behind the palace is a peaceful picnic spot.

Performances of theatre, classical music and dance are held over a period of several days in September during the annual **festival** at the **Shri Purnatrayisa** temple, on the way to the palace. Inside the temple compound, both in the morning and at night, massed drum orchestras perform *chenda melam* in procession with elephants. At night, the outside walls of the sanctuary are covered with thousands of tiny oil lamps to lend the entire spectacle an extra injection of magic. Although the temple is normally closed to non-Hindus, admittance to appropriately dressed visitors is usually allowed at this time.

THE ISLANDS OF LAKSHADWEEP

Visitors to Kochi who really want to get away from it all, and have the time and money to spare, could do no better than to head for **LAKSHADWEEP**, the "one hundred thousand islands", which lie between two and four hundred kilometres offshore, in the deep blue of the Arabian Sea. The smallest Union Territory in India consists of lagoons, reefs, sand banks and 27 tiny coconut-palm-covered coral islands. Only ten are inhabited, with a total population of just over 50,000, the majority of whom are Malayalam-speaking Sunni Muslims, said to be descended from seventh-century Keralan Hindus who converted to Islam. The main sources of income are fishing, coconuts and related products. Fruit, vegetables and pulses are cultivated in small quantities but staples such as rice and many other commodities have always had to be imported. It was the Portuguese who discovered the value of coir rope, a by-product of the coconut. They controlled Lakshadweep during the sixteenth century; when they imposed an import tax on rice, locals retaliated by poisoning some of the 40-strong Portuguese garrison. Terrible reprisals followed. As Muslims, the islanders enjoyed friendly relations with Tipu Sultan of Mysore. That naturally aroused the ire of the British, who moved in at the end of the eighteenth century and remained until Independence, when Lakshadweep became a Union Territory.

At present, only one island can be visited by non-residents of India. The teardrop-shaped uninhabited islet of **Bangaram** welcomes a limited number of tourists at any one time, and expects them to pay handsomely for the privilege. Bangaram is the archetypal tropical paradise, edged with pristine white sands and sitting in a calm lagoon where average water temperature stays around 26°C. Beyond the lagoon lies coral reef and the technicolour world of the deep, home to marine life including sea turtles, dolphins, eagle rays, lionfish, parrotfish, octopus and predators like barracudas and sharks. Islanders come to Bangaram and its uninhabited neighbours to fish and to harvest coconuts.

It's theoretically possible to visit Bangaram all year round; the hottest time is April and May, when the temperature can reach 33°C; the monsoon (end of May to early September) attracts approximately half the rainfall seen in Kerala, and is said to be in the form of passing showers, not a deluge, although seas are rough. The *Bangaram Island Resort* (⑨) accommodates up to thirty couples in simply furnished thatched cottage rooms, each with a verandah; some cane tables and chairs sit outside the simple restaurant on the beach, and a few hammocks are strung up between the palms. "Less is more" might be the management's philosophy; there's no air-conditioning, TV, radio, telephone, newspapers or shops, let alone discos.

Cynics might see such a post-modern attitude as convenient for dollar harvesting, but Bangaram remains staggeringly peaceful, and compared to other resorts, at least attempts to minimize its ecological impact. The tariff, if expensive for India, compares favourably with other exotic holiday destinations; during the peak season (mid-Dec to mid-Jan) it rises to around US$120 per person in a twin-bedded room; in low season (April–Sept except Aug) it may be as much as fifty percent less. A modest restaurant provides buffet meals or barbecues (tariff includes full board; there's nowhere else to go in any case). Fresh seafood is the logical choice, although a limited variety of vegetarian dishes are also on offer; unlike on other Lakshadweep islands, alcohol is available.

Other facilities include scuba diving (from US$40 per dive; lessons with qualified instructor: 1 lesson US$45, course of six US$250); glass-bottomed boat trips to neighbouring uninhabited islands (2hr; $25); and deep sea fishing (Oct to mid-May; US$50–75). Kayaks, catamarans and a sail boat are available free of charge.

At present, the only way to reach Bangaram is on a 20-seater plane from **Kochi** (1hr 30min) to the island of Agatti, 8km southwest. The service is currently operated by NEPC; quite when the planes leave is consistent in its unpredictability. The connecting boat journey from Agatti takes two hours, picking its way through the shallows to avoid the corals; during the monsoon, helicopters are used. All arrangements, including accommodation and the necessary entry permit, are handled by the *Casino Hotel*, Willingdon Island, Kochi (☎340221, fax 340001). Some foreign tour operators, however, offer all-in packages combining Lakshadweep with another destination, usually Goa.

Edapally

The **Madhavan Nair Foundation Museum of Kerala History** (Tues–Sat 10am–noon & 2–4pm), at **Edapally**, 10km from Ernakulam on the NH47 towards Alwaye, runs half-hour "sound and light" shows on Keralan history. The Alwaye bus from near the Ernakulam main boat jetty stops outside the museum. Every year, for eleven days from 23 April, the **Forane church** (founded in the seventh century) at Edapally celebrates a festival dedicated to St George. On the most important day, 1 May, thousands of devotees gather to see the church decorated with lights and, to the accompaniment of bands and fireworks, the statue of St George led in a chariot through the streets.

Accommodation

Despite its romantic atmosphere, **Fort Cochin** holds a regrettably small selection of accommodation. Most visitors end up staying in **Ernakulam**, which is far more convenient for transport connections and general facilities. **Willingdon Island** is a comfortable, but expensive and isolated, alternative.

Ernakulam

Abad Plaza, MG Rd (☎361636). Comfortable business-style high-rise, with restaurant and bar, in the centre of Ernakulam. ⑥.

Basoto Lodge, Press Club Rd (☎352140). Basic, cheap, and dependable. Draws backpackers like flies, so with just 12 rooms it's often full. ①.

Biju's Tourist Home, corner of Canon Shed and Market roads (☎369881). 28 basic but decent rooms, close to the main boat jetty. ①.

Blue Diamond, Market Rd, 1km northeast of the bus station towards the seafront (☎353221). 42 average rooms, some a/c. South Indian restaurant and bar. ②–③.

Durbar Lodge, Jos Junction, corner of MG Rd & Durbar Hall Rd (☎360582). Next door to *Indian Coffee House*. Good, inexpensive Indian-style lodge, often full. ①.

Excellency, Nettipadam Rd, Jos Junction. Close to MG Rd. Recently opened and good value. Some rooms non-a/c. Roof garden, south Indian, western and Chinese food. ②–④.

Grand, MG Rd (☎353211). Two-part hotel near Woodlands Junction in central Ernakulam; the less expensive rooms are in the old part. Restaurant. ④–⑤.

Hakoba, Shanmugham Rd (☎353933). Between Main and High Court boat jetties. Dowdy, but adequate for a night. Restaurant, bar. ②.

Luciya, near KSRTC bus stand (☎354433). Amiable large hotel, with 104 rooms, some a/c. ②–④.

Modern Guest House, Market Rd (☎352130). Basic rooms above Keralan veg restaurant. Cheap, but can get noisy. ①.

Paulson Park, Carrier Station Rd (☎354002). Close to Ernakulam Junction. Recently opened and good value. A/c rooms with *Star TV*. ②–④.

Sangeetha, Chittoor Rd (☎368736). Close to bus and rail stations. All rooms non-a/c. South Indian and Chinese food in restaurant. ③.

Sealord, Shanmugham Rd (☎352682). Modern, comfortable high-rise near High Court jetty. ⑥–⑦.

Woodlands, Woodlands Junction, MG Rd (☎351372). In the centre, an Indian-style middle-class hotel with fine veg restaurant. A/c and non-a/c rooms. ③–④.

Fort Cochin

Elite, Princess St, Fort Cochin (☎225733). Rabbit-warren travellers' haunt, with shared bathrooms and a reasonable veg restaurant. ①.

PWD Rest House, Dutch Cemetery Rd. Near the water. Three gigantic rooms with colonial furniture. Intended for Govt employees, but others can stay when it's not busy. Dilapidated, but cheap. ①.

Seagull, Calvetty Rd (☎228128). Between Mattancherry and Fort Cochin at the water's edge. Assorted rooms, a couple with a/c, but none make the most of the location (stand on a chair to see out of the window). Bar, restaurant. ②.

Tharavadu Tourist Home, Quiros St, Fort Cochin (☎226897). In the road behind the post office. Eight simple, tiny, clean rooms (2 without bathroom) in an old house. Friendly staff, can provide breakfast and cool drinks only. ②–③.

Willingdon and Bolghatty islands

Casino, Willingdon Island (☎340221). 2km from airport, close to Cochin Harbour Terminus railway station. Fairly modern, comfortable, good service, swimming pool, travel agent, restaurants. ⑦.

KTDC Bolghatty Palace, Bolghatty Island (☎355003). Sadly run-down palace in beautiful location, a short hop by ferry from the High Court Jetty, Ernakulam. Huge rooms in main building, built by the Dutch in 1744 and later home of the British Resident, and "honeymoon" cottages in the grounds. Arrive armed with mosquito repellent. As this book went to press it was about to be taken over by a luxury hotel chain, and may be closed for refurbishment. ③.

Malabar, Willingdon Island (☎340010). By Tourist Office Jetty (20min ferry from Ernakulam), 3km from airport, 9km from Ernakulam train and bus stations, near Cochin Harbour Terminus train station. One of the best hotels in India, owned by the *Taj* group. Superb location with waterside gardens and views of old Mattancherry. Two restaurants, swimming pool and excellent service. ⑨.

Eating

Unusually for Keralan cities, Kochi offers a wide choice for **eating out**, from the delicious, if intestinally challenging, fresh-cooked fish by the Chinese fishing nets at Fort Cochin, to the sophistication of the *Malabar Hotel*. Between the two extremes, various popular, modest places in Ernakulam serve real Keralan food.

Ernakulam

Bharat Hotel, Durbar Hall Rd. Good vegetarian lunches.

Fry's Village Restaurant, adjacent to *Mymoor Cinema*, Chittoor Rd. Keralan specialities including Calicut Muslim delicacy *patthri*, wafer-thin rice pancakes, and *idiappam* dumplings. Good value.

Indian Coffee House, corner of MG Rd and Durbar Hall Rd. The usual excellent coffee (ask for "pot coffee" if you don't want it with sugar) and simple snacks such as *dosa* and scrambled egg. There's another branch at the corner of Canon Shed Rd & Park Ave.

Pai's Thattu Dosai, MG Rd. Scores of varieties of *dosa*, rice and wheat pancakes.

Pandhal, MG Rd. Modish, split-level a/c restaurant with bright white walls and western music serving a wide range of seafood and usual generic Indian. Not much for vegetarians.

Sealord, Shanmugham Rd (☎352682). The expensive rooftop restaurant serves absolutely irresistible food – delicious Chinese, all-purpose Indian and sizzlers – but the view is not what it was, since the concrete shopping centre opposite was built.

Travancore Oonu, Four Foods, Shanmugham Rd. Specializes in traditional Keralan dishes, mostly non-veg, particularly fish.

Woodlands, Woodlands Junction, MG Rd. Bargain veg food in functional surroundings.

Fort Cochin

Elite, Princess St (☎225733). Fish curries and "traveller-style" snacks. Cheap.

Chariot Beach, Princess St. Very popular with travellers at night, tables outside. Huge seafood and Chinese menu (155 items), at reasonable prices.

Seagull, Calvetty Rd. Average restaurant, in good postcard-writing location overlooking the water.

Willingdon Island

Casino, Willingdon Island (☎340221). Good lunchtime buffet and evening meals in dark indoor restaurant, and excellent outdoor poolside seafood restaurant, often accompanied by south Indian classical music.

Malabar, Willingdon Island (☎340010). Two restaurants: the *Jade Pavilion* specializes in Chinese and *Rice Boats* serves western, north Indian and Keralan. The latter has tables in a beautiful waterside location. The food is excellent and prices reflect this; the lunchtime buffet is less expensive.

Listings

Bookstores *Bhavi Books*, Convent Rd (☎354003); *Current Books*, Press Club Rd (☎351590); *Higginbothams*, TD Rd (368834); *Paico*, MG Rd (☎355835), Broadway (☎361020), & New Rd (☎225607).

Handicrafts *CI Company*, Broadway (☎352405); plus *Kairali* (☎354507), *Khadi Bhavan* (☎355279); *Khataisons Curio Palace* (☎367472), *Surabhi Kerala State Handicrafts* (☎353063), all on MG Rd.

MOVING ON FROM KOCHI/ERNAKULAM

By Air
Indian Airlines operates daily **flights** from Kochi airport to **Bombay** (1hr 45min; 9.15am); on Tues, Thurs & Sat a second flight leaves at 12.15pm. *East–West* fly twice daily to Bombay (2hr; 7.45am & 12.25pm). *Indian Airlines* also fly to **Delhi** (4hr; daily except Mon; 10.10am) via **Goa** (1hr), to **Madras** (daily; 2hr), via either **Bangalore** (Mon, Wed, Fri & Sun; 11.05am), or **Coimbatore** (Tues, Thurs & Sat; 3.30pm), and, in small 20-seaters, to the Lakshadweep Islands (1hr 30min; Tues, Thurs & Sat; noon).

Indian Airlines have their office on Durbar Hall Rd (☎353901); other **airline offices** include *Air India*, MG Rd, Ravipuram (☎351295); *British Airways*, c/o *Nijhwan Travels*, MG Rd (☎364867); *Cathay Pacific*, c/o *Spencer & Co*, MG Rd (☎369165); *Egypt Air*, c/o *ABC International*, Old Thevara Rd (☎353457); *JAL & KLM*, c/o *Spencer & Co*, MG Rd (☎360997); *Kuwait Airways*, c/o *National Travels*, MG Rd (☎360123); *PIA*, c/o *ABC International*, Old Thevara Rd (☎353457); *Saudia*, c/o *Arafat Travels*, MG Rd (☎352689); *Singapore Airlines & Swissair* c/o *Aviation Travels*, MG Rd (☎367911); *TWA*, c/o *Jet Air*, Warriam Rd (☎369142).

By Train
Unless otherwise specified, the trains below depart from **Ernakulam Junction**.

The fastest of the four daily expresses to **Thiruvananthapuram** is the *Vanchinad Express* #6303 (6am; 4hr 20min), calling at Kottayam (1hr 5min) and Kollam (3hr). The two daily trains to **Alappuzha** – *Bokaro Steel City Express* #8689 (7.25pm; 1hr 20min), and *Madras–Alleppey Express* #6307 (9.15am; 1hr 5min) – are not timed conveniently for backwater trips to Kollam. For **Madras**, the choice is between the *Alleppey–Madras Express* #6042 (4.20pm; 14hr), or the *Trivandrum–Madras Mail* #6320, from Ernakulam Town (6.30pm; 13hr). Another service, *Alleppey–Bokaro Steel City Express* #8690 (6.53am; 14hr), is not all that convenient for Madras itself, but is useful for an early start to local destinations to the north such as Thrissur (1hr 30min), Shoranur (2hr 30min), Palakaad (3hr 20min) and Coimbatore (4hr 45min), the nearest big junction for Ooty and the Nilgiris.

The daily *Kanniyakumari Express* #1082 to **Bombay** VT (12.45pm; 41hr) also calls at Thrissur, Palakaad, Coimbatore, and **Pune** (32hr 35min), while the better of the two trains to **Delhi** is the *Kerala–Mangala Express* #2625/2625a (daily, 2.20pm; 49hr). The daily *Kanniyakumari–Bangalore Express* #6525 leaves Ernakulam Town for **Bangalore** (3.40pm; 14hr 5min). The weekly *Cochin–Ahmedabad Express* #2638 (Fri only) departs Cochin Harbour Terminus at 6.30pm, calls at Ernakulam Junction at 7.05pm, and goes all the way up to **Ahmedabad** in Gujarat (45hr 20min) via Pune.

By Bus
Buses leave Ernakulam's KSRTC Central bus stand for virtually every town in Kerala, and some beyond; most are bookable in advance. Travelling south, around twenty buses per day run to **Thiruvananthapuram** (6hr 30min); most go via **Alappuzha** (1hr 30min) and **Kollam** (4hr), but a few go via Kottayam (2hr).

Travel Agents
Travel agents on MG Road in Ernakulam include *Akbar Travels*, 39/5653 D Vallamattom Estate (☎354912), *Jai Hind Travels* (☎361011), *Kerala Travels* (☎367738), *Sita World Travel* (☎361101), and *Travel Corporation of India*, Telstar Building (☎351645). You could also try *Harrison Malayalam* on Willingdon Island (☎6007).

Hospitals General, Hospital Rd (☎361251); Lissie, Lissie Junction (☎352006); Lourdes, Pachalam (☎351507).

Kathakali Special performances (arrive earlier to see make-up process) are staged for visitors by the following organizations: *Cochin Cultural Centre*, Souhardham, Manikath Rd (☎354162; daily 6.30–8pm); *Indian Performing Arts Centre*, Shanmugham Rd (6.30pm); *See India Foundation*, Kalathil Parambil Lane (☎369471; 7pm).

Photographic Supplies *Fotofast*, MG Rd (☎352619); *Krishnan Nair Bros*, Convent Rd (☎352098); *Royal Studio*, Shanmugham Rd (☎351614).

Visa Extensions City Police Commissioner, Marine Drive (☎31700).

North towards Thrissur

A number of places within easy reach of **Angamali**, a busy nondescript town on the railway line 35km northeast of Kochi, on the edge of the thickly wooded foothills of the Western Ghat mountain range, can be visited as day trips from Kochi. In the hamlet of **Akapparambu**, the Jacobite church holds the best Christian frescoes in Kerala. **Kalady** is the birthplace of the great Hindu philosopher Adi Shankaracharya, and the hilltop Christian church of **Malayattur** nearby draws pilgrims to honour St Thomas.

Regular **buses** run between Ernakulam and Angamali. It is also possible to take the train (3 daily; 1hr) from Ernakulam Junction.

Akapparambu Jacobite Church

According to tradition, the **Mar Sabore and Afroth Church** in **AKAPPARAMBU**, ten minutes' auto-rickshaw ride from the main road at Angamali, was founded in 825 AD on the site of a Hindu temple by two twins, Sabore and Afroth, sent from Syria by a saint to search for two countrymen who had run away to Kerala. The relatives of the runaways kept their promise to build a church when they were found.

The exterior, which replaced the original structure, is typically post-Portuguese, with a pilastered facade, and the multi-curved gables are repeated in the outline of the porch. Metal-hooded cobras on the corners of the overhanging eaves show Hindu influence. Inside, the area around the elaborately carved altar of angels and saints (fairy lights switched on by request) is resplendent with paintings; the lower portions have been damaged, but much remains. Large panels in vibrant colours and simplistic style, separated by floral designs, illustrate episodes from the Bible. To the side of the altar, Sabore and Afroth debate with Nambudiri brahmins; the twins were not priests, but performed miracles that resulted in the conversion of a number of local families. If you find the church locked and there's no one in the offices inside the compound, you can seek out the caretaker, who lives just round the corner. Turn left from the gate and left again at the nearby T-junction. His house is a little way down on the left.

Kalady

An important place of pilgrimage, **KALADY**, on the banks of the River Periyar (10km southeast of Angamali on the highway, MC Rd, and served by regular buses), is the birthplace of the ninth-century Hindu philosopher Adi Shankaracharya (Shankara) who, although he achieved fame through intellectual acumen and debating skill, has accrued enough miracles to secure his status as a fully fledged saint.

The 46-metre, nine-storey **Sri Adi Shankara Keerthi Sthamba Mandapa** (daily 7am–7pm), an octagonal, salmon-coloured concrete tower on the roadside, resembles a quasi-oriental folly that you might find in the garden of an eccentric English aristocrat. Inside, the illustrations of the saint's life may well appeal more to devotees than art lovers. Six floors hold shrines to different deities representing the "six modes of worship approved and encouraged by Shankaracharya".

Away from the road, next to the river, on the site where Shankaracharya found a pregnant frog sheltering from the sun under the hood of a cobra, the **Sringeri Math** (5.30am–noon & 3–8pm) consists of a small complex of temples. Inside is a seven-sided temple to the Sapta Matrikas (the seven mothers) behind a memorial marking where Shankaracharya's mother Aryamba was cremated. Other shrines are dedicated to Ganapati and to Shankara himself. The bathing *ghat* outside, known as the **Crocodile Ghat**, is where Shankara, caught by a crocodile, was not able to free himself until his mother agreed to allow him to take *sannyasi*, the life of an ascetic.

Next door is the **Sri Krishna temple** (5–8.30am & 5–7.30pm), a typical gabled building with a subsidiary shrine dedicated to Ayappa. A little way further west along the river, the **Sri Ramakrishna Advaita Ashram** includes the Universal Temple, three schools (which reserve 70 places for scheduled caste and tribal children), a bookshop, an Ayurvedic dispensary and the Swami Vivekananda Library.

Malayattur

Eight kilometres east of Kalady, and accessible by bus from Angamali, the **Catholic church** of **MALAYATTUR**, on a hilltop overlooking the River Periyar, celebrates one of the most important Christian festivals in Kerala, in honour of St Thomas – the disciple, "Doubting" Thomas, who is said to have introduced Christianity to India. It takes place shortly after Easter when thousands of devotees, chanting prayers, climb the 615m to the church. Ceremonies are held both in the church and the open air.

Thrissur

THRISSUR (Trichur), roughly midway between Kochin (74km to the south) and Palakaad (79km to the northeast) on the NH47, is an excellent base for exploring the cultural riches of central Kerala. Thrissur was once the capital of Cochin state and because of its position, close to the Palghat (Palakaad) Gap – an opening in the natural border made by the Western Ghat mountains – it was on one of the main routes into the region from Tamil Nadu and Karnataka. Thrissur at times fell into the hands of both the Zamorin of Kozhikode and Tipu Sultan of Mysore.

The town is attractively laid out, centering on Kerala's largest temple complex, **Vadakkunatha**, surrounded by a *maidan* (green) that sees all kinds of public gatherings, not least Kerala's most extravagant, noisy and sumptuous festival, **Puram**.

Arrival and information

The principal point of orientation in Thrissur is the Round, a road subdivided into North, South, East and West, which encircles the Vadakkunatha temple and *maidan* at the centre. Once you've established which side of the Round you're on, you can save yourself long walks along the busy pavement by striking out across the green.

Thrissur's **railway station** is 1km southwest of Round South, near the KSRTC (☎0487/21150) **long-distance bus stand**. **Priya Darshini** (also known as "North", "Shoranur" and "Wadakkancheri") bus station, close to Round North, serves Palakaad and Shoranur. The Shakthan Thampuran stand, on Pattalam Rd, 2km from Round South, serves local destinations south such as Irinjalakuda and Kodungallur.

At the KTDC hotel *Yatri Niwas*, Stadium Rd (☎0487/27383), a small tourist office provides local **information**, but keeps erratic hours. The main branch of the *State Bank of Travancore* (Mon–Fri 10am–2pm, Sat 10am–noon) on the first floor next to the Paramekkavu temple, Round East, accepts *American Express* travellers' cheques, but not *Thomas Cook* or *Mastercard*. Opposite the same temple, the *State Bank of India* (same hours) refuses all travellers' cheques but will change dollars and sterling.

Vadakkunatha Temple

Vadakkunatha Temple (closed to non-Hindus), is a walled complex of fifteen shrines, dating from the twelfth century and earlier, the principal of which is dedicated to Shiva. Inside the walls, the grassy compound is surprisingly quiet and spacious, with a striking apsidal shrine dedicated to Ayappa (see p.1007). Sadly, many of the temple's treasures, such as wood carving and murals, are not as well-maintained as they might be.

Once an essential ingredient of the temple's cultural life, but now under-used and neglected, the long, sloping-roofed **Kuttambalam theatre** with carved panels and lathe-turned wooden pillars, is the venue for the ancient Sanskrit performance forms Chakyar Kuttu and Kutiyattam (closed to non-Hindus).

The Town

The **State Art Museum** and **Zoo** (both daily except Mon 10am–5pm) stand together on Museum Rd, ten minutes' walk from Round East, in the northeast of town (turn right at the end of Palace Rd and walk 200m down the right-hand side). Although small, the museum has excellent local bronzes, jewellery, fine wood carvings of fanged temple guardians and a profusion of bell-metal oil lamps. The zoo, however, houses a miserable set of tenants, and although it can be grimly fascinating to observe the variety of snakes that slither locally (king cobra, krait, viper), you may also be expected to watch an attendant prod cobras with a stick so they spit at the glass that separates you from them.

One of the most important churches for Thrissur's large Christian population is the Syrian Catholic **Lourdes Cathedral**, just over a kilometre east of the Medical College Hospital on Round East, along St Thomas College Rd. Three daily masses serve a regular congregation of nine hundred. Like many of Kerala's Indo-Gothic churches, the exterior of dome and spires is more impressive than the interior, with its unadorned metal rafters and corrugated iron ceiling. Among assorted statues of popes and saints is one of Alphonsa, a nun from Kottayam, who died this century and was known for her good works. When the Pope visited in 1986, he declared Alphonsa "Blessed", a preliminary honour before achieving sainthood. Steps lead down from the altar to the crypt, a rather dilapidated copy of the grotto in Lourdes.

PURAM

Thrissur is best known to outsiders as the venue for Kerala's biggest festival, **Puram**, which takes place on one day in April/May. Introduced by the Kochi (Cochin) Raja, Shaktan Tampuran (1789–1803), Puram is today the most extreme example of the kind of celebration seen on a smaller scale all over Kerala, whose main ingredients invariably include **caparisoned elephants**, **drum music** and **fireworks**.

On this day, at the hottest time of year, the centre of Thrissur fills to capacity with a sea of people gravitating towards Round South, where a long wide path leads to the southern entrance of the **Vadakkunatha** temple complex. Two separate processions, representing the Tiruvambadi and Paramekkavu temples in Thrissur, compete to create the more impressive sights and sounds. They eventually meet, like armies on a battlefield, facing each other at either end of the path. Both sides present fifteen tuskers sumptuously decorated with gold ornaments, each ridden by three brahmins clutching objects symbolizing royalty: silver-handled whisks of yak hair, circular peacock feather fans and orange, green, red, purple, turquoise, black, gold or patterned silk umbrellas fringed with silver pendants. At the centre of each group, the principal elephant carries an image of the temple's deity. Swaying gently, the elephants stand still much of the time, ears flapping, seemingly oblivious to the mayhem engendered by the crowds, bomb-like firework bangs and the huge orchestra that plays in front of them.

Known as **chenda mellam**, this quintessentially Keralan music, featuring as many as a hundred loud, hard-skinned, cylindrical *chenda* drums, crashing cymbals and wind instruments, mesmerizes the crowd while its structure marks the progress of the procession. Each kind of *chenda mellam* is named after the rhythmic cycle (*tala* or, in Malayalam, *talam*) in which it is set. Drummers stand in ranks, the most numerous at the back often playing single beats. At the front, a line of master drummers, the stars of Keralan music, try to outdo each other with their speed, stamina, improvisational skills and showmanship. Facing the drummers, musicians play long double-reed, oboe-like *kuzhals* (similar to the north Indian *shehnai*) and C-shaped *kompu* bell-metal trumpets. The fundamental structure is provided by the *elatalam* – medium-sized, heavy, brass hand cymbals that resolutely and precisely keep the tempo, essential to the cumulative effect of the music. Over an extended period, the *mellam* passes through four phases of tempo, each a double of the last, from a majestic dead slow through to a frenetic pace.

The arrival of the fastest tempo is borne on a wave of aural and visual stimulation. Those astride the elephants stand at this point, to manipulate their feather fans and hair whisks in co-ordinated sequence while behind, unfurled umbrellas are twirled in flashes of dazzling colour and glinting silver in the sun. Meanwhile, the cymbals crash furiously, often raised above the head, requiring extraordinary stamina (and causing nasty weals on the hands). The master drummers play their loudest and fastest, frequently intensified by surges of energy emanating from single players, one after another. A chorus of trumpets, in ragged unison, make an ancient noise.

All this is greeted by firework explosions and roars from the crowd. Many people punch the air, some fairly randomly much like heavy metal fans in the west, while others are clearly *talam branthans*, rhythm "madmen", who follow every nuance of the structure. When the fastest speed is played out, the slowest tempo returns and the procession edges forward, the *mahouts* leading the elephants by the tusk. Stopping again, the whole cycle is repeated. At night, the Vadukannatha temple entrances are a blaze of coloured lights and a spectacular firework display takes place in the early hours of the morning.

If you venture to Thrissur for Puram, be prepared for packed buses and trains. Needless to say, accommodation should be booked well in advance. An umbrella or hat is recommended. Women travellers should be aware that the densest parts of the crowd are almost entirely male; Keralan women usually look on from a distance.

Similar but much smaller events take place, generally from September onwards, with most during the summer (April & May). Enquire at a tourist office or your hotel, or ask someone to check a local edition of the newspaper, *Mathrabhumi*, for local performances of *chenda mellam*, and other drum orchestras such as *panchavadyam* and *tyambaka*.

Shopping

Thrissur is a great place to pick up distinctive Keralan **crafts**. The main shopping area is on the Round; on Round West, the *Kerala State Handicraft Emporium* specializes in wood, while a few doors along, a small branch of *Khadi Gramodyog* sells a limited range of handloom cloth. A far better selection of handloom can be found in *Co-optex* at the top of Palace Rd (a one-minute walk from Round East).

At *Chemmanur's*, Round South, near the *Elite Hotel*, you'll find the usual carved wooden elephant type souvenirs, and, on the ground floor, a high-kitsch Aladdin's Cave of nodding dogs, Jesus clocks, Mecca table ornaments and parabolic nail-and-string art. *Sportsland*, further west on Round South, aside from sports equipment, also sells crudely painted wooden toys, such as buses and cars.

Kuruppam Road, which leads south towards the railway station from the western end of Round South, is one of the best places in Kerala to buy **bell-metal** products, particularly oil lamps made in the village of Nadavaramba, near Irinjalakuda (see p.1024). *Nadavaramba Krishna & Sons* and *Bell-metal Craft* both specialize in brass, bronze and bell-metal. Lamps cost from Rs50 to Rs25,000, and "superfine" bell-metal is sold by weight, at over Rs200 per kilo. Continuing south on Kuruppam Rd to the next junction with Railway Station Rd, you'll find a number of small shops selling cheap Christian, Muslim and Hindu pictures etched on metal, and places that supply festival accessories, including umbrellas similar to those used for Puram (see opposite).

Accommodation

Thrissur has a fair number of budget and mid-range hotels, with a real bargain in the *Government Rest House* – if you can get in.

Binny Tourist Home, Round North (☎0487/23203). Very inexpensive, very shabby lodge near the Priya Darshini bus stand. ①.

Casino, TB Rd, near the railway station (☎0487/24699). The poshest of Thrissur's hotels. The management may change travellers' cheques if you eat in their (OK) restaurant (ask first). ⑤.

Elite International, Chembottil Lane, off Round South (☎0487/21033). Pronounced *Ee-light*. Probably Thrissur's first "modern" hotel. Friendly staff and good restaurant, but needs refurbishing. Very central; some balconied rooms overlook the green (booked months ahead for Puram). ③–④.

KTDC Yatri Niwas, off Museum Rd (☎0487/27383). Clean and reasonable place with a beer parlour and "omelette-bread-jam"-style restaurant. ②.

Luciya Palace, Marar Rd (☎0487/24731). Neoclassical fantasy in concrete, falling to bits. Coir-mat floors and cane furniture have seen better days. *Star TV* in a/c rooms only; non-a/c a better deal. ⑤.

Pathan's Lodging, Round South (☎0487/25620). No-frills Indian lodge which is often full. New rooms have a view of the Round, and are excellent spots to watch events on the green. ②.

Ramanilayam Government Guest House, Palace Rd (☎0487/20300). Very inexpensive, huge, clean, comfortable suites with balconies. Bear in mind that it's officially for VIPs, and that they're not obliged to give you a room. It's hugely popular, and often full; if you're alone, the rate doubles after three nights. The (basic) food is by advance order only. ②.

Sree Buddha Tourist Home, Chembottil Lane, off Round South (☎0487/27689). Range of fairly grotty, cheap and very cheap rooms. ①–②.

Surya International, Veliyannur Rd, Kokkalai (☎0487/24774). Modernish Indian hotel, near the railway, KSRTC and Shakthan Thampuran bus stations. ③.

Eating and drinking

Thrissur's big **hotels** offer Indian, western and Chinese food, and Keralan lunches, while several quality, inexpensive "meals" places are clustered near **the Round**. Late at night, on the corner of Rounds South and East, opposite the Medical College Hospital, you'll find a string of *chai* and omelette stalls, frequented by auto-rickshaw *wallahs*, hospital visitors, itinerant mendicants, Ayappa devotees and student revellers.

Bharata Lodge, Chembottil Lane, next door to *Elite Hotel*. Inexpensive, good-quality south Indian breakfasts, snacks and "meals" at lunchtime.

Indian Coffee House, Round South. The better of two in town. Very busy, serving snacks and the usual excellent coffee. The branch on Station Rd is very run down.

Kerala Bhavan, Railway Station Rd. Recommended for breakfast and low-priced regional "meals".

Luciya Palace, Marar Rd (☎24731). Indian and Chinese dishes. The main appeal is that they serve food at night in a pleasant garden illuminated by fairy lights.

Around Thrissur

The chief appeal of exploring the region that surrounds Thrissur is for the opportunities it provides to get to grips with Kerala's cultural heritage. Countless festivals, at their peak before the monsoon hits in May, enable visitors to catch some of the best drummers in the world, **Kathakali** dance drama and **Kutiyattam**, the world's oldest surviving theatre form.

Irinjalakuda

The village of **IRINJALAKUDA**, 20km south of Thrissur, has a unique temple, five minutes walk west from the bus stand, dedicated to **Bharata**, the brother of Rama. Visitors are usually permitted to see inside (men must wear a *dhoti*), but as elsewhere, the inner parts of the temple are closed to non-Hindus. It boasts a superbly elegant tiled *kuttambalam* **theatre** within its outer courtyard, built to afford an unimpeded view for the maximum number of spectators (drawn from the highest castes only), and known for excellent acoustics. A profusion of painted woodcarvings of mythological animals and stories from the epics decorate the interior. On the low stage, which is enclosed by painted wooden columns and friezes of female dancers, stand two large copper *mizhavu* drums, for use in the Sanskrit drama Kutiyattam (see p.1029), permanently installed in wooden frames into which a drummer climbs to play. Traditionally, *mizhavus* were considered sacred objects; Nandikeshvara, Shiva's own rhythm expert and accompanist, was said to reside in them. The drama for which they provided music was a holy ritual, and in the old days the instrument was never allowed to leave the temple and only played by members of a special caste, the Nambyars. Since then, outsiders have learned the art of *mizhavu* playing; some are based near the temple, but the orthodox authorities do not allow them to play inside.

Natana Kairali (☎2129) is an important cultural centre dedicated to the performance, protection and documentation of Kerala's lesser-known, but fascinating and vibrant theatre arts, including Kutiyattam, Nangiar Koothu (female mono-acting), shadow and puppet theatres. Left of the Bharata temple as you leave, it is based in the home of one of Kerala's most illustrious acting families, Ammanur Chakyar Madhom;

NADAVARAMBA BELL-METAL OIL LAMPS

Keralan nights are made more enchanting by the use of **oil lamps**; the most common type, seen all over, is a slim floor-standing metal column surmounted by a spike that rises from a circular receptacle for coconut oil, and using cloth or banana plant fibre wicks. Every classical theatre performance keeps a large lamp burning centre-stage, all night. The special atmosphere of temples is also enhanced by innumerable lamps, some hanging from chains; others, *deepa stambham*, are multi-tiered and stand metres-high.

The village of **Nadavaramba**, near Irinjalakuda, is an important centre for the manufacture of oil lamps and large cooking vessels, known as *uruli* and *varppu*. Alloys made from brass, copper and tin are frequently used, but the best are from bell-metal, said to be eighty percent copper, and give a sonorous chime when struck. Shops in Thrissur that specialize in Nadavaramba ware arrange visits to see the craftsmen at work.

cite that name when you ask for directions. *Natana Kairali*'s director, Shri G Venu, is a mine of information about Keralan arts, and can advise on forthcoming performances.

Irinjalakuda is best reached by **bus** from the Shakthan Thampuran stand at Thrissur rather than by train, as the railway station is an inconvenient 8km east of town.

Kodungallur

Virtually an island, surrounded by backwaters and the sea, the small country town of **KODUNGALLUR** (Cranganore), 35km due south of Thrissur, is rich in Keralan history. The dearth of information regarding the modern town contrasts with tales of its illustrious past, and curious travellers may find that Kodungallur's "sights", with one notable exception, require some imagination to enjoy. The town is easily visited in a day trip by **bus** from Thrissur's Shakthan Thampuran stand (1hr 30min).

Standing on a large piece of open ground at the centre of Kodungallur, the ancient and typically Keralan **Kurumba Bhagavati Temple** is the site of an extraordinary annual event that some residents would prefer didn't happen at all. The **Bharani** festival, held during the Malayalam month of Meenom (March/April), attracts droves of devotees, both male and female, mainly from "low caste" communities previously excluded from the temple. Their devotions consist in part of drinking copious amounts of alcohol and taking to the streets to sing Bharani *pattu*, songs of a sexually explicit nature about, and addressed to, goddess Bhagavati, which are considered obscene and highly offensive by many other Keralans. On Kavuthindal, the first day, the pilgrims run en masse around the perimeters of the temple three times at breakneck speed, beating its walls with sticks. Until the mid-1950s, chickens were sacrificed in front of the temple; today, a simple red cloth symbolizes the bloody ritual. An important section of the devotees are the crimson-clad village oracles, wielding scythe-like swords with which sometimes they beat themselves on the head in ecstatic fervour, often drawing blood. Despite widespread disapproval, the festival draws plenty of spectators.

Cheraman Juma Masjid, 1.5km from Kodungallur town centre, is thought to be the earliest mosque in India, founded in the seventh century. The present building,

---

ANCIENT KODUNGALLUR

Kodungallur has been identified as the site of the ancient cities of **Vanji**, one-time capital of the Chera kingdom, and **Muziris**, described in the first century AD by the Roman traveller, Pliny, as *Primum Emporium Indiae*, the most important port in India. Other accounts describe the harbour as crowded with great ships, warehouses, palaces, temples and *Yavanas* (a generic term for foreigners) who brought gold, and left with spices, sandalwood, teak, gems and silks. The Romans are said to have built a temple in Kodungallur, but nothing remains, though their presence has been shown through finds of coins, the majority of which date from the reigns of Augustus to Nero (27 BC–68 AD). Its life as a great port was curtailed in 1341 by floods that silted up the harbour, leading to the development of Kochi (Cochin).

Kodungallur is also reputed to be the site where the Apostle Thomas ("**Doubting Thomas**") landed in 52 AD, bringing Christianity to the subcontinent. Jews fleeing the fall of Jerusalem arrived in 69 AD, and, although the advent of Islam in India is usually associated with invading land armies arriving from the northwest in the twelfth century, Kerala claims an earlier date. The region had long enjoyed peaceable relations with the Arab world, thanks to its sea trade. **Cheraman Perumal**, the legendary Keralan king who converted to Islam, abdicated, and emigrated to Mecca, is said to have founded the Cheraman Juma Masjid in Kodungallur during the seventh century, making it the earliest mosque in India. The supposed site of his palace, Cheraman Parambu, is easily missable, nothing more than a few broken columns on open ground.

which dates from the sixteenth century, was until recently predominantly made of wood, of a style usually associated with Keralan Hindu temples. Unfortunately, due to weather damage, it has recently had to be partly rebuilt, and the facade, at least, is now rather mundane, with concrete minarets. The wooden interior remains intact, however, with a large Keralan oil lamp in the centre. Introduced five centuries ago for group study of the Koran, the lamp has taken on great significance to other communities, and Muslims, Christians and Hindus alike bring oil for the lamp on the auspicious occasion of major family events. In an ante-room, a small mausoleum is said to be the burial place of Habib Bin Malik, an envoy sent from Mecca by the convert king Cheraman Perumal. Women are not allowed into the mosque at any time ("they pray at home"), but interested male visitors should contact the assistant *mukhari* (*imam*, or priest), KM Saidumohamed, who lives directly opposite and will show you around.

A rather incongruous-looking church, the **Mar Thoma Pontifical Shrine**, fronted by a crescent of neoclassical colonnades at Azhikode (pronounced "Arikode") Jetty (2km) marks the place where the Apostle Thomas is said to have arrived in India, not long after the death of Christ. It's a pleasant enough spot, on the edge of backwaters, but hardly worth a detour unless you're desperate to see the fragment of the saint's wrist bone enshrined within the church.

Guruvayur

Kerala's most important Krishna shrine, the high-walled temple of **GURUVAYUR**, 29km northwest of Thrissur, attracts a constant flow of pilgrims, second only in volume to Ayappa's at Sabarimala (see p.1007). Its deity, **Guruvayurappan**, has inspired numerous paeans from Keralan poets, most notably Narayana Bhattatiri who wrote the *Narayaniyam* during the sixteenth century, when the temple, whose origins are legendary, seems to have first risen to prominence.

One of the richest temples in Kerala, **Guruvayar temple** (3am–1pm & 4–10pm) is from very early morning to late at night awash with pilgrims in their best white clothes, often trimmed with gold. Some visitors find the intense activity of the market around the temple perimeter too commercial, full of glitter and cheap trinkets such as two-*rupee* plastic Guruvayurappan signet rings, but nevertheless there is a palpable air of excitement, particularly when events inside spill out into the streets.

Closed to non-Hindus, the temple has turned away many famous people in its time, including VIPs such as the President of India and, ironically, the most vocal of Guruvayurappan's devotees, the Keralan film song artist Jesudas. Though born into a Christian family (his name literally means "servant of Jesus"), Jesudas has earned

---

THE FOUNDING OF GURUVAYUR TEMPLE

The founding of the **Guruvayur temple** is associated with the end of Krishna's life. After witnessing the massacre of family and compatriots, Krishna returned to his capital, Dvarka, in Gujarat, to end his earthly existence. However, knowing that Dvarka would disappear into the sea on his death, he was concerned that the form of Vishnu there, which he himself worshipped, should be spared its fate.

Krishna invited Brihaspati, also known as Guru, the preceptor of the gods, and a pupil, Vayu, the god of wind, to help him select a new home for Vishnu. By the time they arrived at Dvarka, the sea (Varuna) had already claimed the city, but the wind managed to rescue Vishnu. Krishna, Guru and Vayu travelled south, where they met Parashurama, who had just created Kerala by throwing his axe into the sea (see p.984). On reaching a beautiful lake of lotuses, Rudratirtha, they were greeted by Shiva and Parvati who consecrated the image of Vishnu; Guru and Vayu then installed it, the temple was named after them, and so the deity received the title **Guruvayurappan** ("Lord of Guruvayur").

millions of fans by his sincere rendition of Hindu devotional songs. Many temples, including this one, play his records, but he is not allowed past the door unless he formally converts and produces a certificate to prove it, something he believes should be unnecessary. One of his songs describes how he has, in any event, already had *darshan* of Guruvayurappan "in his mind".

Of the temple's twenty-four **annual festivals**, the most important are Ekadashi and Ulsavam. During the eighteen days of Ekadashi, in the month of Vrischikam (Nov/Dec), marked by frequent processions of caparisoned elephants outside the temple, the exterior of the building may be decorated with the tiny flames of innumerable oil lamps. On certain days (check dates with a KTDC office) programmes staged in front of the temple attract the cream of south Indian classical music artists.

During Ulsavam, in the month of Kumbham (Feb/March), tantric rituals are conducted inside, while on the first day, an elephant race is run outside, some distance from the east entrance. During the ensuing six days, elephant processions take place each morning, afternoon and evening. On the ninth day, the Palivetta, or "hunt" occurs; the deity, mounted on an elephant, circumambulates the temple accompanied by men dressed as animals, who represent human weaknesses such as greed and anger, and are vanquished by the god. The next night sees the image of the god taken out for ritual immersion in the temple tank; devotees greet the procession with oil lamps and throw rice. It is considered highly auspicious to bathe in the tank at the same time as the god. Visitors can take an auto-rickshaw to **Punnathur Kotta**, 4km from the temple, to watch the temple's 44 elephants being fed and bathed.

The **Institute of Mural Painting**, run under the auspices of the Guruvayur Devaswom (the temple authorities), trains students in this traditional art (see p.1012) and gives a fascinating insight into its techniques. Contact the Principal, Mammiyur Krishnan Kutty Nair, to look around. The school can be found just off East Nada (the eastern approach road to the temple), in the Sathram Building.

Practicalities

Buses from Thrissur (40min) arrive at the main **bus stand** at the top end of E Nada St, five minutes east of the temple. **Accommodation** is concentrated along this street; it's often packed to the gills with pilgrims, but the two KTDC hotels are usually good bets. *Hotel Nandanam* (☎04889/6266; ①–③) has both a/c and non-a/c rooms, but can be noisy as it is very near the temple entrance, while *Hotel Mangalya* (☎04889/6866; ②) is a better option, set back from the road near the bus stand. All rooms are non-a/c, but spacious, if a little dowdy. As you'd expect there are plenty of strictly veg "meals" restaurants in town, and a decent *Indian Coffee House* on the southern side of E Nada St serves south Indian snack food.

Cheruthuruthy

Far from big city life, the village of **CHERUTHURUTHY** is an easy day trip 32km north of Thrissur through gently undulating green country. It consists of a few lanes and one main street, that runs south from the bank of Kerala's longest river, the **Bharatapuzha** (pronounced *Bharatapura*). Considered holy by locals, the great river has declined in recent years, leaving a vast expanse of sand. Although of little consolation to locals, who have to deal with the problems of a depleted water supply, it has produced landscape of incomparable beauty.

Cheruthuruthy is famous as the home of **Kerala Kalamandalam**, the State's flagship training school for Kathakali dance drama and other indigenous Keralan performing arts, which was founded in 1927 by the revered Keralan poet Vallathol (1878–1957). At first patronized by the Raja of Cochin, the school has been funded by both state and national governments and has been instrumental in the large-scale revival of interest in

KERALAN RITUAL AND RITUALIZED THEATRE

Among the most magical experiences a visitor to Kerala can have is to witness one of the innumerable ancient rituals, ritualized theatre or dance styles that play such an important, and unique role in the cultural life of the region. The dance drama **Kathakali** is the best known; other less publicized forms, which clearly influenced its development, include the classical Sanskrit **Kutiyattam** and the village hero-worship ritual **Teyyam**.

Many Keralan forms share broad characteristics. A prime aim of each performer is to transform the mundane to the world of gods and demons; his preparation is highly ritualized, involving other-worldly costume and mask-like make-up. In Kathakali and Kutiyattam, this is rigorously codified and part of a classical tradition, whereas the much wilder appearance of Teyyam differs from village to village. One-off **performances** of various types take place throughout the state, building up to fever pitch during April and May before pausing for the monsoon (June, July & Aug). Finding out about such events requires a little perseverance, but it's well worth the effort; enquire at tourist offices, or buy a Malayalam daily paper such as *Mathrabhumi* and ask someone to check the listings. **Temple festivals**, where most of the action takes place, are invariably announced. Tourist Kathakali is staged in Kochi (see p.1019) but to find authentic performances, contact **performing arts schools** such as Thiruvananthapuram's *Margi* (see p.988) and Cheruthuruthy's *Kerala Kalamandalam*. Kutiyattam artists work at both, as well as at *Natana Kairali* at Irinjalakuda (see p.1024).

Kathakali

Here is the tradition of the trance dancers, here is the absolute demand of the subjugation of body to spirit, here is the realization of the cosmic transformation of human into divine.

Mrinalini Sarabhai, classical dancer

Kathakali dance drama, Kerala's most popular theatre form, is recognized as one of the four major classical Indian styles. The image of a Kathakali actor in a magnificent costume with extraordinary make-up and a huge gold crown has become Kerala's trademark, seen on anything from matchboxes to TV adverts for detergents. Traditional performances, of which there are still many, usually take place on open ground outside a temple, beginning at 10pm and lasting until dawn, illuminated by the flickers of a large brass oil lamp centre stage. Virtually nothing about Kathakali is naturalistic, because it depicts the world of gods and demons. Both male and female roles are played by men.

Standing at the back of the stage, two musicians play driving rhythms, one on a bronze gong, the other on heavy bell-metal cymbals; they also sing the dialogue. Actors appear and disappear from behind a handheld curtain and never utter a sound, save the odd strange cry. Learning the elaborate hand gestures, facial expressions and choreographed movements, as articulate and precise as any sign language, requires rigorous training which can begin at the age of eight and last ten years. At least two more drummers stand left of the stage; one plays the upright **chenda** with slender curved sticks, the other plays the *maddalam*, a horizontal barrel-shaped hand drum. When a female character is "speaking", the *chenda* is replaced by the hourglass-shaped *ettaka*, a "talking drum" on which melodies can be played. The drummers keep their eyes on the actors, whose every gesture is reinforced by their sound, from the gentlest embrace to the gory disembowelling of an enemy.

Although it bears the unmistakable influences of Kutiyattam and indigenous folk rituals, Kathakali, literally "story-play", is thought to have crystallized into a distinct theatre form during the seventeenth century. The plays are based on three major sources: the Hindu

Kathakali, and other unique Keralan artforms. Despite conservative opposition, it followed an open-door recruitment policy, based on artistic merit, which produced "scheduled caste", Muslim and Christian graduates along with the usual Hindu castes, something that was previously unimaginable. During the 1960s Kalamandalam's dynamic leadership forged international links with cultural organizations. Foreign students were accepted and every attempt was made to modernize, extending into the way in which the traditional arts were presented. Kalamandalam artists perform in the epics the *Mahabharata*, *Ramayana* and the *Bhagavata Purana*. While the stories are ostensibly of god-heroes such as Rama and Krishna, the most popular characters are those that give the most scope to the actors – the villainous, fanged, red-and-black-faced, *katti* ("knife") anti-heroes. These types, such as the kings Ravana and Duryodhana, are dominated by lust, greed, envy and violence. David Bolland's handy paperback *Guide to Kathakali*, widely available in Kerala, gives invaluable scene-by-scene summaries of the most popular plays and explains in simple language a lot more besides.

When attending a performance, arrive early to get your bearings before it gets dark, even though the first play will not begin much before 10pm. (Quiet) members of the audience are welcome to visit the dressing room before and during the performance. The colour and design of the mask-like make-up, which specialist artists take several hours to apply, reveal the character's personality. The word *pacha* means both "green" and "pure"; a green-faced *pacha* character is thus a noble human or god. Red signifies *rajas*, passion and aggression, black denotes *tamas*, darkness and negativity, while white is *sattvik*, light and intellect. Once the make-up is completed, elaborate wide skirts are tied to the waist, and ornaments of silver and gold are added. Silver talons are fitted to the left hand. The transformation is complete with a final prayer and the donning of waist-length wig and crown. Visitors new to Kathakali will almost undoubtedly get bored during such long programmes, parts of which are very slow indeed. If you're at a village performance, you may not always find accommodation, so you can't leave during the night. Be prepared to sit on the ground for hours, and bring some warm clothes. Half the fun is staying up all night to witness, just as the dawn light appears, the gruesome disembowelling of a villain or a demon *asura*.

Kutiyattam

Three families of the Chakyar caste and a few outsiders perform the Sanskrit drama **Kutiyattam**, the oldest continually performed theatre form in the world. Until recently it was only performed inside temples and then only in front of the uppermost castes. Visually it is very similar to its offspring, Kathakali, but its atmosphere is infinitely more archaic. The actors, eloquent in sign language and symbolic movement, speak in the bizarre, compelling, intonation of the local *brahmins*' Vedic chant, unchanged since 1500 BC.

A single act of a Kutiyattam play can require ten full nights; the entire play forty. A great actor, in full command of the subtleties of gestural expression, can take half an hour to do such a simple thing as murder a demon, berate the audience, or simply describe a leaf fall to the ground. Unlike Kathakali, Kutiyattam includes comic characters and plays. The ubiquitous **Vidushaka**, narrator and clown, is something of a court jester, and traditionally has held the right openly to criticize the highest in the land without fear of retribution.

Teyyam

In northern Kerala, a wide range of ritual "performances", loosely known as **Teyyam,** are extremely localized, even to particular families. They might include *bhuta* (spirit or hero worship), trance dances, the enactment of legendary events, and oracular pronouncements. Performers are usually from low castes, but during the ritual, a brahmin will honour the deities they represent, so the status of each individual is reversed.

Although Teyyam can now be seen in government-organized cultural festivals, the powerful effect is best experienced in the courtyard of a house or temple, in a village setting. Some figures, with painted faces and bodies, are genuinely terrifying; costumes include metres-high headgear, sometimes doubling as a mask, and clothes of leaves and bark.

great theatres of the world, many sharing their extraordinary skills with outsiders; luminaries of modern theatre, such as Grotowski and Peter Brook, are indebted to them. Nonetheless, many of these trained artists are still excluded from entering, let alone performing in, temples, the most popular venue for Hindu artforms.

If you've got more than a passing interest in how this extraordinary technique is taught, don't miss the chance to sit in on the rigorous training sessions, which have to be seen to be believed (Mon–Fri 4.30–6.30am, 8.30am–noon, & 3.30–5.30pm; closed

March 31, June 15, public hols, April & May). Non-Hindus can see Kathakali, Kutiyattam and Mohiniattam performances in the school's superb theatre, which replicates the wooden, sloping roofed traditional theatres, known as *kuttambalams*, found in Keralan temples. For information contact the school office (☎04929/2418).

Practicalities

Cheruthuruthy's only **accommodation** is at the *Government Rest House* (☎04929/2498; ②) near the banks of the river, where eight simple doubles share a verandah. Food may be available by arrangement, otherwise there are simple "meals" tea shops in the village. **Buses** heading to Shoranur from Thrissur's Wadakkancheri stand stop outside Kalamandalam, just before Cheruthuruthy. The nearest **railway** station is Shoranur Junction, ten minutes away by bus or auto-rickshaw.

Palakaad

PALAKAAD (Palghat), known as the "granary of Kerala" because of the surrounding paddy fields, lies on the NH47 between Thrissur (79km) and Coimbatore in Tamil Nadu (54km) and on the railway line from Karnataka and Tamil Nadu. Historically, thanks to the natural twenty-kilometre-wide Palakaad Gap in the Western Ghat mountains, this area has been one of the chief entry points into Kerala. The surrounding country is beautiful, but the town itself barely warrants a stop, unless to break a journey. The well-preserved **fort**, built in 1766 by Haider Ali of Mysore, is the nearest thing to a "sight"; it gets plenty of visitors at weekends, despite having little to offer them.

However, many travellers in search of a **Kathakali** performance find themselves directed here, to the centre of Kerala's cultural heartland. Particularly during April and May, hundreds of one-off events take place in the area. The local Government Carnatic Music College has an excellent reputation, and a small open-air amphitheatre next to Palakaad fort often hosts first-class performances of music and dance.

Practicalities

The **railway station** (☎0491/5231) is 6km northeast of town while the KSRTC **bus stand** (☎0491/27098) is in the centre. Both are well-connected to the rest of Kerala.

Most **accommodation** is in Indian-style lodges. *Kalyan Tourist Home* on GB Rd (☎0491/24206; ①–②) has fifteen basic rooms, a restaurant and bar. Far more upmarket, the modern concrete *Hotel Indraprastha*, English Church Rd (☎0491/24641; ③–⑤), boasts large a/c rooms, a 24-hour coffee shop, garden, restaurant and bar. *Fort Palace*, W Palace Rd (☎0491/24626; ②–③), is also reasonable, with some a/c rooms. The best **places to eat** are the *Fort Palace* which serves Indian food, and *Indraprastha* for its mixed menu of Indian, western and Chinese cuisine.

Kozhikode (Calicut)

The busy coastal city of **KOZHIKODE** (Calicut), 225km north of Kochi, occupies an extremely important place in Keralan legend and history. It is also significant in the story of European interference in the subcontinent, as Vasco da Gama first set foot in India at Kozhikode in 1498. In Keralan tradition, the powerful king Cheraman Perumal is said to have converted from Hinduism to Islam and left for Mecca "to save his soul", never to return. Before he set sail he divided Kerala between his relatives, all of whom were to submit to his nephew, who was given the kingdom of Kozhikode and the title Zamorin, equivalent to emperor. Kozhikode became extremely prosperous and, perhaps because of the story of the convert king, the preferred port of Muslim traders from the Middle East in search of spices, particularly pepper.

Arrival and information

Kozhikode's **airport** (connections only to Thiruvananthapuram, Bombay and the Gulf countries) lies 23km south of the city. The **railway station** is close to the centre, while the most important of the three bus stands is the **KSRTC stand**, Mavoor Rd (☎74596), from where buses run to destinations as far afield as Bangalore, Mysore, Ooty, Madurai, Coimbatore and Mangalore. From the **New Mafussil private stand**, 500m away, on the other side of Mavoor Rd, you can get local buses and services to northern Kerala. The **Palayam stand** is for infrequent long-haul buses and destinations further south, such as Palakaad, Thrissur, and Guruvayur.

The **KTDC Tourist Information Centre** (☎0495/76101) in their *Malabar Mansion Hotel*, at the corner of SM St, can supply limited information.

The City

Few traces remain of the model city laid out in the fourteenth century, which followed a Hindu grid formula based on a sacred diagram containing the image of the cosmic man, Purusha. The axis and energy centre of the diagram was dictated by the position of the ancient **Tali Shiva temple** (closed to non-Hindus), which survives to this day.

Everything, and everybody, had a place. The district around the port in the northwest was reserved for foreigners. Here, a Chinese community lived in and around Chinese St (now renamed Silk St) and, later, the Portuguese, Dutch and British occupied the area. Keralan Muslims (Mappilas) lived in the southwest. The northeast of the city was a commercial quarter, and in the southeast stood the Tali temple. Here too was a palace and fort; all the military *kalaris*, martial art gymnasia, that stood around the perimeter, have now gone.

Considering its history, there is very little to see in Kozhikode, though it is quite good for **shopping**. Around SM St, many good fabric and readymade clothes shops sell the locally produced plain white cotton cloth named calico by the British after their appellation for the city. This district is also a good place to try the local *halva* sweets, especially popular with the large Mappila (Keralan Muslim) community. Some shops also specialize in piping-hot banana chips, straight from the frying pan.

Locals enjoy a promenade on or near the **beach** (3km from the centre) in the late afternoon and early evening. Although not suitable for swimming, it's a restful place, where you can munch on roasted peanuts sold in the many stalls while scanning the seas for jumping dolphins. After dark it's difficult to find an auto-rickshaw to take you back into town, but on the land side of the road regular buses run into the centre.

The **Pazhassirajah and Krishnamenon Museums and Art Gallery** (Tues & Thurs–Sun 10am–12.30pm & 2.30–5pm, Wed 2.30–5pm) stand together 5km from the centre on East Hill. The Pazhassirajah collection includes copies of murals, coins, bronzes and models of the umbrella-shaped, stone megalithic remains peculiar to Kerala, while the Krishnamenon museum houses a collection of memorabilia associated with the left-wing Keralan politician VK Krishnamenon, and a gallery of works by Indian artists. Perhaps the best reason for visiting is to enjoy its peaceful location, with an endless vista of palm trees under which most of the city is hidden.

Accommodation and eating

Kozhikode's reasonably priced **hotels** can fill up by evening, especially during conventions. The beach area is a quiet alternative to the busy city. Your best bet for a proper **meal** is to eat at your hotel, though you can get snacks in town at such places as the usual dependable *Indian Coffee House* on Kallai Rd, and the open-air *Park Restaurant*, by Mananchira tank, which makes an appealing oasis in the evenings in the city centre.

Alakapuri Guest House, Moulana Mohammed Ali Rd (☎0495/73361). Near the train station, 1km from KSRTC bus stand. Built around a flower-filled garden, this must have once been a British guesthouse. Some rooms have huge bathtubs, polished wood and easy chairs; the cheaper, non-a/c, options are rather spartan. The first-floor cafeteria is recommended for south Indian food during the day; in the evening head for the large restaurant on the ground floor. ③.

Diplomat, Railway Station Rd (☎0495/65391). Small hotel near the railway station with restaurant and bar. Most rooms non-a/c. ①–③.

KTDC Malabar Mansion, SM St (☎0495/76101). Modern hotel, near the railway station at the top of the main street. Huge a/c suites, reasonable non-a/c rooms. Beer parlour and restaurant. ②.

Paramount Tower, Town Hall Rd, near railway station (☎0495/62731). Large hotel with some non-a/c rooms. Restaurant, car rental. ③–④.

Sea Queen, Beach Rd, 2km from centre (☎0495/58504). A quiet, comfortable, middle-class hotel over the road from the beach. A/c and non-a/c rooms, plus roof-garden restaurant and bar. ③–④.

North of Kozhikode

The beautiful coast of Kerala, **north of Kozhikode**, is a seemingly endless stretch of coconut palms, wooded hills and virtually deserted beaches. However, the towns hold little of interest for visitors, most of whom bypass the area completely, or zoom right up to the as-yet-unspoilt haven of **Kasargode**. Mahé (65km), the only French settlement on the west coast, and today part of the Union Territory of Pondicherry, is a sleepy coastal town with a reputation for liberal attitudes to alcohol. Marco Polo mentioned **Cannanore** (92km), the ancient capital of the northern ruling dynasty of Kolathiri, as an important source of spices, and Vasco da Gama first visited in 1498. The Portuguese built a fort here in 1505 which still stands, overlooking the sea; nowadays, it's a thriving commercial town with a large Mappila population.

Kasargode and Bekkal

The old-fashioned little town of **KASARGODE** (153km north of Kozhikode, near the Karnataka border) is principally a fishing community – though some say smuggling is not unknown. Though it currently gets few foreign visitors, the number is sure to increase, as it is the nearest town of any size to the beaches and fort at **BEKKAL** (16km south), now earmarked for development. At present, this is as unexploited as you could hope to find, with nary a beachside shack cafe, let alone a five-star hotel.

Bekkal's **fort** stands on a promontory between two long, classically beautiful palm-fringed **beaches**. Although this is one of the largest forts in Kerala and has been under the control of various powers including Vijayanagar, Tipu Sultan and the British, it's nothing to get excited about. The fort's commanding position, with views across the bays to north and south is impressive enough, but only four watchtowers and the outer walls survive. A small temple stands in the entrance. Except for weekends, Bekkal is pretty deserted, and swimming tourists still arouse local curiosity. Caution is advised, as the undertow is very strong. Both beaches are accessible from the fort.

Practicalities

The nearest major town to Kasargode is Mangalore, 50km north in Karnataka, a ninety-minute bus ride away. Long-distance **buses** usually call at both its bus stands, a new one on the outskirts and another in town. Among regular buses along the coast road, those to Kanhangad stop at Bekkal. Kasargode **railway station** is 3km from town.

Accommodation at Bekkal is limited to the *Travellers Bungalow* (☎04995/502; ①), which has two basicrooms in a superb location at the furthest point of the promontory inside the fort. Book through the Kasargode District Collector, Civil Station, Kasargode (☎04995/20666). Near the bus stand in Kasargode, the *Enjay Tourist Home* (☎04995/ 1164; ①–②) has some a/c rooms, a south Indian restaurant and car rental, and *Aliya Lodge* (☎04995/22897; ①–②), also offering a/c rooms, has a restaurant attached. It is best to **eat** at the hotels. Local non-veg delicacies include *meen pathiri* (steamed rice and spiced fish) and stuffed chicken. For sweets and cakes try *City Bakers* in Bank Rd.

CHAPTER TWENTY

KARNATAKA

KARNATAKA, which covers one sixteenth of India, is a diverse state: its two most important cities, the capital Bangalore and the erstwhile capital Mysore, both in the south, could hardly be more different. **Bangalore** is determinedly go-ahead and modern, a leader in technological development and the base for India's space programme. It's a major transport hub, rare in being able to offer good shopping and even pubs, but the few official attractions don't merit a detour. **Mysore**, on the other hand, has enduring appeal, for its old-fashioned ambience, superb palaces, and magnficent **Dussehra** festival (Sept/Oct). At the nearby fortified island of **Srirangapatnam** – the site in 1799 of the bloody battle that finally put the all-important state of Mysore into the hands of the British, by defeating the Muslim military genius Tipu Sultan – parts of the fort, a mausoleum and Tipu's summer palace survive.

Near Mysore, at **Somnathpur** and a little further northwest at **Halebid** and **Belur** are the exquisite temples built by the **Hoysala** dynasty, who ruled southwestern Karnataka from the eleventh to the thirteenth centuries. Both Halebid and Belur are most easily visited from the town of **Hassan**, which can also serve as a base for the Jain pilgrimage centre of **Sravanabelgola**. Here, an utterly amazing eighteen-metre–high hill-top statue of the naked Gomateshvara is one of India's strangest landmarks.

In central Karnataka, scattered over a weird boulder-strewn landscape of austere beauty, the ghost "City of Victory", **Vijayanagar**, also known as **Hampi**, was once the vast capital of a mighty dynasty. Founded in the mid-fourteenth century, it was deserted a mere two hundred years later after a disastrous battle, and the site is now one of the most atmospheric destinations in the country. Further north still, the tiny villages of **Badami**, **Aihole** and **Pattadakal** were the capitals of the **Chalukyas** between the sixth and eighth centuries, and the whole area is scattered with cave temples and literally hundreds of structural temples.

The little-known palm-fringed beaches of Karnataka's western seaboard stretch for over 300km, from Goa to Kerala. Historically important as a centre of the international spice trade, **Mangalore** still processes and exports most of the country's coffee and cocoa, and has rapidly modernized and expanded. Further north, the temple town of

KARNATAKA TRAVEL DETAILS

As this book went to press, the process of changing over Karnataka's antiquated metre-gauge **railway system** to broad-gauge had reached the point where massive disruption had rendered all timetables totally unreliable. It is impossible to predict when services will return to any semblance of normality, or in what form, and for that reason we include no train details below. However, Bangalore especially, as well as other cities in Karnataka, will in theory be better connected than ever with the rest of the country, while the opening of the *Konkan Railway*, running all the way from Bombay to Kerala, may transform the now-quiet coastal regions.

	Buses		Flights	
	Frequency	Time	Frequency	Time
To and from BANGALORE				
Ahmedabad			3 weekly	2hr 5min
Bombay	4 daily	24hr	6–7 daily	1hr 20min
Calcutta			6 weekly	2hr 20min
Coimbatore	2 daily	9hr	4 weekly	40min
Delhi			3 daily	2hr 20min
Goa	7 daily	14hr	1–2 daily	1hr
Hassan	8 daily	5hr		
Hospet	20 daily	9–11hr		
Hyderabad	10 daily	16hr	2 daily	50min
Kochi	3 daily	15hr	1 daily	50min
Madras	21 daily	9hr	2–5 daily	40min–1hr
Madurai	16 daily	15hr		
Mangalore	4 daily	8hr	4 weekly	40min
Mysore	every 15min	3hr		
Pune			3 weekly	1hr 25min
Thiruvananthapuram			5 weekly	60min
Udhagamandalam (Ooty)	12 daily	9hr		

	Buses			Buses	
To and from HOSPET			**To and from MYSORE**		
Badami	3 daily	6hr	Hassan	12 daily	2hr 30min
Goa	1 daily	13hr	Hospet	2 daily	8hr
Hubli	14 daily	3hr 30min	Kochi	3 daily	12hr
Mangalore	3 daily	11hr	Mangalore	8 daily	7hr
Kochi	3 daily	12hr	Udhagamandalam (Ooty)	11 daily	5hr

Note that no individual route appears more than once in this chart; for any specific journey, check against where you want to get to as well as where you're coming from.

Udupi – responsible for another of Karnataka's greatest achievements, the splendid south Indian snack, the *masala dosa* – is an important centre of pilgrimage.

Inland, parallel to the coast, the forested Western Ghat mountains, source of the Tungabhadra, Krishna and Kaveri rivers, offer spectacular scenery such as the towering **Jog Falls**. In the south, **Madikeri** (Mercara), capital of the coffee-growing Kodagu (Coorg) region of the Ghats, is a little-visited town that serves as a base for easy walks and treks in varied, beautiful country. Nearby, the twin wildlife reserves of **Nagarhole** and **Bandipur** are home to a large elephant population, rarely seen tigers and leopards, and many exotic birds.

Karnataka is rich in performing arts. Carnatic classical music and dance, such as *Bharatanatyam*, are regularly staged in the big cities and during Mysore's annual Dussehra festival, but finding performances of folk dance, music or theatre forms such as ritualized *Bayalata* or *Yakshagana*, the region's own vibrant dance drama, requires some detective work. Other than looking in the newspapers, asking at your hotel and in tourist offices, you could enquire at resource centres such as the **Janapada Loka Folk Arts Museum**, between Mysore and Bangalore, or the centre at Udupi.

A little history

Along with much of southern India, Karnataka has over the centuries been ruled by successive Buddhist, Hindu and Muslim dynasties. The influence of Jainism has also been marked; India's very first emperor, **Chandragupta Maurya**, is believed to have converted to Jainism in the fourth century BC, renounced his throne, and fasted to death at Sravanabelgola, now one of the most visited Jain pilgrimage centres in the country.

During the first millennium AD, this whole region was dominated by power struggles between the various kingdoms, such as Vakatakas and the Guptas, who controlled the western Deccan and at times extended their authority as far as the Coromandel coast, now in Tamil Nadu. From the sixth to the eighth centuries, only interrupted by thirteen years of Pallava rule, the **Chalukya** kingdom included Maharashtra, the Konkan coast on the west, and the whole of Karnataka. The **Cholas** were powerful in the east of the region from about 870 until the thirteenth century, when the Deccan kingdoms were overwhelmed by General Malik Kafur, a convert to Islam.

During the early fourteenth century, the great Hindu empire of the **Vijayanagars** was founded by the brothers Harihara and Bukka, who extended their kingdom south

---

BASAVA AND MADHVA

Two important religious leaders emerged in Karnataka during the twelfth and thirteenth centuries. **Viswadharmi Basavanna**, popularly known as **Basava** (1106–67), the founder of the Shaivite **Lingayat** or **Virashaiva** movement, was born into a wealthy *brahmin* family. Distressed as a young child at the inequalities and injustices he saw around him, he was unable to comprehend why his sister was denied a sacred-thread investiture as a *brahmin* merely because of her sex. In protest at this injustice, the eight-year-old Basava refused to go through his own ceremony. Thrown out by his parents, he sought asylum at Kudala Sangama in northwestern Karnataka. After twelve years of study, he obtained a post in the palace treasury of a local ruler, and rapidly rose to the position of finance minister, and then Prime Minister.

Basava quietly started a new religious movement, which was against inequality and the caste system and preached the fatherhood of a benign God; he taught "untouchables", treating them as equals, and rejected the treatment of widows who were forced to cut off their hair and could not remarry. He also opposed childhood marriage and the Hindus' belief in rebirth. He began to draw followers who were greatly attracted by his ideas of equality and to the spiritual messages in his writings, known as **Vachanas**, "sayings". These revolutionary ideas encountered considerable hostility; eventually, after one of the first inter-caste marriages was arranged, violence erupted and the participants, their families and supporters were killed. King Bijala, who had been sympathetic to Basava, was persuaded to reject him and send him into exile (instead of having him killed). Basava accepted his banishment philosophically and returned to Kudula Sangama, where he spent the rest of his days in meditation. The *Lingayat* movement, however, grew and is still a popular form of Hinduism in Karnataka today. Its adherents are easily identified by the *lingams* worn as amulets around the neck, which in essence replace the need for temples.

The second great figure of the period was **Madhva** (1197–1276), from Udupi on the coast. Madhva's staunchly Vaishnavite views challenged the orthodox *advaita*, non-dualist philosophy of Adi Shankara, which reduced the world of experience to illusion. Instead, by writing a commentary on the *Brahmasutras*, he claimed authority from his interpretation of the *Vedas*, while also expounding a popular devotional worship based around the figure of Krishna as revealed in the tenth-century *Bhagavata Purana*. Some aspects of Madhva's thinking are said to have been influenced by the Syrian Christians of the Malabar coast. Unusually among Hindu philosophers he laid emphasis on the "real" nature of dreams. The Madhva cult, centred in Udupi, remains important.

from the River Krishna. They created a new capital, Vijayanagar (**Hampi**), and the empire continued to dominate south India until 1565, when it lost the battle of Talikota to a union of Deccan Sultans. With their power considerably reduced, the Vijayanagars retained some control in the east, for around a hundred years, in what is now Andhra Pradesh and Tamil Nadu, but were finally overthrown by Adil Shahi and Qutb Shahi.

In the south of the state, the independent **Wadiyar Rajas** of Mysore, whose territory was comparatively small, successfully fought off the Marathas. In 1761, however, the brilliant Muslim campaigner Haider Ali, with French support, seized the throne. Haider Ali, and his son Tipu Sultan, turned Mysore into a major force in the south, before Tipu was killed by the British at the **battle of Srirangapatnam** in 1799.

Following Tipu's defeat, the British restored the Wadiyar family to the throne. They kept it until riots in 1830 led the British to appoint a Commission to rule in their place. Fifty years later, the throne was once more returned to the Wadiyars, who remained governors until Karnataka was created by the merging of the states of Mysore and the Madras Presidencies in 1956.

Bangalore

BANGALORE, the capital of Karnataka, is said to be the fastest growing city in Asia, with its population racing towards five million. A major scientific research centre at the cutting edge of India's technological revolution, its trendy high-speed self-image ensures that it is quite unlike anywhere else in south India.

In the nineteenth century, Bangalore's gentle climate, broad streets, and green public parks made it the "Garden City". Until well after Independence, senior citizens, film stars and VIPs flocked to buy or build dream homes amid this urban idyll, which offered such unique amenities as consumer items, theatres, cinemas, and a complete lack of restrictions on alcohol. However, during the last decade or so, Bangalore has undergone a massive transformation. The wide avenues, now dominated by looming tower blocks, are choked with traffic, and for the first time in living memory, the city is suffering from water shortages. Even the "pleasant climate" has been affected.

Many foreigners turn up in Bangalore without really knowing why they've come. What little there is to see is no match for the attractions elsewhere in the state, and the city's very real advantages for Indians are two-a-penny in the west. That said, Bangalore is a transport hub, especially well served by plane and bus, and some visitors enjoy the novelty of a westernized Indian city that not only offers good shopping, eating and accommodation, but is the only place on the subcontinent to boast anything resembling a pub culture.

A brief history

Bangalore began life as the minor "village of the half-baked *gram*"; to this day *gram* (beans) remain an important local product. In 1537, Magadi **Kempe Gowda**, a devout Hindu and feudatory chief of the Vijayanagar empire, built a mud fort and erected four watchtowers outside the village, predicting that it would, one day, extend that far; the city now, of course, stretches way beyond. During the first half of the seventeenth century, Bangalore fell to the Muslim Sultanate of Bijapur; changing hands several times, it returned to Hindu rule under the Mysore Wadiyar Rajas of Srirangapatnam. In 1758, Chikka Krishnaraja Wadiyar II was deposed by the military genius Haider Ali, who set up arsenals here to produce muskets, rockets and other weapons for his formidable anti-British campaigns. Both he and his son, **Tipu Sultan**, greatly extended and fortified Bangalore, but Tipu was overthrown by the British in 1799. The British set up a cantonment, which made the city an important military station, and passed the administration over to the Maharaja of Mysore in 1881. After Independence, the erstwhile Maharaja became Governor of Mysore state. Bangalore was designated capital in 1956, and retained that status when Karnataka state was created in 1973.

Arrival

Bangalore airport, 13km north of the city centre, is served by flights to and from cities throughout south India and beyond; for details of departures, see p.1044. The **KSTDC desk** in the arrivals hall (daily 7am–2pm & 2.30–8.30pm; ☎571467) stocks leaflets on Karnataka and can book hotel rooms. Branches of the *State Bank of Mysore* (daily 8am–7pm) and *Vijaya Bank* (daily 8.30am–12.30pm) **change money**, and there's an STD telephone booth. You can get **into the city** on *KSRTC* buses (Rs12), by taxi (Rs150; book at the pre-paid desk), or by the auto-rickshaws that gather outside.

Bangalore City railway station is east of the centre, near Kempe Gowda Circle, and across the road from the main bus stands (if you plan to stay in the north of the city, get off at Bangalore Cantonment station). As you come into the entrance hall from the platforms, the far left-hand corner holds a **pre-paid taxi counter** (daily 8.30am–2pm & 2.30–5pm) and an **ITDC booth** (daily 7am–5.30pm), where you can book conducted tours. The **KSTDC tourist information office** (daily 6.30am–8pm; ☎70068), to the right, also book tours and accommodation.

Innumerable **long-distance buses** arrive at the big, busy **Central** (*KSRTC*) stand, opposite the railway station. A bridge divides it from **City stand**, used by local services. **City Market**, 2km southeast, has two stands: one for internal buses and one for the surrounding area, while **Shivaji Nagar stand**, in the northeast, is for local services, including the outskirts.

Information

For information on Bangalore, Karnataka and neighbouring states, go straight to the excellent **Government of India Tourist Office** (Mon–Fri 10am–6pm, Sat 9am–1pm; ☎558 5417), in the KFC Building, 48 Church St, a road parallel to MG Rd between Brigade and St Mark's roads. They operate a few worthwhile city **tours**, as well as two-day packages to Mysore and Ooty: quick and convenient if you're pushed for time.

Apart from the desks at the City railway station and airport, the city has two **KSTDC** offices: Badami House, NR Square (☎221 5883 or 221 5869), and in the hotel *Mayura Kempegowda*, Dhanavanthri Rd (☎71759 or 71606). They arrange a wide assortment of tours, ranging from a half-day city tour to long-haul trips to Hampi, Ooty, Goa, and elsewhere. Their useful *Downtown Bangalore* map (Rs30) features bars and restaurants, while for up-to-the-minute information about what's on, restaurants and shops, check the trendy and ubiquitous listings paper *Bangalore This Fortnight*.

The **Post Office** (Mon–Sat 10am–7pm, Sun 10.30am–1.30pm), on the corner of Raj Bhavan Rd and Cubbon St, at the northern tip of Cubbon Park, is about ten minutes' walk from MG Rd. You can **change money** at *Thomas Cook*, 55 MG Rd, on the corner of Brigade Rd, and the *State Bank of India*, 87 MG Rd (Mon–Fri 10.30am–2.30pm & Sat 10.30am–12.30pm). For currency exchange and *Visa* and *Mastercard* encashments – but not travellers' cheques – go to *Bank of Baroda*, 70 MG Rd (same hours).

Cars can be rented from *Dial-a-Car*, 152/1 Anjaneya Complex, Airport Rd (☎572622), or travel agents like *Krishna Travels*, 97/3 E Park Rd, 9th Cross, Malleswaram (☎334 1959; 24hr), and *Varsha Tours and Travels*, 106 GD Park Extn, Vyalikaval (☎368785).

The telephone **area code** for Bangalore is ☎080.

△ Madras

N

0   500 m

BANGALORE

RESTAURANTS:
❶ Kamat
❷ Suvarna Mandir
❸ Shiv Sagar
❹ Shanghai
❺ Konark
❻ Casa Piccolo
❼ Amruth
❽ Coconut Grove
❾ Chit Chat

Bus Stand

British Library

Cash Pharmacy

Technological Museum

Govt Museum

Venkatappa Art Gallery

Cubbon Park

Vidhana Soudha

Racecourse

NIRUPATHUNGA RD

City Bus Stand

Central Bus Stand

City Railway Station

Tipu Sultan's Palace

Fort

City Market

City Market Bus Stand

▽ Bull Temple

HOTELS:
Ⓐ Bangalore International
Ⓑ West End
Ⓒ Tourist
Ⓓ Royal Lodge & Shri Ramakrishna Lodge
Ⓔ KTDC Mayura Kempe Gowda
Ⓕ Minerva
Ⓖ YMCA
Ⓗ Gateway
Ⓘ Nahar Heritage
Ⓙ Imperial
Ⓚ Nilgiris Nest
Ⓛ Victoria
Ⓜ Gautam
Ⓝ Brindavan
Ⓞ YWCA

▽ Mysore

The City

The centre of modern Bangalore lies about 5km east of Kempe Gowda Circle and the bus and train stations. **MG Road** is the focus, where you'll find most of the mid-range accommodation, restaurants, shops, tourist information and banks. Leafy **Cubbon Park**, and its less than exciting museums, lie on its eastern edge, while the oldest, most "Indian" part of the city extends southwards, a rabbit warren of winding streets at their most dynamic in the hubbub of the **City** and **Gandhi markets**. Bangalore's tourist attractions are somewhat spread out; historical monuments such as **Tipu's Summer Palace** and the **Bull temple** are quite a way south of the centre. Most, if not all, can be seen on a half-day conducted tour; if you're determined to explore on foot, be warned that Bangalore has some of the worst pavements in south India.

Although a few characterful buildings still evoke the city's early twentieth-century heyday, most have been replaced or dwarfed by newer blocks. However, **Residency Road**, extending southwest from Gandhi Rd, is lined with old bungalows, the Bangalore Club and *pukka* English schools, along with the landmark *Cash Pharmacy*, an unusual multi-planed tiled-roof building, earmarked for demolition.

Cubbon Park and museums

A welcome green space in the heart of the city, shaded by massive clumps of bamboo, **Cubbon Park** is entered from the western end of MG Rd, presided over by a statue of Queen Victoria. On Kasturba Rd, which runs along its southern edge, the poorly labelled and maintained **Government Museum** (daily except Wed 10am–5pm) features Vijayanagar, Hoysala and Chalukya sculpture, musical instruments, Thanjavur paintings and Deccani and Rajasthani miniatures. Next door, the missable **Venkatappa Art Gallery** (same ticket) has a permanent exhibition of twentieth-century landscapes and abstract wood sculpture, and occasional shows of contemporary art. Further along, the **Technological and Industrial Museum** (daily except Mon 10am–5pm; Rs2) is firmly geared towards school kids, with push-button zoetropes and the like. The star attraction – if it's working – is the Electrotechnic Room where you can play with a "video-phone": a pair of cameras and monitors, with a telephone hook-up.

Vidhana Soudha

Built in 1956, Bangalore's vast State Secretariat, **Vidhana Soudha**, northwest of Cubbon Park, is the largest civic structure of its kind in the country. K Hanumanthaiah, Chief Minister at the time, wanted a "people's palace" that, following the transfer of power from the royal Wadayar dynasty to a legislature, would "reflect the power and dignity of the people". In theory its design is entirely Indian, combining local models from Bangalore, Mysore and Somnathpur with features from Rajasthan and the rest of India, but its overall effect is not unlike the bombastic colonial architecture built in the so-called Indo-Saracenic style.

Lalbagh Botanical Gardens

Inspired by the splendid gardens of the Moghuls and the French botanical gardens at Pondicherry in Tamil Nadu, Haider Ali set to work in 1760 laying out the **Lalbagh Botanical Gardens** (8am–8pm), south of the centre. Originally covering forty acres, just beyond his fort – where one of Kempe Gowda's original watchtowers can still be seen – the gardens were expanded under Ali's son Tipu, who introduced numerous exotic species of plants. The British brought in gardeners from Kew in 1856 and – naturally – built a military bandstand and a glasshouse, based on London's Crystal Palace, which hosts wonderful flower shows. Now spreading over 240 acres, the gardens are pleasant to visit during the day, but tend to attract unsavoury characters after 6pm.

Tipu's Summer Palace

A small two-storey structure built in 1791, mostly of wood, **Tipu's Summer Palace** (9am–5pm), southwest of the City Market, is similar to the Daria Daulat Palace at Srirangapatnam, but in a far worse state, with most of its painted decoration destroyed. Next door, the **Venkataramanaswamy temple**, dating from the early eighteenth century, was built by the Wadiyar Rajas. The *gopura* entranceway was erected in 1978.

Bull Temple

About 6km south of the City bus stand (bus #34 & #37), in the Basavanagudi area, Kempe Gowda's sixteenth-century **Bull Temple** (open to non-Hindus; daily 7.30am– 1.30pm & 2.30–8.30pm) houses a massive monolithic Nandi bull, its grey granite made black by the application of charcoal and oil. The temple is approached by a path lined with mendicants, snake charmers and the like; inside, for a small gratuity, the priest will offer you a string of fragrant jasmine flowers. One of the four watchtowers erected by Kempe Gowda stands 500m west of the temple.

Shopping

For many visitors, the main attraction of Bangalore is **shopping**, with **silk** as the best bargain. Possibly the widest range is sold at *Karnataka Silk Industries Corporation*, Gupte Market, Kempe Gowda Rd, and *Vijayalakshmi Silk Kendra*, on the same road. Numerous ready-made clothes shops include a *Benetton* outlet (much cheaper than in the west) at Copper Arch, 83 Infantry Rd. **Handicrafts** such as soapstone sculpture, brass, carved sandalwood and rosewood are also good value; emporia include *Central Cottage Industries Emporium*, 144 MG Rd (☎558 4083), *Cottage Industries Exposition Ltd*, 3 Cunningham Rd (☎226 8801), and *Gulshan Crafts*, 12 Safina Plaza, Infantry Rd (☎579355). For **silver**, try looking on and around Commercial St (north of MG Rd) and at KR Market, on Residency Rd. At 64 MG Rd, *Natesan's Antiqarts* (☎587427) sells both antiques and beautifully made reproduction sculpture, furniture and paintings.

Bangalore is also a great place to pick up hard-to-find **books**. The first floor of *Gangarams*, 72 MG Rd (☎558 6189), offers a wide selection on India (coffee-table art books and academic) plus the latest paperback fiction. *Higginbotham's*, 68 MG Rd (☎558 7359), is also good. *Premier*, 46/1 Church St (☎558 8570), around the corner from the ITDC office, crams a huge number of books in a tiny space. The shop belonging to renowned publishers *Motilal Banarsidas*, 16 St Mark's Rd, close to the junction with MG Rd, offers a superb selection of heavyweight Indology and philosophy titles.

Accommodation

Budget accommodation in Bangalore is concentrated around the railway station (which has good-value but often full *Retiring Rooms*; ①–④) and Central bus stand. Standards can be very low in the immediate vicinity, but reasonable options line

---

ACCOMMODATION PRICE CODES

All **accommodation prices** in this book have been coded using the symbols below. In principle the prices given are for the least expensive double rooms in each establishment; however, some hotels, usually in category ①, offer rates per bed rather than per room. Local taxes are not included unless specifically stated. For more details, see p.34.

①	up to Rs100	④	Rs225–350	⑦	Rs750–1200
②	Rs100–150	⑤	Rs350–500	⑧	Rs1200–2200
③	Rs150–225	⑥	Rs500–750	⑨	Rs2200 and up

Subedar Chatram Rd, five minutes' walk east, and Dhanavanthri Rd, a little way south. **Mid-range hotels** are more scattered; of the many near MG Rd, the *Victoria* is definitely the most characterful. **Five-stars** are also spread out, with a cluster towards the north of Cubbon Park.

Bangalore International, 2a/2b Crescent Rd, High Grounds (☎226 8011). Range of rooms (some a/c), all with *Star TV*. Bar and restaurant. ④–⑤.

Brindavan, 108 MG Rd (☎557371). Some a/c rooms, close to main shopping area. A good-value restaurant downstairs serves metal-plate *thalis*, paper *dosas*, and south Indian snacks. ③–⑤.

Gateway, 66 Residency Rd (☎544545). Uninspiringly "modern" hotel run by the Taj Group, with two very good restaurants. ⑧.

Gautam, 17 Museum Rd (☎577461). Acceptable rooms for the price, none a/c. ③.

Imperial, 93–94 Residency Rd (☎ 558 5473). Basic lodge, with dodgy bedding but clean bathrooms. Entrance a little back from road. ③.

KTDC Mayura Kempegowda, Dhanavanthri Rd (☎71759). Chain hotel, close to Central bus stand and railway station. Good-value rooms, some with balcony. ③–④.

Minerva, 34 JC (Mission) Rd, near Lalbagh Gardens (☎222 6992). Acceptable, but somewhat over-priced rooms (some a/c) with *Star TV*. Veg restaurant, travel desk. ⑤–⑥.

Nahar Heritage, 14 St Mark's Plaza, St Mark's Rd (☎ 221 3233; fax 226 1468). Comfortable and popular modern business-style hotel near MG Rd. Restaurant. ⑦.

Nilgiris Nest, 171 Brigade Rd (☎577501). Good-size rooms, some with balconies and a/c. Restaurant, bar and exchange. ④–⑤.

Rama, Lavelle Rd (☎221 3381). Clean rooms, some a/c; rates include breakfast. Bar, restaurant. ⑤.

Royal Lodge, Subedar Chatram Rd (☎228951). Clean rooms, all with bath, some with *Star TV*. ③.

Shri Ramakrishna Lodge, Subedar Chatram Rd (☎73041). Large, popular Indian-style lodge. Decent and clean. ②–③.

Tourist, Race Course Rd (☎72381). One of the better budget lodges, all rooms with bathroom. ②.

Victoria, 47–48 Residency Rd (☎558 4077; fax 221 3281). The best mid-range hotel in Bangalore, with plenty of old-world style, set back from a busy road in a leafy compound. Rooms around a pretty garden – deluxe options come with verandah. The airy rattan-seated restaurant serves tasty south Indian food and beer. Small, so book ahead if you can. ④–⑥.

West End, Race Course Rd (☎226 9281). Parts of this hotel date back to 1887; the tiled and gabled roofs are the best examples in the city of the "Bangalore-Gothic" style. Nicest rooms are in older parts, with verandahs overlooking acres of gardens. Several restaurants, including open-air. ⑨.

YMCA, Nirupathanga Rd, Cubbon Park (☎221 1848). Men-only accommodation. Often full. ②–③.

YWCA Guest House, 86 Infantry Rd (☎570997). Women-only, and again, usually booked up. ②–③.

Eating and drinking

Bangalore's eating options range from pizzas, burgers and fried chicken served up at westernized fast food outlets, to delicious Bombay-style *chaat* dishes. If you're after the best of south Indian food, *Coconut Grove* is an essential lunchtime venue; with more to spend try *Karavalli* at the *Gateway Hotel*.

No one could fail to notice the Bangalorean enthusiasm for **beer**, which unlike elsewhere in India, is unbelievably cheap. Draught is widely available, from scores of **pubs** that compete with tacky theme decor and *MTV* video screens, lasers and the like. In 1993, Chief Minister Veerappa Moily imposed a ban on alcohol sales between 2.30 and 5.30pm because of the number of school kids bunking off school to booze; this only seemed to start them off earlier, or had them staying later.

Restaurants

Amruth, St Mark's Plaza, St Mark's Rd. A/c sit-down and fast sections. Good-value south Indian snacks all day and *chaat* from 4pm, north Indian dishes at lunchtime and evenings. Instead of humble "meals", here you get "executive mini-lunches" for under Rs40.

Casa Piccolo, Devata Plaza, 131 Residency Rd. Steps lead down from the road, over the road from *Cash Pharmacy*. Tables outside and flower baskets give the place a European ambience. A dozen different (good) pizzas, *wienerschnitzel*, steaks, fried chicken and ice cream. Patronized by the well-heeled, sunglass-wearing studenty set. Moderate to expensive.

Chit Chat, MG Rd. Trendy fast food and ice creams, set a little back from the road.

Coconut Grove, Church St. A few doors along from the ITDC office. Excellent range of moderately priced, delicious south Indian cuisine and beer on pleasant covered terrace. Noon–3pm & 7–11pm.

Gateway, 66 Residency Rd. Two restaurants: the *Peacock* serves a fairly undistinguished selection of Mughlai and other north Indian dishes, but the *Karavalli* specializes in west coast dishes from Goa to Kerala, including seafood and veg choices. Very attractive room in traditional southern style with wooden ceiling – plus tables outside in the garden. Expensive.

Kamat, 152 JC (Mission) Rd. Standard "meals", south Indian snacks and some north Indian dishes.

Konark, 50 Residency Rd. Indian fast food: *chaat*, south Indian snacks, fruit juices, milkshakes and ice cream.

Sana's Arabian Food, 26 Haines Rd, Egyptian Block, behind Cantonment Bamboo Bazaar. Middle East speciality restaurant, northeast of the centre, serving both veg and non-veg dishes and barbecue items. Expensive and popular.

Shanghai, G3–4 Shiva Shankar Plaza, 19 Lalbagh Rd, Richmond Circle. Good veg and non-veg Chinese restaurant. Excellent beancurd veg soup and Hunan peppered fish, deep-fried with ginger, garlic and spring onions in a black pepper sauce.

Shiv Sagar, 30 Mission Rd. Self-service stand-up and sweet shop on the ground floor, more expensive a/c sit-down restaurant upstairs.

Suvarna Mandir, 76 Mission Rd. Basement restaurant with a good-value selection of south Indian snacks and various kinds of *chaat* (*bhelpuri, dahi batata*), *samosas*, sweets and kulfi ice cream.

Pubs

Black Cadillac, 50 Residency Rd. "American" pub with car fetish decor, and some tables outside. Loud music, snacks and draught beer.

Guzzlers Inn, 48 Rest House Rd, off Brigade Rd. Pub offering *MTV*, *Star Sport* and draught beer.

Nasa, 1/4 Church St. Pub karaoke, space age decor, *MTV* and draught beer.

Pub World, Residency Rd, opposite *Galaxy Theatre*. Four pubs in one; video, music, draught beer.

Listings

Cinemas Among cinemas showing films in English are *Rex*, Brigade Rd; *Sangam*, Tank Bound Rd; and *Bludiamond, Blumoon*, and *Plaza,* all on MG Rd. Billboard fans should head for Kempe Gowda Circle, crammed with the most extraordinarily colourful posters, hoardings and life-size cardboard cut-outs of the latest stars, strewn with spangly garlands.

Emergency Police ☎100; ambulance ☎102.

Pharmacies Open all night: *Al-Siddique Pharma Centre*, opposite Jamia Masjid near the City Market; *Janata Bazaar*, in the Victoria Hospital, near City Market; *Sindhi Charitable Hospital*, 3rd Main S R Nagar. During the day, head for *Santoshi Pharma*, 46 Mission Rd.

Photographic Equipment *Adlabs*, Mission Rd, Subbaiah Circle, stocks transparency film. *GG Welling*, 113 MG Rd and *GK Vale*, 89 MG Rd sell transparency and Polaroid film.

Visa Extensions Commissioner of Police, Infantry Rd (☎75272).

Around Bangalore

Many visitors to Bangalore are on the way to or from Mysore. The **Janapada Loka Folk Arts Museum**, between the two, gives a fascinating insight into Karnataka culture, while anyone wishing to see or study classical dance in a rural environment should check out **Nrityagram Dance Village**. The small hill station of **Nandi Hills** makes a popular day-trip; more unusual, and off-track, are the **Kolar Gold Fields**.

Janapada Loka Folk Arts Museum

After a number of years tucked away in a little-visited suburb of Bangalore, in 1993 the **Janapada Loka Folk Arts Museum** (daily 9am–6pm) reopened on its own plot of land, 53km southwest from Bangalore on the Mysore road. To get there, take one of the many slow Mysore buses (as opposed to the non-stop ones) from Bangalore. After passing the town of Ramanagar, alight at the 53rd km stone by the side of the road.

Created to protect and promote the folk arts of Karnataka, the collection includes an amazing array of agricultural, hunting and fishing implements, weapons, ingenious household gadgets, masks, dolls and shadow puppets, carved wooden *bhuta* (spirit-worship) sculptures and larger-than-life temple procession figures, manuscripts, musical instruments and *Yakshagana* theatre costumes. In addition, 1600 hours of **audio and video recordings** of musicians, dancers and rituals from Karnataka are available for viewing on request. The astonishing variety of performing arts include Madiga drummers, Garudi snake-charmer puppets, Lambani gypsy stick dances, Budubudukye oracles (who sing, play drums and tell the future by listening to birdsong), and the itinerant Jogathi eunuchs who sing songs dedicated to the folk goddess Yelamma.

Plans to put on performances of music, dance, puppetry and martial arts are in the offing. A small **restaurant** serves simple food, and dorm **accommodation** (①) is available. For more details contact the *Karnataka Janapada Trust*, 7 Subramanyaswami Temple Rd, 5th Cross, 4th Block, Kumara Park West, Bangalore (☎362768).

Nrityagram Dance Village

NRITYAGRAM is a purpose-built model village, 30km west of Bangalore, designed by the award-winning architect Gerard de Cunha and founded by the dancer Protima Gauri, who specializes in Orissa's Odissi dance (see p.868). It hosts performances and lectures on Indian mythology and dance, and has **accommodation** for longer stays that promises "oxygen, home-grown vegetables and fruits, no TV, telephones, newspapers or noise". For further information contact their Bangalore office (☎558 5440).

Office – yet another building, this time to the west, accessible from the main road. There are two 24-hour **telephone information** lines; one handles timetable enquiries (☎131), the other reels off a recorded list of arrivals and departures (☎133).

Airline Offices

Air Canada, 131–132 Residency Rd (☎221 5416).

Air France, 68 St Mark's Rd (☎221 4060).

Air India, Unity Buildings, JC (Mission) Rd (☎222 4143).

British Airways, 7 St Mark's Rd (☎221 1205 or 221 4915).

Cathay Pacific Airways, *West End Hotel*, Race Course Rd (☎226 9745).

Damania Airlines, 102–103 Manipal Centre, Dickinson Rd (☎558 8181).

East-West, 1A MG Rd (☎558 7968).

Gulf Air, Unity Buildings, JC (Mission) Rd (☎223 7741).

Indian Airlines, Cauvery Bhavan, KG Rd (☎566233; recorded messages ☎142).

Japan Airlines, Devatha Plaza, Residency Rd (☎221 5091).

KLM, *West End Hotel*, Race Course Rd (☎226 8703).

Kuwait Airways Corporation, 3/4 Unity Buildings, JC (Mission) Rd (☎222 4513).

Lufthansa, 44/2 Dickinson Rd (☎558 8138).

Malaysian Airlines, Richmond Circle (☎221 3030).

Moduluft, *Asipac Travels*, 16 Raheja Plaza, Monsignor D'Souza Circle, Richmond Rd (☎559 2631).

Northwest Airlines, Highpoint, Palace Rd (☎226 8509).

PIA, Brigade Rd (☎558 3074).

Qantas, Westminster, Cunningham Rd (☎226 6611).

Singapore Airlines, 51 Richmond Rd (☎221 2822 or 221 3833).

Swiss Air, 51 Richmond Rd (☎221 1983).

Nandi Hills

Tipu Sultan used the small town of **NANDI HILLS**, 65km northeast of Bangalore, as a summer retreat, building fortifications to back up the formidable natural defence of a steep 300-metre drop on three sides. Nowadays, Bangaloreans flock to this minor hill station to enjoy fine views from the top and the ninth-century **Bhogandishvara temple** at the bottom. The hills are a regular stop on Bangalore's KSTDC conducted tour (see p.1038), or you can get there on one of the three daily buses from Central bus stand. **Accommodation** is available at the KSTDC *Mayura Pine Top* (☎8624; ③), bookable at KSTDC offices in Bangalore. The Department of Horticulture *Rest House* (②) can be booked through the Director of Horticulture, Lalbagh, Bangalore (☎602231).

Kolar Gold Fields

At a depth of up to 2400m, **Kolar Gold Fields**, 98km east of Bangalore, are the deepest mines in the world. Visitors can watch gold extraction on Wednesdays and Thursdays, but it's not an easy business. Consult the ITDC Office in Bangalore to plan a visit, and arrive here the previous evening to get permission from the Office of the Secretary of the Mines. **Accommodation** is available at the nearby *Sylvan Villa* (☎080/333 2837 or 333 0449; ③–⑤), a popular weekend retreat for Bangaloreans, where the staff can help arrange visits to the mines.

Mysore

A centre of sandalwood-carving and incense production, 159km southwest of Bangalore, **MYSORE**, the erstwhile capital of the Wadiyar Rajas, is one of south India's most popular attractions. Considering the clichés that have been heaped upon the place, however, first impressions can be disappointing; like anywhere else, you are not so much greeted by the scent of jasmine blossom or gentle wafts of sandalwood when you stumble off the

Mysore City Railway Station
IRWIN RD
DHANAVANTRI RD
Indra Bhavan
Kwality
KSTDC Mayura Hoysala
Aashraya
Sangeeth
Agrawal Lodge
Metropole
Kings Kourt
Devaraja Market
VINOBA RD
Maurya
Paras
Dasaprakesh
Shilpastri
GANDHI SQUARE
Srikkanth
Central Bus Stand
ASHOK RD
Ritz Hotel
Park Lane
MIRZA RD
City Bus Stand
Maharaja's Palace
0   250 m
N
Lalitha Mahal Palace & Chamundi Hill
▽ Jaganmohan Palace

bus or train, as by the usual cacophany of careering auto-rickshaws and noisy buses, bullock carts, and tongas. Nevertheless, Mysore is certainly a lovely place to visit: an old-fashioned, undaunting town dominated by the spectacular **Maharaja's Palace**, just one of several beautiful residences dotted around the wide, attractive streets. The climb up **Chamundi Hill** makes a pleasant excursion, while the magnificent Hoysala temple of **Somnathpur** lies little more than an hour's drive away.

Mysore's history goes back to the tenth century, when it was the leading town in a district of many villages. The city was ruled from about 1400 until Independence by the Hindu Wadiyars, its fortunes being inextricably linked with those of Srirangapatnam (15km northeast; see p.1051), which became headquarters from 1610. Their rule was only broken from 1761, when the Muslim Haider Ali and son Tipu Sultan took over; in 1799 Wadiyar power was restored by the British Colonel, Arthur Wellesley, later the Duke of Wellington. As the capital of Mysore state, Mysore dominated a major part of southern India. In 1956, when Bangalore became capital of the new state of Karnataka, its Maharaja was appointed Governor.

Arrival and information

Mysore does not have an airport. Karnataka's **railways** are at present in a state of great flux – see p.1035 – but it seems reasonable to assume that three or more daily trains will continue to run from Bangalore to Mysore railway station, 1.5km northwest of the centre, after the city finally joins the broad-gauge network. A **KSTDC** desk at the station provides limited information. Behind the station, the showpiece of the good little **Railway Museum** (daily except Mon 10am–1pm & 3–5pm) is a nineteenth-century royal carriage.

Mysore has three bus stands: all major long-distance *KSRTC* buses pull in to **Central**, close to the centre; the **Private** stand, just a dusty patch of road, is a little way

The telephone **area code** for Mysore is ☎0821.

CONDUCTED TOURS

KSTDC's **city tour** (7.30am–8.30pm; Rs75) makes for a long day, covering Jaganmohan Palace Art Gallery, Maharaja's Palace, St Philomena's Cathedral, the Zoo, Chamundi Hill, Somnathpur, Srirangapatnam and Brindavan Gardens. It only runs with a minimum of 10 passengers, so you may not know for sure whether it will run when you buy your ticket. A **long-distance tour** covers Belur, Halebid and Sravanabelgola (7.30am–9pm; Sun, Tues, Wed & Fri; daily in season; Rs130). Another, exhausting, one goes to **Ooty** (7am–9pm; Mon Thurs & Sat; daily in season; Rs130).

south, opposite the *Ritz Hotel*, and meets buses to and from Somnathpur. Local buses stop at the **City** stand, next to the northwestern corner of the Maharaja's Palace.

Ten minutes' walk southeast of the railway station, on a corner of Irwin Rd in the Old Exhibition Building, the helpful **Tourist Reception Centre** (daily 10am–5.30pm; ☎26349), run by Karnataka's tourist department, will book accommodation by phone and make an effort to answer queries, though there's not much you can take away with you. In contrast, the **KSTDC office** (daily 7.30am–8.30pm), just behind in the same building, is of little use except to book one of their tours (see box). They have another, more helpful office at *Hotel Mayura Hoysala*, Jhansi Laxmi Bai Rd (☎21846).

The main **post office** (poste restante) is on the corner of Ashoka and Irwin roads, and there's a *State Bank of Mysore* on the corner of Sayaji Rao and Sardar Patel Rd.

The City

Quite apart from its official tourist attractions, Mysore is a pleasure simply to stroll around. The characterful, if dilapidated, pre-Independence buildings lining market areas such as **Ashok Road** and **Sayaji Rao Road** give the place a faded grandeur, an appealing counterpoint to the vibrant street life. Souvenir stores spill over with the city's famous **sandalwood**; perhaps the best place to get a sense of what's on offer is the *Government Cauvery Arts and Crafts Emporium* on Sayaji Rao Rd (closed Thurs), which stocks a wide range of local crafts that can be shipped overseas. The **Devaraja Market** on Sayaji Rao Rd is one of south India's most appealing produce markets: a giant complex of stalls groaning with green bananas, luscious mangoes and blocks of tasty bitter chocolate – well worth a browse, even if you're not buying.

Maharaja's Palace

Mysore centre is dominated by the walled **Maharaja's Palace** (daily 10.30am–5.30pm), a fairytale spectacle topped with a shining brass-plated dome surmounting a single tower; especially magnificent on Sunday nights and during festivals, when it is illuminated by no less than five thousand lightbulbs. Designed in the hybrid "Indo-Saracenic" style by Henry Irwin, the British consultant architect of Madras state, it was completed

WILDLIFE SANCTUARIES AROUND MYSORE

Mysore is close to three **wildlife sanctuaries**, all of which require forward planning to get the most out of them. For **Bandipur** or **Nagarhole** (see p.1052), you must arrange transport and accommodation in advance through the Forest Officer, Woodyard Complex, Ashokpuram, 6km south of the city centre (bus #61). For **Mudumalai**, in Tamil Nadu, phone ahead to book hotels and to arrange to be met (see p.976). Forest Department accommodation, however, can only be arranged from Ooty (see p.971).

in 1912 for the twenty-fourth Wadiyar Raja, on the site of the old wooden palace that had been destroyed by fire in 1897. Twelve temples surround the palace, some of them of much earlier origin. Although there are six gates in the perimeter wall, entrance is on the south side only. Shoes and cameras must be left at the cloakroom inside.

An extraordinary amalgam of styles from India and around the world crowds the lavish **interior**, straying well into the realms of kitsch. Entry is through the Gombe Thotti or **Dolls' Pavilion**, once a showcase for the small figures featured in the city's lively Dussehra celebrations and now a gallery of European and Indian sculpture and ceremonial objects. Halfway along, the brass **Elephant Gate** forms the main entrance to the centre of the palace, through which the Maharaja would drive to his car park. Decorated with floriate designs, it bears the Mysore royal symbol of a double-headed eagle, now the state emblem. To the north, past the gate, are dolls dating from the late nineteenth and early twentieth centuries, a wooden *mandapa* glinting with mirrorwork, and at the end, a ceremonial wooden elephant *howdah* (frame to carry passengers). Elaborately decorated with 84kg of 24-carat gold, it appears to be inlaid with red and green gems – in fact the twinkling lights are battery-powered signals to let the driver know when the Maharaja wished to stop or go.

Walls leading into the octagonal **Kalyana Mandapa**, the royal wedding hall, are lined with a meticulously detailed frieze of oil paintings illustrating the great Mysore Dussehra festival of 1930, executed by four Indian artists who worked from photographs of the event over a period of fifteen years. The hall itself is magnificent, a cavernous space featuring cast-iron pillars from Glasgow, Bohemian chandeliers, and multi-coloured Belgian stained glass arranged in peacock designs in the domed ceiling. A mosaic of English floor-tiles repeats the peacock motif. Beyond here lie small rooms cluttered with grandiose furniture, including a pair of silver chairs and others of Belgian cut-crystal made for the Maharaja and Lord Mountbatten, the last Viceroy of India. One of the rooms has a fine ceiling of Burma teak carved by local craftsmen.

Climbing a staircase with Italian marble balustrades, past an unnervingly realistic life-size plaster of Paris figure of Krishnaraja Wadiyar IV, lounging comfortably with his bejewelled feet on a stool, you come into the **Public Durbar Hall**, an orientalist fantasy often compared to a setting from *A Thousand and One Nights*. A vision of brightly painted and gilded colonnades, open on one side, the massive hall affords views out across the parade ground and gardens to Chamundi Hill. The Maharaja gave audience from here; today it serves as a venue for classical music concerts during the Dussehra festival. Paintings by the celebrated artists Shilpi Siddalingaswamy and Raja Rama Varma, from the Travancore (Kerala) royal family, adorn the walls. The whole is crowned by white marble, inlaid with delicate floral scrolls of jasper, amber and lapis lazuli in the Moghul style. Somewhat out of synch with the opulence, a series of ceiling panels of Vishnu, painted on fire-proof asbestos, date from the 1930s. The smaller

---

MYSORE DUSSEHRA FESTIVAL

Following the tradition set by the Vijayanagar kings, the ten-day festival of Dussehra (Sept/Oct), to commemorate the goddess Durga's slaying of the demon buffalo, Mahishasura (see p.919), is celebrated in grand style at Mysore. Scores of cultural events include concerts of south Indian classical (Carnatic) music and dance performances in the great Durbar Hall of the **Maharaja's Palace**. On the last day of the festival, a magnificent procession of mounted guardsmen on horseback and caparisoned elephants – one carrying an elaborate gold *howdah* – marches 5km from the palace to Banni Mantap. There's also a floating festival in the temple tank at the foot of **Chamundi Hill**, and a procession of chariots around the temple at the top. A torchlight parade takes place in the evening, followed by a massive firework display and much jubilation on the streets.

Private Durbar Hall features especially beautiful stained glass and gold-leaf painting. Before leaving you pass two embossed silver doors – all that remains of the old palace.

Nearby, behind the main palace building but within the same compound, a small **museum** run by the royal family shows paintings from the Thanjavur and Mysore schools (see p.947), some inlaid with precious stones and gold leaf.

Jaganmohan Palace: Jayachamarajendra Art Gallery
Built in 1861, the **Jaganmohan Palace** (daily 8am–5pm; no cameras) was used as a royal residence until turned into a picture gallery and museum in 1915 by the Maharaja Krishnaraja Wadiyar IV. Most of the "contemporary" art on show seems to date from the 1930s, when a revival of Indian painting was spearheaded by EB Havell and the Tagore brothers Abandrinath and Ganganendranath in Bengal.

On the ground floor, a series of faded black-and-white photos of ceremonial occasions shares space with elaborate imported clocks, including one – not working – that is supposed to sound drums and play gentle music. Twentieth-century paintings dominate the first floor; Raja Rama Varma's oils show epic themes such as the demon king Ravana absconding with Rama's wife Sita. Games on the upper floor include circular *ganjeeb* playing cards illustrated with portraits of royalty or deities, and board games delicately inlaid with ivory. There's also a cluster of musical instruments, among them a brass *jaltarang* set and glass xylophone, and harmonicas and clarinet played by Krishnaraja Wadiyar IV himself. Another gallery, centring on a large wooden Ganesh sitting on a tortoise, is lined with paintings, including Krishnaraja Wadiyar sporting with the "inmates" of his *zenana* (women's quarter of the palace) during Holi.

Chamundi Hill
Chamundi Hill, 3km southeast of the city, is topped with a temple to the chosen deity of the Mysore Rajas; the goddess Chamundi, or Durga, who slew the demon buffalo Mahishasura (see p.919). It's a pleasant, easy bus trip (#101 from the City stand) to the top; the walk down, past a huge Nandi, Shiva's bull vehicle, takes about thirty minutes. Pilgrims, of course, make the trip in reverse order. Take some drinking water to sustain you, especially in the middle of the day – the walk isn't very demanding, but by the end of it, after 500 steps, your legs are likely to be a bit wobbly.

Seats to the left of the bus give the best views of the plain surrounding Mysore. Don't be surprised if, at the top of the hill, dominated by the temple's forty-metre *gopura*, you're struck by a strange feeling of déja vu – one of the highly educational displays at the **Godly Museum** states that "5000 years ago at this time you had visited this place in the same way you are visiting now. Because world drama repeats itself identically every 5000 years". Another exhibit goes to the heart of our "problematic world: filthy films, lack of true education, blind faith, irreligiousness, bad habits and selfishness". Suitably edified, you can proceed along a path from the bus stand, past trinket, tea and snack stalls, to the temple square. Immediately to the right, at the end of this path, are four bollards painted with a red stripe; return here for the path down the hill.

Non-Hindus can visit the twelfth-century **temple** (daily 8am–noon & 5–8pm; leave shoes opposite the entrance), staffed by friendly priests. The Chamundi figure inside is solid gold; outside, in the courtyard, stands a fearsome, if gaily coloured, statue of the demon Mahishasura. On leaving, if you continue by the path instead of retracing your steps, you can return to the square via two other temples and various buildings storing ceremonial paraphernalia and animal figures used during Dussehra. You'll also come across loads of scampering monkeys, and the odd dreadlocked *sadhu* who will willingly pose for your holiday snaps, for a consideration.

The magnificent five-metre **Nandi**, carved from a single piece of granite in 1659, is an object of worship himself, adorned with bells and garlands and tended by his own priest. Minor shrines, dedicated to Chamundi and the monkey god Hanuman among others, line the side of the path; at the bottom, a little shrine to Ganesh lies near a *chai*-shop. From here it's usually possible to pick up an auto-rickshaw or bus back into the city, but at weekends the latter are often full. If you walk on towards the city, passing a temple on the left, with a big water tank (the site of the floating festival during Dussehra), you come after ten minutes to the main road between the Lalitha Mahal Palace and the city; there's a bus stop, and often some auto-rickshaws, at the junction.

St Philomena's Cathedral

The foundation stone of **St Philomena's** rather gloomy **cathedral**, north of the centre on Ashoka Rd, was laid in 1933 by Mysore's Maharaja. One of the biggest churches in India, it was built in the classical perpendicular Gothic style with twin 53-metre spires. The most arresting features are the stained-glass windows, above the apse, depicting the birth of Christ, the Last Supper, the crucifixion and "breaking the gates of Death".

Accommodation

Mysore attracts a huge number of visitors, and has plenty of hotels to suit all budgets. Cheap lodges are concentrated on and around Dhanavantri Road, a little way south of the tourist office on Irwin Road, and close to Gandhi Square further east. Mid-range to expensive hotels are more spread out, but a good place to start is Jhansi Laxmi Bai Rd, which runs south from the railway station. If you're looking for a palace, then head straight for the *Ashok Lalitha Mahal* or, if it's finally opened, the *Rajendra Vilas*.

Aashraya, Rajmal Talkies Rd, Dhanavantri Rd Cross (☎27088 or 26570). Reasonable lodge; all rooms with attached bathroom and hot water. South and north Indian veg restaurant. ②–③.

Agrawal Lodge, off Dhanavantri Rd (☎22730). Basic lodge; rooms only. ①–②.

Dasaprakash, Gandhi Square (☎24444 or 22821). Large hotel, near the centre, modern and good value. Some a/c rooms, veg restaurant. ②–③.

Govardhan, Sri Harsha Rd (☎34118). Decent budget lodge; deluxe rooms with TV. ②–③.

Highway, New Bannimantap Extension (☎21117). Reasonable rooms (some a/c with TV). Restaurant, coffee shop and bar, travel desk. ④–⑤.

Indra Bhavan, Dhanavantri Rd (☎23933). Simple old lodge, singles and doubles, all with attached bathroom. Veg restaurant. ②.

ITDC Ashok Lalitha Mahal Palace, T Narasipur Rd (☎26316; fax 33398). Set on a gentle slope overlooking the city, and visible for miles around, this white, Neoclassical palace was built in 1931 to accommodate Maharaja's foreign guests. Now it's a Raj-style fantasy; popular with tour groups and film crews on location. Even if you're not staying, indulge in an expensive afternoon tea, a drink in the bar, dinner in the restaurant or a swim in the pool, which is open to non-residents. ⑧–⑨.

Kings Kourt, Jhansi Laxmi Bai Rd (☎25250). Popular, modern place close to the railway station with large rooms (some a/c) , restaurant, bar and currency exchange. ⑤–⑥.

KSTDC Mayura Hoysala, 2 Jhansi Laxmi Bai Rd (☎25349). Near the railway station with good, reasonably priced rooms. Pleasant, simple outdoor restaurant and bar. KSTDC tourist office. ②–③.

Maurya, Hanumantha Rao Rd II (☎26677). Decent budget lodge near Gandhi Square. All rooms with bathroom; restaurant. ②.

Metropole, 5 Jhansi Laxmi Bai Rd (☎20681). Near the railway station, a characterful old-fashioned hotel, once one of the Maharaja's guest houses, with large (some voluminous), comfortable rooms with *Star TV* (some a/c) and verandahs. Restaurant, bar, exchange, travel desk and garden. ⑤–⑥.

Park Lane, 2720 Curzon Park Rd (☎30400). One of the best options in this price range. Very well-maintained with small, comfortable rooms and a good courtyard restaurant and bar. ②–③.

Rajendra Vilas Palace, Chamundi Hill (☎20690). The *Taj Group*'s long-promised refurbishment of this 1930s hill-top palace will, when open, compete strongly at the top end of the market. ⑧–⑨.

Ritz, Bangalore–Nilgiri Rd (☎22668). Comfortable, friendly old hotel, opposite Private bus stand. Pleasant terrace restaurant. Only four rooms; phone bookings accepted up to 15 days ahead. ②–③.

Sangeeth, 1966 Narayana Sastry Rd, near the Udupi Sri Krishna Mandira (☎24693). Rooms, all with bathroom and hot water. No restaurant. ②.

As this book went to press, **train** services from Mysore were impossible to predict, pending the conversion from metre-gauge to broad-gauge. However, work is complete on the line to Bangalore; all the three daily trains (4hr) call at Srirangapatnam. After the changeover, there should be comprehensive services both within and beyond the state; for the moment, if you're contemplating a long-haul train journey, do it from Bangalore.

From **Central bus stand** services include Bangalore (non-stop every 15min, 3hr; numerous stopping buses, 3hr 45min), Hassan (12 daily; 2hr 30min), Ooty (11 daily; 5hr) via Mudumalai and five via Bandipur, Hospet (2 daily; 8hr), Mangalore (8 daily via Madikeri; 7hr). *KSRTC* buses from here go to Ernakulam and Kozhikode. To get to Srirangapatnam, take #125 from the **City stand**.

Eating

Mysore has its fair share of "meals" restaurants, especially around Gandhi Square. You're not likely to get any spectacular gourmet experiences, but plenty of places offer heaps of atmosphere.

Bamboo Grove, *Mayura Hoysala*, 2 Jhansi Laxmi Bai Rd. Simple open-air restaurant and bar.

Dasaprakash, Gandhi Square. Delicious veg "meals"; popular with younger budget travellers.

Metropole, 5 Jhansi Laxmi Bai Rd (☎20681). Recommended more for the characterful setting than the food. Some tables outside in the garden, where there's often an evening barbecue.

Paras, Sayaji Rao Rd, above *Indra Cafe*. At the southern end of the road, the other side from Devaraja market, *Paras* serves tasty, good-value south Indian snacks and meals.

Park Lane, 2720 Curzon Park Rd. Pleasant courtyard restaurant with tasty, not particularly inexpensive, food and bar. Trendy atmosphere.

Ritz, Bangalore–Nilgiri Rd. Nice escape from the streets for a drink or veg and non-veg meals, with best tables in courtyard at the back. Friendly staff.

Shilpastri, Gandhi Square. Another popular travellers' haunt, serving good-value veg and non-veg dishes with some open-air rooftop tables (unlit after dark).

Around Mysore

Mysore is a jumping-off point for some of Karnataka's most popular destinations. At **Srirangapatnam**, the fort, palace and mausoleum date from the era of Tipu Sultan, the "Tiger of Mysore", a perennial thorn in the side of the British. The superbly carved **Hoysala temples** (see p.1054) of Somnathpur, and further out, **Belur** and **Halebid**, are architectural masterpieces. Also near Hassan, the Jain site of **Sravanabelgola** attracts busloads of pilgrims and tourists to see the monolithic naked statue of Gomateshvara.

The Western Ghat mountains are easily accessible from Mysore: just three hours away by road, the capital of the coffee-growing Kodagu (Coorg) region, **Madikeri**, makes an excellent base for country walks and mountain and jungle treks.

Srirangapatnam

The island of **SRIRANGAPATNAM**, set in the River Kaveri, 14km north of Mysore, measures five kilometres by one kilometre. Long a site of Hindu pilgrimage, it is named for its tenth-century Sriranganathaswamy Vishnu temple, which in 1133 served as a refuge for the philosopher Ramanuja, a staunch Vaishnavite, from the Shaivite Cholas in Tamil Nadu. The Vijayanagars built a fort here in 1454, and in 1616 it became the royal capital of the Mysore Wadayar Rajas. However, Srirangapatnam is more famously associated with **Haider Ali**, who deposed the Wadiyars in 1761, and even more so with his son **Tipu Sultan**. During his seventeen-year reign – which ended with his death in 1799, when the future Duke of Wellington took the fort at the bloody battle of "Seringapatnam" – Tipu posed a greater threat than any other Indian ruler to British plans to dominate India.

Tipu Sultan and his father were responsible for transforming the small state of Mysore into a major Muslim power. Born in 1750, of a Hindu mother, Tipu inherited Haider Ali's considerable military skills; unlike his illiterate father, he was also an educated, cultured man who introduced radical agricultural reforms. His burning life-long desire to rid India of the hated British invaders naturally brought him an ally in the French. He obsessively embraced his popular name of the "Tiger of Mysore", surrounding himself with symbols and images of tigers; much of his memorabilia is decorated with the animal or its stripes, and, like the Romans, he is said to have kept tigers for the punishment of criminals.

Tipu's Srirangapatnam was largely destroyed by the British, but parts of the fort area in the northwest survive, including gates, ramparts, the grim dungeons (where chained British prisoners were allegedly forced to stand neck-deep in water), and the onion-domed and minareted Jami Masjid mosque.

The former summer palace, the **Daria Daulat Bagh** (daily 10am–5pm), literally "wealth of the sea", 1km east of the fort, was used to entertain Tipu's guests. At first sight, this low, wooden colonnaded building set in an attractive formal garden fails to impress, as most of it is obscured by sunscreens. However, the superbly preserved interior, with its ornamental arches, tiger-striped columns and floral decoration on every inch of the teak walls and ceiling, is remarkable. A much-repainted mural on the west wall relishes every detail of Haider Ali's victory over the British at Pollilore in 1780. Upstairs, a small collection of Tipu memorabilia, European paintings, Persian manuscripts on hand-made paper and a model of Srirangapatnam are on show.

An avenue of cypresses leads from an intricately carved gateway to the **Gumbaz mausoleum**, 3km further east. Built by Tipu Sultan in 1784 to commemorate Haider Ali, and later also to serve as his own resting place, the lower half of the grey granite edifice is crowned by a dome of white-washed brick and plaster, spectacular against the blue sky. Ivory-inlaid rosewood doors lead to the tombs of Haider Ali and Tipu, each covered by a pall (tiger stripes for Tipu), and an Urdu tablet records Tipu's martyrdom.

Practicalities

The easiest way to see Srirangapatnam is on a **tour** of Mysore (see p.1047). If you prefer to come independently, frequent **buses** run from Mysore Central bus stand, or you can take any Mysore-to-Bangalore **train**. Both buses and trains pull in near the temple and fort. Srirangapatnam is a small island, but places of interest are quite spread out; to avoid long walks, tongas, auto-rickshaws and bicycles are available on the main road near the bus stand. The KSTDC **hotel**-cum-restaurant, *Mayura River View* (☎114; ④), is in a pleasant spot beside the Kaveri, 3km from the bus stand.

Bandipur and Nagarhole

Karnataka's wildlife reserves of **Bandipur** and **Nagarhole** adjoin not only each other but also the reserves of Mudumalai in Tamil Nadu and Wynad in Kerala. **BANDIPUR**, 80km south of Mysore, covers 850 square kilometres, south of the River Kabini, while **NAGARHOLE** stretches over 640 square kilometres from Bandipur's northern border. Prospective visitors to either reserve should first contact the Forest Officer in Mysore or Bangalore, to book forest accommodation and transport and to seek advice on where to go – Nagarhole suffered devastating arson damage in 1992 and was closed in 1993.

Two basic kinds of **jungle** predominate; dry deciduous forest covers most of Bandipur and the southeast of Nagarhole, the rest of which features denser, taller, moist deciduous forest. Here too, open grassy swamps are inhabited by *gaur* (bison) and tiger, its natural predator. More than a thousand elephants are estimated to roam the area, along with seldom-seen tigers and leopards. Bandipur is one of fifteen Project Tiger locations (see p.381). **Birds** range from blue-bearded bee-eater, scarlet miniret and Malabar whistling thrush to the more common ospreys, herons and ducks. You'll also come across crocodiles, monitor lizards and snakes, as well as turtles and frogs.

Roaming around is dangerous and prohibited. Visitors **view the reserves** from either vans or jeeps (book in advance) along well-laid-out tracks that allow you to see as much as possible. At Bandipur, you can also **ride an elephant**, which, though great fun, doesn't give you much opportunity to see the wildlife. Avoid weekends and holidays, when there are likely to be fewer animals and more visitors.

Practicalities

Both parks are normally **open** daily (6–9am & 4–6pm) when forest transport (jeeps, trucks and, at Bandipur, elephants) and guides are available. Five **buses** a day from Mysore to Udhagamandalam (Ooty) call at Bandipur (2–3hr), the first departing at 5.30am. The last bus back to Mysore leaves at 5.30pm, and the road at Bandipur closes at 6pm. Services to Nagarhole are irregular, and should be checked in Mysore.

Accommodation is available at both reserves in **forest lodges** (①–②), which must be booked in advance. Some provide food, at others you must bring your own. Contact the Forest Officer, Forest Department Complex, Ashokpuram, Mysore, or Chief Wildlife Warden, Aranya Bhavan, 18th Cross, Malleswaram, Bangalore (☎334 1993). At Nagarhole, the *Kabini River Lodge* (⑧), an eighteenth-century hunting lodge once owned by the Maharaja of Mysore, offers all-in packages with coracle rides, sailing and forest transport as well as a restaurant, bars and other comforts. Enquiries should be made to *Jungle Lodges and Resorts*, 348/9 Brooklands, 13th Main, Rajmahal Extn, Bangalore (☎36820).

Somnathpur

Built in 1268 AD, the exquisite **Keshava Vishnu temple**, in the sleepy hamlet of **SOMNATHPUR**, was the last important temple to be constructed by the Hoysalas; it is the most complete and, in many respects, the finest example of this singular style (see p.1054). Somnathpur itself, just ninety minutes from Mysore by road, is little more than a few neat tracks and some attractive simple houses with pillared verandahs.

Like other Hoysala temples, the Keshava is built on a star-shaped plan, but, as a triple shrine, represents a mature development from the earlier constructions. ASI staff can show you around and also grant permission to clamber on the enclosure walls, to get a marvellous bird's-eye view of the modestly proportioned temple. The earlier in the day you do this, the better, as the stone gets very hot to walk on in bare feet.

The temple is a *trikutachala*, "three-peaked hills" type, with a tower on each shrine – a configuration also seen in certain Chalukya temples, and three temples on Hemakuta hill at Vijayanagar (Hampi; see p.1066). The only evidence of a tower in earlier Hoysala temples is at the Kedareshvara Jain temple at Halebid, which has since collapsed.

Each shrine, sharing a common *navaranga mandapa* hallway, is dedicated to a different form of Vishnu. In order of "seniority" they are Keshava in the central shrine, Venugopala to the proper right and Jagannatha to the left. The Keshava shrine features a very unusual *chandrasila*, "moonstone" step at its entrance, and, diverging from the usual semi-circular Hoysala style, has two pointed projections.

The Keshava's high plinth (*jagati*) provides an upper ambulatory, which on its outer edge reproduces the almost crenellated shape of the structure and allows visitors to approach the upper registers of the profusely decorated walls. Among the many superb images are an unusually high proportion of Shaivite figures for a Vishnu temple. As at

Halebid, a lively frieze details countless episodes from the *Ramayana*, *Bhagavata Purana* and *Mahabharata*. Intended to accompany circumambulation, the panels are "read" (there is no text) in a clockwise direction. Unusually, the temple is autographed; all its sculpture was the work of one man, named Malitamba.

Outside the temple stands a *dvajastambha* column, which may originally have been surmounted by a figure of Vishnu's bird vehicle Garuda. The wide ground-level ambulatory that circles the whole building is edged with numerous, now empty, shrines.

Practicalities

Very few Mysore buses, if any, go direct to Somnathpur. Buses from the Private stand run to T Narasipur (1hr), served by regular buses to Somnathpur (20min). Everyone will know where you want to go, and someone will show you which scrum to join.

Aside from the odd coconut or watermelon seller, the only **food** and **drink** on offer in Somnathpur is at the KSTDC outpost, *Hotel Mayura Keshava* (no phone; ①), which serves basic snacks until 5pm and meals by arrangement later in the day. Their four

---

HOYSALA TEMPLES

The **Hoysala** dynasty ruled southwestern Karnataka between the eleventh and thirteenth centuries. From the twelfth century, after the accession of King Vishnu Vardhana, they built a series of distinctive temples centred primarily at three sites: **Belur** and **Halebid**, close to modern Hassan, and **Somnathpur**, near Mysore.

At first sight, and from a distance, Hoysala temples appear to be modest structures, compact and even squat. On closer inspection, however, their profusion of fabulously detailed and sensuous sculpture, covering every inch of the exterior, is astonishing. Detractors are prone to class Hoysala art as decadent and overly fussy, but anyone with an eye for craftsmanship is likely to marvel at these jewels of Karnataka art.

The intricacy of the carvings was made possible by the material used in construction: a soft steatite soapstone that on oxidization hardens to a glassy, highly polished surface. The level of detail, similar to that seen in sandalwood and ivory work, became increasingly freer and fluid as the style developed, and reached its highest point at Somnathpur. Beautiful bracket figures, often delicate portrayals of voluptuous female subjects, were placed under the eaves, fixed by pegs top and bottom. A later addition (except possibly in the Somnathpur temple), these serve no structural function.

Another technique more usually associated with wood is the unusual treatment of the massive stone pillars: lathe-turned, they resemble those of the wooden temples of Kerala. They were probably turned on a horizontal plane, pinned at each end, and rotated with the use of a rope. It may be no coincidence that, to this day, wood turning is still a local speciality. Only the central shaft of each pillar seems to have been turned; in the base and capitals, a less precise, presumably handworked imitation of turning is evident.

The architectural style of the Hoysala temples is commonly referred to as *vesara*, or "hybrid" (literally "mule"), rather than belonging to either the northern, *nagari*, or southern Dravidian styles. However, they show great affinity with *nagari* temples of western India, and represent another fruit of contact, like music, painting and literature, facilitated by the trade routes between the north and the south. All Hoysala temples share a star-shaped plan, built on high plinths (*jagati*) that follow the shape of the sanctuaries and *mandapas* to provide a raised surrounding platform. Such northern features may have been introduced by the designer and artists of the earliest temple at Belur, who were imported by Vishnu Vardhana from further north in Andhra Pradesh. Also characteristic of the Hoysala style is the use of *ashlar* masonry, without mortar. Some pieces of stones are joined by pegs of iron or bronze, or mortice and tenon joints. Ceilings inside the *mandapas* are made up of corbelled domes, looking similar to those of the Jain temples of Rajasthan and Gujarat; in the Hoysala style they are only visible from inside.

clean and basic rooms, with bathroom, cannot be booked in advance; you'll have to go back to the cheap "meals" hotels at T Narasipur if you're desperate.

Hassan

The unprepossessing town of **HASSAN**, 118km northwest of Mysore, makes a useful base for seeing the Hoysala sites at **Belur** and **Halebid**, both northwest of the town, and the Jain pilgrimage town of **Sravanabelgola**, southeast.

Arrival and information

Hassan's **bus stand** is in the centre of town, at the northern end of Bus Stand Rd which runs south past the post office to **Narsimharaja Circle**. Here you'll find the *State Bank of Mysore*, where you can change money but not *Thomas Cook* travellers' cheques, and most of the town's accommodation. Winding its way east–west via this junction is the Bangalore–Mangalore Road (BM Rd); along here to the east are the **tourist office** (1km; ☎08172/68026), which won't tell you anything that you can't find out from your hotel, and the **railway station** (2km).

Accommodation and eating

Considering the number of tourists who pass through the town, Hassan is oddly lacking in good accommodation. Most of the budget options are of a pitiful standard: the few exceptions are all within walking distance of the bus stand, around **Narsimharaja Circle**. The best **places to eat** are attached to the hotels listed below.

Amblee Palika, Race Course Rd, near Narsimharaja Circle, off BM Rd (☎08172/66310 or 66307). Comfortable, reliable hotel; arrive early or book in advance as it's often full. Good veg and non-veg restaurant, the *Malanika* (noon–2.30pm & 7–10.30pm), coffee shop, bar and exchange. ③–④.

ITDC Hassan Ashok, BM Rd, near Narsimharaja Circle (☎08172/68731). On the left as you approach from the railway station. Somewhat overpriced posh hotel for tour groups and VIPs. Uninspiring but comfortable veg and non-veg restaurant, craft shops and bar. ⑦.

Kothari Residency, BM Rd (☎08172/67285). New hotel, with spotless rooms and a restaurant planned. Near the railway station (on the right on the way to town), and a longish walk to town. ④.

Mahaveer, BM Rd, near Narsimharaja Circle (☎08172/68885). Cleanish rooms (some with TV) with mosquito nets and good but dilapidated veg restaurant, *Abhiruchi*. ①–②.

Sangam Lodge, Kasturi Bhai Rd (☎08172/68316). Dirty; a last resort. ①.

Sanman, Municipal Office Rd, near Narsimharaja Circle (☎08172/68024). Clean lodge, acceptable for the price, but noisy until the canteen-style restaurant, popular with local youth, closes. ①–②.

Satyaprakash Lodge, Bus Stand Rd (☎08172/68521). Good-value, clean lodge (all rooms with bathroom), just along from the bus stand (turn right). ①.

Vaishnavi Lodging, Harsha Mahal Rd (☎08172/67413). Good budget lodge with decent-sized rooms and veg restaurant. Turn left out of the bus stand, right onto Church Rd and it's on the corner of the first turning left. ②.

Getting from Hassan to Belur, Halebid and Sravanabelgola

The only way to see Sravanabelgola, Belur and Halebid in one day, apart from on a conducted tour from Mysore or Bangalore, is **by car**, which some visitors share; most of the hotels can fix this up for you (at least Rs800). Travelling **by bus**, you'll need at least two days. **Belur** and **Halebid** can be comfortably covered in one day; it's best to take the first (8am; 1hr) of ten daily buses to Halebid and move on to Belur (30min); there's a frequent service back to Hassan (1hr 30min; 6.30am–6.15pm), and some accommodation. **Sravanabelgola**, however, is in the opposite direction, and not served by direct buses; take a bus to Channarayapatna (from 6.30am; 1hr) and pick up one of the regular buses (30min) from there. An early start is recommended.

Halebid

Now a hamlet, **HALEBID**, 32km northwest of Hassan, was once Dora Samudra, the capital of the Hoysala dynasty. Destroyed in 1311 by Delhi Sultanate forces belonging to Ala-ud-Din-Khalji, it came to be known as *Halebid*, "Old Capital". Despite the city's fall, several large Hoysala temples (see p.1054) survive, two of which, the Hoysaleshvara and Kedareshvara, are superb, covered in exquisite carvings. A small **archeological museum** (daily except Fri 10am–5pm) adjacent to the Hoysaleshvara temple houses a collection of Hoysala art and other finds from the area.

The Hoysaleshvara temple

The **Hoysaleshvara** temple was started in 1141, and after some forty years of work remained incomplete; this possibly accounts for the absence here of the type of towers that feature at Somnathpur, for example. It is no longer known which deities were originally worshipped, though the double shrine is thought to have been devoted at one time to Shiva and his consort. In any event, both shrines contain *shivalingams* and are adjoined by two linked, partly enclosed *mandapa* hallways in which stand Nandi bulls.

Like other Hoysala temples, the whole is raised on a high plinth (*jagati*) which follows the complex star-shaped plan and provides an upper ambulatory; the *mandapas* are approached by flights of steps flanked by small free-standing, towered shrines. Inside, the lower portions of the black polished stone pillars were lathe-turned, though the upper levels appear to have been hand-carved to reproduce the effect of turning.

Hoysaleshvara also features many Vaishnavite images. The **sculptures**, which have a fluid quality lacking in the earlier work at Belur, include Brahma aboard his goose vehicle Hamsa, Krishna holding up Mount Govardhana, another where he plays the flute, and Vishnu (Trivikrama) bestriding the world in three steps. One of the most remarkable images is of the demon king **Ravana** shaking Shiva's mountain abode, Mount Kailasa, populated by numerous animals and figures with Shiva and Parvati seated atop. Secular themes, among them dancers and musicians, occupy the same register as the gods. A narrative frieze, on the sixth register from the bottom, follows the length of the Nandi *mandapas* and illustrates scenes from the *Bhagavata* and Vishnu *Puranas*, *Mahabharata* and *Ramayana*.

The Kedareshvara temple

About 600m south of the Hoysaleshvara, a group of Jain *bastis* (temples) stand virtually unadorned; the only sculptural decoration consists of ceiling friezes inside the *mandapas* and elephants at the entrance steps. To the east, a smaller Shiva temple, **Kedareshvara** (1217–21), also built on a stellate plan, is far less famous than the Hoysaleshvara. Unfortunately, due to fears that the ceiling might collapse, it's not possible to get inside. Unlike the Hoysaleshvara, illustrations show that it did, until at least the mid-nineteenth century, have a tower over the shrine. Fine pillars in the *mandapa* were lathe-turned first and then handworked to make them fluted. Two subsidiary shrines flank the main shrine, which must have originally been dedicated to Vishnu, as it is guarded by a pair of Vaishnavite *dvarpala* (door guardians). Many fine images decorate the exterior, including an unusual Krishna dancing on the serpent demon Kaliya – rare in stone, though commonly seen in bronze and painting.

Belur

BELUR, 37km northwest of Hassan, on the banks of the Yagachi, was the Hoysala capital prior to Halebid, during the eleventh and twelfth centuries. Still active (non-Hindus are allowed inside), the **Chennakeshava temple**, a fine and early example of the singular Hoysala style, was built by King Vishnuvardhana in 1117 to celebrate his conversion from Jainism, victory over Chola forces at Talakad and his independence from the Chalukyas of Kalyan.

Built on a star-shaped plan, the temple stands in a huge walled courtyard, surrounded by smaller shrines and columned *mandapa* hallways. Lacking any form of superstructure, terminating at the first floor, it appears to have a flat roof. If it ever had a tower, it would have disappeared by the Vijayanagar (sixteenth-century) period – above the cornice, a plain parapet, presumably added at the same time as the east entrance *gopura*, shows typically Vijayanagar Islamic influences.

Both the sanctuary and *mandapa* are raised on the usual plinth (*jagati*). Double flights of steps, flanked by minor towered shrines, afford entry to the *mandapa* on three sides; this hallway was originally open, but in the thirteenth century, pierced stone screens, elaborately carved with geometric designs and scenes from the *Puranas*, were inserted between the lathe-turned pillars.

The quantity of **sculptural decoration**, if less mature than in later Hoysala temples, is staggering. Carvings on the plinth and lower walls, in successive and continuous bands, start at the bottom with elephants, each different, and then garlands and arches with lion heads; stylized vegetation with dancing figures, birds and animals; pearl garlands; projecting niches containing male and female figures and seated *yakshas*, or spirits; miniature pillars alternating with female figures dressing or dancing; miniature temple towers interspersed with dancers, and above them lion heads. Above the screens, a series of 42 bracket figures, added at a later date, shows full-breasted celestial nymphs hunting, playing music, dancing and beautifying themselves.

Columns inside, each unique, feature extraordinarily detailed carving, with more than a hundred deities on the central **Narasimha pillar**. The inner sanctum contains a black image of Chennakeshava, a form of Krishna who holds a conch (*shankha*, in the upper right hand), discus (*chakra*, upper left), lotus (*padma*, lower right) and mace (*gada*, lower left). He is flanked by consorts Shri Devi and Bhudevi.

Within the same enclosure, the **Kappe Channigaraya temple** has some finely carved niche images and a depiction of Narasimha (Vishnu as man-lion) killing the demon Hiranyakashipu. Further west, fine sculptures in the smaller **Viranarayana** shrine include a scene from the *Mahabharata* of Bhima killing the demon Bhaga.

The KSTDC *Mayuri Velapuri* (☎9; ②), near the temple, has two clean **rooms** with bath and provides meals by arrangement. Nearer the bus stand on Main Rd are two budget lodges with restaurants, *Vishnu Prasad* (☎63; ①) and the smaller *New Gayatri Hotel* (☎55; ①).

Sravanabelgola

The sacred Jain site of **SRAVANABELGOLA**, 49km southwest of Hassan and 93km north of Mysore, consists of two hills and a large tank. On one of the hills, Indragiri (also known as Vindhyagiri), stands an extraordinary eighteen-metre-high monolithic statue of a naked male figure, **Gomateshvara**. Said to be the largest free-standing sculpture in India, this tenth-century colossus, visible for miles around, as well as the nearby *bastis*, Jain temples, make Sravanabelgola a key pilgrimage centre.

Sravanabelgola is linked in tradition with the Mauryan emperor Chandragupta, who is said to have starved himself to death on the second hill in around 300 BC, in accordance with a Jain practice. The hill was renamed Chandragiri, marking the arrival of Jainism in southern India. At the same time, a controversy regarding the doctrines of Mahavira, the last of the 24 Jain *tirthankaras* (literally "crossing makers", who assist the aspirant to cross the "ocean of rebirth"), split Jainism into two separate branches. *Svetambara*, "white-clad" Jains, are more common in north India, while *digambara*, "sky-clad", are usually associated with the south. Truly ascetic *digambara* devotees go naked, though few do so away from sacred sites.

All the *tirthankaras* are represented as naked figures, differentiated only by their individual attributes: animals, inanimate objects (such as a conch shell), or symbols (such as the *svastika*). Each of the 24 is also attached to a particular *yaksha* (male) or *yakshi* (female) spirit; such spirits are also evident in Mahayana Buddhism, suggesting a strand of belief with extremely ancient origins. *Tirthankaras* are represented in either of two postures: sitting cross-legged in meditation, resembling images of the Buddha, save for their nakedness, or *kayotsarga*, "body upright", where the figure stands impassive; here Gomateshvara stands in the latter, more usual posture.

The monuments at Sravanabelgola probably date from no earlier than the tenth century, when a General Chamundaraya is said to have visited Chandragiri in search of a Mauryan statue of Gomateshvara. Failing to find it, he decided to have one made. From the top of Chandragiri he fired an arrow across to Indragiri hill; where the arrow landed he had a new Gomateshvara sculpted from a single rock.

Indragiri Hill

Gomateshvara is approached from the tank between the two hills by around 700 steps, cut into the granite of **Indragiri Hill**, which pass numerous rock inscriptions on the way up to a walled enclosure. Shoes must be placed to the left of the steps; anyone unable to climb the steps can be carried up by chair. Entered through a small wagon-vaulted *gopura*, the temple is of the type known as *betta*, which instead of the usual *garbhagriha* sanctuary consists of an open courtyard enclosing the massive sculpture. Figures and shrines of all the *yaksha* and *yakshi* spirits stand inside the crenellated wall, but the towering figure of Gomateshvara dominates. With elongated arms and exaggeratedly wide shoulders, his proportions are decidedly non-naturalistic. The sensuously smooth surface of the white granite "trap" rock is finely carved: particularly

GOMATESHVARA AND MAHAMASTAKABHISHEKA

Gomateshvara (aka Bahubali), who was the son of the legendary King Rishabdev of Ayodhya (better known as Adinath, the first *tirthankara*), fell into dispute with his elder brother, Bharat, over their inheritance. After a fierce fight, he lifted his brother above his head, and was about to throw him to the ground when he was gripped by remorse. Gently setting Bharat down, Gomateshvara resolved to reject the world of greed, jealousy and violence by meditating until he achieved *moksha*, release from attachment and rebirth. This he succeeded in doing, even before his father.

As a *kevalin*, Gomateshvara had achieved *kevalajnana*, "sole knowledge" acquired through solitude, austerity and meditation. While engaged in this non-activity, he stood "body upright" in a forest. So motionless was he that ants built their nest at his feet, snakes coiled happily around his ankles, and creepers began to grow up his legs.

Every twelve years, at an auspicious astrological conjunction of certain planets, the Gomateshvara statue is ritually anointed in the **Mahamastakabhisheka** ceremony (the last was in December 1993). The process lasts for several days, culminating on the final auspicious morning when 1008 *kalashas* (pots), each with a coconut and mango leaves, tied with coloured thread, are arranged before the statue in the shape of a sacred diagram, on ground strewn with fresh paddy. A few priests climb scaffolding, erected around Gomateshvara, to bathe him in milk and *ghee*, clarified butter. After this first bath, prayers are offered. Then, to the accompaniment of temple musicians and the chanting of sacred texts, a thousand priests climb the scaffold to bathe the image in the water of sacred rivers, sandal paste, cane juice, milk, flowers and other auspicious unguents.

Needless to say, the Mahamastakabhisheka attracts *lakhs* of devotees, Jain *sadhus* and *sadhvis* (female *sadhus*), and the massed cameras of the world. A satellite township, Yatrinagar, is set up close to Sravanabelgola to provide accommodation for 35,000, and eighteen surrounding villages also shelter pilgrims in temporary *dharamshalas*.

the hands, hair and serenely expressive face. As in the myth, ant-hills and snakes sit at his feet and creepers appear to grow on his limbs.

Bhandari Basti and monastery (math)

The road east from the foot of the steps at Chandragiri leads to two interesting Jain buildings in town. To the right, the **Bhandari Basti** (1159), housing a shrine with images of the 24 *tirthankaras,* was built by Hullamaya, treasurer of the Hoysala Raja Narasimha. A high wall encloses the temple, forming a plain ambulatory which contains a well. Two *mandapa* hallways, where naked *digambara* Jains discourse with devotees clad in white, lead to the shrine at the back. Pillars in the outer *mandapa* feature carvings of female musicians, while mythical beasts adorn the entrance to the inner, *navaranga,* hallway.

At the end of the street, the *math* (monastery) was at one time the residence of Sravanabelgola's senior *acharya,* or guru. Thirty male and female monks, who also "go wandering in every direction", are attached to the *math;* normally a member of staff will be happy to show visitors around. Among the rare palm-leaf manuscripts housed in the library, some more than a thousand years old, are works on mathematics and geography, and the *Mahapurana,* hagiographies of the *tirthankaras.*

Next door, a walled courtyard, open to the sky, contains a number of shrines; the entrance is elaborately decorated with embossed brass designs of *yali* mythical beasts, elephants, a two-headed eagle and an image of Parsvanath, the twenty-third *tirthankara,* here shown as Padmavati. Inside, the courtyard is edged by a high platform on three sides, on which a chair is placed for the *acharya.* A collection of tenth-century bronze *tirthankara* images is housed here, and vibrant murals detail the various lives of Parsvanath. In one episode he is pictured deep in meditation in the forest, oblivious to the tigers and deer nearby; another shows visions of the underworld where *himsa,* violence, is represented by fights, below images of *moksha,* or release from rebirth. The hills where the *tirthankaras* stood to gain *moksha* are represented in a model, somewhat resembling a jelly mould, with tacked-on footprints.

Chandragiri Hill

Leaving your shoes with the keeper at the bottom, take the rock-cut steps to the top of the smaller **Chandragiri Hill**. Miraculously, the sound of radios and rickshaws down below soon disappears. Fine views stretch south to Indragiri and, from the north on the far side, across to a river, paddy and sugarcane fields, coconut palms and the village of **Jinanathapura**, where there's another ornate Hoysala temple, the Shantishvara *basti.*

Rather than a single large shrine, as at Indragiri, Chandragiri holds a group of *bastis* in late Chalukya Dravida style, within a walled enclosure. Although the caretakers don't speak fluent English, they will take you around and open up the closed shrines. Save for pilasters and elaborate parapets, all the temples have plain exteriors. Named after its patron, the tenth-century **Chamundaraya** is the largest of the group, dedicated to Parsvanath. Inside the **Chandragupta** (twelfth century), superb carved panels in a small shrine narrate the story of Chandragupta and his teacher Bhadrabahu. Traces of painted geometric designs survive and the pillars feature detailed carving. Elsewhere in the enclosure stands a 24-metre-high *manastambha,* "pillar of fame", decorated with images of spirits, two *yakshis* and a *yaksha.* No fewer than 576 inscriptions dating from the sixth to the nineteenth centuries are said to be dotted around the site, on small pillars and the rock itself.

Practicalities

Sravanabelgola features on the itineraries, along with Belur and Halebid, of organized **tours** from Bangalore and Mysore (see p.1038 & p.1047). However, if you want to spend time looking around it's best to come independently; the most suitable base is Hassan (see p.1055). In Sravanabelgola a few basic pilgrim **lodges** (①) offer accommodation; for information ask the friendly **tourist office** (daily 10am–1pm & 3–5.30pm), left of the steps up Indragiri Hill. A few "meals" **restaurants** line the main street nearby.

Madikeri (Mercara) and Kodagu (Coorg)

Nestling beside a curving stretch of craggy hills, little-visited **MADIKERI** (Mercara), capital of the Kodagu (Coorg) region, is poised 117m up in the Western Ghats. Kodagu is one of India's principal coffee-growing regions, known for distinct cultural traditions and history, with its own language, **Kodagi**, drawing on both Malayalam, the language of Kerala, and Kannada. For much of its history, Kodagu remained more or less independent, ruled by Lingayat Rajas.

Madikeri itself is a pleasant enough town, with red-tiled buildings and undulating roads that converge on to a small, bustling market area. The **Omkareshwara Shiva** temple, built in 1820, features an unusual combination of red-tiled roofs, typical of Keralan Hindu architecture, Gothic elements and Islamic-influenced domes. The fort and palace, worked over by Tipu Sultan in 1781 and rebuilt in the nineteenth century, now serve as administrative offices and a prison; also within the walls, **St Mark's Church** holds a small **museum** of British memorabilia, Jain, Hindu and village deity figures and weapons (daily except Mon 9am–5pm). **Rajas' Seat**, next to *Hotel Valley View*, is a belvedere, said to be the Kodagu kings' favoured place to watch the sunset.

The real attraction of a visit to Madikeri is the surrounding **countryside**, which you can enjoy on quiet, easy walks or more strenuous trekking – both at their best between December and May. Although it's a long way (6km; there's no public transport), the walk to the popular picnic spot of **Abbi Falls** (*abbi* means "falls") is very attractive, passing through domesticated forest with coffee and pepper plantations.

Madikeri practicalities

You can only reach Madikeri by road, but it's an easy three-hour **bus** ride from Mysore (120km southeast), or a little longer from **Mangalore** (135km northwest). The central **bus stand** – little more than a parking place on the main Mysore–Mangalore Road – is also used by local services to Bhagamandala and Nagarhole. The small local **tourist office**, at the *PWD Travellers Bungalow* (daily 10am–5.45pm), is five minutes' walk along the main road towards Mysore. The **post office** is on Kahi Rd.

TREKKING IN KODAGU

Trekking through the Kodagu region takes you through some delightfully varied country. The **north** features rolling hills interspersed with clumps of forest. Near Madikeri, where the hills are closer together, slashed by deep ravines, there is a small amount of forest. Towards the **south** and **southwest**, on the border with Kerala, several kinds of lush forest resemble jungle. In many places, trees rise to heights of over 30m, with dense growth of smaller trees below; sometimes thick vegetation carpets the forest floor, but elsewhere, lack of light, due to the trees' cover, allows little to grow.

Many of the **treks** (usually one or two days) lead through reserved forest and require considerable forward planning, particularly to arrange guides (essential) and overnight stays. It's possible to employ your own guides (around Rs50 per day plus Rs50 for food) with at least three days' notice. If you prefer to join an **organized tour**, the local YHA group organize weekend treks once a month, departing on Saturday and returning Sunday evening. Accommodation is in forest lodges, school halls, temples and the like. For information and advice about all aspects of trekking contact the YHA Group Secretary, B M Rajashekhar, at *Friends Tours and Travels*, College Rd, PB No 51, Madikeri 571201, Kodagu (☎26974).

There's not much choice of **places to stay or eat** in Madikeri. The best place for both is undoubtedly the KSTDC *Hotel Mayura Valley View* (☎6387; ③), which is well away from the main road, next to Raja's Seat, and has excellent views – believe it or not – over the valley. It's worth getting an auto-rickshaw out there, as it's a good fifteen-minute walk from the centre. Rooms are huge and the restaurant, which serves beer, is not at all bad. More basic places, in the centre of town, include the *Anchorage Guest House* (☎6939; ②), *Hotel Cauvery* (☎6292;②) and, a bit more upmarket, *Hotel East End* (☎6496; ③). The romantically named *Hotel Paris* in College Rd is just one of a number of unexciting "meals" places; the menu at the *Hotel Capitol* is more appetizing.

Bhagamandala and Talakaveri

A good bus excursion from Madikeri takes you to the quiet village of **Bhagamandala** (35km west), and from there to the sacred site of **Talakaveri** (9km), said to be the source of the holy Kaveri (Cauvery) River. The hill scenery is superb, and you can opt to walk part of the way back on blissfully quiet country paths.

Wearing something warm, take the 6.30am bus to **BHAGAMANDALA** from Madikeri. You should arrive around 8am, with just enough time to grab a good breakfast at the *Laxmi Vilas* tea shop, right next to where the bus to Talakaveri leaves at 8.30am. At Bhagamandala, the Kaveri merges with two streams, Kanike and Sujyothi, rendering the site of the **Bhagandeshwara temple** auspicious and holy. The temple is a fine example of Keralan-style architecture, with tiled roofs and courtyards.

At **TALAKAVERI** the bus terminates on the slopes of Brahmagiri Hill by the entrance to the sacred tank and **temple**. In October, thousands of pilgrims come here to witness a spring, thought to be the goddess Kaveri, known as Lopamudra, the local patron deity, suddenly spurting into a small well; to bathe in the tank at this time is considered especially sin-absolving. At almost any other time, you're still likely to find wild-haired *sadhus* and groups of bathing pilgrims, the surrounding walls swathed in drying *dhotis* and *saris*. Two small shrines stand at the head of the tank, one containing an image of Ganesh and the other a metal *lingam* with *naga* snake canopy. Steps to the right lead to the peak of **Brahmagiri Hill**, where a red flag flutters. The views are spectacular, with a 360° panorama of surrounding hills.

Coastal Karnataka

The 300-kilometre stretch of Karnataka's palm-fringed and red lateritic **coast** is as yet undeveloped for tourists; although there are beaches, facilities are, with rare exceptions, non-existent. That may well all change when the long-promised and highly controversial *Konkan Railway* finally starts to operate all the way from Bombay to Kerala, with as-yet-unguessable consequences for the fishing villages and long-forgotten fortresses along the way. At present, the only place that sees significant numbers of foreign travellers is the fast-developing port of **Mangalore**, just 15km north of Kerala. There both the Hindu temple, the Manjunatha, which has Buddhist connections, and the Christian St Aloysius College Chapel are worth seeing, while **Udupi**, 58km north, is an important pilgrimage centre for the followers of the Vaishnavite philosopher Madhva (see p.1036), and its Krishna temple is a hive of fascinating ritual activity.

Mangalore

Many visitors only come to **MANGALORE** on their way somewhere else. As well as being fairly close to Madikeri and the Kodagu (Coorg) hill region, it's also a stopping-off point between Goa and Kerala, and is the nearest coastal town to the Hoysala and Jain monuments in the Hassan area, 172km east.

Mangalore was one of the most famous ports of south India. It was already famous overseas in the sixth century, as a major source of pepper, and the fourteenth-century Muslim writer Ibn Batuta noted its trade in pepper and ginger and the presence of merchants from Persia and the Yemen. In the mid-fifteenth century, the Persian ambassador Abdu'r-Razzaq saw Mangalore as the "frontier town" of the Vijayanagar empire (see p.1068) – which was why the Portuguese captured it in 1529. In Haider Ali's time, during the eighteenth century, the city became a shipbuilding centre.

Nowadays, the modern port of Mangalore, 10km north of the city proper, is principally known for the processing and export of coffee and cocoa (much of which comes from the Kodagu region of the Western Ghats), cashew nuts from Kerala, Karnataka and Africa, as well as granite. It is also a centre for the production of *bidi* cigarettes.

Arrival and information

Mangalore's **bus stand** is in the centre of town at the bottom of Lighthouse Hill. Frequent services run south to Madikeri and Kerala and north to Udupi; daily longer hauls include Goa, Mysore, Bangalore and Hassan. **Bajpe airport**, 22km north of the city (bus #47a), is served by *Indian Airlines* flights to Bombay and Bangalore. The airline office is at the *Moti Mahal Hotel*, Falnir Rd (☎0832/4669).

The **railway station**, 1.5km south of the bus stand, in theory (but see p.1035) offers daily services to Delhi, Bangalore, two to Madras, two to Thiruvananthapuram and two to Hassan (not during monsoon). So far, the new *Konkan Railway* only runs as far as Udupi, but if on schedule (extremely unlikely), from 1995 trains will go right up the coast to Bombay via Goa.

KSTDC's **tourist office** at their *Hotel Mayura Netravathi* (☎0832/24192) on Lighthouse Hill is of no use whatsoever. You'd do far better to pick up a copy of the *Sharada Mangalore & Dakshina Kannada* guide book at *Higginbothams*, also on Lighthouse Hill, lower down, nearer the bus stand. You can **change money** at the *State Bank of India*, KS Rao Rd (Mon–Fri 10.30am–2.30pm & Sat 10.30am–12.30pm).

The City

Mangalore is a pleasant city: small and hilly, with a couple of worthwhile sights. Its strong Christian influence can be traced back to the arrival further south of St Thomas (see p.1004). Some 1400 years later, in 1526, the Portuguese founded one of the earliest churches on the coast close to the old port; the present **Most Holy Rosary Church**, however, with a dome based on St Peter's in Rome, dates only from 1910. Fine restored fresco, tempera and oil murals, the work of an Italian artist, Antonio Moscheni, adorn the Romanesque-style **St Aloysius College Chapel**, built in 1885, on Lighthouse Hill, close to the centre.

At the foot of Kadri Hill, 5km north (buses #19, #14, #14a & #48), Mangalore's tenth-century **Manjunatha temple** is an important centre of the Shaivite and tantric **Natha-Pantha cult**. Thought to be an outgrowth of Vajrayana Buddhism, the cult is a divergent species of Hinduism, somewhat similar to certain cults in Nepal. Superb **bronzes** include a 1.5-metre-high seated Lokeshvara (Matsyendranatha), made in 958 AD and considered the finest southern bronze outside Tamil Nadu. Manjunatha's square and towered sanctuary, containing an unusual *lingam*, is surrounded by two tiled and gabled colonnades with louvred windows, showing strong affinity with the temple complexes further south in Kerala. Nine water tanks adjoin the temple. Opposite the entrance to the temple, steps lead via a laterite path to a curious group of minor shrines. Beyond this complex stands the **Shri Yogishwar Math**, a hermitage of tantric *sadhus* set round two courtyards, one of which contains shrines to Kala Bhairava (a form of Dakshinamurti, the southern aspect of Shiva and deity of death), goddess Durga and god of fire, Agni. Nearby, cut into the side of the hill, a tiny unadorned cave is credited with being a "night halt" for the Pandava brothers from the *Mahabharata*.

Two beaches lie within reach to the south; **Ullal** (10km) boasts an attractive resort, while across the Keralan border are the deserted bays at **Bekkal** (50km; see p.1032).

Accommodation and eating

Mangalore's accommodation standards seem to be forever improving; now it even has a modern five-star. The main area for hotels, **KS Rao Rd**, runs south from the bus stand, but you can also stay out of town by the beach in Ullal. The best **places to eat** are in the bigger hotels.

Indraprastha, Lighthouse Hill Rd (☎0832/33756). Serviceable rooms, all with bathroom. ②.

KSTDC Mayura Netravathi, near the bus stand, Lighthouse Hill Rd (☎411192). Good-value rooms (some with balcony and sea views). Average south Indian "meals" and snacks restaurant. ②.

Moti Mahal, Falnir Rd (☎0832/22211). Large hotel (some a/c rooms) with 24-hr room service, bar, pool, shops, exchange, travel desk, 24-hr coffee shop. *Mangala* non-veg and *Madhuvan* veg restaurants serve Indian, Chinese and western food. ⑤–⑥.

Navaratna, KS Rao Rd (☎0832/27941). Some a/c rooms with TV; refurbished and good value. ④.

Navaratna Palace, Navaratna Complex, KS Rao Rd (☎0832/33781). Comfortable modern hotel over the road from the bus stand, with good-value non- and a/c rooms. Two good a/c restaurants, *Heera Panna* for veg and non-veg and *Palimar* for vegetarian dishes. ③–④.

Summer Sands Beach Resort, Chota Mangalore, Ullal, 10km out of town (☎0832/6400). Rooms and cottages (some a/c) near the beach, built in traditional local style. Swimming pool, bar and restaurant serving local specialities, Indian and Chinese food. Bus #44a from town. ③–④.

Vasanth Mahal, KS Rao Rd (☎0832/22311). Basic, cheap lodge. ②.

Welcomgroup Manjarun, Old Port Rd, 2km from railway station (☎0832/26502). Large, modern business hotel; some rooms with sea view and all a/c. Facilities include travel, exchange, swimming pool, bar and 24hr coffee shop. The pricey restaurant, *Galley*, serves Indian and western cuisine. Also *Embers*, a poolside barbecue. ⑥–⑦.

Udupi

One of Karnataka's holiest Vaishnavite centres, **UDUPI** (also spelt Udipi), on the west coast, 58km north of Mangalore, was the birthplace of the Hindu saint **Madhva** (1197–1276). Close to the centre of town, Udupi's **Krishna temple** stands in a square, surrounded by eight *maths* (monasteries) founded by Madhva. It's an important place of pilgrimage; each of an all-but constant round of *puja* ceremonies (5.30am–8.45pm) is conducted by one of the *acharyas*, or pontiffs. The temple fills with a cacophony of clanging bells as the *acharya* approaches the shrine; the crowd divides to let him through, while *brahmin* boys fan the deity with cloths. During the ceremony, the *acharya* chants while flicking a hair whisk. A stone tank in the temple, known as the **Madhva Sarovara**, is the focus of a huge festival every two years, usually in January, when a new head priest is appointed. Outside, in the street, a window in the wall affords a view of the deity; according to legend, a Harijan, or "untouchable" devotee, was denied entry due to his caste. As he worshipped Krishna from outside, the deity turned to face him. A statue of the devotee stands opposite. Nearby, a magnificent gold temple chariot is brought out for processions.

Anyone wishing to know about the wealth of dance, music, theatre and ritual life of the region should head for the **Regional Resources Centre for the Performing Arts**, in the MGM College. The staff can tell you about local festivals and events that take you well off the tourist trail; the collection includes film, video and audio archives.

Udupi's weekend picnic spot, **Malpe beach**, 5km north of the centre, is disappointing, with a huge, unfinished and possibly forgotten modern concrete block that was planned to be a government-run hotel. After wandering around the smelly fish market at the harbour you could take a local boat (Rs400) out to **St Mary's Island**, an extraordinary rockface of hexagonal basalt. Vasco da Gama is said to have placed a cross here in the fifteenth century, prior to his historic landing at Kozhikode in Kerala. A more tempting and virtually empty beach, **Thottam**, is barely 1km north of Malpe.

Incidentally, Udupi also lays proud claim to being the birthplace of the nationally popular **masala dosa**; these crispy stuffed pancakes, made from fermented rice flour, were first prepared and made famous by the Udupi *brahmin* hotels.

Practicalities

City bus stand, in the centre of town, offers a dozen or more daily buses to Bangalore, six to Mysore, two to Panaji and frequent services to Mangalore. With the opening of part of the *Konkan Railway* line, daily **trains** are now available to Mangalore; the rest of the line is optimistically scheduled to open in 1995.

Several decent **places to stay** can be found near the bus stand; rooms at the *Hotel Sharada International* (☎08252/22912; ③–④) range from singles to carpeted a/c ones, and there are veg and non-veg restaurants and a bar. *Kediyoor* (☎08252/22381; ③–④) is much the same, but with three restaurants – the rooftop *Kediyoor Heights* serves tasty tri-cuisine veg dishes and there's an open-air bar – while the *Shri Ramakrishna Hotel* (☎08252/23189; ①–③) also has a good, but slow, non-veg restaurant and bar.

Outside Udupi, another cheap place, *Silver Sands* (☎08252/22223; ①), is on the deserted Thottam beach, 6km north of the centre, just along from Malpe. At the time of writing, they had just two basic cottages offering self-catering or meals by arrangement.

Jog Falls

JOG FALLS, 225km northwest of Mysore, are the highest **waterfalls** in India. Their source, the River Sharavati, is now harnessed to create hydro-electricity, as well as feeding four spectacular falls called the Rani, Rocket, Roarer and the largest, Raja, which drops 250m. Many visitors are disappointed, however; in the driest season, the water more or less dries up, while during the monsoon, mist renders the falls virtually invisible. The **best time to visit** is after the monsoon, from the end of November to the start of January, when you will see not only the water but also wonderful rainbows. If you are sure of foot, walk down the footpath to the bottom of the falls from the *Inspection Bungalow* – beware of leeches if it's wet and misty.

Practicalities

Getting to Jog Falls is not easy. With a **car**, you must make for either Sirsi (52km north), which is 61km over the Ghats from Mirjan, the nearest point on the coastal NH-17, or Shimoga (104km southeast). By **bus**, you can get the single daily service from Karwar (8hr), which is likely to arrive after dark; the same bus returns the next morning. Coming from the south, head for Sagar (30km southeast) and get a local bus to Jog. When this book went to press, all rail services to the nearest railway station of Talguppa, 16km southeast, were suspended during conversion to broad-gauge; eventually there should once again be connections to both Bangalore and Mysore.

Accommodation and eating options are severely limited. The *PWD Inspection Bungalow*, with great views, is invariably full and has to be booked in Shimoga. *Woodlands* (☎22; ②) is unappealing, but has a restaurant, while *Jog Falls Guest House* (②) is a basic lodge run by the Tourism Department.

Hospet

The busy small town of **HOSPET** is of little interest except as a base for the extraordinary ancient city of Vijayanagar/Hampi, 13km northeast. The shops in the main market area, north of the bus stand, can be a mild diversion.

Arrival and information

In theory, Hospet's **railway station**, 1.5km north of the centre, is served by trains from Bangalore (353km southeast), Gadag, Hubli, Badami, Bijapur and Vasco da Gama (about 350km west). However, no trains were running when this book went to press, and if the changeover from metre- to broad-gauge track takes any longer than officially anticipated there may well still be no trains as you read it.

Auto-rickshaws are quite thin on the ground, and often the only available transport from the station into town is cycle rickshaw (Rs10–Rs20). **Long-distance buses** pull into the bus stand, nearer the centre, 250m down MG (Station) Rd, which runs south from the railway station. The most frequent services are from Bangalore and Hubli, but there are also daily arrivals from Mysore, Badami, Mangalore, Kochi and Goa.

You can **change currency** only at the *State Bank of India* (Mon–Fri 10.30am– 2.30pm & Sat 10.30am–12.30pm); the *State Bank of Mysore* (same hours) on MG Rd changes travellers' cheques.

Accommodation and eating

Lodging in Hospet, concentrated around MG Rd, ranges from budget to mid-range. After tramping around Vijayanagar all day, you can work up quite an appetite – fortunately the bigger hotels offer more than plain "meals", and some serve beer. Otherwise, the *Eagle Garden Restaurant*, just behind the enormously popular *Malligi*, is a good place for carnivores and has a lively bar.

KSTDC Mayura Chalukya, Tungabhadra Dam, 5km from Hospet (☎08394/8270). Popular with weekending locals, but difficult for Hampi (16km) without your own transport. ②.

Malligi Tourist Home, 6/143 Jambunatha Rd (☎08394/8101). Two minutes' walk east of MG Rd (from where it is signposted) and the bus stand. Hugely popular, friendly hotel with clean, comfortable rooms (some a/c). They sell the usually hard-to-find illustrated journal *Homage to Hampi*. Pleasant bar and restaurant, opening onto the garden and serving good veg food. Exchange. ②–④.

Priyadarshini, MG Rd (☎08394/8838). Over the road from the bus stand, towards the railway station. Rooms from rock-bottom singles to doubles with TV and a/c (some balconies). Two good restaurants: the veg *Chalukya* and, in the garden, the non-veg *Manasa* which also has a bar. ①–④.

Sandarshan, MG Rd (☎08394/8128). Midway between the railway station and bus stand. Budget lodge, some rooms with bathroom. ①–②.

Shalini, MG Rd. Just across the canal on the right-hand side as you approach from the railway station. Very basic, small lodge, some rooms with bathroom. ①.

Sree Krishna Tourist Home, near the Govt Hospital, l2km west of MG Rd. Very good-value Indian-style lodge; basic, clean and friendly with a veg canteen. Take a rickshaw. ①–②.

Vishwa, MG Rd. Directly opposite the bus stand, so a bit noisy. No-frills budget lodge. *Shanti Restaurant* serves "meals" at lunchtime and south Indian snacks the rest of the day. ②.

Getting to Vijayanagar/Hampi

KSTDC's daily guided **tour** only stops at three of the sites in Vijayanagar and hangs about an inordinate amount of time at the far less interesting Tungabhadra Dam. Even so, it can be worth it if you're very short of time. It leaves from their office at Rotary Circle (Taluk Office Circle), east of the bus station (dep 9.30am, ret 5.30pm; Rs50 including lunch; ☎08394/8537). Frequent **buses to Vijayanagar** run from the bus stand; or, if you arrive late, you could take a taxi or one of the rickshaws that gather outside the train station. The journey takes about thirty minutes. Hotels in Hospet can organize for you to hook up with **trained guides** in Vijayanagar.

Vijayanagar / Hampi

> *The city of Bidjanagar [Vijayanagar] is such that the pupil of the eye has never seen a place like it, and the ear of intelligence has never been informed that there existed anything to equal it in the world. . . . The bazaars are extremely long and broad. . . . Roses are sold everywhere. These people could not live without roses, and they look upon them as quite as necessary as food. . . . Each class of men belonging to each profession has shops contiguous the one to the other; the jewellers sell publicly in the bazaars pearls, rubies, emeralds and diamonds. In this agreeable locality, as well as in the king's palace, one sees numerous running streams and canals formed of chiselled stone, polished and smooth. . . . This empire contains so great a population that it would be impossible to give an idea of it without entering into extensive details.*
>
> Abdu'r-Razzaq, the Persian ambassador, who visited Vijayanagar in 1443.

The magnificent ghost city of **VIJAYANAGAR**, "the City of Victory" (also known as **HAMPI**, the name of a local village), stands on a surreal boulder-strewn plain surrounded by rugged, craggy hills. According to Hindu mythology, Vijayanagar began its days as Kishkinda, the monkey kingdom of the *Ramayana*, ruled by the monkey kings Vali and Sugriva and their ambassador, Hanuman; the weird rocks balanced in perilous arches are said to have been flung down by their armies in a show of strength.

Between the fourteenth and sixteenth centuries, Vijayanagar was the most powerful Hindu capital in the Deccan. Travellers such as the Portuguese writer Domingo Paez, who stayed for two years after 1520, were astonished by the size and wealth of the city, telling tales of its markets spilling over with silk and precious gems, its beautiful, be-

VIJAYANAGAR/ HAMPI

Anegondi

Coracle Jetty

Ruined Bridge

Vitthala Temple

King's Balance

Agni Temple & Kotalinga Complex

Coracle Jetty

Narasimha Temple

Virupaksha Temple

Bus Stand

Rama Temple

HAMPI

Hemakuta Hill

Matanga Hill

Tiruvengalanatha Temple

Narasimha Monolith

Krishna Temple

Guards Quarters

Palace

Gateway

Elephant Stables

Lotus Mahal

Hazara Rama Temple

Madhava Temple

Yellamma Temple

Virupaksha 'Underground' Temple

Mahanavami-Dibba

Palace

Hall of Justice

Chandrashekhara Temple

Queen's Bath

Ganagitti Jain Temple

Bhima's Gate

N

HOTELS:
A Shanti
B Rahul Guest House
C KSTDC Tourist Complex
RESTAURANTS:
1 Shankar's & Rasta Retreat
2 Lotus Mahal

Nageshwara Temple

Kamalapuram Bus Stand

Not to scale

Kamalapuram

Hospet

jewelled courtesans, ornate palaces and joyous festivities. However, in the second half of the sixteenth century, this dazzling city was devastated by a six-month Muslim attack. Only stone, brick and stucco structures survive – monolithic deities, crumbling houses and abandoned temples dominated by towering *gopuras* – as well as the sophisticated irrigation system that channelled water to huge tanks and temples.

Regarded as one of India's holiest cities, Vijayanagar has inexplicably escaped the attention of mainstream tourism. Along with streams of Hindu pilgrims, and tatty-haired *sadhus* who live in the more isolated temple complexes, most visitors are budget travellers straight from Goa. Many find it difficult to leave, and spend weeks chilling out in cafes, swimming in the river and gazing at the spectacular sunsets.

A little history

This was an area of minor political importance under the Chalukyas; the rise of the **Vijayanagar empire** seems to have been a direct response, in the first half of the fourteenth century, to the expansionist aims of Muslims from the north, most notably Malik Kafur and Muhammad-bin-Tughluq. Two Hindu brothers from Andhra Pradesh, Harihara and Bukka, who had been employed as treasury officers in Kampila, 19km east of Hampi, were captured by the Tughluqs and taken to Delhi, where they supposedly converted to Islam. Assuming them to be suitably tamed, the Delhi Sultan despatched them to quell civil disorder in Kampila, which they duly did, only to abandon both Islam and allegiance to Delhi shortly afterwards, preferring to establish their own independent Hindu kingdom. Within a few years they controlled vast tracts of land from coast to coast. In 1343 their new capital, Vijayanagar, was founded on the southern banks of the River Tungabhadra, a location long considered sacred by Hindus. The city's most glorious period was under the reign of **Krishna Deva Raya** (1509–29).

Thanks to its natural features and massive fortifications, Vijayanagar was virtually impregnable. In 1565, however, following his interference in the affairs of local Muslim Sultanates, the regent Rama Raya was drawn into a battle with a confederacy of Muslim forces, 100km away to the north, which left the city undefended. At first fortune appeared to be on the side of the Hindu forces, but there were as many as ten thousand Muslims in their number, and loyalties may well have been divided. When two Vijayanagar Muslim generals suddenly deserted, the army fell into disarray. Defeat came swiftly; although members of his family fled with untold hoards of gold and jewels, Rama Raya was captured and suffered a grisly death at the hands of the Sultan of Ahmadnagar. Vijayanagar then fell victim to a series of destructive raids, and its days of splendour were brought to an abrupt end.

Arrival and orientation

Vijayanagar covers 26 square kilometres on the southern bank of the River Tungabhadra. Due to the size of the site, which is best explored on foot, you should ideally leave at least two full days to see everything. Most of the monuments are spread out between the villages of **KAMALAPURAM**, to the south, and **HAMPI**, to the northwest, and east from Hampi along the banks of the Tungabhadra. North of the river, the ancient village of **ANEGONDI** also holds some sites of interest.

From Hospet (see p.1064), there are two frequent bus services on different routes. Both terminate halfway along the main street in Hampi Bazaar, a little east of the Virupaksha temple. The one via Kaddirampuram is convenient if you're rushed and have to limit what you see. The second route, via Kamalapuram, at the southern edge of the city remains, enables you to visit the museum first and then set out to explore the city from the south on foot. It's a good idea to carry a water supply. Whichever way you tackle this huge site, to **return to Hospet** you can rely on getting buses from Hampi and Kamalapuram until around 7pm.

Information

The **tourist information counter** in Hampi Bazaar might be able to put you in touch with a guide, but not much else; if you're coming from Hospet, you'd do best to organize a guide from there (see p.1066). Rented **bikes**, available in the bazaar, are only really of use if you're planning to explore Anegondi across the river; most paths around Vijayanagar are too rough to cycle. You may be able to **change money** at the *Canara Bank*, near the Virupaksha temple, in Hampi, where there's also a little post office.

The Site

The **"royal" centre** of Vijayanagar, just north of Kamalapuram, includes the remains of palaces, pavilions, elephant stables, guard houses and temples. All the surviving secular buildings show evidence of Indo-Islamic motifs; cut plaster decoration and arches are in the Deccani Islamic style.

Vijayanagar's **most sacred area**, holding the Vitthala and Virupaksha temples, along with a riverside *ghat*, or bathing place, lies north of the royal centre. The area around the **Virupaksha temple** is the original sacred site; both temple and *ghat* are still in use. Some of the attached buildings are very much earlier than the Vijayanagar period. Leading to the temples, the Car Streets were once busy bazaars where temple gods were ceremoniously paraded on huge chariots or "cars"; devotees flung themselves under the wheels, a gruesome death that ended the cycle of rebirths.

Most of the remaining structures were built between the mid-fifteenth and sixteenth centuries; the **oldest parts** of the whole site consist of the core of the Virupaksha temple structure (now hidden from view), certain buildings on the river to the north, a tank between the temple and the river, and the nearby temples on **Hemakuta Hill** to the south. Near many of the temples, scattered in the shade of the trees, you'll see small, engraved rocks that tell poignant tales: those carved with snakes are "fertility stones" left by childless wives; the image of a seated man surrounded by women features on **sati stones**, dedicated to widows who have leapt to their deaths on their husbands' funeral pyres.

Archeological Museum, southern and royal monuments

Approaching from the south, the best place to start is at the **Archeological Museum** (daily except Fri 10am–5pm) at Kamalapuram. Turn right out of the bus stand, take the first turning on the right, and the museum is on the left – two minutes' walk. Among the sculpture, weapons, palm-leaf manuscripts and painting from Vijayanagar and Anegondi, the highlight is a superb scale-model of the city, giving an excellent bird's-eye view of the entire site.

To walk into the city from the museum, go back to the main road and take the nearby turning marked "Hampi 4km". After 200m or so you reach the partly ruined massive **inner city wall**, made from granite slabs, which runs 32km around the city, in places as high as 10m. The outer wall was almost twice as long. At one time, there were said to have been seven city walls; coupled with areas of impenetrable forest and the river to the north, they made the city virtually impregnable.

Just beyond the wall, the **citadel area** was once enclosed by another wall and gates of which only traces remain. To the east, a cluster of monuments include the **Chandrashekhara** and **Saraswati** (sixteenth century) **temples**. Further east, the small *Ganigitti* ("oil-woman's") fourteenth-century **Jain temple** features a simple stepped pyramidal tower of undecorated horizontal slabs. Beyond it is **Bhima's Gate**, once one of the principal entrances to the city, named after the Titan-like Pandava prince and hero of the *Mahabharata*. Like many of the gates, it is "bent", a form of defence that meant anyone trying to get in had to make two ninety-degree turns. Bas-reliefs depict such episodes as Bhima avenging the attempted rape of his wife, Draupadi, by killing the general Kichaka. Draupadi vowed she would not dress her hair until Kichaka was dead; one panel shows her tying up her hair, the vow fulfilled.

Back on the path, to the west, the plain façade of the fifteen-metre-square **Queen's Bath** belies its glorious interior, open to the sky and surrounded by corridors with 24 different domes. Eight projecting balconies overlook where once was water; traces of Islamic-influenced stucco decoration survive. Women from the royal household would bathe here and umbrellas were placed in shafts in the tank floor to protect them from the sun. The water supply channel can be seen outside.

Continuing northwest brings you to **Mahanavami-Dibba** or "House of Victory", built to commemorate a successful campaign in Orissa. A twelve-metre pyramidal structure with a square base, it is said to have been where the king gave and received honours and gifts. From here he watched the magnificent parades, music and dance performances, martial art displays, elephant fights and animal sacrifices that made celebration of the ten-day Dussehra festival famed throughout the land (the tradition of spectacular Dussehra festivals is continued at Mysore; see p.1048). Carved reliefs of dancers, elephant fights, animals and figures decorate the sides of the platform. Two huge monolithic doors on the ground nearby may have once been part of a building atop the platform, of which no signs remain. To the west, another platform – the largest at Vijayanagar – is thought to be the basement of the **King's Audience Hall**. Stone bases of a hundred pillars remain, in an arrangement that has caused speculation as to how the building could have been used; there are no passageways or open areas.

The two-storey **Lotus Mahal**, a little further north and part of the *zenana* enclosure, or women's quarters, was designed for the pleasure of Krishna Deva Raya's queen: a place where she could relax, particularly in summer. Displaying a strong Indo-Islamic influence, the pavilion is open on the ground floor, whereas the upper level (no longer accessible by stairs) contains windows and balcony seats. A moat surrounding the building is thought to have provided water-cooled air via tubes.

Beyond the Lotus Mahal, the **Elephant Stables**, a series of high-ceilinged, domed chambers, entered through arches, are the most substantial surviving secular buildings at Vijayanagar – a reflection of the high status accorded to elephants, both ceremonial and in battle. An upper level, with a pillared hall, capped with a tower at the centre, may have been used by the musicians who accompanied the royal elephant processions. Tender coconuts are usually for sale under the shade of a nearby tree.

East of here, recent archeological excavations have revealed what are thought to have been the foundations of a series of Vijayanagar administration offices, which until 1990 had remained buried under earth deposited by the wind.

Walking west of the Lotus Mahal, you pass two temples before reaching the road to Hemakuta Hill. The rectangular enclosure wall of the small **Hazara Rama** ("One thousand Ramas") temple, thought to have been the private palace temple, features a series of medallion figures and bands of detailed friezes showing scenes from the *Ramayana*. The inner of two *mandapas* contains four finely carved, polished, black columns. Many of the ruins here are said to have been part of the Hazara Rama Bazaar, which ran northeast from the temple. Much of the so-called **Underground Temple**, or Prasanna Virupaksha, lies below ground level and spends part of the year filled with rainwater.

Turning north (right) onto the road that runs to the west of the Underground Temple leads after about 1km to the area of Hemakuta Hill.

Hemakuta Hill and environs

Approaching from the south, you pass two temples facing each other: on the right the **Virabhadra** (1545) is a functioning *lingayat* shrine, while the **Chandikeshvara** is partly ruined. A little further on, in its own enclosure, is one of the treasures of

Vijayanagar: the monolithic, four-armed, seated **Narasimha** (Vishnu as man-lion), an extraordinarily powerful figure standing seven metres high.

The walled **Krishna temple complex**, dating from 1513, although dilapidated in parts, features fine carving and numerous shrines. A fifty-metre-wide processional path leads east from it through what's now a ploughed field, with a straggle of stray remnants of colonnades to each side; once it was the market place of Krishnapura.

Overlooking Hampi Bazaar, on **Hemakuta Hill**, a group of pre-Vijayanagar temples probably date from between the ninth and eleventh centuries (late Chalukya or Ganga). Three are of the *trikutachala*, "three-peaked hills" type, with three shrines facing into a common centre. One small wagon-vaulted shrine, reminiscent of Pallava architecture at Mamallapuram, could date from the late eighth or early ninth century. A natural cave on the hill leads to an ashram. On the slope of the hill, two large mono-lithic sculptures of elephant-headed Ganesh both stand in open *mandapa* hallways. The smaller of the two, 2.5m high, is fancifully called Sasivekalu, or "mustard seed"; the other, almost twice the size, is known as Kadalekalu, "chick pea".

Hampi Bazaar, the Virupaksha temple and the riverside path

Along Hampi's long, straight main street, **Hampi Bazaar**, which runs east from the eastern entrance of the Virupaksha temple, you can still make out the remains of Vijayanagar's ruined, columned bazaar, partly inhabited by today's lively market. Landless labourers live in many of the crumbling 500-year-old buildings.

The functioning **Virupaksha temple** (daily 8am–12.30pm & 3–6.30pm) is dedicated to a local form of Shiva known as Virupaksha or Pampapati. The complex consists of two courts, each entered through a towered *gopura*. The larger gateway, on the east, is approximately 56m high, each storey with pilastered walls and sculptures flanking an open window. It is topped by a single wagon-vault and *kalasha*, pot-shaped finial. In the southwest corner is a large columned *mandapa*; a water channel runs along one side.

A colonnade surrounds the inner court, usually filled with pilgrims dozing and sing-ing religious songs; in the middle the principal temple is approached through a *mandapa* hallway whose carved columns feature rearing animals. Rare Vijayanagar-era paintings on the *mandapa* ceiling include aspects of Shiva, a procession with the sage Vidyaranya, the ten incarnations of Vishnu, and scenes from the *Mahabharata*; the style of the figures is reminiscent of local shadow puppets. Faced by a brass image of Nandi, a *shivalingam* is housed in the small sanctuary, its entrance decorated with painted *makaras*, semi-aquatic mythical animals whose bodies end with foliage instead of a tail. Blue water spouts from their mouths, while above them flicker yellow flames. Just outside the main temple's wall, immediately to the north, is a small earlier temple, thought to have been the "ancestor" of the Virupaksha.

The sacred **ford** in the river is reached from the Virupaksha's north *gopura*. A *mandapa* overlooks the steps that originally led to the river, now some distance away. **Coracles** ply from this part of the bank, just as they did five centuries ago.

To reach the Vitthala temple, walk east from the Virupaksha, the length of Hampi Bazaar. At the end, a path on the left roughly follows the river past numerous shrines, including a Rama temple, home to hordes of fearless monkeys. Beyond at least four Vishnu shrines and the Achutya Bazaar, you can leave the path and see the little-visited waterside **Agni temple** – next to it, the Kotalinga complex consists of 108 (an auspi-cious number) tiny *lingams*, carved on a flat rock. As you approach the Vitthala temple, to the south is an archway known as the **King's Balance**, where the rajas were weighed against gold, silver and jewels to be distributed to the city's priests.

Vitthala temple

Although the area of the **Vitthala temple** does not show the same evidence of early cult worship as Virupaksha, the ruined bridge to the west probably dates from before

Vijayanagar times. The bathing *ghat* may be from the Chalukya or Ganga period, but as the temple has fallen into disuse it seems that the river crossing (*tirtha*) here has not had the same sacred significance as the Virupaksha site.

Now designated a World Heritage Monument by UNESCO, the Vitthala temple was built for Vishnu, who according to legend was too embarrassed by its ostentation to live there. The tower of the principal Vishnu shrine is made of brick – unusual for south India – capped with a hemispherical roof; in front is an enclosed *mandapa* with carved columns, the ceiling of which has partly collapsed. Two doorways lead to a dark passageway surrounding the sanctuary.

The open *mandapa* features slender monolithic granite **pillars**. As in so many Indian temples, guides gleefully make them "sing" by tapping them. Outer columns have characteristic Vijayanagar rearing horses. Although the building is otherwise entirely in the south Indian Dravidian style, its star-shaped plan is similar to northern *nagari*-style temples. The deeply overhanging "S"-shaped eave features incised lotus designs on the corners. Above the eave, also characteristic of Vijayanagar, are parapet niches with small turrets; the ceilings are monolithic slabs carved to look like structured domes, resembling examples in Gujarat, Rajasthan and at the Hoysala temple at Somnathpur, near Mysore (see p.1053). Friezes of lions, elephants and horses on the moulded basement display sculptural trickery – you can transform one beast into another simply by masking one portion of the image.

In front of the temple, to the east, a stone representation of a wooden processional *ratha*, or chariot, houses an image of Garuda, Vishnu's bird vehicle. Now cemented, at one time the chariot's wheels revolved. The three *gopura* entrances, made of granite at the base with brick and stucco multi-storey towers, are now badly damaged.

Anegondi

With more time, and a sense of adventure, you can venture across the Tungabhadra to **ANEGONDI**, a fortress town predating Vijayanagar and the city's fourteenth-century headquarters. The most pleasant way to go is to take a **putti**, a circular rush-basket coracle, from the bathing *ghat* behind the Virupaksha temple. If you rent a bike in Hampi Bazaar, you can take it on the coracle with you; you won't be the only one with such awkward luggage. From the other side, it's a pleasant five-kilometre ride east to Anegondi. Travelling **on foot**, you should cross much further east, from Talavaghat, near the Vitthala temple. This brings you direct to an ancient gateway, close to Anegondi village.

Forgotten temples and fortifications litter Anegondi village and the quiet surroundings. The ruined **Huchchappa-matha temple**, near the river gateway, is worth a look for its black stone lathe-turned pillars and fine panels of dancers. **Aramani**, a ruined palace in the centre, stands opposite the home of the descendants of the royal family; also in the centre, the **Ranganatha temple** is still active. A huge wooden temple chariot stands in the village square. West of Anegondi, off the road, which you pass if you're coming from the Virupaksha crossing, you can clamber up the rocks to Durga fort, temple and royal cremation grounds, from where there are fine views.

Accommodation and eating

Although many visitors to Vijayanagar use Hospet as a base (see p.1064), an increasing number of travellers choose to stay on the site itself, a considerably more atmospheric option. Hampi Bazaar offers a couple of very basic lodges: the *Rahul Guest House* (①), close to the bus stand, and *Shanti* (①), near the Virupaksha temple tank, and some locals rent out lock-up rooms, with minimal facilities. A few such rooms are available across the river, a coracle-ride from the Virupaksha *ghat*; ask at *Shankar's* shack restaurant on the nearest road, which also serves good simple food, or at the hippie hang out on the bank which, cringingly, calls itself the *Rasta Retreat*. At **Kamalapuram**, the

KSTDC *Tourist Complex* (③–④), near the bus stand, has some a/c rooms. Wherever you stay, watch out for mosquitoes, as Hampi is in the malaria zone.

The only **food** you'll get at the makeshift *chai* and coconut stalls dotted around the ruins is biscuits and the odd banana. Hampi Bazaar boasts a number of average "meals" restaurants, some of which offer westernized "travellers" dishes. *Trishul* (aka *Ram Singh's*), on the only side street, serves muesli for breakfast and enormous *thalis*. Amid the antiquities, the KSTDC *Lotus Mahal Restaurant* (daily 9am–4pm), near the Lotus Mahal, serves light meals.

Monuments of the Chalukyas

Now quiet villages, **BADAMI**, **AIHOLE** and **PATTADAKAL**, in northwest Karnataka, were once the capital cities of the **Chalukyas**, who ruled much of the Deccan between the fourth and eighth centuries. The astonishing profusion of **temples** in the area beggars belief, and it is hard to imagine the kind of society that can have made use of them all. Most visitors use Badami, which can offer a few basic lodges, as a base; Aihole boasts a single rest house, and no rooms are available at Pattadakal.

Badami and Aihole's cave temples, stylistically related to those at Ellora (see p.638), are some of the most important of their type. Among the many structural temples are some of the earliest in India, and uniquely, it is possible to see both northern (*nagari*) and southern (Dravida) architectural styles side by side. Clearly much experimentation went on, as several other temples (commonly referred to, in art historical terms, as "undifferentiated") fit into neither system. None is now thought to date from before the late sixth century, but at one time scholars got very excited when they believed the famous Lad Khan temple at Aihole, for example, to be even older.

Although some evidence of **Buddhist** activity around Badami and Aihole exists, the earliest cave and structural temples are assigned to the period of the Chalukya rise to power in the mid-sixth century, and are mostly **Hindu**, with a few Jain examples. The first important Chalukyan king was Pulakeshin I (535–66), but it was Pulakeshin II (610–42) who captured the Pallava capital of Kanchipuram in Tamil Nadu and extended the empire to include Maharashtra to the north, the Konkan coast on the west and the whole of Karnataka. Although the Pallavas subsequently, and briefly, took most of his territory, including Badami, the capital at the end of his reign, Pulakeshin's son, Vikramaditya I (655–81) later recovered it, and the Chalukyas continued to reign until the mid-eighth century. Some suggest that the incursion of the Pallavas accounts for the southern elements seen in the structural temples.

Badami

The village of **BADAMI**, capital of the Chalukyas from 543 AD to 757 AD, extends east into a gorge between two hills, on which stand two ancient fort areas. The south holds cave temples, and on the north are early structural temples. Beyond the village on the east is an artificial lake, Agastya, said to date from the fifth century. Badami is the most convenient base for visiting Aihole and Pattadakal and chronologically, too, it makes sense to see Badami first.

Arrival

Badami **bus stand** – in the centre of the village on Main (Station) Rd, very near two of the four possible places to stay – sees daily services to Gadag, Hospet, Hubli and Bijapur, and frequent buses to Aihole and Pattadakal. The **railway station** is 5km north; buses, tongas and auto-rickshaws are usually available for the journey into town. Services usually include slow passenger trains to and from places further south such as

Gadag, Hospet and Hubli, and Bijapur and Sholapur to the north – but check first because of conversion work on the lines.

Southern Fort cave temples

Badami's earliest monuments, in the Southern Fort area, are a group of sixth-century **caves** cut into the hill's red sandstone, each connected by steps leading up the hillside. About 15m up the face of the rock, **Cave 1**, a Shiva temple, is probably the earliest. Entrance is through a triple opening into a long porch raised on a plinth decorated with images of Shiva's dwarf attendants, the Ganas. Outside, to the left of the porch, a *dvarpala* door guardian stands beneath a Nandi bull. On the right is a striking 1.5m-high image of a sixteen-armed dancing Shiva. He carries a stick-zither-type *vina*, which may or may not be a *yal*, a now-extinct musical instrument, on which the earliest Indian classical music theory is thought to have been developed. In the ante-chamber, a panel on the left shows Harihara (Shiva and Vishnu combined), accompanied by consorts Lakshmi and Parvati and the gods' vehicles Nandi and Garuda. On the right Ardhanarishvara (Shiva combined with Parvati; half male, half female) is accompanied by Nandi and the skeleton Bringi. Ceiling panels include a coiled Naga snake deity, flying couples, and Shiva and Parvati. Inside, a columned hall, divided into aisles, leads to a small, square sanctuary at the back, containing a *lingam*.

A little higher, the similar **Cave 2**, a Vishnu shrine, is approached across a courtyard with two *dvarpala* door guardians at the end. The porch contains a panel to the left of Varaha, the boar incarnation of Vishnu, and, to the right, Trivikrama, Vishnu as a dwarf *brahmin* who inflates in size to cross the earth in three steps. On the ceiling nearby, Vishnu is shown riding his bird Garuda. A central square of the ceiling features a lotus encircled by sixteen fish; other decoration includes *svastika* designs and flying couples. A few traces of painting show how colourful the caves must have been.

Steps and slopes lead on upwards, past a natural cave containing a smashed Buddha image, and steps on the right in a cleft in the rock lead up to the fort. **Cave 3** (578 AD) stands beneath a thirty-metre-high perpendicular bluff. The largest of the group, with a façade measuring 21m from north to south, it is also considered the finest, for the quality of its sculptural decoration. Eleven steps lead up to the plinth decorated with dwarf *ganas*. Treatment of the pillars is extremely elaborate, featuring male and female bracket figures, lotus motifs and medallions portraying amorous couples.

To the east of the others, a Jain temple, **Cave 4**, overlooks Agastya Lake and the town. It's a much simpler shrine, dating from the sixth century. Figures, both seated and standing, of the 24 *tirthankaras*, mostly without their identifying emblems, line the walls. Here, the rock is striped.

After seeing the caves you can climb up to the fort and walk east where, hidden in the rocks, is a carved panel of Vishnu reclining on the serpent Adisesha, attended by a profusion of gods and sages. Continuing from here you can skirt the gorge and descend on the east to the Bhutanatha temples at the lakeside. Before you get to them, there's another rock carving of a reclining Vishnu and his ten incarnations.

North Fort

North of Agastya Lake a number of structural temples can be reached by steps. The small **Archeological Museum** (daily except Fri 10am–5pm) nearby contains sculpture from the region. Although now dilapidated, the **Upper Shivalaya temple** is one of the earliest Chalukyan buildings. Scenes from the life of Krishna decorate the base and various images of him can be seen between pilasters on the walls. Only the sanctuary and tower of the **Lower Shivalaya** survive. Perched on a rock, the **Malegitti Shivalaya** (late seventh century) is the finest southern-style early Chalukyan temple. Its shrine is adjoined by a pillared hallway with small pierced stone and a single decor image on each side: Vishnu on the north and Shiva on the south.

Accommodation and eating

Tourism seems to have made no impact in Badami, and there's very little **accommodation**. Unless you can get into the spartan but clean *PWD Inspection Bungalow*, it's probably best to opt for one of the two basic **lodges** north of the bus stand (turn left as you come out). The KSTDC *Mayura Chalukya* is not recommended. For **food**, your best bet is *Shri Laxmi Vilas* and *Sanman*, a friendly non-veg restaurant near the bus stand, which also serves beer. *Geeta* on Ramdurg Rd does good Indian breakfasts.

PWD Inspection Bungalow, PWD Complex, Ramdurg Rd. Four simple, clean doubles. You're meant to apply to Assistant Engineer, Badami, to get a room, but it's worth asking the caretaker. ①.

Satkar, Station Rd (☎3217). Same management as the *Sanman* restaurant. Very basic, but not bad, with clean sheets and hot water in the morning. All rooms with attached bathroom. ①–③.

Shri Laxmi Vilas (☎3277 or 3329). Seven small doubles with bathroom, plus some singles with shared bathroom. Grotty but acceptable. Friendly staff and good restaurant. ①.

Aihole

No fewer than 125 temples, dating from the Chalukyan and the later Rashtrakuta periods (sixth–twelfth centuries), are found in the tiny village of **AIHOLE** (**Aivalli**), close to the banks of the River Malaprabha. Lying in clusters within the village, in surrounding fields and on rocky outcrops, many of the temples are in a remarkable state of preservation, despite being used as dwellings and cattle sheds. Reflecting both its geographical position and the spirit of architectural experimentation, Aihole holds both northern (*nagari*) and southern (Dravida) temples, as well as unusual variants that failed to survive in subsequent stylistic developments.

Two of the temples are **rock-cut caves**, both dating from the sixth century. The Hindu **Ravanaphadigudi**, northeast of the centre, a Shiva shrine with a triple entrance, contains fine sculptures of Mahishasuramardini (see p.919), a ten-armed Nateshan (the precursor of Shiva Nataraja) dancing with Parvati, Ganesh and the Sapta Matrikas ("seven mothers"). A central lotus design surrounded by mythical beasts, figures and foliate decoration adorn the ceiling. Near the entrance is Gangadhara (Shiva with the River Ganga in his hair) accompanied by Parvati and the skeleton Bringi. A two-storey cave, plain save for decoration at the entrances and a panel image of Buddha in its upper verandah, can be found partway up the hill to the southeast, overlooking the village. At the top of that hill, the Jain **Meguti** temple, which may never have been completed, bears an inscription on an outer wall dating it to 634 AD. The porch, *mandapa* hallway and upper storey above the sanctuary, which contains a seated Jain image, are later additions. You can climb up to the first floor for fine views of Aihole and surrounding country.

The **Durga temple** (*c.* late seventh–early eighth centuries), one of the most unusual, elaborate and large in Aihole, stands close to others on open ground, near the centre of the village. It derives its name not from the goddess Durga but from the Kannada *durgadagudi*, meaning "temple near the fort". Its apsidal-ended sanctuary shows influence from earlier Buddhist *chaitya* halls; another example of this curved feature, rare in Hindu monuments, can be seen in one of the *rathas* at Mamallapuram in Tamil Nadu. Here the "northern"-style tower is probably a later addition, and is incongruously square-backed. The temple is raised on a plinth featuring bands of carved decoration. A series of pillars – many featuring amorous couples – forming an open ambulatory continue from the porch around the whole building. Other sculptural highlights include the decoration on the entrance to the *mandapa* hallway and niche images on the outer walls of the now-empty semi-circular sanctum. Remains of a small and early *gopura* gateway stand to the south. Nearby, a small **Archeological Museum** (daily except Fri 10am–5pm) displays early Chalukyan sculpture and sells the booklet *Glorious Aihole*, which includes a site map and accounts of the monuments.

Further south, beyond several other temples, the **Ladh Khan** (the name of a Muslim who made it his home) is perhaps the best known of all at Aihole. Now thought to have been constructed at some point between the end of the sixth century and the eighth, it was dated at one time to the mid-fifth century, and was seen as one of the country's temple prototypes. The basic plan is square, with a large adjoining rectangular pillared porch. Inside, twelve pillars support a raised clerestory and enclose a further four pillars; at the centre stands a Nandi bull. A small sanctuary containing a *shivalingam* is next to the back wall. Both *lingam* and Nandi may have been later additions, with the original inner sanctum located at the centre.

Practicalities

Regular **buses** run to Aihole from Badami (2hr) via Pattadakal (30min). The only place to **stay and eat** (apart from a few *chai*-shops) in Aihole is the small, clean and spartan KSTDC *Tourist Rest House* (☎Aminagad 41; ①) about five minutes' walk up the main road north out of the village, next to the ASI offices. They've got a "VIP" room, two doubles with bathroom plus two doubles and four singles without. Simple, tasty food is available by arrangement – and by candlelight during frequent power cuts. The *Kiran Bar* on the same road, but in the village, serves beer and spirits.

Pattadakal

The village of **PATTADAKAL**, next to the River Malaprabha, served as the site of Chalukyan coronations between the seventh and eighth centuries; in fact it may only have been used for such ceremonials. Like Badami and Aihole, Pattadakal boasts fine Chalukyan architecture, with particularly large mature examples; and as at Aihole, both northern and southern styles can be seen. The main group of monuments stand together in a well-maintained compound, close to the village.

Earliest among the temples, the **Sangameshvara**, also known as **Shri Vijayeshvara** (a reference to its builder, Vijayaditya Satyashraya; 696–733), shows typical southern features, such as the parapet lined with barrel-vaulted miniature roof forms and walls divided into niches flanked by pilasters. To the south, both the **Mallikarjuna** and the enormous **Virupaksha**, side by side, are in the southern style, built by two sisters who were successively the queens of Vikramaditya II (733-46). The temples were inspired by the Pallava Kailashanatha temple at Kanchipuram in Tamil Nadu, complete with enclosure wall with shrines and small *gopura* entranceway. Along with the Kanchi temple, the Virupaksha was probably one of the largest and most elaborate in India at the time. Interior pillars are carved with scenes from the *Ramayana* and *Mahabharata*, while in the Mallikarjuna the stories are from the life of Krishna. Both temples have open Nandi *mandapa* hallways and sanctuaries housing black polished stone *lingams*.

The largest northern-style temple, the **Papanatha**, further south, was probably built after the Virupaksha in the eighth century. It features two long pillared *mandapa* hallways adjoining a small sanctuary with a narrow internal ambulatory. Outside walls feature reliefs (some of which, unusually, bear the sculptors' autographs) from the *Ramayana*, including, on the south wall, Hanuman's monkey army.

About 1km south of the village, a fine **Rashtrakuta** (ninth–tenth century) **Jain temple** is fronted by a porch and two *mandapa* hallways with twin carved elephants at the entrance. Inexplicably, the sanctuary contains a *lingam*. In the first *mandapa*, on the right, a stone staircase leads up to the roof, where there's a second, empty sanctuary. The porch is lined with bench seats interspersed with eight pillars; the doorway is elaborately decorated with mythical beasts.

Aside from a few village tea shops, "cool drinks" and tender coconut stalls, there are no **facilities**. Pattadakal is connected by regular bus services to Badami (1hr 30min) and Aihole (30min), both of which have simple places to stay.

CHAPTER TWENTY ONE

ANDHRA PRADESH

A lthough Andhra Pradesh occupies a great swathe of eastern India, stretching for over 1200km along the coast from Orissa to Tamil Nadu and reaching far inland from the fertile deltas of the Godavari and Krishna rivers to the semi-arid Deccan Plateau, it's not a place that receives many tourists. Most foreign travellers simply pass through en route to its more attractive neighbours, and it's not hard to see why; exploring Andhra Pradesh takes a lot of time and effort that you may well end up feeling would have been better spent elsewhere. Its infrastructure is rudimentary – in particular, if you don't have your own vehicle you're at the mercy of an extremely poor public transport system.

The state capital, **Hyderabad**, is a run-down but undoubtedly atmospheric city dating from the late sixteenth century. Its endless bazaars, eclectic Salar Jung museum and, nearby, the mighty **Golconda Fort** make it an absorbing place to spend a day or two. By contrast, its modern twin, commercial **Secunderabad**, excels only in characterlessness. **Warangal**, 150km northeast of Hyderabad, has both Muslim and Hindu remains from the twelfth and thirteenth centuries, while the region's Buddhist legacy – particularly its superb sculpture – is now preserved in museums at sites such as **Nagarjunakonda** (south of Hyderabad) and **Amaravati**, the ancient Satavahana capital. In the east, the big cities of **Vishakapatnam** and **Vijayawada** have little to recommend them, though the latter makes a convenient access point for Amaravati. However, the temple town of **Tirupati** in the far southeast – best reached from Madras in Tamil Nadu – is one of India's great Hindu phenomena, a fascinating and impossibly crowded pilgrimage site, said to be more popular even than Mecca.

Although modern industries have grown up around the capital and shipbuilding, iron and steel are important on the coast, most people in Andhra Pradesh remain poor. Away from the Godavari and Krishna deltas, where the soil is rich enough to grow rice and sugar cane, the land is in places impossible to cultivate.

Some history

Earliest accounts of the region, dating back to the time of **Ashoka** (third century BC), refer to a people known as the Andhras. The **Satavahana dynasty** (*c.* second century BC–second century AD), also known as the Andras, came to control much of central and southern India from their second capital at Amaravati on the Krishna. They enjoyed extensive international trade with both eastern Asia and Europe, and were great patrons of Buddhism. Subsequently, the Pallavas from Tamil Nadu, the Chalukyas from Karnataka, and the Cholas all held sway. By the thirteenth century, the Kakatiyas of Warangal were under constant threat from Muslim incursions, while later on, after the fall of their city at Hampi, the Hindu Vijayanagars transferred operations to Chandragiri near Tirupati.

The next significant development was in the mid-sixteenth century, with the rise of the Muslim **Qutb Shahi dynasty**. In 1687, the son of the Moghul emperor Aurangzeb seized Golconda. Five years after Aurangzeb died in 1707, the Viceroy of Hyderabad declared independence and established the Asaf Jahi dynasty of Nizams. In return for allying with the British against Tipu Sultan of Mysore, the Nizam was allowed to retain a certain degree of autonomy even after the British had come to dominate all India.

During the struggle for Independence, harmony between Hindus and Muslims in Andhra Pradesh disintegrated. **Partition** brought matters to a climax, as the Nizam desired to join other Muslims in the soon-to-be created state of **Pakistan**. In 1949 the capital erupted in riots, the army was brought in and Hyderabad state was admitted to the Indian Union. Andhra Pradesh state was created in 1956 from Telegu-speaking regions (although Urdu is widely spoken in Hyderabad) that had previously formed part of the Madras Presidency on the east coast and the princely state of Hyderabad to the west. Today almost ninety percent of the population is Hindu, with Muslims largely concentrated in the capital.

Hyderabad/Secunderabad

A melting-pot of Muslim and Hindu cultures, the capital of Andhra Pradesh comprises the twin cities of **HYDERABAD** and **SECUNDERABAD**. The latter, of little interest to visitors, is the modern administrative city founded by the British, whereas the old city, with its seething **bazaars**, **Muslim monuments** and **Salar Jung Museum** has heaps of charm. Despite this, Hyderabad has been in decline since Independence. While 45 percent of the population inhabit the old city, a mere 25 percent of the city's budget is spent on it, exacerbating a tension that is never far from the surface.

As Hyderabad/Secunderabad is very much the transportation hub for Andhra Pradesh, this chapter has no "Travel Details"; see p.1085 for "Moving On from Hyderabad".

Hyderabad was founded in 1591 by **Muhammad Quli Shah** (1562–1612), beside the River Musi, 8km east of Golconda, the fortress capital of the Golconda empire which by now was suffering from overcrowding and a serious lack of water. Unusually, this new city was laid out on a grid system, with huge arches and stone buildings that included Hyderabad's most famous monument, **Charminar**. At first it was a city without walls; these were only added as late as 1740, as defence against the Marathas. Legend has it that a secret tunnel linked the spectacular **Golconda Fort** with the city, with dome-shaped structures at suitable intervals to provide the unfortunate messengers who had to use it with the opportunity to come up for fresh air.

For the three hundred years of Muslim reign, there was harmony between the predominantly Hindu population and the minority Muslims. Hyderabad was the most important focus of Muslim power in south India at this time; the princes' fabulous wealth derived primarily from the fine gemstones, particularly diamonds, mined in the Kistna Valley at Golconda. In the seventeenth century, Golconda was the diamond centre of the world. The famous **Koh-i-Noor** diamond was found here – the only time it was ever captured was by Moghul emperor Aurangzeb, when his son seized the Golconda Fort in 1687. It ended up, cut, in the British royal crown.

Arrival and information

The old city of **Hyderabad** straddles the River Musi. Most places of interest lie south of the river, while much of the accommodation and the **state bus stand** are to the north. Further north, separated from Hyderabad by the Hussain Sagar Lake, is the modern twin city of **Secunderabad**, where some long-distance trains terminate.

Hyderabad **airport**, 8km north of the city at Begumpet, is served by auto-rickshaws and taxis but no buses. **Hyderabad railway station** (also known as Nampally) is close to all amenities and offers a fairly comprehensive service to major destinations. You can reserve trains here for Secunderabad services, too (see p.1085). The **city bus stand** is about 2km south, close to the north bank of the Musi on Maharani Jhansi Rd.

Hyderabad has a severe lack of **tourist information**. The **APTDC office**, at Yatri Nivas, Sardar Patel Rd, Secunderabad (☎843931), is of little use unless you want to book one of their tours. The best places to **change money** are around Abids Circle, where there's a branch of the *State Bank of India* and the *Andhra Bank*, which appears to be on Nehru Rd although its official address is Sultan Bazaar, and where they'll change travellers' cheques up to US$200 and accept *Mastercard* and *Visa* encashments. For **car rental**, with or without driver, head for *Alpha Motors*, 17 Abids Shopping Centre, opposite *Hotel Emerald*, Chirag Ali Lane, Abids (☎201306). *Hertz* is based at *Hotel Viceroy*, near Tank bund (☎618383 or 618777).

The City

Hyderabad is divided into three: **Hyderabad** the old city; **Secunderabad**, the new (originally called Hussain Shah Pura); and **Golconda**, the old fort. The old and new cities are basically one big sprawl, separated by a lake, **Hussain Sagar**, which was created in the sixteenth century and named after Hussain Shah Wali, who had helped Ibrahim Quli Qutb Shah recover from a serious illness. A huge stone Buddha stands in the centre of the lake.

The telephone **area code** for Hyderabad is ☎040.

The most interesting area, south of the River Musi, holds the **bazaars**, **Charminar** and the **Salar Jung Museum**. It must be a long time since the River Musi amounted to very much. Even after the rains the river is about a tenth the width of the bridge; most of the area under the bridge is grassed over, some planted with palms and paddy. North of the river, the main shopping areas are centred around Abids Circle and the Sultan Bazaar (ready-made clothes, fruit, veg and silk), ten minutes' walk east of the railway station. Abids Circle is connected to MG Rd, which runs north to Secunderabad and metamorphoses into Nehru Rd in the south.

Salar Jung Museum

The unmissable **Salar Jung Museum** (daily except Fri 9.30am–5.15pm), on the south bank of the Musi, houses part of the huge collection of Salar Jung, one of the Nizam's prime ministers, and his ancestors. A well-travelled man of wealth, with an eye for *objets d'art*, he bought whatever took his fancy from both the east and west, from the sublime to, in some cases, the ridiculous. His extraordinary hoard includes Indian jade, Indian miniatures, furniture, lacquer work, Moghul opaque glassware, fabrics, bronzes, Buddhist and Hindu sculpture, manuscripts, and weapons. There are also good examples of *bidri*, decorated metalwork cast from an alloy of zinc, copper and tin, that originated in Bidar in northern Karnataka. Avoid weekends, when it gets very crowded.

Charminar, Lad Bazaar and the Mecca Masjid

A maze of bazaars teeming with people, the old city has at its heart the **Charminar**, a triumphal arch built at the centre of Muhammad Quli Shah's city in 1591 to commemorate an epidemic. It features four graceful minarets, each 56m high, housing spiral staircases to the upper storeys. Although a secular building, it has a mosque (now closed) on the roof; the oldest in Hyderabad, it is said to have been built to teach the royal children the Koran. The yellowish colour of the whole building is thanks to a special stucco made of marble powder, gram and egg yolk.

Charminar marks the beginning of the fascinating **Lad Bazaar**, as old as the town itself, which leads to Mahboob Chowk, a market square featuring a mosque and Victorian clocktower. Lad Bazaar specializes in everything you could possibly need for a Hyderabadi marriage; it's full of bangle shops, old stores where you can buy rosewater, herbs and spices, exotic materials and the more mundane *lunghis*. You'll also find silver filigree jewellery, antiques and *bidri* ware, as well as boxes, plates, *hookah*-paraphernalia and the like, delicately inlaid with silver and brass. Hyderabad is the centre of the pearl trade; **pearls**, so beloved of the Nizams that they not only wore them but apparently liked nothing more than having them ground into powder to eat, can be bought in the markets near the Charminar. Southeast of Lad Bazaar, the complex of **Royal Palaces** includes Chaumahalla, four palaces set around a central courtyard.

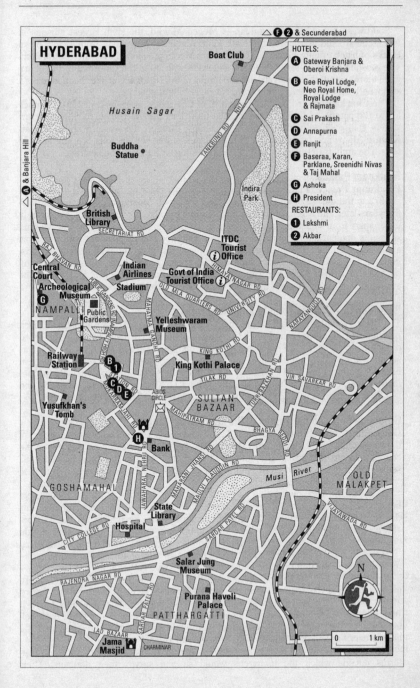

△ **F** **2** & Secunderabad

HYDERABAD

Boat Club

Husain Sagar

Buddha Statue

△ & Banjara Hill

British Library

SECRETARIAT RD

Central Court

RAJ BHAVAN RD

Archeological Museum

G

NAMPALLI

Indian Airlines Stadium

Public Gardens

ITDC Tourist Office ℹ

HIMAYAT NAGAR RD

Govt of India Tourist Office ℹ

OLD MLA QUARTERS RD

UNIVERSITY RD

Yelleshwaram Museum

Railway Station

B 1

STATION RD

C D E

NAKARAMPURA RD

ABIDS CIRCLE

Yusufkhan's Tomb

KING KOTHI RD

King Kothi Palace

TILAK RD

SULTAN BAZAAR

TURREBAZKHAN RD

VIR SAVARKAR RD

MAHIPATRAM RD

BHAGYA REDDY RD

H

Bank

GOSHAMAHAL

△

JAWAHARLAL NEHRU RD

MALLUV ALAUDDIN RD

Musi River

OLD MALAKPET

State Library

Hospital

CITY COLLEGE RD

MAHATMA PHANSI RD

SARDAR PATEL RD

VIJAYAWADA RD

Salar Jung Museum

RAJENDRA NAGAR RD

Purana Haveli Palace

PATTHARGATTI

LAD BAZAAR

Jama Masjid

CHARMINAR

N

0   1 km

HOTELS:
A Gateway Banjara & Oberoi Krishna
B Gee Royal Lodge, Neo Royal Home, Royal Lodge & Rajmata
C Sai Prakash
D Annapurna
E Ranjit
F Baseraa, Karan, Parklane, Sreenidhi Nivas & Taj Mahal
G Ashoka
H President
RESTAURANTS:
1 Lakshmi
2 Akbar

Indira Park

NH9

TANKBUND RD

MAHATMA GANDHI RD

PUBLIC GARDENS RD

NARAYANGUDA RD

Southwest, behind the Charminar, is **Mecca Masjid**, the sixth largest mosque in India, constructed in 1598 by the sixth king, Abdullah Qutb Shah, from locally hewn blocks of black granite. Small red bricks from Mecca are slotted over the central arch. The mosque can hold three thousand followers with up to ten thousand in the courtyard; on the left of the courtyard are the tombs of the Nizams. Outside the mosque is a stall where they will change your torn, cut *rupee* bills at good rates.

The **Charkaman**, or Four Arches, north of Charminar, were built in 1594 and once led to the parade ground of royal palaces (now long gone). The surrounding narrow streets spill over with interesting small shops; through the western arch, **Doulat-Khan-e-Ali** (which originally led to the palace), stores sell lustrous brocade and old *saris*. The arch itself is said to have been once hung with rich gold tapestries.

Faluknam Palace

Faluknam Palace, a little under 2km south of Charminar on Kotti Tur Hill, was built in 1872 to the design of an English architect for a rich Muslim of high rank. Twenty-five years later, the Nizam of Hyderabad bought it to lodge his visitors, but it was rarely used, apart from housing British royalty in 1906. A mixture of classical and Moghul styles, its opulent interiors include a marble entrance hall resplendent with fountains and a superb Italian marble staircase. The official reception room is, perhaps surprisingly, in Louis XIV style. Collections of jade, crystal chandeliers, tapestries and dull portraits of British Governor Generals are also proudly on show. Visits must be arranged in advance, through the Chief of Protocol, Secretariat, Secretariat Rd.

Birla Venkateshwara Temple and Planetarium

The **Birla Venkateshwara Temple** (daily 7am–noon & 3–9pm), on Kalabahad ("black mountain") Hill, north of the Public Gardens, is open to all, irrespective of caste, creed or nationality. Constructed in Rajasthani white marble in 1976 by the Birla Trust, it was set up by the wealthy industrialist Birla family. Although the temple itself is not of great interest, it affords fine views. Nearby, and built by the same organization, is the **planetarium**, whose shows are in English (Mon–Thurs 11.30am, 4pm & 6pm; every 2nd and last Fri from 3pm; Sun 11.35am, 3.45pm & 6pm; closed last Thurs of every month).

Golconda Fort and the Tombs of the Qutb Shahi Kings

Golconda, 122m above the plain and 11km west of old Hyderabad, was the capital of the seven Qutb Shahi kings from 1518 until the end of the sixteenth century, when the court moved to Hyderabad. Its outer wall reached 18m, and the citadel boasted 87 semi-circular bastions and eight mighty gates, four of which are still in use, complete with gruesome elephant-proof spikes.

To get **to the fort**, buses #119 and #80R run from Nampally. Both the #66G direct bus from Charminar and #80D from Secunderabad stop outside the main entrance. **For the tombs**, take #123 and #142S from Charminar. From Secunderabad the #5, #5S, #5R all go to Mehdipattanam, where you should hop onto #123. Or, of course, you could take a rickshaw and spare yourself the bother (agree a waiting fee in advance).

Set aside a day to explore the fort, which covers an area of around forty square kilometres; it's well worth hiring one of the many guides who gather at the entrance.

Entering the **fort**, by the Balahisar Gate, you come into the Grand Portico, where guards clap their hands to show off the fort's acoustics; the claps can be clearly heard at the Durbar Hall at its highest point. Halfway along the steps that lead up to it (reached beyond assorted water channels and wells), you come to a small dark cell named after the court cashier **Ramdas**, who while incarcerated here produced the clumsy carvings and paintings that litter the gloomy room.

The steps are crowned by the three-storey **Durbar Hall** of the Qutb Shahs, on platforms outside which the monarchs would sit and survey their domains. Their

THE QUTB SHAHI DYNASTY

The first king of what became the Qutb Shahi dynasty came from Persia with his uncle to sell horses to the Bahmani kingdom at Gulbarga and Bijapur. Appointed as a governor and well liked by the people, he was given a title by Bahmani ruler Mamu Shbahmani, who changed his name from simply Quli to **Quli Qutb Shah**. By 1518, the dissipation of the ineffectual Bahmanis led Quli to raise an army and declare independence. He ruled for 25 years. His son, **Jamshed**, was keen to take power, but his father favoured a younger son, Ibrahim. Jamshed arranged for his father – then in his nineties – to be beheaded in the mosque while he was praying, and exiled his brothers. When the people came to know that Jamshed had treacherously killed his father, they forcibly deposed him.

Ibrahim Quli Qutb Shah returned to Golconda from exile and became king at the age of eighteen. An educated man, a poet in Urdu and Telegu, he built many important buildings in the Golconda, including the stone fort, which had previously been a Hindu mud construction. His one son, **Muhammad Quli Qutb Shah**, was also a cultured man. The reign was peaceful and prosperous, trading in grains and, it is said, diamonds. Rumour has it that there is a diamond mine in the fort still; only the government knows where it is. They say there used to be a map. . . .

Moghul armies attacked the city in the seventeenth century; the inhabitants surrendered peacefully, and paid their taxes. In 1685 Aurangzeb arrived in Golconda, and two years later brought in a large army. An eight-month battle ensued – eventually, so the story goes, Aurangzeb's son bribed a doorman and the Emperor's troops won.

accompaniment was the lilting strains of court musicians, as opposed to the cacophony of incessant clapping from far below. As you head back down to the palaces and harems, you pass the tanks that supplied the fort's water system.

The ruins of the **queen's palace**, once elaborately decorated with multiple domes, stand in a courtyard centred on an original copper fountain that used to be filled with rosewater. You can still see traces of the "necklace" design on one of the arches, at the top of which a lotus bud sits below an opening flower with a cavity at its centre that once contained a diamond. Petals and creeper leaves are dotted with tiny holes that formerly gleamed with rubies and diamonds; parrots, long gone, had rubies for their eyes. Today visitors can only speculate how splendid it must all have looked, especially at night, when flaming torches illuminated the glittering decorations. At the entrance to the **palace** itself, four chambers provided protection from intruders. Passing through two rooms, the second of which is overgrown, you come to the **Shahi Mahal**, the royal bedroom. Originally it had a domed roof and niches on the walls that once sheltered candles or oil lamps. It is said that the servants used silver ladders to get up there to light them.

There are a total of 82 **tombs** (daily except Fri 9am–4.30pm) about 1km north of the outer wall. Set in peaceful gardens, they commemorate commanders, relatives of the kings, dancers, singers and royal doctors, as well as all but two of the Qutb Shahi kings. Faded today, they were once brightly coloured in turquoise and green; they all have an onion dome on a block, with a highly decorative arcade.

Accommodation

The area in front of **Hyderabad railway station** (Nampally) has the cheapest accommodation, but you're unlikely to find anything basic for less than Rs150. The real **bargains** are more in the mid- to upper-range hotels, which offer better facilities for lower rates than in other big cities. About 2km north of Secunderabad railway station, decent places line **Sarojini Devi Rd**, near the Gymkhana Ground. Unless stated otherwise, all the hotels listed below are north of the river in Hyderabad.

Annapurna Nampally, Station Rd, halfway between station and Abids Circle (☎557931). Large rooms, frayed at the edges, all with *Star TV*. Veg restaurant. ④.

Ashoka, 6-1-70 Lakdi-ka-Pul (☎220105). The rooms (some a/c) are large and fairly clean but badly maintained, and the public spaces are grotty once you leave the ground floor. Room service, travel, car rental. Overpriced. ⑤–⑥.

Baseraa 9-1-167/168 Sarojini Devi Rd, Secunderabad (☎823200). High-standard rooms, all a/c with *Star TV*. Perhaps the lack of grandiose lobby makes it somewhat cheaper. ⑦.

Central Court, Lakdi-ka-Pul (continuation of Raj Bhavan Rd) (☎233262; fax 232737). Smallish, new hotel, 2km from railway, with standard as good as many twice the price. Comfortable rooms with *Star TV* and 24hr room service. Travel desk, coffee shop and restaurant. ⑥.

Gateway Banjara, Road No 1, Banjara Hill (☎222222; fax 222218). Comfortable *Taj* group hotel with usual facilities, overlooking lake, 4km from the centre of Hyderabad on the top of Banjara Hill. Good restaurant and coffee shop. ⑧–⑨.

Gee Royal Lodge, Nampally High Rd, opposite railway station (☎201511). Very basic lodge, all rooms with *Star TV*, some with balconies overlooking the street. ③.

Karan, 1-2-261/1 Sarojini Devi Rd, Secunderabad (☎840191). Somewhat overpriced but rooms are clean and comfortable, all with *Star TV*. Roof garden is a bit neglected but has pleasant view overlooking Gymkhana Ground. Exchange and car rental. Non-veg restaurant. ⑥.

Park, 5-9-110 Public Gardens Rd, opposite Public Gardens and Telegu University (☎243128). Reasonable rooms (some a/c), all with *Star TV* and room service (6am–10.30pm); 2min from railway, 3km from Central Bus Stand. Veg and non-veg restaurant. ④–⑤.

Parklane, 115 Park Lane, Secunderabad (☎84066). Large rooms ("ordinary" and deluxe), with views onto other buildings, very clean bathrooms, *Star TV*, restaurant and friendly staff. ⑤–⑥.

Rajmata, Nampally High Rd, opposite railway station (☎201000). Set back from the road near the various *Royal* lodges. Next door to the *Lakshmi* restaurant. Largish, clean non-a/c rooms. ④.

Ranjit Nampally, Station Rd (☎43225). A bit ropey but basically not bad, although located on a noisy road, 1min from station. Turn right out of station approach road and it's on the left, shares a building with the *New Bombay* bar. All non-a/c, extra charge for *Star TV*. Room service, no restaurant. ③.

Royal Lodge, Nampally High Rd, opposite railway station (☎201194). Decent, basic lodge; all rooms non-a/c with *Star TV*. ③.

HYDERABADI ADDRESSES

Hyderabadis appear to have a deep mistrust of logical, consistent road naming, mapping and addresses. One road merges into another; some addresses refer to nothing more specific than a locality; and others identify themselves as being opposite buildings that no longer exist! Just as confusing are those that have very specific addresses consisting of a string of hyphenated numbers referring to house and plot numbers, incomprehensible to anybody other than town surveyors. All this is somewhat ironic in a city that is home to one of the major sections of the Survey of India.

Sai Prakash Nampally, Station Rd (☎511726/9). Near railway, 2km from bus stand. Modern hotel, complete with capsule lift. Comfortable, carpeted rooms (all with *Star TV*) set around atrium. High standards (non-a/c in particular), and very popular. Good restaurants and bar. ⑤.

Skyline, Ladki-ka-Pul, 2km from railway (☎224644). Small, cleanish rooms, some a/c. ④.

Taj Mahal, 88 Sarojini Devi Rd, Secunderabad (☎812105). Old-fashioned hotel with character, built in 1949, that bears no detectable relation to the Taj Mahal. Rooms are clean, comfortable and spacious, although a bit dark. Veg restaurant with snacks and hot Andhra meals. No bar. ④.

Eating

Plenty of "meals" places around town specialize in Hyderabadi cuisine, such as authentic *biryanis*, or the famously chilli-hot Andhra cuisine, often non-veg.

Akbar, 1-7-190 MG Rd, Secunderabad. Hyderabadi cuisine at moderate prices.

Amaravathi, 3-6-307, Central Chambers, Hyderguda, Hyderabad. Specializes in Andhra non-veg.

Ashoka, 6-1-70 Lakdi-ka-Pul. The *Saptagiri* here is an a/c cafeteria serving south Indian snacks and some north Indian dishes. Good value.

Baseraa, 9-1-167/168 Sarojini Devi Rd, Secunderabad. Two restaurants: the simply furnished *Daawat* serves veg, south Indian snacks, breakfasts and standard north Indian dishes in the evenings. In the basement, the posher *Mehfill* is heavy on Mughlai meat dishes with a few Chinese and western thrown in. It also has a bar.

Central Court Hotel, Lakdi-ka-Pul. *Touch of Class* restaurant serves Hyderabadi, Mughlai, western and Chinese food. Good menu of Hyderabadi non-veg plus some veg options and barbecue kebabs on small patio. Lunchtime buffet, evenings à la carte.

Gateway Banjara, Road No 1, Banjara Hill. *Dakhni* serves excellent, pricey, authentic south Indian cuisine, including Hyderabadi.

Lakshmi, opposite Hyderabad railway station but set back from the road in a little courtyard near the *Royal* and *Rajmata* lodges. Reliable, cheap snacks and meals, both northern and southern.

Park, 5-9-110 Public Gardens Rd, opposite Public Gardens and Telegu University. Morning south Indian snacks, lunch and dinner veg and non-veg dishes.

Sai Prakash, Nampally Station Rd. The *Woodlands* serves good-value veg south Indian snacks and north Indian dishes. *Vintage* is very much posher and pricier, with comfy chairs and imaginative daily specials. Crab, prawns and specialities from Hyderabad and further afield.

MOVING ON FROM HYDERABAD

Domestic airlines serving Hyderabad include *Indian Airlines* (☎140; pre-recorded flight info: ☎142), *East-West* (☎813568), *Jet* (☎840382) and *Moduluft* (☎842054). There's one daily flight to Bangalore (1hr; *Indian Airlines*), six to Bombay (1hr 15min; all four airlines), three daily to Delhi (2hr; *Indian Airlines*, *Moduluft*), two to Madras (1hr; *Indian Airlines*) and three weekly to Calcutta via Bhubaneshwar (2hr 45min; *Indian Airlines*).

From the Central Bus Stand regular services run to Amaravati (one daily; 7hr), Bangalore (10 daily; 13hr), Bombay (8 daily; 17hr), Madras (1 daily; 16hr) and Tirupati (10 daily; 9hr).

Daily services **from Hyderabad** railway station include *Hyderabad Express* #7085 to Bangalore (5.50pm; 17hr); the *Hyderabad–Bombay Express* #7032 to Bombay (7.30pm; 17hr); *Charminar Express* #6060 to Madras (6.30pm; 15hr); *Rayasaleena Express* #7429 to Tirupati (5pm; 16hr); and the *Godavari Express* #7008 to Vijayawada (5.45pm; 6hr). **From Secunderabad**, the daily *Ajanta Express* #7551 runs to Aurangabad (6.30pm; 12hr 15min) and the *Andhra Pradesh Express* to New Delhi (6.30am; 26hr).

The **reservations office** (Mon–Sat 8am–2pm & 2.30–8pm, Sun 8am–2pm) is to the left as you enter the station. Counter #213 (next to enquiry counter) is supposedly for tourist reservations, but it's also used for group bookings and lost tickets. Foreign visitors can make bookings at the Chief Reservation Inspector's Office on platform 1 (daily 9am–5pm). All trains from Secunderabad can be booked from Hyderabad.

Listings

Bookstores *Higginbothams*, 1 Lal Bahadur Stadium, Hyderabad (☎237918); *Gangarams*, 62 DSD Rd, near *Garden Restaurant* in Secunderabad (☎820691).

Crafts *Utkalika* (Government of Orissa handicrafts), House no. 60-1-67, between *Ravindra Bharati* and *Hotel Ashoka*, sells silver filigree jewellery, handloom cloth, *ikhat* tie-dye, Jagannath papier-mâché figures and buffalo bone carvings. *Cheneta Bhavan* is a modern shopping complex a little south of the railway station, stuffed with handloom cloth shops from various states, including Tamil Nadu, Uttar Pradesh, Rajasthan, Madhya Pradesh and Andhra Pradesh. For Kanchi and other silks, head for *Sanchi Kamakshi Silks*, shop no. 4-4-6/1, "Beside Dilshad Talkies" (now demolished) and *Thunga Sambaiah*, "opposite Dilshad Talkies", Sultan Bazaar, Kothi.

Pharmacies *Kanjani Medical Hall*, Nampally Station Rd (☎202233). *Apollo Pharmacy* (☎231380) and *Health Pharmacy* (☎210618) are both 24hr.

Photography and Film *Moorty & Sons*, Gandhi Rd, sells colour film and transparencies and accessories. *Jyoti Foto Emporium*, 5-4-730 Nampally Station Rd (☎553539), sells colour print and transparencies; *Royal Image*, opposite the station, next to the *Royal Lodge* (☎201993), sells print film only.

Travel Agents *Alam Tours and Travels*, 5-9-189/104 1st floor, Lenaine Estate, next to SBH Gunfoundry, Abids Rd (☎203761); *Sita World Travels*, Sita House, 3-5-874 Hyderguda; *Travel Corporation*, 102 Regency House, 680 Somajiguda, Greenlands Rd (☎212722), are all in Hyderabad.

Warangal

WARANGAL – "one stone" – 150km northeast of Hyderabad, was the Hindu capital of the Kakatiyan empire in the twelfth and thirteenth centuries. Like other Deccan cities, it changed hands many times between the Hindus and the Muslims – something that is reflected in its architecture and the remains you see today.

The **fort** (5km north) is famous for its two circles of fortifications: the outer made of earth with a moat, and the inner of stone. Four roads into the centre meet at the ruined temple of **Svayambhu** (1162), dedicated to Shiva. At its southern, free-standing gateway, another Shiva temple, from the fourteenth century, is in much better shape; inside, the remains of an enormous *lingam* came originally from the Svayambhu shrine. Also inside the citadel is the **Shirab Khan**, or **Audience Hall**, an early eleventh-century building very similar to Mandu's Hindola Mahal (see p.391).

The largely basalt Chalukyan-style **"thousand-pillared" Shiva temple** on the slopes of Hanamkonda Hill, north of the fort, was constructed by King Rudra Deva in 1163. A low-roofed building, on several stepped stages, it features superb carvings and has three shrines to Vishnu, Shiva and Surya the sun god. They lead off the *mandapa* whose numerous finely carved columns give the temple its name. In front, a polished Nandi bull was carved out of a single stone. A Bhadrakali temple stands at the top of the hill.

Practicalities

If you make an early start, it's just about possible to visit Warangal in a day trip from Hyderabad. Frequent buses and trains run to the site (roughly 3hr 30min). Warangal's **bus stand** and **railway station** are opposite each other, served by local buses and auto-rickshaws. **Accommodation** is limited; the *Hotel Ashok* (☎85491; ⑤) on Main Rd, Hanamkonda, 8km from the railway and bus stand, has a/c rooms, a restaurant and bar, while basic lodges near the railway include the *Vijya* (☎5851; ②) and *Shanti Krishna* (☎5943; ②) on Station Rd.

Nagarjunakonda

NAGARJUNAKONDA, or "Nagarjuna's Hill", situated 166km south of Hyderabad and 175km west of Vijayawada, is all that now remains of the vast area, rich in archeological sites, submerged when the huge Nagarjuna Sagar Dam was built across the River

Krishna in 1960. Ancient settlements in the valley were first discovered in 1926; extensive excavations carried out between 1954 and 1960 uncovered more than one hundred sites dating from the early Stone Age to late medieval times. Nagarjunakonda was once the summit of a hill, where a fort towered 200m above the valley floor; now it's just a small oblong island near the middle of Nagarjuna Sagar Lake, accessible by boat from the mainland. Several Buddhist monuments have been reconstructed, in an operation reminiscent of that at Abu Simbel in Egypt, and a **museum** exhibits the more remarkable ruins of the valley.

VIJAYAPURI, the village on the shore of the lake, overlooks the colossal dam itself, which stretches for almost two kilometres. Torrents of water flushed through the dam's 26 flood gates produce electricity for the whole region and irrigate an area of almost 800 square kilometres. Many villages had to be relocated on higher ground when the valley was flooded.

Nagarjunakonda and the museum

Boats arrive on the northeastern edge of Nagarjunakonda island, unloading passengers at what remains of one of the gates of the fort, built in the fourteenth century and considerably renovated by the Vijayanagar kings in the mid-sixteenth century. Low, damaged stone walls skirting the island mark the edge of the fort, and you can see ground-level remains of the Hindu temples that served its inhabitants.

Well-kept gardens lie between the jetty and the museum, beyond which nine Buddhist monuments from various sites in the valley have been rebuilt. West of the jetty, there's a reconstructed bathing *ghat*, built entirely of limestone during the reigns of the Ikshvaku kings (third century AD). A series of levels and steps leads to the water's edge; boards etched into some of its slabs were probably used for dice games.

The **maha-chaitya**, or *stupa*, constructed at the command of King Chamtula's sister in the third century AD, is the earliest Buddhist structure in the area. It was raised over relics of the Buddha – said to include a tooth – and has been reassembled in the southwest of the island. Nearby, a towering **statue** of the Buddha stands draped in robes beside a ground plan of a monastery that enshrines a smaller *stupa*. Other **stupas** stand nearby; the brick walls of the *svastika chaitya* have been arranged in the shape of swastikas, common emblems in early Buddhist iconography.

In the **museum** (daily except Fri 9am–5pm), **Buddhist sculptures** include large stone friezes decorated with scenes from the Buddha's life: his birth; his mother's vision of an elephant and a lotus blossom; his renunciation, and his subversion of evil as he meditated and realized enlightenment under the *bodhi* tree. Twelve statues of standing Buddhas – one of which reaches 3m – show the Buddha in various postures of teaching or meditation. Many pillars are undamaged, profusely carved with Buddha images, bowing devotees, elephants and lotus medallions.

Earlier artefacts include 200,000-year-old stone tools, more advanced tools and pots from the Neolithic age (third millennium BC), and metal axe heads and knives (first millennium BC). Among later finds are several inscribed pillars from Ikshvaku times, recording in Prakrit or Sanskrit the installation of Buddhist monasteries and statues. The final phase of art at Nagarjunakonda is represented by medieval sculptures: a thirteenth-century *tirthankara* (Jain saint), a seventeenth-century Ganesh and Nandi, and a set of eighteenth-century statues of Shiva and Shakti (his female consort). Also on display is a model showing the excavated sites in the valley.

Practicalities

An organized **tour** to Nagarjunakonda – taking in the sites and museum, the nearby Ethiopothala Waterfalls and an engraved third-century Buddhist monolith known as the Pylon – leaves daily from Hyderabad at 6.45am and returns at 10.30pm. Bookings can be made at the Hyderabad tourist office. It's all a bit rushed: if you want to spend more time in the area you can take local transport from Hyderabad (5hr) or Vijayawada (6hr; a direct service runs daily at 11am and frequent services leave from Guntur).

Accommodation at Vijayapuri is limited. The APTDC *Vijay Vihar Complex* (☎2125; ③) in South Vijayapuri, near the jetty, can be booked through any APTDC office; it offers clean, spacious a/c and non-a/c rooms with balconies, and excellent south and north Indian food in the restaurant. Another APTDC hotel, *Project House* (☎2040; ①), is more basic and less convenient, 3km from the jetty. Budget options include *Golden Lodge* (☎2348; ①), opposite the hospital and 1km down the hill from *Vijay Vihar Complex* (①), which has simple rooms and a restaurant serving Andhra *thalis*.

Tickets for **boats** to the island (9.30am & 1.30pm; 1hr) are on sale 25 minutes before departure (Rs15). Each boat leaves the island thirty minutes after it arrives, which permits a quick dash round the museum but not enough time to visit the monuments: if you want to spend longer, take the morning boat and return in the afternoon. A cafeteria on the island serves drinks and, occasionally, snacks.

Eastern Andhra Pradesh

Perhaps India's least visited area, **eastern Andhra Pradesh** is sandwiched between the Bay of Bengal in the east and the red soil and high peaks of the Eastern Ghats in the north. Its one architectural attraction is the ancient Buddhist site of **Amaravati**, near the city of **Vijayawada**, whose sprinkling of historic temples is far overshadowed by impersonal, modern buildings. Some 350km north, the major port of **Vishakapatnam** is little better – a crowded, dirty place that barely warrants a stop. For anyone with a strong desire to explore, however, pockets of natural beauty along the coast and in the hills of eastern Andhra Pradesh can offer rich reward. In this sleepy landscape, little affected by modernization, bullocks amble between swaying palms and the rice fields are viridescent against rusty sands. Unless you have the patience to endure the excruciatingly slow public transport system, your own vehicle is essential.

Vijayawada

Almost 450km north of Madras, a third of the way to Calcutta, **VIJAYAWADA** is a bustling commercial centre on the banks of the Krishna delta, hemmed in by bare granite outcrops 90km from the coast. This unattractive city is seldom visited by tourists, but does, however, make the obvious stop-off point for visits to the third-century Buddhist site at **Amaravati**, 60km west.

A handful of temples in Vijayawada merit a quick look. The most important, raised on the low Indrakila Hill in the east, is dedicated to the city's patron goddess **Kanaka Durga** (also known as Vijaya), goddess of riches, power and benevolence. Though it is believed to be thousands of years old, with the exception of a few pillared halls and intricate carvings what you see today is largely renovated (and freshly whitewashed). Across the river, roughly 3km out of town, there's an ancient, unmodified cave temple at **Undavalli**, a tiny rural village set off the main road, easily reached on any Guntur-bound bus, or the local #13 service. The temple is cut out of the granite hillside in typical Pallava style: simple, solid and bold. Each of its five levels contains a deep low-roofed hall, with small rock-cut shrines to Vishnu, Shiva and Parvati, and pillared verandahs guarded by sturdy grey statues of gods, saints and lions. Views from the porches take in a sublime patchwork of rivulets, paddy fields and banana plantations.

Practicalities

Vijayawada's **train station**, on the main Madras–Calcutta line, is in the centre of town. Buses arriving from Vishakapatnam, Guntur, Amaravati and as far afield as Hyderabad and Madras pull into the **bus stand** further east. Specific ticket offices cater for each service, and a **tourist office** has details on local accommodation and sites. Between the bus stand and train station, Ryes Canal flows through the heart of town.

Vijayawada is a major business centre, with a good selection of mid-range **hotels**, all less than 2km from the train station and bus stand. Most have reasonably priced restaurants serving Andhra *thalis* and western food. Budget options include *Monica's* (①), just off Elluru Rd about 500m from the bus stand, or *Bombay Guest House* on Congress Office Rd (☎0866/75353; ①): both are very simple, and slightly grubby. The better-value *Santhi* (☎0866/65056; ②–④), close to *Apsara Theatre* on Elluru Rd, offers extremely clean rooms, private bathrooms with hot water, room service, and excellent food in its veg restaurant. Vijayawada's top hotel is the *Illapuram* on Besant Rd (☎0866/61282; ④–⑦), roughly 1km from the railway station. Its rooms (some a/c) are immaculate, spacious and well lit, with private bathrooms; the carpeted suites are excellent value. Veg and non-veg restaurants on the ground floor serve a wide range of south Indian dishes, and the travel desk arranges tours and transport for guests.

Amaravati

AMARAVATI, a small village on the banks of the Krishna 30km west of Vijayawada, is the site of a Buddhist settlement, formerly known as Chintapalli, where a *stupa* larger than those at Sanchi (see p.336) was erected over relics of the Buddha in the third century BC, during the reign of Ashoka. The *stupa* no longer stands, but its great size is evident from the large mound that formed its base. It was originally surrounded by grey stone railings with a gateway at each of the cardinal points, one of which has been reconstructed in an open courtyard. Its decoration, meticulously carved and perfectly preserved, shows the themes represented on all such Buddhist monuments: the Buddha's birth, renunciation and life as an emaciated ascetic, enlightenment under the *bodhi* tree (see p.789), his first sermon in the Deer Park, and *parinirvana*, or death. Several foundation stones of monastic quarters remain on the site.

Exhibits at the small but fascinating **museum** (daily except Fri 10am–5pm) range in date from the third century BC to the twelfth century AD. They include statues of the Buddha, with lotus symbols on his feet, a head of tightly curled hair, and long ear lobes, all traditional indications of an enlightened teacher. Earlier stone carvings represent the Buddha through such symbols as the *chakra* (wheel of Dharma), a throne, a *stupa*, a flaming pillar or a *bodhi* tree, all being worshipped. The lotus motif, a central symbol in early Buddhism, is connected with a dream the Buddha's mother had shortly after conception, and has always been a Buddhist symbol of essential purity: it appears repeatedly on railings and pillars. Later sculptures include limestone statues of the goddess Tara and *bodhisattva* Padmapani, both installed at the site in medieval times when the community had adopted Mahayana teachings in place of the earlier Hinayana doctrines. What you see here are some of the finer pieces excavated from the site – other remains have been taken to the Madras Government Museum and the British Museum in London.

Practicalities

Only one **bus** daily runs direct from Vijayawada to Amaravati (4.30pm; 2hr), so it's best to take a bus to Guntur (every 30min; 30min), where you can pick up a connection on to Amaravati (1hr–1hr 30min). Buses return to Guntur every half hour, and during the monsoon **boats** gather at the jetty in Amaravati and follow the River Krishna all the way to Vijayawada. The excavated site and museum are roughly 1km from the bus stand. Tri-shaws – miniature carts attached to tricycles and brightly painted with chubby film stars – take tourists to the site and the river bank, where there are several drink stalls. Amaravati has no **hotels**.

Vishakapatnam

One of India's most rapidly growing industrial cities, and its fourth largest port, **VISHAKAPATNAM** (also known as Vizag), 350km north of Vijayawada, is an unpleasant city choked with the smells and dirt of a busy shipbuilding industry, an oil plant and a steel factory. Such is its sprawl that it has overtaken and polluted the neighbouring town of Waltair, once a health resort. Although there's little to warrant a stop at Vishakapatnam – even its wide stretch of beach is not that clean – remnants of older communities lie within a day's journey from the city.

At **Bheemunipatnam**, 30km north, you can see the remains of a Dutch fort and a peculiar cemetery where slate-grey pyramidal tombs are abandoned to nature. **Borra**, 70km inland on a minor road that winds through the Eastern Ghats and the Araku forests, boasts a set of eerie limestone caves whose darkness is pierced with age-old stalactites and stalagmites. You'll need a car to get to **Mukhalingam**, 100km north of Bheemunipatnam, where three Shaivite temples, built between the sixth and twelfth centuries, rest in low hills. Their elaborate carving and well-preserved towering *shikharas* display slight local variations to the otherwise standard Orissan style. There's nowhere to stay in Mukhalingam.

Practicalities

Vishakapatnam's **train station**, on the Madras–Calcutta coastal route, is in the old town, close to the port. The ride to Delhi takes a tedious three days. The **bus stand**, known as "complex", is in a newer area, 3km from the coast. There's also an **airport**, 12km west of town, connected by daily flights to Hyderabad.

If you arrive late by bus, head for the well-maintained **retiring rooms** (①) in the bus stand. Otherwise, most **hotels** are in the old town, near the train station. The best of them is *Hotel Karanths*, 33-1-55 Patel Marg (☎69347; ②), whose spotless rooms have balconies, pressed sheets and attached bathrooms. The downstairs restaurant serves unbeatable *thalis* and *tiffins* at no-nonsense prices. Next door, *Dakshayani* (☎60087; ①) offers simple grotty rooms, some with private bathrooms. Closer to the port in Poorna Market, the *Ashoka* (②) is cleaner and more spacious than the insalubrious surroundings suggest. Vishakapatnam's most presentable upmarket hotel, the *Park* on Beach Rd (☎54861; ⑥), has luxurious rooms, swimming pool, bar and restaurant, and access to the beach; watch for currents if you swim in the sea.

Tirupati

Set in a stunning position, surrounded by wooded hills capped by a ring of vertical red rocks, the **Shri Venkateshvara temple** at Tirumala, a hair-raising drive 700m up in the Venkata hills, 11km from **TIRUPATI** and 170km northwest of Madras, is said to be the richest and most popular place of pilgrimage in the world, drawing more devotees than either Rome or Mecca. If you are not a devotee of Shri Venkateshvar, and not particularly keen on waiting in line for hours at a time, choose the day of your visit with care; avoid weekends, public and school holidays, and particularly special festivals, as you are likely to meet at least ten thousand other visitors.

Arrival and information

The best way of **getting to Tirupati** is by train from Madras; the trip can be done in a day if you get the earliest of the three daily services (3hr 30min). From Hyderabad it takes sixteen hours. An information counter at the **railway station** is accessible from the entrance hall and platform one, where there's a 24-hour left luggage office and a self-service veg refreshment room. Small stands sell English copies of TKT Viraraghava Charya's *History of Tirupati*, and there's a Vivekananda religious bookshop next door.

Tirupati's APSRTC Central **bus station** is about 2km from the railway station. Frequent express services run from Madras (4hr), but the train is far more comfortable, especially as the connecting service to Tirumala and the Venkateshvara temple often requires a lot of waiting in line. An alternative is to go on a **conducted tour** (see below). The easiest option is to take a **taxi**, but be warned that some of the guys outside the railway station are not licensed and your trip may be curtailed by the Tirumala police. APTDC at the railway station can provide tourist taxis.

Local trips to hotels can be made on beautifully decorated **cycle rickshaws**, with silver backs, colourfully painted, some with coverings of appliquéd cloth.

There are several **tourist offices** in Tirupati: *AP Tourism Regional Office*, 139 TP Area (☎232208), *AP Government State Information Centre*, Govindaraja Car St (☎4818) and *TTD Information Centres*, at 1 New Chowltry (☎22777) and the railway station. APTDC (☎20602) runs daily **conducted tours** (10am–5pm; Rs50) from the bus station, which call at the railway station. Places covered include the Srikalahasteswara, Padmavati, Venkataswara, Hare Rama Hare Krishna, Kapilateertham, Govindarajaswamy temples and Chandragiri Fort (not Fri). Where necessary, customers are required to buy "Special Entrance" tickets.

Tirumala Hill, the Venkateshvara temple and Kapilateertham

Not for nothing is there a small shrine to Ganesh at the foot of **Tirumala Hill**. The journey up is hair-raising, to say the least, and any bus or car driver, or passenger for that matter, should say a quick prayer when embarking on it. Overtaking is strictly forbidden, but drivers do anyway; virtually every bend is labelled "blind" and every instruction to drive slowly is blithely ignored. The fearless sit on the left for the best views; the most devout, of course, climb the hill by foot. When you get to the top, you will see barbers busying themselves giving pilgrims tonsures as part of their devotions. This is one of the very few temples where non-Hindus are permitted to enter the inner sanctum, but for everyone *darshan*, a view of the god, is the briefest of brief experiences. Temple funds support a university, hospital, orphanages and schools at Tirupati as well as providing cheap, and in some cases free, accommodation for pilgrims.

The **Venkateshvara Vishnu temple**, started in the tenth century, has been recently renovated to provide facilities for the thousands of pilgrims who visit daily; a rabbit warren of passages and waiting rooms wind their way around the complex in which pilgrims interminably shuffle towards the inner sanctum. Unless your visit is intended to be particularly rigorous, on reaching the temple you should follow the signs for the *darshan* that costs around Rs30 or Rs40. This will reduce the time it takes to get inside by hours, if not days (no *darshan* 10am–noon).

Once inside, you'll see the somewhat incongruous sight of *brahmins* sitting at video monitors, observing the goings-on in the inner sanctum; the constant to-ing and fro-ing includes temple attendants bringing in supplies, truckloads of oil and other comestibles. Huge cooking pots are carried across the courtyard. You may also catch deities being carried past on palanquins to the accompaniment of *nagesvaram* (a south Indian oboe-like double-reed wind instrument) and *tavil* drum, complete with an armed guard. At the entrance is a colonnade, lined with life-sized statues of royal patrons, in copper or stone. The *gopura* gateway leading to the inner courtyard is decorated with sheets of embossed silver; a gold *stambha* (flagstaff) stands outside the inner shrine next to a gold upturned lotus on a plinth. Outside, opposite the temple, is a small museum, the **Hall of Antiquities** (daily 8am–8pm). **Kapilateertham**, a temple at the bottom of the hill, has a gaily-painted little Hindu pleasure garden at the entrance; after the rains, a powerful waterfall crashes into a large tank surrounded by colonnades, and everyone piles in for a bath, ensuing in typically good-natured pilgrim bedlam.

Tiruchanur Padmavati temple

Between Tirupati and Tirumala Hill, the **Tiruchanur Padmavati temple** is another popular pilgrimage halt. A gold *vimanam* tower with lions at each corner surmounts the sanctuary, which contains a black stone image of goddess Lakshmi with one silver eye. At the front step, water sprays to wash the feet of the devotees. A Rs5 ticket allows you to jump the line to enter the sanctuary. If you'd like to donate a *sari* to the goddess, you may do so, on payment of Rs1200. Cameras are prohibited.

Chandragiri Fort

In the sixteenth century, **Chandragiri**, 11km southwest of Tirupati, became the third capital of the Vijayanagars, whose power had declined following the fall of the city of Vijayanagar (Hampi) in Karnataka. It was here that the British negotiated the acquisition of the land to establish Fort St George, the earliest settlement at what is now Madras. The original fort, thought to date from *c*.1000 AD, was taken over by Haider Ali in 1782, followed by the British in 1792. A small **museum** of sculpture, weapons and memorabilia (daily except Fri 10am–5pm) is housed in the main building, the Indo-Saracenic Raja Mahal. Another building, the **Rani Mahal**, stands close by, while behind that is a hill with two free-standing boulders which was used as a place of public execution during Vijayanagar times. A small temple from the Krishna Deva Raya period and a freshwater tank stand at the top of the hill behind the Raja Mahal.

Accommodation and eating

Unless you're a pilgrim seeking accommodation in the *dharamshalas* near the temple, all the decent places to stay are in Tirupati, near the railway and bus stand. The *Bhima* chain are probably the best-maintained hotels in town. **Eating** is recommended in the bigger hotels; there are, of course, cheap "meals" places in town and near the temple.

Bhimas Deluxe, 34-38 G Car St, near railway station (☎08574/20121). Decent, comfortable rooms (some a/c). *Maya* veg restaurant serves south Indian snacks in the morning and north Indian, some Chinese dishes in the evenings. Very reasonable prices. ⑤.

Bhimas Paradise, Renigunta Rd (☎08574/20747). Brand new hotel with spotless, functional rooms (pristine leatherette but no carpets), some with a/c, and tiny balconies. *Star TV*, swimming pool, garden, 24hr coffee shop. The restaurant, *Bharani*, is clean, dark and reasonable, serving veg south Indian snacks, *thalis* and the usual north Indian dishes. ④–⑤.

Mayura, 209 TP Area (☎08574/20901). Well-maintained hotel with some a/c rooms with *Star TV*, exchange and travel desk. The *Surya* restaurant serves reasonably priced south Indian breakfasts, and north Indian evening meals. ④–⑤.

Sri Oorvasi International, Renigunta Rd, 1km from railway (☎08574/20202). Large hotel with a veg restaurant and travel desk. ④–⑤.

Vishnu Priya, opposite Central Bus Stand (☎08574/20300). Dilapidated rooms (some a/c with TV) with views over the bus stand. Veg food, and travel desk. US$ travellers' cheques accepted. ③–⑤.

PART THREE

THE

CONTEXTS

A BRIEF
HISTORY
OF INDIA

The earliest human activity in the Indian sub-continent can be traced back to the Early, Middle and Late Stone Ages (400,000–200,000 BC). Implements from all three periods have been found from Rajasthan and Gujarat in the west to Bihar in the east, from the northwest of what's now Pakistan to the tip of the penin-sula; and rock paintings of hunting scenes can be seen in the Narmada Valley and elsewhere in central India.

These Paleolithic peoples were semi-nomadic **hunters and gatherers** for many millennia. Indeed, some isolated hill tribes continued to be hunters and gatherers or to practice the transitional "slash and burn" type of agriculture into the twentieth century. Five main peoples are known to have been present when the move to an agricultural lifestyle took place, in the middle of the ninth millennium BC: The **Negrito** race, believed to be the earliest; the **Proto-Australoid**; the **Mediterranean** peoples; the **Mongoloid** elements (confined to the north and northeast); and the western **Brachycephals** or **Alpine** peoples.

The first evidence of **agricultural settle-ment**, at Mehrgarh on the western plains of the Indus, is roughly contemporaneous with similar developments in Egypt, Mesopotamia and Persia. Village settlements in western Afghanistan, Baluchistan and the Sind gradu-ally developed over the next five thousand years as their inhabitants began to use copper and bronze, domesticate animals, make pottery and trade with their western neighbours.

The distinct styles of pottery discovered at Nal and Zhob in the Brahui hills of Baluchistan, Kulli on the Makran coast and the lower Indus, and Amri in the Sind indicate the development of several independent cultures. **Terracotta figurines** of goddesses, bulls and phallic emblems echo the fertility cults and Mother Goddess worship found in early agricultural communities in the Mediterranean region and the Middle East; they also prefigure elements which were to re-emerge as aspects of the religious life of India.

THE FIRST GREAT INDIAN CIVILIZATION

From the start of the fourth millennium BC, the individuality of early village cultures began to be replaced by a more homogeneous style of pottery at a large number of sites throughout the **Indus Valley**; by the middle of the third millennium, a uniform culture had developed at settlements spread across nearly 500,000 square miles, including parts of the Punjab, Uttar Pradesh, Gujarat, Baluchistan, the Sind and the Makran coast. Two great cities on the Indus, **Harappa** in the north and **Mohenjo Daro** in the south, were supported by the agri-cultural surplus produced by such settlements. Recent archeological research has unearthed further sites, almost as large as the first two and designed on the same plan, at Kalibangan, on the border of India and Pakistan, at Kot Diji east of Mohenjo Daro, at Chanhu Daro further south on the Indus, and at Lothal in Gujarat.

The emergence of the first great Indian civili-zation, around 2500 BC, is almost as remarkable as its stability for nearly a thousand years. All the cities were built with baked bricks of the same size; the streets were laid out in a grid with an elaborate system of covered drains; and the houses, some with more than one storey, are large. Vast granaries and a citadel built on higher ground with a gigantic adjoining bath at Mohenjo Daro, together with the absence of royal palaces and the large numbers of religious figurines, suggest that it was a theocratic state of priests, merchants and farmers.

By now, farmers had domesticated various **animals**, including hump-backed (Brahmani) cattle, goats, water buffaloes and fowls. They cultivated wheat, barley, peas and sesamum, and were also probably the first to grow and make clothes from **cotton**. Excavations at Lothal have uncovered a **harbour**; merchants were certainly involved in extensive trading by both sea and land, for they imported metals, including gold, silver and copper, and semi-precious stones from the Indian peninsula, Persia, Afghanistan, central Asia and Mesopotamia. While the main export was probably cotton yarn or cloth, they may have exported surplus grain as well. Indus seals found at Ur confirm the continuity of trading links with Sumer between 2300 and 2000 BC.

The sheer quantity of **seals** discovered in the Indus cities suggests that each merchant or mercantile family had its own. They are usually square, and made of steatite (a kind of soapstone), engraved and then hardened by heating. All bear inscriptions, which remain undeciphered, although nearly 400 different characters have been identified. The emblems beneath the inscriptions – iconographic scenes and animals, such as the bull, buffalo, goat, tiger and elephant – are more enlightening. One of the most notable depicts a horned deity sitting cross-legged in an ithyphallic posture, surrounded by a tiger, an elephant, a rhinoceros, a water buffalo and two deer. He appears on two other seals, and it seems certain that he was a fertility god; indeed, he has been called a "**proto-Shiva**" because of the resemblance to Pashupati, the Lord of the Beasts, a major representation of the fully developed Hindu god, Shiva. Other seals provide evidence that certain trees, especially the *peepal*, were worshipped, and thus anticipate their sacred status in the Hindu and Buddhist religions.

No monumental sculpture survives, but large numbers of human figurines have been discovered, including a steatite bust of a man thought to be a priest, a striking bronze "dancing girl", brilliantly naturalistic models of animals, and countless terracotta statuettes of a Mother Goddess. This goddess is thought to have been worshipped in nearly every home of the common people, but the crude style of modelling suggests that she was not part of the cult of the priestly elite.

The sudden demise of the Indus civilization in the last quarter of the second millennium BC used to be explained by invasions of barbarian tribes from the northwest; but recent research has established that tectonic upheavals in about 1700 BC caused a series of floods, and these are now considered primarily to blame.

THE VEDIC AGE 1500–600 BC

The written history of India begins with the invasions of the charioteering **Indo-European** or **Aryan** tribes, which spelt the final collapse of the Indus civilization. This period takes its name from the earliest Indian literature, the *Vedas*, collections of hymns (*samhitas*) composed in Vedic Sanskrit. Though composed between 1500 and 1000 BC, the *Rig Veda* was not written down until as late as 900 or 800 BC. Although essentially a religious text, in use

to this day, it sheds great light on the social and political life of the period.

The Aryans belonged to the barbarian tribes, who broke out of the vast steppeland that stretches from Poland to central Asia to maraud and eventually colonize Europe, the Middle East and the Indian subcontinent from the start of the second millennium BC. They probably entered the Punjab via the Iranian plateau in successive waves over several hundred years; the peaceful farmers of the Indus would have been powerless against their horsedrawn chariots. Aryan culture was diametrically opposed to the Indus civilization, and Vedic literature relates how their war god, Indra, destroyed hundreds of urban settlements.

Semi-nomadic hunters and pastoralists when they first settled the region known as the *Sapta-Sindu* or seven "Induses", from Kabul to the desert of Rajasthan, as the Aryans spread eastwards into the plain between the upper Ganges and the Yamuna, known as the Doab, they adopted the techniques of settled farming from the peoples they had conquered. The tribes began to organize themselves into village communities, governed by tribal councils (*sabha* and *samiti*) and warrior chiefs (*raja*), who offered protection in return for tribute; the sacrifices of the chief priest or *purohita* secured their prosperity and martial success.

The hymns describe the inter-tribal conflicts characteristic of the period, but there was an underlying sense of solidarity against the indigenous peoples, known as Dasas. Originally a general term for "enemies", it came to denote "subjects" as they were colonized within the land of the Aryans (*aryavarta*). The Dasas are described as negroid phallus worshippers, who owned many cattle and lived in fortified towns or villages (*pur*). The Aryans began to emphasize the purity of blood as they settled among the darker aboriginals, and their original class divisions of nobility and ordinary tribesmen were hardened to exclude the Dasas. At the same time, the priests, the sole custodians and extrapolators of the increasingly complex oral traditions of the sacrificial religion, began to claim high privileges for their skill and training.

By 1000 BC, a fourfold division of society had been given religious sanction in a hymn, which describes how the four classes (**varna**, literally "colour") emanated from the mouth, arms, thighs and feet of the primeval man (*purusha*). The *varna* of priest, warrior, peasant and serf (*brahmin, kshatrya, vaishya* and *shudra*) have persisted as the fundamental structure of society to the present day. The first three encompassed the main divisions within the Aryan tribes, which later assumed the status of "twice-born" (*dvija*); the Dasas and other non-Aryan peoples became the *shudras*, who served the three higher classes.

During the later Vedic period, between 1000 and 600 BC, the centre of Aryan culture and power shifted from the Punjab and the north-west to the Doab, whence their influence continued to spread eastwards and southwards. The sacred texts of the *Sama, Yajur* and *Atharva Vedas*, the *Brahmanas* and the *Upanishads* all originate in this period. Like the *Rig Veda*, they tell us much about developments in religious life, but only offer glimpses of the Aryanization of the subcontinent.

One of the *Brahmanas* relates how Agni, the Aryan fire-god, travelled eastwards destroying the jungle until his advance was arrested by the River Gandak. The Aryans refused to cross the river because Agni had not purified the land beyond until the fire-god ordered a warrior called Videgha Mathava to transport him across the river. The story provides an insight into how colonization occurred, both in terms of the gradual progress eastward of Aryan culture, represented by the fire-god, and of the manner in which the jungle was cleared as the migrating tribes established new settlements.

The great epic poems, the **Mahabharata** and the **Ramayana**, and the *Puranas* claim to relate to this period. Though they are unreliable as historical sources, being overlaid with accretions from later centuries, it is possible to extract some of the facts entwined with the martial myths and legends.

The great battle of **Kurukshetra** – the central theme of the *Mahabharata* – is certainly historical, and took place near modern Delhi some time between the ninth and eighth centuries BC. It was the culmination of a dynastic dispute among the Kurus, who, with their neighbours the Panchalas, were the greatest of the Aryan tribes. Archeological evidence has been found of the two main settlements mentioned in

The account of **Hinduism** on p.1117 includes more about the *Mahabharata*, the *Ramayana*, and the development of caste divisions.

the epic, Indraprastha (Delhi) and Hastinapura, further north on the Ganges; the latter was the capital of the Kurus, two of whose kings, Parikshit and Janamejaya, are described as mighty conquerors in the Vedic literature.

By the time of Kurukshetra, the Aryans had advanced into the mid-Gangetic valley to establish **Kosala**, with its capital at **Ayodhya** – according to the *Ramayana*, the realm of Rama, the god-hero. Vedic literature mentions neither Rama nor his father Dasharatha, but does refer to Rama's father-in-law, Janaka of Videha. Certainly the extension of Aryan influence to south India, reflected in the myth of Rama's invasion of Sri Lanka to rescue Sita, did not occur until much later. At this time, the megalithic cultures of Madras, Kerala and Mysore remained untouched by the Aryan invaders. The Aryanization of north India, however, continued throughout the period, and began to penetrate central India as well.

The migrating tribes pushed east beyond Kosala to found the kingdoms of **Kashi** (the region of Varanasi), **Videha** (east of the River Gandak and north of the Ganges), and **Anga** on the border of Bengal. The **Yadava** tribe settled around Mathura, on the Yamuna; a branch of the Yadavas is said later to have colonized Saurashtra in modern Gujarat. Further east, down the Yamuna, the **Vatsa** kingdom established its capital at Kaushambi. Other tribes pushed southwards down the River Chambal to found the kingdom of **Avanti**; some penetrated as far as the Narmada, and by the end of the period Aryan influence probably extended into the northwest Deccan.

This territorial expansion was assisted by significant developments in Aryan civilization. When they arrived in India Aryan knowledge of **metallurgy** was limited to gold, copper and bronze, but later Vedic literature mentions tin, lead, silver and iron. The use of iron, together with the taming of elephants, facilitated the rapid clearance of the forests and jungles for settlement. They now grew a large range of crops, including rice; specialized trades and crafts grew considerably, and merchants re-established trade with Mesopotamia, curtailed since the days of the Indus civilization.

Vedic culture and society was transformed by mutual acculturation between the Aryans and indigenous peoples. By the end of the Vedic period, the Aryan tribes had consolidated into little kingdoms, each with its capital city. Some were republics, but generally the power of the tribal assemblies was dwindling, to be replaced by a new kind of politics centred on a **king**, who ruled a geographical area. His relatives and courtiers formed a rudimentary administrative system – known as "Jewel Bearers" (*ratnins*), they included the chief priest, the chamberlain and palace officials.

Kingship was becoming more absolute, limited only by the influence of the priesthood; a relationship between temporal and sacred power that became crucial. The *Brahmana* literature, compiled by the priests, contains instructions for the performance of sacrifices symbolizing royal power, such as the royal consecration ceremonies (*rajasuya*) and the horse sacrifice (*ashvamedha*). Thus, the priests sustained belief in the association of kingship with divinity through their rituals and assisted new political institutions to emerge.

Not all religious specialists were committed to these political developments, and the evolution of Aryan civilization in the late Vedic period also involved a degree of introspection and pessimism. The disintegration of tribal identity created a profound sense of insecurity, which combined with doubts as to the efficacy of sacrificial rituals led to the emergence of non-conformists and ascetics. Their teachings were set down in the metaphysical literature of the *Upanishads* and the *Aranyakas*, which laid the foundations for the various philosophical systems developed in later periods.

THE AGE OF THE BUDDHA 600–321 BC

The age of the Buddha was marked by great intellectual endeavour and spiritual agitation. Though mystics and ascetics rejected the norms of Vedic society, major political and commercial developments continued; the emergence of kingdoms and administrative systems encouraged rulers to think in terms of empire.

By 600 BC, the association of tribes with the territories they had colonized had resulted in the consolidation of at least sixteen republics and monarchies, known as ***mahajanapadas*** (territories of the great clans). Some, like **Kuru** and **Panchala**, represented the oldest and earliest established kingdoms; others, like **Avanti**, **Vatsa** and **Magadha** had come into existence more recently. The hereditary principle and the concept of divinely ordained kings, tended to preserve the status quo in the monarchies, while the republics provided an atmosphere in which unorthodox views were able to develop. The founders of the "heterodox" sects of Buddhism and Jainism were both born in small republics of this kind (see pp.1124 & 1126).

The consolidation of the *mahajanapadas* was based on the growth of a stable agrarian economy and the increasing importance of **trade**, which led to the use of coins and a script (Brahmi, from which the current scripts of India, Sri Lanka, Tibet, Java and Burma derive) and encouraged the emergence of towns, such as Kashi (Varanasi), Ayodhya, Rajagriha (first capital of Magadha), Kaushambi in the Ganges Valley, and Ujjain on the Narmada. The resultant prosperity stimulated conflict, however, and by the fifth century BC the four great kingdoms of Kashi, Koshala, Vatsa and Magadha and the republic of the Vrijjis between them held sway over all the others.

Eventually, **Magadha** emerged supreme, under Bimbisara (543–491 BC), a resolute and energetic organizer, and Ajatashatru (491–461 BC), who conquered Kashi and Koshala, broke up the Vrijji confederacy, and built a strong administration. Both kings set out to control the trade of the Ganges Valley and its rich deposits of copper and iron.

Magadha expanded over the next hundred years, moving its capital to **Pataliputra** (Patna) and annihilating the other kingdoms in the Ganges Valley or reducing them to the status of vassals. In the middle of the fourth century BC, the **Nanda** dynasty usurped the Magadhan throne; Mahapadma Nanda conquered Kalinga (Orissa and the northern coastal strip of Andhra Pradesh) and gained control of parts of the Deccan. The disputed succession after his death coincided with significant events in the northwest; out of this confusion the first and perhaps greatest of India's empires was born.

Darius I, the third Achaemenid emperor of Persia, had claimed Gandhara in the northwest as his twentieth satrapy, and advanced into the Punjab near the end of the sixth century BC; but a second invasion in the fourth century BC was more significant. **Alexander the Great** defeated Darius III, the last Achaemenid, crossed the Indus in 326 BC, and overran the Punjab. He was in India for just two years and although he left garrisons and appointed satraps to govern the conquered territories, his death in 323 BC made their position untenable. Chandragupta Maurya was quick to take advantage of the political vacuum.

THE MAURYAN EMPIRE
321–104 BC

The accession to the throne of **Chandragupta Maurya**, who overthrew the last of the Nanda dynasty of Magadhan about 321 BC, marked the beginnings of the first Indian empire. He is said to have met Alexander the Great and was probably inspired by his exploits; his 500,000-strong army drove out the Greek garrisons in the northwest, and annexed all the lands east of the Indus. When Seleucus Nicator, Alexander's general, attempted to regain control of Macedonian provinces in India, Chandragupta defeated him and forced the surrender of territories in what is now Afghanistan as a reward.

According to tradition, Chandragupta was assisted by an unscrupulous *brahmin* adviser called Kautilya or Chanakya, the reputed author of the *Arthashastra*, a famous treatise on political economy. The Mauryan empire developed a highly bureaucratic state administration, which controlled economic life and employed a very thorough secret service system. From about 297 BC onwards, Chandragupta's son Bindusara extended the empire as far south as Mysore.

Bindusara was succeeded in around 269 BC by his son, **Ashoka** – the noblest ruler of India, whom the Buddhists called a universal emperor (*chakravartin*). Ashoka's political pragmatism and imperial vision, complemented by his humanity, practical benevolence and tolerance, mark him out as a statesman and a reformer far

ahead of his times. He ruthlessly consolidated his power for the first eight years of his reign, before invading and subduing the tribal kingdom of Kalinga (Orissa), his only campaign of violent conquest, in 260 BC. Two and a half years later, his conversion to **Buddhism** caused Ashoka to espouse non-violence (*ahimsa*), and consequently to abandon territorial aggression in favour of conquest by the **Law of Righteousness** (*dharma*). The fourteen **edicts** in which he laid down its principles were engraved in the Brahmi script on eighteen great rocks and thirty polished sandstone pillars throughout the empire.

Ashoka sought to neutralize the regional pluralism within the empire by his proclamation of the *dharma*, a code of conduct designed to counteract the social tensions created by the *varna* distinctions of class, sectarian conflicts and economic differences. It inculcated social responsibility, encouraged socio-religious harmony, sought to ensure human dignity and expressed a paternal concern for his subjects' well-being and happiness. His social reforms included the restriction of animal slaughter and the prohibition of animal sacrifices in Pataliputra, which encouraged vegetarianism; the cultivation of medicinal herbs and the establishment of healing centres. The system of communications was improved by planting roadside fruit trees and by the construction of wells and rest houses. He also replaced the annual royal hunt with a pilgrimage of righteousness (*dharma yatra*), which gave him the opportunity to visit the distant corners of the empire personally and exhibit himself as the living symbol of imperial unity.

THE EDICTS OF ASHOKA

Edict 1 denounces animal slaughter for sacrifices and festivities, and details the reduced consumption by the royal household from hundreds of beasts to only two peacocks and one deer per day.

Edict 2 records the import and cultivation of herbs, roots and fruits for the treatment of humans and animals, and the building of highways and wells.

Edict 3 instructs *Mahamatras* ("Officers of Righteousness") to carry out *dharma*.

Edict 4 embellishes Edict 3.

Edict 5 requests Ashoka's subjects to aid the families of prisoners and wean criminals away from evil.

Edict 6 says Ashoka is available for council at any time.

Edict 7 recommends self-control and purity of thought so that religious sects may live in harmony.

Edict 8 tells of Ashoka's pilgrimages and acts of charity.

Edict 9 encourages the practice of *dharma* in place of superstitious rites.

Edict 10 praises the modesty brought about by *dharma*, and denounces fame and glory.

Edict 11 propounds the beneficial results of *dharma*.

Edict 12 advises *Mahamatras* to expound the principles of all religions.

Edict 13 apologizes for the devastation at Kalinga.

Edict 14 summarizes the previous thirteen.

His adoption of Buddhism and this new ethical system, however, did not interfere with his imperial pragmatism, and despite his avowed remorse after the Kalinga campaign he continued to govern the newly acquired territory, retained his army without reduction and warned the wilder tribesmen that he would use force to subjugate them if they continued to raid the civilized villages of the empire.

Ashoka's empire extended from Assam to Afghanistan and from Kashmir to Mysore; only the three Dravidian kingdoms of the Cholas, Cheras and Pandyas in the southernmost tip of the subcontinent remained independent. Diplomatic relations were maintained with Syria, Egypt, Macedonia and Cyrene, and all the states on the immediate borders. The Mauryan empire was built on military conquest and a centralized administration – its well-organized revenue department ensured a strong fiscal base – but Ashoka's imperial vision, his shrewdness, and above all the force of his personality and the loyalty he inspired, held it all together.

After Ashoka's death in 232 BC, the empire began to fall apart. While princes contested the throne, the provincial governors established their independence. Inter-regional rivalries and further invasions from central Asia exacerbated matters, and in 184 BC the last of the Mauryans, Brihadratha, was assassinated by his *brahmin* general, Pushyamitra Shunga. The Mauryans had ruled India for nearly 140 years; Ashoka's importance was recognized more than two thousand years later, when Nehru adopted the lion capital of his Sarnath pillar as the emblem of the newly independent India.

THE AGE OF INVASIONS
104 BC–320 AD

Although economic prosperity and cultural enrichment endured for five hundred years after the death of Ashoka, India became politically fragmented. Successive invasions, and the emergence of regional monarchies in the south, reduced Magadha to one of many quasi-feudal kingdoms struggling for regional power.

The dynasty founded by Pushyamitra Shunga ruled Magadha until 72 BC, when the last Shunga monarch was deposed by his servant Vasudeva Kanva. Pushyamitra was an orthodox *brahmin*, but Buddhism continued to be generously patronized; elaborate stone *stupas* were erected at Sanchi and Bharhur

during Shunga times. Magadha still included Bengal, Bhopal and Malwa within its boundaries, though the Punjab and the northwestern territories had been lost.

The Bactrian Greeks, who had asserted their independence from the Seleucids of Syria and recaptured Gandhara (the Peshawar region of Pakistan) in 190 BC, were the first invaders. When the Mauryan empire collapsed, the Indo-Greek rulers occupied the Punjab and extended their control as far as Mathura in Uttar Pradesh. One Indo-Greek king, Milinda or Menander, who ruled the Swat Valley and the Punjab from Sagala (Sialkot) between 155 and 130 BC, became famous for his conversion to Buddhism by the philosopher Nagasena. Another example of acculturation is found on the Garuda pillar at Besnagar (Bhilsa), by Heliodorus, the Greek envoy to the Shunga court, to commemorate the Bactrian conquests of northwestern India. Its inscription proclaimed Heliodorus to be a worshipper of Vasudeva, a god later identified with Krishna, the Lord of the *Bhagavad Gita*.

The next wave of invasions, in the second century BC, saw Parthians (Pahlavas) from Iran take control of Bactria. Soon large-scale movements of central Asian Yueh-Chi nomads had precipitated the migration of the Scythians (Shakas), who displaced the Parthians. During the first century AD, the Kushan branch of the Yueh-Chi in turn drove the Shakas out of northwestern India into Gujarat and Malwa around Ujjain, where they settled and became Indianized, while Kujula Kadphises established the **Kushan** dynasty in the northwest.

The third and greatest of the Kushan kings, **Kanishka**, who reigned for more than twenty years around 100 AD, extended his rule as far east as Varanasi and as far south as Sanchi. Kanishka's empire prospered through control of trade routes between India, China and the west, and his court attracted artists and musicians as well as merchants. Ashvaghosha, one of the first classical Sanskrit poets, wrote a Life of the Buddha (*Buddha Charita*) and is credited with converting the emperor to Buddhism.

While the tribal republics of northern and central India absorbed invaders from the northwest, the kingdoms of Ayodhya and Kaushambi continued to be important in the Gangetic valley; but the first great kingdom of southern India was flexing its muscles. Between the second century BC and the second century AD the **Andhra** or **Satavahana** dynasty, which originated in the region between the rivers Godavari and Krishna, spread its control across much of south and central India.

Having unsuccessfully challenged the Shakas in Malwa and Gujarat, they brought the northwest Deccan under their control and created a capital at Paithan on the Godavari, northeast of Pune in Maharashtra. The Satavahanas overthrew the Kanva dynasty of Magadha in 27 BC and pushed south to the Tungabhadra and Krishna rivers. Their second capital, at **Amaravati** on the Krishna, prospered on trade with Rome and southeast Asia, but by the middle of the third century the Satavahana kingdom had collapsed. The Pallavas took control of their territories in Andhra Pradesh, while the Vakatakas gained supremacy in the central and northwestern regions of the Deccan in the latter half of the third century, only to be subsumed within the Gupta empire by the end of the fourth century.

Further south, the three kingdoms of the **Cheras** on the Malabar coast in the west, the **Pandyas** in the central southern tip of the peninsula, and the **Cholas** on the east coast of Coromandel – together comprising much of present-day Tamil Nadu and Kerala – had been developing almost completely independently of north India. **Madurai**, the Pandyan capital, and still one of the major temple cities of the south, had become a centre of Tamil culture. Between 300 BC and 200 AD, colleges or academies (**sangam**) of poets produced a body of literature which describes an indigenous Tamil culture and society only gradually being influenced by the Aryan traditions of the north. The early kingdoms were matriarchal, and the Dravidian kinship system was endogamous, being based on cross-cousin marriage, in sharp contrast to the Indo-Aryan system of exogamy, which prescribed marriage to outsiders. Society was divided into groups based on the geographical domains of hills, plains, forest, coast and desert rather than class or *varna*, although *brahmins* did command high status. Although agriculture, pastoralism and fishing were the main occupations, trade in spices, gold and jewels with Rome and southeast Asia underpinned the region's prosperity.

The three kingdoms initially balanced individual struggles for political hegemony with alliances to withstand the aggression of their northern neighbours; but after the middle of the first century BC conflicts between themselves became more frequent. This enervating warfare rendered them vulnerable; early in the fourth century AD, the **Pallavas** overran the Chola capital of Kanchipuram, and by 325 AD they were in control of Tamil Nadu. The Pallavas remained a dominant power in the south until the ninth century AD, and thus became one of the longest ruling dynasties in Indian history.

Despite the disintegration of the Mauryan empire and the proliferation of fiercely rival kingdoms from 200 BC to 300 AD, this was also a period of unprecedented economic wealth and cultural development. The growing importance of the mercantile community encouraged the monetization of the economy and stimulated the growth of urban centres all over India. Merchants and artisans organized themselves into guilds (*shreni*), which along with the ruling dynasties, minted their own coins.

External **trade**, overland and maritime, opened up lines of communication with the outside world. The main highway from Pataliputra to Taxila gave India access to the old **Silk Road**, the most important trade route of the time, linking China to the Mediterranean via central Asia. Maritime trade traversed the coastal routes between the seaports in Gujarat and southern India and as far as south Arabia; and Indian merchants established trading communities in various parts of south Asia.

The invasion of foreign peoples, the growth of trade and urbanization together had a considerable impact on the structure of society. Foreign conquerors and traders, who had to be integrated within the *varna* system; the burgeoning importance of the *vaishya* class of merchants and artisans, and the influence of urban liberalism, all presented serious challenges to law and social order. The Law Books (*Dharmashastras*) were composed in this period in an attempt to accommodate these changes and redefine social, economic and legal rights and duties. Important developments in India's religions can also be linked to socio-economic changes. Radical schisms occurred in both Buddhism and Jainism, and may be attributed to the increasing participation and patronage of the *vaishyas*; while the Vedic religion, which had been the exclusive domain of the *brahmins* and *kshatryas*, underwent fundamental transformations to widen its social base.

THE CLASSICAL AGE
300–650 AD

The era of the imperial Guptas (320–550 AD) and the reign of Harsha Vardhana (606–647 AD) of Kanauj, during which north India was re-unified, comprises the **Classical Age** of Indian history.

Chandra Gupta I (no relation to the Mauryan Guptas) struck coins in 320 AD to celebrate his coronation and marriage to Princess Kumaradevi of the Licchavi tribe, which had re-established itself in the neighbouring territory of Vaishali, north of the Ganges. Chandra Gupta I thus established a powerful kingdom, centred on Magadha, Koshala and Ayodhya, in the Gangetic plain, which controlled the vital east–west trade route, and claimed the title of Great King of Kings (*maharajadhiraja*).

His son and heir, Samudra Gupta (*c.*335–376 AD), expanded the frontiers of the realm from Punjab to Assam; an inscription in Allahabad claimed that he "violently uprooted" nine kings of northern India, humbled eleven more in the south and compelled another five to pay tribute as feudatories. The martial tribes of Rajasthan and the Shakas, who had ruled Malwa and Gujarat for over two hundred years, never did more than pay homage; but Samudra had built the foundations for the second largest empire in pre-medieval India, which reached its apogee under his successor.

Chandra Gupta II (376–415 AD) finally subjugated the Shakas in Gujarat to secure access to the trade of the western coast at the end of the fourth century AD, and re-unified the whole of northern India, with the exception of the northwest. He extended his influence by marrying Kuvera, a queen of the Nagas, and marrying his daughter Prabhavati to Rudrasena II of the Vakatakas, whose kingdom included parts of modern Madhya Pradesh, Maharashtra and northwestern Andhra Pradesh.

Fa Hsien, a Chinese Buddhist monk who visited India during the reign of Chandra Gupta II, noted the palaces and free hospitals of Pataliputra and the fact that all respectable Indians were vegetarian. He also mentions discrimination against the untouchables, who carried gongs to warn passers-by of their polluting presence; but generally, he describes the empire as prosperous, happy and peaceful. The Guptas performed Vedic sacrifices to legiti-mize their rule, and patronized popular forms of Hinduism, such as devotional religion (*bhakti*) and the worship of images of Vishnu, Shiva and the Goddess in temples, which were crystallizing during the period; but Buddhism continued to thrive and Fa Hsein mentions thousands of monks dwelling at Mathura as well as hundreds in Pataliputra itself.

Patronage of art and literature under the Guptas facilitated the development of a classical idiom that became the exemplar for subsequent creative endeavours. Secular **Sanskrit literature** reached its perfection in the works of Kalidasa, the greatest Indian poet and dramatist, who was a member of Chandra Gupta II's court. The cave paintings of **Ajanta** and **Ellora** inspired Buddhist artists throughout Asia, and Yashodhara's detailed analysis of painting in the fifth century prescribed the classical conventions for the new art form. In **sculpture**, the images of the Buddha produced in Sarnath and Mathura embodied the simple and serene quality of classicism; but there were also the voluptuous mother goddesses of Hinduism.

The formative stages of the northern style of **Hindu temple**, which became India's classic architectural form, also occurred in this era; a fine example survives at **Deogarh**, near Jhansi in central India. Early Hindu temples were comparatively small and simple; an inner sanctuary (*garbha griha*) housing the deity was connected to a larger hall (*mandapa*), where the devotees could congregate to worship. This prototype of the northern Hindu temple persisted from Gupta times to the present day, but these humble origins subsequently evolved into extravagantly ornate structures.

The era of the Guptas produced great thinkers as well: six systems of **philosophy** (*Nyaya, Vaisheshika, Sankhya, Yoga, Mimamsa* and *Vedanta*) evolved, which refuted Buddhism and Jainism. **Vedanta** has continued as the basis of all philosophical studies in India to this day. In the fifth century, the great **astronomer**, Aryabhata, argued that the earth rotated on its own axis while revolving around the sun, and his terse commentary on an anonymous mathematical text assumes an understanding of the decimal system of nine digits and a zero, with place notation for tens and hundreds. The Arabs acknowledged their debt to the "Indian art" of mathematics; and many western European discoveries and inventions would have been impossible if they had remained encumbered by the Roman system of numerals.

Though the Gupta empire remained relatively peaceful during the long reign of Kumara Gupta, who succeeded Chandra Gupta II, by the time Skanda Gupta came to the throne in 454 AD, western India was again threatened by invasions from Central Asia. Skanda managed to repel White Hun raids, but after his death their disruption of central Asian trade seriously destabilized the empire. By the end of the fifth century, the Huns had wrested the Punjab from Gupta control, and further incursions early in the sixth century were the death blow to the empire, which had completely disintegrated by 550 AD. In the sixth century another wave of central Asian tribes, including the Gurjaras, displaced the older tribes in Rajasthan and became the founders of the **Rajput** dynasties.

After the demise of the Guptas, northern India again split into rival kingdoms; but the Pushpabhutis of Sthanvishvara (Thanesvar, north of Delhi) had established supremacy by the time **Harsha Vardhana** came to the throne in 606 AD. He reigned for 41 years over an empire that ranged from Gujarat to Bengal, including the Punjab, Kashmir and Nepal, and moved his capital to **Kanauj** in the wake of his eastern conquests. Even the king of Assam acknowledged his influence, but his attempts to advance into the Deccan were emphatically repulsed by Pulakeshin II of the Chalukyas. Harsha possessed considerable gifts as well as untiring energy; in addition to his martial achievements and ceaseless touring, he wrote three dramas and found time to indulge a love of philosophy and literature. The life of Harsha (*Harshacharita*) by Bana, his court poet, is the first historically authentic Indian biography.

Harsha's empire was essentially feudal, with most of the defeated kings retaining their thrones as vassals, and when he died without heirs in 647 AD north India once again fragmented into independent kingdoms.

KINGDOMS OF CENTRAL AND SOUTH INDIA 500–1250 AD

After the collapse of Harsha's empire, significant events took place in the Deccan and Tamil Nadu. Aryan influences were assimilated into Dravidian culture throughout the era of the **Pallavas**, which began when they captured Kanchipuram early in the fourth century and

lasted until they were overthrown by a revived Chola dynasty in the ninth century. The upper strata of society increasingly adopted Aryan ideas, but as the indigenous culture reacted to assert itself among the lower strata, a distinctive Tamil culture emerged from the synthesis.

The history of the period was dominated by conflicts between three major kingdoms. The **Pandyas** of Madurai had their own regional kingdom by the sixth century; the **Chalukyas** of Vatapi (Badami in Mysore) had expanded their kingdom into the Deccan when the Vakataka dynasty collapsed in the middle of the sixth century; and the **Pallavas** had supplanted the Satavahanas in the Andhra region and made Kanchipuram their capital.

Under Mahendravarman I, a contemporary of Harsha at the start of the seventh century, the Pallavas came into conflict with the Chalukyas over the region of Vengi in the Krishna-Godavari valley. They remained at war until the middle of the eighth century, intermittently harassed by the Pandyas further south. Both the Pallavas and the Chalukyas enlisted the support of other kingdoms at different times during the protracted struggle – the **Cheras** of Kerala, who made alliances with both sides, avoided direct involvement in the conflict – but their military strength was so evenly matched that neither was able to gain the ascendancy. Eventually the Chalukya dynasty was overthrown in 753 by a feudatory, Dantidurga, the founder of the Rashtrakuta kingdom. The Pallavas survived their arch enemies by about a hundred years, then succumbed to a combined attack of the Pandyas and the Cholas.

The **Rashtrakutas** exploited the instability in the north by attempts to capture the trade routes of the Ganges Valley, and Indra III gained possession of Kanauj for a brief period, but ultimately the campaigns drained the kingdom's resources.

Meanwhile, the **Cholas** were on the ascendant in Tamil Nadu; they conquered the region of Thanjavur in the ninth century, and Parantaka I, who came to power in 907 AD, captured Madurai from the Pandyas. The Rashtrakutas defeated the Cholas in the middle of the tenth century, but when they were replaced by the revived "Later" Chalukyas in 973 AD the Cholas were able to regain their lost territories, and expand further during the eleventh and twelfth centuries.

Rajaraja I campaigned against the allied powers of Kerala, Ceylon and the Pandyas to break their control of western trade and combat competition from the Arab traders, who were supported by Kerala. **Rajendra I**, who succeeded his father in 1014 AD, annexed the southern territories of the Chalukyas, renewing the campaigns against Kerala and Ceylon, and initiating a northern offensive, which reached the banks of the Ganges. Rajendra did not hold his northern conquests for long, but was successful in protecting Indian commercial interests in southeast Asia.

By the end of the eleventh century the Cholas were supreme in the south, but incessant campaigning had exhausted their resources. Ironically, their destruction of the Chalukyas laid the seeds of their own downfall. Former Chalukya feudatories, such as the **Yadavas** of Devagiri in the northern Deccan and the **Hoysalas**, around modern Mysore, set up their own kingdoms; the latter attacked the Cholas from the west while the Pandyas directed a new offensive from the south. By the thirteenth century, the **Pandyas** had superseded the Cholas as south India's major power; the Yadavas and the Hoysalas controlled the Deccan until the advent of the Turkish Sultans of Delhi in the fourteenth century.

Despite constant political conflicts this period was very much the classical age of the south. The ascendancy of the Cholas was complemented by the crystallization of Tamil culture; the religious, artistic, and institutional patterns of this period dominated the culture of the south and influenced developments elsewhere in the peninsula. In the sphere of religion for instance, the great philosophers **Shankara** and Ramanuja, as well as the Tamil and Maharashtran saints, had a significant impact on Hinduism in north India.

REGIONAL KINGDOMS IN NORTH INDIA 650–1250 AD

In north India, Harsha's death was followed by a century of confusion, with assorted kingdoms competing to control the Gangetic valley. In time, the **Pratiharas**, descendants of the Rajasthani Gurjaras, and the **Palas** of Bihar and Bengal emerged as the main rivals.

The Pala king Dharmapala (770–810) was the first to gain the initiative, by taking Kanauj; however, the Pratiharas wrested it back soon after his death. They remained in the ascendant during the ninth century, but were weakened by repeated incursions from the Deccan by the **Rashtrakutas**, who briefly occupied Kanauj in 916. The Pratiharas regained their capital, but the tripartite struggle sapped their strength and they were unable to repel the Turkish invasion of Kanauj in 1018. At the start of the eleventh century the Palas again pushed west as far as Varanasi, but had to abandon the campaign to defend their homelands in Bengal against the Chola king Rajendra.

The struggle for possession of Kanauj depleted the resources of the three competing powers and resulted in their almost simultaneous decline. In northern India, just as in the south, the tendency of feudatories of large kingdoms to assert their independence brought several small states into being. Kingdoms such as Nepal, Kamarupa (Assam), Kashmir, Orissa, the eastern Chalukyas and the Gangas of the east coast developed their own cultural identities. Regional histories and dynastic genealogies were written, local customs and literature were patronized, and the kingdoms competed to outdo each other in building temples.

In **Orissa**, small kingdoms in the Mahanadi and Brahmani valleys had co-existed for nearly five hundred years when the Somavamshi dynasty united western and central Orissa in the eleventh century, and established its capital at **Bhubaneshwar**. The temples they constructed demonstrate a notable continuity from the earliest days in the eighth century, to the magnificent Lingaraja temple, dated around 1000 AD. The royal cult of Jagannath (Vishnu), with its "juggernaut" car festival and the gigantic temple at **Puri** were cultural manifestations of the political unification completed by the eastern Gangas of Kalinga in the twelfth century. The stunning chariot temple dedicated to the sun god Surya at **Konarak** in the thirteenth century represents the aesthetic climax of these regional developments.

The **Rajputs**, so influential in the culture and politics of medieval India, were descended from the sixth-century central Asian invaders. They attained respectability in keeping with the Puranic traditions by acquiring solar or lunar genealogies and adopting *kshatrya* status. By the tenth century, the most important clans, like the Parihares (a branch of the Pratiharas) of south Rajasthan, the Chamanas or Chauhans of

Shakambhari and Ajmer, and the Chaulukyas or Solankis of Kathiawar, had all established regional kingdoms. Rajput clans in western and central India, included the **Chandellas** of Bundelkhand, who produced the magnificent group of temples at **Khajuraho**, the Guhilas of Chittaurgarh, the Tomaras in Haryana, and the Kalachuris of Tripuri near Jabalpur.

The Rajputs fought among each other incessantly, however, and failed to grasp the significance of a new factor, which entered the politics of north India at the start of the eleventh century. **Mahmud**, a Turkish chieftain who had established a powerful kingdom at Ghazni in Afghanistan, made seventeen plundering raids into the plains of India between 1000 and 1027. Mathura, Thanesvar, Kanauj and Somnath in Saurashtra were all looted to enhance the greatness of Ghazni and only the astuteness of the Chandellas of Bundelkhand, who agreed to pay tribute, saved the temples of Khajuraho from destruction.

The three most powerful Rajputs of northern India, Prithviraja Chamana, Jahacchandra Gahadavala and Paramardideva Chandella, were in a state of three-way war when Muhammad of Ghur supplanted the line of Mahmud, seized the Ghaznavid possessions in the Punjab at the end of the twelfth century, and focussed his attention on the wealthy lands further east. **Prithviraja III**, the legendary hero of the Chauhans, patched together an alliance to defeat the Turkish warlord at **Tarain** (near Thanesvar) in 1191; but Muhammad returned the next year with a superior force, defeated the Rajputs, and had Prithviraja executed. Muhammad went home, leaving his generals to complete the conquest and establish what became known as the **Slave Dynasty**.

THE DELHI SULTANATE 1206–1526 AD

The **Delhi Sultanate** was to be the major political force in north India from the thirteenth to the sixteenth century, its power and territories fluctuating with the abilities of successive rulers. Although it never succeeded in welding together an all-India empire, the impact of Islam on Indian culture reverberated for centuries throughout the subcontinent.

Muhammad was assassinated in 1206 within a few years of his return to Ghur. His empire disintegrated, to leave his Turkish slave general, **Qutb-ud-din-Aiback**, as the autonomous ruler of the Indian territories and founder of the first "slave dynasty" of the Sultanate. Aiback died four years later – before the Qutb Minar, his victory tower, in Delhi could be completed – and his son-in-law **Iltutmish** (1211–36) inherited the task of securing the Sultanate's tenuous hold on northern India. When Genghis Khan annihilated the world from which the ancestors of Iltutmish had come, it gave him an added incentive to consolidate his power base in India. Iltutmish had extended the Sultanate's territories from the Sind to Bengal by the time he died in 1236, but the subsequent three decades were critical. His daughter, Sultana Raziyya, succeeded but was murdered in 1240, and not until Balaban, Raziyya's chief huntsman and member of her father's palace guard, took control in 1266 did the Sultanate attain any degree of stability.

Meanwhile, the **Mongols** had returned in 1241. Although internecine strife within the Mongol empire from 1260–61 offered a temporary reprieve, the accession of the Khalji dynasty in 1290 coincided with a renewed threat from the Chaghatai Mongols. Their raids extended beyond the Punjab and even laid siege to Delhi for two months in 1303. Nevertheless, **Ala-ud-din-Khalji** (1296–1315) energetically enforced Islamic rule over the autonomous Hindu states, which were a constant source of aggravation. Having conquered Gujarat and the Rajput fortresses of Ranthambor, Chittaurgarh, Sevana and Jalor in a series of expeditions between 1299 and 1311, he turned his attention to the Deccan and the south where he exacted tribute from the Yadavas of Devagiri, the Kakatiyas of Telengana, and the Pandyas. His aspirations to build a stable empire were dashed, however, when Gujarat, Chittaurgarh and Devagiri all reasserted their independence before his death in 1315.

A fresh imperial impetus came from the **Tughluq** dynasty, which succeeded the Khaljis in 1320. Under **Muhammad bin Tughluq** (1325–51), the Sultanate reached its maximum extent, comparable in size to Ashoka's empire. Unfortunately, Muhammad weakened the empire by his attempts to finance his ambitions. He provoked a peasant uprising in the Doab by increasing the revenue demand to pay for an expedition to Khurasan in central Asia, and later tried to introduce a token currency to pay the troops, which had to be withdrawn. He then made a controversial and abortive attempt to relocate his capital in a more central position at Devagiri (renamed Daulatabad) in the Deccan. Revolts signalled the first phase in the collapse of the Delhi Sultanate: Malabar, Bengal and Telengana all seceded between 1334 and 1339. The Bahmani dynasty became the autonomous rulers of the Deccan in 1347, and the new Hindu kingdom of **Vijayanagar** took advantage of the decline of the Sultanate's authority to extend its influence. From its capital near Hampi, Vijayanagar dominated the region south of the Krishna and Tungabhadra rivers between the middle of the fourteenth century and 1565, when an alliance of Muslim kingdoms brought it down.

Firoz Shah Tughluq (1351–88), who re-established the capital at Delhi, stemmed the tide to some extent with the comparative mildness of his rule. He is credited with an impressive list of public works, including the building of mosques, colleges, reservoirs, hospitals, public baths, bridges and towns – especially **Jaunpur**, near Varanasi, which became a major centre of Islamic culture. However, by reverting to a decentralized administrative system he fostered the rise of semi-independent warlords, who became increasingly antagonistic under the last of the Tughluqs.

Family squabbles over the throne after Firoz Shah's death in 1388 further weakened the Sultanate, and the degeneracy of his successors made it vulnerable to external predators. After **Timur**, the central Asian conqueror known to the west as Tamberlane, sacked Delhi in 1398, autonomous sultanates emerged in Jaunpur, Malwa and Gujarat; the Hindu kingdoms of Marwar and Mewar were established in Rajasthan; and small principalities even nearer the capital appeared at Kalpi, Mahoba and Gwalior. The Delhi Sultanate had been reduced to just one of several competing Muslim states in northern India.

After the death of the last Tughluq, Delhi was seized by Khizr Khan (1414–21), who had been an officer of the governor of Multan and Lahore appointed by Timur before he left India. In 37 years, Khizr's **Sayyid** dynasty lost Multan and were repeatedly harassed by the Sharqi sultans of Jaunpur. The Sultanate experienced a modest revival under the more energetic rule of the Afghan Lodis, especially **Sikander Lodi** (1489–1517), who annexed Jaunpur and Bihar; but his successor, Ibrahim, was unable to overcome the dissension among his Afghan feudatories. Eventually, one enlisted the support of Babur, the ruler of Kabul, who defeated Ibrahim at Panipat in 1526.

By the time of the Sultanate, India had considerable experience of assimilating foreigners; Greeks, Scythians, Parthians and Huns had all been absorbed over the centuries, politically, socially and culturally. However, the Sultanate brought its own theologians and social institutions. **Islam** presented a new pattern of life, far less easy for the xenophobic Hindu social system to accommodate. Nonetheless, a process of mutual acculturation did slowly evolve. Despite the Muslims' iconoclastic zeal, Hinduism found common ground with some aspects of Islam: elements of Sufi mysticism and Hindu devotionalism were combined in the teachings of many saints. **Kabir** (1440–1518), in particular, denied any contradiction between Muslim and Hindu conceptions of god, preached social egalitarianism and was claimed by adherents of both creeds as their own. The replacement of Sanskrit by Persian as the official language of the administration encouraged regional languages; **Urdu** resulted from a fusion of Hindi and Persian using an Arabic script. A stylistically unified architecture began to develop, which flourished under the **Moghuls**; and new social ideas were introduced which became integral to Indian life.

THE MOGHUL EMPIRE 1526–1761

Babur, a descendant of both Timur and Genghis Khan, had gained control of Delhi and Agra by defeating Ibrahim; but his position was threatened by the Rajput confederacy, led by Rana Sanga of Mewar, south of Agra, and by the Afghan chiefs, who had united under the Sultan of Bengal. Babur reacted vigorously by declaring a religious war (*jihad*) against the Rana; he annihilated the Mewar forces at the battle of Kanwaha in 1527, and then turned his attention to the Afghan uprisings in the east. Although he crushed the allied armies of the Afghans and the Sultan of Bengal in 1529, his failing health forced him to retire to Lahore, where he died in 1530.

Babur possessed many talents: as well as a brilliant military campaigner, he was a skilful diplomat, a poet and a man of letters. He constructed a loosely knit empire, extending from Badakshan and Kabul to the borders of Bengal, in just four years. His personal magnetism commanded loyalty and inspired his warrior chiefs to fresh endeavours when they yearned to depart the hot and dusty plains of India for the cool mountains of their homeland. His very readable memoirs, moreover, reveal a man of sensibility, taste and humour, who loved music, poetry, sport and natural beauty.

Humayun, his son and successor, was by contrast a volatile character, who alternated between bursts of enthusiastic activity and indolence. He subdued Malwa and Gujarat, only to lose both while he "took his pleasure" in Agra. **Sher Khan Sur** of south Bihar soon assumed the leadership of the Afghan opposition and after two resounding defeats Humayun had to seek refuge in Persia. Sher Khan set up an administrative system in Delhi, set out to re-assess the land revenue, and continued his campaigns against the Rajputs; but Humayun took advantage of the chaos after Sher Khan's death in 1545 to stage a return. Humayun's armies, led by Bairam Khan and Prince Akbar, crushed Sikander Sur at Sirhund in 1555; but he died the following year after a fall in the Purana Qila in Delhi leaving **Akbar**, his major contribution to the Moghul empire, to succeed where he had failed.

Akbar, aged only 13, was lucky to have Bairam Khan as regent to help him survive the crisis of the first four years. Bairam, a loyal general and an experienced politician, overcame the challenge of the Hindu general Hemu at the second battle of Panipat in 1556, recovered Gwalior and Jaunpur, and handed over a consolidated kingdom of north India to Akbar in 1560. The young emperor quickly established his own control of the government in dramatic fashion; he personally executed Adham Khan, who had murdered the prime minister, and had him thrown from the palace walls.

Akbar's first military campaigns were against the **Rajputs**; within a decade he secured the flank of the Moghul bases at Delhi and Agra by subduing all the Rajput domains except Mewar (Udaipur). Akbar possessed the personal magnetism of his grandfather and was a brilliant general, who above all had the gift of rapid movement. In 1573 he marched his army 600 miles in nine days to defeat astonished insurgents in Gujarat. He had secured Bengal, the richest province, by 1576, and by the end of his reign in 1605 he controlled a broad sweep of territory north of the River Godavari, which reached from the Bay of Bengal to Kandahar and Badakshan, with the exception of Gondwana and Assam.

Akbar was a very clever politician and administrator as well as a successful general. After subduing the Rajputs, he diplomatically bestowed imperial honours on their chiefs by making them military commanders and provincial governors. By giving them autonomy within their own states, he made the Rajputs partners in the empire and thereby secured the acquiescence of the whole Hindu community. His marriage to a Jaipur princess was an important symbolic statement of this partnership.

The imperial service, in which Akbar involved both Moghuls and Rajputs, was carefully crafted to ensure that the nobility were hereditary as an aristocratic class but not as individuals. His officers – *mansabdars*, holders of commands – were arranged in grades that indicated how many troops they were obliged to maintain for imperial service. A commander of five thousand was both an important state official and a noble; but the titles were not hereditary, being conferred by appointment and promotion, and the *mansabdars* salaries were paid in cash so that they lacked a territorial basis for insurrection.

The creation of an administrative framework, which sustained the empire through its efficient collection of revenue, was one of Akbar's most enduring achievements. He collected information about local revenue, productivity and price variations to arrive at a schedule, acceptable to the peasant farmers but also generating maximum profit for the state. Akbar recruited leaders of local communities and holders of land rights (*zamindars*) to collect the revenue in cash.

In addition to involving Hindu *zamindars* and nobles in economic and political life, Akbar adopted a conscious policy of religious toleration aimed at widening the base of his power. In particular, he abolished the despised poll-tax on non-Muslims (*jizya*), and tolls on Hindu pilgrimages. A mystical experience in about 1575 inspired him to instigate a series of discussions with orthodox Muslim leaders (*ulema*), Portuguese priests from Goa, Hindu *brahmins*, Jains and Zoroastrians at his famous house of worship (*ibadat khana*) in Fatehpur Sikri. The discussions culminated in a politico-religious crisis and a revolt, organized by the alienated *ulema*, which Akbar ruthlessly crushed in 1581. He subsequently evolved a theory of divine kingship incorporating the toleration of all religions, and thereby restored the concept of imperial sanctity with which the early Hindu emperors had surrounded themselves, while declaring his non-sectarian credentials.

Akbar was a liberal patron of the arts and his eclecticism encouraged a fruitful Muslim-Hindu dialogue. Music, which he loved, was especially enriched by this mutual acculturation. Akbar ranks alongside Ashoka as one of the great statesmen of the world, and his reign laid the foundations for a century of stable government under the succeeding Moghuls.

The reigns of **Jahangir** (1605–27) and **Shah Jahan** (1628–57) together represent the great age of the Moghuls, whose reputation for magnificence, pomp and luxury did not escape the notice of Europe and is recorded in the writings of Bernier and Dryden. It was a time of brisk economic activity notable for artistic and architectural splendour, as well as the excesses of imperial indulgence.

Despite his reputation for drunken cruelty, Jahangir was a connoisseur of art. It was under his patronage that the art of the **miniature**, imported from Persia, reached its perfection in Moghul painting before being further evolved and enriched by Hindu artists, especially in Rajasthan. Jahangir is best remembered for his great devotion to Nur Jahan, which he celebrated with a special issue of gold coins (*mohur*). Nur Jahan commissioned the building of the beautiful Itmad-ud-Daulah, a magnificent tomb for her parents in Agra, sometimes said to be the blueprint for the Taj Mahal.

In the political sphere, Jahangir settled the conflict with Mewar, extended the empire by subjugating the last of the Afghan domains in east Bengal and Orissa, and restrained the threat from the Deccan by defeating the combined forces of the Nizamshahi kingdom and the Adilshahis of Bijapur in 1620. However, the combination of failing health and political intrigues involving his beloved Nur Jahan prevented him from completing his Deccan campaign, and Persia's capture of Kandahar in 1622 dented the empire's prestige.

When Shah Jahan came to power in 1628, he ruthlessly executed all the male descendants of his brothers and uncles. He displayed all the imperial qualities of administrative and military ability and, like his predecessors, was a great lover and patron of the arts, especially architecture. Delhi's **Red Fort** and **Jami Masjid**, Agra Fort, and the splendid **Taj Mahal**, the mausoleum he created for his wife Mumtaz, are the results of his personal inspiration and artistic direction. Thus he actively participated in the apogee of Indo-Persian culture, although his political achievements were less notable.

Shah Jahan attempted to deal with the ascendancy of the Marathas in the Deccan by conquering the Nizamshahi kingdom in 1636. He then concentrated on extending the empire on the Assam border and the containment of the Uzbek threat in the northwest. He regained Kandahar from the Persians, but it was lost again in 1649. Meanwhile, a crisis was brewing. The revenue schedule had not been reviewed, and the system now tended to enrich local intermediaries at the expense of the empire. Powerful *zamindars* began to resist paying the full revenue to the treasury. The empire's total dependence on the rural aristocrats to collect the land revenue indirectly fostered the agencies of its disintegration.

Shah Jahan governed India firmly for thirty years, but in his later years he became increasingly sensual. He ended his days a pathetic prisoner in the Agra Fort, gazing nostalgically across the Yamuna at the mausoleum of his beloved Mumtaz; a sad old man who had lost everything through self-indulgence.

Aurangzeb, the last of the great Moghuls, seized power in a dramatic civil war, eliminated his brothers, a son and a nephew, and imprisoned his father in the Agra Fort. Though lacking the charisma of Akbar or Babur, he evoked an awe of his own and he proved to be a firm and capable administrator, who retained his grip on the increasingly unsettled empire until his death at the age of 88. In contrast to the pomp of the other Moghuls, his lifestyle was pious and disciplined. In later life the ruthless statesman became an austere sage, who fasted and spent long hours in prayer.

In the first 23 years of his rule, Aurangzeb maintained a continuity with Shah Jahan's administration and ostensibly contained disruptive elements; but he failed to solve the problems which eventually erupted after his death and caused the dissolution of the empire. The **Maratha** chief, **Shivaji**, who humiliated the Moghul army early in Aurangzeb's reign, was a constant threat. Although he was defeated by the Rajput Jai Singh and forced to visit the Moghul court in 1666, Shivaji made a daring escape from Agra, rallied his resources, and was soon again the master of a compact and well-organized kingdom in western India, to which the Muslim kingdoms of Bijapur and Golconda were eager to ally themselves against the imperialism of Aurangzeb.

The militant separatism of the **Sikhs** was brutally suppressed when Guru Tegh Bahadur was executed in 1675 for refusing to embrace Islam; but his son, Guru Gobind, transformed the religious community into a military sect which became increasingly powerful in the Punjab. Aurangzeb's confrontation with the Rajputs over the Jodhpur succession in 1678 resulted in another war, and the alienation of most of the Rajput partners in empire.

Meanwhile, religious and economic discontent turned the passive support of the Hindu community, cultivated by Akbar, into indifference, disdain and even armed conflict. Aurangzeb aligned himself with the orthodox Sunni Muslims of the *ulema*, who rejected the syncretism encouraged by Akbar's non-sectarian policies. Hindu places of worship were again the object of iconoclasm, the tax on non-Muslims (*jizya*) was re-introduced, religious fairs were banned, and discriminatory duties were imposed on Hindu merchants. The Jats and the Satnamis of the Agra-Delhi region rebelled over insufferable increases in land revenue demands, and elsewhere peasant farmers rallied behind Maratha, Sikh and Rajput landholders to oppose imperial exploitation.

Aurangzeb crushed the agrarian rebellions and turned his attention to expansion. He transferred his base to the Deccan in 1681 and spent the rest of his life overseeing the subjugation of the Bijapur and Golconda kingdoms and trying to contain the Maratha rebellion. In 1689, he succeeded in capturing and executing

Shivaji's son, Shambhuji, and by 1698 the Moghuls had overrun almost the whole of the peninsula. The Marathas had been suppressed, but they re-emerged under the Peshwa leadership in the eighteenth century to harass the remnants of Moghul power and even to challenge the political ambitions of the British.

Aurangzeb did manage to extend the empire during his long reign of over 48 years; but the newly acquired lands in the south were difficult to administer, his nobles were divided by factionalism, and the disruptive consequences of his policies were to be critical in the eighteenth-century collapse of the empire.

Bahadur Shah, Aurangzeb's son, succeeded in 1707 and briefly restored the situation, but after his death in 1712 the disintegration of the empire and power struggles between would-be successors dominated events. By the 1720s the Nizam of Hyderabad and the Nawabs of Avadh and Bengal were effectively independent; the Marathas overwhelmed the rich province of Malwa in 1738; Hindu landholders everywhere were in revolt; and Nadir Shah of Persia dealt a serious blow to the empire's prestige when he invaded India, defeated the Moghul army and sacked Delhi in 1739.

The **Maratha** kingdom had by now been transformed into a confederacy under the leadership of a hereditary *brahmin* minister, called the Peshwa. By 1750 the Marathas had spread right across central India to Orissa, had attacked Bengal, and were insinuating themselves in the imperial politics of Delhi. When Delhi was again looted in 1757, this time by an independent Afghan force led by Ahmad Shah Abdali, distraught Moghul ministers called in the Marathas to rescue the situation. The Marathas drove the Afghans back to the Punjab; but Ahmad Shah advanced again in 1761 and overwhelmed them at the third battle of Panipat. Any designs he had on the imperial throne were dashed, however, when his soldiers mutinied for their arrears of pay.

New centres of Moghul culture developed, notably at Murshidabad, Lucknow, Hyderabad, and Faizabad, but the political strength of the empire had fragmented and north India was left in a power vacuum for the next forty years. It was against this background that the European trading companies, and the East India Company in particular, were able to establish their trading posts and develop their ambitions.

THE EAST INDIA COMPANY 1600–1857

The prosperity of foreign trade in India attracted European interest as early as 1498, when **Vasco da Gama** landed on the Malabar coast. During the ensuing hundred years Portuguese, Dutch, English, French and Danish companies all set up coastal trading centres exporting textiles, sugar, indigo and saltpetre.

The **East India Company**, established by eighty London merchants in 1599 and chartered by Queen Elizabeth I on December 31, 1600, arrived in Surat in 1608. The Company had established 27 trading posts by 1647, including **Fort George** on the Coromandel coast, out of which Madras developed. The enclave of Bombay, part of Catherine of Braganza's dowry in her marriage to Charles II, became crown property in 1665, was leased to the Company from 1668, and soon replaced Surat as its headquarters. The Moghul emperor permitted the Company to establish a new settlement at **Fort William**, which grew into Calcutta, and in 1701 the British received a grant of the revenues of the Twenty-Four Parganas near Calcutta from Aurangzeb, in recognition of the growing importance of their trade in the economy of Bengal.

It was in the **south**, however, that European trading initiatives first took on a political significance, after the onset of the War of the Austrian Succession in 1740. Armed conflict between the French and English trading companies along the Carnatic coast developed into a war over the succession of the Nizam of Hyderabad. The British victory and the Peace of Paris in 1763 eclipsed French ambitions in India. Meanwhile, **Robert Clive**'s defeat of the rebellious young Nawab of Bengal at Plassey in 1757 had decisively augmented British power; by 1765 the enervated Moghul emperor legally recognized the Company as an Indian potentate by granting the revenue management (*diwani*) of Bengal, Bihar and Orissa to Lord Clive.

Ironically, the Company's mastery of the rich province soon brought it to the brink of bankruptcy, provoking parliamentary intervention in its affairs. The **Regulating Act** of 1773 appointed a Governor-General of the Company's three provinces in Calcutta, Bombay and Madras; and in 1784 the India Act established a President of the Board of Control in London to oversee the Governor-General in Calcutta.

Warren Hastings, the first Governor-General, made the Company's colony in Bengal politically viable, successfully defending it against the jealous governors of Bombay and Madras, and the internal dissensions of his Council in England. His major achievement was to protect Bombay and Madras against the assaults from a coalition of Marathas, the Nizam of Hyderabad and Haidar Ali, the Sultan of Mysore; but he also laid the foundations of British administration in India by replacing the Indian revenue-collecting deputies with a Board of Revenue in Calcutta and English collectors in the districts. **Lord Cornwallis** completed the reforms by fixing the land revenues in the Permanent Land Settlement of 1793; by dividing Company service into separate political and commercial branches; and by a further Europeanization of the administration.

The Governor-Generals were charged with non-aggression and administrative reform until the end of the eighteenth century, but the Napoleonic Wars allowed **Lord Wellesley** to follow his imperial instincts. His swift defeat of **Tipu Sultan** of Mysore, the company's best organized and most resolute enemy, a confrontation with the Marathas, and the subjugation of the Nizam of Hyderabad resulted in the annexation of considerable territories in Andhra Pradesh, Tamil Nadu, Mysore, the Upper Doab, Gujarat and Maharashtra; nearly all the other rulers in India recognized British suzerainty by 1805. There was a brief respite in the expansion until Napoleon's defeat in 1815; but the last vestiges of Maratha opposition were crushed by 1823, and the absorption of Sind, the Sikh kingdom of the Punjab, Kashmir, Assam, Chittagong and Lower Burma by 1852 established **British supremacy** in India.

The new British dominion, however, was in a state of social and economic collapse as a result of the almost incessant conflicts of the previous hundred years. High revenue assessments had depressed the condition of both peasants and *zamindars*; peasants deserted their lands, land revenue receipts were falling, and there were local revolts and grain riots in the 1830s. Gangs of robbers (dacoits) had reached epidemic proportions, and their activities curtailed commerce between states and towns. The cult of the **Thugs**, who robbed and murdered in honour of the goddess Kali, spread terror all over central and northern India.

Inspired by Burke's ideas, Utilitarianism and the Radical humanism in Europe, **Lord William Bentinck**'s reforms as Governor-General did little to alleviate the situation. The campaign against the Thugs received general approval, but his suppression of the practice of widows joining their husbands on funeral pyres (*sati*) was seen as an attack on the values of traditional Hindu society.

The Company's policy of government patronage for Indian learning was replaced after 1835 by a resolution to promote "European literature and science". Schools and colleges imparting western knowledge through the medium of the English language were established, and English replaced Persian as the official state language. The educated elite and intellectuals like Ram Mohan Roy had already adopted western ideas, but such cultural imperialism aggravated the unrest and distrust of the majority.

James Andrew Broun Ramsey, Marquess of Dalhousie, Governor-General between 1848 and 1856, was a firm believer in the benefits of **westernization**. He promoted western education by initiating plans for the first three Indian universities with Sir Charles Wood, and embarked on a series of public works, including the development of the railway and telegraph systems. These were commendable achievements, but their westernizing influence increased social tension. His controversial policy of annexing dependent but autonomous states, which brought **Oudh**, two Maratha kingdoms and five other states under direct administration, caused considerable resentment among the dispossessed and alarm among the Indian ruling classes.

Against this general background of unease, discontent had been growing in the army, which had been increasingly deployed overseas during the previous two decades – a practice resented on religious grounds by the many *brahmins* it contained. The cows' and pigs' grease on the cartridges of the new Enfield rifle, polluting to both Hindus and Muslims, convinced the soldiers that there was a conspiracy against their religious beliefs and sparked the revolt. The **Indian Mutiny** – the "First War of Independence" – started with a rising at Meerut on May 10, 1857, and Delhi was seized the next day. The last Moghul emperor Bahadur Shah in Delhi, the dispossessed court at Lucknow, and the exiled members of the Maratha court at Kanpur all supported the cause and some landlords participated in the rebellion.

The British authorities were caught by surprise. The Crimean War had reduced the number of their regiments in India, and their forces were concentrated around Calcutta or the Punjab. However, the revolt failed to cut their lines of communication, and crucially the **Sikh** regiments in the Punjab remained loyal. Delhi was retaken by a column from the Punjab in late September, **Kanpur** (Cawnpore) was relieved in the same month, and the final recapture of **Lucknow** in March 1858 effectively broke the back of the Mutiny. The rebels fought on under the leadership of Tantia Topi, and the valiant Rani of Jhansi in central India, until they too were crushed in June 1858. The governing powers of the East India Company were abolished and the British crown assumed the administration of India through an appointed Viceroy in the same year.

THE RAJ AND INDIAN NATIONALISM 1857–1947

India played a key role in the politics of **British imperialism**, especially in the rivalry with France and Russia during this period. Its army became an instrument of British foreign policy, in the Afghan Wars attempting to create a buffer state to block Russia's advance in central Asia, and in the Anglo-Burmese Wars to check the French expansion in Indo-China. It was also used to protect British interests beyond the Indian subcontinent as far afield as Abyssinia and Hong Kong.

As a British colony, India assumed a new position in the world economy. Its trade benefited from the British development of the railways, and Indian businessmen began to invest in a range of industries, including the manufacture of textiles, iron and steel; but India subsidized the British economy as a source of cheap raw materials and as a market for manufactured goods. Its own economy and agriculture remained underdeveloped, and the growth of the gross national product was outstripped by increases in population.

British civil servants dominated the higher echelons of the administration, imposing western notions of progress on the indigenous social structure. Tenurial systems based on ownership rather than land use, irrigation schemes, the suppression of social customs offensive to humanist ideals, the railways and the introduction of a western judiciary often involved policies contrary to existing Indian interests. At the same time, the propagation of the English language and the western knowledge to which it gave access resulted in the emergence of a new **middle class** of civil servants, landlords and professionals, whose consciousness of an Indian national identity steadily increased.

Within thirty years of the Mutiny, the history of the British in India becomes essentially a chronicle of the struggle for **Independence**. By the start of the twentieth century the British conception of empire involved a contradiction between liberal rhetoric and the fact of territorial, economic and intellectual expansion. By World War I, the imperial incentive had been swept away by the realization that Indian independence was unavoidable; the only problem remaining was how to relinquish suzerainty.

Awareness of national identity first found expression in local associations and public demonstrations about specific issues; but when the liberalism of Gladstone was confronted by a growing Indian disaffection while Lord Ripon was Viceroy, the British showed their willingness to conciliate the Indian educated classes by giving their official blessing to the foundation of the first all-India political organization, the **Indian National Congress**, in 1885. It began modestly with only seventy affluent public men as delegates, who advocated limited reforms and a consolidation of union with Britain; but by 1900 Gopal Krishna **Gokhale** and Bal Gangadhar **Tilak**, both Maratha *brahmins*, had emerged as leaders of the Moderates and the Extremists respectively. By 1905 Tilak had persuaded Congress to adopt self-government as a political aim.

Lord Curzon, a romantic imperialist, who believed that it was Britain's duty to protect India's past and educate it for the future, began his second term of office as Viceroy by sending the Younghusband expedition to Lhasa in 1904. When he decided on the equally controversial partition of Bengal in 1905, it precipitated the first major confrontations with the government. There were widespread protests: Tilak proposed a no-tax campaign and a boycott of British goods, and when the government crushed the protests Bengali terrorists employed even more radical tactics.

In 1906, concerns about the predominantly Hindu interests of Congress led to the foundation of the **All-India Muslim League** to represent the Muslims, who made up a quarter of India's population. A Liberal landslide in Great Britain produced the Morley-Minto Reforms in 1909, which paved the way for Indian participation in provincial executive councils and made allowance for separate Muslim representation. Tilak was imprisoned that year for incitement to violence. The reversal of the partition of Bengal was announced at the **Great Durbar** of 1911, held in honour of the new king George V and his queen, and the capital was moved to **Delhi**.

During World War I, the British conflict with the Sultan of Turkey – still considered to be the spiritual head (*khalifa*) of Indian Muslims – provoked further demonstrations. Tilak returned to found a **Home Rule League** in 1916, and made the Lucknow Pact with the Muslims in support of their *khalifa* movement. The British responded with the Royal Proclamation of 1917, which promised a gradual development of dominion-style self-government; and two years later the Montagu-Chelmsford Reforms attempted to implement the declaration. However, legislation authorizing internment without trial, also passed in 1919, seemed to contradict these promises; the Muslim population were alarmed by the collapse of Turkey and the masses were becoming more restless.

At this point, **Mohandas Karamchand Gandhi** – hailed as the Mahatma or "Great Soul" by Rabindranath Tagore upon returning from his campaign of passive resistance against the government in South Africa – took up the initiative. The Indian-style one-day strike (*hartal*) he proposed was organized in all the major cities; but feelings ran so high that there were riots, which were mercilessly crushed by the government. In particular, General Dyer dispersed the Jallianwalla Bagh meeting in **Amritsar** on April 13, 1919 by firing without warning on the unarmed crowd, killing 379 and wounding 1200. The racial bitterness invoked by the atrocity inspired Gandhi's **Non-Cooperation Movement**; but by 1922 further acts of violence induced him to call off the campaign just before he was imprisoned.

Mahatma Gandhi, born in Porbander in Gujarat, had been educated as a lawyer in England. Over the years he was influenced by Christian, Hindu, liberal and humanitarian ideas; but the doctrine of non-violence (*ahimsa*) and the pursuit of truth (*satya*) became the philosophical cornerstones of his endeavours to achieve a united independent India. His belief in the rights of man, and especially his championing of the Untouchables, whom he renamed the Children of God (*Harijan*), put him in opposition to *brahmin* orthodoxy; but he won the hearts of the people in 1921 when he discarded European clothes for the homespun cotton *dhoti* and shawl, to identify with the masses. His personal charisma and all-India appeal inspired the Independence movement throughout the period, whether he was in prison, organizing the rejection of imported cloth in his *swadeshi* campaign, leading acts of civil disobedience, or fasting to bring about the cessation of Hindu-Muslim community violence.

Gandhi was released from prison in 1924. Despite liberal concessions by the British, by 1928 Congress was demanding complete Independence (*purna swaraj*). The government offered talks, but the more radical elements in Congress, now led by the young **Jawaharlal Nehru**, were in a confrontational mood. Their declaration of Independence Day on January 26 1930 forced Gandhi's hand; he responded with a well-publicized 60-mile march from his ashram in Sabarmati to make **salt** illegally at Dandi in Gujarat (see p.527). This demonstration of non-violent civil disobedience (*satyagraha*) caught the people's imagination, leading to more processions, strikes, and the imprisonment of a hundred thousand of his followers by the end of the year. Abortive round-table talks, the Irwin-Gandhi truce, Gandhi's trip to London for further talks, and more civil disobedience culminated in the **Government of India Act** in 1935, which still fell short of aspirations for complete Independence. Congress remained suspicious of British intentions, and despite Gandhi's overtures refused to accommodate Muslim demands for representation.

The idea of a **separate Muslim state** was first raised in 1930 by the poet Sir Muhammad Iqbal and Chaudhuri Rahmat Ali, and a group of fellow students at Cambridge coined the name **Pakistan**, literally meaning "Land of the Pure". **Muhammad Ali Jinnah**, a lawyer from Bombay who assumed the leadership of the Muslim League in 1935, initially promoted Muslim-Hindu co-operation, but he soon despaired of influencing Congress and by 1940 the League passed a resolution demanding an independent Pakistan.

Confrontations between the government, Congress and the Muslim League continued throughout World War II. Mahatma Gandhi introduced the "**Quit India**" slogan and proposed another campaign of civil disobedience; the government immediately responded by imprisoning the whole Working Party of Congress in Pune. Jinnah, meanwhile, preached his "two nations" theory to the educated, and inspired mass Muslim support with his rhetoric against "Hinduization". A spate of terrorist activities left a thousand dead and sixty thousand imprisoned; by the end of the war, the government accepted that complete Independence would have to be negotiated.

British attempts to find a solution that would preserve a united India and allay Muslim fears after the war disintegrated in the face of continued intransigence from both sides, and they gradually realized that Partition was inevitable. In 1946 Jinnah provoked riots in Calcutta with his call for Direct Action, and Hindus retaliated with atrocities against Muslims in Bihar and Uttar Pradesh. The British cabinet appointed **Lord Mountbatten** as Viceroy to supervise the handover of power in 1948. Mahatma Gandhi desperately sought to avert the escalating Hindu-Muslim violence and find a resolution to secure a united India, while Nehru was persuaded that a separate Pakistan would be preferable to the anarchy of communal killings.

Lord Mountbatten brought Independence forward: the subcontinent was **partitioned** on August 15, 1947 and Pakistan came into existence, even though several princely states had still to decide which of the two new countries they would join. The new boundaries cut through both Bengal and the Punjab; Sikhs, Muslims and Hindus who had been neighbours became enemies overnight. Five million Hindus and Sikhs from Pakistan, and a similar number of Muslims from India, were involved in the ensuing two-way exodus, and the atrocities cost half a million lives. Mahatma Gandhi, who had devoted himself to ending the communal violence after Partition, was **assassinated** in January 1948 by Hindu extremists antagonized by his defence of the Muslims. India had lost its "Great Soul", but the profound shock of the Mahatma's last sacrifice at least contributed to the gradual cessation of the violence.

INDEPENDENT INDIA
1947–1994

Jawaharlal Nehru, India's first and longest running Prime Minister, proved to be a dynamic, gifted and extremely popular leader during his seventeen years of premiership. He built the foundations of a democratic, secular state, and guided the first stages of its agricultural and industrial development. Nehru's first task, however, was to consolidate the Union.

His able deputy Prime Minister, **Sardar Vallabhai Patel**, was made responsible for incorporating the 562 princely states within the federal Union. The Nizam of **Hyderabad**, who resisted even though the majority of the state's population were Hindus, had to be persuaded by an invasion of Indian troops. The Hindu Maharaja of **Kashmir** also prevaricated, as three quarters of his subjects were Muslims, and by October 1947 he had to appeal to India for help against a tribal invasion supported by Pakistan. Kashmir's accession to India resulted in the first outbreak of hostilities between the two countries; the United Nations intervened in 1949 to enforce a ceasefire line. The **French** enclaves at Pondicherry and Chandernagar were incorporated in the 1950s; but the **Portuguese** refused to accept the new situation and in 1961 Nehru had to annex **Goa**. The **Naga** people were brought within the federal Union as the Nagaland state in the same year.

The Constitution for India's "Sovereign Democratic Republic and Union of States" became law on January 26, 1950, the twentieth anniversary of "Independence Day". The franchise was made universal for all adults, and with 173 million eligible to vote in 1951 India became the **world's largest democracy**. Hindi was designated the "official language of the Union"; but south India, in particular, was adamant in its opposition to Hindi, and Nehru re-aligned the several state borders on linguistic principles. By 1961 the Union consisted of sixteen states and six centrally administered territories. The Punjabi-speaking Sikhs had to wait until 1966 for their state to be separated from Hindu-dominated Haryana.

Nehru sought to achieve the constitutional aims of justice, liberty, equality and fraternity with a vigorous programme of social and economic reforms. He redressed the iniquities of caste by abolishing "untouchability" in 1955 and radically improved the status of women.

The national average literacy was increased to 23.7 per cent by 1961 and free elementary education became more readily available, although it still fell short of aspirations.

On the **economic** front, Nehru engineered the first three of India's **Five Year Plans** to improve production capability and eradicate poverty. Population growth and the failures of the monsoon in 1952 and 1953 eroded the mainly agricultural aims of the first plan (1951–56); but food grain production increased from 52 million to over 65 million tons by 1956, and to 80 million tons by the end of the second plan (1956–61), which also injected capital into industry. Under the third plan (1961–66), a nuclear energy programme was inaugurated, and foreign aid and technical assistance secured to speed up industrialization.

Foreign policy was Nehru's biggest disappointment. He adopted a policy of non-aligned peaceful co-existence, but **China** threatened his aim of promoting Asian unity. He attempted to dispel the tensions created by the Chinese invasion of Tibet in 1950 by concluding a trade treaty with China in 1954, which included a declaration of mutual respect for each other's territories; but this did not deter the Chinese from building a road across a remote area of Ladakh in 1957, and India sustained losses during a confrontation in 1959. In 1962, sporadic conflicts in the Northeast Frontier Agency (**Assam**) escalated into a war; the Chinese army proved to be far superior and advanced unhindered over India's northeast frontier. Their unilateral decision to withdraw, on November 21, 1962, added humiliation to defeat and spelt the end of India's policy of non-alignment. Nehru immediately made a defence treaty with the US, and set about creating a new elite Border Security Force.

The whole nation, loyal throughout the China crisis, mourned his death in 1964, which prevented him from witnessing the restoration of India's military prestige in the **Second Indo-Pakistan War** of 1965. Indian tanks had advanced to within three miles of a virtually defenceless Lahore when the UN ceasefire was agreed on September 23. Lal Bahadur **Shastri**, who had led the interim government, died shortly after in January 1966 leaving Nehru's daughter, **Indira Gandhi**, to establish her superiority as leader of the Congress left, over Morarji Desai's right wing of the party.

Mrs Gandhi swiftly secured American financial support for India's fourth Five Year Plan (1966–71); but her devaluation of the *rupee* in June 1966 aroused considerable opposition and elections the next year radically reduced her majority. Two years later, Congress split under the pressure of internal dissensions. Mrs Gandhi embraced the socialist principle by nationalizing the banks, and enlisted the support of the Communists, the Sikhs and the Dravidian Progressive Federation (DMK) to form a coalition government. By this time, India had made a spectacular agricultural breakthrough with its **Green Revolution**, as a result of the introduction of high-yield grains, and in 1969 industrial growth was over seven percent. Mrs Gandhi pressed on with her socialist reforms, abolishing the former maharajas' privy purses and privileges after she had consolidated her mandate in fresh elections in 1971.

Meanwhile, Yahya Khan's brutal repression of the struggle for independence in **East Pakistan** had caused a mass exodus of refugees; by April 1971 Bengali civilians were pouring across into India at the rate of sixty thousand a day. Mrs Gandhi astutely waited until she had the moral support of the international community, signed a Treaty of Peace, Friendship and Co-operation with the Soviet Union, and launched simultaneous attacks in West and East Pakistan on 4 December. India had total air superiority, as well as the support of the East Pakistan population, and by December 15 the Pakistani general capitulated and signed the Instrument of Surrender of "all Pakistan armed forces in Bangla Desh".

If the liberation of Bangla Desh was the crowning glory of Mrs Gandhi's premiership, her abandonment of the democratic ideals so dear to her father was its lowest ebb. After widespread agrarian and industrial disturbances and protests against the rate of inflation and corruption within the Congress in 1974, the clamour of protest rose to a crescendo in June 1975, and when the opposition coalition under the joint leadership of JP Narayan and Morarji Desai threatened to oust India's "iron lady", she declared a **State of Emergency** on June 26, which suspended all civil rights, including habeas corpus, and silenced all opposition by internment and strict censorship of the press.

Her administrative and economic reforms had the desired effect of cutting inflation and curbing corruption, but the enforced sterilization of men with two or more children, and brutal slum-clearances in Delhi supervised by her son **Sanjay**, alienated millions of her supporters. When she finally released her opponents and called off the Emergency in January 1977, the bitterness she had engendered resulted in her ignominious defeat in the March elections. The ensuing **Janata** coalition under **Morarji Desai** fell apart within two years, and his premiership was terminated by a vote of no confidence in 1979. Mrs Gandhi, who had rebuilt her Congress-I Party with Sanjay's help, swept back into office in January 1980. Sanjay died in a plane crash a few months later; four years later, Mrs Gandhi made the second, fatal, mistake of her career.

A group of terrorists demanding a separate "nation" – Khalistan – for Sikhs, took control of the **Golden Temple** in Amritsar early in 1984, and organized a campaign of violence from its precincts. Hundreds of Hindus and moderate Sikhs fell victim to terrorist attacks, and the whole nation was calling for positive action to end the atrocities. Indira sent in her tanks in June 1984, but two days of raging combat desecrated the Sikhs' holiest shrine as well as generating the first martyrs of Khalistan. In October that year, her Sikh bodyguards avenged their brotherhood and faith by assassinating Mrs Gandhi at her house in Delhi.

Rajiv Gandhi came to power in December 1984 on a wave of sympathy boosted by his reputation as "Mr Clean", given added meaning by the **Bhopal** gas tragedy just two weeks before the elections. The honeymoon was short-lived; the political accords he reached with the Punjab, Assam and Mizoram deteriorated into armed conflict; more than two years of "peace-keeping" by the Indian army failed to disarm Tamil guerrillas in Ceylon; and allegations of corruption tarnished his image. By the end of the 1980s the opposition had rallied under the leadership of **VP Singh**, a former Congress minister. The December 1989 elections did not give VP Singh's Janata Party a majority, but he managed to form a coalition government with the support of the "Hindu first" Bharatiya Janata Party (**BJP**), led by **LK Advani.**

Singh was immediately confronted by problems in the Punjab and Kashmir, as well as upper-caste Hindu protests against his planned implementation of proposals for a sixty percent reservation of civil service jobs for lower castes and former "untouchables"; but it was an even more emotive issue which brought down his government in less than a year. Advani had assumed the leadership of a popular Hindu revivalist movement, which was demanding that the Babri Masjid mosque in **Ayodhya**, built by Babur in the sixteenth century, should be replaced by a Hindu temple on the supposed site of the birthplace of Rama, god-hero of the epic *Ramayana*.

Singh, utterly committed to secularism, pleaded with Advani to desist; undeterred Advani set off towards Ayodhya in October 1990, seated on a golden chariot pushed by his followers and thousands of devout Hindus, with the avowed intention of destroying the mosque and building a temple for Rama. Singh ordered Advani's arrest; within two weeks the inevitable withdrawal of the BJP support from his coalition government resulted in a vote of no confidence on November 7, 1990. Rajiv Gandhi declined the offer to form an interim government, hopeful that he could improve his party's position in an election. His campaign went well and it was assumed that Congress would win; but then, on a tour of Tamil Nadu in May 1991, he was assassinated by Tamil Tigers seeking revenge for India's active opposition to their "freedom fight" in Ceylon.

PV Narasimha Rao skilfully steered the Congress Party through the elections, and formed a government with the support of the Muslim League, the Communist "Left Front" and Tamil Nadu's most powerful party (AIADMK). At the same time, the BJP ominously increased its seats in the Lok Sabha from 80 to 120, Advani became leader of the opposition, and the enormous popular support for the rebuilding of Rama's temple in Ayodhya encouraged the *Vishwa Hindu Parishad* to take up the crusade. VP Singh countered by leading a march of 500 secularists to Ayodhya; but the BJP had won control of the Uttar Pradesh state government, making them responsible for law and order, and this time it was Singh who found himself arrested and imprisoned.

In 1993, when the situation came to a head again, the central government could not prevent extremists inciting the crowds of fanatical devotees to tear down the mosque in a blaze of publicity (see p.286). The demolition of the Babri Masjid was followed by terrible **riots** in many parts of the country, especially Bombay and Gujarat, where Muslim families and businesses were targetted. A few months later, in retaliation against the extreme Hindu violence, **bombs** were planted in Bombay (see p.577) by underground Muslim groups. As a result of the Babri Masjid episode, the BJP-led state governments of UP, Himachal Pradesh, Madhya Pradesh, Rajasthan and Delhi were suspended. Elections in these states in late 1993 showed that the popularity of the BJP, and its call for the creation of *Hindutva*, a Hindu homeland, was fading. They re-asserted control of Delhi, which has always been a stronghold of the Hindu right, barely hung on in Rajasthan, and lost the rest. Rao and the Congress Party appear for the moment to have weathered the storm.

Dave Crawford

THE RELIGIONS OF INDIA

For the majority of Indians, **Hinduism** permeates every aspect of life, from commonplace daily chores to education and politics. The vast pantheon of Hindu deities is manifest everywhere – not only in temples, but in shops, rickshaws and even on *bidi* packets and matchboxes. Beside Hindus, **Muslims** are the most prominent religious group; they have formed an integral part of Indian society since the twelfth century, and mosques are almost as common as temples. Though **Jains** and **Buddhists** are now a tiny fraction of the population, their impact is still felt, and their magnificent temples are among the finest in India. Both these ancient faiths, like the more recently established **Sikh** community, formed in reaction to the caste laws and ritual observances of Hinduism. In addition, there are small communities of **Zoroastrians**, descended from Iranians, and **Christians**, here since the first century (see p.1004).

Hindu practices, such as caste distinction, have crept into most religions, and many of the **festivals** – see p.59 – that mark each year with music, dance and feasting, are shared by all communities. Each has its own **pilgrimage** sites, **heroes**, **legends** and even culinary specialities, mingling in a unique diversity that is the very pulse of society.

HINDUISM

Contemporary **Hinduism** – the "religion" of over eighty-five percent of Indians – is the product of several thousand years of evolution and assimilation. It has neither founder nor prophet, no single creed, and no single prescribed practice or doctrine; it takes in hundreds of gods, goddesses, beliefs and practices, and widely variant cults and philosophies. Some are recognized by only two or three villages, others are popular right across the subcontinent. Hindus (from the Persian word for Indians) call their beliefs and practices *dharma*, which envelops natural and moral law to define a way of living in harmony with a natural order, while achieving personal goals and meeting the requirements of society.

EARLY DEVELOPMENTS

The foundations of Hinduism were laid by the **Aryans**, semi-nomads who entered northwest India during the second millennium BC, and mixed with the indigenous Dravidian population (see p.1096). With them they brought a belief in gods associated with the elements, including **Agni**, the god of fire and sacrifice, **Surya**, the sun-god, and **Indra**, the chief god. Most of these deities faded in later times, but Indra is still regarded as the father of the gods, and Surya, eternally present in his magnificent chariot-temple in **Konarak** (Orissa), was widely worshipped until the medieval period.

Aryan beliefs were set out in the **Vedas**, scriptures "heard" (*shruti*) by "seers" (*rishis*). Transmitted orally for centuries, they were finally written, in Sanskrit, between 1000 BC and 500 AD. The earliest were the *Samhitas*, or hymns; later came the *Brahmanas*, sacrificial texts, and *Aranyakas*, or "forest treatises".

The earliest and most important *Samhita*, the **Rig Veda**, contains hymns to deities and *devas* (divine powers), and is supplemented by other books detailing rituals and prayers for ceremonial use. The **Brahmanas** stress correct ritual performance, drawing heavily on concepts of **purity and pollution** that persist today, and concentrating on sacrificial rites. Pedantic attention to ritual soon supplanted the importance of the *devas*, and they were further undermined by a search for a single cosmic power thought to be their source, eventually conceived of as **Brahma**, the absolute creator, personified from earlier mentions of Brahman, an impersonal principle of cosmic unity.

The **Aranyakas** focussed upon this all-powerful godhead, and reached their final stage in the **Upanishads**, which describe in beautiful and emotive verse the mystic experience of unity of the soul (*atman*) with Brahma, ideally attained through asceticism, renunciation of worldly values and meditation. In the *Upanishads* the concepts of **samsara**, a cyclic round of death and rebirth characterized by suffering and perpetuated by desire, and **moksha**, liberation from *samsara*, became firmly rooted. Fundamental aspects of the Hindu world view, both are accepted by all but a handful of Hindus today, along with the belief that rebirth is conditioned by **karma**, the force of good or bad actions and intentions.

HINDU SOCIETY

The stratification of Hindu society is rooted in the ***Dharma Shashtras*** and ***Dharma Shutras***, scriptures written from "memory" (*smriti*) at the same time as the *Vedas*. These defined four hierarchical classes, or ***varnas***, each assigned specific religious and social duties known as ***varnashradharma***, and established Aryans as the highest social class. In descending order the *varnas* are: ***brahmins*** (priests and teachers), ***kshatryas*** (rulers and warriors), ***vaishyas*** (merchants and cultivators) and ***shudras*** (menials). The first three classes, known as "twice-born", are distinguished by a sacred thread worn from the time of initiation, and granted full access to religious texts and rituals. Below all four categories, groups whose jobs involve contact with dirt or death (such as undertakers, leather workers and cleaners) were classified as **Untouchables**. Though discrimination against Untouchables is now a criminal offence, in part thanks to the campaigns of Gandhi – he renamed Untouchables *Harijans*, "Children of God" – the lowest stratum of society has by no means disappeared.

Within the four *varnas*, social status is further defined by ***jati***, classifying each individual by family and precise occupation (for example, a *vaishya* may be a jewellery seller, cloth merchant, cowherd or farmer). A person's *jati* determines his **caste**, and lays restrictions on all aspects of life from food consumption, religious obligations and contact with other castes, to the choice of marriage partners. In general, Hindus marry members of the same *jati* – marrying someone of a different *varna* often results in ostracism from both family and caste, leaving the couple stranded in a society where caste affiliation takes primacy over all other aspects of individual identity. There are almost three thousand *jatis*; the divisions and restrictions they have enforced have become, time and time again, the substance of reform movements and the target of critics.

A Hindu has three aims in life: ***dharma***, fulfilling one's duty to family and caste and acquiring religious merit (*punya*) through right living; ***artha***, the lawful making of wealth; and ***karma***, the satisfaction of desires. These goals are linked with the four traditional stages in life. The first is as a child and student, devoted to learning from parents and guru. Next comes the stage of householder, expected to provide for a family and raise sons. That accomplished, he or she may then take up a life of celibacy and retreat into the forest to meditate alone, and finally renounce all possessions to become a homeless ascetic, hoping to achieve the ultimate goal of *moksha*. The small number of Hindus, including some women, who follow this ideal life assume the final stage as ***sannyasis***, saffron-clad ***sadhus*** who wander throughout India, begging for food, and retreat to isolated caves, forests and hills to meditate. They're a common feature in most Indian towns, and many stay for long periods in particular temples. Not all have raised families: some assume the life of a *sadhu* at an early age as *chellas*, pupils, of an older *sadhu*.

THE POPULAR DEITIES

Alongside the *Dharma Shashtras* and *Dharma Shutras*, the most important works of the *smriti* tradition, thought to have been completed by the fourth century AD at the latest, were the ***Puranas***, long mythological stories focused on the Vedic gods and their heroic actions, and Hinduism's two great epics, the ***Mahabharata*** and ***Ramayana***. Through these texts, the main gods and goddesses became firmly embedded in the religion. Alongside **Brahma**, the creator, **Vishnu** was acknowledged as the preserver, and **Shiva** ("auspicious, benign"), referred to in the *Rig Veda* as Rudra, was recognized for his destructive powers. The three are often depicted in a trinity, *tri-murti*, but in time Brahma's importance declined, and Shiva and Vishnu became the most popular deities.

Other gods and goddesses who came alive in the mythology of the *Puranas*, each depicted in human or semi-human form and accompanied by an animal "**vehicle**", are still venerated across India. River goddesses, ancestors, guardians of particular places, and protectors against disease and natural disaster are as central to village life as the major deities.

PHILOSOPHICAL TRENDS

The complications presented by Hinduism's view of deities, *samsara*, *atman* (the human soul), and *moksha* naturally encouraged philosophical debate, and led eventually to the formation of six schools of thought, known as the ***Darshanas***. Each presented a different exposition of the true nature of *moksha* and how to attain it.

Foremost among these was the **Advaita Vedanta** school of **Shankara** (*c.*788–850 AD), who interpreted Hinduism as pure monotheism verging on monism. Drawing on Upanishadic writings, he claimed that they identified the essence of the human soul with that of God (*tat tvam asi*, "that thou art"), and that all else – the phenomenal world and all *devas* – is an illusion (*maya*) created by God. Shankara is revered as saint-philosopher at the twelve *Jyotirlinga*: sacred Shaivite sites associated with the unbounded *lingam* of light, which as a manifestation of Shiva once persuaded both Brahma and Vishnu to acknowledge Shiva's supremacy.

Another important *Darshana* centred around the age-old practice of **yoga** (literally "the action of yoking [to] another"), elucidated by **Patanjali** (second century BC) in his *Yoga Sutras*. Interpreting yoga as the yoking of mind and body, or the yoking of the mind with God, Patanjali detailed various practices, which used in combination may lead to an understanding of the fundamental **unity** of all things. The most common form of yoga known in the west is *hatha-yoga*, whereby the body and its vital energies is brought under control through physical positions and breathing methods, with results said to range from attaining a calm mind to being able to fly through the air, enter other bodies or become invisible. Other practices include *mantra-yoga*, the recitation of formulas and meditation on mystical diagrams (*mandalas*), *bhakti-yoga* (devotion), *jnana-yoga* (knowledge) and *raja*, or royal, *yoga* the highest form of yoga when the mind is absorbed in God.

PRACTICE

The primary concern of most Hindus is to reduce bad *karma* and acquire merit (*punya*), by honest and charitable living within the restrictions imposed by caste, and by worship, in the hope of attaining a higher status of rebirth. Strict rules address purity and pollution, the most obvious of them requiring high-caste

THE MAHABHARATA

Eight times as long as the *Iliad* and *Odyssey* combined, the **Mahabharata** is the most popular of all Hindu texts. Written around 400 AD, it tells of a feuding *kshatrya* family in upper India (Bharata) during the fourth millennium BC. Like all good epics, the *Mahabharata* recounts a gripping tale, using its characters to illustrate moral values. In essence it attempts to elucidate the position of the warrior castes, the *kshatryas*, and demonstrate that religious fulfilment is as accessible for them as it is for *brahmins*.

The chief character is **Arjuna**, a superb archer, who with his four brothers – Yudhishtra, Bhima, Nakula and Sahadeva – represents the **Pandava** clan, upholders of righteousness and supreme fighters. Arjuna won his wife **Draupadi** in an archery contest, but wishing to avoid jealousy she agreed to be the shared wife of all five brothers. The Pandava clan are resented by their cousins, the evil **Kauravas**, led by Duryodhana, the eldest son of Dhrtarashtra, ruler of the Kuru kingdom.

When Dhrtarashtra handed his kingdom over to the Pandavas, the Kauravas were far from happy. Duryodhana challenged Yudhishtra (known for his brawn but not his brain) to a gambling contest. The dice game was rigged; Yudhishtra gambled away not only his possessions, but also his kingdom and his shared wife. The Kauravas offered to return the kingdom to the Pandavas if they could spend thirteen years in exile, together with their wife, without being recognized. Despite much scheming, the Pandavas succeeded, but on return found that the Kauravas would not fulfil their side of the bargain.

Thus ensued the great battle of the *Mahabharata*, told in the sixth book, the **Bhagavad Gita** – immensely popular as an independent story. Vishnu descends to earth as **Krishna**, and steps into battle as Arjuna's charioteer. The *Bhagavad Gita* details the fantastic struggle of the fighting cousins, using magical weapons and brute force. Arjuna is in a dilemma, unable to justify the killing of his own kin in pursuit of a rightful kingdom for himself and his brothers. Krishna consoles him, reminding him that his principal duty, his *varnashradharma*, is as a warrior. What is more, Krishna points out, each man's soul, or *atman*, is eternal, and transmigrates from body to body, so Arjuna need not grieve the death of his cousins. Krishna convinces Arjuna that by fulfilling his *dharma* he not only upholds law and order by saving the kingdom from the grasp of unrighteous rulers, he also serves God in the spirit of devotion (*bhakti*), and thus guarantees himself eternal union with the divine in the blissful state of *moksha*.

The Pandavas finally win the battle, and Yudhishtra is crowned king. Eventually Arjuna's grandson, Pariksit, inherits the throne, and the Pandavas trek to Mount Meru, the mythical centre of the universe and the abode of the gods, where Arjuna finds Krishna's promised *moksha*.

HINDU GODS AND GODDESSES

VISHNU

The chief function of **Vishnu**, "pervader", is to keep the world in order, preserving, restoring and protecting. With four arms holding a conch, discus, lotus and mace, Vishnu is blue-skinned, and often shaded by a serpent, or resting on its coils, afloat on an ocean. He is usually seen alongside his half-man-half-eagle vehicle, Garuda.

Vaishnavites, often distinguishable by two vertical lines on their foreheads, recognize Vishnu as supreme lord, and hold that he has manifested himself on earth nine times. These incarnations, or *avatars*, have been as fish (Matsya), tortoise (Kurma), boar (Varaha), man-lion (Narsingh), dwarf (Vamana), axe-wielding *brahmin* (Parsuram), Rama, Krishna and Balaram (though some say that the Buddha is the ninth *avatar*). Vishnu's future descent to earth as Kalki, the saviour who will come to restore purity and destroy the wicked, is eagerly awaited.

The most important *avatars* are Krishna and Rama. **Krishna** is the hero of the *Bhagavad Gita*, in which he proposes three routes to salvation (*moksha*): selfless action (*karmayoga*), knowledge (*jnana*), and devotion to god (*bhakti*), and explains that *moksha* is attainable in this life, even without asceticism and renunciation. This appealed to all castes, as it denied the necessity of ritual and officiating *brahmin* priests, and evolved into the popular *bhakti* cult that legitimized love of God as a means to *moksha*, and found expression in emotional songs of the quest for union with God. Through *bhakti*, Krishna's role was extended, and he assumed different faces: most popularly he is the playful cowherd who seduces and dances with cowgirls (*gopis*), giving each the illusion that she is his only lover. He is also pictured as a small, chubby, mischievous baby, known for his butter-stealing exploits, who inspires tender motherly love in women. Like Vishnu, Krishna is blue, and often shown dancing and playing the flute.

Popular legend has it that Krishna was born in **Mathura**, today a major pilgrimage centre, and sported with his *gopis* in nearby **Vrindavan**. He also established a kingdom on the far western coast of Gujarat, at **Dwarka**.

Rama is the chief character in the *Ramayana*. Born a prince in Ayodhya, he was denied succession to the throne by one of his father's wives, and was exiled for fourteen years, together with his wife Sita. The *Ramayana* details his exploits during these years, and his defeat of the demon king of Lanka, Ravana. When Rama was reinstated as king in Ayodhya, he put Sita through "trial by fire" to prove that she had remained pure while in the clasps of Ravana. Sita passed the trial unharmed, and is held up as the paradigm of women – faithful, pure and honest.

SHIVA

Shaivism, the cult of **Shiva**, was also inspired by *bhakti*, requiring selfless love from devotees in a quest for divine communion, but Shiva has never been incarnate on earth. He is presented in many different aspects, such as **Nataraja**, Lord of the Dance, **Mahadev**, Great God, and **Maheshvar**, Divine Lord, source of all knowledge. Though he does have several terrible forms, his role extends beyond that of destroyer, and he is revered as the source of the whole universe.

Shiva is often depicted with four or five faces, holding a trident, draped with serpents, and bearing a third eye in his forehead. In temples, he is identified with the *lingam*, or phallic symbol, resting in the *yoni*, a representation of female sexuality. Whether as statue or *lingam*, Shiva is guarded by his bull-mount, Nandi, and often accompanied by a consort, who also assumes various forms, and is looked upon as the vital energy, **shakti**, that empowers him. Their erotic exploits were a favourite sculptural subject between the ninth and twelfth centuries, most unashamedly in carvings on the temples of **Khajuraho**, in Madhya Pradesh.

While Shiva is the object of popular devotion all over India, as the terrible **Bhairav** he is also the god of the Shaivite **ascetics**, who renounce family and caste ties and perform extreme meditative and yogic practices. Many, though not all, smoke *ganja*, Shiva's favourite herb; all see renunciation and realization of God as the key to *moksha*. Some ascetic practices enter the realm of **tantrism**, in which confrontation with all that's impure, such as alcohol, death, and sex, is used to merge the sacred and the profane, and bring about the profound realization that Shiva is omnipresent.

GANESH

Chubby and smiling, elephant-headed **Ganesh**, the first son of Shiva and Parvati, is invoked before every undertaking (except funerals). Seated on a throne or lotus, his image is often placed above temple gateways, in shops and houses; in his four arms he holds a conch, discus, bowl of sweets (or club) and a water lily, and he's always attended by his vehicle, a rat. Credited with writing the *Mahabharata* as it was dictated by the sage Vyasa, Ganesh is regarded by many as the god of learning, the lord of success, prosperity and peace.

Hindus to limit their contact with potentially polluting lower castes. All bodily excretions are polluting (hence the strange looks westerners receive when they blow their nose and return the handkerchief to their pocket). Above all else, **water** is the agent of purification, used in ablutions before prayer, and revered in all rivers, especially the Ganga (the Ganges).

In most Hindu homes, a chosen deity is worshipped daily in a shrine room, and scrip-tures are read. Outside the home, worship takes place in temples, and consists of **puja**, or devotion to God – sometimes a simple act of prayer, but more commonly a complex process when the god's image is circumambulated, offered flowers, rice, sugar and incense, and anointed with water, milk or sandalwood paste (which is usually done on behalf of the devotee by the temple priest, the *pujari*). The aim in *puja* is to take **darshan** – glimpse the god –

DURGA

Durga, the fiercest of the female deities, is an aspect of Shiva's more conservative consort, Parvati (also known as Uma), who is remarkable only for her beauty and fidelity. In whatever form, Shiva's consort is *shakti*, the fundamental energy that spurs him into action. Among Durga's many aspects, each a terrifying goddess eager to slay demons, are Chamunda, Kali and Muktakeshi, but in all her forms she is Mahadevi (Great Goddess). Statues show her with ten arms, holding the head of a demon, a spear, and other weapons; she tram-ples demons underfoot, or dances upon Shiva's body. A garland of skulls drapes her neck, and her tongue hangs from her mouth, dripping with blood – a particularly gruesome sight on pictures of Kali. Durga is much venerated in Bengal; in all her temples, animal sacrifices are a crucial element of worship, to satisfy her thirst for blood and deter her ruthless anger.

LAKSHMI

The comely goddess **Lakshmi**, usually shown sitting or standing on a lotus flower, and some-times called Padma (lotus), is the embodiment of loveliness, grace and charm, and the goddess of prosperity and wealth. Vishnu's consort, she appears in different aspects alongside each of his *avatars*; the most important are Sita, wife of Rama, and Radha, Krishna's favourite *gopi*. In many temples she is shown as one with Vishnu, in the form of Lakshmi Narayan.

KARTTIKEYA

Though some legends claim that his mother was Ganga, or even Agni, **Karttikeya** is popularly believed to be the second son of Shiva and Parvati. Primarily a god of war, he was popular among the northern Guptas, who worshipped him as Skanda, and the southern Chalukyas, for whom he was Subrahmanya. Usually shown with six faces, and standing upright with bow and arrow, Karttikeya is commonly petitioned by those wish-ing for male offspring.

HANUMAN

India's great monkey god, **Hanuman**, features in the *Ramayana* as Rama's chief aide in the fight against the demon-king of Lanka. Depicted as a giant monkey clasping a mace, Hanuman is the deity of acrobats and wrestlers, but is also seen as Rama and Sita's greatest devotee, and an author of Sanskrit grammar. As his representatives, monkeys find sanctuary in temples all over India.

SARASWATI

The most beautiful Hindu goddess, **Saraswati**, the wife of Brahma, with her flawless milk-white complexion, sits or stands on a water lily or peacock, playing a lute, *sitar* or *vina*. Associated with the River Saraswati, mentioned in the *Rig Veda*, she is seen as a goddess of purification and fertility, but is also revered as the inventor of writ-ing, the queen of eloquence and goddess of music.

SANI

Closely linked with the planet Saturn, **Sani** is feared for his destructive powers. His image, a black statue with protruding blood-red tongue, is often found on street corners; strings of green chil-lies and lemon are hung in shops and houses each Saturday (*Saniwar*) to ward off his evil influences.

KHAMDENU

Mention must also be made of the **sacred cow**, Khamdenu, who receives devotion through the respect shown to all cows, left to amble through streets and temples all over India. The origin of the cow's sanctity is uncertain; some myths record that Brahma created cows at the same time as *brah-mins*, to provide *ghee* (clarified butter) for use in priestly ceremonies. To this day cow dung and urine are used to purify houses (in fact the urine keeps insects at bay), and the killing or harming of cows by any Hindu is a grave offence. The cow is often referred to as mother of the gods, and each part of its body is significant: its horns symbolize the gods, its face the sun and moon, its shoulders Agni (god of fire) and its legs the Himalayas.

and thus receive his or her blessing. Whether devotees simply worship the deity in prayer, or make requests – for a healthy crop, a son, good results in exams, a vigorous monsoon or a cure for illness – they leave the temple with *prasad*, an offering of food or flowers taken from the holy sanctuary by the *pujaris*.

Communal worship and get-togethers en route to pilgrimage sites are celebrated with *kirtan* or *bhajan*, singing of hymns, perhaps verses in praise of Krishna taken from the *Bhagavad Purana*, or repetitive cries of "Jay Shankar!" (Praise to Shiva). Temple ceremonies are conducted in Sanskrit by *pujaris* who tend the image in daily rituals that symbolically wake, bathe, feed and dress the god, and finish each day by preparing the god for sleep. The most elaborate is the evening ritual, **arthi**, when lamps are lit, blessed in the sanctuary, and passed around devotees amid the clanging of drums, gongs and cymbals. In many villages, shrines to *devatas*, village deities who function as protectors and may bring disaster if neglected, are more important than temples.

Each of the great stages in life – birth, initiation (when boys of the three twice-born *varnas* are invested with a sacred thread, and a *mantra* is whispered into their ear by their guru), marriage, death and cremation – is cause for fervent prayer, energetic celebration and feasting. The most significant event in a Hindu's life is **marriage**, which symbolizes ritual purity, and for women is so important that it takes the place of initiation. Feasting, dancing, and singing among the bride and groom's families, usually lasting for a week or more before and after the marriage, are the order of the day all over India. The actual marriage is consecrated when the couple walk seven times round a sacred fire, accompanied by sacred verses read by an officiating *brahmin*. Despite efforts to reduce the importance of a **dowry**, a valuable gift from the bride's family to the groom, dowries are still demanded, and among wealthier families may include televisions, videos, and cars in addition to the more common items of jewellery and money. Burning of wives whose dowry is below expectations is still known to occur.

Life transitions are by no means the only cause for celebration among Hindus, whose year is marked by **festivals** devoted to deities, re-enacting mythological stories and commem-

orating sacred sites. The grandest festivals are held at places made holy by association with gods, goddesses, miracles, and great teachers, or rivers and mountains; throughout the year these are important **pilgrimage** sites, visited by devotees eager to receive *darshan*, glimpse the world of the gods, and attain merit. The journey, or *yatra*, to a pilgrimage site is every bit as significant as reaching the sacred location, and bands of Hindus (particularly *sadhus*) often walk from site to site. Modern transport, however, has made things easier, and every state lays on pilgrimage tours, when buses full of chanting families roar from one temple to another, filling up with religious souvenirs as they go.

Perhaps India's single most sacred place is the ancient city of **Varanasi** (also known as Benares or Kashi), on the banks of the Ganges. The river has been sacred since the time of the earliest Aryan settlements, and is personified as the beneficent goddess Ganga. At Varanasi it holds the redeeming quality common to all rivers, but bathing in its waters, and more particularly, dying or being cremated there, is a precondition to entering heaven (*svarga*) and achieving release from rebirth. *Ghats*, steps leading to the water's edge, are common in all river- or lakeside towns, the abode of priests who offer *puja* to a devotee's chosen deity.

The source of the Ganges, high in the mountains of western Uttar Pradesh at **Gangotri**, is held in great reverence, as are the five ancient temples nearby, known as **Panch Kedar**, deep in the Himalaya. Equally important are **sangams**, or **tirthas**, the points where two rivers meet. Every twelve years, when India's largest festival, the **Kumbh Mela**, is held at Allahabad, the *sangam* of the Ganges and the Yamuna, the *ghats* turn into a seething mass of bodies, overrun by near-naked ascetics who are the first of millions to bathe in the holy waters. Lesser *melas* are held at three-yearly intervals at the *tirthas* of Haridwar, Nasik, and Ujjain.

Not only river confluences are auspicious: at Kanniyakumari, the southern tip of India, the waters of the Indian Ocean, the Bay of Bengal and the Arabian sea are thought to merge. Pilgrimages here are often combined with visits to the great temples of **Tamil Nadu**, where Shaivite and Vaishnavite saints established cults, and India's largest temples were constructed. Madurai, Thanjavur, Chidambaram and Srirangam are major pilgrimage centres, representing the pinnacle of the architectural development that began at Mamallapuram. Their festivals often involve the tugging of deities on vast wooden chariots through the streets, a practice most vigorously played out at **Puri**, in Orissa, when Lord Jaganath is taken from the temple during *Rath Yatra* for a foray through the town.

As well as specific temples sacred to particular gods – Brahma in **Pushkar**, Kali at **Calcutta**, or Shiva at the twelve *Jyotirlinga* – historical sites, such as the caves of **Ellora**, and the former Vijayanagar capital at **Hampi**, remain magnets for pilgrims. More than a common ideology, it is this sacred geography, entwined with popular mythology, that unites hundreds of millions of Hindus, who have also been brought together in nationalistic struggles, particularly in response to Christian missionaries and Muslim and British domination.

ISLAM

Indian society may be dominated by Hindus, but **Muslims** – some ten percent of the population – form a significant presence in almost every town, city and village. The belief in only one god, Allah, the condemnation of idol worship, and the observance of strict dietary laws and specific festivals set Muslims apart from their Hindu neighbours, with whom they have co-existed for centuries. Such differences have often led to communal fighting, most notably during Partition, and in 1993 riots all over north India followed the destruction by Hindus of the Babri Masjid mosque in Ayodhya.

Islam, "submission to God", was founded by **Muhammad** (570–632 AD), regarded as the last in a succession of prophets, who transmitted God's final and perfected revelation to mankind through the writings of the divinely revealed "recitation", the **Koran** (Quran). The true beginning of Islam is dated at 622 AD, when Muhammad and his followers, exiled from Mecca, made the *hijra*, or migration, north to Yathrib, later known as Medina, "City of the Prophet". The *hijra* marks the start of the Islamic lunar calendar: the Gregorian year 1995 is for Muslims 1416 AH (*Anno Hijra*).

From Medina, Muhammad ordered raids on caravans heading for Mecca, and led his community in battles against the Meccans, inspired by *jihad*, or "striving" on behalf of God and Islam. This concept of holy war was the driving force behind the incredible expansion of Islam – by 713 Muslims had settled as far west as Spain, and on the banks of the Indus in the east. When **Mecca** was peacefully surrendered to Muhammad in 630, he cleared the sacred shrine, the Ka'ba, of idols, and proclaimed it the pilgrimage centre of Islam.

The Koran, the authoritative scripture of Islam, contains the basics of Islamic belief: that there is one god, Allah (though he is attributed with 99 names), and his prophet is Muhammad.

Muhammad was succeeded as leader of the *umma*, the Islamic community, by Abu Bakr, the prophet's representative, or Caliph, the first in a line of Caliphs who led the orthodox community until the eleventh century AD. However, a schism soon emerged when the third Caliph, Uthman, was assassinated by followers of Ali, Muhammad's son-in-law, in 656 AD. This new sect, calling themselves **Shi'as**, "partisans" of Ali, looked to Ali and his successors, infallible *Imams*, as leaders of the *umma* until 878 AD, and thereafter replaced their religious authority with a body of scholars, the *ulema*.

By the second century after the *hijra* (ninth century AD), orthodox, or **Sunni**, Islam had assumed the form in which it endures today. A collection of traditions about the prophet, **Hadith**, became the source for ascertaining the **Sunna**, customs, of Muhammad. From the Koran and the Sunna, seven major **items of belief** were laid down: the belief in God, in angels as his messengers, in prophets (including Jesus and Moses), in the Koran, in the doctrine of predestination by God, in the Day of Judgement, and in the bodily resurrection of all people on this day. Religious practice was also standardized under the Muslim law, **Sharia**, in the **Five Pillars of Islam**. The first "pillar" is the confession of faith, *shahada*, that "There is no god but God, and Muhammad is his messenger". The other four are prayer (*salat*) five times daily, almsgiving (*zakat*), fasting (*saum*), especially during the month of Ramadan, and, if possible, pilgrimage (*hajj*) to Mecca, the ultimate goal of every practising Muslim.

The first Muslims to settle in India were traders who arrived on the south coast in the seventh century, probably in search of timber for shipbuilding. Later, in 711, Muslims entered Sind, in the northwest, to take action against Hindu pirates, and dislodged the Hindu government. Their presence, however, was short-lived.

Much more significant was the invasion of north India under **Mahmud of Ghazni**, who rampaged through the Punjab in search of temple treasures, and in the spirit of *jihad*, engaged in a war against infidels and idolaters. More Turkish raids followed in the twelfth century, resulting in the colonization of India and the provision of a homeland for refugees pushed out of Persia by the Mongols. The Turks set themselves up in Delhi as **Sultans**, the forerunners of the **Moghuls** (see p.1106).

Many Muslims who settled in India intermarried with Hindus, Buddhists and Jains, and the community spread. A further factor in its growth was missionary activity by **Sufis**, who emphasized abstinence and self-denial in service to God, and stressed the attainment of inner knowledge of God through meditation and mystical experience. In India, Sufi teachings spread among Shaivites and Vaishnavites, who shared their passion for personal closeness to God. Their use of music (particularly *qawwali* singing) and dance, shunned by orthodox Muslims, appealed to Hindus, for whom *kirtan* (singing) played an important role in religious practice. One *qawwali*, relating the life of the Sufi saint Waris Ali Shah, draws parallels between his early life and the childhood of Krishna – an outrage for orthodox Muslims, but attractive to Hindus, who still flock to his shrine in Deva Sharief near Lucknow. Similar shrines, or *dargars*, all over India bridge the gap between Islam and Hinduism.

Muslims are enjoined to pray five times daily, following a routine of utterances and positions. They may do this at home or in a **mosque** – always full at noon on Friday, for communal prayer. (Only the Druze, an esoteric sect based in Bombay, hold communal prayers on Thursdays.) Characterized by bulbous domes and high minarets, from which a *muezzin* calls the faithful to prayer, mosques always contain a *mihrab*, or niche indicating the direction of prayer (to Mecca), a *mimbar* or pulpit, from which the Friday sermon is read, a source of water for ablutions, and a balcony for women. Firm reminders of Muslim dominance, mosques all over India display a bold linear grandeur quite different to the delicacy of Hindu temples. India's largest mosque is the Jami Masjid ("Friday Mosque") in **Delhi**, but magnificent structures, including tombs, schools and substantial remains of cities are scattered throughout north India and the Deccan, with especially outstanding examples in Hyderabad, Jaunpur, Agra and Fatehpur Sikri.

The position of **women** in Islam is a subject of great debate. It is customary for women to be veiled, though in larger cities many women do not cover their head, and in strictly orthodox communities most wear a *burqa*, usually black, that covers them from head to toe. Like other Indian women, Muslim women take second place to men in public, but in the home, where they are often shielded from men's eyes in an inner courtyard, they wield great influence. In theory education is equally available to boys and girls, but girls tend to forgo learning soon after sixteen, encouraged instead to assume the traditional role of wife and mother. Contrary to popular belief, polygamy is not widespread; while it does occur, and Muhammad himself had several wives, many Muslims prefer monogamy, and several sects actually stress it as the duty of Muslims. In marriage, women *receive* a dowry (Hindu women must provide one) as financial security.

BUDDHISM

For several centuries, **Buddhism** dominated India, with adherents in almost every part of the subcontinent. However, having reached its height in the fifth century, it was all but eclipsed by the time of the Muslim conquest. Today Buddhists are a tiny fraction of the population, but superb monuments are firm reminders of the prior importance of the faith, and essential elements in India's cultural legacy.

The founder of Buddhism, **Siddhartha Gautama**, known as the **Buddha**, "the awakened one", was born into a wealthy *kshatrya* family in Lumbini, north of the Gangetic plain in present-day Nepal, around 566 BC. Brought up in luxury as a prince and a Hindu, he married at an early age, and renounced family life when he was thirty. Unsatisfied with the explanations of worldly suffering proposed by Hindu gurus, and convinced that asceticism did not lead to spiritual realization, Siddhartha spent years in meditation, wandering through the ancient kingdom, or *janapada*, of Magadha. His enlightenment (*bodhi*) is said to have taken place under a *bodhi* tree in **Bodhgaya** (Bihar), after a night of contemplation during which he resisted the worldly temptations set before him by the demon, Mara. Soon afterwards he gave his first sermon in **Sarnath**, now a major pilgrimage centre. For the rest of his life he taught, expounding **Dharma**, the true nature of the world, human life and spiritual attainment. Before his death (*c.*486 BC) in Kushinagara (UP), he had established the **sangha**, a community of monks and nuns, who continued his teachings.

The Buddha's view of life incorporated the Hindu concepts of *samsara* and *karma*, but remodelled the ultimate goal of religion, calling it **nirvana**, "no wind". Indefinable in worldly terms, since it is by nature free from conditioning, *nirvana* represents a clarity of mind, pure understanding and unimaginable bliss. Its attainment signals an end to rebirth, but no communion of a "soul" with God; neither exists. The most important concept outlined by the Buddha was that all things, subject to change and dependence, are characterized by **impermanence**, and there is **no self**, no permanent ego, so **attachment** to anything (possessions, emotions, spiritual attainment and *devas*) must be renounced before impermanence can be grasped, and *nirvana* realized.

Disregarding caste and priestly dominance in ritual, the Buddha formulated a teaching open to all. His followers took refuge in the three jewels: *Buddha, Dharma,* and *Sangha.* The teachings became known as **Theravada**, or "Doctrine of the Elders". By the first century BC the *Pali Canon,* the **Tripitaka**, or "three Baskets", had set out the basis for early Buddhist practice, proposing *dana,* selfless giving, and *sila,* precepts which aim at avoiding harm to oneself and others, as the most important guidelines for all Buddhists, and the essential code of practice for the lay community.

Carried out with good intentions, *sila* and *dana* maximize the acquisition of good *karma,* and minimize material attachment, thus making the individual open to the more religiously oriented teachings, the **Four Noble Truths**. The first of these states that all is suffering (*dukkha*), not because every action is necessarily unpleasurable, but because nothing in the phenomenal world is permanent or reliable. The second truth states that *dukkha* arises through attachment, the third refers to *nirvana,* the cessation of suffering, and the fourth details the path to *nirvana.* Known as the **Eightfold Path** – right understanding, thought, speech, action, livelihood, effort, mindfulness

and concentration – it aims at reducing attachment and ego and increasing awareness, until all four truths are thoroughly comprehended, and *nirvana* is achieved. Even this should not be clinged to – those who experience it are advised by the Buddha to use their understanding to help others to achieve realization.

The Sanskrit word **bhavana**, referred to in the west as **meditation**, translates literally as "bringing into being". Traditionally meditation is divided into two categories: **Samatha**, or calm, which stills and controls the mind, and **Vipassana**, or insight, during which thought processes and the noble truths are investigated, leading ultimately to a knowledge of reality. Both methods are taught in Buddhist centres across India.

At first, Buddhist iconography represented the Buddha by symbols such as a footprint, *bodhi* tree, parasol or vase. These can be seen on *stupas* (domed monuments containing relics of the Buddha) built throughout India from the time of the Buddhist emperor Ashoka (see p.1099), and in ancient Buddhist caves, which served as meditation retreats and *viharas* (monasteries). The finest are at **Ellora** and **Ajanta**; like the remarkable *stupas* at **Sanchi**, they incorporate later designs which depict the Buddha in human form, standing and preaching or sitting in meditation, distinguished by characteristic marks, and indicating his teaching by hand gestures, or *mudras.*

This artistic development coincided with an increase in the devotional side of Buddhism, and a recognition of **bodhisattvas** – those bound for enlightenment who delayed self-absorption in *nirvana* to become teachers, spurred by selfless compassion and altruism.

The importance of the *bodhisattva* ideal grew as a new school, the **Mahayana**, or "Great Vehicle", emerged. By the twelfth century it had become fully established and, somewhat disparagingly, renamed the old school **Hinayana**, or "Lesser Vehicle". Mahayanists proposed emptiness, *sunyata,* as the fundamental nature of all things, taking to extremes the belief that nothing has independent existence. The **wisdom** necessary to understand *sunyata,* and the **skilful means** required to put wisdom into action in daily life and teaching, and interpret emptiness in a positive sense, became the most important qualities of Mahayana Buddhism. Before long *bodhisattvas* were joined in both scripture and art by female consorts who embodied wisdom.

Hinayana Buddhism survives today in Sri Lanka, Burma, Thailand, Laos and Cambodia. Mahayana Buddhism spread from India to China, Japan, Korea and Vietnam, where it incorporated local gods and spirits into a family of *bodhisattvas*. In many places further evolution saw the adoption of magical methods, esoteric teachings, and the full use of sense experience to bring about spiritual transformation, resulting in a separate school known as **Mantrayana** or **Vajrayana** based on texts called *tantras*. Mantrayana encouraged meditation on *mandalas* (symbolic diagrams representing the cosmos and internal spiritual attainment), sexual imagery, and sometimes sexual practice, in which the female principle of wisdom could be united with skilful means.

Buddhism was introduced to **Tibet** in the seventh century, and integrated to a certain extent with the indigenous **Bon** religion. Tibetan Buddhism emphasizes teachers, *lamas* (similar to gurus), and reincarnated teachers, known as *tulkus*, and uses elaborate rituals and ceremonies. The **Dalai Lama**, the head of Tibetan Buddhism, is the fourteenth in a succession of incarnate *bodhisattvas*, the representative of Avalokitesvara (the *bodhisattva* of compassion), and the leader of the exiled Tibetan community whose headquarters are in **Dharamsala** (HP). Other parts of Himachal Pradesh, Sikkim and Bihar have been heavily influenced by Tibetan Buddhism.

For Buddhist monks and nuns, and some members of the lay community, meditation is an integral part of religious life. Most lay Buddhists concentrate on *dana* and *sila*, and on auspicious days, such as *Vesak* (marking the Buddha's birth, enlightenment and death), make **pilgrimages** to Bodhgaya, Sarnath, Lumbini and Kushinagar. After laying offerings before Buddha statues, devotees gather in silent meditation, or join in chants taken from early Buddhist texts. *Uposathas*, full moon days, are marked by continual chanting through the night when temples are lit by glimmering butter lamps, often set afloat on lotus ponds, among the flowers that represent the essential beauty and purity to be found in each person in the thick of the confusing "mud" of daily life.

Among Tibetan communities, devotees hang prayer flags, turn prayer wheels, and set stones carved with *mantras* (religious verses) in rivers, thus sending the word of the Buddha with wind and water to all corners of the earth. Prayers and chanting are often accompanied by horns, drums and cymbals.

JAINISM

Though the **Jain** population in India is small – accounting for less than one percent of the population – it has been tremendously influential for at least 2500 years. A large proportion of Jains live in Gujarat, and all over India they are commonly occupied as merchants and traders. Similarities to Hindu worship, and a shared respect for nature and non-violence, have contributed to the decline of the Jain community through conversion to Hinduism, but there is no antagonism between the two sects.

Focused on the practice of **ahimsa** (non-violence), Jains follow a rigorous discipline to avoid harm to all **jivas**, or "souls", which exist in animals and humans, and in plants, water, fire, earth and air. They assert that every *jiva* is pure, omniscient, and capable of achieving liberation, or *moksha*, from existence in this universe. However, *jivas* are obscured by **karma**, a form of subtle matter that clings to the soul, is born of action, and binds the *jiva* to physical existence. For the most orthodox Jain, the only way to dissociate *karma* from the *jiva*, and thereby escape the wheel of death and rebirth, is to follow the path of asceticism and meditation, rejecting passion, wrong view, attachment, carelessness and impure action.

The Jain doctrine is based upon the teachings of **Mahavira**, or "Great Hero", the last in a succession of 24 **tirthankaras** ("crossing-makers") said to appear on earth every 300 million years. Mahavira (*c*.599–527 BC) was born as Vardhamana Jnatrputra into a *kshatrya* family near modern Patna, in northeast India. Like the Buddha, Mahavira rejected family life at the age of thirty, and spent years wandering as an ascetic, renouncing all possessions in an attempt to conquer attachment to worldly values. Firmly opposed to sacrificial rites and caste distinctions, after gaining complete understanding and detachment, he began teaching others, not about Vedic gods and divine heroes, but about the true nature of the world, and the means required for release, *moksha*, from an endless cycle of rebirth.

His teachings were written down in the first millennium BC, and Jainism prospered throughout India, under the patronage of kings such as Chandragupta Maurya (third century BC). Not long after, there was a schism, in part based on linguistic and geographical divisions, but mostly due to differences in monastic practice. On the one hand the **Digambaras** ("sky-clad") believed that nudity was an essential part of world renunciation, and that women are incapable of achieving liberation from worldly existence. The ("white-clad") **Svetambaras**, however, disregarded the extremes of nudity, incorporated nuns into monastic communities, and even acknowledged a female *tirthankara*. Today the two sects worship at different temples, but the number of naked Digambaras is minimal. Many Svetambara monks and nuns wear white masks to avoid breathing in insects, and carry a "fly-whisk", sometimes used to brush their path; none will use public transport, and they often spend days or weeks walking barefoot to a pilgrimage site.

Practising Jain householders vow to avoid injury, falsehood, theft (extended to fair trade), infidelity and worldly attachment. Jain **temples** are wonderfully ornate, with pillars, brackets and spires carved by *silavats* into voluptuous maidens, musicians, saints, and even Hindu deities; the *swastika* symbol commonly set into the marble floors is central to Jainism, representing the four states of rebirth as gods, humans, "hell beings", or animals and plants. Worship in temples consists of prayer and *puja* before images of the *tirthankaras*; the devotee circumambulates the image, chants sacred verses and makes offerings of flowers, sandalwood paste, rice, sweets and incense. It's common to fast four times a month on *parvan* (holy) days, the eighth and fourteenth days of the moon's waxing and waning periods. While reducing attachment to the body, this emulates the fast to death (while in meditation), or *sallekhana*, accepted by Jain mendicants as a final rejection of attachment, and a relatively harmless way to end worldly life.

To enter a monastic community, lay Jains must pass through eleven *pratimas*, starting with right views, the profession of vows, fasting and continence, and culminating in renunciation of family life. Once a monk or nun, a Jain aims to clarify understanding through meditational

THE 24 TIRTHANKARAS	
1 Adinath/Rishabha	13 Vimala
2 Ajitanath	14 Ananta/Anantajita
3 Sambhava	15 Dharma
4 Abinandana	16 Santi/Shantinath
5 Sumati	17 Kunthu
6 Padmaprabha	18 Ara
7 Suparsva	19 Malli
8 Chandraprabha	20 Munisuvrata
9 Puspadanta	21 Nami
10 Sitala	22 Nemi/Neminath
11 Sreyansa	23 Parshva/Parshvanath
12 Vasupujya	24 Mahavira

practices, hoping to extinguish passions and sever the ties of *karma* and attachment, entering fourteen spiritual stages, *gunasthanas*, to emerge as a fully enlightened, omniscient being. Whether pursuing a monastic or lay lifestyle, however, Jains recognize the rarity of enlightenment, and religious practice is, for the most part, aimed at achieving a state of rebirth more conducive to spiritual attainment.

Pilgrimage sites are known as **tirthas**, but this does not refer to the literal meaning of "river crossing", sacred to Hindus because of the purificatory nature of water. At one of the foremost Svetambara *tirthas*, **Shatrunjaya** in Gujarat, over nine hundred temples crown a single hill, said to have been visited by the first *tirthankara*, Rishabha, and believed to be the place where Rama, Sita and the Pandava brothers (incorporated into Jain tradition) gained deliverance. An important Digambara *tirtha* is **Shravan Belgola** in Karnataka, where a 57-feet-high image of Bahubali (recognized as the first human to attain liberation), at the summit of a hill, is anointed in the huge *abhisheka* festival every twelve years.

In an incredibly complicated process of philosophical analysis known as **Anekanatavada** (many-sidedness), Jainism approaches all questions of existence, permanence, and change from seven different viewpoints, maintaining that things can be looked at in an infinite number of valid ways. Thus it claims to remove the intellectual basis for violence, avoiding the potentially damaging result of holding a one-sided view. In this respect Jainism accepts other religious philosophies, and it has adopted, with a little reinterpretation, several Hindu festivals and practices.

SIKHISM

Sikhism, India's youngest "religion", remains dominant in the Punjab, while its adherents have spread throughout northern India, and several communities have grown up in Britain, America and Canada.

Guru Nanak (1469–1539) was the movement's founder. Born into an orthodox Hindu *kshatrya* family in Talwandi, a small village west of Lahore (in present-day Pakistan), he was among many sixteenth-century poet-philosophers, sometimes referred to as Sants, who formed emotional cults, drawing elements from both Hinduism and Islam. Nanak declared "God is neither Hindu nor Muslim and the path which I follow is God's"; he regarded God as *Sat*, or truth, who makes himself known through gurus. Though he condemned ancestor worship, astrology, caste distinction, sex discrimination, auspicious days, and the rituals of *brahmins*, Nanak did not attack Islam or Hinduism – he simply regarded the many deities as names for one supreme God, and encouraged his followers to shift religious emphasis from ritual to meditation.

In common with Hindus, Nanak believed in a cyclic process of death and rebirth (*samsara*), but he asserted that liberation (*moksha*) was attainable in this life by all women and men, regardless of caste, and religious practice can and should be integrated into everyday practical living. He contested that all people are characterized by *humai*, a sense of self-reliance that obscures an understanding of dependence on god, encourages attachment to temporal values (*maya*), and consequently results in successive rebirths. For Sikhs, the only way to achieve release from human existence is to conquer *humai*, and become centred on God (*gurmukh*). The only people believed to have realized the ultimate truth embodied by God are the Sikh gurus.

Guru Nanak, who died in 1539, was succeeded by a disciple, Lehna, known as **Guru Angad** ("limb"), who continued to lead the community of Sikhs ("disciples"), the **Sikh Panth**, and wrote his own and Nanak's hymns in a new script, **Gurumukhi**, which is today the script of written Punjabi.

After Guru Angad's death in 1552, eight successive gurus acted as leaders for the Sikh Panth, each introducing new elements into the faith and asserting it as a separate and power-ful religious movement. Guru Ram Das (1552–74) founded the sacred city of **Amritsar**; his successor, Guru Arjan, compiled the gurus' hymns in a book called the *Adi Granth*, and became Sikhism's first martyr when he was executed at the hands of Jahangir.

The last leader, **Guru Gobind Singh**, was largely responsible for moulding the community as it exists today. In 1699 he founded the **Khalsa Brotherhood**, requiring members to renounce tobacco, *halal* meat, and sexual relations with Muslims, and to adopt the **five Ks**: *kesh* (unshorn hair), *kangha* (comb), *kirpan* (sword), *kara* (steel wristlet) and *kachch* (short trousers). This code, assumed at initiation, together with the replacement of caste names with Singh ("lion") for men and Kaur ("princess") for women, and the wearing of turbans by men, created a distinct cultural identity. Guru Gobind Singh compiled a standardized version of the *Adi Granth*, which contains the hymns of the first nine gurus as well as poems written by Hindus and Muslims, and installed it as his successor, naming it *Guru Granth Sahib*. This became the Sikh's spiritual guide, while political authority rested with the Khalsa, or *sangat*.

Demands for a separate Sikh state – Khalistan – and fighting in the eighteenth century, and later after Independence, have burdened Sikhs with a reputation as military activists, but Sikhs regard their religion as one devoted to egalitarianism, democracy and social awareness. Though to die fighting for the cause of religious freedom is considered to lead to liberation, the use of force is officially sanctioned only when other methods have failed.

The main duties of a Sikh are *nam japna*, *kirt karni*, and *vand chakna*; keeping God's name in mind, earning honest means, and giving to charity. Serving the community (*seva*) is a display of obedience to God, and the ideal life is uncontaminated by the **five evil impulses**: lust, covetousness, attachment, anger and pride.

Sikh **worship** takes place in a *gurudwara* ("door to the guru") or in the home, providing a copy of the *Adi Granth* is present. There are no priests, and no fixed time for worship, but congregations often meet in the mornings and evenings, and always on the eleventh day (*ekadashi*) of each lunar month, and on the first day of the year (*sangrand*). During *Kirtan*, or hymn singing, a feature of every Sikh service, verses from the *Adi Granth* or *Janam Sakhis*, stories of Guru Nanak's life, are sung to rhythmic clapping. The communal meal, *langar*, following prayers and singing, reinforces the practice laid down by Guru Nanak that openly flaunted caste and religious differences.

Gurudwaras – often schools, clinics or hostels as well as houses of prayer – are generally modelled on the Moghul style of Shah Jahan, considered a congenial blend of Hindu and Muslim architecture; usually whitewashed, and surmounted by a dome, they are always distinguishable by the *nishan sahib*, a yellow flag introduced by Guru Hargobind (1606–44). As in Islam, God is never depicted in pictorial form. Instead, the representative symbol *Il Oankar* is etched into a canopy that shades the *Adi Granth*, which always stands in the main prayer room. In some *gurudwaras* a picture of a guru is hung close to the *Adi Granth*, but it's often difficult to distinguish between the different teachers: artistically they are depicted as almost identical, a tradition that unites the ten gurus as vehicles for god's words, or *mahalas*, and not divine beings.

Important occasions for Sikhs, in addition to naming of children, weddings and funerals, are **Gurpurbs**, anniversaries of the birth and death of the ten gurus, when the *Adi Granth* is read continuously from beginning to end.

ZOROASTRIANISM

Of all India's religious communities, western visitors are least likely to come across – or recognize – **Zoroastrians**, who have no distinctive dress, and few houses of worship. Most live in Bombay, where they are known as **Parsis** (Persians) and are active in business, education, and politics; the Tata family are leading industrialists who until recently had a virtual monopoly on Indian truck building, and control many major chemical factories. Zoroastrian numbers (roughly ninety thousand) are rapidly dwindling, due to a falling birth rate and absorption into wider communities.

The religion's founder, **Zarathustra** (Zoroaster), who lived in Iran in 6000 BC (according to Zoroastrians), or between 1700 and 1400 BC, was the first religious prophet to expound a dualistic philosophy, based on the opposing powers of good and evil. For him, the absolute, wholly good and wise god, **Ahura Mazda**, together with his holy spirit and six emanations present in earth, water, the sky, animals, plants and fire, is constantly at odds with an evil power, **Angra Mainyu**, who is aided by **daevas**, or evil spirits.

Mankind, whose task on earth is to further good, faces judgement after death, and depending on the proportion of good and bad words, thoughts and actions, will find a place in heaven, or suffer the torments of hell. Zarathustra looked forward to a day of judgement, when a saviour, **Saoshyant**, miraculously born of a seed of the prophet and a virgin maiden, will appear on earth, restoring Ahura Mazda's perfect realm and expelling all impure souls and spirits to hell.

The first Zoroastrians to enter India arrived on the Gujarati coast in the tenth century, soon after the Arabian conquest of Iran, and by the seventeenth century most had settled in Bombay. Zoroastrian practice is based on the responsibility of every man and woman to choose between good and evil, and to respect God's creations. Five daily prayers, usually hymns (*gathas*), uttered by Zarathustra and standardized in the main Zoroastrian text, the **Avesta**, are said in the home or in a temple, before a fire, which symbolizes the realm of truth, righteousness and order.

Members of other faiths may not enter Zoroastrian temples, but one custom that is evident to outsiders is the method of disposing of the dead. A body is laid on a high open rooftop (or isolated hill) known as *dakhma* (often referred to as a "tower of silence") for the flesh to be eaten by vultures, and the bones cleansed by sun and wind. Recently, some Zoroastrians, by necessity, have adopted more common methods of cremation or burial; in order not to bring impurity to fire or earth, they only use electric crematoria, and shroud coffins in concrete before laying them in the ground.

No Ruz, or "New Day", which celebrates the creation of fire and the ultimate triumph of good over evil, is the most popular Zoroastrian festival; the oldest sacred fire in India, in **Udwada**, just north of Daman in south Gujarat, is an important pilgrimage site.

Harriet Podger

INDIAN CINEMA

Travellers to India cannot help but be struck by the overwhelming presence of the **cinema**. Stridently non-naturalistic film hoardings, in bright primary colours, loom large in the urban landscape, and every city rings with the sounds of the latest popular **film songs** (pop music *is* film music in India), relayed through millions of radios.

Any attempt to understand modern Indian culture must entail coming to grips with the popular cinema, if only on account of the sheer volume of its product. India's film industry is the largest in the world; so large, in fact, that it scarcely makes sense to speak of it as being a single industry. The most obvious factor contributing to its diversity has been the existence, ever since the advent of sound, of a number of **regional language** cinemas. Although the Tamil cinema of Madras is responsible for producing the greatest number of films, the best known and most influential of the regional cinemas is the **Bombay film**. The Hindi market is the largest linguistic market, and one on which the southern studios and stars keep a vigilant eye, through direct production, dubbing regional works into Hindi, and attempting to transform regional stars into national ones.

Indian popular cinema has long been misrepresented and misunderstood, both within India and in the rest of the world. Urban sophisticates obsessed with realist and classical canons of film-making forever charge it with a dependence on simple melodrama, a wilful failure to consider individual pyschology, and an uncontrollable tendency to take recourse in song and dance sequences at every conceivable juncture. In India, such critiques have their roots in the late 1940s and 1950s, and the emergence of an Indian "art cinema", led by **Satyajit Ray**. Ray argued for a cinema that developed its own iconography and addressed the everyday "reality" of Indian life. Quite apart from the universal debate concerning notions of "high" and "low" art, these arguments display a narrow-mindedness as to what may or may not be the "correct" way to portray India, and Indianness.

THE EARLY DECADES

Cinema in India emerged as an art form in the late nineteenth century. As an import from the west, at a time when India was under the political control of the British, it is not surprising that it drew heavily upon European conventions. At the time, Victorian **theatrical melodrama** was one of the most popular and influential forms of entertainment. The earliest Indian films blended melodramatic themes – family conflict, mistaken identity, heart-rending experiences, and a denouement centring on a triumphant disclosure of virtue – with indigenous traditions of narrative and performance. Moral questions, and the role of the family, still tend to be more significant than the secular public domain, and the notions of individual choice and self-determination around which so many western narratives revolve.

Issues of morality and duty permeate what is often referred to as the first Indian feature film, *Raja Harishcandra*, directed by DG Phalke (1913), in which female roles were played by men, as was the custom of the time. Its story, drawn from an episode in the ancient *Mahabharata* epic, details the suffering undergone by the king of the title and his family in order to fulfil a vow of penance. It inaugurated a genre known as the **mythological**, which was to be a staple of popular cinema well into the 1950s.

Despite the occasional gesture, the British never really encouraged the Indian film industry. What little remains of Indian silent cinema up to 1931 barely fills six video-cassettes in the National Film Archives of India, but it is remarkable for the way traditional "theatrical" framing (static characters, faced front on by the camera) is animated by a considerable investment in location shooting, both in natural surroundings and in the city. This is evident not only in *Raja Harishcandra*, but also in historical-cum-stunt films such as *Diler Jigar/Gallant Hearts* (SS Agarwal; 1931) and *Gulaminu Patan/The Fall of Slavery* (SS Agarwal; 1931), and in the international co-productions directed by Himansu Rai and the German Franz Osten. Among these, *Light of Asia* (1925), about the Buddha, and *Shiraz* (1928), about the origins of the Taj Mahal, referred to as **"Romances from India"** by their producers, render "India" as a startling, exotic assemblage: scenes of ancient and medieval court life, attended by the ritual of courtly gesture, and by spectacular processions of elephants and camels, are juxtaposed with a glittering naturalism, impressionist in its capturing of sunlight on leaves as the wind courses through the trees. The orientalist, touristic conception of the Osten/Rai films is underlined in the way *Light of Asia* begins, with a series of views of Hindu, Muslim and Buddhist culture, as they are presented to a group of white tourists. An "oriental" disposition, of worldly renunciation, and unrequited romantic desire is outlined as the ultimate destiny of Gautama (the Buddha) and Shiraz (the artisan who, obsessed with the Empress Nur Jahan, designs the Taj Mahal in her memory). Another aspect of the portrait of "essential" Indian traits is that of the brave Rajput, the warrior caste of north India, who serves to present the past in a heroic, romantic mould.

THE TALKIES

In 1931, India's first talkie, *Alam Ara*, was released, dubbed into Hindi and Urdu. As the talkies emerged over the next decade, so too did a new series of issues. The most prominent of these, of course, was language, and **language markets**; alongside, there are considerations of regional identity, of the different places that separately and together make up India. Many films of the time were produced both in the regional language (Bengali, Marathi), and in Hindi, so that they could be oriented to the larger Hindi-speaking market. However, through the development of a genre known as the **devotional film**, very specific religious and cultural traditions could be addressed by using the **music** of the region. Films like the Bengali *Chandidas* (Debaki Bose; 1932), and the Marathi *Sant Tukaram* (Fatehlal and Damle; 1937) both about popular "saints" from regional devotional traditions that countered Brahmanical orthodoxy, were not released in Hindi versions.

Ironically, the genre that might have added to this sense of specific place and particular custom, the **"social film"**, conceived by the industry to represent contemporary social life, swiftly acquired a pan-Indian homogeneity. While addressing social differences of caste, class and the relations between the sexes, the social films of the 1930s adopted a modern reformist outlook in an essentially converging view of society, and their studio settings

further distanced them from any sense of particular place. Nonetheless, many showed great innovation. The Marathi director, V Shantaram, for example, was alert to world trends in film-making, deploying expressionist effects intelligently in such works as *Amrit Manthan* (Prabhat Talkies; 1934). In what was probably the most important film of the period, *Devdas* (1935), the director Pramathesh Barua created a startlingly edited climax to a tale of love frustrated by social distinction and masculine ineffectuality. Released in Bengali, Hindi and Tamil, *Devdas* created an oddly ambivalent hero for this period (and again, through a Hindi re-make directed by Bimal Roy in 1955), predicated on indecision, frustration and a focus on failure and longing rather than on achievement.

By the 1940s the social film further delimited its focus by excluding particularly fraught issues, especially of caste division. A representative example, prefiguring the kind of entertainment extravaganza that has become the hallmark of the **Bombay film**, was *Kismet/ Fate* (Gyan Mukerji; Bombay Talkies; 1943), which broke all box-office records and ran for more than two years. Family and class become the key issues in the representation of society, and the story's location is an indeterminate urban one. As a child the hero loses a respectable family identity, is precipitated into a life of glamorous crime, and eventually comes to recover his rightful position. Made at the height of **World War II**, in a climate that saw fortunes lost and made thanks to inflation, the film appears to speak to the excitement and anxiety of a new social moment. Social mobility, rather than the rigidity associated with caste, was to become a recurrent theme. However, the melodrama of *Kismet* is woven in with a pageant of nationalist mobilization; social divisions are reconciled by bringing everyone into the family through marriage. Although this became the model for popular cinema, especially after the decline of regional industries in Maharashtra and Bengal by the end of the 1940s, different strains are observable in the Tamil films of the same period.

In the 1930s, the **Tamil cinema** gained national recognition with the costume extravaganza, *Chandralekha*, directed by SS Vasan for Gemini studios, and called by its director a "pageant for our peasants" (a large section of the audience would have been illiterate). Its story, of the conflict for the inheritance of an empire, is laden with overblown set-pieces and crowds of extras. Even more significant than this investment in the spectacular was its "Tamil-ness"; the recognition of a national existence different to that portrayed in the Bombay output. In films inspired by the anti-high caste Tamil nationalist movement, the Dravida Kazhagam, the Tamil region becomes the Tamil nation, distinct from, and frequently oppressed by, the Hindi-speaking north. Such anti-Brahmanical, anti-north ideology is much in evidence in films like *Parasakthi/The Goddess* (1949), although by then some of the radicalism of these positions was already being watered down. From that time onwards, film in Tamil Nadu, and neighbouring Andhra Pradesh, became a key vehicle of politics, facilitating the rise to power of the movie stars MG Ramachandran and NT Rama Rao to the chief ministerships of the two states.

THE 1950s

By the start of the 1950s, Bombay was ascendant in the Hindi film market, while Pune and Bengal were in decline, transformed into struggling regional language centres, and Madras was on the way to becoming a large-scale producer. Calcutta, now disestablished as focus of a thriving commercial film industry, became the vanguard of the art cinema, with the emergence of the **film society movement** at the end of the 1940s and Satyajit Ray's *Pather Panchali/Song of the Road*, produced with West Bengal state government support in 1955.

Post-Independence, despite a relatively sympathetic government enquiry in 1951, the industry became the object of considerable moral scrutiny and criticism, and was subject to severe taxation. A covert consensus emerged between proponents of art cinema and the state, all focussing on the imperative to create a "better" cinema. The Film and Television Institute of India was established at Pune in 1959 to develop technical skills for an industry seen to be lacking in this field. However, active support for **parallel cinema**, as it came to be called, only really took off at the end of the 1960s, under the aegis of the government's *Film Finance Corporation*, set up in 1961 to support new film-makers.

Ironically, this pressure and vocal criticism occurred at a time when arguably some of the most interesting work in popular cinema was being produced. Radical cultural organizations, loosely associated with the Indian Communist Party, had organized themselves as the **All India Progressive Writers Association** and the **Indian People's Theatre Association** (*IPTA*). This latter had produced *Dharti ke Lal/Sons of the Soil* (KA Abbas; 1943), and its impact on the industry can be seen in the work of radical writers such as Abbas, lyricists such as Sahir Ludhianvi, and directors such as Bimal Roy and Zia Sarhady. In addition, directors such as Raj Kapoor, Guru Dutt and Mehboob Khan, while not directly involved with *IPTA*, created films that reflected a passionate concern for questions of social justice.

Largely studio-based, the films of this era nevertheless incorporated vivid stylistic experimentation, influenced by **international currents** in film-making. For example, the expressionist *chiaroscuro* of Hollywood *film noir* was frequently employed to create layers of darkness and light, portraying the shadowy city as a place of economic insecurity and social indignity. Such effects are evident in *Awara/The Vagabond* (Raj Kapoor; 1951; script by KA Abbas), *Awaaz/The Call* (Zia Sarhady; 1956) and *Pyaasa/Craving* (Guru Dutt; 1957). The First International Film Festival, held in Bombay in 1951, showed Italian works for the first time in India; the influence of Neorealism can be seen in films such as *Do Bigha Zamin/Two Measures of Land* (Bimal Roy; 1953), a portrait of father and son eking out a living in Calcutta that strongly echoes the narrative of Vittorio de Sica's *Bicycle Thief* (1948). Mehboob Khan's *Andaz/Style* (1949), an upperclass love triangle founded on a tragic misunderstanding, draws on codes of psychological representation – hallucinations and dreams – that feature strongly in 1940s Hollywood melodrama, especially in what has come to be known as the "women's film".

Mehboob's tendency to make a visual spectacle of his material, and his involvement with populist themes and issues make him a good example of popular cinema of the time. His movies are emblazoned with kitsch ornamentation, and the overall effect of the excesses, the signs of privilege (butlers, valets, cooks, gardeners) and modes of dress (riding clothes, dressing-gowns, sports jackets, ballroom gowns) is that of contamination by the "west".

THE ART CINEMA

India's emergent **art cinema**, led by the Bengali directors Ray, Mrinal Sen and Ritwik Ghatak reacted against such spectacle. **Satyajit Ray**'s world-famous debut, *Pather Panchali* (1955), is based on many of the themes that engaged contemporary popular film-makers of the time, such as loss of social status, economic injustice, uprootment, but sets them within a naturalistic, realist frame which put a special value on the Bengali countryside, locating it as a place of nostalgia, to which the urban and individualist sensibility of its protagonist, Apu, looked with longing.

In Ray's later work on urban middle-class existence, *Mahanagar/Big City* (1963), *Charulata* (1964), *Seemabadha/Company Limited* (1971), *Pratidwandi/The Protagonist* (1970), and *Jana Aranya/The Middleman* (1975), his rational, humanist vision is at the same time at home in the city, and repulsed by it; overarching estrangement is relayed through images of futile job interviews, cynical corporate schemes, murky deals in respectable cafes.

When Ray tries to step out of the cityscape, however, into a broader sphere, he falls flat. The tribal woman character of *Aranyer din Ratri*, played by the glamorous Bombay film star, Simi Garewal, is grotesque; while the director's well-meaning attempt to capture the horror of the great Bengal famine of 1943 through the perspective of a *brahmin* priest, in *Ashani Sanket/Distant Thunder* (1973) , is ineffectual. Films from the latter part of his career, such as *Ghare Baire/Home and the World* (1984), *Ganashatru/Enemy of the People* (1989), *Shakha Proshakha/Branches of a Tree* (1990), and *Agantuk/The Visitor* (1992), show these failings magnified. Wedded to the traditions of the nineteenth-century intelligentsia, he finds society wanting, vilifies it for its ignorance and corruption, and oversees the malignant terrain below with a lofty disdain. In these last works, **women characters**, once his forte, dwindle to assume a conventional moral role, critical of men who wander from the straight and narrow; a great pity, for his *Charulata*, starring the wonderful Madhabi Mukherjee, must stand as one of the great woman's roles of the Indian cinema, subtly evoking the intellectual and erotic frustration that circumscribe the life of the female protagonist in late-nineteenth-century Calcutta. Indeed, Ray's women, such as

the mother, Sarbojaya of *Pather Panchali*, the tomboy Aparna Sen of *Samapti/The End* (1961), Madhabi Mukherjee in *Charulata* and *Mahanagar*, and Kaberi Bose in *Aranyer din Ratri*, are splendidly drawn portraits in the realist tradition.

In contrast to Ray, his contemporaries **Mrinal Sen** and Ritwik Ghatak set out to expose the dark underside of India's lower middle-class and unemployed. Sen, after a phase of uneven, didactic political cinema at the height of the Maoist-inspired Naxalite movement of the early 1970s – marked by the trilogy *Interview* (1971), *Calcutta 71* (1972) and *Padatik/The Guerrilla Fighter* (1973) – made two films, *Akaler Sandhane/In Search of Famine* (1980) and *Khandar/Ruins* (1983), about film-making itself, exploring its inherent distance and disengagement, and the problems entailed in trying to record "reality". In his later works he took on the role of the social raconteur, portraying the claustrophobia, constrained lives and hypocrisy of the lower middle class in a series of interesting films: *Ek din pratidin/And Quiet Rolls the Day* (1979), *Chaalchitra/Kaleidoscope* (1981) and *Kharij/The Court Is Closed* (1982). Bringing the themes together, the intense *Mahaprithivi/This Great Earth* (1992) tells the story of a mother (the remarkable Geeta Sen) who commits suicide after the fall of the Berlin wall; the death of the communist dream seems to have made a mockery of the death of her idealist son in a police firing twenty years earlier.

Perhaps the most outstanding figure of this generation, fulfilling the potential of the radical cultural initiatives of the *IPTA*, was the great **Ritwik Ghatak**. Disruption, the problems of locating oneself in a new environment, and the indignities and oppression of common people are the recurrent themes of this poet of Partition, who lamented the division of Bengal in 1947. Disharmony and discontinuity could be said to be the hallmark of *Nagarik/Citizen* (1952) and *Meghe Dhaka Tara/Cloud-capped Star* (1960), where studio sets of street corners mingle uneasily with live-action shots of Calcutta. There is something deliberately jarring about the rhythms of editing, the use of sound, and the compositions, as if the director refuses to allow us to settle into a comfortable, familiar frame of viewing. In *Aajantrik/Man and Machine* (1958) and *Subarnarekha* (1952;

released 1965) he juxtaposes the displaced and transient urban figure with tribal peoples; placing the human figure at the edge of the frame, dwarfed by majestic nature.

THE 1970s AND 1980s

During the 1960s, popular cinema had shifted its social concerns towards more romantic genres, showcasing such new stars as Shammi Kapoor, Raj's younger brother – a kind of Indian Elvis – and later, Rajesh Khanna, a soft, romantic hero. The period is also notable for a more assertive Indian **nationalism**. Following the Indo-Pakistan wars of 1962 and 1965, the Indian officer, and especially the fighter pilot, came to be a glamorous rallying point for the national imagination in films such as *Sangam/ Meeting of Hearts* (Raj Kapoor; 1964) and *Aradhana/Adoration* (Shakti Samanta; 1969).

However, the political and economic upheaval of the following decade saw a return to social questions across the board, in both the art and popular cinemas. The accepted turning point in the popular film was the angry, violent *Zanjeer/The Chain* (Prakash Mehra; 1973), which fed into the anxieties and frustrations generated by the quickening but lopsided pace of **industrialization** and **urbanization**. Establishing Amitabh Bachchan as the biggest star of the next decade and beyond, its policeman hero is ousted from service through a conspiracy, and takes the law into his own hands to render justice and to avenge his long-dead parents. The considerable **political turmoil** of the next few years, including the railway strike of 1974 and the Nav Nirman movement led by JP Narayan in Bihar and Gujarat, ultimately led to the declaration of Indira Gandhi's Emergency in 1975. It was as if the state and the people had split apart. As the cities grew, so did the audiences. The popular cinema generated an ambiguous figure to express this alienation; whether he represented the state or the people is another question.

At the level of images, there was a greater investment in the stresses of everyday life and, unlike the 1950s, in location shooting. In *Zanjeer*, the casual killing of a witness on Bombay's commuter trains conjures up the perils of life in the metropolis; this is echoed in images of the dockyard, taxi-rank, railtrack and construction site in *Deewar/The Wall* (Yash Chopra; 1975), also starring Amitabh Bachchan.

Here his construction worker takes to a life of crime to maintain his family, and is ultimately killed by his police-officer brother in a rite of moral cleansing that glamourizes the persona of the rebellious outsider. From this period until the present day, popular movies are full of images of a fraught urban scenario, drawing out fantastic and often nightmarish scenes of melodramatic conflict.

The recurrent narrative of these films, of protagonists uprooted from small town and rural families to the perils of the city, is shared by the street children researched by professional sociologists in Mira Nair's *Salaam Bombay!* (1988). It can, however, be argued that Nair's realism, for all its international acclaim, is not an adequate way to represent the experience of the modern city. Here the Bombay film's very excesses, its grand gestures, and the priority it gives to emotion and excitement may more truly reflect the dominant rhythms of urban life in India. At the level of plot and character, however, the Bombay film simultaneously simplifies and collapses our sense of India, reducing the enormous variety of identity – social, regional, ethnic and religious – that makes up Indian society. Where these identities appear, they do so as caricatures and objects of fun. To counter this, the **art cinema of the 1980s** diversified from its Bengali moorings of the earlier period under the aegis of the *Film Finance Corporation*. Works by Shyam Benegal, Gautam Ghose, Saeed Mirza, BV Karanth, Girish Kasaravalli, Mrinal Sen, MS Sathyu, Ray, and Kundan Shah, among others, actively addressed questions of social injustice: problems of landlord exploitation, bonded labour, untouchability, urban power, corruption and criminal extortion, the oppression of women, and political manipulation. Ghatak in particular had addressed many of these issues earlier, but never had there been such an outpouring of the social conscience, nor such a flowing of new images – of regional landscapes, cultures, and social structures. Many of the films may seem didactic and uncomplex, undercutting the attention to form that had marked the earlier period – but not all. Benegal's first two films indicate an unusual concern with the psychology of domination and subordination; *Ankur/ The Seedling* (1974) is particularly striking not only for this and for the open, fluid way it captures the countryside. Among Kannada directors, working in south India, Kasaravalli in *Ghattashradha* (1981) effected an intimate vision of the oppression of widows through the view of a child. And special mention must be made of Kundan Shah's *Jaane Bhi Do Yaaron/ Let Sleeping Dogs Lie* (1984), a wonderful exercise in farce and slapstick that is also a brilliant portrait of Bombay.

THE SOUTH

The most notable of the directors who speak specifically about their own cultures, and about the possibilities of change, are – as well as Kumar Shahani and Mani Kaul, who work in Hindi – Adoor Gopalakrishnan and Aravindan from **Kerala**. A key to their productivity was the overall development of film culture in Kerala, India's most literate state. In his films **Gopalakrishnan** transformed the lush countryside, busy towns and animated culture of Kerala into a strange, dissociated place, fraught with communicative gaps, menacing, inexplicable characters, and an overall sense of the impenetrable. Subjects range from the mounting tragedies that beset a young couple in the city (*Swayamvaram/One's Own Choice*; 1972), and the effete authoritarianism of a declining feudal landlord (*Elippathayam/The Rat-Trap*; 1984), to the mysterious spiritual decline of a popular communist activist (*Mukha Mukham/Face to Face*; 1987). Gopalakrishnan was a markedly controlled director, and his modernist framing of the world could be said either to constrain our vision of it, or to illuminate it from an unconventional angle. *Kodiyettam/Ascent* (1981), his second film about the life of a ne'er-do-well, shot in black-and-white with an eye for the space and texture of the Keralan countryside, breathes more easily in comparison.

The late **Aravindan**, sometime cartoonist and employee of the Kerala Rubber Board, had something of the mystic in him, but went through a range of styles, including a *cinéma-vérité* approach, as in *Thampu/The Circus Tent* (1978), in which circus performers speak direct to the camera. His episode from the *Ramayana*, *Kanchana Sita/Golden Sita*, places the action against the grain of the high Hindu tradition by situating it among tribes in the verdant landscape of the Kerala forests. At his best, his narrative style refuses a didactic approach, generating a whimsical sense of how destinies are shaped.

CONTEMPORARY CURRENTS

In the 1990s, **video**, national and satellite/ cable television have resulted in the development of a prolonged crisis in India's movie industry, where commercial and art films are equally at risk of failing at the box office. The problems of the latter are mainly due to a persistent failure to find distribution outlets; now, more and more film-makers of both streams look to **television**; the state film finance unit (now named the *National Film Development Corporation*) has a major stake in the expansion of the national network.

There have been two responses to this crisis. The first, at the economic level, has been to try and curb film piracy, and to systematize the relationship of film to video. The second is an investment in **new technology**, and in new forms of story-telling. The Telugu and Tamil industries, and directors such as Ram Gopal Varma and Mani Ratnam, are at the forefront of such moves, showing a lively interest in new techniques in American cinema. Varma's *Shiva* (1990) and *Raat/Night* (1991) showcase the use of steadicam – in the latter, to the exclusion of any serious narrative. The technical virtuosity of Mani Ratnam's works, as well as their elegant story-telling and restrained performances have attracted a following among film buffs across the country, who identify with his style and, implicitly, with the image of a dynamic, modern identity. In 1993, Ratnam made an important breakthrough with *Roja*, a love story about a young Tamil peasant woman and her husband, a cryptographer who decodes messages for military intelligence. The couple are transported to Kashmir, presently subject to sustained separatist extremism. Embroiling the Tamil couple in a national issue that might have seemed remote to an earlier generation, the film identified a new pan-Indian field of interest. Dubbed into Hindi, it was a national success, giving rise to the dubbing of a number of southern films. Whether this is a positive development, or will collapse India's many voices into a modern anonymity, remains to be seen.

Ravi S Vasudevan

THE MUSIC OF INDIA

The origin of north Indian (Hindustani) classical music is shrouded in obscurity. There is a tendency in India to attribute the invention of any ancient art form to one of the many Hindu deities, and the resulting synthesis of myth and legend is often taken as literal truth. But in reality north Indian classical music as it exists today is the result of a long process of integrating many diverse cultural influences. Not only is there a rich and varied tradition of regional folk musics, but all through its history India has absorbed the culture and traditions of foreign invaders, the most influential being the Muslim Moghuls.

The introduction of Turko-Persian musical elements is what primarily distinguishes north Indian classical music from its predecessor, Carnatic, now restricted to southern India. The latter is a complex, rich and fascinating musical tradition in its own right, and even an untrained ear can usually distinguish between the two.

TEACHERS AND PUPILS

In the north, both Hindu and Muslim communities have provided outstanding artists. While music recognizes no religious differences – indeed it is something of a religion in its own right – distinguished musicians of Hindu origin customarily take the title of *pandit* (and become known as gurus), while their Muslim counterparts add the prefix *ustad* (meaning "master") to their names. An *ustad* may teach anything – not only his own particular art or instrument. It is not unusual for *sitar* maestros to teach *sarod* or vocal techniques to their pupils.

The **teaching** of north Indian classical music is a subject in itself. One thing that strikes a westerner is the spiritual link between

Features on **music**, **dance** and **performing arts**, scattered throughout this book, include:

teacher and pupil. Quite often the two may be blood relations anyway, but where they are not, a spiritual relationship is officially inaugurated in a ceremony in which the teacher ties a string to the wrist of the pupil to symbolize the bond between them.

Apart from actual musical form and content, north Indian music has various extra-musical traditions and rituals, usually taught through musical families and **gharanas** ("schools"). Traditionally, Indian music is taught on a one-to-one basis, often from father to son. Many academies and colleges of music now follow the modern style, but traditionalists still adhere to the *gharana* system, and great importance is still attached to membership of a musical family or an impressive lineage. A *gharana*, which may be for singing, for any or all kinds of instruments, or for dance, is more a school of thought than an institution. It suggests a particular belief, or a preference for a certain performance style. *Gharanas* differ not only in broad terms, but also in minute details: how to execute a particular combination of notes, or simply the correct way to hold an instrument. They are usually founded by musicians of outstanding ability, and new styles and forms are added by exceptionally talented musicians who may have trained with one particular *gharana* and then evolved a style of their own.

SCALES OF PURITY AND IMAGINATION

Singing is considered the highest form of classical music, after which instruments are graded according to their similarity to the human voice. The two main vocal traditions are *dhrupad*, the purest of all, devoid of all embellishment and entirely austere in its delivery, and *khayal*, which has a more romantic content and elaborate ornamentation and is the more popular today. Less abstract vocal forms include the so-called light classical *dadra*, *thumri* and *ghazal* as well as *qawwali*, religious music of the Sufi tradition. The degree of musical purity is assigned according to a scale which has music at one extreme and words at the other. As words become more audible and thus the meaning of lyrics more important, so the form is considered to be musically less pure.

Indian musicologists talk about two **kinds of sound** – one spiritual and inaudible to the human ear, the other physical and audible. The

MUSICAL INSTRUMENTS

STRING INSTRUMENTS

The best-known instrument is the *sitar*, invented by Amir Khusrau in the thirteenth century and played with a plectrum. It has six or seven main strings, of which four are played and the other two or three are used to supply a drone or a rhythmic ostinato. In addition there can be between eleven and nineteen sympathetic strings. The two sets of strings are fitted on different bridges. Twenty brass frets fastened to the long hollow neck can be easily moved to conform to the scale of a particular *raag*, and their curvature allows the player to alter the pitch by pulling the string sideways across the fret to provide the gliding portamento so characteristic of Indian music.

The *surbahar* ("spring melody"), effectively a bass *sitar*, is played in the same way. Developed by Sahibdad Khan, the great-grandfather of Vilayat and Imrat Khan, it produces a deep, dignified sound. The neck is wider and longer than that of the *sitar* but its frets are fixed. Thanks to its size, and longer strings, the sound can be sustained for longer, and the range of the portamento is wider.

The *sarod* is a descendant of the Afghani *rebab*. Smaller than a *sitar*, it has two resonating chambers, the larger made of teak covered with goatskin, and the smaller, at the other end of the metal fingerboard, made of metal. Ten of its 25 metal strings are plucked with a fragment of coconut shell. Four of these carry the melody; the others accentuate the rhythm. The rest are sympathetic strings, underneath the main strings. The *sarod* was hugely improved by Ustad Allaudin Khan, whose pupils Ustad Ali Akbar Khan and Ustad Amjad Ali Khan are now its best-known exponents.

The *sarangi* is a fretless bowed instrument with a very broad fingerboard and a double belly. The entire body of the instrument − belly and fingerboard − is carved out of a single block of wood and the hollow covered with parchment. There are three or four main strings of gut and anything up to forty metal sympathetic strings. Some claim it is the most difficult musical instrument to play in the world. Certainly the technique is highly unusual. While the right hand wields the bow in the normal way, the strings are stopped not by the fingertips of the left hand, but by the nails. The *sarangi* is capable of a wide range of timbres and its sound is likened to that of the human voice, so it is usually used to accompany vocal recitals. Originally this was its only function, but in recent years it has become a solo instrument in its own right, thanks mainly to the efforts of Ustad Sultan Khan and Pandit Ram Narayan.

The *santoor*, a hammered zither of trapezoid shape and Persian origin, has only recently been accepted in classical music. It has over a hundred strings, pegged and stretched in pairs, parallel to each other. Each pair passes over two bridges, one on each side of the instrument. The strings are struck by two curving wooden sticks. Its most notable exponent is Pandit Shiv Kumar Sharma.

The *surmandal* resembles a zither, and is used by vocalists to accompany themselves in performance. Even though its primary function is to provide the drone, singers sometimes also play the basic melody line on this instrument.

WIND INSTRUMENTS

The *shehnai*, the traditional instrument for wedding music, is a double-reed, oboe-type instrument with up to nine finger holes, some of which are stopped with wax for fine tuning to the scale of a particular *raag*. It demands a mastery of circular breathing and enormous breath control. A drone accompaniment is provided by a second *shehnai*.

The word *bansuri* refers to a wide variety of bamboo (*banse*) flutes, most end-blown, but some, such as Krishna's famous *murli*, are side-blown. Despite offering a range of less than two octaves, it now appears as a solo concert instrument.

DRUMS

The *tabla* is a set of two small drums played with the palms and fingertips to produce an incredible variety of sounds and timbres, in a range of one octave. Its name is short for *tabla-bayan* − the *tabla* is on the right and the *bayan* ("left") on the left. Its invention is attributed to Amir Khusrau, creator of the *sitar*. Both drum heads are made of skin, with a paste of iron filings and flour in the centre, but while the body of the *tabla* is all wood, the *banya* is metal. The *tabla* is usually turned to the tonic, dominant or sub-dominant notes of the *raag* by knocking the tuning-blocks, held by braces on the sides of the instrument, into place.

Pre-dating the *tabla*, the *pakhavaj* is nearly a metre long and was traditionally made of clay, although now wood is more popular. It has two parchment heads, each tuned to a different pitch, again by knocking the side blocks into place. A paste of boiled rice, iron filings and tamarind juice is applied to the smaller head and a wheat flour paste on the larger helps produce the lower notes.

The *pakhavaj* has a deep mellow sound and is used to accompany *dhrupad* singing and *kathak* dancing. A smaller version of the *pakhavaj*, the *mridangam*, is widely used in south Indian music.

inaudible sound is said to be produced from the ether, and its function is to liberate the soul. But to feel it requires great devotion and concentration which the average person can never really attain. Audible sound, on the other hand, is actually "struck" and is said to have an immediate and pleasurable impact.

Indian music always has a **constant drone** in the background, serving as a reference point for performer and listener alike. In north Indian music this drone is usually played on the four-stringed *tambura*. The privilege of accompanying a teacher's performance on the *tambura* is often accorded to advanced students.

Indian music does not so much describe a mood (as some European music does) as help to create that mood, and then explore it to its depths. Where western classical music starts at a particular point and then progresses from it, Indian classical music revolves around the point, probing it from every angle, yet maintaining a dignified restraint. It is this restraint that distinguishes Indian classical music from the carefree abandon of Indian pop and film music.

RAAGS AND RHYTHMS

The mainstay of all north Indian classical music is the **raag** (or *raga*), an immensely intricate system of scales and associated melodic patterns. Each of the 200 main *raags* is defined by its unique combination of scale-pattern, dominant notes, specific rules to be obeyed in ascending or descending and associated melodic phrases. While Indian classical music is renowned for improvisation, this only takes place within the strictly defined boundaries of a particular *raag*. If the improviser wanders away from the main musical form of the *raag* his or her performance ceases to be regarded as "classical" music. The mark of a good performer is the ability to improvise extensively without abandoning the set of defining rules.

Some *raags* are linked with particular seasons; there is a *raag* for rain, and one for spring; *raags* can be "masculine" or "feminine"; and musicologists may categorize them according to whether they are best suited to a male or female voice. Each *raag* is allotted a time of day, a time identified with the spiritual and emotional qualities of the *raag*. *Raags* are specifically allocated to early morning (either before or after sunrise), mid-morning, early

afternoon, late afternoon, early evening (either before or after sunset), late evening, late night and post-midnight. This system causes a few problems in northern latitudes, for there is some argument as to whether a *raag* should be heard by clock-time or sun-time. Purists adhere to the archaic tradition of a "*raag* timeable" even if they're only listening to records.

The performance of a *raag*, whether sung or played on a *sitar*, *sarod* or *sarangi*, follows a set pattern. First comes the *alaap*, a slow, meditative "mood-setter" in free rhythm which explores the chosen *raag*, carefully introducing the notes of the scale one by one. The *alaap* can span several hours in the hands of a distinguished performer, but may only last a matter of minutes; older aficionados allege that most present-day listeners cannot sustain the attention required to appreciate a lengthy and closely argued *alaap*. As a result, performers have felt under pressure to abbreviate this section of the *raag*, to reach the faster middle and end sections as soon as possible. This became customary in the recording studio, although the advent of the CD, which does not force the music to fit into 25 minutes as the LP did, has initiated a move back to longer performances.

In the next two sections, the *jorh* and the *jhala*, the soloist introduces a rhythmic element, developing the *raag* and exploring its more complex variations. Only in the final section, the *gath*, does the percussion instrument – usually the *tabla* or *pakhavaj* – enter. The soloist introduces a short, fixed composition to which he or she returns between flights of improvisation. In this section rhythm is an important structural element. Both percussionist and soloist improvise, at times echoing each other and sometimes pursuing individual variations of rhythmic counterpoint, regularly punctuated by unison statements of a short melody known as "the composition". The *gath* itself is sub-divided into three sections: a slow tempo passage known as *vilambit*, increasing to a medium tempo, called *madhya*, and finally the fast tempo, *drut*.

Just as the *raag* organizes melody, so the rhythm is organized by highly sophisticated structures expressed through cycles known as *taals*, which can be clapped out by hand. A *taal* is made up of a number of beats (*matras*), each beat defined by a combination of rhythm pattern and timbre. It is the unique set of patterns (*bols*) available within a particular *taal* that define it. There are literally hundreds of *taals*, but most percussionists use the same few favourites over and over again, the most common being the sixteen-beat *teentaal*.

The most unfamiliar aspect of *taal* to the western ear is that the end of one cycle comes not on its last beat, but on the first beat of the following one, so that there is a continual overlap. This first beat is known as *sum*, a point of culmination which completes a rhythmic structure, and performers often indicate it by nodding to each other when they arrive at it. Audiences do the same to express satisfaction and appreciation.

Among smaller, more discerning audiences, verbal applause such as "Wah!" (Bravo!), or even "Subhan-Allah" (Praise be to God!), is considered the standard form of appreciation. Only in western-style concert halls, where such exclamations would be inaudible, has handclapping come to replace these traditional gestures of approval.

LIGHT CLASSICAL MUSIC

Many concerts of classical music end with the performance of a piece in one of the styles collectively referred to as "light classical". Although they obey the rules of classical music with respect to *raag* and *taal*, they do so less rigorously than is required for a performance of *dhrupad*, *khayal* or other pure classical styles. The *alaap* is short or non-existent, and the composition is frequently derived from a folk-melody. Indeed, it could be said that light classical music is essentially a synthesis of folk and classical practice. The two most important and widespread types are *thumri* and *ghazal*.

The origin of **thumri** is popularly ascribed to Nawab Wajid Ali Shah, who governed Lucknow (Avadh) from 1847 to 1856. Although little interested in matters of state, he was a great patron of the arts and during his reign music, dance, poetry, drama and architecture flourished. *Thumri* employs a specific set of *raags* and is particularly associated with *kathak* dance; the graceful movements of the dancer are echoed in the lyricism of the musical style. Although classical instrumentalists in concert frequently perform a *thumri* to relax from the intensity of the pure classical style, most *thumri* is vocal, and sung in a language known as Braj Bhasha, a literary dialect of Hindi. The singer is always

accompanied by the *tabla*, as well perhaps as the *tambura*, the *sarangi* or the *surmandal*, and sometimes the violin or harmonium.

The lyrics of *thumri* deal with romance. Love songs, written from a female perspective, they stress themes like dressing up for a tryst, the heartache of absence and betrayal, quarrels and reconciliation, and the joyful return from a meeting with a husband or lover. Such themes are often expressed metaphorically, with references in the lyrics to the (suggestive) flute-playing of the god Krishna, the symbol of young love. Despite the concentration on the woman's point of view, some of the greatest singers of *thumri* have been men, notably Ustad Bade Ghulam Ali Khan. As male singers are frequently middle-aged and overweight, there is a certain initial incongruity about the spectacle of this depiction of the gentle and delicate emotions of a beautiful young woman. Yet a fine artist, fat and balding though he may be, can make a song like this one infinitely affecting: "My bracelets keep slipping off/My lover has cast a spell on me/He has struck me with his magic/What can a mere doctor do?" Her bracelets have slipped off because, while pining for her absent lover, she has starved herself to the point of emaciation.

Still more songlike than the *thumri* is the **ghazal**. In some ways the Urdu counterpart of *thumri*, the *ghazal* was introduced to India by Persian Muslims and is mainly a poetic rather than a musical form. Although some *ghazal* tunes are based on the *raag* system, others do not follow any specific mode. The *taals* are clearly derived from folk music; at times the *ghazal* shades into the area of sophisticated pop song. Indeed, at the more commercial end of the scale – the so-called film *ghazal* – sophistication gives way to mere charm. The *ghazal* has played an important part in the cultures of India, Pakistan and Afghanistan since the early eighteenth century, when it was one of the accomplishments required of a courtesan. Modern *ghazal* singers usually come from a more "respectable" background.

While *thumri* singers take on a female persona, emotions in the *ghazal* are almost always expressed from the male point of view. Some of the finest performers of *ghazals* are women – Begum Akhtar and Shobha Gurtu among them. Many favourite *ghazals* are drawn from the works of great Urdu poets.

A patriotic poem by Faiz Ahmed Faiz, *Mujhse Pehli Si Muhabbat Mere Mehboob Na Maang* (Do not ask me my love, to love you the way I used to love you), proved a milestone in the advance of art poetry into the realm of the film *ghazal*. Sung by the popular Pakistani singer Noor Jehan in her inimitable style, her interpretation is said to have so impressed the poet Faiz that he formally relinquished all claims to it in her favour.

TALES OF THE GOLDEN AGE

Ghazals can be heard every day on the radio or on films either in India or Pakistan or in Asian communities abroad. But pure classical music is, for those who don't get invited to a *mahfil*, most often heard in concert – a far cry from the golden age of Indian classical music, when its chief patrons were nawabs, maharajahs and *zamindar* landlords. At this time Indian classical music was essentially court music, and its forms and practices, perfected within this framework, were clearly aimed at a leisured elite able to appreciate the subtleties that the musicians were developing.

Many traditional tales tell of this period. For instance, the Prince of Mysore would take his court musicians to a neighbouring district, inhabited by deadly snakes. The performers would then play the *poongi*, a kind of wind instrument. As the sounds grew louder, the snakes would venture from their holes and slide towards the musicians. The snakes would encircle the players completely and sway in perfect rhythm, as if intoxicated by the sound. As soon as the music stopped, they would glide away quietly without biting anyone. Another story is that of Tan-Sen, the greatest singer that India ever produced and court musician to the emperor Akbar. Tan-Sen was said to have such extraordinary power over his music that one day, when he began singing a late-night *raag* at noon, the world was plunged into darkness.

If another story is to be believed, there was a singer even greater than Tan-Sen. One day, as Tan-Sen sang the fiery *Raag Deepak*, the whole palace went up in flames. A young water-carrying maiden who happened to be passing by saw the flames, and taking a deep breath began to sing the *Raag Megh* (associated with rain). She sang with such emotion and sincerity that the heavens poured forth torrents and the flames caused by the great Tan-Sen were extinguished. Even in modern times, skilful performers are often credited with averting famine by singing *Raag Megh*. But *Raag Deepak* is superstitiously avoided these days.

Nearly every Indian musician has such tales attached to his or her name. Another one relates to Ustad Imdaad Khan, court musician at Indore and exponent of the *surbahar*. One night, as he accompanied the Maharajah's entourage on a tiger hunt, there was concern about a mad elephant on the rampage. As night set in and everyone prepared to settle down and remain quiet for fear of the elephant, Imdaad upset the whole party by getting his *surbahar* out for his usual practice. When he had been playing a while, a most unusual sight was seen outside his tent – a huge elephant, swaying to the sound of the *surbahar* as though hypnotized. From then on, all through the hunt, Imdaad was ordered to play the *surbahar* each night in order to keep the elephant quiet.

SOUND OF THE SOUTH

Southern India's **Carnatic** classical music is essentially similar to Hindustani classical music in outlook and theoretical background but differs in many details, usually ascribed to the far greater Islamic influence in the north. To the western ear, Carnatic music is emotionally direct and impassioned, without the sometimes sombre restraint that characterizes much of the north's music. For instance the **alaapaana** section, although it introduces and develops the notes of the *raag* in much the same way as the *alaap* of north Indian music, interrupts its stately progress with sparkling decorative flourishes. Often, too, the *alaapaana* is succeeded by a set of increasingly complex elaborations of a basic melody in a way that is more easily grasped than the abstract, sometimes severe improvisations of the Hindustani masters. Compositions, both of "themes" and the set variations upon them, play a much greater role in Carnatic musical practice than in Hindustani.

The *raags* of Carnatic music, like those of Hindustani music, are theoretically numbered in the thousands and musicians are expected to be familiar with them all. In practice, however, only a few hundred are ever played, and probably only fifty or sixty are in common use.

Song is at the root of south Indian music, and forms based on song are paramount, even when the performance is purely instrumental. The vast majority of the texts are religious, and the temple is frequently the venue for performance. The most important form is the *kriti*, a devotional song, hundreds of which were written by the most influential figure in the development of Carnatic music, the singer **Tyagaraja** (1767–1847). He was central to the music, not only for his compositions but also for the development of techniques of rhythmic and melodic variations. Southern India's biggest music festival, held annually near Thanjavur on the banks of the River Kaveri, is named after him.

Although the vocal tradition is central to this music, its singers are perhaps less well known in the west than instrumentalists. MS Subbulakshmi and Dr M Balamurali Krishna are among the famous names, but the most celebrated is probably Ramnad Krishnan, who has taught in America.

The instruments of Carnatic music include the **vina**, which resembles the *sitar* but has no sympathetic strings (Carnatic musicians appear not to like the somewhat hollow timbre that they give to the instrument), the *mridangam* double-headed drum, and the enormous *nadasvaram*, a type of oboe nearly four feet long which takes great experience and delicacy to play. The violin is widely used – listen to the playing of Dr L Subramaniam or his brother L Shankar, better known for his fusion experiments with guitarist John McLaughlin than for his classical recordings. The mandolin is growing in popularity and the saxophone has made a strikingly successful appearance in the hands of Kadri Gopalnath. Among *vina* players look out for S Balachander and KS Nayaranaswami.

Percussion is very important, perhaps more so than in Hindustani music, and percussion ensembles frequently tour abroad. In addition to the *mrindangam* percussion instruments include the *ghatam*, a clay pot played with tremendous zest and sometimes tossed into the air in a burst of high spirits. "Vikku" Vinayakram is its best-known player.

NEW PATHS

In earlier times the job of musician was more or less hereditary: would-be musicians began their musical education at the age of four, and music (as a profession) was considered beneath the dignity of the well-to-do and the academic classes. However, in recent years traditional restrictions have been relaxed, and music is no longer the province of a few families. Many educated Indians are becoming involved in both performance and composition, and as public performance loses its stigma so too the requirement for musicians to begin their training at a very early age becomes less forceful. Women instrumentalists too are making their mark – a startling innovation in a male-dominated musical culture. Two women with particularly high reputations are violinist Sangeeta Rajan and *tabla* player Anuradha Pal, both of whom have recorded in India. Several *gharanas* have been set up abroad, notably the one in California run by *sarod* player **Ali Akbar Khan**, who is probably Indian music's most influential living figure, and there is a steady trickle of westerners who are willing to subject themselves to the disciplines of study.

However, the importance of the old families is barely diminished. Among the younger generation of players are such names as *sarod* player Brij Narayan, son of Ram Narayan, Nikil Banerjee, who studied *sitar* with his father Jitendra Nath Banerjee, and Krishna Bhatt, who studied with Ravi Shankar and also comes from a family of musicians. Other important figures to listen out for are sitarist Rais Khan and vocalist Rashid Khan. These, like the other names mentioned, bear witness to the remaining vitality and richness of the classical music tradition in India and abroad.

FOLK MUSIC OF INDIA

There are very many kinds of **Indian folk**, but the main regional strands are the folk musics of Uttar Pradesh, Rajasthan, the Punjab (spread across both India and Pakistan), and Bengal (including Bangladesh). In the Northwest Frontier Province of Pakistan, folk music shows a definite affinity with that of Afghanistan. Kashmir produces its own distinctive folk sound, and the music of many of India's tribal peoples more closely resembles that of southeast Asia or even Borneo than anything else in the subcontinent. Apart from obvious linguistic differences, the folk songs of each region have their own distinct rhythmic structures and are performed on or accompanied by different musical instruments. Some classical instruments are used, but the following are mostly associated with less formal folk occasions.

In **Rajasthan**, music is always played for weddings and theatre performances, and often at local markets or gatherings. There is a whole caste of professional musicians who perform this function, and a wonderful assortment of earthy-sounding stringed instruments like the *kamayacha* and *ravanhata* that accompany their songs. The *ravanhata* is a simple, two-stringed fiddle that, skilfully played, can produce a tune of great beauty and depth. Hearing it played by a fine street musician behind the city walls of Jaisalmer, it seems the perfect aural background for this desert citadel.

The *satara* is the traditional instrument of the desert shepherds. A double flute, it has two pipes of different lengths, one to play the melody, the other to provide the drone, rather like bagpipes without the bag. The bag is the musician himself, who plays with circular breathing. Local cassettes of these instruments are available in small stores across Rajasthan.

As well as drums, India boasts a variety of tuned **percussion instruments**. The most popular in this category is the *jaltarang* – a water-xylophone – consisting of a series of porcelain bowls of different sizes, each containing a prescribed amount of water. The bowls are usually struck with a pair of small sticks, but sometimes these are abandoned as the player rubs the rims of the bowls with a wet finger.

The small brass, dome-shaped cymbals called *manjira* or *taal* are the best known of the many kinds of bells and gongs.

FOLK AND FILM

There are songs for all kinds of work and play. Almost every activity is represented in song, and there is an extensive repertoire of dance music. Inevitably, film music has drawn heavily from this folk tradition, but sadly has also become a relatively effortless substitute for most of it. In some instances, "pop" adaptations of traditional folk music have served to revitalize and add a fresh lease of life to the original form – *bhangra*, the folk music of Punjab, is a very good example of this. British "*bhangra*-rock" has created a fresh interest in the original *bhangra* of the Punjabi farmers.

Folk music is now beginning to awaken greater interest, particularly with non-Indian record companies, and largely as a result of the growing western interest in different kinds of Indian music. Perhaps this overseas interest has come just in time, for although it is still practised in the old way in more traditional settings and for particular rituals – weddings, births, harvest time and so on – folk music on the whole, if it is to be defined as the "music of the people", has largely been eclipsed by the output of the Indian film industry.

Whereas in the past traditional wedding songs would have been sung by the neighbourhood women all through the festivities, it is now more usual to hear film songs blaring away at Indian weddings. Nonetheless, fears that traditional music is vanishing altogether seem unwarranted: in Pakistan the unique sound of the *sohni* bands – clarinet-led brass bands which play at weddings – fills the air with wild melody, and in Rajasthan members of the traditional musicians' castes still make their living by playing at ceremonies and for entertainment. The radio and cassette player are by no means all-conquering.

Jameela Siddiqi, David Muddyman and Kim Burton

This account has been condensed and slightly altered from articles that appear in the **Rough Guide to World Music** (Penguin, Oct 1994; UK £14.99, Can $25.99, US $19.95). An extraordinarily copious and fully illustrated volume, it includes even more extensive coverage of the music of the Indian subcontinent and the rest of the world, together with recommended discographies.

GREEN ISSUES IN INDIA

As the **population** of India continues relentlessly to rise – one in every seven persons on the planet lives in India – so too does the threat to its **resources**, despite the fact that the average Indian consumes much less than an inhabitant of a typical western country.

A large proportion of Indians live in close contact with nature, meeting their needs directly from the land around them. They draw food from the land; fuel, fodder, building materials and fruit from trees; manure for the fields from animals and composted leaves; and the raw materials for crafts and rural industry from all sorts of different plants. Once land has been denuded or eroded, or a river polluted, people can find themselves unable to earn a living, and there may be little alternative employment. If India is successfully to feed over a billion people during the next century, protecting its natural assets and safeguarding their use by villagers is an essential and urgent task.

Dams and mining have destroyed vast expanses of land, while industrial pollution (of which the **Bhopal** tragedy, see p.328, was a potent example) threatens the quality of life in both rural and urban areas. Almost half the industrial output of India draws on raw materials such as cotton, paper, rubber, jute, tobacco, and sugar. As these industries expand, their demands on land increase and cash crops progressively replace food crops.

The most controversial environmental issues in India today are the uneven distribution of **water**, and the rapid pace of **deforestation**. Since the days of the Chipko movement in the early 1970s (see p.1145), mass protests against state policy have burgeoned. India's fledgeling green movement has achieved striking if limited successes, and attracted international attention.

DAM SCHEMES

The massive post-Independence **river valley projects** of the 1950s – such as the Bhakra-Nangal dam in Punjab, the Tungabhadra project in Andhra Pradesh, the Hirakud dam in Orissa, and the Rihand dam in Uttar Pradesh – affected tens of thousands of people, but encountered little resistance. However, during the 1980s, similar projects from Tehri in the north to Silent Valley in the south, and from Koel Karo in the east to the Narmada Valley in the west, became the subject of bitter criticism. Campaigners argue that government justifications for dam projects invariably over-estimate benefits and under-estimate costs, that siltation rates have usually been much higher than anticipated (and so the life of each reservoir has been shorter), that the construction of large dams seriously disrupts fish breeding and assists the spread of water-borne diseases, and that the high incidence of waterlogging and the wholesale submergence of forests and wildlife is simply unacceptable.

However, above all else, the **social implications** of dam building have evoked the most significant response. Over the last three decades, more than 11.5 million people have been displaced from their homes by development projects, and many of them put into unfamiliar surroundings without appropriate compensation or proper re-housing.

THE NARMADA DAM PROJECT

The 800-mile-long **River Narmada**, the only major Indian river to flow west, rises in the central state of Madhya Pradesh and follows a tortuous route through Maharashtra and Gujarat. Hindus, who believe that its waters spring from the body of Shiva, perform a ritual 1600-mile-long *pradaksina* (ceremonial circumnavigation) by walking all the way along one of its banks, and then back down the other.

The idea of harnessing the river to supply water to some of India's most drought-prone areas, and power to some of its poorest people, was first put forward by Jawaharlal Nehru. The ambitious scheme involves the construction along the entire Narmada Valley of thirty large and over one hundred smaller dams by the year 2025, as well as a huge irrigation project in Gujarat. In addition to providing water for human consumption and irrigation to several million acres of Madhya Pradesh, Maharashtra, Gujarat and Rajasthan, the scheme is intended to alleviate flooding and create up to one million jobs. At the heart of the controversy is the colossal 1.5-kilometre-wide **Sardar Sardovar** dam. Work is already in progress, and the gleaming white spectacle is viewable for miles around.

In theory, up to thirty million people will eventually benefit from the scheme. However, prospects for the rural population, largely indigenous Bhil tribespeople ("tribals") and low-caste Hindus, are far from rosy. As many as 200,000 people may be displaced, with over 100 villages disappearing beneath the waters.

"**Project Affected People**" (PAPs), as the official jargon has it, are to be resettled away from the valley. The *Gujarat Dam Association* has promised that each relocated family will be given a new home, electricity, water on tap, and initial financial support. However, as the dam wall inches upwards, the protest and unrest of tribal peoples has coalesced into a widespread movement. Many villagers have already been forced to leave the "submergence zone" around the village of Manibeli, and often sent to live in temporary tin huts in areas with little or no water, fuel or grazing.

Activists from all over India have participated in mass demonstrations, both in Delhi and in the villages, and been incarcerated for their pains, while hunger strikers have attempted to shame the Indian government into changing its policies.

Only part of the $3.5 billion funding for the dam has been raised. The World Bank, which at first endorsed the project, has pulled the plug on further funding, and decided to hold back $187 million it originally pledged. Ostensibly, this is because the Indian authorities could not guarantee to meet its deadlines, but it seems likely that civil unrest played a part. Cynics argue that by fulfilling the initial tranches of payment, the World Bank has financed the construction of the dam, while withholding the final tranche will mean that the costs of such items as resettlement payments and tree planting cannot be met. As a result of the withdrawal of the World Bank, other major sponsors may well remain jittery; Japan is thought unlikely to release $200 million earmarked for turbines and generating equipment, which was frozen in 1990.

Many local politicians have reconsidered their support for the dam as costs have escalated, and the prospect of its aims being achieved has receded thirty years into the future. The finances of the state of Gujarat have been drained by drought and civil disorder; it was only able to find forty percent of the funds budgeted for the dam in 1993.

In spring 1994, the Indian prime minister Narashlma Rao overruled an order from the Ministry of Environment, which had halted work on the dam on the grounds that the Gujarati government was not fulfilling its commitment to relocate villagers.

The *Narmada Bachao Andalon* movement (Save Narmada Movement, or *NBA*), has long been at the forefront of the campaign against the dam. As this book went to press, protesters were focussing on the actions of project engineers who have defied a court ruling by closing sluices on the dam, which were designed to allow construction to continue without a build-up of water upstream, several months ahead of schedule. Allegedly, this is for reasons of safety; the effect has been to flood villages from which people had not yet been resettled.

THE GREEN REVOLUTION

The much heralded **Green Revolution**, the radical transformation in agricultural practices which followed Independence, has had a profound effect on the environment and on rural lifestyles. Traditionally, Indian agriculture favoured labour-intensive, rotational farming methods; as many as five different crops were grown in a single field, a practice known as **intercropping** which had been refined over many generations. Such diversity ensures that if one crop type fails, not all food production is lost, and also increases nitrogen levels in the soil. Fertility was further retained and enhanced by the use of cow-dung and leaf compost.

After Independence, western aid and government programmes encouraged India to intensify agricultural production. High-yield strains of crops were introduced, along with modern machinery and high-input techniques, such as the purchase of seeds and chemicals and the development of extensive irrigation schemes.

Although successful in the production of large quantities of wheat and rice, which enabled India to survive national drought in 1988, and even to donate food aid during the African Sahelian famines of the 1980s, the longer-term benefits of the Green Revolution are under scrutiny. For example, production of high-protein foodstuffs such as pulses and other cereals – staple food sources for many of India's poorest people – have actually declined.

High-yielding crop varieties can damage the environment, removing nutrients from the soil and producing fewer by-products such as fodder for cattle. The copious irrigation they require often leads to waterlogging and salinization of the soil; in marginal areas, intensive farming practices cause soil erosion. Artificial fertilizers tend to leave high levels of nitrate in the soil, which can pollute water supplies.

The gap between rich and poor farmers has widened in recent years. While better-off farmers have been able to afford new technology such as tractors, farm machinery, high-yielding seeds, and pesticides, this has not been possible for their smaller counterparts, many of whom have ended up in debt, obliged to sell their land to larger businesses. In addition, the high profits and bumper harvests for large-scale farmers have made them want to maximize their land-holdings, and consequently force out their tenants and sharecroppers.

This "shake-down" has had a tremendous impact – there has been a massive trend of **rural to urban migration** in states such as Uttar Pradesh, Haryana, Rajasthan and Madhya Pradesh, as former agricultural workers drift towards towns and cities to find work. Slum settlements adjacent to and within urban areas have mushroomed, placing an ever-greater strain on urban facilities and services.

DEFORESTATION

Prior to the escalation of the dam debate, the exploitation of **forest** resources, by the commercial timber industry, supported by state forestry policy, was the major concern of Indian environmentalists.

In the tribal areas of central India, hunter-gatherers, shifting cultivators, peasants, pastoral nomads and artisans alike depend on forests for fodder, water and fuel – effectively, for their very survival. Until 1864, and the establishment of the Indian Forest Department, there was little state intervention in the management of forested areas; opposition to commercial forestry has grown ever since.

During the 1960s, extensive plantations, often of one sole species of tree (monoculture) were created. Together with development projects such as dams and mines, they served to erode forest areas. Popular protests came to

a head during the 1970s, in formerly well-forested states like Bihar, Orissa, Madhya Pradesh, Maharashtra and Andhra Pradesh, though villagers tended to minimize the element of outright confrontation with authority, and simply continued with the illegal grazing of animals or gathering of fuel wood.

Coherent and widespread opposition was crystallized in 1973 by the emergence of the **Chipko** movement, when the peasants of Mandal, a village high in the Garhwal Himalayas, prevented logging operations in a nearby forest by threatening to "hug" the trees. Campaigners found a common national cause in the coordinated opposition to the government's Draft Forest Bill of 1982, which sought to strengthen the powers of the Forest Department. Dozens of grassroots environmental organizations lobbied hard against the proposed legislation, and the government was finally forced to withdraw it. Popular feeling has also led to notable changes in state forestry policy, such as the abandonment of programmes for the clear-felling of natural forests in order to replace them with plantations of industrially useful exotic species.

Although campaigners stress the importance of returning control of the forests to their inhabitants, it has to be pointed out that a major factor in forest loss is the use of timber to fuel domestic fires. By extension, sheer pressure of population means that the forests are being used up faster than they can hope to regenerate, despite programmes to introduce fast-growing species.

Today, true forest covers around thirteen percent of the total land area of India. Studies in Karnataka have shown a variety of reasons for the ongoing loss, thought to be mirrored countrywide. Among them are the extension of cultivation (30 percent), mining (19 percent), hydro-electric projects (18 percent), direct submersion (16 percent), and the resettlement of displaced persons (11 percent).

Many of India's **mines** are located in forested regions, and the extraction of minerals such as iron ore, bauxite, copper, zinc, gypsum and limestone is increasingly at the expense of the former forest cover. Even more directly, the Indian **paper** industry – India is one of the twenty largest producers of paper in the world – requires the cutting down of several million trees annually.

With forests dwindling by an estimated 15,000 square kilometres per year, competition for living space between the human population and forest **animals** is intensifying. Alarm bells are already sounding for some of the better-known forest creatures. Since the 1930s, the density of the human population per square kilometre has trebled, while the number of tigers has declined to eight percent at best of its previous total. The many forest national parks, may be well protected, but they have become island oases amid intensively farmed land, where nothing goes to waste. At the edges of the forests, farmers spend their nights huddled in flimsy wooden towers, guarding their crops against deer and wild pigs.

On occasion, larger forest animals such as elephants and tigers explicitly threaten the livelihood of farmers. In January 1994, for example, a herd of fifty elephants was driven from their forest in Bihar by forest fires. After blundering through fields, villages and small towns, they were finally driven back to their forest, but not before six people had been trampled to death. Although tigers who spend too much time in close proximity to humans have been known to develop man-eating habits, for many forest creatures avoidance of man and his activities is becoming increasingly difficult.

Indian farmers traditionally view such encroachment onto their land with mistrust. Anti-animal feelings run high; deer are poached, and tigers have been poisoned. Attempts to involve local people with the protection of their forests and its creatures have been encouraged in some areas through the growth of new organizations. In northern India, the Ranthambore Foundation, set up to protect the tigers of Ranthambore, has developed incentives for local people, such as the more efficient management of livestock, the planting of trees and the improvement of local livelihoods.

OVERFISHING

Distinct groups of **fishing** peoples have for millennia worked the rivers and lengthy coastline of India. Until very recently, the coastal fishing economy was controlled by artisanal fisherfolk, operating small, unmechanized craft, and supplying fish to inland markets. In the 1960s, larger businesses realized the potential of fish stocks in Indian waters, and mechanized trawler fleets moved in to exploit the resource. After an initial rapid increase in the quantity of fish landed, stagnation followed, and then the industry began to decline.

The state worst affected by these changes was **Kerala** in the south, where major changes in the ecology and economy of fisheries took place. Some of its fisherfolk were able to make the transition to a more capital and resource-intensive system, but the majority faced the direct competition from the trawler fleets. This conflict gave rise to a widespread movement, in which smaller fishermen pressed for restrictions on the operation of trawlers. Strikes, processions, and violent clashes with trawler owners ensued. The movement also called for a ban on trawling during the monsoon, the breeding season for several major species of fish. When a partial ban was finally imposed in the late 1980s, it did in fact result in an increased harvest following the monsoon months. At the same time, the creation of co-operative fishing villages by many communities has made local people more self-reliant – fish is now marketed co-operatively and money for new boats and equipment is borrowed from within the co-op rather than from outside money-lenders.

In the case of **inland fisheries**, the chief threat to fish stocks is from industrial pollution. However, in some instances, an almost feudalistic control·is still exerted over fishing rights. The best known example of this in recent years has involved fisherfolk in the Bhagalpur district of Bihar, where two families claim the hereditary right to control fishing on a fifty-mile stretch of the Ganga (Ganges). Thanks to an anomaly in the provisions of the law abolishing landlord-ism (*zamindari*), enacted after 1947, these "waterlords" continue to levy taxes on some 40,000 fisherfolk, according to "*panidari*" (water) rights that date back to Moghul times. Since the early 1980s, the fisherfolk have been organized by young socialists into the "*Ganga Mukti Andolan*" (Free the Ganga) movement, but despite a protracted court case they have so far failed to escape their antiquated obligations.

Tony Stones

BOOKS

As we could not possibly hope to provide a comprehensive survey of everything that has been written about India, the following list is a personal selection of the books which proved most useful or enjoyable during the preparation of this guide. Most of them are available in India itself, as are countless inexpensive editions of Indian and English classics.

Unless otherwise stated, all publishers are based in the UK.

HISTORY AND SOCIETY

Alberuni *Alberuni's India* (Norton, US). Lucid and fascinating account by the traveller, adventurer and chronicler in thirteenth-century India – possibly the first guide book on the subcontinent.

AL Basham *The Wonder that was India* (Sidgwick & Jackson). Learned survey of Indian history, society, music, art and literature from 400 BC to the coming of the Muslims.

Judith M Brown *Gandhi and Civil Disobedience* (Cambridge University Press). Pragmatic view of Gandhi's politics, which, refreshingly, doesn't resort to hagiography.

Mary Craig *Tears of Blood* (Harper Collins). Thorough documentation of the Tibetan struggle against the Chinese since the 1950 invasion.

Louis Dumont *Homo Hierarchicus* (University of Chicago, US). Heavy-duty but unique analysis of the caste system, using the techniques of structural anthropology.

Trevor Fishlock *India File* (John Murray). The latest edition of this now classic analysis of contemporary Indian society brings the picture up to date with essays on the Golden Temple siege and the rise of Rajiv Gandhi. Recommended as an all-round introduction, or an enlightening read while travelling.

Tenzin Gyatso (the Dalai Lama) *Freedom in Exile* (Rupa & Co, India/Abacus/Harper Collins). Moving and striking account of the Chinese occupation of Tibet and the forced exile of the Dalai Lama.

Dorf Hartsuiker *Sadhus: Holy Men of India* (Thames & Hudson). The weird world of India's itinerant ascetics exposed in glossy colour photographs and erudite but accessible text.

Gita Mehta *Karma Cola* (Mandarin). Satirical look at the psychedelic 1970s freak scene in India, with some hilarious anecdotes, and many a wry observation on the whackier excesses of spiritual tourism.

Ved Mehta *New India* (Viking/Penguin). An in-depth exploration of the causes and effects of the Emergency, shot through with scathing criticism of Indira Gandhi. The sequel, *A Family Affair* (Penguin), continues in the same spirit to peruse Indian politics after the Emergency.

Prafulla Mohanti *Changing Village, Changing Life* (Viking). An insightful and entertaining portrait of life in an east Indian village through the eyes of an anglicized expatriate. Essential reading if you plan to visit Orissa.

Geoffrey Moorhouse *Calcutta, the City Revealed* (Penguin). Although politically out of date, a fascinating glimpse of the great city around the early 1970s.

VS Naipaul *India: A Wounded Civilisation* (Penguin). Naipaul, a Trinidadian Indian, is one of the country's harshest critics, accusing India of narrow-mindedness and barbaric selfishness amid debilitating poverty and misguided faith; inspired by the revelations of the Emergency. The novelist's latest portrait of the old country, *A Million Mutinies Now* (Minerva), is by far his best yet: a penetrating, superbly crafted mosaic of individual lives from around the subcontinent. Hard going in places, but worth sticking with.

Jawaharlal Nehru *The Discovery of India* (Asia Publishing). Nehru's view of India, its history and its destiny.

Christine Noble *A Home in the Himalayas* (Collins). Life among the hill people of Himachal Pradesh.

Helena Norberg-Hodge *Ancient Futures: Learning From Ladakh* (Rider). The traditional culture and present development dilemmas of Ladakh. A real eye-opener.

John Pemble *The Raj, the Indian Mutiny and the Kingdom of Oudh 1801–1859* (Harvester Press). An honest discourse on the events that led to the Mutiny, and an account of its aftermath.

Janet Rizvi *Ladakh: Crossroads of High Asia* (Oxford University Press). An excellent all-round introduction to Ladakh, past and present: particularly strong on history.

M Singer *Krishna: Myths, Rights and Attitudes* (Princeton University Press, US). A collection of academic discussions which is particularly interesting for Marriott's bungled attempt at studying the festival of Holi.

Percival Spear *Master of Bengal: Clive and His India* (Thames & Hudson). A critical and historical analysis of the adventurer and opportunist who went on to help establish the British Raj.

Romila Thapar *History of India Volume I* (Penguin). Concise paperback account of early Indian history, ending with the Delhi Sultanate. Percival Spear's *History of India Volume II* (Penguin) covers the period from the Moghul era to the death of Gandhi.

Gillian Tindall *City of Gold* (Penguin). Definitive, if rather dry biography of Bombay, from colonial trading post to modern metropolis.

Mark Tully *No Full Stops in India* (Penguin). Earnest, but highly readable dissection of contemporary India by the former BBC correspondent, incorporating personal anecdotes and first-hand accounts of political events over the past twenty years.

Mark Tully and Satish Jacob *Amritsar: Mrs Gandhi's Last Stand* (Jonathan Cape). Aptly named examination of the storming of the Golden Temple and the prime minister's eventual assassination.

Col. Henry Yule and AC Burnell *Hobson–Jobson – a Glossary of Colonial Anglo-Indian Words and Phrases and of Kindred Terms, Etymological, Historical, Geographical, and Discursive* (Munshiram Manoharlal, India). The definitive Victorian reference manual and dictionary on life and customs in India; fascinating on any number of levels.

TRAVEL

Penelope Chetwode *Kullu: The End of the Habitable World* (TBI). A quintessentially English *memsahib* returns to her childhood haunts in Himachal Pradesh. Quirky and nostalgic, with detailed descriptions of PWD bungalows, and the region's temples.

William Dalrymple *City of Djinns* (Flamingo). Modern Delhi vividly brought to life with a wealth of fascinating historical detail.

Alexander Frazer *Chasing the Monsoon* (Penguin). Frazer's wet-season jaunt up the west coast and across the Ganges plains makes a great armchair appetizer.

Norman Lewis *A Goddess in the Stones* (Pan Macmillan). This veteran English travel writer's account of his trip to Calcutta and around the backwaters of Bihar and Orissa includes some vivid insights into tribal India. One of the more accomplished travelogues of recent years.

Joe Roberts *Three-Quarters of a Footstep* (Transworld). A new and deftly written *Englishman Abroad*-style travelogue, mainly focussed on south and central India. Crammed full of anecdotes, literary asides, and rich contextual snippets.

Heather Wood *Third-Class Ticket* (Penguin). A party of elderly Bengalis leave their home village for the first time to tour the subcontinent by train. Absorbing and poignant, though the ersatz fictional style grates after a while.

FICTION

Stephen Atter and Wimal Dissanayake *The Penguin Book of Indian Short Stories* (Penguin). A ragbag of twentieth-century fiction translated from various languages. Widely available (and cheaper) in India.

EM Forster *A Passage to India* (Penguin). Forster's most acclaimed novel, a withering critique of colonialism set in the 1920s. Memorable as much for its sympathetic portrayal of middle-class Indian life as for its perspicacious insights into cultural misunderstandings.

Ruth Prawer Jhabvala *Out of India* (Penguin). One of many collections of short stories, written with brutal and brave honesty that shows India in its full colours: amusing, shocking and thought-provoking. Other titles include *How I Became a Holy Mother, Like Birds, Like Fishes, Heat and Dust*; and *In Search of Love and Beauty*.

Dominique Lapierre *City of Joy* (Penguin). Somewhat melodramatic story of a white man's journey into Calcutta's slums, loaded with anecdotes about Indian religious beliefs and family customs.

RK Narayan *Gods, Demons and Others* (Penguin). Classic Indian folktales and popular myths told through the mouth of a village story teller. Many of Narayan's beautifully crafted books, full of subtly drawn characters and good-natured humour, are set in the fictional south India territory of Malgudi.

Vikram Seth *A Suitable Boy* (Phoenix). Vast, all-embracing tome set in eastern India shortly after Independence; wonderful characterizations and an impeccable sense of place and time make this an essential read for those long train journeys.

Kushwant Singh *Sex, Scotch and Scholarship* (UPSPD, India). Selected short stories demonstrating the best of Singh's wry humour and unusual treatment of topical issues.

Rabindranath Tagore *The Home and the World* (Penguin). Tragic, romantic novel by renowned Bengali poet, focussing on one woman's struggle to escape the confines of her marriage and find happiness with a radical leader.

BIOGRAPHY AND AUTOBIOGRAPHY

JR Ackerley *Hindoo Holiday* (Penguin). During the 1920s, a gay and eccentric pal of EM Forster steps into the bizarre world of an even more gay and eccentric Maharajah seeking a tutor for his eighteen-month-old son. . .

Charles Allen *Plain Tales from the Raj* (Abacus Travel). First-hand accounts from erstwhile *sahibs* and *memsahibs* of everyday British India in the twentieth century.

John Beames *Memoirs of a Bengal Civilian* (Eland Books). The diary of a Victorian civil servant.

James Cameron *An Indian Summer* (Penguin). Affectionate, funny and brutally honest view of the country; the veteran British journalist describes his visit to India in 1972, and his marriage to an Indian woman.

Louis Fischer *The Life of Mahatma Gandhi* (Pan). This meticulously written six-hundred-page biography is the most authoritative currently available.

MK Gandhi *Experiments with Truth* (Penguin). Gandhi's records of his life, including the spiritual and moral quests, changing relationship with the British Government in India, and gradual emergence into the fore of politics. A fascinating read, and valuable insight into the Mahatma's unique mentality.

Jawaharlal Nehru *Nehru – An Autobiography* (Allied Publishers). An insight into the pre-Independence power struggles, written by India's first prime minister.

WOMEN

Elizabeth Bumiller *May You Be the Mother of a Hundred Sons* (Penguin). Lucid exploration of the Indian woman's lot, drawn from dozens of first-hand encounters by American journalist. Subjects tackled include dowries, arranged marriages, *sati*, women's magazines, and female film stars. Recommended.

Sashi Deshpande *The Binding Vine* (Penguin). Disturbing story of one woman's struggle for independence, and her eventual acceptance of the position of servitude traditionally assumed by an Indian wife.

Atia Hossain *Sunlight on a Broken Column* (Virago). A novel set in the 1930s about a Muslim family and the lead-up to Independence.

Patricia Jeffrey *Frogs in a Well* (Zed Press). The meaning of *purdah* in Muslim society, treated from a female perspective.

Anees Jung *New Moon* (Penguin). Revealing and poetic stories woven around interviews with Muslim women from all sectors of Indian society. The same author's *Unveiling India* (Penguin) is a compelling account of the life of a Muslim woman who has chosen to break free from orthodoxy.

Sarah Lloyd *An Indian Attachment* (Eland). Life in a Punjabi plains village through the eyes of a young western woman, whose relationship with an opium-addicted Sikh forms the essence of this honest and enlightening book.

Sara Mitter *Dharma's Daughters* (Penguin). Gripping account of Indian women's lives, influenced by mythical heroines and constrained by social expectations, and the attitudes of women's groups.

Karma Lekshe Tsomo (ed) *Daughters of the Buddha* (Snow Lion). Opinions, concerns and stories gathered from Buddhist women all over the world, compiled after the first International Conference of Buddhist Nuns in 1987.

In Other Words (Kali for Women, Delhi). Collection of stories by Indian women; not all feminist.

THE ARTS AND ARCHITECTURE

William Archer *Kalighat Paintings* (HMSO). A catalogue and introduction to the unique artform that blended indigenous and western traditions and lampooned nineteenth-century society in Calcutta.

Sunil Bose *Indian Classical Music* (Vikas Publishing House, India). Academic discussion of the emotions and history behind Indian classical music, with an appraisal of Indian musicians.

Roy Craven *Indian Art* (Thames & Hudson). The most reasonable and concise general introduction to Indian art, from Harappan seals to Moghul miniatures, with lots of illustrations. Good value, too.

Basil Gray *The Arts of India* (Phaidon Press). Early to modern art forms catalogued in a historical context, and well illustrated.

Mohan Khokar *Traditions of Indian Classical Dance* (Clarion Books, India). Detailing the religious and social roots of Indian dance, this lavishly illustrated book, with sections on regional traditions, is an excellent introduction to the subject.

George Michell *The Hindu Temple* (University of Chicago Press, US). A fine primer, introducing Hindu temples, their significance, and architectural development through the ages.

Andrew Robinson *Satyajit Ray: The Inner Eye* (Andre Deutsch). Auteurist study of Ray's filmmaking.

Christopher Tadgell *The History of Architecture in India* (Architecture Design & Technology Press). Thoroughly illustrated overview of Indian building and sculpting techniques, from the Harappan era to the Moghuls, Rajputs and through to the Raj.

Rabindranath Tagore *Selected Works* (Penguin). Poems, prose and mystical verse penned by the Bengali Nobel-Laureate.

GHR Tillotson *The Rajput Palaces* (Yale University Press, US). Excellent, illustrated catalogue of the history and architecture of northwest India's Rajput palaces.

Bonnie C Wade *Music in India: The Classical Traditions* (Manmohar, India). A scrupulous catalogue of Indian music, outlining the most commonly used instruments (with illustrations and musical scores).

RELIGION

Mary Boyce *Zoroastrians. Their Religious Beliefs and Practices* (Routledge). A survey of Zoroastrian history, both secular and religious.

JL Brockington *The Sacred Thread* (Edinburgh University Press). Academic but thorough overview of Hinduism from its origins to the present.

WO Cole and P Singh Sambhi *The Sikhs: Their Religious Beliefs and Practices* (Routledge). An informative study of Sikh religion.

Paul Dundas *The Jains* (Routledge). Up-to-date, comprehensive study of Jainism.

Diana L Eck *Banaras – City of Light* (Princeton University Press, US). A thorough discourse on the religious significance of Varanasi, and a good introduction to Hindu cosmology in practice.

Richard Gombrich *Theravada Buddhism* (Routledge & Kegan Paul). A history of Theravadin beliefs and practices from their beginnings to the present day.

Trevor Ling *The Buddha's Philosophy of Man* (Everyman). Select Pali texts detailing the Buddha's social outlook and the early ordering of the community.

Ajit Mookerjee *Kali the Feminine Force* (Thames & Hudson). A discussion of the art and beliefs of the *shakti* tradition.

Wendy O'Flaherty (transl.) *Hindu Myths* (Penguin). Translations of popular Hindu myths, providing an insight into the foundations of Hinduism.

Andrew Rippin *Muslims; Their Religious Beliefs and Practices* (Routledge). The essential guide to Islamic history and religious beliefs.

Paul Williams *Mahayana Buddhism* (Routledge & Kegan Paul). A comprehensive study of Mahayana history and philosophy.

RC Zaehner *Hinduism* (Oxford University Press). Lively, accessible and often amusing catalogue of Hinduism history and Indian society.

GLOSSARY

ACHARYA religious teacher.

ADIVASI official term for tribal person.

AGARBATI incense.

AHIMSA non-violence.

AKHANDPATH continuous reading of the Sikh holy book, the *Adi Granth*.

AMRITA nectar of immortality.

ANGREZI general term for westerners.

ANNA coin, no longer minted (16 *annas* to one *rupee*).

APSARA heavenly nymph.

ARAK liquor distilled from coconuts.

ARATA evening temple *puja* of lights.

ASANA yogic seating posture; small mat used in prayer and meditation.

ASHRAM centre for spiritual learning and religious practice.

ASURA demon.

ATMAN soul.

AVATAR reincarnation of Vishnu on earth, in human or animal form.

AYAH nursemaid.

AYURVEDA ancient system of medicine employing herbs, minerals and massage.

BABA respectful term for a *sadhu*.

BAGH garden, park.

BAITHAK reception area in private house.

BAKSHEESH tip, donation.

BANDH strike.

Note that a separate glossary of **Architectural Terms** appears on p.1155; that many **religious** terms are explained in detail in the section which begins on p.1117; and **musical** instruments and other terms on p.1137 onwards.

BANDHANI tie-and-dye.

BANIYA another term for a *vaishya*; a money lender.

BANYAN vast fig tree, used traditionally as a meeting place, or shade for teaching and meditating. Also, in south India, a cotton vest.

BAUL Bengali singer.

BAZAAR commercial centre of town; market.

BEGUM Muslim princess; Muslim women of high status.

BETEL nut chewed in *paan*.

BHAJAN song.

BHAKTI religious devotion expressed in a personalized or emotional relationship with the deity.

BHANG pounded marijuana, often mixed in *lassis*.

BHAWAN (also *bhavan*) palace or residence.

BHOTIA Himalayan people of Tibetan origin.

BHUMI earth, or earth goddess.

BIDI tobacco rolled in a leaf; the "poor man's puff".

BINDU seed, or the red dot (also *bindi*) worn by women on their foreheads as decoration.

BODHI TREE / BO TREE *peepal* tree, associated with the Buddha's enlightenment (*ficus religiosa*).

BODHI enlightenment.

BODHISATTVA Buddhist saint.

BRAHMIN a member of the highest caste group; priest.

BUNDH strike.

BURKHA body-covering shawl worn by orthodox Muslim women.

BURRA-SAHIB colonial official, boss or a man of great importance.

BUSTEE slum area.

CAMISE women's knee-length shirt, worn with *shalwa* trousers.

CANTONMENT area of town occupied by military quarters.

CASTE social status acquired at birth.

CHAAT snack.

CHADDAR large head-cover or shawl.

CHAKRA discus; focus of power; energy point in the body; wheel, often representing the cycle of death and rebirth.

CHANDAN sandalwood paste.

CHANDRA moon.

CHANG liquor distilled from wheat or rice.

CHAPPAL sandals or flip-flops (thongs).

CHARAS hashish.

CHARBAGH garden divided into quadrants.

CHARPOI string bed with wooden frame.

CHAURI fly whisk, regal symbol.

CHELA pupil.

CHIKAN Lucknow embroidery.

CHILLUM cylindrical clay or wood pipe for smoking tobacco or *ganja*.

CHOLI short, tight-fitting blouse worn with a *sari*.

CHOR robber.

CHOULTRY quarters for pilgrims adjoined to south Indian temples.

CHOWGAN green in the centre of a town or village.

CHOWK crossroads or courtyard.

CHOWKIDAR watchman/caretaker.

COOLIE porter/labourer.

CRORE ten million.

DABBA packed lunch.

DACOIT bandit.

DAKKU bandit.

DALIT "oppressed", "out-caste". The term, introduced by Dr Ambedkar, is preferred by so called "untouchables" as a description of their social position.

DANDA staff, or stick.

DARSHAN vision of a deity or saint; receiving religious teachings.

DAWAN servant.

DEG cauldron for food offerings, often found in *dargahs*.

DEVA god.

DEVADASI temple dancer.

DEVI goddess.

DEVTA deity.

DHABA food hall selling local dishes.

DHAM important religious site, or a theological college.

DHARAMSHALA rest house for pilgrims.

DHARMA sense of religious and social duty; the law of nature; truth (Buddhist).

DHOBI man or woman who washes clothes.

DHOLAK double-ended drum.

DHOLI sedan chair carried by bearers to hilltop temples.

DHOOP thick pliable block of strong incense.

DHOTI white ankle-length cloth worn by males, tied around the waist, and sometimes hitched up through the legs.

DHURRIE woollen rug.

DIGAMBARA literally "sky-clad": a Jain sect, known for the habit of nudity among monks, though this is no longer commonplace.

DIKPALAS guardians of the four directions.

DIWAN (*dewan*) chief minister.

DOWRY payment or gift offered in marriage.

DUPATTA veil worn by Muslim women with *shalwa camise*.

DURBAR court building; government meeting.

EVE-TEASING sexual harassment of women, either physical or verbal.

FAKIR ascetic Muslim mendicant.

FENE Goan spirit, distilled from coconut or cashews.

GADA mace.

GADI throne.

GANDA dirty.

GANDHARVAS Indra's heavenly musicians.

GANJ market.

GANJA marijuana in leaf/flower form.

GARI vehicle, or car.

GHAT mountain, landing platform, or steps leading to water.

GHAZAL melancholy Urdu songs.

GONCHA ankle-length woollen robe worn by Ladakhi women.

GOPI young cattle-tending maidens who feature as Krishna's playmates and lovers in popular mythology.

GUNDA ruffian.

GURU teacher of religion, music, dance, astrology etc.

GURUDWARA Sikh place of worship.

HAJ Muslim pilgrimage to Mecca.

HAJJI Muslim engaged upon the *haj*.

HAMMAM sunken bath, Persian style.

HARIJAN title – "Children of God" – given to "untouchables" by Gandhi.

HARTAL strike.

HIJRA eunuch or transvestite.

HINAYANA literally "lesser vehicle": the name given to the original school of Buddhism by later sects.

HOOKAH water pipe for smoking strong tobacco or marijuana.

HOWDAH bulky elephant-saddle, sometimes made of pure silver, and often shaded by a canopy.

IDGAH area laid aside in the west of town for prayers during the Muslim festival Id-ul-Zuhara.

IMAM Muslim leader or teacher.

IMFL Indian-made foreign liquor.

ISHWARA God; Shiva.

JAGHIDAR landowner.

JATAKAS popular tales about the Buddha's life and teachings.

JATI caste, determined by family and occupation.

JAWAN soldier.

JHUTA soiled by lips: food or drink polluted by touch.

-JI suffix added to names as a term of respect.

JIHAD striving by Muslims, through battle, to spread their faith.

JINA another term for the Jain *tirthankaras*.

JOHAR old practice of self immolation by women in times of war.

JYOTRILINGA twelve sites sacred by association with Shiva's unbounded *lingam* of light.

KAILASA Shiva's mountain abode.

KALAM school of painting.

KARMA weight of good and bad actions that determine status of rebirth.

KAVAD small decorated box that unfolds to serve as a travelling temple.

KHADI home-spun cotton; Gandhi's symbol of Indian self-sufficiency.

KHAN honorific Muslim title.

KHOL black eye-liner, also known as *surma*.

KHUD valley side.

KIRTAN hymn-singing.

KOTWALI police station.

KSHATRYA the warrior and ruling caste.

KUMKUM red mark on a Hindu woman's forehead (widows are not supposed to wear it).

KUND tank, lake, reservoir.

KURTA long men's shirt worn over baggy *pajamas*.

LAKH one hundred thousand.

LAMA Tibetan Buddhist monk and teacher.

LATHI heavy stick used by police.

LINGAM phallic symbol in places of worship representing the god Shiva.

LOKA realm or world, eg *deva-loka*, world of the gods.

LUNGHI male garment; long wrap-around cloth, like a *dhoti*, but coloured.

MADRASA Islamic school.

MAHADEVA literally "Great God", and a common epithet for Shiva.

MAHALLA neighbourhood.

MAHARAJA (Maharana, Maharao) king.

MAHARANI queen.

MAHATMA great soul.

MAHAYANA "Great Vehicle": a Buddhist school that has spread throughout southeast Asia.

MAHOUT elephant driver or keeper.

MAIDAN large open space or field.

MALA necklace, garland or rosary.

MANDALA religious diagram.

MANDI market.

MANDIR temple.

MANI STONE stone etched with Buddhist prayers by Tibetans and laid in piles or set in streams.

MANTRA sacred verse.

MARG road.

MASJID mosque.

MATAJI female *sadhu*.

MATH Hindu or Jain monastery.

MAUND old unit of weight (roughly 20kg).

MAYUR peacock.

MEHENDI henna.

MELA festival.

MEMSAHIB respectful address to European woman.

MITHUNA sexual union, or amorous couples in Hindu and Buddhist figurative art.

MOKSHA blissful state of freedom from rebirth aspired to by Hindus and Jains.

MOR peacock.

MUDRA hand gesture used in Vedic rituals, featuring in Hindu, Buddhist and Jain art and dance, and symbolizing teachings and life stages of the Buddha.

MUEZZIN man behind the voice calling Muslims to prayer from a mosque.

MULLAH Muslim teacher and scholar.

NADI river.

NAGA mythical serpent; person from Nagaland.

NALA stream gorge in the mountains.

NATAK dance.

NATYA drama.

NAUTCH performance by dancing girls.

NAWAB Muslim landowner or prince.

NILGAI blue bull.

NIRVANA Buddhist equivalent of *moksha*.

NIZAM title of Hyderabad rulers.

OM (aka *AUM*) symbol denoting the origin of all things, and ultimate divine essence, used in meditation by Hindus and Buddhists.

PAAN betel nut, lime, calcium and aniseed wrapped in a leaf and chewed as a digestive. Mildly addictive.

PADMA lotus; another name for the goddess Lakshmi.

PAISE there are a hundred *paisa* in a *rupee*.

PAJAMA mens' baggy trousers.

PALI original language of early Buddhist texts.

PANCHAYAT village council.

PANDA pilgrims' priest.

PARIKRAMA ritual circumambulation around a temple, shrine or mountain.

PARSI Zoroastrian.

PIR Muslim holy man.

POL residential quarters, common in Gujarat.

PRANAYAMA breath control, used in meditation.

PRASAD food blessed in temple sanctuaries and shared among devotees.

PRAYAG auspicious confluence of two or more rivers.

PUJA worship.

PUJARI priest.

PUKKA correct and acceptable, in the very English sense of "proper".

PUNYA religious merit.

PURDAH seclusion of Muslim women inside the home, and the general term for wearing a veil.

PURNIMA full moon.

PUROHIT priest.

QAWWALI devotional singing popular among Sufis.

RAAG or **RAGA** series of notes forming the basis of a melody.

RAJ rule; monarchy.

RAJA king.

RAJPUT princely rulers who once dominated much of north and west India.

RAKSHASA demon (demoness: *rakshasi*).

RANGOLI geometrical pattern of rice powder laid before houses and temples.

RAWAL chief priest (Hindu).

RINPOCHE highly revered Tibetan Buddhist *lama*, considered to be a reincarnation of a previous teacher.

RISHI "seer"; philosophical sage or poet.

RUDRAKSHA beads used to make Shiva rosaries.

RUMAL handkerchief, particularly finely embroidered in Chamba state (HP).

SADAR "main"; eg. *sadar bazaar*.

SADHU Hindu holy man with no caste or family ties.

SAGAR lake.

SAHIB respectful title for gentlemen; general term of address for European men.

SALABHANJIKA wood nymph.

SAMADHI final enlightenment; a site of death or burial of a saint.

SAMSARA cyclic process of death and rebirth.

SANGAM sacred confluence of two or more rivers, or an academy.

SANGEET music

SANNYASIN homeless, possessionless ascetic (Hindu).

SARAI resting place for caravans and travellers who once followed the trade routes through Asia.

SARI usual dress for Indian women: a length of cloth wound around the waist and draped over one shoulder.

SATI one who sacrifices her life on her husband's funeral pyre in emulation of Shiva's wife. No longer a common practice, and officially illegal.

SATSANG teaching given by a religious figurehead.

SATYAGRAHA Gandhi's campaign of non-violent protest, literally "grasping truth".

SCHEDULED CASTES official name for "untouchables".

SEPOY an Indian soldier in European service.

SETH merchant or businessman.

SEVA voluntary service in a temple or community.

SHAIVITE Hindu recognizing Shiva as the supreme god.

SHALWA baggy ankle-hugging trousers worn by women.

SHANKHA conch, symbol of Vishnu.

SHASTRA treatise.

SHIKAR hunting.

SHISHYA pupil.

SHLOKA verse from a Sanskrit text.

SHRI respectful prefix; another name for Lakshmi.

SHULAB public toilet.

SHUDRA the lowest of the four *varnas;* servant.

SINGHA lion.

SOMA medicinal herb with hallucinogenic properties used in early Vedic and Zoroastrian rituals.

STHALA site sacred for its association with legendary events.

SURMA black eyeliner, also known as *khol*.

SURYA the sun, or sun god.

SUTRA (*sutta*) verse in Sanskrit and Pali texts (literally "thread").

SVETAMBARA "white-clad" sect of Jainism, that accepts nuns and shuns nudity.

SWAMI title for a holy man.

SWARAJ "self rule"; synonym for independence, coined by Gandhi.

TALA rhythmic cycle in classical music; in sculpture a *tala* signifies one face-length.

TALUKA district.

TANDAVA vigorous, male form of dance; the dance of Shiva Nataraja.

TANDOOR clay oven.

TAPAS literally "heat": physical and mental austerities.

TEMPO three-wheeled taxi.

THALI combination of dishes, chutneys, pickles, rice and bread served as a single meal; the metal plate on which a meal is served.

THANGKA Tibetan religious scroll painting.

THERAVADA "Doctrine of the Elders": the original name for early Buddhism, which persists today in Sri Lanka and Thailand.

THUG member of a north Indian cult of professional robbers and murderers.

TIFFIN light meal.

TIFFIN CARRIER stainless steel set of tins used for carrying meals.

TILAK red dot smeared on the forehead during worship, and often used cosmetically.

TIRTHA river crossing considered sacred by Hindus, or the transition from the mundane world to heaven; a place of pilgrimage for Jains.

TIRTHANKARA "ford-maker" or "crossing-maker": an enlightened Jain teacher who is deified – 24 appear every 300 million years.

TOLA unit of weight (11.5g).

TONGA two-wheeled horse-drawn cart.

TOPI cap.

TRIMURTI the Hindu trinity.

TRISHULA Shiva's trident.

TULKU reincarnated teacher of Tibetan Buddhism.

UNTOUCHABLES members of the lowest strata of society, considered polluting to all higher castes.

URS Muslim festival.

VAHANA the "vehicle" of a deity: the bull Nandi is Shiva's *vahana*.

VAISHYA member of the merchant and trading caste group.

VARNA "colour"; one of four hierarchical social categories: *brahmins, kshatryas, vaishyas* and *shudras*.

VEDAS sacred texts of early Hinduism.

WALLAH suffix implying occupation, eg: *dhobi-wallah*, rickshaw *wallah*.

WAZIR chief minister to the king.

YAGNA Vedic sacrificial ritual.

YAKSHA earthly spirit popular in folklore: can be beneficent or evil.

YAKSHI female fertility figure, or a female *yaksha*.

YALI mythical lion.

YANTRA cosmological pictogram, or model used in an observatory.

YATRA pilgrimage.

YATRI pilgrim.

YOGI *sadhu* or priestly figure possessing occult powers gained through the practice of yoga (female: *yogini*).

YONI symbol of the female sexual organ, set around the base of the *lingam* in temple shrines.

YUGA aeon: the present age is the last in a cycle of four *yugas*, *kali-yuga*, a "black-age" of degeneration and spiritual decline.

ZAMINDAR landowner.

ARCHITECTURAL TERMS

AMALAKA repeating decorative motif based on the fluted shape of a gourd, lining and crowning temple towers: a distinctive feature of northern architecture.

ANDA literally "egg": the spherical part of a *stupa*.

BAOLI step-well in Gujarat and western India.

BHAWAN building or house.

BHUMIKA storey.

BIRADIRI summer house; pavilion.

CELLA chamber, often housing the image of a deity.

CENOTAPH ornate tomb.

CHAITYA Buddhist temple.

CHARBAGH quartered garden (Moghul style).

CHAUMUKH an image of four faces placed back to back.

CHHATRI tomb; domed pavilion.

CHORTEN Tibetan equivalent of *stupa*.

CUPOLA small delicate dome.

DARGAH tomb of a Muslim saint.

DARWAZA gateway; door.

DEUL Orissan temple or sanctuary.

DIWAN-I-AM public audience hall.

DIWAN-I-KHAS hall of private audience.

DUKKA tank and fountain in courtyard of mosque.

DURBAR court building, hall of audience, or government meeting.

DVARPALA guardian image placed at sanctuary door.

FINIAL capping motif on temple pinnacle.

GARBHA GRIHA temple sanctuary, literally "womb-chamber".

GARH fort.

GODOWN warehouse.

GOMPA Tibetan (Buddhist) monastery.

GOPURA towered temple gateway, common in south India.

HAMMAM sunken Turkish baths.

HAVELI elaborately decorated (normally wooden) mansion.

IMAMBARA tomb of a Shi'ite saint.

IWAN the main (often central) arch in a mosque.

JAGAMOHANA porch fronting the main sanctuary in an Orissan temple.

JALI lattice work in stone, or a pierced screen.

JANGHA the body of a temple.

KABUTAR KHANA pigeon coop.

KALASHA pot-like capping stone characteristic of south Indian temples.

KOT fort.

KOTHI residence.

KOTLA citadel.

KOVIL term for a Tamil Nadu temple.

LIWAN cloisters in a mosque.

MAHAL palace; mansion.

MAKARA crocodile-like animal featuring on temple doorways, and symbolizing the River Ganges. Also the vehicle of Varuna, the Vedic god of the sea.

MANDAPA hall, often with many pillars, used for various purposes: eg *kalyana mandapa* for wedding ceremonies and *nata mandapa* for dance performances.

MEDHI terrace.

MIHRAB niche in the wall of a mosque indicating the direction of prayer (to Mecca). In India the *mihrab* is in the west wall.

MIMBAR pulpit in a mosque from which the Friday sermon is read.

MINARET high slender tower, characteristic of mosques.

PADA foot, or base, also a poetic metre.

PAGODA multi-storeyed Buddhist monument.

POLE fortified gate.

PRADAKSHINA PATHA processional path circling a monument or sanctuary.

PRAKARA enclosure or courtyard in a south Indian temple.

QABR Muslim grave.

QILA fort.

RATH processional temple chariot of south India.

REKHA DEUL Orissan towered sanctuary.

SHIKHARA temple tower or spire common in northern architecture.

STAMBHA pillar, or flagstaff.

STUPA large hemispherical mound, representing the Buddha's presence, and often protecting relics of the Buddha or a Buddhist saint.

TALA storey.

TORANA arch, or free-standing gateway of two pillars linked by an elaborate arch.

TUK fortified enclosure of Jain shrines or temples.

VAV step-well, common in Gujarat.

VEDIKA railing around a *stupa*.

VIHARA Buddhist or Jain monastery.

VIMANA tower over temple sanctuary.

ZENANA women's quarters; segregated area for women in a mosque.

USEFUL HINDI WORDS AND PHRASES

India has fifteen main languages, and around seven hundred minor languages and dialects. Most Indians are, at least, bi-lingual; **Hindi**, the language of Delhi, is widely spoken and understood everywhere except the far south. **English**, however, remains the language of officialdom.

There are two broad language groups— the older, **southern**, or Dravidian group includes Tamil, Malayalam (spoken in Kerala), and Kannada (Karnataka). The main languages of the **north**, such as Hindi, Bengali, Punjabi, and Gujarati, belong to the Indo-Aryan group and are related to Sanskrit. The odd one out is **Urdu**. (literally "camp"), which developed in the first Muslim camps and settlements in the twelfth century, adding central Asian, Persian, Turkish and Arabic words to the structure of what is now Hindi.

Greetings

Greetings	*Namaste* (said with palms together at chest height as in prayer – not used for Muslims)	Goodbye (to a Muslim)	*Khudaa Haafiz* (may god bless you)
		How are you? (formal)	*Ap kaise hain*
Hello	*Namaskar* (not used for Muslims)	How are you? (familiar)	*Kya hal hai*
		Brother (a common	*bhaaii* or *bhaayaa*
Greetings	(to a Muslim) *Aslaam alequm* in reply – *alequm aslaam*	address to a stranger)	
		Sister	*didi*
		Sir	*Hazuur* (Muslims only)
We will meet again (goodbye)	*phir milenge*	Sir (Sahib)	*Saaheb*

Basic Words

Yes	*han*	You (honorific)	*ap*	Good	*achhaa*	Go	*jaao*
OK	*achhaa*	You (familiar)	*tum*	Bad	*kharaab*	Run	*bhaago*
No	*nahin*	How	*kaise*	Come	*aao*	(also "take a run" or	
Me	*main*	How much	*kitna*	Please come	*aaiiye*	"scram")	

Basic Phrases

My name is . . .	*Mera nam . . . hai*	I don't speak Hindi	*Main Hindi nahin bol sakta hun*
What is your name? (formal)	*Aapka naam kya hai*		
What is your name? (familiar)	*Tumhara naam kya hai*	Please speak slowly	*Aaiste se boliye*
I (male) come from . . .	*Main . . . se aa rahaa hun*	Please forgive me (I am sorry)	*Mujhe maaf kiijiiye*
		It is OK	*Thiik hai*
I (female) come from . . .	*Main . . . se aa rahii hun*	How much?	*Kitna paisa?*
Where do you come from?	*Kahan se aate hain*	How much is this?	*Iskaa daam kyaa hai?*
I don't know	*Maalum nahin*	What work do you do?	*Kya kaam karte hain?*
I don't understand	*Samaj nahin aayaa*	Do you have any	*Bhaai behan hai?*
I understand	*Samaj gayaa*	brothers or sisters?	

Getting Around

Where is the . . . ?	*. . . kahaan hai?*	Which is the bus for Gwalior?	*Gwalior kaa bas kahaanhai?*
I want to go to . . .	*Main . . . jaanaa chaataa hun.*		
Where is it?	*Kahaan hai?*	What time does the train leave?	*Gaarii kab chhutegii?*
How far?	*Kitnaa duur?*	Stop	*ruko*
		Wait	*thero*

Accommodation

I need a room	*Mujhe kamraa chaahiye*	I am staying	*Main ek raat ke liiye tehr rahaa hun*
How much is the room?	*Kamraa kaa bhaaraa kyaa hai?*	for one night	

Medicinal

I have a headache	*Sir me dard hai*	Where is the pharmacy?	*Dawaiikhaanaa kahaan hai?*		
I have a pain in my stomach	*Meraa pet me dardhai*	Medicine	*dawaii*	Nose	*naakh*
The pain is here	*Dard yahaan hai*	Pain	*dard*	Ear	*kaan*
Where is the doctor's surgery?	*Daaktarkhaanaa kahaan hai?*	Stomach	*pet*	Back	*piit*
Where is the hospital?	*Haspitaal kahaan hai?*	Eye	*aankh*	Foot	*paao*

INDEX

HELP US UPDATE

We've gone to a lot of effort to see that *The Rough Guide to India* is accurate and up-to-date. But things change fast – new bars and restaurants appear and disappear, hotels and rooms raise prices or lower standards, sites and museums change their opening hours, extra buses are laid on. If you feel we've got it wrong or left something out, we'd like to know – any suggestions, comments or corrections would be much appreciated, in fact. If you can remember the price, the time, the phone number, so much the better.

We'll credit all contributions, and send a copy of the next edition (or any other Rough Guide if you prefer) for the best letters. Please mark letters "Rough Guide India Update:" and send to:

Rough Guides, 1 Mercer Street, London WC2H 9QJ or

Rough Guides, 375 Hudson Street, 3rd Floor, New York NY 10014.

You are
A STUDENT

You travel
THE WORLD

You want
TO SAVE MONEY

Here's
how

The International
Student Identity Card

Available at Student Travel Offices Worldwide.

Entitles you to discounts and special services worldwide.